THE OXFORD COMPANION TO CHRISTIAN THOUGHT

THE OXFORD COMPANION TO
Christian Thought

EDITED BY

Adrian Hastings

Alistair Mason and Hugh Pyper

WITH

Ingrid Lawrie and Cecily Bennett

OXFORD

UNIVERSITY PRESS

OXFORD
UNIVERSITY PRESS

Great Clarendon Street, Oxford OX2 6DP

Oxford University Press is a department of the University of Oxford.
It furthers the University's objective of excellence in research, scholarship,
and education by publishing worldwide in

Oxford New York

Athens Auckland Bangkok Bogotá Buenos Aires Calcutta
Cape Town Chennai Dar es Salaam Delhi Florence Hong Kong Istanbul
Karachi Kuala Lumpur Madrid Melbourne Mexico City Mumbai
Nairobi Paris São Paulo Shanghai Singapore Taipei Tokyo Toronto Warsaw

with associated companies in Berlin Ibadan

Published in the United States
by Oxford University Press Inc., New York

British Library Cataloguing in Publication Data

Data available

Library of Congress Cataloging in Publication Data

Data available

ISBN 0–19–860024–0

1 3 5 7 9 10 8 6 4 2

Typeset by Tradespools Ltd, Frome
Printed in Great Britain
on acid-free paper by
Butler & Tanner Ltd
Frome, Somerset

CONTENTS

PREFACE

When I was first invited late in 1992 by Michael Cox of Oxford University Press to edit a *Companion to Christian Thought*, to be published in the year of the millennium, I hesitated to agree. It seemed to me altogether too large and demanding a commitment to take on in retirement. Little by little, however, I was converted to the idea, principally by three things. The first was Michael's perseverance in persuasion and his willingness to find ways of making it practicable. The second was the fascination of the project in itself. The more I reflected, the more I felt it a challenge and a privilege I could not decline. The third was the willingness of my old Department of Theology and Religious Studies in Leeds to share the commitment.

It was not until after my retirement in October 1994, however, that we were able to begin the planning of the work in detail, and the very lengthy business of commissioning articles started, and then rather slowly, only in early summer 1995. The editorial team in Leeds was stabilized with Alistair Mason and Hugh Pyper as Associate Editors and Ingrid Lawrie, the Department's administrator, as Editorial Assistant. Alistair and Hugh accepted the additional responsibility of writing large numbers of articles, while without Ingrid's efficiency and near-ceaseless activity, both in handling correspondence with contributors and in sub-editing, it would have been impossible to put the *Companion* together in the time available. The detailed planning of the work, the selection of potential contributors, and the evaluation of articles has been throughout a team activity. In 1997 my sister, Cecily Bennett, formerly Senior Lecturer in Old Testament at St Mary's College, Strawberry Hill, was drawn in, first to translate articles from German and French and then to copy-edit, running her theological eye over the contents as well as the style of entries. While our roles have been different, the work of editing has depended substantially on all five of us and it has seemed most appropriate to recognize that on the title page.

In 1995, Geoffrey Wainwright of Duke University and Philip Quinn of Notre Dame agreed to become Consultant Editors to ensure a full North American participation. Geoffrey's experience in editing the *Dictionary of the Ecumenical Movement* and Philip's as joint editor of the Blackwell's *Companion to the Philosophy of Religion* made them exceptionally well qualified to help us. We are extremely grateful for their prompt response to queries and innumerable suggestions in regard to both headwords and possible contributors.

Many other members of the Department in Leeds, past and present, notably John McGuckin (now Professor at Union Theological Seminary, New York), have contributed to the work, as have other members of the University of Leeds, especially Richard Rastall in Music and Mark Nelson in Philosophy. At the Oxford University Press, Pam Coote and Wendy Tuckey have been the most co-operative, supportive, and friendly of colleagues. OUP sent the initial headword list to Leslie Griffiths, Daphne Hampson, Michael McGee,

Margaret R. Miles, Keith Robbins, Donald W. Shriver, and Janet Martin Soskice for their comments, which considerably helped us revise and extend it. To everyone, I and the rest of the editorial team are most grateful.

Finally, and most of all, we are grateful to our contributors for writing such interesting articles and, quite often, rewriting them in response to our suggestions or criticism. To have experienced so gracious and imaginative a co-operation with 260 scholars across the world has been one of the great pleasures of editing this book, even if at times one has had to plead and cajole in order actually to obtain articles when our deadlines slipped past. But finally everything arrived. If the *Companion* will rightly be judged in part on the principles and priorities which controlled its planning as a whole and for which the editors are responsible, it will be judged still more on the quality of the individual articles and their ability to encapsulate authoritatively and engagingly the way Christians assess their current thoughts and past intellectual history at the opening of the third millennium.

A. H.

Leeds
1 June 1999

INTRODUCTION

The Oxford Companion to Christian Thought has been planned to provide a lively introduction, at once authoritative and accessible, to a living tradition of thought central to the western world and, in modern times, to global civilization. We have given preference to the present over the past while remaining conscious that this is a profoundly historical tradition in which it is quite impossible to understand its present forms without continual reference to how it began, the varied and even seemingly contradictory roads it has followed, the great minds which have influenced its shaping.

Throughout we have tried to be authoritative, but we have also endeavoured to recognize that neither in theory nor in practice is there a single orthodoxy or standard position within modern Christian thought, even though in many areas there is a greater degree of convergence between representatives of the main traditions than may be realized. 'Thought' is not 'fact'. Slippery as the latter can prove to be, the former is much more so. Our contributors are themselves thinkers. Their articles cannot be merely an account of 'thought' as it were from the outside but are expressions of personal thinking reflecting the scholarship and convictions of the authors themselves. Every article is signed and, in the end, remains the responsibility of its author alone, despite the inevitably considerable amount of editorial advice and stylistic rewriting often provided. There are, we hope, significant disagreements and, still more, diversities in stress. That is only to be expected as the contributors number Catholics, Protestants, and Orthodox, including rebels and agnostics of various sorts. Some might well be labelled 'conservative', others 'liberal' or 'radical', some 'catholic', some 'evangelical'. We did indeed endeavour to avoid asking people well beyond the periphery of what appeared as the modern Christian consensus to write major articles on the central doctrinal subjects, but this is not a textbook of contemporary theology for any one church or school of thought. Many things have not been said that could have been, and some would have been if we had chosen different, but no less suitable, contributors. Two hundred and sixty writers from twenty countries, including all the main traditions, both sexes, lay and clerical, veteran emeriti and young postgraduates, nuns, archbishops, journalists, Jesuits, and Quakers, form a crew varied enough. We believe that they provide a pretty fair impression of Christian thought as it flourishes today.

While at times we have asked the same author to treat a number of related subjects so that a deeper and more consistent coverage of their converging themes could be achieved, at most points we have deliberately attempted to balance one writer with another so that a diversity of viewpoint could be reflected without forcing each contributor to maintain an absolute balance. To take one example: Arianism, Athanasius, Alexandria, and the Council of Nicaea are treated by four authors whose very differences assist one's understanding of both the issues at stake and the historical interpretation of one of the most decisive controversies in Christian theology. The very considerable number of articles written by the editors can, it is hoped, be justified in providing an underlying temper to the book as a whole, but the editors are fortunate in that they do not share—at least too evidently—a common viewpoint. In general we have encouraged all contributors to write with sympathy on their own particular topic, Hegel being treated by an enthusiastic Hegelian, Aquinas by a Thomist, monasticism by a monk, Methodism by a Methodist.

Ideas belong to people, and Christian ideas have developed among people within the history of an institutionalized church, itself comprising numerous churches and traditions, often in opposition to one another. There is already a universally acclaimed work of reference for the history of the church and of Christian theology, *The Oxford Dictionary of the Christian Church*, edited by F. L. Cross and E. A. Livingstone (third edition, 1997). In no way does the *Companion* compete with the *Dictionary*. Our entries are often longer, but their number is far smaller, our bibliographies briefer, our style more discursive as well as more personal, our whole purpose different. We have tried to keep to a reasonable minimum the space devoted to factual detail. The *Dictionary* is a handbook for scholars in their own field, its unsigned entries valuable particularly for their weighty bibliographies; the *Companion* is a guide for everyone, an introduction less to facts than to the movement of ideas. We expect readers to want to turn time and again to the *Dictionary* to obtain more factual information than we can offer them, especially about relatively minor figures.

The lengthy survey articles beginning with 'Pre-Constantinian Thought' and ending with 'Twentieth Century: An Overview' provide what is in effect a mini-history of the whole subject, with an article for each century from the 16th. If this series seems over-orientated to the west, there is a parallel series for the east where 'Pre-Constantinian Thought' is followed by 'Greek Theology, 4th–6th Century', 'Byzantine Theology', and 'Eastern Orthodox Theology'. The survey articles are backed up by a considerable number of shorter historical entries on events and movements as well as by the series of entries on individuals. Thus heresies and schisms such as Arianism, Donatism, and Iconoclasm have articles of their own, together with tendencies of thought like Jansenism, Arminianism, or Ultramontanism, and such events as the major ecumenical councils. There is also a series of survey articles treating of various national or regional traditions of Christian thought, focusing particularly on recent times, such as the French, the German, the American, the Scandinavian, the Russian; and another set on denominational traditions, Lutheran, Reformed, Anglican, Baptist, or Quaker. Within the Catholic Church there are comparable entries for the Benedictines, Franciscans, Dominicans, and Jesuits. A companion to Christian thought is almost bound to seem Eurocentric. It has to describe the way things are, but Christianity is less than ever a merely European or western phenomenon, and a series of articles on Chinese, Japanese, Indian, African, and Latin American thought, as well as on the ancient Syriac, Armenian, and Ethiopian traditions should make this clear.

Biblical entries occupy a considerable amount of the *Companion*. It would be impossible to provide a worthwhile introduction to the development of Christian thought without this. Nevertheless, this is not a *Companion* to the bible—Oxford has already published one—and, here again, the selection of what could be included has had to be a careful one, particularly in regard to the Old Testament. Our aim cannot be to offer an introduction to scripture and its individual books for their own sake, but rather to focus on ways in which they have been influential components in the shaping of subsequent Christian thought. Hence we have tried to reduce to a minimum the discussion of dates, authorship, and such matters, asking instead how various writers and biblical themes have been used in the later tradition. It is the Christian history, not the historicity, of Abraham, Job, or Judas that is important here.

We have included a series of short articles on various other building blocks in the construction of the Christian tradition of understanding. One such series is on the most used symbols: water and wine, blood, fire, bread, sheep, light and darkness. Again, we have devoted middle-length entries to various non-Christians who have, nevertheless, deeply influenced the way Christians think: Plato and Aristotle, Marx, Nietzsche, and Jung. A further range of articles is devoted to more methodological themes, under such headings as Reason, Hermeneutics, Postmodernism. Here we come close to the central concerns of the *Companion*, with major articles on theology and philosophy, together with others on more particular approaches—liberationist, feminist, and Black—as well as a group on what might be termed ancillary themes such as language, literacy, biblical translation, publishing, and journalism.

How one behaves is at least as important as what one believes for the characterization of Christianity. Besides general discussions under morality and spirituality, there are a great many articles touching in one way and another on the art of Christian living, its sources in such texts as the Lord's Prayer and the Sermon on the Mount, its use of prayer and fasting, virtues like obedience and chastity, special forms of commitment including asceticism and alternative lifestyles, with major articles on love and mysticism.

In accordance with the *Companion*'s basic orientation we have severely limited the number of pre-twentieth-century thinkers with articles of their own. Those we have included, from Origen to Kierkegaard, are those we believe to remain significant and influential in their own right. In most cases, if not all, their writings continue to be read quite widely. There are, in consequence, many scores of outstanding thinkers whom we have felt unable to include in separate entries. Important in historical terms as the contribution made by Tertullian, Gregory of Nyssa, Duns Scotus, or Bishop Butler undoubtedly was, their direct impact today is rather limited except within the circles of specialists. Many such figures appear in the series of survey articles devoted to centuries or periods, and also in entries on specific themes. For the 20th century we have made a more generous selection of individual figures to illustrate the vast diversity of modern thought. While only a few, for example Barth, Bultmann, Teilhard de Chardin, and Rahner, have been singled out for extensive treatment, almost fifty others have been given short entries intended both to reinforce the thematic articles on recent thought by providing a back-up of biographical and bibliographical information, and to illustrate the range of concern and experience characteristic of 20th-century Christian life. These are by no means all theologians in any narrow sense. Edith Stein and Charles de Foucauld, C. S. Lewis and Kosuke Koyama, among many others, have been chosen as at once influential, each in a special way, and non-normative. It remains an illustrative selection and not at all a comprehensive list. Many distinguished figures, living and dead, have, to our genuine regret, not been included. Limitations of space have forced us to take many hard decisions.

We believe that 'thought' is a great deal wider than philosophy or theology. Spiritual and mystical figures of outstanding influence such as Francis of Assisi and the three Teresas, reformers like the Wesleys, have all been included, together with a small selection of places of exceptional symbolic weight or current influence: Jerusalem, Rome, Alexandria, Constantinople, Geneva, Canterbury, Tübingen, Taizé. While it would be impossible to cover the wider sea of thought at all adequately, we have put a toe bravely in here and there, not only with considerable general articles on science, music, art, poetry, and novels, but with particular studies of Shakespeare, Dante, Bach, and Milton, among other figures.

The Christian contribution to the study and practice of politics has also been considerable. A general article on political theology surveys the scene as a whole but there are also many other entries relating both to Christianity's political involvement in history and to a number of key themes: democracy, kingship, natural law, nationalism, revolution, slavery, socialism, and liberation theology. The wider field of human nature and nurture, gender, and social relations is treated in a further series of entries, of which the most general are those on humanity, sex and sexuality, and the social sciences, but there are further articles on woman, man, motherhood, fatherhood, children, education, friendship, and animals.

Philosophy has occupied a unique position within the history of Christian thought, one closely related to theology which it has much influenced but by which it has in turn been deeply affected. It has, nevertheless, a distinct role, more independent, less clerical. It is, moreover, one that in the last two centuries has seemed to turn increasingly from ally to enemy. Fifty years ago the divorce seemed almost complete, apart from the ranks of Thomists reinvigorated by the leadership of Gilson and Maritain, and the occasional existentialist. Today the position is very different and far more open. Many distinguished philosophers of the latter part of the 20th century have been Christian believers but the relationship between Christian thought and philosophy has recovered none of the relative clarity of previous ages. A series of articles beginning with a major overview of Philosophy and continuing with Natural Theology, Metaphysics, Ethics, and Cosmology, as well as more specific entries such as those on Analogy, Omnipotence, Omniscience, and the Ontological Argument, including discussions of the influence of Plato, Aristotle, and Wittgenstein, have been written by academic philosophers. They provide, we hope, a viable way into fields which, to the outsider, can often seem to have become an almost unenterable minefield of precision.

The central core of articles remains nevertheless the thematic entries of an essentially theological kind: Resurrection, Hope, Justification, Redemption, Eschatology, the Church, Sacrament, the Eucharist, Grace, the Holy Spirit, Christology, the Trinity, God, and many more. Here above all the aim is to provide a way into the subject which is faithful to the historic threads in the tradition while concentrating particularly on the way Christians understand these matters now, including the differences they have among themselves. Written by theologians from widely varied traditions, these articles tackle their subjects in a range of ways. While some include a large measure of history, others are more directly geared to a contemporary account. Nevertheless all indicate the existence of deep diversities in theological understanding, past and present, in regard to every major theme of Christian belief.

Among the thematic articles a considerable number dealing with essentially present-day subjects deserve special notice: global ethics, medical ethics, abortion, reproductive technology, homosexuality, ecology, and many others, treat areas to which a great deal of thought and commitment are currently being given by Christians. However, precisely because they are to a considerable extent new subjects, both in their apparent urgency and in the way they are handled by Christians as well as non-Christians, several of these represent some of the most divisively controversial topics in modern church life. Here nothing like a consensus can be expected. It is hoped that our entries, with a stress upon the quietly informative and the delineation of the issues involved, respect the divided state of the Christian mind in such areas without bypassing the most debated points.

It would be misleading to understand the preceding paragraphs as indicating that the *Companion's* articles can be divided into a precise number of clearly distinct areas. In fact, many key entries are distinctly multidirectional and resist labelling as doctrinal, ethical, historical, or whatever. Thus, to give one example, Fatherhood relates to God, the Trinity, Jesus, and Christology, but hardly less to Motherhood and Feminist Theology, to Children and Family, as well as being exemplific in regard to Metaphor, Analogy, and Language. Biblical studies, theology, philosophy, the history of Jesus, attitudes to personal and family relations, together with a major modern shift in cultural and theological approach are all in question in this one article.

Headwords have been kept as short as possible. To avoid misunderstanding, it is necessary to stress that an article headed Islam, Marxism, or Reason is not intended as an introduction to the subject in itself or its entirety, but only as an account of the impact it has had on Christianity and the way Christian thinkers have related to it.

Almost every article ends with a book list. These lists include works explicitly quoted in the text, unless adequately identified there, but their main aim is to help the reader on the next stage of exploration. They are, therefore, almost all in English and likely to be available in a good library. While we include only what is judged authoritative, we do not include everything authoritative or, even, necessarily the most authoritative. Accessibility and comprehensibility for the near-beginner have been judged the most important qualities in a book, and the lists have deliberately been kept short.

But we also intend that the reading of one article will lead to another. We have included a large number of cross-references, marked with an asterisk, to help readers pursue the links, expected and unexpected, between the articles. In order to intrude as little as possible on the text, where the exact headword does not appear its closest equivalent is asterisked: for example, '*France' indicates a cross-reference to French Christian Thought, '*Hegelian' to Hegel, and so on. Where this has not been possible, the headword is added in brackets in the text, or under 'See also' at the end of the article. Even within the pages of the *Companion* research may thus go a long way: the cross-references encourage the reader to move backwards and forwards between thematic, biblical, historical, and personal articles. Someone looking up Pascal may be led on to Jansenism and Arminianism, back to Augustine or Calvin, across to the general articles on Predestination and Grace, or to the survey article on the Seventeenth Century. Again, a reader wanting to find out about Witchcraft may then turn to Devil and go on to Hell, after tasting Sin and the Fall, as well as Adam and Eve, or may turn instead to Dualism, Light and Darkness, and, more philosophically, to Problem of Evil, and Divine Omnipotence. What seems to be missing under one heading may well be found under another.

Throughout the *Companion*, we hope to convey the sense of a multifaceted tradition of critical belief which is bound to be misunderstood if not perceived in its full complexity. Christian thought is at one and the same time a matter of the contributions of individuals, the complex and subtle histories of words and ideas, institutional doctrines, popular devotion, artistic imagination, all this caught up in humanity's long march across the centuries in search of the meaning of things. We believe that Christian thought has made an unparalleled contribution to that long march while at times losing its sense of direction, bogged down in arcane internal debate. Yet even the disasters are worthy of note. It has been a very fallible tradition. We believe too that this contribution is still continuing. We hope that in the pages of the *Companion* readers will find among much that is enlightening, informative, and even amusing, some things that may well be true.

Adrian Hastings

CONTRIBUTORS

NICHOLAS ADAMS Lecturer, Faculty of Divinity,
University of Edinburgh
Hope

A. M. ALLCHIN Honorary Professor, Department
of Theology, University of Wales Bangor
Compassion, Kenosis, Praise

DIOGENES ALLEN Stuart Professor of
Philosophy, Princeton Theological Seminary
Philosophy

WILLIAM P. ALSTON Emeritus Professor of
Philosophy, Syracuse University
Realism and Antirealism

MARCELLA ALTHAUS-REID Lecturer, Faculty of
Divinity, University of Edinburgh
*Leonardo Boff, José Míguez Bonino, Gustavo
Gutiérrez, Liberation Theology*

REGIS J. ARMSTRONG, OFM CAP. Capuchin Friar,
Editor, *Greyfriars Review*
Francis of Assisi

PAUL AVIS General Secretary, Council for Christian
Unity, and Research Fellow, University of Exeter
*Apologetics, Richard Hooker, Infallibility, Ministry,
Tradition*

EDWARD BAILEY Rector of Winterbourne, Bristol,
and Visiting Professor of Implicit Religion,
University of Middlesex
Folk Religion

R. S. BARBOUR Emeritus Professor of New
Testament Studies, University of Aberdeen
Kingdom of God

BRUNO BARNHART Camaldolese Benedictine
monk of New Camaldoli Hermitage, Big Sur,
California
Bede Griffiths

JOHN BARTON Oriel and Laing Professor of the
Interpretation of Holy Scripture, University of
Oxford
The Bible, Its Authority and Interpretation

STEPHEN C. BARTON Senior Lecturer in New
Testament, University of Durham
Family

RICHARD BAUCKHAM Professor of New Testament
Studies, University of St Andrews
Eschatology

JOANNE C. BECKMAN The Divinity School, Duke
University
Sabbatarianism

KWAME BEDIAKO Director, Akrofi-Christaller
Memorial Centre for Mission Research and
Applied Theology, Akropong-Akuapem, Ghana
African Christian Thought, John Mbiti

R. J. BERRY Professor of Genetics, University
College London, and formerly President of
Christians in Science
Evolution

HELEN K. BOND Lecturer, Department of Divinity
with Religious Studies, University of Aberdeen
John

GERALD BONNER Reader Emeritus in Theology,
University of Durham; formerly Distinguished
Professor of Early Christian Studies, Catholic
University of America, Washington, DC
Pelagianism

SARAH JANE BOSS Director of the Marian Study
Centre, Ushaw College, Durham
Mary

JOHN BOWDEN Editor and Managing Director of
SCM Press
Publishing

FIONA BOWIE Senior Lecturer, Department of
Anthropology, University of Wales Lampeter
*Beguines, Pilgrimage, Chastity, Catherine of Siena,
Teresa of Lisieux*

CARL E. BRAATEN Executive Director, Center for
Catholic and Evangelical Theology, Northfield,
Minnesota
Lutheranism

IAN BRADLEY Senior Lecturer in Practical
Theology, University of St Andrews
Sacrifice

JOHN BROOKE Andreos Idreos Professor of Science
and Religion, University of Oxford
Science

DAVID BROWN Van Mildert Professor of Divinity, University of Durham
Process Theology, Symbolism

PIERRE BÜHLER Professor, Institute for Hermeneutics, University of Zürich
Hermeneutics

DAVID B. BURRELL, CSC Hesburgh Professor of Philosophy and Theology, University of Notre Dame
Jewish–Christian Relations

WILLIAM R. BURROWS Managing Editor, Orbis Books, Maryknoll, New York
David Tracy

JOHN CALDWELL Reader in Music, University of Oxford
Music

EUAN CAMERON Professor of Early Modern History, University of Newcastle upon Tyne
Martin Luther

GEORGE CAREY Archbishop of Canterbury
Evangelism

ROBERT CARROLL Professor of Hebrew Bible and Semitic Studies, University of Glasgow
Biblical Translation

RICHARD J. CARWARDINE Professor of History, University of Sheffield
Revivalism

JOHN CAVADINI Professor, Department of Theology, University of Notre Dame
Latin Theology 300 to 1000

KEITH CLEMENTS General Secretary, Conference of European Churches, Geneva
Dietrich Bonhoeffer

PATRICK COLLINSON Regius Professor of Modern History Emeritus, and Fellow of Trinity College, University of Cambridge
Puritanism, Reformation

CHARLES J. CONNIRY, JR. Director of Doctor of Ministry Program and Assistant Professor of Theology, George Fox University, Portland, Oregon
Conversion

WILLIAM LANE CRAIG Research Professor in Philosophy, Talbot School of Theology
Cosmology, Eternity

PETER CRAMER Winchester College
Anselm of Canterbury

JAMES CRICHTON Formerly parish priest, Pershore, Worcestershire
Penance

HENRI CROUZEL, SJ Formerly Professor of Patristics, Faculty of Theology, Institut Catholique, Toulouse, and Gregorian University, Rome
Origen

COLIN CROWDER Lecturer in Theology, University of Durham
Don Cupitt, Humanity

RONALD CUETO Formerly Reader in Spanish History, University of Leeds
Spanish Catholicism

ADRIAN CUNNINGHAM Emeritus Fellow in Religious Studies, Lancaster University
Carl Gustav Jung

DAVID S. CUNNINGHAM Associate Professor of Theology and Ethics, Seabury-Western Theological Seminary, Evanston, Illinois
Rhetoric

D. LYLE DABNEY Assistant Professor of Theology, Marquette University, Milwaukee, Wisconsin
Jürgen Moltmann

ZDENĚK V. DAVID Librarian, Woodrow Wilson International Center for Scholars, Washington, DC
Huss and Wyclif

ROBERT DAVIDSON Emeritus Professor of Old Testament Language and Literature, University of Glasgow
Covenant, Psalms

BRIAN DAVIES, OP Professor of Philosophy, Fordham University, New York
Thomas Aquinas

GRAHAM DAVIES Reader in Old Testament Studies and Fellow of Fitzwilliam College, University of Cambridge
Exodus

OLIVER DAVIES Professor, Department of Theology and Religious Studies, University of Wales Lampeter
Hildegard of Bingen, Holiness, Saints, Edith Stein

JOHN W. DE GRUCHY Robert Selby Taylor Professor of Christian Studies, University of Cape Town
Apartheid, Democracy

HUGH DINWIDDY Formerly Dean of Makerere University and Lecturer in English Literature
Emily Dickinson

SIMON DIXON Professor of Modern History, University of Leeds
Tolstoy

PETER DOBLE Honorary Lecturer, Department of Theology and Religious Studies, University of Leeds
Education, John Robinson

NIGEL DOWER Senior Lecturer, Department of Philosophy, University of Aberdeen
Global Ethics

AVERY DULLES, SJ Laurence J. McGinley Professor of Religion and Society, Fordham University, New York
Dogma, Faith

JAMES D. G. DUNN Lightfoot Professor of Divinity,
University of Durham
New Testament

ANDREW DUTNEY Senior Lecturer in Theology,
Flinders University of South Australia
Contraception, Reproductive Technology

ANDREAS ECKERSTORFER University of Salzburg,
Austria
George Lindbeck

MALCOLM EDWARDS Independent writer
Gay Theology

CHARLES ELLIOTT Dean and Chaplain, Trinity Hall,
Cambridge
Memory

J. K. ELLIOTT Professor of New Testament Textual
Criticism, University of Leeds
Christian Apocrypha

TROND ENGER Associate Professor of Theology
and Religious Education, Østfold College,
Halden, Norway
Pietism

HOWARD EVANS Formerly Senior Lecturer in
French, University of Leeds
French Christian Thought, Paul Ricœur

DOUGLAS FARROW Associate Professor of Religious
Studies, McGill University, Montreal
Fall

DAVID FERGUSSON Professor of Divinity,
University of Edinburgh
*Divine Foreknowledge and Freedom, Predestination,
Presbyterian Thought, Revelation*

KEVIN L. FLANNERY, SJ Ordinary Professor of
Ancient Philosophy, Pontifical Gregorian
University, Rome
Plato and Platonism

THOMAS P. FLINT Associate Professor of
Philosophy, University of Notre Dame
Problem of Evil

DAVID F. FORD Regius Professor of Divinity,
University of Cambridge
Christology

DUNCAN FORRESTER Professor of Christian Ethics
and Practical Theology, University of Edinburgh
Justice, Social Gospel and Social Teaching, Usury

MARK FOX Lecturer in Religious Studies, Joseph
Chamberlain Sixth Form College, Birmingham
Paranormal

MONICA FURLONG Writer and broadcaster
Thomas Merton

KATHY GALLOWAY Community theologian and
writer in Glasgow, member of the Iona
Community
Alternative Lifestyles

B. A. GERRISH John Nuveen Professor Emeritus,
University of Chicago
John Calvin, Friedrich Schleiermacher

PAUL GIFFORD Reader in African Christianity,
School of Oriental and African Studies,
University of London
Fundamentalism, Prosperity

SHERIDAN GILLEY Reader in Theology, University
of Durham
Oxford Movement

KENNETH E. GOODPASTER Koch Endowed Chair
in Business Ethics, University of St Thomas,
Minneapolis-St Paul
Business Ethics

TIMOTHY J. GORRINGE St Luke's Foundation
Professor of Theological Studies, University of
Exeter
Contextual Theology, Alan Ecclestone, Punishment

ELAINE GRAHAM Samuel Ferguson Professor of
Social and Pastoral Theology, University of
Manchester
Pastoral Theology, Dorothee Sölle

DONALD GRAY Canon Emeritus, Westminster
Abbey, London, and formerly Chaplain to the
Speaker of the House of Commons
Worship

NIELS HENRIK GREGERSEN Associate Professor of
Systematic Theology, University of Aarhus,
Denmark
Providence

STANLEY J. GRENZ Pioneer McDonald Professor of
Theology and Ethics at Carey/Regent College,
Vancouver
Wolfhart Pannenberg

COLIN GUNTON Professor of Christian Doctrine,
King's College London
Authority, Holy Spirit, Protestantism

VIGEN GUROIAN Professor of Theology and Ethics,
Loyola College in Maryland, Baltimore
Armenian Tradition

JOHN HABGOOD Formerly Archbishop of York
Euthanasia, Medical Ethics, Suicide

JOHN HALDANE Professor of Philosophy and
Honorary Professor of Divinity, University of St
Andrews
Analytical Thomism, Aristotle, Natural Theology

STUART HALL Professor Emeritus of Ecclesiastical
History, King's College London
Docetism

NICHOLAS HAMMOND University Lecturer in
French, and Fellow of Gonville and Caius
College, University of Cambridge
Pascal

DAPHNE HAMPSON Reader in Divinity, University
of St Andrews
Post-Christianity

DANIEL W. HARDY Formerly Van Mildert Professor
of Divinity, University of Durham
Church, Joy

JOHN E. HARE Professor of Philosophy, Calvin College, Grand Rapids, Michigan
Immanuel Kant

DANIEL J. HARRINGTON, SJ Professor of New Testament, Weston Jesuit School of Theology, Cambridge, Massachusetts
Mark, Matthew

ELIZABETH J. HARRIS Executive Secretary for Inter-Faith Relations, Methodist Church
Buddhism

CAROL HARRISON Lecturer in the History and Theology of the Latin West, University of Durham
Augustine, Donatism

ANTHONY HARVEY Formerly Lecturer in Theology, University of Oxford, Canon and Sub-Dean of Westminster
Priesthood

SUSAN ASHBROOK HARVEY Associate Professor of Religious Studies, Brown University, Providence, Rhode Island
Syriac Christian Thought

ADRIAN HASTINGS, GENERAL EDITOR Emeritus Professor of Theology, University of Leeds
Abhishiktananda, Anger, Antisemitism, Apostolicity, Blood, Body, Bread, Cathedrals, Catholicism, Christianity, Communion, Conciliarism, Conscience, Constantine, Councils, Charles de Foucauld, Devil, Dialogue, Dionysius the Pseudo-Areopagite, Discipleship, Dualism, Episcopate, Ethiopian Theology, Fire, Freedom, Paulo Freire, God, Hell, History, Incarnation, Jesus, John XXIII, Kingship, Laity, Language, Law, C. S. Lewis, Light and Darkness, Limbo, Donald MacKinnon, Jacques Maritain, Modernity, Morality, Thomas More, Nationalism, Natural Law, John Henry Newman, Orthodoxy, Papacy, Patriarchates, Play, Political Theology, Prayer, Prophecy, Reason, Reconciliation, Religion, Rome, Salvation, Schism, William Shakespeare, Sheep and Shepherds, Subsidiarity, William Temple, Teresa of Calcutta, Theology, Transubstantiation, Truth, Twentieth Century: An Overview, Ultramontanism, Vatican II, Mary Ward, Water, Wine, Witchcraft

BRIAN HAYMES President, Bristol Baptist College
Baptist Thought

BRIAN HEBBLETHWAITE Life Fellow of Queens' College, University Lecturer in Divinity, Cambridge
Immortality, Soul

MARGARET HEBBLETHWAITE Author, and formerly Assistant Editor, *The Tablet*
Base Communities, Exercises of St Ignatius, Motherhood

RONALD W. HEPBURN Professor Emeritus, University of Edinburgh
Religious Experience

EDMUND HILL, OP Formerly lecturer in theological institutions in England, South Africa,

Lesotho, and Papua New Guinea
Tissa Balasuriya

LINDA HOGAN Lecturer in Theology, University of Leeds
Feminist Theology, Elisabeth Schüssler Fiorenza, Rosemary Radford Ruether

E. BROOKS HOLIFIELD Charles Howard Candler Professor of American Church History, Emory University, Atlanta, Georgia
North America: An Overview

MORNA D. HOOKER Lady Margaret's Professor Emerita, University of Cambridge, and Fellow of Robinson College, Cambridge
Paul

CHRIS HUEBNER The Divinity School, Duke University
Alasdair MacIntyre

SEÁN F. HUGHES Department of Theology, University of St Thomas, Minneapolis-St Paul
Sixteenth Century: An Overview

ELIZABETH ISICHEI Professor of Religious Studies, University of Otago, Dunedin, New Zealand
Millenarianism, Montanism

GRACE M. JANTZEN John Rylands Professorial Fellow in the Department of Religions and Theology, and Co-Director of the Centre for Religion, Culture, and Gender, University of Manchester
Julian of Norwich, Teresa of Avila

WERNER G. JEANROND Professor of Systematic Theology, University of Lund, Sweden
Charity, Love, Neo-Orthodoxy

ANDERS JEFFNER Professor, Faculty of Theology, Uppsala University, Sweden
Scandinavian Christian Thought

WILLIE JAMES JENNINGS Associate Dean of Academic Programs and Research Assistant Professor of Systematic Theology and Black Church Studies, Duke University
Black Theology, James Cone

ROBERT JENSON Senior Scholar for Research, Center of Theological Inquiry, Princeton, New Jersey
Trinity

LUKE TIMOTHY JOHNSON Robert W. Woodruff Professor of New Testament and Christian Origins, Emory University, Atlanta, Georgia
Cross and Crucifixion, Sermon on the Mount

ROBERT K. JOHNSTON Professor of Theology and Culture, Fuller Theological Seminary, Pasadena, California
Evangelicalism

WILLIAM JOHNSTONE Professor of Hebrew and Semitic Languages, University of Aberdeen
Moses

GARETH JONES Professor of Religious Studies,
Canterbury Christ Church College
Tübingen

L. GREGORY JONES Professor of Theology and
Dean, The Divinity School, Duke University
Friendship

CHARLES KANNENGIESSER Emeritus Professor of
Theology, University of Notre Dame
Athanasius

JAMES F. KAY Joe R. Engle Associate Professor of
Homiletics and Liturgics, Princeton Theological
Seminary
Rudolf Bultmann

KEVIN KELLY Emeritus Senior Research Fellow in
Moral Theology, Liverpool Hope University
College
Divorce

BONNIE KENT Associate Professor of Philosophy,
Columbia University, New York
Franciscan Thought

JOHN KENT Emeritus Professor of Theology,
University of Bristol
Eighteenth Century: An Overview

FERGUS KERR, OP Regent, Blackfriars, Oxford
Religious Language, Ludwig Wittgenstein

KAREN KILBY Lecturer in Theology, University of
Birmingham
Karl Rahner

URSULA KING Professor of Theology and Religious
Studies, University of Bristol, Visiting Professor
of Feminist Theology, University of Oslo
Pierre Teilhard de Chardin

TIMOTHY KIRCHER Associate Professor of History,
Guilford College, Greensboro, North Carolina
Renaissance

JEFFREY KLAIBER, SJ Professor of History, Catholic
University of Peru in Lima
Latin American Christian Thought

EMMA KLEIN Jewish affairs correspondent, *The
Tablet*, and author of *Lost Jews*
Holocaust

KOSUKE KOYAMA Emeritus Professor of
Ecumenical Studies, Union Theological
Seminary, New York
*Shusaku Endo, Japanese Christian Thought, Kosuke
Koyama*

JONATHAN L. KVANVIG Professor of Philosophy,
Texas A&M University
Divine Omniscience

BERNHARD LANG Professor of Religion, University
of Paderborn, Germany, and University of St
Andrews
Heaven

DAVID R. LAW Lecturer in Christian Thought,
University of Manchester
Existentialism, German Christian Thought

MICHAEL G. LAWLER Amelia and Emil Graff
Professor of Catholic Theological Studies,
Creighton University, Omaha, Nebraska
Marriage

C. HUGH LAWRENCE Emeritus Professor of
Medieval History, University of London
Middle Ages: An Overview, Universities

KENNETH LEECH M. B. Reckitt Urban Fellow at St
Botolph's Church, Aldgate, London
Socialism

HENRIETTA LEYSER Supernumerary Fellow of St
Peter's College, University of Oxford
Mary Magdalene

ANDREW LINZEY IFAW Senior Research Fellow,
Mansfield College, University of Oxford
Animals

JULIUS LIPNER Faculty of Divinity, University of
Cambridge
Hinduism, Raimundo Panikkar

RICHARD LISCHER James T. and Alice Mead
Cleland Professor of Preaching, The Divinity
School, Duke University
Preaching/Homiletics

ANN LOADES Professor of Divinity, University of
Durham
Sacrament

ALASTAIR LOGAN Senior Lecturer, Department of
Theology, University of Exeter
Gnosticism

CLIFFORD LONGLEY Journalist, *The Times, The Daily
Telegraph, The Tablet*
Journalism

GERARD LOUGHLIN Senior Lecturer, Religious
Studies, University of Newcastle upon Tyne
Time

ANDREW LOUTH Professor of Patristic and
Byzantine Studies, University of Durham
*Byzantine Theology, 6th–16th Centuries, Fasting,
Iconoclasm, Iconography, Typology, Virgin Birth*

HUGH J. MCCANN Professor of Philosophy, Texas
A&M University
Creation

DAVID MCCLEAN Professor of Law, University of
Sheffield
Capital Punishment

JAMES W. MCCLENDON, JR. Distinguished
Scholar-in-Residence, Fuller Theological
Seminary, Pasadena, California
Conversion

JAMES MCCONICA, CSB President, Pontifical
Institute of Medieval Studies, Toronto
Erasmus

GERALD A. MCCOOL, SJ Professor Emeritus of
Philosophy, Fordham University
Modern Thomism

BRUCE L. McCORMACK Frederick and Margaret L. Weyerhaeuser Professor of Systematic Theology, Princeton Theological Seminary
Karl Barth

JOHN McDADE, SJ Principal, Heythrop College, University of London
The Development of Doctrine

ALISTAIR McFADYEN Senior Lecturer, Department of Theology and Religious Studies, University of Leeds
Sin

JOHN McGUCKIN Professor of Early Church History, Union Theological Seminary, New York
Council of Chalcedon, Constantinople, Deification, Council of Ephesus, Filioque, Georges Florovsky, Greek Theology, 4th–6th Centuries, Quest for the Historical Jesus, Monophysitism, Nestorianism, Council of Nicaea

DONALD MACKENZIE Lecturer, Department of English Literature, University of Glasgow
John Donne, T. S. Eliot, Gerard Manley Hopkins

JAMES P. MACKEY Director, Graduate School of Divinity, University of Edinburgh
Celtic Christianity

DAVID McLELLAN Professor of Political Theory, University of Kent, Canterbury
Leszek Kolakowski, Marxism, Simone Weil

HUGH McLEOD Professor of Church History, University of Birmingham
Secularization

ERNAN McMULLIN Director Emeritus, Program in the History and Philosophy of Science, University of Notre Dame
Galileo Galilei

PAUL McPARTLAN Lecturer in Systematic Theology, Heythrop College, University of London
Angels, Collegiality, Henri de Lubac, Diaconate, Purgatory, Vatican I

JACK MAHONEY, SJ Emeritus Professor of Moral and Social Theology, University of London
Casuistry

JOHN MARENBON Fellow, Trinity College, Cambridge
Abelard

I. HOWARD MARSHALL Emeritus Professor of New Testament Exegesis, University of Aberdeen
Pastoral Epistles

ALISTAIR MASON, ASSOCIATE EDITOR Senior Lecturer in Church History, University of Leeds
Adventism, Agnosticism, Antinomianism, Arminianism, Baroque, William Blake, Brethren, Charismatic Movement, Samuel Taylor Coleridge, Common Sense Philosophy, Congregationalism, Deism, Dispensationalism, Doubt, Enlightenment, Enthusiasm, Erastianism, Fideism, Gallicanism, Geneva, Jansenism, Liberal Protestantism, Martyrdom, Mormonism, Rudolf Otto, Pilgrim's Progress,

Princeton Theology, Quietism, Reformed Theology, Religious Liberty, Restorationism, Romanticism, Scottish Christian Thought, Temperance, Unitarianism, Universalism

CHRISTOPHER MAUNDER Senior Lecturer, College of Ripon and York St John, and Marian Study Centre, Ushaw College, Durham
Marian Apparitions, New Age, Taizé, Visions

GEORGE I. MAVRODES Emeritus Professor of Philosophy, University of Michigan
Divine Omnipotence

WILFRID MELLERS, Emeritus Professor of Music, University of York
Johann Sebastian Bach

PHILIP A. MELLOR Senior Lecturer in Religious Studies, University of Leeds
Social Sciences

PETER MEREDITH Emeritus Professor of Medieval Drama, University of Leeds
Mystery Plays

PETER MILLICAN Senior Lecturer in Philosophy and Computer Studies, University of Leeds
Abortion, Ontological Argument

ANTHONY MILTON Senior Lecturer, Department of History, University of Sheffield
Seventeenth Century: An Overview

GARETH MOORE, OP Prior, Couvent de l'Épiphanie, Rixensart, Belgium
Homosexuality

ROBERT MORGAN Reader in New Testament Theology and Fellow of Linacre College, University of Oxford
Epistle to the Romans

JOHN MUDDIMAN G. B. Caird Fellow of Mansfield College, and Lecturer in New Testament, University of Oxford
Word/Logos

ROBERT BRUCE MULLIN Society for the Promotion of Religion and Learning Professor of History and World Mission, General Theological Seminary, New York
Miracle

MARK NELSON Senior Lecturer in Philosophy, University of Leeds
Ethics

DONALD NICHOLL Formerly Professor of History, University of Keele
Fyodor Dostoevsky

AIDAN NICHOLL, OP Affiliated Lecturer, Faculty of Divinity, University of Cambridge
Yves Congar, Joseph Ratzinger, Edward Schillebeeckx

EDWARD NORMAN Emeritus Fellow of Peterhouse, Cambridge
Establishment, Revolution

RICHARD A. NORRIS, JR. Emeritus Professor of
Church History, Union Theological Seminary,
New York
Alexandria

EDWARD T. OAKES, SJ Associate Professor of
Religious Studies, Regis University, Denver,
Colorado
Hans Urs von Balthasar

GERALD O'COLLINS, SJ Professor of Fundamental
and Systematic Theology, Gregorian University,
Rome
Redemption

GERARD O'REILLY Senior Assistant Editor, *Oxford
English Dictionary*
Bernard Lonergan

JOHN W. PADBERG, SJ Director and General
Editor, Institute of Jesuit Sources, St Louis,
Missouri
Jesuit Thought

LLOYD G. PATTERSON Huntington Professor of
Historical Theology Emeritus, Episcopal
Divinity School, Cambridge, Massachusetts
Pre-Constantinian Thought

STEPHEN PATTISON Senior Research Fellow in
Practical Theology, University of Wales Cardiff
Health and Healing

CHARLES PINCHES Professor of Theology,
University of Scranton, Pennsylvania
Virtue

GORDON PREECE Lecturer in Ethics and Director
of Centre of Applied Christian Ethics, Ridley
College, University of Melbourne
Work

STEPHEN PRICKETT Regius Professor of English
Language and Literature, University of Glasgow
Poetry

ANNE PRIMAVESI Formerly Research Fellow in
Environmental Theology, University of Bristol
Ecology

HUGH PYPER, ASSOCIATE EDITOR Senior Lecturer
in Biblical Studies, University of Leeds
*Abraham, Adam, Jewish Apocrypha, Archaeology,
Astrology, Cain, Children, Ten Commandments,
Daniel, David, Demythologizing, Desert, Dreams,
Genesis, Humour, Irenaeus, Israel, Jerusalem, Job,
John the Baptist, Jonah, Judas, Kerygma, Søren
Kierkegaard, Literacy, Melchizedek, Messiah, Myth,
Old Testament, Paradise, Paradox, Person, Quaker
Thought, Slavery, Solomon, Song of Songs, The
Temple, Charlotte von Kirschbaum, Wisdom, World*

PHILIP L. QUINN, CONSULTANT EDITOR John A.
O'Brien Professor of Philosophy, University of
Notre Dame
Theories of Atonement, Divine Command Ethics

MARTIN REARDON Formerly General Secretary,
Churches Together in England
Unity

RUTH REARDON Secretary of the Association of
Interchurch Families, London
Interchurch Marriage

DANIEL REES Monk of Downside Abbey, Stratton
on the Fosse
Monasticism

MARGARET A. REES Honorary Research Fellow in
Spanish, University of Leeds
St John of the Cross

DAVID J. REIMER Lecturer in Hebrew and Old
Testament Studies, University of Edinburgh
Exile, Jeremiah

PATRICK REYNTIENS Stained-glass artist and writer
Visual Arts

CECIL M. ROBECK, JR. Professor of Church
History and Ecumenics, Fuller Theological
Seminary, Pasadena, California
Pentecostalism

RICHARD H. ROBERTS Professor of Religious
Studies, Lancaster University
Capitalism, Man/Masculinity

NEAL ROBINSON Professor of Islamic Studies,
University of Wales Lampeter
Islam

JOHN ROGERS Associate Professor of English, Yale
University
John Milton

JOHN W. ROGERSON Emeritus Professor of Biblical
Studies, University of Sheffield
Higher Criticism, Biblical Law

JAMES F. ROSS Professor of Philosophy and Law,
University of Pennsylvania
Analogy

CHRISTOPHER ROWLAND Dean Ireland's Professor
of the Exegesis of the Holy Scripture, University
of Oxford
Apocalypticism, Book of Revelation

ROBERT RUNCIE Formerly Archbishop of
Canterbury
Canterbury

CHRISTOPHER RYAN Professor of Italian, School of
European Studies, University of Sussex
Dante Alighieri

JAMES A. SANDERS President, Ancient Biblical
Manuscript Center; Professor Emeritus of
Biblical Studies, Claremont School of Theology;
Professor Emeritus of Religion, Claremont
Graduate School
Dead Sea Scrolls

JOHN SAWYER Professor of Biblical and Jewish
Studies, Lancaster University
Isaiah

ROBERT P. SCHARLEMANN Commonwealth Professor of Religious Studies, University of Virginia
Paul Tillich

ALFRED SCHINDLER Professor, Faculty of
Theology, University of Zürich
Zwingli

TAD M. SCHMALTZ Associate Professor of
Philosophy, Duke University
Descartes and Cartesianism

SANDRA SCHNEIDERS, IHM Professor of New
Testament and Spirituality, Graduate
Theological Union, Berkeley
Religious Life, Obedience

MATTHEW SCHOFFELEERS Formerly Professor of
Anthropology, Free University of Amsterdam
Anthropology

CAROLINE SCHRÖDER Assistant for Systematic
Theology, University of Bonn
Jonathan Edwards

CHRISTOPH SCHWÖBEL Professor of Systematic
Theology and Director, Ecumenical Institute,
University of Heidelberg
Grace, Judgement, Mercy, Merit

TURID KARLSEN SEIM Professor of Theology (New
Testament), University of Oslo
Luke/Acts, Parable

ANDREW SHANKS Theological Consultant,
Diocese of York
*City, Depiction of Jesus, Georg Wilhelm Friedrich
Hegel, Friedrich Wilhelm Nietzsche, Peace*

PATRICK SHERRY Reader in Philosophical
Theology, Lancaster University
Graham Greene, The Novel,

ROGER L. SHINN Reinhold Niebuhr Professor
Emeritus of Social Ethics, Union Theological
Seminary, New York
Reinhold and H. Richard Niebuhr

A. W. RICHARD SIPE Psychotherapist, researcher,
and author, La Jolla, California
Celibacy

JANET MARTIN SOSKICE University Lecturer in
Theology, University of Cambridge
Fatherhood

BARBARA E. SPENSLEY Teaching Fellow in New
Testament Studies, University of Leeds
*Judaism in the 1st Christian Century, Epistle to the
Hebrews*

T. L. S. SPRIGGE Professor, Philosophy
Department, University of Edinburgh
William James

KENNETH W. STEVENSON Bishop of Portsmouth
Caroline Divines

JACQUELINE STEWART Lecturer, Department of
Theology and Religious Studies, University of
Leeds
Jacques Ellul

R. S. SUGIRTHARAJAH Senior Lecturer in Third
World Theologies, Selly Oak Colleges,
Birmingham
Indian Christian Thought

NIGEL SYKES Consultant and Honorary Senior
Lecturer in Palliative Medicine, St Christopher's
Hospice and King's College London
Death

STEPHEN SYKES Formerly Regius Professor of
Divinity, University of Cambridge
Anglican Thought

EDMOND TANG Lecturer in Missiology, University
of Birmingham
Chinese Christian Thought

MARY TANNER Formerly General Secretary,
Council for Christian Unity, General Synod of the
Church of England
Ordination

NORMAN P. TANNER, SJ Reader in Church History,
University of Oxford
*Inquisition and Holy Office, Council of Florence,
Council of Trent*

MICHAEL H. TAYLOR Professor of Social Theology,
University of Birmingham, and formerly
Director of Christian Aid
Poverty

ADRIAN THATCHER Professor of Applied Theology,
University College of St Mark and St John,
Plymouth
Sex and Sexuality

JAMES THROWER Formerly Professor of the
History of Religions, University of Aberdeen
Atheism

J.-M. ROGER TILLARD Professor of Theology,
Dominican Faculties Ottawa, Vice-Moderator of
Faith and Order
Peter

ALAN TORRANCE Professor, Faculty of Divinity,
University of St Andrews
Justification, Thomas Torrance

MARGARET TRURAN Benedictine nun of Stanbrook
Abbey, Worcester
Benedictine Thought, Virginity

KAREN B. WESTERFIELD TUCKER Assistant
Professor of Liturgical Studies, The Divinity
School, Duke University
*Advent, Calendar, Christmas, Easter, Epiphany, Lent,
Pentecost, Sunday*

CHRISTOPHER TUCKETT Lecturer in New
Testament Studies, University of Oxford
Gospel of Thomas

DENYS TURNER Norris Hulse Professor of Divinity,
University of Cambridge
Mysticism

WERNER USTORF Professor of Mission, University
of Birmingham and Selly Oak Colleges
Mission

PETER VAN INWAGEN John Cardinal O'Hara
Professor of Philosophy, University of Notre
Dame
Metaphysics

MIROSLAV VOLF Professor of Systematic Theology, Fuller Theological Seminary, Pasadena, California
Work

GEOFFREY WAINWRIGHT, CONSULTANT EDITOR Robert Earl Cushman Professor of Christian Theology, The Divinity School, Duke University
Assurance, Baptism, Ecumenical Movement, Eucharist, Faith and Order, Eberhard Jüngel, Methodist Thought, Lesslie Newbigin, John and Charles Wesley

GORDON S. WAKEFIELD Formerly Principal, Queen's College, Birmingham
Lord's Prayer, Forms of Spirituality

MICHAEL J. WALSH Librarian, Heythrop College, University of London
John Paul II

HENRY WANSBROUGH, OSB Master, St Benet's Hall, Oxford, Consultor of the Pontifical Biblical Commission
Raymond E. Brown

GRAHAM WARD Professor of Contextual Theology and Ethics, University of Manchester
Allegory, Michel de Certeau, Metaphor, Modernism, Postmodernism

KALLISTOS WARE Lecturer in Eastern Orthodox Studies, University of Oxford, and titular Bishop of Diokleia
Eastern Orthodox Theology

J. R. WATSON Professor of English, University of Durham
Hymns

FRASER WATTS Starbridge Lecturer in Theology and Natural Science, University of Cambridge
Psychology

CLAUDE WELCH Dean Emeritus and Professor of Historical Theology, Graduate Theological Union
Nineteenth Century: An Overview

ALLAN WHITE, OP Chaplain to Roman Catholics in the University of Cambridge
Dominican Thought

SUSAN J. WHITE Alberta H. and Harold L. Lunger Professor of Spiritual Resources and Disciplines, Brite Divinity School, Texas Christian University
Liturgy

BRIAN WICKER Chairman, Council on Christian Approaches to Defence and Disarmament, and Convenor, 'Commission on Security, Demilitarisation and the Arms Trade', Pax Christi International
Pacifism, War

MAURICE WILES Formerly Regius Professor of Divinity, University of Oxford
Arianism, Creeds, Heresy

MICHAEL E. WILLIAMS Formerly Head of Studies in Theology, Trinity and All Saints College, Leeds
Cinema

ROWAN WILLIAMS Archbishop of Wales
Catholicity, Resurrection, Russian Christian Thought

HADDON WILLMER Emeritus Professor of Theology, University of Leeds
Barmen Declaration, Forgiveness

PATRICK A. WILSON Associate Professor of Philosophy, Hampden-Sydney College, Virginia
Design

VINCENT L. WIMBUSH Professor of New Testament and Christian Origins, Union Theological Seminary, and Adjunct Professor of Religion, Columbia University, New York
Asceticism, Hellenistic World in the 1st Century

LINDA WOODHEAD Lecturer in Christian Studies, Lancaster University
Eve, Woman/Femininity

A. D. WRIGHT Senior Lecturer, School of History, University of Leeds
Counter-Reformation

N. THOMAS WRIGHT Canon of Westminster
Gospels

JOHN HOWARD YODER Formerly Professor of Theology, University of Notre Dame
Mennonite Thought

FRANCES YOUNG Edward Cadbury Professor of Theology, University of Birmingham
Suffering

COMPLETE LIST OF ENTRIES

ABBREVIATIONS

ARCIC	Anglican/Roman Catholic International Commission
CD	Karl Barth, *Church Dogmatics*
col/s.	Column/s
d.	died (with date)
DE	Degree on Ecumenism (Vatican II)
DV	Dei Verbum (Vatican II)
EH	Eusebius, *Ecclesiastical History*
ET	English translation
GS	Gaudium et Spes (Vatican II)
LG	Lumen Gentium (Vatican II)
LXX	Septuagint
NT	New Testament
OT	Old Testament
ST	Thomas Aquinas, *Summa Theologiae*
sv.	*sub verbo* (under the word)
vs.	versus

BIBLICAL REFERENCES

Gen.	Genesis
Exod.	Exodus
Lev.	Leviticus
Num.	Numbers
Deut.	Deuteronomy
Josh.	Joshua
Judg.	Judges
1, 2 Sam.	1, 2 Samuel
1, 2 Kgs.	1, 2 Kings
1, 2 Chr.	1, 2 Chronicles
Ps.	Psalms
Prov.	Proverbs
Eccles.	Ecclesiastes
Isa.	Isaiah
Jer.	Jeremiah
Ezek.	Ezekiel
Dan.	Daniel
Hos.	Hosea
Mic.	Micah
Zech.	Zechariah
Mal.	Malachi
1, 2 Esd.	1, 2 Esdras
Tob.	Tobit
Wisd.	Wisdom of Solomon
Ecclus.	Ecclesiasticus
1, 2 Macc.	1, 2 Maccabees
Sir.	Ecclesiaticus
Matt.	Matthew
Rom.	Romans
1, 2 Cor.	1, 2 Corinthians
Gal.	Galatians
Eph.	Ephesians
Phil.	Philippians
Col.	Colossians
1, 2 Thess.	1, 2 Thessalonians
1, 2 Tim.	1, 2 Timothy
Philem.	Philemon
Heb.	Hebrews
Jas.	James
1, 2 Pet.	1, 2 Peter
Rev.	Revelation

Abelard, Peter (1079–1142). Abelard was the most daring, and probably the cleverest, theologian and *philosopher in Western Europe in the first half of the 12th century; he was also one of the greatest logicians of all time. Born in 1079 at Le Pallet, near Nantes, he had made a name for himself as a teacher of logic by his early twenties. By 1115 he had established himself as master at the cathedral school in Paris. At this time, he had an affair with Heloise, niece of Fulbert, a canon of the cathedral, and a woman renowned for her learning. The affair ended in a secret marriage and Abelard's castration, arranged by Fulbert, who thought he was going to abandon Heloise. Abelard then became a monk and forced Heloise to become a nun. He did not, however, give up teaching, and after a period as abbot of a monastery in Brittany he was again teaching in the Paris schools c.1133–9. His teaching career was brought to an end in 1140 when Bernard of Clairvaux succeeded in having a list of statements, supposedly drawn from Abelard's works, condemned at the Council of Sens. Abelard was given protection by Peter the Venerable, abbot of Cluny, and he died at a dependency of Cluny, reconciled with the church and, possibly, also with Bernard.

Abelard's work is wide ranging: logic (commentaries on the standard logical textbooks by *Aristotle, Porphyry, and Boethius, and an independent treatise), systematic *theology, biblical exegesis, sermons, an ethical treatise and dialogue, letters, and poetry. Four aspects of it are of special, continuing relevance to Christian theology: first, his method in theology and its part in the development of scholastic theological method; second, his views about non-Christians; third, his relationship with Heloise and its effect on his ideas about female *monasticism; and fourth, his positions on particular points of Christian doctrine.

In the late 11th and early 12th centuries, theologians became increasingly concerned with the problematic issues which arose in the course of scriptural exegesis when one passage from the *bible apparently contradicts another. Discussion of these issues led gradually to the development of the question-technique—the method of setting out problems in terms of two contrary views, the arguments for each, and the counter-arguments—which is characteristic of later medieval theology. Abelard played an important part in this movement, although he was not its originator. His *Sic et non* ('Yes and No') is a dossier of passages from the bible and (mainly) the church fathers which are apparently contradictory, arranged problem by problem, so as to show clearly how some answer 'yes' and

some 'no' to the same question. In his *Theology* (Abelard produced three main versions of it: the *Theologia Summi Boni*, 1121; the *Theologia Christiana*, c.1125–6; the *Theologia Scholarium*, c.1133–6) and his commentary on Paul's letter to the Romans, he explores a number of problems where authorities seem to be opposed and argues for what he considers the correct reply.

Abelard's solutions often make use of sophisticated logical analyses, a feature they share with the work of later medieval theologians such as *Aquinas, Duns Scotus, and Ockham. It is wrong, however, to present Abelard, as some historians have done, as a logician who insisted on imposing his logical method on theology and who was concerned merely with the verbal form of theological discourse rather than its content. The links between logic and theology were already well established by the early 12th century, and Abelard was a constructive theologian, for whom the logical analysis of doctrinal statements was never more than a means to an end.

Although Abelard lived in an entirely Christian society, he was very much aware of two different categories of non-Christians: the pagans of ancient Greece and Rome, and the Jews of his own day. He read the classical Latin poets, *Plato's *Timaeus* in Latin translation, and some of Aristotle's logic. He was sure that the great ancient philosophers and poets, and the heroes and heroines they speak of, had been genuinely virtuous and were among the blessed in heaven, although they had apparently lived as pagans. Abelard justified this view, which was clearly in conflict with *Augustine, by explaining that not only did these virtuous people of antiquity worship the one true God, they had also grasped, through their reason, God's triunity; indeed, in his *Theology*, he refers to pagan prophecies of the *Trinity alongside those found in the bible. Abelard went so far as to use the austere lives of the ancient philosophers as a shaming comparison for the dissolute monks of his own day. In his *Collations* (or *Dialogue between a Christian, a Philosopher and a Jew*, c.1125–30), the 'Philosopher', who does not believe in a revealed religion, debates on equal terms with a Christian about the nature of the highest good and greatest evil. Abelard underlines the wide area of agreement between the two men. Perhaps it is not surprising that his own close pupils called him 'the Philosopher'.

Abelard also seems to have been unusually sympathetic to Jews, whom he would have encountered frequently in Paris and whose advice he sought about some points of biblical interpretation (*Jewish–Christian Relations). The Jew in the *Collations* speaks movingly of his people's sufferings. He is made to argue with, not the Christian, but the Philosopher, who claims that the Old Law adds nothing to the natural law all people grasp by reason. Although the Philosopher seems to win the argument, not all the Jew's points are answered.

Traditionally, Abelard's relations with Heloise have been regarded as a subject quite distinct from his work as a theologian and philosopher. An exchange of letters between the two, written about fifteen years after they parted, has become famous as love literature: she apparently remains unrepentantly devoted to him, despite her status as not merely a nun, but now an abbess; Abelard urges her unsuccessfully to love Christ, not him. Yet this exchange has an unromantic and theologically important ending. At Heloise's request (and in line with her detailed instructions), Abelard sends her a history of female monasticism and a new Rule for her nuns. Both these pieces recognize the dignity of *women as human beings and recognize also the need for flexibility in adapting monastic regulations intended for men to female use. Little other writing about women from the time shows such sophistication, which may have been due as much to Heloise's suggestions and influence as to Abelard himself.

Among Abelard's discussions of particular points of Christian doctrine, three are especially important: the Trinity, Christ's work, and the nature of sin. The central concern of his *Theology*, in all its versions, is the Trinity. He holds that, when we talk of *God's power, wisdom, and love, we are talking respectively of the Father, the Son, and the Holy Spirit. He also insists that triunity is a feature of how God really is, not just a reflection of how we understand him, and he struggles to find a way of explaining how something can be at once one and three.

Abelard develops his position on Christ's work—how Christ redeemed humanity—mainly in his commentary on Romans. He rejects *Anselm of Canterbury's view that God demanded the sacrifice of a God-Man. Rather, Abelard argues that by laying down his life for others, Christ gave an example of supreme *love which people could imitate and so be enabled to gain *salvation. It would be wrong however, to draw the conclusion that he thought the *Atonement merely exemplific: Christ's *Incarnation and crucifixion were necessary for human salvation (see CROSS).

In his *Know Thyself* (or *Ethics*), Abelard analyses the concept of *sin. He balances emphasis on the subjective element—sin is identified with contempt for God, as manifest in intended action—with an insistence that through *reason every adult at all times has known many of God's laws. He also recognizes that we often do not wish to perform a sinful act (for instance, murder in self-defence), but we are guilty none the less if we consent to performing it.

Abelard was one of the Christian thinkers who went furthest to adapt Christian teachings to his philosophical views about how a just, benevolent, and omnipotent God orders the universe. It is not surprising that his influence in the *Middle Ages was more on method than in doctrine.   **John Marenbon**

Abelard, P., *Christian Theology* (1948), trans. J. R. McCallum (partial version of *Theologia Christiana*).
—— *Opera Theologica*, ed. E. Buytaert and C. J. Mews (1969–87) (Latin texts of *Theology* (all versions) and of *Commentary on Romans*), i–iii.
—— *The Letters of Abelard and Heloise*, ed. and trans. B. Radice (1974).
—— *Ethical Writings*, ed. and trans. P. Spade (1995) (translation of *Know Thyself* and *Collations*).
Clanchy, M., *Peter Abelard* (1997).
Jolivet, J., *La Théologie d'Abélard* (1996).
Marenbon, J., *The Philosophy of Peter Abelard* (1997).
Mews, C. J., *Peter Abelard* (1995).

Abhishiktananda

Abhishiktananda (1910–73). Henri le Saux was a Breton Benedictine monk at Kergonan where he was ordained in 1935. For years he felt a call to help establish contemplative *monastic life in the *Indian church and in 1948 he joined a brilliant French scholar-priest in Tamilnadu, Jules Monchanin, who shared le Saux's desire to live a monastic life 'in closest possible conformity with the traditions of Indian sannyasa'. 'Total Indianization' was the rule from the start, imitating the 17th-century example of de Nobili and the 20th-century example of Vincent Lebbe in *China. Together they adopted the customs of a sannyasi, sitting and sleeping on a mat, walking barefoot and hatless, while studying Sanskrit, the Hindu scriptures, and Tamil. Visits to one of the great modern *Hindu sages, Sri Ramana Maharshi, in his ashram at Tiruvannamalai proved decisive in shattering any belief that the *Holy Spirit was at work only in the church.

In 1950, le Saux and Monchanin established a new ashram at Shantivanam (grove of peace), at the same time adopting new names, in accordance with Indian tradition. Henceforth le Saux would be Abhishiktananda ('Bliss of the Anointed One, the Lord'). As the years passed, his ever deeper identification with Hindu *spirituality and pursuit of the absolute non-dualism of *Advaita* made him 'too Hindu for Christians' yet still, he complained, 'too Christian for Hindus'. He struggled to be loyal to the heights of both traditions but the 'gulf' between them tore him apart. Feeling intellectually far more 'oriental' than 'Greek', he frequently agonized over whether he was still a Christian or should continue celebrating mass. Even Monchanin found it 'mysterious' that a Christian should insist on taking a Hindu sage as his guru.

Abhishiktananda's spiritual teaching made use, equally well or equally inadequately, of either Christian or Sanskritic terminology. At the end of his life he could write 'all notions about Christ's personality, ontology, history, etc, have disappeared. And I find his real mystery shining in every awakened man, in every mythos', but he daily celebrated mass and a visitor remarked how 'His whole person and all that he did literally radiated the Presence of *God, he was all transparency to the Lord.' Abhishiktananda could be awkward and difficult to live with; no disciples stayed with him for long; yet through the power of his personality, teaching, and multifarious writing in many languages he profoundly influenced a multitude of people to re-explore at the deepest level of personal experience the Christian–Hindu 'gulf'. He represents at its most intense the struggle within *twentieth-century Christianity to identify with, rather than deny, the spiritual depths within non-Christian *religion.

See also GRIFFITHS, BEDE.   **Adrian Hastings**

Abhishiktananda, *Saccidananda: A Christian Approach to Advaitic Experience* (1974).
de Lubac, Henri, *Images de l'abbé Monchanin* (1966).
Mataji, V. (ed.), *Abhishiktananda: The Man and his Message* (1986).
Stuart, James, *Swami Abhishiktananda* (1995).

abortion. The Christian tradition has taken a generally negative view of abortion, but the moral basis and perceived implications of this negative view have varied greatly. In the early church abortion and *contraception were often seen as broadly equivalent, both involving interference with the natural reproductive process. But the tendency to conflate abortion with contraception, and even on similar grounds with male masturbation, declined in the face of the biological discovery of the mother's role as more than just an incubator for the male 'seed'. With the recognition of conception as a distinct and crucial event, abortion was seen as morally far more serious than contraception, involving a threat to life and therefore, arguably, equivalent to homicide. When seen as homicide, abortion has naturally been subject to an almost total prohibition, the only generally agreed exception being where it is necessary to save the mother's life. Within the Roman Catholic communion even this exception has needed the sanction of the doctrine of double effect: where the abortion is not directly intended, but is only a foreseen but unintended consequence of a surgical intervention primarily intended to save the mother's life (e.g. the removal of a cancerous uterus or of a fallopian tube containing an ectopic pregnancy).

The perception of abortion as homicide, however, depended also on the question of 'ensoulment': at what point in its development the foetus becomes animated with a rational human *soul. For many centuries a distinction between 'ensouled' and 'unensouled' foetuses was widely accepted in the western church, based partly on *Aristotelian theory (that the male foetus was 'unformed' until around 40 days after conception, and the female until around 90 days) and partly on a mistranslation in the Septuagint of the one passage in the OT which has a clear relevance to abortion, namely Exodus 21: 22–3 (see Dunstan 1988 for historical background, and Wilkinson 1988: 232, 252–8, for a sober assessment of other biblical passages that have been thought relevant to the abortion debate). No doubt this 'developmental view', which takes the moral gravity of abortion as partly a function of the foetus's stage of development, was also partly motivated by the evident difference between early and late miscarriages: when abortion involves the death of a visibly baby-like being it is natural to see this as a matter of considerable gravity, far removed from the loss of a tiny, unrecognizable embryo.

The Eastern Orthodox church followed Basil in rejecting any developmental view and hence in condemning abortion, from conception onwards, as involving the destruction of a being made in the image of God. Many Roman Catholics and Reformers took a similar view (*Calvin, for example, saw the predestined soul as existing from conception), but in the west the conception was not fully identified as the morally crucial point until the 19th century, influenced in part by the definition of the doctrine of the Immaculate Conception by Pius IX (with the implication that *Mary had a sinless soul from the moment of conception). Such an emphasis on conception implies a sharp moral distinction between abortion and contraception, and although the latter continues to be condemned by some (notably within the Roman Catholic tradition) as contrary to nature, this now tends to be tempered by a generally more positive attitude to *sex as an important element in the marital relationship independently of its reproductive role. Few now would claim that abortion and contraception are morally on a par, though controversy remains regarding methods of 'contraception' (e.g. the intra-uterine device) whose effect is to impede implantation and development of the conceptus rather than to prevent conception.

Not surprisingly, the modern debate on abortion has moved away from questions of biblical and patristic interpretation and theories of ensoulment. Changes in attitudes to sex and broader cultural changes, perhaps most notably the enhanced status of women, increased respect for personal autonomy in moral decisions, and, in particular, the perception of reproductive freedom as a 'right', have emphasized issues other than the individual foetus's 'moral status', which tended to dominate earlier discussions. Biological and medical discoveries have also played an increasingly important role: knowledge of the early development of the foetus has made some traditional positions harder to maintain (e.g. in respect of soul individuation where twinning occurs), while the possibility of prenatal diagnosis of serious genetic and other abnormalities has added a new dimension to the debate by linking it with the issue of *euthanasia in cases where abortion might be thought in the interests of the foetus itself. This link is strengthened by the discovery that a high proportion of fertilized ova are spontaneously aborted in early pregnancy, often owing to chromosomal abnormalities. Such wastage seems in tension with the view that the human soul is created at conception, but it also makes any absolutist prohibition on abortion crucially dependent on the controversial distinction between acts and omissions which has featured prominently in debates on euthanasia. Without this distinction, anyone placing an absolute value on human life from conception seems committed to the saving of millions of prenatally terminated lives.

A less overt but probably more pervasive influence of modern biological knowledge has been that of the theory of *evolution, implying a continuity within the created order which, whilst raising significantly the perceived status of *animals (both in Christian and secular thought), has at the same time tended to lower that of the human foetus by raising questions regarding the traditionally assumed moral precedence of humanity as such. Much of the modern philosophical debate on abortion seems predicated on a desire to avoid pernicious 'speciesism', and accordingly to attribute a special status to the foetus (making its death more morally significant than that of an animal) only if its intrinsic qualities can justify such an attribution. Hence a number of recent writers (Glover 1977; Tooley 1983; Harris 1985) have developed theories of *personhood, arguing that a being's 'moral status' depends not on its species but rather on its possession of such qualities as feelings and desires, rationality, self-consciousness, capacities for action and for relationships. Since a foetus has few if any of these qualities, and none when first conceived, such writers typically see early abortion as morally unproblematic, and late abortion as at worst comparable with the killing of an animal. Some have even been prepared to countenance infanticide.

The standard response to such arguments, not confined to Christian writers but according well with Christian principles, has been to focus not on the human foetus's *actual* properties but instead on its *potential* properties, by which it can clearly be distinguished from an animal and correspondingly accorded far greater moral weight. The main difficulty with this response has been in maintaining a clear line between abortion and contraception, given that the human ovum and sperm, prior to conception, have a similar potential. Attempts to draw such a line have been made (Johnstone 1982; Stone 1987) by appealing to different senses of potentiality, as that the conceptus has the potential to *become* a human, whereas the ovum and sperm have only the potential to *produce* one. Despite these complexities the modern debate has tended to centre around this very traditional issue: is abortion morally similar to contraception or the killing of an animal, or to the killing of a child?

It may be that the only way beyond the extreme polarization which has characterized the abortion debate is to recognize that as a moral issue it is equivalent neither to contraception nor to homicide. It is unique, far less straightforward than commonly represented, and not best judged in the all-or-nothing terms implied by the usual language of 'rights' and 'moral status'. Nowhere else do we find the existence of a determinate living being lacking the familiar morally significant characteristics (sentience etc.) but with a clear potential to acquire them, and in no other circumstance is one living being so totally dependent on another and with so great an impact on her autonomy and life-plans. Viewed in this light, the considerations advanced by both sides can perhaps be seen not as flatly opposed but as complementary, leading back towards the more moderate developmental approach characteristic of the church's thought prior to the 19th century, but based now on moral considerations rather than on theories of soulhood. The anti-abortionists' principle of potentiality, for example, naturally lends itself to a developmental rather than an absolutist interpretation. The pro-abortionists' appeals to personhood do not exclude other developmental moral considerations, including a typically Christian respect for human life and for the affections and perceptions of family and community, which can serve quite properly to distinguish even quite early abortion from the killing of an animal, without objectionable 'speciesism'. These considerations can make even early abortion seriously regrettable without implying that it has the moral gravity of homicide. Very late abortion, on the other hand, might well appear hard to distinguish from the killing of a new-born baby. Most Christians, innocent of philosophical theory and ecclesiastical authority, would probably take such a developmental position, and it is difficult to see how any reasonably broad consensus can be achieved except in this (admittedly complex and messy) middle ground.

See also MEDICAL ETHICS; REPRODUCTIVE TECHNOLOGY.

Peter Millican

Devine, P. E., *The Ethics of Homicide* (1978).

Dunstan, G. R., 'The Human Embryo in the Western Moral Tradition', in G. R. Dunstan and M. J. Seller (eds.), *The Status of the Human Embryo: Perspectives from Moral Tradition* (1988), 39–57.

Dworkin, R. M., *Life's Dominion: An Argument about Abortion and Euthanasia* (1993).

Glover, J., *Causing Death and Saving Lives* (1977).

Harris, J., *The Value of Life* (1985).

Johnstone, B., 'The Moral Status of the Embryo', in W. Walters and P. Singer (eds.), *Test-Tube Babies* (1982), 49–56.

Millican, P. J. R., 'The Complex Problem of Abortion', in D. R. Bromham, M. E. Dalton, J. C. Jackson, and P. J. R. Millican (eds.), *Ethics in Reproductive Medicine* (1992), 161–88.

Stone, J. 'Why Potentiality Matters', *Canadian Journal of Philosophy*, 17 (1987), 815–29.

Tooley, M., *Abortion and Infanticide* (1983).

Wilkinson, J., *Christian Ethics in Health Care* (1988).

Abraham is the first recipient of the promise to *Israel. He is given this name, taken to mean 'father of a multitude', as part of the story in Genesis 17 where *God makes a *covenant with him, promising him countless descendants and the land of Canaan as an everlasting possession. The sign of this covenant is that he should circumcise himself and all the males in his household. The promise is made to him and to his descendants (literally 'his seed') for ever. Under his original name of Abram, he was a dweller in the Mesopotamian city of Ur until, as Gen. 12 relates, God summoned him to leave it for an unspecified destination. At that point, God made him an unconditional promise that his descendants would be a great nation.

No motive is given for the singling out by God of this one man to be the bearer of the promise. The consequences are not simply of benefit to Abraham; he is to become a blessing to all nations (Gen. 12: 3). Herein lies a tension inherent in the Abrahamic traditions between exclusivity and universality which is subsequently taken up in different ways. The *Old Testament is clear that the promise to Abraham and the mission it entails devolve on his descendants, the people of Israel. This motif is one which those writings dealing with the aftermath of the exile, most notably *Isaiah, seize upon as reason to hope for restoration (41: 8) and indeed an exilic origin for the tradition has been suggested. Whatever its origin, it allows the prophet to offer the exiles the consolation that God will not allow Abraham's descendants to lose their unique favour in his sight despite their manifest disobedience. Yet this restoration is not just directed at Israel. It will draw all the nations to worship at Zion.

The problem for Christian thinkers is to show the continuity between this founding promise and the gospel story. This requires them to explain how the promise has been transferred from Abraham's biological descendants to a *church which is increasingly made up of Gentiles. In *Romans 4, *Paul makes much of the Septuagint reading of Gen. 15: 6 that Abraham's faith in God's promises 'was reckoned to him as righteousness'. This allows Paul to argue that belief in itself, not good deeds, is the key to being judged righteous by God. Abraham is not chosen for any special virtue or for his adherence to the Law. Paul also reads this story as implying that circumcision is the seal, not the condition, of Abraham's acceptance. Indeed, Abraham's importance for Christians is that he gives a model of someone who finds favour with God before the institution of circumcision and the giving of the Law, thus demonstrating God's acceptance of those who are not enrolled in the Mosaic covenant (see LAW, BIBLICAL).

But how can Gentile Christians claim to be the heirs to the promise to Abraham? Paul's answer in Galatians depends on interpreting the phrase Abraham 'and his seed' as pointing to one specific descendant as the inheritor, because the word 'seed' is singular (Gal. 3: 16). *Jesus is that descendant. *Matthew's decision to begin his genealogy of Jesus with Abraham (1: 1) may reflect the same desire to demonstrate that Jesus is Abraham's heir.

This gives strength to Paul's central argument that it is those who are baptized in Christ, rather than Abraham's biological offspring, who represent the true sons of Abraham. The baptized Gentile is a participant in the promise of blessing (Gal. 3: 7, 14) by virtue of making the same sort of faithful response that Abraham did and thereby becoming incorporated in Christ.

This concept is taken further when Abraham himself, and therefore all that depends upon him, is assimilated into the gospel story in *John. Jesus' startling claims in that gospel that 'Before Abraham was, I am' and that Abraham 'rejoiced that he would see my day' (8: 58, 56) represent the clearest statements attributed to Jesus himself that imply his pre-existence. They serve to underline the priority of Jesus over any claims of *authority based on antiquity but also bring the whole of the subsequent OT tradition into the embrace of the new dispensation.

While Paul in Romans is careful to insist that Israel retains the privileges of the children of the promise, a further inference is drawn by others. If Christ alone is the seed referred to in the promise, then Israel's claim is void. Passages in the *New Testament deal disparagingly with those Jews who assert that the mere fact of their lineal descent from Abraham makes them the heirs of the covenant. *John the Baptist's retort that God can make children for Abraham out of stones (Luke 3: 8) is a particularly stark example. Subsequent Christian thought was for the most part quite content to follow the logic of this disinheritance.

Here the Christian reworking of the tension between universality and exclusivity becomes manifest. It is the claim to be the true spiritual children of Abraham that allows the church to take to itself the promised destiny of Israel. Abraham, as a 'blessing to the nations', acceptable without circumcision or being bound to the Law, is the guarantor of the claims of non-Jewish Christians to inherit the kingdom. The church has first relied on the universality of that promise to argue for the inclusion of Gentiles as Abraham's heirs. Having staked its claim to represent the true children of Abraham, it has often turned the tables and invoked the exclusive aspect of the promise to argue that those outside the Christian fold, particularly the Jews themselves, now have no claim to Abraham's inheritance (see JEWISH–CHRISTIAN RELATIONS).

To be Abraham's child is, the OT makes clear, not an unalloyed blessing. Ishmael, his son by the Egyptian slave Hagar, is banished to the desert and becomes a *type of those rejected by God, most notably in Paul's most explicit piece of *allegory in Gal. 4: 22–31. Yet the story does also contain the assurance that Ishmael will be the father of a great nation and implies that he is under God's protection (Gen. 21: 18–20).

Isaac, the son of the promise, born to Abraham's elderly wife Sarah, becomes the unwitting focus of Abraham's great test of faith, now often known by its Jewish name, the *Aqedah* (the 'binding' of Isaac). The story as recorded in Gen. 22 hinges on God's command that Abraham should *sacrifice his beloved son. Abraham obeys to the point of raising his knife above the bound body of his son, but at the crucial moment God steps in to reprieve Isaac and restore him to Abraham. For the author of *Hebrews, this restoration is a supreme example of the rewards of faith alone (11: 17). James, by contrast, takes this as the vindication of his insistence that works are necessary to complete *faith (2: 21). Abraham's *obedience is visibly demonstrated. This story becomes a crux in the long-running argument among Christian thinkers over whether faith itself is sufficient for *salvation or whether salvation depends on the accomplishment of loving deeds.

Such a tale of a *father offering up his son at God's command only to be reprieved has deep and disturbing resonances. Beginning with the *art of the Christian catacombs, it has continued to fascin-ate artists and writers but it has features which make it theologically problematic. Even among early Christian thinkers the reference in one version of Hebrews to it as a type of the *Resurrection is not widely explored, though Clement and Tertullian do follow this line. *Augustine sees Isaac carrying the wood for sacrifice as a type of Christ carrying his *cross, but it is the ram, not Isaac, who becomes the type of the crucified Jesus. The implication that Abraham is the crucifier is not developed but this illustrates the awkwardness of the story for later thinkers.

The apparent immorality of this intended murder, whether blamed on God or Abraham, was a stumbling block for many in the acceptance of the OT, as indeed were Abraham's evasions over his marriage to Sarah when danger threatened. In later centuries, *Kant offered a stern reproach to Abraham for supposing that such an immoral order could originate in God and *Kierkegaard's profound if difficult meditation on the story in his *Fear and Trembling* gave rise to his notion of the 'teleological suspension of the ethical'.

Other incidents in Abraham's story have been the subject of Christian interpretation. The three *angels who meet Abraham at Mamre and whom he seems to address at times in the singular as 'Lord' are commonly interpreted as an OT type of the *Trinity, most notably in the *icon by Rublev. His encounter with *Melchisedek is similarly interpreted as a meeting with Christ and a prefiguration of the *Eucharist.

The Lucan parable of the poor beggar Lazarus taken to Abraham's bosom (16: 19–31) together with Jesus' declaration that the God of Abraham, Isaac, and Jacob is a God of the living, not the dead, explicitly imply that Abraham is one of the community of the resurrected (20: 37–8) which gives the patriarch a particular place in the Christian topography of the afterlife. *Protestant piety with its suspicion of saints seems particularly to have taken to this human and fatherly image of the heavenly state. Abraham's story of the individual faithful to God in the face of ancestral tradition has a particular appeal to reformers of every age.

In the late 20th century, Jewish thought in the aftermath of the *Holocaust has turned to the anguish of the *Aqedah* as a potent symbol and has in turn shaped Christian reflection. Abraham has taken on a new significance as the common denominator of the Jewish, Christian, and *Islamic traditions, often bracketed together as the Abrahamic faiths (see for instance, *Vatican II's *Nostra Aetate*, 3–4). This reminder of solidarity is offered by some theologians as the key to developing *rapprochement* between the three communities. The promise that Genesis holds out to the estranged son Ishmael may be a point of contact with Muslims, but the Qur'anic reading of this incident is rather different. The patriarchal narratives of the OT are graphic reminders that being members of one family is no guarantee of mutual tolerance, but also of the forces that lie deeper than rationality and theological debate in the life of religious communities.

Hugh S. Pyper

Kuschel, K.-J., *Abraham: A Symbol of Hope for Jews, Christians, and Muslims*, ET (1995).

Van Seters, J., *Abraham in History and Tradition* (1975).

Wilson, M. R., *Our Father Abraham: Jewish Roots of the Christian Faith* (1989).

Acts of the Apostles, see LUKE–ACTS.

Adam, the first man, is named only in the *creation stories of *Genesis 2–3. Although the creation of *man and *woman forms the climax of Gen. 1, there no names are given. Even in chapters 2–3 it is a matter of dispute as to when the word *adam*, a standard Hebrew term for *humanity in general, should be taken as a proper name. Outside these chapters, the only unequivocal mention of Adam in the *Old Testament is at the head of the great genealogical lists which form the first part of 1 Chronicles. This lack of subsequent reference to a character and a story which became central to Christian thought is quite striking.

Genesis 2–3 recounts how Adam is moulded from earth and given life by *God's breath. He names the animals. From his rib the woman *Eve is created. Together they tend the Garden of Eden until Eve is tempted by the serpent and induces Adam to eat the forbidden fruit of the tree of the knowledge of good and *evil. This leads to their banishment from the garden and the penalty of hard *work in the world.

Modern scholarship is virtually unanimous that these chapters come from a different source from Gen. 1. Although this is a recent critical insight, a sense of some mismatch in the biblical account of human creation has long informed the theological discussion of the nature of Adam. Gen. 1 gives a picture of the human creature made in the image and likeness of God, simultaneously male and female, as the culmination of creation. This seems rather different from that offered in Gen. 2 of a creature made of earth (in Hebrew *adamah*) from whom the woman is later detached. Is Adam the ideal human, or an unfinished creature rough-hewn from clay? How are the two accounts to be read as one?

The Jewish *apocrypha and other non-canonical writings reveal a spectrum of interpretations of the story. Adam is protected by *Wisdom according to Wisdom 10: 1 but Ecclesiasticus 24: 28 makes it clear that his understanding was imperfect. Philo writes of a heavenly Adam who is the type of Adam in the flesh, his *Platonic way of harmonizing Gen. 1 and 2, and the idea of a cosmic Adam, perhaps destined to be restored at the end time, is to be found in *apocalyptic texts and in later rabbinic writings.

It is *Paul who takes up the theme of Adam in the *New Testament, developing a whole theology of *salvation out of the similarities and contrasts between Adam and Christ, or, in Paul's terminology, the Old and New Adams. Adam is a type prefiguring Christ, he argues in Romans 5: 14. In 1 Corinthians 15, the link is made clearer. As all died in Adam, so all will live in Christ (1 Cor. 15: 20); Adam is the man of earth who became a living creature, Christ is the man from heaven who himself has become a life-giving spirit (1 Cor. 15: 45). As Adam is the firstborn of men, so Christ is the first to be resurrected. Indeed, God becomes *incarnate in order to reverse the disaster brought about by Adam's *sin.

This theme is not developed in the rest of the NT, however. Of the *gospel writers, only *Luke mentions Adam in his version of *Jesus' genealogy where the line is traced back to 'Seth, son of Adam, son of God'. This identification of Adam as son of God gives the linear genealogy the completeness of a circle and perhaps implies a cryptic acceptance of Pauline *typology.

Two major strands of theological interpretation of Adam appear in later tradition. Both develop from reflection on Gen. 1: 26, where God announces that humankind is to be made in his own image and likeness, in the light of the stories of Gen. 2–3 . In one under-

standing, this verse is taken to mean that Adam in his original state is the most glorious of created beings, embodying the full image and likeness of his creator, a view which seems to have biblical support in Ecclus. 49: 16. *Augustine, the most influential of those who take this position, lays out Adam's perfections in this unfallen state. He is immortal, incorruptible, morally infallible, and untainted by desire.

The problem then is to account for Adam's *fall from perfection, or in different terms, to give an account which does not leave the risk that even man redeemed in Christ could fall again. Ultimately, most such theologies resort to divine inscrutability as their last word. This account also tends to equate *sexual desire with the fallen state, a position that has wide ethical and *pastoral ramifications. Augustine notoriously argues that through his semen Adam's sin and the guilt it incurs is transmitted to all of his children. His interpretation, which leaves no room for individual freedom to choose or reject the good, was fiercely contested at the time, notably by Julian of Eclanum, but came to be seen as orthodox in the west.

The other approach, more characteristic of the east and best represented by *Irenaeus, gives a different interpretation of the same verse by arguing that the mention of both image and likeness implies some differentiation between these terms. Adam's nature was indeed created free and rational in the *image* of God, but he had yet to attain the perfection in the *Holy Spirit which would constitute true *likeness* to God. The distinction here mirrors the difference between the perfect man of Gen. 1 and the naive gardener of Gen. 2 and 3. The Fall and its consequences then are interpreted as a drastic, and in some views inevitable, schooling for an Adam who is not a perfect being in the sense of being finished but more resembles a *child with its potential for growth.

For much of the course of Christian thought, Adam has held his place as the unique historical ancestor common to every human being, a position enhanced by the traditional view that the transmission of life is through the male alone. He brought sin, *death, and alienation on his children but is honoured as representing our potential while at the same time being condemned for creating our predicament. A fund of legend grew up around him in answer to such questions as: was he circumcised? (Justin Martyr thought not); did he have a navel? (Sir Thomas Browne knew he did not); where was he buried? *Origen began a later much elaborated tradition that Adam's grave was beneath the site of the crucifixion (see Cross) thus reinforcing the typological links between Adam's bringing of death and Christ's defeat of it.

The *myth of the first man came under serious assault from two directions in the *nineteenth century although scepticism over the specifically biblical and legendary account had developed much earlier. Biology produced the theory of *evolution which postulated that humankind arose by natural selection from ape-like ancestors with no act of special creation and, indeed, with no clearly identifiable 'first' human being. At the same time, comparative mythology revealed the similarities in structure and detail between the Genesis story and the myths of neighbouring cultures, in its own way undermining the unique authority of the biblical account.

Some representatives of Christian thought have sought to mount a rearguard action against evolutionary theory, with limited credibility. Denial of the historicity of Adam and the Fall was still condemned in Pius XII's encyclical *Humani Generis* (1950). Otherwise the answer has been one or other modern version of the long-standing interpretation of the Genesis story as an allegory of psychological and spiritual processes at work in each human being. What has proved particularly difficult to retain, however, is the ontological emphasis of earlier theologies. The organic solidarity of humankind as the children of one human father, Adam, is threatened if he is superseded. Even more importantly, the notion of a fundamental human nature in which each of us is ontologically grounded and in which we participate as the children of Adam is lost. *Athanasius, for one, bases his incarnational theology on the concept that by being born in the flesh Christ has taken on and redeemed this fundamental human nature that was warped by Adam's sin. As each human being is a participant in that nature, the Son's *Incarnation brought about the possibility of a radical ontological change in the most concrete terms in every human being. Take away Adam, however, and such ontological claims become hard to defend. This is one part of a complex of philosophical problems in such an account in more recent Christian thought, and finding a way to express this in contemporary terms is a more important theological task than has yet been fully recognized.

Reinstating Adam, however, must also take account of *feminist Christian thinkers who have found Adam an inexhaustible provocation. The creation of Eve from Adam's rib is interpreted in 1 Timothy 2: 13 as giving a natural supremacy to males. To counter this, the Genesis story may simply be abandoned as an outworn myth deliberately created to bolster patriarchy. For those concerned to rescue the biblical tradition, an alternative is to reinterpret it by postulating that the word *adam*, with its derivation from the Hebrew *adamah* ('earth'), may better be translated as an androgynous 'earth being'. Sexual differentiation only occurs when the female is split off, leaving a male remnant. The equality of human beings made male and female in God's image and likeness in Gen. 1 tends to be stressed as a key to the reading of Gen. 2 and 4. The old tension is revisited in a way reminiscent of earlier *Gnostic interpretations.

Adam continues to fascinate *artists and philosophers as a vehicle for exploring human experience in its pristine state. His role as the first namer and user of *language has a particular importance for poets. As a mythic figure, he still informs western culture in its attempts to account for the nobility and perversity of humankind.

Hugh S. Pyper

Cunningham, A., *Adam* (1968).
Kreitzer, L. J., *Prometheus and Adam: Enduring Symbols of the Human Situation* (1994).
Pagels, E., *Adam, Eve and the Serpent* (1988).
York, A., 'Adam' in D. L. Jeffrey, (ed.), *A Dictionary of Biblical Tradition in English Literature* (1992).

Advent, like *Lent, has a complex history. Each apparently developed as a period of preparation for a feast, though Advent's function as a prelude to the *sacrament of *baptism may be questionable. Through *fasting and other *ascetical disciplines, this season generally looked forward to the celebration of the Lord's nativity, hence the use of the Latin *adventus* ('coming') among western Christians. Lectionaries and ecclesiastical legislation from before the 8th century indicate that what became known as Advent could include as many as forty fast days, but by the 11th century it had been almost universally narrowed in the west to the four weeks

before *Christmas. The theme of Christ's first coming in the fullness of *time had by then been broadened to include the expectation of his second coming to *judge the living and the dead. In Advent, therefore, are met the beginning and end of the story of human *redemption.

The twofold aspect of Christ's coming is neatly expressed in the 'Great Os' or 'Major Antiphons' (*antiphonae majores*), anonymous poems written around the 9th century for the pre-Christmas *liturgy, and in the 20th century still utilized as antiphons for the Magnificat at evening prayer during the week before Christmas, and incorporated into the hymn 'O Come, O Come, Emmanuel'. Each of the seven antiphons, beginning with a vocative 'O', connects an invocation of the Expected One of *Israel with a petition for the Saviour's return; 'come' covers the longing expressed for both advents. For example:

> O come, Thou Key of David, come,
> And open wide our heavenly home.

Medieval attention to the second advent was maintained year round in the architecture and ornamentation of church buildings, contrasting the tenderness of the first coming in the nativity with graphic visual reminders that at the end of the age Christ would come again to judge the righteous and the unrighteous. Different artistic media were selected to convey the sense of dread and fulfilment associated with the last day: a large mosaic on the interior west wall at Torcello; the carved tympanum in the south-transept portal at Chartres; and the doomsday mural painting on the chancel arch in St Thomas's church in Salisbury. Some recapturing of this sense of the second advent would provide a corrective to the commercialism of the tinsel Christmas characteristic of late *capitalism.

See also Arts, Visual. **Karen B. Westerfield Tucker**

Alexander, J. N., *Waiting for the Coming* (1993).
Cowley, P., *Advent* (1960).

Adventism. Adventists look for the second coming of Christ to fulfil gospel texts such as Matthew 24 and Mark 13 which refer to it (see Eschatology). The first Christians expected it immediately (1 Thess. 4: 14–18) and the expectation has returned from time to time, sometimes even with a date set for it. Modern Adventists are an organized denomination which arose after a major disappointment. Christ did not come in 1844, though careful arithmetic based on the book of *Daniel had suggested he would. The followers of the *millenarian preacher William Miller (1782–1849) regrouped and carried on. Their close literal reading of the bible also led them to keep the Jewish Sabbath instead of *Sunday, hence Seventh Day Adventists. (There were already Seventh Day *Baptists.) Such breaks with the tradition and scholarship of western Christianity were commonplace in the democratic free-for-all in religion in the new *North American republic.

By 1848 there were Seventh Day Adventist congregations, believing that Christ's coming was 'near', and that the 'cleansing of the sanctuary' expected on earth in 1844 took place then in *heaven. By 1863 they were a formal denomination. They had had a printing press since 1852: these were eagerly expository Christians. Their leading writer was Ellen G. White (née Harmon, 1827–1915), who, half-educated and a chronic invalid, could, when inspired, see 2,000 *visions, preach and lecture fluently, and write large, best-selling books. She was an example of the scope for a creative, assertive *woman in a relatively fluid new denomination in the later 19th century. Contrast her with the similar, but much more marginalized, Joanna Southcott (1750–1814) in Britain. The Adventists were convinced Ellen White was a true *prophet, and had to check themselves by saying that acceptance of her writings was not 'mandatory to church fellowship'.

The collected works of Ellen White amount to 100,000 pages, and shaped Adventist thinking. Their theology shares the commonplaces of its Baptist background, and shows what might be called a Judaizing streak. It has the technical novelty of denying that sinners have immortal *souls. Only Christians shall rise. Adventists pay tithes generously and abstain from some of the minor pleasures of life. Mrs White's interests turned to health reform, and in 1866 she set up the Battle Creek Sanitarium, the first ever. 'Grains, fruits, nuts and vegetables constitute the diet chosen for us by our Creator,' she wrote, so it is apt that the best-known name in Adventism is Kellogg, as in Corn Flakes, though J. H. Kellogg left the Adventists in 1907.

Adventists are pertinacious *missionaries around the globe, with more than 6 million members worldwide. Loma Linda University in California has specialized in training medical missionaries. The Adventist family includes the Worldwide Church of God, which keeps the feasts of the Jewish calendar and whose periodical *Plain Truth* is familiar. Slightly more removed are the Jehovah's Witnesses.

These are Christians who claim to know 'the approximate time of Christ's return', and it is soon. They find the signs of the end in modern *history. Many other Christians sometimes think Adventist thoughts.

Alistair Mason

Ball, Bryan W., *The English Connection: The Puritan Roots of the Seventh Day Adventist Belief* (1980).
Neufeld, D. F. (ed.), *Seventh Day Adventist Encyclopaedia*.
Nichol, Francis D., *The Midnight Cry* (1944).
Pearson, Michael, *Millennial Dreams and Moral Dilemmas* (1990).
Schwartz, Gary E., *Sect Ideologies and Social Status* (1970). *Seventh Day Adventists Answer Questions on Doctrine*.

African Christian thought.

The continent of Africa at the beginning of the third millennium presents a remarkable illustration of the continuing social relevance and intellectual impact of Christian thought. The shift of *Christianity's centre of gravity from the northern continents to the south during the 20th century has seen Africa playing a significant role in the resurgence of the faith. At the start of the century, it was widely held among western *missionaries that the 'traditional' religions of Africa contained no 'preparation for Christianity'. Yet by the 1970s the phenomenal surge of Christian expansion in Africa had led to the view that African Christians might transform Christianity decisively into a non-western religion.

Two distinct trends emerged in African Christian thought from the late 1950s. One, *black theology, a theology of *liberation in the African setting, was the theological dimension to the struggle for the social and political transformation in South Africa, and helped effect the demise of *apartheid in the 1990s. The other, African theology, centred on theological exploration into the indigenous cultures and pre-Christian religious traditions of African peoples. This trend developed in countries where political independence pre-empted the sociopolitical conditions that produced black theology, and aimed to relate the pre-Christian religious experience to African Christian commitment. It is important to recognize, however, that in the African view the two trends were not mutually exclusive, but rather 'a series of concentric circles of which black theology is the inner and smaller circle' (Desmond Tutu).

The theological interpretation of the traditional *religions had the effect of making African theology 'a dialogue between the African scholar and the perennial religions and spiritualities of Africa' (Hastings 1976). In so far as this effort has been pursued as a self-consciously Christian and theological activity, it may be described as having to do with African *Christian* identity. From the standpoint of the writers themselves, the traditional religions belong to the past and their theological importance resides in the fact that they were integral to the religious consciousness of the African Christian, the cultural memory vital for identity.

The nature of African traditional religion and its continuity rather than discontinuity with Christian belief became central. But continuity became a common theme because of a number of factors: the need to respond to the pervasive sense that the western value-setting for the Christian *faith had underestimated the African knowledge and sense of *God; the persistence of traditional world-views as indicating, not a remnant of a 'primitive mentality', but vital realities in the experience of Christians in all churches, and not just the so-called 'independent churches' although these had given the lead in indigenous expression of the faith; and the struggle for a theological method in a field of enquiry which had hitherto been charted largely by western *anthropological scholarship in terminology that African writers found unacceptable. African Christian theologians were approaching the subject 'not as historians of religion do, nor as anthropologists do, but as Christian theologians' (Walls 1996).

Therefore, when they described the traditional religions as 'monotheism' or 'diffused monotheism' (Bolaji Idowu on Yoruba religion), or as a *praeparatio evangelica* (John *Mbiti, reversing the verdict of the 1910 Edinburgh World Missionary Conference), these writers were drawing on their sense of belonging within Christian tradition and using categories which described their understanding of *their* pre-Christian heritage when related to *their* Christian commitment.

So it becomes possible to appreciate how, because of its primary motivation, African theology was shaping a new method that had no counterpart generally in the more recent western Christian thought forged within the context of Christendom. At the heart of it was the issue of identity perceived as a theological category, which entailed the need to confront the question as to how and how far the 'old' and the 'new' in African religious experience could become integrated into a unified vision of what it meant to be Christian *and* African. The theologian was forced to become the locus of this struggle for integration through a *dialogue which, to be authentic, was bound to become personal and intense. For the Christian theologian in modern Africa, as for the Christian apologist in early Hellenistic Christianity, the development of Christian thought became *apologia pro vita sua*.

While the theme of continuity was central, the terms of the argument varied. Idowu's argument for radical continuity, founded on the continuity and the unity of God, was coupled with an equally strong case for a 'radical indigenization of the church'. For so long as it accepted western cultural dominance, the *church in Africa could not develop a tradition of Christian thought that reflected its own original meditation and experience. To remedy this 'predicament of dependence' the African church needed to build its bridges to the 'revelation' given in the pre-Christian traditions. By stressing the 'foreignness of Christianity', this approach tended to minimize the 'newness' in Christianity. Christian experience emerged as merely a refinement of the 'old' religion. Gabriel Setiloane, a South African theologian, shared Idowu's perspective. The Congolese scholar Vincent Mulago Gwa Cikala represented a less radical form of this position. An early vindicator of 'African theology' among Francophone Catholics, Mulago remained convinced of the relevance of the Christian message for Africa, but insisted that the process of forging the new integration could not be viable unless it remained faithful to ancestral traditions while also being judicious in its contact with other peoples and with revealed religion.

At the other extreme of the spectrum was the radical discontinuity postulated by Byang Kato, then representing the thought of African *evangelicals who trace their spiritual heritage to conservative evangelical Faith Missions. Kato (1975) stressed the distinctiveness of the Christian faith to the extent that he rejected all positive evaluations of the traditional religions, considering them a distraction from the necessary 'emphasis on Bible truth'. Kato's insistence on the centrality of the bible for theology must be reckoned an important contribution to African Christian thought. Yet his rejection of the understanding of theology as a synthesis of 'old' and 'new' in a quest for a unified framework for dealing with culturally rooted questions prevented him from providing a sufficient foundation for the creative engagement that the African setting required. Other evangelicals have sought more positive ways to relate Christian faith to African tradition.

However, the dominant approach has been in the middle ground, taking seriously the pre-Christian heritage and recognizing the integrity of African *Christian* experience as a religious reality, on the view that Christianity is not intrinsically alien to Africa, and that the eternal gospel has found a home within the African response to it, with Christ as the integrating presence linking 'old' and 'new' in African experience. This approach, confident that the Christian faith is capable of translation into African terms without injury to its essential content, offered the best prospects for a sustainable Christian thought. The task of African theology came to consist, not in indigenizing Christianity, but in letting the Christian faith not only encounter but also be shaped by African experience. Harry Sawyerr, Christian Baëta, John Mbiti, and Kwesi Dickson exemplified this more settled outlook that helped prepare for the new and self-critical encounter with Africa that followed.

It was rightly stated that in the 1960s and 1970s, 'areas of traditional Christian doctrine which are not reflected in the African past disappear or are marginalized' (Hastings 1976). But an indication that the early concentration on issues of continuity had been appropriate was the fact that the new literature from the 1980s was able to take off from genuinely African categories. This was most marked in relation to *christological discussion, conspicuously minimal in earlier writings. Categories such as 'Christ as Healer', 'Master of Initiation', and 'Ancestor', derived directly from the apprehension of the transcendent within African traditional religions, provided new theological idioms.

African Christian thought was also seriously dealing with issues of theological discourse and methodology, the history of Christian expansion and diffusion, and historical theology, in which issues in modern African Christianity were related to earlier Christian tradition, whilst women's concerns and gender issues began to engage serious attention.

The rehabilitation of Africa's cultural and religious heritage, 'vital for the African's self-respect' (Tutu 1978), had been critical. But the extraordinary feature, from the 1980s, has been the emergence of a theological dialogue in which the two trends in African Christian thought—inculturation and liberation—are engaged in a quest for a 'theology of reconstruction' to address the social and political ills of the continent. Whereas Anglophone and mostly Protestant theologians were the pace-setters in the earlier formative period, the intellectual vitality of this new quest for an 'incarnation-liberation' is found most prominently in Francophone writers, both Catholic and Protestant. A notable feature of this more self-critical African theological literature is its acute sociocultural analysis of the modern 'African condition', within which Christian revelation and tradition are now experienced and tested. The writings of the Cameroonian Jean-Marc Éla, and of the Congolese Kä Mana, both of whom have experience of political exile from their home countries, are significant in this respect.

The era of reaction to western misrepresentation of Africa is past. Ahead lies a critical theological construction that relates the Christian faith more fully to the life-experiences of Africans and to society at large. Here, academic theological discourse needs to connect with the popular Christian responses found at the grassroots where, 'much of the theological activity ... is being done as oral theology, from the living experiences of Christians ...' (Mbiti 1986).

It may well be that it is in modern Africa that Christianity's essential character as culturally 'translatable' will be most notably seen, and the significance of 'the translation principle in Christian history' appreciated afresh (Walls 1996). African Christianity today is inconceivable apart from the existence of the bible in African indigenous languages. This is, probably, the single most important element of the missionary legacy (see BIBLICAL TRANSLATION). It ensured an effectual rooting of the Christian faith in African consciousness and provided the conditions in which an authentic dialogue would ensue between the Christian faith and African tradition in the categories of local languages, idioms, and worldviews.

Hitherto African Christian thought has been expressed, predominantly, in European *languages, the unmistakable result of the western cultural impact. It is an open question how far this linguistic medium determines the content and shape of African Christian thought, and whether 'African theologies should be in the vernacular' since 'language ... is the vehicle for assuming the weight of a culture' (Pobee 1979). The challenge for African Christian thought seems to be, paradoxically, that it should follow the logic of its 'translatable' faith and its translated scriptures. For as the central categories of Christian thought—*God, *Jesus Christ, *creation, *redemption, *history—are transposed into their local equivalents, the scriptures can become the necessary route for sustaining a dialogue between gospel and culture that addresses realistically the elemental forces operating within that culture. As African Christian thought makes its transition from inculturation and liberation into reconstruction, its relevance to African life may lie also with its ability to engage more fully with the mother-tongues in which most of the continent's Christians receive and respond to the faith. Christian apprehension and reflection in African languages, therefore, is set to become more, not less, important, and may well be one of the major means for forging new intellectual categories in the coming decades.

Yet the obligations of African Christian thought may lie also with the challenge of multiculturalism, and within the larger vocation of Christian witness amid pluralism—religious and cultural—as a sequel to the cross-cultural missionary encounter that produced modern African Christianity.

Long before pluralism became a subject of discussion in the west, many Christian communities of Africa had been living and witnessing to their Christian faith in pluralistic contexts. Having had to reflect theologically in the interface of their Christian faith and the spiritualities of their own backgrounds, African theologians recaptured the character of Christian thought as Christian intellectual activity on the frontier with the non-Christian world, and as essentially *communicative* and *missionary*. In this respect, African Christian thought may indicate how the Christian faith may engage, in a missionary sense, with the changed context of the west.

See also ETHIOPIAN THEOLOGY. **Kwame Bediako**

Bediako, K., *Theology and Identity: The Impact of Culture upon Christian Thought in the Second Century and Modern Africa* (1992).
—— *Christianity in Africa: The Renewal of a Non-Western Religion* (1995).
Des Prêtres noirs s'interrogent (1956).
Dickson, K., *Theology in Africa* (1984).
Doré J., *Chemins de la Christologie africaine* (1986).
Éla, J.-M., *African Cry* (1980), ET (1986).
—— *My Faith as an African* (1985), ET (1988).
Hastings, A., *African Christianity: An Essay in Interpretation* (1976).
—— *African Catholicism: Essays in Discovery* (1989).
Idowu, E. B., *Towards an Indigenous Church* (1965).
Kä Mana, *Foi chrétienne, crise africaine et reconstruction de l'Afrique* (1992).
—— *Christ d'Afrique: Enjeux éthiques de la foi africaine en Jésus-Christ* (1994).
Kato, B. H., *Theological Pitfalls in Africa* (1975).
Mbiti, John S., *Bible and Theology in African Christianity* (1986).
Mugambi, J. N. K., and Magesa, L. (eds.), *Faces of Jesus in African Christianity: Experimentation and Diversity in African Christology* (1989).
Nyamiti, C., *Christ as our Ancestor: Christology from an African Perspective* (1984).
Pobee, J. S., *Toward an African Theology* (1979).
Sanneh, L. O., *Translating the Message: The Missionary Impact on Culture* (1989).
Sawyerr, H., *Creative Evangelism: Towards a New Christian Encounter with Africa* (1968).
Tutu, D., 'Whither African Theology?', in E. Fasholé-Luke *et al.* (eds.), *Christianity in Independent Africa* (1978), 364–9.
Walls, A. F., 'Towards Understanding Africa's Place in Christian History', in J. S. Pobee (ed.), *Religion in a Pluralistic Society* (1976), 180–9.
—— *The Missionary Movement in Christian History: Studies in the Transmission of Faith* (1996).

afterlife, see ESCHATOLOGY; HEAVEN; HELL; IMMORTALITY.

agnosticism is a profession of ignorance. An agnostic makes the modest admission that he or she does not know whether there is a *God or not. What gives this controversial bite is that the agnostic is then likely to proceed to assert that, given the nature or scope of knowledge, no one *can* know whether there is a God.

The word came from Greek. A *Gnostic lays claim to more knowledge about God than might bear scrutiny; believers in *revelation or *mystical experience claim to find how the 'unknown god' (*agnostos theos*) has made himself known. But there were no agnostics, calling themselves such, in the ancient world. The term was invented by the scientist T. H. Huxley, popularizer of Darwinism, in 1869, to describe his own position. He claimed to need it for the Metaphysical Society, an élite debating club in London of philosophers, churchmen, and scientists. He knew the Greek overtones, and intended to imply that Christianity is foolishly 'gnostic'. Agnosticism thus began in a world of civilized debate.

> Agnosticism, in fact, is not a creed but a method ... Positively the principle may be expressed: In matters of the intellect, follow your reason as far as it will take you, without regard to any other consideration. And negatively, in matters of the intellect, do not pretend that conclusions are certain which are not demonstrated or demonstrable. This I take to be the agnostic faith, which if a man keep whole and undefiled, he shall not be ashamed to look the universe in the face, whatever the future may have in store for him.
>
> (Huxley)

The comic reuse of the bible and the self-satisfied pose of that final sentence are both characteristic of Huxley. Victorian agnostics should not be assumed to be Victorian *doubters; they were normally confident controversialists, at their least plausible when pretending to wish for belief. A typical expression of late-Victorian agnosticism is Sir Leslie Stephen's *An Agnostic's Apology* (1893).

There is a long history before Huxley of questioning claims that *reason might lead us to God. Reason has limits, according to *Kant, and speculation beyond these limits is useless, though he then allowed us to work on the practical postulate of a God. Agnosticism raises similar questions but works on the practical postulate of no God. Probably Huxley believed less in Kant's critique than in the march of scientific progress.

Logical positivism of the 1930s dismissed all, even agnostic, God-talk as meaningless playing with words. Few philosophers would now accept the cogency of that dismissal but few would accept the theist case as proved either. Agnosticism, strictly speaking, remains the position of all those who say they do not know and do not wish to believe in what they cannot prove. **Alistair Mason**

Cockshut, A. O. J., *The Unbelievers: English Agnostic Thought 1840–90* (1964).
Desmond, Adrian, J., *Huxley: The Devil's Disciple* (1994).
Kenny, Anthony, *What is Faith?* (1992).
Lightman, Bernard, *The Origins of Agnosticism: Victorian Unbelief and the Limits of Knowledge* (1987).

Alexandria, called 'close by Egypt' (*pros Aigupton*) because it was not counted a properly Egyptian city, was founded in 331 BC by Alexander the Great at the western end of the Nile delta, on a neck of land running east and west between Lake Mareotis and the Mediterranean Sea. Just offshore, the island of Pharos created a sheltered harbour (divided in two by the Heptastadion, a mole connecting the city with the island), making Alexandria the port of choice for Egypt's extensive trade.

The city was founded as a Greek-style *polis* with the customary institutions of self-government (soon lost). Its original citizen-body was entirely Greek, though it always had a population of native Egyptians. Alexander's successor in Egypt, Ptolemy I Soter (323–283 BC), made Alexandria the capital from which his Macedonian dynasty ruled Egypt until the advent of Julius Caesar (47 BC). Under Augustus and his successors Alexandria remained the capital, but Egypt was administered by a prefect, a personal representative of the emperor. By this time, the city's population had changed. Greek remained its language, but even the privileged body of 'citizens' was now of mixed Greek and Egyptian ancestry. There was also a large Jewish element (perhaps a third of the population by the time of Claudius) which occupied and overflowed an entire sector of the city, functioning as a semi-independent *politeuma*, with its own ethnarch and board of elders; and it came to be resented by the Graeco-Egyptian population for its size and privileges, and because it appeared to be in alliance with the Roman occupation.

Alexandria was a centre not merely of trade and government but of culture, and for prominence rivalled any Greek-speaking city anywhere. Ptolemy I established the famous Library at Alexandria, in use at least until the third quarter of the 3rd century AD; and Ptolemy Philadelphus (d. 246) founded the equally famous Museum (*mouseion*: 'house of the Muses'), a college of scholars that over the centuries made Alexandria a headquarters of literary and textual criticism, philosophy, and mathematics. Alexandria was a natural centre of Hellenized *Judaism, where the first Greek translation of the Hebrew Scriptures (the Septuagint) was undertaken and where, in the 1st century AD, the Jewish thinker Philo, an adept in Middle *Platonist and Stoic thought, wrote his allegorical commentary on the Books of Moses.

The arrival of *Christianity cannot be dated. Later tradition (Eusebius, *Ecclesiastical History*, 2. 16. 1) attributed it to Mark. It is indeed likely that the Christians arrived early and put down roots in the Jewish community (see Acts 18: 24); but there is no indication of any single founder of an Alexandrian Christian tradition. Christianity probably arrived under various auspices and was initially perceived as a variant of Judaism. Given the variety of outlook within the Alexandrian Jewish community, it is not surprising that the Christianity which grew up there took differing forms, as the range of Christian literature associated with 2nd-century Alexandria attests. The Christian *Gnostics Basilides and Valentinus taught in Alexandria during the first third of the 2nd century, before the latter's move to *Rome, and found opponents there as well as disciples. Perhaps early Alexandrian Christianity was organized around households or congregations that tended to perpetuate distinguishable teaching traditions, or the outlooks of particular masters.

One such 'school' was doubtless that of Pantaenus, known to us through his successor and disciple, Clement of Alexandria. Clement was a learned presbyter and apologist whose writings echoed the outlook of Philo and presented a coherent account of the Christian 'way' from *faith to knowledge and its perfection in *love. Eusebius (*EH* 6. 6. 1) represents him as head of the Alexandrian church's catechetical programme and believes that his work was continued by *Origen. It seems more likely that Clem-

ent's 'school' was one of a number of communities that were indeed centres of study and instruction, but with some of the characteristics of congregations.

The Alexandrian church comes into sharper historical focus at about the time (202) that Clement left Alexandria as a result of the persecutions instigated by Septimius Severus. It now had a single head in the person of Bishop Demetrius (189–232). Eusebius, however, focuses less on the bishop than on Origen and the 'catechetical school' that he founded in the course of a renewal of persecution under the prefect Aquila (*c*.206–10). In face of the church's disarray, Origen supplemented his work as a teacher of grammar by studying the scriptures with persons interested in learning about Christian belief. When Demetrius, who had gone underground with many of his clergy, was again able to take full charge of his *paroikia*, he allowed this work to continue, and later assented when Origen renounced the teaching of grammar to devote himself exclusively to the scriptures, assisted by one of his former students, Heraclas. To this resolution of Origen's we owe not only the completion of his textual work on the Septuagint (embodied in the famous *Hexapla*) but also the flood of commentaries and homilies that issued from his pen when he taught in Alexandria and later in Caesarea Maritima where, after a rupture with Bishop Demetrius, he created yet another school. No doubt Origen had much in common with Clement. Both were heirs of Philo's exegetical methods and his late-Platonist world-view; both were defenders of orthodoxy against the wrong sort of Gnostics; and each practised a different type of Christian *askesis*. It seems unlikely, however, on chronological and other grounds, that Origen was a pupil of Clement or that Clement's 'school' had official or semi-official status, whereas Origen's school seems, after his departure, to have become an established institution—perhaps because three of its heads became bishops of Alexandria.

By the time of Bishop Dionysius (247–65), who brought the Alexandrian church through the persecutions under Decius and Valerian, the importance and authority of that church were growing. Dionysius was influential in the church beyond Egypt, not least because it had become the annual privilege of the bishop of Alexandria to announce to other churches, in a festal letter, the date of the Christian *pascha* (*Easter). With Dionysius one can also see the emerging alliance with the Roman church that was to endure until the Council of *Chalcedon (451), as well as the growing power of the bishop of Alexandria in the affairs of all the churches in Egypt, Libya, and Cyrenaica: a jurisdiction confirmed by Canon VI of the Council of *Nicaea (325).

The prestige and power of the Alexandrian church were severely tested in the opening decades of the 4th century, as much as by the policies of the first Christian emperors as by Diocletian, who in 303 unleashed a persecution that in Egypt endured until 313 and left the churches in disorder. During this time, one Meletius, who had stepped into the shoes of the imprisoned bishop of Lycopolis, ordained clergy in Alexandria and the Nile Delta without reference to the Patriarch (Peter I, in hiding at the time, though later martyred) and thus undermined the unity of the churches in Egypt. His schism continued during the incumbency of Peter's successor Alexander (313–28) and was only settled (in principle) by the Council of Nicaea. By then Alexander's problems had been multiplied by his excommunication and exile of an influential presbyter, *Arius, for teaching that the *Word of God was created 'out of nothing'. Arius found allies in Palestine and Asia Minor, and what might have been a local problem about the interpretation of Alexandria's own school tradition embroiled the whole of the church in the east. Even after the matter was allegedly settled by the Council of Nicaea's dogmatic decree, tension remained. When Alexander died in 328, having refused to receive Arius back into communion, his chosen successor, the youthful *Athanasius, found himself at the centre of a many-sided conflict, involving not only sympathizers with Arius and unreconciled Meletians, but also imperial policy and the religious authority of the burgeoning *ascetic movement in Coptic-speaking Egypt.

In the course of a long episcopate (328–73) including five periods of exile, Athanasius managed to ally 'Greek' Alexandria with the Coptic ascetic movement in opposition both to unreconciled followers of Meletius and to the enemies of the Nicene dogma of the full deity of the divine Word (including the emperors Constantius II, Julian, and Valens). By the time of his death, Athanasius had not only established the authority of the Alexandrian church and its patriarch in the imperial diocese of Egypt, but enhanced its prestige in the church at large as second in honour only to Rome. Further, his defence of the full deity of the Word and insistence that the Word is the immediate subject of Christ's humanity in the *Incarnation established him as the initiator of a new emphasis or focus in the theological programme of the Alexandrian tradition—a focus fully clarified only in the course of the 5th-century *Nestorian controversy.

That controversy turned in part on an issue created by the Council of Constantinople (381), one of whose canons gave the see of *Constantinople, as the New Rome and an imperial capital, the place of honour after the elder Rome. This both violated tradition (which had ranked the church founded by Mark, Peter's disciple, as second after Peter's own see) and wounded Alexandria's self-esteem. The resulting rivalry between Alexandria and Constantinople was played out first between Theophilus of Alexandria (385–412) and John Chrysostom, bishop of Constantinople (398–403). The former exploited Chrysostom's puritan tactlessness in dealing with the imperial court by having him deposed and exiled, largely on trumped-up charges of sympathy with the views of Origen, whom Theophilus now regarded as a *heretic. The same rivalry was played out at the Council of *Ephesus (431) when Cyril, Theophilus's nephew and successor (412–44) joined by Celestine of Rome humbled Nestorius—like Chrysostom, an Antiochene ascetic imported to Constantinople as its bishop. This time, however, the issue was a real one: a conflict between paradigms for the relation of Word and humanity in Christ. Cyril, in the tradition of Athanasius, thought of Christ as the Word living out a concrete human life—bearing a human nature which he 'made his own'. Nestorius, in traditional Antiochene style, thought of the Word as indwelling a particular human being so intimately as to be morally identified with it. Cyril spoke of 'one incarnate nature of the Word of God', Nestorius of 'two natures'.

The subsequent history of the see of Alexandria until the Arab conquest of Egypt (647) simply spelled out the consequences of this controversy. In its second round, under Cyril's successor Dioscorus I, it seemed that the Alexandrian cause might triumph again; for at the Robber Synod of Ephesus (449), called to consider the case of an over-enthusiastic adherent of Cyril's, the church of Constantinople was again humbled in the person of its bishop, Flavian; but in the process the views of Leo I, bishop of Rome, were refused a hearing (for Leo, like Nestorius, spoke of 'two natures' in Christ), and Alexandria's alliance with Rome was dissolved. This became apparent when, at the Council of Chalcedon (451), Dioscorus himself suffered deposition and exile, and Pope Leo's *Tome* became one of the canonical documents of the Council. In the following two centuries, the Alexandrian church remained loyal to Cyril and Athanasius; but even when the 'two natures' doctrine was interpreted in a way arguably consistent with Cyril's teaching, the Egyptian church remained *Monophysite and resisted the rule of 'imperial' Constantinople. The patriarchs of Alexandria were with one exception Monophysite until Justinian imposed a Chalcedonian succession after 537; but around forty years later a rival Monophysite—and Egyptian as opposed to Greek—succession was established, and it was the latter, in the person of Patriarch Benjamin (623–62), that was recognized by the Arab conquerors of Egypt as representing the now subject Egyptian ('Coptic') nation.

The centuries after the Arab conquest (642) saw Alexandria shrink in size and population, but it maintained its status as an active and prosperous port until the 16th century, after which it shrank to the status of a fishing village, only to be revived in the 19th century by a burgeoning trade in Egyptian cotton. Coptic Christianity has survived to the present day, despite intermittent persecutions, decreasing numbers, and the displacement of the Coptic language by Arabic. From c.1050 the patriarchal headquarters has been located in the Arab capital of Cairo. **Richard A. Norris, Jr.**

Arnold, D. W.-H., *The Early Episcopal Career of Athanasius of Alexandria* (1991).

Bell, H. I., *Jews and Christians in Egypt* (1924).

Bowman, A. K., *Egypt after the Pharaohs* (1989).

Frend, W. H. C., *The Rise of the Monophysite Movement* (1972).

Hardy, E. R., *Christian Egypt* (1952).

Kannengiesser, C. (ed.), *Politique et théologie chez Athanase d'Alexandrie* (1974).

Pearson, B. A., and Goehring, J. E. (eds.), *The Roots of Egyptian Christianity* (1986).

Roberts, C. H., *Manuscript, Society and Belief in Early Christian Egypt* (1979).

Steen, G. L. (ed.), *Alexandria: The Site and the History* (1993).

van den Hoek, A., 'The "Catechetical" School of Early Christian Alexandria and its Philonic Heritage', *Harvard Theological Review*, 90 (1997), 59–87.

allegory means speaking of one thing in terms of another. It works by the displacement of identity: A is not A but B or C; or, A is not only A but also B and C. For example, the crossing of the Red Sea is (A) an event in *Israelite history, but it also means (B) Christ's passage through the waters of death to deliver humanity from evil (the Egyptians) and (C) the Christian's passage through the waters of *baptism.

Allegory has three basic forms: as literary *hermeneutic, as a form of writing, and as a metaphysics of creation. Any particular mode may merge two or more of these forms. For example, if the world is perceived in a Stoic or Neoplatonic way, then allegory as hermeneutic is inseparable from allegory as metaphysic. And allegory as a way of writing about the world requires an understanding of the world as other than it appears: what is physically present is meta-physically informed. Hence allegorical representation and *rhetoric are interlaced with philosophical and theological nuances.

As a literary hermeneutic, allegory emerged as a means of inter-preting a text by uncovering concealed meanings. It fostered a philosophical and ethical approach to literature: names, numbers, and events became symbolic. This treatment is employed for simi-lar reasons on biblical texts by Philo in the 1st century, by the 3rd-century Alexandrian *Origen, by the 5th-century Cappadocian Gre-gory of Nyssa, and by *Augustine. For the Christian exegete, the figurative (or spiritual) sense of the text resolves three problems: reception (those scandalized by some scriptural passages), biblical consistency, and textual obscurities.

Allegorical readings were both apologetic and evangelistic: they sought not only to justify the sacred nature of the scriptures, but by doing so to further the dissemination of those scriptures among cultures. Allegory enabled the synthesis of Hellenistic culture first with Jewish (Philo), then with Judaeo-Christian biblical *theology. In the early church, the popularity of allegorical readings was re-lated to the development of the scriptural canon and of Christian *orthodoxy. A *typological understanding of the *Old Testament as prefiguring the gospel wove Judaism into Christianity and con-demned as heretics those who wanted to disregard the OT (the faith's Jewish roots). They also maintained the importance of the historical and concrete against *Gnostic anti-embodiment tenden-cies.

It is just here, where *history meets allegory, that the hermeneu-tical waters become distinctly choppy. The spiritual reading was never in doubt, but the role of the historical was questioned. Some believed that what the words of scripture spoke of was so second-ary to the spiritual meaning that it could be disregarded as value-less: for example, there did not need to be a garden of Eden, only the story of it. Origen, the first to distinguish between the literal and non-literal readings of the *bible and define a set of Christian hermeneutical principles, inclined more towards this view, as did Augustine. Others emphasized that there could be no spiritual meaning dissociated from historical reference: allegorical readings were important but only legitimate because reference was being made to actual people, places, objects, and actions. Gregory of Nyssa, and, later, *Aquinas and Hugh of St Victor held this opinion.

Questions of historical reference are about allegory not only as an exegetical tool but as a metaphysics of *creation. The understand-ing of scripture changed between the early and the medieval church. For Origen, Augustine, and Gregory of Nyssa, scripture and creation were imbued with *God's *Logos, so that a doctrine of the Spirit moving in and through history and interpretation bound the reading of scripture to the triune God's saving *provi-dence. By the time of Aquinas, the two divine texts, scripture and creation, were beginning to separate with the development of nat-ural *science. Scripture was already beginning to be understood as having the autonomy of *revelation that *Protestantism would develop. Exegesis takes on a certain professionalism.

It is within this developing exegetical professionalism that we shift from Origen's threefold interpretation of scripture (where between literal and spiritual there is something rather vague which some scholars have termed 'moral') to the medieval fourfold: historical, allegorical, moral, anagogical. Allegorical meant strictly typological

readings of the OT in terms of the NT. The anagogical read the scriptures in terms of their eschatological fulfilment. But Aquinas observes that allegorical also 'stands for the three spiritual senses' (ST I q. 1 a. 10). What is important with the fourfold sense, as Aquinas presents it, is that we do not graduate from one sense to the other, moving towards states of greater spiritual illumination, as seems to be suggested in Origen's thinking. Rather the fourfold sense corresponds to the relationship of God's salvific relation to *time itself: the historical past, its symbolization in regard to the NT, the moral present, and the fully realized future. In the fourfold sense of scripture, texts constantly transgressed their local and tem-poral limitations.

The move from Origen's understanding of the allegorical sense to Aquinas's (with Augustine equivocally poised between) marks a heightened valuation of the literal meaning. The trend continued through the realist and nominalist debates of the late-medieval period and prepared for the demise of the allegorical reading in favour of the literal in 16th- and 17th-century *Protestantism. Alle-gory did not disappear, but was no longer an exegetical tool. It continued as a form of writing. Bunyan's *Pilgrim's Progress is only one expression of a Protestant allegorical world-view. Seventeenth-century sectarians, in particular, liked readings of history which saw the things of this world in terms of their eschatological significance. But a certain materialist ideology began to emerge towards the end of that century, paralleling the development of secular forms of authority. The material and soon-to-become scientific world-view denounced rhetoric as ornament and allegory as fiction. In the 19th and early 20th centuries this preoccupation with facticity led, in biblical hermeneutics, to a concern with historicity (the *quest for the historical Jesus) and *demythologizing the scriptural text (*Bultmann).

Contemporary fascinations with allegory arise from two sources that feed the exploding interest in cultural studies. The first, in North America, was the attention given to rhetoric following New Criticism (a movement in the literary analysis of texts con-cerned with the technology of style). The second, in France, was the interest in semiotics initiated by Ferdinand de Saussure. In the epoch of *postmodernity, reality is provisional and constituted in and through the exchange of signs, which do not hook up to a world beyond or outside them, but create any world we occupy. These two cultural emphases have returned critical theorists such as Paul de Man to the study of allegory. The postmodern world is a world of *symbols and simulacra, akin in some respects to the pre-*modern world. But the postmodern world view lacks (even de-nies) any theological understanding of creation. The pre-modern allegorical world saw that all symbols and simulacra are caught up within the bringing to fulfilment of the Word, the *Incarnation, in our world, through our words.   **Graham Ward**

Bloomfield, Horton W., Allegory, Myth and Symbol (1992).
Dawson, David, Allegorical Readers and the Cultural Reasoning of Ancient
    Alexandria (1992).
de Man, Paul, Blindness and Insight: Essays in the Rhetoric of Contemporary
    Criticism (1983).
Torrance, Thomas F., Divine Meaning: Studies in Patristic Hermeneutics
    (1995).
Ward, Graham, 'Kenosis and Naming: Allegoria Amoris', in Paul Heelas
    and Linda Woodhead (eds.), Religion, Modernity and Postmodernity
    (1998).

alternative lifestyles. This term may be applied to those forms, styles, and patterns of living which are somewhat or radically different from those of the dominant ideologies and practices, whether political, economic, cultural, or religious, in any given place and time. Within *Christianity, such alternative lifestyles have always existed, many of them as forms of *monasticism. In some parts of the world today, especially where Christianity is a minority faith, to be a Christian is in itself an alternative lifestyle. Though there have always been individuals who choose eccentric or idiosyncratic ways of life (and there is evidence today to suggest that there is a revival of interest in the solitary life, though often not within the context of organized religion) the term is more properly applied to those lifestyles which appeal to sufficient numbers of people to be more than entirely individual, and therefore to constitute a real choice or alternative for other seekers.

Worldwide, there are tens of thousands of households, groups, communities, and networks living alternative lifestyles. Since to be alternative is to be in some senses marginal, going against the prevailing norms, this co-operation is important in offering solidarity and support, opportunities for growth and learning, and for some, the possibility of visibility and outright resistance to the dominant culture.

In countries which have a predominantly Christian tradition, and which are now marked by *secularism and pluralism, particularly in Western Europe and North America, the alternative may be to the economics of free market *capitalism, where people choose to live a simple, even *ascetic, lifestyle with an emphasis on sharing, on resisting conspicuous consumption, and on self-help and fair trading. Others, motivated by an *ecological concern, develop recycling and renewing strategies and the use of alternative technology. There has been a huge growth of such groups around environmental protest and action against, for instance, motorways, airports, and the destruction of natural habitats. Often they adopt a nomadic lifestyle akin to that of gypsies or travellers, and their significant rejection of modern materialism can render them threatening to those living conventional lifestyles.

Others develop their alternative lifestyles as a strategy for inclusion and care of those whom the culture excludes. Such communities as L'Arche (for physically and mentally disabled people), and the Simon, Cyrenian, and Emmaus Communities (for the homeless) offer a characteristic lifestyle where the excluded group and those in solidarity with them live, not as client or patient and professional carer, but as *family.

A new or different way of being family offers an alternative to the dominant nuclear family model, whether it is in extended households or networks of households in a neighbourhood. Though the established churches often have difficulty in relating to such groups, they seem to be a way of reconstructing the traditional extended family through intentionality rather than kinship, in a way that *Jesus himself might readily have recognized.

Though groups such as the above may have their own chosen focus, or may have come into being to respond to a particular social or political need (such as the many concerned with *reconciliation in Northern Ireland) they may share much common ground. With their concern for *justice, *peace, and *creation, they share an integrated and global vision, a commitment to engage with the *world, and, by offering alternatives, to change it.

Alternative lifestyles also proliferated in Eastern Europe during the communist era, when Christianity often provided the only form of alternative identity, the humanizing of impersonal systems, and resistance to Soviet-driven authority. Some of these are determined to hold on to their flexibility, democratic commitment, and resistance to monoculturalism as a continuing faith stance; others, however, have faded, as many lifestyles and groups in all contexts do when that against which they define themselves changes or disappears.

In Central and South America, the *base Christian communities, with their *liberation theology and spirituality, have offered an alternative lifestyle to people already marginalized by *poverty and a different form of totalitarian oppression, and have been a source of inspiration to marginalized groups and peoples worldwide.

All of these could be termed 'communities of contrast'; it is part of their alternative nature to stand over against the norms. But there are also significant numbers of people whose alternative lifestyle is less to do with difference than with intentionality. They choose their way of life to deepen their own commitment, give it greater significance in the midst of conventional patterns. They might be termed 'communities of depth'. Though predominantly lay, many have marked similarities to canonical religious communities; they may be *celibate, or take vows, and are centred on *worship, meditation, and *prayer. Others, such as the Brüderhof, are committed to biblical principles and a recovery of the simplicity and *pacifism of the early church; while such groups as the traditionalist Opus Dei, though not marked by a visibly alternative lifestyle, espouse an alternative conservative viewpoint in their attachment to the cause of the advancement of the Roman Catholic church.

Of a quite different ideology are the Christian *fundamentalist groups found mostly in the United States; predominantly Protestant and sectarian, they are opposed to what they consider to be the secularizing and centralizing tendencies of the liberal democratic state. At the extreme end of this spectrum are the 'survivalist' groups preparing for Armageddon; some of these are militarized and hold doctrines of white supremacy, and their lifestyle is entirely separatist.

But most groups pursuing alternative lifestyles within Christianity are marked by a number of shared characteristics: they are relational rather than institutional, *lay rather than clerical, with a readiness to acknowledge the established churches but a refusal to be controlled by them. They are concerned with openness and exploration, provisional rather than over-concerned with their own survival, and seek to nurture the gifts and insights of their members, especially when these are not related to hierarchical systems. Such inclusive communities are a source of creativity, energy, and vision within the *body of Christ. For many, they offer the only way of being *church, and are communities of *hope.

See also GLOBAL ETHICS. **Kathy Galloway**

Clark, David, *Basic Communities: Towards an Alternative Lifestyle* (1977).
Raiser, Konrad, *To be the Church: Challenges and Hopes for a New Millennium* (1997).
Vanier, Jean, *Community and Growth* (1989).

America, see NORTH AMERICA: AN OVERVIEW; LATIN AMERICAN CHRISTIAN THOUGHT.

Anabaptists, see BAPTIST THOUGHT; MENNONITE THOUGHT.

analogy, the similarity along with difference, among meanings, among sorts of thinking, and among realities. Analogy theory originated with *Aristotle in its three main parts: analogy of meaning, analogous thinking, and analogy of being. There were some antecedents in *Plato, where the names of Forms and of participating things are the same but differ in meaning, and the notion of 'being' is said to differ with what we are talking about, for example Forms versus physical things (Sophist). Systematic use of the three elements to unify philosophy and to resolve problems is, however, Aristotle's invention along with the idea that *metaphor is a species of analogy. Aristotle distinguished what were later called analogies of attribution, based on causation, signs, symptoms, and representations (medical skill, medical supplies; hat/head cover, hat/in picture), from analogy based on proportionality, A : B :: C : D; where the common implicit predicate is related in meaning (supplied food; supplied financing), but not the same in meaning as it is in the arithmetic proportion 4 : 8 :: 8 : 16 (one half). There are two sorts: proper proportionality (a medieval title), such as the pair, 'The aspirin relieved his headache', 'The reinforcements relieved the garrison', and metaphor, such as 'Jove sowed rosy rays on the dawn' vs. 'the farmer sowed wheat in the field'.

Two main uses of analogy were Aristotle's saying that 'being' as exhibited in the ten categories is analogous with a primary sense for substances. Thus the sense in which a human exists is primary and prior to the sense in which we say his weight, height, or colour exists. Aristotle implicitly held that since concepts are abstractions from things and are the meanings of words, analogy of meaning tracks analogy of being. The second main use of proportionality is the adaptation of the 'matter/form' and 'act/potency' distinction, and the like, and of the senses of 'cause' (formal, efficient, material, and final) to varying contexts throughout philosophy of nature, *metaphysics, and moral theory, so for instance, gold is said to be the material cause of a statue of Pericles and flesh and bones the material cause of Socrates. Thus in Posterior Analytics the premises of a demonstration are said to be the cause of the conclusion, and in boat-building the wood is the material cause of the boat.

Similarly, with the rediscovery of Aristotle and the adaptation of his ideas by Albert the Great and Thomas *Aquinas in the 13th century, analogy in all three aspects, of meaning, thought, and being, became a general and fundamental theory which took on a special development in the discussion of the relation of creatures to *God (See NATURAL THEOLOGY). Aquinas adapted what was originally a Platonic and Neoplatonic notion of 'participation', probably from Plotinus and Proclus, to function in an Aristotelian metaphysical context, to explain that the creature's being is a participation in the being of God. The difference is that (1) the being of the creature is its own but is by continuous divine causation and (2) finitely reflects God's infinite perfection. For the history of these ideas, with many citations, see Lyttkens.

So, analogy came as a solution of the dilemma facing religious discourse—that if words we use for creatures apply in the same sense to God, the talk will be mere anthropomorphism and false, but if the words are merely equivocal (unrelated in meaning) then the talk is unintelligible and meaningless—a solution adapted from metaphysics, philosophy of nature, and philosophy of *language, not fashioned for religion in the first place.

Besides inventing his own doctrine of participated being, Aquinas, in opposition to Avicenna, argued for a real distinction between essence and existence in creatures and the absence of such a distinction in God. For Aquinas, existence is related to essence (what-it-is) in creatures as fulfilment to capacity, and thus as act to potency. For him, whatever is related as act to potency is really distinct from it. In God there is no relation of fulfilment to capacity, and thus no real distinction of essence and existence. A consequence is that participated being is the basis for predication of pure perfections (like being, life, intelligence and love—predicates that imply no limitation and are all mutually compatible) of both creatures and God, with carry-over of the content (the res significata) but with a contextual adjustment of the manner of meaning (the modus significandi) that reflects the differences in the manner of being (modus essendi), just as 'really exists' does when applied to substances (cats), quantities (litres), qualities (snub-nosed), and relations (being nearby), as well as pauses, space, *time, and money. Disagreements over whether the term 'being' is univocal or analogous, as applied to God and creatures (Duns Scotus, c.1300, and William of Ockham, c.1320, held that it is univocal), were more intense than disputes about whether predicates applied to God are analogous; that was substantially accepted once it was formulated. And even now, apart from fundamentalists, evangelicals, and *process theorists (Hartshorne) who think God suffers and changes in the same sense that we do, the general position of *theologians is one or another variant, rejected by *Thomists, of the idea that words applied to creatures and to God differentiate in the God-talk, but nearly always with the result that some non-literal form of discourse becomes fundamental for religion: for instance, *Tillich's idea that all true talk about God is 'symbolic', not literal; Karl *Barth's substitution of analogia fidei for Aquinas's analogia entis (in effect, holding that the difference of meaning in common words applied to both creatures and God, for example 'loves', is not explained by the metaphysical differences of the things, but by the role of such words in scriptural narrative, thus holding that words 'gain a proper sense from the revelatory context'); *Ricœur's idea that talk about God involves 'double meaning' characteristic of *symbols and metaphors that forces endless interpretation (*hermeneutics) of the meaning 'in front of religious texts'. Even more uncongenial to analogy theorists are the ideas of Derrida, Barthes, Lacan, and Kristeva, applying to all texts and speech, who claim to find ever self-referring, ever-shifting textures in all, reflecting shifting social conditions, and so on, with no fixed meaning—they all conflict with Aquinas's basic idea that analogies of attribution and of proper proportionality that are at the foundation of our knowledge of God are paradigmatically literal and are derived from our perception of ourselves and of the physical world.

Aquinas also acknowledged varieties of religious discourse, to which the basic theory of meaning involving univocal, merely equivocal, and analogous (both literal and metaphorical) predication, applies. Aquinas distinguished statements 'vantaged' (not his word) in our spatio-temporal condition, statements belonging of necessity to popular piety, for instance 'God knows what I will do tomorrow', 'God will answer my prayers, forgive my sins, and bring me to eternal life', from statements belonging to the 'scientific' (again my word) description of God, for instance 'for God there is no past or future, only one perfect present, no plurality of acts'. He distinguished truths 'according to the appearance of things', as 'The stars are the ornament of the heavens,' said by Moses to an 'ignorant and unlettered people' who would not understand that the stars are the substance of the heavens, the reality of things (*ST* I q. 68 a. 3, and q. 70. a. 1 ad. 3; *De potentia*, 4. 2 ad. 30). He distinguished the legal meaning in the Old Law from the 'spiritual' meaning of its precepts (*Comm. on Hebrews*). He allowed, in the interpretation of the scripture, for allegorical, typical, prophetic, symbolic, and *mystical meanings (*ST* I-II, q. 104 a. 2 ad. 2). So would an analogy theorist today.

Once the 20th-century dispute that originated in logical positivism (consider A. J. Ayer's renowned 1933 popularization of it) about empirical verifiability withered away because the original principle of verification failed its own test and, when revised, excluded nothing as meaningless—a dispute that generated a vast literature, including unwise surrenders to its mistaken assumptions by Braithwaite's and Ian Ramsey's 'empirical placing of religious predicates' and John Hick's 'eschatological pragmatism'—the enquiry returned to how we can talk meaningfully about a transcendent being, one beyond our capacity to experience on our own, and was supplied with various accounts of analogy of meaning (for example Austin Farrer, E. L. Mascall, R. MacInerny, D. Burrell, D. *Tracy). Some others (see J. Ross) emphasize internal linguistic structures that explain the contrasting adaptation of words to diverse linguistic environments, with religious discourse, as well as moral and aesthetic talk, being an orderly, normal, subcase of universal semantic regularities, of 'semantic contagion', not different from what we can find in any craft-bound discourse and anywhere where discourse is adapted to modifying human action and commitment, e.g. 'He answered: /the door/the telephone/the questions/the petition/the complaint.' Still, nonsense is common enough, particularly in philosophy and religion, but in law, medicine, and everywhere else. In fact, analogy of meaning, metaphor, and our ability to make abstractions upon abstractions explains how semantically well-formed utter nonsense can be produced: 'Thingness evokes essential being.'

The basic medieval/Aristotelian principle was that meaning differentiation of a word reflects reality differences in what it is used for, and it is analogical thinking (*analogia rationis*) by which real analogy (*analogia entis*) is recognized, for instance the analogy among the dielectric polarization, mechanical elasticity, and heat capacity of solids; each feature is reversible, each can cause the others to change, and even the quantitative changes are proportional to one another—bending tin will make heat; heating it will bend it. Recognizing verbal and visual analogies marks one's inventive intelligence. Aristotle remarked (*Poetics*, 22. 1459a) 'the greatest thing by far is to be a master of metaphor. It is the one thing that cannot be learned from others.' It is a mark of genius, he said, and (*Rhetoric*, 3. 2) a good metaphor 'puts the matter before the eyes'.

Contrasting meanings do track contrasting realities, but not in the neat and unerring way Aquinas thought, though, of course, some still hold Aquinas's views unrevised. Yet there is no conflict between a more linguistic emphasis in explaining analogy of meaning and still holding a metaphysics of participation between the world and God. It is now unusual for Anglo-American philosophers to say there is something linguistically odd or deviant about talk of God, grace, sin, or salvation, partly because the *Wittgensteinian idea that linguistic propriety and sense is determined entirely by use, by our speech practices, has become well entrenched.

Whatever borderline there was thought to be between 'literal', 'metaphorical', and 'symbolic' meaning was never clear, even among recent writers on metaphor (M. Black, N. Goodman, Eva Kittay, P. Ricœur) and has now disappeared among those who recognize that such terms are contrast-dependent so that a word (drop/a glass) that is literal with respect to another occurrence (drop/a pen) may be at the same time metaphorical in relation to a third (drop/a course). There is no current classification of how the differentiations of meaning for a given word reflect or are responses to differences in reality. That will have to be restarted.

Wittgenstein happened upon the phenomenon that he called 'family resembling terms' but did not explain it or realize that it is universal, law-governed, linguistic regularity (see J. Ross); nor did he remark that the endlessly differentiating senses of 'because', 'knows', 'proves' and everything else philosophers examine may reflect differences in what we talk about, and will defeat any single-pattern Socratic, or even Russellian, contextual definition. Philosophers and theologians have just not caught on to the semantic regularities of analogy, the centrality of analogous thinking, or the importance of analogies in reality. But they will.

See also RELIGIOUS LANGUAGE.   **James Ross**

Barth, Karl, *Church Dogmatics* (4 vols.; 1956–75).
Burrell, D., *Aquinas, God and Action* (1979).
Cajetan, Thomas de Vio, *The Analogy of Names* (1498), ET (1953).
Davies, Brian, *Thinking about God* (1985).
Lyttkens, H., *The Analogy between God and the World* (1952).
Ricœur, P., *The Conflict of Interpretation* (3 vols.; 1984–8).
Ross J., *Portraying Analogy* (1981).
—— 'Semantic Contagion' in A. Lehrer and E. Kittay (eds.), *Frames, Fields and Contrasts* (1992).
Tracy, D., *The Analogical Imagination* (1981).

angels, purely spiritual, created beings. Most depictions of the Annunciation show the Virgin *Mary humbly bowing to the Archangel Gabriel as he bears God's message to her. With biblical insight, however, Leonardo da Vinci has Gabriel kneeling before Mary (in the Uffizi). To emphasize that the incarnate Christ is superior to any angel, the Epistle to the *Hebrews asks: 'to what angel did God ever say, "You are my Son, today I have begotten you"?' (Heb. 1: 5). We may likewise imagine: to what angel did God ever say, 'You are to be the mother of my Son'? Hebrews suggests that the angels stand in awe of the workings of God among humanity. They are designated as 'ministering spirits sent forth to serve, for the sake of those who are to obtain salvation' (Heb. 1: 14). Their very name means 'messenger' (Greek *angelos*, from Hebrew *mal'ak*).

The *Eastern Orthodox liturgy subordinates even the two highest orders of angels to Mary, the Mother of God, in describing her as 'more honoured than the cherubim and incomparably more glorious than the seraphim', and the great hymn of the angels in the heavenly court in *The Dream of Gerontius*, 'Praise to the holiest in the height', is one of wonder at the salvation wrought upon earth. John Henry *Newman believed that the very angels marvel at these human happenings. Gerontius is borne into God's presence by his own angel guardian (cf. Matt. 18: 10), as the angels sing of the drama of the 'second Adam' coming 'to the rescue' of the human race.

The drama arises from the fact that the human being is a complex combination of spirit and matter, not capable of the instantaneous decision for or against God that the angels, as pure spirits, freely and irrevocably make, according to the teaching of Thomas *Aquinas (*ST* I q. 64 a. 2). Because of our corporeal condition, the human decision takes time, it ebbs and flows, and is never sealed until the moment of death. Aquinas's near contemporary in the east, Gregory Palamas (c.1296–1359), maintained that this corporeal condition was precisely the key to human superiority over the angels. 'As pure spirits, the angels are messengers and servants; man is a creative artist, for he has at his disposal the matter of the world and of his own body.' One of the goals of the *Incarnation was 'to venerate the flesh, in order that the proud spirits may not dare to imagine that they are more venerable than man' (P. Evdokimov, *Scottish Journal of Theology* 18 (1965)).

Strictly, angels are not proposed but rather presupposed by divine *revelation. 'The angels are taken for granted; they are simply there, as in all the religions of the world surrounding the bible, and are simply known to exist' (Rahner). Revelation, which culminates in Christ, progressively clarifies that the angels are not divine, but fellow servants of God with humanity, integral even if invisible elements of the cosmos, mightily influencing for good or ill, according to their primordial option, the stage upon which the history of salvation unfolds. Karl *Rahner thinks that such an understanding still has value. 'At the present time when people are only too ready to suppose that because of the tremendous size of the cosmos there be intelligent living beings outside the earth, men should not reject angels outright as unthinkable, provided that they are not regarded as mythological furnishings of a religious heaven, but primarily as "principalities and powers" of the cosmos', in the Pauline phrase.

The meaning of narratives involving angels has often been elusive. Genesis 18–19 is an outstanding example. *Abraham and Sarah receive mysterious guests, identified as God himself (18: 1), but variously described as three men (18: 2; hence Rublev's famous icon of the Trinity), two angels (19: 1), one speaker (18: 10). God is close, but mysteriously so, as also in due course with his people in the *desert. His presence to lead and guard them is variously described as an angel (Exod. 23: 20) and as a pillar of cloud and fire (Exod. 13: 21; 40: 36–8). Somewhat similarly, in medieval Europe, accounts of rulers climbing down from untenable positions indicate that they were often enabled to do so by the intervention of a 'dissociated' person, such a person being variously 'a court jester, an angel', or 'the preacher of a moving sermon' (Mayr-Harting).

In post-exilic biblical texts, angelology became elaborate. A weakening sense of God's nearness (or a growing awareness of his transcendence) prompted the vigorous emergence of angels as advocates and intercessors. In situations of danger, it is angels who protect God's people (Dan. 3: 49; 2 Macc. 11: 6; 15: 22–3). Raphael ('God has healed'), identifies himself as 'one of the seven angels who stand ever ready to enter the presence of the glory of the Lord' (Tob. 12: 15). These seven 'archangels' also include Michael ('who is like God') and Gabriel ('man of God'). Michael is the great Prince, defender of the people in battle (Dan. 10: 13–21; 12: 1;

Jude 5: 9), and later the celestial opponent of Satan (Rev. 12: 7–9; cf. Luke 10: 18), who himself begins as public prosecutor in the court of God (Job 1: 6–12; 2: 1–7) and develops into a tempter (1 Chr. 21: 1), and ultimately into 'the deceiver of the whole world' (Rev. 12: 9) (see DEVIL). Gabriel, the messenger of comfort, interprets *visions (Dan. 8: 15; 9: 21) and announces the birth of *John the Baptist (Luke 1: 11–22) and of *Jesus (Luke 1: 26–38).

Given that, at the time of Jesus, the existence of angels was disputed between the Pharisees and the Sadducees (Acts 23: 8), the gospels can be seen as affirming their existence by frequent mention of them. They comfort Jesus after his temptation (Matt. 4: 11), one strengthens him in his passion (Luke 22: 43). It is angels who tell the women at the tomb of his *Resurrection (Matt. 28: 2–7; Luke 24: 4–7, 23; John 20: 12–13) and then tell the apostles after his Ascension that he will return (Acts 1: 10–11).

Against any Jewish, Hellenistic, or *Gnostic tendencies to divinize the angels, Christian tradition took its cue from Paul's affirmation that they are *created* and subject, like all creation, visible and *invisible*, to Christ (Col. 1: 16; 2: 10, 15; Eph. 1: 21; 3: 10; 6: 12; 1 Cor. 15: 24–8). The angels are not to be worshipped (Col. 2: 18). Indeed, they will be judged by the saints (1 Cor. 6: 3). The Fourth Lateran Council (1215) eventually defined that the one God is 'creator of all things, visible and invisible', 'creator of both kinds of creature, spiritual and corporeal, that is, angels and things of the world' and also of human beings who, being composed of spirit and body, have something in common with both. He is creator of the Devil and the demons, too, for they were created good, but chose evil. Thus were angels finally understood in official church teaching not only as creatures, but also as pure spirits (cf. also Vatican I, *Constitution on the Catholic Faith*). Around the same time, both in literature and in art, there was decreasing emphasis on the angels as 'social agents' who intervene in history to help or to warn, and increasing emphasis on their contemplative function (Mayr-Harting).

Vatican II taught: 'In the earthly liturgy we take part in a foretaste of that heavenly liturgy which is celebrated in the Holy City of Jerusalem' (*Constitution on the Sacred Liturgy*, 8). In this light, the biblical text that continues to exercise the most profound influence upon Christian faith and life with regard to the angels is undoubtedly the call of *Isaiah (6: 1–8), in which the prophet has a vision of seraphs at the throne of God crying: 'Holy, holy, holy is the Lord of hosts, his glory fills the whole earth.' Those words have been and still are uttered, at the Sanctus, by Christians in every eucharistic liturgy, as they expressly blend their voices with the 'unending hymn' of the angels. Lifted into the heavenly worship, Christians, like Isaiah, feel unworthy: 'Woe is me,' he says; 'Lord I am not worthy,' say they. A seraph takes a live coal and touches his lips to forgive his sin. In holy communion, Christians receive the body and blood of the Lord for the forgiveness of their sins.

*Dionysius the Pseudo-Areopagite classified the angels into nine orders in his *Celestial Hierarchy*, each order being an intermediary between what stands above and below: seraphim, cherubim, and thrones; dominations, virtues, and powers; principalities, archangels, and angels (cf. Isa. 6: 2; Ezek. 1: 5; Eph. 1: 21; Col. 1: 16). However, the relatively lowly place given to the archangels, particularly to Michael, seems unbiblical, as also, more fundamentally, is the perpetuation of the idea of mediation.

The biblical message is more direct. The angels serve God and humanity, and especially Christ, God incarnate, the sole mediator. They labour invisibly, throughout the cosmos, to further the final unity of all things, in heaven and on earth, in him.

Paul McPartlan

Barth, K., *Church Dogmatics*, III 3 (1961), §51.
Carr, W., *Angels and Principalities: The Background, Meaning and Development of the Pauline Phrase 'hai archai kai hai exousiai'* (1981).
Daniélou, J., *The Angels and their Mission* (1953), ET (1957).
Mayr-Harting, H., *Perceptions of Angels in History* (1998).
Michl, J., and Klauser, Th., 'Engel', in *Reallexikon für Antike und Christentum*, 5 (1962), cols. 53–322.
Rahner, K., 'Angel', in Rahner (ed.), *Sacramentum Mundi* (1968), i.
Schlier, H., *Principalities and Powers in the New Testament* (1961).
Spinks, B. D., *The Sanctus in the Eucharistic Prayer* (1991).

anger. The wrath of *God is an important and powerful theme in scripture and Christian tradition, but hardly appears in recent thought. Anthropomorphic as it is, it represents God's abhorrence of wickedness. *Israel is the object of God's anger throughout the OT for violating the *covenant, turning to strange gods, and treating the poor unjustly. But God is depicted as violently angry with other nations too: 'Behold the name of the Lord comes from afar, burning with his anger, and in thick rising smoke; his lips are full of indignation and his tongue is like a devouring fire' (Isa. 30: 27). It sounds volcanic. The image of God's anger was a necessary element in Israelite morality; without it human sinfulness and its consequences could not be adequately depicted. *Sin brings divine *punishment, but punishment leads to repentance and so to ultimate divine *forgiveness. 'Circumcise your hearts', declares Jeremiah (4: 4), to escape God's wrath. If the *exile is a 'judgement of wrath', God puts an end to it when Israel has paid her debt.

This very anthropomorphic vocabulary is carried across to the NT though Jesus never personally speaks of God's anger. It is in *Romans and the book of *Revelation that the theme is returned to most emphatically: 'The wrath of God is revealed from heaven against all ungodliness' (Rom. 1: 18). For those who 'obey wickedness', there will be wrath and fury' at the final judgement, 'the day of wrath' (2: 8, 5). 'What if God', asks Paul, 'desiring to show his wrath and to make known his power, has endured with much patience the vessels of wrath made for destruction, in order to make known the riches of his glory for the vessels of mercy?' (9: 22–3). Here is the heart of the matter and Paul's rhetoric may not help. Are there two distinct groups of humanity, 'vessels of wrath' and 'vessels of mercy', or, rather, are not all the first but turned, in Christ, into the second?

Given the appalling character of much human behaviour, we may reasonably think of God as unutterably angry. What Christ seems to show is that this, nevertheless, is a delusion. However badly the prodigal son behaves, his father still awaits his return without a word of reproach. A God characterized by wrath seems in Christian terms a huge misunderstanding, yet one which the preacher of *conversion is naturally prone to appeal to. *Hell fire, self-flagellation to atone for one's sins, and much else are all congruent with the image of an angry God. A good deal in the western *Augustinian tradition has encouraged that way of thinking. Abandon it as unworthy of God, following Ritschl and many another liberal theologian, and one easily abandons a sense of the meaning of sin, and even, as *Barth insisted, of *grace (*CD* IV/1. 490); keep it and, still

more disastrously, a specifically Christian sense of God as revealed in Jesus may be lost. There is no easy way of reconciling 'the wrath of the Lamb' (Rev. 6: 16) with 'Father, forgive them, for they know not what they do' (Luke 23: 24). It remains an unresolved tension in the NT and the entire Christian tradition.

The book of *Jonah depicts its hero forced unwillingly to preach to the people of Nineveh about God's anger and his intention to destroy them. They do penance, God abandons his anger, and Jonah becomes angry in his turn because he had suspected all along that his was a pointless mission, given God's forgiving nature. His prophesying about divine wrath would remain unrealized. The book ends with God chiding Jonah: the inhabitants of Nineveh 'do not know their right hand from their left'. How can one be angry with such people? That is hardly the line most Christian moralists would have followed, yet Jonah may best express the way Paul's 'vessels of wrath' are no less 'vessels of mercy'. The wrath of God, Barth emphasized, can be nothing 'other than the redemptive fire of his love'. 'Throw away thy wrath, O my God,' pleads George Herbert, 'Take the gentle path … Then let wrath remove; love will do the deed.' In Dame *Julian's words, 'There is no wrath in God, but only in ourselves.'

If God's anger was often commended, human anger was generally condemned as one of the seven deadly sins. Yet Jesus appeared very humanly angry at times. It would be against the principle of *analogy to ascribe a quality to God which is always a defect in humanity. If it can be misleading to talk about divine wrath, may it not still be necessary to insist on a human duty of anger faced with injustice and cruelty? The concept of God's wrath was intended to make one realize the evil of human behaviour, stimulating the virtue of righteous anger (2 Sam. 12: 5). Like every virtue its validity depends upon remaining a dimension of love.

Adrian Hastings

Hanson, A., *The Wrath of the Lamb* (1957).
Tasker, R. V. G., *The Biblical Doctrine of the Wrath of God* (1951).

Anglican thought,

the theological and spiritual tradition or ethos characterizing and deriving from the moderate *Reformation of the western Catholic Church in *sixteenth-century England and Wales. The word 'Anglican', as referring to the English nation, has become controversial: 'Episcopalian' is preferred in Scotland and the United States; in *Japan the Anglican Church is called the Nippon Sei Ko Kai (Holy Catholic Church in Japan). But no single alternative has yet generally commended itself. Directly or indirectly, the theological impulses from the English and Welsh Reformations, mediated through various cultural traditions and languages in addition to English, constitute collectively what can be termed 'Anglican thought'.

Anglican thought has the infuriating reputation of being imprecise. At first, with the rejection of the jurisdictional claims of the *papacy, the translation and distribution of the bible into English, and the preaching of the doctrine of *justification by faith, the Church of England appeared to be simply a national *Protestant church. All the major English reformers were in contact with the leading Continental Protestants, but England did not produce a theologian of the calibre or productiveness of *Luther or *Calvin, and there was extensive debate in England about whether the Reformation had proceeded far enough.

The re-establishment of a reformed Church of England under Elizabeth I in 1558, after the initial reforms of Henry VIII and Edward VI, and the return to Roman allegiance under Mary, was by intention moderate and inclusive. In the following century continuing controversy forced a certain self-consciousness upon theological defenders of the Church of England. George Herbert (1593–1633), Anglican priest and poet, praised 'the British Church' for its middle way.

> A fine aspect in fit aray,
> Neither too mean, nor yet too gay,
>   Shows who is best.
> Outlandish looks may not compare:
> For all they either painted are,
>   Or else undrest.

The obvious differences of Anglican *liturgical habit from, on the one hand, Roman Catholics, and, on the other, Independents and *Presbyterians, corresponded to deeper theological differences, which have proved difficult to specify. There are two reasons for this, both concerned with the exercise of *authority in the *church. First, the Church of England never acquired any confessional text comparable to those of the *Lutheran and *Reformed Churches or to the decrees of the Council of *Trent. It did, however, produce a group of documents, the Thirty-Nine Articles of Religion (1571), the Book of Common Prayer (1562), and the Ordering of Bishops, Priests and Deacons (1550), which contain important teaching and are still referred to collectively as its 'inheritance of faith'.

Secondly, the Church of England did not develop an authoritative, contemporary teaching body, comparable to the pope and college of bishops in the Catholic Church. It did assert that the church has authority in controversies of faith (Article XXI), provided that its decisions do not contradict scripture, and its bishops are instructed to be vigilant in the correction of error (The Form of Ordaining or Consecrating of an Archbishop or Bishop).

Hence Anglican thought tends to be both broad in scope and diverse in method. As with other Christian traditions, there exist both church theologies and theologians' theologies. The former are contained in (relatively few) teaching documents, statements, catechisms, or liturgies issued or authorized by bishops and synods. The latter comprise a vast range of theological scholarship and spiritual writing. Though generalization is necessarily uncertain and controversial, certain features can be observed.

First, from the days of the *Apology of the Church of England* (1564), by John Jewel, bishop of Salisbury, Anglicans have claimed that the Church of England is no new invention but the outcome of a restoration of the historic faith of the church, 'confirmed by the words of Christ, by the writings of the apostles, by the testimonies of the catholic fathers, and by the examples of many ages' (pt. 1). 'The Religion of the Church of England ... is the true Primitive Christianity: is nothing new, unless it be in rejecting all that novelty which hath been brought into the Church' (Simon Patrick, 18th-century bishop of Ely).

Secondly, and as a direct consequence, Anglican thought is rooted in orthodox *Trinitarianism. The first five of the Thirty-Nine Articles affirm a Trinitarian incarnational belief. Article VIII insists that the Nicene, Athanasian, and Apostles' *Creeds 'ought thoroughly to be received and believed'. This tradition has been subjected to careful scrutiny since the 18th century, and individual Anglican theologians have occasionally offered radical revisions. But modern Anglican liturgies and theologies remain strongly Trinitarian.

Thirdly, it is affirmed that 'Holy Scripture containeth all things necessary to salvation' (Article VI), a criterion aimed at validating the sweeping away of 'superstitions' and 'novel doctrines'. Public religious practice was greatly simplified, arguably an impoverishment for which the hoped-for study of the scriptures in the vernacular did not fully compensate. But the professed goal was that all members of the church should hear, read, mark, learn, and inwardly digest the holy scriptures for themselves (Collect for the Second Sunday in Advent).

Fourthly, Anglican thought and spirituality was always sustained and informed by its Book of Common Prayer. The sources for its successive editions are various, including moderate Catholic revisions and Continental Protestant service books, blended creatively by the genius of Archbishop Cranmer (1489–1556) on a foundation of earlier, patristic precedents and edifying practice. Anglicans continue to revise these books, and their exclusive use is prescribed by canon law. They function, therefore, both as public prayer and as norms of teaching.

Fifthly, Anglicans characteristically profess that their church is part of the one, holy, catholic, and *apostolic church, believing the catholic faith, celebrating the catholic *sacraments, and handing on the apostolic ministry, subject to the gospel (see CATHOLICITY). Perceived abuses in medieval sacramental theology and practice led to a strong emphasis upon the free, unmerited, justifying *grace of God, an emphasis shared with Continental Protestantism. But Anglicans generally stopped short of denying the efficacy of sacramental and ecclesial means of grace, and insisted that a person justified by grace is also living in *hope and *charity and bidden to do good works.

Finally, Anglicans retained and eventually justified the 'threefold order' of bishops, priests, and deacons (*diaconate), but denied the necessity of being in communion with the pope, for which they inherited some of the *conciliarist arguments (13th–15th centuries). The Articles, however, are cautious about the authority of general *councils. Sixteenth-century Anglican theologians realized that the *Eastern Orthodox had denied the authority of the Council of *Florence in its assertion of the supremacy of popes over councils. Even so, no one metropolitical centre can assert unchallengeable authority over any other—the churches of *Rome, *Jerusalem, *Alexandria, and Antioch are all said to have erred (Art. XIX). The implication is that the councils and synods of the Church of England may also err. Though the orders of bishops, priests, and deacons are said to have been appointed by the *Holy Spirit in the church 'from the Apostles' time', and to have been intentionally continued, reverently used, and esteemed in the Church of England, it is not assumed that plenary inspiration belongs to any one order or all collectively.

The theologian who most notably set these leading characteristics of Anglican thought in a sophisticated, philosophical framework was Richard *Hooker. His main work, *Of the Laws of Ecclesiastical Polity*, was an explicit justification of the Elizabethan settlement including the practice and doctrine of royal supremacy. He opposed the *Puritans' argument that the scriptures must be literally and absolutely followed. He held that human beings were bound to use *reason about the different kinds of material in the scriptures, and that different judgements can and should be made from time to time about controverted points. Such judgements, when made by properly appointed persons in the church, are authoritative but not necessarily infallible. It is better to end strife by a definitive decision, even if sometimes it proves later to be erroneous.

It is typical of Hooker, and some would say of Anglicanism, that, though he rejected the Puritan understanding of scripture, he upheld the Protestant doctrine of justification; and that, though he decried the Roman Catholic view of the church and papacy, he made use of scholastic *philosophy and defended the salvation of Catholics on the grounds of their holding a fundamental belief in Christ.

Hooker died in 1600. In the following century his influence was widely acknowledged, and strongly contributed to the growing sense of a distinctive Anglican tradition. A critical edition of his works appeared in 1836, edited by John Keble, a leader of the *Oxford Movement. It is at this point that the term 'Anglicanism' appears to have been coined. The Oxford Movement looked back to what it considered to be a golden era of Anglican thought, contrasting it with modern infidelity. Hence 'Anglicanism' has tended to be a construct, a selection from the broad streams of Anglican theology and spirituality. The writings of several 17th-century theologians, such as Lancelot Andrewes, were republished in a series, *The Library of Anglo-Catholic Theology*, a venture in which some leaders of the Movement participated, though with decreasing enthusiasm. The *Caroline Divines, as they were called, have assumed a classic status in Anglican thought, though in truth 17th-century Anglican theology was more diverse than the theory of 'Anglicanism' admitted.

*Eighteenth-century *Enlightenment rationalism bore upon Anglican thought, as upon all other western European confessions. John Toland's *Christianity not Mysterious* (1697) denounced as superstitious belief in revelations and the supernatural. Rationality, toleration, and free-thinking were celebrated in Anthony Collins's *Discourse of Free Thinking* (1713). Matthew Tindal's *Christianity as Old as the Creation* (1730) raised an array of problems in biblical exegesis. The Anglican counter-attack was rapid and effective in the writings of Richard Bentley, Daniel Waterland, George Berkeley, and Joseph Butler among others. What was defended was Trinitarian orthodoxy, but undergirded by rational argument. Bishop Warburton, for example, claimed that he had a proof of Christianity little short of mathematical certainty; Bishop Butler argued more modestly for the sufficiency of probability in relation both to natural and, by analogy, to revealed religion. In sermons of lasting distinction, published in 1726, Butler portrayed human nature as a moral synthesis of benevolence and self-interest. The dictates of *conscience, when free from superstition and self-deception, coincide with the requirements of Christian teaching.

Important though these influences were and are on the direction of Anglican thought, a more profound impression was made by the pietism of the *evangelical movement. The evangelical revival sought to recover the experiential content of the doctrine of justification by faith, by a more overt dependence upon scripture, together with the preaching of *conversion and an emphasis on sanctification. Though not at first a fashionable or intellectually distinguished movement, it had grown in strength by the end of the 18th century, and was one of the major strands in the *missionary movement through which the Anglican Communion eventually came into being.

While the sacramental emphasis of 17th-century Anglicanism had not been entirely lost in the 18th, the 19th-century Catholic revival represented a resurgence of this stream in the tradition. Anglican thought and spirituality has been deeply influenced by this revival: by its recovered respect for the teaching of the early church, its positive attitude towards ritual and symbol and its strong doctrine of ordained ministry. A liberal version of the catholic movement grew rapidly in the *twentieth century, attracting such outstanding theologians as Bishop Charles Gore, Archbishop William *Temple, and Archbishop Michael Ramsey. An early work of Ramsey, *The Gospel and the Catholic Church* (1936), contains a fruitful synthesis of a variety of strands of thought.

The Oxford Movement was vital to the development of the worldwide Anglican Communion in asserting the independence of the church and its ministry from the state. When *Newman exhorted his fellow Anglican clergy in the first *Tract for the Times* (1833) to 'exalt our Holy Fathers, the Bishops as the Representatives of the Apostles, and the Angels of the Churches; and magnify your office, as being ordained by them to take part in their Ministry', the political context was the threatened domination of the Church of England by a state intent on reforms. After the consecration in 1784 of Bishop Seabury as first bishop in the United States and the formation of the Episcopal Church there in 1789, the Anglican Communion slowly developed into a worldwide Christian family. In 1867 the archbishop of *Canterbury called the first Lambeth Conference, a meeting of Anglican bishops from all around the world. Henceforth the tendencies of Anglican thought as church theology can be traced in the Conference reports.

The robustness of a tradition tends to be tested under conditions of controversy. What Newman called 'chronic vigour' is a sign of the genuineness of a manifestation of Christian belief; evaluated by that criterion, Anglican thought may well emerge more confidently than Newman (who became a Roman Catholic) allowed. Five controversies in particular have marked Anglican thought in modern times, each imposing strain on the tradition.

The first is biblical criticism. Along with all Protestant denominations, and later Roman Catholicism, Anglican theology had to come to terms with the 19th-century historical-critical study of the bible (see HIGHER CRITICISM). After agonizing controversies, and not without continuing dissent, notably from evangelicals, on the whole Anglicans affirmed openness to such enquiry. The encyclical letter of the bishops at the 1897 Lambeth Conference rather finely declared: 'A faith which is always or often attended by a secret fear that we dare not inquire lest inquiry should lead us to results inconsistent with what we believe, is already infected with a disease which may soon destroy it.' But it was soon discovered that credal and other theological traditions too could not be protected from critical scrutiny. The doctrines of the *virgin birth and the bodily *Resurrection of Christ, and the Trinitarian-Incarnational faith itself, have all come under critical attack from individual Anglican theologians throughout the 20th century. The publication of *Christian Believing* (1976), a report by the Doctrine Commission of the Church of England, spoke of major difficulties in the contemporary reception of the creeds. Since that time the tradition has been powerfully reasserted. In all its recent international and local ecumenical statements the Anglican Communion has consistently affirmed Trinitarian-Incarnational belief and the authority of the Apostles' and Nicene Creeds. But the openness of enquiry poses a perennial difficulty for relations with Christian traditions committed to the view that the church has the authority to pronounce finally on a given subject.

A related issue concerns the progressive deconfessionalization of Anglicanism. The story is full of paradoxes. The Oxford Movement, one of the least tolerant strands of Anglicanism, tended to downplay, even denigrate, the circumstances and theology of the early Anglican Reformation. The Thirty-Nine Articles themselves came under fire as unduly Calvinistic and restrictive. The movement to separate Anglicanism from its 16th-century inheritance can be traced in the Lambeth Conferences from 1867 to 1968, when a hastily constructed motion advising member churches not to print the Articles in their prayer books was passed with few abstentions. But the coalition of forces, embracing both *liberal and Anglo-Catholic theologians, that produced this result was unable to provide any alternative theological basis for the Anglican Communion. In practice, local catechisms and ecumenical statements, together with prayer books, are the principal corporately acknowledged teaching documents in Anglicanism. One notable exception is a series of theological statements produced in the 1980s and 1990s by the Church of England's Doctrine Commission, *We Believe in God* (1987), *We Believe in the Holy Spirit* (1991), and *The Mystery of Salvation* (1996).

Thirdly, liturgical revision has occupied Anglicans since the 18th century. In the early 20th century a major effort to modernize and enrich the Book of Common Prayer encountered fierce evangelical opposition in Parliament. But the liturgical movement beginning in the Roman Catholic Church has had a massive impact on Anglican liturgical books, and has brought about a marked change in sensibility. Though there is still evangelical opposition to the doctrine of a sacrificing *priesthood, a stronger *eucharistic focus is widely acceptable in modern Anglicanism, together with more participatory modes of celebration. The reinculturation of liturgies has proceeded slowly in Asia, Africa, and Latin America, occasionally giving rise to serious questions about the relation of the tradition to local circumstances. Because authorized Prayer Books are among the major teaching documents of the Anglican provinces, their mutual coherence becomes an important issue. This has yet to be tackled with any degree of common acceptability.

Most pronounced of the theological tensions within contemporary Anglicanism are the issues relating directly or indirectly to the *women's movements of the 20th century. Although often spoken of in the singular as *'feminism', there are varied influences and forms. The challenge to the tradition of Christian patriarchy, deeply embedded within the Anglican tradition, was first experienced in relation to *contraception. Artificial means were stubbornly resisted until opposition finally collapsed at the Lambeth Conference of 1958 with acceptance of the report, *The Family in Contemporary Society*.

By then discussion had already begun of the rule restricting *ordination to males. In 1968 the Lambeth Conference declared that the arguments for and against that tradition were inconclusive. By 1978 ordinations of women to the priesthood had already occurred;

by 1988 ordinations to the *episcopate were accepted as inevitable, and the proper business of the separate provinces. A serious and sometimes fragile attempt to combine sharply differing views within a common framework of order is now under way.

The relativity of scriptural patriarchal traditions to their cultural environment and support for equal rights has led to the application of similar arguments to the issue of same-sex relations. The testing of a tradition long hostile to *homosexuality again exposes the problem of authority. Who, and on what grounds, has the right to decide such questions? In practice all Protestant Churches are caught in the toils of the same arguments. Though Roman Catholics may seem to escape by referring them to their central authority, in practice the arguments continue, as does practical disobedience to authoritative statements about contraception.

Fifthly, the *ecumenical movement of the 20th century has also brought its tensions and controversies. Though by intention constituting a comprehensive church, and contributing notably to the early years of ecumenism, Anglicans have commonly found themselves frustrated in recent ecumenical endeavours. This is partly because of their tendency to exempt themselves from the requirements of articulating their own understanding of the church. 'Anglicans have no doctrines of their own' has functioned as a kind of shibboleth, especially in relation to ecclesiology. It has also been common to insist on the retention of episcopacy, but to decline to offer a theological justification for doing so.

Such a stance is dubious in itself and irritating to ecumenical partners. In historical terms it is questionable whether there are literally no doctrines which Anglicans have formulated for themselves. There is, or was, a family of Anglican traditions on eucharistic theology, and the doctrine of justification. It may be argued that no church can function as church without at least an implicit sense of its nature to guide its decision-making. Under the impact of modern ecumenism, such self-imposed reticence is already breaking down. An explicit understanding of the episcopate is articulated in the Porvoo Document, jointly produced by Anglicans of Great Britain and Ireland and Lutherans of the Nordic and Baltic countries. A theology of the church as *communion is a pronounced feature of the work of the Anglican–Roman Catholic International Commission. Such documents are a form of ecumenical church theology; but they are having a progressively significant impact on Anglican thought more generally.

Against the background of the transformation of Anglicanism from a state church to a world communion, and amidst the intensity and complexity of the issues now inescapable for any Christian church, there has continued to be a robust tradition of statement, exploration, and criticism from Anglican sources. Though its capacity to retain and deepen the spiritual and intellectual lives of people of highly diverse convictions and backgrounds was intensely tested in the last decades of the 20th century, Anglican thought continues to be vigorous and productive.   **Stephen Sykes**

Avis, Paul, *Anglicanism and the Christian Church: Theological Resources in Historical Perspective* (1989).

Bradshaw, Tim, *The Olive Branch: An Evangelical Doctrine of the Church* (1992).

Cuming, G. J., *A History of Anglican Liturgy*, 2nd edn. (1982).

Davies, Horton, *Worship and Theology in England* (1961).

Duffy, Eamon, *The Stripping of the Altars: Traditional Religion in England 1400–1580* (1992).

Jacob, W. M., *The Making of the Anglican Church Worldwide* (1997).

MacCulloch, Diarmaid, *Thomas Cranmer: A Life* (1996).

Nockles, Peter B., *The Oxford Movement in Context: Anglican High Churchmanship 1760–1857* (1994).

O'Donovan, Oliver, *On the Thirty-Nine Articles: A Conversation with Tudor Christianity* (1986).

Sachs, William L., *The Transformation of Anglicanism: From State Church to Global Communion* (1993).

Stevenson, K., and Spinks, B. (eds.), *The Identity of Anglican Worship* (1991).

Sykes, Stephen, *Unashamed Anglicanism* (1995).

—— (ed.), *Authority in the Anglican Communion* (1997).

Sykes, Stephen, Booty, John, and Knight, Jonathan (eds.), *The Study of Anglicanism*, rev. edn. (1998).

Taylor, Stephen (ed.), *From Cranmer to Davidson: A Church of England Miscellany* (1999).

Wingate, Andrew, Ward, Kevin, Pemberton, Carrie, and Sitshebo, Wilson (eds.), *Anglicanism: A Global Communion* (1998).

Anglo-Catholicism, see Oxford Movement.

animals.

At first sight, animals might seem an unpromising area for theological enquiry. The usual sources appear rather meagre. There is little direct NT interest in the status of animals. The great systems of Christian thought rarely focus specifically on animals, and those which do usually conclude with Karl *Barth that they constitute a 'marginal' issue (*CD* III/4. 333). Christian ethics, too, has generally been characterized by a neglect—usually not a benign one—of issues concerning animal welfare.

Despite the generally dismissive attitude of the Christian tradition, there have been sub-traditions that have variously highlighted animals as a topic of theological and *moral concern. While these have generally received little prominence, they are testimony to an enduring sense of relatedness to, even kinship with, animals. In relation to contemporary debates, the Christian tradition is still a largely unquarried resource for renewed appreciation of the status of animals.

It is frequently observed that *Jesus said little about the treatment of animals. But what he did say is probably more significant than is often allowed. The 'sparrows' (*strouthia*—little birds) are 'not forgotten by God' (Luke 12: 6)—an exceptional thought given that the *strouthia* were probably bought and sold as little chunks of meat in the Palestinian market. Moreover, Jesus' life and ministry is frequently identified with animals: his ministry begins in the wilderness 'with the wild beasts' (Mark 1: 13); his triumphal entry to *Jerusalem takes place on a humble ass (Matt. 21: 5); unlike the foxes which have their appointed home 'the Son of Man has nowhere to lay his head' (Luke 9: 58); and, most strikingly of all, Jesus is characterized as 'the lamb of God' (John 1: 36).

Proof that these connections were not lost on subsequent tradition can be found in a wide range of *apocryphal material from the 2nd to the 9th centuries. In the *Gospel of Pseudo-Matthew*, an ox and an ass attend the birth of Jesus—a tradition which dates from drawings on the sarcophagi of the 4th and 5th centuries. In the same pseudo-gospel, Jesus makes peaceful relations with dragons, and lions and leopards accompany the Holy Family to Egypt. In the Infancy *Gospel of Thomas*, the boy Jesus creates sparrows from soft clay and revives dead fish (J. K. Elliott (ed.), *The Apocryphal New Testament* (1993), 79–98). In one Coptic fragment, Jesus is pictured healing a mule and admonishing the owner to 'beat it no more, that you may also find mercy' (R. Dunkerley, *Beyond the Gospels* (1957), 144). Two motifs predominate throughout this literature: kinship and *peaceableness. Christian imagination continued for centuries to embellish and supplement the notion, implicit in the canonical gospels, that Jesus' work was inclusive of the animal world.

Subsequent scholastic theology developed many emphases that reinforced theological boundaries between humans and animals. Humans alone are rational, *persons, possessors of an immortal *soul. The dominant effect of these distinctions, however worthy they may be in themselves, was to define *humanity *against* animality, and to abstract humankind from the world of fellow-creatures. Another inevitable result was to eclipse moral solicitude for the non-rational, soulless brutes. Thomas *Aquinas, echoing *Aristotle, reinforced a strongly hierarchical and instrumentalist reading of creaturely relations: 'There is no sin in using a thing for the purpose for which it is. Now the order of things is such that the imperfect are for the perfect ... it is not unlawful if man uses plants for the good of animals, and animals for the good of man as the Philosopher states' (*ST* I. q. 64 a. 1).

However dominant this view has become, it is important to set alongside it other emphases which emerge from hagiography. From the 9th to the 18th century there is an alternative worldview embodied in the lives of innumerable *saints who celebrate animals as fellow-creatures of *God, and who exhibit an inclusive Christlike generosity. The list includes many saints of east and west: from Cuthbert and Columba through to Seraphim and David of Garesja. These stories of fraternal relationships are frequently dismissed as hagiographical gloss but underlying them is a continuity of concern with earlier apocryphal literature. The theological rationale is expressed by Bonaventure writing of *Francis that when 'he considered the primordial source of all things, he was filled with even more piety, calling creatures, no matter how small, by the name of brother or sister because he knew that they had the same source as himself' (Bonaventure, *Soul's Journey into God*).

The recognition of the common origin of all creatures went hand in hand with another related insight that what is created by God deserves our respect. The themes of kinship and peacefulness find continuing expression within, admittedly, a sub-tradition of Christendom. Against the dominant instrumentalist view that animals were here for human use, many saints exemplified relationships of harmony and celebration.

The idea that there was a wider ethic—and that it had specifically Christian authority—was the explicit motivation for the emergence of zoophily or anti-cruelty sensibility in the 19th century, particularly in the Anglo-Saxon world. The Anglican priest, Arthur Broome, who founded the world's first national SPCA (Society for the Prevention of Cruelty to Animals) in 1824, wrote in its prospectus of how the infliction of pain on any living creature was incompatible with divine benevolence. The First Minute Book of the SPCA records that it was founded as a society specifically based on the Christian faith and on Christian principles. That the Anglo-Saxon world should be the principal locus for this rising sensibility is perhaps the result of a specific cultural and theological fusion. The particularly abundant English practice of keeping animals as pets and companions (which dates at least from the 18th century) provided a rich soil in which to plant notions of inter-species fraternity.

Already explicit in the scholastic tradition was the idea that cruelty inflicted on animals could lead to cruel dispositions among the perpetrators. The humanitarianism of the 19th century develops this idea and posits cruelty as undesirable in itself. 'A cruel Christian is a monster of ingratitude,' wrote Humphry Primatt, the prophet of the anti-cruelty movement (*The Duty of Mercy and the Sin of Cruelty* (1776), 20). Although initially marginal, zoophily became mainstream. The sub-tradition that had preserved wider notions of duty itself became institutionalized in the formation of the SPCA and its social acceptability was reinforced by subsequent royal patronage.

While Christian thought remains heavily humano-centric, these sub-traditions have provided some impetus towards the development of a comprehensive theology of animals. Perhaps most significant has been the growing awareness that a strictly theological understanding of animals relativizes humanistic perspectives. The value and worth of other creatures cannot be determined solely by their utility to us. Nothing in *creation can be a subject of indifference to the creator. Belief in a loving creator God requires a positive evaluation of living beings who share the gift of life. Hence the growth of a 'life-centred ethic' expressly inclusive of respect for animals.

Alongside claims for the intrinsic value of other life-forms has gone an increased appreciation that many familiar boundaries between humans and animals are no longer sustainable. Few ethologists now doubt the intelligence, self-consciousness, and emotional complexity of the higher mammals. Most important has been the recognition—especially in philosophical works—of the moral significance of sentiency: that many mammals can experience *suffering in ways analogous to human subjects has led to their firm inclusion within the circle of moral considerability. Arguably this preoccupation resonates with a sensibility to animal suffering which the tradition has, at its best, espoused. John Henry *Newman, among others, highlighted the Christlike innocence of animals. 'Think then, my brethren, of your feelings at cruelty practised on brute animals, and you will gain one sort of feeling which the history of Christ's Cross and Passion ought to excite within you' ('The Crucifixion', *Parochial and Plain Sermons*, VII).

Consolidating these developments has been a thoroughgoing reinterpretation of the meaning of human power over creation. Traditional scholastic opinion appealed to human 'dominion' as if it was absolute or self-justifying. Contemporary scholars, however, have stressed that human dominion—as originally understood in Genesis 1: 28—is a derived, deputized, authority that needs to be exercised in accordance with God's moral will. The notion that 'might is right' has been superseded by a more ecologically friendly (and also more biblically authentic) concept of human responsibility for creation. Some thinkers take this thought to its *christological limit and argue that, as exemplified in the life of Christ, lordship *means* service. Humans are to be not the master species but 'the servant species': their vocation is to express God's care as agents made in God's own image.

The emergence of animal rights philosophy from the 1970s onwards has sharpened still further the older theological issue of moral obligations to animals. Although the language of 'rights' is rejected by many within the Christian tradition, animal rights is—in one sense—a peculiarly theological problem. This is because scholastic theology has been resolute in its *denial* of the rights of animals. Unsurprisingly, animal advocates have therefore latched upon this denial as the cornerstone of 'speciesist' ideology. Rights for animals has become the modern way of expressing the view that what we owe animals is not just a matter of taste, emotion, or philanthropy, but *justice.

While some Christians remain fearful or sceptical, or both, of the language of animal rights, such language addresses in an acute form the issue of moral limits. It challenges Christians in a modern context to recognize the specific claims of animals to just and respectful treatment. Moreover, appeals to animal rights are not without a theological basis. Put theologically, the debate about animal rights can be seen as an issue about the rights of the creator to have what is created treated with respect. The so-called 'Theos-rights of animals' expresses in the strongest possible terms our obligation to respect what is given in creation by the creator.

However valuable rights language may be both rhetorically (in focusing the issue of precise moral limits) and theologically (in registering the prior rights of the creator), it clearly fails to provide a holistic vision of how humans should live with other creatures. Rights language may be essential (in a modern context) but it is not sufficient. Talk of love, empathy, kinship, care, and responsibility are also necessary. Perhaps most important is the notion of moral generosity. Here the sub-traditions of Christian thought and modern sensitivity to animals converge. For what these sub-traditions variously preserve is the christological paradigm of inclusive moral generosity.

At the heart of the gospel narrative is the Christ who identifies himself with the weak and the vulnerable, who makes their cause his own cause—and God's cause too. Indeed those who minister to the needs of the vulnerable and the weak minister to Christ himself (see e.g. Matt. 25: 35–46). It follows that if it is true that this paradigm of generous, costly service is at the heart of the Christian proclamation then it should also be the paradigm for the exercise of human dominion over the animal world. Realization that animals are—like some humans—also vulnerable, unprotected, undefended, morally innocent, and subjects of a special trust compels the response of moral generosity. It may not be inconceivable that future Christian theologizing supplants the notion of a 'preferential option for the poor' with a wider vision of the moral priority of the weak.

See also GLOBAL ETHICS.

Andrew Linzey

Birch, Charles, and Vischer, Lukas, *Living with Animals: The Community of God's Creatures* (1997).

Linzey, Andrew, *Animal Rights: A Christian Assessment* (1976).

—— *Christianity and the Rights of Animals* (1987).

—— *Animal Theology* (1994).

—— *Animal Gospel: Christian Faith as if Animals Mattered* (1998).

Linzey, Andrew, and Cohn-Sherbok, Dan, *After Noah: Animals and the Liberation of Theology* (1997).

Linzey, Andrew, and Yamamoto, Dorothy (eds.), *Animals on the Agenda: Questions about Animals for Theology and Ethics* (1998).

McDaniel, Jay B., *Of God and Pelicans: A Theology of Reverence for Life* (1989).

Murray, Robert, *The Cosmic Covenant: Biblical Themes of Justice, Peace and the Integrity of Creation* (1992).

Pinches, Charles, and McDaniel, Jay B. (eds.), *Good News for Animals? Christian Approaches to Animal Well-Being* (1993).

Salisbury, Joyce E., *The Beast Within: Animals in the Middle Ages* (1994).

Webb, Stephen H., *On God and Dogs: Towards a Christian Theology of Compassion for Animals* (1998).

Anselm of Canterbury

(c.1033–1109). Anselm was born in Aosta. In 1059 he found his way to the abbey of Bec in Normandy, where he was taught by Lanfranc, also an Italian. In 1063 he succeeded Lanfranc as prior, and in 1078 became abbot. Eadmer, in his *Life of Anselm*, gives a vivid account of his reluctance to take office and the care with which he none the less fulfilled his duties as a guide of souls. It was at Bec that he composed the two great theological works, the *Monologion* and the *Proslogion* (1078–9), as well as the earlier among his *Meditations* and *Prayers*, the short treatises *On the Fall of the Devil* and *On Free Will*, and the philosophical works *On Truth* and *On Grammar*. Anselm was consecrated archbishop of *Canterbury in December 1093. Through his troubled tenure as archbishop, and through two periods of exile from England, he kept at his theological work, finishing *On the Incarnation of the Word* in 1095, and his third major work *Cur deus homo* (*Why God became Man*) in Italy in 1098.

His writing was always of unusual clarity and force. It has in it a curious affinity with the thought of *Plato (curious because he can have known at first-hand only the *Timaeus*), has in places the form of a brilliant interpretation of *Augustine's more hesitant speculations (for example on the Trinity), and evoked the interest of *Kant at a time when the thinking of the Middle Ages tended to be the object of condescension.

The *Monologion* is what Anselm calls 'a meditation on the divine essence', and, in its central passages, on the Trinity. In the inward path of its meditation the mind comes upon the 'Highest Good', which it will tend naturally towards because of its own formation 'in the image of God'. Its interpretations are, as it were, tied to the 'Highest Good' or 'Highest Being', and so are in some sense bound to be true to life. The power of discerning what is true is in this way something like an emergence from the chrysalis of solipsism, of meditative introspection, into the daylight of the true being of created things and their creator.

Meditation is, however, also a reflection on words. The *Monologion* is of Anselm's writings the one that owes most to his grounding in grammar, that element in the medieval curriculum occupied with the analysis of *language. In ch. 10, he asks us to recall an experience in the use of words where the mind produces an image of an existing object with such felicity that the image and its object seem to be one. Taking the thought or image as a word, a kind of speaking, Anselm understands such experiences as belonging to language at its most intense and truthful. This is 'the speaking of things' (*locutio rerum*) which appears to be making, or bringing into being, what it says. On the recollection of such moments in the use of words he now constructs his meditation. With scrutiny, the unity between word and thing is seen to be an illusion, for our words do no more than imitate what is already there. They are likenesses of things, not things themselves; like being, but not being itself. For the word which, instead of being 'after' the world, brings it into being, we have to look to the originating word of *God at the moment of *creation, whose quality of unity with what it creates is spelt out in the story of creation from nothing. If God makes the world from nothing, the 'word' with which he does so, since it imitates nothing that goes before it, must bring into being as it speaks. Anselm's thought here is a re-enactment of both the *Timaeus*, with its myth of creation by the demiurge, and of the opening verses of Genesis. Much of what remains of the *Monologion* is a struggle to connect this first word with the many words of our own speech which imitate it.

The guide Anselm takes on his journey is that of 'faith seeking understanding' (*fides quaerens intellectum*), a thread that runs all through his reflections. *Reason here, or understanding, is not external to *faith, as though a separate faculty of mind (as it might be in *Abelard for example), but is implied in it, rather as sympathetic criticism is demanded of its beholder by the interrogative force of a great painting. The kinship of faith and reason has an echo in the perception by some recent philosophers (such as Gadamer, *Ricœur), themselves the heirs of the 18th-century distinction between 'symbol' and 'allegory', that *symbols are not dissolved by analysis but revivified. And it is a kinship borne out in the protrusion of the bible into the argument, despite Anselm's avoidance of quotation in favour of 'the necessity of reason'. The whole book might even be considered a formal reflection on the opening verses of *Genesis and the seeing 'through a glass darkly' of 1 Corinthians 13: 12. With its biblical hinterland, the *Monologion* pushes to its extreme Augustine's discovery that the introspective and the biblical are not distinct. The *Monologion* is thus at bottom radical exegesis, despite its reluctance to quote the bible. Its core is a scrutiny of what it is to speak a word, and if it is exegesis it is exegesis of the bible as word.

Moreover, it is an odyssey, the story of an understanding that waxes and wanes. Towards its end, struck by what he calls 'the indigence of the name of the Trinity'—the helplessness of language before this simultaneity of three and one—Anselm concedes that we have been looking into a mirror: 'through a glass darkly'. It is the sentiment of indigence which prevails as the journey is reviewed. At the height of his odyssey, though, and with an unruffled mastery that borrows from the sublime in his subject, he turns by way of the motif of the birth of the word from its speaker (the Father), to the Trinity. Just as the speech founded in likeness is somewhere indistinguishable from that 'intimate speech' (*intima locutio*) by which God makes the world (or just as the prophet talks back, albeit stuttering, to his inspiration), so, for Anselm, the perception of the Trinity as Father giving birth to Son is not a *metaphor (if metaphor is one thing *indicating* another), but a withdrawal from metaphor. Anselm proceeds by the correction of metaphor, stripping back one metaphor by the introduction of another, on the grounds that the *fatherhood seen in the ascetic light of corrected metaphor is fatherhood as it is: as it is, not in its transient aspect (the fatherhoods of our biographies), but as it is in the perspective of God's art, which is uncorrupted by the passing away of what it produces. And yet this 'as it is' borrows its solidness, its warmth, its exertion of presence, from the familiar lived paternity of human biographies. The effect of these meditations on the Trinity (deepened as they are by a consideration of the *Holy Spirit as the love between Father and Son) is an ascetic joy, which, for all the decline suffered in the concluding pages, is borne out in the substantiality given to the 'divine essence' by the bleakness, both linguistic and moral, felt in the 'indigence of the name of the Trinity'.

The *Proslogion* puts into the form of an argument 'a struggle of thoughts': the 'thought' of the philosophical exhaustion which settles on the mind when the object of its quest, the 'Highest Good' (or the argument which would encompass this 'Highest Good'), endlessly escapes its labours; and the 'thought' which is the mind's inevitable familiarity with God, its inability not to understand God (for it is made in the image of God, a teaching the force of which is known in the act of prayer). This 'inability not to understand' is also glimpsed in that intensest of speaking experiences hit upon already in the *Monologion*, and it is as well to read the earlier work before setting out on the later. 'In this struggle of thoughts, there offered itself what I had despaired of.' The *Proslogion* is not to be read as an argument about God or his existence (see ONTOLOGICAL ARGUMENT). It is rather a rehearsal in the form of an argument of the discovery of God as object (though one in which the object and the process of discovery cannot be told apart). The 'one argument', as Anselm calls it to distinguish it from the less satisfactory 'chain of arguments' in the *Monologion*, is condensed in the definition (also an invocation) of God at the start of ch. 2: 'We believe you to be that thing than which nothing greater can be thought.' On this definition turns the thought, till now hidden within prayer ('When will you light up your eyes? And show us your face? When will you restore yourself to us?') that the most perfect being is also the most real. The phrase 'something than which nothing greater can be thought' is so put together, however, that it throws the mind back into struggle. The 'something' must be greater than can be thought, for otherwise it would be possible to think something greater. Yet it is this side of nothing, and therefore palpable. The mind is caught between quest, and the apprehension of God as *res*, a thing—much as *Job (one might say) recovered from the misery of his incomprehension with the Lord's 'Where wast thou when I laid the foundations of the earth?' And just as Job is made to see with fierce clarity the things of the world, so too in Anselm's philosophical version there is a correspondence between God as thing and world as thing. 'Hast thou given the horse strength? ... Canst thou make him afraid as a grasshopper? the glory of his nostrils is terrible' (Job 38: 4; 39: 19–20). The 'one argument' with which Anselm answers the fool, 'who hath said in his heart, there is no God' (Ps. 14), is perhaps best described as a recognition of what it is to pray. The *Proslogion* is thus a series of Chinese boxes: the exhaustion and revelation of the Prologue; the prayer of ch. 1, where the reality of God presses down in the texture of shame at loss and blindness ('How long wilt thou forget us, O Lord? For ever? How long wilt thou hide thy face from us?' cf. Ps. 13: 1); the objectivity of God discovered in the intellectual quest to unveil his face: 'that than which nothing greater can be thought'. In this way, it might be said that Anselm's response to the fool, who claims that 'that than which nothing greater can be thought' might only be in the mind (*in intellectu*), not in reality (*in re*) outside the mind, is ultimately to displace the fool by the saint, in whom the knowledge of perfection, taken for granted, is repeatedly made surprising, not least to himself, by miracle. The whole course of the argument recalls the delight of the painter who set out to *make* (make up), and then becomes aware that he has *found*. But there is a turn of the screw. The finding and making are put within the frame of a making from nothing (cf. *Monologion*). Perhaps the beauty of the argument is in the end in the

question it poses whether the believer is himself capable of his own belief.

In *Why God became Man*, a dialogue, Anselm gives an account of why it is 'necessary' that God become man in order for man to be saved after the *Fall, a proposition built up in the first place in answer to the scorn of the unbeliever at the humiliation apparently involved in God's being man and bearing the suffering of this particular man (see ATONEMENT). The necessity of God's action is the mark of its dignity, Anselm maintains. It would be unbecoming if God, for example, were to rescue Adam and his kind from their predicament after Eden simply by an unconditional gesture of mercy. For this would suggest that, at least according to our intimations of what justice might really be, injustice, being subject to no law, has more freedom than justice, so that injustice is more like God, who is also not subject to law (1. 12). This line of reasoning (posing more of a problem than it solves: the problem at the centre of *Why God became Man*, how we can say of God he is acting by necessity and yet subject to no law) represents one among many styles of reasoning in the work as a whole. The work, divided into two books, has a disarming freedom, or, perhaps better, grace, which sometimes looks like digressiveness, though it never is (see the long discussion at 1. 16–18 of the restoration to their full numbers of the angels after the fall of Lucifer and his company). It is constructed on a very solid myth, a retelling of the story of reconciliation of man and God. Dismissing as implausible the old 'ransom' myth which has God tricking Satan of his dominion over man by sending his sinless son to die—Satan can have no rights over man, says Anselm, and any patching up is between man and God—Anselm gives the following version: God had to become man because the offence given in the Garden was infinite, the guilty parties finite. Only God has it in him to make it up, only man is obliged to make it up. Hence the God-man. That the offence given to God's honour (as Anselm calls it) is infinite is established with unforgiving exactness—before he ate the fruit, Adam *already* owed all he was and had, his very being, to his maker—for what he is is wholly determined by what he was made for, and that is the beatitude God had in mind for him (1. 22). Everything he might give as recompense (the fear and love which is prayer, the labour of self-denial, forgiveness of others, obedience) he owes as debts of his being at all (1. 20). Worse, what is due to God is being itself, all of being, an impossible situation indeed. 'I think we are living very dangerously,' says Boso, Anselm's interlocutor, after being led to this point. The answer—the only answer Anselm can see, though he is happy to bow to better, or 'more necessary' reasons if he hears them—is a satisfaction by one *who does not owe*, who is not under compulsion of any kind, who has in his possession the gift of being, and, owing nothing, can give it away because he *wishes* to. The infinity of God is recast as the act of will by which he gives what all being other than himself owes (1. 11).

What Anselm wants to get, he tells us, is something solid. He is the painter who paints not on water but on solid stuff (1. 4; 2. 8). And what he paints, we might say, is the solidness of Christ's willing what is necessary. The demonstration that the story must go like this, and our ability to demonstrate this without the help of what we already know of Christ—our ability, given the beginning of the story (the Fall), to complete it by careful reasoning—have convinced us that necessity informs the agony in the Garden and all the 'injuries, insults, griefs' we know to be part of the story (cf. 2. 11). The Christ of *pathos*, very characteristic of Anselm's time, is not Anselm's Christ. Grief, straitened with the precision—the coldness even—of argument, is sublime. Not sublimated: it is still there, harsh as ever, and the sublime is less of Rembrandt's *Deposition* than of Mantegna's *Entombment*.

What, though, can be made of God's acting under necessity? Here, Anselm's view depends on a distinction between necessity of cause and effect (the heavens turn, because the laws of nature turn them), and 'necessity of sequence', where one thing follows or accompanies another, because it is so (you are speaking 'necessarily', because you are speaking). God does not 'lay down his life' because he is forced to by something outside himself; rather, he acts according to a necessity which is at once a refraction of his will and a confession of what is the case. Law, justice, necessity, are not what they seem, but instead the sovereignty evident in harmony, a kind of sureness of touch—so that an eloquent, unstrained gesture gives to each protagonist of this drama (God, Adam, God-man, angels, Virgin) the insistence which is apt to each of them, robbing the drama of tension and admitting between the figures only the most profound connection. At its most profound, the connection is that of the simplicity, the facility of seeing things as they are (and as they have been and will be) and the faith which acts accordingly at a given moment in time—and of the human experience of this the Virgin, made ready to bear God by her own power to guess how the story must end, is the palpable fulfilment (2. 17–19). Perhaps no thinker has so replenished the myths which sustain belief as Anselm with his 'necessary reasons'.   **Peter Cramer**

Anselm, *Collected Works*, ed. F. S. Schmitt (6 vols., 1946–61).

Davies, B., and Evans, G. R. (eds.), *Anselm of Canterbury: The Major Works* (1998).t

Eadmer, *The Life of St Anselm*, ed. R. W. Southern (1962).

Southern, R. W., and Schmitt, F. S. (eds.), *Memorials of St Anselm* (1969).

Ward, B. (ed.), *The Prayers and Meditations of St Anselm* (1973).

Barth, K., *Fides Quaerens Intellectum* (1931), ET (1960).

Campbell, R., *From Belief to Understanding: A Study of Anselm's Proslogion Argument on the Existence of God* (1976).

Evans, G. R., *Anselm and Talking about God* (1978).

Gilbert, P., *Dire l'Ineffable: Lecture du 'Monologion' de S. Anselme* (1984).

Hopkins, J., *A Companion to the Study of St Anselm* (1972).

——*A New Interpretative Translation of St Anselm's Monologion and Proslogion* (1986).

Luscombe, D. E., and Evans, G. R. (eds.), *Anselm, Aosta, Bec, and Canterbury* (1996).

McIntyre, J., *St Anselm and his Critics: A Re-Interpretation of the* Cur deus homo (1954).

Southern, R. W., *Saint Anselm and his Biographer: A Study of Monastic Life and Thought 1059–c.1130* (1963).

——*Saint Anselm: A Portrait in a Landscape* (1990).

anthropology.

Anthropological studies of *religion have focused mainly on primitive religions. Much of the material that the Victorian armchair anthropologists worked from was culled from *missionary publications, and only in the early 20th century did anthropologists begin to undertake fieldwork themselves. The encounter of the two parties in the field gave rise to much mutual criticism, the missionaries being accused of destroying primitive cultures, the anthropologists of trying to keep their tribes primitive. According to Evans-Pritchard (1962) the majority of British anthropologists in his day and before were indifferent, if not hostile, to religion, and only a minority were Christians. The contribution of anthropology to Christian thought can be traced through two specific developments, one starting with the French ethnologist van Gennep, the other with the British anthropologist Frazer.

Van Gennep's unique contribution to anthropology, and indirectly to Christian *sacramental theology, has been the analysis of ceremonies accompanying an individual's life crises, ceremonies which he called 'rites of passage'. Van Gennep observed that typically they consist of three major phases: separation, segregation, and integration. Rites of separation express the neophyte's relinquishment of his former status. Rites of segregation express the fact that he is now cut off from normal community life. Rites of integration express the initiate's acceptance of the new status—adulthood, priesthood, or whatever it may be—and reintegration in the community. Simple as this observation may seem at first, it greatly contributed to the comparative study of such rituals in very diverse settings and texts.

Van Gennep's ideas were further developed by the British anthropologist Victor Turner, an authority on the initiation rituals of the Ndembu people of Zambia. Turner's main interest lay in the segregation phase for which he used the term 'liminal' (from the Latin *limen*, threshold). Liminality is frequently likened to physical death, or to being in the mother's womb. Neophytes may be represented as possessing nothing. Their behaviour is normally passive or humble; they must obey their instructors implicitly, and accept arbitrary punishment without complaint. One recognizes this three-phased movement in the initiation hymn of Christ in Philippians 2: 6–11, and in Paul's *baptismal theology, as set forth in Romans 6: 4. In Africa, where initiation ceremonies are still a regular feature, van Gennep's scheme as elaborated by Turner is successfully used in baptismal catechesis, as it allows for spontaneous identification of the listeners with the person of Christ via their own initiation experience.

Comparing the normal life of an individual with life in a liminal phase, Turner made another important theological contribution by defining these two situations as two major and alternating models for human interrelatedness. The first is of a society as a structured, differentiated, and often hierarchical system, separating people in terms of 'more' or 'less'. The second is of society as an unstructured, or rudimentarily structured, community. 'Communitas', as he calls this, gives recognition to an essential and generic human bond, without which there would be no society. It also implies that the high could not be high unless the low existed, and that those who are high must experience what it is to be low. One recognizes here a fundamental biblical theme, which in the light of Turner's analysis appears to be universally human.

The second anthropological contribution to be considered runs from the Victorian anthropologist James Frazer to the French historian and literary critic Girard. Although Girard is no anthropologist by training, he has made extensive use of anthropological studies, such as Frazer's seminal writings on scapegoat rituals, to develop his theory of religion. Girard sets off from the observation that our desires are to a large degree mimetic. What proves attractive to others may thereby become attractive to us. The next point is that where many people want the same thing, scarcity may be one of the consequences, followed by open conflict and the outbreak of violence. Violence in its turn may escalate to the point at which it threatens the continued existence or viability of a society. One possibility of halting that process is to find a scapegoat, who is then lynched or exiled. Once this has been done and peace has returned, people realize that the scapegoat which was the cause of the crisis has now become the cause of their restored unity as well. This turns the scapegoat into a sacred being whose salutary potential is then regularly activated by the making of *sacrifices. It is one of Girard's contentions that the scapegoat scenario is at the origin of religion, which is then to be defined as a strategy to limit violence. However, the violent origins of religion are kept hidden by a veil of *myth, in which the victim is the guilty party. This mechanism of deceit has been exposed gradually in the Judaeo-Christian tradition and, most supremely, in the *person of Christ.

Girard's anthropological theory of religion has proved surprisingly fruitful and has led to a veritable outpouring of studies in theology as well as other disciplines, particularly in the United States and Western Europe. But both he and Turner have been received with a great deal of scepticism by the majority of anthropologists, which was only to be expected, since the tendency has always been to consider religion as superstition. To be an anthropologist and a professed believer is regarded by most as a contradiction in terms.

See also SOCIAL SCIENCES.   **Matthew Schoffeleers**

Evans-Pritchard, E. E., *Essays in Social Anthropology* (1962).
Frazer, J. C., *The Golden Bough* (1890).
van Gennep, Arnold, *The Rites of Passage* (1909), ET (1960).
Girard, R., *Violence and the Sacred* (1972), ET (1977).
Turner, V. W., *The Ritual Process: Structure and Anti-Structure* (1969).

antinomianism

antinomianism (from *anti*, against, and *nomos*, law) claims that Christians are not bound by moral *law. When Paul said that 'if you are led by the Spirit, you are not under law' (Gal. 5: 8) this was not a licence to be immoral, but it raised a persistent question about the status of law in the Christian life. There has never been an organized body that called itself antinomian.

The word 'antinomian' was first used by *Luther. There is almost a paradox in this, as a belief in *justification by *faith *alone* has underlain much antinomian thought. Johannes Agricola, whom Luther called antinomian, was teaching: 'Are you steeped in sin, an adulterer, and a thief? If you believe, you are in salvation. All who follow Moses must go to the Devil.' Agricola was trying to be a good Lutheran, and he recanted when Luther corrected him. Even Melanchthon, Luther's more cautious heir, could say, 'It must be admitted that the Ten Commandments are abrogated.' *Augustine could seem antinomian to a *Pelagian. There are perhaps occasions when the Christian thing to do is to break a direct commandment: 'You shall not commit murder' (Exod. 20) but *Bonhoeffer joined the plot to murder Hitler. Perhaps 'situation ethics' is the acceptable modern face of antinomianism.

Protestant New England had an antinomian controversy in the mid-17th century, around the teaching of Ann Hutchinson. She was an assertive woman, who trusted the *Holy Spirit in herself over against the duly constituted authorities of New England *Congregationalism. This might seem a good example of the term 'antinomian' being used as a tool of oppression. So-called antinomians do not do what they are told, so their independence threatens the foundations of church and state. She was condemned, not over a reading of justification by faith, but for trusting the Spirit, who will lead us into all truth, even truths the church authorities dislike. Similar libertarians in England in the same period, such as the Ranters, who blasphemed to show their freedom, were more consciously breaking rules for the sake of it.

These might remind us of the medieval Brethren of the Free Spirit, a group of Dutch *heretics around 1450 who believed (if their accusers are right) in free love. The tradition goes back to the *Gnostics of a *dualism saying that, properly understood, the spirit is free, and has nothing to do with the *body. In that case, whatever the body does is irrelevant. That sort of dualism is, however, more likely to treat the body as an enemy, and has more often been a driving force in *asceticism than in antinomianism.

*Blake expresses much of the mystique of antinomianism, while another great imaginative expression of it is in James Hogg's almost contemporary *Confessions of a Justified Sinner* (1824). A thoroughly wicked character presumes he is one of the elect. In practice the besetting sins of those who know themselves *elect are rarely antinomian. They are more often stern moralists. Those who think themselves above the ordinary moral law are more likely to read *Nietzsche than the bible.

Like anarchism, antinomianism is, at first sight, transparently dangerous if not impossible; on further investigation, there might be a truth hidden there. 'To the pure all things are pure' (Titus 1: 15).

Alistair Mason

Adams, C. F., *The Antinomian Controversy*, ed. E. Battis (1976).
Gunter, W. S., *The Limits of 'Love Divine'* (1989).
Hall, D. D., *The Antinomian Controversy 1636–1638: A Documentary History* (1968).
Huehns, G., *Antinomianism in English History* (1951).
Stoever, W. K. B., *'A Faire and Easie Way to Heaven'* (1978).

anti-realism

anti-realism, see REALISM.

antisemitism

antisemitism. Hostility to Jews, often virulent and even murderous, has been a recurrent theme through much of Christian history. Its roots are found in the NT and in a bitter original rivalry for a common name and heritage. Each side in its own view is God's *covenanted people; for each the Hebrew scriptures are sacred; the *psalms of ancient *Israel remain the daily core of the official prayer of both Christians and Jews.

The gospels stress both the Jewishness of *Jesus' life and work and the growing conflict between him and the leading Jewish groups which culminated in his condemnation, for which the Jewish authorities shared responsibility with the Roman governor. This antagonism is in places depicted in terms that have undoubtedly contributed a great deal to fomenting antisemitism. Two passages which seem particularly to do so are *John 8: 44–6 and Matthew 27: 25. In the former Jesus declares 'You are of your father the devil, and your will is to do your father's desires. He was a murderer from the beginning …'. Jesus is here hinting at his own coming murder. In the latter the Jews cry out at Jesus' trial before Pilate, 'His blood be on us and on our children.' Neither of these passages, however, nor anything else in the gospels, can rightly be called antisemitic, for the clear reason that they are all written by Jews inside a prolonged debate between a minority of Jews who believed in Jesus and the majority who did not. Other Jewish sectarian literature of the period is characterized by similarly violent language. Moreover *at the time of the debate* the majority often persecuted the minority: a bitter reaction to persecution can hardly be described as anti-semitism. All the gospels stress that many Jews believed in Jesus and accepted the rightness of the title given to him of 'King of the Jews'. Finally, terrible as the imagined cry at his trial sounds and as Christians have interpreted it across the centuries, placing on the Jews everlasting guilt for Jesus' death, this is certainly not how it should be understood. It seems likely that Matthew, interpreting the destruction of Jerusalem by the Romans in 70 as God's punishment of the wicked city (Matt. 22: 7) envisages the people of Jerusalem, or at least their leaders, as condemning themselves and their children and grandchildren. 'Us and our children' refers neither to universal Jewry nor to endless generations, but to Jerusalem 30–70 AD. This gives us a painfully sectarian and vengeful evangelist, but no excuse for Christian behaviour down the centuries. There is a more attractive interpretation, but it is difficult to attribute it to Matthew himself. Only a chapter earlier, Jesus is reported as affirming that his *blood is to be 'poured out for many for the forgiveness of sins'. The Jewish crowd was praying, despite themselves, for the salvation Jesus died to bring. Even if not intended by Matthew, this does harmonize with Luke's Passion narrative, when the dying Jesus prays 'Father, forgive them, for they know not what they do' (Luke 23: 34). NT denunciations of the Jews, coupled with hope for their subsequent salvation (Rom. 11), were, it must be remembered, very much in line with OT prophetic denunciations.

Three centuries later the situation was entirely different. Christians were now overwhelmingly of Gentile background. They read these texts not from within a Jewish context but from outside. Jews were now seen as a hostile group of people who had blindly persevered in misreading their own scriptures in the face of what Christians had convinced themselves was their obvious sense. The hardening of lines between them established in one situation was transferred to a world where Christians were in power and able to vent their bitterness against those whom they saw as their first persecutors. In the late 4th century there was a revealing incident. A Christian mob led by monks destroyed a synagogue. The Emperor Theodosius ordered the local bishop to repair the damage and punish the perpetrators. Ambrose of Milan, the most politically powerful bishop in the empire, intervened in protest and the emperor accepted his argument. From then on, as medieval Christendom developed, Jews were placed more and more in a position of social exclusion and political deprivation. Theologically they were seen as God-killers, suitably punished by the loss of their country and reduced in consequence to a sort of servitude. Socially, their presence as an absolutely alien element among peoples held together by their Christianity encouraged popular suspicion and wild accusations. Economically, their activity had been in many places almost confined (by Gentile regulations) to *usury, a role needed by Christians but judged sinful. As social outsiders and moneylenders, Jews were obvious objects for outbreaks of popular hooliganism which had little to do with religion.

The medieval church endeavoured to protect Jews, ensuring a minimum level of just treatment, while insisting on their collective guilt for the death of Christ, an insistence which could only stimulate popular hatred. Such is the position of the papal *Constitutio pro judaeis*, first issued in 1061 and often renewed, a sort of protective charter, as of the *Letter to the Duchess of Brabant* of *Aquinas. Actual violence derived from a more popular level. Preparations for the first Crusade led to massacres of the local Jewish population in 1095, especially in the Rhineland. Cologne, Mainz, Trier, and Worms were the worst affected. Anti-Jewish violence appeared a natural concomitant of this new 'holy war'. Rumours that Jews kidnapped and crucified Christian children in ritual murders began a little later, in England in the 12th century. The further charge that they killed Christians to drink their blood appeared in Germany a century later, together with the accusation that they stole and desecrated the eucharistic host. In 1247 Pope Innocent IV, condemning anew the persecution of Jews, explicitly denounced the blood libel, but in place after place such accusations were made and usually resulted in appalling punishment for Jewish communities. In the later Middle Ages, Jews were simply expelled from most West European countries, a natural consequence of popular hatred on the one hand and loss of economic utility on the other as Christians entered the banking and moneylending business.

Although *Luther was particularly gross in his antisemitic expressions, the Reformation brought some change, particularly in the *Calvinist world. Jewish communities flourished in Amsterdam and later in North America. But a greater change came with the *secularization of the 19th century. Jews could now enter into and become integrated with society in France, Germany, England, and elsewhere. This may actually have further inflamed antisemitic attitudes among conservative Christians, opposed to every side of liberalization. Among Catholics in France and Poland, for instance, antisemitism may have grown more intense in consequence. Nevertheless the core of public antisemitism grew more nationalist than religious. The Jew was seen as the ethnically impure element corrupting a nation. While antisemitism long appeared more virulent in France, it would seem to have been this basically *nationalist logic which led in Germany, in the acute reaction to the defeat and humiliation of World War I, to the idea of wiping out once and for all the enemy within.

The *Holocaust was neither the logical nor a likely consequence of Christian antisemitism, given the history of the latter over many centuries and the general secularization of Europe. Nevertheless there is a frightening moral continuity between local medieval massacres and expulsions and the systematic genocide of the Holocaust. Both church leadership and the theological mind were sufficiently infected by antisemitism to offer a highly inadequate protest. Few indeed were the theologians who fully endorsed *Bonhoeffer's emphatic assertion 'only he who shouts for the Jews may sing the Gregorian Chant'. In many cases, leading churchmen kept completely silent or even tended to justify ill-treatment of Jews. The survival of pervasive antisemitic attitudes among Christians made it far easier for the Nazis to obtain the collaboration of ordinary people that they needed. The effect of the Holocaust has been to make Christians aware of the horror of antisemitism within their own tradition in a way never earlier recognized. While Christian antisemitism has not disappeared, it is minute compared with what it was prior to 1939. There have been numerous subsequent condemnations of antisemitism, as in *Vatican II's *Nostra Aetate*, which explicitly rejected the traditional charges made against Jews.

It seems necessary to add that antisemitism is unrelated to the issue of the *conversion of Jews to Christianity. It is sometimes suggested by Christians involved in *dialogue with Jews that any desire to see such conversions is antisemitic. This is not so. Indeed, while any attempted exclusion of Jews from the church or its ministry is certainly antisemitic (and was a cause of the *Barmen Declaration), their inclusion goes counter to the theory and sentiment of antisemitism. It would be, furthermore, impossible without self-betrayal for a religious community all of whose first members were Jews to regard the latter as in any way unsuitable Christians. Moreover, in the 20th century numerous Jewish Christians, such as Raissa Maritain, Edith *Stein, Jean de Menasce, Ulrich Simon, and Hugh Montefiore, have made a major contribution to Christian thought which it would be antisemitic to ignore. Further, while it would be antisemitic to oppose the existence of the state of Israel, it is certainly not antisemitic for Christians to seek equal justice for the Arab inhabitants of Palestine. Radical criticism of Israeli governments is not antisemitic.   **Adrian Hastings**

Hay, Malcolm, *Europe and the Jews* (1950).
Langmuir, Gavin, *History, Religion, and Antisemitism* (1990).
Montefiore, Hugh, *On Being a Jewish Christian* (1998).
Nicholl, Donald, *The Testing of Hearts*, 2nd edn. (1997).
Parkes, James, *The Conflict of Church and Synagogue* (1934).
Poliakov, Léon, *The History of Antisemitism* (4 vols.; 1974–85).
Ruether, Rosemary Radford, *Faith and Fratricide* (1974).
Wigoder, Geoffrey, *Jewish–Christian Relations since the Second World War* (1988).

apartheid

apartheid (Afrikaans) literally means 'separateness'. It refers to the racial policies that were implemented by the Afrikaner National Party after it was elected to power in South Africa in 1948.

The cornerstone legislation was the Population Registration Act which determined racial identity. The Mixed Marriages Act and the Immorality Act were intended to prevent miscegenation; the Group Areas Act and the Pass Laws ensured that people lived in separate racial ghettos; and the Bantu Education Act promulgated racially separate systems of education. Apartheid legislation invariably meant that blacks were economically deprived and subjugated.

Much apartheid legislation had its antecedents in British colonial policy, the segregationist constitution of the Union of South Africa (1909), and the Land Act of 1913. Even so, apartheid had a racist rigidity and totalitarian character that was qualitatively different from previous segregationist policies. In the 1960s, when the government began to establish separate 'independent homelands' (Promotion of Bantu Self-Development Act) for different ethnic groups, apartheid was euphemistically designated 'separate development'.

During the 19th century the Dutch Reformed Church established congregations and synods along ethnic lines. This prepared the way for apartheid and gave it a theological basis. But the main ideological foundations were provided in the 20th century by the pseudo-scientific theories of social Darwinism and eugenics supported by an adaptation of neo-*Calvinist theology. This theology, which originated in Holland, was used to provide divine sanction for the separation of races and cultures. It predominated within Afrikaner church circles from the 1930s. Apartheid ideologists were also influenced by German National Socialism.

Resistance to apartheid, spearheaded by the African National Congress (ANC), was initially peaceful. The 1960 Sharpeville Massacre, however, ushered in a new and violent period of state repression, countered by armed struggle. The Soweto uprising in 1976 led to the designation of apartheid as a 'crime against humanity' by the United Nations. The unbanning of the liberation movements in 1990 signified the beginning of the end of apartheid and paved the way for the non-racial elections in 1994 which were won by the ANC under the leadership of Nelson Mandela.

Churches belonging to the South African Council of Churches (SACC), and church leaders such as Beyers Naudé, Desmond Tutu, and Allan Boesak, played a crucial role in the struggle against apartheid. Support for the anti-apartheid struggle also came from many international and ecumenical church groups, and was central to the Programme to Combat Racism established by the World Council of Churches. In 1968 the *Message to the People of South Africa*, published by the SACC and Christian Institute, declared that apartheid was a 'false gospel'. During the 1970s *black theology galvanized black Christian participation in the liberation struggle. In 1982 the Dutch Reformed Mission Church ('coloured') declared that the theological justification of apartheid was a *heresy. The *Kairos Document*, published in 1986 by the Institute for Contextual Theology and signed by over 200 theologians, provided a 'prophetic theology' which rejected the 'state theology' of the pro-apartheid churches as well as the 'cheap *reconciliation' preached by more liberal churches. It encouraged Christians to resist the apartheid state and to participate actively in the mass *democratic movement.

See also JUSTICE; LIBERATION THEOLOGY; PROPHECY.

John W. De Gruchy

Asmal, K., Asmal, L., and Roberts, R. S., *Reconciliation through Truth: A Reckoning of Apartheid's Criminal Governance* (1996).
de Gruchy, John W., *The Church Struggle in South Africa*, 2nd edn. (1986).
de Gruchy, John W., and Villa-Vicencio, C., *Apartheid is a Heresy* (1983).
Villa-Vicencio, C., *Trapped in Apartheid* (1988).
The Kairos Document (1986).

apocalypse

apocalypse, see BOOK OF REVELATION.

apocalypticism

apocalypticism is the word used to describe the realm of thought similar to that found in the book of *Revelation, whose influence on Christian theology has been immense from the beginnings of the Christianity until the present day. It is the only example of an apocalypse in the *New Testament but its viewpoint is pervasive: *visions and their images enable readers to have another perspective on *God and the *world; and the future hope is depicted in images drawn from the theological outlook of its writers.

The meaning and content of divine *revelation are central issues within NT theology. Thus the impetus for the development of Christianity appears to come through apocalyptic revelations occurring at decisive moments in the lives of significant figures of early Christianity (the baptism of *Jesus, the conversion of Cornelius, the conversion of *Paul). However, at the heart of Paul's theology is the concept of a new, definitive revelation of the divine purposes, coming not as the result of apocalyptic visions or heavenly ascents, as in some contemporary Jewish apocalypses, but through the divine mystery revealed in the crucified *messiah. In the gospel of *John there is a similar theme of the revelation of the invisible God through the Son who has been sent from the Father. The divine mystery is not the prerogative of the apocalyptic seers and their esoteric tradition but is available to all those who see that Jesus of Nazareth is the one who is sent from God and makes the hidden Father known.

The *eschatological dimension of Revelation echoes themes from the prophetic literature of the *Old Testament. Indeed, several prophetic books have contributed widely to Revelation's language, particularly Ezekiel, *Daniel, and Zechariah, whose images are taken up and a deeper meaning found in them. There are differences between Christian apocalypticism and that found in the book of Daniel, the biblical text with which Revelation has some affinities, and from which it borrows some of its key images. Unlike Daniel, the authorship of the book of Revelation is not attributed to a famous figure from the past and in Revelation there is little of the detailed eschatological prediction we find in the later chapters of Daniel.

Apocalypticism still plays a vital part within Christianity. It had a significant impact in the medieval period and has continued, particularly in the context of radical movements with hopes for an imminent change in the political order, though it is equally prevalent today among groups that are largely apolitical. Apocalypticism has affinities with *mysticism, particularly in its quest for the discernment of the most profound divine mysteries, though the mystical texts often lack the eschatological concerns of apocalypticism.

See also MILLENARIANISM.   **Christopher Rowland**

Cohn, N., *The Pursuit of the Millennium* (1957).
Daniélou, J., *The Theology of Jewish Christianity* (1964).
McGinn, B., *The Foundations of Mysticism* (1991).
Rowland, C., *The Open Heaven* (1982).

apocrypha, Christian.

From the 2nd century onwards the proliferation of Christian writings composed in imitation of the literature eventually gathered into the canon of authorized Christian scripture (the New Testament) led the church authorities to disapprove of these secondary *gospels, acts, and *apocalypses. Catalogues of acceptable and unacceptable works were drawn up in west and east, of which 4th-century examples survive in the *Decretum Gelasianum* associated with Damasus I and in the *Stichometry* of Nicephorus of Constantinople. Nevertheless, many of the rejected books survived. They are now often conventionally gathered together under the umbrella title 'The Apocryphal New Testament', where 'apocryphal' means 'spurious' or 'secondary'. It is a heterogeneous collection of writings composed in different parts of the Christian world. Some of the texts are clearly unorthodox, some are tinged with 'heretical' ideas. But, in general, this so-called apocryphal literature may be judged as theologically *orthodox: it testifies to a vigorous literary activity and to the popular, albeit uncritically received, reading matter of the faithful.

While it is conceivable that the *Gospel of *Thomas* includes authentic sayings of *Jesus, scholars should not in general expect from this literature independent, reliable information about 1st-century Christianity, which these works purport to give; the significance of the apocrypha lies rather in revealing the practices and beliefs of Christians in later ages. The development of these writings over many centuries, despite ecclesiastical disapprobation, and their wide geographical distribution gave them a powerful influence on Christian thinking, imagination, and practice.

The five 2nd-century Acts (of Andrew, John, Paul, Peter, Thomas) with their long narratives about the eponymous hero's travels, missionary work, conversions, miracles, prayers, and preaching, kindled an interest which eventually led to the veneration of the earliest *apostles. These stories' identification of an apostle with a particular geographical area influenced belief in patron *saints. Even after ecclesiastical authorities had denounced the use of the apocryphal Acts, clandestine copies or expurgated, catholicized rewritings ensured the survival of many of the stories—especially accounts of the apostle's death, typically by *martyrdom. These and imitative legends developed into ecclesiastically approved lives of the saints, hagiographies, and the *Acta Sanctorum*. The widespread popularity in medieval western Christendom of many of these stories was due to their being retold in the 13th century in Jacob of Voragine's *Golden Legend*.

The often sensational *miracles performed by the apostles in the canonical Acts of the Apostles, and still more in the apocryphal Acts, encouraged believers to seek the intercession of such figures. The *Acts of Thomas* ends with a story in which dust from Thomas's grave effects a cure: such stories fuelled the Christian tradition of venerating relics as panaceas.

The efficacy of intercessory prayer through *Mary in particular is another manifestation of Christian devotion. This practice is reflected in stories found in the Arabic infancy gospel, the traditions in which stretch back to the earliest Christian centuries. There Mary is described in many episodes as a mediatrix and a miracle-worker in her own right. The 2nd-century *Protevangelium of James*, another infancy gospel, is responsible for the story of Mary's upbringing in the *Temple. Arising from this, the Presentation of Mary became one of the Twelve Great Feasts of Orthodox tradition. Belief in Mary's perpetual *virginity is also probably directly attributable to the *Protevangelium*, in which the account of Jesus' birth is followed by the midwives' establishing Mary's continuing virginal condition. Accounts of Mary's death, culminating in her being directly received corporeally into heaven, are found in many apocryphal legends: these widespread traditions led to the doctrine of the Assumption.

The emphasis on virginity as a virtue is accompanied in the apocryphal Acts in particular by an encouragement to *celibacy among Christians and the discouragement of sexual relations, even within marriage (see CHASTITY). Many of these stories revolve around a vengeful pagan husband, who, having lost his wife's favours after her *conversion to Christianity through the apostle's preaching, effects that apostle's death. Common and linked themes in these Christianized novels are the need to abandon conjugal rights and the renunciation of family ties (as in the *Acts of Thomas*, 12).

The Jews' role in Jesus' death exercised Christian imagination from the beginning. As a development of the anti-Jewish themes found in the biblical accounts of the trials and death of Jesus, the apocryphal tradition lays the blame unambiguously on the Jews. The *Gospel of Peter* makes the Jews alone responsible for the crucifixion, and represents the motive for not proceeding with the death-hastening breaking of Jesus' legs (crurifraction) as Jewish malevolence so that he 'might die in torment' (see CROSS). Similarly, in the *Gospel of Nicodemus*, Pilate's letter to Claudius emphasizes that it was the 'envious lies of the Jews' which brought about the crucifixion. Much medieval *antisemitism was doubtless fomented and justified by the stories of hostility found in these legends.

It is in the field of the visual *arts that the influence of the apocryphal legends is strongest. The Anne cycle at Chartres draws on the *Protevangelium*. Giotto's Mary cycle in the Arena Chapel in

Padua depicts the early life of Mary using stories also ultimately descended from this same infancy gospel. Depictions of the Dormition of the Virgin rely on apocryphal texts, as do illustrations of Peter's inverse crucifixion, of John with the poisoned chalice, of Thomas with the builder's T-square, and popular pictures of Jesus' birth in a cave with the ox and ass in attendance. Many such depictions are understandable only when the underlying literary inspiration in the Christian apocrypha is recognized.

In literature and the performing arts too the apocryphal NT was influential. *Dante cites the 3rd-century *Apocalypse of Paul* in *Inferno* 2. 28 and many of his descriptions of the horrors of *hell in the Divine Comedy are taken from it. That apocalypse and its near contemporary, the *Apocalypse of Peter*, contain many lurid scenes of hell and the fate of the wicked. Such images influenced medieval Christendom's imagination, its theological and moral thinking, its sculpture and painting, and particularly its *mystery plays.

Many Christian doctrines and beliefs may have been hammered out at councils and argued for by fathers and schoolmen. But if the patristic writers represent the intellectual cutting edge of the church, the NT apocrypha, which were behind many developments in cult and thought, represent the popular folk religion of the pious in the pew.   **J. K. Elliott**

Elliott, J. K., *The Apocryphal New Testament* (1993).
—— *The Apocryphal Jesus: Legends of the Early Church* (1996).
Koester, H., *Ancient Christian Gospels* (1990).
Schneemelcher, W., *New Testament Apocrypha* (2 vols.; ET 1991, 1992).

apocrypha, Jewish. In a narrow sense, this term refers to those books or parts of books found in the Septuagint, the ancient Greek translation of the *Old Testament, which have no surviving Hebrew equivalent and do not appear in the canon of the Jewish scriptures as subsequently defined by the rabbinic tradition. The contents of the Septuagint seem to reflect the wider range of books in use among the Jewish community in *Alexandria in the 2nd century BC at a time when the boundaries of the canon had not been finally determined. The books in question are: 1 and 2 Esdras, Tobit, Judith, Wisdom of Solomon, Ecclesiasticus, Baruch, the Prayer of Manasseh, 1 and 2 Maccabees, and additions to Esther and Daniel.

More loosely, the term includes a series of late quasi-biblical books which seem to be of Jewish origin, also known as the Pseudepigrapha, which seem never to have been accepted into any canon of scripture. Some of these were, however, referred to by the early fathers. Jude 14–15 quotes 1 Enoch, an Aramaic work now surviving in full only in Ethiopic manuscripts, reflecting its high status in the *Ethiopian tradition.

For the early church, 'scripture' simply meant the Septuagint. It was out of theological controversy with Jews that some disquiet arose over the status of these books; Jewish disputants were unimpressed when arguments were based on proof-texts from works they did not acknowledge. Partly as a result, when Jerome prepared his revised Latin translation of the *bible he extended the term 'apocrypha', which earlier writers had used for books of esoteric doctrine or dubious provenance, to cover those works for which he had no Hebrew text. These he deemed excluded from the canon.

The wider church scarcely registered the relegation of these books to a secondary status and they continued to be used in lit-

urgy, in theological debate, and as a major source of *artistic inspiration. Tobit, with its example of pious resignation enlivened with all the magic and incident of a folk tale, and the chaste and redoubtable warrior heroine in Judith were particular favourites, as was the expression of repentance in the Prayer of Manasseh. The encomium of heroes of the faith in Ecclesiasticus 44–50 still resonates even in secular solemnities. Doctrinally, 2 Maccabees 12: 43–4 provided the main biblical warrant for the practice of prayer for the dead and belief in *purgatory.

The question of the status of these books took on new importance at the *Reformation. The Reformers' stress on *revelation through scripture alone made it imperative to define what counted as scripture. The humanist tradition had already triggered interest in textual criticism and had also revived the study of Hebrew and the rabbinic tradition. Jerome's doubts were raised again. The Reformers' condemnation of the practices and beliefs that were justified from these books further weighted the scales against the apocrypha.

Views quickly polarized. *Luther felt that the apocrypha should not be included in the body of the OT but be clearly labelled and placed between the Testaments. He still commended their reading, however, in contrast to the *Reformed or Calvinist view expressed in the Westminster Confession of 1648 that they had no more authority in the church than any other merely human production. The Catholic church, for its part, at the Councils of *Florence and *Trent formally renewed its commitment to the larger canon including what were more discreetly termed the 'deutero-canonical' books. Avowedly Catholic bibles still retain the Septuagint's contents and ordering.

In the *Anglican communion, the apocrypha had to be included in any authorized bible but were not to be used to prove any point of doctrine. The Calvinist view, however, became more widely adopted across Protestant churches and editions of the bible without apocrypha became increasingly common from the 17th century. By the late 19th century, under the influence of the Bible Societies, they were standard in many Protestant circles.

Increasing ecumenicism and a growing appreciation of the historical and literary interest of the apocrypha has led to a relaxing of attitudes, linked to a wider modern tendency to play down biblical theology. The Common Bible, a modern edition with ecumenical blessing, includes not only the books of the Septuagint but others in use in various branches of the Orthodox Church, while following Luther's practice in printing the apocrypha as a separate section.

                                                                                Hugh S. Pyper

Metzger, B. M., *An Introduction to the Apocrypha* (1957).

apologetics aims to defend and commend the Christian faith, not to apologize for it. It attempts to build bridges between non-Christian faiths and worldviews and the gospel; it defends Christianity against hostile or misinformed criticism. *Paul was engaging in apologetics when he appealed to 'the unknown God' in dialogue with philosophical Athenians (Acts 17: 23). The Christian apologists of the 2nd century, such as Justin Martyr, employed Greek philosophical terms (e.g. Logos, *Word) to make the Christian faith intelligible and acceptable to thoughtful pagans. Apologetics can also take the form of *natural theology as in *Aquinas's Five Ways of establishing the existence of *God without resorting to *revelation.

There is a powerful strand within *Protestant theology that has no room for apologetics or natural theology. *Kierkegaard poured scorn on apologetics. *Barth condemned it as an abdication of the Christian standpoint which is grounded solely in revelation. Brunner, however, continued to look for a point of contact for the gospel and *Tillich developed an elaborate 'answering theology' that correlated existential questions with revealed answers.

In Roman Catholic and some Protestant theology, apologetics has become assimilated to 'fundamental theology'. Traditional Roman Catholic fundamental theology examined the presuppositions of the Christian faith (the existence of God, the fact of revelation and the human capacity to receive it) in connection with the relation of revelation and *reason. But the fundamentals were already given, rather than proposed for enquiry. At its best this approach was 'faith seeking understanding' but, at its crudest, it attempted to prove revelation in an arid, formal way. The current conception of fundamental theology in Roman Catholicism stems from *Rahner's reassessment of it and the encouragement that this approach received from Part One of the *Constitution on the Church in the Modern World* (*Gaudium et Spes*) of *Vatican II. It aims to commend the Christian faith and to establish its credentials by a critical presentation of the *faith in relation to the entire context of contemporary cultural life—a service offered to the believer as much as to the outsider. Within Protestant theology a comparable version of fundamental theology has been proposed that attempts to evaluate the truth of theology in dialogue, not only with other theological disciplines, but with all other sources of information and insight (Ebeling 1979).

Fundamental theology is a truly theological discipline since it is conducted from the standpoint of faith. This distinguishes it from *philosophy of religion which does not presuppose faith and also from traditional apologetics which, while prosecuted from the standpoint of faith, was directed precisely at the non-believer. Fundamental theology is essentially concerned with setting Christian belief within a wider sphere of rationality.   **Paul Avis**

Avis, P., 'Fundamental Theology', in Avis, P. (ed.), *The Threshold of Theology* (1988).

Ebeling, G., *The Study of Theology* (1979).

Fries, H., 'Fundamental Theology', in K. Rahner (ed.), *Encyclopedia of Theology* (1975).

Grant, R. M., *Greek Apologists of the Second Century* (1988).

Metz, J. B., 'Apologetics' and 'Political Theology', in K. Rahner (ed.), *Encyclopedia of Theology* (1975).

Rahner, K., *Foundations of Christian Faith* (1978).

apophatic theology, see BYZANTINE THEOLOGY; GOD; PLATO AND PLATONISM; JOHN OF THE CROSS.

apostolicity.

The word 'apostle' (someone sent) is a specifically Christian term with no real equivalent in Hebrew religion or Greek culture. It suggests a delegate chosen for a special mission, to some extent comparable to an *Old Testament *prophet but without the prophet's basic role of personally receiving a divine message. There is a certain verticality in the prophetic economy to be contrasted with a more horizontal mode in the apostolic. An apostle came to mean someone sent by *Jesus, witnessing to his life and *Resurrection and sharing *authority in his *church. The apostle's status is, however, less clear in the *New Testament than later usage might suggest.

The earliest NT uses of the word are by *Paul. In 1 Thessalonians 2: 7 he talks of himself, Silvanus, and Timothy all as apostles. In Romans 16: 7 he speaks of 'those outstanding apostles, Andronicus and Junias'. At another time, he talks of 'counterfeit apostles, dishonest workmen disguised as apostles of Christ' (2 Cor. 10: 13) but insists on his own claim to be a true one: 'I am an apostle and I have seen Jesus our Lord. You are all my work in the Lord. Even if I were not an apostle to others, I should still be an apostle to you' (1 Cor. 9: 1–2). Acts lists the 'prophets and teachers' in the church at Antioch, including Barnabas and Paul, but when the latter have been elected for missionary work elsewhere it calls them instead 'apostles' (Acts 14: 4, 14) (see LUKE–ACTS).

All this suggests that there was no clear definition or delimitation of apostles to begin with. The word seems to refer to anyone sincerely engaged as a missionary of Christ, who is himself once described as an apostle (Heb. 3: 1). But for Paul he is himself the very model of apostolicity. That, however, is a model different from the one that came to prevail which saw the apostles as essentially a group of twelve chosen in his lifetime by Jesus, 'sent' by him already then (Mark 3: 14), who became the official witnesses of his Resurrection. Paul might be added to them on account of his vision of Jesus and special mission to the uncircumcised (Gal. 2: 8) but there was always tension between the Pauline sense of apostolicity and the defining status of 'The Twelve'.

That Jesus chose twelve *disciples in a special way is one of the most certain things we know about him. He had, of course, many more than twelve disciples, yet it seems unlikely that the Twelve were in his lifetime known specifically as apostles, firm as their identity as his 'twelve apostles' became in subsequent tradition. The last supper Jesus took with them when he instituted the *Eucharist and in doing so also, for much traditional theology, ordained the twelve as *priests is the most significant moment for establishing their identity, but *Mark simply writes, 'when evening came he arrived with the Twelve' (14: 17) and *Matthew, 'he was at table with the twelve disciples' (26: 20). Luke's reference to them as apostles (22: 14) seems to reflect a later terminology. What matters, however, is less the word than the reality. All agree that Jesus chose from among his disciples a group called 'the Twelve' (reflecting the twelve tribes of *Israel) to share his authority and continue his mission. Matthew ends his gospel with the risen Jesus on a mountain in Galilee addressing 'the eleven disciples' (*Judas having fallen away) and commanding them to 'make disciples of all nations'.

At the beginning of Acts, *Peter arranges for the election of Matthias to make up the number of twelve 'apostles' and become an official 'witness' to the Resurrection (1: 22). In the long term this collegial, Petrine view of the apostles comes to prevail, and only Paul is seen as additional to the twelve. Even he had to struggle to establish his right to be so recognized.

It is striking that the early church never saw the office of apostle as continuing. Strictly the apostles had no successors. Only in the early or Pauline sense has anyone since the 'apostolic age' been termed an apostle, as Patrick for Ireland or Boniface for Germany. What remains apostolic as such are not individuals but the church itself. Apostolicity is one of its four defining marks as contained in the Nicene *Creed. Established by the apostles, the church remains faithful to their teaching, their '*tradition'. It does so undoubtedly through a succession of ministers seen as originally appointed by them. The *Letter of Clement* written at Rome *c*.95 is already emphatic that Christ was sent by *God, the apostles by Christ, and a line of ministers ('bishops and deacons') by the apostles. 'Bishops' at this time seem still not to be differentiated from 'presbyters' as in the NT. Collectively they carried on the authority and mission of the apostles, sharing, like the apostles themselves, in a 'college' not restricted to place. When, a century later, *Irenaeus is refuting the claims of *Gnostics by appealing to the 'tradition' of the apostles passed down in each church through a 'succession' of bishops, he points, as an obvious example, to the episcopal succession in *Rome from Peter and Paul to Eleutherus in his own time. Whether he got the list of twelve names quite right does not matter; what does matter was the idea that the church was apostolic because it held to the teaching of the apostles as guaranteed by a succession of ministers. This sense of apostolic succession has remained foundational for a theology of *ministry in east and west. Whether the succession could be continued only by bishops in a narrow sense rather than by presbyters has been a bitterly contested issue between episcopal and non-episcopal churches in the past. The NT and other early evidence, including Clement, suggests that the division between bishop and priest is a post-apostolic arrangement and a matter of ecclesiastical convenience relating to the growing size of local churches. It seems an arrangement dependent upon, and subordinate to, the basic apostolicity of the church it serves. Whether this is so or not, the claim of Rome to be, *par excellence*, the 'apostolic see' as in succession to both Peter and Paul, has been a central fact within Christian history. However apostolicity be interpreted, in *presbyterian, *episcopal, or *papal form, its sense is to provide a guarantee of authority.

What does seem essential in all forms of apostolic succession is the double element of *ordination and jurisdiction, though this distinction was for long only implicitly perceived. While ordination is a ceremony setting someone apart for ministry through a laying on of hands and not to be repeated, jurisdiction means the ongoing authorization by the church and may be lost or renewed. A mere line of ordination passed on from individual to individual without appropriate wider authorization may give valid orders but certainly cannot be seen as apostolic succession. A modern diocesan bishop succeeds both the bishops by whom he is consecrated and his predecessor in the see. Succession is neither purely *sacramental nor purely administrative.

Church history suggests, nevertheless, that apostolic succession, which has featured in much denominational controversy, has taken varied forms and is not easily susceptible to definition. While a succession of individual ministers is certainly an important element within the apostolicity of the church, it remains only part of the church's fidelity to apostolic tradition as a whole. The church's apostolic character signifies a committed fidelity to that tradition as received through historical transmission, but part of that fidelity remains the will to be missionary, to be in fact apostolic in the earliest, widest, and more Pauline sense. The apostolate, in which the *laity share, as even the most clerical Catholic theology now admits, is as much part of apostolicity as is apostolic succession of a ministerial sort. Apostolicity in the end is, then, to be demonstrated not only by what is received, whether orders or creed, but also

through the commitment to communication by latter-day apostles comparable to the Andronicus and Junias whom Paul originally commended.   **Adrian Hastings**

Barrett, C. K., *The Signs of an Apostle* (1970).
Freyne, S., *The Twelve Disciples and Apostles* (1968).
Kirk, K. (ed.), *The Apostolic Ministry* (1946).
Schillebeeckx, E., *Ministry* (1981).
Turner, C. H., 'Apostolic Succession', *Essays on the Early History of the Church and the Ministry*, ed. H. B. Swete (1921), 93–214.

Aquinas, Thomas

Aquinas, Thomas (1225–74). Aquinas is universally agreed to be one of the giants in the history of Christian thought. He has been regarded as a touchstone of Roman *Catholic *orthodoxy since the Council of *Trent (a view of him ratified by Pope Leo XIII, in the encyclical *Aeterni Patris*, and by *Vatican II). As well as being highly respected by generations of Christians of all denominations, his writings continue to be studied by thinkers with no special religious affiliation, many of whom rank him among the greatest of western philosophers.

Born in Italy, Aquinas was sent, aged 5 or 6, to study at the Benedictine abbey of Monte Cassino, where he remained until he was about 15. He then went to the University of Naples, where he encountered the full range of *Aristotle's writings, which had only recently come to be studied seriously in Europe. In 1244 he joined the new *Dominican Order of friars and subsequently lectured at the University of Paris from 1252 to 1259, and from 1269 to 1272. He also taught at Orvieto, Rome, and Naples, writing voluminously all the time. He died at Fossanova on 7 March 1274 *en route* to the second Council of Lyons to advise on relations between the Catholic and Orthodox churches. Ideas associated with him were condemned by ecclesiastical authorities at Paris and Oxford in 1277, but he was never formally censured. He was canonized in 1323.

As well as two long theological treatises, the *Summa Theologiae* and the *Summa contra Gentiles*, Aquinas wrote commentaries on scripture (on which he regularly lectured), a large range of short works on topics in theology and philosophy (the *Opuscula*), and several detailed studies on major theological issues (the *Quaestiones disputatae*). Using newly available translations, he wrote several commentaries on Aristotle, whose teachings he was the first Christian author to employ at length in the service of Christianity (a daring enterprise since many of his contemporaries found Aristotle's thinking inimical to it). He also produced commentaries on Proclus, Boethius, Pseudo-*Dionysius, and Peter Lombard. As 20th-century scholars have come to appreciate, non-Aristotelian sources were as important an influence on Aquinas as Aristotelian ones.

Though always featuring prominently in histories of *philosophy, Aquinas would not have called himself a philosopher. In his writings, 'philosophers' always fall short of the true and proper '*wisdom' to be found in the Christian *revelation and the living of a life properly focused on Christ as the way to perfect happiness (*beatitudo*). But he also thought that, by using their natural ability to *reason, people can arrive at important truths on which those with benefit of Christian revelation can build when talking about the final goal of human living: that they can do this, for instance, when reflecting on people and their behaviour.

On the topic of *humanity in general, Aquinas relates quite especially to recent philosophy. For his views about people (including his philosophy of mind and his *moral philosophy) have little in common with the tradition leading from *Descartes to Hume and beyond, but much in common with the thinking of philosophers such as *Wittgenstein, Ryle, and modern authors at the centre of the contemporary revival of Aristotelian ethical thinking. For Aquinas, people are not incorporeal substances distinct from their bodies. They are not ghosts in or attached to machines. They are human animals with a specific range of powers, activities, and dispositions. He believed that human beings have *souls which can survive the death of their bodies, but these souls are not human individuals. 'My soul is not me', as he writes in his commentary on 1 Corinthians. He takes all living things to have souls (to be animate), for he thinks of the soul as that which is there when something is alive. Human beings are things with a special way of being alive (they have human souls), one which is not simply bodily; so people are more than bodies in motion. Yet they are essentially bodily, and to be the people they are they must be corporeal. 'For as it belongs to the very conception of "this human being" that there should be this soul, flesh and bone, so it belongs to the very conception of "human being" that there be soul, flesh, and bone' (*ST* I q. 75 a. 4). Hence, when speaking of life after death, Aquinas looks forward to the resurrection of the body.

On the question of human action, and concentrating on what we can learn by 'natural reason', Aquinas develops an Aristotelian moral philosophy focused on the notions of *virtue and vice. Virtues are acquired ways of behaving (dispositions) which help us to flourish and be happy. Vices are dispositions which help us to damage ourselves and be unhappy. He is aware that vicious people might say that they are happy, and he regularly insists that those who do wrong must be doing so because they see some good for themselves in what they are doing. On his account, which is somewhat original, there is no sharp distinction to be made between intellect and will (seeing that something is the case, and acting accordingly). Our desires can determine what we see, so we are not always the best judges when it comes to what makes for our flourishing. Our views of what can make for our happiness need to be informed by an understanding of what we actually are as living human animals in a world which includes other people (he has much to say on political matters). Just as doctors will tell us that smoking or excessive drinking is not good for us, Aquinas will say that vices are not good for us. And, just as doctors will advise certain ways of behaving, Aquinas will speak favourably of virtues as things we have reasons to cultivate, reasons which stand on their own without special reference to Christian authorities.

Aquinas also thinks that we have such reasons for asserting the existence of *God (see NATURAL THEOLOGY). He denies that knowledge of God in this life can be had on the basis of anything we might call a direct experience of God (as some of his contemporaries argued, and as some argue today). He also denies that the existence of God can be proved on the basis of an understanding of the meaning of the word 'God'—as, for example, *Anselm and Bonaventure thought, and as some modern philosophers have argued. But we can demonstrate that God exists by reasoning from the world (as effect) to God (as cause).

In a famous passage (*ST* I q. 2 a. 3, often referred to as the 'five ways') he defends this thesis by drawing on largely Aristotelian arguments (though also echoing such authors as Avicenna and Maimonides) and by focusing on change, acting agents, generation and perishing, perfection and being, and the (apparently) goal-directed behaviour of non-rational things (see DESIGN). He argues (as he does in many texts other than the *ST*) that these objects of our experience cannot be fully accounted for in ordinary mundane terms and should lead us to acknowledge a level of causality that transcends any with which we are familiar.

In the 'five ways' and elsewhere Aquinas is particularly intrigued by the fact that there is any *world at all, by the fact that there is something rather than nothing. He explicitly denies that philosophy can show that the world ever began to be (cf. *De aeternitate mundi*), so does not hold that God must exist in order to have got the world going at some time in the past (though he believes that God did this). But he constantly insists that everything we can conceive of or understand is continually dependent on God for its sheer existence (*esse*). The ancient philosophers asked causal questions about things in the world, but some 'climbed higher to the prospect of being as being' and 'observed the cause of things inasmuch as they are beings, not merely as things of such a kind or quality' (*ST* I q. 44 a. 2). If something exists, Aquinas argues, its existence either follows from its nature or is brought about by something other than itself (see CREATION). Aquinas then maintains that there cannot be an endless series of things bringing about the existence of others while themselves being brought about by something else. There has to be something which exists by nature. Following the biblical tradition, he calls this 'God'. In doing so, he was the first Christian author seriously, and in detail, to focus on the notion of existence as of primary importance for reflecting on God, whom he speaks of as 'Being Itself' (*ipsum esse subsistens*).

Among other things, this strand in Aquinas's thinking leads him to insist that free human actions are caused by God. He frequently alludes to arguments suggesting that people cannot be free under God's *providence (cf. *De malo*, 6). He replies to such arguments by affirming that the reality of providence (i.e. the reality of God working in all things as first cause and sustainer) is not incompatible with human *freedom (see PREDESTINATION). People have freedom (a conclusion for which he argues at length); yet God really does act in everything. And since 'everything' includes human free actions, God works in them as much as in anything else.

> People are in charge of their acts, including those of willing and of not willing, because of the deliberative activity of reason, which can be turned to one side or the other. But that someone should deliberate or not deliberate, supposing that one were in charge of this too, would have to come about by a preceding deliberation. And since this may not proceed to infinity, one would finally have to reach the point at which a person's free decision is moved by some external principle superior to the human mind, namely by God, as Aristotle himself demonstrated. Thus the minds even of healthy people are not so much in charge of their acts as not to need to be moved by God. (*ST* I-II q. 109 a. 3)

God 'causes everything's activity inasmuch as he gives it the power to act, maintains it in existence, applies it to its activity, and inasmuch as it is by his power that every other power acts' (*De potentia*, 3. 7). This teaching is not incompatible with belief in human freedom. What is incompatible with that is 'necessity of coercion', the effect of violence, as when something acts on one and 'applies force to the point where one cannot act otherwise' (*ST* I q. 82 a. 1). Freely acting human persons are not under the influence of some other *creature*. They are made to be what they are by God, who is responsible both for freely acting agents and for things which act of necessity. God's will 'is to be thought of as existing outside the realm of existents, as a cause from which pours forth everything that exists in all its variant forms' (*Commentary on Aristotle's De interpretatione*, I 14). Freely acting people are one among many forms of existent. They are free *because of* God, not *in spite of* him.

Aquinas is somewhat reserved in his account of what we can know of God by human reason. 'The knowledge that is natural to us has its source in the senses and extends just so far as it can be led by sensible things; from these, however, our understanding cannot reach to the divine essence' (*ST* I q. 12 a. 12). God 'is greater than all we can say, greater than all we can know; and not merely does he transcend our language and our knowledge, but he is beyond the comprehension of every mind whatsoever, even of angelic minds, and beyond the being of every substance' (*Commentary on Dionysius' Divine Names*, 1. 3. 77). But Aquinas also offers a range of philosophical arguments for the truth of a number of affirmative statements about God. He holds, for example, that God can be proved to be perfect, good, one, living, *omnipotent, loving, changeless, *eternal, *omniscient, and free. Though we cannot know God's essence in this life we can speak of God by using certain words which we normally use when talking of creatures since there is positive reason for doing so and since some words can apply literally to creatures and to God by *analogy, i.e. without signifying exactly the same reality, but without signifying something completely different either (cf. *ST* I q. 13).

But 'man's ultimate happiness does not consist in that knowledge of God whereby he is known by all or many in a vague kind of opinion, nor again in that knowledge whereby he is known in the speculative sciences through demonstration' (*Summa contra Gentiles*, 3. 48). So having explained that God can be known to exist by reason, Aquinas attempts to say how it can be thought that God is *Father, Son, and *Holy Spirit. Then he turns to the *Incarnation. For him, the doctrines of the *Trinity and the Incarnation cannot be demonstrated to be true (he argues that they are demonstrably indemonstrable). But he takes them to be true, and much of his work is an attempt to expound them, to defend them from charges of inconsistency and comparable criticisms, and to indicate their implications.

Aquinas's teaching on the Trinity is partly an attempt to say how God can be three '*persons', though 'God' is not the name of a class of which there can be more than one member. Drawing on what he thinks can be known of God by reason, and echoing such writers as *Augustine, Boethius, and Anselm, he defends the claim that the persons of the Trinity are distinct 'subsisting relations'. Primarily, however (and with much reference to biblical and patristic texts), Aquinas sees the Trinity as a life of knowledge and *love which shares itself with creatures and does so in a special way with people. Absolutely distinct from creatures, the Trinity needs nothing for its perfection. But through the *grace of God people can be brought to share in what it is. There is 'a special love by which God draws the rational creature above its natural condition to have a part in the divine goodness … By this love God, simply speaking, wills for the creature that eternal good which is himself' (*ST* I-II q. 110 a. 1).

Aquinas develops a detailed account of how Christ is the embodiment of God's will in this respect.

Again drawing on truths about God which he takes to be knowable by reason, and with much logical dexterity, he defends the claim that Christ is one divine subject with two natures (cf. *ST* III q. 16). Then he develops an account of Christ as teacher and example to be followed. With an eye on the biblical teaching that 'Christ died for our sins', he also writes at length on the notion of Christ as saviour. Very conscious of human evil and divine goodness, Aquinas is clear that *sin is a barrier between people and God. Unlike many theologians, however, he denies that the obstacle could only be removed by the death of Christ (see ATONEMENT, THEORIES OF). 'Simply and absolutely speaking, God could have freed us otherwise than by Christ's passion, for nothing is impossible with God' (*ST* III q. 46 a. 2).

Aquinas argues that Christ's death deals with sin because it was the death of God incarnate and thus God's expression of his eternal love for sinners. Rare among medieval authors, he maintains that human *redemption is achieved simply by the fact of the Incarnation, though (1) he finds sense in claims that the death of Christ 'satisfies' for the sin of human beings (a notion very prominent in the work of Anselm), and (2) he makes much of the concepts '*priest', '*sacrifice', and 'redeemer' when speaking of Christ's work. His basic position is that Christ, being God, is God drawing people to himself (which is what he means by 'grace'), and therefore saving them simply by existing. Christ's human nature is 'an instrument of the Godhead, even as the body is the instrument of the soul' (*Summa contra Gentiles*, 4. 41). It saves simply by being there, and as long as people conform themselves to what it is and act accordingly. He also stresses that, as well as being a direct cause of grace, Christ is head of the *church. At the centre of his ecclesiology, which is fundamentally a *christology, this thought is developed with a focus on the notion that the merit and grace of Christ is the merit and grace of those who believe in him (cf. *ST* III q. 19 a. 4). Frequently alluding to 2 Peter 1: 4, and resembling Greek rather than western theologians, Aquinas is fond of stressing that the full effect of the Incarnation is the '*deification' of people (cf. *ST* I-II q. 112 a. 1). With this thought in mind, he develops his theories on human virtues noted above to explain how they are crowned by the 'theological virtues' of *faith, *hope, and *charity.

Virtues are dispositions (*habitus*) for living well, and theological virtues are no exception. But, unlike the virtues of which he speaks with acknowledgement to Aristotle, they cannot be acquired and preserved by natural human effort (cf. *ST* I-II q. 112). They are wholly the work of God: they are 'infused'. We have them because grace has been given to us. And they equip us, not for the natural bodily life of rational animals, but for a sharing in the life of God. Although God could have united himself with human beings in a different way, this sharing in God's life is an effect of the life, death, and *Resurrection of Christ and the sending of the Holy Spirit (the establishing of the 'New Law'). Its special mark is the presence of charity, conceived as a *friendship (*amicitia*) with God and a living out of the love which God essentially is as Father, Son, and Spirit (cf. *ST* II-II q. 24 a. 2). Copiously drawing on Aristotle and other ancient philosophers, and with highly sophisticated discussions of topics such as choice, will, emotion, and intention, Aquinas dwells on this thought to offer (especially in *ST* I-II and II-II, which some regard as his greatest achievement) an account of human perfection which reflects what he finds in scripture and patristic sources and which is remarkable for its hugely intelligent weaving together of philosophical and theological ideas and arguments.

Aquinas was one of the greatest thinkers ever produced by the Christian church. His literary achievement was immense, and his impact as a Christian theologian is second only to Augustine's. Yet, in spite of his intellectual strengths, he was clearly opposed to the notion that the powers of human reason are of ultimate significance. He describes the ST as a textbook for beginners who need an uncluttered overview of basic Christian truths. He constantly insists that it is our love of God, not our knowledge of him, which matters in this life, which may account for the fact that he was a profound influence on such writers as *John of the Cross and Meister Eckhart. He was probably the author of the Roman liturgical Office of Corpus Christi (revised in the 15th century), and possibly the author of the popular *hymn 'Adoro te devote'. More people are familiar with these last two works, or at least parts of them, than with his writings as introduced above. This is, perhaps, to use a favourite word of his, fitting (*conveniens*).

See also THOMISM, ANALYTICAL; THOMISM, MODERN.

Brian Davies

Aquinas, Thomas, *Opera Omnia*, Leonine edn. (Rome, 1882–).
—— *Summa Theologiae*, Blackfriars edn. Latin and English with notes and introductions (61 vols., 1964–80).
Bourke, Vernon J., *Thomistic Bibliography: 1920–1940, The Modern Schoolman* (1921).
Chenu, M. D., *Towards Understanding Saint Thomas*, ET (1964).
Congar, Yves, *Thomas d'Aquin: Sa vision de théologie et de l'Église* (1984).
Davies, Brian, *The Thought of Thomas Aquinas* (1992).
Elders, Leo J., *The Philosophical Theology of St. Thomas Aquinas* (1990).
Gilson, Étienne, *The Christian Philosophy of St Thomas Aquinas* (1957).
Ingardia, Richard (ed.), *Thomas Aquinas: International Bibliography 1977–1990* (1993).
Kretzmann, Norman, and Stump, Eleonore (eds.), *The Cambridge Companion to Aquinas* (1993).
Mandonnet, P., and Destrez, J., *Bibliographie Thomiste*, 2nd edn., rev. M.-D. Chenu (1960).
Miethe, Terry L., and Bourke, Vernon J., *Thomistic Bibliography, 1940–1978* (1980).
McDermott, Timothy, (ed.), *Aquinas: Selected Philosophical Writings* (1993).
Torrell, Jean-Pierre, *Saint Thomas Aquinas i. The Person and His Work*, ET (1996).
—— *Saint Thomas d'Aquin: Maître spirituel* (1996).
Weisheipl, James A., *Friar Thomas D'Aquino* (1974); republished with Corrigenda and Addenda (1983).

archaeology.

Scientific archaeology is a relatively young discipline, but, from at least the time of the Empress Helena and her dream-led discovery of the true cross in 326, Christians have had an interest in identifying sites of *pilgrimage and in the discovery of relics. Indeed, remnants of this relic-seeking attitude have tended to infiltrate specifically biblical and Christian archaeology so that academic archaeologists have fought shy of the subject. The caricature of the biblical archaeologist with the bible in one hand and a shovel in the other, bent on confirming the biblical account of ancient Near Eastern history, has had at times a grain of truth. Those trying to reconstruct the history of the ancient Near East express disquiet that the whole debate is skewed by its focus in *Israel, which was only one, rather obscure, political entity in the region.

Any systematic archaeological exploration of the biblical lands had to wait until the beginning of the 19th century when Napoleon's conquests opened up the Levant to western scholars. This led to a revolution in knowledge of the biblical period, not only in the discovery of lost biblical cities such as Nineveh but even more significantly through the decipherment of Egyptian and other ancient languages. Unlooked-for quantities of records from Babylon and other ancient cultures were recovered. The bible, previously the sole record of these periods of history, was thus placed into the context of a bewilderingly rich yet fragmentary literary culture. Later discoveries, such as the *Dead Sea Scrolls and the Nag Hammadi texts, have shed similar new light on the NT period.

An immediate effect of this was to heighten the crisis over *biblical authority. As the only witness to the events it recounted, the bible had been unchallengeable. The new texts and the possibility of uncovering artefacts meant that it could in theory be confirmed or contradicted. The success of the German archaeologist Schliemann in predicting and then uncovering the site of the Homeric city of Troy led to a rather simplistic optimism that similar biblical sites would also be discovered, confirming the bible's historical accounts as Schliemann confirmed Homer. Yet even if archaeology might indicate that a city of Troy had existed, that is far from proof that a Trojan war took place, let alone of the existence and relationships of Homer's heroes.

A biblical case in point is the history of archaeology at Jericho. In apparent confirmation of the account in Joshua 6: 20, an ancient city was discovered on the presumed site of Jericho. When a set of destroyed walls was excavated, this was heralded as proof of the bible's accuracy. Later and more detailed excavations revealed that there were seventeen different sets of destroyed walls. The unique event which correlated site and text at Jericho was suddenly not so unique. Moreover, none of these destructions appeared to coincide with any dates proposed on the basis of biblical chronology for the entry of Israel into Canaan. Jericho's archaeology offered no confirmation that the conquest as recorded in Judges and Joshua had taken place. Indeed, without the biblical account, no archaeologist would be likely to propose that there had been any concerted migration into Canaan from Egypt.

Champions of the bible's historical accuracy are then left with the options of rejecting the archaeological findings or relying on an argument from silence. Alternatively, they may creatively reinterpret the biblical text either by redating it or by treating the Exodus as some kind of symbolic construct. All of these positions have their advocates and their obvious problems.

Tensions are inevitable between those who take it as axiomatic that the biblical account is correct, and those who see the biblical material as only one, highly tendentious, source for the historian of the period. Such tensions remain unresolved, and archaeology alone cannot resolve them. Funding can still be found for expeditions to Mount Ararat to excavate the remains of Noah's ark, much to the dismay of certain academic archaeologists.

Archaeology of the beginnings of the Christian period is particularly difficult. Many sites are of religious significance to some community, making excavation difficult. The situation for sites in Israel is compounded by the sensitivities of Israeli scholars and government authorities. In any case, the period of Christ's life is very short in archaeological terms. Yet there has been a huge growth in knowledge of the period of the Roman occupation of Palestine which allows the context of the NT to be filled out.

Less controversial, but highly informative, has been a massive undertaking in excavating and preserving Christian sites across the whole of Europe, resulting in a much richer understanding of the development of early churches (for instance in Corinth), of the spread of Roman Christianity, and of the spread and daily life of medieval *monastic communities. A much fuller picture of the social context of the development of Christianity is now possible which has again fed into theological controversies over, say, the position of *women in early Christian communities.

Contrary to some expectations, archaeology can very seldom confirm or deny the truth of any biblical incident. Archaeology is an interpretative science. Artefacts and sites must be 'read' just as much as texts and so fail to offer the certain proofs expected of them. In addition, for large tracts of biblical history, the bible remains the only account and no archaeological evidence is available. For instance, there is no uncontroverted evidence from inscriptions or other archaeological sources that *David or his kingdom ever existed. Whether any conclusions at all can be drawn from this silence is another matter.

Archaeology raises rather than answers the question of just what is truly unique in Christian belief and what reflects common cultural assumptions. It also sharpens the question as to how far Christianity's historical claims can or should be relied upon. Its major challenge to Christian thought is its specification of the context within which Christians must interpret their history.

Hugh S. Pyper

Avi-Yonah, M., and Stern, E., *Encyclopaedia of Archaeological Excavations in the Holy Land* (1975–8).

Frend, W. C., *The Archaeology of Early Christianity: A History* (1996).

Mazar, A., *Archaeology of the Land of the Bible* (1992).

Moorey, R., *A Century of Biblical Archaeology* (1996).

Arianism

Arianism has always been regarded as the most basic Christian *heresy. Arius was a presbyter in *Alexandria in the early 4th century who was involved in a dispute with his bishop, Alexander. The dispute spread, involving the other main sees in the eastern church. It was the primary reason for the calling of the Council of *Nicaea, held under the presidency of the Emperor *Constantine, keen to maintain harmony within the church on which he had so recently bestowed imperial favour.

The chief theological issue was the divine nature of the Son and his relation to the *Father. Before outlining the Arian view, it is important to recall earlier attitudes. The *New Testament speaks of *Christ in divine terms, but also as secondary and subordinate to the Father as supreme *God. Christian writers of the 2nd and 3rd centuries continue to reflect these two convictions, and to do so in various ways (see Pre-Constantinian Thought). Some blur the distinction between Son and Father, treating 'Son' as a name for the incarnate presence of the Father. But a greater number insist on the Father and Son as two distinct existents, even speaking on occasion of the Son as a 'second god'. Such language was felt to be consistent with an underlying monotheism, because the Son was also the Logos (Mind or *Word of God); the two were therefore one at the level of will in which the Son was wholly united with the Father.

Arius and his bishop, Alexander, both belonged to this dominant tradition which understood the Son/Logos as a distinct entity alongside the Father. Alexander, in emphasizing the divine status of the Son, spoke of him as co-eternal with the Father. (This was not an entirely new teaching, but had earlier been part of a view, not held by Alexander, which affirmed the eternal nature of all spiritual beings.) To Arius this seemed to involve positing two eternal principles or sources of all existence, and so to be in conflict with a basic monotheistic faith.

It is not easy to outline Arius' own view, since his writings (like those of most early heretics) have not survived, apart from three brief letters, leaving us only those and the hostile comments of his enemies to rely on. But the following summary can be put forward with reasonable confidence. God the Father is uniquely transcendent. The Son is also god (lower case representing the absence of the definite article in Greek), a product of the Father's will which he also fully shares. His derivation from the Father can be spoken of as a process of begetting or of *creation (Prov. 8: 22, which speaks of God 'creating' his Wisdom and which both sides in the dispute took to refer to the Son, provided biblical backing for such usage), but he is different from all other creatures since he is God's agent in the creation of everything else, and thus himself the only direct creation of God. His existence is pre-temporal (since he precedes the universe which gives meaning to temporality) but, being begotten, he is not absolutely without beginning as the Father is. This insistence on the divine, but ontologically secondary, status of the Son was felt to be necessary not only for the upholding of monotheism but also to give truer expression to the divine character of the saving events of the gospel. Those who denied any such distinction between the divinity of the Father and the Son were faced, Arians could argue, with a dilemma. Arius and most of his contemporaries, including his most implacable opponent, *Athanasius, Alexander's successor as bishop of Alexandria, did not explicitly allow for the presence of a distinct human *soul in Christ but saw the Son/Logos as the sole inner reality of Christ's life: hence, if they denied any distinction between the divinity of Father and Son they would be involving God directly in the suffering of the *cross, thereby offending against the almost universal presumption of the impassibility of the supreme deity. If, on the other hand, they affirmed a distinct human soul in Christ, as *orthodoxy came to do, then in ascribing Christ's sufferings to that human soul, they would be undermining the essentially divine character of his death for us.

The Council of Nicaea came down firmly against Arius. Its creed defines the Son as 'true God from true God, begotten not made, of one substance (homoousios) with the Father': in other words, his divinity is the same full divinity as that of the Father and his being begotten from the Father is not a special form of being created but something quite distinct from creation. The point was rammed home by attaching to the creed anathemas against particular tenets of Arius' position; and Arius himself was exiled.

But that was not the end of the matter. The great majority of the leading bishops in the eastern church were unhappy with the precise teaching of Arius, but also with the direction in which the theology of Athanasius was developing, and still more with the way he exercised his ecclesiastical power. So the dispute went on with a wide range of differing accounts of the relation of Father and Son being put forward. Although Athanasius' many opponents did not specifically refer to or draw upon the teaching of Arius, he chose to describe almost any position that did not affirm a full coequality between Father and Son as 'Arian'. Association with the officially discredited Arius was a valuable rhetorical device in the long drawn out polemics of the middle years of the 4th century.

So the term 'Arianism' had an ambiguity built into it from the beginning. It could mean the teaching of Arius, which modern scholarship is still struggling to unravel. It was also used to refer to any position which qualified the ultimately triumphant affirmation of a full coequality of Father and Son. In the west, where knowledge, let alone any influence, of Arius was almost non-existent, old-fashioned views of a strongly biblical provenance which stressed the supremacy of the Father and the subordination of the Son were condemned as 'Arian' by Ambrose to the great indignation of their exponents. In the east the moderate opponents of the developing orthodoxy, whom Athanasius had designated 'Arians', were effectively outlawed by the Council of Constantinople, to which we owe our Nicene *Creed, and by the repressive policy of the Emperor Theodosius on behalf of orthodoxy. But their views continued to flourish for another three centuries as the distinctive form of Christianity practised by the Goths.

In the later history of the church 'Arianism' survived as a term of abuse to be ascribed to almost any deviation from *Trinitarian or *christological orthodoxy, however far it might be from the 4th-century views to which the designation was first applied. That form of 4th-century interpretation was seldom revived, Arius appealing as little as Athanasius to the anti-Trinitarian tradition. The most notable exception was in *eighteenth-century Britain, where there was a strong Arian movement, especially within the Church of England. Its leading exponents, William Whiston and Samuel Clarke, were among the prominent scientists of the day and disciples of Isaac Newton in both their scientific and their theological views. Accepting scripture as embodying divinely given truth, but interpreting it not so much with the aid of tradition as with that of the *reason characteristic of the emerging scientific age, they found themselves impelled in a broadly Arian direction. They objected to the designation 'Arian' if it was intended to link them with Arius himself and his teaching, but not if it linked them with the main body of Athanasius' 4th-century opponents.

The movement died out by the close of the century. One reason for its disappearance was the decay of what had been a widely held belief in an unseen spirit world. A general belief of that kind provided a framework for an interpretation of the *Incarnation as the Incarnation of a pre-existent divine spirit. Without that framework the Arian interpretation of the Son lost much of its plausibility. The conflict of interpretation became one between orthodoxy and *unitarianism. Some contemporary Christians may continue to find difficulty in identifying themselves wholly with the precise doctrine of God that was worked out in dispute with Arius and those given the name of 'Arians', but it is unlikely that Arius or the 'Arians' of the 4th century will prove a persuasive model for any future proposals for an alternative account of the Christian doctrine of God.

Maurice Wiles

Gregg, R. C., and Groh, D. E., *Early Arianism* (1981).
Hanson, R. P. C., *The Christian Doctrine of God* (1988).
Lorenz, R., *Arius Judaizans?* (1978).
Stevenson, J., *A New Eusebius*, rev. edn. (1987), 321–55.
Wiles, M. F., *The Archetypal Heresy: Arianism through the Centuries* (1997).
Williams, R. D., *Arius* (1987).

Aristotle was born in 384 BC in Stagira, Macedonia (in the north of modern Greece). In 367 he went to Athens and became a member of *Plato's Academy. On Plato's death (in 347) he left the city for a dozen or so years, during part of which he served as tutor to Alexander (the Great) in Macedon. In 334 he returned and founded his own school, the Lyceum. Eleven years later the death of Alexander resulted in an anti-Macedonian movement and Aristotle departed for the island of Euboea. He died there in 322 having produced a body of thought that establishes him as one of the two greatest *philosophers of antiquity.

It is difficult to comprehend how anyone could have ranged so widely and produced such profound ideas as are credited to Aristotle. Unlike the writings of Plato, little of what we have appears to be finished work and it is generally supposed that the Aristotelian corpus consists mostly of lecture notes. These explore fundamental issues in *metaphysics, the philosophies of *science and nature, epistemology, logic, philosophy of mind and action, *ethics, politics, and aesthetics. His system has been highly influential during various periods: in antiquity, in the high *Middle Ages, in the 16th and 17th centuries and again in the 20th century both among Christians (especially Catholics) and secular philosophers.

The first works of Aristotle to be widely known, and with which educated Christians would have had some familiarity, were his 'exoteric' writings: semi-popular works aimed at non-specialists. None of these survives intact but they seem to have been early works in which Plato's influence was strong. Subsequently, however, Aristotle rejected the central notion of Platonism, namely the identification of reality with an immaterial realm of timeless, immaterial essences or 'forms'. Plato had been led to postulate these in part because of the search for objects of certain knowledge which the changing, irregular, natural world seemed not to offer. Aristotle agrees with Plato that genuine knowledge is of the abstract universal not the concrete particular, but he sees no reason on this account to reject the natural world or empirical knowledge. Instead, he posits an intellectual capacity, the 'active intellect' by means of which we are able to abstract an intelligible general nature (horseness or gold, say) from experience of its naturally occurring instances (particular horses or pieces of gold).

Aristotle is similarly disposed to naturalism, as against the idealist transcendentalism of Plato, in his account of the *soul and its activities, and of moral, political, and aesthetic values. Whereas Plato repeatedly places divides between matter and mind, empirical fact and norm or value, Aristotle finds ways to harmonize them. On his account the soul is the principle of organization and activity of a living thing, its 'form', and while he contemplates the possibility that the active intellect may be immaterial, for the most part he is inclined to identify reality with empirical nature. Goodness, in his view, is a condition in which the natural being of a thing is realized or 'actualized'. *Morality, like horticulture, is a matter of promoting natural well-being or flourishing.

In the first century or so of *Christianity it was debated whether revealed religion had any need of, or place for, speculative *reasoning. The conclusion—periodically contested thereafter—was that philosophy was an ally of faith. In Justin Martyr (d. *c*.165), *Irenaeus, and Clement of Alexandria (150–215) one may find reasoning traceable back to Aristotle, but the ideas belong to his Platonic phase, and quite generally Neoplatonism was the dominant philosophical influence until the 'rediscovery' in the Middle Ages of the later post-Platonic works of Aristotle.

His writings were received in the *Latin west through two sources. First, through the work of early translators such as Boethius (480–524) and Cassiodorus (490–585) who knew little of the authentic corpus and were themselves Neoplatonists. Ironically, the second and more fruitful source was the *Islamic Arab world. In the 4th century Syrian Christians translated Greek texts into Syriac, and several centuries later their descendants made their way to Baghdad where they began to render these works into Arabic. Muslim philosophers became interested in these and began to produce commentaries upon them. During the 12th and 13th centuries, due in no small part to the Crusades, editions of hitherto unknown Aristotelian works in Greek and Arabic, with accompanying commentaries, began to appear in the west where they were rapidly translated into Latin.

One such translator was William of Moerbeke (1215–86), a contemporary of fellow *Dominican Thomas *Aquinas. Aquinas had been encouraged to attempt a new synthesis of faith and philosophy by the example of his teacher Albert the Great who was excited at the naturalistic orientation of the newly discovered Aristotle. Lacking Greek, Thomas was dependent upon William's translations and consumed and commented upon them as they appeared. Furthermore, he pursued the task of restructuring a Christian vision using Aristotelian philosophy. The result, embodied in a series of works, most famously the *Summa contra Gentiles* and the *Summa Theologiae*, was a system, *Thomism, that by stages became in effect the official philosophy of the Catholic Church.

However, the reception of Aristotle in the 13th century was anything but easy or wholehearted. Within the universities Augustinian Platonism was the favoured approach of secular priests and *Franciscans, and the immediate fate of Christian Aristotelianism was to be attacked on the grounds that it represented a naturalism incompatible with Christian belief. Indeed, in 1270 Bishop Tempier of Paris condemned several propositions associated with Aristotelianism, and similar denunciations were repeated elsewhere. This produced a counter-attack but also encouraged a determined effort to show that, far from being at odds with faith, the central features of Aristotle's system were well placed to support and interpret it.

By the modern period Aristotelianism had found a home within Christian thought. Not all who have been influenced by Aquinas have been Roman *Catholics: the Anglican *Hooker and the Calvinist Grotius (1583–1645) are evidence of this; yet it is the case that Aristotle has been most enthusiastically received by Catholic Christians inspired by the thought of Thomas Aquinas. It is unsurprising, therefore, that in Christian circles Aristotle has been most keenly studied wherever Thomism has been dominant. One example is during the 16th century, when in Italy and in Spain/Portugal powerful Dominican and *Jesuit schools were developed which sought to interpret and apply the thought of Aquinas and Aristotle.

A second example spans the 19th and 20th centuries. In the first of these Joseph Kleutgen (1811–83), a German Jesuit, wrote two massive works in which he argued that only Aristotelian metaphysics could provide a solid basis for Catholic *theology and went on to develop his own version of Christian Aristotelianism. Kleutgen is said to have contributed to a draft of the encyclical *Aeterni Patris* (1879) in which Pope Leo XIII commended Aquinas as providing the surest foundation for Christian doctrine and initiated a phase in Catholic philosophy in which Aristotle was studied as the major fount of pre-Christian wisdom.

The main areas in which Aristotle's thought has been and remains influential are moral philosophy and theology. The original source is his work the *Nicomachean Ethics* but its themes, including the emphasis on *virtue, the emotions, and practical reasoning, were often taken up through reading Aquinas's commentary and the second part of the *Summa Theologiae* (both *Prima* and *Secunda Secundae*).

In this century the cause of Christian Aristotelianism has been championed by several important figures including Jacques *Maritain, Étienne Gilson (1884–1978), and Alasdair *MacIntyre. Maritain and MacIntyre converted to Catholicism, Gilson was born into it. Of the three, MacIntyre is the best known in general philosophical and theological circles for his advocacy of the ethics of virtue and the importance of moral community. In this he has been joined by an American moral theologian in the reformed tradition, Stanley Hauerwas (1933–   ). For all that he is referred to by philosophers, however, MacIntyre's sociological, historical, and religious interests make him something of an outsider so far as mainstream English language philosophy is concerned.

Within the latter community Aristotle is studied and honoured as a great figure; however if there is to be a philosophical appropriation of Aristotle akin to that of the Middle Ages it may well, as then, come from within Christian thought. Aristotle's emphasis upon the reality and intelligibility of the natural order and his account of value as pertaining to the actualization of innate potentialities fits his philosophy very well to Christian doctrines of *creation and *natural law. Once again, then, Aristotle becomes a candidate for retrospective baptism.   **John Haldane**

Ackrill, J. L., *Aristotle the Philosopher* (1981).

Barnes, J. (ed.), *The Cambridge Companion to Aristotle* (1995).

—— (ed.), *The Complete Works of Aristotle* (1984).

Chadwick, H., *Early Christian Thought and the Classical Tradition* (1966).

Haldane, J., 'Thomism', in E. Craig (ed.), *Routledge Encyclopedia of Philosophy* (1998), i.

Lear, J., *Aristotle: The Desire to Understand* (1988).

MacIntyre, A., *Whose Justice? Which Rationality?* (1988).

McCool, G., *The Neo-Thomists* (1994).

Stead, C., *Philosophy in Christian Antiquity* (1994).

Armenian tradition.

Armenian tradition. In 2001 the Armenian Church commemorates the 1700th year of the establishment of Christianity as the official religion of the nation. St Gregory the Illuminator (*c.* 240–332), called the Apostle of Armenia, is credited with having converted King Tiridates III and his court in the early 4th century. Most scholars now place that event in 314, just one year after *Constantine's promulgation of the Edict of Milan, but 301 remains the date of tradition. Whether 301 or 314, the ancient lineage of this church of the Christian east cannot be gainsaid. And it is this lineage that has given cause for the view that Armenia was the first nation to adopt Christianity as the state religion.

Legend and tradition have it that the apostles Thaddeus and

Bartholomew evangelized Armenia in the 1st century. More reliable historical evidence does show that Christian bishops were present in Armenia certainly by the middle of the 3rd century, a result of the missionary outreach of two of the great centres of the early church, Greek Caesarea and *Syrian Edessa. The Armenian Church's spirituality has ever since reflected this combination of influences. Thus, early Armenian Christianity breathed in the great Trinitarian theology of the Cappadocian fathers as well as the asceticism and spirituality of Aphrahat of Persia and Ephrem the Syrian. Armenian biblical exegesis followed the methods of the *Alexandrine school.

Over its first century of existence, the Armenian Church maintained ecclesiastical ties with the church in Caesarea where St Gregory himself had been educated. In 387, however, Armenia was partitioned between Rome and Persia, and the latter exerted strong pressure on the Armenians to dissolve their ties with the Greek-speaking west. The autonomy of the Armenian Church was well under way when the *christological controversy over the fourth Ecumenical Council of *Chalcedon (451) broke out. In 452 Hovsep I was elevated to catholicos (or patriarch), and the end of supervision by the church in Caesarea was formalized. The Armenian Church began its long journey of independence (sometimes in isolation) that over seventeen hundred years has evolved a very distinctive Christian tradition.

The breach that came to separate the churches who adhered to the Council of Chalcedon and those who did not (Syrians, Egyptian Copts, and Armenians) did not entirely cut off the Armenian Church from the mainstream of Christian theology. At the turn of the 5th century, St Mesrob and St Sahak the Great (catholicos c.389–c.438) invented an alphabet and translated the holy scriptures, first from the Syriac and then from the Greek Septuagint text. The Holy Translators and their students also supervised translations of important patristic commentaries and theological works.

Still, there is no question that the Council of Chalcedon marked an important turning-point in Armenian Christianity. The Armenians, who were not in fact present at Chalcedon, were immediately suspicious of Pope Leo's Tome and its influence upon the Council, ultimately seeing in both a taint of the *Nestorian heresy. It was nearly fifty years, however, before a conciliar act was promulgated against Dyophysitism under Catholicos Babgen (490–516) in 506. And it was not until the second and third Synods of Dvin in 554 and 607 that the Council of Chalcedon was formally condemned.

But the issue did not go away. Over the centuries, the record reveals much see-sawing back and forth, as Armenian Church leaders made conciliatory gestures towards *Constantinople and then Rome depending on political circumstances. For example, even in a short space of thirty years after the third Synod of Dvin, on the heels of victory over the Persians, Catholicos Ezra and an entourage of bishops and doctors formally accepted Chalcedon at a synod called together by the Emperor Heraclius. This intercommunion lasted until the end of the century. When the Sixth Ecumenical Council (680) condemned Monothelitism, to which the Armenians heartily subscribed, the shift back to a strong *Monophysite position was completed. This position can be characterized by its emphatic embrace of Cyril of Alexandria's 5th-century formula 'one nature, and that incarnate, of the divine Word', stressing the unity and concreteness of the divine *Word and second Person of the *Trinity who fully assumed our humanity.

In the modern era, this moderate Armenian Monophysitism has proved amenable to compromise in seeking consensus with both *Eastern Orthodox and Roman Catholics. In 1990 representatives of the Armenian Church signed a historic document produced by a Joint Commission of the Eastern and Oriental Orthodox Churches that called for unity and full communion between their churches based upon mutual affirmations of the orthodoxy of their respective christological teachings. And in December of 1996 Catholicos Karekin I of All Armenians (1932-1999), and Pope *John Paul II issued a joint declaration in which they agreed upon a common christological formulation acceptable to both communions.

The strong theopaschal concern of Armenian christology, represented in the church's retention of Peter the Fuller's 5th-century amendment to the Trisagion, 'who was crucified for us', may be of special interest for our time. The emphasis on the suffering of *God is expressed stunningly by the 6th-century Armenian philosopher and apologist David the Invincible (Anhaght) in his short work entitled 'An Encomium on the Holy *Cross of God': 'Now he who laid Himself down indeed did so through and on the Cross. And He who gave Himself on it is still on it and does not distance Himself from it …. Therefore the Cross is the Cross of God and He Himself, the Crucified One, God immortal, uncircumscribable and infinite.' This Armenian christology and doctrine of God has much to contribute to the modern discussion of a crucified God advanced in the 20th century by the likes of Jürgen *Moltmann and Hans Urs *von Balthasar.

The richness and distinctiveness of the Armenian tradition can be found in other quarters as well. Eznik of Kolb championed Armenian *apologetics in the 5th century. His Refutation of the Sects is a mine of information on Mazdean religion and the Marcionite heresy. The Armenian mystical and poetical tradition is represented in its highest form by the 10th-century saint, Gregory of Narek (Narekatsi). His greatest work is entitled The Book of Lamentations, a series of prayers whose tone is strongly penitential. The Lamentations have deeply influenced Armenian piety and spirituality. The theologically rich hymnography of the Armenian Church (this is where Armenian theology may be at its best) reaches its heights in the beautiful and profound compositions of the 12th-century catholicos, St Nerses the Gracious (Shnorhali). The 14th century produced the Armenian scholastic, St Gregory of Datev (Tatevatsi). While he championed Armenian orthodoxy against the Latins, his theology incorporates much of their thinking (notable among these influences are writings of Albert the Great, Thomas *Aquinas, and Bonaventure). He adopted the language of *transubstantiation in his *eucharistic theology and in his discussion of *baptism there is an uncharacteristic accent on original *sin at the expense of a more traditional emphasis on illumination, regeneration, and entrance into the *church and the body of Christ. In any case, the distinctively Latin flavour of St Gregory of Datev's theology lends positive proof of cultural and theological transmigrations between the Christian east and west more widespread than has sometimes been assumed. His best known work is the Book of Questions, written in the style of disputation.

The Armenian Church's *liturgical practices contain some distinct variances from their *Byzantine sources. The prototype of the Divine Liturgy is the Liturgy of Basil of Caesarea but with augmentations from the Liturgy of John Chrysostom and some late Latin influences. The Armenian Church gives communion in both elements, but does not mix water with the wine, and in contrast to the Byzantines uses unleavened bread.

Since the birth of a sovereign Armenian nation in 1991, the church in Armenia has enjoyed religious freedom and special privileges under a new Law on Freedom of Conscience and Religious Organizations. But the Armenian Church lacks the resources effectively to re-evangelize the people. Still, there now is reason to hope that at home and abroad the Armenian Church will recover from the devastating consequences of both the Turkish genocide of over a million Armenians during the First World War and the repression of the Soviet era.

There are over five million Armenians throughout the world, some three million in Armenia and the balance in diasporas concentrated in the old Soviet Union, North America, the Middle East, and Europe. While the Armenian Church is a *de facto* international body, whose leaders have long been active within the *ecumenical movement, both at home and abroad it tenaciously remains a self-consciously national church.   **Vigen Guroian**

Arpee, L., *A History of Armenian Christianity from the Beginning to Our Own Time* (1946).

Guroian, V., *Ethics After Christendom* (1974).

Lang, D. V., *Armenia: Cradle of Civilization* (1970).

Mouradian, C. S., *De Staline à Gorbatchev: histoire d'une république soviétique, l'Arménie* (1990).

Nersoyan, T., *Armenian Church Historical Studies* (1996).

Ormanian, M., *The Armenian Church* (1912).

Sarkissian, K., *A Brief Introduction to Armenian Christian Literature* (1960).

Arminianism

Arminianism is an attempt to dilute the Calvinist doctrine of election. Did Christ die only for the elect, and not for all? How can orthodox *Calvinists preach that '*whosoever* believes in him' shall be saved, if they hold that no real offer is being made to sinners excluded from salvation by predestination? Can one resist *grace? These are Arminian questions.

The word 'Arminianism' comes from Jakob Hermandszoon (1560–1609), a Dutch theologian at Leiden whose name was Latinized as Jacobus Arminius. He had been taught by Calvin's successor, Beza, at *Geneva, and the framework of the Arminian debate was Calvinist.

The Arminian Remonstrance of 1610 was summed up in five points: (1) whoever believes will be saved, and *predestination means that God foresees who *will* believe; (2) Christ died for all men, though presumably in vain for unbelievers; (3) to come to saving belief is a gift of the *Holy Spirit (these are not *Pelagians, who downplayed the role of grace); (4) *but* this saving grace can be resisted; and (5) it may be that Christians can fall from grace. For each of these points there was a Calvinist counter-claim, backed by proof-texts and logic. At the international Synod of Dort (1618–19) the *Reformed Churches refuted, as they thought, the Remonstrance and the Dutch church went on to persecute Arminianism.

The Dutch Remonstrants moved, quite quickly, to a wider challenge to *orthodoxy, with doubts about Christ's divinity and human depravity. Arminianism, in Holland and elsewhere, was often a stepping-stone to rationalist *Unitarianism. The same shift happened in New England a century later.

In 17th-century England, the Puritans' opponents, such as Archbishop Laud, were labelled Arminian (*Caroline Divines). These English churchmen were not, like Arminius, trying to fine-tune Calvinist dogma. The heart of their piety was sacramental, and there is a tension between emphasis on the *sacraments and the doctrine of *election. The official teaching of the Church of England in the 1590s had been Calvinist, so the move away from this attracted the Calvinist label of 'Arminian'.

Christianity as preached, with an offer of grace, tends to Arminianism. Sometimes the drift of men's *preaching contradicts their own creed, but John *Wesley, the great preacher of *revival in the 18th century, knew what he was doing, and was pugnaciously Arminian. The Wesleyans called their journal the *Arminian Magazine*. By the end of the 19th century most officially Calvinist churches had modified their opinions in an Arminian direction. The majority of Christians would like to think that Christ died for all. Few people have ever read Arminius, or reworked the classic debates, but the unconsidered assumptions of most Protestants are now Arminian. There are, however, still Calvinists eager for battle. Who, they ask, is really content with universal *non-efficacious* *atonement and universal *resistible* grace?   **Alistair Mason**

Colie, Rosalie, *Light and Enlightenment: A Study of the Cambridge Platonists and the Dutch Arminians* (1957).

Harrison, A. W., *Arminianism* (1937).

Tyacke, N., *Anti-Calvinists: The Rise of English Arminianism c.1590–1640* (1987).

Wilson, Robert J., *The Benevolent Deity: Ebenezer Gay and the Rise of Rational Religion in New England 1696–1787* (1984).

arts, visual. Art and Christianity seem as inseparable as body and soul. Despite occasional waves of *iconoclasm, for the Christian the clothing of sacred concept in visual form is the extension of the act of *creation. 'No artefacture, no Christian religion' (David Jones, *Epoch and Artist* (1959)).

Before 312, Christian art reflected the seclusion of the catacombs. Its *symbols were not invented, but largely taken from pagan imagery and given a Christian interpretation. Art served as a reminder of truths and attitudes. Inscriptions were personalized; not so art. The Christian *ecclesia* had grown rapidly. Multi-ethnicity encouraged use of easily recognized symbols.

The Catholic church's public role began with the Edict of Milan. *Constantine built St Peter's basilica and others followed. Christians rejected the aesthetic of pagan temples. Their model was the basilica, which may explain the bareness: art was inappropriate for the interiors of courts of law. During the following three hundred years the church enriched its images and decoration. As the corporate memory-structure developed, there was more call for imagery as a reminder of stories and personalities of biblical importance. The style was a pale version of late classicism.

After the transformation of Byzantium into *Constantinople, the art of the east largely concentrated on mosaic and bas-relief. In-the-round sculpture was abandoned. The *liturgy of eastern Rome, composed by John Chrysostom, requires a form of church interior not dissimilar to the classical Greek theatre. The altar is placed behind a screen pierced with three doors. This proscenium is hung with sacred icons in a recognizable schematic order and becomes the *iconostasis* of the *Eastern Orthodox Church.

Iconic forms were finally fixed by the Orthodox Church between the 4th and 6th centuries (see ICONOGRAPHY). They were regarded as a canonical underpinning of the structure of belief parallel to the scriptures themselves. This is why they have not changed in fifteen hundred years, but continue in the exact modes as painted in late antiquity. Icons are subject to transposed *dulia*: they are to be reverenced in the same way as holy persons. Hence they have to be as reliable a representative of the deity or the saint as if the image were an authenticated photograph, so that they can be prayed *through*, the prayer being addressed to the person whom they represent.

Two Christian doctrines, of the *Incarnation and the communion of saints, encourage painted or sculpted representation of real historical persons and are the basis for the whole tradition of figurative art in the west. Christianity does not see the depiction of persons and natural objects as derogating from the glory of God, since in Christ God deigned to become an integral part of his creation. The totally transcendent religions of Judaism and Islam vehemently deny this dogmatic position.

Christianity eventually became confident that the corpus of faith could receive, and baptize for God's use, much of primitive Celtic, pagan, and folkloristic art. Folkloristic art was never to be found in the sanctuary, choir, or nave in the buildings of western Catholic Christianity, but in exterior corbels, capitals, mouldings, and friezes. Very occasionally the details of folkloristic art are found inside a building, but they are assigned a minor role. Folklore added a dimension of richness to an ever more complicated system of visual allusion. Without it the art of the *Middle Ages in the service of the church would have lacked its vigorous and vital character.

The *iconostasis*, the screen signifying the entry into sacred space, was fully used in the west but it was not, as in the east, integral to the performance of the liturgy. It could take the form of a main façade of sculptures, either within or outside the narthex (the porch), a *pulpitum* screen, a reredos, or an eastern-facing stained glass window. In all cases, the space beyond the *iconostasis* was sacred space. It seems as though, in the west, the congregation was sometimes included within this space, sometimes only the celebrants, sometimes neither.

The break with the Romanesque style occurred in the mid-12th century. Abbot Suger, the superior of the royal abbey of Saint-Denis, outside Paris, was obsessed with the construction of a church that would rival Constantinople's Hagia Sophia. The adoption of flatbed masonry as a technique of building enabled the new abbey to dispense with heavy supporting walls and give maximum area to enormous stained glass windows high in the clerestory. Hitherto a minor decorative art, stained glass became the most extensive figurative art of the high Middle Ages. The iconography still had a hint of Byzantium, but the attitudes and gestures of the figures were becoming more lifelike and spontaneous. However, they were simple, hieratic, and, where single large figures were concerned, they radiated austere and dignified authority.

France, together with England, Germany, the Netherlands, and northern Italy, experienced in the 13th century a sudden growth in trade, production, and wealth, and the building of considerable towns for the first time since the Roman empire. This produced a dynamic, optimistic civilization which flowered into an enthusiasm for new forms of art. The rise of the Gothic style was meteoric. Within thirty to forty years, Western Europe was covered with new buildings. More stone was quarried in the course of a hundred years than in the combined architectural activities of the Egyptians, Greeks, and Romans. In this increasingly stable and burgeoning society there was a plethora of opportunities for the sculpted figure on an extended scale: screens, canopies, capitals, cusps, crockets, finials, corbels, all crisply carved, painted, and part-gilded. Wall-painting and tapestry-weaving, stained glass and manuscript illumination, flourished as never before. The density of colour and form must have been very nearly suffocating, as may be guessed by looking at the present restored interior of Sainte-Chapelle, Paris.

At the end of the 13th century, there was a change of aesthetic in France. The ratio between the admission of light, through the stained glass, and the interior elaboration, mostly in wood- and stone-carving, shifted. The increasing pallor of the windows (sometimes involving some 60% white glass) helped the interior sculpture to be seen and the new polyphonic books of choir *music to be read. Sight-reading of elaborate motets came into fashion, hence, perhaps, the new, practical, luminosity of church interiors.

Through the 14th century, owing to the great changes in western society caused by urbanization, the content of art in the church altered dramatically. Because of plagues, and sometimes the decimation of the population, death featured largely in the subject-matter of western Christian art. A sometimes grisly realism, involving crucifixions, flagellations, depositions, entombments, and massacres of the innocents appears in carvings and paintings where no detail was neglected. This tendency for art to shock was partly inspired by the increasingly flourishing drama of miracle and *mystery plays.

During the late 13th and early 14th centuries in Italy, partly as a result of the influence of the *Franciscan Order, there came into being a new realization of the vitality and relevance of everyday existence and its reproduction in art, especially painting. This is best typified by the work of Cimabue and Giotto (master and pupil), based mainly in Tuscany and Umbria. Giotto's paintings are vibrant with observed detail of expression and gesture that mark him out as an innovating genius. The *plein air* feeling to the surroundings of the figures and the landscape is seen for the first time in western art since the height of the Roman Empire.

During the 14th and 15th centuries Gothic became ever more self-referential, absorbed in stylistic innovation. The so-called international Gothic style spread all over Europe, from Bohemia to Spain. However, in the early 15th century there was an exceptional development of painting in Flanders, where the new use of oil-paint for picture-panels produced unforgettable masterpieces by the brothers Van Eyck (the *Adoration of the Lamb* in Ghent) and by other superb painters such as Memling.

The crabbed and inward-turned character of the late Gothic style made it comparatively easy for the 'revived' Roman style (ultimately derived from the stimulus of Giotto) to penetrate throughout Europe during the late 15th and 16th centuries. In southern Italy there had been an urge towards the revival of ancient Roman modes of painting, sculpture, and architecture since the days of the Emperor Frederic II (1194–1250) but this was perhaps countered by the *papal transference to Avignon (1309–1377), which ensured the continued influence of French Gothic. The pope's return to *Rome, the healing of the subsequent schism, and the influence of Greek thought, stemming from refugee Greek scholars and churchmen fleeing from Constantinople (captured by the Turks in 1453) stimulated a yearning for classical revival. The serene realism of the early *Renaissance, which had started in sculpture with the Pisani family in the late 13th century, developed in the early 15th century under the leadership of Ghiberti and Donatello in Florence. Painting secured a fresh lease of life under such masters as Masaccio, with his command of solidity and space, Piero della Francesca, Fra Angelico, Paolo Uccello, and Andrea del Castagno. The clear realism of Florence was balanced by a more hieratic style of great richness which had developed independently in Siena. The greatest master of this school was Duccio. Towards the end of the 15th century in Italy, visual artists became the cynosures of their age. Bramante in architecture, Michelangelo in sculpture, Leonardo da Vinci, Raphael, and Botticelli in painting were quickly famous throughout Europe.

The art of the High Renaissance is fully Christian. It is the fulfilment of an urge that took a thousand years to mature and become fully conscious of itself. The ever-present alien streak of Manichaean disdain for bodily humanity leads to iconoclasm. The exact opposite of this attitude is seen in the art of the Renaissance. This art is evidence of a complete faith in the goodness inherent in God's initial act of creation and in the subsequent assuming of human flesh by God the Son. Hence the great characteristic of the art of the time is the splendour, grandeur, and beauty of the human figure, draped or nude. The nude was celebrated in its own right as something God-given and sacred.

With the discovery of America the hitherto somewhat hesitant civilization of the Iberian peninsula gained enormous confidence. Meanwhile, however, in contemporary northern Europe, especially in parts of Germany, the *Reformation took place. The new invention of printing had made possible a radical revolution in the application of thought processes. Conceptual thought was already a commonplace phenomenon in philosophy, mathematics, and music. But with the invention of printing this mode of dematerialized thinking tended to move sideways into theology and scriptural exegesis. The build-up of memory and concept was no longer directly dependent on visual stimuli or phenomena. Through books people found out things for themselves. This tied in with the *Protestant emphasis on the individual conscience and *justification. In some cases this exclusive cerebral fixation consigned to oblivion all the apparatus of mute visual reminder which had been the reason behind the arts of the Middle Ages and Renaissance. In countries not directly and decisively modified by the spread of typography—Iberia, parts of France and of the Spanish Netherlands, and most of Italy—visual signs in architecture, sculpture, and painting remained unaffected and continued to develop.

There was a period of some confusion among painters as to which persuasion, Catholic or Protestant, they should opt for. The greatest painters of the early 16th century were mostly German: Grünewald (whose masterpiece, the Eisenheimer Altarpiece, is in Colmar, Lorraine), Dürer, Holbein the Younger, and Hans Baldung Grun. Holbein and Cranach seem always to have sided with the reform; later, Jordaens became a Calvinist; Dürer, although not formally a Protestant, was certainly on the best of terms with the Reformers.

By the middle of the 16th century, Europe was broadly divided between Protestant north and *Catholic south. Protestants of the *Zwinglian and *Calvinist persuasions tended to hate and destroy imagery of all sorts, but some, such as the *Lutherans of mid- and southern Germany, had no unease over imagery in church, and their traditional church interiors were not subject to iconoclasm. Catholics in the south continued to subscribe to visual art in religious practice. The disputed doctrine of the *Eucharist is responsible in large part for the difference in visual presentation between Protestant and Catholic. Belief in the real presence of Christ in the blessed sacrament can lead to seeing the body of the church as a throne-room where the King of Heaven reigns, together with his court of angels and saints. If this doctrine is denied then the church is seen simply as a meeting-house for prayer and remembrance. In Protestantism the aural predominates over the visual. In the tradition of Catholic practice there is a melding of aural and visual.

The altarpiece is responsible for the vast majority of larger religious paintings. Introduced into church interiors in Italy in the course of the 14th century, the altarpiece was a reminder of some sacred fact or scene, or group of particular saints, to enlighten and concentrate the minds of celebrant and congregation. It was a newly conceived idea and had little to do with the previous concept of the *iconostasis*. This novelty gave the concept a freedom of treatment that would have been inconceivable and inappropriate for an *iconostasis*. Altarpieces were most often used in side-chapels devoted to semi-private devotion. The form was of a very large picture, appealing to a congregation some distance away. One of the greatest altarpieces, together with that of the *Adoration of the Lamb* by Van Eyck, in Ghent, is the *Assumption of the Virgin* by Titian, in the Frari Church in Venice.

In the reintegration of the Catholic Church as devised by the Council of *Trent there was an attempt to lay down guidelines for artists working for the church. Ultimately ineffective, the art legislation of the Council did kill off the hitherto unquestioned indulgence of folkloristic sidelines. Folkloristic art, curiously enough, subsequently flourished only in England, outside the influence of Rome, where the extreme paucity of religious art between 1550 and 1850 was compensated for by the fecundity and invention of secular tomb-sculpture.

The 16th and 17th centuries were a great period of religious art, either attached to the ceremonies of the church or as exploration of private devotion. Uniquely, El Greco (born Domenico Theotocopuli in Crete, which was then ruled by Venice) combined in a personal way the merits of Greek icon-painting with the discoveries of the Venetians in drawing, aerial perspective, and colour. He went to Spain and flourished. Perhaps his ability to copy his initial and original creations of the Virgin and the saints may be due to this Byzantine heritage with its tradition of unchanging images.

In the late 16th century, the two movements that were uppermost in Christian art were mannerism and the beginnings of realism. Mannerism was distinguished by extreme attitudes in painting and sculpture, so distorted as to call into question the spiritual, aesthetic, and psychological bases of Renaissance classicism. Curious colour-schemes, fitful lighting, odd perspective exaggerations, all render the viewer surprised, confused, alarmed, astonished, and charmed in turn. Pontormo and Parmigianino are major exponents of this style, which spread over Catholic Europe. Tintoretto, a Venetian artist of titanic achievement, was both mannerism's greatest representative and a painter whose originality transcended the limits of that or any movement.

Michelangelo da Caravaggio, the inventor of realism, was uninterested in anything but the depiction of actual reality. His invention and dramatic use of chiaroscuro opened the way to the extraordinary visual inventions of Rembrandt, Velasquez, and, to a lesser degree, Rubens. Rembrandt's series of biblical paintings were not intended for use within the body of the church. They are essentially private devotional pictures for contemplation and spiritual development. They speak directly to the heart and are some of the most unforgettable images ever conceived. They are the perfect art for a Protestant spirituality. Spanish polychrome statuary of the 16th and 17th centuries must be mentioned as some of the most moving images in sculpture ever produced. The intensity of the Spanish sculptural tradition may well have arisen as a reaction against the iconoclasm of Islam.

The greatest painters in the 17th century turned to religious subjects. Even painters of particularly classical bent were able to adopt the current *Baroque church idiom when it came to depicting religious scenes and personalities. Poussin is a perfect example of this. In the mid-18th century, reaction to the 'excesses' of the Baroque took the form of neoclassicism, in Rome under the architect Fuga. It was then adopted by the influential Prussian Lutheran convert to Catholicism, Winckelmann, whose writings revolutionized taste in Europe. All hastened to Rome to imbibe the nectar of the neo-classic. There were difficulties. Secularism and the *Enlightenment coincided with the adoption of the neo-classic, whose easy identification with republicanism, secularism, and atheism demonstrated the style's independence from Christianity.

The arrival of the Gothic revival from the north in the early 19th century put the neo-classical in question (see ROMANTICISM). The Holy See was powerless to take part in, or adjudicate on, the aesthetic norms of the newly arrived Gothic style: its influence on forms in Christian art was over, never to be truly effective again. The Gothic revival, occurring mostly in France, Germany, Great Britain, and Spain, was a mixed blessing. It risked associating the spiritual vision and energy of the 19th century with an essentially backward-looking and defensive stance, so far as Christian art was concerned. There were compensations. Many medieval churches in France were efficiently restored by Viollet-le-Duc; the great uncompleted Gothic *cathedrals of Germany, Ulm and Cologne, were completed after some 400 years; a revived Anglican Church built some of the greatest neo-Gothic churches in existence. Enthusiasm for the Gothic spread to the republican United States of America, producing superb buildings in Washington, New York, and elsewhere.

Architectural activity in 19th-century Europe and America stimulated concomitant decorative arts. Stained glass, sculpture, painting, tapestry-weaving, and woodcarving, all in neo-Gothic style, flourished almost as extensively as in the high Middle Ages, thanks to the unparalleled prosperity of Western Europe, particularly Britain.

In Britain, William Morris, the pre-Raphaelite painters, and their wider circle of admirers and imitators contributed notable paintings and sculpture to the Anglican Church. Later, Alfred Gilbert, an Art Nouveau sculptor of genius, contributed the Duke of Clarence's tomb in Windsor Castle. The turn of the century brought sculptor Eric Gill and painter Stanley Spencer to the fore. Gill's *Stations of the Cross*, in Westminster Cathedral, remain one of the seminal works of religious art of the 20th century. Spencer's masterpiece is the Burghclere Memorial Chapel but his numerous smaller religious paintings and his two enormous *Resurrections* (both in the Tate Gallery, London) hold a religious conviction that other painters of his generation cannot match.

The mass physical destruction and extreme mental and spiritual suffering resulting from the Second World War prompted a temporary recrudescence of art concerned with Christianity. Before that, however, as a result of the general secularization policy of the Third Republic, the church in France was freed from state shackles. The first part of the 20th century witnessed a memorable *RENCH Catholic renaissance and the church was able to commission contemporary artists, painters, and sculptors, between 1906 and 1975, with very significant results. After the war, the Anglican Church and the German churches, both Evangelical Protestant and Roman Catholic, were in the forefront of reconstruction. This resulted in a great revival between 1946 and 1975, especially in the art of stained glass. Many churches in Germany and England became famous for their windows. In spite of the heavy opposition of Communist regimes, the Catholic Church in Poland too succeeded in constructing many significant buildings.

The cultural milieu of the 20th century, particularly by the end, was 'the first atheistic civilization in the history of mankind', to quote Vaclav Havel. It is within this general atmosphere of disbelief that the achievements of Christianity in the arts must be assessed. Concomitantly the church has lost the monetary, political, and physical means to propagate its message in its accustomed mode of the past. The Christian church no longer has the general will of the bulk of civilization to draw upon. Its public manifestations, which include visual art, may become more and more alienated from the assumptions of political and economic society, very much as has already happened to the Orthodox tradition.

In the 1960s the Catholic Church's attempt at self-transformation was deeply affected by the wider revolution in mores, wealth, sexuality, and the whole relationship between faith and culture in a world where Christianity was expanding so rapidly in the southern hemisphere. This was particularly so in the matter of the visual arts. The teaching of *Vatican II in this field (*Liturgy*, 122–30; *Gaudium et Spes*, 62), suggestive of an amateur unattached liberalism towards the forms of visual art, was neither a stimulus nor a help in the European situation, but did provide encouragement for vital new developments in Asia, Africa, and Latin America.

The loss of any securely shared objective foundations upon which to erect a visual art which would have general validity has had the effect of concentrating motivation for the content of painting and sculpture in the subjective personal conviction of the artist. The gain in personal sincerity has gone with loss in dogmatic assurance. The stress on personal choice and witness tended to favour a Protestant approach to Christianity. What it pointed towards, however, has been the restricted themes, and the narrowness of the brackets, within which the best art, applied to Christian worship post-1970, could be found to operate.   **Patrick Reyntiens**

Anderson, W., *The Rise of the Gothic* (1985).
Burckhardt, J., *The Civilization of the Renaissance in Italy* (1860); new edn. intro. Peter Burke (1990).
Daniélou, J., *Primitive Christian Symbols* (1964).
Dhanens, E., *Van Eyck: The Ghent Altarpiece* (1973).
Gimpel, J., *The Cathedral Builders* (1961).

Henry, F., *Early Christian Irish Art* (1954).

Hibbard, H., *Caravaggio* (1983).

Lane, Barbara, *The Altar and the Altarpiece: Sacramental Themes in Early Netherlandish Painting* (1984).

Lasko, P., *Ars Sacra, 800–1200* (1972).

Male, E., *Religious Art in France: The Twelfth Century. A Study of the Origins of Medieval Iconography* (1958), ET (1978).

—— *Religious Art in France: The Thirteenth Century* (1951), ET (1984).

Murray, Peter and Linda, *The Oxford Companion to Christian Art and Architecture* (1996).

Pelikan, J., *Imago Dei: The Byzantine Apologia for Icons* (1990).

Pope-Hennessy, J., *Fra Angelico* (1974).

Reyntiens, P., *The Beauty of Stained Glass* (1990).

Rothenstein, E., *Stanley Spencer* (1962).

Schwartz, G., *Rembrandt: His Life, his Paintings* (1986).

Shapiro, M., *Romanesque Art* (1993).

Watkin, E. I., *Catholic Art and Culture* (1947).

Wittkower, R., *Studies in the Italian Baroque* (1975).

asceticism. The Greek root *askeo* originally meant to practise, exercise, or train (in athletics), to work (raw materials), to create or form (an object by artistic means), to dress (the body with clothing or jewellery). From these root meanings many connotations have abounded, from the neutral one reflecting mundane ancient life contexts to the highly charged symbolic and political meanings that have come to dominate both popular and scholarly religious thinking. Here 'asceticism' is associated with a range of responses to the conviction that reality is divided into two realms—the transcendent and the mundane. Response to the latter ('the *world') has generally been seen in terms of negatives: proscriptions, renunciations, withdrawals, relativization. In spite of the fact that these negatives have been claimed to exist only for the sake of positives (salvation, liberation, enlightenment, a new subjectivity), it is the negatives that have been consistently stressed in historiography, theological interpretation, and popular thinking.

Modern western popular sentiment is so strongly charged in this sense that it is hardly possible for scholarship not to have been infected. The *Oxford English Dictionary*, in a way that both reflects and has affected scholarly and popular engagement with the subject, defines asceticism as 'extreme' and 'severe' abstinence, 'austerity'. The earliest English usage it cites—'Doomed to a life of celibacy by the asceticism which had corrupted the simplicity of Christianity' (Sir Thomas Browne, 1646)—barely hides what must be assumed to be a widely held cultural bias against, even contempt for, the ascetic, especially in relationship to what is understood to be 'authentic' Christianity.

That modern and contemporary scholars have been influenced by such sentiment is clear. Some scholars of the NT and early church, especially in *Protestant traditions, associating asceticism with the corruption of authentic, primitive Christianity, either dismiss it altogether or interpret it as the preoccupation of fanatics. Others who have engaged the topic have uncritically praised particular ascetic traditions, theologies, pieties, or heroic figures, at the expense of critical reconstructive and analytical work. The polemical views and hyperbole that historically have characterized and still characterize interpretation of asceticism make it all the more imperative to seek a more nuanced interpretation.

The earliest extant Christian texts rarely mention the Greek term *askesis*, most often translated as 'asceticism'. (Acts 24: 16 is an exception: RSV translates the verb here as 'take pains'.) But to make much of the lack of occurrences of this one term is to miss the point that the complex phenomena are referred to in many different ways, drawing upon different terminology (cf. 1 Cor 9: 25, where *engkrateuetai* (exercises self-control) functions in much the same way as *askeo*). The widespread and consistent use of the term in early Christian literature in connection with spiritual and moral life begins with the fathers, especially Clement of Alexandria and *Origen, who had been heavily influenced by Greek and Graeco-Jewish moral and philosophical writers. But earliest Christianity could hardly have been without the ascetic impulse. Mark 2: 20 and Acts 13: 2 indicate that the first Christians continued Jewish practices of *fasting. This suggests that besides the problem of rigid, *dualistic thinking on the subject, another hermeneutical problem has characterized the study of Christian asceticism: it has often been delimited by the mere occurrence of the one term (*askesis*) in the texts studied, and by a too limited number of models of piety (for example, the *desert father figure). Not only is it the case that asceticism is consistently represented in texts that never mention any one term in particular, but the names and faces that represent the Christian ascetic include many more than the 4th-century men of the Egyptian desert. The types of practice that qualify as ascetic include much more than those traditions and institutions prominently and dramatically featured in historiography (eremitic or cenobitic *monasticism or stylitism).

Asceticism in Christian traditions, as in all other traditions, must be viewed in terms of complex origins, rhetorical and literary representations, forms and practices, institutionalization, meanings, and power dynamics. Instead of beginning with word studies, lone heroic figures, or histrionic practices, and instead of stressing the idea of the negative as impetus and explanation, it is more appropriate to begin by trying to account for the formation and development of individuals and communities that define themselves by embracing certain world-views and orientations deemed 'other-worldly'. To explain their existence to themselves and to exploit the power inherent in a new social formation, such transcendental communities and individuals have generally had to engage continuously in the work of de-formation and re-formation of 'the world'. Such work is constituted by practices and strategies that function both defensively and offensively: they help communities and individuals not only to take flight—physical, psychical, psycho-social, intellectual, spiritual flight—from 'the world', but also to fend off, critique, and reshape that world. In so far as such communities and individuals define themselves as other-worldly and employ strategies and practices for creating, shaping, and maintaining new identities, communities, and world-views, they and their strategies and practices can be deemed ascetic.

The term 'asceticism' would then actually reflect and help explain some of the complexities of historical and contemporary social and rhetorical formation, including aspects of the formation of the ancient Christian world. Just as words can have different meanings in different contexts, so different practices (renunciations of food and *sex, physical retreat, temperance and moderation, physical torture, psychological withdrawal, *martyrdom/suicide, specialized intellectual and physical regimens and disciplines) can have different meanings among different types of persons (élite males, élite females, slaves and serfs, court philosophers, wandering prophets, and seers) in different sociopolitical-discursive contexts (the desert, urban public square, palace, household, 'church', village, on the road). Even within one community, time, social differentiation (gender, ethnicity, status), power dynamics and conflict, development, institutionalization, affect the meanings of different practices.

In terms of intensity, types of practice, and motivations, the simple renunciatory practices of the primitive Christian communities of 1st-century Syria were different both from Basil's and Benedict's more institutionalized, systematized, and moderate monastic asceticisms (4th century and onwards), and from the daring asceticisms of the Syrian Stylites (5th century and onwards). The rigorous asceticisms of the principled dualistic thinkers among the *Montanists, Manichaeans, and *Gnostics of antiquity and the Cathars and Waldenses of the medieval period were quite different from one another as well as from the urban-, household-, and female-focused asceticisms of the Latin Christianity of late antiquity. The asceticisms of medieval Europe, emphasizing suffering, humility, and poverty, were different from those associated with the piety and ethos of Protestant Reformers and *Renaissance figures; different again from those of many of our own contemporaries (both religious and self-styled secularists) in search of other-worldly retreats.

The list can go on. It is enough to stress that there have always been expressions of the ascetic in Christian practice and thought, there has always been diversity in those expressions, and there has always been conflict about the appropriate expression of Christian asceticism. It needs to be recognized that there has never been a universally agreed upon appropriate or correct understanding or model of it. The concepts of 'mainline', 'orthodox', 'heretical', 'heterodox' do not apply to asceticism; it can be associated with all parties and orientations. What is considered legitimate in one situation can be rendered illegitimate in another. Winners of the various conflicts have generally been in control of the literary and rhetorical spins about the various arguments and practices and their effects.

The acceptance of Christian claims about transcendence necessarily renders the world problematic, a hurdle or stumbling-block, a reality held in contempt that is to be overcome, or at the very least critically negotiated. In spite of the sharp polemic against 'radical', or 'worldly', or simply *different* expressions of ascetic piety over the course of Christian history, it can be argued that there was a common baseline: it was assumed that Christian existence required some sort of expression of the ascetic, of critique and de-formation and re-formation of the world. For most of Christian history, the battle about asceticism has been not whether Christian piety should be associated with it, but about the type, intensity of expression, and meaning of the ascetic that is appropriate or required.

Vincent L. Wimbush

Brown, P., *The Body and Society* (1988).

Clark, E. A., *Ascetic Piety and Women's Faith* (1986).

Elm, S., *Virgins of God* (1994).

Harpham, G., *The Ascetic Imperative in Culture and Criticism* (1987).

Valantasis, R., 'Constructions of Power in Asceticism', *Journal of the American Academy of Religion*, 63 (1995).

Wimbush, V. L. (ed.), *Ascetic Piety in Greco-Roman Antiquity: A Sourcebook* (1990).

Wimbush, V. L., and Valantasis, R. (eds.), *Asceticism* (1995).

assurance is a technical term of controversial theology: the issue has been whether a Christian may properly be certain that he or she presently enjoys the favour of God and/or will attain eternal *salvation. It may be raised at the pastoral level, as when a lady of the imperial court approached Pope Gregory I and received a practical answer in accordance with the principle that 'holy church mingles hope and fear for her faithful children' (*Epistolae*, 7. 25; *Moralium Libri*, 20. 5. 13). Dogmatically, the background questions have been those surrounding *predestination. Is election conditional or unconditional? Is perseverance guaranteed? How may the mysterious will of God be known? Scripturally, the matter is perhaps best located under the work of the *Holy Spirit and the nature of *faith and *hope.

In medieval debate, Thomas *Aquinas held that some might receive an assurance of salvation by the special privilege of a direct *revelation from God (*ST* II-I q. 112 a. 5); but generally one had to be content with a measure of certitude concerning present pardon. In the face of self-delusion on the one hand or agnosticism on the other, the tests were hearing the word of God with joy, readiness to do good, a firm intention not to sin in future, and sorrow for past sins. The Protestant Reformation brought the issue to the fore with *Luther's cry amid the uncertainties of an ecclesiastical system that appeared to make salvation dependent on human works: 'How do I find a gracious God?' Luther's discovery of *justification by *grace through faith alone confuted 'that pernicious doctrine of the papists, that no one can know for certain (*certo scire*) whether he is in a state of grace', whereby they 'utterly ruined the doctrine of faith, overthrew faith, tormented people's consciences, banished Christ from the church, and darkened and denied all the benefits and gifts of the Holy Spirit' (1531, *Commentary on Galatians*, ad 4: 6). The faith which God gives can be described by Luther as 'a living and daring confidence (*Zuversicht*) in the grace of God, so certain that for it one could die a thousand deaths; and such confidence and knowledge of divine grace makes us joyous, bold, and cheerful towards God and all creation' (*Preface to Romans*). Such fighting words provoked the Council of *Trent, in its decree on justification, to reject any 'certitude' about present forgiveness and final salvation that rested on 'faith alone' or '*vana fiducia*'. The moral dangers which Trent saw were presumption and *antinomianism; but behind these stood concern for the loss of ecclesial mediation in the process of salvation.

Meanwhile there occurred controversy on these matters within Protestantism. Luther insisted against the apparent subjectivism of the 'enthusiasts' that salvation remains grounded 'outside of ourselves' in the person and work of Christ and in the *baptism by which God applies it and gives faith. For *Calvin (*Institutes*, 3. 24), objective certainty resides in the divine decrees of predestination and the implied gift of final perseverance; the subjective knowledge of being among the elect is afforded by the Father's call, the gift of faith in Christ, the daily blessings of God and the protection of Christ, and the sealing of the heart by the Spirit of adoption. The matter became controversial again during the Evangelical Revival of the 18th century: *Wesley looked to the witness of the Holy Spirit—both direct in the enabling of believers to cry 'Abba, Father' (Rom. 8: 15–16) and indirect in the evidence of the fruit of the Spirit in their lives (Gal. 5: 22–3)—and considered this present assurance of God's favour ('God is reconciled to me in the Son of his love') the 'common privilege' of believers; but for Wesley, the promises of

God were conditional and held good only so long as a person remained in the faith which it was possible to lose. He distinguished between the 'assurance of faith' (Heb. 10: 22) and the 'assurance of hope' (Heb. 6: 11): 'The plerophory (or full assurance) of faith is such a clear conviction that *I am now* in the favour of God as excludes all doubt and fear concerning it. The full assurance of hope is such clear confidence that *I shall enjoy* the glory of God as excludes all doubt and fear concerning this' (*Explanatory Notes upon the New Testament*; letter of 10 April 1781 to Hetty Rowe). The latter assurance Wesley held to be rarely given and to have no basis in, or provide any basis for, a consistent doctrine of final perseverance.

In late modernity, the question of the assurance of individual salvation is no longer much agitated, whether because of a cool reliance on Heinrich Heine's 'God will forgive me, it's his job', or because of a decline in belief in an afterlife. In face of a diminution in the cultural credibility of Christianity in the west, the more general need of believers is for a 'proper confidence' (Newbigin) in the truth of the gospel as such.   **Geoffrey Wainwright**

Newbigin, L., *Proper Confidence: Faith, Doubt and Certainty in Christian Discipleship* (1995).

Sell, A. P. F., *The Great Debate: Calvinism, Arminianism and Salvation* (1982).

Yates, A. S., *The Doctrine of Assurance* (1952).

astrology, or the art of divination through observing the heavens, is an obvious deduction from most pre-modern accounts of the universe. From earth, we look up to unchanging patterns of light etched on the heavens. Over these, the planets wander erratically but predictably while the sun and moon, with their palpable influences on earthly affairs, show their own mysterious but regular cycles of change. How could all this be merely fortuitous? Any religious system which postulates a *creative will behind natural phenomena is bound to see this order not only as manifesting that creative power but also, in its intricacy, providing a key to understanding divine purposes. These phenomena, unaffected by the vicissitudes of terrestrial existence, seem intuitively closer to the pure world of the divine (see COSMOLOGY).

The Hebrew tradition is no exception. 'The heavens declare the glory of the Lord', says the *psalmist, and the order of the heavens is an earnest of God's enduring faithfulness in many places in the *Old Testament. Where the Hebrew Scriptures differ from the elaborated astronomical and astrological lore of Babylon and Egypt and the later Greek tradition is in their refutation of the claim that these phenomena wield influence of their own other than that willed by their creator. In biblical terms, the heavenly bodies record rather than implement the purposes of God and, in contrast to many other ancient literatures, the Hebrew scriptures take little interest in heavenly portents.

The NT is rather different. The Christian tradition cannot avoid coming to terms with the Star of the Nativity which marks *Jesus' birth and whose significance the magi can read accurately. The book of *Revelation is full of heavenly portents and signs. The fathers, however, reacted strongly against the fatalistic implications of astrology within the prevailing *Hellenistic culture where the publication of popular almanacs was a major industry. Tertullian argues that the natal star was the culmination of an older astrological dispensation which was then ended in Christ's coming.

*Augustine, refuting the influence of the stars, cites the case of Jacob and Esau to show that twins can have entirely different fates and argues that 'the star was not fate for Christ, but Christ was fate for the star'. Yet there is an implication here, as throughout much of Christian history, that such arguments are holding a line against a popular Christian culture that still put store in signs and portents.

The decline of learning in the aftermath of the fall of the Roman empire reduced even popular adherence to astrology, but comets and other celestial portents were still accorded great significance. A more cultivated interest was rekindled when medieval Christendom rediscovered the world of Hellenistic thought where *astrologia* was an integral part of the liberal arts. With this came an anthropology that saw human beings as 'microcosmos', reflecting in their being the structure of the universe. A corollary of this must be that the courses of the stars are keys to human events. Once the church came to terms with *Aristotelianism, it also accepted a modified version of astrology. *Aquinas, for instance, agrees that the heavenly bodies affect the senses and therefore indirectly the intellect, but makes it clear that people are free to resist this influence on their passions. *Dante's *Divine Comedy* reveals the interconnections between medieval Christian and astrological thought.

It is after the revolution associated with Copernicus and *Galileo that it becomes meaningful to distinguish between astrology and astronomy, although the lines are not even then as clearly drawn as one might think. Astrologers attempted to prove their own scientific credentials with at least some rhetorical success. More importantly, the critique of astrology on rational grounds had the concomitant effect of enhancing its status whenever the rational world-view seemed to fail. Amidst the political and religious upheaval of 17th-century England, for instance, there is a great upsurge in the printing of popular almanacs.

The 19th and 20th centuries have been boom times for astrology, perhaps because it combines the mystique of mathematical expertise with a pseudo-scientific claim to predictive value. This resurgence could be tied to the decline in Christian belief, but just as the people of *Jerusalem cooked moon cakes for the Queen of Heaven, much to *Jeremiah's disgust, many Christians know their star sign and will turn to the horoscopes in the popular press, not from any great conviction perhaps, but just in case.   **Hugh S. Pyper**

Garin, E., *Astrology in the Renaissance: The Zodiac of Life* (1990).

Geneva, A., *Astrology and the Seventeenth Century Mind* (1995).

Tester, S. J. S., *A History of Western Astrology* (1987).

astronomy, see COSMOLOGY.

Athanasius (298/9–373). We know little of Athanasius' early years. He records no personal experience of the fierce persecution by Diocletian in his home town, *Alexandria, which continued until he was about 14 years of age. That he was well educated is clear from his later writings, impregnated with the bible and the works of earlier Christian teachers such as *Origen.

Athanasius went with Bishop Alexander to the Council of *Nicaea in 325 as a deacon and secretary and in the summer of 328 was elected to succeed Alexander and so continue his struggle against *Arianism. He was not yet 30 years of age, young enough to give episcopal opponents a convenient pretext for invalidating his nomination. In 335, Emperor *Constantine exiled him to Trier, or, as

Athanasius himself would have said, 'to the end of the world', from where he returned two years later, after Constantine's death, only to be deposed again in 339. This time he found refuge in *Rome, welcomed by Pope Julius I. Back home at length in 346, he enjoyed ten relatively quiet years. Military power, combined with the relentless hostility of some bishops, forced him to flee again in 356, this time into hiding for six years among the *monastic settlements of Egypt's deserts. A fourth and fifth exile of shorter length followed, but Athanasius had outlived all his enemies, becoming in old age a living legend, the most authoritative voice of the Nicene form of *orthodoxy, according to the praise expressed by such younger contemporaries as Basil of Caesarea.

Athanasius never posed as an intellectual of high learning, comparable to Origen or Eusebius of Caesarea. He was born for pastoral action, able to perceive with an independent mind the new opportunities given to the church by the turn of events linked with Constantine's government. His swift reactions and adamant convictions not only demonstrated his natural authority, but generated enduring friendships in the places he visited. From each of his forced exiles his returns to Alexandria gained popular acclaim. On the other hand, he was the most targeted church official of his time, remaining for over two decades under direct attack by a large fraction of the eastern bishops led by the court favourite, Eusebius of Nicomedia, and opposed in his own diocese by a dissident group of clergy and monks.

Best known as the defender of Nicaea, Athanasius contributed more than anyone else to the structuring of an anti-Arian form of orthodox faith. How he did it reveals the true genius of his personal assimilation of the bible. The youthful deacon of 325, called three years later to the episcopal office, had to spend much time during his first five years as a bishop performing pastoral visitations of local churches under his jurisdiction and of monastic groups spread over various desert regions of Egypt and Libya. In the meantime ecclesiastical politics were building up a menacing offensive against the see of Alexandria, with the declared intention of rehabilitating Arius whose condemnation for *heresy had been confirmed at Nicaea by imperial power. By the time Athanasius had completed his prolonged retreats among the monks, he had forged a vision of his own, free from political concerns, but capable of rallying a majority of believers under his leadership. He wrote that vision down in an essay entitled *On the Incarnation of the Divine Logos*.

On the Incarnation is a work of matured pastoral experience engaging in a fundamental rethinking of the theological trends derived from Origen's legacy inside the Alexandrian church, precisely where the heresy of Arius had originated. By a deliberate remodelling of Origen's doctrine of *salvation, Athanasius placed the *Incarnation of the *Word (Logos) centre stage in the world drama of divine *redemption. He could not have demonstrated more effectively, against Arianism, the proper divinity of the Logos than by showing that no one less than *God himself could, as saviour, effect the divinization of *humanity. The aim was not political (when he wrote it he was, unknowingly, on the eve of his first exile), but the truly pastoral and non-polemical thesis of *On the Incarnation* laid the foundation of the incarnational theology that was to prevail in ancient Christianity through the Cappadocian Fathers in the east (see Greek Theology), Ambrose and *Augustine in the west. Into

the theoretical framework of divine revelation and salvific knowledge inherited from Origen, Athanasius introduced a massive array of quotations from Pauline letters focusing on the dialectic of life and death in Christ's mystery (*On the Incarnation*, 8–11), which gave a 'physical' connotation to the traditional idea of the divinizing transformation of human beings.

In exile at Trier or shortly afterwards, Athanasius waded into the fray of the post-Nicene controversy by composing his most important doctrinal exposition, the *Orations against the Arians*. A dating around 340 makes it possible to compare the *Orations* and the many pamphlets, letters, and dogmatic statements issued by the bishop during the next three decades of his long career. The comparison demonstrates the prime value of the *Orations* in the mind of their author, who never tired of multiplying doctrinal variations based on them, the most striking example being the *Letters to Serapion on the Divinity of the Spirit*, written in the late 350s. Orations 1 and 2 (3 may be from another hand) provide a strong articulation of baptismal faith in the divine *Trinity with a central attention given to the substantial relation between *Father and Son in line with the *Creed of Nicaea (one notes that the author never uses the hotly controverted Nicene *homoousios* as part of his own theological vocabulary).

Once more Athanasius updated Origen's thought. By contemplating Trinity in the concrete light of the gospel-event, instead of speculating—in reference to Father and Son—on the nature of the human psyche and its capacity to know divine mysteries, Athanasius succeeded in teaching a consistent theory about the inner life of the three Hypostases, a term Origen had been the first to use in this connection. By playing with the analogy between saved and saviour, Athanasius juxtaposed the experienced reality of baptismal rebirth with the image of the Son in the 'bosom' of the Father (John 1: 18). Thus, the conclusion of the *Johannine prologue became as central for Athanasius' thought as the prologue's initial verses had been for Origen when composing his *Commentary on John*.

Athanasius deepened his anti-Arian position over the years. Much that he wrote was strongly polemical and political but it needs stressing that his political involvement in the imperial scene was from the start *imposed* on him, as was the repeated duress and physical violence against his people. Against his will, Athanasius was kept for over a quarter of a century at the core of a conflict in which political ambitions and theological principles collided. It is no surprise if his writings dating from the 350s and 360s consist mainly in polemical apologies and letters. A distinctive feature of these writings, produced in self-defence, is their documentary exactness; another is the obsessive denunciation by the beleaguered pontiff of all his adversaries as 'Arians'. A welcome diversion from the endless controversies is provided by the synod of Alexandria, 362, a synod for union and reconciliation, the first of its kind, organized by Athanasius with the purpose of harmonizing the doctrinal positions of different pro-Nicene schools of thought.

A more serene image of Athanasius irradiates his pastoral and spiritual writings in which his deeper self finds its genuine expression. Recent hostile historiography has systematically ignored such testimonies, or even denied his authorship of them, as in the case of the *Life of Antony*, without any philological or historical grounds.

The *Festal Letters*, composed each year months in advance by the bishop to announce the dates of *Lent, *Easter, and *Pentecost, are the most original of his pastoral productions. Athanasius transformed the genre of these circular letters, giving them a popular and homiletic twist. In their vibrant exhortations the church leader vanishes behind the spiritual adviser. Through them, as through his influential *Letter to Marcellinus on the Psalms*, the pastor dispensed the biblical riches of his personal culture.

The *Life of Antony* reveals an author perfectly conscious of his composition and purpose, eager to produce a paradigmatic work rich in spiritual significance, but keeping the narrative close to down-to-earth reality. Antony the Hermit, already venerated in his lifetime as an icon and a model by the numerous solitaries who populated the deserts of Egypt from the end of the 3rd century, died in 356. It is probable that Athanasius visited him in the early years of his tenure, and at least once Antony made the trip to Alexandria in support of Athanasius' cause. Before his death Antony bequeathed his only cloak to Athanasius. In the *Life of Antony*, written shortly after 356, the 'Father of all monks' takes on a paradigmatic format, his struggle with the demons inspiring many painters and novelists through the centuries up to the present day. Antony's speeches to audiences of pagan philosophers, Christian ascetics, bureaucrats of the imperial administration, or Alexandrian clergy show rhetorical skills and establish a line of orthodox thought so precisely conformed to Athanasius' own thinking that we cannot but hear the latter speaking through the deceased hermit. The *Life* was destined to become the first Christian best-seller after the bible.

In a global evaluation of Christian thought, as it structured itself through antiquity, the Middle Ages, and modernity, the contribution of Athanasius remains considerable and a painstaking retrieval of his legacy has a special urgency in a time of fundamental doctrinal shifts. To recapitulate: a central aspect of that contribution is the bishop's own *hermeneutical approach towards scripture; a second essential feature is his *political consciousness. His lifelong struggle exemplifies for the first time in Christian history what it means for the church at large to give Caesar and God their proper due. Thirdly, as an intellectual leader engaged in *pastoral ministry, the 4th-century 'pope' of Alexandria showed a *theological* capacity to reformulate the Christian message according to the needs of the church in his time, authoritatively interpreting Nicene orthodoxy for both east and west. Fourthly, Athanasius, a man of the common touch, spontaneously took the lead in the most popular religious revival of his own time, the monastic movement. Long before any other Christian hierarch, he acted in solidarity on *mystical* ground with solitaries and communities, male and female, addressing to them most of his writings.

A man of the bible who wrote no biblical commentaries, Athanasius posthumously 'lent' his name to such exegetical works composed by pious but one-sided admirers. The 'Athanasian Creed', written in his name by a Latin author of the 5th century, reached a quasi-canonical status in western Christianity. His genuine teaching on God's incarnation was to remain seriously vitiated up to the present time by pseudo-Athanasian writings. The discovery of the authentic Athanasius remains a challenge for the historian of Christian thought.   **Charles Kannengiesser**

Arnold, D. W. H., *The Episcopal Career of Athanasius of Alexandria* (1991).
Barnes, T. D., *Athanasius and Constantius* (1993).
Brakke, D., *Athanasius and the Politics of Asceticism* (1995).
Bright, P. (trans.), 'Letter to Marcellinus', in C. Kannengiesser (ed.), *Early Christian Spirituality* (1986).
Gregg, R. C., *Athanasius: Life of Antony and Letter to Marcellinus* (1980).
Grillmeier, A. I., *Christ in Christian Tradition*, 2nd edn. (1975).
Hanson, R. P. C., *The Search for the Christian Doctrine of God* (1988).
Kannengiesser, C., *Arius and Alexander: Two Alexandrian Theologians* (1991).
—— 'Athanasius of Alexandria and the Ascetic Movement of his Time', in V. L. Wimbush and R. Valantasis (eds.), *Asceticism* (1995).
Robertson, A., *Saint Athanasius, Select Works and Letters* (1891; repr. 1952; 1987).
Thomson, R. W., *Contra Gentes and De Incarnatione* (1980).
Widdicombe, P., *The Fatherhood of God from Origen to Athanasius* (1994).

atheism may be differently construed in different religious traditions. It is perfectly possible, for example, to be an orthodox Hindu or an orthodox Buddhist and an atheist—indeed in some forms of Buddhism and in all forms of Jainism it is unorthodox *not* to be an atheist. However, for anyone within the Christian tradition to call themselves an atheist seems, prima facie, somewhat incongruous and' whilst there have been those such as the contemporary American theologian, Thomas Altizer, who have so described themselves, Christian atheism is not a position that has found widespread support within the churches. Yet atheism has played an ambiguous role in Christian thought from the beginning and the 2nd-century apologist, Justin Martyr, found himself having to defend the Christian religion from the charge of atheism brought by the pagan world. The ambiguity of the term is demonstrated by Justin's admission of the charge. He wrote: 'We confess that we are atheists, so far as gods of this sort [i.e. the gods worshipped in the pagan world] are concerned,' although he immediately adds, 'but not with regard to the most true God' (*Apology*, I. 5–6). Justin stands within a tradition of religious atheism that stretches back to the Hebrew *prophets and the Greek philosophers and continues to our own day—a tradition in which one thinker accuses another of atheism on the grounds that the accused does not hold to what the accuser takes to be the true and orthodox conception of '*God'. The 12th-century theologians David of Dinant and Amaury of Bêne, both of whom put forward what today would be called immanentist conceptions of God, were accused by their contemporaries of atheism and in the 20th century theologians such as *Tillich and *Bultmann have also been accused of atheism by those who have regarded themselves as the guardians of Christian *orthodoxy. Yet, as Cornelius Fabro has recognized, the dialectic of the theistic/atheistic debate has, in fact, acted both as a purgative of less than adequate notions of God and as a stimulant to others to develop more adequate conceptions.

However, there are two strains in Christian thought that have led directly if not to outright atheism, to an *agnosticism that comes perilously close to it. The first is that strain in Christian thought known as *fideism, the belief that God cannot be known by *reason, but only by *revelation. In the 20th century it was espoused with particular vigour by the German Protestant theologian Karl *Barth who, denying all forms of *natural theology, saw contemporary atheism as a necessary prelude to the acceptance of that 'Word of God' that speaks through revelation and through revelation alone. That this could lead directly to atheism in those to whom came no such unambiguous Word as came to Barth was recognized by Adolph Harnack in his now famous correspondence with Barth. Harnack, like a number of Roman Catholic and Anglican theologians who take their cue from Thomas *Aquinas, argued that theism must be based on a sound natural theology if *faith in revelation is to be anything other than the expression of subjective opinion. The biographies of many former Barthians who eventually abandoned anything that might be called Christian faith are testimony to Harnack's prescience.

The second strain in Christian thought that leads to an agnosticism bordering on atheism is that known as the *via negativa* or the way of negation. Those who approach knowledge of God in this way maintain that since God is not an object in his own universe he cannot be known by description, but only by *analogy. It is easier to say what God is not than to say what he is. As Umberto Eco has noted, two conceptions of God have dominated Christian thought. On the one hand there is the concept of a personal God who is the fullness of being and on the other a conception of a God who is not 'because he cannot be named, because he cannot be described with any of the categories we use to designate the things that are'. This 'God who is not', says Eco, 'passes through the very history of Christianity'. He hides himself, is ineffable, and can be named only as solitude, silence, and absence and yet, as Eco recognizes, it is this God upon whom the sense of the sacred feeds (Eco 1987: 93).

However, since the 18th century, Christian thought has been confronted by atheism of a different order, one that is absolute in its denial of God and, in the case of Logical Positivism, by the claim that all talk of God is not so much false as meaningless. This may lead, as it did in the thought of one of its leading exponents, A. J. Ayer, to the view that to take up any position—theist, atheist, or agnostic—in the theistic/atheistic debate is impossible as it must imply meaningfulness of the proposition that 'God exists' (Ayer 1936).

The atheism that came into European thinking during the 18th century rejects the claim that God is at all necessary to explain either the existence or the workings of the world. This form of atheism takes the world as given and sees no reason to pose the question how the world itself came into being. Leibniz's disturbing question 'Why is there something and not nothing?', which for Martin Heidegger was the fundamental metaphysical question, is regarded by many philosophers today, as it was by *Kant, as meaningless. This was the impasse reached in the radio debate on the existence of God between Fr. Copleston and Bertrand Russell (Hick 1964). A consequence of this form of atheism has been that men and women and their life in this world are elevated to the level of absolute value and, following Feuerbach and *Nietzsche, such atheism asserts that belief in God and in an afterlife undermines life in this world. Those who espoused this form of atheism have sought to rescue *humanity from the alienation which they believe is endemic to all forms of religion. Feuerbach stated it thus:

> I deny God. But that means for me that I deny the negation of man. In place of the illusory, fantastic, heavenly position of man which in actual life necessarily leads to the degradation of man, I substitute the tangible, actual and consequently also the political and social position of mankind. The question concerning the existence or non-existence of God is for me nothing but the question concerning the existence or non-existence of man.
>
> (Feuerbach 1903: vol. i, pp. xiv–xv)

This form of atheism culminated in the atheism of *Marx and Lenin and was officially enshrined in the policy of the Communist Party of the Soviet Union and its satellite parties. Transposed into a different key, it became the basis of the atheistic world-view and the atheistic ethic proclaimed by Nietzsche who, having announced that God was dead within western culture, but fearful of the consequences, maintained that men and women must themselves become gods if they were to be worthy of living in a godless world. These *Übermenschen*, or 'over-men and women', having overcome themselves, must live affirming life in this world and without an 'afterworld' teleology. 'Remain faithful to the earth', entreats the Nietzschean prophet Zarathustra, 'and do not believe those who speak to you of superterrestrial hopes. They are poisoners whether they know it or not. They are despisers of life, atrophying and self-poisoned men of whom the earth is weary'—although Nietzsche himself was somewhat pessimistic about the possibility of such a breed of men and women taking the place of the all-too-human beings with whom he was familiar. Freud in *Civilization and its Discontents* and in *The Future of an Illusion* expressed similar doubts about the ability of men and women to live without belief in God. Nietzsche's ideal, in principle if not in substance, was reaffirmed in the atheistic *existentialism of Jean-Paul Sartre.

This latter form of atheism is regarded by many theologians as far more subversive of theistic religion than any previous form of atheism. It is also, for some, potentially the most dangerous for, as Jürgen *Moltmann has pointed out, rescuing human beings from alienation from another world, or from God, more often than not simply paves the way for the alienation of men and women by other men and women. He wrote:

> This antitheistic humanism leads unavoidably to anthropotheism, to the divination of man ... If for this atheism 'man is finally man's god', this may be morally fine in face of the situation where man is man's wolf. But a century's experience with such anthropotheism has shown that even these human deities [Moltmann is referring here to the State or the Party] can become man's wolf. If the consequences of Feuerbach's dethroning God is that 'the state is unlimited, infinite, true, perfect divine man', and politics becomes religion, then the history of atheism against theism returns to its beginning, and the old theism would have to be called relatively human ... If God is other than man, then a man can at least not play god over other men.
>
> (Moltmann 1972: 251–2)

This is the central question of our time. Can men and women remain men and women in anything that can be called a human way without the meaning, the purpose, the values traditionally given and guaranteed by theism? Can men and women live in the face of injustice and in the face of *evil without the hope of *redemption either in this world or beyond *time and *history? Marx and his followers said 'yes'; they sought to create a society where happiness and justice would reign supreme and succeeded in creating the very opposite. The western democracies have also said 'yes' and are in the process of creating the kind of world that Nietzsche dreaded—the world of what he called 'the Last Man'—a world where a trivial, self-indulgent individualism replaces the great creative values that, in the past, have been sustained by a belief in a God who created men and women for a destiny beyond that of immediate sensual gratification. The great danger in the foreseeable future is that the death of God in western culture will be followed by the death of the *person. More is at stake in the debate over theism than the existence or otherwise of an, as yet, perhaps, inadequately characterized supernatural being. George Steiner, in his brief but pregnant works *Real Presences* and *Errata* (last chapter), explores in some depth the momentous issues involved in the contemporary theistic/atheistic debate.   **James Thrower**

Altizer, Thomas J. J., *The Gospel of Christian Atheism* (1966).
Ayer, A. J., *Language, Truth and Logic* (1936).
Buckley, Michael J., *At the Origins of Modern Atheism* (1987).
Eco, Umberto, *Travels in Hyper-Reality* (1987).
Fabro, Cornelius, *Encyclopaedia Britannica*, s.v. atheism (1964 edn.).
Feuerbach, Ludwig, *Sämmtliche Werke* (1903–11), i.
Hick, John (ed.), *The Existence of God* (1964).
Moltmann, Jürgen, *The Crucified God*, ET (1974).
Nietzsche, Friedrich, *Thus Spake Zarathustra* and *Joyful Wisdom* in W. Kaufmann (ed.), *The Portable Nietzsche* (1966).
Rumscheidt, Martin H., *Revelation and Theology: An Analysis of the Barth–Harnack Correspondence of 1923* (1972).
Sartre, Jean-Paul, *Existentialism and Humanism*, ET (1948).
Steiner, George, *Real Presences* (1989).
——— *Errata* (1997).
Thrower, James, *Marxist-Leninist 'Scientific Atheism'* (1983).

Atonement, theories of.

According to the doctrine of the Atonement, the life, suffering, and death of *Jesus Christ liberate humans from evil in a unique way. Like the doctrines of *Trinity and *Incarnation, it is distinctively Christian. Unlike them, it was not precisely defined by the early ecumenical *councils. Consequently, the history of Christian thought contains a variety of attempts, each rooted in scriptural motifs, to develop a theory of the Atonement that adequately explains how Christ overcomes *sin and effects human liberation (see also REDEMPTION). These attempts produced theories that have been classified into three main groups: ransom theories, satisfaction theories, and exemplar theories. Contemporary theologians and philosophers continue to appeal to the traditional motifs in framing new theoretical proposals.

Ransom theories

During the patristic period, the dominant view was that the life of Christ was a victorious struggle against personal or impersonal forces of *evil. On the basis of texts such as Mark 10: 45, which speaks of the Son of Man giving his life as a ransom for many, Christ's *death was taken to be a ransom paid to the *devil to liberate human sinners from bondage. To explain why *God did not simply force the devil to release sinners from bondage, some ransom theorists proposed that God had given the devil the right to hold sinners in bondage and so could not justly use force to liberate them. According to a related view, Christ tricked the devil into forfeiting this right. As long as the devil held only sinners in bondage he remained within his rights, but he exceeded his authority when he attacked Christ, who was sinless. Christ tricked him into the unjust attack by hiding his divinity under his humanity. Gregory of Nyssa likens Christ to the bait on a fish-hook; *Augustine likens him to the bait in a mouse-trap. These similes suggest that Christ deceived the devil. Ransom theorists presupposed a high *christology; the victor in the struggle with forces of evil was God incarnate.

The chief difficulty with ransom theories lies with the assumption that God gave the devil the right to hold sinners in bondage or promised the devil control over their fate. Why should God acknowledge any such right? After all, the devil acquires power over sinners unjustly by tempting them to do evil. Why, then, should God be so foolish as to promise the devil control? Another problem is that many modern Christians doubt or deny the existence of the devil. Gustaf Aulén, in *Christus Victor*, argues that 20th-century *theology should use the idea that Christ's life is a victorious battle with forces of evil, but distances himself from some of the less edifying details of literally interpreted ransom theories.

Satisfaction theories

Satisfaction theories were the principal accounts of the Atonement from the high Middle Ages until well into the modern era. *Anselm's *Cur deus homo* contains the first fully developed satisfaction theory: human sin offends God's honour, so sinners owe God a debt of honour. Since the gravity of an offence against honour is measured by the dignity of the offended party and God's dignity is infinite, the debt each sinner owes God is infinite. Because humans owe God perfect *obedience in any case, there is nothing they can do to build up a surplus that would pay even the smallest part of this infinite debt of honour. So human sinners owe the debt but cannot pay it. Being sinless, God can pay the debt but does not owe it. Only someone both human and divine can both owe and pay the debt, and so God must become incarnate if the debt is to be paid. Adopting a notion from Roman law, Anselm describes paying the debt as making satisfaction for sin. Hence the Atonement consists of Christ's making satisfaction for human sin.

Later satisfaction theories view the debt of sin not as a debt of honour but as a debt of *punishment owed to divine retributive *justice. On such theories, known as penal substitution theories, Christ pays a debt of punishment human sinners owe. At one point Martin *Luther declares that Christ is the greatest of all sinners because he assumed in his body the sins of others. If this is taken literally, it means the guilt of human sin is transferred from the sinner to Christ. Other theologians assumed that the guilt of human sin is imputed to Christ but not literally transferred. Anselm's satisfaction theory requires Christ to be God incarnate; other satisfaction theorists also assume that he is.

The chief difficulty with penal substitution theories is that it seems impossible for Christ to pay a debt owed to divine retributive justice because he owes no such debt and it is hard to see how the debts of others can be transferred to him. As Immanuel *Kant puts the point, the debt in question

> is no *transmissible* liability which can be made over to another like a financial indebtedness (where it is all one to the creditor whether the debtor himself pays the debt or whether some one else pays it for him); rather is it *the most personal of all debts*, namely a debt of sins, which only the culprit can bear and which no innocent person can assume even though he be magnanimous enough to wish to take it upon himself for the sake of another.   (Kant 1960: 66)

Satisfaction ideas are sometimes combined with others in a theory of the Atonement. For example, according to *Aquinas, Christ's Passion is a sufficient and superabundant satisfaction for the sins of the whole human race; but it also ransoms us from the devil, though the price is paid to God, to whom it is owed, and not to the devil; and it operates to reconcile us to God by being a *sacrifice acceptable to God (*ST* III qq. 48, 49).

It is also worth noting that some Christians have rejected Aquinas' generous view that the Atonement is a sufficient and superabundant satisfaction for the sins of the whole human race. Doctrines of limited atonement, found in the *Calvinist tradition, restrict the beneficiaries of the Atonement to the elect, those predestined by God to *salvation. As a critic, John McLeod Campbell, points out, such doctrines create a pastoral problem for those who wish to preach Christ to all, while believing he died only for some (Campbell 1959: 79).

Exemplar theories

Pure exemplar theories claim that Christ's life and death are nothing more than an inspiring example of *love and obedience. They are often described as subjective theories because they explain the power of this example wholly in terms of its subjective influence on the minds of sinners. Sinners are moved by the example of Christ to repent of their sins, improve their lives, and become more loving. Pure exemplar theories have become especially popular since the *Enlightenment, perhaps because they cohere well with the view that Christ is only an extraordinary human with no divine nature. Even if Christ is merely, to paraphrase Kant, humankind in its complete moral perfection (Kant 1960: 54), he is indeed an inspiring example.

Hastings Rashdall, a distinguished 20th-century proponent of pure exemplarism, traces the view as far back as *Abelard. But, as Quinn (1993) and others have argued, Abelard is not a pure exemplarist. Though he strongly emphasizes the power of the example of Christ's life and death, like Aquinas, he combines several motifs in his theory of the Atonement. For example, in commenting on Romans 4: 25, which speaks of Christ being handed over to death for our sins, Abelard affirms that Christ removes our sins by enduring the punishment for them.

Critics of pure exemplarism do not deny that Christ is an inspiring example, but they claim that it is not the whole truth about the Atonement. What it leaves out, they argue, is an objective transaction of the sort proposed by rival theories.

Contemporary theories

Contemporary theories of the Atonement pour old wine into new bottles. They combine traditional motifs in new and interesting ways.

Colin Gunton's *The Actuality of Atonement* argues that military, legal, and religious *metaphors identify a divine action in which God remakes broken relationships. The military metaphor of a battle with demons aptly expresses human helplessness in the face of psychological, social, and cosmic forces. The legal metaphor of payment of debts makes vivid the idea that Christ's suffering and death somehow compensate for human default on obligations to God. And the religious metaphor of sacrifice suggests that sin is akin to uncleanness or pollution that is removed from a good creation by Christ's atoning work.

The motif of sacrifice is also central to the theory of the Atonement in Richard Swinburne's *Responsibility and Atonement*. According to Swinburne, ordinary human atonement for wrongdoing normally involves four elements: repentance, apology, reparation, and *penance. Repentance and apology distance the wrongdoer from past wrongdoing. Reparation compensates the victim for the harm done if possible, and penance is a costly gift to the victim above and beyond what is owed by way of reparation. Though God is not harmed by human sin, it is fitting that sinners offer God a costly gift by way of reparation and penance. Since a sacrifice is simply a gift, Christ's sacrifice is his gift of his life and death. That gift is made available to us to offer to God as reparation and penance for our sins if we choose to use it for that purpose. Christ's life 'is a life lived and given voluntarily for that purpose by one who, being God, did not owe God anything, and hence a gift to us' (Swinburne 1989: 154).

It seems that both Gunton and Swinburne have made progress towards accounts of the Atonement that contemporary Christians can accept. Unlike ransom theories, their accounts do not rely on a demonology many Christians now reject. Unlike satisfaction theorists, they do not employ the morally objectionable notion of transferring guilt or liability to punishment from sinners to Christ. Unlike pure exemplar theories, their accounts attribute to the life and death of Christ a significance that goes beyond providing an inspiring moral example. (The fact that they are able to use traditional motifs in new ways suggests that these motifs continue to contain possibilities for creative Christian thought about the Atonement.)

Atonement, it needs to be stressed, means *at-one-ment*, how sinful humans are made again *one* with God, who is sinless. What more philosophical theologians tend to ignore is the centrality to this process of the *Resurrection. The Atonement should not be seen as a way of altering God's attitude to us (the Incarnation presupposes his *forgiveness) but of changing *humanity's attitude to him. Christ does this by adopting human nature in all its spoiledness ('made sin for us'), accepting death as due punishment for that flawed humanity, but then being raised precisely as the New *Adam, glorified humanity, so that in him all who will are reorientated to God. Without a theological sense of the collectiveness (not transference) implied in Christ's being 'Second Adam' the individualist responsibility highlighted by Kant can hardly be overcome. Such a 'transformation' theory of the Atonement may best express the varied motifs found within the biblical material.

Philip L. Quinn

Aulén, G., *Christus Victor*, ET (1931).
Campbell, J. M., *The Nature of the Atonement and its Relation to the Remission of Sins and Eternal Life*, 4th edn., (1959).
Durrwell, F. X., *The Resurrection*, ET (1960).
Gunton, C., *The Actuality of Atonement* (1989).
Kant, I., *Religion within the Limits of Reason Alone*, ET (1960).
Quinn, P. L., 'Aquinas on Atonement', in R. J. Feenstra and C. Plantinga, Jr. (eds.), *Trinity, Incarnation, and Atonement* (1989).
——'Abelard on Atonement: "Nothing Unintelligible, Arbitrary, Illogical, or Immoral about It"', in E. Stump (ed.), *Reasoned Faith* (1993).
Rashdall, H., *The Idea of Atonement in Christian Theology* (1919).
Swinburne, R., *Responsibility and Atonement* (1989).

Augustine, Aurelius, bishop of Hippo (353–430) stands at a watershed in the history of western thought, between the classical world of the Roman empire and the Middle Ages.

Born into a family of minor gentry in the small inland town of Thagaste (modern Souk Arras) in Roman North Africa, son of Monica, a Christian, whom he was to make one of the most famous mothers of history, and Patrick, a Roman citizen, pagan, but converted to Christianity near the end of his life, Augustine enjoyed the distinctive, privileged education which identified and formed the ruling class of the empire. Thus he entered an aristocracy not of birth but of educational formation. At the school of grammar at Thagaste, and then, thanks to a wealthy patron, the schools of *rhetoric at Madaura and Carthage, Augustine was introduced to the intricacies of textual, grammatical study of the classic authors (Cicero, Virgil, Sallust, Terence), and of the disciplines of the liberal arts which reached their goal in the formation of the rhetor—a man practised in the art of teaching, moving, and persuading his audience by eloquence. Augustine exercised his chosen profession, as a teacher of rhetoric, at Carthage (376–83), Rome (383–4), and then at Milan (384–6), the imperial capital, where, in the municipal chair of rhetoric, he had the ear of the emperor. He might not unreasonably have hoped for advancement to a provincial governorship. Instead, in 386, he converted to Christianity.

Faith and reason

Augustine's Confessions, which he began to write ten years later as a bishop, provide us with a retrospective interpretation of the events which led to his conversion (books 1–8). They read as if Augustine was never not a Christian: it is the religion to which he had been born, which he had drunk in with his mother's milk; the religion to which he had been dedicated as a child and from which he had strayed. He rejected Cicero's Hortensius, or Exhortation to Philosophy, which he read in the course of his studies, aged 19, because, although it fired him with a burning desire to find wisdom, 'the name of Christ was not there'. Instead, having briefly examined the Christian scriptures and found them to be rather crudely written for his rhetor's taste, he turned to the Manichees, a religious sect based on revelations given to the prophet Mani (b. 216 AD), characterized by its universal, missionary purpose and its syncretistic, *dualistic, cosmological *myths. The Manichees claimed to possess *truth and to present a rational explanation of the universe, *evil, the *soul, and *salvation. This, together with their impressive literature, *asceticism, communal life, the fact that they criticized precisely those aspects of Christianity that Augustine himself found off-putting (the emphasis upon *faith, anthropomorphic ideas of *God, inconsistencies in scripture), and above all their claim to represent true Christianity, to be integri Christiani, perhaps explains why Augustine remained with them for the next nine years. His enthusiasm was undermined by a growing realization that their claim to truth was no more than pseudo-science, that in fact they did not have the answers; most especially, their dualistic theory of evil raised insuperable problems in relation to the *omnipotence and sovereignty of God. Moreover, their much-vaunted asceticism proved to be a matter more of theory than of practice.

Augustine temporarily despaired of ever finding 'wisdom', and extracted himself from the alluring scepticism of the New Academy only by acknowledging that he could not find the 'saving name of Christ' there. Instead he became a catechumen, one undergoing instruction for baptism in the Catholic Church, following the 'precedent of [his] parents' and while waiting for a 'clear light' to determine his path. The light was to come from two directions, first from Ambrose, bishop of Milan, whose preaching delighted Augustine not only in its eloquence but because his spiritual interpret-

ation enabled him to overcome the problems that the Manichees' literal, rational approach had highlighted. The second direction was from the *philosophy termed 'Neoplatonism' which was being studied and discussed by various individuals at Milan. From one of them he came across some 'books of the *Platonists' (Augustine's vagueness is tantalizing and deliberate—probably some Plotinus, an Egyptian Greek who taught at Rome, author of the Enneads, and maybe some Porphyry, Plotinus' disciple and editor). The revolutionary thing about the Neoplatonists was their teaching that true reality was spiritual. This insight enabled Augustine to break free of the materialism which the Manichees shared with many of the philosophers of the day, from difficult, physical conceptions of God, and gave him an alternative to the Manichees' dualistic explanation of evil as inherent in matter. Rather, he was able to follow Plotinus in teaching the initiative of the good in giving form to matter, and evil as a declining from this order whilst being comprehended by it—a sort of privatio boni (privation of the good) which Augustine attributed, in man, to the free will.

The 'books of the Platonists' also allowed Augustine to 'return into' (Ennead, 5. 1) himself, to appreciate himself as a spiritual being; to find God, true Being, as the foundation of himself, within, and to realize that God transcends him: 'more inward than my inmost being and higher than my highest'. Numerous passages that describe an ascent towards God have prompted some scholars to speak of Augustine's 'spirituality' or 'mysticism', and to evaluate how much this owes to Neoplatonism—for they are undeniably Neoplatonic in form (introversion, ascent from the material world, to the soul, to the mind, and above the mind to God). But Augustine's emphasis on divine initiative and help, and his later emphasis on the need for a mediator, give them a definite Christian colouring. Augustine's later attitude to the Platonists is determined by his doctrine of the *Fall and of Christ's saving work: it is summed up in his observation that, although the philosophers may see the goal, the homeland, the truth, they do not follow the way to it, and will therefore never attain it, for the only way is the way of the *cross (Tractates on John, 28. 5), made possible by Christ the One Mediator (Letter, 118; City of God, 9–10 (against pagan theurgy); On the Trinity, 4. 13). Their presumption and pride are contrasted with Christian confession and humility, their confidence in *reason, like that of the Manichees, with Christian faith in *authority, as the only way to attain truth.

The will

Thus, at least on the basis of the Confessions, it might be argued that Augustine was simply reconciling himself to Christianity. But this was not merely an intellectual reconciliation, it was also a matter for the will. Confessions 1–8 paint a vivid picture of the vitiated and flawed nature of the human will, divided against, and alienated from, itself; willing the good but unable to do it. This was a matter of personal experience (he could not give up his sexual relations with women and embrace the *chastity which, for him, was inseparable from conversion) which Augustine found confirmed by *Paul, whose admonitions in Rom. 13: 13–14 were to precipitate his famous *conversion in the garden at Milan (Confessions, 8).

Augustine's portrait of the vitiated will is not just retrospective interpretation of what he experienced before conversion, but is rather the result of sustained reflection upon the fallen nature of the human will even after conversion. This is first evidenced in a series of works he wrote on Paul, and especially *Romans, during the 390s and which culminate in To Simplicianus, with its uncompromising teaching on the fallenness of man: the Fall of *Adam, humankind as a *massa peccati*, 'one lump in which the original guilt [of Adam] remains throughout' (*Simpl*. 2. 17, 20), the culpability of all, the impotence of the will to do the good, the unmerited *grace of God which can alone (and regardless of faith, reason, or works) inspire a delight in the good. Whilst a doctrine of original *sin was not unknown in African theology, this work, with its application of the Fall to the human will, marks a crucial break with the classical ethical tradition, which tended to uphold humanity's moral and intellectual autonomy, and the attainability of perfection in this life. It also foreshadows his later controversy with the *Pelagians (415 onwards), who represented this late antique viewpoint to their ascetic followers in theological arguments against original sin and the necessity of infant *baptism and in support of the freedom of the will and the possibility of sinlessness by rational observance of the *law. In numerous works to counter these propositions (especially as voiced by Julian of Eclanum, against whom he wrote until his death) Augustine emphasized the double commandment of *love of God and neighbour as the standard of *virtue: a love inspired by God's gracious gift of his *Holy Spirit (Rom. 5: 5) and without which man is simply free to sin. The will is only free in acknowledging its dependence upon God's gracious inspiration, which enables it to delight in and to do the good, and to love in accordance with the true order of reality under God. The logical outworking of his theology of the Fall, original sin, and grace was an uncompromising doctrine of election and *predestination which, for his critics (the monks at Hadrumetum and of southern Gaul), left no room for human initiative or responsibility, but for Augustine expressed the wholly unmerited and gratuitous nature of salvation in circumstances where all justly deserve damnation. Why some are saved and some left to perish he attributed to the unfathomable wisdom of God (Rom. 11: 33). Augustinian realism (or, some would have it, pessimism) as opposed to Pelagian optimism (or, some would have it, realism) and ideas of perfectibility, have been re-expressed in countless different forms in the history of western theology and, as Iris Murdoch (*Sovereignty of the Good*, 1970) forcefully demonstrated, are still manifest in secular philosophical attitudes following the *Enlightenment.

Christian society

For Augustine the Christian life is a social life, a community of people with 'one heart and one mind' towards God (Acts 4: 32). He was convinced that this single-minded devotion was best preserved by chastity (which for him was as much a matter of the mind as the body). From the 'philosophical' retreat with family and friends at Cassiciacum, immediately following his conversion (386), to the lay, celibate, community of 'servants of God' which he established at Thagaste on his return to Africa (388), to the lay and then clerical monastery which he established next to the basilica at Hippo following his ordination as priest (391) and consecration as bishop (396/7) respectively, Augustine aimed to establish a community of like-minded individuals with whom he could live the Christian life. The emphasis (as evidenced in *The Rule* and *On Virginity*) in Augustine's *monasticism is not so much ascetic as upon common life, sharing of goods, friendship, and brotherly love—reflecting a theology in which pride and self-love are the cause of the Fall, and love of God and neighbour are the source, means, and end of grace. This has, not unjustly, been termed a 'spiritual communism', and is the basis for Augustinian communities throughout the world today.

Augustine does not set the *married life in antithesis to the monastic life, rather he sees it as sharing the same ideals, goals, and temporal ambiguities. The married relationship is defined not so much by the sexual bond (this is simply part of the 'friendly fellowship' of marriage and of the duty which spouses owe to one another regardless of procreation) as by unity, harmony, and fidelity; a marriage of minds rather than of bodies. Alone among theologians of late antiquity (with the exception of Ambrosiaster) he entertains the possibility of sexual relations before the Fall and maintains that Adam and Eve were a married couple. The nature of human *sexuality after the Fall comes to prominence in the later debates with Julian on the nature of concupiscence—the violent and irrational carnal feeling which is symptomatic of the disobedient, disordered will following the Fall, and which accompanies the transmission of Adam's sin. Augustine's positive reflections on marriage and sexuality as part of humanity's original creation are often ignored by those who simply wish to regard him as the *eminence grise* of western negative attitudes.

Both the monastic and the married life therefore anticipate for Augustine the perfect community of *unity, mutual love, and *friendship which will be the City of God, but neither, because of man's fallenness, can realize it in this life. Nor, unlike the *Donatists, did he think it could be attained in the *church.

An inordinately large part of Augustine's time and energy as a bishop was consumed by attempts to wipe out the schismatic church of the Donatists which had become so deeply entrenched in North Africa through its claim to have preserved the true church, pure and untainted by the compromise and corruption which, they alleged, had vitiated the Catholic Church during the persecutions. Sermons, treatises, letters, public debate, even a popular song, were used by Augustine to demonstrate the absurdity of the Donatists' position in setting themselves not only against the Catholic Church in Africa but against the universal church. The ecclesiology and sacramental theology expounded in this context has been determinative of the western church ever since. Both sides appealed to African tradition, notably Cyprian, bishop of Carthage, and to the state, to support their position. All else having failed, the Donatists were effectively coerced into defeat by a harsh series of proscriptions in 412 which, in a number of works, Augustine seems to have argued himself into supporting.

The unattainability of perfection in this life is described in world-historical terms in the great work of Augustine's maturity, the *City of God* (413–26). Well before this he had divided human society into two classes, separated by their love of God or of the world (*On True Religion*, 50). In the *City of God*, he develops this division in the context of a consideration of the relation between Christianity and the empire, occasioned by the unspectacular and short-lived, but hugely significant, fall of Rome in 410 to Alaric and the Goths. Were the destinies of the church and empire providentially interwoven, and, if so, in what way? How were the pagans, who blamed the fall on Christianity, to be answered? Augustine's response looks at their historical, political, and social interaction from the perspective of divine *providence and both sets Christianity apart from pagan religion (books 1–5), philosophy (6–10), and *history (15–18) and demonstrates their interdependence at a social, political, and legal level (19) in virtue of the fact that fallen man is simply a pilgrim, a 'resident alien' in a fractured world, where ultimate unity, peace, and harmony cannot be attained, but only longed and hoped for. Here he must respect and use the structures that God's voluntary providence has provided—the church and its scriptures, the empire and its laws—while remembering that they are not the City of God, that the journey ends, for the elect, only in the life to come.

Works

In the intervals of the Donatist and Pelagian controversies, and in the time free from his extraordinarily onerous episcopal duties (as legal arbitrator, preacher, spiritual director, pastoral and theological adviser, and correspondent—in *Letters*, 224. 2, he tells us he devoted the day to one task and the night to another) Augustine produced the largest body of work of any writer in antiquity. A large proportion consists of sermons or works of exegesis, notably the two long series on John's gospel and the Psalms. As well as the *City of God* and the substantial body of controversial works against Manichees, Donatists, and Pelagians, he wrote hundreds of letters, made repeated attempts to interpret the first few chapters of *Genesis, the high point of which is the twelve-book *Literal Commentary on Genesis* (401–14), composed fifteen books on *The Trinity* (399–419, a work which breaks startlingly new ground, and whose psychological analogies have exercised great influence in western tradition), considered the role of classical culture, literary criticism, and rhetoric in *On Christian Doctrine* (396/426, which was tremendously influential in the Middle Ages), wrote numerous treatises on ethical subjects, on Christian instruction, and philosophical questions. There is barely a subject that he leaves unconsidered.

Augustine died in August 430, as the Vandals, conquerors of Roman Africa, were about to occupy and devastate Hippo. His library, however, survived intact.

Western Christian thought can be seen as the history of the assimilation and rethinking of Augustine's legacy. He set the agenda for subsequent thought, and from the moment of his death his influence has been uniquely pervasive and inspiring. This is no doubt partly due to his character, the erudition, eloquence, and coherence of his work, its vast quantity and outstanding quality, his all-embracing interests, and his originality and creativity as theologian, philosopher, controversialist, mystic, and pastor. Medieval reflection on the relation of philosophy and religion, faith and reason, Reformation thought on grace and free will, works and justification, Enlightenment discussions of sin and the possibility of perfection, modern and postmodern theories of language and human motivation, as well as the perennial practice of exegesis, mysticism, and devotion: all bear the distinctive impress of his thought.   **Carol Harrison**

Translations can be found in *Oxford Library of the Fathers, Library of Christian Classics, Ancient Christian Writers, Fathers of the Church* series.

Augustine, *Confessions*, trans. H. Chadwick (1992).
—— *City of God*, trans. H. Bettenson (1972).
Chadwick, H., *Augustine* (1986).
Clark, G., *Augustine: Confessions* (1994).
Bonner, G., *Augustine: Life and Controversies*, 2nd edn. (1986).
—— *God's Decree and Man's Destiny* (1987).
Brown, P., *Augustine of Hippo* (1967).
Burnaby, J., *Amor Dei* (1938).
Madec, G., *Petites Études Augustiniennes* (1994).
—— *La Patrie et la Voie* (1989).
Markus, R. A., *Sacred and Secular* (1994).
—— (ed.), *Augustine: A Collection of Critical Essays* (1972).
O'Daly, G., *Augustine's Philosophy of Mind* (1987).
O'Donnell, J. J., *Confessions*, Text and Commentary vols. 1–3 (1992).
Rist, J., *Augustine: Ancient Thought Baptised* (1994).

authority. The characteristically Christian conception of authority derives from the divine authority attributed to and claimed by *Jesus in the *gospels. Almost all theological disputes derive from differences about what this is and in what measure and form it is transmitted to the community established as a result of his *ministry, death, and *Resurrection. Already in the NT we meet a number of conflicts. One is between *Paul and members of his churches, in which his ultimate appeal is to the authority of the gospel he received and has handed on to them. Another is between the apparently 'charismatic' authority of Paul and the institutional authority of the *Jerusalem church (Acts 15, Gal. 2). A further significant theme is the development of structures of authority evidenced in the late Pauline literature of the *Pastoral Epistles.

Already in the period immediately after the apostles, we find a determined attempt by Ignatius of Antioch to enhance the authority of the *episcopate, while in *Irenaeus of Lyons we find a more nuanced attribution of authority to the churches' shared confession of the rule of *truth as it is handed on by those bishops who maintain loyalty to it. The development of patterns of authority in the following centuries is by no means uniform, but authority in church discipline and doctrinal definition is attributed to ecumenical *councils, representative gatherings of bishops from the whole of the Christian world. At the same time power centres, Antioch and *Alexandria in the east, *Rome in the west, develop a measure of rivalry. The tug of local claims is illustrated by the refusal of considerable minorities to accept the widely agreed *Chalcedonian Definition of the *person of Christ, with *Nestorian and *Monophysite churches remaining outside to this day (see CHRISTOLOGY).

In the east, authority came to be centred on Byzantium, although a relatively diffused conception developed, involving the notion of a number of autocephalous national churches in *communion with one another. In contrast to this, Rome developed a more unitary and centralizing tendency, the stress being placed on the communion of churches with Rome rather than with one another. The development of relations with the civil authorities illustrates problems of disciplinary, as distinct from doctrinal, authority. In the days of persecution, discussion centred on the status of those who desired readmission after renouncing the faith under duress, while after obtaining official status the church came to depend on the state for the repression of *heresy, as early, indeed, as the 5th century.

Thereafter history is dominated by relations with the state. While the Byzantine emperor adopted some of the style of the *priesthood, in the west the *papacy claimed universal jurisdiction over the spiritual realm as the result of a division of powers, later justified by the 8th-century forgery, the *Donation of Constantine*. In Christendom, the church effectively exercised intellectual and disciplinary authority over the whole of European society, vestiges of which remain today in German church taxes and British church schools. The break-up of the system, appropriately symbolized by the exposure of the forgery during the Renaissance, was triggered by a number of forces, papal corruption among them, but also by doctrinal and nationalistic influences.

The *Reformation is paradigmatic for our subject because it raised all the questions of authority in *Christianity. At the centre is a clash over the relative importance of biblical and institutional-churchly authority. *Luther's three 1520 treatises in effect accused the Roman church of wholesale abuses of authority: personal, institutional, disciplinary, and doctrinal. The sale of indulgences focused the complaint. By claiming authority over the spiritual state of believers (even the dead) the church contradicted what Luther saw to be the Pauline teaching that *God's justifying power is mediated by *grace through *faith. But this is not, as it is sometimes made out to be, an opposition of individual to churchly authority. Luther's theology was traditional, his objection to Rome being that the church, for example by withholding the cup from the *laity, wrongly arrogated to itself an authority that was God's alone. Similarly, he had no wish to subvert the church's place in society but to reform her teaching, a reform which he believed the secular authorities had a responsibility to inaugurate.

The differences were sharpened by the Council of *Trent which defined Rome's position against that of the Reformation. That the issue was not simply one of the *bible against *tradition is now clear. Trent had a high doctrine of scripture, while *Calvin's high estimation of the authority (albeit relative) of the great Councils and of the church fathers, especially *Augustine, typifies the mainstream Reformation regard for tradition. The dispute centred on who has the right to define what is the teaching of scripture, and how. While Rome continued to claim the magisterium's final right to decide the interpretation of scripture, the high place in *Protestantism given to church assemblies is shown by the series of Confessions that regional churches, both *Lutheran and *Reformed, have formulated in order to define their doctrinal basis. They are mostly traditionally orthodox in expression. Paradoxically, Rome's strong assertion of ecclesiastical pre-eminence is married with a strong confidence in *reason, albeit reason as traditionally defined by Thomas *Aquinas. This contrasts with Luther's contemptuous rejection of *Aristotle and Calvin's firm subordination of reason to scriptural *revelation. All these positions contrast strongly with that of *Eastern Orthodoxy, which continues to locate *dogmatic authority in the seven ecumenical councils, and has remained relatively untouched by change.

In the west, the differences between and within the churches have been sharpened by the *Enlightenment's emphasis on the authority of reason over against all traditional forms. Until the mid-20th century, Rome's reaction was to develop an ecclesiastical and centralizing conception of authority which itself owed something to the Enlightenment's absolutist tendencies. Rome and the pope's authority was exerted against any movement toward the independence of national churches, while the 19th century witnessed the

peak of that church's unilateral initiation of new dogmatic *developments, notably those of the *infallibility of the pope and the Immaculate Conception of the Virgin *Mary.

In contrast, individualism and rationalism have made deep inroads into Protestant conceptions of authority, leading ultimately to the institutional plurality (some would say, chaotic disorder) of the modern church. The exercise of conceptions of reason deriving from the Enlightenment in biblical and doctrinal criticism have, along with the strongly experiential note introduced by *Schleiermacher, called traditional forms into question. Reflection on these developments led *Newman to a return to dogma and ultimately to Rome, while in the 20th century historic forms of Christian belief owing much to the Reformation have been reasserted by Forsyth and *Barth. The latter's theology of revelation represents a form of biblical and dogmatic authority that attempts both to answer Enlightenment criticisms and to concede the propriety of biblical criticism.

All these differences reflect disagreements in pneumatology. All churches would hold that the *Holy Spirit leads the church into the truth of both doctrine and practice, but the way in which and extent to which that *eschatological reality is realizable in the present is everywhere disputed. Unfortunately, such appeals to the Spirit often appear to be self-justifying. If authority, to use Forsyth's lapidary definition, 'is another's certainty taken as the *sufficient and final reason* for some certainty of ours, in thought or action' (1952: 313), we see all the questions come together. Does the Spirit grant certainty, to whom and how? The Enlightenment sought certainty through the careful employment of reason. What appeared to be a denial of authority, or its concentration in the person of the individual reasoner, was certainly a denial of the church's authority, but in effect led to the establishment of new institutions, the quasi-church of science prominent among them. Modern *Pentecostalism, seeking as it often does the immediacy of spiritual experience, reveals a rather different, but characteristically modern, approach to the crisis.

The authority of an institution and its members oriented to the one who wielded divine authority only by going to the *cross needs to be exercised in the light of Paul's teaching that only at the end shall we know as we are known (1 Cor. 13: 12). That does not forbid an anticipation of eschatological certitude, but does limit the certainty of all human claims. If all authority is finally that of God the creator, room must be found for both the mediation of his authority through Christ and the Spirit and an awareness of the finitude and sinfulness of those who affect to represent that authority on earth.   **Colin Gunton**

Chadwick, Owen, *From Bossuet to Newman* (1957).
Evans G. R., *Problems of Authority in the Reformation Debates* (1992).
Forsyth, P. T., *The Principle of Authority* (1952), 1st edn. (1913).
Luther, Martin, *Three Treatises* (1960), 1st edn. (1520).
Küng, Hans, *Infallible?* (1971).
—— *Structures of the Church* (1964).
McFarland, Ian, *Listening to the Least* (1998).
Whitehouse, W. A., 'Authority, Divine and Human', in *The Authority of Grace* (1981).
Whyte, James, 'The Problem of Authority', *King's Theological Review*, 7 (1984).

B

Babylon, see EXILE.

Bach, Johann Sebastian (1685–1750). J. S. Bach is claimed by many to represent the apex of 'Christian thought' in *music. Thus, for Mendelssohn, the St Matthew Passion was 'the greatest of Christian works'. Albert Schweitzer, both one of the leading theological and missionary figures of the 20th century and a distinguished organist, wrote a two-volume study of Bach, while Nathan Söderblom described him as 'the Fifth Evangelist'. Bach's religious impact on the 19th and 20th centuries has, then, been enormous. For many, he is the supreme Christian composer.

Born at Eisenach in Thuringia, Bach worked for the latter half of his life as a church musician and court composer in Leipzig. He lived on the brink of the age of *Enlightenment yet is ahistorical. For *Luther, 'next to the Word of God, music deserves the highest praise'. Bach was very much a *Lutheran both in finding the heart of his experience in Christ's Passion and the *symbol of the cross, and in seeing music as the best means for communicating faith, but neither story nor symbol differ from the traditional doctrines of the Catholic Church. Again, his orthodox Lutheran devotion was deeply affected by the *Pietism then rekindling German Protestant life, yet Pietism's insistence on simplicity in worship actually devastated the Lutheran musical tradition and was utterly opposed to Bach's complex musical settings. The intensity of his personal religion, the service of God's glory, even the longing for *death, absolutely determine the character of his work. For him, music represented the ultimate reality of *God and constituted a fundamental element of *Christianity. His Passions and Masses were a kind of incarnation of the central mysteries, while his cantatas should be seen as musical sermons to be incorporated into the church's regular liturgy.

Bach's relationship to both Lutheran and Catholic traditional devotion is evident in the two great poles of his religious music—the St Matthew Passion and the Mass in B Minor. Archetypically, the Passion tells the tale, because what Protestantism protested against was precisely the substitution of ritual forms for revealed truth. The Mass—which was not created as a liturgical totality but was a compendium, assembled towards the end of Bach's life, of concepts he had cultivated throughout his career—is a ritual act that contains a story, a comprehensive musical statement of faith combining both Incarnation and Atonement.

There is nothing strange in Bach, a committed 18th-century Lutheran, having composed a Roman High Mass for, as the greatest of Christian composers, he was preoccupied with the heart of the Christian mystery, which is beyond denomination. Luther himself had admitted the Kyrie and Gloria into *Protestant liturgy, and Bach produced four short Masses, with Kyrie and Gloria only, for use in his church's rites. In also completing a full-scale setting of the Ordinary of dimensions so huge that it was unlikely to form part of worship, his unconscious motivation may have been to make an absolute statement of faith comparable in grandeur with his Passions. Like a Catholic Mass, Bach's is divided into Kyrie, Gloria, Credo, Sanctus, Benedictus, and Agnus Dei, though its scope is vastly extended since most sections are subdivided into alternations of contrapuntal or polyphonic-harmonic choruses with operatic arias or ensemble numbers. Although he copied out the score, in his noble calligraphy, at the end of his life, between 1747 and 1748, he composed the Sanctus first in 1724, the Kyrie and Gloria in 1733, for specific occasions, and throughout the work many movements were borrowed from earlier cantatas, usually to German texts. None of these borrowings was prompted by lack of time consequent upon a harried professional life. Bach chose from his prolific output precisely those pieces that were most appropriate, rewriting them subtly and extensively. One might even say, since his musical language was consistent, that the remoulding of earlier sources worked towards rather than against integration, so that the work became both a summation of Bach's life-work and a central musical manifestation of Christian faith.

Bach profited from being born at the 'wrong' time: the High Baroque, an age in which Man as Hero typically was dramatized in the mythological terms of opera. He himself never wrote an opera. None the less, he employed all the contemporary operatic techniques to tell humanity's ultimate story, which proved to be also God's. Baroque opera, ostensibly recounting humanity's triumph, was in fact concerned with a mythology of failure since humans, however grand their aspirations, are mortal. Bach's Matthew Passion, on the other hand, presents a mythology of sublime if painful success, since its hero is at once human and divine. The evolution of the *Passio* as a musical-dramatical-liturgical convention goes back to a need, already latent in the Middle Ages, to humanize the mythological. Long before the *Reformation, this process had been a step towards popularization: the illiterate would more readily assimilate a lesson if it were presented narratively, dramatically, and visually, but it is not fortuitous that in war-ravaged Germany during the 17th century Passion music gradually assumed a dual identity, at once metaphysical and physical, liturgical and theatrical, a development closely connected with the flowering of Protestantism.

The devastations occasioned by Germany's Thirty Years War of religion were appalling but, if a man is strong enough, belief may batten on distress, since he may feel the psychic realities of his nature the more acutely the more the world seems to be passing them by. This was certainly true of one of Bach's greatest precursors, his fellow Thuringian, Heinrich Schütz (1585–1672), who had studied with 'the sagacious Monteverdi', but was for much of his life Court Kapellmeister at Dresden, where he died. In old age Schütz concentrated increasingly on Christ's Passion, incarnating it in musical styles that grew progressively more austere, ending in a vernacular version of plainsong monody, without even a *continuo* instrument and with minimal choric interludes. A narrating Evangelist tells the tale in what the composer himself called 'German recitative', closer to plainchant than to Monteverdian *arioso*. It may, however, accord with Monteverdi's statement that recitative is the language of passion. The Evangelist's monody follows the inflections of vernacular speech, eschewing harmonic support; and if the minor characters are granted snatches of more pliant lyricism and the *turba* is allotted moments of madrigalian harmonic polyphony, Christ himself is not characterized at all. His divinity is made manifest by setting his words for two or three voices, symbolizing the relation of the Son to the Father and the Holy Spirit. Schütz's Passions are thus simultaneously drama and sacrament, and this equilibrium was preserved in the more wide-ranging musical-theatrical techniques in the Passions of his successor.

Bach's Passions were composed half a century later than Schütz's, at the height of the High Baroque. Since the passion in Bach's St John and St Matthew Passions is the human joy and suffering of our pilgrimage on earth, as well as Christ's sacrifice on our behalf, it makes sense that the heart of the experience should be in recitative. Any hint of plainsong intonation has vanished, for Bach's recitative is operatic, growing from the inflections of the German language, reinforced by the stabilities and tensions of the *continuo*'s harmony. We live through the story with a physical and psychological immediacy that is no more than glimpsed in Schütz. The arias, on the other hand, are seldom operatic in effect, but are rather lyrical reflections on what has occurred in the recitative and the narrative and dramatic choruses. The arias, even if wild or fierce, tend to be meditations after the event, the action having taken place during the recitative or even 'off-stage'. In Bach's reinterpretation, the static quality of the *da capo* aria is justified because *this* human story takes place *sub specie aeternitatis* and to Bach's audience, and in a sense to any audience, is literally a matter of life and death. The same is true of the *arioso* sections, which are a halfway house between *secco* recitative and the melodic fulfilment of aria. In Bach's passions *arioso* usually occurs when people are beside or out of themselves with passion, their speech being transcended to lyricism, sometimes with a tacit promise of benediction (for example, Peter's weeping).

The threefold relationship of recitative, *arioso*, and aria is roughly paralleled by the three kinds of choral music that Bach employs.

Just as recitative evokes the immediacy of the personal life, so short, naturalistic outbursts of the *turba* are the public life in turbulent action: 'common' music in being the utterance of people unredeemed. The large-scale polyphonic choruses, on the other hand, present the experience of humanity; usually starting from physical gestures that are topical and local, they become aria-like acts of transcendence, impersonal in their spacious polyphonic flow. The *turba* choruses are thus present action; the polyphonic choruses are simultaneously action and reflection; while choruses of the third type—the originally congregational chorales—remain outside the historical action, since they are meditations by priests and people, in this church, here and now. Their function complements communally that of the personalized arias; in the chorales you and I express our awareness of the story's relevance to us redeemed or redeemable creatures. For the chorale *hymns were literally people's music, gathered together by Luther and his followers for domestic use. Some were newly created by professional composers deliberately making sturdy tunes easy to sing and to memorize; some were recomposed liturgical melodies of the old faith, or more metrical rewritings of composed melodies by the guild musicians and mastersingers; still more were adapted from secular folk-songs often more erotic than pious, since Luther did not believe that the devil should have all the good tunes. By way of his four-part harmonizations—far richer than those of any previous composer—Bach rendered the chorale melodies expressive, even subjective, so that we sense the words' pertinence to him as maker and to us as worshippers. Yet despite this incipiently romantic introversion the strong tunes still function communally, in a manner at once historical and mythological. A parallel has often been traced between a Bach Passion and a Greek tragedy: both tell the story of a dying hero in terms simultaneously dramatic and sacramental; both link the hero's destiny to that of a people, interrelating personal drama with public action.

Bach's position, poised between Christian Passion and humanistically operatic passions, is manifest in his technique, which resolves duality between music's 'horizontal' (linear, polyphonic, contrapuntal) dimension and its 'vertical' (functionally harmonic) dimension. Might we see this as the aural *enactment* of the symbolism of the cross? There is a related paradox in the 'abstract' music of his last years, notably the *Art of Fugue* and the *Musical Offering*, for the mathematics and numerology in this music are at once anciently magical and cornerstones of the scientific universe. The ultimate instance is Bach's final chorale prelude for organ, *Vor deinem Thron tret' ich*, said to have been dictated on his deathbed. Every act in this composition is derived from the Lutheran hymn-tune, *rectus et inversus*, forwards or backwards, in diminution or augmentation. Finally, the music runs down as a dying man's pulse flags, while a sustained inverted pedal note stills the hymn-tune in eternity. There could be no more precise musical metaphor for the identification of death with the will of God, a fit summation of Bach's life-work.

Wilfrid Mellers

Butt, John (ed.), *The Cambridge Companion to Bach* (1997).

Lewis, Anthony, and Fortune, Nigel (eds.), *New Oxford History of Music*, v. *Opera and Church Music 1630–1750* (1975).
Mellers, Wilfrid, *Bach and the Dance of God* (1980).
Schweitzer, Albert, *J. S. Bach*, ET (2 vols.; 1911).
Wolff, Christoph, *Bach: Essays on his Life and Music* (1991).

Balasuriya, Tissa (1924–   ), Sri Lankan Catholic theologian.

After taking degrees in Economics and Political Science (University of Ceylon, 1945), Balasuriya joined the Congregation of Oblates of Mary Immaculate, studied in Rome, and was ordained in 1952. He taught at Aquinas University College, Sri Lanka, was appointed rector in 1964, but resigned in 1971 to establish his Centre of Society and Religion. A founder member of the Ecumenical Association of Third World Theologians, his works include *Jesus Christ and Human Liberation*, *The Eucharist and Human Liberation*, *Planetary Theology*, and *Right Relationships*. His theological concerns centre upon interfaith relationships, especially with *Buddhism and *Islam, and the *liberation of the oppressed.

In 1990, Balasuriya published *Mary and Human Liberation*, for which he was later excommunicated. His aim of replacing the image of a dehumanized *Mary by the Mary of the *Magnificat*, sharing her son's work of liberation in solidarity with the poor, is impeded by over-polemical language, but the Catholic Church authorities' response showed extraordinary disregard for natural justice and due process of *law. The Sri Lankan bishops' committee appointed to examine the book never invited Balasuriya to discuss it, but presented a list of 'errors' to be abjured; the faithful were warned against reading the book. In 1994, the Congregation of the Doctrine of the Faith sent the author their critical observations. His reply was found 'unsatisfactory'; he was required to sign a special 'profession of faith', never imposed on any other Catholic, including the clause that the church had no power to *ordain women. He declined, offering instead to sign Paul VI's *Credo of the People of God*. This being 'unacceptable', the notice of excommunication was published in January 1997.

The book was republished in 1997 in France and England as *Mary and Human Liberation: The Story and the Text*, including all the documentation of the case, which did more than any recent action to bring the Holy See's authority into disrepute. The excommunication was raised in January 1998 after worldwide protests. Balasuriya read aloud Pope Paul's *Credo*, but said nothing about women's ordination.   **Edmund Hill**

Balthasar, Hans Urs von, see VON BALTHASAR.

baptism,

administered in *water in the name of the Father, Son, and Holy Spirit, is the principal rite of admission to the *church. The apostle Paul could count on his addressees having received baptism (Rom. 6: 3–4), and the evangelist Matthew records its institution by the risen Lord (Matt. 28: 18–20). Received on profession of *faith in Christ (Acts 2: 38; 8: 12, 36–8; 16: 31–3), baptism sets the divine seal of the Spirit on those who are being saved (2 Cor. 1: 22; Eph. 1:13–14, 4: 30). In solidarity with sinful humankind, Jesus himself had been baptized by *John the Forerunner at the Jordan, where the Father's voice declared him the beloved Son upon whom the Holy Spirit rests (Matt. 3: 13–17, etc.). After Christ's atoning death and Resurrection, his followers are given a share in that 'baptism' (Mark 10: 38–9) and have their sins forgiven (1 Cor. 6: 11): a people for God's possession (1 Pet. 2: 9–10), Christians are reborn and adopted as sons and daughters of the Father (Rom. 8: 12–17; Titus 3: 4–7; 1 Pet. 1: 1–5), incorporated into the body of Christ, and included in the community of the Holy Spirit (1 Cor. 12: 12–13). As the sign of the evangelized and evangelizing church, baptism has figured historically and theologically as both a *sacra-

ment of *unity and a bone of contention, raising the questions: who has the responsibility and power to baptize? And who may and should be baptized? Baptism and ecclesiology are inextricably linked, for baptism highlights the issue: what is the church, and where is it to be found?

In the type of ecclesiology associated with Cyprian of Carthage, the church is the 'ark of salvation', the would-be sacraments of those separated from the one, visibly united church are null and void, and persons coming from a *schism to the church need to be baptized; some Orthodox and some *Baptists remain closest to this view. In its Augustinian modification, schismatic baptisms are 'valid' (for whether the ministrant be 'Peter', 'Paul', or 'Judas', 'it is Christ who baptizes') but they do not become 'fruitful' for salvation until the persons so baptized come to the one true church; this was for many centuries the dominant view in the Roman Catholic Church. According to ecclesiologies which see schism as somehow internal to the church (as predominantly in Protestantism), or which see 'vestiges of the church' beyond the canonical bounds of the institution held to be the true church or the church in its fullness (as in modern Catholicism), all properly performed baptisms are seen as valid and efficacious.

If these problems associated with the historical fact and theological understanding of schisms affect primarily the question of who may baptize, other controversies concern the appropriate recipients of baptism. Given the clear connection in the NT writings between baptism and faith, there has been a recurrent view that baptism should be received solely upon personal profession of faith. 'Baptists', as they have been designated in modern times, hold that faith cannot be given to infants in baptism, that the future faith of an infant cannot be presumed upon, and that other persons may not stand in for the infant's faith—thereby refuting the three main lines of defence adopted for a practice that is securely attested by the late 2nd century and believed by many to be 'apostolic'. In favour of infant baptism, its advocates variously allege the urgent need to wash away original *sin, family solidarity in the *covenant of *salvation (prefigured in the Old Testament practice of (male) circumcision and possibly reflected in the problematic NT references to the baptism of 'households'), and (in more general terms) the 'prevenience of grace'.

Issues relating to the stewardship of baptism are further complicated by the rite of confirmation and its chequered history. In some episodes in the Acts of the Apostles, water baptism is followed by an imposition of apostolic hands, associated with a coming of the Holy Spirit (8: 12–17; 19: 5–6); and the NT refers also to anointings which may have ritual import (2 Cor. 1: 21; 1 John 2: 20, 27–8). In the ancient church order identified as *The Apostolic Tradition* of Hippolytus (*c.*215), the water rite is immediately followed by the bishop's hand-laying with prayer and unction of the (fore)head. While the *eastern churches have allowed presbyters to administer the unction with episcopally consecrated chrism immediately after the water, the western churches reserved the post-baptismal acts to the bishop; and this eventually led, as Christianity spread so rapidly, to an interval of years between baptisms given to infants by parish priests and the subsequent episcopal 'confirmations'. The latter in fact became regarded as a distinct sacrament, understood as a renewed gift of the Holy Spirit 'to strengthen for the fight' or 'for preaching to others the gift one has received in baptism'.

Confirmation also served—and this was a theme taken up by some of the Protestant Reformers—as an occasion for the catechesis and the personal profession of faith that had been lacking around infant baptism. Continuing differences over the significance of confirmation lead to differences over the age at which it is considered pastorally appropriate to administer it to those already baptized as infants, and over its status as a prerequisite to receiving holy communion. Controversies about Christian initiation, both internally to a church and ecumenically, often involve the relation between baptism and confirmation.

The ecumenical state of play in the late 20th century concerning the understanding and practice of baptism is recorded in the WCC *Faith and Order document *Baptism, Eucharist and Ministry* (BEM) (1982) and the official responses of the churches to that 'Lima text' (*Baptism, Eucharist and Ministry 1982–1990*). After noting its NT 'institution' as 'entry into the New Covenant between God and God's people', *BEM* unfolds baptism's 'meaning' under five heads. First, baptism is 'participation in Christ's death and resurrection', an immersion in the liberating death of Christ, where sins are buried, the power of sin is broken, and the baptized are raised to a new life in Christ. Second, baptism implies 'confession of sin and conversion of heart'; pardoned, cleansed, and sanctified by Christ, the baptized are given 'a new ethical orientation under the guidance of the Holy Spirit'. Third, 'the gift of the Spirit' marks the baptized and 'implants in their hearts the first instalment of their inheritance as sons and daughters of God'. Fourth, baptism brings 'incorporation into the Body of Christ', uniting people in faith to Christ, to each other, and to the church of every time and place. Fifth, as a 'sign of the kingdom', baptism initiates the reality of new life in the midst of the present world and anticipates the universal confession of Christ as Lord to the Father's glory; it is noted that in some traditions the use of the water in baptism is seen to have repercussions 'not only for human beings but also for the whole cosmos'.

On some controversial matters: *BEM* affirms baptism as 'both God's gift and our human response to that gift', looking forward to lifelong growth in faith through the transforming grace of the Holy Spirit; almost all churches welcomed these formulations, although Lutherans still worried lest there remain a danger of *Pelagianism. *BEM* emphasizes that, whether of infants or of those personally professing faith, baptism 'takes place in the church as the community of faith' and expects growth in its understanding; but Baptist responses remained dissatisfied with the commendation as 'equivalent alternatives for entry into the church' of 'a pattern whereby baptism in infancy is followed by later profession of faith' and 'a pattern whereby believers' baptism follows upon a presentation and blessing in infancy'. While *Quakers and the Kimbanguists of Africa do not practise water baptism at all, *BEM* claims that otherwise 'all agree that Christian baptism is in water and the Holy Spirit' (cf. John 3: 3–5; Titus 3: 5–7), but 'Christians differ in their understanding as to where the sign of the gift of the Spirit is to be found' (the water rite itself, chrismation, confirmation, or even glossolalia); the responses to *BEM* demonstrated these differences, but cause for hope is found in the 'increasing awareness that originally there was one complex rite of Christian initiation' whose elements are now being brought together by liturgical reform into 'a unitary and comprehensive process' (*BEM 1982–1990*, p. 112). 'The paschal mystery of Christ's death and *Res-

urrection is inseparably linked with the pentecostal gift of the Holy Spirit' (*Baptism* 14)—and it is the business of the Christian ritual to reflect that.

If there is indeed theological and practical convergence in this last direction, it should help towards the solution of the fundamental problem, namely, the degree to which the various communities claiming to be 'church' can recognize the baptisms performed in other such communities, and then the manner in which, with that baptismal recognition in place, all those various communities can be reconciled in an integrated ecclesial unity.

BEM may point the way when it affirms that, 'in its full meaning', baptism 'signifies and effects' participation in Christ's death and Resurrection as well as reception of the Spirit. 'Signifies and effects' is classical teaching. Trust in baptism as the free 'gift of God' should overcome the fear of some pietist and liberal Protestants lest magic be involved in the passage from 'signifies' to 'effects'. On the other hand, and over against the tendency among the Orthodox to dismiss the notion of 'sign' as expressing a merely extrinsic relation between rite and reality, it may be questioned how far a rite can 'effect' what it fails to 'signify'. To do justice to both the signifying and the effective qualities of baptism requires clarity in ritual performance, a strong theological understanding of what is taking place, and a disciplined practice in the conditions of administration. The most promising moves in that direction have occurred with the post-Vatican II *Rite of Christian Initiation of Adults* and the similar procedures that it has called forth in other churches as well as the Roman Catholic. Inspired by the ritual, doctrine, and discipline reflected in the catechetical lectures and sermons of such great 4th- and 5th-century fathers as Cyril of Jerusalem, John Chrysostom, Theodore of Mopsuestia, Ambrose of Milan, and *Augustine of Hippo, the model process now passes in clear stages from a period of evangelization (enquiry and introduction to the gospel), through acceptance into the catechumenate (when the candidates express and the church accepts their intention to respond to God's call to follow the way of Christ), the catechumenate itself (for the nurturing and growth of the catechumens' faith and conversion to God), enrolment (when the catechumens are deemed ready) for impending baptism, the immediate and intense preparation through purification and enlightenment (typically during *Lent), to the climax (characteristically during the vigil of *Easter) of renunciation of sin, profession of faith, baptism in water, the laying on of hands and anointing with chrism, and sharing for the first time in the eucharistic offering and *communion, with a short period of post-baptismal catechesis or mystagogy to encourage full, active, and conscious participation in the continuing liturgical, evangelistic, and ethical life of the Christian community.

If it is allowed both to inform and be informed by the broader theological dialogue seeking agreement on matters of faith, morals, and communal life, the convergence upon such a pattern of the understanding, performance, and practice of Christian initiation offers prospects for the various historically divided bodies with ecclesial claims to discern the existence of church in themselves and in their neighbours and so be in a position to realize the goal of the *ecumenical movement in the reintegration of unity.

Geoffrey Wainwright

Beasley-Murray, G. R., *Baptism in the New Testament* (1962).
Burnish, R., *The Meaning of Baptism* (1985).

Johnson, M. E. (ed.), *Living Water, Sealing Spirit: Readings on Christian Initiation* (1995).

McDonnell, K., *The Baptism of Jesus in the Jordan: The Trinitarian and Cosmic Order of Salvation* (1996).

Sava-Popa, G., *Le Baptême dans la tradition orthodoxe et ses implications œcuméniques* (1994).

Searle, M., *Christening* (1977).

Schlink, E., *The Doctrine of Baptism* (1972).

Schmemann, A., *Of Water and the Spirit* (1974).

Whitaker, E. C., *Documents of the Baptismal Liturgy*, 2nd edn. (1970).

Yarnold, E. J., *The Awe-Inspiring Rites of Christian Initiation*, 3rd edn. (1994).

Baptist thought.

At the inaugural meeting of the Baptist World Congress in London in 1905 the president called on the assembly immediately to stand and recite the Apostles' Creed, thus affirming and demonstrating that Baptists belong in 'the continuity of the historic church'. It was a sensible and surprising act. Sensible, because Baptists do belong within the tradition of orthodox Christianity. Surprising, because they have been wary of credalism.

Baptist origins are obscure. They are probably to be found in the European *Reformation, inseparably linked with the recovery of the evangelical doctrines of divine sovereignty, *justification by *grace through personal faith, and the authority of the *bible. Most early Baptists were *Calvinists of one kind or another. Historians continue to debate the influence of the Anabaptists of the radical wing of the Reformation. There were contacts between those who were to form the first Baptist Church and Menno Simons (see MENNONITE THOUGHT). Other historians stress the influence of English separatism and *Puritanism. The first Baptist Church on English soil was formed in Spitalfields, London, in 1612 under the leadership of Thomas Helwys. He was to die in prison, claiming freedom in matters of religious belief for all, 'let them be heretics, Turks, Jews or whatsoever'.

English Baptist life began with two streams. The General Baptists were broadly *Arminian in their theology, that is, they argued for the possibility of a free-will decision, open to all, to trust in Christ for *salvation. The Particular Baptists were more strictly Calvinist and argued that only the elect of God were saved by sovereign grace. Theological differences remain a feature of Baptist life.

Theologically, the distinctive doctrine of the Baptists has been that of the *church. Baptists argue, claiming scripture as their authority, that God gathers the church by grace in *covenant love and that the church's membership is composed of those who have truly repented, freely believed, and trusted in Jesus Christ as Lord and Saviour. This is the believers' church tradition, emphasizing the church as a fellowship of believers with Jesus Christ the absolute head. Given this ecclesiology, *baptism is for the believer only, into the name of God in Trinity.

Baptists assert that each local *congregation has, under the lordship of Christ, the liberty to interpret his laws and that no other group of Christians can claim to rule over another church. However, early Baptists emphasized the associating of churches together and this remains an important theological insight. Hence Baptists form themselves into local Associations, Unions, or Conventions. They keep the word 'church' either for the local congregation or for the church universal as the whole company of God's people.

The governance of the church finds expression in the church members' meeting. Church meetings are called for members to seek together the mind of Christ. Since Christ is present with believers they are able, with the leading of the *Holy Spirit, to discern God's will. Of course, Baptists know struggles in the church but whenever they seek power and influence for their own programmes they are untrue to their convictions. Each local church gathered in and by Christ has 'gospel competence' to order its life. The church meeting is itself an affirmation of the theological convictions about the authority of Christ.

Baptists affirm the *priesthood of all believers. They recognize that God gives the gift of ministry to his church (Eph. 4: 11) but they countenance no separated priesthood in the body of Christ. They do however recognize and ordain ministers. There has been a long tradition of pastors, called by local congregations as their ministers, who usually have responsibility for preaching, presiding at the Lord's table, teaching, and pastoral care of the membership and adherents. National Unions have various ways of recognizing those who are called to this ministry. Baptists have sought a theologically trained ministry. However, *ordination to ministry usually only follows upon the call to a local pastorate or other established office. A contemporary debate is between those holding a solely functional view of ministry and those who believe that ministry cannot be reduced to functions but involves a call to 'be' a minister.

Wary of sacerdotalism and sacramentalism, Baptists have spoken of the Lord's Supper and baptism as dominical ordinances. Some, however, have also been ready and eager to use the word '*sacrament', believing that God is active in these actions. Baptism is usually by total immersion, following confession of faith either by public question and answer or personal testimony. Hence Baptists practise believer's baptism and not simply adult baptism. Children are received in services of dedication, blessing, and thanksgiving. The Lord's Supper (*Eucharist) or *communion is usually part of the Sunday worship service, its frequency ranging from weekly to quarterly. Traditionally only the baptized come to the table. More recently the invitation may be to 'all those who repent of their sin and love our Lord Jesus Christ'. The minister presides and the bread and wine are brought to the members by the deacons (chosen members of the church and recognized only in that congregation). This mode of sharing at the Lord's Table reflects the convictions about the church being a gathered community. A form of *Zwinglianism predominates but there are more sacramental understandings of communion among some Baptists.

All Baptists assert the authority of scripture but predictably with differing understandings. A few insist upon a doctrine of inerrancy. However, Baptists have also made a notable contribution to biblical scholarship, for example in the work of H. H. Rowley, G. R. Beasley-Murray, and R. E. Clements. Theologically, British Baptists, in the Declaration of Principle which is the basis of the Union, assert 'That our Lord and Saviour Jesus Christ, God manifest in the flesh, is the sole and absolute authority in all matters pertaining to faith and practice, as revealed in the Holy Scriptures'. The theological precedence here is from Christ, to the bible, to the church. Ultimate *authority for Baptists is found not in a text but in a person.

The emphasis on the authority of Jesus Christ (Matt. 28: 18) is the ground of the Baptist emphasis on *religious liberty. Because Jesus Christ alone is Lord the claims of the state or any other power are relativized. Baptists argue for the separation of church and state.

However, they have seen it appropriate, for the most part, to play a full part in public political life. Baptists continue to press for religious freedom for all, not on the basis of an appeal to human rights but in the light of the absolute authority of Jesus Christ. The sovereignty of God guarantees the freedom of humankind.

The issue of religious freedom relates to the distinction Baptists draw between *creeds and confessions. Creeds are human constructs. No one should be compelled to believe them, nor should freedom of opportunity be diminished because of non-subscription. Confessions were drawn up by local churches and Associations but they were not creeds in the sense that they could be rewritten in the light of further reflection. Confessions were not used as tests of faith so much as teaching resources and ways of explaining being Baptist to others.

Early Calvinistic Baptists showed little interest in *mission. However, in the 18th century there developed a form of evangelical Calvinism, and the Baptist Missionary Society was formed in 1792 with William Carey the first missionary. Theologically mission means participating in the mission of God, and is one of the implications of baptism. The church is a God-ordained agent in the work of the *Kingdom of God. The church is not the same as the Kingdom and does not have a mission of its own but is called to share the mission of God. Thus mission includes the tasks of social *justice. Again relating to their convictions about the authority of Jesus Christ, Baptists have worked for human rights and freedom.

Theologically Baptists have always known diversity among themselves. The diversity can be seen in American Baptists of this century who have included in their number people as diverse in their theologies as Walter Rauschenbusch, Harry Emerson Fosdick, Martin Luther King Jr. (see BLACK THEOLOGY), Harvey Cox, and William (Billy) Franklin Graham. The local Baptist church may be *fundamentalist, *charismatic, *liturgical, radically political, or almost anything else you could mention under the contemporary theological sky. However, the majority stand in the *evangelical tradition of the faith.

Present theological tensions among Baptists are really old issues in new light. Thus there are disputes about authority, leadership, and power; the proper interpretation of the bible; the status and significance of the *ecumenical movement, shunned by some and eagerly embraced by others. There is a new interest being shown in the radical *discipleship of the Anabaptist traditions and in the theology of covenant. There are over 42 million Baptists worldwide according to the 1996 Baptist World Alliance Directory.

Brian Haymes

Beasley-Murray, G. R., *Baptism in the New Testament* (1963).

Freeman, C. W., McClendon, J. W. Jr., and Velloso Da Silva, C. R., *Baptist Roots* (1999).

McBeth, H. L., *A Sourcebook for Baptist Heritage* (1990).

Maring, N. H., and Hudson, W. S., *A Baptist Manual of Polity and Practice* (1991).

Payne, E. A., *The Fellowship of Believers*, enlarged edn. (1952).

Walker, M., *Baptists at the Table* (1992).

Barmen Declaration.

The Synod of Barmen's 'Theological Declaration about the Present Situation of the Church', 31 May 1934, has become a landmark in modern Christian thinking and a classic text for the *German *Protestant tradition. Here German Protestant theology in a most vital form (represented for example by *Barth in the early stages of *Church Dogmatics*) responded to issues raised for the *church, not so much by the Nazi regime itself as by the errors of the variegated 'German Christians', who in their enthusiasm for Hitler's seizing power (1933), seen as the advent of the 'German hour' of salvation, used all means, including force, to gain control of the German Evangelical Church. In the process they drastically modified evangelical theology and preaching to develop a religion of praise, thanks, and trust for Hitler as *God's present *revelation for Germany.

In 1933, church leaders sought primarily to defend the freedom of the church from such politicizing interference, so the churches were forced to consider the grounds on which they might refuse to accept the Hitlerian God of *history without being unpatriotic. For the significant minority of German Protestants who formed the Confessing Church (*Bekennende Kirche*), those grounds were found, after intense debate and drafting, to be succinctly stated in the Barmen Declaration.

It affirmed that the church lives by obedient attention to the one Word of God, *Jesus Christ as witnessed to in scripture, who is God's 'vigorous announcement of his claim upon our whole life'. Since the church's distinctive task is to live fully in Christ, it is not available to be shaped and used by the prevailing political ideas of the day. The church does not have special leaders (*Führer*) but offices through which the whole community exercises servant ministry. The church was thus distinguished not only by a doctrinal profession but by organizing itself according to the *gospel. Although this stance protected the church from absorption by a totalitarian regime, it did not explicitly require a general political or ethical opposition to totalitarianism on behalf of all its victims.

Unsurprisingly, in view of the church's tradition of being 'above party', the Declaration responded to the crisis with a recall to constitutional order, in the Lutheran tradition of the doctrine of the Two Kingdoms in which church and state have separate and complementary functions. The state was appointed by God to the humanly limited task of maintaining *justice and *peace, using force, while the church was, through the *ministry of the *Word and *sacraments, to draw attention to the *Kingdom of God and the responsibility of rulers and ruled. At the cost of limiting the political action of the church, this controversial clause bridged divisions within the Confessing Church, between authoritarians and democrats, *Lutherans and *Reformed, even Nazis and anti-Nazis. The Declaration did not produce a church united in opposition to Hitler, let alone Nazism's removal, the morally necessary basic political project of the time. The Declaration says nothing about the early concentration camps and the elimination of constitutional politics, plainly visible in 1934. There is no theologically based commitment to *democracy, though the door is left open for those who wish to read it in that way. There is no comment on the regime's active *antisemitism, which had already affected the churches through the dismissal of Jews from public office; the protest of the Pastors' Emergency League in 1933 had been partly provoked by the dismissal of pastors of Jewish descent, but the far-reaching significance of the issue was not perceived.

The Declaration called for the confessional groups of churches (Lutheran, Reformed, United) to 'work out a responsible interpretation of it on the basis of their confessions'. Thus the primary interpretations are to be discerned in the practice, as much as in the theorizing, of the Confessing Church in the Third Reich; some were merely traditionalist, others penitent and innovatory; *Bonhoeffer lived to the end within the parameters of Barmen so as to discover new ways of being Christian. After 1945, Barmen was honoured by some as part of a heroic or sacred past; some who took it to be a still contemporary word calling for radical critical obedience were prepared for it to validate unwelcome conflict in the church in order to realize a true penitent church, in which the failures of the past were not repeated. For them, the Stuttgart 'Guilt declaration' (October 1945) was an essential chapter in the continuing Barmen tradition.

The Declaration was not solely Barth's work, but its afterlife was dependent to a degree on the popularity of his post-war theology of *politics, which was based on the one universal Lordship of Christ and the 'humanity of God'.

In South Africa, the Declaration helped many to see their situation under *apartheid as a 'church struggle', where the church must spell out the political implications of its confession of faith, if it was to continue to be church in a real sense. Thus, apartheid was eventually identified not merely as political folly or moral evil, but as *heresy—and therefore an intolerable threat to the church's faithfulness to its essential service of the Word of God, or gospel. Elsewhere, nuclear weapons were seen by some Christians as a 'blasphemy threatening all life' which, on the same principle, the church as church could not tolerate. With explicit reference to Barmen, Ulrich Duchrow argues that the injustice of the world economic system, in which churches are involved, puts the credibility of their confession of faith in God into question.

Haddon Willmer

Ahlers, Rolf, *The Barmen Theological Declaration of 1934: The Archaeology of a Confessional Text* (1986).

Barnett, Victoria, *For the Soul of the People* (1992)

Clements, Keith, *Learning to Speak* (1995)

de Gruchy, J. W., *Bonhoeffer and South Africa* (1984).

Duchrow, U., *Global Economy: A Confessional Issue for the Churches?* (1987)

Jüngel, E., *Christ, Justice and Peace* (1992).

Nicolaisen, C., *Der Weg nach Barmen: Die Entstehungsgeschichte der Theologischen Erklärung von 1934* (1984).

baroque.

Look up in a great baroque church, perhaps one of the pilgrimage churches of Bavaria or Austria. The walls vanish into clouds and a painted sky, with *saints and *angels floating upwards above us. Our hearts lift with the delight of it. This was what was intended; baroque *art sets out to move us. So, if we are in a bad mood, or the painter was not a very good one, we notice that we are unmoved, and talk about tawdry theatricality, and overdrawn emotionalism. The word 'baroque' had these overtones from the first.

'Baroque' is a technical term in the history of art, architecture, and *music. Bernini, Borromini, Rubens, Murillo, Vivaldi, *Bach are all names in the history of baroque. With a slight uneasiness, and more on the continent of Europe than in English-speaking countries, the word also has uses in the history of literature, and of the whole culture from which such art, music, and literature spring. Some *postmodernists, discovering a fellow-feeling with the theatricality and artifice of baroque, find new types of baroque today. Our concern here is with the religious overtones of the baroque art of nearly two centuries after about 1570, at its peak around 1660.

Baroque art is overwhelmingly *Catholic. The emotions it intends to evoke are normally religious emotions. Because it seeks to catch movement rather than settled repose, it is filled with the gesticulations of ardent feeling. St *Teresa opens her arms in helpless abandon to the angelic dart. Eyes are habitually turned up to heaven, and the mechanics of *martyrdom are dwelt on in shuddering detail. At its worst, there was misplaced eroticism, sadism, and total emotional unreality.

There is no doubt that baroque is theatrical. *Puritan England, in distrust, closed the theatres, though Calvinist Holland did not. Theatricality goes beyond theatres. The Spanish playwright Calderón ends his *Great Theatre of the World* on this very theme, with a mass on stage. A great baroque church, and the ritual within it, achieved high drama. So did the ritual of a public funeral, or of a public execution, or, above all, of a royal court. This was not an age when people were self-conscious in public; when performing a stated role they liked being watched. Baroque piety brought new standards of order to processions and *pilgrimages, and even to conduct on one's deathbed, or as a widow, or as an ordinary *dévot*.

Kings loved baroque. The style seems to lend itself to absolutism. There is no obvious theology in gilt and curlicues, yet *Counter-Reformation Roman Catholicism was, in theological terms, absolutist. Prague was filled with baroque churches to cow a formerly Protestant people. The baroque can be read as triumphalist, and somehow bullying, and fake. Who is ever deceived by a painted sky as a ceiling? Charles I of England, trying to be a baroque king, had his father painted floating skyward on the ceiling of the royal Banqueting House at Whitehall. The airborne king looks uneasy, and from that room his son later went out to his execution. It seemed fitting to his enemies. The Divine Right of *Kingship is baroque theology at its least approachable.

Is there a baroque Christianity? The Catholicism shaped by the Council of *Trent and by the new religious orders of the Counter-Reformation found its characteristic form in the baroque. Ecclesiastically, *Rome is above all a baroque city, with Bernini its typical architect. It is difficult to apply terms of art to doctrines, but such a devotion as the cult of the Sacred Heart, a matter of posing and pointing, a stylized emotionality, belongs clearly to its period. Could we say that *Jesuit spirituality was baroque? Most patrons of the baroque learnt their Christianity, and much else of their culture, in Jesuit schools. The Society of Jesus, greatest of Counter-Reformation religious orders, gave a physical expression to baroque Christianity without really trying. They knew what shape of church they wanted for convenience; they rather disliked showiness; in theory they liked approval from the centre for new building schemes. In practice, many Catholics for centuries thought that there was a standard, showy, baroque norm for Jesuit churches everywhere. Though this was not true, the expectation was enough. And some of the more juvenile aspects of baroque piety become more comprehensible when we remember that the Jesuits' primary task was the schooling of the young.

Baroque music, like baroque art, strove to surprise—sudden voices from another gallery somewhere behind you in the church—and to express and arouse emotion. In such pieces as Monteverdi's *Lamento d'Arianna* a single voice leads us to tears. More often the simple melody line is overwhelmed by harmonic ornamentation, and composers did everything they could to provide experiences of dramatic contrast. In music, as in Caravaggio's paintings, there is chiaroscuro, thrilling light in exaggerated shadow. The world of opera, a baroque art form, is utterly unlike the real world. We miss the point unless we see that the baroque imagination does not want to settle for ordinary reality. Everything is heightened. For great festivals the chancel of the Gesù, the mother church of the Jesuits in Rome, was filled with soaring trompe l'œil architecture as a stage-set for biblical tableaux. Even when, as if we were following the Spiritual *Exercises of St Ignatius Loyola, we are invited to visualize something concrete and real, it is dramatized. The actual saints of the Counter-Reformation, such as Ignatius, were low-key, natural, anything but posturing, but the baroque piety that was built on them, and the paintings their devotees made of them, were larger than life and splendidly theatrical.

A puritan critic might deplore the artificiality of the baroque. Carnival is to northern visitors the most disturbing aspect of baroque culture, all the more because of the contrast it plays up with Lent. The sight of Christians in masks, whether a visor at a Venetian ball, or the pointed hood of a Spanish penitent, upsets Protestant individualists. The baroque taste for flattery and panegyric as a literary form, so appropriate for absolute monarchies, rings false. German cultural historians argue that a taste for appearance against reality lies at the heart of baroque. A moral indictment is building up.

We should however recognize that Christianity can take a baroque form, that all ways of encountering the transcendent are under question, and those that undercut themselves and their own claim to seriousness and stability may give more of a clue to something beyond. Painted skies and stretching saints floating upwards in unearthly light are a laughably stilted and inadequate heaven, but those who know better are often pompous fools.

There is a Protestant baroque, somewhat less ostentatious, but recognizable. The case has been made for seeing *Milton as a baroque poet. In Paradise Lost we are caught up into a drama on a cosmic scale, with the sharpest conceivable contrasts, heaven and hell; even Lucifer's court is filled with high-flown flattery fit for an archangel. There might be more of the baroque if we look for it, even in Puritanism. Not all *preaching was in a plain style. There are Protestant parallels to the Sacred Heart. Cotton Mather's Magnalia Christi Americana has some of the magnificence and massy ornamentation fit for the taste of an earthly king.

We need not include all that is creative between 1570 and 1740 under the heading baroque. Each country has its own variations on the theme, and Christian missionaries took baroque architecture to Mexico and South India. There has seldom been a Christian art so filled with pleasure in this-worldly beauty, and yet which has pointed beyond itself. If we found their tasteful expositions of the vanity of all human achievements lacking in conviction, we would be wrong. It is a different idiom, but one worth learning.

Alistair Mason

Angoulvent, A.-L., L'Esprit baroque (1992).
Hart, Clive, and Stevenson, K. G., Heaven and the Flesh (1995).
Martin, J. R., Baroque (1977).
Roston, Murray, Milton and the Baroque (1980).
Schloder, J. E., Baroque Imagery (1985).
Skrine, Peter N., The Baroque (1978).
Wittkower, R., and Jaffe, I. B. (eds.), Baroque Art: The Jesuit Contribution (1972).

Barth, Karl

Barth, Karl (1886–1968), arguably the greatest theologian of the *twentieth century; a thinker in whose work the unresolved problems resident in the *Schleiermacherian tradition in dogmatic theology were finally overcome and that tradition found its most self-consistent expression.

Barth was born in Basel, Switzerland, of *pietistic parents. His father, Johann Friedrich (Fritz) Barth, became a lecturer in NT and early church history at Bern when Karl was 2. Known as a 'positive' theologian, Fritz Barth confounded conservative expectations by embracing moderately critical approaches to the investigation of scripture. He took a strong interest in social issues (the *women's rights movement, for example) and was well acquainted with the concerns of the Christian Socialist movement.

On the eve of his confirmation at the age of 15, Barth made the momentous decision to become an academic theologian so that, as he said later, he might discover what the *creed was all about. He began his university studies at Bern. After completing his initial battery of qualifying exams, he followed the common practice of going abroad to study. A semester in Berlin was spent listening to Adolf Harnack, Julius Kaftan, and Hermann Gunkel. After another Bern semester, he spent the year 1907/8 in *Tübingen and Marburg. Marburg meant, above all, study with the greatest dogmatic theologian of the time, Wilhelm Herrmann. It also afforded contact with the neo-*Kantianism of Hermann Cohen, a Jewish philosopher whose influence on Barth would be discernible throughout his career. Following the completion of his studies, Barth served as editorial assistant to Martin Rade, whose Die christliche Welt was the leading 'liberal' theological journal of the day.

After serving a Vikariat in a German-speaking church in *Geneva, in July 1911 Barth became pastor in Safenwil, a small town whose leading industry was textiles. He had already encountered poverty in *Calvin's city. But at that time, he regarded social ills fatalistically, as an unfortunate necessity of nature. In Safenwil, he very quickly (and to his own astonishment) found himself siding with the *socialists. Barth's sudden theological/political transformation shortly after his arrival there provoked consternation in his family and disapproval on the part of friends and mentors in Marburg. A first address to the local Workers' Union (the base organization of the Swiss Social-Democratic Party in that area) three months after his arrival was followed by a highly provocative and well-publicized address in December with the title 'Jesus Christ and the Social Movement'. In the face of mounting criticism, Barth defended himself by saying that he could no longer preach a 'neutral "gospel"'. He had to take a decisive stand on practical issues like *capitalism. We see in this early episode in Barth's pastorate a level of practical engagement which would remain characteristic of his entire career. Barth's theology had to eventuate in *ethics; that was a matter of internal necessity.

The outbreak of war in August 1914 and the endorsement by his beloved theological mentors in Germany of the war policies of Kaiser Wilhelm became the catalyst for a new departure in Barth's thought. Most biographers have treated this crisis in Barth's theological existence as a 'break' with *liberal theology and even with 'modernity', to the extent that the two terms were regarded as synonyms. And there can be no question that Barth experienced his shift as a rupture with the past and always interpreted it as such. With hindsight, however, we have to say that the 'break' was not as complete as Barth thought. Recent studies have shown that Barth's anti-modern rhetoric often served to conceal how thoroughly modern his new theology was. And even the 'break' with so-called 'liberal' theology was never complete. With Schleiermacher and Herrmann, particularly, Barth stood in a relationship characterized by both continuities and discontinuities. His departure from the theology of his teachers is best described as a move from an experientially based theology to a theology grounded in a dialectically conceived model of *revelation.

In the summer of 1916, Barth began work on what would become the most significant theological work since the publication of Schleiermacher's *Speeches*: his commentary on *Paul's epistle to the *Romans. The first edition was published in November 1918, as the First World War came to an end. It belongs to a body of *apocalyptic/utopian literature which emerged in that year of political and cultural convulsions: Ernst Bloch's *Geist der Utopie*, Oswald Spengler's *Decline of the West*, and Franz Rosenzweig's *Stern der Erlösung*. Written in an expressionistic style, it differed from the more famous second edition primarily through its affirmation of the possibility of experienceable irruptions of the *Kingdom of God in history.

When the possibility of reissuing the commentary arose in late 1920, Barth found that a number of factors had conspired in the interim to force a complete rewrite. Intellectual influences (the 'critical idealism' of Barth's brother Heinrich and Franz Overbeck's apocalyptic reading of the NT and early church history) moved Barth to a more radical *eschatology that rendered connections between the Kingdom of God and this *world tenuous. Hence, the second edition of *Romans* has been rightly described as a 'violent' work (Steiner 1978: p. ix); 'violent' in the sense that the *judgement of God is pronounced against the world in its totality. But the anger which comes to expression in the work has to be seen against the horizon of hopefulness that governs the whole. The judgement of God is everywhere understood to be in service of God's graciousness. *Grace kills only in order to make alive. And the quasi-idealistic rendering of the critical negation to which the world is subjected is relieved, here and there, by the realistic affirmation of the bodily *Resurrection of *Jesus from the dead as a prolepsis of a final transformation of the world.

In 1921, Barth accepted a chair in *Reformed theology at Göttingen. Five semesters of preparatory teaching in historical theology and biblical exegesis eventuated in Barth's first dogmatics lectures in the summer of 1924. *The Göttingen Dogmatics* marked a decisive move forward in Barth's thinking through his appropriation of the ancient *christology of the post-*Chalcedonian church and his use of it to lend coherence to his claim that revelation reaches into history without becoming a predicate of history. Barth's dogmatic method—which he continued to employ in the *Church Dogmatics* with little modification—was a function of the material decisions he made at this time in the areas of *revelation, christology, and *Trinity.

In 1925, Barth was called to Münster as a regular professor of dogmatics and New Testament exegesis, and in 1930 he succeeded Otto Ritschl as professor of systematic theology in Bonn. The Bonn

years were notable, above all, for the role played by Barth in the 'Church Struggle' against the Nazi regime. Though Barth later acknowledged he should have been more alert to dangers posed to the Jews (see ANTISEMITISM), his public defence of the freedom of the church to proclaim the gospel made him a leader of the resistance and a natural choice to pen the *Barmen Declaration in May 1934. Barth was suspended from his teaching responsibilities in November of that year for refusing to give an unqualified oath of loyalty to the *Führer*. His dismissal the following month left him free to return to his native Basel in 1935.

His return as professor of systematic theology allowed Barth to devote himself to his *magnum opus*, the *Church Dogmatics*. A work whose contents first saw the light of day as lectures to students, its situationally driven interest in current issues in both church and society is lost to sight today without considerable archaeological labour. Its freedom from complete allegiance to any one philosophical scheme has enabled the work to remain relevant to church audiences long after the philosophies of its day were rendered outdated. Barth retired from teaching in 1962.

At the heart of Barth's theology lies a single conviction. *God is in eternity (in himself) the mode of his self-revelation in time. The content of revelation (its 'what') is identical with its mode (its 'how'). The significance of this conviction may be seen through a brief comparison with Schleiermacher's theology.

In his *Christian Faith*, it was Schleiermacher's intention to overcome all speculative foundations in theology by means of a strict concentration upon the Christian's pious self-consciousness (i.e. that religious consciousness wherein the 'feeling of absolute dependence' has been *modified* by the redemption accomplished in Jesus of Nazareth). Much of his doctrine of God, however, was established by means of an idealistic derivation of grounds in God for the 'feeling of absolute dependence' *considered formally* (apart from all historical, lived modifications). Given that Schleiermacher's 'feeling of absolute dependence' has no existence in reality in the absence of modifications on the level of what he called the 'sensible' self-consciousness, he ought not to have been able to treat the religious self-consciousness *at any point* without regard for the specifically Christian experience of it. Or, if he thought he was justified in treating the doctrine of God and his relationship to the world without regard to specifically Christian experience, then he could not legitimately claim (as he did) that John 1: 14 is the basic text for all dogmatics. The unresolved problem in Schleiermacher's dogmatics is the extent to which things are said of God which reach beyond the limits established by history and, as a consequence, perpetuate the weaknesses of classical *metaphysical theism. Judged from that standpoint, Schleiermacher is rightly seen as a transitional figure with only one foot in the modern world.

The significance of Barth's work lies in his ability to close the door firmly on speculation about an abstract eternal being of God 'in himself' (i.e. essentialism). For Barth, God's being is constituted by his free decision for the incarnation of the Son and the outpouring of the Spirit in time. Hence, even before these things take place, God is in himself (by way of anticipation) what he has freely determined himself to be in time. The result is that when God incarnates himself, no change is effected in the divine being. The economic Trinity therefore becomes wholly disclosive of what God truly is in and for himself. There is no state of existence in the triune life of

God which lies beyond the reach of what might be known of God in and through his self-revelation in time. And this means, in turn, that the epistemological limits placed on the human knower by history are not violated in knowing a transcendent (supramundane) God. For this reason, Barth's theology does justice to the historicizing tendencies of more than a century of theology before him (even as it establishes the proper limits of those tendencies). And in overcoming the idealistic elements in Schleiermacher's approach to dogmatics, Barth also fulfilled the promise contained in the former's adumbration of a more christocentric grounding of theology.

How did Barth arrive at these conclusions? Two doctrines were materially decisive, both developmentally and in terms of internal systematic integration. The doctrine of revelation was elaborated and honed over a period of twenty-two years (1915–36). The doctrine of election then provided the divine ontology which would ground and render fully coherent his doctrine of revelation.

With respect to the doctrine of revelation, the key concept is that of the relation of indirect identity which is established in the event of revelation between the being of God and the creaturely medium through which that being is revealed. The language of 'indirect identity' refers to the idea that, in revealing himself, God makes himself to be fully and completely present *in* a creaturely reality without divinizing that creaturely reality. In the absence of such divinization, the creaturely reality which serves as a medium of God's act of self-revelation can never become directly revelatory; the divine reality lies hidden 'beneath the surface', so to speak. If the divine reality in the medium is to be recognized, it must be revealed by the *Holy Spirit. Revelation is, thus, a Trinitarian event. God the Father reveals himself in the Son through the power of the Holy Spirit. This much of Barth's doctrine of revelation was largely in place in the two commentaries on Romans. What he added in *The Göttingen Dogmatics* was a christological explanation. The meaning of the Incarnation is that the eternal Son assumed a *human 'nature' and lived a thoroughly and completely human life without detriment to his deity. Basic to Barth's elaboration of this claim was his rejection of the thought that the hypostatic union of the divine and human natures in one person (or subject) gave rise to a transference of divine attributes to the human nature. Thus, the concern sounded in *Romans* remained in place: no divinization of the creature in revelation! What he could not yet explain was how the living of a human life did not produce change in God on a fundamental, ontological level.

It was in Barth's mature doctrine of election that he was finally able to advance a divine ontology which would provide the realistic ground of the whole of his theology. God, he was now able to say, is a self-determining subject who freely and eternally chose to be God in a covenant of grace with the human race and to be God in no other way. In that God made this 'primal decision', he assigned to himself the being he would have from everlasting to everlasting. There was never a time when God's being was not already determined for this covenant—and that means that the idea of an undetermined, abstract mode or state of being in God above and prior to election has been completely eliminated. God *is* in eternity what he has determined himself to be in time.

With his divine ontology firmly in place, Barth could then go on (in later volumes of the *Church Dogmatics*) to construct a human ontology consonant with it. What God and the human 'are' is defined by the *covenant of grace which constitutes the material content of God's primal decision (election). God is the Lord of the covenant; we humans are his covenant-partners, chosen and created for lives of free covenant fidelity before him. Jesus Christ is the one human in history in whom this true humanity is perfectly realized. Through the reconciliation achieved in his life, death, and Resurrection and our assimilation to it by the transforming power of the Holy Spirit, our humanity is brought, moment by moment, into conformity with Christ's own.

In spite of the fact that Barth disdained a positive employment of the concept of an 'analogy of being' between God and humanity after 1929, such an *analogy is implied. Formally, the analogy consists in the fact that both divine being and human being are understood by Barth to be a being-in-act (i.e. both are conceived in actualistic terms). Materially, both are structured by the covenant of grace. The dissimilarity in the analogy lies in the fact that God gives himself his being whereas we receive our being from him. The similarity lies in the fact that as and when our being is brought into conformity to Christ's own, it is made to be like his in *holiness. And it is in holiness, finally, that the true positive analogy between God and the human is to be found. Admittedly, this last emphasis is drastically underdeveloped in Barth's own work and collides, in some respects, with his treatment of the *imago Dei*. Still, that his work implies an analogy of being on something other than traditional Catholic terms (i.e. as a function of created faculties or a created relation) has been largely overlooked by Barth scholars.

Barth had no interest in repristinating old theological trains of thought, though he sought to interpret them generously. For that reason, traditional characterizations of his theology as neo-orthodox are misleading. What is true is that Barth showed, more than anyone else, what being orthodox under the conditions of modernity might entail. He rejected the 'metaphysical way', which was basic to all classical forms of Christian theism, without sacrificing real knowledge of God in himself. And he did so by understanding God in himself as the mirror reflection of the God disclosed in the history of Jesus of Nazareth through the outpouring of the Holy Spirit.

At every stage of his development after 1915, Karl Barth was a cultural outsider. Even when he forsook the expressionistic style of writing in his dogmatic works, his work continued to express the 'son's revolt against the father' (Peter Gay)—embodied, above all, in the person of Schleiermacher but extending to the whole of modernity. He remained, throughout his life, strongly countercultural and combative, working out a positive vision that would do justice to the critical concerns of earlier years. Of a domestication of theology by the later Barth there can be no talk. His was the single most anti-dogmatic dogmatics produced in the modern period; anti-dogmatic in the sense that his doctrine of revelation, centred as it was in the dialectical relation of God to every medium of that revelation, would not allow for domestication. Rarely has that been fully grasped and misunderstandings abound in the stock criticisms directed against Barth's theology.

From the *Romans* period on, his rejection of *natural theology made him the target of vehement opposition. What is forgotten today is that Barth's rejection of natural theology is of a piece with a lengthy history of uneasiness with natural theology which, starting with Hume and *Kant, included notables like Schleiermacher and Ritschl. What made Barth a special target during his lifetime was the fact that he radicalized the critique of natural theology by defining it more broadly than previously, as any theology that failed to recognize that God is in himself the mode of his self-revelation in time. Revelation *is* God himself, speaking in person. If inferences drawn from observations of nature could produce knowledge commensurable with the self-revelation of *this* God, then Barth would have had to concede the legitimacy of natural theology. But he could not convince himself that this was possible. Debates with Barth's attitude towards natural theology which do not realize that his position can only be defeated by taking on his doctrine of revelation in its entirety (including christology, election, and Trinity) will always fail to rise above the level of a superficial quibble. To suggest that his view was a function of a necessary but transcendable polemic against Nazi ideology is completely to miss the point.

Second, Barth awakens suspicions because he is able to make such definite assertions about subjects that late-19th-century theology had taught the church it could say nothing about (e.g. election). Even where Barth speaks of subjects which are *meta*-physical in the strict sense, however, the way he takes in gaining access to them is not the metaphysical way. His 'metaphysics' (understood as a region of discourse) were strictly 'anti-metaphysical' (understood as a methodology), resting on an epistemology that respected the limits of history.

Third, Barth arouses hostility today because of his 'Christocentrism'. That was not so much of a problem in his own lifetime: virtually everyone wanted to be 'Christocentric' in some form—as the classical liberal tradition demonstrates. But today, concerns for the world religions, not to mention the desire on the part of many Christian theologians to construct an independent doctrine of the Holy Spirit, make his 'Christocentrism' an affront. The 'exclusivity' of Barth's 'Christocentrism', however, is inherently inclusive in that every human is, for him, elect in Jesus Christ. We need to recognize that today's debates over approaches to the issue of 'inclusivity' reach to the very heart of what it means to be genuinely Christian in the realm of theology. On this issue, at least, Barth would have had the whole of the classical liberal tradition on his side. It is worth pondering whether today's 'liberals' have not taken a turn that amounts to a break with their own tradition, thereby stepping out of the realm of Christian theology altogether.

In the English-speaking world, Barth's impact has yet to be assimilated fully. It may well be that the period of his greatest influence lies in the future. It was, after all, the 'first postmodernity' in Germany (Roberts 1991: 170) which created the conditions needed for his influence in Europe. Though not himself postmodern in any sense, his non-metaphysical revelational approach to providing foundations for knowledge made him attractive to many. So also today, in a period in which the putative lack of foundations for knowledge make us vulnerable to nihilism, reassurances based on optimistic assessments of human nature are not going to satisfy. What is needed is a theology that, without violating newly accepted canons of postmodern reflection, is able to address the situation created by those canons. Many are finding such a theology in Karl Barth.

See also KIERKEGAARD, SØREN; VON KIRSCHBAUM, CHARLOTTE; PREDESTINATION.   **Bruce L. McCormack**

Barth, Karl, *Church Dogmatics* (13 vols.; 1936–69)
—— *The Epistle to the Romans* (1933).
—— *The Göttingen Dogmatics: Instruction in the Christian Religion* (1991).
Busch, Eberhard, *Karl Barth: His Life from Letters and Autobiographical Texts* (1976).
Gay, Peter, *Weimar Culture* (1968).
Hunsinger, George, *How to Read Karl Barth* (1991).
McCormack, Bruce, *Karl Barth's Critically Realistic Dialectical Theology: Its Genesis and Development, 1909–1936* (1995).
—— 'Beyond Nonfoundational and Postmodern Readings of Barth: Critically Realistic Dialectical Theology', *Zeitschrift für dialektische Theologie*, 13 (1997).
—— 'Grace and Being: The Role of God's Gracious Election in Karl Barth's Theological Ontology', in John B. Webster (ed.), *Cambridge Companion to Karl Barth* (2000).
Roberts, Richard, *A Theology on its Way? Essays on Karl Barth* (1991).
Steiner, George, *Martin Heidegger*, 2nd edn. (1978).
Webster, John, *Barth's Ethics of Reconciliation* (1995).

base communities.

base communities. Within the Catholic Church after *Vatican II there was a mushrooming of highly active small groups which saw themselves as 'a new way of being church'. These base communities, which began in *Latin America among the poor, were the form of *church that led to *liberation theology, and to which liberation theology led. Both sprang to life under the impact of Vatican II upon a highly Catholic continent particularly short of priests and in need of social revolution.

The groups have been variously named base communities, basic Christian communities (the early name), basic ecclesial communities (a later, more theological title), and small Christian communities (the preferred name in Africa). They read the bible together and discuss how its message applies to the community; and they undertake common projects in response to local social needs. A church of base communities draws its energy from its roots—the poor and the *laity—instead of waiting for instructions from the top of the tree.

Ordinary people in the base communities take on many tasks once left to the clergy, but that does not mean that they see themselves as independent of the hierarchy. On the contrary, the encouragement of the priest and the bishop has proved crucial in building confidence and providing training for local leaders, and communities have multiplied most rapidly where they have been part of a diocesan pastoral plan. In Europe, however, the term 'base community' has sometimes been used for middle-class, ecumenical groups which cut free from the restrictions of the institution.

The roots of base communities are found in Brazil in the 1950s and 1960s but the high period of growth was triggered by the General Conference of Latin American Catholic Bishops in Medellín, Colombia, in 1968, which proclaimed the church's 'option for the poor'. The budding communities were identified, named, and affirmed in the words: 'The Christian base community is the first and fundamental ecclesial nucleus', and it is 'a primordial factor in human promotion and development today'.

Further encouragement was given by the bishops' next meeting at Puebla, Mexico, in 1979, which declared that the communities—now dignified with the name CEBs (basic ecclesial communities)—were 'an important ecclesial event that is peculiarly ours'.

Base communities in Latin America have suffered a decline since liberation theology fell out of official favour in the mid-1980s. New bishops of a more conservative disposition have paid lip-service to their value, but in practice they have changed the emphasis from the social to the devotional.

Yet the worldwide thrust continues. Many bishops in Asia, Oceania, and Africa continue to promote the formation of base communities, though with a more cautious vision than before. Further, the inspiration of what can be done by the poor, armed only with a bible, has left an indelible mark on pastoral practice in all mainline Christian churches, in First and Third World alike.

Margaret Hebblethwaite

Hebblethwaite, M., *Base Communities: An Introduction* (1993).

Marins, J., Trevisan, T., and Chanona, C., *The Church from the Roots: Basic Ecclesial Communities*, 2nd edn. (1989).

Torres, S., and Eagleson, J. (eds.), *The Challenge of Basic Christian Communities* (repr. 1982).

Beatitudes, see SERMON ON THE MOUNT.

Beguines.

Women calling themselves Beguines were first recorded in the diocese of Liège (Belgium). They may have acquired the name through association with a group of pious women inspired by the church reformer Lambert le Bègue (d. 1177), or from the Old French *li Beges* after their grey penitential dress. The Beguines represented a new experiment in *women's *religious life. They earned their own living, and avoided the constraints of both marriage and *monastic enclosure. They had no founder, leader, common rule, or geographical focus, although they became most numerous and acquired their greatest degree of organization in the Low Countries and Rhineland. The origin of the Beguines should be sought in the upsurge of religious piety in 12th-century Europe, characterized by the *vita apostolica* and the intense personal devotions known as 'bridal mysticism'. They lived in their own homes, in shared houses ('convents'), or in larger communities (beguinages), and promised to remain chaste while living as a Beguine.

Beguines wrote some of the earliest vernacular religious prose and poetry in Europe. It is personal and affective, making use of both biblical material (particularly the *Song of Songs) and popular secular genres (pre-eminently courtly love, troubadour poetry). Among the most celebrated Beguine writings are Mechthild of Magdeburg's (*c.*1212–85) account of her spiritual journey, *The Flowing Light of the Godhead*, and the letters, poems, and unitive visions of Hadewijch of Brabant (written *c.*1221–40).

Although Beguines had their admirers, their extra-regular lifestyle caused unease to many churchmen, and they became associated with an *antinomian *heresy said to characterize a group known as the Free Spirit. The explicit condemnation of Beguines and their male counterparts, the Beghards, at the Council of Vienne (1311–12), led to the forced closure of many Beguine houses. Wherever they lacked powerful patrons Beguines were forced into marriage, became Franciscan or Dominican Tertiaries, or enclosed members of established orders. The larger, more organized communities, the vast majority of which had been founded between 1230 and 1270, offered the greatest protection. Beguinages were most fully developed in Flanders and Brabant, where they sometimes achieved the status of separate parishes. Individual Beguines were more vulnerable than those in community. In 1236, for instance, a Beguine called Aleydis was executed on a charge of heresy, and in 1310 Marguerite Porete was burned in Paris for continuing to circulate her book *The Mirror of Simple Souls*, which was considered heretical. After a period of decline in the 15th and 16th centuries, Belgian beguinages experienced a second period of rapid growth in the 17th century. A small number of women continue to live as Beguines today. Contemporary interest in Beguines has focused on the model they provide of semi-autonomous, women's religious communities, and on their affective, intense, and at times erotic, vernacular writings.

Fiona Bowie

Bowie, F. (ed.), *Beguine Spirituality* (1989), American edn. (1990).

McDonnell, E. W., *The Beguines and Beghards in Medieval Culture, with Special Emphasis on the Belgian Scene* (1954).

Benedictine thought.

The Rule of St Benedict, written in the second quarter of the 6th century for monks but always used by nuns as well, has proved a Christian text of immense significance. The model for western *monasticism since the 9th century and a formative influence on *religious life generally, it has had an incalculable impact on the intellectual and social history of Europe. No subsequent monastic rule has superseded it.

Compiled at Monte Cassino, Italy, and until recently considered Benedict's original work, the Rule is almost certainly, however, dependent on a text of the previous generation, the *Rule of the Master*. The handing down of monastic wisdom was taken for granted, a process reflected in the genesis of the Rule. By pruning luxuriant detail, changing or inserting passages, and adding several chapters at the end, Benedict produced a document of overall sanity and balance with a cast of mind often quite different from its predecessor's.

The opening echo of the OT book of Proverbs places the Rule in the genre of *Wisdom literature; its teaching is experiential and has to be lived in order to be understood. The monk is handed the gospel as his guide, provided with basic Christian and monastic maxims as 'tools of good works', and given instruction, supported by scripture, on the traditional monastic discipline of *obedience, silence, and humility. Recommending the teaching of other legislators to those who want to move on to 'loftier heights', Benedict locates the Rule, presented as a guide for 'beginners', in the mainstream of monastic thought.

The Rule sets forth a monk's vocation as a dynamic journey towards *God. Desire for true life is its springboard, its motivation love of Christ, humility the means, and mutual service in community the harmonious expression of that love and humility. One basic attitude is required of a novice, 'Is he really seeking God?' If he stands firm in his purpose and goes forward to profession, he makes three lifelong promises: stability, introduced for the first time in monastic legislation as a vow, which roots a monk in his community; *conversatio morum*, fidelity to the monastic way of life; and obedience, not external compliance with authority but the responsiveness of someone who has 'the ear of his heart' attuned to the promptings of the *Holy Spirit. 'Nothing is to be preferred' to love of Christ. The maxim found in the *Rule of the Master* becomes the fulcrum of the Rule, the factor which transforms obedience or a difficult relationship, so bringing a monk to perfect love and humility.

The idea of the monk striving to be constantly mindful of the presence of God is central. Desire for God, in itself a foretaste of heaven, imbues monastic theology with a sapiential, contemplative quality, evident in the writings of *Anselm and Bernard. Benedict inserts a passage to stress that this mindfulness, already the first and last step on the ladder of humility, is an essential disposition for the Work of God, the daily round of *liturgical *prayer over which nothing should take precedence.

The principle that God comes first ensures not only balance and order but also a certain suppleness and flexibility since everything else is subject to a more important consideration. Keeping the further horizon in view gives monastic life a *sacramental dimension: the monastery is not an institution but a school of the Lord's service; monks want to obey the abbot, seen to hold the place of Christ in the monastery, and even to obey one another since it is by way of obedience that they will go to God. The emphasis on mutual service, mentioned only in passing by earlier legislators but at the heart of the teaching in the chapters added at the end of the Rule, constantly reminds the monk that obedience is more than a matter of practical organization.

Benedict's development of thought on this issue springs from a less *ascetic approach to monasticism and markedly more positive view of community life than that of his predecessors. What may seem harsh at the outset, he explains, is there to serve other ends and the monk who perseveres faithfully will find in monastic life a sweetness of *love beyond telling. His last chapters tackle community life from the angle of human difficulty and weakness, revealed as opportunities to trust in God's love and to show that love to others. The teaching on mutual service is extended to the superior in a chapter inserted on the abbot, chosen normally by all or some of his monks rather than appointed by his predecessor, the prevalent practice. His office is a stewardship, placing him not above his monks but in a position to serve them.

Despite the attention paid to life in community, Benedict leaves a monk with the option of proceeding to 'the single combat of the desert' as a hermit. The Rule's fundamental openness to diversity and modification in the light of other factors of time, place, and character makes it not only eminently adaptable but capable of varied application. Cistercian and eremitical reformers of the 11th and early 12th centuries both cited the Rule in justification of their position. Benedict expected monks to remain within the enclosure but also legislated for times when this would not be possible. At one point he himself, according to the biography attributed to Pope Gregory the Great, evangelized the pagan countryside around Monte Cassino. Benedictines, from the 8th-century Apostle of Germany, Boniface, to the St Ottilien and Tutzing Congregations in the 20th century, have not been slow at times to follow his example in their understanding of monastic life.

The *worship of God, the central action in a Benedictine monastery, has always impinged on Christian life outside. Their public prayers gave the 10th-century monks of Cluny a professional standing in society. The liturgical spirituality of Gertrude the Great three centuries later made her the earliest exponent of devotion to the Sacred Heart. In the 19th century the monks of Solesmes, attentive to the aesthetic dimension, began the restoration of Gregorian Chant in the church's liturgy. Beuronese monks devoted themselves to its theology and stimulated the liturgical movement in the years preceding Vatican II.

The last hundred years have witnessed a wider Benedictine impact. Foundations made to serve the local church in mission territories led to an expansion of monastic life in Africa, Asia, and Latin America. Benedictines engaged in *dialogue with the eastern churches and fostered ecumenical relations with the religious communities emerging in the *Anglican tradition. *Bede Griffiths and Henri le Saux, alias Swami *Abhishiktananda, pioneered interchange with non-Christian monasticism, a development now officially recognized under the title Monastic Interfaith Dialogue. Benedictine scholarship, while remaining typically liturgical, patristic, and monastic, found a forum through the publication of major journals, notably *Worship* (Liturgical Press, Collegeville, Minnesota), *Revue Bénédictine* (Maredsous, Belgium), and *Studia Monastica* (Montserrat, Barcelona).

The Rule's outreach today is evident in the growing number of Benedictine secular oblates and the popularity of monastic retreats and weekends. Many people are struck by the sense of peace flowing from the integrity of monastic relationships, whether with God, the community where there is no private ownership and everything is held in common, oneself, or with creation; the Rule respects natural factors of daylight, climate, and harvest time. The rhythm of a day balanced between prayer, *lectio divina*, and *work, and of a liturgical order which recognizes *Sunday, the day of the Resurrection, as the first day of the week, is a reminder that *time does not necessarily revolve around the weekend and the return to work on Monday. New books testify that the monastic discipline of *lectio*, the art of reading a spiritual text not for information or to make it serve our purpose, but to let its words have their full impact and even change us, is being rediscovered as part of Christian life. The writings of the Cistercian Thomas *Merton and Cardinal Basil Hume, formerly abbot of Ampleforth, have introduced the insights of monastic *spirituality to a worldwide readership.

The secret of the Rule's continuing contribution to Christian life and thought lies in its synthesis of a teaching close to the heart of the gospel, ability to discern between the essential and the contingent, and insistence on the primacy given to God.

Margaret Truran OSB

Butler, Cuthbert, *Benedictine Monachism*, 2nd edn. (1924).

de Vogüé, Adalbert, *The Rule of Saint Benedict: A Doctrinal and Spiritual Commentary* (1983).

Eberle, Luke, *The Rule of the Master*, ET (1977).

Fry, Timothy, (ed.), *RB 1980: The Rule of St Benedict in Latin and English with Notes* (1981).

Gregory the Great, *The Life of Saint Benedict*, commentary by Adalbert de Vogüé (1993).

Holzherr, George, *The Rule of Benedict: A Guide to Christian Living* (1982), ET (1994).

Kardong, Terrence G., *Benedict's Rule: A Translation and Commentary* (1996).

Leclercq, Jean, *The Love of Learning and the Desire for God* (1978).

Rees, Daniel, *et al.*, *Consider Your Call: A Theology of Monastic Life Today* (1978).

bible, its authority and interpretation.

All Christians agree in ascribing *authority to the bible. But this authority is differently conceived, and has a different role, within different Christian communions.

Biblical authority in the churches

In traditional *Catholicism, the bible's authority is intimately bound up with that of church *tradition and the authority of the church's teaching magisterium. *Truth is seen as having been entrusted to the church, which through its teaching organs such as the *papacy makes that truth known afresh in each new generation. The bible, in one aspect, is the record of the church's earliest teaching, and cannot be separated therefore from the tradition handed down in subsequent centuries. But more than that, as the deposit of the original teaching of the church and hence of Christ's first *apostles the bible also has a regulative aspect: subsequent teaching must conform with it. This does not mean, however, that scripture can be appealed to as a separate source of truth over against the church's tradition, since the indefectibility of the church (defined in more recent times as its *infallibility) means that what the church authoritatively teaches always will be in conformity with the teaching of scripture, since *God himself is the guarantor of both. In modern times, since the rise of biblical criticism (see HIGHER CRITICISM) and especially since *Vatican II, Catholic thought has tended to allow somewhat more place to the autonomy of the bible as a source of doctrine, and many modern Catholic theologians grant that in some cases the church's teaching needs to be reformed in the light of scripture. Nevertheless the authority of scripture continues to be seen as a subset of the authority of tradition, not as something radically separate from it.

In *Protestantism the bible is generally conceived as something set over against the church, by which the church's teaching is to be judged. The source of authority for Christians is defined as scripture alone (sola scriptura): the message of the bible, which comes from God himself, is prior to all human—including ecclesiastical—tradition. If we then ask how the meaning of the bible is to be known without some accredited human agency of interpretation (which might seem to allow the church's magisterium in through the back door), the Protestant answer is that scripture 'is its own interpreter'. This in practice can turn interpretation into a matter for the individual believer, but in principle none of the major Protestant denominations has understood this to be the case. It is the *church, the whole assembly of all faithful Christians, to which the word of God in the bible is addressed, and it is as this word is heard faithfully that its meaning becomes apparent. When it does so, its effect is to judge the church, to challenge its traditions and its authorities in the light of the higher authority of God himself, who speaks through the human words of the text. Protestant Christians differ in how much authority they continue to ascribe to church tradition. *Anglicans, for example, have traditionally spoken of scripture and tradition as two (possibly equal) authorities, together with *reason; and *Lutherans interpret sola scriptura to mean not that only what scripture teaches can be true, but that nothing is to be accepted if scripture actually contradicts it—a softer position than that usual in *Reformed tradition. But all Protestants agree that scripture, however it is to be interpreted, has a regulative function over against ecclesiastical tradition essential to the preservation of Christian truth.

Features of scriptural text

A common feature uniting these various assessments of the role of the bible is that they all ascribe to it a special status which means it is not simply like any other collection of documents, ancient or modern. In this Christianity is not unusual. All three of the great monotheistic religions, Judaism, Christianity, and Islam, ascribe a special status to their scriptures—indeed, the word 'scripture' in itself implies documents with such a special status. Hindus, Buddhists, and Sikhs also recognize sacred writings which are not read in the same way as other books. At least four features can be recognized as characteristic of the interpretation of holy books in many different religious systems, and all can be found in Christian reading of the bible.

1. Perhaps most obviously, scriptural texts are normally interpreted as *meaningful*: it is not an allowable option, within the religious system which acknowledges their authority, to claim that texts are vacuous, self-contradictory, or simply incomprehensible. It may be freely allowed that texts are *difficult*, and indeed in some religions difficulty is itself a mark of religious authority—some early Christians argued that the difficulty of the bible was a special commendation of its sanctity. But the difficulty must always be capable of explication. Nonsensical texts are not permitted; or, to put it another way, apparent nonsense in texts calls for interpretative skill to show that it is, indeed, only apparent. This is only a heightened form of the so-called 'principle of charity' with which readers approach all texts, expecting to find meaning in them; but it never allows the principle to be frustrated.

2. Closely linked to the belief that scriptural texts are meaningful is a commitment to their *relevance*. Christians do not read the bible for antiquarian reasons, but because they believe it has things to say which are pertinent to their lives today. This relevance which the bible is perceived to have may take many forms. In the early church, the bible was often thought to be able to answer the questions then being posed about the nature of *Jesus in his relationship to God (*christology) and about the nature of the Godhead itself (*Trinitarianism). At the *Reformation the text was combed for references to the nature and proper organization of the church. Nowadays the bible is commonly appealed to in support of various political ideals (e.g. in *liberation theology) and is also read devotionally, that is, as bearing on the personal religious life and concerns of the individual Christian. All these varied interests are united by a conviction that the bible speaks to each new situation in which Christians find themselves, and that it offers resources from which guidance may be found for whatever issue may be uppermost in their minds.

3. A third mark of the bible is its *consistency*. This operates both at the level of the individual book—books are not read as self-contradictory—and also at that of the whole bible. One of the major difficulties in reconciling critical reading of the bible with a traditional religious use of it is that critical reading discloses many examples of inconsistency between one book and another, so that it is hard, if not impossible, to present 'the biblical view' on any given issue. Traditional Christianity, both Protestant and Catholic, has treated the bible as a unity, and looked for ways of reconciling (apparent?) differences within it. One difference that was important at the Reformation is the discord between *Paul's epistles and the epistle of James on the question of *justification by *faith. Because James appears to oppose this doctrine, *Luther, who saw it as the 'article by which the church stands or falls', proposed that James should be removed from the biblical canon—in his German translation he printed it as an appendix to the bible. But majority opinion in both Protestantism and Catholicism has been that, since James *is* in the bible, it is impossible that it should really be opposed to

something which is a central doctrine in Paul. Accordingly Paul and James have traditionally both been read in a way that involves no clash between their different opinions, but at worst a difference of emphasis appropriate in different circumstances.

4. Finally, scriptures the world over are read as *profound*. It is not acceptable to religious believers to interpret them in such a way that their message appears to be trivial. In church tradition one sees this belief in the fact that much of the teaching of the early church fathers is presented as commentary on scripture, which, as well as being meaningful, relevant, and consistent, is also held to have depths which can never fully be fathomed. In the modern world it can be seen in the great proliferation of biblical commentaries, which bear witness to a conviction that these ancient texts are worthy of sustained and detailed attention, that they have something momentous to tell us. It would be fatal to the authority of any scriptural book if it could be shown to be really trivial in its content. However, the tradition of regarding all the books of the bible as profound perhaps militates against this ever becoming a possibility: believers have a built-in imperative that dictates that they should look for profundity, not triviality, in scripture.

It should be noted that these four marks of scriptural books are shared fully by Catholic and Protestant interpreters, and, for that matter, by Christians in the *Eastern Orthodox churches; they are not controversial. They form the background against which all biblical interpretation in the churches is carried on.

The two Testaments

Judaism and Islam both possess a single scriptural book or collection of books which is fairly obviously from their own religious tradition, but Christianity is in a slightly more complicated position. The Christian bible consists of two parts. By far the longer part, the *Old Testament, was inherited from Judaism, so that only the (much shorter) *New Testament can be called 'Christian scripture' pure and simple. Furthermore, much of the NT involves interpretation of the OT—in other words the question of scriptural interpretation arises already *within* the canon of scripture, not just from the point of view of the church once faced with the complete bible. The early Christian claim was that Christ 'fulfilled' the OT, and this produced an attitude towards it which faced in two directions at once: on the one hand the church affirmed the OT, since Christ had done so by becoming its goal and true meaning; on the other, it declared the OT superseded as a definitive statement of God's purposes and intentions, since Christ had now declared these more fully and completely. This dual attitude may be seen as summed up in Paul's expression 'Christ is the end of the law' (Rom. 10: 4). He is the goal to which it points, and therefore vindicates it; yet he is also the abolition of that which existed *only* to point to him, which has now discharged its function and so can be dismissed.

Christianity has never found a stable answer to the question of the relation between Old and New Testaments, but has oscillated between wholehearted affirmation of these older scriptures and virtual rejection of them, though never (in orthodox faith) going all the way to either pole. There have been and are Christian denominations which regard the OT as still binding on the Christian in something like its Jewish understanding—an example would be *Adventism, in which observance of the biblical food laws is still widely practised; in others, as in some branches of Lutheranism, the

OT has been practically ignored because it has been identified with the 'law' in the negative sense that term sometimes has for Paul. *Allegorical and *typological interpretation, as practised in the early and the medieval church, offers one way of integrating the two testaments, and is still popular in Catholicism. Lutherans tend to read the OT as a foil for the NT, and many modern theologies of the OT, written from a basically Lutheran perspective, tend to follow this direction, presenting the OT as building up to a climax in Christ, who fulfils all that is good in it but also makes good its defects. Reformed Christians have on the whole had a less problematic relationship with the OT than have other Christians, seeing the two Testaments together as forming the foundation document for the Christian church, and regarding both as part of the law of Christ.

The grounds of biblical authority

While all Christians accept that the bible is authoritative, there is a surprising range of opinions about why this is so. One explanation, common in Catholic Christianity, traces its authority back to its *authorship*. The NT was written by apostles (Paul, Matthew, John) or the companions of apostles (Mark, Luke), and, since it was to them that God revealed the truth about Jesus, the NT is authenticated by having them as its authors. Similarly the OT was written by *prophets (this is also a common Jewish view) who in their own day enjoyed a similar privileged access to divine secrets. This explanation has proved difficult to sustain in the light of modern biblical criticism, which tends to regard it as unlikely that (for example) the author of the fourth gospel was *John the apostle or the author of Mark a friend of Peter. Biblical critics also see many OT books as mostly the product of centuries of growth, so that it is impossible to speak of them as having 'authors' in any straightforward sense.

A second explanation (not incompatible with the first) is to appeal to the idea of *inspiration*. Such a line of thought takes as its basis 2 Peter 1: 21: 'no prophecy [meaning, scriptural text] ever came by the impulse of man, but men moved by the Holy Spirit spoke from God'. Inspiration has been the standard account of authority in many brands of Protestantism, and is especially common in *evangelicalism, where it is sometimes but by no means always associated with the idea of dictation—the idea that God himself wrote the scriptures, using human authors (as Quenstedt put it in 1685) merely to provide the 'tongue and pen'. Other Protestants often deny that inspiration should be seen so 'literally' as this, maintaining instead that God inspired the minds of the biblical authors but that the actual words they used were their own. This position has proved somewhat unstable: is it a matter of indifference in what words thought is expressed, and, if not, can there be any inspiration of texts which is not somehow verbal, since it is of words that texts are made?

The usual Protestant assumption has been that the biblical texts are infallible precisely because they are inspired by God, who cannot lie. But it is possible to hold a kind of verbal inspiration in which the texts are *fallible yet still inspired*: God wants us to have precisely these texts, yet does not want them to be inerrant in every particular since he desires us to have faith in him, not infallible knowledge of him. A theory of this kind was developed in Catholic *modernism at the end of the 19th century, though it was suppressed by the church authorities. It has the effect of making biblical criticism licit while still according to the bible the authority Christians do accord to it.

In modern times there have been attempts at a more historically viable theory of scriptural authority, which have seen the bible as important chiefly as a *historical witness*. Biblical books are not themselves divine *revelation, but record the reactions of those who were witnesses of God's actions in ancient times. Revelation is thus located not in the texts but behind them, in the events to which the texts testify. On such an understanding inspiration is not a characteristic of the texts, but more of the underlying events. Thus, for example, God is to be encountered in the *Resurrection of Christ: Paul's epistles, such as 1 Corinthians which in ch. 15 testifies to the truth of the Resurrection, are reliable witnesses to this, not a locus of divinely revealed truth in themselves.

Authority and interpretation

Finally, it may be asked: does the authority of scripture depend on how it is interpreted, or does its interpretation depend on its authority? As we have seen, the perceived authority of the bible has in the past constrained interpreters to read it in certain ways. It has been normal to begin with the divine character of scripture, and let that dictate what kinds of interpretation are acceptable. It is only with the rise of biblical criticism since the Enlightenment that people have begun to ask pragmatically what kind of authority the bible can have, given that it has the character that biblical critics (rightly or wrongly) attribute to it. It is fair to say that theorizing about biblical authority in the church has even now not caught up with this wholly different way of putting the question. A theory of biblical authority that takes seriously the reality of historical biblical criticism is still not available.

Despite this, the majority of biblical critics are members of a faith community, Christian or Jewish, and do not perceive their commitment to biblical criticism as being at odds with their commitment to their faith. Rather than having a thoroughly worked-out theory of biblical authority, they tend to have found, pragmatically, that their detailed work on the text of the bible does not diminish but rather heightens its stature—which one might expect, if it does indeed have in some sense a divine origin. What remains mysterious is the particularity of the bible, its extremely heterogeneous contents and very diverse religious character. This has become much more apparent through the work of biblical criticism, and critics who have a religious commitment to the bible therefore tend to see Christianity itself as a highly complex and many-sided thing. It is fair to say that there is a great difference between the faith of most biblical critics and that of people who have not learned to study the bible in the way they have, yet the sense of belonging to a shared faith-community is usually stronger than these differences. Few, perhaps, come to have a religious faith through their study of the bible, but many find that such study strengthens rather than weakens the faith they already have.   **John Barton**

Abraham, W. J., *The Divine Inspiration of Holy Scripture* (1981).
Barr, J., *Holy Scripture: Canon, Authority, Criticism* (1983).
Barton, J., *People of the Book? The Authority of the Bible in Christianity*, 2nd edn. (1993).
—— *The Spirit and the Letter: Studies in the Biblical Canon* (1997).
Brown, R. E., *The Critical Meaning of the Bible* (1981).
Bruce, F. F., and Rupp, E. G., *Holy Book and Holy Tradition* (1968).
Burtchaell, J. T., *Catholic Theories of Biblical Inspiration since 1810* (1969).
Dodd, C. H., *The Authority of the Bible* (1929; repr. 1960).
Kelsey, D. H., *The Uses of Scripture in Recent Theology* (1975).
Muddiman, J., *The Bible: Fountain and Well of Truth* (1983).
Reid, J. K. S., *The Authority of Scripture* (1957).

bishop, see EPISCOPATE.

black theology

black theology is both a critique of western Christianity by African American Christians and a Christian interpretation of African American life. It expresses Afro-Christians' criticisms of western Christianity in a world largely constituted by *slavery and colonialism. It is also the continuing attempt of Christians of *African descent to understand a world not of their own making, one constricted by race and racism. Because of its location in academic *theology it involves the attempt of Christian theologians to re-order western theology. As seen by black theologians, this requires an awareness of the *contextual origins and emancipatory purposes of theological discourse.

Black theology was shaped not only by the modernism at work since the turn of the century in American academic theology but also by the civil rights and black power movements of the 1960s. These movements challenged white hegemony, expressing with a new intensity the African American tradition of social protest, going back to the beginnings of slavery in the western hemisphere. They were clearly part of the social protest sweeping the western world during the 1950s and 1960s, but in *North America this era of protest opened new visions of social inclusion or rebellion for African Americans. This was due partly to the tenor of the time, but also to the fortuitous alignment of socially progressive people within and outside the African American community. The tragedies of the 1960s are especially significant for African Americans: the many killings, especially the assassination of Martin Luther King Jr., and the violent and repressive governmental responses to the civil rebellions arising in many urban centres. These tragedies showed both the intractable power of racism and the need to resist white supremacy to the death, never losing hope in the real possibility of transforming American society. At the same time, the 1960s saw a great interest among academic theologians in divine *revelation, culture, and the relation of theology to the *social sciences, raising urgent questions about theological method. Academic theology was examining its own conditions and foundations. Black theology arose from these two dynamics, social and academic. It begins with the work of James Hal *Cone.

Martin Luther King Jr. was killed in the spring of 1968. Within a year, James Cone wrote his first book, *Black Theology and Black Power* (1969), amidst cultural and civic upheaval, followed one year later with *A Black Theology of Liberation*. These texts introduced the struggle of African Americans for *justice and *freedom into the theological arena. Cone was not the first to do this. Vincent Harding, Benjamin E. Mays, Howard Thurman, and several others stand in the immediate background. But what is significant is the level at which Cone engaged the theological world. Cone wrote with the urgency of the moment, while making a concise critique of European and Euro-American theological methods. This gave him conceptual leverage with which to propose the liberation of African Americans from the dominant paradigms of European theology.

Cone's *The Spirituals and the Blues* (1972) and *God of the Oppressed* (1975) clarified the central issues which continue to shape discussions within black theology, and issues raised more recently to a large extent build on the foundation of these two texts. Cone's response to the constructive criticisms of his earlier work sharpened his critique of white theology and outlined a fuller agenda which was to become the guiding force of black theology. His intellectual trajectory is already discernible in his dissertation on Karl *Barth's anthropology, which explored the conditions necessary for authentic knowledge of God and the human being. But it is these later texts which weave together the two central concerns of black theology: (1) a fundamental rethinking of the conditions necessary for doing theology, and (2) a sustained theological reflection on the realities of African American life.

What makes this possible is Cone's use of material from Barth and Paul *Tillich, who provide conceptual pillars on which to construct a theory of black experience. With it Cone recast the issues raised by his critics so as to supply a *hermeneutical principle, explicate a theological method, and inscribe an African presence in systematic theology. Black experience is the epistemological starting-point. Knowledge of *God begins with the experience of *Jesus Christ as one with black people in their struggle to be free. Out of this experience arises self-reflection as the basis of theological discourse. Cone's paradigm is structured by the thought of both Barth and Tillich. With Barth he rejected any possibility of a natural knowledge of God, a knowledge without specific conditions. With Tillich he excluded any theological discourse that is not an essentially cultural performance. The combination establishes a *christologically-shaped vision of black culture, rich in both its theological implications and its response to white supremacy. Black experience is by its very nature a critique of white Christianity and white theology while reflecting its own theological vision. Cone saw black experience as constituted by its particular story (slavery, *suffering, disenfranchisement), but made it into a powerful principle ensuring the emergence of a long-ignored black presence in theological discourse.

He achieved a remarkable reversal. Theological reflection, long authenticated primarily by internal factors—philosophic consistency, intellectual rigour, adherence to a tradition—was now judged by its emancipatory impact and its authenticity in terms of cultural and social realities. He had exposed theological discourse to the critique of the marginalized. African Americans gained access to theology: they could now pose critical questions to white theology itself.

Cone anticipated the correlation of worldwide *liberation struggles with the new focus among academics on the conditions for theological reflection. The outcome of currents of thought going back to the turn of the century, it has been intensified by growing interest in social, historical, psycho-analytical, and cultural studies. Cone captured the intellectual mood of the time while remaining engaged in a genuinely theological enterprise, but this achievement, together with the work of other black theologians, has raised further issues that continue to define black theology.

How does theological discourse result from particular cultural experiences? This is the question raised by the correlation of theological discourse with black experience. Once theology is understood as formed by a cultural and social context, it becomes in an important sense a cultural performance. But what is the status of that performance? Here black theology has had to confront a number of issues.

How does it relate to the black *church? As early as 1972 Cecil W. Cone (James Cone's brother) raised this question in *The Identity Crisis in Black Theology*. He pointed to a tension between black theology's dependence on European theology and its basis in African American experience, a tension also noted by Henry Mitchell in *Black Belief* (1975), *Black Preaching* (1970), *The Recovery of Black Preaching* (1977), and later a co-authored text, *Soul Theology* (1986). Black theology needed to speak to the black church to represent authentically the experience of African Americans. They identified its problem as arising from its very nature as academic theology. In a sense it was guilt by association and location. Genuine theology, they argued, must be done 'on the ground' among those for whom and to whom it wishes to speak. The real way black people live in faith must be the guiding principle for doing black theology.

Clearly this concern continues to be a major issue. While great efforts are made to show this connection to the black community, black theologians also assert the need for a critical attitude towards the black church. They wish to speak not only *for* the church but also *to* the church: there is a deep tension between the two aims, each having its own set of concerns. On one hand, proponents of black theology claim an abiding connection to the black church, conferring ecclesial authority on their theological pronouncements. On the other in the academic context they often operate in intellectual traditions critical of Christian faith and theology in general, and specifically of the church. Hence their work, if noted at all, is often looked on with not-unjustified suspicion. Many people deeply involved in the black church have noted black theology's remoteness from the everyday practices of black church people, a level at which it remains remarkably silent.

Where black theology has most clearly interacted with the church is in the analysis of *preaching. There is a growing body of work focused on this vital connection which also discloses the fact that black theology functions most easily in the field of theological method—consideration of the conditions for doing theology. Thus black homiletics shares with black theology a focus on the hermeneutic presuppositions and epistemological foundations of their respective subjects, and both must live with constant challenges to the authenticity and comprehensiveness of their analysis.

Another important concern has been the relation of black theology to African and African American religious studies. In the latter half of the 20th century scholarly attention has focused on the lives of the slaves, including their religious life. This attention was linked to the growing interest of cultural *anthropology and the other social sciences in African cultures and societies. At one level, this interest in African and slave religious life merged with black theology in a common focus on black experience. But at another level questions arose over the appropriateness of Christianity for interpreting that religious experience. Gayraud S. Wilmore, *Black Religion and Black Radicalism* (1973) and Charles H. Long, *Significations* (published in 1986, but containing essays from as early as 1967), examined this tension in terms of the relation of black *religion to black theology. What is required is recognition of an African religious consciousness as a foundation for understanding black theological reflection.

A number of important historical studies, especially John Blassingame's *Slave Community* (1972) and Albert Raboteau's *Slave Religion* (1978), reinforced the point, as did such African scholarly work as John *Mbiti's *African Religions and Philosophy* (1969), *Concepts of God in Africa* (1970), *New Testament Eschatology in an African Background* (1971), and *Biblical Revelation and African Beliefs* (1969) edited by Kwesi Dickson and Paul Ellingworth. These texts sought to bring systematic articulation to African beliefs, revealing their inner connection to Christian theology. But the chief concern was not with this connection but with the transformation of African religious consciousness in the new world of slavery and oppression. Scholarly interest in slave religion and African religious consciousness had little concern with the desire for liberation, informed by Christianity, as an essential part of black experience. It focused rather on the multiple transformations affecting African religion in the new world, and the hybrid religious forms developing in the colonialist context. Here black theology often seemed scientifically at fault, unable to contribute to further understanding of black experience, especially in terms of the slave narratives. In response black theologians sought to establish their right to interpret these narratives in terms of their essentially emancipatory character.

This conflict highlights the difficulties inherent in placing so much conceptual weight on black experience. It has served black theology well in its subversion of white hegemony in Christian theological discourse, but has kept adherents focused on the epistemological foundations of black religious consciousness. This has given the motif of liberation added significance. The desire for emancipation was seen as what actually constituted black experience. Liberation, as the link between theology and sociopolitical agendas, has always been an important concept for black theology. It naturally became a point of reference in differentiating black theology from black religious studies.

But seeing the concept of liberation as the link between theology and sociopolitical agendas has its own problems. Attention was first drawn to them in the debate between James Cone and J. Deotis Roberts. The year 1971 saw the publication of Roberts's *Liberation and Reconciliation: A Black Theology*, largely a response to Cone's *Black Theology and Black Power*. Roberts agreed with the importance of liberation for African Americans but argued that reconciliation between whites and blacks must also be central to the social and political agenda: God's action of liberation must be one with God's action of *reconciliation. Cone responded in *God of the Oppressed*, insisting that liberation must precede reconciliation: the tremendous imbalance of power between whites and blacks must be addressed before reconciliation becomes viable. The argument exposed the ambiguity in the theological concept of liberation.

A black theology of liberation presupposes advocacy of black freedom, but in what sense is that advocacy theological? The Cone–Roberts debate sought to clarify the point but the theological status of liberation was profoundly challenged in William R. Jones's *Is God a White Racist?* (1973). Jones argued that liberation, seen as a divine action in which we are called to participate, makes no sense given the terrible history of black suffering. He proposed a humanism freed from christology, liberating blacks to work for their own freedom. His book exposed the conceptual dissonance between theological discourse and any sociopolitical programme. Black theology constantly needs to justify its existence in terms of its pro-

motion of the social advancement of the marginalized. One such justification was made in the early work of Cornel West. His *Prophesy Deliverance* (1982) suggested that a black theology of liberation must evolve into an analysis and critique of western *capitalism, its ideological structures and oppressive practices. West accepted the (black) Marxist critique of (black) Christianity and offered a constructive integration of *Marxism with Christian theological vision.

In another direction, black theology was already being appropriated in the African context as a way to address racism and the history of colonialism. Allan Boesak's *Farewell to Innocence* (1977) and *Black and Reformed* (1984) signalled South African appropriation of black theology (see APARTHEID). The year 1977 also saw the historic Pan-African Conference in Accra, Ghana. The conference papers were published as *African Theology en Route* (1979). Both conference and book focused on the status of (Christian) theology in Africa in relation to the struggle for liberation, further explored by two of Cone's students, Josiah Young, *Black and African Theologies: Siblings or Distant Cousins?* (1986) and Dwight Hopkins, *Black Theology U.S.A. and South Africa* (1989). Black theology crossing the Atlantic became a further justification for its existence, asserting its usefulness to the advancement of oppressed Africans. Yet it has also intensified the question of the theological status of liberation. F. Eboussi Boulaga's *Christianisme sans fétiche* (1981; ET, *Christianity without Fetishes*, 1984) questioned the status of Christian theology in African theological discourse. While not directly linked to the introduction of black liberation theology to Africa, Eboussi Boulaga articulates the two questions raised: (1) What is the function of Christianity in a theology committed to the authentic liberation of Africans from all forms of western captivity? (2) Is not liberation a culturally specific notion requiring the context of local theologies and politics? In response, black theology has had to clarify the status of Christianity itself in its vision of liberation. This clarification presents Christianity as simply one tradition-specific resource, one result being to make a black theology of liberation even more purely a matter of theological method.

Methodological issues have also dominated the critique of black theology by black women. Beginning with Jacquelyn Grant, *White Women's Christ and Black Women's Jesus* (1989), and Katie Cannon's *Black Womanist Ethics* (1988), a new level of critique was brought to bear on the constructions of both black theology and white *feminist theology. Grant and Cannon noted the absence of black women from the theological treatment of white oppression and terrorism and suggested a theological orientation reflecting the experience of black women. They initiated a rethinking of oppression and marginalization from the standpoint of women of colour. Black and white theology were shown to be joint participants in black women's oppression. However, womanist theology (a designation borrowed from the novelist Alice Walker) still builds on the methodological foundations established by black theology.

Mercy Amba Oduyoye's *Hearing and Knowing* (1986) and *With Passion and Compassion* (1989), edited jointly with Virginia Fabella, and Delores S. Williams's *Sisters in the Wilderness* (1993), reveal these foundations and their concomitant problems. This black women's critique of theology is part of a wider critique brought by theologians of African descent, such as those from the Caribbean and *Latin America, who find their experiences overlooked in black theology's agenda. Black theology has been faulted for implicitly claiming a uniformity in the experience of oppression and the desire for liberation. The critique of black theology by womanist scholars also sharpens the questions concerning the status of Christianity in an authentically black theology. Womanist theology surmises that the absence of black women from both the critique of white oppression and the reflection on black experience indicates much more far-reaching methodological problems, such as the profound influence of patriarchy. A fundamental reconstruction of theology is needed, based on the experiences of black women in a world shaped by racism and patriarchy.

Womanist theology draws on black theology, but expresses more clearly its methodological emphasis, pressing black theology for a clearer set of methodological commitments. Do the different experiences of black men and black women present different epistemological regimes demanding fundamentally different theological agendas? What is the status of Christian tradition in terms of dogma, creeds, and confessions? Is there a christological or soteriological foundation on which black (womanist) theology must build? While the critique of western theology from a Christian position by black and womanist theology has been substantial and ground-breaking, the need now is for more theologically constructive proposals.   **Willie James Jennings**

Cannon, Katie, *Black Womanist Ethics* (1988).
Cone, Cecil W., *The Identity Crisis in Black Theology* (1972).
Cone, James H., *A Black Theology of Liberation* (1970).
—— *God of the Oppressed* (1975).
Grant, Jacquelyn, *White Women's Christ and Black Women's Jesus* (1989).
Kretzschmar, Louise, *The Voice of Black Theology in South Africa, 1971–1980* (1982).
Torres, S., and Appiah-Kubi, K. (eds.), *African Theology en Route* (1979).
Wilmore, Gayraud S., and Cone, James H. (eds.), *Black Theology: A Documentary History 1966–1979* (1979).
Young, Josiah, *Black and African Theologies: Siblings or Distant Cousins?* (1986).

Blake, William (1757–1827).

All his life, Blake saw *visions. This was his everyday reality, and whether it was his dead brother, or an OT *prophet, he would ask them questions, or, if need be, paint their portraits. His neighbours knew this and thought him somewhat mad. Those who knew him well assure us that otherwise he was sane. With a longer perspective, and the evidence of his *art and *poetry, we could well ask whether he was even more than sane.

William Blake was a tradesman's son from London. His family were *Protestant dissenters with radical views on politics, so Blake knew his bible, had little formal education, and all his days had the home and lifestyle, only slightly adjusted, of a London tradesman. Though he studied at the new Royal Academy, he went on to earn his living as an engraver. This was an obsolescent art, as printing improved, and Blake, a fiercely independent man, spent his life being under obligations to patrons and to more successful artists. He was poor at keeping to contracts, too innovative for his commercial good, and his best-known work in his lifetime had been handed over to a more fashionable engraver to make it saleable. His was a life of unacknowledged genius—nobody came to look at his exhibition in his brother's shop—but not of heartrending misery. He had an excellent wife; though he quarrelled with his patrons

they did their best for 'poor Blake'; and in his old age a group of young painters made him their guru. One patron carried him off for three years to the seaside in Sussex as his 'secretary', which did not work; London was his city. He liked to be able to see the Thames from his bedroom window, but he had no time at all for Wordsworthian ideas about learning from nature. 'Whoever believes in Nature', said Blake, 'disbelieves in God—for Nature is the work of the Devil.' We might have to investigate what values he put on '*God' and '*Devil', but certainly what mattered to Blake were the eyes of the imagination: 'Mental Things are alone Real'.

Blake was self-taught, and very much an original. Nevertheless, like all artists, he had a historical context. If we look at his paintings we can see a kinship to his friend and contemporary Fuseli, whose art is full of hunched, muscular, nightmarish figures. Training as an engraver, Blake was sent to draw the tombs in Westminster Abbey. He loved the Gothic, and often in his figures' poses there is the mannered curve of medieval art. There is also Michelangelo: Blake's *Vision of the Last Judgement* reworks the east wall of the Sistine chapel, and there is much more. He also had a negative context: he defined himself against the classic tradition of Sir 'Sloshua' (Joshua) Reynolds, the most fashionable court painter of his age. Blake was temperamentally a rebel.

The context of his *poetry is more contentious. Two poets of his own day who clearly influenced him were both purveyors of the fake antique. Chatterton pretended to have discovered medieval poems which he had written himself. Macpherson used oral tales and fragments of Gaelic poetry to construct an epic of a mythical past which he claimed to have translated directly from Ossian, an ancient Celtic bard. Some of the names and some of the misty grandiloquence of these Ossian poems are there in Blake's longer works. 'I believe both Macpherson & Chatterton, that what they say is Ancient, Is so …' Blake often rewrote history; he thought that Joseph of Arimathea brought Gothic architecture to England. On such historical detail any critical reader can pounce. But Blake is full of allusions to strange lore, where history is less precise.

It would help to know what sort of Protestant his parents were. There are passages in Blake very like the Diggers and the Ranters of Commonwealth England, radical *millenarian and anti-establishment groups of a century before. There were still similar groups in London early in the 18th century, but not much evidence later. His mother's surname comes up in the Muggletonians, who were radically dualist, distrusted reason, and met in public houses. Certainly Blake's attack on religion, brusque, combative, and earthy, resembles radical dissent, but such ideas may come up spontaneously, and have no sense of precedent. There is no proof of continuity between Blake and the Commonwealth time, but one feels there ought to be. Blake was engrossed by *Milton, the Commonwealth poet, who was nearer the Ranters than was once thought, perhaps indeed, in Blake's words, 'a true poet and of the devil's party without knowing it'.

Blake certainly joined the Swedenborgians. Emanuel Swedenborg (1688–1772) was a wide-ranging Swedish scientist who saw visions, many visions, and set up the New Church. Anyone who saw visions struck a chord with Blake; he loved *Teresa of Avila too. Swedenborgianism is complex, but liberating. Over the door of its London chapel was 'Now it is allowable'. Blake preferred this to the orthodox alternative. He says in *Songs of Experience*:

And the gates of this Chapel were shut
And 'Thou shalt not' writ over the door.

However, he quarrelled with the Swedenborgians as they became more structured, and *The Marriage of Heaven and Hell* has hostile jokes that depend on a knowledge of Swedenborg's habitual turns of phrase. But there are still Swedenborgian ideas in his later poems.

To *mystics, Swedenborg is too concrete and too modern. They find earlier sources for Blake in the tradition that includes Plotinus, Paracelsus, and Boehme. Blake met Paracelsus and Boehme in a vision, and left Swedenborg. We need not patronize Blake: he read eagerly, could learn languages without trouble, and had a sharp intelligence. Nevertheless, he was self-taught, something of a magpie, and the scholarly apparatus now available for his writings fits him too smoothly into a learned mystical counter-tradition. On the shelves where he must have found Boehme he would also find Ranters, and Blake is as much a Ranter as a Neoplatonist.

How much was he a Christian? Blake hated rules. 'The Gospel is Forgiveness of Sins & has No Moral Precepts.' The threatening God of orthodox Christianity is 'Nobodaddy'. This resembles *Gnosticism. Blake can gleefully turn everything upside down. 'This angel, who is now become a devil, is my particular friend; we often read the Bible together in its infernal or diabolical sense, which the world shall have if they behave well.' In passages such as this in *The Marriage of Heaven and Hell*, Blake is teasing us, and solemn words such as 'dialectic' miss this. Consider the comic timing in 'Christ he said—he is the only God—But then he added—And so am I and so are you'. Or the rival visions of Christ:

Thine has a great hook nose like thine
Mine has a snub nose like to mine.

Blake was a happy subversive, and it can be liberating to read him.

Students should try to see modern replica editions of Blake's own works, where the poetry and the paintings are interwoven on the page. The grinning Tyger perhaps adds little to the poem, but such strong visual images as Urizen may lead us into long-lined epic poems that otherwise seem off-putting. Alongside a great deal of the familiar imagery of the bible, Blake set himself to create his own mythology. Who are Urizen and Orc and Los? Urizen ('your reason') is the false god that sums up all that is wrong in Britain. This challenged prevailing philosophies—Blake hated the 'reason' of Locke and Newton—but his ideas were politically subversive too: 'I wander through each charter'd street', and every charter, in giving rights, excluded others less fortunate. The *Songs of Experience* speak of dark experience and a passionate hatred of oppression and injustice.

Among Blake's writings are some that seem to offer an alternative religious system—tracts such as *All Religions are One*, *There is No Natural Religion*, and the *Everlasting Gospel*. The scheme is, in technical language, immanentist and pantheist. Swedenborg had said 'God is very Man', and Blake believed in the 'human form divine': 'God is Man and exists in us and we in him.' There is in Blake a biting hostility to the norms of English religion:

And they blessed the seventh day, in sick hope:
And forgot their eternal life.

There is also a sense that 'everything comes into being through conflict'. Think again what his well-known poem *Jerusalem* means: 'Bring me my bow …'.

English Christianity, however, can domesticate almost anything, and some of Blake's *Songs of Innocence* found their way into Victorian anthologies. *Jerusalem* was given a stirring tune by Parry, and by an irony of history became almost a second national anthem, adopted by the establishment Blake so despised. His *Tyger* is known to almost every English-speaking child and, familiar as it is, still strikes the reader as hot from the furnace of Blake's visionary genius. Others have seen overtones of Marxist dialectic or *Jungian archetypes in him. None of the systems fit, but anyone who saw *angels as Blake did opens *heaven to us. 'When the Sun rises do you not see a round Disk of fire somewhat like a Guinea O no no I see an Innumerable company of the Heavenly host crying Holy Holy Holy is the Lord God Almighty'.

See also HELL.   **Alistair Mason**

William Blake, *The Complete Poetry and Prose*, ed. David V. Erdman, commentary by Harold Bloom (1982).

Ackroyd, Peter, *Blake* (1995).

Morton, A. L., *The Everlasting Gospel: A Study in the Sources of William Blake* (1958).

Raine, Kathleen, *The Human Face of God: William Blake and the Book of Job* (1982).

Thompson, E. P., *Witness against the Beast: William Blake and the Moral Law* (1993).

blood provides a primary *redemptive *symbol, ultimately derived from the *sacrificial practice of many religions. Its Christian use depends most directly on the passover rite, annually commemorating the Israelites' escape from Egypt, when they were commanded to smear the blood of a sacrificed lamb on their houses. 'When I see the blood I will pass over you … and you shall escape' (Exod. 12: 13), while the firstborn of Egypt would be slain. Again, when God later renewed the *covenant with *Israel, it was sealed sacrificially while *Moses declared 'This is the blood of the covenant' (Exod. 24: 8).

These two passages provide the textual key for interpreting the death of *Jesus preceded by a supper, seen in passover terms, at which he shares a cup of *wine, declaring 'this is my blood' of the covenant, a passage appearing in the NT no fewer than four times (1 Cor. 11: 25; Mark 14: 24; Matt. 26: 28; Luke 22: 20). For Christians, Jesus is the lamb whose blood has bought men for God (Rev. 5: 9) and, in a lengthy theological discussion of the theme, *Hebrews insists that 'if there is no shedding of blood there is no remission' (9: 22). Christians are both washed in the blood of the lamb, and drink it.

If the OT provides the basic framework for a theology of blood, symbolizing redemption and covenant, the NT transforms this symbol in various ways. First, the Johannine account of the issuing of 'blood and water' from Jesus' side on the *cross (John 19: 34) is taken to signify the way Jesus' death brings life, the *waters of *baptismal regeneration flowing out on the world. Secondly, the *eucharistic cup, 'the blood of the covenant', while ensuring that Christ's blood will continually reach believers, *sacramentalizes it into wine. While the *Temple worship involved a daily slaughter of animals, there will in Christianity be no blood-shedding. It is over once and for all. Thirdly, the 'sacrifice' of Jesus, which brings bloody sacrifice to an end, is in reality murder, simply violence. Unlike its OT predecessors, it has no divine authorization. A religion of bloody sacrifice is not only fulfilled, it is also subverted.

Henceforth, instead of blood there will be only wine. The paradoxical achievement of the Christian transformation of the religious theme of bloody sacrifice is to ensure that it remains present within its absence. If we want sacrifice, we must make do with *bread and wine. There has, however, been recurrent failure to make do with this. Hebrews already spells out an account in which the fact of Jesus' death as murder is glossed over within a priestly theme of self-offering. In late medieval and *Baroque art, the reticence in depicting the crucifixion manifest in early Christian times gives way to very gory scenes. Orders of flagellants and Good Friday rituals with flagellating processions suggest a thirst for actual blood, while a preoccupation with Christ's blood perceived rather unsacramentally led in the Catholic Church to the establishment of the Feast of the Precious Blood (1 July) in 1849. 'There is a fountain filled with blood drawn from Emmanuel's veins, And sinners plunged beneath that flood, lose all their guilty stains,' wrote Cowper (1779) in a popular hymn. This harping on blood is repugnant for many Christians, but, for others, such as the *evangelicals in the East African Balokole '*Revival' movement, 'The Blood' is Christianity's dominant symbol. In the 1950s, Balokole, refusing to swear the blood oaths of the Mau Mau movement, declared, 'I have drunk the blood of Christ, how then can I take your blood of goats?' They were martyred in consequence.

In 4th-century *Constantinople, John Chrysostom, in his third instruction to catechumens, asked 'Do you want to know the power of Christ's blood?' and proceeded from Moses via the cross to the Eucharist. In modern times, both newly instructed catechumens in Kenya and theorists of sacrificial symbolism from Evans-Pritchard to René Girard wrestle with the power of blood and its continued meaning.   **Adrian Hastings**

body.
'This is my body' is highly unusual as a sentence which appears identically in four places in the NT (Matt. 26: 26; Mark 14: 22; Luke 22: 19; 1 Cor. 11: 24). This in itself suggests its extreme importance for the *church. When *Paul wrote his first letter to the Corinthians some twenty years after *Jesus' death, its regular use in their weekly gatherings was something already established. It has been, ever since, at the heart of Christian worship in all the main traditions, linking the present both with the past, the final memory of the *disciples communing with their master, and with the *resurrected Christ alive at the Father's right hand. Precisely because the breaking of *bread sacramentalizes at the same time the body of Jesus as he sat with his disciples, his body hanging on the *cross 'given for you', and his resurrected body, there is clearly no question of a physical identity in the sense that Christ's body comes from there to here if only one could see it. The *eucharistic bread is a sign making present the Christ whose one body was alive, endured *death, and experienced Resurrection. Theological interpretation of 'this is my body' has led to centuries of often bitter discussion about the 'real presence', *transubstantiation, and the nature of a *sacrament. Nothing divided the *sixteenth-century church more intractably.

'You are the body of Christ and individually members of it' (1 Cor. 12: 27). Paul repeatedly likened the church to Christ's body.

A body has many diversified members—eye, ear, foot—so has the church many members with different functions. There are *apostles, and *prophets, and teachers, but Christ is the head. Clearly this is a *metaphor usable in a variety of ways. As head, Christ is part of the body, but he can also be seen as separate, loving his body, the church, as a bridegroom loves his bride (Eph. 5: 23–33). While employing the metaphor of a physical body or a human relationship of love, this usage suggests chiefly a social body, comparable with other social groups, united but diversified. In 1 Cor. 10: 16–17, however, a deeper, more *mystical—but also more physical—explanation is provided for the concept of the church as Christ's body: it is made so by eating the eucharistic body. 'The bread which we break, is it not a participation (koinonia, communion) in the body of Christ? Because there is one bread, we who are many are one body, for we all partake of the one bread.' If the church is a social body, it is one of a very special kind, a *communion.

This might well be claimed as the key ecclesiological text of the NT, so influential did it prove for the central traditions of both east and west. The church is made the body of Christ by eating the body of Christ. Christians become what they receive. In patristic theology the body of Christ was seen in consequence in three ways: his physical body which lived, suffered death, and is now in glory; the sacramental body received in communion; the mystical body which is the church. This remained fairly standard terminology for a thousand years. However, in the west it changed in the high Middle Ages. As popular devotion to the sacramental body increased, notably with the feast of Corpus Christi established in the 13th century, it came to take over the term 'mystical body'. In the same period, with the organizational development of the western church under papal rule, the church itself came to be seen less as a mystical unit and more as a social and governmental one headed by the *papacy. Visibility was stressed. In consequence a sacramental understanding of the church's nature, together with the dynamism inherent in the relationship of the three modes of Christ's body, fell by the wayside. Against this organizational visibility the reformers of the 16th century stressed the invisibility of the church constituted by *faith, *predestination, *grace, or *love, but mostly without questioning that visibly it is constituted by preaching and the sacraments.

A more traditional understanding of the church's bodiliness (never lost in the east) began to be recovered in the Catholic west with the work of Johann Adam Möhler of the *Tübingen school in the 19th century under both Protestant and patristic influence. In England, Henry Edward Manning was a striking protagonist of the church as 'mystical body'. This recovery became more widespread, both in Catholicism and Anglicanism, from the 1930s. A powerful force here was the two-volume work on the *Mystical Body of Christ* by the Jesuit Émile Mersch (1933; ET 1938). In the Church of England a school of writers including A. G. Hebert, Dom Gregory Dix, Lionel Thornton, and Eric Mascall produced a series of books portraying the church as the body of Christ, while in 1943 Pius XII's encyclical *Mystici Corporis* encouraged the revival of 'Mystical Body' theology while still defining it firmly in terms of an institutional unity dependent on its papal headship. It is noteworthy that the encyclical never referred to 1 Cor. 10: 16–17. In contrast, the next year *de Lubac's *Corpus Mysticum* explored with immense learning the traditional teaching on how the eucharistic body 'makes' the ecclesial body.

*Vatican II followed de Lubac rather than Pius XII. It not only repeatedly emphasized the doctrine of the church as Christ's body but stated this in eucharistic terms. Thus 1 Cor. 10: 17 was quoted twice in ch. 1 of *Lumen Gentium*. The difference between these two views is considerable in itself and of great practical consequence. In the one the unity of the body with Christ is assured through the church's 'head', the pope as vicar of Christ, and is defined in terms of papal communion; in the other, unity with Christ is assured eucharistically and, therefore, locally. Communion flows upwards, not downwards.

A fully sacramental theology of the body has necessarily to be a theology of flesh. If for Paul the eucharistic bread is a participation in 'the body of Christ', the main NT commentary upon its meaning is in John 6, where Jesus proclaims himself 'the bread which came down from heaven' but then identifies that bread more specifically with 'my flesh' which must be eaten to give life. The eucharist thus becomes an extension of the *Incarnation. In 1 John (4: 2) the writer attacks 'false prophets' who deny that 'Jesus has come in the flesh' while *Irenaeus, a century later, argues against *Gnostics for 'the salvation of the flesh' rather than 'salvation from the flesh', by insisting that the materiality of the Eucharist guarantees that our bodies, the 'substance of our flesh', and not only a soul within us, can be saved. 'The resurrection of the flesh' ('body' in most English usage) was the final article in the early Roman creed and became part of the Apostles' *Creed.

Modern and *postmodern preoccupation with embodiment and the sociology and anthropology of the body can be seen as a reaction to the separation of mind and meaning from materiality and particularity characteristic of Cartesianism (see DESCARTES) and the *Enlightenment, a separation perhaps reflecting earlier Protestant insistence on the invisibility of the church. The significance of the theology of the body of Christ is both that it held Christian *asceticism back from any outright attack of a *dualist kind on the goodness of bodiliness, and that it united the physical and the spiritual in so profound a way as to undercut the enlightened tendencies which the modern concern with embodiment is countering. It is to be noted that this theology of the body was not a product of 'medieval' conditions; it dates from the very beginning of the Christian tradition, an extension of the theology of the Incarnation.

Adrian Hastings

Brown, Peter, *The Body and Society: Men, Women, and Sexual Renunciation in Early Christianity* (1988).

de Lubac, Henri, *Corpus Mysticum* (1944).

McPartlan, Paul, *The Eucharist Makes the Church: Henri de Lubac and John Zizioulas in Dialogue* (1993).

Mascall, Eric, *Corpus Christi* (1953).

Mellor, Philip A., and Shilling, Chris, *Re-forming the Body: Religion, Community, and Modernity* (1997).

Boff, Leonardo

(1938–   ), Brazilian *Franciscan theologian. Boff, who studied theology and philosophy in Brazil (Curitiba and Petrópolis) and in Germany (Munich), is a prolific writer, with more than twenty books and numerous articles and essays to his credit. He developed the *christology of *liberation theology, as well as contributing extensively to a variety of themes relating to ecclesiology, *spirituality, and *ecology. Boff's christology was a first attempt to produce an authentic *Latin American reflection on Christ. He gave priority to the *humanity of Christ and to the historical *Jesus, highlighting the liberative praxis of the *gospels. According to Boff, Jesus' death was the product of a coherent life serving the poor and denouncing injustices. Jesus died as a result of confronting structures of *sin. To follow Jesus means to be committed to liberating the poor (see POVERTY). Boff also dedicated his work to the *basic ecclesial communities which he considers a legitimate expression of the *church of the poor in Latin America. He identifies the role of the Roman Catholic Church as a '*sacramental sign' of universal *salvation. The church's *mission is to defend and encourage the goodness of human initiatives such as social movements, even if these seem to be outside the church. This is Boff's 'Theology of Captivity' where the church, faced with difficult situations, must consider alliances with movements which promote human dignity and rights. It was his ecclesiology, based on charisms rather than hierarchical structures, that led in 1985 to his silencing by the Vatican for one year. In 1992 he resigned from the *priesthood and left the Franciscan order, declaring that he was forced to do so by the continuous restrictions and punishments he was suffering from the church.

See also BONINO, JOSÉ MÍGUEZ; JUSTICE; POLITICAL THEOLOGY.

Marcella Althaus-Reid

Boff, L., *Jesus Christ Liberator* (1980).

—— *Church: Charisma and Power* (1985).

Boff, L., and Elizondo, V., *Ecology and Poverty* (1991).

Bonhoeffer, Dietrich

(1906–45), *German *Lutheran theologian. Bonhoeffer has proved one of the most provocative and seminal influences on Christian life and thought since the Second World War. His story is full of paradoxes. His native Lutheranism had inculcated in generations of German Protestants a sharp divorce between the realms of *faith and *politics, and bred an attitude of quiescent obedience to the state. Yet Bonhoeffer was hanged by the Nazis for his part in the conspiracy against Hitler. He was deeply devout, his daily routine fed by *prayer and biblical meditation, but has become famous especially for his writings from prison which call for a 'religionless Christianity' to be practised in a 'world come of age' where human questions can be answered 'without God'.

Bonhoeffer was brought up in Berlin where, after studying in *Tübingen and Rome, he completed his theological studies. His first published works were his doctoral and post-doctoral theses, respectively *Sanctorum Communio* and *Act and Being*. These sought to pull together Karl *Barth's emphasis on the unique self-*revelation of the transcendent God through his *Word, with an understanding of human existence as essentially social. Revelation becomes earthed in the church as a human community. Indeed, 'The Church is Christ existing as community.' After a student pastorate in Barcelona, and a year as an exchange student in New York, Bonhoeffer took a lecturing post in Berlin in 1931. By now he was querying the traditional Lutheran interpretation of the *Sermon on the Mount as an unrealizable 'ideal', and seeing it instead as the command of Jesus to be obeyed concretely: above all, in the command to *peace and non-violence. He became active in the ecumenical peace movement. Hitler's arrival in power in 1933 and the onset of the Church Struggle saw Bonhoeffer an unequivocal supporter of the Confessing Church, above all in its rejection of the 'Aryan clause' which would have meant exclusion of pastors of Jewish descent (see BARMEN DECLARATION).

From late 1933 to 1935 Bonhoeffer was pastor of the two German congregations in London, and then returned to Germany as director of one of the Confessing Church's illegal seminaries at Finkenwalde on the Baltic coast. Here his teaching became extremely biblically focused, as seen in his classic *The Cost of Discipleship* and his exposition of Christian community, *Life Together*. In the summer of 1939, faced with the prospect of conscription into Hitler's army, Bonhoeffer accepted an invitation to work in the USA. Within days of arriving in New York he decided to return home, despite the obvious dangers, to be in solidarity with his church and his people. In war-time Germany, through the offices of his brother-in-law Hans von Dohnanyi (who was masterminding much of the civilian side of the conspiracy against Hitler) Bonhoeffer was drawn into the resistance, aiming to use his *ecumenical contacts abroad (such as his great English friend Bishop George Bell) for communication between the resistance and the allies. In this context he wrote his *Ethics*, a series of profound reflections on responsibility before God in a world of unsurpassed *evil where even attempts to do the good are infected with ambiguity. Bonhoeffer, who had earlier espoused near-*pacifism, knew he was now faced with the choice between becoming guilty through complicity in a plot which would involve violence against the *Führer*, or becoming guilty in the complicity of inaction over the unspeakable fate of millions of innocents, above all the Jews (see HOLOCAUST). In the light of the crucified Christ, 'real innocence shows itself precisely in a man's entering into the fellowship of guilt for the sake of other men' (*Ethics*, p. 210).

Bonhoeffer was arrested in April 1943 and placed in Tegel Prison, Berlin, where he began his remarkable clandestine correspondence with his friend Eberhard Bethge. From the end of April 1944 his letters took a radically new theological turn in struggling to answer his own searching question 'Who is Jesus Christ, indeed who is God, for us today?' Transported south in early 1945, he was still searching, and still praying, when he was hanged at Flossenbürg barely a month before the end of the war.

Precisely because, for all his Lutheranism, he so decisively rejected sheer acquiescence in the state as a divine ordering, Bonhoeffer presents a unique challenge to Christianity to take a prophetic stance towards any misuse of political power. As early as April 1933, little more than two months after Hitler came to power, Bonhoeffer had asked his fellow-Lutherans whether the plight of the Jews might not require the church to do more than question the state about its actions, or to aid the victims of its oppression, but actually 'to put a spoke in the wheel itself'. It was seven years before Bonhoeffer himself began active involvement in the political conspiracy. But the question was always there and was eventually more than adequately answered. If the plot against Hitler, which reached its climax on 20 July 1944, had succeeded, Bonhoeffer would have demanded that the church's first response be to read from all pulpits a confession of its own guilt by acquiescence and silence in face of the Nazi terror, and above all in the fate of the Jews.

Successively, from his early dissertations to his prison writings, Bonhoeffer reorganized his theology to meet new situations. In each context, major ingredients of his theology remain the same. The constants are: with Karl Barth, the transcendent, 'wholly other' God known only in his word in Jesus Christ; an equal emphasis upon the truly *incarnate, wholly human, nature of that Christ whose existence is wholly 'for us', as portrayed in *Luther's theology of the *cross; and the irreducibly social nature of human existence which finds (or should find) its fulfilment in the communal life of the church where people, *forgiven and forgiving, live for each other. In the prison writings, the context of the modern world at large, which finds 'God' increasingly unnecessary and irrelevant, forces Bonhoeffer back to his basic theological elements in a quite new way.

Hitler had appealed to vast numbers of Protestants and Catholics by lacing his rhetoric with pious allusions to '*Providence' and 'protecting Christianity'. For Bonhoeffer, the acid test about claims to Christianity lay in what was happening to one's neighbour, of whatever race or belief. It should be no surprise then, that in his prison writings '*religion' should be such a suspect word. Karl Barth had already sharply contrasted the *gospel with 'religion' seen as a kind of innate human capacity for the divine, an attempt to evade the truly divine *judgement and *grace. Bonhoeffer agrees with Barth but feels that he has not gone far enough. It is all very well to say that God can only be known in Christ. But *who* is this Christ for us today, asks Bonhoeffer, and where and how may he be found? Christianity seen as a 'religion' has answered: God is to be found 'beyond' this world, in the hereafter, or in the shrinking area of unsolved 'problems' as yet unexplained by science, or in the shadowy recesses of the individual soul being probed by *existentialism or psychotherapy. Religion calls on God as a last resort for succour.

Increasingly, Bonhoeffer argues, humankind has for centuries been learning to do without such a God, thanks to the natural and human *sciences. Religion, as an individualistic, metaphysical concern for survival beyond this world is no longer a real option in a world 'come of age'. People must now accept responsibility for themselves and their world and live 'as if God were not given'. But paradoxically, it is with precisely such recognition that God is encountered anew: 'Before God and with God we live without God. God lets himself be pushed out of the world on to the cross' (*Letters and Papers from Prison*, p. 360). It is the God who thus suffers in Christ, 'the Man for others', who transforms us by calling us to share his own *sufferings and be caught up in his own existence for others. That is the true experience of 'transcendence', in all its worldliness. Religion resorts to God as an answer to human weakness. Christ confronts humanity in its strength and maturity, in the call and offer of a new life for others. This has radical implications for the church, which must adopt a new way of serving people at the heart of their existence, rejecting the temptation either to seek domination over people, or to retreat to the 'religious' margins of modern life.

For all their fragmentariness, few modern theological writings have had such widespread appeal as Bonhoeffer's prison letters. His posthumous influence is in fact very varied. At one level there is simply the pervasive effect of his witness as one who took on the *twentieth century at the very heart of its greatest trauma and out of that cauldron called for a fresh look at the meaning of Christian faith. Equally, he is susceptible to misuse. He can be so admired as a shining example of Christian heroism that the simple question may be forgotten: why were there so few Bonhoeffers in Nazi Germany?

Certain specific and important ways in which he has been influential can be identified. For example, Bonhoeffer was greatly influential in the 'radical' and *'secular' theology movements in western Protestantism in the 1960s, especially through his emphasis on 'the world come of age'. Bishop John *Robinson made much use of him (alongside *Bultmann and *Tillich) in his best-selling *Honest to God* (1963). Whether Bonhoeffer would have recognized his intentions in the works of such authors is another matter. For one thing, Bonhoeffer was not seeking to provide the usual *liberal apologetic which tries to make God 'acceptable' to 'modern thought' (there he was uneasy with Bultmann). Rather, he sought to confront and challenge the modern world with something quite new in the 'worldliness' of Jesus and the gospel. For another, Bonhoeffer in his prison writings calls for a period of silence about Christian doctrine, a 'secret discipline' whereby Christianity confines itself to prayer and righteous action until it has found the right interpretation of the doctrinal tradition for the modern world. It is therefore ironic that his writings were exploited with so much verbosity in the rush for a new interpretation by 'secular theology', however creative.

Bonhoeffer has greatly influenced ecumenical life and thought, with his vision of the international Christian community as a witness for peace among the nations, and his recognition that the true mission of the church lies not in its own upbuilding but in the preservation, *reconciliation, and healing of the world. The Programme to Combat Racism which the World Council of Churches set up in 1968 shocked many white, western Christians in the north, but many in the Third World saw it as an answer to Bonhoeffer's challenge. Equally, the WCC's late-1980s programme, Justice, Peace and the Integrity of Creation, owed much to a rediscovery of Bonhoeffer's call in the 1930s for the convening of a great ecumenical council of the churches to summon the world to peace and to the rejection of *war.

But Bonhoeffer's influence has nowhere been so conspicuous as in his challenge to the churches to stand up to politicized evil in specific situations. He was deeply important, for instance, in the struggle against *apartheid in South Africa—where the parallels with Nazi Germany in racism, militarism, and a conformist Christianity could hardly be missed. That will not be the last context to which the imprisoned Bonhoeffer says so much in so few words: 'The church is the church only when it exists for others'.

Keith Clements

Bonhoeffer, D., *The Cost of Discipleship*, ET (1959).
—— *Ethics*, ET (1955).
—— *Letters and Papers from Prison*, ET (1971).
Bethge, E., *Dietrich Bonhoeffer* (1970).
Feil, E. (ed.), *International Bibliography on Dietrich Bonhoeffer* (1998).
Gruchy, J. de, *Dietrich Bonhoeffer: Witness to Jesus Christ* (1988).

Bonino, José Míguez

(1924–   ), Argentinian Protestant theologian, born in Santa Fe. Bonino graduated in Theology from ISEDET (Evangelical Higher Institute for Theological Studies), Buenos Aires, and worked as a Methodist minister in parishes in Bolivia and Argentina for more than a decade, before obtaining a doctorate from Union Theological Seminary, New York. He became a lecturer in Christian ethics and rector of ISEDET.

Bonino was one of the first theologians to develop a Protestant theology of *liberation and was an observer during *Vatican II. He was also one of the founder leaders of ISAL (Movement for Church and Society in *Latin America). Bonino elaborates on the *political praxis and concrete commitment that is required from liberation theologians. This praxis mediates in the relation between the *Kingdom of God and the historical task demanded of Christians when confronting structures of oppression. Liberation theology cannot claim political neutrality and must acknowledge the historical and ideological mediations to which it is subjected. There is a *hermeneutical need to be specific in the denunciation of injustices, based on a sociopolitical analysis which should include *Marxist theory, differentiating between scientific Marxism and Marxist ideology. Political and *social sciences provide the theoretical framework of analysis to understand the people's experience in their struggle against oppression. Finally, Bonino demands from theology a sense of concreteness when referring to *poverty, and the search for a faith which must be efficacious beyond rhetoric. During the 1970s Bonino was active in confronting issues of human rights violations in Argentina. His work has undoubtedly been deeply influential in providing a bridge between liberation theology and Protestant circles, both in Latin America and in the wider world.

See also BOFF, LEONARDO; JUSTICE.   **Marcella Althaus-Reid**

Bonino, J. M., *Revolutionary Theology Comes of Age* (1975).
—— *Christians and Marxists* (1976).
—— *Towards a Christian Political Ethics* (1983).

bread. 'I am the bread of life', declares the *Jesus of *John's gospel (6: 35) in the most extensive of its *symbolic tracts, triggered off by the miracle of five barley loaves feeding the five thousand. At his last supper, Jesus took bread and blessed it, saying 'this is my body' (1 Cor. 11: 24; Mark 14: 22 and parallels). Bread becomes the central *eucharistic symbol of his ongoing presence and activity. It was at the breaking of bread that the disciples at Emmaus recognized the Lord (Luke 24: 30–5). But the bread–*body equivalence is ecclesiological as well as christological. *Augustine's remark that when a priest holds up the bread at mass saying 'This is my body', he refers both to the bread (sacrament of Christ's physical body) and the congregation (his mystical body), becomes a recurrent theme. The ease with which the idea of bread as nourishment can come to represent the nourished body ties in with *Paul's insistence on the *church as an organic body when coupled with his 'because there is one bread, we who are many are one body, for we all partake of the one bread' (1 Cor. 10: 17). This is reflected in the early 2nd-century prayer of the *Didache*, 'As this bread that is broken was scattered upon the mountains, and gathered together, and became one, so let the church be gathered together from the ends of the earth.'

In medieval devotion the consecrated bread became supremely symbolic of Christ's earthly presence, in the pyx where the sacrament was reserved for the sick and in the processions of the feast of Corpus Christi; yet the very insistence upon the reality of the presence came, in the doctrine of *transubstantiation, to threaten its symbolic foundation in the reality of bread. Furthermore, the neat, unleavened form of the wafer could add to the symbolic confusion. While transubstantiation denied the enduring 'substance' of bread, the form of wafer could obscure the 'accidents'. Yet at the end of the day this has to be the 'bread of heaven', or both doctrine and ritual were undermined.

If bread has both christological and ecclesiological connotations, this significance still grows out of a basic humanitarian one. Bread is a matter of human need and productivity: 'Give us this day our daily bread'. The verbal identity between *Lord's Prayer and eucharistic formula is vital. Bread in the former signifies food at its most basic, but still 'the product of human hands'. Ecclesiastical insistence that the eucharistic bread be wheaten must undermine that identity in climates where wheat cannot be grown. 'Bread for the World' is the name of one of the largest modern Christian charities, referring to something not only universally needed but also obtained only through human production, much as we may pray for it. Bread's linkage of meaning stretches from basic foodstuff and human productivity to the presence of Christ in the world and the form of the church as a society breaking bread together.

Adrian Hastings

Brethren, archaic form of 'brothers'. Christians who call themselves Brethren live in close-knit congregations and refuse to conform to the *world.

There were friars (which means brothers) and Brethren of the Common Life in medieval Catholicism, the Moravian *Unitas Fratrum* (Unity of Brothers) predated the Reformation, but the German Brethren started in 1708. In the Rhineland Palatinate, led by Alexander Mack, 'eight persons agreed to establish a covenant of a good conscience with God … united with each other as brothers and sisters in the covenant of the cross of Jesus Christ as a church of Christian believers'. Under pressure, the church moved to tolerant Pennsylvania, and became Pennsylvania Dutch (*deutsch*, German).

These Brethren fall between Anabaptists and *Pietists. They practise adult baptism, with three dips in the threefold name, so earning their nickname Dunkers. But they never had a ban on dissidents as did the Anabaptists, though some Brethren practised avoidance. They were less suspicious of civil government than Anabaptists, but like them distrusted alcohol. Unlike Pietists, they withdrew from large churches. They saw no need for an educated ministry, and so their differences were not explained or rationalized in terms of abstract theology. Quarrels were seldom over theology, rather over how to copy Christ and the apostles. In foot-washing, for example, can one person wash and another dry, if Christ did both? Their eucharist is a bread-breaking after a supper, a real meal round a table, which begins, like the Last Supper, with foot-washing.

There were Pennsylvania Dutch folk customs—the fringe of beard without a moustache, the anti-war testimony, the deliberate simplicity, and antique dress. When they split, the middle way between Old Order and Progressive called themselves Conservative. Many of their people went over to the *Universalists (the Brethren had a rather embarrassed belief that all would be saved) and to 19th-century *Restorationism, which resembles Brethren 'restitutionism' (copying the apostles) but was much more eager to recruit members. Slowly, however, the German Brethren became Americanized, more educated, more willing to be *revivalist in their methods, more ecumenical. There is a traditionalist fringe, of Old German *Baptist Brethren and others, who have scruples about accepting social security benefits, or using translations other than the King James Version. Inward-looking, they explain that 'Go ye into all the world' refers specifically to the twelve apostles, not to them. The bible says we should 'greet one another with a holy kiss', and so 'the brethren greet the brethren and the sisters the sisters, and between the sexes we greet with a handclasp'.

In Britain, the term refers to Plymouth Brethren, who arose *c.*1829. Like Restorationists in America, they had no intention of setting up a denomination. The word 'Brethren' meant they were just Christians, meeting informally in small groups, and expecting Christ's imminent second coming. Their leader, John Nelson Darby (1800–82), was an Anglican clergyman whose sacrificial saintliness was evident to the Catholic peasantry of Ireland as he tramped round their villages preaching. The Brethren became a denomination, or rather a number of denominations, splitting and splitting again. In America the census labelled the varieties P.B. I to VIII, as the groups refused to take distinctive names. The first organization, and the first division, was in Plymouth, in the south-west of England. The Brethren celebrated the Lord's supper together, weekly, in private houses, and split, in 1848, between Open and Exclusive, on whether the table should be open to all professed Christians, or only to those belonging to other, exclusive, meetings. Darby became the theologian of the Close or Exclusive wing. His theology was basically Calvinist, though Brethren do not have formal creeds. Technically, he taught 'pre-tribulation pre-*millenarianism', that Christ would come at the start of the end-times, which was soon, and the 'rapture of the saints' ('one shall be taken and the other left').

Brethren ideas, from Darby, and from Fred Grant's *Numerical Bible*, underlay much of *Dispensationalism. The shift in large sections of *evangelical opinion during the second half of the 19th century from a post-millennial hope that the conversion of the world, even the Jews, was on its way, to the gloomy pre-millennial belief that we were heading swiftly to catastrophic judgement was very largely due to Brethren influence. Though Darby was not one of the Open Brethren, they were agents in spreading his ideas, particularly in the 20th century through entering pan-evangelical work, such as Inter-Varsity associations and Billy Graham crusades. They played a part in publishing *The Fundamentals* too (hence '*fundamentalism'). The Open Brethren have had influence far beyond their numbers.

Some Exclusive Brethren drew apart from the world, worrying about being 'unequally yoked with unbelievers'. They would withdraw from professional associations, and avoid sitting down for meals with people, even family members, not in the meeting. The rigorist, autocratic claims of Jim Taylor Jr. split the Brethren in the 1960s. They risked new ideas on *christology: 'in person He is God, in condition He is Man'. The basic tradition remains of a very biblical lay piety in small meeting-halls with 'If the Lord will, the Lord's Word will be preached' on the board outside.

The word 'Brethren' is not copyright. In Africa the Brethren are revivalist. There were surviving Lollards calling themselves Christian Brethren in England in the 1520s. The Brethren from Germantown in Pennsylvania and from Plymouth have little in common beyond the name. They both have rigorist wings, with something of the spirit of the elder brother too apparent. Even to outsiders, there is also undeniable simplicity and goodness. Catholics see churches like these as resembling married religious orders. In the

1720s at Ephrata a celibate community of mystics arose from the Brethren. Both Brethren traditions make more of the Lord's Supper than many Protestants, but still the central fact is that both are steeped in the Bible.

See also MENNONITE THOUGHT.   **Alistair Mason**

Bowman, Carl, *Brethren Society: the Cultural Transformation of a 'Peculiar People'* (1995).

Coad, F. Roy, *History of the Brethren Movement* (1968).

Durnbaugh, D. F., 'Brethren in Early American Church Life', in F. E. Stoeffler (ed.), *Continental Pietism* (1976).

—— (ed.), *The Brethren Encyclopaedia* (1983).

Rowdon, H. H., *The Origins of the Brethren* (1967).

Sandeen, E. R., *The Roots of Fundamentalism: British and American Millenarianism, 1800–1930* (1978).

Brown, Raymond E. (1928–98).

A leading figure in Roman *Catholic biblical scholarship, Raymond Brown combined a sharp critical mind with an unswerving loyalty to church teaching. A long-serving member of the Pontifical Biblical Commission, he insisted that the bible must be read within the tradition of the church. Despite his formidable scholarship, attested by more than 25 honorary doctorates and his unique triple presidency of the Catholic Biblical Society of America, the Society of Biblical Literature, and the International Society of New Testament Studies, his approach was notably pastoral. He made a point of wearing clerical dress when lecturing, devoting himself to the diffusion of the findings of biblical scholarship among non-specialists. He lectured widely all over the English-speaking world, giving popular courses as well as academic seminars, becoming well known to an even wider audience by the ready distribution of tapes of his courses.

His published output included volumes of exhaustive research, notably the Anchor Bible *Gospel according to John* (1966; 1970), *The Birth of the Messiah* (1977; re-edited 1994), *The Death of the Messiah* (1994), and finally *An Introduction to the New Testament* (1997). Arguably more important and stimulating were the frequent smaller works, such as *The Churches the Apostles Left Behind* (1984). He was also one of the three editors of the important one-volume *Jerome Biblical Commentary* (1969; 1990).

A valued element of his work was its ecumenical dimension. He was the first Catholic to hold tenure at Union Theological Seminary, New York, where he was Auburn Professor for two decades. During *Vatican II he was the first Catholic to address the *Faith and Order Commission of the World Council of Churches, and for 25 years was a member of that Commission. This work issued in two ecumenical studies of which he was co-editor, *Peter in the New Testament* (1973) and *Mary in the New Testament* (1978).

Henry Wansbrough

Buddhism.

When Christians meet Buddhism, it is not a case of one Christianity meeting one Buddhism. Buddhism contains within itself different language worlds, historical legacies, and cultures—Chinese, Japanese, Tibetan, South Asian—and its transposition to the west is creating yet new forms. Each context contains a different dynamic of encounter. Yet, in all contexts, well-known signposts may be missing for the Christian: a creator God, a Saviour, forgiveness for sin. The two *religions might seem to inhabit different worlds. Yet, potential touching points are numerous. Both Buddhism and Christianity look back to one, charismatic, historical

figure. Both recognize a radical dislocation at the heart of existence caused by greed and selfishness and affirm the importance of self-lessness, *compassion, non-violence, and social harmony. Both use silence as entry into the spiritual life and respect the voluntary *poverty of *monasticism.

Christian encounter with Buddhism stretches back to the early years of Christianity, as Buddhism travelled north from India along trading routes. A Christianized version of the biography of the Buddha actually entered the medieval Christian calendar in the figure of St Josaphat (or Joasaph), known for his *asceticism and awareness of suffering. Few records of this early interaction exist. In more recent times, European expansionism combined with *missionary activity brought Christians face to face with Buddhism through observation, *dialogue, and textual study. By the end of the 19th century, attitudes had polarized. Condemnation of Buddhism as degrading, nihilistic, *atheistic, and morally impotent was widespread, influenced by figures such as Robert Spence Hardy (1803–68), Methodist missionary to Ceylon. Yet, there were also Christians who praised Buddhism as gentle, rational, and life-giving. Sir Edwin Arnold's poem, *The Light of Asia* (1879), which claimed that the Buddha gave Asia 'light that still is beautiful, conquering the world with spirit of strong grace' and the positive attitude of missionaries such as Timothy Richard (1845–1919) in China and Arthur Lloyd (1852–1911) in Japan contributed to this.

In the 20th century, negative appraisals of Buddhism continued to fuel mistrust among Buddhists towards Christians in several countries. Buddhist monks in Sri Lanka boycotted a visit by Pope *John Paul II in January 1995 because of the characterization of Buddhism in his book, *Crossing the Threshold of Hope*. Yet there has been increased recognition of the value of Christian–Buddhist *rapprochement*. One western pioneer was Thomas *Merton, who called for an international and inter-religious monastic, spiritual encounter. Since his premature death at the 1968 Bangkok meeting of 'L'aide à l'implantation monastique' (AIM), an international network of groups involved in Buddhist–Christian inter-monastic dialogue has developed, inspired by his vision.

In the 1960s, Christians in several Asian countries were also reaching out towards Buddhism. In *Japan, H. M. Enomiya Lassalle and J. Kachiri Kadowaki, *Jesuits, were discovering that Zen meditation could contribute positively to Christian spirituality. In Sri Lanka, a group of young priests was attempting to reverse the legacy of mistrust left by western missionaries. Yohan Devananda, Anglican, had formed a Christian ashram influenced by Buddhist practice. Lynn de Silva, Methodist, called for informed debate so that, 'right understanding can be the basis of unity' (*Daily News*, Sri Lanka, 2 August 1966). Aloysius Pieris, Jesuit, was immersing himself in Buddhist religiosity and calling other Christians to a similar baptism. Similar movements could be seen in other countries.

In the 1970s, academic research into Buddhist–Christian relationships grew through institutions such as the Ecumenical Institute for Study and Dialogue in Sri Lanka and the Roman Catholic Nanzan Institute for Religion and Culture in Japan. Particularly important was the East–West Religions Project, started in 1980 by the University of Hawaii Department of Religion. This gave rise to a series of international Buddhist–Christian conferences from which regional initiatives arose, such as a Japan chapter of the project (1982) and the North American Buddhist–Christian theological encounter group under Masao Abe and John Cobb (1983). The 1987 Conference gave birth to the Society for Buddhist–Christian Studies. A parallel organization, the European Network of Buddhist–Christian Studies, was formed in 1997.

A spectrum of attitudes towards Buddhism is present within these developments. Some Christians stress similarity at the expense of difference, particularly at the level of *spirituality, often through contact with Zen meditation practice with its emphasis on non-dual, direct perception of reality. Some of these would wish to call themselves Buddhist–Christians. Others recognize difference and yet seek to transcend it either in joint social action based on common values or through shared silent meditation practice. Yet others prefer to probe differences and similarities at a conceptual level.

Topics which arise as a result include: resurrection and the concept of 'the deathless'; the figure of Buddha and the figure of Jesus; *sunyata* (emptiness) and *kenosis (self-emptying); *liberation theology and socially engaged Buddhism; agape and compassion; nirvana and the *Kingdom of God; religion and violence; 'other power' and 'own power'; redemption and liberation.

Within such exploration, some Christians seek doctrinal convergence, for example acceptance that nirvana and the experience of God could be the same at the level of ultimate reality. Others such as Michael von Brück in Germany and Aloysius Pieris in Sri Lanka stress not only that difference must be respected but that the differences are an opportunity for the remaking and enriching of both traditions as each helps the other to rediscover and interrogate itself. Hence, the Buddhist practice of meditation can help Christians rediscover their own contemplative tradition and the lack of a creator God concept could help Christians detect abuses in their own concept of God. Each encounter between the two religions then becomes part of a dynamic process of change, which could have profound consequences for both religions. Within this spectrum the consensus is that the meeting between Buddhism and Christianity is an exciting one.   **Elizabeth J. Harris**

Cobb Jr., J. B., and Ives, C. (eds.), *The Emptying God* (1990).
MacInnes, E., *Light Sitting in Light* (1996).
Pieris, A., *Love Meets Wisdom: A Christian Experience of Buddhism* (1988).
Smart, N., *Buddhism and Christianity: Rivals and Allies* (1993).
von Brück, Michael and Walen Lai, *Buddhismus und Christentum: Geschichte, Konfrontation, Dialog* (1997).

Bultmann, Rudolf

Bultmann, Rudolf (1884–1976). The 20th century's most influential interpreter of the New Testament, whose controversial programme of *demythologizing largely set the terms for theological discussion throughout the 1950s and early 1960s.

Born into a *Lutheran parsonage in Wiefelstede, Germany, Bultmann began his university studies in 1903 in the centres of the reigning Protestant *liberalism, first *Tübingen, then Berlin (under Hermann Gunkel and Adolf Harnack), and finally Marburg (under Adolf Jülicher, Wilhelm Herrmann, and Johannes Weiss). Encouraged by Weiss to pursue a doctorate in NT, Bultmann stayed on in Marburg, immersing himself in the comparative methods of the history of *religions school typified in Wilhelm Bousset.

While teaching in Breslau in 1916, Bultmann gave the first open sign, in a letter to Martin Rade, of his break with liberal theology. His disenchantment came with the realization that the liberal 'lives' of *Jesus, biographies written to inspire faith, had now been rendered untenable by scholarly research that squarely placed the gos-

pels into the context of the *myths and cult-dramas known to the Graeco-Roman world.

In 1921, Bultmann published his monumental form-critical study, *The History of the Synoptic Tradition*, still a standard today. This coincided with his return to Marburg, where he began his 30-year tenure (1921–51) as professor of NT. Here, he published his volume on the message of Jesus (1926), his theologically profound, if now historically dated, commentary on the Fourth Gospel (1941), his commentary on Second Corinthians (1976), and his four volumes of collected essays (1933–64).

Bultmann's tenure at Marburg overlapped the rise and fall of the Third Reich (1933–45). With Karl *Barth and others, Bultmann was openly part of the Confessing Church, organized in 1934 in opposition to Hitler. But even as early as May of 1933, amid the full flush of Nazi enthusiasm, Bultmann had lectured to his classes that no nation is so 'pure and clean' that its will can be equated with that of God, and he called for *theology to serve the nation by exercising *prophetic criticism. That same fateful year, Bultmann drafted a declaration by the Marburg theological faculty opposing any extension of the new Nazi laws that would have excluded 'non-Aryans' from church office, and he vigorously defended this position in the theological press. Similarly, in 1934, he threatened to resign the editorship of a prestigious academic series if the dissertation of his Jewish student, Hans Jonas, were blocked from publication. Thus, Jonas's book on Gnosticism became one of the few by Jews published in Germany during the Nazi period. In such ways as these, Bultmann attempted a faithful Christian witness under totalitarian conditions.

Throughout his career, Bultmann consistently wedded the *Kierkegaardian concept of the 'wholly other' God with the distinctive terminology of Martin Heidegger, who described human existence (or *Dasein*) as radically 'fallen' into 'inauthenticity'. Bultmann set forth his own *existentialist theology and *hermeneutical programme most comprehensively in his 1941 lecture 'New Testament and Mythology', which Schubert Ogden called 'perhaps the single most discussed and controversial theological writing of the century' (Ogden, p. vii).

Bultmann's retirement in 1951 was crowned by the completion of his *magnum opus*, *Theology of the New Testament*, and his visit to the United States where he gave the Shaffer Lectures at Yale, later published as *Jesus Christ and Mythology*. In 1953 he delivered the Gifford Lectures in Edinburgh on the theme of 'History and Eschatology'. By the early 1960s, which witnessed the zenith of his transatlantic influence, Bultmann was engaging in lively, at times pained, debates with former students such as Ernst Käsemann, Günther Bornkamm, Hans Conzelmann, and Gerhard Ebeling. In opposition to their Marburg mentor, these 'post-Bultmannians' all urged a renewed *quest for the historical Jesus, a task Bultmann consistently argued was misguided on both historical and theological grounds.

Bultmann held that Jesus Christ matters decisively for each individual's transition from inauthentic to authentic existence. Moreover, he was convinced that believing in Jesus Christ as one's Lord and Saviour does not mean believing in the prescientific cosmology found in the NT. Christian faith is neither a leap out of *modernity, nor a retreat from intellectual honesty. One does not have to profess the mythical frameworks and formulas of yesterday in order to confess Jesus Christ today. Thus, the aim of Bultmann's theology was to show how one could responsibly embrace Christian faith in a modern age whose canons of knowledge were shaped by science.

This apologetic aim shows the kinship between Bultmann's thought and that of Protestant liberalism. Indeed, Bultmann learned from his liberal teachers that the NT accounts of Jesus intertwine historical sources and traditions with mythical motifs widely found throughout the ancient Near East and the Graeco-Roman world. With this discovery, liberalism sought to unbind the historical Jesus from the constrictions of myth by eliminating them from its dogmatics and preaching. These included a number of traditional tenets such as Jesus' *virgin birth, vicarious *atonement, and bodily *Resurrection. No longer handicapped by these orthodox 'absurdities', liberalism was free to emphasize the incomparable personality of the historical Jesus and to join him in proclaiming a *Kingdom of God progressively developing within the historical process. Faith was interpreted to mean coming under the redeeming influence of Jesus' personality as it continues to guide humankind towards the realization of God's rule in human affairs.

Bultmann believed liberalism was right to distinguish between the historical and the mythical elements in the NT, but went on to show where, with the best of intentions, it had gone wrong. The error was in its failure to recognize that the saving significance of Jesus is never understood in the NT in a historicist sense, as a fulfilment of the world's latent possibilities; rather, it understands Jesus in an *eschatological sense, as one whose coming marks the final judgement, or end of the world. This is expressed in the *apocalyptic language of Paul's *cross–Resurrection message or *kerygma (which the Synoptic Gospels narrate) and in the *Gnostic-derived concepts and framework of the Fourth Gospel, which tell of the divine Logos who comes into the world 'from above'. In other words, while the Jewish prophet Jesus of Nazareth, who proclaimed the Kingdom of God, is the historical presupposition of Christianity, it is the proclaimed destiny of this Jesus as crucified and risen, or God's eschatological salvation event, that is the real source and norm of Christian faith. The proclaimer (of the Kingdom) has become the proclaimed (of the church), and Christian faith only arises from this latter proclamation. Therefore, when the liberals eliminated apocalyptic and Gnostic myth from their portrayals of Jesus, they unwittingly eliminated the eschatological essence of the Christian faith and, hence, the significance of Jesus for salvation.

The resultant problem was how the church could continue to proclaim its eschatological understanding of salvation when that understanding was expressed in mythological language. Bultmann answered by arguing for an existentialist interpretation of NT eschatology. The point was not to eliminate the Christ-myth which expressed Jesus' saving destiny, but to translate it so that it could truly be heard as a call to authentic existence. This apologetic aim led Bultmann to advocate his famous hermeneutical programme known as 'demythologizing'.

This programme assumes that the real referent of NT mythology is not the objectivized realities of which it literally speaks—heaven, hell, Satan, atoning sacrifice, reanimated corpses, or virgin births—but rather the understanding of existence that such mythological constructs symbolize. Thus, interpreters of the NT, especially preachers of the gospel, must proceed by translating outmoded cosmological categories into modern existentialist ones. For example, Paul's mythology of the cosmic powers, which the cross of Christ overcomes (1 Cor. 2: 6–8; cf. Col. 2: 13–15), is a way of speaking of one's bondage to the norms and patterns of this world, to the past, and to vain attempts to secure existence ever threatened by suffering and death. Hence, to be 'crucified with Christ' (Gal. 2: 19–20; 5: 24; 6: 14) means to accept God's judgement on our worldly dependence and to accept God's freedom to embrace the future without fear of death.

The word that judges our past and extinguishes our old life is simultaneously the word that re-creates us; it is 'the power of God unto salvation' (Rom 1: 16). Faith means entering here and now into eschatological existence, into love for our neighbours, and into the freedom of no longer being always determined by the power of death. This message or 'the word of the cross' (1 Cor. 1: 18) is thus 'the word of life' (Phil. 2: 16). The Resurrection of Jesus is not about the resuscitation of a corpse. Such mythological language, rooted in Jewish apocalyptic, is really a way of saying that when the word of the cross is proclaimed as an appeal for authentic existence, as a call for the decision of faith, it comes alive in its hearers and effects in them the very judgement and grace it proclaims. Jesus' Resurrection is simply a 1st-century way of symbolizing the performative power of the Christian message. This is why Bultmann could agree with the formulation, hurled at him in criticism, 'Jesus has risen into the kerygma.'

Since the 1970s, commentators have noted the precipitous decline in Bultmann's popularity. In some ways, the very comprehensiveness of his theological proposals, drawn from NT exegesis and theology, history of religions, hermeneutics, systematic theology, and philosophy, has been eroded by further developments in these disciplines. Many scholars now question Bultmann's historical assumptions (e.g. that a Gnostic Redeemer myth provides the Johannine conceptuality for Jesus' saving significance), his existentialist theology (e.g. that the cosmological referents in NT eschatology can be translated without remainder into existentialist concepts), and his philosophy of language (e.g. that language is primarily the expression of existential self-understanding).

Thus, Bultmann's continuing influence does not stem from a surviving school of thought bearing his name, since the synthesis he achieved has unravelled. Rather, his continuing influence is seen (1) wherever the NT is approached through historical and comparative methods involving other ancient texts and parallels known to the history of religions; (2) wherever the saving significance of Jesus Christ is identified not with historical reconstructions but with the preaching of the Christian gospel or 'word of the cross'; and, (3) wherever talk of God is understood as revealing the self-understanding of the faith (and faith communities) out of which it emerges. This hermeneutical turn in modern theology, with its concern for the 'situation' or 'context' in which theological *language arises and to which it is addressed, is Bultmann's most enduring legacy in our postmodern period.   **James F. Kay**

Bultmann, R., 'New Testament and Mythology: The Problem of Demythologizing the New Testament Proclamation,' in S. M. Ogden (ed.), *New Testament and Mythology and Other Basic Writings* (1941), ET (1984).
—— *Theology of the New Testament* (2 vols.; 1949–51), ET (1951–5).
—— *Jesus Christ and Mythology* (1958).

Fergusson, D., *Bultmann* (1992).

Kay, J. F., *Christus Praesens: A Reconsideration of Rudolf Bultmann's Christology* (1994).

Morgan, R. 'Rudolf Bultmann,' in D. F. Ford (ed.), *The Modern Theologians: An Introduction to Christian Theology in the Twentieth Century*, (2nd edn. 2 vols.; 1997).

Bunyan, John, see PILGRIM'S PROGRESS.

business ethics.

Is there a distinctive contribution made by Christian thought to business life, historically and in contemporary discussions of *ethical practices in business?

'A distinctive contribution by Christian thought' could mean an explicit influence of Christian thought and values on business decision-making or on government regulation of business. Indirectly, it could mean that ethical norms of western society, many of which are founded on Christianity, have influenced business conduct. Glenn Tinder (1989) asks, 'To what extent are we now living on moral savings accumulated over many centuries but no longer being replenished?', implying that modern *secular norms derive indirectly from a Judaeo-Christian faith tradition, ethical 'capital', which may run dry. Since medieval times, Christian influence on business and commerce has evolved from the direct to indirect.

From *usury to weights and measures, from living wages to unionization to *work and *family issues, Christian reflection has concerned itself with commerce and business activity. The core Christian message of *love—embracing the cardinal virtues of *justice, *temperance, prudence, and fortitude—inevitably has a bearing on changing economic relationships, the transition from agricultural to manufacturing economies, and polarizations between factory owners, workers, and the state.

One of the most comprehensive windows on Christian concerns about 19th-century business conduct is Leo XIII's 1891 encyclical *Rerum Novarum*, which applied NT reflection to the changes wrought by the Industrial Revolution (*c*.1750–1850). Its principal exhortations to business owners were to recognize the dignity of the worker, to give workers and their families a living wage, and to acknowledge workers' rights to form voluntary associations. To governments, the message was that, besides reinforcing these exhortations, they should consider the right to own property as inherent in workers' personal dignity.

Exactly a century later (15 May 1991), *John Paul II issued a Christian review of business conduct for the 20th century: communism was collapsing and *capitalism seemed over-confident about its moral credentials. This encyclical, *Centesimus Annus*, was addressed both to Catholics and to persons of good will everywhere. Like *Rerum Novarum* it paid close attention to work and the family, but also raised broader concerns about marketing and the media, and their effects on education and culture. Highlighting the dignity of human *persons not only as workers but as consumers, the encyclical says:

> In singling out new needs and new means to meet them, one must be guided by a comprehensive picture of man which respects all the dimensions of his being and which subordinates his material and instinctive dimensions to his interior and spiritual ones... Of itself, an economic system does not possess criteria for correctly distinguishing new and higher forms of satisfying human needs from artificial new needs which hinder the forma-

tion of a mature personality. Thus a great deal of educational and cultural work is urgently needed, including the education of consumers in the responsible use of their power of choice, the formation of a strong sense of responsibility among producers and among people in the mass media in particular, as well as the necessary intervention by public authorities

Christian concerns about business or commercial ethics in the modern period, as in the Middle Ages, have centred on the most vulnerable participants in economic transactions in the spirit of 'What you do to the least of my brethren, you do unto me' (Matt. 25: 40). Dealing with usury, this meant condemning predatory loan rates; dealing with factory-based manufacturing, it meant calling for living wages and decent working conditions. If the logics of market forces and commercial law ignore the dignity of the vulnerable, Christianity can offer a faith-based reaffirmation of that dignity. Interpreting the Protestant Christian perspective, Glenn Tinder says:

> Christians [are and have been] deeply suspicious of the maxim that the invisible hand of the market is always to be trusted in preference to the visible hand of government. Such a maxim has a look of idolatry. The principle that only God, and never a human institution, should be relied on absolutely suggests a far more flexible and pragmatic approach to the issue.

Has the conduct of business life developed to the point where Christianity's concerns can be heard by business leaders and thus make a difference in decision-making? The mid-20th century saw the emergence of the idea that considerations other than profit maximization could and should influence business decisions: that corporations, like individual persons, should have a *conscience in their decision-making.

The evolution of corporate law in the United States, and increasingly worldwide, is towards legitimating the interests and rights of the whole range of stakeholders (employees, customers, suppliers, local communities), not only stockholders, as relevant decision factors for corporations. Indirectly, this trend manifests the Christian concern for parties affected by economic transactions, particularly the most vulnerable.

Central to stakeholder thinking is the analogy between moral expectations we have of individual persons and those we have of organizations, what is called 'the principle of moral projection' (Goodpaster and Matthews 1982). Whether such a stakeholder approach to private enterprise carries *socialistic implications is a matter of considerable debate. On the face of it, encouraging corporations to institutionalize conscience is very different from advocating the socialization of capital and control.

The global expansion of commercial activity, facilitated by modern technologies, has increased our need for transcultural ethical principles to guide business conduct. The economically vulnerable are less-developed nations as well as individual citizens. Groups like the Caux Round Table, based in Switzerland but including business leaders from North America, Europe, and Asia, have articulated such transcultural principles, acknowledging that, *indirectly* at least, they build upon Christian foundations.

Perhaps Christianity's most distinctive contribution to the conduct of business life may lie in what T. S. *Eliot called 'knowing how to ask questions'.

See also GLOBAL ETHICS.   **Kenneth E. Goodpaster**

Brady, Bernard, Goodpaster, Kenneth, and Kennedy, Robert, 'Rerum Novarum and the Modern Corporation', in F. P. McHugh and S. M. Natale (eds.), *Things Old and New* (1993).

The Caux Round Table Principles for Business (1994).

Goodpaster, Kenneth, and Matthews, John, 'Can a Corporation Have a Conscience?', *Harvard Business Review* (Jan.–Feb. 1982), 132–141.

Novak, Michael, *The Spirit of Democratic Capitalism* (1982).

—— *The Catholic Ethic and the Spirit of Capitalism* (1993).

Tinder, Glenn, *The Political Meaning of Christianity* (1989).

Walton, Clarence, *The Moral Manager* (1988).

Byzantine theology, 6th–16th centuries.

Byzantine theology was shaped by three distinct, though intertwined, traditions: the *ascetic or *monastic tradition, the developing dogmatic tradition (*Trinitarian theology and, especially, *christology), and a continuing philosophical tradition, mainly *Platonic and Neoplatonic in complexion (see GREEK THEOLOGY). The philosophical tradition, with its pagan roots, was often referred to, dismissively, as 'exterior' (*exothen*), a usage that goes back to the Cappadocian fathers; the complementary terminology of an 'interior' (*esothen*) tradition came later, and was claimed by the monks. The 6th century saw decisive developments in all these three traditions.

By the end of the 6th century a considerable body of monastic literature had developed: the assembling of the traditions of the fathers of the Egyptian desert was still taking place at the beginning of the century, though by this time the centre of gravity of Orthodox monasticism had moved to Palestine and Sinai, whence stems the single most influential Byzantine monastic treatise, the *Ladder of Divine Ascent*, written perhaps at the turn of the 6th/7th century by John, Abbot of St Catherine's Monastery, Sinai, whom tradition identifies as simply 'of the Ladder', *tou Klimakos*. This monastic tradition of ascetic wisdom was deeply indebted to the great 4th-century theorist of the Egyptian eremitical life, Evagrius, himself much influenced by *Origen; it owed no less a debt to the experiential tradition of the Macarian Homilies. Origenism had been anathematized at Justinian's instigation in the 6th century—by imperial edict in 543 and at the Fifth Ecumenical Council in 553—but nonetheless it continued to appeal to many in monastic circles.

The dogmatic tradition also emerged from the 6th century with distinctive features. The Council of *Chalcedon (451) had deeply divided Christians in the eastern provinces, and though Justinian's attempts at bridge-building failed, he marked forever the Byzantine dogmatic tradition. The Fifth Ecumenical Council endorsed the Cyrilline reading of the Chalcedonian definition for which Justinian had pressed. Henceforth that definition was read subject to the following qualifications: (1) the person (*hypostasis*) who became incarnate is identical with the second person of the Trinity, (2) Cyril's favoured expression—'one incarnate nature of God the Word'—was acceptable, if properly interpreted, (3) 'theopaschite' language about 'God suffering in the flesh' was endorsed.

As for the philosophical tradition, with Justinian's closing of the Platonic Academy at Athens in 529, public teaching of pagan philosophy was outlawed. However, the impact of this must be qualified, first, by the fact that much Platonic thought had already been absorbed into Christian theology (not least in the ascetic tradition), and secondly, by the growing popularity of the works ascribed to *Dionysius the Areopagite from the 6th century onwards. This body of writings, the *Corpus Dionysiacum*, although ascribed to the apostle Paul's Athenian convert, was probably composed in the early years of the 6th century. It gave expression to a powerful cosmic vision, drawing on much earlier Christian theology (notably that associated with the Cappadocian Fathers and John Chrysostom), but clothed this in the terminology and concepts of the late Athenian Neoplatonism of such as Proclus (d. 485) and Damascius (the last head of the Platonic Academy). Through the influence of Dionysius, and through the interest of lay intellectuals in pagan philosophy which surfaced from time to time, Neoplatonism continued to influence Byzantine theology.

The 7th and 8th centuries saw a further refining of the dogmatic tradition, but, even more significantly, the creation of an enduring synthesis of these traditions in the thought of Maximos the Confessor and the epitomizing genius of John of Damascus. The refining of the dogmatic tradition occurred as a result of principled rejection of both the final attempt to heal the rifts caused by Chalcedon, and the imperial prohibition of religious imagery. In the 7th century, the Byzantine emperor was seeking to heal the politically weakening divisions in the church exposed by the Persian invasion of the eastern provinces in the 610s and 620s; he hoped, by means of this policy, to win back the provinces lost to the Arabs in the 630s and 640s. Concurrently, the final refinement of Orthodox christology was being fashioned, principally by Maximos, called 'Confessor' as his stubborn resistance to the imperial will led to suffering and exile that cost him his life. The imperial compromise—monenergism and later monothelitism—built on the Cyrilline Chalcedonianism of the 6th century, and tried to achieve union with the *Monophysites on the basis of the confession of one activity (or energy), or one will, in Christ: a single composite activity or will—divine-human, 'theandric'. Maximos, no less committed to Cyrilline Chalcedonianism, saw in this compromise a complete betrayal of the theology of the *Incarnation, for if God the creator did not respect the integrity of *creation in his saving of humankind, then Christian theology, with its conviction of a God who creates out of love, is bankrupt. This conviction of the integrity of God's creation, even after the *Fall (the effects of which he does not underestimate), lies at the heart of Maximos' synthesis of the several strands of Byzantine theology. For Maximos the cosmos and humankind reflect each other: the human being is a little cosmos, in whom all the divisions of the cosmos meet, while the cosmos is like a great human being, manifesting God's glory and, through *humanity, created in the image of God, drawn back into the unity of God. The fall of humankind has shattered this harmony, which can only be restored by the Son of God's taking on himself human nature and thus fulfilling the work of *reconciliation that is the intended role of humankind, as 'bond of the cosmos'. The work of the Incarnation is accomplished in the cosmos through the attempts of each human being, through faith in the Incarnate One, to achieve unity in its own 'little cosmos' by ascetic struggle, and also by the grace of the sacraments, especially the *Eucharist. The cosmic dimension of the Eucharist is expressed in the structure of the church building, which reflected the idea of the *church as an image of the cosmos. In Maximos' theology, these ascetic, liturgical, and dogmatic strands are woven together in a vision of the cosmos, expressed in the philosophical language of Neoplatonism, drawn from Dionysius.

It was not in Byzantium proper, *Constantinople, that Maximos' theological synthesis first came to be assimilated, for there the traditions of the imperial theological compromise that Maximos opposed still held sway. Rather it was in Palestine, where Christians now found themselves politically powerless under the Muslim Umayyads, that the Maximian synthesis became the basis of the theology of those who accepted the tradition of the Byzantine Ecumenical Councils, including the Sixth (Constantinople III, 681) which had endorsed Maximos' christology. Deprived of imperial support, Byzantine Christians in Palestine had to defend their position against Monophysites, Monothelites, and other Christian heretics (who reviled them as 'Maximians'), as well as Jews and Muslims. This process, belonging to the 7th and 8th centuries, reached its culmination in the theology of John of Damascus, onetime Umayyad civil servant, who spent the last decades of his life (he died c.750) in one of the Palestinian monasteries, by tradition the Great Lavra, the monastery of Mar Saba. His greatest work, the *Fount of Knowledge*, is an epitome of the Maximian theological synthesis. The first two parts—the *Philosophical Chapters* and *On Heresies*—provide the logic and clearly defined terminology needed to state and defend Orthodoxy, and an account of one hundred typical misinterpretations. The final part, *On the Orthodox Faith*, expounds that faith in a hundred chapters, mostly drawn from the writings of revered fathers of the church. This exposition of the faith covers not only doctrinal matters, but also matters of cosmology and the structure of human nature, both physiological and psychological (which John regarded as profoundly interlinked). This short work was to be translated into most Christian languages, including Church Slavonic and Latin, the former nourishing the Slavs who, from the 9th century onwards, embraced Byzantine Christianity, the latter providing both a convenient summary of the patristic dogmatic tradition for the scholastics, and a pattern for their *Summas*. In John's own time this theological synthesis received its first testing in the *iconoclast controversy, for clearest amongst the voices opposing the imperial decree was that of the monk John.

As well as being concerned with the place of religious imagery, the iconoclast controversy led to clarification of other theological matters, not least in the matter of eucharistic doctrine, where the iconoclast idea of the Eucharist as itself a symbol led the Orthodox to insist that the presence of Christ in the Eucharist is not symbolic but involves a real ontological change. In other ways, too, the iconoclast controversy marked a watershed in Byzantine theology and *religious life. On the one hand, the ending of iconoclasm coincided with a renewal of the monastic life, heralded by the Studite reform of Theodore in the interlude between the first and second periods of iconoclasm. Its final ending was marked by the issuing of the *Synodikon of Orthodoxy*, a piece of performance art, consisting of acclamations and anathemas, read henceforth on the first Sunday of Lent, the 'Sunday of Orthodoxy'. All this had the effect of underlining the Orthodoxy of the Byzantine Church.

The renewal of monasticism led to a deepening sense of the importance of the inner wisdom represented by the monks. A pivotal figure in this, controversial in his time, was Symeon the New Theologian (949–1022). His *theology, expressed in monastic catecheses, centuries of 'chapters', and poems, lays stress on the experience of God as the heart of theology. Theology is, as the monastic tradition had long maintained, experience of God, healing and transfiguring

human nature. This led Symeon to stress that feature of the monastic tradition that tended to subordinate the priestly hierarchy to the experiential authority of the ascetic. Going back to the 3rd-century Alexandrian theologians, Clement and Origen, this tradition is found both in Dionysius and in monastic tales such as those in John Moschus' *Spiritual Meadow*, where we read of priest-monks who celebrated the Eucharist only after receiving a divine vision during the preparation. For Symeon this principle applied to spiritual direction, including the sacrament of *penance, which was the preserve of the holy ascetic rather than the priest. The authority of (monastic) *holiness was fostered by the monastic foundations contemporary with Symeon, especially those on the holy mountain of Athos (where the Great Lavra was founded by Athanasios the Athonite in 963).

The *Synodikon of Orthodoxy* received only minor modifications in the 9th and 10th centuries, but from the accession of Alexios Komnenos in 1081 it was used to bolster the fragile authority of the Komnene emperors by presenting the emperor as the guardian of Orthodoxy. With the flourishing humanism of the 11th century, there had been renewed interest in pagan philosophy and Neoplatonism (including magic and *astrology), especially in the circle of the learned layman (and occasional monk), Michael Psellos. For mainly political reasons, Michael's pupil and successor as 'consul of the philosophers', John Italos, was condemned at a trial in 1082, an event commemorated by a new section of the *Synodikon*, embodying a comprehensive condemnation of the 'exterior wisdom'. Alexios' grandson, Manuel, continued this process with theological debates, held under his aegis, about questions connected with the theological issue that was to dominate politics as long as the Byzantine empire survived: that of relations with the west. The two debates, the conclusions of which were appended to the *Synodikon*, were on the question of whether the eucharistic sacrifice was offered to God the Father, or to the Trinity, and whether the interpretation of Christ's saying 'The Father is greater than I' is Trinitarian or christological. Both concerned issues raised by theologians in the west as part of the renewal of theological activity associated with the 12th-century renaissance. After the fall of Constantinople to the crusaders in 1204, the problem of relations with the west became even more urgent. Byzantine emperors accepted humiliating terms at union *councils at Lyons (1274) and *Florence (1438–45), but these had little impact on the Byzantine Church, nor did these concessions find their way into the *Synodikon*. Perhaps the most important theological issue dividing east and west was the *filioque controversy: does the *Holy Spirit proceed from the Father (as the creed endorsed by the Second Ecumenical Council affirmed) or from the Father and the Son (as the Latin version of the creed came to affirm by the addition of the term *filioque*)? This was first raised against Latin theologians in 7th-century Constantinople, and made a public issue by the patriarch of Constantinople, Photius, in the 9th, though many Byzantine theologians regarded the dispute as evidence of a lack of subtlety in western theology due to the deficiencies of the Latin language rather than anything more serious, at least until the 13th century.

The 'official' line of Byzantine theology, represented by the *Synodikon of Orthodoxy*, and the monastic tradition converge in the last major theological controversy of the Byzantine empire. This concerned hesychasm, a monastic movement that traced its tradition back through Symeon the New Theologian and laid emphasis on the transforming nature of *prayer. The word 'hesychasm' derives from the Greek word for quietness, *hesychia*: hesychasts devoted themselves to solitary quietness in which they prayed for the acquisition of the Holy Spirit, and maintained that the goal of such prayer was a transforming vision of God, in which they beheld the uncreated light of the Godhead, and were deified. Although the hesychasts came to represent a theological position opposed to the scholasticism of the contemporary west, the origins of the dispute lay entirely within the tensions of Byzantine theology, and in particular involved the interpretation of Dionysius the Areopagite. Those opposed to the hesychasts interpreted the negative, apophatic theology of Dionysius in intellectual terms: the utterly transcendent God is known through negations, in the sense that he is beyond knowledge altogether, including the experiential knowledge claimed by the hesychasts. The hesychasts themselves maintained that apophatic theology was a theology, or experience of God in prayer, that, by denying the adequacy of all that we affirm about *God, reaches beyond any knowledge about him to an encounter (or union) with God himself; and they accused their opponents of interpreting Dionysius in terms of the exterior wisdom or pagan philosophy. A further factor in the dispute was the use of techniques of prayer—use of the Jesus prayer ('Lord Jesus Christ, Son of God, have mercy on me, a sinner'), its recitation synchronized with one's breathing, and even a crouched posture—which were ridiculed by the opponents of hesychasm, especially Barlaam, a Greek monk from Calabria. The greatest defender of the hesychasts was Gregory Palamas (*c.*1296–1359), who had himself been a monk on Mount Athos, and eventually became archbishop of nearby Thessalonica. At the centre of his defence of hesychasm was the distinction he drew between the essence and the energies of God: the essence is unknowable, but the energies are knowable, yet both essence and energies are equally God, and uncreated. He defended the experience claimed by the hesychasts of being transfigured in the uncreated light of the Godhead, the very same light that radiated from Christ on the Mount of the Transfiguration, and even the use of physical techniques (though he laid little stress on these, regarding them as sometimes useful for beginners). Gregory was supported by the monks of Athos, but not, to begin with, by the authorities in Constantinople. However, with the accession of John Kantouzenos to the imperial throne in 1347, Gregory was vindicated at synods in the capital, and canonized in 1368 within a decade of his death. The principles of his defence of hesychasm are enshrined in the final addition to the *Synodikon of Orthodoxy*. Hesychasm was, however, a movement embracing more than monastic practice: one of Gregory's supporters, a layman called Nicolas Kavasilas, expounded his understanding of the Christian life both in a commentary on the divine liturgy, and also in his *Life in Christ*, which roots that life in the sacraments. Hesychasm, or Palamism, represents the deepest assimilation of the monastic and dogmatic traditions, combined with a repudiation of the philosophical notions of the exterior wisdom. Although Palamism had little immediate impact on Orthodox theology after the fall of Constantinople in 1453, Orthodox theological reflection being then too bound up with defining itself in largely western terms in relation to Catholicism and Protestantism, the hesychast revival associated with the *Philokalia* of Nikodimos the Hagiorite and Makarios of Corinth (published 1782), its reception by Slav Orthodoxy, and its importance for the Paris school of Orthodox theology in the 20th century have led to hesychasm's becoming definitive for modern Orthodox theology as never before.

As well as the controversy over hesychasm, the final decades of the Byzantine empire saw an unparalleled renewal of Byzantine humanism: interest in Plato, *Aristotle, and the Neoplatonists revived, as well as in contemporary movements in western theology and philosophy (*Aquinas's *Summa contra Gentiles* was translated into Greek in 1354). This had little lasting effect on Byzantine theology, and indeed had less impact on the emerging Italian *Renaissance than is often claimed. It was the monks with their interior wisdom, not the scholars with their exterior wisdom, who survived the final collapse of the Byzantine empire to the Turks, and it was among the monks that traditions of Byzantine theology were preserved most faithfully, and among them that the seeds of renewal took root and eventually bore fruit.

See also EASTERN ORTHODOX THEOLOGY.   **Andrew Louth**

Krivochéine, B., *Dans la lumière du Christ: S. Syméon le Nouveau Théologien 949–1022: Vie—Spiritualité—Doctrine* (1980).
Lossky, V., *The Mystical Theology of the Eastern Church* (1957).
Louth, A., *Maximus the Confessor* (1996).
Meyendorff, J., *St Gregory Palamas* (1964).
—— *Byzantine Theology* (1974).
—— *The Byzantine Legacy in the Orthodox Church* (1982).
Pelikan, J., *The Spirit of Eastern Christendom (600–1700)* (1974).
Runciman, S., *The Last Byzantine Renaissance* (1970).

Cain. 'Am I my brother's keeper?' With these familiar words in Genesis 4: 9, *Adam's son Cain, who has killed his brother Abel because the Lord accepted Abel's sacrifice rather than Cain's, seeks to deny responsibility for his actions. Cain's punishment for the murder is to wander across the face of the earth with a mark upon him which protects him from the vengeance of others. He founds the first *city which is thus built on blood and on his denial of human solidarity. The problem of where the other people to fill this city come from has exercised Christian exegetes throughout the centuries but may point to an original context for the story removed from the account of Eden.

Cain's story raises fundamental questions for subsequent interpreters about the nature of *evil, of *forgiveness, and of divine election. Why should two sons of one family turn out so differently? Why should Cain be permitted to live when his brother's blood cries out from the earth for vengeance? For the writer of 1 John, Cain, unlike Abel, was 'from the evil one', the first of the line of children of the *devil.

*Augustine takes up this theme in a more elaborated way, when he points to Cain as the founder of the earthly city, the ancestor of those who live by human, not divine, standards. Yet even he is not able to explain definitively what it was about Cain or his actions which led God to reject his sacrifice.

This uncertainty has had two effects on subsequent theological discussion. On the one hand, Cain has been interpreted as having a predisposition to evil, something discernible by God but not by human understanding, or something God himself had inscrutably foreordained (see PREDESTINATION). Cain becomes the type of the reprobate who is arbitrarily but incontrovertibly rejected by God. As the killer of the innocent shepherd Abel, Cain is further identified by Augustine and other writers with the Jews as killers of the Good Shepherd, Jesus. The figure of the Wandering Jew, so prevalent in medieval literature, has the wanderer Cain at its root. Exile and banishment are equated with God's rejection.

By the 18th and 19th centuries, however, the spread of *Arminianism and its extension of the potential of salvation to everyone means that Cain, the archetypal sinner, is also seen to be redeemable. For writers such as *Blake and Byron, Cain rather than Abel should be seen as the victim, in his case of an erratic and partial deity. He becomes a forerunner of the doomed *Romantic hero driven to desperate action. This more favourable view of Cain may have a long ancestry if *Irenaeus' reference to a sect of 'Cainites' is taken at face value.

Cain's anomalous survival in the face of unequivocal biblical insistence on the execution of murderers has its own significance. If *capital punishment was not applicable for the first of all murderers, why was it applicable for others? What is the true Christian attitude to the sinner? What is the nature of *justice in a Christian state? Cain's story embodies the tension between justice and *mercy which the Christian vision of a loving, omnipotent, and moral *God entails.

Hugh S. Pyper

Melinkoff, R., *The Mark of Cain* (1981).
Quinones, R., *The Changes of Cain* (1991).

calendar. The daily, weekly, and annual *prayer of the *church is shaped according to a calendar of times and seasons, feasts and *fasts. Undergirding the construction of the liturgical calendar is the belief that *God acted and acts within *time and place, *Jesus Christ being the pivotal point, for 'when the time had fully come, God sent forth his Son' (Gal. 4: 4). This event provides the outline for an annual cycle that retraces the biblical chronology of Christ's birth, ministry, Passion and death, Resurrection, Ascension, bestowal of the Holy Spirit, and expected return. The temporale, or sequence of christological observances, follows a regular course, with some dates fixed by the solar year and others—*Easter and days related to it—determined through a complex system of calculation that depends also upon lunation. Existing alongside the temporale is another annual series, the sanctorale, which has specified days to mark remembrances of the *apostles, *martyrs, and *saints who, through the power of the Spirit, witnessed to Christ by their lives and deaths.

Although the events observed in the temporal calendar assume a linear-historical progression, the conceptual underpinnings for the entire calendrical system are theological rather than simply chronological. At the heart of the calendar is the paschal mystery, the Christian Pascha or Passover, which encompasses the obedience of Jesus unto death as an atonement for human sin, his subsequent *Resurrection and exaltation (cf. Phil. 2: 6–9), and his ongoing work for the salvation of humankind. The paschal mystery embraces more than a past historical occurrence; it pertains to the redemption unbounded by time that was obtained from the sacrifice at Calvary. Christ's salvific achievement celebrated at Easter is the central proclamation of the church from which radiate the other emphases of the calendar—and the entire liturgical life of the church.

The calendar, therefore, is not to be understood as a static device, but as a dynamic means of encountering and reappropriating the gospel message. It has both historical and eschatological aspects which stand in tension in enabling the community to 'proclaim the Lord's death until he comes' (1 Cor. 11: 26). The annual repetition of feasts and fasts invites recollection of the past through an active remembering (*anamnesis*) by which historic occasions become contemporaneous (see MEMORY). At the same time, the yearly cycle moves the Christian community closer to the consummation. By the invocation (*epiclesis*) of the Holy Spirit, the earnest of the end, God's future impinges upon the present—which, mysteriously, also helps to bring it about.

Study of Christian heortology—the meaning and observance of festal days and seasons—reveals two basic characteristics of the calendar: (1) that the development of the calendar was from simplicity to complexity, with occasional movements to restore relative simplicity; and (2) that, even from the earliest periods, there has been diversity within the church regarding the formulation of the detailed calendar, with the basic christological structure of the temporale the most generally uniform.

In the apostolic period, the primary celebration of the Christian community occurred each *Sunday, the day of the Lord's Resurrection, at which the redemptive work of Jesus Christ was recalled and lauded. The annual festival of Easter, the oldest among Christian feasts, which appears originally to have been set to coincide with the celebration of the Jewish Passover on 14–15 Nisan, reiterated and intensified the theme of redemption obtained by Jesus' death and displayed in his Resurrection. By the 4th century, when the date for Easter was uniformly established on a Sunday (Council of *Nicaea, 325), the dual focus on *cross and Resurrection came to be distributed between Good Friday and Easter Day. Every Sunday was a 'little Easter'; Easter was the 'Great Sunday' which, in some regions, was not confined to one day, but was extended by as many as fifty days. Culmination of the paschal celebration on the fiftieth day, *Pentecost, eventually led to its establishment as a feast celebrating the universal mission of the church inaugurated by the outpouring of the Spirit.

Festivals and fasts articulating specific themes or concepts related to the redemption wrought in Jesus Christ evolved from the 4th century onwards at different rates and in various regions. Some emerged from theological debates or were included to enforce doctrinal principles; for example, *Epiphany in the east and *Christmas/Nativity in the west grew in response to controversies about the nature of Christ's Incarnation. Others, such as *Lent and *Advent, developed as periods of preparation before the more significant festivals. Still others were introduced in imitation of a local custom or because of devotional popularity: the practice in Jerusalem of visiting the supposed locations of the events of Holy Week and Easter gave rise in other areas to the separate observances of Palm Sunday, Maundy Thursday, and Good Friday; and the doctrinal feast of the Trinity in the west (the first Sunday after Pentecost) was officially established in the 14th century after existing for generations at the folk level. Many of the now-standard components of the temporale first appeared as local experiments which over time

gained wider acceptance. And while the basic framework—consisting of the two main festal cycles of Lent–Easter–Pentecost and Advent–Christmas–Epiphany with intervening 'ordinary' periods—has changed little over the past millennium, the dynamism characteristic of the calendar continues to allow variations as new concerns confront the church and as future generations give their testimonies of faith.

The use of the calendar varies among the churches. The fullest expressions of the temporale and the sanctorale have always been found among the Catholics and the Orthodox. The churches of the *Reformation objected to the current sanctorale because of perceived superstitions and abuses associated with the cult of the saints. Nevertheless, *Lutherans and *Anglicans kept a commemorative sanctorale that was at first almost entirely limited to biblical figures (though with a comprehensive feast of All Saints on the customary date of 1 November); and as time went by they added post-biblical saints to their list. On the other hand, the *Reformed, *Methodist, and Free Churches generally have never followed a sanctorale. Protestants as a whole, however, have been more attentive to the temporale (at least in its simplest form), and in the 20th century, under the impetus of the liturgical and *ecumenical movements, even churches that historically ignored the temporale have adopted a calendar or looked at one with increasing interest. Ecumenical co-operation has also yielded calendars and related lectionaries to be shared across confessional lines.

At the level of world history, it remains remarkable that current time is most commonly reckoned from the assumed year of Christ's birth, *anno Domini*.   **Karen B. Westerfield Tucker**

Adam, A., *The Liturgical Year* (1979), ET (1981).
Frere, W. H., *Studies in Early Roman Liturgy, i. The Kalendar* (1930).
McArthur, A. A., *The Evolution of the Christian Year* (1953).
Perham, M., *The Communion of Saints* (1980).
Talley, T., *The Origins of the Liturgical Year* (1986).

Calvin, John (1509–64).

The Reformer of *Geneva and one of the foremost theologians of the *Reformation era, Calvin became the leading spokesman of the *Reformed, as distinct from the *Lutheran, churches. His influence on the course of the Protestant Reformation reached far beyond Geneva through his correspondence and disciples. His achievements as a biblical commentator and theologian have given some of his writings the status of enduring classics of Christian literature.

French by birth, Calvin was sent to Paris for his education and was expected to enter the service of the church. But his father's plans for him changed, and he moved to Orléans and Bourges to study law. When the father died (1531), Calvin returned to Paris and embarked on the literary career of a classical scholar, publishing his first book in 1532, a commentary on Seneca's *De clementia* ('On Clemency'). Two years later he wrote his first statement of evangelical faith, an elegant preface to the French translation of the *New Testament by his cousin Pierre Robert (Olivetari). Sometime between 1532 (probably) and 1534 he had undergone the 'sudden conversion' of which he wrote in the autobiographical preface to his *Commentary on the Psalms* (1557). He continued to see himself as a writer, though now in the cause of 'pure religion', and in the summer of 1535, at the age of 26, he handed the first edition of his *Institutes* to a printer in Basel. But the following year a detour on a journey from Paris to Strasbourg took him to Geneva and changed the course of his life, forcing the reserved scholar to become a man of action. Hearing of his presence in the city, William Farel enlisted his services in the cause of the Genevan reformation with the warning that God would curse his quiet, scholarly life if he refused. Save for a brief interruption when Farel and Calvin were both dismissed by the civil authorities, Calvin devoted the rest of his years to the reform of Geneva.

Calvin's literary productivity was by no means impeded by his labours as a reformer. He was far from being a man of a single book, but his reputation rests largely on the work familiarly known as his *Institutes*. (The Latin title, *Institutio Christianae religionis*, properly means 'Instruction in the Christian Religion'.) The first edition (1536) might be described as a manual for enquirers, but the time of its appearance, during persecution of the French Protestants, lent it also the character of an apology. A modest volume of six chapters, it was evidently modelled on Martin *Luther's catechisms (1529). Luther had added to the traditional expositions of the Ten *Commandments, the *Creed, and the *Lord's Prayer two chapters on the *sacraments. Calvin departed from him in treating the two evangelical sacraments together and devoting a separate section to the five spurious 'Roman' sacraments. He then concluded with a remarkable chapter, very much his own, on Christian *freedom in relation to ecclesiastical power and the civil government. Preoccupation with the sacraments and church order was to remain a distinctive mark of Calvin's theology, and the prefatory address to the French king, Francis, attests another characteristic: the ease with which Calvin could marshal the opinions of the early Christian fathers in support of the Reformation cause.

The second main edition of the *Institutes*, published while Calvin was living in Strasbourg (1539), was greatly enlarged and had a different readership in mind. In seventeen chapters Calvin offered interpretations of key biblical concepts (providence, faith, Christian freedom, and so on) to help theological students find their way in the scriptures. His model now was the *Loci communes* (theological 'commonplaces') of Luther's associate, Philip Melanchthon, first published in 1521.

The definitive edition of the *Institutes* (1559) adopts a quite different arrangement, in eighty chapters. The correlative knowledge of *God and knowledge of ourselves, in which nearly all our wisdom consists, is ordered by the distinction between knowing God as *creator and knowing God as *redeemer. Knowledge of the creator is the theme of book 1. Books 2–4 deal with God the redeemer from three perspectives: redemption through Christ, faith in Christ, and the means of *grace. The order intended, however, is not the actual order of knowing. Calvin held that a sound knowledge of God the creator is possible only for believers, redeemed by Christ. An experiential sequence, then, would need to begin with book 4 and end with book 1—reading the *Institutes* backwards, so to say. It was partly the weight of tradition that led Calvin to follow the order he did, and it has often been pointed out that the sequence of the four books corresponds roughly to the order of the Apostles' *Creed.

Attempts have been made to identify a central dogma in Calvin's *Institutes* that is regulative of everything else, or even serves as the 'principle' from which everything else is deduced. Their failure has sometimes given rise to a forthright denial that Calvin was a sys-

tematic theologian at all. But the reaction is unwarranted. Calvin was manifestly concerned to see every part of his *Institutes* in the context of the whole; failure to take note of what is surely a systematic concern accounts for some of the mistakes that have plagued Calvin's critics and friends alike to this day. It is essential to ask, not simply what Calvin said on any given topic that happens to interest the reader, but also how it fits within the total design; and it is better to seek the links between topics in recurring metaphors rather than in some elusive central dogma.

God, humanity, and redemption

Calvin's thinking about God and God's relation to *humanity is dominated by two favourite images: God is the fountain of good and the *Father who cares for his children. The two images say the same thing, the one by a *metaphor drawn from nature, the other by a metaphor from personal relationships: that whatever good we possess has its sole source in the abundant goodness of God. To acknowledge that this is so is what Calvin understands by piety, and where there is no piety we cannot properly say that God is known. The security of the 'pious' lies in their confidence 'that the heavenly Father so holds everything in his power … that nothing falls out unless by his design'.

The vocation of humanity—their unique role in the created order—is to render continual thanks to the Father and fountain of good. They live in the world as privileged spectators in a theatre of God's glory and accordingly should live in thankfulness, like mirrors reflecting the glory of God's goodness. But the shame of *Adam was that he spurned the bounty God had lavished on him and so diminished God's glory. His descendants now sit like blind men in the theatre; they enjoy the gifts but do not see the hand of the giver. Calvin's remarks on human depravity offend our modern sensibilities. However, they do not express disgust with humanity, but rather with human ingratitude, which abandons piety for unbelief or transforms it into *impietas*, a servile dread of God that seeks to placate him with sacrifices.

Calvin perceives even *impietas*, though it is only a vain shadow of religion, as a confused knowledge of God. Hence the remedy, which is the *word of God in scripture, can be compared to corrective lenses that assist our weak vision and focus our otherwise confused perception of God. Just how it was possible for Calvin to think of God's word as like a pair of spectacles is immediately clear from his understanding of the *faith that receives it: faith is resting on the word of God's mercy or goodwill in Christ—that is, the gospel. Faith does what Adam's descendants can no longer do without the help of God's word: it recognizes God in his true character as the Father who means well to his children. Calvin can make the same point with his other favourite metaphor (in his *Commentary on John*, for example) when he speaks of Christ as the one who opens up access to the fountain. But the familial metaphor is particularly striking: often he simply identifies faith with the recognition of God's fatherhood, opposing it to the servile dread that God may be against us.

The cardinal Reformation doctrine of *justification by faith is interpreted accordingly. It means that, being reconciled to God through Christ, we have a gracious Father in heaven instead of a judge. Calvin presents the passage from a servile to a filial consciousness of God most eloquently in his chapter on Christian freedom, which he introduces as an appendix to justification, intended to help us understand its 'power'. Servants, who are under the yoke of the law, are afraid to face their master unless they have done exactly what is demanded of them. But children do not hesitate to show their father unfinished projects that they have scarcely begun, or even have spoiled a little, confident that he will like them, 'however small, rough, or imperfect they may be'. The concept of 'merit' is thereby excluded. When scripture speaks of 'reward', it does not mean a servant's pay, but a child's inheritance.

It was Calvin's belief, however, that the grace of adoption was not for everyone. Scripture and experience concur that not all hear the gospel; and of those who do, not all receive it in faith. The difference between those who believe and those who do not cannot be attributed to human freedom without undermining the cardinal conviction that every good comes solely from the goodness or *mercy of God, including the faith by which the gift of eternal life is received. Faith must be grounded wholly in God's freedom, not ours: there is an 'eternal election' by which God has *predestined some to eternal life, others to destruction. As Calvin saw it, this *election was the final, conclusive testimony to the utter gratuitousness of God's grace; hence it was also the foundation of both the assurance and the humility of the elect. Double predestination was not the centre of Calvin's theology, but it did qualify his understanding of the gospel: the restoration of humanity to prelapsarian piety was not intended for *all* humanity. Calvin's interest was in the recovery of Adamic piety, not in the fact (as he supposed it to be) that many would be excluded from it. But he was honest enough to admit that God's 'awe-inspiring decree' gives rise to 'great and difficult questions', which he tried energetically to answer from the scriptures, arguing that since no one deserves to be saved, God cannot be charged with injustice if he grants salvation to some and not to others.

The means of grace

The gift of faith is given through the word preached and made visible in the sacraments. Calvin attributes to *preaching itself the kind of efficacy the medieval church ascribed to the sacraments. The word not only evokes faith; it is 'the instrument by which Jesus Christ, with all his graces, is dispensed to us'. But as adjuncts to the word the best of fathers has provided signs or figures of the grace that the word conveys: *baptism is the sign of adoption into the Father's household; in the Lord's Supper (*Eucharist) he gives his children a pledge of their continual nourishment with the bread of life, which is Jesus Christ. Both participate in the sacramental efficacy of the word.

Calvin's sacramental theology rested on *Augustine's distinction between sign and reality. Luther had accused Huldrych *Zwingli of misinterpreting Augustine, for whom a sign was the bearer of a present reality, not, as Zwingli thought, a reminder of something done in the past. Calvin's view was truer to Augustine's: though a sign is not itself the reality, it attests and brings the reality it signifies. The sign presents what it represents; if it were not so, God would be a deceiver. Such a sacramental theology posed obvious difficulties for an evangelical understanding of baptism, which is normally administered to infants. If salvation is by faith, how can an infant incapable of faith receive the grace that baptism signifies? The Calvinist teaching seemed to imply that there are, after all, two

ways of being saved. Some even of Calvin's friends have doubted if he solved the problem. He insisted that baptism is administered only to the infant child of believing parents (in recognition of its birth within the *covenant) and that it does require the future faith of the baptized if it is to become effective. But he did not hesitate to speak of infant regeneration as the sacrament's effect at the actual time of its administration.

In his teaching on the Eucharist Calvin became a leading advocate of the mediating position that emerged after the disastrous clash between the Lutherans and the Zwinglians at Marburg (1529). At a ground-breaking conference between Bucer and Melanchthon in December 1534, the bread and wine of the sacrament were identified as 'exhibitive' signs, 'which being proffered and taken, the body of Christ is proffered and taken at the same time' (Wittenberg Concord, art. 2). Calvin agreed. Since he rejected the Lutheran doctrine of the ubiquity of Christ's *body, it was difficult for him to explain *how* *communion with Christ's life-giving flesh takes place in the sacrament. He was content, he said, to feel what he could not understand. But from Romans 8: 9–11 he concluded that participation in Christ must be the work of the *Holy Spirit. The sacramental signs are efficacious as the Spirit's 'instruments'. Though Calvin often used the language of simultaneity, according to which the reality is given *when* the sign is enacted, instrumentalism was more characteristic of him: the Spirit gives the reality *through* the sign.

Calvin devoted a chapter to what he perceived as the medieval perversion of the sacrament. The Lord's Supper, as the name implies, is a meal and not a *sacrifice. It is indeed true that the body once offered on the cross is offered daily, but for nourishment not for propitiation: it is God's gift to the *church, not the church's sacrifice to God. The Roman mass did twofold violence to the sacrament: it turned the gift of God into a human work, and it dissolved the ecclesial community by reducing communion to the solitary deed of a priest. There is, to be sure, a eucharistic sacrifice since believers are consecrated by the sacrifice of Christ to an answering sacrifice of praise, which includes all the duties of love to their brothers and sisters. The sacrament is a liturgical enactment of this continual thanksgiving by God's people—a collective act of what Calvin understood by 'piety'. But it has nothing to do with appeasing God's *anger.

The church and the civil government

Calvin's ideal was co-operation between church and state, each having its own constitution. But the dividing line between them was not wholly clear in principle, much less in practice. It is remarkable that civil government appears, alongside the church and the sacraments, under the general rubric 'The External Means or Aids by Which God Invites Us into the Society of Christ and Keeps Us Therein'. The civil magistrates are God's deputies; they occupy a holy office, which includes the responsibility of establishing true religion and preventing public blasphemies against God's truth. Their office extends to both tables of the Decalogue.

Perhaps because he saw the civil government as the institution responsible for the outward worship of God—public religion—Calvin spoke of the church mainly in terms of personal nurture. The church is the Mother of believers: as Cyprian said, having God for Father requires having the church for Mother. There is no other way to enter into life than for Mother Church to give us birth and care for us until we lay aside our mortal flesh and become like the angels. It is true that the church has the means for discipline as well as education and nurture in its fourfold *ministry of pastors, teachers, elders, and deacons. But it is the civil government that wields a sword.

The significance of Calvinism for the political and economic institutions of the western world has been keenly debated (see POLITICAL THEOLOGY; DEMOCRACY). The questions are not in the main about Calvin's own opinions on economic and political affairs. His reflections on economic activity are mostly concerned to impose moral limits on the pursuit of monetary gain, not to encourage a free market. And the fact that his political ideas seem capable of development in opposite directions reflects his explicit intention to hold a middle course between those who renounce the civil order and the flatterers of princes, who praise their power too much.

Calvin's thoughts on civil government, summed up in the concluding chapter of the *Institutes*, were shaped by his location in republican Geneva and by his special concern for the Reformed minority in his native land; the use made of his political ideas was shaped in turn by the later fortunes of the Reformed churches both in and beyond France. His explicit point of departure in the chapter on church and state, however, is the characteristic assertion that the existence of the divinely ordained political order is yet another reason for gratitude to God. He has already (in book 3) invoked the 'two kingdoms' doctrine as a warning not to apply the gospel's teaching on spiritual freedom to the political order. In the chapter on civil government he now lays heavy emphasis on the duty of *obedience to those in authority, even when their authority is abused: the obligation of subjects to obey is not contingent on the success with which rulers meet their obligation to rule for the good of their subjects.

It is true that Calvin shows himself suspicious of the absolute power of *kings and expresses a preference either for aristocracy or for a mixed constitution in which not even the 'best men' have the sole voice. Hence he espouses the view that abuse of power at the highest level can and should be challenged by inferior magistrates if the existing constitution allows for it. Moreover, he believes that, as *Daniel defied the edict of King Nebuchadnezzar (Dan. 6), even the private citizen who holds no constitutional office should not obey the civil government if obedience to human authority would mean disobedience to God. Plainly, however, there is no straight line from these qualifications of total passivity to the later Calvinist doctrines of active resistance and legitimate tyrannicide. Calvin thought subjects should be grateful if the form of government under which they lived was beneficent; but if not, they were to suffer it rather than attempt to change it. His horror of shedding the blood of the civil authorities, ordained as they were by God, prevented his views on the limits of compliance from ever becoming a defence of the right to armed resistance. The best the pious could do, whether lower magistrates or private citizens, was to hope that God would exercise the unique divine right of raising up an avenger to punish the injustice of the tyrant.

Calvin's intellectual legacy is not to be measured simply by his influence on western culture. His theology was first and foremost a contribution to Christian thought, and his achievement in the *Institutes* was his construction of a comprehensive interpretation of the Christian faith, an interpretation that continues to provide resources for theological construction today. Unfortunately, his achievement has been overshadowed by dislike of his personality and an obsessive preoccupation with a few issues—or even just one issue—torn from the total fabric of his thought. Calvin did not invent the practice of executing heretics. He had little if anything new to say on the Christian doctrine of election or predestination. The trial and execution of Servetus for denying the Trinity took place at a time when deviant believers were being put to death by the hundreds. And it is a serious failure of understanding when Calvin's treatment of election, which he placed at the end of the third book of the *Institutes*, is discussed with little regard for anything he has said before. The prominence of double predestination in later Calvinism tells us less about its place in Calvin's own thinking than about the points at which opponents outside and inside the Reformed church directed their sharpest criticisms.

Calvin's contribution to Christian thought can be fairly assessed only when seen as a whole. He stands in the company of such masters as *Aquinas and *Schleiermacher. Though he lacked the precision of the one and the originality of the other, his rhetorical style kept him closer than either of them to the immediate language of the believing community. To some, this may seem to be one of his special virtues.

See also SIXTEENTH CENTURY: AN OVERVIEW.   **B. A. Gerrish**

Butin, Philip Walker, *Revelation, Redemption, and Response: Calvin's Trinitarian Understanding of the Divine Human Relationship* (1995).

Davis, Thomas J., *The Clearest Promises of God: The Development of Calvin's Eucharistic Teaching* (1995).

DeVries, Dawn, *Jesus Christ in the Preaching of Calvin and Schleiermacher* (1996).

Gerrish, B. A., *Grace and Gratitude: The Eucharistic Theology of John Calvin* (1993).

Hesselink, I. John, *Calvin's Concept of the Law* (1992).

Jones, Serene, *Calvin and the Rhetoric of Piety* (1995).

McGrath, Alister E., *A Life of John Calvin: A Study of the Shaping of Western Culture* (1990).

Parker, T. H. L., *Calvin: An Introduction to his Thought* (1995).

Puckett, David L., *John Calvin's Exegesis of the Old Testament* (1995).

Rainbow, Jonathan H., *The Will of God and the Cross: An Historical and Theological Study of John Calvin's Doctrine of Limited Redemption* (1990).

Schreiner, Susan E., *The Theater of His Glory: Nature and the Natural Order in the Thought of John Calvin* (1991).

—— *Where Shall Wisdom Be Found? Calvin's Exegesis of Job from Medieval and Modern Perspectives* (1994).

Steinmetz, David C., *Calvin in Context* (1995).

Tamburello, Dennis E., *Union With Christ: John Calvin and the Mysticism of St. Bernard* (1994).

Zachman, Randall C., *The Assurance of Faith: Conscience in the Theology of Martin Luther and John Calvin* (1993).

Calvinism, see REFORMED THEOLOGY.

canon, see APOCRYPHA, CHRISTIAN; BIBLE, ITS AUTHORITY AND INTERPRETATION.

canon law, see LAW.

Canterbury, now a comparatively modest urban centre in Kent, the symbolic focus of the *Anglican *Communion. Its continuous history begins before the Romans occupied Britain. It became the capital of a powerful Anglo-Saxon Kentish kingdom,

hence its role in the mission to the English (597) sent by Pope Gregory I under the leadership of the monk Augustine. Augustine established himself there rather than in London, the former Roman capital of Lower Britain (Gregory's original choice) and although the Kentish kings soon lost their leading role in England, archbishops continued to reside at Canterbury, eventually extending their rule over most of England and Wales, and gaining formal precedence as 'Primates of All England' over the northern English archbishops of York ('Primates of England'). Their monastic *cathedral was rivalled by the nearby monastery of St Peter and Paul (also founded by Augustine, his burial-place, and from 978 known by his name) until the monastic dissolutions in 1538.

The murder of Archbishop Thomas Becket during a church–state clash with King Henry II (1170) triggered a *pilgrimage cult of European significance and financed rebuilding which made the cathedral one of Europe's most magnificent. Becket's cult was suppressed and his shrine destroyed by Henry VIII in 1538, and although Henry preserved the cathedral under a secular dean and chapter, the *Reformation much reduced Canterbury's importance. In any case, the archbishops had long shifted their real headquarters to Lambeth Palace, on the Thames in London, to be near the centre of English government.

Canterbury regained significance in the 19th century, when the Church of England became increasingly conscious of being at the centre of a worldwide Anglican Communion, much of which was beyond the boundaries of the British empire. Lambeth, closely associated with the power of the English state, made a less appropriate focus for Anglican familial unity than Canterbury. From 1897 archbishops re-established a home in the cathedral close. Since then the cathedral has played a major part in Anglican *ecumenical thinking. It has come both to present the external face of Anglican identity and to re-emphasize its cosmopolitan history, symbolizing the ties of English religion and identity with continental Europe: its medieval archbishops included Italians (Augustine and *Anselm) and a Greek (Theodore of Tarsus), much of the building is of purest French Gothic, and since the Reformation a French Protestant congregation has worshipped in its crypt. It has re-established warm links with the *Benedictine Order which served it for centuries; it was the setting for the Anglican welcome to Pope *John Paul II on his British visit in 1982, and in 1986 hosted the signing of the agreement to build the Channel Tunnel linking Britain with the rest of Europe.

From 1867, successive Lambeth Conferences of Anglican bishops from the worldwide communion have met at 10-year intervals. In the beginning they always made a pilgrimage and held a symbolic service at Canterbury. Since 1978 they have been able to spend three weeks in residence together at Canterbury. This has now become established custom and an important international church conference.

Canterbury's role as an episcopal centre beside *Rome, *Constantinople, and Moscow encapsulates the commitment of modern Anglicanism to act as a middle way (via media) in the task of healing the historic divisions of Christianity. In the closing years of the 20th century the medieval pilgrimages to Canterbury were revived but their individualist piety transformed into shared expressions of religious devotion and a common search for Christian *unity.

Robert Runcie

Brooks, N., *The Early History of the Church of Canterbury: Christ Church from 597 to 1066* (1984).

Carpenter, E., *Cantuar: The Archbishops in their Office*, 3rd edn., enlarged by A. Hastings (1997).

Collinson, P., Ramsey, N., Sparks, M. (eds.), *Canterbury Cathedral* (1995).

Runcie, R., *Authority in Crisis? An Anglican Response* (1988).

capitalism. The word 'capitalism' is contentious, and difficult to define without giving offence to the many vested interests that have disputed for or against this, a dominant reality of our time. For present purposes, capitalism may be defined, albeit in a limited way, as: an economic system that sanctions the private and corporate accumulation, exchange, and deployment of wealth as a means of organizing the *work of others from whose labour it is possible to extract a surplus, a profit which may in turn be reinvested in the original or other enterprise, or be otherwise directed.

The history of economic analysis indicates that classical capitalism appeared in the course of the late 18th century and was first theorized in its classic form by Adam Smith in the *Wealth of Nations* (1776). Max Weber conceded that capitalism understood simply as great individual financial undertakings is as old as history, whereas R. H. Tawney (glossing Weber) argued 'Capitalism, as an economic system, resting on the organization of legally free wage-earners, for the purpose of pecuniary profit, by the owner of capital or his agents, and setting its stamp on every aspect of society, is a modern phenomenon' (Weber 1930: I (c)). Capitalism, properly so-called, is therefore that mode of production and exchange initially associated with the industrial revolution, political economy, and emergent *modernity. The impact of industrialization and the concomitant growth in urban population was to be felt across Europe (and then more widely) in ways that were to have a powerful impact not only upon both *Protestant and Catholic forms of Christianity, but now for all practical purposes upon all sociocultural contexts and religions of the world. Since Weber, capitalism has, of course, enormously developed and diversified. There are many new globalized markets and innovative ways of manipulating capital for profit, and there are, besides, many cultural adaptations of capitalism.

According to Weber, the *mentalité* associated with the capitalist mode of production had historical connections and elective affinities with this-worldly Protestant asceticism, and it is therefore customary (but not undisputed) to link the nascent spirit of capitalism with the much-disputed Protestant ethic, and, above all, with the *Reformed Christian tradition (Ray 1987). Weber explores the affinities between the single-minded pursuit of God and an equally focused desire for profit. It is not by chance that Weber uses the Latin scholastic ascription of *God as supreme good, when he analyses this distinctive mind-set and hints at its wider implications:

> In fact the *summum bonum* of this ethic, the earning of more and more money, combined with strict avoidance of all spontaneous enjoyment of life, is above all completely devoid of any eudaemonistic, not to say hedonistic, admixture. It is thought of so purely as an end in itself, that from the point of view of the happiness of, or utility to, the single individual, it appears entirely transcendental and absolutely irrational. Man is dominated by the making of money, by acquisition as the ultimate purpose of his life. Economic acquisition is no longer subordinated to man as the means for the satisfaction of his material needs.

(Weber 1930/1977: 53)

In *Religion and the Rise of Capitalism* (1926), the historian and economist R. H. Tawney applied Weber's insights to 17th-century England, and provided a powerful, but indirect critique of the *laissez-faire* liberal capitalism that foundered in the economic crisis of the interwar period. Later, further British explorations of the processual metaphor of the 'rise' of capitalism were extended by V. A. Demant (1952) to its 'decline', and its 'persistence' by R. H. Preston (1979). Following the Second World War, the creation of a partially state-managed capitalism, spelt out by John Maynard Keynes in the *General Theory* and other writings, enabled the 'Butskellite' political consensus that underlay the ethos of the Welfare State, but this had minimal theological impact. In short, capitalism was largely evaluated in terms of its practical impact upon the distribution of wealth and social benefits, in what Tawney had called the 'acquisitive society'. Now, in an era of resurgent capitalism, it is possible to see that this assimilation and application of Weberian perspectives was somewhat narrow in scope. Recent work by, for example, Donald Hay, Douglas Meeks, and others has provided Christian theologies of 'God the Economist' and discussions largely founded upon the ethics of distribution, rather than involving critical consideration of capitalism as such. Within the ambit of North American capitalism, *prosperity theology, with its uncritical endorsement of capitalism, remains a popular theological genre.

Consideration of the full theological significance of capitalism and its most trenchant critique in *Marxism is related to, but not to be identified with, the creation of biblically based discussion of economic theory characteristic of Hay and Meeks. Beyond the confines of mainline Protestant Christian theology of the *twentieth century, public understanding of capitalism as a cultural phenomenon was often dominated by the critique generated by revisionist Marxism. Rather in the way that the polemic of early Christianity furnishes major information about heresy, so the representation of 'capitalism' was constitutively influenced by Marx's hostile accounts, most notably as found in the *Communist Manifesto* (1848) and *Capital* (1887). Informed theological evaluations of both capitalism (perceived as a system in crisis) and Marxism (a set of doctrines terminally tainted for many Christians by the events of the Russian Revolution of 1917 and its aftermath) were rare in the interwar period. It was only after the Second World War and with a gradual thaw in the ensuing Cold War that this situation changed. In Germany, *political theology, which involved a variety of syntheses between Protestant theology and various strands of revisionist Marxism, developed in the 1960s and 1970s. Insights from political theology were transplanted to Central and *Latin America, where, after *Vatican II and the Medellín Conference of 1968, *liberation theology emerged in the context of rapid industrialization and urbanization similar to the conditions Marx and Engels had observed in the Rhineland in the 1830s. This theology drew perspectives from Marxist analysis of society and its critique of the distribution of wealth, but sidestepped the *atheistic aspects of Marxism highlighted by the Sacred Congregation in Rome. Liberation theology developed its most radical critique of capitalism with the representation of the imbalanced distribution of wealth in the *global economy as a confessional issue.

A notable exception to the relative theological ignorance of the full implications of capitalism and of its socialist critique is to be found in Roman Catholic social teaching. After lengthy consultation provoked by the changing socio-economic conditions of the 19th century, *Rerum Novarum*, the first of a series of papal encyclicals, was published in 1891. Mindful of the fate of the Catholic Church in revolutionary France (and later of the Orthodox Church in Soviet Russia), the position of the church with regard to the historic struggle between capital and labour was defined in terms of a conflict between the competing rights and obligations of owners and of workers, over which the church was to exercise a moderating role. Both parties to this conflict were to recognize the mutuality of their rights and obligations, and yet to relativize these through acknowledgement of the beatific vision as the sole and legitimate goal of humankind, thus resisting the Weberian slippage (under conditions of *secularization) from the spiritual worship of God to the practical service of Mammon. The church sought to maintain this position. During the pontificate of *John Paul II, and with the publication of the encyclical *Centesimus Annus* in 1991, a deeper level of cultural analysis of both Marxism and capitalism has become apparent. Papal teaching had made a concerted attempt to defend the integrity of the human agent against the depredations of both Marxist *socialism and unrestrained capitalism; both are represented as aspects of a destructive, secular modernity in need of comprehensive re-evangelization.

Neither Protestantism (with its historic associations with urbanization and the ethos and practice of capitalism) nor Roman Catholicism (with its reluctant adjustments to the modern world) has fully come to terms with the transformatory character of resurgent capitalism, which, during the Reagan–Thatcher era, was informed and driven by a New Right version of political economy. The collapse of Marxist socialism in 1989–90 removed what was regarded by some as the final barriers to the triumph of capitalism. Thus encouraged, Francis Fukuyama proposed 'the End of History' in which the unfettered enactment of capitalism is attended by the managerial regularization of the whole world. For Fukuyama, capitalism has triumphed, and, in the light of this, both Christianity and socialism are in effect superseded. The exceptional few, contemporary entrepreneurs represented as a *Nietzschian élite of 'Last Men', must draw upon the pre-Christian *thumos* (manly virtue) depicted in *Plato's *Republic*, in order to lead a global mass humanity domesticated by the disciplines of managerial capitalism. Christian thought has yet adequately to respond in an informed and comprehensive way to the normalization of the world in accordance with the requirements of resurgent capitalism.

Fukuyama's vision of the historic closure that attends the emergence of a world in which capitalism has no rival leaves unasked many of the questions which arose in Marx's critique of capitalism. As rebellious atheistic Jew, Marx understood the theological implications of capitalism, albeit expressed in the antireligious polemic of his early thought and later parodic 'anti-theology' of the *Grundrisse* (1857/8). With both historical understanding and prescience, Marx was able to attack the residual, alienated theology of West German idealism, and its displaced surrogates, the state and the accumulated power of money in dynamic, world-transforming capital. In the *Communist Manifesto* (1948), Marx paradoxically expressed a profound admiration of the achievements of the bourgeois revolution and its ability through technology to master and harness nature to the service of man; rightly controlled, this would lead to the abolition of human need. The alchemic potency of capitalism was such that, as Marx ironically observed, the ugly man who was rich became handsome. Money as mediation, and labour as the source of value (as opposed to land or precious metals) had the power to transmute *all* aspects of human life into commodities and exchange values in an ever-extending market, increasingly dominated by monopolies. Marx's concern was to destroy the form of mediation itself, the accumulation of capital based on the right to private property, and to invest the future of humankind in the 'concrete universal' of the enslaved proletariat, the societal analogue of the Hegelian bondsman (the *Knecht*), a 'negation of the negation' through which total societal emancipation would be effected.

In recent years the market has expanded into the remaining interstices of the human condition and commodification has correspondingly extended in ways scarcely foreseeable. The velocity of capital circulation has increased through the use of information technology to the point that time-compression has profound cultural consequences. Now globalization (and the problematic interface between the global and the local) has augmented class struggle within nations with an asymmetry of opportunity and outcomes between competitors in a core–periphery world system. For those at the heart of this system, capitalism is becoming 'soft' and reciprocally infused with transformative cultural power. Under these conditions *religious language and even theological vocabulary have become a conceptual resource for the representation of that which now enacts those modes of omnipresence, omnipotence, omniscience, and instantaneity formerly attributed to the God who subsisted at the core of western consciousness.

This is now the era of what the American Catholic writer and apologist, Michael Novak, has called 'magic capitalism'. In his comprehensive inversion of Marxist socialism, Novak has argued that humankind has to abandon the naive and infantile 'dreams' (that is, the false consciousness) of socialism and to recognize the universality of necessary alienation. Experience of the latter is a universal rite of passage in which each must encounter the 'empty shrine' of 'democratic capitalism' (Novak 1982/1991: 53). So matured, humankind may then draw upon *spirituality, *theology, and religious values (taken from Christianity and Judaism) for strength to compete and survive in the face of the *Nihil* in the 'empty shrine' of capitalism; according to Novak, this is our contemporary 'dark night of the soul'.

There are, however, further dimensions of contemporary capitalism that require fundamental theological appraisal. In a globalized world system in which the consciousness of humanity (and its virtual enhancement) is refracted through the World Wide Web and the Internet, the parameters of the human and the natural are displaced in ways only remotely foreshadowed by Marx and others. There is no one single 'new' spirit of capitalism; but there is evidence of increasingly intimate synergetic interactions between religions, innovative spiritualities, and the cultures of capitalism. Moreover, the classic secular asceticism analysed by Weber has been complemented and challenged by celebration of the consuming and expressive self in an expanding global market of human—and inhuman—opportunities. It is not at present clear how Christian thought with its perceived collusions, including those with patriarchal capitalism, will respond to these new cultural configurations. The all-encompassing and transformatory power of contemporary capitalism requires an equally comprehensive theological response. This is the more urgent since the collapse of Marxism, and the apparent elimination of any residual critical standpoints external, as it were, to the system.　　**Richard H. Roberts**

Duchrow, U., *Global Economy: A Confessional Issue for the Churches?* (1987).
Entemann, Willard F., *Managerialism: The Emergence of a New Ideology* (1994).
Fukuyama, Francis, *The End of History and the Last Man* (1992).
Green, D. G., *The New Right: The Counterrevolution in Political, Economic and Social Thought* (1987).
Hampden-Turner, Charles, and Trompenaar, Fons, *The Seven Cultures of Capitalism: Values Systems for Creating Wealth in the United States, Britain, Japan, Germany, France, Sweden, and the Netherlands* (1993).
Hay, D. A., *Economics Today: A Christian Critique* (1989).
Lash, Scott, and Urry, John, *Economies of Signs and Space* (1994).
Meeks, M. D., *God the Economist: The Doctrine of God and Political Economy* (1989).
Novak, M., *The Spirit of Democratic Capitalism* (1982/1991).
Ray, Larry, 'The Protestant Ethic Today' in R. J. Anderson, J. A. Hughes, and W. W. Sharrock (eds.), *Classic Disputes in Sociology* (1987), 97–125.
Roberts, R. H. (ed.), *Religion and the Transformation of Capitalism: Comparative Perspectives* (1995).
Thrift, Nigel, 'The Rise of Soft Capitalism', *Cultural Values*, 1/1 (1997), 29–57.
Weber, Max, Tawney, R. H. (ed. and foreword), *The Protestant Ethic and the Spirit of Capitalism* (1930).

capital punishment. Recent decades have seen a marked decline in the use of capital punishment. It has been abolished or has fallen into disuse in many countries, but in some it has been reintroduced after abolition or applied after a long period during which no executions were carried out. There are pronounced regional variations: capital punishment has virtually disappeared in Western Europe and Latin America but remains in use in Islamic countries (as part of, or under the influence of, *Shari'a*), in many Asian and African countries and those formerly part of the Soviet Union, and in most of the United States and the Caribbean. In the United Kingdom it was retained for treason until 1998 but was effectively abolished in 1965 in all but Northern Ireland, and there in 1973. It was provided for in the law of the Vatican City State until 1969. A number of international conventions in the field of human rights contain provisions excluding the use of the death penalty, at least in peacetime.

Christians have been notably reluctant to identify capital punishment as a matter on which the spirit of the New Testament contradicts the letter of the Old. Christian thought has not been able wholly to shake itself free of the *lex talionis*, 'a life for a life' (Exod. 21: 23) (see LAW, BIBLICAL). Although the *lex talionis* was deprecated in the *Sermon on the Mount (Matt. 5: 38–41), the Christian duty to *forgive was not interpreted as precluding the imposition of capital punishment by the state. So *Augustine, writing to urge that the torture and execution of priests should not be met by exact retaliation, noted that the execution of criminals as a result of charges brought by the secular power was not a matter to which objection need be made (*Letters*, 133). In England, the Thirty-Nine Articles declared that 'the Laws of the Realm may punish Christian men with death, for heinous and grievous offences' (Article 37), and the current Catechism of the Catholic Church affirms the right of the state to punish criminals with appropriate penalties 'not excluding in cases of extreme gravity, the death penalty'.

Other early Christian writers were opposed to capital punishment: Tertullian doubted whether a Christian could accept public office if it involved sitting in judgement on a capital charge (*De idololatria*, 17), and Lactantius thought it neither lawful nor just to bring a capital charge, for the commandment against taking life applied to a *punishment as to the original crime (*Divinae institutiones*, 6. 20).

Capital punishment was, however, an entrenched part of the practice of rulers, one from which many Christians suffered during times of persecution (see MARTYRDOM). In later centuries, Christians did not hesitate to impose capital punishment on one another in the context of disagreements as to doctrine or authority within the church.

For centuries the bishops of the Church of England supported a wide application of the death penalty even for offences, such as theft of five shillings from a shopkeeper, which could scarcely be regarded as heinous or grievous. Their clergy were engaged in the pastoral care of the condemned; the joyful confidence with which some of the condemned faced death was cited in support of capital punishment.

If there has been a shift in the balance of Christian thought on the matter, it must be admitted that it has tended to follow rather than lead informed opinion.

The 20th century saw a gradual loss of confidence in the arguments which had sustained capital punishment. So, statistical studies cast doubt on the deterrent effect of capital punishment as compared with that of lesser penalties; the United States Supreme Court in *Gray* v. *Georgia* (1976) found that there was no convincing statistical evidence either way on that issue. Belief in the death penalty as a supremely effective deterrent was further weakened by more sophisticated analysis of the mental element in the crime of murder, and of the circumstances in which homicide typically occurs: circumstances of anger, fear, or excitement, inimical to reasoned reflection on the sanctions of the penal system.

The most commonly advanced arguments for the use of capital punishment speak of its retributive, denunciatory, or symbolic value. In the words of the court in *Gray* v. *Georgia*, it is 'an expression of society's moral outrage'.

Against retributive theories of punishment must, however, be set the demands of *mercy and forgiveness as well as evidence of the frailty of human systems of criminal justice. Capital punishment is irreversible and there are cases in which innocent men have been executed. There is a growing body of evidence of inconsistency, and in some countries racial bias, in the imposition of the death sentence. The Fraser Committee reporting in Jamaica in 1981 described the death penalty as bearing 'unequally and irrevocably on the poor, on minority groups, and on opposition groups within the population'.

In recent decades, the churches have supported the abolitionist cause, primarily in the human rights context, with theological points of reference not only in ideas of the *Kingdom but in OT prophecy; though the abolitionist views of church authorities are not always shared by the majority of church members. Late 20th-century Catholic teaching on capital punishment was expressed in Pope *John Paul II's encyclical *Evangelium Vitae* (1995; para. 56). He followed Lactantius in considering the issue in the context of the commandment 'Thou shalt not kill'. He argued that punishment

should not go to the extreme of executing the offender except in cases of absolute necessity: in other words, when it would not be possible otherwise to defend society. Such cases 'are very rare, if not practically non-existent'. Other forms of punishment were more in conformity with the dignity of the human *person.

See also CONSCIENCE; LAW; NATURAL LAW.   **David McClean**

Bedau, H. A., *The Death Penalty in America*, 3rd edn. (1982).
Hood, R., *The Death Penalty: A World-wide Perspective*, 2nd edn. (1996).
Schabas, W. A., *The Abolition of the Death Penalty in International Law* (1993).

Caroline Divines.

Caroline Divines. This term describes those theologians who set out to show the Church of England of the *seventeenth century as both *Catholic and *Reformed. 'Caroline' is first known to have been used as a referent to King Charles I, but theologians of the school are often taken to embrace the reign of Charles's father, James I (1603–25), as well as of his two sons, Charles II (1660–85) and James II (1685–8). They may represent the most extensive attempt within the first century of the *Reformation to reclaim the full theological and spiritual legacy derivable from earlier periods.

The main characteristics of this school consist of the defence and elucidation of the principles inherent in the Book of Common Prayer, which was itself an evolving tradition; the study of the early fathers, particularly those of the east; the application of *reason as a critical and imaginative faculty in the discernment of religious *truth, pioneered by Richard *Hooker and developed by others; and concern with applying Christian devotion to daily *discipleship. As masters of English writing as well as of a restrained spirituality, their influence is perhaps most popularly expressed in the poetry of George Herbert (1593–1633), who wrote both a treatise on the work of the country parson and such classics of religious poetry as 'Let all the world in ev'ry corner sing' and 'King of glory, King of peace' which stress the *providence of God in the ordinary things of life. Jeremy Taylor (1613–67) was a prolific devotional writer, whose *Rules and Exercises for Holy Living* (1650) has been constantly reprinted. One of its main features is the 'embodied' life of God in human nature, giving rise to such expressions as 'we are cabinets of the mysterious Trinity'.

The Caroline Divines are often regarded as the founding fathers of *Anglican thought. Among those with the most lasting influence is Lancelot Andrewes (1555–1626), who, like many of them, was a parish priest and also a distinguished academic, and later became a bishop. In 1629, 96 of Andrewes' sermons were published, nearly all of them *preached before the court of King James I at the festivals. These sermons are rich in biblical exposition, vivid imagery, patristic learning, and practical devotion. The 1617 Whitsun sermon on Luke 4: 18–19, 'The Spirit of the Lord is upon me…', applies the text to the 'coming of the Spirit'; to the life of the Trinity, 'to retain to each person, his own peculiar, his proper act, in this common work of the all'; to the spiritual freedom of being able to 'return to the heart' (Isa. 46: 8 LXX—a favourite *Augustine motif); as well as to the *Eucharist itself: 'the memorial, or mystery of which sacrifice of Christ's, in our stead, is ever… the top of our mirth, and the initiation of the joy of our jubilee'.

These writers went a long way to rescue the Church of England from becoming narrowly inward-looking through their wider vision of Anglicanism, which was rekindled in the *Oxford

Movement in the 19th century. More significantly, they continue to fascinate scholars of other churches, including Roman Catholic and *Eastern Orthodox, in the ecumenical climate of the later 20th century.   **Kenneth W. Stevenson**

Lossky, Nicholas, *Lancelot Andrewes The Preacher (1555–1626): The Origins of the Mystical Theology of the Church of England* (1991).

McAdoo, H. R., *The Eucharistic Theology of Jeremy Taylor Today* (1988).

Stevenson, Kenneth, *Covenant of Grace Renewed: A Vision of the Eucharist in the Seventeenth Century* (1994).

Cartesianism, see DESCARTES.

casuistry is the study of relating general *moral principles to particular cases; especially analysing predicaments which appear to involve a conflict of principles, such as whether it is permissible to lie to protect a confidence, or to alleviate a patient's pain by giving drugs which will also accelerate death (see MEDICAL ETHICS). Not exclusively a Christian activity, as Cicero's *De officiis*, 3, illustrates, the study of moral 'cases of *conscience' nevertheless has been a continuing concern of Catholic moral theology, especially from the 16th century, in its attempt to keep pace both with the *church's requirement of private confession of *sins and with the continuing need to assess traditional morality in the light of changing reality.

Casuistry acquired the bad name from which it still suffers in some quarters, and in some dictionaries ('2. Reasoning that is specious or oversubtle', *Collins Concise Dictionary*), by becoming linked with the theory of probabilism, a systematic method for solving problems of moral uncertainty. Probabilism claimed that if in a particular case one was in doubt as to the right course to pursue, one could take any course which had good arguments for it, even if the case for taking the opposite line was stronger. Starting as an attempt to respect the individual's freedom of conscience against automatic compliance with *authority and moral rules, probabilism became in the hands of some theologians a recipe for minimalism, rationalization, and moral permissiveness. As such it fell foul of the powerful *Jansenist movement of reform and rigour in the 17th-century church in France; and it was brilliantly, if unfairly, pilloried by the Jansenist sympathizer, *Pascal, in his *Provincial Letters*, for the widespread moral 'laxism' which he and others charged Jesuit theologians and confessors with encouraging.

Casuistry, however, survived the excesses of probabilism and the attacks of Jansenism, especially when the latter movement was itself officially discredited by Rome and when the system of probabilism shed its irresponsible extremes. Indeed, the popularity of analysing typical 'cases of conscience' as an aid to individuals in various personal or professional situations, especially in a changing society, was not confined to Roman Catholic theologians; it flourished also among Protestant, Anglican, and Puritan writers, with the added advantage of being written in the vernacular languages rather than Latin and thus being much more accessible to *lay people. Interestingly, however, non-Catholic casuists accepted the strictures of Pascal on probabilism (and on the Jesuits), and in their study of cases generally gave the benefit of any doubt not to the individual, but to the *law or the moral precept which might appear to be in question.

Old casuistry, new case studies. As the sciences, social and behavioural as well as physical, have added more new and increasingly complex features to every area of modern living, there has also been a dramatic increase in the new issues challenging hitherto generally accepted moral principles and straining traditional morality. In such fluid circumstances the modern popular approach of moral exploration by way of case studies is replicating the characteristics of historical casuistry in two ways. By requiring painstaking factual analysis of the typical or individual situation being considered, the casuistical, or case study, approach aims to respect human reality in its complexity, and to identify all the morally relevant features of the case which will contribute to a realistic solution. And by playing off these facts against the moral principle or principles which the case appears to invoke or involve, the method institutes an interplay between facts and principles which might shed new light on the deeper meaning and extension of the principles while at the same time establishing moral priorities and providing justification for a particular solution to the dilemma.

It is to the merit of casuistry that it does not envisage all moral reasoning as the deductive applying of a general principle to a particular situation (lying is wrong; this is a lie; so this is wrong). Nor is it, as some modern writers hold, the ignoring of principles in preference for appealing to paradigm cases or for arguing by *analogy from case to case (it was all right in that case; so it should be all right in this one). For the feature which a particular new case may share with others, enabling them to be appealed to as precedents or analogues, can often be formulated as a new generalization or principle applying to the whole class of such cases.

In fact, the value of casuistry as a heuristic moral activity is best found in its providing a dialectical form of exchange between, on the one hand, what appear to be the facts of a particular case and, on the other, one or more generally accepted moral principles which appear to be relevant to this case. Casuistry is thus viewed not as the study of applying general moral principles *to* particular cases, but as the study of applying principles *in* particular cases as judged appropriate. Such a continuing exercise of moral reflection, which brings respect and a critical approach both to new reality and to moral tradition, not only enables moral justice to be done to new situations; it can also provide a basis for appropriate new moral insights and new and refined moral principles.   **Jack Mahoney**

Bedau, H. A., 'Casuistry', in L. C. and C. B. Becker (eds.), *Encyclopedia of Ethics*, (1992), i.

Ciulla, J. B., 'Casuistry and the Case for Business Ethics', in T. J. Donaldson and R. E. Freeman (eds.), *Business as a Humanity* (1994).

Jonsen, A. R., and Toulmin, S., *The Abuse of Casuistry: A History of Moral Reasoning* (1988).

Keenan, J. F., 'The Return of Casuistry', *Theological Studies*, 57 (1996), 123–39.

Mahoney, J., 'The Meaning of Exception', in *Seeking the Spirit: Essays in Moral and Pastoral Theology* (1981).

—— *The Making of Moral Theology: A Study of the Roman Catholic Tradition* (1987).

cathedrals are the most powerful visual expression of Christianity's central, Catholic, tradition, but they would have made little sense to early Christianity, while for many sectarian and more intensely *Protestant movements they were objects of suspicion, the pointless ostentation of a worldly *church. In the Scottish *Reformation several were abandoned and fell into ruins as also in England's Cromwellian period, after which severely damaged buildings like Durham and Lichfield required massive restoration.

If the greatest, most prolific, period of construction lay between the 12th and 14th centuries, cathedrals were arising already in the age of *Constantine, the 17th century saw the construction of some very magnificent ones in Latin America, the 19th the building of many more in North America, Africa, and elsewhere, while even the second half of the 20th century provided a number of entirely new ones.

The basic reasons for the cathedral's existence are clear enough: the nature of the *Eucharist as Christianity's public weekly ritual and of the local *episcopate as presiding over the Eucharist and gathered church. The Eucharist presupposes the attendance and participation of all Christians; hence, once the number of Christians much increased in the 4th century, large assembly places were needed within urban society. Moreover, as each *city was seen as forming a single 'church' presided over by its bishop, this assembly place obtained a necessarily episcopal character. At its east end a large raised chair, a *cathedra*, was built for the local bishop: hence a 'cathedral'. The large pillared hall of Roman law courts (basilicas) provided a convenient model and soon 'cathedrals' of varying sizes were rising wherever there was a bishop. In *Rome St John's Lateran Basilica and St Peter's Vatican Basilica, both built by Constantine, became archetypes for an institution denoting the public presence, even social ascendancy, of Christianity. While, strictly speaking, the Lateran was Rome's cathedral and St Peter's a *pilgrimage church above Peter's *memoria*, the nature of the latter inevitably gave it also a cathedral character, representing the pope's larger authority.

While many cathedrals were fairly small, a contagious example was set by the greatest—St Peter's for the west, Hagia Sophia, built by Justinian in *Constantinople, for the east. Witness the Ottonian cathedrals, such as Speyer, of 11th-century imperial Germany. The political message of Speyer, the royal burial-place, was clear. Nothing could be too magnificent for the cathedral of a great imperial city and for the highly complex *liturgy which developed within such churches, different indeed from the simplicity of an early Eucharist. Here great numbers of people could experience the church as a worshipping reality, at once aesthetically, spiritually, and politically magnificent. 'We knew not whether we were in heaven or on earth. For on earth there is no such splendour or such beauty, and we are at a loss how to describe it. We know only that God dwells there among men.' Such was the reaction of a group of *Russians sent from Kiev in the 11th century on witnessing the liturgy of Hagia Sophia (*The Russian Primary Chronicle: Laurentian Text*, ed. S. H. Cross and S. H. and O. O. Sherbowitz-Wetzor, 1953). Western pilgrims visiting St Peter's in Rome would have felt something similar. It was a sense of earth opening onto *heaven, recalling Jacob's dream at Bethel of the ladder reaching to heaven and his comment upon it: 'This is nothing less than the house of God; this is the gate of heaven' (Gen. 28: 17), a text used in the Introit of the common for the dedication of a church and repeated time and again in sermons at cathedral consecrations, as in 1649 when Bishop Palafox dedicated the great Mexican cathedral of Puebla.

The first cathedrals of medieval northern Europe were simple enough but the incentive to vie in splendour became enormous. As conditions stabilized and building expertise improved, an extraordinary wave of magnificent churches arose across medieval Europe. From the late 11th century remarkable engineering developments led to the evolution of the 'Gothic' style with its pointed arches, high ribbed vaults, slender clustered pillars, ever-larger windows, and flying buttresses. The engineering expertise required to make these churches possible (and still stable in many cases eight centuries later) is seldom fully appreciated. They were by far the most significant buildings of their age, in size, daring design, aesthetic satisfaction, and spiritual *symbolism. While they varied considerably between themselves, so that English Gothic, for example, is markedly different from French, German, or Portuguese, they shared a common *élan*. If the greatest formal perfection may be claimed for Chartres or Bourges with their extreme simplicity of plan, and intense verticality, English cathedrals like *Canterbury, York, or Salisbury have an alternative fascination in the very complexity of their plan. Compare the transept-less unity of Bourges with the double transept model of Salisbury and its resultant multiplication of spaces, corners, and chapels, and one has two divergent pictures of how a cathedral was envisaged and used.

While essentially achievements of architecture, they depended for their full effect on a wide range of *arts, most important of which were stained glass and stone-carving, but also cast bronze, the wood-carving of stalls and screens, floor and wall tiles, wall-painting. In one or another form, every possible biblical and theological theme could be depicted. Yet the art closest to the functional heart of the cathedral was *music. This was the case at least from the time of Ambrose and Gregory the Great. The English musical tradition, in particular, owes a huge debt to cathedral music, from Merbecke, Tallis, and Byrd in the 16th century to the cathedral choirs and schools, the choral evensong, of the present, despite a protracted lack of interest in the 18th and early 19th centuries.

Enriched in so many ways, cathedrals constituted an extraordinary aesthetic ensemble at the heart of medieval Christianity, expressive of the way it had the power to make use of everything for worship and instruction. In Lethaby's words, 'In these buildings all may be explained as devised for ritual use and for the instruction of the people; all as material and structural necessity; all as traditional development; all as free beauty and romance in stone.' Of course, cathedrals were not alone in this. Numerous other churches, especially those of monasteries, shared some of the same characteristics.

The heart of the cathedral remained the celebration of mass and office, and this was still the case with post-Reformation cathedrals like Wren's St Paul's or 20th-century examples such as Coventry and the two cathedrals in Liverpool, but as the understanding of the way the Eucharist should be celebrated has altered, so has the structuring of cathedrals, from the elongated to the circular, from the mysterious to the participatory. Yet the scale of the greatest cathedrals has to be explained in more political terms. Hagia Sophia manifested the transcendence of imperial Byzantium, Michelangelo's St Peter's the uniqueness of the *papacy, St Paul's a religious space at the centre of the capital of a growing empire and great commercial city, Protestant yet episcopal. Others obtained their special function and funds from the cult of a local saint or, like Chartres, Marian pilgrimage. Their social usefulness could also be considerable. Many an English parliament met in a cathedral chapter house. Every such building required vast financial resources and, in consequence, a commitment as much lay as clerical. It was a shortage of money which explains the long delays in completion which many of them suffered.

The purpose of these churches became, nevertheless, increasingly problematic. They can appear as an exercise in competitive grandiosity. With the development of a full parochial system and the effective demise of the conception of a diocese as a eucharistic community, they almost lost their basic role. Eucharistic meaning goes with intimacy rather than magnitude. Even the bishop's *cathedra* largely lost its point as well as its place, although the medieval cathedral could well be seen as retaining a largely educational function, maintaining a school which might rival an early *university and providing the informed sermons seldom offered in parishes. As a wide gap developed between the 'Lord Bishop' and his cathedral, the latter fell increasingly into the hands of dean and chapter which, at best, signified an extensive collegial ministry, liturgical, educational, scholarly, and pastoral, but often became instead a narrow oligarchy engrossed in the administration of something which had lost any clear *raison d'être*. The petty but long-lasting feuds and Trollopian Bonapartes that can so dominate the life of a cathedral close are not, unfortunately, something wholly of the past.

The engineering and architectural achievement of one generation can become the white elephant of another, though in reality the building and rebuilding of many of the most historic cathedrals is something which has continued generation after generation across the centuries. Their survival, even physically, requires never-ending and costly attention dependent in modern times upon financial support from either the state or a ceaseless tourist influx. The challenge of the cathedral today is how to be more than a historical monument or tourist attraction. It has to link the provision of space for eucharistic and choral celebration of rather a special kind with vast availability for wider religious, artistic, educational, and civil activities. Cathedrals dominated the townscape until the coming of skyscrapers and tower-blocks; in many places they still do, and there is a memorableness about the dominance of Durham, Lincoln, or Salisbury's spire vastly beyond that of any tower-block. Can they continue to find a comparable socially encompassing role? The rebuilding of Coventry Cathedral, destroyed by wartime bombs, was an essentially national act. Its design by Basil Spence, dominant Graham Sutherland tapestry of *Christ in Glory*, baptistery glass by John Piper and Patrick Reyntiens, and, perhaps most striking of all, the first performance of Benjamin Britten's *War Requiem* on 30 May 1962 when the church was reconsecrated, all demonstrated that a 20th-century cathedral could still provide the focus for the moral and cultural life of a nation. Moreover, Coventry's continuing *ecumenical work and German links suggest ways in which a cathedral's ministry may be uniquely reconciliatory. Effectively it seems that a cathedral needs to be a highly multi-purpose and ecumenical reality. Now as in the past there is a tension between unity and multiplicity, verticality and horizontality. While the former may provide the greatest spiritual and aesthetic perfection, it is also least hospitable to a more secular diversity. The danger for the cathedral today is simply to be dead for nine-tenths of the time, a survivor from another age, touristically attractive through its very otherness. It is true that a cathedral may offer tourists a sense of something deeper than does a castle or palace. Witnessing to otherness has its own intrinsic value. Cathedrals may remain, even through tourism, a major link between Christianity and post-Christian society, and tourism may even recover a sense of pilgrimage. But the difficult challenge remains to do still more than this and

achieve some sort of living translation, so that cathedrals continue to witness to the creative enlistment of human arts and sciences in the service of God. It is something impossible to realize without the dedicated co-operation of a great many people, most of them unpaid.   **Adrian Hastings**

Campbell, Louise, *Coventry Cathedral* (1996).

Collinson, P., Ramsay, N., and Sparks, M. (eds.), *A History of Canterbury Cathedral* (1995).

Hastings, Adrian, *Elias of Dereham* (1997).

Lethaby, R. R., *Medieval Art* (1904).

Murray, Peter and Linda, *The Oxford Companion to Christian Art and Architecture* (1996).

Tatton-Brown, Tim, *Great Cathedrals of Britain* (1989).

von Reinhard, Bentmann, and Lickes, Heinrich, *Churches of the Middle Ages* (1979).

Catherine of Siena (1347–80) is known as a *mystical writer, faithful daughter of the church, exemplar of *charity and self-denial, stigmatic, *visionary, and *miracle worker. Born Caterina Benincasa, the twenty-third out of twenty-five children, her *spirituality can only be understood in the context of her family experiences. She alone of the Benincasa children was successfully nursed by her mother. Her twin sister, sent out to a wet nurse, died, like most of her siblings, in infancy. Catherine grew up with the knowledge of being a privileged child, the one who was given her mother's breast and survived. She certainly had a strong internalized guilt, blaming herself for the death in childbirth of her elder sister Bonaventura. Catherine determined not to marry and developed an *ascetic spirituality which included daily *fasting, flagellation, sleep deprivation, silence, and *prayer. Her iron will and determination to punish her body appear to be linked to a pact in which she asked God to be allowed to suffer in return for the salvation of her family. The despised body became a vehicle with which to imitate Christ and win salvation both for herself and others.

The 14th century saw a flowering of new religious forms of expression, and in her late teens Catherine was admitted to the *Mantellate* (precursors of Dominican tertiaries), widowed matrons who devoted themselves to charitable works. They accepted Catherine on the grounds that she was both sincere and plain. She continued to live at home and became known for her prodigious generosity, usually at her father's expense, which included a determination to feed others whilst denying herself. In 1374 the Dominican Raymond of Capua became Catherine's spiritual director, and later her biographer. In around 1378 Catherine completed her book (*The Dialogue*) in which the saint petitions God for four graces: to be allowed to suffer in *atonement for *sin; for the reform of the church; for peace among Christians; and for divine providence.

As Catherine's public life and reputation for sanctity grew she dictated numerous letters of advice and admonition to leading figures of her day, which give us a vivid picture of a charismatic and determined woman. She played a part in persuading the reluctant Pope Gregory XI to leave Avignon for Rome. For Catherine the pope (whom she referred to as 'Daddy') was both a father and Christ on earth. Gregory's successor, Urban VI, proved unpopular and the cardinals elected an alternative candidate, initiating the Great Schism, which saw rival papacies established in Rome and Avignon. Catherine felt that she had failed and sought to increase her sufferings on behalf of her family and the church. Eventually refusing water as well as food, Catherine died on 3 April 1380 aged 33. She was canonized in 1461 and in 1970 was accorded the title 'Doctor of the Church'.

Catherine is remembered now as a woman who spoke her mind, even to popes, for her twin passion for God's love and institutional reform, but also as a victim of a medieval model of female sanctity in which suffering and self-sacrifice could merge with self-hatred, and in which the desire to love was framed within a personal life-and-death struggle for autonomy and self-control. Why she was declared a 'Doctor of the Church' remains enigmatic.

Fiona Bowie

Catherine of Siena: The Dialogue, ET (1980).
I, Catherine: Selected Writings of Catherine of Siena, ET (1980).
The Life of Saint Catherine of Siena by Raymond de Capua, ET (1980).
Bell, Rudolph M., *Holy Anorexia* (1985).
Bynum, Caroline Walker, *Holy Feast and Holy Fast* (1987).

Catholicism

Catholicism signifies the central public form which Christianity has assumed in history. 'Catholic' means 'universal' and the term was very early assumed as a title for the *church to refer not only to its wide geographical extent but also to that common character shared between otherwise diverse local churches upon which their unity depended. It contrasted with the unacceptable beliefs or practices of any separatist group deviating, in the view of the *episcopate, through *heresy or *schism.

Historically, the characteristics and developing meaning of Catholicism may best be described by considering its different phases. 'Early Catholicism' refers to the character of the *church as it assumed a fairly firm shape in the course of the 2nd century (see Pre-Constantinian Thought). It was structured as a network of local churches or dioceses, each led by a bishop assisted by presbyters and deacons, focused upon the weekly celebration of the *Eucharist and entered into by the rite of *baptism. The network of local churches saw itself as a single church, the Body of Christ, God's holy people, spread out across the world and called into existence from both Jews and Gentiles. Its rule of faith depended upon the teaching believed to have been passed down from the apostles and enshrined particularly in the group of writings set canonically apart as 'scriptures', along with those of the Jews, which it retained as God's word foretelling the coming of Christ (see Bible). *Creeds, used at first chiefly at baptism for newcomers to affirm their belief in set form, were also important in establishing identity. Episcopate, the *sacraments of Eucharist and baptism, scriptures, and creeds together provided the core of early Catholicism, a shape hammered out in contestation with *Gnostic appeals to other revelations, and defended on grounds of *apostolicity: it was through the legacy of the apostles, both the scriptures they had authenticated and the episcopal authority derived from them, that the church was linked visibly to Christ. If anyone in particular was responsible for the convincing delineation of this early Catholicism—but not for its creation which essentially preceded him—it was *Irenaeus of Lyons, the greatest theologian of the 2nd century. To these central pillars of Catholicism there was already added a cult of apostles and *martyrs and a great respect for the practice of *virginity. A very other-worldly religion in the goal it pursued and the moral practices it most revered, it no less insisted upon the

goodness of the material *creation dependent upon God and upon the goodness of the 'flesh' of humanity assumed by God's Son.

Early Catholicism was at the same time very diverse. It had no central working *authority; its traditions of cult and theology varied considerably from place to place, although there could be unease if the diversity was judged seriously inconvenient in regard to such matters as the date of *Easter. It was a church wedded to no particular language; Greek for the most part, it always had a *Syriac branch and welcomed the use of Latin and then Coptic in communities speaking those languages. While special respect was already given to the Church of *Rome, where both Peter and Paul had been martyred, any sense of a wider authority deriving from this special apostolicity, as witnessing with particular reliability to the apostolic mind, was as yet unformulated.

The Catholicism of the *Middle Ages derived directly from early Catholicism but had developed in a number of ways, some of which were common to the Greek and Latin traditions but others characteristic only of the west. East and west shared a certain openness, an ability to absorb considerable elements in the pre-existent cultures of the peoples converted to Christianity, whether the 'high' culture of the *philosophers or the popular culture of illiterate communities. This was not an uncritical absorption, rather a process of sifting and transforming in which there were many warning voices. Yet Catholicism as a system proved able over the centuries to integrate into itself a great deal that had no origin in the bible or the apostolic church, providing the ground for the wealth of literature, *music, and *art which Catholicism has fostered. East and west shared a great extension both in the veneration of the *saints and in the organization of the *monastic life as a central element of Christian living, a regularized shaping of a life of *prayer and *asceticism for large numbers of people which had grown out of the early dedication of virginity. They also shared a marked growth in the complexity and solemnity of worship, especially as regards the Eucharist but also in many ancillary rites performed chiefly in cathedrals and monasteries. With this went an increase in the number of 'sacraments' and 'sacramentals', including rites which had been practised since very early times but not in so precise a way as when, by the Middle Ages, the western church had decided that the sacraments were seven in number. Beyond all this, western medieval Catholicism was also greatly and permanently affected by the development, particularly in the 11th and 12th centuries, of the authority and power of the *papacy and, with it, increased separation between clergy and *laity as well as an ever-greater distancing of *women from the sacred and ministerial. With the 11th-century Gregorian reform of the church, Catholicism came to claim a specifically 'Roman' character, marked by a growth in administrative centralization and the complexity of canon *law. Thus the canonization of saints ceased to be a matter of popular acclaim and became instead one of papal decree. Latin increasingly assumed an almost sacred character as the official language of Catholicism. By the later Middle Ages this Romanization had effectively distinguished the Catholicism of the west from the 'Orthodoxy' of the east and produced in the former a degree of uniformity hitherto unknown in Christianity, together with the growth of new, papally authorized, practices such as 'indulgences', as well as legal insistence that priests and deacons must be 'unmarried'.

Catholicism's next form, that of the *Counter-Reformation, as represented especially by the Council of *Trent, was characterized by its emphatic rejection of the principles of the *Reformation. In response to the *Protestant attack on many of the beliefs and practices of the medieval church, it mounted an explicit defence of all the major medieval developments. Catholicism came thus to be characterized by its contrast with Protestantism and by certain insistences, such as on a *celibate clergy, a Latin liturgy, the denial of the cup to the laity, a multiplication of 'private' side-altar masses and, behind all this, an even greater stress on papal authority. *Ultramontanism in the 19th century further sharpened the sense of contrast with Protestantism, while discrediting *Gallicanism and reducing the degree of diversity hitherto surviving within Catholicism, and in 1870 putting the capstone on the edifice of Roman Catholicism with the definition of papal *infallibility. Insistence upon the teaching of scholastic philosophy and theology further enhanced the image of Catholicism as permanently caught in a medieval time warp. Nevertheless it is important to remember that the majority of all Christians remained Catholic, and that in practice Catholicism included large interior diversity between its practice, say, in Bavaria and Mexico, or in Croatia and Portugal, as also between the spiritual and intellectual traditions of the principal orders—*Benedictine, *Franciscan, *Dominican, and *Jesuit.

The *Eastern Orthodox and Protestant Churches have never, it needs to be remembered, abandoned the claim to be themselves part or whole of the 'Catholic Church' as expressed in the creeds. Moreover, in the *Anglican tradition and elsewhere within Protestantism, especially following the *Oxford Movement, there has been in the 19th and 20th centuries a prolonged and partially successful endeavour to reclaim aspects of early and even medieval Catholicism rejected or underrated at the Reformation while distinguishing this from anything specifically Rome-centred. Such developments, Anglo-Catholic and other, have often adopted much even from the theology and spirituality of post-Tridentine Rome and have helped fashion a concept of Catholicism at home in the post-Reformation churches but sympathetic, if not to Roman power, at least to the deeper direction of Christianity that Rome has fostered.

The final form of Catholicism may be dated from *Vatican II and has, to the surprise of many Catholics and non-Catholics, in many ways reversed the trends of a thousand years. Some of the criticisms of the *sixteenth-century reformers have at last been met and numerous aspects of a pattern of religious life little changed since the early Middle Ages were quite rapidly abandoned, causing considerable confusion. In principle, the diversity between local churches grounded on language and culture has been welcomed in place of an ultramontane stress upon the uniformity of one 'Roman' church. This reflects the immense expansion of Catholicism in Asia, North and *Latin America, and *Africa, which has, for instance, made Brazil the country with the largest Catholic population in the world. From the late 1960s Latin quickly disappeared in most places from both the public liturgy and priestly training, 'private' masses were replaced by concelebration, communion of the cup was restored to the laity, and married men could be ordained as deacons though not—at least as yet—as priests. Women who had been so largely relegated to the margins of the Catholic system became 'eucharistic ministers' and entered in many other ways into the active life of the church. Catholicism no longer appeared as

something in necessary contrast with Protestantism. On the contrary it could again be understood, not as one rather uniform and one-sided tradition within Christianity, but as signifying a wholeness within which the values of Protestantism and Orthodoxy might be included. In practice this is far from fully achieved within the Roman Catholic communion. In consequence, Catholicism at the beginning of the third millennium can mean either a diversified fullness of historic Christianity, reincorporating in modern form long-separated traditions in a unity of *communion without insistence on detailed uniformity, or it can mean a far more closely regulated type of church, which has incorporated the more specific outward reforms of Vatican II into a still highly centralized papal system, in close continuity with the Catholicism of the medieval and Tridentine periods. For both models, however, Catholicism stands for the recognition of historic continuity with all periods of Christian history, claims to be a truly universal and visible communion, and roots its fidelity to Christ and the gospel not simply in the scriptures but also in the authority of the *collegial episcopate centred upon the Petrine see of unity.

The strength of Catholicism lies in its inclusiveness of the values of nature, *reason, and culture, and its openness to development, but these have for centuries been partially negated through clinging to one rather ossified form of such inclusiveness and excluding the purificatory processes represented by the Reformation.

Adrian Hastings

Corbishley, T., *Roman Catholicism* (1950).
Daniélou, J., and Marrou, H., *The First Six Hundred Years* (1964).
de Lubac, H., *Catholicism* (1950).
Hastings, A. (ed.), *Modern Catholicism* (1991).
—— 'Catholicism and Protestantism', in *The Shaping of Prophecy* (1995), 97–109.
Holmes, J. D., *The Triumph of the Holy See* (1978).
McBrien, R., *Catholicism* (1994).
Morris, C., *The Papal Monarchy* (1989).
Ramsey, A. M., *The Gospel and the Catholic Church*, 2nd edn. (1956).

catholicity. The adjective *katholikos*, formed from the Greek phrase *kath' holon*, 'according to the whole', applies to qualities held in common between individuals of a group as opposed to qualities distinguishing one individual from another. In late classical Greek, *katholikos* means 'general' or 'universal', applied to a generally true proposition or a universal history. It does not occur in the NT (its use for the epistles of *Peter, James, and Jude, not addressed to any local church, is late 2nd century), but appears in the correspondence of Ignatius of Antioch in the 2nd century: 'where the bishop appears, there let the congregation be—just as, wherever Jesus Christ is, there is the catholic church' (*To the Smyrnaeans*, 8). This has usually been taken to refer to the *church as a whole; but the phrase suggests something more, to do with fullness of *faith or teaching. Later in the 2nd century, in the letter of the church of Smyrna about the martyrdom of Bishop Polycarp, we find the same ambiguity: the 'catholic church' is dispersed throughout the world, and one can speak of the local communities *of* this church; but Polycarp is bishop of the 'catholic church' in Smyrna, making catholicity a feature of the local church. Clearly the adjective has more than a geographical reference. *Greek and *Latin writers of the 4th and 5th centuries use it to underline the integrity of the church's teaching and *sacramental life: the 4th-century Cyril of

Jerusalem (*Catechetical Discourses*, 18. 23) defines catholicity as universality, teaching the fullness of *doctrine, including all sorts of human beings, dealing with all kinds of sin, and showing all the fullness of Christian virtue. *Augustine likewise refers to the completeness of Christian doctrine as part of the word's meaning (*Epistulae* 92. 7). From at least the late 3rd century, 'catholic' could be applied to faith or teaching as well as to the church, again suggesting a more than geographical sense.

Both Greek and Latin credal formularies (see CREEDS) refer to the 'catholic church', and in the 4th century the 'catholic faith' was identified as the teaching of *Nicaea and the later synods that endorsed it, as against the beliefs of the *Arians. We now first find 'catholic' as synonymous with 'orthodox Christian', and distinctions drawn between 'catholic' bishops and others (of suspect *orthodoxy).

Differentiation between the senses of 'universal' and 'integral' or 'all-inclusive' was not explored during the centuries following but it became polemically helpful in the *sixteenth century, when the *Reformers wished to distinguish between a church and a faith that were, as a matter of fact, geographically widespread and a church and faith that could claim authenticity or integrity. It made perfect sense to ask whether adherents of the Pope's jurisdiction could really be called Catholics, since, in the Reformers' eyes, they failed to teach the true and *apostolic doctrine. Both apostolicity and catholicity, as qualities or notes of the church and its teaching, were sharply separated from considerations of numerical prevalence, geographical universality, and institutional continuity: what mattered was the completeness of biblical faith. The continuity or universality that mattered was continuity with the primitive church and with what had always been believed *even when* overlaid with later additions and corruptions (thus Melanchthon, for example, but also many English Reformed theologians such as Bishop Jewel). To be 'catholic' was to strip away what had accumulated around the faith of the apostles.

This directly contravened the western medieval formula that communion with the bishop of *Rome was the test of catholicity (i.e. of orthodox belief and canonical good standing). Gradually the debate about catholicity came to be dominated by issues of order and sacramental validity, rather than the limits of true catholic *faith*. This was probably inevitable, since the *authority* to determine the limits of faith was a matter of profound disagreement, raising questions about the legitimacy of different kinds of church order. By the *nineteenth century, discussion of the 'catholicity' of non-Roman Catholic communities in the west was largely about validity and legitimacy, especially in the debates between the Anglican and Roman Catholic communions.

*Twentieth-century theology has shown increasing dissatisfaction with this approach. The earlier concern with catholicity as 'qualitative', connected with the wholeness or integrity of faith, has been revived, most notably and freshly in *Eastern Orthodox theologies. The *Russian *émigré* Vladimir Lossky devoted several essays to reconstructing the idea of catholicity as an integral relation to the living truth of God rather than something capable of institutional checking or validating. He argues that the church's character as *apostolic* is the guarantor of legitimacy: arguments about order, especially sacramental authenticity, properly belong there. Catholicity requires a more profound analysis. The church must be cath-

olic even when not universal in a geographical sense: otherwise one of its four crucial marks will depend on historical contingency. Catholicity is bound up with *communion: it is our communion with the Son of God (and therefore our endowment with everlasting life), our union with his eternal relations within the *Trinity. In virtue of this union, we are set free for a different level of communion with each other, living in interdependence. Because of this interdependence, the Christian's consciousness is altered: s/he is attuned to the wholeness of Christian experience, in time and space. This is 'catholic' consciousness; and the church's catholicity is this dimension of its life. There is a close link between catholicity and the work of the *Holy Spirit who breaks open our individualist self-definitions to make us truly *personal*: that is, existing in the likeness of the personal communion that is the very life of God. In each subject, the Spirit realizes Christ's image in a distinct way; yet each such realization is a moment in a closely woven web of *mutual* definition of the distinct vocations that Christians live out. Thus in each believer the wholeness of the new humanity in Christ is fully present, though, as in the life of the Godhead, this fullness can exist only in *koinonia*, loving communion.

Catholicity is clearly a spiritual quality, not an external mark subject to canonical or juridical criteria. While this vision is indebted both to the Greek fathers and the 19th-century Russian philosophers who developed a complex doctrine of cosmic interdependence in Christ, it is also remarkably in tune with the early work of the Jesuit Henri *de Lubac, who argued in *Catholicisme* (1947) for the same notion of the full presence of Christ in each believer as the foundation of catholic identity, which has the form of unity in mutuality or complementarity. Each believer is the whole church 'in miniature'; and the gift of unity with Christ frees us from the bounds of individualism to equip us for communion with the whole creation, enabling us to give sacramental meaning to our entire environment. De Lubac looks to the Greek fathers for inspiration, and his work has been an important point of contact with modern Orthodox theology for Roman Catholics and others. More recent Greek theologians, especially Christos Yannaras and John Zizioulas, have continued similar lines of reflection, with Yannaras developing insights about 'catholic personality' as a *mode of being* (so that Christianity is an existential or ontological change before it is a new doctrine to be accepted), and Zizioulas outlining a highly influential theology of the *Eucharist as the realizing of catholic wholeness in each local Christian community gathered around its bishop, the sign of the Christ who is to come and reunite all creation.

These theologies of catholicity reflect a general modern concern to spiritualize or internalize it, filling out the early Christian insight that catholicity is integrity or 'integrality' of faith with the corollary that catholic identity is a particular kind of personal and spiritual integrity and openness. Something of this can be seen in the Anglican report *Catholicity* (1947) and the 1950 response from the British Free Churches, *The Catholicity of Protestantism*, as also in the careful *Vatican II statement (*Lumen Gentium*, 8) that the Catholic Church 'subsists in the Roman Communion', allowing the recognition of some kind of catholicity in other ecclesial communities, even if full realization requires communion with Rome. The joint RC/World Council of Churches statement of 1968 on *Catholicity and Apostolicity* repeats the emphasis on catholicity as a spiritual quality and even admits that *no* ecclesial body realizes it entirely this side of the eschaton, although there may be argument about degrees of fullness. These developments have continued to stimulate *ecumenical dialogue; but, more importantly, they have reinforced the necessity to connect theologies of the church and its integrity with the central doctrinal commitments of Christian faith (the *Incarnation and the Trinity) and with the analysis of Christian *holiness and maturity. **Rowan Williams**

Abbott, E. A., *et al.*, *Catholicity: A Study in the Conflict of Christian Traditions in the West* (report to archbishop of Canterbury) (1947).

Congar, Yves, *Diversity and Communion* (1984).

de Lubac, Henri, *Catholicism* (1962).

Dulles, Avery, *The Catholicity of the Church* (1987).

Florovsky, Georges, 'The Catholicity of the Church', in *Bible, Church, Tradition: An Eastern Orthodox View* (1972), 37–55.

Lossky, Vladimir, *In the Image and Likeness of God* (1974).

McPartlan, Paul, *The Eucharist Makes the Church: Henri de Lubac and John Zizioulas in Dialogue* (1993).

Ramsey, Michael, *The Gospel and the Catholic Church* (1936).

Staples, Peter, 'Catholicity', *Dictionary of the Ecumenical Movement* (1991), 134–7.

Tavard, George, *The Quest for Catholicity* (1963).

World Council of Churches–Roman Catholic Joint Theological Commission 'Catholicity and Apostolicity', *One in Christ*, 6 (1970).

Yannaras, Christos, *Elements of Faith* (1991).

Zizioulas, John, *Being as Communion* (1985).

celibacy is generally understood as a state of non-*marriage and/or abstinence from *sexual activity. Confusion results if religious celibacy is limited to this definition since one can be unmarried but sexually active or married and sexually abstinent. Christian celibacy demands greater specificity. It presumes lived reality. Religious celibacy is a freely chosen, dynamic state, usually vowed, that involves an honest and sustained attempt to live without direct sexual gratification in order to serve others productively for a spiritual motive.

Christian tradition assumes that *Jesus Christ was not married, but there are no clear teachings about celibacy in the gospels. Traditionally, Jesus' comment about being a eunuch 'for the sake of the kingdom' (Matt. 19: 11) has been used as a scriptural support for clerical celibacy, but more current exegesis relates these words to their context of marriage and *divorce.

*Paul gives witness to his choice of a personal celibate dedication in his epistles where he also commends temporary sexual abstinence for married couples who want to devote themselves to a period of prayer; and cautions the unmarried and the married to remain in their current status in expectation of the imminent eschaton (1 Cor: 7). Some Roman Catholic scholars have argued that all the apostles devoted themselves to celibacy after Pentecost, but this is in direct contradiction to Paul's claim that, like other apostles, he had a right to a wife, and to the standards for bishops (see EPISCOPATE) he enumerates in other letters (1 Tim. 3: 2, 12; 4: 1–5; Titus 1: 6–9).

Hermits and monks (see MONASTICISM) developed the best-defined practice and theory of celibacy as a mode of spiritual discipline and awareness in the early Christian centuries. John Cassian (360–435) in his *Conferences* reflects the most astute and enduring analysis of the nature and meaning of religious celibacy. His explorations confront directly the inextricable relationship between human sexuality and celibacy. He acknowledges a celibate process distinguishing between continence, restraint from sexual activity, and *chastity, a total transformation of sexual activity on all levels of internal desire and expression. Divine *grace, contemplation, *fasting, and study are indispensable to religious celibacy.

Celibacy for intellectual and scholarly motives was well known; already in 529 BC Pythagoras established a community of celibate philosophers. Other *Platonic and Stoic *philosophers held that teachers ideally ought to be unmarried. Early Christian writers were emphatic that the ideal, motivations, and dynamics for Christian celibacy were distinct from those of the philosophers. Some proponents applauded celibacy at the same time as denigrating marriage and demonizing *women.

Early Christian writers extolled celibacy as a mythopoetic equivalent of *martyrdom. The admiration for religious celibacy is grounded in its witness of a gospel *love so encompassing that one is willing to sacrifice anything or everything in the service of others. Without doubt, the *asceticism and *spirituality recorded in Christian lives and literature has centred around celibate love as a pre-eminent way of imitating Jesus and dealing with human sexuality. The durability of religious celibacy as a mode of spiritual witness, insight, and dedicated service, proves itself in the two millennia of Christian tradition as well as the centuries-older Hindu and Buddhist practice.

The 1st and 2nd centuries of Christianity were centred around *family and homes. Sexual righteousness was always a consideration for laity and presbyters alike but celibate practice was not formalized. An ever stricter split developed between clergy and laity during the 3rd and 4th centuries. At that time hot debates ensued about whether or not celibacy should be required of priests as a mark of unalloyed dedication and proof of a spirituality worthy of wielding ecclesiastical power and service.

The earliest records of a local church synod—Elvira 309—imposed a requirement of sexual abstinence on its deacons, priests, and bishops, married or not. Thirty-eight of the eighty-one canons of that synod regulate sexuality and consider sexual transgressions by laity and clergy. An urgent and prominent concern of the synod fathers was to eliminate the disbursement of church property to a cleric's family.

Even the first ecumenical Council of *Nicaea in 325 debated the question of obligatory celibacy for clerics. The ideal had already forged strong bonds with the priesthood, but Paphnutius, himself a celibate, argued convincingly against mandatory celibacy for clergy. Throughout history many popes and bishops, and most clergy, were married until universal legislation for the Latin Rite was promulgated by Rome. Questions about a married priesthood were legislated out of practical existence at the second Lateran Council (1139) which declared that any marriages of men ordained subdeacon, deacon, or priest were and would be invalid, and married men would not be ordained to the priesthood. The *eastern Christian church had settled the question of clerical celibacy for itself at the Council of Trullo in 691 by declaring that bishops must be unmarried and sexually abstinent. Married men can be ordained priests; single men, however, must agree to remain unmarried and abstinent in order to be ordained to the priesthood.

The *Protestant reformers relied more on the biblical foundations of Christian ministry than *tradition and believed that the medieval insistence on clerical celibacy was wrong and corrupt. The question of an unmarried or married clergy became a litmus test for both Protestants and Roman Catholics. Catholic orthodoxy required belief in the real presence in the *Eucharist, celibacy for its ministers, and submission to the authority and supremacy of the Pope. Protestant Christians judged that it was a good thing for clergy to marry and rejected papal claims to authority.

By far the greatest opprobrium levelled against religious celibacy throughout the centuries has been aroused by those who profess to be celibate but whose behaviour turns out to be neither celibate nor religious. Sexual failures of clergy that involve hypocrisy and violations of truth are a perennial religious concern. The media in the 20th century exposed a great deal of sexual activity by clergy worldwide and contributed to a sense of crisis surrounding mandated celibacy for priests. Legitimate debate is fuelled by moral failures of those expected to be celibate who prove to be sexually active. Current debates have a familiar historical ring. They reflect a crisis of ecclesial authority since clerical celibacy is a church mandate. Arguments for optional celibacy for priests also involve the Eucharist because the number of men willing to subject themselves to a celibate lifestyle has diminished to the point where the *sacraments are unavailable to large numbers of Catholics.

But the reality of religious celibacy is far more significant than the debates of mandatory or optional celibacy for Catholic priests. These will be settled in time. Religious celibacy is a Christian charism and will endure throughout the ages, but it cannot be legislated. Celibacy should be available and supported wherever it is inspired in any Christian. Religious celibate dedication offers insight into spiritual reality and provides a human service that is inestimable. Gandhi wrote that any nation is poor without such persons.

A. W. Richard Sipe

Lea, Henry, *An Historical Sketch of Sacerdotal Celibacy*, 2nd edn. (1884).
Schillebeeckx, Edward, *Celibacy* (1968).
Sipe, A. W. Richard, *A Secret World: Sexuality and the Search for Celibacy* (1990).
—— *Celibacy: A Way of Loving, Living and Serving* (1996).
Stewart, Columba, *Cassian the Monk* (1998).

Celtic Christianity.

Modern studies in world Christianity are dominated by the theme of inculturation, as a great variety of non-western cultures still seek to reassert themselves against the political, economic, and general cultural domination of Europe, the USA, and Russia. Christians in such cultures often realize the importance of continuing to 'inculture' western Christianity in their own surviving religious forms. Yet many overlook the parallels with that first massive and, to this day, most successful inculturation of Christianity, which occurred when a version of a Near-Eastern religion called Judaism became incorporated in the imagery, thought patterns, rituals, codes, and institutions of a Graeco-Roman empire. That process is repeated in the subsequent inculturations of a thoroughly Graeco-Romanized Christianity in the cultures of peoples to the north-west of the empire, amongst them that family of peoples whom the Greeks had already called the 'Keltoi'.

The task of uncovering early Celtic versions of Christianity is almost impossible in most of the territories once settled by Celtic peoples: ancient Gaul, the Iberian Peninsula, parts of Italy, Galatia even. Although *archaeological remains are available, there is no native contemporary literature to help interpret them; a lack that is only minimally and questionably compensated for by comments in the language of the colonizing Romans. The task is less difficult in the case of the Goidels or Gaels, for in their language, Gaelic (basically Irish and derivatively Scots Gaelic), we have the earliest substantial vernacular literature of Europe; and to this must be added an even more substantial literature from them in what is called Hiberno-Latin. The next best prospect comes from Brittonic people whose somewhat later literary remains survive in the Welsh language.

Partly because of the wandering, or *pilgrimage, of Celtic monks (*peregrinatio pro Christo*) and of other scholars from the 6th century onwards, the manuscripts in which the relevant literature is contained are scattered from Poland to the Caucasus, and the work of collecting, editing, and translating them is still far from complete. Nevertheless, if one can avoid any repetition of those forms of political and ecclesiastical chauvinism which have plagued this question (as when, for example, the Synod of Whitby in 664 is described as the beginning of the end of Celtic Christianity, or when early Gaelic culture and its early 'non-Roman' Christianity was 'rediscovered' in the 18th and 19th centuries as the foundation myth of Protestant nationalism in Ireland and *Scotland) some genuinely distinctive and significant features of an early Celtic Christianity can be sketched; which can be checked, in part at least, against elements of survival to the present day.

Begin, then, with the central feature of any *religion, namely, the experience and understanding of divinity; and take the case of Brigid. She was a pan-Celtic divinity, (triune) daughter of the Dagda, the Great Good God who was All-Father. She was the divine source of poetry, arts, and crafts (that is to say, of those *visionary and creative functions that make for life and life more abundant—hence her attribute of fire), of healing, fertility, and plenty: in short, she was the continuous creator. She is attested in place-names all over the Gaelic-speaking areas (as in Brittonic realms), particularly in the names of churches and wells, and around such places she is still prominent in prayers and in folk rituals. She was adopted as a Christian abbess and *saint, and in particular in Ireland as the legendary foundress of the Abbey of Kildare, undoubtedly one of her most important pre-Christian sites. Her Christian feast-day coincides with the ancient Celtic quarter festival of Imbolc, which celebrated the first burgeoning of new life in a dead, frozen world. For, as the saint or saintly abbess, she retained her original divine creative functions, as extant *Lives* of Brigid amply illustrate.

In contrast, say, to some Latin American peoples who, on Christianization, merged the Pachamama (creator goddess of the earth) with *Mary, the Gaels neither modelled Brigid on Mary nor merged them. Rather they made Brigid the foster-mother of Jesus. In Celtic divine hero myths, the foster-mother is more the 'real' mother (*muime*, mummy) than the biological mother is (*mathair*, mother). In these terms Jesus is a hero who rides into the world on his *cross to defeat our enemies. And so a very high goddess finds a central role in one version at least of Celtic Christianity.

In the resulting experience and understanding of divinity, then, the strict orthodoxy of Christian monotheism is preserved. *God the Father–Son–Spirit alone is God. At the same time, God's creative, life-giving power is experienced in and indeed as a *woman. Add the wider Celtic context, in which the divine is immanent in all agents and elements of the created world, and one has simultaneously an alternative to the narrow theism of the 'Wholly Other' to which so much modern humanism takes exception, and a key to the *spirituality of collections of surviving Celtic prayers and songs such as the *Carmina Gadelica*, a spirituality which encounters divinity directly in all ordinary life.

*Monasticism from the deserts of Egypt arrived in the Gaelic realms via ancient Gaul and the Brittonic churches, and by other seaways and settlements. The groupings (*familiae*) of principal and client monasteries and their lands formed a distinctive church structure alternative to that of bishops and dioceses, which was modelled on the structures of Gaelic kingship, with high kings and client kingships, their system of landholding and protocols of succession, and so on. The manner in which a Christian community structures itself can be as crucial for people's experience of God and of God's ways with the world as can creeds and doctrines. The benign influences of the Christian 'way' were more effectively transmitted to the old Gaelic social structures as a result of the similarity of structure in their 'church–state' relationships.

Further, the great abbots in these alternative ecclesiastical structures were influential leaders who could take their own distinctive views of an already entrenched Roman primacy. Columbanus, who ruled his Continental monastic *familia* finally from Bobbio in the early years of the 7th century, has no problem with Roman primacy. But he is very clear on the basis, nature, and proper exercise of that primatial *authority. It is not based upon any mere protocol of accession or succession in that office. 'Power remains in your hands just so long as your principles remain sound; for he is the appointed key-bearer of the kingdom of heaven, who opens by true knowledge'; so Columbanus informs Pope Boniface, 'For amongst us it is not a man's station but his principles that matter' (Letter 5).

Finally, since these monastery churches were in lieu of parish churches also for all who lived in or near their lands, a version of their athletic Christian spirituality, spare and highly disciplined, was designed for lay consumption. And this gave ordinary Christians a means of treating this world's goods and pleasures as no better, but also no worse, than sustaining elements on our journey to our true home; but with a corresponding appreciation for them in this role, in contrast to an Augustinian *dualism that lumps the world and the flesh with the devil under the sign of the originally sinful and corrupt.

The older tradition of Celtic Christianity today presents an uneven image of survival and revival. Survival is found on the Celtic fringes, in the forms of ancient customs, rituals, and prayers that cluster round sacred places (wells, islands, hilltops) and festivals long Christianized. The revival element broadens as collections of such hymns and prayers are added to surviving scripture homilies and apocrypha, hagiography, and so on, published by a growing scholarly community specializing in Celtic Christian Studies. These are eagerly taken up by quite disparate groups of people, ranging from parishes, perhaps enclosing an ancient sacred site, to *ecologists seeking a sense of God's immanence in all things, or *feminists wanting a real experience of God as feminine, or *New Age believers who are less interested in strict 'authenticity' than in a more creative and syncretistic spirituality. More generally still, this revival reflects and reinforces a widening sense that Christianity as a world religion must escape the narrowness of imperial, colonizing patterns and structures, and rediscover the richness of truly incultured forms; particularly in the case of those cultures which still retain enough native strength to oppose that dominant materialism that is the more recent imposition of the west upon the rest of the world.

See also CONTEXTUAL THEOLOGY **James P. Mackey**

Carmichael, Alexander, *Carmina Gadelica* (1928–).
Condren, Mary, *The Serpent and the Goddess* (1989).
Herbert, Maire, *Iona, Kells and Derry* (1988).
Low, Mary, *Celtic Christianity and Nature* (1996).
McCone, Kim, *Pagan Past and Christian Present* (1990).
Mackey, J. P. (ed.), *An Introduction to Celtic Christianity*, 2nd edn. (1995).
—— 'The Theology of Columbanus', in P. Ni Chathain and M. Richter (eds.), *Ireland and Europe in the Early Middle Ages* (1996).
Richter, Michael, *Medieval Ireland: The Enduring Tradition* (1983).
Sancti Columbani Opera Omnia, ed. and trans. G. S. M. Walker (1957).

Chalcedon, Council of,

fourth ecumenical *council, held in 451. After the debacle of the Council of *Ephesus, 431, a fragile reconciliation was negotiated between the Egyptian and *Syrian churches. In their respective spheres, however, the theologians of the two traditions continued to denounce each other, leaving a further explosion of conflict inevitable. For the *Alexandrians, if a true union of the divine and human took place at the *Incarnation, then it was on the basis of a single divine personal subject, and it precluded any subsequent talk of abiding dualities in the one Christ. For the Antiochene and Roman theologians, such logic seemed to abolish a necessary distinction of natures and was redolent of the earlier *heretic Apollinaris, who argued that the humanity of the incarnate *Word (Logos) was an incomplete, mindless vehicle. At least it betrayed the full reality of *Jesus and his solidarity with the race. Important linguistic distinctions between 'natures' and 'subjects' could not always be clarified by the parties involved.

After Cyril of Alexandria's death in 444, the conflict between the churches was rekindled. The deposition of the monk Eutyches was the immediate cause. The Alexandrians elevated him as a champion, after Constantinople and Rome denounced him as a heretic. His appeal was heard in council at Ephesus in 449. There the Alexandrians suppressed the opposition so violently that the Emperor Marcian was forced to call a legal review, and summoned another council to Chalcedon in 451. This suburb of *Constantinople was chosen so that proceedings could be policed vigorously. Daily affairs were organized by an imperial commission which kept the bishops focused on the task in hand. As a result, Chalcedon is the most dense of all synodical processes, always seeking out an eirenical concord. Its thinking is entirely dominated by Greek conceptions of nature and subjectivity and how they can express the doctrine of incarnate *redemption. It is obsessively careful about semantics.

The sessions of the first week tried to reach agreement on the basis of a core of authoritative texts. This was soon pared down to Cyril's Second Dogmatic Letter, and the Tome of Pope Leo, but many were unhappy about the compatibility of these two approaches. At the very turbulent fifth session the commissioners tried to draw up a new draft agreement (now lost) that tactfully described Christ as composed 'out of two natures', leaving it unresolved whether one could speak of one or two *after* the Incarnation. This avoidance of the issue failed badly. After several committee sessions the final draft dropped the 'out of two' and taught that Christ existed 'in two natures.' It was composed, like a mosaic, from Cyril's writings, the Formula of Reunion, and Leo's Tome.

Against Nestorius the Chalcedonian statement stressed the oneness of Christ's subjectivity by using the recurrent term, 'the self-same'. Against Apollinaris it affirmed Christ's perfect *humanity. Against Eutyches, it affirmed the essential identity of that humanity with our race. Turning to the vexed issue of nature language it concluded: 'One Christ, perceived in two natures', and it went on to specify how those natures were made known: 'unconfusedly, unchangeably, undividedly, and inseparably'. The first two adverbs excluded *christological theories of a synthetic fusion of natures, the last two excluded *Nestorianism. The formula, having thus been devised to impose a truce on the warring schools, went on to offer a more positive statement.

Leaning on the Tome of Leo, it argued that there could be a unity that surpassed *duality and yet retained differentiation: 'the distinction of natures is not done away with because of the union, but the characteristics of each nature are preserved and concur in one person and subsistence'.

Although Chalcedon was intended to be a reconciliation of differences, it became, in the east, one of the greatest causes of continuing disunity. In the west, the council was elevated to pre-eminent status, but its interpretation was entirely channelled through Leo's Tome. In Byzantium it was to be substantially nuanced by the Council of Constantinople of 553. The Egyptian churches refused to acknowledge Chalcedon at all, and to this day the christology of the ancient churches of Africa (the Copts and *Ethiopians) follows the path of Cyril's early theology (so-called *Monophysitism) only. Important Syrian thinkers also came to adopt the anti-Chalcedonian cause. *Armenia never acknowledged the synod. The disruptions caused by Chalcedon set hard as the Islamic invasions of the 7th century permanently detached Syria, Egypt, and Africa from the imperial church. In recent times the World Council of Churches sponsored a dialogue among the eastern churches which led to a recognition of the substantial agreement existing between the Byzantine, Roman, and Oriental traditions, despite the apparent diversity of 'One Nature–Two Nature' languages.

The elevation of Chalcedon to 'classical status' in the Greek and Latin worlds probably resulted in a less dynamic model of Christ than was desirable. The artificialities of the settlement became fixed as dominant categories. The static idea of a nature attached to a person no longer commanded a central role in post-Enlightenment thought; but christological thinkers were slow to meet new challenges. Nineteenth- and 20th-century christologies which attempted to skirt round the prescripts of Chalcedon often fell back into forms of those 'excessive' positions that Chalcedon had been trying to reconcile. The issue of articulating a christology that summarizes the past faithfully enough, yet is also sufficiently liberating and diverse to express the church's multicultured faith in Christ, remains a most pressing need.   **John McGuckin**

Gray, P. T. R., *The Defense of Chalcedon in the East (451–553)* (1979).
Gregorius, P., Lazareth, W., and Nissiotis, N. (eds.), *Does Chalcedon Divide or Unite? Towards Convergence in Orthodox Christology* (1981).
Grillmeier, A., *Christ in Christian Tradition*, 2nd edn. (1975).
Sellers, R. V., *The Council of Chalcedon: An Historical and Doctrinal Survey* (1953; 1961).

charismatic movement.

Charismatic phenomena are there at the beginnings of Christianity. In 1 Corinthians 12–14, Paul puts them in their place behind *love. They disappeared for centuries, but historians looking closely, particularly among the disinherited, see occasional recurrences of 'wildfire'. In the 20th century there have been *Pentecostal churches, with baptism of the *Holy Spirit, speaking in tongues, and miraculous healings as the staple of their religious experience. They had almost nothing to do with the mainstream churches, being anti-ecumenical, distrustful of academic *theology, and overwhelmingly churches of the poor.

In the 1960s and 1970s all the characteristic phenomena of Pentecostalism appeared in mainstream churches, including American Episcopalians and Roman Catholics, churches with a tradition of stately decorum in their public worship. The charismata were not immediately intruded upon church services; instead there were cell meetings for prayer and bible study. Precedence is normally given to Dennis Bennett, an Episcopalian priest in California, who claimed in 1960 to have experienced the baptism of the Spirit, and had to find another parish. Catholic Pentecostalism began in 1966–7 with a group on the staff of Duquesne University, reading *The Cross and the Switchblade*, a Pentecostalist account of the Spirit at work in downtown New York. Barrett's *World Christian Encyclopaedia* claimed that by the late 1970s there were 20 million charismatics, and the numbers continue to grow, more even in Catholicism than in Protestantism. By the 1980s the movement had papal blessing. Christian theology generally had a bad conscience about forgetting the Spirit, and was willing to encourage specialists in charismatic renewal.

The first wave of charismatics was overwhelmingly middle-class, and they had to break down class inhibitions to let themselves go with the Spirit. It is slightly reminiscent of the way that with rock-and-roll the thrills of Black popular culture found a wider appeal. Imperceptibly, the charismatic movement gentrified Pentecostalism. There were pentecostals, notably David Du Plessis, who were anxious to make links with mainstream Christianity, but the pentecostal churches were, for some time, largely suspicious and at a loss when confronted with unabashed imitations of their own beliefs and practices. By the late 1980s, however, there were pentecostal/charismatic congresses in North America. Theologically the two strands were very near. Some quite rigorous theology of the Holy Spirit was done, helping to win acceptance in mainline churches.

A new movement, claiming special gifts from the Spirit, is liable to split congregations, and might have been expected to lead to schism. In practice it scarcely did. Charismatics were more theologically accommodating than pentecostals, *evangelical rather than *fundamentalist, and largely stayed in their churches and developed *ecumenical links. Their network of flourishing congregations sometimes resembles a denomination within the wider denomination.

In the 1980s and 1990s other forms of charismatic Christianity, somewhat more sectarian, developed. These are detached from other churches, more centred on individual leaders, and sometimes have a more authoritarian structure. Examples might be seen in

John Wimber's Vineyard Christian Fellowship, or the Lauderdale Five and the 'shepherding movement', or the *Restorationist 'house-church' movement in Britain. Most Latin American Protestantism is now charismatic. In many ways it is nearer in style to classical Pentecostalism, including, very often, a habit of confrontation with Catholicism. There are questions about the political consequences of charismatic piety, which in Third World countries tends to be supernaturalist and emotional rather than politically engaged. The influence of charismatic renewal on Christian thought, rather than Christian body language and liturgy, has been conservative.

See also BLACK THEOLOGY.   **Alistair Mason**

Burgess, S. M., and McGee, G. B. (eds.), *Dictionary of Pentecostal and Charismatic Movements* (1989).

Harper, Michael, *Charismatic Crisis: The Charismatic Renewal, Past, Present and Future* (1980).

Hocken, P., *Streams of Renewal* (1986).

Martin, D., *Tongues of Fire: The Explosion of Protestantism in Latin America* (1990).

charity is the attitude Christians are expected to develop toward God and neighbour. The term is derived from the Latin *caritas* which in turn stands for the Greek *agape* in the NT. Today *caritas* and *agape* are both usually translated as 'love'. Charity and *love have sometimes been used synonymously, but in modern usage love generally refers to the nature of God and of Christian relationship, whereas charity tends to be used in a more restricted sense for benevolent action in support of the poor (see POVERTY), and victims of violence, war, and natural catastrophes. Thus the biblical definition of God's nature as *agape* (1 John 4: 16) is translated as 'love', not 'charity'. 'Charity' is also used in a secularized context, with reference to benevolent actions and attitudes in general: philanthropy, *compassion, care, almsgiving, solidarity, aid to the underdeveloped world.

Charity, together with *faith and *hope, is one of the three theological *virtues discussed by Paul, most prominently in 1 Corinthians 13: 13 but also in 1 Thessalonians 1: 3, Galatians 5: 5–6, and Colossians 1: 4–5. He names charity as the greatest of these theological virtues, which later theology has distinguished from natural virtues. Charity is seen as a virtue within the context of God's gracious plan of *salvation and *redemption, so that it is characterized by an *eschatological orientation: it is both fruit of and witness to God's emerging reign on earth.

'Christian charity' is also an expression for the complex network of individual and corporate social services within Christian churches and groups. Inspired by the gospel commands to respond to human need by treating every human being as if he or she were Christ himself (Matt. 25: 31–46; Luke 10: 25–37), Christians down the centuries have developed a great number of patterns of individual and structural response to social needs in and beyond the churches. Christians and churches have co-operated with state authorities, and more recently with other religions, international organizations, and political institutions such as the International Red Cross and the United Nations, in their effort to meet individual, social, and structural needs throughout the world. In the process, some Christian concerns have been institutionalized by the emergent welfare state, or taken over by non-governmental agencies and voluntary associations. Christian churches and communities have no monopoly of caring for groups of people whose needs they may have been the first to identify: the sick, the handicapped, the dying, prisoners, orphans, widows, refugees, outcasts, exploited women and children, underdeveloped nations, victims of tyranny and torture. Moreover, Christians must be on the look out for new needs and be sensitive to the special dialectics of charity.

A number of questions need to be asked concerning the motivation and effect of Christian charity. Is there a danger of reducing human beings to mere recipients of charity? Are people in need to be defined exclusively by their needs? Should Christians concentrate on aiding victims or should they also become involved in the struggle for better and more just structures in this world? Should Christians develop bureaucratic structures to meet present and future needs or should their work for the needy remain *ad hoc*? Should Christians co-operate with non-Christian organizations? Should Christians insist on a spiritual dimension in their efforts to meet various needs? Should Christian charity be explicitly Christian and thus related to confessional requirements and *missionary activities? How should one balance self-love and love of God, love of the other and love of God's creation, at a time when all the needs of the world are brought to our constant and immediate attention through the mass media? What does Christian *discipleship mean in such a situation of conflicting needs?

Supposed manifestations of 'Christian charity', which do not respect the personal integrity of the recipients as created and loved by God, result from a misunderstanding of the Christian vocation to love. Every opportunity we have to meet the needs of others is itself a gift of God. So, Christian charity must be seen and developed within the framework of faith in God's *grace and of hope for God's emerging reign on earth. The ultimate criterion for judging expressions of Christian charity is willingness to serve human beings—while respecting their dignity as God's creatures—and not one's own ego and its intricate projects. Thus Christian charity constantly requires both spiritual nourishment and self-critical examination.

Of recent years, Christian moralists, third-world theologians, *feminist theologians, and other socially engaged people have drawn attention to the intricate relationship between charity and *justice. They have warned against offering mere charity when what is needed is justice. The development of a natural and social environment which safeguards justice, in terms both of equal respect for individuals and of the fair distribution of available goods and services, is better than 'acts of charity', especially if these are expressions of technocracy and paternalism. The ambiguity of charity calls for much further reflection on the nature of Christian action in the world.

See also GLOBAL ETHICS; KINGDOM OF GOD.

                                          Werner G. Jeanrond

Hauerwas, S., *A Community of Character* (1986).

Jeanrond, W. G., *Call and Response* (1995).

Küng, H., *Global Responsibility* (1990), ET (1991).

Metz, J. B., *Faith in History and Society* (1977), ET (1980).

Outka, G., *Agape: An Ethical Analysis* (1972).

chastity (*castitas*, 'purity') has retained a double meaning in Christian thought. It refers to the purity of heart which enables the individual to see God (Matt. 5: 8), and as such is both a gift and a discipline, acquired through temperance and self-control. More narrowly, chastity is defined as abstention from *sexual intercourse, often associated with a denigration of *marriage and distaste for the *body, linked to an implicit or explicit misogyny.

*Paul, writing to the Corinthians at a time when the return of Jesus was considered imminent (*c*. 55), expressed a clear preference for *celibacy for the unmarried, conjugal chastity for the married, and continence for the widowed (1 Cor. 7: 1–40). In Matthew's gospel (19: 9) chastity is referred to in the context of marital fidelity (a man who divorces his wife for reason other than her lack of chastity is guilty of adultery). Both chastity and *virginity are seen in the NT as a gift from God and as a witness to the *eschatological hope of the *church (cf. Matt. 19: 11–12).

Although the Essenes extolled the virtues of continence, it was *Gnostic, rather than Jewish thought, which had the greatest influence on Christian teaching. Among the early fathers chastity is usually equated with celibacy and virginity, rather than marital fidelity. The meaning and value of *enkrateia* ('self-containment') was hotly contested in 2nd-century Alexandria. The 'Encratites' adopted the position that marriage (*gamos*) was itself sinful, and incompatible with Christianity, despite the condemnation of this position in 1 Timothy 4: 1–5. A more moderate version of *enkrateia* considered all sexual contact corrupt, but recognized that weaker Christians would marry. Virginity represented a more perfect Christian calling (a view which has remained dominant in both eastern and western churches, and which owes much to Paul's Corinthian address). The Jewish understanding of procreation as the primary purpose of the creation of human beings (Gen. 1: 28) was replaced in much Christian thought with the notion that sexual activity departed from God's original plan for humanity and was brought about, or caused by, the *Fall. Tertullian, for instance, under *Montanist influence, regarded sex within marriage as fornication, and forbade remarriage for widowed Christians. Gregory of Nyssa (d. 395) and John Chrysostom (d. 407), for instance, held that procreation by means of sexual intercourse was a consequence of the Fall. Jerome (d. 419/420) declared that the only good in marriage was that it brought forth virgins, and any sensual pleasure in marriage was condemned (*Letter to Eustochium*).

In medieval Latin *castitas* was synonymous with celibacy. In the Rule of St *Benedict chastity is described as an instrument of good works, although it did not require a specific vow. Marriage was seen as necessary for the procreation of children, but remained an inferior form of Christian discipleship. Thomas *Aquinas affirmed this hierarchy of perfection. Virgins had pride of place, followed by the (sexually continent) widowed and, finally, married people. The Council of *Trent (Canon 10) anathematized anyone who held that marriage was equal to celibacy or virginity, and named chastity as one of the three evangelical counsels, along with *poverty and *obedience—which together formed the obligatory vows of the *religious life. The voluntary abstinence from sexual intercourse within marriage was encouraged by many churchmen, including Francis de Sales, and the attitude that married people are second-class citizens persists in some parts of the Catholic Church. The presence of a married clergy in both *Eastern Orthodoxy and Protestantism has meant that these churches have tended not to equate chastity with celibacy, or to regard marriage quite so negatively. Luther regarded both celibacy and marriage as 'works', and there-

fore irrelevant in spiritual terms (cf. 'Sermon on Marriage', 1531, and the 'Schmalkaldic Articles', 1537). The Book of Common Prayer (1662) repeats the view of marriage set out by Augustine in *De bono conjugali*. Marriage is 'ordained for the procreation of children', 'a remedy against sin', and for 'the mutual society, help, and comfort, that the one ought to have of the other, both in prosperity and adversity' ('Solemnization of Matrimony').

The *Catechism of the Catholic Church* (1994, paras. 2337–59) defines chastity as 'the successful integration of sexuality within the person and thus the inner unity of man in his bodily and spiritual being' (2337). It is seen as an aspect of 'temperance' 'which seeks to permeate the passions and appetites of the senses with *reason' (2341). The *Catechism* cites St Ambrose's three forms of the virtue of chastity—that of spouses, widows, and virgins (*De viduis*, 4. 23), adding that those who are betrothed to be married and people in *homosexual relationships should practise continence, and condemning masturbation. The 1991 report by the House of Bishops of the General Synod of the Church of England, *Issues in Human Sexuality*, recognizes that prohibitions relating to sex outside marriage (whether homosexual or heterosexual) are widely ignored by Christians. The more controversial report *Something to Celebrate: Valuing Families in Church and Society* (Working Party of the Board of Social Responsibility of the Church of England, 1995) also acknowledges that the church's teaching on chastity as a prohibition on sexual intercourse outside marriage is widely ignored, and calls for a new pastoral approach, particularly to single (and male and female homosexual) people.

Contemporary Christian teachings on chastity can be illustrated by looking at attitudes to single people. The *Catechism*, in a paragraph on 'the sacrament of matrimony', states that single people are 'especially close to Jesus' heart and therefore deserve the special affection and active solicitude of the Church' (para. 1658). It is difficult to avoid the impression that the single person who has not chosen celibacy as a way of life or virginity as a vocation cannot be easily fitted into the Catholic Church's vision of society. *Issues in Human Sexuality* reminds Christians that *Jesus was single, and therefore any idea 'that to be unmarried is to fall short as a human being is totally false'. Singles are required to be 'chaste', while being blessed with the 'special gift' of *friendship (3. 10–13). *Something to Celebrate* is altogether more positive and less prescriptive in its evaluation of singleness. Single and married life are affirmed as equally valid, and the definition of what constitutes a *family is left to single people themselves. It is clear that a Christian ethic of chastity that is relevant for both married and single people, the sexually active and celibate, is urgently needed.

Fiona Bowie

Brown, P., *The Body and Society: Men, Women, and Sexual Renunciation in Early Christianity* (1988).

Maloney, F., *A Life of Promise: Poverty, Chastity and Obedience* (1984).

O'Loughlin, T., 'Marriage and Sexuality in the *Hibernensis*', *Peritia*, 11 (1977), 188–206.

Ranke-Heinemann, U., *Eunuchs for Heaven: The Catholic Church and Sexuality* (1990).

Selling, J. A., 'You Shall Love Your Neighbour: Commandments 4–10', in M. J. Walsh (ed.), *Commentary on the Catechism of the Catholic Church* (1994), 367–94.

Stuart, E., and Thatcher, A., *People of Passion: What the Churches Teach about Sex* (1997).

children have an ambivalent status in Christian thought, one which is reflected in the different connotations of the adjectives 'childlike' and 'childish'. *Jesus enjoined his listeners to 'become as little children' (Matt. 18: 3), for 'of such is the *Kingdom of Heaven' (Matt. 19: 14); *Paul, however, 'put away childish things' (1 Cor. 13: 11) in his growth to maturity as a Christian and berates the Corinthians for remaining 'babes in Christ' (1 Cor. 3: 1). Perhaps the seeming contradiction is lessened if it is recognized that to *become* as a child does not mean one should remain as a child. It demands becoming mature enough to be born again rather than making a virtue of immaturity.

Jesus himself was a child who, as Luke's gospel stresses, 'increased in wisdom and in stature' and was obedient to his parents (Luke 2: 52). This not only brings the *paradox of God made man starkly into view (the maker of heaven and earth 'contracted in a span'), it also heightens the tension between human development over time and the *eternity and changelessness of *God. It was the scandalous idea of God being born which provoked *Nestorius to protest over the title *Theotokos* (God-bearer) being applied to *Mary. Orthodoxy as defended by Cyril of Alexandria insisted on the paradox but the conclusions drawn from this as to the nature of children and the child Jesus have varied. Where Victorian piety may have cooed over the picture of God as an innocent and loving baby, Byzantine art depicts the child as a rather stern miniature man, his divinity displayed precisely in his rationality even as an infant (see ICONOGRAPHY).

The differences reflect three basic attitudes to children identifiable in Christian tradition, with antecedents both in biblical teaching and in Greek thought. The first regards the child as unspoiled, trusting, and innocent, the model of loving dependence on God. Clement of Alexandria gives a sustained account of the child as the apex of Christian perfection in his *Paidagogos*. A second sees the child as pre-rational, a *tabula rasa* to be schooled into the responsibilities and possibilities of adulthood. The common view in the ancient and medieval worlds was that 7 was the age at which a child could be deemed rational, with the age of maturity, indeed marriageability, set at 14 for boys and 12 for girls. The third model presents the child as the prey of original *sin and the fruit of the base *sexual instincts, a reminder of mortality, and a distraction from the spiritual life. *Augustine saw the helplessness of infants as a grim penalty exacted for their inherited sinfulness and spoke of his own younger self as 'so small a child and so big a sinner'.

These attitudes are reflected in the tradition's ambivalence over the desirability of having children at all. In the *Old Testament, God's first instruction to the humans he creates in Genesis 1 is that they should be fruitful and multiply. Children, especially sons, are the great sign of blessing, but what is most desirable about them is what they may become, the props of their parents in old age and the bearers of the *memory of their name once they have died. Childhood itself is not a focus of interest, although the OT offers several vignettes of the early life of its heroes, most notably Samuel, *Moses, and *David, much beloved of writers for children in later centuries.

By contrast, despite the high regard for children in the *New Testament, childbearing is if anything discouraged. The one justification offered for it seems to be that children keep potentially wanton *women occupied (1 Tim. 5: 14). In the expectation of an imminent end-time, there was no need for progeny. As Christianity became woven into the fabric of society, this attitude to childbearing changed. The raising of children for the Lord's service became a duty and vocation for those not gifted with the grace of *celibacy.

In later thought, the most important theological question over childhood is at what point the child becomes an autonomous moral agent capable of conscious faith, and the significance of this for determining its fitness to be fully incorporated into the life of the church. The vexed question of infant *baptism and the related but distinct one of children's participation in the *Eucharist are clearly bound up with the divergence of views over the status and capacities of children. A religion that stresses belief and conscious moral choice was bound to have a problem with children, but also a vested interest in their *education and training, a feature of church life from the earliest decades, one formalized in organized schooling whether by the *Jesuits or Dr Arnold of Rugby.

Changing attitudes to children may be reflected in the gradual increase in devotion to the child Jesus in the early Middle Ages, much of it fuelled by the writings of Bernard of Clairvaux and the visions of St Birgitta of Sweden (see SCANDINAVIAN CHRISTIAN THOUGHT), which climaxes in *Franciscan spirituality and its introduction of tableaux of the nativity, or cribs, into churches. The poverty and simplicity of the circumstances of the Saviour's birth is one stimulus to this interest, as is the development of Marian piety. As the modern age dawns, a new appreciation of the individuality of the child seems to come about, together with the emphasis on the *family as an autonomous unit. Children become their parents' possessions rather than public property and are increasingly segregated into defined compartments of life, the nursery and the school. The stress on *reason and the loss of the sense that baptism in itself cleansed from original sin mean that, as humanism and enlightenment take hold, the generally tolerant earlier attitude to the weaknesses of young children is replaced by a much harsher discipline and training from an early age.

It is in the 17th and 18th centuries that the adaptation of Christian thought and writing for the specific consumption of children began in earnest, much of it sternly moralistic in tone. Victorian literature reflects a new interest in children and a new sense of the need to protect them from exploitation by the adult world. Childhood becomes a distinctive stage of life to cherish. Part of this may be linked to the falling levels of child mortality and a tendency towards smaller families which may have intensified the relationships between parents and children. In the later 19th and 20th centuries, the work of educationalists and child *psychologists made more apparent the differences between the child's view of the world and that of adults and offered a greater understanding of child development. This, linked to Freud's uncovering of the powerful ambivalences of relations between children and adults and their far-reaching effects, has led to a new sensitivity to the needs of children, which some would also see as a crisis over adult responsibility. Christian thinkers have still to work through the impact of these changes on their view of the child.

See also FATHERHOOD; MOTHERHOOD.   **Hugh S. Pyper**

Ariès, P., *Centuries of Childhood*, ET (1962).
Cunningham, H., *Children and Childhood in Western Society since 1500* (1996).
Pyper, H. S. (ed.), *The Christian Family: A Concept in Crisis* (1996).

Chinese Christian thought.

Christianity has been on Chinese soil on and off for fourteen centuries. In four separate periods Christian missionaries were in China but most of these encounters with Chinese culture resulted in very little lasting influence or development of indigenous theological thought. Not until the 20th century was there sufficient Christian presence among the Chinese for theological thinking by Chinese Christians to begin.

The first Christians to arrive were *Nestorians. A stone monument erected in 781 recorded the official arrival of a Nestorian mission in 635 led by the monk Alopen from Persia, probably aimed at providing pastoral care to Persian merchants using the Silk Road to China. The Chinese empire was at the height of its power, covering a huge area from Central Asia to the Pacific. Many peoples were under its rule and the imperial court was confident enough to allow foreign cultures to flourish, even encouraging the translation of Nestorian manuscripts in the imperial library.

Nestorian missionaries did not hesitate to borrow Chinese religious concepts. God the creator was described as the one who set 'the original breath in motion and produced the two principles … he made and perfected all things'; the two principles being yin and yang in Taoist thought. The Nestorians, however, never gained sufficient ground to have a lasting influence and were, like Buddhism, banned in 845.

After a short-lived *Franciscan mission in the 14th century under the Mongols, Christian missionaries, *Jesuits this time, were back in China in the early 17th century. These were men steeped in the learning of the *Renaissance. In China they encountered neo-Confucianism at its height: sophisticated metaphysics, a spiritual discipline based on lifelong learning and a cultivated taste for art and literature. This high Chinese culture was in turn interested in the philosophy, geography, mathematics, and science brought by Matteo Ricci and his companions.

Ricci's approach to Chinese culture was based on the assumption that the Confucian classics contained a '*natural law'. He believed that this ancient tradition was aware of a Supreme Being, Tianzhu, and that human beings are able to reason from the nature of the universe to the existence and nature of God, and to develop a moral life accordingly. It was therefore legitimate to accommodate the gospel to Chinese mentality, and to accept the Chinese cultural system and quasi-religious rites. The theological and moral principles of Confucianism, once purified and supplemented by biblical revelation, could become an integral part of the Christian faith in China. Ricci was able to befriend and convert highly placed Chinese intellectuals such as Paul Hsu (Xu Guangqi) who helped to introduce western scientific thought as well as Christian thinking to the Chinese.

The rival Franciscan and *Dominican orders, as well as some of Ricci's own Jesuit successors, challenged Ricci's approach. For them, *conversion to Christianity implied the obligation to abandon Chinese intellectual traditions. The argument came to a head in the Rites Controversy. Two major issues were involved. The first had to do with the Chinese name for the Christian God. In identifying *tian* and *shangdi*, 'heaven' and 'lord of the above', with Jehovah, Ricci and his companions were open to the accusation that they compromised with idolatry. The second issue concerned participation in the ancestral cult. Ricci did not consider these ceremonies fundamentally superstitious since Confucianism was itself agnostic about the afterlife, but as harmless expressions of filial piety. In the end Rome decided against Ricci's position. As a result Christians went through several periods of persecution. Christianity was prohibited by the Qing government in 1724. Missionaries were expelled, but the church, though persecuted, survived. Although the Jesuit mission failed in the end, defeated as much for political reasons as for doctrinal differences, their approach to Chinese culture highlighted the theological issues that Chinese Christians had to deal with in later generations.

What Ricci and his companions failed to achieve by friendship and *dialogue the 19th-century missionaries tried to do with the help of gunboats and diplomatic pressure. The Opium Wars forced open China's door to the west. The 'unequal treaties' gave westerners, including missionaries, legal status in the Chinese empire. Theology gave way to the struggle for political as well as cultural and religious supremacy. Most of the missionary writings in this period were apologetic in character, either attempting to refute the doctrines of *Buddhism or to develop a *natural theology in response to Confucianism. However, neither reformed theology, which was the principal influence among Protestant missionaries, nor a rigid Catholic doctrinal system imposed by Rome was suited to cultural dialogue. The door of China was forced open, but was there a corresponding opening in the Chinese mind towards western ideas and religion?

The social dysfunction caused by the impact of western economic and political domination led to a revolt of the peasantry against foreigners and the rise of *nationalism among the intellectuals in the early 20th century. This hostility was directed especially at Christians. Against this background of social and intellectual hostility some far-sighted church leaders and missionaries began appealing for a thorough Sinicization of Christianity. First, leadership positions were gradually turned over to Chinese nationals. In 1926 the Pope consecrated six Chinese bishops. In 1927 the Church of Christ in China was established with the aim of forming a purely Chinese church guided by the principles of self-government, self-propagation, and self-support. Secondly, Chinese theologians felt called to develop a Chinese apologetic. Thus the problem of indigenization, on both the institutional and theological levels, was to become a dominant theme of Chinese Christianity in the 20th century.

On the issue of theological indigenization, there were two outstanding questions. The first concerned the western character of Christianity and its ties with imperialism. Chinese theologians tried to show that Christianity was a universal religion, not necessarily linked with any particular culture but at home in all cultures, including the Chinese traditions. The second question concerned national reconstruction: to what extent could Christian values be part of the spiritual construction of the Chinese nation?

Vincent Lebbe, Célestin Lou, and John Wu were among Catholics calling for such reforms, but the most representative theologian of the period was T. C. Chao (Zhao Zichen). From the 1920s to the arrival of the Communist government, Chao was the leading theologian of Protestant Christianity and was elected one of the six presidents of the World Council of Churches in 1948 (see ECUMENICAL MOVEMENT). Chao believed that the Chinese church must go through a double purification, institutional and doctrinal. Institutional purification meant rejecting the trappings of denominationalism and alien forms of worship introduced by western missionaries. Doctrinal purification meant conforming the tenets of the faith to rational and scientific world-views. 'Unscientific' concepts such as the virgin birth, the resurrection of the body and miracles in general must be purged from the Christian faith (see DEMYTHOLOGIZING). Only then will the person of Jesus and the event of the cross shine forth, not as *atonement for humanity's sins, but a means by which sacrificial love triumphed over evil. Jesus' death on the cross should motivate Christians to identify with those who are suffering and participate in the programmes of social reconstruction and nation building.

Chao also believed that Christianity must engage with Confucianism, which he considered to be a *revelation of God 'akin to some of the OT prophets'. To him, this revelation was not different from the biblical revelation in kind but only in degree. As he fulfilled the promises of the OT Jesus would also fulfil other human aspirations as well as bringing to light the transcendental and religious nature of the Confucian tradition.

Many Chinese theologians of this period believed, like Chao, that the essence of Christianity could easily be detached from its cultural forms. Subtract western culture from a western Christ and we obtain the essential Christ. This essential Christ can then be grafted to Chinese culture to produce a Chinese Christianity. But before this theological attempt could arrive at a deeper synthesis, it was overtaken by political events. Decades of civil war compounded by total social and cultural disintegration had made Chinese society ready for more radical reforms. Dialogue with Confucianism became irrelevant as it was accused of being the source of China's feudal system. The attempts to relate Christian morality to national construction also suffered from a fundamental weakness: they started from an idealist perspective, lacked a vigorous social analysis, and did not develop a viable social programme.

The establishment of Communist China in 1949 changed both the locus and focus for Chinese theologians. Besides the government's attempt to bring all religions under its control, two sets of circumstances had put the churches in a double dilemma. On the one hand the *pietist theology inherited by Chinese Protestants from evangelical missionaries hampered any positive engagement with the new developments. On the other hand, traditional liberal theology was silenced by the practical achievements of the early Communists who were more efficient in bringing about the social changes that the church had preached.

Church leaders and theologians were divided along these two lines. Leaders such as Ni Duosheng (Watchman Nee) and Wang Mingdao opposed the new government from a theological perspective. They and their followers bore the brunt of the government's harsh censures. Others, influenced by the *Social Gospel movement, tried to come to terms with the new social reality. Most of them were activists, not trained theologians, such as Y. T. Wu, the leader of the Three-Self Movement. Intuitively they believed in the cause of *Socialist Revolution and its affinity with the Christian vision, but in seeking an accommodation of the Christian gospel with Communist ideology they were not able to articulate the distinctive identity of their Christian faith or its special relevance.

The most significant attempt to bridge this gulf was made by K. H. Ting, the leader of the Protestant church since it resurfaced in the late 1970s after the Cultural Revolution. For Ting, the theo-logical enterprise for China must consist of three corrective stages: a positive evaluation of *atheism; a new understanding of sin and grace; and a rediscovery of the Christlike God. For Ting, the idea of the 'Cosmic Christ', so clearly expounded in the writings of Paul and John, has been hidden by rational and historical theologies for centuries. Traditional *christologies fail to bridge the enormous gulf between the Judaeo-Christian tradition and Chinese culture, and similarly between an institutional church and the revolutionary movements in society. An understanding of Christ not bound by history or institution is therefore needed to free the Chinese Church so that it can engage with Chinese culture and society. It will point Chinese Christianity in the right *eschatological direction, where the cosmic dimension is the principal hermeneutical key to the mystery of God's action in the world. It also extends the domain of Christ beyond the church to include secular values and allies in society.

After the death of Mao Zedong and the end of the Cultural Revolution, Deng Xiaoping ushered in a period of economic reforms leading to a greater openness to new ideas and influences. Against the background of a 'spiritual void' and a society devoid of a coherent system of values, the thirst for spiritual values is evident. Churches and temples are full. Religious books find their way to best-seller lists, as a cursory visit to Chinese bookshops will convince even a sceptic. The intellectual world has also been speaking of a new group of 'culture Christians' in China. They are not Christians in the ordinary sense of the word. Most are academics but there are also writers and artists. Only a few are baptized and most do not frequent the Chinese churches. Yet they share a common empathy for the gospel and the Christian humanist tradition. Rather than a curious anomaly, their existence is a sign of the deep malaise in Chinese society, but also of a deep searching. Not since Ricci and his Jesuit colleagues has Chinese society been so receptive to Christianity. A new Chinese theology may be born outside the confines of the church.

See also CONTEXTUAL THEOLOGY.   **Edmond Tang**

Chinese Theological Review (1985–).

Covell, Ralph R., Confucius, the Buddha and Christ: A History of the Gospel in China (1986).

Criveller, Gianni, Preaching Christ in Late Ming China: The Jesuits' Presentation of Christ from Matteo Ricci to Giulio Aleni Taipei (1997).

Dunne, George H., Generation of Giants (1962).

Gernet, Jacques, China and the Christian Impact (1985).

Hunter, Alan, and Chan, Kim-Kwong, Protestantism in Contemporary China (1993).

Lu, Cheng-Lsiang, Ways of Confucius and of Christ (1948).

Tang, Edmond, and Wiest, Jean-Paul (eds.), The Catholic Church in Modern China (1993).

Wang, Xiaochao, Christianity and Imperial Culture: Chinese Christian Apologetics in the Seventeenth Century and their Latin Patristic Equivalent (1998).

Whyte, Bob, Unfinished Encounter: China and Christianity (1988).

Christianity is best understood as comprising the entire range of beliefs and practices which, across two thousand years, the followers of *Jesus have subscribed to as defining their following, or as consequent upon it. The sense of *discipleship as fundamentally constitutive of Christianity has made it continually debatable whether a 'true Christian' is primarily identifiable in terms of belief or in terms of *loving, but many seemingly contradictory things have been taken for granted by Christians as characteristic of their *religion: the multiplication of ritual yet profound suspicion of ritual; a passion for icons yet hardly less passionate waves of *iconoclasm; *pacifism yet a cult of military honour; glorification of *virginity and *celibacy yet the hardly less absolute glorification of monogamous *marriage; intense internationalism yet hardly less intense involvement in *national identity. The list could well be extended. How can Christianity at different times and places be perceived as including so many diversities without self-evidently being untrue to itself?

The followers of Jesus came to be called 'Christians' very early, according to Acts in the first years at Antioch (11: 26). This has, ever since, been their unquestioned primary name and it indicates this movement's one irremovable character: their religious identity derives from Christ (a title which quickly turned into a name, but which Jesus himself may well not have used). One may admire Jesus and his teaching as one admires Socrates or Rousseau. That does not make one a Christian. The criterion of Christianity, and indeed the only one, appears to be acceptance of Jesus as Christ, signifying Master, Lord, Saviour, or *Word of God. Christianity, however, is more than a matter of individual commitment. From the start it included the sense of belonging to a public community, fellowship, or *church, the *body of Christ. Many people have sought and many still wish to add further necessary qualifications, or to define some more specific essence of Christianity—a 19th-century pursuit, encouraged by *Schleiermacher—but this will always represent some particular *theology rather than *history, phenomenology, or existential reality. For these it seems impossible to add anything significant. Thus one could be tempted to add belief in the divinity of Christ, the practice of *baptism and the *Eucharist, or acceptance of the authority of the scriptures (see BIBLE). But to insist on acceptance of Christ's divinity must certainly exclude numerous highly committed Christians, past and present; to insist on any *sacramental practice excludes *Quakers, while the inclusion of the scriptures in a *sine qua non* may seem self-evident to many Christians, *evangelicals especially, but is actually even more problematic. As regards the *Old Testament, Christians even now do not agree in regard to which books are canonical; moreover, some Christians have denied that any OT work, subsequent to Christ's *Resurrection, retains formal authority. Again, if some authority be granted, there is absolutely no agreement as to what sort of authority it is. As regards the *New Testament, several generations of Christians had passed before it was seen to exist as such. Insistence on the formal necessity of accepting the NT scriptures paradoxically excludes the originally named Christians from being Christian because at the time they were so named not one book of the NT had been written. It must then surely be mistaken to define Christianity formally in such terms, important as they are within its central tradition.

Why is Christianity so open a historical reality? The answer would seem to lie in its origins. If its defining authority is lodged in Christ, he himself wrote nothing and provided no clearly coherent body of doctrine or law. The distance separating the Word from the words which followed, whether of *apostles, evangelists, or whomever, has provided almost immeasurable space. The very diversity of the *gospels, irreducible to a single master text, has often exasperated scripture scholars and theologians anxious to get

closer to Christ. He continually eludes us, not because he is wholly unknown or unknowable—*Bultmann's dismissal of the 'Jesus of History' (see QUEST FOR THE HISTORICAL JESUS) fails to convince either historically or theologically—but because he remains perennially ungraspable yet still decisive. The contrasts between the gospels, together with the still wider diversity within the NT as a whole, demonstrates that any and every presentation of Christian truth is integrally dependent on presenter, place, and time. It is precisely because *Pauline, *Matthean, *Petrine, and *Johannine Christianities are already recognizably distinct, placeable against different cultural and personal contexts, that as time and place further changed so did Christianity's forms. Inherent in this process is the principle of *translation, something actually intrinsic to Christianity's essence, a movement not just from *language to language but from mind to mind and culture to culture. It is here crucially important that translation already took place prior to the writing of any NT work—from Aramaic to Greek. We do not and cannot have a pre-translated text. Jesus precedes translation but the texts do not. If it does not alter the ultimate authenticity of the Word's words that they were pronounced in Aramaic to Galilean fishermen but written down thirty years later in Greek for the townsmen of Antioch, Ephesus, or Rome, their authenticity is not diminished by further translation into Latin, Coptic, Armenian, or, eventually, Esperanto. If it is of the essence of following Jesus Christ not to have an 'essence' discoverable behind and apart from its varied formulations, Pauline, Johannine, Catholic, Protestant, or whatever, it equally has no privileged language or culture.

Christianity can, then, only be understood, as a matter both of fact and of theology, as everything that Christians, with or without the guidance of the *Holy Spirit, have made of it. It must then be defined inclusively, not exclusively, as a living oscillation between a series of contrasting poles rather than one single straight and narrow *via media*, legal or doctrinal. The following of Jesus can, however, be claimed to be most authentically and fully Christian when it best integrates the polarities which have constantly reappeared in its history—*incarnation with transcendence, the New Testament with the Old, the synoptics with John, Paul with Peter, Martha with Mary, marriage with virginity, church with kingdom, *mysticism with *social responsibility, *faith's leap with *reason's argument, this *world with the next.

See also CHRISTOLOGY; PARADOX.   **Adrian Hastings**

Bettenson, H., and Maunder, C. J., *Documents of the Christian Church*, 3rd edn. (1999).
Edwards, David, *Christianity: The First Two Thousand Years* (1997).
Hastings, A. (ed.), *A World History of Christianity* (1999).
McManners, J. (ed.), *The Oxford Illustrated History of Christianity* (1992).
Sanneh, L., *Translating the Message* (1990).
Smart, N., *The Phenomenon of Christianity* (1979).
Sykes, S., *The Identity of Christianity* (1984).

Christmas, perhaps the most widely celebrated of Christian festivals, is observed on 25 December, and traditionally continues for the twelve days following until the feast of *Epiphany on 6 January. Although *Russian and Slavic churches appear to keep Christmas on a different day (at present 7 January), that date is in fact 25 December according to the Julian calendar.

Christmas commemorates the nativity of *Jesus in Bethlehem—his birth as the *incarnate one, 'God with us' (Matt. 1: 23; cf. Isa. 7:

14), the *Word made flesh (John 1: 14). The infancy narratives in the gospels of *Matthew and *Luke, along with OT passages believed to prophesy the coming of the *Messiah, and the placement of the festival in the northern hemisphere's winter season, have all contributed rich images to the *liturgy, *carols and *hymns, *art, and *folk religion. Maternal and natal motifs in particular have inspired the development of various cultural expressions surrounding the festival, which in turn have encouraged its popularity among non-Christians as well as Christians. The custom of gift-giving, originating in imitation of, and thanksgiving for, the gift of the Son, has in some places become so commercialized that the Christian associations of the practice and of the Christmas season itself are feared lost. Efforts to purge secular accretions and restore Christian integrity have had mixed success.

In fact, Christmas, which the Philocalian Chronograph of 354 shows was celebrated in *Rome on 25 December at least by the early 4th century, may have its roots in non-Christian practice. One theory for placing Christmas on 25 December suggests that the motivation for a Christian observance came from the pagan birth-feast of the unconquered sun (*dies natalis solis invicti*) which the Roman emperor Aurelian, in 274, ordered to be held annually throughout the empire on the day of the winter solstice, determined then to be 25 December. According to this 'apologetics' or 'history of religions' hypothesis, the church at Rome adopted the day of pagan festivities for its own purposes, providing a Christian alternative by celebrating instead the birth of the true 'sun of righteousness' (see SUNDAY); the heathen content of the festival was reinterpreted and its date retained.

Another theory explaining the origin of the date of Christmas discounts entirely the possible associations with a pagan festival, and looks rather to the practice of computing the date of Jesus' birth from an accepted date of his Passion and death, 25 March, the spring equinox. Because Jesus lived a perfect, complete life (Heb. 5: 9; cf. Jas. 1: 4), his conception would have occurred on the same day of the year as his death; and with a perfect nine-month gestation, his birth would be 25 December. This 'calculations' hypothesis potentially establishes 25 December as a Christian festival before Aurelian's decree, which, when promulgated, might have provided for the Christian feast both opportunity and challenge.

The festival of Christmas spread quickly from the 4th century onwards. It allowed for a liturgical counterpart to the theological conclusion reached at the Council of *Nicaea which, in condemning *Arianism, affirmed that Jesus Christ was the eternal and only-begotten Son of the Father, humanly born of *Mary (recognized by the Council of *Ephesus as the 'God-bearer', *Theotokos*). In the words of Charles *Wesley:

> Who gave all things to be,
> What a wonder to see
> Him born of his creature, and nursed on her knee.

See also CALENDAR.   **Karen B. Westerfield Tucker**

Roll, S., *Toward the Origins of Christmas* (1995).
Schmidt, L. E., *Consumer Rites: The Buying and Selling of American Holidays* (1995).

christology

christology usually refers to the doctrine of the *person of *Jesus Christ, but may also include the doctrine of the work of Christ (soteriology). It is commonly recognized that the person (who he was and is) is inseparable from the work (what he did and does), because the *gospels mainly identify Jesus through his work: his words, actions, *suffering, and *death. The key christological issue has been his full divinity and full *humanity.

Biblical testimony

Jesus Christ is for Christians both a historical figure and alive now, to whom they relate in faith, hope, and love. This ongoing relationship identifies him both as a particular person and in corporate form as the *church, the new humanity, the *body of Christ, the *poor. For all these modes of identification, testimony is crucial. The *New Testament gives explicit testimony to him, but does so drawing pervasively on the *Old Testament and on other elements of Jewish experience and tradition. One of the major contributions of 20th-century scholarship has been to relate Jesus more thoroughly to his Jewish tradition and its setting in the Roman empire of his time. But there is little direct early evidence about Jesus himself outside the NT, which thus remains the main source for discussion about him.

What role should *historical argument play in christology? The question has become acute since the rise of modern critical historical methods (see QUEST FOR THE HISTORICAL JESUS). Answers have varied from proposing for belief only what can be proved according to strict historical criteria, to refusing to admit the relevance of any historical critical examination of the NT. Most theological positions come between those extremes, granting a role to historical investigation but allowing that it cannot adjudicate the whole *truth of the biblical testimony.

Is the historical probability of the NT testimony sufficient for christology? The testimony to Jesus as a real historical person must be at least in principle falsifiable, and should preferably be supported as reliable in its main lines. Scholarly opinion is divided on many issues, and the NT itself offers diverse accounts often involving differing christologies. The following account of Jesus Christ draws on elements of the Synoptic Gospels which a wide range of scholars consider historically well supported, its aim being to draw out the testimony of his relationship to *God.

Jesus was born around 4 BC, brought up in Galilee, and known as Jesus of Nazareth, after his home town. He was associated with the prophetic ministry of *John the Baptist. At the heart of his own *ministry was his announcement of the *Kingdom of God, which was above all about who God was and what God was doing. He gave good news of God's overwhelming generosity, *forgiveness, and *compassion, with special emphasis on how this embraced those usually thought to be beyond *salvation. He acted this out in his own controversial practice of table fellowship with prostitutes and tax collectors.

Jesus saw his ministry as embodying what *Israel was meant to be, and this communal dimension involved choosing twelve *disciples, symbolizing the twelve tribes of Israel. His *prophetic teaching called for radical *obedience to God, willingness to go beyond the written requirements in imitation of God's *love and *mercy.

Jesus did not follow the line of any of the main parties in the *Judaism of his day and was therefore provocative to each of them. His vision was *apocalyptic in the sense that it took up intense expectations of God's bringing about a great turn-around, transforming the world, and Israel's place in it. He saw a crisis looming, and he announced *judgement, but also the opportunity to repent and be part of God's Kingdom. In this context, two features of his message were especially distinctive: he saw the Kingdom of God breaking in already, according to the will of a generous, welcoming God, and saw it as connected inextricably with his own person.

Those two features are crucial for christology: its central concern, the relation of the God of Israel to the person of Jesus Christ, is rooted in his life and ministry. For all the differences between the gospels, the inextricability of God from Jesus' message, ministry, and person is perhaps the most deeply embedded structural element in their testimony. This both entails historical claims and goes beyond them by referring to God. But one historical claim that seems most reliable is that Jesus referred his whole teaching, ministry, life, and death to God, whom he addressed as *'Father' or 'Abba'. This faced both the original witnesses and later generations with a radical challenge, to which christology is one response.

The gospels show God's interconnection with the message, activity, and person of Jesus through the stories of his birth, baptism, and transfiguration; through use of such titles as the Son of Man, Christ, Lord, and Son of God; and through his claims to authority in teaching, healing, exorcism, and forgiveness. The interconnection reaches its greatest intensity in the climax of the story in *Jerusalem, focused on what happens to him and on actions by which he put his life on the line. The Romans and the priestly aristocrats seem to have combined to have him arrested, tried, and executed on charges of sedition identifying him as a *messianic claimant who forecast the destruction of the *Temple.

In an event reminiscent of many biblical prophetic actions, Jesus, before he died, sealed the knot between his mission, his person, and the God of Israel at a 'Last Supper' with his disciples, linking *covenant and forgiveness with his own death, to be remembered in a meal that identifies *bread and *wine with his *body and *blood (see EUCHARIST). This and other elements of the gospels show how he understood his own suffering and rejection as related to the salvation of Israel; he approached his death as a fulfilment of his mission and expected God to vindicate him.

The *Resurrection was seen by the NT authors as Jesus' vindication. It sets the horizon for all they wrote and is central for christology. The event to which they testify can be interpreted in many ways, and the most searching cross-examinations have failed to resolve the difficulties and reach consensus (see DEMYTHOLOGIZATION). This is hardly surprising, because what is at stake is not only whether to believe the witnesses to an extraordinary event but also a whole understanding of reality (including life, death, history, and God), and a call to live life trusting in the crucified and risen Jesus Christ. In the NT the main point about the Resurrection is that it is a God-sized event, whose content is Jesus Christ and which generates a community of witnesses. It is not about resuscitation, but about Jesus being made alive by God in a way that was both new and yet continuous with the person who celebrated the Last Supper. The risen Jesus is still himself, free to be present, communicate, and act; he lives in unity with his Father, with no question of further death; and he is understood as involved in the origins and future of the whole of *creation and history.

The theological structure of the Resurrection is: God acts; Jesus appears; people are transformed by the *Holy Spirit coming from the risen Jesus. Here are the beginnings of what became the doctrine of the *Trinity: the Resurrection was essential to the development of that distinctively Christian conception of God. At the heart of that development were the christological debates of the early centuries, which can be interpreted as working out theologically the implications of the unique relationship of Jesus to the God of Israel as in the NT testimony.

Classical christology

There is no overall NT christology. As the church developed, certain fundamental questions, especially concerning the relationship of Jesus to God, provoked diverse answers. Key elements which continue to be significant for Christian thought are noted here. It is striking that the thoroughness of the engagement with the person of Jesus Christ by Christian thought in its *Greek, *Latin, and *Byzantine settings has meant that the main options in christology were explored during the first seven centuries and variations on them have continually recurred.

Christology was worked out in an explosion of oral and written communication by Christians, including profound disagreements, and accompanied by intense pressures from political authorities and surrounding cultures. The considerable consensus among the network of Christian communities spread through the Roman empire and beyond was focused on their common allegiance to Jesus Christ. Agreement, often hard-won, developed on vital aspects of what this meant: faith in the God of Israel; receiving the Jewish scriptures as Christian (with Jesus identified as the Messiah); consensus on their own most authoritative writings, which became the NT; forms of church order, discipline, and consultation; short summaries of their faith which eventually became *creeds; forms of initiation (teaching, or catechesis, leading to *baptism in the name of Father, Son, and Holy Spirit, followed by admission to the Eucharist); and, above all, regular participation in the Eucharist and other *worship. These factors shaping ordinary Christian life are the essential background for understanding how vital the christological debates were: Jesus Christ was pivotal for scripture, *authority, teaching, discipleship, worship, and a whole world-view. Classical christology was largely an attempt to articulate, in the face of new questions, what was already being affirmed in those formative discourses and practices. So the life of the early church, especially its worship, is essential for interpreting the *developments of doctrine.

*John's gospel played a pivotal role in those developments. It was written in gospel form, stressing the importance of historical testimony to Jesus; but it also, in telling the story, spelt out the theological implications of his life, death, and Resurrection, paying special attention to his person. It shaped christological discussion by its explicit identification of Jesus as God. Its prologue, 1: 1–18, calls Jesus the *Word (Logos), identifies the Word with God, and makes the basic statement of *Incarnation: 'The Word became flesh' (1: 14). 'Logos' was a key term both in the Septuagint and in Greek and Hellenistic culture, so this term became crucial for the articulation of Christianity in that culture.

In the *pre-Constantinian period, the main theological focus was on various versions of Logos christology, the central core being that Jesus Christ was the pre-existent Son of God and Word of God, through whom the world was created and who became incarnate. In opposition to *Docetism (the contention of some *Gnostics that

Jesus Christ only apparently became human), the reality of his flesh and the goodness of creation were affirmed. In opposition to the Ebionite or Adoptionist contention that Jesus Christ was a man on whom divine qualities were conferred, it was affirmed that he was the Word who was with God from before creation. Against modalism (the contention that the Father, Son, and Spirit were successive 'modes' of the one God), it was affirmed that the Logos was (with the Spirit) eternally coexistent with the Father.

Debates about Logos christology culminated in the *Arian controversy. The critical question was where to place Jesus in relation to the line between creator and creation, and Arius was concerned lest God be identified with the weakness, passibility, and vulnerability to temptation of the NT Jesus. In opposition to Arius, *Athanasius affirmed that the Son is intrinsic to the being of God, and that in the Son God acts directly to save humanity from within creation in union with humanity. He rejected a created mediating saviour as not doing justice to the full involvement of God in salvation. The Council of *Nicaea decreed, in line with Athanasius, that Jesus Christ, the Son, is eternally begotten from the Father and is the same in substance or being (homoousios) as the Father. This innovative, unbiblical terminology was an attempt to maintain the continuity of faith in the face of new circumstances and challenges.

The Council of Nicaea introduced the crucial phase of christological debate leading up to the Council of *Chalcedon. Defining Jesus Christ as fully God stimulated discussion of how he was also fully human, and how the two could be held together. Both divinity and humanity were reconceived by thinking through the significance of Jesus Christ in the context of the God of Israel and the whole of creation. It was not that a predefinition of God was laid alongside a predefinition of humanity and then an attempt made to reconcile them. The revolution consisted in thinking through afresh what God means if Jesus Christ is intrinsic to who God is (the answer was the doctrine of the Trinity), and what being human means if the criterion of humanity is Jesus Christ (there has never been an answer comparable to the doctrine of the Trinity). The critical point of doctrinal decision was at Chalcedon, where the union of true divinity and true humanity was affirmed as 'without confusion, without change, without division, without separation' in 'one and the same Son and only-begotten God, Word, Lord Jesus Christ'.

In the debates leading up to Chalcedon the main schools of thought were associated with *Alexandria and Antioch. The Alexandrines stressed the divinity of Christ and the unity of the divine and human in him; the Antiochenes emphasized the humanity of Christ and the importance of distinguishing divinity from humanity in him. Chalcedon did not solve the christological problem, and the church has remained split over it ever since, with churches labelled *Monophysite representing an Alexandrine rejection of it and those labelled *Nestorian an Antiochene rejection. However, for most Christians in east and west Chalcedon offered an enduring framework for christological discussion which continued intensively and with increasingly refined terminology. Key issues concerned union and division in Christ, as related both to soteriology and to the Trinity.

Overall, the debates of the first seven centuries at their best set the standards within mainstream Christianity for contributions to christology, which have operated even when conclusions have differed:

thorough, enquiring engagement with scripture, tradition, and worship; critical sensitivity to ecclesial, cultural, political, and religious contexts; engagement with contemporary philosophies and world-views; and, at the heart of it all, a focus on the particular human being Jesus of Nazareth as intrinsic to who God is.

Three contributions of special significance for later centuries were:

1. The Byzantine *iconoclastic controversy which faced the question of the visual representation of Christ in images and their use in devotion. The question recurred in the *Reformation, is a continuing issue between religions (Judaism and Islam being aniconic), and has been sharpened by the proliferation of images in modern communication media. Theological discussion of the testimony to Jesus Christ through the visual and other *arts is still underdeveloped despite their importance in shaping conceptions of his person and significance (see Jesus, Depiction of).

2. Medieval theology in the west, which developed Chalcedonian christology in important ways. In 1098 *Anselm of Canterbury produced a new integration of the person and work of Christ in Cur deus homo (Why God Became Man). Scholastic theologians, especially Thomas *Aquinas, conceptually refined the related doctrines of the Trinity and christology. Aquinas especially develops a 'negative christology' affirming the hypostatic union of God and humanity as unique and as the highest of a hierarchy of unions between God and creation, but always insisting on the inadequacy of human *language to express this. Medieval theology also, in association with spirituality and art, showed a rich appreciation of the suffering humanity of Jesus Christ, especially exemplified in the life and teaching of *Francis of Assisi.

3. The Protestant Reformation was content with classical christology, and reflected some of the debates leading up to Chalcedon: *Luther tended towards Alexandrine christology; *Calvin, and even more *Zwingli, to Antiochene. But the Reformation's fresh engagement with the bible meant rethinking the person of Jesus Christ, with the main emphasis on salvation. The Reformation's chief contribution was the integration of christology and soteriology, as seen especially in Calvin's doctrine of the 'three offices' of Jesus Christ (prophet, priest, and king), and in the doctrine of Christ's 'two states' in humiliation and exaltation. Best understood as a supplement to 'two natures' christology, the two states refer especially to Philippians 2: 5–11. They offer a dynamic, cross-centred conception of Jesus Christ in relation to both God and humanity.

The focus on the Philippians passage continued, and in the 19th and 20th centuries was intensified in *kenotic christologies, emphasizing the self-emptying of God in becoming human. Kenoticism has repeatedly questioned and subverted classical christology. Its strength has been in doing justice to the humanly limited figure of Jesus in the gospels; its main problem has been how to reconceive God. This tension has been typical of much western christology since the *Renaissance, and has often given it, in classical terms, an Antiochene bias towards stressing the humanity of Jesus rather than his divinity.

Modern christology: five types

The period since the 18th century has seen intensive christological critique and attempted reconstruction, while Christianity has been expanding globally and becoming inculturated in an unprecedented variety of contexts. The biblical testimony has been criticized with regard to its authority, historicity, morality, portrayal of *God, mythological world-view, cultural specificity, and irrelevance due to historical distance. Classical christology has been criticized in similar terms, and also as wedded to Greek philosophical views of God, creation, and humanity. Especially in the 20th century, critiques interrogated the role of christology in the persecution of Jews (*antisemitism), in western imperialism, in oppression of *women, and in exploitation of nature. The context for these critiques has been massive transformations in most areas of life and understanding. These have sharpened the problems of trying to offer an understanding of Jesus Christ which is both true to biblical and classical christology and accessible to intelligent faith today.

A wide range of solutions has been proposed and the following typology, drawing on that of Hans Frei, suggests a way to map the variety of modern christologies. Its main criterion is the way a particular christology relates contemporary frameworks, philosophies, or practical agendas to the figure of Jesus as portrayed in the gospels and affirmed in mainstream Chalcedonian Christianity. There are five basic types, though many of the most interesting christologies cannot be fitted neatly into one.

Type 1 gives priority to some contemporary philosophy, framework, method, culture, or agenda, and Jesus Christ has to fit in with that. Anything about him that does not fit is rejected, so he becomes an illustration or external support for a position arrived at independently of him. One of the most powerful such positions in modern times has been that of Immanuel *Kant, whose principal criterion for judging Christianity was his own philosophical ethics. For him there is a universal ethical *religion whose rational archetype cannot be fully embodied in one individual. It can be exemplified allegorically by Jesus Christ, but the more general framework, by which Jesus Christ is judged, is a morality based on autonomous *reason.

Others have used criteria based on different philosophies, a worldview appealing to the natural or human sciences, historical-critical methods, specific cultures, political commitments, a vision of human or *ecological well-being, feminist concerns, sexual orientation, or a different religious faith. Any of those may be important elsewhere in the typology, but in Type 1 one or more of them acts as the overall conception of reality in which Jesus Christ has no decisive voice.

At the other extreme, Type 5's christology consists in appropriating the NT's way of describing Jesus Christ. It sees all reality in these terms, rejecting all contemporary research, frameworks, and agendas as irrelevant. Such *fundamentalist positions may hold that the bible alone is the clear, inerrant, inspired Word of God for all times and places, simply to be believed and acted upon, while other versions of fundamentalism may supplement the bible with later doctrinal statements or with a particular liturgy or tradition, but the distinguishing feature is that external descriptions or criteria of intelligibility and truth have no validity or relevance: Christianity's self-description is all-sufficient. A more sophisticated version suggests that christology based on the NT and church tradition is a 'language game' with its own 'rules', and cannot be understood in terms of other language games (see WITTGENSTEIN). Theologians should make clear what sort of language game christology is and draw the consequences for 'playing' it, but it is pointless to try to justify Christian faith in alien terms.

The three types in between embrace most christology in mainstream Christianity.

Type 2 takes external frameworks seriously but also engages with what is distinctive about Jesus Christ. If, for example, one finds a philosophy which suits Christian faith better than others, one might use it to show how Jesus Christ makes sense and is relevant today. Rudolf *Bultmann does this with *existentialist philosophy. He accepts its analysis of the human condition in terms of *Angst*, with the constant temptation to seek security in ways that enslave us and take away our freedom and authenticity. He sees NT faith meeting this condition with a proclamation (*kerygma*) that challenges hearers to depend entirely on God for their security. To decide for the gospel is to have a new self-understanding and to be freed to live in faith, love, and hope before God, a condition Bultmann describes as 'eschatological existence'. But if this existential freedom in faith is what the NT is really about, then it is necessary to disentangle its message from inessentials, such as its 1st-century world-view or its tendency to objectify and mythologize Jesus Christ. So Bultmann unites his existential analysis with historical critical scholarship in order to identify and interpret what he sees as the core of the gospel and to prune away the rest as 'mythological'. This core is about the practical transformation of people; it is not about the person of Jesus Christ. So Bultmann gives soteriology priority over christology, and is interested neither in the quest for the historical Jesus nor in the classical christological emphasis on his person. What matters is the possibility of transformed existence through faith.

A very different version of Type 2 is offered by Wolfhart *Pannenberg. His key idea is that God is revealed indirectly through history, and that this knowledge of God 'from below' has to be tested and developed using historical critical and philosophical methods. Theological claims have to be argued for in rational, general, universal terms. At the heart of his christology is an understanding of the Resurrection of Jesus as the key to universal history. It is the event which anticipates the consummation of history and sets the horizon for understanding all reality in relation to God. Beginning from a historical critical account of the Resurrection he argues for the divinity of Jesus Christ and develops a doctrine of the Trinity. In contrast with Bultmann, he insists on reaching through the existential meaning of the NT to find the historical Jesus and the person of the risen Christ.

Many christologies labelled 'liberal' or 'revisionist' might also be seen as Type 2 in their concern to reinterpret christology as thoroughly as possible in modern terms. *Religious experience, or a human capacity for it, has often been the basic reality in terms of which Jesus is related to life today, and this has also been a way of integrating christology with other religious traditions.

Type 3 is what happens when no framework such as the human capacity for religious experience, Pannenberg's conception of universal history, or Bultmann's existentialism is allowed an overall integrating role. It is in the middle of the spectrum because it does not allow that any single framework is adequate. It takes issues raised in relation to Jesus Christ by the NT and correlates them (*Tillich's key term) with a variety of approaches.

*Schleiermacher's christology is (at least according to many commentators) of this type. Jesus Christ can be described as a particular historical person using various academic disciplines, and also as the mediator of Christian experience of *redemption in the church. He finds these external and internal descriptions—later called the 'Jesus of history' and the 'Christ of faith'—to be in harmony, but they are distinct, and there is no overarching theory or general framework within which to integrate them.

Correlating Jesus Christ as understood by historical critical methods with the understanding given by the NT, classical christology, and Christian tradition became one of the main concerns of christology in the 19th and 20th centuries. Correlational theologians have engaged in many other dialogues too: with natural scientists about *miracles and resurrection; with philosophers about appropriate conceptualities for divinity and humanity, or about criteria for truth and goodness; with ethicists about the *Sermon on the Mount and the implications of Jesus Christ for *morality; with Jews about messiahship; with psychologists about the *psychology of Jesus and of faith in him; with those in politics about Jesus as prophet or liberator; with various cultures around the world; and with other religious traditions about divinity, humanity, salvation, ethics, and so on.

The Protestant Paul Tillich and the Roman Catholic Edward *Schillebeeckx have developed different correlational christologies taking account of a wide range of dialogues without any general integrating theory or framework. Many *feminist christologies are also of this type, keeping Jesus Christ in critical dialogue with feminist concerns, and especially suspicious of male-dominated frameworks which have shaped much christology. Some christologies labelled *postmodern (including some with gender as a leading theme) revel in a lack of overview or systematic coherence, to the extent of seeing Christ as sponsoring the coexistence of radical differences.

Type 4 accepts the desirability of a range of dialogues, but believes that Christian faith does propose an integrator: Jesus Christ. It insists (against Types 1 and 2) that no outside framework should dictate our understanding of the contents of Christian faith; it also refuses to see the relationship of Jesus Christ to other conceptions of reality in as open or indeterminate a way as Type 3. It gives overall priority to Christian self-description. It is 'faith seeking understanding', basically trusting the main lines of classic Christian testimony, but also open to dialogue. It stands within Christian tradition, rejecting any neutral stance for dialogue.

The most substantial and influential 20th-century christology, that of Karl *Barth, is largely of Type 4. He was deeply disturbed to see Christianity compromised by its alliances with modern western thought, culture, politics, and civilization. At the heart of his *Church Dogmatics* is a christology which integrates afresh the Reformation themes of priest, king, and prophet not only with the two states of humiliation (servanthood) and exaltation (Lordship), but also with the whole classical dogmatic tradition of Christianity. In this he is both an example of the coinherence of each major doctrine with all the others, and a leading advocate of the determinative role of christology. Perhaps his most original contribution is his complete integration of the person and work of Jesus Christ, culminating in *CD* IV/3 where the living Jesus Christ is understood as the 'light of life', moving through history as the one who makes sense of it and calls the church and each person to his or her true vocation.

The influential christology of the Roman Catholic Karl *Rahner is one (among many) which is difficult to categorize in this typology, showing both its usefulness and limitations. Some of his writings use the framework of 'transcendental *Thomism' as a general framework to show how the life, death, and Resurrection of Jesus Christ make sense, as in Type 2. He also engages in a wide variety of unsystematic dialogues and correlations, as in Type 3. Yet it is argued that the overall thrust of his theology is 'faith seeking understanding', as in Type 4, with Jesus Christ as the unsurpassable integrator.

Finally, another christology which in far briefer compass displays features of the central three types but with a bias to the fourth is that of Dietrich *Bonhoeffer. The reason for its brevity, Bonhoeffer's execution for taking part in the 20 July 1944 plot against Hitler, also raises a perennial issue affecting the testimony to Jesus Christ by communities as much as by individuals: the relation of that testimony to the life of those who give it.   **David F. Ford**

Barth, Karl, *Church Dogmatics* (1936–69).
Bockmuehl, Markus, *This Jesus: Martyr, Lord, Messiah* (1994).
Boff, Leonardo, *Jesus Christ Liberator* (1978).
Bonhoeffer, Dietrich, *Christology* (1971).
Bonino, J. Míguez, *Faces of Jesus: Latin American Christologies* (1984).
Bultmann, Rudolf, *The Theology of the New Testament* (2 vols.; 1952–5).
Cullmann, O., *Christology of the New Testament* (1959).
Dunn, J., *Christology in the Making* (1980).
Fiorenza, Elisabeth Schüssler, *In Memory of Her* (1983).
Ford, David F., *The Modern Theologians: An Introduction to Christian Theology in the Twentieth Century*, 2nd edn. (1997).
Frei, Hans W., *Types of Christian Theology* (1992).
Grant, J., *White Woman's Christ and Black Woman's Jesus* (1989).
Grillmeier, Aloys, *Christ in Christian Tradition*, 2nd edn. (1975).
Küng, Hans, *On Being a Christian* (1977).
Loades, Ann, *Feminist Theology: A Reader* (1990).
Moltmann, Jürgen, *The Crucified God* (1974).
—— *The Way of Jesus Christ* (1989).
Nyamiti, Charles, *Christ as our Ancestor: Christology from an African Perspective* (1984).
Pannenberg, Wolfhart, *Jesus—God and Man* (1968).
Pelikan, Jaroslav, *The Christian Tradition: A History of the Development of Doctrine* (1989).
Rahner, Karl, *Foundations of Christian Faith* (1978).
Sanders, E. P., *The Historical Figure of Jesus* (1993).
Schillebeeckx, Edward, *Jesus: An Experiment in Christology* (1979).
—— *Christ: The Christian Experience in the Modern World* (1980).
Sobrino, J. *Christology at the Crossroads: A Latin American Approach* (1978).
Sugirtharajah, R. S. (ed.), *Asian Faces of Jesus* (1993).
Tillich, Paul, *Systematic Theology* (1957), ii.
Vermes, G., *Jesus the Jew* (1973).
Williams, Rowan, *Arius: Heresy and Tradition* (1987).
Young, Frances M., *From Nicaea to Chalcedon* (1983).

church.

Thinking about the church today involves the conception of the church as such; its situation in a world for which it is not normative; and the variety of disciplines used to consider it.

Introduction

Christian *faith is held by Christians in common ('our faith'), and their commonness, constituted by the substance of the faith that they hold, is what is called 'the church'. Christian faith is itself formative of the church because its content is social, derived from the *communion within the *Trinitarian *God. In God Christians find the true basis for the social life of humanity, its true sociality, realized in *heaven (the church triumphant) and in the *world (the church militant). This is what existing churches, despite their differences, their inadequacies, and their sin, have to exemplify. As a descriptive term, therefore, 'the church' is a collective designation for the varying social embodiments of Christian life in the world, as each differently approximates the godly basis of true sociality. Implicit in this variety is a major theological question: how does God's Trinitarian self-determination for humanity bring a true society in and through the diversity of the churches? This is the question to which *ecumenical efforts have repeatedly been directed, especially in periods of disruption.

Though 'the church' includes a significant proportion of the world's population, it is often not capable of exemplifying God's true sociality, either because of its own failures or because it is not considered normative (or even a significant contributor) for the societies in which it is present. This raises questions of how its own constitution relates to other configurations of social life, such as particular governments, cultures, or religions, and corresponding questions as to what response is appropriate, whether mutual exclusion, constructive *dialogue, assimilation, or mutual reinterpretation: the choice is often determined by how a particular church understands itself. Although exclusivist strategies seem more simple and attractive in times of challenge, engaging with the problems and vitalities of non-Christian societies has brought important developments for the churches. New forms of ecclesial thought and practice have frequently resulted from addressing issues of politics, inculturation, liberation of the oppressed, and the influence of other religions. The overarching theme is the question of *mission: what value is to be assigned to other configurations of social life, and how is a true sociality arising from the fullness of humanity's relationship with God in Christ to be embodied in these forms of society?

The third aspect requiring attention is modern academic study of the church, using norms developed outside the churches. Various disciplines—sociological, anthropological, legal, cultural—have been deployed to consider the church. Although often naturalistic (in practice if not intent) and limited by their 'interests', they frequently prove informative and illuminating about worldly features of church life, chiefly by their searching analysis of parallels in other forms of social life. They can be problematic when used to give a fundamental account of the church as a society, since they displace the study of the *theology of church life. If they are not to be discarded, in the name of 'theology as itself a *social science, and the queen of the sciences for the inhabitants of the *altera civitas*' (Milbank), the question is how the church can engage with them in the understanding and practice of true sociality. This is a highly significant issue for present-day Christians, who find the truth of social unity in God and yet find themselves in a world understood in other terms.

An adequate response to these issues will come only from a fuller understanding of the common tradition of Christian sociality, of normative conceptions of the church and of the possibilities for critical reappropriation of the idea of the church.

Redescribing the common tradition of church understanding

The church began by understanding itself as the continuation of God's people of *Israel, the people whose life together is constituted by their *covenant with God, as manifest in their *history with God, their common *worship and scriptures, and in *laws governing their social life. Their history shows 'God's method of bringing unity to the human race beset with the disorder of sin' (Ramsey) and his intention to extend this to the nations of the world. For Christians, this is fulfilled in the life, death, and *Resurrection of Christ, in whom the church is constituted as the new Israel, and God's purposes for human society are accomplished. There all human beings and *nations—every nation, Jew and Gentile, male or female, bond or free (Gal. 3: 28)—are to be brought into unity.

Historically, then, the question of the nature of the society proper to Christians begins with the constitution of the people of God in the *Old Testament covenant. Taking account of the truth, loyalty, and uprightness of *Abraham and *David, God promises to adopt David as his son and unconditionally to grant him and his heirs a 'house' and a 'kingdom' forever, including a dynasty, land, and peoples. It is this promise that constitutes these as a people, with a place and political continuity in the world, and norms for social behaviour.

While still the continuation of the covenant people of God, the church owes its special character to the concentration of the relation of this people to God in the life, death, and Resurrection of Jesus Christ. Christ came to gather God's people in anticipation of the feast of the Lord in the latter days (cf. Isa. 2: 2; Zech. 14: 16; Matt. 9: 36; 12: 30; 16: 18), fulfilling the Jewish Passover by his death and Resurrection, and sending the *Holy Spirit to the disciples assembled together on *Pentecost (Acts 2). In this New Covenant the people of God are reconstituted as the *messianic community in which the blessing of God in Jesus Christ is realized for the sake of the coming *Kingdom.

As thus envisaged, the church has an implicit Trinitarian basis. God's *Word is the constitutive principle of the church (Heb. 1: 1; 2: 3, 4; Matt. 28: 20; John 14: 26; 16: 23; 1 Cor. 14: 37), and the Holy Spirit is its life (John 14: 16–18; Rom. 8: 9), through which it is protected and sent in mission to the world as the anticipation of the Kingdom. From its participation in the death and Resurrection of Christ, the church as his body receives its 'marks' (one, holy, *catholic, and *apostolic) as new, redeemed *humanity, and its vitality comes from the life-giving power of the Spirit (Rom. 8: 9–11; John 14: 16–17). The promise of the Father in the Son is fulfilled in the spirit-filled life of the people of God, and in the special gifts by which the church praises God, nurtures its members, and witnesses to the world.

The church was not initially an idea or a doctrine but a practice of shared faith. The consolidation of this faith, its preservation from the divisive effects of *heresy, and its missionary spread through unified, vital communities, were sufficient, making a fuller doctrine of the church unnecessary at first. There was none until the Middle Ages, when both the basis and the commonality of faith were rendered problematic by alternative perceptions of truth and social divisions. The four 'marks' of the church identified in the *Nicene *Creed were in the first place practical norms, expressing the full dynamics of the church. It was to be self-consistent, the embodiment of the *holiness of God in Jesus Christ, the fullness of his *salvation for all peoples, and to exercise its *ministry in conformity with the apostles.

These norms were performed through practices such as common worship, discipline, virtuous living, *forgiveness, and *reconciliation, *compassion, care for the oppressed, and witness to the new society implicit in these. Hence, faith in Jesus Christ took the form of certain practices of inter-human life, which in turn constituted a distinctive kind of society whose purpose was the fulfilment of all social life in anticipation of the Kingdom of God.

These practices distinguished the church from other societies, and also stimulated engagement with them. They made the church 'another sort of country, created by the Logos of God' (*Origen, *Contra Celsum*, 8. 75), a new people, race, or city, of which others were seen as approximations or distortions which could be brought to true realization only by the spread of the church. Thus living as the church brought responsibility in wider society, although this in turn raised important questions about the meaning and finality of the *redemption of human society achieved by Jesus, and the extent to which Christians could participate in unjust and violent activities.

It is significant that what the apostles established were small communities whose practice signified true sociality in the pagan world. Their practice was what made them notable and persuasive: 'let us confess him in our deeds, by loving one another, by not committing adultery, nor speaking one against another, nor being jealous, but by being self-controlled, merciful, good' (Clement of Alexandria). The unity of belief and practice (rhetorical, artistic, theological, behavioural) accounts for the astonishing growth of *Christianity in early times.

The need to consolidate such beliefs and practices in communities brought other requirements: control of corporate *memory; establishment of boundaries of participation; education, formation and discipline of members; arrangements for corporate social life (polity). Hence, a canon of authoritative writings was established, and their implications interpreted in *preaching and catechesis for the guidance of the communities (see BIBLE). A determinative place was given to *sacraments of initiation (*baptism) and incorporation into the sacrifice of Christ (*Eucharist), which included people in the benefits of Christ's life, and served to enact the kingdom thus brought into being. An appropriate polity was developed to distribute responsibilities within the sociality established in Jesus. The truth of Christ in the church was regarded as sign ('sacrament' in discussions today) of a new society anticipating the *eschaton.

Conceptions of the church today

Does the church's understanding of itself permit it to discern the social content of Christian faith, to embody this fully in the presence of other configurations of social life, and to engage with other ways of understanding (and practising) sociality? This is a serious question for the body that is the active social correlate of the triune God's self-giving for the world in Christ.

If the theological implications of the common church *tradition are taken seriously, it is the social content of their faith, deriving from the Trinity, which brings Christians together. Historically, the 'basis' of this content has been explained in a number of different ways, which all have limitations even where modified by the traditions originating from them. Four types can be identified: ontological, actualist, *mystical, and historical.

In the *ontological* way, associated with traditional Roman Catholicism, the existence of natural society is willed by God who created human beings, to enable them to attain their full stature, while the church exists to help them secure their supernatural well-being. The church derives its being from the action of God in the Incarnation of Jesus Christ; it is the abiding presence of Christ in the sacraments that makes it a sign of the kingdom. Its social constitution thus arises from its continuity (Matt. 16: 18–19) with the church of the apostles (apostolic succession). This is manifest in its sacramental life, hierarchical structure (a point considerably modified since *Vatican II), governance (canon law), doctrinal authority (magisterium), and virtuous life.

In the *mystical* way, associated with the *eastern churches, the church is constituted by its participation in the inner dynamism of the endless *love of the triune God, and therefore in the divine economy awakening fallen creation to participate in salvation and fulfilment, making human nature divine and immortalizing nature. In that 'divinization', the divine and the created interpenetrate and co-operate, each according to its own measure. Church life and theology are properly centred where this dynamic is most fully found, in the *liturgy, in scripture, in the fathers of the church, and in the practice of love in concrete local situations. These emphases lead to a church polity which disperses authority in regions and localities.

In the *actualist* way, found typically in churches of the *Reformed traditions, the premiss is that 'God's action is always the condition of the possibility of all human action' (Schwöbel, 'The Creature of the Word', in C. Gunton and D. W. Hardy (eds.), *On Being the Church*). The church is an assembly that is always being reconstituted by the Word of God, by the gracious act of God (election), received in faith. This Word alone is the law of the church, just as God's Spirit alone gives life to the church. Properly speaking, therefore, the church is defined as God sees it, as invisible. The visible church is constituted by gathering around the Word proclaimed, and is not in itself a guarantee of salvation. Yet it is the 'condition' which makes the mediation of revelation possible (see BARTH), and should be the place where the Word of God is purely preached, the sacraments properly celebrated, and church discipline faithfully exercised.

For the *historical* way, found typically in *Anglicanism, the church is constituted by the fullness of biblical and traditional Christian belief and practice maintained through its social dynamic in history. The diverse positions found in the other 'ways' are embraced in the development of the church as a visible society through interacting traditions of common worship, reason, and practice. In a communion of regional churches developing in their own particular historical circumstances, God's justifying grace permeates and transforms the human condition, private and public.

All these conceptions of the church are strongly tied to notions of what is most real. Questioning of the authoritative basis of such views has led to the (phenomenological) suggestion that churches are best understood as rule-governed forms of life or 'systems of signs' governed by biblical or theological categories. Whether the church is seen as a symbolic body mediating Jesus Christ, as in Vatican II Roman Catholic thought, or as 'cultural-linguistic' (George *Lindbeck, *The Nature of Doctrine*), it redescribes the world in Christian terms, reversing modern tendencies to conform the church to external worldly realities. These conceptions have brought a new openness to other forms of society, but the question is whether they incorporate a full view of sociality, divine or human, or provide a basis for engagement with other configurations or understandings of social life.

Critical reappropriation of the common tradition

The common tradition of church understanding finds the basis of true social life, not only for Christians but for humanity, in the history of the covenant of God with Israel focused in the new covenant made in Jesus Christ through the Holy Spirit and continued in the church. In so far as the church fulfils this mandate, it is the primary manifestation of the 'economy of salvation' and embodies the intensity of God's Trinitarian life in the extensity of social life in the world, both in time and in eternity.

The character of this embodiment deserves attention. The intensity of God's Trinitarian life is his pattern for the creation, redemption, and perfection of human life in the world. As God determines himself by a movement of love that calls forth reception, he forges the possibilities of human social life by the movement of love between people. That is, God establishes and fulfils human sociality—its *unity, holiness, catholicity, and apostolicity—not from without but by awakening the possibilities of human beings themselves by justifying grace. When Jesus, as a human being fully in relation to others, both reconstitutes these possibilities and maximizes them through restoring communion with God, he transforms human social life from within, both relatively to sin and absolutely. The church, in heaven and on earth, is the unfolding of what was accomplished in him for all human existence.

A major issue is the quality of this extensity in social life over time, and how far it attains the scope appropriate to the limitless possibilities of God's self-determination. The church needs continually to learn to be the church through its critical reappropriation of the implications of God's Trinitarian self-determination for humanity in the world. The danger is that in its task of realizing itself, in its missionary engagement with other social configurations, and in its interaction with modern ways of understanding and promoting society, it will be severely restricted by its own self-conception and practice. If the church is to avoid the dictum that 'society can exist only as a self-referential system' (N. Luhmann, *Essays on Self-Reference*), it needs to relearn its sociality from the true sociality inherent in God's Trinitarian life. To do so, in a continuous engagement with God and the world, will continually reform it (*ecclesia semper reformanda*). To do less will assimilate it to what is less.

Daniel W. Hardy

Avis, P. D. L., *The Church in the Theology of the Reformers* (1981).
Barth, K., *Church Dogmatics* IV (1956–61), §§ 62, 67, 72.
Bonhoeffer, D., *Sanctorum Communio* (1931; 1998).
Ellacuria, I., and Sobrino, J. (eds.), *Mysterium Liberationis* (1993).
Farley, E., *Ecclesial Man* (1975).
Küng, H., *The Church* (1976).
Lohfink, G., *Jesus and Community* (1985).
Milbank, J., *Theology and the Social Sciences* (1990).
Rahner, K., *The Church and the Sacraments* (1965).
Ramsey, A. M., *The Gospel and the Catholic Church* (1956).
Schmemann, A., *The Eucharist: Sacrament of the Kingdom* (1987)
Schweizer, E., *The Church as the Body of Christ* (1964).

cinema has effected a shift in the locus of Christian theology, which is no longer an exclusive domain for theologians or even believers, but is now present in the global market-place. As one of the mass media, cinema addresses itself to the public at large in all its cultural diversity of belief and unbelief. This is not only a challenge to Christians who often see themselves and their faith made a spectacle to the world, but puts the gospel itself to the test. It has to ask itself how its claim to be a faith for all nations can be sustained in the light of this new accessibility. Moreover, film is a special medium. It does not rely on the written or spoken word. Images on the screen are more evanescent and less precise than words on the page or in the ear, but their power of communication can be greater since they go beyond mere information.

The figure of Christ has appeared in many films since *From the Manger to the Cross* (1912). In their quest for historical accuracy filmmakers have sometimes adopted a *fundamentalist interpretation of the scriptures. At other times they have given us a very personal and idiosyncratic portrait in order to pose particular questions. Pasolini's *The Gospel According to St Matthew* (1964) attempts to follow the account of a single gospel narrative and restrict the spoken text to actual citations from that gospel, while *The Last Temptation of Christ* (1988) speculates on the nature of Christ's temptation and suggests that it was an invitation to come down from the cross, live an ordinary *human life, and not play the martyr hero.

Apart from screen lives of the historical *Jesus and re-creation of biblical scenes, we often come across characters in films who bear a strong resemblance to Christ. Sometimes this is intentional: Carl Dreyer's *Joan of Arc* (1928) is a Christ figure in her trial and sufferings and so is the fictional character in *Jesus of Montreal* (1989). A more implicit Christ figure is the character played by Terence Stamp in Pasolini's *Theorem* (1968). Such is the impact of the visit of this stranger on father, mother, son, daughter, and housemaid that each of their lives is transformed. The power of love leads the maid to *mysticism and the father to give all his possessions to the workers at his factory. *Theorem* and *The Gospel According to St Matthew* form an interesting pair.

It is possible to take parallels between Christ and film characters too far, but at least anyone who makes such a comparison has already formed some opinion as to the *person of Jesus. However, it is in one of the consequences of the *Incarnation, the importance of everyday human events, that the presence of Christian values in cinema is most commonly found. This became apparent after the Second World War in films associated with neo-realism. At the specifically religious level, Bresson's *Diary of a Country Priest* (1950) considers the feelings of inadequacy and failure besetting a good and conscientious *priest. *Le Défroqué* (1948) deals with loss of faith and *Dieu a Besoin des Hommes* (1951) with communities deprived of a resident pastor. These are problems that have increased rather than diminished with the years. In the 1960s the films of Ingmar Bergman, with their soul-searching about the ultimate reality of death and the transitoriness of love, have a particular resonance because of his own Christian culture and upbringing. In *The Seventh Seal* (1957) and *Through a Glass Darkly* (1960) there are references to classical Christian writers. On the other hand, directors such as Buñuel and Fellini take a more critical stance, their films reflecting their dissatisfaction with their Catholic upbringing. In *The Milky Way* (1969), Buñuel succeeds in his satirical attempt to illustrate scenes from the history of Christian theology. More recently, *Babette's Feast* (1987) tells how a Christian community in a remote part of Europe, devoted to a frugal life of work and prayer, experience the joys of a common celebratory meal, illustrating how in the

Christian life *word and *sacrament are complementary. Kieslow- ski's *Decalogue* (1988) is not a biblical account of the giving of the law but an application to contemporary life of the Ten *Command- ments. In ten episodes he probes questions of guilt and *punish- ment in reference to the death penalty and rather mischievously suggests that stamp collecting can manifest a form of covetousness.

The extent to which a visual medium like cinema can convey the idea of transcendence depends on one's understanding of the rela- tion between matter and spirit and the Christian doctrine of *cre- ation and *Fall. Different responses may be given according to whether one is in the Catholic or the Reformed tradition, but most Christians would agree that the Spirit of God is abroad in the *world and its presence is not always heralded by spectacular events. This does not mean that science fiction has nothing to offer. Such films as *Solaris* (1972) and *2001: A Space Odyssey* (1968) entertain the possibility of intelligent life higher than that of humankind. Ridley Scott's *Bladerunner* (1982) and James Cameron's *Terminator* (1984) pose serious questions about the nature of the human race and what distinguishes human beings from artificial intelligence. *Terminator 2: Judgement Day* (1991) is worthy of special mention because this film asks whether the future is fixed or whether we are able to determine our fate by our actions now so that judge- ment is in the present. The context of the enquiry may be a world of fantasy but the question asked is familiar territory for the Chris- tian theologian.

The challenge of cinema is that it is a relatively new medium. In previous generations, the *church made use of current modes of artistic expression and philosophical argument. Today, there is a *language specific to film that must be learnt and spoken if the church is to communicate effectively and respond to the needs and aspirations of the contemporary world.

See also NOVEL, THE.   **Michael E. Williams**

Butler, I., *Religion in the Cinema* (1969).
Malone, P., *Movie Christs and Antichrists* (1990).
Marsh, C., and Ortiz, G. W. (eds.), *Explorations in Theology and Film* (1997).
Martin, J. W., and Ostwalt, C. E., Jr. (eds.), *Screening the Sacred* (1995).
Pavelin, A., *Fifty Religious Films* (1990).

city. Christianity originates as a primarily urban movement, ap- pealing to a widespread disaffection from the prevailing civil norms. In this disaffection, it was very much at one with the dom- inant schools of *Hellenistic *philosophy. Cynics, Epicureans, Stoics, all in different ways also rejected the 'superstition' of the local cults, participation in which played such an important role in shaping people's sense of civic belonging. The early Christians re- sembled the Epicureans in their *missionary impulse, whilst they shared the Stoics' recoil from the extreme subjectivity of the Epi- cureans' appeal to the criterion of pleasure. But their rejection of Roman civil *religion went deeper, not only because it was clothed in an *apocalyptic view of history, but also by virtue of being em- bodied in a form of organization finely honed to survive actual persecution by the civil authorities.

A persecuted community urgently needs the sort of *unity that the early *church's *martyr-cult and horror of *heresy provided. The great problem, however, comes when an institution formed in this way, essentially to cope with such pressures, has to adapt to the very different circumstances of life in professedly Christian cities.

*Augustine is the key thinker for this transition. The 'city of God', to which Christians owe their whole allegiance, is decisively distin- guished by Augustine from both the Christian 'earthly city' and the institutional church, as they actually exist. However, it is first and foremost the church that is called to represent this ideal, over against the earthly city. The medieval *cathedral-builders, as Richard Sennett put it, effectively 'translated Augustine's religious vision into urban design': erecting vast *symbols of divine order within the initially higgledy-piggledy disorder of the earthly city, which later town-planners then sought to organize around its churches.

Long before Augustine, the Stoics had developed the metaphys- ical notion of a divine cosmopolis. In the later Stoic conception, this cosmopolis includes among its citizens, along with the gods, all human beings in so far as they live their lives according to the rational laws of nature. But Zeno's earlier version had also resem- bled Augustine's in confining citizenship to a small élite. Augus- tine's main source, though, is the biblical tradition regarding *Jerusalem. He himself cites the *Psalms (*The City of God*, II. 1) and Galatians 4: 21–31 (15. 2). And his opposition between the two cities echoes the book of *Revelation, in which all the negative symbolism previously associated with Egypt and with Nineveh, for instance, is concentrated into the figure of the earthly Babylon, once the power responsible for *Israel's exile, now effectively iden- tified with imperial *Rome—and dramatically overthrown by the heavenly Jerusalem.

What is momentously new with Augustine is his (partial) de- apocalypticizing of the difference between the two cities, and his reinterpretation of it in terms of the outworkings of two forms of *love: 'the love of God carried as far as contempt of self' and 'self- love reaching the point of contempt for God' (14. 28). In itself this distinction might be merely banal; but it gains its cutting edge from his reading of the Roman historian Sallust, and in particular Sallust's critical analysis of Roman decadence as the product of a ravenous *libido dominandi*, lust for domination. The earthly city is both driven by corporate *libido dominandi* and riven by the personal *libido dom- inandi* of its politicians. It 'loves its own strength shown in its powerful rulers'; that is, the dominated take a masochistic pleasure in their condition. What it honours as the noble-minded quest for glory is mostly just *libido dominandi* in disguise. Augustine differs from the whole preceding tradition of *political philosophy in his complete indifference to the question of the ideal constitution. He is interested only in defining the ideal civil *ethos*: a certain quality of inter-subjectivity. Moreover the corrupt ethos of the earthly city, so defined, is not confined to paganism; it may equally appear in Christian form. However, Augustine's critique of Christendom re- mains very largely restricted to its purely civil—as opposed to its (orthodox) ecclesiastical—aspects. Indeed, he relished his allotted role as bishop. An institution shaped by the imperatives of survival under persecution all too easily becomes a self-righteously perse- cuting agency itself when it comes to power; and, in relation to the *Donatists, Augustine also becomes an apologist for persecution— quite oblivious, it seems, to the possibility that that too might be a veiled expression of *libido dominandi*.

Perhaps the sharpest 20th-century critic of the mainstream Augus- tinian tradition in Christian political thinking has been Hannah Arendt. Arendt's first book was a study of Augustine, and she remains to the end a great admirer of his achievement. Yet her primary project is to draw the moral from the story of that ultimate explosion of *libido dominandi*, the nightmare of totalitarianism in its Nazi and Stalinist forms. And, as she sees it, the historic dominance of the Augustinian vision within western Christendom is very much part of the long-term problem.

Thus, for Arendt, the chief thing we need to learn from the catastrophe is truly to love that which totalitarianism most immediately destroys: 'politics' in the original sense, the spirit paradigmatically embodied in the civil culture of the ancient Greek polis, and above all in that of Athens. In other words, not politics as an art of ruling, but politics as that free-spiritedness that systematically minimizes the rulers' scope for ruling; the maximum spontaneous participation of as many citizens as possible in all properly public affairs. But not only did the Christian church, in its decisively formative period, never enjoy any real experience of free-spirited civil life in this sense, it also inherited the Greek philosophical tradition's collective revolt against the older polis-ethos, in its decline. As a contemplative activity, philosophy necessarily belongs to a different order of life from politics. With regard to its own self-interest, all it is inclined to demand from its urban environment is a maximum of tranquil stability. Hence, when it comes to public affairs, the natural preoccupation of the philosopher, as such, will always tend to be with the question of what constitutes good rule, rather than with the very different virtues of politics. Augustine, as a Christian philosopher, likewise ranks the contemplative life above the active. And so—Arendt argues—in the end, his notion of the heavenly city is just too heavenly.

Under what circumstances does it actually become possible for 'politics', in the strict Arendtian sense, to flourish? It would seem that it requires either a thriving, not too large, single-city context, as in ancient Athens, or else the clear differentiation, from the state and all its works, of a vigorous pluralistic 'civil society', in a permanently critical relationship to government.

There have indeed been several examples of the former in post-Augustinian church history, where Christian public-spiritedness really does appear to break free from the institutional self-interest of both church and state, as rival entities, to merge instead into a quite straightforward expression of civic pride. The cities of later medieval Western Europe developed a vibrant 'political' life, through the mediation of their devoutly religious trade-guilds and confraternities (see MIDDLE AGES). In *North America, Philadelphia—'the city of brotherly love'—was originally intended by its *Quaker founders in the 1680s very much as an experiment in free-spirited Christian civility. Or, again, there is the particular contribution of—above all—the English Dissenting tradition to the burgeoning municipal life of the leading cities of the Industrial Revolution: the work of the *Congregationalist minister R. W. Dale in mid-19th-century Birmingham, for example.

Arguably the most promising source of hope for the future of Christian urban mission, however, lies in the current transformation of civil society into a new political arena, one fundamentally set apart from the interplay of actual or would-be governmental ideologies. This is the world of pure 'consciousness-raising politics': a plethora of single-issue lobby groups and solidarity networks, exploiting the unprecedented communications potential of the turn-of-the-millennium city.

There have been numerous different types of positive Christian response. These include campaigning organizations on a national or international scale—often *ecumenical, building secular alliances. Many more localized diaconal initiatives have acquired a political edge, promoting the self-organization of particular disadvantaged groups. The *base communities of *Latin America and elsewhere are local projects of political self-organization among the inhabitants of slums and shanty-towns, with a strongly ecclesial character. Hence they have become the subjects of their own theology of *liberation. Certain forms of consciousness-raising industrial mission—in the UK and other parts of the Anglo-Saxon world, Scandinavia and Germany—clearly also belong in the same general category. And then there are the strategies of 'broad-based organizing', seeking so far as possible to draw whole parish congregations, and other local community groups, into campaigning federations.

Even apart from such initiatives, church congregations often play a crucial role in helping preserve at least some rudiments of community spirit in the poorest and most anarchic parts of contemporary cities. In Britain, the Church of England report *Faith in the City*, published in 1985, was both a celebration of that role and a politically significant 'call for action by church and nation' in response to urban decay.

The corporate soul of a city may be said to consist in its processes of public debate. All of the above are examples of the church working to enrich that debate by helping otherwise submerged voices gain a proper hearing. They are thus direct attempts to heal Augustine's 'earthly city' of the malign consequences of its *libido dominandi*, and so to help save its soul.   **Andrew Shanks**

Arendt, H., *Love and Saint Augustine* (1929), ET (1996).
—— *The Human Condition* (1958).
Cox, H., *The Secular City* (1965).
Hawkins, P. (ed.), *Civitas: Religious Interpretations of the City* (1986).
Tonna, B., *Gospel for the Cities* (1982).

Coleridge, Samuel Taylor (1772–1834), poet and philosophical theologian. Some of his best *poetry was fragmentary, his theology even more so; his life was a mess. Nevertheless, every fragment gives some sense of a divine unity that he was seeking.

The son of an Anglican clergyman, he was to have a major impact on 19th-century Anglicanism. But first he became a *Unitarian, a radical young preacher, welcoming the ideals of the French Revolution. Like his disciple, F. D. Maurice, he came back to orthodoxy while still upholding free enquiry, which puzzled both uncomplicated Unitarians and orthodox.

He was a *Romantic poet, making the high claims for the divine inspiration of poetry common to Romantics. His best poems certainly do not preach; he came to regret 'the obtrusion of the moral sentiment so openly' in his *Rime of the Ancient Mariner*. His writings came more easily when he was young. As his opium habit took hold, he postponed and prevaricated, drew up vast schemes which came to nothing, wrote pot-boilers, often plagiarized pages at a time from German, his best ideas emerging in footnotes as asides, and he exploited and quarrelled with his friends. He wallowed in guilt.

Some modern scholars discover, nevertheless, a great philosophical scheme in Coleridge's thought, reworking *Kant, Schelling, and

Schlegel. Readers seeking this are easily lost in seemingly cloudy abstraction, filled with numerical patterns and neologisms. But it is still possible to see what 19th-century readers found in Coleridge's prose. The *Confessions of an Enquiring Spirit*, a clear and approachable book, made the case against the verbal inspiration of scripture. The bible *finds* a man: people do not need evidence of inspiration before they read it. Though he could approach self-parody as an idealist philosopher, Coleridge nevertheless wanted reality rather than notions. 'Christianity is not a Theory or a speculation; but a *Life*. Not a *Philosophy* of Life, but a Life... TRY IT.'

There are clues to Coleridge's system of theology in *Aids to Reflection*, which shows his characteristic pattern of an open and enquiring mind combined with a strong sense of humanity's need for a redeemer. Most free thought makes for dry religion; most balm for sinners is opposed to thought. Reason and revelation must combine. 'My principle has ever been that Reason is *subjective* Revelation, Revelation *objective* Reason. If I lose my faith in *Reason*, as the perpetual revelation, I lose my faith altogether. I must deduce the objective from the subjective Revelation.'

Coleridge was a discoverer of unities. When he wrote on church and state, early Christian *Socialists, such as Maurice, Kingsley, and Ludlow, took their cue from him. Some thinkers, such as *Newman, who defined themselves against the Broad Church tradition which honoured Coleridge, had more in common with Coleridge than they believed. He provides a clue to most 19th-century English theology.   **Alistair Mason**

Barth, J. Robert, *Coleridge and Christian Doctrine* (1969).

Jasper, David (ed.), *The Interpretation of Belief: Coleridge, Schleiermacher and Romanticism* (1986).

——*Coleridge as Poet and Religious Thinker: Inspiration and Revelation* (1985).

McFarland, Thomas, *Coleridge and the Pantheist Tradition* (1969).

Prickett, Stephen, *Romanticism and Religion* (1976).

collegiality,

the doctrine finally hammered out at *Vatican II according to which the bishops form a college which, together with its head, the pope, governs the *church. 'The order of bishops is the successor to the college of the *apostles in their role as teachers and pastors, and in it the apostolic college is perpetuated. Together with their head, the Supreme Pontiff, and never apart from him, they have supreme and full authority over the universal church' (Dogmatic Constitution on the Church, *Lumen Gentium*, 22) (see EPISCO-PATE; PAPACY).

After *Vatican I it was generally thought that the pope, whose primacy and *infallibility had now been defined, would not need to summon the bishops for any further ecumenical *councils. He could rule alone. It is understandable, therefore, that, when Pope *John XXIII actually called a new council, reasserting the church's ancient conciliar way of life, one of its centrepieces should turn out to be a vigorously debated doctrine of the collegiality, or shared responsibility, of the bishops. The doctrine brought a settlement of sorts to the long-standing western debate on the relative powers of bishops and pope. The debate produced the doctrine of *conciliarism, which reached the peak of its influence at the Council of Constance (1414–18), at which the thirty-year-long scandal of rival popes was brought to an end.

Conciliarism and Constance viewed a council over against a pope or popes. At the other extreme, Vatican I so highlighted the author-ity and doctrinal infallibility of the pope that the role of bishops was obscured and councils almost disappeared from church life. An integration of pope and bishops was needed to overcome the constant threat of polarization.

With its pyramidal understanding of the church, Vatican I taught that the pope has 'ordinary' and 'immediate' 'episcopal' jurisdiction over the whole church, whereas each bishop has 'ordinary and immediate episcopal jurisdiction' over 'the particular flock' assigned to him. In other words, each one looks after his own church and the pope himself looks after the whole. Regarding matters quite otherwise, Vatican II said that the pope and the bishops *together* look after the whole.

Crisis votes of 30 October 1963 turned the tide and collegiality was strongly endorsed. However, at the last moment, in November 1964, just a week before the final acceptance of *Lumen Gentium*, Pope Paul VI added an 'Explanatory Note' that emphasized the essential role of the pope within the college: 'there is no such thing as the college without its head', it said; moreover, the pope regulates the exercise of collegiality 'as he sees fit' (n. 3).

Lingering tensions between primacy and collegiality are evident in that note. Significantly, Vatican II needed to stress that the bishops are all truly 'vicars and legates of Christ' and not 'vicars of the Roman Pontiff' (*LG* 27). However, as recently as 1996, retired archbishop John Quinn complained that the papal curia too often considers itself as superior to the college of bishops and so hinders the development of collegiality (*The Tablet*, 6 July 1996, p. 879). As yet, there are few collegial structures, apart from an ecumenical council. The synod of bishops established by Pope Paul VI (*Apostolica Sollicitudo*, 15 September 1965) simply advises the pope: 'it is not a collegial organ of leadership for the universal church' (Ratzinger 1988: 46).

Scriptural and liturgical scholarship underpinned the doctrine of collegiality. Scripturally, it is clear that *Peter is not isolated from the other foundational apostles. Together they form 'the Twelve', in succession to the twelve tribes of Israel. Liturgically, by his study of the early *ordination rites, it fell to Bernard Botte (1893–1980), to open the door for Vatican II on collegiality (Ratzinger 1988: 11). The *Apostolic Tradition* (*c.*215) of Hippolytus, believed lost until identified early in the 20th century, was not available to Vatican I. Its prayers reveal, first, an understanding of the bishop as the 'high priest' of his people (*LG* 21), offering the gifts. Unlike the juridical governor of later scholasticism, such a bishop was the priestly celebrant of the central act that fundamentally unites all the local churches and makes them one, namely the *Eucharist (*LG* 26). Correspondingly the bishops themselves were one. The ministry of the pope himself has, since the council, increasingly been seen eucharistically.

Secondly, ancient practice, endorsed by the Council of *Nicaea, required at least three bishops for the ordination of a new one. Episcopal ordination was shown thereby to be something not passed from individual to individual, but rather conferred by reception into the episcopal college, three members constituting a quorum. Not just between individual Christians, but also between local churches and their bishops, the Lord's words apply: 'where two or three are gathered in my name, I am there in the midst of them' (Matt. 18: 20).

Collegiality is therefore but an aspect of the *communion or *koinonia* that is fundamental to Christian life, reflected in synods, conferences, and congregational fellowship throughout the Christian churches and rooted ultimately in the communion that is the life of the *Trinity, shared with the human race by Christ.

Paul McPartlan

Congar, Y., et al., *La Collégialité épiscopale* (1965).

McPartlan, P., *Sacrament of Salvation* (1995).

Philips, G., et al., 'Dogmatic Constitution on the Church', in Vorgrimler, H. (ed.), *Commentary on the Documents of Vatican II* (1967), i. 105–37, 186–217, 297–305.

Ratzinger, J., 'The Pastoral Implications of Episcopal Collegiality', *Concilium*, 1/1 (1965), 20–34.

—— *Church, Ecumenism, and Politics* (1988).

Commandments, Ten.

The Ten Commandments (also known, from the Greek, as the Decalogue) appear in two slightly different versions in the OT, in Exodus 20: 2–17 and Deuteronomy 5: 6–21. According to Exod. 19, they are written by *God on tablets of stone and delivered on Mount Sinai to *Moses, who smashes them in anger when he discovers the Israelites worshipping the golden calf. The laws are then rewritten by God. This direct divine authorship gives the collection a unique authority within the biblical record and it is the implications of this that will be discussed here.

The Catholic and Protestant traditions make different use of the commandments. At least all agree there are ten, although even here two ways of reckoning are found. *Augustine counted the prohibitions against worshipping alien gods and making images as one command, but regarded the prohibitions against coveting one's neighbour's house and goods and coveting his wife as two separate commandments. In this he was followed by Catholics and Lutherans. Other Christian traditions reverse these decisions, arriving at the same total.

The biblical tradition itself shows changing attitudes to the commandments. They are not specifically alluded to in the OT outside the Pentateuch. In the NT, *Paul asserts that the commandments are all subsumed in the single injunction to 'Love your neighbour as yourself' (Rom. 13: 9–10). He recognizes that the final commandment against covetousness differs from the others in its concern with an inner disposition rather than an act and gives it a special place in his discussion of the nature of *sin and law (Rom. 7: 7–25) (see Law, Biblical).

This emphasis is reflected in the gospels. *Jesus is never represented as rescinding the commandments but is prepared to modify them. Intentions rather than deeds become the sphere of transgression. The prohibition of adultery becomes a prohibition against looking with lust on a woman; not just the act of killing but *anger against one's brother is condemned. Honouring one's father and mother has to be set aside in the service of the *Kingdom of God. In Matt. 22: 37–40, Jesus declares that the law and the prophets can be summed up in two commandments: to love God and to love one's neighbour. Post-Reformation theology on this basis divides the ten between two tables of the law. The first to fourth commandments deal with our duties to God while the remainder treat duties which undergird human society.

In subsequent Christian thought, the commandments become a bench-mark for *ethical prescription, but their precise function is bound up with theological arguments over the status of *natural law. Theologians in the Catholic tradition for the most part see the Ten Commandments as a divinely sanctioned confirmation of the common stock of *moral precepts which human beings can rationally derive for themselves. Their undoubted similarities to codes of law or moral precepts in other ancient cultures only serve to bear this out.

In this tradition, the commandments are the basis for judging when specific infractions of the natural moral order have occurred so that due *penance can be done, or, positively, set the standard for behaviour which helps to fit one for salvation. Scholastic theology thus becomes intent on unravelling the complexities of applying the commandments to the sad ingeniousness of human misdemeanour. The commandments, as a revelation of the natural law, were of universal application as distinct from the gospels' 'counsels of perfection' which bore directly only on those dedicated to the *religious life.

*Luther's understanding of sin meant that transgressions against the first table of the law, summed up as defiance of God, took precedence over the specific sins formulated in the remaining commandments which occupied Roman Catholic thinkers. He argued that the Christian is no longer bound by the commandments as such, because the work of salvation implanted the new law in the human heart. However, they remain valid as a civil code. While in broad agreement with this shift of emphasis, *Calvin placed more weight on their continuing role in the life of the Christian. He writes of them as a 'whip' to the 'stubborn ass of the flesh' in the struggle for sanctification. For their part, radical reformers refused the idea of counsels of perfection and applied the gospel standard to all Christians, to some extent displacing the commandments in the process.

For all Christians, however, they remain important in *dialogue over ethical matters with non-Christians. Augustine popularized the use of the commandments in catechesis and both Catholic and Protestant traditions continue to use them in the education of children and prospective converts. The *Catechism of the Catholic Church* produced in 1994 devotes nearly 100 of its 700 pages to the commandments. This confirms their importance but also reflects the fact that they are couched in the most general terms. This fits them for universal application but inevitably leads to disagreement over their scope. 'Thou shalt not kill', for instance, has been interpreted by some as an injunction to *pacifism or vegetarianism, whereas others cite the evidence of OT practice to restrict the ban only to premeditated murder. Protestant churches particularly have found themselves engaged in heated internal controversy over such matters.

In broader terms, the role of the commandments as at least part of a civil code of morality still persists. Politicians in countries with a Christian heritage are liable to appeal to the Ten Commandments as the common foundations of ethical behaviour in society, rather leaving aside the theological underpinnings. This begs important questions as to their *authority and continuing validity. Recent scholarship has also pointed out that, rather than being universally applicable, the commandments presume a particular audience of male householders in an ancient society. Women, children, and servants appear only as responsibilities, not as responsible agents in their own right. For many Christians, however, the commandments' divine origin makes them unchallengeable, even if sometimes puzzling, as the foundations of a Christian ethic.

See also Abortion; Capital Punishment; Euthanasia; Family;

FATHERHOOD; ICONOCLASM; MARRIAGE; MOTHERHOOD; SABBATARIAN-
ISM; SEX AND SEXUALITY; SUNDAY; WAR.   **Hugh S. Pyper**

Childs, B. S., *Exodus* (1974).
Clines, D. J. A., *Interested Parties* (1995).
Gustafson, J. M., *Protestant and Roman Catholic Ethics* (1978).
Johnstone, W., ' "The Ten Commandments": Some Recent Interpret-
ations', *The Expository Times*, 100 (1988–9).
Nielsen, E., *The Ten Commandments in New Perspective* (1968).

Common Sense philosophy

*Scottish Common Sense Realism was the predominant *philosophy in the United States for much of the 19th century. Earlier it had a strong impact in Germany, and, crossing the Protestant–Catholic boundary, was much in favour in *France before about 1850. Though somewhat reminiscent of *Thomism, it was distrusted by those in the scholastic tradition. Its Catholic followers were nearer Malebranche. A philosophy largely devised by clergymen, it was unthreatening to orthodox Christianity. Traces can still be seen in popular evangelical argument.

Philosophy can lead to surprising conclusions. Berkeley challenged the material reality of things, Hume the workings of cause and effect. Other lines of argument can undercut our sense of being individual free agents. Scottish Common Sense will have none of this. Thomas Reid (1710–96), a Presbyterian minister teaching at the universities of Aberdeen and Glasgow, argued for common sense, but it is difficult to find arguments for things that you already see as self-evident. His usual line of attack was that, whatever philosophers say, in ordinary life they live as if common sense works.

Common sense is not simply what most people at the time think, though it can easily slide into that. Reid wished to think that it is what everybody finds self-evident, except that, annoyingly, some philosophers, such as Hume, do not, so he has to say that all our language fights against Humean scepticism. You cannot talk it, let alone live it. Reid saw the root of the problem in Locke who says we have 'ideas' in our mind showing us how to see things. Reid said that what we see, we see: these are 'natural signs', and all else is 'enchantment of words'. This is philosophical *realism. As a theory it is of some interest to philosophers, and Reid is more impressive than his colleague Beattie, who claimed to refute Hume on *miracles. Dugald Stewart (1753–1828), professor at Edinburgh, disliked the popular overtones of 'common sense' and spoke instead of 'the fundamental laws of human belief'.

The giver of these fundamental laws is God. Sceptical philosophy is, at least in theory, a threat to morals. With a Common Sense philosophy, we are responsible beings in a world that is as it seems. Ministers can avoid being side-tracked by clever arguments, and concentrate instead on sinful humanity and its need for a redeemer. Reid and Stewart became set books in training clergy. Scottish Common Sense Realism was taken to *North America by John Witherspoon (1723–94), president of *Princeton, and those he taught shaped the new republic.

There is something democratic about a 'common sense' theory. 'In a matter of common sense, every man is no less a confident judge than a mathematician is in a mathematical demonstration' (Reid). It arose in the Moderate party of the Church of Scotland, but suited their Popular opponents too. In its early days in America it was a liberalizing force. Later, however, it became linked with defensive orthodoxy, and more distinctly clerical. In Scotland, Sir

William Hamilton (1788–1856) blended realism with *Kant, and the tradition lost in popular appeal what it gained in subtlety.

Alistair Mason

Davie, George, 'The Social Significance of the Scottish Philosophy of Common Sense', in *The Scottish Enlightenment and Other Essays* (1991).
Grave, S. A., *The Scottish Philosophy of Common Sense* (1960).
Kuehn, M., *Scottish Common Sense in Germany, 1768–1800* (1987).
Lehrer, K., *Thomas Reid* (1989).

communion

is a key word within *Christianity's special terminology, one without which much that matters cannot be well understood. Its basic sense is to translate the Greek *koinonia*, meaning fellowship, association, partnership. The two fundamental NT texts using this term are Acts 2: 24 and 1 Corinthians 10: 16. In the former the early *church is described as people devoting themselves 'to the apostles' teaching and fellowship (*koinonia*), to the breaking of bread and the prayers'; in the second Paul asks 'the cup of blessing which we bless, is it not fellowship (*koinonia*) in the blood of Christ? The bread which we break, is it not fellowship (*koinonia*) in the body of Christ?'

The fellowship of the first Christians is depicted as a brotherhood of *love, of shared *prayer and material possessions, united both by acceptance of the *apostolic teaching and by what soon became a regular weekly experience, the breaking of *bread, the *sacrament of the Lord's presence through the memorial repetition of his Last Supper, an experience in which 'the Lord was known to them' (Luke 24: 35). In hard fact, as the church developed in different places, the breaking of bread, soon to be called the *Eucharist (thanksgiving), was the only thing that necessarily brought Christians together on a regular basis. Their fellowship was, sociologically, a communion, an eating and drinking society. But this communion was not simply a horizontal one. Still more fundamentally, it was a vertical *koinonia* in the *body and *blood of Christ, unification with Christ, and it was this that gave the associating of Christians its essentially supernatural character, establishing the very nature of the church. Thus 'communion' signified at one and the same time the sacramental relationship established with the Lord through the mystery of the Eucharist and the ecclesiological relationship of Christians with one another, and of each local church with its neighbour churches. Christians received the Lord in communion but they were also and consequentially in communion with one another. The word 'communion' thus provided the best technical term to describe the specific type of visible, associational relationship that made the church what it was.

This fundamental causative and verbal relationship between Eucharist and church has remained at the heart of Christian experience and public history, something insisted upon by countless patristic and medieval writers. In the words of the Anglican scholar, Gregory Dix, 'It is by the unity of communion in that one Sacramental Body that the Church is one' (Hebert 1937: 122), or of the *Eastern Orthodox theologian Georges *Florovsky, describing the theology of the early church, 'communion and an integral unity were exact correlatives' (Baillie and Marsh 1952: 57). This common doctrine of east and west is well demonstrated by *Aquinas (*ST* III q. 73 a. 4) when he quotes John Damascene to explain why the Eucharist is called communion 'because through it we communicate with Christ … and through it we communicate and are united with one another'. Every conflict or *schism was seen as rupturing communion and when, in later history, some such ruptures became permanent, each side still saw itself as a communion, even as the sole communion to constitute the church: a theology of non-communicating communions implies self-contradiction.

Nevertheless in the western church especially this eucharistic conception of church *unity was little by little replaced by a more juridical and governmental one—submission to *episcopal or *papal *authority. The church came to be seen as comparable to the state. In reaction to this juridical visibility the *Reformation came to redefine the church in far more invisible terms, of right *faith and *grace. Visibility did not disappear, but became secondary and contingent. Communion unity itself had, of course, in traditional theology, like all sacraments, to be validated in 'invisible' terms, the terms of what as sacrament it signifies—a communion of love, faith, and *hope. In this it shares in the common nature of Christianity, as a construction of visible signs denoting invisible realities, signs capable of being left void or otherwise misused.

The signs can also be retained while being interpreted one-sidedly. Thus 'communion' remained the common term for the Eucharist but was widely understood as signifying only a sacramental and spiritual relationship between the receiver and Christ, intense as that might be. It may indeed be that as the ecclesial dimension of communion faded from view, the affective union with Christ, symbolized by eating his body and drinking his blood, grew in the intensity of devotion with which it was conceived. *Corpus Christi, salva me, Sanguis Christi inebria me* (Body of Christ, save me, Blood of Christ inebriate me) are among the invocations of the much-used early 14th-century prayer, the *Anima Christi*, which came later to be placed by Ignatius Loyola at the opening of his Spiritual *Exercises*. Even if the reception of communion, for many devout people both Catholic and Protestant, became a rare—perhaps merely annual—event, it had all the more to be very carefully prepared. This applied particularly to a young person's first communion, a rite whose celebration might become a public feast of considerable proportions, yet remained at heart intensely individualistic, a quality well expressed in *Hopkins's evocative poem, *The Bugler's First Communion*.

The revival of a full sense of the Eucharist–church identity (both being the body of Christ) owed much between the 1930s and 1950s to *de Lubac, Dix, Florovsky, and the Catholic *nouvelle théologie* generally. It powerfully influenced much of the theology of *Vatican II (particularly *Lumen Gentium* and the decree on Ecumenism) but the full flowering of a renewed theology of communion is really characteristic of the post-conciliar years, though it was already central to two late pre-conciliar books published in English in 1963, Jerome Hamer (a French Dominican and, later, cardinal), *The Church is a Communion* and A. Hastings, *One and Apostolic*. Frequent reference to *koinonia* and its implications are characteristic of the ARCIC statements (particularly that of 1976 on 'Authority in the Church') and of the International Joint Commission between the Catholic Church and the Orthodox Church which declared (Munich, 1982) 'the one and unique church finds her identity in the *koinonia* of the churches'. It has been recognized, especially since Vatican II, that communion can be 'partial' rather than all or nothing—perhaps, indeed, it always is partial, the ideal always circumscribed by human weakness. In consequence a theology of the church as one communion can be harnessed to assisting the reality of still-divided churches in a way acceptable to all sides. While a traditional theology of communion seemed simply to unchurch all Christians outside a single fellowship on grounds of their being in schism, it can now be used positively to link bodies hitherto divided, even going so far as Paul VI's description of the Orthodox Churches as being in 'almost complete' communion with Rome (Letter to Patriarch Athenagoras, 1971). Communion has become in consequence probably the most used term in the *ecumenical ecclesiology of the late 20th century, benefiting greatly from a sense that a church thus conceived reflects the internal communion of the *Trinity, but still grounded, both verbally and experientially, in the Eucharist: communion in the one sense creates communion in the other.   **Adrian Hastings**

Baillie, D., and Marsh, M. (eds.), *Intercommunion* (1952).
de Lubac, H., *Corpus Mysticum: L'Eucharistie et l'église au Moyen Age* (1949).
Hamer, J., *The Church is a Communion* (1963).
Hastings, A., *One and Apostolic* (1963).
Hebert, A. G., *The Parish Communion* (1937).
Wright, J. R. (ed.), *A Communion of Communions: One Eucharistic Fellowship, The Detroit Report of the Episcopal Church* (1979).
Zizioulas, J. D., *Being as Communion: Studies in Personhood and the Church* (1985).

compassion. A passage on this subject from a 7th-century *Syriac monastic writer, Isaac of Nineveh, has become comparatively well known in the last quarter of the 20th century, quoted in many places, and included in anthologies.

> An elder was once asked, 'What is a compassionate heart?' He replied, 'It is a heart on fire for the whole of creation, for humanity, for the birds, for the animals, for demons and for all that exists. At the recollection and at the sight of them such a person's eyes overflow with tears owing to the vehemence of the compassion which grips his heart ... This is why he constantly offers up prayer full of tears, even for the irrational animals and for the enemies of truth ... He even prays for the reptiles as a result of the great compassion which is poured out beyond measure, after the likeness of God, in his heart.'

This is a passage which speaks of a universal compassion, that extends not only to our friends, but to our enemies, not only to our fellow believers, but to those whom we might think of as the enemies of truth. Indeed it extends to the whole *animal *creation, to the whole world; finally it includes the demons. The writer is not afraid of the thought that we should pray for the restoration of all things in the *love of *God.

This passage from Isaac is not an isolated or eccentric one. It could be paralleled in others of the school of Syriac writers to which he belonged, and also more widely in *Eastern Orthodox spiritual writing where the belief that we may at least pray and hope for the *salvation of all is deeply rooted in the mainstream of the church's consciousness (see UNIVERSALISM). In the west such a universal, all-embracing compassion is also to be found at times, especially in some of the great *women *mystics of the Middle Ages, notably for instance *Julian of Norwich. But on the whole a more *dualistic view of the last things has been characteristic of western teaching, and too often it has been assumed that while the saved will be few the damned will be many.

In Christianity the thought of an all-embracing compassion, where it prevails, is rooted in a belief in the human ability to suffer with another's *suffering. This itself is seen as reflecting God's divine compassion, a compassion evident already in the OT prophets; God suffers in the suffering of his people. In the NT this vision takes flesh. The human capacity for compassion is understood as flowing from the compassionate love of God in Christ.

This theme is also to be found in other religious traditions, most notably in the case of *Buddhism, where the thought that universal compassion is a characteristic of the Buddha-nature is found in many different schools, from Tibetan Buddhism to Japanese Zen. In *Islam, faith in God as the merciful and compassionate one can lead to the idea that the believer is also to mirror these qualities, though here the idea of a shared suffering is less prominent.

A. M. Allchin

Allchin A. M. (ed.), *The Heart of Compassion: St Isaac of Syria* (1989).
Brock, Sebastian, *The Syriac Fathers on Prayer and the Spiritual Life* (1987).
Clément, Olivier, *The Roots of Christian Mysticism* (1993).

conciliarism, the view that the authority of *councils is above that of popes. Through most of the 14th century the popes were French and lived at Avignon. This abandonment of *Rome by the bishops of Rome became a cause of increasing dismay. In 1377, Gregory XI was persuaded by *Catherine of Siena to return to his diocese. He soon died and was succeeded by Urban VI who, unfortunately, quickly showed signs of insanity. In consequence, most of the cardinals withdrew and elected one of their number as Clement VII. He returned to Avignon. For the next 30 years there were two lines of popes—Urbanists in Rome, Clementists in Avignon—with Europe split between them. This disastrous situation highlighted the problem of whether there is anything in the church superior to the pope. Earlier medieval theologians, faced with the ever-growing power of the *papacy, had raised the issue more theoretically: what if a pope taught heresy, as John XXII (1316–34) came close to doing? Now the existence of two popes, each with his own college of cardinals, and each enjoying strong national support, encouraged the development of a doctrine of conciliarism, appealing to the practice of the patristic period and asserting the supremacy of councils over popes. Most of the best Catholic minds of the time (Jean Gerson, Pierre d'Ailly, and Nicholas of Cusa) accepted this in some form and a body of conciliarist theology developed, grounded in the knowledge that the first ecumenical councils were not convened by the pope.

In 1409, the Council of Pisa, convoked by a group of cardinals, declared itself ecumenical, deposed both popes and elected Alexander V, but, as the two refused to retire and retained some support, there were now three popes: the situation seemed worse than ever. Nevertheless, Pisa paved the way for the Council of Constance (1414–18) at which, under pressure from the Emperor Sigismund, all three popes then alive—Gregory XII (Urbanist), Benedict XIII (Clementist), and John XXIII (the Pisa line)—were finally compelled to resign. In the decree *Haec Sancta*, the Council declared the pope bound to obey it and, in a further decree, *Frequens*, arranged for the holding of councils every ten years. A new pope was elected, Martin V, who frequently reaffirmed the Council of Constance's authority, upon which indeed his own depended.

Once a single pope was firmly re-established in Rome, the old papal supremacy quickly returned in practice, though the Council of Basle in 1431 was convoked in fulfilment of *Frequens*, and Basle continued the line of Constance until it became discredited through ineffectiveness. Pius II, who in earlier life had been a convinced conciliarist, condemned any appeal from pope to general council by the decree *Execrabilis* (1460). In practice, 15th-century councils were torn too fiercely by national rivalries and political pressures to govern the church effectively, but the failure of the conciliar movement to establish constitutional limits to papal autocracy prepared the way for the Reformation. The principles of conciliarism at that point went underground within the Roman Catholic Church to surface once more, in restrained form, in the doctrine of collegiality approved by Vatican II.

Adrian Hastings

Alberigo, G., *Chiesa Conciliare: Identita e significato del conciliarismo* (1981).
Crowder, C. M. D., *Unity, Heresy, and Reform, 1378–1460: The Conciliar Response to the Great Schism* (1977).
Oakley, F., *Council over Pope? Towards a Provisional Ecclesiology* (1969).
Tierney, B., *Foundations of the Conciliar Theory*, repr. (1968).

Cone, James Hal (1938–   ). Cone is one of the progenitors of *black theology. Born in Fordyce, and raised in Bearden, Arkansas, in the ecclesial context of the African Methodist Episcopal Church (AME), Cone matriculated in 1954 at an AME school, Shorter College. He studied at Philander Smith College (BA 1958), at what became Garrett Theological Seminary (BD 1961), and Northwestern University (Ph.D. 1965). He was appointed Charles A. Briggs professor of systematic theology at Union Theological Seminary, New York, in 1969, after short teaching stints at Philander Smith College and Adrian College in Michigan.

Cone's work is characterized by his experiences of growing up in America's pre-Civil Rights era and his profound desire to bring formal Christian theological discourse into conversation with the complex existence of African Americans. *Black Theology and Black Power* (1969) and *A Black Theology of Liberation* (1970) introduced the dual concerns of his literary witness. First, western theology has been marked by negation of an *African presence, part of the wider consequences of *slavery and colonialism. This negation produced a methodological blindness in western theologians to matters of race and culture. Second, theology is in an important sense a cultural performance requiring all theologians to recognize their own context, and for which the contributions of people of African descent have been ignored. *The Spirituals and the Blues: An Interpretation* (1972) and *The God of the Oppressed* (1975) completed Cone's critique of western theology and outlined a theology displaying the cultural performance of African Americans, a black theology. *My Soul Looks Back* (1982), *For My People* (1984), *Speaking the Truth: Ecumenism, Liberation, and Black Theology* (1986), and *Martin & Malcolm & America: A Dream or a Nightmare* (1991) reiterated the critique and further clarified an authentically black theology.

See also LIBERATION THEOLOGY; NORTH AMERICA: AN OVERVIEW.

Willie James Jennings

confirmation, see BAPTISM.

Congar, Yves (1904–95). The foremost Catholic ecclesiologist of the 20th century, Congar's influence on the formulation of the mystery of the *church at *Vatican II, as well as in establishing principles for 'authentic' ecumenism and church reform, was recognized in his honouring as a cardinal in 1994. Though holding no academic position, since his life as a *Dominican friar was spent in research, writing, and teaching in the study houses of the order in *France (and in 'exile' during the 1954 worker-priest crisis, in Jerusalem and England), his encyclopaedic studies of patristic, medieval, and early modern theology stimulated much fresh academic interest in ecclesiology and its relation to other theological disciplines and topics. In *Divided Christendom* (1937; ET 1939), Congar worked out principles for Catholic ecumenism in the light of the differing conceptions of the church's essential nature, and her unity, entertained by liberal Protestants, Anglicans, and Eastern Orthodox. In *Vraie et fausse réforme dans l'Église* (1950), lamenting contemporary Catholicism's inadaptation to the *world to which preaching was addressed, he proposed a reform of the church by return to the sources, 'true' rather than 'false' because avoiding disruption both of the continuity of her history and of the peace and charity of her members. In *Lay People in the Church* (1953; ET 1957) he produced a theology of the *laity, who have the task of mediation between church and world by the exercise in their distinctive sphere of the threefold office of Christ as *prophet, *priest, *king. In *Tradition and Traditions* (1960–3; ET 1966) his attention began to shift from a *christologically ordered picture of the church to one which, though by no means neglecting dominical determination, gave greater weight to the mission of the *Holy Spirit, by whose agency Christ's gifts to the church are concretely realized. Two major chronicles of the history of ecclesiology, *L'Ecclésiologie du haut Moyen Age* (1968) and *L'Église: de saint Augustin à l'époque moderne* (1970), prepared his systematic synthesis, *L'Église une, sainte, catholique, apostolique* (1970).

The closing years of his life were devoted to the creation of a tripartite pneumatology, *I Believe in the Holy Spirit* (1979–80; ET 1983) which ranged from a Catholic assessment of the *charismatic renewal, via an attempted solution of the *filioque dispute with the Orthodox East, to a portrait of the church's life as a prolonged prayer for the Spirit's advent.   **Aidan Nichols, OP**

Jossua, J.-P., *Yves Congar: Theology in the Service of God's People* (1968).
Nichols, A., *Yves Congar* (1989).
Vauchez, A. (ed.), *Cardinal Yves Congar 1904–1995* (1999).

Congregationalism

Congregationalism believes in a gathered *church. This is not to disbelieve in 'one holy catholic and apostolic church' which is not visible now but will be revealed, but to challenge the way the word has been used for large corporations, the ecclesiastical wing of secular governments, and generally to include those who might some day be Christian but are not yet visibly so. A gathered church can seem excessively élitist, as does the old language of 'visible saints' and the 'elect', but the gathering together in love of people who know each other by name is still the best manifestation of 'church' available on earth. Wider structures and support networks might have their place, but the normative unit of Christian life is neither the individual, nor the diocese, nor the national or international church, but the congregation. In practice, some variant on this is the lived experience of many or indeed most Christians, though they are patronized by the official theology of their traditions for being limited in their perspective.

Historically, the theology of the gathered church goes back to the Tudor *Puritans. 'The kingdom of God was not to be begun by whole parishes, but rather of the worthiest, were they never so few'

(Robert Browne, *c*.1583). These Separatists were driven out of England to Holland and *North America. The main Congregationalist tradition, less judgemental about the Church of England, more eager to affirm the positive rightness of a congregational church government, arose later in the 17th century. Independency (its other name in England) was Oliver Cromwell's tradition, and Independents were among the ministers dismissed from English parishes at the Great Ejection of 1660. Congregationalism was the leading church of New England, the legal establishment in some of the colonies. There was clearly no retreat from the responsibilities of civil life to a holy huddle there. There were problems: secularists looking back shudder at the thought of rule by killjoy saints; the expedient of the Half-way Covenant (for church attenders whose religious experience fell short), and even the surprising movement of the Spirit in the Great Awakening, were ways of coping with the consequences of treating the congregation of the visibly elect as the focus of civil government. Since the American Revolution, Congregationalism is nowhere established. Other forms of church government, using central planning and itinerant ministries, have proved more effective, certainly in the short term, in recruiting large numbers. Nevertheless, if one adds in the *Baptists, there are many millions of Christians with a congregationalist form of government.

The original claim of Congregationalism was not simply the pragmatic one, that people naturally fall into congregation-size clumps. The belief was that, in the church so constituted, God's Spirit spoke, and no external authority had a right to overrule it. There used to be a fairly clear line between the two great Reformed strands, the *Presbyterians, who solemnly subscribed to *creeds, and the Congregationalists, who safeguarded *orthodoxy by listening to individuals' personal testimony in their own words as they joined the church. This was never a claim for complete theological liberty (though some individual congregations in America have become *Unitarian), nor, democratic as the churches were, a belief in the God-given rights of a majority vote.

Congregationalism, in England a Union in 1832, became a Church in 1966, and then the major component of the United Reformed Church in 1972. The World Alliance of Reformed Churches unites Presbyterians and Congregationalists. Most United churches (like those of Canada, South India, Zambia, and Australia) have a congregationalist component, and the tradition of *ecumenism and union continues.   **Alistair Mason**

Atkins, G. G., and Fagley, F. L., *History of American Congregationalism* (1942).
Jones, R. T., *Congregationalism in England 1662–1962* (1966).
Sell, A. P. F., *Saints: Visible, Orderly, and Catholic: The Congregational Idea of the Church* (1986).

conscience

conscience is often a vaguely used term but it is, nevertheless, the key to Christian *morality, accepted as such in all ages and most traditions. It signifies the informed personal judgement on what in actual circumstances is right or wrong and its *authority is absolute. Its inescapable presence hints at the existence and authority of *God but it is a moral authority internal to the person, correlative to *natural law. Indeed, it is the only way one can directly ascertain natural law and its obligatoriness. Never can one rightly go against one's conscience but it is inherent in Christian understanding that conscience represents a person's response to objective moral law, that is to say it must be informed. Having an informed conscience means that one has sincerely sought for and pondered whatever reliable guidance is available from nature, *revelation, church teaching, or serious moral discussion of any sort. Conscience then decides. One can never wholly escape one's conscience and its judgement on one's behaviour. Nevertheless its voice can be drowned, if habitually disregarded, just as it can be sharpened, if carefully followed. While, strictly speaking, it refers to the individual act of moral judgement, it may also be used to refer to one's habitual moral culture, out of which individual decisions are made, often almost instantaneously. Without a sense of conscience as one's personal moral perception shaped over time by a variety of influences and decisions acted upon, it would indeed be impossible to understand the moral authority of the individual act of conscience and why it must be followed even when erroneous. Not to do so places a person in conflict with her whole moral identity.

A good conscience is always a safe guide, indeed the only safe guide, even if objectively its decision is mistaken, that is to say not in accord with divine law. Again, another person's conscience can never, as such, provide a rule for oneself. Conscience is something essentially personal: though the conscientious decisions of someone else can certainly be a factor fed into one's own moral reasoning, one will be judged by God in accordance with conformity to one's own informed conscience and not in accordance with what anyone else has done or with any *law, positive or even divine.

Conscience does not, however, excuse one from the penalties of civil or ecclesiastical law. If someone conscientiously decides to kill a deformed baby or assassinate a dictator, Christian theology does not suggest that the law should allow this to happen or not punish the deed. On the contrary, it is inherent in the theology of conscience that we accept the possibly grave consequences of our actions if they violate civil or religious law. On the other hand, Christian legislators should ensure that evidence of good conscience is accepted as a mitigating factor and, furthermore, where possible, formulate laws which allow space for conscientious objection in contentious areas such as military action. Law not tempered to provide fair protection for tender consciences or reasonable conscientious disagreement is bad law.

The basic conception of conscience as the interior judge of right behaviour is clear in the NT, for instance in Paul's instruction 'You must obey, therefore, not only because you are afraid of being punished, but also for conscience sake' (Rom. 13: 5) or 'Do not hesitate to eat anything that is sold in butchers' shops; there is no need to raise questions of conscience' (1 Cor. 10: 25). In the NT, as later, reference is only made to it when the right moral course might be disputed. The clearer the latter is, the less need to advert to the role of conscience in acknowledging it, but acknowledgement may be needed not so much because of lack of clarity as of difficulty. The authority of conscience is implicit in many of the *acta* of the early *martyrs, but as Speratus, leader of the martyrs of Scilli (180 AD) replied to the proconsul judging them, 'When the right is so clear, there is nothing to consider.' They rejected the offer of additional time in which to reconsider their decision and went to immediate execution.

The teaching of *Aquinas on conscience has a special importance in clarifying its role. He insists that the moral duty to follow one's conscience allows no exceptions, which does not negate the duty to ensure that one's conscience is well informed. If one culpably fails to ensure a knowledge of what is objectively wrong, the authority of conscience is undermined, but, so long as that is not so, then it is right and necessary to obey one's conscience, even when it contradicts public law. Thus where Peter Lombard, the standard early medieval theological authority, held that if there is a conflict between what the church teaches and what conscience upholds, then one must follow the former, Aquinas commented categorically, 'Hic magister falsum dicit' (Here the master is wrong): it is better to die excommunicated than to violate one's conscience. Nevertheless there has been a recurring tendency in all ages on the part of ecclesiastical leaders, spiritual writers, and ordinary church people to follow Peter Lombard, play down the authority of conscience, and stress instead the duty of *obedience to any clear command given by a recognized authority in church or state.

This doctrine of the primacy of conscience was shared by Catholics and Protestants. The words that *Luther is said to have pronounced at the Diet of Worms, 'Here I stand. I can do no other,' express exactly the position as set out by Aquinas. Cranmer's final recantation of his recantations shortly before execution was of 'the great thing which so much troubleth my conscience'. The hymn line 'Dare to be a Daniel, dare to stand alone' might be thought to express the quintessence of Protestant individualism, but it is actually no less a Catholic obligation. Thomas *More has often, and rightly, been seen as expressing explicitly and repeatedly the primacy of Christian conscience. To it he insistently appealed when refusing to swear an oath abjuring the pope's authority while stressing that he did not 'condemn the conscience of any other man'. When it was put to him that as he did not condemn their consciences he could not be so sure of his own and should, then, 'leave the doubt of your unsure conscience in refusing the oath and take the sure way in obeying your prince', More could only reply that he had not 'informed' his conscience suddenly or slightly.

*Newman, in the chapter he devoted to 'the supreme authority of conscience' in his 1874 *Letter to the Duke of Norfolk*, stressed, correctly, that Catholics and Protestants were in full agreement on the subject of conscience. Thus Catholic theologians, like Protestants, insisted time and again on the absolute duty to obey one's conscience and disobey the pope if convinced in conscience that the pope's commands were morally wrong, and all agreed this to be a possible scenario (see PAPACY). It is true, however, that what one may call the characteristic Catholic regime has developed on the assumption that this was so unlikely as to be practically disregardable. Both the Tridentine and *ultramontane church itself and countries such as Spain claiming to be based on Catholic principles in practice left little if any room for the exercise of a dissenting conscience. It was taken for granted that within a Catholic society any public disagreement with *orthodoxy, however seemingly conscientious, was either morally culpable because manifestly 'uninformed' or so socially subversive that it could not be allowed. In this there was for a long time a great divide between Catholic and Protestant positions, a divide only overcome with the Declaration on *Religious Liberty of *Vatican II, one of the council's most intensely contested documents. The Declaration was masterminded by the American Jesuit John Courtney Murray, and piloted through the council chiefly by Bishop de Smedt of Bruges and the

Secretariat of Christian Unity. 'It is through his conscience that man sees and recognizes the demands of divine law. He is bound to follow this conscience faithfully in all his activity ... Therefore he must not be forced to act contrary to his conscience. Nor must he be prevented from acting according to his conscience, especially in religious matters' (para. 3). The Declaration spelt out the implications of this teaching in considerable detail as did *John Paul II in his message of January 1999, when referring to the 50th anniversary of the Universal Declaration of Human Rights; 'Individuals must be recognized as having the right even to change their religion if their conscience so demands. People are obliged to follow their conscience in all circumstances and cannot be forced to act against it.' Decisive as these statements are, they contrast with Catholic practice over many centuries. There may be no other comparable U-turn in modern Roman Catholic teaching.

See also INQUISITION AND HOLY OFFICE.   **Adrian Hastings**

Baylor, M. G., *Action and Person: Conscience in Late Scholasticism and the Young Luther* (1977).

Callahan, S., *In Good Conscience: Reason and Emotion in Moral Decision-Making* (1991).

Curran, C., and McCormick, R. (eds.), *Readings in Moral Theology No. 3: The Magisterium and Morality* (1982).

D'Arcy, E., *Conscience and its Right to Freedom* (1979).

Delhaye, P., *The Christian Conscience* (1968).

Graves, S. A., *Conscience in Newman's Thought* (1989).

Kirk, K. E., *Conscience and its Problems* (1927).

Pierce, C. A., *Conscience in the New Testament* (1955).

Potts, T., *Conscience in Medieval Philosophy* (1980).

Constantine was the first Christian emperor and responsible for a profound alteration in Christianity's relationship to the political. The son of the Emperor Constantius, he was proclaimed emperor by the troops in York on his father's death in 306, and marched south to enforce his claim. His decisive victory over his rival, Maxentius, at the Battle of the Milvian Bridge made him master of *Rome. In 313 he and Licinius, emperor in the east, agreed to divide the empire between them, at the same time ending all persecution of Christians by the Edict of Milan.

For Licinius, this was a purely pragmatic decision, for Constantine it was far more. At some point prior to the Milvian Bridge, he had undergone an experience of *conversion to the Christian *God, to whom he attributed all his success. He began immediately to involve himself quite intimately in church affairs, while restoring former ecclesiastical property and granting much more. In 324 he defeated Licinius, restored the empire's unity of government and founded a new capital, *Constantinople, on the Bosphorus. He built great churches, convoked church *councils, and made Sunday a public holiday. Hailed by such admirers as Eusebius of Caesarea as the thirteenth apostle, but guilty of many crimes, he put off *baptism until his own deathbed in 337.

Constantine was one of the most powerful, decisive, and successful rulers in human history. His adopting and privileging of Christianity transformed within a single generation the practices and attitudes of what had hitherto been an almost apolitical community, lacking more than local ecclesiastical leadership and a handful of rich or powerful members. His impact may be summarized under four headings. First, he ended the period of intermittent persecution which had so considerably controlled the Christian

mentality hitherto. Secondly, he politicized Christian experience and thought. While the Edict of Milan did not make Christianity the empire's established religion—that would be done by Theodosius seventy years later—Constantine, followed by his sons, Constantius and Constans, ensured that a whole range of new politico-moral issues, such as the use of power, the treatment of dissidents, the justification of *war, required to be faced by Christians.

Thirdly, by intervening in doctrinal disputes, calling the first ecumenical council at *Nicaea, and banishing bishops who opposed imperial policies, Constantine pressed the church towards developing central structures of decision-making and to accept, especially in the Greek world, a measure of *Erastianism. This bonding of ortho-dox Catholicism and the empire had considerable repercussions for Christians both outside the empire (e.g. Persia) and in potentially dissatisfied areas inside (e.g. Egypt).

Finally, by constructing Constantinople as the new and explicitly Christian capital of the empire, a role it would exercise for eleven hundred years, he set it on a line of development in which its church became the central see of the Greek-speaking world, in almost inevitable rivalry with that of *Rome.

While it was probably unavoidable that Christianity would become a state religion sooner or later (it happened in *Armenia at almost the same date) the suddenness and decisiveness of the Constantinian revolution, following the great persecution, remains a crucial turning point in Christianity's historic evolution.

Adrian Hastings

Barnes, T. D., *Constantine and Eusebius* (1981).

Baynes, N. H., *Constantine the Great and the Christian Church* (1929), 2nd edn. (1972).

Hastings, A. (ed.), *A World History of Christianity* (1999).

Kee, A., *Constantine versus Christ* (1982).

Constantinople. After gaining absolute control of the Roman empire in the civil war of 324, *Constantine the Great marked his victory with the foundation of a city that would bear his name. Because of the instability of the 3rd-century imperial successions, the locus of the administrative centre of the empire had long been drifting eastwards. Constantine's awareness, after the battle of the Milvian Bridge, of the strategic defects of Rome induced him to invest this new foundation with a dynastic and strategic importance that allowed Constantinople soon to become the dominant capital of the newly Christianized empire. Its role as a great Christian city, situated at the gate of Europe and Asia and poised on the axis point between the Slavs and the Semites, gave it an immensely influential role in the dissemination of ideas within the wider *church. The impact of this 'New Rome' on Christian life may be marked out in four phases.

The Age of the Founders: 4th–6th centuries

In its original design, Constantinople was a particularly elaborate example of a late antique city. Constantine conducted a foundation ceremony on 4 November 324. He chose the site of the colony of Byzantium (hence *Byzantine), attracted there because of the town's commanding geographical position, its strong defence capability, and its excellent potential as a trade port. His building programme favoured the erection of Christian churches. By 328 the walls on the only side of the city exposed to land attack had enclosed three square miles, and in 330 he presided at the dedication ceremony. To glorify his new capital, Constantine commandeered the greatest of the ancient world's sacred and secular statuary, which provoked Jerome's trenchant remark: 'Constantinople dedicated: all the world stripped bare.' The siting of these venerable works in the open streets may be read as one of the first essays in the desacralization of the old religion, a programme that would continue apace under Constantine's Christian successors.

Constantinople's early fortunes as an ecclesial centre were inauspicious. In the time of the *Arian crisis it allied itself with anti-*Nicene factions, and in the time of Theodosius almost all its churches had to be forcibly reappropriated by troops and given back to the tiny Nicene party. Gregory Nazianzen had preached in the city throughout 380 to attempt to re-establish the Nicene cause. His *Five Theological Orations* afterwards became a classic exposition of christological and Trinitarian orthodoxy. While he delivered them, however, he complained of being stoned by the populace. By the early 5th century the see of Constantinople had risen in power by association with the imperial court, and in the time of its charismatic bishop John Chrysostom it was awarded a large ecclesiastical territory comprising much of Asia Minor. Chrysostom's political downfall was partly orchestrated by provincial synods resistant to his claims to extend Constantinople's jurisdiction. Not until the late 5th and into the 6th century did the city finally establish itself as the undisputed ecclesial centre of the east, much to the disadvantage of *Alexandria. At the Council of *Chalcedon in 451 the ambiguously phrased Canon 28 was added to the Acts confirming the city's pre-eminence after *Rome. Constantinople understood that to mean a successor's parity with Rome, while Rome reluctantly took it to mean subsidiarity. Therein lay the seeds of much bitter dispute between the churches. In the 6th century the bishops of the imperial city claimed the title Ecumenical *Patriarchs, meaning the chief bishops of the 'civilized (Roman) world', which further aroused the *papacy's hostility. The claim was advanced on the notion that the church's jurisdictional power ought to reflect the civil imperial divisions of administration: a principle of eastern church governance in place from the time of Valens in the 4th century. Whereas the Roman tradition emphasized ecclesial superintendence based on apostolic founders (primarily Rome itself), the Greek tradition saw any church in harmony with apostolic doctrine as 'apostolic' and the jarring of these two principles for envisaging ecclesiological order would result in centuries of conflict between the sees, and ultimately in division between eastern and western Catholicism.

The city enjoyed the benefits of the recovery of the empire in the 6th century under Justinian. There followed a magnificent phase of new building, including the surviving churches of Hagia Sophia, Hagia Eirene, and Saints Sergius and Bacchus. Hagia Sophia was then the world's largest cathedral, and even today in its denuded condition creates a stunning evocation of the lost glories of Byzantium. After Justinian, the finances and political stability of the empire moved into a long winter.

The Static Age: 7th–12th centuries

This extensive hibernation of the capital was not an isolated phenomenon. The entire Roman world was shaken from its earlier embodiment as a city-based international culture. The decline of the cities marks the advent of the medieval age in Byzantine affairs.

By the end of this period Constantinople and Thessalonike alone had any claim to be great cities in the East Roman world. The loss of large and rich provinces to Islamic expansion had the effect of isolating Constantinople while simultaneously magnifying its importance, for it now served as a magnet to draw in all manner of Christian talent. From its earliest days the eastern capital had attracted monks. At first they settled outside the walls, but as Constantinople expanded rapidly the new phenomenon of city *monasticism came about. In the 5th century the city monastery of St John of Studios was founded, and was to flourish for centuries as one of the most important monastic centres in the Christian world. In the 9th century minuscule writing is thought to have originated there, making transcription cheaper and facilitating the transmission of both Christian and antique classical texts to later generations. As early as the 6th century there were no fewer than eighty-five monasteries in Constantinople, and monastic spirituality, born in the wilderness, came home to have an influence at the heart of Christian imperium. The close proximity of a strong monastic party within the capital, together with the clerical staff of the Great Church around the patriarch, created the vital synthesis between monastic patterns of *prayer and a splendid imperial *liturgy which was to form the future character of *eastern Christian worship. Between the 8th and 9th centuries serious conflicts in Constantinople over the issue of iconic art and sacramental theology (see ICONOCLASM), resulted in victory for the city's intellectual and artistic élites, and in this period Constantinopolitan writers such as Theodore Studite and Patriarch Germanos issued important works of symbolic and aesthetic theology.

The late Byzantine flowering: 13th–15th centuries

In 1204 the armies of the Fourth Crusade, mortgaged to the Venetians and led on by hopes of plunder, after abandoning their journey to the Holy Land turned to the attack and looting of Constantinople, inflicting massive depredations. For a time the city fell under Latin rule, while the Byzantine emperors relocated to Nicaea. This experience of the Fourth Crusade introduced a new and long-lasting element of bitterness into the way in which the Byzantines related to western Christianity. A programme for the recovery and renovation of the capital was attempted in the mid-13th century under Michael VIII, the founder of the last Byzantine imperial dynasty of the Paleologans. The twilight of the 13th century witnessed a brilliant flourishing in art, architecture, and literature in Constantinople. The surviving church of St Saviour in Chora, with perhaps the most magnificent works of mosaic ever created, is a symbol of this Indian summer (see ICONOGRAPHY). The same period also witnessed the rise of an important and distinctive spiritual tradition in Byzantine monasticism: the Hesychast school, with centres in Constantinople, Thessalonike, and Athos, which stressed a *mystical and direct awareness of God's luminous energies. And yet the continuing loss of territories, the ensuing financial chaos, and the concomitant neglect of the armed forces, made the city's conquest by Mehmed II in 1453 an inevitability. Thereafter some churches survived in Christian usage, and many continued in a new guise as mosques, but Constantinople's role as a centre of Christian culture was afterwards only a shadow of what it had been. The last emperor of the Romans, Constantine XI, died fighting at the St Romanos Gate. In Greek thought he became the

Immortal Emperor, turned to marble, asleep until the time of the Christians would return and the 'Great City' be won back.

Constantinople as a Christian centre under the Ottomans

After the Ottoman conquest, ironically, the fortunes of Constantinople as a Christian city positively revived from their low point. The new ruler, Mehmed II, was determined to repopulate his captured prize, and transferred a large number of Greek Christian subjects to Constantinople. After the conquest had ended the eastern Christian imperium, the Ottoman rulers transferred to the patriarch the rights and duties of 'ethnarch', dealing with him as the religious and political overlord of all Christian subjects of an Islamic empire that was soon to stretch across a vast expanse. Several patriarchs met a brutal end under the sultans because of this, and during the 19th-century Greek War of Independence one was even hanged from his own palace gate (now permanently welded shut at the patriarchate in his memory). Even so, the patriarch's prestige and power as the leading bishop in the eastern Christian world continued and was fostered by the Ottomans. In Constantinople, the suburban area of the Phanar (Lighthouse) gave the patriarchate a new home, and so became the vital centre of the large Greek community. 'Phanariot' Greeks became an international aristocracy of Christians in the Ottoman territories. The Greek War of Independence brought about a sea-change in the affairs of Christian Constantinople, for it led to a resurgence of Greek nationalism on a wider front. The collapse of Ottoman power after the First World War was the occasion for a Greek military attempt to seize Constantinople as the restored capital of Hellenism. The Turkish armies frustrated the manœuvre, but mass expulsions of Turks and Greeks from each other's territories followed in the bitter aftermath. The effect of this hostility was particularly marked in Constantinople, where a rapid and massive reduction in the number of Christians occurred, particularly among those holding significant political and economic positions, who were now closed out from Attaturk's movement of national reconstruction. He symbolically removed the Turkish capital from Constantinople to Ankara, renaming the old city Istanbul. Hagia Sophia was decommissioned as a mosque and reclassified as a museum. Its status, like the holy places in Jerusalem, remains freighted with international tension. The Treaty of Lausanne (1923) committed the Turkish state to protecting the remaining Christian minority, though henceforth the patriarch could be elected only from among Turkish citizens. The long decline of the numbers of Orthodox in the city continued until the final decades of the 20th century, all of which has left the Christian community in Constantinople merely of symbolic and historic interest. The decrepitude of the surviving churches, and the squalor of the once brilliant Phanar district are mute testimonies to that decline. To this day, however, the ecumenical patriarch still serves as a strong focal point for wider Hellenic Christian identity. His position as the senior bishop in the Orthodox world is expressed not so much in juridical terms, but in a collegiality within Orthodoxy where he is 'first among equals'. Even so, he has direct ecclesiastical jurisdiction over Mount Athos and over large, articulate, and wealthy diaspora Orthodox communities in America, Australia, Canada, Western Europe, and Britain, making his role as one of the leading voices of the Orthodox world more than merely symbolic in international ecumenical debate. Patriarch Athenagoras

(1886–1972) was perhaps the most notable holder of the office in the 20th century, renewing the international ecclesiastical prestige of the patriarchate by his (generally) successful summoning of the Orthodox families of churches to greater co-operation and harmony. These efforts resulted in the Pan-Orthodox Conferences, first held at Rhodes in 1961. The historic meeting between Athenagoras and Pope Paul VI in Jerusalem (1964) led in the following year to the revoking of the mutual anathemas existing between the churches of Rome and Constantinople since the 11th century. The new conditions of freedom which the Slav families of Orthodox churches found themselves able to enjoy after the collapse of Soviet Communism will undoubtedly come to be reflected in a renewed international role for the other Eastern European patriarchates, some of whom still preside directly over massive Orthodox populations. How this qualifies the future development of the ecumenical patriarch's international role remains to be seen.

John McGuckin

Buckton, D. (ed.), *Byzantium: Treasures of Byzantine Art and Culture* (1994).
Every, G., *The Byzantine Patriarchate 451–1204* (1947), rev. edn. (1962).
Hetherington, P., *Byzantium: City of Gold, City of Faith* (1983).
Krautheimer, R., *Three Christian Capitals* (1983).
Mathews, T. F., *The Byzantine Churches of Istanbul: A Photographic Survey* (1976).
Sevcencko, I., *Society and Intellectual Life in Late Byzantium* (1981).
Talbot-Rice, D., *Constantinople: Byzantium–Istanbul* (1965).

contextual theology has three senses. It is frequently used as a synonym for *liberation theology, and refers to that theology's methodological insistence on beginning with experience. This method is contrasted with an earlier seminary theology, often neo-*Thomist and deductive rather than inductive in emphasis. Liberation theology insists that *theology is a 'second step', which follows commitment and action. Theology thus conceived is 'critical reflection on praxis' and not in the first instance an account of *dogmatic or biblical principles. The priority of experience is associated with the educational methods of Paulo *Freire, widely used throughout *Latin America. Consciousness-raising *education seeks to harness the existing experience of participants and elicit questions relevant to their situation rather than to begin with the transmission of information. Western theology, it is claimed, has largely divorced doctrine and life and made action secondary to reflection. Contextual theology insists on their dialectical unity.

It is clear that *Marxist discussion of the sociology of knowledge is in the background here and contextual theology may be understood, secondly, to recommend a particular *hermeneutic practice. In *The German Ideology* Marx insists that it is life that determines consciousness and not vice versa, and that it is essential to realize that all ideas ('superstructure') have to be understood in relation to the position in society and material concerns of their authors ('base'). In this sense contextual theology is opposed to idealist modes of theology which are concerned primarily with the history of ideas, and represents the insistence that we cannot understand ideas of any sort unless they are properly contextualized against their social, economic, and political background.

The critique of idealism is also part of a post-colonial critique of cultural domination of the south by the north. This provides our third sense. The claim to universality implicit in most forms of

Christian theology up to the present century is said to prevent it from taking non-western experience seriously. The phrase 'contextual theology' is also commonly used to speak of what was earlier in the 20th century called indigenous theology or inculturation. These terms were criticized as too static and essentialist a way of envisaging the process of what happens when the gospel takes root in a non-Christian culture. Rather, recognizing that culture is always changing, the demand is that the theologian must seek to discern where God is at work in the light of the tradition, and articulate a theology sensitive to the local context. These ideas have been seized on by those responding to *postmodernity, with its emphasis on plurality and difference, and 'local theology' has been urged as the proper response not just to major non-western cultural traditions, but to regional differences within western cultures. Here the demands of liberation theology for the empowerment of the local community and the priority of experience find a western home.

See also AFRICAN, CHINESE, INDIAN, JAPANESE CHRISTIAN THOUGHT; BLACK THEOLOGY.　　　　　　　　　　　　**T. J. Gorringe**

Bevans, S., *Models of Contextual Theology* (1994).
Bujo, B., *African Theology in its Social Context* (1992).
Schreiter, R., *Constructing Local Theologies* (1985).

contraception is the intentional prevention of sexual intercourse from resulting in pregnancy. Christian teaching on contraception has been remarkably consistent in all periods except for the *20th century when, in a single generation, the churches moved from almost universal disapproval of contraception to almost universal acceptance of its moral legitimacy.

The bible contains no explicit judgement. The OT is generally pro-natalist, reflecting in religious terms the natural preoccupation of the ancient Hebrew people with fecundity (of flocks as much as families). The tone of the NT is different. It is an overstatement to call the NT anti-natalist, as some have done recently, but its lack of interest in procreation and equivocation on the appropriateness of *marriage for Christians makes it at least non-natalist. The traditional condemnation of contraception is related to the understanding of *sexuality. Drawing on Stoic ethics, Clement of Alexandria taught that sexuality existed solely for the purpose of procreation. This was applied more radically by *Augustine of Hippo who specifically condemned contraception as a sinful misuse of sexuality. Medieval scholars such as Thomas *Aquinas were more moderate, accepting that sexual intercourse was not legitimated solely by procreation but was acceptable even in marriages which were infertile or past their procreative potential. Critical to their teaching was the appeal to the order of nature which required semen to be deposited in the vagina. Not only a contraceptive practice such as withdrawal, but also masturbation and oral or anal intercourse were condemned on these grounds. In the 16th century Protestants maintained the opposition to contraception, although their attack on clerical *celibacy and reassertion of the intrinsic value of marital sexuality laid the basis for the dramatic reversal that would come. Their arguments against contraception focused on possible harm to the woman or a foetus, but not on the sinfulness of a couple engaging in sexual intercourse without wanting to conceive.

By the 19th century in Catholic France contraception was widespread, leading to conflicts between priests and people, and fuelling anticlericalism. In 1930 the Lambeth Conference created heated debate by becoming the first authoritative church body to endorse the use of contraception if there is 'a clearly-felt moral obligation to limit or avoid parenthood and where there is a morally sound reason for avoiding complete abstinence'. Lambeth's innovation was all the more startling since it had upheld the traditional condemnation of contraception as recently as 1908 and 1920. Reacting to the Anglican reversal, Pope Pius XI reasserted the traditional position in *Casti Connubii* (1930). By the 1960s virtually all the Protestant churches had followed Lambeth's lead, with leading theologians such as Emil Brunner, Reinhold *Niebuhr, and Karl *Barth giving substance to the new teaching. By contrast, controversy erupted in the Catholic church in 1968 over the encyclical *Humanae Vitae*, in which Paul VI again condemned contraception. The dismay in the church was caused not only by the fact that by then many Catholic people approved or made use of contraceptives, but also by the disappointment of hopes aroused by the shifts which had taken place in *Vatican II's theology of marriage and the subsequent recommendation of a papal commission that the church's teaching on contraception be changed.

Anglican and Protestant arguments favouring the use of contraception have generally begun by recognizing that marital sexuality is given primarily to nurture the love of the couple, not just to propagate the species. This may sometimes require the temporary or even complete avoidance of pregnancy. Parental obligations to existing children may also require postponing or forgoing further pregnancies. The role of family planning in the struggle against *poverty and in the improvement of women's and children's health was recognized very early. More recently the necessity of human population regulation for the global *ecology has been a topic of *ecumenical discussion. In all of this emphasis is placed on the human vocation to co-operate with the creator in responsible governance rather than passively submit to nature and history. The *Eastern Orthodox churches have become generally accepting of the use of contraception on similar grounds, adding the observation that in fact none of the ecumenical *councils made a definitive statement of opposition to contraception.

Humanae Vitae remains the key statement of Roman Catholic teaching on contraception. It too recognizes that it is appropriate to distinguish between 'the unitive and the procreative meaning' of marital sexuality, but insists that the two cannot be completely separated. According to *natural law 'each and every marriage act must remain open to the transmission of life'. It agrees that being responsible parents sometimes requires a couple to limit or space their children, but not by 'artificial' means. Avoiding sexual intercourse during the fertile days of the woman's cycle is an acceptable means of family planning since it respects and co-operates with nature. The encyclical identifies dangers in the use of 'artificial birth control' including the encouragement of promiscuity, the reduction of women to sex objects, and the potential for misuse by a totalitarian government. While the dispute gathered momentum in the Catholic church, and some theologians argued that loyal Roman Catholics could legitimately dissent from the encyclical's teaching, *John Paul II took up the theme of warning and made it his own. In *Evangelium Vitae* (1995) he argued that the use of contraception fosters a 'contraceptive mentality' in which the lives of the weakest are devalued, making *abortion and *euthanasia more acceptable. Indeed it is a key component in the 'conspiracy against life' which involves not only individuals and couples 'but goes far beyond, to the point of damaging and distorting, at the international level, relations between peoples and states'. This approach to population policy brought official Catholicism into surprising alliances with Islam and some ecofeminists.

See also GLOBAL ETHICS.   **Andrew Dutney**

Bratton, Susan Power, *Six Billion and More: Human Population Regulation and Christian Ethics* (1992).

Noonan, John T., *Contraception: A History of its Treatment by the Catholic Theologians and Canonists*, enlarged edn. (1986).

Ranke-Heinemann, Uta, *Eunuchs for Heaven: The Catholic Church and Sexuality* (1990).

conversion is at once the most common and the most controverted of Christian concepts. Because it has been exaggerated by some and diminished by others as a dimension of Christian life, to show its central place while reflecting the varieties of Christian teaching and practice about it remains a difficult task. On the positive side, there is no account of saintly (or model) Christian life that does not include an account of that life's beginning—that is, of conversion to Jesus Christ and to his rule or *Kingdom. Jesus' first *disciples, *Paul, Lydia, Perpetua, *Augustine, *Francis of Assisi, *Catherine of Siena, *Luther, *Teresa of Avila, Menno, Sarah Edwards, John Henry *Newman, Charles Spurgeon, Dorothy Day, Dag Hammarskjöld, Mother *Teresa—all these apostles, *saints, *mystics, and *martyrs not only had to endure to the end but had also to begin the life of faith, and the name of that beginning is conversion. How is it, then, that conversion remains a disputed dimension of Christian existence? The explanation lies in a turbulent history of Christian expansion and change in which more than one road was taken by the major actors and thinkers.

The Hebrew *shub* and Greek *epistrophe* (and the corresponding verb *epistrepho*) both connote, broadly, a 'turning' or 'returning'—such as God's turning his anger to or from Israel (cf. Num. 25: 4; Josh. 7: 26; 24: 20), Israel's turning to or away from God (Deut. 4: 30; 1 Sam. 15: 11), and the Gentiles' turning to Christ in faith (Acts 15: 3). The call to conversion comprised a principal theme in the preaching of Paul, for, when one turns to the Lord, the veil that lies over one's mind is removed and one is able to see the reflected glory of the Lord. This results in a transformation into the same image—from one degree of glory to another (2 Cor. 3: 17–18). Such transformation leads to devoted service to *God and the joyful expectation of Christ's return from heaven (1 Thess. 1: 9–10). Likewise in Acts, the Apostle Peter calls upon his listeners to repent and turn to God so that their sins may be wiped out (Acts 3: 19). The residents of Lydda and Sharon who beheld the physical restoration of a paralytic turned to the Lord (9: 35). Moreover, a conversion event is suggested in the action of Jesus' first disciples, who left all to follow him (Mark 1: 16–18), and in the call Nicodemus received to be born again (John 3: 3). Jesus required such life-transforming change of all who would be his disciples (Luke 9: 23–4)—a challenge that was to be reiterated whenever and wherever new disciples are made (Matt. 28: 19–20).

The successors to the apostles valiantly carried out the *missionary assignment they had received: the good news was for all; its claim upon the life of the convert was a total one. In obedience, Christian witnesses pressed to the limits of the Roman empire and beyond. A crucial document both for its representation of typical conversion in antiquity and for its paradigmatic role is the *Confessions* of *Augustine of Hippo. Having related his life story with its religious quest up to a critical point, Augustine tells how his time of preparation for Christian commitment came to its term. He heard Ambrose proclaim the gospel in the cathedral of Milan, he agonized over whether to accept it, struggling with his unchastity; then in a moment of distress he heard a child's singsong voice across a garden wall repeating *tolle, lege*, that is, 'take up and read'; Augustine opened 'the book' and his eye fell on the words of Romans 13: 13–14. Light flooded his heart; he was converted. Harvard historian Arthur Darby Nock (1933) links this story with others to show the shape of conversion in the Roman empire in the early centuries.

By this time, though, Christian practice already faced a profound difficulty. The *Constantinian church-state arrangement had ended official persecution of Christians wherever Roman power prevailed; it had legitimized Christianity and in course of time made it popular. A phenomenal spread of Christianity followed. In these circumstances, the practice of *baptism in infancy became normative and seemed to many to remove the need for conscious conversion, even though in NT narratives baptism itself had been a conversion rite (as had the baptism of *John the Baptist). Now for many, however, infant baptism took the place of individual conversion, and this revision has governed many Christian communities up to the present.

In the new situation, two strategies seemed possible. The first detached confirmation from baptism and then, in modern times, made it the occasion for Christian instruction at an age when the recipient could understand what was involved. In happy cases this instruction with ritual chrism might be treated as a sort of stylized conversion. In popular understanding, however, all Europeans (and later, all Europeans in America) were considered Christian from birth, or from their infant christening, so that no conversion was in order for them. Only pagan outsiders (and Jews, willing or unwilling) needed conversion if they were to be saved. In the west this strategy sufficed for most Catholics and Protestants. Meanwhile the Christian east never went even so far. Confirmation was not detached from baptism. Infants were confirmed as soon as they were immersed. The second strategy appeared in various reform movements through the centuries; it held that *faith and discipleship must be self-chosen. The blight of sin could not be escaped by formal rites alone, but only by lively, deliberate conversion to Christ. In some such movements, for example 16th-century Anabaptism (see MENNONITE THOUGHT), the needed turn was authentic only if it led to membership in a free community of fellow-believers. Often this was marked by returning to the primitive initiation practices, principally 'believers' baptism'. In other movements (notably 17th and 18th-century *Pietism and *Methodism), however, reform entailed no necessary break with the baptismal rites of the established church, but born-again believers met in supplementary assemblies with other true believers to practise a piety fixed not on external forms but on converted hearts. Thus today conversion, like baptism itself, remains a disputed aspect of Christian life. Is conversion necessary? Is it only the gradual change that accompanies any developing life? Or does Christian existence demand a conversion, a 'crossing over from death to life' (cf. 1 John 3: 14) that can be sensed and celebrated, however protracted the journey to its climax may be?

Christian thought in every age interacts with its setting. In an age in which the human sciences (*psychology, *anthropology, etc.) have developed richly, there is abundant material to compare with traditional Christian conversion accounts. In this perspective, conversion is seen as a recurrent natural event for human beings. Typically, it involves a change in the self over a period of time, though recognition that one is converted may focus upon a few inner choices or outward events. It is more than a mere development or series of developments, however. It is a transformation of the human self and its world that issues in a change of course and direction. All life is comprised of growth and change, but growth and change compressed constitute turns, sometimes sharp ones. Conversion in this sense is admittedly neither supernatural nor novel. In common speech, 'conversion' describes a precipitous occurrence that is evidenced by an improved condition of one sort or another. Starting with this, philosopher and psychologist William *James suggested that in conversion a disunited self is united. While conversion is necessarily personal, it is not on that account isolated. Typically, the converted nurture one another in their new life. Moreover, the form of conversion in a given community is transmitted from one generation to the next, and its form may migrate from one cultural milieu to another. For the individual, conversion shapes the convert's world-view, directing judgements and forming character. As a communal and historical phenomenon, conversion imparts to a group or movement a thematic character by which it explores its origins and measures its developments, successes, and failures. The intensity, vividness, and disruption entailed by a given conversion will probably vary in proportion to the environment in which it takes place (Wallace 1956).

Theologians and teachers today use sociological and psychological material of the sort just noted in their attempts to interpret Christian conversion while adding to it the teaching of scripture and church. Three such approaches are noted here:

1. Canadian Roman Catholic theologian Bernard *Lonergan found the concept of conversion central to his interpretation of the human task of knowing and understanding. He analysed conversion into three elements or stages: intellectual conversion, in which one's thinking undergoes profound reorientation, moral conversion, in which one's lifestyle is altered, and religious conversion, in which one's relation to God becomes paramount. Some have seen this analysis as too narrowly individualist; must there not be a ritual dimension of conversion as well (cf. believers' baptism)? Others have questioned the existence of any one of these stages without the others in authentic Christian experience. To do justice to Lonergan, it needs to be insisted that he regarded conversion in its several dimensions as necessary to each faithful traveller on the Christian path. There could be no authentic Christian knowledge without Christian conversion.

2. Karl *Barth warns in the last completed part-volume of his *Church Dogmatics* against treating conversion in a triumphalist manner as the redeemed sinner's own achievement even while emphasizing its biblical place as a 'commissioning and sending'—his view with regard to baptism as well.

3. James McClendon has tried to mediate the enduring debate over conversion by locating it among several stages or elements in a pattern of Christian spirituality that includes (a) preparation (which may be linked to the church's guidance of those not yet ready for the grand transformation itself); (b) conversion itself, properly marked by baptism; (c) discipleship or following, understood as the ongoing obedience of the converted and properly marked by participation in eucharistic worship; and finally (d) 'soaring', a term alluding to those higher reaches of Christian life recognized by John *Wesley as 'perfect *love'—an earthly foretaste of *heaven.

Recent theologians recognize in conversion not a fixed outward form but an end, attaining by *grace the new way of Jesus. Christian conversion turns on this attainment and thereby becomes the turn of turns. Attempts simply to equate this turning with outwardly similar phenomena fail to provide a reliable index of conversion to Jesus Christ. It is something that precipitates antitheses between oneself and one's internalized and parental and social values, setting 'a man against his father, a daughter against her mother' (Matt. 10: 35). The convert to Christ may be not easier but harder to live with (cf. Acts 9: 29), and may discover that it is more difficult to live with himself or herself as well. The dynamic which brings peace with God often brings the *world's enmity. Christian conversion is a turn to Christlikeness: a new-found relation with the living God fosters a radical alteration of one's orientation to life. Individuals co-operate to meet one another's needs as well as those of the (unconverted) world. Such born-again converts become disciples, and disciples comprise churches united by a shared solidarity in Jesus Christ.

James William McClendon, Jr.
Charles J. Conniry, Jr.

Barth, Karl, *Church Dogmatics*, IV/3 (1962); IV/4 (1969).
James, William, *The Varieties of Religious Experience* (1902).
Lonergan, Bernard, *Method In Theology* (1972).
McClendon, James William, *Doctrine: Systematic Theology* (1994), ii.
Nock, A. D., *Conversion* (1933).
Rambo, Lewis, *Understanding Religious Conversion* (1993).
Wallace, A. F. C., 'Revitalization Movements', *American Anthropologist*, 58 (1956).

cosmology is that branch of physics which studies the structure and *evolution of the universe as a whole. It comprises both cosmogony (the origin of the universe) and *eschatology (the fate of the universe). It is probably the field of *science which intersects most directly with *theology, given the commitment of the Christian church to the biblical doctrine of *creatio ex nihilo* and, hence, to a temporal beginning of the universe.

'In the beginning God created the heavens and the earth' (Gen. 1: 1). With majestic simplicity the author of the opening chapter of *Genesis thus differentiated his viewpoint from that of the ancient *creation myths of *Israel's neighbours. For the author of Genesis 1, no pre-existent material seems to be assumed, no warring gods or primordial dragons are present—only God, who is said to 'create' (*bara*, a word used only with God as its subject and which does not presuppose a material substratum) 'the heavens and the earth', a Hebrew expression for the totality of the *world or, more simply, the universe). Moreover, this act of creation took place 'in the beginning' (*bereshith*, used here as in Isa. 46: 10 to indicate an absolute beginning). This sentence is without parallel in ancient creation *myths. The usual form of these myths was 'When——was not yet, then God made …' The first clause expressed the state of things prior to God's action, the second clause God's subsequent activity in making something out of that state. We find this typical form in

Gen. 2: 5–7: 'When no plant of the field was yet in the earth and no herb of the field had yet sprung up... then the LORD God formed man ...' The author of Gen. 1 took the typical 'When——was not yet' and made it v. 2 and then took the typical 'then God ...' and made it v. 3; then he prefixed both of these by his own sentence in v. 1. Hence, v. 1 is not a temporal subordinate clause; it lies outside the typical structure and is the author's own formulation. Nor is v. 1 merely a title or heading, since it is connected with v. 2 by *waw* (and), indicating a relation of connection between God's primary and subsequent acts of creation. In a construction of *waw* plus a non-predicate *cum* predicate, the preceding clause furnishes either background or circumstantial information. Whenever this construction precedes the main verb, as it does in v. 2, then it is background information which is given. Accordingly, v. 1 is not simply a heading, but a historical statement which constitutes the background to v. 2. According to the most likely exegesis of the text, then, the author of Genesis 1 gives us to understand that the universe had a temporal origin and thus implies *creatio ex nihilo* in the temporal sense that God brought the universe into being without a material cause (that is, in the absence of any physical substratum) at some point in the finite past.

This is certainly how later biblical authors understood the Genesis account of creation (see e.g. Prov. 8: 27–9; John 1: 1–3; Col. 1: 16, 17; Heb. 1: 2–3; 11: 3; Rev. 4: 11). Moreover, the doctrine of *creatio ex nihilo* is implied in various places in early extra-biblical Jewish literature. And the church fathers, while heavily influenced by Greek thought, dug in their heels concerning the doctrine of creation, sturdily insisting, with few exceptions, on the temporal creation of the universe *ex nihilo* in opposition to the eternity of matter (see, for example, the *Shepherd of Hermas*, 1: 6; 26: 1; *Irenaeus, *Adversus haereses*, 3: 10, 3). In 1215, the Catholic church promulgated temporal *creatio ex nihilo* as official church doctrine at the Fourth Lateran Council, declaring God to be 'Creator of all things, visible and invisible... who, by his almighty power, from the beginning of time has created both orders in the same way out of nothing.' This remarkable declaration not only affirms that God created everything out of nothing, but even that *time itself had a beginning. The doctrine of creation is thus bound up with temporal considerations and entails that God brought the universe into being at some point in the past without any material cause.

For nearly two millennia the church stoutly affirmed, first in the face of Greek *philosophy and then of modern materialism and idealism, the traditional doctrine that the universe had been brought into being out of nothing by God a finite time ago. The idea of the eternality of the universe had all the same become so entrenched in the secular mindset that Albert Einstein, upon discovering in 1916 that the application of his newly formulated General Theory of Relativity to the universe as a whole implied a universe either in a state of cosmic collapse or cosmic expansion, felt obliged to introduce into his equations a 'fudge factor', the so-called cosmological constant, to ensure a static universe. Einstein's universe was, however, radically unstable to the slightest perturbation and would quickly dissolve into an expanding or collapsing universe. Models of the universe involving a cosmic expansion from a point of origin in the finite past were developed independently by Friedman and Lemaître. Then in 1929 the Friedman–Lemaître model received empirical confirmation by Hubble's discovery that the light from all other measured galaxies is shifted towards the red end of the spectrum to a degree proportionate to their distance from us, thus implying a decelerating, isotropic expansion of the entire universe. The startling implication of Hubble's discovery was that the common assumption of the universe's eternality was wrong, for a time-reversed extrapolation of the expansion implied an origin of the universe at some point in the finite past. Physicist John Wheeler registers some of the impact of that discovery when he writes, 'Of all the great predictions that science has ever made over the centuries, was there ever one greater than this, to predict, and predict correctly, and predict against all expectation a phenomenon so fantastic as the expansion of the universe?' ('Beyond the Hole', in H. Woolf (ed.), *Some Strangeness in the Proportion* (1980), 354).

As one traces the expansion back in time the universe becomes progressively denser until one arrives at a state of infinite density called a singularity. Whether the universe is spatially finite or infinite makes no difference to its past temporal finitude. In either case this singular state marks the beginning of the universe; literally nothing exists before it, that is, it is false that anything exists before this state. The universe simply appeared out of nothing a finite time ago.

A good many scientists were none too happy about this development. After all, in the absence of a transcendent creator, the absolute origin of the universe out of nothing seems evidently absurd. Thus, the model raised questions of profound *metaphysical—and maybe even theological—significance. Fred Hoyle, a Cambridge astronomer who found any such suggestion repugnant, derisively characterized the alleged origination as 'the Big Bang', and, ironically, the name stuck.

Nevertheless, the term 'Big Bang' and the attendant imagery of an explosion can be very misleading. It is important to understand that the standard Friedman model does not posit simply an expansion of the material cosmos into a previously existing empty space which has endured throughout infinite time. Rather the postulated expansion is the expansion of space itself, and the initial state marks not only the origin of all matter and energy, but even of physical space and time themselves. The galaxies are conceived to be fixed in space and simply to ride along with the expansion of space, just as buttons glued to the surface of a balloon are fixed and yet recede from each other as the balloon is inflated. Thus, there existed no place or time at which the Big Bang occurred, for space and time themselves come into being in the Big Bang. It represents truly an origination *ex nihilo*.

The evident metaphysical problems associated with such an absolute origination fuelled attempts to find alternatives to the standard model which do not imply a beginning of the universe. As the prominent Russian cosmologist Andrei Linde confesses, 'The most difficult aspect of this problem is not the existence of the singularity itself, but the question of what was *before* the singularity ... This problem lies somewhere at the boundary between physics and metaphysics' ('The Inflationary Universe', *Reports on Progress in Physics*, 47 (1984), 976).

Hoyle's self-confessed hostility towards theism motivated him to propose with Bondi and Gold in 1948 the alternative Steady State model of the universe. In this model, the universe never had a beginning but has always existed in the same overall state. As the galaxies recede from one another, new matter comes into being in the regions vacated by the retreating galaxies, so that the basic state of the universe remains unchanged. Although it never secured a single piece of experimental verification, the Steady State model remained a competitor to the Big Bang theory until the 1960s. Then in 1965, A. A. Penzias and R. W. Wilson discovered that the entire universe is bathed with a background of microwave radiation, which is most plausibly explained as a vestige of an earlier very hot and very dense state of the universe. Since according to the Steady State model no such state could have existed, that model has now been abandoned by virtually all scientists.

The Friedman model presupposed boundary conditions of homogeneity and isotropy for the universe, conditions which are remarkably approximated by our universe over large scales. But during the 1960s some theorists hoped to avert the initial singularity by denying that those conditions obtained in the early universe. It was hypothesized that if a contracting universe were not perfectly homogeneous and isotropic, then the converging particles would not coalesce, but would in part pass each other by, so that after reaching a certain minimum radius the universe would begin to re-expand. If each expansion were preceded by a contraction and each contraction by an expansion, then the universe would never have begun to exist. Thus was conceived the Oscillating model of the universe, which became for ideological reasons the darling of certain Soviet physicists and was popularized by Carl Sagan, who held that 'the Cosmos is all that is or ever was or ever will be' (*Cosmos* (1980), 4). The discovery in 1968 by Stephen Hawking and Roger Penrose of the singularity theorem which bears their names constituted a major blow to the Oscillating model, for that theorem revealed that in any expanding universe meeting certain very general requirements an initial singularity was inevitable. According to Hawking, the Hawking–Penrose singularity theorem 'led to the abandonment of attempts (mainly by the Russians) to argue that there was a previous contracting phase and a nonsingular bounce into expansion. Instead almost everyone now believes that the universe, and time itself, had a beginning at the big bang' (Hawking and Penrose 1996: 20).

Subsequent attempts to avoid an absolute origination of the universe sought to relativize the beginning by placing our universe in the context of a wider reality. Since we have no evidence of the existence of such a wider reality, these models constitute what one theorist has called exercises in 'metaphysical cosmology' (A. Vilenkin, 'Birth of Inflationary Universes', *Physical Review D*, 27/12 (1983), 2854). The first of these was proposed by Edward Tryon in 1973, what we may call the Vacuum Fluctuation model of the universe. On the analogy of the spontaneous emergence of a virtual particle from the quantum mechanical vacuum, Tryon suggested that our universe originated—along with countless others—through a vacuum fluctuation in the energy of a wider, empty space, which is itself eternal. Thus, while our mini-universe began to exist, it was spawned by a wider universe which never had a beginning. A fatal shortcoming in this model, however, is that for any point in the wider space there is within any finite interval of time a non-zero probability of a universe-generating fluctuation occurring. Given an infinite, past, wider time, universes will thus be spawned at every point, and as they expand they will begin to collide and coalesce. Thus, we should observe either an infinitely old universe

or 'worlds in collision', which we do not. Thus, vacuum fluctuation models were very quickly scrapped and nothing much has been done with them since (Isham 1988: 387).

The suggestion by Alan Guth that the universe may have experienced a brief period of super-rapid, or inflationary, expansion in its early history has prompted Linde to champion his Chaotic Inflationary model of the universe as a viable means of avoiding an absolute origin of the universe. On this scenario, inflation produces a multiplicity of universes like ours and never ends and never begins. Rather than being like the expansion of a single balloon, the evolution of the wider universe is more like a froth of bubbles, which eternally begets new bubble universes. Vilenkin and Borde, however, have very recently shown that even Linde's Chaotic Inflationary model must posit an initial singular beginning of space-time: models in which inflation is eternal in the future 'must necessarily possess initial singularities'; therefore, 'inflation does not seem to avoid the problem of the initial singularity .... [This] forces one to address the question of what, if anything, came before' (A. Borde and A. Vilenkin, 'Eternal Inflation and the Initial Singularity', *Physical Review Letters*, 72 (1994), 3305, 3307).

Perhaps the most speculative models of all are the Quantum Gravity models of Hartle–Hawking and Vilenkin, which postulate the origin of the universe in a space-time in which time is imaginary, that is, imaginary values such as $\sqrt{-1}$ are assigned to the time variable in the equations. On such models the universe is finite in the past but does not have a beginning point, since the imaginary space-time in which it originates is the four-dimensional analogue of the surface of a sphere and so has no edge. Apart from technical difficulties, Quantum Gravity models face severe interpretative problems. If we construe them instrumentally, then they actually serve to support an origination of the universe *ex nihilo*, in that they posit a finite imaginary time on a closed hyper-surface prior to the Planck time (10^{-43} second after the Big Bang in the standard model) rather than an infinite time on an open surface. They are merely redescriptions using the formalism of quantum mechanics of a universe which really has an absolute beginning; when one translates back into real numbers the singularity reappears. This is the way in which Hawking apparently construes his model, as he espouses anti-realism and employs a similar re-description in analysing electron-positron pair creation (Hawking and Penrose 1996: 53–5). On the other hand, if, in order to avert the beginning of the universe, we construe such theoretical descriptions realistically, then these models seem to be both physically unintelligible, since it is wholly mysterious what could be meant by intervals of 'imaginary time', and also metaphysically objectionable, because the assigning of imaginary values to the time variable eliminates any distinction between time and space, which are evidently distinct in that time is uniquely and essentially ordered by the *earlier/later than* relations.

Thus, despite every effort, many of them extremely speculative, to eliminate it, the initial cosmological singularity remains with us, a reminder of the contingency of time and space, matter, and energy. In fact Penrose has argued adamantly that it is misguided to try to eliminate the singularity because without it the chances of the initial conditions of the universe requisite for thermodynamics as we know it today would be about $1:10^{10^{(123)}}$, a number which is unparalleled in physics (R. Penrose, 'Time Asymmetry and Quantum Gravity', in C. Isham (ed.), *Quantum Gravity*, 2 (1981), 249). The traditional doctrine of *creatio ex nihilo* is therefore remarkably consonant with contemporary physical cosmology.

The doctrine that God created the universe—indeed, space and time themselves—out of nothing has profound implications for God's relationship with time. It has been alleged by opponents of theological creationism that the Big Bang cannot have a cause because causes precede their effects, whereas there was no time prior to the Big Bang. But the creator may be conceived to be causally, not temporally, prior to the Big Bang, such that his act of causing the universe to begin to exist is simultaneous with its beginning to exist. Philosophical discussions of causal directionality deal routinely with cases in which cause and effect are simultaneous, the challenge being to discern which event is the cause of the other. In the case of creation and the Big Bang, God's action and the origination of the universe are plausibly simultaneous, and it is obvious which is the cause and which the effect, since it is metaphysically impossible for God to have a cause. Such a view implies that God exists timelessly *sans* the universe and becomes temporal at the moment of creation and the origin of time. Creation thus expresses a determination on God's part to take on a temporal mode of existence, a mode God could have foregone by freely refraining from creation.

William Lane Craig

Craig, W., and Grünbaum, A., 'Creation and Big Bang Cosmology', 'Comments', 'Response', *Philosophia naturalis*, 31 (1994).
Craig, W., and Smith, Q., *Theism, Atheism, and Big Bang Cosmology* (1993).
Hetherington, N. (ed.), *Encyclopedia of Cosmology* (1992).
Hawking, S., and Penrose, R., *The Nature of Space and Time* (1996).
Isham, C., 'Creation of the Universe as a Quantum Process', in R. Russell *et al.* (eds.), *Physics, Philosophy, and Theology* (1988).
——'Quantum Theories of the Creation of the Universe,' in R. Russell *et al.* (eds.), *Quantum Cosmology and the Laws of Nature* (1993).
Kanitscheider, B., *Kosmologie* (1984).
Leslie, John (ed.), *Modern Cosmology and Philosophy* (1998).
Sailhammer, J., *Genesis* (1990).
Westermann, C., *Genesis 1–11* (1984).

Council, see CHALCEDON; EPHESUS; FLORENCE; NICAEA; TRENT; VATICAN I; VATICAN II; CONCILIARISM.

councils. *Vatican II was, in the official Roman Catholic view, the twenty-first Ecumenical Council. What constitutes such a council and what are its powers? Central as councils have been to Christian history, that question remains curiously under-studied. While ecumenical councils have made all the main dogmatic decisions, it would be hard to find any dogmatic definition of an ecumenical council or the nature of its *authority.

The NT provides a model in Acts 15: 1–29 and, undoubtedly, this example has encouraged the church throughout history to settle problems by calling a meeting. In this so-called Council of Jerusalem, certain elements can be distinguished as a model for subsequent conciliar decision-making. First, a contested issue: do Gentile Christians need to be circumcised? Second, a meeting (of 'apostles and elders') held to resolve the issue, in which various views are expressed by members of local churches. Third, a decision arrived at *collegially and with practical unanimity, but actually proclaimed by James, head of the host church. Fourth, complete confidence in the rightness of the decision: 'It has been decided by the *Holy Spirit and by ourselves'.

Councils of local bishops in considerable numbers were already held in the 3rd century at Antioch, Carthage, and *Rome. The church, then, recognized this as the appropriate instrument for decision-making, something already available for the Emperor *Constantine to turn to when seeking to resolve conflicts between Christians. He did so first with a council at Arles, called to decide about the *Donatist–Catholic dispute in Africa, and then in 325 at *Nicaea to resolve the disagreement over *Arianism. Nicaea was followed by numerous other councils, all convoked by emperors, several of which came eventually to be accepted like Nicaea as 'ecumenical', and definitive for the church as a whole, while Arles among others was held to be merely regional. Nicaea was followed by Constantinople I (380), *Ephesus (431), *Chalcedon (451), Constantinople II (553), Constantinople III (680–1), and Nicaea II (787). While the first four were placed in a class of their own and even compared with the four gospels, these seven were accepted by both east and west, although the western church was barely represented at most of them and their moral status varies considerably. While Nicaea I appears to have been adequately free and reasonably representative of the church of the time, Constantinople II, for instance, had no more than 165 bishops, quite unrepresentative of even the non-Latin church of the 6th century. Moreover, its decisions were forced through by the Emperor Justinian against direct condemnation by Pope Vigilius, who was later browbeaten into agreement.

The twenty-one councils recognized as ecumenical by Rome include a number of medieval synods of such limited size and weight (Lateran II of 1139 is particularly insignificant) that it is hard to take seriously their claim to ecumenicity, unrecognized at the time. The Catholic list was only established in the 16th century and makes little sense in terms either of history or of the way modern Roman canon law defines an ecumenical council. However, once it is recognized that a 'twenty-one councils' model is difficult to sustain, it becomes almost impossible to decide which gatherings of bishops, if any, should be credited with a unique 'ecumenical status'. The theological implications are immense. Clearly, for instance, the dogma of papal *infallibility depends upon the ecumenicity of *Vatican I, yet there are serious grounds for questioning whether it had sufficient freedom, whether it arrived at sufficient consensus, or whether its membership was sufficiently wide, given the absence of *Eastern Orthodox representation.

While councils dominated the doctrinal history of the high patristic period, their role diminished as papal authority advanced. In the west they were revived as little more than a convenient tool for implementing papal policy, until in the late Middle Ages the *papacy discredited itself disastrously with the concurrent claims of two, and then three, popes. This led to *conciliarism, which endeavoured to right the situation by asserting the superiority of councils over popes. The Council of Constance (1414–18), accepted as the sixteenth in the series, actually decreed its own superiority to the pope but, after the schism was ended, the papacy rejected any such view.

The Orthodox Churches have never accepted more than seven ecumenical councils, while most Protestants agree to only four and only then, it seems, to their teaching rather than to any intrinsic authority. *Luther appealed to an ecumenical council against papal condemnation, but then decided that councils too could be wrong, and the Thirty-Nine Articles of the Church of England agree that they 'may err and sometimes have erred'. It seems theoretically questionable to place just seven, or four, councils in a different category from other gatherings.

Much of the difficulty may derive from a somewhat fundamentalist wish to treat the declarations of ecumenical councils as expressions of ecclesiastical infallibility (encouraged, perhaps, by Acts 15: 28). But rejecting fundamentalism need not destroy the significance of ecumenical councils, while making both their status and the authority of their pronouncements more relative. The authoritativeness of group decision-making in the church is continually recognized, whether through diocesan or episcopal synods, annual assemblies, or the Lambeth Conference. The more a council genuinely represents the whole church and listens to the Holy Spirit, the more it behaves in a truly reasonable and Christian manner, free from political pressure or bullying of any kind, the more ecumenical it is, the more its conclusions may be accepted as truly authoritative. But it appears crucial to any theory of conciliar authority that it includes the element of 'reception'. Only if the wider church, freely and across the years, recognizes a council's decisions as representing the mind of the whole body, can they be seen as fully authoritative. If this has too seldom been the case, it can only be concluded that ecumenicity is easier to claim than to achieve.

Adrian Hastings

Bermejo, Luis M., *Church, Conciliarity and Communion* (1990).
Dvornik, F., *The Ecumenical Councils* (1961).
Jedin, H., *Ecumenical Councils of the Catholic Church: An Historical Outline* (1960).
Tanner, N. P., *Decrees of the Ecumenical Councils* (2 vols.; 1990).

Counter-Reformation.

This term was not known to western European Christians of the *sixteenth and *seventeenth centuries in any language. It was coined by later historians, originally to denote a *Catholic reaction, from the mid-16th century onwards, to the *Protestant *Reformation. This negative reaction was supposed to be essentially defensive, as a product solely of the Reformation. An alternative term, the 'Catholic Reformation', has sometimes been used in the 20th century to reassert the independent origins of institutional and individual spiritual reform in later medieval western Christendom (see MIDDLE AGES), as a movement from which emerged the protagonists of continued internal reform within the traditional church as well as eventual Protestant leaders such as *Luther. The original term, used in a way that accommodates this point, has nevertheless largely held its own, not least because of an undisputedly reactionary element in, for example, the decrees of the Council of *Trent, many of which controvert specific Protestant doctrines. Beyond the Tridentine decrees, however, the Christian thought of the Counter-Reformation is much less obviously reactionary. Ignatius Loyola drew on existing Christian thought, medieval as well as humanist (see EXERCISES). *Teresa of Avila and *John of the Cross, for example, also reflected at least partly existing traditions of Christian mysticism, rather than being anti-Protestant in inspiration.

Thus the Oratorian Baronius (1538–1607) stressed in his *Annales Ecclesiastici* the unbroken continuity of Christian belief and practice still found in the traditional western church, though his church history was in fact a response to the Protestant *Centuries* published under the direction of Flacius Illyricus as a defence against charges

of innovation and disruption. On the other hand the *Jesuit Robert Bellarmine (1542–1621) systematized Catholic doctrine, substantially clarified at the Council of Trent, in works including both apologetics against Protestant polemic and summaries of Catholic teaching intended to consolidate true belief among the faithful. The catechetical confirmation of the faith was further popularized by another Jesuit, Peter Canisius (1521–97). His catechisms remained in fact more influential among Catholics, immediately and in the long term, than the Roman Catechism published in Latin by Pope Pius V in 1566 and addressed to parish priests rather than directly to the faithful. In the following year the same *Dominican pope elevated Thomas *Aquinas to the status of Doctor of the Church. But this again involved by definition a pre-Reformation not an anti-Protestant theological tradition. Moreover the papal decision also reflected unresolved internal tensions between Dominican and other Catholic tendencies, not least that of the newly founded Jesuits. These had not been fully settled at Trent, and were to become more evident in the decades before and after 1600.

Indeed, by that date, Jesuits and Dominicans, particularly in Spain, had clashed over the true nature of Thomist teaching itself. A Jesuit interpreter, Francisco Suarez (1548–1617), was subsequently to prove influential in a wider development, that of international *law, building on earlier foundations provided by the Dominican Francisco de Vitoria (1483–1546). But an unmodified Thomism was defended by the Dominican John of St Thomas (1589–1644), and by 1600 Jesuits were charged with innovation in Christian thought not only by Protestant critics but also by opponents within Catholicism. This internal hostility increased rather than diminished with the influence of *Jansenism during the 17th and 18th centuries. Other aspects of Catholic Christian thought seem even less the result of conscious response to Protestant challenge. The pastoral austerity of Charles Borromeo of Milan (1538–84), the model post-Tridentine bishop, especially in his guidance to confessors, had some long-term impact, most obviously among the French Jansenists, but a contrasting stress on Christian peace and joy was inculcated by Philip Neri (1515–95), whose own sense of discipline nevertheless helped to shield the Oratorians from the contemporary accusations of pastoral laxity which the Jesuits came to face. The conservatism, rather than reaction, maintained by the post-Tridentine popes, between 1564 and 1789, was thus intended not least to preserve a fragile equilibrium and the image of unity among Catholic theologians themselves. Despite contrary pressures, the papacy in that period retained the theology of Trent, refraining from positive and binding dogmatic formulations with regard, for instance, to either the Immaculate Conception or a personal papal *infallibility. Twentieth-century use of the term 'Counter-Reformation' however has not always avoided the conflation of later Catholic teaching (such as that of the First Vatican Council) and the specifically post-Tridentine.

A truer continuity, until the period since the Second Vatican Council, was perhaps the centrality in the Counter-Reformation of *casuistry. In the pristine sense this meant the distinguishing of cases of *conscience, in which confessors were trained, in order to provide better spiritual direction to their penitents, as the Tridentine and post-conciliar church stressed the merits of regular sacramental confession as a means of grace, and not merely as an annual obligation of the church's law (see PENANCE). Though the term 'casuistry', through selective use of evidence by its critics, came to be identified with equivocation, not least as attributed to Jesuits, true casuistry in the Counter-Reformation undoubtedly suggested a care for discipline, institutional and individual, contrasted with the alleged licence of the varieties of Protestantism. Indeed, despite the continued controversies among professional theologians, it was the clarification of orthodox belief in the Tridentine decrees that allowed the subsequent systematic catechizing of the people of Catholic Europe on a comprehensive basis beyond the capability of the pre-Reformation western church. Some recent historical interpretations have suggested that such stress on individual responsibility for faith and practice, rather than reliance on family and social ritual, transformed medieval western Christianity almost as much as did the Protestant Reformation, but this assessment is questionable. In any case, despite a stress on individual responsibility, and the individualist mysticism of Teresa of Avila or John of the Cross, the Tridentine decrees and the consequent catechetical campaigns emphasized the corporate identity of the one true *church in Catholic thinking. This visibility of the church already potentially triumphant, though still militant on earth, was celebrated in the ecclesiastical art and architecture of the *Baroque in Catholic Europe.

The preservation of orthodoxy was certainly a fundamental aim of Counter-Reformation Catholicism, but papal diplomacy for a while concentrated even more on the traditional confrontation with *Islam, sustained to the early 18th century, than on attacking Protestant rulers. The chronology of overseas *missionary expansion, in the Americas and the Far East, from the late 15th century onwards, also establishes that this was not in origin a response to Protestantism nor initially intended to replace with new converts the numbers lost to heresy in Europe. Though responsibility for such expansion had at first been devolved by the papacy to the Iberian monarchies, the belated attempt, begun by Gregory XV in 1622, to recover greater Roman direction of overseas mission reasserted the importance of *evangelism which the Council of Trent had defined as the prime duty of Catholic bishops. Internal dispute in Catholic Europe, over both pastoral practice and doctrinal definition, nevertheless influenced later popes, by the 18th century, in their ultimate condemnation of innovative missionary methods among non-Europeans, adopted above all by Jesuits in *India and *China.

Within Catholic Europe the Church's opposition to publication of heterodox ideas, and a related hostility to unauthorized vernacular versions of the scriptures or even of liturgical texts, were not precisely Counter-Reformation phenomena, despite preliminary work at the Council of Trent to consolidate a definitive Index of prohibited literature. There was already a call for systematic censorship at the Fifth Lateran Council (1512–17), in response not to Luther but to the preceding spread of printing. In the post-Tridentine church the close relationship, in the Italian peninsula, between papal *authority and the Roman *Inquisition as revitalized from the mid-16th century, could not be reproduced elsewhere. The Iberian monarchies had their own, largely independent Inquisition and Index. Other Catholic states refused to admit unlimited exercise of papal authority in their territories. The difficulties encountered by Pope Urban VIII and his successors in the mid-17th century when confronted by persistent war between the major secular powers of Catholic Eur-

ope affected the development of Roman reaction to Jansenism in the longer term, as well as Urban's immediate response to *Galileo. But the distinct forms of Counter-Reformation in the Iberian peninsula, France, and German-speaking Catholic lands meant that Roman equation of perfect obedience to papal authority with true Catholicism was never universally established.   **A. D. Wright**

Bossy, J., *Christianity in the West 1400–1700* (1985).
Delumeau, J., *Catholicism from Luther to Voltaire* (1977).
Dickens, A. G., *The Counter Reformation* (1968).
Evennett, H. O., *The Spirit of the Counter-Reformation* (1968).
Fenlon, D., *Heresy and Obedience in Tridentine Italy: Cardinal Pole and the Counter Reformation* (1972).
O'Malley, J. W., *The First Jesuits* (1993).
Wright, A. D., *The Counter-Reformation: Catholic Europe and the Non-Christian World* (1982).
—— *The Early Modern Papacy: From the Council of Trent to the French Revolution 1564–1789* (1999).

covenant is the normal translation in English of the Hebrew word *berit*, which in the *Old Testament describes a wide variety of human relationships: for example Jonathan and *David's solemn pledge of *friendship (1 Sam. 20: 11–1), treaties between states (1 Kgs. 5: 12), and *marriage (Mal. 2: 14). Such covenants were often entered into with due legal formality and with religious rites such as *sacrifice, with the gods of the contracting parties invoked as guarantors of the covenant (Gen. 31: 44–54). The most common uses of covenant, however, describe the relationship between *God and his chosen people. It features in several different traditions. In the Mt. Sinai tradition (Exod. 24: 1–8) it emphasizes the obligation of *Israel to an exclusive loyalty to the Lord whose saving act at the *Exodus was the foundation of the community's existence; an exclusive loyalty which had ethical as well as religious implications (Exod. 20: 1–17). This tradition provided the context in which were placed the regulations, social and ritual, which were to govern Israel's life. The covenant with *Abraham appears in two traditions, one in Gen. 15, the other in Gen. 17. Both stress the element of promise, in Gen. 15 the promise of the land to Abraham and his descendants, in Gen. 17 the promise of innumerable descendants, with circumcision the sign of what is described as the everlasting covenant between God and his people. The covenant between God and the Davidic royal family has similar features; an everlasting covenant guaranteeing that the Davidic dynasty will continue forever (2 Sam. 7: 8–13; Ps. 89). The covenant with Noah (Gen. 9) is again essentially promissory, a covenant with humanity that never again will the earth be destroyed by a flood. The original provenance of and the relationship between these varied traditions is a matter of considerable debate. The very fact, however, that covenant appears in a variety of traditions shows the important place it held in the religious thinking of ancient Israel. The repeated failure of the people to live in obedience to their obligations under the Sinai covenant led to several attempts to renew that commitment, notably under Hezekiah (2 Chr. 29: 10) and Josiah (2 Kgs. 23) when on the basis of the discovery of the book of the covenant, probably part of Deuteronomy, when repairs were being undertaken to the Jerusalem *Temple, the king and people 'made a covenant before the Lord' in an act of recommitment. It is theologically important to notice, however, that in each tradition, whatever the stress on obligation, the initiative in establishing the basic covenant relationship lies with God. It is the gift of God's *grace. The same emphasis probably lies behind the way in which the Greek translation (LXX) and the NT consistently render *berit* not by the usual classical and Hellenistic word for an agreement, *suntheke*, but by *diatheke*, a word which can mean order or institution, but more commonly is a technical term meaning last will or testament.

Covenant provided the basic paradigm of Judaism, one God and one people of God. This paradigm has remained across the centuries. In rabbinic teaching the people's obligation was to obey all the commandments given by God and enshrined in Torah (Genesis to Deuteronomy). The implications of such obedience for everyday life were spelled out in *halakah*, the correct way to live, in the Mishnah (2nd century AD) and the later Talmuds (see LAW, BIB-LICAL). In a different context, whether we look at the attempt of Philo of Alexander in the 1st century to build a bridge between *Judaism and *Hellenistic thought or Maimonides' concern to use contemporary philosophic and scientific thinking in the 12th century in *The Guide for the Perplexed*, the starting-point is the same, what God has revealed to the Jewish people and what he expects from them in terms of the covenant. Although there may be division and sometimes bitter debate between Orthodox, Conservative, and Reformed Jews today as to how far certain provisions of *halakah* can be applied literally in modern life, all would accept that the fundamental relationship in which the Jew stands is still that of the covenant (cf. Borowitz). The precise nature of that covenant, however, has been variously understood, Martin Buber, for example, in the context of his I–Thou philosophy, insisting that it should be seen not as a legal contract, but rather as similar to a marriage between parties linked in mutual trust. Various elements within the covenant traditions have led to lively contemporary debate, not least whether the promise of the land in the Abraham covenant justifies the existence of the state of Israel and its claim to the whole of Judaea and Samaria as a Jewish homeland by divine right. More radically, voices have been raised questioning whether it is still possible to believe in the God of the covenant in the aftermath of the *Holocaust.

But covenant may also be used in a more exclusive sense. If covenant provides the paradigm for the people of God, then groups, such as those from whom the *Dead Sea Scrolls came, tended to claim the covenant for themselves. They alone were the true people of God. The *Community Rule* stipulates that those admitted to membership of the community, after due examination, 'entered the covenant', taking upon themselves the commitment to observe the laws of *Moses as interpreted by the leadership of the community. Some of these interpretations clearly separated the community from the rest of Judaism. They were 'the children of *light' and all others outside the community were 'the children of darkness'. Thus covenant ideology nourished sectarianism.

Within this framework we must understand the use of the covenant concept in the NT and the early church. The Synoptic Gospels put on the lips of *Jesus in the context of the Last Supper the description of the cup to be shared as 'the blood of the (new) covenant' (Mark 14: 24; Matt. 26: 28; Luke 22: 20). This tradition is confirmed by *Paul in 1 Corinthians 11: 25 in the words, 'This cup is the new covenant in my blood', precisely echoing the words of Moses in Exod. 24: 8, 'this is the blood of the covenant'. The sharing in the meal, therefore, symbolized the new relationship with God

that Christians claimed came into being through the death and *Resurrection of Jesus. *Hebrews twice refers to Jeremiah 31: 31–4 which looks forward to a new covenant that, through a new act of God's grace, will make possible that obedience for which the *prophets looked in vain, and claims that this new covenant has come into being through the unique *priestly ministry of Jesus. Paul in Galatians appeals to the Abraham covenant tradition with its emphasis upon the blessing to come to the nations to justify the admission of Gentiles into the new people of God without the necessity of their becoming Jews (Gal. 3), while in an *allegory in ch. 4 he places side by side and contrasts two covenants, the one representing Judaism, the other representing the new Christian community. The seeds were thus sown of what was to become an increasingly bitter Christian–Jewish confrontation over who could rightly claim to be the true covenant people. It was not helped by the fact that, provoked by Marcion's claim that the God of the Hebrew Scriptures was not the God of Jesus, the church affirmed the unity of scripture but divided it into OT and NT, 'testament' being the Latin form of 'covenant'. All too soon there developed a Christian sense of superiority and arrogance which was to have fateful consequences for the Jewish community; a superiority and arrogance rooted often in a failure to understand the theological basis of covenant in Israel and an oversimplified contrast between law and *gospel. Historical, social, and religious factors were to combine to transform into persecutors a community which had begun life as a Jewish sect persecuted by Jewish authorities.

The new covenant passage in Jeremiah 31: 31–3 has posed theological problems. Within Judaism it has always been seen as a yet unfulfilled hope. The Christian claim of fulfilment in Jesus leaves many questions unanswered. *Calvin, in face of the denigration of Israel by Servetus and the Anabaptists (see BAPTIST THOUGHT), insisted on continuity between the covenants. 'The covenant made with the patriarchs is so much like ours in substance and reality that the two are actually one and the same. They differ only in the mode of dispensation' (*Institutes*, 2. 10). In his *Commentary on Jeremiah* he regards the new covenant passage as hyperbolically pointing to the gospel, but he refuses to accept that the words 'no longer shall they teach one another' imply, as the Anabaptists argued, the end of all teaching ministry.

In *Reformed Confessions of Faith, notably the Westminster Confession of Faith, God's covenant with humanity had a twofold aspect: (1) a covenant of works with *Adam, the failure of which through Adam's disobedience led to transmitted original *sin, and (2) the covenant of grace in Jesus Christ, set forth in the whole bible, in terms of law in the OT and grace in the NT. In the political and religious struggles of the post-Reformation era, however, covenant came to the fore to describe the actions of people who solemnly bound themselves together for specific purposes. Two examples will suffice. The 'Bands subscribed by the Lords' in 1557 was the forerunner of many such covenants in *Scotland. The National Covenant of 1638, while recognizing the authority of the king, condemned *episcopacy, asserted the sovereignty of the Scottish Parliament over against papal interference, and proclaimed the intention 'to recover the purity and liberty of the gospel'. It was to be followed by 'The Solemn League and Covenant' of 1643. Such covenants assumed that Calvinistic *Presbyterianism was to be the religion of Scotland and beyond, and that force could legitimately be used to ensure this. In the ensuing period of the Covenanters in the second half of the 17th century, religion and politics were inextricably interwoven, and bloody deeds besmirched the name of both. Covenant theology was also deeply influential among the *Puritans of New England. It provided the social and ethical context in which the individual lived and worshipped. Its roots were in the covenant of grace between God and the individual, but it united the Puritan settlements not only in a spiritual bond but in a civil society which affected every part of their daily lives.

Covenant ideology has also played a role in contemporary *ecumenical thinking. The Nottingham *Faith and Order conference of 1964 invited members of the British Council of Churches 'to covenant together to work and pray for the inauguration of union by a date [which]... we dare to believe should be not later than Easter 1980'. It was to be a forlorn hope. In the light of continuing ecumenical discussions there was published in 1976 'Ten Propositions' for a Covenant of Unity. In its final form such a covenant of unity came before the Church of England Synod in 1982 and failed to gain acceptance.

Covenant ideology has therefore had a long and varied history since it first appeared in the revelation to ancient Israel. It has been central to the debate between Judaism and Christianity. It has, within both Judaism and Christianity, been the banner under which enthusiasm, sectarianism, and intolerance have flourished. It has not always succeeded in holding together the prevenient grace of God and the responsive obedience of the people of God which characterize many of the OT covenant traditions.

See also JEWISH–CHRISTIAN RELATIONS.   **Robert Davidson**

Borowitz, E. B., *Choices in Modern Jewish Thought* (1983).

Dupre, L., and Saliers, D. E., *Christian Spirituality: Post Reformation and Modern* (1989).

Eichrodt, W., *Theology of the Old Testament* (2 vols.; 1961; 1967).

Küng, H., *Judaism* (1992).

Neusner, J., *The Way of Torah: An Introduction to Judaism* (1979).

Nicolson, E. W., *God and His People: Covenant and Theology in the Old Testament* (1986).

Sanders, E. P., *Judaism: Practice and Belief 63 BCE–66 CE* (1992).

Vermes, G., *The Dead Sea Scrolls: Qumran in Perspective* (1977).

Watt, H., *Recalling the Covenanters* (1946).

creation, the activity by which *God confers existence on the universe. The belief that the *world owes its existence solely to the creative activity of God is inherited by Christianity from Judaism. According to traditional doctrine, creation is *ex nihilo*: the world is not made out of anything, nor is its production a process in which anything pre-existing changes. Creation is, moreover, entirely the activity of divine will; there may be evil forces in the world, but they do not participate in its production. And although the products of creation have their being 'in' God (Acts 17: 28), they are not components of him. Rather, the classic account takes the creator to be completely simple—to be identical, in fact, with the single act by which he both creates and knows the universe—whereas the products of creation are diverse and complex.

A number of foundational disputes turn at least in part on how creation is understood. The *Genesis account has God creating the world over a six-day period 'in the beginning', following which he rests. The world, however, continues to exist, and no further activity on God's part is presented as required for that. Rather, God's concern after the initial creation is with the well-being of humankind, with whom he interacts, and to whose stubborn misdeeds he responds with patience and *forgiveness, culminating in the purchase of our *salvation through the sufferings of *Jesus Christ. Once created, on this portrayal, the world is ontologically independent of God: it stands on its own, and both secondary and agent causes exercise real power. Because this is so, humans can be held responsible for actions freely undertaken, and for any evil those may involve. And while God holds great power and majesty on this view, he is not the simple and impassible pure act of the classical theologian. On the contrary, he is as changeable as we are: he observes, finds things out, and adjusts his plans to respond to new events.

Why should such a view have been thought unsatisfactory? In part, because it presents God as less than the completely perfect being classical theology demanded. The anthropomorphic God of most of scripture is subject to *time: experientially, the past is as lost to him, and the future as unreachable, as they are to us. And if the future contains undetermined and independent exercises of will by moral agents, then both God's knowledge and his sovereignty over creation appear compromised. More generally, to the extent God's role in the world is reduced to that of an observer, his *providence is made less pervasive; and if there are events he does not control his ends must be achieved reactively—by stratagem rather than fiat, which seems inconsonant with what is said elsewhere in scripture, that he has wrought all our works in us (Isa. 26: 12).

The *ex nihilo* doctrine also suggests a more involved God. Most theists would claim that even if the world had no beginning in time, a creator would still be necessary to explain its existence. But if, once present, the world sustains itself, it is hard to see what role a creator would have. And if the world did have a temporal beginning, there could still have been nothing short of the *being* of the world that was the product of divine fiat, since the *ex nihilo* doctrine rules out there being a *process* of the world coming to be. But if the first existence of the world requires a creator, then why not the rest? Indeed, the whole idea that the world sustains itself seems to be without foundation. Surely there is no activity by which it does so, and a mere disposition to continue in existence has no explanatory power. The disposition could not be grounded in any other descriptive feature or characteristic structure of things, lest we wonder in turn how that is sustained, and it could have no manifestation other than the continued being of the world—the very phenomenon that was thought to require explanation. So the idea of self-sustenance comes to nothing. It is simply a restatement of what we knew all along: that the world does continue to exist. If we are to have a genuinely explanatory account of the continued being of things, God's creative activity cannot be confined to a primordial time. He must be just as responsible for the universe lasting another moment as for its existing at all.

This need not be taken to imply that God creates the world anew at each instant: He is simply responsible for its entire existence. Creation and sustenance are the same activity, and have the same result—namely, being. But if divine action is responsible for the entire existence of the world, secondary causes may appear problematic. Popular understanding often treats natural causation as a productive relation, grounded in *scientific law, by which the world somehow bootstraps itself into the future, later states of affairs receiving their existence from earlier ones. If, by contrast, the existence of everything is directly caused by God, it can seem either that things are always overdetermined as to their existence, or that secondary causes are not truly efficacious.

Secondary causation need not, however, be taken as an operation that confers existence on things. As Hume pointed out, we observe no causal nexus in the world, and it is hard to see what such a thing would consist in. As for scientific laws, they are propositions, and propositions do not ground physical realities. It is the other way around: realities are needed to ground the truth of propositions. Moreover, it is not obvious that the fundamental principles of nature are diachronic. In classical physics, at least, action and reaction are simultaneous, not sequential, and laws measure relationships between variables that coexist rather than succeeding one another. If that is correct, then secondary causation is not a matter of the past conferring existence on the future. It is a matter of dynamic interaction, in which *conserved* quantities—momentum, energy, and the like—assume new, determinate manifestations. There is nothing unreal or redundant about secondary causation thus understood, and if we assume the world will persist, the predictive force of scientific laws remains untouched. All we need to surrender is the idea that the world persists by its own power.

Perhaps more troubling, from a religious perspective, are the implications of such a view of creation as regards human *freedom, God's knowledge and sovereignty, and the problem of *evil. If as creator God is directly responsible for all that is, then he should be responsible for the character and behaviour of the things in the world as well as their existence. And that would presumably include human behaviour. This squares with the scriptural passages which suggest the 'elect' are *predestined for salvation (Rom. 8: 29; Eph. 1: 4), since it places all human conduct under God's immediate sovereignty and providence. It also offers a satisfying account of *omniscience, since God's knowledge of the world is made complete simply by being founded in his intentions as creator. But this view appears to undercut human freedom and responsibility: if our actions occur by his own will, how can God find fault with us (Rom. 9: 19)? Rather, it would seem, God is the author of our sins, and so bears primary responsibility for moral evil.

One way to avoid this outcome is to abandon the supposition that lies at the heart of this problem: namely, that the exercise of God's will in creation is ontologically distinct from the moral choices of created agents, so that, if our decisions fall under his will, there must be some further decision on his part that stands as an independent, determining condition of them. The view of creation implicit in this supposition is analogous to the picture on which, once created, the world somehow bootstraps itself into the future. That is, we imagine that God first issues a creative command, and the command then causes the world to be. But this is just more bootstrapping. We have no concept of a process by which a command on God's part can produce anything. If there were such a process, moreover, God could retain sovereignty over it only by having created it as well. That would require a further command on his part, and we would be headed for an infinite regress. Better, then, for God simply to create the world, in such a way that *it*, not some imagined command, is the first expression of his creative will.

But if that is how creation works, moral agency can fall under divine providence without the decisions of created agents being caused, even by a decision on God's part. God and his creatures would be too closely united for that. Creaturely decisions, together with their defects, would still be predicated of created wills: it is we who decide as we do. But they would also be an expression of God's will, since it is he who creates us deciding as we do. Yet, because they are created directly, our decisions would be the *first* expression of God's will regarding them, and God's will is free. Thus, our decisions also would be free. Our deciding as we do counts as the *content* of God's will, not a consequence of it, and so is able to belong to the providential order without being determined by it. We might, indeed, still question that providence. We may wonder why God would choose to create a world in which creatures freely choose to do evil. But that is just the problem of evil, which was going to be a problem in any case.

A final issue concerns how God's own will in creation can be free. If we imagine God creates by selecting among preconceived 'possible worlds', it may not be, since his goodness might compel him to select the best. On the other hand, it may be that there is no best possible world, or that God is free to choose among a number of equal alternatives. Or, this deliberational model of creation may itself be mistaken, being more suited to moral choice than to anything we would ordinarily call creation. In human terms, creation is above all a matter of art—which need not, and in the end cannot, be confined to a plan. Perhaps, then, God's creative activity should be likened to spontaneous acts of human artistic creation, so that what comes first in the created order is not a plan but the reality itself. There is, after all, no need to guard against error.

Hugh J. McCann

Aquinas, Thomas, *Summa contra Gentiles*, 3. 64–102.
Calvin, John, *Institutes of the Christian Religion* (1559).
Edwards, Jonathan, *The Great Christian Doctrine of Original Sin Defended* (1758).
Freddoso, Alfred J. (ed.), *The Existence and Nature of God* (1983).
Helm, Paul, *The Providence of God* (1994).
Malebranche, Nicolas, *Dialogues on Metaphysics* (1688), ET (1980).
Morris, Thomas V. (ed.), *Divine and Human Action* (1988).

creeds are a peculiarly Christian phenomenon. Other faiths may have their systems of belief, but they do not express them in the same concise style or give the same religious importance to any formulation of them. One reason why Christianity differs from other *religions here is probably the distinctive way in which it defines itself in terms of the past events of Christ's life, *death, and *Resurrection, understood as *God's decisive act in *history. Furthermore in the early centuries of its life the *church lived in a hostile environment in which it struggled to define its identity over against Judaism, Roman religion, and many syncretistic forms of Hellenistic religion.

Three 'ecumenical' creeds, dating from those early centuries, still figure in the formularies and the worship of many churches today—the Apostles' Creed, the Nicene Creed, and the Athanasian Creed. The three are very different in their origins, their characters, and their roles, but one thing they do have in common: in each case the title is liable to mislead. The Apostles' Creed (despite ancient legends) was not composed by the Apostles; the Nicene Creed is not the creed adopted at the first Ecumenical Council at *Nicaea in 325; and the Athanasian Creed was not written by *Athanasius.

The earliest record we have of the Apostles' Creed in the precise form in which it is now used dates from the 8th century, but very similar forms can be traced back to 4th century Italy. It was used in *baptism, but that is the earliest evidence we have of the use of declaratory creeds in baptism. More indirect, but generally accepted, evidence points to the use of very similar words in an interrogatory form (spoken by the officiant rather than the baptisand) in use at baptisms at Rome in the 2nd century. The church at that period, though making much use of succinct statements or 'rules' of faith, was not worried by divergent formulations where the basic intent was the same. Our Apostles' Creed is thus a relatively late example of a family of baptismal creeds, widely used in the western church, whose origins can be traced back to the 2nd century. These credal forms were, no doubt, used not only at the actual baptism itself but also served as the basis for the catechetical instruction that preceded it. Very soon after its comparatively late appearance the form we know began to replace all other variants through the influence of Charlemagne. It also began to be used in the daily offices, as well as at baptism, at about the same time.

Our Nicene Creed, though not the actual creed adopted at the Council of Nicaea, belongs to the same family of creeds as the one promulgated by the Council. Its precise origin is obscure. The Council of *Chalcedon (451) refers to it as the creed of the second Ecumenical Council of Constantinople (381), though its exact relation to that council is not clear. Like the creed of the Council of Nicaea itself, it is a development of a typical baptismal creed of the eastern church, designed for the explicit purpose of excluding *Arian *heresy. It thus has the same threefold structure as the Apostles' Creed, but differs in style and ethos from it by the addition of negative emphases ('begotten not made') and more technical language (*homoousios* or 'of one substance with'). Despite this more explicit anti-heretical intention expressed in language not so obviously appropriate for *liturgical use, it began to be used in *eucharistic worship in the east in the 5th century, though it was not used in that way at Rome until the beginning of the 2nd millennium. The form that came to be adopted in the western church differed in one respect from the original eastern form. The addition of the one word *filioque asserted the procession of the *Holy Spirit from the Father *and the Son* instead of from the Father only. This was fiercely objected to by the eastern church. The change does represent a difference of theological approach between east and west, but the bitterness to which it gave rise probably derived more from disagreement about the *authority for making such changes than from the theological substance of the change itself.

The Athanasian Creed is a composition of a very different kind. It is a concise summary of orthodox teaching on the *Trinity and the *Incarnation for the guidance of teachers, emanating from southern Gaul in the 5th century. Its anti-heretical intentions are far more explicit than those of the Nicene Creed, and are reinforced by its introductory 'damnatory' clauses, affirming belief in the *faith taught in the Creed to be necessary for *salvation. It was never officially accepted in the east, but in the west it found its way into the liturgies of the Roman Catholic, Lutheran, and Anglican churches, despite not having been intended and being wholly unsuitable for such a role. Today such use, though not formally rescinded, is very rare indeed.

The story of the three creeds shows the diverse reasons that led to the development of creeds and the diverse uses to which they have been put. First and foremost they are designed to express the basic faith commitment of every believer, to which he or she subscribes at baptism. In eucharistic worship and the daily offices the creed follows the scripture readings and acts as a recollection of and a response to the whole gospel of which some section has been read. The creeds can also serve as a syllabus of instruction and a way of insisting on uniformity of doctrine. In that last role they have often functioned as instruments of political or ecclesiastical control. It is no accident that it was Charlemagne who secured the monopoly of the final form of the Apostles' Creed, and that it was Constantine at Nicaea and Theodosius at Constantinople who were most insistent on the need for a formula of belief that would exclude heretical dissension within their domains.

While the Catholic, *Eastern Orthodox, and Protestant churches have valued and used creeds in these various ways, there have also been groups stemming from the *Reformation that have been opposed to them altogether. Some, who have exalted the role of scripture as the utterly distinct Word of God, have classed all creeds in the category of human words which have no right to control the believer's faithful reading of scripture. Others, as in the *Quaker tradition, have objected to creeds as exercising an unacceptable restriction on the free movement of the Spirit. Today even those who judge the creeds overall to have provided a much-needed shape to Christian faith, exercising a salutary check on the vagaries of Christian understanding that are only too evident in the record of the church's history, are faced with new questions about the role and appropriate use of creeds in the present age.

Such uncertainty about the role of creeds has many roots. Most fundamentally we are more conscious than most previous generations of the difference of world-view between us and our forebears. This makes it more difficult for us to use formulations of a past age directly to give expression to our own deepest convictions. The early creeds were designed to summarize and safeguard the true understanding of scripture. But our recognition of the diversity of views within scripture makes us less certain of the viability of that goal; changes in the understanding of *revelation make that a much less plausible expectation today than it was in the past. Moreover, in pursuing that goal the framers of the creeds were inevitably and properly influenced by the particular concerns of their own age; thus the Nicene Creed was specifically directed to deal with the issues of the Arian controversy, where both sides were operating with presuppositions very different from those of the present time. Finally the frequent abuse of the creeds by civil or ecclesiastical authority to enforce conformity raises moral as well as intellectual doubts about the way creeds have been and might be used.

Reflections such as these do not rule out the use of creeds altogether, but they do suggest certain general principles about an appropriate attitude to them. It no longer seems reasonable to regard creeds as formulating unquestionable *truths from which no deviation is to be permitted. The way in which religious knowledge is attained does not allow for the possibility of truths of that kind. To treat creeds in that way serves the interests of institutional control rather than those of Christian truth.

But creeds still have a place in baptismal and other liturgical contexts, and in the teaching of the faith, provided it is the overall thrust of their affirmations rather than the detail of the letter to which appeal is made. Seen in that light they give expression to a continuity of structure in Christian faith down the ages. It is that with which we align ourselves in Christian worship, while acknowledging that there are bound to be major differences in the understanding of that faith between us and earlier generations—as there will also be between us and future believers. The original form of the Nicene Creed begins with 'We believe' rather than 'I believe', a form which better expresses the corporate rather than purely individual nature of credal formulations. In the teaching of the faith the Apostles' Creed is often, and appropriately, used as the framework for the teacher's exposition. But when used in that way it is more like a syllabus to be worked at than a set of propositions known to be true and calling only for expansion and clarification.

Maurice Wiles

Kelly, J. N. D., *Early Christian Creeds* (1950).
—— *The Athanasian Creed* (1964).
Küng, Hans, *Credo: The Apostles' Creed Explained for Today* (1992).
Pannenberg, Wolfhart, *The Apostles Creed: In the Light of Today's Questions* (1972).
Ritter, Adolf M., 'Creeds', in I. Hazlitt (ed.), *Early Christianity* (1991), 92–100.
Vinzent, M., and Kinzig, W., *Creeds and Credal Formulae of the Early Church* (forthcoming).
Young, Frances, *The Making of the Creeds* (1991).

cross and crucifixion,

cross and crucifixion, respectively, the instrument and manner of *Jesus' *death, which became, in turn, the most universally recognized iconographic *symbol of Christianity, and traditionally the paradigm of authentic *discipleship.

A combination of *torture and slow asphyxiation, crucifixion was a distinctively though not exclusively Roman method of execution, whose cruelty was matched by its shamefulness. That Jesus was killed by this means under Roman authority, the most certain historical fact about him, is embedded in the statement of the *creed, 'crucified under Pontius Pilate, he suffered, died, and was buried', and is expressed ritually by the 'sign of the cross' inscribed by Christians as a sign of their identity. 'The cross' stands as shorthand for the way in which God's victory over *sin and death is accomplished through the *incarnate Son's *obedient *suffering for others. The feast of the Exaltation of the Cross, traditionally celebrated on 14 September, expresses the remarkable way in which one of the ancient world's most grisly symbols of cruelty was transformed into a symbol of God's power.

The *paradox of God's good news of *salvation coming through a criminal's death is at the heart of *Paul's theology (Rom. 1: 16–17; 3: 21–6). Paul insisted that the experience of transforming power that came from the *resurrected Lord must always be held in tension with the suffering of the cross. In 1 Corinthians 1: 18–31 he grounds the unlikely existence of the Corinthian community in the surprising character of Jesus' *messiahship. The death of Jesus confounded the expectations of the world: its weakness and shamefulness contradicted the standards of divine power and honour valued by Greek wisdom. More decisively, for Jews who might have sought in Jesus the signs of messiahship, this mode of death was decisive negative proof, for Torah itself declared 'cursed be every man who hangs upon a tree' (Deut. 21: 23). That God raised Jesus in power meant that every human standard of judgement is put in question.

The cross becomes, for Paul, the fundamental paradigm for God's work of *reconciliation through Christ (2 Cor. 5: 16–21). God's wis-

dom and power is revealed through foolishness and powerlessness, so that the power can be seen as God's and not as human: 'Let the one who boasts, boast in the Lord' (1 Cor. 1: 31; 2 Cor. 10: 17). The way God worked through Jesus also becomes the pattern for Christian ministry. Discipleship and weakness, foolishness, *poverty, death, and even sin itself, are revalued in the light of the cross of Jesus: 'For our sakes God made him who did not know sin to be sin, so that in him, we might become God's righteousness' (2 Cor. 5: 21). For Paul, this exchange was accomplished by Jesus' obedient death on the cross: 'Christ has delivered us from the law's curse by becoming for us a curse, for it is written, "cursed be everyone who hangs upon a tree"' (Gal. 3: 13). Life is therefore now to be understood as life for others, even at the risk of the most dramatic loss to oneself. Having 'the mind of Christ' (1 Cor. 2: 16; Phil. 2: 1–11) means living according to what Paul calls 'the law of Christ', which he spells out as 'bearing one another's burdens' (Gal. 6: 2).

That the salvific and exemplary significance of Jesus' death is not simply a Pauline preoccupation is shown by such other early epistles as 1 Peter (see 2: 21–5) and Hebrews (see 9: 23–8; 13: 12), but above all by the canonical gospels, in each of which the Passion of Jesus—that part of the story extending from the Last Supper to the burial (see Mark 14: 1–15: 47; Matt. 26: 1–27: 66; Luke 22: 1–23: 56; John 13: 1–19: 42)—is not only a lengthy and detailed climax to the narrative, but also one prepared for by multiple literary anticipations (e.g. Mark 8: 31; 9: 31; 10: 33–4, and parallels; John 3: 14–15; 7: 33–9; 10: 17–18).

Although in general the accounts of Jesus' Passion have a historical basis, they are scarcely neutral reportage. They are written from the perspective of Christian belief in God's vindication of Jesus through Resurrection, and bear the evident marks of a community's reflection on Jesus' scandalous death in the light of scripture, especially texts such as Isa. 52–3 and Pss. 21 and 69 (LXX), which were not only now read in the light of Jesus' death, but were themselves used in the narrative to clothe the naked facts with the garments of scripture, so that, in the gospels, Jesus' death truly becomes, in Paul's words, how 'Christ died for our sins in accordance with the scriptures' (1 Cor. 15: 3). The meaning of Jesus' death is expressed most eloquently in the account of the meal, where Jesus gives his followers *bread as his *body and *wine as his *blood 'to be poured out on behalf of many' (Mark 14: 22–4; compare 1 Cor. 11: 23–5). The exemplary character of Jesus' sacrificial death is shown, in turn, by the demand on his disciples that they must 'drink the cup' that he has drunk (Mark 10: 38–45), and must 'take up the cross and follow' in his path of suffering for others (Mark 8: 34 and parallels; compare John 13: 15; 15: 9–17).

The cruciform character of discipleship was emphasized in the orthodox battle against various forms of *Gnostic Christianity in the 2nd century that tended to downplay both the *Incarnation and the suffering of Christ. Ignatius, Polycarp, Felicity, Perpetua understood authentic discipleship as following literally in the way of Jesus, and this *martyr piety extended itself, after the cessation of persecution, into the *ascetical life of *monasticism. Eusebius's account of *Constantine leading his soldiers into battle with a cross of gold and precious stones in response to a *vision suggests that the triumph represented by this symbol was not immune to political aggrandizement (*Life of Constantine*, 28–30).

Veneration of the cross is attested in *Jerusalem as early as the 4th century by the *Pilgrimage of Etheria* and has remained an element in the services of Good Friday. The centrality of the cross through the period of Christendom was evident in the forms of Christian architecture, in the choreography of the *liturgy, especially in the celebration of the *Eucharist, in the entire *sacramental system, and in every form of *art. Representations of the cross varied considerably, from crossed lines scratched on catacomb walls through realistic depictions of the tortured body to ornate and bejewelled celebrations of *Christus Victor*. The *Reformed tradition, reacting against Catholic *iconography, adopted an empty cross as symbol in place of the crucifix, and this can still distinguish a Protestant from a Catholic place of worship. The difficulty of actually living out a cruciform discipleship was expressed by Thomas à Kempis, *The Imitation of Christ*, 2. 11: 'Jesus has many who love his kingdom in heaven, but few who bear his cross … many admire his miracles, but few follow him in the humiliation of his cross'.

The Protestant *Reformation, especially in Martin *Luther, sought to restore the 'theology of the cross' to the heart of Christian identity in place of a culturally accommodating 'theology of glory' that was thought to have pervaded Catholicism. Thus, Luther on Gal. 5: 11: 'Therefore it is unavoidable that, when the Gospel flourishes, the stumbling block of the cross will follow; otherwise it is sure that the devil has not really been attacked but only been gently caressed' (*Lectures on Galatians*, 1535). In such 20th-century theologians as *Barth and *Tillich, the cross stood as the challenge of faith to human endeavour even in the form of religion itself: 'Christianity claims that in the cross of Christ the final victory in this struggle has been reached, but even in claiming this … that which is rightly said about the cross of Christ is wrongly transferred to the life of the church, whose ambiguities are denied …' (Tillich, *Systematic Theology*, iii. 104).

In the late 20th century, the central place of the cross within the Christian tradition has come under severe historical and ideological criticism. The passion narratives of the gospels have been criticized for their portrayal of Jewish involvement in the death of Jesus. More fundamentally, some scholars challenge the assumption that all of earliest Christianity was equally characterized by a death and Resurrection *christology. Is it possible that the Pauline fascination with death and Resurrection triumphed over other equally early versions of the 'Jesus movement' that focused on Jesus the teacher? The passion accounts are therefore understood not as interpretations of events but rather as fictions that retroject mythic understandings of Jesus back into history. A variety of theories have thus suggested 'trajectories' of development from hypothetical gospel sources untouched by death and Resurrection christology (such as, purportedly, 'Q'), to Gnostic writings such as the Coptic *Gospel of Thomas*. Such theories have little to recommend them beyond the pleasures of supposition, but in an atmosphere in which the traditional canon of scripture (see BIBLE) itself is regarded as an instrument of ideology susceptible to revision, they become calls for the reconsideration of Christianity on another basis than that of the cross.

Another form of ideological criticism challenges the theological appropriateness of the cross in an age of liberation. Based at least in part on a supposed connection between images of the crucifixion, masochism, and violent pornography, *feminist and womanist theologians in particular have considered the cross a symbol too easily co-opted by the forces of oppression as an instrument by which the downtrodden (in particular women and people of colour) can find a meaning in their subjugation, thus preventing them from seeking positive social change. In this reading, the cross stands as a stumbling-block to full human actualization, and as a symbol too freighted with negative connotations for contemporary Christians. Such a view is based on an attenuated understanding of symbol as well as the odd premiss that the cross is simply one malleable or disposable symbol among others, rather than the essential pointer to God's revelation through Jesus Christ.

While neither the sad examples of pathology passing as piety nor the human capacity to manipulate symbols should be minimized, it still seems that the contemporary discomfort with the symbol of the cross derives primarily from an alienation from the classic Christian tradition, which regarded the cross not as an excuse for passivity and will-lessness, but rather as a paradoxical sign of the greater life that can come from the most radical sort of self-donation. The sign of the cross is a sign of hope in God's power to rule the world with righteousness. Just as the cross confounded ancient Jews and Greeks by contradicting their conventional wisdom about God, so does it remain an obstinate challenge to every age that seeks to identify God's rule with human comfort.

Luke Timothy Johnson

Brown, R.E., *The Death of the Messiah: From Gethsemane to the Grave, a Commentary on the Passion Narratives in the Four Gospels* (2 vols.; 1994).
Guenon, R., *Symbolism of the Cross*, ET (1958).
Hengel, M., *Crucifixion in the Ancient World and the Folly of the Message of the Cross*, ET (1977).
Pelikan, J., *Jesus through the Ages: His Place in the History of Culture* (1985).
Schneider, B., *Kreuz, Kruzifix: Eine Bibliographie* (1973).

Cupitt, Don (1934–). The work of the notoriously prolific philosopher-theologian Don Cupitt has been redrawing the boundaries of radical religious thought for more than twenty years. Cupitt was born and raised in Lancashire, and after his ordination in the Church of England he served there as a priest between 1959 and 1962, but returned to Cambridge University (where he had studied both natural sciences and theology) in 1962 and has taught there ever since. As a Fellow of Emmanuel College, Cambridge, from 1966, and later as University Lecturer in the Philosophy of Religion, he has influenced generations of students, but his impact on contemporary *theology owes far more to his many books, essays, articles, and broadcasting, above all to the BBC television series *The Sea of Faith* (1984). Each of his works has represented a new stage in an intellectual and spiritual journey away from *orthodoxy, embracing a series of increasingly radical theological positions.

In *Taking Leave of God* (1980), perhaps his best-known book, Cupitt parted company with 'theological *realism'—that is, belief in God as 'an actually-existing independent individual being'. Cupitt argued that theism, in this sense, was not true, but was much more interested in arguing that it did not work: it was surplus to religious requirements, at best, given Cupitt's understanding of the *spirituality appropriate for a 'fully-unified autonomous human consciousness', and in practice it subverted them, as it took away the possibility of a genuine 'disinterestedness'. The alternative to theological realism was 'expressivism', or 'subjectivism', in which 'belief in the God of Christian faith is an expression of allegiance to a particular set of values'. This position is now widely known as 'non-realism', because of its critique of realism, but this can be misleading: Cupitt's claim was not that God was not 'real', but that 'the sense in which God is real is given in the language and practice of religion' and nowhere else. Moreover, Cupitt was moving towards a universal non-realism in which *all* meanings, truths, and values (not just religious ones) were seen as the product of human creativity. In *The Sea of Faith*, Cupitt called this 'radical humanism', and it is this idea that he has pushed further in each of his books since then. As *Kant's influence has given way to the influence of *postmodernist philosophers in Cupitt's works, however, the old notions of the *human have gone the same way as the old notions of the divine, and in the 1990s his writings have progressively *'demythologized' the human subject.

Cupitt's ever more radical reflections, inseparable from a characteristically polemical, playful, often dazzlingly inventive style, have been extensively criticized not only by traditional realists of various kinds, but also by those who read postmodern theory and culture very differently. Nevertheless, few would deny that Cupitt has succeeded in raising questions that have become central to contemporary theological debate, and his answers, if sometimes infuriating, are never less than fascinating.   **Colin Crowder**

Cupitt, D., *The Sea of Faith*, 2nd edn. (1994).

—— *After All: Religion Without Alienation* (1994).

Crowder, Colin (ed.), *God and Reality: Essays on Christian Non-Realism* (1997).

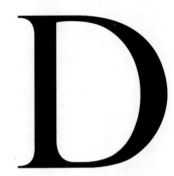

damnation, see HELL; JUDGEMENT.

Daniel, book of. In Christian bibles, the book of Daniel appears among the major *prophets whereas the Jewish tradition regards it as one of the Writings, the third and least authoritative division of scriptural books. This fact in itself indicates the book's distinctive importance for the development of Christian thought. The Jewish and many Christian traditions also disagree over its contents. The Septuagint, the ancient Greek translation that became the first scriptures of the nascent church, contains additional stories and prayers in Daniel accepted as canonical by Orthodox and Catholic Christians but regarded by Protestants as *apocryphal.

The book falls into two clear sections. Chapters 1–6 recount various adventures of Daniel and his friends as members of an intellectual Jewish élite living in exile in Babylon. As well as being a model of pious resistance to an alien and God-defying ruling power, and of the missionary importance of faithful witness to the one God, Daniel is presented as a divinely gifted interpreter of other people's *dreams and *visions whose wisdom raises him to the highest offices of state. Chapters 7–12 move into a different realm as they recount the visions accorded to Daniel himself concerning the rise and fall of future kingdoms and God's final judgement of the dead.

The vivid exemplary tales in the first part of Daniel have inspired a rich tradition of artistic representation. His rescue from the lions' den (Dan. 6), the writing of the message *Mene mene tekel upharsin* on the wall (Dan. 5), and, from the Greek text of Daniel, the vindication of the chaste Susannah from the accusations of the lecherous elders (Dan. 13) have formed part of Christian *iconography from the Roman catacombs to the latest children's interactive CD Rom.

Together with the book of *Revelation, which itself draws heavily on Daniel, the second half of the book, with its complex *angelology and vision of a final battle, is a key source of the characteristic imagery of Christian *apocalypticism. With its direct engagement with the problems of understanding visions and texts, the book also acts as a sanctioned model for the *allegorical and *typological interpretation of scripture which so shaped the thought-world of the Christian church. When Daniel reinterprets *Jeremiah's prophecy of a 70-year gap until the restoration of the *Temple as meaning seventy *weeks* of years (Dan. 9: 1–24; Jer. 25: 11), the way is opened to an unending quest by subsequent interpreters to unlock the secrets of the enigmatic numbers and allegorical beasts which abound in the visionary chapters of Daniel itself.

Traditionally, the book is taken at face value as Daniel's own work arising from the Babylonian *exile. His prophetic powers in predicting the later history of the Greek and Roman empires act as a guarantee that the yet to be fulfilled prophecies of the end-time the book contains are accurate in turn. On this view, to doubt the historicity of Daniel undercuts the authority of scripture and blinds us to the awful warnings of imminent disaster which the book contains and which successive generations have succeeded in applying to their own times, so far to be proved wrong.

As early as the 3rd century AD, however, the anti-Christian polemicist Porphyry alleged that the book was a pseudonymous product of the Maccabean period and that most of its prophetic portions were actually written after the event. Most modern biblical scholars would agree, albeit with some refinements. The issue of Daniel's authorship is as clear a point of divergence between incompatible approaches to the *biblical text as will be found within the Christian fold.

Leaving aside such questions, the influence of Daniel on Christian thought is considerable. *Jesus' frequent references to himself as the Son of Man hark back to the one 'like a son of man' in Dan. 7: 13 who is given eternal dominion over all peoples. This link has provided fuel for the cosmological and eschatological development of *christology. The last chapter of Daniel contains the only explicit reference to a bodily *resurrection followed by judgement to be found in the Hebrew canon of the OT. This passage is crucial for the historical development of the Christian doctrine of the resurrection of the body.

In many ways, Daniel is set apart from the other books of the canonical Hebrew bible. The Christian tradition has drawn on these unique features to ground and advance its own characteristic development.

See also FUNDAMENTALISM. **Hugh S. Pyper**

Casey, M., *Son of Man: The Interpretation and Influence of Daniel 7* (1979).
Collins, J. J., *Daniel* (1993).
Davies, P. R., *Daniel* (1985).

Dante Alighieri (1265–1321). By common consent, Dante's *Divine Comedy* is a masterpiece of world literature; it is also, patently, a Christian work, welling up from the writer's conviction that he is called to recreate the gospel message for his own day.

Following biblical precedents, the *Comedy* takes full account of the human instinct to respond to a good tale. The narrative is simple in outline: it opens with Dante lost, physically and spiritually; it purports to be the veracious account of how the poet was rescued from his plight by being led through the three realms of the afterlife—*hell, *purgatory, and *heaven—and culminates in the fulfilment of Dante's will after a vision of the *Trinity and of Christ within it. The unfolding of the plot is carefully staged to take account of the differing abilities of readers. The journey through hell brims with incident, and the characters met there are often portrayed with an astonishing blend of subtlety and horrific vigour. As befits the realm of the painful recovery of pristine beauty, purgatory is distinguished by a quietly meditative tone, where express reflection on some of the major issues involved in the journey begins to be heard. Readers intellectually confident enough to venture beyond purgatory are rewarded by an account of a journey through heaven that is full of movement of every sort, as the pilgrim shoots through the realm of the stars: there he meets a wide panoply of *saints, and refines his mind and heart as he increasingly penetrates central Christian mysteries before finally glimpsing directly the triune God and being granted a fleeting understanding of how the divine and the human can be united in the Son.

The attraction the *Comedy* has exercised is not, however, due simply or even principally to its being a tale well told. In broad outline and often in minute detail the poem is the product of a powerful, passionate, yet disciplined religious imagination, which, despite the multiplicity of its creations, sets itself throughout to explore two basic questions: what does it mean to be human? and, how is the divine to be found in the human?

It is significant that Dante sets out to answer the former question first, for the degree of success of that attempt tells us much about the poet's Christianity. It is striking that Dante's guide throughout hell and purgatory is the Roman poet Virgil. The choice of this figure is motivated in part by sheerly poetic considerations: Dante never ceased to believe that *poetry, with its rhythmic and imaginative power, could carry persuasion where cold prose might fail. Operative too, however, is the political conviction that the author of the *Aeneid* would by his very presence signal the importance of the worldwide empire centred in Rome that alone, to Dante's mind, could curb and channel the wild passions that disfigured the societies of Europe, of Italy in particular. Most of all, though, the choice of a pagan guide signalled Dante's belief that the *moral realm was humanity's special province, the area where, even after the *Fall of *Adam and Eve, human beings could through their own powers achieve due mastery in theory and practice. Indeed the vehemence of Dante's recurrent strictures, and the at times almost overpowering horror of the scenes depicted in hell, are scarcely intelligible unless one sees in them the frustration and anger of a man convinced that human beings could have shaped immeasurably better their individual lives and the societies in which they played out those lives, if only they had had the will to do so.

Supremely civilized though he may be, Virgil is from the outset of the *Comedy* a fatally flawed figure, his limitation serving to illustrate the plight of humankind when left to its own devices, without the benefit of Christ. For however much the human being may strive for self-perfection within society, without the revelation of Christ he or she will not attain to belief in the Trinity or to baptism, both necessary for salvation. The benefits of Christianity are indicated, negatively, in the state of eternally unfulfilled desire to which even the most virtuous of pagans are condemned in *limbo, the uppermost circle of hell—a point of which we are continually reminded in the wistfully attractive figure of Virgil throughout the first two parts of the poem. Positively, heaven is portrayed predominantly as an extended hymn to the joy experienced as the intellect expands its horizons through increasing knowledge of God and his ways and the will delights in the deeper knowledge thus gained.

Theoretical explanation plays an increasing role as the journey to God progresses, with much of the *Paradiso* given over to discourses on major points of doctrine. None the less, the poem makes its overwhelming impression mainly through the myriad encounters with memorable personalities—whether, in hell, twisted by evil even when they retain more than a vestige of tragic grandeur; or, in purgatory, immensely human in their yearningly unfulfilled state; or, in heaven, unfailingly courteous as they reflect both the light of God and concern for the wayfarer's unceasing questions. Here native talent and central conviction match, for if we owe it to Dante's skill as a narrator of genius that so many characters from his poem now people our imagination, that skill seems to have worked on and been nourished by the belief that God is to be met above all (or his absence to be felt) in human personalities. This conviction is epitomized in the figure of Beatrice, who takes over as Dante's guide when Dante approaches the heavenly realm from which Virgil is eternally excluded.

The reunion of the poet with the woman whom he had loved at a distance since they were both children is a moment of intense, and for Dante, painful surprise: having toiled down into the depths of hell and then up the stark ridges of Mount Purgatory, and having been led by Virgil to expect a joyful welcome from Beatrice, the poet is scornfully greeted with the question: 'What are you doing here?' (*Purg.* 30. 74). She drives home sharply and relentlessly the point that Dante has largely remained a spectator to the suffering caused by sin: he must now repent of his own specific waywardness, must be purged of and actively will the opposite of the sinful tendencies which had blocked him from heaven. This is no external moralizing, for to enter heaven (which is the next stage of Dante's journey) is to become part of a society whose members delight in reflecting the creative goodness of God. Dante is prepared for the final vision of the Trinity and of the God-man by becoming accustomed to the variously dazzling goodness of the saints encountered: the elegantly affectionate courtesy of Beatrice herself, for instance; the judicious lucidity of Thomas *Aquinas; the plain, even rough, rhetoric of Dante's soldier ancestor Cacciaguida; and the fiery anger of St Peter as he contemplates the radical unfaithfulness of his recent successors on the papal throne.

The *Comedy* continues to draw an immense readership. All, whether believers or not, are attracted by the poem's outstanding literary qualities. Many, though, return to the work time and again precisely because it nurtures their faith, because it presents in its essence a Christianity with which they can identify and by which they can be profoundly and authentically challenged. Often in the course of history Christianity's *apologists have chosen to extol the value of *grace by denigrating the human nature which that grace purports to heal and elevate. Dante, however, was an ardent champion of the strength and beauty of human nature: to the literary centrality of human personality corresponds the intellectual centrality of his belief in the presence and importance of free will. He twice calls freedom of the will God's greatest gift to humankind (*Par.* 5. 19–22 and *Mon.* I. 12. 6), and he embodies the same belief in his placing of lengthy discourses on free will at the heart of the *Comedy* (*Purg.* 16–18); indeed this view is strikingly if implicitly present in the opening narrative of the *Comedy* proper (*Inf.* 3), which portrays the ceaseless yet useless running of those who in life had been so pusillanimous as never to have moved themselves to decide for or against good. The Christianity of the *Comedy* continues to attract because the grace it preaches is one which nourishes and brings to fulfilment a human nature in which God already delights.

There is never the slightest danger in the *Comedy* that the championing of human nature will degenerate into sentimentality. It scarcely could, when its author penned the entire poem during his permanent exile from Florence, imposed by factional politicians with no interest in justice. It is a sobering thought that Dante's imaginative richness is owed in no small measure to the material poverty which forced him for almost the last twenty years of his life to criss-cross Italy absorbing the diversity of its language, culture, and peoples. It is, in fact, an enduring strength in Dante's greatest work that it combines qualities not often linked: to the poet's sensitivity is allied the political exile's realism; to linguistic flair is added breadth of experience; and vivid imagination is coupled with an admirable capacity for abstract thought and a scholarly concern for precision of philosophical and theological expression. In many of these skills Dante had trained himself before or alongside the writing of his poetic masterpiece. To his early years belong most of his lyric poetry and the elusively charming *Vita nuova* (*New Life*), in which a number of love poems are gathered within a narrative and critical framework. During the first years of his exile, Dante in *Il Convivio* (*The Banquet*) set out to make available in the vernacular some of the philosophical truths which he had previously only hinted at in his allegorical poetry; about the same time he began a theoretical discussion of language and poetry in his quest for the best form of Italian (*De vulgari eloquentia*, *On Eloquence in the Vernacular*). In his later years he argued at length, in the *Monarchia*, for the independence of the political authority of the emperor against the papalists who would see it as deriving from the religious authority of the pope.

Dante's mind was not formed principally by Christian *theology in the technical sense. He was steeped in the bible, through reading and through participation in the *liturgy; and he had more than a passing acquaintance with some of the works of several giants of the theological tradition, notably *Augustine, Boethius, Bernard of Clairvaux, *Anselm, and Aquinas. The two authors who most nourished his thought, however (leaving aside the special case of the bible), were *Aristotle and Virgil. His devotion to these two, together with his extensive acquaintance with the Latin and vernacular poetic traditions, gives an eclectic richness to his thought. Though no wide-eyed optimist, his belief in the fundamental capacity of human beings to shape their destiny contrasts with the dominance of Augustinianism in the professional theology of his day. Dante's views are often likened to those of Aquinas, whom he greatly admired; broadly speaking the comparison is apt, but in

significant ways the poet went further than the theologian in attributing a relative autonomy to nature *vis-à-vis* grace.

Christopher Ryan

Dante Alighieri, *The Divine Comedy*, ed. and trans. with notes, by R. M. Durling and R. L. Martinez (3 vols.; 1996–).

Charity, A. C., *Events and Their Afterlife: The Dialectics of Christian Typology in the Bible and Dante* (1966).

Foster, K., *The Two Dantes and Other Studies* (1977).

Gilson, E., *Dante the Philosopher* (1939; ET 1948).

Imbach, R., *Dante, la philosophie et les laïcs* (1996).

Mastrobuono, A. C., *Dante's Journey of Sanctification* (1990).

Ryan, C., 'The Theology of Dante', in R. Jacoff (ed.), *The Cambridge Companion to Dante* (1993).

Singleton, C. S., *Dante's Commedia: Elements of Structure* (1954).

——*Journey to Beatrice* (1958).

darkness, see LIGHT.

David, the shepherd boy and harpist who, according to the biblical account, became king of united *Israel, gave it its capital in *Jerusalem and inaugurated its *Temple worship, is a figure with many resonances in Christian tradition. God's pledge of an eternal kingdom to David and his descendants in 2 Samuel 7 gave rise to the expectation of a *messiah in Israel when the dynasty itself fell. In the NT, *Jesus is identified as the heir to that promise to David and addressed as Son of David, but the gospels also distance themselves from this tradition, whether through an anxiety that Jesus should not be cast too much in David's mould or through genuine difficulties over substantiating such claims. The way David appears in the genealogies of Jesus shows this. In both Matthew and Luke the line is traced from David to Jesus, but through Joseph, raising obvious problems in the context of the concurrent claim of a virgin birth. Whatever the reality of this genealogical relationship, David is certainly adopted as a type of Christ. His kingship, with its vicissitudes and triumphs, foreshadows the perfection of Christ's rule. That rule, however, is shown to be a radically different thing from the establishment of an earthly kingdom.

David's place in the development of Christian thought is also ensured by the Jewish tradition that made him the author of the book of *Psalms. This makes him a patron and a source of inspiration for both poets and musicians. His role in the inauguration of Temple worship, at least according to the book of Chronicles, also gives him an honoured place in the development of Christian *liturgy. As the author of a biblical book, David is enrolled in the ranks of the *prophets. This opens the way for the long tradition of messianic interpretation of the psalms which the NT adopts and elaborates, reading them as texts where Jesus' royal ancestor foresees the humiliation and glory of his successor.

All this leads to the picture of the pious and kingly musician who so often appears in illuminated manuscripts of the psalms. However, David's human frailty is made plain in 2 Samuel, especially in the account of his adultery with Bathsheba and his hand in the death of her husband Uriah. Piety may lead to the suppression of this episode in favour of the image of an ideal king. It also gave rise, however, to a tradition that laid stress on David as the exemplary penitent, an impression reinforced by the confessional spirit of many psalms. For some writers, for instance Ambrose, his sin is almost justified in that it leads to his turning to God. This became the dominant reading of his character in the medieval period and reinforced the status of the psalms in personal devotion and the practice of *penance.

In this emphasis on David as a model of personal piety, we must not forget his political significance. For the rulers of Christendom, David's God-given kingship was a model to be envied. Several royal houses had legends of Davidic descent and others adopted Davidic ceremonies and titles as evidence of their divinely favoured status. Conversely, David's rise from humble origins and his campaigns against his predecessor Saul can inspire more democratic and even revolutionary sentiments. The boy David, with his youthful vigour and charm, who defeats the giant Goliath through a combination of cunning, courage, and divine favour becomes a byword for the victory of the underdog. He also becomes an exemplar for Christian youth in his obedience and enterprise. In portraying the young David, Michelangelo and other *artists of the *Renaissance found a way of bringing the classical tradition's Apollonian ideals of beauty and athleticism into the Christian mainstream.

The character of David still holds its fascination, as the steady supply of novels, plays, and films based on the biblical account attests. Contemporary writers are more likely to be inspired by the complexity and contradiction of the remarkable character in Samuel than with the more sanitized versions that traditional piety has produced. His relationships with Saul, with his own sons, with his wives and with his beloved *friend Jonathan display the ambivalences of love, hate, and power in a way that has seldom been matched. Indeed, it has been claimed by Robert Alter that David as depicted in Samuel is the first rounded character in world literature. As such, his importance in the development of the literary tradition in Christian cultures and therefore for contemporary conceptions of both *humanity and *masculinity has yet to be fully explored.

Hugh S. Pyper

Brueggemann, W., *David's Truth in Israel's Imagination and Memory* (1985).

Frontain, R.-J., and Wojcik, J., *The David Myth in Western Literature* (1980).

Heym, S., *The King David Report* (1973).

Dead Sea Scrolls

Dead Sea Scrolls is the popular name given to the manuscripts written in Hebrew, Aramaic, and Greek on animal skin, papyrus, and copper that were discovered between 1947 and 1961 along the west littoral of the Jordan fault. A more appropriate name reflects Modern Hebrew usage: Scrolls of the Judaean Desert. The core of the discoveries was found in eleven caves ranging slightly west and up to nearly 3 kilometres north of the Wadi Qumran on the barren north-west shore of the Dead Sea. Other scrolls, basically unrelated to Qumran, were found in the Zealot fortress at Masada and in caves elsewhere. The eleven caves are numbered in order of discovery. Caves One (Spring 1947) and Eleven (February 1956) yielded the best preserved scrolls while Cave Four contained over 10,000 fragments. The total number of manuscripts recovered is over 800, a remarkable *archaeological find by any count.

The regnant theory is that, with the probable exception of Caves Three and Seven, the Qumran caves contained the remains of a library belonging in antiquity to a discrete Jewish community that some scholars identify as Essenes, others as Sadducees or Zealots, and yet others as a heretofore unknown Jewish sect. The library

may have contained as many as 1,000 scrolls by the time that the community building, located just north of the wadi, was destroyed by Vespasian's Roman troops in the spring of 68 AD. The fact that all the scrolls in Cave Four were found in fragments, many no larger than a thumbnail, may indicate the discovery of this presumably seditious literature by the soldiers and a subsequent attempt to destroy it. It is also the main reason for the long delays in publication of the bulk of the Cave Four material.

The only serious challenge to the library theory is one that claims that the scrolls were brought down to this desolate area from a range of sources in Jerusalem to secure them from just such destruction by the Romans. The fact that not a single fragment was found in the ruins of the community building and that only in one or two cases is the same scribe's handwriting in evidence in all the plethora of manuscripts might support this challenge. Against it are the facts that all the Qumran literature indicates a solar calendar of 364 days, whereas the calendar operative in Jerusalem at the time was lunar, and that the theology expressed in the scrolls is broadly coherent and distinct from other known forms of *Judaism at the time.

All the Qumran literature is religious or theological—a remarkable find for that reason alone. The library contains three basic kinds of Jewish literature: books known from the standard (Masoretic) tradition of the Jewish scriptures (nearly one-third of the scrolls); non-Masoretic or *apocryphal books known up to now only in translations preserved by the church (about a quarter); the rest representing hitherto unknown literature, much of it expressive of a cohesive and distinctive set of beliefs and polity.

The first fifty years of study of the scrolls had an impact on current understandings of the origins of Christianity in a number of ways. The most important of these was a dramatic revision in the history of early Judaism out of which first Christianity and then Rabbinic Judaism arose in the 1st century of the common era. Prior to their discovery it was commonly thought that early Judaism in the centuries before Christ had one normative expression, Pharisaism, and a few heterodox parties enumerated by Josephus and Philo. Now it is universally accepted that Judaism in the Second Temple period was quite diverse. This raises questions as to the historical accuracy of the portrayal of early Judaism within the NT.

It appears also that many Jewish communities in the period were highly *eschatological, even *apocalyptic in thinking, expecting God to intervene in *history to combat evil and establish a reign of righteousness. When Pharisaism was viewed as normative for the period it was thought that adherents to Judaism believed that *prophecy or *revelation had ceased at the time of Ezra and Nehemiah in the mid-5th century BC when the Torah was brought from Babylon. Far more Jews than Pharisaic doctrine indicates believed that God continued to reveal the divine will. Indeed, the Qumran Scrolls may imply that this emphasis on divine intervention was one response to a much more oppressive Roman regime than either Josephus or the NT seems to portray. The NT gives some evidence of the harshness of the occupying power, but shows more animus towards the parent Jewish community than against the empire.

The discovery for the first time at Qumran of some books of the apocrypha and pseudepigrapha in the original languages confirms that these writings, which were ultimately excluded from the Hebrew bible, had a wide circulation during this period. Their presence reinforces the impression that the canon of scripture at Qumran was open-ended. Although the Torah and the prophets had been accepted in their present form probably by 400 BC, the other writings were quite fluid. Even within the accepted canon, the text itself was not standardized until the end of the 1st century of the Christian era.

Study of the scrolls has also clarified the considerable impact of *Hellenism on Judaism. A major reason that the community at Qumran separated itself was the extent to which the priesthood and government in Jerusalem had been influenced by Greek ways, yet even Qumran was minimally influenced by Greek culture and thinking.

In their own view, however, they were the community of the renewed *covenant, the true *Israel that faithfully reflected the original desert community at the foot of Mount Sinai. The Qumran community believed that their mission was in part to maintain a landing strip for angelic armies whom they would join in the final battle to defeat the forces of evil on earth. They were a priestly people, believing in two *messiahs, of Aaron and of David. They took their clues for self-understanding and community organization from their particular interpretations of scripture, focusing especially on the biblical laws of purity and holiness (Lev. 17–26). They firmly believed that scripture addressed the end-time, that they lived in the eschaton and that therefore scripture spoke directly to them, interpreted by a special key revealed by God to their founding leader, the Teacher of Righteousness.

Similarly the scrolls have also shown that the text of Jewish scripture, like that of the NT, was comparatively fluid until the concept of verbal inspiration in the 1st century replaced earlier prophetic views of shamanistic inspiration. Stabilization towards a proto-Masoretic Hebrew text was not complete until the end of the 1st century of the common era, hence the considerable fluidity in the texts of scripture quoted and paraphrased in NT literature.

After fifty years' study of the Judaean Desert Scrolls it is clear that they are indeed the most important discovery of modern times for understanding the bible, though perhaps not in ways that might be imagined. While they contain nothing directly pertaining to early Christianity, or indeed directly to Rabbinic Judaism, they have considerably altered understanding of what early Judaism, which gave rise to those two religions in the 1st century of the common era, was really like. They have shown how oppressive the Roman occupation of Palestine was and the circumstances that caused both the rapid Hellenization of Christianity and the equally strong resistance to Hellenization established by the emerging Rabbinic Judaism. They have shown how deeply Jewish the *New Testament was even in its polemic against Pharisaic/Rabbinic expressions of Judaism. Finally, they have clarified the remarkable reliability of the Hebrew text of the *Old Testament at the same time as they have shown how adaptable the text was to new emerging expressions of Judaism in the period before the fall of *Jerusalem to Rome in 70 AD.

James A. Sanders

Carr, David M., 'Canonization in the Context of Community: An Outline of the Formation of the Tanakh and the Christian Bible', in Richard D. Weiss and David M. Carr (eds.), *A Gift of God in Due Season: Essays on Scripture and Community in Honor of James A. Sanders* (1996).

Evans, Craig A., *Jesus and His Contemporaries: Comparative Studies* (1995), 83–154.

Flint, Peter W., 'Of Psalms and Psalters: James Sanders's Investigation of the Psalms Scrolls', in Weiss and Carr (eds.), *A Gift of God in Due Season* (1996), 65–83.

Martinez, Florentino Garcia, *The Dead Sea Scrolls Translated* (1994).

Reed, Stephen A., Lundberg, Marilyn J., Phelps, Michael B., *The Dead Sea Scrolls Catalogue: Documents, Photographs and Museum Inventory Numbers* (1994).

Sanders, James A., 'The Impact of the Scrolls on Biblical Studies', *The Proceedings of the 1996 International Conference on the Dead Sea Scrolls* (1999), 47–57.

Scanlin, Harold, *The Dead Sea Scrolls and Modern Translations of the Old Testament* (1993).

Stegeman, Hartmut, *The Library of Qumran* (1994).

Wise, M., Abegg M., Cook, E., *The Dead Sea Scrolls: A New Translation* (1996).

death is the one inevitability facing every person, and it appears to be natural to fear it. Such fear attaches to death itself, to what might lie beyond it (see HEAVEN; HELL), or to the sense that, if death is the end of all consciousness, achievements in this life have no lasting meaning, and wickedness and injustices go for ever unrecompensed. Fear also attaches to the process of dying, especially in an age when, at least in the developed world, witnessing a death is rare: fantasies about what dying might be like are more frightening than reality.

At the heart of all *religions is a solution to the problem of death. For Christians death is definitive, occurring 'once only' (Heb. 9: 27). Reincarnation, either to undergo a repetition of the same life, or in a different form contingent upon the moral quality of one's previous existence, has never been part of the Christian answer to the unresolved nature of human life. Resolution is achieved by union with *God, made possible through Christ's death and announced by his *Resurrection. Christianity is unique in that its solution is brought about by the death of its central figure, indeed of God himself, a death which is ignoble and yet graphically described. Christians not only have an assurance of the redemption obtained by Jesus' sacrifice but also a model of Christian dying (see CROSS AND CRUCIFIXION).

This model has always been both disturbing and reassuring to Christians, disturbing because its squalor and God-forsakenness is offensive to those who emphasize *Jesus' divinity. Indeed it was disturbing to the disciples (Luke 24: 17) until their experience of the risen Christ showed them its significance. Most famously this disturbance led to *Docetism, the denial that Christ truly suffered in his dying, condemned as heretical by *Irenaeus and other fathers of the early church. Conversely the model is reassuring because Christ shared the fears which people have about their own death.

Jesus was afraid of death. In Gethsemane he prayed to be spared the conviction and execution that lay ahead. His death was heralded by a desolate cry to God, from whom he apparently felt utterly separated. He died before the thieves who were crucified with him, but there is no sense that this was because he accepted or embraced death. His dying was full of physical and mental anguish: it was thoroughly human. Christians facing death can have the consolation that if they fear what lies ahead, if they fear humiliation, physical pain, or spiritual separation, so did their saviour.

Subsequent generations cultivated the ideal of a calm approach to death in full assurance of *faith in God and at peace with him. The example for this was not Jesus but the early *martyrs, especially Stephen, the first martyr. 'Stephen, filled with the Holy Spirit, gazed into heaven and saw the glory of God, and Jesus standing at God's right hand. As they were stoning him, Stephen said in invocation, "Lord Jesus, receive my spirit"' (Acts 7: 55, 59). The emphasis is on the action of the *Holy Spirit in someone *obedient to the will of God. Stories of holiness maintained in the face of agonizing deaths grew more elaborate: St Lawrence (d. 258) is said to have lain 'broiling upon the burning coals, as merry and quiet as though he lay upon sweet red roses'. The more authentically attested ability of Thomas *More to joke with his executioners as he was led to the scaffold ('I pray you to see me safe up, and for my coming down let me shift for myself') carries the same message.

Calmness in the face of death manifested a clear conscience stemming from a life rightly lived. It implied that this person was ready to meet God and would be received into eternal life in heaven. This involved a link with judgement, a link which grew gradually stronger during the Middle Ages. In the 15th century appeared the *artes moriendi*, illustrated exercises of preparation for dying in which the sick person is presented as experiencing a deathbed presentation of the events of his past life. The reaction, of contrition or pride, determines the nature of the person's reception by God.

How often Christians of former times achieved, or were granted, this ideal death cannot be known, but believers can still feel that their death ought somehow to be better than that of someone without faith. Nevertheless, the example of Jesus himself shows that faith and a life lived in prayerful obedience do not necessarily take away the fear of death.

This is not to say that the Christian message is no help in facing this inescapable event. The story of Jesus shows us that our weaknesses in the face of death are accepted by God. We are not expected to relish the thought of leaving behind this life which, whatever its trials, will for most people have brought pleasure in relationships and in the experience of the physical world. It is the only existence we have known and few can give it up lightly, even in extreme age. The Judaeo-Christian God is presented throughout the bible as the creator who is committed to an ongoing renewal of an intimate relationship with his *creation. The created world is not rejected but taken seriously as a context for the working out of his plans for *humanity. The world of matter is not merely an antechamber to the world of spirit, although it is certainly a place of preparation for it.

Sadness at losing the familiar people and things of this life is legitimate. So is anguish at a sense of failure and consequent meaninglessness to life, which could be redeemed by the restoring touch of a God who, however, might not accept us or might even not be there. Any life of faith must be subject to *doubt and that doubt is liable to be strongest in facing death, because faith then has the double challenge of belief in the presence of God now and in the fulfilment of a new life with him hereafter. Even Jesus at his death experienced alienation from his Father, despite intimate prior knowledge of his *love and faithfulness. Yet Christ's Resurrection demonstrated that his Father was with him after all, and not as one uniquely privileged but as the first to trace a path that all Christians can now follow.

Christ's death involved physical as well as mental and spiritual *suffering. Even if people do not fear death they often fear dying, because of the physical symptoms, indignity, and loss of control that might accompany it. Jesus experienced all these things. It is not appropriate to conclude from this that suffering is to be welcomed or left unrelieved. Paul writes ambiguously of the linkage of his own bodily suffering with that of Christ (Col. 1: 24), but it is inconsistent with the NT presentation of a loving God concerned for the well-being of all his creatures to imply that he seeks our suffering. Christian moral theology has never prescribed extraordinary means to extend a life made burdensome by ill health and, as a corollary, would expect the use of all available skills to ease that burden.

A life after death which is more than a shadow existence makes its first appearance in *Daniel (12: 1–3) and the second book of Maccabees. The distinctive nature of this life by contrast with Greek or Egyptian ideas of *immortality is the survival of a person as a complete mind–body entity, not merely a *soul, but with a *body that is transformed by its creator despite physical mutilation or disintegration (2 Macc. 7: 11; John 20: 27). This is the consequence of the encounter between God, who is entirely life, and death, which is entirely creaturely. This encounter was made possible by God's *Incarnation in Christ in which he took on humanity and the death inseparable from it.

The possibility of eternal life has traditionally had a defining influence on a Christian's approach to death. Today, many western churchgoers apparently have little faith in an afterlife and, because of the increased numbers who die at an advanced age, death is now often of those whose mind is considerably faded. Therefore preparation for death must be different from the medieval ideal. Without a clear *hope (and it can be no more) of an afterlife in the eternal God, *Paul's claim that through Christ death has lost its sting (1 Cor. 15: 55) loses its force. There is no longer scope for resolution of the injustice and senselessness which are such features of human life on earth. Neither is there any compensating gain in relief from fear and uncertainty regarding death.

On the other hand, Christ's example in dying remains valid, in the sense that he has been through the experience before us and legitimizes our apprehensions about it. Moreover, the fact that death has been overcome by life means that life itself must not be impaired. It follows that Christian faith in the Resurrection has implications which are of practical use for people facing death whether or not they share the same beliefs. Two recent instances are the growth of the modern hospice movement and the work of Mother *Teresa of Calcutta's Missionaries of Charity. St Christopher's Hospice in London, founded by Cicely Saunders, declares in its founding statement that it 'was established as a Christian Foundation, not simply in terms of its care but from a belief that God revealed in Christ shared and shares the darkness of suffering and dying and has transformed the reality of death'. About half of British hospices would say something similar.

In each case, although many of those cared for have no explicit Christian faith, the sense on the part of the founders that death, although shrouded in mystery, is not necessarily the end allows it to be lived with and talked about without fear. Hospices in particular have recognized that though the sick and those who love them can find new strength through suffering which can be enriching for themselves and those who witness it, suffering is intrinsically ungodly and there is a Christian duty to relieve it. Hence work must continue on the medical management of symptoms, and Mother Teresa was criticized for her workers' inattention to medical care of the 'poorest of the poor' whom they rescued from destitution.

However, both these models of care recognize that the promise of Christ is not that all human suffering will be relieved but that 'I am with you always, to the end of time' (Matt. 28: 20). It is not possible to remove all suffering from human existence, in sickness or in health: to expect otherwise leads only to *suicide or *euthanasia. What is possible is to stay with the other person even when it seems that there is nothing else that can be offered. There is a relief in being accompanied along the path of dying, in knowing that others are attempting to understand one as an individual. God's concern for each of us in our uniqueness (Matt. 10: 29–30) must be reflected in the way we deal with each other, especially at times of great need.

The spiritual dimension of care is integral, but it is defined in terms of questions about meaning, which may or may not have a religious answer. Yet the example of these two initiatives in caring remains a modern testimony to the contribution that Christian faith, thought, and motivation can make to the practical support of people facing death and of those whom they leave behind.

Nigel Sykes

Aries, P., *The Hour of Our Death*, ET (1981).
Cope, G. (ed.), *Dying, Death and Disposal* (1970).
Holloway R., *Anger, Sex, Doubt and Death* (1992).
Küng, H., *Eternal Life?*, ET (1982).
Schillebeeckx, E., *The Layman in the Church* (1963).

de Certeau, Michel (1925–86). Having read classics and philosophy in Grenoble, Lyons, and Paris, Certeau joined the Society of Jesus in 1950, hoping to embark upon *missionary work in China. Priested in 1956, in 1960 he obtained from the Sorbonne his doctorate for research on the origins of the *Jesuit order, which introduced him to the work of the 17th-century mystic Jean-Joseph Surin. His interests broadened beyond historiography to the *social sciences, semiotics, and psychoanalysis. He taught at the Institut Catholique in Paris, the University of California, and the École des Hautes Études en Sciences Sociales in Paris.

Certeau's work covers very diverse themes, the central one to be summed up in a book, planned but not completed, on the anthropology of believing. One essay from his collection *The Practice of Everyday Life* (1980; ET 1984) is entitled 'Believing and Making People Believe'. His colleague Luce Giard edited a posthumous volume of essays from this latter work, *La Faiblesse de croire* (1987). In the late 1960s, Certeau became interested in the clash between the religious and the *secular in early modernity, exploring 'cultural studies'. Central to books such as *La Possession de Loudon* (1970) and *The Writing of History* (1975; ET 1988) is the politics of interpretation: who writes the account of events and from what perspective? *The Practice of Everyday Life* reflects these concerns, as do the essays collected and translated by Brian Massumi, *Heterologies: Discourse of the Other* (1987).

With his last work, *The Mystic Fable*, i. *The Sixteenth and Seventeenth Centuries* (1982; ET 1992), Certeau returned to spiritual writing. The concern for the Other, the excess of meaning that transcends all our attempts to write about and domesticate it, has had throughout a theological tenor. The voice of the mystic sings of somewhere else. The one who is true to that Other voice embarks on a *pilgrimage, an *Abrahamic journey into *exile. The Other questions continually, calling each out to another place, a future not yet written. Certeau's desire to become a missionary is realized in intellectual and spiritual enquiry. It is, ultimately, the Jesuit emphasis upon vocation that organizes the whole of his *œuvre*.   **Graham Ward**

Ahearne, Jeremy, *Michel de Certeau: Interpretation and Its Other* (1995).
Bauerschmidt, Frederick, 'Introduction to Michel de Certeau', in Graham Ward (ed.), *The Postmodern God* (1997).
Ward, Graham (ed.), *Michel de Certeau S. J.*, *New Blackfriars* Special Issue (November 1996).
—— (ed.), *The Certeau Reader* (1999).

deconstruction, see POSTMODERNISM.

de Foucauld, Charles (1858–1916). A thoroughly dissipated and generally dissatisfied young French cavalry officer, trained at Saint-Cyr, de Foucauld set out in 1882 without leave on a secret exploration of Morocco, disguised as a rabbi from central Europe. From this expedition came both his *Reconnaissance au Maroc*, for which he was awarded a gold medal by the French Geographical Society, and a personal rediscovery of *religion: '*Islam produced in me a profound upheaval.' The sight of faith as found among ordinary Muslims led to a total personal reorientation. De Foucauld was temperamentally an extremist. Reconverted to Christianity, he spent seven years as a Trappist monk in the *monastery of Akbès in Syria (1890–7), but, finding this insufficiently demanding, left to become for three years a servant of the Poor Clare nuns in Nazareth, leading a life of extreme *poverty and *prayer. The silence of Jesus' life at Nazareth was ever afterwards his model. Ordained a priest, he set out to be a solitary in the Sahara, settling finally at Tamanrasset far into the *desert among the Tuareg people whose language he learnt and whose life he shared. His wider influence depended upon an extensive correspondence, much of it later published. In 1916 he was murdered during a Tuareg rising against the French.

In life Brother Charles, as he was always called, gained no *disciple of any sort yet he had written careful rules for both 'Little Brothers' and 'Little Sisters' of Jesus. In the 1930s various groups of Little Brothers and Little Sisters began to be founded, in both North Africa and France, by René Voillaume, Madeleine Hutin, and others under the inspiration of de Foucauld's writings and life. They have since spread, with hundreds of 'fraternities', into every part of the world. For all its apparent eccentricity, de Foucauld's *spirituality has proved deeply appealing to modern Christians. It is one which entirely eschews verbal *evangelism in favour of presence and silence, a life shared with the very poor, renewing that of the Holy Family at Nazareth as well as that of the desert fathers. De Foucauld sought continuously to implement Jesus' words 'Whatsoever you do to the least of my brethren you do to me' (Matt. 25: 40), words which, he claimed, had overturned his life. He combined complete *ecumenical openness, embracing Muslims, Christians, and Jews alike, with an intense devotion to *Jesus and his *eucharistic presence. He wanted to 'cry the gospel with his life' in a way quite different from all contemporary *missionary groups and his example, like that of *Francis of Assisi, while almost impossible to imitate in the full starkness of its *asceticism, has proved irresistible to many.

His essentially spiritual and *mystical approach to Islam proved intellectually influential. Louis Massignon, greatest of French Christian Islamic scholars, felt deeply indebted to him. Louis Gardet, joint author with the Egyptian Dominican, G.-C. Anawati, of the magisterial *Mystique musulmane* (1961), was a Little Brother, while Jacques *Maritain, when old and widowed, became one too. When the WCC commissioned a series of books, *Christian Presence*, on interreligious relations, the first by Kenneth Cragg, *Sandals at the Mosque* (1959), opened with a quotation from de Foucauld, which is indicative of how the influence of this strange Saharan solitary had permeated Christianity.

See also RELIGIOUS LIFE.   **Adrian Hastings**

Preminger, M., *The Sands of Tamanrasset* (1961).
Quesnel, R., *Charles de Foucauld: Les Étapes d'une recherche* (1966).
Spink, Kathryn, *The Call of the Desert: A Biography of Little Sister Magdeleine of Jesus* (1993).
Voillaume, R., *Seeds of the Desert* (1955).

deification is a powerfully evocative term in Christian theology that connotes the believer's ultimate union with the Godhead. The idea first appears in 2 *Peter 1: 4. ('participants (*koinonoi*) in the divine nature') where the *Hellenistic notion of merging with deity (*apotheosis*) is boldly evoked and yet countered with a new and corrective sense of access to the divine granted as a grace through the power of *Jesus' mediation. The Hellenistic uses of the term had ranged from crudely conceived *myths of humans becoming demi-gods to the more subtle philosophical usage of late Stoicism, where it tended to mean the ascent of a *soul in a purified moral state until it could perceive the godhead more clearly. Both the synagogue and the early church had castigated a theology of divine access based on the former principles, where the dividing line between the creature and the Uncreated Lord was not sustained, but early *Christianity boldly pressed the philosophical concept further than the mere moral significance of assimilation to *God's will through moral refinement.

From Clement and *Origen of *Alexandria onwards, the notion of deification (*theosis, theopoiesis*) came to be used by Greek theologians to synopsize the dynamic effect of the divine encounter with humankind through the incarnation of the *Word (Logos). *Athanasius set it out clearly as the centre of his theology of *Incarnation: the divine Logos assumed flesh so that all humankind could be lifted up into the mystery of his divinity. He conceived the Incarnation as a concretely physical *atonement, a mystical reconciliation of the hitherto disparate natures of God and *humanity. Cyril of Alexandria pressed and clarified his implications further. That which could not happen, that is the 'natural' (or ontological) reconciliation of divinity and humanity, had in effect been demonstrated, in the incarnation of the Logos as the God-Man Jesus Christ. Cyril further argued that this whole mystical transaction 'in the natures' came about not merely in the person of Christ or for Christ's sake, but rather for the human race, and as no less than the divine re-creation of the foundations of human nature. Greek patristic thought thus conceived the Incarnation as having recon-

stituted the human *person as a divinely graced mystery. This dynamic approach of incarnational theology was soon diffused in the Christian mainstream. The language of deification was perhaps never quite as dominant in the west, where it did not carry the main burden of *redemption theory as it did with the Greek fathers, but it frequently emerged as a salutary counterbalance to the *Augustinian pessimism over the extent of nature's corruption, and was repeated in the very words of 2 Peter in each celebration of the Roman Mass (*divinitatis consortes*). Medieval *mystical theology found it a natural concept through which to express the rhapsodic and ecstatic sense of union with God, to the growing concern of ecclesial authorities who felt the dividing line between Servant and Lord had been eroded. For such reasons the *Reformation tradition decisively moved away from the richness of the tradition of deification theology.

In modern times it has re-emerged as a dominant notion among *Eastern Orthodox theologians, has proved important in recent Catholic *sacramental theology, and has received a more sympathetic hearing in Protestant circles as having positive and fundamental implications for *ecological thought and *creationist theologies.   **John McGuckin**

Gross, J., *La Divinisation du Chrétien d'après les pères grecs* (1938).
Lossky, V., *The Vision of God* (1963).
Mantzaridis, G., *The Deification of Man: St. Gregory Palamas and the Orthodox Tradition* (1984).
Nellas, P., *Deification in Christ* (1987).

deism is a form of belief in God. In the late 16th century, Christian writers were using the word 'deist' of opinions they disliked. This caricatured a tendency rather than pinpointed individuals. 'Deists' relied more than their opponents liked on *natural theology, so they might be followers of *Erasmus, cheerful moralists with an anticlerical streak, or they might be early Socinians (see UNITARIANISM), doubting whether Jesus is God revealed. Sometimes when people are given a name as an insult they wear it with pride. By the middle of the 18th century, it was possible to publish an anthology of deist writings. Even then, most of the memorable deists refused the name. Some were 'theists', some were 'Christian deists', and at least one claimed to be a pantheist. But their opponents named them, and history has accepted the name. Deist views continued, but the 'deist controversy' was *eighteenth-century, and there deism belongs.

Deism was more at home in coffee-houses than in churches, a world of good-humoured discussion and common sense, sharply aware of the evils of religious intolerance. It was not a martyr faith, but some deists died in jail, and others were much travelled and very evasive. The principled dislike of any aggressive *orthodoxy is a form of religious witness, but much deism seemed at the time, and since, simply antireligion. Deists had a taste for reading the bible looking for petty inconsistencies. Even Voltaire can be boring as a biblical exegete. Admittedly they sometimes made discoveries which anticipated later scholars. And if deists were critical more often than constructive, their Christian contemporaries wrote millions of words refuting them.

Among the English deists, the name usually mentioned first is Lord Herbert of Cherbury (1583–1624), brother of George Herbert the poet, and an *Anglican. He compiled a famous list of the five points that all *religions have in common: there is one God over all; to him worship is due; virtue is a main part of that worship; sins should be repented of; and there is a future judgement. It is only a step from here to say that these are the heart of the matter, and that we can work them out for ourselves. Not usually recognized as deists are Alexander Pope, the poet, a practising Roman Catholic, but his 'Essay on Man' and his 'Universal Prayer' (to 'Jehovah, Jove or Lord') are memorably expressed deism, and John Locke the philosopher, whose *Reasonableness of Christianity* is not far off. His title is reminiscent of the two major deist works, *Christianity Not Mysterious* by John Toland (1670–1722), and *Christianity as Old as the Creation* by Matthew Tindal (1657–1733). Their critics would say the reasonable religion they describe, however admirable, is not Christianity. If Toland was, as he claimed, a pantheist, we might wonder whether the conventional picture of a lazy and remote god of deism is fair.

The deist controversy was English, but great writers elsewhere were deist. There is not much constructive deism (he called it 'theism') in Voltaire, perhaps more in Rousseau's *Confessions of a Savoyard Vicar*. *Kant's *Religion within the Limits of Reason Alone* is probably as far as intellectual acumen and moral integrity can go along the deist line. Deism has been a useful sparring-partner for Protestant Christianity, but standing alone as one of the world's monotheist religions it is a shadowy creature.

See also ENLIGHTENMENT.   **Alistair Mason**

Baird, William, *History of New Testament Research*, i. *From Deism to Tübingen* (1992).

Betts, Christopher J., *Early Deism in France* (1984).

Lemay, J. A. Leo (ed.), *Deism, Masonry, and the Enlightenment* (1987).

Sullivan, Robert E., *John Toland and the Deist Controversy* (1982).

de Lubac, Henri

de Lubac, Henri (1896–1991; cardinal, 1983), French *Jesuit theologian and pioneer of *Vatican II. 'The Eucharist makes the Church', a principle now widely espoused ecumenically, often presumed to be patristic, was coined by de Lubac in *Corpus Mysticum* (1944). *Surnaturel* (1946) precipitated ten years of enforced silence in the wake of the papal encyclical, *Humani Generis* (1950), rumoured to have been directed at de Lubac and others of the *nouvelle théologie*. What was '*nouvelle*' was his understanding that we theologize in *history and that teaching on nature and *grace, as on *church and *Eucharist, has changed over the years. On the former, de Lubac wished to correct later scholastic deviations from *Aquinas's authentic teaching on the 'natural desire for the vision of God'; on the latter, to reinstate patristic perspectives. All of this was present in embryo in *Catholicisme* (1938). He greatly encouraged the patristic revival, so evident in the documents of Vatican II and important across the churches, by founding the series, *Sources Chrétiennes* (1942).

Drafted into the preparations for Vatican II by Pope *John XXIII in 1960, de Lubac's influence particularly affected the texts on *Revelation (cf. *Exégèse Médiévale* (4 vols.; 1959–64)), the Church (cf. *Méditation sur l'Église* (1953)), and the Church in the Modern World (cf. *Le Drame de l'humanisme athée* (1944); *Athéisme et sens de l'homme* (1968)). A loyal friend of *Teilhard de Chardin, he wrote several books in his defence. Under continual Roman suspicion in Pius XII's pontificate, de Lubac was revered by subsequent popes and created a cardinal in his eighties.   **Paul McPartlan**

d'Alverny, M.-T. *et al.* (eds.), *L'Homme devant Dieu* (3 vols.; 1964).

de Lubac, H., *At the Service of the Church* (1989), ET (1993).

Komonchak, J., 'Theology and Culture at Mid-Century: The Example of Henri de Lubac', *Theological Studies*, 51 (1990), 579–602.

McPartlan, P., *The Eucharist Makes the Church: Henri de Lubac and John Zizioulas in Dialogue* (1993).

von Balthasar, Hans Urs, *The Theology of Henri de Lubac* (1991).

democracy

democracy. The roots of democracy in the western world may be traced to ancient Athens, medieval Europe, and *Renaissance Italy. But democracy as we now know it developed only gradually after the Enlightenment, notably in the United States, France, Britain, Switzerland, and elsewhere. It became the polity of *modernity. At the same time, the vision of social equality, *freedom, and *justice that democracy seeks to embody through political structures and policies may be traced back to the 8th-century BC Hebrew *prophets and the messianic hope of biblical *eschatology. Despite this historical connection between the prophetic tradition and the aspirations of democracy, the relationship between Christianity and democracy has frequently been ambiguous and at times antagonistic.

There is general agreement that democracy is the 'rule of the people by the people for the people', but there is considerable disagreement about what this means, and about how 'popular power' should be structured politically. The debate about democracy has usually distinguished between direct, participatory democracy and representative democracy, and has been influenced by whether its advocates stand within the liberal or *socialist traditions. Although socialism cannot be equated with communism (see MARXISM), the demise of the latter in the late 20th century has meant that liberal democracy has become dominant, with a strong emphasis on the free market as an integral element.

Contemporary struggles for democracy and the theoretical debates they have evoked, particularly with regard to gender, ethnicity, culture, and economic issues, have made it necessary for us to go beyond the arid confines of the debate between liberalism and socialism. Democracy must be contextually embodied and developed. The democratic struggle is not simply a matter of extending liberal western democracy to places where this does not exist; nor can democracy flourish today and serve the cause of justice, equality, and freedom if it remains encrusted in past expressions, even though it will embody many of the same principles. It is therefore necessary to distinguish between democracy as a *vision* of what society should become, and democracy as a *system* of government that seeks to enable the realization of that vision within particular contexts.

By democratic system is meant those constitutional principles and procedures which have developed over the centuries, largely but not only in the west, and which have become an essential part of any genuine democracy whatever its precise historical form. By democratic vision is meant that hope for a society in which all people are truly equal and yet where difference is respected; a society in which all people are truly free, yet where social responsibility rather than individual self-interest prevails; and a society which is truly just, and therefore one in which the vast gulf between rich and poor has been overcome. Democracy, put differently, is both a specific way of structuring society, and an open-ended process which seeks to become more inclusive, more just, and more truly global. It is an ongoing project whose success is contingent upon the development of people able to participate fully in the body politic, and therefore upon the development of institutions which allow and foster such participation. Democracy is, in fact, dependent upon a viable civil society of interlocking institutions which are not controlled by the state. Democracy needs constant revitalization if it is to fulfil its promise.

Until recent times Christians have frequently regarded democracy as inimical to good government and, particularly in Europe, as the handmaiden of *revolution. None the less Christendom historically provided the womb within which modern democracy gestated. Many of its original exponents (e.g. John Locke) were deeply rooted in those verities that derived from Christian faith, even if some of them had already moved beyond the parameters of the church and its theological claims.

At least five trajectories within Christian tradition have made significant contributions to the development of democratic theory and praxis. Our point of departure must be the witness of 8th-century prophets of social righteousness, notably Amos, *Isaiah, and Micah, and the way in which this witness is affirmed and taken further in the proclamation of the reign of God in the life and death of Jesus Christ. The democratic vision has its origins in the messianic hope which longs for liberation from oppression, affirms human equality, and seeks social justice. Utopian as it may be, it is this prophetic vision which has been, and often remains, the driving force behind the struggle for democratic transformation across the world, even if it can never be fully realized and embodied adequately in systems of government.

The second trajectory, which emerged in various ways within medieval Catholicism, encouraged the development of civil society through the formation of trade guilds, and representative forms of government. Key notions derived from *Aristotelian political philosophy in support of such developments, such as the common good, were placed on a Christian basis. The Christian Democracy movement in Europe after the Second World War embodied this tradition, which may also be described as 'personalist'.

The third trajectory is the *covenantal. This derives from the *Reformed or *Calvinist tradition and stresses the need for human responsibility before God and towards others on the basis of God's reign in Jesus Christ. In certain respects this corresponds with the secular doctrine of the social contract. However its binding force is not just a sense of obligation, but one of commitment to others within the body politic under the authority of God. This leads to a strong emphasis on accountability not only to an electorate but to God. The covenantal tradition played an important role in the shaping of democracy in the United States in its formative stages.

The fourth trajectory, the liberal, which we find expressed variously in the heirs of the Radical Reformation and Calvinism, notably English Nonconformity (the Free Churches: Baptists, Independents, or Congregationalists), and liberal Protestantism in North America, affirms the dignity of the individual, human rights, the freedom of *conscience, separation of church and state, and religious toleration. Liberal Christians have insisted on the God-given value of the individual and the rights of individual dissent over against both the will of the majority and the power of the state.

The fifth trajectory has been variously embodied within the Christian Socialist tradition, for instance the alliance between the English Free Churches and the Labour movement, and finds contemporary expression in various forms of *liberation theology. It stresses that there can be no democracy without a just economic order. Key concerns here are human solidarity, participation in the democratic process, and economic justice.

Each of these trajectories emerged within specific historical contexts as Christians of different traditions sought to express their faith within the public arena on the basis of the dominant theological motifs and insights of the time. All of them have rejected tyrannical government, though they have developed different strategies for opposing it; all have acknowledged that human sinfulness leads to political corruption, though some are more optimistic about human nature than others; and all have eschewed selfish individualism and sought to develop forms of community as the place within which human beings find fulfilment. Yet the trajectories, though complementary, are not identical in the way in which they have understood or influenced democracy. The personalist trajectory has a more organic understanding of society than the liberal; the liberal has clearly affirmed individual freedoms and given its support more readily to a free-market style economy; the socialist regards economic democracy as a priority. Different Christianities have thus led to different rationales for democracy, and have supported different kinds of democracy.

*Ecumenical Christianity, especially after the 20th-century experience of Nazi and Stalinist totalitarianism, now appears to be committed to the retrieval of democracy as essential to its vision of a just world order. Indicative of this is the fact that Catholic social teaching (see SOCIAL GOSPEL AND SOCIAL TEACHING) has come out strongly in support of democratic forms of government. This can be seen, for example, in *John Paul II's *Centesimus Annus*. The same is true of documents emanating from the World Council of Churches. Yet it is also the case that many churches continue to resist democracy, giving their support to authoritarian governments instead.

Christianity does not sanction any political system as divinely ordained, democracy included. But this does not mean that all systems of government are equally acceptable to Christian faith. While the establishment of a democratic order will not usher in the *Kingdom of God, it is the best form of government that human beings have yet been able to construct in the interests of human equality, freedom, and justice. In this regard, the message of the Hebrew prophets provides a constant critique and challenge to society and to the witness of the church within it.

From the beginning of the Christian movement the role of the *church in society has been not only to proclaim the message of the reign of God but to be a sign of that reign within its own ecclesial life and structures. If genuine democracy should enable human fulfilment and flourishing, how much more should the life of the church enable its members to discover an even deeper fulfilment and freedom in Christ. For this reason there is currently a debate about democracy in the life of the church itself. The issues are complex because for some traditions hierarchy is of the essence of the church whereas for others the goal is an egalitarian community. All church traditions would insist, of course, that the final authority for the church is not the will of the majority but the will of God as revealed in Jesus Christ. None the less from the beginning the idea of participation has been central to all forms of church government. This is symbolized most dramatically by the sacrament of *baptism which declares that all those who are baptized, irrespective of gender, social class, or ethnicity, are united as equals within one body and share together in the mission of the church in the world.

Theologically speaking, the church can never be regarded as simply another non-governmental organization within civil society. Its *prophetic witness to the reign of God, and to the gospel of *forgiveness, *reconciliation, and transformation, requires that it always retain a critical distance from both political and civil society. If that critical distance is surrendered the church does not become more but less relevant within society. Yet the church is also a significant institution within civil society and, just as it may provide a model for society, it can also provide space within which those engaged in the struggle for democracy can find solidarity and a home.

Democracy by its very nature is a fragile form of government. In some western countries which have had a long democratic tradition, democracy seldom fulfils its ideals even though political leaders invariably pay them lip service. Moreover, the transition from an authoritarian to a democratic order, such as has occurred in many countries at the end of the 20th century, is invariably beset with enormous problems. These include large-scale inequalities, a lack of resources, and an inadequate education and preparation for democratic participation.

Irrespective of whether other people are buoyant about political developments or tired and cynical, despairing of an end to the struggle for justice, Christians 'hope against hope', interpreting what is happening in the light of God's promise. Unless this hope is kept alive there can be no commitment to the struggle for a democratic society because the ecumenical vision of a renewed and transformed cosmos has been surrendered. This is why some writers insist that democracy is ultimately dependent upon the development of a spirituality in which human freedom, genuine community, and a willingness to share, undergird political programmes and action.

See also POLITICAL THEOLOGY.   **John W. De Gruchy**

Barth, Karl, *Community, State and Church* (1960).
Bellah, Robert, *et al.*, *The Good Society* (1991).
Berman, Harold J., *Law and Revolution: The Formation of the Western Legal Tradition* (1983).
de Gruchy, John W., *Christianity and Democracy* (1995).
Dunn, John (ed.), *Democracy: The Unfinished Journey, 508 BC to AD 1993* (1992).
Gifford, Paul (ed.), *The Christian Churches and the Democratisation of Africa* (1995).
Hauerwas, Stanley, *A Community of Character: Toward a Constructive Christian Social Ethic* (1981).
Maritain, Jacques, *Christianity and Democracy* (1986).
Niebuhr, Reinhold, *The Children of Light and the Children of Darkness* (1944), new edn. (1960).
O'Brien, David J., and Shannon, Thomas A., *Catholic Social Thought: The Documentary Heritage* (1992).
Provost, James, and Walf, Knut, *The Tabu of Democracy within the Church* (1992).
Witte, John (ed.), *Christianity and Democracy in Global Context* (1993).

demythologizing is a term most often associated with the work of Rudolph *Bultmann. He used the equivalent German word (*Entmythologisierung*) to describe what in his view was the necessity of recovering the *kerygma, the existential demand of the biblical message, from the vocabulary and assumptions of the biblical writers' outmoded world-view. For example, when the book of Acts describes Jesus' 'ascent' to heaven, it is assuming, according to Bultmann, the picture of a three-tier universe with a flat earth covered by the dome of heaven and floating on the waters. Upwards is literally Godwards. To use the old categories confuses rather than convinces modern would-be believers. What is still a valid experience is the *existential and transforming encounter with a 'risen' Christ. In Bultmann's opinion, such existential truths are best expressed in the categories of Heidegger's philosophy of authentic being.

*Cosmology, *psychology, and *philosophy have made radical changes in the modern view of not only the physical but the spiritual and mental worlds. For instance, much of what the gospels describe as demonic possession may now be explained as epilepsy or mental illness. There are those who back the biblical accounts against the discoveries of *science, but unless one takes an uncompromising biblicist view, uncomfortable choices have to be made as to which results of modern thought are to be taken on board and which rejected. There are few today who concur with the biblical account of astronomy in which the stars and planets are lamps moving across a dome arched over a flat earth, even if they profess to accept other aspects of biblical cosmology. Paradoxically, rather than falling into the half-way house of paying lip-service to the *bible's authority while redefining its terms to accord with modern scientific description, Bultmann allows us to recover the coherence of the biblical world-view.

For many, all this represents a profound attack on traditional religion and the authority of the bible. Its proponents would argue that on the contrary it is the only way to give them any credence in contemporary society. Another line of defence, however, itself biblical, can be adduced. It can be argued that the biblical tradition itself engages in a drastic programme of demythologizing the common theological and cosmological inheritance of the ancient Near East. In place of the dramatic battles between gods and the personified forces of nature in the *creation myths of Babylon and Egypt, *Genesis opens with a series of stark statements. No opposing power has any part to play. Details such as calling the sun and moon the greater and lesser lights can be interpreted as part of a deliberate stance against deifying the heavenly bodies or any natural object. Even the sabbath cycle of seven days can be seen as an attempt to impose a mathematical rhythm on life, rather than relying on the phases of the moon with its *mythic associations.

Elsewhere in the bible, the prophetic denunciation of idolatry and polytheism is a clear counter to the elaborate mythical cycles of contemporary cultures. Even *Israel's own myths are not above attack. The sacrificial cult of the Temple is decried in favour of the reformation of the heart, and Ezekiel and other prophets instruct the people at times *not* to follow in the way of their fathers, or to rely on the story of past glories, but to await an event of radical transformation. *John the Baptist and *Jesus, with their call to repentance and to a change of heart more fundamental than adherence to any priestly structure or elaborated mythology, may be seen as Bultmann's precursors, as may all those reformers throughout the history of the church who have stressed the importance of the transforming experience of God over against systematization and ritual.

Yet the church elaborated a complex myth around the person of Jesus. Is this Christian myth a betrayal of the simple ethical call of a 1st-century rabbi, an outdated construct which now must be discarded? Bultmann has been charged with inconsistency in his affirmation of the centrality of Christ and the reality of God. Why should these features be retained rather than embracing Heidegger's humanism completely?

The other side of the coin may be that mythopoesis, the making of myths, is intrinsic to human thought and culture. Whether or not there is such a thing as naked experience underlying all systems of *language and thought is one of the unresolved questions of the late 20th century. Even if there is, to communicate any experience presupposes shared assumptions about the nature of the physical and spiritual environment within which communication takes place, assumptions which are made by everyone, academically trained or not, and few of which are susceptible to proof. We live by myths, in that sense, and they 'flesh out' experience in a way that the central Christian claim of *Incarnation seems to reflect. Far from being fairy tales or just plain untruths, as popular usage might lead us to believe, myths may be the only way we have of speaking truth.

In this view, all so-called demythologizing is inevitably remythologizing, redescribing something in terms of a different, but by definition mythical, world-view. Heideggerian categories may be no more fundamental than anyone else's and two thousand years from now may need demythologizing themselves. Perhaps, indeed, the idea that demythologization can succeed is itself, in the popular sense of the word, a myth, but so too is the idea that any form of Christian expression is free from cultural particularities. Christian thought, as in so many areas of concern, has long had to cope with a deep ambivalence about mythical categories. **Hugh S. Pyper**

Bultmann, R., *Jesus Christ and Mythology* (1958).
Macquarrie, J., *The Scope of Demythologizing: Bultmann and his Critics* (1960).
Painter, J., *Theology as Hermeneutics: Rudolf Bultmann's Interpretation of the History of Jesus* (1987).
Thiselton, A. C., *The Two Horizons* (1980).

Descartes and Cartesianism.

The term 'Cartesianism' denotes either the views of the French philosopher, mathematician, and physicist René Descartes (1596–1650), or the defence and development of these views in the writings of *les cartésiens*, an eclectic group of *seventeenth- and *eighteenth-century European intellectuals. The term, from the Latin *Cartesius*, seems to have been introduced into English by the Cambridge Platonist Henry More. Descartes is perhaps best known today for the method outlined in his first published work, the *Discourse on the Method* (1637), one which involves the use of radical *doubt to clear the way for the discovery of the first *truth accessible to the reflective self, namely, the famous *Cogito ergo sum* (in the *Discourse*, *Je pense donc je suis*). Descartes is often called the father of modern *philosophy, and for many it is his method of doubt and his reflections on the *cogito* that provide the key to his *modernity.

Descartes is also popularly associated with 'substance dualism', the thesis that mind and *body are distinct substances. Some form of *dualism was already established in Christian thought by the beginning of the modern period, but what is distinctive about Descartes's version of the doctrine is that it identifies mind with thinking substance, and body with extended substance. In his dedicatory letter to the Faculty of Theology in Paris prefacing his *Meditations on First Philosophy* (1641), Descartes himself emphasized that his definition of mind solely in terms of thought provides firm support for the Christian doctrine of the *immortality of the *soul. Yet his view that the self inhabiting a body is an immaterial thinking substance, which Gilbert Ryle ridiculed as the doctrine of the 'ghost in the machine', is counterbalanced to some extent by his doctrine of the soul–body union. Anticipating the charge that he adopted the *Platonic definition of a *human being as a soul using a body, Descartes urged in the *Meditations* that the human soul is something which is 'closely joined with and, as it were, intermingled with' its body 'so as to form a unit'. While many have seen the doctrine of the union as an attempt to overcome problems with mind–body interaction, Descartes himself appealed to it primarily in order to distinguish human experience from 'pure' thought. His most sustained attempt to come to terms with the distinctive character of human experience is in his final published work, the *Passions of the Soul* (1649).

However, Descartes was best known in the early modern period neither for his method of doubt nor for his understanding of mind. Defenders and critics alike emphasized rather that his definition of body as extended substance required the systematic displacement of explanations, deriving from the work of *Aristotle, of natural phenomena, then predominant in both Catholic and Protestant schools on the Continent. In the *Principles of Philosophy* (1644), Descartes proposed as an alternative to Aristotelian explanations in terms of prime matter, substantial forms, and final causality his own more austere explanations in terms of extension, its modifications, and purely mechanistic laws. There were other critics of the Aristotelianism of the schools, most notably in France, Pierre Gassendi (1592–1655) and the Gassendists. Nevertheless, Descartes's followers proved to be more adept than the Gassendists at packaging the new mechanistic science. Even so, it is understandable that Cartesian *science is less known now than Cartesian epistemology and theory of mind, given the decisive refutation of Descartes's particular brand of physics in the work of Henry More's student, Isaac Newton (1642–1727).

*Theological issues also dominated discussions of Descartes's system in earlier centuries in a way no longer current. Such issues were of immediate practical concern to Descartes himself, who encountered fierce theological resistance not only in France but also in the United Provinces (the Netherlands), where he lived for most of the second half of his life. He failed in his attempt to infiltrate the Catholic French universities at least partly because Aristotelian traditionalists saw his system as a threat to the Catholic dogma of the miraculous conversion in the *Eucharist of the substance of bread and wine into the body and blood of Christ (*transubstantiation). Descartes fared somewhat better in the *Calvinist United Provinces. Even in this region, however, orthodox Calvinists urged that his insistence on the essential difference between mind and body conflicts with the Aristotelian position that the soul bears a natural relation to a certain body in virtue of being its substantial form. Overlooking Descartes's own assertion of the substantial union, these critics emphasized the threat that his system posed to Christian doctrines such as the *resurrection of the body and the unity of the *incarnated Christ. Both before and after Descartes's death, moreover, critics attempted to gain an advantage over Cartesianism by linking it to heterodox theological views. Before his death the connection was typically to the doctrinally tolerant Dutch Remonstrants while after his death it was to a very different group, the rigorist French *Jansenists (enemies of the Jesuits) who were targeted in large part because of the work of the Port-Royal Cartesian Antoine Arnauld.

There was a strong inclination among French Cartesians to counter theological objections by invoking the authority of *Augustine. There were two general approaches, reflected in the distinction of the scholar Henri Gouhier between 'Cartesianism augustinized' and 'Augustinianism cartesianized'. The augustinized Cartesians, including Descartes's literary executor Claude Clerselier and the physician Louis de la Forge, were concerned to bolster Cartesian natural philosophy by stressing the ways in which Descartes's proofs of the existence of God and of the immateriality of mind complement Augustinian spirituality. The defence of a 'cartesianized' theology, on the other hand, was pursued with disastrous consequences by the Benedictine Robert Desgabets (1610–78), whose development of Descartes's account of the Eucharist provided the impetus for the prohibition of the teaching of Cartesianism in France two decades after Descartes's death.

The cartesianized Augustinians tended to emphasize not Descartes's infrequent forays into theology but rather his more common insistence that theological issues are outside his jurisdiction in so far as they require recourse to *revelation. In controversy with the Jesuits, theologians such as Arnauld appealed to Descartes's insistence on this to safeguard a 'positive' or dogmatic theology devoted to explicating Augustinian views on matters of faith. Dutch Cartesians also attempted to insulate Cartesian philosophy from theology, though for them the concern was less to promote Augustinian purity in theology than to honour the distinction of the disciplines in the universities. This interest in making Descartes fit for the schools also explains the emphasis in the work of these Cartesians on the similarities between Aristotle and Descartes. This 'scholasticized' Cartesianism was exported from the United Provinces to Germany soon after Descartes's death, and provides the background for the attempt by the German theoretician Gottfried Wilhelm Leibniz (1646–1716) and later Leibnizians to reform and reconcile Aristotelian *metaphysics and the new mechanistic (but no longer Cartesian) science.

The fact that Leibniz also was concerned to defend the rationality of divine providence bespeaks the influence on his thought of the distinctive form of Cartesianism in the writings of Nicolas Malebranche (1638–1715), a member of the Oratory in Paris. Malebranche attempted with other French Cartesians to link Descartes to Augustine; in Malebranche's case the result was a synthesis that stressed the dependence of creatures on God's rational activity. His system included the view, anticipated in the work of La Forge and others, that bodies serve as the non-causal occasion for God to distribute motion in accord with the most economical laws. Malebranche extended this view to theology, arguing that God distributes *grace in accord with simple general laws. This upset his former ally Arnauld, who saw it as a dangerous philosophical incursion into theology. None the less, the opening salvo in his protracted and increasingly bitter dispute with Malebranche was his critique of Malebranche's doctrine that 'we see all things in God', that is, that we know the bodies we see through the idea of extension in God that represents them. Arnauld appealed to Descartes in defence of the alternative position that representative ideas are merely modes of our soul. This defence, well known among early-modern intellectuals, was taken up by Pierre-Sylvain Régis (1632–1707). Unlike Arnauld, however, but like Desgabets, whom he admired, Régis challenged Malebranche's claim that since ideas or eternal essences are identical to divine reason, one must reject Descartes's assertion that God has freely created the eternal truths.

Arnauld won over the Cartesians in the battle with Malebranche on the nature of ideas, but Malebranche was ultimately successful in his campaign against the creation doctrine, as shown by the fact that Régis was the last major Cartesian to endorse it. Even so, scholars have recently revisited this doctrine (see, for instance, Marion's *Sur la théologie blanche*) which belies the characterization of Descartes as a strict 'rationalist' given its connection to his position that God, as the infinite 'ground' of created reality, including our own rationality, is fundamentally incomprehensible. If we are to understand completely the philosophical and theological significance of Descartes for modern thought, we must consider his *creation doctrine as well as his views on doubt, the *cogito*, and dualism. Some 350 years after his death, however, we have yet to take the full measure of this foundational doctrine.   **Tad M. Schmaltz**

Clarke, Desmond M., *Occult Powers and Hypotheses: Cartesian Natural Philosophy under Louis XIV* (1989).

Des Chene, Dennis, *Physiologia: Natural Philosophy in Late Aristotelian and Cartesian Thought* (1996).

Gaukroger, Stephen, *Descartes: An Intellectual Biography* (1995).

Gouhier, Henri, *Cartésianisme et augustinisme au XVIIe siècle* (1978).

Lennon, Thomas M., *The Battle of the Gods and Giants: The Legacies of Descartes and Gassendi (1655–1715)* (1993).

Marion, Jean-Luc, *Sur la théologie blanche de Descartes: Analogie, création des vérités éternelles, et fondement*, 2nd edn. (1991).

Verbeek, Theo, *Descartes and the Dutch: Early Reactions to Cartesian Philosophy, 1637–1650* (1992).

desert. In the eastern Mediterranean lands, the desert is a powerful and inescapable presence. Life-threatening yet liberating in its unbounded spaces and solitudes, for the biblical tradition it stands in contrast to the orderliness of the *city, which may represent security but can also be claustrophobic, violent, and decadent. Civic life needs the desert to sustain it. Leviticus 21 acknowledges this in the ritual of the scapegoat which, sent out into the desert, carries away the *sins of the people, enabling human society to continue. The desert is a liminal space where the constraints of social life are stripped away and both destruction and transformation are possible. It is in the desert that *Moses, Elijah, *David, *Israel in the *exodus and *exile, *John the Baptist, and *Jesus himself are faced with the refiguring of their existence and of their relationship to God.

The desert offers both asylum and threat. Human violence may be evaded by fleeing into its solitudes, but not so the assaults of the demonic. This is most graphically depicted in the tradition of Jesus' confrontation with the *devil in the desert (Luke 4: 1–13). This ambivalence over the purity and yet danger of the desert is formative for Christian *monasticism. The desert fathers, *ascetic monks who fled the lure and the persecuting zeal of the Roman city for the Egyptian wilderness, found there silence, solitude, and peace, an unencumbered access to God in the life of *prayer. There, too, they engaged in titanic struggles against the devil and his temptations and buffetings. The desert represents the true battleground of the soul, where the consolations and distractions of human intercourse are stripped away. In modern times, figures such as Charles *de Foucauld have continued this tradition.

Throughout Christian history, individuals and communities have sought by withdrawing from the structures of the society around them to recover the pristine purity of spiritual experience which the desert signifies. Others have found themselves driven involuntarily into the desert, whether literally or metaphorically, by some disaster. In either case, the nuanced account of the desert in Christian thought has allowed space both to free oneself from overbearing social or theological structures and to renew them.

The desert may also represent the sense of abandonment by God which some of the most profound spiritual teachers in Christianity have experienced. Again, the duality of the tradition offers the hope of transformation out of emptiness. If the desert is the place of death, it can also be the place of rebirth. Contemporary *spirituality draws on this duality in talking of 'the desert in the city'. Negatively, this refers to the spiritual emptiness of modern industrial life. Positively, the phrase holds out the possibility of creating uncluttered space to commune with God in the midst of civic clamour.

Hugh S. Pyper

Burton-Christie, D., *The Word in the Desert* (1993).
Louth, A., *The Wilderness of God* (1991).
Seale, M., *The Desert Bible* (1974).

design presupposes a designer, so the question of discerning design in the *world amounts to distinguishing the true design of intentional agency from the merely apparent design that results from non-intentional, naturalistic processes. What makes it easy to confuse merely apparent design with true design is that explanatory alternatives to design are always available and that our insights into a putative designer's thoughts and intentions depend on problematic analogies with our own thoughts and intentions. Arguments for design, however convincing, can thus be no more than probabilistic. Christian thinkers appealing to design in the world, or to the design of the world as a whole, on the lines of Thomas *Aquinas or William Paley, must realize how intrinsically difficult it is to recognize a designer's handiwork.

An obvious alternative to design, one that underscores the probabilistic nature of all arguments for design, is chance. The probability is always more than zero that a 'chance' meeting of long-lost friends, for example, is literally a chance meeting, due to no one's design. On the other hand, the probability that a monkey randomly hitting a keyboard will produce a novel within a year, while also non-zero, is so low—and the independent significance of novels so great—that design by an intelligent author is clearly the better explanation of novels. As an alternative to design, chance is always available though not always plausible.

A more subtle alternative concerns the fact that the very conditions for observation sometimes make what is observed appear designed (the 'Anthropic' principle). There need be no design in the fact that we do not find ourselves in the infernal centre of a star or adrift in the cold, uninhabitable reaches of space, for, if our immediate environment were uninhabitable, we could not observe it in the first place. Many of earth's hospitable features, being necessary conditions for our existence as observers, require no further explanation.

The fact that there are habitable planets at all, or that the basic structure of the universe permits their formation, is another matter. If the strength of gravity were different by only a tiny factor, for example, the universe might well have been devoid of stars, planets, and life of any sort. Had this been the case, the point about observers necessarily finding themselves in habitable environments would have been moot, for no environments would have been habitable and there would have been no observers. The probability that the universe's basic parameters fall within the extremely narrow range of habitability appears to be low enough to rule out chance as an explanation. To invoke design would be premature, however, before determining whether the universe's defining parameters can randomly vary in the first place and before deciding whether the physical requirements of anthropomorphic observers are, in the scheme of the universe, significant enough to call for explanation.

For living organisms, natural selection constitutes the most powerful alternative to design (see EVOLUTION). A mindless winnowing of deleterious mutations, though inefficient, parallels a designer's rejection of unsuitable designs. In the classic example of the eye, one finds an arrangement of parts and an adaptation of means to ends so exquisitely complex that, at first glance, the organ looks obviously designed for seeing, the work of a brilliant engineer with a masterly plan. But there are numerous ways to effect an eye, some of the primitive ones perhaps actual precursors of complex eyes. The evolution of every part of a complex eye can be traced, conceptually if not historically, through a continuous series of predecessors, each having visual or other functionality adequate for its selection. Only to the extent that (1) unbridgeable gaps remain in the best evolutionary account of an organ's formation, (2) insufficient time has elapsed for the accumulation of beneficial variations, and (3) the organ's functionality evidences a degree of optimality beyond what is necessary for survival, does design gain an advantage over natural selection as explanation. Conversely, vestigial organs such as hip bones in whales, homologies like that between ear bones in mammals and jaw bones in reptiles, and flawed designs such as the panda's 'thumb'—as well as the consilience of evidence from palaeontology, molecular biology, comparative anatomy, and other fields—favour mindless natural selection over design.

Perhaps the human tendency to read design into the world before considering the alternatives is itself evidence of design, namely, of *God's desire for humans to see his handiwork. In that case, the awe inspired by the world's multiple levels of order and complexity would constitute a religious experience. On the other hand, the naturalistic view holds that we see the world resembling our own creations because doing so requires less mental and emotional strain than estimating probabilities and following complicated arguments. Our tendency to infer design, on this view, tells us nothing about the world but something about ourselves.

Wherever design really does recommend itself over the alternatives, one must scrutinize one's assumptions about the purported artefact's purpose and about the purported designer's thoughts and intentions. Because highly complex objects in particular do not wear their purposes on their sleeves, it is perfectly possible to infer that an object is designed while being unable to determine exactly for what it is designed. An elaborate and unfamiliar scientific instrument found lying on a heath, for example, might be clearly designed though its purpose is unknown. Alternatively, its purpose might seem clear, although its designer had in mind other purposes that elude our immediate grasp. To claim to know that an artefact's purpose is what its designer intended is to claim insight into the designer's abilities, beliefs, and intentions. Because inferences about the purposes of artefacts and the minds of designers become riskier the further one departs from human artefacts and human designers, arguments about the design of the universe are the riskiest of all.

See also COSMOLOGY; PHILOSOPHY; SCIENCE.

Patrick A. Wilson

Barrow, J. D., and Tipler, F. J., *The Anthropic Cosmological Principle* (1986).
Dawkins, R., *Climbing Mount Improbable* (1996).
Dennett, D. C., *Darwin's Dangerous Idea* (1995).
Mackie, J. L., *The Miracle of Theism* (1982).
Swinburne, R., *The Existence of God* (1979).

deutero-canonical books, see APOCRYPHA, JEWISH.

development of doctrine. The two issues raised are (1) the coherence of Christian teaching as it unfolds across the centuries, and (2) the relation of later teaching to *revelation and the *biblical witness. The issues are central to *Reformation debates: does doctrinal amplification extend the biblical norms of Christian belief without sufficient warrant (the *Protestant challenge), or, because there is a continuum of inspired understanding (*tradition) between early and later interpretations, is the emergence of later normative doctrine integral to what God brings about as a guided response to his revelation in *Jesus (the *Catholic claim)? Although this remains an important issue in *ecumenical relations, the modern discussion of development is more concerned with how to characterize the continuity of Christian understanding as it takes shape in different contexts which contribute new factors and intellectual possibilities to the formation of Christian teaching.

Vincent of Lérins (d. 450) is the patristic point of reference for later discussion: on the one hand, he was universally quoted for his assertion that Christian teaching is 'what was believed everywhere, always and by all': hence no doctrinal interpretation was to be accepted which was not supported by a universal consensus of the ancient *church. But he also spoke of a progress of the Christian religion, like the growth of the human body, 'so that it may be consolidated in the course of years, developed in the sequence of time and sublimated in age, while remaining incorrupt and unimpaired, complete and perfect in all the proportions of its parts and in all its essentials' (*Commonitorium*, 22–3). Is the fixity of the first statement compatible with the growth model of the second? 'The latent contradiction will work itself out in later history' (Walgrave 1972: 89).

Vincent's image of doctrinal growth was picked up in *nineteenth-century theology, notably by the Catholic theologians of *Tübingen and by *Newman. They described the emergence and amplification of Christian doctrine as a process of 'development', a quasi-organic evolution in which what develops later is the flowering of what was contained at the inception of revelation: as living things grow to fullness without surrendering their identity, so does Christian faith in its intellectual dimension. (*Holiness, strangely, does not seem to increase as the years go by.) Möhler offers the classic image of organic growth: 'Development cannot but be an unfolding of something which from the start is given in its fullness, in such a way that the later originates from the earlier in a living, gradual transition' (Walgrave 1972: 290).

Unlike Bossuet, for whom the church never expresses new articles of faith, but only finds new and clearer ways of saying what she already knows, Newman uses the analogy of development to argue that while new and later formulations of teaching emerge in the life of the church, they still arise within the dynamic of God's founding revelation and share in its authority. 'New', therefore, does not mean 'extraneous' and 'later' does not imply secondary status. The church's permanent contact with revelation—the presence of the risen Christ and the *Holy Spirit—brings gifts of mind and heart expressed in a trajectory of later teaching continuous with earlier faith.

If, as Newman preached in one of his last Anglican sermons, 'Scripture begins a series of developments which it does not finish,' the completion can only be in the understanding to which the church is led by God. As a great social or cultural idea becomes an active principle in society by initially engaging minds, hearts, and imaginations and only subsequently giving rise to a reasoned consideration of its consequences, so revelation sets in motion a process of engagement, response, reflection, and judgement in which *creeds and *dogmas come to be formed under God's infallible guidance. The church, encountering God's revelation and subject to its illuminating presence, forms statements about what it understands, 'till what was an impression on the Imagination has become a system or creed in the Reason' (Newman 1843). If, as one poet put it, 'a writer creates his own audience', so God's revelation creates the conditions for its reception and interpretation by giving rise to doctrines by which it is communicated, preserved, and approached.

For many modern writers, 'development' may be an unavoidable way of designating the issue, but neither it nor any other single analogy can be an adequate characterization of the process. Can the *continuity* between 'then' and 'now', and all points in between, be adequately described by a single category (e.g. development, homogeneous evolution, logical implication, implicit knowledge becoming explicit) and still respect the elements of *discontinuity* and transformation that history introduces? To treat the process as linear and cumulative, without any significant variation or change, is to write an unrealistic history. The challenge of any theory of development is to see historical change as the matrix within which Christian identity is consistently reappropriated in a living stream of tradition.

The NT itself is the first witness to this process. Unlike Rabbinic Judaism which developed a limited theological framework in relation to Torah-observance, the earliest Christian thought is characterized by rapid development in three related areas: the person of Christ, his saving function (*redemption), and the character of *God. These pressed for attention because Christians had to think through the implications of a historical moment in which God reveals himself and illuminates human destiny in Christ.

Recent scholarship emphasizes the Jewish, rather than Hellenistic, roots of these developments: patterns in *Judaism in the 1st Christian century, rather than an importation of Hellenistic ideas, provided the conceptual resources of the early communities. The initial roots of doctrinal development are exegetical and imaginative: reading the Jewish scriptures in the light of Christ enabled the NT writers to see biblical themes brought to realization and fulfilment in him. Post-biblical developments build upon what was achieved in this initial stage, and although Hellenistic concepts enabled the formulation of *Trinitarian and *christological teaching, the decisive steps antedate Hellenistic influence.

Both early and later stages are governed by a rule that *Lindbeck calls 'Christological maximalism': every possible importance is to be ascribed to Jesus and the highest possible estimate is to be reached of Christ's significance and identity, in ways that respect the oneness of God and full human reality in Christ. Nicene and Chalcedonian *orthodoxy arises from 'the process of adjusting Christian discourse to the world of late classical antiquity in a manner conformable to regulative principles that were already at work in the earliest strata of the tradition' (Lindbeck 1984: 94–5).

Lindbeck's approach identifies regulative principles within Christian faith-experience which impel *theology to take the shape that it does; at any period, these principles intersect with the interpretative possibilities offered by a culture (for example, Palestinian religion, Neoplatonism, Baroque aesthetic). Thus due weight can be given both to a continuity of principles directing Christian thought and to the varying modes of discourse in different cultures which shape the church's formulation of doctrine. In similar vein, Jossua proposes an interaction of *structured* elements (*idées-force*, or 'master-themes') which recur in the tradition (e.g. proclamation of salvation, humanity and divinity of Christ, grace and nature) and the structuring elements drawn from a given cultural milieu. The structured element (revelation and faith) is never expressed without a relationship to *structuring* elements (linguistic, conceptual, and cultural factors). Doctrinal development can then be viewed as a history of successive structurings, some of which, because of their centrality to revelation, come to assume normative status for the church's faith.

Newman anticipates these approaches with some remarks which are undeveloped in the theoretical part of his *Essay*: 'An idea not only modifies, but is modified, or at least influenced, by the state of things in which it is carried out, and is dependent in various ways on the circumstances which surround it'. Join this to his consideration, later in the *Essay*, of the distinctive principles within Christianity deriving from 'the central truth' of the Incarnation which generate doctrinal development, and the approaches of Lindbeck and Jossua are not far away. 'If it be true that the principles of the later Church are the same as those of the earlier, then, whatever are the variations of belief between the two periods, the later in reality agrees more than it differs with the earlier, for principles are responsible for doctrines' (ibid. 353).

When the articulation of doctrine develops through time, a fundamental continuity is maintained through the impulse of dynamic and regulative principles throughout the process. Newman identifies 'development' as one such principle which gives Catholic teaching 'a unity and individuality' (ibid. 326). Among such principles we might also include: the unsurpassable *self*-communication of the one God in Christ; God's universal saving will; full human reality in Christ; continuity of revelation from OT to NT; unitive grace and sanctification; the relation of divine and human *freedom; the goodness and sacramentality of *creation; the reality of moral *evil. Such principles are, we might say, the *cantus firmus* on which the melody of doctrine develops.   **John McDade, SJ**

Chadwick, O., *From Bossuet to Newman: The Idea of Doctrinal Development* (1957).

de Lubac, H., 'The Problem of the Development of Dogma', in *Theology in History* (1996).

Jossua, J.-P., 'Immutabilité, progrès ou structurations multiples des doctrines chrétiennes?', *Revue des sciences philosophiques et théologiques*, 52 (1968), 173–200.

Lash, N., *Change in Focus: A Study of Doctrinal Change and Continuity* (1973).

Lindbeck, G., *The Nature of Doctrine* (1984).

Newman, J. H., 'The Theory of Developments in Religious Doctrine', in *University Sermons* (1843).

——— *An Essay on the Development of Christian Doctrine* (1845, 1878).

Nichols, A., *From Newman to Congar* (1990).

Rahner, K., 'The Development of Dogma', *Theological Investigations*, 1 (1961).

Walgrave, J. H., *Unfolding Revelation: The Nature of Doctrinal Development* (1972).

devil. The devil has a complicated history. The OT has remarkably little to say on the subject. Only in the later books are there hints about him and his function (Satan, being by nature an *angel, has no sex, but in this case feminists are unlikely to complain about consistent use of the male pronoun). Satan's best-known appearance is in the temptation of *Job but he does this in obedience to God, whose minister he is. Satan as 'accuser' in Zechariah 3: 1 seems no different; however, when 2 Samuel 24: 1, 'The anger of Yahweh blazed out against Israel and incited David against them', was rewritten in 2 Chronicles 21: 1 as 'Satan rose against Israel and incited David', it does suggest a Satan seen as disengaged from divine control. There is little else. In particular there is no reason internal to *Genesis for thinking the serpent in the Garden of Eden (3: 1–15) was a spiritual being in disguise (see FALL). It was simply a snake. However, it would subsequently become an image of Satan just as the strange passage about 'the sons of God' who saw that the 'daughters of men' were beautiful (Gen. 6: 1–4) would much later help the development of an account of the 'fall of the angels'.

In the post-exilic, intertestamental period Satan entered Jewish religious consciousness far more fully, and the idea of an evil spirit, warring against God, mysterious in origin, fearful in power, began to take shape. While the concept may have been borrowed from neighbouring, more *dualistic religious systems, Babylonian or Persian, it did not undermine the fundamental monism of Hebraic ontology: Satan is not an alternative principle but a 'fallen' creation of Yahweh. The first work to describe the fall of Satan at any length, and attribute it to pride, is 2 Enoch but the date of this book, which survives only in medieval Slavonic, is unsure.

The NT appears to take the existence and power of Satan and a multitude of lesser devils absolutely for granted, but it does more than that. The devil becomes a principal protagonist in the story. Devils are cast out by *Jesus and, when accused of doing this by the power of Beelzebub, he replies unhesitatingly, 'How can Satan cast out Satan?' (Mark 3: 23). On the contrary, he suggests, 'no one can make his way into a strong man's house... unless he has tied up the strong man first... Only then can he burgle his house.' Jesus is the burglar who has entered Satan's house and tied him up. Somehow, then, the *world can be seen as Satan's kingdom until, with Jesus, 'the prince of this world is overthrown' (John 12: 31, cf. 14: 30). Paul can even call him 'the god of this world' (2 Cor. 4: 4). Moreover in Luke's account of Jesus' temptation, the devil declares 'I will give you all this power and the glory of these kingdoms for it has been committed to me and I will give it to whom I will' (Luke 4: 6). Of course, one must beware of believing anything the devil says, as the Johannine Jesus remarks: 'he is a liar and the father of lies' (John 8: 44). That may well be the most important point the NT makes about him. If he claimed so much power over the world, was that true? The NT paradox is that it appears to agree with him, though that agreement only provides the backdrop for its account of Jesus' achievement in smashing the devil's power so utterly: 'By his death he could take away all the power of death, that is the devil, and deliver all those who had been held in slavery all their lives by the fear of death' (Heb. 2: 14–15). One theory of the atonement, popular with the fathers, saw it precisely as ransom paid to the devil as 'lord of this world'.

The problem remains that, despite this victory, the battle goes on. Satan turns up even within the Christian community in all manner of forms (Acts 5: 3; 1 Cor. 7: 5; 2 Cor. 2: 11). Defeated he may be, put out of action apparently not. Much of the book of *Revelation is given up to the wildest images of ongoing spiritual warfare between Christ and 'the great dragon ... that ancient serpent, who is called the Devil and Satan' (Rev. 12: 9), warfare which is seen as continuing through the Christian era.

With such a legacy, the Christian church was bound to be highly devil-conscious. Exorcism was a crucial element of *baptism and exorcists abounded in each local church. Some of the fathers, Tertullian especially, were intensely concerned with Satan. Nevertheless, the central doctrinal preoccupation, from *Irenaeus to *Augustine, was to deny any sort of ontological dualism. The devil must then come from God, whatever power he has obtained to defy God. Essentially it was an exercise in limiting his significance. Clement and *Origen of Alexandria even thought the devil might ultimately be converted, becoming again what he had once been. The very idea cut him down to size even more.

By the Middle Ages he has already become for some a figure of fun and yet the most fearsome period of Christian demonology began in the 14th century with the attack on *witchcraft whereby, it was claimed, large numbers of people made a pact with the devil, whom they worshipped in secret 'sabbats' while receiving power to harm their neighbours. Perhaps a Christian root of this idea is to be found in John 13: 27: Satan 'entered' *Judas Iscariot. The *Inquisition, wrestling in the 13th century with dualist Catharism, came to identify *heretics with servants of the devil and moved on from there to the idea, which hitherto the church had emphatically rejected, that the witches of popular imagination really existed and must be tracked down without mercy. The theme of a pact with the devil fascinated the early modern mind, producing the figure of Marlowe's Dr Faustus and Goethe's romanticized Faust. In 1487, two German inquisitors published the *Malleus Maleficarum*, the

standard textbook for the witch-craze which swept Europe for the next 150 years, for reasons sociopolitical as much as religious, which largely baffle the historian, despite a huge amount of modern scholarly research. Sixteenth-century theologians, *Luther especially, had much to say about the devil, but it was the tying of belief in the devil so closely to the witchcraft idea which led, as the irrationality and horror of the witch trials became evident in the course of the 17th century, to a rapid decline in effective concern with, or belief in, the devil.

Yet the mid-17th-century turning-point also produced the most magnificent literary expression of the 'Christian' devil in *Milton's *Paradise Lost*. Here the cosmic battle between the NT 'Prince of this world' and God is rewritten poetically with unflinching orthodoxy and yet a panache which transforms Satan into the tragic hero of modernity whose 'mind and spirit remains invincible' moved by 'th'unconquerable will' never to submit to God and so enabled slyly to appear 'Patron of liberty'. Never was the devil portrayed as more nasty to Christian minds yet more subtly appealing, even so human. Diabolical sin is here recast to prefigure the humanist *atheism about to offer a public challenge to divine authority in the name of human autonomy. In more modern literature, a sense of the cosmic, dualist struggle between the devil and the servants of God may best be caught in the writing of C. S. *Lewis, both the science fiction trilogy and the Narnia sequence. In mainline, increasingly *liberal, Protestantism the devil faded into invisibility. Exorcism was largely abandoned even before that happened. It was, however, long retained by Catholics who continued to experience the devil as a personal reality: Jean-Marie Vianney (1786–1859), the *curé d'Ars*, was buffeted by Satan as realistically as Luther or *Teresa of Avila three centuries earlier. Yet by the mid-20th century, without any official change in teaching, the devil had faded almost as completely from Catholic consciousness and exorcism from the church's practice. That is why Archbishop Milingo's ministry with its regular exorcisms, belief in the existence of witches, and claims to converse with devils (A. Hastings, *African Catholicism* (1989), 138–55) proved so unacceptable to Rome that he was compelled to resign the see of Lusaka in 1982. Exorcism, on the other hand, was powerfully revived in Protestant *fundamentalist circles among which belief in diabolical possession grew rapidly in the late 20th century.

What are we to make of this history? Internally the theology of the devil remains problematic in various ways. First, the devil's origin and character. There is remarkably little in scripture as to where he came from, his fall, or his future, at least outside the book of Revelation. The church has also been extremely parsimonious in dogmatizing in this area. Old Testament texts point to a Satan somewhat unpleasant but not absolutely inimical to God. Giovanni Papini could still argue in the mid-20th century that the devil might finally be converted and humans, if considerate, even help 'contribute to restore him to his original nature'. In the NT only Jude and Revelation, both arguably marginal works, hint at the devil's prehistory—and somewhat enigmatically. Neither was generally accepted as canonical for several centuries. The impact of *Gnostic dualism may have contributed to shaping a sense of diabolic power, but the necessity of arguing against Gnostics that there is only one creator of all things 'visible and invisible' forced development of a coherent theory of an angelic fall in order to explain how such evil beings could exist. But the development of the idea of a 'fall before the Fall', so poorly grounded in scripture, presents problems of its own.

The second internal problem lies in a tension between power and powerlessness. There is absolutely no consensus as to what the devil can do, especially after Christ's coming. In some interpretations, particularly Revelation and dependent texts, he is hugely potent, in others unable to do anything much but act as a buffoon, or so dependent upon divine permission that he becomes simply (as with *Calvin) an executor of his judgements, the 'minister' of God's wrath, returning very nearly to the role of Satan in Job. All Satanology is an attempt to explain the reality of evil in terms which avoid implicating God but equally escape any full-blooded dualism. Whether it succeeds is questionable and mainline Christian thought has certainly moved away from it in modern times, though it may be argued that the devil, as supreme liar, finds belief in his non-existence actually helpful!

The main argument for Christian belief in Satan remains undoubtedly the large place he occupies in the NT, but it is less clear that this is true of Jesus' own thought; it may owe more to his interpreters. Nowhere is it more difficult to decide whether, within a culture which took a certain belief for granted, the Christian message could use its terms without finally being committed to their literal meaning. If there is no 'personal' devil, as most modern Christian thinkers would probably claim, what, others enquire, are we saved from? 'No devil, no God', said *Wesley. Yet the personal status of the devil is irrelevant to the reality of evil, to its power in the human heart and society. Whether or not the devil is a 'personal' reality or a *symbol appropriate within a society which believed in the existence of a multitude of invasive invisible beings, the power of evil is unchanged together with the Christian duty to resist it. That the 'devil', shorthand for evil at its most potent, truly exists is unquestionable. 'He' was present throughout the witch-craze but in the hearts not of its victims but its inquisitors. He was present at Auschwitz. His face appears only too often in the daily papers. The danger in demonology is not that it has overemphasized the need to struggle with the 'powers of darkness' but that, too often, it has misplaced and perhaps even belittled the extent of their true identity. For *hermeneutics, *demythologization, and the *development of doctrine alike, Satan remains a primary candidate for explanation.   **Adrian Hastings**

Bruno de Jesus-Marie (ed.), *Satan*, ET (1951).
Forsyth, Neil, *The Old Enemy: Satan and the Combat Myth* (1987).
Messadie, Gerald, *The History of the Devil* (1997).
Papini, Giovanni, *The Devil* (1955).
Ricœur, Paul, *The Symbolism of Evil* (1967).
Russell, Jeffrey Burton, *The Devil* (1977).
—— *Satan: The Early Christian Tradition* (1981).
—— *Lucifer: The Devil in the Middle Ages* (1984).
—— *Mephistopheles: The Devil in the Modern World* (1986).
Wink, Walter, *Naming the Powers* (1984).
—— *Unmasking the Powers* (1986).
—— *Engaging the Powers* (1992).

diaconate. The Lima Report on *Baptism, *Eucharist and *Ministry (1982) by the *Faith and Order Commission of the World Council of Churches (see ECUMENICAL MOVEMENT) states that the threefold *ordained ministry of bishop, presbyter, and deacon 'may serve today as an expression of the unity we seek and also as a means for achieving it' (*Ministry*, 22) (see also EPISCOPATE; PRIESTHOOD).

One indication of the need for widespread change in order to realize the potential of the threefold pattern is the great variety of current understandings of the diaconate. In *Lutheran churches, deacons are generally not ordained but are commissioned as *lay ministers for parish work and social service; *Calvinist deacons are ordained as part of the fourfold ministry of pastor, teacher, elder, and deacon, to give leadership in caring for the poor and the *suffering; whereas many *Catholics and *Anglicans still think of the diaconate simply as a step on the way to presbyteral (priestly) ordination, rather than as a distinct ministry in its own right. The latter view actually originated in the 5th century and in the 6th the permanent diaconate became virtually extinct.

*Vatican II envisaged restoring the diaconate 'as a proper and permanent rank of the hierarchy', able to be conferred 'even upon married men', because the functions of deacons 'are so extremely necessary for the life of the church' (*Lumen Gentium*, 29). Pope Paul VI duly restored the permanent diaconate in the Catholic Church (*Sacrum Diaconatus Ordinem*, 1967). However, the restoration has been patchily implemented, because of lingering uncertainty about what a deacon actually is. This combination of enthusiasm and uncertainty is widespread and has prompted much ecumenical discussion of the diaconate in recent times (cf. the Anglican–Lutheran 'Hanover Report'), and a renewed awareness that, for instance, there were women deacons in the early Christian east. There have been women deacons in the Anglican Communion since the 1940s, succeeding the deaconesses whose introduction in the 1860s was influenced by the 19th-century Lutheran revival of nursing and teaching deaconesses at Kaiserwerth.

Catholics and Anglicans tend to dwell on the limited *liturgical usefulness of deacons in comparison with priests. Deacons can baptize, officiate at marriages and funerals, proclaim the scriptures, in particular the gospels, sing the Easter *Exsultet*, and preside at worship and prayer, but not at the most vital celebration, namely that of the *Eucharist. However, the deacon is *not* simply a minister who can perform fewer sacred actions than a priest. Correctly viewed, he or she is a different kind of minister altogether, whose few sacred actions are part of a ministerial portfolio which *bridges* the potential gap between the sacred and the secular. The deacon, who is also fundamentally dedicated 'to works of charity and functions of administration' (*LG* 29), uniquely embodies the Christian conviction that the sacred and the secular are not separate categories. Worship flows out into *work and work flows back into worship.

In ancient times, the twofold flow was liturgically expressed by the deacons' role as go-between, linking the bishop who presided at the liturgy, surrounded by the presbyters, with the people gathered round. The deacons presented the people's gifts to the bishop to be offered to God, prepared the gifts of bread and wine upon the altar, and then took those gifts consecrated back to the people for communion. In all their works of charity and administration outside the formal setting of the liturgy they could be said to be helping the people to prepare the gifts they will most fundamentally bring to the liturgy, namely their own holy lives and their strivings in the world. If it is the laity's task, 'worshipping everywhere by their holy actions' to 'consecrate the world itself to God' (*LG* 34), then the deacons are their prime enablers.

Deacons first appear in the NT as facilitators, so to speak, between the apostles (later succeeded by the bishops) and the people. After murmuring had occurred because some of the widows were 'neglected in the daily distribution', the Twelve directed the Christian community to pick out 'seven men of good repute, full of the Spirit and wisdom' to perform the practical tasks and thereby free the apostles for their own proper ministry of preaching the word. One of those chosen, Stephen, gave brave witness to his faith before the high priest and was stoned (Acts 6–7). The first Christian *martyr was a deacon.

*Paul describes the qualities required of deacons (1 Tim. 3: 8–13) and both Ignatius (*c.*100) and the *Didascalia Apostolorum* (early 3rd century) highlight the nobility of their calling as imitators and examples of Christ in his primary quality as *servant* (*diakonos*), even to the shedding of his blood (cf. Matt. 20: 26–8): 'whoever would be great among you must be your servant'. According to the *Apostolic Tradition* (*c.*215), the deacon is to 'acquaint the bishop with such matters as are needful'. For the *Didascalia*, he is 'the bishop's ear, mouth, heart and soul'!

Next to the bishop, in the 3rd century, the deacons were the most influential figures in the local church, more so than the part-time presbyters. This drastically changed with the great rise in Christian numbers in the 4th century. In the newly established parishes, presbyters became the regular eucharistic presidents. Both in their practical care for the people and in their representation of the bishop they now eclipsed the deacons. Some deacons were ordained to the presbyterate, for which their ministry began to appear simply as a preparation.

The Lima Report says, on behalf of many traditions, that 'by struggling in Christ's name with the myriad needs of societies and persons, deacons exemplify the interdependence of worship and work in the Church's life' (*Ministry*, 31). The struggle to perceive the deacons' role for today and relaunch their ministry across the churches is surely worthwhile.   **Paul McPartlan**

Anglican Consultative Council and Lutheran World Federation, *The Diaconate as Ecumenical Opportunity* (Hanover Report, 1996).

Barnett, J. M., *The Diaconate: A Full and Equal Order*, 2nd edn. (1995).

Collins, J. N., *Diakonia: Re-interpreting the Ancient Sources* (1990).

Hall, C., *The Deacon's Ministry* (1991).

McCaslin, P., and Lawler, M. (eds.), *Sacrament of Service* (1986).

Plater, O., *Many Servants: An Introduction to Deacons* (1991).

dialogue.

Imitating, perhaps, the Socratic model, Justin wrote a *Dialogue with Trypho*, a Jew (*c.*135), *Augustine several dialogues at Cassiciacum in his early philosophical period after baptism, and *Abelard a *Dialogue between a Christian, a Philosopher, and a Jew*. Nevertheless, both the literary form and the underlying idea of dialogue were for centuries of marginal significance for the history of Christian thought, though it could be claimed that in reality a dialogue with Greek philosophy was always central to it and that the long commentaries, for instance, of *Aquinas on *Aristotle's ethics and politics were essentially examples of dialogue.

In the early post-Reformation years there were numerous attempts to restore unity between *Catholics and *Protestants, or between *Lutherans and *Zwinglians, through theological dialogue as in the colloquies of Marburg (1529), Worms, and Ratisbon

(1540–1), and the Interim of Augsburg (1548). Unquestionably the best proponent of dialogue at that time was Melanchthon (1497–1560), most conciliatory of Lutherans. For the 19th century one might refer to Pusey's *Eirenicon* and *Newman's response, 'A Letter Addressed to the Rev. E. B. Pusey' (1864), even if Newman could remark, not unfairly, 'you discharge your olive-branch as if from a catapult'.

The emergence of the concept of dialogue, however, owes more to extended contact between *missionaries and the great *religions of Asia. Little by little, especially from the late 19th century and particularly at the time of the Edinburgh Missionary Conference of 1910, increasing appeals were made to replace a model of strident *evangelization of peoples seen as sunk in error and evil custom by an approach in which it was accepted that *Hinduism, *Buddhism, and *Islam were profound bearers of spiritual wisdom which could best be approached as partners in dialogue through which much could be learnt, as well as imparted. While this did not necessarily rule out hopes of *conversion, it introduced a new element into missionary work which might well become a dominant one. Despite a strong reaction against such an approach, stimulated by the advance of *Barthianism and, in particular, Hendrik Kraemer's uncompromising *The Christian Message in a Non-Christian World*, written especially for the International Missionary Council's 1938 conference at Tambaram (India), dialogue became a dominant theme both for interreligious relations and for interchurch *ecumenical relations during the latter part of the 20th century. Catholics, previously forbidden to take part in dialogue with other Christians, were encouraged by *Vatican II to enter enthusiastically into 'frank dialogue' with people of other religions or none: 'Such dialogue, conducted with appropriate discretion and tending to truth by way of love alone, excludes nobody' (*Gaudium et Spes*, 92). In consequence there has been a plethora of organized dialogues between different churches and religions as well as numerous instructions about dialogue, mostly emanating from Rome (e.g. 'On Dialogue with Unbelievers', August 1968, and 'Reflections and Suggestions Concerning Ecumenical Dialogue', August 1970). Numerous theological works have also been produced of a deliberately dialogical sort, one of the most distinguished examples being Hans *Küng's study of *Justification* in the work of Karl Barth, his doctoral thesis first published in 1957.

In one way and another, dialogue has as a result profoundly altered the entire character of the way Christian thought develops, at least in areas affected by interchurch and interreligious issues. There remains, however, much disagreement about the character, presuppositions, and fundamental justification of dialogue. Does it undermine or negate any point in mission seen as evangelization? Can one continue to believe both in dialogue and in the point of conversion from one religion or church to another? For many people committed to an evangelistic mission of a traditional sort, the pursuit of dialogue is betrayal, a sentiment strongly expressed, for instance, at the fifth assembly of the WCC at Nairobi in 1975. Dialogue involves an openness to learning from the other side and changing one's mind but it would be mistaken to suggest that it necessarily requires a conscious willingness to abandon any previous certainty. Useful dialogues may actually have quite limited goals, the aim of establishing not full agreement but shared understanding of some specific topic. While the ecumenical movement long favoured multilateral dialogue, from the 1960s, under the influence of the Roman Secretariat of Unity, there was a mushrooming of bilateral commissions appointed for official dialogue with the aim of producing agreed statements, of which the ARCIC reports between Anglicans and Catholics may be the best known. It has become increasingly clear, however, that there is a limited value in what can become a somewhat artificial activity, especially when the 'final' reports seldom prove to be final or are actually implemented. More important is an open dialogical sharing of minds at many levels from that of scholars to neighbourhood community groups.

It would be a mistake to attempt a definition of authentic dialogue in any precise way or to expect all dialogues to take a common form or start with identical presuppositions. While the aim of dialogue is always mutual understanding, not conversion, dialogue is not the whole of life. Parallel activities are possible within a single body, or even a single person, and a commitment to serious dialogue cannot be held to imply a rejection of the idea of conversion in any circumstances. Basically it does, nevertheless, symbolize a vast intellectual change affecting the way many Christians think both about Christian traditions other than their own and about other religions and views of life. It is a way correlative to recognition that the world is highly pluralistic and that many of our own traditionally held beliefs are less well founded than might be imagined. Moreover, dialogical theology has to be open, not only to other religious traditions but also to the whole range of intellectual disciplines just as it was traditionally to Greek philosophy. The road of dialogue does not imply or lead to absolute relativism but it does point to acceptance of a larger measure of relativism than most believers thought tolerable in the past and its rejection remains characteristic of almost every form of *fundamentalism.

See also CHINESE CHRISTIAN THOUGHT; INTERCHURCH MARRIAGE.

Adrian Hastings

Cracknell, Kenneth, *Justice, Courtesy, and Love: Theologians and Missionaries Encountering World Religions 1846–1914* (1995).

Kinnamon, M., *Truth and Community: Diversity and its Limits in the Ecumenical Movement* (1988).

Samartha, S. J. (ed.), *Faith in the Midst of Faiths* (1977).

Sheard, R. B., *Inter-Religious Dzialogue in the Catholic Church since Vatican II* (1987).

Dickinson, Emily

Dickinson, Emily (1830–86). 'I'm nobody, who are you?' A direct question posed by Emily Dickinson in the first line of a poem written from her self-imposed isolation in The Hermitage, Main Street, Amherst, Massachusetts. Of the 1,775 poems, including fragments, her sister Vinnie garnered after her death, only seven were printed in her lifetime, none in their original form.

There was a quality of burning ice that cut through pretension, and which spurred the expression of an intensely private inner life. 'I'd rather undress in public than have my poems published,' she wrote to a friend. Like her close neighbour, the philosopher and poet Ralph Waldo Emerson, she knew *poetry was 'heart language'. It was to the literary journalist Thomas W. Higginson at their first meeting, after eight years of correspondence, that Emily confided, 'If it makes my body so cold no fire can warm it, I know *that* is poetry.' Never, he told his wife after the meeting, had he been so drained of nervous energy—by her intensity.

Inevitably, as she wrote, she saw 'New Englandly', and that included living in the shadow of her father, prominent citizen, rock of the establishment, an elder of his Calvinistic church (see REFORMED THEOLOGY), from which Emily separated in 1848 following a religious crisis. This came about from a love affair ending in death, and an overdose of 'the dry wine' of Calvinistic logic imbibed at the Mount Holyoke Female Seminary. Nineteenth-century New England culture, though white Anglo-Saxon Protestant, was nevertheless generations on from classical Calvinism. Mount Holyoke had a tone of warm evangelical *revivalism, and in itself, as a women's college, challenged tradition. Emerson had begun his career as a minister of the *Unitarian church, a long-standing deviation from, and challenge to, Calvinism, before embracing Transcendentalism, an eclectic form of religious monism. In some very broad sense, Dickinson, like Emerson, was part of the delayed American encounter between religion and *Romanticism, as well as between Christianity and disbelief. Her poetry represents in consequence an intensity denuded of all dogmatic content, the expression of a post-Christian religiosity still feeding upon a powerful legacy of New England Protestantism.

Like Emerson before her, Emily passionately sought for a freedom of spirit. Even on 'the deplorable question of Slavery' Emerson wrote, in his massive journal, 'I have quite other slaves to free ... to wit, imprisoned spirits, imprisoned thoughts far back in the brain of man' ... For him 'dogmas' became 'the measles and the mumps of the soul'. It was these that Emerson and then Emily were to replace with the poetic voices of the purified and chaste 'soul' of mankind. She was to find that these could be equally tyrannical.

Much concerned with the intensities of death she first half-parodies the righteous, 'Safe in their alabaster chambers' ... 'Rafter of satin, | And roof of stone,' before taking her own carriage of death. This 'held just ourselves | And immortality' whose 'horses heads | Were toward eternity'. Thus the path of the carriage may be seen as a symbol of the intersection of time and eternity, a theme central to *Eliot's 'Four Quartets', in which Lyndall Gordon traces echoes of Dickinson in her *Eliot's New Life*.

Both poets retained a love/hate relationship with New England. Both, with Emerson, retained their *Puritan selves. On the day her father died in 1874, she was prostrated on her bed. 'His heart was pure and terrible', she wrote: she did not attend his funeral. Though all her life she had been absorbed with the mystery of *death, her 'soul-belief' enabled her to be almost casual about her own: 'I heard a fly buzz when I died.' There had been affinities with Emily Brontë and, at her request, the bold Brontë poem, 'Last Lines', was read at Emily's funeral. It was Mr Higginson who obliged.

Hugh Dinwiddy

Johnson, Thomas H. (ed.), *The Poems of Emily Dickinson* (3 vols.; 1955).

Johnson, Thomas H., and Ward, Theodora (eds.), *The Letters of Emily Dickinson* (3 vols.; 1958).

Levi, Barton, *Emily Dickinson and Her Culture: The Souls Society* (1984).

Dionysius the Pseudo-Areopagite

Dionysius the Pseudo-Areopagite. Dionysius, the author of a number of remarkable theological works, most probably lived in Syria in the early 6th century. His principal writings are the *Celestial Hierarchy*, the *Ecclesiastical Hierarchy*, the *Divine Names*, and the *Mystical Theology*. Profoundly affected by Neoplatonism (see PLATO), they offer the most co-ordinated account of theology as a whole written until then in the east. Their combination of systematization and profundity ensured a vast influence both in the *Byzantine east and, later, in the west, particularly in the high Middle Ages, affecting both academic theologians and spiritual writers. Areas in which they have had most influence include the negative, apophatic, knowledge of *God, the orders of *angels, the union with God or *deification of creation, the nature of the *church, especially the *symbolism of the *sacraments and of numbers, the shaping of the life of *prayer, in particular *mystical prayer.

The authority of these works was, however, vastly increased by the belief that they had been written by 'Dionysius the Areopagite' whom Paul converted at Athens (Acts 17: 34). This gave them almost *apostolic standing, still further enhanced by the western legend that Dionysius later became the first bishop of Paris (and patron saint of France). Their 1st-century date was challenged by 16th-century scholars and their 6th-century date convincingly demonstrated by 19th-century ones but the influence of the Dionysian writings on the development of Christian thought remains profound.   **Adrian Hastings**

Louth, Andrew, *Denys the Areopagite* (1989).
von Balthasar, Hans Urs, *The Glory of the Lord* (1984), ii. 144–210.

discipleship

discipleship is a striking feature of the gospel story and a historically reliable one. *Jesus called individuals to follow him, sharing his peripatetic and unstable life, and imbibing his teaching. The calls to Simon and Andrew, James and John, Levi and others to 'follow me' represent the true start of his ministry, while the discipleship which resulted from their obeying the call provides an enduring model for Christian life. Jesus' teaching was given, primarily, to them. It was teaching about the *Kingdom of God and how to respond to it, not about himself. Nevertheless the frequently asserted dichotomy between Jesus' focus on God and the church's subsequent focus on Jesus can be misleading because his call to the disciples was to 'follow me'. Subsequent christocentrism is not simply a post-*Resurrection phenomenon. Its root lies in the nature of discipleship. 'Lo, we have left everything and followed you' (Mark 10: 28). The idea of discipleship is a reflection of Jesus' strangely emphatic assertion of personal *authority. Following meant sharing his ideas, his moral imperatives and, in due course, his fate: 'Who ever does not bear his own cross and come after me, cannot be my disciple' (Luke 14: 27) for a disciple is not greater than his master. While discipleship included a measure of imitation, it was still more a matter of *obedience and of placing loyalty to Jesus above every other human tie.

It is noteworthy that the word 'disciple' did not last long within the Christian community. It represented too close a relationship with Jesus in the flesh; moreover, even in that meaning, the word 'apostle' came to be preferred. The twelve *apostles were now seen as those closest to Jesus, but it is noticeable in Mark and Matthew that even at the Last Supper, a vital moment for later theologies of the apostolate, the word 'disciple' is used. 'He sat at table with the twelve disciples.' Luke changed that to 'he sat at table and the apostles with him'.

Discipleship plays a particularly poignant role in *John's gospel which actually claims to be written (21: 24) by 'the disciple whom Jesus loved', who lay close to the bosom of Jesus at the final supper (symbolic of son and heir, cf. 1: 18), received the mother of Jesus into his home after the crucifixion, and outpaced Peter in running to the empty tomb (13: 23; 19: 26–7; 20: 2–10). Traditionally this disciple was John, son of Zebedee, something hard to gainsay as he would otherwise go unmentioned in this gospel for no explicable reason, but what matters here is rather his symbolic role, precisely that of disciple. In this as in everything in the fourth gospel, the frontier between history and *symbolism is impossibly difficult to trace, and every commentator charts it differently, but the beloved disciple would seem to signify the believing Christian as distinct from the pastoral Peter. Discipleship is subtly preferred to apostleship, yet does not challenge it. The disciple is closest to Jesus in love, cherishes his mother, remains until Jesus returns, but still defers to the authority of the hierarchy, whose ministry the risen Christ confirms in his final words to Peter recorded by the disciple. However, as the church grew in hierarchical differentiation, the word 'disciple' became archaic, to be replaced by 'Christian' (Acts 11: 26). Essentially the meaning was identical; a Christian is a disciple of Jesus. The continuity of identity between the pre- and post-Easter community is assured by the following of Jesus Christ.

The theme remains a constant one in Christianity, though often overshadowed by other institutional or moral preoccupations, always damagingly. For Paul Christian life was a matter of being changed into the likeness of Christ (2 Cor. 3: 18). *Francis of Assisi represents at its most striking the *spirituality of becoming almost an icon of Jesus. The 15th-century classic *The Imitation of Christ* of Thomas à Kempis sought to do the same, if less dramatically. No book apart from the bible can compare in extent of spiritual influence throughout the Christian world. It was translated no fewer than 33 times into English before 1900, John *Wesley and the Catholic Bishop Challoner producing two of the best versions, both in the 1730s. Nothing illustrates better the centrality of a sense of personal discipleship to Christian life. One of the classics of modern spiritual writing, *Bonhoeffer's *The Cost of Discipleship*, written when he was struggling against the Nazi state, strikingly revivified this sense. In the early 19th century too a group of American Christians, seeking to escape institutional denominationalism, began a movement that sought to restore the spirit of NT Christianity, once more calling themselves Disciples. The Disciples of Christ became a distinct communion in 1832 (see RESTORATIONISM).

Often forgotten behind the heavy institutional structures which have developed from the apostolate, discipleship is at one and the same time another name for Christian *morality and a marker of the essential equality between Christians while witnessing to the continuity of experience linking Jesus' own community with the subsequent community of the church.   **Adrian Hastings**

Bonhoeffer, D., *The Cost of Discipleship* (1937), ET (1959).
Freyne, S., *The Twelve: Disciples and Apostles* (1968).
Lawrence, K. (ed.), *Classic Themes of Disciples Theology* (1986).
Robinson, John, *The Priority of John* (1985).
Teegarden, K., *We Call Ourselves Disciples* (1979).

Dispensationalism

Dispensationalism is a method for taking the *bible literally. It does so by 'rightly dividing' it, so that apparently contradictory passages belong to different 'dispensations'. Thus prophecies will all come true, but we must not muddle the ones that claimed to refer to *Israel with those that refer to the *church. Christians for centuries have blurred these distinctions, so dispensationalists sometimes sound more modern, more like the historical critics whom they dislike, than one might expect.

The first dispensationalist was John Nelson Darby (1800–82), first leader of the Plymouth *Brethren. He rightly stressed how much *apocalyptic material there is in the bible, expected Christ's sudden return and the 'rapture of the saints' into the air, leaving the rest of us to the Tribulation, and, with literal-minded logic, worked out a scheme where God's promises to Israel of a messianic *kingdom on earth would also come true. This characterizes Dispensationalism. 'God is pursuing two distinct purposes: one related to the earth with earthly people and earthly objectives involved which is Judaism; while the other is related to heaven with heavenly people and heavenly objectives involved, which is Christianity' (Chafer, *Systematic Theology*).

Dispensationalism spread far beyond the Brethren, possibly helped by an ecclesiology which disparaged all organized churches, but canonized para-church pressure-groups. Devout young Presbyterians, Congregationalists, and Baptists learned Dispensationalism at Bible Conferences, like the ones that started at Niagara in 1876, and colleges like the non-denominational Moody Bible Institute. They read the bible using dispensational bible courses, and above all, they bought the *Scofield Reference Bible* (1909) which sold more than two million copies.

The word 'dispensation' is used in several places (particularly see 1 Cor. 9: 17; Eph. 1: 10; 3: 2; Col. 1: 25) in the Authorized Version, translating the Greek *oikonomia*. Economy is the art of running a household; other schools of theology too have talked of God's economy in giving us, for example, spiritual milk or meat as appropriate. Dispensationalism looks back through *history, and finds that God spoke differently in the past. This was not a new insight. 'The divine institution of sacrifice was suitable in the former dispensation, but is not suitable now' (Augustine). Earlier Christians than Darby, such as Isaac Watts, the 18th-century hymn-writer, had compiled a list of divine 'dispensations'. But Darby gave them emphasis and centrality. A dispensation is a 'well-defined time-period' and one 'during which man is tested in respect to obedience to some *specific* revelation of the will of God'. Scofield lists the dispensations: (1) innocence (Adam before the fall); (2) conscience (until Noah, and God's promise with the rainbow); (3) human government (until the call of Abraham); (4) promise (until the two-way covenant with Moses); (5) law (until Christ's death, which did away with the law); (6) church (including the present); and (7) the millennium. Each dispensation begins with a new covenant from God. Dispensationalists find they have to explain that Christ is relevant to all stages, not just the last two.

The willing amateur is thus given a framework with which to do bible study. One can go quite far with elementary logic and the literal sense of the words. Behind 19th-century Dispensationalism lay Scottish *Common Sense realism, and alongside it the rationalistic scientism of popular unbelief, all three strong on sense and weak on mystery.

Dispensationalism arose in a historically minded period, and is an attempt to explain change in history, and every word in the bible within a precise, fixed scheme of things. It rejects the historian's taste for development and evolution (theologically dangerous words) and sees nothing promising in change. 'In every instance, there was total and immediate failure as regarded man' (J. N. Darby). In each dispensation the only hope is for God to intervene unexpectedly. Christ will come on the clouds. The political consequence of such beliefs is detachment, or indeed a cynical hostility to reform. However, dispensationalists do tend to see God's hand at work in the new state of Israel in 1948, and so some, like Pat Robertson and Jerry Falwell, have tried to influence American foreign policy to help Israel. Dispensationalists want to convert Jews (Jews for Jesus) but Israel, Jews as Jews, excites them in a way unknown in earlier Protestantism, which saw itself as the Israel of God.

The movement breeds disciples, and wordy magisterial scholars, such as C. I. Scofield (1843–1921) and L. S. Chafer (1872–1952), who wrote an 8-volume *Systematic Theology*. It has developed over time. Some dispensationalists are seen as having made one division too many, like E. W. Bullinger, who thought that baptism and the Lord's supper belong in a different dispensation from ours. Some gave the impression that the Sermon on the Mount really belonged to the forthcoming messianic kingdom. (Are we *literally* expected now to turn the other cheek?) At one time it was usual to separate what Christ said about the 'kingdom of God' from what he said about the 'kingdom of heaven'. Charles C. Ryrie (1925–) set himself to rework or remove such problems as these, and his *Ryrie Study Bible* of 1978 has largely supplanted Scofield.

The tradition has broadened with the years. There are 'progressive dispensationalists', with a social conscience and a scholarly distaste for the 'speculation and sensationalism' of such fashionable apocalyptic as Hal Lindsay's *Late Great Planet Earth* (1970). On the other hand, the old contrast with *Adventism, with its search for 'signs of the times', as opposed to Dispensationalism's insistence that until Christ comes the prophecies are not fulfilled, has become blurred. However, many bible students round the world still want the literal reading that Dispensationalism offers.

Alistair Mason

Blaising, Craig C., and Bock, D. L., *Progressive Dispensationalism* (1993).
Marsden, George M., *Fundamentalism and American Culture* (1980).
Ryrie, Charles C., *Dispensationalism Today* (1965).
Sandeen, Ernest R., *The Roots of Fundamentalism: British and American Millenarianism 1800–1930* (1978).

divine command ethics claims that part or all of *morality depends in some fashion on the will of *God as promulgated by divine commands. This claim has an important place in the history of Christian thought. Both *Augustine and *Aquinas appeal at times to a divine command conception. As the selections in Idziak (1979) indicate, divine command theories are found in the *Franciscan ethics developed by John Duns Scotus and William of Ockham; they are also found in the work of disciples of Ockham such as Pierre d'Ailly, Jean Gerson, and Gabriel Biel; both Martin *Luther and John *Calvin endorse divine command ethics; and in modern British thought, prominent divine command theorists include John Locke, George Berkeley, and William Paley. The last three decades of the 20th century saw a revival of divine command ethics. Among the philosophers who made significant contributions to the revival are Robert M. Adams, Janine M. Idziak, Philip L. Quinn, and Edward R. Wierenga.

The recent revival of divine command ethics has devoted its energies to three tasks. The first is finding precise formulations of various versions of divine command ethics. The second is defending the theories thus formulated against objections. And the third is building a positive case for a divine command ethics. There has been progress in carrying out each of these tasks.

Formulating divine command ethics

Divine command ethics is best understood as an account of the deontological part of morality, which consists of moral requirements (obligation), permissions (rightness), and prohibitions (wrongness). On a divine command conception, actions forbidden by God are morally wrong, actions not forbidden by God are morally right, and actions commanded by God are morally obligatory. The present discussion focuses on the link between moral wrongness and divine prohibitions.

There has been disagreement about the nature of that link. Adams (1973) initially proposed that being contrary to the commands of a living God is part of the meaning of being morally wrong in the discourse of some Jewish and Christian believers. He later abandoned that proposal but argued for identifying moral wrongness with being contrary to the commands of a loving God (Adams, 1979). Quinn (1979) and Wierenga (1989) have proposed theories in which moral wrongness depends causally on divine prohibitions. Informally stated, Wierenga's idea is that an action is morally wrong only when God forbids it and God's forbidding an action causes it to be morally wrong.

Causal divine command theories are consistent with more than one account of moral knowledge. Just as we sometimes infer ordinary causes from their effects, we might come to know what God has forbidden by first coming to know what is morally wrong. A *natural law theorist, for example, could hold that we first come to know by the use of *reason what is contrary to natural law and then infer what God has forbidden from that knowledge. Hence it is possible for theorists such as Aquinas consistently to combine natural law thinking with divine command thinking. But just as we sometimes infer ordinary effects from their causes, we might also come to know what is morally wrong by first coming to know what God has forbidden. Divine command theorists could also hold that we first come to know what God has forbidden from the *revelation recorded in scripture and then infer what is morally wrong from that knowledge. And these two views can be consistently combined. Perhaps the most plausible view for a divine command theorist to adopt is that in some cases our knowledge of what is morally wrong is prior to our knowledge of what God has forbidden but in other cases our knowledge of what God has forbidden is prior to our knowledge of what is morally wrong.

Defending divine command ethics

There are many objections to divine command ethics. It is incumbent on its defenders to consider each of them on its own merits. The recent revival of divine command ethics has produced successful defences against several weighty objections.

Probably the most familiar objection is that divine command ethics would lead to moral nihilism if there were no God. According to divine command ethics, actions are morally wrong only if God forbids them. Hence nothing would be morally wrong if there were no God. But surely, the objector claims, murder would still be wrong even if God did not exist. One reply to this objection appeals to the traditional theological doctrines of God's necessary existence and essential moral perfection. God could not fail to exist and could not fail to be morally perfect, and so God could not fail to forbid murder and murder could not fail to be morally wrong. The objector is correct in thinking that murder could not fail to be morally wrong but does not see that this is because God could not fail to exist and to forbid it. More generally, the moral perfection of the divine nature acts as a constraint on what God can and cannot command. Divine commands are not arbitrary fiats.

Supporting divine command ethics

Successfully defending a theory against objections does not, of course, provide any positive reason for thinking the theory is true. And there is probably no single argument that proves the truth of any divine command theory. Yet divine command ethics can derive support from diverse considerations that add up to a strong cumulative case argument. Four such considerations support divine command ethics in a way similar to that in which the legs of a chair support the weight of a seated person. No leg supports all the weight, but each leg contributes to supporting it.

The first consideration comes from philosophical theology. According to the doctrine of divine sovereignty, all contingent things depend on God's creating and conserving power for their existence. Theoretical unity and simplicity make it attractive to extend the scope of divine sovereignty from human existence to human morality and to say that morality too depends upon the power of God.

Another consideration derives from the way in which a Christian exegetical tradition deals with the so-called 'immoralities of the patriarchs' in the Hebrew bible, most notably, the divine command to Abraham to slay Isaac recorded in Genesis 22: 1–2. Augustine (City of God, i. 21) maintains that Abraham's consenting to kill Isaac, which would have been wrong in the absence of the command, was not wrong given its presence. Aquinas (ST I-II q. 100 a. 8 ad. 3) argues that because God, who is Lord of life and death, commanded the slaying of Isaac, Abraham did not consent to murder when he consented to slay Isaac. Similar arguments by Bernard of Clairvaux and Andrew of Neufchateau are discussed in Quinn (1992).

A third consideration is that the ethics of love set forth in the gospels makes love the subject of a command. Matthew 22: 37–40 records Jesus as saying that we are commanded to *love God and the neighbour. In Works of Love, Søren Kierkegaard argues that there are two reasons to suppose that Christian love of neighbour is an obligation imposed by divine command. The first is that only a dutiful love can be sufficiently extensive in scope to embrace everyone without distinction, even one's enemies; the second is that only a dutiful love can be invulnerable to changes in its objects, a love that does not 'alter when it alteration finds'.

Finally, often enough in Christianity the rule for *prayer is also the rule for belief (lex orandi, lex credendi). After citing some examples of divine command ideas in Christian hymns and prayers, Idziak argues that divine command ethics formalizes an important theme of Christian spiritual life, namely, conformity to the divine will (Idziak 1997: 457).

Thus divine command ethics is both defensible and positively supported by a cumulative case argument. Though it competes for the allegiance of Christians with rivals such as natural law ethics and virtue ethics, it continues to be a valuable resource for Christian ethical thought.   **Philip L. Quinn**

Adams, R. M., 'A Modified Divine Command Theory of Ethical Wrongness', in G. Outka and J. P. Reeder, Jr. (eds.), *Religion and Morality* (1973).

—— 'Divine Command Metaethics Modified Again', *The Journal of Religious Ethics*, 7 (1979).

Idziak, J. M. (ed.), *Divine Command Morality: Historical and Contemporary Readings* (1979).

—— 'Divine Command Ethics', in P. L. Quinn and C. Taliaferro (eds.), *A Companion to Philosophy of Religion* (1997).

Kierkegaard, S. A., *Works of Love*, ET (1995).

Quinn, P. L., *Divine Commands and Moral Requirements* (1978).

—— 'Divine Command Ethics: A Causal Theory', in J. M. Idziak (ed.), *Divine Command Morality: Historical and Contemporary Readings* (1979).

—— 'The Primacy of God's Will in Christian Ethics', in J. E. Tomberlin (ed.), *Philosophical Perspectives*, 6 (1992).

Wierenga, E. R., *The Nature of God: An Inquiry into Divine Attributes* (1989).

divorce. In virtually all cultures over most of history *marriage was predominantly a patriarchal institution. Within this institution divorce was the procedure by which a husband could rid himself of an unsatisfactory wife. A wife's role was functional: to bear and nurture *children to continue her husband's lineage; to satisfy the *sexual needs of her husband; and to look after the home. Although there were variations between cultures, in general if a wife failed to satisfy these criteria, especially the first and second of them, she could be divorced.

Even in the Christian era patriarchy continued to have an impact on the institution of marriage, although likening the fidelity of the husband to Christ's fidelity to his *church (Eph. 5: 25–33) transformed the whole concept of the relationship and implied that it is on the husband that the primary obligation to fidelity lies. A wife came to be seen more as a *person in her own right and the mutuality of rights and obligations could be recognized (1 Cor. 7: 2–5 is extremely careful to stress mutuality). Consequently, divorce lost its *raison d'être* as an escape clause for dissatisfied husbands. In a society where divorce was exceedingly common, Christians were fully aware that Jesus had condemned it emphatically (Mark 10: 1–12). Not divorcing was one of Christianity's most notable characteristics.

Yet it was also recognized that in some circumstances the marriage relationship could be judged unsustainable, especially for a wife. For instance, if she becomes a Christian and her husband refuses to live at peace with her, *Paul has no qualms in declaring her free (1 Cor. 7: 15). Marriage is not meant to be destructive of persons, he argues. In cases of infidelity, *forgiveness is the order of the day but even here, in the absence of any real repentance, the Matthean community (Matt. 19: 9) would seem to have accepted the possibility of divorce. Neither of these *pastoral solutions was seen as denying the challenge of the words of Jesus, 'What God has joined together, let no one put asunder' (Matt. 19: 6). How that challenge works out in practice came to be interpreted differently in east and west. The church in the east held it in creative tension with Christ's words about *compassion and forgiveness. Hence, in unhappy and ambiguous situations affected by human failure and *sin, the possibility of healing and new life coming through another marriage could be accepted, provided there is genuine repentance.

In the Latin church a combination of Roman law and a classical mindset helped lead to a more absolute stance against divorce. Marriage as a contract, enacted by the couple's consent, created an ontological bond between them which, in the case of Christians in a consummated marriage, was absolutely indissoluble. However, a too-literal interpretation of the words of Jesus, 'What God has joined together, let no one put asunder' actually led to the conclusion that 'putting asunder' (divorce) was a possible option, but something reserved to God alone. Only God could divorce a couple. A high doctrine of the papacy began to claim that God had delegated the same power in certain circumstances to the pope by virtue of the power of the keys (the 'Petrine privilege'). The irony here is that divorce, described in the *Catechism of the Catholic Church*, n. 2385, as 'a plague on society', is implicitly recognized as a divine activity, even though, in the same breath, it is denounced as intrinsically person-injuring and community-destabilizing! Such a position is hard to reconcile with Christian common sense. On the other hand, if it is admitted that divorce, even if followed by a second marriage, can sometimes bring healing and new life out of a human situation which has become destructive for all involved, then in such cases it would seem to be a legitimate exercise of the church's healing *ministry. The church in the east opted for this second interpretation. In the west many have begun to move in the same direction, though approaching it via a slightly different route.

Recent statistics show that in the USA one in two marriages, and in the UK one in three, ends in divorce. Behind these disturbing figures lie numerous stories of personal pain as couples find their dream of a shared life together shattered and the investment of their persons in an enterprise of mutual affirmation and growth gradually turn into a nightmare of disillusionment. The accepted wisdom has come to be that it is better for a couple to divorce than to remain in a destructive relationship. While it is the children of a marriage who often suffer most from a divorce, it does not necessarily follow that it would be better for them to continue in a *family unit where the antagonism of their parents is severe.

That divorce involves a *moral failure due to an inability or unwillingness to live up to a freely made personal commitment is agreed by most churches. They also recognize that divorce is a social evil causing immense suffering. However, the way to tackle a social evil is not to penalize its victims. Millions of Christians now live in second marriages. It is not condemnation they need, but support, encouragement, affirmation, and practical down-to-earth help in rebuilding their lives. This must be the principal thrust in any policy of pastoral care for the divorced.

Increasingly for many churches pastoral care is being based on the belief that, for some at least, a new marriage can be an occasion of *grace and even a kind of resurrection experience. It is perfectly true that many second marriages fail, perhaps in part precisely because most churches do so little to make them a success. Instead of offering the preparation needed to give them the skills and confidence to build a more successful relationship this time, many churches are not prepared to involve themselves in second marriages. The official policy of the Roman Catholic church, for instance, is to refuse any semblance of celebrating a second marriage after divorce and the couple concerned are officially debarred from receiving the *sacraments. It is claimed that this is not meant to imply that they are living in sin at a personal level but is because their lifestyle 'objectively' contradicts Christ's total fidelity to the church celebrated in the Eucharist. Nevertheless, for those on the receiving end, this is rarely experienced as pastoral care but as an unforgiving and even punitive attitude. Invitations to them to change their unacceptable lifestyle and live together as brother and sister only serve to deepen their feelings of being condemned and rejected.

Here as elsewhere in the moral life the basic issue may be whether the primary moral obligation of a person can be encapsulated in some 'objective' pattern of behaviour or whether it consists in being as loving as possible within the existing circumstances, in part created by their own past failings. The exclusion from *communion of Christians doing their best within a committed second marriage seems contradictory to Christian morality as a whole, and may epitomize better than any other current issue the basic divide: is Christianity a religion of law or one of *love?

Kevin T. Kelly

Kelly, Kevin T., *Divorce and Second Marriage: Facing the Challenge*, 2nd edn. (1996).

Pospishil, Victor, *Divorce and Remarriage* (1967).

Roberts, William P. (ed.), *Divorce and Remarriage: Religious and Psychological Perspectives* (1990).

Steininger, Viktor, *Divorce* (1969).

Docetism is an early view of the person of *Jesus Christ in which his human nature, especially his *body and *sufferings, are not real but apparent. The term derives from the Greek *dokein*, 'seem', and is a term of abuse: no one ever called himself a Docetist. The tendency is already resisted in New Testament texts, where Jesus proves his body is real (Luke 24: 36–43) or it is asserted that he 'came in the flesh' (especially later texts; John 20: 24–9, 1 John 4: 1–6). Ignatius of Antioch denounces the view that Jesus suffered and rose only 'apparently' (*to dokein*), which calls in question the sufferings of the martyrs.

That Jesus' body is spiritual, especially after the *Resurrection, might seem to follow from biblical incidents, like walking on water, going through closed doors, disappearing when pursued, or not needing food. In a 2nd-century apocryphon, Jesus' body is not always substantial and he walks leaving no footprints (*Acts of John*, 93). Marcion, some so-called *Gnostics (especially the Valentinians), and the Manichees held such views. To them the transcendent nature of the ultimate Spirit from whom Christ came did not permit contamination with a physical *body: Christ came to manifest the true life of the spirit, and to awaken the victims of flesh and darkness to their true nature and destiny. Other notions are sometimes regarded as 'Docetic', as when Cerinthus and others distinguished the spiritual or divine element in Jesus from the physical man, suggesting that the divinity entered him at baptism and left him before the crucifixion. Some Basilideans held that Simon of Cyrene was crucified instead of Jesus, and, in *Acts of John*, 97, Jesus' true self talks to John while the body is crucified (see CROSS).

The term 'Docetists' (*doketai*) is first used by Serapion of Antioch (c.180) of the *Gospel of Peter*, where Christ's divine power forsakes him before the crucifixion. Such ideas are consistent with a view of human destiny (coherent with current *Platonism) as escape from the world and flesh into a realm of pure knowledge and spirit. Its critics, such as *Irenaeus and Tertullian, held that the one true God

made this world good, and humanity in it, and that the purpose of Christ's coming was precisely to save the physical world, and human beings in their psychosomatic totality, from the corrupting effects of sin. It was of central importance that Christ lived a fully human life and that his death and Resurrection were physical, like those of other human beings. With human *salvation would come a new heaven and a new earth.

The term 'Docetic' reappears from time to time in theology, as in criticism of Apollinaris (4th century) who held that Jesus Christ's mind was that of God the *Word, and not of a created man, and Julian of Halicarnassus (6th century), who held that the divine presence in Christ's flesh made it incorruptible, for which he was dubbed 'aphthartodocetic' (incorruption-docetist). Although ancient and condemned, Docetism is still remarkably resilient. There seems to be a recurrent tendency, both in popular Christianity and in some theology, to spiritualize the man Jesus to the point of dehumanizing him.

See also CHRISTOLOGY; INCARNATION; PRE-CONSTANTINIAN THOUGHT.

Stuart G. Hall

Grillmeier, Aloys, *Christ in Christian Tradition*, 2nd edn. (1975).

Elliott, J. K., *The Apocryphal New Testament* (1993).

dogma as a term has many meanings. In Greek and Roman secular usage, it generally referred to an opinion or decision as to what seemed true (see TRUTH) and good. In ancient philosophy the Stoics were called 'dogmatists' because, unlike the Academics, they professed certain beliefs and did not resign themselves to scepticism. In the Greek bible and the Vulgate Latin translation 'dogma' generally means 'ordinance' or 'edict' (Esther 4: 3; Dan. 2: 13; 6: 12, 16; Luke 2: 1; Acts 16: 4; 17: 7; Eph. 2: 15; Col. 2: 14). In the early church, conciliar decrees (usually practical directives) were occasionally called 'dogmas' (e.g. eighth canon of Nicaea). In patristic and medieval Latin theology the term 'dogma' generally meant a tenet. It could be true or false, revealed or unrevealed. While the 'false' or 'perverse' dogmas of the heretics were repudiated, the 'true' and 'heavenly' dogmas of the Catholic Church were treasured. The Council of *Trent distinguished between dogmatic decrees, pertaining to faith, and reform decrees, pertaining to morals and conduct. Since the 18th century, 'dogma' has become a technical term, generally meaning a propositional truth that is authoritatively taught in the *church as revealed by God and as binding on all members of the community.

Although dogma as a technical term is relatively new, the idea that certain beliefs are matters of *faith and may not be contested in the community has ancient roots. The OT, for example, teaches the necessity of acknowledging the one true God who delivered Israel from its captivity (e.g. Deut. 6: 4–25). The NT teaches the obligation to believe in Jesus Christ as the Son of God (1 John 4: 15), the only Lord (1 Cor. 8: 6), and the sole mediator of salvation (1 Tim. 2: 5). The apostolic tradition concerning the *Resurrection is proposed as a matter of faith (1 Cor. 15: 1–11). Anathemas are invoked on all who preach 'another gospel' (Gal. 1: 8–9). Those who fall away from 'the doctrine of Christ' (2 John 9–11) are to be shunned. The early *councils in their determinations of the faith (Greek *ekthesis* or *pistis*) gave definitive answers to the *Trinitarian and *christological questions with which they dealt. The first seven councils of the first eight centuries are accepted in most of the Christian world. Since the split between the east and west at the end of the first millennium there have been no councils having the same ecumenical recognition.

In *Eastern Orthodoxy, dogmatic authority is attributed to binding doctrinal formulations issued by ecumenical councils of the 'undivided' church and received by the church as a whole. Roman *Catholics generally hold that, since the church of Christ 'subsists' in the Roman Catholic communion, medieval and modern western councils (including Trent, *Vatican I, and *Vatican II) can be ecumenical and, as such, can proclaim dogmas. Since the concept of dogma was imprecise in earlier centuries, and since papal *infallibility was slow in gaining recognition, it is difficult to determine which declarations of medieval popes and councils deserve to be called dogmas in the modern sense.

Vatican I, following certain theological developments since the *Reformation, understood dogmas to be revealed truths authoritatively taught by the church as requiring the assent of Christian faith. The council distinguished between two classes of dogma: those defined by a 'solemn judgment' of popes and councils and those taught by the 'ordinary and universal *magisterium*'—i.e. the bishops in communion with Rome. The same council solemnly defined papal infallibility as a 'divinely revealed dogma'.

Vatican II reaffirmed the doctrine of papal infallibility and added that the whole body of Catholic bishops, especially when gathered at an ecumenical council, can teach the faith infallibly (*Lumen Gentium*, 25). Vatican II, however, refrained from proclaiming any new dogmas. Like Vatican I, it taught that popes and councils can proclaim as dogma only what is contained, at least implicitly, in the word of God as transmitted through scripture and tradition. But these councils also specified that the magisterium of the church is able to expound the deposit of faith authoritatively, speaking in the name of Jesus Christ (*Dei Verbum*, 10 and 12). *Heresy, in modern Catholic usage, is considered to consist in obstinately doubting or denying a dogma, and is thus correlative with dogma (cf. *Profession of Faith* of 1989 and canon 751 of the *Code of Canon Law* of 1983).

Even within the Catholic Church the official concept of dogma is not uncontested. Hans *Küng, influenced by Karl *Barth, questioned the infallibility of popes and councils. His position was repudiated by the Congregation for the Doctrine of the Faith in the Declaration *Mysterium Ecclesiae* (1973). More recently August Hasler and Luis Bermejo have questioned whether the bishops at Vatican I spoke with the freedom and unanimity that would be required for their teaching on papal infallibility to be recognized as authentic dogma. John Henry *Newman at the time of Vatican I experienced similar difficulties, but was able to resolve them on the ground that the bishops after the council accepted the definition of papal infallibility. Some Catholics today argue that Vatican II freely and unanimously received the teaching of Vatican I.

Generally speaking, the concept of dogma has been less central to Protestant than to Catholic thinking. *Liberal Protestants such as Adolf Harnack regarded dogma as deformation resulting from the reception of the gospel on Hellenistic soil. While objecting to the 'Hellenization of the gospel', Harnack was even more strenuous in his denunciation of the modern Catholic concept of dogma, which he regarded as authoritarian and legalistic.

Other Protestants, however, are willing to accept 'dogma' in a broader sense, as a definitive statement of Christian truth that finds general acceptance in the community. Julius Kaftan (1848–1926) called for a new concept of dogma corresponding to the faith of the Reformation and consonant with Immanuel *Kant's conception of practical reason. Karl Barth in his *Church Dogmatics* proposed a more biblically grounded concept of dogma. For him dogmas are doctrinal propositions acknowledged and confessed by the church as being contained in the word of God. They have relative authority, but are in need of being tested against the event of *revelation, which comes to us through the bible as the written word of God. In the Lutheran tradition, 20th-century ecumenists such as Edmund Schlink, Wolfhart *Pannenberg, and George *Lindbeck have accented the confessional and doxological aspects of dogma and have noted the historical and cultural factors that have conditioned the church's formulation of dogma. For Lindbeck, dogmas are communally authoritative rules governing discourse in the church. While irreversible in their original context, dogmas, Lindbeck holds, can lose their binding force as the cultural setting shifts.

The universal and permanent character of dogmatic definitions is often challenged because, on the one hand, divine mysteries transcend the power of the human intellect and, on the other hand, human concepts and *languages are conditioned by the cultures of various times and places. Consideration of these difficulties can bring a necessary refinement to the concept of dogma. The human mind cannot conceptually grasp the mysteries of revelation except as filtered through limited human apprehensive powers. Dogmas reflect particular aspects of revelation and depend on the *analogy of things known by natural experience. But these limitations do not prevent dogmas from being true and certain so far as they go.

Dogmatic pronouncements are further limited by the conceptual patterns and linguistic usages of the culture in which they were formulated and by the limited context of knowledge available at the time. The contemporary meaning and value of ancient formulations may require explanation. New formulations must sometimes be substituted for old ones that have become obscure and confusing. Such substitutions do not mean that the dogmatic teaching of the church in the past was false but only that it was expressed in outdated concepts or language or in a limited framework that has been transcended.

Beginning with the earliest credal confessions, such as those found in scripture, the objectification of faith has progressed through the baptismal *creeds of the first three centuries, the more elaborate creeds of Nicaea and Constantinople, conciliar decisions such as those of *Chalcedon, and finally, modern dogmas such as those promulgated by Vatican I and by recent popes. Some development seems inevitable, since the human mind cannot assimilate any teaching without reflecting in new contexts on the meaning and significance of what has been taught. It does not seem possible to limit the contents of faith to explicit biblical teaching or even to the teaching of the early centuries.

Dogmatic *development is spurred on by a variety of motives. The Christian message, originally cast in Semitic thought-forms, has to be made intelligible in other cultures. As time goes on, the church has to respond to new questions not explicitly answered in the earliest sources. In order to ward off heresies, the church has to explicate certain beliefs that were previously held in a vague or tacit manner. Then again, devotional interests may prompt the church to celebrate God's gifts by solemn proclamation. To show the legitimacy of the process by which any given doctrine has developed would require a detailed historical study of that doctrine in particular. Newman, in his *Essay on the Development of Christian Doctrine*, laid down seven criteria of authentic development and applied them to a number of the Catholic teachings that were being challenged in his day. For him the developments met the criteria.

To promote better *ecumenical relations between churches that differ regarding the concept of dogma, it is important to bear in mind that Christian faith does not signify, in the first instance, assent to dogmas. It goes out primarily to the God who reveals himself in the person of Christ, in history, and in experience. Revelation does not come to us, originally, in the form of dogmas, but rather in the vivid, non-technical, and primarily narrative language of scripture. Credal and dogmatic formulas are hammered out in subsequent reflection and are intended to summarize and clarify what was previously believed, though perhaps indistinctly. While the dogmatic heritage of the past is enriched and reinterpreted in the context of increasing knowledge, teachings that were formerly regarded as dogmas sometimes come to be reclassified as doctrines of a lower order.

Dogmas, then, must not be regarded as the primary objects of Christian faith, but rather as aids for focusing faith on God as Lord and saviour. The central dogmas relating to God and Christ are shared by most Christians. Dogmas, as partial refractions of the revealed mystery, should never be taken in isolation. They have their true meaning in the context of the total revelation, which is mediated by scripture and by the *liturgy, *prayer, and life of the church. Because human language depends on created analogies, dogmas always fall short of capturing the divine reality. Properly understood, however, they can help the Christian people on their journey towards the vision of God, in which there will no longer be any need for dogmas. In relation to that vision all dogma is 'provisional'.

Avery Dulles, SJ

Barth, Karl, *Church Dogmatics*, I/1, *Doctrine of the Word of God* (1936), ET (1975).

Deneffe, August, 'Dogma: Wort und Begriff', *Scholastik*, 6 (1931).

International Theological Commission, 'On the Interpretation of Dogmas', *Origins*, 20 (1990).

Lindbeck, George, *The Nature of Doctrine: Religion and Theology in a Postliberal Age* (1984).

Newman, John Henry, *An Essay on the Development of Christian Doctrine* (1845).

Pannenberg, Wolfhart, 'What Is a Dogmatic Statement?', in his *Basic Questions in Theology* (1970), i.

Sullivan, Francis A., *Creative Fidelity: Weighing and Interpreting Documents of the Magisterium* (1996).

von Harnack, Adolf, *Outlines of the History of Dogma* (1893).

Dominican thought.

The Dominican Order was founded by Dominic of Caleruega, a Spanish cleric, in 1215. Originating in an itinerant *preaching group combating the Albigensian *heresy in 1205, it was transformed over the next twenty years, with papal encouragement, into an international religious order. Its mission was the defence of orthodox Catholic doctrine through preaching, teaching, and the disciplined study of *theology in the context of a modified *monastic discipline. The friars were to communicate the fruits of their ascetic contemplation in the exercise of their preaching ministry, hence their official name, the Order of Preachers.

By 1300 Dominicans were present in all the major European university towns and had attracted large numbers of university-trained clerics to their ranks. The work of Albert the Great (*c*.1200–80) and his pupil, Thomas *Aquinas, transformed scholasticism, giving the speculative and dogmatic outlook and method of the Dominican Order an abiding intellectual cast.

The Dominican vision focuses on *God as the First Truth and orders experience and life in accordance with that *truth. The basic doctrines of the Christian faith cannot be established by *reason alone, but the intellectual integrity of Christianity demands that they be shown not to conflict with reason. In the Dominican scheme, the critical intellect is applied to the revealed truths of the faith in order to demonstrate their internal coherence. Intellectual enquiry is undertaken in the context of a life of *prayer and *worship marked by the vocation of Christian *discipleship.

Dominican theological endeavour, bolstered by the appropriation and Christianization of the metaphysical structure of *Aristotelian thought, engages positively with the objectivity of material reality, accepts the movement of divine *revelation, and holds all knowledge as valuable because it leads ultimately to God. The communication of this 'divine wisdom' is an exercise of compassionate intelligence that recognizes in every partner in theological dialogue an actual or possible Christian disciple. This approach accepts and incorporates what is true in an opposing argument, admitting the position of the other as the initial field of encounter.

Dominican thought is theocentric, seeing God as Alpha and Omega, the origin and fulfilment of all things and Christ as the way 'who showed in his own person that path of truth which, in rising again, we can follow to the blessedness of eternal life' (Aquinas, *Summa Theologiae*, Prologue, III). Beginning in opposition to a metaphysical, *dualist heresy which taught that the material world is evil and the product of an evil anti-God, it answered this challenge by proclaiming that the world is essentially good, that *humanity is flawed and fallen but not totally corrupt, and that human beings are marked by an innate desire for God. This desire is often imperfectly satisfied by fixation on what is less than God. The integration and edification of this desire is achieved through the attentive contemplation of the objectivity of reality, which leads to a delight in the luminous divine intelligence whose essential simplicity informs the complex beauty of the natural and human creation.

In 1313 the General Chapter of the Order declared that all Dominican teachings must be in accord with the Thomist synthesis. A major revival of Thomist studies followed in the work of John Capreolus (*c*.1380–1444) and de Vio Cajetan (1469–1534), who was to become the standard commentator on Aquinas. He is also known for his confrontation with *Luther in 1518. The University of Salamanca took up the Thomist standard under the inspiration of Francisco de Vitoria (1483–1546) who opposed nominalism and shifted the focus of theological study from the *Sentences* of Peter Lombard to the text of Aquinas. Confronted by the imperial expansion of Spain's Golden Age, he attempted to apply the principles of *natural law and *justice to the political, ethical, and moral questions raised by the conquest of the Indies. He is often called the father of international *law for his work on questions of the just *war, the power of states, his doctrine of citizenship, and his advocacy of the rights of the native Americans. All of this was constructed on the application of Thomistic moral and political principles. Another tireless defender of native American rights was Bartolomé de Las Casas (1484–1566); a priest and colonial landholder, he underwent a profound personal conversion, began to contest the Spanish colonial system, and joined the Dominican Order. His demands for reform were partly successful in the promulgation of the New Laws of 1542–3 which prohibited Indian slavery and attempted to reform the colonial administration. Up to his death in 1566 he continued to plead the cause of justice and anti-*slavery with limited results.

Dominicans and the word of God

Reliable versions of the sacred texts are indispensable to the preacher. Hugh of St Cher (1200–63) drew up one of the first concordances of the Vulgate and composed other works relating to biblical textual study. Nicholas of Gorran (1232–95) followed by preparing a series of influential scriptural commentaries. Albert the Great always insisted on working on the best texts available, while Aquinas's scriptural commentaries are a major and unappreciated part of his œuvre. Sixteenth-century concern for the integrity of texts was expressed in the *bible translation of Santes Pagninus (d. 1536), whose fidelity to the original caused some anxiety to his contemporaries. The 19th-century Dominican, Marie Joseph Lagrange (1855–1938), was amongst the first Catholic scholars to engage with biblical *higher criticism, establishing the École Pratique d'Études Bibliques at Jerusalem in 1890, and two years later the Revue biblique. Despite being suspected of *modernism at the outset of the 20th century, he was able to present a case for the reconciliation of critical methods of interpretation with the inspiration and inerrancy of the bible. His work influenced papal encyclicals on sacred scripture and the Decree on Revelation of *Vatican II.

The living word of God must be embedded in particular historical and cultural forms and woven into the vital tradition of the people of God. Expressions of this vision can be found in the work of the popular 14th-century Italian preachers Venturino of Bergamo and John Dominici who founded the reformed convent at Fiesole outside Florence from which sprang the Florentine priory of San Marco in 1436. San Marco numbered amongst its 15th-century members Antoninus Pierozzi, a social reformer, a confidant of Cosimo de Medici, and subsequently archbishop of Florence; the artist Fra Angelico (Giovanni da Fiesole); and Girolamo Savonarola, an apocalyptic preacher whose utopian evangelical vision led to his eventual excommunication by Pope Alexander VI, and execution by the commune of Florence.

Dominicans and the Inquisition

The papacy quickly channelled Dominican expertise into the support of the *Inquisition, whose formal organization coincided with the appearance of the Mendicant Orders. Gregory IX promulgated its fundamental constitution in 1231, and Dominicans soon found themselves entrusted with the work of the new tribunal in Germany, France, northern Italy, and Spain. The most notorious representative of the Spanish Inquisition was Tomás de Torquemada (1420–98) whose severity has become a byword for fanaticism and cruelty. The expulsion of the Jews from Spain in 1492 may be partly attributed to his influence. Dominicans continued to hold office in the various tribunals until the final suppression of the Spanish Inquisition in 1834.

The challenge of the 20th century

Pope Leo XIII fixed on *Thomism as the classical synthesis of Catholic doctrine best endowed to provide an *apologetic structure for answering the threat posed by liberalism and scepticism. In 1894 he established the Leonine commission to produce a critical edition of the works of Aquinas. Over a century later, the commission continues its work. A challenge to the classical neo-scholastic Thomist synthesis was posed by the work of Marie-Dominique Chenu (1895–1990) of the French Dominican theological school at Le Saulchoir outside Paris. Chenu's principal opponent in the debate was his former teacher and fellow Dominican, Réginald Garrigou-Lagrange (1877–1964), professor at the Angelicum, the Dominican University in Rome, regarded as the leading Thomist theologian of his time. Chenu appealed for the contextualization of theological study, situating Aquinas only in the context of his time and against the contemporary intellectual background. He implicitly criticized Garrigou-Lagrange and his disciples, who represented a Roman neo-scholastic orthodoxy, for presenting an absolutist Thomism abstracted from any time and place and applied in quasi-Gnostic fashion as an apologetic tool for the defence of the faith. At times such a method resembled *Enlightenment rationalism with its indifference to history. Chenu was quickly accused of modernism and his approach denounced as crypto-*Hegelian.

Despite temporary eclipse, Chenu decisively influenced Yves *Congar and the Flemish Dominican Edward *Schillebeeckx. Both were his pupils and were influenced by his method. Their approach advocated the sympathetic examination of theological tradition in the light of contemporary experience. Resources for this project were drawn from 19th-century Catholic theologians such as Johann Adam Möhler and John Henry *Newman. Möhler's view of the *church as a living organism animated by the eternal principle of the Holy Spirit exercised a strong influence over Chenu, Congar, and their students, shifting the principle of significance in the theology of the church from idea to life. According to this view, the church is always embodied, not an intellectual construct, and must be studied as such. European Dominican theologians thus made space within Catholicism for a deeper appreciation of the principle of doctrinal *development, of the role of the imagination and experience in the theological task, and of the function of the liturgy and magisterium in the articulation of the faith.

The drift of 20th-century Dominican thought has been bifocal: an attentive and contemplative scouring of tradition and an attention to the spiritual and doctrinal needs of the age. It rests on the belief that as God has revealed himself in Word and Sacrament his providential purpose is also unfolded in the 'signs of the times'. In the 1940s and 1950s the *French Dominicans attempted to respond to the crisis presented to French Catholicism by *secularization and industrialization by providing a theological and dogmatic framework for the worker-priest movement, an association that was ended under Roman pressure in 1954. They were pioneers in the ecumenical field and in the dialogue with *Eastern Orthodoxy, establishing the Istina institute in Paris. The Institute for Islamic Studies in Cairo, founded and staffed mostly by French Dominicans, continues the work of study and dialogue with Islam begun in the 13th century by Raymond of Peñafort.

The emphasis on the return to the well-springs of tradition in the hope of renewing liturgical, dogmatic, spiritual, and social life was not without its critics. In 1950 Pius XII condemned what was called the 'New Theology' in his encyclical *Humani Generis*. Condemnation by the Vatican led to years of isolation for Congar amongst others. This ended for him with his appointment as an expert at Vatican II when his work was incorporated into the documents on Revelation, the Church, and Ecumenism. He was named cardinal in 1995. The influence of Chenu at Vatican II, on the other hand, is to be seen above all in the *Constitution on the Church in the Modern World, (Gaudium et Spes)*.

As 13th-century Dominican thought was marked by an openness to Aristotelianism so Dominican thought, as exemplified by Schillebeeckx and his supporters and opponents, struggles with the problems of *hermeneutics. The Thomist vision, whilst perennially valid, is no longer accorded exclusive status but is exposed to the challenge of biblical exegesis, philosophy, politics, and sociology. In this endeavour a tension is maintained between text, contemporary reality, and history itself in the creative development of tradition.

Allan White, OP

Ashley, B. M., *The Dominicans* (1990).
Chenu, M. D., *Une École de théologie: Le Saulchoir* (1937), 2nd edn. (1985).
Lehner, F. C., *St Dominic: Bibliographical Documents* (1964).
Hinnebusch, W. A., *The History of the Dominican Order* (2 vols.; 1966; 1973).
Kennedy, P., *Schillebeeckx* (1993).
Nichols, A., *Congar* (1985).
—— *Dominican Gallery* (1996).
Tugwell, S., *The Early Dominicans* (1982).
—— *The Way of the Preacher* (1979).
Vicaire, M. H., *Saint Dominic and his Times* (1964).

Donatism was a *schism in the North African Church which originated during the 'Great Persecution' of 303–5. Those clergy who had compromised, by obeying Diocletian's edict that all copies of the scriptures should be handed over to the Roman authorities, were regarded by rigorists as *traditores* (traitors), and as thereby having excluded themselves from the true Catholic church in Africa.

When Mensurius, bishop of Carthage, died (311), the church elected his unpopular archdeacon, Caecilian, to take his place. The rigorists, represented by Secundus of Tigisi, primate of Numidia, and seventy bishops, opposed the election on the grounds that one of the consecrating bishops, Felix of Apthungi, was himself a *traditor* and therefore his ministry was invalid. They elected their own candidate, Majorinus, who was quickly succeeded by Donatus, whose name the schism bears. The church had experienced numerous schisms based on rigorist ideals of perfection and purity. Donatism was exceptional, however, in its localized character, its social, political aspect, and its fierce tenacity over a number of centuries.

Despite imperial opposition, the schism soon became entrenched in North Africa, and in 336 Donatus was able to call a council of 270 Donatist bishops. Only with the Emperor Honorius' *Edict of Unity* (405), which applied anti-heretical laws to the Donatists, and the concerted attack of Aurelius of Carthage and *Augustine of Hippo, did Donatism begin seriously to falter. The Conference of Carthage in 411, attended by 285 Donatist bishops and 286 Catholic bishops, sealed the fate of the Donatists when the imperial tribune, Marcellinus, found against them and instituted a harsh series of laws (412) designed to coerce them into unity with the Catholic Church.

There is, however, evidence of Donatist activity as late as Gregory the Great.

Our main sources of evidence are Optatus of Milevis' *De schismate donatistarum* (rev. c.390) and Augustine of Hippo's many treatises and letters against them (which are also the source for most of the Donatist works now known to us), as well as legal, archaeological, and epigraphical evidence.

Political, social, economic, and geographical, as well as religious, factors have been suggested to explain the origin and extraordinary tenacity of the schism. The uncompromising, traditional, conservative religion, and the popularity of the cult of the *martyrs, in the villages of inland Numidia and among Berber nomads, combined with a strong sense of social injustice due to the system of taxation and the increasing sedentarization of the land, is thought to lie behind the rise (from 340 on) of the extreme and violent wing of Donatism, represented by the fanatic Circumcellions, and of their support of political revolts such as those by Firmus (372) and Gildo (398). The Donatists, however, also embraced educated laymen, notably Tyconius.

The Donatists considered themselves to be the true, uncompromised, Catholic Church in Africa—the true inheritors of the African fathers, Tertullian, who had propounded a very similar doctrine of perfection in the church, and Cyprian of Carthage. To the latter they appealed to support their emphasis upon the holiness and purity of the clergy, especially the bishops, on which they believed the validity of the *sacraments to depend. They therefore stressed the necessity (maintained by Cyprian against Pope Stephen) of rebaptism for anyone baptized by a heretic or schismatic. They were supported in their ideals by a strong martyr spirit which emphasized the necessity of preserving purity, and of *suffering for the cause of righteousness, against the hostile forces of the world, often represented by the persecuting state which was now allied with the Catholic Church ('What has the Emperor to do with the Church?', Donatus, in *Optatus*, 3. 3).

Their main opponent was Augustine of Hippo. He argued against them on the basis of carefully researched factual, historical detail, as well as theological doctrine. He pointed out that in schism they were separating themselves from the Universal Church throughout the world ('securus iudicat orbis terrarum' (*C. ep. Parm.* 3. 4. 34), a text which had great significance in precipitating the conversion of *Newman in the 19th century); that the *holiness of the Church, its ministers, and its sacraments derives not from any personal, ritual, or institutional purity, but from Christ; that the sacraments therefore have an intrinsic sanctity, integrity, and value; even when administered by a schismatic they are valid when performed in the name of Christ and according to the proper formulae (though they are ineffective—since faith and the operation of the Holy Spirit are lacking); that the church is a mixed body, containing wheat and tares, that will only be separated at the last judgement; that coercion is a justified means of dealing with the threat the Donatists posed (though he only gradually came to this position). The ecclesiology, and theology of the sacraments and priesthood, thus elaborated, have remained influential in the west ever since.

The conflict between Donatists and Catholics essentially represents two different views of the role of the church in society: the one uncompromising, perfectionist, exclusive, and usually local; the other comprehensive, catholic, universal, and inclusive.

These two attitudes, and their resultant religious groupings, have been clearly manifest throughout the history of church divisions. Further, in challenging the church's relation to the secular state and its use of coercion, the Donatists touched upon a nerve which is still sensitive in the present day.   **Carol Harrison**

There is a selection of Augustine's anti-Donatist treatises in the Nicene and Post-Nicene Fathers; Monceaux reconstructs Donatist texts from Augustine's work in vol. v (see below); Donatist literature has been gathered together by J.-L. Maier, *Le Dossier du Donatisme* (1987–9).

Crespin, R., *Ministère et sainteté, pastoral du clergé et solution de la crise donatiste dans la vie et doctrine de Saint Augustin* (1965).

Frend, W. H. C., *The Donatist Church: A Movement of Protest in Roman North Africa* (1952), new edn. (1985).

Monceaux, P., *Histoire littéraire de l'Afrique chrétienne*, (1922), iv–vii.

Willis, G. G., *Saint Augustine and the Donatist Controversy* (1950).

Donne, John

Donne, John (1572–1631). Donne first captures our attention as a 1590s poet-about-town: abrasive, satirical, with a bent for dialectical drama and *paradox; he ends his career as dean of St Paul's, and a leading and flamboyant Anglican preacher.

The massive expositions of his *Sermons* can be counter-balanced by the exploratory drama of his best *Divine Poems*, and of the *Devotions upon Emergent Occasions*, composed after a near-fatal illness in 1623. In all of them his theology draws much of its power from its engagement with the *world evoked in his secular *poetry. It is a world turbid with conflicting religious claims compounded by the impossibility of severing religion from national and international politics. Donne, born into a Catholic family that had suffered much for its faith, knows such conflicts from the inside. His own experience of conflicting claims—not only in religion—can fissure into a sense of the world as teeming and fragmented; and fragmentation can spiral, in turn, into an awareness of radical contingency, focused in a phrase from the *Sermons*: 'this occasional world'. His predilection for dialectic can, similarly, darken into a vision of human existence as fundamentally ambivalent, self-perplexed.

The religious conflicts of the *sixteenth century could breed authoritarian solutions or scepticism. Donne's first religious poem, *Satire III* (probably mid-1590s), attacks both. Its central lines on *truth combine the need for oblique and strenuous quest with the promise of mastery. Its close rejects the destructive submission of religious belief to political power in favour of naked trust in God.

In its engagement with conflicting claims *Satire III* prefigures the *casuistic works of Donne's bleak middle years. Those comprise the commissioned prose polemic *Pseudo-Martyr*, seeking to persuade Catholics to take the oath of allegiance to James I; an unpublished private treatise on *suicide, *Biathanatos*; and the long semiliturgical poem, *A Litanie*, which sifts moral and religious extremes in its pursuit of a tempered middle way. Though little read, Donne's casuistic works deserve mention, for casuistry can mesh several aspects of his sensibility: the awareness of alternative and multiple perspectives; a relish for twists of argument and analysis; his legal training; and a moderation which is not cautious or placid but rigorous in its balancing.

What such works and responses cannot encompass are, on the one hand, Donne's jagged extremism of mind and temperament, and on the other his desire to integrate and master experience. His late religious works in poetry and prose give scope to both, as also

to his responsiveness to the complexity of experience. Their achievement can be focused in three areas: Donne's handling of grace, of sin and evil, of death and resurrection.

The *Sermons* meet the contingency of an occasional world with an answering contingency of *grace. Donne can stress discontinuities: not only between nature and grace but between former grace and future; or (as in his Christmas sermon of 1621) between *Christ the essential *light and all other lights. Yet the same sermon works to orchestrate the different lights it discriminates. If Donne upholds an absolute divine *freedom, it is the freedom of God's groundless *love, and a freedom that has yoked itself in *covenant through Christ. Against the more extreme forms of *Calvinist *predestination he wages a recurrent pastoral campaign, urging the logic of worship ('never propose to thyself such a God as thou wert not bound to imitate'), the inter-reflection of God and *humanity based on the creation in God's image, and the need to find a God who is *Deus Noster*: who has made himself ours in his *Incarnation and made us his in his own glorification.

On *sin and *evil, Donne brings to bear a crisp knowledge of the world and a serpentine accuracy in tracking the movements of temptation and self-deception, but mounts beyond these to engage with *metaphysical issues. The ontological concept of sin as privation is braced into conscious paradox: sin is nothing and there is nothing but sin. *Metaphor can be deployed to insinuate a theodicy or to evoke an awareness of sin as inherent in humanity and, simultaneously, alien.

Paradox and dialectical drama find their grandest play in the handling of *death. The threefold structure of the *Devotions* focuses the ironic ambivalence of human life with a concentrated brilliance (Meditations), releases that ambivalence in questioning and *typology (Expostulations), and gathers it into intricate pattern (Prayers). *A Hymn to Christ* moves through an exploration of *sacrifice to the strange exultation of its close: 'And to scape stormy days I choose | An everlasting night'. *A Hymn to God the Father* mobilizes Donne's inveterate punning on his own name to articulate the deep fears and ambivalences in his relationship with God. The *Sermons* can present death as macabre or bizarre or, plangently, as the universal leveller. But they are at their most potent when evoking it as inherent in all the processes of life; and *resurrection itself as pivoted on the experience of death. This is marvellously enacted in the *Hymn to God, my God* where the imagination sweeps out from the deathbed to encompass a world possessed in the moment of its loss, then centres itself in a typological fusion of extremes—*Paradise and Calvary, first *Adam and last—by which the speaker is incorporated into a baroque image of the crucified and victorious Christ.

It is through such incorporation that the acutely self-analytic and self-dramatizing Donne achieves a transcendence where the self is not negated but swallowed up in the potently impersonal. This can occur in the *Devotions'* famous Meditation on the solidarity of mankind in death; or in a sermon which presents the preacher as only 'Vox, voyce; not A voyce, but The voyce' to the one Word which is Christ. For the modern reader it may be in such moments of self-transcendence that Donne, working in the idioms of his own Jacobean culture, speaks most commandingly.

See also SHAKESPEARE.   **Donald Mackenzie**

Carey, J., *John Donne* (1981).

Mueller, J. M. (ed.), *Donne's Prebend Sermons* (1971).
Webber, J., *Contrary Music* (1963).

Dostoevsky, Fyodor

Dostoevsky, Fyodor (1821–81), *Russian writer and, in the judgement of many, Christianity's greatest novelist. It seems appropriate to start at the end. For Dostoevsky, 1880 was a year of triumph. *The Brothers Karamazov* was nearing its completion, its instalments reaching an ever wider public and causing readers to exclaim, 'You are a prophet. We have become better human beings since reading *The Brothers Karamazov*,' praise echoed a century later when Yves *Congar remarked that every Catholic theologian should read the *Legend of the Grand Inquisitor* once a year. As soon as the *novel was complete, Dostoevsky died. The weight of all the *suffering he had endured, the humiliation inflicted upon him in the late 1840s by Turgenev amongst others, the mock execution by firing squad to which he was subjected by Tsar Nicholas I, the years in the Siberian prison camp, the years of desperate grasping for a woman's love, his addiction to gambling (which he conquered), his lifelong financial difficulties, his constant bouts of epilepsy, his worsening emphysema, had all exhausted his body. Yet the timing of his death has a fittingness strikingly parallel to that of the poet with whom he was often compared, *Dante Alighieri.

Dante's whole life had been a preparation for the *Divine Comedy*. At its culmination he died, even before the last cantos had been published: he had completed his work and in the process had become as integrated a human being as he could be. The same can be said of Dostoevsky's death in January 1881, for, as Mochulsky (1973) has claimed of *The Brothers Karamazov*, 'Never in all world literature has Christianity been advanced with such striking force as the religion of spiritual freedom'. The parallels between the life and work of Italian poet and Russian novelist are worth attention because Dostoevsky himself was conscious of them. In 1863, for instance, he wrote that for years he had been contemplating the great novel which the 19th century direly needed: 'Such a great work of art will have to give voice to the aspirations and characteristics of our own age just as the *Divine Comedy*, for example, expressed fully and for ever the beliefs and ideals of medieval Catholicism.'

Dostoevsky's writings and the *Divine Comedy* share a further characteristic. Just as it would be a misreading, particularly of the *Inferno*, to think of the characters as external to Dante himself, for the *Divine Comedy* is actually a confession, so is this true of Dostoevsky. The characters in his many writings reflect the vices, temptations, betrayals, despair, and unbelief of his age by all of which he was touched. But he was at the same time able to incorporate them into what many have seen as the greatest and most hopeful novel in world literature.

The Russian saying *konets venchaet dela*, 'the end crowns the deed', was a truth that Dostoevsky never lost sight of, which is why he was always so concerned to shape the endings of his novels to throw light on everything that has happened previously. 'Reality is not to be exhausted by what is immediately at hand,' he wrote in one of his notebooks, 'for an overwhelming part of this reality is contained in the form of a still latent, unuttered future word.' Once Dostoevsky's own life is seen in this light it presents us with what in Russian spirituality is termed a *podvig*, which can be translated as 'a great heroic deed', though that hardly conveys its full resonance in the Russian spiritual tradition. One exploit often described as a

podvig was the undertaking to go on *pilgrimage; another, less common, was to take upon oneself the vocation of *iurodvi* (holy fool). The form which Dostoevsky's *podvig* took was still less common: it was writing itself.

Dostoevsky was brought up in an atmosphere of profound, traditional Russian piety. His father, Mikhail, a doctor in the Mariinsky Hospital for the Poor on the outskirts of Moscow, came from a long line of priests and had himself received a seminary education. Fyodor was only 8 when he read the book of *Job, which left a profound impression upon him because of Job's daring to question God's claim to be just in the face of innocent suffering. The image of Job and his suffering, which placed both Job and God in an agonizing dilemma, runs through the whole of Dostoevsky's life. When, in his notebooks, Dostoevsky wrote 'The one thing in the world is spontaneous compassion. As for justice, that is a secondary matter,' he was revealing something about himself which goes far to account not only for the extraordinary depth of his insight into the feelings of all creatures but also for some of the excesses into which his intense feelings led him. The man who in his youth could say to his brother Mikhail, 'I intend to become a fool,' already had a presentiment that he was never to be comfortable amidst the pretence and hard-heartedness of polite society, which in return was time and time again to treat him as a *iurodvi*.

Six years in the Army Engineers were followed by the start of Dostoevsky's literary life and his adoption of *atheism under the influence of Russia's leading critic, Vissarion Belinsky. However, while he often doubted God's existence, he never wavered in his devotion to Christ. As he was to say, in a much quoted statement,

> I have shaped for myself a *Credo* where everything is clear and sacred for me. This *Credo* is very simple, here it is: to believe that nothing is more beautiful, profound, sympathetic, reasonable, manly, and more perfect than Christ; and I tell myself with a jealous love not only that there is nothing, but there cannot be anything. Even more, if someone proved to me that Christ is outside the truth, and that *in reality* the truth were outside Christ, then I should prefer to remain with Christ rather than with the truth.

The statement has often been misunderstood. Even Dostoevsky never elucidated it in the language of philosophy, but he did so through his artistic creations, refusing to accept the either/or choice demanded of Job: 'either God is just and you, Job, are guilty or you are innocent and God unjust'. Job's answer, 'I know that my redeemer liveth,' an answer transcending the choices offered by both the comforters and the rationalists, and one only to be realized centuries after Job, in the person of Christ, is the answer given by Dostoevsky when Ivan Karamazov, the rationalist, is trying to destroy the faith of his brother, Alyosha. Alyosha accepts that he cannot answer Ivan's logical assault upon the claim that God is loving and just; he can only point to the way of practical *love as embodied in Father Zosima.

Anyone reading Dostoevsky's writings in chronological order notices how the author slowly, searchingly, feels his way along a series of his own creations. There is the figure of a proud woman making her plight worse through the *egoism of suffering* (little Nellie in *The Insulted and the Injured*), who is embodied in Polina (*The Gambler*), then in Nastasya Philippovna (*The Idiot*), and finally in Katerina Ivanovna of *The Brothers Karamazov*. A similar line, his figure of the character who sets himself aside from the common herd and takes pride in his isolation, runs through Raskolnikov (*Crime and Punishment*), to Stavrogin (*The Devils*), and finally to Ivan Karamazov. Probing along such lines could not be done simply by taking thought but required years of personal maturing.

Dostoevsky's method for discerning the true way through his forest of *symbols was rooted in his own singular personality, which always led him to allow an experience to penetrate his heart and mind to its extreme end, never to abort it. 'As for myself,' his *Underground* man says, 'in my life I have pushed to the extreme what you yourselves have never dared to take even half way. Because you have constantly mistaken your cowardice for prudence and have constantly deceived yourselves with comforting reflections. The truth is that I have been more *alive* than you.'

Dostoevsky pushes ideas, as well as emotion, to the extremity, as in his celebrated *pro et contra* arguments, for and against. The outstanding illustration is in *The Brothers Karamazov*: the whole of one of its twelve books is headed *Pro et contra* and contains the famous *Legend of the Grand Inquisitor*, where the arguments against the idea of a loving *God are stated so powerfully that the over-procurator of the Orthodox Church, Pobedonostev, was alarmed. To him Ivan's atheistic arguments seemed unanswerable—as they were, indeed, to Dostoevsky at the level of logic and psychology. But by then Dostoevsky had long realized a truth later stated succinctly by one of his most gifted commentators, Vyacheslav Ivanov: 'Denial of God and faith in God are not two different interpretations of the same world, but two essentially different worlds of the spirit, existing side by side, like an Earth and a counter-Earth.' The great difference between those two worlds is that whereas one may easily drift into denial of God, one can only enter into the world of faith through a conscious, whole-hearted response to the *Holy Spirit. By the time Dostoevsky emerged from the prison camp at Omsk, he had already, however inchoately, responded to the Spirit.

His release in 1854 was, nevertheless, followed by years of great wildness. While his return to religious faith may be dated to the death of his first wife in 1864, it was only in 1867, with his second marriage to Anna Snitkin, and departure for four years to western Europe, that a measure of calm returned. Those years of moving around Germany, Switzerland, and Italy were by no means comfortable. But in spite of all their hardships, Anna weaned Dostoevsky from his gambling addiction. He was able to write *The Idiot* and work out the scheme for *The Devils*. But, above all, Anna's reliability, her common sense, and unpretentious piety steadied Dostoevsky and helped to ground his emotions upon the soil of family happiness. As Nikolai Strakhov, who knew him well, wrote, 'There is no doubt that it was precisely abroad, in that setting, amid those long, serene reflections, that the peculiar revelation of the Christian spirit which had always dwelt in him, was consummated.' Strakhov predates 'the consummation' of Dostoevsky's 'particular revelation of the Christian spirit', because it took the remaining ten years of life to achieve it. But it points to the fact that those last ten years are best understood as one continuous 'public civic *podvig*', as Dostoevsky himself expressed it.

As one sign for understanding those years as a whole, there is none better than the word which has played such a profound role in expressing and shaping Russian spirituality: *sobornost*. *Sobornost* derives from *sobor*, 'cathedral', and refers to the feeling experienced in the cathedral or church when the *liturgy brings all the worshippers into unity so that each feels he or she belongs to everyone else there and to the organic whole which they form. The ultimate derivation is the verb *sobirat*, 'to gather together', which expresses exactly what Dostoevsky was attempting to do. He grieved over the separation between sections of Russian society and longed to gather them together: parents and children; peasants and merchants; rich and poor; Orthodox and Old Believers; revolutionaries and monarchists; Westerners and Slavophiles; women and men; educated and ignorant; living and dead, gathered together in a spirit of *forgiveness and *reconciliation which he dared to describe as 'universal communion in the name of Christ'—a new form of church where all peoples will be gathered 'in a great universal brotherly fellowship in the name of Christ'.

Dostoevsky set about his task soon after returning to Russia by 'preparing to write a very big novel', which would both express and promote *sobornost*. All his writings since the publication of *Poor Folk* in 1846 can be seen as preparation for *The Brothers Karamazov*, but with it we move into a new dimension, a new atmosphere of spiritual *freedom and *joy. But if it was *The Brothers Karamazov* that most perfectly expressed *sobornost* for his Russian readers then and continues to do so, it was the *Diary of a Writer* that taught him how to achieve that 'public civic *podvig*'. When he started to issue his *Diary* in 1873 he did something unprecedented in Russian life: by breaking the barrier between the writer and his readers he established an intimacy enabling him to speak to them, and encouraging them to write to him. The openness with which he expressed his convictions and fears called forth similar openness in his readers who, in their hundreds, confided their fears and hopes to him, almost as though they were making their confessions to a priest. As soon as the *Diary* began to appear, the readers sensed an urgency in Dostoevsky's writings missing 'in the aristocratic landowners' literature' of Turgenev and *Tolstoy. There was need, Dostoevsky maintained, for 'a new word' that could help redeem the tragic situation of Russia; and *he* was called to pronounce that word. For Russia was on the edge of an abyss, as he had tried to demonstrate in *The Devils*: Russia had become possessed by *devils like the man in the gospel story of the Gadarene swine. There is no doubt that Dostoevsky saw himself as a prophet of healing and reconciliation. It was no accident that in these years, whenever he was asked to do a public reading, he invariably included Pushkin's *The Prophet*, a poem invoking the prophet *Isaiah in words taken from church Slavonic.

His readers must have been quite startled by his long articles on the many criminal cases in which he took such a deep interest—not merely attending the courts but going to visit the accused, both in prison and, in the case of Katerina Kornilov, in her home. While pregnant, she had thrown her small stepdaughter out of the window in a fit of rage with her quarrelsome husband. The stepdaughter survived. But when the case came to court and it seemed that Katerina would be sent to Siberia for 17 years, Dostoevsky intervened, raising the case in his *Diary*. By a powerful description of the morbid psychology frequently encountered in pregnant women, he convinced the jury to acquit Katerina.

Dostoevsky's use of the term 'The Russian Christ' in no way implies that Russians enjoyed an exclusive understanding of Christ (see CHRISTOLOGY). Dostoevsky specifically rejected any such exclusive claim, as made by Danilevsky and the Slavophiles, because it limited Russia's universal mission to share its unique historical experience of Christ with all humanity. It was rather that Dostoevsky had been born again into Christ through the Russian folk whose sufferings he shared in the prison camp, so that his sense of Christianity had fused the age-old faith of the peasantry with the insights of a modern psychologist.

It has rightly been said that the feeling of a new period of forgiveness and reconciliation dawning in Russia, marked by the completion of *The Brothers Karamazov*, was the crowning of Dostoevsky's life. That feeling did not last, yet for a moment it was sustained and even deepened by his death. Dostoevsky's death and burial seemed to confirm the feeling of Russians as a people gathered together. From the day of his death until the moment of his interment, in Petersburg and throughout Russia, an outpouring of spontaneous grief took place such as had never been seen, even at the death of a tsar. As one who was present at his funeral wrote, 'This was no burial. It was a celebration of life, the resurrection of life.'

Donald Nicholl

Dostoevsky, Fyodor, *Crime and Punishment, The Idiot, The Devils*, trans. C. Garnett and D. Magarschak (1951; 1955; 1953).
—— *The Diary of a Writer* (1979).
—— *The Brothers Karamazov*, trans R. Pevear and L. Volokhonsky (1992).
Berdyaev, Nicholas, *Dostoevsky* (1957).
Frank, Joseph, *Dostoevsky* (4 vols.; 1976; 1984; 1987; 1995).
Gibson, A. Boyce, *The Religion of Dostoevsky* (1973).
Mochulsky, Konstantin, *Dostoevsky* (1973).
Pascal, Pierre, *Dostoievski et Dieu* (1995).

doubt.

doubt. 'It is an awful moment when the soul begins to find that the props on which it has blindly rested so long are, many of them, rotten, and begins to suspect them all' (F. W. Robertson, a 19th-century English liberal preacher). Doubt appears as quintessentially Victorian. In *Protestant, and pre-eminently in Anglo-Saxon, cultures, many Christians went through agonies of doubt, as they felt their faith slipping away. The agonies were genuine, and present a challenge to 20th-century sympathies. The Christianity they had doubts over was clear-cut, *missionary, and pugnacious, and saw doubt as a *sin. It was prepared to make an intellectual defence of much that later might be seen as not worth defending, and Victorian doubters fastened their intensity of feeling on matters that might well now be seen as mere difficulties. When compared with *existential *Angst*, 19th-century doubt seems over-intellectualized. However, as we read Victorian doubters, we can come to feel something of the moral revulsion that fuelled their intellectual doubt. Many could no longer reconcile a good God with *hell or a substitutionary *atonement. The 18th-century resort to a benevolent God revealed through reason and natural theology was also questioned, however. Tennyson, in his *In Memoriam*, agonized over 'nature, red in tooth and claw', in view of the new evidence that whole prehistoric species of animals had been wiped out.

For social reasons, doubt often was lived through in secret. People did not want to see certainties crumble: '[If] we turn to our next neighbour, and put to him some searching or testing question, we shall, in nine cases out of ten, discover him to be only a Christian in his own way... and that he doubts of many things which we ourselves do not believe strongly enough to hear doubted without

danger' (Ruskin). Nevertheless, they felt hypocritical when they continued to pay lip-service to their old beliefs, they were likely to encounter horror and dismay if they opened the subject with their loved ones, and they had frequent bouts of nostalgic longing for the simple certainties of childhood. Perhaps the saddest experience was that of clergymen, formally committed to preaching a Christian gospel. Two good fictional accounts of this can be found in William Hale White's *Autobiography of Mark Rutherford* (1881), and Mrs Humphrey Ward's *Robert Elsmere* (1888).

The standard Victorian cure for doubt was healthy-minded activism: 'Feed on Nature, and do not *try* to understand it.... Look round you much. Think little and read less. Never give way to reveries' (Charles Kingsley, to his wife). When we consider how active the Victorian churches were, we might think that this therapy was tried very often.

Even in Victorian England, the suspicion grew that thorough-going certainty is not the essence of Christianity. Bishop Westcott, the NT scholar, thanked for making everything clear, replied in horror, 'I do hope not.' It became possible to question Christian orthodoxy. Tennyson's words

> There lives more faith in honest doubt
> Believe me, than in half the creeds

were seized on by some confident doubters. Alternative positions to Christianity could, in a still largely Christian society, present their total scepticism as polite doubt. Perhaps they did doubt: even Herbert Spencer cannot have been as certain on everything as he seemed. But he is a far cry from a real doubter like A. H. Clough, with that pathetic double negative in:

> And when we lift up holy hands of prayer
> I will not say they will not give us aid.

Doubt was not invented by the Victorians. There were religious and philosophical precedents. It is possible to argue that one distinguishing mark of *Israelite religion from its neighbours was the zest with which the Jews doubted God. An inevitable part of the narrative of God's ways with his people is their distrust. The *Resurrection needs a doubting Thomas. 'He that never doubted, scarce ever well-believed,' wrote the English poet William Austin (d. 1634). It may well be that classic Victorian doubt was a basically religious reaction to a cut-and-dried argumentative orthodoxy that tried to rule out the ups and downs of human experience.

There is also a philosophy of doubt. In 1879 the future British prime minister, A. J. Balfour, wrote *A Defence of Philosophic Doubt*, though by then it was dogmatic science rather than dogmatic Christianity that challenged free-thinkers. Doubt had long been a philosophic method: we need only think of Cartesianism. Behind *Descartes there is *Augustine's 'For if I doubt, I am.' If it is true that he doubts, there at least is one truth. Later, John Henry *Newman's own philosophical tradition was sceptical British empiricism. Yet his 'Ten thousand difficulties do not make one doubt' points us away from quibbling scepticism to something deeper. The *Apologia* is a book full of beautifully relived doubt over whether to continue as an Anglican.

Since the Victorians, Christians have found more positive ways of handling doubt. It is now a religious insight to say that 'Lord, help my unbelief' can be prayed in two ways. The 20th-century theologian Paul *Tillich takes the Protestant principle as far as it will go:

'no one can say of himself that he is in the situation of faith... Every theologian is committed *and* alienated; he is always in faith *and* in doubt.' It could well be argued that what makes faith different from knowledge is that faith is of necessity accompanied by its twin, doubt. Yet those who make an easy merger of faith and doubt may become, far more than the earnest Victorians ever were, 'light half-believers in our casual creeds' (Matthew Arnold). Modern theologians still return to Arnold's poem, *Dover Beach*, that most poignant expression of Victorian doubt, as if, on the shingles there, we would find something of an authenticity present even in his loss.   **Alistair Mason**

Houghton, Walter E., *The Victorian Frame of Mind* (1957).
Jay, Elizabeth, *Faith and Doubt in Victorian Britain* (1986).
MacGregor, Geddes, *God Beyond Doubt* (1966).
Parsons, Gerald (ed.), *Religion in Victorian Britain*, ii. *Controversies* (1988).
Willey, Basil, *More Nineteenth Century Studies: A Group of Honest Doubters* (1956).

dreams are regarded rather ambivalently in the Christian tradition, in keeping with the tension it holds between rationality and inspiration. In the OT, prophets and patriarchs receive messages through dreams. Joseph and *Daniel represent a long tradition common to ancient Near Eastern cultures both of the prophetic dream and of the art of the dream interpreter (see PROPHECY). That young men will see visions and old men dream dreams is for Joel (2: 28) one of the signs of the coming day of the Lord. Yet there are always caveats, and the deliberate seeking of inspiration through dreams which was so much part of Mesopotamian and Egyptian culture is at times roundly condemned.

The NT also has a tradition of the revelatory dream. *Matthew in particular, no doubt emulating the OT model, includes several warning dreams in the early part of his gospel. In Acts, where Joel is cited, *visions rather than dreams are the norm but the distinction is not always easy to maintain.

Despite the doubts expressed by *Aristotle over the role of inspiration in dreaming, the Graeco-Roman world had a flourishing literature of dream interpretation and a Christian counterpart was not long in developing. Several of the *apocryphal *apocalypses hover on the verge of being dream accounts. The most influential of the early Christian treatises on the subject was written by Tertullian to give a theoretical justification of the prophetic qualities of dreams. He also exonerates dreamers from blame for sins committed in their dreams. *Augustine discusses the nature of the knowledge to be gained from dreams in his *De genesi ad litteram*, and elaborates the classification put forward by the pagan commentator Macrobius in terms of his own tripartite distinction between corporeal, spiritual, and intellectual vision. This explains how the dreams of both saint and sinner who share the same median spiritual nature can veer towards either carnal images or celestial revelations.

Throughout Christian history, the *church was caught in the double bind of preaching the revelatory value of the dreams of patriarchs and *saints while trying to control the superstitious reliance on spurious and perhaps even demonically inspired dreams and interpretative practices. Medieval writers drew mainly on Augustine and indeed Macrobius to temper Aristotelian scepticism. Books of dream interpretation continued to be produced and widely circulated while canon law sought to discourage any such divinatory practices. Writers such as *Dante and, much later, Bunyan

(see PILGRIM'S PROGRESS) use the liberty of the dreamer to write about spiritual realms normally closed to the living.

The rise of rationalism tended to exclude revelation gained through dreams from responsible theological discussion. In the 20th century, both Freud and *Jung revived interest in the divinatory power of dreams but as a manifestation of repressed desire rather than of divine communication. In contrast to this, the *Pentecostal movement has sought to reclaim the direct inspiration of the early church and the gift of prophetic dreaming gained new weight as one of its manifestations.

Traditional societies, on the other hand, often have no trouble in assimilating aspects of the life of the early church that may seem remote to western Christians. For many *African Christians, dreams are a crucial part of their *conversion experience or the call to *ordination and this grew to be accepted by western missionaries, who were rationalist by temperament; an early example of the Africanization of Christianity. For many Christians around the world whose cultural expectations are less touched by western scientific realism, dreams remain a potent channel for divine inspiration, offering warnings, secret information, and consolation to believers.

See also MYSTICISM.   **Hugh S. Pyper**

Campbell, J., *Myths, Dreams and Religion* (1988).
Freud, S., *The Interpretation of Dreams*, ET (1953).
Jędrej, M. C., and Shaw, R., *Dreaming, Religion and Society in Africa* (1992).
Kruger, S. F., *Dreaming in the Middle Ages* (1992).

dualism divides any given area of reality into two contrasting and, probably, conflicting elements. 'The spirit is willing but the flesh is weak' (Mark 14: 38). *Jesus' comment in Gethsemane on his disciples suggests a dualism between spirit and flesh of a moral rather than ontological kind, but *Paul's words in *Romans are more emphatic: 'To set the mind on the flesh is death, but to set the mind on the Spirit is life and peace' (8: 6). By the 'flesh', Paul explains, he means that 'I am carnal, sold under sin ... I know that nothing good dwells within me, that is, in my flesh ... if I do what I do not want, it is no longer I that do it, but sin which dwells within me' (7: 14–20).

It was possible to conclude from such remarks that there is some ontological conflict between spirit and flesh, deriving from opposed principles and that human beings are caught in the middle, belonging to two different worlds. The material world of flesh is seen as inherently evil, something in which we are entrapped, but from which *Christ and his *Holy Spirit deliver us. Dualist ontologies of this sort derived from Persia and Mandaeanism, and their impact on Judaism can be seen in the Qumran community (see DEAD SEA SCROLLS). Such too was the *Gnostic position and it inevitably followed that the material world was not made by the good God at all but by some other, evil, power. Gnostic ontology and cosmology could be exceedingly complicated but were necessarily at variance with the insistence in *Genesis that there is only one God who is good, creating everything so that matter too is good, or again with the NT insistence that this same God sent his Son, or Word, to become the man Jesus, and thus be 'made flesh' (John 1: 14). While Paul may occasionally sound Gnostic (as Marcion claimed), it should be clear that he was not. What he called 'flesh' was not the material side of human nature but some deep, mysterious, force within us, leading humans to do evil rather than good, but which can be overcome for the *salvation of both *soul and *body.

Nevertheless the Gnostic temptation to ontological dualism, a temptation which inevitably required one to deny that the *Word became flesh and hold instead a *Docetism according to which only an appearance of flesh was taken, presented a great challenge to early Christianity, just because it looked in some ways so similar to Christian *asceticism. When the author of 1 John warned 'By this you know the Spirit of God: every spirit which confesses that Jesus Christ has come in the flesh is of God' (4: 2; see also 2 John 7), he was warning against Gnostic dualism. The flesh could not be rejected as evil because Christ had come in the flesh. Despite occasional rhetorical flourishes, the NT is emphatically anti-dualist at the level of being, of flesh, and spirit. All comes from God and, despite the mysterious power of *sin, all is reconcilable through the enfleshment of God's son.

Gnosticism fades from Christian history after the 2nd century, out-argued especially by *Irenaeus with his very anti-dualist vision of the 'recapitulation' of all things in Christ, but dualism reappears in the 4th century as Manichaeism and, later in the Middle Ages, as Bogomilism and Catharism, the beliefs of the Albigensians of southern France, so ruthlessly persecuted by the 13th-century church. The attraction of this whole line of thought was very powerful. It provided a clear answer to the problem of *evil but it did so by undermining the basic unity of *creation, *redemption, and the *sacraments. Instead of seeing the body as a channel of the spirit, fortified by such sacraments as the *Eucharist and *marriage, such a dualism insisted that the way to divinity could only be through progressively escaping from the flesh.

Yet if Christian orthodoxy perennially rejected that belief, did it not all the same necessarily maintain a still deeper dualism—not between spirit and matter but between good and evil, God and the *devil? A stark binary symbolism is built up across the biblical narrative—*Israel and Egypt, Jehovah and Baal, *light and darkness, *life and *death. Evil is evil. The *psalms contrast the good and the wicked again and again, even if the devil, as an existent personal evil of exceptional power, only makes a clear appearance at the very end of the OT period. Certainly the judgement scene in Matthew 25 in which Christ describes the separation of sheep and goats, one group destined to enter the kingdom of God, the other to endure eternal punishment, suggests a very decisive moral dualism, which leads back to an almost ontological one, once *hell is set against *heaven. Given the lack of any clear biblical explanation as to the why or what of the devil, his very presence on the scene prior to humanity, with some sort of hell as his home, is bound to make

reality look dualistic, so that, if dualism is not countenanced at the start of the story, it is there at its end.

Yet Christian thought has always sat with even this sort of dualism very uneasily, despite the fearful imagery of some *art and some *preaching, particularly of the late medieval and Reformation period. If the cause of the sinfulness Paul laments so powerfully in Romans was located in *Adam's *fall, it is significant that he sees that sin as fully conquered by the New Adam. The first Adam is carried to heaven by the second Adam, and his very sin becomes in the triumphant exordium of the Easter liturgy no more than a *felix culpa*: 'O truly necessary sin of Adam, O happy fault'. The very dualism between sin and *grace seems here overcome, the ultimate triviality of the one swallowed up in the overwhelming love of the other, just as the binary divide of death/life is overcome by the *Resurrection: *Dux vitae mortuus regnat vivus* (the lord of life, once dead, now lives and reigns). Even darkness becomes not the negation of life but rather the blessed night in which the Resurrection took place, a necessary route to union with God, a 'dark night of the soul' traversed by every mystic. In Ephesians, Paul could declare that Christ who descended is he who ascended, 'that he might fill all things' (4: 10). Nothing is to be left out. All this does not remove a sense of moral battle here and now, often described in highly dualistic terms. Christian thought has continually oscillated between the unitary and the dualistic—the one more central to the *Greek tradition, the other to the *Latin, being especially strong in its North African roots. Upon the one side lies the grim recognition of the power of evil, the image of a devil sometimes portrayed as rather too potent, an eternal hell, and upon the other side the more tentative defence of an ultimate *universalism by Clement of Alexandria, *Origen, and Gregory of Nyssa in ancient times, *Schleiermacher, F. W. Farrar, W. Michaelis, *Teilhard de Chardin, and others more recently. *Barth wrestled with the problem when discussing the betrayal of *Judas in his *Church Dogmatics*, II/2. Do not Paul's assertion that Christ's grace brings 'life for all men' (Rom. 5: 18), abounding further than Adam's sin, and the plea of Jesus from the cross, 'Father, forgive them for they know not what they do' (Luke 23: 34) both actually require a universal fulfilment unlimited by any final dualism?   **Adrian Hastings**

Lambert, M. D., *Medieval Heresy: Popular Movements from Bogomil to Hus* (1977).

Logan, A., *Gnostic Truth and Christian Heresy* (1996).

Minns, D., *Irenaeus* (1994).

Pétrement, S., *Le Dualisme chez Platon, les Gnostiques et les Manichéens* (1947).

—— *Separate God* (ET 1991).

Strayer, J. R., *The Albigensian Crusades* (1971).

Wakefield, W. L., and Evans, A. P., *Heresies of the High Middle Ages* (1969).

E

Easter, the oldest annual festival of the *church, celebrates the deliverance from *sin and the promise of eternal life obtained for humankind by the *Resurrection of *Jesus Christ from the dead. The highly *joyful tone expected for the feast is expressed by the Easter proclamation (*praeconium paschale*) or *Exsultet* which has been used in some form by the western church at Easter since perhaps the 5th century. This paean of praise heralds Christ's victory over the powers of darkness: 'Rejoice, heavenly powers! Sing, choirs of angels! Exult, all creation around God's throne! Jesus Christ, our King, is risen! Sound the trumpet of salvation!'

At first, Easter was a Christianized passover (*pasch*) that held Christ's *death and Resurrection together as constitutive of the new *exodus by which came liberation from bondage. From the 4th century onwards, as christological feasts and *fasts were added to the *calendar, a more distributive chronology turned Easter from a unitive festival of the entire redemption into more of an anniversary of the Resurrection that had occurred on *Sunday, the first day of the week. Events from Christ's Passion were eventually assigned to the 'holy week' preceding Easter, beginning with the Palm Sunday commemoration of Jesus' triumphal entry into *Jerusalem.

In many communities, the ceremonies and rituals of Holy Week were rich in symbolism and pathos as Christians confessed their complicity in Christ's betrayal, *suffering, and sacrifice. Remembrance of the Last Supper and the institution of the *Eucharist were attached to Holy Thursday, as was also the custom of footwashing in imitation of Jesus' washing of the disciples' feet and in obedience to his 'new commandment' (*mandatum* = 'Maundy'; cf. John 13: 1–20). The commemoration of Christ's trial, scourging, crucifixion, and death on Good Friday moved believers to profuse demonstrations of sorrow and grief: fasting, readings of the scriptural accounts of the Passion, the acceptance of reproaches put into the mouth of Christ, veneration of the *cross, *tenebrae* (a service of shadows, held also on Holy Wednesday and Thursday), and dramatic and musical re-enactments of the story figure among the practices Christians have employed. Holy Saturday, a day of introspection and fasting, imitated the silence of Christ's repose in the tomb, with the hush finally broken by the good tidings of Easter.

In the 20th century, efforts to recover in the rites of the church the ancient and unitive aspects of Easter owed much to *liturgical theologians such as Odo Casel who emphasized Christ's redemptive work as a kind of primal *sacrament, the accomplishment of the 'mystery' of God's saving purpose. Concentration on the paschal mystery of human *redemption has the additional benefit of placing in appropriate context the *metaphors of spring and new life that have historically reinforced the themes of Easter in the northern hemisphere, but which cannot be shared (directly) by Christians of the southern hemisphere or the tropics.

The paschal mystery is now expressed liturgically by renewed attention to the interconnection of the three days from sunset on Holy Thursday to Easter Day (the *Triduum*) and by a restored paschal vigil, held during the night from Holy Saturday to Easter Day, when participants pass from darkness to *light aided by the kindling of a new fire and the lighting of a paschal candle. At the vigil new Christians are made by dying and rising with Christ through the waters of *baptism and receiving the first Eucharist, bringing to a conclusion a period of catechesis often begun in *Lent, but anticipating continuing mystagogy and nurture in the faith.

Although the day of Resurrection is marked as Easter Day, the festival of Easter continues for the next fifty days, when alleluias are sung, and fasting, along with kneeling for prayer, is traditionally forbidden—all as witness to the anticipated participation in the kingdom of heaven. In the early church this entire season was designated as *Pentecost; only in the 4th century was the term used more frequently to identify the fiftieth day which developed as a distinct, though related, feast. Following the chronology of the Acts of the Apostles (1: 1–11), the church observes during this joyful period the feast of the Ascension, held on the fortieth day (a Thursday) after Easter: Christ now reigns at the right hand of the Father and intercedes for humankind (Rom. 8: 34; and the Epistle to the *Hebrews).   **Karen B. Westerfield Tucker**

Casel, O., *The Mystery of Christian Worship*, 1st edn. (1932), 4th edn., ET (1962).
Greenacre, R., and Haselock, J., *The Sacrament of Easter* (1989; 1995).
Tyrer, J. W., *Historical Survey of Holy Week* (1932).

Eastern Orthodox theology.

The Orthodox Church, largely isolated from the west until the 20th century, has begun during the last hundred years to exercise a limited yet significant influence upon western thinking. Following the fall of the Byzantine empire (1453), Orthodox Christianity in the Greek lands and the rest of the Balkans entered its 'dark ages', the period of Ottoman domination, extending until the 19th century; this allowed little opportunity to eastern Christians for creative development of theology. In Russia, however, outside Turkish rule, there emerged from the 1840s onwards an independent and at times strikingly original approach to religious questions. It was in 19th-century Russia that the first serious encounter occurred between Orthodoxy and *Enlightenment and post-Enlightenment thought.

*Russian religious thought in the 20th century continued to display exceptional vitality, first in Russia itself until the 1917 Revolution, thereafter in the western world. The main intellectual centres of Russian émigré theology have been the Institute of St Sergius in Paris, which enjoyed an era of great brilliance between the two World Wars, and more recently St Vladimir's Seminary in New York. From the 1960s onwards theologians of international stature appeared also in Greece and Romania. Orthodox debates in the 19th and 20th centuries concentrated upon three major topics: the nature of *theology, the doctrine of *creation, and the essence of the *church. Relatively little attention has been given to biblical studies.

How should we theologize? *Byzantine thought, especially towards the end of the empire, tended to be highly conservative. 'The great men of the past', observed Theodore Metochites (1270–1332), 'have expressed everything so perfectly that they have left nothing more for us to say.' Yet especially in the realm of *mystical theology Byzantium continued to produce original thinkers of the first rank such as Symeon the New Theologian (959–1022) and Gregory Palamas (1296–1359). The Turkish period, however, was marked by an inflexible theological traditionalism. As Patriarch Jeremias II of Constantinople stated in 1590, 'It is not the practice of our church to innovate in any way whatsoever, whereas the western church innovates unceasingly.'

Nevertheless this conservatism was counterbalanced by a strongly westernizing trend within Orthodox thought during the 17th and 18th centuries. The absence of Christian universities in the Ottoman world meant that most Orthodox theologians obtained their training in the west, under Roman Catholic or Protestant teachers, and inevitably this led them to adopt western terminology and styles of argument, resulting in what the Russian theologian Georges *Florovsky has termed a 'pseudomorphosis'.

It was the Russian Slavophiles in the mid-19th century who first strove to break free from this 'Babylonian captivity' (Florovsky's phrase). Ivan Kireevsky (1806–56) rebelled against what he saw as the rationalism of the west, its excessive reliance upon discursive argumentation. 'Rome', he affirmed in somewhat sweeping terms, 'preferred the abstract syllogism to sacred tradition, which is the expression of the common mind of the whole Christian world, and in which that world coheres as a living and indissoluble unity' (Collected Works (1911), i. 226). Truth for the Slavophiles was not to be attained by the isolated individual relying solely on the reasoning brain's logic, but could be discovered only within the organic life of the church, through shared experience and interpersonal communion. 'The knowledge of the truth is given to mutual love,' said Aleksei Khomyakov (1804–60).

Fundamental to all religious understanding, according to Khomyakov, is the spirit of sobornost (literally 'catholicity'), by which he meant unanimity in freedom, the grace-given possibility whereby the church's members, without sacrificing personal liberty, are enabled to attain a common mind. The Slavophiles took as their model the corporate consciousness to be found (so they believed) in the Russian peasant commune; in Turgenev's phrase (originally applied to Herzen), they 'sought salvation in a sheepskin coat'. But their sources were not exclusively Russian: they were influenced also by German Idealist philosophy, especially by *Hegel and Schelling.

Leading Russian theologians in the 20th-century emigration, Florovsky and Vladimir Lossky (1903–58) for example, agreed with Kireevsky and Khomyakov in repudiating undue dependence upon the west, but they reacted sharply against the Slavophile attempt to identify a specifically Russian approach to theology. They advocated instead a return to the *Greek fathers. Florovsky, a firm upholder of 'Christian Hellenism', summed up his theological programme in the phrase 'neo-patristic synthesis'. He meant, not simply mechanical repetition of the words of the fathers, but rather a creative recovery of the 'patristic mind'. The fathers are to be treated not as voices from the distant past but as contemporary witnesses; they are to be not only quoted but questioned, for holy tradition represents the critical spirit of the church.

For Florovsky and Lossky, as for a later generation of émigré Russian theologians including Alexander Schmemann (1921–83) and John Meyendorff (1926–92), the notion of the 'patristic mind' signified above all the integral link between theology and *prayer. In the much-quoted words of the 4th-century desert father Evagrius of Pontus, 'If you are a theologian, you will pray truly; and if you pray truly, you are a theologian' (On Prayer, 60). All authentic theology is therefore liturgical and mystical. 'Far from being mutually opposed,' stated Lossky, 'theology and mysticism support and complete each other. One is impossible without the other.'

A similar approach is evident in contemporary Greek writers such as John Romanides (b. 1927) and Christos Yannaras (b. 1935). Yannaras, influenced by Heidegger as well as Lossky, rejects the 'academic scientism' which in his view dominates the work of older Greek theologians. Theology is 'not an intellectual discipline but an experiential communion, a participation'. It is 'a fruit of the interior purity of the Christian's spiritual life', to be 'identified with the vision of God… with the personal experience of the transfiguration of creation by uncreated grace'.

Yannaras's reference to cosmic transfiguration brings us to a second dominant theme in modern Orthodox theology: the doctrine of creation. Here two main tendencies are apparent. There is first the school of Sophiology, represented by three Russian thinkers, Vladimir Soloviev (1853–1900), Pavel Florensky (1882–1937), and the former Marxist Sergii Bulgakov (1871–1944), who understand the relationship between God and the world in terms of Sophia or Holy *Wisdom. In Bulgakov's thought, which is complex and frequently obscure, Sophia is both divine and creaturely. Divine Sophia (not a person or hypostasis) signifies God's eternal plan of creation, and more particularly the uncreated freedom which enables the divine life to empty itself in the act of creation and to mirror itself in that which is not God. Self-emptying or *kenosis, a pivotal concept for Bulgakov, is to be seen not only in the Incarnation of the Son but also in God's decision to create the world and even in the eternal life of the Trinity. On the creaturely side, Sophia denotes creation's response to God, the impulse within all created things towards harmony and order, their longing or eros for divine

Beauty. Uncreated and created Sophia are united supremely in the person of Christ.

Turning to the second tendency, we find the sophiological approach vehemently repudiated by the 'neo-patristic' group. Bulgakov was attacked above all by Lossky, who maintained that he had confused the levels of person (*hypostasis*) and nature (*physis*). Kenosis, Lossky argued, involves the Second Person of the Trinity, the incarnate Logos, but it cannot be equated with the divine nature. To interpret the relationship between God and the world, the neo-patristic group preferred the cosmological teachings of Maximus the Confessor (*c*.580–662) and Gregory Palamas.

The Romanian theologian Dumitru Staniloae (1903–93) has drawn especially upon Maximus' notion of the immanent *logoi*. Within each created thing the creator Logos has implanted a *logos* or inner principle which makes that thing uniquely itself, and which at the same time draws it to union with God. Thus the world is a theophany, a sacrament of God's presence; all created things are God's 'garments', and each is a divine 'word' spoken to us personally. The human being, as high priest of the creation, has the vocation of rendering these *logoi* manifest, and so of transfiguring the cosmos. 'Man puts the seal of his understanding and of his intelligent work on to creation, thereby humanizing it and giving it, humanized, back to God. He actualizes the world's potentialities. Thus the world is not only a gift but a task for man' (*Sobornost*, 5. 9 (1969), 665).

In his understanding of the creation, Staniloae also employs, as do Florovsky, Lossky, Meyendorff, Romanides, and Yannaras, the essence–energies distinction developed by Palamas. The divine essence denotes God's transcendence, the energies his immanence. God's essence remains for ever radically unknowable to all created beings, not only in the present age but in the age to come. The energies, on the other hand—which are not an intermediary or a created gift but God himself in his direct, unmediated action—permeate the universe, filling all things with uncreated grace and glory.

By using this distinction between divine essence and divine energies, the neo-Palamites seek to affirm without compromise both God's otherness and his nearness. The apophatic mystery of God is safeguarded, but the creator is also seen as everywhere present: not pantheism, but pan*en*theism. Some western theologians, both Roman Catholic and Anglican, consider that the essence–energies distinction impairs God's simplicity and indivisibility, but others have incorporated it in their own thinking. Manifestly the theological categories of Palamism differ from those of *Thomism; each system deserves to be judged by its own criteria.

Closely linked with Palamite theology, although not identical, is the hesychast tradition of mystical prayer (*hesychia* meaning inner silence, stillness of heart). The classical expression of hesychasm is the *Philokalia*, a vast collection of spiritual texts edited by Macarius of Corinth (1731–1805) and Nicodemus of the Holy Mountain (1748–1809). First published in 1782, it has enjoyed a growing popularity among both Orthodox and non-Orthodox Christians during the last fifty years. In the eyes of many, this hesychast renaissance, with its devotion to the Jesus Prayer, represents the most dynamic element in contemporary Orthodox spirituality.

We turn now to the third theme, the church. For the Slavophiles the decisive factor in ecclesial life is not power of jurisdiction but mutual love. In the words of Khomyakov's disciple George Samarin (1819–79), 'The church is not a doctrine, nor a system, nor an institution. She is a living organism, the organism of truth and love, or rather she is truth and love as an organism.' The corporate consciousness or *sobornost* of the church is manifested above all in *councils. A church council, while attended primarily by the hierarchy, acquires ecumenical *authority only if 'received' by the whole body of the church, including the *laity.

Orthodox theologians in the 20th century have criticized Slavophile ecclesiology for its lack of precision, its diminution of the teaching *charisma* of the *episcopate, and its failure to emphasize the *sacramental character of the church. Khomyakov's notion of *sobornost*, based as it is upon the sociological model of the Russian peasant commune, reduces supranatural church communion to a naturalistic level. Following Ignatius of Antioch (d. *c*.107), the Russian Nicolas Afanassieff (1893–1966) and the Greek John Zizioulas, Metropolitan of Pergamon (b. 1931), prefer to envisage the church not in sociological but in *eucharistic terms. In full agreement with the Roman Catholic writer Henri *de Lubac, they maintain that it is the Eucharist that makes the church; participation in holy communion actualizes the church as the body of Christ and maintains it in unity. The Eucharist can take place only locally, and so the local church possesses crucial significance. The title 'catholic' applies not primarily to the church as a worldwide association, but to each local assembly at which the Eucharist is celebrated.

Zizioulas has employed the concept of communion not only in his ecclesiology but also in his understanding of the *human *person. Our humanness is realized through interpersonal relationship; there is no true person unless there are at least two persons in communication with each other. Created in the image of the triune God, we become genuinely human only through reciprocal love after the model of Trinitarian perichoresis. Such is also the viewpoint of Staniloae, who writes: 'The Trinity alone assures our existence as persons.'

It is a striking fact that, since the First World War, the growing-points of Orthodox theology have been not so much in the traditional Orthodox lands as in the west, in Paris and New York, for example. Orthodoxy can no longer be regarded as exclusively 'eastern'. The fall of communism opened up fresh and exciting possibilities in Russia and eastern Europe, and perhaps the centre of intellectual influence will now shift back eastwards; but the pattern of the future remains uncertain. For Russian Orthodoxy, as for the Orthodox world in general, this is an unsettled era, a time of danger but also of great hope.

Kallistos Ware

Blane, A., Raeff, M., and Williams, G. H., *Georges Florovsky: Russian Intellectual and Orthodox Churchman* (1993).

Bulgakov, Sergii, *Towards a Russian Political Theology*, ed. Rowan Williams (1999).

Lossky, V., *The Mystical Theology of the Eastern Church* (1957).

McPartlan, P., *The Eucharist Makes the Church: Henri de Lubac and John Zizioulas in Dialogue* (1993).

Nichols, A., *Light from the East: Authors and Themes in Orthodox Theology* (1995).

Pain, J., and Zernov, N., *A Bulgakov Anthology* (1976).

Sopko, A. J., *Prophet of Roman Orthodoxy: The Theology of John Romanides* (1998).

Staniloae, D., *The Experience of God* (1994).

Williams, R., 'Eastern Orthodox Theology', in D. F. Ford (ed.), *The Modern Theologians*, 2nd edn. (1997).

Yannaras, C., 'Theology in Present-Day Greece', *St. Vladimir's Seminary Quarterly*, 16/4 (1972).

Zernov, N., *The Russian Religious Renaissance of the Twentieth Century* (1963).

Zizioulas, J. D., *Being as Communion: Studies in Personhood and the Church* (1985).

ecclesiology, see CHURCH.

Ecclestone, Alan (1904–92), English parish priest, writer on *spirituality, communist. At school Ecclestone encountered Conrad Noel's vehemently anti-imperialist egalitarian Christian *socialism. Despite brilliant academic prospects, and a Cambridge double First in history and English, these convictions led him from university teaching into parish ministry, the bulk of which was spent in industrial Sheffield. Here he pioneered the Parish Meeting, which understood the *church as a form of *base community which met each week not just to worship but to discuss national and local politics and to turn this into action. A lifetime's commitment to the Worker's Educational Association kept history, art, and literature on the agenda; for Ecclestone, Christianity was concerned with fullness of life. The task of the church was 'to nurture the human soul'. In 1947 he joined the Communist Party and stood six times as a candidate for local elections, which created scandal. Ecclestone was at the centre of the Christian–*Marxist dialogue of the late 1960s. On retirement in 1969 he wrote a series of fine books, including *Yes to God* (1975) and *The Night Sky of the Lord* (1980), a passionate plea for Christian penitence and respect for the integrity of Judaism (see JEWISH–CHRISTIAN RELATIONS). *Yes to God* was ground-breaking in abandoning conventional approaches to *prayer, understanding it instead as the attempt to refract daily experience in the light of God's reality. Simone *Weil's 'prayer consists in attention' was at the heart of it and led Ecclestone to see art and poetry as training in prayer. The profound account of the spirituality of *sexual relationships was grounded in his marriage to Delia Abraham, apart from which his life and work cannot be understood. His insistence on experience, and his suspicion of *theology, reflected both the strength and weakness of much contemporary Anglicanism.

T. J. Gorringe

Gorringe, T., *Alan Ecclestone* (1994).

ecology (from the Greek *oikos*, 'household') is a *scientific discipline which investigates the relationships interlinking all members of the Earth household. The term originated with the German biologist Ernst Haeckel, who, in 1866, defined it as 'the science of relations between the organism and the surrounding outer world'. In 1909, the biologist Jacob von Uexküll used the word *Umwelt*, environment, to denote that surrounding world. Functional relationships (such as food chains and food cycles) are seen as the central organizing principle of biological communities, where organisms and their physical environments interact as an ecological unit. The British plant ecologist A. G. Tansley coined the term 'ecosystem' to characterize this network of interaction and interdependence.

While remaining a practical scientific discipline, ecology and its concepts have influenced many other fields of learning. The ecosystem concept fosters a systems approach in the analysis of the character and function of relationships within different types of community. It emphasizes the whole system over its parts, and its processes, such as negative and positive feedback loops, over its structure. Feedback loops, studied extensively in cybernetics, posit a circular arrangement of causally connected elements, in which an initial cause propagates around the links of the loop, so that each element has an effect on the next, until the last 'feeds back' the effect into the first element of the cycle. The cyclical exchange is sustained by pervasive co-operation rather than competition. Small fluctuations are amplified, some to the point where new structures emerge as a basis for development, learning, and *evolution. This creative generation of new forms within the stability of the main structure is a key property of all living systems. Its presence reflects the flexibility and diversity which enables ecosystems to survive disturbances and adapt to changing circumstances (Fritjof Capra, *The Web of Life* (1996), 32–70).

Consideration of these processes leads to an important ecological tenet: ecological wholeness does not imply an immutable homogeneity but rather the opposite—a dynamic unity of diverse elements. In nature, balance and harmony are achieved by ever-changing differentiation, by ever-expanding diversity which supports ecological stability. In human organizations, including Christian ones, both formal and emergent structures are always present, with the latter seen as expressions of the community's collective creativity and its ability to adapt to changing conditions.

Ecological emphasis on multifaceted relationality resonates with *process thought, based on the philosophy of Alfred North Whitehead, in which every organism, including the human, is constituted by its particular set of relations with the rest of the world. The eco-philosopher Arne Naess reiterates this by saying that relationships between entities, whether physical, cultural, religious, political, or economic, are an essential component of what those entities are in themselves (Merchant 1994: 120–4; 322–6).

In such ways, the ecosystem model has become a methodological tool by which different groups focus on particular aspects and functions of relationality. The natural environment's functional relations are taken as pattern and precondition of organizing principles in human societies. Within these societies, human ability to exist in freedom depends on the stability of the natural ecosystems in which societies are embedded, ecosystems which are much too variegated to be subordinated to human domination. For many social ecologists, this freedom in interdependence is bound up with the transposition of non-hierarchical principles from ecology to society. It too can be viewed as a circular, interlacing nexus of plant–animal relationships rather than a stratified pyramid with *humanity at the apex, a hierarchical view typical of philosophies, theologies, and policies of domination.

Social ecology's underlying premise is that there is an integral relationship between *global economic policies, which at present create an ever-widening gap between rich and poor individuals and nations, and global ecological crises. Therefore solutions in one sphere presuppose solutions in the other, in the form of a radical transformation of *capitalist production relationships from competitive systems to co-operative ones (Merchant, 163–72). The search for this radical transformation focuses on three areas which in turn distinguish three broad ecological movements. Eco-*feminism highlights connections between environmental degradation, violence against *women, and the feminization of *poverty. The environmental justice movement sides with the poorest communities, usually marked by race and class, whose environments often suffer a disproportionate share of negative environmental impacts (air pollution, soil degradation) resulting from economic policies. Anti-consumerist movements within civil society take the culture of conspicuous consumption as reflecting a materialism which comes close to idolatry.

These broadly differentiated, but ultimately coinciding, movements balance and complement each other by regarding the whole Earth household as an internally connected moral order. Increasingly, their concerns form and inform the agenda of major Christian charities and aid agencies worldwide. They too have discovered that economic and environmental injustices are inextricably linked, and employ economists and ecologists to help them deal with the results of economic and environmental policies that are not, and never were, morally neutral.

Environmental philosophers, eco-theologians, and activists see human domination of non-human nature as dependent on a presumed separation of humanity from nature, correlating to the separation of capital from labour, of executives from workers, of mind from body. Separation of internal human nature, epitomized as instrumental *reason, from the external natural world, reduces nature to an object, with reason as controlling instrument. By endorsing and technologizing instrumental reason, the domination of external nature and of many aspects of society is made possible and legitimized (ibid. 28–207).

Some significant intersections with Christian thought emerge from this brief discussion of ecological concepts and their theoretical evolution. The use of domination as a defining category in critical ecological theory coincides with a major charge against Christianity, formulated by Lynn White, Jr., in 1967. He argued that the Jewish and Christian mandate expressed in Genesis 1: 28 to 'increase, multiply, replenish the earth and subdue/dominate it' has made Christianity the most anthropocentric religion the world has ever seen. This anthropocentric world-view sees heaven and earth as made for the sake of human beings, as the place where they are given the right, indeed the duty, to procreate without limit, and implicitly, without regard for other life forms. The male human being, epitomized in Christ, is installed as the crown of *creation, with male rationality/instrumental reason at the apex of hierarchical rule. 'Subdue the earth' can be viewed as another divine command—a command to dominate nature, to conquer the world, and rule over it.

Jürgen *Moltmann, taking the charge seriously, reflects that this unbridled striving for power was believed to make human beings like their *God, 'the Almighty'. They invoked God's mighty powers to furnish a religious justification for their own. Allied with the reductionist view of nature implicit in modernist, mechanistic science, itself a product of western Christian culture, the tools for domination were made refulgent with religious fervour. The results have left many peoples and their environments devastated, especially in those continents simultaneously colonized and converted in the name of an all-conquering Christ and a 'higher' as opposed to a 'primitive' religion (Moltmann, 1985: 20–1).

The relatively recent ecological challenge to Christianity has, as yet, met with rather unstructured, generally revisionist responses (Hessel 1996: 7–8). All rely on either the acceptance or rejection of *natural theology's premiss, namely, that the natural order, as disclosed to us today by science, can be revelatory of God's will for us alongside God's self-revelation in Jesus Christ. How Christians align themselves on this issue affects their use of doctrinal, scientific, and other resources. Accepting the premiss, the Flood narrative in *Genesis, read as a *covenant between God and humankind for the preservation of all living creatures, endorses scientific warnings about the loss of biodiversity, turning it into a moral as well as an environmental issue. Similarly, when secular analyses of society single out the poor, indigenous peoples, women, and children as most at risk from, and most powerless to do anything about, the effects of environmental degradation, this resonates for some Christians with prophetic calls for *justice and with the messianic vision of the *Kingdom of God proclaimed by Jesus. For them, his promise of liberation from poverty and of a Sabbath for all creation, and his death under imperial rule, place him with those oppressed today by global capitalism and ecosystem destruction. Legitimation of domination in the name of God, however and wherever manifested, becomes a matter for repentance and reform, and an impetus towards interfaith *dialogue, especially with those religions, such as *Buddhism, which inculcate non-violence and compassion towards all living beings. The cultural specificity of concepts and imagery for God and for Christ originating in the post-Constantinian empire are radically critiqued for their militaristic, imperial, and triumphalist character. Forms of racial, gender, economic, and class oppression are set against the background of the primary oppression of nature, and the science of the Earth household translated into a vision of the planet as a temple of the Spirit, a dwelling place for all beings (Hallman 1994: 227–83).

Responding to the ecological challenge has other notable effects on Christian imagery. There is a definite metaphoric shift to the language of process, with an emphasis on relationality and mutuality evident in common use of terms such as system, interdependence, larger wholes, mutual relations, structural change. The notion of *sin as transpersonal and structural, rather than as simply a personal offence against God, signals a shift from 'supernatural' to natural processes as a Christian way of comprehending and describing our lives (Suchocki 1994: 16–64; Gottlieb 1996: 182–345). The old dividing lines between living and non-living, between mind and matter, between a self-aware humanity and a non-aware environment break down, and with them, the idea of the human species inhabiting an alien and indifferent physical universe (Wallace 1996: 133–70).

Ecology teaches that causal relations are real but far from unilinear. Each event in an ecological system is made possible by a complex interaction of antecedent events. No one of the antecedents is 'the cause', but all play a causal role. These ecological relationships are not peculiar to biological phenomena but are universal. Causal efficacy is a mode of immanence and of participation which has ethical implications. One's concern for the well-being of another in whose existence one participates is both for the sake of the other and for one's own sake. An extension of the sense of participation to the whole of nature brings a realization that the whole of nature participates in us and we in it. We are diminished by every death, wounded by the misery of the felled redwood tree and the starving child (Cobb and Griffin 1976: 154–5).

For Christians who acknowledge the role of natural causal efficacy (including our participation) in the world's evolution, God's continuing active role in events and process is not diminished. Chance, emergence, lawful causes (such as natural laws in which, for example, DNA plays a decisive role in shaping the physical structures of organisms) and human agency are not alternatives to, or exclusive of, a definitively divine presence. All are constitutive of each event throughout history. God's purposes are expressed not only in the relatively unchanging structural conditions of life, such as night following day, but more specifically in relation to changing patterns and situations. This suggests a God of persuasive love rather than coercive power, a God who influences and is influenced by the world, who desires freedom in humanity and spontaneity in nature, is involved in the world and participates in its amazing evolution (Barbour 1990: 175).   **Anne Primavesi**

Adams, C. J., *Eco-Feminism and the Sacred* (1993).
Barbour, I. G., *Religion in an Age of Science* (1990).
Cobb, J. B., Jr., and Griffin, D. R., *Process Theology* (1976).
Gottlieb, R. S., *This Sacred Earth* (1996).
Hallman, D. G. (ed.), *Ecotheology* (1994).
Hessel, D. T. (ed.), *Theology for Earth Community* (1996).
Merchant, C., *Ecology* (1994).
Moltmann, J., *God in Creation* (1985).
Primavesi, A., *From Apocalypse to Genesis* (1991).
Santmire, H. P., *The Travail of Nature* (1985).
Suchocki, M., *The Fall to Violence* (1994).
Wallace, M., *Fragments of the Spirit* (1996).

ecumenical movement

ecumenical movement is the name given to the 20th-century search to restore Christian *unity. The adjective derives from the Greek *oikoumene* or 'inhabited earth', which in secular Hellenistic usage carried the connotation of 'the civilized world' or 'the Graeco-Roman empire'. Ecclesiastically, the word signified 'Christendom' from the 4th century onwards, and 'ecumenical' institutions and decisions were those that affected the entire *church. The Roman Catholic and Orthodox traditions continued to make that claim for themselves. Among Protestants, the 18th-century revival stimulated both a recovered obligation to universal *mission and a sense of Christian fellowship transcending nations and confessions. The 20th-century ecumenical movement retained the twin thrusts towards global *evangelism and ecclesial unity, their interconnection being epitomized in the motto *ut omnes unum sint*: the Lord's prayer for his disciples 'that they all may be one' envisaged the goal 'that the world may believe' (John 17: 21).

Recognizing such precursors as the Evangelical Alliance (1846) and the World Student Christian Federation (1895), the modern ecumenical movement conventionally dates itself from the World Missionary Conference at Edinburgh in 1910. While overwhelmingly Protestant and Anglo-Saxon in composition (with the American Methodist layman John R. Mott, 1865–1955, in the chair), this meeting was significant for the coalescence of leading figures determined on worldwide mission, the encouragement of self-governing, self-supporting, and self-propagating churches in every region, and the development of practical co-operation through institutional forms. These concerns were then pursued through the ever more widely representative International Missionary Council between 1921 and 1961.

In the eyes of some, divisions among Christians were not simply a practical impediment to mission; they amounted to 'the scandal of disunity': communities living unreconciled among themselves undercut the credibility of the gospel as the world's *reconciliation to God (2 Cor. 5: 19) and *schisms between parties claiming ecclesial status inflicted wounds on the body of Christ, if they did not indeed dismember it. Thus the ecumenical movement in its fullness demanded the 'reunion' of the Church. Here the *Anglican contribution was important, epitomized in the letter from the bishops at the Lambeth Conference of 1920 'to all Christian people'. The American bishop Charles Brent played a formative part in launching the *Faith and Order movement which held a first world conference at Lausanne in 1927 and devoted itself to the matters of doctrine, *worship, and pastoral structures that would need to be settled among the churches on the way to fuller unity; and the continuing agenda was in large part set by the Chicago–Lambeth Quadrilateral of 1886–8 with its proposal of the scriptures as 'the rule and ultimate standard of faith', the Apostles' and Nicene *creeds as sufficient for confession and teaching, *baptism and the Lord's supper or *Eucharist as 'the two sacraments ordained by Christ himself', and 'the historic *episcopate, locally adapted' as a unifying *ministry.

The year 1920 saw also the publication by the Orthodox Patriarchate of *Constantinople of an encyclical letter 'to the churches of Christ everywhere' proposing, by analogy with the incipient League of Nations, a 'fellowship of churches' that would foster *rapprochement* among them through study and co-operation and enable them to bear witness together in face of the social consequences of the First World War. Simultaneously, the Swedish *Lutheran archbishop Nathan Söderblom (see SCANDINAVIAN CHRISTIAN THOUGHT) began preparing for the Universal Christian Conference on Life and Work that would take place in Stockholm in 1925 and carry forward the movement for 'practical Christianity' devoted to the concerns of *freedom, *peace, and *justice in national and international affairs. While Stockholm operated with the slogan 'doctrine divides, service unites', the attempt to find a basis at least in theological ethics marked the second conference on Life and Work at Oxford in 1937, with its theme of 'Church, Community, and State'.

Faith and Order also held its second world conference in 1937 in Edinburgh, its dominant theme being the presence of *grace and its signs in the church. The personal overlap between the Faith and Order and the Life and Work movements finds an emblem in William *Temple, archbishop of York and then of Canterbury. From the side of Life and Work came an initiative, accepted with some hesitation on the part of Faith and Order, to establish a World Council of Churches. After the testing times of the Second World War, the founding assembly of the World Council (WCC) took place at Amsterdam in 1948, where no less a figure than Karl *Barth contributed to the theme of 'Man's Disorder and God's Design'. With a continuing tension between a futurist European focus on the *Kingdom of God as still to appear and a more 'realized' North American one on its present signs, the eschatological orientation was pursued at the second assembly, held at Evanston near Chicago in 1954, under the title 'Christ—the Hope of the World'. The cohesion of the WCC in its early decades owed much to W. A. Visser't Hooft, its Dutch Reformed General Secretary (1948–66).

The classic high point of the ecumenical movement in its WCC form occurred with the third assembly, at New Delhi in 1961, dedicated to 'Jesus Christ—the Light of the World'. This is where the concern for direct evangelization, represented by the International Missionary Council, became institutionally integrated with Faith and Order and the life-and-work interests by then labelled 'Church and Society'. Membership in the WCC was expanded by the entry of the Russian and several other *Eastern European Orthodox Churches. The organization's original constitutional basis was strengthened by a mention of the scriptures and of the doxological vocation of the churches in the service of the Triune God: 'The WCC is a fellowship of churches which confess the Lord Jesus Christ as God and Saviour according to the scriptures, and therefore seek to fulfill together their common calling to the glory of the one God, Father, Son, and Holy Spirit.' The New Delhi assembly also adopted a description of 'the unity which is both God's will and his gift to his Church': it

> is being made visible as all in each place who are baptized into Jesus Christ and confess him as Lord and Saviour are brought by the Holy Spirit into one fully committed fellowship, holding the one apostolic faith, preaching the one Gospel, breaking the one bread, joining in common prayer, and having a corporate life reaching out in witness and service to all and who at the same time are united with the whole Christian fellowship in all places and all ages in such wise that ministry and members are accepted by all, and that all can act and speak together as occasion requires for the tasks to which God calls his people.

At this time, ecumenism enjoyed mutual reinforcement with the movements for biblical theology, patristic revival, and liturgical renewal; and many of these interests came together in the third world conference on Faith and Order, at Montreal in 1963, with its texts on 'Worship and the Oneness of Christ's Church' and 'Scripture, Tradition, and traditions'.

Meanwhile, and not by chance, the Roman Catholic Church was overcoming the suspicions it had officially displayed towards the ecumenical movement of Protestants and Orthodox since Pius XI's encyclical *Mortalium animos* of 1928 had forbidden participation in it for fear of religious 'indifferentism'. The 'spiritual ecumenism' of Paul Wattson (1863–1940) and Paul Couturier (1881–1953)—consisting chiefly in prayer for unity 'as Christ wishes and by the means he desires'—and the pioneering theology of Yves *Congar, author of *Chrétiens désunis* (1937), bore fruit in the Council of *Vatican II, conducted in the presence of observers from other churches. The conciliar decree on ecumenism, *Unitatis redintegratio* (1964), recognized that other Christians are, by *faith in Christ and the *baptism that signifies it, set into some measure of *communion, albeit imperfect, with the (Roman) Catholic Church; and that, while the one Church of Christ 'subsists in' the (Roman) Catholic Church, other churches and ecclesial communities—defective though they may be in some matters of doctrine, sacraments and order—are nevertheless 'not without significance in the mystery of salvation'. Retaining its own ecclesiological claims, the Roman Catholic Church became henceforth a major player on the ecumenical scene, under the aegis of the Secretariat (later Pontifical Council) for Promoting Christian Unity, headed first by Augustin Bea (1881–1968), and then Jan Willebrands (b. 1909).

The entry of the Roman Catholic Church brought into prominence a relatively new ecumenical procedure—the conduct of 'bilateral *dialogues' between that church and several other worldwide families of churches (Orthodox, Lutheran, Anglican, Reformed, Methodist) as well as between those communions themselves in various permutations. These dialogues, which still continue, have concentrated chiefly on dogmatic matters such as the nature of the gospel and of faith, ecclesiology, *sacraments, ministry, tradition, and *authority. They have sought both to establish broad common perspectives and to achieve agreement on more precise questions that have historically been controversial between the respective partners. Considerable interaction has taken place between these dialogues and WCC Faith and Order, with the latter body facilitating a regular forum to bring together participants in the various dialogues across the board as well as pursuing its own projects such as 'Baptism, Eucharist and Ministry' and 'Confessing the One Apostolic Faith'.

The WCC itself, however, has been engaged in something of a 'paradigm shift' (K. Raiser) since around its fourth assembly, at Uppsala in the revolutionary year of 1968. Hitherto guided by a view of the history of salvation with Christ at its centre (the dominant thrust at Vatican II also), the WCC now underwent the paradoxically related influences of the theology of *secularization of the mid-1960s, on the one hand, and an increasingly positive approach to religious pluralism, on the other. Interest in the *redemption of humankind began yielding to the preservation of the natural creation; and the concern for evangelization was diverted towards dialogue with 'people of other living faiths and ideologies'.

In 1990 the editors of the WCC-produced *Dictionary of the Ecumenical Movement* could still give a positive reading to the three principal streams in the ecumenical movement, faith and order, life and work, mission and evangelism:

> At its best, the ecumenical movement has been a search for unity in the truth as it is found in Jesus (Eph. 4: 21), and into which the Holy Spirit leads (John 16: 13). It has not been a matter, on the one hand, of creating a super-orthodoxy uniformly formulated or, on the other, of doctrinal compromise or indifferentism. Rather the churches have together searched the Scriptures, the venerable Tradition of the Church, and the belief and practice of contemporary communities with the aim of reaching a 'common expression of the apostolic faith today' (to adopt the title of a Faith and Order study).... At its best, the ecumenical movement has embodied a search for the will of God in every area of life and work. It has been a matter neither of a pretentious 'building of the kingdom' nor of a quietism that remains unmoved by the world's needs. Rather the churches have sought to engage in studies and action for the furtherance of 'justice, peace and the integrity of creation' (to use the title of the programme set out by the Vancouver assembly of the WCC in 1983).... At its best, the ecumenical movement has sought to discern, proclaim and participate in the Triune God's eternal and constant purpose for humankind and the mission of God to the world. It has not been a matter either of weakening witness to Jesus Christ or of refusing the truths that can be found outside the institutions of Christianity. Rather, the participating churches, whether members of the WCC or not, have 'confessed the Lord Jesus Christ as God and Saviour' and looked to 'fulfill together their common calling to the glory of the one God, Father, Son and Holy Spirit' (to use the words of the membership basis of the WCC).

Nevertheless, the WCC assembly at Canberra in 1991 provoked a strongly critical statement from the Orthodox participants concerning 'an increasing departure from the Basis of the WCC': 'We miss from many WCC documents the affirmation that Jesus Christ is the world's Saviour. We perceive a growing departure from biblically-based understandings of (a) the Trinitarian God; (b) salvation; (c) the "good news" of the gospel itself; (d) human beings as created in the image and likeness of God; and (e) the Church.' Similar concerns figured in the post-Canberra letter written by evangelical Protestants, whom the WCC has sought to woo. From two quite different quarters, therefore, the WCC was being called back to its original purposes. During the 1990s the WCC in fact worked hard at framing afresh 'a common understanding and vision', but few at the Harare assembly of 1998 considered that the vision had been granted to the organization.

How, then, are the achievements and prospects of the ecumenical movement to be evaluated at the turn of the century? The 20th century unquestionably witnessed a growth in mutual charity among confessionally and institutionally divided Christians. They meet, pray together, and engage in joint action for practical service of the needy and sometimes even in common evangelistic witness. At the level of doctrine, they have found convergence and even agreement on many important topics, as illustrated by the joint statement on *Baptism, Eucharist and Ministry* and many of the reports from bilateral dialogues. Their liturgies now often share the same basic structures and at points even common wordings. Informally, some Christians practise sacramental intercommunion across institutional lines, and some churches have officially declared eucharistic hospitality or entered into agreements of communion with other churches. But the untidiness of the situation at this level betokens remaining disagreements over the nature of the church and its unity. Institutional reunions have for the most part taken place within particular families, especially Methodist and Reformed/Presbyterian, or across those two family lines (as in Canada, Australia, and Zambia). In South India (1947), the Anglicans also joined, and in North India (1971), the Baptists and *Brethren, too; and in those two cases, the uniting church adopted 'the historic episcopate' as practised by Anglicans. Theologians in the Roman Catholic and Orthodox Churches are struggling to find an ecclesiological account of the presence of Christians outside their own respective boundaries; and the accounts finally given will affect the ways in which reunions may take place.

In his significant encyclical of 1995, *Ut unum sint*, Pope *John Paul II expressed the 'irrevocable' commitment of the Roman Catholic Church to ecumenism and affirmed the common obligation of all Christians to evangelization. He recognized the measures of doctrinal agreement achieved so far by Faith and Order and the bilateral dialogues and looked for further progress on the basis of 'Sacred Scripture as the highest authority in matters of faith' and 'Sacred Tradition as indispensable to the interpretation of the Word of God' (a formulation of canonical authority and hermeneutical location very much in line with the principles adumbrated by Faith and Order at Montreal in 1963). The Pope affirmed the 'effective presence' of 'the one Church of Christ' beyond Roman Catholic boundaries (opening a more attractive perspective for others on reunion than that of a 'return' to Rome) and offered the see of Rome (see PAPACY) as a universal 'ministry of unity' to be exercised in ways that should be the object of further dialogue.

It is clearly both premature and problematic to speak, as some do, of entering into a post-confessional or post-denominational age. The positive heritage concerning the truths of faith and the forms of their embodiment continues to require acknowledgement and assimilation, and the controversial heritage to require settlement. Moreover, new issues arise, new participants join in, and the terrain changes. It would be foolhardy to forecast what configurations of Christian unity and gospel mission will develop in the 21st century as the existing churches face up to such ecclesial issues as the *ordination of women, such moral issues as *abortion, *homosexuality, and *euthanasia, such denominational trends as the decline of hitherto mainline Protestantism and the spread of *evangelicalism and *Pentecostalism, such geopolitical events as the apparent demise of Soviet communism and such demographic features as the southward shift in the church's centre of gravity.

Geoffrey Wainwright

Evans, G. R., *Method in Ecumenical Theology: The Lessons So Far* (1996).

Fey, H. E. (ed.), *A History of the Ecumenical Movement (1946–68)*, ii (1970).

Kinnamon, M., and Cope, B. (eds.), *The Ecumenical Movement: An Anthology of Key Texts and Voices* (1996).

Limouris, G. (ed.), *Orthodox Visions of Ecumenism: Statements, Messages and Reports on the Ecumenical Movement 1902–1992* (1994).

Lossky, N., *et al.* (eds.), *Dictionary of the Ecumenical Movement* (1991).

Meyer, H., and Vischer, L. (eds.), *Growth in Agreement: Reports and Agreed Statements of Ecumenical Conversations on a World Level* (1984).

Newbigin, L., *The Household of God* (1953).

—— *The Reunion of the Church* (1948); rev. edn. (1960).

Raiser, K., *Ecumenism in Transition: A Paradigm Shift in the Ecumenical Movement?* (1991).

Rouse, R., and Neill, S. C. (eds.), *A History of the Ecumenical Movement* i. 1517–1948 (1954).

Stormon, E. J. (ed.), *Towards the Healing of Schism: The Sees of Rome and Constantinople: Public Statements and Correspondence between the Holy See and the Ecumenical Patriarchate 1958–1984* (1987).

Visser't Hooft, W. A., *Memoirs* (1973).

Wainwright, G., *Worship With One Accord: Where Liturgy and Ecumenism Embrace* (1997).

education is a slippery word: some aspects of its slipperiness can be grasped in one brief Victorian episode in Christian education. When the Irish bishops invited him to establish a Catholic University in Dublin, J. H. *Newman entered a decade (1850s) of educational striving. He needed first to clarify his *concept* of education (*The Idea of a University*); to relate that concept to *institutions* (his work in Dublin, the Oratory School in Birmingham, his involvement with adult education); to decide on appropriate *curricula*; in the matter of Catholic parochial schools, to examine *relations between church and state*; to explore the concord of *religion and education*; finally, to advocate a fuller role for the *laity in the church's educational thinking and practice. Newman's six issues still confront Christian educators.

What is education for? Newman affirmed that one purpose was to equip people to live in the real world, to be socialized into their cultures, and skilled to earn their keep. This required attention to a rapidly broadening and deepening stream of human knowledge. He was equally sure that another prime purpose was to nurture persons—in particular, gentlemen—who were genuinely human, sensitive, and cultured. These two ends remain in tension. Throughout the world, funders of education insistently demand the functional approach: costly education must deliver a skilled workforce for market economies. So, on independence, every African government undertook huge investment in public education, thereby encountering Catholic and Protestant educators who had different, mixed notions of what education should be for. Missionaries had established schools and other institutions to produce Christians: 'neglect your churches to perfect your schools' was accepted mission wisdom.

Many educational philosophers, however, following Paul Hirst, judge this 'religious' end to be as functional as the market's: for them, 'education' must never have a qualifier; only a disinterested, rational education can produce truly autonomous people. Although Christian commentators have responded that such 'education' conceals its own qualifier and has its own interested agenda, the question persists of the purposes of Christian educators, and the word 'indoctrination' hangs in the air.

Is education schooling? Newman planned both *university and school, institutions anciently generated on foundations of *monastic learning; he was also much concerned for the education of the poor and of adults. Schools have long been at the heart of the church's enterprise. In the African missions, as in most of India and Latin America, primary education was basic; rudimentary teacher education followed. Schools were at the heart of Christian communities; *children matured in *family, church, and school. Such schools were similar to those established in English parishes 'to educate the children of the poor in the principles of the Established Church'. Yet church schools appear not to promote faith better than secular ones; they may offer education within a faith context; they may be faithful communities successfully delivering a civilizing curriculum; but, according to Fowler, substantially anticipated by Dewey in 1903, faith development depends on longer and wider experience within the community of faith than schools can or do offer. If Dewey is right, then a major problem for church schools is that they may try to deliver more than a child can digest, inhibiting the very end they seek to achieve. Lifelong learning, firmly based on the learner's own problem-solving, accommodates the scale of human development. This insight has led churches to explore the potential of post-institutional education: in Bangladesh, John Hastings established adult *literacy and numeracy programmes to furnish adults with tools for self-improvement; the Brazilian Paulo *Freire's theoretical work in education focused on what education was for—domestication or liberation? For Freire, education was the practice of freedom.

What of the curriculum? In recent years, educators have debated whether there can be a 'Christian curriculum'. Some 'Christian schools', drawing inspiration and materials from the USA, adopted a confessional approach to the whole curriculum, especially to matters of controversy: Noah's Ark allows for both two and seven times tables; the study of human origins must be confined to Genesis (see EVOLUTION), but Newman's wider, humane curricular approach has nothing to do with such rejection of the world. The changing, post-*Enlightenment world remained God's, however unfamiliar. While there is no Christian mathematics, it is now clearer that subjects such as history and literary criticism are not neutral: people always learn from within world-views.

Consequently, Newman's Oratory School at Birmingham was to be 'like Eton, without the wickedness, and with the inculcation of Catholic faith'. In 1599 the *Jesuits had produced their meticulous *Ratio Studiorum*; in 1668, Comenius his *Unum Necessarium*, which anticipated later developments by accenting personal growth—forming persons in the image of Christ—and by insisting on understanding as a precondition for genuine learning.

But, if the state pays for much of the schooling, who decides on the curriculum? It was this issue which led churches in Zambia to withhold their support when government, having first nationalized the schools, later asked the churches to take them back; why, they reasoned, should they labour for ends not their own?

Given a world of nation-states, how might churches relate to the state's provision for education? (see ESTABLISHMENT). For Newman and his peers, the pressing issue was government grants for Catholic schools for poor children. In France, the *Code Napoléon* had taken public education into state control; in the USA, the constitution, formally separating religion from state, ensured that public funding should not support the teaching of religion in schools, even though much higher education derived from religious foundations.

The collapse of Christendom thrust a form of this question into focus around the world. Historically, the foundations and instruments of education had been religious. Schools and universities once equipped church and state with functionaries. Modern nation-states, often multiracial and multifaith, have yet to face scarcely broached questions about the relations between education, faith, and culture, questions racking the consciences of faith communities which scarcely know how to cope with the effects of a *secularizing and internationalizing popular culture. The defence of the church school has been a long rearguard action.

How, then, might 'religion' be thought to relate to 'education'? Tertullian's earlier, bluff response was 'What has Athens to do with Jerusalem? What concord is there between the Academy and the Church?' (*De praescriptione haereticorum*, 7. 9). Salvation was crucial and philosophy could never replace revelation in getting it. Archbishop *Temple, a former headmaster, was more cautious: 'An education which is not religious is atheistic … If you give to children an account of the world from which God is left out, you are teaching them to understand the world without reference to God.' From his letters on the Tamworth Reading Room (1841) to his *Idea of a University*, this was also Newman's perspective; in varying forms, it still focuses Christian approaches to education: 'Christianity, and nothing short of it, must be made the element and principle of all education. Where it has been laid as the first stone, and acknowledged as the governing spirit, it will take up into itself, assimilate, and give a character to literature and science' (*Discussions and Arguments* (1872), 274–5). Certainly, a thoroughly secular curriculum indoctrinates as surely as a religious, though less obviously. Christian educators point out that they, for their parts, have clearly indicated their axioms; many are sceptical about the purposes of secular societies' arrangements for the inculturation of the young.

Much of Europe still permits the presence of religious education in varying kinds: Germany's largely confessional approach is an add-on to the curriculum; Britain's 1996 Education Act confirmed the schools' responsibility for spiritual, moral, social, and cultural development of pupils. It ignores the relation of this responsibility to the locally agreed syllabuses of religious education in non-church schools, whose usual aim is 'understanding' rather than 'belief'. Yet underlying all education is a purpose and a world-view, disclosed or secret, understood or not.

One of Newman's major preoccupations long antedated *Vatican II's conciliar decree on the Church. He was insistent that the church, the *laos* of God, was primary, and he strongly resisted the clericalism that confined laypeople to hunting and similar activities, while financially supporting the clergy: bishops, priests, and laity together comprised God's *laos*. This insight came during his study of *Arianism, when he realized that it was not the clergy who had defended the truth. It was deeply resented in the Catholic Church in Newman's time, but there is now an insistent, worldwide search for ways to educate laypeople for their apostolic, apologetic role: training days, correspondence courses, video- and audio-tapes, easily accessible publications, computer software, are all deployed in this development. Gains from 'secular' education contribute to this process, especially Comenius' and Dewey's accent on understanding in order to learn: didacticism is out, discovery in. Education is generally conceived as more than instruction and quite other than indoctrination.

Since churches exist as communities of faith within nation-states, Christian lifelong learning will probably increase in relation to education received in schools and colleges, while Christians will need increasingly to witness to the profoundly moral, social, and political dimensions of all education: a process nurturing *persons within communities of persons, created for the glorious *freedom of the children of God.
                                                                    Peter Doble

Astley, J. and Francis, L. J. (eds.), *Christian Theology and Religious Education: Connections and Contradictions* (1996).

Culler, A. D., *The Imperial Intellect* (1955).

Erricker, C. (ed.), *Teaching Christianity*, 2nd edn. (1995).

Felderhof, M. C., *Religious Education in a Pluralistic Society* (1985).

Fowler, J. W., *Stages of Faith: The Psychology of Human Development and the Quest for Meaning* (1981).

Freire, P., *Pedagogy of the Oppressed* (1970).

Gates, B. (ed.), *Freedom and Authority in Religions and Religious Education* (1996).

Jackson, R., *Religious Education: An Interpretive Approach* (1997).

King, U. (ed.), *Turning Points in Religious Studies* (1990).

Newman, J. H., *The Idea of a University* (1852–59).

——— *Discussions and Arguments* (1872).

Edwards, Jonathan

Edwards, Jonathan (1703–58), considered by some the greatest theologian of the 18th century. The leading preacher and champion of the First Great Awakening, Edwards wrote works on theology, philosophy, and ethics aimed at upholding Christian *orthodoxy in the age of the *Enlightenment. He was born in East Windsor, Connecticut, and educated from 1716 to 1720 at Yale. Having spent a short time serving a small *Presbyterian congregation in New York, he returned to Yale as a tutor. In 1727 he married Sarah Pierrepont from New Haven; they had eleven children. In the same year, Edwards began his ministry in Northampton, Massachusetts, first as assistant to his ageing grandfather, the influential Solomon Stoddard, and later as sole minister; it ended with his unfortunate dismissal in 1750. The following years (1751–7) were spent in Stockbridge, a frontier settlement at the western edge of Massachusetts, where Edwards was in charge of a small community of white settlers and of the local mission to a Houssatonic band. In 1757 he was voted president of the College of New Jersey in Princeton. He had some hesitation in accepting the offer, for his years in Stockbridge, initially a kind of exile, had become very productive. Here he had written his major philosophical works, including *Freedom of the Will* and *The Nature of True Virtue*. He had hoped to work on a more systematic account of Christian doctrine. But only a few weeks after his departure from Stockbridge and his induction as president he died as the result of a smallpox inoculation.

In Edwards's boyhood he had been fascinated by 'flying spiders'. Years after recording his observations of them, he used the spider-image in his most famous sermon, 'Sinners in the Hands of an Angry God', preached at Enfield, Connecticut, in 1741. The dangling spider represented the unconverted sinner hanging over the pit of hell. The resulting sense of imminent threat is intensified when one discovers that *God is both one's enemy and one's saviour. Edwards forces his congregation to see itself, unbearably, as without Christ: in the midst of death, held only by the slender thread of life, which is no more than God's temporary restraint of his will to leave the sinner to eternal destruction. But despite Edwards's determination to confront his contemporaries with the shattering reality of the will of God, he was not a typical *revivalist. The moderate style of his *preaching, the depth of his thought and its wide horizon distinguish him from such itinerant preachers as George Whitefield and James Davenport, whose charismatic impact left their audiences fired with religious enthusiasm. Unfortunately, later generations seem to have had selective memories: they remembered and abhorred Edwards as preaching hellfire sermons, and affirming God in a way that diminishes humanity. Both his opponents and his friends have created him according to their own ideas. He is seen as the tragic hero of an outmoded European *Calvinism, or, on the contrary, as an early example of new, modern America: sometimes as the father of transcendentalism, sometimes even as belonging to the world of *postmodernity. Some of his writings, such as the *Life of David Brainerd*, *A Faithful Narrative*, *Religious Affections*, and *A History of the Work of Redemption*, made a strong impact on 19th-century *evangelicalism, with its interest in *mission, its *millennialist hopes, and its emphasis on personal sanctification. Questions about Edwards's personal life preoccupied a number of scholars. His private notes, the *Miscellanies*, edited by Thomas Schafer, were expected to reveal some secret about a man whose thoughts and writings often looked like pieces of a puzzle that did not fit together.

In *God Glorified in Man's Dependence*, his first sermon to be published, Edwards expresses what was to be central to his theology: God's sovereignty, not matched by any human effort. His emphasis on the asymmetry and immediacy of the relationship between God and the human being was puzzling to an audience accustomed to the mediating arrangements of *covenant theology. The sermon expresses another aspect of Edwards's theological *realism: *faith is a sense of what is real in the work of *redemption, which later helped him to steer the vessel of *religious experience between the Scylla and Charybdis of *Antinomianism and *Arminianism.

In *A Divine and Supernatural Light* we encounter the keyword of Edwards's religious psychology: the gift of a new 'sense'. He shows a *mystical tendency in favouring the metaphor of *light. What a truly religious person knows is beyond notional knowledge, being based on an experience similar to an actual sensation. It is an immediate grasp of the beauty of God's work of redemption, and is more effectual than reason or education in disposing human beings to accept it. In short: true religion is a matter of the heart and its affections, but the human heart tends to self-deception and hypocrisy, so affections which claim to be religious must be tested by a number of reasonable criteria. Religious Affections, Edwards's last defence of the Awakening against growing criticism, is impressive evidence of his unwillingness to reduce religion to an emotionalism that encourages people to rely solely on their own 'extraordinary' experiences and immunizes them against questioning by the community of the *church.

Edwards inherited from his grandfather Solomon Stoddard a set of problems focused on the church as the visible community of saints. Originally only the children of church members were admitted to *baptism, and to be accepted as a member one was expected to undergo and publicly declare some kind of *conversion experience. There was a great deal of uncertainty about the nature of this experience and the accounts given of it before the congregation. Conversion can simply be seen as the moment when the Christian doctrine of salvation is taken personally: whereas up till now I have been a more or less indifferent member of the audience, I now discover myself as an actor in the drama itself. According to the ecclesiology of 'visible saints', a minister's primary responsibility was the pastoral care of those still only in the audience, who needed to be guided into the story of salvation. Now came the questions to which Edwards, like any other minister of the *Puritan tradition, had to find answers: Is there such a thing as guidance? Does people's experience of conversion follow a fixed pattern? Are there any steps we can take preparatory to that life-changing moment when saving faith first emerges? Do we know anything about human nature that helps us to initiate the process? From his own experience, Edwards knew that all these pastoral efforts towards stimulating conversion were misleading. When the first revivals occurred in his parish in 1734, he understood them as God's own testimony to the doctrine of *justification by faith alone. The beginning of the Awakening in Northampton can be seen as the first blow struck against the compromise of the Half-way Covenant, with its tacit implication that public and visible religion is simply morality. The Half-way Covenant, introduced in 1662 and favoured by Stoddard and many others, allowed the children of the growing number of unconverted parents to be baptized: parents who could not claim any conversion experience were treated as people sincerely longing for true religion and therefore on their way into the church. But the Awakening proclaimed that there is no area for 'half-way-Christians'. The middle ground between *world and church, the distance between 'total depravity' and true religion, cannot be measured. It is God's immediate presence that creates something entirely new, both in personal and in public life, and invalidates all the means by which we order and manipulate our lives before God and our fellow human beings.

In Freedom of the Will Edwards declares that the only *freedom necessary for human beings to be considered moral agents is freedom in the sense that one is able to do as one wills: that one's behaviour is a coherent expression of who one is. People are free to behave as they are, not free to choose who and what they are: their nature, habits, and inclinations are part of the biography given to them before and beyond any specific act of will. Hence his controversial achievement was to establish a concept of human freedom by which a person is seen as both totally dependent upon God's providence and fully consistent with her own nature. The expression of that freedom, emphasizing both determinism and responsibility, was the ambiguous notion of 'moral necessity' as the basic structure of human life in general, and one of the few qualities that the regenerate and unregenerate have in common.

Edwards's purpose was to show that a certain religious liberalism had taken root in American soil, which undermined the doctrinal fortress built in 1618 by the Synod of Dort to protect the sovereignty of God and its foremost expression, the doctrine of *predestination, against the Arminians. He opts for an anthropology of total depravity both in Original Sin, and in the The Nature of True Virtue, in which he exposes humanity's moral capabilities before regeneration, however impressive, as inconceivably distant from the true beauty of a spiritual and virtuous life. He stands for 'unconditional election', questions the meaning of preparation, and interprets the Awakening as God's testimony to the doctrine of justification by faith alone. We find him holding on to the doctrine of 'limited atonement' when he addresses his congregation with the urgency of a revivalist for whom the final division of humankind into two irreconcilable camps is a given and indisputable fact. We see him alluding to John Locke's 'simple idea' in support of the tenet of 'irresistible grace' and comparing religious experience with the supernatural gift of a new sense. Finally, we see his increasing concern for the 'perseverance of the saints' when he insists that good dispositions and works spring from faith as good fruit grows on a good tree. When the revivalist preacher loses his initial naivety and becomes a critic of the Awakening in general and of his congregation in particular, he is responding to people's self-centred interest in sensational experiences exalting them above the duties of their daily unobtrusive lives. True religion is not one among many aspects of human reality. It disrupts the hopeless habits of a person's and a society's life, in ways that human beings cannot foresee as the millennium breaks through the structures of history. But it needs to be more than a mountain-peak experience of incommunicable emotions. That experience demands expression in intelligible words and in a life that can be recognized as according with what the church knows of the will of God.

See also NORTH AMERICA: AN OVERVIEW.   **Caroline Schröder**

Cherry, C., The Theology of Jonathan Edwards. A Reappraisal, new edn. (1990).

Conforti, J. A., Jonathan Edwards: Religious Tradition, and American Culture from the Second Great Awakening to the Twentieth Century (1995).

Fiering, N. S., Jonathan Edwards's Moral Thought and its British Context (1981).

Guelzo, A. C., Edwards on the Will: A Century of American Theological Debate (1989).

Jenson, R. W., America's Theologian: A Recommendation of Jonathan Edwards (1988)

Lee, S. H., The Philosophical Theology of Jonathan Edwards (1988).

Lesser, M. X., Jonathan Edwards (1988).

——Jonathan Edwards: An Annotated Bibliography, 1979–1993 (1994).

Miller, P., Jonathan Edwards (1949).

Miller, P., and Smith, J. E. (eds.), The Works of Jonathan Edwards (1957–).

Murray, I. H., *Jonathan Edwards. A New Biography* (1987).

Schroeder, C., *Glaubenswahrnehmung und Selbsterkenntnis: Jonathan Edwards's* theologia experimentalis (1998).

Stein, S. J. (ed.), *Jonathan Edwards's Writings: Text, Context, Interpretation* (1996).

eighteenth century: an overview.

The 'long 18th century', which stretches from the 1660s to as late as the 1830s, from the impact of the ideas of Locke and Newton on European society in the later *seventeenth century to the time when Europe was slowly assimilating the consequences of the French Revolution, is a historian's convention, but it is relevant to the history of western Christianity because these were the years in which the Christian churches first found their social and intellectual position in European society threatened by the critical assaults of an aggressive *modernity. The medieval western church had divided into Protestant and Roman Catholic institutions in the 16th century; in the 18th, as the importance of that break-up declined, organized Christianity faced new sources of conflict. In this context the 18th-century *Enlightenment was above all a series of challenges to long-accepted authorities, religious, scientific, and philosophical: changing ideas, especially in the fields of physics and historical studies, deeply affected the churches as well as society as a whole. There was no simple black-and-white conflict, but a long drawn-out sifting of traditional certainties.

From this point of view the 18th century may easily seem to have been disastrous for the Christian churches. The French historian, Delumeau, thought that by the end of the 18th century the running-down of successive Protestant and Catholic campaigns to convert the ordinary people of Europe to Christianity, which had been going on ever since the *Reformation, had become clear; and Vovelle has written of the 18th century as a time of 'dechristianization', at any rate in France. This was not the whole of the story, however. In the case of Christian worship, for example, Protestant church music was transformed by Johann Sebastian *Bach and Georg Friedric Handel, while congregational singing entered a new era through the *hymns of Isaac Watts and the *Wesley brothers. Between the late 17th and the mid-18th century there was a tremendous outbreak of Protestant *revival *preaching, not dissimilar, on the practical level, to the older *Jesuit methods of mission-preaching, though the theologies involved differed. This was the basis of what is usually called the *Evangelical Revival, through which Protestantism, which had seemed in danger of falling to pieces in the later 17th century, regrouped, and rapidly acquired a new and vitally important power-base in *North America. This revivified popular *Protestantism, in both its German and British forms, firmly retained a belief in the authority of the Christian scriptures as a final divine self-revelation. Both John Wesley and his fellow-Anglican, the philosophical theologian Joseph Butler, sought in different ways to assert the absoluteness of a Christian understanding of creation in which the human race depended for its ultimate happiness on salvation from sin through Christ. And European Catholicism not only survived the fiery tests of the 1790s, but successfully relaunched itself in the following century.

Nevertheless, the Enlightenment bulks large in any account of the religious history of the period. The Enlightenment is often described as a radically anti-Christian, though not necessarily anti-

religious, movement among a relatively small number of 18th-century intellectuals, who are said to have shared an over-optimistic belief in the capacity of human society, guided by *reason, *science, and education, to make progress towards perfection. Among the 18th-century thinkers typical of the Enlightenment looked at as a movement for intellectual freedom were such French intellectuals as Denis Diderot, editor with d'Alembert of the subtly anti-Roman Catholic *Encyclopédie*; Jean-Jacques Rousseau, who invented his own civic religion, the purpose of which was to give moral stability to the ideal political community of his *Social Contract* (1762); and Voltaire, a pessimistic theist, who thought that society needed to be saved from the Christian churches. The greatest figure of the German Enlightenment, Gotthold Lessing, attacked Christianity as intellectually intolerant and was himself inclined to pantheism, in the style of the Jewish philosopher, Baruch Spinoza. The work of these men was characteristic of what in the course of the 18th century became a self-conscious intellectual movement, whose leaders saw themselves as possessing a liberated, hopeful, non-Christian, and, in the case of some of them, atheistic understanding of the present position and future possibilities of humanity. But this was not a revolutionary political movement: there was no direct link between such writers and the Jacobins of the French Revolution. For the handful of people most passionately involved no political revolution was necessary: they thought in terms of reason's gradual, irresistible advance towards greater and greater clarity. They identified Christianity with darkness and superstition: Edward Gibbon, the English historian, for example, described the thousand years between the end of the Roman empire in the west and the fall of Constantinople in 1453 as the triumph of barbarism and religion.

The Enlightenment, however, was not simply an affair of intellectuals which broke out suddenly as the *ancien régime* entered the 'enlightened despot' stage of its struggles to modernize. What also caused many 18th-century people to think of theirs as an enlightened age was a broad pattern of social and intellectual changes which had been going on in Europe and also in the Americas between the 16th century and the French Revolution of 1789, and which modified the way in which many ordinary educated people thought about human nature and *religion. One of the more remarkable examples of how the general view of the supernatural was altering by the end of the 17th century in much of Europe and North America was the quite sudden shift of opinion against holding *witchcraft trials, and against the consequent execution of both men and women on the ground that they were witches. However one explains the great witch-panics, the Christian churches had largely accepted this magical world-view as part of their theological environment. There had been no real doubt about the existence of demonic forces, and both theologians and ecclesiastical authorities had been involved in the trials of alleged witches. Nevertheless, both trials and executions became socially unacceptable by the end of the 18th century. This does not mean that there was an overall decrease in the amount of human cruelty: the Jacobins executed people wholesale on political grounds, and this has been seen as an indirect outcome of the Enlightenment.

The disappearance from most of Europe of witchcraft as a serious social and religious problem went with a shrinking of the hold on the imagination of the more educated classes of the Christian doctrine of *providence, which is concerned with the divine government of the creation. What many people began to doubt was the possibility of supernatural intervention in nature, thought of as the world of physical experience, and witchcraft offered a crude example of alleged supernatural activity. There is no agreed explanation of how the change came about, though it is clear that those who administered justice became less and less confident about the nature and quality of the 'confessions' that were put before them, and about the use of torture in the legal system to extort them. From a practical point of view the protest against judicial torture was summed up by a leading figure of the Italian Enlightenment, Cesare Beccaria, in his book, *On Crime and Punishment* (1764), and the roots of Amnesty International are to be found in the enlightened view of the rights of the individual over against all forms of social and political power. In Tuscany, Beccaria's influence led to the abolition of the death penalty, a unique action in the 18th century. Modern, by no means universally successful, protests against *capital punishment have depended heavily on the typically 'enlightened' fear of error, of executing an individual who should not have been executed. In England, the 16th-century law that sanctioned prosecution for alleged witchcraft was repealed in 1736; the last European execution of someone charged with witchcraft may have been in Poland in 1793. At much the same time it was becoming socially impossible to execute people on the ground that they were heretics or blasphemers, though imprisonment remained a possibility in many countries.

The move toward greater reliance on human reason was as much a social product as the by-product of philosophical argument. One direct source of increased 'enlightenment' was the steady accumulation of fresh evidence about human life and its environment. This evidence often clashed with what had been transmitted by tradition, or asserted on the basis of a combination of scriptural statements and classical philosophical categories. The relationship between classical antiquity and the European present changed steadily between 1600 and 1800. It became absurd to suggest, as John Wesley, for example, still did in the later 18th century, that 'modern' music, by which he meant the music of Bach and Handel, had much less power over the human soul than the music of the Greeks; but when J. W. Goethe visited Assisi in 1786 he deliberately ignored the Franciscan basilica and went instead to look at the surviving portico of the Roman temple which was now used as a Catholic church. Geographical and astronomical discovery, Newtonian physics, and Harvey's demonstration of the circulation of the blood were among changes of scientific perception which led a broad section of the educated élites of Europe and America to modify their world-view. They accepted the essential accuracy of the new information, and they were not easily tempted into a theological assessment of their widening knowledge. They were therefore gradually ceasing to treat either the bible or the Christian churches as the major source of their understanding of the physical universe, the planet itself, or the history of the diverse human races inhabiting it. When Diderot, for example, poured scorn on the assumption that because a French naval expedition in the 1770s had set foot on Tahiti the French were entitled to annex the island and enslave its inhabitants, he made it clear that he did not think that the French could plead a superiority in religion as part of their justification. The Tahitians were entitled to their own world-view.

Behind these changes of attitude lay a shift in the European world-view, the growth of the belief that the individual human being did not, in order to think and act correctly, have to submit to external, traditional *authority, even when authority came in the written form of alleged divine self-revelation, as in the case of the Jewish and Christian scriptures, or to the religious institutions established on the basis of such an authority. As early as 1678 the Catholic scholar, Richard Simon, in his *Histoire critique du Vieux Testament*, was seeking to establish the right of biblical criticism, as it was later called, to question the limits set by ecclesiastical authority to free discussion. Simon himself was anathematized by the church, but his book was still read. In the long run the 'enlightened' scholar insisted on the freedom to construct his/her own version of the text and of its 'original' meaning. In the 19th century *Liberal Protestantism continued the 'enlightened' approach, as did Catholic *modernism at the beginning of the 20th century. As in Simon's case, both groups of scholars met considerable ecclesiastical resistance.

This more critical attitude to the *bible was symptomatic of the way in which the European cultural situation had been changing since the 16th century. There was a decrease in the number of people who assumed that the Christian 'revelation' could be used to provide final definitions of human nature, its purpose, and its fate. The philosophical theology of the great figures of 17th-century *philosophy, René *Descartes, Thomas Hobbes, and John Locke, already related much more to human reason than to divine *revelation. These 'enlightened' tendencies were expressed with extreme boldness between 1690 and 1730 in the writings of the English *deists, a small group of intellectuals, among them Anthony Collins, whose best-known book was entitled, significantly, *A Discourse of Freethinking* (1713), Samuel Clarke, and John Toland, who published *Christianity not Mysterious* in 1696. They were deeply alienated from traditional Christianity, and, although they have often been underrated, they should be included in the general picture of the British Enlightenment. They thought that the individual's own reason, whether thought of as God-given, or as somehow the natural product of a basic substance or matter, should be his fundamental guide, and reason was understood as primarily a free, critical instrument, depending on knowledge, logic, and judgement for its results. Among these results might be the knowledge of God and of the moral behaviour which he required, though Collins was probably an atheist and Toland became a pantheist. There was no need for a specifically Christian revelation; there was talk of 'natural religion' and of a 'moral sense'. As for the Anglican George Berkeley, his brilliantly obscure anti-materialist apologetic had no effect on his contemporaries in the great wave of enthusiasm for Newtonian science.

Eighteenth-century Britain offers an example of 'enlightenment' as a kind of 'conservative modernism' (J. G. A. Pocock). There was no tremendous tension, but *freedom of thought, freedom of religious belief, freedom of publication, freedom of political action, all quietly increased and became part of an attitude which looked back to an idealized classical city-state more than it looked forward to modern experiments in mass democracy. Religion was valued if it helped to stabilize society. The cautious, ironical, sceptical philosopher, David Hume, extended the normal Protestant rejection of alleged latter-day *miracles back into the NT, but he made no direct challenge to the Anglican apologist, Joseph Butler, who had argued that the first converts became Christians in terms of miracles, and that their testimony was the same kind of evidence as if they had put it in writing and these writings had survived (*The Analogy of Religion* (1736), 257).

A major consequence of the Enlightenment was a widening gap between 'popular' and 'official' Christianity. In the case of the Protestant churches the cultural effects of the Reformation directly contributed to the spread of what came to be called 'enlightened' attitudes. In some parts of the 18th-century Catholic Church there was a distinct reaction against *Counter-Reformation piety. In Italy, for example, L. A. Muratori, one of the founders of the modern (enlightened) approach to historical scholarship, criticized popular enthusiasm for a definition of the doctrine of the Assumption of the Virgin Mary, and was answered by Alphonsus Liguori in *The Glories of Mary* (1750). The Habsburg emperor, Joseph II, who ruled between 1765 and 1790, tried to reduce what he regarded as superstition among the less educated of his subjects. At the popular level, therefore, belief in Christianity as a source of supernatural intervention in ordinary life had to find new means of expression, and from this point of view Protestant evangelical revivalism, which in its early creative phase was a search for supernatural power, and which rejoiced in what were regarded as 'special providences' of God on the individual's behalf, has to be interpreted as 'counter-Enlightenment'.

Yet another major element in this gradual transformation of attitudes in Europe and the Americas was that by the end of the 17th century the struggle between the Roman Catholic and the Protestant Churches had reached a point at which it became clear that Protestantism would survive the long Catholic counter-offensive. Both parties continued to affirm that theirs was the pure form of primitive Christianity, but the educated élites of Europe ceased to think of the choice as a major intellectual issue. There were still many people who, for various reasons, accepted the view that the state had the right to choose and impose a particular version of Christianity on its subjects, but the approach was breaking down in favour of some concept of religious toleration. The most sustained example of the traditional policy was the relentless anti-Protestant drive of the ageing Louis XIV, determined (and failing) to make France a totally Roman Catholic country, but it was the subtle arguments in favour of an absolute toleration of religious deviance by a French Protestant exile in Holland, Pierre Bayle, which pointed to the future. The demand for freedom of thought and publication, though often challenged since the 18th century on the grounds that public welfare cannot indefinitely tolerate the extremes of free human expression on such themes as racism or religious belief, was a vital element in the Enlightenment's legacy. There was a shift of power as 'public opinion', which in the 18th century meant 'enlightened opinion', became an independent force demanding official acceptance as a legitimate part of cultural and political processes. Society increasingly rejected constraint by religious institutions and presuppositions, as well as by the arbitrary will of government. From this point of view, it is difficult to argue that modern western culture draws its vitality principally from the Christian tradition.

In the history of the Enlightenment's influence on 18th-century religion the American Revolution (1776) is more important than the French (1789). At the heart of the American rebellion lay a deter-mination to break with the authority of both the Church of England and the Hanoverian dynasty. The American leaders happily claimed that God had created all men equal, but they were no longer concerned to impose any specific version of deist or Christian doctrine as the basis of a sound commonwealth. This was a more profound and permanent break with the past than anything achieved in 1789, and was sustained without the morally destructive device of the Terror, which rejected the essential spirit of 'enlightenment'. The assumption that the Protestant churches and other forms of Christianity should have no direct political power, that a republican United States of America should be created with no official commitment to a particular form of Christianity, was accepted without much resistance. This was a sign of a growing acceptance of the 'enlightened' view, that the toleration of several unofficial forms of Christianity was better for the social system than the imposition of a single form by the state. In practice, there was a de facto Protestant hegemony in the new United States that lasted well into the 20th century, and which did not depend upon the authority of the state.

The French revolutionaries, on the other hand, retained the belief of their monarchist predecessors that the ideal state should be reflected in an ideal ecclesia. At one stage they tried to 'reform' the French Catholic Church, at another to introduce the worship of a Supreme Being. Van Kley argues that a central tragedy of the French Revolution was that Roman Catholicism was driven into adopting a role on the right of post-revolutionary European politics. Neither the Vatican nor the French Catholic Church could accept either the Jacobin assertion of lay independence from clerical authority, or the implication that in the modern state Christianity should continue only as part of the individual's private life. The anti-Enlightenment religious and political tradition, which caricatured the Enlightenment as a conspiracy of intellectuals and Freemasons against God, his church, and monarchical government, may be dated from the 1790s, and became as important as the 'liberal individualism' against which it raged.

Important as these developments turned out to be, one should not allow one's interpretation of 18th-century religion to be dominated by the history of the French Revolution. A new, relatively optimistic view of human nature, at odds with the pessimistic side of the Christian tradition, became widespread both inside and outside the churches in the course of the century and survived the excesses of the Jacobins. Those who talked about an 'enlightened age' were claiming that Europeans now knew more and saw more clearly than their predecessors, and where science was concerned this was true. The French naturalist, Georges-Louis Buffon, for example, was already examining the evidence that suggested that the world as it was might not have been *created by divine agency all of a piece and not very long ago, as Christian teaching had maintained, but had developed, both in geological and biological terms, over a vast space of time. The classical argument for the existence of God from *design, which argued from order in the world to a supernatural designer, was sharply criticized by David Hume in the *Dialogues Concerning Natural Religion* (published posthumously in 1779), and although the Anglican theologian, William Paley, in his *Natural Theology* (1802), produced a very popular restatement of the belief that the universe could not have occurred by accident, a future containing Darwin, Marx, and Nietzsche's exultant 'There is no such thing as purpose—we invented purpose' was not far away.

Nevertheless, the fact that the churches seemed to be losing support in the 18th century does not oblige one to think in terms of a one-way *secularizing process of modernizing 'enlightenment'. There were those in the churches who set out to revive traditional beliefs and practices, and others who wanted to reform religious institutions along lines suggested by 'enlightened' influences. In Italy, for example, in the 1780s the Habsburg duke of Tuscany, Leopold, briefly gave state support to the would-be reformer, Scipione de Ricci, bishop of Pistoia in northern Italy. The synod of Pistoia in 1786, the high point of 'enlightened' influence in Roman Catholicism before the French Revolution, protested against parish missions, a characteristic Jesuit method of seeking to revive local religion by bringing into the parish powerful and ultimately centralizing forces from outside. On the other hand, the Synod was as much ducal as episcopal when it proposed to shift power in the church from the centralizing Vatican and the ubiquitous male and female orders to national churches in which the dynamic role would be that of the local parish priest. In the parish church there would be one plain altar, and, in a flight of fierce reaction against contemporary church architecture and decoration, the role of statuary would be reduced to a minimum; ideally, the mass would be said in the vernacular and the congregation would always communicate. One is suddenly looking at proposals which, while not in themselves 'enlightened', shared something of the 'enlightened' search for personal, existential certainty (both Diderot and Rousseau come to mind here); proposals which would play their part in the slow formation of an effective Catholic reform movement, whose breakthrough came at *Vatican II.

This was a radical ecclesiastical reaction to the problems of 18th-century cultural change, and one sees something similar in the unsuccessful attempt made in England in 1772 to relax compulsory clerical subscription to the Anglican foundation-document, the Thirty-Nine Articles. In *German Protestantism, on the other hand, there was more emphasis on the application of historical criticism to the documentary basis of Christianity as such. Johann Semler historicized the development of the biblical canon and so weakened its authority; and Samuel Reimarus, whose work was posthumously published by Lessing himself, showed once and for all how it was possible to argue that the text of the NT was made up of different layers of material, not all of which were even aimed at the same audience. Reimarus left the professional study of the life of *Jesus in permanent disarray, but at the same time unintentionally offered 'radical' Christians a way of remaining within a Protestant culture.

These 18th-century solutions to the problems set by the Enlightenment had as yet no widespread support. In the *Analogy of Religion*, however, Joseph Butler produced a subtle and long-lasting restatement of orthodox theology. He started from the argument that 'natural religion', the alternative theological system that 18th-century Enlightenment theists offered, could not cope with 'the wretched state of the world', which was 'in ruin'. Butler argued that human repentance, the deist response to the moral requirements of the creator, was simply not enough, that one must accept the revelation of the NT, confirmed by the miraculous history of Christianity, that it needed divine intervention and the propitiatory

sacrifice of Christ to restore creation. The argument from the 'ruined' state of the world was and remains emotionally powerful, and Butler's willingness to speak of Christ's redemptive acts as a mystery which we could not fully understand added to his appeal. John Wesley, on the other hand, while he was more intellectually conservative than Butler, was emotionally much less restrained: he moved beyond general ideas of repentance and redemption to the possibility of men and women being so utterly transformed in an individual experience of 'the power of the Spirit' that they might be described as being in a state of 'Christian perfection'.

When the German philosopher, Immanuel *Kant, summed up in the 1790s what he took to be the essence of 'enlightenment', he described it as the individual's achievement of maturity, that is, of having the courage to think for oneself. In religious terms, this meant not only rejecting the churches' demand for conformity to a particular theological tradition, a demand still sometimes backed by the power of the state, but also refusing to submit to the emotional pressures that Kant saw at work in the Protestant *Pietism of his day. Whereas John Wesley encouraged his followers to expect a conscious experience of divine power as the confirmation of the truth of Christianity, Kant argued that right conduct was the essence of religion, and dismissed what we might now call 'popular religion', whether Protestant or Catholic (*Religion within the Limits of Reason Alone*, 1794). His belief that one could trust one's understanding of the moral nature of the universe more safely than one could trust one's alleged religious experience, whether in the eucharistic service or in the revival meeting, that one's 'moral sense' was a more reliable guide than one's 'religious sense', set out a position on which one side of *nineteenth-century humanist western culture was to rely heavily. Kant did not settle the argument. The idea that human beings are capable of an intuitive or mystical apprehension of a supernatural order was not so easily swept aside, either in philosophy, theology, or popular religion.

*Romanticism reversed the trend, preferring existential faith to scepticism, distinguishing, rightly or wrongly, imagination from science. At the same time, however, the release of social, economic, and intellectual energy which had been reflected in self-conscious talk of 'enlightenment' continued to transform both society and the environment, and so confirmed the importance which the 18th century attached to unrestricted scientific investigation. As Hans Blumenberg has said (1966), what was losing plausibility was the Christian doctrine of providence.

In the 18th century it became clear that Christianity as the source of very specific theological world-views and ethical systems no longer dominated the intellectual life of western culture. Nevertheless, and despite the sociopolitical shocks of the American and French Revolutions, the churches emerged from apparent decline with renewed determination in the 19th century. Some of the sources of this recovery may be found in the part played by women in the 18th-century churches and, more broadly, in popular religion. But whatever the source, already before 1800 there were clear signs of the fresh *missionary campaigns that would carry both Roman Catholic and Protestant Christianity all over the world in the following hundred years.   **John Kent**

See also BLAKE, WILLIAM; EDWARDS, JONATHAN; ENTHUSIASM.

Adorno, T. W., and Horkheimer, M., *Dialectic of the Enlightenment* (1947), ET (1972).

Blumenberg, H., *The Legitimacy of the Modern Age* (1966), ET (1983).

Bolton, C. A., *Church Reform in 18th Century Italy (The Synod of Pistoia 1786)* (1969).

Butler, J. *The Analogy of Religion Natural and Revealed, to the Constitution and Course of Nature* (1874).

Byrne, J., *Glory, Jest and Riddle: Religious Thought in the Enlightenment* (1996).

Carroll, M. P., *Madonnas that Maim: Popular Catholicism in Italy since the Fifteenth Century* (1992).

Champion, J. A. I., *The Pillars of Priestcraft Shaken: The Church of England and its Enemies* (1992).

Chartier, Roger, *The Cultural Origins of the French Revolution*, ET (1991).

Chatellier, L., *The Europe of the Devout: The Catholic Reformation and the Formation of a New Society* (1987), ET (1989).

Delumeau, J., *Catholicism between Luther and Voltaire* (1971), ET (1977).

Diderot, D., *Supplément au Voyage de Bougainville* (1796), in *Œuvres*, ed. A. Billy (1951).

Dupront, A., *L. A. Muratori et la société européenne des pré-lumières* (1976).

Furbank, P. N., *Diderot: A Critical Biography* (1992).

Gay, P., *The Enlightenment: An Interpretation: The Rise of Modern Paganism* (1967).

Haakonssen, K. (ed.), *Enlightenment and Religion: Rational Dissent in Eighteenth-Century Britain* (1996).

Harrison, P., *'Religion' and Religions in the English Enlightenment* (1990).

Hume, D., *The Natural History of Religion*, ed. H. E. Root (1957).

Koselleck, R., *Critique and Crisis: Enlightenment and the Pathogenesis of Modern Society* (1959), ET (1988).

Labrousse, E., *Bayle* (1983).

Locke, J., *The Reasonableness of Christianity*, ed. I. T. Ramsey (1958).

Pailin, D. A., *Attitudes to Other Religions: Comparative Religion in Seventeenth and Eighteenth Century England* (1984).

Pocock, J. G. A., 'Clergy and Commerce: The Conservative Enlightenment in England', in *Eta dei Lumi: studia storice sul settecento Europeo in onore di F. Venturi* (1985).

Porter R., and Teich, M. (eds.), *The Enlightenment in National Context* (1981).

Sharpe, James, *Instruments of Darkness: Witchcraft in England 1550–1750* (1996).

Toland, J., *Christianity not Mysterious*, ed. G. Gawlick (1964).

Ugrinsky, A. (ed.), *Lessing and the Enlightenment* (1986).

Van Kley, Dale K. *The Religious Origins of the French Revolution: From Calvin to the Civil Constitution 1560–1791* (1996).

Vovelle, M., *Piété baroque et déchristianisation en Provence au xviii siècle: Les Attitudes devant la mort d'après les clauses des testaments* (1973).

Ward, W. R., *The Protestant Evangelical Awakening* (1992).

election, see PREDESTINATION.

Eliot, T. S. (Thomas Stearns, 1888–1965). Eliot, who was raised a *Unitarian, and, when he composed *The Waste Land* (1922), was strongly attracted to Buddhism, proclaimed himself 'Anglo-Catholic in religion' in *For Lancelot Andrewes* (1927). Poet, critic, and dramatist, his work assimilates influences as diverse as modern *anthropology, *Dante, eastern *religions, and the music-hall. Although a trained philosopher, and a probing critic of culture and society, his richest contribution to Christian thought is in his *poetry. This is not to ignore his prose with its magisterial formulations on tradition, or its *aperçus* on the different levels of belief, and the relation of belief to scepticism or to ritual.

Much of his work is driven by the quest to integrate and redeem a world characterized by what he claimed it was a poet's 'essential advantage' to be able to see: 'beneath both beauty and ugliness … the boredom, and the horror, and the glory'. His pre-conversion poetry, culminating in *The Waste Land*, maps the descent of ennui into an isolation that becomes a horror of disintegration and sterility amid the squalors of the modern *city and the fragmentation of modern culture. The glory that can pierce boredom and horror is apprehended in haunting visionary moments of *memory or transfiguration (as in the 'hyacinth girl' passage of *The Waste Land*), never as a comprehensive vision.

Eliot's conversion rechannels, without mitigating, the bleakness of this world-view. *Humanity's bondage to self-dramatizing, self-deception, intellectual laziness, appetites, and excitements now enforces an astringent summons to a purgative Christian life. Even when this astringency does not become corrupted into spiritual snobbery, in *The Idea of a Christian Society* (1939) or the 1947 play *The Cocktail Party*, it generates a Christianity aridly polarized between an élitist sainthood and an ordinary life of tradition and routine. *The Idea* is, in the end, more valuable for its critique of liberal individualism and its resilient pessimism about *history than for the positive ideal it sketches.

Eliot's later poetry explores the way of purgation with a subtlety and resource not possible in polemical prose. The *Four Quartets* (1935–42) recast much of his earlier work, especially *The Waste Land*, marshalling disruptive moments of visionary encounter, and the cyclic vanity of human existence, towards a glimpsed *incarnational redemption. Their discipline of negation (drawing on *John of the Cross and the *Hindu traditions of the *Bhagavadgita*) orchestrates Eliot's lifelong preoccupations: the intersection of the temporal by the timeless; the integration of past with present; the dialectic of interpretation and experience; the writer's toil with language. The fourth, *Little Gidding*, marries *purgatorial *fire with the tongued fire of *Pentecostal revelation to climax in an incantatory dance of echoes where ends and beginnings, *paradisal innocence and beatific vision, fuse to evoke a world finally integrated in 'A condition of complete simplicity | (Costing not less than everything)'.

See also ETERNITY; TIME.   **Donald Mackenzie**

Bush, R., *T. S. Eliot: A Study in Character and Style* (1983).

Edwards, M., *'Eliot/Language' and 'Renga': Towards a Christian Poetics* (1984).

Gardner, H., *The Art of T. S. Eliot*, 4th edn. (1968).

Kojecky, R., *T. S. Eliot's Social Criticism* (1971).

Ellul, Jacques (1912–94), French Protestant polymath. Ellul's contribution to theology is difficult to localize. He was academically active in sociology, politics, and law; one of his books on history was a standard text in French universities. He was also a theologian in the Reformed tradition, and the key to understanding his wide-ranging interests is the influence of *Barth. The dialectic structure of reality suggested by Barth, in which *God interrogates *humanity's proposals, informed Ellul's thinking as well. In political terms, he was sympathetic to *Marxism. He supported the Resistance in Bordeaux during the Second World War, and became deputy mayor at the Liberation. He was well known locally for his activities, which included pioneering post-war work in the rehabilitation of young offenders and the later *ecological alliance with Bernard Charbonneau. He wrote a weekly column for the Bordeaux newspapers for most of his life. His books, of which there are over fifty, follow his explicitly expressed dialectical pattern in that a sociological or political study usually has a theological counterpart. The most significant theological works are: *The Presence of the Kingdom* (1951), *The Meaning of the City* (1970), *The Politics of God and the Politics of Man* (1972), *The Theological Foundation of Law* (1961), *Violence* (1969), *The Humiliation of the Word* (1985), *The Subversion of Christianity* (1986). The theological tone of all his work is set by *The Presence of the Kingdom* where he is concerned to establish the priority that God has over all human evasion of the call to *justice. He warns against the human tendency to conceal the true ends of political activity by substituting discussion of the means. He attacks the creation of a technological world-view in a series of books better known in the English-speaking world than most of his work, *The Technological Society* (1964) being the first. A simplistic evaluation of this work from a sociological perspective alone has led to him being classed as a modern Luddite, but an appreciation of the theological agenda informing his rejection of the confusion of the end with the means would help readers avoid this mistake.

Jacqui Stewart

Troude-Chastenet, Patrick, *Lire Ellul* (1992).

Endo, Shusaku (1923–96).

Born in Tokyo, Endo was baptized into the *Catholic faith at the age of 11. Early he became attracted to the thought of Jacques *Maritain. In 1956, Endo received Japan's coveted literary accolade, the Akutagawa Prize, for his *novel *The White Man*. *Silence* appeared in 1966, to be translated and published in English in 1969, and in Swedish, Norwegian, French, Dutch, Polish, and Spanish in 1972. In 1981 he was created a member of the prestigious National Art Academy (Geijustu-In) of Japan.

The spiritual and intellectual orbit of Endo is determined by the tension caused by the encounter between Japan's nature-oriented culture and the nature-disturbing culture of the west under the influence of Christianity. The motif of continuity (predictability, equilibrium) is central to the former, that of discontinuity (unpredictability, disequilibrium) to the latter. A similar tension existed between the ancient cultures of the predictable Nile and the unpredictable Tigris-Euphrates. More distinctly, this pattern of encounter can be observed wherever Semitic monotheism (Judaism, Christianity, *Islam) encounters the cultures of pantheistic-polytheistic orientation (see ECOLOGY). This is what makes Endo's works dramatic and unsettling. Scenes of nature, all embracing, all beautifying, and all forgetting—sunshine, cloud, rain, snow, wind, trees, sea, and mountains—are set in contrast to scenes of the agonizing deaths of the Japanese Kirishitan *martyrs.

The orientation towards discontinuity creates the *beyond nature* possibility of apostasy (*korobi*) or martyrdom. This was a new possibility, unknown to the Japanese until the arrival of the Catholic *mission in the 16th century. Endo's consuming interest in these themes gives a distinct theological character to his writing. Deftly he deploys *symbols, *myths, and human faces, creating a map of the soul in which his theological insights are cogently expressed. Endo does not preach. He does not give easy answers. He holds his readers in the grip of new questions.

What he is asking is whether such an intense religion that takes its followers beyond the security of nature's embrace, and ultimately brings them to face the possibility of apostasy or martyrdom, has had any qualitative impact on *Japanese culture. He suggests that it has not. He observes the contradictory character of the Japanese

mind. The Japanese are arrogant yet humble. They are incapable of transcendent thinking, yet they are capable of suffering martyrdom. Beneath this contradiction is Endo's judgement that Japan is a religious swamp that swallows all things indiscriminately.

Endo describes the agonizing moment of apostasy as the Kirishitans trample on the image of Christ before the officials of the inquisition. Those who trampled on the image were spared their life. In *Silence*, Christ's sad eyes beckon to the frightened prisoner; 'Go ahead, trample!' Then comes a brief exchange; 'Lord, I resented your silence.' 'I was not silent. I suffered beside you.' This dialogue reveals the heart of Endo's understanding of culture, religion, and theology.

To the cultural tradition of Japan in which 'silence' signified tranquillity of soul, Endo introduced a drastically disturbing image of silence. Japanese people are fascinated by this contrast. By intersecting these two types of silence Endo challenged the Japanese people and helped them to form their intercultural self-identity.

Kosuke Koyama

Williams, Mark, *Shusaku Endo: A Literature of Reconciliation* (1999).

Enlightenment.

In the *eighteenth century this movement of thought had influence throughout western civilization. Few of its leaders, men such as Voltaire, Hume, Gibbon, and Lessing, were Christian. The precepts of the Enlightenment often challenged Christianity: dare to be adult and let go of the church's apron-strings; trust your own *reason and measure *revelation against it; be prepared to use your reason critically in any context. The Enlightenment was in many ways a dangerous antagonist to Christianity.

Nevertheless, the polarity is misleading. The Enlightenment had Christian roots. The saying, beloved by the Cambridge Platonists, 'The mind of man is the candle of the Lord,' is a mystical expression of the Christian belief in human reason, whence it follows that educated people can be convinced by argument (see SEVENTEENTH CENTURY). Recent historians, quite rightly, have played down the real impact of the handful of *deist or *atheist philosophers on a largely Christian Europe. But they have often not done justice to the wider Christian Enlightenment, frequently depicted as fellow-travellers with unbelief. In some real sense, 18th-century Christian Europe accepted the Enlightenment, and in fact made many changes later Christians do not regret. This was the age that came to see *witch-hunting as cruel and pointless. Increasingly, Christians since have accepted *religious liberty as actually preferable to 'persecuting privileged orthodoxy'. Some Christians were leaders of Enlightenment; for example, the leaders of the Scottish Enlightenment, apart from Hume, were almost all clergymen.

Even with this proviso, much of Christianity then and since has defined itself against Enlightenment. The *Romantic Revival rediscovered the *Middle Ages, and with that the case for medieval Catholicism. In the battle between 'Greeks' and 'Goths' over the true architecture of Christianity the Goths won, and dark interiors and pointed windows became for a time almost the Christian norm. In theology, *Schleiermacher specifically dismissed reason and ethics as the core of Christianity in favour of the feeling of dependence, which scarcely seems a statement of adult autonomy. He was, however, more *Kantian than he sounds, eager for each person to discover his own religion, appealing to individual experience rather than any tradition, and the liberal theology that looks back to him still owes much to the Enlightenment.

German idealist philosophy, particularly that of *Hegel, tried to digest or historicize the Enlightenment, rather than renounce it. Hegelian theology, which attempts to synthesize divine and human, and, for that matter, darkness and *light, has different priorities from the Enlightenment. Later 19th-century *Liberal Protestantism, with the Kantian moralism of Albrecht Ritschl, opting for a religion of moral values and not facts, probably deserved to be called, as it sometimes was, the 'new Enlightenment'. But there were strands in German thought that saw the Enlightenment as typically French, and in some sense a symptom of decay.

Karl *Barth, in affirming *neo-orthodoxy, showed his characteristic relish in building up the human achievement of Enlightenment, just to say that it gets us nowhere. Nothing human beings can do works towards real progress. Half his *Protestant Theology of the Nineteenth Century* is about its Enlightenment precursors. To him *Pietism and rationalism, the two opposed forms of 18th-century Christianity, are in fact twins, because both are basically human and vehicles of bourgeois morality. There is a non-condemnatory truth here, of how much *evangelicalism does owe to the Enlightenment, including its own traditional philosophy of *Common Sense Realism, and perhaps its almost total immunity to *antinomianism.

Some modern theology is in the Enlightenment tradition. *Tillich's lucid fair-mindedness and openness to modern thought (and the small quantity of dogma in his belief-system) are a good example. But others see it as an enemy. Lesslie *Newbigin, fearing attempts in India to remove the uniqueness of Jesus by incorporating him within a *Hindu thought-world, felt that something equivalent had happened in Europe 'domesticating the gospel within the reigning plausibility structure', and that it was the Enlightenment which had provided our local scheme of rationality. Christianity, *the* truth, is betrayed if another standard of truth is used to judge it, or if it is merely allowed its place in the 'religious preference' niche of a wider order. Newbigin follows the post-critical philosopher Polanyi in hunting out the more subtle expressions of enlightened hegemony. He warns us that we should not trust the characteristically modest tone, which goes back at least to Lessing, of the enlightened person confronted with varieties of religion; in Newbigin's view 'the emphatic admission of our fallibility only serves to re-affirm our claim to a fictitious standard of intellectual integrity'. In other words, the reasonable admission of ignorance simply enshrines reason as the final arbiter. In the postmodern age, however, the biting phrase 'fictitious standard' can be turned on anyone with pretensions to intellectual integrity, Newbigin included.

No one can deny that there are varieties of religion. That fact might seem to suggest that the Enlightenment rejection of tradition and its authority has triumphed. We all now are, and have to be, choosers in a bazaar of faiths; as Berger says, there is a heretical imperative. But many, perhaps most, practising Christians in the 20th century preferred to stay with the givenness of tradition. They did not want enlightened autonomy, and opted away from it as soon as possible.

On the level of technical systematic theology, such writers as Gunton, Jenson, and Thiemann focus on the individualism of the Enlightenment. When Kant says 'dare to know', they notice that the command is in the singular form. The villain of the piece, however, is often *Descartes, individual suspicion of authority carried to a principle of philosophical practice. Descartes predated the Enlightenment, and he did not dominate its thought, but writers in systematic theology very often see the Cartesian individual, with the principle of *doubt and even more the achievement of a place to stand, as the beginning of enlightened autonomy. These scholars use reason, but as a tool, never as a starting-point. In particular they dislike any sense that there are some ideas that are just true, or foundational, from which we can argue. They also, following Polanyi, question the Enlightenment's detached view of how the mind works, god-like in its assumption of pure objectivity.

*Postmodernism, following the Frankfurt school of Adorno and Horkheimer, radically deconstructs the Enlightenment's claim to a single rational order. There are postmodernists (like Derrida) who theologize, and a wide range of theologians who use postmodernist gambits. All understanding is unveiled as imperialist: what is understood is commodified, measured, and controlled. Control is the clue. Reason, they claim, is based on assumptions that are really only the assumptions of power, and the reasoning individual is uncovered as the bourgeois hungry for power. Such arguments, turning on its head the Enlightenment's critique of religion as a plot by greedy priests, can serve simply to clear the way for a revamped traditionalism. Having got rid of the so-called 'reason' of the Age of Reason, they can return to a completely Christian discourse, with the divine Logos as the norm.

*Feminist theology, and other theologies of the oppressed, which have good reason for suspicion of the confident certainties of bourgeois males, can also join in a critique of the Enlightenment, which went only so far in liberating the groups they represent. Other theologians, perhaps more consistently postmodern, such as Mark Taylor and Don *Cupitt, have certainly not returned to pre-Enlightenment modes of thought, but, in trying to articulate post-Enlightenment thought, puzzle most Christians. These are some of the very varied ways of doing post-Enlightenment theology.

For two hundred years the Enlightenment has been an antagonist of choice for Christian theologians. As might be expected, this has done much to shape theology. It is unlikely that recent tendencies towards post-Enlightenment will bring the dialogue to an end.

Alistair Mason

Cragg, G. R., *Reason and Authority in the Eighteenth Century* (1964).
Dyson, A. O., 'Theological Legacies of the Enlightenment', in S. W. Sykes (ed.), *England and Germany* (1982).
Gunton, C. E., *Enlightenment and Alienation* (1985).
Michalson, G. E., *Lessing's Ugly Ditch: A Study of Theology and History* (1985).
Newbigin, Lesslie, *The Gospel in a Pluralist Society* (1989).
Young, B. W., *Religion and Enlightenment in 18th Century England* (1998).

enthusiasm.

'Sir, the pretending to extraordinary revelations and gifts of the Holy Ghost is a horrid thing, a very horrid thing.' Thus one of the greatest Christians of the 18th century rebuked another. Bishop Butler thought that John *Wesley was an enthusiast, and Wesley, whenever the subject came up, was anxious to prove he was not. 'It is the believing those to be Miracles which are not, that constitutes an Enthusiast,' he wrote. The trouble was that

Wesley's standard of proof for *miracles was rather low. His life was surrounded by special providences: if the rain held off, or if some opponent dropped dead suddenly, this was a sign of God's favour. Many of his less-educated followers certainly were enthusiasts.

On the other hand, Wesley and his fellow *Methodists were alive with Christianity, and some of their Anglican critics were narrow and unpleasant. Around 1750 Bishop Lavington wrote a book called *The Enthusiasm of Methodists and Papists Compared* where he speaks of 'the most nasty, ridiculous, crack brained, nay wicked saints … such as the saints Francis, Dominic, Ignatius'. These wicked enthusiasts are all now with John Wesley in the calendar of saints of the Church of England, and the bishop is forgotten. In the 20th century Monsignor Ronald Knox revived the religious use of the term with his book *Enthusiasm*, tracing the history of ecstatic religion through the centuries with deftness and *humour. This was before the *charismatic renewal in the Roman Catholic church, and he measures everything against a cut-and-dried orthodoxy not so unlike Bishop Lavington's. Already in the 18th century the contrast was made between harmless enthusiasts and bigots, and enlightened people preferred enthusiasts.

'Enthusiasm' and its family of words comes from ancient Greek. *En* is 'in', and *theos* is 'god', so the enthusiast has a god who has come into her and taken her over. We think with a shudder of the devotees of Dionysus who in a drunken frenzy tore in shreds whoever came in their way. Or we think of the oracle of Apollo at Delphi, possessed by the god who speaks through her. Sixteenth-century Protestants rediscovered such terms to put down radical Anabaptists claiming special gifts of the *Holy Spirit.

In the 17th century the idea of enthusiasm was already losing its supernatural overtones. Henry More, the Cambridge Platonist, wrote *Enthusiasmus Triumphatus* in 1656 against the early (quaking) *Quakers. He was not so much interested in spirit-possession as in personality types. What was it that 'disposes a man to listen to the Mystical Dictates of an overbearing *Phansy* [his spelling, relating 'fancy' to 'phantasm'], more than to the calm and cautious insinuations of free *Reason*'? Perhaps there were medical or even climatic reasons. In any case, a lively fancy or imagination is not a disastrous gift: 'a poet is an enthusiast in jest, and an enthusiast is a poet in good earnest'.

The third Earl of Shaftesbury (1671–1713) did more than anyone else to give enthusiasm its modern positive sense. As a philosopher, he was light-hearted and easy to read, and so had great influence. He is not to be confused with his descendant the seventh earl, the evangelical (even enthusiastic) Victorian philanthropist. The third earl published *A Letter Concerning Enthusiasm* in 1708. It was an apt time, because all London was talking about the French Prophets, Huguenot refugees whose reaction to persecution was to rediscover primitive charisms. They prophesied, they rolled about in convulsions, there were strange signs from the sky, they even, with thousands of Londoners, stood round a grave after three days waiting for one of their company to rise again. These were classic enthusiasts, the sort that embarrassed serious Christians and intrigued the general public. Should they be put down? Shaftesbury said no: we should 'never punish seriously what deserved only to be laughed at'. 'Good-humour is not only the best security against enthusiasm, but the best foundation of piety and true religion.' The moderate piety of the age of *reason owed much to Shaftesbury, as did the enthusiasts whom they teased and tolerated.

Christianity can cope with being laughed at. Shaftesbury himself recognized that we can run a worthwhile risk of being comic in handling great matters. 'Something there will be of extravagance and fury, when the ideas or images received are too big for the narrow human vessel to contain.' This resembles Wesley's line of thought: 'whatever is spoken of the religion of the heart, and of the internal change of the Spirit of God, must appear enthusiastic to those who have not felt them'. Enthusiasm for anything is funny to an outsider, but we would be cold creatures without it. As Shaftesbury said 'all sound love and admiration is enthusiasm'. The concept is not simply religious: 'there have been enthusiastical atheists'. And as for religion, it is too hard to draw the line between inspiration, orthodox and approved, and enthusiasm, misguided and reprehensible. 'Inspiration is a real feeling of the Divine Presence, and Enthusiasm is a false one. *But the passion they raise is much alike*' (author's emphasis).

Outside religion, enthusiasm became a good word, but not within. Quakers and Methodists wore their old nicknames with pride, but no group claimed to be enthusiasts. There have been enthusiastic Christians from *Montanists to the recipients of the Toronto Blessing, and it is easy to find parallel phenomena in other religions. What they see as gifts of God may seem comic to outsiders, but those who oppress them seem comic too. In 1814 the keynote of the consecration sermon of the first Anglican bishop for Asia was 'Put down enthusiasm'. Perhaps mercifully, he failed.

Alistair Mason

Cooper, Anthony Ashley, Third Earl of Shaftesbury, *Characteristics of Men, Manners, Opinions, Times* (1711), Bobbs Merrill edn. (1964).

Knox, Ronald, *Enthusiasm: A Chapter in the History of Religion, with Special Reference to the Seventeenth and Eighteenth Centuries* (1950).

Rack, Henry D., *Reasonable Enthusiast: John Wesley and the Rise of Methodism* (1989).

Tucker, Susie I., *Enthusiasm: A Study in Semantic Change* (1972).

Ephesus, Council of, 431 AD, the third of the seven ecumenical *councils. Its central concern was to consider how the divine *Word could have lived an authentic human life on earth. The controversy occasioning it was Cyril of *Alexandria's attack on the teaching of *Nestorius of Constantinople, who had opposed the use for *Mary of the term *Theotokos*, preferring *Christotokos* (Mother of Christ). Unaware that Nestorius' doctrine was regarded as 'traditional' by large sections of the oriental church, Cyril accused him of *heresy in having divided Christ into two personal subjects, only 'associating' the man Jesus with the divine Word in honorific terms (see Christology).

By 430 Cyril had secured Rome's agreement to the condemnation of Nestorianism and the Emperor Theodosius II was forced to convoke an international synod. Despite military opposition, Cyril assumed its presidency and called for a trial of his opponent. Nestorius had arrived early, but his supporters in the *Syrian church's delegation were much delayed and Cyril began proceedings without them. After excerpts had been read from his own works and from Nestorius' sermons, he secured the latter's condemnation by a large majority. When the Syrians arrived they condemned Cyril in an alternative minority synod, but could not persuade the majority to reconsider their verdict. It took two years of imperially sponsored mediations before the Syrian and Alexandrian churches would sign a joint agreement. From antiquity this 'formula of reunion' has been designated the *symbolum Ephesinum*, the 'creed' of Ephesus.

The council of Ephesus was one of the first Christian debates where technical terms of *theology and patristic proof-texts were central to the case; most particularly the concept of 'hypostatic union' which became the classical confession of the relation of the divine and human in Christ. Cyril applied the term *hypostasis* to connote individual subjectivity. Accordingly, the *Incarnation involved the choice of the divine hypostasis of the Word to assume a human nature in order to live an earthly, human, life. But he did not assume a human hypostasis: the Word was the only personal subject in Christ's incarnate life, who united in himself the human and divine conditions. Cyril summarized this by his slogan: Mary is the mother of God (*Theotokos*).

Cyril argued that the hypostatic union had the effect first of *deifying* the body of Jesus and that, thereafter, this destiny of transfiguration was given as a grace to the church. The concept of *deification* by *grace dominated all subsequent eastern thought on the Incarnation. The issues raised by this debate, particularly those concerning the dynamics of *salvation, the psychological unity of Christ, and the transcendent nature of *personhood, remain as important questions for christology, and much modern discussion has been stimulated by reassessments of the Ephesus controversy.

John McGuckin

Camelot, T., *Éphèse et Chalcédoine* (1962).
Hall, S. G., *Doctrine and Practice in the Early Church* (1991).
McGuckin, J. A., *St. Cyril of Alexandria and the Christological Controversy* (1994).

Epiphany,

traditionally observed on 6 January, is the festival of the *Incarnation which emphasizes the appearance (Greek, *epiphaneia*) of the long-awaited Saviour and his manifestation to the world.

The original impetus behind the selection of 6 January is unknown. As with the younger feast of *Christmas, scholars speculate: that the day was a Christianization of what originally had been pagan worship, in this case a water, wine, or solar festival, or the celebration of a local deity; that the day was calculated from other, predetermined dates; or that some combination of these two theories is most accurate. Although 6 January was recognized as the day of Epiphany, the festival often continued for eight days (the 'octave'). For some Christians today, the Sunday nearest 6 January, and not the day itself, has absorbed the focus of the feast.

Epiphany is attested in the east from at least the 3rd century as a unitive celebration of Christ's birth which, for Egyptian Christians in *Alexandria, also included commemoration of his baptism. By the second half of the 4th century, Christmas had been introduced in the east, and Epiphany in the west, with the majority of churches apparently keeping both festivals; exceptions included the Jerusalem church which did not adopt Christmas until the beginning of the 6th century, and the *Armenian church which still observes only Epiphany. Various combinations of themes witnessing to the manifestation of God in Christ (*theophaneia*) came to be attached to the celebration of Epiphany. Peter Chrysologus, archbishop of Ravenna in the early 5th century, identifies at Epiphany (Sermon 160)

three demonstrations of the divinity of Christ: the gifts of the Magi (Matt. 2: 1–11); the testimony of the Father at Jesus' baptism (Matt. 3: 16–17); and the changing of the water into wine (John 2: 1–11). The Roman rite's Epiphany antiphon for the Benedictus weaves these subjects together in a nuptial image:

> Today the church is joined to her celestial bridegroom,
> for, in Jordan, Christ washed her sins away;
> the Magi hurry with gifts to the royal wedding,
> and the guests are made glad with water turned to wine.

These three themes have continued to be associated with Epiphany, if not on 6 January, then on nearby Sundays, each identifying a significant aspect of Christ's person and work.

The visitation of the Magi from the east signals Christ's manifestation to the Gentiles: the gospel was extended to all the nations of the earth, and not just the Jewish community. Tradition has made the wise men of Matt. 2 into three kings; around the 6th century they were popularly ascribed the names Balthasar, Melchior, and Gaspar in the west, and later they came to be depicted as representatives of the world's races and of the different stages in the human life span from youth to old age. A favourite subject of western *artists and *poets (e.g. T. S. *Eliot's *Journey of the Magi*, with its first line 'A cold coming we had of it'), the story of the sages and their gifts was seen to foreshadow the destiny of the child in the manger: the gold signified his royal dignity, frankincense, the divine priest-victim in the sacrifice of the cross, and myrrh, his death, burial, and Resurrection.

The baptism of Jesus (see JOHN THE BAPTIST) reveals his divine sonship through the descent of the *Holy Spirit upon him in the form of a dove and the voice from heaven which declares him to be the 'beloved Son'. Jesus' willingness to receive baptism at John's hands indicates his complete identification with sinful *humanity; his baptism was not for his own *sin, however, but for the purpose of human salvation. The church, as the beloved of Christ, is washed by water and the *Word. As the dome mosaics of the Ravenna baptistries suggest, every Christian *baptism stands under the sign of Christ's baptism; and as his baptism heralded the beginning of Jesus' public ministry, so Christian baptism likewise inaugurates the service expected of all believers.

Jesus' first *miracle at the wedding feast in Cana 'manifested his glory' (John 2: 11)—a glory become radiant when later he is transfigured before his disciples and a heavenly voice again declares him to be the chosen one (Matt. 17: 1–8; Mark 9: 2–9; Luke 9: 28–36). In the sign itself Christ is revealed as the one who supplies a new wine (Luke 5: 36–8), the wine of his own blood shared at the *Eucharist in anticipation of the *messianic banquet when the bridegroom will sup with his bride, the church.

See also CALENDAR.   **Karen B. Westerfield Tucker**

Lemarié, J., *La Manifestation du Seigneur* (1957).
McDonnell, K., *The Baptism of Jesus in the Jordan* (1996).

episcopate.

In several NT books there is a reference to *episcopoi* and *presbyteroi* (Acts 11: 30; 14: 23; 1 Tim. 3: 1–7; 5: 17; Titus 1: 5–9). It seems clear, however, that these are not two distinct functions but two names for the 'elders', whether *apostolically appointed or otherwise chosen, who presided over a Christian community in any place where it had come into stable existence. This early local leadership of the *church appears to have been a group one. Where there was a single president, his function was not at first named differently from that of his colleagues. However, quite soon, a pattern of ministry was stabilized in which a single 'bishop' (*episcopus*) was assisted by a group of 'presbyters', as well as by another group of deacons (*diaconate) who had already a distinct identity within the NT. It was for the bishop to preside at the celebration of the *Eucharist and it was probably that presidency which underlay his primacy within the *ministry.

It appears mistaken to claim any straight historic link between the function of apostles and that of bishops. Between the two there is, at least in most places, a time gap. Moreover, the role of the former as witnesses of the *Resurrection was not transferable. We know little of the way local churches and their ministry developed in the first generations after the apostolic period and it is possible that the kind of delegation we find in Paul's letter to Titus of personal authority over a particular area, in this case Crete, provided a pattern used more widely. The historical details do not matter greatly. Apostolic *authority was understood to have been passed on, exercisable within, but also above, individual churches. While it may, initially, have been held by a group rather than an individual, by the mid-2nd century it was normally held by a single bishop in each local church; nevertheless the group element remained precisely in the joint authority of bishops of local churches acting collectively to recognize, reprove, or even expel individuals. The group dimension being always essentially there, it was natural for its shape to be extended when Christianity grew larger and new problems arose, first through local *councils of bishops and then, in the 4th century, through 'ecumenical' ones. The apostolic authority of an individual bishop was thus contained within, and finally subordinate to, the apostolic authority of the episcopate as a whole, representing the church as a whole.

If the 4th century made clear the limitation of episcopal power by the increasing use of councils, it also saw the bishop's local ministry reshaped through the development of parishes within a single diocese, whereby presbyters became the regular presidents of the eucharistic assembly in churches other than the bishop's *cathedral. In early times the multiplication of congregations produced a multiplication of dioceses, but with the vast increase of Christians in a single town it became necessary to subdivide dioceses into parishes, a process begun in the 3rd century. If the presbyter was now, for most Christians, their regular pastor and Eucharistic celebrant, the bishop became a pastor to the pastors. His characteristic sacramental function was no longer the celebration of the Eucharist but the *ordaining of other ministers. He also became a powerful political figure. This had already begun by the Constantinian era. By the time of *Augustine, a bishop was laden with secular responsibilities of all sorts, but the normative form of episcopacy was now firmly established and common to the Greek and Latin worlds. Men like Augustine and Basil have provided the episcopal ideal ever since, particularly for the *Eastern Orthodox world where, while priests can be married, insistence upon the *celibacy of bishops has permanently monasticized the episcopate.

When the Roman empire collapsed in the west, the secularization of episcopacy developed still more. By the Middle Ages, bishops were typically members of the ruling class, holders of a great deal of land, living in castles or palaces. While there were many excellent pastoral bishops, their image became one of power and wealth, from which even the holiest could hardly escape. In consequence, while the priesthood still looked more or less like a NT ministry (clearly visible, for instance, in Chaucer's ideal parish priest described in the *Canterbury Tales* Prologue), the episcopate did not.

Most of the 16th century *reformers preferred to abolish the episcopate as a medieval aberration. Where it survived within a *Protestant church, most notably in England and Sweden, it was chiefly because the sovereign thought it easier to control the church with bishops than without them. In the Catholic *Counter-Reformation, bishops such as Charles Borromeo and Francis de Sales set a high standard of personal holiness and pastoral care and, in many places, the political role of the episcopate declined, although elsewhere, notably in some German states, bishops continued to rule their own principalities until the 19th century, hardly appearing as fathers in God to the local church. Almost everywhere they were chosen, as they had been since the Middle Ages, by the kings or leading aristocratic families of their area. There seemed only one way of escaping this political control and that was through papal control. Where *Gallicanism and its equivalents held the episcopate within the political system of France or wherever, it was increasingly challenged by *ultramontanism, which sought ecclesiastical independence through reasserting the power of the *papacy. The French Revolution led to the collapse of Gallicanism and a huge surge in ultramontanism. This reached a climax in *Vatican I, 1870, with its definition of the pope's ordinary and immediate jurisdiction over the whole church. It could appear that, henceforth, bishops would be no more than papal delegates, 'satraps dispatched to their provinces', as Bishop Goss of Liverpool bitterly prophesied.

*Vatican II was exceedingly keen to do away with any such impression and, in the third chapter of the dogmatic constitution *Lumen Gentium*, stressed the authority of the episcopate in its own right. It did so by affirming its ordinary, not delegated, jurisdiction; by developing a doctrine of *collegiality whereby the supreme authority in the church was perceived as resting in a college of all the bishops under the presidency of the pope; and by affirming that 'the fullness of the sacrament of orders is conferred by episcopal consecration'. In these ways Vatican II did much to remove the impression provided by Vatican I that the constitution of the church was essentially a papal one. Most of what it said was welcome to both Eastern Orthodox and Anglicans. Nevertheless it passed over the evidence that in the early church there was no decisive difference between episcopate and presbyterate, the differentiation having come rather as a matter of convenience in organizing a growing community. It did, of course, also ignore the non-episcopal experience of most Protestant churches. However, almost all Protestant churches have in point of fact been moving over the years in a moderately episcopal direction by institutionalizing a difference between local pastors and regional supervisors who need to act especially as pastors to the pastors, a development comparable to that of the early church. There may be little substantial difference between most churches about the way the ministry needs to be organized today; *Methodists in America, for instance, have long been episcopal. The Church of South India united Anglicans, Methodists, and others in 1947 on the basis of accepting the episcopate but no particular theological interpretation of it. For few people is the medieval model now attractive, though traces of a monarchical 'Lord Bishop' still survive.

There is good evidence that even in the high Middle Ages ordination to the priesthood by non-bishops was allowed in some cases; hence it would seem that even on the most severe Roman Catholic theological principles there is no decisive reason against accepting the validity of lines of ordained ministry in churches which have lacked an episcopate. In the Church of England there was for long an argument as to whether the episcopate was of the *esse* of the church, as Anglo-Catholics claimed, thus denying that non-episcopal Protestants formed part of the visible church, or only of the *bene esse*—a useful but not essential tool. It would seem that both may have been right. The historic episcopate can exist without being named, just as it did in the primitive church. If the presbyterate exists, *ipso facto* so does the episcopate. Nevertheless pastoral good order calls for a measure of functional differentiation traditionally expressed in the threefold division into bishops, priests, and deacons. The episcopate is best understood as constituted by the principal pastors of local churches throughout the world, to whom collectively the supervision of the apostolic mission remains entrusted.   **Adrian Hastings**

Brown, R., *Priest and Bishop: Biblical Reflections* (1970).
Carey, K. M. (ed.), *The Historic Episcopate* (1954).
Colson, J., *L'Épiscopat catholique* (1963).
Halliburton, J., *The Authority of a Bishop* (1987).
Kirk, K. E. (ed.), *The Apostolic Ministry* (1946).
Swete, H. B. (ed.), *Essays on the Early History of the Church and the Ministry*, 2nd edn. (1921).

Epistles, see HEBREWS; PAUL; PASTORAL EPISTLES; PETER; ROMANS.

Erasmus, Desiderius (c.1467–1536). Inventor of his own name, he was a reforming humanist and controversialist who influenced profoundly the discourse and theology of the *Reformation whilst maintaining, within the Catholic Church, a stance of critical distance from either side. Although his family was of Gouda in the Netherlands, he was possibly born at Rotterdam, and definitely of unmarried parents, a fact doubtless responsible for the uncertainty attending all record of his origins, family name, and early life. His schooling at Gouda, Deventer, and s'Hertogenbosch provided the foundations of remarkable erudition in the literature of antiquity which dominated his life, in conjunction with a commitment to the renewal of Christendom through the fruits of humanistic scholarship applied to the sources of the Christian faith. Acquaintance with those sources would, he believed, transform the life and very being of the believer and thus renew the church. Two magisterial projects summarize this achievement, the *Adagiorum chileades* (first edition 1508) and his edition of the *New Testament, first published in 1515. The former was a compendium of the learning and moral wisdom of antiquity, the latter the first printed text of the Greek NT accompanied by a new Latin translation and by extensive critical annotations. Developed through many editions, they were the core and foundation of a mass of educational works, scholarly editions, satires on abuses in church and state, treatises to nourish the *lay vocation of the following of Christ—the '*philosophia Christi*'—and controversies with critics both Catholic and Protestant. His mature life was divided between England, Italy, Louvain, and Basel chiefly, but the fame of his writings along with his correspondence took his name and his views to every corner of western Christendom. He died in Basel where the Froben Press had become his effective seminar and home.

As influential in his day as was Voltaire in his, Erasmus remains a towering figure in the history of Christian scholarship, but he has escaped relegation to the past through the continuing relevance of his reforming outlook. To modern *ecumenists he seems a prophetic figure. He was a pioneer in promoting the enfranchizing vocation of the *baptized as the foundation of the church; he deplored confessional disputes which obscured the essentials of the faith and (as he saw it) frustrated the tuition of the human family by the *Holy Spirit; he assailed the greed and enmity of *nations as inimical to Christian *peace. He used the weapons of satire—most famously the *Praise of Folly*, dedicated to his friend, Thomas *More—to expose hypocrisy and self-deception amongst clergy and laity alike, and insisted on the highest standards of scholarship in the interpretation especially of Christian scripture and the fathers. Wherever the cause of international peace, irenicism, scholarly integrity, and devotion to the Christ of scripture is admired, his legacy is alive.

James McConica

McConica, J. K., *Erasmus* (1991), reissued (1996).
Rummel, E. (ed.), *The Erasmus Reader* (1990).
Schoeck, R. J., *Erasmus of Europe: The Prince of Humanists 1501–1536* (1993).

Erastianism. If the final decision in choosing bishops for the Church of England lies with the prime minister, critics call this Erastianism. The powers that be are ordained of God, but have they the authority to rule the church? 'Erastianism' is a term of reproach.

Erastus himself did not deserve it. Thomas Lueber, Lieber, or Liebler (to give him his German name), born in 1524, was the Swiss court physician to the elector of the Palatinate, teaching medicine at Heidelberg. The *Calvinist reformers there were 'fencing the tables', granting admission to communion only to visible saints. Erastus hated the use of excommunication. 'Who but God is the judge of men's hearts?' He believed that Christ came for sinners, and if they approach his table we should not turn them away. If we have a godly king, like the Elector Palatine, then real wickedness is dealt with by the civil courts. The church need not set itself up as another coercive power alongside the state. For such views as this, he was himself excommunicated. When a new elector decided to make his country Lutheran instead of Reformed, Erastus went back to Switzerland, where he died in 1583. If he had been a real Erastian, believing that kings know best, he would have stayed.

'I see no reason why the Christian magistrate at the present day should not possess the same power which God commanded the magistrate to exercise in the Jewish commonwealth.' That was the opening sentence of thesis 73 of Erastus's 75 *Theses on the Communion*, the first where he deals with 'Erastian' matters. He carefully said that he thought the magistrate should consult the experts on doctrine, and must himself be Christian. The *Theses* were first published in 1589, after his death, probably in England, and with the support of Archbishop Whitgift, more Erastian than Erastus. They influenced *Hooker and helped to justify the 'royal supremacy' over the Church of England (see ANGLICANISM).

*Lawyers and political theorists make real Erastians. Marsilius of Padua in the Middle Ages argued that ecclesiastical power is merely borrowed from civil power, and that a general council, which is above any pope, should be lay as well as clerical. The great lawyer Grotius writing in 1614, and Thomas Hobbes in *Leviathan* (1651), clearly subordinated church to state. Governments and those who justify them habitually encroach and it is not only England where they have had a hand in appointing bishops.

What of a mystical view of God's dealing with a nation as a whole? Hooker saw the Church of England as the people of England at prayer. If a people is Christian, he claimed, then it is fitting for their church to be subject to their civil rulers. They are different aspects of one reality. 'Holy Russia' is a more lasting example of the same belief. A *nationalist view of the church is almost necessarily Erastian and typically, like Erastus himself, appeals to the OT example.

See also ESTABLISHMENT.   **Alistair Mason**

Figgis, J. N., 'Erastus and Erastianism', in *The Divine Right of Kings* (1914 edn.).

McDonald, L. C., *Western Political Theory* (1962).

Niebuhr, H. Richard, *Christ and Culture* (1951).

eschatology (from the Greek *eschatos*, meaning 'last') concerns the ultimate destiny of *God's *creation, including the future of individual people beyond *death, of human *history, and of the whole *cosmos. Christian faith understands the world by means of a 'meta-narrative': a grand, all-encompassing story, giving the meaning of all reality in narrative form. It is the story of the whole world and of God's relationship with it from its creation to its end. The bible begins with God's creation of all things in *Genesis 1–2 and ends with God's renewal of all things, described in terms which echo Genesis, in *Revelation 21–2. The *creeds also refer both to creation and to the eternal destiny which awaits us, and tell the story of *Jesus Christ as concluding only when 'he will come again in glory to judge both the living and the dead, and his kingdom will have no end'.

This meta-narrative provides for Christians the overall framework within which everything else is to be understood. *Memories of the past, experiences of the present, and hopes for the future are all given their Christian meaning by their context within it. It includes reference to historical events, such as the history of *Israel, the life of Jesus, and the history of the *church, but necessarily extends beyond historical narrative in its account of the world's beginning and its final destiny. Since they lie wholly outside the experience of human beings in history they cannot be literally described, but only pictured imaginatively or defined abstractly. For the meta-narrative to have adequate meaning it must, like all stories, have an ending. We cannot understand God's purposes in history without some indication of the goal towards which they aim and how they will be completed. This does not mean that the future is wholly determined. It does mean that in essence the final destiny of the world is not in doubt. Christians trust God's promise that in the end God's good purpose will overcome all *evil in creation and take this redeemed creation into a new and eternal form of existence, beyond death and transience and in union with God's own life. This hope gives meaning to the struggle against evil and *suffering now and in the face of death.

In the *tradition, eschatology was represented primarily by the 'four last things' (*eschata*): *resurrection, *judgement, *heaven, and *hell. These concern the ultimate fate of all human persons. All who have ever lived will, at the end of the world, be raised from death; their fate will be decreed at the last judgement; and all will be assigned either to eternal bliss with God in heaven, or to eternal punishment in hell. The great influence and imaginative impact of this expectation can be gauged from the artistic tradition of last judgement scenes, which dominate many medieval churches. The prominence of judgement and the symmetrical presentation of the two destinies, heaven and hell, gave much medieval eschatology the character of fearful warning, as much as, or even more than, promise and *hope.

Both in this broad outline and in much specific detail Christian eschatology has been both determined by the bible and influenced by extra-biblical sources which transmitted the themes and images of early Jewish eschatology to the church. It has also been significantly influenced by Greek *philosophy, especially *Platonism, in the patristic and medieval periods, and by the historical progressivism of the *Enlightenment in the modern period. The former promoted a spiritualizing, the latter an historicizing, of eschatology. These will be best explained in relation to four polarities: (1) personal eschatology and historical and cosmic eschatology; (2) thisworldly and other-worldly expectations; (3) immanence and transcendence; and (4) the present (the 'already') and the eschatological future (the 'not yet').

1. Christian eschatology concerns the end of all creation: an end in which the whole course of human history will reach its God-given conclusion. It also speaks of the destiny of all human persons in their *bodily as well as spiritual reality. It speaks of the eschatological future in terms of human community as well as individuality, and of the *redemption and fulfilment not only of God's human creatures, but also of the non-human creation, which God will renew in eternal glory. These are all aspects of a theocentric goal for the whole creation. In each case creation is given its fulfilment in union with God's eternal life (except for those evil or unrepentant creatures, *devils and humans, who must suffer *eternity without God). The future of individuals is a central concern of Christian eschatology, but it is placed within the wider context of corporate, historical, and cosmic eschatology. This is why the resurrection of the dead occurs only at the end of history: individuals are raised to share in the corporate future of God's people and the cosmic future of God's whole creation.

This holistic eschatology, uniting personal, historical, and cosmic, has not always been fully maintained. In the NT, and in many later periods of lively expectation of Christ's imminent coming to bring history to its end, there has been little difficulty in holding personal and historical eschatology together. But at other times, the future of the individual after death has often been emphasized at the expense of the future of the world. This emphasis was fostered by the influence of Platonism in earlier periods and later by modern individualism. Platonism, with its strong matter/spirit dualism, maintained a purely spiritual and individual eschatology: the human spirit, which is the real person, is liberated at death from the body and its passions, which entangle the soul in the material *world. Such a fully Platonic eschatology is not found in the mainstream Christian tradition. The patristic and medieval church limited Platonic influence by tenaciously upholding the doctrine of bodily resurrection, which affirmed the body as integral to human being and preserved the connection between the attainment of human destiny and the consummation of all things. But the influence of Greek dualism on the mainstream theological tradition can be seen in the belief in the inherent *immortality of the *soul, which survives death and is reunited with its body at the resurrection. Only in the 20th century has this belief been gradually abandoned by many theologians who have recognized its Greek origin and seen the understanding of the human person as a psychosomatic unity as both more biblical and more consonant with modern scientific views.

In the modern period these two aspects of eschatology (individual and historical/cosmic) have often been completely separated from each other. On the one hand, in theology influenced by the 19th-century idea of progress, and in some recent *liberation theology, the utopian goal of history is understood in an immanent historical way which precludes the participation of the dead. Theologians and believers who take this view might also hope for eternal life for individuals after death, but without relating this to the future of the world. On the other hand, in the existentialist theology of Rudolf *Bultmann, to take a notable example, eschatology is limited to the subjectivity of individuals and has nothing to say of history or the non-human world. But since Bultmann an influential trend (initially called 'theology of hope'), finding its fullest expression so far in Jürgen *Moltmann's *The Coming of God*, has sought to transcend these reductions and to articulate an eschatology that encompasses the whole of creation: individual and social, personal and historical, material and spiritual, human and non-human. Initially, in opposition to individualized and spiritualized eschatologies, this trend emphasized the future of human history and the sociopolitical relevance of hope for the future of the world. Only more recently has *ecological consciousness led to the recognition that non-human nature should not be subsumed into human history but considered in the light of its own future in the new creation. Thus the cosmic aspect, which in traditional eschatology rarely gained much attention, has finally come into its own.

2. Eschatological expectations can take the form either of perfected versions of the life experienced in this world (for example, paradisal abundance of nature; a fully just society in which all are treated equally); or of a radically different kind of world: eternal life beyond the reach of death and beyond worldly *time; the immediate presence of God. These are not strict alternatives but the poles of a spectrum. Most versions of Christian eschatology combine elements of both, though with varying emphases. The more that eschatological images are understood as imaginative portrayal of what cannot be literally described, the easier it is to combine both types of expectation. The new creation can be understood as the sphere of fulfilment of many human aspirations which cannot be fully satisfied in this world.

More this-worldly forms of expectation have often found expression in *millenarianism, with its hope for an earthly kingdom of Christ and the saints. The millennium is properly a transitional period of earthly perfection, intervening between the end of history and the new creation of all things, but where millenarian hope is strong the millennium itself naturally forms the focus of expectation, rather than the more distant eternity beyond. By promising that unjust social structures and the harsh conditions of ordinary people's lives will be replaced by utopian conditions, the millenar-

ian tradition has often brought Christian hope into touch with popular concerns and aspirations. Its this-worldly hope has made it a potentially disruptive and subversive force, often viewed with suspicion by church authorities, and condemned for offering too material and unspiritual a hope. For much of Christian history the mainstream view of human destiny has been predominantly otherworldly.

Two major eschatological images which typify the more this-worldly and the more other-worldly forms of hope are the *Kingdom of God and the vision of God. The latter, which has biblical and Jewish as well as Platonist backgrounds, is a theocentric image of *worship and contemplation, which has often been understood in intellectualist or purely spiritual and individualist ways. The former is a social and political image of a world whose conditions and ordering perfectly reflect the righteousness and goodness of God. That the two images can complement each other and cohere can be seen in the portrayal of the New *Jerusalem in the book of Revelation (21–2) and in *Augustine's understanding of the vision of God as inclusive of the corporate and the material (*City of God*, 12. 29). But we can also see the polarization of the other-worldly and the this-worldly in the dominance of one or other of these images, the former especially in the medieval period, the latter especially in the modern. While the vision of God is the other-worldly goal of a contemplative and *ascetic piety, the Kingdom of God is the historical goal of progressive or liberative praxis in this world. Before the modern period the Kingdom of God was often identified with the church and so tended to make ecclesiology a kind of realized eschatology. With the influence of the modern idea of progress, the Kingdom was often seen as coming about through the progress of history towards utopia. In a more dialectical or *Marxist form, the idea that the struggle for political *justice builds the Kingdom of God informs much liberation theology. Elsewhere, as in Moltmann's theology, the future coming of the Kingdom in God's eschatological transformation of the world inspires and motivates hopeful praxis in anticipation of the Kingdom.

3. It is possible to think of the final future of the world as the goal towards which the historical process is moving and the result which that process will produce. This is how philosophies and theologies of historical progressivism in the modern period have thought. But it is not how the eschatology of the bible and the Christian tradition understands the end of history. Rather this is a divine act of new creation or renewal of creation, in which God will make of the world what it has no immanent capacity of its own to become. A transcendent eschatology of this kind introduces a radical discontinuity between history and the new creation, where a more immanent eschatology envisages continuity between historical progress and its ultimate result. Continuity is, of course, also important for transcendent eschatology. God will renew *this* creation, not simply replace it by another. But the continuity is given by God in God's transformation and glorification of creation, bringing to completion God's own work, redeeming creation from all evil, and delivering it from transience and mortality by giving it eternal life. Fulfilment, restoration, and glorification are different aspects of God's eschatological renewal of creation. Although this will end historical time, it is not simply what happens to the world as it will be at the end of history: it happens to the *whole* of history. All who have ever lived will rise from the dead.

The distinction between transcendent eschatology and the Enlightenment's progressivist view of history is important, because Christian eschatology in the modern period always stands in some kind of relationship, negative or positive, to the progressivism of the age. The distinction is often played down when it is said that the Christian tradition provided the linear idea of history moving irreversibly towards a future goal which the modern idea of progress has taken over in secularized forms. There is truth in this, provided it is recognized that *secularization made a radical difference. In place of hope for the transcendent God's creative and redemptive action, human activity working in harmony with some kind of inherent teleology in the historical process would bring about utopia through a cumulative and continuous progression. Hope derives from confidence in human rationality and in the inherent direction of the historical process towards utopia. Evolutionary views of the world have helped very much to bolster the idea of historical teleology, as can be seen in the work of *Teilhard de Chardin, probably the most thoroughgoing attempt to Christianize the progressivist world-view.

The idea of progress historicized eschatology in the sense that much of what Christian eschatology expected from God was now to be expected from incremental historical progress. Humanity was to be perfected by *reason and *education, and the world re-created through the great modern project of technological mastery of nature. The evils and sufferings of past history would be redeemed by the glorious future that will in the end emerge. But it is now clear that the idea of progress laid on history an eschatological burden it cannot bear. It prevented realistic recognition of the limits of human capacities and of the resources of nature. It minimized the significance of evil and transience. The attempt to achieve utopia by mastering the future has not only failed, as the unprecedented horrors of 20th-century history make unambiguously clear, but has itself become a threat to the future of humanity and the earth, as the development of weapons of mass destruction and the looming ecological catastrophe show. Historicized eschatology is inevitably Promethean, courting disaster in overreaching itself.

Christian eschatology in the modern period has frequently been to a greater or lesser extent assimilated to Enlightenment progressivism. By playing down transcendence and interpreting progress—whether gradual or revolutionary—as the God-ordained task of humanity, such theologies have baptized Prometheanism and ignored the sorely needed sense of limits that transcendent eschatology can provide. But two factors have precipitated a recovery of transcendent eschatology in much 20th-century theology. One is the realization, initially by Johannes Weiss and Albert Schweitzer, that the Kingdom of God in the gospels is not the immanent progressivism of 19th-century liberal theologians, but truly eschatological, the discontinuous act of the transcendent God. The other factor is the horrors of 20th-century history, beginning with the First World War, which have shown not only that progress is a myth, but also that assimilation to liberal progressivism deprives theology of its critical power. Even more importantly they have highlighted the evil and the pain of history in such a way as to make any justification of the historical process intolerable. No future utopia can compensate for the *Holocaust. Meaning cannot be found within the process but only beyond it.

Eschatological transcendence was first reasserted in Karl *Barth's early dialectical theology, but here, as in *Bultmann's *existentialist and *demythologized eschatology, eschatology loses any reference to the future of the world. In reaction against any kind of progressivist teleology, eschatology is taken to refer to the moment in which the human and historical is set in crisis by the divine eternity impinging 'vertically' on this world. Only with the 'theology of hope', developed in the 1960s by *Pannenberg, *Moltmann, and others, did an eschatology that speaks of a transcendent future for the world become influential again in the theological mainstream. By envisaging the future as not merely *futurum* (the future that develops out of the present in continuity with it and can therefore be extrapolated) but as *adventus* (the future that comes to us out of the infinite possibilities of the future), Pannenberg and Moltmann made it possible to think of the final future of the world as God's gift and the proximate future as the sphere in which the coming Kingdom can be anticipated. In Pannenberg's work the stress is on the eschaton as the completion of the historical process giving meaning to the whole of history, while Moltmann's more dialectical approach, with a stronger emphasis on the problem of evil, stresses the redemption of history and the world from evil, suffering, and transience. Moltmann's most recent work adumbrates what is now urgently needed: a transcendent eschatology contextually situated in the contemporary collapse of the ideology of progress and the collapsing of future into the extended present of *postmodernity.

Transcendent eschatology need not lead to fatalism or *quietism, as though nothing can be done short of God's eschatological act of new creation. Christian hope need be neither Promethean nor quietist. It should neither attempt what can only come from God nor neglect what is humanly possible. Sustained by the hope of everything from God, it attempts what is possible within the limits of each present. It seeks appropriate anticipations of the coming Kingdom, but does not burden itself with the impossible task of achieving it. Nor does it value what can be done only as a step in a linear progress to a goal. It does what can be done here and now for its value here and now, confident that every present will find itself, redeemed and fulfilled, in the new creation.

4. Perhaps the greatest impact of NT study on 20th-century eschatology was the realization that in a NT perspective eschatology cannot be confined to the eschatological future. For the earliest Christians the end had already begun in the events of the ministry, death, and Resurrection of Jesus, and they themselves were living in the end-times of history in which God was at work to fulfil God's ultimate purposes for creation. That in some sense the fulfilment of God's eschatological promises was already under way is clear because of the Resurrection of Jesus and the coming of the Spirit. Since resurrection, in Jewish expectation, was an event of the end of history, the Resurrection of Jesus ahead of other people must be understood as a kind of trail-blazing for the resurrection of those who through Christ would share in the resurrection to eternal life at the end. The presence and activity of the *Holy Spirit in the early church was understood as the life of the new creation already present under the conditions of this world, a kind of first-fruits of the eschatological harvest to come.

One effect of this NT perspective has been the realization that eschatology cannot be confined to the last chapter of dogmatics, but must be seen as a dimension of the whole of theology. Christology, pneumatology, and soteriology especially need to be understood in an eschatological perspective. This restores a sense of the continuity of God's activity in Christ in past, present, and eschatological future. This is the continuity of God's eschatological redemption of history, which itself is notably discontinuous with the ordinary course of history marked by transience and evil, as the Resurrection of Jesus shows. Another significant result of the revised perspective has been a more christological understanding of eschatology than was common in the past. The Parousia (Second Coming) of Jesus Christ as Saviour and Judge was central to the traditional understanding of the end of history, but with relatively little connection with the Christ-event of the past. Some recent theologians, such as Karl *Rahner, go so far as to maintain that Christian eschatology can never be more than an extrapolation from events of the life, death, and Resurrection of Jesus, spelling out what they imply for the future of the world to which they promise new life on the model of Jesus' resurrection out of death. This may go too far in neglecting that Jesus himself still has a future with the world to which he will come at the end. But a christological focus in eschatology is certainly faithful to NT theology and helps to prevent the eschatological imagination straying into merely speculative fantasy. The eschatological future of the world is not any conceivable future, but specifically that future which God has opened up for the world in raising the crucified Jesus to new life.

The recognition of a 'realized' aspect to NT eschatology has led to considerable debate about its theological interpretation, debate which has also involved the issue of the so-called delay of the Parousia. For Bultmann and others the fact that the Parousia did not happen soon, as the first Christians expected, discredits their eschatological expectation entirely. The issue has been met both by the contention that eschatology should be understood as wholly realized in the Christ-event (C. H. Dodd) or that, since the decisive acts of salvation have already occurred in Christ, the theological weight lies on the past rather than the future, and what remains to be fulfilled in the future is no more than the necessary consequences of the Christ-event (O. Cullmann). In place of the polarity of 'realized' or 'future' eschatology, the notion of 'inaugurated' eschatology has become quite common as a means of recognizing both the 'already' and the 'not yet' of the NT's eschatological discourse. But even this kind of formulation needs to be protected from misinterpretation along the familiar lines of modern historical progressivism. It is not a matter of a merely linear, still less cumulative historical process that will in time produce the new creation. It is a matter of God's coming to God's creation to redeem, to complete, and to transform it.   **Richard Bauckham**

Bauckham, R. (ed.), *God Will Be All in All: The Eschatology of Jürgen Moltmann* (1999).

Bauckham, R., and Hart, T. A., *Hope Against Hope: Christian Eschatology in Contemporary Context* (1999).

Daley, B. E., *The Hope of the Early Church: A Handbook of Patristic Eschatology* (1991).

Hebblethwaite, B., *The Christian Hope* (1984).

Hick, J., *Death and Eternal Life* (1976).

Körtner, U. H. J., *The End of the World: A Theological Interpretation* (1988), ET (1995).

Küng, H., *Eternal Life?* (1982), ET (1984).

McDannell, C., and Lang, B., *Heaven: A History* (1988).

Moltmann, J., *Theology of Hope* (1965), ET (1967).

—— *The Coming of God: Christian Eschatology* (1995), ET (1996).

Runia, K., 'Eschatology in the Second Half of the Twentieth Century', *Calvin Theological Journal*, 32 (1997).

Travis, S. H., *Christian Hope and the Future of Man* (1980).

establishment. In western tradition the legitimacy of all government derives from a moral foundation. The exercise of sovereignty by the state is thus expected to be defensible by reference to an identifiable system of moral teaching. It is also within western tradition that this teaching should have the sanction of religion, and in historical terms this has meant that the state maintains some kind of formal relationship with institutional religion. Christianity for its part was from the start prepared to recognize the authority of the state as God-given, as Paul made clear in Romans 13. It was the conversion of the Emperor *Constantine I, after the Battle of Milvian Bridge in 312, and his progressive extension of toleration and then of official patronage to the Christians, which 'established' Christianity (in succession to the Roman civic religion) as the moral basis of the state. Now an establishment of religion exists where there is a connection between *law and religious opinion. It is not essential for this—though it has been normal in practice—that a single *church or religious tradition should be the repository of the state's moral authority. It is possible to have a constitutional relationship between government and a number of religious bodies or institutions. Thus in some European countries, in Switzerland and some of the German states, for example, government allocates designated tax income to the different denominations; and in Britain during the 19th century there was an extended debate about what contemporaries called 'concurrent endowment', whereby the state was to retrieve the public resources for religion (the incomes, buildings, and so forth) and to redistribute them among the various Christian denominations on the basis of numerical following.

The balance within the partnership of church and state has not usually been easy either to define or to stabilize. Sometimes the leaders of the church have laid extensive claims to authority over the civil power: tendencies to theocracy, in this sense, had their clearest institutional expression with the states of the church in Italy, where until the later years of the 19th century virtually all civil government issued from the *papacy. Sometimes, on the other hand, the civil authority has sought or imposed a relationship with the church in which the subordination of the clergy was spelled out in concrete constitutional provisions; the parliamentary *Erastianism of the English *Reformation was of this order. Occasionally, as in the Soviet Union under Lenin's decrees, and in Mexico under Calles and Cardenas in the 1920s and 1930s, a kind of establishment of religion existed even in an *atheist state. There the ruling *Marxist parties, through departments of religious affairs, supervised the churches and so perpetuated a relationship of church and state which was explicitly intended to diminish the influence of the clergy.

Establishment of religion has been undermined in modern times by two developments: the growth of ideological opposition to religious belief, and the recognition of religious pluralism. The first is of less importance. The assault upon Christianity that accompanied the French Revolution, with its later parallels in Spain during the Civil War in the 1930s and in the eastern bloc Communist regimes in the 1950s, has not been sustained. The idea of establishment has much more typically come under attack from within Christianity itself. The development of religious pluralism within the populations of some Christian countries led first to movements for toleration and then, by the middle years of the 18th century in the case of the thirteen American colonies, and by the middle of the 19th century in the case of Britain, to demands for actual disestablishment. The motive was not the creation of a *secular polity in any militant sense, but fair treatment by the state of the various denominations. It was, indeed, precisely because disestablishment, when it came, was the work of those who had no vision of an alternative to a Christian state, and who sought only the removal of religious inequality before the law, that the separations of church and state created as many ideological problems as they solved. According to the ancient confessional theory of the state, the church was established because of the inherent truth of Christianity. According to the principles enunciated by reformers, in contrast, an establishment could only be defended (if it could be defended at all) on the basis of majority support. The growth of religious dissent appeared to indicate that some churches—such as the Protestant establishments in some of the American colonies, or the Church of Ireland in Catholic Ireland—did not enjoy popular support. Even when an establishment could arguably be said to retain a majority following, as was the case with the Church of England itself, it was in practice diminished as a constitutional reality by piecemeal political concessions to dissenters. During the 19th century a series of *ad hoc* reforms, making constitutional concessions on such matters as civil marriage, release from payment of taxes for the support of the established church, and the qualifications to take part in legislation, in practice left the establishment as a species of constitutional anomaly. And so, both in England and in Scotland, it has remained to this day: formal establishments of religion, one Anglican and the other *Presbyterian, while in England the church is still in possession of the national religious endowments, but in no real sense consulted by the state in the conduct of national affairs.

There appears to be no coherent philosophical alternative sanction available to legitimize modern western governments, and problems about the diminution of establishment remain unresolved—and are often unrecognized. Indeed, modern politicians who speak of 'the high moral ground' often go on to suggest a Christian basis—a clear link of government to religious opinion, or establishment in its most basic sense. In the United States since the 1960s there has been a series of Supreme Court decisions in which secularists have managed to outlaw public reference to religious belief, thus giving an extremely rigorous interpretation to the constitutional separation of church and state. Yet American public life remains full of Christian resonances. Even in Russia, since the demise of the Communist state, senior figures of the Orthodox Church have reappeared in official functions. Establishment, in some sense or other, seems to defy the logic of modern secularism, and to survive—at least until an ideologically sympathetic alternative is available. **Edward Norman**

Coleridge, S. T., *On the Constitution of the Church and the State* (1830).
Hastings, Adrian, *Church and State: The English Experience* (1991).
Niebuhr, H. Richard, *The Social Sources of Denominationalism* (1929).
Troeltsch, Ernst, *The Social Teaching of the Christian Churches* (1911), ET (1931).

eternity. Divine eternity signifies *God's attribute of being without beginning or end of existence. Attested frequently in Christian scripture, God's being eternal is entailed by his status as a necessary being, for if his non-existence is impossible, he can neither begin nor cease to exist.

But is divine eternity to be understood as omnitemporality (everlastingness) or as timelessness? The scriptures most often speak in terms of God's beginningless and endless temporal duration (Ps. 90: 1–4; see, however, Gen. 1: 1; John 1: 1; Jude 25), but such language may be anthropomorphic. It may be reasonably doubted whether the reflective context of the authors of scripture included the philosophical question of the nature of divine eternity. Under the influence of Neoplatonic *philosophy (see PLATO)—particularly of Plotinus, whose ultimate metaphysical principle, the One, is atemporal—church fathers such as *Origen, *Augustine, and Boethius construed God's eternity in terms of his complete transcendence of *time. The tradition of divine timelessness was championed by medieval scholastics like *Anselm and *Aquinas but, after drawing incisive criticism from Scotus, receded in late scholastic theology as represented by Ockham. In our own day a temporalist construal has been greatly advanced by Whitehead and Hartshorne's *process theology, which sees development and, hence, temporality as essential to God. On the other hand, the rise of Big Bang *cosmology has served to reinvigorate the atemporalist view, since in the standard model time itself is finite in the past, so that God, as beginningless, must somehow transcend time.

What arguments might be offered for and against divine timelessness or temporality respectively? God's timelessness could be directly deduced from divine simplicity or immutability, since a temporal God would have to be changing in certain respects, for example, in knowing what events are simultaneous with any moment of his existence. But as these doctrines are even more controverted than the doctrine of divine timelessness, they do little to commend it. Perhaps the best argument in favour of divine atemporality is the claim that the fleeting nature of temporal life is inherently defective, since one is constantly losing the past and has not yet acquired the future, a state of affairs inappropriate for a most perfect being. Anyone who has experienced life's 'walking shadow' will appreciate the force of this argument; but God's attribute of *omniscience, which affords him full recall of the past and anticipation of the future, may blunt the force of this consideration. With his ability to experience the past and future as vividly as the present, a temporal God's experience of time's flow may not be so melancholy an affair as it can be for finite beings.

Against divine atemporality, it has been objected that the concept of an atemporal *person is incoherent, since persons engage in essentially temporal activities such as remembering, anticipating, and so forth. But it is far from evident that such activities are essential to personhood. There is nothing inherently temporal about self-consciousness or about activities such as knowing and willing, which seem essential to personhood, so long as these are unchanging. Thus, while a timeless being would lack some of the incidental characteristics of temporal persons, it could possess the essential properties of personhood and so, accordingly, could be personal.

In favour of divine temporality, it has been argued that God's real relation to the temporal world implies that God is temporal. For example, in creating the universe God comes into a new relation at the moment of *creation, which we may express as his coexisting with the universe or his sustaining the universe. He thereby undergoes at least an extrinsic change, in virtue of which he must be temporal. For anything that changes even extrinsically endures through a 'before' and an 'after' and so must be *in* time. Aquinas averted this conclusion only at the expense of denying that God has real relations with the world (though the world is really related to God). This is an extraordinarily difficult doctrine. For not only does it seem unbiblical and counter-intuitive to say that God does not stand in the relation of knowing, willing, and loving his creatures, but Aquinas's position makes it unintelligible why creatures exist at all. For in every broadly logically possible world, God's knowledge, will, and *love are absolutely similar, since he has no real relation to creatures, and creatures thus make no difference to him. The only salient difference between possible worlds in which creatures exist and those in which only God exists is not to be found in God but in the real relation creatures have to God. But why creatures exist at all remains mysterious, since God is absolutely the same in worlds in which they do exist and those in which they do not. Recent attempts by certain analytic philosophers of religion to argue that God is really related to the world but is none the less timeless turn out upon analysis to be based upon explanatorily vacuous accounts of 'eternal–temporal simultaneity' relations (Stump and Kretzmann) or upon category mistakes such as postulating a zero spatial distance between God and creatures and thus a 'frame of reference' in which nothing changes relative to God (Leftow).

It has also been argued on behalf of divine temporality that God, as an omniscient being, must know tensed facts such as what is *now* happening in the universe or that Columbus's discovery of America is *past*. But a timeless being cannot know such facts. At most he can know which events occur earlier than, simultaneously with, or later than certain other events—but such knowledge comprehends only tenseless facts, not tensed facts. A timeless being's knowledge of the universe has been aptly compared to a film producer's knowledge of every frame in a movie film as it lies in the film can, in contrast to a moviegoer's knowledge of what frame is now being projected on the screen. A timeless God will know only the tenseless facts concerning events in the *history of the universe but will be ignorant of what is now going on in the world, which is incompatible with his maximal cognitive excellence.

Probably the only way for a defender of divine timelessness to escape the force of the above two arguments is to reject the metaphysic of time which they tacitly presuppose. In the philosophy of time there are two radically opposed views of the nature of time, variously characterized as the dynamic versus the static, or the tensed versus the tenseless, or (borrowing the terminology of J. M. E. McTaggart, who first carefully delineated the two views) the A-Theory versus the B-Theory. Partisans of the dynamic, tensed, or A-Theory of time maintain that the distinction between the past, present, and future is a non-relational, mind-independent feature of time and typically regard temporal becoming as real, things coming into and passing out of existence as they come to be and cease to be present. By contrast, proponents of the static, tenseless, or B-Theory of time regard only the distinction between earlier and later as objective, the difference between past, present, and future being either purely subjective or else merely relational

with respect to any arbitrarily selected date. Temporal becoming is typically regarded as an illusion of consciousness, all events in time being on an ontological par.

It is clear that the above two arguments for divine temporality presuppose the A-Theory of time, for they assume that temporal becoming is real and that there are objective, tensed facts. But given the B-theory of time, these assumptions are erroneous. According to that theory, the four-dimensional space-time manifold, even if finite in the *earlier than* direction, never comes into or goes out of being: the entire 'block universe' simply exists (tenselessly). God does not exist within the space-time manifold but transcends it and sustains it timelessly in being. He knows all the tenseless truths about it, such as that some event E occurs (tenselessly) at some time t. Moreover, in a single, unchanging act, God can act in history to cause E to occur (tenselessly) when it does, and so with every event. Thus, given a B-Theory of time, the doctrine of divine timelessness becomes perspicuous.

Defenders of divine timelessness have argued against God's existing in time by noting that according to the Special Theory of Relativity there is no unique worldwide 'Now' or edge of becoming, but a multitude of times each associated with a different reference frame. Accordingly, they ask, if God is in time, whose time is he in? Relativity seems to imply a schizophrenic God with a now-consciousness associated with every reference frame. This objection, however, overlooks two important considerations. First, the classical defenders of divine temporality would distinguish, with Newton, between time itself (God's time, a metaphysical reality) and our empirical measures of time (time as it plays a role in physics). Relativity theory properly describes, not time, but our physical measures thereof, which are relative to reference frames. Only a defunct verificationism would permit one to conclude that because absolute time and relations of absolute simultaneity are not detectable by our empirical measures therefore they do not exist. Second, as its name implies, the Special Theory is a restricted theory which governs only reference frames in relative uniform motion. In order to deal with accelerated and rotational motion, one must turn to the General Theory of Relativity, which is not, properly speaking, a theory of relativity at all, but a theory of gravity. When the General Theory is given a cosmological application, it turns out that there exists in the universe a worldwide cosmic time which is not relative to reference frames but is the same for every hypothetical observer and which registers the duration of the universe as a whole. Cosmic time could well be thought to be an appropriate, rough measure of God's time as well, at least since the beginning of the universe.

The defender of God's timelessness might at this point raise the age-old problem of why God, if he existed for infinite time prior to the creation of the universe, did not create the universe sooner. For at any moment of time prior to creation God at that moment consciously delayed creating the universe. It is plausible that as a supremely rational being God would not delay creating unless he had a good reason for doing so. But in such an infinite time there can be no good reason for postponing creation at every moment. Thus God could not have endured for infinite time prior to his creating the universe. This conclusion is underlined by traditional cosmological arguments against the possibility of traversing an infinite past to arrive at the present and against the possibility of an actually infinite multitude (in this case, past events).

The proponent of divine temporality is not without recourse, however. The above objections strike against God's infinite past duration, not divine temporality *per se*. One could hold that God *sans* creation exists either timelessly or in a geometrically amorphous time in which distinct moments cannot be differentiated and that subsequent to creation God exists in our familiar, metric time. So long as these two states are not thought of as temporally related (perhaps God's timeless state can be thought of as the boundary of his temporal state), there is no incoherence in such a hybrid view.

Thus, it seems that whether one construes divine eternity in terms of temporality or timelessness is apt to depend upon whether one embraces an A- or a B-Theory of time. Given the static conception of time in the B-Theory, divine timelessness is a coherent doctrine. But if one accepts the objective reality of tensed facts and temporal becoming, as posited by the A-theory, then one is compelled, it seems, to conclude that God is temporal—at least since the moment of creation.   **William Lane Craig**

Helm, P., *Eternal God* (1988).
Leftow, B., *Time and Eternity* (1991).
Lucas, J., and Hodgson, P., *Spacetime and Electromagnetism* (1990).
Mellor, D. H., *Real Time* (1981).
Padgett, A., *God, Eternity and the Nature of Time* (1992).
Smith, Q., *Language and Time* (1993).
Stump, E., and Kretzmann, N., 'Eternity', *Journal of Philosophy*, 79 (1981).
Wierenga, E., *The Nature of God* (1989).
Yates, J., *The Timelessness of God* (1990).

ethics.

Christianity is an ethical religion. This does not mean that Christians are especially good people; indeed, much wickedness has been and is done in the name of Christianity. It means that one cannot characterize the Christian view of *God, the *world, and the relation between them, without reference to ethical ideas, such as good and bad, right and wrong, *virtue and vice.

All serious thinking about ethics tries to give an account that makes sense of the elementary things we think and do, offers guidance on practical decisions, and answers to the special needs of its moment in history. Christian thinking about ethics also tries for such an account, but one that does justice to teachings of *church and scripture and to the life of Christian communities. Given the variations over nearly two thousand years in Christian thinking about God, world, church, scripture, *tradition, and *reason, and differences in its cultural settings, Christian thinking about ethics has been, not surprisingly, extremely diverse. Christian accounts of ethics have, however, attempted the same tasks: an understanding of the moral attributes of God, the relation between God and human *morality, and, most importantly, a reflective account of the content of human morality as lived, or aspired to, by Christians.

Christian thinking about the content of human morality tries to offer an account of how we are to live, and why this is the case, including: (1) a theory of *moral psychology*, of how humans act, and how actions affect character and vice versa; (2) a theory of *obligation*, of what actions are right or wrong; (3) a theory of *value*, of what things are good or bad. Typically, one of these accounts takes priority over the others, and the rich diversity in Christian ethics reflects this.

A long and influential tradition in Christian ethics is based on the teleological moral psychology of *Plato and *Aristotle. On this view, all human action is directed towards some end, and the ul-

timate end for humans is happiness. What is true human happiness? According to Plato and Aristotle, it is a life befitting our human nature as 'rational animals', and requires certain habits of character, or virtues, such as self-control, bravery, *wisdom, and *justice. According to Christians, ultimate happiness is everlasting life with God, and the 'theological virtues' of *faith, *hope, and *charity must be added to the 'cardinal virtues' mentioned above in order to attain this end. Ethics, then, is largely an account of what these virtues are, how they are related to human nature, and how, under the grace of God, we cultivate them. This approach finds full expression in *On the Morals of the Catholic Church* by *Augustine, and in the *Summa Theologiae* of Thomas *Aquinas, still the basis for much Roman Catholic teaching on the subject. It suits the idea of God as the 'author of nature' (including human nature) and has enjoyed a remarkable resurgence in English-speaking *philosophy and *theology in the last quarter of the 20th century.

With the rise of the Protestant *Reformation in the 16th century, and of mechanistic *science in the 17th, the desire arose for an ethics that was neither Aristotelian nor teleological, and which would guide the rational choices of conscientious individuals. In some such accounts, the idea of duty takes priority, as in *Kant's *Groundwork of the Metaphysics of Morals*, which argues that one's duty is to act on principles that one could consistently will to be universal laws. This duty, known as the 'categorical imperative', requires one to treat *persons as autonomous 'ends in themselves' and never to use them as mere 'means'. Kant is not ordinarily thought of as an orthodox Christian, and his preoccupation with autonomy seems at odds with Christian obedience and humility, but he was partly motivated by a *pietistic Christian upbringing, and made God and *immortality necessary postulates in his ethical system. Moreover, many Christians have seen Kant's emphasis on *law as congenial to the Judaeo-Christian emphasis on law, and his emphasis on universality as the rational expression of the Golden Rule (Matt. 7: 12). In any event, his work has influenced virtually all subsequent Protestant thinkers, including *Schleiermacher.

Equally, some thinkers have held that the theory of value should take priority. On this view, we must identify what is intrinsically valuable and produce as much of it as possible. If the valuable is what people do in fact value, and if, as Jeremy Bentham held, humans ultimately value pleasure and the absence of pain, then right actions will be those that 'maximize utility', or produce the greatest balance of pleasure over pain for everyone affected over the long run. This approach reached its high-water mark in the 19th century, in the works of Bentham and J. S. Mill. Utilitarianism has often been regarded as a secular moral philosophy, though Mill's *Utilitarianism* presents it as compatible with Christianity, on the assumption that God desires the happiness of his creatures. Christians such as William Paley have held versions in which obedience to God's laws maximizes utility, and utilitarianism is nothing more than the NT command to 'love one's neighbour as oneself' writ large (Mark 12: 31). Other Christians have objected, however, that utilitarianism arrogates to humans the divine responsibility for ensuring best overall results in the universe.

Christians have not always been enthusiastic about borrowing secular philosophical frameworks. Thus, some have tried to minimize philosophical speculation by holding the apparently simple-minded view that ethics must be based directly on God's will as revealed in scripture. Obligatory actions are those which God commands (such as observing the sabbath), wrong actions those which God forbids (such as killing), and permissible actions those which God has not forbidden. This *'divine command' view is attractive for several reasons: besides avoiding non-biblical accretions upon church teaching, it is accessible to ordinary people, fits with Christianity's Judaic conception of God as sovereign lawgiver, and expresses the widely held conviction that 'If God is dead, then everything is permitted.' Simple versions of this view face problems, though, in depicting God's will as arbitrary or inexplicable, offering no guidance on issues where scripture is silent, and making covert or uncritical use of precisely the philosophical commitments they hope to avoid. Sophisticated versions of this view were defended by Peter *Abelard and William of Ockham, and in the later 20th century by Philip Quinn. These avoid many of the problems of simpler versions, but belie the idea that the divine command theory is somehow innocent of philosophical or theological commitment.

One finds a similar degree of diversity in Christian thinking about particular ethical problems. In many controversies, it is hard to find *the* Christian position at all. Regarding *contraception, for example, some Christian 'consequentialists' endorse it on the grounds that the consequences of permitting contraception are better than those of not permitting it. Some Christian Aristotelians oppose it on the grounds that it frustrates the natural end of sexual activity, which is procreation. Some divine command theorists permit it on the grounds that God has not explicitly prohibited contraception in scripture; others could oppose it as incompatible with the biblical ideals of love and marriage. Even on issues such as the intentional killing of the innocent, which Christians tend to judge absolutely wrong, one finds variation in the application of absolute principles. For example, many Christians oppose *abortion on the grounds that it is the intentional killing of innocent persons, while Christians who permit abortion often do so on the grounds that the foetus is not a *person, or that the intention in abortion need not be to kill the foetus, but simply to save the life of the mother.

There have also been serious attempts at Christian ethics in terms of *existentialism, phenomenology, *Marxism, even *postmodernism; and there are many other practical problems where differences between various Christian approaches play themselves out in interesting ways. Despite this bewildering variety of methods, styles, and conclusions, one can make the following high-level generalizations about Christian ethical thinking:

1. In contrast to subjective accounts that view the truth about morality as dependent on human beliefs, choices, or attitudes, Christian accounts of ethics tend to be *objective*, viewing the truth about morality as dependent on something beyond the subjective states of humans. This 'something' may be creaturely natures, rational principles, or the will of God, but it is objective as far as humans are concerned.

2. In contrast to relativist or 'situationist' accounts that hold that any type of action may be permissible in some situation or other, Christian accounts tend to be *absolutist*, holding that certain actions, such as idolatry or the intentional killing of the innocent, are never permissible. These absolute prohibitions have been explained as befitting the holiness of God or the image of God in humankind, and supported by reference to Paul's implied injunction in Romans 3: 8 'not to do evil, that good may come'.

3. In contrast to sceptical approaches that deny the possibility of moral knowledge (either because there are no ethical truths to know or because we lack sufficient information to know them), Christian accounts tend to be *non-sceptical*, holding that some degree of ethical knowledge is possible. They may disagree over whether this knowledge comes through human reason or through divine *revelation, but agree that, in God's providence, we have enough knowledge of right and wrong for practical purposes, and to convict us as morally responsible for our *sin.

4. In contrast to egoist approaches, that hold that human actions are, or ought to be, primarily *self-regarding*, Christian approaches to ethics tend to be *other-regarding* in their emphases on *agape* (self-giving love of God and neighbour) and on *justice*. This is not to say that Christianity requires utter disregard for oneself; Jesus' command to love one's neighbour as oneself presupposes some interest in one's own well-being. Nevertheless, even those who see the Christian life as leading to their ultimate happiness tend also to see the holiness of God and the welfare of their neighbour as separate sources of value and obligation.

There have been exceptions to these generalizations throughout history, and intellectual pressures toward subjectivism, relativism, scepticism, and egoism are stronger than ever. One source of these pressures is 'scientific naturalism', the widespread view that reality must be understood in purely natural (that is, non-supernatural) terms. On this view, ethics must squeeze itself into the world of facts as revealed by science, or be trimmed to fit the space. If objectivity would require supernatural value entities, then the pretence to objectivity must be dropped. If absolutism would require unfashionable Aristotelian 'natures' or a commanding God, then absolutism must be dropped. If the possibility of moral knowledge would require non-empirical sources of knowledge, then moral scepticism becomes inevitable. If the only intelligible reason for action is the gratification of one's biologically or psychologically given urges, other-regarding action is exposed as illusory.

Some Christians have been tempted to accept the reduced ethics left over after the squeezing and trimming; others have tried to meet these objections on their own ground by defending moral objectivity, absolutes, knowledge, and altruism in empirical, scientific terms; still others have denied that Christian ethics need be vindicated on terms set by scientific naturalism, with its dubious empiricist framework and barely concealed secular bias.

Mark Nelson

Beaty, M., Fisher, C., and Nelson, M., *Christian Theism and Moral Philosophy* (1998).
Field, D., and Atkinson, D., *Dictionary of Christian Ethics and Pastoral Theology* (1995).
Gustafson, J., *Christ and the Moral Life* (1968).
Holmes, A., *Ethics: Approaching Moral Decisions* (1984).
Lewis, C. S., 'Christian Behaviour', in *Mere Christianity* (1952).
Long, E. L., *A Survey of Christian Ethics* (1967).
—— *A Survey of Recent Christian Ethics* (1982).
Mavrodes, G., 'Religion and the Queerness of Morality', in R. Audi and W. Wainwright (eds.), *Rationality, Religious Belief, and Moral Commitment* (1986).
McInerny, R., *Ethica Thomistica* (1982).
MacIntyre, A., *A Short History of Ethics* (1966).
Quinn, P., *Divine Commands and Moral Requirements* (1978).
Ramsey, P., *Deeds and Rules in Christian Ethics* (1965).

Ethiopian theology.

'Ethiopia shall stretch out her hands to God' (Ps. 68: 31) provides a biblical grounding for Ethiopian Christianity as does the account in Acts (8: 26–39) of the conversion of the eunuch, an officer at the court of the queen of Ethiopia. Ethiopia in these texts meant black Africa, especially that part of it closest to the Middle East, not so different geographically from modern Ethiopia. For centuries the name was used in Europe for Africa as a whole.

The kingdom of Aksum on the Red Sea coast was converted to Christianity in the 4th century by Frumentius, consecrated as bishop by *Athanasius of *Alexandria. In later centuries the kingdom spread further inland, becoming less Semitic and more evidently African in culture (rectangular churches, for instance, gave way to round) but Aksum Cathedral always remained its ecclesiastical centre where the kings were crowned. Until the 20th century its church remained dependent upon the see of Alexandria, its *liturgy was basically Alexandrian, and its bishops mostly Egyptian monks. This did not prevent profound indigenization and the development of a perhaps unrivalled *contextual theology, made inevitable by the extent to which for centuries Ethiopia was cut off from contact with the rest of the Christian world, particularly after the rise of Islam which came effectively to surround it.

Its identity and survival depended largely on the *translation of the bible into Ethiopian by the end of the 5th century, together with some other literature, mostly Alexandrian theology. It was above all in *monasteries that the bible and liturgy were passed on as the core of an Ethiopian tradition of Christianity in which *Marian devotion, choral music, and a dominating sense of a providential national identity as the New *Israel were the most striking characteristics. The link, often tenuous, with Alexandria ensured a minimum communion with the wider Christian world, strengthened by the stubborn presence from the early Middle Ages of an Ethiopian monastery in Jerusalem which helped to provide some further translation of western Christian literature; but the tradition was shaped predominantly by its internal momentum.

According to the powerful national myth enshrined in the *Kebra Nagast* (whose content appears to go back at least as far as the 6th century) the Ethiopian kingly line descends from the son of *Solomon and the Queen of Sheba, Menelik I, who when grown up carried off the Ark of the Covenant to Aksum where it remained, indisputably establishing the Israelite character of Ethiopia, both as kingdom and as church. Probably more than any other traditional part of Christianity, the Ethiopian Church treasured its continuity with the OT. Some of this, such as the observance of the 'two sabbaths' (Saturday and Sunday), may date only from the Middle Ages, but the wide 'Hebraic' character of Ethiopian Christianity is striking. The almost complete absence of Greek or Latin intellectual influence may help explain this greater commitment to the OT heritage. Ethiopia in its isolation lacked adequate academic tools to defend or evaluate its religious heritage and doctrinal position, although in the 16th century, faced with severe challenges from *Islam on the one hand and *Jesuit Portuguese missionaries on the other, the monk Enbaqom responded remarkably well in his *Angasa Amin* to the one and King Galawdewos in his *Confession* to the other. But each of these works is uncharacteristic. The threat from both directions made Ethiopia withdraw still further into isolation, not helped by the arrival of *evangelical missionaries in the 19th century with their horror of Marian devotion (even Catholics were insufficiently fervently Marian in Ethiopian eyes). Strange as the Ethiopian tradition has appeared to some western Christians, it has survived across fifteen centuries as striking evidence both of the tenacity of Christianity in a non-western world and of its capacity to take a diversity of forms. It can hardly be doubted that it was its religious and literary tradition that enabled Ethiopia to survive with a continuous political identity through history in a way unique in Africa.

In modern times its symbolic power has been important for Africa as a whole: a political unit which, unlike every other, withstood the 19th-century western scramble for Africa and drove off an Italian invasion at the battle of Adowa (1895). Crushed very brutally by Mussolini in the 1930s, it was quickly resurrected in the Second World War. In the 19th century the word 'Ethiopian' came to signify movements of political unrest coupled with literacy and ecclesiastical independence in both south and west Africa. Missionaries and colonialists alike tended to abhor the spirit of 'Ethiopianism'. Bengt Sundkler in his classical study of the multiplying independent black churches, *Bantu Prophets in South Africa* (1948), distinguished a little too simply between 'Zionists' who were 'prophetic' and 'Ethiopians' who were schismatic, but in general it remains true that the name 'Ethiopian' was adopted most often by Christians little affected by the prophetism characteristic of 20th-century Africa. Nevertheless the greatest of such prophets, the Liberian evangelist William Wadé Harris, declared proudly, 'I stand up for the Ethiopian'. Ethiopia has signified, continent-wide, the vision of an Africa undominated by Europe but a no less Christian Africa with biblical validation and a documented history across many centuries.

Adrian Hastings

Beshah, Girma, and Aregay, Merid, *The Question of the Union of the Churches in Luso-Ethiopian Relations* (1964).

Cerulli, E., *Scritti teologici etiopici dei secoli XVI-XVII* (2 vols.; 1958; 1960).

—— *Tiberius and Pontius Pilate in Ethiopian Tradition and Poetry* (1973).

Haile, G., 'Materials on the Theology of Qebat or Unction', in G. Goldenberg (ed.), *Ethiopian Studies* (1988).

—— *The Mariology of Emperor Zära Ya'eqob of Ethiopia: Texts and Translations* (1992).

Hammerschmidt, E., *Studies in the Ethiopic Anaphoras* (1961).

Hastings, Adrian, *The Church in Africa 1450–1950* (1994), chs. 1, 4, 6.

Kaplan, Steven, *The Monastic Holy Man and the Christianization of Early Solomonic Ethiopia* (1984).

Ullendorff, Edward, *Ethiopia and the Bible* (1968).

Eucharist,

from the Greek word for thanksgiving, is now the name most widely favoured for the rite celebrated in the various parts of Christendom as the mass, the divine liturgy, the Lord's supper, or the holy communion. The rite derives from the actions recorded of *Jesus at the Last Supper, when he took *bread and *wine, gave thanks over them, and, identifying them with the *body and *blood of his impending self-sacrifice, distributed them to his disciples to consume, with the instruction that they should henceforth do this in memory of him (Matt. 26: 26–9; Mark 14: 22–5; Luke 22: 14–20; 1 Cor. 11: 23–5). Down the centuries its celebration has continued as, in the words of an important text from WCC *Faith and Order, 'the central act of the church's worship' (*Baptism, Eucharist and Ministry* or *BEM, Eucharist*, 1).

The very centrality of the Eucharist to the *church has made of it both the sign of *unity among Christians and yet also a focus of the divisions that have arisen among them. Differences in the understanding and practice of the Eucharist have often been symptomatic of other differences in doctrine and life that have entailed the breaking of *communion among divergent communities all claiming to be church. The modern *ecumenical movement has made considerable progress in resolving these differences and thus approaching the restoration of mutual communion. It has become possible to compose a theological account of the Eucharist that finds broad support even while acknowledging that some points of contention remain only partially settled and so still prevent complete mutual acceptance among the churches.

Such an account might take its cue from the declaration of the apostle *Paul to the Corinthians that 'as often as you eat this bread and drink this cup, you proclaim the Lord's death until he come' (1 Cor. 11: 26). Five points can be made here. First, it may be noted that Christ is called 'the Lord', a title associated especially with his *Resurrection from the dead and his present sovereignty (see CHRISTOLOGY). From the beginning, Christians have *encountered their living Lord* in the context of a meal. Meals were significant already in the days of Jesus' earthly ministry, for they enacted his fellowship with sinners and his calling of them to repentance (Matt. 9: 10–13 = Mark 2: 15–17 = Luke 5: 29–32; Matt. 11: 19 = Luke 7: 34; Luke 15: 1–2; 19: 1–10), and they were occasions for him to feed the crowds who were otherwise like *sheep without a shepherd (Mark 6: 30–44; 8: 1–10; Matt. 14: 13–21; 15: 32–9; Luke 9: 11–17; John 6: 3–15). The risen Christ made himself known to the two at Emmaus 'in the breaking of the bread' (Luke 24: 13–35), appeared again to his disciples in Jerusalem while they were at table (Luke 24: 36–49; Acts 10: 41), and prepared breakfast for them on the seashore (John 21: 1–14). In their continuing assemblies, the early Christians acclaimed or invoked Christ's presence: 'Maranatha', 'Our Lord has come' or 'Our Lord, come' (1 Cor. 16: 22; cf. Rev. 3: 20; 22: 20).

The eucharistic *presence of Christ* has been a constant confession of the church, even though Christians have differed sharply in their accounts of the manner in which he is 'both host and food'. Controversies have fixed on the status and role of the bread and wine. The eastern churches have affirmed their 'change' (*metabole* in Greek) into the body and blood of Christ while often discouraging speculation as to how this occurs. The western churches have a long history of debating, under several guises, the 'real' versus the 'symbolic', the 'intrinsic' versus the 'extrinsic' relation between Christ himself and the chosen elements. That goes back as far as Paschasius Radbertus against Ratramnus in the 9th century and the case of Berengar in the 11th. In the 16th century, the *Anglicans considered that the Roman doctrine of *transubstantiation 'overthroweth the nature of a sacrament', and the *Lutherans were just as keen to maintain the integrity of the created elements; for *Calvinists and *Zwinglians, the issue was the distance set from earthly events by Christ's Ascension. In the 20th century, ecumenical theology has alleviated the problems by emphasizing, as in fact Orthodox and Calvinists respectively did, the role of the *Holy Spirit in bringing about Christ's presence to the church in the *sacrament: most newer liturgies contain in some form an *epiclesis*, or invocation of the Holy Spirit, upon the assembly and the bread and wine which the participants will consume at Christ's command. This move is reflected in *BEM*; but while that document's affirmation of 'Christ's real, living and active presence' (*Eucharist*, 13) has been

unanimously welcomed, the official evaluations of the text by the churches show many of them still unwilling or unable to find their own and others' more specific accounts accommodated in it.

Second, it may be noted that Paul speaks of the Eucharist as a proclamation of the Lord's *death. Christ's death lies at the heart of the *redemption of humankind for which the church gives thanks to God in the Eucharist. The biblical and traditional interpretation of Christ's death as a *sacrifice ensures that the Eucharist, as its commemoration, bears a *sacrificial character*; but again, Christians have differed in their accounts of it. In particular, this has been a bone of contention between Catholics and Protestants. In the 16th century, the Reformers charged that 'the multiplication of masses' was the ritual outcrop of a system whereby human action was thought to supplement, replace, or repeat what Christ alone had achieved for our salvation on Calvary. Theology in the 20th century has reworked the category of 'remembrance' (in Greek *anamnesis*, as in Luke 22: 19–20 and 1 Cor. 11: 24–5), against the background of ritual memorial in the OT (root *zkr* in Hebrew), in order to recover the notion that significant moments in the history of salvation can, at the divine command and by divine grace, be 'made present' for the inclusion of other generations into the story—and that without entailing a repetition of the event or, on the other hand, a merely mental recollection (see MEMORY). While scholarly debate still surrounds this notion at least in details, it has proved a valuable interpretative tool in the matter of eucharistic sacrifice, as again *BEM* shows. It can now be agreed that the Eucharist is a 'sacrifice of praise and thanksgiving' for the work of Christ on the cross and a prayer for the application of its benefits through the continuing intercession of Christ, and that in Christ Christians are enabled to offer themselves in worship and service to God. Yet once more we find hesitation as to the complete adequacy of such an account: for Lutherans in particular worry lest *BEM* should place too much stress on the 'upward' movement of the eucharistic action, while the Roman Catholic Church doubts that the role of Christ as intercessor gives sufficient expression to the eucharistic representation of his self-offering (Thurian 1988: vi. 20–1).

Third, we find in Paul that the Eucharist proclaims the Lord's death *until he come*. With varying degrees of emphasis the traditional liturgies of the church have viewed Christ's sacramental presence as a projection into the here and now of his future and final advent, and the Lord's meal as the sacramental anticipation of the heavenly banquet in the definitive *Kingdom of God. Following such OT expectations as Isaiah 25: 6–9, Jesus in his parables and sayings pictured God's reign as a feast (Matt. 8: 11 = Luke 13: 29; Matt. 22: 1–13; 25: 1–13; Luke 14: 16–24), where his own followers would join him at his table (Matt. 26: 29; Mark 14: 25; Luke 22: 14–18, 28–30), so that the joy of *salvation could take shape as 'the marriage supper of the Lamb' (Rev. 19: 6–9). Eucharistic theology and practice in the 20th century has recovered this *eschatological* dimension of the Lord's supper as part of a more general turn to *eschatology. One indication is an awareness of the transgenerational character of the church as the Eucharist embodies not only union with the Lord but also, in the words of *BEM* (*Eucharist*, 11), 'communion with all the saints and martyrs' (visually expressed in the icons that surround the liturgical action in Orthodox churches). Another indication is the perception of the Eucharist as what *BEM* calls 'precious food for missionaries, bread and wine for pilgrims on their apostolic journey' (ibid. 26): what participants receive as a 'promise' and 'foretaste' nourishes the eucharistic community for its witness to the new reality into which they are on God's behalf to invite the entire world. While theologians nuance differently their accounts of the relations between present and future, the 'already' and the 'not yet', the churches' evaluations of *BEM* do not appear to consider these differences doctrinally divisive.

Fourth, the apostle Paul makes clear that the eating and drinking of the eucharistic meal is properly an act of the Christian *community*: by their abusive behaviour in that respect the Corinthians are running counter to the very nature of the Lord's supper (1 Cor. 11: 17–34). It is the one body of Christ that is shared by the breaking of the bread, and Christ's blood that is shared in the cup of blessing, and 'because there is one bread, we who are many are one body, for we all partake of the one bread' (1 Cor. 10: 16–17). The 'cup of blessing' is the 'cup of the new covenant in [Christ's] blood' (1 Cor. 11: 25; cf. Matt. 26: 27–8), whereby participants are integrated into God's people (cf Eph. 2: 11–22; Heb. 13: 20–1). On that basis it is common Christian teaching that the Eucharist, in the words of Pope Innocent III (1198–1216), both 'signifies' and 'effects' *churchly unity*: it expresses the communion already existing among members of the body of Christ, and the grace afforded through its celebration also maintains and furthers such communion. That is why, negatively, serious disruptions in fellowship lead to and are sealed by the rupture of eucharistic communion between the disputing churches, and why, then, the restoration of eucharistic communion must be part of any reconciliation. That has been recognized in the modern ecumenical movement, although the churches have not yet reached a common mind as to what remaining or regained measure of unity in faith and life justifies the resumption of eucharistic communion so that the shared sacrament may play its part in deepening and strengthening that unity. What is clear is that persistence in 'unjustifiable' divisions among Christians is 'inconsistent in face of the reconciling presence of God in human history' (*BEM*, ibid. 20).

Fifth, the 'eating of the bread' and the 'drinking of the cup' locate the divine work of salvation celebrated in the Eucharist firmly amid the *material creation* and *embodied humanity*. The NT calls Christ's death an 'exodus' (the Greek word at Luke 9: 31) and Christ himself 'our passover' (1 Cor. 5: 7: cf. John 19: 36), and the new covenant in Christ inherits the concreteness of the Passover and Exodus in the old (cf. 1 Cor. 10: 1–4). The *cosmological* and *cultural* reference of the Eucharist, while long dormant in much western theology and practice of the sacrament, has found expression in the offertory prayers of the missal of Paul VI (1969): 'Blessed are you, Lord, God of all creation. Through your goodness we have this bread to offer, which earth has given and human hands have made. It will become for us the bread of life … Through your goodness we have this wine to offer, fruit of the vine and work of human hands. It will become our spiritual drink.' The Eucharist can in fact serve as a paradigm in the *ecological and economic areas to which contemporary Christianity devotes much attention: a responsibly celebrated Eucharist shows the right use of earthly resources as gifts from God to be taken as the matter of communion with the creator; it also exemplifies *justice in the distribution of those gifts, for those who hunger and thirst for righteousness are all equally welcomed by the merciful Lord into his table fellowship and all share

together in the fruits of redemption and in the foretaste of the new heavens and the new earth in which right will prevail (cf. 2 Pet. 3: 13). Living eucharistically, human beings begin to fulfil the divine vocation of humankind to be, as the Orthodox theologian Alexander Schmemann puts it, 'the priest of the cosmic sacrament': to receive the world from God and to return the world to God, having found its place and function in the loving purposes of God (*For the Life of the World*, 1973).

The nuanced agreements displayed in such a theological account of the Eucharist as this are reflected in the ritual convergence that has occurred in the course of the 20th-century ecumenical movement and the often overlapping liturgical movement. It remains the case that the styles of eucharistic celebration may vary greatly between and within the different ecclesial traditions, depending on such things as the degree and type of ceremonial used, the processions, gestures, postures, and table manners of the officiants and other participants, the arrangement and furnishing of the gathering place, and the amount and mode of music employed. Likewise, the remaining doctrinal differences will come to subtle expression in the detailed phrasing of the prayers that have been composed in a time of rarely paralleled revision of service books. Yet there has been a remarkable *rapprochement* among the churches both in the basic structure of the eucharistic liturgy and in the expectation that the Lord's people will gather each Lord's day to hear the Lord's word and share in the Lord's meal. The model has become again what Justin Martyr described as the practice of the Roman Christians around the middle of the 2nd century: On Sunday, the first day of the week (the beginning of creation and of the new creation inaugurated by Christ's Resurrection), all assemble from town and country to listen to 'the writings of the prophets' and 'the records of the apostles' (OT and NT), to hear those scriptures expounded and be exhorted to appropriate conduct, to pray for the church and for the world, to present the bread and the wine over which the presider gives thanks as Christ commanded in remembrance of his saving work, and then to receive again that food and drink as the body and blood of Christ, taking care that the sick and the needy are not neglected either spiritually or materially (Justin, *First Apology*, 65–7).

Geoffrey Wainwright

Allmen, J.-J. von, *The Lord's Supper* (1969).
Baptism, Eucharist and Ministry: Faith and Order Paper No. 111 (1982).
Davies, H., *Bread of Life and Cup of Joy: Newer Ecumenical Perspectives on the Eucharist* (1993).
Heron, A., *Table and Tradition: Towards an Ecumenical Understanding of the Eucharist* (1983).
Jasper, R. C. D., and Cumming, G. J., *Prayers of the Eucharist: Early and Reformed*, 3rd edn. (1987).
Jeremias, J., *The Eucharist Words of Jesus* (1966).
Just, A. A., *The Ongoing Feast: Table Fellowship and Eschatology at Emmaus* (1993).
Léon-Dufour, F. X., *Sharing the Eucharistic Bread: The Witness of the New Testament* (1987).
Macy, G., *The Theologies of the Eucharist in the Early Scholastic Period* (1984).
Marshall, I. H., *Last Supper and Lord's Supper* (1981).
Mazza, E., *The Eucharistic Prayers of the Roman Rite* (1986).
Power, David N., *The Sacrifice We Offer: The Tridentine Dogma and its Reinterpretation* (1987).
Reumann, J., *The Supper of the Lord: The New Testament, Ecumenical Dialogues, and Faith and Order on Eucharist* (1985).

Rubin, M., *Corpus Christi: The Eucharist in Late Medieval Culture* (1991).

Schmemann, A., *The Eucharist: Sacrament of the Kingdom* (1988).

Stone, D., *History of the Doctrine of the Holy Eucharist* (2 vols.; 1909).

Thurian, M., (ed.), *Churches Respond to BEM: Official Responses to the 'Baptism, Eucharist and Ministry' Text* (6 vols.; 1986–8).

Wainwright, G., *Eucharist and Eschatology* (1971).

euthanasia is a deliberate medical intervention undertaken with the express intention of ending a life to relieve intractable *suffering. What has sometimes been called passive euthanasia is best referred to as the withdrawal of, or failure to initiate, treatment, which then has had the secondary effect of shortening life. Either course of action may be described as voluntary or non-voluntary, depending on whether the patient was competent to give informed consent. Involuntary euthanasia is the killing of a person competent to give consent who has not in fact given it, and is indistinguishable from murder.

It was only in the second half of the 20th century that euthanasia, as distinct from *suicide, became a major topic of *ethical concern. Three factors contributed to this change of perception. First, a growing sense of personal autonomy has led many to believe that neither *God nor man can take away their right to choose the manner of their *death, just as they choose the manner of their life. In particular they look for a death which is appropriate to their life, and is neither degrading nor unnecessarily distressing. If it is permissible to interfere with natural processes by lengthening life, why should it not be permissible to shorten it?

Secondly, medical advances have added to many people's fears that they may be kept alive beyond the point at which life has ceased to have any meaning for them, and in circumstances which rob them of their dignity. Even such a simple advance as the control of pneumonia, once known as 'the old man's friend', raises difficult questions about whether it should always be treated, particularly when increasing anxieties about litigation encourage doctors to be overcautious.

Thirdly, and against these two tendencies, the Nazi programme of involuntary euthanasia has acted as a cautionary tale about what can happen when the normal taboos against killing people are broken, and when the state can make decisions about who shall live.

Until recently most Christians have been firmly opposed to euthanasia on the grounds that it is a form of suicide. Life is a gift from God which is not at our disposal, but is to be revered and cherished. Our duty is to care for the dying, and to be with them, not to abandon them. This duty need not entail excessive or demeaning attempts to keep them alive at all costs. But to cross the line between killing and letting die is to trespass on what properly belongs to God, as well as to strike at the basis of *law in its protection of the person, and at the basis of medicine in its commitment to do no harm.

Much use is also made of the slippery slope argument. There are fears that permitting euthanasia, even under strict safeguards, could lead to a euthanasia-minded society, on a par with our present *abortion-minded society. To the objection that it is always possible to erect legal barriers, it is replied that, in matters so emotionally complex and so dependent on nuanced clinical judgements, legal barriers and the definitions on which they rely can be relatively ineffective, as has proved to be the case with abortion. Further-

more, do we really want lawyers haggling over our deathbeds? Nor is it hard to imagine the pressures on some old people, conscious of using up scarce resources, who might be driven to feel that euthanasia was their duty.

Others, including some Christians, have questioned whether *compassion does not require a greater willingness to look at the actual distress and suffering experienced by some terminally ill patients, and to ask whether palliative medicine, excellent though it now is, can cope with all the symptoms. Some also doubt the validity of the distinction between killing and letting die, especially when the latter involves pain-relieving treatment, one consequence of which may be the shortening of life. Massive doses of morphine, for instance, may be needed to keep the pain of terminal cancer under control. But morphine can also hasten death, though not always; indeed in some cases the relief it brings can actually prolong life. Ethical dilemmas about such risks to life are usually resolved by appeal to the principle of double effect, according to which an unpredictable and unintended secondary effect does not invalidate the primary *moral intention of an action. In other words, if a doctor intends to treat pain or distress, and uses drugs appropriate for that purpose, then even if there is a risk of adverse consequences, he or she is not culpable. But if the treatment is certain, or almost certain, to cause death, the principle of double effect cannot operate, and the distinction between such treatment and euthanasia vanishes.

Philosophically minded critics have on the whole been suspicious of such fine distinctions, and have argued that it would be more honest to permit euthanasia than to hide it under the guise of treatment. Those who have to make difficult decisions about actual patients tend to disagree, and most are reluctant to cross a line which in clinical practice seems real enough.

Some of the hardest problems are posed by the condition known as persistent vegetative state, in which the boundary between life and death is hard to define. A judicial decision that it may be in the best interests of such patients to discontinue feeding, on the grounds that they no longer have any interests, has caused disquiet among some Christians. Action of this kind, which ensures death rather than simply permitting it and is based on suppositions about a patient's quality of life, cannot be defended on the principle of double effect. The fear is that it could open the door to similar judgements, made in less dire circumstances, which might more obviously breach the principle that life should not be taken deliberately.

See also HEALTH AND HEALING; MEDICAL ETHICS.

John Habgood

Church of England, *On Dying Well* (1974).

Dunstan, G., *et al.*, *Euthanasia: Death, Dying and the Medical Duty* (1996).

Gormally, L., *Euthanasia, Clinical Practice and the Law* (1994).

House of Lords, *Report of the Select Committee on Medical Ethics* (1994).

John Paul II, *Evangelium Vitae* (1995).

evangelicalism. The variety and vitality of worldwide evangelicalism defies easy description. It is best understood as an umbrella category which includes under its spread a wide range of otherwise disparate churches, movements, and ministries. To grasp both evangelicalism's centre and the full extent of its reach, readers need to consider evangelicalism (1) sociologically, (2) theologically, and (3) historically.

Sociologically

Evangelicalism should be viewed as a diffuse subculture within world Christianity that stretches across theological and denominational traditions by means of a loosely linked network of leaders, teachers, speakers, literature, music, prayer networks, missions organizations, para-church agencies and activities, and the like. Evangelicals sing the same choruses through much of the world; emphasize the same fads and trends in Christian experience; support the same para-church ministries; and look to the same colleges and seminaries for education. One tongue-in-cheek definition of those who are evangelical has been 'all who find Billy Graham and his theology acceptable.'

Since the Second World War, much of this evangelical 'culture' has had its origin in the United States. Fuller Theological Seminary, *Christianity Today*, the Billy Graham Association, Young Life, Youth for Christ, Campus Crusade for Christ, Wycliffe Translators, World Vision—the American evangelical network has extended its ministry worldwide. But evangelicalism's influence has also proved multidirectional (cf. British biblical scholarship, Korean prayer conferences, Latin American evangelists). Seen in this light, evangelicalism is an international, 'transdenominational community with complicated infrastructures of institutions and persons' (George Marsden, *Evangelicalism and Modern America* (1984), p. ix).

Not all evangelicals have been comfortable with the leadership of this evangelical coalition. Some, as at the worldwide Lausanne II consultation in Manila in 1989, have found American influence oppressive. Others have thought evangelicalism to be controlled by those who stress the conceptuality of *Reformed orthodoxy over a commitment to renewed life. Still others have complained about the obverse, that evangelicalism has ignored *theology in the interest of cultural relevance and evangelistic utility.

Rather than be delimited either by those who desire evangelicalism to be primarily truth-oriented or by those who see evangelicalism pragmatically as simply conversion-oriented, others have desired evangelicalism to centre around its spiritual orientation (many *Pentecostals and *Wesleyans) and/or its service orientation (those in the Anabaptist traditions). Though all evangelicals are concerned with *truth, *conversion, piety, *and* service, emphases vary among the sub-traditions that fit under evangelicalism's spread. Despite evangelicalism's popularity and influence, differing priorities have produced a growing disunity.

Evangelicalism is more than a network of ministries and ministers, however. The word can also be used to describe a loose grouping of denominations and theological traditions, all holding to certain core convictions and experiences, as well as to a common *Protestant ('protesting') tradition. Pre-millennialism, *fundamentalism, Pentecostalism, *Adventism, the *holiness movement, the *restorationist churches, the *Black churches, the *Baptists, *Pietism, the Anabaptist churches, the self-consciously Reformed, and conservative *Lutheranism should all be considered part of evangelicalism. Despite significant differences in ethos and theology, and in the absence of real institutional connectedness, these theological strands share enough common direction to be called a movement.

While laity in these various church bodies easily identify themselves as 'evangelical Baptists', or 'evangelicals who are Nazarene', not all church leaders are equally comfortable with this conjoining. Those from churches rooted in the Reformed tradition tend to make use of the label more often, while some in the pietistic and Wesleyan traditions feel misunderstood by it. But despite such reservations, all bear a sufficient family resemblance to be called 'evangelical'. A second tongue-in-cheek definition that has been offered of an evangelical is 'someone other evangelicals are willing to call an evangelical'. Each of these traditions fits that description.

Such 'denominational' descriptors prove too narrow, however, for they leave out many in the mainline Protestant denominations (e.g. *Anglican, *Presbyterian, *Methodist). There are millions of persons in these denominations worldwide who agree theologically with those in the more independent and explicitly evangelical denominations. Moreover, there are increasing numbers of Roman Catholics, many of whom have been influenced by the *charismatic movement, who define their faith in terms of personal *salvation, the authority of the *bible, and other evangelical priorities. Taken together, these additional groups make up the majority of evangelicals in some contexts. It is for this reason that descriptions of evangelicalism have moved beyond the sociological to include the theological.

Theologically

Evangelical Christians may also be described as those with 'a dedication to the gospel that is expressed in a personal faith in Christ as Lord, an understanding of the gospel as defined authoritatively by scripture, and a desire to communicate the gospel both in evangelism and social reform. Evangelicals are those who believe the gospel is to be experienced personally, defined biblically, and communicated passionately' (Robert K. Johnston, *The Variety of American Evangelicalism* (1991, 261).

It is, however, important to understand what is, and what is not, being suggested here. Each of these three gospel affirmations will be developed by evangelicals in a variety of ways. Evangelical Lutherans, for example, will make their authoritative appeal to the *gospel* of scripture while evangelical Presbyterians will root their theology in the *scripture* of the gospel. But ultimate appeal will always be made to or through authoritative biblical teaching.

Secondly, such a listing of evangelical Christianity's central convictions will be ordered differently depending on one's particular theological tradition. Those from pietistic and Pentecostal church communities, for example, will move in their theology from *Holy Spirit to *Word, from life to truth. Thus, in the Evangelical Covenant Church, the primary question has been, 'How is your walk with the Lord?' Those from Reformed and Baptist contexts will begin with one's knowledge of God through scripture and then turn to the experiential dimensions of the faith. They move from Word to Spirit, from truth to life.

Thirdly, evangelicalism's core beliefs will be reformulated contextually by those in the worldwide evangelical family. The foundational, soteriological, and missiological aspects of evangelical theology have always found new voice among different peoples and in different times. To give but one example, evangelical Christians in north-east Thailand, where Confucian teaching concerning a 'works-righteousness' pervades the culture, have focused their theology of conversion exclusively on the *grace of God, not wanting one's human response to be considered an achievement.

Regardless of nuance, however, evangelicals are known worldwide for a triad of beliefs and practices the wider contemporary church has tended to undervalue or challenge—personal conversion, biblical authority, evangelical witness. Here are evangelicalism's axiological convictions.

There are those who, while accepting this threefold description of what is essential to evangelicalism, would add one or two other elements. Some would define evangelicalism to include the importance of a spiritually transformed life. Here might be mentioned the ongoing, transformative work of the Holy Spirit, or personal holiness, or Christian *freedom, or perhaps the importance of Christian community. Others would want evangelicalism's core commitments to include certain fundamental doctrines—human sinfulness, the virgin birth, Christ's substitutionary Atonement, the bodily Resurrection, the personal return of Christ, and so on. What is assumed in such enumerations is that there is a relatively fixed body of doctrine which can be referenced as summarizing basic, biblical truth.

Such extensions to evangelicalism's core convictions concerning 'heart, head, and hands' are affirmed in principle by all evangelicals. Evangelicals desire their Christian faith to be behaviourally expressed and biblically defined. A life of holiness and a set of theological convictions (what Wesley called our 'knowledge and vital piety') are the natural implications of such commitments. But the particular formulations of these additional descriptors remain contested within evangelicalism.

Those who tend towards the credal in their descriptions of either evangelical truth or piety often fail to give adequate account of evangelicalism's range. For example, some charismatics and Pentecostals define the work of the Spirit in ways that exclude others who are less 'Spirit-filled'. (The early 'signs and wonders' movement made this mistake.) Similarly, some Reformed evangelicals limit their understanding of the Atonement in ways that exclude those in the holiness tradition. One particularly egregious example of this is a Reformed theologian's dismissal of 19th-century evangelist Charles Finney as a foe of evangelicalism. Both doctrine and Christian living remain essential for the whole of evangelicalism, but particular formulations of these remain disparate among evangelicals.

Historically

The word 'evangelical' derives from the biblical term *euaggelion* (gospel, good news) and is thus appropriately used to describe all Christians. It has, however, been used in three historical eras to delineate particular 'protest' movements within wider Christianity.

At the time of the Reformation in the 16th century, the term came to be used to describe those Protestants who held to *justification by grace through faith and to the final authority of scripture. (These are labelled the material and formal principles of Reformation theology.) Rather than base their theology on the church's tradition, the reformers considered the *euaggelion* their standard. If 'the priesthood of all believers' is added to *sola gratia* and *sola scriptura*, one hears already in the reformers' theology the triad of beliefs that have become evangelicalism's continuing centre.

Two notes need to be added here. When understood against the backdrop of the Reformation, the term 'evangelical' is largely equivalent with 'Protestant' and is used as such in parts of the world. In Latin America, *evangelico* has often simply meant Protestant, perhaps because Protestants have been until the last quarter of the 20th century a small protest group against the dominant Roman Catholic church. As the Pentecostal church has burgeoned, however, additional distinctions among Protestants are now beginning to be noted. Similarly, the word *evangelisch* is used to label German Protestants, especially Lutherans.

Secondly, the Reformation gave rise to two divergent traditions: the *reformatio* and the *restitutio*. Both the reformers and the restitutionists (the radical reformers) 'protested' against aspects of the Catholic tradition, grounding authority in scripture and salvation simply in grace through faith. In this sense, they together are the precursors of modern evangelicalism. But those in the *restitutio* tradition approach scripture as a source book or divine code for restoring the original purity of the church. They are, thus, more radical in their ecclesiology than the reformers. Moreover, they can be seen as less *Augustinian in their view of human nature, valuing human initiative and involvement in the soteriological process and denying forensic righteousness. Today, both the Anabaptist and the Campbellite churches continue these *restitutio* emphases while belonging to the modern-day evangelical movement.

A second use of the term 'evangelical' looks back to the 17th, 18th, and 19th centuries and embraces the Pietists (Francke and Spener) and the Puritans (Owen and Edwards), the Methodists (Wesley) and the revivalists (Finney). If the primary focus of the reformers was on soteriology, here the emphasis is on a vital Christian experience and an active mission in the world. If the children of the reformers fail to stress the importance of religious experience in doing theology, the Pietists and Methodists ground their theology there.

For these evangelicals, what is important is one's new life in Christ. Their focus is on sanctification, on empowerment by the Holy Spirit, and on acts of love. Prayer, bible study, charitable activity, a life separated from immorality and 'worldly' pleasure, missionary endeavours, education, social activism—Pietists stress a practical Christian lifestyle. We might call these evangelicals Christian pragmatists. Like their forebears, they have turned from scholastic debate to conducting revivals, deepening discipleship, and reforming society. Conservative Methodists, Baptists, Scandinavian Pietists, the holiness churches, even Pentecostals—such evangelical movements trace their roots to these earlier renewals.

A third historical expression of the term 'evangelical' is associated with 20th-century American fundamentalism. If 16th-century evangelicals focused on the way of salvation, and those in the next centuries on a deepening of spirituality particularly through a renewed sense of mission, evangelicalism's early 20th-century expression centred on the bible as the source of religious *authority. Thus, the soteriological, missional, and foundational dimensions of evangelicalism's core belief structure each find priority within a particular historical model.

American fundamentalism continued evangelicalism's posture as a protest movement. But whereas the reformers were reacting to error in the Catholic church and the Pietists and revivalists to a perceived dead orthodoxy in the Protestant churches, fundamentalists saw as their target the modern scepticism of the *Enlightenment as manifest in *liberals in the church and secularists in the broader society. Such modernists exalted science over religion, particularly as they accepted biblical criticism. To an aggressive commitment to soul-winning, fundamentalists thus wedded a militant defensiveness concerning literal interpretations of the bible.

Key to the early fundamentalists' battle was their commitment to the final authority of scripture as evidenced in a traditional interpretation of its account of the *creation of the world. When the fight turned against them, fundamentalists retreated from public life and separated from what they believed to be an apostate church. Dispensational pre-millennialism provided theological support for their separatism, as well as for their anti-intellectualism and societal non-involvement.

This description of evangelicalism's history is widely accepted by students of evangelicalism. However, the use which one makes of this history has been the occasion for ongoing controversy. Central to the discussion has been the debate between two evangelical historians, George Marsden and Donald Dayton. Put most simply, those who have found in the 20th-century modernist—fundamentalist debate the context for the rise of modern evangelicalism have tended to take a more intellectualized approach (scripture has been the touchstone). They have most often been oriented towards a reformed theology, particularly, that of the Old *Princeton. A 'conservative–liberal' paradigm for evaluation has been the result. Scholars from the Methodist, holiness, and Pentecostal traditions have sometimes attempted an alternative reading, concentrating on evangelicalism's spirituality. They have more often used a paradigm of 'orthodoxy–radicalism.' Neither perspective needs to be understood exclusively, both readings being in fact helpful. Evangelicals can be understood as combining a commitment to biblical truth with a focus on the Christian life—on personal conversion, spiritual renewal, and active service and witness.

Contemporary evangelicalism

By the 1940s, some fundamentalists began to distance themselves from the militancy and defensiveness that plagued the movement. These neo-evangelicals sought reform on three fronts. They rejected their colleagues' separatist ecclesiology and instead favoured greater dialogue with the whole church; they sought to move beyond a prevalent anti-intellectualism as they began new seminaries and reshaped existing ones; and they opposed the cultural isolationism and escapism which had characterized the previous generation of fundamentalist evangelicals, seeking societal involvement instead. Carl F. H. Henry was the first to express this agenda clearly in The Uneasy Conscience of Modern Fundamentalism (1947). Modernism and theological liberalism remained the 'enemy', but the battle would be waged in new arenas. Present-day evangelicals such as theologian David Wells and sociologist James Davison Hunter continue this agenda of first-generation evangelicalism into the present.

By the mid-1960s, a new generation of evangelicals emerged who no longer had as their agenda reforming fundamentalism. Arising worldwide from all three historical strands of evangelicalism (reformational, pietistic, and fundamentalistic), these more progressive evangelicals were uncomfortable with what Edward Carnell labelled evangelicalism's regnant 'status by negation'. They sought new ways in their contemporary scholarship to relate orthodox Christianity to modern scientific thought, particularly through biblical criticism, *psychology, and *anthropology.

For many of these second-generation evangelicals, 'inerrancy' no longer seemed the best language with which to speak of biblical authority. A concern with *apologetics and a desire to root out *heresy largely gave way to a desire for a more robust, contextually sensitive proclamation of the gospel, through both word and deed. In still more recent decades, progressive evangelicals have more actively encouraged *dialogue with a wider Christianity; explored ecclesial and community-based theological discourse; and recognized certain insights from modern and postmodern thought, even while maintaining a commitment to an active, personal, biblical faith. David Hubbard and John Stott are representative figures of this more progressive evangelicalism.

As modern-day evangelicalism enters its third generation, issues such as the role of *women in the church and the home, the utility of a wide range of biblical critical methods, the nature of evangelical social ethics, the desirability of ecumenical dialogue, the nature of God's responsiveness to human initiative, the place of the Spirit in life and witness, the use of other traditions in theological formation (for example, post-liberal, process, Orthodox), and the value and limitations of contextual theology continue to spark controversy.

Given current debates, some have wondered if the evangelical coalition is not breaking apart. But evangelical unity has always proven elusive with regard to particular theological issues. This is perhaps to be expected of any 'protest' movement. The edges of evangelicalism will remain fuzzy and particular issues and doctrines will spark controversy, but evangelicals will continue to be distinguished within the wider Christian communion by a cluster of commonly held affirmations. Evangelicals remain those who have (1) a personal faith in Jesus Christ, (2) a belief in the bible as final authority, and (3) a vital commitment to Christian mission.

Robert K. Johnston

Bebbington, David, Evangelicalism in Modern Britain (1989).

Carnell, Edward John, The Case for Orthodox Theology (1959).

Dayton, Donald, and Johnston, Robert K. (eds.), The Variety of American Evangelicalism (1991).

Dayton, Donald, Discovering an Evangelical Heritage (1976).

Elwell, Walter (ed.), Handbook of Evangelical Theologians (1993).

Henry, Carl F. H., The Uneasy Conscience of Modern Fundamentalism (1947).

Hunter, James Davison, Evangelicalism: The Coming Generation (1987).

Johnston, Robert K., Evangelicals at an Impasse (1978).

McGrath, Alister, Evangelicalism and the Future of Christianity (1995).

Magnuson, Norris, and Travis, William, American Evangelicalism: An Annotated Bibliography (1990).

Marsden, George, Understanding Fundamentalism and Evangelicalism (1991).

Noll, Mark, Between Faith and Criticism (1986).

Noll, Mark, Bebbington, David, and Rawlyk, George (eds.), Evangelicalism (1994).

Quebedeaux, Richard, The Young Evangelicals (1974).

Rawlyk, George, and Noll, Mark (eds.), Amazing Grace: Evangelicalism in Australia, Britain, Canada and the United States (1993).

Sweet, Leonard (ed.), The Evangelical Tradition in America (1984).

Weber, Timothy P., 'Fundamentalism Twice Removed', in Jay Dolan and James Wind (eds.), New Dimensions in American Religious History (1993).

Wells, David F., and Woodbridge, John D. (eds.), The Evangelicals (1975).

evangelism. The whole *mission of Jesus is summed up in his own declaration that he was sent to proclaim the 'good news' (*euaggelion*) of the *Kingdom of God (Luke 4: 18). The character of his ministry expresses the nature of mission, founded as it is in the yearning love of God: it is like a fisher of men, like a shepherd seeking lost *sheep, like a mother caring for her children, like a merchant seeking after treasure, like a woman frantically searching for a lost coin, and like a father aching for a wandering son.

Two shifts of meaning in the concept of '*gospel' are discernible in the *New Testament. First, the 'good news' was the message which Jesus himself brought. He came 'preaching the gospel of God and saying "The time is fulfilled and the Kingdom of God is at hand, repent and believe the gospel" ' (Mark 1: 14). His call to repentance (Greek *metanoia*) meaning a change of mind or direction, implied that those first believers were invited to turn their backs on the old life and to follow Jesus Christ as his *disciples.

However, the cross and Resurrection formed the watershed in the growth of the church. From these momentous events the *apostles did not merely repeat what Jesus said—they preached Jesus himself. For them, he was the gospel and the kingdom. Thus, Paul later proclaimed, possibly citing an early baptismal confession, 'If you confess with your mouth that Jesus is Lord and believe in your heart that God raised him from the dead, you will be saved.'

The 'good news', then, is that through the life, death, and Resurrection of Jesus Christ God has reconciled humankind to himself and has established his kingdom of righteousness, love, and peace. The responsibility of the church is to 'preach the gospel to all the nations' and to call people to baptism (Matt. 28: 18).

The church has never treated evangelism as merely '*preaching' the gospel. It is certainly true that *apologists, missionaries, and evangelists have been significant channels of proclamation through which people have been brought to baptism. Indeed, every Christian is called to share in the church's task of making disciples. All the gospels include the commission to evangelize the world: Matt 28: 18; Mark 13: 10; Luke 24: 47–9; John 20: 21. While the task is entrusted in the first instance to the apostles, it is towards the entire church that the command is directed. Whilst not everybody is called to be an evangelist all are expected to be witnesses (Greek word-stem *martur* from which the word '*martyr' comes).

But evangelism cannot be sharply divided off from God's total activity in reconciling and redeeming all things—which theologians call 'the mission of God' (*missio Dei*). Matthew's treatment of the ministry of Jesus reveals three clear elements: teaching in the synagogues, preaching the good news of the kingdom, and *healing all kinds of diseases (Matt. 9: 35). The *compassion of Christ for the sick, the poor, the downtrodden, and the helpless is the key to God's mission and helps us to hold word and action together. As Pope Paul VI's apostolic exhortation *Evangelii Nuntiandi* (*On Evangelization in the Modern World*) puts it: 'evangelization consists of liberation from everything that oppresses us'. This includes not only the bondage of *sin but all that oppresses human beings and stops them responding fully to God's love. The Exhortation calls on Christians to engage in God's mission: 'The first means of evangelization is the witness of an authentically Christian life … the witness of poverty and detachment, of freedom in the face of the powers of this world, in short, the witness of *sanctity.'

And the form of sharing in God's mission or evangelization may vary according to the needs of those to whom the gospel is lovingly put. For some it will be in terms of 'presence' as we sit with a dying or troubled person; for others it will take the form of teaching and nurture as through many different ways the faith is taught; and for others it will be the sacrificial care for the sick, the physically and mentally handicapped. And the most basic way of all will be through the devoted care of priests and people in maintaining church life, administering the sacraments, and 'being there' for people wherever there is human need. Indeed, the evangelistic power of the worship of the church should never be underestimated.

Mission, then, is wider than evangelism although it includes it. God's mission is to encompass all and bring all things to him: 1 Corinthians 15: 20–8; Colossians 1: 20. Mission denotes the total activity of the church as it reaches out into the world. Such is the interrelatedness of evangelism and mission that we can say that 'evangelism which ignores the poor and marginalized and mission which fails to call people to baptism and new life fall short of Jesus' own practice'. Contemporary distinction between the terms 'evangelism' and 'evangelization' is hard to convey neatly in theological terms although it does remind us of the multifaceted nature of our task. *Evangelism* may be understood as the task of proclaiming Christ in word and deed, whereas *evangelization* suggests the process as people are led on that journey and *pilgrimage towards Christ. Whatever word is chosen, all Christians are called to 'witness' to the love of God shown in Jesus Christ who came to establish the kingdom of God.   **George L. Carey**

Abraham, W., *The Logic of Evangelism* (1989).
Bosch, D., *Transforming Mission* (1991).
Green, M., *Evangelism Through the Local Church* (1990).
Moltmann, J., *The Church in the Power of the Spirit* (1975).
Paul VI, *Evangelii Nuntiandi* (1975).

Eve illustrates well the way in which Christian thought is often shaped around persons and narratives rather than concepts. Though she makes only a brief appearance in the bible, she has attained an almost archetypal significance in Christian cultures. Within theology, the figure of Eve has had particular significance in relation to thought on *womanhood and the origins of *evil.

In Genesis 2–3, Eve is painted in both light and dark shades, the one always serving as counterpoint to the other. Identified at first simply as 'woman' (Gen. 2: 23), thus establishing her generic connection with all women, she is part of God's good *creation, a companion fit for *Adam, destined to be 'one flesh' with him (Gen. 2: 24). Tempted by the serpent, however, the woman and the *man disobey God's will. Together they are cursed and exiled from the garden. Yet even at this darkest moment, east of Eden, some light returns. The woman is given her name 'Eve', 'because she was the *mother of all living' (Gen. 3: 20). As mother of the human race, Eve is able to serve God's purposes despite her *sin.

Though subsequent Christian reflection on Eve has reproduced both the light and dark shades of the Genesis narrative, the darkness has often overshadowed the light. Generally speaking, the most negative reflections appear within the context of writings which seek to justify female subordination to men. 1 Timothy sets the tone by (1) suggesting that Eve's creation out of Adam implies that female subordination was part of God's creative will, and (2) attributing greater blame for the *Fall to Eve than to Adam (1 Tim. 2: 13–14). Some of the most misogynist writings about women within the Christian tradition recapitulate this early reflection on Eve, including Tertullian's notorious description of woman as 'the *Devil's gateway', and Jankyn's comment on Eve in Geoffrey Chaucer's *Wife of Bath's Prologue*: 'that womman was the los of al mankynde'.

It would be wrong, however, to suggest that Eve has been made to bear the whole weight of blame and guilt for the Fall throughout the Christian tradition. In the context of reflection on Christ's redeeming work, for example, it tends to be Adam who is identified as the guilty party through being made the type of Christ 'the second Adam'. Such *typological symmetry was also applied to Eve in two ways. First, Eve, mother of the living, has been seen as the type of the *church, mother of the saved. Second, Eve has been presented as the type of *Mary, a symmetry which finds its most concise expression in a wordplay on the Latin 'Ave' ('Hail!') of Gabriel's greeting to Mary construed as a reversal of the disobedience of 'Eva'.

A more positive interpretation of Eve (and so of woman) appears sporadically within Christian thought, usually within reflection on Eve's prelapsarian graces (as in *Milton's *Paradise Lost*), or on her postlapsarian role as mother of all living (as in the thought of the *Reformers). It is only since the 19th century, however, that attempts have been made to present Eve as a wholly admirable figure. Such attempts have been particularly prominent within *feminist theology and *biblical exegesis, beginning with Elizabeth Cady Stanton's interpretation of the Genesis narratives in the *Woman's Bible* (1895–8). More recently, in *God and the Rhetoric of Sexuality* (1978), the biblical scholar Phyllis Trible has made an influential attempt to reread the Genesis narrative in a way that emphasizes the mutuality of the two sexes.

Christian feminists have been prominent in the attempt to rehabilitate the figure of Eve because of their awareness of Eve's wider significance for Christian understandings of womanhood. Many feminist theologians believe that a more positive view of woman necessitates a more positive understanding of Eve. Yet it seems artificial to separate the story of Eve from the wider story of human origins and the origin of sin. Much feminist theology merely glosses over these wider issues, betraying an unreflective dependence upon a post-Romantic belief in original goodness and progress rather than in sin and Fall. The more difficult but more important challenge for future Christian thought is to interpret Eve in ways which are not collusive with the male domination of woman, yet which are also nuanced enough to do justice to the subtle lights and shades of the Genesis narrative's depiction of the human condition.

Linda Woodhead

McColley, D. K., *Milton's Eve* (1983).

Meyers, C., *Discovering Eve: Ancient Hebrew Women in Context* (1998).

Norris, P., *The Story of Eve* (1998).

Phillips, J., *Eve: The History of an Idea* (1984).

Trible, Phyllis, *God and the Rhetoric of Sexuality* (1978).

evil, problem of. Evil has often been cited as strong evidence against the existence of *God. For if God were as perfect as Christians traditionally have maintained, would he not produce a universe perfect in every respect? The evil our *world contains, then, shows us that there is no God.

Though the core of the problem of evil can be simply stated, it can be fleshed out in several different ways. Some critics of theism, claiming that the existence of evil is utterly incompatible with the existence of God, contend that evil allows us to fashion a solid *deductive* argument for the non-existence of God. Other opponents of theism, though admitting that evil may not be literally incompatible with God's existence, insist that it renders it unlikely that there is such a deity. For these critics, then, there is a good *inductive* (or *probabilistic*) argument from evil against theism. Many people, however, find the challenge posed by evil to be a matter not of investigating theoretical questions but of maintaining a vibrant faith and trust in God given the evils they actually experience. This struggle might be referred to as the *experiential* problem of evil.

In this article, each of these three variants of the problem—the deductive, the inductive, and the experiential—is examined. Our initial and chief concern, though, is with the deductive argument, for this form of the problem has occasioned both the strongest attacks upon and the most innovative defences of traditional *Christianity.

The deductive argument from evil

In its simplest form, the deductive argument from evil claims that there is no possibility that God exists if evil exists. Surely there are possible worlds (that is, ways in which things could be) in which evil is absent? So why did God not make such a world? If he is *omnipotent, he surely had the power to do so; if *omniscient, the requisite knowledge could hardly be lacking; and if perfectly good, he certainly would have wanted such a world. The presence of evil thus conclusively proves that there is no God.

This basic argument can be modified in two principal directions. Some proponents maintain it is not the mere existence of evil, but the exorbitant amount of it (as evidenced, say, in the *Holocaust) that causes the problem. Others point not to the amount of evil, but rather to particularly horrendous instances of it (such as the torture and death of a small child) as being incompatible with the God Christians profess.

Theists have offered many responses to these deductive arguments. Some have denied that evil exists, either because evil is merely a negation (the absence of goodness), or because evil is merely an appearance, and what seems evil to us would not so appear from a wider perspective. Other theists have denied one or another of the three divine attributes (omniscience, omnipotence, or perfect goodness) upon which the deductive argument is based. But the dominant theme among Christian apologists has long been that God allows evil for the sake of some greater good. And the good most often cited is human *freedom. The importance and value of free will, they suggest, provide us with the best defence against the deductive argument.

The free will defence

Why might freedom be seen as offering such a defence? Because of the intimate connection between freedom and *morality. Beings who are not genuinely free, it is maintained, are incapable of acting either virtuously or viciously. Robots who do as they are programmed are not fit subjects of moral praise or moral blame. Had

God made a world containing only such robotic extensions of his will, he would have sacrificed something of enormous value: free beings who on their own choose to do good. Perhaps God concluded (the free will defence continues) that the existence of such creatures was too great a good to forgo, and so decided to make people with free will. Once he had made this decision, though, the possibility of evil became inescapable. For if creatures are truly free in a morally significant sense, then the decision to do good is theirs, not God's. The existence of evil suggests that some of God's creatures used their freedom poorly, but that (the argument concludes) is the price God had to pay to create a world with virtuous creatures.

Critics of this defence have offered a number of responses. Some question the libertarian notion of freedom (roughly, the claim that genuine freedom is incompatible with external or prior internal causal determination of an agent's actions) that is presupposed by the free will defence. However, since this notion of freedom has deep and widespread (though hardly universal) support among Christians, this criticism has limited effect. Two more lines of attack, though, seem more promising. First, some maintain that the free will defence offers an explanation for the existence only of *moral* evil—of evil resulting from vicious free actions. Since much of the evil we encounter (for example, human and animal suffering connected with natural disasters) cannot plausibly be seen as the consequence of human freedom, appealing to the value of freedom fails to justify such evil. Secondly, others ask, is the existence even of moral evil really explained by the free will defence? Are there not worlds in which God's creatures consistently use their freedom correctly? As John Mackie famously wrote, 'If there is no logical impossibility in a man's freely choosing the good on one, or on several occasions, there cannot be a logical impossibility in his freely choosing the good on every occasion' (1955, p. 209). But if there are worlds where moral virtue but no moral vice is exhibited, then a good God surely would have created one of them. 'Clearly', concludes Mackie, 'his failure to avail himself of this possibility is inconsistent with his being both omnipotent and wholly good.'

These two challenges to the free will defence are serious indeed. But Alvin Plantinga has argued that they are not fatal. With regard to the first point, it is possible that *all* evil is moral evil. Much pain and suffering clearly are the result of human malevolence; could it not be that the remaining evil, which appears to be non-moral, actually results from the vicious activities of other, non-human free creatures—for example, of *devils?

In response to the second criticism, Plantinga does not deny the possibility of worlds containing free creatures who always act virtuously. Rather, he questions the assumption that an omnipotent God would necessarily be able to create any world that is possible. If a creature is significantly free, then the situation in which it is placed does not determine any particular action on its part; it can decide in that situation to do good, or to do evil. But even if God knows how a particular creature would act in a certain situation, there is a world God cannot create. Suppose God sees that Adam, if created in Eden in certain circumstances, circumstances leaving him free with respect to eating the apple, would freely decide to do so. In that case, God sees that the world in which Adam in those circumstances freely *refrains* from eating the apple is one he cannot bring about, because Adam would not co-operate with him in

making it actual. Worlds, then, can be possible but not *feasible*—that is, not such that God can create them.

Why is the distinction between feasible and possible worlds relevant for our second objection to the free will defence? Because God could not simply decide which worlds were, and which were not, feasible. Feasibility is a function of what free creatures would do, and what they would do is for those creatures, not for God, to decide. Hence, it could be that all those worlds in which free beings always do what is right were infeasible—they simply were not among the worlds God could decide to bring about. Thus, it may be that God had no choice, if he wanted to make a world with moral good, but to make one that included evil too.

This type of free will defence can evidently be extended to counter deductive arguments based on the amount or particular types of evil. Perhaps God saw that, though there are better worlds with less evil or fewer horrendous evils than ours, all such worlds are infeasible. In other words, perhaps he saw that ours is the best (or among the best) of the feasible worlds.

The inductive argument from evil

Though elements of the free will defence (for example, the assumption made in many versions of the defence that it can be known what free beings would do if placed in various circumstances) have elicited heated debate, there is a general consensus that the deductive argument constitutes much less of a threat to Christian belief than was commonly believed in earlier generations. But this hardly means that evil is no longer viewed as a problem. As many see it, the means of ushering the deductive argument from centre stage have simply shifted the spotlight to the inductive argument from evil.

Consider, for example, two of the claims made in support of the free will defence: that apparently non-moral evils might be the result of demonic activity, and that all those better worlds with much less evil than ours might be infeasible. Even many who would agree that these are possibilities, and that they tend to cripple the deductive argument, would insist that they are extremely unlikely possibilities. Evil, then, still provides us with significant reason to renounce Christianity, for it renders the existence of God exceedingly unlikely.

Theists have taken two general approaches in responding to this inductive argument. Some contest the claim that the probability that God exists, given the existence of evil, is low. Belief in demonic forces, for example, may be less popular now than in previous ages, but do we really have good reason to deny the maleficent endeavours of Satan and his understudies? More generally, is not calculating probabilities in this area simply impossible? Probability theory may offer us pellucid answers to questions (for example, concerning the odds of various poker hands) where the necessary evidence is on the table and where its connection to the issue at hand is patent. But in this case, our evidence is so limited, and the connections so obscure, that no honest investigator could view evil as clearly rendering God's existence improbable.

On the other hand, some theists would grant that evil does tend to make questionable the existence of God. Were evil our *only* relevant evidence, we would indeed have to judge Christianity improbable. But, they insist, once we add to our evidence base the order, beauty, and goodness that the world also exhibits, we see that we have no reason to think it improbable, given *everything* that we know, that God exists.

The experiential problem of evil

Even should the deductive and inductive arguments from evil be deemed unsuccessful, the experiential problem remains. For many theists have found that dismantling the theoretical arguments from evil does not save them from floundering in feelings of estrangement and abandonment in the wake of particularly crushing instances of evil.

In many ways, this is probably the most grievous form of the problem of evil. Philosophical reflection, pastoral assistance, continued participation in the shared life of the Christian community, and private prayer may eventually serve to restore one's sense of God's presence, but clearly there is no magic formula. Christians profess that *faith and *hope are gifts; nowhere, perhaps, is this more evident than in such cases.   **Thomas P. Flint**

Adams, Robert, 'Middle Knowledge and the Problem of Evil', *American Philosophical Quarterly*, 14 (1977).
Dostoevsky, Fyodor, *The Brothers Karamazov* (1879–80) ET (1992).
Howard-Snyder, Daniel (ed.), *The Evidential Argument from Evil* (1996).
Mackie, John, 'Evil and Omnipotence', *Mind*, 64 (1955).
Plantinga, Alvin, *The Nature of Necessity* (1974).
Wiesel, Elie, *Night* (1960).

evolution ('descent with modification'). The theory of evolution has been traced to ancient Greece (Thales, Anaximander, and others), appears in Gregory of Nyssa and *Augustine, and was assumed in the 18th century by Leibniz, Maupertuis, and Diderot. None of these thinkers was truly an evolutionist in the modern sense: although they accepted progress from 'lower' to 'higher' forms of life, they did not profess biological change (and extinction) as now understood, because it was generally believed that the earth was either unchangeable or relatively young. Only in the later 18th century did independent calculations of the earth's age extend it significantly beyond biblical reckoning, hence allowing time for gradual change.

Jean Baptiste Lamarck (1744–1829) was the first serious protagonist of converting the long-acknowledged hierarchy of beings into a line of descent, but he had no clear proposal of a mechanism for this process; Charles Darwin (1809–82) claimed he did not gain a single idea from Lamarck. Notwithstanding, Lamarck provoked evolutionary thinking, notably in France by Cuvier (1769–1832), in Austria by Unger (1800–70), and in Britain by Darwin's grandfather, Erasmus Darwin (1731–1802), and particularly by Robert Chambers (1802–83). Chambers's *Vestiges of the Natural History of Creation* (1844) argued that God had instituted laws which had produced evolutionary change, and sparked controversy which paved the way for *On the Origin of Species* (1859).

Charles Darwin's major contribution to evolution was to suggest a plausible mechanism (natural selection) by which adaptation could take place without divine intervention. Since adaptation (the precise fit of organism to environment) was the observation underlying much of the prevailing *deism (summarized in William Paley's *Natural Theology* (1802)), Darwin's ideas were a mortal blow to this way of thinking and the idea of God as 'Divine Watchmaker'. Christianity, however, cannot be equated with deism. In-

deed, Darwinian ideas were rapidly accepted by many Christians, especially evangelicals who saw evolutionary mechanisms as compelling evidence for *providence. Frederick Temple (archbishop of Canterbury 1896–1902) followed Chambers by asserting in his 1884 Bampton Lectures that Darwin had not damaged Christianity since God had made the laws which produced evolutionary change. In *Lux Mundi* (1889), Aubrey Moore declared that Darwin had done the work of a friend in the guise of a foe, by destroying the credibility of belief in an absentee landlord who interfered in his estate on rare occasions, and brought God back into the world he had made. Evolution accounted coherently for so many disparate facts (fossil sequences, geographical distributions of organisms, vestigial organs, biological classification) that no serious doubts about its occurrence have had wide credence since that time. Even the well-known debate in 1860 between Samuel Wilberforce and Thomas Henry Huxley was not primarily about *science versus *religion; it was an attack by the bishop on anything that seemed to legitimize progress and by Huxley on authority and privilege. The myth of a persisting science–faith conflict centred on evolution was illegitimately but sadly successfully sustained by two American books, J. W. Draper's *History of the Conflict between Science and Religion* (1874) and A. D. White's *History of the Warfare of Science with Theology in Christendom* (1896).

Although the *fact* of evolution has not been challenged seriously since the 1870s, there are continuing and proper scientific debates about the relative importance of different evolutionary *mechanisms*. In popular writing, these are frequently and wrongly portrayed as 'doubts about evolution'. There have been four main periods of debate:

1. Objections expressed in Darwin's own time and largely anticipated and dealt with in *On the Origin of Species*, about the apparent rarity of species transitions, the effectiveness of natural selection, and the origin of novelty;

2. Biometricians and Mendelists (or geneticists), following the rediscovery of Mendel's work in 1900, and the finding that genetic changes (mutations or saltations) were abrupt and large in effect, implying that evolution was driven by means other than slow adjustments in the genetic material;

3. Palaeontologists versus geneticists in the 1920s and 1930s, with long-continued evolutionary trends in fossil sequences being claimed as evidence for an internal organizing force (*orthogenesis*), under various guises including *Teilhard de Chardin's later speculations, since they seemed incompatible with the random and largely deleterious changes described by geneticists. This phase culminated in the neo-Darwinian (or neo-Mendelian) synthesis (named from Julian Huxley's *Evolution: The Modern Synthesis* (1942)) prompted by work on the effects of gene substitution by R. A. Fisher, E. B. Ford, Theodosius Dobzhansky, and others, which showed that previous theories were based on misleading interpretations from artificial laboratory conditions. Unfortunately the difficulties and associated unfashionability of Darwinism between 1900 and 1930 appeared in three widely read histories of science (by Nordenskiöld (1928), Singer (1931), and Radl, ET (1931)), resulting in the synthesis being commonly ignored or misunderstood;

4. Neutralism versus selectionism: quantitative biochemical methods of measuring amounts of variation from 1966 onwards implied more variation than could apparently be tolerated by selec-

tion. This was resolved by a better understanding of the interface between genetics and *ecology.

The conclusion from more than a century of research and argument is that Darwin's ideas have had to be little changed from their original formulation, although they have been refined and expanded through incorporating discoveries in a range of disciplines. It has been a failure to integrate ideas that has led to many disputes over evolution, well illustrated by the neutralism–selection debate, and by current arguments over punctuated equilibrium (evolution in occasional spurts, rather than long-continued and progressive change). Leaving aside scientific debates which are only relevant because they are sometimes falsely used to claim uncertainty among scientists, there are four areas of disagreement that impinge on Christian thought:

1. *Philosophy.* It is sometimes mooted that the theory of natural selection is tautologous since 'survival of the fittest' means only that the fittest survive, which is a mere truism. This is no more than confusion about terminology: 'fitness' in biology is a measure of reproductive success, not health. More serious has been the assertion by Karl Popper that evolution is not truly scientific, because it is non-falsifiable. Popper later recognized that this was a product of an overrestrictive and artificial definition of science, and he later retracted it, accepting that different sciences have different methodologies.

2. *Human nature.* Traditionally *humans have been regarded as special creations, qualitatively distinct from other animals. However, we share 98.4 per cent of our DNA (or genes) with chimpanzees, and it is difficult to maintain that we do not share a common ancestry with other apes, particularly in the light of a reasonable fossil record for humankind. However, the significant point for Christians is that humans alone are in God's image, which should not be conceived in anatomical or genetic terms. It is an unresolved question whether this image evolved in the same way as other traits or was somehow imparted at a time in history. Humanists such as G. G. Simpson, J. S. Huxley, and C. H. Waddington do not disagree with Christians that we operate in a *moral realm very different from that of any other animal. There is no evidence for the suggestion of Richard Dawkins that culture and religion are determined by virus-like particles, 'memes'.

3. *Ethics.* It was long assumed (including by Darwin) that natural selection could foster only selfishness, and that altruistic behaviour could not therefore evolve as an adaptive trait. However J. B. S. Haldane showed in 1932 that if an organism behaved so as to increase the breeding success of its close relatives, the genes affecting the behaviour could increase in frequency in future generations even though it had a reduced success itself. In other words, altruism could be selected and spread within that family and its descendants. This idea was later formalized as 'inclusive fitness' or 'kin selection'. It achieved popularity (and notoriety) in E. O. Wilson, *Sociobiology* (1975), where he extrapolated from the inheritance of behaviour in (mainly) insects to human beings. He then expanded this naturalistic assumption in later works, and his thesis has been largely accepted by some ethicists as removing the need for any extrinsic or supernatural basis from ethics. This raises moral issues only if it is accepted that inherent tendencies cannot or should not be controlled by conscious will, that is if the person concerned has no choices. There is no evidence whatsoever for such determinism in humans. As knowledge about genes and gene action has grown, it has become increasingly possible to affect the expression of inherited traits in various ways. The notion of an irrevocable genetic determinism owes more to the imagination of such writers as Aldous Huxley (*Brave New World*) than to scientific understanding.

Likewise the idea that an evolutionary ethic can be derived from the course of evolution itself can be dismissed as yielding to a naturalistic fallacy. Although theists may claim that evolutionary change is subject to the providence of God, it is not true that such change indicates the proper basis for an ethic. Nor should it be assumed that evolutionary change (and by implication the inherited factors on which the change depends) should necessarily be assisted or opposed; on these grounds, genetical engineering is not intrinsically evil.

4. *Creationism.* A literal interpretation of the *Genesis *creation stories had become rare among both scientists and theologians well before 1900. Even the very conservative *Princeton theologian Charles Hodge, who coined the phrase 'What is Darwinism? It is Atheism', was not against evolution as such, but against the assumption that Darwinism demolished divinely controlled purpose: 'He [Darwin] denies design in any of the organisms in the vegetable or animal world … and it is the feature of his system which brings it into conflict not only with Christianity but with the fundamental principles of nature religion' (*What is Darwinism?* (1874), 176–7). Even the authors of the *Fundamentals* (1910–15) were largely agnostic about evolution. In his contribution, B. B. Warfield, unreserved apologist for the authority and inerrancy of the bible, wrote that evolution could supply a tenable 'theory of the method of divine providence' in the creation of mankind; he regarded *Calvin's understanding of the creation, 'including the origination of all forms of life, vegetable and animal alike, including doubtless the bodily form of man [as a] … very pure evolutionary scheme'.

Modern creationism seems to have clearer sociological than scientific or theological origins. In the USA it was partly a frustrated response in rural areas to technological progress elsewhere, linked with suspicion about intellectualism and encouraged by the social Darwinism of Herbert Spencer (1820–1903). Laws banning the teaching of evolution were passed in four states during the 1920s. In 1925 John Scopes, a schoolteacher, was tried under such a statute in Tennessee and found guilty. The negative publicity from this 'monkey' trial led to a retreat of organized creationism for 30 years until the publication of the *Genesis Flood* (1961) by theologian John Whitcomb and hydrologist Henry Morris. They argued that a worldwide flood had laid down most of the geological strata; the authors asserted 'the real issue is not the correctness of the interpretation of various geological data, but simply what God has revealed in His Word concerning these matters' (cited by Numbers, 1992: 207). This led to the founding of a Creation Research Society (1963) followed by an Institute for Creation Research (1972), dedicated to the spread of 'scientific creationism' and linked with demands for 'balanced treatment in the teaching of creation-science and evolution-science'. However, an Arkansas court ruled in 1984 that creation-science was religion and not science, and could not legally be taught in public (state) schools.

Creationists have concentrated their attacks on evolution mainly on philosophical grounds claiming that evolution is merely an *interpretation* of facts (or theory) and is a paradigm in the Kuhnian sense which may be overturned. Attempts to challenge scientific data (such as claims that the speed of light has changed through time or that radioactive dating of rocks is invalid) have not gained credence. In the 1990s, creationist sympathizers have argued for an Intelligent Design Theory on the grounds that known Darwinian mechanisms are inadequate to explain complex adaptations at the biochemical and cellular level. In principle this is no different to objections dealt with by Darwin himself and more recently demolished by Richard Dawkins.

Some argue that evolution excludes the possibility of a creator God; others that evolution cannot be true, since God is the creator. Most commentators deny that such an antithesis exists: traditional Christian understanding can affirm God as an active agent in the evolutionary process whilst at the same time acknowledging him by faith as creator (Heb. 11: 3). The most positive result of evolution–creation debates has been to destroy the credibility of the wholly transcendent God of deism, and hence focus attention on the interaction of God and his world; their most negative result has been to detract attention from the human role in creation care, and divert Christians from the task of responsible conservation (or sustainable development, as it has come to be known).

R. J. Berry

Berry, R. J., *Neo-Darwinism* (1982).

Clark, R. W., *The Survival of Charles Darwin* (1984).

Dawkins, R., *The Blind Watchmaker* (1986).

Godfrey, L. R. (ed.), *Scientists Confront Creationism* (1983).

Kitcher. P., *Abusing Science: The Case against Creationism* (1982).

Larson, E. J., *Summer for the Gods: The Scopes Trial and America's Continuing Debate over Science and Religion* (1997).

Livingstone, D. N., *Darwin's Forgotten Defenders: The Encounter between Evangelical Theology and Evolutionary Thought* (1987).

Mayr, E., *The Growth of Biological Thought* (1982).

Mayr, E., and Provine, W. B. (eds.), *The Evolutionary Synthesis* (1980).

Moore, J. R., *The Post-Darwinian Controversies* (1979).

Numbers, R. L., *The Creationists: The Evolution of Scientific Creationism* (1992).

Skelton, P. (ed.), *Evolution* (1993).

Ward, K., *God, Chance and Necessity* (1996).

Whitcomb, J. C., and Morris, H. M., *The Genesis Flood* (1961).

exegesis, see HERMENEUTICS.

Exercises of St Ignatius,

the first and still the standard basis for structuring a retreat, deriving from the saint's own guidelines (written between 1522 and 1541) for helping others in their *prayer. Ignatius Loyola's 'Spiritual Exercises' are enthusiastically welcomed by many as a classic foundation for the spirituality of an active life, even though others have associated them with an outdated and even harmful sequence of devotions. The use of military metaphor can be off-putting to modern sensibilities: Ignatius pictures Christ as the commander-in-chief of an army, calling men to fall in behind his flag. And there are meditations on *sin and *judgement, so out of harmony with the modern mood of holistic piety.

The originality of Ignatius' vision was that the receiver of the Exercises (whom Ignatius called the 'exercitant') should proceed at his or her own speed, and that the giver of the Exercises ('director') should adapt and modify the retreat according to individual need. The 'Spiritual Exercises' should authentically be given in private one-to-one discussions, not preached to a group. Above

all, they were never intended as a book to be read, but more as a folder of suggestions for the director.

The Exercises are divided into four 'weeks' of unequal length, and in their complete, original form they are 'made' over about 30 days in silent withdrawal from ordinary life. The 'weeks' follow a traditional rhythm of *spirituality, such as may be observed also in the *liturgical year: repentance for sin; meditations on the life of Christ; on his passion; and on his *Resurrection. Reflections on the exercitant's own life are interspersed, so that people sort out their priorities in the light of their relationship with God. The purpose of the Exercises, wrote Ignatius, is 'the ordering of one's life … in freedom from any ill-ordered attachment'.

Ignatius drew on earlier devotional traditions, such as the *Benedictine idea of spiritual reading, and the various ways of praying described by Ignatius are so broad that almost any prayer tradition finds an echo somewhere. But one particularly characteristic Ignatian method is the imaginative contemplation on a gospel scene: the exercitant pictures himself or herself to be present in a story from scripture, while imagining the sights, sounds, feelings, smells, and even tastes of the moment.

From the late 1970s there was an explosion of interest around the world in the 'Spiritual Exercises', with many adaptations and developments. In addition to the full Exercises and the 8-day directed retreat, there were shorter residential retreats, day retreats, weeks of directed prayer in parishes, and a host of books and tapes all owing some degree of influence to Ignatius. 'Ignatian spirituality' became one of the most popular approaches to prayer, not only among *Jesuits and Catholic religious, but among lay people of all denominations. **Margaret Hebblethwaite**

S. Ignatius of Loyola, *Personal Writings*, ed. J. A. Munitiz and P. Endean (1996).

Hebblethwaite, M., *Way of St Ignatius*, 3rd edn. (1999).

Ivens, M., *Understanding the Spiritual Exercises* (1998).

exile, the period of the Babylonian captivity of Judah during the 6th century BC. Despite first impressions, the boundaries of the exile are not easy to fix. The period begins with two deportations spaced a decade apart (*c.*597, 587 BC) and ends with the takeover of Babylon by Cyrus the Persian in 539, although this event seems to have had little immediate impact on those living in exile. 'Exile', then, refers both to the historical period—which is often said to be the defining moment for the Hebrew bible and constitutive for Judaism as a religious system—and to a symbol of spiritual alienation.

Two problems obscure its particular influence in Christian thought. First, already in the OT exile and restoration are bound up with the idea of the *exodus (cf. Jer. 23: 7–8; Ezek. 20: 33–8) with the result that the two themes are closely connected, sometimes almost fused, in later tradition. Second, 'exile' is deeply embedded in human experience in all times and places, further complicating the business of discerning what derives especially from the Babylonian exile of the bible.

The importance of the Babylonian exile is reflected in several ways in the NT. In Jesus' genealogy (Matt. 1: 11–12, 17) it provides the major structural element in historical terms. Amos 5: 27, which speaks of an 'exile beyond Damascus', becomes a 'removal beyond Babylon' in its citation in Stephen's speech (Acts. 7: 43). This association with Babylon holds special significance for the later development of 'exile' as metaphor. *Isaiah 13–14 (cf. Isa. 21: 1–10) and *Jeremiah 50–1 contain oracles against Babylon that provide a source for the apocalypse of *Revelation 17–18 and its frightening image of Babylon as the Great Whore (Rev. 18: 2). The combination of the metaphors of alien residence and 'Babylon' in 1 Peter (1: 2; 2: 2; 5: 13) helps to shape Christian identity and lifestyle (cf. Jas. 1: 1), a more positive role than in early Jewish usage (cf. e.g. 2 Macc. 1: 27).

Among the pseudepigraphical writings, the Jewish/Christian *Testaments of the Twelve Patriarchs* (2nd century AD) contain a significant thread of references to the exile. Eight of the twelve 'testaments' contain some reflection on the nature of exile, the reasons for it, and prospects following it. Usually, references to exile in the *Testaments* conform to the 'sin–exile–restoration' pattern. At times 'exile' refers to physical scattering or captivity; at other times it means estrangement not only from land but also from God.

*Augustine in his *City of God* contrasts the heavenly and earthly 'cities'. Although the Babylonian captivity is included in his historical survey of Jews and Gentiles (18. 25), Babylon more significantly serves as the prototype of the earthly *city of death and confusion (18. 42). Augustine makes the connection through Babylon to the Tower of Babel (Gen. 11: 1–9) which itself foreshadows the later city (the names in Hebrew are identical) and is also a symbol of alienation from God.

The Avignon *papacy (1308–78) was termed the 'Babylonian captivity' of the papacy by critics, notably *Dante and Petrarch, who preferred the papal court to reside in Rome. Here, the suggested parallel with the Judaean exile is not a strong one, and the negative theological judgement implied by the metaphor is contestable. However, it is important to notice the *symbolic value of the association even while precise historical parallels are lacking. This kind of terminology is most famously associated with *Luther's early work, *The Babylonian Captivity of the Church* (1520), which contains an attack on the Catholic doctrine of the *sacraments. Again, the analogy to the historic Judaean exile is rather loose, and Luther does not pursue it in the treatise. Still, Luther intended the title to associate the symbolism of captivity with his perception of 'the papacy in the kingdom of Babylon' (*Luther's Works*, xxxvi. 10).

Clearly, the symbol of alienation is at the forefront of Christian usage of the *metaphor of exile. This dimension has been authoritatively pursued by Northrop Frye in *The Great Code*. Frye perceives in the flow of biblical history a repeating pattern of falls and rises as, for example, Eden, the promised land, and Zion serve as points for descent into the wilderness, Egypt and Babylon respectively. Among these the Exodus event is 'the primary and model form' (p. 171). As these moments are identified in the bible itself, thus the move can be made from Israel in Egypt or the Jews in Babylon to the 'human situation generally' (p. 190). The narrative movements found in these shared metaphorical movements of descent and restoration symbolize wider human experience. Similarly, the condensed biblical history offered by Ernst Bloch (*Principle of Hope* (1986), ii. 496–9) makes a close connection between exodus and exile in contrasting mass exploitation and a utopian social order.

Use of the language of exile commonly neglects the aspect of restoration. It might seem that the call to develop a 'post-exilic' theology in post-*apartheid South Africa reverses this trend. Itumeleng J. Mosala, *liberation theologian from South Africa, resists this move. While he concedes that the release of Nelson Mandela was a harbinger of hope, he argues that changes in government do not necessarily bring deep-seated social change. It appears that alienation engendered by exile persists at many levels. This observation surfaces repeatedly in the OT theology of Walter Brueggemann for whom 'exile' is a guiding metaphor. Not only is the Hebrew bible itself a textual response to the historical exile, he claims, but 'exile' symbolizes social, moral, and cultural displacement and the dominance of false powers and values. The metaphor, then, reveals the danger inherent for 'aliens', which can be interpreted as the church in the *world, of exchanging their true identity conferred by God for that promoted by the dominant culture. In this way, 'exile' is not merely a historical datum, but a paradigm of the condition of modern faith communities.

David J. Reimer

Brueggemann, W., *Cadences of Home: Preaching Among Exiles* (1997).
Frye, Northrop, *The Great Code: The Bible and Literature* (1981).
Hollander, H. W., and de Jonge, M., *The Testaments of the Twelve Patriarchs: A Commentary* (1985).
Knibb, M. A., 'The Exile in the Literature of the Intertestamental Period', *Heythrop Journal*, 17 (1976), 253–72.
Mosala, I. J, 'Bible and Liberation in South Africa in the 1980s', in D. Jobling *et al.* (eds.), *The Bible and the Politics of Exegesis* (1991), 267–74.
Scott, J. M. (ed.), *Exile: Old Testament, Jewish, and Christian Conceptions* (1997).

existentialism describes a diffuse group of thinkers who take the existence of the single, individual human being as the starting-point of their philosophizing and theologizing. 'Existence' here is not mere factual existence but a qualitative type of existence described by Søren *Kierkegaard as 'becoming a self' and by Martin Heidegger (1889–1976) as 'authentic existence'. It is not a fixed quality given to each individual, but a *possibility* which the individual may or may not realize. This idea lies behind Sartre's (1905–80) (in)famous claim that 'existence precedes essence', meaning that there is no predetermined or God-given blueprint for human existence; human beings create themselves by choosing the self each wishes to become.

In taking the human subject as their starting-point, the existentialists stand in the Cartesian–*Kantian tradition, but, unlike *Descartes and Kant, they explore human subjectivity in the concrete situations and crises of everyday existence. This gives rise to one of the most characteristic features of existentialist thought, its concern with phenomena generally considered outside the domain of philosophy, such as anxiety, despair, finitude, guilt, alienation, and *death. These 'boundary-situations', as Karl Jaspers (1883–1969) calls them, have the potential to shake the individual out of absorption in the 'crowd' (Kierkegaard), the 'herd' (Nietzsche), or 'the They' (Heidegger), confronting him or her with the possibility of authenticity.

In its broadest sense, the term 'existentialist' is used to identify writers and thinkers who show such interest in concrete human existence, particularly its crises. Consequently, the term has been applied to such figures as Blaise *Pascal, regarded by many as a forerunner of existentialism, Fyodor *Dostoevsky, Albert Camus (1913–60), and a host of other writers. More narrowly the term is confined to those thinkers who have been influenced by Kierkegaard, justifiably considered the father of existentialism.

Kierkegaard presents a variety of existential possibilities and attempts to lead the reader to what he regards as the highest form of existence, Christian existence, by showing how other modes of existence ultimately break down. In the process he develops a series of concepts significant in existentialism, the most important of these probably being his concept of anxiety, which he describes as 'a sympathetic antipathy and an antipathetic sympathy' in which we are both drawn to and repelled by our freedom.

Existentialism after Kierkegaard divides into three camps. First, there are avowed *atheistic existentialists such as *Nietzsche, Sartre, and Camus. Some argue that this is the purest form of existentialism, for in rejecting God these thinkers seem to place even greater emphasis on human autonomy than their theistic counterparts. Secondly, thinkers such as Heidegger and Jaspers claim to be neither theistic nor atheistic. For Heidegger the *human being or *Dasein* is the prism through which we can view and answer the question of Being. Because it is the human being who raises and answers this question, Heidegger's *Being and Time* (1927) has been regarded as an existentialist work despite its author's rejection of the designation. The third group consists of theologians who make use of existentialist insights and concepts in constructing their theologies. They have tended to draw on existentialism in two ways. The first approach understands human existence to point beyond itself to God, authentic existence being attained only when the human being comes to sustain a relationship with God. This form of Christian existentialism, in the tradition of Pascal and Kierkegaard, is found in the Russian Orthodox Nikolai Berdyaev (1874–1948), the *French Catholic Gabriel Marcel (1889–1973), and the Scottish Anglican John Macquarrie (b. 1919). The second form of theistic existentialism employs existential concepts to unpack the meaning of Christian doctrine, understanding the latter as a description of the existential state of human beings and of what is required to attain to authentic existence. The leading representative is Rudolf *Bultmann, who draws on Heidegger's concepts in interpreting the NT *kerygma. For Bultmann, that kerygma is a call to decide for or against authentic existence but is expressed in the NT in *mythological terms. If the existential content of the Christian gospel is to be recovered, a programme of *demythologization is needed. Only so will the gospel's meaning and significance become understandable for contemporary people.

Existentialism has had its critics. *Bonhoeffer condemned it as a 'spiritual subterfuge', an attempt, in a world from which God has been banished, to retain the divine in the sphere of the personal. Harvey Cox has described it as 'the last child of a cultural epoch, born in its mother's senility' and castigates it as 'anti-technological, individualistic, romantic, and deeply suspicious of cities and of science'. Adorno, in his *Jargon of Authenticity*, takes Heidegger to task for the obscurity of his language and attacks the philosophical foundations upon which existentialism is based. Far from being a description of human existence, existentialism is merely, in his view, the reaction of the bourgeois spirit to the crises of the 20th century. Existentialism has also been accused of being so centred on the individual as to ignore the community. Though there may be some justification for this criticism as regards Kierkegaard, thinkers such as Marcel and the Jewish philosopher Martin Buber (1878–1965) have attempted to redress the balance by developing existentialist analyses of interpersonal relations.

Existentialism's role as a major player in theological debate seems to be over, at least for the present, although certain aspects of it have been taken up and employed in other theological and philosophical approaches. It has lost its cult status, a role that seems to have been taken over for the time being by *postmodernism. Theologians today seem to prefer to turn to other categories and systems to explain the nature of the human individual, and that individual's relation to God. Reports of existentialism's death have been greatly exaggerated, however, and to those capable of looking beyond immediate theological fashion it continues to provide an important resource for understanding human existence and for constructing theologies which take the human self as their starting-point.

David R. Law

Cooper, D. E., *Existentialism: A Reconstruction* (1990).
Macquarrie, J., *Existentialism* (1972).
Warnock, M., *Existentialism* (1970).

Exodus, the second book of the Pentateuch, or Torah. It contains the story of the oppression of the Israelites in Egypt, their escape, and their journey to Mount Sinai, where a *covenant is made (and renewed) between them and Yahweh, the Law is revealed, and a tent-shrine (the 'tabernacle') is constructed according to a divinely revealed plan.

The central place of the exodus story, and the theology embedded in it, within the OT election traditions is borne out in several ways. Liturgically it is a major theme of certain *psalms, including three associated with the northern kingdom of *Israel (77, 80, and 81) and several from post-exilic times (105, 106, 135, and 136), as well as some possibly older Judaean psalms (78, 99, and 114). There was a growing tendency to make it the focus of all the major Israelite festivals and other rituals (most obviously the Passover: Exod. 12). It became a central motif of prophetic teaching (for example Amos 3: 2; 9: 7) and Deutero-*Isaiah used it as a pattern for the new deliverance from Babylon which he announced (Isa. 51: 10–11; 52: 11–12). In the theology of the Deuteronomic literature the exodus was the act of Yahweh *par excellence*, which defined his nature and the beginning of his relationship to Israel (Deut. 4: 20). The law given at Horeb (as Sinai is called in Deuteronomy) was the basis of the covenant (Deut. 5: 2–21) and *Moses received his commission as a lawgiver there (5: 22–33).

In the NT the passages most quoted from Exodus are the call of Moses (Matt. 22: 32, etc.) and the Decalogue (Matt. 5: 21, 27, etc.). Several passages make use of a substantial portion of the Exodus narrative, whether as a basis for criticism of the Jews (Acts 7: 17–44) or as a warning to Christians (1 Cor. 10: 1–11) or to present Moses and the Israelites as examples of faith (Heb. 11: 23–9). A number of individual episodes in Exodus are regarded in a somewhat ambivalent way, as both prefiguring NT themes and being transcended by them: the Passover (1 Cor. 5: 7), the departure from Egypt (Matt. 2: 15), the manna (John 6: 30–58), Sinai (Gal. 4: 21–5: 1), the covenant (2 Cor. 3: 1–18), and the tabernacle (Heb. 9: 1–5, 11, 24). In the Lucan story of the Transfiguration of Jesus, Moses and Elijah are said to have spoken with him about 'his departure [Greek *exodos*], which he was about to accomplish in Jerusalem' (Luke 9: 31), which many commentators have taken to imply an explicit *typological parallel between the exodus from Egypt and Jesus' death and *Resurrection. Elsewhere statements in Exodus, like other OT passages, are regarded by Jesus and the NT writers as guides to belief and behaviour. The reference to Yahweh as 'the God of *Abraham, the God of *Isaac, and the God of Jacob' in the call of Moses (Exod. 3: 6) is seen as an argument for life after death (Matt. 22: 32 par.), and the explanation of the name of God as 'I will be' (Exod. 3: 14), in its Greek rendering 'he who is', lies behind part (or perhaps the whole) of the description of God as he 'who is and who was and who is to come' (Rev. 1: 8). *Paul bases his teaching on divine sovereignty in Romans 9, in part, on the example of Pharaoh (Exod. 9: 16) and on words addressed to Moses in Exod. 33: 19. In several passages (see above) one or more of the Ten *Commandments is cited as a guide to right behaviour: presumably this is why Paul can describe the law as 'holy and just and good' (Rom. 7: 12) and as being summed up in love of one's neighbour (13: 8–10), as well as being the means by which sin is known (3: 20; 7: 7).

Through many centuries of Christian history these responses to the Exodus text have been taken up and extended in a great variety of ways, in sermons, theological treatises, liturgy, commentaries, and art. From early times the exodus came to be understood as an *allegory of the soul's spiritual journey from bondage to freedom and life. Following the lead of 1 Cor. 10: 2, Christians saw the crossing of the Red Sea as a type of their *baptism and also of the Resurrection of Christ himself, hence the use of the Song of Moses (Exod. 15: 1–18) as an *Easter anthem and the many allusions to it in Easter hymns. Above all, the description of the desert shrine or tabernacle in Exod. 25–31 was interpreted in symbolic terms, both as embodying the secrets of the natural world and, more often, as a typological foreshadowing of the whole of the Christian dispensation. The Ten Commandments formed a core of Christian moral and religious instruction and were incorporated into Cranmer's Holy Communion service and exhibited on plaques in many churches and chapels. The laws of the Book of the Covenant, too, while widely regarded as having no lasting significance, were taken up in the post-Reformation period as a model of an ideal polity by the *Puritans and the 'Laws and Liberties of Massachusetts' (1648). Scenes from Exodus were regularly illustrated in stained glass, both in narrative sequence (as in the East Window of York Minster) and in typological pairs with NT scenes (as in King's College Chapel, Cambridge). There are also many paintings of individual scenes, especially the discovery of the baby Moses, the crossing of the Red Sea, and the presentation of the stone tablets of the Law.

In the modern period the book of Exodus, like the rest of the bible, has been the subject of intensive historical and literary-critical study. Allegory and typology were banished and attention was focused on a historical, geographical, and scientific explanation of the text. Source-criticism attempted to distinguish between more and less authentic parts of the book and the Priestly narrative strand, including the description of the tabernacle, came to be seen as a late and unhistorical element. But the historicity of an 'exodus event', generally dated in the 13th century BC, has rarely been called in question, however much scholarship has played down the miraculous events in the story. In modern biblical theology 'exodus faith' as represented in the early poems in Exod. 15 has been seen as both source and paradigm of Israel's supposedly distinctive belief in a God who 'acts in history' for the deliverance of his people. This and the Sinai covenant of Exod. 19–24 became the twin pillars of many presentations of OT theology in the mid-20th century. Serious questions have, however, been raised about the relationship between history and the tradition that bears witness to it. There is a growing tendency to approach the text as story rather than history, but Exodus is a part of a larger narrative that begins with creation and finds its climax and meaning in true worship. The latter can be seen in the reference to a 'sanctuary' in 15: 17 and in worship at Mount Sinai (18: 10–12; 24: 9–11). In the Priestly strand the tent-shrine is clearly envisaged as a prototypical *Temple, designed to be a place where Yahweh will 'dwell' in the midst of his people (25: 8) and meet with them (25: 22). The theology of Exodus is therefore as much a theology of divine presence and worship as a theology of salvation and covenant.

The book of Exodus, at least its first part, has not surprisingly played a prominent part in modern *black and *liberation theology. An anticipation of this political approach can be seen in 19th-century Negro spirituals, the literature of the American Civil War, and some anti-Nazi writing in Germany. In the *Latin American form of liberation theology, the oppression in Egypt has been equated with the policies of right-wing governments and their external supporters. The validity of such interpretations remains a matter of debate, even in Latin America itself. There are signs that human history is not amenable to an exclusively liberationist interpretation and the bible itself suggests a range of models for understanding history which is not limited to the Exodus paradigm.

G. I. Davies

Carroll, M. D., 'God and his People in the Nations' History: A Contextualised Reading of Amos 1–2', *Tyndale Bulletin*, 47 (1996).

Childs, B. S., *Exodus: A Commentary* (1974).

Clines, D. J. A., *The Theme of the Pentateuch* (1978), 2nd edn. (1997).

Croatto, J. S., *Exodus: A Hermeneutics of Freedom* (1978), ET (1981).

Iersel, B. van, and Weiler, A. (ed.), 'Exodus: A Lasting Paradigm', *Concilium*, 189 (1987).

Johnstone, W., *Exodus* (1990).

Reventlow, H. G., *Problems of Old Testament Theology in the Twentieth Century* (1982), ET (1985).

Terrien, S. L., *The Elusive Presence: Towards a New Biblical Theology* (1978).

exorcism, see DEVIL.

faith, as understood in Christian theology, is the fundamental response of the believer to the *God who reveals himself and his plan of *salvation pre-eminently in his Son, *Jesus Christ. Theologians commonly distinguish between particular acts of faith and the abiding disposition or 'habit' of faith, which marks one as a believer. They also distinguish between faith as a subjective stance (the faith *by which* one believes) and the content or object (the faith *that* is believed). Some distinguish further between faith as a response to a specific *revelation, recognized as such, and faith as a positive disposition to accept a revelation if and when it comes. Our concern here is primarily with faith as an acceptance of God's word as communicated in Christ and mediated by the Christian community.

In the Hebrew Scriptures faith is frequently designated by terms connected with the root *'mn*, which connotes firmness or constancy. Such firmness is pre-eminently an attribute of God, who can be relied on to keep his covenant promises. Faith is also demanded of Israel, in order that it may believe the truth of those promises, trust in God's faithfulness, and faithfully live up to the terms of the *covenant. Faith, as a kind of 'amen' to God's initiatives of love, involves intellectual assent, trust, and obedience. Assent is indicated, for example, in the basic creeds of Israel (Exod. 15: 1–18; Deut. 6: 4–9; 26: 5–10). Trust is illustrated by *Abraham's confidence that he will become the father of many nations (Gen. 15: 4–6; 17: 2–8, 15–21). Obedience is illustrated in Abraham's compliance with God's order to leave his ancestral home (Gen. 12: 1–4) and his willingness to sacrifice his son Isaac (Gen. 22: 2, 12, 16). Deutero-*Isaiah emphasizes the vocation of Israel as a believing community to bear witness to God's fidelity (Isa. 43: 10–12; 44: 6–8).

The NT inculcates the same faith-relationship to the God of Israel but adds the conviction that God has acted definitively in Jesus Christ, who is to be believed, trusted, and obeyed as divine Lord and saviour. In the Synoptic Gospels faith (*pistis*) generally signifies trust in the power of Jesus to heal and rescue from all danger. In the Johannine writings the power of Jesus to bestow eternal life is viewed as a primary datum of faith. In Acts and the Pauline letters faith is frequently depicted as an adherence to the basic Christian message, the *kerygma* preached by the apostles. For *Paul acceptance of the *kerygma* and a corresponding trust in Christ as saviour are decisive for *justification and salvation (Rom. 10: 9–10). Faith places the whole life of the believer under the lordship of Christ.

Faith without *love is useless (1 Cor. 13: 2–4); what avails for salvation is 'faith working through love' (Gal. 5: 6). The Epistle of James, rejecting the salutary value of 'faith alone', insists on the necessity of good works for justification and salvation (Jas. 2: 14–26). The Epistle to the *Hebrews, in a passage later Christians accepted as an inspired definition, describes faith as 'the assurance of things hoped for and the evidence of things unseen' (Heb. 11: 1).

The Greek Fathers, beginning with Clement and *Origen, contrast faith, as a kind of trustful assent, with knowledge (*gnosis*), which perfects faith through personal experience and understanding of faith's content. Later Greek fathers, notably Pseudo-*Dionysius and Maximus the Confessor, celebrate the power of faith to effect a spiritual union with God whereby believers are initiated into mysteries that lie beyond the realm of rational discourse. In the west *Augustine made a profound psychological analysis of the relationship between knowledge and love in the assent of faith. Faith, as a loving assent, enhances *reason, enabling it to understand what would otherwise elude it, and faintly anticipating the beatific vision reserved for the saints in heaven. Against the *Pelagians Augustine insisted that faith is a free gift of God and that human effort, unassisted by *grace, cannot achieve even the beginning of faith.

Medieval western theology systematized the teaching of scripture and the church fathers, especially Augustine. Monastic authors such as *Anselm of Canterbury, Bernard of Clairvaux, and Hugh of St Victor probed the affective and experiential aspects of the life of faith. Thomas *Aquinas, while reaffirming the essential teaching of Augustine, recast the theology of faith in terms of the epistemology and psychology of *Aristotle. He described faith as an infused intellectual habit having as its object the divinely revealed truth. 'To believe', he wrote, 'is an act of the intellect assenting to divine truth by virtue of a command of the will, which is moved by God through grace so that the act rests on a free decision directed toward God' (*ST* II-II q. 2 a. 9).

The emphasis of the 16th-century *Reformers was very different. Martin *Luther centred his discussion of faith on the question of justification. With special reliance on certain texts from Paul, especially from *Romans, he held that faith enables sinners to place their entire hope of salvation in Jesus Christ, who takes our sins upon himself and bestows his merits upon us. In his 1522 *Preface to Romans* he declared: 'Faith is a living, daring confidence in God's grace, so sure and certain that the believer would stake his life on it a thousand times'. Melanchthon systematized Luther's teaching, giving particular emphasis to the element of trust or confidence. 'Faith is not merely a knowledge of historical events but is a confidence in God and in the fulfillment of his promises... We should understand the word faith in the scriptures to mean confidence in God, assurance that God is gracious to us, and not merely such a knowledge of historical events as the devil also possesses' (*Augsburg Confession*, art. 20). *Calvin took essentially the same position, except that he showed greater concern for the 'firm and certain knowledge' upon which trust in God's promises must be founded. The certainty of faith comes from the interior testimony of the *Holy Spirit. In a famous sentence he wrote: 'We shall possess a right definition of faith if we call it a firm and certain knowledge of God's benevolence toward us, founded upon the truth of the free promise in Christ, both revealed to our minds and sealed upon our hearts through the Holy Spirit' (*Institutes of the Christian Religion*, 3. 2, 7).

Responding to Luther and Calvin, the Catholic Church sought to reaffirm the Augustinian and scholastic heritage. While agreeing with the Reformers that faith is a free gift of God and is essential for salvation, the Council of *Trent diverged from them by teaching that faith does not justify except when animated by supernatural love (*charity), which gives rise to good works.

In the polemics of the ensuing period Catholics contended that faith is a free assent having as its object the truth of God's word. Protestants generally accented the fiducial and existential aspects, holding that faith involves confident trust in the forgiveness of one's own sins. The Calvinists frequently linked faith with a sense of *assurance that one is predestined for eternal salvation.

In inner-Catholic literature, controversies arose regarding the motivation of faith. It was asked how one can attain full and unshakable certitude that a given truth is guaranteed by the authority of the revealing God, the motive of faith. Some, like Juan de Lugo, argued that even before making the act of faith the mind can achieve a kind of supernatural intuition of the fact of revelation. Others, with Suarez, held that the fact of revelation is itself accepted in faith.

With the discovery of the New World and a fresh awareness of the peoples of Asia, the problem of the salvation of infidels took on new actuality. The *Jansenists, like many Protestants, held that no pagans, Jews, or Muslims could have justifying faith unless they became Christians. Many orthodox Catholic theologians, such as Melchior Cano, Domingo Bañez, and Gregory of Valencia, took a similar view. But some Catholic theologians, such as the Dominican Domingo de Soto, the Franciscan Andrea Vega, and Jesuits such as Jacobus Payva d'Andrada, Juan Martinez de Ripalda, and Juan de Lugo, held that virtuous unevangelized persons could by God's grace arrive at an inchoative or implicit faith in the true God and in Christ, sufficing for justification. This latter view eventually prevailed in official Catholic teaching.

In the *Enlightenment a new challenge to Christian faith arose through rationalism in its various forms, notably that of *deism. Some theologians conceded to the rationalists that all the necessary *truths of religion could be known without revelation and faith, but more orthodox thinkers, both Protestant and Catholic, held that while reason could discover a certain number of religious truths, other essential doctrines, such as the *Trinity and the *Incarnation, could not be established except by faith in the revealing word of God. They depicted faith primarily as a free and loving submission to the authority of God the revealer. This view of faith was canonized for Catholics in the teaching of *Vatican I. A few theologians, reacting against rationalism, spoke as though faith were contrary to reason, but the council discountenanced this extreme position.

In the early 20th century the problem of faith and history came to the fore. Liberal Protestants, such as Albrecht Ritschl and Adolf Harnack, relied on historical method to reconstruct the original message of Jesus, which they identified as a purely ethical teaching. Faith for them was not an acceptance of doctrine but confidence in the indestructible power of love. Catholic Modernists, sceptical about the *quest for the historical Jesus, sought to separate faith from history. They regarded faith as a quasi-mystical consciousness arising from inner experience of the divine.

Towards the middle of the 20th century personalist *existentialism made its impact on the theology of faith. Protestant dialectical theologians, such as Karl *Barth, depicted faith as a self-involving response to God's word—especially the Incarnate Word whereby God takes our sins upon himself and freely communicates his justifying grace. Many Catholics, influenced by personalist phenomenology, depicted faith primarily as a welcome of God's grace or 'inner witness' and only secondarily as an assent to doctrine. Transcendental theologians, such as Karl *Rahner, took a similar position. For them the primary constituent of faith was not an assent to a preached message but an acceptance of God's offer of grace given in interior experience.

These and other recent trends, however, have not supplanted the classical issues. Evangelical Protestantism, perpetuating the themes of Luther and Calvin, retains a strongly biblical orientation. In Catholicism, the tradition of Augustine and the medieval scholastics continues to be living and fruitful.

The Catholic Church, at *Vatican II, made an effort to overcome the old Protestant–Catholic polemics and to return to a more biblical and personalist position. The *Constitution on Divine Revelation* declared: 'The revelation of God calls for the "obedience of faith" (Rom. 16: 26; cf. 1: 5; 2 Cor. 10: 5–6), by which one commits one's whole self freely to God, offering "the full submission of intellect and will to God who reveals" [Vatican I] and freely assenting to the revelation given by him' (*DV* 5). This text affirms the element of assent but subordinates it to obedience and personal trust. Elsewhere Vatican II speaks more fully about the initiative of the Holy Spirit as the awakener and sustainer of faith and the freedom of the will in responding. The council makes it clear that faith is not a monopoly of Roman Catholics but a universal force that tends to draw all Christians, and indeed all peoples, into *unity. People of every time and place are viewed as recipients of God's offer of salvific faith; all religions are seen as reflecting rays of divine truth. The council seems to imply that faith is present in some measure in the various religions and that the dynamism of faith, properly followed, can bring adherents of different religions into closer communion.

Within the broad ecumenical consensus expressed by Vatican II and subsequent dialogues, Catholics and Protestants generally preserve their own distinctive emphases. Protestants, without denying the freedom of faith, characteristically emphasize the primacy of God's gracious gift, while Catholics, taking grace as a presupposition, devote greater attention to the freedom of the human response. The Protestant position is centred on the *bible as an inspired record of revelation, whereas Catholics insist more on the mediation of the church as the corporate carrier of Christian faith. For this reason Catholics frequently speak of the church's *dogmas as 'revealed truths' calling for an assent of divine faith, whereas Protestants commonly limit the contents of faith to the teaching of scripture. Protestants, using a broad biblical concept of faith, regard faith as sufficient for justification, while Catholics, distinguishing between the 'theological virtues' of faith, hope, and charity, contend that faith does not justify in the absence of the other theological virtues. Finally, the Protestants, accenting the fiducial aspect of faith, emphasize personal trust in the God who forgives our sins. Catholics, by contrast, emphasize intellectual assent and participation in divine life. The differences, aggravated though they are by disparities of terminology, seem to reflect diverse perspectives. Granted the complexity of the mystery of faith, the differences are in some cases complementary rather than mutually exclusive.

The nature of faith can be further illuminated by reference to the classical problem of faith and reason. The following dilemma is sometimes presented: either the truth of what we hold by faith is rationally demonstrable, in which case faith is unnecessary, or it is not demonstrable, in which case faith is irrational. Theologians grappling with this dilemma generally reply that unaided reason can achieve the judgement that it would be reasonable to believe (the judgement of credibility) but that to say 'I do believe' demands an intervention of the will assisted by grace. Yet faith is not irrational, because reason can discern sufficient motives for believing and because the grace of God illumines the mind as it finds its way to faith.

Something analogous to the 'free certitude' of faith is experienced in human relationships when we rely on the testimony of a trusted *friend. Our loving familiarity with the other person sometimes helps us perceive the credibility of that person's testimony. So too, religious faith contains an existential or interpersonal component, since it depends upon the believer's being well affected towards God. According to many theologians, grace produces a kind of connaturality, disposing us to perceive the credibility of God's word. The certitude of faith therefore differs in kind from the certitudes of mathematics and the physical sciences.

Because it arises through a personal relationship with God, faith is closely connected with the life of *prayer. Prayer is a constant exercise of faith, since in praying we acknowledge who God is and who we are in relation to God. To utter the petitions of the *Lord's Prayer, for example, is already to profess faith in God's goodness, power, and other attributes. The contents of revelation are mysterious and obscure, but the obscurity itself becomes luminous when contemplated by the eye of love. Prayerful contemplation solidifies faith by discerning the splendour of divinely revealed truth shining radiantly in the face of Christ.

In its higher degrees faith leaves behind all creaturely supports and clings nakedly, as it were, to the word of God. The individual enters into what *John of the Cross described as a 'dark night'—a darkness, paradoxically, more luminous than the day. Purification from natural motives seems to be a necessary condition for entering into the mystical union to which faith points. Having passed through an agony of 'unknowing', the mind is ready to plunge into the blinding light of the unseen God.

The modern world presents challenges to all faith-traditions, including Christianity. The empirical *sciences and technology tend to fix our attention on inner-worldly realities that can be seen, measured, and manipulated, rather than on the divine. Some traditional beliefs that have been regarded as matters of faith have been exposed by modern science as false or superstitious. The social supports for religion seem to be crumbling in many traditionally Christian lands. The times seem to call for a more personal and explicit adherence rather than an 'implicit faith' in what the community professes.

Some contend that the new-found ability of humanity to shape its own destiny makes religious faith less relevant and credible. But the problems of constructing a just and peaceful society can also sharpen the sense of religious need. In the face of poverty, oppression, and anonymity, many individuals are drawn by the sense of community and the comforts and hope provided by faith. Economic and political development, if it is not to be destructive, calls for a clearer vision of the purposes of human existence, such as faith can provide. The current success of missionary efforts in many parts of the world suggests that the testimony of faith, if delivered with sincere conviction, can still be powerful and effective.

Avery Dulles, SJ

Alfaro, Juan, *Fides, Spes, Caritas: Adnotationes in tractatum de virtutibus theologicis*, new edn. (3 vols.; 1963).

Aubert, Roger, *Le Problème de l'acte de foi*, 2nd edn. (1950).

Capéran, Louis, *Le Problème du salut des infidèles* (2 vols.; 1912), rev. edn. (1934).

Clark, Gordon H., *Faith and Saving Faith* (1983).

Dulles, Avery, *The Assurance of Things Hoped For* (1994).

Ebeling, Gerhard, *The Nature of Faith* (1961).

Hermisson, Hans-Jürgen, and Lohse, Eduard, *Faith* (1981).

Lee, James Michael (ed.), *Handbook of Faith* (1990).

Mooney, Michael, *et al.* (eds.), *Toward a Theology of Christian Faith: Readings in Theology* (1968).

Newman, John Henry, *Fifteen Sermons Preached before the University of Oxford 1826–43*, 3rd edn. (1871).

Tillich, Paul, *Dynamics of Faith* (1957).

Faith and Order

Faith and Order represents one stream in the modern *ecumenical movement, dealing with matters of doctrine, *worship, and ecclesial structures as the divided churches seek the restoration of *unity among Christians. Its world conferences—held at Lausanne (1927), Edinburgh (1937), Lund (1952), Montreal (1963), and Santiago de Compostela (1993)—have been at their respective moments the most widely representative gatherings possible of theologians, first in terms of confessional spread and later also in terms of geographical origin. Since 1948 Faith and Order has been institutionally located in the World Council of Churches, where it has the constitutional function 'to call the churches to the goal of visible unity in one faith and one eucharistic fellowship, expressed in worship and in common life in Christ, in order that the world may believe'. The Faith and Order Commission comprises some 120 members: the Orthodox, Anglican, Reformation, and Free Church representatives have been joined since 1968 by twelve Roman Catholic members, even though the Roman Catholic Church does not belong to the WCC. Faith and Order's main style of continuing work is that of thematic studies undertaken by specialist groups.

While the early decades of the movement were largely occupied with the self-presentation of the various confessional traditions and *church families (as seen, for instance, in the volumes on *The Nature of the Church*, on *Ways of Worship*, and on *Intercommunion*, all prepared for Lund 1952), an important shift in perspective and method occurred when the Lund conference decided that the time had come to move from mutual comparisons made around the circumference of a circle to a common concentration on the Christ who is at the heart of 'God's dealings with his whole people'. This move chimed with the then prevalent interests in biblical, patristic, and dogmatic theology set within the perspective of 'the history of salvation' (*Heilsgeschichte*). It found formal expression in the *rapprochement* reached on the relations between 'Scripture, Tradition, and traditions' at Montreal in 1963 and substantially underlay the work of the next two decades that prepared the text on *Baptism, Eucharist and Ministry* unanimously approved by the Faith and Order Commission at Lima in 1982 as 'mature' for submission to the churches.

Some 200 official responses, in the most participatory of ecumenical processes yet, showed wide measures of convergence and agreement among the churches regarding the three topics of 'the Lima text'; but it also became clear that the issues of the Church's nature, identity, and location needed to be addressed all the more urgently, and ecclesiology became again the dominant theme of Faith and Order in the 1990s, under the watchword since the 1993 Santiago conference of *koinonia* or *communion. Complementary work continues on doctrine (*Confessing the One Faith* (1991)), worship (*So We Believe, So We Pray* (1995)), and 'ecumenical hermeneutics', which is the current form taken by the constant concern that the gospel must be proclaimed in the present and in very varied contexts.   **Geoffrey Wainwright**

Baptism, Eucharist and Ministry 1982–1990: Report on the Process and Responses (1990).

Gassmann, G. (ed.), Documentary History of Faith and Order 1963–1993 (1993).

Vischer, L. (ed.), A Documentary History of the Faith and Order Movement 1927–1963 (1963).

Fall,

the event or process in which *creation, or some part of it, deviates from the good and is corrupted.

Traditional doctrines of the Fall postulate a discrepancy between creation as we know it and creation as originally given, a discrepancy introduced by the sin of angels and of the first humans, and by the divine *judgement or curse that followed it. Some modern versions (stressing both a continual creation and a continual Fall) point only to a discrepancy between divine goals for creation and creaturely outcomes.

The older idea has two significant roots. One of these can be traced back to *Genesis 3, which completes that book's rejection of any account of creation that attributes it to strife between the gods, or between good and evil principles. Responsibility for the tragedies and evils which mar human existence lies with humankind, not with its creator. This is the tradition carried forward by Paul (Rom. 1: 18–23; 5: 12–14; 8: 18–23) and also by *Irenaeus who did battle with *Gnostic pessimism by insisting that the *world is not the defective product of a defective deity. Freely created *ex nihilo*

(from nothing) by the one true God, it is a good world. It is corrupt only by reason of *sin, not because it is finite, diverse, and subject to change.

The other main root can be found in *Augustine's response to *Pelagius' optimism about human nature, which posed a more subtle threat to the biblical world-view. It was a false optimism, since it implied that our fallen condition is something natural to us. It had to be countered (as the *reformers also believed) by a strong emphasis on the Fall. Because of that emphasis Augustine is often contrasted with Irenaeus, who appears almost to excuse the Fall as something the first humans, in their naivety, could hardly avoid. The contrast is mistaken since for Irenaeus too the Fall was a devastating event, turning humanity 'backwards' and away from God, hence also from its true vocation in the world. The real difference between these theologians lies in how forcefully they reject the Hellenic tendency to associate fallenness with finitude. For Irenaeus there is nothing suspect about temporal and material being, which is neither the cause nor the consequence of the Fall. But Augustine in his early writing is less clear on this point, leaving an opening to those critics of the traditional doctrine who mistakenly accuse it of pessimism about the natural world, forgetting that its purpose is always to highlight the danger posed by sin to a good creation.

The roots of the modern dilution of the doctrine are also two. The first developed slowly from the medieval church's compromise with Pelagius. The idea of *grace as in some way conditional upon human behaviour combined with the other-worldliness inherited from Hellenism to produce a system of piety that succeeded only in oppressing *consciences, keeping them subject to the clerical apparatus for *penance and absolution. In response, the reformers went one way and the humanists another. The former sought to break the logic of the system by pointing to the corruption of the human will and to grace as strictly unconditional; the latter turned cautiously towards a more thoroughgoing Pelagianism. After the scientific revolution, the tide of *Enlightenment optimism swept away all caution. The doctrine of the Fall, in so far as it claimed that all people were implicated in, and corrupted by, the act of their first parents (that is, by original sin), was itself seen as a form of perversion. It was a doctrine inconsistent with human dignity and *freedom, not to speak of divine justice. Moreover, it was the prop holding up a corrupt and repressive institution. For *Nietzsche, it lay like a cancer in the bowels of an entire civilization.

The other source of modern thinking on the doctrine appeared more abruptly. In the Enlightenment a break was made with the concept of salvation history, and with it the idea of special *revelation, as incompatible with respect for the laws of nature and for *reason as 'the very voice of God'. Salvation history came under attack at its beginning, middle, and end: the *parousia* was regarded as a failed hope; the *Resurrection as an experience not of the dead *Jesus but of his living *disciples; the Fall as a purely *mythical story told to account for the origin of evil. The work of the geologists and of Darwin confirmed widespread doubts about any historically real situation of 'original righteousness', lost in some ruinous moral disaster. Genesis 3 was now seen as the stuff of *psychology or comparative *religion. Unlike the gospels, it did not retain even a limited element of historicity.

But the modern option, though motivated and shaped by these negative considerations, does not reduce to no option at all, for tradition can always be reinterpreted. When *Kant speaks of 'radical evil', is he not postulating another form of original sin? He understands it as the propensity of the human will, evident but inexplicable, to prefer a lower good (that of the senses) to a higher (that of the rational nature), and thus to subvert its own freedom. He differs from Augustine chiefly by refusing to allow that this propensity is inherited, or in any way externally conditioned, which would make it an actual bondage; each individual Fall is a new event. *Hegel, to take a second example, is rather bolder. He transforms the story of the Fall into an account of human consciousness as such, and the tradition's *felix culpa* motif into an affirmation of the Fall as a necessary moment in the ascent or deification of man: 'Paradise is a park, where only brutes, not men, can remain. For the brute is one with God only implicitly .... The Fall is therefore the eternal Mythus of Man—in fact, the very transition by which he becomes man' (*Philosophy of History* (1956), 321–2).

Modern examples of such reinterpretation might well be multiplied. What binds them together is that original righteousness and original sin are consistently seen as non-temporal structures qualifying all human situations, rather than as historic states of affairs. This view is endorsed by leading Protestant theologians from *Schleiermacher to *Tillich, and by some Roman Catholics too. On the other hand, it is regularly rejected in papal encyclicals and other official documents (see, for example, the recent *Catechism of the Catholic Church*). What exactly is at stake here, apart from any formal question about the status of church dogma?

First, the meaning of the biblical claim that creation is good, indeed very good. To de-historicize the Fall is to allow moral failure and other occasions of human tragedy to come into collision with that claim, threatening to nullify it. The only alternative, hardly an improvement, is to agree with *Origen that the claim is made not of *this* creation but of some other. (Origen taught that we have fallen from an eternal world, which is good in itself, into a temporal and finite one, which is good only in the sense that a reform school may be good. Modernity's tendency to connect sin with finitude shows more than a trace of the same ambivalence.)

Second, the meaning of *redemption. A de-historicized doctrine of the Fall invites a de-historicized soteriology. If the Fall, in the last analysis, is but an aspect of our self-consciousness, why not deliverance *from* the Fall too? Redemption will then not be grounded objectively in the event of the Incarnation, but internally in each human subject. Of course, this implies that salvation is more an affair of the mind than of the body, hence more private than public. The scope of Christian *hope, and of Christian *eschatology, is also at stake.

Third, the question about Christ and about God. If the Fall is not a particular event in history which is met and answered by another particular event in history, it is easy to conclude with Troeltsch (or, more recently, with Maurice Wiles) that incarnational *christology rests on a mistake, and the doctrine of the *Trinity with it.

Fourth, the question of theological method. Is the standpoint of original righteousness still in principle available? If so, then the fallen may hope to understand their Fall and reverse it. If not, they are in the position to which *Kierkegaard's Climacus points: they require the solution before they can even grasp the problem. 'We must know Christ as the source of grace in order to know

*Adam as the source of sin', insists the *Catechism of the Catholic Church* (1994, para. 388). But this is not just a question about method. It is also a question about the nature of sin and of grace, and about the meaning of human freedom.

Fifth, issues in *moral theology. One merit of the traditional view, it is sometimes said, is that it allows us to affirm that the world is created good without denying that it is also corrupt. This in turn disallows any hastily drawn connection between the so-called facts of nature and right human behaviour (we cannot argue, for example, from 'natural' *abortions to 'therapeutic' abortions). Such connections, however, are already illegitimate for reasons unrelated to the doctrine of the Fall. Moreover, abandoning the traditional doctrine more often leads to war with nature, to a determination to overcome nature, than to a false compliance with it. Nature, even our own nature, is viewed as a barrier to human advance: this hubris generates a host of ethical and ecological dilemmas.

In sum, there is very little of importance in Christian theology, hence also in doxology and praxis, that is *not* at stake in the question of whether or not we allow a historical dimension to the Fall. But what shall we say about the resulting clash of world-views? Can there be any alternative to the modern view for a modern person?

As we stand at the end of *modernity, looking back on, *inter alia*, the *Holocaust, we might turn the question around and ask whether it is not now clearly perverse to say as little about falling and fallenness as Kant, or Hegel, or Schleiermacher have said. But we might go even further than that. Noting that various ancient theologians have also tried to speak of the simultaneity of creation and Fall, we might ask whether the underlying problem is really a modern one at all. Perhaps the refusal to allow Genesis 3 to stand, like its fabled cherubim, at the border between myth and *history (that is, to be both myth *and* history) betrays a preference for one of the already existing alternatives to the world-view of Genesis. Does it not reveal a human tendency, already transparent to the author of the story of the Fall, to cover our embarrassment over sin with an ontological or cosmological fig-leaf? To make some lame interjection about the delicacy of the human constitution, or the difficulty of thinking universally, when what is needed is a confession of disobedience?

But this would not let us off the hook altogether, since we have learned through modern science not to read Genesis with the chronological naivety of an earlier generation. In order to maintain the historicity of the Fall we would have to break, not merely with the closed universe of the *deists and the ambiguous world of the pantheists, but also with a simple linear view of history. We would have to recover something of the complexity of Irenaeus' christological and anthropocentric understanding of *time, the understanding implicit in his doctrine of recapitulation. Courage renewed, we might then continue his project of thinking about the Fall by working backwards from a centre in Jesus, who for our sake descended *without* falling and (holding to the good) also ascended into glory.

Douglas Farrow

Barth, Karl, *Church Dogmatics* IV/1 (1956).
Bonhoeffer, Dietrich, *Creation and Fall* (1959).
Brunner, Emil, *The Christian Doctrine of Creation and Redemption* (1952).
Hall, F. J., *Evolution and the Fall* (1910).
Pannenberg, Wolfhart, *Systematic Theology* (1991), ii.

Schwarz, Hans, *Evil* (1995).

Suchocki, Marjorie, *The Fall to Violence* (1995).

Tennant, F. R., *The Sources of the Doctrines of the Fall and of Original Sin* (1903).

Tillich, Paul, *Systematic Theology* (1957), ii.

Williams, N. P., *The Ideas of the Fall and of Original Sin* (1927).

Williams, R. R., 'Sin and Evil', in P. Hodgson and R. King (eds.), *Christian Theology* (1982).

Willimon, W. H., *Sighing for Eden* (1985).

family. The family and *marriage have been Christian concerns from the earliest days of the church. From ancient Israel and Judaism, Christianity inherited sacred writings and an ethos in which tribal and clan relations, and law and custom relating to extended family life, bulked large. From the Graeco-Roman world, Christianity inherited political ideals and patterns of social organization that accorded the patriarchal household a central role as the city-state in microcosm. The NT and other early Christian writings bear witness to the pervasiveness of concerns related to marriage and the family. Examples include: the teaching of Jesus prohibiting *divorce (in part to protect women from unjust, summary dismissal by their husbands), the sayings about *children and becoming 'like a child', the hard sayings in which Jesus summons followers to leave their families behind or to become 'eunuchs' for the sake of the kingdom, stories of *conversion by household, the practice after the Resurrection of gathering for worship in 'house-churches', apostolic instruction for household members including advice for spouses in 'mixed marriages', and stories in the *apocryphal Acts and elsewhere about the sometimes catastrophic effect of conversion on family ties. In general, a rigorous marriage discipline enjoined upon men and women alike, the advocacy and practice of *celibacy in certain quarters, and a strong but 'Christianized' household order were potent ways of representing the new life of the *Kingdom of God. In addition, such teaching sought to deflect accusations from outsiders that the Christian movement was socially irresponsible and politically subversive.

Contemporary Christianity contains a wide spectrum of thought on marriage and the family. This spectrum is the result of many factors. One such is the effect of historical developments from the origins of Christianity through the *monastic movement beginning in the 4th century, the 'papal revolution' of the 11th century and the birth of the discipline of canon *law, the movements of religious reform in the 16th century, the appeal to *reason and scientific method in the 18th century *Enlightenment and, most recently, the cultural revolt against totalizing metanarratives known as *postmodernism. A second factor is the impact of developments in Christian doctrine especially to do with the *sacraments, *priesthood, ecclesiology, Mariology, *holiness, and *sexuality, all of which were affected in turn by trends in theology and biblical interpretation. Then there is the impact of movements in the contemporary world, such as *feminism with its critique of patriarchy and the environmental movement with its concerns about the *ecological effects of overpopulation. Technological developments have played their part also. These include mass-produced artificial *contraception, *in vitro* fertilization, clinical *abortion, and genetic engineering (see REPRODUCTIVE TECHNOLOGY). Finally, there is the effect of the widely acknowledged anxiety about the future of the family caused by social trends such as high divorce rates, the increase in lone-parent families, the increase in the number of children born out of wedlock, and a greater variety of family forms, itself related to multiculturalism and moral pluralism.

In general, it can be said that marriage and the family play a central part in Christian thought about the nature of society and the church and what it means to be truly *human. But they do not play the only part. In the central Catholic tradition, there has been a significant variety of ways of living the Christian life from the start. The hard sayings of Jesus and the practice of singleness for the sake of the kingdom of God became part of venerable eremitical and monastic traditions in which the family image was carried beyond the biological family. For example, religious orders, especially *Benedictines and *Franciscans, made much use of the symbolism of family ties to constitute themselves as spiritual families. At the same time, it is possible to trace a development in *Catholicism from teaching and practice which (originally in reaction to pagan sexual mores) exalted *virginity and sexual *asceticism as the way of Christian perfection through the cultivation of the image of the Holy Family (Jesus, *Mary, and Joseph) especially from the 17th century, and fostered by the immensely popular paintings of Murillo, to the position of *Vatican II which declared the celibate and married states equally holy human vocations. In Roman Catholic thought today, itself rooted in the teaching of *Augustine and later *Aquinas on the 'three goods' of marriage, the family has considerable spiritual and practical significance as part of the natural order given by God for the good of society and for the procreation of children. In doctrinal terms, marriage is a *sacrament. It is a means by which a *man and a *woman become a blessing and source of divine grace both for each other and for the community of which they are a part. The family, in turn, is understood as the foundation of society, and emphasis is placed on the equal dignity of every member, children as well as husband and wife. In its own right, the family is a special kind of community where moral and religious formation take place. The Christian family in particular is thought of as a domestic church. Its common life expresses the *communion within the life of the Trinity and involves the practice of the faith, life, and mission that characterizes the church as a whole. This fundamentally ecclesial vision of the family is also shared by the Orthodox Church.

In Protestantism, the understanding of marriage and the family has its roots in *Luther's critical principle of 'scripture alone' (*sola scriptura*) and the central doctrines of justification by faith, the priesthood of all believers, and the freedom of the Christian. On this basis, Luther rejected as unscriptural the sacramental understanding of marriage, clerical celibacy, and the Church's traditional exaltation of virginity over marriage and sexual fulfilment. The place of the monastery and nunnery was taken now by the family. Protestant clergy married and raised families, many aspects of the marital legislation and custom of the medieval church were reformed (including widening the grounds for divorce and permitting remarriage), the contribution of women to the shaping of society by their roles in the household was emphasized, and the place of children was given stronger emphasis. In the Lutheran doctrine of the 'two kingdoms', marriage was understood as one of the three social estates of the earthly kingdom, alongside the clergy and the magistracy. In the *covenantal theology of *Calvinism, marriage was conceptualized as a covenantal association within the civil and ecclesiastical order. *Anglicanism regarded it as a domestic 'commonwealth' within the church and commonwealth of England. The overall, gradual effect of these changes was to reduce the role of the church and to increase the role of the state in marriage and family life. As a move from a sacramental to a social and ultimately contractual model of marriage and the family, it could be argued that this represents a step in the direction of the secularization of the family and society which reached its culmination in the Enlightenment and the values of *modernity.

In the *evangelical movement of the 19th century and subsequently (a movement that cuts across the Protestant denominations), the family is seen as part of the natural order, the will of God as revealed above all in the bible. It is the intimate community where parents and children are nurtured physically and spiritually. It is important also as a symbol of social stability and moral virtue. Especially among *fundamentalists, it becomes a divinely ordained haven from the moral ambiguities, individualism, and experimentation of a modern world which is seen to have lost its way. In line with what is understood as biblical teaching, strong emphasis is placed on male headship, the subordination of women, and the responsible exercise of parental authority in the nurture of children. The family, in some cases even more than the church, is seen as the basic institution for the induction of children into the beliefs, values, and skills necessary for godly living. Sexual fidelity within marriage and a conservative position on divorce and remarriage are practices that should mark Christians out from the secular world.

Significantly different in certain respects is the approach of *liberal theology. Liberalism (ironically like evangelicalism in this respect) is in part the heir of a Reformation theology that played down the sacramental interpretation of marriage and family in favour of a more social and civic interpretation. It brings the tradition of the church into dialogue with contemporary ideas and experience and modifies or reinterprets it in the light of reason. Here, the family is above all a focus for the development of human individuality, religious sensibility, and mature *personhood, and strong emphasis is placed on the rights of the individual, including those of the child. In this tradition more than in the Roman Catholic and conservative Protestant traditions, there is more flexibility in marriage disciplines, and greater tolerance of cohabitation and same-sex relationships. This is due in part to a re-evaluation of Christian tradition and traditional notions of authority, including the respective authority of marriage partners. It is due also to a greater sympathy towards developments in modern knowledge, including the *social sciences and the various schools of psychotherapeutic thought and practice.

A more recent development in Christian thought comes from *liberation and *feminist theologies. Where liberal theology gives centre-stage to the individual, liberation theology focuses on the needs of oppressed classes and groups, not least impoverished families. It challenges church and society to recognize how much family life and values in the west are shaped by prior commitments of race, class, property, and political economics. Feminist theology shares with liberation theology the character of a theology of protest and a commitment to unmask injustice, but in relation to the experience of women in particular. In feminist theology, the 'traditional' nuclear family is seen as an instrument of the patriarchal oppression of women. Rather than offering a sacred haven from the macho world of work and politics, the family is implicated in issues of gender and power in quite profound, though usually unacknowledged, ways. The starting-point for this theology is women's experience of exclusion, silencing, and abuse both in public and domestic life. In its various forms, feminist theology calls for radical change: imaging God in ways that go beyond God as Father, being the *church in ways that enable the empowerment of women, and developing patterns of family life that transcend patriarchy.

Predicting the future of Christian thought about the family is a hazardous task. Some find in postmodernism an opportunity to go beyond both pre-modern options that tend to exalt a particular ('Victorian') form of the family and modern options which tend to subordinate the family to the demands of consumer individualism. It is argued that, because of its attention to the identity and interests of particular communities and traditions, postmodernism offers a space for Christians in different places and from diverse traditions to work out for themselves (but not necessarily in isolation) what it means to live as families in the eschatological family whose life is the life of God and whose identity is formed by ongoing participation in the story of Israel and the church.

See also ALTERNATIVE LIFESTYLES; FATHERHOOD; MOTHERHOOD; RELIGIOUS LIFE. **Stephen C. Barton**

Barton, S. C. (ed.), *The Family in Theological Perspective* (1996).

Brown, P., *The Body and Society* (1989).

Browning, D. S., *et al.*, *From Culture Wars to Common Ground: Religion and the American Family Debate* (1997).

Cahill, L. S., *Sex, Gender and Christian Ethics* (1996).

Clapp, R., *Families at the Crossroads* (1993).

Familiaris Consortio (Apostolic Exhortation of Pope John Paul II, 1981).

Moxnes, H. (ed.), *Constructing Early Christian Families* (1997).

Osiek, C., and Balch, D. L., *Families in the New Testament World* (1997).

Peters, T., *For the Love of Children: Genetic Technology and the Future of the Family* (1996).

Pyper, H. (ed.), *The Christian Family: A Concept in Crisis* (1996).

Witte, J., Jr., *From Sacrament to Contract: Marriage, Religion and Law in the Western Tradition* (1997).

fasting is a practice common to all the world religions, even if it is not a prominent feature of modern western Christianity. It is practised as a sign of penitence (see PENANCE), and also as a preparation for a deeper communion with the ultimate, which might take the form of *visions (cf. Dan. 10: 2–9). The evidence from the NT about fasting is ambivalent. On the one hand, it is taken for granted as a Christian practice (cf. Matt. 6: 17; Acts 13: 2); on the other, fasting seems not to have been a practice among Jesus' disciples (Mark 2: 18–22 and parallels). The early church, however, practised fasting, and there is evidence of Wednesday and Friday set apart as days of fasting (*Didache*, 8, in conscious distinction from Jewish practice). Eventually there were additional periods of fasting in preparation for *Easter (*Lent: from the 4th century lasting forty days), before *Christmas (called *Advent in the west), and (in the east) before the feasts of Peter and Paul, and the Dormition of the Mother of God (*Mary), as well as on the vigils of certain great feasts. Fasting during these periods meant not eating until evening (or late afternoon), and restricting one's diet. In current *Eastern Orthodox practice, which is certainly ancient, the diet on fast days excludes meat, fish, dairy products (including eggs), wine, and oil. Until later in the Middle Ages, the rules in the west were very similar (save that Saturdays during fasting periods were observed with full rigour, in contrast to the east); from the early modern period the fast came to exclude only meat, and since *Vatican II most countries have abandoned any dietary fast.

Such periodic fasting (and feasting) is a powerful factor in forging corporate identity. The variety in such customs marked out, in a tangible way, the difference between Jews and Christians (and eventually Muslims) in late antiquity, and in the Middle Ages between Latin and Greek Christians. In a modern secular society, Orthodox Christians find that the shaping of time by feast and fast is a valuable factor in articulating the identity of an often much-dispersed community. But the principal purpose of fasting is religious: it involves the *body and affects the body, it may induce weariness, a kind of fragility that deepens awareness of human dependence on God, but beyond that is discovered a sense of lightness, wakefulness, *freedom, and *joy. Fasting is not something to be practised on its own, but together with *prayer and almsgiving: the increased consciousness of dependence on God disposes one to prayer, and active charity towards others is to fill the spaces, and use the resources, made available by fasting. But periods of fasting lead to periods of rejoicing: in particular, the Lenten fast leads into the joy of celebrating the *Resurrection. In that way it prepares the Christian to appropriate more deeply the meaning of the feasts. It is also customary to fast from all food before receiving holy communion, traditionally (and still in the Orthodox East) from rising; in the Catholic west the eucharistic fast has recently been reduced to one hour.   **Andrew Louth**

Deseille, P., and Sieben, H.-J., 'Jeûne', in *Dictionnaire de Spiritualité* (1974), viii.

Ware, K., 'The Meaning of the Great Fast', in Mother Mary and Archimandrite Kallistos Ware, *The Lenten Triodion* (1978).

fatherhood.
No divine title has been more central in the history of Christian thought and worship than that of Father, yet in modern times the fatherhood of *God has been at the centre of dispute.

In the NT *Jesus teaches his disciples to pray to God as Father and nowhere, with the exception of the cry of dereliction from the *cross (Mark 15: 34), does Jesus address God by any other name. By contrast in the OT God is styled as 'Father' only eleven times, a reticence which may, in the early texts, reflect a desire to dissociate the God of Israel from those gods who were held to be 'fathers' and 'mothers' of their peoples in some biologically generative way. That Israel might one day call God 'Father' as a title of intimacy is suggested in the prophetic writings (see Jer. 3: 19–20) and it may be that Jesus, in calling God 'Father', was suggesting that this hour had arrived.

It is mistaken, however, to view Jesus' preference for calling God 'Father' in an intimate way as a disavowal of more distant and austere Jewish understandings of God. It is better seen in a tradition of divine names in the Hebrew bible which stress the closeness of God to Israel. 'Father' becomes a relatively common title for God in Rabbinic *Judaism (1st–5th centuries AD) and whether Jesus was the pioneer, or one of the first to speak in this way, is unclear. What is noteworthy and was regarded as such by the early Christian theologians is his preference for this title (occurring over 170 times in the gospels).

The 'fatherhood' of God suggested to the early Christians a web of kinship metaphors. In one of the earliest Christian writings *Paul expands upon the idea that the Christian is no longer a *slave but a son of God—a contrast also drawn by the rabbis—'the spirit of sons … makes us cry out, "Abba, Father"' (Rom. 8: 15; see also Gal. 4: 4–6). The paternal *metaphor, then, suggests not simply a relation of parental intimacy but a relation to an authority ('father' rather than 'master'). 'Father' is not readily replaced by 'mother' in these contexts, since fathers and mothers did not have the same social status. 'Divine *motherhood' has a different set of resonances. The extension of the *familial metaphors, begun already by Paul, suggested to early theologians that the Christians are '*children' or 'sons' of God by virtue of being one with Jesus, for whom God was 'Father'.

What the 'fatherhood' of God might mean in conjunction with the conviction that Jesus was the *messiah and himself divine posed its own problems. For some early theologians to call God 'Father' suggested the subordination of the Son to the Father, on the model of then customary relations in human families. Some *Arians moved from a literalistic insistence that God is the Father and Christ is the Son to the conclusion that the Son must have been non-existent before begotten (see INCARNATION). This subordinationism was unacceptable to the emergent *Trinitarian orthodoxy which insisted on the equality and co-eternity of Father, Son, and *Holy Spirit. The titles 'father' and 'son', it was observed, were relational. *Origen argued that there must always be the Son if there is always the Father, for the Father is not Father without the Son. *Athanasius developed the notion that the Father was eternally generative of the Son. Despite subsequent refinements of Trinitarian theology there remains a tension between the affective ascriptions of 'Father' and 'Son' in the NT, and the more metaphysical formulations of these titles in subsequent Trinitarian thought.

Greek philosophy also made reference to the 'fatherhood' of God. *Plato speaks of God as fatherly in his generative powers and contrasts passive, 'maternal' matter with the active and creative male principle. Philo, a Hellenized Jewish contemporary of Paul, writes of God in a way more indebted to Plato's *Timaeus* than to the OT as 'the Father who as its begetter and contriver made the Universe'. The Platonic extension of the fatherhood metaphor, with its stress not on affective relations but on generation and governance, while not obviously influential on NT notions of fatherhood, did influence subsequent Christian theology.

The modern period has seen concern amongst theologians and the Christian faithful about the *symbolic and psychological outworkings of the 'fatherhood of God'. The criticisms are particularly associated with *feminist theologians, but are by no means exclusive to them. Mary Daly's *Beyond God the Father* is a *locus classicus*: Daly writes, 'The biblical and popular image of God as a great patriarch in heaven, rewarding and punishing according to his mysterious and seemingly arbitrary will, has dominated the imagination of millions over thousands of years' (p. 13). While Daly notes that 'sophisticated thinkers' have never identified with God a Superfather in heaven, nevertheless 'if God is male, then the male is God. The divine patriarch castrates women as long as he is allowed to live on in the human imagination' (pp. 17, 19). Carter Heyward (1982: 156) sketched an 'idolatrous' God in even stronger terms as an 'impassive unflappable character who represents the headship of a universal family in which men are best and women least … the eternal King, the Chairman of the board … the Husband of the Wife …'

The Christian churches are coming to terms with a past in which unquestioned acceptance of a natural subordination of women shaded at times towards active misogyny. The question now is whether 'the fatherhood of God' as found in scripture and tradition must inevitably yield a patriarchal Christianity in which women are held in low esteem. Does 'fatherhood' always imply dominance and oppression? While every human being has a biological father, what 'fatherhood' means at the social and symbolic level varies greatly across cultures and historical periods. Not every Christian who identifies with feminist aspirations finds the 'fatherhood of God' to be an oppressive notion as is evidenced by some womanist theologians who point out that they do not have the same difficulties with 'father' language as do white feminists.

The modern preacher, perhaps especially in the west, faces a pastoral and a pedagogical challenge. 'Father' is a central term in the NT writings and closely associated with the teaching of Jesus. If it is the case that the 'fatherhood' of God has been used as a template for oppressive human relations in Christian churches and societies, then it must also be said that there seems little warrant for this in the use Jesus in the gospels made of the title. This use was above all affective, and suggested an intimacy which the Christians were to enjoy as a new family of God, not by blood but by Spirit. As such this new family was subversive, as various early martyrologies attest, of the loyalties of the biological family and the biological father. In this NT use, unlike that of the Platonists, there is no correlative and subordinate female principle with which the male creative and generative principle is contrasted. The 'fatherhood' model in Christianity moves within the affective, and not the biological, extensions of the metaphor.

And finally, within developed Christian theology, 'Father' must be seen as above all a Trinitarian title. The 'Father' is father of the 'Son'. Christians are one with the Father, through the Spirit, in the Son. The Father cannot be within the Trinitarian economy a sole and solitary ruler or an autocratic emperor without collapse into monarchianism.

See also MAN/MASCULINITY.   **Janet Martin Soskice**

Barr, James, 'Abba Isn't Daddy', *Journal of Theological Studies*, NS 39 (1988).
Daly, Mary, *Beyond God the Father: Toward a Philosophy of Women's Liberation* (1973).
Heyward, Isabel Carter *The Redemption of God: A Theology of Mutual Relation* (1982).
Kimmel, Alvin F. (ed.), *Speaking the Christian God: The Holy Trinity and the Challenge of Feminism* (1992).
Metz, J. B., and Schillebeeckx, E. (eds.), 'God as Father?' *Concilium* (1981).
Weinandy, Thomas G., *The Father's Spirit of Sonship* (1995).
Widdicombe, Peter, *The Fatherhood of God from Origen to Athanasius* (1994).
Williams, Jane, 'The Fatherhood of God', in Alasdair Heron (ed.), *The Forgotten Trinity* (1991).

femininity, see WOMAN.

feminist theology developed out of the conviction that Christian thought and practice radically excludes *women's experi-

ence. Although in the early years of the women's movement (early 1960s) it had been commonplace to reject all mainstream religious traditions as inherently patriarchal, a small number of women, notably Mary Daly and Rosemary Radford *Ruether in the United States, and Kari Børresen and Elisabeth Gössmann in Europe, began to challenge their churches to be more inclusive of women. This nascent reform movement was strongly influenced by the *liberation theology emerging in Latin America. Feminists drew on liberation theology's conviction that Christianity necessitates political involvement and work for the poor and oppressed groups in which women form a major part. By the late 1970s this new synthesis had evolved from being a branch of the women's movement into a distinct theological approach combining the political activism of feminism with a critique of the Christian tradition. But as feminist theologians began to write women's experience back into *theology, the diverse nature of that experience became apparent. In particular, women of colour have argued that early forms of feminist theology simply represented the concerns of white, middle-class, western women. As a result of this critique, initially from Afro-American women, feminist theology has moved away from a simple concern with gender to examine the complex interaction of theology with race, class, ethnicity, and gender. It is now more appropriate to speak of feminist theologies, including womanist (articulated by women of colour, mainly Afro-American), *mujerista* (Hispanic), and *minjung* (Asian) perspectives (see BLACK THEOLOGY).

When feminists examine the Christian tradition they are confronted with sacred texts which are sexist and misogynistic. Many passages in the OT and NT convey a belief in women's inferiority. The first letter to Timothy is a case in point. The author (traditionally said to be *Paul although scholars today deem this unlikely) instructs the community thus: 'Let a woman learn in silence with all submissiveness. I permit no woman to teach or to have authority over men; she is to keep silent. For *Adam was formed first, then *Eve; and Adam was not deceived, but the woman was deceived and became a transgressor. Yet woman will be saved through bearing children, if she continues in faith and love and holiness, with modesty' (1 Tim. 2: 11–15). This and many similar biblical texts both create and reinforce the subordination of women in the Christian church. Patristic, medieval, and later theologians can be similarly criticized for misogyny. Jerome's *On the Apparel of Women* has assumed almost iconic status in feminist theology. This text unites an unambiguous belief in the inferiority of women with an association of woman with evil. Jerome addresses women directly:

> Do you not know that you are each an Eve? The sentence of God on this sex of yours lives in this age, the guilt must, of necessity, live too. You are the devil's gateway. You are the unsealer of that forbidden tree. You are the first deserter of the divine law. You are she who persuaded him whom the devil was not valiant enough to attack. You destroyed so easily God's image, man. On account of your guilt … even the son of God had to die. (1. 1)

These themes are replicated and elaborated elsewhere in the Christian tradition. Kari Børresen's *Subordination and Equivalence* (1968) was a pioneering work in that it attempted to analyse the anthropology of *Augustine and *Aquinas. Books such as Ruether's *Religion and Sexism*, Mary Daly's *The Church and the Second Sex*, and Phyllis Trible's *Texts of Terror* are examples of the many works that now catalogue the tradition of misogyny central to Christian *history. Feminist theologians insist that this radical anti-woman strain in the sacred texts and traditions of Christianity must be acknowledged and that its continued impact needs to be investigated.

One of the central and recurring questions arising out of this historical work is whether Christianity is *irredeemably* patriarchal. Feminist theologians disagree about the ethical viability of a religion that has systematically excluded women from full participation in its liturgical, theological, and administrative life. Many, following Mary Daly, argue that 'the medium is the message': the message of Christianity cannot be separated from its patriarchal texts, traditions, and practices. Daphne Hampson extends this argument, seeing Christianity as a *historical religion inextricably bound to a sexist past. The sexism of the biblical texts is particularly problematic because the *bible is read as *revelation, reinforcing the sexism by divine sanction. Such criticisms have spawned a small but significant grouping of scholars, calling themselves *post-Christian, who recognize their indebtedness to the Christian tradition but have attempted to articulate a spirituality and a corresponding theology free of sexism. Carol Christ, Mary Daly, and in the 1990s Daphne Hampson have each advocated the rejection of Christianity because of its unethical treatment of women. They have also begun the process of creating new religious forms, focusing variously on goddess spiritualities (Carol Christ), radical feminist philosophy (Daly), or a combination of *Enlightenment philosophy and French feminism (Hampson).

Feminists who still want to be identified as Christian have rejected this dismissal of Christianity as absolutist, while repudiating what they see as a naive search for non-patriarchal starting-points, either in the past or present. Christian feminists argue that Christianity, despite containing much that is objectionable to women, has a central message of liberation. This debate continues to dominate much feminist theological thought. Rosemary Radford Ruether bases her defence of Christianity on what she calls 'a canon within the canon'. She contends that at the heart of Christianity is the '*prophetic *messianic principle of biblical religion', and that this principle is not purely marginal or arbitrary but central to the character of biblical faith. It enables Christianity to critique all forms of religious and social oppression, including any patterns of discrimination existing within the Christian tradition itself. The bible is thus a source of liberating paradigms, and all Christian texts and traditions must be evaluated on this basis. Most Christian feminist theologians, while not necessarily agreeing with Ruether's methodological approach, endorse the view that Christianity is essentially liberative and compatible with the expressed goals of feminism.

In defending their stance that Christianity has internal mechanisms enabling it to address its patriarchal past, Christian feminists have engaged in the retrieval of 'the lost history of women'. Elisabeth Schüssler *Fiorenza's *In Memory of Her: A Feminist Historical Reconstruction of Christian Origins* (1982) argued convincingly that women exercised significant leadership in the early church. They were missionaries, preachers, and teachers and, she insisted, often presided over the shared meal which later evolved into the church's *eucharistic celebration. The perceived absence of women in the tradition is not a true reflection of their importance but a product of the patriarchal writing of Christian history. Women did not play as public a role as men, but the contributions which they did make are often neglected or forgotten in mainstream historical scholarship. At a superficial level this may reflect the problems of androcentric language. The letters of Paul, for example, address only brothers and sons when clearly the Christian communities included sisters and daughters. Translations from Hebrew and Greek often compound the problem. Feminist scholars have advocated a *hermeneutics of suspicion in relation to all such texts. One should not assume that they reveal the true extent of women's involvement in Christian history.

Feminist historians have also turned their attention to the much neglected stories of powerful and religiously significant women in the OT such as the prophet and judge Deborah (Judg. 4) and Miriam, the sister of Moses and Aaron (Exod. 15). The history of women's work as scholars, *mystics, and foundresses in patristic and medieval times is also important. The range of texts composed by women from the earliest centuries which feminist historians have uncovered highlights the neglect of these sources by traditional scholarship. Detailed studies of the lives and works of women have been made: Perpetua the *martyr, *Hildegard of Bingen, Marguerite Porete (burned as a heretic in Paris in 1310), Hadewijch, and *Teresa of Avila. Others like Dhuoda (9th century) and Hrotsvitha (10th century) are only beginning to be seriously examined, and many are still neglected. Even in the case of Hildegard it is estimated that only 10 per cent of her writings are available in satisfactory modern editions and many of her letters remain unedited. This research gives a more complete picture of the history of Christianity, and an insight into the diverse and important roles that women have played.

Feminist theologians have also been revising traditional theological themes in ways that take seriously the experience of women. This includes reformulations of the concept of *God, of *christology, and of *sin and *redemption. Christian *ethics, both theoretical and applied, also comes under scrutiny as does ecclesiology and *liturgy. These doctrines and practices have tended to convey assumptions about women's inferiority. The main concern in rethinking them is to develop Christian doctrine in an inclusive manner and thereby enhance the standing of women in the churches.

Reconceptualizing the doctrine of God has been one of the main preoccupations. Although it is a commonplace in Christian tradition that God is neither male nor female, in daily liturgy, preaching and catechesis, 'male is what God is'. Christianity does not have a public discourse which acknowledges the possibility, still less the appropriateness, of speaking of God as female. This exclusion of the female from public speech about God reinforces social norms that systematically exclude women. From a feminist perspective, traditional speech about God (classical theism) is both oppressive and idolatrous. It is not the maleness of the language *per se* which is problematic, but the difficulties which arise when these images are used exclusively, literally, and patriarchally. This analysis has given rise to a variety of proposals concerning how best to create a more inclusive understanding of the Christian God. Ruether suggests that Christians should speak of God\ess, Daly proposes Be-ing (a verb not a noun), McFague speaks of God as Mother or God as Friend. Others advocate retrieving the occasional female images of God from the bible and tradition, as for example maternal metaphors such as God's womb or God's breasts which occur throughout the tradition (Isa. 46: 3–4; 49: 14–16; 66: 7–13). Yet another strategy involves restoring the feminine gender of the Hebrew noun *ruah* (spirit) in the doctrine of the Trinity. Catherine LaCugna and Margaret Farley put their faith in emphasizing the relational character of the triune God. Perhaps the most innovative suggestion comes from Elizabeth Johnson. In *She Who Is: The Mystery of God in Feminist Theological Discourse* she reinterprets the 'I Am Who I Am' (Exod. 3: 14) relationally, historically, and in a feminist manner. The Christian God, she claims, can be addressed as She Who Is. She argues that linguistically this is possible, theologically it is legitimate, and religiously it is necessary, if speech about God is to shake off its idolatrous leanings (see FATHERHOOD; MOTHERHOOD).

Christological and soteriological doctrines are also, inevitably, called into question. This is because of the perceived problem that the *Incarnation in male form poses for feminists. Ruether famously asked 'Can a male saviour save women?' This issue revolves around the importance of the maleness as distinct from the *humanity of *Jesus. The Vatican *Declaration Concerning the Question of the Admission of Women to the Ministerial Priesthood* (*Inter Insigniores*, 1976) ascribes theological significance to the maleness of Christ, insisting that the Incarnation in male form is in harmony with the entirety of God's plan. Furthermore it argues that the presider at the Eucharist must be a man, 'for Christ himself was and remains a man'. Elisabeth Schüssler Fiorenza has contested this point by appealing to the soteriological axiom, 'What is not assumed is not healed, but what is assumed is saved by union with God.' The early christological disputes established the theological and salvific importance of the full humanity, not merely the maleness of Jesus. Fiorenza suggests that by turning its back on this central doctrinal principle the Vatican declaration 'risks heresy'.

Christian feminists have almost unanimously answered Ruether's question by saying that a male saviour can save women only if the maleness of Jesus is *not* elevated to a theological principle. Feminist christologies have focused instead on the liberating praxis of Jesus (Jacquelyn Grant, Chung Hyun Kyung), on his *discipleship of equals (Fiorenza), and on Jesus as Sophia Incarnate (Johnson) (see WISDOM). Edwina Sandys's sculpture of the *Christa*, a statue of a female Jesus in a cruciform position, symbolically represents much of this christological thinking.

The reinterpretation of these key Christian symbols has also occasioned related discussions of ecclesiology, ministry, liturgy, and in particular Mariology. The key question is whether *Mary's role in the life and theology of the church challenges or reinforces the male domination of Christianity. Some argue that she represents a strong female presence, with vestiges of earlier goddess worship. Others suggest that she is merely a handmaid of patriarchal religion.

The issue that has had most impact remains that of the *ordination of women. Most churches have now admitted women to the eucharistic ministry (if sometimes reluctantly), but as yet the question is unresolved in the Catholic church, as in Orthodoxy. Above all else this exclusion is seen as symbolic of the patriarchy inherent in Christianity.

Feminist theology has already made a lasting impact by recovering a long-suppressed history of the crucial role of women in Christian life and thought. As it develops it is likely to be concerned less with the past treatment of women and more with the continued reinterpretation of Christian thought and practice in an inclusive manner.   **Linda Hogan**

Cannon, K., *Black Womanist Ethics* (1988).
Christ, C., and Plaskow, J., *Womanspirit Rising: A Feminist Reader in Religion* (1979).
Fiorenza, Elisabeth Schüssler, *In Memory of Her: A Feminist Theological Reconstruction of Christian Origins* (1983).
—— *Searching the Scriptures* (1994–5), i and ii.
Hampson, D., *After Christianity* (1996).
Isasi-Diaz, A., *Mujerista Theology: A Theology for the Twenty-First Century* (1996).
Jantzen, G., *Power, Gender and Christian Mysticism* (1995).
King, U., *Feminist Theology from the Third World: A Reader* (1994).
Loades, A., *Feminist Theology: A Reader* (1990).
Miles, M., *Carnal Knowing* (1989).
Moltmann-Wendel, E., *I Am My Body: A Theology of Embodiment* (1995).
Ruether, R. R., *Sexism and God-Talk* (1983).
Russell, L., and Clarkson, J., *Dictionary of Feminist Theologies* (1996).
Trible, P., *Texts of Terror: Literary-Feminist Readings of Biblical Narratives* (1984).

fideism.

Can a Christian put too much reliance on *faith? 'Fideism', from the Latin *fides*, 'faith', is a term normally used in a hostile sense of Christians who (it is thought) refuse to think, who make a virtue of believing as many impossibilities as possible before breakfast, and who disdain to give an answer for what they believe.

The word is most often used by Catholics. Protestants have 'faith alone' in their heritage, though there faith is contrasted with works, and the keen Protestant sounds *antinomian. In fideism, faith is contrasted with *reason, and the fideist sounds irrational. There have been irrationalist strands in Christianity, such as Tertullian, in the early church, glorying in *paradox, and William of Ockham, in the Middle Ages, logically pulling apart reason and faith. These found their critics, though the word 'fideism' was not used. Faith, the trust in God in times of darkness, and the lived experience that *Pascal knew of the God of Abraham and Isaac and Jacob rather than the god of the philosophers, was so clearly self-authenticating and Christian that the church was slow in using the word to provide the label for a *heresy.

The word 'fideism' was first used by liberal *French Protestants in the 1870s as a term of approval. These were Christians post-Kant and post-Schleiermacher, who had no time for proofs of God's existence, and relied on religious experience. Somehow the heart moves to God, and this has nothing to do with accepting dogmas, which are only symbolic in any case. The best-known book from this school is Louis Sabatier's *Religions of Authority and the Religion of the Spirit*.

Very soon in the 1880s French Catholics took over the word, using it negatively. Catholic encyclopaedias identify very many different ways of being fideist. It is there in 12th-century Islam in al-Ghazali's *Destruction of Philosophers*, in Protestantism as such, in *Schleiermacher, in *Kant, in *existentialism, in the French Catholic school called 'traditionalism', in fact in anything that seemed to cast doubt on the rational credentials of the faith.

In practice many 19th-century Catholics had not had great success in arguing unbelievers into faith. Many retreated to what might be called pragmatic or naive fideism, a siege mentality, determined to accept what the church taught without question. Gifted and promising thinkers looked again at what makes one person believe and another not. Louis Bautain (1796–1867) came to earn, retrospectively, the label of fideism for the main thrust of his work. Bautain was concerned about human need. 'When we speak of God, the question is not to prove that it is impossible he should not exist; the problem is to make men feel that he does exist.' How reminiscent this is of *Coleridge, weary of evidences of religion when what we need is to taste it. Proofs might give us *deism or pantheism, but it is God's revelation that works faith. Knowledge is born of belief, not the other way round; consider the old saying, 'believe in order to understand'. The psychology of belief goes deeper than logic: 'It is not from reason, properly speaking, but from *the centre of the human being*, from that which is profoundest, most mysterious in man, that judgements come.' All this is worked out in a philosophical scheme much indebted to *Plato and somewhat to Kant, where reason deals with the world of the senses, whereas 'intelligence', personally redefined, speaks of a higher 'intelligible' world. An authoritarian church pushed Bautain into recanting, and by 1840 he had agreed that reason can prove everything, and he then gave up publishing original ideas. But the church might have done better to listen.

In the 1840s, and so contemporary with Bautain, but in the completely different theological world of Lutheran Denmark, Søren *Kierkegaard went much further. He encountered a different type of rationalism, the German idealism of *Hegel, a great incorporating scheme that could swallow any contradiction, including anything that might claim to be distinctive in Christianity. So Kierkegaard has sharp boundaries. There is a shocking contradiction between the ethical and the religious. *Fear and Trembling* (1843) looks long and hard at what *Abraham's willingness in faith to sacrifice Isaac means. '[What] a tremendous paradox is faith, a paradox which can transform a murder into a holy act pleasing to God, a paradox by which Isaac is returned to Abraham, a paradox which no thought can encompass because faith begins where thought leaves off.' Christians who talk of paradox and the 'leap of faith' might be called fideist. Kierkegaard, almost unread in the 19th century, seems to speak to the existential condition of many modern Christians.

In the modern philosophy of religion there is a less ardent type of fideism. It may be that it is in the nature of *religious language not to mesh easily with other forms of discourse, and we should not worry about this. This school of thought has been called 'Wittgensteinian fideism'. The philosopher Ludwig *Wittgenstein talked about 'language games', and the need to know what game a particular utterance was in before you could make sense of it. Is there a religious language-game? Thinkers such as D. Z. Phillips claim there is, and that faith-statements, as such, cannot and need not be justified or explained: 'the magical and religious beliefs, unlike the metaphysical statement, the neurosis or the superstition, are not forms of language of which it makes sense to ask, "Why are you speaking like that?"' The believer and the non-believer are just not seeing the same picture. 'If one characterizes the lack of belief as believing the opposite one falsifies the character of belief and the character of non-belief.' Critics of such arguments as this, not themselves simple rationalists, are ungrateful for what seems to be no more than a licence for a private language.

Those called fideists thus often reason well to show where reason

cannot go, whether in uncovering the motives of our hearts, or in acknowledging the difference between God-talk and other discourses.   **Alistair Mason**

Kierkegaard, S., *Fear and Trembling* (1843).
McCool, G. A., *Catholic Theology in the Nineteenth Century: The Quest for a Unitary Method* (1977).
Phillips, D. Z., *Religion without Explanation* (1976).
Reardon, B. M. G., *Liberalism and Tradition: Aspects of Catholic Thought in Nineteenth Century France* (1975).

filioque, Latin 'and from the Son', referring to the double procession of the *Holy Spirit. Christian pneumatology was one of the last elements of the classical architecture of *doctrine formally to emerge in the patristic era. It was only at the very end of the *Arian controversy that *christological statements on the coequality of the Son of God were extrapolated to refine the church's understanding of the *person and status of the Spirit of God. Accordingly the Nicene *Creed, which had been elevated in the early 4th century as a main standard of right belief, was seen at the end of that century to be defective in its expressions about the Holy Spirit. Originally the creed's pneumatological element read only: 'And we believe in the Holy Spirit'. At the Council of Constantinople in 381, however, the fathers affirmed the full divine status of the Spirit by adding the significant developing clauses: 'And we believe in the Holy Spirit, the Lord and Life-Giver, who proceeds from the Father, who with the Father and Son is co-worshipped and co-glorified; who has spoken through the prophets.' Such was the final form of the Niceno-Constantinopolitan creed which thereafter became the standard of *orthodoxy for east and west alike, soon regarded as a sacrosanct expression of the ancient catholic faith.

The *filioque* clause refers to a later addition to the western version of that creed, which became popularly diffused in the west in Carolingian times. To the clause 'who proceeds from the Father' (a biblically inspired description taken from John 15: 26) unknown Latin apologists in 6th-century Spain (probably determined to defend *Trinitarian orthodoxy in the face of a renewed Arian apologetic) added the term 'and from the Son'.

When the additional phrase first came to the notice of the east, being introduced into the Latin churches at *Constantinople, the learned Patriarch Photios censured it as an unauthorized addition to an ecumenical *council's definition of the faith. He communicated with the papacy, and disagreement ensued over the theological orthodoxy of the addition. Western theologians argued that the theology of double procession exemplified by the *filioque* clause was a précis of the Trinitarian theology of *Augustine. Greek theologians, led by Photios, contended that it was a *heretical confusion of a fundamental principle of the internal cohesion of the divine Trinity, wherein the Father was the sole cause of both the Son and the Spirit. The medieval papacy refused to accept that the *filioque* was heretical, but resisted all attempts to add it formally to the creed until the 11th century, by which time it had become a standard element of western catholic confession.

On many occasions, both ancient and modern, notably at the councils of Lyons (1274) and *Florence (1439), the matter has been discussed, for it is regarded as a substantive cause of ecclesial division. The eastern churches continue to regard the *filioque* as doubly objectionable: first in having been intruded into an ecumenical statement and thus unwarrantedly elevating a local *theologoumenon* into a universal dogma; secondly in having at best dubious theological justification, or at worst committing the western churches to an erroneous form of basic confession. Any future dialogue between *Eastern Orthodoxy and the western Catholic churches will need to address this issue.   **John McGuckin**

Howard, G. B., *The Schism between the Oriental and Western Churches with Special Reference to the Addition of the Filioque to the Creed* (1892).

Kelly, J. N. D., *Early Christian Creeds*, 3rd edn. (1972), 358–67.

Vischer, L., *Spirit of God, Spirit of Christ: Ecumenical Reflections on the Filioque Controversy*, WCC, Faith and Order Paper, 103 (1981).

Fiorenza, Elisabeth Schüssler (1938–).

An internationally renowned scholar, Fiorenza has combined scholarship on *biblical interpretation with innovative work on *feminist *hermeneutics and theology. She has published widely in German and English and her books have been translated into several languages. She gained her licentiate in practical theology and her doctorate in New Testament studies in Germany, but her academic career has been mostly in the United States. She has lectured at the University of Notre Dame, the Episcopal Divinity School in Cambridge, and since 1988 has been Krister Stendahl professor of scripture at the Harvard Divinity School. She was the first woman president of the Society of Biblical Literature, is on the editorial boards of many major journals, and has received numerous awards and honorary doctorates.

Fiorenza's theology involves two interrelated projects, each of which was introduced in her ground-breaking *In Memory of Her* (1983). She has argued that the early church was a 'discipleship of equals' and has engaged in *archaeological, textual, and *historical research to demonstrate that much of *women's participation in Christian history has been neglected. This has involved the articulation of a feminist biblical hermeneutics in which questions of the authority of biblical texts and their use in the church today, together with more textually based issues, are examined. Her second concern has been to formulate a new vision and theology of Christian praxis, which draws its inspiration from the early church. The future *ekklesia* must be a democratic community of women and men who envision new ways of being Christian. Fiorenza pioneered, and herself exemplifies, this combination of historical reconstruction and advocacy which has become an important methodology for feminist theology.   **Linda Hogan**

Fiorenza, E. S., *Bread Not Stone* (1984).

—— *Discipleship of Equals* (1993).

—— *Jesus: Miriam's Child, Sophia's Prophet* (1994).

—— *Revelation: Vision of a Just World* (1991).

fire.

Despite its high *symbolic power in many religions, fire has seldom been effectively integrated into the Christian symbolic system. God's self-revelation to *Moses ('I am who I am') in the burning bush that remained unconsumed (Exod. 3: 1–15) made fire irrevocably an image of divine presence. 'Our God is a consuming fire', wrote the author of *Hebrews (12: 29), quoting Deuteronomy 4: 24. The message here seems aimed at inculcating fear: God's displeasure can burn one up. But the gospel use of fire suggests a wider perspective. Jesus, said John, 'will baptize you with the Holy Spirit and with fire' (Luke 3: 16) 'It is fire', Jesus declared, 'that I have come to spread over the earth' (Luke 12: 49). Hence, tongues of fire descend on the apostles at *Pentecost (Acts 2: 3), symbolizing the

descent of the *Holy Spirit, transforming them into courageous, outgoing evangelists able to talk in a multitude of languages and convert a multitude of listeners. While the rite of lighting the new fire to signify the *Resurrection has remained part of the Easter vigil liturgy, it is not always performed very excitingly. In practice the symbol of fire has largely been captured by the *devil and his cohorts or, at least, by a multitude of hellfire *preachers, though essentially the fires of *hell are simply the achievement of divine justice implementing the message of Hebrews. The fires of purgatory do the same more constructively: 'Learn that the flame of the Everlasting Love doth burn ere it transform,' as *Newman put it in *The Dream of Gerontius*. But the effective transfer of ownership of fire from the Holy Spirit to Satan by late medieval artists and evangelical preachers has been part of a larger evacuation of a theology of the spirit for many centuries prior to 20th-century *Pentecostalism.

Fire may be too unpredictable to be a safe symbol for internal use within a highly controlled ecclesiastical or sacramental system. Its principal use was, instead, for the public execution of *heretics and *witches, again a matter of inculcating fear. This too was a late-medieval development. Joan of Arc in 1431 at Rouen, Servetus in 1553 in *Calvin's *Geneva, Cranmer in 1556 at Oxford, and Giordano Bruno in Rome in 1600 were among thousands burnt at the stake. It may be hard for the church to look fire in the face after such a history.

A positive use of the symbol remains most apt to express areas of religious life uncontrolled by the institution. When George Fox denounced 'the bloody city of Lichfield' on a famous occasion he felt 'the fire of the Lord … all over me'. Perhaps he recalled how, forty years earlier, Edward Wightman had been burnt at Lichfield for claiming to be the paraclete. Fire speaks of the passion and unexpectedness of *prophecy, of uncontrolled *enthusiasm, of sudden violent movements of *conversion and *revival, of all the things which the first Christian Pentecost experience hinted at but which tend to be excluded in the regularity of an orderly church. 'The fire that breaks from thee then', wrote *Hopkins in *The Windhover: To Christ our Lord*, 'a billion | Times told lovelier, more dangerous, O my chevalier!'   **Adrian Hastings**

flesh, see BODY; INCARNATION.

Florence, Council of (1439–45).

For the western church this *council is important because it both sounded the death knell of the *conciliar movement and achieved partial reunions with the Greek (Orthodox) and other eastern churches. For easterners it is largely a mirage concocted by the west and affecting little the sorry story of *schism between the churches (see EASTERN ORTHODOX THEOLOGY).

The council came about because Pope Eugenius IV rejected the wishes of the majority of the Council of Basle and ordered its transfer to Italy. Eugenius had been hostile to that council from its beginning, chiefly because it asserted the superiority of a general council over the pope, and he sought an opportunity to dissolve it or transfer it to a city which would be more under his control. At a vote on 7 May 1437, two-thirds of the members of the council voted for remaining at Basle, one-third voted for the pope's proposed transfer. Those who voted to remain preserved a council at Basle, and later at Lausanne, until it finally dissolved itself in 1449, but it gradually lost out in the struggle with the rival papal council. Conciliarism never fully recovered in the medieval period.

Eugenius transferred the minority council briefly to Ferrara and then in 1439 to Florence. This council occupied itself partly in issuing condemnations against the continuing council at Basle, partly in negotiations for reunion with the Greek and other eastern churches. For the discussions about reunion, the delegation of the Greek church, from *Constantinople, was persuaded by Pope Eugenius to come to Ferrara and later to Florence, not to Basle; their choice was a major reason for the demise of the council at Basle.

At Florence, in July 1439, after much discussion, a formula of reunion was agreed upon. The decree, which was promulgated in both Latin and Greek, is usually referred to in the west by the opening words of the Latin version, *Laetentur Caeli*. Agreement was reached on four issues. First, the Greeks accepted the legitimacy of the addition of the *filioque* clause in the western *creed but they were not obliged to include it in their own creed. Diversity of practice was also accepted in the type of *bread used in the *Eucharist: leavened bread by the Greek church, unleavened by the Latin. *Purgatory, thirdly, was recognized but in the sense of 'cleansing pains' and without mention of fire, which was objectionable to the Greeks. Finally, the latter accepted *papal primacy, including plenitude of jurisdiction, but with the saving clause 'as is contained in the acts of ecumenical councils and in the sacred canons'.

The reunion was not a sell-out to the western church. Eugenius IV, knowing that reunion would be a major victory in his struggle with the Council of Basle, made considerable concessions, certainly greater than had been made by any of his predecessors as popes since the start of the schism in the late 11th century. All the members of the Greek delegation, including its leader, the emperor John VIII Palaeologus, signed the decree of reunion except the metropolitan of Ephesus, Mark Eugenicus. The patriarch of Constantinople, Joseph II, who had been present at the negotiations, died shortly before the signing. Nevertheless the reunion was not received within the Greek church. Several members of their delegation, in addition to Mark Eugenicus, voiced reservations on the sea voyage back to Constantinople, and the emperor John VIII never formally promulgated the decree of reunion within the Byzantine empire. The whole project was overtaken by the capture of Constantinople by the Turks in 1453.

The reunion, therefore, has been of historical interest rather than of lasting theological significance. In the renewal of discussions about reunion in recent years, attention has focused more on the possibility of returning to relations between the two churches before the original split in the 11th century. Still, the decree of Florence has formed part of the background of recent discussions and it may have potential for the future, especially since it illustrates the willingness of the papacy to compromise.

The rejection of the reunion by the eastern church was not immediately apparent in the west, so that *Laetentur Caeli* appeared to be a triumph for the papacy. Thereafter the council, which moved to Rome in 1443 for the final two years of its existence, occupied itself in further condemnations of the Council of Basle and in reunions with four other churches: *Armenians, Copts, Chaldaeans, and Maronites of Cyprus. In each case only a small group within the church entered into communion with Rome and the reunion

meant, for the most part, a submission to Roman claims rather than a negotiated settlement. The decrees of reunion with the Armenians and Copts were very detailed and they exercised considerable influence upon Roman Catholic theology in later centuries, defining the seven *sacraments and asserting the impossibility of *salvation outside the church.

Another aspect of the council, which influenced the European *Renaissance, was the arrival of Greek scholars from *Byzantium. Most prominent among them was John Bessarion, who as archbishop of Nicaea attended the council as part of the delegation from Constantinople. He accepted the reunion, was created a cardinal by Pope Eugenius and made his home in Italy, where he acted as a patron to other Greek scholars.

The council came to be included in the Roman Catholic Church's traditional list of ecumenical councils. But its ecumenicity, and therefore its authority, may be questioned on the grounds of both its rejection by the Greek church and the abstention of the Council of Basle from its proceedings.   **Norman Tanner**

Concilium Florentinum: Documenta et Scriptores. Editum consilio et impensis Pontificii Instituti Orientalium Studiorum (11 vols.; 1940–70).

Alberigo, G. (ed.), *Christian Unity: The Council of Ferrara-Florence 1438/ 9–1989* (1991).

Gill, J., *The Council of Florence* (1959).

Hussey, J., *The Orthodox Church in the Byzantine Empire* (1986).

Tanner, N. P. (ed.), *Decrees of the Ecumenical Councils* (1990), i.

Florovsky, Georges

Florovsky, Georges (1893–1979), *Russian church historian, *ecumenist, and philosopher-theologian. Florovsky was a member of that circle of Russian intellectuals (including Bulgakov, Lossky, and Berdyaev) which first brought *Eastern Orthodox theology back to the attention of western thinkers in the early and mid-20th century.

Florovsky spent the major part of his active life in representing the Orthodox voice in the *Faith and Order movement and the World Council of Churches. Challenged by the hermeneutics of international dialogue he argued that only a 'Neo-Patristic Synthesis' in theology could restore a common language to ecumenical discourse. For him, the creative yet faithful translation made by the patristic age of the biblical discourse rooted in Jewish culture had not only evangelized the Greek world but in the process had created the distinctive culture of Christianity. Florovsky offered this reconciliation of cultural paradigms as a model for theologians to elaborate a systematic that reached out to modernity (with its own nexus of philosophical understandings) and yet was always in harmony with that continuity of Christian experience witnessed in the *conciliar tradition. His positive approach to historical theology as revealed wisdom contrasted starkly with the agenda of *Protestant systematics in his own day.

*Symbolic antinomies much characterized his mind. He described Christianity as ever poised between the poles of *creation and *eschatological experience. He thought Roman Catholicism tended to overstress the first, and Protestantism the latter; whereas a patristic-led Orthodoxy sought the balance, and might thus serve to facilitate an ecumenical reconciliation. His full range of writings became widely available in English only after his death. Today his influence is mainly felt among younger Orthodox theologians of western education. His major work on the *Ways of Russian Theology* still stands as a definitive achievement.   **John McGuckin**

Florovsky, G., *The Collected Works* (14 vols.; ET 1987).

Blane, A. (ed.), *Georges Florovsky: Russian Intellectual—Orthodox Churchman* (1993) (with full bibliography).

Neimann, D., and Schatlein, M. (eds.), *The Heritage of the Early Church: Essays in Honour of G. V. Florovsky, Orientalia Christiana Analecta*, 195 (1973).

folk religion. This term, as a way of referring to part of the religious interface between canonical traditions and particular human concerns, pinpoints problems that confront Christian *orthodoxy whenever it combines *mission with inculturation. As is the way of such expressions, its use is both ambiguous and emotive.

The term originates with students of peasant cultures, and of their transplants and 'survivals' in industrial societies (see ANTHROPOLOGY). In this matrix, folk religion is part of a package that includes other aspects of life such as folk-dancing and folklore. American usage of the term tends to be at the level of such folk arts. Patronizing or admiring, the interest that inspired such studies has encouraged a recovery of confidence among the 'folk' themselves, as well as the adoption of many such traditions by outsiders.

English usage, on the other hand, has been more judgemental. In the 1960s, Anglican clergy especially began to refer in this way to the desire of non-churchgoers to have children baptized, or to have a church wedding or funeral. However, by the 1980s, when the term became generally recognized, it could also be seen as a tactful way of obtaining a place on ecclesiastical agendas for serious consideration of the variety of possible reasons for requesting such 'occasional offices'. The 'occasional' recourse to orthodox rites was then seen as being (necessarily) infrequent, without necessarily being casual.

Between these two usages, which might be described as the social and the ecclesiastical, lie a more productive pair, from the realm of religious studies. Japanese scholars (writing in English) describe as folk religion that congeries of individual and familial practices which lies beneath any major tradition that is also popular. Just as we have learnt to look at the great traditions of world *religions without prejudging them as 'idolatry', so this approach lets us consider the 'little', or more popular, traditions without prejudging their value or their motivation as mere 'superstitions' or 'insurance policies'. The term only differs from 'popular religion' by its emphasis upon practices that tend to be widespread, and yet private, as against practices that are collective and public. Both are responses to human felt needs, but 'folk religion' is more appropriate when people are making use of a tradition in which they no longer seem to play an unbroken part.

Nordic and Germanic scholars, on the other hand, use 'folk religion' to highlight the corporate continuity of those peoples that trace their identity back to the conversion to Christianity of an invading *Volk* in the first millennium. This approach has the advantage of emphasizing the historical dimension of folk religion, explaining why universal concerns find different forms of expression. This usage overlaps with that of civil religion. However, the latter tends to be used of what is civic rather than civil, official rather than popular, formal rather than collective, expressive of particular corporations rather than itself corporate, and so is less expressive of the concerns of ordinary folk.

'Folk religion' came into general Christian usage at the end of the 20th century, as those formally involved in Roman Catholic or Protestant missionary activity increasingly distinguished religion from culture, faith from context. There used to be a tendency to criticize 'others' for turning icons into idols, sacraments into fetishes, scriptures into spells, rites into magic. Recently, though, those who are most active in western mainline evangelism have become increasingly aware of the ambiguities that are present, both within other religions and cultures, and within their own. Sectarian critics, however, tend to dismiss such sophisticated questioning as indicating either a loss of specifically Christian faith, or as part of a general failure of nerve. Such criticisms are, indeed, also to be heard within all the mainline denominations.

However, the issue is widely seen as having a long history. The example is frequently cited of Augustine of Canterbury, asking whether the native English temples should be razed (and thus erased); and Pope Gregory the Great's reply, recommending that they be converted into churches. A similar issue regarding the proper relationship between new revelation and old cloth may be seen in the First Council of Jerusalem (Acts 15) regarding the need (or otherwise) for circumcision, and in Jesus' saying that he came, not to abolish the Law, but to fulfil it.

Christian thinking on the issues referred to by the term tends towards three conclusions. The first is that no single, simple, uniform, universal answer is possible. Precedent for a variety of responses may be found in the example of Jesus himself, who at different times either avoided or accepted the contemporary Jewish ('folk-religious') title of *Messiah. The second conclusion is that the issue in every case is not the outward form (architectural, musical, ritual, etc.), but its spiritual significance (bearing in mind the observers, as well as the actors). To discern this requires extreme sensitivity, but it remains crucial.

Lastly, Christian belief does not consider the relevance of the gospel to every human concern as abrogated by the equivocal, partial, or spasmodic character of people's adhesion to it. The God and Father of Jesus Christ is seen as more, not less, concerned than humankind with matters such as birth and death, health and sickness, prosperity and poverty, justice and injustice, peace and war, safety and risk. Christian faith, indeed, often draws its metaphors, if not its entire meaning, from precisely such experiences. 'In good faith', therefore, Christian discipleship often runs the risk of 'compromising the Gospel', in order to communicate the faith.

Edward Bailey

Carr, A. W., *Brief Encounters: Pastoral Ministry through the Occasional Offices* (1985).

Clark, D., *Between Pulpit and Pew: Folk Religion in a North Yorkshire Fishing Village* (1982).

Davies, D., et al., *Church and Religion in Rural England* (1991).

foreknowledge (divine) and freedom. Divine foreknowledge refers to *God's knowledge of events prior to their occurrence. It is usually dealt with in discussions of God's *omniscience. Scriptural resources for a doctrine of divine omniscience may be found in Psalm 139, in the contention that information about the future is imparted to *prophets, and in repeated references to God's *providential rule over nature and history. Further arguments refer typically to the omnipresence and *omnipotence of God. Nothing is excluded from the divine vision. To limit God's knowledge is to place God on a level with creatures whose faculties are severely limited. Omniscience, moreover, is a necessary condition of God's sovereign rule over the cosmos.

The most serious difficulty for any doctrine of divine foreknowledge concerns its compatibility with creaturely *freedom. If God knows the course of the future then the outcome of all human actions must already be fixed. Various attempts to resolve this difficulty can be identified in the history of Christian thought. As early as Justin Martyr it is argued that since divine foreknowledge is of future free actions, the latter are guaranteed by the former. Thomas *Aquinas claims that although it is necessary that God foreknows future events, those events themselves are not necessary occurrences. The necessity attaches only to God's knowledge. The difficulty with this manœuvre is its tendency to deprive human action of the element of indeterminacy necessary at the time of our free choices. Thus if God already knows for certain—as opposed to having informed beliefs or making reasonable guesses—what I shall do on 1 January next year, my choices seem to be deprived of freedom. If I am genuinely free in what I do on that day, then is there nothing which determines the outcome of my decisions in advance. There is consequently nothing by virtue of which God can fully comprehend the future, since the future, at least in part, is unsettled. This objection presupposes a strong libertarian account of freedom. However, if one works with a thesis in which freedom and causal determinism are compatible (sometimes referred to by philosophers as 'soft determinism' or 'compatibilism') then one may adhere to this resolution of divine foreknowledge and human freedom.

An alternative solution is to maintain the *timeless nature of God's knowledge. This notion of divine timelessness is found in Boethius and *Anselm, and is the preferred solution of Aquinas to the problem of foreknowledge and freedom. God does not foreknow the future since the divine mode of existence transcends temporal categories. Past, present, and future are simultaneously present to God's eternal vision. The past is not so much foreknown as known timelessly. While commanding significant assent in the history of Christian thought, this proposal has been subjected to vigorous criticism in recent *philosophy of religion. The principal objections are that timeless knowledge of temporal events may involve a contradiction and that a timeless God is incapable of genuine intention, action, and involvement in the drama of creation. The view thus emerges that divine foreknowledge must be limited by the bestowal of genuine freedom upon creatures. Even God cannot know for certain the precise shape of the future, although this does not preclude God having keen insight into what we are likely to do and exercising a providential rule of the world.

See also ETERNITY; PREDESTINATION.   **David A. S. Fergusson**

Fischer, John Martin (ed.), *God, Foreknowledge, and Freedom* (1989).
Swinburne, Richard, *The Coherence of Theism* (1993).
Taliaferro, Charles, *Contemporary Philosophy of Religion* (1998).

forgiveness

forgiveness takes various forms according to context. Some are simple, known through everyday life. So, for example, forgiving operates when hurt, insult, and injustice are not revenged, but good is returned for evil. Genuine goodness works for *reconciliation with the wrongdoer. Any viable reconciliation will involve forgiving, both as *freedom from past offence and in sustaining new relations with one's fallible fellow-beings. Not executing *punishment for an offence may be a form of forgiving, though it can also arise from carelessness about *justice or a lack of power to punish. Pardon for guilt embodies a refusal to let the wrong done determine the future freedom of the wrongdoer. The remission of debt, an early model for forgiveness in the Christian tradition (as in the *Lord's Prayer and *parables of Jesus, e.g. Matt. 18: 23–35), shows that forgiving is not purely spiritual, but operates in social and economic practicalities. Where the mechanisms and *morality of society insist that debtors must fulfil their obligations to the last farthing, the poor will be enslaved and crushed. To correct such oppression, Leviticus 25 prescribed the restoration of alienated property every fifty years; the international campaign for the cancellation of the unpayable debts of the world's poorest countries by the year 2000 took its title from this Jubilee (see POVERTY).

Forgiving, as pardon of guilt or remission of debt, liberates from the past. This liberation is sometimes seen as analogous to forgetting: God in forgiving 'remembers your sin no more'. Some forgetting is inevitable in human life; it may preserve sanity and to some degree support forgiving, but it is not a clue to its essence: forgiving is always a way of reckoning *truthfully with what is wrong and hence is a way of remembering, in which the past wrong is not denied but deprived of its power to shape the future. It is not pure remembering, in which the past stays with us, but a remembering which enables the transformation of the past so that it no longer destroys *joy, *peace, and *love. Wrong may determine the future and thus block forgiveness in more than one way. It may operate as the accepted basis for future action (as though the wrong were right) or it may be the object of obsessive attempts to punish and revenge (in which case, the wrongness of the wrong is admitted, but allows opponents and victims no freedom to do anything but react to it). When forgiving is effective, wrong is remembered, but no longer sets the agenda for the future or consumes people's lives. Where forgiveness is understood as intrinsic to reconciliation, remembering is especially inescapable, for the persons being reconciled do not have identity without *memory. This applies equally to personal relations, to relationships within the family, and to larger societies and organizations. In post-*apartheid South Africa, as elsewhere, working for reconciliation has involved bringing truth to light, even when it is hidden in shame and pain. Beyond acknowledgement of truth, there is the problematic concept of the healing of memories. It is at least clear that interpreting *history can play an important part in forgiveness.

A truthful future free from determination by past wrong is not only the product of forgiveness, but also its dynamic incentive and justification. Forgiveness is more than remembering or mere evolution from the past; it reaches out for, welcomes and is sustained by imagined or promised futures. Forgiveness is the restoration of a free spirit (Ps. 51: 10) in relation to God and *conscience.

Where the future comes from, if it does not evolve from the past, is mysterious. Its openness may be seen as the gift of the living God and/or the challenge to persons and *human communities to take freedom as the presupposition for living. Disputes about repentance are concerned with the moral relation between past and future in forgiveness. Repentance is commonly regarded as a prerequisite of forgiveness: the wrongdoer must turn from the past, with contrition and reparation, before forgiveness can be granted. In this case the burden of change falls on the penitent, so that there is little for the forgiver to do beyond accepting the change achieved by the penitent. But another view sees forgiveness as a costly initiative creating a new undeserved opportunity for the wrongdoer; repentance then occurs when the wrongdoer goes through the door opened by forgiveness. Repentance is the reshaping which happens through living within the forgiveness (or 'embrace' as Volf puts it) on offer. This second account of repentance reflects the priority and recreative authority of God's forgiving. Jesus invited people to repent by welcoming and living in accord with the coming *Kingdom of God; repentance was less from past *sin, more towards the future. This way of thinking does not minimize repentance, but it does prevent its being turned into a moral precondition dispensing the forgiver from risking the generous pioneering inventiveness of forgiving. It obviates the fashionable pious error which sees forgiving as holy impotence rather than the exercise of power to effect liberating and humanizing change.

Many examples of these modes of forgiving are to be found in the bible. There, they are held within and serve to build up a cumulative narrative of God's relations with his people, in which his forgiving, or withholding forgiveness, is a critical issue. Since God chose ordinary wayward people to be his own and to carry his reputation (name) in the world, forgiving is more than non-judgemental generosity to wrongdoers. It becomes the only way by which God can faithfully sustain the *covenant and show that he is Lord against all his enemies who despise and maltreat his people (Ezek. 36: 13–38). So the return from *exile is itself forgiveness (2 Chr. 6: 24, 25): divine forgiving operates on a grand historical scale, to be discerned and sought in public, collective practice. It is because God forgives that he is to be feared, honoured as truly God (Ps. 130). In the Christian prolongation and early readings of this narrative, God's forgiving was concentrated in the central event of the *sacrificial *death and *Resurrection of Jesus and thereby universalized. All humanity sins in *Adam and is restored in Christ (Rom. 5), the Lamb of God, who takes away the sin of the world (John 1: 29).

Forgiveness in the Christian account is not a purely transcendent divine act, done once for all at the *Cross or at the final *judgement. God's forgiveness is enacted humanly. The gospel unites God and humanity in forgiving. When Jesus forgave the paralytic, and was charged with usurping God's place, he responded not by saying he was God, but that authority had been given to the 'Son of Man' to forgive sins on earth (Mark 2: 1–10). Jesus in turn gave the disciples the authority to forgive and retain sins. The church is a community constituted by the forgiveness of sins. Forgiveness is the practice by which it holds together as a community, facing and resolving conflicts, and including the awkward, strangers, and sinners as Jesus did in eating with them. The basic principle is spelt out in the Lord's Prayer and in parables of Jesus: we are forgiven as we forgive (Matt. 18: 15–35; 6: 12).

The communication and management of forgiveness thus became a prime responsibility of the church, as it understood itself on the basis of Matt. 16: 19 and John 20: 22–3: the dominical commission of the disciples gives them the power to remit and retain sin. This ministry of forgiveness was achieved through *preaching and *baptism. Since baptism identified with Christ, the *eschatolo-

gically perfect sacrifice for sin, sin after baptism was especially wrong: indeed some thought it ontologically impossible and others unforgivable. To cope with post-baptismal sin, the sacrament of *penance developed and, throughout the medieval period, became progressively less severe and more encouraging to sinners. The piety of western Christianity especially revolved around the forgiveness of sin. Increasingly, the Mass was focused by it; *purgatory and indulgences grew in importance in order to give hope of forgiveness in the face of the final judgement of God. The *Reformation modified rather than broke with this tradition: it was emphasized that God's forgiveness was already accomplished in Christ, and therefore should be a sure foundation for life rather than a hoped-for end. Preaching rather than penance became the way it was communicated. In *evangelicalism, *conversion rather than baptism became the locus of the definitive reception of forgiveness.

The forgiveness which really counted was God's, at the final judgement. Intra-human forgiving was often presented as a condition for being forgiven by God and so attaining eternal salvation. It was less often seen as actual participation in God's forgiving. Thus the universal narrative of forgiveness was not applied to the whole of life. It was recognized that much normal practice in the *world was not forgiving and the church did not expect to transform or reorder this world. The limitation is not to be explained wholly by people's inability ever to be fully forgiving. It was also the effect of the way the church managed forgiveness. *Universalism (the inevitable final salvation of all human beings) has rarely been seen as an implication of the universal narrative: *Origen represents a minority in expecting even the *devil to be finally redeemed by forgiveness. Some, like *Barth, have risked, but also qualified, universalistic language in order to be faithful to the triumph of *grace over sin. Mostly, Christian thought has been in tension, glorifying the amazing grace of divine forgiving while being cautious lest justice, *virtue, and order are undermined by too much of it. The tension is eased by compartmentalization: forgiveness is consigned to the relation of persons with God, and to some degree to uninstitutionalized interpersonal relations, but excluded from the methods and responsibilities of social organization. At most forgiveness becomes the exception to the rules rather than the essential good which the rules should respect and implement. *Luther was typical of this tradition when he systematized its restriction of the scope of forgiveness by distinguishing rigidly between the two modes of God's rule of the world, through *law and sword without forgiveness on the one hand, and grace and word (gospel), and so forgiveness, on the other. This systematization could not, however, accommodate all Christian belief and experience of forgiveness. Since in Christendom church and civil society were closely related, the need for forgiveness to repair social peace was continually and pragmatically evidenced. It was understood that if people do not forgive each other, they will often destroy each other. Already in the NT this prudential argument for forgiving was put and its operation in a pre-modern parochial Christendom is exemplified by the Communion Service and its accompanying pastoral discipline in the *Anglican Prayer Book of 1662.

Though it is a human necessity, not a Christian peculiarity, forgiveness became, in the history of the west, especially associated with the church, and so was vulnerable to criticism and marginalization as secularization in the modern period reduced the church's influence. The *realpolitik* of Machiavelli, the strict moralism of *Kant, and *Nietzsche's anti-Christian humanism of strength variously belittled forgiveness. *Science and technology order power efficiently with an implicit promise that mistakes can be reduced, if not quite eliminated; they hint at utopias where forgiving is redundant, as people are perfectly—chemically or socially—adjusted to their environments. Reconciliation and forgiveness were eschewed by *revolutionaries who were sufficiently confident in their projects to make a new world even when that involved being murderously unforgiving to all who represented the old. It is only with the discrediting of these projects in the late 20th century that there is a renewed openness to forgiving as a practical wisdom for life, rather than as religious idealism or even sentimentality.

Modernity, however, has not been unambiguously hostile to forgiveness. Tolerance and forgiveness are indeed to be distinguished, but not separated: tolerance will be fragile where there is no readiness to forgive and forgiveness needs tolerance as one of its instruments. In education and psychotherapy, the understanding has grown that, even though they are complex and questionable, human beings must be affirmed rather than condemned if they are to do well. So forgiveness has been reinterpreted as 'acceptance' by oneself, by others, and by whatever serves as God (as in *Tillich and Frank Lake's clinical theology). Though this translation runs the risk of confusing forgiveness with narcissistic self-indulgence, it also shows the continuing relevance of the idea and the experience of forgiveness.

In the darkness of 20th-century history, the question whether human beings can accept and live with themselves has not been an idle one. In view of the record, it is impossible to affirm the worth or dignity of humanity if there is no embracing narrative of forgiveness whose truth is supported by historical, if partial, demonstrations. Admittedly, it remains as easy as ever for the righteous to affirm themselves by directing their fire at the unforgivably wicked 'other'; this may give divisive comfort, so long as the self-righteous can protect themselves from exposure as flawed hypocrites, unfit to cast the first stone. It is not surprising that recent study recovers and works afresh from the biblical potential for understanding forgiveness as divine and human together.

In the 21st century, it will be necessary to understand and practise forgiveness in new ways. The overarching *ecological crisis teaches us how much human beings depend on forgiveness for life itself. For most of its history, humanity has been able to trust the natural world to be resilient in recovering itself, whatever the damage caused to it by aggressive exploitation. In that sense, humanity has been able to take for granted the forgivingness of its natural environment as a whole system. Now there is reason to fear that humanity has stretched this natural forgivingness to breaking-point. Does it matter if humanity is in the end discarded and unforgiven by the total environmental system (Gaia)? Since Christian thinking is committed to a belief in *creation which includes the worth of human beings as the image of God, it cannot be indifferent to humanity's proving to be finally unforgiven. The only way forward is for human beings deliberately to share practical responsibility for nurturing and maintaining the forgivingness which sustains their existence.   **Haddon Willmer**

Jones, L. Gregory, *Embodying Forgiveness: A Theological Analysis* (1995).
Mackintosh, H. R., *The Christian Experience of Forgiveness* (1927).
Moore, Sebastian, *The Crucified is No Stranger* (1977).
Shriver, Donald W., *An Ethic for Enemies: Forgiveness in Politics* (1995).
Telfer, W., *The Forgiveness of Sins* (1959).
Tournier, P., *Guilt and Grace* (ET 1962).
Volf, M., *Exclusion and Embrace* (1996).
von Campenhausen, H., *Ecclesiastical Authority and Spiritual Power in the Church of the First Three Centuries* (1969).
Wiesenthal, S., *The Sunflower* (1969).

Franciscan thought. The life of *Francis of Assisi posed for his followers many of the same problems that the life of Christ posed for early Christians. Choosing to own nothing but the clothes on his back, Francis exemplified the ideals of absolute *poverty and humility. He was, by his own description, an *idiota* (an unlearned one). Though educated persons were welcome in the order Francis founded, he discouraged the friars from studying and would not permit them to own books. Someone with books would yearn for a quiet place to read, then for even more books, and so would become dissatisfied with poverty. Worse, he would tend to feel superior to the illiterate. Francis wanted his followers to avoid such temptations. To his mind, people have only as much knowledge as they can put into practice, and they can preach only as well as they act. He accordingly urged the friars to preach mainly by concrete example, to do good works, as the saints did, instead of merely talking about them.

The Franciscans saw in their founder's life a faithful imitation of the life of Christ. At the same time, they encountered grave difficulties when they tried to follow Francis's example to the letter. Their burgeoning number alone made it hard to preserve the ideal of absolute poverty. When a dozen friars beg for food and shelter, they may serve as an evangelical inspiration to the Christian community. When the number rises to hundreds, the community faces some of the same problems presented by the homeless in our own day. The practice of begging easily becomes less inspiring than annoying, or even threatening. The backlash increased owing to the *apocalypticism of many Franciscans during the 13th century. Those who believed that the end of the world was quite near, though usually the closest to Francis's ideal of wandering mendicancy, also tended to favour drastic institutional changes distressing to established authorities. If it were going to survive, the order had to acquire greater discipline and stability.

The ban on owning books and on study in general proved highly controversial even during Francis's lifetime. Many of his followers sought greater latitude in *preaching. They thought it important to preach not only by example and through moral exhortation but also on scripture and matters of doctrine. To do so, they would need to learn theology, an exercise difficult to reconcile with Francis's efforts to discourage his followers from educational pursuits.

Does learning truly have no spiritual value? Is it only a temptation to pride and a step on the road to acquisitiveness? The task of finding a place for study in the life of the friars fell to Bonaventure, who came to be known as the second founder of the Franciscan order.

Bonaventure believed that in struggling to follow Francis, as in struggling to imitate Christ, one needs to distinguish between those works intended for imitation and those intended for instruction. If we were expected to imitate Christ in all respects, would we not be expected to perform miracles? Francis himself, according to Bonaventure, intended preaching as the chief work of the friars. Poverty was part of Francis's ideal, but it was not the ideal itself. In *The Journey of the Mind to God* (1259), Bonaventure explains that we need not repudiate the sensible world, for it reflects the goodness, wisdom, and power of its creator. We must, however, move beyond contemplation of sensible things to contemplation of the *soul as *God's image and the attributes of God himself. Learning has a place in this ascent: the labour of the mind is no less *work than the labour of the body. Yet learning must always be pursued with humility, as part of a morally upstanding life. We shall never be able to see the image of God in human beings unless the mirror of our own souls has been cleaned and polished. All we would see reflected is our own pride and vain ambitions.

Bonaventure lived to see realized at the University of Paris some of his worst fears about the abuse of learning. As *Aristotle's works gained in popularity, certain masters took to defending his teachings as if they represented the crowning achievement of human reason. In three series of Lenten sermons (*collationes*) beginning in 1267, Bonaventure attacked the sheer folly of following blindly where an ancient author leads. Since human *reason is doomed to go astray unless illumined by *faith, all pagan philosophers made serious mistakes. Aristotle himself believed that the world is eternal, not created; he could see neither the effects of original *sin nor our need for God's *grace; he was ignorant of Christ, the key to our reconciliation and reunion with God; he knew nothing of the perfect happiness of the afterlife.

Though Bonaventure expresses a certain sympathy for the ancients, who lacked the benefits of *revelation, he sharply criticizes contemporary *university masters who have such benefits and yet choose to philosophize as if they were pagans. To forget that the ultimate end of human life lies in enjoyment of the highest good, and that this good lies above us, in our union with God, is to misunderstand true happiness and the very purpose of learning. When a Christian loses a sense of its higher purpose, education becomes self-defeating.

Bonaventure's *Retracing the Arts to Theology* explains the divisions of human knowledge in a way intended to demonstrate their interrelations and proper order. Such arts as agriculture and navigation have their place, just as logic has its place. There is no branch of knowledge without some contribution to make. Nevertheless, we need to keep an eye trained on the larger picture. Even as we pursue our own callings, we should bear in mind that our ultimate aim is not to be a good navigator, or a good philosopher, or even a good theologian, but rather a good human being—and hence, in Bonaventure's view, a good Christian. Few things would be more abhorrent to him than modern educational systems where *Christianity is considered a private matter, to be excluded from one's work as a student and a teacher.

Bonaventure's later works, strongly influenced by Neoplatonic and mystical writings (see PLATO AND PLATONISM), elaborate on the idea that the whole of creation proceeds from, mirrors, and returns to its source. Christ is both the ladder by which we return to God and the exemplar or pattern of all creation. In the supernatural order Christ serves as the model of every grace, *virtue, and *merit; but even the natural world mirrors him, so that it too,

when properly understood, leads us back to God. Nature has its own ways of sharing in God's goodness. Although no creature can attain the full perfection of Christ, we must remember that imperfection is a lesser good, not the contrary of perfection.

During Bonaventure's lifetime, the Franciscans and Dominicans were still struggling to gain full acceptance in the universities. By the early 14th century, they were firmly entrenched. Some of the leading theologians of the day belonged to the mendicant orders. The *Dominicans' works display a high degree of consistency because the order had already bound itself to teach and defend the thought of Thomas *Aquinas. Among the Franciscans there was no such uniformity. The order did not have then, nor does it have now, one master singled out for intellectual reverence and emulation. While Bonaventure enjoyed a good deal of respect, his successors John Duns Scotus and William of Ockham likewise gained followings, and the influence of all three extended well into the modern period. Scotus argued against some of Bonaventure's teachings; Ockham argued against Scotus as well as Bonaventure. Reading the works of these Franciscan theologians, one cannot but recall the thoroughgoing individualism of the order's founder. We might also see some justification for the quip that there is no opinion likely to escape criticism by a Franciscan, especially if another Franciscan defends it.

Scotus is best remembered for his *metaphysics—for example, his teachings on the transcendentals, and on the formal distinction, which falls roughly midway between a real distinction and a purely mental one. To him goes the credit for what might well be the longest, most elaborately structured argument for the existence of God ever produced (*A Treatise on God as First Principle*). The daunting sophistication of Scotus's thought helps to explain how he could be ridiculed by 16th-century humanists and reformers for pointless, nearly maniacal complexity (hence the word 'dunce'), though he wins praise in our own day as the *Kant of the Middle Ages.

Ockham's fame derives in part from his rejection of traditional metaphysics, which regards universals such as 'human nature' as somehow real. Founding father of the school later known as 'nominalism', Ockham argued that universality is a property only of signs, of the way in which we talk about and refer to individual things. So, to put it crudely, the traditional question of how universals are individuated is not a genuine problem; because only individuals exist in reality, the problem is rather to give an account of universals.

Ockham is equally well known for arguing that whatever God wills, just because he wills it, is *right*, as well as for his defence of God's absolute power to do whatever does not involve a contradiction. These doctrines, together with the attack on realistic metaphysics, are usually reported with disapproval in works on medieval thought. Ockham, probably more than any other scholastic, has been blamed for undermining 'the Thomistic synthesis' of Augustinianism and Aristotelianism, of theology and philosophy. We can indeed see in Ockham's emphasis on the individual, on God's power, and on God's will as all that is strictly necessary for *salvation certain contributions to what became the covenantal theology of the *Reformation. The connections are not merely conjectural: Martin *Luther himself was schooled in nominalism. On the other hand, one might consider it an open question whether the Thomistic synthesis succeeded, or whether the internal tensions were such that the separation of Christian theology from Aristotelian philosophy was virtually inevitable.

Given the Franciscans' academic success, along with their penchant for arguing among themselves, it might be hard to discern anything that the order's leading theologians have in common with each other, much less with the simple, bookless, self-described *idiota*, Francis. None the less, there is. Whether one reads Bonaventure, Duns Scotus, or William of Ockham, one finds a steady emphasis on practical knowledge, the importance of the will, and the primacy of *charity. Few, if any, Franciscans valued speculation as highly as the Dominicans did. Even the order's intellectuals typically argued that *love is higher than knowledge, volition more distinctive of human beings than cognitive activity, and beatitude (the enjoyment of God, the ultimate end of human life) more dependent on the will than the mind. They believed that learning has some spiritual value; they taught in universities; and yet they seem never to have forgotten the example of their founder.

See also MIDDLE AGES: AN OVERVIEW; RELIGIOUS LIFE.

Bonnie Kent

Bonaventure, *The Works of Bonaventure*, ET (1960–70).
—— *The Journey of the Mind to God*, ET (1993).
Duns Scotus, John, *God and Creatures: The Quodlibetal Questions*, ET (1975).
—— *Duns Scotus on the Will and Morality*, ET (1986).
—— *Duns Scotus: Philosophical Writings*, ET (1987).
Ockham, William of, *Quodlibetal Questions*, ET (1991).
Adams, M., *William Ockham* (1987).
Bougerol, J., *Introduction to the Works of Bonaventure*, ET (1993).
Freppert, L., *The Basis of Morality According to William Ockham* (1988).
Gilson, E., *The Philosophy of St. Bonaventure*, ET (1965).
Moorman, J., *A History of the Franciscan Order* (1968).
Wolter, A., *The Philosophical Theology of John Duns Scotus* (1990).

Francis of Assisi

Francis of Assisi (c.1182–1226) unquestionably continues to capture the hearts and imagination of people throughout the world. The small collection of his known writings, directed mainly to his followers, reveals a man in awe of the implications of the Incarnate Word and burning with the desire to live authentically the new life of *baptism. Within two years of his death, Pope Gregory IX canonized Francis of Assisi and in preparation for the event commissioned Thomas of Celano to prepare an official account of his life. In fulfilling the papal mandate, Thomas unwittingly unleashed one of the great struggles of hagiographic literature, that of identifying the historical Francis. His *Life of Saint Francis* borrows heavily from previous hagiography as do the writings and a more condensed life prepared by Julian of Speyer between 1232 and 1235 for the liturgical celebrations of the new *saint's feast. While all of these initial texts clearly focused on the saint, Francis of Assisi, they left unanswered many questions concerning the events of his life.

Between March 1240 and August 1241 John of Perugia, a close companion of Giles of Assisi, composed recollections that seem to come from Giles and other early followers of Francis. In 1243 Crescentius of Iesi, General Minister of the friars, ordered the collection of all similar information. Two texts, *The Legend of the Three Companions* and *The Legend of Perugia* or the *Assisi Compilation*, reflect the contributions of 'we who were with him', that is, those close to the saint. The reliability of all three texts has been debated by later scholars. Their influence, however, is evident in the second

work of Thomas of Celano, *The Remembrance of the Desire of a Soul*. In its first section, Thomas reveals details provided by John of Perugia and the *Legend of the Three Companions*, and, in its second, focuses on the ideals portrayed by 'we who were with him'. After approval of this second work in 1247, Thomas provided a third work, *The Treatise on the Miracles of Saint Francis*, completed in 1250 and approved by the friars in 1254.

In 1260 the friars entrusted Bonaventure of Bagnoreggio with the task of compiling 'one good legend of blessed Francis from all those already in existence'. Three years later, Bonaventure presented two works: the *Major Legend*, a finely articulated theological portrait of the saint, and the *Minor Legend*, a shorter companion piece whose principal purpose was liturgical in nature. In both instances, he relied on the earlier works of Thomas of Celano and Julian of Speyer. At their next General Chapter the friars ordered 'under obedience that all the legends of Blessed Francis that have been made should be removed'. The Friars Preacher had enacted a similar measure in 1260 after Humbert of Romans, the Master General, had compiled from existing works a legend of St Dominic. The Friars Minor were far more exacting in decreeing that all earlier legends be *deleantur* (removed). If all the reasons for their sweeping decision are unclear, the result is not. For the next five centuries Bonaventure's official portrait dominated the *Franciscan landscape; the others written before 1266 remained hidden, presumed to have been destroyed.

A Book of Praises of the Blessed Francis, a devotional introduction to the biographies of the first General Ministers of the Order, was the work of Bernard of Besse who wrote shortly after Bonaventure's death in 1274. *The Mirror of Perfection* appeared in 1318. Based on the *Assisi Compilation*, it was composed by an unknown author in a more pedagogical way to present 'a mirror of perfection of the state of a lesser brother'. Ten years later Hugolino of Monte Giorgio collaborated with an unknown friar and produced the *Deeds of Blessed Francis and his Companions*, a collection of 'little flowers' or stories rooted in both the written and oral Franciscan tradition. The text became more appealing when its seventy-six chapters were reduced to fifty-three and translated into Tuscan Italian. The *Fioretti* or Little Flowers achieved a popularity unparalleled in Franciscan literature. In addition to popularizing Francis, it highlighted his *prophetic role and underscored his conformity with Christ, a theme that eventually culminated in another of the great Franciscan classics, Bartholomew of Pisa's *The Conformity of the Life of the Blessed Francis to that of the Lord Jesus Christ*. Written between 1385 and 1390, Bartholomew's work was an ambitious study of the life of Francis in the light of that of *Jesus, making it clear that Francis was truly an *alter Christus*.

While these 14th-century portraits of Francis existed, that of Bonaventure was most influential. In 1651, however, Daniel Papebroch, SJ, discovered in Perugia a manuscript of the work of John of Perugia which was eventually published in 1768 by Cornelius Suyskens, SJ, in the *Acta Sanctorum*. During that same period, Suyskens discovered a manuscript of the *Life of Saint Francis* by Thomas of Celano. The 19th century witnessed a storm of scholarly controversy in which, as other manuscripts of the pre-Bonaventure works began to surface, the Italians, Germans, and French discussed the 'authentic' portrait of the saint. Towards the end of the century, Paul Sabatier challenged all Franciscan scholars to develop a more critical approach in understanding Francis. His *Vie de saint François d'Assise* marked the beginning of the 'Franciscan Question', a controversy centred on which texts about Francis were the earliest and most reliable.

Modern scholarship has been assisted by the work of the Friars Minor of Quaracchi, Florence, whose publication of the 'official' portraits of Thomas of Celano, Julian of Speyer, and Bonaventure provided a scholarly approach to these works. Others, for example Brooke, Desbonnets, Di Fonzo, Bigaroni, published critical editions of the 'non-official' works such as the *Assisi Compilation* and *Legend of the Three Companions*. In 1976 and 1978, Kajetan Esser published two scholarly, detailed editions of the writings of Francis. All these texts were analysed electronically at the Catholic University of Louvain and published in the *Corpus des sources franciscaines*, a work that gradually changed the ways in which scholars examined these texts.

While every age has attempted to determine the core of the distinctiveness of Francis, much of that attempt has been undertaken without an in-depth consultation of his own writings. Esser's critical edition and the proliferation of translations of his findings altered that approach. Francis's writings reveal a profound *Trinitarian *spirituality in which the *revelation of Christ became the focal point. A practical result of this was a relational spirituality in which an all-embracing spirit of fraternity inspired Francis to view all creatures as his brothers and sisters. In addition to those men and women who came to follow him, his *Canticle of the Creatures* addresses sun, moon, water, etc., in sibling terms. Moreover, the sense of *humanity that pervades Francis's writings is unquestionably one of their most distinctive and appealing qualities. The embrace of a leper that initiated his conversion undoubtedly prompted him to find God among the outcasts and poor of society and, in imitation of Christ, to develop experientially a spirituality of living *sine proprio*, without anything of one's own. This life of fraternity in *poverty is the most distinctive element of Francis's vision. Unlike *monastic or Augustinian communities, living poorly and simply as itinerant or eremitical brothers and sisters, dependent on God and one another, characterized Francis's followers. The result is a spirituality that is neither monastic nor apostolic but one in which internalizing and expressing the word of God became the central enterprise. For this reason, the image of the stigmatized Francis, that is, the one totally conformed to Christ, became the central icon of the Franciscan tradition.

See also RELIGIOUS LIFE.   **Regis J. Armstrong**

Francis of Assisi: Early Documents, ed. Regis J. Armstrong, J. A. Wayne Hellmann, and William J. Short (3 vols.; 1999).

Armstrong, Regis J., *Saint Francis of Assisi: Writings for a Gospel Life* (1994).

Dalarun, Jacques, *La malavventura di Francesco d'Assisi: per un uso storico delle legende francescane* (1996).

Van Khahn, Norbert Nugen, *Teacher of His Heart*, ET (1992).

freedom. 'You were called to freedom, brethren', *Paul told the Galatians (5: 13). 'The freedom for which Christ has set us free' was, in Paul's argument, release from the law of circumcision in particular and of all the ritual requirements of Jewish law (see LAW, BIBLICAL) in general—'You observe days, and months, and seasons, and years!' (Gal. 4: 10) he scathingly remarked. Pauline freedom is linked with the interior realities of *faith, *love, and the *Holy Spirit, 'Where the Spirit of the Lord is, there is freedom' (2 Cor. 3: 17) but Paul has to insist that freedom is not licence. If believers are no more slaves to the law, they are slaves to Christ instead (1 Cor. 7: 22). But Paul's rhetoric appeals to wider horizons: the whole of creation is now to enjoy 'the glorious liberty of the children of God' (Rom. 8: 21).

All this is reflected clearly enough in the gospels. The synoptics emphasize stories in which *Jesus violates details of the law or defends his *disciples for so doing, especially in regard to the sabbath, in a way intended to be symbolic of a far wider freedom. 'The sabbath is made for man, not man for the sabbath' (Mark 2: 27) is a principle profoundly significant for the development of an ethic of freedom. It is not that the gospels suggest that Jesus was an *antinomian, but they certainly do portray someone of an exceptionally free disposition in his way of life, a religious teacher without being either a scribe or an ascetic, who has abandoned any home, pays no attention to his family, but gladly sits down to a meal in many houses, who has many women friends, chats with a Samaritan woman at a well, and insists that children should not be prevented from coming to him, who often appears extreme in the remarks he throws out while being a wonderful storyteller, who enacts mysterious symbolic actions, and insists on returning to Jerusalem despite the manifest danger. Jesus was an intensely free person. He communicated a sense of freedom but did not define what it was to be free. When in *John's gospel he is reported as saying, 'You will learn the truth and the truth will make you free' (8: 32) we are disposed to believe him because he exemplifies it himself. But the freedom he possesses comes from being God's son and that is what he passes on—'if the Son makes you free, you will be free indeed'. The alternative is to be enslaved. It is striking how close to John is Paul's principal discussion of freedom in Galatians 4: 5: we are free, not slaves, because we share the sonship of the Son.

Freedom means different things to different people and can be discussed in philosophical, ethical, psychological, political, or economic terms. The specifically Christian sense of freedom does not, however, belong to any of these categories, though it presumes indeterminism: what human beings do is not wholly or necessarily controlled by forces within the created order external to themselves, or by their internal material components. Choice is a moral reality. But the NT idea of freedom is less concerned with choice than with the new life empowered by divine sonship. God is supremely free and participation in the sonship of Christ means sharing that freedom through faith and love, a state which somehow releases one from being dominated by earthly things, whether temporal power, wealth, *law, or *sin. Paul's immediate preoccupation is freedom from the obligation to be circumcised, but this stands for so much more that the lyrical rhetoric seems justified. 'Where the Spirit of the Lord is, there is freedom' (2 Cor. 3: 17).

How does such an intuition of freedom relate to more down-to-earth matters? It has no obvious or immediate political consequences. Paul does not denounce the institution of *slavery. If in Christ 'there is neither slave nor free' (Gal. 3: 28) that is very much 'in Christ'. Paul sends the escaped slave Onesimus back to his master Philemon but with instructions which are in reality revolutionary: 'No longer as a slave but more than a slave, as a beloved brother … receive him as you would receive me' (Philem. 16–17). Clearly, for Paul, continuance of the former master–slave relationship 'in Christ' is simply inconceivable but it would take many centuries for Christians to grapple with working out Christian freedom in political terms, not just for one favoured person but for all society. Again, we find no straight answer to the question whether, if humankind was created in the image of God and therefore free by nature, that freedom was forfeited by sin and only recovered in Christ or whether, while wounded, it remained a reality. How far is the freedom of sonship a 'natural', how far a 'supernatural' reality? Catholic theology tended to the former, Protestant to the latter. Again, how is human freedom reconcilable with divine *omnipotence, with Paul's image borrowed from Isaiah of the potter and the pot (Rom. 9: 19–24) or, hardest of all, with a full doctrine of *predestination? In classical theology this was the area where human freedom, or lack of it, was most in evidence.

The excitement a sense of freedom generates is strongest in *revolutionary movements. A settled church or state lives by law, tying freedom down, channelling it in acceptable and conventional directions. That is what the medieval church tried so hard to do. Canon law arranged Christian life securely from the cradle to the grave. There was little room for freedom in so well-structured a church, at least in theory. Every grace and sin could be catered for by sacraments and monasteries, penances and pilgrimages, indulgences and relics. *Luther, exploding in rebellion, wrote *The Freedom of a Christian Man*, one of his epoch-making trilogy of 1520. But once freedom was thus let out of the bag, it led to all sorts of things that horrified Luther: Spirit-led chaos exemplified in Münster where the city, seized by Anabaptists, proclaimed communism and polygamy and John of Leiden was declared the king of New Zion. Here, as again in England in the civil wars of the 17th century, the anti-slavery campaigns of the 18th, or America in its civil war of the 19th, the NT celebration of freedom provided inspiration for all sorts of other freedoms, social and political as well as ecclesiastical, sound and silly, all of them defended at times by appeal to the guidance of the Spirit. There remains no agreed way to translate the one into the other and hasty attempts to do so lead usually to disillusionment. 'Liberty hath a sharp and doubled edge, fit only to be handled by just and virtuous men,' concluded *Milton, previously as eager as any to support the English Revolution. Moreover, those most outspoken about the tyranny of others, such as the Independents of 17th-century England, could, when they got their way, as in New England, set up a system in itself intolerant enough. Nevertheless, looked at as a whole, the *Protestant experience from the 16th to the 19th century can fairly be seen as one in which the elusive sense of Christian freedom, if never sufficiently realized in any church or community, was not only refusing to be stifled but also doing much to stimulate the reshaping of both churches and societies in more tolerant directions. *Religious liberty and the rights of *conscience were increasingly respected. Yet the frequent explosion of new 'Free' churches, free, that is, from state control, often led intellectually to a greater stifling than was imposed in the state churches.

Christian freedom, then, seems more a symbolic dream than a social or ecclesiastical reality. Its power is in the soul rather than in the structures. For centuries it was almost outlawed in Roman *Catholicism as dangerous folly. *Ultramontanism valued *authority and *obedience far more. This generally applied to the state as well as to the church. In the first half of the *twentieth century,

however, Catholicism was largely reconverted to a respect for civil freedom, especially under the influence of the church in North America, and French liberals like *Maritain. Almost inevitably, this led to reflection on the need for freedom within the church as well, a primary theme of Catholic history in the later 20th century. It produced in the 1960s probably the most hard-fought battle of *Vatican II before the Declaration on Religious Liberty was finally passed on the last day of the council. That did not prevent stringent measures being taken subsequently by the successor to the *Inquisition against several of the more adventurous Catholic theologians of the late 20th century: Hans *Küng, Leonardo *Boff, Tissa *Balasuriya. The 1960s were, in their way, another revolutionary epoch, culturally and politically still more than religiously. It seems hardly surprising that they produced the most sustained attempt to theologize in terms of freedom, political, cultural, and economic, in *liberation, *black, and *feminist theology. It is noticeable that the models they apply are culled from the OT more than the NT. While the points they make may be valid, they are far from encapsulating what Christian freedom really signifies. That may always elude one, just as the figure of the free man *par excellence*, Jesus of Nazareth, will do so.

In *Dostoevsky's marvellous parable of the Grand Inquisitor in *The Brothers Karamazov* that is what happens. Jesus returns to the city of Seville just after an *auto da fé* in which numerous heretics have been burnt by the Inquisition. The Grand Inquisitor locks him up at once, denouncing the disastrous consequences of the freedom for which Jesus stood on earth which is so unsuited to most people and contrasting it with the controlled order and happiness that the church has created. The masses 'themselves have brought us their freedom and obediently laid it at our feet'. That could be true, too, of many a monastery, as of the millions who watch the television screen. Jesus, declared the Inquisitor, 'instead of taking over men's freedom, increased it, and forever burdened the kingdom of the human soul with its torments'. Throughout the parable Jesus says nothing but, in the end, kisses the Inquisitor's aged lips and goes away. This is by universal consent one of the great parables of Christianity. Yves *Congar said that every theologian should reread it yearly. If it suggests how far the institutional church was able, almost inevitably and so speciously, to depart from its founder's spirit, it hints still more provocatively at how indefinable and even impractical Christian freedom itself really is. May not the Grand Inquisitor be right to insist on the 'torments' of the soul that it is only too likely to bring with it? Paul's 'glorious liberty' may be vital for Christianity, but it cannot be painless.   **Adrian Hastings**

Bainton, Roland, *The Travail of Religious Liberty* (1951).
Guardini, Romano, *Freedom, Grace, and Destiny* (1961).
Küng, Hans, *The Church and Freedom* (1965).
Murray, J. C., *The Problem of Religious Freedom* (1965).
Rahner, K., 'Freedom in the Church', *Theological Investigations* (1963), ii. 89–107
—— (ed.), *Sacramentum Mundi*, ii. Freedom (1968), 349–62.
Thielecke, H., *The Freedom of the Christian Man* (1963).

Freire, Paulo (1921–97). A Brazilian from Recife, Freire was outstanding both as practitioner and theorist of popular *education. He first made his reputation as organizer of mass *literacy campaigns and in 1963 was given national responsibility for this by President Goulart. Freire's success lay in seeing such campaigns, and all good education, as an exercise that must truly enter into the social and mental world of the learners, part of a discovery of personal and social awareness, of *freedom. Education should not be a means of imposing upon the poor, while imparting technical skills, the values of the dominant. Following the right-wing military coup of 1964, Freire was imprisoned and exiled after interrogation: 'Do you deny that your method is like that of Stalin, Hitler and Mussolini... an attempt to turn the country Bolshevist?' While in prison he began his first book, *Education as the Practice of Freedom*. In exile as a visiting professor at Harvard, Freire wrote his world-renowned *Pedagogy of the Oppressed* (1970). Students must be encouraged in 'rebellious doubt, a curiosity not easily satisfied', an approach familiar enough for the well-heeled élite universities of the west, but revolutionary for the impoverished masses of the Third World.

In subsequent years Freire was based in *Geneva working especially with the World Council of Churches. His work proved profoundly influential in many countries, especially India. Eventually allowed to return to Brazil in 1979, he was appointed in 1988 at the age of 67 Education Secretary for the city of São Paolo. His twenty-six books are a major contribution not only to the philosophy and practice of education but to the theology of *liberation. It is characteristic of the latter to stress the priority of 'praxis'. Freire, a married Catholic layman, really was a practitioner, sharing 'freedom' by the way he taught, a freedom both personal and socio-political. His approach, at once educational and theological, was summed up in a word popularized by his warm supporter, Archbishop Helder Camara of Recife, 'conscientization'.

See also LATIN AMERICAN CHRISTIAN THOUGHT; BOFF, LEONARDO; BONINO, JOSÉ MÍGUEZ; GUTIÉRREZ, GUSTAVO.   **Adrian Hastings**

French Christian thought.

The *seventeenth century was the great age of French Catholicism. After the religious civil wars of the 16th century, ended by the Edict of Nantes (1598), guaranteeing certain rights to Protestants (the Huguenots), the French church revived, taking over the moral leadership of Catholicism from a declining Spain. Led by such pastorally minded saints as Francis de Sales, Jane Frances de Chantal, and Vincent de Paul, it produced new styles of religious life and spiritual literature, and stimulated numerous missionaries to leave for North America and Asia. It was an age of creative religious philosophy and exact scholarship. *Descartes, *Pascal, and Malebranche were its most outstanding minds, while Tillemont and Richard Simon pioneered a rigorous new *historical and biblical scholarship. The conflicts over *Gallicanism, *Jansenism, and *quietism, troublesome as they were, witnessed to both the tensions and the vitality of a classical moment in Catholic history, comparable with nothing else for two hundred years. Nevertheless, the Revocation of the Edict of Nantes (1685) and subsequent persecution of Protestants may have helped stimulate the growth of a profound intellectual dissatisfaction with Catholicism manifest in the *Enlightenment, the Revolution, and the intense anticlericalism which dominated so much of later French intellectual and political life.

In the 18th century the *ancien régime*'s 'union of throne and altar' purported both to care for the spiritual needs of the faithful and to maintain an absolutist social structure. While the Jansenist controversy continued within the church, Catholicism was confronted by

Voltaire's deism and Rousseau's natural religion. The Revolution brought cataclysmic changes. Throughout the 19th century and beyond, Catholicism was in conflict with the principles of the secular state whose foundation was laid in 1789, the pervading belief in science and progress (and its philosophical expression in Positivism), and the new socio-economic ideologies of capitalist liberalism and socialism. French Protestantism was, for historical as well as doctrinal reasons, less embroiled in these controversies.

After religious persecution during the Revolution, the restoration of the French church by the 1801 Concordat and the Organic Articles unilaterally imposed by Bonaparte placed the church (and the Protestant churches) under the effective control of the centralized state. During the Restoration (1814–30) attempts by the ultra-royalists to repeal the Concordat and give back to the church its pre-Revolutionary influence and prestige led to a surge of anticlericalism that remained a permanent feature in France for many years. For the reactionary, theocratic Joseph de Maistre and Louis de Bonald all the evils in French society stemmed from the Revolution and the 'subversive' ideas of the 18th century. They advocated a return to the principles of authority based on the tradition of the church and the monarchy of divine right. The Abbé Félicité de Lamennais in his early writings denounced the 'incredulity' of the 18th century, individual reason leading only to scepticism and doubt. Only 'general reason', embedded in human nature and expressed in the authority of the church, could provide certainty and truth. But later he came to see the only hope for the regeneration of society not in a restored Gallican church but in an alliance of the papacy with the people in their yearning for freedom. With a small group of disciples he founded in 1830 a journal, *L'Avenir*, which adopted the revolutionary ideas of popular sovereignty, separation of church and state, and freedom of conscience, the press, education, and association. *L'Avenir* was condemned by the Vatican, as was Lamennais's prophetic and revolutionary *Paroles d'un Croyant* (1834).

Nevertheless, liberal preachers such as Dupanloup and Lamennais's former comrade, Lacordaire, with charismatic figures such as Jean-Marie Vianney, the *Curé d'Ars*, had considerable influence. Further signs of spiritual renewal were the increase in vocations, the rapid development of religious (in particular women's) orders, and the development of Catholic social action with the creation in 1833 by Frédéric Ozanam of the Society of St Vincent de Paul, which organized personal assistance to the poor. From the middle of the century papalist *ultramontanism prevailed over nationalist Gallicanism and the influential Catholic press was dominated by the virulent ultramontane intransigence of the *journalism of Louis Veuillot in *L'Univers* and the Assumptionists' *La Croix*.

Throughout the 19th century and indeed until the separation of church and state in 1905, controversy raged over church/state relations, between a form of clericalism inherited from the pre-Revolutionary period and what came to be called *laïcité*. The term came into common usage during the Third Republic, but the concept can be traced back to political thinkers of the 17th and 18th centuries. In legal terms it signifies freedom of conscience, neutrality of the state towards all recognized religions, and the absence of religion from the state education system, and as a corollary the non-involvement of churches in the political and administrative machinery of the state. Having lost, to a very large extent, its combative, anticlerical associations, it has come to be accepted by all Christian churches in France.

The final years of the 19th century and the early years of the 20th were of crucial importance for Catholicism in France. It was a time of major anticlerical legislation: of Leo XIII's call for *ralliement* to the Republic, only grudgingly accepted by many Catholics; and of Catholic support—inspired by militant *nationalism and *anti-semitism—of the army's refusal to admit the innocence of Captain Dreyfus, a Jewish officer condemned on patently false evidence for spying. Yet against this background a new intellectual vitality could be perceived. At the same time as the *modernist crisis, there emerged (1) a flowering of literature of essentially Catholic inspiration, (2) an important Social Catholic movement, Marc Sangnier's *Sillon*, and (3) Charles Maurras's reactionary *Action française*.

1. Rejecting the dominant literary naturalism, and in a climate of virulent religious conflict, the 'reactionary revolution' in French literature during this period was marked by religious traditionalism, prophetic mysticism, a sense of the reality of evil, belief in the efficacy of vicarious suffering, and the rejection of the modern world. The ravages of positivism were denounced and traditional moral values reaffirmed. Many of the writers were converts. Léon Bloy was to influence many later Catholic writers and thinkers, including Jacques *Maritain. Paul Claudel's plays show the struggle between Christian purity and physical desire, resolved by God's saving love. Charles Péguy's polemical prose writings and poetry decisively marked successive generations of French Catholics including Maritain and Emmanuel Mounier. In his early years a self-proclaimed anticlerical and an ardent defender of Dreyfus, Péguy espoused a personal form of socialism while attacking what he saw as the parliamentary politicking of French socialists and radicals, their vacuous phraseology, petit-bourgeois sympathies, and religious intolerance. He condemned as a threat to France's cultural and religious heritage the modern, materialistic, bourgeois-dominated world with its emphasis on money. As war approached, patriotism became dominant in his writings although he refused the overtures of the royalist extreme right. Return to the Catholicism of his childhood was marked by the publication in 1910 of his epic and mystical *Mystère de la Charité de Jeanne d'Arc*.

2. In 1894, with the impetus provided by Leo XIII's social encyclical, *Rerum Novarum*, Marc Sangnier founded *Le Sillon* (The Furrow), a crucial element in the history of Christian *democracy and social Catholicism in France. Like Lamennais's writings two generations earlier, it aimed to reconcile Catholicism and democracy, which Sangnier defined as 'the social organization most fit to harness everyone's civic conscience and responsibilities'. It was condemned by Pius X in 1910 on the grounds that it concerned itself with politics at the expense of spirituality.

3. At the opposite extreme, Charles Maurras founded Action française in 1899. An adversary of the Reformation and the Revolution, he advocated traditionalism, integral nationalism ('France first and foremost'), monarchy, and antisemitism. Although Maurras was an agnostic, rejecting the metaphysical dimension of Christianity and the possibility of any religious motivation in political choices, he admired the traditional hierarchic structure of the Catholic church and defended it against the republic. His books and his journal, *Action française*, found an answering note among many clergy and bourgeois traditionalists. When in 1926 the Vatican placed his writings on the Index and excommunicated the members of Action française, many Catholics experienced a grave crisis of conscience, not least among them Maritain. The Vatican condemnation of Maurras can now be seen as a turning-point in French Catholic thought and social action.

The inter-war years set in train developments that were subsequently to affect the deliberations of *Vatican II, when French theologians acted as some of the most influential experts. A group of priests and laymen, of whom Maritain was the most prominent, restored Christianity to an important place in French intellectual life. The Maritains' home at Meudon was between the wars the meeting-place of philosophers, theologians, writers, and artists, both Christian and agnostic. Maritain was one of the foremost proponents of the *Thomist revival in France and the United States. He broke with Maurras and Action française in 1926, publishing in 1927 *Primacy of the Spiritual* (in opposition to Maurras's 'politics first'). In this and other works, he argued for a reconciliation of Christianity with the values of the Enlightenment and for a new non-clerical Christendom critically receptive to some of the values of the modern world. He encouraged and participated actively in the founding of the 'nonconformist' reviews of the 1930s, Emmanuel Mounier's *Esprit*, the Dominicans' *Sept*, and *La Vie intellectuelle*. He was one of the few French Catholics (with Mounier and the *novelists Georges Bernanos and François Mauriac) to side against Franco in the Spanish Civil War. He was almost alone in France in alerting public opinion to the threat posed by Nazi antisemitism and in February 1939 he attempted to awaken Christian consciences to 'the deafening screams rising from the concentration camps', only to be met by widespread scepticism. Maritain was politically in the succession of Lamennais and Sangnier and his 'progressism' was frequently the object of Vatican suspicion. However, in 1945 he was appointed French Ambassador to the Vatican, a post he held until 1948; in Rome he became a close friend of Mgr. Montini, the future Paul VI.

Gabriel Marcel (1889–1973) the philosopher and dramatist, was another convert. While rejecting the term 'Christian existentialism', he provided a Christian response to the atheistic *existentialism of Camus and Sartre prevalent in the 1940s and 1950s. Among theologians who opened up new avenues for Christian thought in France (most of whom were regular visitors to Meudon), mention should be made of the influential *Dominican theologian Marie-Dominique Chenu (1895–1990), condemned by the Vatican in 1942 for 'philosophical and theological relativism'; the Dominican Yves *Congar, one of the pioneers of ecumenism and a theology of the *laity, removed from his post at the order's theological school of Le Saulchoir in the worker-priest crisis; the *Jesuit Jean Daniélou (1905–74), proponent of the patristic renewal and an active supporter of Jewish–Christian dialogue. Another Jesuit, Henri *de Lubac, like many of his Christian contemporaries influenced by *Kierkegaard and *Dostoevsky, was during the wartime German occupation one of the main architects of 'spiritual resistance' (in the clandestine *Cahiers du Témoignage Chrétien*). The impact of Simone *Weil's experience of the divine gift of affliction and of *Teilhard de Chardin's creation theology provided further new dimensions to the spiritual vitality of the period.

Témoignage Chrétien pursued its career after the war, advocating nuclear disarmament, decolonization, Algerian independence, and supporting the worker-priest movement (in which priests became full-time industrial workers to break down the alienation from the church of the working class); it continues to adopt a constructively critical position towards the church. *Esprit*, founded in October 1932 by Emmanuel Mounier, played a major role among the intellectual élite in 20th-century Christian thought in France. Mounier brought together the strands of Bergsonism, Péguyism (Péguy's 'La Révolution sera morale ou ne sera pas' became his motto) and utopian socialism. He saw personalism as an alternative to *Marxism. Mounier's reluctance to translate principles into proposals for action led to accusations of non-commitment and to controversy over his attitude towards Pétain's Révolution nationale. Under Mounier until his death in 1950 and under successive editors, *Esprit* has continued as a forum for religious debate in France.

The second quarter of the 20th century saw the flowering of a literature of Catholic inspiration with Paul Claudel, François Mauriac, Georges Bernanos, and Julien Green. In different ways all depict the tragic conflict between evil and grace, passion and faith.

Protestants with, among others, Jacques *Ellul and Paul *Ricœur, have made a significant contribution to French Christian thought. Throughout the 19th century Protestantism was marked by a strong *pietist current and divided by the conflict between orthodox and liberal Protestants. Having obtained religious freedom in 1787, Protestants supported republicanism and, in line with their belief in the primacy of conscience, were active proponents of *laïcité*. In the 20th century the theology of Karl *Barth was a major influence in French Protestant thinking. Faith and social action have become inseparable for many Protestants: in the 1930s antisemitism was condemned by Denis de Rougemont and after 1940 Protestants—with Pastor Marc Boegner in the lead—were the first Christians in France to condemn publicly Vichy's anti-Jewish measures. Protestant communities played an important role in sheltering Jews during the Occupation. Protestant leaders, at the risk of prosecution, were later active in condemning the French use of torture in the Algerian war.

Christian thought in France at the end of the 20th century presented a striking contrast with the optimistic vitality of fifty years earlier. Catholic thinkers such as Maritain, Daniélou, and de Lubac, who had led the way for intellectual renewal and had much influenced Vatican II, became disturbed at its consequences, though this did not apply to Congar and Chenu. As this generation passed away it was not replaced. For the first time since the 17th century France appeared to have lost its intellectual leadership in world Catholicism. What may be as important, given the racial tensions within French society, is the progress achieved in interfaith *dialogue, pursuing the commitment to interreligious contacts of Maritain's friend, the Islamist Louis Massignon, and in the degree of Protestant/Catholic *reconciliation achieved at Taizé and in L'Arche communities for the mentally disadvantaged. But, half a century after the publication of Abbés Godin and Daniel's *La France, pays de mission?*, a book that made a great impact in the post-war world, it was clearer than ever that France is less a traditionally Christian society than missionary territory. **Howard Evans**

Barre, Jean-Luc, *Jacques et Raïssa Maritain: Les Mendiants du ciel* (1995).
Cholvy, Gerard, and Hilaire, Yves-Marie, *Histoire religieuse de la France contemporaine*, i. *1800–1880* (1985); ii. *1880–1930* (1986); iii. *1930–1985* (1988).
Cooper, J. W., *A Theology of Freedom: The Legacy of Jacques Maritain and Reinhold Niebuhr* (1985).
Fouilloux, Étienne, *Une Église en quête de liberté: La Pensée catholique française entre modernisme et Vatican II, 1914–1962* (1998).
Gibson, Ralph, *A Social History of French Catholicism* (1989).
Griffiths, Richard, *The Reactionary Revolution: The Catholic Revival in French Literature 1870–1914* (1966).
Halda, Bernard, *Bernanos ou la foi militante et déchirée* (1981).
Irving, R. E. M., *Christian Democracy in France* (1973).
Kelly, Michael, *Pioneer of the Catholic Revival: The Ideas and Influence of Emmanuel Mounier* (1979).
McManners, John, *Church and Society in Eighteenth Century France* (2 vols.; 1998).
Maritain, Jacques, *The Peasant of the Garonne: An Old Layman Questions Himself about the Present Time* (ET 1968).
Poulat, Émile, *Où va le Christianisme à l'aube du iiie millénaire?* (1996).
Quoniam, Theodore, *Du Péché à la rédemption* (1984) (on Mauriac).
Vidler, Alec, *Prophecy and Papacy: A Study of Lamennais, the Church and the Revolution* (1954).

friendship has a complex yet rich history as a topic in Christian thought, even though it has not been discussed much in modernity. Gregory the Great offers a succinct definition: a friend is the guardian of one's soul, *custos animae*. This notion, which has roots in both ancient philosophy and the bible, has influenced many subsequent conceptions of the importance of friendship.

At the same time, however, there has been resistance within Christianity to recognizing the importance of friendship. Friendship stresses particular bonds, and also involves mutual affection; yet the gospel entails universal commitments, and *agape* suggests that Christians ought to love without regard for mutuality, loving even our enemies. Hence, Christians have from time to time worried whether the particular bonds of friendship are compatible with the more generalized vocation of Christian *love.

Friendship was an important topic in the ancient world. In particular, it is central to such famous texts as *Aristotle's *Nicomachean Ethics*, Plato's *Lysis*, and Cicero's *On Friendship*. It was seen as a bond that significantly shapes people's lives and their outlooks, and as a good in itself. A friend was taken to be a mirror that aided self-knowledge, and friendship was often taken to be a crucial foundation for political community.

Many Christian discussions of friendship have drawn on these authors as well as several key biblical references. In the OT, for example, Proverbs 18: 24 indicates that 'Some friends play at friendship but a true friend sticks closer than one's nearest kin' (see also Eccles. 4: 9–12). In both Isaiah (41: 8) and James (2: 23), Abraham is described as being a friend of God.

In the NT, *Jesus' ministry is characterized in several places in reference to friendship. He is described somewhat derisively as a 'friend' of tax collectors and sinners because he associates with them and eats with them (see Luke 7: 34). He also describes his disciples as friends (see Luke 12: 4). However, it is in John's gospel that some of the most decisive references appear. Jesus describes his own death with reference to friendship: 'No one has greater love than this, to lay down one's life for one's friends. You are my friends if you do what I command you. I do not call you servants any longer, because the servant does not know what the master is doing; but I have called you friends, because I have made known to you everything that I have heard from my Father' (15: 13–15).

The Epistle of James also has a passage that draws together the biblical emphasis on being a friend of God with the Graeco-Roman emphasis on how friendship marks a person's identity. Referring to the world as that realm of sin that rejects knowledge of God, the writer warns: 'Do you not know that friendship with the world is enmity with God? Therefore whoever wishes to be a friend of the world becomes an enemy of God' (4: 4). Though this passage can be taken to suggest the importance of removing oneself from the world, it can also be read as indicating that one's involvement in the world must be defined by a formative friendship with God.

The bible also contains stories that emphasize particular friendships. Especially noteworthy are the friendships of Ruth and Naomi, David and Jonathan, Jesus and John.

Friendship continues to be a prominent theme in patristic and medieval writing. For example, Gregory Thaumaturgus praises *Origen's friendship and the role it played in his own Christian formation and education. *Augustine also stresses the importance of friendship, though primarily in the context of loving God and loving friends in God. Thomas *Aquinas describes charity as friendship with God, charity being also the form of the virtues that shapes Christian friendship with others. The most striking medieval account is to be found in Aelred of Rievaulx's *Spiritual Friendship*. Aelred actually characterizes God as friendship, and sees the monastic vocation in terms of spiritual friendship. This conception of 'spiritual friendship' indicates a friendship in the Spirit, and is in no way tied to gender-specific connotations or to sexual expression. It suggests a focus shaped primarily by the vocation to friendship with God and to see others as friends in God.

Friendship has not been a significant topic in most modern philosophy or theology, with the exception of some significant treatises by such figures as Montaigne and *Kierkegaard, but in recent years there has been a revival of interest in its theological significance. In part, this is attributable to revived interest in Aristotle's moral philosophy and Aquinas's moral theology. It is also the result of the attempt to do greater justice to the particularities of people's lives, especially in relation to the emotions and to embodiment.

There is now an emerging consensus among philosophers and theologians that, whatever the challenges to universal demands of love and justice, friendship remains morally and theologically significant. What is needed are ways to narrate the tensions between the universality of love and the particularity of friendship such that the demands of each are honoured.

Some have suggested that friendship is a 'special relation' that is justified by human finitude, even though people ought continually to be striving towards the obligations of *agape*. Others have suggested, more persuasively, that friendships are a primary bond for learning the virtues which continually expand into concern for what all 'neighbours' require. It is clear, then, that friendship both helpfully describes the human vocation in relation to God as well as other people, and requires the expansive requirements of *agape* to ensure that we learn to recognize all human beings, even strangers and enemies, as beloved creatures—and hence as potential friends—of God.   **L. Gregory Jones**

Hunt, Mary E., *Fierce Tenderness: A Feminist Theology of Friendship* (1992).
Kierkegaard, Søren, *Works of Love* (1847).
Lewis, C. S., *The Four Loves* (1960).
McGuire, Brian Patrick, *Friendship and Community* (1988).
Meilaender, Gilbert, *Friendship* (1981).
Wadell, Paul J., *Friendship and the Moral Life* (1989).

fundamentalism.

fundamentalism. The term 'fundamentalist' most properly applies to particular groups of *Protestants in *North America, the product of a specific conjuncture of circumstances. In the last decades of the 19th century the north-eastern cities of the United States were experiencing considerable social and cultural transformation, intensifying through the First World War and its aftermath, with the 'red scare' and Wilson's attempt to bring America into the League of Nations. Urbanization, industrialization, immigration (from non-Protestant lands) were affecting the taken-for-granted nature of American Protestantism. On a more theological level, German *higher criticism was reaching America, as was Darwin's *evolutionary thinking. During these decades, Protestantism also underwent considerable institutional realignment. *Revivalism, creating an ethos of *evangelism and piety, was providing a new network of structures for people not otherwise linked. Other non-denominational institutions were gaining importance: the bible institute, the bible and prophecy conference, new periodicals, and publishing houses. Not the least significant effect of these new institutions was the promotion of premillennialism, particularly John Nelson Darby's *dispensationalism, widely diffused through the burgeoning prophecy conferences, and in the *Scofield Reference Bible*, published in 1909.

During these years the mainline denominations of the northern states were gradually adapting to the changing context, accommodating evolutionary thinking, absorbing biblical criticism, even advocating a *social gospel. By contrast, many conservative Protestants denounced these accommodations as *modernism or *liberalism. They opposed modern biblical criticism's supposed denial of prophecy and of the miraculous and supernatural generally. Such opposition, in its most theologically rational form, drew on the *Princeton theology of Charles and A. A. Hodge and Benjamin Warfield. It was during these years of struggle, about the time of the First World War, that fundamentalism emerged with its own distinct identity. Between 1910 and 1915 appeared a series of pamphlets, *The Fundamentals*, published by the World's Christian Fundamentals Association, founded in 1909. In 1920 the editor of the Baptist *Watchman-Examiner* called 'fundamentalists' those who, like him, were prepared to take their stand on the 'great fundamentals', normally understood to be five: the authority of scripture (explained in terms of inerrancy, infallibility, or plenary inspiration); the virgin birth; the substitutionary atonement; the bodily Resurrection; and Christ's divinity (or sometimes his second coming).

In these early years, it was not only Protestantism that the religious conservatives fought to reclaim, but American culture generally. By the mid-1920s, however, it was obvious that these fundamentalists or *evangelicals (the terms were for a while interchangeable) had failed on all fronts. They failed in their attempts to take control of the Northern *Baptists and *Presbyterians. Their wider cultural defeat was epitomized in the 'monkey trial' in Tennessee in 1925, when a young teacher was prosecuted for teaching evolution. The prosecution succeeded, so strictly speaking the conservatives won, but they attracted so much public ridicule that they withdrew from public involvement.

They did not disappear, however. In succeeding decades, away from the public eye, these Christians reorganized. The religious, educational, and missionary institutions that had been slowly strengthening over the previous half-century came to carry the movement. Denominational allegiances may have been largely transcended, but another source of division arose, and by about 1950 the strains could no longer be contained. One sector (personified by Billy Graham) opted for some form of cultural relevance; another (epitomized by Bob Jones) chose cultural separation. The former tended to avoid the label 'fundamentalist', preferring 'evangelical'. Thus the distinction between evangelical and fundamentalist on the North American scene has been one of style rather than theology. (Marsden's popular definition catches this well: 'A fundamentalist is an evangelical who is angry about something.') The separation widened throughout the 1950s and 1960s.

The fundamentalists re-emerged into the public arena about 1970, driven both by the strength of their institutions and the rising wealth of their members, and drawn by the cultural changes taking place: the civil rights movement, the women's movement, the Vietnam War and Watergate, the Supreme Court decision in 1963 against prayer in schools, and the 1973 ruling to legalize *abortion. With some encouragement from political fixers in the Republican Party, they mobilized to contest the public realm, in such organizations as Christian Voice, the Religious Roundtable, the American Coalition for Traditional Values, and, the most high-profile of all, Jerry Falwell's Moral Majority, founded in 1979. The September 1985 edition of *Time* devoted to 'Fundamentalism in the US' featured Falwell on the cover. Domestically they targeted abortion, gay rights, the equal rights amendment, 'welfare', the teaching of evolution in schools, New Age movements, and more generally the 'secular humanism' of the Supreme Court, the media, and the educational system. Overseas, they denounced communism and supported Israel. Through these groups fundamentalism made its presence inescapable, especially as they began effectively to monopolize Christian radio and television. To their other institutions they added the National Religious Broadcasters, deemed significant enough to be addressed by President Reagan.

In the 1960s and 1970s the South was being transformed. Its religious homogeneity crumbled in the face of desegregation, industrialization, urbanization, and immigration from the North. No longer taken for granted, Southern conservative Christianity aggressively turned itself into Southern fundamentalism. Now the intra-denominational struggles, unsuccessful in the North half a century before, became possible here; and here the fundamentalists had more success. They took control of the *Lutheran Church, Missouri Synod, in the mid-1970s, and after a long struggle controlled the Southern Baptist Convention by the mid-1980s. This 'Sunbelt Fundamentalism' is now for many the primary expression of the movement.

Behind fundamentalism there lies a theological vision, a stress on human *sinfulness, and the need for redemption, the conviction that this has been achieved by Christ and is appropriated through personal faith, an emphasis on individual *salvation and personal morality, a low view of the church and sacraments. All these elements have a long history in Christianity. The high view of scripture as all-sufficient and uniquely constitutive of doctrine also has an impeccable pedigree; even the use of isolated decontextualized verses. Nor are doctrinal exclusiveness, heresy, and excommunica-

tion new. But despite these obvious continuities, and despite its own claims to be Christianity as it always was and would be still but for liberalism and the apostasy of the mainline denominations, the strain of Christianity to which the label 'fundamentalist' is best applied is essentially a modern phenomenon. Its revivalism can be traced back to *Wesley and Whitefield (and, like Wesley, fundamentalism has tended to be *Arminian rather than *Calvinist). It was in the 18th century that there appeared the loss of confidence in existing church institutions as the sphere in which salvation is to be found. About the same time some began to hold that one could work with a simplified list of essentials rather than theologies and complicated intellectual doctrinal systems. The fundamentalist conception of truth is derived from a scientific age. Several observers have noted the link with Scottish *Common Sense Philosophy, or with a view of science going back to Francis Bacon (1561–1626). The fundamentalist theological method is formed on the analogy of natural *science, and natural science as seen in the Newtonian mould. Fundamentalists tend to have a 'scientific' view of the bible; a series of hard 'facts' apprehendable by the common sense of the sincere believer. They presuppose a 19th-century materialistic emphasis on the mere happening of events, rather than on their significance, as the central form of truth. The stress on the accuracy of the bible in its material physical reporting separates modern fundamentalism from older theology like that of *Luther and *Calvin. The fundamentalist notion of biblical inerrancy in history and science is inconceivable without modernity. The precise emphasis on the bible as a set of prophecies of the end-time, and the dispensationalist scheme of Darby, are recent developments. Fundamentalism's approach to the bible is something new, adopted in reaction to the new situation brought about by the rise of biblical criticism. It is this new context that is all-important. Richardson has expressed this well:

> The position of a man who insists after the Copernican revolution that the sun goes round the earth is not really the same position as that of the pre-Copernican astronomers. He has in fact taken up an attitude to evidence which the pre-Copernicans had not been able to consider … His attitude to the authority of Ptolemy is quite different from theirs; for them Ptolemy was the only known standard of truth, and accepting Ptolemy did not involve rejecting Copernicus.
>
> (*Cambridge History of the Bible* (1963), iii. 310)

Some of the views most immediately associated with fundamentalism in public perception have in fact little necessary connection with the religious vision, being essentially cultural. The most obvious is the 'hyper-American patriotic anti-communism' (Marsden), which stems from a dualistic mindset fairly widespread in the USA. There is an affinity between this and premillennial dispensationalism, but paradoxically, although it was in large part the millennialism that fuelled fundamentalists' anti-communism and support for Israel, their very involvement in politics has tended to move their millennialism from centre position, as they have come to adopt a more engaged ('dominion', 'kingdom', or even 'reconstructionist') theology.

The fundamentalists' political involvement of the last decades of the 20th century attracted enormous publicity and academic attention, but their significance has proven much less than they have claimed (or their critics feared), partly because their attempts to build coalitions (with, say, Catholics and *Mormons against abortion, with *Pentecostals in support of Israel) have alienated much of their natural constituency. Marion (Pat) Robertson, strictly a Pentecostal rather than a fundamentalist, who ran for the US presidency in 1988 in the hope that he could mobilize this constituency of the Religious Right, failed spectacularly.

'Fundamentalism' primarily refers to a recognizable form of Christianity emerging from a specific context, cultural and political as much as religious. It has come to be applied to a theology, in isolation from the wider and original context. Even in North America this extended usage can be confusing. North America's *Black churches, for example, though sharing roughly the same doctrinal position, have traditionally been understandable more in terms of ethnic cohesion than of the shifting relation to North American culture outlined above. Pentecostalism, which may now be the more significant sector within the Religious Right, is uncompromisingly fundamentalist in doctrine, but the stress falls less on orthodoxy of doctrine, as in fundamentalism, more on personal experience. Outside the USA, the label 'fundamentalism', although widely used of theological strands especially within Anglo-Saxon Protestantism, becomes even more problematic. Here the label usually connotes 'a constellation of differing positions disposed around the centrality and inerrancy of the bible' (Barr 1977). It conjures up a set of family resemblances: a strong emphasis on the inerrancy of the bible; an unremitting hostility to modern theology and to the methods, results, and implications of modern biblical criticism; an assurance that those who do not share a particular religious viewpoint are not 'true Christians'. The word has come to be extended beyond Protestantism to cover aggressively traditionalist Catholics, but Catholicism has such a different relation to the bible that such terms as 'ultramontane' or 'integrist' convey the Catholic dynamic much better.

Since American fundamentalist agencies form a large part of the Christian missionary enterprise today, they have influenced a good deal of Third World Christianity. But, even when a daughter church has been founded by and is still linked to a North American fundamentalist agency, the characterization is best avoided. Most Third World Christians of this sort are best described as pre-critical rather than anti-critical. The theology and attitude to the bible of much Third World Christianity may appear similar to that of fundamentalism, but the cultural baggage is usually quite different.

In recent times the word has been applied more widely yet, to other religions. Its most frequent use today is for 'Islamic fundamentalism', but, since virtually all Muslims believe that the Qur'an is inerrant, having been revealed directly by God to Muhammad, its application is unsatisfactory. A term such as 'Islamic Radicalism' would better capture the passion of political involvement, without confusing the picture with an essentially different relation to scripture. When applied to other religions, the term conjures up still other sets of family resemblances, such as defensiveness on the part of a traditional culture under threat; discontent, reaction, counter-attack, perhaps even militancy; a selective appropriation of the past, a quest for authority, a flight from ambiguity or ambivalence, even the adoption of a new identity through the formation of a new community.   **Paul Gifford**

Ammerman, Nancy T., *Bible Believers: Fundamentalists in the Modern World* (1987).

Barr, James, *Fundamentalism* (1977).

Bruce, Steve, *The Rise and Fall of the New Christian Right* (1988).

Marsden, George M., *Fundamentalism and American Culture* (1980).

—— *Understanding Fundamentalism and Evangelicalism* (1991).

Marty, Martin, E., and Appleby, R. Scott (eds.), *Fundamentalisms Observed* (1991).

Sandeen, E. R., *The Roots of Fundamentalism* (1970).

fundamental theology, see APOLOGETICS.

Galilei, Galileo (1564–1642), Florentine physicist and mathematician. Galileo was one of the principal originators of that century-long transformation of human thinking about nature called the Scientific Revolution. His most notable contributions lay in mechanics, philosophy of *science, and *cosmology.

But it is not these major achievements that his name conjures up for most people today. In 1609, Galileo turned his newly fashioned telescope to the skies. The discoveries he made (an earth-like lunar surface, sunspots, four moons circling Jupiter, and, most significant, phases of Venus like those of the moon showing the sun to be at the centre of Venus's orbit) led him to assert the correctness of the heliocentric system of the world proposed by Copernicus in 1543. This directly contradicted *Aristotelian cosmology, dominant in the *universities of the day. The Aristotelians, under sharp attack, called on their colleagues in theology for aid.

A century earlier or later, theologians might have responded very differently. But the debates about the proper interpretation of scripture occasioned by the Protestant *Reformation had led to a growing literalism in scriptural interpretation among Protestants and Catholics alike. In Rome, the reaction to the Copernican theses was sharply negative. Galileo composed a treatise on the proper handling of apparent disagreements between scripture and natural science, the *Letter to the Grand Duchess Christina* (1615); the *hermeneutic principles advocated there, he emphasizes, all find a precedent in *Augustine's *De Genesi ad litteram*. He did not advert to a significant tension within his principles: one of them conveys that the *bible is simply not relevant to scientific issues, but another seemed to imply that justification of a non-literal interpretation of a scriptural text requires *demonstration* of the conflicting scientific claim. This is the principle that Galileo's theological opponents, notably Cardinal Robert Bellarmine, would point to. And they were quite certain that he had not demonstrated (and, Bellarmine evidently believed, could not possibly demonstrate) the truth of the Copernican theses.

Early in 1616, the Congregation of the Holy Office (*Inquisition) submitted these theses to an advisory committee which reported back that the proposition that the sun is at rest at the centre is 'absurd in philosophy and formally heretical'; that the earth is in motion is also philosophically (scientifically) false and 'erroneous in faith'. Within a few days, the Congregation of the Index banned Copernicus's *De revolutionibus* 'until corrected', its claims about the

earth and sun being 'false and altogether opposed to Holy Scripture'. The decree did not mention Galileo, but it was agreed that he should be enjoined to 'abandon these opinions'; if he refused, he was to be given a solemn injunction to abstain from teaching, defending, or even discussing the prohibited doctrine.

This was the decisive phase of the 'Galileo affair'. Once the Roman authorities had committed themselves so unequivocally against Copernican cosmology, it would have been difficult to go back. The subsequent trial of Galileo was, in terms of *doctrine, no more than a footnote, but it is what lingers in popular memory and has become so entwined in myth.

With the election of his friend, Cardinal Barberini, as Pope Urban VIII in 1623, Galileo saw an opportunity to reopen the debate. The new pope allowed him to proceed with the book he had long planned, on the understanding that the Copernican system would be treated as 'hypothesis only'. When Galileo's *Dialogue on Two Chief World Systems* was published in 1632, arguing effectively for the falsity of Aristotelian cosmology, and, with some plausibility, for the truth of its Copernican rival, Urban felt betrayed. Galileo was brought to trial before the Holy Office in 1633. That he could not produce a *demonstration* of the Copernican view was taken by the tribunal to be sufficient to warrant the church's maintaining the literal reading of the disputed biblical texts. He was declared 'suspect of heresy' and ordered to recant publicly. After this recantation, he was sentenced to permanent house arrest.

It is important to recognize that what was at stake here was not primarily a cosmology. Had a handful of biblical references to the sun's motion and the earth's stability not existed, there would have been no 'Galileo affair'. The issue was the authority of scripture and the matter of who should be allowed to interpret it. The disagreement between the Reformers and the defenders of the *Counter-Reformation on this very issue was at its most intense precisely in those years. To the Roman theologians, Galileo's claim to reinterpret the disputed biblical phrases on his own authority must have seemed perilously similar to the Protestant challenge.

Galileo's condemnation had a far more profound effect on public opinion than had the prohibition of Copernicus's book. It became a symbol of an irreconcilable difference between the traditional church and the new science. Rome for long remained intransigent about its proscription of Copernicanism. The works of Galileo and Copernicus still appeared on the *Index of Prohibited Books* as late as

1819. Pope *John Paul II established a commission of inquiry into the affair in 1981, finally in 1992 declaring that the theologians of Galileo's day erred and 'the Bible does not concern itself with details of the physical world'. Galileo was definitively, if tardily, exonerated.   **Ernan McMullin**

Fantoli, A., Galileo: For Copernicanism and for the Church, 2nd edn. (1996).
Finocchiaro, M., The Galileo Affair: A Documentary History (1989).
McMullin, E., 'Galileo on Science and Scripture', in P. Machamer (ed.), The Cambridge Companion to Galileo (1998).

Gallicanism is the strand in *French Catholic thought that distrusts *papal power. The French church (ecclesia gallicana), unlike the English, resisted the impulse to break away from *Rome. Nevertheless, there have been tensions, often a Gallican spirit, and sometimes a case argued for the liberties of the French church, a case linked with a wider *conciliarism.

The high point of Gallicanism came in 1682 when Bossuet, bishop of Meaux, a pillar of Catholic *orthodoxy, drew up the four Gallican Articles to be the official teaching of the French church. The first upheld the rights of *kings against popes, civil against ecclesiastical jurisdiction. The second reaffirmed the decrees of the Council of Constance, and hence subordinated the pope to a general council. The third claimed that the ancient laws and customs of the Gallican Church were inviolable. The fourth said that though the pope was the ultimate teaching authority, his judgements, without the consent of a council, were not irreformable. By 1693 the pope had succeeded in having these articles withdrawn. Nevertheless, their influence continued.

While a large part of Gallicanism was concerned with the rights of French kings, a Catholic *Erastianism, it also asserted the ancient rights of the French bishops, the Sorbonne, and the French legal system, countering the Donation of *Constantine with creative rewritings of the ecclesiastical career of Charlemagne. More impressively, it included an early theology of the *church as the whole people of God. The medieval clashes between popes and emperors were refought in France, and in 1516 the kings of France gained papal permission to choose bishops. The French church was distinct: 'France does not receive the tribunal of the *Inquisition.' It might seem odd that Louis XIV went no further, and instead withdrew support from the Articles. Other Catholic monarchies also sought control of their national churches: there was regalism in Naples, Febronianism in Vienna. *Ultramontanist history drew too dark a picture of such movements.

With the French *Revolution, the Civil Constitution of the Clergy established a Gallican church in France, unrecognized by the pope. When Napoleon merged the Constitutional Church with the church loyal to Rome, it was (on his instigation) the pope who dismissed all the bishops of both sides, to start afresh: a complete denial of the ancient liberties of the French church. There was now no king, and a supreme pope. But Gallicanism, or neo-Gallicanism, still lingered. There had to be a name for the natural conservatism that opposed the new ultramontanes. Archbishop Affre (d. 1848) of Paris could still claim that 'in France the pope reigns but does not govern'. The ultramontanes seemed to win: the papalism of the *Infallibility decree of 1870 was very ungallican. But the principle of *collegiality, and much else in *Vatican II, was not. Gallicanism

cannot be simply dismissed as a greedy, unprincipled policy in the service of long-dead kings.   **Alistair Mason**

Gough, Austin, Paris and Rome (1986).
Martin, V., Les Origines du Gallicanisme (1939).
Rothkrug, L., Opposition to Louis XIV: The Political and Social Origins of the French Enlightenment (1965).

gay theology. Quite apart from their efforts to offer an ethical justification of *homosexuality, many lesbian, bisexual, and gay theologians have also articulated critiques and reconstructions of the Christian tradition based on their experience of living as gay people. Gay theology is concerned not with whether Christians can live homosexual lifestyles, but with the ways in which living a homosexual lifestyle might encourage individuals and communities to reconstruct their theologies. The considerable convergence of opinion among gay theologians is, however, due as much to their common intellectual heritage in the *liberal tradition as to their shared sexuality. Many of those who are most vocal in the field form a close academic community and are influenced by the same seminal texts, for example Carter Heyward's The Redemption of God. 'Gay theology' means both theology written from a gay perspective and, more specifically, theology written by this distinct group.

Central to gay theology has been the contention that many of the classical Christian doctrines are opposed to the liberation of lesbians, bisexuals, and gay men. The doctrines of *God, Christ, *salvation, and *humanity are all reviewed to reveal the heterosexist assumptions on which they are based and the homophobic power structures implicit within them. These structures include the belief, criticized by *feminist and *liberation theologians, that it is better to exercise power over people than to work with them in order to empower them. Drawing on the experience of working with the poor and the oppressed, gay theologians point out that whereas external aid keeps people in a position of powerlessness and dependency, genuine aid consists in working alongside them, helping them to help themselves (see POVERTY).

Heterosexist power assumptions are most evident in the doctrine of God's transcendence, which is virtually equated with a position of 'power over'. Gay theologians therefore characteristically focus on divine immanence, often equating the divine with the power for resistance to oppression that exists within each human being. Divine impassibility (Greek apatheia) is also rejected, on the grounds that a God who does not know *suffering cannot care about those who suffer and is above such petty matters as politics and the struggle for survival and liberation. An impassive God is seen to be apathetic in the modern sense of uninvolved and callous.

Drawing on the insights of liberation theology, gay theologians focus on the humanity rather than the divinity of *Jesus. Jesus is not a saviour who comes to us from without but a fellow human who works and suffers alongside the oppressed. The term 'Christ' is not used exclusively of Jesus, but is applied to the experience of healthy empowerment (Christic experience) wherever this is found. Heyward also criticizes the incarnational model of *Chalcedonian christology because in it Jesus' humanity has no choice in being united with divinity. This is seen as yet another instance of 'power over'.

As regards the doctrine of salvation, it is axiomatic for gay theology that salvation comes from within rather than without. Jesus' role in salvation is to teach us how to realize our own full potential, to release the power within ourselves that enables us to overcome our experiences of powerlessness. It is this power, referred to as *eros*, which is the ultimate fount of salvation.

In continuity with the liberal philosophical tradition on which it depends, gay theology has a highly optimistic view of humanity. Although liberal individualism has failed, gay theologians believe that by co-operating in communities, humans are able to work towards *justice without supernatural aid. There is little place here for developing a doctrine of original sin seen as a tendency towards racism, sexism, and heterosexism, perhaps because the term has become inextricably linked in the lives of gay people with guilt about their *sexuality.

In its versions of each of these central doctrines, gay theology has been heavily influenced by liberal theology. Although it is at pains to reject liberalism's individualism and power-blindness, its dependence in terms of *christology and salvation is striking. One of the questions which must surely arise, therefore, is the extent to which gay theology is able to prosper where the liberal paradigm is less influential than in certain US seminaries. Although there are theologians whose doctrinal position is more orthodox, the liberal heritage of gay theology maintains a strong hold by virtue of the priority given to experience.

Gay theology, in common with many other theologies that are based on group identities, presupposes that individuals who claim an identity have, to a significant extent, common experiences. For some authors these experiences are primarily social: the experience of coming out of the closet (publicly affirming one's sexuality), for instance. For others, they are internal, private experiences: some would claim that gay people possess a special spiritual awareness or artistic sensitivity. From these common experiences flow shared beliefs about the nature of divine reality.

Even if it is allowed that gay and lesbian people share certain experiences, it is still an open question whether these experiences can or should lead to a common theology. According to Michel Foucault, the tendency in modern society to see sex as the essence of humanity and the basis of knowledge is overwhelming, and encourages us to focus on sexuality where other factors such as personal temperament, intellectual background, and spiritual heritage may be equally significant. It is the importance of factors such as these that accounts for the wide diversity which gay theologians now recognize but cannot as yet adequately theorize.

If a common sexual identity does not lead to a shared theology, what sense does the phrase 'gay theology' make? Perhaps the most that it is possible to say is that certain people who have chosen to self-identify on the basis of their (homo)sexual orientation have a tendency to bring common questions to theological discussion.

Malcolm S. Edwards

Cleaver, R., *Know My Name* (1995).
Comstock, G., *Gay Theology Without Apology* (1993).
Goss, R., *Jesus Acted Up* (1993).
Heyward, C., *The Redemption of God* (1982).
Stuart, E., *Just Good Friends* (1995).

Genesis, the first book of the OT, has had a particularly important role in shaping Christian thought, which, as part of its inheritance from *Platonism, has a profound interest in beginnings. The first three chapters contain the only sustained accounts in the biblical canon of the *creation of the universe, the nature of *humanity and its predicament, and the founding relationship between *God and human beings. They have thus had to bear more theological freight than any others in the OT. The *Incarnation requires Christian thinkers to apply themselves to just these questions as they insist on the identity between the God of creation and the Father of Jesus Christ in the face of *Gnostic denials, and try to give an account of the nature of God and humanity faithful to both the OT witness and the reality of Jesus.

The book contains a wealth of narratives and *mythical imagery which can be turned to *typological ends. Noah's ark, for instance, became a type of the church as the rescuer of souls. The action is set before the giving of the Law and so offers the church examples of individuals and societies who are found acceptable to God without being bound to the Mosaic code (see LAW, BIBLICAL).

Despite the diversity of material and the complex editorial processes that critical scholars have discerned in Genesis, it is held together by the motif of the divine promise worked out through *family relationships and the birth of children, hence the prevalence of genealogies. The great family sagas of the patriarchs, apart from their literary appeal, provide models of continuity and change in human society. The recurrent theme of the younger son who ousts the older gives concrete examples for later consideration of the mystery of election and rejection.

Though the promise is threatened by human folly and sometimes even by inexplicable divine action, it nevertheless remains in force even if its fulfilment is deferred and oblique. *Adam and *Eve are banished from the garden, *Cain murders his brother, *Abraham is told to sacrifice his son, Jacob deceives his blind father and tricks his brother Esau out of his inheritance and in turn is cheated by his father-in-law Laban, and yet the line continues.

The book ends with the cycle of stories about Joseph, masterly tellings of the adventures of the abandoned favourite son who becomes effective ruler of Egypt, setting the scene for the disaster and triumph of the *exodus. Yet it is the bizarre and seemingly intrusive episode in chapter 38, where Judah unknowingly fathers children on his daughter-in-law Tamar, which carries the story beyond the bounds of Genesis to his descendant *David and through him to Jesus. Tamar herself appears in *Matthew's genealogy of Jesus (Matt. 1: 3), a character from Genesis witnessing in the NT to its message of the arbitrariness, ambiguity, and certainty of God's blessing.

See also HIGHER CRITICISM.   **Hugh S. Pyper**

Alter, R., *Genesis* (1996).
Armstrong, K., *In the Beginning* (1996).
von Rad, G., *Genesis* (1972).

Geneva is set in a natural tight corner, where the Alps come down to the Rhône, flowing out of a lake. It was a frontier post in Caesar's time, and had a history of playing off powerful neighbours. Historically, the Genevans did not see themselves as French or as (German) Swiss. The 'national' church is the church of Geneva.

When it was most famous, Geneva had a population of fewer than 15,000. A very visibly fortified town, in 1526 it had rebelled against the dukes of Savoy and expelled its bishop. In 1536 the city voted to 'live henceforth according to the law of the gospel and the Word of God, and to abolish all papal abuses'. The magistrates accepted Geneva's role as a city of refuge, the south-west corner of *Protestant safety, and the religious ministrations of refugee French Protestant clergy, led by *Calvin. They, and not Calvin, imposed on the city the godly discipline that made it a school of saints. It was never a theocracy, although, once the Libertine opposition was crushed, Calvin's personal ascendancy was seldom questioned. Geneva's rules were not unusually strict for the period, but they were diligently enforced without respect of persons. Some rules, biblically based, were progressive and humane; men said Geneva was a '*women's paradise'.

For about 30 years from the 1550s, Geneva dominated the *Reformed churches of Europe, as refuge, arbiter of *orthodoxy, supplier of books and ministers, and model of a Christian city. The principal reason for this supremacy was Calvin, who, however, would never admit that he or the city had any special status. Later in the century, under military threat, the city was able to raise funds from as far away as Transylvania and Scotland, but this was an effect of nostalgia, not of current power. Geneva just managed to fight off both the *Counter-Reformation and the duke of Savoy. Francis de Sales, Geneva's best-known Catholic bishop, appointed in 1602, was only once able to visit it. Based in France, he represented the Counter-Reformation in its gentlest form, supporting the religious advancement of women, writing the famous *Introduction to the Devout Life* intended for lay people, and remarking that flies are more attracted by a spoonful of honey than a barrel of vinegar. Calvin's successor, Beza, could no longer supply ministers to France, and feared that the world thought that 'in Geneva everyone is a banker'. Geneva had no influence at international Calvinism's greatest council, the Synod of Dort, in 1612.

Geneva was the city of Rousseau, and knew Voltaire. Henri Dunant, a Genevan, inspired the foundation of the Red Cross and instigated the Geneva Convention (1864). Through his influence, Geneva had the office of the World's Committee of the Young Men's Christian Associations (YMCA). Reflecting the spirit of the League of Nations, inaugurated in the 'Salle de la Reformation' in 1923, there came the headquarters of the World Student Christian Federation, and, from 1938, of what was to become the World Council of Churches (see ECUMENICAL MOVEMENT). Other transnational headquarters followed. The WCC, with its international task and large bureaucracy, serves in some ways as non-Catholic Christianity's *Rome. It has more continuity with the Red Cross than with Calvin.   **Alistair Mason**

Monter, E. William, *Calvin's Geneva* (1967).
Naphy, William G., *Calvin and the Consolidation of the Genevan Reformation* (1994).
Prestwich, Menna (ed.), *International Calvinism 1541–1715* (1985).
Roney, J. B., and Klauber, M. I., *The Identity of Geneva* (1998).
Visser't Hooft, W. A., *Memoirs* (1973).

German Christian thought.

Christianity was brought to Germany by the Anglo-Saxon missionary monk Boniface (*c*.680–*c*.754), the 'Apostle of Germany', commissioned in 718 by Pope Gregory II to preach the gospel to the German tribes. There were some significant German thinkers in the late Middle Ages, notably the *Dominican *mystic Meister Eckhart (*c*.1260–1327), the first theologian to write extensively in German. It was possibly the difficulty of expressing the reality of the mystical experience that led to suspicions against his orthodoxy and the posthumous condemnation of some of his teaching. He was, however, always defended and revered by his disciples, fellow-Dominicans, and fellow mystics Johann Tauler (*c*.1300–61) and Henry Suso (*c*.1295–1366). It is probably wrong to interpret Eckhart, as some have, as leaning to pantheism. His teaching was in fact in the Dominican scholastic tradition. Tauler's sermons were greatly valued by *Luther.

It was with the *Reformation that German Christian thought began to acquire a distinctive character, with the rediscovery of the Pauline doctrine of *justification by *grace through *faith alone. Luther interpreted it to mean that human beings enter into a right relationship with *God not through moral effort or good works but through God's gracious gift of righteousness to the believer. A second important doctrine was *sola scriptura*: that the church is subordinate to scripture and only doctrines and practices grounded in scripture are binding upon believers. These two doctrines have continued to inform German *Protestant thought to the present day, but perhaps the most significant impact of the Reformation was its division of Germany into *Lutheran, *Reformed, and *Catholic camps. From the Reformation onwards theology in Germany was done along denominational lines. Only in the 20th century with the rise of ecumenism and the Leuenberg Concord of 1973 did these divisions begin to lose their force.

An unforeseen consequence of the Reformation was the close tie German Christianity developed with the political establishment. Luther's two kingdoms doctrine, contrasting the *Kingdom of God and the kingdom of this world, led Lutheran clergy to concern themselves with the former and neglect the latter. Furthermore, the Reformation needed the support of the German princes to survive. The importance of the political establishment was confirmed in the Treaty of Augsburg (1555), which gave the German princes the right to determine their subjects' denomination (*cuius regio, eius religio*).

In the 18th century, the challenge facing German theology was posed by the *Enlightenment, especially its claim that beliefs must be rationally justified. Where this was accepted in *theology, it resulted in large-scale rejection of *dogma. The attack on the rational credibility of Christianity was extended by *Kant's *Critique of Pure Reason* (1781, 1787), which undermined the metaphysical foundations upon which Christian theology had been based. The Enlightenment critique of Christianity also forced reformulations of *christology. Growing scepticism concerning *miracles removed one of the traditional arguments for Christ's divinity, and the two natures doctrine came to be regarded by many thinkers as an absurdity. The claim of H. S. Reimarus (1694–1768) that the central Christian doctrines were created by the disciples to save *Jesus' movement after the failure of his political mission, and the argument of G. E. Lessing (1729–81) that history cannot convey rational truths, raised the problem of the relationship between the Jesus of history and the Christ of faith which has exercised theologians ever since.

The common solution to the Enlightenment critique was to emphasize the *moral* content of Christianity on the grounds that *morality is untainted by dogma and *metaphysics, and is accessible to *reason. Many Enlightenment thinkers came to regard morality as the final meaning and content of religion and Christ as a teacher or exemplar of morality. One consequence was a shift from christologies 'from above', taking Christ's divinity as their starting-point, to christologies 'from below', which begin with the man Jesus and attempt to establish in what sense he can be spoken of as divine.

The 19th century saw the unification of Germany and its rise to a great power. After destroying the Holy Roman empire in 1806, Napoleon organized Germany into thirty states. Corresponding to this, thirty provincial churches (Landeskirchen) were established and this has remained the basic structure of German Protestantism. The head of each provincial church was the local monarch, which strengthened Lutheran political and social conservatism. Napoleon's reorganization incorporated many Catholic regions into predominantly Protestant states, reducing Catholics to a disadvantaged minority. This minority status was accentuated still further by the unification of Germany under Protestant Prussia in 1871, resulting in Protestant domination of government, bureaucracy, and army. This, coupled with the theological conservatism of the *papacy, meant that Catholicism had little impact on the cultural and intellectual life of 19th-century Germany. The main exception was the *Tübingen school; its chief representatives, J. S. Drey (1777–1853) and, above all, J. A. Möhler (1796–1838), advanced a theory of doctrinal *development that acknowledged the necessity of the growth of doctrine. A further significant development in German Catholic thought was the rise of social Catholicism, resulting from the disadvantaged status of Catholics, who made up the bulk of the poorer classes in Germany.

The most significant developments in the *nineteenth century, however, took place in Protestant circles. Lessing and Kant had created a new and highly problematic context for Christian theology and thrown up the two fundamental problems with which theology has had to grapple ever since: the epistemological status of religious *truth-claims and the relationship between theology and *history. Furthermore, Enlightenment scepticism concerning supernatural events forced biblical scholars to search for new ways of defending the authority of the *bible. Their commitment to sola scriptura made this a particularly acute problem for Protestant theologians, which accounts for the intensity with which they searched for and developed new methods of biblical interpretation. Their acute awareness of the challenge posed by the Enlightenment, and the creativeness of their attempts to meet it, accounts for the dominance of German theology in the 19th and early 20th centuries.

A leading characteristic of post-Enlightenment German Protestant theology was the 'turn to the self', the first great representative of which was *Schleiermacher. He responded to the theological problems posed by the Enlightenment by grounding theology not in the analysis of dogmatic propositions but in the examination of the subjective consciousness from which such propositions were derived: religion is 'neither a Knowing nor a Doing, but a modification of Feeling, or of immediate self-consciousness'. This 'feeling' is one of absolute dependence. Schleiermacher identifies it as a pre-reflective consciousness of our being in relation to God. As the archetype and historical manifestation of pure God-consciousness, Christ is the originator and source of the Christian community's consciousness of *redemption.

*Hegel attempted to map out the historical process in which Geist (Spirit/Mind) comes to know and articulate itself ever more fully. Christianity forms an important part of this process since Christ expresses the principle of divine–human unity and thereby marks a progression in the self-consciousness both of Absolute Spirit and of humanity. *Religion, however, expresses this self-consciousness in Vorstellungen, sensuous representations produced by feeling and imagination. The task of *philosophy is to articulate in philosophical concepts (Begriffe) what is intuitively grasped but inadequately expressed by religion.

Although Hegel's speculative philosophy rapidly fell out of favour after his death, certain aspects of his thought exerted considerable influence on subsequent theology. His distinction between Vorstellung and Begriff underlies the way that D. F. Strauss (1808–74) interprets the NT in terms of *myth, understanding 'myth' as the sensuous representation of an inadequately articulated concept. By interpreting the NT in this way, Strauss eliminated the need to defend the *gospels' reports as historical records of supernatural events or to discern what natural occurrences are being thus described. In doing this, however, he seemed to many to undermine the basis of the Christian faith.

F. C. Baur (1792–1860) criticized Strauss and Schleiermacher on the grounds that their theologies could not establish an essential connection between the historical Jesus and the Christ of Christian dogma: only through historical-critical study of the origins of Christianity can the significance of Jesus be established and christology constructed. This emphasis on historical-critical study of the NT was one of the factors that led to *liberal Protestantism, a somewhat diffuse 19th-century theological approach. It responded to the Enlightenment critique by taking the historical Jesus as its starting-point, maintaining that a modern, undogmatic christology can be constructed by treating Jesus' life as a human life and tracing its development. This led to the *quest for the historical Jesus, an attempt to penetrate through the layers of church dogma to the historical figure allegedly concealed beneath them. The resulting christologies stress above all the message of Jesus and tend to understand it in terms of morality. A common feature of the theologies of Albrecht Ritschl (1822–89), Wilhelm Herrmann (1846–1922), and Adolf Harnack (1857–1930) was that they understood Jesus as a teacher of morality, the founder of a community of moral values.

Towards the end of the 19th century, liberal Protestantism was subjected to major criticism. By showing that *Mark had organized his material according to his theological interests, Wilhelm Wrede (1859–1906) undermined the view that Mark's gospel could be seen as an objective historical report of Jesus' life, that provided a firm historical basis for constructing an undogmatic christology. Johannes Weiss (1863–1914) and Albert Schweitzer (1875–1965) showed that, far from giving a picture of the 'real' Jesus, the liberal Protestant view is fundamentally unhistorical, for it discards the *eschatological contents of Jesus' message. Martin Kähler (1835–1912) held that since Christ is not a historical but a 'suprahistorical figure', the 'Christ of faith' should be the starting-point of theology. It is not the historical Jesus who is important for faith and theology but Christ active in the lives of believers now. Ernst Troeltsch (1865–1923) threatened liberal Protestantism from a rather different perspective by arguing that Christianity should be interpreted in relation to its cultural environment, which undermined Christianity's claim to absoluteness. Both historical and sociological approaches were rejected by Rudolf *Otto in favour of a view of religion grounded in the experience of the 'holy' or 'numinous'.

The major theological movements of the *twentieth century can be regarded as attempts to find a more adequate basis for theology than was offered by the historicism and anthropocentrism of the 19th. Whereas the 19th century made human subjectivity, idealist philosophy, or history the starting-point for theology, the 20th century was characterized by a swing back to the Christ of faith, a rediscovery of eschatology, a return to Trinitarianism, and a recovery of Luther's theology of the cross. The crucial turning-point was the advent of 'dialectical theology' or 'theology of crisis', also called *neo-orthodoxy, its most important representatives being Friedrich Gogarten (1887–1967), Emil Brunner (1889–1966), Rudolf *Bultmann, Paul *Tillich, and, above all, the Swiss Reformed theologian Karl *Barth.

Barth's *Römerbrief* (Commentary on the Epistle to the Romans; 1st edn. 1919; 2nd edn. 1922) transformed the German theological landscape. For Barth, theology since Schleiermacher had taken the wrong direction. Jesus had been subsumed into the historical nexus, into human culture, and subordinated to human thought. By contrast, Barth emphasized the 'infinite qualitative difference' between God and humankind, and the eschatological content of the gospel. God is the 'wholly other', who comes to us not in continuity with human culture but 'vertically from above' when he speaks his *Word, a Word that confronts humankind with divine judgement and that can only be received by the 'impossible possibility' of faith.

Barth's emphasis on the radical distinction between God and *humanity and his interpretation of biblical eschatology in terms of divine *judgement made a deep impression on a generation traumatized by the First World War and a number of other young theologians soon made common cause with him. Gogarten joined the fray in 1920 with his lecture on 'the crisis of our culture', in which, like Barth, he emphasized the radical distinction between God and the world. His 1920 essay *Zwischen den Zeiten* (*Between the Times*) was regarded by many as the manifesto of dialectical theology and gave its name to the journal founded by Barth, Gogarten, Eduard Thurneysen, and Georg Merz in 1922. Another early supporter of dialectical theology was Barth's fellow-countryman and Reformed theologian Brunner, whose book *The Mediator* (1927) was the first major work on christology by a dialectical theologian. Brunner rejects all attempts to ground Christ's significance in history or human experience, developing instead a high christology centring on the *Incarnation and Christ's role as mediator between God and humankind.

Dialectical theology caused considerable controversy in 1920s Germany and gave rise to an important debate between Harnack and Barth. In the January 1923 edition of *Die Christliche Welt* (*The Christian World*) Harnack addressed fifteen questions to the 'despisers of scientific theology', raising especially the question of the foundations of the Christian faith, which he believed could be established only by historical-critical investigation. Barth answered that it is the Risen Christ of faith who is the starting-point for theology, not a Christ established by historical investigation, which cannot provide secure foundations for Christianity.

After about 1930 dialectical theology began to disintegrate as a coherent movement. Barth's estrangement from Gogarten began as early as 1927, when Gogarten welcomed Barth's *Christian Dogmatics in Outline* in a way that Barth found theologically unacceptable. The final break came in 1933, with Barth's essay, 'Departure

from *Zwischen den Zeiten*'. He wrote that Gogarten's increased anthropological orientation showed that their co-operation had been a mistake. The controversy with Brunner concerned *natural theology. In 1934 Brunner published *Nature and Grace*, in which he argued that the fact that human beings, despite their sinfulness, are made in the image of God provides a point of contact between God and humankind making possible the construction of a natural theology. Barth's response was an angry 'No!' The human being possesses no point of contact with God except what God himself establishes. The only source of knowledge of God is God himself when he imparts his Word to us, which he has graciously done in Jesus Christ.

The backdrop to these debates, and one of the reasons for Barth's vigorous opposition to his former theological allies, was the ominous political scene in 1930s Germany and the increasing pressure exerted by the Nazi regime on the churches. Because of their close relations with the political hierarchy, the collapse of the German empire in 1918 had been most keenly felt by the Protestant churches. Political conservatism and antipathy towards the Weimar Republic resulted in many Protestant clergy initially welcoming Hitler's seizure of power, some even regarding it as a divine miracle. Hitler strove to eliminate any resistance to Nazi rule that the churches might offer. Resistance from the Roman Catholic Church was weakened by the Concordat between Hitler and Pope Pius XII in 1933, apparently undermining disapproval of the Nazi regime. Hitler attempted to control the Protestant churches by supporting the pro-Nazi German Christian Faith Movement and uniting the *Landeskirchen* under a single Reich bishop, Hitler's protégé Ludwig Müller. Barth's disputes with Gogarten and Brunner stemmed in part from his fear that theological anthropology and natural theology could provide support for the political status quo. Only a theology showing God standing over and against the world in judgement of it could provide the resources for resisting Nazism. It was his concern to resist Nazi pressure on the Protestant churches that prompted Barth, at the Reformed Synod at *Barmen in 1934, to draw up the 'Declaration on the Right Understanding of the Reformation Confessions in the German Evangelical Church Today', which became the manifesto of the 'Confessing Church', the anti-Hitler bloc within the Protestant churches.

Bultmann had been profoundly impressed by the second edition of Barth's *Römerbrief* and took Barth's side in his debate with Harnack. Both agreed that Christian theology must be based on the Christ of faith. To base theology on the historical Jesus is, as Bultmann puts it, to base it on 'Christ according to the flesh', whereas theology should be concerned with 'Christ according to faith'. But, though initially allies, they became increasingly alienated from each other after the publication of Barth's book on *Anselm (1931). The point of contention concerned the anthropological dimension of theology and Bultmann's use of Heidegger's philosophy, which in Barth's opinion subjected Christianity to a criterion outside itself.

It was the cultural and theological crisis brought about by the First World War that attracted Tillich to dialectical theology in the early 1920s. Unlike Barth and Gogarten, he was concerned to find new ways of relating theology to culture, as is indicated by his 1919 lecture 'On the Idea of a Theology of Culture'. Evident here are the beginnings of his 'method of correlation', which sees theology as responding to the questions raised by the age in which it finds itself. Tillich's differences with dialectical theology became apparent in his 1923 debate with Barth and Gogarten on *paradox. Barth sums up their differences thus: whereas for dialectical theology 'Christ is *the* salvation history … for Tillich he is the presentation of a salvation history which more or less occurs always and everywhere with completely symbolic power'. Whereas dialectical theology holds 'to the indissoluble correlation of the theological concept of truth with the concepts of "church", "canon", "*Holy Spirit*" ', Tillich relates or, from the perspective of dialectical theology, subordinates theological truth to non-theological spheres of discourse.

In 1925 Tillich began work on his *Systematic Theology*, although the first volume did not appear until 1951 in the USA. However, the publication of *The Religious Situation of the Times* in 1926 made him widely known in Germany. *The Socialist Decision* (1932) led to his dismissal by the Nazis and his emigration to the USA in 1933, where he played a major role in *North American theology until his death in 1965.

After the disintegration of dialectical theology as a movement, its members went their separate ways. Brunner's later work is influenced by the personalist interpretation of the human being's encounter with God as an 'I–Thou' relationship. Brunner took up this understanding of the divine–human relationship in *Truth as Encounter* (1938) and in the second volume of his *Dogmatics* (1950), in which he interprets faith as a personal encounter with God in the person of Jesus Christ.

In Barth's later period the infinite qualitative difference of the earlier writings is replaced by emphasis on dialogue between God and humankind: a very one-sided affair, for the initiative in the divine–human relationship lies solely with God. God is the subject who addresses his Word to humankind, who are called upon to receive it in *obedience. By giving such pre-eminence to God and reducing the role of the human being to obedience, Barth believes he is able to remove the need for anthropology in theology. A key work in this development is his book on Anselm, in which he argues that God's Word has its own rationality, which cannot be subsumed into human rationality but stands in opposition to it. This Word of God is Jesus Christ, and it is the theologian's task to articulate and unfold this Word, something which Barth attempts to do in his uncompleted *magnum opus*, *Church Dogmatics* (1932–68). The Trinitarianism of this work has played a significant role in renewing the theology of the *Trinity after its neglect in 19th-century German thought.

In his mature period, Bultmann constructed a theology centred on the *kerygma, the early church's teaching concerning Jesus. Despite his immense contribution to the historical criticism of the *gospels, Bultmann believed that the historical foundations of the kerygma are impossible to establish and are in any case of no importance. What is significant is only 'the That' (*das Daβ*) of Jesus, the fact that he existed, and the faith elicited by the individual's encounter with the kerygma. But the kerygma is clothed in mythological language and the 20th-century view of the world is radically different from that of the 1st century. If the NT is to be intelligible today, it must be translated into a form that can address modern people. This is the subject of Bultmann's lecture, 'New Testament and Mythology' (1941), which introduced the term *demythologizing into Western theology. Drawing on Heidegger's philosophy,

Bultmann attempts to strip the eschatological message of the NT of its mythological garb and recover its *existential meaning. He sees the kerygma as confronting each human being with the possibility of authentic existence by creating an existential crisis that demands a decision.

Although profoundly influenced by Barth, particularly in his early period, Dietrich *Bonhoeffer was concerned at Barth's lack of concreteness and critical of his 'revelatory positivism'. Bonhoeffer develops a theology of sociality in which he relates a Barthian type theology of revelation to concrete reality in order to bring to the fore the communal dimension of Christianity. It is, however, his letters from prison that have had the greatest theological impact. Here he speaks of the problems facing Christianity in a 'world come of age' and the necessity of 'religionless Christianity,' ideas that subsequently influenced Bishop John *Robinson's *Honest to God* (1963), as well as 'Death of God' theology, and the secular gospel. Bonhoeffer was not claiming that God did not exist or demanding the reduction of Christianity to secular moral teaching, but advocating the reworking of Christianity so as to address human beings in a way which respects their autonomy. In place of 'religion' the church must transform itself in accordance with Christ's example and 'live for others'.

The experiences of the Third Reich and the Second World War led to a new relationship between church and state in post-war Germany. The Protestant churches in the Federal Republic abandoned the relationship with the state that had dominated German Christianity for so long and adopted the role of benevolent critic of government policy. Catholics were integrated into West German society more than ever before and came to play a leading role in the nation's political life. In East Germany the churches provided a focus for opposition to the communist regime, contributing to the dissolution of the German Democratic Republic in 1989–1990.

In the immediate post-war period, Barth and Bultmann continued to dominate German theology. However, Bultmann's historical scepticism and his severing of the link between the historical Jesus and the Christ of the kerygma were increasingly challenged by many of his pupils. For Ernst Käsemann, Ernst Fuchs, Günther Bornkamm, Hans Conzelmann, and Gerhard Ebeling, it was essential to uphold the relationship between the historical Jesus and the Christ of faith lest the latter become merely a product of the Church's faith with no historical grounding. This led to the 'new quest for the historical Jesus', which aimed to show that the source of the kerygma is not the early church but Jesus himself, and that there is an essential connection between Jesus' life and message and the kerygma.

The publication in 1961 of *Revelation as History*, a collection of essays edited by Wolfhart* Pannenberg, offered another way of attempting to ground the significance of Jesus Christ by advancing an eschatological interpretation of history. History, Pannenberg argues, can only be understood as a totality when viewed eschatologically, from the perspective of the eschatological event of God's self-disclosure that will bring history to its conclusion at the end-time. This divine eschatological self-disclosure is proleptically actualized in Christ through whom alone an understanding of history becomes possible, because only in Christ is God's eschatological self-disclosure available. It is the need to defend the historicity of the divine self-disclosure in Christ that motivates Pannenberg's christology, expressed in his *Jesus: God and Man* (1964), in which he attempts to provide a historical grounding for Christ's significance and argues for the objective reality of the Resurrection.

The importance of eschatology in 20th-century German Christian thought is also evident in the theology of Jürgen *Moltmann. In his *Theology of Hope* (1964) and *The Crucified God* (1972), Moltmann sees the crucifixion as God's self-identification with the world's god-forsakenness and Jesus' Resurrection as God's promise of a new creation of the world of negativity represented in the crucified Jesus. But the crucifixion is a significant event not only for human-kind but for God himself, for in the *cross human suffering is taken up into the history of God: something which must be understood in Trinitarian terms and entails the rejection of the impassible God of classical theism. Although Christians look forward to God's eschatological fulfilment of the promise contained in Jesus' Resurrection, Moltmann emphasizes that the Christian *hope is not other-worldly or utopian. The eschatological dimension is a call to action, a challenge to transform the world from what it is at present into what it should and one day will be. This emphasis on praxis has influenced *political and *liberation theology.

Like Bonhoeffer, Eberhard *Jüngel is concerned with the problem of speaking of God in a world where God seems to be absent, and like both Bonhoeffer and Moltmann he regards Luther's *theologia crucis* as an essential resource for doing so. God is the mystery of the world, both present and hidden in the cross, and yet the eye of faith sees him in the apparent godforsakenness of the crucified Jesus. God's self-identification with the crucified Jesus necessitates the positing of a distinction in God, expressed in the NT in terms of God the Son (the Crucified One) and God the Father (he who raises the Crucified One from the dead). This distinction forms the basis of Jüngel's understanding of the Trinity and his critique of mono-theism, metaphysical theism, and *atheism, all of which arise from the failure to think of God in Trinitarian terms.

The recommendation by Leo XIII of *Thomism as the philosophical framework for theology and the condemnation of *modernism by Pius X did much to stifle Catholic thought in the late 19th and early 20th centuries. However, the second half of the 20th saw the re-emergence of Catholic theology as a major force in contemporary German Christian thought, notably with Karl *Rahner and J. B. Metz. Two Swiss nationals, Hans *Küng, who has spent his academic life at Tübingen, and Hans Urs *von Balthasar have also exerted a significant influence on German theology.

Perhaps the most significant work to be published in the 1990s was Pannenberg's three-volume *Systematic Theology*. However, Barth's thought continues to be influential and to provide the resources for creative theological work. Of interest is Ingolf Dalferth who provides a philosophical grounding for a theology of the Word and addresses the epistemological, ontological, and linguistic issues raised by Christian doctrine. A further development in recent German theology has been the attempt by F. Wagner to map out the transcendental presuppositions and conditions of religious belief by means of insights drawn from German idealism. Liberal Protestantism is represented by F. W. Graf and *feminist theology by Elisabeth Moltmann-Wendel, Dorothee *Sölle, and Luise Schottroff. While German thought dominates world theology less than in the first half of the 20th century, it remains its most powerful single constituent.   **David R. Law**

Barth, Karl, *Protestant Theology in the Nineteenth Century: Its Background and History* (1973).

Ford, D., *The Modern Theologians*, 2nd. edn. (1997).

Heron, A., *A Century of Protestant Theology* (1980).

Hirsch, E., *Geschichte der neuern evangelischen Theologie im Zusammenhang mit den allgemeinen Bewegungen des europäischen Denkens* (5 vols.; 1949–51).

McGrath, Alister, *The Making of Modern German Christology* (1986).

Macquarrie, John, *Jesus Christ in Modern Thought* (1990).

Welch, C., *Protestant Thought in the Nineteenth Century* (2 vols.; 1972–85).

global ethics

global ethics (or world ethics) signifies the exploration of the complex of moral values, norms, and responsibilities that we acknowledge in regard to the relations between states and the relations individuals have with one another and the natural *world on a global scale. A global *ethic will have two components: first, certain values and norms that are universal, in that they are applicable to all human beings everywhere, and second, certain duties or responsibilities that are global in scope, in the sense that individuals, states, and other bodies have, in principle, duties towards all others in the world, such as respecting rights, and aiding those in need. Any such global ethic is called a form of *cosmopolitanism*.

The basic idea behind cosmopolitanism is that we are all citizens of the world, not in the sense in which human beings are citizens of particular political communities, but as members of one global society, with duties towards one another. This idea originally came into prominence through the Stoics who contrasted the contingency of the particular community into which one was born with the more basic fact that one was a citizen of the universe. National borders and identities, therefore, are not of ultimate moral significance. Many theories support a cosmopolitan conception, such as *Kant's 'kingdom of ends', a moral realm of all rational agents; utilitarianism which says that all beings affected by one's actions should be considered in calculating the greatest balance of good over evil; or human rights theories, arising from the *natural law tradition, which assert certain features of well-being—subsistence, security, liberty—to which all have a right, with corresponding duties to respect, protect, and promote these features for others.

The Christian ethic as a global/cosmopolitan ethic

On this basis, almost all Christians would accept the idea of a global ethic, since the very idea of *God as *omnipotent, *omniscient, and benevolent creator suggests that all human beings are of equal status as God's children, that the same basic values underlying well-being and the same moral norms apply to all human beings, who are neighbours in the fellowship of *humanity, towards whom we owe, in some form, the duty of *charity. Christians may also hold to an *eschatological vision of human *history culminating in a time when humans will live at *peace in a truly global society. Nevertheless there are considerable variations over the importance attached to this global aspect of ethics, over its content, and over its implications in the real world of separate states and societies. But in so far as there is an acceptance of real and active obligations as citizens of the world, Christian ethics are cosmopolitan in character.

What is it about the modern world that makes the assertion of a global ethic particularly important? First, there are clearly *global problems*: apart from two world wars, there have been numerous large-scale conflicts in most parts of the world, and the nuclear arms race still risks destruction on a global scale. Despite international efforts, the gap between rich and poor countries has grown in the last fifty years, and one billion people, one-fifth of the world's population, live in absolute *poverty. The pressures of economic growth, combined with increasing populations, continue to degrade our natural environment and use up its resources. Second, the technological revolutions of communication and transportation are turning the world into a 'global village', leading to a breakdown of the traditional nation-state system and transforming relations between people. These changes open up new possibilities for effective action to address global problems. Whether we tackle them effectively depends on many factors, including whether we accept a global ethic at all, and what global values are acknowledged. Four areas of concern illustrate this: *war and peace, development, environment, and population.

Christianity may lend support to a global ethic, but it should be noted that there are powerful alternatives to the very idea. The validity of ethics in international relations is questioned by some forms of realism, because in a world of fearful and hostile states the right of *national survival must take precedence. Then there is a form of the internationalist tradition that endorses a 'morality of states', sanctioned by custom and tradition, but centred on the rights of sovereignty. Though some Christians have been drawn into the realist fold, this kind of realism runs counter to Christian insights about the status of all human beings. It was out of the 'natural law' traditions of Christian Europe that the internationalist tradition itself arose. In so far as the latter approach has subsequently become resistant to the idea of positive obligations between states and peoples, many Christians would see it as a betrayal of the very principles of natural *justice underlying the development of the idea of international *law by Vitoria and Grotius. Such principles now require a global ethic that both radically criticizes the behaviour of states and inspires individuals to become engaged global citizens.

Peace

The maintenance of peace and order has always been a central concern of international society. Apart from the *pacifist rejection of all forms of fighting, it was generally recognized that wars could be fought legitimately. Today, many of the assumptions about maintaining peace and about legitimacy have come to be questioned. Nuclear war and deterrence through the threat of it have been seen by many Christians as morally problematic, partly because such war would involve disproportionate destruction (including damage to other countries, future generations, and nature). Perhaps more significantly, greater emphasis is now put on seeking the conditions of peace and thus avoiding the need for just wars. Attempts to restrict or regulate the arms trade exemplify one kind of committed social action, support for the United Nations (perhaps requiring reform) exemplifies another. This change of approach shows itself in the greater emphasis placed upon accommodation and mutual respect between cultures: the concerted attempt to forge a consensual global ethic and thus 'peace amongst the *religions' through the World Parliament of Religions (1993) is significant.

World poverty

This brings home the relevance of a global ethic. Modern technology has made the extent of world poverty more immediately apparent, and makes practical responses easier. All we need is the will. While some Christians might not accept a significant duty of aid, most recognize that we have duties of charity, if not of justice, to respond to global poverty. The fact that poverty exists in another country is no reason for ignoring it. Even if some Christians, for example some right-wing groups in the USA, do deny any duty to give aid, it is not usually because they reject the idea of a global ethic, but because they accept a libertarian framework that emphasizes economic liberty and apply this to social policy at home as much as in the world outside.

Although most Christians would accept a duty to aid those suffering from poverty or other causes, such as human rights abuses, in other parts of the world, there will be disagreements about the extent of this duty, and how it is understood and justified. Many would accept a standard secular ethical justification in terms of Kant's theory, or utilitarianism, or human rights, with religious faith providing the inspiration and motivation for action. Others will turn to more specific versions of Christian theology or appeals to biblical authority. Thus, the basis may be Christian charity (as a duty not an optional extra), or an evangelical appeal to biblical texts (as with Sider's *Rich Christians in an Age of Hunger*), or a conception of a just society as one in which the basic needs of all are properly met (as in the papal encyclical *Populorum Progressio*); or demands for radical redistribution and the 'option for the poor' in *liberation theology.

The exercise of global responsibility can take many forms, including supporting charities such as Oxfam, Christian Aid, and CAFOD. Political action may also be taken; though we cannot directly be citizens of a global democracy, we can influence the political processes in our own countries so that governments pursue more cosmopolitan policies. Thus a key issue is the size of the foreign aid budget, and many Christians are involved in trying to increase aid to 0.7 per cent of GNP, to which governments of rich countries committed themselves at the beginning of the 1970s. The further issue of improving the quality of aid arises in several forms; at its most basic level, it involves not linking aid to military contracts, using it to prop up oppressive governments, or supporting the kind of economic growth that does not alleviate poverty. Many Christians raise further, more subtle, questions about the nature of the development which is being aided. Standard conceptions that equate development with economic growth are questioned, partly because they place insufficient emphasis upon distributive or social justice, partly because they underestimate environmental problems, and partly because, with an emphasis upon free markets and material consumption, the spiritual and moral dimensions to human well-being are ignored. Quite apart from such perspectives, the issue of aid cannot be treated in isolation. The whole structure of economic relations between the north and the south needs to be critically assessed and challenged in the light of basic Christian principles of fairness and social justice, as in Duchrow's critique of what is now called the 'global economy', the increasingly integrated global market, dominated by transnational companies and informed by the values of the free market.

Environment

*Ecology is perhaps the most obvious area for global ethics, since many of the major environmental problems of the second half of the 20th century have been global in scope—resource shortages, pollution in land, sea, and atmosphere, and population pressures on areas with limited carrying capacity.

Christian thinkers have responded in a number of different ways. Some environmentalists have tried to blame the problems on Christianity itself, instancing the importance in *Genesis of humans having *dominion* over nature, and more generally the idea that humans, as separate from the rest of *creation because they alone have rational *souls or are made 'in the image of God', can exploit nature for their own ends. Genesis has, however, been defended as being about responsible *stewardship* over the rest of nature; since nature is created by God, it has a value over and above its usefulness to humans.

For global ethics the more important challenge relates to what may broadly be seen as the finiteness of the planet—its non-renewable resources, its limited capacity to absorb the effect of human activity without deleterious change, and the finite areas of land and water capable of producing in a sustainable way resources such as food. Whether we are concerned because of the effect of our activities on other living things or merely on human beings (present or future), the need for significant changes in our lifestyles is recognized by many, along with the need to change our technologies (to expedite the 'greening of industry'), and to find ways to pursue sustainable development. Specific policies will be based partly on factual estimates that could be wrong. But in so far as Christians accept the environmental predicament, they will accept that the reasons for altering the way we live have to do with the welfare of all human beings, both present and future, and with our duty as stewards to care for nature. Many have sought earnestly to combine concern for human well-being and justice with proper care for the environment, as witnessed in the World Council of Churches' 1970s call for the 'just and sustainable society' and the recent initiative 'Justice, Peace, and the Integrity of Creation'. Many Christians have been active in movements of ethical consumerism and ethical investment, which encourage people to be concerned about the history of the goods they buy (who made them and under what conditions), and to ensure that moneys invested are in banks or companies that either do positive good or at least do not themselves engage in unacceptable practices, either at home or abroad (see BUSINESS ETHICS).

Population

The interface between development and environment is nowhere better illustrated than here. Whether and how to limit populations are amongst the most contentious issues facing Christians. At one level, the question of acceptable numbers turns on what is ecologically the carrying capacity of an environment. At another level the issue is over what numbers can be sustained, given the expectations of the population in terms of material comfort and well-being. Optimists argue that the planet is nowhere near its carrying capacity, and that with appropriate social and economic policies, rising populations will stabilize by the middle of the 21st century at a satisfactory sustainable level. Pessimists see this as out of touch with reality. Poverty in the south already exists on a vast scale, causing land degradation. Northern affluence, producing unacceptable levels of pollution, is already unsustainable. Thus radical action is needed, including deliberate reduction of family size, supported by public policies. Most, however, would accept that attempts to limit family sizes *on their own* are unlikely to be successful. Only if appropriate supplementary public policies are in place, such as health care and pensions for old age, will people be motivated to have smaller families.

While some Christians may be unperturbed by population trends and pressures, and take the view that we should still accept the injunction 'go forth and multiply' (and perhaps leave what happens in the future to God's *providence), most accept that, given the world as it is today, there is some obligation to limit family size or to find ways of encouraging people to have fewer children. What deeply divides them is the means to do so. *Abortion is seen by very many as wrong (either simply wrong, or wrong in all cases where there are no special reasons, such as a threat to the mother's life). *Contraception and sterilization are more widely acceptable but are still rejected by significant voices, especially the Catholic Church, as unnatural. Again there may be a division of opinion over the extent to which governments should try to control family size, either by regulation or by incentives and disincentives, since the freedom of the individual is a central value for most Christians. Few will countenance policies such as those pursued by, for instance, the Chinese government.

Agreement on these issues does not determine the acceptance of a global ethic. Two Christians may be equally committed to a global ethic, but disagree about some of the values which they accept as part of it. To a Christian who sees contraception as acceptable and an obvious way of limiting family size, the position of another unwilling to use or advocate contraception may seem lacking in serious commitment, but that would be to misread the position.

Conclusion

What the population issue brings out very strongly is that while most Christians would accept that they had a global ethic (though they might not use the term), and that this involves accepting obligations towards others throughout the world, the detailed content of that ethic varies considerably. Almost all will accept the need to tackle extreme poverty, oppose the violation of basic rights, work for peace and *reconciliation, and protect our common environment. But there are also differences, partly over the means for pursuing these agreed goals, partly over other values also seen as important. These other values include the theological implications of one's own form of Christian belief. Both the pacifist and the just war theorist work for peace, but have different views on how to go about it. Both believers in contraception and their opponents may see the need to limit populations by voluntary means. How far can Christians work with those with whom they partly disagree, including people from other religious traditions? Questions like this are important in practice but they are asked within the framework of global ethics, the need for which few Christians would in principle question.   **Nigel Dower**

Attfield, R., *The Ethics of Environmental Concern* (1983).
Barbour, I. G., *Technology, Environment and Human Values* (1980).
Beitz, C. R., *Political Theory and International Relations* (1979).

Brown, C., *International Relations Theory: New Normative Approaches* (1992).

Dower, N., *World Ethics—The New Agenda* (1998).

Duchrow, U., *Europe in the World System 1492–1992—Is Justice Possible?* (1996).

Goulet, D., *Development Ethics—Theory and Practice* (1995).

Hall, D. J., and Radford Ruether, R., *God and the Nations* (1995).

Küng, H., *Global Responsibility* (1990).

Küng, H., and Kuschel, K.-J. (eds.), *A Global Ethics: The Declaration of the Parliament of the World Religions* (1993).

Macquarrie, J., *The Concept of Peace* (1973).

Nardin, T., and Mapel, D. (eds.), *Traditions in International Ethics* (1992).

Nelson, J. A., *Hunger for Justice: The Politics of Food and Faith* (1981).

Shue, H., *Basic Rights: Subsistence, Affluence and US Foreign Policy* (1996).

Sider, R., *Rich Christians in an Age of Hunger* (1978).

Gnosticism

Gnosticism is the modern designation of an apparently widespread religious phenomenon of late antiquity which in some ways is similar to the *New Age movements of today, not least in difficulty of definition. Debate about its nature and origins still continues to rage. The terms *gnostic* and '*gnosis*' (cf. 1 Tim. 6: 20), in ancient sectarian texts and the writings of their Christian opponents, heresiologists such as *Irenaeus of Lyons, refer to a certain kind of *knowledge*. This involves understanding one's original divine nature and its fall and entrapment in this inferior realm of matter. The material *creation is seen as the work of an ignorant lower deity, the demiurge, and his minions, the *archons*. 'Knowledge' gives the key to escape back from matter to the unknown, true God through an awakening saving call or the revelations of a redeemer. This redeemer is sometimes identified with Christ but the phenomenon would seem to most scholars to predate Christianity in pagan and Jewish circles, later influencing nascent Christianity, especially *Paul and *John. Thus a distinction is usually made between Gnosis (or pre- or proto-Gnosis, consisting of elements of the later developed phenomenon) and the Christian Gnosticism of the early second century onwards with its developed *mythological systems and profound challenge to Catholic Christianity. The latter is the target of Christian *heresy-hunters.

Although some would see this earlier Gnostic phenomenon as an independent religion (as evidenced, for instance, by Manichaeism), most would consider it as an essentially parasitic and syncretistic movement which claims the ultimate answers to fundamental questions, particularly those involving cosmology (the One and the Many) and theodicy (the nature of and justification for *evil). Whereas earlier scholars emphasized oriental influences, recent scholarship has highlighted the fundamental Jewish elements in Gnosis/Gnosticism. However, the lack of incontrovertible evidence of pre-Christian Gnostic texts and systems, the testimony, however biased, of the earliest and apparently most trustworthy heresiologists such as Irenaeus, and the obvious reliance of Gnostic sects such as the Valentinians on Christian scriptures and concepts, have led some to argue that Gnosticism only arose after the spread of Christianity. The classic Gnostic myth, detectable in Irenaeus' accounts of the 'Barbelognostics' and 'Ophites' (*Against Heresies*, 1. 29–30) and, according to him, the basis of the Valentinian system, does seem to be rooted in mainstream Christian beliefs and sacramental practices.

Irenaeus himself traces 'the falsely so-called *gnosis*' back to Simon Magus (cf. Acts 8), including in his genealogy (*Against Heresies*, 1.

23–31) such disparate figures as Basilides, the Ebionites, and Marcion. The term may be better limited to those groups who used it of themselves and present or presuppose a developed myth and rite of salvation. These include Irenaeus' Barbelognostics, the Naassenes of the *Refutation of all Heresies* of Hippolytus of Rome (160?–235), and the Valentinians. Here we find, first, not Marcionite rejection but sophisticated exegesis of the OT. The subordinate creator and his prophets are the unwitting vehicles of *revelation. New Testament authors, particularly John and Paul, are also appropriated as scriptural support. An appeal is made to a Gnostic succession of teachers and secret oral tradition deriving from Jesus and his true Gnostic apostles. One example is the Valentinian Ptolemy who was active in Rome in the mid-2nd century and Irenaeus' main target. In his *Letter to Flora* on the three sources of the OT law, he appeals to his sect's tradition as received from the apostles. This, he claims, is provable by comparison with the teaching of Christ himself (Epiphanius, *Panarion*, 33. 3. 1–7. 10).

Second, we find a sophisticated treatment of the doctrines of creation, *Fall, and *redemption showing evident signs of *Platonic influence. Thus the Gnostic myth of the origin and fall of heavenly Sophia (*Wisdom) is developed to explain the existence of this evil world and the presence of the elect in it, using a reinterpreted Genesis 1–9 to illuminate the paradox of the Gnostic predicament. Humans are made by the demiurge in the outward image of a divine being. They are trapped in an earthly body, subject to sex, law, and fate, but this world is necessary as 'a vale of soul-making' for the divine element. The creator is not evil, but by his arrogance and ignorance he is responsible for evil. Human salvation is apparently 'by nature' according to some texts, yet it has to be worked out by *ascetic effort; it remains a matter of grace and can be lost or rejected. Thus the basic stance is ascetic reflecting the need to exist in this world without being affected by it, until death. The attainment of true 'gnosis' allows the ascent of the *soul through successive stages, each requiring its password, to union with the unknown supreme God, made possible by the knowledge revealed by his Son. Christ is central to this Gnostic myth as the archetype of our experience of initiatory rebirth and ascent. Gnostic *eschatology is futurist. The ultimate goal is the unscrambling of the mixture of divine and material creation and the restoration (*apokatastasis*) of everything to its original state. Later critics such as Clement of *Alexandria (150?–215?) reappropriated Gnostic elements and the title 'Gnostic' for Catholic Christianity.

Until 1945 the principal sources for our knowledge of the Gnostics were Irenaeus and the heresiologists largely dependent on him (Tertullian of Carthage (160–225?), Hippolytus, and Epiphanius of Salamis (315–403)), with a few fragments of original texts (e.g. the excerpts of the Valentinian Theodotus preserved by Clement of Alexandria). But the discovery of a collection of Coptic texts, including the famous Gospel of *Thomas, the *Apocryphon of John*, presenting three versions of Irenaeus' Barbelognostic myth, and Sethian and Valentinian 'gospels' and treatises, near Nag Hammadi in Upper Egypt in December 1945 has transformed the situation. Now we have a variegated collection of original writings, 'gospels', apocalypses, letters, treatises—even pagan texts (Platonic and Hermetic), dating to the mid-4th century but with some items much earlier. Whether the collection represents a library of Gnostic sectarians or Pachomian monks is debated. When used as a control for the accuracy of the heresiologists' accounts, it tends to confirm the accuracy of Irenaeus' depiction of the Barbelognostics and Valentinians, but is difficult to square with the classifications of later heresiology.

Thus the latter has been impugned as false and even the existence of actual Gnostic sects denied. The very term 'Gnosticism' and the definitions offered in its support have been rejected as inadequate to describe the variety and plurality of the phenomenon, an alternative classification of 'biblical-demiurgical' movements being suggested. This would include possible pre-Christian movements within Judaism and new movements within Christianity, most of which died out. But there is sufficient evidence of the existence of Gnostic and related later sects and systems to allow the continued use of the term to describe a blend of distinctive universal myths of salvation constructed from biblical, Jewish, Christian, and Platonic elements to answer fundamental questions about the self as divine and about the problem of evil. Movements that distinguish the supreme God from a creator demiurge and reflect a basic spirit—matter *dualism, together with pessimism about the cosmos and contemporary history, arise at various points. Among these one can include Manichaeism, the medieval Bogomils and Albigensians, and the Mandeans of southern Iraq, the only surviving example of an ancient Gnostic religious movement. What gives rise to such movements is not so much direct influence from earlier Gnostic traditions, but rather a combination of similar religious, political, and social factors. Modern New Age movements are not direct descendants of the Gnostics but are akin to them in their understanding of the self and its divine potential.

Arising within Judaism and Christianity, Gnosticism had its greatest and most obvious effect upon the latter. Gnostics have been claimed by some scholars to be the true heirs of Jesus, persecuted by ecclesiastical orthodoxy, and Gnostics undoubtedly understood themselves as the only authentic interpreters of Christianity. Furthermore, Gnosticism's profound challenge to Catholic Christianity in terms of *authority and its interpretation (scripture and tradition; charism and *apostolic succession), theology (creation, Fall, and redemption/apokatastasis), ministry, and ethics, provided the main stimulus for the formation of Catholic orthodoxy from Irenaeus and Tertullian onwards. The need to resist Gnostic tendencies gave rise to the canon of scripture, the *creeds, and the theology of recapitulation. Particularly in its dualist, Manichaean forms, Gnosticism continues to haunt Christian theology still.

See also BIBLE, ITS AUTHORITY AND INTERPRETATION.

Alastair H. B. Logan

Filoramo, G., *A History of Gnosticism* (1990).
Jonas, H., *The Gnostic Religion*, 2nd edn. (1992).
Logan, A. H. B., *Gnostic Truth and Christian Heresy* (1996).
Pagels, E., *The Gnostic Gospels* (1980).
Perkins, P., *Gnosticism and the New Testament* (1993).
Pétrement, S., *A Separate God: The Christian Origins of Gnosticism* (1991).
Robinson, J. M. (ed.), *The Nag Hammadi Library in English*, rev. edn. (1988).
Rudolph, K., *Gnosis: The Nature and History of Gnosticism* (1983).
Williams, M. A., *Rethinking 'Gnosticism'* (1996).

God.

*Jesus and all his *disciples and first interpreters were Jews. However much he and they came to take issue with some aspects of contemporary *Judaism or to supersede it by virtue of a new and final *covenant, they wholly accepted the Jewish understanding of God as revealed in the Hebrew scriptures: God the creator in *Genesis, the chooser of *Abraham, the liberator of *Israel from Egypt, the God whose *justice and *love were proclaimed by the *prophets, the God who was prayed to in the *psalms, the *Temple, and synagogues. A Christian doctrine of God can only begin with this profound continuity. Aspects of the God of the OT, such as the *anger and the punishments, the command to wipe out the inhabitants of Palestine and the apparent baffling narrowness of the God of all creation being so preoccupied with little Israel, made Marcion in particular contrast the NT God of love with the OT God of law (see LAW, BIBLICAL), but this was a position wholly unacceptable to the early *church as a whole (see PRE-CONSTANTINIAN THOUGHT). The God in whom Christians believed was not conceived in any way other than that of the Hebrew scriptures, a God who intervened in *history, a person who could be addressed as 'thou'.

Nothing is more integral to early Christian *orthodoxy. What most absolutely holds the two covenants together is precisely God. Moreover some of the finest passages of *New Testament *theology are little more than quotes from the *Old Testament. Take, for example, *Paul's marvellous conclusion to the central argument of *Romans: 'O the depths of the riches and wisdom and knowledge of God! How unsearchable are his judgements and how inscrutable his ways! For who has known the mind of the Lord or who has been his counsellor? Or who has given a gift to him that he might be repaid?' (11: 33–5). The first half of this is Paul's own composition, but the second part consists of quotations from *Isaiah and *Job. Genesis and Isaiah, the Psalms, Job, and much else in the OT would always remain fruitful sources for the Christian doctrine of God. Yet, just as the OT conception of God had gone on evolving with every new experience of Israel and everyone who wrote about him, so did the Christian conception of God incorporate a series of further developments within a continuous tradition of belief. The OT was read throughout by Christians with Christ as the interpretative key to its meaning; so too was God reinterpreted in the light of Christ, the Son of God. There were three main phases of this reinterpretation. The first was that of Jesus' own life; the second the apostolic and early sub-apostolic age in which the NT was written; the third, the period of definitive doctrinal formulation centred around the Council of *Nicaea.

'No one knows the Father except the Son and anyone to whom the Son chooses to reveal him' (Matt. 11: 27). Such an assertion is revolutionary in its implications for the knowledge of God and all the more significant coming in a synoptic *gospel rather than in *John. Jesus is here claiming to be so much the interpreter of his Father that without him we cannot really know God. In what ways could this be justified? The first was precisely in the sense of personal sonship. The idea that God could be seen as the father of Israel was not new; nevertheless no one had stressed the specific divine character of *fatherhood so repeatedly, so intensely, or so personally. No one, it seems, had addressed God directly as 'My Father', while Jesus did so almost invariably, as all the gospels affirm, using the Aramaic abba (Mark 14: 36) in so personal a way that it is almost the only Aramaic word to be retained in the recording of what he said. While not being a childish form of address, it was deeply familiar, reflecting the closeness and warmth of relationship illustrated throughout the gospels. When Jesus extends this personal sense of sonship to his disciples by instructing them too to address God as Father (Matt. 6: 7–9), he is laying down something fundamental for the Christian sense of God ever after, the consciousness of a personal relationship true for every believer. The sense of continuity in this was such that Christians continued to address God as *Abba* in Rome and elsewhere, though they spoke Greek (Rom. 8: 15; Gal. 4: 6). The God of Abraham, Isaac, and Jacob (Mark 12: 26; Acts 3: 13) has become, primarily, the Father of Jesus and, in consequence, of every disciple of Jesus. Fatherhood has become his most striking characteristic: an identity that involves loving care, understanding, willingness to forgive, even the type of equality that must exist between parent and child.

What fatherhood meant for Jesus is well illustrated by that *parable which is most pre-eminently about God, the parable of the prodigal son (Luke 15: 11–52). Its point is often mistaken, like its name, because it is not really about the son but about the father, the man who, while his repentant son was yet at a distance, 'saw him and ran and embraced him and kissed him', who hardly even listened to his son's confession of guilt, so intent was he on celebrating the prodigal's return and demonstrating *forgiveness: 'Let us eat and make merry, for this my son was dead, and is alive again, he was lost and is found.'

Jesus not only creates a new sense of God as Father, he provides a new model of God in action, revealing in himself what that means. 'He who has seen me has seen the Father: how can you say "Show us the Father"?' (John 14: 9). This gentle rebuke to Philip indicates another essential way in which Jesus alters the understanding of God. Awkward as it is *philosophically to think of God in terms of the reported behaviour of a human being, that is what his teaching drives one to do: radical *truthfulness, openness to every sort of person, an experience of *freedom, a love that sacrifices self for others, the forgiveness even of one's murderers, these are the human indicators of what God is. They 'show us the Father'. They can, moreover, all be joined in the one word 'love'. 'God is love' (1 John 4: 8 and 16). While this simple affirmation comes late in the NT, it may be thought the most succinct summary of its theology.

Early Christians, however, had a further, different, problem to face. If Jesus expressed the nature of God so authoritatively and perfectly, could he really just be a man? Did his own words, if deeply pondered, not signify a far closer relationship with God? If he was God's very *Word for the *world, did that not imply that he was divine as well as human? Very quickly such questions were answered in ways that suggested he must indeed be more than man. But, if so, what? He could not easily or quickly be called 'God' (*theos*), because it was a term which in the NT was generally used with reference to the Father. Moreover, Jewish monotheism, which shaped the mind of the first Christians, could only react in horror to a claim that a man was God. Such a claim had much to overcome. Inevitably, all sorts of formulas were tried to find ways whereby the relationship of Christ to God could be expressed, ways that did not, and for long could not, simply affirm his divinity and yet tended more and more to imply it (see INCARNATION; CHRISTOLOGY).

It is relatively easy to see how the memory of Jesus and what he said of himself, coupled with the experience of the *Resurrection

appearances, could lead in the direction of some sort of 'binity'. What appears more surprising is the quick emergence instead of belief in a *Trinity: not only Father and Son but *Holy Spirit. Reference to the Spirit of God is frequent in the NT, but it is not strikingly out of line with that in the OT, signifying the presence, power, inspiration of God, but not implying anything like a distinct divine 'person'. Nevertheless, certain rather special passages, such as the promise of Jesus in the fourth gospel that 'the Counsellor, the Holy Spirit, whom the Father will send in my name, he will teach you all things' (John 14: 25), do suggest that the Spirit is on a par with the Father and the Son. Even more decisive are the final lines of *Matthew's gospel (28: 19–20) in which the risen Christ instructs the disciples to baptize 'in the name of the Father and of the Son and of the Holy Spirit'. This text provides the clearest NT witness to the Trinity and its importance is immense. It indicates that when the gospel was written, probably not later than the 80s, the Trinitarian formula for *baptism was already firmly established in the churches for which Matthew was written. Once this gospel was generally accepted in the course of the 2nd century, these final words of Jesus, closing the opening book of the canon, made a doctrine of the Trinity virtually inevitable.

The word 'Trinity' itself was first used in the late 2nd century. While there was much discussion about terms and relationships before the Councils of Nicaea and *Constantinople affirmed the basic Trinitarian *dogma, it would be mistaken to regard it as essentially an open question until the 4th century. There was, given the NT material, no convincing alternative. That, however, leaves open numerous questions as to how Father, Son, and Spirit are to be understood in human concepts. The distinction between the three is certainly revealed in terms of their relationships to the world and, especially, the work of Son and Spirit in *salvation. Could these three names then be regarded as defining modes of divine action towards creation (an 'economic Trinity') rather than as expressing the ontological and eternal (immanent) nature of God himself? As both Son and Spirit are described as 'sent' by the Father, are they subordinate to the Father? Such questions naturally arose and were not resolved before the 4th century and perhaps not then. Thus while *Latin thought customarily began with the unity of the divine nature and, that presupposed, moved on to consider the relation of the three persons, *Greek thought began rather with the persons, that is to say with the Father, and moved thence to consider the unity of nature. Christian thought about God continues to veer back and forth between an emphasis on monotheism, modified by some sort of Trinitarian 'modalism', and a Trinitarianism which at times, at least in popular devotion, may sound like tritheism. Much of the most thoughtful theological writing in the 1970s, such as Maurice Wiles's *The Remaking of Christian Doctrine* (1974) and Geoffrey Lampe's *God as Spirit* (1977), look modalist and hardly Trinitarian at all, while in the following decades the theological pendulum swung back to a far more decisive Trinitarian affirmation.

The main case against Trinitarianism would seem to derive from a feeling that the first Christians ontologized *metaphors unduly. *Symbols of divine action became substantial in their own right. While this may be hard to deny in terms of a movement of thought and *language, the underlying question remains open as to whether it was a justified movement; whether, for instance, the writer of the fourth gospel correctly divined the true meaning of Jesus and his message or whether he corrupted it, finding a depth of significance that was not really there. If Trinitarian doctrine is rejected, it is hard to avoid the conclusion that both the NT itself and the subsequent development of Christian thought in its central stream have been dangerously misleading.

It is part of the deep attraction of the idea of the Trinity that affirming God as a communion of persons makes it easier to think of him in terms of realized knowledge and love (on Augustine's 'psychological' model); easier to see human fellowship in general and the communion of the church in particular as a reflection of, and participation in, God's being; easier to avoid a philosophical coldness and detachment, a sense of impersonality which, once monotheism has passed beyond ideas of an 'angry' God intervening anthropomorphically in human history, leads it into *deism. It is hard to see how a *unitarian God could be thought to be 'Love', unless the nature of God is held to require a world to love, in which case God becomes naturally dependent upon the world. Furthermore, Trinitarian belief responds in its way to the plea of polytheism that plurality as well as unity needs somehow to be affirmed within divinity. It thus suggests that polytheism, so prevalent in human culture, is not simply to be condemned as false.

It would be mistaken to see Christian thought about God as static, fixed once for all in the 4th century, apart from the periodic upsurge of *heresy, usually of a unitarian kind. It is wiser to see it as a continuous dialogue about mysteries which, because of their ultimacy, no one can understand, no formula encapsulate, but in which a diversity of evidences, experiences, and authorities have all to be included, and in which different writers approaching the doctrine of God from a variety of backgrounds—scriptural, philosophical, historical, or mystical—will offer different, even seemingly incompatible, emphases.

One approach has been to stress themes of justice, anger, and *judgement. Just as the *atonement has been explained in terms of divine justice requiring the God-man's sacrifice as expiation for human sin, so, despite the atonement, God has been perceived by numerous theologians as condemning the great majority of his children to an eternity of punishment. He has been seen too as patron of authoritativeness in both church and state, satisfied with the infliction on deviants of the most appalling punishments, and the blesser of numerous conflicting *nationalisms, to be thanked with a Te Deum for every petty military victory. In all this as much else man has enthusiastically constructed God in his own image yet, however widespread such beliefs have been, they remain deviant to an authentic Christian sense of what God signifies.

Philosophy and *mysticism have for centuries had the major impact. Christian thought about God between the 12th and the 20th centuries may well be seen as a wrestling match between biblical personalism and the impersonal insistences of philosophic argument, a match in which mysticism played a role on either side, upon the one hand providing the fruits of an intensely personal experience of union with God, on the other sharing with much philosophy a commitment to the via negativa, denying the possibility of positive verbal affirmation about God's being.

While Greek philosophy was much in use in the theological debates of the 4th century, it was essentially involved as a linguistic handmaiden of scriptural exegesis. By and large this remained the

case until the 12th century. *Anselm may be the last great mind for whom in the formulation of a theological system there was such an absolute unselfconscious assurance of the revealed God that *reason's role was simply to provide tools for the exposition of *revelation in a context of prayer. The Renaissance of the 12th century, the recovery of *Aristotle, and the development in the new *universities of a far more secular study of both philosophy and theology changed all that for ever. Philosophy recovered a truly independent role so that it became necessary to ask: do we know God by reason or by revelation? Can philosophy show that God is and, if it can, does that prevent God from being an object of *faith? If it cannot, are we in a world in which the knowledge of God has been edged into or beyond the margin of knowledge as such? There is, for Christian thought about God, a huge, if for many an invisible, gulf separating all that came later from the unquestioning confidence in God, the God of the NT, which had prevailed up to then. Yet in the post-12th-century world, it remained of great importance that the NT itself witnessed to the possibility, even the universality, of a natural knowledge of God, if of an almost buried sort. Recognition of this by Paul in Romans 1–2 as in the Areopagus speech (Acts 17: 22–30) has been used to ground rational knowledge of God, even if Paul's point was that it proved a fruitless knowledge: 'Although they knew God they did not honour him' (Rom. 1: 21). While the God who is the Father of Jesus Christ has very different characteristics from a God of philosophy or natural religion, still, Paul is saying, it is the same God and he is in some way knowable and known apart from revelation.

Is it the same God? And was Paul talking about a rationally grounded knowledge and not just a superstitious one? *Aquinas, basing himself on Paul, answered a firm yes to both questions. He rode the knife-edge of the gulf between ancient and modern brilliantly but, inevitably, dangerously. The one small article in the Summa Theologiae which asks 'Is there a God?' (I q. 2 a. 3) and answers yes by means of the 'five ways', each of which argues from effect to first cause, may well be the most succinct philosophical statement ever made in comparison with the amount written about it, in commentary, vindication, or refutal. The danger appears to be that it establishes a narrow gate of rationality through which alone one can enter into the sure knowledge of God, even into faith. If the cogency of its arguments is denied, is one then necessarily left outside? Aquinas surely did not think so, but that could well be drawn as a conclusion, and often has been. Is belief sane, if the best arguments that can be mounted for God's existence are not fully cogent? *Barth would reply that the question is pointless: the use of natural theology is a total mistake for the grounding of a Christian knowledge of God; but few would fully agree with him. Others, such as *Rahner, would respond that such arguments, convincing or unconvincing, do not in any case arrive at the God who was revealed as the Father of Jesus Christ. So, whether or not we can establish rationally the existence of a God of philosophy, the Christian God is still a matter of faith.

It is Aquinas's firm progression from the five ways to the nature of God in its unity and then on to the Trinity which, while faithful to the traditional western approach to the knowledge of God, has provided a baseline for *Catholic systematic theology ever since. The theology of the Trinity is encapsulated within a doctrine whose shape is determined philosophically.

Two aspects of Aquinas's doctrine seem particularly significant. The first is the principle he lays down between q. 2 on God's existence and q. 3 on God's simplicity that we cannot know what he is but only what he is not, the *via negativa*. Aquinas owed this especially to Pseudo-*Dionysius upon whose work he wrote an extensive commentary, as did many western medieval theologians. When this is followed by detailed discussion of God's goodness, limitlessness, unchangeableness, or *omnipotence, one might conclude that it is more a matter of theory than of practice, as is often claimed. It can, then, be valuable to consider what this principle signifies. Much that we say of God sounds positive enough, but is, on close examination, simply a denying of creaturely qualities which clearly cannot be predicated of God. The question is what, if anything, is left. It is easy enough to see how the principle applies to materiality or complexity. To declare that God is spiritual or simple cannot purport to provide actual knowledge of how he is, but is only a denial of what he is not, because we know nothing of spiritual or simple beings from experience. Anything imagined about a spirit is pure surmise. It is more difficult to claim full application of the *via negativa*, however, when it comes to such things as life, *personhood, knowledge, or love. When we say that God is love we mean far more than to deny that he hates people. We move here from the method of negation to that of *analogy. God is everything that we mean by personhood or love, but in a way so much beyond what we can conceive that the application to him of such terms, used primarily for creatures, is analogical, not univocal. But it is not merely negative.

The second aspect is the assertion that God is pure existence, the heart of Aquinas's philosophy of God. Everything that we know has a nature other than its existence. That is something integral to creatureliness. We can conceive of anything else as not existing. God alone cannot *not* exist. Every nature that we can imagine is a way in which something does or might exist, and each such way is limiting: x is such and such—and no more. But God exists in no identifiable way because subject to no limitation. He simply exists; everything else that exists does so because he gives it existence. For Aquinas this is the most profound thing one can say of God. Every type of conceptual quality one attributes to him must always suggest a definable God, contained by his 'essence' or identity. Sheer existence avoids that trap and also carries one back to the bible's best definition when God spoke to *Moses from the burning bush: 'I am who I am' (Exod. 3: 4). 'Say this to the people of Israel, "I Am has sent me to you."'

Attempts to define what divine *omniscience or omnipotence signifies tend to pass from the *via negativa* to a rather firm use of analogy, but must inevitably fail because they essentialize God, making him intelligible according to a model that limits his being to our perception. The teaching of the mystics is important at this point to restrain the overconfidence of philosophers: nevertheless Aquinas's doctrine of God as pure existence suggests that philosophy too, in line with the bible, can at its peak pass beyond every essentialist discussion to assert not that God is such and such, but simply that God is God.

If, however, there is through revelation a second basic principle for Christian theology, it is that God is love. An emphasis upon this is what the NT adds most decisively to the OT. It is interesting that Barth, in his massive account of the Doctrine of God in the two-part second volume of the *Church Dogmatics*, begins it with two great affirmations. The first affirmation about the reality of God is 'God is', the second that he is 'the one who loves', he 'wills as God to be for us and with us who are not God'. But 'love' may here, Barth insists, 'take on a meaning which is fulfilled in a way which breaks up and reforms its meaning' (*CD* II/1. 276), a Barthian way of talking about analogy.

The relationship between a biblical conception of God and a philosophical conception would remain determinative of Christian understanding in two ways. The first concerned the very possibility of the latter. Even in the later Middle Ages, Nominalism, derived from William of Ockham and called at the time the *via moderna*, denied the validity of the 'five ways' and the philosophical knowability of God. Theology, intricately logical as it remained in Ockham's writings, could depend only on faith and revelation. *Luther was much influenced by Nominalism but some *Protestants, notably Bishop Butler in *The Analogy of Religion* (1736), held to the basic position of Thomism in this field. The struggle to retain a convincing philosophical basis for theism took varying forms. Thus both *Descartes and Leibniz attempted to revivify Anselm's *ontological argument. *Kant, while rejecting traditional *metaphysics, proposed instead a moral argument: the inescapability of moral obligation postulates the existence of an ultimate moral reality, God. For many people this has remained convincing. However, there is a growing recognition that no argument exists able to convince with formal certainty on a subject so difficult but also so intertwined for everyone with questionable assumptions of one sort or another, and that this applies to all arguments in this field, atheistic as much as theistic. Yet conviction of some sort is still needed. The shaping of one's life depends upon it. What is appropriate in such circumstances may be not one or another precise piece of logic, but the consideration of probabilities, in a way *Newman attempted in *A Grammar of Assent*, following Butler's premiss that 'probability is the very guide of life'. Nevertheless, from the *Enlightenment onwards, western philosophy became increasingly inimical to granting any validity to rational thinking about God. Despite *Hegel's attempt to reunite philosophy and theology in a radical new synthesis, the divorce became increasingly absolute, particularly in the middle years of the *twentieth century under the impact of logical positivism and linguistic analysis, entailing the rejection of any sort of metaphysics. If by the end of the century metaphysics had recovered a measure of credibility, and forms of *natural theology, often influenced by Aquinas, some of their earlier attraction, yet theistic philosophy of any sort remained on the defensive.

The second way is more intrinsic to Christian understanding of God. It relates to the fact that aspects of philosophical theism appear almost incompatible with biblical theism, even though both have been integrated within classical theology. A daunting example is the immutability of God. Classical philosophical argument may demonstrate easily enough the apparent contradictoriness in admitting any possibility of change in God, but this makes biblical history, which reads as a relationship in *time between humans and God, into a story only about humans. This is particularly problematic in regard to the Incarnation. To claim, as Aquinas does, that as God is immutable this can bring no change whatsoever to God but only to a human nature now united with the Word of God is strange enough; but when it is remembered that in the Incarnation, as classically conceived, the divine person of the Son becomes the person of Christ who is born, dies on the *cross, and rises again, so that there is no other person of whom these things can be predicated, then to say that the person of the Son is absolutely immutable appears quite contradictory.

Is it also philosophically unnecessary? *Process theologians, led by Alfred Whitehead and Charles Hartshorne, have thought so. If by the *via negativa* we can deny change in God, may we not also deny changelessness? Rather than use it to exclude only a certain limited range of more obviously mundane characteristics, negative theology may be applied, as often by mystical writers, to insist that in human terms we really do know nothing of God. Arguments such as 'Things in change are always composite. Now God is not at all composite, but altogether simple. Clearly then he cannot change' (*ST* I q. 9. a. 1) use human reason to analyse the nature of God inappropriately if we cannot know his nature. All we can affirm unreservedly about God is the great *Daβ*: He is. Yet it would be pointless to affirm God's existence but not his role as creator or his quality of goodness. That much must go together. It would, however, be hard to argue, apart from revelation, as to what this goodness really implies. It is not that we cannot or should not think deeply about God. No question is more important; yet the history of *religion, philosophy, and culture shows that innumerable answers can be given for almost every question to do with divinity. This is not because of a failure in the thinkers, though that may be real enough, but because of the profound incomprehensibility of God.

The modern Christian understanding of God has been much affected, not only by such problems and the pressures of western philosophy but by the wider evolution of culture, the advance of *science, the theory of *evolution, the critical analysis of the scriptures (*hermeneutics), the social process of *secularization, and a far greater awareness of the religious experiences of non-Christians. Thus much that could be attributed to divine intervention in a pre-scientific age is now attributed to natural causes.

It would have been impossible for Christian thought about God not to enter a great state of flux in the modern age, short at least of terminal decline. Its resources remain the scriptures, the experience of personal *prayer, *conversion, faith, and the life of the church, as well as an ongoing tradition of rational thought sharing in the wider experience of *humanity. Out of this mix it has brought forth almost every model from the biblical *neo-orthodoxy of Barth to the *existentialist *modernism of *Tillich, from forms of unitarian deism, in reality if not in name, to a determined Trinitarianism as well as an array of *fundamentalist and *charismatic theologies in which the action of the Holy Spirit in *pentecostal possession or immediate divine response to prayer with the most this-worldly aims—financial prosperity, even a place in a car-park—seem to matter most. Christian thought about God is, then, in considerable confusion and the more bizarre forms may appear also the most newsworthy. It has to face, moreover, the avowed *atheism of many leading thinkers in the western world and the *agnosticism of many more. *Nietzsche, one of the strangest and most powerful prophets of modernity, announced the 'Death of God' and in the free-for-all 1960s a number of theologians developed a 'Death of God' theology. Since then the 'Sea of Faith' network, a group of Christians following the lead of the Cambridge theologian Don *Cupitt, whose *Taking Leave of God* appeared in 1980, have attempted to develop a coherent 'non-*realist' view of God as a symbolic spiritual ideal and focus of aspiration. This seems, however, to turn God into an entirely individualist notion in which the deliberate lack of objectivity makes any symbol as valid but as private as any other.

Among the relatively new issues which loom large in thought about God at the beginning of the third millennium, two may be singled out for consideration: the question of gendered language and the relation of the God of Christian belief to the world as a whole and non-Christian religion in particular. This article has consistently used 'he' for God, following almost universal Christian tradition. Yet gender is something meaningful only for physical beings. God cannot be gendered, but God-language has been, with the resulting stimulation of male images for what God is like. Can we, should we, substitute 'she', given that some pronoun is required (however hard some theologians try to manage without one) and 'it' would violate a sense of God as personal? For philosophical theism there can be little problem with this and the same may be true for OT theism. But for Christian theism it is more difficult, given that its conception of God is centred upon the 'Father' of Jesus. While it is perfectly acceptable for Christians to apply to God feminine images characteristic of *motherhood and to use the pronoun 'she' at times, including in prayer, since all our language is metaphorical or analogical, it remains true that privileging the idea of divine fatherhood, and other related gendered language, derives from the main root of specifically Christian theism. Its eradication would threaten linguistic and spiritual continuity with Jesus, unappealing as this conclusion may be to some forms of *feminist theology.

That God is both creator and redeemer provides the heart of Christian theism, yet most theologians have been overwhelmingly preoccupied with the relationship between God and believers, both collectively as church and individually, within the biblical and ecclesial 'history of salvation' or *redemption. His ongoing relationship with the world as a whole in all its physical complexity and forms of life, or, equally, with the vast non-Christian majority of the human race received extraordinarily little attention before the 20th century. It was widely accepted that all non-Christians were necessarily excluded from salvation. But reflection on the way other religions fit into the divine scheme and relate to God's love has recently brought about profound changes in Christian theism. Thus John Hick has claimed a 'Copernican revolution' in presenting a God-centred rather than a Christ-centred scheme for belief, in which Christ becomes but one of a number of comparably significant religious figures such as the Buddha and various Avatars. While this may provide the discipline of religious studies with an uncontroversial base, it involves complete abandonment of the central beliefs of Christianity, and with rather little reason, especially as it is hard to see how it could lead to any even moderately coherent alternative position, other than a devout agnosticism. One basic objection to Hick's innovation is that it is no innovation. Christianity has always been God-centred and Christ can only be central in so far as he is God. On the other hand much Christian theology has gravely failed to be consistent with its deepest principles. If God is love, it should be clear that none of the children he has created are excluded involuntarily from his loving care. Christ as saviour can be the *sacrament of God's salvation for the whole world but hardly the creator of a new 'middle wall' (Eph. 2: 14) dividing the saved from the non-saved, Christian from non-Christian.

Even more central to modern Christian thought about God remains the perennial problem of the relationship of biblical to philosophical theism. John *Robinson in *Honest to God* (1963), following in the steps of Tillich a generation earlier, was attempting to sketch a modern liberal form of philosophical theism. Process theology or such thinkers as *Moltmann in *The Crucified God*, on the other hand, have been struggling with the help of various traditions, *Eastern Orthodox, *kenotic, and *evangelical, to escape conceptions of God locked into a seemingly iron frame of philosophical unchangeability, so as to restore both a sense of the meaningfulness of Trinity and of the involvement of God in a world of *suffering. Can theology combine coherently a biblical sense of the personal involvement of God with humanity with philosophical or rational categories, concepts, and arguments of any sort? Here may lie the most decisive issue facing the future of Christian thought, precisely because it is the most foundational and final. Theology has, first and last, to be thought about *Theos*, God.

Yet it must be living thought, something people actually *live* by, and act out. If one asks in the modern world whether God is or what he is like, many different Christian answers will be given, all of them partially true and all inadequate. But just as Jesus could say to Philip, 'Who has seen me has seen the Father' so this may remain the best mode of verification and still be true of those who, being children of God, truly love God and one another. Perhaps the best answer may then be simply to point to the most God-conscious of modern Christians, to Simone *Weil or Mother *Teresa, Dietrich *Bonhoeffer, *John XXIII, Donald Nicholl, or numerous other believers in every land and race and say of any of them 'who has seen these has seen God'.   **Adrian Hastings**

Barth, Karl, *Church Dogmatics*, II. *The Doctrine of God*, 1 and 2 (1957).
Brown, David, *The Divine Trinity* (1985).
Crowder, Colin (ed.), *God and Reality: Essays on Christian Non-Realism* (1997).
Davies, Brian, *Thinking about God* (1985).
Friedman, R. E., *The Disappearance of God: A Divine Mystery* (1995).
Gilson, Étienne, *God and Philosophy* (1941).
Hartshorne, Charles, *A Natural Theology for our Time* (1967).
Hick, John, *God and the Universe of Faiths* (1973).
Kenny, Anthony, *The Five Ways* (1969).
Küng, Hans, *Does God Exist? An Answer for Today* (1980).
Lampe, Geoffrey, *God as Spirit* (1977).
McCabe, Herbert, *God Matters* (1987).
Mascall, Eric, *He Who Is* (1962).
Moltmann, Jürgen, *God in Creation* (1985).
Rahner, Karl, 'Theos in the New Testament', *Theological Investigations* (1961), i. 79–148
Robinson, John, *Honest to God* (1963).
Swinburne, Richard, *The Existence of God* (1979).
—— *The Christian God* (1994).
Taylor, A. E., 'Theism', *Encyclopaedia of Religion and Ethics*, ed. J. Hastings (1908–26), xiii.
Torrance, T. F., *The Trinitarian Faith: The Evangelical Theology of the Ancient Catholic Church* (1988).
Turner, Denys, *The Darkness of God: Negativity in Christian Mysticism* (1995).
Ward, Keith, *Rational Theology and the Creativity of God* (1983).

gospels.

Within sixty years of the death of *Jesus of Nazareth, at least four separate books about him were in circulation. These 'gospels' are considered here as a whole, and the questions of what they are, why and how they came into existence, how they were used and regarded subsequently, are addressed even though it is impossible to ascertain when, where and by whom the gospels were written.

The four gospels in the NT canon present themselves as the story of Jesus of Nazareth, focusing on his short but striking public career, and describing in detail the events leading to his violent death. All end with the story of his *Resurrection (or at least, in Mark's case, the discovery of his empty tomb). This narrow focus, combined with the apparent pre-literary shaping of units of material to meet the needs of the early Christian community, led earlier scholars to deny that the gospels were 'biography'. This denial, however, is itself refuted by ancient classical biographies, where such a concentration on short periods of the subject's life, including the events surrounding his death, is quite compatible with biographical genre and intent. Likewise, the fact that the gospels are not mere chronicles, but have been (as their material had already been at the pre-literary stage) selected, adapted, and arranged for theological, literary, and/or practical purposes, provides no reason to deny that their authors intended, among other things, to describe an actual person and the events in which he was involved (see QUEST FOR THE HISTORICAL JESUS).

The relation of the 'gospels' to the 'gospel' itself helps to explain what the gospels themselves are. The Greek word translated 'gospel' (*euaggelion*) occurs frequently in *Paul, where it draws together two strands of meaning. Paul's 'good news' (the meaning of the older English 'gospel') was the announcement that the prophetic promises of Israel's God had at last been fulfilled: the redemption of *Israel, and hence of the world, had occurred in Jesus. Second, this 'gospel' was the heraldic proclamation of Jesus as a royal figure. This offered a challenge to other royal announcements, including those of other would-be *kings of the Jews, and those of pagan rulers such as the Roman Caesars. Paul's 'gospel' declared that Israel's hope had been fulfilled in the *Messiah, Jesus, and summoned the pagan world to submit, through him, to the creator God, the God of Israel.

The four canonical 'gospels' do not call themselves by this name. Even *Mark, which opens with the words 'The beginning of the gospel of Jesus Christ', probably means by this not 'this is where the book called "the gospel" begins', but 'this is how Jesus began to announce "the gospel message"'. Later scribes added superscriptions including the word 'gospel' to the canonical gospels, but the word does not occur in this sense in the original texts. It is, in fact, entirely absent from *Luke and *John, and is used sparingly in Mark (seven times), *Matthew (four, three of which are parallel to Marcan passages), and Acts (twice). (Luke does, however, have ten occurrences of the verb *euaggelizomai*, 'to announce the gospel', which also occurs frequently in Acts.) However, the canonical gospels correspond quite closely, but in extended narrative mode, to the Pauline 'gospel'. In their different ways, they narrate the messianic career of Jesus, through which Israel's history has reached its climax, and by which, for that reason, the one true *God has issued his challenge and summons to the whole world.

This explains the complexity of the gospels, and shows that, for their inner theological dynamic to make sense, it mattered that the events they were describing really did take place. The history of Israel, which (they believed) had reached its culmination in the events to do with Jesus, concerned actual places, people, and politics, not abstract ideas or spiritualities. The rulers of the world, who (they believed) were challenged by God's Messiah, Jesus, were real people and power-structures, albeit with spiritual 'counterparts'. The implied readers of the canonical gospels were people whose own stories, personal and communal, had been changed and reshaped by the story of Jesus: they were, the gospels imply, the true Israel, through whom the one God was making himself savingly known, as he had promised, to the whole world. Precisely because the gospels were written in and for such communities, to ground and order their life, to sustain them through suffering and persecution, and to energize them for mission, they were intended, as were the individual stories of which they consisted, to be about the actual person Jesus of Nazareth, not about a shadowy cipher of that name, the mere embodiment of the ideals or faith of later believers. The message of the canonical gospels for their own generation, which so determined their shape and content, had to do precisely with the biography of Jesus of Nazareth.

Several other documents, sometimes called 'gospels', stand out as distinct from the canonical four (and, to some degree, from one another). Some of these are small fragments, possibly from works somewhat like the Synoptics. Other, fuller writings include the Gospel of *Thomas: this, however, with some others, is not a narrative, but a collection of sayings. Nothing in it indicates that Israel's history has reached its climax, or that the creator God is calling the world to account. On the contrary, the Jewish dimension of the Christian message is screened out; and, instead of offering a challenge to the world, readers are encouraged to escape from it. Much of this material, in fact, exhibits a *Gnostic world-view which is not otherwise known to have existed until the 2nd century at least.

Some have proposed, nevertheless, that some or all of these works represent a strand of theology, community, and spirituality that goes back to Jesus, and which was subverted by the canonical gospels' development of a Jewish-style narrative about him. Most scholars, though, regard them as secondary and derivative, with little relation to Jesus himself. For the most part, they are not 'gospels' in the sense explained above, but only in the wider sense of 'collections of material purporting to be about Jesus'. They do not offer good news, but, at best, good advice. It is quite feasible, however, to suppose that some of the sayings of Jesus in them, otherwise unknown, might be authentic.

In addition to actual surviving documents, it is sometimes considered that the hypothetical sources behind the four canonical gospels are themselves to be seen as 'gospels'. This question belongs with the wider one: how did our four canonical gospels come into existence?

It is obvious even to a casual reader that Matthew, Mark, and Luke share a family likeness which John does not. They can be, and often are, displayed in parallel, giving them the name 'synoptic' ('seen-together') gospels. The relationship between them and John is a matter of continuing debate. Some suppose that the author of John knew some or all of the synoptic traditions, but chose to ignore or heavily adapt them; others think that John, even where more or less parallel to the synoptics, had access to independent traditions. Within John itself, some scholars have suggested that we can detect, and isolate, a 'signs source', or even a 'signs gospel', consisting of the accounts of the *miraculous 'signs' of Jesus (starting with John 2: 1–11, the changing of water into wine). On this theory, the author has combined the 'signs' source with discourses and other material to form the book we now have. This theory remains, however, unproved and probably unprovable. As to content, opinions range widely from those who regard most of John as unhistorical (though perhaps still theologically valuable) to those who see it as historically complementary to the synoptics.

The Synoptic Gospels themselves have generated complex theories of literary interrelationships. Almost all scholars agree that Matthew, Mark, and Luke were not simply independent collectors of oral tradition. Luke, after all, mentions using written as well as oral sources (1: 1–4). The close similarities between the Synoptics at several points, particularly in the sayings of Jesus, can be partially explained by strong oral traditions and memories in the early church. But it is extremely likely that they are also related at a literary level.

After two centuries of debate, the most popular theory is that Mark was used by both Matthew and Luke, both of whom also had access to another document, known as 'Q' (for the German Quelle, 'source'), from which they obtained the material in which they overlap with each other but not with Mark. Some now even treat Q as a 'gospel', whose theology and community can be reconstructed through several stages. However, some envisage quite different scenarios: for example that Mark used Matthew, and possibly also Luke; and/or that Luke's Q material is in fact his own adaptation of Matthew, thus rendering the Q hypothesis unnecessary. The complexity of the material, and our scanty knowledge of early Christianity, mean that all such theories fall short of proof, and that simplifications are inevitably misleading.

The canonical gospels are usually dated between 60 and 90. Some have suggested that their writing represents a failure of nerve in the early church: on this theory, the earliest Christians looked forward to Jesus' return, but the second generation looked back to a (possibly imaginary) past, a golden age. It is, however, more historically probable that the committing of lively and plentiful early Christian traditions to writing came about because of the Jewish war (66–70), which fragmented the original storytelling communities. It remains perfectly possible, though, both that some written material was produced considerably earlier than this, and that one or more of the canonical gospels was not completed until towards the end of the century. Despite popular impressions, the gospels' historical value does not depend on their dating, or, indeed, on the authors' locations and identities, which, notwithstanding some claims, remain as uncertain after centuries of research as they were to begin with.

Already by the early 2nd century, Christian writers were referring to the four gospels as authoritative. By around 150 they were read in public worship alongside the Jewish scriptures. By 200, Christian writers were distinguishing them from non-canonical alternatives, and developing theories as to why, in God's providence, there were four gospels rather than some other number. Around the same time, the 'New Testament' was so called for the first recorded time. The narratives of Jesus as Israel's Messiah, and Lord of the world, were thus woven deeply into the pluriform spirituality of

*Christianity from a very early stage. The gospels were on their way to becoming, within developing eucharistic liturgy, a symbol of the presence of Christ.

The subsequent formal canonization of the four gospels, especially after the conversion of *Constantine, has sometimes been taken to imply that they advocated a quiescent, politically subdued, or socially conformist type of religion, which made them a more attractive alternative to other, more radical forms which they supplanted. This is highly misleading. The four gospels were in fact accepted as normative at a time when, in keeping with the story they told, the rulers of the world were deeply hostile to the subversive movement they sustained. Their canonization constituted a striking claim: that, under the guidance of the *Holy Spirit, these books enabled the church truly to tell the story of Jesus and thereby truly to celebrate and implement his *Kingdom in the world.

N. T. Wright

Burridge, Richard A., *What are the Gospels? A Comparison with Graeco-Roman Biography* (1992).

—— *Four Gospels, One Jesus? A Symbolic Reading* (1994).

Farmer, William R., *Jesus and the Gospel: Tradition, Scripture, and Canon* (1982).

Koester, Helmut, *Ancient Christian Gospels: Their History and Development* (1990).

Sanders, E. P., and Davies, Margaret, *Studying the Synoptic Gospels* (1989).

Schnackenburg, Rudolf, *Jesus in the Gospels: A Biblical Christology* (1993), ET (1995).

Stanton, Graham N., *The Gospels and Jesus* (1989).

Talbert, Charles, H., *What is a Gospel? The Genre of the Canonical Gospels* (1977).

Tuckett, Christopher M., *Q and the History of Early Christianity: Studies on Q* (1996).

Wright, N. T., *Christian Origins and the Question of God*, i. *The New Testament and the People of God* (1992).

grace. In the Christian tradition 'grace' sums up the relationship of the triune *God with *creation. It depicts this relationship as grounded in the *freedom of God's *love and as directed towards the perfecting of God's *communion with creation. Since God overcomes the contradiction of his will by *sin and evil, grace includes God's *judgement on sin for the benefit of the sinner. Christian doctrine, worship, and life are shaped in all their dimensions by the way in which grace is understood. Since the concept of grace determines our understanding of divine action and its relationship to human action it is a highly contentious concept. The history of Christian doctrine and pastoral practice could well be written as a history of debates on the interpretation of grace.

Biblical traditions

Debates about the meaning of grace constantly refer to the use of the concept in the bible. In the Hebrew bible the concept is expressed mainly by three groups of words: the noun *hesed* focuses on the faithful maintenance of a covenantal relationship; words derived from *hanan* express the gratuitous gift of affection; those deriving from *raham* denote mercy and compassion, including forgiveness for the violation of a relationship. As applied to God, grace is interpreted as his motive for the election of *Israel and the *covenant with Israel. The fundamental manifestation of grace is the *torah* (see Law, Biblical) given in the covenantal relationship, so grace in all its forms is intrinsically connected to fulfilling or ignoring the law. God re-establishes his broken relationship with Israel by forgiving those who have violated it. In the post-*exilic period the understanding of grace is both universalized to include the whole creation and personalized to relate to particular *persons in their individual circumstances.

In the NT writings the definitive manifestation of grace is the *revelation of God in Jesus Christ through the *Holy Spirit which liberates humanity from bondage to sin and death. This is the common focus of a rich diversity of expressions in which the death of Christ is interpreted, from the perspective of faith in his Resurrection by God, as vicarious penitential suffering (1 Cor. 15: 3; Rom. 3: 24), as *reconciliation (2 Cor. 5: 19), as *redemption from the powers of darkness, and as liberation (2 Cor. 3: 17; Gal. 5: 1) (see Atonement, Theories of). The NT writers appropriate both the universal and personal dimensions. God's grace is interpreted as the actualization of his original intention, formed before creation, to include the whole of creation and its history. In its personal dimension grace is the renewal, transformation, and perfecting of persons included in the actualization of God's universal will. While in the Hebrew bible the *torah* is the means by which God's grace is realized, it is now Jesus Christ, his person, and destiny that is the content and medium of God's grace and the all-encompassing criterion by which the relationship of God to the world in all its aspects is understood.

Early church

The issue of grace was not immediately in the foreground in early doctrinal discussions, though it played an important role in interpreting the divine economy and in the development of the doctrines of the Trinity and the person of Christ (see Pre-Constantinian Thought). *Irenaeus interpreted the whole divine economy as structured by God's gracious will. God creates the world and human beings in order to enable them to participate in eternal divine life. But *Adam and *Eve fail to achieve their destiny because of their immaturity. So God recapitulates their story in Christ, who succeeds where they failed and thus restores humanity's destiny to be eternally in communion with God.

From the 4th century onwards, theological reflection in the east focused on the theme of *deification but in the west concentrated on how God's grace becomes effective for the individual person in overcoming sin. The latter process was triggered by the teaching of *Pelagius and Caelestius that the church's proclamation and sacraments are there to serve as an aid to the correct use of human freedom, impeded by the *Fall, but not lost, and hence capable of being restored by following the example and law of Christ. In response to this view, which threw doubt on the baptism of infants for the remission of sins, *Augustine of Hippo developed a comprehensive theory of grace which provided the matrix for all further debates by focusing on three related issues: the human need for grace, the efficacy of grace, and the ultimate ground of grace.

The *human need* for grace is rooted in hereditary sin. Although humans were created with freedom of choice and were directed towards the good by an additional divine aid so that they had the ability not to sin, Adam, motivated by pride and self-love, turned away from God. Having lost the divine help which gave direction to his will he is henceforth ruled by material desires (concupiscence). He has lost the freedom of choice. This depravity of human nature is passed from generation to generation by sexual reproduction. Descended from Adam, all humanity is burdened with hereditary sin; it is a 'mass of perdition' condemned to eternal death. The *efficacy* of grace is grounded in Christ, who confronts the condemned sinner in the proclamation and sacraments of the church. Grace inspires *faith, which is the re-creation of the love of God. Through faith the sinner receives forgiveness of sins. *Justification by the grace of Christ heals the depravity of human nature. Grace is both *gratia operans*, initially causing the will to choose and intend the good, and *gratia cooperans*, co-operating with the will so that those good intentions can be made effective. God's grace enables the will to intend to do good and to follow this intention; it creates perseverance in pursuing the good, and gives completion to all good actions. In so far as grace does not re-create the freedom of choice but replaces it, it is, in effect, irresistible. Hence, for the *ultimate ground* of grace, Augustine can only point to God's *predestination.

The church only partially accepted Augustine's teaching. The doctrine of hereditary sin as the inability to do good, the necessity of grace for willing the good, the healing effect of God's grace and the lifelong dependence of the justified sinner on grace were received and acknowledged at synods at Carthage (418) and Orange (529). However, the church did not accept Augustine's view of the final loss of freedom of choice, the irresistible character of grace, and the doctrine of predestination.

Middle Ages and Reformation

This partial reception of Augustine's doctrine in the official teaching of the Catholic Church, which could be called Semi-Augustinianism, is the reason why subsequent discussions focused on the relationship between nature and grace or between human and divine freedom. In rejecting the thesis of Peter Lombard (1100–60) that grace is the direct indwelling of the Holy Spirit in the believer, most theological schools worked with a distinction between uncreated grace (God's act) and created grace (the effect of that act in humans). For *Aquinas grace restores the goal-directedness of human reason towards God lost in the Fall. This is achieved through the infusion of grace, which constitutes the supernatural habit of the soul (clothing the soul like a garment), by which sins are forgiven and the will is reoriented towards God in *faith, *hope, and love. Thus established, grace co-operates with those human acts of which it is the ultimate cause and which are deemed to be meritorious. The relationship between divine and human freedom is based on the axiom that grace does not destroy nature, but supports and perfects it.

In the younger *Franciscan school (Duns Scotus and William of Ockham) the freedom of the will is seen as an essential characteristic of human nature which was not lost in the Fall. On this view, human beings are guilty because they have abused the capacities of their nature (hereditary guilt). They could remove the stain of guilt by using their will appropriately. Scotus and Ockham avoid an outright relapse into Pelagianism by stressing the order of grace that has been ordained and revealed by God and is taught in the church. God wants the suffering of Christ to bring forgiveness of sin and removal of guilt for all people. Therefore he will acknowledge as meritorious only such acts as are rooted in habitual participation in the grace of Christ as mediated in the *sacraments. However, the sacraments can only be effective if those receiving them are disposed to acknowledge their efficacy. Such a disposition is effected either by the sacraments themselves, or by acts which are meritorious in the sense that God will not withhold his reward for them, treating them as a preparation for grace. God then confers the habit of grace, enabling justified believers to do the good works that constitute a real claim on divine rewards.

Over against this teaching, which provoked the radical protest of the *Reformation, the Council of *Trent confirmed a mediating position along the lines of Aquinas. It taught that grace is necessary for *salvation and already at work preparing human nature for receiving justifying grace. But against the Reformers' doctrine of the bondage of the will, Trent asserted the existence of human free will both before and after the Fall, so that humans can co-operate with God's grace both before justification and in receiving it. This co-operation, though always enabled by grace, is meritorious and necessary for growing in grace and receiving eternal life.

In response to the abuses to which the late medieval theology of grace had led in the pastoral practice of the church, *Luther proposed an extensive modification of the doctrine of grace as the basis for reforming the church. He revived the radical Augustinian position that after the Fall human nature is completely unable to will the good, let alone do it. What is needed is a complete transformation of the human heart governing the use of the will. It is brought about by a profound change in the relationship between God and the human person. This occurs through the proclamation of the gospel in word and sacrament, which offers sinners the assurance of God's grace. This promise has as its content the unconditional justification of the sinner that takes place when the Holy Spirit freely discloses the truth of the gospel of Christ and so constitutes faith as unconditional trust in God. At the heart of Luther's doctrine of justification is a precise distinction between God's work and human action. Grace is God's work alone, humans cannot contribute anything to their salvation apart from trusting God's promise. But the passivity in which the promise of God's justification is received is the basis for doing God's will in faith. For Luther, the capacity of the word and sacraments to communicate God's grace is entirely dependent on the free action of God. In the word of preaching and the sacraments of baptism and the Lord's supper we encounter, whenever and wherever God wills, the self-giving of the triune God. The distinctive emphases of Luther's view of grace are expressed in the 'exclusive particles' of Reformation theology: the sinner is justified by grace alone (*sola gratia*) which neither needs to be nor can be supplemented by good works; by Christ alone (*solo Christo*), because the death of Christ is all-sufficient for salvation; and by faith alone (*sola fide*) because faith is the total response of the justified sinner to God's grace.

Early and late modern discussions

While Luther expounded his insights in occasional writings, lectures, sermons, and academic disputations, *Calvin offered a systematic reconstruction of the reformed doctrine of grace in his *Institutes of the Christian Religion*. For Luther, God's predestination can only be known as it is disclosed in the certainty of salvation in faith, and this existential insight cannot be developed into a general theory of predestination. While Calvin still maintained the doctrine's pastoral function in comforting the troubled conscience of the believer, later generations of Calvinists turned it into a fully fledged theory of double predestination. This had at an early stage provoked the critique of the 'Freewillers' in England. The doctrine of predestination seemed at first to carry the day, being stated as Article XVII in the Thirty Nine Articles (1563). William Perkins (1558–1602) defended a Calvinist soteriology at Cambridge, where he was challenged by the Lady Margaret Professor, Peter Baro (1534–99), whose teaching prepared the ground for *Arminianism in England. Jacobus Arminius had been a prolific critic of the Calvinist doctrine of the irresistibility of grace and the theory of double predestination. While the Arminian position, which sought to avoid the alternative of grace without freedom or freedom without grace, was condemned at the Synod of Dort (1618/19), it became highly influential in England in the 17th century and received support from the *Caroline Divines. John and Charles *Wesley both adopted an Arminian view of grace in spite of their admiration for Luther. While Luther had emphasized that the believer is simultaneously wholly justified (by God's judgement) and wholly a sinner (as a matter of empirical reality apart from God's grace), the Wesleys understood the believer to be partly sinful, but partly justified. This led them to see the justification of sinners as being completed in their sanctification, even their 'entire sanctification' (see HOLINESS).

The debates in the Roman Catholic church on the teachings of *Jansen show a surprising similarity with central aspects of the inner-Protestant debate. In his doctrine of grace, published posthumously in his main work *Augustinus* (1640), which was condemned as heretical two years later by Pope Innocent X, Jansen followed a line not far removed from that taken by the *Dominican Domingo Bañez (1528–1604) against the *Jesuit Luis de Molina (1535–1600), in what came to be known as the *De Auxiliis* controversy. Molina had taught that divine grace becomes effective through its co-operation with human free will, whose acts are foreknown to God by his 'middle knowledge' of future contingent events. According to Jansen's interpretation of Augustine, God's commandments cannot be kept without the aid of divine grace, which operates irresistibly as the only source of good actions. In accordance with their view of grace as the inner transformation of the human heart, the Jansenists proposed a rigorous understanding of *penance, concentrating on the true remorse of the heart, to be distinguished from repentance motivated by fear of divine punishment. Their acerbic debate with the Jesuits documents the connection between the doctrine of grace and the exercise of power in the church. Condemned by a series of papal bulls from 1641 (*In eminenti*) to 1713 (*Unigenitus*), the Jansenists were forced into submission in France but survived in the Netherlands, where their views survived in the Old Catholic Church which separated from Rome in 1724. The Jansenist emphasis on the interiority of the operation of grace in the transformation of the human heart has continued to exercise a distinctive influence both in Roman Catholicism and Protestantism through the writings of *Pascal, whose *Pensées* summarize the Jansenist view on grace, faith, and morality.

Over against the creed of human autonomy proclaimed by the European *Enlightenment (the very core of the self-understanding of *modernity), important representatives of 20th-century theology have attempted to recover the understanding of grace as incorporating the essence of Christian faith. *Tillich applied the doctrine of justification to epistemology as well as to the social situation of the proletariat, and developed a concept of radical acceptance as the foundation for the 'courage to be'. *Barth interpreted the doctrine of grace through the radical christocentrism of his theology, in which Christ is seen both as the electing God and as elected humanity. *Küng supported this view from a Roman Catholic position, stressing that grace is God's favour towards humanity and not a quasi-physical entity in the human subject. For *Rahner grace can only be adequately understood as the correlation between divine self-communication and human self-transcendence. In the late 20th-century renaissance of Trinitarian theology, theologians from different confessional backgrounds have interpreted grace as God's threefold self-giving, relating to creation, *reconciliation, and redemption. The common denominator in modern reconstructions of the understanding of grace is a critique of the tendency, prevalent in some strands of the tradition, to treat grace as a semi-material, 'infused' substance; this is corrected by a stronger emphasis on grace as God's personal self-communication. In the ecumenical dialogues between the Roman Catholic church and the Lutheran churches there has been a growing convergence in the interpretation of justification by grace alone, but there is also a remaining difference about the acceptance of grace by faith alone. A further remaining matter of dispute concerns the implications of the growing convergences and remaining divergences for understanding the church and its structure. The ongoing debate over the doctrine of grace seems to indicate that it is indeed the nerve-centre of Christian doctrine, Christian worship, and Christian life. This would seem to suggest that there is life in Christian theology as long as conversation about God's grace does not come to a dead end.

See also PROVIDENCE; EASTERN ORTHODOX THEOLOGY.

Christoph Schwöbel

Braaten, C., *Justification* (1990).

Fransen, P., *The New Life of Grace* (1969).

McGrath, A. E., *Iustitia Dei: A History of the Christian Doctrine of Justification* (2 vols.; 1986).

Moeller, C., and Phillips, G., *The Theology of Grace and the Ecumenical Movement* (1961).

Oman, J., *Grace and Personality* (1917), repr. (1961).

Whitehouse, W. A., *The Authority of Grace: Essays in Response to Karl Barth*, ed. Ann Loades (1981).

Yarnold, E. J., *The Second Gift* (1974).

Greek theology 4th–6th centuries.

The Greek-speaking Christian world between the 4th and 6th centuries experienced one of the most vital periods in the history of Christian *theology, experiencing factions and conflicts, both political and intellectual, which at times threatened the *church's coherent long-term survival. The intellectual demands made upon Christian thinkers of that period, however, led to the adoption and development of basic positions that would characterize *Christianity for many centuries. This can be seen both in the intellectual methods of argument adopted to resolve difficulties, and in those structural forms of organization and procedure the church came to favour. Many of the foundations of these positions had been laid down in the cultural movement from Semitic to more overtly Greek forms of thought and expression that accelerated throughout the church of the 2nd and 3rd centuries. It is in the period under consideration, however, that we see refined and tested centrally important understandings of the nature of *God and God's involvement with the world; the dynamic significance of the person and work of *Jesus; the concept of *Trinity; the ways deemed appropriate of reading the scriptural foundations of Christian thought; the forms of the churches' *liturgical and *sacramental life; and the infrastructures of Christian local and global ecclesiastical organization. Many of these matters were not to be thought about seriously again, or challenged in their essential structure, until the late *Middle Ages.

Exegetical foundations

Much of the pattern for 4th-century Christian thought had been laid down by *Origen of Alexandria. Even his enemies could not ignore him. His metaphysical speculations were increasingly downplayed in subsequent centuries, but he determined the agenda in terms of the doctrine of Christ's salvific work and his relation to the divine absolute for almost all the leading thinkers of the 4th century. The chief intellectual issue driving the whole of Origen's time, and much of the century following, was the problematic relation of the absolute God to a contingent *world. Several of the *Hellenistic schools, especially the Stoics, Middle-*Platonists, and Neo-Pythagoreans, had challenged Christians to think out more fully the *metaphysical and *cosmological implications of theology that were so notably absent from their biblical accounts. Origen had responded by focusing his thought on the crucial issue of the relation of the One to the Many, and by positing Christ, both as the eternal *Word (Logos) and the historically realized teacher Jesus, as supreme mediator between the worlds. The refining of this cosmic *christology became the master theme of 4th-century thought. To illustrate the mediating role of the Logos made flesh, Origen systematized a method of interpreting the scriptures that allowed eternal meaning to be drawn from apparently relativized historical texts, by a manner of *allegorical and *typological (spiritualized) readings. The approach was enthusiastically adopted by the church of the next century, and greatly simplified in the process. The great change from a 3rd- to a 4th-century context, however, can be seen in the different manners of approaching the result of those exegeses. Many times, where Origen speaks tentatively and speculatively (addressing a circle of scholars and disciples), the 4th-century theologians wished to proceed to a more definite expression of truth. The methods appropriate to the small groups of advanced readers for whom Origen wrote had given way to a universalized doctrine meant for a greater mass of hearers in the churches. The age of doctrinal formulation had arrived with a flourish, and was advanced by key figures and teachers who wove together in their biblical expositions the insights they had gained from extensive classical *rhetorical educations. The introduction, in this period, of *philosophical key terms to elucidate theological arguments is very noticeable. The pace of the intellectual exchange in the 4th century was undoubtedly fuelled also by the extraordinary opportunities afforded to Christians after their emergence from a long period of political disapproval, if not active persecution, into the (relative) sunlight of the Constantinian dynasty.

Christological disputes

The 4th century was a period of great conflicts and internal confusions among Christian teachers, centred round the two primary disputes over christological and Trinitarian theology. Both issues were rooted in the ways that different schools approached scriptural exegesis. In the early part of the 4th century the *Arian con-troversy over the status of Christ had found opposing parties appealing for contradictory conclusions to the selfsame body of texts. If such a massive conflict in basic conclusions was all too obvious, how could the church ever deduce coherent *doctrine from such a disparate collection as its biblical canon? The controversies of this era were equally issues of how to nuance the fundamental problem of addressing the manner in which the Absolute God approached a contingent world, and thus almost all the disputes that racked the 4th-century church can be seen as the working out of the corollaries of Logos theology.

Here again the legacy of Origen, who had taught both the pre-temporal origination of the Logos, and his subordination to the supreme God, was central. This question of how a mediating Logos could itself be an absolute had been tormenting the church in the early decades of the 4th century. Though the idea first came to prominence in *Alexandria where a forceful hierarch had anathematized the presbyter Arius for his subordinationist theology, many parties now perceived these twin aspects of Origen's system to be contradictory, and threatening to disrupt the coherence of the larger *communion of churches in the east. The Arian crisis ran far beyond the issues raised by Arius and his bishop Alexander, but his case had already divided the eastern church for several years before *Constantine called an international synod at *Nicaea in 325, to settle the christological dispute (as he hoped) once and for all. *Athanasius had been a young deacon then, but he inherited the see of Alexandria shortly afterwards and propagated a hardline defence of Nicene christology as the only authentic inheritor of the biblical and apostolic faith. At the outset he regarded the party-word 'consubstantial' (the Logos was *homoousios*, that is of the same essence of God, and thus truly God in every significant nuance of that title) as a dispensable factor if the sense was agreed (it was controversial to many because it was not a biblical designation), but as synod succeeded synod throughout the first half of the 4th century, factionalizing the churches, he soon came to realize that attachment to the word (bringing with it the support of western Christians) would be a useful policy, both to simplify the debate and offer a rallying-point of unity. Athanasius' own understanding of the christology of *homoousios* was soteriologically led; he saw the descent of the Logos to earth as an act of the redemption and re-creation of *fallen creatures. As God became human, he argued, so humans might become divine. The *Incarnation was a *deification of the body of the Logos, and thereby an archetypal pattern for the deification of all *humanity by *grace. Athanasius saw the cosmic battles fought in the sacred body of Jesus, for example the fight with, and conquering of, death in the flesh, as an ontological victory for all humankind. Only later in his life did some of the negative implications of such a powerful 'divine-agent christology' become apparent. Because of the context of his apologetic, Athanasius was thought by several of his contemporaries (and most modern commentators) not to have laid sufficient emphasis on the human soul of Jesus. More fundamentally, Christian thinkers of the generation after Athanasius began to worry about the whole rationale of a consubstantial christology, just at the moment its future seemed secure—at the very end of the 4th century when the Emperor Theodosius I positively proscribed Arianism at the Council of Constantinople in 381 and held up Nicene orthodoxy as the future standard for the Christian empire.

The theologians of the generation after Athanasius, who subscribed to the Nicene tradition, were faced with a great dilemma: if Christ was as coequally absolute as the Father, had not the whole point and purpose of a Logos christology (wherein the Logos functions as a subordinate divine mediator between the realms of absolute and contingent) been thoroughly disrupted? It was a younger generation of Asia Minor thinkers who took his christological effort forward with significant adaptations, the Neo-Nicenes, pre-eminent among whom was a circle of friends and relations: Basil of Caesarea (330–79), his brother Gregory of Nyssa (c.331/40–395), and the learned Gregory Nazianzen (c.329–90). Together with the latter's cousin, Amphilokius, and Basil's *ascetic sister Macrina, these are collectively known as the Cappadocians. The bishop theologians among them were stimulated to their argument by the late and radical school of anti-Nicene theology known as Neo-Arianism, or Eunomianism.

In the 350s and 360s the dialectician Aetius, aided by his devoted pupil Eunomius, had emerged as a rallying-point for all radical opposition to the various Nicene parties and the Homoiousians, those parties willing to go halfway towards the Nicene position merely stating the Son's fundamental likeness to the Father, though without having necessarily to elaborate a Trinitarian theology, or disrupt the principle of having only one absolute divine person. Taking their cue from the majority Arian faction known as the Homoians (who argued that the Son was simply 'like the Father') whom they regarded as time-serving compromisers, the Neo-Arians elaborated a theology of the Son's radical 'unlikeness' to God (hence they were named Anomoians). In 359 Aetius proposed a dense, syllogistical synopsis of theology, his *Syntagmation*. He argued that the scriptural texts reveal God as fundamentally 'the Unbegotten Cause' of all. As the Son is defined by scripture to be begotten he is, therefore, caused, and thus no part of the Father, though related to him as a primary effect of the divine will. Although the Son issues from before *time, he is a contingent part of creation. Eunomius, after his teacher's death, was to press forward this theology with even greater stress on the revelatory force of names and titles in scripture. The latter further argued that correctness in doctrine was not merely an essential prerequisite for *holiness, but was itself constitutive of holiness. The sharply dialectical method of the school, and its logical development to a view of God who was perfectly self-revelatory, and logically consistent, led many to hold them in disdain. Their premises brought about many of the characteristic traits of the Cappadocian theologians who opposed them, in particular their stress on two fundamental insights opposed to the Neo-Arians: first that the scriptural titles possessed merely a dynamic force—that is when names such as Father and Son are used in scripture they function as suggestive analogies rather than absolute revelants (and so an authentic method of scriptural exegesis has to be contextually sensitive and multivalent); and secondly, over and against Aetius' view of a perfectly cogent self-revealing God, that God was essentially incomprehensible, and obscure even in his acts of revelation. The net result of the Cappadocian theology was to raise a severe warning about the limits of systematic reason in the face of the nature and person of God, and this was to set a dominant tone for centuries of eastern Christian theology to come.

This defence of christology left the Cappadocians with the diffi-

culty of explaining how one knew, at any given instance, whether a scriptural text carried the full weight of a metaphysical revelation about the nature of God, or was merely an illustrative analogy; whether it referred to the ideal world or the contingent; whether it described God in himself, or simply evoked God in his dealings with the world: to meet this problem they argued that the role of the interpreter was critical. Such a man (presumed to be an educated and ascetically purified bishop) would have been tested and refined in the rigours of spiritual *askesis* so that all arbitrary and sense-bound elements of his mind would have been clarified. He would thus be an archetypal teacher of the truth in line with the ancient gospel tradition. This stress on the purified nature of the true interpreter was the main subtext of the massively influential *Five Theological Orations* by Gregory Nazianzen (*Orations*, 27–31), which he delivered at Constantinople in 380 as a synopsis of the Neo-Nicene faith in God as Trinity. It was meant to (and did) become a standard synopsis of orthodox theology for subsequent generations.

The stress on the purified interpreter might seem curiously individualistic for a church emerging from a generation of crises caused by conflicts of schools, but it signalled the lack of faith in the solution proposed in the early 4th century: synodical consensus as a guide to truth. During the main era of the Arian crisis so many *councils had been held, mutually anathematizing each other, that any belief in the usefulness of this method for identifying and promulgating authentic Christian tradition had been severely shaken. In the aftermath of the Council of Constantinople (381) Gregory Nazianzen dismissed the whole affair as 'quacking geese' and concluded that 'nothing good' could ever come from such meetings. The Cappadocians, setting asceticism as a necessary prelude for theological accuracy, tried to restrict the development of theological speculation considered as a philosophical quest. In this they largely succeeded. Monastic ascetical communities would serve henceforth as a fostering community for theologians, and would check their philosophically speculative range.

The Cappadocian era is especially notable for its contribution to the theology of Trinity. *Augustine would contribute a large element of the picture later, in his *De Trinitate*, but his influence would extend only over the west. In the eastern church the Cappadocians were the unchallenged masters of this fundamental Christian teaching. Among them Gregory Nazianzen is the most explicit. God, he says, is to be acknowledged as being one in nature, and three in hypostasis. The three hypostases (persons, or subsistent entities) are each possessed of the same nature (or being). The diversity appears in the manner in which the contingent world experiences the unapproachable God. God is unapproachable in his essence, but reaches out to the created world by means of his hypostases. Thus, the Father who 'begets' the Logos, and 'sends out' the *Holy Spirit is the solitary cause of the Trinity. This justifies Christians claiming to believe in only one God. The Father's hypostatic existence is explained as the sole cause of the other two, and as such he is the ground of unity of the divine being. The Son and Spirit come in discrete ways from the one Father to express the divine power of outreach (thus although God is unknowable and unapproachable he also expresses himself as desiring to be known and approached) and to effect the salvation among earthly beings that will realize this revelation of the true God among them. For Gregory, as the hypostases of Son and Spirit share the single divine being of the Father, all three are coequal and coeternal, and yet the rationale of the threefold process of Trinity is assured by the inner logic of the Trinitarian dynamic movement. The Father, being sole cause of the other hypostases, effects the movement within the Godhead that results in the outreach to all creation. Yet the Father, understood as cause of all within the eternal life of Godhead, remains beyond all external movement that can be considered as contingent. God is thus the Unmoved Mover. The Trinity is fundamentally the outreach of its cause: that is the Father's dynamic concern to draw all creatures back to himself, through the Son, in the Spirit. In its original design and intent, therefore, Trinitarian theology was an essay in biblical soteriology as much as a metaphysical speculation on the nature of the relation of the divine to the cosmos.

The complexity of this doctrine, which became the capstone of a Christianity now able to explicate, to itself and to others, why it offered supreme veneration to Jesus, was to be an intellectual handicap in the hands of lesser minds than those as versed in bible and philosophy as the Cappadocians. This was especially true in the face of the advance of Islam in the eastern provinces from the 7th century onwards, where a radically simple doctrine of God was set in opposition to a difficult and nuanced Christian position. Nevertheless, the genius of the Cappadocian approach was that it managed, finally, to resolve the problems of the relative status of the divine Logos and the Spirit, and to affirm clearly that Christians worship Jesus as God without idolatrously elevating a man to divine honours. It also served to reconcile a doctrine of an absolute God with the biblical sense of a God who loves and cares for a people of his own in a highly involved relationship. In a real sense, the Cappadocian doctrine of Trinity created from the forge of two centuries of bitter Christian controversies a final synthesis of the Judaic and Hellenistic insights into theology: the God who acts in *history, and the God who is beyond all movement. Even though, after the 4th century, it was hardly developed much again, theologians being content to repeat the formularies of the earlier writers, the concept of Trinity was dynamically maintained in the doxologies and prayers of the eastern church.

Liturgical developments

After Constantine came to power he dispensed large grants to the Christians, partly in compensation for properties confiscated. Several key building projects resulted, most notably the great new churches at *Rome, *Constantinople, and *Jerusalem, which came to have a stimulating effect on the development of Christian *liturgy and a reflective theology of the cult. At the Church of the Holy Sepulchre the various sites within the same complex—the tomb of Jesus, the Anastasis, the place of Calvary, and the baptismal pool—led to a style of ceremonial which, together with that of the imperial capital in later centuries, would prove highly influential. There survives from one of the bishops of the Jerusalem Church in the 4th century a set of liturgical homilies, or Catecheses. Their author, Cyril of Jerusalem (d. 387), was a leading protagonist in the Arian struggles, whose sympathies at various times both Nicenes and anti-Nicenes thought they could command. He delivered his Catecheses through *Lent for the benefit of candidates for baptism. He is also the probable author of a series of lectures on the *sacraments. In these works Cyril presents the Christian rituals as awe-some mysteries, and lays down the basis for a more solemn structuring of the liturgical life of the church than had been previously witnessed. From his time onwards the liturgy was to grow in magnificence, and his association of ritual and sacramental meaning was to be immensely influential in the establishment of an enduring liturgical theology.

Graeco-Syrian influences on the east-Christian tradition

Close neighbours to the north, the *Syrian Church's literature had from earliest times been marked by ascetical interests. Writers such as Aphrahat and Ephrem (c.306–73) had laid down a body of literature that was rich with biblical symbols, hymnal and rhapsodic in character. They worked out a theology less apologetically driven than their Greek-speaking neighbours, and more explicitly concerned with the great themes of an ascetical return to *paradisal bliss. By the end of the 4th century, this Syrian tradition was at home in the literature of the Greeks, though it was never to lose its sensitivity to the local traditions and traits that had made Syrian thought distinctive. At this period it produced a great school of exegesis, in Syriac and Greek, with such luminaries as Diodore of Tarsus (d. c.390), his younger contemporaries and disciples Theodore of Mopsuestia (c.350–428) and John Chrysostom (c.347–407) (the latter becoming one of the most influential models of 'Greek' Christian rhetoric), and, in the early 5th century, *Nestorius and Theodoret of Cyrrhus (c.393–457) who were to witness a massive attack launched on their traditions of christology by Cyril of Alexandria (c.375–444), a barrage that would be responsible for the posthumous synodical condemnation in 553, under the emperor Justinian, of the leading Antiochene teachers.

The Syrian tradition influenced the Greek world mainly through its approach to scripture, which adopted a critical distance from much of what Origen had recommended. Lucian of Antioch (d. 312) founded a school of interpretation that, much more markedly than the Alexandrians (who preferred a transcendental exegesis of the texts), was more carefully attentive to the social and historical significance. Lucian drew a devoted circle of admirers round him. His edition of the Septuagint became the standard text received in all the churches of the east, and his edition of the NT is the foundation of what is now the Textus Receptus. Lucian's biblical method was taken forward by Diodore of Tarsus. In his time Diodore was one of the leading Christian opponents to the emperor Julian's policy for the revival of paganism, and worked tirelessly to produce philosophically sensitive treatises attacking the anti-Christian factions of his day. He founded a monastery and school near Antioch and was there the teacher of Theodore Mopsuestia and John Chrysostom, who spread the exegetical traditions to Constantinople and throughout the east, after their elections as bishops. Diodore's approach to the biblical text deliberately undermined the readings preferred by Origen. He followed a consistently historical reading, from which he wished to demonstrate higher significances. Allegorical interpretation, he argued, abused the literal sense and therefore could not rise to a higher veracity. In his treatment of the Blessings of Jacob, or the first fifty *Psalms, on which he comments, it is noticeable how only those passages are accepted as 'messianic' that traditional Jewish exegesis had already accepted as such. This amounted to a very few texts indeed (in this case only Gen. 49: 10–12; and Pss. 2, 8, and 44). This was in stark contrast to the general tendencies already witnessed in the mainstream of Christian interpretation that gave *messianic readings to a much larger body of biblical loci. The practical results can be seen most visibly in his christology. He was an avowed opponent of Apollinaris (c.315–92), his opposite pole, who taught that Jesus was a divine being inhabiting a veil of flesh, not needing to commit himself to a fully human life in so far as his divine power absorbed and 'included in' anything necessary for a visitation of humankind on earth. Diodore held any form of monist christology such as this in horror. He urged, rightly, that it presented the death of incarnation theology in favour of an epiphanic theology of Jesus that was more akin to earlier *Docetic thought, where Jesus' real status as a human being was undermined. Yet, as a result of his apologetic intent, his language often seemed to others outside his school to be too heavily dualist. He spoke of christology in terms of 'Two Sons': one Son before the ages, the other a Son within time. It was a language that was to lie behind much of his disciples' work, and even lasted into the 5th century, providing the backdrop to Nestorius' bitter opposition to Cyril.

Theodore Mopsuestia was, in the late 4th century, an eminent practitioner of the methods of Diodore. He was regarded in his own time as the leading Syrian theologian, but his reputation was fatally damaged in the aftermath of the 5th century christological controversy and finally he was posthumously condemned in 553 when Justinian's council anathematized him as a 'forebear' of the *heresy of 'Nestorianism'. Theodore's biblical commentaries were firmly focused on the literal reading, and he only lightly touched on the issue of the NT as a typological fulfilment of the OT. Instead he stressed that the individual Christian believer looks to his type in Christ. Part of the reason for this is that he has a firm doctrine of successive ages of *revelation: the first given to the pagans, the second to the Jews, the last to the Christians. The NT stands only partly in relation to the OT. It complements it, but does not unerringly fulfil it, since it often supersedes it, and thus its meaning cannot be explicated out of the OT text, as if both were a seamless robe in the manner Origen had looked on them. Through Chrysostom's work which popularized many of these approaches, though in a less radical form, and which became staple reading in the East, the Syrian influence came home to have a permanent impact on Greek Christian thought.

The 5th-century controversies

Throughout the 4th century Christian asceticism had been growing in extent. The classic forms of *desert *monasticism had already been subjected to much variation as communities grew up in the cities and villages. Monasticism, at first a wilderness experience often at odds with hierarchical authority, had become urbanized, and ascetic teachers were more and more sought out as bishops of important cities. By the 5th century a pattern of theological process that is rooted in askesis and looks to past precedent for its doctrinal formulations becomes clearly observable. Now, it is the nexus of monastic parties and communities that does much to determine the successful outcome of great intellectual issues. By the 5th century the appeal to scripture had evolved into a procedure that wished to amass as many proof-texts as possible. In this era one can also see that system extended from the scriptures as authoritative sources and into the works of theologians from earlier generations who

have now come to be seen as standard-bearers of orthodoxy, and to whom is given the title 'Abbas' or 'fathers'. This century is the age, properly speaking, of 'patristic' theology. Nowhere are the issues more clearly seen than in the greatest of the controversies of the 5th century, the christological dispute that flared up between the great sees of Alexandria and Constantinople in the persons of their respective archbishops Cyril and Nestorius. It was a dispute that was to constitute the agenda for all the christological debates of the 6th century too.

Whereas Nestorius argued that christology ought to be marked above all else by clarity of thought and language, Cyril appealed to the essential 'mystery' of the Christ event (and consequent necessary mysteriousness of theology). Above all, Cyril called on a whole dossier of patristic authorities which he had his chancery scribes assemble. This method in theological argumentation, the compiling of the patristic authorities who support one's opinion about scriptural exegesis and dogmatic formulary, became the standard form of Christian theological method from this time until the medieval scholastic period. It can be first seen in its full legal and scholastic process in the procedural documentation of the Council of *Ephesus 431. The christological solution proposed at Ephesus made Alexandrian premises the chief starting-point for reflection on the role of Jesus. But what the Syrian and Western churches thought to be an excessive monism in the Alexandrian pattern of thought ensured that the conflict would occupy much of the 5th and 6th centuries, in a string of imperially sponsored councils and decrees. The decision of the Council of Ephesus, affirming that Jesus the Christ was a single and coherent divine person inhominated, was further extrapolated at the Council of *Chalcedon (because of Syrian and Roman pressures) to affirm that this single person was also endowed with two complete natures (divine and human) united under a single personhood (hypostasis). This came to be known as hypostatic christology and was adopted as the standard of orthodoxy by most of the churches.

Sixth-century conflict and resolutions

Many of the Alexandrian school of theologians thought that the Syrian-influenced stress on the duality of natures in Christ had strayed into a revival of Diodore's excessive dualism. In the semantics of the time there was a fine line between the notion of person and that of nature, and the Greek terms used in the debate contributed to the confusion. Many thought that Chalcedon was propounding a hopelessly artificial view of Christ. Several important theologians in Egypt and Syria began a protest movement against the council and its doctrine of two natures (Dyophysitism). They came, therefore, to be known as the *Monophysites.

Severus of Antioch (c.465–538) was perhaps the greatest intellectual among them. Their main points were taken from the works of Cyril of Alexandria, and were meant to advance a mystically coherent vision of Jesus as a divine being who had deified the flesh that he had assumed. They attempted to rehabilitate the transcendent aspects of Alexandrian christology while avoiding the defects of Apollinaris. The arguments that ensued over fine points of christology radically disrupted the peace of the eastern Christian world at every level. Monasteries were almost at war with each other throughout Palestine, and in Egypt and Syria the cohesion of the hierarchies was substantially damaged. Imperial efforts to enforce agreement, under one or another emperor, were sometimes subtle and sometimes heavy-handed throughout the 5th and 6th centuries. In 544 the court of Justinian issued an explicit condemnation of the dualistic christology of three of the leading Syrian authorities: Theodore, Theodoret, and Ibas of Edessa, in an attempt to appease and reconcile the Monophysite party. This edict, known as the Three Chapters, was reaffirmed at the imperially sponsored Council of Constantinople II in 553. This too attempted a reconciliation between the Dyophysite and Monophysite factions on the basis of a more nuanced interpretation of Chalcedon. It was an effort that was largely in vain. The social effects of the ecclesiastical divisions in the east were finally resolved only when the most troublesome provinces of Syria and Egypt were lost to imperial control in the Arab advances of the 7th century. The theological differences have remained to this day as the leading cause of division among eastern Christians, and comparable, as far as they are concerned, to the fractures consequent on the Reformation controversies later in the west.

As the 6th century drew to a close, in an eastern empire that was increasingly stretched to preserve its political integrity and fiscal sufficiency, a highly influential figure was born, who in many ways was a precursor of times to come. Maximus the Confessor (580–662) was destined to be the great representative link between the late antique period and the flourishing of *Byzantine theological thought in the centuries ahead, in the east. For all his brilliance, however, and the cosmic range and character of his speculative intelligence, he is to all intents and purposes a great systematizer of what has gone before. He is a commentator, a scholiast, an explicator, and in this represents the slowing down, if not the closure, of a great era of active and frequently disruptive theological debate in the east Christian world. After him the world of late antiquity is definitively over and early medieval Byzantium beckons.

John McGuckin

Barnes, T. D., *Athanasius and Constantius: Theology and Politics in the Constantinian Empire* (1994).

Frend, W. H. C., *The Rise of the Monophysite Movement* (1972).

—— *The Rise of Christianity* (1984).

Grillmeier, A., *Christ in Christian Tradition*, 2nd edn. (1975), i.

Hanson, R. P. C., *The Search for the Christian Doctrine of God* (1988).

Kelly, J. N. D., *Early Christian Doctrines* (1958).

McGuckin, J. A., *St. Cyril of Alexandria: The Christological Controversy* (1994).

Meyendorff, J., *Byzantine Theology* (1975).

—— *Imperial Unity and Christian Divisions* (1989).

Norris, R. A., *Manhood and Christ: A Study in the Christology of Theodore Mopsuestia* (1963).

Pelikan, J., *The Christian Tradition*, i. *The Emergence of the Classical Tradition* (1974).

—— *Christianity and Classical Culture* (1993).

Rousseau, P., *Basil of Caesarea* (1994).

Simonetti, M., *Biblical Exegesis in the Early Church* (1994).

Young, F., *From Nicaea to Chalcedon* (1983).

Zaharopoulos, D. Z., *Theodore of Mopsuestia on the Bible* (1989).

Greene, (Henry) Graham (1904–91), English *novelist, playwright, and essayist. He travelled widely, and lived in France from 1966. In 1926 he joined the Roman Catholic Church, and came to be regarded as a leading Catholic writer. In his later years, when his links with the Church became more tenuous, he described him-self as a 'Catholic *agnostic'; yet one of the lighter works of his last period, *Monsignor Quixote* (1983), based probably on a Spanish priest friend, is Catholic enough. More important in religious terms, however, are the novels of his middle period, which interweave ideas of *sin, guilt, *grace, *redemption, and sanctity in powerful and dramatic narratives.

These themes emerge outstandingly in *The Power and the Glory* (1940): a nameless Mexican priest goes from place to place carrying out his ministry at a time when the church is being persecuted, and eventually dies a *martyr. He is an alcoholic, has an illegitimate child, and is often weak and faltering. Yet he is also depicted as open to *God's grace, and, in a powerful scene in prison, as coming to a genuine love of his flock. Through his analyses of the priest's thoughts and feelings, Greene manages to point a contrast between how people seem to themselves and to others, and how they stand in God's eyes.

The Heart of the Matter (1948) makes similar explorations of motive and emotion. Its main figure, Scobie, is a policeman in West Africa during the Second World War: he has an adulterous affair, then is drawn into corrupt dealings with a local merchant. Eventually he sees death as the only solution to his dilemma, and commits suicide. Although Scobie regards this as the ultimate sin, the priest's words of comfort to his widow, appealing to the mystery of the human heart and to God's *mercy, indicate that Greene felt that a Christian verdict on Scobie's action is not clear-cut.

The End of the Affair (1951) also starts with an adulterous relationship. During the London blitz Sarah Miles promises God that if her lover, Bendrix, survives a bombing raid, she will renounce her adultery. Bendrix is miraculously spared; Sarah, though still in love with him, fulfils her part of the bargain. The rest of the book explores the themes of conversion, sanctity, and the miraculous.

Greene's novels are striking both for their psychological penetration and their theology, especially the delineation of salvation within sin and seediness. Many of his works are marked by their illumination of the conflicting motives in the hearts of sinners. Critics, however, have accused Greene of having a Manichaean sensibility, sometimes making too stark a contrast between nature and grace, world and religion. This accusation finds support in his ambiguous attitude to sexuality, as in *Brighton Rock* (1938) and *The Heart of the Matter*.

Patrick Sherry

Lodge, David, *Graham Greene* (1966).

Sherry, Norman, *The Life of Graham Greene* (3 vols.; 1989–   ).

Stratford, Philip, *Faith and Fiction: Creative Process in Greene and Mauriac* (1964).

West, W. J., *The Quest for Graham Greene* (1998).

Griffiths, Bede (1906–93). Turning from the industrialized modern west with its one-sided rationality, Bede Griffiths sought a renewal of Christianity through integration of the ancient and universal spiritual wisdom that he saw as 'the perennial philosophy'. Drawn first to the intuitive, imaginative world of the English *Romantic poets, Griffiths followed the trace of wisdom eastwards to India, studying the *Hindu Vedanta in the simplicity of an ashram life. His autobiography, *The Golden String* (1954), recounts this spiritual journey through a conversion and twenty years as a Benedictine monk in England, until just before his permanent move to southern *India in 1955. There Griffiths would become a pioneer in the inculturation of Christian *spirituality. In his enchanting *Return to the Centre* (1976), Griffiths looks exclusively inwards, backwards, and eastwards. *The Marriage of East and West* (1983) brings together the theological worlds of the Hindu and Judaeo-Christian traditions, still with a strong bias towards the east. By the time of his full encounter with the 'new science' in 1982, Griffiths was already looking westwards, assimilating the holistic and organic perspectives that resonated with his own vision. His fullest synthesis, *A New Vision of Reality* (1990), brought the ancient religious traditions of Christianity and the east together with conceptions of contemporary physics, *cosmology, and transpersonal *psychology in a new evolutionary perspective. Still, personally rooted in Christ through his faith, Griffiths centred his thought more and more explicitly in the trans-temporal non-dual Absolute that he understood as the core of every religion. This unitive principle binds together the three worlds of spirit, of psyche/consciousness, and of matter. Griffiths's bold intuitive thought, advancing swiftly along lines of affinity, brings everything forward into the light of the One.

See also ABHISHIKTANANDA.   **Bruno Barnhart**

Du Boulay, S., *Beyond the Darkness: A Biography of Bede Griffiths* (1998).

guilt, see SIN.

Gutiérrez, Gustavo (1928–), Peruvian Catholic theologian, who studied medicine and philosophy at the University of Lima, and psychology in Louvain, Belgium. Gutiérrez graduated in theology from Lyons, France, and the Gregorian University in Rome. Ordained in 1959, he works as a priest in Rímac, Peru, and directs the Bartolomé de Las Casas Centre in Lima. Considered to be the father of *liberation theology, he defines it as a critical reflection on Christian praxis done in the light of the *Word of God. He advocates a new way of doing theology in which the social engagement of the Christian in the struggle against oppression comes first, and theology comes second as reflection on such actions. Gutiérrez addresses his theology to the oppressed masses whom he calls the 'non-human beings' of history (*Hombres Cactus*, literally 'cactus people'). These are the victims of conditions of exploitation which have stripped them of the right to have a human and dignified existence. A theology of liberation is one that defines the message of Christianity in relation to the active solidarity with the poor that the gospel requires. The term 'liberation' in Gutiérrez has political and historical meaning but also implies liberation from *sin. The social dimension of sin is stressed because *poverty is a collective phenomenon and the result of class exploitation. Poverty is akin to *death. To announce the message of *Resurrection implies denouncing structures that seek to destroy human life while announcing the good news of the *Kingdom of *God working in solidarity with the poor. This praxis of solidarity is the 'option for the poor' and is the fundamental premiss of liberation theology.

See also BOFF, LEONARDO; BONINO, JOSÉ MÍGUEZ; FREIRE, PAOLO; JUSTICE.   **Marcella Althaus-Reid**

G. Gutiérrez, *A Theology of Liberation* (1988).
—— *The God of Life* (1991).
—— *Las Casas: In Search of the Poor of Jesus Christ* (1993).

H

health and healing have been of intense practical concern to Christians, as well as others, over the last two millennia. Although closely related to such profound theological issues as the nature of *suffering and *evil, they have not often directly elicited the best intellectual efforts of theologians (this despite the widespread use of *metaphors associated with illness and health in many theological works). Extensive practical efforts to overcome the ill-effects of disease by all available means have mainly been underwritten by the belief that God provides in nature and by the use of human efforts, including medicine, the means of healing and *grace that are needed to combat illness. The evangelist *Luke, traditionally characterized as a physician who might therefore have used both 'natural' and 'supernatural' methods of healing, acts as an icon for an eclectic, pragmatic approach to theological thought about healing and health, something presupposed, for instance, in the work of Thomas *Aquinas.

The vast majority of contemporary Christians in this age of relative biomedical security, following the majority western and Thomist tradition, regard scientifically based medicine as the main divinely given source of healing. Some see the progress of medicine as a sacrament of divine care and *providence that renders distinctively religious healing methods unnecessary. Others argue that biomedical science can be supplemented or amplified with explicit religious activities such as participation in the traditional ecclesiastical *sacraments of the *Eucharist, laying on of hands, anointing, or confession. Finally, there are those, particularly in the *charismatic *revivalist tradition, presently undergoing a renaissance, who see spiritual and religious means of healing such as exorcism, laying on of hands, and *prayer, as the main way to attain healing of body, mind, and spirit. These positions might be labelled liberal humanist, sacramentalist, and fundamentalist charismatic revivalist. Individuals are often eclectic in adopting beliefs and practices; this has been the position throughout history in seeking to find an effective response to disease and suffering.

Christian theological thought about health and healing in the light of the practical dominical imperative to heal the sick (Matt. 10: 8) has remained rudimentary. It is often easier to point to omissions and basic conflicts in Christian thought about healing and health than to profound, well-developed insights. Certain issues, attitudes, and lines of thought that have accompanied a variety of practices and acted as rationalizations for them can, however, be identified.

One way of documenting some of these is to trace their roots in, and their development from, Jesus' healing work.

An important part of Jesus' activity was that of healing and exorcism. His healings were interpreted by the gospel writers as authenticating signs of the inbreaking of the rule of God and of the advent of *salvation (Luke 4: 16–22; 7: 18–23), and they provided much of the impetus for early Christianity to be a healing movement. Many of the issues and disputes that surrounded Jesus' healing *ministry have continued to influence and shape Christian thought on healing and illness, such as it is, until the present day.

Throughout the last two millennia, Christians have speculated upon, and argued about, the causes, meanings, and appropriate religious responses to disease. In particular, there has been much dispute about the relationship between *sin, illness, and *punishment with some arguing that illness may be a direct divine punishment for sin or a way of disciplining or improving people. This kind of controversy is plain in the ministry of Jesus (John 9: 2), as is the association between *forgiveness and healing (Mark 2: 5), and that between healing and salvation. Where people are healed they are literally 'saved' (Mark 5: 34). There is a related controversy about whether, therefore, illness should be alleviated or healed as a sign of sins forgiven, or whether it should be borne with fortitude. The desire to interpret illness as a manifestation of divine justice has frequently resurfaced. For example, some Christians have suggested that AIDS should be seen as the natural punishment for sexual immorality.

While those around Jesus are presented as disputing the origins and meanings of disease, Jesus takes a pragmatic approach, seeking to cure rather than explain it, perhaps because he saw it as a manifestation of the powers of evil. Jesus probably saw himself as being directly involved in a war against Satan (Mark 3: 20–30). This practical, anti-intellectual, *dualistic, and combative attitude has contributed to Christianity's involvement with practical care and cure, such as setting up hospitals. It has, perhaps, also contributed to intellectual foreclosure on the causes, nature, and meanings of illness. The emphasis on the war against disease perceived as an unmitigated evil has also meant that little thought has been given to the positive meaning and promotion of health. Christianity, like modern biomedicine, has tended to remain fixated upon *post hoc* negative aspects of pathology and cure of illness rather than upon wider factors of cause and prevention. Furthermore, little attention has been given to the experience of illness or the voice of sufferers except in so far as they might contribute cautionary tales or witness to divine cure. This has been particularly problematic in the case of people with mental health problems who may even now be regarded as demon-possessed.

While Jesus' healings and exorcisms may be interpreted as signs of the inbreaking of a sociopolitical reality, the *Kingdom of God, and some recent thinkers have tried to emphasize their corporate and communal significance, the locus of healing was an individual sufferer. This inevitable individualism has helped to ensure that Christian thought has often not addressed the wider social causes and constraints bearing upon health and healing. So, for example, many Christians pray for the sick and the medical personnel who attend them, but they do not ask for the demise of the tobacco industry which causes epidemic disease. Social and political factors are largely excluded from articulated Christian thought about healing and health. Although Christians have often been active in social reforms that have had beneficial effects on the health of the population at large, for example in 19th-century England, they have been inspired perhaps more by general Christian social thinking than by any developed theology focused on healing and health (see also TEMPERANCE).

Jesus' healings and exorcisms are presented as helping to authenticate his ministry as an agent of the Kingdom of God. Subsequently, the power to heal has often been used to imply a divine guarantee for the truth of agents, words, and assertions within Christianity. Healing *miracles abound in the lives of the *saints. Charismatic individuals, such as the *Quaker George Fox, and many modern *revivalist groups, often point to the healings that are associated with their words and works to gain audience, credibility, and social influence. Disputes about the authenticity of healing have lain at the heart of many ecclesiastical controversies. Mainstream churches have often attempted to regulate the activities of healers of all kinds. Thus, the Roman Catholic church sought at various times to control as well as to promote certain kinds of healing practice, including licensing all medical practitioners. It continues to maintain strict monitoring over time-honoured, overtly religious healing methods such as visiting the shrine at Lourdes. Many Christians remain deeply sceptical and rejecting of religious healers and their methods while those who adopt them often fail to subject them to any kind of critical intellectual analysis. The question of who should be 'allowed' to heal people, and how, remains a key matter of debate as it was when attempts were made to discredit Jesus as an agent of Beelzebul (Mark 3: 20–30).

Jesus employed several means of healing and exorcizing people, ranging from anointing (probably—see Mark 6: 13), through the use of linguistic formulae, to physical means such as spittle and dust, or laying on of hands. Sometimes the *faith of the sick person or those around them is deemed to be crucial (Mark 5: 34; 6: 5–6), at other times it is presented as unnecessary (Mark 3: 9–10). Some of the means used, therefore, seem to be entirely supernatural and miraculous, others seem to owe something to what was known of medical knowledge or even to magic. The issue about what means may legitimately be used in healing has continually dogged Christian thinking. Some *dispensationalists maintain that the age of supernatural miracles concluded with the end of the apostolic era and the establishment of the church. Others, notably modern cha-

rismatic revivalists, regard this as faithless. There is an unresolved debate about the use of natural versus 'religious' means of healing and so about what putting one's faith in God in time of illness means. The issue of whether people fail to recover when religious means are used continues to raise the question of whether and to what extent personal or group faith in, and *obedience to, God determines the outcome of acts of religious healing such as laying on of hands or exorcism.

Healing in the gospels was a sign of the advent of the Kingdom and the realization and authentication of salvation, often closely linked to forgiveness (Mark 2: 9–12). The precise nature and content of salvation is not spelt out in the NT, nor is healing practised in consistent ways with definite, unambivalent meanings. Although the concept of wholeness or salvation is present (Mark 5: 28, 34) and it might be seen as pointing towards a wider concept of 'health', that is, something more comprehensive and significant than the elimination of physical illness, modern concepts of health can only be implicated in this with strenuous efforts. While the Christian tradition of thought and practice can probably truly be said to point towards some kind of integration between concepts of healing, health, and salvation, this relationship, while important, remains, at best, vague and inferential. Christian thought has only very poorly articulated ideas of health and its relation to salvation, so the contribution that it might make in this area has been limited.

The ambiguities and controversies explored here continue unresolved. While many Christians probably do not think much about healing and health, others adopt positions largely unilluminated by critical theological thought. Christians continue to make important contributions to the theory and practice of health care, for example in the creation of hospices and by participating in debates about *medical ethics. Gradually, it is becoming possible for Christians to think about the positive, preventative, communal, social, and political aspects of these issues and to begin to contribute to a positive vision of health. The sacrament of anointing is now seen as a sacrament of healing and *reconciliation with the living human community and not merely as the viaticum for those close to *death. However, the attempts some Christians make to contribute to contemporary debates about healing and health are largely unsupported by theology that is informed about up-to-date knowledge about these topics from the medical and *social sciences. Meanwhile, signs, wonders, and miracles continue to flourish amongst revivalist groups in an age which has never been more biomedically secure. These evoke awe and amazement, not critical thought, social and political action, or the provision of mass health care.

Christians are not alone in being ignorant and confused about the nature of illness, health, and healing. These are complex issues and the range of practical and intellectual responses appropriate to them remains immense.   **Stephen Pattison**

Conrad, L. I., Neve, M., Nutton, V., Porter, R., Wear, A., *The Western Medical Tradition* (1995).
Kee, H. C., *Medicine, Miracle and Magic in New Testament Times* (1986).
Kelsey, M., *Healing and Christianity* (1973).
Lambourne, R. A., *Community, Church and Healing* (1963).
Maddocks, M., *The Christian Healing Ministry* (1995).
Marty, M. E., and Vaux, K. L., *Health/Medicine and the Faith Traditions* (1982).
Pattison, S., *Alive and Kicking: Towards a Practical Theology of Illness and Healing* (1989).

Percy, M., *Words, Wonders and Power* (1996).
Wilson, M., *Health is for People* (1975).
—— (ed.), *Explorations in Health and Salvation* (1983).
Woodward, J., *Encountering Illness* (1995).

heaven is the traditional name of the abode of *God, the *angels, *saints, the blessed among the dead believers, and, eventually, redeemed humankind. The bible locates heaven at the top level of a three-tiered structure composed of netherworld (below the earth), earth, and heaven (above the sky). As a powerful symbol denoting a superior realm, this location has survived modern revisions of this archaic *cosmological description. In Christian thought and language, heaven figures prominently in two traditions that may be termed 'visionary' and '*eschatological'. The visionary tradition is about the experience of some people who report their being admitted to heaven in *dreams, *visions, or rituals. The eschatological tradition is about life after death which Christians hope to spend in the abode of God.

The visionary tradition

Today, few Christians would claim to have access to heaven there to experience God in special *mystical moments. In the past this has been different, and one can identify at least two rich visionary cultures: that of the Old and New Testaments, and that of the medieval mystics.

In biblical times, *prophets, *priests, and leaders were thought to have access to heaven. Some visionaries experienced how special blessings were conferred on them; they also witnessed certain scenes of cosmic significance, for human history may be initiated in the heavenly realm. *Moses and the elders are reported to have ascended to the holy mountain where they 'beheld God, and they ate and drank' (Exod. 24: 11); this legend may echo little-known rituals celebrated in the *Temple of Jerusalem in which the deity was thought to be visible in a kind of mirror made of sapphire stone. The prophet *Isaiah was admitted to the heavenly throne-room and cleansed for his office, as was the high priest Joshua (Isa. 6; Zech. 3: 1–5). In a dream *Daniel witnessed a heavenly scene of the judgement of wicked powers and the investment of an angel with authority over the nations (Dan. 7). In the NT, visions figure prominently. At his *baptism by John the Baptist, Jesus saw the heavens open and heard a heavenly voice (Mark 1: 10–11). A similar experience is reported of Stephen, who saw heaven open when being martyred (Acts 7: 55–6). In the gospel of Luke, Jesus reports an experience in which he 'watched Satan fall from heaven like a flash of lightning' (10: 18). Jesus' vision may be related to those described in the book of *Revelation, where the seer witnesses a heavenly war between the angel Michael and a being called the dragon. During this war, the dragon is thrown down to the earth and eventually cast into a lake of fire (Rev. 12: 9; 20: 10). The book of Revelation ranks as the classic document of the visionary tradition; its visions have been variously interpreted as literary fictions, experiences of the early Christian seer John of Patmos, or experiences reported in the circle of John the Baptist and Jesus. More subdued is the visionary tradition in the letters of *Paul, but he describes, in quite unambiguous terms, how he experienced a heavenly journey 'whether in the body or out of the body I do not know'. On this journey he was 'caught up into *Paradise and heard things that are not to be told, that no mortal is permitted to repeat' (2 Cor. 12: 3–4).

Indicating that he had this experience fourteen years earlier, Paul implies that heavenly visions are rare. The gospel of John declares that 'no one has ascended into heaven except the one who descended from heaven, the Son of Man' (John 3: 13); this may indicate strong scepticism about visions like that reported by Paul or express belief in the fact that no one can enter heaven without Christ's consent.

With the waning of early Christian *enthusiasm, much of the visionary culture was lost. It was not before the high Middle Ages that a new visionary culture emerged in the monasteries. The classic reports of heavenly visions that generally include scenes of the soul's entering Christ's bridal chamber can be found in the writings of two 12th-century nuns, Mechthild of Magdeburg and Gertrude of Helfta. Associated with, though not part of, the medieval visionary culture is *Dante, who in the third part of his Divine Comedy (1308–21) writes about himself as someone who is allowed to travel through the various spheres that make up the created universe. Eventually he arrives in heaven, where St Bernard helps him to gaze into the divine light. Dante's vision is fictional, but precisely as fiction it survived the culture in which it was created.

After the medieval period, heavenly visions did occur, but they tend to be isolated rather than forming part of a flourishing visionary culture. When in the 18th century Emanuel Swedenborg filled many books with his descriptions of heaven, he made a tremendous impact on many of his readers, but failed to initiate a new visionary culture (see also BLAKE, WILLIAM).

The eschatological tradition

In OT times, three mutually exclusive ideas vied with each other: (1) the view that the dead, far from joining God in heaven, actually sleep as shadowy beings in the netherworld (Eccles. 3: 19–21; 9: 5); (2) the notion that the dead could ascend to heaven, if not in the body like Enoch and the prophet Elijah (Gen. 5: 24; 2 Kgs. 2: 11), then at least in some other form we may describe as the *soul (Ps. 49: 15; 73: 24); (3) the idea of bodily *resurrection and participation in a new kingdom of those who had died a violent death, especially from persecution for faith in the Jewish God (Dan. 12: 2–3; 2 Macc. 7).

In the NT, the first of these notions is utterly rejected, both by Jesus and all his early followers. The gospels suggest that Jesus held the second view. According to Jesus, angels would transport a deceased person's soul to a place where that person would stay 'in the bosom of *Abraham', i. e. with Israel's ancestors. In this transcendent realm, human persons are no longer subject to human needs nor involved in an earthly social network; marriage does not continue in heaven (Luke 20: 27–40). They are like angels, spiritual beings that live close to God and for the service of God. Paul casts Jesus' doctrine in a more traditionally Jewish framework that includes a period of sleeping in the grave, an eventual resurrection of the body, the transformation of the resurrected body into a spiritual one, and a heavenly ascension of those who are worthy to spend everlasting life with God and Christ in heaven (1 Cor. 15: 1 Thess. 4, 17). The Pauline view corresponds to the second OT notion referred to above; but Paul also includes bodily resurrection—the third OT notion—in his eschatological scenario, albeit only as a very brief prelude to spiritual transformation (1 Cor. 15: 52).

In Christian thought and teaching, the two (OT) notions of heavenly ascension and resurrection vie with each other and are often combined. In the notion of heavenly ascension, a mystical impulse coming from the visionary culture can be felt. Theologians who felt close to its legacy transformed biblical notions of seeing God into philosophical notions of the 'beatific vision'. They insisted that all eternal bliss derives from 'seeing God'. In the rival notion of resurrection, a political impulse deriving from the ancient Jewish theology of *martyrdom can be felt, and found its most dense expression in the doctrine of Christ's bodily Resurrection and his empty tomb. Those theologians who felt close to this political tradition expected a bodily resurrection of all the faithful and an ensuing this-worldly *millennium ruled by Christ. After most theologians had abandoned millennial ideas, the resurrection paradigm emerged in a new form. Starting with Cyprian of Carthage, certain theologians came to see the heavenly kingdom as a place where people meet their relatives and friends and form a society with them.

The ascension-related theocentric tradition with its emphasis on the beatific vision came to be characteristic of medieval scholasticism and *Reformation theology. The resurrection-related anthropocentric tradition with its emphasis on meeting again flourished in the theology of the Italian Renaissance, Swedenborg, and much of 19th-century theology and Christian fiction. Twentieth-century theology has not been very kind to the notion of heaven as the abode of the blessed. While in certain circles, 19th-century notions of heavenly homes persist and are even revitalized, most theologians (such as *Rahner, *Barth) describe heavenly existence in minimalist fashion as eternally being with God; thus they support theocentric notions. Some radical theologians have gone as far as denying individual life after death altogether or they are content with vague notions of individual human biographies being forever stored in God's eternal *memory.

See also HELL; LIMBO.   **Bernhard Lang**

Barker, M., *The Risen Lord* (1996).
McDannell, C., and Lang, B., *Heaven: A History* (1988).
Russell, J. B., *A History of Heaven* (1997).

Hebrews, Epistle to the.

It is widely acknowledged by scholars that Hebrews constitutes one of the most powerful and distinctive pieces of *theological writing in the NT and, along with *Romans, the nearest thing to a theological treatise to be found there. Whoever the author was (certainly not *Paul), he was one of the great theologians of his time. The contents of Hebrews reveal a man skilled in Graeco-Roman *rhetoric, able to communicate in good literary Greek, with an extensive knowledge of the Jewish scriptures, of Jewish cultic traditions, and of the literature of Hellenistic *Judaism. Still more important, he was a Christian of profound spirituality, a creative thinker with a penetrating intellect who wrote with authority to his church, from which he was temporarily absent. He probably wrote before the destruction of the *Temple in 70 AD, making his work one of the earliest NT writings.

The recipients, probably Hellenistic Jewish Christians, are recent converts, located possibly in Rome. More important for an understanding of the letter is the situation that precipitated it. Apparently a group within the church, having misunderstood some fundamental elements of Christian teaching, have taken a course of action which is leading to apostasy, and the community to division. The group-members are especially concerned about post-baptismal *sin and have lost faith in the eternal saving efficacy of Christ's *death; instead they are seeking *atonement in the ritual practices of Judaism, deserting Christian assemblies for the synagogue, and failing to live the Christian life with its goal of perfection exemplified in Jesus. This church is in crisis!

Authoritatively, yet with sensitivity, the author addresses this situation with profound theological teaching and exhortation. In doing so he provides evidence for the existence of a strand of NT theology not otherwise known. It focuses on the significance of Christ's death in a way that goes beyond anything else in the NT, producing sophisticated and distinctive perspectives on both the person of Christ and the Christian life.

Just as the writer assumes the readers' familiarity with the term 'Son of God', so he assumes their awareness of traditional Judaeo-Christian teaching about *God. God is the 'living God' (3: 12; 9: 14), judge of all (4: 12; 12: 23), who spoke formerly through *prophecy, and now has spoken in his Son (1: 1–12), who bears the stamp of God's nature (1: 3b). The Son shares God's eternal sovereignty (1: 13, cf. 13: 8) and reflects his glory (1: 3a).

Interwoven with this concept of the exalted Son is that of the authenticity of *Jesus' human nature. He, the eternal Son incarnate (2: 14), shared on earth the suffering, temptations, and weakness of mankind (4: 15; 5: 2) yet was sinless (4: 15). Through suffering he learned *obedience and attained perfection (2: 10; 5: 7–9), being perfect for ever (7: 28). It was his death, a necessary death, which, by God's *grace, delivered *humanity from death and from fear (2: 9; 2: 14–15) and led ultimately to his *Resurrection (13: 20) and exaltation into heaven itself where he sits at God's right hand.

To sharpen the readers' understanding, the writer introduces the distinctive *christological motif of Jesus as 'a high *priest after the order of *Melchizedek' (5: 10), a great high priest who has passed into God's presence (5: 6; 7: 24; 13: 8, cf. Ps. 110: 4), having made purification for sins (1: 3). Jesus' full humanity qualified him to become 'a merciful and faithful high priest' (2: 17) and his unique sinlessness (4: 15; 7: 26) enabled him to make the eternally valid expiatory *sacrifice of himself (1: 13), his dual role thus effecting universal access to God's presence (8: 2; 10: 20). By using Melchizedek, who antedates Levi (Gen. 14) as a model of non-Aaronic priesthood, the author is able to present not only the priestly function of Jesus, the son of God, of Davidic (royal) descent (cf. Ps. 110: 4), but also his superiority over the Levitical high priests and the sacrificial system of the Temple. Thus a new order replaced the old order (8: 13) and Jesus, the perfect Son and high priest, is the surety of a better *covenant (7: 22; 8: 6–13), while maintaining the essential faith of Judaism (11: 39–40). The writer is revealed here as a radical innovator with respect to his thinking about Jesus, a characteristic which is found in other aspects of his theology. This is 'high' christology at a very early stage in the development of Christian thought.

The overall picture in Hebrews of the Christian life is similar to that of other NT writers. However, the understanding of *faith, shown especially in the encomium in chapter 11, is distinctive. Here it involves an attitude of absolute trust in and dependence upon God, his words and his promises; it involves living in the present in total confidence that the goal of life in its fullness will one day be reached. Jesus the 'pioneer' and perfecter of faith (2: 10; 12: 2) has, as the forerunner and pathfinder (6: 20), successfully completed the race that Christians are called to run. The writer maintains that their sure hope will enable them to endure the inevitable suffering of the Christian way without which they would not learn obedience and become true sons of the Father (12: 5–7).

Hebrews has influenced both the *liturgy and the developing theology of the church throughout the centuries. No discussion, past or present, about the nature of the *ministry, the meaning of the *Eucharist, or the divine–human nature of Jesus, can ignore it.

Barbara Spensley

Attridge, H. W., *The Epistle to the Hebrews* (1989).
Ellingworth, P., *The Epistle to the Hebrews* (1993).
Hagner, D. A., *Hebrews* (1990).
Lane, W. L., *Hebrews* (2 vols; 1991).
Lindars, B., *The Theology of the Letter to the Hebrews* (1991).
Wilson, R. McL., *Hebrews* (1987).

Hegel, Georg Wilhelm Friedrich

(1770–1831), Christian philosopher. The son of a civil servant of the duchy of Würtemberg, as a young man (1788–93) Hegel studied at the *Lutheran theological seminary in *Tübingen, where he became a close friend of two fellow students, the future philosopher Schelling and the future poet Hölderlin. Thereafter he worked as a private tutor, in Bern and Frankfurt, before joining Schelling as a lecturer at the University of Jena in 1801. His career was severely disrupted by the chaos of the Napoleonic wars. Following the battle of Jena in 1806 he lost his job, becoming first a newspaper editor and then a schoolteacher, in Nürnberg. Eventually, however, in 1816 he was appointed professor of philosophy at Heidelberg; and then in 1818 moved to the University of Berlin. Here he was a colleague of *Schleiermacher's, with whom he had a rather uneasy relationship. His Berlin years brought him widespread fame and recognition.

Hegel's mature *philosophy of religion has been interpreted in a bewildering variety of ways. He himself claimed that it amounted to a systematic philosophical vindication of orthodox Lutheran faith; and this was the way his 'right-wing' disciples also interpreted it. *Kierkegaard's hostile polemic is a response to the flourishing of right-wing Hegelianism in the Danish Lutheran church of the 1840s. But his portrait of Hegel as a straightforward apologist for 'Christendom'—simply seeking, by philosophical means, to render faith easier for the liberal bourgeoisie—is nevertheless quite clearly a grotesque caricature.

Others of Hegel's immediate admirers, on the other hand (the 'left-wingers') have tended to regard his profession of religious orthodoxy as a regrettable veneer, overlying the deeper critical truth of his teaching. The most notable *nineteenth-century representatives of this attitude included such thinkers as D. F. Strauss, Feuerbach, and *Marx. Some have even gone so far as to suggest that Hegel himself was really a covert *atheist. Certainly, one may well question just how orthodox a Lutheran he was: in terms of theological heritage, he is actually perhaps more a follower of the *mystic Jacob Boehme than of Luther. Already in his lifetime he was being accused, by more conservative theologians, of being a pantheist, a charge to which he responded with scorn, questioning whether the term 'pantheism' ever has any real value in philosophical discussion. His own formula for the relationship of his philosophy to Christian religion is that it shares an identical content, but in another form. Arguably, however, Hegel is in fact not only the most radically philosophical of Christian thinkers, but also the

most profoundly Christian of philosophers, who developed a distinctive *christology.

Thanks to the survival of a number of early manuscripts, dating from the period 1793–1800 and unpublished in his own day, we are able to trace the original gestation process of Hegel's thought. These early writings are not yet the work of a philosopher; rather, Hegel writes here as a would-be religious reformer. Indeed, they constitute a savage indictment of church Christianity in general, resting on two main objections. In the first place, he urges the desirability of a true *folk religion. This would be the self-expression of a politically free-spirited people, by means of a richly celebratory representation of their *own* culture and history. At this stage, he sees the paganism of ancient Greece as an ideal model of folk religiousness. And bible-bound contemporary Christianity suffers badly from the contrast, in that its sacred narratives derive from a world that is alien to that of the actual worshippers.

Then, secondly, he has an *Enlightenment rationalist line of argument. He invokes the authority of *Jesus against the *church. In his writings of 1795–6 especially, he portrays Jesus essentially as a teacher of pure *Kantian ethics. Later, in *The Spirit of Christianity and Its Fate* (1798–9), he turns against Kant, because of the lack of an adequate 'folk-religious' element in Kantian theology. But throughout these early writings Hegel's basic diagnosis remains the same: the tragedy of Christianity is that the world of Jesus' day was not yet ready for the purity of his teaching. In *The Spirit of Christianity* we are told that what Jesus established was a community grounded in pure love, alone; but that that could not be sustained; and so the doctrine of *Incarnation emerged, simply in order to provide another, more effective basis for church unity, albeit at the cost of a complete sacrifice of rationality. It is only after Hegel became a philosopher, in his Jena years, that he came to see that the Incarnation might, after all, have another meaning.

Yet there is a sense in which his whole philosophy then takes shape, fundamentally, as an elaborate strategy for explicating that other meaning. The first formulation of Hegel's mature christology comes right at the end of his Jena text, *Faith and Knowledge* (1802), where he defines the very essence of philosophic truth as a 'speculative Good Friday'. This is further associated with a description of his own age as one which is, as never before, haunted by the feeling that 'God is dead'.

The main argument of *Faith and Knowledge* is a critique of three philosophical responses to this crisis—what might be called theological *agnosticism in its Kantian and Fichtean forms, and what might be called the *fideism of Jacobi, also associated with Schleiermacher—all of which, in Hegel's view, fail because of a lack of adequate historical self-awareness. But for the post-Enlightenment 'death of God' to be transformed into a 'speculative Good Friday' requires the truth of theological tradition to be resurrected in quite another mode of philosophy: one which would, by contrast, be absolutely exposed to all the vicissitudes of history, inasmuch as it defines the wisdom at which it aims precisely as the most deeply considered, and most comprehensively articulated, registering and reconciliation of all the various opposing spiritual pulls of the age. Such absolute exposure, or vulnerability, of thinking to historical experience is just what Hegel henceforth terms 'absolute knowing'. 'Speculative' becomes his technical term for a thinking which refuses to rest content with the sort of hard-and-fast distinctions giving fixed answers to questions whose real significance shifts, depending on context. He completely repudiates any other foundation for metaphysics. And this is also the basic sense in which he thinks philosophy will always need religion: since it is, above all, at the level of religious experience that the shocks are first felt, which philosophy then has to deal with.

The dogma of the Incarnation thus becomes in the first instance, for Hegel, a *metaphor for the necessary self-emptying of true speculative thought; its systematic abandonment of any defence mechanisms, against even the most immediately traumatic of new insights. Hence, too, his revival of the doctrine of the *Trinity. The whole structure of his explicit discussion of Christian theology is Trinitarian: in the *Phenomenology of Spirit* (1807), in the *Lectures on the Philosophy of Religion* (1821–31), and again in Part 3 of the *Encyclopaedia of the Philosophical Sciences* (1830). Hegel's Trinitarianism is a direct development of his commitment to the idea of a 'speculative Good Friday'.

Already in the earliest patristic versions of Trinitarian doctrine, *God the Father is not only the God of *Israel to whom Jesus prayed but also, for the most part implicitly, the God of *Platonist philosophy, set over against the Son and the *Holy Spirit somewhat as the pure conceptual thinking of philosophy—oriented towards the eternal and unchanging universal first principles of thought—is set over against the particular stories and images of popular faith. (In this respect the roots of the doctrine are actually in the pre-Christian Jewish Platonism of Philo.) Even though he does not himself discuss the early historical emergence of the doctrine as such, Hegel for the first time renders that implicit dynamism fully explicit.

For him, the life of the Trinity consists of the dialectical interrelationship between three modes of thought. In the 1831 *Lectures on the Philosophy of Religion* he expresses this in terms of three kingdoms. The 'immanent Trinity' is not just posited as existing, unthinkably, prior to the revelation of the 'economic Trinity' in salvation history. Instead, it appears as the specific truth of 'the kingdom of the Father', the domain of pure philosophic universality. Salvation history, for him, simply *is* the interplay between pure philosophy—the first kingdom—and that which is religiously other to it, in the other two. This otherness is, on the one hand, the truth of 'the kingdom of the Son': a thinking that is, as it were, incarnate in the passions of religious experience, as codified by theological dogma. And on the other hand it is the truth of 'the kingdom of the Spirit', emerging in and through the practical life of the community of faith, as that community has interacted with its environment, and so also with the challenge of pure philosophy.

The point is that to think about God is to think about authentic thinking; and vice versa. In Christian terms, thinking at its ethically most significant is a 'speculative Good Friday'. But in order to grasp this, in its full significance, it has to be thought through in all three of these modes. First, the fixed formulaic answers of un-'speculative' metaphysics have to be dissolved. Secondly, an appropriate language must be found, for thoughtful religious faith. Thirdly, against that twofold background, it is necessary for the thinking of each generation to orient itself as clearly as possible to its own distinctive historical situation.

Three modes of thought, three tasks. Hegel pursues the first task, systematically, in his *Science of Logic* (1812–16) and in the first two parts of the *Encyclopaedia*, on logic and philosophy of nature. The third task is really the dominant concern underlying his various Berlin lecture series—on the philosophy of *history, the history of philosophy, aesthetics, and religion—and his *Philosophy of Right* (1821). His handling of the second, more specifically christological, task is less clearly demarcated in textual terms than the other two.

Nevertheless, it remains pivotal. The key text in this regard is the *Phenomenology of Spirit*. At first sight the christological elements here may seem peripheral; yet appearances are deceptive. For, right at the heart of his argument in this work, Hegel moves on beyond the notion of the 'speculative Good Friday' to another, supplementary, level of christological interpretation. In effect, he sets out to answer the question first rigorously posed, and answered, by *Anselm: *Cur deus homo?* Why a God-man; what exactly is it about the human condition that required God to become incarnate, as the necessary means of our salvation? Hegel does not directly discuss the Anselmian doctrine, as such. But his is arguably the classic alternative answer to Anselm's.

The *Phenomenology* is an extraordinarily difficult work, seeking as it does to explore the processes of *Geist* (spirit/mind, both human and divine) at every level of experience, from the simplest and most private to the most complex of cultural constructs. But, throughout, the basic issue remains the same. *Geist* is the drive towards open-mindedness. What Hegel presents is a linked series of portraits, depicting various types of mentality, each one in terms of the limitations it tends to impose upon one's actually learning from one's own experience. One of the most fundamental requirements of *Geist*, however, is clearly the sheer elementary self-confidence to trust one's own experience, even when it conflicts with culturally reinforced prejudice. Hegel's term for this is 'freedom of self-consciousness'. And his name for the mental servitude it overcomes is 'unhappy consciousness'.

Unhappy consciousness may be either religious or irreligious in form, but it appears at its clearest where the false inner censor-self projects itself in the image of a despotic Lord God. Hence its clearest overcoming would be in a theology that decisively did away with that image. It is not enough for freedom of self-consciousness to be expressed in a merely abstract philosophizing, like that of Stoicism; nor is it enough for it to take shape as a merely playful all-encompassing scepticism. It needs religious embodiment. And that is why it is necessary for the Lord God to become *kenotically incarnate in a human individual; in the Pauline formula, 'taking the form of a servant'.

Thus, the truth of the Incarnation is a universal truth about human individuality in general: 'the infinite value of the individual as such'. But the problem is that by its very nature religious *symbolism particularizes, and the universal truth is all too easily concealed behind the particularity of the representative Individual. So it becomes the essential vocation of Christian philosophy to point beyond that particularity to the universal truth it represents. For Anselm, by contrast, the necessity of the Incarnation lies in the absolute difference of Christ from all other mortals: only his sufferings, as suffered by God, are infinite, and therefore adequate by way of compensation for the strictly infinite gravity of human sinfulness as an offence against God. But Hegel's educational, rather than juridical, soteriology has diametrically opposite implications.

There is no direct reference in the original passage on unhappy consciousness either to God or to Christ. This reticence is imposed by the sheer universality of the phenomenon. Yet the whole discussion is filled with more or less veiled allusions to Christian history, since that is where the issue most directly comes to a head. And then in the penultimate chapter of the *Phenomenology* unhappy consciousness reappears, this time explicitly associated with late Roman paganism, in its '*death-of-God' despair, preparing the way for Christian faith.

In his overall philosophy of history, Hegel sets out to construct a fully comprehensive account of the emergence of freedom of self-consciousness to full articulacy. The Incarnation forms the 'speculative mid-point' of this larger story, which moves from the beginnings of civilization right up to its culmination in the historical context that had, at long last, rendered possible Hegel's own clarification of the gospel. Of each form of civilization, Hegel's underlying question is: to what extent has it provided a truly effective cultural framework for the corporate affirmation of such freedom? Here, the religious-reforming impulse of his earliest essays resurfaces, transmuted into philosophical form. Ultimately, he now argues, the ideal context for freedom is a Christian culture organized in the form of a liberal secular state; with a strongly rooted religiousness, purged of unthinking traditionalism by the cumulative shocks of the *Reformation, the Enlightenment, and the French Revolution.

On the basis of subsequent historical experience, one may well question the durability of this actual conclusion. But the abiding challenge of Hegel's thought surely lies not so much in his historically limited conclusions as in his formulation of the basic criteria for theological truth, and in the way he thereby systematically opens the tradition up to creative further development.

See also GERMAN CHRISTIAN THOUGHT.   **Andrew Shanks**

Hegel, G. W. F., *Faith and Knowledge* (1802), ET (1977).
—— *Phenomenology of Spirit* (1807), ET (1977).
—— *Early Theological Writings*, ed. T. M. Knox (1948).
—— *Lectures on the Philosophy of Religion*, ed. Walter Jaeschke (1983–5), ET (1984–7).
Fackenheim, E., *The Religious Dimension in Hegel's Thought* (1967).
Houlgate, S., *Freedom, Truth and History: An Introduction to Hegel's Philosophy* (1991).
Jaeschke, W., *Reason in Religion: The Formation of Hegel's Philosophy of Religion* (1990).
Küng, H., *The Incarnation of God* (1987).
Lauer, Q., *Hegel's Concept of God* (1982).
O'Regan, C., *The Heterodox Hegel* (1994).
Shanks, A., *Hegel's Political Theology* (1991).
Toews, J., *Hegelianism: The Path Towards Dialectical Materialism, 1805–1841* (1980).
Walker, J., *History, Spirit and Experience* (1995).
Williamson, R. K., *Introduction to Hegel's Philosophy of Religion* (1984).
Yerkes, J., *The Christology of Hegel* (1983).

hell may be defined as a state (or place) belonging to rational beings who have totally rejected God or are rejected by God. There is little about this in the OT. Perhaps the closest it comes is the final verse of Isaiah (66: 24): 'They shall go forth and look on the dead bodies of the men that have rebelled against me; for their worm shall not die, their fire shall not be quenched, and they shall be an abhorrence to all flesh.' But this is little more than the provision of *symbolism for ideas still to come. The NT is very different, sharing in the common understanding of later Judaism. Hell (Hades or Gehenna), like the *devil to which it is home, is frequently mentioned. It is a place of *punishment for the wicked, torment, *fire, 'outer darkness', everlasting loss (Mark 9: 43–8; Matt. 5: 29–30; 22: 13; Luke 16: 23–31, etc.). It is especially the *judgement scene as described in Matt. 25: 31–46, one of the most influential of biblical passages, which has established the doctrine of hell, both theologically and for public imagination: 'Depart from me, you cursed, into the eternal fire prepared for the devil and his angels' (25: 41, cf. Rev. 20: 10–15). As Johann Michl concluded as late as 1970, 'Any attempt to mitigate the grave and terrible implications of the reality of hell... is bound to fail in view of the absolute clarity of scripture on this subject.'

Some of this, however, is less clear than it may seem. Thus if Luke 16 places the rich man in Hades, in insufferable heat, it suggests that he retains sentiments of *compassion for others incompatible with a developed theology of hell. Many of these passages represent highly coloured moral admonition rather than teaching about any final condition of sinners. Early Christianity was certainly not unanimous in recognizing any 'absolute clarity'. *Origen, its greatest theologian, held that hell might not be everlasting and *Augustine's arguments in reply (*City of God*, 21. 17, 23, and 24) make clear that Origen was not alone. Nevertheless, Origen's opinions were condemned by the fifth ecumenical council (553), whose authority, however, remains questionable. Augustine's very uncompromising view of hell and the multitudes committed to it prevailed for centuries, yet a retreat from it in stages seems undeniable. A first stage was medieval. Augustine held that all unbaptized babies went to hell and suffered 'mild' pain as punishment for original *sin. Aquinas rejected this conclusion. For him, original sin was not a fault meriting punishment, but only a lack of supernatural grace. Unbaptized babies were sent in consequence not to hell but a *limbo of natural happiness. Furthermore, the development of the doctrine of *purgatory helped establish the idea that people not holy enough at death to go to heaven need not go to hell, but could escape by undergoing a purifying fire.

Nevertheless, the majority of human beings, most theologians agreed, do end up in hell, including, the Council of *Florence insisted, all Jews, *heretics, and *schismatics unless they become Catholics before they die. 'Many are called, but few are chosen' (Matt. 22: 14) was quoted generation after generation as proof that only a minority ever reached heaven, despite the difficulty of reconciling this with the love and saving intention of God in Christ. After the *Reformation, Protestants, having rejected purgatory, were left once more with a stark heaven or hell choice. Perhaps the difficulty of believing that many people apparently unready for heaven necessarily went to everlasting punishment or that the latter was consonant with divine goodness and *mercy, made some question the doctrine. By the late 17th century, doubts were mounting, an Origenist *universalism re-emerging, and by the late 19th century Protestants were clearly divided between liberals who denied the doctrine of an everlasting hell, and conservatives who insisted that the NT left no doubt about the matter. Catholic theologians agreed with the latter. Hellfire sermons remained a central feature of every parish mission.

Only in the mid-20th century did Catholic theology move on to a new stage, as it came to be recognized that the 'many are called' text had been gravely misinterpreted in a typically fundamentalist way and provided no indication about how many people might be damned. Quite quickly the whole approach altered. Hell was no longer seen, except by *fundamentalists, in terms of satisfying divine justice by the imposition of vindictive punishment, but rather in terms of the inherent *freedom of the rational creature to say a final 'no' to God's truth and love. If there is no absolute reason to believe anyone is in the state of hell, one cannot rule out that possibility, given human power to be definitively autonomous: 'Better to reign in hell than serve in heaven', the conclusion of *Milton's Satan. Hell, Rahner insists, is no more than a possibility. But heaven is a reality. Yet, as truth and goodness are synonymous with being, their final rejection may rather signify a return to non-existence. In the light of divine goodness, is it plausible to think that God could allow anyone an eternity of misery on account of decisions taken in one brief life? It is sad that the symbols of NT teaching were used through an over-rationalized theology to make God appear a cruel tyrant and so justify comparably cruel punishments on earth. Indeed, it was often argued that the doctrine of hell was needed to restrain the wicked and ensure civil order. Nevertheless, the fading of hell strains traditional *eschatology to an extent seldom admitted. **Adrian Hastings**

Barth, K., 'The Determination of the Rejected', *Church Dogmatics*, II 2 (1957), 449–506.

Farrar, F. W., *Eternal Hope* (1878).

Küng, H., *Eternal Life?* (1995), 129–42.

Michl, Johann, 'Hell', *Encyclopedia of Biblical Theology*, ed. J. B. Bauer (1970), i. 369–71.

Rahner, K., 'The Hermeneutics of Eschatological Assertions', *Theological Investigations* (1966), iv. 323–46.

Rowell, G., *Hell and the Victorians* (1974).

Walker, D. P., *The Decline of Hell* (1964).

Hellenistic world in the 1st century.

The world within which the first three generations of the Christian movement were located and within which they defined themselves was Greek in cultural orientation in many different respects. After a history of imperial domination, first Greek, then Roman, the challenge faced by most of the peoples of the 1st century in their various states, kingdoms, and social formations around the Mediterranean was not *whether* to be of Greek orientation, but *in what ways* and *to what degrees* to be and remain Greek *and* whatever else they were in their traditional local cultures and societies. It was not so much that the peoples around the Mediterranean in the centuries immediately following Alexander's conquests simply became Greek. Hellenization (*hellenizein*) meant a much more complex set of phenomena affecting either directly or indirectly almost everyone in that area at that time. Within the new political economies that were the Greek and Roman empires almost everyone—Greeks and non-Greeks, Romans and non-Romans—became something different, with Greek culture as the dominant catalytic cultural force or template on which, in the light of which, or over against which, the transformations took place.

So the history of dominance that stretches back at least to the military conquests of Alexander in the 4th century BC must be the presupposition for the social and cultural transformations that had already taken place and that continued to take place among peoples and groups around the Mediterranean in the 1st century. Although

Greek culture also changed and developed in the new situation, most Greeks and Romans and most of Rome's 1st-century subjects doubtless understood the process as a one-way phenomenon—the Hellenization of the non-Hellenized world. Although it is argued here that this is too simple an explanation, it is none the less clear that it was Greek culture (Roman military-economic-political hegemony notwithstanding) that provided the dominant constructs within which the new social and cultural transformations were worked out.

The first three generations of the Christian movement should also be interpreted as creative sociocultural (trans)formation(s). They were nuanced translations and re-formations of 1st-century Hellenistic *Judaisms, both Palestinian and diasporic, which were themselves sociocultural transformations inspired and provoked by the new situation brought on by the Greek and Roman empires. Three of the arguably most important facets of Greek culture that influenced and reflected the formation and development of early Christianity are:

1. Language

Language is the basic reflector and transmitter of culture. The first generations of Christians thought about themselves and the world, talked and wrote to and about one another and others, in Greek. This situation was a given, not a mere reasonable option. Greek was the lingua franca of the Hellenistic kingdoms in the 1st century. Those who wanted to communicate beyond traditional local groupings, those who wanted to be a part of the local and regional markets and the Mediterranean-wide commerce that the *pax Romana* allowed, needed to communicate in Greek.

It is important to note that while Greek was lingua franca throughout the east, local and regional languages continued to be used. It was not simply that knowing, speaking, writing in Greek transformed individuals into Greeks. It was rather the fusion of the Greek language and culture with native languages and cultures that led to transformations, into something other than either Greek or traditional culture.

Adding to the complexity was the fact that the Greek language in question was not the Greek of the peoples of ancient Greece (*Attikos*). It was already another Greek, the language of the many (*koine*). Consider what it means that the texts of the NT are written in Greek, mainly the common Greek of the east: for the earliest Christians to speak and write Greek meant not simply becoming Greek; it meant negotiating and experimenting with new formations and identities, with 'Greek' as linguistic, rhetorical, and cultural springboard and main frame of reference.

2. Literary genres and rhetorical forms

As the springboard and main frame of reference for creative reconceptualizations, for the communication of new ideologies and the consolidation and development of the realities behind the ideologies, the common Greek of the eastern Roman empire inspired different literary genres and *rhetorical forms, and creative manipulations of such forms, in the centuries leading up to and including the 1st century. The earliest Christians were among those inspired. In fact, they became noteworthy and legendary, even in late antiquity, as a rhetorically creative and literarily productive group, both imitating older strategies and creating their own strategies of argumentation and persuasion. They borrowed quite a bit and experimented and adapted quite a bit. Their argumentation and efforts to persuade dramatically reflected the changed situation for rhetoric and politics involved in the change from the more culturally homogeneous Greek city-state to the less homogeneous Hellenistic and Roman empires. This involved, among other things, the change from reflecting on and responding to issues demanded by the narrowly constituted assembly (*ekklesia*) or council (*boule*), which called for deliberative, judicial types of speech. Now the need was to respond to the many different issues that the larger, more diverse and complex empires inspired and provoked.

Narratives of different types: 'gospels' as a type of biography and as a type of ancient history; letters: some dialogical, occasional, or circumstantial linked to specific historical situations, some general or monological connected loosely or not at all to such situations; apocalypses; homilies; hymns; handbooks; apologies; treatises; gnomic sayings; parenesis; oracles; laws: all these among the major rhetorical and literary genres functioned, differently but collectively, as the 'grammar' for expressing the earliest Christianities.

Long before the 1st century the various distinctively Greek forms of expression had already become hybrid—different translations, nuancings, and manipulations of rhetorical formations and literary genres had already taken place on the local and regional levels. For example, Jewish communities throughout the Mediterranean had already rather dramatically engaged and translated Greek forms of expression for their own purposes, not so much in order to become Greek as to be Jewish in response to specific challenges of empire. Their influence upon Christian engagements of such forms was the earliest, most prominent and, perhaps, most determinative. Such influence alone is enough to make the point that the engagement of different 'Greek' and other forms of expression is not simple.

3. Philosophical and religious formations and orientations

The Hellenistic kingdoms and the Roman empire also inspired and provoked on the local level a great deal of social and religious ferment and experimentation. There were social formations that were, if not entirely new, certainly intensifications or exaggerations of older formations or collectivities. These collectivities functioned as resocialization media for those for whom the comings and goings of empires were felt as the displacement, relativization, even destruction, of traditional societies.

Some of the social formations most often mentioned in efforts to characterize the social and religious character of 1st-century Christianities—households, clubs and voluntary associations, synagogues, mystery religions, philosophical schools, bands of wandering popular moralists—were already in evidence centuries earlier among Greeks, Romans, and others. Yet what these social formations meant among the Christians was reflective of their particular interests and anxieties as new groups. One example, the household, can illuminate the point. Among Greeks the household was the site of socialization, identity formation, and role assumption for free-born kindreds (wife, children, and father as head) at the centre and servants or slaves on the periphery. Christians (and other new peripheral groups) took this model and translated it into a site for the cultivation of fictive kinship relationships, *reso-cialization*, identity *reformation*, and other-worldliness. It was not so much that all things were new: some social and other differences and hierarchies still obtained. But these differences and hierarchies

were justified and commended on a different basis altogether: *en christo*, that is on the basis of the new world and the other-worldly orientation it requires.

It is in comparison with popular philosophical and religious movements of the Hellenistic-Roman period that earliest Christianity appears most other-worldly, and most dynamic and innovative in its employment of Greek traditions. The Hellenistic and Roman periods ushered in some intensifications and modifications, some developments and changes in religious cultic practices and in philosophical teachings and movements. By the 1st century there was already much evidence of such developments and changes. The preoccupation with the metaphysical and the physical on the part of the Academy and *Platonism and to a lesser extent the Stoa had given way to emphasis on practical matters: on ethics, or what form of life was most appropriate for the wise individual. While official traditional cults did not altogether disappear, they found themselves pressured to be more sensitive to personal religious sensibilities and yearnings. More emphasis was placed on personal salvation, on personal and rigorous forms of piety, and on personal relationships with divine figures. The new situation encouraged the mixing of the old gods and goddesses and the old cults with new cults and new divine figures. Thus, there was an atmosphere in which there was much borrowing and imitation, translation and reformulation. There was also movement away from entrenched and long-standing tradition toward acceptance of the claims of innovation (social, political, hermeneutical), reform, and new and different sources of authority. There was movement away from emphasis on systems and formal schools towards popular morality and ethics, especially towards other-worldly orientation.

It was just such orientation that came to distinguish Christians from among other critics of society in late antiquity. It was not that they were the only group so oriented; there is evidence of a whole subculture of other-worldly individuals and groups accused of misanthropy and of being 'enemies' of the empires. Apocalyptic seers and diviners, prophets, magicians, *astrologers, popular moralists, philosophers, self-styled pneumatics, and ascetics—these were some of the types of individuals and groups that modelled such orientations.

Christianity represented one of several types of Hellenistic-Roman other-worldly orientations. Christians were deemed by many to be more other-worldly than other groups because they were deemed more threatening. They were more threatening because they were more successful in drawing others into their fold and because they were of mixed social constitution, without clear or single ethnic identity or ancient roots. It was clear enough to both insiders and outsiders that the Christians, for all their diversity, were those most consistently and dramatically 'not of this world'. Yet even on this matter of being other-worldly, the early Christians proved themselves part of that world: they were other-worldly precisely in ways and forms inspired and delimited by the Greek (and Roman) world.

See also Pre-Constantinian Thought.   **Vincent L. Wimbush**

Aune, D., *The New Testament in its Literary Environment* (1987).
Balch, D. L., and Stambaugh, J. E., *The New Testament in its Social Environment* (1986).
Bowersock, G. W., *Hellenism in Late Antiquity* (1990).

Bulloch, A., Gruen, E. S., *et al.* (eds.), *Images and Ideologies: Self-Definition in the Hellenistic World* (1993).

Cohen, S., *From the Maccabees to the Mishnah* (1987).

Gruen, Eric S., *The Hellenistic World and the Coming of Rome* (1984).

Mack, B., *Rhetoric and the New Testament* (1990).

Meeks, W. A., *The Moral World of the First Christians* (1986).

Peters, F. E., *Harvest of Hellenism* (1970).

heresy was a dominant issue in the life of the early *church, and has continued to figure prominently throughout most of its subsequent history. The struggle between *orthodoxy and heresy is a witness both to the intellectual seriousness of the main Christian tradition and also to its fatal tendency to demonize its opponents, especially internal opponents; heretics were generally regarded as worse than outsiders, since they had some acquaintance with Christian *truth and yet set themselves in opposition to it.

The traditional account of the emergence of heresy is that the church began with a firm hold on Christian truth and that all heresy was later deviation from that original faith. Such deviations were often ascribed to the pride or ambition of the founder of the particular heresy, and, more significantly, in many cases explained as due to the malign influence of some particular philosophical school.

That picture no longer holds. The earliest churches are now seen to have been relatively diverse in belief and practice. Orthodoxy was something to be achieved rather than simply maintained. On this understanding heresy and orthodoxy alike were seeking to make sense of the faith in relation to the basic ideas of their milieu. Heresies are the attempts that were judged to have failed. The motivation of heretics was not significantly different from that of the orthodox, and they can even be seen as a necessary element in the difficult process of how best to articulate the faith in relation to the surrounding culture. In some cases indeed the fault of the heresy can better be seen as an unwillingness to adapt in the face of new ideas rather than as moving away from established truths.

Where churches, or groups within churches, were at loggerheads, a distinction was drawn between *schism and heresy. A schism was a split caused by personal rivalries or differences of practice, not involving any difference of belief, which was the distinguishing mark of heresy. The distinction was important but not absolute (if persisted in, schism implies a false doctrine of the church and thus falls over into heresy). Those entering the church from a schismatic body did not have to undergo *baptism, because they had been baptized in the true faith expressed by the Trinitarian name used in the rite of baptism, even if outside its proper context of the one true church. But heretics had to be baptized just like those coming into the church from paganism, because whatever baptismal formula might have been said over them it was not expressive of the true faith.

Many of the most important heresies of the early period involved divergent ways of speaking about the divinity of Christ in relation to God the Father or in relation to Christ's humanity (*christology). *Arianism, Apollinarianism, *Nestorianism, *Monophysitism, and Monothelitism all fall into this category. Christians were determined to understand the central point of their faith—the man *Jesus as divine saviour—at the deepest level. But this commendable concern was marred by the conviction that differing interpretations—on issues of ever-increasing precision—represented denials of the true faith that necessarily excluded those who held them

from the fellowship of the church and from salvation. That attitude towards heresy antedates the close links between church and state that began with the emperor *Constantine, but once those links were forged the power to act punitively against the perpetrators of heresy was greatly enhanced. In 386 AD Priscillian became the first person to be put to death for heresy.

The demonization of heresy had many unfortunate consequences. The early struggle between orthodoxy and heresy (for all its shortcomings) does bear witness to the intellectual vitality of early Christianity, but once the differences were institutionalized into Catholic church against heretical sect, serious engagement with the issues between them could much more readily give way to *rhetorical denunciation by a process of labelling opponents with the now well-established names of heresies from the past. Moreover, different understandings of the faith often went hand in hand with differences of a social or ethnic character. The *Donatist–Catholic divide in North Africa was partly of this kind, and the Arianism of Gothic Christianity was an added barrier between the Goths and the Catholic empire. Thus those very divisions, which like that between Jew and Gentile the gospel should have been helping to overcome, were in fact exacerbated by the fact that each group viewed the other as not merely misguided, but as wicked heretics.

In the medieval world, with the church's more unified and extensive control, dissident groups could quickly be designated heretical and the full weight of the church's disciplinary powers might be brought to bear against them, with the firm conviction that to do so was to fulfil the divine will (see INQUISITION). Nor did the Reformation break the mould. Not only did the traditional attitude towards heresy provide a basic framework for the justification of the intense hatred between Catholic and Protestant, but the same pattern quickly established itself between the differing forms of Protestantism. Michael Servetus' death by burning for heretical beliefs about the Trinity in *Calvin's *Geneva in 1553 was only one example of many such actions.

Capital punishment for heresy became much rarer in the centuries that followed. The last person to be executed for heresy in England was Edward Wightman in 1610. But the concept of heresy kept its hold on the mind of the church much longer. In most churches today there is an embarrassment about invoking it but also a reluctance to abandon it altogether. To appeal to it seems to align the church with a past divisiveness it is keen to disavow; to abandon it seems to imply indifferentism, a lack of serious concern for truth.

Underlying this ambivalent attitude is the deep division among Christians about the nature and sources of Christian truth. For those who believe that specific truths, necessary to human salvation, have been explicitly revealed by Jesus, through scripture or in the teaching of the magisterium, it is an essential part of the church's task (especially in an age of *secularism and widespread lack of belief) to maintain those God-given truths with clarity and firmness, excluding those who question or reject them. For those who understand *revelation in less clear-cut terms and see truth more as the goal of the church's search under the guidance of the Holy Spirit than as a deposit to be guarded, the category of 'heresy' (with all the unacceptable baggage it carries with it from the past history of the church) appears as a hindrance to the securing of truth rather than a means of preserving it. It is appropriate that the wider church should assess and express its mind on any new and divergent teaching that may grow up within it, but such judgments need to be, and to be seen to be, provisional and not absolute in character. There are too many cases from the past of teaching condemned in one generation that has become the orthodoxy of the next. The concept of 'heresy' implies a finality of judgment on the part of the church in matters of belief which is hard to justify.

Maurice Wiles

Bauer, W., *Orthodoxy and Heresy in Earliest Christianity* (1972).

le Boulluec, A., *La Notion d'hérésie dans la littérature grecque, IIe–IIIe siècles* (1985).

Rahner, Karl, 'What is Heresy?', in *Theological Investigations* (1966), v.

—— 'Heresies in the Church Today?', in *Theological Investigations* (1974), xii.

Wakefield, W., and Evans, A. P., *Heresies of the High Middle Ages* (1969).

Wiles, Maurice, 'Orthodoxy and Heresy', in I. Hazlitt, (ed.), *Early Christianity* (1991), 198–207.

hermeneutics derives from the Greek *hermeneuein*, to make intelligible, which has various shades of meaning: (1) to say, to express something, the sense in which it is used by *Aristotle in *On Interpretation*; (2) to translate from one *language into another; (3) to interpret, understand. Hermeneutics, as developed in modern times, means the critical theory of interpretation, its principles, rules, methods, and limitations. It first appears in the title of a work produced in 1654 in the context of *Protestant orthodoxy: J. C. Dannhauer's *Sacred Hermeneutics, or the Method of Expounding the Sacred Scriptures*. At the beginning of the 19th century *Schleiermacher conferred upon it the status of a discipline, recognized in theology and philosophy.

Its proper object can be defined in wider or narrower terms: as having a bearing only on the interpretation of written texts, making it a part of philology; or, with Schleiermacher, as concerned with the understanding of all human discourse, written or oral; or, with Dilthey, as dealing with every manifestation of the human spirit throughout history, in science, literature, or art. For Heidegger, hermeneutics becomes a fundamental procedure for understanding the structures of human existence. Today its meaning tends to be further and further extended, into a general theory of signs, or a general philosophy for interpreting all phenomena, making it difficult to define its boundaries with linguistics or epistemology. Depending on the degree of extension given to it, hermeneutics has a bearing on numerous disciplines, but it is chiefly relevant in the fields of philology, *philosophy, *theology, *history, jurisprudence, *psychology, and the *social sciences. While it has become an academic discipline, we must not forget that it is rooted in lived experience. We frequently put the hermeneutical question in everyday conversation: What do you mean by that? How am I to interpret your remarks? Did you understand what I told you?

Hermeneutical reflection plays an important part in religious tradition, for interpreting foundation-narratives, sacred texts, rites, doctrines, and rules of piety. This is particularly true of what are called the religions of the book, Judaism, Christianity, and Islam, each of which has developed its own rules of interpretation for its authoritative texts. Today, thanks to interreligious dialogue, we are able to measure more precisely how much the hermeneutical question has mattered in relations between these three religions, in particular between Judaism and Christianity when interpreting what one of them calls TaNaK (Torah-Nebiim-Ketubim) and the other the Old Testament.

For Christian thought, the roots of hermeneutics are to be found in the NT. Luke's gospel repeatedly shows Jesus interpreting (*dihermeneuein*) the scriptures to his disciples, notably on the road to Emmaus. In his encounter with the Ethiopian eunuch reading the prophet Isaiah, Philip the deacon puts the hermeneutical question *par excellence*: 'Do you understand what you are reading?' (Acts 8: 30). Writing to the Corinthians on the subject of speaking with tongues, Paul lays stress on the importance of the charism of interpretation (*hermeneia*, 1 Cor. 12: 10 and 14: 26–8). Primitive Christianity was clearly confronted from the start by the hermeneutical problem: first by concrete questions about translation and the handing on of tradition, then more particularly by the need to give Christian interpretations of OT texts and to relate the two testaments to each other. For this purpose, 2 Cor. 3: 6 ('the letter kills but the spirit gives life') became a hermeneutical rule, establishing the fundamental distinction between the literal sense, given in the very letter of the text, and the spiritual sense, hidden behind or beyond the letter. Patristic hermeneutics elaborated this distinction into various theories of the senses of scripture, the most thoroughgoing being those of *Origen in the east and *Augustine in the west. Both models also have ontological and anthropological implications: their idea of the reading process forms part of an essentially Neoplatonist concept of reality and of human nature.

The Middle Ages set about systematizing the patristic heritage, translating it into a fourfold scheme of the senses of scripture. This first appears in Cassian (5th century) and remains the guiding principle for centuries of *biblical exegesis. The four senses consist of the literal sense and three spiritual senses: *allegorical, tropological or moral, and anagogical. Nicholas of Lyra's mnemonic formula (14th century) defines them thus: *littera gesta docet, quid credas allegoria, moralis quid agas, quo tendas anagogia*. The letter teaches 'events and deeds', historical facts; the allegorical sense reveals in the texts 'what you are to believe', the church's doctrines; the moral (tropological) sense, 'what you are to do' (i.e. ethical exhortation); the anagogical sense, 'whither you are going', is the secrets of the end-time.

Under the influence of *Renaissance humanism, with its principle of 'back to the sources', *Reformation Protestantism gradually freed itself from the medieval scheme and brought about a vigorous renewal of hermeneutical reflection. The reformers integrated philological and historical work into their exegesis and focused attention once more on the literal sense, making it the criterion by which all interpretations should be judged. The letter of the text is important because in it is made manifest the full meaning of the word of God, which does not hide behind or beyond the letter but is clearly revealed there and nowhere else. This belief in the letter as the place in which the Spirit operates becomes the principle of *sola scriptura*, 'scripture alone', which is primarily a hermeneutical principle: scripture is its own interpreter and understanding it means entering into its own process of interpretation so as to be, in the end, interpreted by it.

This hermeneutical reflection on the part of the reformers was to make it possible, during the 17th and 18th centuries, for Protestant faculties of theology to meet the challenge of modern hermeneutics. But in the meantime, hermeneutics went through a phase of doctrinal hardening within Protestant orthodoxy. Orthodox theologians reaffirmed the *authority of scripture by identifying it literally with the word of God. This made it a sacred text in the absolute sense, infallible and divine in origin, requiring its own hermeneutics, *hermeneutica sacra*, as opposed to profane hermeneutics. Underlying such a reading is the dogma of verbal inspiration of the scripture (extending to the very vowel-signs of the Hebrew OT).

This *hermeneutica sacra* is the target attacked by the new movement of historical criticism in the 17th and 18th centuries. Its champions demanded the right to read the biblical texts like any other text (the principle of universality, often called the 'Semler principle', after an 18th-century German exegete). The historical approach seeks to interrogate the text critically, without presupposing any commitment to what it proclaims; to discern the origin and historical context of the biblical texts, the opinions they convey and the traditions they transmit. The emergence of this kind of critical thinking could not fail to provoke violent conflict with the representatives of orthodoxy, comparable with today's debate with *fundamentalism (see, for instance, the Chicago Declaration).

The implications of this new manner of reading are not fully developed until we come to Schleiermacher's hermeneutics at the beginning of the 19th century. Taking as his starting-point the basic human phenomenon of understanding, Schleiermacher laid the foundations of a general hermeneutics which Dilthey developed about a century later as an epistemology of the human sciences, historical science in particular. For Schleiermacher, working within the perspectives of German *Romanticism, understanding involves two stages: grammatical interpretation, bearing on the general structure of the language, and psychological interpretation, which seeks to delve into the author's inner world so as to enter into communion with him or her across all the intervening centuries.

In the 20th century hermeneutics has undergone a renewal by its encounter with *existentialist philosophy, beginning in the 19th century with *Kierkegaard. Inspired by Heidegger's analysis of the structure of existence, Rudolf *Bultmann developed the method of historical criticism into his programme for an existential interpretation of the biblical texts. What matters is the effect of the text on the person who receives it: the true goal of understanding is only reached when it becomes the reader's self-understanding in the light of the text. Bultmann's approach marks an important reorientation as against Schleiermacher: the centre of interest shifts from the author to what the text is really about, its 'thing' (*die Sache*), which, following Kierkegaard, Bultmann often calls the existential message of the text, or its *kerygma. From 1941 onwards, Bultmann was struggling to give this existential interpretation a concrete realization in his programme of *demythologizing, which provoked extremely lively debate. If the biblical texts are to be able to involve 20th-century man, he said, they have to be freed from the mythological picture of the world in which they are framed and given a different linguistic embodiment, accessible to modern readers.

Bultmann's NT hermeneutics has been developed by Gerhard Ebeling into a hermeneutics of dogma, rooted in the fundamental structure of proclamation (*Wortgeschehen*). Ebeling sees dogma as the effort of Christian faith to carry out its task of understanding

itself, assuming responsibility for itself, and expressing itself in intelligible discourse.

Bultmann's stress on the *Sache* of the text, its 'thing', has had an effect on philosophical hermeneutics, as can be seen in both Gadamer and *Ricœur, with very different perspectives. In *Wahrheit und Methode* (1960), Gadamer insists that understanding must be set within the fundamental continuity of tradition, stressing the importance of what has been effected in *history (*Wirkungsgeschichte*). Understanding strives to transcend all distortions of the truth by a progressive fusion between the horizon of the person understanding and the horizon of what is being understood. For Ricœur, on the contrary, the primary task is to take patient account of whatever 'othernesses' leap out as alien when confronting the text's 'thing'. They have a salutary distancing effect, guarding against hasty and over-direct assimilation of the message. The hermeneutical effort must lead to other strategies (explicative, reductive, critical) if the loosening and shifting of perspective is to bear its proper fruit.

Turning to today's challenges, we find that, after a long period during which the method of historical criticism and its derivatives have held a monopoly, the reading of biblical texts now displays a plurality of approaches, some complementary, some in competition with each other. Within this current scene, we often find patristic and medieval methods making a reappearance, if in new forms. We can say with Ricœur that our situation is one of a 'conflict of interpretations', in which he has already initiated a dialogue between three methods: (1) historical criticism, which tries to grasp the historical dimension of the texts, their origins, and the contexts in which they are rooted; (2) structuralism, a method which aims at discerning the inner linguistic structures of the text while abstracting from its context and history; (3) psychoanalytic interpretation, which looks for reflections in the text of psychic mechanisms, so as to enable the reader to discover his or her own psychic structure in the light of the text. Still other methods have developed in recent decades, some of which are outlined below.

Sociopolitical interpretation always focuses on two connected aims: to lay bare the relations of power and oppression reflected in the biblical texts and, at the same time, to find in them the potential for conscientization and political struggle. This type of interpretation forms part of the theology of *liberation. *Feminist readings, a variant of the above, put questions to the text about the relations between the sexes. Here there is the same double perspective: to expose the oppression of *women which the bible has legitimized or which it demonstrates indirectly, and to realize the potential which it nevertheless has for the liberation of women.

In contrast with these two models based on ideological conviction, there are others inspired by methods of reading. In recent decades literary studies have focused particularly on the nature of story and the narrative strategies which it calls into play. We now find this emphasis when approaching biblical texts, which are mostly narratives. How is a story able to express theology? What narrative strategies are employed in proclaiming the gospel? How does a story convey its message to its readers? After a long period of concentrating on the author, the text, and its context, interest is now being shown in the reader: the reader's response has a bearing on the meaning that he or she extracts from a text. Hence hermeneutics is concerned with various theories about the act of reading and the aesthetic reception of the text.

Taking a critical view of the method of historical criticism, seen as linked too unilaterally to certain presuppositions of the modern era, some kinds of hermeneutics are now trying to adopt *postmodern ideas and use them theologically, for instance by bringing out the ambiguity of the biblical texts, the shifts in meaning that they display, or, in the style of Derrida, by deconstructing the ultimate certainties at work in them.

All this plurality is stimulating. It forces hermeneutics to re-examine critically various points which had until recently been regarded as established, and faces it with a number of current challenges. For a long time it was assumed that a text has just one primary meaning which it is possible to ascertain. Now we are asking ourselves whether there is not rather a plurality of meanings in a text, so that it is hardly possible to fix the one true meaning, and we may have to be content with determining the limits of what we can make it say. It was once possible to think that the meaning was all there, complete, in the text and that all we had to do was to get it out. Today we have rediscovered the reader's part in constructing the meaning: meaning emerges in the constant interaction between the text acting on the reader and the reader's way of receiving it. Such a perspective involves a call to hermeneutics to reflect on an ethic of interpretation.

It is necessary to look critically at the universalist principles with which modern hermeneutics has worked: today we are asking questions about the necessary contextuality (social, political, cultural, etc.) of the process of interpretation. The interpreter (or, rather, the interpreting community) is not an abstraction but a concrete reality which hermeneutics needs to examine critically.

As against the traditional aim of arriving at what the text itself intends, recent methods invite us to interrogate texts about what they tend to hide or to present in truncated or alienated form. This leads us to consider putting into practice what Ricœur calls the hermeneutics of suspicion. Postmodern work has made us aware of how texts connect with other texts, of how they reinterpret and comment on each other. This prompts us to give fresh consideration to the question of intertextuality. The interpreter cannot abstract from the interplay of texts with each other, but is part of that interplay, and, if he or she does not take full account of it, will fall victim to it. These points suffice to show that today, more than ever, hermeneutics is a wide-open task.

It is obvious that theological hermeneutics has had a strong and permanent influence on the general hermeneutics of western culture. But for nearly two centuries hermeneutics has become an autonomous discipline, fed by numerous contributions from other disciplines. This means that theological hermeneutics should not turn in upon itself and shut itself into its own traditions, a temptation which has been strengthened in our day by the reappearance of various forms of fundamentalism preaching uncritical and often servile readings of the text. Theological hermeneutics needs to enter into interdisciplinary dialogue; only on this condition can it continue to make its voice heard in the chorus of hermeneutical research. What is at stake is, as always, the human being, summoned to know and discover him- or herself before God in the act of reading. 'You are the man!' (2 Sam. 12: 7) remains forever the challenge which the interpreter must face.   **Pierre Bühler**

Bühler, P., and Karakash, C. (eds.), *Quand interpréter, c'est changer: Pragmatique et lectures de la Parole* (1995).

Bultmann, R., 'New Testament and Mythology: The Problem of Demythologizing the New Testament Proclamation', in S. M. Ogden (ed.), *New Testament and Mythology and Other Basic Writings* (1941), ET (1984).

—— 'Das Problem der Hermeneutik' (1950), in *Glauben und Verstehen*, 5th edn. (1968), ii.

Caputo, J. D., *Radical Hermeneutics: Repetition, Deconstruction, and the Hermeneutic Project* (1987).

Ebeling, G., 'The Significance of the Critical Historical Method for Church and Theology in Protestantism' (1950) and 'Word of God and Hermeneutics' (1959), both in *Word and Faith* (1963).

Eco, U., *Limits of Interpretation* (1990).

Gadamer, H.-G., *Truth and Method* (1989).

Gusdorf, G., *Les Origines de l'herméneutique* (1988).

Jeanrond, W. G., *Theological Hermeneutics: Development and Significance* (1991).

Laks, A., and Neschke, A. (eds.), *La Naissance du paradigme herméneutique: Schleiermacher, Humboldt, Boeck, Droysen* (1990).

Patte, D., *Ethics of Biblical Interpretation: A Re-evaluation* (1995).

Pyper, H. S., *David as Reader: 2 Samuel 12: 1–15 and the Poetics of Fatherhood* (1996).

Ricœur, P., *Conflict of Interpretations: Essays in Hermeneutics* (1969), ET (1989).

—— *From Text to Action: Essays in Hermeneutics* (1991).

Thiselton, A. C., *New Horizons in Hermeneutics: The Theory and Practice of Transforming Biblical Reading* (1992).

Tracy, D., *Plurality and Ambiguity: Hermeneutics, Religion, Hope* (1987).

higher criticism, a term used interchangeably with historical criticism in *nineteenth-century biblical studies, its counterpart being lower, or textual criticism. Modern usage prefers the term historical criticism. There are two views on its origins: that it arose within the 17th-century legal and classical humanist tradition, or that its seeds were present in the critical attitudes to the bible of *Luther and *Calvin and bore fruit in 18th-century German Protestant *Pietism. There is truth in both positions, the underlying issue being whether historical criticism is alien to Christian theology or a product of it.

Critical attitudes to the bible were fostered by the humanist Dutch lawyer Hugo Grotius (1583–1645) who regarded OT law (see LAW, BIBLICAL) as incomplete and archaic, and by Baruch (or Benedict) Spinoza (1632–77), a Dutch Jew who was repudiated by his co-religionists and who drew attention to repetitions, contradictions, and inconsistencies in the OT. A French Catholic priest, Richard Simon (1638–1712), rejected traditional views of the authorship of the OT books and attributed their composition to scribal schools. The *deists in Britain attacked the immoral behaviour of model characters such as *David, and the absence of a belief in *immortality in the OT.

These critical impulses from differing countries and traditions indicate that no single theory can account for the rise of historical criticism. However, particular social conditions were necessary for it to become professionalized, and these were found in the twenty or so Protestant theological faculties in German universities from 1750. Aspiring scholars were required to undertake original research to gain a doctorate or licentiate, the results of research being communicated through scholarly journals. These social conditions were supplemented by a willingness in certain German Protestant circles to re-express Christian doctrine in terms drawn from contemporary *philosophy, which meant in practice the critical philosophy of *Kant. German Pietism, with its stress on experience and indifference to doctrine, was also a factor. By 1800 historical criticism in Germany had reached the point where *Genesis had been divided into two or more sources, the unity of authorship of *Isaiah and *Daniel had been disputed, the interdependence of the first three *gospels had been demonstrated, and *miraculous elements in the OT and NT had been explained as resulting from the primitive or pre-scientific outlook of the biblical writers.

A decisive advance occurred in 1806–7 with the publication of the *Beiträge zur Einleitung in das Alte Testament* (*Contributions to OT Introduction*) of W. M. L. de Wette (1780–1849). This was the first work to use historical criticism to propose a version of *Israel's religious history radically at variance with the account given in the OT itself. De Wette was simply trying to make sense of contradictions such as that Deuteronomy, attributed to *Moses, requires Israelites to offer sacrifice only at a single, central sanctuary, whereas it is apparent from other parts of the OT that such people as Samuel, Elijah, and Amos were unaware of such a command. De Wette's solution was that the laws said to have been given by Moses at the beginning of Israel's history came from much later periods.

Criticism openly acknowledged to be influenced by *Hegel's philosophy appeared in 1835–6 in the *Biblische Theologie* of W. Vatke and in D. F. Strauss's *Life of Jesus* (see QUEST FOR THE HISTORICAL JESUS). Vatke gave greater precision to de Wette's position, while Strauss attacked the credibility of *John's gospel as a historical source for the words and works of *Jesus. He also maintained that the gospel tradition was '*mythical', that is, so profoundly shaped by 1st-century Jewish expectations and pagan mythology that it was evidence only for how Jesus' earliest followers understood him, not material from which a historical Jesus could be recovered. F. C. Baur (1792–1860) attempted to restore credibility to the history of Christian origins seeing the NT as the synthesis of the dialectical opposition between *Pauline and Jewish Christianity.

It has been fashionable to reject Hegelian-inspired biblical criticism simply for being Hegelian. However, many of its proposals arose from tensions in the bible itself and some of its conclusions, for instance that John's gospel is essentially 'spiritual' or that the NT owes something to the clash between Pauline and Jewish Christianity, have become commonplace in academic biblical scholarship, in a modified form.

That historical criticism is not inherently inimical to Christian belief is shown by the case of William Robertson Smith (1846–94), a member of the Free Church of Scotland and a pioneer in establishing the final form of the position first outlined by de Wette and classically stated in 1883 by Julius Wellhausen in his *Prolegomena zur Geschichte Israels* (*Prolegomena to the History of Israel*). As a convinced *evangelical Smith believed that historical criticism was a continuation of the *Reformation's recovery of the bible, and a necessary tool to enable intelligent churchgoers to make sense of it. A similar view was powerfully advocated a generation later by the Primitive *Methodist biblical scholar A. S. Peake (1865–1929). Both denied strongly that accepting historical criticism involved rejecting the supernatural origins of Christianity. Catholic resistance to historical criticism was overcome by the pioneering work of the French *Dominican M.-J. Lagrange, first director (1890) of the École Biblique in Jerusalem, and by the *Jesuit Augustin Bea, who played a vital part in the publication of the papal encyclical *Divino afflante spiritu* (1943) sanctioning historical criticism.

While historical criticism has been influenced by many factors its prime source is the biblical text and the problems it contains for readers with critical awareness. In the hands of non-believers it can be pressed to positions that may be embarrassing to traditional Christian belief. It is not, however, inherently hostile to Christianity but potentially liberating for Christians who wish their faith to be intelligently grounded and intellectually honest.

J. W. Rogerson

Greenslade, S. L. (ed.), *The Cambridge History of the Bible* (1963), iii.

Kümmel, W. G., *The New Testament: The History of the Investigation of its Problems* (1973).

Reventlow, H. G., *The Authority of the Bible and the Rise of the Modern World* (1984).

Rogerson, J. W., *Old Testament Criticism in the Nineteenth Century: England and Germany* (1984).

Hildegard of Bingen (1098–1179).

Few medieval figures enjoy as much popularity in the contemporary world as Hildegard of Bingen, and her current influence reflects exactly the combination of authentic discovery and creative misreading which so often characterizes modern appropriations of the *spiritual past. She appears in some ways to be very much a 12th-century phenomenon, in her rationalistic optimism, her persistent interest in questions of cosmology, her openness to the use of *art in the service of theological truths. Much of this is true too of the school of Chartres, especially the work of Bernard and Thierry of Chartres. Hildegard may also have been influenced by some of the same Platonic texts that were read at Chartres, most notably *Plato's own *Timaeus* and works by Scotus Eriugena. From another perspective however, she seems to stand alone. Her creativity, curiosity, and the strongly personal coloration of her spiritual and artistic vision recommend her work to us today—in suitably abbreviated form—as a foundational part of the western tradition. Of particular interest is the way in which she felt able to explore distinctively feminine aspects of the revelation, or to approach Christianity at times from a distinctively feminine perspective. The former is apparent in her imaginative and repeated use of feminine imagery to express the dynamic and creative qualities of *God, while the latter is shown in her facility for bringing the experience of *women to bear at least to some extent on some of the major moral and doctrinal themes of the day. For this we have reason to be grateful. But the very freedom which allowed Hildegard to develop in this way is again a reminder of the extent to which she belongs as a phenomenon to the 12th century, to a period before the rapidly increasing centralization and clericalization of the *church and the rise of the universities.

Hildegard herself presents the figure of a complex and intriguing personality, an abbess imperious towards kings and popes but not free of self-doubt, deeply touched by God but not free of social inhibitions (a certain snobbery perhaps). Although essentially a conservative figure, indebted to the spirit of orthodoxy and deeply committed to her work as a didactic proclamation of the Christian gospel, Hildegard also transcends the parameters of her age. Most interestingly, we sense in her writings the conflict of controlling and liberating paradigms, especially where issues to do with the nature and equality of women are concerned, and we cannot fail to be moved by what is essentially a far-ranging systematic theological vision, centred upon the theme of the fertility and fecundity of God. It is this that constitutes the unity of her work, finely expressed in the recurrent image of *viriditas*, or 'greenness', which denotes life-giving *grace as a quality of God and the saints, of the church and the sacraments, and of the living body of the earth.

Oliver Davies

Bowie, Fiona, and Davies, Oliver (eds.), *Hildegard of Bingen: An Anthology* (1990).

Lautenschläger, Gabriele, *Hildegard von Bingen: Die theologische Grundlegung ihrer Ethik und Spiritualität* (1993).

Newman, Barbara, *Sister of Wisdom: St Hildegard's Theology of the Feminine* (1987).

Hinduism,

like Christianity, stands for a range of religious ways of life, some reaching back to great antiquity. Both Hinduism and Christianity are now world *religions each numbering many millions of adherents. Both—but especially Hinduism—display a marked internal diversity, and they have developed in very different cultural milieus.

A distinction must be made between attitudes towards Hinduism that Christians have expressed *as Christians*, involving an underlying theology, and attitudes professed by Christians in other capacities; as politicians, scholars, administrators, and so on. This article focuses on the first of these, though the distinction has often been blurred, with important consequences.

Those known as St Thomas Christians represent the earliest noteworthy Christian presence in (south) India, from about the 4th century, but they took little interest in Hinduism. It was the arrival of Europeans in appreciable numbers (Portuguese in the west in the 15th century, British in several locations in the 17th) and their interaction with Hindus and Hinduism that stimulated Christian theological approaches to Hinduism. These approaches can broadly be classified as Catholic and Protestant, though the labels cover a range of variously nuanced, and sometimes significantly overlapping, views.

Early European non-Catholic approaches, generally evangelical in character, tended to depict Hinduism as an irredeemable mixture of the repellent and the bizarre, a characterization persisting among evangelical theologians to the present day. The *Baptist *missionaries of Serampore (Srirampur) in the Bengal area in the early 19th century are typical of this approach. Nevertheless, the famous debates about the nature of God between one of their number, Joshua Marshman, and the educated Hindu, Rammohun Roy, led to a new appreciation of Christ among the westernized Bengali élite as an ethical ideal in a unitarian context, with far-reaching consequences for indigenous social and political reform.

Early Roman Catholic thinking, whilst also condemnatory to some extent, showed a tendency to distinguish 'natural' truths of reason from practices upon which truths of revelation, and supernatural grace, could exercise their leavening effect. Seventeenth- and 18th-century *Jesuit activity in India, by Italian and French Jesuits respectively, tended to be adaptive of Hindu customs. A notable practitioner was the Italian Jesuit Roberto de Nobili, who tolerated the hierarchy of caste as part of the natural order, and worked with some success to evangelize Brahmins within this framework. There is still ambiguity in Catholic missionary strategy on this matter, with recent *dalit* theology in particular, both Cath-

olic and Protestant, vigorously repudiating caste discrimination (see INDIAN CHRISTIAN THOUGHT).

In the 19th century, with most of the subcontinent falling under British hegemony, Christian attitudes developed on the basis of a more comprehensive and scholarly grasp of Hinduism. British administrators and scholars allowed Christian presuppositions to shape their understanding of Hinduism as a tradition which may have had a commendable past but had markedly degenerated in the present. This assessment was accepted not only by evangelical Christian missionaries but also by westernized Christian converts, both Protestant and Catholic. Nevertheless, in both camps in the late 19th and early 20th centuries there were influential voices seeking to rehabilitate aspects of Hinduism in terms of some form of fulfilment theology. Among prominent Protestant thinkers were Krishnamohan Banerjea, who contended that ideas of *sacrifice in the Sanskrit scriptures, the Vedas, bore witness to a primitive divine *revelation prefiguring the true revelation of Christ, and J. N. Farquhar, who argued that Christian faith was *The Crown of Hinduism* (the title of his outstanding work). Catholic voices include the Jesuit monthly *The Light of the East*, whose theme was the fulfilment of Hindu religion—more particularly, aspects of the Sanskritic tradition—in Christian faith, and the influential Brahmabandhav Upadhyay, who maintained that as a Hindu Catholic he could (and should) be a Catholic by faith but Hindu by culture.

In the context of Indian independence, both Protestant and Catholic thinkers showed an increased tendency towards *dialogue with Hinduism, on an intellectual or practical basis. As scholarship on Hinduism has become methodologically more mature, this trend has become more marked. Swami *Abhishiktananda and Sister Vandana are representative of a more contemplative approach, while V. Chakkarai, R. De Smet, P. Devanandan, I. Hirudayam, E. Lott, R. *Panikkar, and S. Samartha are some names among many who have entered into dialogue at a more theoretical level. Jyoti Sahi is noteworthy for incorporating Hindu themes into his Christian paintings. Much, however, remains to be done if Christians are to shake off the charge, still current, that their faith is something alien to India.

In the latter half of the 20th century the rise of *dalit* theology, the *politicized theology of the oppressed or most marginalized groups, shows a new trend in Christian attitudes. Most Indian Christians belong to *dalit* communities, and the theology formulated in their name seeks to incorporate many hereditary beliefs and practices in an attempt to affirm *dalit* history and to identify the Sanskritic tradition as the source of their traditional oppression.

See also CONTEXTUAL THEOLOGY; GRIFFITHS, BEDE; THOMAS, M. M.

Julius Lipner

Ballhatchet, K., *Caste, Class and Catholicism in India, 1789–1914* (1998).

Forrester, D., *Caste and Christianity: Attitudes and Policies on Caste of Anglo-Saxon Protestant Missions in India* (1980).

Lipner, J., *Brahmabandhab Upadhyay: The Life and Thought of a Revolutionary* (1999).

Massey, J., *Towards Dalit Hermeneutics* (1994).

Panikkar, R., *The Unknown Christ of Hinduism* (1981).

Sharpe, E. J., *Faith Meets Faith* (1977).

history

is basic to Christian belief and self-understanding. The evocation of remembered events and an interest in historical method have been characteristic of Christian life in almost all periods. Like so much in Christianity, this began in part as an inheritance from Judaism. The long march from *Adam and *Abraham via *Moses, *David, and the *exile to Second *Temple Judaism was incorporated within the Christian *memory and remained paradigmatic for further historical understanding, but a wholly new dimension was provided by belief that the historical life and death of *Jesus, while fulfilling the meaning in that long march, inaugurated a new age. It would be centuries before the usage of chronicling history in terms of AD (the years of the Lord, beginning with the birth of Jesus) and, still later, BC (before Christ), was invented, but this decisive reshaping of history in terms of Jesus was implicit in Christian belief from the start. It already appears in the opening lines of one of the earliest Christian writings, *Hebrews: 'In many and various ways God spoke of old to our fathers by the prophets; but in these last days he has spoken to us by a Son.' The *apostles are identified as eyewitnesses of events that have actually happened and a sense of the way in which precise historical particularities had become of central importance is suggested by another early text, *Paul's insistence in 1 Corinthians that 'the Lord Jesus on the night that he was betrayed took bread' (11: 23).

But it is in *Luke–Acts that Christian history is first related to general history in so deliberate a way as to suggest a relationship of mutual significance. Thus the account of Jesus' birth begins 'in those days a decree went out from Caesar Augustus that all the world should be enrolled' (Luke 2: 1), while that of his ministry again starts with a Roman reference: 'In the fifteenth year of the reign of Tiberius Caesar, Pontius Pilate being Governor of Judaea, and Herod tetrarch of Galilee … the word of God came to John' (Luke 3: 1–2). This linkage does not end with Jesus' life. Acts provides a first history of Christianity, the springboard for all later histories of the church, but it too is written quite emphatically within this larger context and the story ends, not accidentally, in *Rome with Paul's arrival there.

Yet, as a whole, the NT, while in most of its books clearly regarding the memory of things that actually happened as central to its subject, leaves the relationship of Christian history to general history unexplored. *Revelation, perhaps the least historical and most confrontational of NT literature, may regard Rome and all earthly civilizations under the rubric of 'Babylon', an empire of the *devil, Luke–Acts may hint already at an affinity between church and empire, but in general it is more a sense of simple otherness that prevails: the things of God as proclaimed by Jesus and cherished by early Christians have little in common with the things of Caesar. Christian thinkers seeking a paradigm for the interpretation of public and political history have always had to turn to the OT far more than the NT.

The greatest historian of early Christianity, Eusebius of Caesarea (260–340), wrote his *History of the Church* in the early days of the Christian empire. He had himself been imprisoned during the 'great persecution', became Bishop of Caesarea shortly after it ended, and set himself to chronicle the church's entire history across persecution and heresy to 'the kind and gracious deliverance accorded by our Saviour', that is to say the peace of the church following the Edict of Milan. When *Constantine became emperor of the east as well as the west in 324, Eusebius became a great Constantinian, and the final chapter of his history is a eulogy to the 'mighty victor, pre-eminent in every virtue' who had reunited the empire and so established Catholicism that empire and church could now enjoy a common history. He followed this with a *Life of Constantine*, and the *Tricennial Oration* in honour of the thirtieth anniversary of the emperor's accession to power. In these writings Eusebius established a model for Christian history, a model building upon the Lucan approach but going vastly beyond it: divine *providence had prepared the empire for Christ and his church. Secular history is thus absorbed providentially within a Christian history through the perceived mission of the empire which takes on the 'chosen' role accorded in the OT to *Israel. Constantinople, capital of the Christian empire, fuses Jerusalem with Rome. This provided the standard *Byzantine view for many centuries and passed to Moscow, self-understood as 'third Rome'. Such a philosophy has also been powerful in the west but has here been in contention with a very different approach, shaped by *Augustine.

In 410 the Goths sacked Rome and many people blamed this disaster upon Christianity and the abandonment of the empire's traditional gods. In reply Augustine composed across many years the vast, rambling, twenty-two books of the *City of God*, in which Rome with its mixture of good and bad qualities became one among many empires, subject to the law of rise and fall of all earthly powers, essentially distinct from a far more mysterious reality, the 'City of God'. General history was thus secularized, even accepted as cyclic, and Constantine became of slight significance. Ever since, these two models of history, Eusebian and Augustinian, have jostled within the Christian tradition, though the regression of Orosius, Augustine's disciple, in his much-used *Historia adversus paganos*, towards a more distinctly Eusebian view helped ensure that even in the west secular history has frequently been sacralized. Again and again a great 'Christian' empire has been hailed by its upholders as providential centre-point for historical understanding, a new chosen people replacing Israel. Spaniards saw the greatness of 16th-century Spain blessed by God with the discovery and riches of America in this light; Bossuet defined Louis XIV's France similarly in his *Discourse on Universal History*, written for the education of the dauphin. Here universal history culminates in the French monarchy, the empire having been carried through Charlemagne from Rome to the Franks. The English began to believe the same of themselves in the Elizabethan age and became still more convinced of it in the Victorian; once again Christianity, this time in *Protestant guise, and a world empire had come together in an unmistakably providential way, enabling a new *missionary movement to penetrate throughout the world. America with its sense of 'manifest destiny' and global power has been seen by many of its citizens in the same way in the 20th century. It may be noted that *liberation theology, while turning this imperialist theology of history on its head, has maintained a comparable paradigm: the 'chosen people' of the OT is replicated but precisely among the poor and oppressed, not the rich and powerful.

Sixteenth-century Spain, 17th-century France, 19th-century Britain, and 20th-century America have all been great producers of foreign missionaries. Each has thus enjoyed a religious centrality extending beyond its political power. It would be hard to deny all plausibility in such a providential reading of the course of world history, one combining Augustus, Constantine, Charlemagne, Philip II, Louis XIV, Victoria, and the America of Billy Graham in an ongoing divine conspiracy for the spread of Christianity, but the secular historian and the critical theologian are unlikely to be convinced. History is a more confused, less unilinear matter than that. Augustine seems a safer guide when the particularities of history's ceaseless ins and outs, stripped so far as possible of the simplifications of mythology, are analysed.

Seventeenth-century France was the initial home for just such a scientific approach, pioneered by some of the greatest of Christian historical scholars, Tillemont and Mabillon. Also among them Richard Simon, an Oratorian, extended the field of historical sciences to the OT and came to deny that Moses wrote the Pentateuch. Bossuet, aware of an incompatibility between his views of history and Simon's, demanded unsuccessfully that the latter's works be burnt. In fact they led the way for the modern study of the bible. The development of the historical study of both the bible and early Christianity in the 19th century, above all in Germany, from F. C. Baur to Harnack, while undermining many earlier Christian presuppositions, was faithful to Christianity's inherent preoccupation with history rather than *myth. It did much to ground the whole modern scientific approach to history in the most exacting scrutiny of documents, but it also brought about fundamental shifts in theological understanding. The latter has acquired in consequence an inescapably historicist sensitivity to everything within its own tradition, despite attempts by Protestant *fundamentalists, Catholic *ultramontanes, and others to depict truth, biblical or ecclesial, as somehow capable of escaping historical context. While general history, for Bossuet, was still something capable of encapsulation within a rigid biblical frame extended to include the French monarchy, history is now itself the frame within which both *revelation and church have to be interpreted. This, however, may be less a capitulation to modern secularist history, seen as something alien to the Christian tradition, than the outworking of fidelity to Augustinianism and even to the inner logic of *Incarnation.

Christians have continued to contribute immensely to the enterprise of historical writing, in practically every field, most of it far from polemical, and in the footsteps of Simon rather than Bossuet. It has become a naturally ecumenical area. It is sufficient to recall the names of three outstanding Regius Professors of Modern History in the University of Cambridge in the second half of the 20th century: David Knowles, a Catholic, Herbert Butterfield, a Methodist, and Owen Chadwick, an Anglican. Congruence of mind between historian and Christian believer remains a significant element within modern Christian thought.

It is noticeable that Christians were far from quick to develop a chronology of history based on the birth of Christ, in contrast with Muslims who, beginning six centuries after Christianity, were actually the first to establish a religious era, basing it on the hijra, Muhammad's flight from Mecca to Medina. This was done within a decade of his death in 632. Unlike Islam, Christianity had no inherent commitment to a public reshaping of human society in theocentric terms. For the most part, imitating Luke's 'in the fifteenth year of Tiberius Caesar', Christians were happy to use one or another of the secular Graeco-Roman systems, most often based on the reigns of emperors. It was only when in the west the Roman order had quite collapsed so that dating years by consulates or the reigns of emperors had become wholly anachronistic that Bede, writing in 8th-century Northumbria, popularized a system based on an approximate but inaccurate dating of Christ's birth. It was a

pragmatic rather than a theological move and yet reflected a vision of Christ's centrality in history present from the start.

If historical science is the pursuit of truth within a field where the subtle analysis of probabilities can get one very far but mathematical certainty is unattainable, one can never simply move from history to *faith, but history can make some forms of faith possible only for the irrational. While history cannot decide what is theologically true, it can do much to tell us what cannot be true, what is merely bad *dogma, deriving from past failings of understanding. *Newman's recognition, both as theologian and historian, of something he called '*development', an inevitable evolution in belief and its formulation across the centuries, historicized dogma, undercutting most previous attempts to formulate the dynamics of doctrine, Protestant or Catholic, and led to his disillusion with Anglicanism. The two most forthright Catholic opponents of papal *infallibility in 1870, Ignaz Döllinger and Lord Acton, were both outstanding historians. For Döllinger at least his historical judgement brought disillusionment with Roman Catholicism. Catholics and Protestants alike have used the appeal to history to throw doubt on beliefs they disagree with, at times very convincingly, while numerous agnostics from Gibbon on have used history as a stick to hammer belief of any sort. 1845, the year history brought Newman into the Catholic Church, was the year that Renan left it, convinced that history undermined Catholicism. The inter-involvement of history, conceived in modern terms, and belief may constitute the most central and persistent theme in Christian thought throughout the 19th and 20th centuries.

Can history whittle away belief in a historical religion almost to vanishing point? Is it impossible, as Lessing claimed, to find in 'the accidental truths of history' the 'necessary truths of reason'? If Adam and Abraham never existed, if there was no massacre of the innocents at Bethlehem, if Jesus did not actually walk on the water or rise in the air to be hidden by a cloud, has 'salvation history' turned into no more than 'salvation myth'? Or can enough remain, if only 'suffered under Pontius Pilate', to maintain the claim that Christian belief, even if much enriched by myth, is still focused on history of a basically secular sort, on something that actually happened? Plenty of sound historians think that enough does remain, but the history of historians remains a micro-history, seldom quite sufficient for theologians still persuaded of the need for a grand, non-cyclic, macro-historical scheme.

In the original scheme, if Adam was at the beginning and Christ at 'the fullness of time', everyone afterwards must live *eschatologically awaiting 'the end'. In practice this was often modified, as we have seen, by a focus on some new sort of preliminary 'end', whether it be Constantine's empire or Louis XIV's. Loss of credibility in such constructions throws one back on the question: what sort of theological history do we live in? *Hegel attempted an answer with a beguiling rewrite of Christian belief in terms of a philosophy of history which few have found fully convincing. Effectively the historical dimension in theology seems to depend on the strength of its eschatology and it is striking that it has reappeared, with theologians such as *Moltmann and *Pannenberg, in an eschatological context. The key to the theology of history, Pannenberg insists, must lie in a mysterious future we still await, God's future, but proleptically already present in Jesus' *Resurrection. It is a conviction Augustine would share.   **Adrian Hastings**

Aubert, R. (ed.), *Church History at a Turning Point*, CONCILIUM (Sept. 1970).

Barnes, T. D., *Constantine and Eusebius* (1981).

Bossuet, J.-B., *Discourse on Universal History*, ET (1976).

Butterfield, Herbert, *Christianity and History* (1949).

—— *Writings on Christianity and History*, ed. C. T. McIntire (1979).

Chadwick, O., *Catholicism and History* (1978).

Frykenberg, R., *History and Belief: The Foundations of Historical Understanding* (1996).

Hinchliff, P., *God and History* (1992).

Markus, R. A., *Saeculum: History and Society in the Theology of St Augustine* (1970).

Moltmann, J., *Theology of Hope* (1967).

Niebuhr, Reinhold, *Faith and History* (1949).

Pannenberg, W., *Revelation as History* (1986).

holiness.

holiness. The modern English word translates a number of different ancient terms and embraces a range of concepts to do with the otherness of God and the character of a human life which is ordered so as to be consciously centred on him and his service. In the OT, it usually represents the Hebrew noun form *qodes* which derives from the Semitic root *qds* signifying separation. It first appears in Exodus, where it is associated primarily with land (cf. Exod. 3: 5 and the 'holy ground' that surrounds the burning bush). Increasingly *qodes* comes to take on specific cultic resonances, and is linked with the *Temple, with *Jerusalem, and with the *priesthood. Through the influence of the *prophets, however, and the development of the notions of God's 'holy name', 'holy word', and 'holy spirit', the concept, especially in its adjectival form of *qados*, also takes on a more personalist and ethical sense, signifying *Israel's fidelity to God's act of having set Israel apart. Importantly, Israel's holiness is based upon that of God: 'You shall be holy, for I the Lord your God am holy' (Lev. 19: 2).

In the NT the term used to translate *qados* is *hagios*, following Septuagint usage. This is a clear attempt to avoid the pagan associations of the alternative Greek word *hieros*, which was widely used in the mystery religions. God the Father is *hagios* in the appellation *pater hagie*, 'Holy Father' (John 17: 11). A passage from 1 Peter 1: 15–16 repeats the admonition from Leviticus to 'be holy' 'as he who called you is holy'. In general, however, the NT presumes the holiness of God, and the focus shifts to establishing the equal holiness of Jesus and also, though here matters are more complex, of the *Holy Spirit, as we can see in the angel's words to Mary: 'The Holy Spirit will come upon you, and the power of the Most High will overshadow you; therefore the child to be born will be holy' (Luke 1: 35). The unclean spirits moreover recognize Jesus as 'the Holy One of God' (Mark 1: 24 and Luke 4: 34).

The application of *hagios* to *Jesus leads to the attribution to him of the power of sanctification or making others *hagios*. This is particularly developed in the Epistle to the *Hebrews, in association with the notion of redemptive *suffering (especially ch. 9). In the 4th century Basil the Great argues that the Holy Spirit itself must be of God if it is the 'origin of sanctification'. By baptism and 'renewal' and 'rebirth' through the Spirit, the individual Christian is made part of the church, which is called 'a chosen race, a royal priesthood, a holy nation' (1 Pet. 2: 9). The church is called to be 'holy and without blemish' (Eph. 5: 27), while individual Christians are to present their bodies 'as a living *sacrifice, holy and acceptable to God' (Rom. 12: 1). Holiness, which is the characteristic of the 'saints' in the local churches (*hagioi*; cf. Phil. 1: 1; Col. 1: 2), is defined as 'purity' (1 Tim. 1: 5), 'wisdom', and 'innocence' (Matt. 10: 16); and a holy life is one consecrated into the holiness of Christ, lived out in the mutual love, fidelity to God, and hope for the *Kingdom which is the foundation of the church.

In the post-biblical period, the more general notion of holiness is bound up with the dominant *ascetical and spiritual ideals of the day. Thus during the patristic period holiness is seen as flowing from the *liturgical life of the church and is particularly expressed in the radical ascetical Christianity of *monasticism as a life 'set apart'. It is in this period that we see the emergence of the distinction between the 'active' and the 'contemplative' life, thus thematizing the distinction between holiness as a category of being and as a category of action. This returns in the 13th and 14th centuries in the dialogue between the embrace of *poverty as an ascetical lifestyle and the advocacy of poverty of spirit as an inner state of being that realizes our likeness to God. In both cases, however, the concept of holiness looks back to biblical models in that it is seen as humanity's conforming to the prior holiness of God. An intense preoccupation with holiness is apparent during the Middle Ages in the many manuals of spiritual guidance and the practice of *prayer, expressing a range of pragmatic and contemplative approaches.

During the post-Reformation period, discussion of 'piety' and 'godliness' formed part of the sometimes confrontational dialogue between a new Protestant scholasticism that stressed purity of doctrine and a contrasting appeal to the ethical and experiential dimensions of Christianity. The advocates of the latter show some continuities with medieval *spirituality in their occasional use of medieval *mystical motifs and their predilection for devotional handbooks. The Reformation character of the pietistic literature of the late 16th and 17th centuries resides in its emphasis upon biblical reading, family devotions, and meditation upon Christ as personal saviour, while the tradition of hymnody, from the *hymns of Paul Gerhardt to those of the *Wesleys, has remained an important expression of the intimacy of Protestant worship and spiritual life.

Late 16th-century *Lutherans such as Martin Moller and Stephen Praetorius drew upon and adapted certain Catholic mystical writings for their themes, as the early Luther had done, while radical Lutherans such as Philip Nicolai, author of *Mirror of Joy* (1599), and Johann Arndt, author of *True Christianity* (1605), inaugurated a more clearly Reformation spiritual tradition, though still stressing the indwelling of Christ and the notion of the Christian vocation as a passage into a deepening christocentric life. During the 17th century, the trend towards sensibility and personal commitment in Lutheranism found expression in the *Pietist movement led by Philip Jacob Spener and August Hermann Francke. In 1675 Spener published his *Pia Desideria*, which combined Arndtian spirituality with a more richly *eschatological urgency, and he sought to realize his goal of a purified church by establishing *collegia pietatis* or 'conventicles', where lay people could meet for biblical reading and the sharing of their life in Christ. In England the *Puritan movement similarly looked back discreetly to earlier tradition in certain ways but laid particular emphasis upon a biblical and doctrinal spirituality and upon the marks of true conversion. Among the many influential works of Puritan piety, John Bunyan's *Pilgrim's*

Progress (1678), with its simple though profound analysis of the journey of the soul into spiritual maturity, holds a special place.

The Anglican tradition has reflected different understandings of holiness in different contexts, frequently in *dialogue with other traditions. The piety of the Book of Common Prayer of 1552 itself shows a combination of Catholic and Protestant trends. A number of *Anglican writers and theologians, including Lancelot Andrewes, George Herbert, and Henry Vaughan, looked back to elements in medieval and indeed patristic tradition in the articulation of Anglican tradition (see CAROLINE DIVINES). Jeremy Taylor's classic *Holy Living* (1650), followed a year later by his *Holy Dying*, reflected his Anglican concern with an ordered piety, stressing the benefits of moderation and sobriety. His work, like that of Andrewes, Herbert, and Vaughan, was also characterized by the very highest qualities of expression and style.

Among modern treatments of holiness, *The Idea of the Holy* by Rudolf *Otto, which first appeared in German in 1917, has played a particularly important role, stressing holiness as the numinous presence of the wholly other expressed as the *mysterium tremendum et fascinans*. Mary Douglas's work *Purity and Danger*, written from an *anthropological perspective, has also shown the way in which notions of the holy serve to maintain categorial systems of separation and distinction within society. Contemporary Christian engagement with the holy has in general sought to strip away the world-denying resonances of the term. This results in part from the modern understanding of the self as an agent in the construction of the social order, and thus looks to some dimension of social, political, and world-transforming engagement in definitions of what constitutes Christian holiness. In the modern period, devotional practices and schools of spirituality have also become detached from their original contexts and are more readily accessible to all. This is evident in the popularity of the Ignatian *Exercises among groups other than the Jesuits, and in a widespread familiarity among western Christians of an *Eastern Orthodox devotion to *icons and the use of the Jesus Prayer.   **Oliver Davies**

Burton-Christie, Douglas, *The Word in the Desert: Scripture and the Quest for Holiness in Early Christian Monasticism* (1993).

Chavchavadze, Marina (ed.), *Man's Concern with Holiness within the Anglican, Catholic, Reformed, Lutheran, Orthodox Traditions* (1972).

Douglas, Mary, *Purity and Danger: An Analysis of Concepts of Pollution and Taboo* (1966).

Dupré, Louis, and Saliers, E. (eds.), *Christian Spirituality: Post-Reformation and Modern World Spirituality* (1989).

Otto, Rudolf, *The Idea of the Holy*, ET (1923).

Miles, Margaret M., *The Image and Practice of Holiness: A Critique of the Classic Manuals of Devotion* (1989).

Nicholl, Donald, *Holiness* (1981).

Sheldrake, Philip, *Images of Holiness: Explorations in Contemporary Spirituality* (1987).

Holocaust,

the systematic extermination of six million Jews by the Nazis during the Second World War, took place in the heart of Christian Europe. The ultimate genocide, the *Endlösung* (final solution), has forced Christian theologians radically to re-examine traditional assumptions about Jews and Judaism and the nature of God's intervention in human history (see JEWISH–CHRISTIAN RELATIONS). Many have expressed shock that centuries of Christian civilization not only failed to prevent nearly two million Jews

from being gassed to death at Auschwitz alone but may actually have contributed to the cataclysm. For adhering to a theological perspective seen as revolutionary and subversive at the time, a few such as Dietrich *Bonhoeffer shared the *martyrdom of their Jewish brothers and sisters.

After the war, newsreels of the liberation of the extermination camps changed the mindset of many ordinary people in the Christian world towards Jews and their struggle to establish a Jewish state in Palestine, inspiring a few clergymen and academics to engage in *dialogue with their Jewish counterparts. No substantial breakthrough in Christian thinking emerged for another two decades. By then, the existential and political reality of the state of *Israel, accepted in the wake of the Holocaust by a majority of Christian countries, challenged the long-standing image of a peculiar and accursed people condemned, following Hadrian's destruction of Judaea, to wander or be confined to the ghetto.

Recognizing this new reality, the *Vatican II document *Nostra Aetate* absolved the Jewish people of the charge of deicide and affirmed that God had always remained faithful to his *covenant with Israel, thereby undermining Christianity's traditionally supersessionist stance towards its parent faith. Individual theologians were coming to terms with the effects of centuries of anti-Jewish teachings perceived as originating in the gospels and grappling with the Jewishness of *Jesus in the light of the extermination camps. Ulrich Simon, one of the first to tackle the subject, sees the defamation of the Jewish people in the gospel of *John as 'an incitement to corporate murder'. Roy and Alice Eckardt, who have made perhaps the most radical theological response to the Holocaust, start with the premiss: 'Had the Jew Jesus of Nazareth lived in the "right" time and "right" place, he would have been dispatched to a gas chamber.'

Many theologians felt compelled by the Holocaust and the existence of the state of Israel to reject the replacement theology which saw a triumphalist church assume the mantle of the 'true Israel' at the expense of the unconverted Jews. Gregory Baum finds 'Auschwitz and the participation of the nations' a sign that 'it is the Christian world that is in need of conversion'. Expressions of repentance for *sins of omission and commission during the Holocaust have been made by various church bodies. Statements by the French and German bishops that point the finger at the church's long-standing tradition of anti-Judaism, and criticize their predecessors as bishops, have been more candid than the Vatican document which attributes responsibility to the shortcomings of individual Christians.

Inconsistency has not been uncommon in post-Holocaust theology, with several Christian thinkers jettisoning certain traditionally *antisemitic assumptions and retaining others. Some decry antisemitism but continue to embrace a triumphalist *christology. Others express great solidarity with the Jewish people provided that Jews demonstrate the exemplary moral and ethical standards of Jesus Christ. Support for Israel, more forthcoming when the Jewish state has been perceived as weak or in danger, has often been based on such preconditions.

Problems persist for Christians who believe that salvation can come only through Christ. A number in more obscurantist societies, where the message of *Nostra Aetate* and subsequent church documents has failed to percolate, view Jewish suffering as a punishment for having rejected Jesus. Others, of an equally traditionalist stamp, treat the Holocaust as part of the divine plan that would lead to the ingathering of the Jews in their land and usher in the Second Coming.

In contrast, several theologians have located the Holocaust within the continuum of texts on *suffering that challenges the key principles of theodicy, running from the books of *Jeremiah and *Job in the Hebrew Scriptures to the passion of Christ. Some believe that God has renounced his *omnipotence and withdrawn from his creation to make space for the world to exist autonomously. Many see God in the suffering of the victim, whether on the *cross or in Auschwitz. Dorothee *Sölle characterizes God as 'our mother who cries about what we do to each other' and who 'can console but not "magic away" '. Paul van Buren suggests that as the death of Jesus hurt God, so the death of six million of God's children hurt God even more.

Indeed, a few revolutionary theologians imbue the Endlösung and Auschwitz with the significance of a new Golgotha, demanding nothing less than metanoia, a wholesale revision of the concepts of crucifixion and *Resurrection. 'Who has the right to talk of the Cross in a post-Auschwitz world?' Alan *Ecclestone demands. For van Buren, Auschwitz questions the formulation that the cross 'was once for all', while Alice Eckardt finds the cross in Auschwitz, with the crucified Christ suffering the Holocaust with his brethren.

The Resurrection's victorious undertones have led the Eckardts to throw doubt on its physical reality. They suggest that this will be witnessed by Christians in the *messianic era when the dead, including the martyrs of the Holocaust, are resurrected. Roy Eckardt intimates that the state of Israel may be the 'special historical event' that redeems 'the victimizing resurrection', while Jacobus Schoneveld sees the Resurrection as 'the vindication of Jesus as a Jew' and 'the vindication of the Jewish people as God's beloved people'.

See also EVIL, PROBLEM OF.   **Emma Klein**

Ecclestone, Alan, The Night Sky of the Lord (1980).
Eckardt, Alice and Roy, Long Night's Journey into Day, 2nd edn. (1988).
Pawlikowski, John, The Challenge of the Holocaust for Christian Theology (1978).
Pergamon Press, Remembering for the Future (3 vols; 1988).
Simon, Ulrich, A Theology of Auschwitz, 2nd edn. (1978).
van Buren, Paul, Christ in Context (1988).

Holy Office, see INQUISITION.

Holy Spirit.
There is an apparent reference to the Spirit of *God in only the second verse of the bible. Although 'The spirit of God was moving over the face of the waters' (Gen. 1: 2) could be translated 'the wind of God', it is implausible, because all other uses of the Hebrew expression are clearly references to the Spirit. Along with them, this verse founds a way of speaking of divine action in and towards the *world, a form of action sometimes characterized in terms of the mysterious unpredictability and power of the wind, as perhaps definitively in Ezekiel 37: 1–14. Here, a sustained pun on the different meanings of the Hebrew ruah as wind, breath, and spirit, clearly anticipates later biblical descriptions (John 3: 8), as well as dogmatic definitions of the Spirit as the giver of life. (See also Ps. 104: 30 for a more general reference.) Other OT themes relevant for the later development of a theology of the Spirit are the inspiration of *prophecy, sometimes involving ecstatic behaviour, and the promise in Joel of an *eschatological outpouring on all flesh

in the end times. The OT in general reveals a wide range of forms of divine action through the Spirit, everyday and *miraculous alike, in relation to all forms of being.

The opening chapters of Luke's gospel combine the giving of new life in the womb of *Mary with the inspired prophecy that accompanied the conception and birth of the saviour. The Synoptic Gospels indicate the presence of the Spirit to *Jesus at crucial stages of his ministry, his *baptism and temptation in particular, while *Hebrews (9: 14) teaches that it is through the eternal Spirit that Jesus offered himself to God the Father. Similarly, some traditions have taken *Romans 8: 11 to imply that it was by his Spirit that God raised Jesus from the dead, another link with the giving of life that is expanded in the final verses of 1 Corinthians 15.

Many NT references focus on the gift of the Spirit to the *church. Acts 2, with its allusions to Joel and the overcoming of Babel, uses traditional imagery of wind and *fire to describe the creation of a new community at *Pentecost, a point made differently in John 20: 21–2. There is, however, a difference of focus in the teaching of these two books. Acts presents the Spirit as the one whose action is to be seen in crucial new steps taken by the church, often validated by ecstatic experiences. *John's teaching, more reflectively theological, places the Spirit in *Trinitarian perspective, teaching that just as, during his *Incarnation, the Son reveals the Father by doing his work, so afterwards he will ask the Father to send 'another paracletos' to continue, and, indeed, intensify that work by witnessing to Jesus as the truth and enabling the church to do 'even greater things'. This and the linking of the Ascension with the giving of the Spirit's gifts in Ephesians 4 help to found the notion of the Spirit as *personal.

The Fourth Gospel's careful expression of the Spirit's self-effacing action in relation to the Son who is the way to God the Father is anticipated less clearly in earlier writing, especially that of *Paul, who is sometimes said not to distinguish between the risen Christ and the Spirit. In Romans 8: 9–10a, they are virtually indistinguishable, sometimes even apparently conflated. Gordon Fee has argued in great detail against such a conflation, but clearly any systematic treatment will require not the playing of proof-texts against each other but an enquiry into whether it is right to discern a second distinct focus for the mediation of God the Father's action in the world. For this it is necessary to focus on two features that the tradition has tended to neglect: the transcendence and eschatological orientation of the Spirit's characteristic forms of action. So familiar have become notions of the Spirit within the church and the believer that it is sometimes forgotten that it is the Son who is characteristically immanent—in Incarnation—while the Spirit as Jesus' 'other' relates him, and subsequently believers, to the Father in anticipatory fulfilment of eschatological promise.

Early debate about the nature of the Christian God concentrated on the person of Christ, not surprisingly in view of the fact that the divinity of God's Spirit is less likely to be in contention than that of a man. *Irenaeus described the Son and the Spirit as the 'two hands of God', two personal mediators of God the Father's action in the world. There is a distinction of function, the Son becoming incarnate and the Spirit serving as the focus of eschatological activity consequent upon Jesus Christ's recapitulation of Adam's story. This clearly implied the divinity of both Son and Spirit as well as their close relation. In opposition to the *Gnostic view that divine action in the material world is mediated by deities lower in the scale of being than the supreme deity, Irenaeus, in continuity with biblical ways of speaking, insisted that both the hands of God are God himself in action.

For the next two centuries, however, there develops a tendency, influenced by Neoplatonism (see PLATO), to treat the Spirit as the lowest of three *hypostases* in a hierarchy of being. For *Origen, the Spirit is a creature, albeit a supreme one, ranking below the Son. More than a century later, challenges to the divinity of the Spirit compelled theologians to express their pneumatology more clearly. But they trod a knife-edge. Too strong an emphasis on the fact that the Spirit was 'one in being' with God the Father led to suspicions of Sabellianism; too weak, and the Spirit appeared to be placed on an ontological hierarchy. Basil of Caesarea's treatise on the Holy Spirit is sometimes said to tread a middle course, though there is no doubt that he writes in defence of the Spirit's divinity. *Athanasius characteristically contended strongly in favour of the Spirit's divinity, which had apparently been affirmed at the Council of *Nicaea in 325.

The confession of the Spirit's divinity raised other questions, chiefly that concerning the difference between the Son's and the Spirit's relation to the Father in the Godhead. The doctrine that while the Son is *begotten* the Spirit *proceeds* signalled a distinction in relationship, but one that is sometimes charged with being uninformative. It also leaves unanswered questions about the Spirit's personal character. *Pannenberg has recently sought to broaden the conceptions beyond the relations of origin into relations of reciprocity. He has argued that the Son and the Spirit are defined by their differing self-distinction from the Father and their relations to him. The Spirit is thus identified as one who is given by the Father to the Son to empower his work and in turn teaches us to confess the Son's lordship (*Systematic Theology*, i. 321).

Pannenberg's is one of several proposals designed to heal the schism between Rome and *Byzantium centred on the doctrine of the Spirit. Dated formally to the early 11th century, it had its roots far earlier in the differences between *Augustine's and the Cappadocians' Trinitarian theology (see GREEK THEOLOGY). While *Eastern Orthodoxy, following the Cappadocians, holds that the Spirit proceeds 'from the Father', the west unilaterally adopted the addition, 'from the Father and the Son' (the *filioque* clause). Ecumenical opinion now seems to incline towards accepting a version or modification of the eastern view. By subordinating the Spirit to the Son, it is held, the western addition diminishes the Spirit as little more than the one who applies to the believer the benefits of Christ. Eastern theologians criticize the excessive christocentrism of western theological discussion, attributing it to this source. Moreover, it is charged, the principle of double procession encourages modalism by inviting the positing of an underlying and impersonal divine substance to account for the unity of the being of Father and Son.

The important question underlying the disputes concerns whether the world and human beings are the product of an intrinsically personal God, or whether some impersonal and unknowable substrate underlies the three persons. The west's perennial temptation to monistic and pantheistic forms of theology provides some support for the eastern view, and for the modern Orthodox John Zizioulas's insistence that the Father is the cause of both the being and the divinity of the whole Godhead. A typical western rejoinder is that the east correspondingly cuts off the Spirit from the Son, and encourages a non-incarnational *mysticism.

Augustine's doctrine of the Spirit is determinative for later western teaching, Catholic and Protestant alike. The predominant model is of the Spirit as the bond of *love uniting the Father and Son, generating an idea of God as a closed circle and a unitary agent related to the world as one substance to another. Can a bond be a person? The outcome was an identification of the work of the Spirit as the means of God's causal action upon us rather than free personal relation with us. More seriously, in some Catholic theology, *grace, conceived as a semi-substantial reality poured into the believer, came to displace many of the Spirit's functions, so that it sometimes appeared that the Spirit's work was restricted to the church as an institution, and, indeed, according to Protestant charges, regarded as within the control of the church.

Protestant criticisms did at least perform the service of eliciting something of a renaissance in pneumatology, particularly in the theology of *Calvin, who attributes to the Spirit functions both in *creation and towards the believer. A similar service was performed unconsciously by the anti-Trinitarian reaction resulting from the Wars of Religion after the Reformation. In defending the divinity of Christ, the *Puritan John Owen paid close attention to the Spirit's relation to Jesus and was enabled to maintain both that Jesus was the incarnate Son of God and that, as truly a man, he was related to the Father by the Spirit. This distinction between Incarnation and inspiration became the basis of a pneumatologically construed link between Christ and the believer, something exploited by Puritan spiritual writers, and in the 19th century by Edward Irving. A recent Roman Catholic contribution to the discussion (Del Colle) has similarly shown how a critique of causal conceptions of the Spirit's action in favour of more personal ones opens new possibilities for *christology.

One unfortunate consequence of the retrenchment that took place on both sides of the Reformation divide was a move into a rather wooden conception of the relation of the Spirit to scripture (see BIBLE). From the rather ambiguous claim that 'all scripture is God-breathed' (2 Tim. 3: 16) onwards there had been difficulties over the concept of inspiration. Philo, Origen, and Augustine founded a theory of *allegory which enabled great freedom of interpretation, though Origen's concept of inspiration also encouraged interpreters to seek inspired meaning in every verse. A reaction against allegory in favour of the literal sense of the text, encouraged by *Renaissance humanism and the Reformers alike, ultimately gave rise to a rather literalistic equation of inspiration and *revelation. The effect on Rome is shown in the Council of *Trent's teaching that the whole of Scripture had been given 'at the dictation of the Holy Spirit', and one has only to recall the disputes about Darwinism and creationism to become aware of something of the effect of similar Protestant rigidity (see EVOLUTION).

In other respects, however, the Reformation debates reveal deep differences between the churches. It is little oversimplification to say that whereas Rome tended to locate the Spirit's action within the institutional church, the Reformation, in effect if not in intention, came to attribute it to the individual. When universalized this gave rise to two characteristic modern phenomena, rationalism and experientialism, both of which in different ways locate the Spirit's action *within* human being. The rationalist turn, quintessentially in *Hegel, uses the concept of rational spirit to characterize the inner workings of reality: *Geist* is that which works out its being in the dialectical processes of history. A less subtle development is to be found in Lampe's *God as Spirit* (1977), according to which a *unitarianly conceived Spirit-deity manifests himself historically in various forms, paradigmatically in Jesus as an inspired human being.

The experiential development is represented by *Schleiermacher's theology of inwardness, according to which the Spirit becomes closely identified with human religiosity. As in so many other developments, the transcendence of the Spirit is lost to a generalized indwelling. This is not the Spirit who drove Jesus out into the wilderness, but a somewhat tamer force which wells up from the depths of history and the person, a concept that returns in some strands of *Tillich's theology.

Schleiermacher's background in Moravian *Pietism, with its strongly experiential tone, points forward to modern *Pentecostalism, whose early form is well represented by Edward Irving around 1830. Desperate for experiential evidence of the Spirit's working, Irving was attracted to manifestations of tongues and healings, in his own congregation and elsewhere. The last century in particular has witnessed the rapid rise, outside and within the mainstream churches, of Pentecostal forms of Christianity with their stress on the direct experience of the Spirit (see CHARISMATIC MOVEMENT). This marks the theology of, for example, Welker. To some extent in continuity with outbreaks of *millenarianism and sectarianism in previous centuries, Pentecostal movements are various, dynamic, and growing, particularly in Latin America where they threaten the hegemony of Roman Catholicism.

Despite its tendency sometimes to neglect christology, Pentecostalism provides implicit witness to endemic weaknesses in the western tradition. However, much Pentecostalism could also be said to replicate a widespread weakness of traditional theology by limiting the Spirit's action to the human realm. A more broadly biblical conception, drawing on Ezekiel 37 and Romans 8 especially, would pay more attention to the cosmic functions of the Spirit. Relevant is Basil's differentiation of the distinctive forms of activity of the three persons of the Trinity: 'the original cause of all things that are made, the Father; the creative cause, the Son; the perfecting cause, the Spirit' (*On the Holy Spirit*, 15. 38). The Holy Spirit is on such an account the person of the Trinity to whom is attributed the eschatological function of enabling the created order to become that which it was created to be. In this light the twin tendencies of internalizing and spiritualizing the work of the Spirit can be seen to derive from the loss of the eschatological dimensions of his action, from the creation of the church as the community of the last days to the drawing of all created reality into the sphere of human redemption (Rom. 8).

Something of a universalizing of the Spirit's action has been attempted by *Moltmann, who unfortunately tends to lose the very eschatological note for which he is so well known in favour of a rather Neoplatonist emanationism, ironically replacing Augustine's Platonizing construction of the inner Trinity with an equivalent outward reduction of the relation of God and the world. By blurring the boundaries between God and the world, such emanationism endangers the distinctive reality of both.

And so we return to the 'otherness' of the Spirit. Attention to the eschatological character of the Spirit's activity in the economy—his drawing of the world forwards, to completion—will suggest that the Spirit is not the person of the Trinity who closes the circle of the divine being, but rather the one who perfects divine eternity by being the focus of God's movement outwards. God's immanent reality, his being in communion of love, thereby becomes the basis of the expression of that love outwards in creation, Incarnation, and redemption. By thus closing the oft-lamented breach between the immanent and economic Trinity, we return to the beginnings of Trinitarian theology with a renewed notion of the Son and the Spirit as the 'two hands of God': mediators of divine action within and towards the created world.

A greater stress on the Spirit's eschatological otherness will also have much bearing on the topics mentioned. We have already seen something of possibilities for a new conception of the divinity and humanity of Christ. Similarly, by opening up a space between divine action and the writing of scripture, it guards against both narrowness and scepticism. Inspiration is the enabling of human agency, not its reduction to automatism. Perhaps most importantly, the notion of the Spirit's transcendence generates an alternative to rigidly institutional views of the church by changing the relation of christology and pneumatology. Crucial here is Zizioulas's view that while the Son institutes the church, it is the function of the Spirit to constitute it ever anew in the present as the *body of Christ. This rules out doctrines that the Spirit empowers an already given institution as well as conceptions according to which the Spirit merely inspires individuals who may or may not form into community. The Spirit is the one who empowers the *worship and life of the whole church by bringing it as a community of faith to God the Father though the living presence of his Son. Consequent upon this is a theology of the church as open to responding to the Spirit's action wherever it is found.

Colin Gunton

Badcock, Gary, *Light of Truth and Fire of Love: A Theology of the Holy Spirit* (1997).

Del Colle, Ralph, *Christ and the Spirit* (1994).

Fee, Gordon, *God's Empowering Presence* (1994).

Gunton, Colin E., 'God the Holy Spirit', in *Theology through the Theologians* (1996).

Jenson, Robert W., 'The Holy Spirit', in C. E. Braaten and R. W. Jenson (eds.) *Christian Dogmatics* (1984), ii.

Moltmann, Jürgen, *The Spirit of Life* (1992).

Owen, John, *ΠΝΕΥΜΑΤΟΛΟΓΙΑ or, A Discourse Concerning the Holy Spirit* (1674), in W. H. Goold (ed.), *Works* (1965), iii.

Pannenberg, Wolfhart, *Systematic Theology* (1991), i.

Smail, Thomas, 'The Holy Trinity and the Resurrection of Jesus' in A. Walker (ed.), *Different Gospels*, 2nd edn. (1993).

Vischer, Lukas (ed.), *Spirit of God, Spirit of Christ* (1981).

Wainwright, Geoffrey, 'The Holy Spirit', in C. E. Gunton (ed.), *The Cambridge Companion to Christian Doctrine* (1997).

Welker, Michael, *God the Spirit* (1994).

Zizioulas, John, *Being as Communion* (1985).

homiletics, see PREACHING.

homosexuality.
Although different societies vary considerably in their attitude to homosexuality, modern research indicates that same-sex relationships exist in most societies today and were also widespread in the past. Homosexuality appears to be, in this empirical sense, part of human nature. While most people establish *sexual relationships with a member of the other sex, there are

considerable numbers of men and women who are by nature inclined to seek a partner of their own sex. For homosexuals, as for heterosexuals, such a relationship often involves a strong emotional commitment which invests the sexual activity with great significance; the sexual union is understood as the physical expression of the emotional bond that exists between the partners, and of their shared life.

In earlier ages, when homosexuals had no public voice, the voice of the church was uniformly condemnatory. Both scripture and *natural law seemed to speak loudly against homosexual acts. The biblical texts standardly cited then and now are Genesis 19, Leviticus 18: 22, Romans 1: 26–7, 1 Corinthians 6: 9, and 1 Timothy 1: 10. Apart from scripture, nature seemed to show that God intended sex for procreation, so that any sexual activity which excluded procreation, as did homosexuality, was against nature and its divine author, and its practitioners were rebels against God. Today homosexuals are able to speak more for themselves, and there is both a growing general awareness of the ordinariness of homosexuals and a corresponding increasing tolerance of homosexuality, which is now understood less as a perversion of a heterosexuality supposedly natural to all people, and more as a natural variant of human sexuality. There are many devout homosexual Christians, including ministers, living in sexual relationships, who see their sexuality and their partner as gifts from God. The earlier blanket condemnation of homosexuality no longer seems tenable or desirable, and there are signs in all the mainstream churches of an effort to move away from the earlier condemnatory tone. The Church of England document *Issues in Human Sexuality* (1991) goes so far as to see committed homosexual relationships as a valid option for Christian living. Christian homosexuals who accept their sexuality positively, as well as other Christians who desire to adopt a more understanding and welcoming attitude, are confronted with the problem of how to remain faithful to their biblical heritage and to the Christian faith in God as creator and the author of nature. Writers such as the Roman Catholic John McNeill and the Episcopalian Norman Pittenger were among the first to work on this question, and they have been followed by a growing number of theologians and exegetes in the major churches. The general drift of their work has been to try to show, negatively, that the earlier biblical and theological arguments against homosexuality are weak, and positively, that homosexuals can aim at and achieve worthwhile goods in their sexual relationships, and that these relationships are compatible with profound Christian values as found in scripture and tradition.

Concerning the biblical texts, it is often argued that they do not in fact mean what they have been taken to mean in the past. The exegetical arguments involved are necessarily detailed and cannot be entered into here, but they have at the very least thrown much doubt on the earlier anti-homosexual interpretation. Some have identified a deeper problem: the social values presupposed by these biblical texts are not Christian ones. As the work of Michel Foucault and others makes clear, sexual activity of one kind or another is normally invested with a meaning that depends on wider social structures and institutions, particularly those concerning gender relations and the *family. A sexual hierarchy was deeply embedded in Israelite and Jewish society throughout the biblical period: men dominate and possess, women are the submissive possessions of men. Sexual relationships were accordingly understood

in terms of domination and possession. It is this understanding of sex that gives the various laws and stories concerning homosexuality their sense: briefly, sex between men (sex between women is not even mentioned in the OT) upsets the 'natural' hierarchy by treating a superior man as an inferior woman. But this hierarchy is perceived in modern times as incompatible with the sexual equality proclaimed by Christianity, in which 'there is neither male nor female; for you are all one in Christ Jesus' (Gal. 3: 28). Christians reject both the social context and the resulting understanding of sexual relations which give these texts their meaning, and this, it is claimed, makes it impossible to use the texts in a Christian argument about homosexuality.

The classical natural law argument can be summarized briefly. God is the author of human nature, and sex is designed by God for procreation, as can be seen by observation: there is a clear empirical link between sexual activity and procreation. Further, it is only by reference to procreation that our sexual nature, the fact that humanity is divisible into two sexes, can be understood. Hence, any sexual activity which is incompatible with procreation violates nature and the will of God. There are a number of drawbacks to this position. First, the premiss that God designed sex for procreation, though it once seemed obvious, is, when questioned, difficult to justify either by empirical observation or by reason. Empirically, much sex does not result in conception; indeed, many kinds of sex cannot do so (this is precisely the complaint of traditional moralists). Even if it is clear that there is a fundamental link between human sexuality and reproduction, it does not follow that sexual activity should always be of the reproductive type (see CONTRACEPTION). The argument also tends to present nature as a given to which human beings must simply submit, and this does justice neither to human creativity nor to the Christian freedom which is a central theme of the NT. Again, this theory, like the biblical texts, puts too much stress on acts, and neglects the relational aspect of sex; to many Christians, if there is a God-given purpose of sex, it is to be found rather in the possibilities it offers for expressing and building love between the partners, so that what we need is not a narrowly focused theory about sexual acts, but rather reflection on the role sex plays in the life of people, their development, and their love.

This last observation is the basis of a newer approach adopted by thinkers on both sides of the argument about homosexuality. According to this approach, the important question to be asked is not whether a particular act is condemned in the bible or can be biologically fertile, but whether a sexual relationship helps those concerned to grow and develop as people, to become more loving and fulfilled. This shift in the argument does not mark an abandonment of the bible, but a concentration on more fundamental biblical values. It also depends on its own style of natural law argument, since conceptions of human nature have an important place in it. Those who regard homosexuality as compatible with Christianity appeal to broad observations on human nature and to the fundamental place of *love in the teaching of *Jesus. When Jesus says: 'whatever you wish that men would do to you, do so to them; for this is the law and the prophets' (Matt. 7: 12; see also 22: 35–40), he preaches a radical *freedom, replacing obedience to law with loving concern for others as the fundamental principle of a life pleasing to God. There is no reason, it is argued, to suppose that homosexual relationships make those involved any less lovingly concerned for others. In fact, there is reason to think the opposite. Modern thought, both secular and Christian, stresses the importance for personal development of successful intimate human relationships, including sexual relationships. While some may be called to a life of *celibacy, most are not, and for this large majority a lack of an intimate bond with another is a misfortune that may well render it more difficult for them to relate to others with the generous love demanded by the gospel. The bible attests that 'it is not good that the man should be alone' (Gen. 2: 18). If this is true for people in general, it is also true for homosexuals. While most people will seek an intimate relationship with a member of the other sex, a fact reflected in the story of the creation of Eve (Gen. 2: 21–4), some are so constituted by God that they look to their own sex. But this is a matter of secondary importance; it is the place of love in a sexual relationship that matters, not the sex of the people involved. The gospel demands that all Christians accept in love the sexual diversity that God wills in his creation and in his church. This will require a certain creativity: homosexual Christians have inherited a bible and a tradition which do not take into account their sexuality, so they must create a new framework for their lives and relationships; but if a faithful and generous love is central to their lives in the way demanded by Christ, they remain true to the deepest biblical and traditional teaching. The church, in order to remain faithful to the same teaching, must include homosexuals fully within its life; this may mean evolving ways of invoking God's blessing on homosexual partnerships, and accepting the existence of openly homosexual ministers (see MARRIAGE; ORDINATION).

There are still many Christians for whom such a programme would be a betrayal of the gospel. For these, love is indeed the fulfilment of the law and the prophets, but this does not mean that the law and the prophets have to be abandoned; on the contrary, it shows that the deep meaning of the biblical attitude to homosexuality is that homosexual practices are of their nature incompatible with Christian love. When God saw that it was not good for the man to be alone, he precisely made a woman to be with him. This is not a secondary matter. Human sexual duality is stressed again in Gen. 1: 27—male and female he created them—and is basic to our relationships. This duality is not only the biological basis of human reproduction; it is also the basic form of 'otherness', and openness to the 'other' is an essential element of love. The homosexual, in rejecting the otherness and complementarity represented by the other sex, cannot truly love. Homosexual attraction and homosexual relationships reflect a fundamentally narcissistic search for what is the same as oneself and are therefore unfulfilling. The Christian tradition's rejection of homosexuality is a direct consequence of its commitment to love, and is meant in part to encourage the homosexual towards that love and away from his or her narcissism.

There is still much sifting of arguments to be done on this question. But it should be remembered that there is always a presumption of freedom: an act or relationship is presumed acceptable unless good reason can be shown why it is not. The burden of proof is on those who claim that homosexual relationships are illegitimate. In this light, it has to be asked, not which side of the argument is on balance the more convincing, but rather how convincing the newer arguments against homosexuality are. Here, there are grounds for considerable doubt. Empirically, it does not seem true that their sexual relationships tend to make homosexuals unfulfilled and unhappy, especially if these relationships are stable and faithful. Neither is it true that not wanting a sexual partner of the other sex implies rejection of the other sex; non-sexual love and *friendship remain possible, and many homosexuals have deep friendships with people of the other sex. Further, there are many kinds of difference between people other than sexual ones, and the argument ignores these. It might be argued that the fundamental difference on which love depends is not the sexual difference between men and women but the irreducible difference between two *persons regardless of their sex, and this difference is involved in all human relationships. Any love, homosexual or heterosexual, respects and cherishes this difference.

See also BIBLICAL LAW.   **Gareth Moore**

Boswell, John, *Christianity, Social Tolerance and Homosexuality: Gay People in Western Europe from the Beginning of the Christian Era to the Fourteenth Century* (1980).

Foucault, Michel, *The History of Sexuality* (3 vols.; 1979–88).

Hanigan, James P., *Homosexuality: The Test Case for Christian Sexual Ethics* (1988).

McNeill, John, *The Church and the Homosexual* (1977).

Moore, Gareth, *The Body in Context: Sex and Catholicism* (1992).

Pittenger, Norman, *Time for Consent* (1976).

Scroggs, Robin, *The New Testament and Homosexuality* (1983).

Vasey, Michael, *Strangers and Friends* (1995).

Hooker, Richard (1554–1600), classic *Anglican theologian. Little is known about Hooker's life, and Izaak Walton's account of the henpecked, unworldly scholar rocking the cradle or tending the glebe while reading the classics has been demolished by Sisson as legend. Hooker was born at Exeter and educated at Oxford, before becoming a parish priest and Master of the Temple. He is regarded as the greatest Anglican theologian and the chief architect of Anglican ecclesiology, though seldom studied by Anglican clergy today. His reputation rests on one substantial work, *Of the Laws of Ecclesiastical Polity*, in eight books, of which three were published posthumously (though they lack the final polish of books 1 to 5, their authenticity is now established beyond reasonable doubt). Hooker's style, though sublime, is complex and demanding.

Much of Hooker's thought can be paralleled elsewhere and he draws on a vast range of learning. In philosophy *Aristotle and *Aquinas are dominant influences; in *theology he draws freely on patristic, medieval, and *Reformation sources. He welds them into a theological synthesis of striking intellectual power. 'Hooker's outstanding characteristic as a thinker is his eclecticism' (Cargill Thompson 1972: 21).

The *Laws* is a polemical work, though the elevated tone of the argument partly disguises this. Hooker fights by fair means and foul and the *Puritans were unable to answer his arguments. Every book is directed against some tenet of Puritan theology and the overall aim is to legitimate the arrangements for the reinstatement of the reformed Church of England under Elizabeth I (the 'Elizabethan settlement'), whereby major features of the pre-Reformation Church, particularly *episcopacy, were perpetuated, together with minor but symbolic medieval features, such as the surplice, and the ring in marriage. Hooker is a *Reformed theologian, with a powerful sense of *grace given in *justification and sanctification, but he has no time for biblical literalism or the notion that the

Church of England must eschew anything used by the Church of Rome.

Hooker grounds his argument in first principles: the realm of *law permeating the universe and reflecting the nature of God. Divine law is inscribed in the scriptures and interpreted by human *reason under the guidance of *tradition. The realms of nature and of grace are integrated in Hooker's thought and here he stands in the tradition of Aquinas. For Hooker the church is not purely the creation of *revelation—it is not merely supernatural, the 'mystical' church—but is also a political body, with structures of government that should reflect the received wisdom of political philosophy. Therefore it is inappropriate to look for precise biblical precedents for the outward aspects of the church. These are governed by human, positive law and every particular (national) church has the authority to regulate its life according to reason and the sense of what is appropriate to the circumstances. There is an element of expediency and pragmatism in Hooker's system that is justified by his taxonomy of law: divine and human, *natural and positive, immutable and mutable. Thus episcopacy is to be retained since it goes back to the apostles, but the church could do without bishops in an emergency. The royal supremacy (see KINGSHIP) is a God-given institution but the sovereign rules by consent and is subject to the law. Hooker is an inheritor of the pre-Reformation *conciliar movement which stressed that authority resided in the whole church of *laity as well as clergy and was exercised constitutionally and representatively.

The church is thus both a 'politic society' and a 'supernatural society' where we are brought into fellowship with 'God, *angels and holy men'. The church is distinguished from other religious societies by the profession of the essential revealed faith centred on the salvation brought by Jesus Christ. 'The visible Church of Jesus Christ is therefore one in outward profession of those things which supernaturally appertain to the very essence of Christianity and are necessarily required in every particular Christian man' (3. 1. 4). Hooker's definition of the church is inclusive and tolerant. Societies and individuals are deemed to belong to Christ's church if they make the profession of faith. Hooker's approach is in tune with Queen Elizabeth's claim that she would make no windows into men's hearts and secret thoughts. Unlike the Puritans, he does not believe that Roman Catholics (including pre-Reformation English people) were excluded either from the church or salvation: they were 'our fathers' after all. In his important sermon 'Of Justification', Hooker argues that Rome does not teach that we can be saved by meritorious works alone. He believes that, though Rome obscures and corrupts the gospel, it does not negate its essential message, that salvation is by the grace of Christ. While deploring Rome's corruption and superstition, Hooker nevertheless regards her as belonging to the family of Christ.

Hooker was equally discriminating in his view of the Continental Reformers. He is hostile to extreme Calvinism and, in his emphasis on reason, moral discipline, and sacramental grace, he has more in common with the *Arminian *Caroline Divines of the following century. He punctures the cult of *Calvin himself showing that Calvin's programme at *Geneva was dictated by a prudent response to circumstances, rather than an implementation of divine revelation. His method of evaluating the Genevan regime on its merits was offensive to the Puritans. However, it can be shown that in his view of the authority of scripture, tradition, and reason Hooker has much in common with the magisterial Reformers. Too relaxed about episcopacy for later High Churchmen and too insistent on the visible society of the church for evangelicals, Hooker remains the paradigm of the Anglican middle way.

Paul Avis

Hooker, R., *Works*, ed. W. S. Hill *et al.* (6 vols.; 1977–93).

Avis, P. D. L., *Anglicanism and the Christian Church* (1989), ch. 4.

Cargill Thompson, W. D. J., 'The Philosopher of the "Politic Society": Richard Hooker as a Political Thinker', in W. S. Hill (ed.), *Studies in Richard Hooker* (1972).

d'Entrèves, A. P., *The Medieval Contribution to Political Thought: Thomas Aquinas, Marsilius of Padua, Richard Hooker* (1939).

Evans, G. R., and Wright, R. J. (eds.), *The Anglican Tradition: A Handbook of Sources* (1991).

Rowell, G. (ed.), *The English Religious Tradition and the Genius of Anglicanism* (1992).

Sisson, C. J., *The Judicious Marriage of Mr Hooker and the Birth of the Laws of Ecclesiastical Polity* (1940).

hope, in Christian understanding, is a learning to look forward, confident in the *memory of what God has already achieved in Jesus Christ, to the fulfilment of *God's *creation. This brief statement encapsulates what is peculiar to Christian *eschatological hope and clearly distinguishes it from other possible hopes which do not have God's creativity as their object. It is, however, clear from many of the discussions of hope in the 20th century that it is an important *philosophical theme shared by Christians and non-Christians and that hope has provided a space for many fruitful engagements between different traditions. To consider Christian hope is to be drawn into the particularity of Christian patterns of thought and *worship at the same time as encountering the points of contact it has, especially in public life, with its neighbours.

The Christian eschatological hope has a continuity with Jewish hopes for the *Messiah. Israel's trust that God's people will be set free is transformed in the Christian vision into an understanding that the *redemption of all people has been begun in the life, death, and *Resurrection of *Jesus Christ. On the basis of this memory, handed down the generations, Christians look forward in hope for the completion of that redemption. Christian hope is not gained as a result of looking around in the world for unambiguous grounds for optimism. It is learned by understanding the partiality of all our current seeing and knowing, and by anticipating the fullness of our life in God that is yet to come. Something like this informs *Paul's encouragement in the well-known King James translation: 'For now we see through a glass, darkly; but then face to face: now I know in part; but then shall I know even as also I am known. And now abideth faith, hope, charity, these three; but the greatest of these is charity' (1 Cor. 13: 12–13). Christian hope is thus characterized by an awareness that human knowing is unavoidably provisional and that faith in God is, partly, a trust that what God will make possible is not constrained by what women and men are able to imagine or plan. God's possibilities cannot be seen in advance; they are often surprising. It is in this light that one can perhaps best interpret another of Paul's encouragements: 'For in this hope we were saved. Now hope that is seen is not hope. For who hopes for what he sees? But if we hope for what we do not see, we wait for it with patience' (Rom. 8: 24–5).

According to *Augustine the essentials of Christian *faith, hope, and *charity find their brief formulation in the *Creed and in the *Lord's Prayer. In considering how these three so-called theological virtues relate to each other, about which much has subsequently been written, Augustine establishes a model that has largely been adopted by his successors. The relationship between faith, hope, and charity is basically triadic: there is no love without hope, no hope without love, and neither hope nor love without faith. No simple linear model does justice to the interrelationships. Of these three, hope takes the form of prayer, particularly the Lord's Prayer. In this prayer Christians hope both for absolute redemption ('Thy Kingdom come') and for the necessities of life here and now ('give us this day our daily bread'). These two are not separate, for Augustine: the request for daily *bread and the anticipation of God's coming *Kingdom are indivisibly bound together in one prayer. It is this indivisibility of worldly needs and the world's redemption that has made hope one of the most important themes in theological reflections on issues of politics and *justice.

In the *Summa Theologiae*, *Aquinas treats hope most famously in two places: in his discussion of human acts (where hope is considered one of the passions) and in his discussion of Faith, Hope, and Charity. In the first, Aquinas says that hope concerns that which is future, yet to come. The object of hope is a future good, difficult but possible to attain (*ST* I-II q. 50 a. 1). It is contrasted with despair (whose object is something impossible to attain) and fear (whose object is evil rather than good). One of Aquinas's more significant reflections concerns the relationship between hope and experience. Experience cannot be said straightforwardly to cause hope: it will depend on what kind of experience it is upon which one draws, and experience can be a cause of despair as well as of hope. More pertinent, for Aquinas, are the experiences that arise from one's education: 'hope is caused by everything that makes man think that something is possible for him; and thus both teaching and persuasion may be a cause of hope. And in this way also experience is a cause of hope, in so far as it makes him consider something possible which before his experience he looked upon as impossible' (I-II q. 50 a. 5). Hope is thus something one has to learn. What one takes to be possible is influenced not primarily by everyday experience but by what one is taught is possible. It follows from this that hope is well founded to the extent that what one has been taught is sound. In the discussion of Faith, Hope, and Charity, Aquinas builds on this general insight in his treatment of the specifically Christian quality of the theological virtues. A virtue is theological if it has God as its object. Thus if the object of hope is God, then hope is a theological virtue (II-II q. 17 a. 5). Christian hope is consequently dependent on experience of God, on who one understands God to be; this is a matter, amongst other things, of teaching, because one has to learn how to recognize God. For this reason Aquinas agrees with Augustine that hope is not possible without faith. Most important of all, perhaps, is Aquinas's insistence that the virtue of hope is not strictly speaking a passion but a habit of will (II-II q. 18 a. 1), and this has a number of significant implications. The future good which is difficult but possible to attain, to which Christians look forward, is God. Christians cannot attain this future good by themselves: it is God's gift. The Christian future good is God's self-offering. A Christian has to learn the habit of responding to this self-offering and in this way learns the habit of hoping for God. As Karl *Barth was later to put it, the Church's 'own hope, the

goal of its faith, stands or falls with the acceptance of this offer' (*CD* II/2. 281). The habit that Christians must learn is dependent on understanding who God is. Christians know God through an education that focuses upon the person of Jesus Christ, and so their response to God is a response to the life, death, and Resurrection of Jesus Christ. The basis of the habit of hope, and that which makes it possible, is Christ the risen Lord. Hope is a habitual response to a memory of the future promised in Jesus Christ.

These formal characteristics of Christian hope shape Christian understandings of everyday thoughts, words, and deeds in various ways. Human beings cannot achieve God's future unaided: if they could, they would be God. It is God who establishes the future for which Christians hope. Yet God's creativity does not make humans idle. All Christian statements of hope are unavoidably self-involving in the same way that all Christian action is a participation in God's creativity. Because human beings are God's creatures, the power they exercise belongs to God. This does not mean that they should not exercise it; indeed God commands that they should. It means that they should exercise it responsibly and obediently. The human exercising of God's power is understood by Christians to be part of their habitual hoping for God's future.

If, as Augustine believes, human desire for God's coming Kingdom is bound up with asking for our daily bread, one would expect theologians in the 20th century to engage with the work of Karl *Marx. Marx's writings, like those of many Christians, are saturated with questions of human hoping and their relation to future material goods; moreover, his language is heavily indebted to eschatological formulations concerning a coming release from need. Hope is a theme treated extensively by the heterodox atheist Marxist Ernst Bloch, whose work was one of the many points of contact for a group called the *Paulusgesellschaft*, a European forum in which Christians and Marxists met in the 1950s and 1960s to consider their shared concerns. The *Paulusgesellschaft* discussions have been influential on the work of the German Protestant theologians Jürgen *Moltmann and Wolfhart *Pannenberg, and the Catholic theologians Karl *Rahner and J. B. Metz, as well as upon *liberation theology. Marx's thought has also been treated in detail by the English theologians Nicholas Lash and Denys Turner. Despite the important differences between these engagements with Marx, all share one common concern: how best to characterize the relationship between political practice in the public sphere and hope for the future. What differentiates Christian contributions to this debate from those of Marxists and others is an explicit understanding of the absolute future not as a process immanent within nature (however understood) but as God's self-giving in the completion of creation. The basis for this understanding is contained in the presuppositions and self-understandings that form part of Christian education. For Christians it is not men and women who create the new transformed future that is different from the often unhappy reality of the present, but God. Christians understand their hope as a participation in this divine transforming creativity. It is for this reason that a theologian like Rahner can insist that although no finite human vision or plan can exhaust the infinity of God's creativity, Christians are called by God constantly to exercise their imaginations in planning finitely for the future in the light of God's inexhaustible self-giving. God's self-gift is, in fact, what makes such provisional planning possible in the first place, and what sustains it. In considering whether hope is an individual or a social matter, theologians such as Rahner insist that Christian hope is my recognition that my freedom lies in being in God's control, and that this recognition's context is the wider body of the church: its languages and its social practices.

As Moltmann (1965: 16) puts it, Christian hope 'embraces both the object hoped for and also the hope inspired by it'. The memory of the freedom of Jesus Christ, which Metz calls a 'dangerous memory', encompasses not only the past but also the future. The Christian hope is the futural discourse of God's enabling grace. At the same time it embraces, in Aquinas's terms, hope as a human act: an existential orientation towards that future. For Christians this orientation is primarily one of unconditional trust in God's freely given graced self-communication. Hope is, in Rahner's words, 'the name of an attitude in which we dare to commit ourselves to that which is radically beyond all human control' (1973: x. 250). For a Christian this means a habitual commitment to God revealed in Jesus Christ. The particularity of Christian hope is a consequence of the particularity of its memory. The Christian hope is indivisible from the Christian memory. Its memory is its hope.   **Nicholas Adams**

Barth, K., *Church Dogmatics*, II/2 (1957).
Bloch, E., *The Principle of Hope* (1986).
Lash, N., *A Matter of Hope* (1981).
Metz, J. B., *Faith in History and Society* (1980).
Moltmann, J., *Theology of Hope* (1965).
Pannenberg, W., 'The God of Hope', in *Basic Questions in Theology* (1971), ii.
Rahner, K., *Theological Investigations* (1973), x.
Turner, D., *Marxism and Christianity* (1983).

Hopkins, Gerard Manley (1844–89).

Hopkins, though hailed in the wake of posthumous publication (1918) as a pioneer of 20th-century poetry, now seems deeply mid-Victorian: in his Ruskinian attention to detail, whether in nature or church architecture; his passion for amateur philology; his recoil from industrialism; his romanticizing of soldiers. His distinctive achievement is to ground these Victorian preoccupations in a christocentric theology and a sketched philosophy of being.

God's Grandeur answers the miseries of industrialism with a vision of divine immanence. If the romanticizing of soldiers produces the problematic *Bugler's First Communion*, it can also feed into Hopkins's revitalizing of the ancient concept of *Christus Victor* in the final movement of *The Wreck of the Deutschland*. His response to detail is articulated in terms of inherent shaping pattern (inscape) and the shaping two-way activity of perception (instress). Hopkins undergirds both by an emphasis on individuation (*haecceitas*) which he takes from Duns Scotus; and poems like *The Windhover* celebrate magnificently the individual being of created things (see also FRANCISCAN THOUGHT).

Correspondingly, it is masterful individuality that attracts him in artists such as *Milton and Purcell. His own is expressed in innovations of syntax, diction, and rhythm which can snarl themselves in the idiosyncratic. Such masterfulness can waken the conflict he registers between his activity as poet and his vocation as priest. As a *Jesuit, Hopkins's religious thinking is moulded by the Ignatian *Exercises and their foundation statement: man was created to praise, reverence, and serve God our Lord. But his Notes on the *Exercises* infuse into them his exploration of selfbeing as an absolute

and irreducible experience. His terminology in this area—'pitched', 'selved', 'stress', 'flush'—signals his central intuition of being as action, structure as patterned energy. His poetry enacts this in coinages that fuse noun or adjective with verb: 'the just man justices'; 'all his hallows'; 'leaves me a lonely began'.

*Praise, for Hopkins, is inseparable from sacrifice. He holds, with Scotus, that the Incarnation was not a response to the Fall but that the universe was created as a field for Christ to enact his sacrifice of praise to the Father. If Christ plays 'to the Father through the features of men's faces' he also configures by his passion the suffering of martyrdom or shipwreck. Hopkins's poetry of *sacrifice matures from the aesthetic religiosity of some of his early Oxford pieces to the tempered protest of the late sonnet *Thou art indeed just, Lord*. This belongs with the sonnets of conflict, written during his last frustrating years in Dublin, which recreate, in a modern idiom, the wrestling of *Job or the *psalmists with a God experienced as fearful or baffling. These constitute one pole of his work, the poems of celebration the other. Together they establish his achievement, for all its comparative smallness of bulk and frequent idiosyncrasy, as classic.   **Donald Mackenzie**

Ellsberg, M. R., *Created to Praise* (1987).
Storey, G., *A Preface to Hopkins*, 2nd edn. (1992)
von Balthasar, Hans Urs, 'Hopkins', in *The Glory of the Lord* (1962), ET (1986), iii.

humanity.

The church has never formulated an official doctrine of human nature, comparable, for example, to the Chalcedonian Definition of 451, which affirmed that in Christ one *person existed in two natures, divine and human, without confusion, change, division, or separation. The Council of *Chalcedon, however, was attempting to bring to an end a century of *christological controversy, and the fact that the church produced no anthropological dogma in the patristic era might say something about the extent to which theologians of the age shared a common understanding of what it was to be human. On the other hand, it is hard to imagine theologians before the modern era being prepared to put humanity centre-stage. Thomas *Aquinas, in his defence of the unity of theological science, was following a long tradition in subordinating questions concerning humans and other created beings to questions concerning *God as such: 'Sacred doctrine is not concerned with God and the creatures equally. It is concerned with God fundamentally, and with the creatures in so far as they relate to God as their beginning or end.' (*STI* q. 1 a. 3) It is only relatively recently that humanity has secured its own particular place on the theological agenda under the heading of 'theological anthropology'.

The significance of this development should not be overlooked. There is nothing like an explicit doctrine of humanity in the *creeds and confessions of the earliest churches, and not much in the writings of their theologians that could be described in this way without imposing the categories of modern *theology in an anachronistic manner. Yet their work as a whole bears witness to sustained and searching reflection on the nature and destiny of human beings, making it possible to reconstruct a distinctive account of what it is to be human from material which is distributed across the entire spectrum of Christian doctrine. In other words, the characteristically Christian vision of humanity was, for many centuries, inseparable from other doctrines—not simply the theology of *creation, as is often acknowledged, but also the theology of *redemption, of the *church, of 'the last things' (*eschatology), and so on, including the theology of the *Incarnation, given that this necessarily raised questions concerning the nature of the humanity with which God was united in Christ. The theologians of the early churches took different views on these matters, and it is not surprising that there are corresponding differences between their various understandings of human nature. The fundamental perspective, however, is remarkably consistent, and consistently 'theocentric' (God-centred), and to this extent is determined by the way in which the bible speaks about human existence. There is no systematic theology of human being (or, for that matter, of anything else) in the bible, but as Richard Norris says, 'The scriptural "way of talking" about human beings is systematically *theological* in the sense that human individuals are identified and understood as such through their relationship to God. Their being, to use one of Luther's favourite phrases, is *coram Deo* [before God]. "God" is the name of the ultimate context in which and to which they are responsive.' (1989: 80).

It is this theocentric 'way of talking' that governs Christian thought on human existence for most of its history, from the church fathers to the Reformers and beyond. The idea, for example, that knowledge of the self and the knowledge of God are very closely connected with one another is present in the work of Clement of Alexandria (*c*.150–*c*.215), even more so in the work of *Augustine, and *Calvin sets it at the very beginning of his *Institutes of the Christian Religion*. 'Yet', Calvin adds, 'however the knowledge of God and of ourselves may be mutually connected, the order of right teaching requires that we discuss the former first, then proceed afterward to treat the latter' (*Institutes*, 1. 1. 3). To some extent this echoes the position of Aquinas, and there is nothing especially original in the way in which Calvin aims to relate questions concerning humanity to more fundamental questions concerning God. For Calvin, as for most of his predecessors, the possibility of articulating a theological interpretation of humanity structurally independent of the doctrines of creation and redemption, and so on, never really arises. It is only with the emergence of theological anthropology, as a semi-independent theological 'locus', or topic, in *Protestant systematic theology, that this possibility becomes a reality. The expression itself had been in use since the 16th century, but the discipline that it names was only established in the middle of the 19th century as theologians sought to respond to the intellectual challenge presented by *Enlightenment philosophy. The emergence of theological anthropology as a special discipline, therefore, is bound up with the 'turn to the subject', commonly associated with the philosophical methods of *Descartes, and perpetuated in a variety of ways by the philosophies of the Enlightenment, and post-Enlightenment movements such as *Romanticism. The task of the theological anthropologist, now as then, is to construct a Christian interpretation of human existence, through identifying and investigating significant concepts in the Christian tradition and relating them to one another and to the perspectives of other disciplines—*philosophy, of course, but in principle any discipline concerned with what it is to be human, and in the 20th century theologians have been obliged to engage more and more with the perspectives of the biologist, the *psychologist, the sociologist, and so on (see Social Sciences). The sheer sophistication of

contemporary theological anthropology reflects the fact that its practitioners do not confine their attention to philosophical accounts of subjectivity, as was once normally the case, but often reflect upon dimensions of human existence investigated by one or another of the natural and human sciences. As if all this were not enough, they must also come to terms with *postmodern critiques of 'the modern subject'—the academic shorthand for a fundamental vision of human existence, primarily concerned with the autonomy of the individual subject in relation to knowing the world and acting within it, which is shared by many modern philosophical movements. Critiques of this kind present theological anthropologists with significant opportunities; but in undermining the legitimacy of the moves that precipitated the rise of theological anthropology in the first place, they can (and perhaps should) make its practitioners question the terms of their own enquiries.

Yet it is often assumed that theological reflection on human existence, far from being sophisticated, is little more than the restatement of a primitive *mythology (that is, the first chapters of the book of *Genesis), and as such must be committed to a pre-critical belief in the descent of the entire human race from *Adam and *Eve. Quite apart from anything else, to think in this way is to adopt (as the *fundamentalist 'creationists do') a narrow and unimaginative approach to Genesis that obscures more serious problems for the Christian tradition. Adam has *always* been interpreted as a type or paradigm of human nature, even when most believers would have happily affirmed his historical existence as well, and it is far from controversial to suggest that the church found new ways of expressing this conviction through the technicalities of Greek philosophy.

This philosophical influence, however, has been a mixed blessing for Christian thought about humanity. On the one hand, it supplied a new vocabulary for the articulation of ideas embedded in the scriptures, traditions, and liturgies of the churches. On the other hand, it committed Christianity to a strict separation between the *soul and the *body—that is, to a *dualism—which the scriptures, traditions, and *liturgies of the churches did not warrant, and which is now widely considered to have been entirely discredited. It is arguable that it is the church's investment in dualism, rather than its investment in a literal reading of Genesis (which, even when universal, was often theologically incidental), that has proved to be the more problematic legacy. That the Jewish and Christian scriptures presuppose some kind of duality in human nature is undeniable, and even in the account of the formation of the first human from 'dust from the ground' and 'the breath of life' (Gen. 2: 7) there is a hint of this view. The NT speaks of 'body' and 'soul', and 'spirit' too, and these concepts are central to the work of later theologians seeking to identify and isolate different components of human nature. In early Christian theology, therefore, there is some conflict between 'dichotomists', who contrasted the soul with the body, and 'trichotomists', for whom a distinction between the soul and the spirit was just as important. The trichotomist view (which provided the anthropological theory for the 4th-century christological *heresy of Apollinarianism) was officially condemned at the Fourth Council of Constantinople (869–70), but it has never disappeared entirely, and the dichotomist view has flourished through the centuries in a variety of different forms. Recently, however, it has come under sustained attack from various quarters, not least from biblical scholars, who have studied the anthropological vocabularies of the Jewish and Christian scriptures and concluded that dualism (with its characteristic opposition of the spiritual to the material) misrepresents the Hebrew and Greek terms translated as 'flesh', 'body', 'soul', 'spirit', and so on, and biblical thinking about the nature of humanity generally. In consequence, for many theological anthropologists, it is now axiomatic that the original Christian vision of humanity followed the Jewish tradition in affirming human life as a 'psychosomatic unity', distinguishing, but never separating, the soul and the body as different dimensions of human existence. What is distinctive about the Christian vision of humanity, therefore, is not that it posits the existence of an additional entity, the soul, not recognized by other anthropologies, but that it posits the existence of an additional relation—a relation to God, as creator and redeemer—which encompasses all the other relations which define us as individuals. The insistence that the human being is an 'embodied soul' or an 'ensouled body', and not a soul somehow occupying a body, is now not just the conclusion of arguments in theological anthropology but also the premiss of arguments in some other theological disciplines, and this is one measure of the success of the campaign against dualism in the second half of the 20th century. (It is significant, for example, that although Christian belief in life after death was for many centuries articulated through two sets of ideas—one concerning the destiny of the soul and one concerning the *Resurrection—few contemporary theologians are willing to see anything of value in the first of these perspectives.) Whether the theological critics of dualism have given sufficient credit to the philosophers is open to question—the theologians have often overestimated the dualistic tendencies of ancient Greek philosophy and of the Christian philosophers of the Middle Ages, and underestimated their own debts to 20th-century philosophers whose criticisms of dualism had helped to create the intellectual 'space' for modern theology. In this context, however, it is more important to note the degree to which the bible, including the creation narratives of Genesis, has been utilized to counteract movements in post-biblical Christian thought, especially in so far as the latter contributed to the separation of a true self, the soul, from the body, from others, and from the natural world.

There is some truth, then, in the idea that Christian thinking on humanity is bound up with the creation narratives in a particular way. Yet even 'creation' itself is only one of the themes that govern reflection on human existence in the Christian tradition. In fact, what unites Christian thinking on humanity is not so much a concept of human existence as a conviction that human existence must be understood as *created*, *fallen*, and *redeemed*. These perspectives determine the shape of Christian discourse concerning humanity, and the perspective of redemption (which involves more than a restoration to a created state or the reversal of a fallen state, however these are to be conceived) is essential. It is a reminder that Christian reflection on human existence, throughout its history, has always been not only *protological*, but *eschatological* too—that is, it has been concerned not just with beginnings but with ends, and so has never reflected on human nature, on what we are, without also reflecting on human destiny, on what we should and might yet be. One particular concept links Christian thinking on created, fallen, and redeemed human existence more than any other, and that is the concept of the *imago Dei*, the image of God. The idea that

human beings are made in the image of God is introduced in the creation narratives—'Then God said, "Let us make man in our image, after our likeness…"' (Gen. 1: 26)—and invoked in other passages in the Jewish and Christian scriptures. There is little agreement concerning its meaning in these texts, and the proliferation of interpretations down the ages gives some indication of the complexity and diversity of Christian theological reflection on humanity. In relation to creation, theologians have tended to interpret the image as a capacity, such as rationality, *conscience, or *freedom of the will, or as a function, such as the 'dominion' over the earth that is emphasized in the passage in which the idea of the image is first introduced. Others, including Augustine, have interpreted it as a relationship, in which humanity is united with God in a specific way. Contemporary theological anthropologists typically reject the first style of interpretation, which they characterize as 'static', 'individualistic', and 'dualistic', and insist upon the relational model, which, they argue, integrates the different dimensions of human existence and recognizes that this existence is essentially social. Given these various approaches to the image in the context of creation, it is not surprising that theologians have differed concerning the degree to which the image is distorted, damaged, or destroyed through the *Fall (however this is understood). Some have followed *Irenaeus in distinguishing between the 'image' and 'likeness' in Genesis 1: 26, so that the former (as a natural capacity) survives the Fall, even though the latter (as a supernatural gift) does not. This move, however, has long been deemed illegitimate; but no alternative way of resolving the question (which has been central to disputes about freedom, *sin, and *grace, from the *Pelagius–Augustine controversy to the Reformation and Counter-Reformation and beyond) has commanded universal acceptance. But the question is one that cannot be answered without reference to a third context, that is, in relation to redemption, and it is here that christological concerns become particularly important. Christ, characterized as the 'second Adam' by Paul (Rom. 5: 12–21) is *the* image of God (2 Cor. 4: 4; Col. 1: 15), and it is through participation in Christ that the image is renewed and perfected. This christological determination of the idea of the image is taken up by many theological anthropologists today, who understand the idea in terms of men and women being called in Christ to reflect the dynamic interrelatedness of God the *Trinity in their relations with one another and the world.

One of the reasons why this kind of account is so popular, across a broad spectrum of theological positions, is that it reflects philosophical and psychological interest in the ways in which our identity is constituted by networks of relations. In this respect it could be said to be as much a product of its time as any theological anthropology of the 19th and 20th centuries, and yet it is often presented as something new, a perspective that guarantees the theological character of theological anthropology. Some theologians are profoundly suspicious of any attempt to ground their discipline in a general analysis of human existence informed by the natural and human sciences, and are particularly critical of the attempt to construct a new *natural theology through the identification of certain aspects of our lives as 'signals of transcendence'. On the other hand, other theologians are profoundly sceptical about any attempt to derive the most fundamental truths about human existence from christology and the doctrine of the Trinity, and are particularly critical of the idea, associated with Karl *Barth, that 'true' humanity is revealed exclusively in the person of Jesus Christ. No account of what it is to be human is purely empirical, in that our existing frameworks of interpretation always determine, in part, the phenomena of human life that we find significant in the first place as well as the specific significance that we attach to them. This does not mean, however, that the theological anthropologist is entitled to deduce an account of human existence from the theologies of the Incarnation and the Trinity, as if separating theological enquiries from all others was a straightforward enterprise. Christian thinking about humanity has always represented the product of conflict and resolution between different sets of concepts, *symbols, and narratives, and there is no reason to believe that it could, or should, become anything else now. The task of the theological anthropologist, therefore, includes not only criticizing the reductionism of sociobiologists or cultural materialists when they transgress the methodological limits of their own discipline, but also confronting the tendency of theological anthropology to underestimate, not overestimate, the challenges to its own existence presented by a particular discipline, discourse, or intellectual movement. The current enthusiasm for 'the death of the subject', 'the end of the Enlightenment project', and so on, is a good example, and compares interestingly with the general failure of the discipline to come to terms with the seriousness of the charges made against it by *feminists over the past thirty years. At its worst, Christian thought on humanity has served to legitimize the oppression of women (and others) and the destruction of the natural world; at its best, however, its resources may help us to resist new negations of our common humanity. These resources, however, are not restricted to the conceptual, nor even the symbolic, but also include the complex of practices in which, in different cultures, the Christian vision of humanity is most fully embodied.

See also MAN/MASCULINITY; WOMAN/FEMININITY.

Colin Crowder

Anderson, Ray S., *On Being Human: Essays in Theological Anthropology* (1982).

Cairns, David, *The Image of God in Man*, 2nd edn. (1973).

Farley, Edward, 'Toward a Contemporary Theology of Human Being', in J. William Angell and E. Pendleton Banks (eds.), *Images of Man* (1984).

Graff, Ann O'Hara (ed.), *In The Embrace of God: Feminist Approaches to Theological Anthropology* (1995).

Hill, Edmund, *Being Human: A Biblical Perspective* (1984).

Kelsey, David H., 'Human Being', in Peter C. Hodgson and Robert H. King (eds.), *Christian Theology: An Introduction to its Traditions and Tasks* (1982).

Kerr, Fergus, *Immortal Longings: Versions of Transcending Humanity* (1997).

McFadyen, Alistair I., *The Call to Personhood: A Christian Theory of the Individual in Social Relationships* (1990).

Macquarrie, John, *In Search of Humanity: A Theological and Philosophical Approach* (1983).

Morea, Peter, *In Search of Personality: Christianity and Modern Psychology* (1997).

Norris, Richard, 'Human Being', in Geoffrey Wainwright (ed.), *Keeping the Faith: Essays to Mark the Centenary of Lux Mundi* (1989).

O'Neill, Mary Aquin, 'The Mystery of Being Human Together: Anthropology', in Catherine Mowry LaCugna (ed.), *Freeing Theology: The Essentials of Theology in Feminist Perspective* (1993).

Schwöbel, Christoph, and Gunton, Colin (eds.), *Persons, Divine and Human* (1991).

Taylor, Charles, *Sources of the Self: The Making of the Modern Identity* (1989).

Ward, Keith, *Religion and Human Nature* (1998).

human rights, see ANTISEMITISM; APARTHEID; DEMOCRACY; JUSTICE; LIBERATION THEOLOGY.

humour. 'If you want to make God laugh,' advises the American comedian Woody Allen, 'tell him your future plans.' Christian thinkers, often seen as a dour company, are likely to be engaged in the even more ludicrous activity of attempting to tell people God's future plans. Their seriousness compounds the absurdity and may account for the neglect that the fundamental *human experience of laughter has suffered in Christian thought.

After all, God does laugh on occasion in the OT. The experience is, admittedly, not particularly funny for his targets who are laughed to scorn. Human laughter is not often heard in the bible. Both *Abraham and Sarah laugh when they hear she is to bear a child, but as much from bitter incredulity as pleasure, so it appears, and the life of their son Isaac, whose name means 'he laughed', is no joke. The *Wisdom books, particularly Ecclesiastes and Proverbs, equate laughter with folly and warn against both.

*Jesus is never recorded as having laughed and neither is anyone else in the NT. Mockery is another thing. Jesus is often the target of derision, most notably in his passion. The one positive reference to laughter is in Luke's beatitudes which promise laughter to those who now weep (6: 21), but the accompanying woes condemn those who laugh now to subsequent weeping (6: 25). James takes up this theme and admonishes us to turn our present laughter to mourning (4: 9). This might seem effectively to condemn humour as at best frivolous.

That said, the books of the OT are shot through with a peculiarly dark humour when human self-confidence and ambition fail in the face of divine decree. The *prophets abound in this ironic *Schadenfreude*. Parody, puns, and satire are their literary stock in trade. There are lighter moments too: it is hard to read of the punctured pomposity of *Jonah or the resourceful improvisations of Esther and other biblical women without suspecting a comic intention. Even so crucial a passage as the call of *Moses reads as an increasingly ludicrous series of excuses. Edwin Good's *Irony in the Old Testament* was a pioneering study which has been followed by a number of other explorations of this phenomenon in the biblical canon.

The NT also contains many episodes that can be read as comic: Jesus' image of the camel squeezing through the eye of the needle or the devastating straight-faced naivety with which the man cured of blindness deals with the Pharisees in John 9 are only two. John in particular can raise a smile through the aptness of his characterization; the mildly flirtatious tone of the encounter between Jesus and the woman at the well is beautifully caught. The smile evoked is one of recognition, its evocation a trait that marks out the great writer of any age.

Nor should this surprise us. If we adopt Koestler's analysis of humour which sees it as the creative realization of unsuspected congruence between hitherto unrelated aspects of life, then what could be a better source of humour than the idea of God become man? The mismatch between human aspiration and human achievement is either comically endearing or exasperating, or perhaps both.

The later NT, however, shows itself much more concerned with maintaining a proper gravity. The *Pastoral Epistles are very solemn. This is not only a matter of an increasing authoritarianism which cannot countenance the anarchic tendencies of humour. There is also an involuntariness in laughter which cuts against self-discipline and detachment, something the Greek tradition warned against. Imbued with a consciousness of human *sinfulness, the seductiveness of worldly pleasure, and the certainty of impending *judgement, the fathers in their turn see much more profit in tears than in laughter, pointing out again and again that Jesus wept, but never laughed. A writer such as Tertullian does not lack a vein of mocking sarcasm but there is little sense of a compensating ability to laugh at himself. Socrates Scholasticus gives us an account of the more endearing figure of Sisinnius, a Novatianist bishop in Constantinople at the time of John Chrysostom. Charged by the bishop of Ancyra with disregarding repentance, Sisinnius replied that no one repented more heartily than he did—of coming to see the bishop. By Socrates' account, Sisinnius was much loved and admired for his repartee. No doubt it reads better in Greek.

Yet we have to hunt to find even these traces of humour. In *monastic rules such as *Benedict's there are strong warnings against any trivial gossip which might provoke laughter and therefore distract monks from their duties. Later Bernard of Clairvaux would voice the strongest discouragement from laughter. Umberto Eco's novel *The Name of the Rose*, though hardly a work of Christian thought, explores the hostility to humour in early medieval Christian theology in an illuminating way. Laughter is subversion, a threat to *authority, and so must be suppressed.

However, there is a parallel tradition of the carnivalesque which has been brought to modern critical attention through the work of Mikhail Bakhtin. Practices such as the election of boy bishops and the long tradition of *risus paschali*, 'Easter laughter', where preachers in German-speaking countries presented the Easter story as amusingly as they could, were surprisingly prevalent. The comical treatment of figures such as Noah's scold of a wife and the suspicious St Joseph in the miracle and *mystery plays can still amuse an audience, and medieval cathedrals are replete with gargoyles and grotesque misericords and roof bosses. Perhaps they speak of a world with sufficient confidence to allow the release of humour. *Aquinas, with *Aristotle to back him up, recognized that Jesus' *humanity made him 'risible' in the sense of 'capable of laughter'. Chaucer and Boccaccio combine bawdry and a mockery of clerical pretension with an unaffected piety.

As that world cracks, humour becomes more dangerous and therefore something to be suppressed. *Erasmus's urbane but effective satire on the church in *The Praise of Folly* is answered by the brutal earthiness of *Luther's excoriations of Erasmian compromise, though elsewhere Luther displays genuine humour. The *Reformation is not otherwise marked by wit. On the Catholic side, however, a figure such as St Philip Neri, the founder of the Oratory, was celebrated and appreciated, if not by all, for his practical jokes and his unconventionality, and Thomas *More was a noted wit. Something of this character, but far less knowing, is to be found in the Russian tradition of the *iurodvi*, the holy fool, whose innocent, perhaps even simple-minded, frankness and fearlessness is a re-proach to the worldly and sophisticated. *Dostoevsky's work brought this notion to wider attention in the west.

Later Christianity has had its humorists, partly through a renewed appreciation of the rhetorical power of humour and partly because the church has often been an easy target for jokers and there is sense in fighting fire with fire. Sydney Smith (1771–1845) through his letters became the archetype of a certain urbane Anglican drollery coupled with a sharp and by no means shallow understanding of human foibles. In the early part of this century, the writings of G. K. Chesterton had a wide appeal which still continues, as did Ronald Knox's debunking of theological pretension. C. S. *Lewis's *Screwtape Letters*, where a devil instructs his nephew in the arts of temptation, is one of the better examples of the use of comedy to attract a wider audience. Among 20th-century Christian writers, one might single out Flannery O'Connor, who powerfully uses her particular brand of black comedy to point out the absurdity of modern self-preoccupation. Her sometimes grotesque stories have an avowed rhetorical purpose, seeking to shock a spiritually apathetic readership into a response (see NOVEL).

Theologians have had their moments. *Kierkegaard, for instance, can be genuinely funny, *Newman had an ear for satire, and Karl *Barth's writings on Mozart show a real appreciation of the importance of the comic. Specific attempts to think theologically on the topic of humour are rare; Kuschel and Berger may be evidence of a new awareness of its importance.

Humour is an ambivalent and dangerous thing. Christian thought has for the most part been wary of trivializing both the human condition and the majesty of the divine. Human pretension may need cutting down, and nowhere more so than in the church at times, but the risk of pride in the one who does the cutting is strong. Humour can be penetrating and yet it can also be a means of deflecting the important question. It can mock folly and also embrace folly; it can laugh at and laugh with. In that sense, it is a capacity that depends upon and reveals our judgements about what folly and wisdom may be, who should be respected and who need not be. It may seem to be the ultimate resource of shallow relativism.

And yet Christian thought insists that the darkness of this world is overcome and that a *reconciliation with God is already under way. *Dante writes a *Divine Comedy*, not as a work full of laughs, which it is not, but one which points to the *joy of the Christian promise where 'all will be well', in the words of *Julian of Norwich. Essentially, Christianity has a comic vision in the technical sense of a plot which leads to restored harmony. In so far as humour testifies to and can lead towards this joy below tears, it has a place in Christian thought.

See also PLAY.   **Hugh S. Pyper**

Berger, P. L., *Redeeming Laughter: The Comic Dimension of Human Experience* (1997).

Good, E. M., *Irony in the Old Testament* (1965).

Koestler, A., *The Act of Creation* (1964).

Kuschel, K.-J., *Laughter: A Theological Reflection* (1994).

Screech, M. A., *Laughter at the Foot of the Cross* (1997).

Whedbee, J. W., *The Bible and the Comic Vision* (1998).

Huss and Wyclif

Huss and Wyclif. A paradoxical relationship has linked the Czech reformer John Huss (c.1370–1415) and the English *bible *translator and theologian John Wyclif (c.1320–84). For his dramatic refusal to submit passively to an absolute authority in a highly visible public forum, Huss rose from his ashes to historical immortality as a champion of human *freedom. Wyclif has earned the appellation 'Morning Star of the Reformation'. Active as a popular and charismatic *preacher and theology professor in Prague after 1400, Huss shared in the Czech reform movement, launched by John Milíč of Kroměříž and others, who aimed at reducing the material wealth and secular power of the clergy and the monasteries. The heterodox writings of Wyclif, late reclusive and choleric Oxford theologian, were brought by students to Prague, and bolstered the Czech reformers' efforts after 1398. Huss's involvement in national causes, such as fostering the vernacular language, augmented his local fame and prestige. Accused of teaching *predestination and the *Donatist *heresy (both under Wyclif's influence), he faced excommunication by Pope John XXIII in 1411. Arriving at the Council of Constance to clear his name in 1414, he was arrested despite assurance of safe conduct from the Emperor Sigismund and burned at the stake on 6 July 1415, for refusing to condemn certain of Wyclif's teachings unless their falsity was demonstrated by recourse to the bible and patristic literature.

Huss's relation to Wyclif has been a crucial issue in the assessment of his work and legacy, together with the related issue of his links (largely through the Taborite movement) to the Protestant *Reformation and particularly *Luther. The link to Wyclif became exaggerated by two factors, (1) the efforts of 19th-century scholars, like Johann Loserth and Constantin Höfler, to demonstrate the purely derivative character of Huss's teaching; and (2) the prominence of Wyclifite issues at his trial. Recent scholarship has drastically reduced the alleged dependence on Wyclif by emphasizing that Huss cherished his English precursor's moralism, not his dogmatic *theology. To shed light on the trial at Constance, Francis Oakley, in agreement with Paul de Vooght, maintains that Huss became the victim of his own 'gratuitous acts of bravado', such as employing provocatively Wyclifite terminology on predestination and the *Eucharist when formulating perfectly orthodox ideas. Huss eschewed Wyclif's other innovative doctrines, such as the rejection of the episcopal rank, the placing of the *laity on an equal footing with the priesthood in the exercise of the ministry, and the rejection of auricular confession and priestly absolution in *penance. On the highly visible matter of indulgences, Huss questioned only their specific misuse by Pope John XXIII for a war on King Ladislas of Naples in 1412, not their ultimate basis as did Wyclif, who denied the very existence of a reservoir of excess merit in the church at the disposal of the pope to distribute.

The largely artificial link between Huss and Luther owed much of its origin to the tactics of the diplomats of the Roman Curia in combating the German Reformation. Initially they tried to use the charge of Czech 'Hussitism' against Luther, to discredit him by relying on the Germans' dislike of influence from abroad. Though this nationalist gambit failed, Catholic propagandists perpetuated the idea that the extremism of Huss's challenge to Rome arose from the magnitude of his heresy. But whereas there was indeed something epochal in Huss's denunciation of the ecclesiastical governance, he nevertheless adhered to the doctrines of medieval Christianity and contradicted such touchstones of Luther's teaching as sola scriptura and sola fide. Ironically, however, Wyclif's subsequent Protestant fame would be linked with the martyrdom of orthodox Huss rather than with any direct influence on Protestant Luther, who had reason to regard Wyclif as a heretic for equivocating on the all-important (to Luther) issue of the real presence.

In reality, while Huss remained within the limits of a renewed Catholicism, Wyclif crossed the line to proto-Protestantism. Hence Wyclif can be seen as preparing the way via the Lollard groups for the explicitly Protestant currents in England, especially *Puritanism. Huss became one, perhaps the chief, protagonist of 16th-century Czech Utraquism, so called because of its belief in communion in both kinds (sub utraque specie) for the laity, including infants and small children. In the long run, the Utraquists represented a via media between Rome and Wittenberg. It is misleading, however, although it is often done, to call the church in Bohemia 'Hussite'. Huss was its best-known member but not its originator, rather fitting in with a pre-existing movement. The Utraquists, moreover, did not consider themselves a new creation but a direct continuation of the medieval *church. The Utraquist Church, like the Ecclesia Anglicana of the Elizabethan settlement, defended scripture, *reason, and tradition. The Habsburg-sponsored *Counter-Reformation in Bohemia and Moravia suppressed the 200-year-old Utraquist movement in the wake of the Battle of the White Mountain (1620), although its libertarian spirit survived in the political culture of the Czechs, who consider Huss a national hero.

Wyclif's influence was much more definite and unambiguous within the Taborite movement that arose to challenge mainline Utraquism during the religious wars in Bohemia (1420–34), following the death of Huss. Instead of drawing, like Huss and his colleagues, on the orthodox Bohemian Reformation of the late 14th century, the Taborites embraced (1) the totality of Wyclif's teachings, as communicated from Oxford to Prague by Peter Payne, and (2) the clearly anti-canonical doctrines of the German Waldensian and French Picard sects. Moreover, Taborite radicalism and chiliasm conferred on the wars of the Bohemian Reformation the character of a major social upheaval, so that historians have viewed them (under the label of the Hussite Revolution) as an early specimen, if not the first link, in the chain of revolutions in the Euro-Atlantic world of the early modern period: the Dutch, English, American, and French revolutions. After disappearing briefly, this Taborite trend partially revived in 1457 in the Bohemian *Brethren (Unitas Fratrum), a small, but devout sect, which attracted the attention of Reformation luminaries, including Bucer, *Calvin, Luther, and Melanchthon, as a rare specimen of a Proto-Protestant church. It survives in the contemporary world under the names of the Moravian Church (mainly in North America and the Caribbean), or the Church of the Bohemian Brethren (mainly in Central Europe).

Zdeněk V. David

David, Z. V., 'The Strange Fate of Czech Utraquism: The Second Century, 1517–1621', Journal of Ecclesiastical History, 46 (1995).

Holeton, D. R., 'Wyclif's Bohemian Fate: A Reflection on the Contextualization of Wyclif in Bohemia', Communio Viatorum, 32 (1989).

Hudson, A., The Premature Reformation: Wycliffite Texts and Lollard History (1988).

Kaminsky, H., A History of the Hussite Revolution (1967).

Kenny, A. (ed.), Wyclif in His Times (1986).

Spinka, M., John Hus: A Biography (1968).

Vooght, P. de, L'Hérésie de Jean Huss, 2nd edn. (1975).

hymns are theology for all. Apart from the *Lord's Prayer, they are the best-known and most widely practised form of religious discourse, used in *worship throughout the world, and uniting people and churches of different beliefs and persuasions in a common practice of adoration and sacred song. The versification of belief is an art that requires careful attention to the craft of line and verse (see POETRY); and the writing of tunes to carry the words, or words to fit the tune, is a serious challenge to the composer or writer. When the *music and words fit together, and the results are sung with full heart and voice, the praise of God becomes, in Isaac Watts's phrase, 'duty and delight'.

But hymns are more than theology. They are also records of the inner life, of the movement of the *soul, of awe and wonder, of penitence, fear, *joy, or peace. A hymn such as 'Abide with me' or 'The day thou gavest, Lord, is ended' has the power to touch the hearts of those for whom *preaching is irrelevant or ineffective. As George Herbert noticed, 'a verse may find him, who a sermon flies'. In addition, hymns versify the bible, preserving it and interpreting it in ways that can illuminate the original text and give value to it. So Charles *Wesley will take an obscure verse from Leviticus (6: 13) and turn it into a hymn of dedication and service, 'O thou who camest from above', addressed to the *Holy Spirit. John Ellerton's 'The day thou gavest' begins with Genesis 1, 'Let there be light', and ends with Revelation, 'Till all thy creatures own thy sway'. *Blake's dictum that 'the Old and New Testaments are the great code of art' could well be applied to hymns, for congregations often sing coded messages, as in

> How Judah's lion burst his chains,
> And crushed the serpent's head …

This hymn, by Fulbert of Chartres (d. 1028), is a reminder of the antiquity of the tradition. The early church took over the Jewish practice of singing *psalms, and created its own hymns, such as the verses of Philippians 2. The eastern church developed a tradition of short hymnic prayers, or *troparia*, later elaborated into more complex forms; while the Latin church tradition, encouraged by Ambrose (c.340–97) in Milan, produced not only the *Te Deum* but also masterpieces such as *Corde natus ex parentis* ('Of the father's love begotten') and *Pange, lingua, gloriosi* ('Sing, my tongue, the glorious battle'). These Latin hymns were used and added to during centuries of *monastic worship, and after the *Reformation they achieved a new life in translations such as John Cosin's 'Come, Holy Ghost, our souls inspire' and 19th-century renderings by John Mason Neale.

The Reformation led to the development of German hymns, beginning with *Luther and continuing with devotional poets such as Paul Gerhardt and Joachim Neander (later superbly translated into English by Catherine Winkworth). In Britain hymns were slower to develop, because of the Puritan attachment to metrical psalms: not until Isaac Watts (1674–1748) was there a writer who could confi-

dently unite the orthodoxy of psalmody with the urgency of personal expression (as in 'When I survey the wondrous cross'). He showed the way forward to writers such as Philip Doddridge and Anne Steele, and to the *Methodists: Charles Wesley's huge output builds on Watts, but is different in its energy and controlled enthusiasm. After Wesley, hymns became particularly associated with the *Evangelical Revival, in the hands of Toplady ('Rock of Ages'), Newton, and Cowper (*Olney Hymns*, 1779). The main body of the Church of England remained suspicious of the emotionalism associated with these hymns (and with Methodism), until hymn-writing was made respectable by Reginald Heber ('Holy, holy, holy') and Henry Hart Milman ('Ride on, ride on in majesty'). Heber became a bishop, and Milman a dean, so their examples were hard to criticize, even for the prejudiced; a parish priest, Henry Francis Lyte, followed them with some very fine hymns ('Praise, my soul, the king of heaven'). The full glory of Church of England hymnody was embodied in *Hymns Ancient and Modern* (1861), which with its various supplements and additions became the bench-mark hymn book of the Victorian age.

By this time, hymn-writing had grown from the pursuit of the few to the obsession of the many (Fanny Crosby is supposed to have written three hymns a week for twenty years). At the end of the 19th century, there were probably some 400,000 hymns in existence, covering every kind of eventuality: children's hymns (Mrs Alexander), gospel hymns (Sankey's *Sacred Songs and Solos*), hymns against drink (Hoyle's *Temperance Hymns*), and hymns about nature ('All things bright and beautiful') or about national life ('Rejoice, O land, in God thy might'). The 20th century saw the arrival of two major books, *The English Hymnal* and *Songs of Praise*; and the 'hymn explosion', beginning in the 1960s, has produced some fine new hymns.

This suggests that there is a continuing life for hymns as an important element in worship. And in spite of some misguided clergy who claim that hymns are unsuitable for the present age, they have shown an extraordinary ability to survive over the years and may continue to do so, if only because they have the power to express theology and religious emotion with truth and feeling, and because they can speak to ordinary people in a way that sermons often cannot. They will surely continue to be an inspiration to those who can feel their power, who value their insights, and who have come to regard them with affection and love.

See also LITURGY.   **J. R. Watson**

Adey, Lionel, *Hymns and the Christian 'Myth'* (1986).
Benson, Louis F., *The English Hymn* (1915).
Bradley, Ian, *Abide with Me* (1997).
Davie, Donald, *The Eighteenth-Century Hymn in England* (1993).
Newman-Brooks, Peter, *Hymns as Homilies* (1997).
Routley, Erik, *Hymns and the Faith* (1955).
Watson, J. R., *The English Hymn* (1997).

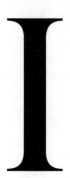

iconoclasm, the breaking of (usually religious) images. Iconoclasm was imposed in the *Byzantine empire by imperial edict in 730 (or possibly 726) and continued to be imperial policy, with a break from 786 to 815, until 843. The historical sources in the east for this controversy are entirely from the side of those who supported the veneration of *icons (the iconodules, or iconophiles), so reasons adduced for iconoclasm must be speculative. From the opponents of Leo III's first edict (Germanus, patriarch of Constantinople, who resigned in 730, and John Damascene, then a monk in Palestine), it would seem that Leo's objection to icons was that they infringed the second commandment and were thus tantamount to idolatry. The Orthodox response, which drew on earlier defence of Christian *art against Jewish objections, argued that the OT itself enjoins religious art, even figurative art, despite the second commandment, and that the manifestation of God in human form in the *Incarnation anyway alters the situation, making what was perhaps only permissive now imperative. John Damascene explains that veneration of religious images is a way of venerating not the images themselves but what they depict, though he affirms, too, that the use of matter in Christian art is an extension of the principle of the Incarnation of the One 'who became matter for my sake, and accepted to dwell in matter, and through matter worked my salvation' (*De imaginibus*, 1. 16). Perhaps in response to this, under Leo's son, Constantine V, the argument of the iconoclasts became *christological: if the nature depicted in the icon of Christ is his human nature, separate from the divine, then *Nestorianism is entailed, if it is a composite 'divine–human' nature, then *Monophysitism, and it cannot be the divine nature, for that is uncircumscribable. The final Orthodox response to this argument, not clearly articulated until the 9th century, is that what the icon depicts is not the nature, but the *person. A further argument used by the iconoclasts was that any true icon must be consubstantial with its archetype (as when the Son is called the image of the Father), something patently not true of a work of art. However, there is, the iconoclasts argued, an image that is consubstantial with Christ—the *Eucharist: that, and the form of the church building (both of which could be controlled by the hierarchy), and the sign of the *cross (with its imperial associations) were the only images admitted by the iconoclasts. For the Orthodox consubstantiality is not a characteristic of images encountered in Christian art, rather an image is relational, and refers to its archetype. In reaction against the icono-

clast affirmation of the Eucharist as the true image, the Orthodox came to insist that the Eucharist is not an image of Christ, but involves a real ontological change: in the Eucharist, Christ is truly present.

The first phase of iconoclasm was endorsed by a council held at Hieria in 754, which was rejected by the council held in Nicaea in 787, which is deemed the Seventh Ecumenical Council. The attitude of the western church to all this was mixed: the pope was not prepared to remove images in obedience to the imperial edict, but neither did the west invest images with the theological significance the eastern iconodules ascribed to them—religious art was valued, but not venerated. The response of the Carolingian theologians to the definition of the Seventh Ecumenical Council was even more negative, at least owing partly to the poor Latin of the version they had: at Frankfurt in 794 they rejected Nicaea II. It may be partly because of this that the iconodule arguments in the second stage of iconoclasm (815–43) focus on justifying, less the existence of icons, than their veneration. Both Theodore of Stoudios (759–826) and Nikephoros, the patriarch of Constantinople who resigned in 815, defend the notion of 'relational veneration' (*sketike proskynesis*), utilizing the *Aristotelian notion of relation. The restoration of the veneration of icons in 843 was presented as the 'Triumph of Orthodoxy' and henceforth, in Byzantine Christianity (which came to include the Christianity of the Slavs), the use of icons, both public and in private use, became imperative—a defining mark of Byzantine Orthodoxy.

The link between the icon as a depiction of the person and the theology of the person as the image of God, a link already adumbrated by John Damascene, became a fundamental axis of Byzantine theology. As eastern and western Christendom drew apart over the Middle Ages, the Byzantines articulated a theology of icons that excluded western practice, in particular the use of three-dimensional statues in the west, so that 'icon' came to be restricted to flat images—frescoes, panel paintings, or mosaics—a restriction foreign to the 9th and earlier centuries.

Later iconoclasm, notably at various stages in the Protestant *Reformation, is a simpler phenomenon than Byzantine iconoclasm, in that religious art was destroyed as idolatrous. Nor did the defence of religious art in the early modern period develop a theology of the image as did the Byzantine iconodules. Perhaps the deepest contrast between Byzantine iconoclasm and comparable phenomena in the west is that in Byzantium the argument was entirely about visual imagery, whereas in the west visual imagery was opposed to the word, whether the 'silent word' of the elevated host or the preached word of the Protestants.

In the 20th century, *Eastern Orthodox theologians have stressed the humanism implicit in veneration of the person disclosed through the face in the icon, a humanism deepened by a theology of the human person as the image of God, and sometimes set this ideal up in opposition to the erasure of the face in much modern art.

Andrew Louth

Belting, H., *Likeness and Presence* (1990), ET (1994).

Besançon, A., *L'Image interdite: Une histoire intellectuelle de l'iconoclasme* (1994).

Bryer, A., and Herrin, J. (eds.), *Iconoclasm* (1977).

Campenhausen, H. von, 'The Theological Problem of Images in the Early Church', in H. von Campenhausen (ed.), *Tradition and Life in the Church* (1968).

Grabar, A., *L'Iconoclasme byzantin: Dossier archéologique* (1957), 2nd edn. (1984).

Ouspensky, L., *The Theology of the Icon*, 2nd edn. (2 vols.; 1992).

iconography, the art of painting, or, as Orthodox say, *writing*, icons. The term icon, in religious *art, refers nowadays exclusively to the religious art of the *Eastern Orthodox tradition. It derives from the Greek word, *eikon*, meaning image, which was the normal word for a picture or any other artistic representation (statue or mosaic) in classical Greek. Nowadays an icon is most commonly a painting on a wooden panel (though frescos are common, too), but in the *Byzantine period the term *eikon* was not so restricted, and also embraced mosaics, carved ivory, illustrated manuscripts, and even statues (though very few religious statues survive). The origins of the characteristic style of Byzantine religious art, which has been perpetuated in Orthodox iconography, are not thoroughly understood. Antecedents have been sought in the sacred style of art, probably of Neoplatonic inspiration, that developed in late antiquity in contrast to the realism of hellenistic art, or in the tradition of Egyptian funerary masks (most notably those preserved at Fayum). But the Christian conviction of the *resurrection meant that those men and women whom Christians depicted in art—besides Christ and his mother, the patriarchs and prophets of the OT, and the apostles and martyrs of the NT—were regarded not as dead, but as having passed to the fullness of the risen life. Consequently they were depicted as alive in the age to come, and icons came to be seen as pointing from this world to that. Such an understanding of the icon was fostered by the resonances of the word *eikon*, image, for the *human being was regarded as created in the image of God, and, in the generally (Neo-)*Platonist intellectual atmosphere of late antiquity, the word *eikon* suggested something that represented an eternal archetype. Icons thus acted as a focus for devotion to Christ, the Mother of God, and the saints, and they themselves became symbols of the care and compassion of those whom they depicted. Such devotion was banned during the periods of *iconoclasm in the 8th and 9th centuries, but the final condemnation of iconoclasm in 843 had the effect of solemnly confirming the veneration of icons, so that such veneration became a distinctive part of Byzantine Christianity. When the Slavs embraced Chris-

tianity, with liturgy and scriptures translated into Slavonic, icons, because they passed unscathed through the linguistic filter, assumed even greater significance. Post-iconoclast art developed a subtle language of colour and form, and an increasingly standardized pattern of internal church decoration; the icon screen (iconostasis), nowadays found in all Orthodox churches, was a *Russian development that made its way back to Byzantium. Because of the deepening schism between eastern and western Christendom, the Byzantine and Slav tradition of iconography was shielded from the developments in western art from the 13th century onwards. Not that iconography did not develop—there is remarkable development in the Byzantine tradition from the 10th to the 14th century, in the Russian tradition from the 13th to the 17th century, and in Romania from the 14th to the 18th century—but these developments preserved an essential continuity, rather than leading to what has been called the birth of art as object in the west.

From the 17th century onwards, the living tradition of iconography foundered, largely because of the influence of western styles of art, and the tradition was preserved only in a mechanical form by handbooks, the most famous being that by Dionysios of Fourna (18th century). In the 19th century, even that mechanical link with tradition was severed. But in the gathering dusk of iconography, theory, like the owl of Minerva, took flight, and at the turn of the 19th/20th century, various Russian thinkers, notably Evgeny Trubetskoy and Pavel Florensky, sought to give expression to the characteristic genius of Orthodox (especially Russian) iconography. This theory of the icon made much of the apparently stylized depiction of saints in icons, the use of reversed perspective; it developed a symbolism of colour, and deliberately contrasted the use of light in iconography with the western technique of chiaroscuro.

It is hard to tell how far this represents anything in the mind of the Byzantine iconographers, but its starting-point is what is central to the tradition of iconography: icons are not works of art, but objects of devotion and *prayer. The saints are depicted as our companions and helpers in prayer; Christ is depicted as one to whom prayer is addressed; Mary points us to Christ, and protects us with her intercession. The icon invites us into their company. One of the icons most prized by these Russian theorists, and one that has touched the hearts of many, is Andrei Rublev's icon of the Holy *Trinity, which was singled out as a pattern at the council of Moscow in 1551. This famous icon, which represents the Trinity under the form of the three angels to whom *Abraham offered hospitality at the Oak of Mamre (Gen. 18), depicts the three angels seated round a table, turned towards those who pray before the icon, so that they are drawn into the communion of the Holy Trinity. This attempt to discover the nature of the icon has led to a rediscovery of the lost art, and there have been several fine icon painters in this century, some inspired by Leonid Ouspensky, one of the finest being the monk Gregory Kroug, and in Greece Photios Kontoglou. Icon painting (or writing) is held to be a way of prayer, demanding *asceticism and purity of heart from the artist. Although apparently highly stylized, with no room for expression of the artist's ego, an icon must be written with a spontaneity inspired by the Holy Spirit. Even a trace of this spiritual authenticity (as preserved in reproductions) has immense power: testimony to which is the popularity of icons among non-Orthodox, and even non-Christians.

See also JESUS, DEPICTION OF.   **Andrew Louth**

Evdokomov, P., *The Art of the Icon: A Theology of Beauty*, ET (1990).

Florensky, P., *Iconostasis* (written in 1922 and published in Russian in 1972), ET (1996).

Ouspensky, L., *Theology of the Icon* (2 vols.; 1992).

Ouspensky, L., and Lossky, V., *The Meaning of Icons* (1952), new edn. (1982).

The Painter's Manual of Dionysius of Fourna, translated by P. Hetherington (1974).

Quénot, M., *Icons: A Window on the Kingdom* (1992).

Ignatius Loyola, see Exercises of St Ignatius.

Imitation of Christ, see Discipleship.

Immaculate Conception, see Mary.

immortality. The term means 'not being susceptible to death'. In antiquity the immortals were the gods, by contrast with human beings, who, like other inhabitants of the earth, are mere mortals. This usage was transferred to the *God of the Christians, of whom is sung, 'Immortal, invisible, God only wise …'.

But treatment of immortality is more usually concerned with the question of whether *human beings, despite appearances, in fact survive *death. No one doubts that humans, like other *animals, die. But, throughout recorded history, it has been widely held that death is not the end, and that, in one way or another, human beings live beyond death. In this sense immortality is not to be contrasted with *resurrection. Resurrection would be a species of the survival of death and thus a species of immortality. Immortality is here the wider term, and is not restricted to some future disembodied state. As a matter of cultural history in the west, however, immortality has been bound up with *soul–*body *dualism and predicated of the immaterial soul, while resurrection has been associated with more holistic, or even physicalist conceptions of human beings as complex animal organisms. In this sense there is, after all, a contrast between immortality and resurrection.

Strictly, only God's immortal nature is intrinsic—being an integral aspect of God's independent and necessary being. All creatures depend on the Creator both for coming to be and for remaining in being. Deprived of God's act of *creation they would cease to exist. But there is still a distinction between the idea of some creatures—*angels, for example, and perhaps human souls—possessing a relatively indestructible, and therefore intrinsically immortal nature, and that of all creatures on earth, including human beings, being composite and destructible, thus requiring a fresh creative act of transformation or even replication in another mode, if ever some of them are to acquire immortality.

Outside the context of theism, arguments for immortality tend to centre on the idea of the soul as a simple and therefore indestructible substance. We find this in *Plato and, surprisingly, in the 20th-century atheist philosopher John McTaggart. In both cases the argument was held to work as much for pre-existence as for post-mortem existence, an implication foreign to the Christian tradition, apart from *Origen. The Christian mind was too determined by the doctrine of creation to countenance the idea of pre-existence. But the argument for immortality from the soul's God-given simplicity reappears throughout the Christian centuries, in Thomas *Aquinas and in Bishop Butler, for example.

Empirical arguments for immortality, based on parapsychology, are difficult to evaluate. While it shows prejudice simply to ignore them, the possibility of alternative explanations—physiological, *psychological, even *paranormal (telepathic)—makes it very difficult to accept such narratives as hard evidence. Nor is the kind of survival suggested easy to interpret theologically.

Where soul–body dualism is rejected, as in many strands of contemporary Christian *theology, arguments for immortality (in this context immortality as resurrection) are overtly theological, not *philosophical or *anthropological. It is God's nature, his *love and his *justice, that are the principal grounds for belief in life beyond death. Issues in theodicy feature strongly here: the *suffering of the innocent makes no theological sense if this life is all there is. Indeed it can be argued more widely that God's creation of such profound, yet short-lived and fragile, values as those exemplified in human life and culture makes no theological sense if those values have no lasting future in God's *eternity.

These theological arguments, presupposing belief in a just and loving creator, have not wholly displaced anthropological arguments based on human experience. It can still be suggested that there are intimations of immortality in the values themselves that, on any reckoning, have emerged in the course of *evolution on this planet, as poets like Wordsworth and *Coleridge have shown. *Kant's moral *argument* for immortality as a postulate of practical reason is very different from such intimations. It is derived rationally from his conception of the highest good which it is our rational nature not only to pursue but to attain.

Philosophical interest has in fact shifted from arguments for immortality to the coherence of any conception of life beyond death. Where the idea of a future disembodied state is under consideration the question is certainly one of intelligibility. How could such finite, immaterial, souls be identified? How could they communicate? Valiant efforts to answer these questions have been made, notably in the speculations of H. H. Price, but these have not won widespread assent. Indeed Eastern conceptions of loss of individuality as the soul is released or absorbed into the world soul might appear more intelligible.

Christian theology today is inclined to share these doubts over the intelligibility of disembodied existence and to prefer the language of immortality as resurrection. Here the main problem is continuity. Given present-day knowledge of the nature of the stuff that constitutes a human body, resurrection can hardly mean the reassembly of the particles. But new creation in another mode looks more like the creation of an immortal replica, whose identity with the *person who lived on earth is hard to defend.

Perhaps the most plausible defence of the idea of a future life requires a combination of immortality and resurrection. The new resurrection 'body' provides the conditions—in the resurrection 'world'—of identity and communication beyond the grave, but the soul or spiritual subject, formed here on earth through its experiences, personal growth, and unique history of interpersonal relations, is the bearer of continuity across the boundary of death.

So far only humans from among earth's creatures have been deemed appropriate candidates for immortality or resurrection. The reasons for this are bound up, in the Judaeo-Christian tradition, with the view that humans alone are made in the image of God, endowed with the rational and interpersonal capacities that make them spiritual beings, thus *capable* of being made immortal. On this view, the belief that the higher animals, with their developed sentience and awareness and their quasi-personal qualities of character and affection, deserve a place in *heaven, would be rejected as merely sentimental. However, it might be argued that, if immortality means resurrection, and if resurrection means translation into a resurrection 'world', then through their association with the life stories of humans, animals may, after all, form part of that resurrection 'world'. Whether this is a real possibility depends on whether the idea makes sense—whether, that is, the nature of the higher animals allows for such translation.

One reason why the idea of immortality, even for *humans*, is often rejected today not only by *atheists but by some religious people stems from the modern sense of human life as an essentially bounded affair—the boundaries of birth and death prescribing the very nature and conditions of human existence in its finitude and temporality. This view found philosophical expression in the work of Heidegger, who insisted on 'being towards death' as a defining characteristic of the human. While this is understandable from an anthropological perspective, it can hardly be allowed to determine theology. From a theological perspective the *hope of immortality is inextricably bound up with God's nature and with the demands of theodicy.

A more theologically respectable reason for questioning the traditional Christian hope of immortality, at least when construed as life after death, is bound up with the notion of eternity as timelessness. If God is outside *time, then to be taken into God's eternity is to be removed from all temporal sequence. There can thus be no question of life 'after' death. Sometimes this conception of our ultimate destiny is represented as a matter of our being held in God's *memory*. But, quite apart from 'memory' being itself a temporal term, this does scant justice to the actuality of our own real presence in God's eternity. Increasingly, theologians and *philosophers of religion today are coming, rather, to question the idea of eternity as timelessness. God's 'sempiternity' is that of boundless life, and the hope of immortality is the hope of future participation, by God's recreative act, in God's own endless future. To the objection that endless life would be tedious, Aquinas had an unanswerable reply: 'Nothing that is contemplated in wonder can be tiresome, since so long as the thing remains in wonder it continues to stimulate desire. But the divine substance is always viewed with wonder by any created intellect. So it is impossible for an intellectual substance to become tired of this vision.'   **Brian Hebblethwaite**

Hick, J. H., *Death and Eternal Life* (1976).
Lewis, H. D., *The Self and Immortality* (1973).
Penelhum, T., *Survival and Disembodied Existence* (1970).
—— (ed.), *Immortality* (1973).
Price, H. H., *Essays in the Philosophy of Religion* (1972).
Taylor, A. E., *The Christian Hope of Immortality* (1930).
Tugwell, S., *Human Immortality and the Redemption of Death* (1990).

incarnation is central to the beliefs most characteristic of *Christianity in all its main traditions, eastern and western, Catholic and Protestant. It is the principal trigger of *Trinitarian doctrine on the one hand and of the ways in which *redemption has traditionally been conceived on the other. Christianity without the doctrine of the Incarnation, *Unitarianism, for instance, looks rather like a type of reformed Judaism, the consequence of a remarkable prophet simplifying the law and opening wide the doors of Judaism—as earlier prophets had suggested—to all humanity.

In its strict form it is wholly dependent on the prologue to *John's gospel, a powerful piece of poetry starting 'In the beginning was the Word; the Word was with God and the Word was God', and continuing, moving from eternity to time, through a reference to John the Baptist, to the key assertion, 'The Word was made flesh and dwelt among us, full of grace and truth; we have beheld his glory, glory as of the only Son of the Father' (1: 1, 14). This text provides the most unambiguous affirmation of the divinity of Jesus Christ to be found in the NT, and the whole of the fourth gospel can be read as a commentary upon it. It is also the only text to use *Word in this sense, the only text to use the phrase 'became flesh', and one of the very few texts to affirm the pre-existence of him whom the world knew as *Jesus. This is made clear precisely by the use of 'Word' to identify the son in his pre-human state. Without this text there could have been no doctrine of the Incarnation in the precise terms that came to characterize it. Nevertheless the 'hymn' in *Paul's letter to the Philippians, a far earlier text, is almost as explicit: 'Christ Jesus who, though he was in the form of God, did not count equality with God a thing to be grasped, but emptied himself, taking the form of a servant, being born in the likeness of men' (2: 5–7). While the terminology is different, the sense is close. The Johannine terminology has become standard, the Pauline slightly eccentric until the modern revival of *kenotic theology. Both represent attempts to use complex *metaphors (word, flesh, emptied himself, the form of a servant) to express what, if true, was a mystery beyond the reach of standard language.

The letter to the Colossians (either by Paul or by an early disciple) is almost equally emphatic: Jesus Christ is 'the image of the invisible God, the first-born of all creation; for in him all things were created, in heaven and earth, visible and invisible ... all things were created through him and for him' (Col. 1: 15–16). While we do not find such extended statements in Paul's early letters, nevertheless both 1 Corinthians (8: 6) and Romans (8: 3) imply the same; God 'sent' his son, 'through whom we exist'. Again, the letter to the *Hebrews, not part of the Pauline corpus but almost as early (probably pre-70 AD), begins with a no less firm assertion: 'In many and various ways God spoke of old to our fathers by the prophets; but in these last days he has spoken to us by a Son, whom he appointed the heir of all things, through whom also he created the world. He reflects the glory of God and bears the very stamp of his nature, upholding the universe by his word of power' (1: 1–3). In the Synoptic Gospels too we find at times almost comparable texts such as Matt. 11: 25–7. While the basic title 'Son of God', used so often from the opening verse of *Mark onwards, may be understandable in a less than fully incarnational way, it is still in a unique way grounded in the elevation of Jesus subsequent to crucifixion and *Resurrection. But the two ways quickly merge: for early Christian thought he 'came down' from the Father and he 'returned' in the glory of the Resurrection to the Father. The identity of meaning between 'God' and 'Father' made it almost impossible to use the first term unambiguously for Christ even if the believer accepted his divinity. This only changed when the doctrine of the Trinity evolved in a later stage of development.

Following their experience of the Resurrection, the *disciples of Jesus hailed him at once as the Christ (*Messiah). This identification was so absolute and so quick that Christ soon became more of a name than a title and the disciples themselves became 'Christians'.

As a title it was replaced or extended by *Kyrios*, Lord. While used for kings, this was also a divine title. Like 'Son of God', it retained a measure of ambiguity. Collectively the evidence available suggests that a basically incarnational theology asserting the divinity of Christ was already part of Christian belief in the first generation after his death and too widely spread to be judged a personal invention of Paul. Yet it was almost certainly not part of anything Jesus explicitly said (his discourses in John's gospel must be regarded as a later meditation upon the mystery of Jesus and his teaching). What is certain is that the NT as a whole shares this development.

But it is no less clear that the phraseology in which Jesus' divine character is referred to is remarkably diverse, using a considerable range of images and models. While it cannot be questioned that in the subsequent centuries most Christians held firmly to the divinity of Christ as well as to his humanity, it was easy to disagree about what this meant. Thus, for instance, if he was 'first-born of all creation', was he himself part of creation? Was the Son less *God than the Father? It is hardly surprising that it proved hard to express the nature of Christ in any one agreed formula when this was attempted, not by mere repetition of scriptural verses, but in the philosophical language fashionable in the church after the peace of Constantine. The consequence was a series of intense disagreements and conciliar definitions in metaphysical terms unknown to scripture ranging from *Nicaea I (325) to the condemnation of monothelitism (the doctrine that, though there were two distinct natures in Christ, there was a sole 'will') at Constantinople III (681). What seems unquestionable, already in the NT but still more in subsequent doctrinal history, is the way that, though the full *humanity of Jesus was regularly insisted upon, against every attempt to conceive him in an almost purely divine way, with humanity hardly more than a disguise, nevertheless what we may call a working humanity disappeared. While the Christ of classical *christology was not ontologically *Docetist, he was so experientially. His human life was seen as effectively swallowed up by the consciousness of divinity. That was already, one might think, the weakness of Johannine christology. Thus it was generally accepted and insisted upon by *Aquinas, for instance, that Christ's human soul enjoyed throughout his life the joy of the beatific vision of God as possessed by the saints in heaven. It is hard to make any psychological sense of the agony in the garden and on the cross if that were so.

The doctrine of the Incarnation may be assessed at various levels. The first is that of scripture, where it is formulated in a wide variety of ways, most of them at least partly poetic and metaphorical. The second is the classical account centred upon the teaching of *Chalcedon that Christ was a single *person possessing two distinct natures, divine and human. This formulation was both required and controlled by the conflicts of that period, particularly between the *Alexandrian and Antiochene traditions. It would be absurd to claim that Christianity has for ever to think of Christ in the terms of 5th-century *Greek theological philosophy. Moreover, it is certainly not necessary to hold that the Chalcedonian formula answered every problem, even in its time. In fact, while intended to protect Christ's humanity against absorption in the divinity, it remains true that almost all the christology of that age leaned heavily to the divine side, making much in the gospel account of Jesus unnecessarily hard to understand. Only in the 19th and 20th cen-

turies, with the rise of kenotic theology and other approaches, have there been serious attempts to assert the truth of the Incarnation as a necessary truth of Christianity but in ways that do justice to Jesus' humanity as a functioning reality. In previous ages attempts to achieve the latter seem to have led almost invariably to a denial of his divinity and on to Unitarianism.

Where does this leave us today? What now, as in the past, seems regularly overlooked is the necessary incomprehensibility of the Incarnation. Human understanding depends on the general, not the particular, on classes of things and comparisons, on what we can measure experientially. None of this is available for the Incarnation. We do not know God and therefore we cannot conceivably understand what it may or may not imply for God to be man. Here is something by definition unique. In the assertion that Christ has two natures, one word is used to cover two quite different things. There is no class 'nature' to which the divine and the human both belong. Moreover, the distinction between 'nature' and 'person' seems questionable. Is not being a person an intrinsic part of human nature? The idea that a divine person exists 'in' a human nature but that there is no human person appears to contradict the further Chalcedonian statement that 'Christ is like us in all respects'. We are unable to formulate in either ontological or experiential terms what it means for Jesus of Nazareth to be so united with God's 'Son' or 'Word' that they must be considered one single 'person', a word that again cannot mean the same thing in regard to divinity as it does to humanity. Again, it is simply impertinence to attempt to prescribe the kind of knowledge that Jesus the man must have had by reason of this union. We do not know. The union was strictly, as many dogmatic statements have stressed, 'incomprehensible'. What we do know is that Jesus, the son of Mary, a craftsman from Nazareth, was fully human. Believing in the Incarnation has nothing to do with knowing what consciousness Jesus had of being God's son or when that consciousness began, except in so far as we can build on historical evidence. Like Paul, Christians believe that 'God was in Christ reconciling the world to himself' (2 Cor. 5: 19), like Luke they believe that 'Jesus increased in wisdom and in stature' (2: 52), but modern Christians may be more agnostic than their predecessors about the formulation in ontological terms of what 'God was in Christ' means, just as they may have a greater concern for the significance of 'increased in wisdom'.

Paul's formula 'reconciling the world' is important. In the NT and the classics of incarnation theology, such as the *De incarnatione* of *Athanasius and the *Cur deus homo* of *Anselm, the decisive interpretative theme remains the redemption: Christ needed to be of such and such a nature in order to be the appropriate vehicle of God's redemption of humanity. Nevertheless, while incarnation theology acquired a rather rigid structure, redemption theology never did so. Thus there is no agreement on whether the Incarnation, as the achieved union of God and humanity, should already be seen as redemptive or whether it is rather a precondition for redemption achieved on the cross. There has always been a range of models for conceiving the *atonement and they do not all logically require the same kind of incarnation. While the Athanasian and Anselmian models stressed the divine character required in the redeemer, other more expressive or exemplarist models may need for credibility a redeemer more autonomously human in his consciousness, experience, and knowledge, yet still the definitive *sacrament of God. If God's merciful love is to be made manifest in a human figure it must be one that can really be taken seriously by other humans, psychologically as well as ontologically a creature.

Much of the significance of incarnation theology lies in its wider implications. Take 'flesh' first. In the OT it meant humanity in its mortality, weakness, and sinfulness contrasted with God, immortal, strong, holy. Man as flesh is certainly not evil but rather a field of battle between the spirit of God and the spirit of iniquity. This remains the case in the NT, but whereas in the OT 'flesh' stood for humanity as such, in the NT under Hellenistic influences a usage grew dividing human nature into two elements: flesh and spirit (later *body and *soul). There is at times a hint that flesh is bad, spirit good. We find it in Paul. 'To set the mind on the flesh is death, but to set the mind on the Spirit is life and peace' (Rom. 8: 6). God, Paul affirms, sent 'his own son in the likeness of sinful flesh and for sin, he condemned sin in the flesh' (8: 3). This is ambiguous but could be read to mean that the flesh is inherently sinful and that the son only seemed to be enfleshed. There was certainly a beguiling wave of *Gnostic *dualism flowing through the Christian community in late apostolic and post-apostolic times, making for such interpretations. John's letters are written to warn against it, appealing for a fully incarnational gospel, something 'we have seen with our eyes and touched with our hands' (1 John 1: 1). 'Many false prophets have gone out into the world. By this you know the Spirit of God: every spirit which confesses that Jesus Christ has come in the flesh is of God' (4: 1–2). Because God has 'become flesh', the goodness of the material, the bodily, is ensured. Powerful as the tendency was for *asceticism to take an unmitigatedly anti-flesh form, it could never quite succeed. On the contrary, John's eucharistic doctrine of the 'bread of life' given to the world to eat as Christ's flesh (6: 51) is an extension of the Incarnation and pervades the understanding of the church's central ritual. Similarly Christian orthodoxy always insisted on the goodness of *marriage. The Incarnation was thus a way of emphatically affirming the goodness of the flesh in particular and *creation in general. While fully in line with the OT, it greatly intensified that sense of goodness by affirming God's union with 'flesh'. This is seen especially in the thought of the first absolutely major post-apostolic theologian, *Irenaeus, who continually defends the significance and goodness of flesh against the Gnostics and formulates his theology in terms of a 'recapitulation' of creation in the Incarnate Christ, establishing thereby a sense of the way nature is taken up by grace which would remain crucial for Catholicism. As Christ is supremely the 'New Adam', the Incarnation establishes perfect humanity as divine. 'God became man that man might become God', Irenaeus insisted, a remark taken up by *Augustine and later by Aquinas. 'My me is God, I do not know my selfhood save in him', declared the 15th-century mystic Catherine of Genoa. Unique as the Incarnation looks, it transforms one's sense of everything.

One danger in the use of 'flesh' in incarnation theology was to suggest that what was united with the Word was not full humanity, a body but not a mind. While that misunderstanding was impossible within a Hebrew thought context, it was easy when the term survived in a Hellenized one. Apollinaris, a close friend of Athanasius, denied the presence of a human mind or soul in Christ. After Athanasius died, Apollinarianism was condemned. Thus a terminology originally intended to assert the absoluteness of the Son of

God's unity with humanity could be used instead to imply that he was far less than fully man.

Would there have been an Incarnation if there had been no *Fall, no need of redemption? No, said Aquinas; yes, said Scotus, for whom the Incarnation was primarily not a way of rescuing humanity from sin but of bringing creation to its divinely intended fulfilment. Here as in much modern theology there is an unresolved struggle between deeply diverse theological philosophies: how are Incarnation and crucifixion related? While redemption and cross long dominated the western tradition, Protestantism especially, the Incarnation remained more central to the eastern. Much modern western theology, particularly English, has sought to become more incarnationalist.

In the 19th and 20th centuries the Incarnation, like other doctrines, has come under heavy liberal attack as a 'myth', damaging true understanding of the historical Jesus, as an import from 'mystery' religions, and as in principle unacceptable in imputing unique significance to a single individual within history. It represents a 'scandal of particularity', claiming absolute authority for a particular person, and thus violating G. E. Lessing's assertion that an 'ugly ditch' divides the 'accidental truths of history' from the 'necessary truths of reason'. In the words of one theologian, affirming a typical post-*Enlightenment position, 'it is not possible with consistency to ascribe an absolute authority to a particular section of experience within the world, such as the life of Jesus' (Maurice Wiles, The Remaking of Christian Doctrine (1974), 48).

The first objection may be met more easily than the last. While acceptance of the Incarnation is essentially a matter of faith, not history, there is arguably sufficient continuity between the historic Jesus, so far as we know him, NT writing, and subsequent Christian belief to base a claim that the doctrine was there in embryo from the start and that a convincing *development holds the process together. Without some acceptance of the idea of development, later christological orthodoxy is clearly indefensible. It can, furthermore, be claimed with reasonable confidence that an explanation of belief in Christ's divinity in terms of the impact of other religions is unconvincing, given the brief period between the death of Jesus and clear evidence of that belief.

One cannot respond so easily to philosophical rejection of the claim that a single individual, one poor Jewish male, living 2,000 years ago, could be uniquely significant for all time. Many people, notably the Russian émigré philosopher Berdyaev, happy to believe in the potentiality of incarnational religion in general, are incredulous faced with a claim to any absolute incarnational particularity, however much that claim is made in connection with a theology of universal divinization. In *Hegelian understanding the Incarnation becomes a matter of a vast evolutionary process in history as a whole, the coming together of divinity and humanity. Undoubtedly a great leap in faith is needed if the particularity is to be maintained. There is however no reason, despite Wiles's affirmation, to accede to Lessing's theory. Almost all our values derive primarily from particular experience, beginning with a mother's loving care. There is no philosophical or experiential necessity to deny that the most important of truths can come to us through historical particularity. The Incarnation cannot be denied on general grounds because its claimed uniqueness puts it in principle beyond the reach of general laws. The question is whether faith in something so extraordinary can be backed by a sufficient degree of plausibility. That may be found in three things. First the mysterious impact Jesus made on his disciples and the rapid expansion of their community. Secondly, the impact the NT depiction of Jesus as a whole can continue to make on the reader. Here is something wonderful enough to be divine; nowhere else do we find anything quite comparable. Thirdly, in the fact that 2,000 years later there are many millions of Christian believers in every part of the globe. The vitality, endurance, and expansion of faith in Christ could be proposed as evidence of its correctness.

Abandon the uniqueness, regard Jesus as one of the world's exceptionally holy men and no more, perhaps a Hindu avatar, and the inner integrity of both the NT and Christianity's ongoing shared tradition of creed and liturgy simply falls apart. Accept the distinctive ultimacy of Christ, and one can still admit that all the terms used to express this incomprehensible reality are and must be inadequate. The very range of titles and forms of expression, all borrowed from somewhere, used of Christ in the NT already suggests that. The theologians of the councils could not escape a comparable predicament. The Incarnation itself remains both a word compounded from a metaphor and the reality of God's presence in Jesus of Nazareth, transcending all formulas and continually fertilizing incarnational religion by the very freedom it provides for those who, knowing or unknowing, constitute in the world and in the flesh an extension to the body of the Incarnate Lord.

Adrian Hastings

Dunn, James, *The Christ and the Spirit*, i. *Christology* (1998).
Hebblethwaite, B., *The Incarnation* (1987).
Hick, John (ed.), *The Myth of God Incarnate* (1977).
Jenkins, David, *The Glory of Man* (1967).
Morgan, R. (ed.), *The Religion of the Incarnation: Anglican Essays in Commemoration of Lux Mundi* (1989).
Moule, C. D. F., *The Origin of Christology* (1977).
Pannenberg, W., *Jesus, God and Man* (1968).
Rahner, Karl, 'Current Problems in Christology', *Theological Investigations* (1961), i. 149–200.
Robinson, John, *The Human Face of God* (1973).
Torrance, Thomas F., *Space, Time, and Incarnation* (1969).
—— (ed.), *The Incarnation* (1981).

inculturation, see CONTEXTUAL THEOLOGY.

Indian Christian thought.

The three major Christian missionary impacts in India, establishing the oriental churches from the 2nd century AD, Roman Catholic from the 16th, and the Reformed from the 18th, generated little indigenous theology until the possibility of a post-imperial Indian Christian identity was prompted by the emerging national consciousness in the 19th century. The first Indians to engage in the rooting of Christian thought in the Indian soil were not Indian Christians, but Indian Hindus of the reform movement Brahmo Samaj, such as Rajah Rammohun Roy (1772–1833), P. C. Mozoomdar (1840–1905), and Keshub Chunder Sen (1838–84), who worked out innovative ways of interpreting Christ. Interestingly, none of them felt the need to confess the Christian faith. These Hindus not only set the parameters for Indian Christian theology but also inspired Indian Christian converts to utilize their own cultural resources creatively, resources denounced by missionaries as heathen, and to use these very resources to elucidate their new-found faith.

Modern Indian Christian thought arose as a result of English-educated, middle-class Indian converts trying to reconcile their new faith with their national identity, and to come to terms with the colonial presence, revitalized textual *Hinduism, and aggressive denominational theologies that saw their task as rescuing and civilizing the natives. Thus, it was in response to these that the early converts began to define a Christianity that would be genuinely indigenous and at the same time true to the catholic nature of Christian faith. Arumainayagam (1823–1919) in the south, K. M. Banerjea (1813–85), and Lal Behari Dey (1824–94) in the east, were pioneers in their attempts to overcome their alienation by consciously integrating themselves in the newly constructed notion of India. Brahmabandhav Upadhyaya (1861–1907) spoke for many when he wrote: 'In short, we are Hindus as far as our physical and mental constitution is concerned, but in regard to our immortal souls we are Catholics. We are Hindu-Catholics' (Baago 1969: 125).

The emotional need for cultural belonging continued even after independence, when Indian theologians saw their task as helping to build the nation after the end of the colonial era. The theological writings of Vengal Chakkarai (1880–1958), Paul Devanandan (1901–62), and M. M. *Thomas bear witness to their patriotic consciousness. These theologians engaged in the task of applying the Christian message to nation-building after the ravages of colonialism. The title of Michael Amaladoss's book, *Becoming Indian: The Process of Inculturation* (1992), is an indication of how crucial this question is, and how it continues to plague Indian Christians.

Indian Christian thought can be classified in two overarching clusters: religio-cultural, which takes the spiritual and philosophical heritage seriously, and sociopolitical, which focuses on inequalities and seeks liberation from oppressive social structures. These categorizations are not clear-cut and compartmentalized divisions, but often overlap and interact.

Religio-cultural

This has two discernible interpretative bases—Vedic Hinduism and vernacular traditions. The former finds its favourable climate in Sanskritic textual tradition represented by the *Vedas*, the *Upanishads*, and the *Bhagavadgita*, and sees them as normative for theologizing. If Sanskritists emphasized the Vedanta, the vernacularists focused on the *bhakti*, devotional tradition; but both were involved in the task of tracing Christian ideas in the Hindu thought-world; and in their construction of theology they went beyond and at times bypassed Semitic and Hellenic images. The Vedic Christian theology drew selectively from ancient writings a spiritualized and metaphysical Hinduism, and was preoccupied with the task of translating Christian faith into one of the Hindu philosophical traditions. For instance, Brahmabandhav Upadhyaya sought to accommodate Upanishadic understanding of Brahman as *sat-cit-ananda* (reality, consciousness, bliss) with the Christian notion of Trinity; Chenchiah saw Jesus as the *Adi purusha* (primeval person). Among others, Pierre Johanns, Swami *Abhishiktananda (Henri le Saux), and R. *Panikkar undertook an intensive reading of the Vedanta to make the gospel relevant to the Indian context and in the process enriched Christianity. S. Jesudason, Ernest Forrester-Paton, and J. C. Winslow, and much later Bede *Griffiths adopted the ashram ideals to build bridges between Hinduism and Christianity. The initial combative and contrastive practice later gave way to the acknowledgement of the complementarity of Hindu and Christian traditions. Even before the World Missionary Conference at Edinburgh in 1910 and *Vatican II in the 1960s popularized the notion of positive elements embedded in the other faith traditions, K. M. Banerjea believed that providence had been preparing Hindus to receive the teachings of the ultimate revelation of all—the Christian faith. He argued that the bible had been anticipated in the Vedas, and the sacrifice of Jesus had been foreshadowed by *Prajapathi* (The Lord of the Creation). The implication was that Christian faith, far from being a foreign *religion, is a fulfilment of the Vedas. The current writings of Amaladass, Aleaz, and Sr. Vandana, among others, fall within the Sanskritic paradigm.

Vernacular theology is prompted by regional languages and narrative styles and is sustained by literary traditions of the mother-tongue. One of the distinctive features of vernacular theology is its mode of presentation. Its method is not analytical or dialectical, but devotional and synthetic. Instead of producing treatises, it uses the medium of devotional *poetry or, as in the case of Sunder Singh (1889–1929) in Punjab, storytelling. Narayan Vaman Tilak (1862–1919), in Marathi, H. A. Krishnapillai (1827–1900), and Vedanayagam Sastriyar (1774–1864), in Tamil, were formidable interpreters who imaginatively assimilated ideas and *ragas* (melodies) from *Saivite* and *Vaisnavite bhakti* poets and made use of them profitably for Christian apologetics. Inspired by the lyrics of the great Telugu composer Thiyagaraja, who praises the noble birth and sterling qualities of Rama, Vedanayagam composed similar lyrics extolling the superior qualities of Jesus.

Vernacularists are often castigated for their claims to recover an ancestral purity, their cultural narcissism and inscriptions of overtly evangelical zeal. There were nevertheless interesting strands in their writings. Even before it had become fashionable to ascribe feminine qualities to God in western theology, Tilak, following in the Hindu *bhakti* tradition of Tukaram and others, wrote:

> Tenderest Mother—Guru mine,
> Saviour, where is love like Thine?

Krishnapillai similarly employed the imagery of God as *mother. Another example of what appears to western theology as theological radicalness, but for which there are numerous antecedents in India, can be seen in Mayuram Vendanayakar's interreligious lyrics. He composed over 190 of them (*The Sarva Samaya Samaraca Kirtathanikal: Lyrics of all Religions in Reconciliation*, 1878), without a single reference to the names of Jesus, Christ, or God or to the Judaeo-Christian tradition, which could be sung by adherents of all faiths.

Sociopolitical

Encouraged by Latin Americans, Indians have worked out their own version of *liberation theology, but one which takes into account both the rich religious culture and deep spirituality of the people, and also existing liberative themes in Indian religions, particularly in *Buddhist and *bhakti* traditions. Sebastian Kappen, Aloysius Pieris, and M. M. Thomas have been at the forefront in working out a theology of liberation. Each in his own way has been trying to weave the emancipatory aspects in the gospel with radical elements in Indian religious traditions, and positive elem-

ents in Marxism. Thomas even went on to identify the liberative potentiality of brahminical tradition. I. Jesudasan and T. K. John have developed a theology of liberation utilizing Gandhian insights.

Recently, however, there has been a number of new voices offering counter-theology to the dominant Sanskritically based theology and also to the mainstream liberation theology. The most vociferous and vibrant are the *dalits*, the tribals, and Indian women. These groups have their own distinctive histories of pain and rejection, and they come from varied socio-economic and political backgrounds. What is common to all of them is that they have been marginalized and alienated by the ideological and theological conceptions of the prevailing Christian theology.

Once known variously as 'untouchables' or *harijans*, the present day *dalits* ('broken', 'crushed', 'trampled upon') perceive the traditional Indian theology as patronizing and a convenient tool to legitimize their low status. They seek liberation from their economic deprivation, but more importantly, from social stigma. In their earlier attempts Christian *dalits* naturally turned to biblical resources to facilitate their struggles (A. P. Nirmal). As lifelong servers in Indian society, the idea of the suffering servant envisioned by *Isaiah resonates with their plight. Similarly Jesus' identification with the socially handicapped and stigmatized Galileans has a natural appeal. Recently, however, there has been an attempt to go beyond the biblical vision and find strength and value from their own symbols, myths, gods and goddesses, and historical heroes and martyrs. The revisioning of Saguni-Ranga, a *dalit* god, as a friend and servant (V. Devasahayam), and the recovery of the religious dance, the *Song of Pottan Teyyam*, which advocates common humanity and common destiny for all in spite of caste differences, are cases in point (A. Ayrookuzhiel).

Though Indian women have yet to come up with distinctive terms equating with 'womanist' or *mujerista* to identify their cause and struggles, they are equally vigorous in negotiating their role. Inspired by such attempts, Indian women have delineated their own route drawing critically from both Christian and Hindu sources. More practical than theoretical, Indian *feminist theology sees its task as transforming both secular and ecclesiastical structures. While celebrating the recent spurt of Indian feminist discourse, one needs to pay attention to the earlier pioneers, especially Panditha Ramabhai (1858–1922). She was not only at the forefront of anti-colonial agitation but also committed herself to the improvement of Indian women. Her major contribution was in her *translating efforts. Dissatisfied with the missionary versions of the Marathi Bible which were full of Sanskrit, Arabic, and Persian words which went beyond the reach of the ordinary people, she produced her own version which made the Bible accessible to children, women, and the poor, thus surpassing the hermeneutical scope even of Elizabeth Cady Stanton.

India has a tribal population of 60 million whose identity is marked by their symbiotic relationship with the earth and the environment, and their egalitarian social system. Until recently, and following Hindu precedent, tribal culture was seen as inferior and glossed over by mainstream Indian theological thinking. However, the recent awakening of the tribals to their cultural identity has resulted in a reinvention of their values. For instance, the tribal opposition to greed and pride stands in stark contrast to caste pride and consumer greediness (Paulus Kullu). Significantly these values are seen as being endorsed by the bible. They also draw on their own festivals and folklore to articulate their faith.

India has celebrated the golden jubilee of her independence. As she moves into the new millennium, what will be the future markers of Indian Christian theology? There seem to be three options. One is to long for a time when Indian Christian theology will triumph over its rivals and the entire subcontinent will confess the name of Christ. This was the *missionary expectation, but the relatively small numerical success to date, and the reinvigoration of the other major religions, make this only a continuing utopian dream. The second is to hold on to its institutional system, but to try to get rid of a western image by superficially infusing Christian doctrines and rituals with Indian ideas. The third is to undergo an enormous reassessment, give up Christianity's claim to be the sole conveyor of truth, and renegotiate its role built on differences. Rather than striving to redeem India, its future would lie in its ability to evolve a hybridized style of identity. Its relevance will be measured not by its ability to invoke lost authenticities of ancient India or to superintend the purity of the gospel, but in creating an allegory of theological hybridity. In this way it could be accepted as complementary to other religious discourses in India and a companion in the search for truth and religious harmony. The very survival of Indian Christian theology, or for that matter the Indian church, may depend on its capacity to respond to a society that is at times tolerant, but often sceptical of a minority community committed to a religion with foreign origins and linked with recent colonialism.   **R. S. Sugirtharajah**

Amaladass, A. (ed.), *Christian Contribution to Indian Philosophy* (1995).
Baago, K., *Pioneers of Indigenous Christianity* (1969).
Boyd, R., *An Introduction to Indian Christian Theology* (1969).
Gnanadason, A. (ed.), *Towards a Theology of Humanhood* (1987).
Massey, J. (ed.), *Indigenous People: Dalits. Dalit Issues in Today's Theological Debate* (1994).
Patmury, J. (ed.), *Doing Theology with the Poetic Traditions of India* (1996).
Puthanangady, P. (ed.), *Towards an Indian Theology of Liberation* (1986).
Sugirtharajah, R. S., and Hargreaves, C. (eds.), *Readings in Indian Christian Theology* (1993), i.
Wilfred. F. (ed.), *Leave the Temple: Indian Paths to Human Liberation* (1992).

infallibility is the prerogative of being guarded by divine intervention against error. There are in Christianity three candidates for infallibility, apart from Christ himself: the *bible, general *councils representing the church, and the *papacy. Infallibility rests on the assumption that God would not reveal himself definitively to the world without providing entirely dependable information about that *revelation.

Biblical infallibility or inerrancy was assumed in medieval theology, but softened by the *allegorical method of interpretation. The literal inerrancy of scripture, in a sense that cannot be reconciled with scientific and historical knowledge, is a modern notion, developed in response to biblical criticism. The Roman Catholic Church was committed to it until the encyclical *Divino Afflante Spiritu* in 1943, since when a variety of *symbolic modes and literary genres have been acknowledged in scripture. *Vatican II, acknowledging the human as well as the divine element in the bible, insisted only that it teaches without error the truths that God intended to be inscribed 'for the sake of our salvation'. In Protestantism a doctrine of biblical inerrancy was elaborated by the *Princeton

school of *Reformed theology in the 19th century (B. B. Warfield). Biblical infallibility is held by many conservative *evangelicals, though others are content to insist on the basic reliability of scripture.

The infallibility of the *church, expressed in a general council, has been held by the eastern and western churches. It goes considerably beyond the generally held belief in the church's indefectibility—the doctrine that the church's faith cannot ultimately fail. For the Roman Catholic Church, general councils consist of the bishops (see EPISCOPATE) convened in union with the pope. For *Eastern Orthodoxy, the infallibility of general councils manifests the infallibility of the whole church and is not dependent on the papacy. *Anglicans also recognize general councils as the church's supreme *authority, but do not accept that it is the pope's prerogative to convene them, preside at them, and ratify their conclusions or that they are necessarily infallible.

The doctrine of papal infallibility was first developed by *Franciscan theologians in the early 14th century. Held by some theologians, rejected by others, it became by the 19th century the touchstone of *ultramontanism. The circumstances in which papal pronouncements are made infallibly were meticulously defined by *Vatican I, called by Pius IX, against concerted opposition. Bishops (Dupanloup), historians (Döllinger), and theologians (*Newman) regarded it as an abuse of a general council to make a gratuitous definition of *dogma when the infallibility of the church, with the pope as its mouthpiece, had been accepted for centuries. Vatican I nevertheless decreed that it was 'a dogma divinely revealed' that when the pope, as the successor of *Peter, 'speaks *ex cathedra*', when as 'pastor and doctor of all Christians … he defines a doctrine regarding faith or morals to be held by the universal church', he possesses the infallibility that Christ bestowed on his church. Therefore such definitions are 'irreformable of themselves, and not from the consent of the church.' Ultramontane as this definition appears, it is important to recognize that papal infallibility is still defined explicitly within the context of 'the infallibility that Christ bestowed on his church' and that its use is hedged around in a way the ultramontane lobby never intended.

The only agreed case of a formally infallible papal definition, since 1870, is the 1950 dogma of the bodily Assumption of the Blessed Virgin *Mary to heaven. There are about a dozen serious candidates for infallible papal statements in the entire history of the church, but there is no means of deciding for certain which do qualify. Within the Roman Catholic communion, in the 1970s papal infallibility was contested by *Küng and subtly redefined by Chirico and others. Some Catholics are concerned about 'creeping infallibility' whereby fairly routine examples of papal teaching are claimed to be irreformable. In Roman Catholic–Anglican dialogue (ARCIC), infallibility has been assimilated to the uncontroversial doctrine of indefectibility. Thus the pope can articulate the mind of the church after extensive consultation and provided this is received generally by the faithful (*sensus fidelium*). This is an interpretation congenial to many liberal Roman Catholics, but hardly acceptable to ultramontanes. In reality, papal infallibility remains a subject about which there is no Christian consensus.   **Paul Avis**

Barr, J., *Fundamentalism* (1977).
Butler, C., *The Vatican Council 1869–1870* (1930; 1962).
Chirico, P., *Infallibility: The Crossroads of Doctrine* (1977).

Farrer, A. M., Murray, R., et al., Infallibility in the Church: An Anglican-Catholic Dialogue (1968).

Küng, H., Infallible? (1971).

Tierney, B., Origins of Papal Infallibility (1972).

Inquisition and Holy Office.

The Inquisition conjures up, for our modern sensibilities, one of the most unpleasant ghosts of the Christian past: inquiry into religious beliefs and practices, areas thought to be very personal and private; extraction of information, often about other people, by various means of pressure including torture; physical *punishment for these beliefs and practices, including capital punishment.

The Inquisition with a capital 'I' must be distinguished from inquisition. Inquiry (inquisitio) into religion, notably through the enforcement of emperor worship, was a feature of the Roman empire into which Christianity was born and within which it lived for several centuries. Indeed it has been a feature of most societies, more or less pronounced. Christianity took over many features of the Roman empire's procedures of religious inquiry when it emerged as the official religion of the empire from the early 4th century onwards, enshrining them most notably in Book 16 of the Theodosian Code (438/9). In the following centuries uniformity of religion, including inquiry and coercion, were features, with varying degrees of intensity, of most communities that became predominantly Christian.

The beginning of the Inquisition is usually dated to the reign of Pope Gregory IX (1227–41), often to the bulls issued by him in 1231, though his pontificate witnessed a crystallization of existing trends rather than a sudden change of policy. In a series of measures the pope reserved the investigation of *heresy to officials appointed by him, thereby withdrawing the matter from the authority of both secular rulers and the bishops of the locality. Part of the context was the growing threat of the neo-*Gnostic Cathar heresy in southern Europe. Usually friars of the two mendicant orders, *Dominicans and *Franciscans, were appointed as the inquisitors, and gradually a body of recognized procedures and penalties grew up. Historians debate to what extent there was an institution rather than just ad hoc commissions to individuals. The commissions were confined to certain countries, notably France, Germany, and northern Italy, so that in many others, including England, the Inquisition never functioned and the prosecution of heresy remained in the hands of the local bishops and other ecclesiastics. In *Spain a separate Inquisition, known as the Spanish Inquisition, was established in 1478, approved by the pope but under royal control.

Torture was authorized by Pope Innocent IV in 1252. Penalties ranged from mild penances to imprisonment, scourgings, and the ultimate sanction, usually reserved for relapsed or obstinate offenders, of being handed over to the secular authorities, which meant death normally by burning at the stake. Indeed, church and state usually co-operated closely in the matter. While there was a genuine desire for the *conversion of the sinner and mercy was often preferred, nevertheless corporal punishment was frequent and many people were put to death. In part there was a desire to protect other members of the Christian community from what was regarded as the infection of heresy, partly there was a sense that the Christian gospel is self-evidently true so that anybody who has seen the light and then rejects it must be gravely at fault.

The Inquisition survived the Reformation. In 1542 Pope Paul III centralized its authority in Rome as Sacra Congregatio Romanae et Universalis Inquisitionis seu Sancti Officii. It was given supreme authority, under the pope, in doctrinal matters and it issued decrees on most topics in debate within the Roman Catholic Church in the following centuries, often with beneficial effects. However, its condemnation of the heliocentric theories of the astronomer *Galileo in the early 17th century was an error of judgement that took centuries to reverse, and its decree Lamentabili against *modernism in 1907 damaged the credibility of the church.

The Spanish Inquisition was finally abolished in 1834. The Roman Inquisition's name was changed in 1908 to Congregatio Sancti Officii (The Holy Office) and in 1965 to Congregatio pro Doctrina Fidei (Congregation for the Doctrine of the Faith). Decrees and spiritual penalties continue to be promulgated by it—the excommunication of Tissa *Balasuriya of Sri Lanka as recently as 1997—but corporal punishment has not been attempted for some time. Pope Paul VI in 1965, moreover, gave it the task of promoting good theology and sound doctrine, not just safeguarding them. Cardinal Joseph *Ratzinger became its energetic head (prefect) in 1981. It continues to occupy the building designed for it in the late 16th century, in the Piazza del S. Uffizio next to the basilica of St Peter.

Some monitoring of *orthodoxy is necessary. To some extent, too, the Inquisition may be explained by historical and cultural conditions, particularly the emergence of a predominantly single-religion (Christian) society in the *Middle Ages. Nevertheless, in terms of its involvement in coercion, it may be regarded as one of the saddest deviations in the whole of Christian history and partly accounts for the fact that Christianity has been perhaps the most intolerant of all world religions. There was always a minority of Christians who opposed at least its coercive measures and physical punishments, mostly among the *laity, illustrating once again that their instincts are often better than those of the clergy. Even in recent times its image has been too negative and condemnatory, insufficiently promoting theology according to the mind of Pope Paul VI: though its merits and its effort to preserve the brilliance of Christian *revelation should also be appreciated.

Norman Tanner

Denzinger, H., and Hünermann, P. (eds.), Enchiridion Symbolorum, Definitionum et Declarationum de Rebus Fidei et Morum, 37th edn. (1991), for the decrees of the Holy Office and the Congregation for the Doctrine of Faith.

Hamilton, B., The Medieval Inquisition (1981).

Kieckhefer, R., 'The Office of Inquisition and Medieval Heresy: The Transition from Personal to Institutional Jurisdiction', Journal of Ecclesiastical History, 46 (1995).

Lea, H. C., History of the Inquisition in the Middle Ages (3 vols.; 1888).

Reese, T. J., Inside the Vatican (1996).

interchurch marriage.

This term is applied to mixed *marriage between Christians, often to marriage between a Roman Catholic and a Christian of another communion. Traditionally strongly discouraged by all churches, since 'marrying out' threatens the identity of any group, such marriages are increasingly common. Often neither partner practises his or her faith, or only one does so; but cases in which both partners are practising, although a minority, have an *ecumenical significance out of all proportion to their number.

*Vatican II called the *family the domestic *church, and the

American Catholic bishops have told families that 'you are the church in your home'. This can be applied to mixed marriages between *baptized Christians. Such a marriage thus forms a domestic church that spans a denominational divide. The theology of the domestic church cuts right across denominational divisions. A church requires the *Eucharist to build up its common life; this is true for the domestic church as for any other church community. Some couples and families have expressed their intense need and desire to share communion; this felt need is authenticated by Catholic ecclesiology.

Theological insights are translated into canonical possibilities in a piecemeal way. On the basis of the 'real but not fully realized communion' which binds all baptized Christians to the Catholic Church, eucharistic sharing in certain cases and under certain conditions is not only permitted but commended. From the Catholic perspective, marriage between baptized Christians sacramentally deepens the bond of *communion in a unique way. Thus the Roman Catholic Church could identify mixed marriages between baptized Christians as a circumstance of need for eucharistic sharing in its *Directory for the Application of Principles and Norms on Ecumenism* in 1993.

But this unique identification has wider ecumenical significance. It is a response to the urgent need *of the married couple* to share the Eucharist. It moves beyond a response to the need of an *individual* cut off from the ministry of his or her Christian community. The Vatican II constitution *Gaudium et Spes* described the married couple as a 'community of life and love'. An interchurch couple is therefore seen as an ecumenical community of life and love. It is not so much different in kind from other groups, and indeed whole church communities. Where it may be different is in the intensity of the partners' commitment to love one another—an intensity experienced just because their community is so small and intimate. Their one domestic church is related to two different churches (denominations and local congregations) not in communion with one another, and belongs to both.

Moreover as parents the couple share a common mission. If they decide to bring up their children within the life of both their church communities, those children have an experience of 'double belonging' which goes further than that of their parents. In their Christian nurture they have never known what it is to grow up exclusively within the life of one denomination. When these children ask that their Christian commitment be acknowledged by a joint celebration of confirmation, they raise more difficult questions for the divided churches than their parents' request for eucharistic sharing. The churches are beginning to acknowledge that the questions raised by interchurch families, out of their experience of Christian living, are ecclesiological questions that cannot be avoided.

Ruth Reardon

Churches Together in England, *Churches Together in Marriage: Pastoral Care of Interchurch Families* (1994).

Hurley, M. (ed.), *Beyond Tolerance* (1975).

Interchurch Families, a biannual journal (1993–).

Kilcourse, G., *Double Belonging* (1992).

Irenaeus (c.130–c.200) retains a particular importance as the first exponent of a *catholic Christian *orthodoxy. In contrast to most earlier Christian writers, his arguments are not directed against Judaism or paganism, but at defining Christianity against *heretics, chiefly various *Gnostic groups who acknowledged *Jesus as Saviour. Irenaeus saw their arcane doctrines of emanations and heavenly secrets as a betrayal of the Christian message. His *Adversus haereses* (*Against the Heretics*) remains a vital source of information on their teachings which at times he satirizes with some wit.

As a boy in Smyrna, Irenaeus was deeply influenced by the aged Polycarp who himself had been a follower of the apostle *John. After spending some time in *Rome, Irenaeus embarked on a mission among the Gauls, becoming bishop in Lyons. He is reported to have met a *martyr's death.

Irenaeus' fundamental conviction is that there is a consistent, true *tradition of Christianity which can be traced back to Jesus and which it is the church's office to preserve. The *Holy Spirit's gift of truth has been consigned to the *apostles and their successors and anyone else who claims it is to be opposed. Any Gnostic notion of a secret tradition not taught by the apostolic church is a wicked fancy. The ancient churches and their bishops (see EPISCOPATE), among which Rome has primacy, are the authorities who can resolve difficulties of interpretation. Irenaeus is the first writer who treats the NT books as canonical scriptures and he preserves early traditions about the composition of the *gospels and development of the canon. He makes it clear that there must be four and only four gospels, bolstering his argument with analogies from the four winds and the four beasts of the book of Revelation. Whatever we may think of that argument, Irenaeus gives authority to a long-lasting tradition of distinctively Christian exegesis. A plurality of gospels is preserved which can be used to illuminate difficult passages, but these cannot be supplemented by other books. He reads the OT as prophetic record of the coming of the Son of God. Unlike the earlier apologists, he has some sense of the narrative sweep of scripture rather than simply regarding it as a repository of proof-texts, but is also given to some rather strained *allegorical interpretations (see BIBLE, ITS AUTHORITY AND INTERPRETATION).

The teaching most often associated with Irenaeus is his doctrine of 'recapitulation', a term derived from Ephesians 1: 10. This develops the *Pauline teaching of Jesus as the second *Adam. Adam when first created was, in Irenaeus' view, a spiritual infant whom God sought to train as a son of God, but who was led into disobedience by the *devil (see FALL). To undo the consequences of this, Jesus took flesh from the Virgin *Mary to live a life of *obedience, reversing at each stage of human life the effects of Adam's transgression. In defence of this idea, Irenaeus maintained that Jesus was well over 40 when he was crucified, the age when one 'declines into seniority'. All human experience is thus 'recapitulated' and set right in Jesus' earthly life. This is a powerful soteriological image, although it has left a problematic heritage. In particular, there are difficulties in understanding how Jesus then represents *women, whose experience he did not retrace, and whom Irenaeus certainly never mentions in this regard.

Irenaeus' absolute conviction that the Father of Jesus Christ is the *creator spoken of in the OT, one of his main points of issue with the Gnostics, is at one with his insistence on the reality of the *Incarnation. He relies heavily on the prologue to John's gospel for its teaching that Christ as *Word coexisted with the Father, definitively differentiating him from any Gnostic emanation. The Word took on real human flesh and this is guaranteed by the transformation of the humble elements of bread and wine into Christ's *body in the *Eucharist. All these doctrines interact to shape his understanding of the positive relationship between the material and spiritual universe and allow him to defend the bodily *resurrection with vigour.

Irenaeus ties this scheme in its turn to the guaranteed authority of the apostolic succession of bishops, giving shape to the formidable ecclesiology that has sustained the institutional *church throughout the centuries. It has also only too often tempted the church to regard institutional structures and their survival as its priority at the cost of the freedom of the Spirit. There can be no doubt that Christianity has been profoundly shaped by his legacy, one often overshadowed by the rather different emphases of *Augustine.

See also PRE-CONSTANTINIAN THOUGHT.   **Hugh S. Pyper**

Grant, R. M., *Irenaeus of Lyons* (1997).
Minns, D., *Irenaeus* (1994).
Nielsen, J. T., *Adam and Christ in the Theology of Irenaeus of Lyons* (1968).

Isaiah has always played a unique role in the history of Christianity. Alone of all the biblical *prophets he was believed from early times to be, as Jerome puts it, 'more evangelist than prophet because he describes all the mysteries of Christ and the church so clearly that you would think he is composing a history of what has already happened rather than prophesying about what is to come'. The frequency of quotations from Isaiah in the NT suggests that this goes back to the very beginning, possibly to Jesus himself.

Since the 1st century, texts from Isaiah provided scriptural authority for much of the language and imagery of Christian writers, as well as for many of the beliefs and practices of the church. The Immanuel prophecy in 7: 14 (LXX) and the *suffering servant passage in chapter 53 are two of the most obvious examples; but there are hundreds of others, including the wolf dwelling with the lamb, a voice crying in the wilderness, a light to the nations, good news to the poor, the key of David, the Mighty God, the Prince of Peace, and a new heaven and a new earth. The frequent use of texts from Isaiah by Clement, Justin, Tertullian, and others to support their teaching on the *Trinity (6: 3; 42: 1), *baptism (1: 16; 12: 3), the *Eucharist (55: 1; 65: 13), and even bishops (60: 17 LXX), confirms Isaiah's role as a key component of Christian scripture before the formal canonization of the *gospels and *Pauline epistles.

Details in the traditional story of the life of Christ, some not given in the gospels, originate in Isaiah. The 'ox and the ass' (1: 2) in the nativity scene and the fall of the idols in Egypt (19: 1) come from Isaiah, as do some of the gruesome details of Christ's passion added in the Middle Ages, such as the traditions that no part of his body was free from injury (1: 6) and that all his hair was pulled out until he was bald (Latin *calvus*: hence Calvary) (50: 6; 53: 7). Some interesting iconographical and literary links were also made with the *apocryphal *Martyrdom of Isaiah*. The libretto of Handel's *Messiah* is largely based on a selection of passages from Isaiah.

The cult of the Virgin *Mary found in Isaiah, especially in the Latin Vulgate, a rich source of imagery. In addition to 7: 14 (*Ecce virgo concipiet* ..., 'Behold a virgin shall conceive ...'), the verse most often associated with Isaiah in Christian iconography, 'the rod (*virga*) from the root of Jesse' (11: 1) was frequently interpreted as a reference to Mary. References to the *virgin birth ('as dew in April | That falleth on the grass') were found in 45: 8; 53: 2; 66: 7

and elsewhere, while the church fathers frequently found scriptural authority for the mystery of the *Incarnation in 63: 8.

Isaiah has always been very popular in Judaism too. Known as 'the prophet of consolation', he provides the three sentences with which prayers in the house of the bereaved conclude (66: 13; 60: 19; 25: 8), and no less than half the readings from the prophets in the annual lectionary. The language of Isaiah has also been prominent in the history of modern Zionism. Yet ironically Isaiah also supplied the church with scriptural authority for much of the language of hatred and rejection directed at the Jews. The church fathers cite Isaiah's vitriolic attacks on Judah when they call the Jews blind and stubborn (ch. 6), dogs (56: 10), drunkards (29: 9), 'citizens of Sodom and Gomorrah' (1: 10), and a people with blood on their hands (1: 15). Chapter 65 has been particularly prominent in *antisemitic polemic even until modern times.

One of the mottoes of Martin *Luther's followers was *Verbum dei manet in aeternum*, 'the word of God remains for ever' (40: 8), interpreted to proclaim the eternal authority of the *bible as the word of God. Protestant polemic against idols, both Roman Catholic and pagan, made much use of Isaiah too, especially such passages as 2: 8; 40: 18–20, and 44: 9–20, and the frequently repeated monotheistic formula 'besides me there is no god' (e.g. 45: 5, 6, 14, 21, 22). Isaiah's global perspectives also provided Protestant missionaries of the 18th and 19th centuries with much of their inspiration. The reference to the 'land of Sinim' (49: 12) sent missionaries to China, and 'the ships of Tarshish bringing thy children from afar, their silver and gold with them', cited earlier in relation to Christopher Columbus, justified the winning combination of Christianity and commerce in missionary enterprises to India and South East Asia. Quotations from Isaiah are disproportionately frequent in 19th-century *evangelical *hymns.

*Liberation theologians found scriptural authority for their 'option for the poor' in the prophet's appeals for social justice (1: 17; 16: 3–5; 32: 1), interpreted according to their own political and economic principles. Thus the sins of Sodom and Gomorrah attacked by Isaiah (1: 10) are 'pride, surfeit of food, and prosperous ease ... they did not aid the poor and needy' (cf. Ezek. 16: 49). The Vatican II statement (Gaudium et Spes, 78) on *justice and *peace took as its starting point a verse from Isaiah, which (in the Vulgate) contains the words *opus iustitiae pax*, 'peace is an enterprise of justice' (1975 translation). 'Swords into ploughshares' (2: 4; cf. Mic. 4: 3) and the 'peaceable kingdom' (11: 6–9) have now become two of the commonest images in modern political discourse.

Christian *feminism has also found authority and inspiration in the unique concentration of 'God as *mother' passages in Isaiah. The following prayer derives all its imagery from Isaiah: 'God our mother, | you hold our life within you, | nourish us at your breast, | and teach us to walk alone' (cf. Isa. 46: 3–4; 49: 14–15; 66: 7–13). The female image of the 'daughter of Zion' in Isaiah (chs. 40–66), traditionally overshadowed by the 'servant of the Lord' passages, has also in recent years been given more prominence as a powerful and poignant expression of *women's experience of God, and Lilith, now a symbol of radical feminism, has her only scriptural appearance in Isa. 34: 14 (NRSV).

Modern historical-critical scholarship, typified by J. C. Döderlein's recognition of a Second Isaiah (Deutero-Isaiah) and Bernhard Duhm's discovery of the four Servant Songs (42: 1–4; 49: 1–6; 50:

4–9; 52: 13–53: 12), did much to undermine traditional Christian interpretations of Isaiah by maintaining that only the original meaning of the Hebrew text could claim any kind of authority. More recently, scholarly interest in the final form of the text, the literary and theological unity of the book as a whole, reader-response, reception history, and the history of interpretation, together with a more positive attitude towards *patristic exegesis, has had the effect of shifting the emphasis away from what the original author intended and focusing instead on how people down the ages, Jews and Christians, have actually used and interpreted the text.

See also HIGHER CRITICISM.   **J. F. A. Sawyer**

Conrad, E. W., *Reading Isaiah* (1991).

Knibb, M. A., 'The Martyrdom and Ascension of Isaiah', in J. Charlesworth (ed.), *Old Testament Apocrypha* (1985), ii.

Miranda, J. P., *Marx and the Bible: A Critique of the Philosophy of Oppression* (1977).

Ruether, R. R., *Faith and Fratricide* (1974).

Sawyer, J. F. A., *The Fifth Gospel: Isaiah in the History of Christianity* (1996).

Schökel, Luis Alonso, 'Isaiah', in R. Alter and F. Kermode (eds.), *The Literary Guide to the Bible* (1987).

Trible, P., *God and the Rhetoric of Sexuality* (1978).

Islam. In common with Christians, Muslims believe in one *God who is the sole creator. Like Christians, they hold that he has sent a series of messengers—including *Abraham, *Moses, and *Jesus—to give religious and moral guidance to humankind; that Jesus was conceived by a virgin, worked miracles, and ascended into heaven; and that the dead will be resurrected to face the judgement. Nevertheless, there are some significant doctrinal differences. Muslims maintain that the series of messengers culminated in the Prophet Muhammad, to whom Gabriel brought the Qur'an, God's definitive *revelation. The Qur'an censures Christians for regarding Jesus as the Son of God, and denies that he was crucified.

Within a century of Muhammad's death in 632, Islam had expanded far beyond the confines of Arabia to form a vast empire extending from Spain to the Indus valley. Orthodox Christians living in the former *Byzantine territories conquered by the Muslims, and in the beleaguered Byzantine capital *Constantinople, developed a fiercely polemical approach to Islam. The tone was set in the works of John of Damascus (d. before 753), who referred to Islam as 'the forerunner of the Antichrist'. He regarded Islam as a *heresy and alleged that Muhammad was a false prophet who had a garbled and superficial knowledge of the bible and who had learned about Christianity from an *Arian monk. The Qur'an was not divine revelation but his own invention, as was clear from the many absurdities that it contained and the sexual licentiousness which it permitted. John acknowledged that the pre-Islamic Arabs had been idolaters, and that Muhammad preached monotheism, but in his view the Muslims were 'mutilators of God' because of their rejection of the *Trinity.

A more eirenic approach was fostered by the Arabic-speaking *Nestorian Christians of Iraq, whose catholicos resided in the former capital of the Persian empire. Having become accustomed to minority status under the Persians, the Nestorians were deferential to their Muslim overlords. Not long after the Abbasids moved the Islamic capital to Baghdad in 763, the Catholicos Timothy I transferred his see there in order to have easier access to the corridors of power. In a celebrated dialogue with Caliph al-Mahdi, Timothy acknowledged that Muhammad had a divinely inspired mission to the Arabs to teach them the unity of God and to lead them away from the worship of idols. He affirmed that, like the Hebrew prophets, Muhammad commanded his people to do good and avoid evil, and that like them he bore witness to Christ. Timothy none the less stopped short of acknowledging that Muhammad was actually a *prophet, for to have done so would have exposed him to criticism for not becoming a Muslim. He therefore cautiously suggested that Muhammad 'walked in the way of the prophets'.

Compared with their eastern counterparts, Christians in western Europe long remained lamentably ignorant of Islam. When Pope Urban II called for the First Crusade at the Council of Clermont in 1095, nobody present can have known even the name Muhammad, or anything about the beliefs of Muslims. It was simply assumed on the basis of the bible that the Saracens were the descendants of Abraham's illegitimate son Ishmael and that Christians, as Abraham's true heirs, had a right to the promised land. A further half-century elapsed before Peter the Venerable, the abbot of Cluny, commissioned Latin translations of Arabic texts in order to defend the church against Islam. The Cluniac Corpus included Peter of Toledo's translation of an anti-Muslim tract, the *Apology of al-Kindi*. This had a section on the life of Muhammad which contained accurate information drawn from Islamic sources but selected for its polemical utility and presented in a hostile manner. Subsequent medieval biographies of Muhammad were written in a similar vein. He was generally depicted as an opportunist who married an older woman for her money; an impostor who pretended to receive revelations; a lecher who invented a religion which pandered to men's baser instincts; and a warmonger motivated by an insatiable appetite for booty.

One occasionally encounters medieval writers who espoused a more positive attitude to Islam—men like Ramón Llull (1233–1315), who was active as a missionary in Spain but who acknowledged his debt to the Sufis and considered Islam closer to Christianity than to any other *religion. Such men were, however, rare exceptions. Despite long-standing European admiration for Islamic philosophy, medicine, and science, Islam as a religion was generally held in low esteem by Christians until comparatively modern times. Furthermore, Christians tended to rely uncritically on earlier polemical works. For instance, in the 16th century the Cluniac Corpus was published with a preface by Martin *Luther; and as late as 1882 Muir translated the *Apology of al-Kindi* into English for use by Protestant missionaries in India.

Although the polemical approach to Islam is still encountered in some quarters, most Christian Islamicists now have more enlightened views. In Roman Catholic circles, this is due largely to the influence of the French orientalist Louis Massignon (1883–1962), who was himself influenced by Charles *de Foucauld. There are three focal points to Massignon's Christian vision of Islam. First is his conviction that Islam is an Abrahamic religion like Judaism and Christianity. He stressed that although Hagar and Ishmael were driven out after the birth of Isaac, Ishmael had previously received God's blessing in response to Abraham's prayer (Gen. 17: 18–23). The rise of Islam among Ishmael's descendants, the Arabs, should therefore be interpreted as the fulfilment of God's promise to make him a great nation. Moreover, Muhammad shared the faith of Abraham because like him he left his homeland in order to serve the one true God. Second, because Muhammad did not experience *mystic union he was not imbued with *love in the full Christian sense of the term. He was thus unable to understand the inner workings of the divine life, which is why the Qur'an—which Massignon viewed as a sort of truncated Arab bible—denies the Incarnation and Christ's death on the cross. Third, unlike Muhammad, some of the Sufis did experience mystic union and their lives are consequently evidence that the *Holy Spirit is at work within Islam, bringing it to perfection. Against earlier scholars who attributed the rise of Sufism to the external influence of other religions including Christianity, Massignon argued that Sufism was authentically Islamic. He was deeply attracted to a Sufi called al-Hallaj, who uttered the words 'I am the Truth' while he was in a state of ecstasy and who was crucified in Baghdad in 922 to cries of 'his execution will be the salvation of Islam; may his blood fall on our necks'. Massignon maintained that al-Hallaj was a genuine mystic; that he died in ecstatic participation in Christ whom he knew about exclusively from Islamic sources; and that his death summons Islam to admit that Christ's crucifixion was a reality.

Despite the attractiveness of Massignon's approach, it is not without difficulties. Abraham undeniably plays an important role in the Muslim imagination. Nevertheless, there are historical grounds for questioning whether the Arabs are really the descendants of Ishmael, or whether Abraham and Ishmael did in fact build the Kaabah in Mecca as the Qur'an alleges. We should therefore be cautious about labelling Islam as an Abrahamic religion. Massignon's attitude to Sufism is even more problematic. Muslims themselves are divided as to whether Sufism is the true heart of Islam or whether it is an aberration, but many Sufis view al-Hallaj with suspicion and all would reject Massignon's implicit claim that he is a more important figure than Muhammad.

Massignon's influence may be detected in the references to Muslims in the official documents of *Vatican II. *Lumen Gentium* asserts that 'the plan of salvation also includes those who acknowledge the Creator, in the first place amongst whom are the Muslims: these profess to hold the faith of Abraham, and together with us they adore the one merciful God, mankind's judge on the last day'. *Nostra Aetate* mentions the church's esteem for Muslims who 'strive to submit themselves without reserve to the hidden decrees of God, just as Abraham submitted himself to God's plan, to whose faith Muslims eagerly link their own'. It lists the key beliefs that Christians and Muslims have in common; draws attention to the Muslim stress on prayer, fasting, and charity; and calls on everyone to forget past hostilities and strive for mutual understanding in order to promote peace, liberty, and social justice. Neither document actually refers to Islam as an 'Abrahamic religion'. In fact 'Islam' is nowhere mentioned. Instead, the emphasis is on 'Muslims' and their own perceptions of the relation of their faith to that of Abraham. Nevertheless, these statements represent a revolution in the church's attitude and have done much to improve Christian–Muslim relations.

Although the World Council of Churches has sponsored Christian–Muslim dialogues since 1969, neither the WCC nor any other Protestant body has issued statements of comparable importance (see ECUMENICAL MOVEMENT). This is not surprising in view of the fact that contemporary Protestant thinkers have widely divergent attitudes to Islam, ranging from the intransigent exclusivism of those who draw their inspiration from *Barth to the radical pluralism of Cantwell Smith, Hick, and others. The most influential figure however, is, undoubtedly Kenneth Cragg, who occupies the middle ground between these two extremes. Cragg combines a grateful acknowledgement of Islam's witness to God, and a celebration of all that Christians and Muslims have in common, with a persistent and sensitive Christian critique of Islam. He acknowledges the revelatory status of the Qur'an but insists that it was historically conditioned and that Muhammad was not simply a passive recipient of the message. He regards him as a prophet whose supreme achievement was to bring about 'a vast human practice, or ruling consciousness of God's reality as Lord'. The Muslim and Christian scriptures speak about the same God, but their understanding of him differs. Cragg wishes neither to blur the distinction between the two faiths nor to exaggerate it. For instance, unlike some Christian apologists, he admits that the Qur'an denies that Jesus was crucified. None the less, he stresses that it affirms man's evil intention of crucifying him and implies his willingness to die—two important elements in the Christian understanding of what happened. In the last analysis however, the Qur'an's silence about the crucifixion as 'an act of God in grace' has serious consequences. God's majesty and transcendence are so emphasized in the Qur'an that any real engagement on his part with human *sin and *suffering are rendered impossible. When his messengers fail in their educative role, the only option is coercion: Muhammad the persecuted Meccan prophet therefore becomes the Medinan head of state and military leader. Cragg admires the former but has reservations about the latter. Despite the perspicacity of his work, it has limited appeal to most Muslims because he wrestles with the Qur'an in a very 'Protestant' way, often assuming the right to interpret it without reference to subsequent Islamic tradition.

There would appear to be four prerequisites for a viable Christian 'theology of Islam'. First, because conflicts between Christians and Muslims are usually caused by political and economic inequalities rather than by differences in belief, theologians need to become aware of the extent to which extrinsic factors of this sort distort their own perceptions. Then, in view of the media's tendency to stigmatize all Muslims as dangerous '*fundamentalists', they must learn to discern between genuine Islamic revival and the more demonic forms of political Islam. Next, because Islam is rich and varied, they must resist the temptation to describe it as a static system of beliefs and practices which may be criticized from a Christian perspective. Finally, while holding to the centrality of Christ, they should develop such empathy for Muslims that the legitimate fears and aspirations of the latter become in large measure their own.

Neal Robinson

Cragg, K., *The Call of the Minaret* (1956).
—— *Muhammad and the Christian* (1984).
Daniel, N., *Islam and the West* (1997).
Robinson, N., *Christ in Islam and Christianity* (1991).
—— 'Massignon, Vatican II and Islam as an Abrahamic Religion', *Islam and Christian-Muslim Relations* (1991), ii. 182–205.
Sahas, J. D., *John of Damascus on Islam* (1972).

Israel is the name of at least six entities in the Old Testament: a biblical character, a people, a land, the united kingdom of Saul, *David, and *Solomon, the northern kingdom alone, and a religious community. The fluidity of usage testifies to a crucial feature of the OT tradition: its ability to assert continuity in difference. A tribal confederation can be reinvented as a monarchy and then as a religious party and still be Israel. Promises which seem to have failed can be reapplied to very different circumstances. Indeed, it could be said that the question informing the entire biblical tradition is the exploration of what it means to be Israel, a community seemingly arbitrarily singled out by God—but why and for what end? From another angle, this becomes the equally compelling question of who is included in Israel.

The bible explores this identity most directly under the forms of the *covenant between Israel and its *God. In this regard, Deuteronomy 7: 4–6 is a key passage. There Israel is told that it has been chosen to be a *priestly people and to come under God's special favour, not because of its size or virtue, but because God *loves it. The circularity of the reasoning underlines rather than softens the arbitrariness of the choice. However, Israel is put under the obligation of obedience to the law (see Law, Biblical), although Deuteronomy predicts that they will fall away and reap their just punishment. It is quite unprecedented that the defining text of a people should contain such forthright condemnations of their failings.

The intimacy and emotional passion of the biblical depiction of the stormy relationship between a jealous God and the endlessly fickle Israel is striking. Israel is both bride and child to God. God himself is customarily referred to as the God of Israel and seldom spoken of outside the sphere of this relationship. Israel's story is the story of this engagement, which the OT presents as worked out in a *historical experience of abandonment and restoration.

Partly because of this theological investment, contemporary scholarship is divided over how far the OT can be relied on as a source for the history of ancient Israel. For much, the OT remains the sole witness, not the ideal basis for historical research. All but the most extreme on either side would agree that the texts reflect a range of theological and ideological recastings of historical material. The disagreement is to what extent there is a recoverable core of fact and what bearing this has on the credibility and interpretation of the theological claims for Israel found in the biblical text. In the light of the continuing claims to the land and to historic continuity with ancient Israel, this controversy has repercussions well beyond academia. Doubt has been cast on the very existence of the Davidic monarchy, as well as on the biblical account of the *Exodus and conquest. The consequences of this critical study, however, have come late to the debate. For most of its history, Christian thought has accepted the biblical version.

As the bible presents the story, Israel as a people was, in line with wider ancient Near-Eastern thought, conceived of as a family descended from an eponymous ancestor, Jacob, who was renamed Israel ('he wrestled with God') in *Genesis 32: 28 after his struggle with the divine messenger. 'The Children of Israel' became the standard designation for the twelve tribes descended from him. Forged into a unity by the experience of the Exodus from Egypt and the leadership of *Moses and Joshua, the people of Israel conquered the land promised to them by God and the name Israel

came to mean the united kingdom built up by Saul, David, and Solomon. When the kingdom divided, however, the ten northern tribes retained the name while the two southern tribes were known as Judah. After the northern kingdom fell to the Assyrians in 722 BC, the name was reapplied to the hoped-for restored kingdom.

The *prophets warn, however, that only a remnant of Israel will be saved. Israel is seen as constantly threatened by the apostasy of its people corrupted by the idolatry of their neighbours. The true Israel becomes a religious rather than a political entity which explicitly does not include all those who profess the name as their ethnic or national identity. As the longed-for restoration was deferred, the name increasingly took on a more restricted use to mean a particular group in favour with God. Not surprisingly, there were rival candidates for the title, especially as the point at issue is the legitimacy of potential heirs to the promises made to Israel. In Ezra and Nehemiah, for instance, it seems clear that there is a tension between the returning exiles and those who had been left in the land as to which had the best title to the name. The later NT assertion that it is the emerging Christian communities that represent the true Israel can be seen to have precedents in the struggles for a Jewish identity in the post-exilic community.

*Paul makes an explicit appeal to such lines of thought in chapters 9–11 of *Romans where he argues that 'not all who are descended from Israel belong to Israel' (Rom. 9: 6). The descent is rather to the children of the promise. Characteristically, Paul then turns the standard argument on its head. Those who receive the promise define Israel, he asserts, rather than membership of Israel, however defined, being the condition for receiving the promise. Yet Paul then makes the strongest possible statement that the stubbornness of the descendants of Israel is a providential mercy to the Gentiles who otherwise have no claim to Israel's inheritance. Far from marking the disinheritance of Israel, the admittance of the Gentiles to his mercy is how God has planned to bring about Israel's salvation which remains his central purpose.

In the *gospels, Jesus' mission is clearly presented as being primarily to Israel. 'I was sent only to the lost sheep of Israel' he tells a Canaanite woman (Matt. 15: 24) but her faithful response and that of other Gentiles contrasts with the stubbornness of the Israelites. Luke's gospel begins with the testimony of the most impressive representatives of Israel—John, Anna, and Simeon—and Jesus' birth is seen as a fulfilment of the prophecies to Israel, but as the book progresses the scope of his mission widens. His first sermon is in the synagogue in Nazareth but its message is that God's salvation reaches beyond the bounds of Israel. The same pattern can be seen in *Acts, where the apostles preach first to the people of Israel and only then turn to the Gentiles. However, this pattern is read by later commentators in the light of the gospels' fierce condemnations of the Pharisees and Jewish leaders which are transferred to Israel as a whole. Most damningly, the incident where Jesus curses the fruitless fig tree (Matt. 21: 19–21) is taken by early interpreters as his final judgement on Israelite religion.

The NT's polemics over who is the true Israel must be read in the context of the history of internal dissent in Judaism, a point that quickly became lost as the early church reacted to persecution and became increasingly Gentile in its composition. The destruction of the *Temple and the crushing of Jewish resistance seemed to confirm to most Christians that Israel as a political and religious entity outside the church had had its day and had come under divine judgement. Dispossession of the land was then seen as a just punishment for the rejection of the *Messiah and the Jews were regarded as condemned to a life of homeless wandering.

From then on, the Christian tradition appropriates the identity of Israel with hardly a glance at continuing Judaism. The *liturgical use of the *psalms in particular and the retention of the OT as a whole both required and reinforced this identification. The fluidity of application which was such an asset to the survival of Judaism now allows the church to identify itself as seems fitting either with the triumphant kingdom, or, in times of persecution, with the heartfelt pleas for the promised restoration. The promises relating to the land are transposed to the heavenly realm. The actual land retains its holiness but now as the place where Jesus' life, death, and Resurrection took place, and any Jewish claim was regarded as rescinded.

The political aspect of the biblical Israel, however, was never entirely suppressed. The founding myths of the Exodus and the *exile, read as stories in which a nation is forged by maintaining its ideological and racial purity in the face of an oppressive great power, enter into the rhetoric of *nationalism throughout European history, but most especially in the Protestant countries and among smaller nations. The concept of a chosen people beset by the corrupt and ungodly has been twisted to many ends by American Puritans and South African Calvinists among others (see APARTHEID). Yet an alternative, more inclusive model, represented perhaps by *Jonah and *Isaiah, that sees Israel as a priestly people, a servant dedicated to the *reconciliation and blessing of the nations, is also traceable through Christian thought about the relationships of nations and peoples, a model always vulnerable to the fanaticism of others.

The establishment of the state of Israel in 1948 brought a new factor into the equation. This secular Israel complicated the spiritualized picture familiar to most Christians and indeed caused problems for some religious Jews. Intractable conflicts over competing claims to the land and international law were compounded by being conducted in the aftermath of the horrors of the genocide of European Jewry (see HOLOCAUST). Many western Christians sought to express solidarity with those whom they have increasingly come to speak of as their elder brothers in faith. Others, particularly those who held a premillenarian view, vested the Israeli state with their own brand of theological significance, seeing it as a harbinger of the *apocalypse. The churches of the east, with a different history, were less inclined to revise their traditional supersessionist position. Those at Vatican II who framed the document *Nostra Aetate*, which in 1965 for the first time committed the Catholic Church to fraternal *dialogue with Judaism as well as with the other major world religions, expressly omitted any mention of the state of Israel under the influence of objections from Christian and other groups in the Middle East. For many Jews, this failure to acknowledge the religious and existential significance of the Israeli state was evidence that the gestures of reconciliation with Judaism were only partial and that age-old prejudices still in fact held sway. *Jewish–Christian dialogue on the issue remains tense. Whatever the outcome of this politically fraught situation, it does at least mean that Christians have had to think again about their appropriation of the name of Israel. Paul's words in Romans, so often misapplied in Christian thought, can be read once more as a call to Gentile Christian humility.

See also ANTISEMITISM.   **Hugh S. Pyper**

Barth, M., *Israel and the Church* (1969).

Ecclestone, A., *The Night Sky of the Lord* (1980).

Kenny, A., *Catholics, Jews and the State of Israel* (1993).

Reventlow, H. G., *Problems of Biblical Theology in the Twentieth Century*, ET (1986).

Richardson, P., *Israel in the Apostolic Church* (1969).

Soggin, J. A., *An Introduction to the History of Israel and Judah*, 2nd edn. (1993).

Whitelam, K. W., *The Invention of Ancient Israel* (1996).

J

James, William (1842–1910), American philosopher/psychologist. William James had a medical training and was a professor of (successively) physiology, *psychology, and *philosophy at Harvard University. Henry James, the novelist, was his brother, and his father, Henry James, Snr., was an independent religious writer of private means.

A religious quest was always at the heart of James's philosophy. In his paper 'The Will to Believe' (1896) he argues that we have a right to adopt a belief whose *truth-value cannot be settled empirically or logically, provided it is 'momentous', 'live' (a genuine option for us), and forced (we must live either as accepting or rejecting it). In such a case it is legitimate to adopt the belief that is most helpful to us psychologically. These conditions are met for many by the belief that *God exists.

His Gifford lectures, *The Varieties of Religious Experience* (1902), form his most thorough treatment of religion. Here he distinguishes between personal *religious experience and institutional religion. Controversially, he thinks the latter a second-hand version of the former, and that the student of *religion should study reports of first-hand religious experience rather than *creeds or denominations (though these certainly affect its description).

Religious experience is, *prima facie*, a felt encounter with something not of this world to which the appropriate reaction is *joyful but solemn, and through relation to which alone one can escape from one's ordinary defective nature. Its typical characteristics are a sense of connection with a wider life than our normal petty little interests, of willing self-surrender to control by it, and immense elation as the outlines of selfhood melt away. Its fruits (most complete in genuine saintliness) are *asceticism, increased strength of character, purity, and *charity.

James contrasts the religious experience of the 'healthy minded' with that of 'sick souls'. The first is a joyous sense of the divine with no preceding period of tribulation and self-contempt; the second is only reached after a 'dark night of the soul' and a strong sense of personal unworthiness and surrounding *evil. The second is the deeper and more significant. This is illustrated by reports of a wide range of religious experiences (mostly by Christians) ranging from the quite ordinary to the most richly *mystical.

Philosophical and theological arguments for God's existence and nature are flawed; theory must rest on the evidence of religious experience, personal or reported. There is enough in common between mystical experiences across cultures to conclude that they are encounters with the same genuine reality. A pantheistic interpretation seems the most initially promising, but the problem of evil and other considerations suggest that in religious experience we encounter a personal force for good vastly greater than ourselves, but neither including, nor in total control of, the universe as a whole. This is James's 'finite God'. Our point of contact with this divine being (or possibly beings) is through our subconscious.

James has little to say about *Jesus and seems Christian only in holding that in western culture experience of the divine has typically been interpreted in the language of Christian belief.

T. L. S. Sprigge

Levinson, H. S., *The Religious Investigations of William James* (1981).
Myers, G., *William James: His Life and Thought* (1986).
Sprigge, T. L. S., *James and Bradley: American Truth and British Reality* (1993).

Jansenism began as a rediscovery of *Augustine in *seventeenth-century Catholicism. Cornelius Jansen (c.1585–1638), a professor at Louvain, and briefly bishop of Ypres, left for posthumous publication his *Augustinus*, reasserting the depth of human *sin and the invincibility of divine *grace, topics bitterly disputed at the time between *Jesuits and *Dominicans. Five propositions drawn from the book were condemned by Innocent X in 1653. The book's defenders struggled to avoid the condemnation, on the grounds of fact, that these individual propositions were not actually in the *Augustinus*, and that what was condemned was *Calvinism, with which no Jansenist agreed. Both sides were disingenuous in argument. The propositions did sum up Jansen's ideas, and the distinction between Jansen's position and Calvinism is almost entirely unreal. On the other hand, Jansen and Calvin were much better Augustinians than Innocent X. The Catholic church ever since *Aquinas and other medieval theologians had been turning away from full Augustinianism towards a more semi-*Pelagian viewpoint. The *Jesuits had gone farthest in this.

Jansen was Dutch, but his sympathizers, who became known as Jansenists, were mostly French, a remarkable group of people centring round the nunnery of Port-Royal in Paris under their abbess, Mère Angélique Arnauld. The appeal of Jansenism lay not in his theology but in the lives of godly intensity of those denounced as Jansenist. The devout nuns of Port-Royal had no copy of the *Au-

gustinus in their library. The book that did shape the Jansenist mind was one by Mère Angélique's brother, Antoine Arnauld, *On Frequent Communion*, whose rigorist teaching kept generations of Catholics away from communion. Could a lady receive communion the day she went to a ball? The Jesuits said yes, the Jansenists, no. Catholicism seemed in confrontation with unworldly devotion. *Pascal, the greatest of Jansenist controversialists, a close friend of Port-Royal where his sister was a nun, spent a little time in his *Provincial Letters* making Augustine palatable, but much more in sharp-edged mockery of the lax morality countenanced by the Jesuits. Both Port-Royal and Pascal transcend Jansenism, but they also express it, as one distinctive devotional mindset.

In 1713, in another purge of Jansenism, the papal bull *Unigenitus* went even further away from Augustinianism in condemning Pasquier Quesnel, an edifying biblical commentator, for such views as 'only love speaks to God; God listens to love only'. Jansenism was indeed rigorist, but this is a rigour that desires *love, not fear. *Eighteenth-century French Jansenism, under persecution, turned to miracle cures (famously well authenticated) and then to the sort of religious experience that looks like hysteria. It also found its way into opposition politics, and certainly had a hand in the suppression of the Jesuits. Outside France, the word 'Jansenist' was used of *Enlightenment-minded reform.

Jansenism is often unfairly blamed for anything rigorous in Roman Catholic practice, its use comparable with that of *Puritanism among Protestants. In *nineteenth-century France something of Jansenism continued in some French seminaries, sombre, reverent, and internalizing. Pius X's insistence on frequent communion in 1905 was really what brought the longer Jansenist age in Catholic devotion to a close.

See also PREDESTINATION.   **Alistair Mason**

Crichton, J. D., *Saints or Sinners?* (1996).
Kolakowski, Leszek, *God Owes Us Nothing* (1995).
Sedgwick, Alexander, *Jansenism in Seventeenth-Century France* (1977).
—— *The Travails of Conscience* (1998).
Van Kley, Dale, *The Jansenists and the Expulsion of the Jesuits from France* (1975).

Japanese Christian thought.

The coming of the *Jesuit Francis Xavier to Japan in 1549 marks the historic encounter between Christian humanism (Matt. 16: 26) and Japanese Buddhist–Confucian–pantheistic culture. By 1570 there were 30,000 Kirishitans. This remarkable success of the Jesuit *mission was countered by the political authorities: in 1616 the Tokugawa Shogunate banned the Kirishitan religion. In 1639 a seclusion law closing Japan to the outside world was put into force, not to be repealed until 1854. Only a few years later, in 1861, a Russian Orthodox mission came to Japan. The first Protestant church was formed in Yokohama in 1872 and the ban on Christianity was finally lifted in the following year. But the 1889 Constitution of the Empire of Japan, focusing on the exclusive glory of the emperor's person, was not coached in enlightened, universal language. Not until the 1946 Constitution of Japan, born of the devastation of a war waged against 52 nations, did Japan begin to invoke the principle of universal morality based on the value of the human *person.

In 1945, when Hiroshima was annihilated, the government-sponsored ideology of a divine land, home of a morally superior, chosen people, abruptly disappeared. It was, in truth, a national experience of emancipation: out of slavery to Japanese chauvinistic particularism into *democratic universal humanism (see NATIONALISM). That 'no nation is responsible to itself alone, but that laws of political morality are universal' is a line in the preamble to the post-war constitution, witnessing to a moment of historical repentance and a determination to be responsible to history. Thus defeat in war provided a major moment for the reception of the gospel.

In 1946 Shigeru Nambara, the Christian president of Tokyo University, in his public address on 'The Creation of a New Japanese Culture', pointed out the need for spiritual reform towards universal human values. In 1967 came the 'Confession on the Responsibility of the United Church of Christ in Japan during World War II', in which a Japanese theology of *history was given distinctive expression. Kiyoko Takeda, in her 1978 study of the imperial system, gave theologians reliable historical information on the basis of which they could form an educated judgement about the clash between the imperial system and Christian theology.

Since it first contacted Christian preaching in Xavier's day, the Japanese mind has focused on two basic Christian thoughts: the transcendent yet historically engaged God, and salvation in God incarnate. Responding to these ideas, Japanese Christian thought has continued the great theological tradition of accommodation of the gospel, realising that it is God's incarnation which gives accommodation its ultimate validity (see CONTEXTUAL THEOLOGY). Responses have been given in this century by such representative writers as Masahisa Uemura (1858–1925, Protestant minister, theological educator), Kanzo Uchimura (1861–1930, founder of the Mu-Kyokai (Non-Church) movement), Tokutaro Takakura (1885–1934, Protestant minister, theological educator), Yoshihiko Yoshimitsu (1904–45, Catholic theologian), Ken Ishihara (1882–1976, Protestant historian), and Yoshitaka Kumano (1899–1982, Protestant systematic theologian). They are inspiring in their spiritual commitment, their critical appreciation of Japanese culture, and the keen ecumenical vision with which they have engaged in theological work. They have proclaimed the closeness of God, the Holy One, as a theological and cultural 'shaking of the foundations', which summarizes the theological substance and mission of Japanese Christian thought since Xavier. This theological challenge may be seen as central to Japanese theology in the 20th century. In a powerful Christian dialectic, the Lutheran Kazoh Kitamori, in his *Theology of the Pain of God* (1946), invited his war-devastated compatriots to experience the astonishing closeness of God.

The significance of this dialectic must be seen against the background of Japanese culture, in which, as Masao Maruyama points out, the idea of 'next' (*tsugi*) or 'next-next' (*tsugi-tsugi*), signifying continuity, is basic. Since 1945, when the Japanese people experienced a radical national discontinuity, the Christian concept of the closeness of God has been in tension with the enduring Japanese metaphysics of continuity. The dialectical discontinuity hidden in the closeness of God may be kept meaningful, without losing its own distinctiveness, if Japanese Christians take seriously the issue of theological accommodation, or contextualization as it is often called.

Christianity in Japan, predominantly Catholic and Protestant, has been influenced by the German, British, and American expression of the faith. Uemura and Uchimura creatively used and subordinated western theology when conducting their own biblical studies within the Japanese cultural context. Their biblically informed language intimates the tension between the biblical discontinuity/paradox and the indigenous spirituality of continuity. The distinction accorded to the Catholic writer Shusaku *Endo derives from his perceptive interpretation of the theological and psychological depth of this tension.

For all the abundant literature on Hiroshima/Nagasaki, no major Japanese theological work has focused on this unprecedented event, or on the International Military Tribunal for the Far East (1946–8). Since 1945 there has, however, been a sustained theological criticism of the imperial system. In 1990, in an open letter to the Japanese government, the United Church of Christ criticized the government's attempt to revive the ideology of the divine emperor.

Today, the lively fronts of theological thought are in the areas of the welfare of minority groups, of evangelism and mission, of interreligious *dialogue (between Christians and *Buddhists), and of Japan's self-identity among the family of nations. While the number of Christians is estimated at 1 per cent of the total population, Christianity has exercised a significant social and educational influence. Theologians such as Yoshinobu Kumazawa (1929–), Yasuo Furuya (1926–), and Akio Dohi (1927–) are studying the theological and sociological implications of this minority status combined with Christianity's paradoxical strength.

Kosuke Koyama

Furuya, Y. (ed.), *A History of Japanese Theology* (1997).

Kumazawa, Y., and Swain, D. L. (eds.), *Christianity in Japan, 1971–90* (1991).

Maruyama, M., 'Rekishi Ishiki No Kosoo' ('Ancient Layer of Japanese History Perception') in *Rekishi Shiso Shu* (*Thought on History*), ed. M. Maruyama (1972).

Jeremiah is associated with the turbulent period surrounding the fall of Judah (587 BC) and the transition from monarchy to *exile. The book bearing his name is the longest of the *Old Testament prophetic books. Chief among the influential ideas from the Jeremiah traditions are the seventy years (Jer. 25: 11; 29: 10; later developed in *Daniel 9: 2), the 'righteous branch' (23:5; cf. 33: 15), the person of Baruch (Jeremiah's scribe), and especially the 'new *covenant' passage (31: 31–4). More important than any oracle, however, is the persona of the *suffering *prophet.

Among *New Testament writers, only Matthew names the prophet explicitly, twice as the origin of a fulfilled prophecy (Matt. 2: 17; 27: 9) and once, curiously, preceding the confession of *Peter (16: 14). The writer to the *Hebrews uses the 'new covenant' passage (Heb. 8: 8–12; 10: 16–17) to widen his argument from the person of *Jesus to larger religious structures in making his case for Christian supersession of Judaism. Jeremiah's language of the 'new' prompts him to call the Mosaic covenant 'old', thus contributing to the notion of 'old' and 'new' testaments. The precedent set by this polemical language inevitably attracted later Christians writing against Jews, since Jeremiah's 'new covenant' provided an authority within the OT itself for not regarding the Law of Moses as final. In the east, such documents as the *Doctrine of Jacob* and Pseudo-Andronicus I Comnenus's *Dialogue of a Christian and a Jew against the Jews* made repeated use of the Jeremiah text, while in the west writings by Walter of Tournai (*Against the Jews*), Peter the Venerable (*Against the Hardness of the Jews*, c.1144–7), and Peter *Abelard (*Dialogue between a Christian, a Philosopher and a Jew*) make plain the

predominantly polemical use of this text. John *Calvin carried this forward in the Reformed tradition, where Jer. 31: 31–4 again serves to demonstrate that the OT is literal and inferior to the superior and spiritual NT. Calvin, however, makes a connection to 2 Cor. 3: 6–11 rather than to Hebrews, and points out that *Paul's negative depiction of the law goes beyond Jeremiah's (*Institutes*, 2. 11. 7).

The most important aspect of the Jeremiah traditions for the history of Christian thought is the depiction of the suffering prophet. Both the 'laments', some of the most outspoken passages in the bible (11: 18–23; 12: 1–6; 15: 10–21; 17: 14–18; 18: 18–23; 20: 7–18), and the accounts of his mistreatment by the Judaean authorities contribute to this profile. Jeremiah may well have served as a model for the gospel depiction of Jesus. The *Temple sermon (chs. 7 and 26) parallels Jesus' cleansing of the Temple: both wept over *Jerusalem; both were brought to trial; both are men of sorrow who experienced a 'dark night of the soul', rejected by those to whom they were sent. This suffering persona also dominates artistic presentations of the prophet. These are few prior to the 6th century, but two of the most famous from later times, Michelangelo's Sistine Chapel frescoes (1508–12) and Rembrandt's 'portrait' (1630), are strikingly similar. The prophet gazes disconsolately into the distance, weary and worn. Alone among Michelangelo's 'writing prophets' (unless *Jonah should be included), Jeremiah lacks a book or scroll. A more recent artistic representation is found in the poetry of Robert Burns (1759–96). His paraphrase of Jer. 15: 10 poignantly conveys the rejection of the suffering prophet:

> Ah, woe is me, my mother dear!
> A man of strive ye've born me:
> For sair contention I maun bear;
> They hate, revile, and scorn me.

A century later, Gerard Manley *Hopkins made an explicit link to Jeremiah in his 'terrible sonnets'.

The book of Lamentations is found after Jeremiah in Christian bibles, as the prophet has traditionally been identified as its author. The Jewish liturgical use of Lamentations in the commemoration of the destruction of Jerusalem on the 9th of Av is paralleled in Christian tradition by selections from Lamentations in the Holy Week liturgy for Maundy Thursday, Good Friday, and Holy Saturday. Texts from Lamentations have been set to music by both Leonard Bernstein and Igor Stravinsky.

Jeremiah's career has been associated with the German theologian Dietrich *Bonhoeffer in his stand against Nazism. In an early lecture delivered in the United States on 'Distress and Hope in the Contemporary Religious Situation: The Tragedy of the Prophets and its Lasting Meaning' (13 November 1928), Bonhoeffer 'projected himself into the minds of the major prophets, identifying himself with them to an almost impermissible extent, lingering particularly on Jeremiah, who was already his favourite' (E. Bethge, *Dietrich Bonhoeffer: Theologian, Christian, Contemporary* (1970), 82). But in his *Letters and Papers from Prison*, Bonhoeffer identifies several times rather with Baruch, whose life served to guarantee Jeremiah's oracles against Judah and who became an important figure in the pseudepigraphic writings. 'I can never get away from Jeremiah 45', Bonhoeffer wrote; it became for him a theological shorthand for letting go of one's life in the face of God's demands.

In recent biblical scholarship, Jeremiah has provided one of the sharpest debates on biblical historicity. The 'minimalist' case has been most strongly made by Robert Carroll: since Jeremiah is the creation of the Deuteronomists whose ideology the book promotes, there can be no access to a historical prophet within the book. Although this conclusion has been contested, Carroll's suggestion resonates with the traditional use to which the book has been put: the rhetorical profile of Jeremiah consistently overshadows his book's contribution to history.   **David J. Reimer**

Carroll, Robert, *From Chaos to Covenant* (1981).

Curtis, A. H. W., and Römer, T. (eds.), *The Book of Jeremiah and its Reception* (1997).

Hillers, Delbert, *Lamentations*, 2nd edn. (1992).

Hopper, S. R., 'The "Terrible Sonnets" of G. M. Hopkins and the "Confessions" of Jeremiah', *Semeia*, 13 (1978), 29–73.

Heimann, Adelheid, 'Jeremias', in E. Kirschbaum (ed.), *Lexikon der Christlichen Ikonographie* (1970), ii. cols. 387–92.

Williamson, H. A., 'Jeremiah and Jesus', *Expository Times*, 34 (1922/3), 535–8; 35 (1923/4), 39–42.

Wolff, Christian, *Jeremiah in Frühjudentum und Urchristentum* (1976).

Jerusalem, *David's city, the site of the *Temple and the scene of the climactic moments of *Jesus' earthly ministry, retains a unique importance in Christian thought. Its violent history has been the result of the passions that it has engendered, both of devotion and hatred. Originally a Jebusite stronghold conquered by David to provide a neutral capital for his new kingdom and a central site for the cult, the city was always somewhat set apart from the rest of the land. The writers of the OT alternate between praising it as the 'joy of all the earth' (Ps. 48: 3), the place where God deigned to permit his Temple to be built, and calling down God's wrath upon it for its faithlessness, lamenting thereafter its destruction and yearning for its restoration. In the *prophetic books there is already a divergence between the city's future as the divinely appointed centre of a restored kingdom and its present position under judgement for the intrigue and faithlessness of its inhabitants and their rulers.

A similar disjunction can be found in the NT, where the two aspects are even contrasted linguistically: the Greek Hierosolyma is used in geographical references, whereas the Hebraic form Jerusalem almost always indicates the spiritual city. Jesus famously mourns over the city's unwillingness to hear his message and foretells its destruction. It is there that the events of his Passion occur. Politically, this was inevitable, as it was the seat of government and justice, but theologically for the NT writers it is also fitting that the radical redefinition of *kingship, *priesthood, and prophethood which his *death and *Resurrection represents should happen in the site of their power.

The gospel records span the period of the destruction of the Temple and city by the Romans in 70 AD which may account for some ambivalence in the NT traditions over the role of the city. The book of Acts gives us to understand that the earliest church groups met in Jerusalem, attending the Temple services. Under the leadership of James, the brother of Jesus, the Jerusalem church seems to have taken its primacy for granted. *Paul, however, although he urges his correspondents to contribute to the upkeep of the Jerusalem community, stands for the cosmopolitan church in the diaspora which soon breaks free of Jerusalem's dominance. John, writing after the destruction, records Jesus as saying that

*worship is to be in spirit and in truth, not bound to any sacred site.

The followers of the king whose kingdom is not of this *world looked to a city which is not of this world, the New Jerusalem of *Revelation 21 which will descend from *heaven, where God will reign directly and where the Temple will no longer be required. This vision of the new spiritual Jerusalem meant that for many Christians the destruction of the city could be seen as a just punishment of the unbelieving Jews and a vindication of Jesus' prophetic powers. This also confirmed an irreversible shift of power away from Jerusalem and from those Christians who sought to preserve their Jewish identity through practice of the law (see Law, Biblical) and Temple worship.

Christian hopes become fixed on Jerusalem as a spiritual reality. As such, it provides a standard example for centuries of exegetes of the importance of *allegorical interpretation of the scriptures. The promises and praises directed to Jerusalem could no longer be credibly applied to the despoiled city. To the spiritual interpreter, biblical references to Jerusalem spoke of the church, the individual human soul, or the heavenly city of God. The elaborate descriptions of the city with its gates of precious stone were further fuel to the allegorical imagination. This meant that *psalms could still be sung in praise of the might and beauty of Jerusalem, while the city stood ruined as a stern reminder of the supersession of Judaism, all the more so when it was rebuilt by the Romans as a pagan city and renamed Aelia Capitolina.

This attitude began to change, however, under the reign of *Constantine. Makarios, bishop of Aelia, outmanœuvred his rival, Eusebius, bishop of Caesarea, at the Council of *Nicaea and had his ancient claim to primacy recognized, though its *patriarchate never approached the importance of *Constantinople or *Alexandria. The espousal at Nicaea of *Athanasius' *incarnational theology to counter *Arian leanings may have contributed to a new interest in the actual sites of Jesus' earthly existence, as may a growing sense that Christianity now had a stake in the political and material life of the empire. Makarios persuaded Constantine to allow the temple of Aphrodite in Aelia to be demolished so that the tomb of Christ could be excavated, thus reinforcing a tradition of *pilgrimage to such sites which continues to this day. The city which saw the crime of the crucifixion was, after all, also the place of *Resurrection and *salvation. Constantine's own mother Helena identified many other sites and new shrines began to proliferate.

By the end of the 4th century, the city was filled with monks and nuns. They and the many pilgrims who came to Jerusalem sought in great processions to reenact Jesus' last journeys during Holy Week. Its bishop, Cyril, left a valuable record of the liturgical practice of the time. This tradition of encounter with the *humanity of Jesus may explain why in the later quarrels over *Nestorianism and *Monophysitism the Jerusalem church stood out for *Chalcedonian orthodoxy. Throughout the political vagaries of the following centuries, which included the sacking of the city by the Persians and its later conquest for Islam, pilgrimage continued. For the most part, Islamic rulers respected Christian sites, but resentment grew and continued war with Byzantium led to uprisings and reprisals. Nevertheless, sizeable communities of Coptic and *Armenian Christians developed alongside the Orthodox and Latin churches. Strife between Christian groups added to the air of tension.

This came to a head in the Crusades. The western church, incensed by attacks on increasingly wealthy pilgrims, many responding to the urging of monks of Cluny, and drawing on an old tradition that the Emperor Charlemagne had been given rights over the sacred sites, gave its blessing to the attempt to wrest the city from Islamic rule. Despite the establishment of a Latin Kingdom of Jerusalem, which for many recalled prophecies that in the latter days a king from the west would rule in Jerusalem and there battle the Antichrist, the several Crusades over the next 200 years brought about little but bloodshed and misery and a lasting antipathy between western Christendom and the Islamic world, and hastened the eventual collapse of the Byzantine empire. For all the shabbily mixed motives of many crusaders, however, they witness to a powerful sense in Christian thought of the time of the importance of the concreteness of Jesus' human existence and to a willingness to undergo appalling suffering, as well as to inflict it, in his cause. The city's conceptual importance is reflected in the fact that early medieval maps place it unquestioningly at the centre of the world.

Once Islamic rule was re-established, the west was represented in Jerusalem by a group of *Franciscan friars, who developed a special devotion to the Via Dolorosa, the reconstructed route of Jesus' journey with the *cross, but who also had a tendency to seek *martyrdom by insulting the Prophet. Their presence was resented by other Christian groups, and under the Ottomans the patriarch of Constantinople used his access to the sultan to gain concessions. Squabbles between different Christian communities over the possession and the rights of access to the holy sites involved their various protecting powers and shaped international diplomacy. As late as 1854, the Crimean war could be traced back to a quarrel in the Church of the Nativity which drew in France and Russia in defence of opposing parties. A Muslim family still holds the key to the Church of the Holy Sepulchre as no Christian group could trust any of the others to keep to the agreed times of services. In the meantime, Jerusalem sank into economic decline, though still a centre for pilgrimage, mainly from the east.

A new type of visitor began to appear in the 18th century. The enlightened *Protestant tourist usually professed nothing but scorn for the tawdry elaboration of the sacred sites and the ritual infighting of the rabble of monks, but brought a different sense of *history and of the importance of the man Jesus. Jerusalem as museum or *archaeological site was an irresistible draw once access became easier in the 19th century. Where better to *quest for the historical Jesus? The search began for more authentic, less tainted sites. General Gordon's discovery of the simple 'Garden Tomb' is a good example of the attempt to repristinate Jerusalem. Much of this effort and especially the high-handed excavation of holy places seemed sacrilegious to other communities, and archaeological investigation of many of the most important sites is still impossible. A further factor was the Protestant, indeed *Calvinist, emphasis on the importance of the OT *covenant and of the role of the Jews in the history of salvation. In 1842, the first Protestant bishop arrived in Jerusalem, announcing his intention to convert the Jews. Successive western missionary projects mainly served to alienate both the Jewish population of an overwhelmingly Arab city and the members of the ancient Christian communities.

Jerusalem passed out of Ottoman control into British protection in 1916, bringing a regime informed by a Protestant ideal that favoured the return of the Jews to their homeland. The establishment of the state of *Israel in 1948 and the annexation of Eastern Jerusalem after 1967 meant that the city came under Jewish control for the first time in many centuries, itself a sign of millennial significance for various Christian groups. Tensions remain, and the attitudes of western leaders to the problems of the city seem to many still coloured, whether consciously or residually, by the centuries of Christian engagement with the place.

While the actual city of Jerusalem exerted this continuing influence on Christian thought, the ideal of the heavenly Jerusalem was at least as important. *Blake voices it most memorably in his poem of the name, where he pledges not to rest until Jerusalem is built in England's green and pleasant land. Long before he wrote, however, Christian emperors and kings had proclaimed their capitals the New Jerusalem, from Aksum in *Ethiopia to *Rome and Charlemagne's Aachen. The same ideal fired the pilgrims to the New World, where a New Jerusalem could be forged, a city of justice and harmony run on godly lines. Modern *Africa contains numerous 'New Jerusalems' founded by prophets, such as Simon Kimbangu's village of Nkamba.

For the contemporary city, holy in three faiths and the disputed capital of a secular Jewish state, the difficulty of living out the clash between the mundane reality of urban life and the conflicting ideals of a whole variety of religious systems is still unresolved. Relations between Christian groups are still strained and their relationship to the Israeli state can be fraught. The ancient churches of the region still feel ignored or at best patronized by the powerful churches of the west. Individuals claiming to be the harbingers of Jesus' second coming, or to be Jesus himself, appear there with great regularity. Moves to have the city placed under international protection meet fierce opposition from many Israelis who see it as an inalienable part of their identity. It remains, however, a unique focus of hope, in the beauty of human aspiration, and of despair, in the intransigence of human folly; a potential flashpoint for war and yet the place to which all nations may one day be drawn in peace, as *Isaiah's towering vision proclaimed when the fortunes of the earthly city were at a nadir.

See also JEWISH–CHRISTIAN RELATIONS.   **Hugh S. Pyper**

Armstrong, K., *A History of Jerusalem: One City, Three Faiths* (1995).
Gilbert, M., *Jerusalem in the Twentieth Century* (1997).
Peters, F. E., *Jerusalem* (1985).
Walker, P. W. L., *Holy City, Holy Places? Christian Attitudes to Jerusalem and the Holy Land in the Fourth Century* (1990).
——*Jesus and the Holy City: New Testament Perspectives on Jerusalem* (1996).

Jesuit thought

Jesuit thought draws its substance from the Society of Jesus. Ignatius of Loyola and nine companions received formal recognition of the Society as a Roman Catholic religious order in 1540. The major influences in the development of Jesuit thought have been the Spiritual *Exercises, the Jesuit Constitutions, and the interaction of the members of the Society with the various milieus in which they lived and worked.

Because every Jesuit in the course of his life 'makes' the Spiritual Exercises regularly and because the spirituality of the Exercises has been the basis of Jesuit training, they have played a pervasive part in Jesuit thought. The Exercises both presuppose and further inculcate certain attitudes and convictions characteristic of the Society. Among them are the necessity for inner *freedom in making choices, the use of the imagination, the conviction that God can and does act directly upon his creatures, the importance of reflection upon one's personal experiences, the desire to follow Christ, and the awareness that God can be found in all things (or, as the Jesuit poet Gerard Manley *Hopkins put it, 'The world is charged with the grandeur of God'). The Jesuit Constitutions structure the Society 'to serve the Lord alone and the Church, his Spouse, under the Roman Pontiff, the vicar of Christ on earth' (Formula of the Institute). These attitudes and convictions and this clear but generally stated purpose underlie the specific Jesuit contributions to Christian thought.

Because the Society of Jesus was meant in principle to be open to any form of service, it has undertaken a wide variety of works that have contributed to the diversity of views also characteristic of Jesuit thought. Early in its history, the Society took on especially the works of missionary evangelization, education, preaching, and spiritual direction. Carrying out these tasks contributed greatly to Jesuit thought.

Missions worldwide, from Canada to Cochin, from Paraguay to *Japan, enlarged Jesuit horizons. Especially important were the missionary enterprises in places such as *India with Roberto de Nobili and *China with Matteo Ricci and their successors because Jesuits became participants in sophisticated non-European cultures, asked questions of their experiences therein, and responded imaginatively.

The Society had not been founded specifically as a teaching order but Jesuit educational institutions expanded rapidly from their beginnings in the late 1540s to schools all over Europe, Asia, and the New World. These schools demanded Jesuits expert in fields far beyond simply the philosophy and theology customary for priests. The 'all things' in which God could be found increasingly included as objects of Jesuit research and teaching almost every field of western scholarship. They ranged from anthropology to mathematics, from history to astronomy, from ancient languages to ballet, from optics to theology, from law to architecture. Men such as Athanasius Kircher and Rudiger Boscovich were polymaths; many others became specialists, for example Christopher Clavius in mathematics. The defence and propagation of the faith made Jesuits authors of catechisms (Peter Canisius) and devotional works such as *The Christian Directory* (Robert Parsons) that profoundly influenced Christian life, thought, and prayer. Although not founded to oppose Protestantism, the Society was enlisted by the papacy in the recovery of Catholicism and the countering of the *Reformation. As a result, much Jesuit thought from the later 16th through the 18th century centred on theology and its related disciplines. These efforts involved questions such as the relationship of free human choice and divine action (Luis Molina), and the nature of the *church, its relation to the state, and the prerogatives of each (Robert Bellarmine). The theories of Molina were denounced by the *Dominicans while the Jesuit development of *casuistry in moral theology incurred the wrath of *Pascal and other *Jansenists.

The extraordinary variety of Jesuit engagement makes it difficult specifically to isolate Jesuit thought except in the sense of the attitudes and convictions that impelled them to such works. The papal suppression of the Society in 1773 under the threat of schism by the Bourbon courts put an end to these deeds and words which had often subjected Jesuits to charges at least of rashness if not of heterodoxy.

From its restoration in 1814 until about the middle of the 20th century the Society was understandably much more cautious and conservative in thought and action than it had previously been. Its members strongly supported papal claims; its philosophers participated prominently in the revival of *Thomism; its theologians helped develop the theoretical and historical bases for teachings such as papal *infallibility and primacy as defined at the First *Vatican Council.

During the last fifty years the general characteristics of Jesuit thought have come prominently into play as Jesuits have engaged vigorously in what might be called a series of conversations with the thought of contemporaries both within the Christian church and outside it. The Society has engaged especially in four such conversations. Its partners have been the secular world in all its variety and complexity, its own Roman Catholic church and the wider Christian community, the Society itself in the persons of the successive generations of its own members, and men and women of other cultures, traditions, and religious experiences.

Jesuits carry on the first of those conversations, with the contemporary world, especially through their almost two hundred institutions of higher education which have more than a million students; through their publications which range from the scholarly, such as *Theological Studies*, to journals of opinion such as *The Month*, *America*, *Études*, or *Civiltà Cattolica*; through research scholars such as Walter Ong in cultural studies, and others in fields that range from astronomy to history to psychoanalysis to public policy; and through centres for social thought and action established around the world.

With its own Roman Catholic church and the wider Christian community the Society in the last decades of the 20th century has conversed in three areas above all. First, its specifically ecclesiastical institutions of higher education, such as the Pontifical Biblical Institute and the Gregorian University in Rome, Heythrop College in London, or the two US Jesuit Schools of Theology in Cambridge, Massachusetts, and Berkeley, California, have been at the forefront of scholarship on the whole range of Christian thought. Secondly, individual Jesuits have greatly influenced the Christian church's self-understanding, theologians such as Karl *Rahner, John Courtney Murray, Henri *de Lubac, Bernard *Lonergan, patristic scholars such as Jean Daniélou, philosophers such as Joseph Maréchal, liturgists such as Joseph Jungmann, and the palaeontologist Pierre *Teilhard de Chardin. Christian spirituality has been the third area of such conversation within the church. Scholarly study of that spirituality, the recovery of the tradition in the Spiritual Exercises of the personally directed retreat, and the training of clergy, religious, and laity in the art of spiritual direction have markedly affected how Christians individually and as groups have conceived of and lived the Christian life.

Within its own ranks and as a stimulus to its own self-understanding, the Society has carried on conversations with its past, present, and future. In critical text editions of the *Monumenta Historica* and in the major vernacular languages it has made widely available the important original source documents that told of its origins and detailed its past history within Christianity. The present and future have been the subjects of the four Jesuit general congregations, the highest governing body of the Society, held since *Vatican II from 1965 to 1995. These, the 31st to 34th congregations, gathered elected and ex-officio Jesuits from all over the world. The first, held during and after Vatican II, went far towards adapting the internal life of the Society and its works to the visions of church and world that came out of the council. The next or 32nd congregation was best known for stating that the perennial mission of the Society as expressed in appropriate contemporary circumstances was primarily the service of the faith with the promotion of *justice as an absolute requirement of such service. The following congregation's principal task was to elect a new general superior.

Most recently the 34th congregation, while explicitly reaffirming the intellectual dimension of Jesuit ministries, has situated all of those ministries in a fourfold context of a service of the faith, a commitment to justice, an entry into other cultures (see CONTEXTUAL THEOLOGY), and a *dialogue both with differing religious traditions and with non-believers. Putting those decisions into practice will, it is hoped, generate both further conversations in new and different milieus of Jesuit activity and further contributions to Christian thought in which the general characteristics of Jesuit thought will be operative.

See also COUNTER-REFORMATION; RELIGIOUS LIFE; DE CERTEAU, MICHEL.   **John W. Padberg, SJ**

Bangert, W. V., *A History of the Society of Jesus*, 2nd edn. (1986).

de Guibert, J., *The Jesuits: Their Spiritual Doctrine and Practice* (1953), ET (1964).

Donohue, J. W., *Jesuit Education: An Essay on the Foundations of its Idea* (1963).

Letson, W., and. Higgins, M., *The Jesuit Mystique* (1995).

Loyola, I., *The Spiritual Exercises and Selected Works*, ed. G. Ganss (1991).

O'Malley, J., *The First Jesuits* (1993).

Jesus. What do we know of Jesus? In the *New Testament there appear four *'gospels', each of which provides a biography of sorts. They agree in the broad lines, but disagree over numerous details. The three Synoptics even share much material. Does this strengthen or weaken their general reliability? All four were probably written between thirty-five and seventy years after Jesus' death, in places far removed from where he lived and in a language different from the Aramaic he had mostly (or entirely) used. It is uncertain whether any of their authors had ever seen him. They were writing, moreover, with strong theological convictions and to serve the needs of young churches very different from Jesus' own community.

In these circumstances, can their accounts, or parts of them, be judged reliable as *history in a modern sense? No question has been more debated. Up to the 18th century almost no Christian questioned their absolute correctness, and it remains unquestioned by very many Christians today. But since the 19th century the *quest for the historical Jesus, a search for the real Jesus behind the formal *christological doctrines of the church and the already heavily charged documents of the NT, has produced many thousands of books, mostly attempting to analyse the latter with scientific rigour but all still influenced by the beliefs or disbeliefs of their authors. By the mid-20th century it looked as if the quest had led to the conclusion that we can say next to nothing with any confidence of Jesus' life and teaching. For *Bultmann, most influential biblical

scholar of that period, this was almost an asset. The historical Jesus was of no importance for his *kerygmatic, existential theology. Christianity is a matter of *faith, and not in Jesus the Palestinian, but in Christ as preached through the ages.

Since the 1950s, however, the position has greatly changed. Few theologians would share Bultmann's lack of interest in Jesus the man but, more important for us now, few careful historians would take such a negative view of the evidence. While much in the gospels is historically dubious, it appears a great mistake to reject wholesale the claim that they give us much reliable information. It is fundamentally implausible to think that early Christians were uninterested in what Jesus actually said and did. The very existence of the gospels in the form they took is evidence to the contrary. Some people in 70–90 AD will have remembered him, or those who knew him. The stretch of *memory required is not enormous. Moreover, the gospel writers certainly made use of shorter documents written considerably earlier. While the communal process of remembering and forgetting was unquestionably influenced by the developing concerns of Christian communities, there is no evidence to suggest that this completely controlled the writing of the story, and much to the contrary. Thus, important as the 'church' was becoming by then, the word appears only twice in the entire gospels; there is no attempt to present Jesus as giving instructions for its shaping. Equally, some of his recorded sayings and doings were likely actually to embarrass Christians, yet they were not excluded. The criterion of embarrassment is one of the more reliable in assessing authenticity. Furthermore, the gospels include much detail which fits Palestine too well to have been simply invented by writers elsewhere. It must have been passed on, orally or in writing, by people for whom the factual history of Jesus greatly mattered.

What follows is intended to give as sound a summary as possible of what even a non-believer should accept as historical truth about Jesus. Admittedly, scholars still do not agree and never will. There is no entirely neutral history. Every historian is affected by personal assessments about significance, probability, and authenticity. Nevertheless there has been a noticeable and carefully grounded movement away from the extreme scepticism of the past. This account focuses on what appears most sure; much more may be added as possible or even probable, but it needs to be consonant with what is comparatively certain.

The most ancient tradition is enshrined in two short summaries which Paul claimed some twenty years after Jesus' death to have received and passed on to his converts, 1 Corinthians 11: 23–5 and 15: 3–5. *Mark, probably the earliest of the canonical gospels, begins with *John the Baptist's preaching and his baptism of Jesus. *Matthew and *Luke insert opening sections on Jesus' birth at Bethlehem and his infancy. These hardly tally between themselves, sharing only a few basic details. Matthew's infancy narrative is driven too obviously by a desire to show the fulfilment of OT texts to inspire confidence in its historicity. While it is conceivable that Luke at least includes some historically reliable material, in the scholarly field that is not widely accepted. It seems likely that Jesus was born at Nazareth, but the historical story has to begin with his baptism by John.

Again, there is good reason to think that the fourth gospel includes much genuinely historical detail. Indeed, many would regard it as factually the most reliable of the gospels. Nevertheless, the history of Jesus was here more than anywhere else subordinated to its theological presentation. Thus it is hard to believe that the same person spoke in the way Jesus speaks in the Synoptics and the way he does in *John, even though just occasionally (e.g. Matt. 11: 26–7) the former sounds remarkably like the latter. Nevertheless, John's long meditational texts can best be read as an amazing re-write of Jesus' teaching, reflected through the mind of a great theologian, faithful to the kernel of the master's ideas but developing it in a way that people in his lifetime failed to perceive and shaping the whole narrative to reflect the author's interpretation. Very little of this can be used to establish what Jesus said or did, except in so far as it confirms other evidence. There is much else in the Synoptic Gospels that has to be judged dubious in historical terms, including, for instance, such 'nature miracles' as walking on water. Probably more important to stress is the way in which genuine sayings of Jesus are extended or interpreted by the evangelists. Thus the parable of the sower in Mark 4: 3–8 is probably authentic, but the interpretation put into the mouth of Jesus (4: 10–20) inauthentic, representing the way the Christian community had come to view his words many years later. The same seems true of the parable of the weeds in Matt. 13: 24–30, 'explained' in 36–43. Here, as elsewhere, Matthew's preoccupation with punishment is imposed on Jesus' teaching.

Even without the infancy narratives, most of John's gospel, and various other passages, we are still left with a considerable body of material on which to base a history of Jesus. It covers a period of very few years, ending with the crucifixion in *Jerusalem, in or around 30 AD. Most of the events took place in or near Galilee, apart from the final, perhaps only, visit to Jerusalem but they have been put together in an order that is not primarily chronological. We cannot construct a chronological history of Jesus' ministry, nor even imagine what happened in his thirty or so previous years, apart from knowing that he had been a craftsman in Nazareth, the son of Mary. His brothers and sisters were well known (Mark 6: 3). In the past, and still today, reputable scholars as well as popular journalists and pious writers have tended to jump beyond the evidence through first adopting an idea of Jesus—moral reformer, political revolutionary, Palestinian peasant, charismatic rabbi, even the son of God—and then reconstructing his story to fit the idea, including suppositions about his intentions and consciousness. A very long history of unconvincing interpretation suggests that to typecast him first and construct a story second will never work. The historical Jesus evades any easy classification.

Jesus was a Palestinian Jew living entirely within a Jewish society. There was no way his mind, teaching, and behaviour could do other than reflect Palestinian *Judaism, and everything he thought and said must have had some parallel or source within his world. He could read and write but was not a scribe and did not speak like one. He identified with very ordinary people, particularly the poor and marginal, starting where they started. He was seen as a *prophet, and behaved like one, both in word and symbolic action. He was a 'holy man' who healed people and performed *miracles—nothing is more certain than that. He was also an itinerant teacher and controversialist, wandering almost ceaselessly from place to place, calling a group of people individually to follow him, and, usually, they did. Most of these disciples came from Galilee. In

Jerusalem he felt himself on less sympathetic territory, but it still represented the heart of Judaism and the point where his mission had to culminate. He appeared remarkably unascetic, liked eating and drinking with friends; he had much to say about *women and there were some among his followers in a society where women were almost invisible; he liked *children, he was happy to mix with people accounted sinful or otherwise excluded from good society. He seems never to have travelled far outside Jewish Palestine or had much to do with Gentiles yet he seemed inimical to barriers.

John the Baptist was an *ascetic, calling people to repentance, a sedentary figure in the *desert, who baptized. Jesus was not an ascetic, seems not to have greatly stressed repentance, was not sedentary, ministered in ordinary populated places, and did not baptize. Yet John baptized Jesus. For Christians, this later seemed a fact awkward to explain; baptism symbolized cleansing from sin and Jesus had no sin. So why be baptized? The fact that Mark and Matthew still report it is good evidence of its historicity and for the way history could prevail over theology in gospel writing.

The *Kingdom of God was Jesus' central message. What did it mean? Was it something already present or a future reality to be awaited? It seems too undefinable to be susceptible to any precise either/or. However, while its location in the near future was for long central to scholarly interpretation, it seems more likely that its 'already here if only you can see it' quality is as important. Jesus was a teacher of present wisdom, of an unconventional, subversive sort, in which the use of *apocalyptic phraseology to refer to coming events did not imply expectation of an imminent end to a space-time universe. One may get nearest to a sense of the kingdom with some of the simplest and most authentic *parables: the sower, the lamp hidden under a bushel, the mustard seed, the yeast, the treasure hidden in a field, the pearl of great price (Mark 4; Matt. 13: 31–46). There is a homely, rural, almost democratic imagery here and a noticeable absence of any royal, military, or civic idiom to characterize Jesus' kingdom: not the kind of imagery townsmen in Corinth or Rome would have created two generations later. It goes with an exceptionally demanding, yet unlegalistic, *morality, insisting upon the commandments of *love, emphatically extended even to one's enemies and formulated with that tendency to verbal exaggeration that might be claimed as Jesus' signature tune: 'If your right hand cause you to sin, cut it off', 'Let the dead bury the dead', 'Do not be anxious about tomorrow'. 'Who are my mother and my brothers?', he asked when told that his family was asking for him; 'anyone who does the will of God, that person is my brother, and sister, and mother' (Mark 3: 34–5)—again a saying not altogether in line with the culture of the early church. Jesus' teaching was wholly *God-centred. It was what God was doing or would do that mattered; the actual shape of that doing remained vague but it certainly entailed a great new divine initiative in the light of which previous concerns, whether legal details, past sins, or, even, the *Temple itself, were somehow almost irrelevant.

All this was said with a sense of great personal *authority which struck listeners and contrasted with the kind of authority that the scribes exercised. The 'I' in many of Jesus' statements has profound significance. Who then was Jesus? What did he claim to be? The answer is that he seems to have made no comprehensive claim about his own identity. Almost certainly he did not use or encourage either '*messiah' (Christ) or 'lord', which became his regular titles in early Christianity. Instead he called himself the 'Son of Man'. The literature on the meaning of this term is vast, yet it remains enigmatic. Possibly that is what he intended: 'I am who I am', perhaps no more than 'a man like you', but perhaps hinting at 'one like a son of man' whom in a vision *Daniel saw 'coming on the clouds of heaven' to be given 'sovereignty, glory, and kingship' (Dan. 7: 13). But that may be to read back into his self-description more than he intended. We shall never be sure. It was not a title Christians used later, making its repeated presence in the gospels good evidence of historicity.

The Son of Man was also son of God. That was not so much a title as a statement of fact. Jesus continually referred to God as *abba*, father, 'my father'. Certainly, God as father was not an idea hitherto unheard of, but there is no precedent for Jesus' regular, personal use of it, and it was precisely this sense of personal relatedness to God that grounded his confidence in personal authority. Yet it was a sonship that he could share with his disciples. 'When you pray, say: Father, may your name be held holy, your kingdom come' (Luke 11: 2).

A prophet often taught by signs, and central to Jesus' work was a series of symbolic actions, all highly mysterious, but hugely significant for him personally, significant too for his disciples, even if they seldom quite understood them, but probably not too significant for any larger audience. The five that mattered most were the appointment of 'the Twelve' (see APOSTOLICITY), the entry into Jerusalem, the disturbance in the Temple, the final supper, and Jesus' actual death (see CROSS). Each of these was a profoundly prophetic action. It was in them that we come nearest the heart of what we may call Jesus' developing strategy, and it is just because of this that Christian believers, the evangelists, and especially John could subsequently further elaborate this symbolic pattern without any fundamental betrayal of historicity. The Twelve signified a new people of *Israel replacing the twelve tribes, entry into Jerusalem on an ass suggested that the messianic moment had arrived with the entry of a very unmilitaristic king—but still a king—into David's city, the overturning of tables in the Temple seems to have symbolized its destruction and replacement rather than its cleansing, the meal in the upper room celebrated the new *covenant fellowship (*Eucharist) he was inaugurating by his death. Most mysteriously and contentiously of all, his death itself signified the road to life whereby God's kingdom would arrive. The evidence that he foresaw death, facing it with deliberation when he went up to Jerusalem that last time, is considerable. It was the 'cup he had to drink', both a ruthless extinction of his ministry by his enemies and the last and most difficult of his prophetic actions, but one integrally connected with all the signs he had constructed since arriving at Jerusalem.

Historically, there is no reason to question that the Jewish authorities had decided he needed to be removed. His teaching and actions threatened their position, at least potentially, and could lead to an uprising which the high priests were anxious to avoid. The accusation at his trial that he had spoken of the destruction of the Temple almost certainly suggests that their resolve was related to what he had done in the Temple, but it was in terms of a political danger that he was handed over by them to the Roman governor, Pontius Pilate, and executed as 'King of the Jews', a title written on the placard placed above his cross, surely a piece of authentic infor-

mation. Mentioned in all four gospels, it is not a title Christians later used of Jesus. That none of his disciples was executed with him makes it clear that Jesus was not seen as leader of an actual political insurrection, but the shouts of an excited crowd, 'Save us, Son of David', when he entered the city could have been enough to convince a nervous procurator that the high priests were right: there was a serious threat to law and order. Their viewpoint was essentially the same.

The gospels end with an empty tomb and a Risen Lord. The apparition accounts are far from consistent, yet persuasive of something even by their very variety. It is certain that within fifteen years of Jesus' death his *Resurrection and appearances were already a shared belief among his disciples. It is likely too that his tomb really was found empty, though that is more open to dispute. The earliest surviving form of Resurrection account is Paul's summary in 1 Cor. 15: 3–8. The first apparition may well have been to *Mary Magdalene or to a group of women. That would be consonant with much in Jesus' story. The appearances to *Peter and the Twelve came later, probably in Galilee, but their accounts were regarded as the ones that mattered. It is impossible to claim the same sort of historicity for these experiences, especially for any individual account. Yet collectively it is hard on grounds of evidence to discount it, basic as the experience was to the immediate rationale of an expansive little community confident in its claim to have seen the Risen Lord. There is an inscrutability here which faith can work with and reason overleaps itself to dismiss—confident as the rationality of the Enlightenment was to do just that—but the Resurrection appearances go well beyond the historically ascertainable life of Jesus of Nazareth, which has been our subject here. It would seem a life open to a variety of interpretations. For most of his Jewish contemporaries, many of them intelligent and sincerely religious, a high interpretation in any way consonant with the church's later christology was unacceptable. If Jesus was a good man, he was also dangerously deluded. Many people today, presented with the evidence available, come to the same conclusion. Nevertheless, Jesus continues two millennia after his death to be a personal influence in the lives of millions of people, something extraordinary, especially for someone who wrote not a word. There is a strange strength in what he said and did that breaks through any normal defining lines. His life as we know it does not appear to rule out a fully Christian interpretation, a matter of faith as that has always been. There is no reason for the believing Christian to shut out of mind the historian's conclusions. Christology and the secular evidence of sound history are not incompatible.

Adrian Hastings

Chilton, Bruce, and Evans, Craig (eds.), *Studying the Historical Jesus: Evaluations of the State of Current Research* (1994).

Crossan, J. D., *The Historical Jesus: The Life of a Mediterranean Jewish Peasant* (1991).

Dodd, C. H., *The Founder of Christianity* (1970).

Harvey, A. E., *Jesus and the Constraints of History* (1982).

Meier, John P., *A Marginal Jew*, i (1991); ii (1994).

Riches, John, *Jesus and the Transformation of Judaism* (1980).

Robinson, John, *The Priority of John* (1985).

Sanders, E. P., *Jesus and Judaism* (1985).

Theissen, Gerd, and Merz, Annette, *The Historical Jesus: A Comprehensive Guide* (1998).

Vermes, Geza, *Jesus the Jew* (1973).

Wright, N. T., *Jesus and the Victory of God* (1996).

Jesus, depiction of.

The earliest images of Jesus, in the rough catacomb art of the 3rd to the 5th centuries, show him as a beardless youth. Often he is the good shepherd, with a *sheep slung round his neck; a good biblical image, but also found in pagan art depicting Hermes, god of *compassion. Elsewhere he appears as Orpheus, charming the *animals. A vault-mosaic in the necropolis under St Peter's shows him as the chariot-driving sun-god Apollo. Why were these models abandoned? However great paganism's spiritual decay, no one could deny the magnificence of its monuments. Christian *art clearly *could* have continued borrowing from that heritage for ever, in more and more sophisticated ways. Yet it did not.

The reason seems to be that Christianity stands in a more complex relationship to art than did paganism. The religious art of ancient Greece and Rome is a straightforward celebration of human life; the gods represent that life at its most beautiful, vigorous, healthy, and serene. Therein lies their whole divinity. But Christianity introduces a new element of social criticism, which, in turn, gives a far greater role to the narrative content of religious tradition, as defining the historic conflict between divine and human will. Whereas the *myths concerning Greek and Roman gods symbolically *illustrate* their divine vitality, the divinity of Jesus is *revealed* in and through his life-story.

One consequence is a new preference for painting. Sculpture offers greater possibilities for the imposing embodiment of a blissful divine ideal, as we see in pagan statuary. Painting has greater narrative capacity, and so becomes the primary form for Christian art.

But the Christian depiction of God *incarnate tends to become overloaded with meaning. In so far as it focuses on the particularity of the *gospel story, it depicts intense vulnerability and passion, the exact opposite of the pagan vision. Yet the whole point of the story lies in the paradoxical conjunction of that redemptive passion with the eternal serenity of the divine. These two aspects may well be reconciled in the richly dialectical inwardness of Christian faith, but Christian *art* is called to exteriorize the reconciliation: which, at the highest level of artistic ambition, proves impossible.

The *iconoclasm of the 8th century and the post-*Reformation period may have been an overreaction to the resultant problems. Nevertheless, there surely is an important element of truth in *Hegel's observation that for thoughtful Christians, 'art, considered in its highest vocation, is and remains … ' (*Aesthetics*, p. 11). Art's 'highest vocation' is the essentially unproblematic, and hence central, role it played in depicting the gods of ancient paganism, as a 'religion of art'. No Christian art could ever be so boldly definitive; or so definitively bold. The bolder it is, in the naturalistic representation of its own ideal reality, the more it is embroiled in contradiction.

One way to resolve the problem is to eschew boldness. The *iconography of eastern Christendom, stemming from *Byzantium, does this: icons are deliberately low-voltage art. With their carefully formalized primitivism, halfway between naturalistic representation and hieroglyph, they modestly point beyond themselves. Nothing could be further from the splendid ideal-naturalism of classical antiquity. But compare the art of the *Re-

naissance. Sensuous, perspectival, full of lavish theatrical effects, high Renaissance painting is art at its boldest. And so the contradictions emerge. Take the work of three painters from the early 16th century: Michelangelo, Grünewald, and Raphael.

Michelangelo is the Christian artist who comes closest to reviving the religious exuberance of pagan antiquity. A sculptor as much as a painter, he sculpts the dead Christ, on his mother's lap, as a monument of noble repose. However, in his Last Judgement in the Sistine Chapel, Christ appears as an Olympian figure, of absolute serenity, yet all action.

Contrast Grünewald's vision of the crucifixion (see CROSS): here we have the starkest antithesis. Equally far removed from the spirit of Byzantium, it is a depiction of pure passion. Christ's body hangs twisted and savagely wounded; an image of grief beyond all grief, in violent colour. It was the tendency of northern European Renaissance painting, unlike that of Italy, to accentuate the cruelty of the event, especially in scenes of Jesus' flagellation. Grünewald carries that tendency to its furthest extreme. His masterpiece, the Isenheim altarpiece, was painted for a hospital, and partly, no doubt, conceived as a response to the suffering of the sick. Perhaps it also reflects the mood of anguish shortly to issue in the upheavals of the Reformation. Grünewald himself became a follower of *Luther.

Entering into Grünewald's nightmare world, one sees how theologically one-sided Michelangelo's approach is, for it is a powerful display of everything in the gospel that Michelangelo has turned his back on. But what is the outcome? A no less one-sided abandonment of serenity. The Isenheim altarpiece includes the *Resurrection; the risen Christ still bears the stigmata, yet otherwise appears quite unrelated to the crucified one. His face is a lurid yellow glow. It is a disturbingly feverish picture; given the nature of the adjoining crucifixion, some such effect is probably inevitable.

Raphael represents a third vision. Unlike Michelangelo, he paints the Incarnation in terms of a tenderly transfigured vulnerability; unlike Grünewald, he does so with serenity and charm, but only by concentrating on one much-repeated theme: the image of Madonna and Child. By abstracting Christ's Incarnation from the drama of his Passion, this image effectively eludes the artistic contradictions deriving from that drama (so Hegel called it 'the most perfect subject' for Christian visual art). But, when one looks at Raphael's painting of the Passion, one can only say that, compared with Grünewald, it appears emotionally lightweight. The style that works so well with the Madonna and Child seems altogether less convincing when applied to the heavier symbolism of divine adulthood.

Yet in the western art of the succeeding centuries Raphael's way prevailed. Worshippers in Byzantine churches had been confronted by the formidable, imperial image of Christ Pantocrator, spread across the apse or dome; in the *Baroque period, by contrast, Christian art increasingly became an exercise in *seduction*. Amidst an intoxicating swirl of angels, saints, and sinners, Jesus stands out as the personification of sweet gentleness.

Rembrandt, in the 17th century, adds something genuinely new, of some theological interest: for the first time, a Christian artist with a sense of history paints Jesus as a Jew, in an orientalized world where the wealthy wear turbans. But in the following period, the chief factor determining the image of Jesus is an impulse to mass popularization, as the Jesus of conventional Baroque art, like that of

Guido Reni, is transformed, for instance, into the kitsch-imagery associated with the Sacred Heart.

It is significant that the most powerful Christian painting of the 19th century, that of Hegel's contemporary Caspar David Friedrich, no longer involves any direct depiction of biblical scenes. Friedrich recoils from the clichés of such art, preferring to paint esoterically symbolic Baltic or Alpine landscapes, with Jesus depicted only at second-hand, in wayside crucifixes in the snow or on mountain-tops. Then the Pre-Raphaelites attempted a revival of Renaissance piety, and Holman Hunt's allegorical painting 'The Light of the World' still continues to enjoy extraordinary popularity; which is only the success of an (admittedly brilliant) Victorian sentimentality.

What now? In response to the mass-production of devotional kitsch, it is surely the primary task of Christian art to reopen our imaginations: the more discordantly, perhaps, the better. More than ever before, the universal representativeness of Jesus becomes an issue. As the Rastafarians forcefully complain, the kitsch-portrayal of Jesus carried by white *missionaries to the subject-peoples of western imperialism assumes the ideological function of represent-ing a 'white God'. He needs to be depicted in every other sort of ethnic identity. *Feminist theology, likewise, has started to inspire representations of a female Christ, or 'Christa', such as the crucifix by Edwina Sandys which hung for a time in New York's Anglican Cathedral.

The 20th century witnessed an efflorescence of highly individua-lized *christological visions, as modestly primitivist as Byzantine icons, yet released from their conventional restraints. Stanley Spen-cer set the gospel story in the Berkshire village of Cookham, paint-ing scenes of bizarre comedy yet also, on occasion, of ferocious grief, as in his portrayal of a crucifixion in the high street. The non-Christian Marc Chagall has portrayed the crucified Jesus as a fellow-sufferer of Jewish affliction (though in his later work, to the con-sternation of some Jewish critics, the theme is universalized). Emil Nolde has painted numerous NT scenes, with all the vivid turbu-lence of German Expressionism, while Georges Rouault's expressi-vist paintings of a quietly sorrowing Jesus stand alongside his savage depictions of corrupt judges and tragic prostitutes. Thus Christian modernist art has declared open war on the perceived complacency of more conventional portrayals of the saviour.

Andrew Shanks

Alexander, S., *Marc Chagall* (1979).

Courthion, P., *Georges Rouault* (1977).

Hegel, G. W. F., *Aesthetics: Lectures on Fine Art* (2 vols.; 1820–9), ET (1975), i.

Maas, J., *Holman Hunt and the Light of the World* (1984).

Pople, K., *Stanley Spencer* (1991).

Quenot, M., *The Icon: Window on the Kingdom* (1991).

Selz, P., *Emil Nolde* (1963).

Jewish–Christian relations.

That *Jesus himself and all his disciples were Jews, and that his message of the *Kingdom was initially preached to his own people, are facts that were soon eclipsed by history, as the mission of *Paul and his companions to other peoples of the Roman empire quickly took precedence. Paul's relation to his own people was one of agonized involvement, as Romans 9–11 eloquently testifies. Yet that same Paul was unequivo-cal in denouncing 'Judaizers' among the fledgling communities that he was forming 'in Christ', as Galatians clearly testifies.

So a twofold tension emerged from the beginning: first between those Jews who recognized Jesus as the 'one who was to come' and 'of whom Moses spoke' (John 1: 45, referring to Deut. 18: 18) and those who did not, a conflict reflected in the gospels themselves, notably in their polemical stance regarding Pharisees and the Sab-bath. The second tension emerged within the fledgling community itself, reflected in Acts 15, between Jews who had recognized Jesus and new converts from paganism: should these be circumcised or not? The decision not to require this condition for admission into the new community, established by consensus in Jerusalem, had the effect of detaching Paul's mission from *Israel, the original 'people of God'. So began a process whereby that people came to be seen as those who *had* been given a divine promise, designed to prepare for the good news to be effected in Jesus for the salvation of the entire world: 'not for the nation only, but to gather into one the children of God who are scattered abroad' (John 11: 52). Similar sentiments are forthrightly expressed in the letter to the *Hebrews, long thought to have been authored by Paul. Citing Jeremiah 31: 31, 'The days will come, says the Lord, when I will establish a new *covenant with the house of Israel and with the house of Judah', the letter goes on to announce: 'In speaking of a new covenant he treats the first as obsolete' (8: 13); and then placing the words of Psalm 40: 8, 'Lo, I have come to do thy will', in Jesus' mouth, clearly asserts that 'he abolishes the first [covenant] in order to establish the second' (10: 9).

Hence the dominant outlook that came to characterize Christian reflection on Israel: supersession. After saying that 'in speaking of a new covenant he treats the first as obsolete', the author of Hebrews continues 'and what is becoming obsolete and growing old is ready to vanish away' (8: 13). It must be remembered that in that period what was old was considered proven and better: the perspective introduced here was turning the tables on that convention as well. A different reading of the situation can be gathered from Paul's agonized reflections on his own people in Rom. 9–11, culminating in the insistence that 'the gifts and the call of God are irrevocable' (11: 29), but the bulk, to date, of Christian–Jewish history was to elapse before that perspective would have even a chance to prevail.

The destruction of the *Temple and burning of Jerusalem in 70 AD was easily read by Christians as confirmation of the demise of the Jews as God's people, and even as divine punishment for their collective failure to acknowledge Jesus as the one sent by God and already promised by *Moses. The Acts of the Apostles chronicles Paul's preaching to the world beyond Jewry: again and again he begins his catechesis with the Diaspora Jewish communities in each locale, only to be rebuffed and so turn to the uncircumcised Gen-tiles, who receive the message. These turned out to be no less vacillating in their adherence to the gospel than Jews had been with the Torah, as Paul's own letters illustrate; but some among them were eager to hear this unexpected 'good news' that faithful Jews tended to reject as a novelty.

This was an entirely comprehensible reaction, and one that Paul might have recognized from his own case. But, when coupled with the stern warnings and condemnations of the Hebrew prophets found in the scriptures, it was a response that tended to harden each group's attitude to the other. Moreover, each represented a subcommunity within the Roman empire, vulnerable to persecution by guardians of the dominant religious beliefs that subserved the imperial interest. So after *Constantine, when Christianity was first tolerated and then officially promoted, Christians were before long exploiting their new-found recognition by celebrating the superiority of the revelation in Jesus over its parent faith.

Yet that 'people of God' had recovered its identity in the wake of the Roman destruction of the Temple, when its leaders assembled at Javneh to focus the community on book and prayer rather than Temple sacrifice. The 'Judaism' that emerged embodied an understandable set of defensive reactions to this Christian movement that had spread so widely so quickly.

So the stage was set for a conflict fought with increasingly acerbic *rhetorical tools during the patristic era. Apologists wielded powerful *metaphors drawn from the pervasive Neoplatonic culture ('flesh/spirit', 'shadow/reality'), to bring the two covenants into confrontation, always to the detriment of the Torah. They dealt a kind of conceptual *coup de grâce* to the liturgical pattern of promise/fulfilment, effectively evacuating the promise in the light of its fulfilment. Thus they denigrated its richness and negated the obvious fact that the two are inherently related. For who can recognize a fulfilment without having been imbued with its promise? And is not fulfilment within the course of history always equally the bearer of a promise? To regard the NT as *having* fulfilled the promise entirely overlooks the 'fear and trembling' with which Paul characterized Christian faith, and the extent to which the gospel is always proclaimed to a community seeking (and failing) to fulfil its stringent demands. This attitude, later known as 'triumphalism', was buttressed by the negative image of 'the Jew', as that community continued to subsist in the midst of an ostensibly Christian world (see ANTISEMITISM). It is this assertive anachronism, the survival of a tradition that was supposed to have gone into eclipse, that seems to have been particularly offensive to Christians, as shown in John Chrysostom's defensively vitriolic rhetoric. The continued existence of a Jewish community was provocation enough, but the fact that it could pose an attractive alternative for baptized Christians was intolerable. The severity displayed by early writers such as Melito of Sardis and Justin Martyr towards Jews and their worship, and later by such figures as Ambrose and *Augustine, can best be explained by observing that Christian pastors sensed a threat in the witness of such an integral community.

The advent of *Islam on the scene created a three-body problem that appears to have opened new possibilities for Christian–Jewish relations. Jews remained 'infidels in our midst', as well as a community that would not go away, but one that could become an interlocutor, unlike this aggressively new *revelation with its whole new book that claimed to be addressed, as the gospel was, to all mankind. Judaism remained truncated according to the Christian appropriation of the bible, but here was an entirely new revelation, claiming to present God's way of superseding both covenants, and not content with doing battle rhetorically. In the Christian east, Islamic hegemony soon reduced both Jews and Christians to religious enclaves, respected but officially superseded by a dominant culture based on the Qur'an. Jews living in the midst of western Christendom might even see themselves and be seen as allies on the side of the bible against this new religious reality, which also claimed *Abrahamic lineage. Yet they remained an alien religious faith, threatening by their very presence the worldwide mandate to spread the gospel. The second of these attitudes was manifested in the ensuing Crusades to liberate Jerusalem, which could also produce violence against Jewish populations in their wake. The first bore fruit in intellectual circles (as indeed from as far back as Jerome) with scripture scholars actively seeking the expertise of rabbis in understanding the holy book shared, at least in part, by both communities.

In the high Middle Ages, particularly under the influence of the kingdom of Naples, thinkers of all three traditions can be seen tackling the philosophical implications of their shared faith in the free creation of the universe by one God. While the relative maturity of Islamic culture over that of the Christian west meant that the best Islamic thinkers predated those in the west, later thinkers could certainly profit from earlier ones: Moses ben Maimon (Maimonides) from the work of al-Ghazali, and *Aquinas from both of them, as well as from the Islamic philosophers Ibn Sina (Avicenna) and Ibn Rushd (Averroës). Indeed, the bridge figure here proved to be Maimonides, whose intellectual location in the midst of Islamic culture allowed him to assimilate its philosophy in such a way as to contribute effectively to Aquinas's cognate project of reconciling faith with reason. This period of Mediterranean culture represents a high point in the illumination of western Christian philosophy by Islamic and Jewish thought, notably in Andalusia, where the three Abrahamic traditions found themselves engaged in building a culture at once popular and intellectual. In subsequent centuries, Christian and Islamic civilizations resorted to geographical partition or military stand-off, while the increasing intolerance of a more politically triumphant Christendom made such endeavours of mutual illumination less likely, as witnessed most palpably in the Iberian peninsula. An ambivalence similar to the earlier one can be seen in the 16th-century turn to scripture, with *Erasmus seeking out Jewish biblical scholars for assistance in reading original texts, while *Luther's law/gospel polarity offered an ideological reading of Paul that went beyond even the patristic metaphors of contrast and conflict between the covenants. Such a theological position inevitably licensed political leaders to marginalize Jewish communities both by legislation and by communal practices.

The intellectual and political structures of the *Enlightenment worked to foster some *rapprochement* between the nominally Christian communities dominant in Europe and the Jewish subgroups in their midst, with a new watchword of 'tolerance'. This attitude received a sympathetic intellectual response in figures from Moses Mendelssohn to Martin Buber, whose more irenic writings sought ways to collaborate across the divide of differing faiths. This promising new chapter was brutally terminated by the Nazi machine, whose 'final solution' to the 'Jewish problem' transformed a theological conflict into an exercise of power unrelieved by any humane religious constraints. In retrospect, the *Holocaust can be seen to represent the furthest reaches of ideological 'rationalism' as much as a dark unleashing of forces kindled down the centuries by a rhetorical conflict that consistently demeaned the Jews. It has been in the wake of that tragedy that Christian–Jewish relations have become increasingly articulate, as dramatized in the *Vatican II document, *Nostra Aetate*, which expressly substituted Paul's insistence that 'the gifts and the call of God are irrevocable' (Rom. 11: 29) for the widely disseminated *supersessionist* position of Christianity with respect to Judaism. On the Jewish side, the reaction has been varied, but is most vocally dominated by a Zionist ideology giving prominence to the state of Israel as a safe haven for Jews and a platform for Jewish cultural and intellectual life. However, many voices can be heard within it, from those inspired by Martin Buber to those speaking with the accents of Jabotinsky (whose 'revisionist Zionism' inspires the Israeli right.) The latter insist that what happened at Auschwitz shall never happen to *us* again, while the former work to see to it that it should never happen to *anyone*, with political strategies corresponding to these very different attitudes.

At the same time the unmistakable stimulus which Israel has given to Jewish cultural life has encouraged Jewish thinkers to look again at Jesus and those who purport to follow him. Such scholars as Geza Vermes and David Flusser have been mining the figure of 'Jesus the Jew', to invite Jews and Christians to reflect together on their origins. Moreover, since Jews who grow up in Israel find themselves no longer briefed about Christians in a defensive manner, fascinating new perspectives are emerging from which the two communities may overcome their centuries-old stand-off. At the same time, the realities of political power have put Jews and Judaism into an arena never experienced in the centuries of Christian hegemony, at a time when the Christian faith appears less and less relevant to political decisions in the world at large. So new alliances will emerge, although they will doubtless be affected by age-old images.

How should Christians, in such a climate, take stock of their relation to the Jewish faith? As thinkers and believers in *dialogue with their Jewish counterparts, for only a dialogue of living persons can elicit the kind of self-criticism that assures that the two traditions acknowledge the ways they can learn and have learned from each other. Only the capacity for self-criticism keeps a religious tradition from hardening into an ideology, and dialogue is a strategy by which each can try to incorporate the other's perspectives. These perspectives are often unwelcome especially where a history of disdain has poisoned the capacity for give and take which dialogue must embody. Yet the combined capacities of scripture and human reason ought to supply these two traditions with rich resources to do just that. On the Christian side, the verses following immediately upon Paul's reminder that 'the gifts and the call of God are irrevocable'—'O the depth of the riches and wisdom and knowledge of God! How unsearchable are his judgments and how inscrutable his ways!' (Rom. 11: 33)—should forcibly remind us that the relation between the two covenants has never been clearly articulated, so any form of triumphalism will be tantamount to a denial of the good news of Jesus. But even on the Jewish side, nothing, not even Auschwitz and the genocide, can give exemption from the task of self-criticism and the scrutiny of one's own tradition. Jewish thinkers like Amos Elon are able to criticize a process whereby 'the Holocaust [has been] mystified to become the center of a new civil religion and used to justify Israel's refusal to withdraw from occupied territory'. That kind of resolute challenge to the idolatries endemic to each tradition will be using biblical tools to forge what can be an ongoing relation between those holding the faith of each of the covenants. Nothing less will do, and the resources of each community should foster thinkers and people of faith able to meet such a challenge.

David B. Burrell, CSC

Abulafia, Anna Sapir, *Christians and Jews in the Twelfth-Century Renaissance* (1995).

Chazan, Robert, *Daggers of Faith: Thirteenth-Century Christian Missionizing and Jewish Response* (1989).

Cohen, Jeremy (ed.), *Essential Papers on Judaism and Christianity in Conflict: From Late Antiquity to the Reformation* (1991).

Conzelman, Hans, *Gentiles, Jews, Christians: Polemics and Apologetics in the Greco-Roman Era* (1992).

Croner, Helga, *Stepping Stones to Further Jewish–Christian Relations: An Unabridged Collection of Christian Documents* (1977).

Davies, Alan (ed.), *Anti-Semitism and the Foundations of Christianity* (1979).

Fisher, Eugene, *Visions of the Other: Jewish and Christian Theologians Assess the Dialogue* (1994).

Lewis, Bernard, *Cultures in Conflict: Christians, Muslims, and Jews in the Age of Discovery* (1995).

Mann, Vivian, *et al.* (eds.), *Convivencia: Jews, Muslims, and Christians in Medieval Spain* (1992).

Novak, David, *Jewish–Christian Dialogue: A Jewish Justification* (1989).

Prior, Michael, *Bible and Colonialism: A Moral Critique* (1997).

Thoma, Clemens, *A Christian Theology of Judaism* (1980).

van Buren, Paul, *A Christian Theology of the People Israel* (1983).

Vermes, Geza, *The Religion of Jesus the Jew* (1993).

Wilken, Robert, *John Chrysostom and the Jews: Rhetoric and Reality in the Late Fourth Century* (1983).

Job, a maverick among the *Wisdom books of the OT, tells the story of the pious and wealthy Job who becomes the subject of a wager between *God and Satan (see DEVIL) as to whether his piety is genuine or merely a result of his *prosperity. To test this, Job is deprived of his goods and his children and smitten with disease. He accepts all this patiently, saying, to the disgust of his wife, 'The Lord gives and the Lord takes away; blessed be the name of the Lord' (1: 21). Thus far, the story reads like a folk-tale. However, the book then opens out into a cycle of poetic speeches as Job's silence breaks and he enters into a debate with his three friends, the proverbial Job's comforters. They attempt to account for Job's seemingly undeserved *suffering by arguing in various ways that he did deserve it. Job not only protests his innocence but, between complaints that God's inaccessibility denies him a proper hearing, hurls violent accusations against God of callous indifference and wanton cruelty. The cycle is broken by the voice of youth, Elihu, and then by God's answer, an astonishing but baffling display of virtuosity both by the all-powerful creator of the cosmos who points up the wonder and strangeness of his *creation and by the master of poetic imagery who wrote the book. The result is that Job, now reduced once more to silence, has his goods more than restored, while his friends are rebuked for their impertinence.

Critically speaking, the book sits oddly in the Hebrew Scriptures. Perhaps not even originally composed in Hebrew, perhaps the end product of a long process of accretion and editing as different theological viewpoints were stressed or repressed, its hero is not Jewish and its *theology depends little on the bible's historical traditions. Yet it is one of the few books in the Hebrew Scriptures where something like explicitly theological argument is conducted, revolving around a complex of issues concerning the meaning of suffering in a world made and sustained by God's action and the relationship between divine *justice, divine *mercy, and human desert.

For the writer of the epistle of James, it was Job's patient resignation that earned him God's favour and which seems to have already become proverbial (Jas. 5: 11). Patristic and medieval commentators saw Job's undeserved suffering and final restoration as an antitype of Christ's passion. Particularly significant was Gregory the Great's work *Moralia in Iob*. Job 19: 25–6, 'I know that my redeemer liveth and that he shall stand at the latter day upon the earth: and though after my skin worms destroy this body, yet in my flesh shall I see God,' was taken to show Job's stature as the prophet of the *Resurrection and second coming of Christ and as a witness to the resurrection of the body. The oddity of this translation hallowed by the authority of the King James bible makes it plain that the underlying Hebrew is peculiarly ambiguous.

This *typological reading, however, inevitably plays down the element of protest in the book. The *Romantic sensibility of William *Blake, for instance, led to his depicting Job as an archetypal rebel in his series of illustrations to the book. As historical criticism developed, so awareness of the ambiguity and structural peculiarity of the book increased as did appreciation of its sheer poetic power. The 'happy' ending, beloved of earlier Christian commentators, became an embarrassment and was even interpreted as the pious addition of later editors unable to cope with the naked force of the poetic chapters. Job then can be read as the champion of those who uphold the tragic dignity of the human spirit by refusing to bow to implacable and insuperable arbitrary power. It is his *impatience* which makes him a hero. For *Jung in his *Answer to Job*, Job's defiance teaches God what it is to be human.

The book remains an enigma. Often appealed to now in discussion of theodicy, the relationship between God and *evil, it refuses an answer. Is God's speech merely a sneer, as George Bernard Shaw put it, or an acknowledgment of the human right to protest? Is James Barr right to see the book's central affirmation as God's verdict that the 'impious' Job is a better theologian than his pious friends? Does the ending endorse the theology of ultimate prosperity of the good, which experience, our own and Job's, otherwise contradicts? Or does it move to some realm beyond morality into what the novelist Muriel Spark has called 'anagogical humour', where the *paradox is that suffering is all-important and yet unimportant?

After all, the only explicit explanation of Job's plight in the book is that it is the by-product of a wager in heaven; not a particularly edifying piece of theological speculation. Yet Job articulates something of the human plight of the survivor, the man who lives on beyond reason, kept alive—who knows why?—by a God who sustains him only, it seems, to prolong his pain, who is intimately involved with him and yet will not render an account of himself. Such questions became all the more poignant for theologians in the light of the *Holocaust. The steady stream of theological and artistic interpretations of the book testifies to its enduring power to face us with these dilemmas.   **Hugh S. Pyper**

Gordis, R., *The Book of God and Man* (1965).
Perdue, L. G., *Wisdom in Revolt* (1991).
Zuckerman, B., *Job the Silent* (1991).

John. The fourth canonical gospel has had a profound impact on Christian tradition through its distinctive *christology, striking poetic *metaphor, and its emphasis on community and *love.

Precisely where it was written is uncertain: the majority of commentators still accept the traditional location of Ephesus, though Alexandria or a Hellenistic city of lower Galilee are also possibilities. What is certain, however, is that the thought-world in which the gospel was composed was predominantly Jewish: OT motifs lie behind many of the author's expressions; there are several references to the Passover and other Jewish festivals; the author stresses that both Moses and the OT scriptures in general pointed to the coming of *Jesus; and both the prologue (1: 1–18) and the christology of the gospel as a whole evoke ideas from Jewish *Wisdom literature. The strikingly dualistic outlook of the gospel too finds parallels within other branches of 1st-century *Judaism, particularly that of the *Dead Sea Scrolls.

Given this clear Jewish provenance, it is rather surprising to find several extremely derogative references to Jews within the gospel. The phrase 'the Jews' is often used of Jesus' opponents; they are equated with the hostile 'world' which often (though not always) rejects Jesus and his followers. Though himself a Jew, Jesus distances himself from his opponents, referring to 'your law' and 'your synagogue'. This bitter hostility manifests itself most openly in chapter 8 where Jesus accuses his opponents of being children of the *devil (8: 44). These two contradictory elements—John's Jewish heritage and his apparent anti-Jewishness—can be understood only by an appreciation of the situation of the 'community' or group of churches for which the gospel was written. The gospel itself offers a small but significant clue here. Unlike the other gospels which frequently refer to various groups within 1st-century Judaism, John's gospel portrays the Pharisees alone as the undisputed leaders. Furthermore, there are references in the text to the Pharisees expelling followers of Jesus from the synagogue and persecuting Christians (12: 42; 9: 22; 16: 2). These references seem to reflect conditions after the fall of the *Temple in 70 AD, when the Pharisaic party became dominant and synagogue authorities were more anxious than ever before to define the boundaries of Judaism. Although primarily the story of Jesus and his ministry, the gospel, on another level, outlines the history of the Johannine 'community' and its turbulent relationship with the Jewish synagogue. It reflects the harsh experiences of Jewish converts to Christianity and attempts to strengthen them in their faith. Nicodemus and Joseph of Arimathaea may represent 'crypto-Christians', followers of Jesus who are still within the synagogue but do not have the strength to make their allegiance known openly; the evangelist may want to encourage such people to make the traumatic break. The gospel fits well into the late 1st-century situation when the growing hostility between followers of Jesus and the parent synagogue led to the parting of the ways. For this reason a date of about 80–100 seems the most likely, though the gospel was probably worked over by one (or perhaps several) authors before reaching its present form. The negative references to 'the Jews', therefore, have to be read in their historical context. Israel and the OT scriptures are still of paramount importance and it would be anachronistic to regard the book as anti-Jewish (see ANTISEMITISM).

The sense of exposure and alienation felt by the Johannine Christians may account to a large extent for the gospel's greatest contribution to Christian thought: its distinctive portrayal of Jesus. Throughout he is depicted as a stranger from heaven: he is sent by God and descends to an alien and often hostile world for a short time before withdrawing once more to his Father. He is the divine Logos, the *Word and agent of God in creation and *redemption, and is completely in control of his destiny. Sure of his role and his unity with the *Father, he discusses his status with his opponents and speaks openly of his mission, a mission which is to reveal the Father to those living in a world characterized by darkness, death, slavery, and sin (see ch. 17 in particular). Paradoxically, this revelation reaches its greatest height at the crucifixion (see CROSS). This is the hour of Jesus' glorification, the time when he will be 'lifted up' and his glory and that of the Father will be revealed. It is the supreme moment of God's *revelation and, at the same time, his judgement of all people. The whole account of Jesus' ministry has built up to his death, right from the prologue (1: 11). Many elements which form part of the passion narrative in the other gospels have been narrated at an earlier stage in John's gospel: the cleansing of the temple (2: 13–22), the Jewish 'trial' (10: 22–39), the meeting of the Sanhedrin and the decision to execute Jesus (11: 47–53), all of which heighten the immediacy of the Passion and underline its central place. For the evangelist, it is only with Jesus' *death that his ministry can be properly understood. Yet this death, with its images of revelation and cosmic judgement, also has a personal touch in that Jesus dies for his friends (10: 1–16; 15: 13). His death prepares the way for the Paraclete, a distinctively Johannine term for the *Holy Spirit who will continue Jesus' revelation amongst his followers. Believers must accept the revelation that Jesus brings and, like him, prepare to suffer the world's rejection.

John's portrayal of Jesus is very different from the Jesus encountered within the Synoptic Gospels (*Mark, *Matthew, and *Luke). The following are some of the more fundamental differences:

1. Most obviously, the style of the Fourth Gospel is quite different from that of the others. The Synoptics are series of short stories and sayings—each, no doubt, carefully reworked and ordered by its author—but, even so, a mosaic of Jesus' teaching and ministry. John, however, has woven together a much more coherent narrative. His Jesus is prone to long discourses and sustained philosophical discussion; *parables have given way to extended *metaphors. Some of the most memorable of these metaphors are the 'I am' sayings, taking their background from Exodus 3: 14 and providing some of the most striking *symbols in Christian art and reflection: Jesus is the good *shepherd, the *light of the world, and the way, the *truth, and the life. The author skilfully uses the techniques of irony and misunderstanding to further the plot. Recent literary studies of the gospel (such as those of Culpepper and Stibbe) have added even more to our understanding of the richness of the narrative and the creativity of its author.

2. The timing of events is also different. Jesus' ministry in the Synoptics lasts for only one year while in John it lasts for at least two. The crucifixion also takes place a day earlier in John: in the Synoptics, Jesus is crucified after he has celebrated the Passover with his disciples; in John he dies on the day of preparation, thus being presented theologically as the new paschal lamb.

3. All three synoptics show Jesus as a *miracle worker; in John, miracles are replaced by a few carefully chosen 'signs'. It would be hard to overlook the theological significance of these signs—for example, Jesus gives sight to the blind (ch. 9) and life to the dead (ch. 11). They are intended to show Jesus' identity and to induce belief (20: 30–1). However, exorcisms have completely dropped out of John's narrative, perhaps because the evangelist sees Jesus' death as achieving a cosmic victory over the forces of Satan.

4. References to the *Kingdom of God/Heaven which were so prominent in the Synoptic Gospels have given way in John's gospel to talk of 'eternal life'. John is often said to have a 'realized eschatology' since eternal life is not something that the believer will have 'on the last day' but something which is already a present possibility. John appears to avoid 'Kingdom' language, preferring instead to talk of a community of those who faithfully abide in Jesus and remain faithful to one another through mutual love and humility.

5. Some scholars have suggested that the fourth evangelist has little interest in *sacraments. He describes Jesus' last meal with his disciples at length without mentioning the institution of the *Eucharist and has little to say on the subject of *baptism. Against this view, however, his clear sacramental allusions at 6: 52–9, 3: 5, and 13: 1–11 suggest that baptism and the Eucharist were practised within his community.

6. The narrative of the Fourth Gospel involves several characters unknown in the synoptic tradition, such as Lazarus, Nathanael, and Nicodemus. One of the most interesting Johannine characters is the unnamed Beloved Disciple. He appears only in the second half of the gospel and is always portrayed as a model of true *discipleship; often he is contrasted favourably with Peter. While it is possible that the Beloved Disciple was a historical person (often he is equated with John son of Zebedee who is not otherwise referred to except at 21: 2), it is more likely that this disciple is a literary construct, an idealized figure who shows the reader what true discipleship entails. It is also quite striking that the *women of John's gospel are similarly represented as paradigms of discipleship, often at the expense of their male counterparts. In this gospel it is Martha and not Peter who confesses 'Yes, Lord; I believe that you are the Christ, the Son of God, he who is coming into the world' (11: 27).

In the face of these differences is there any connection between John and the Synoptics? Did John know one or more of the other gospels, or was he heir to a quite different set of traditions? From the rise of historical criticism until the early part of this century, it was taken for granted that John used the Synoptics. John, it was assumed, wrote his own, spiritualized account. From the 1940s onwards, however, the differences between the two led to a shift in scholarly opinion in favour of Johannine dependency on separate traditions and sources. Although this is still the dominant position, an increasing number of scholars are beginning to go back to the earlier view that John knew at least Mark's gospel. The author is certainly not slavishly dependent upon the earlier work, but many of his discourses and symbols may be reflections on Marcan themes.

Related to John's sources is the question of historical accuracy. It used to be fashionable to regard John's gospel as more 'theological' and the Synoptics as more 'historical'. Nowadays it is widely recognized that all the gospels have their own *theological biases that have shaped their portrayal of Jesus and the gospel story, John no more than any of the others. Though few would uphold the historicity of the whole of John's gospel, many elements may reflect historical reality, in particular the two- to three-year ministry, the mission to the Samaritans, the Roman soldiers at Jesus' arrest, and some of the sayings of Jesus. Any reconstruction of the historical

Jesus needs to take the Johannine portrayal seriously (see QUEST FOR THE HISTORICAL JESUS).

One remaining question is that of authorship. The gospel has traditionally been linked with John, son of Zebedee (and so, by some, with the Beloved Disciple). Modern criticism doubts that the gospel was written by an eyewitness, though the son of Zebedee may well have had a connection with the community and their traditions at an early period of its history (as 21: 24 seems to claim). Another suggestion is that the author was John 'the elder' of 2 John 1 and 3 John 1. The similarities in vocabulary and theological outlook suggest that the Johannine epistles come from the same Johannine 'community' or 'school', but the significant differences between them and the gospel (particularly the lack of OT quotations in the epistles, their future eschatology, and their emphasis on the death of Jesus as a sacrifice), suggest that they do not share an author. The epistles appear to date from a later stage in the history of the community: the high christology of the gospel seems to have led to some form of *Docetism and the opponents are no longer 'the Jews' but those who were formerly part of the community. The authors of the Johannine literature remain unknown.

The distinctive message of John's gospel has greatly enriched the *church over the centuries. Many fundamental doctrines are derived to a large extent from its christology. One of its most striking and influential assertions, 'the Word was made flesh' (1: 14), is perhaps the best-known phrase in the whole NT and is central to the theology of the *Incarnation. It is from John too that the concept of Jesus as God's 'only begotten son' is derived (1: 18). The great stress upon the person and work of the Spirit-Paraclete in John also contributed significantly to the later development of *Trinitarian thought. Individual passages have fired the imaginations of interpreters throughout the ages: the 'Bread of Life' discourse in chapter 6 has been a rich source for eucharistic theology, while Jesus' last prayer to his Father in chapter 17, with its overriding concern for Christian *unity, has provided the most regularly quoted texts for the modern *ecumenical movement. The gospel also says something important about the nature and use of *tradition: tradition is not static but needs to be reinterpreted and moulded so that it is challenging and life-giving in each new situation. Finally, the poetic images and metaphors of the fourth gospel have attained a unique place in Christian art and reflection. Not surprisingly, church tradition has often linked the sublime character of the gospel with the soaring flight of an eagle.

Helen K. Bond

Ashton, J., *Understanding the Fourth Gospel* (1991).
Barrett, C. K., *The Gospel According to St John*, 2nd edn. (1978).
Brown, R. E., *The Gospel According to John* (2 vols.; 1966, 1970).
——*The Community of the Beloved Disciple* (1979).
Culpepper, R. A., *Anatomy of the Fourth Gospel: A Study in Literary Design* (1983).
——*John the Son of Zebedee* (1994).
Hengel, M., *The Johannine Question* (1989).
Kysar, R., *John's Story of Jesus* (1984).
Martyn, J. L., *History and Theology in the Fourth Gospel*, 2nd edn. (1979).
Moody Smith, D., *The Theology of the Gospel of John* (1995).
Rensberger, D., *Overcoming the World: Politics and Community in the Gospel of John* (1989).
Schnackenburg, R., *The Gospel According to John*, ET (3 vols.; 1968–82).
Scott, M., *Sophia and the Johannine Jesus* (1992).
Sloyan, G. S., *What are they Saying about John?* (1991).
Stibbe, M., *John as Storyteller* (1992).

John XXIII (1881–63) may well have had a wider impact on the course of 20th-century Christian thought than any other person. Born to a farming family near Bergamo, Angelo Roncalli entered a seminary aged 11, and was ordained in 1904. After acting as secretary to his bishop and as military chaplain during the First World War, he spent 30 years in the papal diplomatic service in Bulgaria, Turkey, and France, before becoming patriarch of Venice in 1953. His scholarly interest lay in editing the *Acts* of Charles Borromeo's pastoral visit to the diocese of Bergamo in 1575, published in five volumes (1936–58). His spirituality was old-fashioned, his temperament optimistic and open. He sensed that the *church greatly needed a face-lift, which he described as *aggiornamento* (modernization) responding to what he called 'the signs of the times'.

In 1958, on Pius XII's death, Roncalli, now 77 years old, was elected pope, taking the irenic-sounding name of John. Many saw it as the choice of a kindly, conservative stopgap. They were mistaken. Within three months Pope John had announced the calling of an ecumenical *council designed to define no doctrine, pronounce no anathemas, but modernize the church and work for the reunion of Christians. The latter years of Pius XII, following the 1950 encyclical *Humani Generis*, had been ones of repression, in which leading theologians, including *Congar and *de Lubac, had been banned from teaching. The contrast under John was startling, demonstrating a new papal willingness to listen, to theologians not only in Rome but in France and Germany, and even to non-Catholics. The 1960 visit of Geoffrey Fisher, archbishop of Canterbury, began a transformation in Anglican–Catholic relations.

Preparations for *Vatican II, which opened in October 1962, were, nevertheless, largely left in curial hands. John seemed unaware of how acute the underlying theological cleavages were. In consequence the council was prepared in two ways—officially with highly conservative draft documents produced in Rome; unofficially but worldwide by a spate of theological publications and public discussion. Yet John put the cat among the pigeons by establishing in 1960 a new Roman Secretariat of Christian Unity, headed by the German *Jesuit biblical scholar, Cardinal Bea. This, the most important appointment he made, helped to ensure that, when the council opened, almost all the preparatory drafts were effectively rejected. Not a single decree was approved in the first session, the only one John lived to see.

Meanwhile he published two encyclicals on social matters, *Mater et Magistra* (1961) and *Pacem in Terris* (1963). Both related rather optimistically to the 1960s, encouraging the welfare state, approving the nationalization of key industries, stressing the rights of *conscience and *freedom of worship. The welcoming assertion of *Pacem in Terris* that 'the part women are now playing in public life is everywhere evident' struck a different note from most papal remarks about the role of *women. Most quoted is his judgement that 'in this age which boasts of its atomic power, it no longer makes sense to maintain that *war is a fit instrument with which to repair the violation of *justice'.

In five years Pope John transformed the image of papal authority, even in Protestant eyes, both by the way he spoke and by the revival of *conciliarity. He hugely enlarged the acceptable frontiers of Catholic theological discussion, and established a public *dialogue between Catholics and other churches. All of this has made the post-Johannine world of Christian thought extraordinarily different from what had gone before.   **Adrian Hastings**

John XXIII, *Journal of a Soul* (1965).
Hales, E. E. Y., *Pope John and his Revolution* (1965).
Hebblethwaite, Peter, *John XXIII, Pope of the Council* (1984).

John of the Cross (1542–91), Carmelite *mystic. This Spanish

saint, born Juan de Yepes in rural Fontiveros, Avila, and reared in the near-destitution of a one-parent family, spearheaded the reform of the Carmelite Friars and was made a Doctor of the Universal Church. Inspiring such diverse 20th-century luminaries as Salvador Dalí, T. S. *Eliot, and Thomas *Merton, his teaching rings out today with a challenge as powerful as when it was first heard.

The theory that nothing can be defined except by its opposite might have been designed with John in mind. His biographers often comment on the contrasts inherent in his native Castile, symbolizing for the Greek *poet Kazantzakis the two extremes of the Spanish spirit—'Nada' (nothingness) and passion. It is strange that a spiritual teacher known for kindness and gentleness, as affectionate and accessible to Juana, a servant-girl, as to the great *Teresa of Avila herself, should today cause even religious from his own order—though perhaps more friars than nuns?—to shy away in alarm. Some of his writings are felt to seem repellent, striking a deadly chill in the first-time reader. Perhaps those who approach him through the sensual richness of his poetry may react differently to those making his acquaintance in his theological prose. Nevertheless it is true that his most quoted lines (paraphrased by Eliot in *East Coker*) are an extremely 'hard saying', recommending that to have pleasure in everything we should desire to have pleasure in nothing. He urges us always to choose not the easiest, but the most difficult. Yet this is the ecstatic poet whose soul exults that the heavens and the earth, God and Christ, are all his and for him.

This apparently paradoxical figure, whom Merton nevertheless describes as 'the Church's "safest" mystical theologian' (Merton 1976: 13), was indeed firmly rooted in theological tradition. After a patron had provided him with education at the *Jesuit College in Medina del Campo, his joining the Carmelite order led to four years at Salamanca University, then one of the brightest beacons of learning in Europe. The air was buzzing with new ideas, propagated by the writings of Bartolomé de Las Casas for example, but in the lecture room John acquired a solid doctrinal basis of Thomism (see AQUINAS). Like Teresa of Avila, he was never to deviate from the church's orthodox teaching. In the Catholic Monarchy's territories these were heady and dangerous times, with exploration and great achievement in every sphere of human activity, including the spiritual. John soared to such a peak of awareness of God's presence that he has been called the mystics' mystic, yet he is adamant that ecclesiastical *authority is paramount. Not for him the *quietism of the *Alumbrados* ('enlightened ones'), crushed by the *Inquisition. What his experiences do provide is teaching that is still, today, a practical handbook for religious and laity alike on the pitfalls encountered in a life of prayer.

With individual experience added to orthodox learning, he became one of the greatest apophatic theologians, in the tradition of Gregory of Nyssa, describing God by what God is not. Yet, Hans

Urs *von Balthasar points out, he could 'exalt the vertical to such a degree only because [he] never let go of the horizontal', becoming with *Dionysius the Pseudo-Areopagite one of the 'most decidedly aesthetic theologians of Christian history' (*The Glory of the Lord: A Theological Aesthetics* (1982), i. 124–5).

Von Balthasar also calls John 'one of the world's great simplifiers' (ibid. iii, 133 n. 124) and his writings, while deep enough to keep theologians endlessly occupied, have a crystalline clarity that makes them available to any reader. But they do make difficult and stark demands. Three poems which are among the greatest in Spanish—*Dark Night*, *The Spiritual Canticle*, and *Flame of Living Love*—gave rise to commentaries requested by nuns or by a laywoman, Ana de Peñalosa. *The Ascent of Mount Carmel* (1578–63) and *Dark Night* (begun 1579) both gloss the one poem; *The Spiritual Canticle* and *Flame of Living Love* on the other two were written in 1584. These, with shorter pieces and letters, make up the corpus of his work. Soon the apparently violent contrast between gloom and dazzling *light in John's teaching clarifies into a unified plan—illustrated in his well-known diagram of the ascent of Mount Carmel—for making progress in *prayer.

As a psychologically skilful personal trainer, he keeps his eye on nothing less than the gold medal, and the training is rigorous. At first we are plunged into the 'dark nights' associated with his name. John was no stranger to the darkness of physical deprivation and spiritual suffering. In 1577 'calced' Carmelite monks, objecting to the discalced reform which he led, imprisoned him for nine months in a cell scarcely large enough to hold this diminutive 'Senequita' (little Seneca), as Teresa called him. Here he knew the sensory deprivation and mental torture that present-day hostages describe. Yet it was in this fetid cell that his great poems began to flower.

Before plunging into the first dark night it is as well to remember that some of John's advice was aimed specifically at nuns and friars in a contemplative order. However, the active steps towards *asceticism which he took long before his imprisonment are to be followed universally. It is a question of what Ayurvedic thought describes as 'object-referral', that habit of identifying ourselves with objects (whether things, circumstances, or relationships) that is seen as the cause of all problems. With John this is far from being the negative asceticism that the modern world finds disturbing. It is true that he teaches detachment from all earthly pleasure and preferences and, as the nights deepen, even from spiritual consolations and 'favours'. *Visions and voices are to be disregarded. As well as the 'active' nights of purification of the senses and the spirit there are the 'passive' nights, a desert of spiritual dryness, in which we can do nothing but in which God is at work. John provides tests and reassurances along the way, but he warns, in terms reminiscent of *Dante's *Hell, that if the nights of the senses are bitter and terrible, the nights of the spirit are even more horrific.

All this seems to justify John's forbidding reputation and make readers turn to those apparently gentler Carmelite Doctors, Teresa of Avila and Thérèse (*Teresa) of Lisieux. In fact John's nights are the nights of the lover and lead to a sunburst of ecstatic *joy. This saint who delighted in nature and human company teaches that, once the soul is wholly concentrated on *God, pleasure in his created world is restored, and indeed intensified, since right perspective has been restored. A computer scan of John's writings might well show that words associated with gloom are outnumbered by the vocabulary of light and joy as the soul climbs the 'mystic ladder' of divine *love to union with God. The only illumination by which we climb is *faith, which is itself a darkness, and our love must be for a God unseen and not felt. This is love as the Neoplatonists (see PLATO) saw it, going so far as to equalize the lover and the beloved in unity with each other. In this splendid state the Christian enjoys everything. Anything to which he turns his hand prospers and nothing can prevail against him. Occasionally ecstasy almost reduces John's usual clarity to a rhapsodic stuttering. It is no wonder that two commentaries come to a sudden end, language failing him to describe the heights of oneness with the divine.

Commenting on The Spiritual Canticle, John mentions the garlands offered by the church to Christ, its Bridegroom: virgins' white flowers, martyrs' red carnations, and also the splendid blooms of 'the holy doctors', and in 1926 he himself was recognized by Pius XI as a Doctor of the Church. He is a stern but understanding and, above all, an experienced and immensely practical guide to issues as vital now as in the *sixteenth century. More important still, his life shows that he put into practice what he preached. Persecuted by colleagues in his last years, stripped of office, and exiled to a remote spot, he wrote to a nun: 'Where there is no love, put love, and you will draw love out' (letter to M. María de la Encarnación, 26 July 1591).   **Margaret A. Rees**

Brennan, G., St John of the Cross: His Life and Poetry (1973).
Leeds Papers on St John of the Cross (1991).
Matthew, I., The Impact of God: Soundings from St John of the Cross (1995).
Merton, T., The Ascent to Truth (1976).
O'Donoghue, N., Mystics for Our Time: Carmelite Meditations for a New Age (1989).
Peers, E. A., Spirit of Flame (1943).
Thompson, C. P., The Poet and the Mystic: A Study of the 'Cántico Espiritual' of San Juan de la Cruz (1977).
Turner, D., Darkness of God: Negativity in Christian Mysticism (1995).

John Paul II

John Paul II (1920–   ), pope. Born Karol Jozef Wojtyla, in Wadowice, near Cracow in Poland, at the age of 18 he entered Cracow's Jagellonian University to study Polish philology, but his university career and ambitions towards acting were cut short by the German occupation. In 1942 he entered the clandestine seminary in the palace of the archbishop of Cracow. After the the end of the Second World War he went to *Rome for doctoral studies on *John of the Cross under the direction of the conservative *Thomist theologian Réginald Garrigou-Lagrange. He began a second doctorate after his return to Poland, on the philosophical *ethics of Max Scheler. These studies introduced him to personalism and phenomenology. He was appointed to lecture in philosophy at the Catholic University of Lublin, which he continued even after being made bishop in 1958. He attended *Vatican II, though he played only a small part in its proceedings. He became Archbishop of Cracow in 1965, and a cardinal two years later. He was elected pope on 16 October 1978.

His major work of philosophy, The Acting Person, appeared in English translation only after his election, but the Polish version had been published a decade earlier. This is a work of a phenomenologist, in which Wojtyla analyses the human act where, he says, is to be found the fullest expression of the *person. For him the person develops in a relationship with others: the self precedes the community, but the self needs the solidarity of community in order

to be fulfilled. Individuals, when exercising free will and choosing to act, must do so with reference to objective *truth: only in that way will they achieve their full potential. Even for the phenomenologist, therefore, Thomist teaching on absolute truth was inescapable. As one commentator remarked, 'I often have the impression of banging into scholastic steel as I wander through the phenomenological fog' (John J. Conley in McDermott, 1992: 28).

The theme of The Acting Person reappeared in the pope's first encyclical, Redemptor Hominis, issued in March 1979. As was to become a commonplace, he examines the situation of the *church in the light of the coming of the millennium. He speaks also of *God and of Christ, but in the central section of the encyclical discusses 'Man' (inclusive language has not figured large in Vatican utterances in Pope John Paul's pontificate) who is, the pope insists, not an abstract individual but part of a society characterized by solidarity which he distinguishes from collectivism. It is Man's task to make life more human, to achieve full dignity. *Freedom is the condition of this dignity, but freedom is under threat from *atheism, from a misunderstanding of human rights, from consumerism, and from materialism. True dignity can be achieved only if Man enters into the mysteries of the *Incarnation and the *Redemption.

Similar topics occur in many of the encyclicals, especially in the two addressed specifically to *moral issues, Veritatis Splendor (1993) and Evangelium Vitae (1995), both of which attacked what the pope regarded as moral relativism. In both of them there was an implied criticism of the democratic process. There had, he said in the earlier encyclical, been an abandonment of any sense of good and evil. *Democracy was only to be praised if it kept in view objective moral values. In the aftermath of the collapse of communism in Eastern Europe, John Paul was prepared to praise *Marxism for its concern for the poor.

Society's obligations towards the poor, and the achievement of greater *social justice, were addressed in three encyclicals in particular: Laborem Exercens (1981), Sollicitudo Rei Socialis (1987), and Centesimus Annus (1991). Each stressed the need for solidarity if human dignity is to be preserved and advanced. Sollicitudo caused controversy because it was said to describe *capitalism and communism as morally equivalent. Four years later, however, Centesimus Annus attributed the collapse of communism not only to its atheism and disregard for workers' rights, but to its economic inefficiency in comparison to capitalism. Though in his many travels John Paul II constantly championed the poor and criticized the abuse of human rights, it is difficult to construct a consistent social theory on the strength of the encyclicals.

It is still more difficult to construct a theology. Much of what passes for theological writing is philosophical in tone, though bolstered by constant reference to the bible. Scripture, however, he treats meditatively rather than with regard to modern scholarship, somewhat to the despair of exegetes. He was, however, influenced theologically by Henri *de Lubac and Hans Urs *von Balthasar, both of whom he created cardinals.

Although John Paul II frequently cites the *authority of Vatican II, as he did in detail in Sources of Renewal, a work based on a diocesan synod he held when archbishop of Cracow, his vision is much more authoritarian, and conservative, than the Council's theology led many to expect. He pays lip-service to Vatican II's doctrine of *collegiality, but acts in a way that suggests he considers all authority in the church to reside in himself. He has appointed to bishoprics throughout the world, and to his Curia in Rome, those of similar outlook. One such, Cardinal Joseph *Ratzinger, head of the Congregation for the Doctrine of the Faith, the successor of the Holy Office, has been the Church's doctrinal watchdog. Several leading theologians have been disciplined: the Swiss theologian Hans *Küng had his licence to teach as a Catholic professor withdrawn, one liberation theologian, the Brazilian Leonardo *Boff, was first silenced, and then felt obliged to leave the priesthood, another, the Sri Lankan Tissa *Balasuriya, was even excommunicated.

*Liberation theology, with its roots in Marxist social analysis, has been an especial target for condemnation.

See also PAPACY.   **Michael J. Walsh**

Wojtyla, K., *The Acting Person* (1979).
—— *Sources of Renewal* (1980).
Buttiglione, Rocco, *Karol Wojtyla: The Thought of the Man who became Pope John Paul II* (1997).
McDermott, J. M. (ed.), *The Thought of Pope John Paul II* (1992).
Walsh, M. J., *John Paul II: A Biography* (1994).
Williams, G. H., *The Mind of John Paul II* (1981).

John the Baptist,

John the Baptist, Jesus' kinsman, is his first witness, leaping in the womb when the pregnant *Mary visits his mother Elizabeth, and the culmination of the *prophetic line of the OT. The NT accords him high respect but also makes it plain that he himself acknowledged his role as merely the herald of one greater to come. This may reflect negotiations between the early Christian community and a continuing group which looked to John as the expected prophet (cf. Acts 19: 1–7), but he is also a key figure displaying the relationship between the OT traditions and the Christian gospel. He is accorded his own birth narrative by Luke, which recapitulates all the typical features of the birth stories of OT heroes but which serves all the more to heighten the contrast with the unique circumstances of the *virgin birth of Jesus.

John's rough mantle of camel hair and his solitary existence in the desert link him *typologically with Elijah, the expected forerunner of the *messiah, and also with *Isaianic prophecy. The austerity of this life, memorably epitomized in his diet of locusts and wild honey, served as a model for the *desert fathers, and John became the archetype for the *ascetic ideal in general. This is no disengaged piety, however. His recorded preaching echoes prophetic calls for social justice and plain dealing. It was John's public condemnation of incest in the royal family of Herod Antipas that resulted in his arrest (Mark 6: 14–29). His rectitude and simplicity are starkly contrasted with the luxury and lasciviousness of court life in the story of the machinations of Herodias who won her husband Herod's assent to John's execution through the seductive allure of her daughter. He is an exemplar of the incorruptible believer, assailed by both male tyranny and female sexual wiles, who bravely denounces decadent power. Martyred for his righteousness by beheading, John is represented in medieval sources, including *Piers Plowman*, as once more Jesus' forerunner, announcing his coming to the patriarchs in *limbo.

John's *baptism of repentance for sins clearly relates to early Christian practice, especially as Jesus himself consents to undergo it. If historical, it is unique in Jewish practice in being linked to a promise of regeneration from sin which undercuts the sacrificial and priestly system of the Temple and decries an easy reliance on *Abrahamic descent. Theologically, it is a problem why the sinless Jesus should consent to John's baptism, and the differing accounts of the gospel writers reflect different solutions. In the fourth gospel, there is no explicit mention of a baptism. Instead the Baptist proclaims Jesus as the Lamb of God. In all this, John's function in the Christian tradition is to remind the believer of the inadequacy of even the most righteous human aspiration confronted with Jesus. The Baptist's words 'He must increase, but I must decrease' (John 3: 30) form a fittingly humble motto for Christian thinkers in subsequent centuries.   **Hugh S. Pyper**

Tatum, W. B., *John the Baptist and Jesus* (1994).
Webb, R. L., *John the Baptizer and Prophet* (1991).
Wink, W., *John the Baptist in Gospel Tradition* (1968).

Jonah.

Jonah. In Matthew 12: 39–41, Jesus himself refers explicitly to the 'sign of Jonah' as the only sign the scribes and Pharisees will have from him. The Son of Man will spend three days in the earth, just as Jonah spent three days in the belly of the great fish before his reappearance. The sign of Jonah is also alluded to in Luke 11: 29–32, but here the sign seems to be related to the effect of Jonah's preaching on the people of Nineveh in bringing about their repentance.

The mention of the fish in Matthew's version has led to a strong and continuing concern in the tradition of commentary to vouch for the historicity both of Jonah and his being swallowed. If Jesus quoted the story, then it must be historically accurate. Conversely, if it is proved false, Jesus' credibility is at stake. Both ancient pagans and post-Enlightenment sceptics have had a hard time swallowing the whale and much ingenuity has been spent by Christian *apologists in its defence either by invoking the miraculous or by rationalizing the account; for instance, the 'Great Fish' has been interpreted as the name of a ship which rescued Jonah. Such endeavours seem to others to underestimate the ability of a master *parable-teller such as the author of Jonah to make use of pious fiction.

From another angle, the church fathers made much of the symbolic and *allegorical richness of this little book in line with the Matthean reading. Episodes from Jonah's story appear frequently in the earliest Christian art. Jonah is read as a type of Christ who was 'shipwrecked' on the cross, entombed and triumphantly delivered. Other commentators, notably Jerome, recall that 'Jonah' is the Hebrew word for 'dove', making a connection to the form of the *Holy Spirit or else to the use of 'dove' as a simile with reference to Israel. Jonah's flight and entombment in the fish can then be read as allegories of the captivity of Israel. His fury over the repentance of the Ninevites alludes to *Israel's rejection of the salvation of the Gentiles.

The *Reformers rejected such allegorical interpretation and emphasized instead the human drama of the disobedience of Jonah in contrast to the *mercy of God. Subsequent scholarship has increasingly read the book as a satirical or parodic work. In one view, Jonah is set up as a representative of the intolerance of the prophetic or post-exilic tradition, opposed to the universal saving work of God. Alternatively, the book is dealing with the apparent arbitrariness of a God who will save Nineveh, but abandons Jerusalem. The book's importance now becomes its masterly allusiveness, its testimony to a sense of *humour in the biblical tradition and the humanity of its portrayal of a fallible and irascible prophet. The tension between these varied readings is typical of the problem of reconciling historical specificity and universal applicability in Christian thought.   **Hugh S. Pyper**

Bowers, R. H., *The Legend of Jonah* (1971).

Magonet, J., *Form and Meaning: Studies in the Literary Technique of the Book of Jonah*, repr. (1983).

Miles, J. A., 'Laughing at the Bible: Jonah as Parody', *Jewish Quarterly Review*, 65 (1974/5).

journalism.

Religious institutions and churches have responded slowly and grudgingly to the important and sometimes decisive role that the mass media play in their affairs. Opinions may differ as to whether the press belongs to the world, the flesh, or the devil, but not many Christian voices have been raised suggesting it belongs to the realm of the Spirit, even less that it has a place in building the *Kingdom of God. At the same time, major ecclesiastical institutions from the Vatican and World Council of Churches down to local dioceses have put in place facilities to enhance their relations with the press; information offices, press officers, and, increasingly, outlets on the Internet. Their practice has therefore moved some way ahead of their theory. This has left their mass media policies lacking in coherence and strategy.

A worked-out theology of the press (which would include broadcast journalism) has been conspicuous by its absence, though an exception must be made for the Roman Pastoral Instruction *Communio et Progressio*, published in 1971. It attempted systematically to analyse the role of 'the means of social communication' as instruments for fostering solidarity and social *justice. These being what God wills, the media were judged to be among the 'gifts of God'. They have an honourable place allotted to them in the history of creation, incarnation and redemption.

It is useful to introduce a distinction here between 'journalism' as a subject suitable for critical Christian reflection in terms of social justice and professional *ethic, and journalism as itself a vehicle for Christian reflection which takes for granted the internal logic of the medium and uses it to elucidate and publicize theological debate and exploration, as for instance concerning ecclesiastical attempts to suppress the work of controversial theologians such as *Küng or *Balasuriya.

The 1971 Roman document says that in the domain of professional journalistic ethics, practitioners must display 'sincerity, honesty and truthfulness' and adds that public opinion 'is an essential expression of human nature organised in a society'—something church authorities themselves have not yet entirely acknowledged. Partly this is because the idea of openness is anathema to conservative and authoritarian institutions, not least because of the implication that there is, in internal church matters, such a thing as a 'right to know'. There is no doubt that public opinion does have a significant impact on developments within church institutions, whose representatives cannot ignore publicity for wrongdoing, abuses of *authority, attempts to suppress debate or discipline wayward individuals, and so on, much as they might like to.

Magazines and journals, secular and religious, provide a forum mostly beyond the control of church officials in which issues of interest can be debated, views exchanged, and attention drawn to matters that might otherwise be known only to a few. The strength of a journal like *The Tablet* lies in its very freedom from clerical control despite its Christian commitment. It may seem hardly surprising that the mass media are often, perhaps inevitably, in a state of tension with official church authorities. *Communio et Progressio* recognized a 'right to information' and avoided the common but mistaken assumption that journalists who belong to a particular church have a duty to protect its interests, or even to advance the Christian message in general. They have no such duty; if they acted thus it would undermine the very credibility of their work. Their primary duty is truth-telling, come what may. The integrity of their relationship with their audience or readers demands that they treat all material, damaging or otherwise, with professional detachment; if necessary, in the teeth of disapproval from religious authorities.

But *Communio et Progressio* failed to grasp the extent to which activities so characteristic of the modern world are bound to be shot through with the flaws of that world: domination by market forces, tendency towards multinational monopoly, manipulation of public opinion, oversimplification, relativism in moral judgements, pandering to the lowest levels of taste, preoccupation with other people's personal failings, and so on. It is these shortcomings that tend in practice to dominate Christian approaches to the mass media, sometimes leading to an exaggerated distrust of the press.

But it is a fact that most churches have relatively weak internal communications, and must depend on the mass media to shape individual members' perceptions of their church's policies beyond the immediate experience of parish or congregation. For instance, western European churches, responding to grass-roots pressure, have at times had to question their participation in such bodies as the World Council of Churches because of adverse media publicity for that body's activities.

The sense of cohesiveness and identity in the internal life of a church has come increasingly to depend on the mass media, by which the lifeblood of information and communication, including new *theological thinking, circulates beyond the control of the church's official agencies. That fact alone is of ecclesiological significance. The ability of the churches to create, restrict, and use information about themselves is reduced; they have to rely upon institutions outside their own orbit of control. It is largely through the work of secular journalists that the majority of Christians heard of, and were inspired by, international figures like Mother *Teresa of Calcutta and Martin Luther King, Jr. (see BLACK THEOLOGY). Without such journalists few Christians would have much idea of the personality or policy even of a pope or archbishop of Canterbury. A participative model of *lay involvement in church affairs necessarily requires that the mass media be taken seriously as a key influence, both positively and negatively.

None of this does justice to the radical and fundamental function that the press performs in public affairs, which it is possible to perceive in religious terms. That the 'truth shall make you free' (John 8: 32) is not confined to doctrine as narrowly defined. Other forms of *truth can also loosen the bondage of the 'structures of *sin' in society of which all churches, in their social teaching, have become increasingly aware. Political or social truth has a liberating, even salvific, power in that it can move an individual or group from a false to a true consciousness.

This is a continuous process, progress on one front often being offset by retreat on another. But the 'naming of evils' is an essential element in confronting them, and can properly be described as part of the process of *evangelization. This is an essential service to the community that the press routinely performs, even though it is often itself caught up in the evils it describes.

See also FRENCH CHRISTIAN THOUGHT; SPANISH CATHOLICISM.

Clifford Longley

For *Communio et Progressio* see A. Flannery (ed.), *Vatican Council II: The Conciliar and Post-Conciliar Documents* (1992), i. 293–349.

joy. Although often overlooked, joy is fundamental to believing as a Christian, to finding God in faith, and to the anticipation of the *Kingdom of God. It is the sign of each person's and community's well-being when established in this faith, in which the gifts of *creation and *salvation, the fruits of God's own joy in the world, are fulfilled. Its great significance is shown by its wide use in scripture, and its dynamics identified there by the close etymological link between the bestowal of this joy (*chara*) by God through *grace (*charis*), the gifts which arise therefrom (*charisma*), the resulting expression of gratitude (*eucharistia*), and the act of giving freely to others (*charizomai*).

In common usage, joy is 'a vivid emotion of pleasure [or state, source, object or expression of such] arising from a sense of well-being or satisfaction' (*OED*), in contradistinction to pain. As used in Judaism and Christianity, joy denotes a deeper affirmation of God in no matter what circumstances. In favourable situations, it appears as exultation and healing. Where there is vulnerability and sorrow it still appears, but adversity alters its character to self-giving, trust, and perseverance (Luke 21: 5–19). In either case, without such joy life is turned in upon itself, and becomes self-limiting.

The Christian conception of joy is 'based on the truth' of God: 'that is the authentic happy life, to set one's joy on you, grounded in you and caused by you' (*Augustine, *Confessions*, 10. 32). As the presentation in human pleasure or pain of the all-goodness of God shown in Jesus Christ and enlivened by the Holy Spirit, it is fully natural and human, appearing in all aspects of ordinary life, even where the full implications are not recognized. It is normal for life to be sustained by exultation and contentment, and normal to seek through the action of God in Jesus Christ to extend the joy already present in life. There is a deep affinity between 'natural' life, with its cultural expressions, and Christian expressions of joy (*Christmas and *Easter, for example); and between ordinary aspirations for harmony, freedom, and joy on the one hand and the joyful mystery of God's freedom to love within human life and through suffering on the other. But there is also a tension between such 'natural' practices and a full understanding of what belongs to Christian joy. Without an awareness of these deeper implications, preoccupations with pleasure or pain arise which are incompatible with joy (cf. Rom. 14: 17).

Both affinity and tension arise because of three main characteristics that make Christian joy both attractive and demanding. First, it is more fundamental in its origins than its natural counterpart, being grounded in God's overflowing truth, goodness, and beauty: 'if you find God, you will find complete and everlasting happiness … and the perfect enjoyment of this good', whether on earth or in the kingdom of God (Jonathan *Edwards, *Religious Affections* (1746), I. 8). In a world rooted in this truth, its scope is extraordinarily encompassing: in Judaeo-Christian tradition, God's good purposes are found in nature (fertile or barren), social life (God's chosen and aliens), personal life (all human faculties), historical complexity and adversity, law and freedom, etc. Through discipline and dedication to this God, ordinary life provides intimations of goodness: in the world, the true constitution of *humanity, the harmony of creation; and correspondingly, of joy.

Second, it is more radical in its implications for human life. The dynamics of God's good will in Christ—'the laws of Christ, the gospel by which he governs, [as] wonderfully gracious, exceedingly tending in their own nature to the peace, comfort, joy and happiness of his people' (Edwards)—show the full scope of good life, including the joy proper to human life. To live according to this inner movement is the precondition of true joy for the Christian, as all creation moves through salvation to the Kingdom of God. The very words and work of Jesus have as their purpose the transference to those who follow him, of the joy of the Father's purposes; they provide joy even in pain and weeping.

Third, Christian joy is more available, because it is mediated through actual historical life. In the inmost character of history itself, the course of the world is changed for good (redeemed) by God. In the history of the Jews, those who steadfastly rely on God and his 'path of life' find the fullness of joy (Ps. 5: 11; 17: 11). For Jesus, in whom this history culminates, joy is directly associated with right response to the Kingdom of God: the word of the Kingdom must be 'sown on good soil' and bear fruit, not merely elicit a quick response of joy (Matt. 13: 20, 23). The Kingdom of God and its attendant joy is found through the incorporation of humanity in Jesus' suffering, dying, and being raised by God. Those who live from the resurrected Jesus are 'filled with joy and with the Holy Spirit' (Luke 24: 52; Acts 13: 52).

This life continues by joining believers into the company of the church; and the joy of the Resurrection is perpetuated as they work together (2 Cor. 1: 24) and communicate joy to each other (2 Cor. 2: 3). The effect of the Resurrection, as the basis of the church, is sustained through sacraments which recapitulate it and anticipate the fullness of joy in the coming Kingdom of God. The preaching of the word and the sacraments of baptism and Eucharist, by which the common life of the people of God coheres and extends itself in witness to the world, are properly marked by the outpouring of joy amongst them, releasing them from alienation to serve and give freely to others. Thus the joy of their common life in the world is the social counterpart of their praise of God, both attracting and guiding others to the true meaning of joy. **Daniel W. Hardy**

Barth, K., *Church Dogmatics*, II/1. para. 31 (1957).
Bonaventure, *The Life of St. Francis* (1263/1978).
Edwards, J., *A Treatise Concerning Religious Affections* (1746; 1959).
Kittel, G., *Theological Dictionary of the New Testament*, ed. G. Bromiley (1985).
Moltmann, J., *Theology and Joy* (1973).

Judaism, see ANTISEMITISM; ISRAEL; JEWISH–CHRISTIAN RELATIONS.

Judaism in the 1st Christian century.

The 1st century AD encompasses, from a Jewish perspective, late Second Temple Judaism and the beginning of the rabbinic period. The transition came with the Jewish War, 66–70, when the Jerusalem *Temple was destroyed. The war, which was precipitated by an uprising of Palestinian Jews against Roman imperial power, the culmination of long-standing guerrilla action and sporadic unrest, ended with Jewish defeat. These events were of immense significance for all Jews, both in Palestine and the Diaspora, since the centre of Jewish life shifted from Jerusalem with its sacrificial cult to Jamnia with its rabbinic academy.

Although there was a common core of beliefs and practices, pre-war Judaism contained a rich diversity of groups, or Judaisms, each with distinctive characteristics. Equally diverse are our sources consisting, for example, of Jewish pseudepigrapha, *Dead Sea Scrolls, works by Philo of Alexandria and Josephus, the NT, and later rabbinic texts. The gradual process of compiling and systematizing the oral traditions, previously preserved and transmitted by the Pharisees, which was undertaken by the rabbis of Jamnia after 70 AD, eventually led to a more united Judaism.

The sources demonstrate that all 1st-century Jews were ethical monotheists, worshippers of one *God, Yahweh, *creator of the cosmos, who acted in history to save, revealing himself to man, and with whom Jews had, as God's elect, a *covenant relationship. At the heart of the covenant lay Torah (Genesis to Deuteronomy), God's directions, binding on all Jews, and visibly signified by circumcision and sabbath observance. Recognized as scripture, although not yet within a closed canon, were the rest of what are now known as the Hebrew Scriptures (OT). Prior to 70, sacrificial worship took place in the Jerusalem Temple while non-sacrificial worship was conducted in the synagogues, which, after 70, became the only centres of Jewish worship.

The Pharisees, probably the largest of the pre-war Judaisms, followed by a majority of the people, and the Sadducees, recognized as leading political figures by Rome, both emerged during the Maccabaean Revolt of Jews against Greeks in the 2nd century BC. The former, who included many scribes and rabbis, were devoted to both written Torah and oral traditions, their preservation and interpretation; strictly upholding the sabbath and dietary laws and those concerning ritual purity. Like the Essenes, they held in tension a belief in man's free will and a belief in divine *providence and *foreknowledge. Using the whole of the Hebrew Scriptures as a basis, they developed an elaborate angelology and demonology and beliefs in bodily resurrection, life after death, and the expectation of the coming of a Davidic messiah sent by God in the last days. These beliefs were not shared by the Sadducees.

It is impossible to establish the precise composition of the Sadducees although many of them were priests and certainly they took responsibility for Temple ritual and traditions. They based their beliefs on the written Torah, having their own interpretative tradition; however, since there is no extant Sadducean literature, identifying their beliefs is difficult. Politically they were upholders of the status quo, hence their antagonism to popular messianic movements and to the rebellion of 66 AD. After the destruction of the Temple with its sacrificial cult, they disappear from history as do the Zealots, who were primarily responsible for precipitating the war. Zealots followed Pharisaic teaching, but their belief that God helps those who help themselves led them into guerrilla warfare and later into military action against Rome in preparation for the messiah and the last days. It may be that another group of activists,

the *sicarii* (knifemen), who held Masada, were a subgroup of the Zealots.

Essene Judaism, including the Qumran community, which probably produced the Dead Sea Scrolls, was also eschatologically orientated and anticipated the coming of a prophet and two messiahs, of Aaron and David, and a final conflict between 'the sons of light' and 'the sons of darkness'. In preparation they, the redeemed elect, practised daily rituals of purification, copied and interpreted the scriptures, waiting upon God. They lived ascetic, disciplined lives in hierarchically structured communities, maintaining a minimal connection with the Jerusalem Temple, whose authorities they regarded as corrupt. The Therapeutae, an ascetic group living in community, described by Philo, were similar to or possibly a subgroup of Essene Judaism. Various pietist groups, characterized by intense devotion to God and the strict observance of purity laws, such as that which produced the *Testament of Moses*, could have been similarly placed. Perhaps John the Baptist and his followers could be included here, although John's practice of baptizing other Jews, signifying repentance and forgiveness, is unique.

It is evident that there were other Judaisms and also currents of thought that permeated one or more of these discrete groups. There was, for instance, the distinctive and uniquely well-documented Judaism of Philo of Alexandria, a fusion of Hellenistic philosophy with the Jewish faith, and there were many *apocalyptists, concerned with unveiling the end-times, who expressed their beliefs in graphic visions of God's judgement and final victory over evil on a cosmological scale sometimes through the agency of a supernatural Son of Man. The Jewish Book 4 of the *Sibylline Oracles* (probably post-70), seems to indicate the existence of a strand of thought emphasizing salvation through baptism and repentance that would replace the Temple cult. Then there were Jewish mystics, contemplatives and visionaries, whose thinking later penetrated some rabbinic circles.

That Judaism, especially but not exclusively Pharisaic and Essene Judaism, had an immense formative influence on the beliefs, way of life, and organization of early Christianity, is clearly demonstrated by NT writers. Indeed, many Jewish Christians continued to participate in the religious life of Judaism until, in about 95 AD, they were officially excluded.   **Barbara Spensley**

Barclay, J. M. G., *Jews in the Mediterranean Diaspora* (1996).
Grabbe, L. L., *Judaism from Cyrus to Hadrian*, 2nd edn. (1994).
Macoby, H., *Judaism in the First Century* (1989).
Sanders, E. P., *Judaism: Practice and Belief, 63 BCE–66 CE* (1992).
Schiffman, L. H., *From Text to Tradition* (1991).
Stone, M. E. (ed.), *Jewish Writings of the Second Temple Period* (1984).

Judas.

The gospel tradition that Judas, one of Jesus' own choosing, betrayed his master reveals that the possibility of failure among Christian leaders is recognized from the start. Whatever the historical truth of Judas' actions, and the gospel accounts differ significantly, his story has functioned to ensure that the inevitable human lapses and treacheries of those in places of trust in *church communities have an acknowledged place in the Christian view of the world. Such incidents become a mark, not of the failure of the church, but of its authenticity as it suffers betrayal by its friends as did its Lord.

However, if this affords a way to cope with betrayal, it is at the expense of the repudiation of the scapegoated figure. Judas, whose name means simply 'the Jew', has provided a figure onto which ill-feeling against Jews in general could be vented. The ignominious death he suffers as punishment for his betrayal has often found its dire counterpart in the fate meted out to Jews and Jewish communities who have been vilified as themselves traitors to Christ.

Jesus' statement that it would have been better for the one who betrayed him if he had not been born (Matt. 26: 24; Mark 14: 21) seems to leave little room for Judas' salvation. When this is set in tension with the gospels' portrayal of Judas' act of betrayal as a necessary and fore-ordained precursor to the Passion, central questions about *freedom, election, and *guilt are raised. A fascinating theological exploration of Judas as the exemplar of those rejected by God and thus a counterpart to Christ is offered by *Barth. This may, however, give Judas more significance in the drama of salvation than gospel evidence would warrant. But Judas is more than just a sinner. His *sin is compounded by his despair which, in Matthew's gospel, leads to his death by *suicide, and for much of Christian history the church's horror of suicide and excommunication of its perpetrators could be justified by association with this reviled character.

Modern discomfort at *antisemitic stereotypes and the 19th- and 20th-century penchant for tragic heroes may explain recent attempts to redeem Judas as a victim of forces beyond his control or as a misguided but well-meaning zealot. As an extreme case, Jorge Luis Borges writes half-seriously of a fictional theologian who regards Judas as the true messiah who bore not just death, but eternal damnation and vilification, as his part in the drama of the Passion.

However the story is now read, Judas has provided the church with a figure through which to deal with the treatment of the 'insider become outsider'. Whether this has led to complete rejection of the outsider or conversely to a breakdown in the rigid application of these categories has depended on the theological and political confidence of particular Christian communities.

Hugh S. Pyper

Barth, K., 'The Election of the Individual: The Determination of the Rejected', in *Church Dogmatics* II/2 (1957), 498–563.
Borges J. L., 'Three Versions of Judas', in *Labyrinths* (1970).
Klassen, W., *Judas: Betrayer or Friend of Jesus?* (1996).
Maccoby, H., *Judas Iscariot and the Myth of Jewish Evil* (1992).

judgement.
Discourse about the judgement of *God refers to the response of God's *justice to all actions which human beings perform and for which they are responsible. The notion of God's judgement presupposes that in relation to God, creator and Lord of creation, being human means being *responsive*, answering God's call, and being responsible before God's judgement. In the Hebrew bible discourse about God's judgement is focused on the connection between deed and consequence, based on the order that God instituted in creation. God's judgement can refer both to individual persons and to communities. In the prophetic tradition images of a lawsuit are employed to illustrate God's judgement. God can appear as prosecutor or witness for the prosecution (Mic. 1: 2; Mal. 3: 5). Accusations against *Israel may be incorporated into accusations against other nations. The people of all nations, as well as heaven and earth, may be called upon to act as a tribunal (Isa. 1: 2–3; Mic. 6: 1–2; Ps. 50; Jer. 2: 12). The cosmic dimension of God's judgements is emphasized when God takes his place in the court of heaven to sit in judgement over the gods because they 'judge unjustly' (Ps. 82). Only in the book of *Job does an individual person summon God to court (Job 9: 16); equally rare are instances of individuals brought to trial by God (Ps. 143: 2; Job. 22: 4).

God's judgement is directed against all *evil and against all violations of the divinely established order of creation. The prophets Amos and *Isaiah proclaim the 'day of the Lord' (Amos 5: 18–20), a 'day of wrath' (Isa. 13: 6–9) for the whole world. However, where God's judgement brings destruction, this is not an end in itself, but serves to bring about God's salvation. The remnant of Israel (Amos 5: 15; Isa. 6: 13) shall be acquitted. The connection between God's judgement and the *eschatological purifying fire (Isa. 1: 25; Jer. 9: 6; Isa. 48: 10) makes a similar point. God's judgement is part of God's rule, subduing the forces that rebel against him, and is understood to cleanse his people from all that separates them from God.

In the Jewish *apocalyptic literature the image of God's judgement is extensively developed in the image of a last judgement where individual persons, all nations, even angels and demons are brought to trial. The last judgement is the final victory of God's justice over all injustice. At the last judgement, *history has run its course, and from the end everything will be revealed in its true character. It is thus the ultimate disclosure of truth. The hope of *resurrection means that everyone, living and dead, can be brought before the judgement seat of God.

In the NT, discourse about God's judgement is focused on the expectation of the last and universal judgement. It comes on a day that God has fixed. It occurs not in history, but at the end of history. Even where the final judgement is understood as happening now (as in John's gospel), it is, like the last judgement, eschatological in character. Since God's judgement is universal in character it presupposes the resurrection of the dead. There are two images of the final judgement, not easy to reconcile: it is seen either as the final separation of the saved from the condemned (Matt. 13: 40–3, 49–50) or as a trial of the whole of humankind including believers (Matt. 25: 31–46; Rom. 2: 5–11).

The specific character of God's judgement in *Jesus' proclamation can be understood by comparison with the preaching of *John the Baptist. While John preaches the imminent coming of the day of judgement that will bring the *anger of God on all those who do not repent, Jesus' proclamation of the *Kingdom of God is focused on the present coming of the Kingdom. Jesus' message contains an implicit theology. The judgement of God is salvation for all those who trust unconditionally in God's justice as the *salvation of the *sinner. It also contains an implicit *christology: ultimately, people's relationship to God is determined by their relationship to Jesus. Whether they accept the truth of Jesus' message and so accept him as the one in whom God acts decisively for the salvation of humankind decides people's fate in God's judgement.

The early Christian communities, who understood the Resurrection of the crucified Jesus as the victory of God's righteousness and the validation of the witness of Jesus' life, continued to speak of God's judgement but gave it a new christological content. Christ is both judge and saviour. Humanity is judged by the one in whom God's ultimate judgement on the world is already spoken. The last judgement nevertheless remains real for believers, just as their resurrection is still to come. As those who are reconciled with God

(Rom. 5: 1) believers live in hope supported by the *Holy Spirit as the firstfruits of the harvest to come (Rom. 8: 23–4). For *Paul righteousness by faith alone and the divine judgement of 'the secrets of the human heart through Christ Jesus' (Rom. 2: 16), forms no contradiction. Both, *justification and judgement, are seen as constitutive elements of Christian faith.

In the history of Christianity the theme of judgement has been a powerful stimulus to popular piety, expressed in vivid pictures of God's judgement upon the world. The contrast between the fate of believers and that of unrepentant sinners is variously and imaginatively developed.

Patristic theology developed the theme of the last judgement. Thus *Irenaeus argues that the second coming of Christ must occur together with a universal judgement, otherwise the world and its history would be of no significance for God. For *Augustine, God's judgement already begins during our life on earth and becomes apparent in the things that happen to us. The last judgement is the last day of God's judgement, when we shall be able to discern the true character of every person and event, and all God's ways with the world will become plain.

In medieval times theological reflection abounds concerning God's judgement, its character, and the order of events leading up to it. Following Peter Lombard and Bonaventure, *Aquinas sought to justify both a particular judgement upon each individual person and a general judgement on the whole of humanity. Since every human being is an individual, he or she will be judged immediately after death; as members of the human race they will be judged at the end of time when the good and the wicked are finally separated. The idea of a particular judgement supported the doctrine of *purgatory as a place or state where those who have died in the grace of God experience the punishment still due to forgiven transgressions. This teaching, defined at the Councils of Lyons (1274) and *Florence (1439), provided the background for the controversy on indulgences which became one, though not the only, reason for the *Reformation. An indulgence was understood as the remission of temporal penalties for forgiven sins to be endured in purgatory. The pastoral problems caused by fear of divine judgement and by the facile assumption that somehow the alleviation of punishment could be 'bought', even for the dead (suggested by the practice of selling indulgences to raise funds for the building of St Peter's in Rome) form the background of *Luther's doctrine of justification.

God's justification of the sinner, on account of Christ and by grace alone in *faith, is for the Reformers the eschatological judgement. God works out his judgement upon the world by his justifying grace for those who accept it unconditionally by faith alone. Faith as radical trust in God's *grace is therefore the certainty of salvation for believers, who no longer have to fear the last judgement. God's judgement is understood as the condemnation of sin by pardoning the sinner. Luther could therefore speak of the last judgement as the day of salvation when all the tribulations that plague the believer here and now will be overcome and God's truth which is now grasped in faith will be evident for all to see.

Modern Protestant theology has developed this approach to radical conclusions. For Karl *Barth everything speaks against the possibility of a last judgement, because humanity has already received its sentence in Christ. He is the judge who is sentenced in our place and in this way he enacts his judgement over humanity. The judge-

ment of Christ is the only real judgement. The notion of a last judgement is merely a sign of divine judgement pointing to Christ as its content. Thus God's judgement is identical with his reconciliation with humanity. Barth seriously questions all conceptions of a division between those destined for eternal salvation and those destined for eternal damnation. *Hell as a place of eternal punishment would make evil and suffering eternal and thus call into question the ultimate victory of grace.

Whereas Barth's teaching on judgement can be seen as a radical reformulation of the Reformers' view that the justification of the sinner is God's eschatological judgement, the official teaching of the Roman Catholic Church as summarized in the World Catechism maintains the distinction between the particular judgement after death and the last judgement after the resurrection. In the particular judgement everybody receives 'eternal retribution' according to their works and faith. Everybody will either be led through a process of purification (purgatory), or be immediately admitted to eternal bliss, or condemn himself or herself forever. The last judgement after the general resurrection will disclose the true relationship of all human beings to God and will reveal the ultimate consequences of the good they have done or not done during their lives on earth.

The difference between these views on God's judgements point to a continuing tension within Christianity that does not only concern the doctrinal dimension but also extends to the dimensions of worship, personal piety, and ethics. While the one view focuses on the justification of the sinner as God's eschatological judgement and thereby relates the expectation of the last judgement to the present certainty of salvation in faith, seen as the necessary and sufficient basis for righteous action, the other focuses on the last judgement as the final disclosure of the believer's relationship to God, so that faith's experience of the grace of God needs to be maintained and nurtured in righteous action. The former is most clearly, though not only, represented by the tradition of the Reformation, the latter most distinctively, though not exclusively, by the Roman Catholic Church. This continuing tension seems to suggest that the main emphases distinguishing the two views should not be understood as strict alternatives, but as constituting a polarity that cannot be completely resolved—until the day of judgement. Both views, however, have to face the challenge of views which see God's judgement as no longer significant for the fundamental orientation of human life.

Any reassessment of the understanding of God's judgement today will have to take into account that the *Enlightenment ousted Christ from the judgement-seat, replacing him with human *reason. This is particularly evident in the question of theodicy, where God is put on trial for the suffering and evil in the world, which seem incompatible with either divine goodness or divine *omnipotence or both. Theodicies attempt to justify God in the court of reason. But when the idea of God as judge of the world is lost and the state of things in the world does not even provoke the question of theodicy, human judgement becomes the final court of justice. The need of human beings to justify themselves takes the place of God's judgement and justification. Theodicy is replaced by what has been called 'anthropodicy', the constant need for human self-justification.

Against this backdrop there are good reasons for reassessing belief in the divine judgement of the world. If God is seen exclusively as a God of *love whose love does not include judgement upon injustice, the world becomes a godless place. Belief in God's judgement upholds an understanding of God as not only the ground and end of all being, but also as the ultimate standard of justice. The conviction that God's judgement is the ultimate disclosure of *truth about everything and the end of all deception limits the claims made for human judgement, and this conviction serves as a reminder that no human judgement can escape responsibility before the judgement-seat of God. Whereas God's judgement of human actions is the ultimate declaration of truth about all human deeds, his judgement of human persons is their ultimate transformation for communion with him. The conviction of Christian faith that everybody will be brought to account before the judgement seat of Christ should strengthen our trust that while our actions will be judged for what they truly are, we have already received our judgement in the cross and Resurrection of Christ, which defines God's justice once for all as *mercy on those who could not hope to leave the divine court of justice with a verdict of 'not guilty'.

Christoph Schwöbel

Hick, John, *Death and Eternal Life* (1976), repr. (1985).
Küng, Hans, *Justification: The Doctrine of Karl Barth and a Catholic Reflection* (1964).
Pannenberg, Wolfhart, *Systematic Theology* (1998), iii. 608–30.
Rahner, Karl, *On the Theology of Death* (1973).
Ratzinger, Josef, *Eschatology: Death and Eternal Life* (1988).

Julian of Norwich,

the 14th-century *mystic and theologian, is better known today than she has ever been. She was born in 1342, probably somewhere in the English East Midlands, and became an anchoress (a hermit with a fixed place of residence) attached to the Church of St Julian in Norwich, from which she took her name. Little is known of her early life: not so much as her given name survives. Neither is it known when or why she became an anchoress, nor when she died. Virtually the only source of information about her is her remarkable book of *Showings*, sometimes also called *Revelations of Divine Love*, which is one of the earliest books written in Middle English vernacular. In it she is forthright about the most intimate details of her life as they impinge on her theme and utterly silent about everything besides.

That theme is the *love of *God as Julian came to understand it through a series of *visions given to her during an acute illness when she was 30 years old. The visions did not come from nowhere. Julian explains that in her youth she had made three prayers. Her first prayer was for 'recollection of the Passion', by which she meant a participatory vision of the *suffering of Christ on the *cross. The second was for a bodily illness so severe that she and all those around her would think she was dying. She recognized that these prayers were unusual, and asked that they be granted only if they would be to her spiritual benefit; and then, she says, she forgot all about them. Her final prayer, which she prayed 'urgently, without condition', was for 'three wounds … the wound of true contrition, the wound of loving compassion, and the wound of longing with my will for God'.

During her thirtieth year Julian did indeed become severely ill. The priest who came to attend her death held a crucifix before her eyes, and as she gazed at it, 'suddenly I saw the red blood running down … just as it was at the time when the crown of thorns was pressed on his blessed head'. There followed sixteen visions, centred on the love and *compassion of Christ. Julian recovered from her illness and wrote an account of her visions known as the Short Text. She then pondered them for a further fifteen years or more, after which she wrote a second account, known as the Long Text, which incorporates most of the Short Text and adds her intervening reflections. By comparing the two versions one can observe her increasing confidence in writing as a *woman, and her growing theological depth.

Julian is insistent throughout that 'I am not good because of the revelations, but only if I love God better.' That love is measured not by keeping a monastic rule of poverty, chastity, and obedience (which she significantly never mentions) but by compassionate care for oneself and others. Although Julian speaks of *sin, she sees it as a bitter scourge rather than as something for which we should be blamed. There is no *anger in God but only in ourselves, and the divine love changes it to *peace and gentleness, turning the wounds we suffer as a result of sin into badges of honour just as the nailprints in the hands and feet of Jesus are now the marks of his glory.

A striking difference between Julian and many other medieval spiritual writers is her positive attitude towards the *body. This is coupled with her emphasis on the *Incarnation. The terms she uses are 'substance' and 'sensuality', which correspond roughly to our true self or essence, which is always grounded in God, and our empirical self (which Christ took on in the Incarnation) which can become disoriented and fragmented. Growth in spirituality means bringing the substance and the sensuality into union, bringing the wounds of the fragmented sensuality to healing through the gentle love of God.

A great problem for Julian is how there could be such suffering and *evil as she saw about her, not only in physical respects such as the Black Death which was then ravaging Europe, but also in terms of sin, for which the church declared the doctrine of eternal *hell. This she found incompatible with the absence of wrath in God; and repeatedly asked God to explain it to her. She was given the assurance that 'all shall be well'; but though she found herself dissatisfied with this assurance, she could do nothing beyond trust in the love of God as she experienced it and accept that she remained in ignorance about these matters.

One of the themes that has attracted considerable recent interest is Julian's discussion of God as Mother. She was by no means the first to write in these terms, but she developed the theology of divine *motherhood far beyond any previous writer. She saw God's motherhood in three respects: in our initial creation, in our *redemption (in which Christ through his labour brings us to new birth), and in our spiritual nourishment and upbringing which includes both nurture and admonition. Throughout, her message is one of encouragement and love. Pondering the meaning of her visions, she was given the response: 'What, do you wish to know your Lord's meaning in this thing? Know it well, love was his meaning.'

Grace M. Jantzen

Julian of Norwich, *Showings*, ET (1978).
Baker, Denise Nowakowski, *Julian of Norwich's* Showings: *From Vision to Book* (1994).
Jantzen, Grace, *Julian of Norwich: Mystic and Theologian* (1987).
Pelphrey, Brant, *Christ our Mother: Julian of Norwich* (1989).

Jung, Carl Gustav

Jung, Carl Gustav (1875–1961). Jung was a close associate of Sigmund Freud and first president of the International Psychoanalytic Association until his break with mainstream psychoanalysis in 1912–13. Based in Zurich all his adult life, he travelled and lectured extensively.

Since for Jung the drive for meaningfulness of life was the key to *psychological understanding, religious issues were a constant preoccupation, and his complex relation to Christian tradition has met with comparably diverse responses.

He came to a radical view of Freud's founding insight that medical symptoms have meaning and that this meaning can be located in the individual's struggle to come to terms with the forces of aggression and *sexuality. Where Freud saw religion as the displaced or disguised expression of such inevitable conflicts, Jung shifted the emphasis to the ways in which religious or spiritual struggles may be entangled or confused with disturbances of an apparently non-religious kind. The quest for a satisfying ultimate personal meaning, in a sense properly called spiritual or religious, thus has a decisive autonomy *vis-à-vis* other psychological data. It is the keypoint of classical Jungian theory and practice. The weight given to the individual quest (individuation), the variety of symbolic sources it may draw upon, and the tendency to elide the terms religion, spirit, and psyche have both attracted and repelled theologians.

Overall, Jung's work may be seen as a series of responses to the disenchantment of the world accompanying the process of modernization and the consequent doubt cast over the possibility of objectivity of judgement, of ultimate certainty, in either *science or *religion. Amidst the chaotic forces of endless relativism and subjectivity, Jung sought for recurrent patterns and themes in the record of human experience rather than any determinative revealed or discovered *truths. With regard to the diversity of individual perspectives, Jung developed a theory of personality types to illuminate the differences and similarities. As elaborated by Myers and Briggs, this was readily adopted in various forms of Christian religious formation. With regard to the religious content of these ways of seeing, Jung claimed to find recurrent figures and motifs, patterns he called archetypal, in the repertoire of the world's mythologies. Traditional *myths and *symbols, including biblical ones, together with their spontaneous and private analogues in the world of *dreams can thus provide the prime resources for the discovery or construction of personal religious identity.

One major line of critical engagement with Jungian thought is represented by the *Dominican theologian and therapist, Victor White, a valued friend of Jung's until their estrangement in the late 1950s over the latter's *Answer to Job*. White's *God and the Unconscious*, censured by Vatican authorities, and the more systematic *Soul and Psyche* broke new ground. Drawing on the philosophy of *Aquinas, White saw substantial agreement between the theological vocabulary of the *soul and the contemporary Jungian understanding of the psyche, a controversial correlation at the time. White also placed Jung's work on the drive for meaning and the resources of universal symbolism in the traditional providential framework of a latent inherent Christianity in the human soul. There was fierce disagreement over the question of *evil, whether this was indicative of a division within the divine sphere as Jung implied, or a reality to be finally subsumed in the supreme good-

ness of God as orthodox theology uniformly argued. An even more basic disagreement was whether theology and philosophy could retain their autonomy in the wider vision of Jung's psychology, whether anything meaningful could be said of or revealed by God as beyond the Self, the source and goal of psychological growth from Jung's position. With the profound changes in Catholicism attendant on *Vatican II, the theological context White had operated in shifted and there was something of an eclipse of this major form of engagement with the Jungian world-view.

A second major stream of Christian response to Jung, of which the Anglican writer Don *Cupitt may be taken as a radical representative in the 1980s and 1990s, seems closer to what in reality was Jung's own position. The essential emphasis of this may be seen in a dream of 1947, shortly before the explosive creativity of the *Answer to Job*. Jung was with his father, a minister in the Swiss Reformed Church, before 'the highest presence'. Whilst the father bowed his head to the floor, 'I could not bring my forehead quite down to the floor—there was perhaps a millimetre to spare. But at least I had made the gesture with him.' Jung commented that he had been visited by a premonition, long present in humanity, that 'the creature surpasses its creator by a small but decisive factor' (*Memories, Dreams, Reflections* (1963), 208–10).

Jung shared with many of his contemporaries a powerful if cloudy evolutionary and vitalist belief in the power of 'Life itself' driving towards self-realization and fuller self-consciousness. Comparable sentiments and phrases may be found in sources as diverse as the Jesuit *Teilhard de Chardin, the writings of D. H. Lawrence, parts of the rhetoric of both communism and fascism. For Jung it is in the drama of individual development that the purpose of the life process is either advanced or retarded. The religious myths and symbolic systems of the world had in the past provided the public framework in terms of which this personal quest can be located and extended. Jung saw the Christian myth as a failing one, and psychoanalysis as both a contemporary mode of spiritual discovery for those who could no longer believe and, more widely, as a force contributing to a more inclusive myth containing and surpassing Christianity. Thus he looked to compensatory factors on the margins of mainstream Christianity, *Gnosticism and alchemy, that might supplement and correct the deficiencies of Christianity, especially with regard to the role of nature, of evil, and of the feminine. It is in this sense that Jung has been aptly characterized as 'treating' Christianity as he would a patient in therapy, and as the father of *New Age spirituality.

In this context it is powerfully ironic that one of the most influential post-Jungians, James Hillman, claimed that Jung never finally escaped the monotheism of his heritage and underestimated the kaleidoscopic and polytheistic reality of the human psyche. In questioning the sense of individuation as development through a hierarchy of archetypal stages, Hillman struck at the overarching intentionality of the Self as 'God within', crucial to Jung's project. From this perspective many of Jung's formulations on the religious function of the psyche share the datedness of such sympathetic Christian critics as White. The Canadian analyst and theologian John Dourley was one of the few to try to meet this challenge.

Responses such as Cupitt's 'taking leave of God' while attempting to retain the imaginative and spiritual resources of Christian myth and metaphor may be seen as a radical version of the *liberal Protestant stance deriving from *Schleiermacher at the very end of the 18th century and a potent influence in Jung's early milieu. Schleiermacher's appeal to the individual and universal experience of a sense or feeling of absolute dependence at the core of our identity produced an ambiguous heritage. In this view what we ultimately depend upon and 'God' are interchangeable. If so, then an atheistic humanism like that of Feuerbach—where what we ultimately depend upon is other human beings—is a consistent and plausible alternative to Christianity. Similarly, if, in Jung's view, we are taken to depend upon a collective unconscious expressive of 'Life itself', then any Christian or other decisive theological claims are necessarily marginalized.   **Adrian Cunningham**

Heisig, J. W., *Imago Dei: A Study of Jung's Psychology of Religion* (1979).

Lammers, A. C., *In God's Shadow: The Collaboration of Victor White and C. G. Jung* (1994).

Ryce-Menuhin, J. (ed.), *Jung and the Monotheisms* (1994).

Stein, M., *Jung's Treatment of Christianity* (1985).

Jüngel, Eberhard

Jüngel, Eberhard (1934—), *Lutheran theologian. Born in Magdeburg, Jüngel left his East German base in 1966 and has been since 1969 a much frequented teacher at the University of *Tübingen. His early studies took place in the tension between the schools of *Barth and *Bultmann, and his independent and original work continues to address *dogmatic and *hermeneutical questions together. The western metaphysical tradition, after it had made God merely the 'necessary' guarantor of the human subject (so Jüngel on *Descartes and Cartesianism), finally ran out in *atheism. The gospel, by contrast, is that the *God who exists and acts in sheer gratuity has 'come to speech' in the *incarnate *Word, *Jesus Christ, and above all in his *cross and *Resurrection, which, as 'the unity of life and death to the advantage of life', is the enactment of the *love which God is (1 John 4: 8). This divine self-*revelation is what makes it possible for human beings to 'think' God, to 'speak' God, and to act, suffer, and hope 'correspondingly', in the way of 'discipleship' (*Nachfolge*)—and so become, not divine, but more truly *human; for, although God is from all eternity 'turned towards' humankind, God's distinction remains and is indeed the ground of his creative and redemptive action. Jüngel holds firmly to the Lutheran doctrine of *justification by *grace through *faith alone and draws from this certain consequences in the realms of ecclesiology (against Roman Catholicism he resists any notion of the 'agency' of the *church in the mediation of a *salvation that is received in entire passivity), *anthropology (he sharply distinguishes between persons and their works and on this ground opposes, for instance, capital punishment), and politics (which are limited to earthly welfare, *Wohl*, without trespassing on salvation, *Heil*). A forceful contemporary expression of classical Protestant theological themes, Jüngel's demanding work has not received much attention in the English-speaking world; but his *magnum opus* was rendered as *God as the Mystery of the World* (1983), and J. B. Webster has translated two volumes of his provocative *Theological Essays* (1989, 1994).   **Geoffrey Wainwright**

Webster, J. B., *Eberhard Jüngel: An Introduction to his Theology* (1986).

——(ed.), *The Possibilities of Theology: Studies in the Theology of Eberhard Jüngel in his Sixtieth Year* (1994).

justice is the subject of vigorous and sometimes confusing debate today. This discussion draws on two ancient ways of understanding justice—the *philosophical and the *biblical—that have interacted with one another in various ways down the ages.

Philosophical accounts of justice spring from the thought of *Plato and *Aristotle in particular. Both saw justice as simultaneously the architectonic principle of a decent society and a cardinal virtue in human behaviour. Justice, Plato taught, should be expressed in the structure of society and in the individual soul. It is justice that holds a decent society together and is the central characteristic of the good *soul. For both thinkers, justice might be hard to grasp intellectually, and the doing of justice was only possible as the result of strenuous discipline and education; but justice was believed to be an objective reality grounded in the nature of things. For Plato, and to a lesser extent Aristotle, justice stands in *judgement on the existing order of society and of the soul, and demands radical change both in the structure of society and in the character of its citizens. Only so may a just society be established in which just individuals flourish. Justice is more than giving to each person what is due. For Plato it is the harmony of the parts of the soul or of the society, so that they work together and find their fulfilment in the service of the good of all. Aristotle introduces important distinctions within the understanding of justice, between general and particular justice, and distributive and rectificatory justice, the latter distinction corresponding roughly to the modern categories of social and criminal justice. For Aristotle, as for Plato, justice is both the supreme or comprehensive virtue in an individual, and the basic principle of cohesion for a decent society.

Greek thought, on justice as on other topics, was aristocratic and élitist, and excluded whole categories of people (*women, manual workers, and *slaves, for example) from the discussion. Socrates is reported to have said that injustice is the greatest of evils to the doer of injustice, and that doing injustice is a greater evil than suffering injustice. This exclusion of the victims and their insights from the discussion made it partial and distorted; for whole dimensions of the reality of justice are only available to the victims of injustice.

In the biblical tradition, justice is an attribute of *God, an essential component of God's being, intimately associated with the divine *love that provides a similar language to speak of God, for God is love. As with the Greeks, the parallel biblical ideas of justice (*tsedeq*) and righteousness (*mishpat*) are comprehensive and complementary values, being rooted in the very being of God. Doing justice, or loving, are sometimes spoken of as ways to know God, and as such love and justice share in the reality or objectivity of God.

God's justice is expressed most clearly in the *covenant, and the covenant community is called to be faithful to God's justice. To act unjustly is to turn away from God; in acting justly God is known and obeyed. God's justice in the biblical tradition involves a special care for the victims—the weak, the poor, the marginalized, the stranger, and the oppressed—for the divine justice vindicates them against their oppressors (Exod. 22: 21–2; Deut. 10: 18; 14: 29; 15: 7; Ps. 82: 3–4; 103: 6; 140: 12; etc.).

In the NT justice is a central characteristic of the reign of God that is proclaimed as imminent. Jesus calls people to seek first the reign of God and its justice (Matt. 6: 33). In Jesus' teaching and parables of the *Kingdom a distinctive understanding emerges: justice heals relationships and restores community. This is a proactive understanding of justice as setting things right, overcoming offence, and creating relationship. God's justice brings us all to judgement, it is true, but in judgement God's *mercy is to be found. In this understanding, as Portia declared in *The Merchant of Venice*, 'earthly power does then show likest God's when mercy seasons justice'. Indeed in this great play *Shakespeare seems intent to contrast the generous, merciful, 'feminine', and Christian justice of Belmont with the mechanical, retributive, and 'masculine' justice of Venice.

The bible early became a resource for more sustained reflections on justice, in constant dialogue with secular philosophies, and increasingly with an eye to the guidance to be given to rulers, judges, and magistrates. *Augustine drew a clear distinction between the relative and partial justice that was possible in the earthly city, and the true justice of the heavenly city. True justice must measure up to the divine justice and love revealed in Jesus Christ and realized fully only in the heavenly city. But without something of this justice, earthly cities become demonic, simply bands of robbers (*De civitate dei*, 3. 4).

In the Middle Ages elaborate accounts of justice were developed which arose out of the dialogue between Aristotle and the biblical tradition. On this basis 'mirrors for princes' and manuals for their confessors were developed, and sophisticated and influential theories of justice in relation to economic life (just price and just wage) and warfare and conflict (just war) emerged. In more recent times this intellectual tradition has shaped the development of Catholic *social teaching from the late 19th century; and from this teaching the concept of 'social justice' emerged in the 20th century. Today *liberation theology in its various forms articulates the cry of the victims of injustice and demands justice in the political and economic orders.

The *Reformation arose from a renewed understanding of *justification—that God accepts us as just even while we are still sinners. *Luther himself found that in his experience of justification his understanding of God's justice was transformed. He now realized that the justice of God had at its heart 'grace and sheer mercy', and the justice that had filled him with hate and fear was now 'inexpressibly sweet in greater love'. But Luther developed a theory of the two kingdoms that was often used to suggest that this kind of justice had its proper locus in the soul and in the church, and had no bearing upon 'the *world', where hard, impersonal, retributive justice was to prevail: God's 'strange work' as against his 'proper work' of love and acceptance. Calvinists, on the other hand, were strongly committed to seeking to realize in the temporal order something of the justice of God. The conflict between Lutheran and Calvinist views became a major issue in the German church's struggles in the 1930s, when Karl *Barth (particularly in *Rechtfertigung und Recht*, 1937) accused the more conservative Lutherans of exempting Hitler and the Nazis from prophetic critique because they believed they had no mandate to speak of the justice of God in the temporal realm, whose standards of justice were beyond theological scrutiny.

In more recent times, especially since the publication of John Rawls's *A Theory of Justice* (1971), there has been a vigorous but remarkably inconclusive debate about the nature of justice. The context for this debate among liberal thinkers was not dissimilar to that out of which Plato's great work on justice, the *Republic*, emerged many centuries before: a pluralistic society in which there was pervasive uncertainty about justice and *ethics. The main difference is that while Plato / Socrates assumed that although it was very hard to discover what justice was, it existed as an objective reality to be discovered and to which one should be obedient, today's theorists, almost unanimously, believe they must set aside any *metaphysical or religious assumptions and produce purely rational accounts of justice, based on the 'considered convictions' of most people in a modern liberal democratic society (Rawls), or on some kind of general consensus. Justice then becomes, for thinkers such as Ackerman or Hayek, the establishment of a social structure that gives individuals the maximum possible *freedom to pursue their own individual goods, while the society as such recognizes no common good, no common goal. Rawls himself produces a more egalitarian account of justice, involving redistribution of resources and providing a kind of justification for a welfare state. It has accordingly proved very attractive to many left-of-centre radicals as providing a rationale for their social practice. Being founded, however, on no more than a consensus (what most people believe in a modern liberal *democracy), Rawls's theory is very vulnerable to a demonstration that this consensus does not exist. It is easy to show that Robert Nozick, Alasdair *MacIntyre, and Friedrich Hayek, to take only three prominent examples, reject most of the assumptions about human beings and the good life that are crucial for Rawls's theory.

Not all the contributors to the present debate would accept the liberal label. Communitarians such as MacIntyre, Stanley Hauerwas, Michael Sandel, and Charles Taylor reject the individualism and the negativity towards tradition characteristic of the liberals. In addition most of them take religion and theology seriously. A community of shared faith generates, refines, and criticizes over time common understandings of social ordering and thus produces understandings of justice. There is in fact, they argue, no way to rise above such socially conditioned understandings to a timeless, objective view. Out of the richness of a community of faith inheriting a great tradition of reflection, commitment, and action comes an understanding of justice that may be recognized as true or at least constructive even in 'the desolation of reality that overtakes human beings in a post-religious age that has grown too wise to swallow the shallow illusions of the enlightenment' (John Gray).

Jürgen Habermas, while believing that religious insights are to be excluded on principle, and accepting that no overarching vision of the good is possible today, develops a suggestion that there is a procedure for deciding on what is just that contributes to the development of a just society: that is by involving all the concerned people. Deciding what is just in a particular situation is not the task or privilege of an educated and powerful élite. Such people cannot, *pace* Plato, know what is good for others. Only in a debate open to everyone affected, and lacking any coercion, intimidation, pressure, or fear, is a true consensus on what is just likely to emerge. The very process of the discourse makes the community itself more just. This is more than a procedure for deciding what it is just to do. Abstaining from coercion and attending to what people say even if they are powerless are pointers towards the qualities that are needed if a society is to be just.

*Feminist thinkers such like Okin, Nancy Fraser, and Carol Gilligan have argued that almost all theorists, being male, have drawn a sharp, and characteristically masculine, distinction between the public realm, where justice should hold sway, and *family life, which is subject to different, more affective principles such as love and care, altruism and generosity, not believed to be applicable in public life. These thinkers suggest that just families, and justice in the domestic realm, are necessary if succeeding generations are to learn how to be just. Furthermore they argue that the domestic/public distinction should be reassessed so that a more adequate account of justice might emerge, allowing for care, altruism, and generosity. There is a gap that needs to be bridged between a universalizing justice expressed primarily through large-scale structures and processes, impersonal, impartial, and general in its operations, and a justice that stresses the claims and needs of the concrete neighbour and the specific situation. In some cases care, generosity, and mercy are best delivered through large-scale mechanisms. Some needs of our neighbours are most appropriately met while allowing them to retain the dignity of being strangers to those who ultimately assist them. These are fundamental principles of the welfare state, surely a serious attempt to embody social justice. These feminist thinkers are in harmony with deep springs of the Christian account of justice in advocating something broader, richer, and more complex than the accounts produced by most male secular theorists.

Christian thinkers tend to find the major secular positions in today's debate about justice thin, narrow, and resting on weak foundations, however impressively argued. While there is much sympathy for a communitarian position it is recognized that some communitarians advocate styles of community which involve excessive abrogation of freedom. Hayek is at least partially right in suggesting that 'teleocratic' societies with a dominant commitment to a precisely defined common good have a tendency to become oppressive. Theories of justice that on principle eschew theological and metaphysical considerations easily end up too mechanical and narrow to play the central role in social order that justice should play. An adequate account of justice needs to be capable not only of constraining selfishness, dealing with offences and distributing goods and penalties; a decent society needs a justice which is concerned with the healing of relationships, with the restoration of fellowship, and with escape from the cycle of retribution; with *reconciliation, in short. Such an understanding of justice as healing, relational, restorative has deep roots within the Judaeo-Christian tradition. That it is challengingly relevant to the realities of today's world is demonstrated, among numerous instances, by the work of the Truth and Reconciliation Commission in South Africa, chaired by Archbishop Desmond Tutu.   **Duncan Forrester**

Benhabib, Seyla, *Situating the Self: Gender, Community and Postmodernism in Contemporary Ethics* (1992).

Forrester, D. B., *Christian Justice and Public Policy* (1997).

Heller, A., *Beyond Justice* (1987).

MacIntyre, A., *Whose Justice? Which Rationality?* (1988).

Okin, Susan M., *Justice, Gender, and the Family* (1989).

Rawls, J., *A Theory of Justice* (1971).

—— *Political Liberalism* (1993).

Sandel, Michael J., *Liberalism and the Limits of Justice* (1982).

Walzer, Michael, *Spheres of Justice* (1983).

justification.

justification. The Greek word *dikaioun*, meaning 'to put in the right' or 'to place someone in the right', can be used in both a positive and a negative sense. Since the realization of the ends of justice may involve the exposure of a person's guilt, it was widely used in Greek to mean 'condemn'. However, in the Septuagint and the *New Testament the word is generally used in its more positive sense to denote justification, vindication, or treating someone as just. In *Paul, it is used almost exclusively of *God's *judgement and again, in the positive sense, of the acquittal of men and women, of their being pronounced and treated as righteous—being liberated to become righteous. Thus, at the heart of Christian *theology there is to be found a profoundly positive concept of justification which, none the less, takes full account of the negative implications (*katakrimata*) of attributing righteousness to an alienated *humanity. The gospel teaches 'the justification of the ungodly', which means putting the ungodly in the right in such a way that we are justified in and through our very condemnation. Thus both the positive and the negative aspects are held together. In Christ, we are both exposed in our guilt and also made righteous, we are judged and condemned, and at the same time vindicated.

When Karl *Barth affirmed that 'there never was and there never can be any true Christian church without the doctrine of justification', he could be taken as speaking on behalf of the *church catholic. The question of 'justification' (the placing of human beings in a proper relationship with God) is central to the church's doctrine. Nevertheless, history bears witness to widely differing interpretations and profound divisions on how the doctrine is to be understood. Barth himself clarified this statement by emphasizing that the '*articulus stantis et cadentis ecclesiae* is not the doctrine of justification as such, but its basis and culmination: the confession of Jesus Christ … the knowledge of his being and activity for us and to us and with us'. This points to an essential continuity with what *Irenaeus said in the 2nd century: 'He took what was ours that we might have what is his.' But it also presents us with a critical question: what is the relationship between Christ's *objective* fulfilment of righteousness and the *subjective* righteousness of the faithful? How does the righteousness of the life of Christ relate to the life of the church as a whole and to the lives of individual believers? Barth's restatement of the doctrine strives to hold the two poles in balance while placing the emphasis firmly on the objective, *christological pole as denoting a complete, unconditional, and once and for all event. Any emphasis on subjective justification must derive from the objective, christological content of the doctrine. Moreover, the human appropriation of righteousness, whether by good works or some subjective act of *faith, must never be seen as a condition of the significance or extent of Christ's establishment of righteousness on behalf of humanity: both the Roman Catholic and Protestant interpretations of the doctrine have tended to introduce such an element of contract. Barth restates the doctrine thus:

> The right of God established in the death of Jesus Christ, and proclaimed in his resurrection in defiance of the wrong of man, is as such the basis of the new and corresponding right of man. Promised to humanity in Jesus Christ, hidden in him and only to be revealed in him, it cannot be attained by any thought or effort or achievement on the part of humanity. But the reality of it calls for faith in every human being as a suitable acknowledgement and appropriation and application.

Of the various discussions which took place in the early history of the church concerning the nature of *salvation and human righteousness, it is *Augustine's detailed exposition of the theology of justification in debate with *Pelagius that sets the scene for those which were to follow. Augustine insisted that justification is a pure act of God's *grace, entirely free and unmerited by fallen humanity, and reposing on nothing except God's gracious promises. Indeed, due to the *fallenness of human nature through natural descent from *Adam, all forms of human righteousness and all good works are the direct result of God's working in and through fallen human nature. The justification of humanity does not and cannot derive in any way from any capacity or facet of human nature but purely from God in fulfilment of the divine promises. Consequently, it is Christ alone who justifies and it is solely in him that we find our justification through faith: 'inasmuch as it is he that justifies the ungodly, to the man who believes in him … his faith is imputed for righteousness'. It was thus Augustine's exposition of justification by grace alone, together with his emphasis on the importance of faith, which furnished the categories for the *sixteenth-century debates which were to divide the church in the west.

It was *Luther's redefinition of the church's understanding of justification that initiated the major debates of the *Reformation era. When he later looked back on the course of his life, he attributed his reforming zeal to a discovery of far-reaching theological significance: the meaning of the phrase 'the righteousness of God' in Romans 1: 17. In his early years this phrase had come to fill him with dread, since he saw it as denoting a righteousness that could only oppress us and compound our sense of guilt because, as Augustine had shown, it was unachievable by humanity. The virtuous works and especially the virtuous intentions that he had been taught to view as the necessary precondition of justification were simply unrealizable and condemned humanity to the bondage of a sense of its own guilt. After much theological reflection, however, he came to see that when Paul speaks of the 'righteousness of God' he is not referring to a divine righteousness that condemns humankind from afar, but to God's refusal to leave humanity lost in its unrighteousness and condemned to the vain and hopeless task of struggling to deliver itself from this state. Paul is referring to 'that by which the righteous person lives by the gift of God (faith)'—a righteousness which, far from condemning humanity to the bondage of guilt, frees it for a life of *joyful faith. The righteousness of God denotes that 'passive righteousness, by which the merciful God justifies us by faith'. Thus, a phrase which had previously induced fear became 'the very gates of paradise for me'. There then emerges what is to become an increasingly christocentric interpretation of the righteousness of God focusing on the humanity of Christ, in whom the righteous requirements of the law are fulfilled on our behalf. In his sermons on John, he describes the righteousness of God as a righteousness which is 'far different from that acknowledged by the world'. This 'alien righteousness' Christ identifies 'exclusively with himself' denoting his reign and Kingdom. It is 'entirely outside and above us; it is Christ going to the Father, that is, his suffering, Resurrection and ascension'. It is grasped exclusively 'by faith in the Word preached about him which tells us that he himself is our righteousness … in order that before God we may boast not of ourselves but solely of the Lord'. Believers are thus incapable of self-justification and actually remain sinners, but God reckons them righteous by imputing to them the righteousness of Christ. 'Christ our righteousness' is the essential clue to Luther's understanding of justification. Through faith, believers repose on Christ's righteousness which is counted by God as theirs. Thus, before God the believer is reckoned righteous though never ceasing to be a sinner being 'at one and the same time righteous and a sinner'—simul iustus et peccator.

Luther's understanding of imputed righteousness was developed by Melanchthon into the doctrine generally referred to as 'forensic justification' which emphasized that the sinner is pronounced righteous under God's judgement in the heavenly court, in foro divino, hence 'forensic'. This development of Luther's thought led to a sharp distinction between 'justification' on the one hand, and 'sanctification' or 'regeneration' on the other. Its primary weaknesses are the concept of law informing its forensic interpretation and its individualistic, subjective orientation. It shows a concern with the salvific requirements of the individual rather than a Pauline emphasis on participation by the power of the *Holy Spirit in Christ. Moreover, by emphasizing that our appropriation of justification is by faith alone, it tended to turn faith into a work. This opened an obvious and easy line of attack on the Reformers' theology: that making justification conditional upon faith grossly overestimated faith as the sole human virtue at the expense of all other human virtues.

*Calvin's discussion (Institutes, 3. 11–13) reflects his perception of the potential deficiencies of such an approach and in his exposition of justification he sought to restore a proper balance. First, he insisted that faith cannot contribute anything whatsoever to our justification—'nihil afferens nostrum ad conciliandum Dei gratiam'. Faith is not a habitus nor a quality of grace infused into humans. To believe is to come to God entirely empty, and, since God's justification concerns precisely what we lack, there is no point in enquiring into the extent and adequacy of our faith. Second, he was concerned that, if we simply identify 'the righteousness of God' with a 'righteousness from God', we will fail to perceive that it is precisely the human righteousness of Christ that justifies humanity. The Lutheran tendency to interpret justification as a righteousness imparted directly from God (understandably motivated by a fear of introducing notions of conditional acceptance) could all too easily short-circuit the human righteousness of Christ and so focus away from the person of Christ to the work of God through the *cross—a weakness that has continued to characterize Protestant *evangelicalism! Calvin sought instead to expound justification in a manner that, while establishing an objective focus on the righteousness of God, interpreted it in terms of Christ's human righteousness. He stressed that the righteousness of God in Christ was emphatically not a divine righteousness infused into Christ but a genuinely human righteousness. As the Second Adam, Christ assumes our humanity and thereby realizes and fulfils all righteousness in our place and on our behalf as the truly human righteousness of the one who is flesh of our flesh and bone of our bone. Human justification is established in the person of our kinsman redeemer who thereby restores us to our lost inheritance: righteous communion with God.

While Calvin was to oppose any dichotomization between justification and sanctification resulting from an insufficiently christological focus, the concern of the Council of *Trent was that Luther and his followers failed to hold them together at the anthropological level. Summoned in 1545, the first of the Council's two main periods (the Imperial Epoch) was directed towards the Lutheran doctrine of justification. Following the traditional western ordo salutis (plan of salvation), it begins by expounding humanity's fallenness and consequent inability to justify itself, while affirming that human free will is 'in no way extinct' (ch. 1). Justification denotes the state of grace resulting from our transition and the consequent transformation of our disposition from our original fallen state. This 'bath of regeneration' is attributed to God's prevenient grace which awakens, assists, and disposes men and women 'to turn to their own justification by freely assenting to and co-operating with that grace'. Much is said from which the Reformers would not wish to dissent, but the Council of Trent is more anthropological, indeed subjective, in its focus, and this reflects a difference in theological direction. Chapter 7 opens: 'This disposition or preparation is followed by justification itself, which is not the remission of *sins but the sanctification and renewal of the interior man through the voluntary reception of grace and of the gifts, whereby from unjust man becomes just, and from enemy a friend, that he may be "an heir in hope of eternal life" (Titus 3: 7).' There is a somewhat Pelagian ring about this exposition of the God–human relationship which the notion of 'infused justice' is intended to offset.

So where precisely are we to locate the differences between Trent and Calvin? One particularly interesting way of highlighting the similarities and differences is in their contrasting application of the scholastic categories of causality to the doctrine of justification. For Calvin (citing John 3: 16) the formal or instrumental cause is 'faith' and the material cause is 'Christ, with his obedience, through which he acquired righteousness for us'. Trent prefers to speak, more contractually, of a 'meritorious cause' which is 'our Lord Jesus Christ who merited for us justification by his most holy passion on the wood of the Cross and made satisfaction for us to God the Father'. The formal cause is 'the justice which we have as a gift … and by which we are spiritually renewed'.

Perhaps the most fundamental theological question that emerges from the Reformation debates is how far the doctrine of God (and thus the language of justification) is informed by the *Incarnation. To interpret justification in terms of Christ's meritorious satisfaction of the Father's justice, as this has characterized trends in both Catholic and Protestant thought, seems to suggest that the Father has to be conditioned into being loving and so into forgiving his alienated creatures (whereas John 3: 16, 1 John, and much else suggest that God is, by nature, love). Does not the projection of such a contractual arrangement into the relationship between Father and Son undermine the doctrine of the *Trinity? Does it make sense to see Christ, as the one in whom the fullness of the Godhead dwells bodily with and for humanity, as having to *merit the Father's *forgiveness on behalf of humanity? Does not conceiving of the work and death of Christ as meritorious satisfaction of the Father's demands threaten to reduce the Pauline en Christo to a propter Christum—'on account of Christ' instead of 'in Christ' (see ATONEMENT)? The theological irony here is the extent to which both of these tendencies can be seen to characterize evangelical Protestantism as much as Tridentine Roman Catholicism in their expositions of God's plan of salvation and human justification. If Catholics tended to make justification conditional upon faith and works, Protestants have too often made it conditional upon faith (and repentance) conceived as a work.

In conclusion, one might point to ingredients contributing to an ecumenical exposition of justification today. Recent studies of Rabbinic Judaism show that to interpret the Jewish law, torah (see Law, BIBLICAL) and the *covenant, berit, in terms of western notions of forensic, contractual *law (lex) and contract (foedus), or to interpret Jewish righteousness (tsedaqu) as iustitia, is to do serious damage to the whole structure of thought underlying Judaism and NT Christianity. Justification has to be interpreted in terms of God's unconditioned and unconditional love for humanity in Christ: a covenant commitment, to which juridical categories of interpretation do not apply, not a contract. If, as Tom Wright has suggested, God's righteousness is to be interpreted as the completion of the covenant in Christ, then both the objective and the subjective, the theological and the anthropological dimensions have to be interpreted christologically. The fear that interpreting both the justification and sanctification of humanity as completed 'in Christ' may lead to an *antinomian playing down of moral obligations may be addressed by a more strongly Trinitarian interpretation of the doctrine as offered by the modern Lutheran Robert Jenson. For him justification is 'the underived event of communal faithfulness in God, as this is directed as love and is actual in the reality of the incarnate Son. That we are justified simply means that we, as the body and spouse of the Son, are included.' Clearly, this chimes with the view emerging in NT studies that to be justified is to hear the affirmation that one is a full member of the community of promise. To participate by the Spirit in this community will surely translate into the lived recognition and endorsement of what Barth calls 'the right of God established in the death of Jesus Christ, and proclaimed in his Resurrection in defiance of the wrong of humanity'.

Alan Torrance

Barth, Karl, Church Dogmatics, IV, ET (1956).
Jenson, Robert, 'Justification as a Triune Event', Modern Theology, 11/4 (October 1995).
Küng, Hans, Justification: the Doctrine of Karl Barth and a Catholic Reflection ET (1964).
McGrath, Alister E., Iustitia Dei: A History of the Christian Doctrine of Justification (2 vols.; 1996).
Neuner, J., and Dupuis, J. (eds.), The Christian Faith in the Doctrinal Documents of the Catholic Church, 'Foreword' to the Decree on Justification of the Council of Trent (1983).
Newman, J. H., Lectures on the Doctrine of Justification (1838).
Rupp, E. G., The Righteousness of God: Luther Studies (1953).
Torrance, T. F., 'Justification: its Radical Nature and Place in Reformed Doctrine and Life', in Theology in Reconstruction (1965).
Wright, N. T., The Climax of the Covenant (1991).
Yule, George, 'Luther's Understanding of Justification by Grace Alone in Terms of Catholic Christology', in George Yule (ed.), Luther: Theologian for Catholics and Protestants (1985).

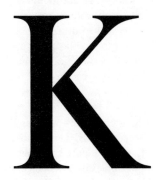

Kant, Immanuel (1724–1804). The question of Kant's relation to *Christianity has been controversial from his own time to the present. While the view offered in this article is responsible to the texts, there is no consensus among Kant scholars. He nowhere tells us about his personal religious beliefs, for example whether he believed that Christ rose from the dead. He does, however, tell us that certain religious beliefs are required for the practice of the moral life, and others are 'vehicles' by which moral faith is transmitted to us. Sometimes interpreters talk of Kant as being tactful about Christianity, disguising his distaste to appease the Prussian authorities, but a more straightforward approach is adopted here.

Kant grew up in a pietist *Lutheran family, and had pietist Lutheran schooling. We need to read his work, especially in the *philosophy of religion, as constantly engaged in discussion with *Pietism. Comparing Kant with one of its great figures, August Hermann Francke, reveals that both emphasize the primacy of practice over theory in the life of faith. Both change the emphasis from history to what God wants to do in every human heart. Both insist that we have no natural ability to destroy the root of *evil in our souls. Both distrust the natural inclinations, but think they can be trained to serve God either directly or indirectly. Finally, both have the vision of a worldwide *moral and spiritual renewal, and think of the visible *church as a potential hindrance to this. But Kant also defined himself in some ways in opposition to the pietists. He was against what he calls 'fanaticism', and objected to the claims some pietists made to being supernaturally favoured by God. 'To claim that we *feel* as such the immediate influence of God is self-contradictory, because the Idea of God lies only in reason.' Kant did not attend religious services, even as rector of the university, perhaps because of his experience of Christianity's tendency to become what he calls 'dictatorial'. But this opposition to Pietism is also characteristic of Lutheranism in his day, though of a different branch. Kant's combination is idiosyncratic; but, without further evidence, we should not place him outside Christian *orthodoxy.

In the *Critique of Pure Reason*, Kant argues that we cannot, on his restrictive view of knowledge, *know* that God exists; for we could not possibly experience his existence with the senses. God is a thing-in-itself, a *noumenon*, beyond the range of our sensory intuition of *phenomena*. Accordingly he criticized the traditional proofs of God's existence—such as the *ontological, cosmological, and teleological arguments—as overstepping the limits of the human understanding. This is part of Kant's 'Copernican revolution'. Copernicus had suggested that we could understand our observations of the movements of the heavenly bodies as a function of our own movement. In the same way, Kant suggests that we can see the a priori principles of human knowledge as a function of the limits to which our sense-experience has to conform. But pointing to human limits does not, for Kant, imply scepticism. He wants to limit knowledge to make room for *faith. In the *Critique of Practical Reason* he argues that we have to *believe* that God exists, because we continue throughout our lives to desire our own happiness in everything else that we desire. There is nothing wrong here. What is wrong is our inborn condition in which we put the desire for our own happiness *above* the desire to do our duty. If by some revolution of the will this priority can be reversed, we shall still be desiring our own happiness. Hence if we are to persevere in the moral life, we have to believe that it is consistent with our own happiness: that we do not have to do what is morally wrong in order to be happy. This is not the justification for the moral life, for that would turn it into a means towards happiness; whereas we should do our duty for its own sake. But we do have to believe that our attempts at virtue are rewarded by happiness, which in turn requires us to believe in someone who can do the rewarding, namely God. Kant has a similar argument for the need to believe in personal immortality. The moral law requires us to be committed in this life to the pursuit of *holiness. But we do not see such a pursuit even near to fulfilment in this life, and to sustain our endeavour we need to believe that the pursuit can be continued in the next. Finally, in the *Critique of Judgement*, he argues that *reason has to ask why nature exists, and cannot answer without imagining a being who, in creating nature, gave it an ultimate end.

We should think of our duties as God's commands. God is the head of the kingdom of ends, and we are members in this same kingdom. In this kingdom of ends, we treat all other rational beings as ends in themselves, not as mere means to our ends. To treat another person as an end in herself is to make her ends our own ends, as far as the moral law allows. The *kingdom of which God is head is thus a system of morally permissible ends shared by all rational agents. The possible realization of this kingdom (required for its normativity) is produced by God's headship of it, just as in the political realm the possible realization of the *polis* (again required for its normativity) is produced by the exercise of political authority. There is, in our relation both to God and to political authority, an autonomous submission, which is not liable to Kant's objections to heteronomy. Heteronomy means making something other than our respect for the moral law (for example, fear of punishment) the ground of our action. Kant thought that some pietist versions of *divine command theory were guilty of this, but that his own view, that we should see our duties as God's commands, is not.

Kant's relation to the *bible is an area in which his interpreters disagree. Some call him a *deist, in the sense that he does not accept special *revelation. It is better to take him, in his own term, as a 'pure rationalist': he accepts special revelation but does not think this acceptance necessary to rational religion. In the prologue to the second edition of *Religion within the Limits of Reason Alone*, he suggests that we see revelation as two concentric circles. The historical revelation (to particular people at particular times) lies in the outer circle; the revelation to reason (which Kant takes not to be historical in this sense, but the same in all people at all times) lies in the inner one. He then takes the central items of the historical revelation (*creation, *Fall, *redemption, and Second Coming), to see if they can be translated into the language of the inner circle in the light of moral concepts. Since Kant is a pure rationalist, we can expect him, by this translation, to demonstrate the consistency of the historical faith with the religion of pure reason, but also to deny that the historical faith is the only possible way to reach a saving faith. He thinks it possible to lead a life sufficient for God to decree salvation even though it is lived outside the geographical and historical reach of the Christian scriptures. But for Kant himself and his contemporaries in Christian Europe, the Christian scriptures have been the 'vehicle' of saving faith.

Despite being a pure rationalist, Kant also concedes that we may have to believe some item in the outer circle, even though we cannot make use of it with our reason either theoretically or practically. An important case is raised by what he calls 'Spener's problem', referring to the great pietist and his treatment of the Christian doctrine of original *sin. According to Spener we are born with the disposition not to *love God with all our hearts, minds, souls, and strength and not to love our neighbours as ourselves. Nor can we get ourselves out of this disposition by our own devices. Spener's problem was how, given this incapacity, we can change; 'how we can become *other* men and not merely better men (as if we were already good but only negligent about the degree of our goodness).' Kant agrees with Spener (and *Luther) that human beings are born in bondage to radical evil: in Kant's terms, with an innate tendency to prefer our own happiness to our duty. But then how can we change to the opposite preference, as required by morality? Kant thinks that 'ought' implies 'can'; if we cannot live under the moral law, then it is not the case that we ought to do so. But he is sure that we ought, and therefore he has to be able to assert that we can. He concedes, however, that we cannot bring about by our own devices the required revolution of the will. In his terms, the propensity to evil is radical, and is therefore inextirpable by human powers, 'since extirpation could occur only through good maxims, and cannot take place when the ultimate subjective ground of all maxims is postulated as corrupt.' This is Spener's problem. And Kant's solution is also Spener's; he appeals to divine assistance. We

must believe that it is God who works in us, by negative and positive helps, to bring about the revolution of the will. 'Ought' implies 'can'; but 'ought' does not imply 'can by our own devices'. What we can accomplish depends upon what kind of assistance is available to us. This doctrine of the availability of divine *grace is both something Kant thinks we have to accept if we are to sustain the moral life and something he cannot translate without remainder into the language of the inner circle.

Kant's philosophy of religion has been immensely influential. The greatest influence has been from the Copernican revolution, and the accompanying project of reconciling *science and moral life. The influence goes through *Hegel (who saw himself, like Luther, as a reformer of Christianity) and *Kierkegaard (who repeats, in the figure of Judge William, Kant's translations of Christian doctrine into ethical terms). In Christian theology, *Schleiermacher (to mention only the most important name of the *nineteenth century) was deeply immersed in Kant, as were in the *twentieth century *Otto, *Tillich, and *Barth (though all three partially define themselves in opposition to him). The *liberal Protestantism of Ritschl was also neo-Kantian in inspiration. In philosophy, the influence can be felt both in the Continental tradition, through *Nietzsche and Heidegger, and in the analytic tradition through Russell and Austin. It is interesting to see how secular the Kantian tradition becomes even though in Kant himself there are still strong moorings in Christianity. His reconciliation project, together with its Christian basis, is widely perceived to have failed. This author believes that the project is bound to fail when detached, as it has been, from its traditional base; but this cannot be argued here.   **John Hare**

Kant, I., *Practical Philosophy*, ET (1996).
—— *Religion and Rational Theology*, ET (1996).
—— *Critique of Pure Reason*, ET (1956).
—— *Critique of Judgement*, ET (1987).
Hare, John E., *The Moral Gap: Kantian Ethics, Human Limits, and God's Assistance* (1996).
Michalson, Gordon, *Fallen Freedom: Kant on Radical Evil and Moral Regeneration* (1990).
Reardon, Bernard M. G., *Kant as Philosophical Theologian* (1988).
Rossi, Philip J., and Wreen, Michael (eds.), *Kant's Philosophy of Religion Reconsidered* (1991).
Schneewind, Jerome, *The Invention of Autonomy* (1998).
Wood, Allen W., *Kant's Moral Religion* (1970).
—— *Kant's Rational Theology* (1978).

kenosis, emptying, derives from a Greek word in Philippians 2: 7, where it is said that Christ Jesus, though he was in the form of God ... 'emptied himself, taking the form of a slave'. Philippians 2: 5–11 is amongst the most important passages in *Paul's letters and has been the source of an immense amount of thought. 'However it is interpreted, it is agreed that this passage is an invaluable witness to the rapid development of "advanced" claims for Jesus, and of formulas to express these claims, presumably for use in worship and teaching' (J. L. Houlden, *A Dictionary of Biblical Interpretation* (1990), 541).

One of the many fascinating things about the passage is, as Houlden hints, that it seems to be in poetic form, and so may be understood as a quotation from a hymn, possibly of Paul's composition, or more probably a text already in use in the early Christian congregations. So, its form as well as its content may speak of the remarkable rapidity with which 'advanced' claims for *Jesus had become part of the faith and *prayer of the earliest believers.

The passage speaks of the humility and *obedience of Christ, not in terms of incidents taken from the course of his life, or of speculations about his psychological motivation. What we have is an affirmation of more than temporal and local import. Christ freely and willingly exchanges equality with *God for the form of a slave. He moves from the divine realm to the human, from the world of eternity to the world of time, making himself open and vulnerable to death, death on the *cross. As a direct consequence of this God raises him up, giving him the name and honour which is due to God alone (cf. Isa. 45: 23, 'To me every knee shall bow, every tongue shall swear.'). This exaltation, far from taking away from the divine glory, is itself 'to the glory of God the Father'; the fulfilment of an eternal design.

In the context of the epistle the passage emerges from an exhortation to the Christians to be of one mind, united in one *love. They are to have amongst themselves the mind which was in Christ Jesus. In its original setting, therefore, the purpose of the passage was practical rather than speculative. Its formulations arise out of the context of Christian prayer and praise.

So through the centuries, the idea of the divine self-emptying has continued at times to receive powerful and poetic doxological expression, as in Charles *Wesley's lines.

> He left his father's throne above—
> So free, so infinite his grace—
> Emptied himself of all but love
> And bled for Adam's helpless race.
> 'Tis mercy all, immense and free,
> For, O my God, it found out me.

In the last hundred years or so, however, the idea of kenosis has come to play a more considerable part in dogmatic and apologetic theology. Already in the mid-19th century, German Lutheran writers such as Thomasius began to open up this line of approach. In Britain the kenotic theory expressed by Charles Gore in his 1891 Bampton Lectures, *The Incarnation of the Son of God*, and developed further by him in subsequent books, had considerable influence. The question was being discussed in a situation in which much in classical *christology, the idea for instance that Jesus constantly enjoyed the beatific vision, or that he possessed infallibility not only in ethical but also in factual matters, seemed altogether at variance with the gospel evidence for his *humanity. Could the Jesus of classical christology, it was asked, really have uttered the cry of abandonment recorded by Mark (15: 34)? Part of the deep uneasiness felt in this period emerges from the modern tendency to think in historical and psychological categories, as opposed to the ontological categories taken for granted in much early theology.

Another more recent theological exploration of the idea of kenosis has arisen within the *Eastern Orthodox tradition, in particular in the writing of Vladimir Lossky and John Zizioulas. It is particularly significant that this discussion should arise within the Christian tradition which most prizes its faithfulness to the patristic heritage. In this view the self-emptying and obedience of the Son is seen as showing the ultimate characteristic of all true personal being. The *person is one who can go beyond him/herself in a movement of total self-giving. So in a paradoxical way God goes beyond his own nature, transcends himself in order to enter into his own creation, and in doing so opens the possibility for his human creation to transcend itself, to go beyond itself, in a responsive movement of total self-giving.

In this approach the concept of kenosis thus becomes central to our understanding of what it is to be human, made in the divine image and likeness, in order to be caught up into the exchange of love of which Paul speaks in the passage in Philippians.

See also INCARNATION.   A. M. Allchin

Carpenter, James, *Gore: A Study in Liberal Catholic Thought* (1960).
Henry, P., 'Kenose', *Dictionnaire de la Bible*, suppl. 5 (1957), cols. 7–161.
Jenkins, D. E., *The Glory of Man* (1966).
Lawton, J. S., *Conflict in Christology: A Study of British and American Theology 1889–1914* (1947).
Lossky, Vladimir, *The Mystical Theology of The Eastern Church* (1957).
Zizioulas, John, *Being as Communion* (1985).

kerygma, which means 'proclamation' or 'announcement' in Greek, came to be applied in 20th-century theology to the essential message preached in the NT. This usage develops *Paul's reference to the word in Romans 16: 25 where it appears in parallel to *gospel and to 'the *revelation of the mystery long hidden but now made known'. Modern writers who endorse the term are seeking some timeless core of Christian teaching that is immune to the assaults of historical or cultural criticism. For *Bultmann, its most famous advocate, the kerygma is not to be defined in terms of any content, but rather can be identified by its effect of bringing about the transformation of the hearer, or the experience of *redemption. Support for this view is found in Paul's apparent lack of interest in the historical *Jesus. Others, for instance C. H. Dodd, insist that even for Paul there is a historical bedrock in Jesus' life, death, and *Resurrection that is common to all Christian *preaching and part and parcel of the kerygma.

On either account, there is a presupposition that a unified essence can be discovered either in the NT or in some reconstructed earlier stage of oral proclamation. Furthermore, by implication the business of the *church is to transmit this essential message. The faithful transmission of the kerygma, however, may depend on abandoning the historical and linguistic trappings in which it has been handed down. What brought an ancient audience to belief may leave contemporary hearers unmoved or even alienated. Bultmann's programme of *demythologization is one response to this perception.

Such assumptions can be challenged. The focus on preaching reflects a Protestant emphasis that downplays the importance of traditions conveyed through the communal practice of the church and particularly in the sacraments. Karl *Rahner's account redresses the balance to some extent here. The effort to find a unified kerygma risks failing to take account of the NT's diversity. In practice, one element in this variety tends to receive privileged treatment while others are in danger of being distorted to fit this preconception. At work here is a variant of the genetic fallacy, which seeks to ground the authority and unity of the Christian community in one generative experience underlying all the confusions and accidents of the human and historical. The focus on kerygma also fosters a rather individualistic vision, concentrating on the isolated experience of transformation. Pushed too far, this leads to the *Gnostic conception of the gospel as a key to enlightenment. A contrary line can be taken which sees the mission of the Christian community as something expressed in its continual grappling with human diversity through time.

The concept of kerygma served as a useful rallying-point for those theologians who sought to recover the living engagement with the biblical text that both *liberalism and *fundamentalism tend to bypass. As with all correctives, however, it proves inadequate when made the linchpin of theological thought.

Hugh S. Pyper

Bultmann, R., *Jesus and the Word* (1935).
Evans, C. S., *The Historical Jesus and the Jesus of Faith* (1996).
Lemcio, E. E., *The Past of Jesus in the Gospels* (1991).
Rahner, K., and Lehmann, K., *Kerygma and Dogma* (1969).

Kierkegaard, Søren (1813–55).

It has been claimed that all western philosophy consists of footnotes to Plato; it seems quite as justifiable to assert that the history of 20th-century theology and philosophy largely arises from conflicting readings or misreadings of Kierkegaard. *Barth, Buber, *Bultmann, Derrida, Heidegger, Levinas, Marcel, Sartre, *Tillich, *Wittgenstein are only a few of the diverse thinkers who acknowledge their debt to Kierkegaard, although that debt is often greater than the acknowledgement would indicate.

It is striking that the idiosyncratic works of a *Scandinavian theological writer in a minority language have been so influential. These very features of his authorship, of course, increase the possibility of misreading. For most of his readers, Kierkegaard has been accessible only in translation. His virtuosic use of Danish and the poetic and literary values intrinsic to his style are obscured. Another consequence is that his carefully planned output was published piecemeal in other languages. For instance, the fact that the posthumous polemic, the *Attack upon Christendom*, was the first work of Kierkegaard's to appear in German tended to brand him for German scholars as the champion of an individualistic and headily radical Christianity. Also obscured is the context: the philosophical, theological, and social debates of Copenhagen in its Golden Age, to which Kierkegaard was a witty, ironic, sometimes scathing, always controversial, but above all passionately engaged contributor.

Yet even for his Danish contemporaries the sheer quantity of his writing, much of it produced in an astonishing burst of creativity in the last ten years of his life, formed an obstacle to comprehending his message. In addition to twenty-five published works, his papers and journals run to some thirty thousand pages. This mass is compounded by its variety. Kierkegaard deploys a whole cast of pseudonyms. The relationships between these figures and how representative they are of his own positions have remained vexed questions. Only too often, later authors have cited quotations from the pseudonymous works as a simple statement of Kierkegaard's own views whereas he specifically pleads that they should be attributed to the pseudonyms. This highly self-reflexive view of authorship, with its roots in German *Romanticism, extends also to the writings under his own name which are shot through with *humour and irony, often missed by earnest commentators.

All this matters the more because at the heart of Kierkegaard's authorship is a concern with the process of communication itself. If we are to believe his own account in the posthumously published *Point of View of my Work as an Author*, his whole literary production was designed from the beginning as an exercise in communicating the Christian message to those who are hardest to reach: those nominal Christians who make free with the words of the gospel without taking on board the radical challenge of its claims to the whole basis of their existence. How was the full force of its impact to be recovered? For all his *philosophical and literary interests, Kierkegaard was at heart a preacher, or better still, in the true sense of the word an evangelist, although he always insisted that he wrote as one 'without authority'. His work is often at its most original where he turns to a particular problematic biblical text and teases out its implications.

In wrestling with these issues, Kierkegaard's prime resource was his own experience. Hence, it is hardly surprising that many students of his work regard his writings as a treasure trove of *psychological insights into the man and reduce his most startling insights to particular comments on his own circumstances. So much writing on Kierkegaard has been bedevilled by this that it is necessary briefly to review his life if only to sound this note of caution.

He was born and died in Copenhagen. Apart from a couple of brief sojourns in Berlin, his whole life was spent within the limited world of the Danish capital. Yet out of the events of a seemingly unexciting life he managed to create a vast body of writing, endlessly poring over his own melancholy. This he felt was inherited from his father and it was the reason he confided to himself for the seminal event of his existence—his deliberate adoption of a devil-may-care persona to provoke his fiancée Regina Olsen into breaking off their engagement. This distressing but hardly earth-shattering event fills countless pages of his journals and appears in many guises throughout his writings.

The other event of comparable impact was his dispute with the *Corsair*, a satirical journal. He complained that he was the only honourable man in Copenhagen not to be lampooned and then became, unsurprisingly, the target of a fierce attack that concentrated on the fact that his trouser legs were never of the same length. Again, this seems trivial, but Kierkegaard spoke of the horror of being 'trampled to death by geese'.

One can read his publications as a brilliant but pathologically obsessive reworking of his peculiar psychic reactions. It is at least as possible, however, that it was precisely the cast of his theological and philosophical genius that laid him open to these experiences. In any case, it is well to be wary of Kierkegaard in confessional mood. 'Kierkegaard', as much as any of his pseudonyms, may be the product of his literary imagination. What unifies these events, moreover, is that they revolve around the ambivalence of communication between the multiple personae which we adopt or have forced upon us, and demand reflection on the nature of the self in its relations to others and to God.

Central to Kierkegaard's work is his insistence on the absolute qualitative difference between God and the human. Any notion of a synthesis between the two which would open the way for an assimilation of the Christian life to the civil and ecclesiastical establishment is anathema to him. Such a radical difference, however, would seem to make any communication between God and the human impossible. For Kierkegaard, it is precisely that impossibility that came about in the *Incarnation. *Jesus is the absolute paradox of the conjunction of divine and human, the God-man. Like *Anselm in *Cur deus homo*, Kierkegaard bases his *christology on the fact that only such a figure could allow for communication between God and humanity.

In this refusal to soften the paradox, Kierkegaard is standing out against the prevailing Hegelianism of the young Danish intellectuals of his day. *Hegel's central theological insight was to see the reconciliation of the difference between God and man in the synthesis that Jesus represented. For Hegel, God is free because he is able to manifest the qualities intrinsic to his nature; Kierkegaard's God is free because he has infinite possibility. *The Sickness unto Death* makes explicit a further implication: 'since everything is possible for God, then God is this—that everything is possible'.

Paradoxically, it is the *impossibility* of Jesus as the God-man that Kierkegaard sees as constituting his salvific role. As the concrete instance of the impossible actualized, he bursts the bonds of the necessity that masquerades as possibility in the Hegelian account. As Kierkegaard remarks in *Judge for Yourselves!*, considered as mere possibility, Christianity seems easy, attracting the plaudits of the crowd. What an illusion, however, if someone imagines that by instantiating this possibility he would draw even greater acclaim. The gospels show that the presence of God in Jesus did not lead to universal recognition of his power, but on the contrary to scandal and offence, culminating in charges of blasphemy and the crucifixion.

This means that Kierkegaard denies that there is any effect of *time on this response. The eyewitness to Jesus' earthly life or the 19th-century theologian with the benefit of nearly two thousand years of reflection are alike in the difficulty they face in comprehending the scandalous fact of God become man. The much-quoted phrase from the *Concluding Unscientific Postscript* that 'truth is subjective' comes into play here. In context, this does not mean that it is up to each individual to determine *truth with no regard to evidence, as if to say, 'Jesus is God if I choose to believe he is.' Kierkegaard is not a simple relativist. It is rather that even given the evidence, human beings can manifestly stand in front of the objectively presented crucified Jesus and still refuse to acknowledge the consequences for themselves of what is happening before their very eyes.

The common error is to suppose that the Kierkegaardian subject has some form of true existence prior to the fact of God's coming in Christ and is thus capable of making some objective decision. One is only a subject because one has acknowledged that coming. Truth is subjective because truth constitutes the subject. This differs crucially from the existentialist misapprehension that it is choice itself that constitutes the subject.

For Kierkegaard, the self is a process that is incomplete without the relationship to God. 'Man is not yet a self,' he declares. His insistence on the necessity of becoming an individual, which can be read as carrying a tone of *Nietzschian defiance, is actually a call for the surrender of the self in any narrowly egotistic sense. Nor is it in the end a call to repudiate society and human relationships, although sometimes he seems close to advocating this. It is only as an individual in this sense that one can hope to enter into meaningful relationships. What Kierkegaard attacks is the illusion of sociability that he calls the 'mass'. Only by extracting oneself from the mass can one begin to build a truly human social life.

The failure to become a self brings on despair, prompted by the feeling of *Angst*, translated 'dread' or 'anxiety'. Two of his most profound psychological studies, *The Concept of Dread* and *The Sickness unto Death*, explore the relationship between angst, sin, and despair in a dizzying virtuosity of insight. Fundamentally, however, these also relate to the ideas of possibility and necessity. Angst arises out of the awareness of the possibility of choice. Even before they sinned, Adam and Eve felt angst, because the existence of the forbidden created a possibility that they could not grasp. But both possibility and necessity carry the potential to reduce the existing individual to despair because both seem to reduce the scope for meaningful choice. Too much possibility leads to anxious indecision, too much necessity to anxious fatalism. The only cure for such despair is the much-quoted 'leap of faith' (an expression not often used by Kierkegaard) whereby trust in the infinite possibility of God reorients and indeed brings about authentic existence.

Once again it is maintaining the right relationship between possibility, necessity, and actuality that is the key to much of Kierkegaard's thought. His account of the development of the individual is a case in point. Commentators often lift this as a system straight from complex pseudonymous works; all our earlier caveats should be recalled. The system extracted lays out a series of stages of life: the aesthetic, the ethical, and the religious, the latter sometimes subdivided into 'religiousness A', a general religiousness and 'religiousness B', the seizing of the *paradox of Christianity. These relate once again to the notions of the possible and the actual. The aesthetic stage is one in which the world seems all possibility, all play, because of a profound scepticism over the notion that any possibility can truly become actualized. The roles and poses of the aesthetic stage are so many masks that can have no real transforming effect on the unreality of the human being. The ethical stage, however, believes in choice. Possibilities can and must be actualized, not simply by reference to the individual, but to the universal consequences of the choice. Here, however, the figure of *Abraham in *Fear and Trembling* interposes, Abraham who shows his trust in God by preparing to sacrifice his son, an act that no ethical system could condone. The religious stage, however, is the one that truly lives out the claim that 'God is that all things are possible', and, in particular, that the dead can be restored to life or that, in choosing between two possibilities and renouncing one, one can gain the benefit of both possibilities.

The temptation felt by many to seek a coherent philosophical system in Kierkegaard's work is liable to lead to frustration. He himself always maintained that his role was to be an irritant and a corrective, the pinch of pepper in the stew. It is certainly possible to criticize his writings for irrationalism, for a defective doctrine of the Holy Spirit, for what may seem clear misogyny and unpalatable *antisemitism, and he is the last person who would accept being excused as a child of his time. These criticisms can be debated and at times answered, but his real significance is not in his systematics so much as in the mode of communication he adopts, or, more truthfully, in his awareness of the inextricable links between these two.

Many partial readings have led to many Kierkegaards. He has been seen as the champion of an ahistorical approach to Christianity who allows later thinkers to leap the chasm between the historical *Jesus and the religious experience of contemporary believers.

In the face of biblical criticism and historical doubt, he provides an alternative concept of truth. It is not much of a step for others to read him as a champion of the idea that Christianity is an expression of psychological needs and constructions with no connection to objective truth. On the other hand, he has been read as the radical champion of the true absurdity of Christianity in the face of the structures of established religion: the young Barth especially was fired by the iconoclasm of his later works. His hermeneutics have been heralded as deconstructionism *avant la lettre* yet also taken up by biblicist Protestants inspired by his reverence for the scriptures. Yet others have taken him as the 'melancholy Dane', the forerunner of the analysis of despair and alienation that so characterized 20th-century thought. He is claimed as the hero or villain, depending on one's point of view, who most clearly sounded the battle cry for the individual, either the defiant champion of true *freedom or the tortured guru of the fractured and destructive solipsism so often bewailed in modern theology.

The current resurgence of interest in his work may reflect an uneasiness about the various projects of *demythologization, secularism, liberalism, *neo-orthodoxy, and *fundamentalism that came to the fore in the 20th century. All these have been profoundly influenced by readings of Kierkegaard's work that have fallen to one side or another of the paradox that he insisted on holding in tension. As the projects of the 20th century peter out, the prospect of new shoots from that common root will form a vital resource for the Christian thinkers of the new millennium.   **Hugh S. Pyper**

A complete annotated edition of Kierkegaard's works is in preparation under the editorship of H. V. and E. H. Hong (Princeton University Press).

Ferguson, H., *Melancholy and the Critique of Modernity* (1995).

Gouwens, D. J., *Kierkegaard as Religious Thinker* (1996).

Hannay, A., *Kierkegaard* (1983).

King, G. H., *Existence, Thought, Style* (1996).

Matuštík, M., and Westphal, M. (eds.), *Kierkegaard in Post/Modernity* (1995).

Pattison, G., *Kierkegaard and the Crisis of Faith* (1997).

Kingdom of God.

According to the first three gospels, the central theme of the preaching of *Jesus was that the Kingdom of *God had drawn near, and in some sense had actually arrived. But in what sense, and what did Jesus mean by the phrase? Debate on those questions has been intense over the last 150 years. Jesus apparently assumed that his hearers would understand the phrase 'Kingdom of God' (or 'Kingdom of Heaven'—'Heaven' is a synonym for God): it is therefore worth asking what it meant in the OT and in Jewish writings of the period to the time of Jesus. From the establishment of the Israelite monarchy, and possibly earlier, God was thought of as king over his people or, as in *Isaiah 40–66 and elsewhere, over all peoples. He manifested his *kingship mainly in two ways: through his 'mighty acts' in the history of *Israel from the *exodus onwards and, in a cosmic context, as creator and king whose assumption of his throne was probably celebrated annually in the worship of the second *Temple.

In the subsequent writings of Judaism the same themes reappear, but in altered form. God's 'mighty acts' tend more and more to be connected with his hoped-for future intervention to restore the broken fortunes of the people and defeat its enemies, world empires included; and, in their concentration on their own sad state, the people think more of God's permanent sovereignty as it manifests itself in their *obedience to his law (see LAW, BIBLICAL), which rabbis refer to as 'taking upon oneself the yoke of the kingdom'. The researches of G. Dalman showed conclusively a century ago that God's Kingdom (*malkuth* in Hebrew, *basileia* in Greek) refers primarily to his kingly rule, his activity in the world, rather than to any area over which he reigns. The phrase is rare in the writings of the time just before Jesus, but in the Aramaic Targum (paraphrase) of Isaiah, which may have been known to him, it refers to God's intervention on behalf of his people in their restoration from *exile. Similarly with Jesus: the summary of his proclamation in Mark 1: 15, 'the time has arrived; the Kingdom of God is upon you,' speaks of God acting in strength. The best commentary on it is Jesus' announcement in the corresponding context in Luke 4: 16–21, where he quotes the programme of God's servant in Isaiah 61: 1–2a, and says 'today in your hearing this text has come true'.

Because this theme of God's action was so central to Jesus, the Kingdom of God has tended to become a cover-phrase for varied understandings of that action in the world. This is evident in the story of research over the last 200 years. In the optimistic evolutionism of the latter part of the 19th century it was easy to equate God's rule with the growth of communities (including especially the *church) where his will was done. Albrecht Ritschl, perhaps the most important figure in this movement, insisted also that God's love 'reached out beyond' all 'this-worldly' possibilities, and Adolf Harnack could speak of the Kingdom as 'God himself, in his power'. A totally 'this-worldly' conception of the Kingdom thus never quite captured the field. It was Ritschl's son-in-law, Johannes Weiss, whose work revealed instead a Jesus whose expectation was of a wholly 'other-worldly' kind: Jesus announced a Kingdom that 'would come down to earth and abolish this world', a Kingdom that humans could never establish although they could enter it (e.g. Matt. 5: 20; 7: 21; Mark 9: 47; 10: 23) and that would be the end of the present age and the beginning of a wholly different 'age to come'. Weiss and Albert Schweitzer effected a revolution in the understanding of the Kingdom which has had enduring effects. Jesus was not an *apocalypticist, one who believes that he has been given the secrets of God's drastic future shake-up of the world, but his preaching and his life were wholly *eschatological, that is concerned with the 'last things', with God's great final act of rescue, which could never be undone or superseded, and which was beginning with him, his deeds, and his words.

That eschatological nature of Jesus' whole ministry made it seem totally alien to the modern world, in the view of Weiss and Schweitzer. The next generation of theologians, *Bultmann, *Barth, and others, accepted the eschatology but found ways of circumventing its apparent expectation that this world would rapidly come to an end. The early Christians undoubtedly believed that the ascended Christ, who was Son of Man, would soon return (1 Thess. 4: 16–17; 1 Cor. 15: 51–2, etc.) and it seems that Jesus himself shared this expectation (e.g. Mark 9: 1; 13: 30 but cf. 13: 32). Jesus must have proclaimed a Kingdom that was both present (e.g. Matt. 12: 28, Luke 11: 20) and future (e.g. Mark 14: 25 and the prayer 'Thy Kingdom come') but the relation between present and future remains hard to elucidate, and is bound up with the interpretation of his *parables, their meaning for the early Christians, and their possible meaning for him.

To summarize Jesus' teaching on the Kingdom in a few sentences is impossible. But it is vital that it discloses a conception of God's rule that can be illustrated from ordinary processes and events in the Galilee Jesus knew, and to that extent there must be a continuity between this age and the age to come. God is going out of his way to rescue sinners and the poor; this is his *joy (Luke 15). His rule, which he alone can bring, demands reception but can be rejected; this, and other features of Jesus' teaching, already qualify the thoroughgoing eschatology that has sometimes been attributed to him. The integration of his hopes and beliefs—hopes for the restoration of Israel, as recent scholars have stressed, and for the coming of the Gentiles into God's Kingdom too—with his deeds and his fate, his death and *Resurrection, is no easy matter either, and at this point interpretation of the texts and theological evaluation are inextricably intertwined. Are we today to think of Jesus himself as the Kingdom (as *Origen said), or does this obscure his own proclamation of its essential futurity?

Since the Resurrection Christians have spoken both of a present or future (that is, *millenarian) kingdom (reign) of Christ and of a present and future Kingdom of God. The understanding of the former depends in part on the interpretation of such passages as 1 Corinthians 15: 20–8 and the pictorial allusions in the book of *Revelation. The understanding of the latter has always also depended on other historical and cultural factors. Sometimes the two have been identified.

In the early centuries *Augustine's City of God was the most influential exposition of what the Kingdom of God could mean, on earth and beyond it; he related it closely to but did not identify it with, the church. In medieval times the two became identified; later thought has sundered them. Since the *Reformation much Christian political thought has been concerned with the relation between the Kingdom of God and the kingdom(s) of this world; are the two to be thought of as in some sense parallel, even independent, realms (as in the *Lutheran tradition), or are the latter rather subordinate to or enclosed within the former (Barth and others)?

All modern discussions of the Kingdom have been influenced by the eschatological understanding of Jesus. God is king, and his kingship is expressed in a real but also an anticipatory way, in the present exaltation of Jesus which constitutes the hope of his final triumph. The Resurrection is an act of new creation, and as such is in itself a thrust towards the fulfilment of God's rule everywhere, both within historical processes, where liberation of the oppressed is the work of God who liberated Israel and liberates everyone in Christ, and beyond all historical process, when the true meaning and reality of the Kingdom of God will at last become clear. For many modern Christians a concern for the 'Kingdom', relating to the world in all its dimensions, prevents over-preoccupation with the fortunes of the 'church'. Indeed the two are easily contrasted though a critical interplay between them may be both what best represents the NT as a whole and what the inner exigencies of contemporary Christian life require. Theologians of *hope and of *liberation in particular have found it essential to speak of the Kingdom in such a way that Jesus' words and deeds two millennia ago can become his words and deeds for today. Nor does the fact that monarchy—the rule of one person—is unfashionable in a *democratic world make the image of the Kingdom irrelevant: God remains one, and personal, and active.   **R. S. Barbour**

Barbour, R. S. (ed.), *The Kingdom of God and Human Society* (1993).
Beasley-Murray, G. R., *Jesus and the Kingdom of God* (1986).
Gutiérrez, G., *The God of Life* (1982).
Lundstrom, G., *The Kingdom of God in the Teaching of Jesus* (1963).
Moltmann, J., *The Trinity and the Kingdom of God* (1980).
Perrin, N., *The Kingdom of God in the Teaching of Jesus* (1963).
Pixley, G. V., *God's Kingdom* (1981).
Sanders, E. P., *Jesus and Judaism* (1985).
Wright, N. T., *Jesus and the Victory of God* (1996).

kingship represented, until late modern times, the supreme expression of earthly power. As such, it was persistently sacralized. It was sanctioned by divinity, mediated divinity, and symbolized divinity, in numerous ancient Near-Eastern, African, and Asian cultural systems. As mediator the king was endowed with *priestly character; thus the Canaanite *Melchizedek encountered by *Abraham was both 'king of Salem' and 'priest of God most High (El-Elyon)' (Gen. 14: 18). Kings were divinized at their death and, in some societies, in life as well; the whole order of nature might be seen as dependent upon the king's health. The rituals of kingship, continually emphasizing its divine or sacred character, were equally fertility rites both for humankind and for nature. Moreover, the kingship of the earthly ruler symbolized and modelled that of the heavenly and it would be hard to establish which derived from which.

It is uncertain whether the Israelites gave the title of king to God until they themselves possessed kings. Israel's demand for a king is portrayed in 1 Samuel 8 as desertion of divine *authority, but something none the less sanctioned by God through Samuel's consecration of Saul. Israel's demand in this was to 'be like other nations', but its emphatic monotheism excluded divinization of the king though not a considerable royal *mythology centred upon *David and his predicted *messianic descendant. The establishment of the monarchy paralleled a developing cult of Yahweh as king, demonstrated especially in the 'psalms of accession to the throne' (47; 93; 96–9): 'Yahweh is king' was something to 'proclaim to the nations'. It remained better to have Yahweh as king than a king thought to be 'divine', for Yahweh's rule was universal.

If the teaching of Jesus centred upon the coming of God's kingdom, it is clear that the two strands in Israel's kingship—Yahweh's and the human Davidic succession—came together in early Christian belief about him. Especially in later NT literature, the '*Kingdom of God' becomes increasingly the kingdom of Christ. Already in Matthew 13: 14, the Son of Man will judge 'his kingdom', something clearly no different from the 'kingdom of heaven'. For *Paul we have been taken into 'the kingdom of the Son' (Col. 1: 13), while 2 Peter, one of the latest NT works, can speak of 'the eternal kingdom of our Lord and Saviour Jesus Christ' (1: 11). This transition is made easier by Jesus' inheritance of the earthly Davidic kingship stressed at the start of both Matthew's gospel (2: 2) and Luke's (1: 32). Jesus is supremely king because he is son both of God and of David, but in John's gospel, under Pilate's interrogation, he reinterprets his kingdom away from power to being a matter of witnessing to *truth (18: 37).

The kingship of Christ has ever after been central to Christian faith; he is both king and 'lord' (again traditionally a title at once royal and divine). The feast of Christ the King is, admittedly, a modern one, instituted by Pius XI in 1925, to challenge the mostly far-from-Christian powers of the contemporary world, to assert Christ's total sovereignty and become a rallying-point for 'Catholic Action' within the secular realm. The affirmation of Christ as King of life and *love has, however, been a constant in Christian devotion. On one side there is the powerfully triumphalist *Christus vincit, Christus regnat, Christus imperat*, sung at English coronations from the 11th century, on the other the image of a man crowned with thorns.

Where did all this leave Christian kings? When Christians first came to power in the 4th century, in the Roman empire and elsewhere, kings had to steer a course that avoided the formal divinization of earlier Roman emperors, yet retained as much sacralization as possible. The prototype was provided by *Constantine, who ensured that the legacy of a 'divine' Caesar survived with an *apostolic, quasi-*episcopal, face-lift, and then by Charlemagne. In Rome on Christmas Day 800 at the beginning of the papal mass Charles arose from praying before St Peter's tomb to be crowned by Leo III who then knelt before him in homage, the only pope ever to do obeisance to a western emperor. Charlemagne was both Caesar and the 'New David'.

The Israelite example would be regularly appealed to hereafter. Coronations were made as awe-inspiring and *sacramental as possible; consecrated kings in a state of grace were held to possess quasi-miraculous powers of healing; royal authority could be claimed as unchallengeable precisely because it was both received directly from God and existed as a sort of sacrament of God's own kingly authority. The consequent tension between claim and reality is superbly drawn in *Shakespeare's *Richard II*. As a theory the 'divine right of kings' was hammered out to counter the medieval *papacy with its own monarchical claims symbolized by the triple crown, a model of theocratic government that necessarily cut down the authority of emperors and kings.

'Divine right' as argued in anti-papal texts such as *Dante's *Monarchy* began to prevail from the 14th century as the main working theory for Christian government, most especially in France and England. In the post-*Reformation world it became the accepted politico-religious orthodoxy for Catholics, high-church *Anglicans, and *Lutherans alike. This was especially true for the 17th century, when it was upheld by James VI and I in *The True Law of Free Monarchies*, by Robert Filmer in *Patriarcha*, and by the *Gallican Articles* (1682). When the Roman Catholic James II was deposed in 1688, William Sancroft, archbishop of Canterbury, and five other Protestant bishops were so committed to the doctrines of divine right and non-resistance that they left office rather than accept his Protestant successor. While in the Catholic Church belief in divine right had long been a mark of Gallicanism, in the 19th century it revived for a while in the work of de Maistre and others in an alliance with *ultramontanism against the advance of liberal and secular views of political authority.

*Calvinists were never sympathetic to a doctrine of the divine right of kings and it waned wherever Calvinism prevailed, as it did, more widely, in the face of the advance of more consensual and *democratic models of political order. Among Catholics too, leading *Jesuit theologians like Bellarmine and Suarez had never accepted it. From the end of the 18th century, the American example of republicanism helped demonstrate that monarchy was not needed for good government. If Catholics were slow to come to terms with these developments, the 20th century saw them too move away, under the influence of *Maritain and others, from monarchical to democratic models for political society.

Where does that leave the theology of kingship? Firmly underpinned, as it was, by the practice of earthly monarchies, it both employed their symbols and appeared in their light as an appropriate and comprehensible expression of divine authority. That comprehensibility has now all but disappeared. In a world where kings have either ceased to exist or become insignificant, the analogy of royal power provides nothing to assist the appreciation of divinity. In practice, without being formally discarded, royal attributes are used less and less in the imaginative depiction of God and may even be a burden for *contextual theology in a modern, post-monarchical world. Yet in Jesus himself the kingly image involved not enhancement of the glories of earthly monarchy but discontinuity: the man hailed as a king when mounted only on a donkey (Matt. 21: 5), his crown only one of thorns. The point of his kingship, set against that of temporal kings, may remain unaffected by their passing precisely because it was so paradoxically different. Such a kingship could still be that of God.   **Adrian Hastings**

Figgis, J. N., *The Theory of the Divine Right of Kings*, 2nd edn. (1914), repr. (1965).

Filmer, Robert, *Patriarcha and other Writings*, ed. J. P. Sommerville (1991).

Johnson, A. R., *Sacral Kingship in Ancient Israel* (1955).

Sommerville, J. P., 'From Suarez to Filmer: A Reappraisal', *Historical Journal*, 25 (1982), 525–40.

Ullmann, W., *Principles of Government and Politics in the Middle Ages* (1961).

Kirschbaum, Charlotte von, see von KIRSCHBAUM.

Kolakowski, Leszek (1927–). Born in Radom, Poland, Kolakowski studied philosophy at Lodz University and then entered the philosophy faculty at Warsaw. He was a member of the Communist Party, and his early publications were of an orthodox *Marxist nature, dealing with medieval and contemporary Catholic philosophy. However Kolakowski soon became critical of party doctrine and was influential in the development of intellectual liberalization which led to the Polish 'spring' of 1956. Increasingly disenchanted with Marxist orthodoxy, Kolakowski was one of the major proponents of intellectual dissent in eastern Europe. Expelled from the Communist Party in 1966 and from his Chair at Warsaw University in 1968, he moved to the west, where he has been based at All Souls College, Oxford, and the University of Chicago.

As a philosopher of religion, Kolakowski's major scholarly work is *Religious Consciousness and Church Affiliation*, published in Warsaw in 1965, a study of *mystical and heterodox movements in 17th-century Europe with emphasis on the irreconcilable dialectic between *grace and *law, individual conscience and institutional necessity. During the 1970s Kolakowski settled accounts with his past in the magisterial three-volume *Main Currents of Marxism* (1978), in which he traces the increasing bankruptcy of the Marxist tradition. Returning to his first interests, he produced a highly original treatise entitled *Religion* (1982), which combines his deep knowledge of the history of *natural theology with an *existentialist approach reminiscent of *Dostoevsky. Kolakowski is a brilliant essayist, and his more recent collection *Modernity on Endless Trial* (1990), particularly the third section on the dilemmas of the Christian legacy, offers the best introduction to his thought,

Fundamental to Kolakowski's philosophy of religion is his emphasis on the is/ought dichotomy. He is despairingly fair to both sides and insists on the vanity both of attempts to give religious faith a rational foundation and of the claim that the rules of empiricism and rationalism are themselves any more than matters of faith. For him, 'the search for an ultimate foundation is as much an unremovable part of human culture as the denial of the legitimacy of this search'. A stoic, even tragic, philosopher in the mould of *Pascal, on whom he has written in *God Owes us Nothing: Brief Remarks on Pascal and on the Spirit of Jansenism* (1995), Kolakowski is at his most impressive in pointing up the unpleasant and insoluble dilemmas present in the human condition and the consequent necessity of moderation in the drive for consistency.

David McLellan

Koyama, Kosuke (1929–), theologian and educator.

Koyama was born in Tokyo, educated both in *Japan and in the United States (Ph.D. from Princeton Theological Seminary in 1959), and began his professional career as a missionary of the United Church of Christ in Japan at Thailand Theological Seminary in Chiang Mai, Thailand (1960–8). He was dean of the South East Asia Graduate School of Theology (1968–74), senior lecturer in religious studies at University of Otago in New Zealand (1974–9), and professor of ecumenics and world Christianity at Union Theological Seminary, New York, from 1980 to his retirement in 1996.

As a boy growing up and listening to the biblical stories narrated by his grandfather, his early mental world was informed by the *dialogue between the culture of the bible and the nature-oriented culture of Japan. The John R. Mott Lectures given by Visser't Hooft entitled 'Accommodation, True or False', at the Asian Faith and Order Conference in Hong Kong in 1966, had a decisive impact upon Koyama's theological thought. In his first book *Waterbuffalo Theology* (1974; revised and expanded edition, 1999) he searches for a way to communicate the gospel in the context of the Buddhist—animistic culture of Thailand. This search was engaged at the converging of Japan devastated by war, Christian America under Eisenhower, and Thailand of Theravada *Buddhism.

The focus of Koyama's theology is *theologia crucis*, theology of the *cross, in which Jesus Christ, the central person, goes to the periphery. This perspective was sharpened in the encounter with *feminist, *black, and Jewish theologies during his days in New York. In the *theologia crucis* he finds the basis to refute the idolatry

that destroyed his country in 1945 and has caused countless tragedies in human history. Culture cannot provide the principle by which one can criticize idolatry. The theme of idolatry is the connecting link between Koyama's theology and his ethics.

Kosuke Koyama

Koyama, K., *Mt. Fuji and Mt. Sinai* (1984).
Irvin, Dale T., and Akinade, Akintunde E. (eds.), *The Agitated Mind of God: The Theology of Kosuke Koyama*, Festschrift (1996).

Küng, Hans (1928–), professor emeritus, University of *Tübingen.

Küng has been one of the most influential Roman Catholic voices in the 20th century. After his formative years as a student in Rome and Paris and as an officially appointed *peritus* (theological expert in attendance) at *Vatican II, the Swiss-born priest and theologian quickly became known for his ecclesiological works, beginning with an immediately pre-conciliar best-seller, *The Council and Reunion* (1960; ET 1961). In the light of a critical rereading of the gospels Küng proposed a thorough reform of the Roman Catholic *church, its teachings, and its hierarchical leadership. His book *Infallible? An Enquiry* (1970), in which he challenged the biblical and theological foundations of the *papacy, caused a major debate and eventually led the church authorities in 1979 to withdraw his teaching licence, needed by every state-appointed teacher of the Roman Catholic religion in Germany. However, Küng was able to continue his teaching and research in an independent institute within the University of Tübingen until his retirement in 1996.

Besides his ecclesiological concerns, Küng's theological project includes reflections on the major aspects of the Christian faith as well as on the relationship between the world *religions and on their common search for a *global ethic. Most of his books, such as *On Being a Christian* (1974), *Does God Exist?* (1978), *Eternal Life?* (1982), *Christianity and the World Religions* (1984), *Global Responsibility* (1990), *Judaism* (1992), and *Christianity* (1994), have been translated into many languages and reached a wide audience. Küng's attempt to demonstrate the reasonableness of faith in the God of Jesus Christ, to listen to the intellectual, cultural, ethical, political, and economic challenges of our time, to address the plurality of religious expressions in our world, and to develop an approach to *theology in which *faith and *world are critically co-related and, if necessary, contrasted, make him an important companion for many men and women searching for a critical faith.   **Werner G. Jeanrond**

Häring, H., *Hans Küng: Breaking Through* (1998).
Häring, H., and Kuschel, K-J., *Hans Küng: New Horizons for Faith and Thought* (1993).
Nowell, R., *A Passion for Truth: Hans Küng, A Biography* (1981).

laity. A theology of the laity is a well-intentioned mistake, chiefly a Roman Catholic and Orthodox mistake. Laicism in all its forms is always a response to clericalism, one mistake spawning another. The mistake arose as follows. Little by little, especially in the Middle Ages, every sort of activity proper to a Christian became confined by canon *law to the clergy, defined not theologically by *ordination but legally as those who, having received the tonsure, were subject to the church's courts. The more the church was clericalized the more it was fundamentally divided into two parts: active clergy and passive laity. The latter inevitably resented clerical pretensions, so much so that Boniface VIII with accustomed exaggeration declared in the Bull *Clericis Laicos* (1296) that it was a matter of history that lay people had always been opposed to the clergy.

When *Luther reasserted the idea of the *priesthood of all Christians, he undermined the doctrinal clericalism that had created the negative category of 'laity', that is to say, non-clergy. Instead he was affirming that all Christians share the same basic religious responsibilities, although in practice a quite considerable clergy–laity divide survived in most post-Reformation churches and was actually exacerbated by tendencies, such as the *Oxford Movement, to re-catholicize Protestantism. Within the Catholic Church, *par excellence*, the laity were expected to say their prayers and contribute money as needed, but otherwise to exercise no ecclesiastical role whatsoever. 'What is the province of the laity?', asked Mgr. Talbot, Pius IX's adviser on English affairs and Archbishop Manning's regular correspondent, 'To hunt, to shoot, to entertain.' From such a viewpoint, *Newman's essay 'On Consulting the Faithful in Matters of Doctrine' seemed dangerously bizarre. But then, in a modern, often hostile, world, the church increasingly found it needed its laity to do all sorts of things of a more *apostolic kind. Between the two world wars there developed in particular something called Catholic Action, which was defined in Rome as 'the participation of the laity in the apostolate of the hierarchy'. This heavily centralized attempt to mobilize the laity to defend the church's position in public life, while maintaining the theory that anything the laity did was essentially a delegation from the hierarchy, never really worked outside Italy and some *Latin American countries. Apart from Catholic Action, other forms of lay apostolate were, however, being promoted, grounded in a rediscovered recognition that it was of the essential nature of all Christian life entered through baptism

and confirmation to be active rather than passive. But such activity is not specifically lay, it is simply Christian.

*Vatican II came at a moment when 'Lay Apostolate' enthusiasm was running at a high and it was felt essential to say something thoroughly positive. Yet for the first two years not a single lay person was brought into the drafting commission and an idea of the laity profoundly shaped by clericalism remained dominant. The Council came to struggle with two conflicting models, both of which can be seen in its two principal texts on the subject—chapter 4 of *Lumen Gentium* and the *Decree on the Apostolate of Lay People* (*Apostolicam Actuositatem*). It was now generally agreed that the laity had 'their' apostolate and were not simply permitted, when things got rough for the church, to 'participate in the apostolate of the hierarchy'. But where did that apostolate come from, and in what did it consist?

One model still wanted the lay apostolate to be sharply contrasted with that of the clergy: the latter had a 'sacred ministry' concerned with 'salvation' and the church's own life; the laity, on the other hand, 'live in the world' and have a 'secular' task of 'engaging in temporal affairs' and achieving 'the renewal of the temporal order'. This disastrous dichotomy derived from the traditional definition of a mission of 'evangelization and sanctification' committed to the clergy and the consequent need to seek something 'other' for the laity. The Council's second model is very different. In this view the laity, like all the people (*laos*) of God, share in the priestly, prophetic, and kingly office of Christ. By *baptism and confirmation the *mission of *evangelization and sanctification belongs to everyone. It is, essentially, a mission 'in the world'. There is no area of apostolate from which the laity can rightfully be excluded, nor are they to be defined over against the clergy. There are, rather, a number of 'ministries', 'charisms', or 'vocations' to which different Christians are called, some involving ordination, others not. Moreover, the clergy have always shared responsibility for the 'renewal of the temporal order'. It is simply fantasy to speak of some people 'living in the world' while others are occupied in a different 'sacred' sphere. What, after all, could be more worldly than the activities of the Vatican Bank and so much else carried on within the Roman Curia?

These two theologies, while totally incompatible, remain inextricably entangled in the Council's documents, but also in the wider thinking of all Christianity's more clericalist traditions. The first model dominated the early drafts for the conciliar decree (drafts to which no lay person contributed); but the second model steadily advanced in the course of the council and is ascendant in the final text. It is found best, perhaps, in article 3 of the Decree, a late addition. However, it is no less clear that the first model returned to favour in some later Roman directives, particularly in the pontificate of *John Paul II. It is to be found, for instance, in canon 207 of the new Code of Canon Law as in the particularly retrograde and clericalist 'Instruction on Certain Questions Regarding the Collaboration of the Non-Ordained Faithful in the Sacred Ministry of the Priest' of 13 November 1997. The stated presupposition of this Instruction, explicitly approved by the pope, was that lay activity in the pastoral, preaching, and sacramental fields can only be justified by a shortage of priests. Canon 207 unambiguously declares that 'By divine institution, among Christ's faithful there are in the church sacred ministers, who in law are also called clerics; the others are called lay people'. There should be no 'others'. Just as the ordained are called to serve justice and community in the world, and only in that context can they also fulfil their evangelistic and sacramental ministries, so the laity, that is to say all members of the church, defined not as non-clerics but as Christians, are empowered by baptism and confirmation to participate actively in the full priestly and prophetic mission of the church, and only in that context can they also fulfil their 'royal' role of furthering justice in temporal affairs. As a matter of hard fact, the clergy and their monopolistic pretensions are fast fading away in Roman Catholicism as elsewhere. Such documents represent an anachronistic medieval model, sadly out of touch with the reality, shared by most churches, of an increasingly declericalized Christian life in which the category of 'laity' has become basically redundant.   **Adrian Hastings**

Congar, Yves, *Lay People in the Church* (1965).
Doohan, Leonard, *The Lay-Centred Church* (1984).
Klostermann, Ferdinand, 'Decree on the Apostolate of the Laity', in H. Vorgrimler (ed.), *Commentary on the Documents of Vatican II* (1969), iii. 273–404.
Parent, Rémi, *A Church of the Baptized* (1987).
Rademacher, William, *Lay Ministry* (1991).

language

language is the first great achievement of culture and the foundation of every subsequent achievement. Everything else in civilization, economy, politics, and *religion depends on the use of language in all its vast complexity. Moreover, every language in the world is roughly comparable in its range of subtlety, though not in its range of subjects nor in the subtlety with which each subject is addressed.

The beginning of *Genesis, echoed by the beginning of *John's gospel, portrays *God in terms of the spoken word, first to creation, then to *humanity. The language used was divine, *paradisal, or Adamic. The multiplicity of languages as we know them is depicted as originating with Babel (Gen. 11): a multitude of discordant tongues, none of them privileged. The discord is symbolically overcome with the first Christian *Pentecost (Acts 2) in terms of a unity of understanding despite a continued multiplicity of languages. The Pentecost experience suggests that no tongue is exclusively sacred for *Christianity. The church did, after all, meet the Hebrew Scriptures chiefly in their Greek Septuagintal form. The inspiration of scriptures, old and new, is felt to survive any leap of *translation, though theologians have argued over how far that could be so. In practice it is accepted as remaining in any honestly translated text, whether the language be Greek, Latin, Syriac, or Coptic. Only 'Amen' and 'Alleluia' would remain unchanged, anchoring all Christian speech, particularly *liturgical speech, in a single shared language community.

Christianity is, then, from the start, a multilingual community, but is soon made aware that there is no straight equivalence between any of the languages it uses. Moreover, all the languages we encounter or reconstruct share the inadequacies of the post-Babel situation, a matter of confusion and misunderstandings, never entirely overcome. Nowhere do we hear the divine *Word in a divine language but have to struggle to understand it while shaping human words for realities that surpass them. Yet the experience of scripture translation into hundreds of languages across two millennia justifies the conviction that meanings are communicable across any language barrier.

Each language, however, has its own agenda. Greek with its *philosophical inheritance forced the asking of questions and the use of a vocabulary different from the Hebrew. Yet it did not provide an agreed vocabulary. Thus terms relating to being, nature, and personal individuality such as *ousia, physis, hypostasis,* and *prosopon* were brought into theological use to explain the relationship of Son to Father in God, or of humanity to divinity in Christ, but with no single preceding meaning. Schools of thought, non-Christian or Christian, could define them as they chose. Moreover the comparable vocabulary in Latin, such as *substantia, natura,* or *persona,* offered no precise equivalence, any more than did any other language past or present. Accuracy in word usage depends, furthermore, on precise sense experiences, verification, or comparison. The more you move into realms where these are unavailable, the more language reflects personal or *poetic insight, never precisely replicated. *Metaphor, *allegory, and *analogy become central to language games, sharp but slippery tools for constructing worlds of meaning where the subjective, the imaginative, and the intuitive prevail over the demonstrable. But such areas of language depend more than any other on the particular culture of a society or individual.

Religious belief and its theological expression are, then, of necessity located within the most variable of linguistic areas. This can only be partially gainsaid by tying religion to a single culture or language, as to a considerable extent has been the case for Islam, and as happened to some extent with medieval Latin *Catholicism as well as Greek Orthodoxy. Christianity as a whole, on the contrary, because of its commitment to multiculturalism, translation, and, indeed, the inherent development of human thought, theology included, remains exceptionally open to the inherent relativity of language use in both *metaphysical and poetic modes.

It is not surprising that the doctrinal conflicts of the 4th and 5th centuries were largely about the use of words. If the agreed conciliar solutions—the *homoousios* (consubstantiality) of Father and Son proclaimed at *Nicaea and the 'one person in two natures' definition of *christology at *Chalcedon—were using an essentially non-biblical language to define what the bishops saw as biblical truth reformulated for a Greek Christian empire, they were demonstrating the ongoing dilemma of Christianity in regard to language use. The employment of all such terminology is not mistaken in principle but it is inherently contextual to a culture.

That does not make it merely subjective but it does mean that the subjective, culture-bound dimension of language is not removable from any formulation so as to allow a 'pure' statement of truth in a divine, pre-Babel tongue. The theology of the *via negativa* has always wisely insisted that language is inherently incapable of providing positive accounts of God because of the divine uniqueness and otherness. Much the same has to be true of both the hypostatic union and Christ's *eucharistic presence. In each case the mistake is to press language further than it can go in regard to explaining or describing the unique.

The way language controls Christian thought and expression is much more than a matter of certain classical formulas. The fact that Greek and Latin had the words *anthropos* and *homo* for the human being, quite distinct from the sexually distinguished *man (*andros*, *vir*), contrastable with *woman (*gune*, *mulier*), while modern European languages mostly use a single word for the two senses, has had fateful consequences. While *homo* fully embraced the sexes in their diversity, 'man' cannot do so without exceptional strain. Thus the credal proclamation that the Word became *homo* sounds very different in English where *homo* is replaced by 'man', the word used elsewhere to translate the very different *vir*. The semantic shift leads easily to the claim that a woman, not being a man (*vir*), cannot 'represent' Christ, 'who became man' (*homo*). In general, the use of male or female pronouns, required by most European languages, has reinforced the masculinization of God, something completely absent in, say, a Bantu language. The deep structures of language are clearly inescapable though it remains possible, with an effort, to surmount them in specific cases by insisting, for instance, when speaking in English, on the absolutely ungendered nature of God. For the most part, however, we think and express ourselves unconsciously and inevitably within the parameters of a given language.

As a matter of history Christian thought has greatly benefited from a series of dominant languages, which have contributed an important unifying dimension: Greek in the early centuries, Latin by the Middle Ages, then German until the modern dominance of English. Significant variant traditions have, however, also been firmly language-based: *Syriac in the patristic era, *Ethiopic, then both French and Russian as set against the 19th-century German hegemony. Will *Chinese become a principal vehicle of Christian thought in the 21st century? The more tongues of very different language trees are used creatively for the expression of Christian thought, the more the openness of Christianity to the shaping influence of language becomes not an impoverishment but a source of strength and renewal.

See also RELIGIOUS LANGUAGE.   **Adrian Hastings**

The Encyclopedia of Language and Linguistics, 'Christianity', by John Sawyer et al. (1993).

Hastings, A., The Construction of Nationhood (1997).

—— 'The Choice of Words for Christian Meanings in Eastern Africa', African Catholicism (1989), 98–121.

last things, see ESCHATOLOGY.

Latin American Christian thought: an overview.
Twentieth-century Christian thought in Latin America is deeply influenced by 16th-century realities, especially the conquest and the subsequent clash between the dominant European culture on the one hand, and, on the other, the cultures of the Indians, the blacks, and the mestizos who made up the majority of the population. Modern Catholic conservatives look back with nostalgia on their version of colonial society, which, like the medieval ideal of European Christendom, was a corporate community in which whites, Indians, blacks, mestizos (the mixed races), and creoles (native-born whites) lived in harmony, each in their own social sphere, and all under the paternal guidance of the king and his viceroys. The Peruvian intellectual and politician, José de la Riva-Agüero (1885–1944), held that Peru had only experienced real progress when it was under the benevolent leadership of authoritarian élites such as the Incas and the Spanish.

But modern Catholic progressives point to another heritage: that of radical utopianism, which was also part of the colonial experience. Bartolomé de Las Casas, the *Dominican priest who passionately championed Indian rights, was a forerunner of *liberation theology. In New Spain (Mexico) Vasco de Quiropa, a humanist who became a priest and the first bishop of Michoacán, used Thomas *More's *Utopia* as his principal guide for founding two colonies for Indians, one in Mexico City and the other in his diocese. The *Franciscans who evangelized New Spain dreamed of creating a society of Christianized Indians who would be free of the contaminating influences of the Old World. The founder of Peruvian *Marxism, and a contemporary of Riva-Agüero, José Carlos Mariátegui, pointed to the *Jesuit reductions in Paraguay as a model of what might have been for all of Latin America. The feminist voice may be heard in the writings of the Mexican religious Sor Juana Inés de la Cruz (?1651–95). In her poetry Indians and black *slaves play a prominent role, and *women mock the *machismo* of overbearing clerics.

These contrasting views, one advocating progress under the benevolent tutelage of enlightened élites, and the other calling for a society based on democratic solidarity, are the two principal currents that have influenced Christian thinkers from the 16th century to the present. In the 18th century, when the winds of independence began stirring throughout Latin America, the king of *Spain and most bishops denounced challenges to the established order as antireligious. Nevertheless, creole priests, well versed in the writings of the French philosophers and impressed by the American *revolution, everywhere took up the banner of independence. These clergymen aimed to forge a synthesis between their Christian faith and the *Enlightenment. While they espoused *democracy and human rights, they did not agree with the violent anticlericalism of the French Revolution.

In Mexico the Dominican priest José Servando Teresa de Mier (1765–1827) questioned some aspects of the story of the Virgin of Guadalupe and suggested that St Thomas had pre-evangelized America. In so doing he undermined Spain's claim to rule in the name of Christianity. In Argentina, Gregorio Funes (1749–1829), the dean of the Cathedral of Cordoba, openly supported the May revolution of 1810 and became a founding father of the new nation. The exiled Peruvian Jesuit, Juan Pablo Viscardo y Guzmán (1744–89), called upon the British to assist Túpac Amaru in his revolution and help liberate all of Latin America.

These progressive clergymen, like their fellow creole laymen, were inspired principally by the western *natural law tradition as expounded by Thomas *Aquinas, Robert Bellarmine, and Francisco

Suarez. In contrast to this more rationalistic view, the utopian radicalism of the 16th century resurfaced in the many *messianic Indian rebellions of the 18th century. In Peru in 1780, Túpac Amaru, the Indian leader of Inca nobility whom Viscardo y Guzmán wished to aid, set off the greatest Indian rebellion in all of colonial history. Túpac Amaru, who had studied under the Jesuits, cited the bible to compare himself with Moses and David. He called for the creation of a new Christian Inca order in which Indians, blacks, and creoles would live in harmony. In Mexico in 1810, Miguel Hidalgo, the parish priest of Dolores, summoned the Indians to fight for independence in the name of Mexico and under the banner of the Virgin of Guadalupe.

In the 19th century the church found itself embroiled in battles with liberalism, which by mid-century had grown increasingly critical of the church. For the liberals, the church, with its properties and great influence, was the principal obstacle in the way of social progress. Although most liberals considered themselves Catholics, few attempted to forge an intellectual dialogue between their liberal faith and *Catholicism. One who did was the Peruvian priest, Francisco de Paúla González Vigil (1792–1875), a staunch critic of religious and political authoritarianism. Vigil called upon Latin Americans to resist the encroachments of the Roman Curia and to return to the practice of pristine Christianity. Although excommunicated in 1851, he did not reject Catholicism.

But most churchmen held views similar to those of Bartolomé Herrera (1808–64), a Peruvian priest who used the pulpit to attack liberalism, which for him was the principal cause of contemporary social disorder. He called for a new social order based on respect for law and legitimate authority. In particular, he praised Spain for all the benefits it had brought to the New World. In so doing, he became a forerunner of Hispanism, the ideological and literary current which extols the Spanish heritage to the detriment of other cultural traditions.

Finally, the church found its defenders in the *caudillos*, the colourful strongmen who seized power and rewrote the constitutions of their different republics in their image and likeness. These self-appointed rulers frequently used religion to justify their rebellions. In 1829 the Argentinian dictator Juan Manuel de Rosas (1793–1877) led his mounted gauchos into Buenos Aires with the cry, 'Death to the impious Unitarians', an allusion to the liberals who dominated the port city. Ecuador's conservative leader, Gabriel García Moreno, crowned his presidency (1861–5; 1869–75) by having the country solemnly consecrated to the Sacred Heart of Jesus.

At the beginning of the 20th century the church was in full intellectual retreat throughout all Latin America. Liberals and positivists dominated the universities and intellectual circles. But by the 1920s and 1930s the church experienced a vigorous intellectual and religious reawakening. The social teachings (see SOCIAL GOSPEL AND SOCIAL TEACHING) of Leo XIII, and the call of Pius XI to create Catholic Action, infused new life into a dormant Catholicism. Although few in number, Catholic Action militants made up in enthusiasm what they lacked in numbers. They earnestly studied the social teachings of the church, organized eucharistic congresses, and engaged in public polemics with liberals and anticlericals.

For all the external signs of harmony, however, this new Catholic militancy covered deep differences. Many Catholic militants were conservatives and even integralists: that is, believers who held that

no changes could ever occur in the church or in its teachings without threatening the very foundations on which Catholic Christianity rests. The Catholic integralists also tended to be authoritarian and sectarian in the political sphere. Many admired Mussolini, and, even more, Francisco Franco. For them, Catholicism was an essential element in the identity of Latin America; new and extraneous forces such as *Protestantism or Communism were seen as threats to that identity and cultural unity. But other Catholic militants went on to found the Christian Democratic parties of Latin America. Although they, too, esteemed their Catholic culture, they believed that democracy and tolerance of spirit were essential qualities of a modern Catholic. Most of them looked to the French philosopher, Jacques *Maritain, as their mentor and guide.

In Peru, José de la Riva-Agüero was the leading Catholic conservative. But his friend and contemporary, Víctor Andrés Belaunde, who rose to become president of the General Assembly of the United Nations (1959), called for a Christian social order based on democracy. In Brazil, Jackson de Figueiredo (1891–1928), founder of the Dom Vital Center in Rio de Janeiro, championed the cause of a militant anti-liberal and anti-communist Catholicism. He was the forerunner of other integralist movements which culminated in Tradition, Family, and Property, founded in 1960 by Plínio Correa de Oliveira. The other side of the coin is represented by Alceu Amoroso Lima (1893–1983), who originally shared many of Jackson de Figueiredo's views. But after the military coup of 1964 he became a vigorous defender of human rights and democracy, and sympathized with liberation theology.

In Chile, a group of dissidents within the Conservative Party founded the National Phalanx, which evolved into the Christian Democratic Party in 1957. One of their leaders was Eduardo Frei Montalva, who became president of the country between 1964 and 1970. The principal Christian voice among Chilean workers was Clotario Blest, president of the United Workers' Union. In general, the Chilean social Christians led the way for other Catholic Action groups and Christian Democrats in the rest of Latin America.

In Colombia, Argentina, and Mexico no significant middle of the road Christian Democratic party emerged as an alternative to highly polarized extremes. The leading voice of Catholic conservatism in Colombia, Laureano Gómez, became president of the country (1950–3), but was overthrown by the military partly because of his own authoritarian tactics. Argentina represents an extreme case of Catholic integralism which was characterized by a special alliance between the church and the military. Excluded from this pact were liberals, communists, and other voices in favour of social change. The Peronist movement in particular captured the imagination of the workers and peasants, but the church, fearing the loss of influence over the lower classes, closed ranks with the upper class and the military against Perón and his wife, Evita. This church–military alliance was reaffirmed during the 'Dirty War' (1976–83) when the military used state terror to persecute and murder thousands of people suspected of leftist tendencies.

Christian thought should also include protest thinkers and leaders who, although not connected with the official church, conveyed their message through reference to religion and biblical redemption. Two important examples were Víctor Raúl Haya de la Torre and José Carlos Mariátegui, the founders of the Peruvian left and the standard-bearers of an entire generation of Latin Americans.

Haya de la Torre (1895–1979), of middle-class origins from the northern coastal city of Trujillo, became a university student reform leader in Lima. His most famous initiative was to lead a protest march against the consecration of Peru to the Sacred Heart in May 1923. Haya, supported by Protestants and Masons, denounced the close association between the church and the dictator, Augusto B. Leguía. He founded the Aprista movement (from the acronym APRA: Popular Revolutionary Alliance for America) in Mexico as a multi-class front to combat imperialism and to forge a new united Latin America. He returned as a presidential candidate in 1931, and almost won. Imprisoned in 1932 by the military dictator, Luis Miguel Sánchez Cerro, Haya was freed in 1933 after the dictator was assassinated. In public addresses he consoled the Apristas who had suffered persecution by comparing his movement with the crucified Christ. In so doing he also cast a messianic aura around himself and his party. More than any political leader on the left in that period, Haya forged a populist alliance that combined elements of Marxism, nationalistic capitalism, and popular Christianity. After being denied the presidency twice by the military, he was elected president of Peru's 1978 constitutional assembly.

José Carlos Mariátegui (1894–1930) was of quite a different cast. Born into the lower middle class of Lima, he did not follow formal university studies and chose journalism as his profession. A devout Catholic in his youth, he won a prize for his description of the great Lord of Miracles procession that takes place in Lima every October. Exiled by President Leguía in 1919, he went to Italy and became a Marxist, returned to Peru and founded the first socialist party in 1928. He subsequently abandoned the practice of religion, but, unlike most socialists of his time, he never criticized religion itself. In his most important work, *Seven Interpretative Essays on the Peruvian Reality* (1928) he held that both religion and revolution stem from humankind's innate desire for a better world. In fact, Mariátegui esteemed religious faith as a necessary factor in the human quest for utopia. He was the first Latin American socialist to praise religion as a positive force in history; in so doing, he became one of the most important forerunners of the liberation theology, which developed from the late 1960s to become a major intellectual contribution to world Christianity, and of which *A Theology of Liberation*, by the Peruvian Gustavo *Gutiérrez (1971) was a first, and classical, expression.

Until the 1960s Protestants exerted little intellectual influence beyond narrow confessional lines. One important exception was John Mackay (1889–1983), a Scottish Presbyterian minister who studied under Miguel de Unamuno in Spain before arriving in Peru in 1916. Mackay received his doctoral degree at San Marcos University in Lima, and founded the Anglo-Peruvian High School. He befriended many avant garde and leftist intellectuals, including Haya de la Torre who taught in Mackay's school. Author of *The Other Spanish Christ* (1932) Mackay highlighted the Christian elements in the protest thinkers and leaders in the Latin culture. After sixteen years in South America he went on to become president of Princeton Theological Seminary and editor of *Theology Today*. Another exception was Moisés Sáenz (1888–1941), a Protestant and a disciple of John Dewey, who influenced educational trends in the Mexican revolution in the 1920s. Sáenz was especially concerned about fostering education for the Indians. At the same time that the Catholic church experienced a new awakening following *Vatican II, some

Latin American Protestants also turned more ecumenical and social-minded. Two Protestant theologians in particular, Rubem Alves, a Brazilian, and José Míguez *Bonino, an Argentinian, stand out for their contribution to liberation theology.   **Jeffrey Klaiber, SJ**

Cleary, Edward L., *Crisis and Change: The Church in Latin America Today* (1985).

Dussel, Enrique (ed.), *The Church in Latin America 1492–1992* (1992).

Hanke, Lewis, *The Spanish Struggle for Justice in the Conquest of America* (1949; 1965).

Ivereigh, Austen, *Catholicism and Politics in Argentina, 1810–1960* (1995).

Kantor, Harry, 'Catholic Political Parties and Mass Politics in Latin America', in Donald Eugene Smith (ed.), *Religion and Political Modernization* (1974).

Klaiber, Jeffrey, *Religion and Revolution in Peru, 1824–1976* (1977).

—— *The Church, Dictatorships, and Democracy in Latin America* (1998).

Levine, Daniel H. (ed.), *Religion and Political Conflict in Latin America* (1986).

MacCormack, Sabine, *Religion in the Andes: Vision and Imagination in Early Colonial Peru* (1991).

Mackay, John, *The Other Spanish Christ* (1932).

Mariátegui, José Carlos, *Seven Interpretative Essays on Peruvian Reality* (1928), ET (1971).

Phelan, John L., *The Millennial Kingdom of the Franciscans in the New World* (1956).

Richard, Pablo (ed.), *Raíces de la teología latinoamericana* (1985).

Vallier, Ivan, *Catholicism, Social Control, and Modernization in Latin America* (1970).

Véliz, Claudio, 'Latitudinarian Religious Centralism', in *The Centralist Tradition of Latin America* (1980).

Latin theology, 300 to 1000.

The 4th century witnessed the flowering of early Latin theology as Christianity made its transition from a *religio illicita*, the subject of periodic persecution, to established religion, the beneficiary of legal privilege, while the old Roman polytheism became the target of punitive legislation. The 4th to the 6th centuries witnessed the sharpening of features that would come to characterize Latin theology over against its *Greek counterpart. Engagement with the questions and controversies exercising the east begins to be eroded by a loss of fluency in Greek in an increasingly isolated west, and, more positively, by attention to categories and issues native to the west. Over this transition towers the figure of *Augustine, whose influence dominates nearly the whole of our period, both a source of inspiration and a sign of contradiction as his legacy was interpreted and contested. We must refuse the temptation to view either western or eastern theology as inherently superior, recognizing instead their complementary genius and their underlying unity.

Hilary of Poitiers (c.300–c.367) represents a style of Latin theology well acquainted with Greek language and with the controversies of the east. Elected bishop of Poitiers; deposed for anti-*Arian activity; exiled to Phrygia (356); he became deeply acquainted with *Origen's works and with members of the *homoeousian* party, who described the Son as 'of like nature' with the Father, rather than 'of the same nature' (*homoousios*). He admired these men, and even, for a time, represented them (at Seleucia in 359). His *De trinitate* (356–60) combines the legacy of Tertullian and Novatian (see PRE-CONSTANTINIAN THOUGHT) with strong anti-Sabellian and anti-Arian theologies. It shows a sympathetic confluence of homoeousian and homoousian concerns, arguing as much by appeal to biblical passages as by dialectics. His earlier exegesis (*Commentary on Matthew*) attests the state of western exegesis before Origen was much known in the west, but his *Commentary on Psalms*, written after his exile and thoroughly indebted to Origen, served to introduce Origenian themes into western theology.

Ambrose (c.339–97) follows Hilary in his engagement in anti-Arian polemic and in his ability to read Greek sources, including Origen, Philo, and, now, Plotinus (see PLATO AND PLATONISM). Ambrose, elected bishop of Milan (373 or 374) before he was baptized, gradually persuaded the Emperor Gratian to adopt anti-Arian instruction and policy, culminating in anti-heretical sanctions and in the treatises *De fide* and *De Spiritu Sancto*, which show the influence especially of Basil and of Didymus. In addition to doctrinal treatises and moral/ascetic works (including the *De officiis* on the priesthood, and the *De virginitate*), much of his output was exegetical, mostly OT commentary (and one on Luke). These show the influence of Origen and (though Ambrose consistently denigrated philosophy and philosophers as possessed of half-truths wholly derivative from the bible) the pervasive influence of Plotinus, a source untouched by Hilary but increasingly influential in the west. Ambrose was a prominent member of the circle of Milanese Christian Neoplatonists (including Marius Victorinus) who exerted lasting influence on Augustine.

Contemporary with Ambrose are Jerome (c.347–419) and Rufinus (c.345–410), friends who, with others, embarked upon a joint ascetical and scholarly enterprise at Aquileia. Jerome copied the works of a growing canon of Christian Latin literature: Cyprian, Hilary, Tertullian; but, when Rufinus moved east with Melania (373), visiting the Origenist monks in Egypt and eventually establishing a monastery himself on the Mount of Olives, Jerome left for Syria, where he studied Hebrew and Greek and was ordained priest at Antioch. He returned to Rome (c.382) where Pope Damasus made him his secretary and supported his project of correcting the extant Latin translations of the gospels and the psalms. After Damasus's death, Jerome left Rome and established with Paula a monastery at Bethlehem, having visited Origen's library at Caesarea on the way. Beginning in 393, he made direct translations from the Hebrew of the psalms and other biblical books. Together with his own and Rufinus the Syrian's translations of the NT, these eventually became the Vulgate, perhaps the single most influential work of the patristic Latin west.

Jerome was progressively alienated from Rufinus, Melania, and their Origenist patron, Bishop John of Jerusalem, because his own protector and friend, Epiphanius, was vehemently anti-Origenist, though Jerome's exegetical works continued to depend (more discreetly) on Origen's. Rufinus returned to Rome in 397, beginning a career of translation which, together with translations by Jerome, saved most of what remains today of Origen. When Theophilus of Alexandria condemned Origen in 400, Jerome saw to it that Pope Anastasius would repeat this condemnation (which he did in two letters), and this effectively cut off appeal to Origen's systematic theology in the west (though his exegesis was read in all centuries). Thus the 4th century ends with the eclipse of Origen's delicate synthesis of Middle Platonism and Christian faith, with its tracing of the origin of evil and balancing of 'nature' and 'grace' (as they would later be called in the west). As knowledge of Greek ebbed, the sophisticated syntheses of Origen's eastern heirs, the Cappadocians, became equally unavailable for sustained theological use.

Augustine of Hippo was to have the problem of forging a new synthesis of Christian faith and reason without much benefit from earlier solutions. He began his theological career in an anti-Manichaean mode, following the lead of Ambrose in using the philosophical monism of Neoplatonism to combat Manichaean *dualism. Augustine's insistence that all being, *qua* being, is good, and that evil is not being but rather the corruption of being, unites him with all Platonist theologians of antiquity. Increasingly, however, tensions inherent in the Neoplatonic anthropology, tensions that Ambrose tended to overlook and that traditionalist Origenist theologians such as Jerome solved in other ways, began to bother Augustine. In his earliest works, he repeats Porphyry's injunction that 'Everything bodily must be avoided,' and interprets the creation of the sexes in Genesis 2 allegorically. But once ordained (392) and working as a pastor, he began to acquire greater familiarity with and sympathy for scripture, so that these strategies, anti-Manichaean in intent, came to seem Manichaean themselves. Augustine's study of St Paul just after his consecration as bishop of Hippo (395) refined his sense of *sin as interior conflict within the soul, rather than conflict between soul and body. His theology begins to emphasize the positive character of bodily nature as originally created, and (in reaction against Jerome's radically ascetic views), of marriage and sex even after the *Fall.

Instead of focusing on the body as the origin of sin, Augustine focused on the will, its freedom vitiated in the pride of Adam and Eve, who wished to create and hold on to a fellowship with each other independent of God, replacing, in effect, God's central place in the universe with their own. Human societies obsessively re-enact this prideful desire to find in themselves a self-sufficient good. Individuals inherit a nature vitiated by the effects of original sin and can be healed only by the special, predestined intervention of God's *grace. The *Incarnation of the Son, the *Word and *Wisdom of God, is a moving act of humility on God's part, and this spectacle of God's abject humility moves those whose hearts have been restored to health by grace; though for others the proclamation of the gospel will, even if heard, fall on deaf ears. The controversy with *Pelagius (411–17) and its vigorous afterlife in the controversy with Julian of Eclanum did not substantially alter Augustine's position, though it refined his understanding of the precise operation of grace.

The change in Augustine's theology from Neoplatonic optimism based on theories of human perfectibility is often regarded as disillusionment or as a turn towards pessimism about the human condition, but it can also be viewed in opposite terms: his sense of the insidious complicity in evil which binds all humanity together and constitutes its 'original sin' makes him more sensitive to the life of the Christian believer as one of continuous healing and transformation rather than one of static perfection. Growth in the spiritual life is not restricted to a philosophic few, but is equally available to those in any walk of life, regardless of distinctions of education, class, or marital status. Augustine certainly thought *virginity superior to *marriage, but both were equally liable to succumb to temptation (marriage to lust and virginity to pride), and transformation and healing were available equally to both in Christ. As one comes to identify one's sufferings and trials with the sufferings of the Word made flesh, all people can find in the active life the beginning of the contemplative vision of God's Wisdom. The Neoplatonic 'ascent' from consideration of creatures to contemplation of God needs no special philosophical training; in fact it is possible only by clinging in faith to the 'wood', the cross of Christ, in which God's humble Wisdom is fully revealed. Bonaventure (see FRANCIS-CAN THOUGHT), *Dante, and other theologians of the high medieval period would develop this theme further.

Against the *Donatists, Augustine had argued that the *sacraments belong to Christ, not to the minister of the sacrament, and their efficacy depends not on the moral character of the minister but on the valid celebration of the sacrament and its reception in faith. In receiving baptism (for example), one places one's faith in Christ, not in the minister (whose character is, in any event, hidden from us). Such an 'objective theory' of the operation of the sacraments may seem in tension with Augustine's theory of grace imparted internally and specially, but they are actually complementary. Anti-Donatist and anti-Pelagian arguments both pictured a church composed not of the perfected but of those being healed from imperfection, the 'inn' which the Good Samaritan Jesus had founded for our cure. The Eucharist in particular, as the universally celebrated sacrifice of Christ, is the locus of continuing re-formation. Both the anti-Donatist and the anti-Pelagian polemic emphasize the 'mixed' character of human life, in the church (where those predestined to life and those not so predestined exist together); in the individual (where faith prompted by grace is always operative in the midst of competing desires and motivations); and in society at large (where even the best of cultural activity, e.g. the liberal arts, is not free from the corruption of pride and cannot lead anyone to God apart from the preaching of the gospel, the sacraments, and the inner working of grace). Augustine's theology thus affirms that the best in social and cultural reality can be transformed in the hands of those converted by grace, but he retains a critical distance from any particular cultural system. This is a direct result of his theology of grace which was to distinguish theology in the west from eastern theologies more inclined to identify themselves with particular cultures. In the conviction that all human nature, no matter how vitiated by sin, could be transformed by grace (even if not all would be) as in the deepening of the sense of hope for transformation available to all, one sees the completion of Augustine's original anti-Manichaean polemic, contrary to charges both ancient and modern that he returned to Manichaean dualism in his rather physical analysis of the transmission of original sin. The sense that the wonder of grace restores the wonder of nature echoes resoundingly in later theology from *Hildegard to Bonaventure to *Pascal.

Augustine recognized a canon of western Christian authors (Hilary, Ambrose, and those mentioned in De doctrina, 4) though he rarely felt the need to appeal to any of them as authorities unless his opponents had. He anticipated his own inclusion in the canon, cataloguing a library of his own writings. They were immediately anthologized, beginning with Prosper of Aquitaine, whose Sententiae excerpted passages for use against John Cassian (c.360–435), Faustus of Riez (c.400–c.490), and other semi-Pelagians. These agreed with Augustine on the universal necessity for baptism and for direct interior infusion of grace, but disagreed on the extent of the damage done by original sin, admitting some remaining natural capacity for initiating (but not completing) salvation in advance of grace. The 5th-century dispute over the Augustinian theology of grace was resolved at the Council of Orange (529), which upheld Augustinian teaching on the necessity and prevenience of grace, condemning semi-Pelagian teachings without explicitly condemning the semi-Pelagians as heretics, and disowning double *predestination (predestination to damnation as well as to salvation), always a pitfall in Augustinian doctrine.

Cassian had lived in the Egyptian desert, and Faustus had been both monk and abbot at Lérins, established by Honoratus on principles observed on his own journeys east, so both had roots in eastern *monastic spirituality. This was based on eastern views of the Fall as less serious: an evil but immature mistake of childlike beings who even before sin needed to be educated to a higher, freer state. The Rule of St Benedict (c.530) may be regarded as a resolution, on the spiritual level, of the 5th-century debates on grace; perhaps the most enduring resolution of all, one of the few places where east and west met so fruitfully. It embraces the developmental view of Cassian and Basil, but in the conviction that the central act of *asceticism is the formation of a community of mutual love and service and that only grace can call such a community into being out of the 'nothing' of an assortment of individuals of varying temperament and unequal social rank, we recognize the legacy of Augustine.

Augustine was influential in other 5th- and 6th-century debates and movements. Vincent of Lérins' Excerpta anthologized passages for use against *Nestorianism, and Eugippius's Excerpta collected passages on a variety of topics. In North Africa Fulgentius of Ruspe excerpted and glossed Augustine's trinitarian works in controversy with the Vandal Arians. Augustine's De doctrina, with its insistence on the utility of secular learning for Christian exegetes and its catalogue of great Christian stylists, inspired Cassiodorus, whose Institutes chartered a vision of education to which all the great educators and encyclopedists of the 7th–9th centuries were heirs: Bede in Britain, Isidore in Spain, Rabanus Maurus in Germany, Alcuin in Gaul, Remigius of Auxerre, and Odo, founder of Cluny. These and other early medieval writers were heavily dependent not only on Augustine, but on Jerome and Gregory the Great (c.540–604) as well. Gregory's exegesis (Moralia in Job; 40 Gospel Homilies; homilies on Ezekiel and the Song of Songs) and pastoral theology (in the Letters and Pastoral Rule) were especially influential and were themselves anthologized.

The early medieval centuries are often underestimated by historians who scorn the theology and exegesis of the period as wholly derivative. But to see the true creativity of the period, one must look at the use of sources. The scriptural commentaries of Bede, Alcuin, Rabanus, and others may cite long passages from the church fathers word for word, but selecting and editing citations is a process of interpretation: it both establishes the fathers as authoritative tradition and seeks to clarify their meaning, especially in view of contemporary questions. For example, Alcuin's huge Commentary on John is drawn mainly from Augustine's, yet Alcuin's skilful work of redaction gives his edition an entirely new cast, concerned less with the self-disclosure and hiddenness of God, and more with the question of how Christ is both divine and human, reflecting Alcuin's role in the Adoptionism controversy. This controversy, which began in Spain in the 8th century as an argument between Elipandus of Toledo and Beatus of Liebana, spilled over into Carolingian realms when Alcuin attacked Felix of

Urgel, accusing him of Nestorianism, that is of teaching that Jesus was adopted as God's Son and so exists as a second person beside the eternal person of the Word. One could regard this dispute partly as concerned with interpreting western christological sources such as Leo I (see CHALCEDON) and (especially) Augustine. Similarly, the hostile western reception of the decisions of Nicaea II (787), resolving the eastern *iconoclast controversies in favour of the veneration of icons, was due partly to a bad translation of the decrees and partly to increasing tension between east and west over issues such as the insertion of the *filioque into the creed. But it was also due to a conviction culled from western sources that icon-worship (which the bad translation made Nicaea II seem to be approving) was wrong. The Libri Carolini (late 780s) drew heavily upon previous western sources, especially Augustine's De doctrina and Gregory the Great's letter to Serenus.

Ninth-century controversies between the monk Gottschalk and Hincmar of Rheims over predestination represented another attempt to interpret the patristic inheritance. Gottschalk, arguing an exaggerated Augustinian position, was condemned and imprisoned. Hincmar relied partly on Hilary of Poitiers' Commentary on the Psalms to rebut Gottschalk, and thus, perhaps without knowing it, mitigated extreme Augustinianism by appeal to Origen, whose work inspired Hilary's Commentary and who could now affect the controversy under the unimpeachably authoritative name of Hilary. A similar creative appeal to authorities characterizes Hincmar's De una et non trina deitate, defending, against Gottschalk and Ratramnus, his replacement of the hymn phrase 'trina deitas' as promoting tritheism. Another controversy, between Paschasius Radbertus and Ratramnus, both monks of Corbie, on the Eucharist, is often thought to foreshadow Reformation debates, with Radbertus upholding a more 'realist' view and Ratramnus a more 'symbolic' one. In fact, both defend what we would call the Real Presence, but the language chosen to describe this, and the precise bodily presence in question, were the issues under debate as both sides, especially Ratramnus, claimed Augustine as warrant.

The most daring and creative intellect in the whole period between the collapse of the western empire and the year 1000 is John Scotus Eriugena (c.810–77), whose Periphyseon was an attempt to synthesize eastern and western sources into a unified theology. This was preceded by his translation into Latin of what would come to be, after Augustine, the single most influential theological source in high medieval theology, the works of Pseudo-*Dionysius (5th–6th centuries). The Periphyseon uses Greek sources (Dionysius, Gregory Nazianzen, Gregory of Nyssa, Maximus, etc.), attempting to integrate Augustine into their outlook. The results are not as forced as one might think. Eriugena is skilful in finding and emphasizing points of contact and in handling areas of genuine ambiguity in Augustine in ways that emphasize the harmony between the two thought-worlds. The Periphyseon was condemned for pantheistic tendencies, perhaps partly through misunderstanding by theologians not acquainted with eastern theologies.

A treatise of Alcuin, On the Faith of the Holy and Undivided Trinity, may sum up the concerns and achievements of early medieval Latin theology. Written partly as a response to the Adoptionist controversy, it is a three-book summary of the Catholic faith, admired and copied in all succeeding centuries up to the advent of printing. It is mostly derivative, consisting of often lengthy passages

from the fathers, unattributed and sometimes merged directly with passages drawn from other sources or with sentences in which Alcuin himself speaks. It is thus a work of synthesis and harmonization. It is certainly too strong to say that it is the creation of *tradition. But, while concerned to preserve the very language of the fathers as authoritative and not to innovate beyond them, it nevertheless subordinates all their individual voices in its attempt to find its own voice and to articulate precisely what the authoritative tradition of the fathers is saying. In this attempt, it is a true antecedent of the scholastics of the high *Middle Ages.

John Cavadini

Chadwick, H., The Early Church (1967).
di Berardino, A., Encyclopedia of the Early Church (1992).
Evans, G. E., Philosophy and Theology in the Middle Ages (1993).
Frend, W. H. C., The Rise of Christianity (1984).
Ganz, D., Corbie in the Carolingian Renaissance (1990).
Hall, S., Doctrine and Practice in the Early Church (1991).
Jedin, H., A History of the Church (1964; 1980), ii–iii.
Kelly, J. N. D., Early Christian Doctrines (1978).
Knowles, D., The Evolution of Medieval Thought (1962).
Marenbon, J., From the Circle of Alcuin to the School of Auxerre (1981).
Pelikan, J., The Emergence of the Catholic Tradition (100–600) (1971).
—— The Growth of Medieval Theology (600–1000) (1978).
Quasten, J. Patrology (4 vols.; 1950–86).
Southern, R., Western Society and the Church in the Middle Ages (1970).

law occupies a curiously ambiguous position within Christianity, which unlike Judaism or Islam, is not a religion of law. It possesses no obvious primary legal code to refer to; moreover, both *Jesus and *Paul seemed to take up almost anti-legal positions. It is true that Jesus is reported as saying that 'not one iota, not a dot, will pass from the law until all is accomplished' (Matt. 5: 18) but the final qualifying clause introduces ambiguity: when will all be accomplished and how? Has it been accomplished with Jesus' death? Challenged by the Pharisees to explain how his disciples can do on the sabbath 'something that is forbidden', Jesus claims to be 'master of the sabbath' (Matt. 12: 1–8). The point is not whether such a discussion actually took place, nor whether it is probable that such small infringements of the law helped lead to Jesus' death. Such stories should rather be seen as *parables illustrating the conviction of early Christians that he was not a legally minded man. There is no suggestion that he flouted the law, but, whereas other religious zealots of his time actually added to the multiple small obligations of Jewish legal orthodoxy, Jesus is portrayed as pointing in quite a different direction. 'Fulfilling the law' will be realized, not by multiplying minutiae, but by getting back to its central commandment of *love practised in a quite unritualistic way (see LAW, BIBLICAL).

The early church soon decided to reject a demand 'to keep the law of Moses' (Acts 15: 5) and required only a minimalist set of obligations that did not even include keeping the sabbath. While the latter was of enormous importance to Jews as one of the Ten *Commandments, it was quickly abandoned by Christians. Nor can it be said that the Jewish sabbath was simply transferred to the Christian Sunday, for all that many later Christians have seen it thus. Almost everything special in 'keeping the sabbath' simply went. Paul's rhetoric could go still further: Christians are 'dead to the law', 'discharged from the law' (Rom. 7: 4–6), not because the law is bad but because in Christ they have entered a new kind of existence whose morality is that of a 'new' and simpler 'law of love'. NT Christianity was not *antinomian, even if occasionally it sounded like that. In fact its combination of moral earnestness and lack of any extended initial law of its own made it particularly open to both embracing and developing other law systems that appeared not too discordant with its own ideals. At the same time, the larger and more complex its own life and organization became, the more it needed an internal ecclesiastical or canon law to regulate its affairs.

Four different legal developments were the result. The first was a taking over of Roman law, once the emperors were Christian, as the central civil law of the Christian community. This was not difficult, given Paul's teaching in Rom. 13 about subjection to the governing authorities and the deeply law-abiding character of the early Christian community. Roman law was codified by Christian emperors, notably Theodosius II and Justinian, while being adapted to Christian susceptibilities. Secondly, in other societies where there had been no written law, Christian influence quickly produced one. Thus the English legal tradition begins with laws of Ethelbert of Kent who was converted by Augustine. Written law was spread by Christianity, just as *literacy itself was. Thirdly, the canons of *councils and decretals of popes already constituted a considerable core of canon law by the fourth century, but the decisive systematization of church law was made by a monk, Gratian, in the 12th century, a work soon followed by the development of the *University of Bologna, for both civil and canon law. There are more surviving manuscripts of Gratian's *Decreta* than of any other book, apart from the bible. Fourthly, if Christians took over civil law from the Romans, they took over a concept of *natural law from the Greeks, both Stoic and *Aristotelian, that is to say the idea that a system of *moral right and wrong is embedded within the rational nature of humankind, something Paul appears to recognize already in Rom. 1 as reflecting divine law. The idea linked with the doctrine of creation and explained why basic morality did not depend on revelation, the Ten Commandments indeed being seen as binding precisely because they were an expression of natural law. It was, above all, the work of *Aquinas, making full use of Aristotle, to develop a rounded conception of natural law, something which has remained central to catholic theology.

By the time of Aquinas, the study of both civil and canon law had become a major element of ecclesiastical culture and in the later Middle Ages its authority grew ever greater. Most bishops and popes were trained lawyers rather than theologians, and the Roman Curia, in particular, came to be dominated by a legal mentality. Much theology became little more than an extension of law; this was especially true of moral theology and of ecclesiology where the canon law relating to papal sovereignty, developed so extensively in the Middle Ages, provided the norm for understanding the church and conducting its affairs. While the great age of church law-making undoubtedly improved the subtlety of all law, it resulted in much church history becoming a matter of prolonged litigation in diocesan and Roman courts. The enormous volume of Roman canon law was finally synthesized into a single-volume *Codex*, as late as 1917. Revised in 1983, it continues to dominate the life of the Catholic Church, while comparable, if less extensive, codes apply elsewhere as in the revised (1969) *Canons* of the Church of England.

In this way a religion which began with absolutely no equivalent

to Islamic Shari'a was in possession, fifteen centuries later, of the most complex religious law the world has ever seen, a system however in which equity remained underdeveloped. If the *Reformation was in part a protest against the church's enmeshment in legalism, in few places did it in effect reduce the legalism. Indeed, abolition of the sacrament of *penance could much increase the legalism with which sins and failings were treated.

Preoccupation with the pope's monarchical authority and the obedience it requires also led to a preference for similar absolutist systems in the state, while the Lutheran doctrine of 'two realms' left the absolutist state largely uncriticizable by the church. The excessive and gruesome *punishments provided by civil law in the early modern period went unchallenged by the church, Catholic or Protestant, and modern legal reforms relating to due process, humane punishment, and much else have owed little to pressure from the churches.

Yet Christianity has ample resources for humanizing law and challenging immoral law both from NT priorities and from the natural law tradition. Paul's injunction in Rom. 13 to obey the governing authorities since all government comes from God did not necessarily imply a quiescent attitude towards bad law. While the Christian is by conviction a law-abiding person, as the 2nd-century epistle to Diognetus already insisted, that does not exclude struggling to embody the higher values of *love, *justice, *mercy, and *freedom within positive law so far as possible. Moreover, for the theologian of natural law, positive law exists only for the common good. It must in some way embody natural law, itself an expression of divine law. Laws which in no way serve the common good are invalid and cannot command conscientious obedience. It is right, Aquinas insists, to rise up against tyranny. Where a law is enacted that manifestly benefits only a group, to the severe disadvantage of other citizens, such as the anti-Jewish laws in Nazi Germany, or racially discriminatory laws in *apartheid South Africa, there may well be a moral obligation not to obey the governing authority. If many laws, while not self-evidently against the common good, appear moderately unjust, then it can be a Christian duty, not to disobey, but to contest them in any way constitutionally allowed. The character and purposes of punishment, the immorality of *capital punishment, and conscientious objection to military service (see PACIFISM) are among the areas with which modern Christians, especially minority groups like the *Quakers, have engaged in their endeavour to improve positive law. While positive law is a necessity for every society, and it can never fully embody a gospel ethic, it can almost always be rendered more humane, more convincingly just. The less fair a law is, the more it should be contested; the better a law is, the more it should be cherished. While there will always remain a gap between a merciful fairness on the one hand and positive law on the other, the task of the Christian lawyer is to reduce that gap to the minimum and ensure that positive law does effectively serve the persons who form society and the common good they share. **Adrian Hastings**

d'Entrèves, A. P., *The Medieval Contribution to Political Thought* (1939).
Finnis, John, *Aquinas: Moral, Political, and Legal Theory* (1998).
Mahoney, John, *The Making of Moral Theology* (1987).
Sanders, E. P., *Jewish Law from Jesus to the Mishnah* (1990).
Ullmann, Walter, *Law and Politics in the Middle Ages* (1975).

law, biblical. Biblical law, although found throughout the bible, is concentrated in the OT in three main blocks: Exodus 21: 1–23: 19; Leviticus 1: 1–27: 33; Deuteronomy 12: 1–26: 15. According to their narrative setting these laws were given by *God to *Moses on Sinai and during the wilderness wanderings after the *exodus. Modern critical scholarship dates the material from roughly the 9th to the 5th century BC.

The laws in Exod. 21–3 imply an agricultural, slave-owning society in which the property rights of land-holders need to be safeguarded. Parallels between these laws and sections of the laws of Hammurabi (king of Babylon, 1792–1750) have been noted since the latter's discovery in 1901–2. However, there is a distinctive emphasis upon *compassion in the Exodus laws, grounded in the need to imitate God's graciousness in freeing the Israelites from *slavery in Egypt. Slavery is restricted to six years for males (Exod. 21: 2), money lent to the poor must not require interest to be paid (22: 25) and the chief beneficiaries of the law forbidding work on the sabbath are the domesticated *animals (23: 12). The emphasis on compassion is reinforced in Deuteronomy whose laws originated in the reform of King Josiah of Judah in 622 BC. Women are included in the six-year restriction on slavery (Deut. 15: 12), a three-yearly tithe is introduced whose yield is to be used to support those on the margins of society (14: 28–9), and the power of kings is made subject to the observance of God's laws (17: 14–20). These laws have been described by modern scholarship as an attempt to legislate the demands of the 8th-century *prophets for social *justice.

Leviticus is devoted mainly to regulations about *priesthood, *sacrifice, and ritual purity. In chapter 25, however, it introduces the Jubilee or fiftieth year, a year in which property that has been sold because of need is to be returned to the original owners, and slaves are to be set free. Whether or not it was ever observed, the Jubilee affirms a theological principle that those who belong to a people redeemed by God should not be enslaved in any way (Lev. 25: 42). (See also POVERTY; FORGIVENESS.)

A striking feature of the OT laws is their incompleteness. The laws of Hammurabi contain sections on marriage, divorce, adoption, the rights of prisoners-of-war, how to gain redress against a physician or a house-builder. These matters are largely ignored in the OT. This incompleteness of OT law has led some commentators to argue that the material illustrates the *ethics or theology of the OT rather than its laws. It has also been an important factor in differing Christian attitudes to biblical law, as well as in the development of Judaism.

One of the most important strands within the Judaism at the turn of the Common Era was that which adapted the OT laws into a comprehensive system for knowing and observing the will of God in every aspect of daily life. This was justified by the belief that God had given two laws to Moses on Sinai, a written law (in the bible) and an oral law that had been passed down from Moses through the judges and prophets to the forerunners of the rabbis in the late Second Temple period. After the fall of *Jerusalem in 70 AD this strand became the dominant one in Judaism and, from the 3rd century AD, the oral law began to be collected in the Mishnah and the Tosephta, and it was further established and elucidated in the Babylonian and Jerusalem Talmuds. The incomplete biblical law was thus supplemented by a recorded oral law.

Christianity originated within the broad stream of 1st-century *Judaism that included groups for whom strict observance of the law was fundamental to their religion. According to the *gospels *Jesus did not share this view. He is presented as violating the sabbath by healing (Mark 3: 1–6; John 5: 2–18), and by not rebuking his disciples when they plucked ears of grain (Mark 2: 23–8). In the *Sermon on the Mount, he both radicalizes and sets aside parts of the written OT law (Matt. 5: 21–48).

It is clear from the *Pauline letters and the Acts of the Apostles that the question of the observance of the OT law fundamentally divided the early church. The main issue was whether non-Jews who became Christians should be required to observe the law. One party, led by James the brother of Jesus (Gal. 1: 19; 2: 12), insisted that non-Jewish Christians should be circumcised and should obey the law, although in what form or to what degree is not stated in the extant sources. The opposite view was held by Paul who believed that Christ had opened the way to God for the whole human race and that the requirement that Gentiles should observe the Jewish law militated against this. Acts 15 records a council at Jerusalem at which it was agreed that non-Jewish Christians should observe only three things: to abstain from meat sacrificed to idols, from meat from which the blood had not been drained at slaughter, and from unchastity, i.e. fornication (Acts 15: 20, 29). Although this meeting probably did not take place (Paul never refers to the Apostolic Decree in his letters), Acts 15 is nevertheless evidence for opinion in the Pauline churches; and it was the Pauline viewpoint that prevailed as Christianity spread into the Gentile cities of the *Hellenistic-Roman world.

The NT makes little reference to the Jewish law. The letter to the *Hebrews argues that the priestly and sacrificial laws of Leviticus have been fulfilled and abrogated by the death and Resurrection of Jesus. There are references to the Ten *Commandments in the teaching of Jesus and in Paul (Mark 10: 19; Rom. 13: 8–10); but there is also the belief that the law can be summarized in the two commandments of *love to God and one's neighbour drawn from Deut. 6: 5 and Lev. 19: 18 (see Mark 12: 28–34; Rom. 13: 9–10). Where ethical instructions are given in letters such as Ephesians and Colossians, they draw upon 'household codes' from the Graeco-Roman world (Eph. 5: 21–6: 9; Col. 3: 18–4: 6).

The early church had a paradoxical view of the OT and its laws. It was regarded as scripture, and believed to have foretold the coming of Jesus, whose words and works had fulfilled it; but he had also abrogated its laws. This ambiguity was to become and remain a source of division in the churches over their attitude to biblical law.

The striking thing about the Christian writings of the 2nd century is their almost complete neglect of the OT law. Two writings which set out to guide Christians in how they should live, the *Didache* (date uncertain) and the *Shepherd of Hermas* (c.140) do so without the aid of biblical law, while there are robust repudiations of the Jewish law in the letters of Ignatius of Antioch (died c.115?) and the *Epistle of Barnabas* (c.130). Barnabas justifies the Christian neglect of the observance of the Sabbath, which in the OT is built into the story of creation itself (Gen. 2: 3). The verse is taken not as a command but to refer to the coming again of God's Son after six days (interpreted as 6,000 years) to bring an end to wickedness (*Barnabas*, 15: 4–5).

A more positive attitude towards the OT resulted from the need to defend it against Marcion (c.85–160) who proposed to reject it entirely. The Alexandrian interpreters Clement (c.150–215) and

*Origen rehabilitated OT law by allegorizing it. There were also moves to make parts of it literally applicable to Christians either by dividing it into the categories of ceremonial, civil, and moral laws, of which only the latter were binding on Christians, or by saying that all laws subsequent to the incident of the Golden Calf (Exod. 32) were binding only on the Israelites in order to correct their apostasy. At the same time, Christian *moral theology was developing the idea of *natural moral law to cover the many areas not dealt with by biblical law.

The work of *Aquinas is a high point in Christian understanding of the use of the Jewish law, and noteworthy because it is indebted to the *Guide of the Perplexed* (1190) of the Jewish philosopher Moses Maimonides. Aquinas accepts that the OT law was fitting and appropriate for the Israelites in their historical setting. He also believes that its sacrificial regulations point, typologically, to the work of Christ. While its moral commandments are binding on Christians this is because they embody the natural moral law.

The *Reformation brought sharp divisions. Whereas the Lutheran tradition re-emphasized the Pauline hostility to the law, the Reformed tradition rehabilitated it to a degree hitherto unparalleled, aided by rigid theories of the verbal inspiration of the bible. Within *Puritanism, OT law was believed to constitute a *covenant of works that had not lost its commanding power under the Christian dispensation. One of the marks of those *predestined to salvation was that they had the power to keep the law (2 Pet. 1: 10). This particular tradition survives today in Christian reconstructionist and theonomist movements that seek to incorporate as much biblical law into contemporary legal systems as modern moral sensibilities will allow. It is also found in fundamentalist and holiness movements which believe that Christians have the moral power and duty to observe the biblical law. These movements usually support *capital punishment (Gen. 9: 6) and what they regard as traditional personal and *family moral values. They reject any suggestion that OT laws and practices are immoral and they employ traditional methods of *apologetic to argue that biblical laws are God's revealed instructions for how humanity is to live.

The *liberal Christian tradition derives from the *Enlightenment attack upon the traditional understanding of the OT, directed against its laws and morality, which were denounced as those of an unenlightened Semitic tribe. Two strategies were employed by liberal defenders of the OT law. The first was the theory of progressive revelation or education, according to which the OT was evidence for ancient Israel's moral evolution from lower to higher levels of understanding. The non-sacrifice of Isaac in Genesis 22 (see ABRAHAM) was cited as an example of this evolution. The other strategy was to put the *prophetic and priestly traditions in the OT in sharp opposition. The prophetic calls for ethical monotheism and social justice were regarded as the heart of the religion of Israel, while the emphasis on priesthood, sacrifice, and observance of the law was considered to be a late development and part of a decline into 'Judaism'.

Current liberal debate about Christian attitudes to biblical law has been affected by *feminist and *liberation theologies, and the differing approaches within them. Thus, there are feminist and liberation writers who argue that the OT is unusable because it is the product of the oppressing classes in a patriarchal society. An opposite view draws attention to OT laws that require compassion for the poor and marginalized, including *women.

The attitude of the churches to biblical law has varied greatly throughout history, and has depended upon prior theological interests. While there are still many fundamentalist churches that seek to adhere to biblical law, at least as far as this affects personal and family life, the broader Christian tradition has always accepted that there are various sources for Christian moral teaching, and that the contribution made by biblical law is at the level of the spirit rather than the letter.   **J. W. Rogerson**

Birch, B. C., *Let Justice Roll Down: The Old Testament, Ethics, and Christian Life* (1991).

Kaiser, W. C., *Toward Old Testament Ethics* (1983).

Rogerson, J. W., 'The Old Testament', in J. Rogerson, C. Rowland, B. Lindars, *The Study and Use of the Bible* (1988).

—— 'The Old Testament and Christian Morality', *Heythrop Journal*, 36 (1995).

Urbach, E. E., *The Sages: Their Concepts and Beliefs* (1975).

law, natural, see NATURAL LAW.

Lent, the season of forty days preceding *Easter, is observed by *fasting, almsgiving, acts of penance, and other forms of disciplined spiritual devotion. In current practice, the emphasis does not fall predominantly on the Passion and death of the Lord, but rather on human mortality and *sin transformed by the redemptive love of God in Christ. The solemnity and seriousness of Lent is traditionally betokened in corporate worship by the absence of joyful music or alleluias, and by the omission of the *Gloria in excelsis* and the *Te Deum*.

Historically, Lent has a complex origin. In ante-Nicene Egypt, the observance of the Lord's baptism at the feast of the *Epiphany was followed by a period of fasting in imitation of the wilderness fasting of Jesus. More generally, a period of fasting at this time of year developed rather as part of the preparation of baptismal candidates. In the west, this season soon became connected also with the public expulsion and subsequent restoration of penitents guilty of serious sin. Earlier of variable length, Lent took on by the 4th century a six-week duration approximating the example of the forty-day fasts of *Moses (Exod. 34: 28), Elijah (1 Kgs. 19: 8), and the Lord himself (Matt. 4: 2; Mark 1: 12–13; Luke 4: 1–2). A total of forty pre-Easter fast days, first known in Jerusalem, became normative in the Roman church in the 7th century. Because *Sundays, as days celebrating the Resurrection, were not figured among the number of fast days, Lent was calculated to begin on the seventh Wednesday before Easter: on 'Ash Wednesday' ashes were sprinkled on penitents and, from early in the 2nd millennium, upon all the repentant faithful, who were marked on their foreheads in the sign of the cross.

With widespread preference increasingly given to the *baptism of infants from the 6th century onwards, emphasis on Lent as baptismal preparation for adult converts declined in favour of general penitential practices and fasting. The Lenten fast initially was quite strict: one daily meal was eaten, usually in the evening, and dietary restrictions were imposed, among them abstinence from meat, eggs, dairy products, and alcohol. Although from the 9th century food prohibitions were often relaxed and the breaking of the fast came earlier in the day, fasting and limitation of consumption have persisted to the present day as characteristic Lenten disciplines.

Historic baptismal associations and practices of Lent—along with the vigil at Easter—have been reclaimed for contemporary Christians from the liturgical model provided in the *Apostolic Tradition* of Hippolytus (*c*.215), and from descriptions in the 4th-century catechetical sermons of Ambrose of Milan, Cyril of Jerusalem, Theodore of Mopsuestia, and John Chrysostom. Lent has become a time of intense preparation for catechumens anticipating Easter baptism, who continue their learning about and experience of the Christian faith (*catechesis*) as they move through ritual stages towards the sacraments of admission to the *church.

See also CALENDAR.   **Karen B. Westerfield Tucker**

Schmemann, A., *Great Lent* (1974).

Lewis, C. S. (Clive Staples) (1898–1963).

C. S. Lewis was one of the most interesting and widely influential Christian writers of the 20th century. Born in Belfast and brought up in Protestant Ulster, which he came to dislike intensely as 'Puritania', he turned to *atheism during schooling in England but discovered at the same time the fascination of *mythology. In 1917 he entered Oxford University to study classics for a few months before conscription into the army. Wounded in the battle of Arras in April 1918, he returned to Oxford in 1919. In 1924 he became a fellow of Magdalen College and tutor in English Literature until in 1954 he was appointed to a professorship in Cambridge, but Oxford remained his home.

Lewis only fully recovered Christian faith, following a long quest, in 1931, much helped by J. R. R. Tolkien and other friends, mostly Roman and Anglo-Catholics. His beliefs, as represented by a series of small theological works written mostly in the 1940s (*The Problem of Pain*, 1940; *The Screwtape Letters*, 1942; *Beyond Personality: The Christian Idea of God*, 1944; *The Great Divorce*, 1946; *Miracles*, 1947; *Mere Christianity*, 1952) were firmly *orthodox, of a conservative kind, avoiding issues that divided Catholics and Protestants. Their clarity and readability are characteristic of all Lewis's work. This was the period of his presidency of the Socratic Club, where wartime and post-war undergraduates learnt to discuss theology under his enriching influence.

Lewis's mastery of his academic field is shown in his massive *English Literature in the Sixteenth Century Excluding Drama* (1954) and in two earlier works bordering on the religious field: *The Allegory of Love: A Study in the Medieval Tradition* (1936) and *A Preface to 'Paradise Lost'* (1942). His first major publication, *The Pilgrim's Regress: An Allegorical Apology for Christianity, Reason, and Romanticism* (1933), already set forth the true programme of his life's work as a Christian *apologist: the renewal of *allegory as a vehicle of religious expression. He subsequently demonstrated this with extraordinary imaginativeness in two series: the science-fiction trilogy (*Out of the Silent Planet*, 1938; *Perelandra*, later renamed *Voyage to Venus*, 1943; *That Hideous Strength*, 1945) and the Narnia series, beginning with *The Lion, the Witch and the Wardrobe* (1950).

Powerfully stimulating as these fictional works are, with lively narrative, passages of great spiritual insight, and the evocation of central Christian themes, most notably the conflict between heavenly and satanic powers, Lewis's most mature contribution to Christian thought may be found in three books of his final period: two autobiographies, *Surprised by Joy* (1955), an account of his early life, and *A Grief Observed* (1961, published pseudonymously), the story of his marriage late in life to a woman dying of cancer, and *Till We Have Faces* (1956), an allegory based on the myth of Eros and Psyche, a beautiful but often overlooked work.

Lewis is a paradoxical figure. Subject of the brilliant play and film, *Shadowlands*, of an eight-foot high stained glass window in an Episcopal church in California, and of countless semi-hagiographical works including no fewer than six journals devoted to his work, Lewis was throughout life a heavy smoker and drinker; a famed academic, he fought *modernity tooth and nail, delighting in being a 'dinosaur' as he described himself in his Cambridge inaugural. A Christian apologist largely disregarded by contemporary theologians as a reactionary amateur, he has survived in his work and wide-ranging influence better than they.   **Adrian Hastings**

Carpenter, Humphrey, *The Inklings: C. S. Lewis, J. R. R. Tolkien, Charles Williams and their Friends* (1979).

Wilson, A. N., *C. S. Lewis* (1990).

liberal Protestantism.

For the last two centuries, individual Christians have existed, often unwillingly, on a spectrum between liberal and conservative. Many have used 'liberal' as a term of abuse for those further to the 'left' than themselves.

'Liberal' is not a specifically religious word. Historically, liberalism was the dominant political philosophy of the 19th century, upholding individual freedom and the ideals of the American and French Revolutions. Political liberalism itself had religious roots in the struggles of *Protestant dissenters. A movement of deeply sincere Christians, trying to gain freedom to be Christian in their own way, had secularizing side-effects. They themselves learnt a political language. Some creatively misread religious language: *Luther's, 'Here I stand, I can do no other,' became a slogan of individualism. In the modern world, people found the virtue of free trade in religion as in goods. Many Christians since have watched unhappily as new sects gave the customers what they wanted, and wondered if the customer does know best. Liberal optimism about human nature lays itself open to mockery. Moreover, liberal tolerance of Christian variety leads inevitably to tolerance of irreligion. John Stuart Mill's *Essay on Liberty* makes what is to liberals an unanswerable case that to hold an idea you have to understand it, and to grasp the best case possible against it, and that no one, even if judged wrong, should be silenced. One direct consequence of this is, as Mill surely hoped, organized articulate unbelief. The alternative, societies where a conservative church fought to silence all doubts, in practice had revolutions and evoked an *atheist anticlericalism, often indeed calling itself liberal, though illiberal on religious matters.

In churches, as in society, organized parties arose. Individuals may resist stereotyping, but two-dimensional 'left' and 'right' became the normal way of placing one's neighbours. John Henry *Newman, who in Anglicanism had defined the *Oxford Movement against liberalism, was a liberal in the eyes of *ultramontane Catholics. There is no *absolute* liberalism. This becomes very clear when we look at the set-piece battles between liberal and conservative parties in the 19th-century churches. More often than not, even if defeated at the time, the liberal opinion went on to become commonplace and normative. Conservative Christians of a later generation took it in their stride, and battle was joined elsewhere. It said little for the sense of history of conservative Christians that they seemed not to draw any moral from this pattern. On the other hand, what was called 'march of mind' liberalism, eagerly attuned to the spirit of the age, could sound very dated after a few years had passed.

It may be that liberalism prospers in peaceful, stable societies with some economic growth, where progress is a sensible hope. Some theologies, and schools of political thought, say that such eras are fraudulent. They question whether there is ever either true peace or a progress visible in human history as God 'working his purpose out'. Critics of liberalism say it lacks a sense of human *sin, and of the tragedy of the human condition. Liberals, traditionally soft-hearted, are moved by this reproach, and their best theologians are full of feeling and concern. Nevertheless, liberalism is basically cheerful. God's goodness is all around us, and he can speak to us through anything. 'Miracle is another name for event,' said the father of liberal Protestantism, Friedrich *Schleiermacher. His *Speeches on Religion* (1799) probably remain the greatest summary of liberal Protestant ideas. A theologian of Christian experience, he brought innovation and freedom to his readers.

The other leader of German liberal Protestantism, Albrecht Ritschl (1822–89), was different. Schleiermacher had been eager to differentiate the *religious experience from *ethics, Ritschl summed up religion in ethical 'value judgements' as against facts. Both found ways of talking about the essence of Christianity that seemed to hold together the person of the historical *Jesus and lived human experience. Some liberal theologians, like F. C. Baur and D. F. Strauss, spoke the language of the great philosophers, *Kant and *Hegel. Some, like Adolf Harnack (1851–1930), talked about a timeless essence, the simple faith of Jesus, rather than the creeds about him. It is unjust to select only three or four names from 19th-century Germany. Dorner's account of progressive *incarnation, or Thomasius's *kenotic christology, or Herrmann's account of the Christian's communion with God in Christ are all impressive works of a theology that tried to be a 'true mediation' between historic Christianity and contemporary culture.

At its best, liberal Protestant theology sounded both fresh and relevant. Just as Sabatier's liberal life of *Francis of Assisi made him live for modern Christians in a way that no conservative revisionism can ever destroy, so the liberal *quest of the historical Jesus was the most convincing christological move for centuries. '[I]n the human Jesus we have met with a fact … which makes us so certain of God that our conviction of being in communion with him can justify itself at the bar of reason and conscience' (Herrmann). All *christology from below, based on the 'man for others', the man from Nazareth, is characteristically liberal.

The 18th-century ancestors of liberal Protestantism, trying to avoid being tied down by inherited *creeds, had taught that the *bible alone was the religion of Protestants. But traditional biblical Protestantism in time proved too narrow, and later liberal Protestants reread the bible in interesting ways. They read it as any other ancient text, trying to find out what actually happened, imputing motive and character to the writers, finding evidence in the text for a development in the religious insight of the Israelites. The achievements of biblical critics are real and solid. They have liberal presuppositions, and were fought every inch of the way by opponents eager to stress every incoherence, every risky hypothesis. The bible

as given to us by liberal Protestantism, a collection of ancient documents, some pseudepigraphical, some more legend than history, some ethically dubious, all of their time, nevertheless in its day spoke more compellingly of God than the bible shielded from critical scholarship. Liberal bible scholars such as William Robertson Smith and Charles Briggs were hunted down as heretics, and dismissed, but their ideas continued.

English-language liberal Protestantism was often less magisterial than German. Even in professorial chairs, English liberals were happy to come up with suggestive ideas, or to undercut received commonplaces, rather than lay down the law. Bishop Westcott was once horrified when a student told him he had made everything clear. There is, nevertheless, an English liberal tradition, including the loose 'Germano-*Coleridgean' school, the Oxford Noetics, the writers of *Essays and Reviews* (1860), and, in a more catholic idiom, but perceptibly liberal, the *Lux Mundi* (1889) school. In *North America there was a great variety of liberal strands, some, like the New Haven theology or Horace Bushnell, reusing much of traditional orthodoxy, others, like the *Unitarian Channing, boldly innovative. There were those who gladly spoke of a 'new theology'. The early Chicago School, led by Shailer Mathews, was not gadflyish, like the English, but had a systematic programme and a 'socio-historical method'.

The First World War was a great blow to liberal Protestantism, which now seemed superficial, blandly optimistic, blind to human wickedness, a 'culture Protestantism' that muddled (suddenly unconvincing) Western progress with God-given destiny. The most prominent liberal German theologians, led by Harnack, had cheerfully affirmed the Kaiser's war. Liberalism was rightly chastened by this experience.

The great tradition of German systematic theology, as it continued in the 20th century, is even so interwoven with liberalism. Theologians such as *Otto and *Tillich were perceptibly liberal, but both *Barth and *Bultmann, who defined themselves against it, are incomprehensible without liberalism, and, in a wider perspective, nearer to it than they admitted.

A historical account such as this is likely to be liberal. Conservatives believed that they held to timeless truths while the whole essence of liberalism consisted in adopting the intellectual fashions of the day. Liberals themselves believed that they held to the heart of the matter (that favourite word 'essence', so difficult to give an agreed content to) and that a living Christianity will be restated in each age. Though some liberals have had a dogmatic streak—there has often been a willingness to write off whole traditions as hidebound—the typical liberal dislikes any *dogma, and any hint of authoritarianism. 'Think it possible you may be mistaken.' Liberals do not damn other Christians who disagree with them; they are more likely to canonize variety. Such *ecumenism as has been achieved is much indebted to liberalism. Given Protestantism's broken history, a plausible Protestant theology of the church is safer built on the liberal acceptance of fallibility and variety.

Liberalism was, and is, ethical. The liberal critique of traditional dogma was indebted to the various philosophies of the day, but much more to a real effort towards human maturity and goodness. More was owed to *novels—more was owed to *family life—than to abstract thought. And from insights learnt in human experience arise questions about the ways of God. The doctrine of the *atonement as popularly presented was a bloodthirsty *myth. No good father would deal thus with his children. The best theologian of 19th-century Scotland, McLeod Campbell, raised such questions as this to challenge his ancestral *Calvinism. God came to be reshaped in our better image.

Christianity is the religion of Christ. Liberal Protestantism went back to the historical Jesus. Good scholars since have said this was impossible to do. But after centuries of more-or-less *Docetic christology, where Jesus was a god appearing on earth, the effort was creditable. Forget the metaphysics and miracles; Jesus was a real person, with real moral dilemmas like ours, with a sense of God his father like ours, and of course we remake him in our own image, but we are remaking ourselves in the process. The human Jesus of liberal Protestantism, felt to be a true revelation of God just because he was human, has in the last two centuries caught the imagination of ordinary people well beyond the boundaries of organized Christianity. *Liberation theology, though disliking political liberalism, is theologically much indebted to liberal Protestantism.

Nevertheless, speaking generally, liberal Protestantism has not had mass appeal. The poor preferred sensation—miracles and black-and-white dualism. Liberal Christianity struggled to break out of its increasing suburban captivity, and, like political liberalism, had its reforming successes. The troubled conscience of middle-class Christianity raised many millions of pounds and dollars for action against social evils. 'What would Jesus do?', the title of a liberal Protestant best-selling novel, characterized the imaginative drive of such work. Theologically, this practical aspect of liberal Protestantism is best seen in the *social gospel. Walter Rauschenbusch, its theologian, was a Ritschlian with a strong sense of historical process and (evidence against the caricature of liberalism as sentimentally unrealistic) of the institutionalized structures of sin.

The tradition continues, though to call oneself liberal sounds oldfashioned. In each generation there is a challenging radicalism, like that of John *Robinson or David Jenkins, (neither as radical as their critics thought), which fights the old liberal battles. Catholic theologians such as Hans *Küng are very reminiscent of liberal Protestantism. The almost necessary presupposition of any pluralist divinity faculty must be liberal. Though there are post-liberals (see LINDBECK, GEORGE) as there are *postmodernists, many other strands in modern theology are still clearly liberal. The old spectrum between liberal and conservative still exists on ethical issues, like gay rights. The liberal tradition goes on, seriously and subtly engaging with ethical questions, always wanting to express love and freedom and not the letter of the law.   **Alistair Mason**

Clements, K. W., Lovers of Discord (1988).
Gerrish, B. A., Traditions and the Modern World (1977).
Hinchliff, P., God and History (1992).
Hutchison, W. R., The Modernist Impulse in American Protestantism (1976).
Rupp, G., Culture Protestantism (1977).
Smart, N. et al, Nineteenth Century Religious Thought in the West (1985).
Stephenson, A. M. G., The Rise and Decline of English Modernism (1984).
Tillich, P., The Protestant Era (1948).
Welch, C., Protestant Thought in the Nineteenth Century (1972–85).

liberation theology as a term was originally applied to a *contextual *theology originating in *Latin America. The term tends to be used now to describe any contextual or *political theology which either comes from the Third World or is developed in the First World under Third World inspiration (for instance, Scottish liberation theology). However, the Latin American experience remains the decisive one and needs to be understood in the context of wider movements occurring in the continent at the end of the 1960s, including the Education for Liberation Movement (Paulo *Freire, Brazil), the project of the Philosophy of Liberation (Enrique Dussel, Argentina), and the Psychotherapy of the Oppressed (Alfredo Moffat, Argentina). The Latin American social climate was one of increasing awareness of the need to change cultural, philosophical, and economic models in order to overcome the almost endemic *poverty and economic dependency of the continent. The word 'liberation', as opposed to the traditional concept of 'development', came into common use; it was a generative word that did not arise from intellectual circles but from the streets. During these years many countries in the region were suffering under dictatorial regimes. The triumph of the Cuban revolution in 1959 marked a new period of hope for many Latin Americans, who saw a country ready to take seriously the issue of national sovereignty and self-determination. The failure of the US-inspired Alliance for Progress, a developmentalist project powerless to overcome the economic and political dependency of Latin America, produced an awareness of the need for a deep structural transformation. Development became an obsolete concept. Liberation expressed the aim of Latin Americans. In the Roman Catholic Church, many priests took an active role in denouncing national and international structures of injustice, as well as organizing communities to struggle for their rights. Such was the Movement of Third World Priests. Some followed the example of Fr. Camilo Torres in Colombia, who went to fight with the guerrillas. The Movement was repressed, and its members identified as 'revolutionary priests', opposed by governments and the official church.

Key historical moments of liberation theology are associated with the meetings of *Vatican II, the Second General Assembly of CELAM, the Latin American Episcopal Council (Medellín, Colombia, 1968), the meeting of theologians in El Escorial (Spain, 1972), the Third General Assembly of CELAM (Puebla, Mexico, 1979), and the Fourth General Assembly of CELAM (Santo Domingo, 1994), but chronologies are deceptive here. Gustavo *Gutiérrez held a conference on liberation theology in 1968 after many years of work and reflection with poor communities. The process of liberation theology took place in action long before any books were published. From the beginning, the aim was not to reproduce a systematic theology from a Latin American perspective, but *to do* theology. It was said that a letter written by a community demanding one tap for clean water in a neighbourhood had more value than a book on dogmatics.

Main characteristics of a theology developed from praxis
Liberation theology presents a proposal for a *Christianity that is political and culturally decentralized. This involves, first, the acknowledgement that Christianity has always, consciously or not, supported ideological structures of power; hence theology cannot claim neutrality or political indifference. Moreover the bible does not, and *Jesus himself did not, claim such political neutrality in their message. Secondly, Christianity can no longer be reduced

culturally to a Eurocentric reflection, nor confined within the boundaries of a particular *philosophical tradition, such as that of the Greeks. Liberation theology wants to liberate theology from the constraints of methodological assumptions that ignore the importance of the culture of the oppressed and the historical experience of their struggle. This style of theologizing is a 'God-Walk' (Caminata) rather than 'God-Talk'. Its main characteristics are:

1. *Non-neutrality*. Every theology is ideologically biased and supports a social configuration of the world and political structures. Liberation theology claims that theologians should be aware of the interests they support, by declaring them at the moment of doing theology and also be aware of the consequences of such ideologies. Liberation theologians usually start their reflections by making explicit their experiences and their political standpoint, and declaring their presuppositions. This does not mean that such presuppositions cannot be challenged. On the contrary, by making them public, they open themselves to *dialogue with different perspectives and experiences.

2. *Option for the poor*. Liberation theology is issue-based, starting its reflection from the realities of human life. In Latin America, the situation of chronic poverty, social injustice, and political dependency has provided the locus for theological reflection. The option for the poor means that liberation theology acknowledges, first of all, that according to the testimony of the scriptures and early church *God has always been inclined towards the poor. The bible shows the poorest of the poor as God's favoured people. The mystery of the *Incarnation of Jesus makes this message even clearer. God became a poor man in a country under foreign occupation, as a testimony to God's own identification with the exploited. Liberation theology does not romanticize the poor, but sees in them a collective *prophetic voice, denouncing the injustice of *humanity through their suffering. This understanding gave rise to a new ecclesiology, represented in the movement of the *Basic Ecclesial Christian Communities which became a model for the *church of the poor.

3. *The concept of 'realidad'*. Literally translated as 'reality', *La realidad* implies not only a reflection upon the actual circumstances in which we are living but also an analysis of the historical causes of those circumstances. *Realidad* is a concept that reunites past and present. Sometimes it means '*truth'.

4. *Praxis*. This refers to the process of action and reflection that operates in this way of doing theology. Theological praxis combines elements of social engagement; by reflection upon a previous action, strategies can be elaborated to transform the conditions of oppression in the people's *realidad*.

5. *Orthopraxis*. The non-neutrality of theology implies that any theology, even in the more apparently detached forms, carries a responsibility for the social conditions in which people live. Traditional theology can be a powerful ally of the status quo, either showing indifference to structures of human oppression or opposing social changes that may threaten the privileged position of the church. Theology thus becomes a mere instrument for sacralizing structures of oppression. Liberation theology tries to discern which theological actions support or alternatively challenge structures of oppression. Thus *orthopraxis* (right action/reflection) becomes the criterion of veracity for *orthodoxy* (right dogma). It is not that dogmas have no place in liberation theology. They do, but as a

critical rediscovery of the challenges calling for actions of transformation which lie at the core of the Christian faith.

The concept of traditional theology as a reflection on the existence and nature of the divine revealed in the world is reversed. In liberation theology the reflection is first of all upon the world, and only then is it considered how God has manifested Godself in the historical events of humankind's liberation. This process is known as second-act theology. The first act will always be to analyse the socio-economic and political situation of some particular people in order to discover the roots of oppression and injustice. Here liberation theology uses mediatory disciplines such as sociology, psychology, economics, ethnology, etc. Then comes reflection on actions in order to produce new actions of social transformation (praxis). Faith must find its own efficacy, through a prophetic process of denouncing injustices and announcing changes for transformation, especially to structures of oppression.

6. *Structures of sin*. Without denying the reality of individual *sin, liberation theology concentrates on the structural aspects of sin, that is the macro-structures that perpetuate social injustice, poverty, and violence around the world. International trade agreements and the economic system are identified as sinful since they are responsible for the collective poverty of people in Third World countries, and also convey images of what is right and acceptable that often contradict the Christian meaning of life. Consumerism, greed for wealth, and the reduction of economic activity to the pursuit of profit are some of the values thus made acceptable, which induce people to sin. Related to structures of sin is the concept of 'structures of human sacrifice', developed by Franz Hinkelammert. This denounces the idolatry of the present economic system, which costs so many lives that it can be seen as a massive structure of human sacrifice. For instance, the children who are born in a country under the constraints of external debt are born to be sacrificed, since their quality of life will be reduced by misery and exploitation.

The hermeneutical circle

This refers to liberation theology's methodology. It was originally developed by J. L. Segundo, J. Severino Croatto, and C. Boff amongst others, but it is a permanent process of action and reflection which is constantly enriched by people's experience. The philosophical basis of the *hermeneutical circle comes from phenomenology (Paul *Ricœur) and Paulo Freire's education for liberation. From Ricœur it has taken the organization of the circle of interpretation itself, the theory of *symbols, and the dynamics of *myth; from Freire, the methodology of conscientization. The circle of interpretation is basically organized in four moments, although these are not linear but in a dynamic relation.

1. *Reading reality from the community's experience*. Starting with the concept of the community as interpreter and interpreted, the initial perspective is materialist, that is, issue-based, an interpretation of the community's *realidad*. At this early stage dogma and scripture are not the starting-point. The community works together to identify key issues in its social reality. This step may sometimes include the rebuilding of a community around issues of solidarity and *justice. The methodology of conscientization is used at this stage to 'decode' structures of oppression that have been internalized and remain unchallenged, often because of theological concepts such as

resignation and acceptance of poverty as part of God's will in one's life. The communities understand themselves as co-workers with God for the kingdom announced by Jesus. This process of starting with *realidad* and proceeding to the scriptures has been called *eisegesis* by Croatto and other biblicists, in contrast to exegesis (but C. Boff uses *eisegesis* with negative connotations in his struggle to reconcile the spontaneity of popular interpretation with the normative role of Roman Catholic traditions).

2. *The dialectic scripture / realidad.* This is a moment of analysis, where liberation theology uses *social sciences and political theory. *Marxism has been a key conceptual framework for such analysis but is by no means the only one. Although there have been different Marxist positions in liberation theology, it can be said in general that it has an Althusserian perspective, by which the Marxist scientific approach and its economic analysis is differentiated from Marxist political ideology. Gutiérrez made a distinction during the early 1970s between Marxist dialectical methodology based on the analysis of the class struggle, and the atheist Marxist world-view. Liberation theology took elements from Marxist theory in order to become a critical theology, which addressed questions to the dialectic of action / reflection (praxis) and the place of Christian faith in such praxis. There has been no homogeneity in the interpretation of Marx, and while some insisted on the need for a *revolutionary struggle (Camilo Torres in Colombia and Ernesto Cardenal in Nicaragua), others such as Gutiérrez and Segundo have accepted the class struggle but rejected the strategy of class war. However, the *realidad* of the class struggle has been a starting-point for the reading of the scriptures in the context of the life of the poor. 'Liberation' was used as the hermeneutical key in the reading of the scriptures as can be seen in Cardenal's *The Gospel in Solentiname.* The poor communities identified themselves with the prophetic voices denouncing structural sin in the bible. Croatto used structuralist approaches to subvert biblical texts that had become domesticated in the service of structures of oppression. Popular biblicists, such as Carlos Mesters, found ways of conveying the basics of a materialist / structural approach to the bible to illiterate peasants. The community discussion of key issues in their lives, together with a reading of the bible that liberated the text from the constraints of orthodoxy, becoming closer to an orthopraxis, transformed biblical exegesis. New translations of the bible such as *La Biblia Latinoamericana,* couched in terms from Latin American culture, has references identifying the struggle of *Israel with modern agrarian reform or God's condemnation of dictatorial regimes and human rights violations. This political reading of the bible led to persecution of Christian communities by the authorities.

3. *Understanding the text in community.* This is the moment in the process of the hermeneutical circle when the text becomes part of the historical experience of the community reading it. The actions of liberation portrayed in the scriptures are subjected to new reflections. It is a moment of critical engagement challenging not only the traditional reading of the bible, but also the ideological construction of Christianity and the church in Latin America. To understand the text, people's own experience in situations of historical oppression, and *their* priorities are taken seriously. The development of liberation theology in new areas of praxis such as *feminist theology, eco-theology, *mestizo* theology, Maya and Andean theology have come from this critical engagement that goes beyond the explanation of biblical texts set in present contexts. This is a critical hermeneutical theology, engaged in a continuous process of interpreting *realidad* and the Christian faith in order to produce a praxis of social transformation.

4. *Appropriation of the text.* The popular exegeses made in the context of liberation theology are validated in practices for change towards a Christian vision of an alternative society. The text that has been read must produce a change at the level of consciousness of the community who have interpreted it. This may be seen at different levels, from the self-confidence that a community can acquire for the struggle for its own rights, to solidarity and participation in the organization of religious or secular movements towards *peace and justice. The best of liberation theology exegeses have never been written down or published. They have become actions illuminating a new community reading of the bible, thus arriving at discernment and inspiration for new actions of transformation. Thus, the hermeneutical circle is completed and begins anew.

Liberation theology at the end of the century

In its strictest form, liberation theology reflects a moment in Latin American experience almost past, but in a wider sense it represents one of the most powerful influences in modern theology, flowing out into numerous other areas and forms. From Gutiérrez's *Towards a Theology of Liberation* until now, Latin America has gone through a series of political changes, reflected in liberation theology, such as:

1. The triumph of an unrestrained *capitalism in the world and the global policies of the new economic order have produced in Latin America a new group of people who fall beyond the category of merely poor. These are the excluded masses of economically marginalized people for whom even exploitation could well be a kind of privilege. The option for the poor has become the option for the marginalized, those excluded from society because they have no participation in economic processes.

2. Changes within the structures of the church, produced by the Vatican, have been responsible for a widespread dismantling of Basic Christian Ecclesial Communities (BECs) and a general decline in support for them. However, the BECs have given rise to a new development known as the 'popular movements'. Such is the Movement of the Landless People which has the support of Brazilian bishops, and which is a coalition between the church, the peasants, and professional people who give their expertise to help people to obtain land to live on and cultivate. This, with other popular movements, such as ecological groups and the Children of the Street movement, today represent liberation theology in action.

3. New theological paths have been developed in liberation theology. *Women, *black, and indigenous people have reclaimed their right to be subjects of theology, and have started reflections from their specific circumstances. The concept of 'the poor', for instance, used to be treated as if the experience of poor women in patriarchal Latin America were no different from the experience of poor men. Gender, class, and race need to be part of the analysis. Recognition of the poor's religious experiences has also led liberationists to see the need for a dialogue between gospel and culture,

taking into account the role of traditional religions in the continent.

Marcella Althaus-Reid

Aquino, M. P., *Our Cry for Life: Feminist Theology from Latin America* (1993).

Boff, C., *Theology and Praxis: Epistemological Foundations* (1987).

Boff, L., *Ecology and Liberation. A New Paradigm* (1995).

Boff, L., and Boff, C., *Introducing Liberation Theology* (1987).

Cardenal, E., *The Gospel in Solentiname* (2 vols.; 1977–82).

Cook, G. (ed.), *New Faces of the Church in Latin America* (1994).

Croatto, S., *Exodus: A Hermeneutics of Freedom* (1981).

Dussel, E., *Ethics and Community* (1988).

Freire, P., *Pedagogy of the Oppressed* (1972).

Gebara, I., and Bingemer, M. C., *Mary, Mother of God, Mother of the Poor* (1987).

Gutiérrez, G., *A Theology of Liberation* (1973).

—— *The Power of the Poor in History* (1983).

Míguez Bonino, J., *Doing Theology in a Revolutionary Situation* (1975).

Miranda, J., *Marx and the Bible* (1974).

Segundo, J. L., *The Liberation of Theology* (1976).

Sobrino, J., *Christology at the Crossroads* (1978).

Sobrino, J., and Ellacuría, I. (eds.), *Mysterium Liberationis* (1990).

light and darkness are probably the most pervasive of all Christian and biblical *symbols. The Christian use of the *metaphor of light draws profoundly upon the OT where, again and again, *God is described as our 'light and salvation' (Ps. 27: 1) in whose 'light do we see light' (Ps. 36: 9). God's justice is 'a light to the nations' (Isa. 51: 4) while Israel is called to 'walk in the light of the Lord' (Isa. 2: 5). The relationship between God and light goes back to the first lines of *Genesis: 'God said "Let there be light" and there was light' (1: 3). He saw that the light was good, separated it from the darkness and called the one day, the other night. While this establishes a special God–light relationship from the start, it also makes clear that the night too belongs to him. He gives names to both.

In later Judaism, however, from about the 2nd century BC, light and darkness became contrasted in a near-ontological *dualism as appears in various *apocrypha and, especially, the *Dead Sea Scrolls where the 'sons of light' are at war with the 'sons of darkness' ruled over by an *Angel of Darkness. Nowhere may the NT seem closer to Qumran than here. For Matthew (4: 16), quoting Isaiah (9: 2) 'the people who sat in darkness have seen a great light'. Simeon hails Jesus as the 'light to lighten the Gentiles' (Luke 2: 32). Jesus' true nature is revealed in the brightness of the Transfiguration light. All three synoptics stress that at the crucifixion there was darkness over the whole land, while the angelic witnesses to the *Resurrection were dazzlingly white. *John's gospel begins in Genesis style with an account of the coming of light to the world, a light that enlightens everyone (1: 9), a light that Jesus declares to be himself (John 8: 12 and 9: 5). This light is emphatically contrasted with darkness: 'Men loved darkness rather than light, because their deeds were evil' (3: 19); walk not in darkness, but in light that you may be 'sons of light' (12: 36). This dualistic contrast is to be found as strongly in *Paul as in John. 'What fellowship has light with darkness? What accord has Christ with Belial?' (2 Cor. 6: 14–15).

This symbolic legacy, at once NT and OT, has permeated the whole of Christian thought, from dogma to popular liturgy and literature. The Nicene *Creed proclaims Christ 'light from light'. Popular religion established the moment of Christ's birth as that of the winter solstice, so that it would, like the sun, bring light to the world at its darkest moment. *Dante's *Divine Comedy* is almost a poetic theology of light; in Henry Vaughan's *The World*, eternity is portrayed as 'a great ring of pure and endless light', prepared by the bridegroom for the bride, while all the 'small lights' of the world—from sun and moon to sanctuary and altar lamps—point for T. S. *Eliot to the 'light invisible'.

A religious culture's underlying symbolic structure shapes the way the world is viewed and behaviour formed in all sorts of ways. Christianity's preoccupation with light has, inevitably, to wrestle with and apply the tension between monism and dualism already biblically present. Thus much Victorian thought, especially *missionary expression, was couched in terms of a very simple struggle with darkness, whether found in industrial slums, Roman superstition, or 'darkest Africa', and it was easy enough to see those dark areas as especially subject to Satan, Prince of Darkness (see DEVIL). Light could appear as pre-eminently a characteristic of 'enlightened' northern Europeans, 'white' in skin, Protestant in faith, and progressive in civilization. *Blake's 'Little Black Boy' mixes up some of this well enough: 'I am black but O, my soul is white! | White as an angel is the English child. | But I am black, as if bereaved of light.' Misapplications of the symbolism of light often went dangerously far, especially in regard to race (see APARTHEID), but Blake was himself struggling in his poem to find a positive meaning in blackness.

Christian thought has never wholly surrendered darkness to Belial. The conviction that 'the darkness falls at thy behest' (as in John Ellerton's well-known hymn) undercuts any exaggerated dualism. It is part of a God-given world, with its own positive significance. For *John of the Cross, 'the greater the darkness wherein the soul journeys… the greater its security.' If it is 'night' when the betrayer leaves Jesus, as John's gospel emphasizes (13: 30), the nights of Jesus' birth and Resurrection are none the less holy and hymn-worthy. Light and darkness coalesce rather than conflict within the totality of Christian symbolism.

Adrian Hastings

limbo is a theological term for a place or state of the dead that is neither *heaven, *hell, nor *purgatory. It lacks at once the heavenly vision of God and the pains of hell or purgatory. There have, historically, been two limbos. The first was the 'place' where the just who died before Christ were thought to await *redemption. It appears to be referred to in a (probably 4th century) line of the Apostles' *Creed, 'Christ descended into hell', an idea derived from 1 Peter 3: 18, he 'went to preach to the spirits in prison'. Both phrases are enigmatic and their meaning is disputed. At best they can do no more than *symbolize the universality of Christ's redemptive effect, in regard not only to present and future but also to the past.

The second 'limbo' was allotted to infants dying unbaptized. While *Augustine reluctantly consigned them to hell, as *baptism is the sacrament of *salvation, subsequent theology found this too hard and constructed instead a place of natural happiness appropriate for rational beings who have neither sinned, nor, through baptism, been granted supernatural grace. This became a stable element in Catholic teaching for many hundred years. In the 1950s it was suddenly eroded through recognition that if unbaptized babies were prevented from sharing salvation as a consequence of original *sin derived from *Adam then *Paul's assertion in Romans 5, the principal source for the doctrine of original sin, that 'where sin abounded, grace did more abound' would be untrue: the impact of the First Adam would extend further than that of the Second. Since then limbo has simply faded. It remains unmentioned in the, fairly conservative, *Catechism of the Catholic Church* of *John Paul II which simply affirms that God's great *mercy and the tenderness of Jesus towards *children 'allow us hope that there is a way of salvation for children who have died without baptism' (p. 321).

Adrian Hastings

Gumpel, P, 'Unbaptized Infants: May They be Saved?', *Downside Review*, 72 (1954), 342–458.

Hastings, A., 'The Salvation of Unbaptized Infants', *Downside Review* (Spring 1959), 172–8.

Van Roo, W., 'Infants Dying without Baptism', *Gregorianum*, 35 (1954), 406–73.

Wilkin, V., *From Limbo to Heaven* (1961).

Lindbeck, George

Lindbeck, George (1923–), American Protestant theologian. Lindbeck was born in China where his parents were *Lutheran missionaries. He was educated at Yale University where he taught theology and philosophy from 1951 to 1993. Throughout his career, Lindbeck was intensively engaged in *ecumenical discussions, particularly with Catholics, and most notably as an observer at *Vatican II; from 1968 to 1987 he was co-chairman of the international Joint Roman Catholic/Lutheran Commission.

In his writings Lindbeck espouses a 'catholic Protestant' position which holds that the heirs of the *Reformation should strive for reunion with Rome, since the Reformers intended to launch a reform movement *within* the *church. Accordingly, characteristic of Lindbeck's publications is a high ecclesiology with a strong confessional/*credal component and an emphasis on doctrinal issues.

Lindbeck is best known as the principal architect of 'postliberal theology', sometimes known as the Yale School. With the late Hans Frei, his colleague at Yale, he pioneered a Protestant *theology that self-consciously attempts to halt the erosion of Christian identity and effectiveness in the modern era by focusing on the internal logic of faith within particular traditions. Reflecting communal Christian practice, theology should seek to transmit the church's belief system in its distinctiveness through ever-changing cultural contexts, and it has to resist the temptation of translating the faith into secular conceptual frameworks.

Lindbeck has been particularly attentive to biblical matters. In what he regards as the postliberal (*postmodern) age, it is crucial for the Christian church and for theology to retrieve critically a premodern *hermeneutics of the bible that stresses its canonical unity and reads the so-called historical narratives as something more akin to a realistic novel. Such a 'classic' intratextual pattern of biblical interpretation has a unique potential to build consensus and community and absorb the contemporary world into the text, not vice versa.

Andreas Eckerstorfer

Lindbeck, G., *The Future of Roman Catholic Theology* (1970).

—— *The Nature of Doctrine: Religion and Theology in a Postliberal Age* (1984).

Marshall, B. (ed.), *Theology and Dialogue: Essays in Conversation with George Lindbeck* (1990).

literacy

literacy. As a religion of the book, Christianity has depended on readers and writers to transmit its insights. It is hard to estimate the degree of literacy in any early society but *Paul could rely on letters as a means of communication as he travelled between his churches, even if only a proportion of his congregations could actually read them. In this way a sense of a wider Christian community could be maintained. Even isolated churches could sustain their spiritual identity through possession of the sacred books.

After the fall of Rome in 410, the situation changed drastically. Levels of literacy in the general population tumbled, and it was in the *scriptoria* of *monastic communities that literacy survived in the west. It is clear that some copyists were themselves barely capable of reading what they wrote, but an ember was tended that was rekindled by the resurgence of literary culture in the 12th century and beyond.

As reading spead, it became more difficult for the church to control what was read or how it was interpreted. The *Reformation went hand in hand with the advent of printing which allowed the dissemination of bibles and tracts in unprecedented numbers, to little avail if there had not been substantial numbers of readers who were eager and able to take advantage of this. The Reformers drew on *Augustine's profound reflections on reading in their belief that the bible was open to all to interpret and profit from as a road to salvation. This encouraged the development of schools for a much wider range of the population. Until well into the 19th century, it was from the bible that children learned to read. The first printed work in many European vernacular *languages was the bible, often leading to the development of a standard literary form of the language.

This trend has continued as missionaries bring the bible to non-literate peoples, supplying an alphabet and a written literature for languages never before transcribed. Such enterprises go back at least as far as Cyril and Methodius, who in the 9th century devised the Cyrillic alphabet to *translate the bible into Slavonic languages. With the bible the technology of literacy arrives in oral societies.

Theorists of literacy have argued that a literate society functions very differently from an oral one, and that literate people conceive of themselves in an altered way. The ability to stand back from and revise one's own words allows a different level of self-awareness and it has been suggested that some of the social and psychological characteristics of *Protestantism are as much a product of its stress on literacy as any more directly spiritual or theological policy. If this is so, then the effect on Christian thought of the new electronic media with their recovery of aspects of oral transmission along with the fluidity of hypertext may be further-reaching than we yet imagine.

See also JOURNALISM; PUBLISHING.   **Hugh S. Pyper**

Gamble, H. Y., *Books and Readers in the Early Church* (1995).

Jeffrey, D. L., *People of the Book* (1996).

Ong, W. J., *Orality and Literacy* (1982).

Stock, B., *Augustine the Reader* (1996).

liturgy

liturgy is the public *worship of the *church, the body of communal religious rituals that gives structure, definition, and expression to the relationship between *God and the company of Christian believers. Although traditional definitions stress the qualities of ceremonial precision and formality, liturgy happens wherever *religious experience evokes particular, patterned human responses. At the heart of the Christian liturgy is the experience of what the apostle Paul describes as 'that harvest of righteousness that comes through Christ Jesus for the glory and praise of God' (Phil. 1: 11), and liturgical *prayer, along with ethics, *spirituality, and doctrine, becomes a basic component of the church's self-definition in any particular circumstances. The story of the liturgy, then, is essentially the story of the ways in which complex social, cultural, and theological forces have shaped the various ritual responses to the experience of God in Christ.

Any attempt at a broad survey of the Christian liturgy is complicated by a number of factors. Not only is there very little direct textual evidence for many periods of liturgical history, but the relationship between liturgical texts and liturgical practice is often uncertain. Christian diversity makes most conclusions about the nature of the liturgy tentative and generalizations few. But since a 1st-century congregation of urbanized Jews undoubtedly would have assimilated Jewish cultic practices in a very different way from a rural church made up of former devotees of Isis or Asclepius, the debate about the continuity of Jewish and Christian liturgy in the 1st century continues. But despite its diverse forms and intentions, some general things can be said about the Christian liturgy even in its early period. From the very beginning, Christian communities of all kinds seem to have taken it for granted that *water *baptism was the method by which new members were incorporated into the *Body of Christ. It is not surprising, given the missionary character of the documents, that there are more NT references to baptism than to other forms of Christian worship, and in the Acts of the Apostles the constituent elements of water bath, forms of instruction, and the laying on of hands (as a sign of the power of the *Holy Spirit in the life of the newly baptized) are described (see, for example, Acts 8: 26–39). In addition, a number of theological motifs begin to coalesce around the practice of baptism: the *forgiveness of *sin, rebirth into the community of the redeemed, and entry into the messianic era.

A second ubiquitous element of early Christian liturgy is the ritual meal, consisting at first of a full supper with a *bread and cup ritual appended to it. Patterned loosely on *Jesus' final meal with his friends, the supper was usually referred to as the 'Lord's supper' or the *agape* (love feast), and the bread and cup ritual was usually called either by the Jewish term 'the breaking of bread' or by the Greek word *Eucharist (*eucharistia*), meaning 'thanksgiving'. Historical associations with the Last Supper are fairly clear in early descriptions of the meal (such as in 1 Cor. 11), and eating and drinking was understood as a way of coming into the presence of Jesus Christ and remembering his sacrificial life, death, and *Resurrection. Participation in the meal also foreshadowed the coming reign of God and established *communion both with God and among members of the Christian fellowship.

It is likely that certain other liturgical rites and practices were also a part of this earliest layer of Christian life. Anointing of the sick is mentioned in James 5: 14–15, and the singing of 'psalms and hymns and spiritual songs' during gatherings for worship is recommended to the Christians at Ephesus. We also know that *preaching was probably a part of most worship services, and there is some suggestion that Christians, like Jews, may have punctuated the day with formal prayers, convinced that *time itself was a potential locus for divine revelation. After about 150 we begin to find evidence for rites for the reconciliation of those who have sinned, and

later there are others for *ordination, burial, and *marriage. Later still is mention of a liturgical *calendar, centred on *Easter, with *Pentecost and *Epiphany and seasons of preparatory *fasting also beginning to be established.

With few exceptions, then, the basic components of all future Christian liturgy were very probably in place by the time of the Council of *Nicaea: baptism; the Eucharist (the *agape* meal having become detached); rites of *reconciliation and *penance, ordination, and healing; daily prayer; *hymn- and *psalm-singing; the liturgical recitation of the bible, *creeds, and responsive prayers; preaching; the beginnings of a Christian calendar. In addition, most of these elements were taking on the overall shape that they would retain for at least the next 1200 years. As the church came to terms with its growing respectability, the liturgy moved from a domestic to a public setting, adopting the trappings of imperial court ritual. But there remained an improvisational quality about liturgical prayer that would not be completely lost until the Middle Ages. Roles within the assembly were also gradually regularized, and the liturgical ministries of bishop, *priest, and deacon were, with certain local variations, being reflected in the theological content of the rites of ordination (see EPISCOPATE; DIACONATE).

At the same time, the rise of Christian *monasticism was having a profound impact on the shape of the liturgy. Beginning with the Egyptian ascetics in the 4th century, and continuing with the establishment of various cenobite traditions, the liturgy was increasingly understood as a vehicle for self-discipline, contemplation, and penitence. The Rule of Saint *Benedict prescribes eight services (offices) of prayer throughout the day, with the recitation of the psalms the core of their content.

Gradually the liturgy, particularly the eucharistic liturgy and daily office, became the province of religious professionals, both monks and clergy, while the *laity were increasingly distanced in various ways from the liturgical action. The retention of Latin in the west as the language of the liturgy, the growing awe and reverence towards the eucharistic bread and *wine, the physical distancing of the altar from the main body of the church, the decline of preaching, and the elaboration of liturgical rites and ceremonies all conspired to make the liturgy increasingly something for the laity to observe rather than to engage in as a participant. This trend towards the professionalization of the liturgy is perhaps best symbolized by the prohibition of the laity from receiving the cup at the Eucharist, due to fear of insufficient reverence and of spilling the eucharistic wine.

In the *Reformation of the 16th century, the liturgy again became the most visible indicator of theological and ecclesiastical change. The Continental Reformers shared a passionate belief that lay people had been denied full participation in the liturgy, and that abuses of both the spirit and the letter of the liturgical canons had multiplied.

The liturgical experiments of Martin *Luther, Huldrych *Zwingli, and John *Calvin, while differing in the degree to which they departed from their medieval predecessors, are all shaped according to principles that mark them as 'Protestant': emphasis on the reading and preaching of scripture, the use of the vernacular, and the regular reception of communion by all members of the congregation (instead of by clergy only). In addition, all agreed that baptism, as an act of the whole church, should always be conducted in the ordinary Sunday service, and insisted on the removal of all 'undue ceremonial'. The eucharistic liturgy was the object of the Reformers' special attention, and was the cause of division between *Lutheran and *Reformed Protestants, the latter believing that the Lutheran rites had not been revised radically enough and still provided occasions for idolatry and abuse.

Reacting to the threat of liturgical anarchy, the Council of *Trent reinforced the ideal of uniformity in the practice and interpretation of the liturgy. The institution of all seven *sacraments by Jesus, the *sacrificial character of the Eucharist, the doctrine of *transubstantiation, the denial of the chalice to the laity were affirmed and the church's liturgy was standardized according to the Council's decrees. The rites of the Council of Trent formed the official liturgy of the Roman Catholic Church until *Vatican II authorized a new round of revisions four centuries later.

As the Reformation spread westwards, Protestant liturgy became more eclectic, shaping itself according to the particular political and theological situation within which it developed. In two successive editions of the *Anglican Book of Common Prayer (1549/1552), for example, Lutheran, Zwinglian, and Calvinist theological tendencies in liturgical and sacramental practice are evident, which make the texts controversial to this day. Various purifying movements in the centuries which followed (*Puritans and *Quakers in the 17th, *Methodists in the 18th, Anglo-Catholics in the 19th) also made reform of the liturgy part of their agenda, and Christian missionaries to other continents sought to provide revised rites in support of the task of evangelization.

The 19th century was marked by the rise of liturgical scholarship and a renewed search for the ancient roots of the Christian liturgy. But with old liturgical lines of demarcation being dissolved and new ones laid down, the conditions for a degree of liturgical flexibility and freedom were also established in this period. By the turn of the 20th century, *Protestantism had again divided, this time not along denominational or confessional lines, but rather over the question of where authentic religious experience was to be found. The profound impact on the liturgy of *evangelicalism on the one hand and *Romanticism on the other is embodied in the church buildings each subgroup occupied: the brightly lit auditorium-like churches dominated by the central pulpit inspired by the evangelical revival, and the dim and lofty, altar-centred neo-Gothic churches that expressed the new sacramentalism (see ARTS, VISUAL). More recently, Pentecostalist and *charismatic influences have affected all liturgical traditions, creating room for spontaneity and for the outpouring of the gifts of the Spirit on the congregation.

Academic study of the liturgy has raised a number of significant issues about the place of corporate worship in the religious lives of Christian believers. In what ways do such things as saying marriage vows, confessing our sin, or exchanging gestures of reconciliation allow us to establish and maintain a lively and compelling relationship with God and one another? How does the recitation of liturgical prayers help us to create structures of religious meaning? Can an encounter with the *symbols of fire, water, bread, be life-changing? As theologians and liturgists have considered these questions, tentative proposals have emerged for understanding the specifically religious value of the Christian liturgy.

First, many observers comment on the importance of the liturgy in harnessing the power of human *memory and imagination. At its most basic level, the liturgy is the occasion for Christians to gather publicly to relate and ritualize the core narrative that binds us together as a body of believers. In so doing, we not only recall that story, with all its myriad associations and connections, we also imagine ourselves as inserted in that narrative as actors in our own right. This process creates what Walter Brueggemann has called a 'zone of possibility' within which we can not only envision alternative futures, but act upon them.

While the ability to act out of an imagined future is important to the religious life of both individuals and groups, it is also important in establishing a sense of social and psychological location. 'Knowing our place' in a rapidly changing world is a difficult thing, and keeping our place in a situation of profound fragmentation, isolation, and alienation is equally challenging. The second important religious value of the Christian liturgy, then, is that it gives participants a lively sense of where they stand in relation to the world, to one another, and to ultimate reality. Where 'seeing is believing' may have been the *Enlightenment paradigm for Christian faith, the model for the third millennium will more likely be 'belonging is believing'. To engage in patterns of ritual behaviour with others plays an essential role in the process of belonging.

Susan J. White

Bradshaw, Paul, *The Search for the Origins of Christian Worship* (1992).
Bradshaw, P., and Hoffman, L. (eds.), *The Making of Jewish and Christian Worship* (1991).
Fink, Peter (ed.), *New Dictionary of Sacramental Worship* (1990).
Jones, C., Wainwright, G., Yarnold, E., and Bradshaw, P., *The Study of Liturgy*, rev. edn. (1992).
Lee, Bernard J. (ed.), *Alternative Futures for Worship* (7 vols.; 1986).
Wainwright, Geoffrey, *Doxology* (1980).
World Council of Churches, *Baptism, Eucharist, and Ministry*, Faith and Order Paper, 111 (1982).
White, James F., *Protestant Worship: Traditions in Transition* (1992).
White, Susan J., *Groundwork of Christian Worship* (1997).

Logos, see WORD.

Lonergan, Bernard (1904–84), Canadian philosopher-theologian and methodologist. Born in Buckingham, Quebec, Lonergan joined the *Jesuits in 1922 and studied in Canada, England, and Rome, becoming a priest in 1936. He taught dogmatic theology in Montreal (1940–7), Toronto (1947–53), and Rome (1953–65), until lung cancer intervened. After surgery and convalescence, he resumed work in North America, and continued teaching until 1983.

His publications included ground-breaking interpretations of Thomas *Aquinas (*Verbum*, exploring his implicit epistemology, and *Grace and Freedom*) and Latin textbooks on *christology and the *Trinity. Other subjects he worked on include logic, philosophy of history, education, and macroeconomics (a 22-volume *Collected Works* is in progress). But *Insight* (1957) and *Method in Theology* (1972) represent the core of his work. Several research centres, societies, and periodicals exist to promote Lonerganian studies.

Lonergan believed that theology's task of making a religious tradition intelligible in ever-changing cultural contexts required new philosophical foundations, which could be discovered by investigating one's empirically, intelligently, and rationally conscious experience of enquiry (the structured three-level process which, he held, generates knowledge by transforming experience via insights into validated judgements). He argued that self-commitment to the inescapable norms governing this process contains an implicit affirmation of the intelligibility of reality and reveals a fourth level (responsible consciousness) to ground a rich understanding of objectivity as not excluding subjectivity but demanding sustained authentic subjectivity. *Method* treats religious *conversion (fundamentally an experience of unrestricted being-in-love) as a transforming gift on this fourth level. Lonergan's deeply considered *ecumenical model of methodical theology as a collaborative two-phase process of critical retrieval and (for believers) committed elaboration of a religious tradition systematically relates his four-level structure of authentic subjectivity to the tasks and conflicts of theologians, and calls for far-reaching personal and communal development. **Gerard O'Reilly**

Crowe, F. E., *Lonergan* (1992).

Morelli, M. D. and E. A. (eds.), *The Lonergan Reader* (1997).

Tracy, D., *The Achievement of Bernard Lonergan* (1970).

Lord's Prayer.

Lord's Prayer. When *Jesus taught *prayer he did not prescribe techniques of meditation but gave a form of words to enter into conversation with *God whom his disciples were to approach as children approach their father, though the degree of intimacy which the name 'Abba' represents has been disputed. The words are few, with no heaping up of phrases or long lists. God knows our needs before we ask and we address him in simple trust. The prayer Jesus gives is probably not intended as an unchanging form of words for solemn repetition but a pattern, a *model* for prayer.

There are two versions in the gospels, Matthew 6: 9–13, part of the *Sermon on the Mount, and Luke 11: 2–4. The shorter form is more likely to be the original, which would give priority to Luke. It is clear that the prayer found in Matthew has been filled out *liturgically, some manuscripts even adding a doxology, 'For thine is the kingdom, the power, and the glory, for ever and ever, Amen', essential if the prayer was to be used in *worship. Luke's setting is also more convincing, the prayer given in answer to a request. Jesus had not appeared as a traditional teacher of prayer and the disciples wanted him to take on this role. However, Luke's fourth petition, 'Forgive us our sins, for we forgive everyone who is indebted to us,' seems an attempt to make the Matthean debts and indebtedness more spiritual and perhaps less primitive. The Lucan 'sins' obscures the probably original parallelism between the clauses. Certainty here is not possible.

Most important is that the Prayer is thoroughly Jewish and that it is a petition. There has been a tendency to regard petition as one of the 'lower levels' of prayer, to be outgrown by meditation and contemplation leading to *mystical union. This is certainly to go one better than Jesus, for whom prayer was, above all, a personal relationship with God, our Father, and experience of our dependence on him.

The heart of the prayer is 'Thy kingdom come'. We may interpret this difficult phrase, in the words of Ronald Gregor Smith's epilogue on Prayer in his *Secular Christianity* (1966), 'Prayer is to be understood as the anticipation in the whole of our existence of that one end which is the reality of God … It is the engagement of the whole life in the hope of the End in Christ.'

There are two especially difficult clauses, 'Give us this day our daily bread' and 'Lead us not into temptation'. In the former, *epiousion*, translated 'daily', is unknown outside the prayer and its citations. Five fathers of the church, from Tertullian to *Augustine, gave five different interpretations. Reference to the *bread of the *Eucharist became prominent, hence the inclusion of the Lord's Prayer in liturgies after the Prayer of Consecration. Modern translators prefer 'Give us today bread enough for tomorrow', but are divided as to whether this means what we need for earthly subsistence, sufficiency not luxury, or a foretaste of the bread of heaven, the age to come. 'Lead us not into temptation' raises other theological problems. This is so much the traditional translation in English that both the Revised Standard Version and the Church of England Alternative Service Book retain it. However, the original does not refer to temptation to sin, but to the trials and disasters that it was believed would herald the inauguration of God's *Kingdom, as in Mark 13. Therefore the Revised English Bible and the New Jerusalem Bible translate 'Do not put us to the test', and the New Revised Standard Version 'Do not bring us to the time of trial'. For Christians today this could be a request to be saved from persecution or malignant illness.

There are those who object to the language of paternalism and *kingship. However, these are *metaphors with value because Christ used them and because, as Paul *Ricœur said, it is the children who make the Father and in the Son's death the distinctive nature of *fatherhood is established, while God's kingly rule, the end for which the universe was made, is that shown in the love of Calvary (see D. Ihide (ed.), *The Conflict of Interpretation* (1974), 468).

The Lord's Prayer in fact plants the *cross at the heart of Christian prayer, for effectively it is the prayer of Jesus himself in the garden. 'Pray that you may be spared the test.' 'Father if it be your will take this cup from me. Yet not my will but yours be done' (Luke 22: 41, 42). As they pray it throughout the ages, Christians watch with Christ in Gethsemane. It represents the quintessence of Christianity, both the teaching and the practice of Jesus.

Gordon S. Wakefield

Duquoc, C., and Florestan, C. (eds.), *Asking and Thanking* (1990).

Evans, C. F., *The Lord's Prayer*, 2nd edn. (1997).

Jeremias, J., *The Prayers of Jesus* (1966).

love.

love. Christian thinkers agree that love is the central concept of *Christianity. Love refers both to the nature of *God and the divine nature of relationship, thus covering a broad network of interdependent relationships: between God and the universe, God and *humanity, God and the *church; between human beings and God, between one human being and another, between human beings and the universe, between each human being and his or her self. However, throughout Christian history there have been many different attempts at discussing this all-embracing notion of love and its role in Christian life. The use of 'love' in ordinary language further complicates Christian reflection upon it.

In ordinary language 'love' may mean a feeling of mutual attraction between persons or a person's desire of, sentiment for, or attachment to a particular object. A person may love her home, her country, her children, her friends, her parents, her cat, her car, her money, her holiday. Love is used synonymously with friendship, desire, loyalty, attachment, feeling, and liking. In English 'making love' is also a term for *sexual intercourse.

Concepts of love, its experience, and significance, are by no means confined to Christianity. The use of the word and its changing role within Christian life and thought derived from the Hebrew Scriptures, the Septuagint translation of them into Greek, the various strands within the NT, and the discussions on love in classical Greek philosophy and literature.

In the Hebrew Scriptures, love can be for things as well as for persons, as in modern English, but the various words translated as 'love' are also used for the divine–human relationship. The most common expressions, the verb 'aheb and the noun hesed, are used in a religious context. 'aheb occurs in the Shema, Deut. 6: 4–5: 'Hear, O Israel: the Lord our God, the Lord is one. Love the Lord your God with all your heart and with all your soul and with all your strength.' It is also used in the command to love neighbour (Lev. 19: 18) and stranger (Lev. 19: 34). With reference to God's *covenant, 'aheb refers to God's love for his people, despite *Israel's failure to love God (Jer. 31: 3). Hosea compares God's love for his people to the love of a husband for his wife or of parents for their child. In contrast to 'aheb, hesed is never used with reference to inanimate objects; it refers to actions resulting from a particular kind of personal relationship. God's hesed means that God is committed to Israel by covenant, even when Israel is disobedient. Hence forgiveness is part of his love. Hesed is also used to express human love for God (especially in Hosea) or for other human beings (cf. Mic. 8: 8). Hesed affirms commitment of the partners in a relationship, and in particular what they do for each other in situations of need. It also stresses the freedom of the lover towards the beloved.

'aheb and hesed express God's relationship to his people and his invitation to Israel to respond in love. Hence the model of love in the Hebrew Scriptures is a relationship between persons, a relationship characterized by *freedom, election, covenant, commitment, and faithfulness, and thus understood in terms of action, not only in terms of desire.

Neither Hebrew nor English has a special word for sexual love, but classical Greek offers a distinction: agape for love as a general attitude or *virtue, eros for passionate, erotic love. The Septuagint translators of the bible preferred agape (or the verb agapo) for the various Hebrew words for love, but classical Greek philosophy considers love in terms of desire (eros) for the eternal and ultimate. Originally, in both Greek and Roman culture, eros belonged in the religious realm: it meant the vital and ecstatic forces of nature as expressed in *myths, symbolized by divine figures, and celebrated in cults.

For *Plato the ultimate object of love was the transcendent God. Eros is the force that moves souls to search for the good, the beautiful, and the *true. Love allows human beings to transcend themselves; human nature is thus essentially a striving for knowledge and possession of the good. *Aristotle applied this terminology to his own metaphysical reflection upon the cosmos, whereas he saw human love and *friendship (philia) as rooted in self-love. Understanding God as the unmoved mover, he says that God is loved by all, but loves only himself. In this matter, emergent Christianity differs sharply from the Greeks. The NT speaks of love mostly as agape, never as eros.

The different texts and traditions within the NT treat love according to their particular experiences and theological orientations. In the Synoptic Gospels, love is *Jesus' primary relationship to God and to the people he meets on his way, and is central to his proclamation of God's reign. All three Synoptic Gospels (Mark 12:

29–31, Matt. 22: 37–40, Luke 10: 25–8) give the dual command to love God and neighbour as the greatest commandment. This quotation of Deut. 6: 5–6 and Lev. 19: 18 links the Christian and Jewish understanding of love. While it underlines the distinction between love of God and love of neighbour, it warns against separating them. The gospels offer the abstract definition of either love, but let Jesus' life, proclamation (especially through the *parables), and sacrificial *death demonstrate the meaning of love. Jesus shows that God's love is limitless; it longs for all people, including sinners, to turn to God's healing and redeeming presence in the world. Hence love provides the paradigm for the hope and faith praxis of Jesus' disciples as they await God's coming *Kingdom.

The Pauline and Johannine texts offer more explicit reflection on love as the principle of Christian relationships. Paul does not make moral or psychological comments on love, but treats it theologically. Love, the gift of the *Holy Spirit, must determine the entire life of the individual Christian and the community (cf. Rom. 5: 5, Gal. 5: 22). In his prose-poem in 1 Corinthians 13, Paul names *faith, *hope, and love (the three theological virtues) and praises love as the greatest. The Johannine texts provide further thinking on love. *John's gospel depicts love as a communication between God and human beings in which God's essence is revealed. God is the cause of love and communicates his love in different ways to the world (John 1). Jesus embodies this divine love and invites his disciples to participate in a mutual bond of love. Love is here the dynamic of personal relationship within the Christian community, without much regard to *ethics or to the outside world. The Johannine letters, however, add some ethical reflections on love for the brothers and provide an explicit definition: 'Whoever does not love does not know God, because God is love' (1 John 4: 8). Knowledge of God is linked to the dynamics of love (1 John 4: 12). Love points to God's creative, salvific, and unifying presence in the world, mediated by Jesus and available as a divine gift to his followers.

Despite different emphases, the whole NT shows Jesus as the norm of Christian love. He proclaimed God's love and lived in it unto his self-giving death on the *cross. God has accepted Jesus' love and confirmed it through the *Resurrection. The NT texts make various attempts to conceptualize love, while showing an increasing tendency, especially in the 'catholic' epistles, to apply the principle of love to all relationships: divine–human relationship, family relations, between *marriage partners, among friends, towards enemies and outsiders, within the Christian community, towards the poor and needy, hospitality, works of *charity. There is also a tendency to reduce the all-embracing love that Jesus proclaimed to an exclusive love between Christians. Moreover, neither the expression of burning longing for God and God's presence found in some of the *Psalms (eg. 42 and 63) nor the passion of the *Song of Songs is to be found in the NT.

Under the influence of Neoplatonist thinking, the passionate desire for union with God returned to Christian thinking most prominently with *Augustine. Union with God was not seen as somehow competing with the gospels' proclamation of God's reign (the Synoptics) or eternal life (the Fourth Gospel). On the contrary, the desire for union with God was understood precisely as flowing out of the divine love which the gospels proclaim as the essence of Jesus' message, ministry, death, and Resurrection.

Christian *mysticism has continued to develop this Augustinian insight ever since.

Augustine followed Paul in setting love (in Latin *caritas*, or sometimes *dilectio*) as the highest of the virtues, culminating in his famous dictum 'Love and do what you will' (*On the Epistle of John*, 7). The ability to love God and other human beings is God's gift. Augustine distinguished between *cupiditas* (self-love) and *caritas* (selfless love). He called *caritas* the motion of the soul towards the enjoyment of God for his own sake, and the enjoyment of one's self and of one's neighbour for the sake of God, whereas he defines *cupiditas* as a motion of the soul towards the enjoyment of one's self, one's neighbour, or any material thing for the sake of something other than God (*On Christian Doctrine*, 3. 10. 16). Hence all true love is directed to God from whom it originates.

Thomas *Aquinas too saw God as the reason why human beings love each other. But he also stressed the transformative dynamics of love: what is loved perfects the lover in the act of love. This seems to mean that all authentic love includes concern for oneself. Moreover, one must also love one's enemies, because in them too God's gift of love is to be found. Supernatural love, Aquinas insists, draws to itself, without absorbing, all honest natural loves, among which conjugal love is properly the most intense (*ST* II-II q. 26 a. 11). For Aquinas, love, the central theological virtue, is the basis of all Christian *morality whose aim must be a gradual realization of love.

Martin *Luther distinguished sharply between God's love and human love. God's love is free, creative, and unearned. Human love is directed towards an object in which human beings always seek their own good: so human love is never free from self-interest. It is not that Luther denigrates human love. He praises its different manifestations—between married partners, friends, parents and children, love for animals. To love God's good gifts can never be bad: only their evil use is bad. But Luther wishes to emphasize the ambiguity of human love: even when directed towards God and God's good creation, it is not free from selfishness.

Distinguishing between authentic and inauthentic love has continued to occupy Christian thinkers. Søren *Kierkegaard distinguished Christian love not so much from the human desire for union with God as from ordinary love between married people or friends. Such love is selective, and because it hopes for love in return it is ultimately self-centred, whereas genuine Christian love is directed, without qualification, to what is best for our neighbour; it does not hope for love in return. Only genuine Christian love, which comes to us as a command and must be met with *obedience, reflects God's gratuitous love.

Anders Nygren (1890–1978) contrasted *eros*, understood as the human desire for union with God, with *agape*, genuine Christian love. He interpreted Christian discourse on love from Augustine onwards as a wrong development. Only with Luther do we come back to the genuine essence of Christian love. For Nygren, *eros* and *agape* are irreconcilable categories. Either one follows one's own egocentric desire for union with the divine realm, as in *eros*, or one submits oneself totally to God's love, *agape*, taking no account of any human creativity or value. Nygren made this distinction between the two forms of love in the context of *justification as seen in *Reformation theology: only God can justify human beings; human beings can never justify themselves. *Eros* always aims at establishing one's own way to God, one's own righteousness. So Nygren rejected Augustine's synthesis between *eros* and *agape*, and saw Luther alone as true to the heights of Pauline and Johannine love. Nygren's interpretation of Luther and his sharp distinction between human desire and divine love have been challenged. While Christian thinkers have agreed that God's love is a selfless gift, Nygren's firm categorical distinction between *eros* and *agape* has been rejected on the grounds that God is the creator of the human desire to love and is creatively present in it. All true love comes from God. Karl *Barth, for instance, defended human love for one's neighbour as being true love, love for the sake of love, against Nygren's categorical treatment of *agape* (as against Kierkegaard's legalistic treatment of love). It must be added that Nygren's *agape* lacks both the dynamics of free mutuality and, related to this, respect for the freedom and otherness of the other, whether human or divine.

Paul *Tillich drew attention to both the complexity and the ambiguity of love. He saw in all acts of love an inbuilt desire, and he defended this erotic quality. But he warned against any form of love that ignores the demands of *justice. Separated from responsibility and justice love is reduced to mere aesthetic enjoyment. Tillich affirmed the complementarity of *eros* and *agape*. *Agape* sanctifies both *eros* and the selectiveness of love (as in friendship) by loving love itself, in everybody and beyond everybody.

Karl *Rahner emphasized the dialogical character of love and saw a loving God as present wherever one human being offers love to another. Human love is always a response to God's *grace, and hence cannot be fully grasped by any definition or attempted conceptualization. God's *agape* consists ultimately in his free self-giving to his creation, culminating in the *Incarnation. Love is the mystery of God's creative presence in his creation and in its history. His love does not remain a mere sign of his lordship, but communicates itself in a personal way to his creatures, allowing them to enter freely into the mystery of God's perfecting work.

C. S. *Lewis drew a distinction between divine gift-love and human need-love. He analysed the different forms of human love without denigrating them, while insisting both on the radical difference between human loves and God's love and on the fact that all human gift-love comes from God. He transcended the dichotomy between *eros* and *agape* by attributing to God an awakening in the human heart of a supernatural appreciative love, directed towards himself. 'This is of all gifts the most to be desired.'

More recent discussions of love in Christian theology have centred on regard for the self as well as for the other and on the social dimension of Christian love. *Feminist critics have argued that the radical stress on overcoming or sacrificing the self in Christian love has sanctioned the continuing oppression of women in church and society. Every unqualified call for the surrender of selfhood endangers the process of becoming a *person able to relate in love to God, to other people, to the world, and to one's own fragile self. It is not only selfishness and possessiveness that are obstacles to the development of Christian love, but the very lack of self too. Feminist theologians have therefore stressed the mutuality in any genuinely loving relationship.

Further, the question of how far Christian love is free requires deeper reflection on the conditions for participation in relationships. How is the dignity of each individual safeguarded? When does a person become able to love? How can one develop a context for education in Christian love? Thus theological attention has come to focus on the *social* context of Christian love.

The tendency to consider Christian love only in terms of one-to-one relationships has been criticized by theologians of political, *liberationist, and *ecological orientations alike. Love must not be reduced to a private sentiment, nor to a mere object of belief (J. B. Metz). Love must inspire and guide Christian faith, hope, and action for the coming of God's Kingdom (Gustavo *Gutiérrez). A criterion for the authenticity of Christian love will be the pursuit of justice and equality for all human beings and the affirmation of the universe as God's creation through appropriate action. The kingdom of God proclaimed by Jesus has at least three features: freedom from any kind of oppression; radical equality of all its members; and God's gratuitous, creative, and surprising presence. Any social manifestation of Christian love will need to be evaluated against this proclamation. Moreover, while Christian love must always transcend the boundaries of any Christian community or church, it must be firmly rooted at the heart of the Christian community. In prayer, worship, liturgy, contemplation, theological reflection, critique, and self-critique the community must constantly seek to renew its understanding of God's love, to develop a pattern of personal and social love in the world, and to shape its actions accordingly.

Finally, attention to the other as other is a crucial dimension of Christian love. Respect for God's divinity, for the otherness of the human other, but also for the otherness of one's self is a precondition for the dynamic and creative development of loving relationships in which God's transforming grace is at work. Attention to the dynamics of God as triune love will require any Christian approach to love to measure itself against the generosity of God's gracious acts of self-communication in the creation, redemption, and perfection of all his creatures. God's love has created human beings as free subjects able to relate in love to God, to one another, to the created universe, and to themselves. The Christian believer and the believing community, the church, are invited to contemplate this mystery and respond to it in their lives.   **Werner G. Jeanrond**

Brümmer, V., *The Model of Love* (1993).

Jeanrond, W. G., *Call and Response* (1995).

Johnson, E., *She Who Is: The Mystery of God in Feminist Theological Discourse* (1993).

Lewis, C. S., *The Four Loves* (1960).

Nygren, A., *Agape and Eros*, ET (1953).

Outka, G., *Agape: An Ethical Analysis* (1972).

Tillich, P., *Love, Power, and Justice* (1954).

Luke–Acts.

Luke–Acts. Two NT writings have been ascribed to the author whose name is given as Luke: the third *gospel and the Acts of the Apostles. They probably belong together despite the fact that no known manuscript contains them consecutively. The two-volume work is today often referred to as Luke–Acts.

The gospel was written first, probably, in the early 80s. The work is likely to stem from an urban environment where Hellenistic *Judaism was influential, perhaps Syrian Antioch or somewhere in Asia Minor. Luke refers to other accounts of *Jesus, and comparison of the texts indicates that he knew a gospel of *Mark and another source (Q), known also in some version to *Matthew. Luke

has besides a rich reservoir of material including some of the best-known gospel stories, for example the birth and childhood narratives and also great *parables such as the Good Samaritan and the Prodigal Son.

Language and style reveal a well-educated author, master of the literary conventions of his time. The literary genre seems to resist rigid classification. It has a historical orientation, but includes novelistic features and theological and edifying interests. There are apologetic features: Roman authorities are presented in a favourable light and reassurances given that Christians are not a subversive group. Luke stresses the public character of the Christian proclamation—what they say and do is done openly.

Early tradition identified the author with Luke 'the beloved physician', *Paul's co-worker (Col. 4: 14; Philem. 24 and 2 Tim. 4: 11). Modern scholarship doubts this, but accepts that the author represents a tradition for which Paul was important. Paul is the protagonist in the latter part of Acts. His own testimony in his letters has often been read within the framework of Luke's reconciling version, placing Paul within the common mind of the early church. Luke's Paul is assimilated to a common pattern. His voice usually echoes Stephen's or *Peter's, and he lacks the distinctive character shown in his letters as he proclaims without compromise that *justification is by *faith. Luke defends Paul without sharing his most burning theological concerns; this has made it questionable whether he could possibly have known him, other than remotely.

In later Christianity, Paul's address to the Greek philosophers on the Areopagus (Acts 17) has been treasured as a masterpiece of *missionary advocacy to an intellectual élite. It speaks of the transcendence of the one *God, *creation, the preservation of the world, and humanity's religious potential.

As regards church structure, Paul's farewell speech to the Ephesian elders (Acts 20) has been seen as authorizing a ministry of oversight to protect against distortion of the message, while the account of the apostolic *council in *Jerusalem (Acts 15) has provided a model of conciliar decision-making. *Apostleship belongs historically to the post-Resurrection period; it has probably been transposed back into Jesus' ministry and applied to the twelve *disciples whom Jesus selected and commissioned. In Luke–Acts this identification is so absolute that not even Paul is recognized as an apostle (apart from his linking with Barnabas as *apostoloi* in Acts 14: 4 and 14). Luke's presentation of the *collegium* of twelve has decisively influenced later Christian tradition, providing a biblical basis for the later notion of apostolic succession. But in Luke's account the commissioning of the twelve is directed to the twelve tribes of *Israel. The twelve are witnesses in Jerusalem for a certain period of time during which the *collegium* has to be complete. After the Apostolic Council the twelve disappear from Luke's story without any mention of successors.

Luke–Acts expresses a Christianity deeply embedded in Jewish tradition, while presenting a defence for itself on Graeco-Roman terms. It is an interesting case of religious and cultural hybridization, for which Hellenistic Judaism has prepared the way. Luke repeatedly appeals to the history of the Jews. This serves to legitimate Christianity as a religion with ancient roots since, in Graeco-Roman culture, the age of a tradition was a criterion of its truth. In theological terms, it interprets *history as *salvation history marked by a recurring pattern of prophecy and fulfilment, the divine promises being successively fulfilled, and the prophecies proving that events happened according to the will of God.

Jesus is both the fulfilment of *prophecy and a prophet himself. His mission is to restore the people of God, albeit in ways that involve division. Luke accepts Israel's privileged position in salvation history. The Jews may divide over Jesus, but they remain the people of God and are not replaced by a Gentile church. The account in Acts of the early church shows it as first a church of Jews, then of Gentiles. It shows how God in faithfulness ensures that the history of God's people continues towards its universal purpose. The salvation of all people was God's plan from the beginning and part of God's promises to Israel, as we see in the words of Simeon, who recognizes the child Jesus as the salvation which God has prepared for all peoples (Luke 2: 31–2).

The geography of Luke–Acts reflects this plan of salvation. The gospel narrative gravitates towards Jerusalem, beginning and ending there in the *Temple. Much of Jesus' public activity happens while 'his face is set to go to Jerusalem' (Luke 9: 51–19: 19). In Acts the movement goes out from Jerusalem to 'the ends of the earth' (Acts 1: 8), ending, in fact, in *Rome, capital of the empire. This geographical design gives a strong sense of purposeful movement; what Christians call themselves in Acts is 'the Way' (9: 2; 19: 9, 23).

Luke's historical orientation means that the end of *time is no longer perceived as imminent. Luke–Acts is an early example of how Christians adjust to ongoing life in a world whose termination is postponed. As they draw strength from the memory of God's past actions and are guided by the *Holy Spirit in the present, *eschatological excitement is tempered by moral and philosophical discourse. But Luke also intensifies the demand, common to the synoptics, of voluntary commitment to an *asceticism involving *sexual renunciation. *Chastity is a sign of angel-like immortality, and hence a state of constant eschatological readiness. The focus shifts from the future to the present, but this present life is marked by similarity to the life of the eschaton. The gospel of Luke became a favourite of ascetics; a prologue added later to the gospel stated that Luke himself died childless and unmarried.

In the early church many *women were attracted to the ascetic life as an alternative to their submission in *marriage and *family. In Luke–Acts women exhibit a peculiar independence and play a significant role in the book. One of Luke's compositional devices is parallel patterns, some of which are 'gender doublets' in discourse and narrative material. They highlight the explicit mention of 'men as well as women' among the believers. There is no doubt that there were women among Jesus' followers (Luke 8: 1–3), and the continuous presence and witness of the 'women from Galilee' form the link connecting Jesus' ministry, through his *crucifixion, to the message of his *Resurrection at the empty tomb. The problem is that the women are not believed, and in Acts women appear merely on the margin of a narrative concerned primarily with Christian witness in the public realm, where visibility and accountability were a male prerogative. This intrinsic ambiguity in Luke–Acts has made it a battleground of *feminist discussion. Some claim that Luke more than most NT writers included traditions from women and gave them a rare visibility in a variety of roles; others that his strategy was to silence and subordinate women, thereby effectively contributing to the oppression of women in the church.

Luke has a special compassion for the poor and outcast (see Pov-

ERTY). The Magnificat (Luke 1: 46–55) announces a divine reversal of social distinctions and status, and Jesus' public ministry begins with a speech (Luke 4: 16–30) proclaiming good news to the poor, release to captives, and *freedom to the oppressed. Within *liberation theology these have become key passages. Luke addresses both poor and rich, but while his message may comfort and encourage the poor, he confronts the rich with the inescapable demand to provide for the needs of all, envisaging a model of radical redistribution. One main characteristic of the first, ideal community in Jerusalem is a sharing of possessions where everyone receives according to need (Acts 2: 44–5; 4: 34–5), implementing the divine reversal in which beneficence expects no return. Ultimately the benefactor will be repaid by God, who is the great benefactor and source of all gifts (Luke 14). Thus God is the protector of the poor and needy, and all gratitude is to be directed towards God.

Turid Karlsen Seim

Cadbury, H. J., *The Making of Luke–Acts* (1927).

Conzelmann, H., *The Theology of St Luke*, ET (1982).

Esler, P., *Community and Gospel in Luke–Acts: The Social and Political Motivations of Lucan Theology* (1987).

Fitzmyer, J. A., *The Gospel According to Luke I–II*, Anchor Bible, 28–28A (1981–85).

Haenchen, E., *The Acts of the Apostles: A Commentary*, ET (1982).

Jervell, J., *The Theology of Acts* (1996).

Keck, L. E., and Martyn, J. L. (eds.), *Studies in Luke–Acts* (1980).

Maddox, R., *The Purpose of Luke–Acts* (1982).

Seim, T. K., *The Double Message: Patterns of Gender in Luke–Acts* (1994).

Luther, Martin (c.1483–1546), theologian and preacher who inaugurated the *Reformation of the 16th century, and founding figure of the *Lutheran churches.

Luther to c.1520

Martin Luther was born in Eisleben in the county of Mansfeld, to a family involved in leasing the copper-mining businesses of the region. He was schooled in Mansfeld, Magdeburg, and Eisenach, and in 1501 entered the University of Erfurt. In summer 1505, after some sort of mental crisis and contrary to his family's wishes, Luther abruptly entered the house of reformed Augustinian Eremites at Erfurt. Ordained priest in 1507, he began to study theology, and quickly acquired the minor degrees in the discipline. In 1510/11 he made a brief visit to Rome on his order's business. Soon afterwards he transferred permanently to the monastery and university at Wittenberg in Saxony, where he had already taught briefly, and took his doctorate in theology there. Thereafter he served as a professor of theology and preacher in Wittenberg for the rest of his life.

Luther began to deliver twice-weekly lectures from winter 1513/14 onwards. Notes from his lectures on *Psalms* (1513–15), *Romans* (1515–16), *Galatians* (1516–17), *Hebrews* (1517–18), and a further series on *Psalms* (?1518/19–21) survive, though these cannot all be dated with absolute precision, and some other lectures may have been lost. Through Luther's lectures, scholars have shown how he gradually emancipated himself from the theology of his training, then shaped a challenge to late medieval *Catholicism (see MIDDLE AGES). Luther was educated in the *via moderna*, derived from the 14th-century Oxford theologian William of Ockham. Many in this tradition resolved the paradox of divine *grace and human response in *justification by reasoning that God's grace lay in his promise to reward, especially through the *sacraments, people's inadequate but 'semi-meritorious' efforts to love God. By its stress on the initial effort of the pious *soul, this school encouraged the voluntary acts of devotion popular in the contemporary church.

Luther grew progressively more dissatisfied with this view, perhaps influenced by some within his Augustinian Order who argued for the spontaneous work of divine grace within the believer. By 1515–16 he taught that God's indwelling grace 'healed' the soul, in a manner reminiscent of Augustine's anti-*Pelagian tracts. In 1516–18 he attacked the 'scholastic' theology of his early training. By 1518–19 his thought had moved further, reaching its mature form by 1520–1.

In conversations later in life, and in his 1545 autobiographical sketch, Luther described a sudden flash of insight, in which he had realized that 'God's righteousness … revealed [in the Gospel]' (Rom. 1: 17) meant not God's terrifying righteous condemnation of sin, but the divine gift of innocence or acquittal, offered through faith. This flash of insight, sometimes called the 'tower-experience' (Turmerlebnis) cannot be dated securely on the basis of the contemporary lectures or correspondence. Luther appears, with hindsight, to have invented a spiritualized oversimplification of his prolonged spiritual development.

While Luther was developing his personal theological perspective, a relatively peripheral issue forced him into public view. In autumn 1517 sales of the great indulgence to support the rebuilding of St Peter's basilica in *Rome were renewed in the territory of the archbishop-elector of Mainz, partly to help the newly elevated Archbishop Albrecht of Brandenburg recover the costs of his installation. Papal indulgences exempted living people, on payment of an individually assessed fee, from *penances imposed at previous confessions. However, since around 1480 indulgences had been extended to departed souls presumed to be in *purgatory, in the belief that they might also shorten or terminate penances in the hereafter. Mainz territory included Erfurt, adjoining Saxony, and Luther was asked to give an opinion on the claims of the indulgence preachers.

On 31 October 1517 Luther wrote to the archbishop a respectful request that he restrain and correct his preachers' over-enthusiasm, and enclosed ninety-five 'theses' (short academic propositions) for disputation on the power of indulgences. It is not certain that the theses were also, as tradition claims, fixed to the door of the Wittenberg castle-church and formally disputed. Luther did send them privately to his friends, and soon single-leaf printed versions appeared in at least four cities. However pugnaciously phrased, the ninety-five theses were technical propositions in school Latin, not a populist manifesto. They stirred up a storm because the *Dominican Order saw Luther's criticism of its indulgence-preachers as a slight, and immediately sought his condemnation at Rome as a *heretic.

The *papacy responded with heavy-handed authoritarianism combined with diplomatic appeasement of Luther's prince, the elector of Saxony, and a failure seriously to address the theological issues. Luther, called on simply to recant by the papal legate Cajetan in October 1518, without being given convincing reasons, instead questioned the basis for the pope's *authority. Accused by the Ingolstadt theologian Johann Eck at the Leipzig disputation (June 1519) of repeating the heresy of the Bohemian John *Huss, Luther also lost confidence in church councils like the one where Huss had been condemned. Pope Leo X provisionally excommunicated Luther on 15 June 1520. Summoned to the German Reichstag at Worms in April 1521, Luther refused to withdraw his writings, unless shown to be in error according to 'Scripture or evident reason'.

Though soon afterwards condemned by the church and outlawed by the emperor, Luther's reputation prospered in Germany because of the discredit and ridicule in which many of his opponents were held, especially by advanced intellectuals influenced by the northern *Renaissance. His accessible style in Latin and German won him a readership even among those who had not grasped the core of his ideas, nor foreseen their destructive impact on traditional religion.

Luther and the Reformation challenge c.1520–1

Before appearing at Worms, Luther issued pamphlets and manifestos that won him support, at least partly because he appeared to echo calls for change already widely expressed. In To the Christian Nobility of the German Nation, written in the summer of 1520, Luther cut the knot which had prevented the political leaders of German society from redressing faults in the church, despite repeated protests made by the Reichstag to Rome since the 1450s. The clergy, he argued, had claimed that they, the ordained, sacrosanct *priesthood, were the *church: that they alone could govern, discipline, or reform themselves. Yet this claim was 'deceit and hypocrisy'. All Christians were equally 'spiritual', though differing in their functions. Consequently, a priest was merely a representative of the shared 'priesthood' inherent in the whole community. Luther then concluded that the community should go ahead and reshape its religious life without reference to pope or hierarchy.

Secondly, Luther's programme appealed to Renaissance intellectuals who had learned, especially under the influence of *Erasmus, to be sceptical of the materialism of popular piety, and to despise contemporary theology. Luther's attack on indulgences reached readers who already doubted whether time to be spent in purgatory could be calculated precisely. He proposed that the local shrines of Germany, such as those of the bleeding eucharistic hosts at Wilsnack or the miraculous image of the Virgin at Regensburg, should be demolished; many intellectuals already mocked bogus *miracles. Above all, Luther's campaign to reform academic theology, by replacing medieval scholastic systematizers with the early fathers and literary exposition of the *bible, struck a chord with contemporary Christian humanism.

However, the resemblances with anticlerical, nationalistic, or humanist programmes were superficial. Luther's critique of contemporary sacerdotalism rested on a fundamentally new definition of the 'righteousness' that saved the soul. This definition was expressed in its mature form (in the opinion of most recent scholars) in the sermon 'On twofold righteousness' of 1519, lyrically and accessibly in On Christian Freedom, written in October 1520, and with greatest technical precision in Against Latomus, written in 1521 during his protective custody after the Worms Reichstag. A very influential statement of Luther's view appeared in the first edition of the Common Places published by Luther's younger Wittenberg colleague Philip Melanchthon, also in 1521.

Whereas recent theology usually viewed justification in terms of inner purification through grace and sacrament, Luther defined justification as the merciful *forgiveness of God given to those who were really still sinners. Righteousness was a 'cloak', something extrinsic or 'alien' to the soul, draped over its continuing sinfulness, and apprehended through faith. One who trusted in this forgiveness was free from the obligation to perform 'works' that tried to 'earn' salvation. However, those who were saved would naturally overflow in acts of love towards God and their neighbour, even though this 'sanctification' was incomplete and inadequate. The sacraments (reduced from the traditional seven to two, *baptism and the *Eucharist, by Luther's *On the Babylonian Captivity of the Church* of 1520) offered tangible seals and pledges of justification.

These teachings wielded astonishing power to destroy old modes of thought and alter the priorities of the religious life. Late medieval western Catholicism leaned heavily on the objective value of pious works—sacramental penance, masses for the soul, the veneration of *saints, and the cult of relics and other 'holy things'. Luther's teaching exploded this whole edifice. In its place he stressed the reading and exposition of scripture, to learn, understand, and trust the promises of the gospel. Scripture, he argued, was authoritative of itself and by itself, because of the message of Christ contained in it. No tradition of approved Catholic exegesis, or extra-scriptural revelation, was admitted. Luther's German *translation of the bible, issued in parts from 1522, was by no means the first vernacular version, but soon superseded earlier translations wherever his message was received. He urged communal worship, private prayer, and neighbourly charity. Private masses were soon abolished; worship took place in the vernacular, though Luther made this change deliberately slowly.

The abandonment of the Catholic principle, that divine power is mediated through a reliable church, abolished sacral priesthood. It justified assimilating clerics into *lay society, something eagerly embraced by city and princely governments alike. The estate of the clergy turned into the qualified profession of married, often middle-class, and endogamous parish pastors. The hierarchy was drastically simplified; *monastic orders were abolished. The visible church became coterminous with the lay political community, whether a city-state, principality, or kingdom. Lay authorities took responsibility for social tasks formerly the church's preserve, such as education and the relief of the poor. Luther did not have a high view of the state's role in religious matters. In his *On Secular Authority* of 1523, he regarded the realm of the spiritual Christian as quite separate from political life: faith could not be coerced, and secular powers could not legislate in the spiritual sphere. Nevertheless, his rejection of political power for the 'clergy' led inescapably to lay management of the visible church (see POLITICAL THEOLOGY).

These changes did not take place at once, though many communities, especially German city-states, took some decisive steps in these directions by the mid-1520s. The ideal of the self-governing lay community assuming spiritual responsibility for its priesthood was appropriated by some articulate leaders of the peasant uprisings which began in Swabia in autumn 1524 and flared up across Germany in the spring of 1525. The literate adaptation of this ideal for the peasants' programme owed something to the reformers of southern Germany and Switzerland, more influenced by *Zwingli than Luther. Luther observed the peasant revolt in the violent *millenarian form which it assumed in nearby Thuringia. Quite literally believing the *devil to be at work there, he urged secular rulers to use extreme force against recalcitrant rebels. After the brutal suppression of the revolts in 1525–6, while popular reformation movements continued, especially in the cities, the tone changed subtly. Fewer lay people published spontaneously on religious themes; recognized authority tightened its grasp on the movement.

The definition and characteristics of Lutheranism

In the later 1520s Luther's task changed. Rather than produce new insights of shattering importance, he had to define his position precisely; to contradict 'false brethren' among the reformers whose teachings threatened to outflank and supersede his own; and to respond to the untidy exigencies of the political context. In none of these contexts was he at ease. As a group of cities and princes coalesced in 1529–30 as the core of the 'Lutheran' states, a foundation document was produced, the *Confession of Augsburg* submitted to the emperor and the *Reichstag* in 1530. This conciliatory document was drawn up not by Luther (though he approved it) but by Philip Melanchthon. The *Instructions to the Visitors* of 1528, which laid much of the groundwork for the Saxon church, were also Melanchthon's work. Melanchthon was more confident than Luther in the work of church-building, and more ready to accept princes as fellow-workers in reform. Another associate, Johann Bugenhagen, performed similar work for the churches of north *Germany and *Scandinavia. However, as the visitations of 1528 revealed the appalling ignorance of priests and people, Luther wrote in 1529 two *Catechisms*, a short version for rote learning and a long one to inform preachers, both definitive for the Lutheran tradition.

Luther gave the 'Lutheran' churches a distinctive character through controversy. The debate provoked by Erasmus's *On Free Will* of 1525 had little historical significance: most humanists had already taken a stance *vis-à-vis* Luther's message. The controversy with Oecolampadius and Zwingli over the sacraments, especially the Eucharist, in 1527–9 was momentous. Luther's response to those who denied a physical, bodily presence of Christ in the Eucharist was fatefully determined by his earliest confrontation on this subject with an estranged colleague, Andreas Karlstadt. Thereafter he could not respect anyone whose views resembled Karlstadt's. Luther needed to believe in a physical, objective presence of Christ as the guarantee of justification. He regarded rational argument that expounded away the words 'this is my body' as an arrogant misuse of 'harlot' *reason. Philip of Hesse's effort to bring Luther to agree a common position with Zwingli and the Swiss at the Colloquy of Marburg in 1529 failed on this issue, alone of all the topics discussed. Followers of Luther, especially Johannes Brenz, would develop the doctrine of the 'ubiquity' of Christ's risen body, and the insistence that even the unworthy truly ate the body, and keep the Lutheran and Calvinist traditions at a hostile distance well into the next century.

Luther bequeathed to the Lutheran churches a style of worship that distinguished them from the south Germans and Swiss. He was a liturgical conservative in communal worship: he insisted on teaching the people before introducing changes. His German mass-order (1525–6) stripped out any suggestion of propitiatory sacrifice, but left such traditional elements as were not clearly offensive. He objected to the ritual destruction of images and legalistic objection to pictures, found in the Swiss reformations. Lutheran churches retained much of their medieval ornamentation; Lutheran religious books used illustrations quite freely. Luther made a vital contribution to the *musical heritage of the Protestant churches. In contrast to Calvinism, where scriptural texts and above all the *psalms formed the core of sung worship, Luther readily wrote new *hymns of his own and encouraged others to do so. By the late 1520s Luther had written some two dozen hymns, including the famous *Ein feste Burg*. The richness of later German church music may safely be traced to his influence.

Luther's personal qualities

In certain respects Luther's personal preferences and attitudes were not normative for the Lutheran churches, and posed problems in his own lifetime and after. Recent scholarship has shown how Luther viewed the world as the theatre of a cosmic struggle between divine and demonic spirits. In controversy he opposed not just his adversary, but the 'spirit', the 'devil', which he saw behind the adversary. He saw 'diabolical' assaults from within his own camp as proof that the true gospel was being preached. This led him to assimilate his opponents to each other, and not to take their subtleties seriously.

Luther may also have regarded this cosmic struggle of the gospel and the devil as a sign of the imminent end of the world (especially in 1520, 1531, and c.1540). In this context, Luther saw his role as being to preach the gospel in the face of the devil's assaults, until Christ appeared as the true 'reformer'. If this view of Luther is correct, his *apocalyptic outlook does account for Luther's relative indifference to outward forms, and his sublime lack of concern for the political security of the Reformation.

Luther's spirituality could be highly subjective. Having arrived at his understanding of the gospel through an immense inner struggle, he had no respect for others whose consciences were not similarly 'captive to the Word of God', if this meant that they could play with the meaning of scripture in their sacramental theology. He regarded the 'true Christians' in this world as a minority, lost among the majority of the indifferent. Yet the reluctance of so many either to heed his preaching, or to show any improvement in their lives after hearing him, also caused him fits of depression (for instance in 1527) and prompted him to abandon preaching entirely for a time (in 1529–30).

Concern at the limited impact of the gospel may also help to explain his abusive writings against the Jews (see ANTISEMITISM), which reached a peak in 1543. These seem to have been motivated by a fear that Jewish exegetes of the OT might shake the faith of Christians. Luther's hostility, however, focused on the religious teaching of Judaism, not the mythical child-murders which were the stuff of contemporary anti-Jewish fantasy. Luther used increasingly foul and abusive language in many of his later polemics, whatever the target, apparently as a calculated and deliberate tactic.

Assessment

Luther died in 1546, just before the Emperor Charles V won a military victory over the Lutheran League of Schmalkalden. Military defeat, and the ambiguity of Luther's legacy, provoked a thirty-year split in the Lutheran churches between moderate revisionists led initially by Melanchthon, and a hardline faction that exaggerated many of Luther's personal idiosyncrasies. Up to the Reformation centenary celebrations of 1617 and beyond, he became more and more of an icon, a miraculous figure revered and canonized by his followers.

Luther's core insight, in various ways rediscovered or reinvented in all the Protestant traditions, decisively shifted the paradigm of Christian thought in northern Europe away from the Catholic concept of divine grace transmitted through Holy Church, and changed the whole religious culture built on that concept. The insight, and its expression through exegesis and *preaching, mark Luther as a theologian of genius. Without his tenacity and conviction, this insight, 'the Word' as he saw it, might not have achieved its effect. Yet the converse side to Luther's nature, his apocalyptic vision, his almost Manichaean attitude to opponents, left his church with a difficult inheritance. His heirs, in Lutheran and Reformed traditions alike, have often found it expedient to use his legacy selectively.

See also PROTESTANTISM; 16TH CENTURY: AN OVERVIEW.

Euan Cameron

Althaus, P., *The Theology of Martin Luther*, ET (1966).
Brecht, Martin, *Martin Luther: His Road to Reformation, 1483–1521* (1981), ET (1985).
—— *Martin Luther: Shaping and Defining the Reformation, 1521–1532* (1986), ET (1990).
—— *Martin Luther: The Preservation of the Church 1532–1546* (1987), ET (1993).
Cargill Thompson, W. J. D., *The Political Thought of Martin Luther*, ed. P. Broadhead (1984).
Edwards, Mark U., *Luther and the False Brethren* (1975).
—— *Luther's Last Battles: Politics and Polemics, 1531–46* (1983).
Harran, Marilyn J., *Luther on Conversion: The Early Years* (1983).
Hendrix, Scott H., *Luther and the Papacy: Stages in a Reformation Conflict* (1981).
Oberman, Heiko A., *Luther: Man between God and the Devil* (1982), ET (1989).
—— *The Reformation: Roots and Ramifications* (1986), ET (1994).
Steinmetz, D. C., *Luther and Staupitz: An Essay in the Intellectual Origins of the Protestant Reformation* (1980).

Lutheranism is the name given to the movement initiated by Martin *Luther to reform the Roman *Catholic Church in the 16th century. The term 'Lutheran' was first used by Luther's Catholic opponents as a nickname to indicate the movement's purely human origin, thus deflating the cause of the *Reformation. Luther did not intend to found a new community named after himself; his basic intention was to renew the one holy catholic church according to the gospel. Luther said:

> I ask that no reference be made to my name; let them call themselves Christians, not Lutherans. After all, the teaching is not mine. Neither was I crucified for anyone. St. Paul, in I Corinthians 3, would not allow the Christians to call themselves Pauline or Petrine, but Christian. How then could I—poor stinking maggot-fodder that I am—come to have people call the children of Christ by my wretched name? Not so, my dear friends; let us abolish all party names and call ourselves Christians, after him whose teaching we hold.

Lutheranism retained core elements of the Catholic tradition, specifically the canonical scriptures, ancient *creeds, *liturgical rites, *sacraments of *baptism and holy communion (*Eucharist), and an *ordained clergy. Yet, in spite of its evangelical and catholic intention Luther's reforming movement led to the division of the western church and gave rise to a variety of *Protestant communities around the world. New ecclesiastical structures, at first intended as interim arrangements until unity could be restored, eventually became permanently established in separation from the Roman Catholic Church. By the end of the 16th century Lutheranism had spread from its birthplace in *Germany to the *Scandinavian countries, embodying itself in the national churches of Denmark, Sweden, Norway, Iceland, and Finland. In Eastern Europe Lutheranism took shape in minority churches, often suffering persecution at the hands of the political and ecclesiastical leaders of the Catholic majority. Lutherans reached *North America early in the 17th century, but their numbers did not swell until the mass immigrations from Europe between 1870 and 1910. The 19th-century *missionary movement contributed greatly to the planting of Lutheran churches throughout Africa, Asia, and Latin America. Statistically the total number of Lutherans in the world at the end of the 20th century lay somewhere between 60 and 75 million.

From the beginning Lutheranism was shaped both by its understanding of the gospel as articulated in its confessional writings (e.g. *The Book of Concord*) and by its struggles to define itself against Roman Catholicism (see TRENT, COUNCIL OF), humanistic critics such as *Erasmus of Rotterdam, Anabaptists (e.g. Thomas Müntzer), and the Swiss Reformation led by Huldrych *Zwingli and John *Calvin. The history of Lutheran self-definition continued in the generations to follow, notably in the ongoing and often fierce polemics between 17th-century orthodoxy, stressing pure doctrine, *Pietism, calling for experiential faith, and the *Enlightenment with its rationalistic criticism of religion.

Luther had been a professor of Bible at the University of Wittenberg. In his lectures on the Psalms, Romans, Galatians, and Hebrews he articulated a radical understanding of the gospel that subsequent Lutheranism framed by its three famous solas—*sola gratia*, *sola fide*, and *sola scriptura*. Sola gratia—by *grace alone—means that a person receives *salvation solely by the free and sovereign will of *God, without any co-operation from the human side. Sola fide—by *faith alone—means that a person becomes righteous in the sight of God solely through an act of trust in Christ apart from works of the law. Sola scriptura means that the Old and New Testaments are the final *authority by which all church teaching must be judged. The core of these solas may be summed up in one phrase—*solus Christus*. Christ is the sole basis of the Christian hope of salvation.

Lutheran theology developed out of the emergency situations in which Lutheran pastors and congregations found themselves. Their model was the picture of Luther at the Diet of Worms in 1521, standing alone, bible in hand, confronting the authorities of empire and church. The Lutheran confessors claimed that they were teaching nothing contrary to what the church had taught from ancient times. True theology is bound to scripture because it conveys the gospel of Christ. The principle of *sola scriptura* was deemed necessary to set the word of God over all church teaching and human opinion. However, the controversy between the Reformation and Rome led increasingly to an inflation of the doctrine of scripture in Protestantism. The idea of scripture's *infallibility and inerrancy was set in opposition to the rising claim of papal infallibility in Roman Catholicism and the authority of the magisterium.

The Lutheran interpretation of the scripture principle has always gone hand in hand with a strong emphasis on the Ecumenical Creeds and the Lutheran Confessions as the true exposition of the *Word of God in all matters of faith and life. When the church has faced acute difficulty the relevance of its Creeds and Confessions has come into play. In modern times this happened in the German church struggle against National Socialism, especially in opposing the Aryan heresy of the 'German Christians' (see BARMEN DECLARATION).

Lutheran churches have retained for the most part the liturgical and sacramental traditions of western Christianity. Article 24 of the Augsburg Confession expresses a basic conviction: 'Actually, the Mass is retained among us and is celebrated with the greatest reverence.' But Luther's reformation did bring about certain reforms in *worship. For example, private masses were abolished; the idea of the mass as a priestly *sacrifice was also removed; communion in both kinds for all the people was restored. The chief Lutheran concern was faithful communication of the saving presence of God in Jesus Christ through the preaching of the Word and the administration of the sacraments.

Luther's personal religious question of 'how to find a gracious God' has indelibly left its mark on Lutheran spirituality. The Christian life involves at one and the same time a deep awareness of *sin and a triumphant *joy in the gospel. *Paradoxically the Christian is simultaneously 'saint and sinner'. God's grace is both favour and gift, received though a faith active in doing deeds of *love. Every Christian is called through the *forgiveness of sins to serve God and neighbour in all the worldly contexts of daily life—in *family, *work, and government. This outlook had the historical effect of undercutting *monasticism as the ideal form of Christian service.

After the Reformation Lutheran piety often tended to accommodate changing patterns of cultural life. For example, the *spirituality in 17th-century Protestant orthodoxy reflected sentiments of the *Baroque period—pessimistic, even fatalistic, attitudes towards life in this world. In Pietism spirituality cultivated the inner feelings of the regenerated Christian, reflecting new interest in psychology. At the same time many pietists worked to create conditions for a better society. In the 19th century the High Church Movement restored a sacramental piety among Lutherans, entailing love of the church, its liturgies, and ministerial orders. In America Lutherans have adapted to a more socially active style of piety typical of the *social gospel movement.

For some traditions church order is constitutive of their identity. The name of each reflects a particular order considered to be essential, such as *Episcopal, *Presbyterian, *Congregational, even Roman. Questions of order have never played a comparable role in Lutheran ecclesiology. Doctrines of the gospel and not orders of ministry have been the common bond of fellowship among Lutherans around the world. For Lutherans the ordained ministry exists to serve the gospel; the forms of that ministry may vary from church to church. For example, the churches of Sweden and Finland retained the historic episcopacy; the churches of Germany, Denmark, Norway, and Iceland did not. Yet many intramural controversies in Lutheranism have revolved around the doctrine of the ministry. Two incompatible concepts of ministry have co-existed in Lutheran *theology. The disputed question is whether the ordained ministry was instituted by Christ through the *apostles or derived instead from the *priesthood of all believers.

Lutheran personal *ethics has been shaped by the doctrine of *justification by faith and its social ethics by the doctrine of the two kingdoms. On the one hand, the Christian life is based on a new relationship brought about by God's justifying grace in Christ. Good works are not the condition of justification but the fruits of faith worked by the *Holy Spirit. Every situation calls for a faith active in love towards the neighbour. On the other hand, the Christian lives simultaneously in two realms (kingdoms), the one civil in which God rules politically through the law, the other spiritual in which God rules religiously through the gospel. Luther taught that theology is the fine art of drawing the proper distinction between law and gospel.

This duality of law and gospel is linked to other pairs: God hidden and revealed, the left hand and the right hand of God, the strange work of God's wrath (see ANGER) and the proper work of God's love. While intersecting all dimensions of life the two kingdoms should be neither separated nor equated, but always properly distinguished, otherwise massive confusion results. Historically Lutheranism cannot claim always to have succeeded in properly distinguishing such things. A typical failure has been so to separate the two kingdoms that the gospel has nothing to do with life in the everyday world of politics and business, resulting in a split between the personal and social dimensions of life. The most notorious example of such a dichotomy between the private and the public realms, faith and society, church and state, was that of the official church in the Third Reich, a position supported by many pastors and theologians (see POLITICAL THEOLOGY).

The conflicts between orthodoxy, Pietism, and Rationalism in the 17th and 18th centuries left Lutheran theology weak and confused. However, in the 19th century various personalities and schools contributed to a renewal of Lutheran theology, especially in Germany and Scandinavia, characterized by two lines of development, one *liberal, the other conservative. Along the liberal line: (1) the *Tübingen School, headed by Ferdinand Christian Baur (1792–1860), followed *Hegel's dialectical philosophy in its reconstructions of biblical history and the history of Christianity; (2) Albrecht Ritschl (1822–89) interpreted the Christian faith in terms of *Kant's moral philosophy, as did Wilhelm Herrmann and Adolf Harnack; and (3) the History of Religions School of Ernst Troeltsch relativized the place of Christianity among world *religions. Along the conservative line: (1) the Erlangen School, led by J. C. K. von Hofmann (1810–77), integrated the new findings of biblical scholarship, the data of Christian experience, and the doctrines of tradition in a system of Christian truth; (2) the theology of repristination, exemplified by Ernst W. Hengstenberg (1802–69), aimed to restore and preserve the treasures of Holy Scripture and church tradition in a

pure and undiminished form; and (3) the mediating theology of Isaak A. Dorner (1809–84) for example, endeavoured to reconcile reason and revelation, philosophy and theology, Christianity and modern thought.

To the north were two intellectual giants, contemporaries and bitter rivals, N. F. S. Grundtvig (1773–1872) and Søren *Kierkegaard. Grundtvig's thought centred in the life of the church, its credal and sacramental tradition, as they found expression in the culture of the Danish people. Kierkegaard went in the other direction, setting Christianity in opposition to culture, faith to reason, eternity to time. His sense of radical *discipleship drove him to attack the Danish church and its cultural accommodation. Kierkegaard's idea of the 'infinite qualitative difference' between God and the world, the infinite and the finite, found its 20th-century champion in the dialectical theology of Karl *Barth, especially in his *Romans Commentary*.

Twentieth-century Lutheran theology is characterized by radical pluralism, from Rudolf *Bultmann's existentialist theology, Paul *Tillich's dialectical theology, the neo-confessional theology of Werner Elert and Paul Althaus, the Swedish School of Gustaf Aulén and Anders Nygren, the theology of secularization of Dietrich *Bonhoeffer and Friedrich Gogarten, the hermeneutical theology of Ernst Fuchs and Gerhard Ebeling, the eschatological theology of Wolfhart *Pannenberg, to the narrative theology of Eberhard *Jüngel, to mention only a few of the leading figures. Despite their conspicuous differences, they all bear a clear family resemblance to their Lutheran heritage.

In the 20th century Lutheranism has been deeply committed to *ecumenical *dialogue with all major Christian traditions. Every six years representatives of Lutheran churches gather together for meetings of the Lutheran World Federation. Most Lutheran churches are members of the World Council of Churches. The issue of their common Lutheran identity looms all the larger as they strive with non-Lutherans to reach the ecumenical goal of church *unity.   **Carl E. Braaten**

Bergendoff, Conrad, *The Church of the Lutheran Reformation: A Historical Survey* (1967).

Braaten, Carl E., *Principles of Lutheran Theology* (1983).

Elert, Werner, *The Structure of Lutheranism* (1962), i.

Gritsch, Eric W., and Jenson, Robert W., *Lutheranism: The Theological Movement and its Confessional Writings* (1976).

Kolb, Robert, *Confessing the Faith: Reformers Define the Church, 1530–1580* (1991).

Nelson, Clifford E., *The Rise of World Lutheranism: An American Perspective* (1982).

Preus, Robert D., *The Theology of Post-Reformation Lutheranism* (1978).

M

MacIntyre, Alasdair (1929–). Born in Glasgow, Scotland, MacIntyre was educated in classics and philosophy. Having taught at universities in Britain and America, he has been at Duke University since 1995. Although his many writings are wide-ranging and defy easy disciplinary classification, there is a unity to MacIntyre's work that consists in a rejection of the universal and timeless notion of *morality as such that exists in abstraction from concrete social and historical particularities. In its place, MacIntyre attempts to provide a more socially and historically sensitive understanding of *ethics, claiming, in short, that every ethic presupposes a particular sociology.

In his most widely influential work, *After Virtue* (2nd edn., 1984), MacIntyre argues that modern moral *philosophy is best understood as a series of fragments that have survived from an older, more unified moral scheme, and that the absence of a systematic account of the *virtues leads to interminable moral disagreement. Accordingly, the task of *After Virtue* is to defend an *Aristotelian account of the virtues as qualities of character that sustain particular goal-directed practices and, more generally, socially embodied traditions of moral enquiry. In *Whose Justice? Which Rationality?* (1988) and *Three Rival Versions of Moral Enquiry* (1990) MacIntyre argues that ethics is best understood in terms of *Aquinas's synthesis of Aristotle's teleological account of practical rationality and the genesis of human action with an *Augustinian understanding of the deformed will (*mala voluntas*) and the theological conception of *grace required to overcome it. Moreover, he appeals to the dialectical structure of Aquinas's *Summa Theologiae* in arguing that a Thomistic approach to philosophy is the best exemplification of a broadly historicist conception of rationality as tradition-constituted enquiry. Thus, while he initially rejected Christianity in general as underwriting just the kind of ahistorical conception of ethics that his account of the virtues was designed to overcome, MacIntyre has more recently come to argue that a version of Christian philosophy associated with Aquinas escapes such an objection.

Chris Huebner

Horton, John, and Mendus, Susan (eds.), *After MacIntyre: Critical Perspectives on the Work of Alasdair MacIntyre* (1994).
Knight, Kelvin (ed.), *The MacIntyre Reader* (1998).

MacKinnon, Donald (1913–94). A devoutly Episcopalian Scottish Highlander, an Oxbridge don whose heart rested in Oban and Aberdeen, a professional *philosopher whose impact was mainly theological, a paragon of donnish eccentricity yet most affectionate of husbands, MacKinnon is hard to classify. He wrote little that was lengthily systematic, his strength lying in the width of his interests and often agonized and many-sided analysis of particular historical or ethical issues aimed at discerning some central truth, but only after working through an almost impossibly extensive series of qualifications. His impact could be strongest when lecturing.

MacKinnon was born at Oban, studied in Oxford and was tutor in philosophy there at Keble College, 1937–47, before becoming professor of moral philosophy in Aberdeen. In 1960 he was elected to the Norris-Hulse Chair of Divinity in Cambridge and retired back to Aberdeen in 1978. Most of his best theological work is to be found in a series of collections, *Borderlands of Theology* (1968), *The Stripping of the Altars* (1969), *Explorations in Theology* (1976), and a final volume published in his seventy-fifth year, *Themes in Theology: The Threefold Cord* (1987).

MacKinnon was a realist, political radical, anti-establishmentarian, and a man who, despite the sometimes excessively convoluted nature of his expression, had an incomparable personal influence among British theologians of the 20th century. He could not be a systematician because his heart lay in probing *existential particularity and the prevalence of tragedy, realities which he faced with the absolute particularity and tragedy of *Jesus always central to his thought. He combined philosophical precision with the passion of a lay believer. It is unsurprising that one of his last writings was a small piece on Jesus as 'Son of Man', in which he appealed to the Loch Ness monster, the queen in Parliament, and Frege's *Foundations of Arithmetic* to argue against much NT scholarship that would not allow Jesus 'any element of genuine creativity'. Instead we should see that here 'the tragically human is being allowed to penetrate the arcane of the mysteriously transcendent', a fair summary for all MacKinnon sought to illuminate throughout his writing.

Adrian Hastings

Surin, K. (ed.), *Christ, Ethics and Tragedy* (1989).

man/masculinity. Whilst there is much prima facie contemporary evidence to indicate that male identity is in crisis (examples might well include male crime rates, mass rape in the former

Yugoslavia, the widespread exposure of sexual abuse, the departure of men from the Christian church, and the 'feminization' of Christianity), it would be possible for this to over-determine any assessment of Christian views of 'man' and 'masculinity'. The representation of the latter within the Christian tradition raises many issues going far beyond the basic questions surrounding the semantic identifications of such words as *homo, vir,* and *anthropos.* The rediscovery of viable Christian images of man and masculinity from within the tradition is an important task, not least because recent *feminist interrogations of the 'patriarchal' western tradition as a whole become particularly intense when confronted with that tradition's Jewish and Christian roots. There is, however, a wide spectrum of views within the feminist critique, ranging from demands for the correction of historic injustice and the modification of gender bias, through calls for a deeper interrogation of the dynamics of gender and male identity on the part of men, on to outright rejection of Christian representations of maleness and of *God revealed in the *humanity of the man *Jesus Christ.

Christianity is not simply founded upon the message of the *Kingdom of God proclaimed by one male individual, Jesus Christ, nor is it simply a spiritual discipline modelled upon the life, teachings, and actions of a man, who, as it happens, is not recorded as having been married or as having had sexual relationships of any kind. The ideological and ontological core of classical Christianity is the *Incarnation, a powerful and enduring construct founded upon belief in the unique and unrepeatable collocation of divinity and humanity in the person of Christ. Despite the representation of the historical Jesus in the Synoptic Gospels and the Fourth Gospel as a man unusually, indeed scandalously, positive towards women by comparison with Jewish and Roman attitudes and practices of the time, subsequent developments, stemming especially from the teaching of the later epistles attributed to the apostle *Paul, seem to have overwhelmed and suppressed this theme. Christian tradition includes both institutional patriarchy and an intense sensitivity to the dangers of *sexuality focused in the female, the 'other'. This is not a new problem that arose only in the sexually aware culture of the late 20th century. As Judaism and Christianity struggled for self-definition in the first four centuries of the Christian era, the Jewish tradition of *marriage as the normative state was opposed by a Christian ideal of the 'angelic way': life lived without the travails of sexuality (Brown 1988; Lane Fox 1988).

A gender-conscious reading of such classic works as *Athanasius' *De incarnatione* and *Augustine's *De trinitate,* two texts peculiarly relevant to the development of *christology and the doctrine of the *Trinity, reveals a comprehensive tacit masculinity. The saving humanity of Christ that Athanasius expounds is the contingent male humanity of the incarnate *Word, which makes it a bearer of patriarchy. But it is presented as encompassing the whole of humanity, whereas some argue that gender and sexual difference are not peripheral to human existence, but central issues. Augustine's triadic analogies also transcend such differences, which promotes a curiously ungendered and asexual implicit masculinity. The suppression of sexual difference in the Christian representation of God has had fateful consequences when seen from the standpoints of depth psychology, feminism, and contemporary spiritual developments (Eilberg-Schwartz 1994).

The male-created origins of the central Christian doctrines of

Christ and of God as Trinity are thus bearers not so much of explicit as of an implicit masculinity. The facts that the Incarnation of the Word took place in a male body, and that the apostles were all men offered no counter to the linguistic and cultural identifications of the key terms for 'man' and 'mankind' as used in both Latin and Hellenistic culture. This tended to reinforce unquestioned assumptions of male priority and superiority. These linguistic identifiers were employed in patristic theology in both east and west, and in the subsequent culture of Christendom. The contingent particularity of the hypostatic union of the divine and human natures in the God-man Jesus Christ came to be seen as a universal, all-comprising 'manhood', *sacramental participation in which was mediated and regulated by a hierarchical *church. The *Reformation challenged the power and authority of the Roman Church, but neither then nor later was there adequate interrogation of Christian theological reliance upon ideas of divine *fatherhood in the Hebrew bible, nor of the long-term consequences of the prolonged struggle with the notion of 'nature'—what the *Gnostics repudiated in their flight from the flesh; nor of the deep-rooted fear of sexuality as embodied in *women, the female 'other' perceived as daughters of the temptress *Eve; nor of the Augustinian account of the transmission of original *sin through concupiscence and the sexual act itself. It has been the historic task of 20th-century theological feminism to uncover what has to be regarded as a problematic Christian masculinity.

At a deeper level than that of obvious sexual and gender differentiation is the ineluctable conflict between western concepts of 'virtue' (and the ancient Greek *thumos*), traceable deep into Greek and Roman culture, and Christian paradigms of self-giving *love enacted in the life and death of Jesus Christ, which offers another way of exposing and articulating implicit masculinity. The German Jewish philosopher Karl Löwith sketched this out as an opposition within western consciousness between Prometheus and Christ, represented as two alternative, indeed incompatible, ways of being human—and male (Löwith 1949). As Simone de Beauvoir and other feminist theorists have recognized, the aggressive modernity of European thought and male domination reached a peak in the parable of the Lord and Bondsman in the *Phenomenology of Mind* (1807). *Hegel here presents a daunting spectacle of Promethean and Faustian masculinity: a bullying *mentalité* schizophrenically coexists with the trembling insecure, 'unhappy consciousness … divided and at variance within itself' (Baillie 1910: 251). This disintegrative image of masculinity has been exploited in a remarkable way within feminist theory following Simone de Beauvoir's articulation of identity as domination (Weir 1996: ch. 1).

A range of recent Christian theological responses to the dilemmas presented by images of contemporary masculinity is apparent. A first option is exemplified by the German Reformed theologian Jürgen *Moltmann, who has produced an 'open christology' operating in a community of 'brothers', 'sisters' and 'mothers'—but not 'fathers'. The 'fatherhood of God' is effectively bleached out; male identity draws upon an archetype that has, for better or worse, been 'feminized' by inclusion in a maternal concept of 'daddyhood', the one to whom 'Abba' is addressed (Moltmann 1990). Another strategy is to reconstruct masculinity through a return to tradition and the reassertion of an 'orthodox' Christian patriarchy, providing a role-model for an initiative-taking, committed, unifying, sacrificing, zealous fatherhood. Given Christ's apparent sexlessness and his problematic relationship with the paradigm of *family life, writers such as the idiosyncratic American Weldon Hardenbrook have abandoned the figure of Jesus and renewed the archetype of male existence through the image of *Job represented as the 'survivor of great suffering (and) an incomparable image of manhood' (Hardenbrook 1987: 119). A third approach is to embrace the body-centred mode of identity-construction favoured by some forms of third-wave feminism. Thus James Nelson presents Jesus as both Christ-bearer and 'Christ-barer' and unfolds masculinity out of the latent possibility of sexual wholeness seen as the basis of a mature male identity comprising both strength and weakness (and as it were divinity and humanity). He maintains that to be a man means 'embracing the fullness of the revelation that comes through our male bodies' in a 'mutuality which can be enriched by other life without losing its centre' (Nelson 1992: 110). Such, however, is the over-sexualization of globalized world culture that it may be less than easy to give full value to the Christian *celibate tradition even in its most appealing form as represented by such figures as Philip Neri, Francis de Sales, and Vincent de Paul.

Contemporary Christian accounts of masculinity indicate that much recent reflection is driven by reactions to theological feminism. This reactive posture would indicate that (like the pre-feminist woman) contemporary Christian male consciousness has yet to come to an adequate understanding of existence in and for itself, and also for the female *Other*. Whilst a wide range of Christian theological and cultural resources is potentially available, in comparison with feminist theological endeavour the male Christian response to the questions presented by the legacy of patriarchy is seriously underdeveloped.   **Richard H. Roberts**

Brown, Peter, *The Body and Society: Men, Women, and Sexual Renunciation in Early Christianity* (1988).

Eilberg-Schwartz, Howard, *God's Phallus and Other Problems for Men and Monotheism* (1994).

Hardenbrook, Weldon M., *Missing from Action: Vanishing Manhood in America* (1987).

Hearn, Jeff, and Morgan, David (eds.), *Men, Masculinities and Social Theory: Critical Studies on Men and Masculinities* (1990), ii.

Hegel, G. W. F., *The Phenomenology of Mind* (1807).

Lane Fox, Robin, *Pagans and Christians* (1988).

Löwith, K., *Meaning in History: The Theological Implications of the Philosophy of History* (1949).

Moltmann, Jürgen, *The Way of Jesus Christ: Christology in Messianic Dimension* (1990).

Nelson, James, *The Intimate Connection: Male Sexuality, Masculine Spirituality* (1992).

Thompson, Keith, *To Be a Man: In Search of the Deep Masculine* (1991).

Weir, Allison, *Sacrificial Logics: Feminist Theory and the Critique of Identity* (1996).

Marian apparitions

Marian apparitions are *visions in which people report seeing, hearing, and even touching the Virgin *Mary. She is sometimes accompanied by the infant *Jesus or *angels. Such phenomena have been widespread and popular in both western and eastern Christianity throughout the centuries; in Roman *Catholicism particularly they have enjoyed a special significance.

Apparitions of Mary occur in hagiography; Zaragoza claims such a vision to St James. Although this is legendary, it is clear that visions of Mary have played their part in Christian life from at least the 4th century. In medieval times, apparitions were often important elements in the foundation stories for popular shrines, such as Le Puy, France, and Walsingham, England. The best-visited shrine of all is Guadalupe, Mexico, founded after the Spanish conquest in the 16th century. The Guadalupe story features a vision of a dark-skinned Mary to an Indian peasant on a hill associated with the local goddess; the ensuing cult played its part in the Christianization of the region. In 19th-century France, a wave of Catholic and Marian renewal set the scene for a modern apparition cult, with new shrines—Rue du Bac and its 'Miraculous Medal', La Salette, Lourdes, and Pontmain—taking precedence over medieval predecessors. Bernadette Soubirous's visions at Lourdes in 1858 led her to discover a grotto spring, claimed to have miraculous healing powers. The Lourdes story has passed into the popular consciousness of people of all faiths and none.

If there is one thread linking apparition phenomena from the late medieval period to the present, it is probably communal anxiety and crisis. The visionary messages testify to the ever-present hopes for physical healing, deliverance from famine and war, reassurance about *salvation, renewed *pilgrimage, and religious *conversion. Apparitions do not always have a reactionary implication, as they are interpreted in many, often contradictory, ways; neither do visionaries consistently conform to the stereotype of the rural Catholic expressing fears about the loss of traditional lifestyles. However, anxieties about the violence of social change or the growth of irreligion do underpin many of the most famous cases. In Ireland in the 1980s, the outbreak of visionary and moving statue phenomena was seen as a divine response to an intensifying of the *secularization process. Some visions are concerned with particular issues, such as *abortion, the focus of the continuing visions at Surbiton, England.

Over the last two centuries, great numbers of visions have been reported, but only a few have enjoyed the support of Catholic bishops. These include the French cases, Knock (Ireland), Fatima (Portugal), Beauraing and Banneux (Belgium), and, more recently, Betania (Venezuela). Since the Council of *Trent, the local bishop has had the formal responsibility of evaluating and approving new visions and shrines; in practice, the Vatican is normally asked to endorse his judgement. Many modern apparitions have been ignored or suppressed by bishops: notably, Marpingen (Germany), Ezkioga (Spain), and, since the 1960s, Garabandal (Spain), San Damiano (Italy), and Medjugorje (Bosnia-Hercegovina). Nevertheless, pilgrims to the last three shrines have persevered, and episcopal disapproval is being tempered by a non-committed pastoral oversight. Some other cases, such as Palmar de Troya (Spain) and Bayside (New York), have led to schismatic movements.

Many 20th-century apparitions have been of the *apocalyptic type, with threats and promises of chastisements and *miracles. Common themes include warnings of social and environmental disaster and an urgent summons to a renewed *spirituality. Prophecies are claimed to have been fulfilled; for example, those of the seer Lucia dos Santos of Fatima, whose 'secrets' were revealed from 1929. Lucia prophesied that 'Russia will be converted', a message that has been interpreted as referring to the collapse of communism in 1991. Yet the original context of the Fatima visions in 1917 was the First World War, and the belief that praying the rosary would bring peace. However, Marian visitations are not necessarily to be welcomed. At Medjugorje and Kibeho (Rwanda), the apparitions and their desperate pleas for peace and tolerance in the 1980s were followed (in both cases) by genocide.

Apparitions, at least the more profound cases, may best be understood as 'charismatic gifts' in the spirit of 1 Corinthians 12–14. Visionary experiences and support for them are, for the most part, explicable in terms of the sociopolitical and ecclesiastical context. Nevertheless, another dimension can be discerned: a charism of *prophecy that serves to confirm the general Catholic belief in the presence and healing power of Mary.

The visions evoke interest beyond Catholicism: some *New Agers see proof of the (undefined) supernatural guidance of humanity; some Protestants, signs of a living God acting according to the subjective expectations of the locality; some *feminists, the continuing importance of the ancient Goddess, present among springs, grottos, trees, and on mountains; some Muslims, devotion to the mother of Jesus linked with the name of Muhammad's daughter, Fatima.

For Catholics, however, apparitions are often contentious, setting conservative against liberal. For the former, they reveal a Mary visiting the world to support a besieged papacy, for the latter, they represent a backward-looking, superstitious, and socially naive attitude. At their most profound, Marian apparitions are more complex and mysterious than either of those rationalist views would suggest. They express a yearning for an alternative history, one in which peace triumphs over war, in which God is at the centre of life, and in which healing and companionship, as seen at shrines like Lourdes, have the last word over sickness and suffering. They also confirm the continuing need for the powerful and maternal protection of Mary.   **Chris Maunder**

Apolito, Paolo, *Apparitions of the Madonna at Oliveto Citra: Local Visions and Cosmic Drama*, ET (1998).

Blackbourn, David, *Marpingen: Apparitions of the Virgin Mary in Bismarckian Germany* (1993).

Carroll, Michael, *The Cult of the Virgin Mary: Psychological Origins* (1986).

Christian, William, *Visionaries: The Spanish Republic and the Reign of Christ* (1996).

Laurentin, René, *The Apparitions of the Virgin Mary Today*, ET (1991).

Zimdars-Swartz, Sandra, *Encountering Mary: From La Salette to Medjugorje* (1991).

Maritain, Jacques (1882–1973).

*French *Thomist philosopher. Brought up a liberal Protestant, Maritain studied philosophy under Henri Bergson. Jacques and his wife Raissa, a Russian Jewish poet, became Catholics together in 1906 and enthusiastic Thomists. He taught philosophy for many years at the Institut Catholique in Paris, but after 1933 spent much time (including the Second World War years) in North America, principally at Toronto and *Princeton. He and Étienne Gilson, both laymen, were the most effective protagonists of the Thomist revival. While Gilson excelled in historical interpretation, Maritain concentrated on a more contemporary thematic approach, applying Thomism in the fields of social and political philosophy, art, and culture. He wrote more than sixty books, of which *The Things that are not Caesar's* (1931), *The Degrees of Knowledge* (1932; ET 1959), and *Integral Humanism* (1936; ET 1938) were particularly influential.

Increasingly liberal, Maritain was one of the few leading Catholics to support the anti-Franco side in the Spanish Civil War. A persua-sive defender of *democracy, his writing did much to transform Catholic political attitudes, especially in the post-war period. His appointment as French ambassador to the Vatican (1945–8) symbolized the *reconciliation of the French state, the Catholic Church, French Catholicism, and democracy after long years of estrangement from one another. His influence was extremely wide, through both friendships and teaching, within the French Catholic renaissance of the first half of the 20th century, but also across the world, particularly in North America. Perhaps more than anyone else, he presented internationally a new and attractive face for the Catholic intellectual community. Raissa's account of their many friendships, *Les Grandes Amitiés*, provides part of the explanation.

After Raissa's death in 1960, Maritain went to live with the Little Brothers of Jesus (see DE FOUCAULD) in Toulouse, where *Aquinas is buried. Eventually he joined the brotherhood. By then in his eighties he felt alarm at the apparent disintegration of traditional *Catholicism in the aftermath of *Vatican II, lamenting it in a final work, *The Peasant of the Garonne* (1966; ET 1968).   **Adrian Hastings**

Maritain, Jacques, *Son Œuvre philosophique* (1949).

McInerny, R. M., *Art and Prudence: Studies in the Thought of Jacques Maritain* (1988).

Tamosaitis, A., *Church and State in Maritain's Thought* (1959).

Mark.

The shortest and probably the earliest canonical *gospel is traditionally ascribed to 'Mark'. This was a common name in antiquity, but some connection may be intended to John Mark of Acts 12–13 and/or the Mark described by Papias as *Peter's interpreter at *Rome (Eusebius, *Ecclesiastical History*, 3. 39. 15). Mark's gospel assumes a situation of crisis and persecution, and so an association with Rome around Nero's time or shortly afterward (70 AD) fits the gospel's content well. That it was written for a largely Gentile community is suggested by the apparent need on the evangelist's part to explain Jewish customs (see 7: 3–4). Some scholars, however, place the gospel's composition in Galilee and link it to the destruction of the *Jerusalem *Temple by the Romans in 70.

Mark was the first to provide a narrative framework or plot for the traditional sayings and stories related to *Jesus of Nazareth. Thus he invented the Christian literary genre known as 'gospel', and was followed closely by *Matthew and *Luke. Mark developed his narrative about Jesus according to geographical and theological principles. After a prologue (1: 1–13) establishing Jesus' superiority to *John the Baptist and his identity as the Son of God, the episodes in the first half of the gospel (1: 14–8: 21) take place mainly in Galilee. The first part of the Galilean ministry (1: 14–3: 6) describes Jesus' call of his first disciples and his successes as a powerful healer and a wise teacher capable of avoiding the plots of his opponents. The second part (3: 7–6: 6) takes positive and negative reactions to Jesus as the occasion for *parables about the mixed reception given to his proclamation of God's *Kingdom. Despite the manifestations of Jesus' power over the storm, demons, illness, and death, he encounters rejection even in his home town. The third part (6: 7–8: 21) begins with Jesus sending his disciples to share his mission and ends with his exposing their failure to understand him. In between are an account of the death of John the Baptist (6: 14–29), two cycles of *miracles (6: 30–56; 7: 24–8: 10), and two controversies (7: 1–23; 8: 11–13).

The second half of the gospel (8: 22–16: 8) moves from Galilee to

Jerusalem. Along the way (8: 22–10: 52) Jesus instructs his *disciples about who he is (see CHRISTOLOGY) and what it means to follow him. Between two stories about blind men receiving their sight there are three cycles (8: 27–9: 29; 9: 30–10: 31; 10: 32–45) in which Jesus prophesies his death and Resurrection, his disciples misunderstand, and Jesus provides them with further instructions. Jesus' activity in Jerusalem is recounted in the form of a week culminating in the Passion. In the first days (11: 1–13: 37) he enters the city, offers prophetic teachings, debates with his opponents, and tells what is to happen in the future. The passion narrative proper (14: 1–16: 8) describes the anointing of Jesus and the Last Supper, his prayer in Gethsemane and arrest, trials before the Sanhedrin and Pontius Pilate, crucifixion and *death, and empty tomb. (The appearance stories in 16: 9–20 are generally recognized as a 2nd-century compendium of texts from other gospels.)

Mark's portrayal of Jesus of Nazareth not only directly influenced Matthew and Luke, but has shaped all of subsequent Christian theology. More than a chronicle of Jesus' public ministry, Mark's story of Jesus conveys a theological portrait. There is no infancy narrative (as in Matthew and Luke), and the account breaks off with the empty tomb. Jesus is identified as the Son of God both at the outset of the Gospel (1: 1) and at the moment of his death when a centurion says, 'Truly this man was God's Son' (15: 39). In between Mark presents Jesus as a miracle-worker who heals the sick, frees individuals from demonic possession, and manifests power over nature and even death. He also portrays Jesus as an authoritative teacher ('A new teaching—with authority!', 1: 27), though in comparison with the other gospels he gives relatively little of Jesus' teaching. Throughout the narrative, Jesus is further identified as the Son of Man, Son of David, Lord, *Messiah, or Christ, and other exalted titles already attached to Jesus by Mark's time. Nevertheless, Jesus' identity, according to Mark, can be properly understood only with reference to his death on the *cross. Jesus dies with the opening of Psalm 22 on his lips ('My God, my God, why have you forsaken me?', 15: 34). The passion narrative interprets Jesus' death with reference to the biblical motif of the righteous sufferer (see Ps. 22, Isa. 53). In his *suffering and death, Jesus is not only faithful to God and to his mission from God ('not what I want, but what you want', 14: 36) but also gives his life as 'a ransom for many' (10: 45).

Mark also develops the themes of *faith and faithlessness, thus providing the Christian tradition with models to be followed and to be avoided. Throughout the narrative, Jesus is the perfect example of faithfulness to God and to others. In the first half of the gospel the disciples respond enthusiastically to Jesus' invitation to follow him and to share his lifestyle and ministry. Nevertheless, by the end of the Galilean ministry the disciples become less perceptive. During the journey to Jerusalem they fail to understand Jesus' three passion predictions. And in the passion narrative they desert Jesus, and Peter denies him three times (14: 66–72).

During the Galilean ministry Jesus faces opposition from the Pharisees and Herodians, and from the people of his home town. In Jerusalem he debates with the chief priests, scribes, elders, Pharisees, Herodians, and Sadducees. His execution is the result of a conspiracy linking one of his own disciples (*Judas), the Jewish leaders (chief priests, elders, Sanhedrin), the Roman prefect (Pontius Pilate), and the soldiers under him.

The *women of Mark's passion narrative provide a positive ex-

ample of faithful discipleship. By anointing Jesus (14: 3–9) an unnamed woman identifies him as the 'Messiah' and prepares his body for burial. Whereas the twelve flee, the women remain with Jesus throughout his suffering and death on the cross. They see where Jesus was buried, and they discover his tomb empty on Easter Sunday.

Christian life, according to Mark, involves responding to Jesus, being with him, sharing his mission, and following his example. It calls for faithful service after the pattern of Jesus and for accepting the cup of suffering (14: 36). Finally it demands constant vigilance in hope for the full coming of God's kingdom even though its precise time remains unknown.   **Daniel J. Harrington**

Anderson, J. C., and Moore, S. D. (eds.), *Mark & Method: New Approaches in Biblical Studies* (1992).
Hooker, M. D., *The Gospel According to Saint Mark* (1991).
Kermode, F., *The Genesis of Secrecy* (1979).
Neirynck, F. (ed.), *The Gospel of Mark: A Cumulative Bibliography, 1950–1990* (1992).
Taylor, V., *The Gospel According to St. Mark*, 2nd edn. (1966).
Telford, W. R. (ed.), *The Interpretation of Mark*, 2nd edn. (1995).

marriage, and thinking about marriage in the west, has been controlled by an imperial Roman definition: a 'union of a man and a woman and a communion of the whole of life'. Marriage is taken to be, at least in theory, a natural, lifelong union of love between one man and one woman. Though the Christian understanding of marriage is not to be exclusively identified with natural marriage, neither are they to be totally separated. The passage in Ephesians (5: 21–33) which ties together the Genesis text (2: 24) about natural marriage, the high mutual love expected of married Christians, and the very relationship between Christ and the *church, establishes the range, moral significance, and mystical dimensions that have always characterized the central tradition of Christian thought. Marriage is both a natural and a religious reality, a Catholic *sacrament and a Reformed *covenant binding spouses not only to one another but also to God, a Lutheran social estate, and an Anglican little commonwealth established for the good of the spouses and the glory of God.

The Roman definition of marriage leads many to the uncritical judgement that the monogamous marital union between a man and a woman is 'natural' and 'biblical', but that would be oversimplistic. Though they may not necessarily practise polygamy on a large scale, so many cultures have accepted it in one or another form that it can hardly be 'unnatural'. The polygamous families depicted in the OT, those of Jacob (Gen. 29), Gideon (Judg. 8: 30), David (1 Chr. 3: 1–9), Solomon (1 Kgs. 11: 3), and a host of lesser Israelites indicate that polygamy is also not 'unbiblical'. Both polygamy and monogamy respond to political, social, economic, and religious needs and processes within different cultures.

Though marriage is a worldwide institution, there is thus no single marital structure. That monogamy has been taken for granted in the west and in Christianity is not sufficient warrant for the claim that it is the structure demanded in all circumstances by human nature and, still less, by God.

Two questions arise in the modern context. How more unnatural or unbiblical is simultaneous polygamy, multiple wives at the same time, than the serial polygamy, now widely practised in the west and largely accepted by the churches? If such serial polygamy can be accepted, why not simultaneous polygamy in certain circumstances? The circumstance most frequently discussed, and most pressing, for instance, in the churches of *Africa, is that of the polygamously married man seeking *baptism. Historically, most churches have required such a man to remain a catechumen for life or to divorce all but one of his wives, not necessarily the one he married first. Is it not possible to acknowledge that this man and all his wives, married in good faith according to the legal requirements of their culture, could be accepted for baptism? There is no biblical text that either prescribes monogamy or proscribes polygamy.

In almost every culture, provision is made for *divorce, as sanctioned release from unhappy or abusive marriages. However only in the west has divorce become so widespread, leading some to assume, contrary to the evidence, the demise of marriage as an institution. The rate of marriage has in fact decreased only slightly in the last fifty years, and some 75 per cent of those who divorce remarry, 50 per cent of them within three years of their divorce. Though they endeavour to promote stable marriages and oppose divorce, the major world religions such as Judaism and Islam all provide for divorce, as does civil law in the societies which they control. The Christian NT, specifically the gospel words of Jesus, appears the great exception, but again there is widespread debate.

The gospels report in four places Jesus' words about divorce *and* remarriage: Mark 10: 11–12, Matthew 5: 32 and 19: 9, and Luke 16: 18: 'Everyone who divorces his wife *and* marries another commits adultery.' In this, Luke's redaction, the saying is an isolated one, but in Mark and Matthew it is situated in the setting of a 'discussion' with Pharisees, highlighting both its importance and its difficulty. Matthew's version is significantly different in including twice an exemptive clause, 'except in the case of *porneia* [probably meaning adultery, but the sense is unclear]'. The precise meaning of this phrase has been endlessly debated but perhaps still more important is its origin. Did the exemptive clause originate with Jesus or later with Matthew responding to the needs of his community? Most scholars hold to the latter. Being fully aware of Jesus' *logion* about divorce *and* remarriage, Matthew did not hesitate to interpret and apparently modify it in the light of the needs of his Jewish-Christian community. Nor did Paul. In 1 Corinthians, written before any of the gospels, *Paul acknowledges the charge from the Lord about divorce *and* remarriage (7: 10–11). But in a situation then common at Corinth and still common in predominantly non-Christian cultures, that of a recently baptized Christian married to a non-baptized spouse unwilling to live with the Christian, he makes an exception on his own authority ('*I* say, not the Lord', 7: 12).

There is a flexibility but also a hesitancy in Paul's instructions about marriage in 1 Corinthians 7 which is revealing. He recognizes the goodness of marriage yet thinks it even better not to marry. He admits that he has 'no directions from the Lord' as to *celibacy, but recommends it from his own experience. He also accepts that widows may remarry. The early church developed an increasingly severe approach towards *sexuality, some people even disagreeing with Paul in rejecting any second marriage: monogamy must be absolute. In general the preference for celibacy steadily grew, especially under the influence of *monasticism, in practice devaluing the married state, yet the goodness of marriage was insisted upon against various forms of *dualism, even though some theologians,

*Augustine included, found it hard to see sexual intercourse in a fallen world as ever entirely sinless. With medieval theologians like *Aquinas and Bonaventure that would decisively alter.

Throughout its history, and perhaps more than in any other side of life, the Christian church has wrestled with the problems inherent in relating marital practice to its ideal model. Thus the *Eastern Orthodox Church follows its most revered theologian, Basil, in the strategy of *oikonomia* (pastoral prudence). Though marriages are intended to be lifelong they sometimes die, and when they die, *oikonomia* judges, it makes no sense to argue that they continue ontologically. The Orthodox Church, therefore, permits divorce and, in certain circumstances, also blesses remarriage. The *Reformation Churches also permit divorce and remarriage in certain circumstances, following *Luther's doctrine about marriage, that it is a purely natural and secular institution regulated by secular laws and, under the proviso of Matthew's exemptive clause (19: 9; 5: 32), regarded as a genuine word of Jesus authorizing divorce and remarriage. The one exception to the permission of divorce *and* remarriage appears to be the Roman Catholic Church, but again that exception is more appearance than reality. Thus it sanctioned the Pauline approach to dissolving a valid marriage from the 12th century, naming it the Pauline Privilege. But it has also extended this approach to include other valid and consummated marriages, so long as they are not between two Christians, calling the power to dissolve such unions the Petrine Privilege. Furthermore it claims the power even to dissolve valid sacramental marriages so long as they have not been consummated. Roman law decreed that mutually free consent made a marriage. Northern European law, on the other hand, held that it was made by the first sexual intercourse after the giving of consent. This debate was settled in the 12th century by a compromise proposed by Gratian of Bologna: consent *initiates* a marriage, subsequent sexual intercourse *consummates* it and makes it indissoluble. This compromise remains enshrined in both western civil and Roman canon law. Thus two Catholics can be validly married but not yet indissolubly married; unconsummated, a Christian marriage is already a sacrament yet dissoluble by the Catholic Church 'for a just reason'.

There are cases, therefore, in which even the Catholic Church dissolves valid marriages, that is, grants divorces: the case of the Pauline or Petrine Privilege and the case of a valid but unconsummated Christian marriage. The church states its law unequivocally: 'a marriage that is ratified [as sacrament] and consummated cannot be dissolved by any human power or by any cause other than death'. Absolute indissolubility is thus claimed not for marriage as such but only for Christian marriage. The question is naturally asked: on what is this claim to be based? Clearly not on any saying of Jesus, with or without the Matthean qualification, because Jesus was expressly speaking of marriage 'from the beginning', not, therefore, the sacramental marriage of two Christians.

It is fashionable in modern societies to be cynical about marital consent 'until death do us part,' not only because divorce statistics seem to belie it but also because, it is argued, unconditional promises covering periods of up to fifty years are just not possible. Only those marital promises made on the condition that there be no change in either spouse, the argument runs, are morally binding. But it is perfectly possible for couples to commit themselves unconditionally, for commitment is a statement of present, not future, intention. It is perfectly possible that principles, freely chosen and willingly embraced now, can continue to be freely chosen and willingly embraced fifty years hence in changed circumstances. Practice proves this to be true.

What is marriage *for*? From earliest history, under the influence of a physicalist paradigm that took for granted that sexual intercourse was for the generation of children, marriage has been held to have two purposes: a social purpose, the procreation and nurture of *children, and an interpersonal purpose, the loving communion of the spouses. The medieval church classified those two purposes as primary and secondary respectively, the procreative purpose taking precedence. Until the first part of the 20th century, that hierarchical arrangement dominated discussions of marriage and the regulation of births in marriage. In the course of the century, however, the physicalist paradigm gave way to a new *personalist paradigm, in which the two purposes were seen as equally significant. This perspective led the Lambeth Conference in 1930 and again in 1958, and indeed most of the Christian churches, to admit the justifiability of artificial *contraception under certain circumstances.

It could appear that the Roman Catholic Church is an exception to that general trend, but again this is more appearance than reality. The ordering of the purposes of marriage was hotly debated at *Vatican II, which, in keeping with the 20th-century personalist approach, taught that the generation of children 'does not make the other ends of marriage of less account' (*Gaudium et Spes*, 50). The matter was placed beyond Catholic doubt when the primary-secondary language was removed from the revised *Code of Canon Law* in 1983. The personalist approach, in which the mutual good of the spouses is an equal purpose of marriage with the procreative purpose, is now taken for granted. What that will do ultimately to the question of artificial contraception, and to the Catholic approach to sexual matters in general, remains to be seen.

The root of Christian ideas about the sacramentality of marriage goes back to the prophet Hosea's enthronement of marriage as a prophetic *symbol of the covenant between God and Israel. On a superficial level, the marriage of Hosea and his wife Gomer was like many another marriage. On a deeper level, however, Hosea cast it as a symbol which reveals in representation the steadfast covenant between God and Israel. Gomer left Hosea for other lovers as Israel left Yahweh for other gods. Hosea faithfully waited for Gomer's return and took her back without recrimination as Yahweh waited for and took back Israel. The divine and human covenants are both threatened, but Hosea's action mirrors and reveals Yahweh's. His prophetic action reveals in secular reality his faithfulness to Gomer and in symbolic reality Yahweh's faithfulness to Israel.

Contemporary *feminists rightly object to any patriarchal reading of the story that casts Hosea, and every husband, in the role of the faithful God and Gomer, and every wife, in the role of faithless Israel. However, the parable is not about two people, it is about God and God's fidelity. Marriage is a natural, secular, universal institution, but it can also be a religious symbol, representing the union between God and God's people. Paul, or whoever wrote the letter to the Ephesians, critiques the absolute authority of any one Christian over any other, of a husband, for instance, over a wife. He highlights an attitude required of all Christians, an attitude of giving way (5: 21). As all are to give way to one another, it is no surprise

that a wife is to give way to her husband (5: 22). What is a surprise, then and now, is that a Christian husband is to give way to his wife. Paul's instruction is not that 'the husband is the head of the wife,' but rather '*in the way* that Christ is the head of the church is the husband the head of the wife' (5: 23). This *way* is clear: it is the way of service (Mark 10: 45; Matt. 20: 28). *Authority modelled on Christ is always service, never domination. Spouses are invited to imitate Christ by establishing their marriage as a sacrament or symbol of the servant relationship between Christ and his church.

To say that a marriage between Christians is a prophetic symbol is to say it has two dimensions. In its secular dimension, it remains the union of life and love between a woman and a man. In its religious and symbolic dimension, it points also to the union of life and love between Christ and Christ's church. Every couple marrying says, 'I love you and I give myself to and for you.' A Christian couple seeking to create a specifically *Christian* marriage says that too, but they also say more. They say, 'I love you as Christ loves his church, steadfastly and faithfully.' A Christian marriage is a natural marriage with an added, religious dimension.

The conscious presence of Christ, that is, of *grace in its most ancient Christian meaning, is not something extrinsic to Christian marriage. It is something essential to it, something without which it would not be *Christian* at all. Christian marriage reveals the love of the spouses for one another; but, in the image of their love, it also reveals the love of God and of God's Christ for them. It is in this sense that, in the Catholic tradition, it is said to be a sacrament of the presence of Christ and of the God he reveals. It is in this sense also that, in the Reformation Churches, following Calvin and Luther, it is believed to be a covenant, a God-willed, holy, and sanctifying vocation.

The practice of Christian marriage has often been dour, patriarchal, and one-sided, even dominated by considerations of property and inheritance. It succumbed too easily to the gender inequalities of every society and culture. Nevertheless, its ideal form challenges its own practice with two basic assertions, rooted in the story of *Jesus and developed in Christian experience. The first is of the equality and mutuality of the spouses, something Paul clarified by insisting, surprisingly for his time, that 'the wife does not rule over her own body, but the husband does; likewise the husband does not rule over his own body, but the wife does' (1 Cor. 7: 4). It is really this insistence on reciprocity which from Christian origins ruled out acceptance of polygamy. The second assertion is that marital partnership should be lifelong, providing a security that gives freedom to be human and imperfect without the danger of rejection. Each of these assertions admits, as we have seen, of possible modification given special circumstances or human failing, but each emphatically belongs to the nature of Christian marriage in its moral, symbolic, and passionate fullness, a spirit well expressed in a 14th-century English poem *Cleanness* (or *Purity*) in which God declares,

> I set them a natural power and secretly taught them its use,
> And held it in mine ordinance singularly dear,
> And placed love therein, the sweetest of joys,
> And the play of passion I depicted myself
> And made thereto a manner merrier than any other,
> When two true ones had tied them together.

See also FAMILY; INTER-CHURCH MARRIAGE.   **Michael G. Lawler**

Brooke, C. N., *The Medieval Idea of Marriage* (1989).

Eels, H., *The Attitude of Martin Bucer towards the Bigamy of Philip of Hesse* (1924).

Hastings, A., *Christian Marriage in Africa* (1973).

Hillman, E., *Polygamy Reconsidered: African Plural Marriages and the Christian Churches* (1975).

Lacey, T. A., *Marriage in Church and State*, rev. edn. (1959).

Lawler, M. G., *Marriage and Sacrament* (1993).

Mackin, T., *What is Marriage?* (1982).

Parmisano, Fabian, 'Love and Marriage in the Middle Ages', *New Blackfriars* (Aug. 1969), 599–608; (Sept. 1969), 649–60.

Report of a Commission Appointed by the Archbishop of Canterbury, *Marriage, Divorce and the Church* (1971).

Schillebeeckx, E., *Marriage: Secular Reality and Saving Mystery* (1965).

Witte, J., *From Sacrament to Contract: Marriage, Religion and Law in the Western Tradition* (1997).

martyrdom. 'The noble army of martyrs' stands in the hierarchy of the *Te Deum* along with *apostles and *prophets, as a distinct group praising God. Two questions require attention: what is a martyr? and what is the contribution of martyrdom to the formation of Christian faith and practice?

Martyr, from the Greek *martur*, means a witness, one who bears testimony or gives evidence. Being a witness of the ministry of Jesus from the beginning, and especially of his *Resurrection, is the qualification of apostles (Acts 1: 22; 1 Cor. 15: 8, 9). Such a one is able to testify to those events that constitute the substance of *faith and Christian belonging (John 1: 14, 15; 1 John 1: 1–5). In the NT, especially *John's gospel, giving witness to Jesus was God's action, in what Jesus did and was, and by the *Holy Spirit, the prime witness.

Jesus was controversial, even in death; the witness was involved in conflict, and met scepticism and more hostility. Some early Christian witnesses were killed, the first being Stephen, and the lengthy account of his killing in Acts 7 became the classic text for what martyrdom signifies. Even the later adage that 'the blood of the martyrs is the seed of the church' is fulfilled in the conversion of Saul who had participated in Stephen's death. Before long, the martyr was seen less as a witness giving testimony to audiences open to hearing truth, than as one willing to die rather than deny the Lord; to whom, as the early martyr Polycarp said of himself, he had been faithful for eighty-two years. The will for total *sacrifice became the defining mark of the martyr. No longer eyewitnesses of Jesus, martyrs were evidence of courage and charity and even imperviousness to pain in his name. In some early martyrdoms the dying martyr was seen in the form of Christ. This is true of the *Acts of Perpetua* and her companions, where every vivid detail of the trials and dreams and suffering of these North African martyrs (around 200) is preserved (see MONTANISM). The martyr is one with Christ in dying: this unity is both a comfort for the sufferer, an assurance of immediate *salvation, and a witness to friends and enemies in the world.

There were martyrs for faith before, such as the Jewish Maccabees, but the fully developed martyr theology needed both the judicial customs of the Roman empire and Christian ideas of vicarious sacrifice. The martyr is a figure of human powerlessness in the face of hostile governors or crowds, who yet acts defiantly in the assurance of the ultimate victory: faith in God will not be denied, but rather God is confessed as the judge who will punish the persecutor.

Martyrdom early attracted certain people, fascinated by pain and *death and seeking a quick and certain way to salvation. The *church could not disown martyrdom but it nevertheless needed to control its immense spiritual power. Martyrdom was not to be sought; indeed it was legitimate to flee in persecution, to avoid being martyred if faith was not at stake. A martyr also had to be *orthodox, to be dying for the true faith, if the martyrdom was to be of value.

The call of Jesus to his disciples, to take up their *cross in following him, has not always been interpreted as implying that discipleship requires dying for the faith; taking up the cross has other forms. Yet it renders Christianity spiritually and imaginatively susceptible to the attraction of the zealous passion and total self-sacrifice of the martyr. There are martyred ways of living, on various moral levels. A good 19th-century fictional example of such willed, and ethically troubling, self-sacrifice is the character of Dorothea in George Eliot's *Middlemarch*. Some martyrdom is effectively a *suicidal gesture to put the other completely in the wrong. There is also a risk that the *art of depicting martyrdom, and the literary art of martyrology, have sometimes strayed towards providing sado-masochistic thrills, particularly in representing female martyrs.

Jesus is the prime martyr, though not often given the title. There are aspects of much martyr culture that are sub-Christian, and appear so when compared with how Christians normally speak of Christ. Sometimes, the martyr looks for vengeance (Rev. 6: 10; 11: 1–19); martyrdom carries on war by supernatural means. But Jesus, followed by Stephen (Acts 7: 60), prayed for his persecutors to be forgiven, thus freeing the future from the obligation of revenge. Yet Christians have sometimes been vengeful in both theory and practice, especially in relation to the Jewish people, and even when speaking of Christ (see ANTISEMITISM). Martyrs as foci of religious chauvinism and group formation are very questionable but very powerful.

Some of the finest, most Christlike spirits in the tradition have desired to witness to the positive substance of faith without getting involved in the psychological, cultural, and relational complications of violent argument, threats of vengeance, all or nothing confrontations with unbelievers which bring about death by martyrdom. Witness by persuasive argument, in reliance on the Logos, was characteristic of both Justin and *Origen; since both were martyred, they are not evidence for a dichotomy between a reasonable Christianity, playing down the idea of dying for the faith, and a Christianity that embraces martyrdom.

After the 4th century, the church itself became a persecutor at times, so that it was not merely being given martyrs but making them for others: John *Huss for the Hussites, for instance, among others. The two traditions of Protestant and Catholic in England inherited rival martyrologies after Tudor persecutions. Protestants remembered 'Bloody Mary' and read Foxe's *Book of Martyrs*, Catholics had dark memories of Henry VIII and Elizabeth, and sang feelingly of 'Faith of our Fathers'. There were resemblances in their English ways of showing courage, but on each side the *memory of martyrs could stimulate feelings of hostility to fellow Christians many generations later.

The main tradition continues into the modern period, with governments from right and left making martyrs. Every strand of Christianity has its martyrs. But there are complications, especially when martyrs are made in the encounter between European and other cultures, perhaps nowhere so sensitively explored as in the work of the Japanese Shusaku *Endo. And there is still the question of what qualifies as martyrdom—*Bonhoeffer is counted by some as a martyr, though he did not himself think so. Where is the distinction between being killed for a Christianly inspired, but essentially human, moral political opposition to an evil regime and dying for the explicit confession of faith? Many modern martyrs, like Archbishop Oscar Romero, are not killed for admitting to the name of Christian, but for preaching the faith in a way that threatens vested interests. Their murderers are likely to portray them as turbulent priests interfering in matters that did not concern them. Very few modern martyrs are given the platform of a public trial to explain their witness. The witness itself needs witnesses who understand what has happened. It was not traditional martyrdom when in the 1990s a bishop in Pakistan committed suicide to gain international press attention for the persecution of Christians there, but evidence that a visible, comprehensible testimony grows harder to make in a world of modern media.

See also SAINTS.

Alistair Mason
Haddon Willmer

Bowersock, G. W., *Martyrdom and Rome* (1995).
Chenu, Bruno, *et al.*, *The Book of Christian Martyrs* (1990).
Cooper, Kate, 'The Voice of the Victim: Gender, Representation and Early Christian Martyrdom', in Grace Jantzen (ed.), *Religion, Gender and Representation* (1998).
Droge, A. J., and Tabor, J. D., *A Noble Death* (1992).
Frend, W. H. C., *Martyrdom and Persecution in the Early Church* (1965).
Kolb, Robert, *For All the Saints* (1987).

Marxism.

Karl Marx (1818–83) himself was extremely hostile to *religion in general and *Christianity in particular. His approach to history was materialist and consequently tended to equate the *truth value of a belief with its historical origins and social function. This led him to discuss religion as an illusion that at best told us something about human aspiration and at worst acted as a diversion from the struggle to establish a fully human society.

But Marx's approach is in practice more flexible than his few dismissive comments on Christianity might suggest. The fact that Marx never used the expression 'historical materialism' (still less 'dialectical materialism') is not merely a linguistic point: it indicates the open-ended nature of his approach to *history, which he preferred to call 'the materialistic conception of history'. The key to this approach was the idea that the essential element in an understanding of human history was a comprehension of the productive activity of human beings. This fundamental activity was the way they obtained their means of subsistence by interaction with nature—in short, their labour. Marx summed up in *Capital* his view of labour as the instrument of human self-creation: 'Labour is a process in which both man and nature participate, and in which man of his own accord starts, regulates, and controls the material reactions between himself and nature … By thus acting on the external world and changing it, he at the same time changes his own nature. He develops his slumbering powers and compels them to act in obedience to his sway.' This self-creation through labour was the primary factor in history, and the ideas and concepts—political, philosoph-

ical, or religious—through which people interpreted this activity were secondary. History was not the result of accident, nor was it shaped by the acts of great men (still less by supernatural powers): history was the—mostly unconscious—creation of labouring individuals, and it was subject to observable laws.

Perhaps the most vital point in any understanding of Marx is that when he called himself a materialist he meant quite simply that in order to understand human history it was essential to begin with the material conditions of its production. Thus Marx was not an empiricist: he did not believe that insight could be gained from a collection of dead facts; he drew distinction between essence and appearance; and he poured considerable scorn on 'common sense', which he considered as poor a guide in history and economics as it would be to the question of whether the earth moved around the sun. Nor was Marx a materialist in the rather metaphysical sense of someone who believes that the world consists only of matter. Indeed, Marx's most detailed account of his materialist conception of history was contained in *The German Ideology*, which was intended to distinguish his views from those of Feuerbach on precisely this question.

There were, of course, elements in Marx's thought that tended to overemphasize aspects of necessity and predetermination in his view of society. Indeed, some interpreters have read into Marx a kind of economic determinism, supposing him to have said that other elements in the historical process were uniquely determined by the economic one; or even that the only important economic factor was the actual instruments of production. It is true that Marx sometimes narrowed down the determining factor in such statements as 'the hand mill will give you a society with the feudal lord, the steam engine a society with the industrial capitalist'. It has been strongly argued in criticism of Marx that any theory of historical materialism that separates the base from the superstructure is invalid, since the base necessarily involves elements from the superstructure—for example, it is impossible to conceive of any economic organization of society without some concept of rules and obligations. But it is doubtful whether Marx ever formulated his theory as the strict causal one implied by this criticism. The most that could be said is that for Marx technological change was a necessary, though not a sufficient, condition of social change. Nor is the language used to describe the relationship of the base to the superstructure always precise: sometimes Marx uses the term 'determine', sometimes the milder 'condition', sometimes again the phrase 'correspond to'—which conveys a rather different idea. Thus Marx's theory is best regarded as intended to supply a series of flexible structural concepts through which to interpret the development of past and present societies.

It is also clear that Marx assigned a positive role to non-economic factors in society. Indeed, he sometimes included the *workers themselves among the instruments of production and even called the revolutionary class 'the greatest productive power of all the instruments of production'. It is significant that in his usual formulation what is said to determine consciousness is not simply 'being' but 'social being'. Yet ideas, for Marx, were definitely of secondary importance in the understanding of society. He warned that just as we would be chary of judging an individual by what he thought of himself, so we should not rely on the self-interpretation of a particular epoch. To take a particular example: the rights of man as proclaimed in the French Revolution and the United States Constitution United States were not eternal truths about the nature of humanity which happened to be discovered at that particular time, as those who proclaimed them imagined; they could be fully understood only if viewed in the context of demands by new commercial groups for the end of feudal restrictions and for free competition in economic affairs. It was in this sense of ideas propagated to serve a particular class interest that Marx usually used the term 'ideology'.

Given this materialist and, by implication, *atheist account of things, it is not surprising that Marxism met with initial hostility from organized Christianity. Pre-Marxist *socialists were, on the whole, sympathetic to Christianity: Lamennais, Blanc, and Cabet were all believers and held to Robespierre's anathema of godless philosophy. And the flexible *Hegelian origins of Marxist thought left room for fruitful dialogue that would be exploited in the 1960s. But the Christian churches grew increasingly conservative as the 19th century progressed, a high point being reached with the condemnation in Pius IX's *Syllabus Errorum* of liberalism, progress, and *democracy. And the Hegelian elements were squeezed out of mainstream Marxism just at the time, in the 1890s, when it became the dominant type of socialism and acquired, under the name of dialectical materialism, a metaphysical materialism foreign to its initial impetus. This applied much more to the continent of Europe than to Britain where the pluralism of religious tradition, allied perhaps to a native distrust of over-systematic thought, has permitted a more fruitful relationship between some varieties of religion and politics.

With the advent of mass Marxist parties and their accession to power, particularly in Russia, institutional Christianity saw established Marxism as a rival pseudo-religion. Nikolai Berdyaev, the first Christian writer to take seriously the revolutionary aspect of the Marxist challenge, expounded at length the idea that it was the religious character of communism that made it anti-Christian. Pius XI in his 1937 encyclical *Divini Redemptoris* followed the same line, condemning 'atheistic communism' for its false messianism, its materialism, and its promulgation of the class struggle that undermined traditional morality. And the Cold War only served to reinforce in some theologians, such as Emil Brunner, this absolute rejection.

On a more intellectual and nuanced level, Christian reflection has concentrated not on institutional Marxism but on its deficiencies as an account of the human condition. And here two main criticisms emerge. First, it is said that Marxism is not radical enough: Marx merely generalized the function of much religion in mid-19th-century Western Europe to become the function of religion in all societies and reduced the significance of religion to that of the economic conflicts it was held to reflect. As befitted a Rhineland intellectual, Marx conserved a strong element of *Enlightenment rationalism in his view of the world. This led him, and his followers, to underestimate the cognitive importance of non-rational modes of discourse. But the religious mode, like the artistic, can refresh parts that more rational modes cannot reach. Such a criticism of Marxism would not concentrate on its atheism, but on its inadequate grasp of human nature, and this not in the banal sense that socialist projects neglect some supposedly ineradicable individual self-interest. On the contrary, the criticism would be that Marxism is too narrow, too exclusive, too short-sighted in its conception of human potential. Second, and linked, is the Marxist view of the dispensability of religion. Inherent to Marxism is the facile assumption of the disappearance of religion under communism. There is a strong parallel between the Marxist view of the transparency of human relations under communism and the Christian tradition of the disappearance of religious symbols and images in the *Kingdom of God. But unlike Christianity, Marxism's whole *raison d'être* lies in worldly success. For Marxism *reason and reality must in the end coincide and therefore worldly failure is, for Marxism, ultimately dispiriting, whereas for Christianity it should serve as a salutary warning.

However great the antipathy, it is also true that Christianity has been much influenced by Marxism. It has often been said that Marxism is the *secularized child of Christianity—and a wise parent has much to learn from her children. In general terms the increasing information available about the world during the 20th century has meant that Christians have been made aware of the vast gap between rich and poor together with the waste of resources on weaponry and luxury goods—an awareness that has prompted a desire to denounce these injustices coupled with a realization that past efforts in terms of *charity, appeals to the powerful, and merely political changes have been ineffectual. Marxism, by contrast, seemed to offer an explanation for this failure, a vision of a just future society, and a strategy for getting there. In the United States the importance of the Depression had led theologians such as *Niebuhr and *Tillich, building on the *social gospel movement, to be open to Marxist influences in their reflections on society. More specifically, the changed climate of the post-war years allowed the appearance of what came to be known, in the vernacular of the time, as a Marxist–Christian dialogue. The coincidence of the 20th Congress of the Communist Party of the Soviet Union and *Vatican II lessened the attraction of dogma for its own sake. The enthusiasm for *dialogue came mainly from the Christian side, and in particular from energetic German Protestant theologians. This dialogue was given fresh impetus by *John XXIII in his 1963 encyclical *Pacem in Terris* which recognized at least the possibility that Marxism might express the legitimate aspirations of humanity. A distinctively *political theology emerged in the writings of theologians such as Jürgen *Moltmann and J. B. Metz. This stressed that God is revealed inside history, promising a new earth as well as a new heaven, and that the church must become an 'institution of social criticism' acting for the sake of the world. The growing *liberation theology movement, particularly in *Latin America, tried to integrate into its reflection the Marxist tradition of historical materialism and develop a theology that was both critical and materialist. It is the Marxist emphasis on practice and experience that many Latin American Christians have used to evaluate and transform their religious heritage. To liberation theologians it seemed that Marxism contained certain views that Christianity in some more impoverished versions had ceased to propagate: of human beings as essentially social, of solidarity with the poor and outcast, of taking history seriously, and of looking towards the future. Although finding little favour with the Vatican, such an approach is likely to be of continuing relevance. The relations of Marxism to new *feminist, *black, or green theologies is a matter of some debate but the collapse of communism means the further advance of *capitalism with all its destructive potential. And Marxism still offers the best available critical analysis of capitalist society. As such, it will continue to be of interest to Christians concerned with issues of social justice. To turn Marx's own saying on its head: his followers may not have had much success in changing the world, but they still provide its best interpretation.   **David McLellan**

Bentley, J., *Between Marx and Christ* (1982).

Hebblethwaite, P., *The Christian–Marxist Dialogue and Beyond* (1977).

Kolakowski, L., *Main Currents of Marxism* (3 vols.; 1978).

Lash, N., *A Matter of Hope: A Theologian's Reflections on the Thought of Karl Marx* (1981).

McLellan, D., *Marxism and Religion: A Description and Assessment of the Marxist Critique of Christianity* (1987).

Mojzes, P. (ed.), *Varieties of Christian–Marxist Dialogue* (1980).

Thrower, J., *Marxist-Leninist 'Scientific Atheism' and the Study of Religion and Atheism in the USSR* (1983).

van Leeuwen, A., *Critique of Heaven. Critique of Earth* (2 vols.; 1974).

West, C., *Communism and the Theologians* (1958).

Mary is the name of the mother of *Jesus in the Synoptic Gospels (Matt. 1–2, Mark 6: 3, Luke 1–2). Synoptic agreement on her name suggests that this is ancient tradition and likely to be accurate. Beyond this, it is hard to ascertain what concerning Mary is factual and what symbolic. Since *Luke's gospel contains information that could have been known only to Mary, she has been seen traditionally as herself the source for Luke's conception and infancy narratives. Current scholarship tends to focus on the theological purpose of these stories rather than on their possible historical basis.

The primary biblical source for the cult of the Virgin is Luke 1 and 2, especially the narrative of the angel Gabriel's annunciation to Mary and her virginal conception of Jesus. Modern Catholic commentaries have pointed out that Luke presents Mary as *Israel, welcoming the Saviour into her midst. Zephaniah (3: 14–17) greets the 'Daughter of Zion' with the word 'Rejoice!' and the news that her salvation is at hand. But Luke goes further; his annunciation narrative echoes Genesis 1. The spirit of God broods over the face of the deep; the Holy Spirit overshadows Mary. The waters of creation are 'without form and void'; Mary's womb is virginal. God's word creates the world; the conception of Christ occurs in accordance with the angel's 'word'. The whole world is recreated in Christ from his conception, accomplished by God in and through Mary.

*Liturgy has also associated Mary with God's work of creation. OT *Wisdom texts have been used for Marian feasts since the 8th century. Proverbs 8: 22–31 came to be the lection for the feast of Mary's conception, suggesting that she was conceived in the mind of God before the beginning of the world, the most perfect of created beings and the image of creation's final completion.

Throughout the early and medieval periods, Christians took it that Gabriel's message asked for Mary's assent. She had the option of refusing but chose to say, 'Be it done to me according to your word.' Hence *Irenaeus calls her the 'New Eve', as Christ is the 'Second Adam'; where the first *Eve's disobedience brought death, Mary's obedience brought salvation. She is thus a moral agent in the work of *redemption.

*John's gospel mentions 'the mother of Jesus' twice: at the wedding feast at Cana and the crucifixion (2: 1–11; 19: 25–7). From the 12th century, Christ's act of entrusting his mother and the beloved disciple to one another has been taken to signify Mary's spiritual *motherhood of all Christians. John 19 also underlies the cult of Our Lady of Sorrows, popular in the later Middle Ages. By sharing Mary's *suffering, the worshipper is brought near to the Saviour's own suffering. Conversely, Mary is seen as close to those who suffer, and thus a source of strength in times of distress.

Divine maternity

The *Atonement requires that the Saviour be both truly God and truly human. Since it was Mary who gave him his flesh, it is not only her free assent to Gabriel's message, but also her physical maternity that is necessary to the world's redemption. As the bearer of God incarnate, Mary is given in Greek the paradoxical title of *Theotokos*, 'Godbearer' (Latin *Deipara* and *Dei genetrix*), usually translated as 'Mother of God'. Following a challenge to the orthodoxy of this title, the Council of *Ephesus declared it the true teaching of the church. Cyril of Alexandria explains: 'because the holy virgin bore in the flesh God who was united hypostatically with the flesh, for that reason we call her mother of God … This was not as though he needed … for his own nature a birth in time … but in order that he might bless the beginning of our existence' (*Third Letter of Cyril to Nestorius*). Thus the *Incarnation is not merely the necessary condition for salvation, it is itself salvific. God already redeems the human race by taking flesh and being born of a human mother. The Word of God is united to the whole human race by becoming the child of a particular woman, Mary. This makes her representative of the human race and, since the Incarnation unites Christ to the whole created order, of the entire creation in its right relationship with God.

In the Christianity of the Catholic, Orthodox, and pre-Chalcedonian churches, to be in a right relationship with God means being a vehicle of God's presence in the world. In the case of a moral agent, it also means co-operating freely with God's will. Mary supremely fulfils these criteria and is the type and forerunner of the church and all the redeemed. According to Karl *Rahner, to be perfectly redeemed would be 'to conceive Christ in faith and in the flesh'. Much Protestant theology has rejected this understanding of the right relationship between God and creation, and consequently found no place for Mary in theology or devotion. Since all goodness is from God's grace alone (*sola gratia*), it is idolatrous to venerate created beings. If a person does God's will, it is only by God's grace and not by any independent human choice. Mary's miraculous God-bearing is not a cause for devotion to her; talk of her 'assent' denotes a failure to recognize that the incarnation is solely God's work. For Karl *Barth, 'she is simply man [*sic*!] to whom the miracle of revelation happens' (*CD* I/2. 140).

Catholic teaching willingly confesses that all *holiness is from God and that the capacity to co-operate with God is itself a work of God's grace, but does not object to reverencing a creature. Within the Reformed Churches, some, sharing this understanding, are happy to honour Mary for her active part in the Incarnation. Thus, the *Caroline divine, Lancelot Andrewes: 'To conceive is more than to receive. It is so to receive as to yield somewhat of our own also. A vessel is not said to conceive the liquor that is put into it. Why? Because it yieldeth nothing from itself. The Blessed Virgin is, and therefore is because she did. She did both give and take' (*Ninth Sermon for Christmas Day*).

The divine motherhood is the foundation of all Marian doctrine and devotion. The apocryphal *Gospel of James* (possibly late 2nd century) narrates Mary's life until the exile in Egypt. It presents her as being prepared before her conception to be the Lord's mother and is a major source for stories of her life as depicted in art and commemorated in liturgy, including her presentation in the temple and her betrothal to Joseph.

The earliest known prayer to Mary (John Rylands Gk. Pap. 470, *c*.3rd–5th century) calls her *Theotokos* and asks for her compassionate assistance. Later devotion saw her as Queen of Heaven, second only to Christ, her intercession more powerful than that of any other saint. Appeals to her compassion became common in the Middle Ages, and have remained popular. Christ, who in justice might condemn the human race to hell, will be merciful because he has been human and knows our weakness. Since Mary gave him his flesh, her intercession recalls his humanity and thus evokes his mercy. However, it must be acknowledged that appeals to her compassion can turn into Mariolatry if they imply that Mary is more ready to be merciful and loving than the Saviour himself.

Within the first few centuries it became common belief that Mary remained perpetually a *virgin, a tradition retained in the Orthodox and Catholic Churches today. It seems to be influenced by the idea of Mary as the sacred vessel who carried the word of God: as a chalice should be used for no purpose other than the sacred one for which it was made, so Mary's womb never bore another child. The belief that her hymen remained unbroken has been called into question by some modern authors (for example, Karl Rahner, 'Virginitas in Partu', *Theological Investigations*, 4), but the concomitant understanding that she did not suffer pain in labour has made her popular as an intercessor on behalf of women in childbirth.

Immaculate Conception and Assumption

The doctrine that Mary was conceived without *sin had one of its principal origins in the liturgical celebration of her conception. The beginning of the flesh that would be united with the Word of God was seen as a cause for celebration. The feast was observed in the east by the 8th century, and in the British Isles by the 11th century at the latest, whence it spread to mainland Europe. Some, like Bernard of Clairvaux, opposed it on the grounds that everyone is conceived in a state of sin, since sexual intercourse is inevitably sinful (a view that persisted for centuries), and it is wrong to celebrate a sinful act. But others defended the feast as meaning that Mary was conceived without original sin, that is, in a state of grace. The arguments nearly all refer to the divine maternity: for example, that since God has given Mary the greatest imaginable privilege in making her the mother of his son, he will surely not have withheld from her any possible blessing.

John Duns Scotus was the most important champion of the doctrine. Against such authors as *Aquinas who contended that it would mean that Mary had no need of Christ's redemption, Scotus argued that to be preserved from sin was a more excellent form of redemption than to be cleansed of it. During the post-Tridentine period, Mariology became a recognized branch of Catholic theology, its most important exponent being the Jesuit Francisco de Suarez (1548–1617). Henceforth, the Immaculate Conception increasingly became normal Catholic teaching. Promotion of the Immaculate Conception has been strongly influenced by the experience of women visionaries. The Revelations of Birgitta of

Sweden (1303–73) were cited in its favour (see SCANDINAVIAN CHRISTIAN THOUGHT). The modern iconography of the doctrine derives in part from the *visions of Beatrice de Silva (d. 1490), and the apparitions to Catherine Labouré in 1830 led to the striking of the popular Miraculous Medal, showing Mary 'conceived without sin'. In 1854 Pius IX defined the doctrine as an article of faith, and Bernadette Soubirous's visions of Mary as the Immaculate Conception, at Lourdes in 1858, were taken as heavenly endorsement of his action.

The only other Mariological doctrine to be declared by a pope is Mary's assumption into heaven, proclaimed by Pius XII in 1950. Various accounts of Mary's death or dormition are found from the 4th century onwards, with slight differences between east and west. The eastern tradition holds that Mary's body was taken to *paradise, to be reunited with her soul on the last day, while the western tradition maintains that her body and soul have already been joined in *heaven. While the Catholic Church celebrates the Assumption, the corresponding Orthodox feast celebrates the Dormition.

The 20th century

The period 1830–1960 was one of intense Mariological discussion, with theologians sometimes pressing for a definition of Mary as coredemptrix, and of fervent Marian devotion, sustained by the writings of Louis de Montfort (1673–1713) and Alphonsus Liguori (1696–1787). However *Vatican II did not promote such an elevated Mariology as some had hoped. By a narrow vote, the Council fathers decided to include teaching on Mary in the document on the church (*Lumen Gentium*, ch. 8) not in a separate document, thus underlining the church's understanding of Mary as one of the redeemed, and allaying some of the anxieties of Reformed Christians who had feared that Catholics might compromise the doctrine of Christ as sole mediator and redeemer. *Lumen Gentium* repeats the Catholic Church's received teaching on Mary, leaving controversial questions open. The Council initiated a considerable *rapprochement* between Catholics and Protestants and there have been shared discussions on such topics as Mary as type of the church, or Mary in the NT.

Mary's relationship to the church can be interpreted in different ways. She is the church's *type* and the believer *par excellence*, in whom divine *grace can be fully operative. Where 'church' means a hierarchical institution, she may embody the docility and subordination required of its members, particularly female. However, for *feminist and *liberation theologians, such as Rosemary Radford *Ruether, Ivone Gebara, and Maria Clara Bingemer, 'church' means its ordinary members, and Mary is seen as a sign of *hope to the oppressed: she is the woman who sings the *Magnificat* and enjoys the fullness of redemption that Christ offers to all.

Throughout the centuries, Mary's presentation has been as much *artistic as theological or liturgical. No religious subject has been more popular. From the nobility of a Romanesque *Virgin in Majesty*, to the pain of a German *Lament of the Virgin*, or the idealized beauty of a Raphael *Madonna*, Mary has been the means for expressing a wealth of religious experience.

The two decades following Vatican II saw a decline in Marian theology and devotion in northern Europe and North America. This began to change in the late 1980s, with a worldwide revival of interest in *Marian apparitions, and a renewed movement for

Mary to be formally defined as co-redemptrix. There is a divergence of views between those Catholics whose main concern is to remain close to scripture and form bonds with other Christians, and those who believe that the Holy Spirit is working through the visible presence of Mary to lead the church more deeply into the mystery of Christ. It is not clear what will be the future of Marian doctrine and devotion; but this itself may signify something of the nature of the church at the end of the 20th century, since it demonstrates the variety of strands existing within orthodoxy and comprising catholicity.   **Sarah Jane Boss**

Allchin, A. M., *The Joy of All Creation: An Anglican Meditation on the Place of Mary* (1993).

Boss, S. J., 'The Virgin Mary and Other Women', in L. Osborn and A. Walker (eds.), *Harmful Religion* (1997).

Brown, Raymond E., *The Birth of the Messiah: A Commentary on the Infancy Narratives of Matthew and Luke* (1993).

Gebara, Ivone, and Bingemer, Maria Clara, *Mary, Mother of God, Mother of the Poor* (1989).

Graef, Hilda, *Mary: A History of Doctrine and Devotion* (1985).

Hirn, Yrjö, *The Sacred Shrine: A Study of the Poetry and Art of the Catholic Church* (1958).

Jugie, Martin, *La Mort et l'assomption de la Sainte Vierge: Étude historico-doctrinale* (1944).

Laurentin, René, *Mary's Place in the Church* (1965).

Miegge, Giovanni, *The Virgin Mary: The Roman Catholic Marian Doctrine* (1955).

O'Carroll, Michael, *Theotokos: A Theological Encyclopedia of the Blessed Virgin Mary* (1982).

O'Connor, Edward (ed.), *The Dogma of the Immaculate Conception: History and Significance* (1958).

Pelikan, Jaroslav, *Mary Through the Centuries: Her Place in the History of Culture* (1996).

Rahner, Karl, 'Le Principe fondamental de la théologie mariale', *RSR* 42 (1954), 481–522.

—— 'The Immaculate Conception', *Theological Investigations* (1961), i. 201–13.

Roschini, Gabriel, *Mariologia* (4 vols.; 1947–8).

Ruether, Rosemary Radford, *Sexism and God-Talk: Towards a Feminist Theology* (1983).

Warner, Marina, *Alone of All Her Sex: The Myth and the Cult of the Virgin Mary* (1985).

Mary Magdalene, that is 'from Magdala', a fishing village four miles north of Tiberias, has two distinct, albeit closely related, roles in the *gospels. In *Luke 8: 2–3 she is among that group of *women whom Christ healed—he is said to have cast seven devils out of her—and who subsequently accompanied him and his disciples on tour, 'providing for them out of their own resources'. In this capacity she was present at Christ's crucifixion, watching from a distance with women 'who had followed him and looked after him when he was in Galilee' (Mark 15: 40–1, cf. Matt. 27: 55–6) and, in Mark's account, it is with two of these women that Mary goes to anoint Christ on the following Sunday (Mark 16: 1–3). According to *John (20: 14–18) and the continuation of *Mark (16: 9), Mary is then singled out for special favour, for it is to her that the Risen Christ first appears. In John, Mary at first mistakes him for the gardener; as she recognizes him she seeks to embrace him but is forbidden, while being charged to spread the news of his coming ascension.

Much ink and paint have been spilt over Mary's gospel roles. Christ's injunction to her in John, *noli me tangere* (do not touch me), has inspired artists but troubled theologians. Why is Mary denied her embrace while Doubting Thomas is enjoined to put his hand in Christ's side? Why should it have been to a woman that Christ first appeared? Did this in some way redress the sin of *Eve? Or was the testimony of a 'hysterical woman', as the pagan Celsus (2nd century) would have it, grounds for dismissing the whole account of the *Resurrection? In this century, *feminist theologians have considered the role of the group to which Mary belonged. What kind of ministry did they exercise? Of notable relevance is the testimony of 2nd-century *apocryphal scriptures, in particular the eponymous *Gospel of Mary*, a *Gnostic text that both attributes to Mary special knowledge of Christ and portrays her in direct competition with *Peter for leadership of the nascent Christian community.

Important as such issues are to current debates on the position of women in Christianity today, they bear little relation to Mary as the repentant prostitute; yet in the western (though not in the eastern) church it is as such that she has been best known, the result of a conflation of gospel women. In Luke 7, a nameless prostitute anoints Christ's feet with myrrh; in John 12, Mary of Bethany, sister of Martha and Lazarus, likewise anoints his feet. From the time of Gregory the Great (*c.*540–604) until the 16th century, when critical objections were raised, these two and Mary Magdalene merged into one figure, not to be officially unscrambled by the Catholic Church until 1969. Feminist theologians have argued that this long association of Mary Magdalene with *sin and *sex worked to reinforce clerical misogyny, all the more given the emphasis the medieval church placed on the perpetual virginity of *Mary, the mother of Christ. Whatever the validity of this view, it is worth stressing the richness of the medieval legends attached to Mary Magdalene, legends that are more significant than any binary polarity between the two Marys might suggest. Such legends made Mary Magdalene the bride of the wedding feast at Cana, her groom none other than John the Evangelist; when John left her to follow Christ she was so piqued that she became a prostitute until Christ converted her. After the crucifixion Mary and seventy-two disciples left the Holy Land to preach the gospel in France; her last years she spent as a hermit in a cave in Provence, her nakedness covered only by her hair. Variations on these stories led to considerable competition for the Magdalene's relics, the winner being Vezelay where her feast day is still kept on 22 July.

Mary Magdalene's putative adventures have been a constant source of inspiration for artists, writers, and philanthropists. In the Middle Ages, she was traditionally depicted as a weeping penitent, a jar of ointment in her hand. More sensual and more sentimental images followed. In the 17th and 18th centuries it became the vogue for aristocratic women to be painted as Magdalenes; in the 19th, pre-Raphaelites portrayed her as beautiful and desirable, while social reformers founded Magdalene-homes for repentant prostitutes. In the 20th century Mary Magdalene remained a figure of paradox and controversy, reclaimed by some as an *apostle of the early church, portrayed by others as Christ's lover.

Henrietta Leyser

Haskins, Susan, *Mary Magdalen: Myth and Metaphor* (1993).

Jansen, Katherine Ludwig, 'Maria Magdalena: *Apostolorum Apostola*', in Beverley Mayne Kienzle and Pamela J. Walker (eds.), *Women Preachers and Prophets through Two Millennia of Christianity* (1998), 57–96.

Saxer, Victor, *Le Culte de Marie Madeleine en Occident des origines à la fin du moyen age* (1959).

masculinity, see MAN.

mass, see EUCHARIST.

Matthew.

The first book in the NT canon is the Gospel of Matthew. Its precise relation to the apostle Matthew (9: 9; 10: 3) is not entirely clear, and the tradition of an Aramaic or Hebrew original prior to the Greek text (Papias in Eusebius, *Ecclesiastical History*, 3. 39. 16) raises more questions than it solves. The Gospel of Matthew appears to have been composed in Greek after the destruction of the *Jerusalem *Temple in 70 AD (see 21: 41; 22: 7; 27: 25), probably around 85 to 90. A city with mostly Greek speakers and a substantial Jewish population (Antioch in Syria, Damascus, Caesarea Maritima) seems most likely as its place of composition. As sources, the evangelist used *Mark's gospel and a collection of Jesus' sayings which scholars have hypothesized to exist and named Q, as well as special Matthean traditions. Thus his gospel can be regarded as a revised and expanded edition of Mark.

As a second edition of Mark, Matthew's gospel follows the basic Marcan outline of *Jesus' public ministry in Galilee, his journey to Jerusalem, his (short) ministry in Jerusalem, and his Passion and death. Matthew provides an infancy narrative (1–2; cf. Luke 1–2) and *Resurrection appearances (28: 9–20), features not present in Mark's narrative. His most obvious contribution to the Marcan outline, however, is the inclusion of five major speeches developed mainly from Q and the special material: the *Sermon on the Mount (chs. 5–7), the missionary discourse (10), the *parables (13), the community instruction (18), and the *eschatological discourse (24–5). Thus Matthew adds considerable material concerning the content of Jesus' teaching. The result is five cycles of narratives and speeches, bracketed by the infancy narrative (1–2) and the Passion-Resurrection narrative (26–8).

In Matthew's gospel Jesus appears as the authoritative teacher, indeed the only teacher (23: 8). The epitome of his teachings known as the Sermon on the Mount (chs. 5–7) presents him as having come 'not to abolish but to fulfil' the Law (see LAW, BIBLICAL) and the prophets (5: 17). The six antitheses ('You have heard … but I say', 5: 21–48) show how Jesus insists on going to the roots of the biblical commandments. The instructions about performing acts of piety—almsgiving, *prayer, and *fasting—stress their goal of serving God rather than gaining public notice (6: 1–18). Throughout his instructions Jesus insists on the traditional Jewish connection between knowing and doing (7: 21). Even his summaries of the Law and the prophets—the golden rule ('do to others as you would have them do to you', 7: 12) and the great commandment ('You shall love the Lord your God … you shall love your neighbour as yourself', 22: 37, 39)—are concerned to offer a perspective on the whole Jewish tradition rather than to abolish it.

The horizon of Jesus' teachings and actions according to Matthew is the 'kingdom of heaven'. Both John the Baptist and Jesus call for repentance in view of the approaching *Kingdom (3: 2; 4: 17). The heart of Jesus' own prayer (the *Lord's Prayer, 6: 9–13) is the hope for the fullness of God's kingdom: 'Thy kingdom come!' The beatitudes look for a future reversal in which the poor in spirit will possess the kingdom in its fullness. The parables in chapters 13 and 24–5 look forward to the fullness of the kingdom. But they also assume that there is already something at work (the 'seeds' of God's kingdom) in the ministry of Jesus the teacher and healer sent from God. Because the fullness of the kingdom is not yet, there is need for constant vigilance on the part of Jesus' followers in the present (24: 32–25: 46). And much of Jesus' ethical teaching is concerned with showing people how to enter and live in the present phase of the 'kingdom of heaven'.

Matthew's gospel has greatly influenced Christian understandings of the *church. Jesus as Emmanuel ('God with us', 1: 23) remains with his *disciples in all ages as the risen Lord (28: 20). His followers constitute the people of God (21: 33–46) and so carry on the heritage of *Israel. The disciples are portrayed by Matthew somewhat more positively than they are by Mark, though the expression 'little faith' applied to them is hardly a ringing endorsement. As a paradigm of the Matthean disciples, *Peter illustrates the meaning of 'little faith' in his failure to continue walking on the water (14: 28–31). Nevertheless, Peter is blessed as the recipient of a divine revelation about Jesus, is designated as the rock on which the church is to be built, and is given the power to 'bind and loose' (16: 17*b*–19; cf. 18: 18). The promise to Peter has been invoked by the Roman church to apply to the bishop of Rome, thus furnishing the biblical foundation for the *papacy. But whether the promise went beyond Peter, and applied perpetually to the popes as Peter's successors, has been vigorously contested throughout Christian history.

Matthew's gospel is often called the most Jewish gospel, and thus an appropriate bridge between the Testaments. The genealogy that opens it places Jesus in the context of Israel's history from *Abraham through *David and the exile to Joseph and *Mary. The inclusion of *women in the genealogy—Tamar, Rahab, Ruth, and the wife of Uriah—prepares for the surprising mode of Jesus' own birth from the Virgin Mary (1: 18–25). Throughout the gospel, Matthew gives the already traditional *christological titles some distinctive directions in the light of Jewish traditions: the Son of God as the representative of Israel, the Servant of God who takes our infirmities upon himself, the healing Son of David, and so forth. In the passion narrative Matthew increases the already strong Marcan emphasis on Jesus' suffering and death as fulfilling the Jewish scriptures (especially Ps. 22).

Matthew's gospel is sometimes also called 'anti-Jewish'. Besides supplementing Mark in the light of additional sources, Matthew spoke to the crisis facing Jewish Christians and all other Jews after 70: how to preserve and reconstitute *Judaism after the destruction of the Jerusalem Temple and Israel's loss of political identity. In contrast to the *apocalyptic (4 Ezra, 2 Baruch) and early rabbinic (written down to some extent in the Mishnah and Tosefta around 200) solutions, the early Jewish Christian response expressed in Matthew's gospel was that authentic Judaism is best carried on by Jesus the teacher and those gathered around him. Thus Matthew emphasizes that Jesus fulfilled the Jewish scriptures and shows that his teachings spoke to debates within late 1st-century Judaism. This historical setting also explains the heated polemics against the religious and intellectual leaders of other Jewish groups (23: 1–39).

Throughout Matthew's gospel there are debates with the representatives of 'their synagogues' in which the parallel Marcan pericopes are adapted to fit late 1st-century controversies within Judaism about *sabbath observance (Mark 2: 23–3: 6; Matt. 12:

1–14), ritual purity and food laws (Mark 7: 1–23; Matt. 15: 1–20), and marriage and *divorce (Mark 10: 1–12; Matt. 19: 1–12). The so-called anti-Jewish statements (23: 1–39; 27: 25) are best read as part of the late 1st-century conflict within Judaism regarding the future of Judaism. When taken out of that historical setting, they have the potential to foment and justify *antisemitism, as history shows. Matthew's gospel, originating very much within the context of Judaism, has been read as 'anti-Jewish' by non-Jews ignorant of that context.   **Daniel J. Harrington**

Davies, W. D., and Allison, D. C., *A Critical and Exegetical Commentary on Matthew* (1988; 1991; 1997).

Harrington, D. J., *The Gospel of Matthew* (1991).

Luz, U., *The Theology of the Gospel of Matthew* (1995).

Neirynck, F., Verheyden, J., and Corstjens, R., *The Gospel of Matthew and the Sayings Source Q: A Cumulative Bibliography 1950–1995* (1998).

Saldarini, A. J., *Matthew's Christian–Jewish Community* (1994).

Stanton, G. (ed.), *The Interpretation of Matthew*, 2nd edn. (1995).

Mbiti, John

Mbiti, John (1931–). Born in Kenya, Mbiti has achieved international recognition as a creative theologian and writer. After doctoral studies in the University of Cambridge, he became professor of religious studies in Makerere University, Uganda, and director of the Ecumenical Institute in Bossey, Switzerland. His major publications include: *African Religions and Philosophy* (1969), *Concepts of God in Africa* (1970), *New Testament Eschatology in an African Background* (1970), *The Prayers of African Religion* (1975), and *Bible and Theology in African Christianity* (1986).

Mbiti's significance lies in his positive contribution to the development of *African theology. His early perception that African theology could not be artificially created, but would evolve spontaneously from the life and witness of the African church in context, was soon advanced by a differentiation between indigenous Christianity that 'results from the encounter of the gospel with any given local society', and the gospel, which is 'God-given, eternal and does not change'.

But the turning-point came when Mbiti rejected the quest for the indigenization of Christianity because it assumed that 'Christianity is a ready-made commodity which has to be transplanted'. He now saw the gospel as genuinely at home in Africa, apprehended in terms of African religious experience understood as 'preparation for the gospel'. Since God is One, 'God, the Father of our Lord Jesus Christ' was 'not a stranger in Africa prior to the coming of missionaries' (see Mission). They did not bring God, God brought them, so that through the gospel African people might be enabled 'to utter the name of Jesus Christ … that final and completing element that crowns their traditional religiosity and brings its flickering light to full brilliance'.

By the 1980s, Mbiti's theological approach had established him as the leading African theologian. Mainstream developments in African theology have built on his foundations.   **Kwame Bediako**

Bediako, K., *Theology and Identity: The Impact of Culture upon Christian Thought in the Second Century and Modern Africa* (1992), 303–46.

Olupona, J., and Nyang, S. S. (eds.), *Religious Plurality in Africa: Essays in Honour of John S. Mbiti* (1993).

medical ethics.

medical ethics. All professional work depends on trust. This is especially true in medicine, where intimate contacts and invasive procedures are tolerable only if those performing them can be trusted to do so with integrity, and with the good of the patient as the overriding motive. The necessity for medical *ethics, therefore, precedes any particular religious commitment. Understandably, though, all the major religions have shown concern for *health and healing. The theme is prominent in the bible and in the teaching of *Jesus, where health is seen as a gift from *God. Its frequent link with *forgiveness is a reminder that healing involves the whole *person, not just a body or a disease. The command to heal the sick gradually became institutionalized by the 4th-century church in the provision of hospitals and hospices. There is a biblical presumption that doctors are responsible moral agents whose work should be honoured (Ecclesiasticus 38: 1), and the tradition that *Luke was a physician has undoubtedly added lustre to the profession in Christian eyes. However until the mid-19th century when medicine began to become more systematically experimental, and hence more effective, there were few instances of Christian concern with medical ethics as now understood. The term referred primarily to internal professional standards rather than to the wider ethical implications of professional practice.

A major scandal in Germany in the 1850s, sparked off by experiments on patients deliberately infected with syphilis, was an early warning of what might happen as the new, more scientifically grounded medicine began to flex its muscles. The need for external ethical review became increasingly apparent. In the latter half of the 20th century the stream of discoveries and consequent difficult moral decisions became a torrent, so much so that medical ethics in its new broader sense now dominates much of the public ethical agenda. There are few other topics with such a potent combination of rapid innovation, intimate personal concern, and incalculable social consequences.

Christians have on the whole been cautiously welcoming towards medical advances. At the heart of Christian ethics lie beliefs about what it is to be human, as revealed in the life and teachings of Jesus. This concern for true *humanity entails a positive attitude towards all that sustains human life and dignity, makes for human flourishing, strengthens human relationships, and allows the exercise of human creativity. The human condition implies both a physical necessity of *suffering as part of the animate mortal world, and moral necessity to struggle to remove or overcome it. Healing is no less a gift from God for being a human responsibility requiring the use of the best possible medical techniques. Yet there are limits to what can be done, and reasons for caution. God allows the world, humanity included, to be inherently frail and passing, subject to the laws of physical existence and *death. This entails acceptance of a certain givenness in the human condition, a need to acknowledge human weakness and finitude, and not to shrink from the possibilities of growth through suffering. To be made in the image of God imposes on human beings a delicate balance between creativeness and creatureliness.

In retrospect some examples of excessive caution can seem ludicrous. Early opposition to vaccination on the grounds that it could 'animalize' human beings looks now like baseless scaremongering. But it has its modern counterpart in the worries felt by some about the use of animals' organs for human transplants, if and when these are deemed to be medically safe. Doubts about the directions taken by *reproductive technology—and the word 'technology' is itself revealing—centre on the belief that some distinctively human qualities are in danger of being lost. The wholeness of the reproductive process, rooted in *love, sustained by faithfulness, expressed in intimacy, consummated in *sex, and fulfilled in the birth of a child within the nurturing environment of a *family, is increasingly under threat. Christians differ in their perceptions of the seriousness of this threat. Some see the fragmentation of the process, say by the use of donor sperm, as a small price to pay for the satisfaction of having a child. For some the integrity of the whole reproductive process is more important than individual wishes. Others see the heart of the problem as lying in a culture that sedulously fosters unreal expectations.

Roman Catholic moral theologians have often tried to give detailed guidance to the medical profession, based on the principles of *natural law. The belief that nature itself, when made the object of rational reflection, can provide the basis for normative principles has strong attraction, not least in offering the hope of a universal *morality. Furthermore, if there are moral absolutes that can be seen as grounded in the way things are, these can act as a bulwark against creeping moral relativism, which creeps ever faster as one technological triumph succeeds another. Nevertheless natural law tradition has its difficulties, among them the fact that nature itself has a history. A belief that every natural object can be described in terms of some fixed essence sits uncomfortably with an understanding of the natural world as the product of an *evolutionary process that carries no guarantee that all its results will be good. The notion of God-givenness thus appears less secure, both as a description and as a source of clear-cut moral insights. To say precisely what an embryo is, for example, and hence what its moral status should be, entails making some more or less arbitrary decisions about the significance of different moments or stages in what is in fact a continuous process.

Some versions of the natural law tradition have also had an unfortunate tendency to concentrate on the moral evaluation of particular acts, say a surgical intervention such as sterilization, or on particular functions, say the use of the reproductive organs, in virtual isolation from their contexts and possible consequences. Such individually labelled acts, whether described as intrinsically good or intrinsically evil, seldom relate easily to the real world in which decisions have to be taken. It has been said that just as there are few atheists in foxholes, there tend to be few absolutists at the bedside.

The hard edges of absolutism can to some extent be blunted by the principle of double effect. Actions may have several consequences, some of which may be undesirable and unintended. According to the principle, undesirable consequences do not invalidate the morality of an action whose primary intention was good. An operation on a mother may result in the inadvertent death of a foetus, for instance, but this does not mean it was necessarily wrong to attempt it.

The two main principles that in practice guide most doctors are to preserve life and to prevent suffering. Decision-making is at its most difficult when, as not infrequently happens, they are in conflict. Current interest in *euthanasia reflects such conflict, which led to a Christian-inspired response in the form of the hospice movement. Other conflicts may be less capable of resolution. Thus Christian emphasis on the value of every human life is not the sole consideration in dilemmas about the treatment of the newborn and the elderly. How does one weigh the risks and traumas of serious intervention against the hopes of marginal improvement? Is

it a good idea to operate for cancer on a 75-year-old, who shows signs of succumbing to Alzheimer's disease?

Nothing can diminish the ultimate accountability of medical professionals in the face of such issues. However, the sheer difficulty of making principled decisions has led to increasing reliance on procedural devices. This is one reason why emphasis on the necessity for informed consent is now in the forefront of medical ethics. It is, of course, more than a procedural device and is based on a proper recognition, congenial to Christian thinking, that patients share responsibility with their medical advisers. Everybody has a right and duty to make decisions about their own treatment, and to care for their own minds and bodies as gifts from God. This emphasis on patient autonomy has been a major factor in the changing ethos of medical practice in the latter half of the 20th century, and has led to a healthy reduction in paternalism. It is also a way of asserting the inviolability of personhood. Nobody has an automatic right to use invasive techniques on another person's mind or body, or to manipulate them as persons against their will, except in those circumstances where they are a danger to others or, as in psychiatry, to help restore their powers of rational decision-making.

But even these admirable aims are not without their difficulties. Patient autonomy can be asserted to the point at which it becomes a kind of consumerism, backed by threats of litigation if the customer is dissatisfied. In Christian thinking autonomy has always to be qualified by a recognition that choices affect other people, and therefore have to be made with wider relationships in mind, including the relationship with God. *Suicide, for instance, is one of the ultimate expressions of autonomy, but has repercussions far beyond the person committing it. A decision about *abortion is always a decision about a family or potential family, as well as about an individual. Most directly of all, genetic testing provides information, possibly unwanted, about a person's blood relatives as well as about him- or herself. Furthermore each choice contributes to the cultural context in which others have to make their decisions. An accumulation of unethical choices can, in Pope *John Paul II's words, create 'a culture of death'.

There is a telling example in the British Human Fertilization and Embryology Act (1990) illustrating the extent to which informed consent can appear to obviate the need for making decisions about matters of principle. The moral and legal status of embryos is left undefined, and the requirement to respect them is set out entirely in terms of the consents that have to be obtained before anything is done to them. This procedural approach is in direct contrast to traditional Catholic moral theology in which precise definition, logical deduction, and firm prescription are of the essence. It may fit better, however, with a style of Christian thinking in which the emphasis is on individual *conscience and the circumstances of particular cases, and which acknowledges that many choices are messy and uncertain (see CASUISTRY). Procedures may help to define the area within which choices must be made, but there is no guarantee that all the insights of moral theology will necessarily point the same way.

Central to Christian ethics, whether in medicine or in any other field, is the notion of restraint. Allegiance to the God who, in the name of love, limits himself to our human condition, accepts suffering, and triumphs over death, entails a willingness to live hopefully and creatively within the limits of our humanity. Nature may not have a fixed essence from which it is possible to deduce unarguable moral principles, but there is nevertheless a wisdom in respecting what is given, without wantonly transgressing its boundaries. The possibilities of genetic manipulation provide a particularly sharp test for such an orientation. When the mapping of the human genome is complete, the scope for using this vast reservoir of genetic knowledge will be enormous, not only as at present in the diagnosis of abnormalities, but in exercising greater 'quality control' over who is born. The elimination of the few thousand known hereditary diseases caused by defects in single genes is the first objective. This could be done by selective abortion, or embryo selection during *in vitro* fertilization. But defective genes could also be replaced by germ-line therapy, in which a new gene is substituted for a defective one, thereby eliminating the defect from all future generations. A further step might be the replacement of genes or gene segments that are not specifically linked with clearly identifiable disease, but which play some part in predisposing a person to, say, alcoholism or some other health hazard. This would be a much more risky procedure because the interactions between genes are largely unknown, and it would be difficult to predict the precise consequences of any interference.

Germ-line therapy of either kind would entail experimenting with embryos destined to become fully developed persons, and with all their descendants. Christian opinion, as indeed that of most responsible researchers, has been unanimous in rejecting this possibility, but not always for the same reasons. Some concentrate on the practical hazards, including the social dangers of trying to trim humanity to our own design. Others regard any non-therapeutic interference with an embryo's genetic constitution as being in itself wrong, a denial of God-given individuality. At stake here are questions about whether personhood is to be understood as somehow already 'given' in a set of genes; or whether it is a developing reality, initiated by a particular set of genes, that is not itself sacrosanct, but that comes into being through a process of interaction and interrelationship, grounded in and sustained by God, and having a different moral significance at different stages. Similar disagreements about how and when persons are formed underlie different Christian attitudes to abortion.

There is no dispute among Christians, however, about the moral status of even highly impaired personalities once independent life has started. Inherited defect, disease, accident, and slow degeneration can all impair or reduce qualities of personhood, most devastatingly when the brain itself is damaged. In some cases, as in the persistent vegetative state, the line between life and death is difficult to draw, and there is disagreement over whether such patients should be regarded as possessing bodily functions only, which should be allowed to cease, or whether they should continue to be treated as living persons, albeit without any possibility of regaining consciousness. In all other cases, where some degree of conscious personhood remains, Christian belief points strongly in the direction of respecting and cherishing such lives, on the grounds that they are loved and held in being by God who alone knows their potential in this life and beyond it. It is frequently said that the quality of a society is judged by the way it treats its weakest and most vulnerable members.

When doctors themselves discuss ethical issues, resource allocation is usually near the top of the agenda. While it is easy to accept in principle that highly impaired people should have as much care as those with good chances of recovery, if not more, in practice difficult choices have to be made. It is not surprising that the leading edges of medical technology should attract more funding than geriatrics. There are no simple Christian answers to such dilemmas beyond constant reminders that all people are God's children, whether they seem to be deserving or not. Furthermore because Christianity is a universal faith, Christian concern about health and healing ought to have a global perspective. The realization that primary health care and the accessibility of very simple remedies are still the greatest needs in large parts of the world puts in perspective the worries created by some of modern medicine's more esoteric dilemmas.

See also GLOBAL ETHICS. **John Habgood**

Beauchamp, T., *et al.*, *Principles of Biomedical Ethics* (1994).

Duncan, A. S., *et al.*, *Dictionary of Medical Ethics*, 2nd edn. (1981).

Dunstan, G. R., *et al.*, *Doctors' Decisions* (1989).

Habgood, J. S., *Being a Person* (1998).

Poole, J., *The Harm We Do* (1993).

Reiss, M. J., and Straughan, R., *Improving Nature?* (1996).

Smith D., *Life and Morality: Contemporary Medico-Moral Issues* (1996).

Melchizedek. In the letter to the *Hebrews, Christ is designated as 'a high priest after the order of Melchizedek' (5: 6–10). This picks up the claim in Psalm 110: 4 that the *Davidic *king is a 'priest after the order of Melchizedek' which may itself reflect an earlier attempt to legitimate the new Jerusalem Temple and the priestly status of the Davidic monarchy against the traditional establishment. Melchizedek first appears in *Genesis 14: 17–20, where as 'king of Salem' and 'priest of God Most High' (*El Elyon*) he greets *Abraham after the latter's victory over the kings of the land. He brings out bread and wine and blesses him, whereupon Abraham delivers to him a tenth of his spoils.

Nothing is known of Melchizedek's antecedents, and this very fact is used by the writer of Hebrews as evidence of his eternal nature. His name and title are explained as 'King of righteousness' and 'King of peace', both *messianic titles. For the writer to the Hebrews, Melchizedek represents an order of *priesthood older than and superior in authority to Abraham, the recipient of the covenant. As a priest in this line that outranks the Levites and the Temple cult, Jesus renders the Temple superfluous.

Both priest and king, Melchizedek provides a model for the writer of Hebrews that explains the union of these two offices in Christ. This counters the expectation in some apocalyptic circles of two messiahs, a kingly one from the line of David and a priestly one from the line of Aaron.

Writers in the intertestamental period portray Melchizedek as a cosmic figure. Philo saw him as a representation of the Logos and in the *Dead Sea Scrolls he appears as an angelic eschatological being. Thus the use of Melchizedek in Hebrews to underpin Christ's role as cosmic high priest represents a Christian adaptation of a complex figure that had a long tradition of use in legitimating claims to priesthood against the established hierarchy.

Later Christian tradition builds on Melchizedek as a type of Christ. His association with bread and wine has obvious *eucharistic resonances, as noted by Clement of Alexandria, and his offering is seen as a counter to the animal sacrifices of the Temple. Melchizedek foreshadows the universal scope of Christ's priesthood in that he is not part of the Jewish covenant community. The importance of this eucharistic understanding is shown by the fact that his name appears in the canon of the Roman Catholic Mass.

In a typical move, the apologists of the *Reformation use Melchizedek to establish their claims against the Roman priesthood, repeating a pattern of argument that may perhaps have been used to legitimate the seeming novelties of the Davidic monarchy and the early church in their day. The radical Reformers use this argument in turn in their polemics against *Luther and *Calvin. Melchizedek is always available to the tradition to be enlisted as the legitimating forerunner for an alternative priesthood.   **Hugh S. Pyper**

Horton, F. L., Jr., *The Melchizedek Tradition* (1976).

memory. From *Augustine onwards, Christians have been interested in memory, not only because the whole Judaeo-Christian tradition depends critically upon *remembering* the past, but also because memory defines—or helps to define—the self, and thereby constitutes the identity of the believer before God. Indeed, for Augustine memory is the high road to a more authentic reality that can, in part, recapture prelapsarian innocence (*Confessions*, 10). Given this high doctrine of memory that Augustine, drawing on both *Plato and *Aristotle, bequeathed to Christian *philosophy at least until the 19th century, some may find modern emphasis on the *plasticity* of memory unnerving. As recent studies of the memories of forensic witnesses (i.e testimonies) have shown, *time, interest, bias, and even the company and location in which the remembering is done all influence what is remembered.

When we apply what is now known about memory to our interpretation of the *bible, we find traditional assumptions challenged. Thus in the OT a superficial view would be that it is *Israel's memory of crucial events in her *history that forms her self-identity as a chosen nation. The difficulty with this account is that it leaves the nature of memory uncontested. There is ample evidence that much of the 'remembering' was cultic in origin; the cult formed the process by which the *nation was constantly reminded of the (cultic officials' view of) its formative history. In this context recent research on the way in which 'social memory' functions is instructive. In many (but not all) societies, oral history is not, as some classic accounts of memory (including those of both Plato and Augustine) imply, the repetition of an unwavering formula—the so-called wax tablet account—but is, rather, deliberately refashioned, reshaped, artfully crafted for a particular purpose and/or a particular audience. One way of making this contrast would be to oppose *stimulus* and *control*. The cult acted as both. It stimulated the reshaping of memories to fit a particular situation but simultaneously acted as a control within which that reshaping took place.

In the NT we are in a world that is the same but different. It is the same in the sense that the community knows that its central memories, of the life, death and *Resurrection of this man, *Jesus, are cardinal. Without them, the community is one more among many aberrant sects of orthodox Judaism. It is the memory of Jesus that makes the community special, in exactly the same way that it is the memory of *exodus and *covenant that makes Israel special. Different, however, are three things. First, the remembering community is small, scattered and, certainly initially, critically impaired. Second, among the orthodox Temple worshippers and the occupying power, the memories held dear by the community are either unwelcome or subversive. Third, and perhaps most important of all, the foundational memory, that of the Resurrection, runs counter to common sense and experience and is therefore most open to the charge of excessive poetic crafting.

The fourth evangelist, significantly writing later than the allegedly more historical gospel writers, seems especially aware of these difficulties. It is he who has Jesus, in the last discourses, lay such emphasis on the work of the *Holy Spirit in 'bringing all things to [the] remembrance' of the young community (John 14: 26). This is revealing because it suggests that the community John was writing out of or for felt the need for some transcendent guarantee of the theo-historicity of its memories. By making more central and explicit a theme that is fleetingly glimpsed in the OT, John assures his readers that any doubts they may have about the 'truth' (John 14: 17) of the memories incorporated in his gospel—and presumably by extension in the others—are redundant. In a very specific sense, they are inspired.

In this context, the role of Jesus' explicit charge to his disciples at the Last Supper to 'do this in remembrance (*anamnesis*) of me' (Luke 22: 19; 1 Cor. 11: 24) is especially significant. This phrase, known as the *anamnesis*, is central to every *eucharistic liturgy. Here, if anywhere, we seem to be in contact with the very words of Jesus, his *ipsissima verba*, a 'hard', cultically embedded, and action-stimulated memory that has a number of intriguing features. First, it refers back to the OT memory of the covenant: it makes a new covenant. Second, it is intentionally mnemonic: its purpose is to remind the community of Jesus' life and death. Third, it is set within a ritualistic framework, the Passover, and therefore links the memory of Jesus to the memory of the great deliverance. Fourth and in some ways most telling, it is developed by the community not just as an act of remembrance, but also, by drawing on a deeper religious tradition, as a representation of the thing remembered. In this sense, the *anamnesis* is a proleptic remembering in which the participants both *remember* the event and *become participants* in it. In the process they are themselves re-membered, for by receiving the life of Christ, they are made one with him.

In OT and NT, then, we have layers of different types of remembering and memorizing, none of which can be guaranteed to present to us (as time- and culture-embedded recipients) *what actually happened*. We are (usually) in a shifting world of poesis rather than a solid world of wax-tablet or memory chip. Does that matter? In *law, we think not. The contingency of the memory of witnesses does not render them unreliable. The 'whole truth' they tell may not be *demonstrable* but we acquit or condemn on its basis without any sense of violating truth. That does not imply that they may not have been honestly mistaken or dishonestly lying. It does mean that we accept their testimony in good *faith* (sic), because overall we judge them and their memories to be at least good guides to the *truth. We respect their characters, and therefore their account of 'what happened', even when their memories are not wholly mutually consistent. So it is in religion.

The Christian tradition has developed the idea of memory in three main ways: in eucharistic theology, the themes of memorial/re-presentation/sacrament have been well worked over, often, it must be said, with little discussion of the nature of the memories incorporated in the *anamnesis*. In biblical theology, the great debates have been on historicity (and therefore, by implication, of the nature of the remembering implied in written history), and the reliability (and even ontological status) of oral tradition. More recently, there has been much interest in the way the text is received by the reader. In that context, the prior memories the reader has as s/he approaches the text may determine and will certainly influence what s/he finds there. This area of interest leads naturally into a new field of study that seeks to illuminate the *unconscious* memory material at work in the reading of the text. In ecclesiology, many of the debates about *authority in the church can be read—though they have not usually been expressed—as debates about who determines which memories are kept alive to become part of the living tradition, and how they are crafted in the process. This has been of particular interest in the *Catholic Church, both historically in the process of canonization and contemporaneously in the context of *liberation theology. An important appendix to that whole debate is the rediscovery of 'lost' memories and the analysis of why (at whose behest) they have been lost, a theme introduced by *Nietzsche's interest in 'forgetting'.

Two other dimensions can be mentioned in conclusion. The first is in the devotional life of the church. From Augustine to Ignatius of Loyola to contemporary advocates of 'memory-work', there is a long tradition, consistent with John's account of the work of the Paraclete, of seeing the memory as a faculty through which God can draw the soul of the Christian into closer communion with himself. The second is the theme of the gospel as a collection of 'dangerous memories' that challenge the status quo both ecclesiastically and politically. Especially associated with the name of Jean-Baptiste Metz, the theme has become popular with all those who want to read the memories of the early church *against the grain* of contemporary society. They emphasize that the memories that the early church seems to have been especially assiduous in preserving are of the rights and dignity of the dispossessed. In this sense, both the memories of the early church as expressed in the gospels and the way in which we interpret those memories, in the light of the memories we have, for example, of *Holocaust or *apartheid or oppression, become together dangerous to those who advocate a status quo that flies in the face of the *Kingdom of God.

Charles Elliott

Butler, Thomas, *Memory, History, Culture and the Mind* (1989).
Cohen, Gillian, *Memory in the Real World* (1989).
Connerton, Paul, *How Societies Remember* (1991).
Elliott, Charles, *Memory and Salvation* (1995).
Falconer, Alan D. (ed.), *Reconciling Memories* (1988).
Fentress, James, and Wickham, Chris, *Social Memory: New Perspectives on the Past* (1992).

Mennonite thought.

In the 16th-century *Reformation, state-church theologians chose the pejorative terms 'anabaptist' (or 'catabaptist') to designate a variety of more radical Reformers who called for *baptism of adult believers upon confession of *faith, and who thereby broke with the medieval unity of church and society. They also denied that civil rulers were qualified to reform and govern churches. Movements of this kind spread rapidly between 1525 and 1540, forming viable communities especially in the upper Rhine basin, in the Netherlands, and in Moravia.

Menno Simons (c.1496–1561) did not found any of these movements. Originally a Frisian parish priest, he was baptized ('rebaptized' from the Catholic perspective) c.1536 and was soon called to leadership within Dutch Anabaptism. He helped consolidate the movement in and beyond the Netherlands, especially by clarifying internal differences, so that his name came to be used to designate the non-violent and biblicist strands of Anabaptism, as they were increasingly distinguished from other less sober radical groups, some of them socially violent and some *apocalyptic. Menno's name thus became a label for communities in areas where he had never worked and where his writings were hardly known.

Half the Mennonites in the world today are ethnically descended from those first European communities. They survived and prospered, especially in the Netherlands where persecution first ended, spreading from there to the Vistula basin, and then in the 1790s to the Ukraine where they were invited as colonizers. Political change forced some of them to move again from the Ukraine to the prairies of the USA and Canada in 1874, and there was another exodus after the Soviet revolution. Later migrations established colonies in Brazil and Paraguay.

The Swiss and South German communities lived a different history. They were persecuted longer than the Anabaptists in the north, and socially discriminated against longer still, but survived quietly as tenant farmers in the countryside from the canton of Bern to the Palatinate, migrating gradually from all those regions to settle in colonial North America.

A third strand of Anabaptism survived from the 16th century, also non-violent and biblicist. The 'Hutterian brethren' in Moravia took their name from Jakob Hutter, who consolidated their commitment to community of goods as a part of the gospel. The Hutterians had a similar migration experience, also finally settling in the USA and Canada, and co-operating in some ways with Mennonites.

Mennonites in the Netherlands, north-west Germany, and the Vistula basin became broadly involved in the life of their societies, losing some of their sense of separateness, and becoming leaders in education, the arts, and commerce. Those further south in Europe and those in Russia and North America were slower to open themselves to outside influences, but they were affected by *Pietism and various *evangelical revival movements, beginning their own overseas *missions in the 19th century, and founding schools, publishing houses, and hospitals. As a result of this missionary activity half the Mennonites in the world today are not descended from the Germanic parent cultures of the 16th century. There are strong self-governing communities of over 15,000 members each in Indonesia, India, Ethiopia, Mozambique, Tanzania, Zaire, Paraguay, and Mexico, and smaller churches in a score of other countries, joining the 400,000 in North America (plus about 40,000 Hutterian Brethren) and 45,000 in Western Europe to total roughly a million baptized members worldwide.

Polity patterns vary from the *congregationalist to the loosely synodical. Regional and national 'conference' structures administer common concerns (missions, schools, publications), but it is not held that any particular form of '*church' above the congregational level is theologically imperative. While divisions that occurred in Switzerland in the 1690s (the Amish), and others that arose in the Ukraine and in 19th-century frontier America, have not been fully overcome, most groups share in centrally administered relief and service programmes. A consultative World Conference meets every six or seven years.

Together with *Baptists, *Disciples, *Pentecostals, and others

Mennonites continue to reject the baptism of infants in favour of baptism upon personal confession of faith, constituting communities independent of civil authorities. The age at which children of member families may request baptism varies from the early teens to the twenties. Mennonites have found little success in their efforts to achieve *dialogue with the large communions about the age of baptism or the meaning of membership, although many people within the traditionally paedobaptist communions now find themselves reconsidering the practice of infant baptism for their own reasons, and on a world scale the proportional numerical weight of churches baptizing on confession of faith (*Adventist, Baptist, Pentecostal) is growing.

Among Mennonites, theological understanding of the Lord's supper (*Eucharist), as well as the practices of weekly *worship, devotional life, and Christian education, usually resemble those of the more general evangelical culture. Ministerial leadership is not understood as a sacrament. Although today many local congregational leaders have been trained in Bible Colleges or seminaries, over the centuries most have been locally called and not academically trained.

Believers' baptism correlates with a vision of the Christian life often called 'discipleship' or 'holiness': a process of moral change, rapid or gradual or both, sustained by community life. This moral seriousness, allied to decentralized 'conference' structures and lay leadership, has fostered the vitality of conservative regroupings variously known as 'old order', reacting against urbanization and modernization, or 'old colony'. In some North American regions such conservative groups (perhaps a fifth of the total North American membership), contribute to the image of Mennonites as avoiding civilization. At the same time, especially in Canada, there is growing involvement in commercial and political leadership, the arts and education, similar to what had long ago prevailed in the Netherlands and northern Germany.

The original Anabaptist and *Quaker advocacy of *religious liberty, costly and even heroic in the early centuries, may seem in the west to be a battle that is won and hence redundant; yet there are many parts of the world where religious establishments and religiously ratified ethnocentrism still seek to enforce uniformity, and where standing for religious liberty can still require heroism.

Historians and ecumenical and service agencies group Mennonites with Friends and *Brethren under the label 'historic peace churches' (HPC) because of their shared rejection of participation in *war. Their *pacifist commitment has in some places been a reason for persecution and for emigration to more tolerant host countries, mostly the Americas. European Mennonites had largely forgotten the pacifist strand in their identity since the Napoleonic age, but it has been retrieved in recent generations, and become a theme for *ecumenical dialogue.

In the 20th century the HPC led in developing civilian service activities as alternatives to military service. Such work extended into relief for victims of war, post-war reconstruction and development, and domestic disaster relief. These are the activities for which HPC churches are best known to the public. They have developed 'conflict transformation' as a form of social science, and as a social service ministry, in situations of large- or small-scale social tension, and as a challenge to pathologies in the field of criminal justice. They have sent 'peacemaker brigades' to serve as mediating observers in troubled societies. They have shared in efforts to foster ecumenical dialogue about the moral issues of Christian participation in *nationalism and war. In missionary settings Mennonites have tended to relate co-operatively to both evangelical and ecumenical networks, and to seek to integrate spiritual and social ministries, in the face of pressures (both intellectual and institutional) to pull these dimensions of witness and mission apart.

John Howard Yoder

A Declaration on Peace: In God's People the World's Renewal has Begun (1991).

Durnbaugh, Donald F. (ed.), *On Earth Peace: Discussions on War/Peace Issues* (1978).

Dyck, Cornelius J. (ed.), *Introduction to Mennonite History* (1993).

Hershberger, Guy F. (ed.), *The Recovery of the Anabaptist Vision* (1957).

Mennonite Encyclopedia (1955–90).

Mennonite Quarterly Review.

mercy. In the Christian tradition 'mercy' denotes both an important attribute of God and a form of human action that is both enabled and called for by God's mercy. Although the English word comes from the Latin *merces*, meaning reward, wages, recompense, 'mercy' means *compassion towards those who have no claim to kindness and from whom no recompense can be expected, as in the case of offenders unable to offer compensation for the damage they have caused. This significant shift in meaning was introduced by Latin spiritual writers as early as the 6th century. Just as the English word 'mercy' overlaps with *grace, compassion, clemency, and leniency, so mercy is expressed by a variety of words in the biblical traditions. In the Hebrew bible being 'merciful and gracious' (Exod. 34: 6) is a self-predication of God, closely linked to the identity expressed in his name. God freely shows mercy even to those who have violated the relationship with him and who have no means of restoring it, so that they can only call on God's mercy. Returning to God and receiving his mercy means being reinstated in a relationship which secures life and well-being. Accepting God's mercy obligates and enables the recipient to act in accordance with this relationship.

In the *Pauline letters of the NT the emphasis is on mercy as an attribute of 'God the Father of our Lord Jesus Christ, the Father of mercies, and the God of all comfort' (2 Cor. 1: 3). The sovereign freedom of God's mercy is underlined in his turning to those who are to be saved, be they Jews or Gentiles (Rom. 9: 15–18). Mercy as the distinctive feature of God's character is the ground for all-encompassing salvation, so that Gentiles who have no claim on God 'might glorify God for his mercy' (Rom. 15: 9). In many instances the meaning of mercy seems identical with grace, although they can also be distinguished (Heb. 4: 16).

In the Synoptic Gospels the focus is on the way in which God's mercy calls for mercy in human relationships. Jesus is described as defining his mission in debate with the Pharisees by quoting: 'I require mercy, not sacrifice' (Hos. 6: 6), 'I did not come to call the virtuous, but sinners' (Matt. 9: 13; cf. 12: 7). Mercy takes the place of sacrificial rites. In a manner reminiscent of the prophetic criticism of the cult 'justice, mercy, and good faith' are described as the more difficult demands of the law (Matt. 23: 23). The attitude and form of action enabled and demanded by God's mercy is summarized in the beatitudes: 'Blessed are those who show mercy; mercy shall be shown to them' (Matt. 6: 7). Mercy finds its highest expression in love of enemies (Luke 6: 35), which is only made possible for humans by being conformed to the pattern of God's mercy: 'Be therefore merciful, as your Father is also merciful' (Luke 6: 36).

The Christian ethos is therefore based on God's mercy: 'Therefore, my friends, I implore you by God's mercy to offer your very selves to him: a living sacrifice, dedicated and fit for acceptance, the worship offered by mind and heart' (Rom. 12: 1). Calling upon God by saying 'Lord have mercy', a much-used invocation in the liturgy both of the eastern and western churches, not only means asking for God's kindness as one who neither deserves it nor can offer recompense for it, but also implies being conformed to the pattern of God's mercy. Not as autonomous independent subjects but as themselves dependent on God's mercy, believers can let their attitudes and actions be transformed by mercy, as Isabella pleaded in *Shakespeare's Measure for Measure. So the Christian ethos responds to the misery of those who suffer by taking their place and exercising solidarity with them. Being merciful as those who themselves depend on mercy means defining one's course of action not by a principle of moral independence but by one's experience of one's need of the other. Stoic ethics reject mercy as having no place in an ethos guided by wisdom. For *Kantian ethics it means doing good to the undeserving and should have no place in moral human interaction. In *Nietzsche's view mercy is a pathological affect. In contrast to all these views, a Christian ethos of mercy can be described as ecstatic in a twofold sense: it depends not on the moral independence of those exercising it, but on their dependence on God's mercy; and it is motivated not by an ethical principle but by the need of one's fellow creatures. Jesus' story of the good Samaritan displays an ethos of mercy as the only one that can meet the needs of those who suffer (Luke 10: 29–37). Those who are conformed to the pattern of God's mercy can hope to become channels of God's mercy.   **Christoph Schwöbel**

Macky, Peter, W., 'The Metaphors of God's Mercy and Judgement in the New Testament', *Proceedings, Estn. Gt. Lakes and Midwest Bibl. Soc.* 9 (1989), 231–45.

Murphy, Jeffrie, and Hampton, Jean, *Forgiveness and Mercy* (1988).

Sobrino, Jon, 'The Samaritan Church and the Principle of Mercy', *Trinity Seminary Review*, 13 (1990), 3–12.

merit. The notion of merit is based on the equivalence of deed and consequence. In the *wisdom literature of the Hebrew bible this divinely instituted pattern is interpreted as governing the social and cosmic order. However, if God rewards good works this is an act of grace, freely corresponding to the human expectation of a fair reward for acting according to the law of righteousness. The assumption that the *election of *Israel and its gaining possession of the land is based on merit is explicitly rejected (Deut. 9: 4–5). Not Israel's merit, but God's *love and faithfulness in keeping his promises to the forefathers (Deut. 7: 8) determines Israel's fate. The sovereignty of God's *grace and *mercy excludes any claim on God based on human merit. 'I shall be gracious to whom I shall be gracious, and I shall have compassion on whom I shall have compassion' (Exod. 33: 19).

*Apocalyptic literature, systematically developing the idea of merit, struggles with the problem that God's order of righteousness can no longer be verified in experience, since the righteous suffer and the wicked flourish. By fulfilling the demands of the law the righteous acquire a treasure of merits in heaven which God records

in a book (2 Esd. 7: 77), just as God keeps a record of human transgressions (Syriac *Apocalypse of Baruch* 24: 1). Merits and transgressions are weighed in the last judgement, which will reveal the true character of every human agent.

In the NT the sovereignty of God's grace overrules the equivalence of deed and merit (cf. Matt. 20: 1–16), overturning any order defined by claims based on merit. *Paul's criticism of the *law as a way of salvation is based on a rejection of the idea of merit in the divine–human relationship. Because the broken relationship between God and humanity is restored in Christ, the law does not have the function of making it possible to acquire merit before God. It only serves to reveal the inability of sinful humanity to meet its demands and so points to God's action in Christ as the ground of salvation.

In the early church *Augustine's doctrine of grace excludes any real idea of merit from the divine–human relationship. One can speak of merit only in a figurative, almost ironic sense, since God's goodness is so overwhelming that he regards as merits what are really his gifts. The schoolmen distinguished between a *meritum de condigno*, which constitutes a real claim to a divine reward because it is acquired by the justified believer through good works of salvific relevance, and a *meritum de congruo*, which does not constitute such a claim because no merit could be proportional to God's reward. However, God graciously regards these good works as merits in preparation for grace. Against the view of some late medieval theologians, that even before receiving grace the good works of human nature can create a disposition for receiving it, the *Reformation revived the radical Augustinian view that sinners are justified by grace alone, on account of Christ and through faith. Good works are never conditional for God's grace, but always consecutive upon his grace.

While reflection on merit has all but vanished in modern theology it has reappeared in secular guise as the idea of a meritocracy, a society based exclusively on achievement and merit and not on inherited privileges. The secular quest for merit, often pursued with religious fervour, is as much in need of criticism in the light of God's free grace which grants dignity to every person regardless of merit, as was the older religious quest for merit as a preparation for God's grace.   **Christoph Schwöbel**

Heinz, Johann, *Justification and Merit: Luther vs Catholicism* (1984).

Küng, Hans, *Justification: The Doctrine of Karl Barth and a Catholic Reflection* (1964).

Wawrykow, Joseph Peter, *God's Grace and Human Action: 'Merit' in the Theology of Thomas Aquinas* (1995).

Merton, Thomas (1915–68).

Trappist monk, writer, and poet, Merton became famous in 1948 when he published an autobiography, *The Seven Storey Mountain*, which described his conversion to Catholicism while an undergraduate at Columbia, and his experiences when he joined the Trappist community at Gethsemani, Kentucky. The book, which painted the *religious life in glowing terms, created something of a boom in *monastic vocations, not least at Gethsemani itself, which became seriously overcrowded. Merton went on to write a number of books on *spiritual themes.

He was to change a great deal in the years after the book was published, not least in coming to see the Roman Catholic Church and his own order in far less ideal terms, and it was this inner change which caused him to ask more profound questions, not only about his faith, but about the usefulness of the monk in the modern *world. Merton found the 'busyness' of American Trappists hard to endure and this, and his problems with *authority, brought him near to breakdown. When later appointed as Novice Master, his work with the younger monks, together with extensive reading of post-war writers, helped him to reorientate within his own order, and by the 1960s he was full of new energy and ideas.

He started living as a hermit in a cinder hut away from the monastery in order to understand more about solitude. He developed a view of the monk as a contemplative on the margin of *church and society, free because he had nothing to lose, and detached enough to be perceptively critical. From this stance he wrote of the Cold War, of Hiroshima and atomic weapons, and of preparations by the USA for war with Russia. He felt that it was important to try to make sense of the horror of the death camps and of the Gulags, how in the extreme of 'irreligiousness' what he called 'abstract thinking' took over, and people became no more than faceless units, who could then be transported in trucks and killed in gas chambers. He did not think that the Roman Catholic church was innocent of some kinds of abstract thinking.

His writing focused increasingly on the overcoming of divisions—between the Soviet bloc and the west, between eastern and western *religions, and, closer to home, on racial and religious divisions. He conducted a small revolution in Kentucky, inviting Southern Baptists, Episcopalians, Jews, and others to Gethsemani for discussion. He was profoundly interested in Eastern religions, particularly *Buddhism, and he practised Zen meditation and calligraphy.

Without leaving Gethsemani until the last two years of his life, Merton managed to be part of the thinking of the 1960s, influencing some of the leaders of the Civil Rights Movement, including Martin Luther King, Jr., trying to persuade fellow monks to take *ecological concerns seriously at home in their own fields and woods. In the last year of his life he was permitted by a new abbot to make a long journey to the east, where he visited India and Thailand, talked with the Dalai Lama, and Hindu and Buddhist holy men. He died by accidental electrocution at Bangkok just after delivering a remarkable speech about the coming together of east and west.

Monica Furlong

Merton, T., *The Seven Storey Mountain* (1948; 1990); abridged version, *Elected Silence* (1949).
—— *Conjectures of a Guilty Bystander* (1966).
Furlong, Monica, *Merton: A Biography* (1980; 1995).
Mott, Michael, *The Seven Mountains of Thomas Merton* (1984).

messiah, a transcription of the Hebrew word for 'anointed one', which can be translated literally into Greek as *christos*. In the Old Testament, the word is applied to anointed kings and high priests but also more widely to those chosen by God to bring about the restoration of *Israel. Cyrus, king of Persia, who allowed the return from Babylon and the rebuilding of the *Temple, is given this title, for instance (Isa. 45: 1), but more usually it refers to *David and his descendants.

The prophetic tradition and the royal *psalms, however, foresee a scope and majesty in the rule of the messiah that no anointed leader of Israel ever obtained. When the Davidic kingdom and the Davidic line disappeared, such descriptions were applied to a future restorer of Israel who would re-establish the throne of David in *Jerusalem. Later Judaism developed a more *eschatological understanding whereby David's descendant would usher in an age of tribulation that would lead to the establishment of God's *Kingdom. The tradition was very fluid: the *Dead Sea Scrolls look forward to two messiahs, one from the Davidic line and one from the priestly line.

Applied to *Jesus, the title undergoes a profound transformation. Whether he accepted it himself and what he understood by it are matters of scholarly dispute. His humility, crucifixion, and *death seem flagrant contradictions of the messianic ideal. For the gospel writers, and particularly for *Paul, it is the *Resurrection that vindicates Jesus as God's anointed in a way that confounds contemporary expectations. Elements from the suffering servant of *Isaiah and the Son of Man in *Daniel, never linked to the messianic concept before, are called on to round out a new understanding of *salvation as brought about through the messiah's redemptive death.

The writers of the NT can suppose that their readers will have some knowledge of the underlying traditions. As the gospel spread into the Gentile world, the understanding of the term *christos* as explanatory of Jesus' authority diminished and it came to be regarded as a name. A tension still persisted, however, as the world carried on its old way with no unambiguous sign that the promised messianic age had come about. The 2nd-century apologist Justin Martyr countered this by developing the influential idea that the OT indicated that the messiah would appear twice, first in humility and the second time in glory.

This allows Christianity the best of both worlds in that it acclaims Jesus as the fulfilment of the OT promises of the messiah, yet can still maintain hope for a future consummation in the face of the continued injustice of the present age. It also means that a door is open to the rise of messianic movements that proclaim their leader as the new Christ. Some indigenous African churches, for instance, begin with the appearance of a messianic figure, such as the Zulu Isaiah Shembe, who announces the arrival of the kingdom but is later reinterpreted as a *prophet by followers when the kingdom once more is delayed and the movement becomes concerned to stress its Christian orthodoxy. All Christian thought has to take its stance between proclaiming a messiah who has come and a kingdom not yet fully realized on earth.   **Hugh S. Pyper**

Beuken, W., Freyne, S., Weiler, A., *Messianism through History* (1993).
Juel, D., *Messianic Exegesis: Christological Interpretation of the Old Testament in Early Christianity* (1988).
Kaiser, W. C., *The Messiah in the Old Testament* (1997).
Neusner, J., Green, W. S., Frerichs, E., *Judaisms and Their Messiahs at the Turn of the Christian Era* (1988).

metaphor is a figurative use of *language in which one term is viewed through the associations of a second term. The philosopher and literary critic I. A. Richards called the first term the tenor and the second the vehicle. So, in the phrase 'the ship ploughs through the water' the ship is the tenor and its movement through the water is described through the vehicle, 'ploughs', with all the associations of that agricultural action. A certain transferral of meaning takes place through the act of association. The relationship between the two terms in a metaphor is not strictly comparative. A simile, employing 'like' or 'as', establishes a comparison between two terms—'to swim like a fish': the two terms remain as separate entities. But in a metaphor the second term transfers its significance to the first. There is then only one entity in a metaphor, the object which is being viewed through things associated with something else. In the phrase 'God is our shield' the metaphor centres upon the nature of *God; it does describe two items, but one *in terms of* the other.

The metaphoricity of theological language, which draws theological discourse into the orbit of *poetic discourse (and therefore literary analysis), has generated much excited attention in recent years. In part this is a result of earlier movements. Romantic hermeneutics divided experience from expression and pointed up how language mediates our understanding of the world. This emphasis upon mediated representation accepted figurative language as necessary and unavoidable. By contrast, in the 17th century, following the Protestant demand for a literal understanding of the scriptural word, the first Fellows of the Royal Society held that clear thinking must be mirrored in clear expression. The tendency of *Enlightenment thinkers was to value the lucid use of language in which words acted as windows of transparent glass, and metaphor was classed as unnecessary ornament, a deviation from what was literally meant. In reaction, *Romanticism stressed that, since our experience of the world is mediated and no word hooks up to the world directly, all language involves translation and comparison. The question of what, therefore, the 'literal sense' really meant began to emerge; and in its wake came the 20th-century obsession with the nature of language. *Wittgenstein famously illustrated, through his analysis of language games and family resemblances between the use of the same word in different contexts, a basic linguistic truth: to understand what a word means one has to study how it is used, and its use will change with every new iteration. In so far as all language is iterative—for it is only its repeated use that familiarizes us with a word and enables it to gain social accreditation—any use of language involves the transferral of a word employed in one context into another, dissimilar, context. Viewed like this, all language becomes metaphorical. The very concept of meaning and reference itself begins to be a problem. This affects the way we read and understand texts.

*Liberal Protestantism, with its attention to *myth and *symbol, its programmes of *demythologizing and deliteralizing, has long encouraged examination of the literary nature of scriptural and theological texts, distinguishing *revelation and *kerygma from their human and historically embedded expression. The work of Paul *Ricœur builds explicitly on *Bultmann's legacy. His contribution to the concept of metaphor lies in emphasizing, like the Romantics, the intrinsic creativity involved in the production of metaphors. We, like the poet or writer beforehand, participate in the linguistic transaction whereby one level of meaning is erased *in the metaphorical process* to create another. As readers, and re-performers, of the metaphorical text, we participate in an ontological unfolding of meaning or Logos. It is the restoration to discussions of metaphor of this ontological and existential purchase that characterizes Ricœur's contribution to this field of enquiry. Poetic texts do not mirror but recreate, opening the reader to new revelatory experiences. Readers experience a transcendence of themselves and their accustomed ways of viewing the world.

Furthermore, Ricœur, recognizing how metaphors generate networks of other metaphors and building upon Max Black's work on metaphors as models enabling us to see things differently, extended his analysis of metaphor into work upon narrative. Attention to narrative associates existential analyses of metaphor with the experience of reading and temporality.

Ricœur's work on metaphor, that views the metaphorical as generative, participatory, and revelatory, drew inspiration from Mircea Eliade's work in religious anthropology. But it has been David *Tracy and Sallie McFague who have done most to promote the roles of metaphor and metaphoricity in Christian *theology. Tracy developed Ricœur's work on the experiential function of metaphor into his own understanding of how to read the religious classics. McFague saw the potential for *feminist and *ecological theology of viewing theological language as metaphorical and creative of new ways of seeing and living. The problem of the *fatherhood of God and all patriarchal language is transformed from a theological to a linguistic one. The metaphors can be changed so that new gender-inclusive and eco-friendly models for God can arise. If Ricœur's work, following Bultmann's, develops a theology of the symbol (and metaphors are linguistic symbols for Ricœur), then with Tracy and McFague a metaphorical theology begins to emerge. It is not without its critics: those who point to its dangerous *Gnostic tendencies, who are suspicious of the move from one level of experience to another through metaphor, who draw attention to its theological liberalism, and the various modes of self-transcendence that are not necessarily experiences of the transcendent God. These critics (Hans Frei is probably the best known) call for reaffirmation or redefinition of the literal sense, not at the expense of the metaphorical, but as a way of grounding the metaphorical in the historical and concrete. In another direction, the work on metaphor by Janet Martin Soskice has sought to emphasize the cognitive content of metaphor. In religious language, metaphors set up models whereby we can picture what we do not know or cannot apprehend directly: they have an intellectual as well as an affective function.

Graham Ward

Frei, Hans, 'The "Literal Reading" of Biblical Narrative in the Christian Tradition: Does it Stretch or Will it Break?', in *Theology and Narrative* (1993).
McFague, Sallie, *Metaphorical Theology* (1983).
Ricœur, Paul, *Interpretation Theory: Discourse and the Surplus of Meaning* (1976).
Soskice, Janet Martin, *Metaphor and Religious Language* (1985).
Tracy, David, *The Analogical Imagination* (1981).
Ward, Graham, 'Biblical Narrative: The Theology of Metonymy', *Modern Theology*, 7/4 (July 1991).

metaphysics. It is notoriously hard to provide a satisfactory account of what metaphysics is. Certain 20th-century coinages such as 'metaphilosophy' and 'metapsychology' encourage the impression that metaphysics is a study that somehow 'goes beyond' physics. In reality, however, the Greek phrase *ta meta ta phusica*, from which our word 'metaphysics' is derived, is the term that the early editors of *Aristotle's corpus used to refer to his book (from their point of view, his 'books') on what he called first *philosophy. And this phrase means only 'the ones [books] that come after the ones about nature'.

As is often the case, therefore, etymology is no guide to meaning.

And it could be argued that an examination of the history of the applications of the word 'metaphysics' is not a much better guide, because different authors have applied the word to studies that vary widely in subject-matter and method. Nevertheless, this history of applications is all we have, and perhaps some general tendencies can be discerned in examining some of these applications.

1. Some studies are purely descriptive: they are content to describe carefully the way things appear to observers. Others are content to construct hypotheses or theories that 'save the appearances'. That is, they offer 'models' of the unobservable aspects of the world that generate appearances, but—as a deliberate matter of policy—they raise no questions about these models beyond the question whether they make correct predictions about the aspects of the world that *can* be observed. It is of the essence of metaphysics not to rest content either with 'phenomenology' (the careful description of appearances) or with 'saving the appearances'. Metaphysics attempts to get behind all appearances and to describe things as they really are. An example may be helpful. There are available two 'interpretations' of quantum mechanics. One, the standard 'Copenhagen' interpretation, implies that particles such as electrons in passing from an emitter to a target do not in general follow 'trajectories', continuous paths through space. The other interpretation, the work of David Bohm, implies that particles do follow trajectories. It can be shown that these two interpretations are empirically equivalent: they make the same predictions about the outcomes of all possible experiments. This fact has led many physicists and philosophers to say that the question which interpretation (if either) describes the way particles really behave is a metaphysical question. The two theories both 'save the appearances'—or at least, if either fails to save the appearances the other will fail as well, and in the same way—but they are obviously not 'the same'. Assuming that the concept 'following a continuous path through space' is a coherent concept, particles must, as a matter of logic, either follow continuous paths through space or not. Therefore, both interpretations cannot be correct descriptions of the real behaviour of particles, although they could both be incorrect. It could be argued that the question which (if either) is correct is impossible to answer and therefore idle. But that is not the same as saying it has no answer. If it is a meaningful question it has an answer, and if 'follows a continuous path through space' is a meaningful phrase, the question is meaningful. The anti-metaphysical attitude is typified by the scientist who is willing to make use of each of two logically inconsistent theories that make the same predictions about possible observations, and deprecates as idle or meaningless the question whether either theory describes things as they really are.

2. In the last analysis, the productions of the metaphysician are declarative sentences. They are public, not private. Anyone who claims a private, incommunicable knowledge of the reality that lies behind appearances is speaking as a mystic, not as a metaphysician (though the same individual might speak as a metaphysician in some contexts and as a mystic in others). The metaphysician aims at producing sentences that strictly and literally describe reality and which can, with sufficient effort, be understood by anyone whose intellect is equal to the task. *Metaphor may play a heuristic role in metaphysics—as in physics or economics or comparative linguistics—but must be banished from the metaphysician's 'finished product'. (The metaphysician may begin by calling space a receptacle or time the moving image of eternity, but these metaphors must be replaced at some point in the metaphysician's investigations with language that is meant to be taken literally. Or, at any rate, if a metaphysical work depends essentially on metaphor, it must be regarded as inherently incomplete, a sort of work in progress.) To say these things is not to say that the metaphysician is (necessarily) hostile to claims to mystical insight or (necessarily) regards the metaphorical as inferior to the literal; it is merely to demarcate what belongs properly to metaphysics.

3. Metaphysics is a very general study. The thesis that all Greeks are mortal may be (as far as it goes) a correct description of the reality that lies behind all appearances—it may well be that there really are such things as Greeks, and that all of them really do have the property 'mortality'. (But if, as many metaphysicians have insisted, neither individuality nor time is real, then neither of these things would be the case.) And, obviously, 'All Greeks are mortal' is a declarative sentence, intelligible to anyone who knows English, and it contains no figurative language. Nevertheless, that all Greeks are mortal is not a metaphysical thesis because it is insufficiently general: even if it does, in a sense, describe the reality that lies behind all appearances, it describes a very special aspect of that reality. It is, however, very difficult to spell out the sense of 'general' in which metaphysics is a 'very general study'. It will not do to say that a metaphysical thesis must be 'general' in the sense of being 'about everything'. First, it is not easy to say what it is for a thesis to be 'about everything'. According to the logicians, 'All Greeks are mortal' is 'about everything', since it is equivalent to the thesis that everything is mortal if a Greek; and if the logicians have an inadequate conception of what it is for a thesis to be 'about everything' it is by no means evident what an adequate conception would be. Secondly, there are incontrovertibly metaphysical theses that would not seem, intuitively, to be 'about everything'. For example: that every event has a cause; that *God is a necessary being; that there could exist two objects that were perfect duplicates. (The third example is not a trivial thesis: it has been asserted by *Kant and is the negation or denial of Leibniz's Principle of the Identity of Indiscernibles.) We can perhaps do no better than to give an illustrative list of metaphysical theses and hope to convey thereby the sense in which metaphysical theses are 'general'.

Everything is such that it might not have existed.

Change is impossible unless there exists something unchanging that persists through change.

Every thinking being is immaterial.

Mathematical objects exist in a different sense of 'exist' from the sense in which material objects exist.

The physical world does not have an infinite past.

The order of things that we observe in nature can be explained only on the hypothesis that nature is a product of intelligent design.

Moral qualities such as 'good' and 'wrong' are objective features of the world.

Persons confronting a choice between two alternatives are

sometimes able to choose the one and also able to choose the other.

Statements about the future are either true or false.

Since the denial or negation of a metaphysical thesis will itself be a metaphysical thesis, one could 'double' this list at a stroke—to include, 'There is something such that it is false that it might not have existed', and so on.

From the *content* of metaphysics, we move to its *method*. Metaphysicians do not, after all, simply assert metaphysical theses, any more than geologists simply assert geological ones. How do metaphysicians attempt to establish, ground, argue for, or support the metaphysical theses they favour? Perhaps more importantly, how should they? Although philosophers have, individually, said much about the question of method in metaphysics, it would seem that most of what they have said has been tendentious in the extreme—designed to set a test that their own writings will pass and the writings of their competitors will fail. For example, it has been said that metaphysics must be a purely a priori discipline, and that the metaphysician must therefore not draw upon the findings of the empirical sciences (except *per accidens*, as a source of illustrations of theses whose truth or falsity is independent of the findings of the empirical sciences). And it has been said that the arguments of the metaphysician must depend on human reason and observation alone, and that the metaphysician must therefore not draw upon any premises (supposedly) known by revelation. But each of these proposed restrictions is without merit.

Consider the first. One metaphysical thesis, as we have seen, is 'The physical world does not have an infinite past' (cf. the 'Thesis' of Kant's 'First Antinomy of Pure Reason' in *The Critique of Pure Reason*). It would be absurd to suppose that current physical *cosmology was irrelevant to the question whether the world had an infinite past. It may be plausible to suppose that physical cosmology, by itself, can never absolutely settle the question whether the world has an infinite past. Perhaps some sort of philosophical evaluation of the data and theories of physical cosmology would be a necessary component of any responsible attempt to answer this question. But if that is so, the fact remains that the data and theories of physical cosmology must in some extremely important way figure in any responsible attempt to answer this question.

Consider the second. Imagine someone proposes an account of the nature of possibility such that it follows trivially from this account that there can be no necessary being—no being 'such that it is false that it might not have existed'. Hume has in fact proposed an account of possibility that has this consequence. If I believe that God exists and is a necessary being, why should I not reject Hume's account of possibility for that reason alone? And if my belief that God is a necessary being is based essentially on what I (think I) know on the basis of *revelation, am I somehow barred by that fact about the source of my belief from using it as a premiss in my *reasonings about the nature of possibility? Or should one say that when I conclude that Hume's account of possibility is wrong, this conclusion is 'theological' rather than 'metaphysical' (despite the fact that an atheist might well agree—and many atheists do believe this—that Hume's account of possibility is wrong)? There would seem to be no good reason to insist that if one employs premises that one claims to know on the basis of revelation, then one is *ipso*

facto not a metaphysician. If one does employ such premises, of course, one will find that one's arguments will be of interest mainly to those who agree with one about the content of revelation—and this would seem to be the only thing that could motivate those metaphysicians who believe in revelation not to appeal to revelation in their metaphysical writings: the desire for a broader audience. There is, sadly, little that can be said about method in metaphysics beyond these purely negative remarks.

Is metaphysics possible? There are two sorts of argument for the impossibility of metaphysics. One purports to show that there is something about the human mind that unfits it for metaphysics. Kant, for example, argued that metaphysics is an attempt to take concepts whose role in human cognition is to structure appearances and to apply them to the reality that lies behind experience—a misapplication of these concepts that invariably leads to irresoluble contradictions. Arguments of the other sort purport to show that the concept of a reality that lies behind all appearances is in some way a defective concept. The logical positivists, for example, argued that the meaning of a statement is entirely a function of the experiences that would verify it, and that statements that supposedly describe a reality that lies behind all appearances are by definition unverifiable by experience and are therefore meaningless. Most philosophers would agree that no argument of either sort has been a success. Arguments of the Kantian type proceed by ascribing certain features a priori to the mind; it all too often turns out that the mind does not have these features. Arguments like those of the logical positivists, and of current 'anti-*realists', seem invariably to suffer from 'self-referential incoherency'. Consider, for example, the logical positivists' central thesis about meaning. What experiences would verify, 'The meaning of a statement is entirely a function of the experiences that would verify it'? None, it would seem—and therefore this statement is either meaningless or says of itself that it is false.

No one seriously asks whether physics and pure mathematics—the two sciences metaphysicians have most often regarded as models—are possible. In the face of their impressive achievements, scepticism about their 'possibility' would be absurd. But metaphysics has no impressive achievements to its credit, and there has for many centuries been a respectable body of opinion holding that metaphysics is impossible. And yet there seem to be no arguments for its impossibility with any force at all. Whether metaphysics is possible therefore remains an open question.

Christian attitudes toward metaphysics have varied considerably. Paul says (Col: 2: 8), 'Take care lest anyone steal you by philosophy and empty deceit, according to human tradition, according to the elements of the cosmos, and not according to Christ.' Tertullian asks derisively, 'What has Jerusalem to do with Athens?' In the Middle Ages, however, philosophy was seen as the handmaid of *theology, and most traditionally minded universities, especially Roman Catholic ones, continue to give philosophy a central place in their undergraduate curricula. It should be emphasized that what Paul and the medievals mean by 'philosophy', and what Tertullian alludes to as 'Athens', is largely metaphysics. When, therefore, a pre-modern writer attacks or praises 'philosophy' one might say that he is attacking or praising metaphysics. The attitudes that Christian writers have expressed towards metaphysics would seem to be a function of whether they perceived metaphysics as essentially an autonomous attempt to give an account of the world and humanity's place in it. Any such autonomous enterprise must be in competition with Christian revelation, and it must contain much that is dangerous and erroneous because the human intellect is finite and corrupted by original sin. But many Christians have believed that metaphysics—even the writings of pagan metaphysicians, if read with the eye of faith—can be 'baptized', that it can be, in *Anselm's words, 'faith seeking understanding'. Whether metaphysics can indeed be a servant of the church is a question of speculative theology, and Christian opinion about its proper answer has been as diverse as Christian opinion about most speculative theological questions.   **Peter van Inwagen**

Beaty, Michael (ed.), *Christian Theism and the Problems of Philosophy* (1990).

Loux, Michael, *Introduction to Metaphysics* (1997).

Miller, Ed L., *God and Reason: An Introduction to Philosophical Theology* (1995).

Morris, Thomas V. (ed.), *Philosophy and the Christian Faith* (1988).

——(ed.), *Divine and Human Action: Essays in the Metaphysics of Theism* (1988).

Stump, Eleonore (ed.), *Reasoned Faith* (1993).

Swinburne, Richard, *Faith and Reason* (1981).

van Inwagen, Peter, *Metaphysics* (1993).

Vesey, Godfrey (ed.), *The Philosophy in Christianity* (1989).

Methodist thought

Methodist thought sounds, to Lutheran and Reformed ears, like an oxymoron: Methodists allegedly 'feel', not think. It is true that Methodists have not characteristically engaged with the great philosophical systems. If, say, Schubert Ogden and John Cobb are ranked with *process theology, they do not make much in their writings of their Methodist allegiance, although some may detect a natural affinity through the high value placed on human agency by both Whiteheadians and Wesleyans; it is only belatedly that Cobb, in his *Grace and Responsibility* (1995), attended to *Wesley in claiming to produce 'a Wesleyan theology for today' which knowingly departs from the eponym's substantive position on certain matters. Much scholarly effort among Methodists, mindful of Wesley's self-description as *homo unius libri*, has been devoted, from Joseph Benson (1749–1821) and Adam Clark (1760–1832) onwards, to the scriptures: the 20th-century line of biblical exegetes stretches from A. S. Peake and W. F. Howard through W. F. Albright, Vincent Taylor, N. H. Snaith, C. K. Barrett, Morna Hooker, Howard Marshall, and D. M. Smith to R. L. Hays. Yet Methodism has also produced theologians concerned for the intellectual integrity and systematic coherence of the teaching presented in their ecclesial tradition. Typically, their dogmatic interests have aimed at serving the church in what Wesley recognized as its primary tasks of worshipping God, evangelizing the world, and loving the neighbour—and this in an ecumenical spirit that affirms Methodism's place in a church recognized to be wider than itself. A fine current example is found in the comprehensive volume by the German Methodists Walter Klaiber and Manfred Marquardt, *Gelebte Gnade: Grundriss einer Theologie der Evangelisch-methodistischen Kirche* (1993).

In Britain, the principal comprehensive dogmatics (so Langford, 1983) have been, first, Richard Watson's *Theological Institutes* (1823–9), which defended *revelation against *deism and, as the *missionary movement gained momentum, stressed the universal scope of Christ's redeeming work; then, William Burt Pope's *Compendium of Christian Theology* (1875–6), which was offered as one of the 'various systematizations' of the faith that Methodism holds in common with 'the catholic evangelical tradition of the church'; and, third, Geoffrey Wainwright's *Doxology* (1980), that seeks to clarify the church's direction towards 'the praise of God in worship, doctrine, and life'.

In the United States, where a rapidly expanding Methodism entered into an intellectual and social symbiosis with the culture to become in the 19th century the most representative form of Christianity in *North America, Robert Chiles (1965) detected a long-term transition whereby what had been secondary poles in a Wesleyan ellipse became the more prominent foci in a shift of emphasis 'from revelation to reason', 'from the sinful predicament to moral character', and from 'free grace to free will'; the names on that trajectory run from Daniel Whedon (1808–85) and John Miley (1813–95) to Harris Franklin Rall (1870–1964) and Albert Knudson (1873–1953). American Methodism has continued to bear a strongly anthropocentric character, but various reversions to more balanced positions can be found as part of what Americans consider the *neo-orthodoxy movement of mid-century (J. R. Nelson, *The Realm of Redemption*, 1951; R. E. Cushman, *Faith Seeking Understanding*, 1981) and more recently Thomas Oden's intentionally patristic and classical *Systematic Theology* (1986–92) and his *John Wesley's Scriptural Christianity* (1994). A further interesting development is the re-entry of the smaller 'holiness' communities and their thinking into wider Methodism (with Donald Dayton as an advocate).

There are many examples from the past half century of the healthy orientation of Methodist theology to one or more of the primary ecclesial tasks—evangelistic, ethical, euchological. On the missionary front, the classic thrust of Wesleyan evangelism was represented by the Sri Lankan D. T. Niles (*Upon the Earth*, 1962). Methodism supplied the World Council of Churches with two general secretaries who for long kept the proclamation of the gospel on that institution's theological agenda: the West Indian Philip Potter (1972–84) and the Uruguayan Emilio Castro (1984–92).

In the matter of spreading 'scriptural holiness', the tendency of Methodist ethicists has been to see sanctification not so much as an individual process with social consequences but rather as a corporate process in which Christians are integrated into an ecclesial community that bears a witness to, and perhaps even seeks to transform, the human world in which it is set. To note are the very varied North Americans Paul Ramsey (*Basic Christian Ethics* (1950); *Deeds and Rules in Christian Ethics* (1967)), Stanley Hauerwas (*Character and the Christian Life* (1975); *A Community of Character* (1981); *The Peaceable Kingdom* (1983)), James *Cone (*A Black Theology of Liberation* (1970); *God of the Oppressed* (1975)), M. Douglas Meeks (*God the Economist* (1989)), and L. Gregory Jones (*Transformed Judgment: Toward a Trinitarian Account of the Moral Life* (1990); *Embodying Forgiveness* (1995)), as well as the Argentine liberationist José Míguez *Bonino (*Doing Theology in a Revolutionary Situation* (1975); *Toward a Christian Political Ethics* (1983)), and the younger Singaporean R. George Eli (*Social Holiness* (1994)).

In the area of *worship and *prayer, A. Raymond George, a leader in the liturgical movement, set out his biblical base in *Communion with God in the NT* (1953). John Lawson has surveyed all the classical topics of dogmatics in his *Wesley Hymns as a Guide to Scriptural Teaching* (1987). Geoffrey Wainwright's sacramental interests were put to service in *Faith and Order's *Baptism, Eucharist and Ministry* (1982) and are reflected in his *Eucharist and Eschatology* (1971) and *Worship With One Accord* (1997). Theodore Jennings has written on *Life as Worship: Prayer and Praise in Jesus' Name* (1982) and *The Liturgy of Liberation: The Confession and Forgiveness of Sins* (1988), and Don Saliers on *Worship as Theology: Foretaste of Glory Divine* (1994).

Drawing on Wesley's 'catholic spirit' of openness without indifferentism, Methodists have made a practical and theological contribution to the *ecumenical movement throughout the 20th century. The American layman John R. Mott, formative in the student movement with its motto of 'Ut Unum Sint' and its drive towards 'the evangelization of the world in this generation', chaired the Edinburgh Conference of 1910 from which the ecumenical movement is conventionally dated, and continued active in the ensuing International Missionary Conference/Council and in Faith and Order. The British theologian R. Newton Flew gave leadership to the ecclesiological study of Faith and Order between the world conferences of Edinburgh 1937 and Lund 1952, first shown in his own *Jesus and His Church* (1938) and then in his editing of *The Nature of the Church* (1952).

A watershed in the Methodist contribution to ecumenical theology occurred, however, when the Australian Colin W. Williams responded to a challenge to state the distinctive witness that Methodism has to offer the church at large in the search for Christian unity: his *John Wesley's Theology Today* (1960) returned to the thought and practice of Methodism's principal founder and related it in systematic form to questions currently undergoing ecumenical exploration. Such a 'return to the sources' with a contemporary application was prepared for by 'the rediscovery of John Wesley' (to borrow G. C. Cell's 1935 title), which had begun when the Belgian Catholic Maximin Piette, in *John Wesley and the Evolution of Protestantism* (originally 1925), provocatively interpreted Methodism as a 'Wesleyan reaction' against 'the crazy solafidianism of Luther'. Other theological readings of Wesley varied considerably. Cell himself made the most of Wesley's own declaration that he came 'to the very edge of Calvinism'. Without going so far, William Cannon's *Theology of John Wesley* (1946) located his subject firmly in the Protestant range of Anglican opinions on the key doctrine of *justification. Franz Hildebrandt, whose *From Luther to Wesley* (1951) carried an autobiographical ring, presented *Christianity According to the Wesleys* (1956) with a strong Lutheran coloration.

The watershed of 1960 was accompanied and followed by historical studies by Albert Outler and Gordon Rupp that brought out the eclectic character of Wesley's thought and claimed for it the character of a convincing synthesis from eastern, western Catholic, Continental Protestant, and Anglican elements (a trend maintained also in Randy Maddox's systematically ordered *Responsible Grace: John Wesley's Practical Theology* (1994)). These studies have fanned out into examinations of Wesley's teaching on particular themes: christology: J. Deschner (1960); pneumatology: L. M. Starkey (1962); anthropology: J. Weissbach (1970); sacraments: O. E. Borgen (1970); social ethics: M. Marquardt (1977); Christian antiquity: T. Campbell (1991); and scripture: S. J. Jones (1995). The theological interest in Wesley is supported by the 35-volume critical edition of *The Works of John Wesley* (in course since 1975). Paradigmatic appeal to Wesley has become a substantive and methodological commonplace in the bilateral dialogues held under the auspices of the World Methodist

Council with the Roman Catholic Church, the Lutherans, Reformed and Anglicans, and the Orthodox Churches (Wainwright 1995). In this way Wesley assumes the role of a 'father', serving as Methodism's access to and representative in the greater tradition of the church.

Internal to Methodism (particularly in the United States and the United Methodist Church), but with ecumenical implications, recent debate has centred on the factors that shape faith, doctrine, and theology. The 1972 *Book of Discipline* of the UMC spoke of a 'living core' of 'Christian truth' that is 'revealed in scripture, illumined by tradition, vivified in personal experience, and confirmed by reason'. The quick dubbing of this as a 'quadrilateral' (with the suggestion of equal sides on a single plane) led to an obscuring of the relative importance and varied functions of the named factors. Subsequently, the primacy of the scriptures has been reaffirmed, but anthropological interests continue to promote 'experience' ('feeling', after all?). William Abraham has pleaded that debates on theological method should give way to the recovery of canonical and Wesleyan substance (*Waking from Doctrinal Amnesia* (1995)).

Worldwide, an important manifestation of Methodist thought has been the Oxford Institute of Methodist Theological Studies, which has brought together every four or five years since 1958 a hundred or so participants from around the globe. The first meeting was devoted to 'Biblical Theology and Methodist Doctrine', and later themes are signalled by the titles of the volumes subsequently published: *The Doctrine of the Church* (1964), *The Finality of Christ* (1966), *The Living God* (1971), *The Holy Spirit* (1974), *Sanctification and Liberation* (1981), *The Future of the Methodist Theological Traditions* (1985), *What Should Methodists Teach? Wesleyan Tradition and Modern Diversity* (1990), *The Portion of the Poor* (1995). **Geoffrey Wainwright**

Chiles, R. E., *Theological Transition in American Methodism 1790–1935* (1965).

Langford, T. A., *Practical Divinity: Theology in the Wesleyan Tradition* (1983).

—— *Wesleyan Theology: A Sourcebook* (1984); useful especially for 19th and early 20th-century America.

—— (ed.), *Doctrine and Theology in the United Methodist Church* (1991).

Oden, T. C., *Doctrinal Standards in the Wesleyan Tradition* (1988).

Outler, A. C., *The Wesleyan Theological Heritage*, ed. T. C. Oden and L. R. Longden (1991).

Wainwright, G., *Methodists in Dialogue* (1995).

Middle Ages: an overview.

Besides a rich literary and liturgical legacy, the Christianity of late antiquity made two particular bequests to the medieval church: *Romanitas*, the culture of classical Rome, and *monasticism. Both profoundly influenced its institutional development and permeated its spiritual life.

The most conspicuous heir to the Roman tradition was the pope, the bishop of the ancient capital of the west. After the lapse of a Byzantine imperial presence in Italy, the *papacy remained the repository of the imperial idea until it materialized in a new, very different, western empire: in 800 Pope Leo III conferred an imperial crown on Charlemagne, king of the Franks, inaugurating the Christian empire of the Middle Ages under Germanic leadership. The papal claim to dispose of the empire, ignoring Byzantium's claim to be the authentic successor of *Rome, was supported by a tradition that *Constantine had, in quitting Italy for his eastern capital, conferred on Pope Sylvester I the imperial regalia with dominion over the western empire. In the 8th century, partly to counter Byzantium's claims over Italy, the legend was committed to writing in what pretended to be an imperial diploma.

The legend of Constantine's 'donation' enjoyed a long life, but the hierocratic claims of the medieval papacy to temporal authority over Christendom's rulers rested upon a deeper basis. It derived not from the imperial status of Rome but from the foundation of the Roman see by *Peter, to whom Christ entrusted the keys of the kingdom of heaven: a unique commission to teach, protect, and govern the Lord's flock. The bishop of Rome was Peter's successor and heir to his office. In medieval eyes this unique spiritual authority was reinforced by the Roman church's possession of the body of Peter, whose shrine, in the basilica Constantine had built over it, was a focus of *pilgrimage from all over Christendom.

In the early Middle Ages veneration for the Apostolic See existed without support from any governmental organization. Men went to Rome, 'threshold of the Apostles', as pilgrims or petitioners, and came back with books and relics. Occasionally they appealed to the pope to vindicate their doctrine or defend their episcopal rights, as they had in antiquity. Following a precedent set by the southern English church, planted by missionaries dispatched by Pope Gregory the Great, archbishops sought papal ratification of their appointment and collected the *pallium* from St Peter's tomb. Otherwise the northern churches did not look to Rome for government or direction. The work of evangelizing northern Europe and creating bishoprics proceeded under the direction of local missionaries and princes. As yet the papacy lacked any administrative apparatus through which it could oversee the affairs of local churches.

The Gregorian Reform movement of the 11th century initiated an expansion of papal government that, over time, transformed the western church into a centralized monarchy under a uniform system of canon law. This movement, inaugurated by Leo IX (1048–54) and brought to a climax by the radical programme of Gregory VII (1073–85), was a reaction against the widespread secularization of ecclesiastical office. Its object was to renew the church by restoring what the reformers regarded as the proper hierarchical order of Christian society, found, they believed, in the primitive church. This involved exalting the *priestly office, as having the task of directing God's people to their eternal salvation, and repressing the claims of secular authorities to a voice in spiritual matters. The church was to be rescued from the abuses of lay control symbolized by the designation and investiture of bishops by lay princes. Zealous bishops would be chosen through a process of 'free and canonical election' by the clergy of the church concerned. High on the agenda was the exaltation of the Apostolic See and the assertion of its right and duty, implicit in the Petrine commission, to oversee and direct the life of the universal church.

The plan required the creation of a disciplined clergy, conscious of their sacred calling, protected by immunity from the jurisdiction of the secular courts, and following a way of life that would detach them from lay preoccupations and distractions. To this end, the reformers revived the canons of late antiquity forbidding *marriage to those who served the altar. Clerical marriage, common in the early Middle Ages, came under mounting attack. A series of Roman councils decreed that *celibacy was required of clergy in the major orders of priest, deacon, and subdeacon. The rule was made absolute by the first Lateran Council (1123): no clerk in major orders

could contract a valid marriage. Enforcement of the law was necessarily slow and difficult; at the level of the rural parish clergy it never achieved more than partial success. Although it fell short of turning the clergy into a sacred caste, it had profound legal and social consequences for medieval church and society.

In the 12th and 13th centuries, the Gregorian Reform was promoted by a variety of agents, including papal legates dispatched to regional churches and a series of ecumenical *councils, culminating in the fourth Lateran (1215) summoned by Pope Innocent III. It legislated on a wide range of religious observances, ecclesiastical discipline, and eradication of abuses. But the main vehicle through which the post-Gregorian papacy established its supremacy over the entire western church was canon *law.

In response to Gregory VII's demand for restoration of the 'ancient law', meaning the order and discipline of the early church, fresh collections of the early canons were compiled, culminating in Gratian's *Concordance of Discordant Canons*, c.1140. Combining a systematic collection of early texts with legal discussion, it became at once a standard text for commentary in the Bologna law schools and laid the foundation of a new science of canon law. It was subsequently supplemented and updated by official collections of later papal decretals. The texts established the pope as supreme lawgiver. As heir of St Peter, he was the 'universal ordinary'—everyman's bishop, to whose tribunal all, however humble, might have access—and the ultimate source from whom the spiritual jurisdiction of his brother bishops was derived.

The consequences of the doctrine of papal sovereignty were inexorably realized in the later Middle Ages and beyond. Papal supremacy materialized in a multitude of ways: an ever-growing flood of petitioners to the papal Curia, taxation of clerical incomes, and papal provision to benefices, a practice extended by the Avignon popes of the 14th century to bishoprics and archbishoprics, thus effectively extinguishing the electoral rights of *cathedral chapters. Adopted for fiscal reasons, the practice generally accommodated the wishes of lay rulers, whose nomination of bishops was usually accepted. Thus, in the three centuries after Gregory VII, the western church was welded into a single juridical organism with a centralized government. The Roman Curia developed into a complex bureaucracy. Papal administration was shared by the cardinals, the original archpriests and deacons of the city who, with the bishops of the seven suburbican sees nearest to Rome, came to be recognized in the 11th century as a collegiate body entrusted with the election of the pope. This elaborate structure survived the removal of the Curia to Avignon from 1305 to 1377, when French domination of the Sacred College posed a threat to the international status of the papacy, and emerged intact from the Great Schism (1384–1429), when rival popes contended for the allegiance of Christendom, stimulating the development of *conciliarism. It remains essentially that of the Roman Catholic church today.

One aspect of the mental and structural changes produced by the Gregorian papacy was the hardening of polemic between the Latin church and the Greek Orthodox churches of the east. Differences in language, liturgy, and culture widened the separation of Rome from *Constantinople, and in the 11th century controversy arose over the *filioque*—the procession of the Holy Spirit from the Son—which western tradition had added to the Nicene creed. The dispute was embittered by a collision between the Greek and Latin churches in southern Italy and by the uncompromising claims of the papacy to universal sovereignty. An embassy led by the over-bearing Cardinal Humbert, sent to Constantinople in 1054 to re-solve points of conflict, ended disastrously with the legates excommunicating the Greek patriarch, Michael Cerularius, and the legates in turn being excommunicated by the Greek synod. Subsequent efforts to heal the schism led, after long negotiation, to public affirmations of unity at the Second Council of Lyons (1274) and the Council of *Florence (1439), but because they were accept-ed by the Greek emperors for reasons of political expediency, with no general support from the eastern clergy, they proved ephemeral.

One of antiquity's most formative bequests to medieval Chris-tianity was monasticism. Originating in Egypt and Syria, it was transmitted to the west both in its eremitical form, derived from the example of the *desert hermits, and in its cenobitical form of organized *ascetical communities. In the 6th century the monastic ideal received its classical western exposition in the Rule of St *Benedict, which gradually gained acceptance until in the Carolin-gian age, with the help of imperial patronage from Charlemagne and Louis the Pious, it came to be regarded as the norm of western monastic observance. In the centuries that followed, the great abbeys, nurseries of saintly bishops and scholars like *Anselm and Bernard of Clairvaux, established a cultural hegemony over the collective mentality of Christian society. Their intellectual leader-ship was reinforced by the fact that monastic scriptoria possessed a near monopoly of book-production until the rise of university sta-tioners at the beginning of the 13th century.

The spiritual impulse that moved not only princes but people of every rank to endow religious communities was a desire to associ-ate themselves with the round of liturgical *prayer forming the framework of the monastic day. The impulse derived its force from the doctrines of vicarious merit and satisfaction. The notion of satisfaction to be rendered for *sin was fostered by the practice of private auricular confession and the use of penitentials: these listed a tariff of penances for every sin, involving *fasting and other ascetical exercises to be performed for a specified number of days, weeks, or even years, according to the gravity of the sin. The burden of these fearsome documents long haunted the practice of the confessional, but from the 10th century it was increasingly alle-viated by indulgences—commutation by bishops of specified periods of canonical *penance for prayers, almsgiving, pilgrimage, or other recognized good works. Indulgences came to hold an important place in the popular piety of the late Middle Ages.

These features of the penitential system explain the eagerness of the landed classes to found and endow monasteries. Monks were 'the poor of Christ', renouncing all personal possessions to follow the Lord. Supporting them could remit a long period of penance. More important, through their penitential life of fasting and prayer they acted as surrogates for their benefactor, performing satisfac-tion on his behalf, which, as a deathless society, they would always continue to do. For many centuries assumptions about the nature of the Christian life were dominated by monastic theology. From Cassian to St Bernard, the monastic ideal of renunciation and with-drawal from the world was presented as the perfect realization of the gospel counsels, indeed the only authentic model of the Chris-tian life. In a *world that seemed irremediably sinful, the cloister

offered the only sure path to salvation. 'Acknowledging the enor-mity of my sins', runs a charter of the 11th century, 'and fearing the dread condemnation of the reprobate, I fly to the harbour of safety.' The harbour referred to was Cluny, then approaching the zenith of its grandeur and influence, with hundreds of dependent abbeys and priories. Arnaldus, the charter's author, donated both the church he owned and himself to Cluny, where he proposed to take the habit. For others, oppressed by the need to do penance, but unable thus to commit themselves, the best hope of salvation seemed to lie in sharing in the merits of a monastic community through admission to confraternity—a privilege much sought by both clerical and lay benefactors.

The consensus that monastic life provided the sole paradigm of Christian perfection was reinforced by the images of sanctity dis-seminated by hagiography—apart from martyrs, most saints in the calendar of the church were prelates or monks. But the monastic ideal was challenged and slowly deprived of its exclusive validity by changes overtaking the church and the whole western world in the 12th century.

An urban renaissance, driven by population growth and expan-sion of international trade and industry, produced a more affluent and more mobile society. New forms of *religious life arose in response, some of them the outcome of tensions within the mo-nastic world itself. At the same time, an exuberant scholastic move-ment centred in cities, culminating in the creation of the first *universities at Bologna, Paris, and Oxford, transferred intellectual leadership from the cloister to the schools of the secular clergy.

A feature of this more complex society was the spread of *literacy among lay people, engendering a new kind of spirituality. The idea of vicarious merit dependent upon the prayers of professional as-cetics was unsatisfactory for an articulate town-dwelling *laity in search of personal religion. One aspect of the religious enthusiasm of this time was the *dualist *heresy of the Cathars, whose élite combined a life of poverty and rigorous asceticism with itinerant preaching. Although Catharism, with its rejection of the flesh and its repudiation of the Catholic sacraments, bore a resemblance to early Manichaeism, modern scholarship gives more importance to the failings of orthodox teaching than to oriental influence in fos-tering the heresy. By the middle of the 12th century it had won the allegiance of significant numbers of people in the Languedoc and in the towns of northern and central Italy. It posed the most formid-able challenge to the church's spiritual authority until the *Hussite rebellion of the 15th century.

Religious toleration was not considered a virtue by the medieval church or by society at large. Religious dissent endangered not only the soul. Since church and state were two arms of the same body, heresy was an attack on the polity, and it was the recognized duty of rulers to repress it. This consensus underlay the draconian pen-alties decreed against heretics by 13th-century rulers. It was the bishops' duty to detect heretics and delate the unrepentant to the secular power for *capital punishment by burning. The spread of Catharism and the failure of local bishops to cope with it persuaded Pope Innocent III to invoke a crusade of the northern knighthood against the Languedoc to depose Count Raymond of Toulouse, who had protected the heretics; and in the 1230s Gregory IX set up the papal *inquisition—special commissioners, independent of the local hierarchy, whose task was to investigate those suspected of heresy and persuade them to recant. The few who proved obdurate were to be handed over to the lay power.

Out of the spiritual ferment of the 12th century arose new kinds of religious organization, answering the desire of lay people for active Christian discipleship. Such were the Humiliati, a devout penitential fraternity, with many adherents in the cities of Lombardy and the Veneto, and the group of mendicant lay preachers founded by Waldes, a rich cloth merchant and banker of Lyons. A common inspiration of these movements was the model of the primitive community described in the Acts of the Apostles, epitomized by the term *vita apostolica*, 'the apostolic life'. Monastic tradition had long invoked this to justify the cenobitical life of monks; but now the term acquired a fresh and dynamic meaning. The true apostolic life involved not withdrawal from the world, but engagement with it; its authentic marks were voluntary *poverty modelled on the poverty of Christ, mission to the unconverted, and service to the poor. The idea was exemplified by the Breton Robert of Abrissel, who abandoned his clerical career to become a homeless wandering preacher and gathered a throng of disciples, mostly women, in the forests of Maine.

This model of the apostolic life found enthusiastic converts among both the secular clergy and the literate laity. For lay people it offered an ideal of sanctity and a programme that could be realized, without abandoning marriage or worldly responsibilities, in the penitential confraternities that appeared in many Italian towns. These groups, organized and run by lay people, combined a devout life of prayer and ascetical discipline with works of *charity. The idea came to its ultimate fruition in the orders of mendicant friars that sprang up in the first decade of the 13th century. The two first and greatest both had discernible roots in the 12th-century ideology of the apostolic life. The *Franciscans or Friars Minor originated in the literal and uncomplicated vision of a layman. The *Dominicans or Order of Preachers were founded by a Spanish Augustinian canon, and their internal regime bore the stamp of their monastic origin. But both represented a revolutionary departure from monastic tradition by abandoning the principle of enclosure to pursue an active *preaching apostolate among the people, and by rejecting corporate ownership of property. Both wrote the ideal of evangelical poverty into their statutes and relied for support upon organized begging.

This new version of the religious life deeply affected the way people thought about the Christian vocation. No subsequent religious order could escape its influence. During the 13th century, this observance was imitated by the Carmelites and Augustinian hermits and other new orders of friars; houses of Mendicants were established in practically every European town. The enthusiasm with which they were welcomed and supported by rulers and townspeople throughout Europe showed that they embodied an idea whose time had come: that it was possible for a committed *disciple of Christ to be in the world, but not of it, that the proper condition of those who aspired to spiritual perfection was one of voluntary poverty, and that the imitation of Christ involved an active mission of evangelization either by preaching or personal witness and service to the poor.

To lay people dissatisfied with their role as passive spectators of religious observances and hungry for guidance in personal religion, the friars offered a new theology of the secular life: personal sanctification was within the reach of people in secular trades and professions, even merchants, whose occupation was generally censured by monastic theologians. This new optimism was the directing principle of a new genre of sermon in which the friars excelled, sermons *ad status*, addressed to the spiritual needs of different classes and occupations: sermons for knights, merchants, scholars, masters and servants, rulers, and married people, taking full account of their state and responsibilities. The devout lay person took his or her place alongside the monk and the secular priest as an authentic Christian.

The friars' first century was a turning-point in the history of popular piety. An intense devotion to the humanity of Christ, a concern with the details of his earthly life, and a compassionate regard for his sufferings were features of a new orientation of western religious sentiment that had its roots in the monastic spirituality of the 12th century. Compassion or imaginative identification with the sufferings of Jesus was an important theme in the writings of St Bernard and the Cistercians. It was largely through the teaching of the Franciscans that in the 13th century it emerged from the cloister and became a central theme in the religious experience of the ordinary Christian. *Francis himself became the supreme example, his experience validated by the imprint on his body of the stigmata of the crucified Christ. This change in people's intuitive and emotional response to the story of *redemption was expressed in such popular devotions as the crib, the rosary, and the Office of the Passion. It was also reflected in western *art. In the century separating Bernard from Bonaventure, the passionless triumphant Christ of Romanesque art is replaced by the contorted figure of the Man of Sorrows hanging on the cross.

One of the major services the friars rendered the church was their contribution to education. The medieval church never devised institutions to train the secular clergy outside the annual meetings of the diocesan synod. The majority of parish clergy were recruited locally from the free peasantry; and, apart from an educated élite absorbed by the schools and ecclesiastical administration, their education was barely above that of their rustic parishioners. The diocesan seminary was an invention of the 16th century. This gap in the pastoral equipment of the church was filled by the friars. Recognizing that a mission to the articulate people of the towns, especially those touched by the Cathar heresy, required theological education and mental agility, they created a scholastic system of their own. Every friary had a classroom, where the brethren were taught by a lector and practised the art of disputation. Their ablest pupils proceeded to schools of their order in the universities, where they succeeded so brilliantly that their teaching and written works dominated the study of western theology for more than a century. By opening their schools to outsiders, the mendicants also made a significant contribution to improving the educational standards of the parish clergy.

The 12th-century intellectual renaissance took many forms and flowed into many channels, but at its heart was the recovery of a great part of Graeco-Arabic philosophy and science, through Latin translation and the revived study of classical Roman law. In the course of the century these discoveries revolutionized both the content and methods of learning. *Aristotle's works on logic, metaphysics, and natural science, and his Arab commentators, confronted scholars with a new world of scientific knowledge and speculation, seeming to offer for the first time the possibility of a rational understanding of the physical universe and the place of man in relation to God and the moral order. If not everything was known or even knowable, everything was at least intelligible in principle and open to rational enquiry, including God's plan for humankind as revealed in the person of Jesus Christ. The scholastic method consisted of the application of dialectic or analytic logic to the study of authoritative texts. The status of recognized authorities rested upon the premiss that the teacher's task was to recover the lost wisdom of the ancients. As Bernard of Chartres told his pupils, 'we are pygmies standing upon the shoulders of giants', a dictum illustrated for posterity by the 13th-century glass-maker of the south transept of Chartres Cathedral, who depicted the evangelists seated on the shoulders of the gigantic prophets of the OT. Every discipline had its recognized authorities. The law doctors of Bologna lectured on the *Code* and *Digest* of Justinian, the canonists on Gratian and the later papal decretals.

For theologians, the authoritative text was the Latin Vulgate bible, and the fundamental task was the exegesis of the inspired text. With the advance of theological inquiry in the Paris schools, stimulated by the teaching of *Abelard, an additional prescribed authority was found in the *Sentences* of Peter Lombard, a coherent conspectus of Christian doctrine, providing a more systematic treatment of doctrinal questions than was possible within the framework of the biblical lecture. The use of the *Sentences* as a course-book was pioneered by the friars teaching theology at Paris in the years 1230–45. Peter Lombard's book made possible the rise of *theology as a science, based upon the rational exploration of the data of revelation. It paved the way for the great *summas*—the systematic compendia of doctrinal questions composed by leading schoolmen like Alexander of Hales, Albert of Cologne, and *Aquinas.

For several centuries scholasticism was a bond uniting an international community of learning in a common enterprise. In universities throughout western Europe schoolmen studied the same texts and debated in a common scholastic idiom. Their aim was the enlargement of man's understanding of his place in the universe through rational enquiry. It was an enterprise with severe limitations in the field of physical science: the Ptolemaic model of a universe of geocentric spheres would not be superseded in popular consciousness until the 17th century; but scholasticism gave to western theology and canon law much of their conceptual framework. Its language and concepts continued to dominate the discourse of both Catholic and Protestant polemicists during the Reformation and beyond.

The impact of scholastic thought was evident in several forms of religious observance in the later Middle Ages. One was devotion to the 'real presence' of Christ in the mass, focused especially upon the elevation of the host following the words of institution. This devotion, which found expression in Corpus Christi guilds and public processions as well as in private worship, was inspired by the scholastic concept of *transubstantiation—the use of Aristotelian categories to elucidate the eucharistic mystery—given formal approval by the Lateran Council of 1215. Another preoccupation of late medieval piety inspired by scholastic theology was a concern with *purgatory. The Paris schoolmen of the 13th century clarified and defined the inchoate belief of earlier ages in a state of purgation

after death, involving transitory suffering, which could be alleviated by the suffrages of the living. This belief inspired innumerable private devotions as well as the Office of the Dead, masses, charitable bequests, and chantry foundations.

More than is commonly appreciated, lay piety of the Middle Ages was nourished by scripture. The immense cost and time involved in medieval book-production precluded the possession of a complete bible. The popular one-volume bible was an invention of printing. Individual books and sections, such as the Pentateuch, the gospels, and the Pauline epistles, were used in the schools and circulated more widely. Daily use of the psalter was common among literate lay people of both sexes. In response to the growth of lay literacy in the 12th century, *translations of the gospels and epistles began to appear in French and Provençal, and Anglo-Norman versions appeared in England. The Augsburg Bible of 1350 provided a High German translation of the whole NT. In 14th-century England, Middle-English versions of the bible made by John Wyclif's followers, being tainted by the Wyclifite heresy, drew from Archbishop Arundel the first official condemnation of unauthorized translations of scripture (see HUSS AND WYCLIF). But both vernacular and Latin versions of the psalms and the Passion narratives continued to circulate ever more widely in the primers or books of hours. Vernacular versions of the 12th-century *Historia Scholastica* of Peter Comestor, one of the most influential of the Paris schoolmen, disseminated knowledge of the events and figures of the OT.

Although from the 11th century onwards an increasing body of vernacular literature was aimed at the needs and tastes of *women, who shared in the spread of literacy among the upper classes and the urban bourgeoisie, women had no part in the scholastic movement of the 12th and 13th centuries. In accordance with the tradition it received from antiquity, the secular church of the Middle Ages excluded them from any official role. Not only sacramental acts but all ecclesiastical functions, including teaching, were confined to men. By contrast, women had filled a conspicuous role in the monastic church. In the Germanic world of Merovingian Gaul and Anglo-Saxon England, their high status was reflected in their prominence as monastic founders and royal abbesses of nunneries and double monasteries ruling both men and women with the self-assurance that was their birthright. Abbesses, including Hilda of Whitby and Gertrude of Nivelles, were among the most influential religious leaders of their generation. But in the aristocratic society of the 11th and 12th centuries, where legal arrangements and modes of thought were conditioned by the military fief, women were reduced to a subordinate role. They played no part in the initiatives that launched new monastic movements like Cîteaux and Prémontré. Similarly, ecclesiastical tradition and social convention denied an active role to the women devotees of the *vita apostolica* and the mendicant ideals of the 13th century, so that the female branches of the Franciscan and Dominican friars were strictly enclosed, contemplative orders of a traditional monastic type. Nevertheless, both the *Beguine movement and the 'third orders' linked with the friars provided space for women in and after the 13th century to be committedly 'religious' yet unenclosed. Within the constrictions of monastic institutions, and more often outside them, women had always figured among the leading *mystics and teachers of the contemplative life. In the crises that afflicted the church of the later Middle Ages, some, like the Beguine Marie d'Oignies and the

Dominican tertiary, *Catherine of Siena, emerged as solitary prophets, exerting a decisive influence upon the ecclesiastical leaders of their time.

In a multitude of ways the thought and experience of the medieval centuries have left their impress upon the Christianity of the modern world. The medieval structure of ecclesiastical government and law has shaped the institutions of all episcopal churches. The writings of the medieval mystics and speculative theologians continue to nourish religious sentiment and spirituality transcending all confessional boundaries. Besides compelling paradigms of sanctity, the Middle Ages bequeathed to Christendom a huge treasury of liturgical prayer in the eucharistic liturgies and the eightfold daily offices, traces of which are clearly visible in all service-books, Protestant as well as Catholic, that derive from the medieval tradition.

See also DANTE; JULIAN OF NORWICH.   **C. H. Lawrence**

Brooke, C. N. L., *The 12th-Century Renaissance* (1969).

Chenu, M.-D., *Nature, Man and Society in the Twelfth Century*, ET (1968).

Dvornik, F., *Byzantium and the Roman Primacy* (1966).

Knowles, M. D., *The Monastic Order in England* (1949).

Lambert, M., *Medieval Heresy: Popular Movements from Bogomil to Hus* (1977).

Lawrence, C. H., *Medieval Monasticism: Forms of Religious Life in Western Europe in the Middle Ages*, 2nd edn. (1989).

—— *The Friars: The Impact of the Mendicant Movement on Western Society* (1994).

Leclercq, J., Vandenbrucke, F., and Bouyer, L., *The Spirituality of the Middle Ages: A History of Spirituality* (1968), ii.

Little, L. K, *Religious Poverty and the Profit Economy in Medieval Europe* (1978).

Moore, R. I., *The Origins of European Dissent*, 2nd edn. (1985).

Renouard, Y., *The Avignon Papacy*, ET (1970).

Smalley, Beryl, *The Study of the Bible in the Middle Ages*, 3rd edn. (1983).

Southern, R. W., *St Anselm and his Biographer* (1963).

—— *Western Society and the Church in the Middle Ages* (1970).

—— *Scholastic Humanism and the Unification of Europe* (1995).

Tellenbach, G., *Church, State and Christian Society at the Time of the Investiture Contest*, 3rd edn. (1989).

Vauchez, A., *La Sainteté en occident aux derniers siècles du moyen-age* (1984).

Ullmann, W., *A Short History of the Papacy in the Middle Ages* (1972).

—— *The Growth of Papal Government in the Middle Ages* (1955).

millenarianism. In the Christian tradition, millenarianism refers to the expectation that Christ will reign on earth for a thousand years, which tends to go with a belief that this is near at hand. It sometimes refers to a more general anticipation of an approaching end-time. More loosely, in non-Christian or marginally Christian contexts, millenarianism refers to a general *apocalyptic reversal of the status quo. The sociologist Bryan Wilson calls Melanesian cargo cults 'Commodity Millennialism' (*Magic and the Millennium*). Faiths as diverse as the Unification Church, the Rastafarians, and Soka Gakkai (in Japan) have been called millenarian, as have the writings of *Marx.

Early Christians believed that the Second Coming was imminent, and read apocalyptic texts such as the *Shepherd of Hermas*. The only such work to become part of the canon of scripture, and hence the basic source for Christian millenarianism, is the book of *Revelation. Apocalyptic belief fostered detachment from *worldly goals and values and endurance in persecution. As time went on, a radical Jesus movement at odds with the values of the wider society became a *church that absorbed many of the latter's values. Millennial beliefs tended to become the province of fringe movements, such as the *Montanists, who believed that the New Jerusalem would appear in Phrygia (in modern Turkey).

Hippolytus made the first of many attempts to calculate the date of the Second Coming on a scriptural basis; he suggested 500. Some of the church fathers, among them Tertullian and *Irenaeus, believed in an earthly millennium, when the saved would enjoy a period of happiness on earth. *Origen, however, believed that Revelation should be understood *allegorically. The realities of *eschatology were spiritual, and concerned the fate of the individual soul.

*Augustine devoted much attention to the subject, especially in Book 12 of his *City of God*. It was impossible to calculate the date of the End. 'To all those who make ... calculations on this subject comes the command, "Relax your fingers and give them a rest."' The reign of the *saints had already begun; the Kingdom of God consisted not of the church, but of the saved within it, who would be known only on the last day.

It has been said that millenarianism has an ancient, but not a continuous, history. In the high Middle Ages, there was a widespread belief that, in the words of Heloise, 'the world is now growing old', that the end-time was near, a belief reflected in medieval Doomsday paintings in parish churches. One other dark and continuing element in Christian apocalyptic was the belief that the millennium would be preceded by the reign of Antichrist, identified with many political figures, including Napoleon III.

Joachim of Fiore (1145–1202) elaborated a more optimistic and extremely influential eschatology. He divided history into three ages, of the Father, Son, and Holy Spirit. He calculated that between 1200 and 1260 the third and last age would dawn, and the world would be peopled with saints until the last judgement. He has been regarded by some as one of the most influential exponents of the shape of future history. But his followers were progressively marginalized, and persecuted as *heretics.

Millennial and apocalyptic beliefs, which offered a miraculous reversal of the status quo, have always had a special appeal to the poor and marginalized. They were characteristic of many heretical movements in the Middle Ages, including the *Hussites and Lollards, and continued to flourish during and after the *Reformation. In some cases, apocalyptic expectations fuelled militant action. Thomas Müntzer believed that Antichrist, in the form of the Turks, must rule the world, after which the elect could usher in the millennium by a just war. When the nobility were deaf to his appeals he turned to the poor. His militant, millenarian vision can be counted among the complex and disputed causes of the Peasants' Revolt of 1525. The Anabaptist rule in their New Jerusalem of Münster in 1533–5 was also millenarian.

*Puritan eschatology was closely linked with political action. An analysis of writings by Independent and Presbyterian divines during the English Civil War found that 70 per cent expounded millenarian ideas (see SEVENTEENTH CENTURY). The Fifth Monarchy Men (with an eschatology based on *Daniel) attempted to usher in the reign of King Jesus in unsuccessful risings in 1657 and 1661. After the Restoration, this millenarianism faded away. There is, nevertheless, a striking parallel with the imagery of Julia Ward Howe's *Battle*

Hymn of the Republic, which sprang from the experience of a different Civil War: 'Mine eyes have seen the glory of the coming of the Lord ... Let the Hero, born of woman, crush the serpent with His heel.' This continues the long-standing millenarian tradition of the 'manifest destiny' of the American New World.

*Revolutions, American and French, were welcomed as a sign by post-millennialists. Theirs is an optimistic faith, not unlike that of Joachim; it postulates a gradual Christianization of society and fitted well with 18th-century concepts of progress. Pre-millennialism, on the other hand, anticipates a succession of calamities, until Christ bursts into history, and brings the Golden Age. Wars, earthquakes, and epidemics herald the approaching End. Nineteenth-century millenarianism, not rooted in persecution or deprivation, nevertheless became predominantly pre-millennial. Sandeen has argued, 'Fundamentalism ought to be understood partly if not largely as one aspect of the history of millenarianism.' Thus the Rapture, a distinctive element in much contemporary American *fundamentalism, owes its origins to John Nelson Darby (1800–82), best known as one of the founders of the Plymouth *Brethren. His (pre-millennialist) eschatology was reproduced in the best-selling 1909 Scofield Bible and is called *dispensationalism, because it divides history into successive epochs, or dispensations. In the Rapture, true believers will be suddenly taken up into heaven (cf. 1 Thess. 4: 17). A modern exponent describes the carnage on the motorways, when Christian drivers are suddenly removed from their moving cars.

Many millenarians remained within mainstream churches, but there also arose a considerable number of new denominations, among them the small (Irvingite) Catholic Apostolic Church, and the much larger Seventh Day *Adventists and Jehovah's Witnesses. Millenarianism has often been linked with *mission work, and with the concept that the Great Commission must be fulfilled before Christ comes. It has sometimes been linked with Zionism, since it is thought that the Jews must return to Israel before the millennium can begin.

Millenarian movements are often short-lived; some, like the Fifth Monarchy Men and the Anabaptists of Münster, have been suppressed by authority. More fundamentally, they face a crisis when the expected End fails to appear. Surprisingly often they cope with this. In 19th-century America, a Baptist layman, William Miller, decided from a study of Daniel and Revelation that the world would end in 1844. Many of his followers, after the Great Disappointment, went on to become Seventh Day Adventists. The visionary Ellen White spiritualized the Disappointment: Christ did come in 1844, but to heaven, not earth, and his return to earth would take place shortly.

Charles Taze Russell (1852–1916), influenced by other Adventists, founded the Watch Tower Bible and Tract Society (renamed the Jehovah's Witnesses in 1930) in 1881. He taught that the soul is mortal; only the Witnesses will live on in glory, in the millennium. He predicted the Second Coming in 1914; his successor postponed this first to 1918 and then to 1925. Like many millenarians before them, the Witnesses believe that existing churches and states are evil, which is why, for instance, they refuse to salute the flag. This negative approach is widespread—if the end of the world is imminent, there is little point in trying to improve it. In Africa, by contrast, millennial expectations became once more a consolation for the disinherited. Watch Tower spread widely in southern Africa in the early 20th century, often in indigenized forms the parent body did not recognize. Today, there are 1.5 million Witnesses in the world, a quarter of a million of them Africans.

Many contemporary North American evangelicals hold millenarian views. The millennium will be preceded by a cataclysmic conflict; in the days of the Cold War, this was understood as war with the USSR. Hal Lindsay's *The Late Great Planet Earth* (1970) was a best-seller. Millennialism is often found in association with social conservatism and the support of militarism. Disasters such as famines and epidemics tend to be regarded less as human problems that demand human solutions than as indicators of the approaching end.

Elizabeth Isichei

Brouwer, Steve, Gifford, Paul, and Rose, Susan, *Exporting the American Gospel* (1996).

Clouse, R., *The Meaning of the Millennium, Four Views* (1977).

Cohn, Norman, *The Pursuit of the Millennium*, rev. edn. (1970).

O'Leary, S. D., *Arguing the Apocalypse* (1994).

Reeves, Marjorie, *Joachim of Fiore and the Prophetic Future* (1976).

Sandeen, E. R., *The Roots of Fundamentalism: British and American Millenarianism 1800–1930* (1970).

West, Delno C., and Zimdars-Swartz, Sandra, *Joachim of Fiore* (1983).

Milton, John

Milton, John (1608–74). Author of the Christian epic poem *Paradise Lost* (1667), Milton has long been considered the greatest religious *poet to have written in English. The common western understanding of the story of the fall of Satan (see DEVIL) from *heaven, and of the subsequent *Fall of *Adam and *Eve from their *paradisiacal state in the Garden of Eden, has been indelibly marked by the Miltonic imagination. While often scrupulous in its adherence to the *Genesis narrative of the Fall, Milton's poem also expands its scriptural original by situating the story within the classical literary form of the epic established by Homer and Virgil. An updated, Christian example of such epics as the *Iliad*, the *Odyssey*, and the *Aeneid*, *Paradise Lost* is arguably the west's last great poem in this tradition. Milton also wrote a sequel, *Paradise Regained*, as well as the tragic drama *Samson Agonistes* and many shorter lyrics.

He identified himself first and foremost as a poet, a figure whose literary genius could rival that of his favourite English writers, Edmund Spenser and William *Shakespeare. But unlike those Elizabethan predecessors, Milton was also one of the most voluble participants in the heady religious, social, and political controversies of his age. Educated at St Paul's School and later Cambridge University, where he wrote his first great English lyric, *Ode upon the Morning of Christ's Nativity*, he had by his mid-twenties swerved from his early ambition to become an Anglican clergyman and thrown himself into the reformist *Puritan movement. An independent, self-disciplined young man, he burst onto the English intellectual scene in the early 1640s with a series of fiery polemical treatises that pushed for the liberal reform of the hierarchically organized Church of England. He soon followed these with an even more scandalous series of treatises: one group of works defended *divorce and even polygamy; the treatise *Areopagitica* defended the freedom of the press from state censorship; and a later cluster of tracts defended the right of the English people to rise up and execute Charles I, the monarch considered a tyrant by so many Puritans. It was for these controversial works of social, religious, and political protest that Milton was best known in his own time. When

Paradise Lost appeared in 1667, many years after he had established himself as one of the century's most eloquent voices of the left-leaning Independent movement, it proved difficult for his contemporaries, as it is for many today, to disentangle the sublime poetry of the epic from the boisterous political daring Milton had exercised in his polemical prose.

While a source of comfort and inspiration to readers of all kinds, Milton's prose and poetry have tended to exercise the greatest impact on Christian thought during periods of social and political turmoil. Avidly read during both the American and French Revolutions, his writing has long nourished the social and aesthetic values of reformers and revolutionaries. The libertarian ideas as well as the poetic cadences of *Paradise Lost* left a particularly deep mark on the most radical of the British *Romantic poets, William *Blake, as well as on William Wordsworth, Percy Bysshe Shelley, and John Keats. Blake would offer in *The Marriage of Heaven and Hell* a theory of the composition of the epic that resonated not only with his own generation of Romantics, but with the majority of Milton's readers thereafter: 'Milton wrote in fetters when he wrote of Angels & God, and at liberty when he wrote of Devils & Hell … because he was a true Poet and of the Devil's party without knowing it.' Blake was wrong to suggest that Milton did not write with passion of the loyal *angels who served *God in the sumptuously represented court of *heaven, but he correctly identified the most powerful of Milton's characterizations: Satan, whose rebellion against an allegedly tyrannical God had many, perhaps awkward, affinities with Milton's own efforts during the Puritan revolution. The extreme individualism expressed by Satan, for whom 'the mind is its own place, and in itself | Can make a Heav'n of Hell, a Hell of Heav'n', has tended to attract or repel readers depending on their sympathy with Milton's generally libertarian stance.

The radical associations of Milton's epic poem were established even more firmly in 1823, when a manuscript of his theological treatise, *De doctrina christiana* (*On Christian Doctrine*), was discovered and soon thereafter published. Probably written during the same years as *Paradise Lost*, the treatise was considerably more heterodox than most readers had expected. Not only did Milton continue to marshal theological arguments in favour of divorce and polygamy, but he argued clearly and forcefully that Christ was not an equal member of the *Trinity (a capital offence in 17th-century England), equivocated on the importance of Christ's satisfaction for man's sins (the *Atonement), denied the efficacy of all *sacraments, and insisted on the corporeality of the human *soul, which, he conjectured, mouldered with the body in death until its resumption at the Last Judgment. This largely wayward theology turned out to resemble in many respects the views of his younger contemporaries, the political philosopher John Locke and the scientist Isaac Newton, who joined Milton in their surreptitious sympathy with Socinianism, the heretical sect that paved the way for modern *Unitarianism.

In the early part of the 20th century, there was a concerted effort by many conservative literary scholars to demote this radical from his esteemed position in the pantheon of English poets. Extending their instinctive antipathy for Milton's republican politics and his low-church religion, F. R. Leavis and T. S. *Eliot began to argue, influentially, that Milton's verse, particularly *Paradise Lost*, was morally and aesthetically hollow. Not only were Milton's ideas repug-

nant, but, for Eliot, the empty 'organ voice' of his long, Latinate verse paragraphs was a barbaric bastardization of normal human speech. Milton's poetic reputation did not fully revive from these spirited attacks until C. S. *Lewis argued in 1942 that the great epic poem bore no trace of the heretical views expressed in *De doctrina christiana*, and, further, that the poem was fully in line with the Anglican orthodoxy to which Lewis himself subscribed. Lewis was wrong about the implicit theology of Milton's epic, but his commentary on the poem did have the effect of drawing a new generation of readers back to Milton. Joining Lewis in this effort was his contemporary G. Wilson Knight, who asked his countrymen, in the troubled years of the Second World War, to draw strength from the defence of liberalism so persuasively presented in Milton's poem.

Readers of *Paradise Lost* today are generally divided on the question of the degree of consonance between the values expressed in the poem and the dominant strains of mainstream Christian thought. Many have followed the poet and critic William Empson and the Marxist historian Christopher Hill, both of whom praised the poem not in spite of, but because of, its heretical daring: the intelligent questioning of the rebellious Satan and the proto-feminist *Eve is for these readers one of the central attractions of the poem, which can still be seen to inspire religious-minded radicals throughout the culture. But many readers, too, have followed in the footsteps of Lewis, insisting that the grandeur of the poem be distinguished from the poet's detestation of kings and criticism of Christian orthodoxy. A group of Milton scholars in the 1990s have in fact taken even further Lewis's attempt to decontaminate Milton's reputation: they have attempted vigorously, if unsuccessfully, to prove that Milton could not have written *De doctrina christiana*, the rediscovered manuscript of which remains the primary evidence for the heretical extremes of Milton's religious views. The anti-monarchist whose rousing arguments for the right to divorce and the freedom of the press are still cited enthusiastically today most probably did write the theological treatise which questions with such audacity many of the central tenets of Christian orthodoxy. But debates concerning the content of Milton's theology and the implicit message of *Paradise Lost* will no doubt continue to rage for many years. That poem, whose compelling narrative and lush poetic beauty are no less powerful now than at their initial appearance in 1667, sought, in Milton's words, 'to justify the ways of God to men'. The nature and the complexity of Milton's justifications remain matters of dispute.   **John Rogers**

Milton, John, *The Complete Prose of John Milton*, ed. D. M. Wolfe *et al.* (8 vols.; 1953–82).
——— *The Riverside Milton* (1998).
Eliot, T. S., *On Poetry and Poets* (1957).
Empson, William, *Milton's God* (1965).
Hill, Christopher, *Milton and the English Revolution* (1977).
Hunter, William B., *A Milton Encyclopedia* (9 vols.; 1978–83).
Knight, G. Wilson, *Chariot of Wrath: The Message of John Milton to Democracy at War* (1942).
Leavis, F. R., *Revaluation: Tradition and Development in English Poetry* (1936).
Lewis, C. S., *A Preface to Milton* (1942).
Rogers, John, *The Matter of Revolution: Science, Poetry, and Politics in the Age of Milton* (1996).

ministry may best be understood as any work for the *church that is recognized by the church. It occurs when a person, whether *lay or *ordained, performs a task on behalf of the community that is recognized by the community. But it has often been restricted to a narrower, clerical sense. The most used NT term for ministry, *diakonia*, contains ambiguity that has led to contrasting emphases on either lay or ordained ministry (see DIACONATE).

The 'lay' interpretation starts from the literal meaning of *diakonia* as service. Every Christian is called to serve God and the community, therefore every Christian has a ministry. This view tends to locate ministry within the ethical sphere of general service or benevolence and carries the danger of detaching it from its theological basis in the divine commission bestowed upon the church as a body and attaching it instead to the ethical obligations common to individual Christians. The 'clerical' interpretation starts from the official recognition rather than the semantics of *diakonia* and emphasizes the aspect of commissioning and *authority. It reflects the historical experience of most churches in which the 'ministry' has long been synonymous with the work of the ordained though in the early church 'orders' included such 'lay' posts as acolyte and door-keeper.

Ministry, whether lay or ordained, is grounded in certain ecclesiological principles: (1) All ministry is that of Jesus Christ in his church. Ministry is simply Christ at work through the presence of the Holy Spirit, leading, teaching, sustaining, and governing his body through unworthy human instruments. Because ministry manifests Christ, the servant king, it embodies both authority and the spirit of service. (2) Ministry is grounded in baptism, the foundational sacrament of the church, because it is through baptism that Christians are united with Christ in his death and Resurrection and share in his threefold office as prophet, priest, and king. As prophets Christians discern and proclaim the word of God. As priests they offer spiritual sacrifices of prayer, praise, gifts, and ultimately themselves. As a royal priesthood they play their part in the governance of Christ's kingdom. Baptism incorporates a believer into the ministerial community, in which, however, there is a variety of gifts and services, every limb of the body of Christ having its own role to play (1 Cor. 12). (3) Ministry is representational in that it consists of public actions, owned by the community, that manifest the nature and life of the community. The public ministers of the church represent both Christ and the church (Christ-in-the-church), not in the vicarious sense that they take the place of an absent Christ, but in the realist sense that they make Christ truly present and show forth the true nature of the church as his body. The ministry leads the way in doing what the church must do and acting as the church must act.

Some locate the representational role of the ordained ministry in the *persona* of the minister and see him or her as an icon of Christ, grounding this in the 'character' bestowed at ordination and the authority that goes with it. This ontological view sees little scope for lay representational ministry and may be linked with the notion that only males can represent Christ, since there must be a natural resemblance between Christ and the priest. Others adopt a more functional view of ministry, locating the representation of Christ in the actual performance of the tasks committed to the church: proclaiming the gospel, administering the sacraments, providing *pastoral care, and facilitating conciliarity. Both points of view have something to offer. The first presumably would not insist that a minister who never preached, presided, or pastored still represent-

ed Christ. The second presumably would not recognize that Christ was represented by someone who took it upon himself, without authority and charism, to exercise the functions of public ministry.

The connection and distinction between the ministry or royal *priesthood of all the baptized and the ministry or priesthood of the ordained remains, nevertheless, a major *ecumenical issue and its resolution is a precondition for further progress towards interchangeability of ministries between churches. It has not yet been clarified sufficiently. *Vatican II stated that the 'common priesthood of the faithful and the ministerial or hierarchical priesthood' are different 'in essence and not only in degree', though they are related by being 'each in its own special way ... a participation in the one priesthood of Christ' (*Lumen Gentium*, 10). Anglican–Roman Catholic dialogue (ARCIC) followed suit in separating but not integrating the two. Other ecumenical dialogues have had difficulty with this. Adopting an insight from the eastern tradition, we may say that the ordained ministry (priesthood) is a divinely instituted *economy* within the whole priestly body: a limitation of public priestly functions to a part for the benefit of the whole.

Paul Avis

Avis, P., *Christians in Communion* (1990).
Collins, J. N., *Are All Christians Ministers?* (1992).
O'Meara, T. F., *Theology of Ministry* (1983).
Osborne, K. B., *Ministry: Lay Ministry in the Roman Catholic Church, Its History and Theology* (1993).
World Council of Churches Faith and Order Commission, *Baptism, Eucharist and Ministry* (1982).

miracle. Miracles are generally understood in Christianity as extraordinary actions by God in the physical world, standing over against the normal order of nature for a religious purpose. Various Hebrew and Greek words have been used to identify miracles: in Hebrew *oth* (sign), and *mopheth* (wonder) occur; and in Greek *semeion* (sign), *teras* (wonder), *ergon* (work), and *dunamis* (power) are used. Each term reflects a key element of the traditional understanding of miracle. Miracles are 'signs' pointing to a greater reality; they are 'powers' emanating from forces not usually associated with nature; they are 'wonders' leading humans to reflect upon greater things; and they are 'works' because they are seen as being in some way connected to the greater work of God.

Accounts of miracles are found in both the biblical record and in ecclesiastical history. In the OT they are generally clustered into two cycles: one in the narratives concerning the *exodus and the Israelite sojourn in the wilderness, and a second in the stories associated with the prophets Elijah and Elisha. In the NT they are found in both the gospels and Acts. The Synoptic Gospels have many of these stories in common, while *John includes accounts (such as the miracle at the marriage feast in Cana and the raising of Lazarus) that are recorded nowhere else. Students of the gospels have offered various classifications for these miracle accounts. Some, such as the *Virgin Birth and the *Resurrection, serve to frame the earthly ministry of *Jesus. Others are directed towards human beings as miracles of *healing or restoration, including exorcisms. Still others are nature miracles, such as the walking upon the waters (Mark 6: 45–52 and parallels) and the stilling of the storm (Mark 4: 35–41 and parallels). The book of Acts contains numerous miracle stories associated with the early mission of the church and interprets such signs as reflective of the presence of the *Holy Spirit in the life of the early community. The role of the miraculous is less prominent in the epistles, but some Christian traditions have interpreted the anointing and healing referred to in James 5: 14 as miraculous, and Paul, in 1 Corinthians 12: 10, lists the doing of miracles as one of the charismatic gifts.

Until the 17th century, Christian speculation concerning miracles largely focused on the relationship between miracles and the order of nature, and the question of post-biblical or ecclesiastical miracles. While writers such as *Origen attempted to interpret miracles in the light of the orderliness of nature, others, like Tertullian, saw them as flying in the face of *reason. There was also a lack of consensus about post-biblical miracles, and by the end of the 2nd century *Irenaeus suggested that they were passing away.

The Christian view of miracles was decisively changed in the 4th century, both by popular piety and through the influence of *Augustine of Hippo. On the popular level post-biblical miracles, associated with *saints and holy persons, became viewed as important vehicles in the Christianization of the Roman empire. Augustine formulated a classic understanding of the miraculous, as well as an interpretation of the relationship between biblical and post-biblical miracles. For Augustine the great miracle was *creation, since it reflected the creative nature of God. Thus the proper distinction between God's actions in nature and miracles was that the latter, being unusual, produced the effect of wonder. Nature and miracle were part of the same divine work. Hence for Augustine miracles were not contrary to nature (contra-naturam) but only supra-naturam, or outside of what human beings knew of nature. By late in his life Augustine also gave support to the interest in the post-biblical miracles of saints and *martyrs. From this developed another key element in the traditional Christian understanding of miracles, the belief that they functioned as signs of *holiness. The association of miracles with holiness was given official sanction in Latin Catholicism by the 11th century, when miracles became a part of the formalized canonization process of saints.

Thomas *Aquinas offered a further (and different) refinement to the understanding of the miraculous. Whereas for Augustine an act was miraculous because of the religious wonder it produced, for Aquinas a miracle was understood through its relationship to nature. A miracle was an event that happened outside the entire order of created nature, and hence was truly supernatural. The miraculous became a far more objective category from the *Thomist perspective than it had been in Augustine, and this Thomistic objective view has continued to be the official Catholic position.

The *Reformers and their successors recast the understanding of miracle. Reacting against the accumulation of miracle stories associated with saints and shrines, the Reformers largely rejected both ecclesiastical miracles and the long-standing association of miracles with holiness. Instead, as writers like *Calvin argued, miracles confirmed the authority of the gospel. Accordingly as the gospel became established they passed away. By the late 17th century, writers such as Hugo Grotius and John Locke had turned the argument into a strict evidentialist view of biblical miracles. Miracles offered evidence for the truth of revelation. They were like the credentials of an ambassador, giving *authority to his words. Thus for several hundred years the Protestant position on miracles was twofold: a vigorous defence of biblical miracles coupled with a sceptical rejection of all ecclesiastical miracles.

The rise of the *scientific world-view during this same century, however, inaugurated a fundamentally new phase in the discussion of miracles. Baruch Spinoza argued that miracles were incompatible with the inexorable nature of *natural laws. *Deist writers also attacked the credibility of miracle stories and of apostolic testimony. These two critiques came together in David Hume's classic argument against miracles. Hume argued that since the testimony of witnesses could never be more sure than the uniformity of natural laws, such testimony could never serve to establish the occurrence of a miracle. In his work, Hume turned the long-standing Protestant scepticism of ecclesiastical miracles against all miracle claims.

If the 18th-century debate pitted Christian defenders of miracles against deist critics, by the 19th century the debate had become an intra-Christian one. In Germany, Friedrich *Schleiermacher rejected both the basing of Christian claims upon miraculous evidences and any objective view of miracles. Like Augustine, he claimed that any event that produced wonder was a miracle. Such views also found voice in America among Transcendentalists like Ralph Waldo Emerson, and in Samuel Taylor *Coleridge in England. But many 19th-century writers gave the Augustinian understanding of miracle a new thrust by linking it with developing views of science and *history. If, as scientists and historians posited, nature and history were governed by uniform natural forces (the principle of uniformity), there was no place for 'supernatural' events. Accordingly, one must necessarily question the facticity of any reported miracle for which no natural cause could be posited. The end of the 19th century witnessed a great intra-Protestant debate over the reality of the nature miracles. Catholics remained largely aloof from this debate. *Vatican I affirmed the 'objective' quality of miracle events, and in places such as Lourdes miracles continued to be reported and evaluated to examine whether they were indeed truly supernatural.

Christians at the end of the 20th century and beginning of the 21st approach the question of the miraculous within the context of this two-thousand-year discussion. Modern views of the natural order are certainly far less mechanistic than those presupposed by the 19th-century advocates of uniformitarianism. But whether modern physics makes the universe more friendly to miracle claims is questionable, since if the uncertainty principle makes extraordinary events more possible, it also makes it more difficult to classify them as miraculous acts of God. Although classic evidentialist arguments about miracles are still occasionally found among some conservative Protestant *evangelicals, most modern theological writers acknowledge that the question of miracles depends on a belief in a personal God. One must start with such a belief if miracle claims are to be plausible. In this sense 'miracle' is pre-eminently neither a scientific nor a philosophical category, but a religious one. Yet in the modern discussion one continues to hear the echoes of Augustine, Aquinas, Hume, Schleiermacher, and even Tertullian. This discussion largely focuses on two areas. The first concerns the appropriateness of the classical understanding of a miracle as a divine intervention. For some, such a view of a God transcendent from creation is archaic and rests upon an ancient notion of a multilevelled universe, in which God 'breaks in' from the heavenly realm. The rejection of such an understanding by science, it is argued, necessitates the abandonment of it by Christian theology.

When such language occurs it must be *demythologized or translated into modern categories. Proponents of such an agenda further argue that the language of supernatural intervention was not part of Jesus' original message but was either added as Christianity expanded into the Gentile world or had some social or anthropological function. Others, however, have continued to maintain the idea of a transcendent God. For them, the language of intervention, whatever its intellectual problems, is crucial for the idea of a personal God. Furthermore they claim that the miracle stories of the gospels are essential parts of the narrative and cannot be demythologized. This debate was vigorously carried on in the early decades of the 20th century, only to recede at mid-century during the heyday of *neo-orthodoxy, with its distinction between faith and knowledge. The debate has reappeared at the turn of the century, fuelled by a new attempt to discover the 'historical Jesus'.

But if some Christians question whether the category of miracle is meaningful to modern minds, others emphasize not only their scriptural importance but their present reality. Considerable interest in modern miracles was one of the surprising ironies of the late 20th century, brought about through a largely silent revolution in which Protestant and Catholic views of the miraculous were drawn more closely together. From the middle of the 19th century there was a large scale erosion of the traditional Protestant view of a limited age of miracles, now held by only a minority of Protestant believers. If this led some to question the reality of biblical miracles, it led others to argue that modern miracles are as plausible as biblical ones. This new Protestant interest in modern-day signs and wonders was most vividly seen in the growth of *Pentecostalism which originated in the United States at the very beginning of the 20th century. Pentecostals believe that the *charismatic gifts mentioned in 1 Cor. 12 (prophecy, tongues, interpretation) have been restored as a mark of the church, and one of these is the gift of miracles. Faith healing has played an important role in the growth of Pentecostalism. But interest in modern miracles has not been limited to Catholics and Pentecostals. Survey polls of the United States of America, for example, showed that at the century's end almost 70 per cent of Americans continued to believe in miracles.

The vigour of both of these discussions suggests that the question of miracles for Christian thinkers is profoundly *paradoxical. As a concept, 'miracle' remains an ambiguous and difficult term, difficult to integrate into other parts of a modern world-view. Yet at the same time it remains a powerful and attractive religious belief, one cherished by believers both past and present.

Robert Bruce Mullin

Brown, C., *Miracles and the Critical Mind* (1984).
Burns, R. M., *The Great Debate on Miracles* (1981).
Crossan, J. D., *The Historical Jesus* (1991).
Lewis, C. S., *Miracles* (1947).
Meier, J. P., *A Marginal Jew* (1994), ii.
Monden, L., *Signs and Wonders* (1960), ET (1966).
Moule, C. F. D., *Miracles: Cambridge Studies in Their Philosophy and History* (1965).
Mullin, R. B., *Miracles and the Modern Religious Imagination* (1996).
Swinburne, R., *The Concept of Miracle* (1970).
Wright, C. J., *Miracle in History and in Modern Thought* (1930).

mission signifies (1) historically, the deliberate attempt of indi-

viduals, groups, or churches to evangelize non-Christian societies and otherwise act in a Christlike way towards strangers or people living beyond their boundaries, religious, cultural, social, or other; (2) theologically, the flowing outwards of God's inner life in the history of creation and *salvation, particularly in the history of humanity's redemption through God's continuing self-giving in its struggles, sufferings, and hopes. Christianity since *Paul and the Gentile breakthrough has crossed many boundaries and generated varieties of agents, forms, and definitions of mission. The age of discovery defined mission as 'expedition', a meaning still to be found in Christianity's vocabulary; but since the Willingen conference of the International Missionary Council (1952) and the *Vatican II *Decree on the Church's Missionary Activity* (*Ad Gentes*, 1965), attempts have been made to reclaim the term for denoting God as the sending and the sent one (*missio Dei*). A single term thus holds together a diversity of concepts.

At the beginning of the third millennium of Christian history, two initial points may be made. First, today's image of the missionary as the spiritual agent of white supremacy corresponds with some justification to what K. M. Panikkar called the Vasco da Gama epoch of history, stretching from the 1490s to the middle of the 20th century and covering the era of colonialism, the *padroado* (under the control of the Spanish and Portuguese crown), *slave trading, and aggression. The modern missionary movement was particularly closely related to the social dynamics of western culture: *Enlightenment and abolitionism, *capitalism and industrialization, liberalism and the self-organization of the working class, social and cultural pluralism. It both internalized these trends and opposed them. The colonialist model of mission can well be understood by referring to Defoe's *Robinson Crusoe*, in which a stranger is baptized and his alienness consequently negated. Crusoe, regarding this alien as a wiped slate (*tabula rasa*), provides him with a new identity (Friday) wholly belonging to Crusoe's world. Symbolically, the baptism stands not only for Friday's access to God's salvation, but also for the loss of his own tradition and for his non-equal status in the new *orbis christianus* (he becomes and remains the servant). Secondly, the modern image of mission as the religious side to the introduction of a new, western, world order is neither historically nor theologically inevitable; it was firmly rejected already in the 17th century by the instructions of Propaganda Fide (the Vatican department in charge of missionary work) and in the 19th by leading thinkers such as G. Warneck. There is a chain of individual figures in western mission history, from Bartolomé de Las Casas, Matteo Ricci, and Roberto de Nobili, to Vincent Lebbe in *China and Placide Tempels in the Congo, who opposed westernization and made human equality a principle of mission work. It remains true, however, that the practical overcoming of this image has been achieved only in the period of decolonization, especially by the quest for *liberation in the churches of the south who now account for 60 per cent of Christians worldwide.

It is all the more important to rediscover an alternative history of mission both western and non-western, such as that of the Celtic mission carried out from the 6th to the 8th centuries in northwestern Europe. The approach to mission of Celtic Christianity was characterized by the model of *peregrinatio*, *pilgrimage: spending one's life 'as a pilgrim for love of our Lord' (Bede). Again, it is arguable that from the 6th century for nearly a millennium the

Church of the East was the most missionary of all. Stretching from Persia and the Arabian peninsula to China, Mongolia, Manchuria, and south India, the (so-called) *Nestorian mission was related neither to a Christian empire, nor to conquest, colonization, nor claims of superiority. The Nestorian way represented a *dialogical model of mission, working side by side with the advance of *Islam and *Buddhism. Today such models are of interest for all those contexts where Christians live as a minority. Aspects of the pilgrim and dialogue models (including a theological option for a place for all *religions in God's salvation) are to be found in the documents of Vatican II (besides *Ad Gentes* see *Lumen Gentium*, 1964, and *Nostra Aetate*, 1965) and have been taken up by recent Roman Catholic mission statements such as *Dialogue and Proclamation* (1991), and even in the more cautious papal adhortation *Evangelii Nuntiandi* (1975) and the encyclical *Redemptoris Missio* (1990).

The Greek NT does not offer one overall definition of mission, but, in highlighting witnessing to the *truth, living in loving fellowship, and caring for those in need, it uses more than a hundred different terms (among them *apostellein*, to send, and *apostolos*, the one sent for the sake of humanity; *martyrein*, to give witness; *keryssein*, to announce the good news). There is one case (Heb. 3: 1) where *Jesus Christ himself is called 'the *apostle', therefore seen as the plumb-line of mission. The 'Great Commission' at the end of Matthew's gospel (28: 18–20), emphasizing the importance of missionaries and their role as teachers, is only one of a variety of phrases, but it became the most favoured for legitimizing mission work and church expansion in the modern era. Today, there is a tendency to focus on Luke 4: 18 and Acts 10, emphasizing the importance of liberation, social *justice, the *conversion of the missionary as well as of the missionized, and God's acceptance of the vernacular and local culture. Since the establishment of missiology as an academic discipline in the 19th century, the definition of mission, its aims, and its methods have been argued over. David Bosch has shown that the biblical texts do not tell once and for all what mission is, and that an understanding of it is always constructed in accordance with a given cultural-historical and church context. The *church has not been missionary always and everywhere. Initially, some of the *Calvinist churches, because of their emphasis on *predestination, did not develop a missionary consciousness, and, as late as the 17th century, *Lutheran orthodoxy opposed demands for an overseas mission on theological grounds, among them that the existence of Jews, Muslims, and other non-Christians was ordained by God. The theological status of the Jewish people, in particular, proved to be a stumbling-block in the missionary movement.

The interrelation of the three elements of missionary activity: *kerygma* (proclaiming the message of God's salvation in Christ), *koinonia* (sharing the fellowship, unity, and equality of all believers in *communion with the Father and Son through the Holy Spirit), and *diakonia* (serving the secular needs of other people, rooted in and modelled on Christ's service), proved somewhat diverse in practice. The three elements were hardly ever given equal attention at the same time. Traditionally the conversion of individuals and the establishment of new local churches took priority. Some have regarded mission as a one-way spiritual process with an emphasis on individual soul-saving (freelance and charismatic missionaries); others expected the congregations established through mission to enrich the knowledge of God in ecumenical recognition

(N. Zinzendorf and the philanthropic Moravian lay missionaries of the 18th century); others again (19th-century Protestant mission societies) aimed at establishing a model church overseas, often intended to be supra-denominational: a sort of mini-Christendom, free from the agnosticism in the old heartlands of Christianity. The medieval and 19th-century idea of Christianizing whole nations survives in a modified way in the emphasis on converting homogeneous groups of people (as advocated by the church growth school centred in Pasadena, California). On the Catholic side, the 20th-century school of Louvain (Pierre Charles) restated the meaning of mission as 'planting' the church. This was by no means wholly new, being basically a reassertion of Propaganda Fide's perennial instructions, but the continuing dependence of overseas Christianity on generations of foreign missionaries and their concentration on preaching and service required a reassertion of priorities: 'planting' means enabling the local church to take over full responsibility for its own life and mission. *Diakonia*, in the form of social emancipation and medical and educational work, has a long tradition in the practice of the missionary movement, but less so in its theory. It resurfaced in 1932 in W. Hocking's *Rethinking Missions* as a genuine form of mission and led to a radical reformulation of 'mission from below' by J. Hoekendijk (1952) who refused to see the world as an ecclesiastical training ground and declared that *shalom*, not the formation of churches, was the aim of mission, and the task of missionaries was to participate in people's struggle for justice and integrity.

The late 20th-century restructuring of northern mission agencies has had three aims: giving the primary responsibility for mission to the local church (in the north as well as in the south); the sharing of financial resources between north and south; and equal participation in decision-making. Leading the way in the 1970s were the Protestant Paris Mission and the London Missionary Society, now multi-church organizations (Evangelical Community for Apostolic Action, Council for World Mission). Contrary to public opinion, while the number of missionaries of a traditional sort leaving Europe in particular has greatly fallen, the overall number of missionaries of all kinds at work in countries other than their own, including a rising number of non-westerners, was increasing in the last decades of the 20th century (up to 415,000 by mid-1999, according to not very specific or reliable estimates).

Two major factors, however, have fundamentally changed missionary topography and perhaps subverted the received perspectives. First, missionary outreach and the *translation of the bible have not only made Christianity, in its majority, a non-western religion and multiplied groups and denominations across the globe (among them *Pentecostals, non-denominationalists, and African Instituted Churches), but have thereby tapped into thousands of languages and cultures. There is a heritage of different memories (of colonialism, or of the suffering caused by an imposed world market); there are different metaphysical and religious backgrounds, different *symbol systems, *iconographical traditions, and sacred texts, different types of social behaviour. All this obliges world Christianity to go beyond the received theological terminology and navigate with a plethora of new symbolic maps and charts. Particularly in *Africa and Asia, there is a trend to appreciate and redefine at least part of the local religio-cultural heritage or even to regard it as a genuine medium of divine revelation. This process of reinventing Christianity has led to the construction of new theological categories to elucidate and challenge Christian belief. It has highlighted the fundamental issue of the relationship between other religions and Christianity. Secondly, this need for a theology of culture and religions coincides with a simultaneous theological quest for truth in the west. The practical relativity of Christianity's claim to be the truth has been brought home to us for quite some time by the way the church in parts of the old homelands of Christianity has become effectively marginal. Y. Daniel and A. Godin's *France—A Mission Country?* (1943) was one of the first studies to investigate the haemorrhage of the church in Europe. The Mexico City mission conference (1963) labelled western society a 'mission field'; but none of the re-evangelization campaigns so far has halted the trend towards marginalization. The development of a missionary response capable of understanding the double issue of post-Christian *agnosticism and new religious sensibility, and thus capable of speaking the language of *postmodern culture, is still to be awaited. The interpretation of all religion and the interpretation of postmodern culture are both fundamental theological questions the answer to which will impact on the understanding of mission.

The current tendency in world Christianity, including a large part of its western branch, is to insist that Christianity does not save anybody, only God does, and mission belongs essentially to God. This perception makes it impossible to force mission back into the straitjacket of a western-tribal religion. It may take a long time, perhaps centuries, before the theological implications of Christianity's mutation into a world religion, inclusive of its post-Christian trend, will finally be worked out, so there is reason to exercise a humble agnosticism *vis-à-vis* God's plans. The parochialism of much western theological thinking has become obvious, but there is now the opportunity for an ecumenical and intercultural redrawing of the theological map by crossing the borders of established systems of thought. This is precisely what mission studies is all about, and missionary thought today is characterized by remarkable vitality, not least in the areas of research and publication, as witnessed in journals such as the *International Bulletin of Missionary Research* (USA, 1977–), *International Review of Mission* (Switzerland, 1912–), and *Missionalia* (South Africa, 1973–). Yet the revitalization of mission studies has not, strangely enough, been matched by a revitalization in the mission involvement of many churches.

See also Black Theology; Contextual Theology; Hinduism; Japanese Christian Thought; Jewish–Christian Relations; Latin American Christian Thought; Universalism.

Werner Ustorf

Anderson, G. H. (ed.), *Biographical Dictionary of Christian Missions* (1998).

Bosch, D., *Transforming Mission* (1991).

Hoekendijk, J. C., 'The Church in Missionary Thinking', in *International Review of Mission*, 41 (1952), 324–36.

Jongeneel, J. A. B., *Philosophy, Science, and Theology of Mission in the 19th and 20th Centuries* (2 vols.; 1995–7).

Müller, K., *et al.* (eds.), *Dictionary of Mission* (1997).

Newbigin, L., *The Open Secret* (1978).

Rzepkowski, H., *Lexikon der Mission* (1992).

Scherer, J., and Bevans, S. B. (eds.), *New Directions in Mission and Evangelization* (2 vols.; 1992–4).

Schreiter, R. J., *The New Catholicity: Theology Between the Global and the Local* (1997).

Verstraelen, F. J., *et al.* (eds.), *Missiology: An Ecumenical Introduction* (1995).

Walls, A. F., *The Missionary Movement in Christian History* (1996).

Woodberry, J. D., *et al.* (eds.), *Missiological Education for the 21st Century* (1996).

modernism. If the thesis of Hans Urs *von Balthasar is accepted, the cult of the new, the up-to-date, the modern has been surfacing within western European culture since the late medieval period. In 15th-century philosophy, the fashionable *via moderna* (following Ockham) was contrasted with the *via antiqua* (following *Aquinas or Scotus). Modernism, understood as the claim that the contemporary, the now, the avant-garde is more true or authentic than the traditional or received, has a history. The narrative of its beginning, unfolding, and possible termination (in postmodernism) is termed *modernity. There are key moments in the history of the modern: the fight over the role of tradition and, most significantly, classicism, between the ancients and moderns in the early 18th century; the French Revolution and the denunciation of the *ancien régime*; the crises of the modern and concerns about cultural decline which begin to emerge in Germany from the 1870s; and *fin-de-siècle* decadence. The latter constitutes the immediate precursor to the early 20th-century movement which we now call modernism.

*Catholic modernism was specifically a trajectory pressing for the Roman Catholic faith to take account of its contemporary moral and cultural setting. Calling for changes in the way traditional teaching was understood in the light of new scientific research and developing methods of biblical and historical criticism, it was a trajectory rather than a movement, since its main exponents did not view their work as interdependent and forming a coherent system. The two leading voices, Alfred Loisy and George Tyrrell, corresponded, but they never met. In the wake of an *ultramontanist reaction against 19th-century political liberalism (expressed most intensely in the centralization of authority and the confirmation of papal infallibility in 1870), these modernists developed a theological liberalism concerned with making Catholicism culturally relevant, whereas ultramontanist reaction only widened the gap developing between church and society, theology and science. The parallel Protestant form of theological *liberalism, concerned with similar syntheses between Christianity and modern areas of knowledge, was far more successful and long-standing, culminating in the work of Rudolf *Bultmann and Paul *Tillich. Ironically, Alfred Loisy's 1903 volume *The Gospel and the Church*, an important landmark in Catholic modernism, was offered to the public as not only a new Catholic *apologia*, but a refutation of the liberal Protestantism of Adolf Harnack's *The Essence of Christianity*. Harnack had laid down the challenge by soundly condemning Catholicism for its distorted expression of the Christian faith, its appeal to past tradition, and its obscurantism, all overcome by the Reformation, he argued, which returned the Christian faith to its essentials. But Catholic modernists and Protestant liberals shared the view that every expression of the Christian faith is historically situated and coloured, so that its teachings need to keep pace with the movement of history. The doctrines and the institutions of the Christian church must therefore be modified with time, and develop. In fact, a Catholic account of tradition could sit more easily with this radical historicism—as Loisy was quick to point out. Both Catholic modernism and liberal Protestantism in making their rebarbative claims espoused a series of fundamental *dualisms (experience and its expression; truth and its representation; transcendent content and its symbolic form) and tended towards immanentism. Tyrrell was perhaps most radically immanentist, denying *revelation as a fixed body of truths and wishing to emphasize in a *Hegelian manner the movement of the spirit or idea of Christianity. Most modernists were not so immanentist as to deny the reality of the supernatural, though Loisy, after his excommunication, eventually came to reject Christian theism. In biblical criticism, both Catholic modernists and liberal Protestants appealed to a general rather than a theological *hermeneutics: methods of interpretation believed to be independent of dogmatic considerations and more scientifically objective.

Catholic modernism's heyday lay between 1890 and 1910. It found support mainly in *France and Italy, and a little in Germany and England, but not in any organized way. Its theses were condemned by Pius X in the papal encyclical *Pascendi* in 1907 on several grounds, in particular the question of authority with respect to scriptural exegesis, a certain non-realism concerning the text of the bible and theological formulas, and the timelessness of Catholic orthodoxy. No reform or appeal to the spirit of the age was believed necessary, because the eternal truth of the faith, the *depositum fidei*, was founded upon divine revelation and passed on for all time to the church of the apostles. Besides condemning the movement, the encyclical established codes of practice for its effective suppression, the success of which further demonstrated papal absolutism. This papal stand (along with Leo XIII's official endorsement of the teaching of Thomas Aquinas in 1879) led to the dominance of *Thomistic and neo-scholastic theologies and philosophies in 20th-century Catholicism until the emergence of the *nouvelle théologie* and the turn to patristic studies led by Jean Daniélou and Henri *de Lubac.

How Catholic modernism relates to the aesthetic movement termed 'modernism' is a complex question. Cultural critics disagree on the meaning of 'modernism' in its aesthetic sense; the characteristics of a modernist work are so varied. Proto-modernism is seen in the rejection of realism evident in the poetry of Mallarmé and Huysmans's novels. But the main period for the avant-garde—the search for a new style with an accompanying enthusiasm for the experimental and the novel—is 1907–25. The movement, which would include the writer Virginia Woolf, painters of the Dada and Futurist schools, the music of Stravinsky, poets *Eliot and Rilke, and, later, architects such as the Bauhaus school and Le Corbusier, countered the conventional even to being iconoclastic. It might be seen as the last great flourish of the liberal dream: individualism, self-expression unfettered by the past. But for all its appeal to aesthetic purity and the transcendence of the sublime (witness Malévich's paintings or Schoenberg's music) it reflected profound existential anxieties: alienation, isolation, even madness. Catholic modernism, which predated this aesthetic movement, shared some of its characteristics: those common to a European liberal culture, such as historicism, humanism, and the mediation of the real. It shared some of aesthetic modernism's vitality, but little of its daring. Catholic modernism sought reform not revolution; synthesis not subversion.   **Graham Ward**

Barmann, Lawrence F., *Baron von Hügel and the Modernist Crisis in England* (1972).
Bradbury, Malcolm, and McFarlane, James (eds.), *Modernism* (1976).
Ranchetti, Michele, *The Catholic Modernists: A Study of the Religious Reform Movement 1864–1907*, ET (1969).
Reardon, B. M. G. (ed.), *Roman Catholic Modernism* (1970).
Sagovsky, Nicholas, '*On God's Side': A Life of George Tyrrell* (1990).
Vidler, Alec R., *A Variety of Catholic Modernists* (1970).

modernity began as an idea, it would seem, in the 15th century, with the naming of two related movements, both of which had started in the previous century: the *devotio moderna* in spirituality and the *via moderna* in philosophy, the former derived from Gerhard Groote, a Dutch priest, the latter from William of Ockham, an English *Franciscan philosopher. Here, people began to contrast the 'modern' with the 'ancient' or pre-modern, and the *via moderna* with the *via antiqua*, a catch-all title for everything from *Plato to *Aquinas and Duns Scotus. The characteristic notes of the modern here seem to have been interiority, secularity, and a divide between rationality and *faith. This is the first example of a claimed contrast between two ways of thinking, modern and pre-modern, that would subsequently remain a permanent element in western thought. It was an appropriate moment for the idea to begin, just as printing, modernity's supreme tool, was being invented.

A conviction about the significance of this contrast was greatly strengthened in the 18th and 19th centuries. An ever-growing body of scientifically grounded ideas derived from an *Enlightenment perspective constituted the assuredly 'modern' against which all previous ideas were to be judged and many discarded as 'primitive', unacceptable to rationality. So Hume dealt with *miracles. *Religion in any supernaturalist form could easily be characterized as inherently pre-modern, essentially primitive, part of a world-view untenable in the light of modern *science. One finds the 20th-century development of this contrast at its most strident in Lucien Lévy-Bruhl's *La Mentalité primitive* (1922). Lévy-Bruhl stressed the 'prelogical' and 'mystical' way 'primitive' people think. For him, such thinking included all religion and differed completely from the way 'modern' people think. Subsequent *anthropologists, notably Edward Evans-Pritchard (*Theories of Primitive Religion* (1965)) and Claude Lévi-Strauss (*The Savage Mind* (1962; ET 1966)), argued that this is not so and that all thought systems function in a more or less logical manner, while beginning from different presuppositions. It is quite possible to understand and work within thought-worlds that seem at first profoundly alien. Nevertheless, the sense of a fundamental division between modern and pre-modern has remained a presupposition of most western thought, and is particularly characteristic of 'modernist' social theorists like Anthony Giddens, even though the decisive characteristics of modernity are redefined again and again. The point of division is generally located at the Enlightenment, though *Descartes is often seen as the progenitor. If this sense of division is correct, given that the scriptures and early Christian literature were written by people taking for granted a pre-Enlightenment thought-world, is it possible for a modern, post-Enlightenment person really to enter into and believe them, at least without sacrificing the cultural commitments of modernity? This is, it could be claimed, the central question in *nineteenth- and *twentieth-century *theology, and numerous entries in this *Companion*, from *Bible, its Interpretation and Authority* to *Hermeneutics, Demythologizing, Development of Doctrine*, and many others from *Miracle* to *Devil* tackle it in a variety of ways. One can come to understand another thought system without believing it, as an agnostic biblical scholar can do; alternatively, one may accept it in part, transforming its more peripheral aspects. Thus the *Genesis *creation story presupposes a flat earth. Pre-modern Christians quickly accepted a Ptolemaic round earth without difficulty, reading the creation story accordingly. When the Copernican view replaced the Ptolemaic, it was quickly accepted despite the determination of ecclesiastical authority to make itself look foolish (see GALILEO). The pre-modern *cosmology which the scriptures presupposed could thus be twice abandoned without affecting the doctrine of creation.

That is, however, a marginal case. Is Christianity in other ways so deeply embedded in pre-modern conceptions of reality that Christian belief today either forces one into a fundamentalistic rejection of modern cultural commonplaces or requires so complete a transformation of what Christianity has in the past claimed to be true that continuity and unity of belief with the past cannot honestly be asserted? Is it possible to be a genuinely modern believer?

One must insist that there is in historical reality no single divide between modern and pre-modern, wherever located, but a continuing series of divides. The question, moreover, applies to all areas of knowledge and consciousness. We cannot think or feel quite as our parents and grandparents did. Anyone seriously studying even Victorian culture must become aware of its alienness, of a vast if subtle divide in understanding between then and now. The longer the distance in *time and space, the greater the divide is likely to be. And yet we are also aware that we can not only understand the mind of the other but also be enriched by that understanding within a communion of thought, which is never one of straight identity. To suggest that there is an insuperable divide between, say, *Shakespeare and ourselves, or even Plato and *Aristotle and ourselves, so that they cannot decisively teach us is to be false to our own experience. The supreme quality in human intelligence is precisely an ability to cross such divides, just as it is to cross other divides, discovering the enriching truth in, say, many a non-literate religion and culture.

In claiming that biblical and Christian thought can be reassimilated within a modern context, then, one is not claiming anything in itself unique. A great deal of past 'thought' is, undoubtedly, wholly abandoned with the march of time, but some is not. The only effective test of survivability is survival. If biblical and Christian thought cannot be translated in a way that modern minds find compelling, then it must die. But there is no convincing evidence of this at present. Numerous leading thinkers in the modern age have found keys to truth in *John's gospel, *Augustine's Confessions, Aquinas's Summa, and so much else. All are pre-modern, confined within the culture of their own time and place, yet continue to speak convincingly in other contexts. Any concept of an evolving human culture requires this.

The question is, however, rendered still more complex by the impact of *postmodernism. Whereas the modernist holds to an objective unity of understanding, grounded in the Enlightenment's conviction of the universal clarity of *reason, so that there can and should be in principle a single discourse acceptable to the modern world as against the multiple discourses of religious faiths and regional cultures, the postmodernist challenges any such imperialist hegemony of a single world-view. The confidence of 'modern man' in the unified intelligibility of reality is hereby undermined. If the most modern cultural understanding is, then, postmodern, even anti-modern, where does that leave our argument? Christianity may well be claimed to cohere with both modernism and postmodernism: with the former because its inherent realism, its belief that God is *truth, that one truth cannot contradict any other, and its conviction that it is in principle a universal faith, all tie in with the rational objectivity and claim to universality of the Enlightenment. From this viewpoint, the Enlightenment was indeed merely reasserting the pre-modern position of Aquinas. On the other hand, the Christian commitment to the absolute significance of particular events, to faith as going beyond reason and, thereby, opening up truths not verifiable by reason, as well as its recognition that much knowledge is negative, mystical, and partial, point to a world of understanding different from and more varied than the clarity and generality of the Enlightenment paradigm. The *Reformation reaction against scholasticism and the *Romantic reaction against the Enlightenment, while in reality each retaining many of the characteristics of what they were reacting against, nevertheless included a reassertion of the multiformity of understanding, poetic, artistic, or religious, comparable to postmodernism's reaction to modernism. It may be that any attempt to establish a human 'science of everything' is so bound in its hubris to fail that it must needs generate a reaction in favour of the particularities of story, imagination, or faith. This is the reaction of *existentialism to essentialism, and of theologies based on experience and narrative to systematic philosophical theology.

It could, then, be a mistake to accept the idea of a single 'modernity' according to which Christianity must be ordered or die. Modernity is as transient and variable as the pre-modern, and much that was claimed in its time as modern, from the via moderna onwards, would now be dismissed as pre-modern. While it is obvious enough that Christian belief in the 21st century cannot be the same as Christian belief in the 1st or the 11th, that recognition in no way resolves the issue of whether the one is genuinely in succession to the other. Nor does it clarify just what elements in earlier belief need to fall by the wayside, as many have already done in the doctrine of all the main churches. The more the scriptures and tradition are approached fundamentalistically the more evident the difficulty; the more it is accepted, instead, that development has been at work throughout Christian history, in line with a wider evolution of culture, the more the perennial challenge of modernity, in ever new guise, ceases to be a threat. The challenge remains, however, and calls Christian thinkers to a scrupulous and frank examination of the ways in which such development has taken place and continues to do so. **Adrian Hastings**

Badham, Paul, The Contemporary Challenge of Modernist Theology (1998).
Berman, M., All That is Solid Melts into Air: The Experience of Modernity (1982).
Cascardi, A. J., The Subject of Modernity (1992).
Giddens, A., The Consequences of Modernity (1990).
Habermas, J., Theory of Communicative Action (1981), ET (1984), i.
Hastings, A., 'On Modernism', Modern Believing, 40/2 (1999).
Pattison, George, Art, Modernity and Faith (1998).
Tracy, David, On Naming the Present (1994).

Moltmann, Jürgen (1926–).

Moltmann, born in Hamburg, professor at *Tübingen since 1967, is the most important *Protestant theologian of his generation. His work can be divided into three periods. In the 1950s, beginning with his dissertation, he examined the history of *Reformed theology. The high point of the second period, the 1960s and 1970s, was the trilogy *Theology of Hope* (1964), *The Crucified God* (1972), and *The Church in the Power of the Spirit* (1975). The last period, dating from 1980, has as its centrepiece a series of texts he terms 'Contributions to Systematic Theology'. Five have appeared thus far: *The Trinity and the Kingdom* (1980), *God in Creation* (1985), *The Way of Jesus Christ* (1989), *The Spirit of Life* (1992), and *The Coming of God* (1996). These eight books constitute the conceptual core of his vast literary production to date.

Moltmann's influence on theological discussion since the mid-1960s has been pervasive. His work is marked by a commitment to biblical theology, to the Reformed heritage, to *ecumenical theology, and to the task of bringing Christianity to a clearer awareness of the *social implications of the gospel. The theme that runs through all his thought is *eschatological *hope. A matter of existential discovery in the Allied prisoner-of-war camps where he became a Christian, this theme was the central concern of his theology in the post-Second World War years. In conversation with the neo-*Marxism of Ernst Bloch, he fashioned a thoroughly eschatological theology, structured as a dialectic of the *cross, and calling for a Christian praxis of social transformation. Moltmann's self-described '*political theology' has subsequently had a profound impact on all the forms of *liberation theology that have arisen in the past generation. In his insistence that eschatology be understood 'horizontally' in relation to history, that history be interpreted by the cross on which Christ gave voice to the hopeless cry of the oppressed, and that sociality belongs to the *Trinitarian life of God, theologians throughout *Latin America and Asia as well as North America and Europe have found a set of conceptual tools that they have been able to use to good purpose in their own contexts of seemingly hopeless oppression. This is seen perhaps most immediately for Moltmann himself in the work on *feminism that he has done in partnership with his wife, Elisabeth Moltmann-Wendel, who was one of the first in Germany to write on the subject, and whose *Autobiography* has recently appeared.

In addition Moltmann has made important and creative contributions to many of the classical questions of doctrine as well as to such contemporary questions as that of history, *ecology, and social ethics. In doing so, he has never shunned controversy. Early on he was criticized by the right as too politically radical and the left as too theologically conservative. Later he was accused of compromising divine sovereignty with his insistence that God is defined in the suffering of the cross, and of undermining human efforts to achieve social utopia with his insistence that God is the ultimate hope for human redemption. More recently his doctrine of the social Trinity has been characterized as tritheistic by those who champion the western over the eastern Trinitarian tradition. In the face of each of these criticisms, Moltmann has remained steadfast in pursuing his own theological agenda of speaking of hope to the hopeless.   **D. Lyle Dabney**

Bauckham, Richard, *The Theology of Jürgen Moltmann* (1995).
Dabney, D. Lyle, 'The Advent of the Spirit: The Turn to Pneumatology in the Theology of Jürgen Moltmann', *Asbury Theological Journal*, 48 (1993).
Meeks, M. Douglas, *Origins of the Theology of Hope* (1974).

monasticism can be described as the explicit, direct, and single-minded pursuit by men and women of union with God in Christ and in close association with like-minded seekers by means of a structured community life comprising various practices: silence, simplicity, *celibacy, *obedience, *prayer in common, manual *work, *lectio divina*, and community building—many of which were recommended in the NT and have proved their value as means of opening a human life more fully to the initiatives of God. The renunciations of property, family, and self-determination obviously run counter to the usual springs of human behaviour and entail a certain distance from the *world, and that is the feature that differentiates monasticism most clearly, though this detachment from the world at the surface level should be accompanied by a deeper rediscovery of and commitment to it when it is seen in its relationship with God, a sensitivity that Thomas *Merton saw should come to the monk in so far as he is a 'marginal man'.

Such a quest for the absolute is widespread also in other *religions. This gives rise to the question whether Christian monasticism is but one instance of a universal human phenomenon or a uniquely Christian witness to the compelling and radical impact of encountering Christ, particularly in so far as in its lifelong vows it bears a note of 'for ever' not to be found elsewhere. The vision of the absolute also differs from one religion to another, although the means of attaining it are very similar, and the *dialogue between monks and nuns of different faiths has been one of the most successful ventures in today's wider ecumenism.

In Christian antiquity, *monachos* carried a freight of different meanings. Routinely it described those who for the sake of the gospel remained unmarried, often too those who lived alone as hermits. Subsequently its application became more interior and psychological, denoting a man who sets out to unify his inner life (see ORIGEN; DIONYSIUS THE PSEUDO-AREOPAGITE) or who has made God alone his goal (Theodore the Studite). The communitarian discipline comes to the fore when *Augustine relates it to the 'one heart and one soul' of the early Christian community at Jerusalem which had all things in common (Acts 4: 32).

This nostalgia for the primitive church underlies John Cassian's contention that monasticism originated with the apostles. This claim seems to be more for an ideal than for a historical pedigree. While there may have been monks, even monasteries, in the very early church, the first monk to achieve historical recognition is Antony of Egypt (*c*.251–356). His *conversion, resulting from a conviction that the words of Christ summoning to total renunciation were addressed to him personally and brooked no delay or compromise, would be replicated in the lives of many peasants in Egypt just recently Christianized who felt that the gospels simply meant what they said. Thus monasticism was an indigenous Christian movement and not, at this stage, as sometimes alleged, an invasion of Christianity by the contemplative ideals of *Platonism.

Though the original impulse behind the rush to the *desert was to the life of a hermit, some community structure inevitably followed if new disciples were to be saved from the excesses of the inexperienced by apprenticing themselves to a spiritual father. The master—disciple relationship evolved into the highly organized monasticism of Pachomius (290–346) while the monasteries Basil set up in Asia Minor were focused unreservedly on communitarian rather than eremitical ideals. Basilian monasteries were often located in cities, were closely linked to the local bishop, and undertook works of social welfare. The Rules of St Basil are still normative for all *Eastern Orthodox monasteries.

John Cassian (c.360–430) was the bridge between Western Europe and the Egyptian tradition which he wrote up in his *Institutes* and *Conferences*. For him the aim of monasticism was to arrive at purity of heart by which men shall see God. The form of monastic life that was ultimately to prevail in the west was that proffered by the Rule of St *Benedict (c.480–547) which was a balanced, flexible, and discerning distillation of the whole monastic tradition, fusing the eremitical aspirations of Egypt with the call of Basil and Augustine to brotherly union and mutual service. For long it was but one rule among many, but in 817 Louis the Pious ordered that it should be the universal norm for the monks of his empire.

During the Dark Ages, monastic *scriptoria* preserved and transmitted the works of classical and patristic authors, but always with a view to the better understanding of the bible. A 'monastic theology' emerged which was to hold the field until the onset of scholasticism. It ruminated on scripture in a spirit of faith, receptivity of the tradition, and reverence for the mystery, but *Abelard challenged it for allowing little scope for human reason. Simultaneously the monastic movement emanating from Cluny awakened the aesthetic senses by the splendour of its chant, *liturgy, and architecture. This engendered a reaction towards simplicity in the Cistercian reform begun in 1098 which called for a return to the desert. The Cistercians interpreted the Rule strictly according to the letter, revived manual labour, admitted lay brothers, and in the *Carta Caritatis* devised an effective instrument for the collaborative government of their many monasteries.

In this violent age there was a widespread conviction that only in a monastery could Christians live their ideals integrally. The world was a sinister force to flee from rather than to redeem, and those engaged in it might just make salvation if they were supported by the monks' prayers. This outlook explains why the Gregorian Reform imposed on the secular clergy a lifestyle very similar to that of the monks. But the arrival of the *Franciscans (1209) and *Dominicans (1220), who intermingled with the world and were at home in the heady atmosphere of the nascent *universities, meant that the monastic order was no longer the only form of *religious life and certainly not the one most in vogue. Though it remained very numerous and fairly observant, it receded into the background of the later *Middle Ages.

*Luther's personal experience convinced him that monasticism even at its best was a semi-*Pelagian system for getting right with God through human works rather than through faith responding to grace. The vows, the evangelical counsels of celibacy, *poverty, and obedience, the notion that monasticism was a 'state of perfection', all fostered the impression of a spiritual aristocracy to which he opposed the priesthood of all believers, sanctifying themselves in their family and civic duties rather than by flight from the world. Nor did monasticism fare any better with the thinkers of the *Enlightenment for whom it was one of the major forces of obscurantism. Inevitably the French Revolution completed the work of the Reformation in obliterating monastic institutions almost totally from the map of Europe.

Their refoundation in the course of the 19th century was at first governed by the spirit of a restoration tinged with romanticism and antiquarianism and a defiance of the spirit of the age, but in its more mature phase it set into motion many of the forces that issued into the mentality of *Vatican II: liturgical reform, ecumenism, the return to the sources biblical and patristic, acculturation of Christianity in the world outside Europe, *subsidiarity and *basic communities, the option for the poor, and the rediscovery of contemplative values. The local autonomy of which monastic families are so tenacious ensured that they provided space and freedom for many currents of Christian life and expression before they were accepted universally. Remarkable too has been the emergence and official acceptance of monastic communities in the *Anglican and *Reformed Churches. The magnetism of *Taizé comes from its being generally perceived as a vibrant monasticism but one with a care for the problems of the world and of the hour. The religious orders of the Church of England, beginning as eccentric and barely tolerated associations, are now much valued and have earned for themselves a quasi-official standing, with representatives in the Synod.

Vatican II required a major overhaul, not just to update obsolete practices, but also to recover the original inspiration and charism. This proved to be a laborious and untidy process, coinciding with a time of declining recruitment. As far as the future prospects of monasticism are concerned, the general picture is a patchy one and visibility ahead is very low, but the many vicissitudes of their history have trained monks and nuns to expect surprises, especially frequent in a form of life where dependence on God is to be a felt reality.
Daniel Rees

Butler, C., *Benedictine Monachism*, 2nd edn. (1924).

Colombas, G. M., *Tradicion Benedictina* (6 vols; 1989–).

de Vogüé, A., *Histoire littéraire du mouvement monastique* (4 vols., 1991–).

Kirk, K. E., *Vision of God* (1931).

Le Maître, G., *et al.*, *Théologie de la vie monastique* (1961).

O'Neill, J. C., 'The Origins of Monasticism', in R. Williams (ed.), *The Making of Orthodoxy: Essays in Honour of Henry Chadwick* (1989), 270–87.

Ramsey, B., *John Cassian: The Conferences* (1998).

Rees, D., *et al.*, *Consider your Call: A Theology of Monastic Life Today* (1978).

Monophysitism,

Monophysitism, a confused and redundant description of a most complex period in *doctrinal controversy, designating all those who refused to regard the Council of *Chalcedon as authoritative. It was meant to bear the pejorative sense of *heretical, and from the perspectives of Chalcedonian orthodoxy it labelled all those who affirmed that in the incarnate *Word (Logos) there was only 'one nature'. The Chalcedonian position is therefore designated, in opposition to this, as Dyophysite. Many Chalcedonians, past and present, have erroneously gone on from the basis of this hostile and rather simplistic summation of their opponents' beliefs to conclude that such a single nature of Christ must, of necessity, be a hybrid or 'mingled nature' of God-manhood. The implications, forcefully expressed in many earlier studies, are that Dyophysite thought represents *christological clarity where the one divine *person of the incarnated Logos presides directly over two distinct natures; whereas Monophysitism represents muddy thinking where deep piety (affirming Christ's unquestioned divine status) underestimates the full authentic range of his human experiences. Some of the opponents of Chalcedon undoubtedly did follow a line of thought that paid less than sufficient attention to Christ's human actuality. Following in varying degrees in the steps of Apollinaris of Laodicea, they often believed that to affirm human limitation was a disservice to the divine Christ. Thinkers such as Julian of Halicarnassus represented extremes of this confused piety. There were others, however, such as Philoxenus of Mabbug, Timothy Ailouros, and Severus of Antioch, who cannot be reduced to this level (see SYRIAC CHRISTIAN THOUGHT).

The major argument, if hostile apologetics can be cleared away, turns around two closely related issues: first that Cyril of Alexandria (who had become a towering authority on christology in the east) had used certain terms simultaneously in two senses. Chalcedon, for the sake of clarity, wished to move towards one agreed technical vocabulary and had vetoed some of his expressions. His followers (not least the entire Egyptian church) refused to accept such a veto. Cyril had spoken of the seamless union of divine and human activity in a single Christ under the party slogan: 'One *Physis* of the Word of God incarnate'. Here he applied *physis* in the antique sense of 'one concrete reality', which was more or less a synonym for the central idea of his (and Chalcedon's) christology that there was only 'one hypostasis'. The second aspect was that Cyril felt such graphic language was necessary, for he was worried that those parties who ostensibly wished to defend the authenticity of human experience in Christ, and the differentiated spheres of human and divine actions in his life, had actually strayed into such a polarization that the Incarnation had become artificial; a disunion rather than a union of God and man. Cyril's followers, labelled as Monophysites, saw their defence of the 'Union of Natures' as a last stand for the belief in the *deification of the human race that came from the Incarnation of God. In turn they regarded the Chalcedonians as no better than defenders of *Nestorianism. In this they were quite wrong, but the semantic confusions extended the controversy for centuries, and after the Muslim seizure of Syria and Egypt in the 7th century the possibilities of reconciliation with the Byzantine and Roman traditions became increasingly slight.

Today the ancient churches of Africa, the Copts and the *Ethiopians, follow the radical, Cyrilline, anti-Chalcedonian, tradition. Other ancient churches, such as the *Armenian, also have a very similar tradition from the common root of Cyril's theology, though they were not so much involved in the refusal of the decrees of Chalcedon, as simply not aware of its transactions until much later, and then did not wish to afford it the same authority as had Rome and Constantinople, who had elevated it as the fourth of the ecumenical synods.

It was not until the 1950s that a serious scholarly reassessment began in earnest. In the late decades of the 20th century active ecumenical dialogues were begun with the non-Chalcedonian churches instigated, independently, by Rome and the patriarchate of Constantinople. Both sets of dialogues issued in eirenic statements that there was no substantive ground for disagreement over doctrinal matters. The issues of confused terminology, however, have made the explication of those dialogues to non-specialists a more difficult matter, and the problem of how to approach the matter of the major 'saints' of both sides who have been anathematized by the ancient synods of the other side remains a bone of contention among *Eastern Orthodox Christians who attribute to the decrees of ecumenical councils the status of revealed truth.

Outside this narrowly ecumenical domain (which still has large implications for the health of many eastern Christian churches in unsympathetic political climates) the controversy has continuing relevance in modern christological discussion, from which it has been almost universally excluded. The rise to prominence of *kenotic and historically based christologies in western Christianity over the last century and a half (christologies 'from below'), has convinced many scholars that there is little substantive difference between the Monophysites and Chalcedonians. Both doctrines are rooted so fundamentally in a transcendental concept of the incarnate Word that the most important issue may be the identification of points of contact between them and recent alternative christologies. But whether christological discourses need to be, or can be, connected at all, is also a point in dispute that made the latter half of the 20th century one of the most fertile periods of christological discussion for centuries past.   **John McGuckin**

Frend, W. H. C., *The Rise of the Monophysite Movement* (1972).
Grillmeier, A. (with T. Hainthaler), *Christ in Christian Tradition* (1996), ii. pt. 4.
Luce, A. A., *Monophysitism Past and Present: A Study in Christology* (1920).
Meyendorff, J., *Christ in Eastern Christian Thought* (1975).
Robertson, R. G., 'The Modern Roman Catholic–Oriental Orthodox Dialogue', in *One in Christ*, 21 (1985), 238–254.

Montanism,

an *apocalyptic movement dating from 156–7 (according to Epiphanius) or from 172 (according to Eusebius). Its founder, Montanus, was a recent convert; it is possible, though the evidence is slender, that he had been a priest of Cybele. The movement's heart was in Phrygia (now inland Turkey) and its members were called Cataphrygians by opponents. Montanists themselves spoke of the New Prophecy. There had been Christians in Phrygia from the dawn of church history (Col. 4: 13 refers to the Phrygian town of Hierapolis; also cf. Acts 18: 23). The Montanists believed that the New Jerusalem would descend at the Phrygian village of Pepuza, an endearing manifestation of local patriotism!

Phrygia had a tradition of Christian *prophecy, and of woman prophets. The four prophet daughters of Philip were buried at Hierapolis and the tradition was continued by Ammia and Quadratus of Philadelphia. The Montanists believed that they were the heirs of this tradition; their critics, interestingly, accepted the authenticity of the earlier prophets but not of the Montanists. Montanus himself was closely associated with two women who became leading missionaries of the movement. Such was the importance of Priscilla and Maximilla that the three names are usually found together.

Tertullian (see PRE-CONSTANTINIAN THOUGHT) was a convert, first to Christianity, and later, from *c*.207, to its Montanist form. He condemned other Christians, whom he called Psychics, and praised the spirit-filled Pneumatics. His works *On Monogamy, An Exhortation to Chastity, On Fasting*, and *On Modesty* are the only Montanist sources that survive in full; the rest are found only in extracts in the work of their opponents. This is, however, the Montanism of Carthage, not of Phrygia, and authorities differ as to the relationship between the two.

The Montanists believed that the end of the world was near; they stressed the role of the *Holy Spirit, disapproved of those who evaded *martyrdom, advocated severe *fasts, and condemned the remarriage of the widowed. Montanus seems to have prophesied in a trance state; his Oracles (as the recorded sayings of the Montanists are known) include such statements as, 'I am the Lord God, the Almighty dwelling in man' (Epiphanius, *Panarion*, 48. 11), meaning not that he was divine, but that God spoke through him.

All these emphases were found among many other contemporary Christians. In what sense were the Montanists *heretical? As *Origen pointed out (*On the Epistle to Titus*), 'Some have properly raised the question whether those who have the name Cataphrygians ought to be called a heresy or a schism.' Because their views were not unusual, it is not easy to know who was and who was not a Montanist. This is a real difficulty in interpreting the inscriptions on Phrygian Christian tombs, a precious supplement to the literary record. A few are indisputably Montanist, but there is a large grey area. There are tombs carrying the inscription 'Christians for Christians', which has been seen by some as Montanist, but this is unsupported by hard evidence. The martyrs of Lyons (a Christian community with strong Asian and Phrygian connections) who died in 177 had much in common with the Montanists.

Perpetua was a young woman who died a martyr's death in Carthage in 203; some have seen Montanist influences in her prison journal, and it has often been suggested that it was Tertullian who wrote the introduction and conclusion of the extant text. But perhaps it is more likely that Montanism and the outlook of the Lyons and Carthage martyrs are independent manifestations of a similar outlook.

The Montanists came into conflict with local bishops Melito of Sardis and Apollinaris of Hierapolis. Pope Zephyrinus (199–217) condemned them, after some hesitation, in order to be consistent with his predecessors.

There was, in the 2nd century and later, a tension between church *authority—pope, bishop, and presbyter—and the authority claimed by confessors, visionaries, and (prospective) martyrs. Saturus, who died with Perpetua, recorded a *vision in which he and Perpetua were asked to settle a dispute between bishop and presbyter. Despite persecution, the Montanist movement survived until the 6th century; their headquarters was at Pepuza, and they had a hierarchy of bishops and priests which included women.

Some modern commentators have interpreted Montanism as a new form of the ecstatic cult of Cybele. Others saw it as a return to the values of the early church, which were becoming eroded. To Ronald Knox, Montanism was one in a long series of manifestations of an (undesirable) *enthusiasm, 'a naked fanaticism, which tried to stampede the church into greater severity'. He says of Tertullian's Montanist conversion, 'It was as if *Newman had joined the Salvation Army.' He did not intend this as a compliment!

Montanism, like *Gnosticism, looms large in contemporary *feminist Christian thought, on the grounds that in response to a church increasingly dominated by male authority, women found a place to feel at home on the margins. Women church leaders were prominent in the various Gnostic movements, and Sophia, Lady *Wisdom, was often central to their theology. Two of Montanism's three founders were women. Montanists appealed to much the same biblical precedents as do modern feminists—Miriam, Deborah, Huldah, Anna, the daughters of Philip. Priscilla had a vision of Christ in the form of a woman; this has been reclaimed by contemporary women confronting the problem of a male saviour. Often, their quest has taken them to Sophia.

Elisabeth Schüssler *Fiorenza's influential chapter in Rosemary Radford *Ruether and Eleanor McLoughlan, *Women of Spirit: Female Leadership in the Jewish and Christian Traditions*, is entitled 'Word, Spirit and Power: Women in Early Christian Communities'. This comes from words attributed to Maximilla: 'I am pursued like a wolf from the sheep. I am not a wolf. I am word and spirit and power.'   **Elizabeth Isichei**

Frend, W. H. C., 'Montanism: A Movement of Prophecy and Regional Identity in the Early Church', *Bulletin of the John Rylands University Library*, 70 (1988).
Heine, R. E., *The Montanist Oracles and Testimonia* (1989).
Knox, R., *Enthusiasm* (1950).

morality. Is there a Christian morality? Is it to be found in the NT? Does it derive, in some comprehensible way, from *Jesus himself? Perhaps surprisingly, many scholars would respond more or less negatively to all these questions. There is no agreement on this subject as a whole though there was a great deal of movement in ideas in the latter part of the 20th century. The traditional schools of Catholic moral theology have largely fallen apart, but despite a lively debate involving philosophers, biblical scholars, and radical moral practitioners, there is no new consensus. Nevertheless the interpretation of Christian morality here presented, answering an emphatic yes to our initial questions, is derived from an integral assessment of the modern debate in all its dimensions.

It is unquestionable that the Jewish community at the time of Jesus was an intensely moral society. It is equally unquestionable that, a generation later, the early Christian community was no less self-committedly moral and yet its moral system was profoundly different from that of the Jews. How did this happen? Where did the new system come from, and in what, chiefly, did it consist? The central characteristic of Jewish morality was that it was one of law—*divine command, developed and interpreted over the generations by countless jurists and administered in religious courts (see LAW, BIBLICAL). The law itself was furthermore extended with material, added by the Pharisees, of a typically legal sort though not legally enforceable. These developments would lead on to the Talmud. The quality of moral concern in this is not in question, but the form that it took was a preoccupation with a multitude of precise rules involving minute avoidances and ritual practices. Somewhat later Islam would appear as another monotheistic religion dependent upon a complex body of law. Its development too would lie in the interpretation of law and the addition of further laws.

Unlike Judaism and Islam, Christianity is emphatically not a religion of law. In its origins and early development it entirely lacked any formulated moral law comparable to theirs, its morality being of an essentially different kind. This was already so in the apostolic period. *Paul with his exceptionally sharp eye for primary issues endeavoured in both Romans and Galatians to formulate the contrast he saw in terms of a dichotomy between law or *grace and *faith, but it was not basically a Pauline invention. It was simply a characteristic of Christian life evident in all four gospels. It seems impossible to believe that so complete, quick, and smooth a change happened by accident, but if by design or as an inevitable part of a basic religious shift, it is implausible to see anyone other than Jesus as ultimately responsible. It was also a gradual development. Jesus and his disciples certainly conformed for the most part to the moral and ritual norms of their society, even while he was subtly suggest-ing a profoundly different system. After his death the situation did not immediately change. The process of realizing that the entire Judaic legal system had become in principle anachronistic in the light of Jesus' teaching, death, and Resurrection inevitably took the disciples some years. It was hastened by two things. The first was the sharp mind and evolving theology of Paul; the second the in-crease of Gentile Christians. Together they ensured recognition of the moral implications of faith in Jesus in a way that did not fully happen in the predominantly Jewish Christian communities of Palestine. But a basic realization of release from any detailed law underlies the somewhat mysterious decision of the 'Council of Jerusalem' (Acts 15) 'to lay upon you no greater burden than these necessary things: that you abstain from what has been sacrificed to idols and from blood and from what is strangled and from unchas-tity'. And even that far-reaching instruction was something of a halfway house, as is clear from Paul's advice to the Corinthians about eating what may have been sacrificed (1 Cor. 10: 23–30).

There is a striking fundamental consistency in the moral teaching of Matthew, Luke, John, and Paul and the early apostolic church which should be unmistakable but has in fact frequently been ques-tioned or denied. It is dependent directly upon Jesus whose moral system comes to us in three parts. The first is the commandment of *love; the second the very demanding instructions to be found in their most concentrated form in the *Sermon on the Mount (Matt. 5–8) but which in fact pervade all the gospels, particularly Luke; the third is the concept of *discipleship, the moral duty to imitate Jesus.

The commandment of love is given in all three synoptics (Mark 12: 28–34; Matt. 22: 34–40; Luke 10: 25–8) and recapitulated at length in the final superb meditational text in John (13–17) which begins with Jesus' washing of the feet of the disciples at their Last Supper. The importance of this passage in which Jesus puts together Deu-teronomy 6: 4–5 on the love of God and Leviticus 19: 18 on the love of neighbour is stressed. In Mark the scribe comments, 'this is far more important than any holocaust or sacrifice', and the evangelist adds decisively 'after that no one dared to question him any more'. In Matthew Jesus adds 'on these two commandments hang all the law and the prophets' and in Luke 'do this and life is yours'. Each comment possesses its own finality, as does John's four-chapter long recapitulation. Luke, moreover, follows it at once with the parable of the good Samaritan to explain who your 'neighbour' really is: it is not the person of your own kith and kin who lives next door. On the contrary it is the foreigner who believes differ-ently from you and whom you have never met before, a note different from that of Leviticus. One does not need to think that people saw at once the full significance of what Jesus had said. Indeed the gospels themselves suggest that its revolutionary signifi-cance could only be comprehended little by little. It would take time to arrive at the full realization: 'Let us love one another. To love is to live according to his commandments. This is the com-mandment which you have heard since the beginning, to live a life of love' (2 John 5–6). The divine command remains but its legal codification does not.

Was this a 'new' commandment? The writer of 1 John considers the question and is clearly confused about the answer. It is not new and yet it is new. Jesus was, after all, only quoting OT texts. He added nothing and yet it was, as a system of morality, so incredibly new that it took its hearers years to understand its implications. In the OT these two verses, located apart and never verbally merged into a single message, remained part of a highly complex legal system. They represented its underlying spirit, summed up what it was all about, but in no way displaced it. On the contrary, the system with its courts, ritual observances, and commentaries grew ever more complicated and continued to do so, after Jesus' time, in Mishnah and Talmud. Jesus follows a diametrically opposed path to the Mishnah. Instead of refining the law with a complexity of pro-posals to tie up every aspect of life, he reduces it to one supreme principle, love. Everything else simply falls away as Christians enter spiritually into this breath-taking *freedom of their new inherit-ance. It was a falling away already hinted at in Jesus' radical pro-nouncement in Mark 7: 15: 'Nothing that goes into a man from outside can make him unclean; it is the things that come out of a man that make him unclean.'

The point of love is that there are no limits to it. It is something only definable in its fullness and in its fullness it is a matter of total self-giving in all directions. God is its best definition. The complete model is not love of neighbour 'as yourself' but 'as I have loved you', which overturns the balanced middle-class sanity of 'as your-self', difficult as that already is. It may mean accepting the cross for oneself to bring life to one's neighbour.

Love cannot be defined, decreed, or prescribed. It does not have rules. It can only be described, hinted at in terms of its most au-thentic expression, but the more authentic, the more seemingly impossible. That is what the Sermon on the Mount and much else in Jesus' teaching attempts to do. While these attempts ranged over a variety of topics, the most striking is undoubtedly the insistence on loving your enemies and practising unlimited forgiveness. There is no strict OT precedent for Jesus' command to 'love your enemies and pray for those who persecute you' (Matt. 5: 44). This and everything else in the Sermon on the Mount is not, in any strict sense, a commandment, any more than 'if your right eye should cause you to sin, tear it out' is a commandment. It fits the tradition of wisdom sayings, not that of law-making; but while wisdom lit-erature tended to be safe, middle-of-the-road, and prosaic in the guidance it offered, Jesus' words have again and again a manifest radicalism to them, an exaggerated phrasing offered to make a point memorably, which puts them in a class of their own. Collect-ively, they suggest a model of loving beyond anyone's grasp, but not quite beyond one's occasional reach, something continually beckoning onwards, essentially limitless. 'Lord, how often must I forgive my brother if he wrongs me? As often as seven times?' Jesus answered 'Not seven, I tell you, but seventy-seven times' (Matt. 18: 21–2). There is no suggestion that any of this is directed at a few select souls only. It simply represents Jesus' moral teaching for anyone willing to listen.

The third element is that of imitation, the following of Jesus. It is sometimes claimed that there is little stress in the NT that Jesus should be imitated. It is to misunderstand the literature. It is, of course, impossible to imitate Jesus in many things. He is essentially the initiator of a new *Kingdom. No one else can do that. Never-theless it is inherent throughout the gospels that the point of the story is to produce disciples, followers, who will also be imitators. 'Follow me' is one of the most repeated themes of the gospels and the example of Stephen (Acts 7) is presented as of someone who did just that. But Christians are repeatedly instructed to imitate Jesus, itself a way of imitating God. 'Shoulder my yoke and learn from me, for I am gentle and humble of heart' (Matt. 11: 29). 'A disciple should be like his master' (Matt. 10: 25). 'If anyone wants to be a follower of mine, let him renounce himself and take up his cross' (Mark 8: 34). 'Here am I as one who serves' (Luke 22: 30). John takes up that last line from Luke elaborating it into a full account of the washing of the feet—'I have given you an example' (John 13: 15), essentially an example of love, 'as I have loved you, so are you to love one another' (15: 2). The imitation is not a matter of particulars but of the underlying spirit. There is complete continuity here with Paul: 'It is not an order that I am giving you; I am just testing the genuineness of your love against the keenness of others. Remember how generous the Lord Jesus was' (2 Cor. 8: 8–9). 'The Lord has forgiven you; now you must do the same' (Col. 3: 13). 'In your mind you must be the same as Christ Jesus' (Phil. 2: 5). Just as the lack of limits to Jesus' love is illustrated in the gospels by the marginal people—lepers, tax collectors, Samaritans, prostitutes—whom Jesus befriended, so it is shown more theoretically in Paul's superb assertion 'neither Jew nor Greek, neither slave nor free, neither male nor female' (Gal. 3: 28). All are one. Love includes them all. This is not just a theological point about redemption or the church. It is a moral one, part of a consistent moral doctrine permeating the NT.

Universalism; love of enemies; unlimited willingness to forgive: it is all part of the pursuit of perfection. 'You must be perfect just as your heavenly father is perfect' (Matt. 5: 48). The imitation of Jesus is the road to imitation of God, already a Jewish ideal. Surely this cannot be a morality, it is just asking too much? Scholars have sometimes tried to explain it in terms of a belief that the *eschaton was about to arrive and, therefore, modifiable once that did not happen. But there is little reason to link the two. Again, Christians have frequently tried to cope with such teaching by regarding it not as morality but as spirituality, something to which a small number of specialist people are called, while everyone else gets on with a workaday morality discovered not in the NT but somewhere else. Such an explanation has proved disastrous for the general understanding of Christian life but there is not the slightest reason to think that it is how NT teaching was meant to be understood. Of course, none of it has the precision of law. It is something different, an imagining within human life of divine perfection, but it is still offered as the only replacement of the old law available to the Christian.

Paul sums it up in 1 Corinthians in a rhapsody on love that can fairly be read as a restatement of the Sermon on the Mount using the different style of Greek society. There is the same sense of the perfect and unlimited: but nothing less than this can ever be proposed as properly Christian. Prophecy, faith, total self-sacrifice, if not founded in love, are all, he insists, of no use whatever. 'Love is patient and kind; love is not jealous or boastful; it is not arrogant or rude. Love does not insist on its own way; it is not irritable or resentful; it does not rejoice at wrong but rejoices in the right. Love bears all things, believes all things, hopes all things, endures all things. Love never ends' (13: 3–8).

Early Christian writers such as Justin and Tertullian regularly appealed to love as characteristic of the Christian community. *Augustine threw out the fantastically confident *ama et fac quod vis*, love

and do what you like. *Aquinas centred his entire moral theology upon the principle that love alone unites us with God because God is love. It is the form of all the virtues and without it no virtue is possible. Every other virtue is then in reality simply a way of shaping love from a specific point of view. Between the gospels, Paul, and Aquinas there is an essential coherence.

Nevertheless, how was Paul or any other Christian teacher actually to advise ordinary Christians about their behaviour in regard to the multitude of daily problems and human relationships? In practice, for relatively unimaginative people a code of what love might lead one to do and to avoid remained necessary. In principle the guidance offered was neither the moral law of the OT nor the moral customs of Graeco-Roman society, underpinned by a philosophical concept of *natural law and the authority of *conscience. In practice, however, that is what it largely was, all the more so as Jewish law and Greek, mostly Stoic, philosophy were seen to be largely in conformity with one another. A correlation between Christian morality and natural law is happening already within the NT (see Rom. 2). There was no other way of formulating a code of behaviour for Christians, the implementation of love in daily life, than to run it, so to speak, along the tracks of natural law. It could be expected to go well beyond what others would see as natural law requirements, but it had to fulfil the latter in order to be credibly moral in non-Christian eyes. It would have appeared irrational to practise love in terms deemed to violate natural morality. However, the more this was taken for granted, the more the idea could take root that Christian morality was in principle natural law morality or, alternatively, Ten *Commandments morality. The tool was mistaken for the hand. This led on to the reinterpretation of the evangelical model of morality, comprising the Sermon on the Mount, the following of Jesus and the primacy of love, as not a matter of morality as such but of spirituality, a path of perfection for the few who were committed to it through a special vocation. This development was greatly assisted both by the mass conversion of the rural peoples of Europe and the growth of monasticism after the 4th century, creating a vast gap between the two groups of Christians. Faced with the task of Christianizing a multitude of illiterate people the church fell back on a morality of law, based on the Ten Commandments, and an essentially juridical system of enforcement developed canonically. Moral theology came to be constructed around the sacrament of *penance, administered judicially and heavily dependent upon the rulings of an ever-expanding canon *law. This was particularly striking with the Catholic moral teaching of the post-Tridentine period developed by generations of *Jesuit and Redemptorist theologians. The commandments rather than the virtues were central to this exercise and the science of *casuistry was carefully refined to cope with it. The underlying motivation of this whole process was a judicial one—the perceived need in the sacrament of penance to judge sins as a violation of law and impose appropriate penance. The supreme master of this theology, which dominated Catholicism to an extraordinary extent between the 17th and 20th centuries, was Alphonsus Liguori (1696–1787), founder of the Redemptorists. With Liguori casuistry is seen at its kindest; nevertheless the difference between this and the *virtue-based moral theology of Aquinas was immense.

It is noteworthy that the Thomist tradition in morality was best preserved by Anglicans, notably the *Caroline Divines of the 17th century, but in general Protestants distrusted too much formalization of morality. It was part of what *Luther had rebelled against. Without the pressure of the confessional, Protestant moral thinking was less individualistic and juridical than Catholic, but it became far more dominated by philosophical ethics. Barth, in reaction to this, developed in his *Church Dogmatics* a powerful morality specific to the kingdom of Christ.

In the second half of the 20th century a great deal changed. The Catholic approach to Christian morality was decisively transformed under the influence of Bernard Häring and other writers of the Vatican II era; the standard textbooks were scrapped. In general the need was seen to escape the intense individualism of confessional-orientated textbooks together with the dominance of canon law in particular and any predominantly law-based model in general. All this was to be replaced either by a direct return to the NT or to the virtue-centred and *Aristotelian-grounded tradition of Aquinas, enabling the separated fields of morality and spirituality to be reunited around the concept of virtue and the primacy of love. Comparable developments were taking place in the Protestant world, led by authors like John Howard Yoder and Stanley Hauerwas, strong particularly in their stress on the public, political dimension of morality, something linked with the expansion of *political theology. Central here was the pursuit of *peace through non-violence: 'Blessed are the peacemakers' (Matt. 5: 9).

The weakness of a moral tradition originating in love alone appears to lie in the diversity and seeming contradictoriness to which it has left Christian thought and practice open across the centuries. But its strength lies both in the very simplicity of its basic premiss, which makes excellent theological sense, and in the way that it has left room for development in moral awareness and practice, avoiding the legalistic fundamentalism which results from the staking out by any religion of an extensive and unchangeable initial code of conduct. An integrated Christian moral theology may well need to make extensive use of the moral tradition of the OT, natural law theory, and an Aristotelian approach to the virtues, as well as incorporating new insights coming from philosophy, science, and human experience. Nevertheless the central and all-embracing principle that provides its distinguishing and unitive character remains the NT assertion, derived directly from Jesus, of the unique requirement of love.

Adrian Hastings

Ford, J. Massyngbaerde, *My Enemy is my Guest: Jesus and Violence in Luke* (1984).

Fuchs, J., *Christian Morality: The Word Becomes Flesh* (1987).

Gilleman, G., *The Primacy of Charity in Moral Theology* (1959).

Guroian, Vigen, *Incarnate Love: Essays in Orthodox Ethics* (1987).

Gustafson, James, *Protestant and Roman Catholic Ethics* (1978).

Harvey, A. E., *Strenuous Commands: The Ethics of Jesus* (1990).

Hauerwas, Stanley, *The Peaceable Kingdom: A Primer in Christian Ethics* (1983).

McAdoo, H. R., *The Structure of Caroline Moral Theology* (1949).

McCabe, Herbert, *Law, Love and Language* (1968).

Mahoney, J., *The Making of Moral Theology* (1987).

Meeks, W. A., *The Origins of Christian Morality* (1993).

O'Donovan, O., *Resurrection and Moral Order* (1986).

Riches, John, *Jesus and the Transformation of Judaism* (1980).

Tinsley, E. J., *The Imitation of God in Christ* (1960).

moral theology, see CASUISTRY; ETHICS; MORALITY.

More, Thomas (1478–1535). A London lawyer, who became Speaker of the House of Commons, Chancellor of the Duchy of Lancaster, High Steward of the Universities of Oxford and Cambridge, and Lord Chancellor, More was an immensely successful public man, hard-working, efficient, and honest, someone everyone trusted, 'the king's good servant'. It would be hard to doubt that he enjoyed power, success, and the wealth that went with them. Yet More was also a man who wore a hair-shirt beneath his fine robes, gave lectures in his parish church on *Augustine's *City of God*, was remembered as a judge for his concern for the poor, and finally abandoned every earthly fortune because, with a handful of clerics, he refused to accept that king and parliament could alter the law of the universal church, or reject the pope's *authority. For this he was executed on Tower Hill.

More remains a somewhat inscrutable figure, perhaps especially in his almost ceaseless flow of dry wit. For Samuel Johnson in the 18th century he was 'the person of greatest virtue these islands ever produced'. For English Catholics, he has always been the very standard-bearer of their tradition. But in the 20th century his reputation grew more than ever. He was canonized by Pius XI in 1935. In the 1960s, Robert Bolt's play *A Man for all Seasons* proved extraordinarily popular. Biographies and studies, including Peter Ackroyd's striking *Life of Thomas More* (1998), have multiplied. A thriving More Society, based in France, produces the journal *Moreana*, while Yale University has published the definitive edition of his works in fifteen volumes. While much of the biography, beginning with the memorable short life by his son-in-law, William Roper, is hagiographical, there has always been an alternative hostile stream, focusing on his persecution of Protestants, represented most recently by Richard Marius, *Thomas More* (1984). More's repudiation of the underlying principles of unlimited national sovereignty and an *Erastian church has made him the supreme counter-figure to England's central political and ecclesiastical orthodoxy.

A close friend of *Erasmus, More laughed at scholasticism, loved the Greek and Latin classics, and wrote *Utopia*, an enigmatic work of political philosophy. While its second book describes an imaginary communistic society, its first discusses very realistically whether philosophers should enter into practical politics. More's favourite adjective was 'merry', reflecting a home life where he played the lute with his wife, and insisted on his daughters and foster-children learning the classics and philosophy. Margaret, his eldest daughter, became the most learned woman in England. Holbein's famous paintings of both More and his *family offer a captivating impression of firmness and affection. In all this More was quintessentially a *Renaissance man and, like many of his friends, keen on the reform of the church. But when the *Lutheran *Reformation broke, he defended Catholic doctrine with a near fanatical intensity and used his brief authority as Lord Chancellor in a vain attempt to prevent Lutheran literature from entering the country. Those he condemned to death were almost all directly connected with the importation of books that he believed must lead to the devastation of the religious and social order. It is ironic that, in the brief period—hardly more than a year—he was doing this, the king himself was increasingly falling under Protestant influences.

More's significance rests in his lay fusion of Catholic faith and spirituality, learning, family life, high politics, and even humour. When things fell apart, he insisted on the obligation to follow *conscience, a word to which he constantly returned. He spent his months in prison composing *A Dialogue of Comfort against Tribulation*, finest of his English works. His last letters to his beloved daughter Margaret are singularly moving. Called by Erasmus 'a man for all seasons', More described himself on the scaffold as 'the King's good servant, but God's first', summarizing both the duality in his life and the primacy within it. **Adrian Hastings**

Chambers, R. W., *Thomas More* (1935).
Fox, Alistair, *Thomas More: History and Providence* (1982).
Kenny, Anthony, *Thomas More* (1983).

Mormonism.

In 19th-century Protestant *North America there was a *prophet, a new scripture, a new *Israel which went out through persecution to a promised land. The prophet was Joseph Smith, the scripture was the Book of Mormon, the people were 'the Church of Jesus Christ of Latter-Day Saints', and the promised land, 'Deseret', became the state of Utah. There are now about six million Mormons, with some of the features of a nation as well as a *church, a stable and prosperous society with strong *family values. The relationship of Mormonism to Protestant North American Christianity is ambiguous.

Joseph Smith came from upstate New York, called the 'burnt-over district' because of its many religious revivals. An outsider would say that the narrative supposedly by Mormon, the last of an American lost tribe of Israel, which Smith translated behind a curtain and published in 1830, supplementing the Old and New Testaments, was full of all the religious concerns of Smith's own time. His people found there a prehistory, going back to the Tower of Babel, and in some ways a more liberal code. Smith went on to gather his people into communities, under the 'law of Consecration and Stewardship', and to build a *temple. In a land of religious free enterprise and communitarian experiment, the Mormons were unlike others largely in their unpopularity. When they were driven from Ohio, Nauvoo in Illinois became a Mormon theocracy, with Smith as king, declaring he would stand for President of the USA. Instead, a lynch mob killed him and his brother in 1844.

Brigham Young, one of Smith's twelve apostles, led the exodus through the Rockies to set up Salt Lake City. There they made the desert blossom, and built a temple for their secret ritual. In their own territory their previously secret polygamy was openly practised, shocking other Americans, and many Mormons. (The minority Reorganized Church was more conventional.) In 1890 the US government forced the Mormons to outlaw polygamy. Utah became a state of the Union, and Mormons ordinary Americans. They now marked the boundaries by forbidding alcohol and tobacco, tea and coffee, and by rules about dress. Their eclectic theology, which its leaders, when inspired, can adjust, of a self-made finite deity, plurality of gods, eternality of matter and also of *marriage, remains distinctive, but in a nation of 'behavers' rather than 'believers' (M. Marty, *A Nation of Behavers* (1976)) does not seem greatly to excite them or others by its difference.

Young Mormons spend time as missionaries, encountered normally as pairs of young men in suits knocking on doors. The church has masterly genealogists to facilitate their custom of retrospectively baptizing the dead. Everything in their practice is family-minded; shifts from patriarchy come slowly. Alongside, rather than in debate or fellowship with American Christianity, the Mormons show interesting parallels, in handling their scriptures and in adjusting to change in society. **Alistair Mason**

Brodie, Fawn, *No Man Knows My Story* (1945).
Hansen, Klaus, J., *Mormonism and the American Experience* (1981).
Shipps, Jan, *Mormonism: The Story of a New Religious Tradition* (1985).

Moses

is the chief human figure in the biblical books *Exodus to Deuteronomy. In a richly diverse narrative, he plays a number of key roles: leader of *Israel in their exodus from slavery in Egypt and during their subsequent wandering through the wilderness towards the promised land; recipient of the law (see Law, Biblical); mediator of the *covenant; *prophet *par excellence*. Yet Moses' status has to be seen in theological perspective. *Miracle predominates in the narrative (the crossing of the sea, striking water from the rock, etc.); the decisive initiatives and actions are God's. Already in the opening sections of the story the initial acts of Moses lead only to reverses (Exod. 2: 11–22); deliverance, it becomes clear, depends wholly upon the intervention of God (2: 23–5). In the end, Moses is denied entry into the promised land because of his failures (Deut. 1: 37; Num. 20: 12; 27: 14). This limitation on Moses' standing is in line with Jewish tradition: the 'diminished hero' of the biblical narrative (D. J. Silver's phrase, *Images of Moses* (1982)) scarcely figures, for example, in the passover *seder*. It also agrees with the findings of modern scholarship. The 'historical Moses' is difficult to locate precisely in time: the naming of the cities where the Israelites laboured as slaves in Exodus 1: 11, which seems to point to the Ramesside period of the Egyptian New Kingdom beginning in the late 14th century BC, is the only specific reference to external circumstances, but its firmness may be more apparent than real; the account of Moses' death and burial in Deut. 34: 5–6 seems designed to draw a veil of mystery over events. The historical data are few and ambiguous, probably deliberately so: the significance of Moses and all that he stands for is universal, it is not confined to, or exhausted by, one period; least of all is there to be a cult of a mere human personality.

In OT outside the Pentateuch Moses is most frequently referred to as an authority figure, not least in connection with 'The Law of Moses' (e.g. 2 Kgs. 14: 6). Yet, while there would be no doubt among biblical, and post-biblical, writers about the authority of Moses—as mediator but not originator—behind the law in its oral and written forms, there was from early times a concept of the 'unfolding of Torah' (cf., for example, the figure of the rabbi as the spring welling up ever more strongly in *Aboth*, the 'Sayings of the Fathers'). This, too, is in conformity with the dominant view of modern scholarship: the composition of the Pentateuch spanned many centuries and passed through perhaps two major phases of collecting and editing of manifold oral and written sources: one in the 6th century BC in response to the crisis of the Babylonian *exile; the other in the post-exilic period, perhaps even as late as the early 2nd century BC, when, in disillusion after centuries of varying political fortunes, hopes of the dawn of the reign of God came to be expressed in terms of an idealized portrayal of origins.

The NT use of the figure of Moses is also multilayered. At its most direct, the OT story of Moses is simply presupposed (as example of rejection by his people in Acts 7: 20–44) and is used as a model of faith (especially *Hebrews 11: 24–9). This acceptance leads also to the inferring of details of the life-story not included in OT and to some embroidery, as in Jewish *haggadah*: the assumption that, in his youth, Moses must have been 'schooled in all the wisdom of Egypt' (Acts 7: 22); the names of the magicians, Jannes and Jambres, who were Moses' (actually more particularly Aaron's) rivals at Pharaoh's court (2 Tim. 3: 8); and the struggle for the soul of Moses between archangel Michael and the devil (Jude 9). The schema 'prophecy and fulfilment', which emphasizes continuity between the two Testaments on the time-line, is used in connection with the promise that God will 'raise up a prophet like me [Moses]' (Deut. 18: 15, 18), interpreted in individual terms as Jesus (Acts 3: 22; 7: 37; cf. the narrative of the transfiguration, Matt. 17: 3). 'Fulfilment' is also understood in terms of 'filling out to its fullness' the content of the original; thus, in the deliberate patterning of Matthew's gospel, the *Sermon on the Mount is the 'fulfilment' of the revelation at Sinai, with the repeated, 'It has been said … but I say' (Matt. 5: 17–48). A development of this approach is *typological interpretation, whereby the OT material is but the foreshadowing of greater things to come: thus crossing through the Red Sea becomes the type of Christian baptism (1 Cor. 10: 2); manna in the wilderness a figure for the bread of life offered by Jesus as in the *Eucharist (John 6: 32); the bronze serpent of Numbers 21: 8–9 a prefiguration of Christ's crucifixion (John 3: 14); the tabernacle revealed to Moses according to the heavenly prototype itself but a shadow of the full realization of that prototype in the priestly work of Christ (Heb. 8: 5). But the NT is above all witness to the profound theological issues raised, not least in connection with Moses, in particular with the Law of Moses, by the opening of the Kingdom of God to the Gentiles. One of the most contentious issues is the function of the Law of Moses within the new community, as seen especially in *Paul's discussions on '*justification' in *Romans and Galatians. The Law of Moses is displaced as the foundation and framework of the new community by the prior basis of the *faith of *Abraham. None the less, the Law remains as the statement of what is required of the community of faith, yet not in a literalist way: the change of basis brings with it the necessity for observing the 'spirit' above the 'letter', as, for example, the controversy about the need for circumcising Gentile converts makes clear (e.g. Acts 15; contrast Exod. 12: 43–9).

The figure of Moses as presented in OT or as interpreted in NT has been repeatedly applied typologically in connection with events great and small in the subsequent history of Christianity, not least in modern times. The victory of *Constantine at the battle at the Milvian bridge in 312, for example, which led eventually to the acknowledgement of Christianity as the official religion of the Roman empire, is interpreted by the contemporary church historian Eusebius as a new crossing of the Red Sea. Other instances include the Pilgrim Fathers' arrival in the New World in the 17th century and the emancipation from *slavery and the struggle of African Americans for racial equality as in Martin Luther King's celebrated sermon at Mason Temple, Memphis, in 1968. The transposition of the Moses story into the idiom of contemporary thought, pioneered by the 1st-century Jewish thinker Philo of Alexandria, is illustrated by the Neoplatonist interpretation of Moses in Gregory of Nyssa's *Life of Moses: or Concerning Perfection in Virtue*, c.390, by *Luther's 'rediscovery' in the 16th-century German *Reformation of Paul's doctrine of justification, or by *liberation the-

ology developed in relation to the poor especially in *Latin America in the second half of the 20th century.

The fragility of many such applications is indicated not just by frequently one-sided adoption (e.g. the desire for political freedom without the accompanying covenantal obligations) but by celebrated influential misinterpretations. For example, the presentation of Moses in western medieval art as 'horned', most famously in Michelangelo's statue of Moses (c.1513–15) in S. Pietro in Vincoli, Rome, is based on the rendering of Exod. 34: 29 in the Vulgate ('his face *was horned* from the conversation of the Lord'); the almost certainly correct sense of the Hebrew verb 'radiated' (cf. LXX), underlies Paul's interpretation in 2 Cor. 3 of the dazzling glory of the revelation to Moses, which the Christian can now read 'unveiled'. Sigmund Freud's psychoanalytical study, *Moses and Monotheism* (1939), is based on far-reaching embellishment (the supposed influence on Moses of the 14th-century BC Pharaoh Akhenaten's monotheism) and inference (E. Sellin's conclusion that Moses was murdered by his own people). There is constant need for return to the canonical biblical picture as standard for correction and refreshment.

See also HIGHER CRITICISM.   **William Johnstone**

Classic 'biographies' of Moses have been written in the modern period by M. Buber (1946); E. Auerbach (1953); G. von Rad (1960).

Allison, Dale C., Jr., *The New Moses: A Matthean Typology* (1993).

D'Angelo, M. R., *Moses in the Letter to the Hebrews* (1979).

Daniélou, J., *From Shadows to Reality: Studies in the Biblical Typology of the Fathers* (1960).

Hafemann, S. J., *Paul, Moses, and the History of Israel: The Letter/Spirit Contrast in the Argument from Scripture in 2 Corinthians 3* (1995).

McBride, S. Dean, et al., *Interpretation*, 44 (1990).

Martin-Achard, R., et al., *La Figure de Moïse: Écriture et relectures* (1979).

Mellinkoff, R., *The Horned Moses in Medieval Art and Thought* (1970).

Van Seters, J., *The Life of Moses: The Yahwist as Historian in Exodus— Numbers* (1994).

motherhood is a state of life imbued with significance in Christian thinking. Not only have mothers been held in special esteem (though this has sometimes been tinged with keeping *women in their place), but motherhood has been used as an image for the nurturing of Christians by the *church, by its pastors, by *Jesus, and by *God.

The first mother of scripture was *Eve, whose version of the original curse was that she would bring forth children in pain, and that her husband would rule over her (Gen. 3: 16). Strong biblical matriarchs then walk through the pages of the OT. Though they attract less coverage than the patriarchs, mothers such as Rebecca, who secured the chief blessing for her favourite son by trickery, or Hannah, whose tenacity in prayer earned her a son after years of barrenness, present an image of the mother which is determined and beautiful, loving and faithful. A famous passage in Isaiah presents maternal love as the most powerful reflection of God's faithful *love that can be thought of: 'Can a woman forget her nursing child, or show no compassion for the child of her womb? Even these may forget, yet I will not forget you' (49: 15).

Moving to the NT, Matthew's gospel begins with a genealogy of Jesus in which, curiously, four mothers figure amongst the long line of *fathers. It is commonly suggested that these four mothers have been chosen precisely because in their sexual activity they risked their own condemnation: Tamar was a childless young widow who seduced her father-in-law; Rahab was a prostitute and a Gentile; Ruth was a foreign widow who engineered a sexual union with a Jew; and the wife of Uriah was an adulteress who married her husband's murderer and bore his child. When Mary, and then Jesus, are placed at the end of this line, a rather more challenging context is given to their family backgrounds than conventional piety might suggest.

*Mary, the mother of Jesus, is the woman most spoken of in the gospels, particularly in the infancy stories of Luke, where she is marked by her submission to God's will and her grateful joy in the *grace shown to her. While mainstream Christian tradition has exalted the obedience of her fiat to the angel—'let it be done to me according to your word'—*feminists are cautious of presenting submission as a specifically motherly 'virtue'. It has even been suggested that Luke portrays Mary too much as a dependent, self-sacrificing woman who never initiates any action.

The other gospels include hints of a more ambiguous tradition, suggesting that Jesus' mother did not always understand her son's mission, and was sometimes slighted by him (Matt. 12: 46–50, Mark 3: 21, 31–5, John 2: 4). John includes a sentence from Jesus on the *cross to his mother and the beloved disciple that has carried great significance in the understanding of Mary's role vis-à-vis the church: 'Woman, here is your son…. Here is your mother.' Whatever its original intent, it has been interpreted as showing Mary as Mother of the Church, a title formally confirmed by Pope Paul VI in 1964. The most important motherly title that has been given to Mary, however, is Mother of God (Greek Theotokos, God-bearer), affirmed at the Council of *Ephesus in 431.

The suspicion of *sinfulness that was thought to hang over *sexual relations is observable in the great value that the church has traditionally placed on the belief that Mary was simultaneously a *virgin and a mother. Only in the mother of Jesus was it thought that one and the same person could unite these two most valued, and normally incompatible, states of womanhood.

While Mary may be seen as mother of the church, the church itself is habitually spoken of as a mother who nourishes and guides her *children. Mother Church is an extension of the old *Jerusalem, spoken of in scripture as a mother who nurses and comforts her children (Isa. 66: 11–13). Nor does the maternal imagery stop with the church. Abbots and pastors are urged by the 12th-century Bernard of Clairvaux to be mothers to those in their care, showing affection and letting their breasts swell with the milk of encouragement and of sympathy. Jesus himself is called a mother by many *mystics, most famously by the 14th-century *Julian of Norwich, who develops the idea from the life-giving labour pains of the Passion, and from the way Jesus feeds us on himself through his *body and *blood, as a mother feeds her child on herself through her milk. 'This fair lovely word "mother",' writes Julian, 'is so sweet and so kind in itself that it cannot truly be said of anyone or to anyone except of him and to him who is the true mother of life and of all things' (Showings, ch. 60).

For Julian, as for many others, the mother image is no less applicable to God, in complement to God as *father. A recent authority to do this was John Paul I, who said 'He is a father; more than that, he is a mother.' He was following in a long tradition exemplified by, for example, the 3rd-century Clement of Alexandria, and *Teresa of Avila. There is also a tradition among the eastern fathers of calling the *Holy Spirit a mother. The 4th-century Gregory of Nyssa speaks of 'the dove' of the Spirit as 'gentleness, who gives birth to many children', which are the virtues. Despite such impeccable sources, it remains controversial to call God mother, though the *language is increasingly common in feminist liturgies. There was scandal in 1982 in the Church of Scotland when a prayer by the liturgist Brian Wren was read in public, beginning: 'God our Mother, you give birth to all life, and love us to the uttermost.'

Hostility to placing female alongside male imagery for God may be connected with a desire to keep mothers in the home and away from public life and ecclesiastical ministry, attitudes at times bolstered up with extravagant praise for the mystique of motherhood. A classic example of someone who elevates motherhood in such a way, while adamantly opposing a *priestly role for women, is Pope *John Paul II, a man who lost his own mother when he was a young child, and so has reason for placing a particular value on the role of a mother. In his letter on women's dignity (Mulieris Dignitatem, 1988) he writes: 'Motherhood implies from the beginning a special openness to the new person: and this is precisely the woman's "part". In this openness, in conceiving and giving birth to a child, the woman "discovers herself through a sincere gift of self"…. It is commonly thought that women are more capable than men of paying attention to another person, and that motherhood develops this predisposition even more' (para. 18).

*Pastoral developments arising out of this 'high' view of motherhood may include a valuing of large *families as a sign of greater generosity, and a distrust of *contraception as a failure to be open to the transmission of life. An interesting pastoral evolution is the changing attitude of Christians towards the unmarried mother, from a figure of shame for bringing an illegitimate child into the world, to a figure of virtue for placing her child's right to life above her own freedom.

But arguably the 'highest' view of motherhood sees God as the supreme mother. While this has been an occasionally recurring strand of devotion, it has been kept in the background by the emphasis on Mary's motherhood, leaving the Godhead with an unduly male concentration of imagery that sits uneasily with the doctrine that God transcends sex. This language has had a profound effect on attitudes: fathers have modelled themselves on God, with a sense of *authority; mothers have modelled themselves on the private woman whose role was defined by her relationship to a public *man. But when God is imaged as mother, the balance of sex roles changes: women are no longer the second sex; mothers lead rather than support.

When seen as a reflection of God's own nature, motherhood becomes connected with innovative creativity, because human life originates in the mother's body; with powerful protection, because the womb is the safest of environments; with painful transformation, because the mother gives birth through labour; and with life-giving love because the mother feeds the child on herself at the breast. These qualities, intrinsic to the Christian concept of God, receive a womanly association when God is spoken of as mother. Women in turn discover the dignity of being made in the image of God. **Margaret Hebblethwaite**

Bynum, C. W., Jesus as Mother (1982).
Carr, A., and Schüssler Fiorenza, E. (eds.), Motherhood: Experience, Institution, Theology, Concilium, 206 (1989).

Mollenkott, V. R., *The Divine Feminine* (1984).

Newsom, C. A., and Ringe, S. H. (eds.), *The Women's Bible Commentary* (1992).

music as an aspect of Christian thought may be considered under three headings: as an abstract concept; as an element in *liturgy; and as a cultural phenomenon able both to draw on and to transmit a Christian ideology.

Abstract concept

The ancient Greeks were unusual in having a word—*mousike*—to describe the art in its totality. While it could and often did mean 'music' in roughly its modern sense, it ideally also embraced *poetry whether sung or spoken. For *Plato, its three constituents were 'harmony' (pitch-content), rhythm, and text (*logos*); other writers used different terms and included the dance, but essentially their views coincided. The word also came to be used without qualification as a subject of study rather than for the thing itself.

The Semitic languages have no exact equivalent to this word: Jewish and early Christian writers tended to discuss music more concretely in terms of the activity involved (singing or playing) or with reference to musical instruments. However, the Greek bible uses the adjective *mousikos* (Dan. 3: 5; Sir. 44: 5); and the early fathers were able to draw both on this tradition of Hellenized Judaism and (in some cases) ancient authors directly when discussing music. Pagan authors, for their part, were as likely to discuss song, dance, and instrumental playing as they were 'music' in the abstract.

Although there was clearly an overlap between Greek and non-Greek ideas about what we call music, it is important to bear in mind the terms in which arguments were conducted if early Christian writers are to be correctly understood. Outright condemnation of music is usually to be interpreted in reference to the theatres, banquets, and taverns of the pagan world, or else to the fables of pagan mythology (Tatian, Clement of Alexandria). Another line of thought was *allegorical. The rich *Temple liturgy was destroyed for ever in 70 AD, and it became an irrelevance, even an embarrassment, to Christian writers. The musical instruments described in the bible were often interpreted allegorically, for example by Clement of Alexandria (*Paidagogos*, 2. 4., on Ps. 150). Even song is often described in terms that are either clearly allegorical or at best ambiguous. *Paul enjoined the Ephesians and Colossians to 'sing in your hearts', though his wording does not exclude the possibility of real song (Eph. 5: 19–20; Col. 3: 16–17). The apostolic fathers, such as Clement of Rome and Ignatius of Antioch, often speak in a similar fashion. Jerome, commenting on the epistle to the Ephesians, advises those whose office is to make melody in the church: 'Sing to God, not with the voice, but with the heart'; even a *kakophonos* can be a good singer. 'Singing' is a spiritual activity going beyond the mechanics of 'making melody'.

The study of music, the proper province of the 'musician' according to late antique ideas, also exercised the minds of early Christian writers. For a writer like Cassiodorus (6th century), it could be justified by the need to understand the musical references in the bible. This theme resounds through the *Middle Ages, for example in Roger Bacon. Another, more productive idea was to understand in a Christian sense the Pythagorean notion of the universe as founded upon number. *Augustine, who began his *De musica* be-fore his baptism but completed it thereafter, taught that the numerically ordered world of heard music was a reflection of the potential inherent in God's *design, to which humans could attain through ascending levels of perception. While philosophical *myths of creation, such as that put forward by Plato in his *Timaeus*, could not survive literally in a Christian world, their basis in the idea of divine order had already been harmonized with biblical doctrine in such works as the Wisdom of Solomon (11: 20): 'thou hast arranged all things by measure and number and weight'.

One other element of pre-Christian thought retained its usefulness: the idea that different types of music had different effects on the *soul. For Plato music was to be judged according to its moral effect; not only the words but the musical style (*harmonia*) affected the hearer. In the Middle Ages and even later, this doctrine was often reduced to a formula by which each musical mode or scale was assigned a particular character. The tunes by Tallis given in Archbishop Parker's Psalter (1567), each in a different mode, are prefaced by a rhyme beginning 'The first is meek: devout to see. The second is sad: in majesty.' Christian moralists who have objected to music have usually done so on more general grounds: that it is at best a useless activity, at worst conducive to depravity, comments applied to both performers and their audiences. As an ornament of *worship music has been attacked on the grounds of its complexity, for example by the English Cistercian Aelred in the 12th century, by Pope John XXII in the 14th, and later by the Lollards, or because it obscures the words. This argument was put forward by both Catholic and Protestant theologians in the 16th century, and the most elaborate types of late medieval polyphony were indeed finally abandoned about then.

But if music has often been attacked, it has also had its warm defenders. They were hardly needed in the early Middle Ages, when plainsong of considerable intricacy was an inherent part of the liturgy and believed to have been composed in large part by Pope Gregory I. The defence of elaborate polyphony later on took the tacit form of ecclesiastical provision of the resources required to produce it. Much church music of this period was privately commissioned, but it still had to be consistent with prevailing norms. The anonymous *Praise of Musick* (1586) is a characteristically learned defence of music in Christian worship at a time of strong *Puritan sympathies. In the 18th century, when *evangelical churchmen took a 'low' view of music in worship, their high church counterparts published pamphlets and sermons such as Thomas Bisse's *Musick the Delight of the Sons of Men*, preached at the Three Choirs Festival at Hereford in 1726.

In the early Middle Ages the study of music lost its undesirable pagan connections, partly because of its association with Boethius (*c*.480–*c*.524), and partly because of its revival in the context of the church. From that time until the 17th century, music tended to be considered as either speculative (theoretical) or a practical discipline. The former restated the age-old Pythagorean principles of 'harmony', preserved for Latin readers by Boethius, while the latter served the needs of cantors and others who taught the practice of music in church. Although the *Reformation reduced the scope of musical education by eliminating the monasteries and many other foundations in which the subject had been taught, in Germany at least a thriving tradition of Latin-based teaching in the schools continued. An English choir-school education was less formal, but it provided, and still provides, a grounding in music in a clearly Christian context to set against the secular training that always existed (as apprenticeship, for example) but has predominated since the middle of the 17th century.

Liturgy

While singing was evidently practised in the church from the outset, it seems not to have been formalized before the 4th century, when religious toleration finally permitted the construction of solidly built basilicas and sanctuaries. The original context was not the synagogue, as was once thought, but the private house, where Jewish family worship took place and where the early Christians met for their own rites. The singing of a hymn at the Last Supper—possibly the *Hallel*, the group of psalms used at Passover—is a symbolic starting-point for music in Christian worship, although it cannot be followed up by exact parallels in the early Christian era. However, it seems clear that the *psalms continued to be sung, enhanced perhaps by new compositions such as the *Odes of Solomon* and the fragments of poetic material found in the NT.

The terms psalm, *hymn, and song seem to have been used interchangeably, and one must not look for precise distinctions at this stage. However, the 3rd-century fragment discovered at Oxyrynchus in Egypt of a Christian hymn with its music testifies to a diversification by that stage; it is written in Greek in an ancient metre with music in the ancient Greek notation. It may have been no more than an exercise or technical demonstration, but its words are paralleled by a hymn written by Clement of Alexandria and by those of Synesius of Cyrene (375–430). Other Christian hymns are rhythmically free and closer to psalmody: examples are the morning hymn 'Glory to God in the highest', originally in Greek, and the Latin *Te Deum* (part of which also survives in Greek). Latin writers also produced metrical hymns for singing (Ambrose, Hilary of Poitiers) or reading (Prudentius).

Hymn-singing must originally have been practised in informal contexts. Hymns of the Ambrosian type became part of the *monastic liturgy set out by St *Benedict (6th century), and by the early Middle Ages were an intrinsic feature of the divine office everywhere. In the eastern church hymnody played a still larger part. Psalmody was a much older feature of daily *prayer; under monastic influence it came to involve the recitation at least once a week of the complete psalter, though this was not always sung. Probably the simple melodic formulae vouched for by medieval sources from the 9th century, or something like them, were in use from an early date. With the psalms were sung short refrain-like interludes known in the west as antiphons and in the east as *troparia* or *stichera* (in the east the antiphon is a responsorial form complete in itself).

The earliest descriptions of the *eucharistic liturgy (for example by Justin Martyr, c.150) do not refer to psalmody or to singing of any kind. Possibly the *agapai* or communal (originally pre-eucharistic) meals, which died out in the 3rd century, included song. Singing became an intrinsic feature of the Eucharist in the 4th century, when responsorial psalmody, the forerunner of the gradual, is attested for the first time. In due course the items comprising the proper of the western mass appeared: introit, gradual, tract, alleluia, offertory, and communion. Non-Roman rites in the Latin west had comparable forms, while in the east there were fewer and their music seems less elaborate. We can get an idea of liturgical outlines from as early as the 4th century in the *Peregrinatio Egeriae*, a western abbess's description of her pilgrimage to Jerusalem and of the liturgy she encountered. However, her account of musical forms is imprecise, and we can learn little about them before the appearance in the 9th century of notated manuscripts in both east and west. Though the notation is not directly decipherable, the outlines are clear enough as regards the length and elaboration of the melodies. By that time, too, liturgical documents are far more plentiful and explicit.

The liturgy continued to be enhanced in both east and west by new material—in the east (including the non-Greek oriental rites) by hymns to adorn the office, and in the west, from the 9th century, by accretions known as sequences and tropes. The study of eastern liturgical music is complicated by the problems inherent in its transmission, both written and oral, and is not discussed here. In the west, many of the tropes by which certain forms were extended have also been lost except in outline. The majority of sequences (extensions to the alleluia of the mass) survive, however, because their texts remained in use for longer and early melodies were frequently set to new texts. An important new development, also of the 9th century, came with the addition of other parts to the existing liturgical melody: an ecclesiastical form of polyphony. At first all liturgical polyphony (the only kind surviving from before the 13th century) was based on an existing melody, but by the 12th century it was possible to write completely new music in parts.

The application of polyphony to liturgical purposes does not mean that the use of plainsong came to an end. On the contrary, it predominated until the Reformation, when in the *Protestant churches it was superseded by analogous forms in the vernacular (the *Lutheran church being the most traditional in this respect). In the Catholic church it long continued, in a somewhat curtailed form, though it has played a considerably smaller role since the introduction of the vernacular liturgy in the 1970s. Polyphony was originally a speciality of monastic foundations and a product of their enthusiasm for liturgical adornment. More austere orders such as the Cistercians did not use it. In the 12th century it passed to non-monastic churches—*cathedrals and parishes—now the product of the enthusiasm of paid singers and their clerical and lay patrons. The music of Notre Dame in Paris in the 12th and 13th centuries became famous all over Europe and was, given the technical resources of the period, of enormous elaboration. In the 14th century there was a reaction: John XXII produced a bull forbidding complexity in church music, and composers concentrated on more straightforward settings of the ordinary of the mass, with motets for ceremonial occasions.

Musical settings of the ordinary of the mass usually include the Kyrie eleison, Gloria, Credo, Sanctus, and Agnus Dei, though there are examples with fewer and more movements. There is no intrinsic reason why these texts collectively should have given rise to a single musical form, since apart from the Kyrie and Gloria they are not heard successively in the liturgy. At the earliest stage, composers simply set these texts individually and scribes copied them into separate manuscripts, though they sometimes brought settings of the separate movements together adventitiously. The *Messe de Nostre Dame* by Guillaume de Machaut (c.1300–77) is unique for its time in being considered by its composer as a coherent work, though unlike most later masses it is not unified by thematic material. Such unity was at first attained between pairs of movements, such as the Gloria and Credo, or Sanctus and Agnus Dei, though the scribes initially kept them separate. The strongest form of unification was through the adoption of the same plainsong tenor in each movement, and was first achieved in complete four- or five-movement cycles by the English composers Lionel Power and John Dunstable in the early 15th century.

By far the commonest method of unification in the 15th and 16th centuries was the adoption of the same pervading material throughout the mass, as we may now call this musical form. This material was not necessarily plainchant or even sacred in origin. The tenor parts of secular songs were often used as the basis of masses until the Council of *Trent tried to stop the practice, which continued, though more discreetly, for some time afterwards. A mass could also be based on existing sacred or secular polyphony, using some or all of the original voice-parts in various ways in the different movements. This method of composition fell into disuse after about 1600, though Claudio Monteverdi published an example, based on a motet by the early 16th-century composer Nicholas Gombert, in 1610. From that point it became usual to supply an instrumental accompaniment for liturgical music of all kinds—either a skeleton organ part (a bass with figures to indicate the chords) or a more elaborate accompaniment. In the 18th century a full orchestral accompaniment was permitted by an edict of 1746, and this led to the symphonic style cultivated especially by Haydn, Mozart, Beethoven, and Schubert, a tradition still maintained in the days of Anton Bruckner. But the tendency since the 18th century has been towards a greater simplicity in Catholic church music, as in Lutheran music, which with J. S. *Bach and his contemporaries had achieved a similar degree of elaboration.

In Germany the 19th-century Cecilian movement embraced the revival of 16th-century polyphony and a renewed cultivation of plainsong in its post-Tridentine form. But the restoration of the medieval chant tradition by the monks of Solesmes from the middle of the century came to inspire a new, modally inflected form of composition in the music of Fauré, Tournemire, Duruflé, and others, that for long represented an ideal in Catholic church music. The great legacy of the Protestant churches, on the other hand, has been the cultivation of congregational metrical psalmody and hymnody in the vernacular.

Victorian church music, largely unaffected by the plainchant revival, sought a new directness of appeal in both simple and more elaborate styles, leading often to sentimentality but on occasion to music that is both dignified and moving. The music of C. V. Stanford escapes any charge of sentimentality, but it was not until the later generation represented by Herbert Howells that a genuine renewal based on an expanded musical language could occur. Unfortunately the finest modern composers, British and otherwise, have written only a small number of works for regular liturgical use: Benjamin Britten's *Missa brevis* for boys' voices and organ is exceptional.

Cultural phenomenon

Many of the forms just discussed gave rise to concert music that is Christian in a more general sense. It will have a wholly or partially Christian content, and may be to a certain extent inspired by the liturgy, but will not have been composed with any thought of liturgical performance. In between come such works as Bach's Mass in B minor and Beethoven's *Missa solemnis*, which were intended for liturgical performance but never achieved it, at least in their composers' lifetime. The same is true of Mozart's C-minor Mass and his Requiem, both unfinished at his death. The Requiem in particular, as completed by his pupil Süssmayr, became a model for occasional or concert works like those of Berlioz, Verdi, and Dvořák. (The Requiem mass, cultivated as a musical form from the 15th century, omitted the Gloria and Credo but added various movements of the proper and sometimes additional movements at the end. Mozart and those who came after him, except for Fauré, usually included the *Dies irae*.) The mass and the Requiem have continued to inspire 20th-century composers: two striking British examples are Herbert Howells's *Missa Sabrinensis* (1954) and Britten's *War Requiem* (1962). The latter intersperses the liturgical texts with Wilfred Owen's war-poetry to create a challenging and at times disturbing work.

Another liturgical form to have inspired modern composers is the Passion. Originally this simply provided polyphonic music for the part of the *synagoga*, the parts of the text not assigned to Christ or the narrating evangelist, in the readings of Holy Week. A similar method was adopted by Heinrich Schütz in his four passions for Lutheran use. But already more elaborate schemes had been devised, and by the time of J. S. Bach the German Passion included a selection of hymns (the 'chorales') and a series of meditative texts set as recitatives and arias in addition to the passion narrative itself, which took the form of recitatives and short choruses. Modern composers have treated the passion material in various ways. While some have retained a liturgical or quasi-liturgical form, others, such as Penderecki's St Luke Passion, are essentially concert works.

Yet another liturgical form to have reached the concert-hall is the *Eastern Orthodox Vespers, set by both Tchaikovsky and Rachmaninov. These were intended for the liturgy itself, but their length and complexity, especially in the case of Rachmaninov, has limited their liturgical usefulness. The modern English composer John Tavener has been much influenced by Orthodox spirituality, as were others in the 20th century such as Stravinsky (*Symphony of Psalms*).

When music of this kind reaches the concert-hall it becomes assimilated to the oratorio and sacred cantata in their widest sense. The oratorio (originally Italian for an oratory or chapel) began as a kind of prayer-meeting under the aegis of Philip Neri in Rome, enlivened by spiritual songs known as *laude*. During the 17th century the term came to be applied to sacred works of various kinds, since they were originally performed in oratories founded by or similar to those founded by Neri. Many were dramatic in form, resembling an opera, but not acted. Composers in Italy from Carissimi to Vivaldi created a large number of such works, while in Germany comparable forms emerged under the same designation: these had a considerable influence on the development of the passion and other quasi-liturgical narrative forms (as represented for example by Schütz's *historiae* on the Resurrection and nativity). But the most far-reaching development occurred when Handel took up the form in England.

Handel was familiar with the German and Italian precedents, and had written an Italian oratorio himself, but he stumbled on the

English form by accident. He had composed *Esther* as a 'masque' for private performance but, stung by an unauthorized revival, revised it himself as a theatrical performance without scenery or action. The success of this encouraged him to write others, mostly dramatic in form but similarly unacted, though he did not immediately abandon Italian opera or other forms of choral music. Eventually he wrote fourteen sacred dramatic oratorios, together with a few secular examples and some non-dramatic religious works. The most successful of his oratorios was the non-dramatic *Messiah*, its texts drawn entirely from the bible: it has continued to be performed regularly, for example with the unusually large forces amassed for the Handel commemorations of 1784 and subsequent years. It influenced both Mozart, who reorchestrated it, and Haydn, whose *Creation* preserves much of the spirit of Handelian choral writing.

Oratorio in the wake of Handel has taken many different forms. It has tended to shed its dramatic structure, partly because of a more relaxed attitude to sacred subjects on the stage, for which oratorio had often provided a substitute, and partly because narrative and meditative elements have come to be an equally important part of its appeal. Elgar's *Dream of Gerontius* (1899–1900) is unusual in setting an imaginative dramatic poem by Cardinal *Newman in a way that recalls operatic methods without ever suggesting the stage. Much commoner in the 19th century was the biblical narrative, Mendelssohn's *St Paul* and *Elijah* being among the best of their kind. Brahms's *German Requiem* uses a selection of biblical texts to create a large-scale work of an essentially meditative nature.

Modern oratorio has drawn on a wider range of sources. In France, Gounod's *La Rédemption*, first heard in London *c*.1882, may be taken as the starting-point of a tradition leading to Messiaen's *La Transfiguration* (1969), in which the text is selected from the bible, the Roman missal, and Thomas *Aquinas. British oratorio since Elgar is represented by only a small number of significant works, some not explicitly Christian. Tippett's oratorios, *A Child of our Time* and *The Vision of St Augustine*, adopt an essentially humanistic framework, though the former has Christian overtones and the latter, a meditation on the perception of *time, takes as its starting-point a moment of spiritual intensity in Augustine's *Confessions*. More outwardly conventional, though they cannot conceal their composers' ambivalence, are Vaughan Williams's *Sancta Civitas*, based on the book of *Revelation, and Walton's *Belshazzar's Feast*, which draws on the book of *Daniel. Vaughan Williams, while actually omitting the Holy Name from his final sentence ('Amen, even so, come Lord'), does convey a sense of eternity, while Walton's work seems devoid of spirituality.

Large-scale choral works are but one aspect of an immense range of modern western music that to varying degrees expresses some form of Christian idealism. Hindemith's *Das Marienleben* (poems by Rilke) and Britten's *The Holy Sonnets of John Donne* are two outstanding examples of religious song-cycles, while Britten's church parables (*Curlew River*, *The Burning Fiery Furnace*, and *The Prodigal Son*), though not exclusively Christian or biblical in content, place his subject-matter in the context of the worshipping community.

How has it come about that Christianity, alone of world religions, has found expression in a wealth of sophisticated art-music impinging on and interacting with that of the secular sphere? To some extent the answer lies in the origins of western musical thought in the Carolingian scholarship of the 8th and 9th centuries. The Carolingian theorists set in train the processes that led first to an unambiguous notation of pitches, then to that of durations, and this in turn to the art of written composition. Initially these developments were the product of a Christian, and for the most part a monastic, milieu. The church held the monopoly of written composition (for even secular written music was largely the work of clerics) prior to the 16th century, by which time a vast heritage of compositional procedure had grown up. The hold of the church on the techniques and subject-matter of music weakened thereafter, but it has remained a powerful stimulus for both.

It is therefore the specifically western Christian context that has yielded this phenomenon, and only in modern times has Eastern Orthodoxy, for example, under western influence produced comparable artefacts. Similarly it is only fairly recently that an art-music inspired by a specifically Jewish liturgy and religious culture has grown up, for example in the work of Ernest Bloch and the technically radical Arnold Schoenberg, while Islam has not attempted a similar development. Needless to say these religions have long had their traditions of functional liturgical music, as have the eastern churches, but the growth of a religious art-music is bound up with western culture and its expansion into many other parts of the world. At the same time the simple forms of religious song have kept their place and have themselves developed through acculturation. The clearest example of this is in America, where from the music of the black slave population (itself profoundly affected by European missionary activity in Africa) there emerged the spiritual, the gospel-song, and the revivalist hymn, all of them *re*imported into the Europe where their musical essentials had originated. Modern western Christian music is indeed a transatlantic phenomenon and is represented across the entire range of sophistication on both sides of the ocean. There are, moreover, few parts of the world where an intrinsic connection between western music and Christianity would not be recognized, at least by the intelligentsia, even if not always welcomed.

If explanations, however provisional, can be found for the phenomenon of a Christian music and its expansion worldwide as an intrinsic part of the western musical heritage, it is harder to say what it is that music has contributed to Christianity. Theologians and philosophers have tended to regard music, if not as a dangerous pursuit, then at best as an attractive coating on the surface of the religious fabric. *Vatican II, it is true, goes beyond this, describing the musical tradition of the church as 'a treasure of inestimable value, greater even than that of any other art' because in combination with words 'it forms a necessary or integral part of solemn liturgy' (*Sacrosanctum Concilium*, 112, cited in *Catechism of the Catholic Church*, 1156). The *Catechism* goes on to quote Augustine's description of the emotional effects on him of the church music of his day (*Confessions*, 9. 6) without however referring to his subsequent reservations (ibid. 10. 33).

But these comments strive only to validate music—of an appropriate kind, presumably, though nothing is said about what that might be—in a liturgical context. Catholic theology is brought into line with long-standing Protestant opinion in declaring music to be above all the province of the assembly of the faithful. Is it possible nevertheless to argue that music *per se* is capable of expressing religious truth? If it is, then the question might be dealt with at either the emotional or the intellectual level. In the case of the former it seems axiomatic that a religious response must be dependent on verbal content. We may be moved to tears by any music, sacred, secular, or instrumental; it is on a narrow view the verbal element alone, or on a broader view the particular way in which it and the musical are combined, that qualifies our emotion as religious or otherwise. Such a response, moreover, is highly subjective: the same combinations of words and music may leave another person completely unaffected.

At an intellectual level it could be argued that music by its very nature stands in some kind of relation to absolute (and hence, from the Christian perspective, religious) *truth. Its composition is inherently a form of mathematics; that is to say, its composition represents a selection, arbitrary in itself, from a series of possibilities of universal applicability. While this selection is normally conditioned by the inherited preconceptions that determine style, and while its ideal form is usually somewhat disguised by the exigencies of performance, it can nevertheless be evaluated with reference to such criteria as order, coherence, appropriateness to its context—all of them representative of the moral rightness that in Christian thought is intrinsic to created being. The imperfections of human music are due to the fact that nature, including especially humanity, has fallen from grace; composition and performance, however, in striving for perfection are a reflection of humanity's ultimate and God-centred goal. Such a conclusion is entirely consistent with the neo-Pythagoreanism espoused by Augustine in his search for absolute truth.   **John Caldwell**

Blume, F., *Protestant Church Music: A History* (1975).

Brown, H. M., *Music in the Renaissance* (1976).

Grout, D. J., *A History of Western Music*, rev. C. Palisca (1996).

Hiley, D., *Western Plainchant: A Handbook* (1993).

le Huray, P., *Music and the Reformation in England 1549–1660*, 2nd edn. (1978).

McKinnon, J., *Music in Early Christian Literature* (1987).

Schueller, H. M., *The Idea of Music* (1988).

Smither, H. E., *A History of the Oratorio* (3 vols.; 1977–87).

Strunk, O., *Source Readings in Music History* (1950), new edn. in 5 vols. (1981). See especially vol. i for early Christian material.

Temperley, N., *The Music of the English Parish Church* (2 vols.; 1979).

Yudkin, J., *Music in Medieval Europe* (1989).

mystery plays. This term has popularly been used to cover all types of vernacular medieval religious drama: biblical and *apocryphal narratives, *allegorical debates, *saints' lives, narratives of saints' posthumous *miracles or of miracles of the sacrament. It is perhaps most usefully restricted to the biblical and apocryphal narratives, though the French use of *mystère* covers saints' lives as well.

Medieval religious drama has had two lives, one ending in the 16th or 17th century, the second starting in the 20th. Some plays spanned the gap, adapting to changes of secular attitude or religious belief. Some simply survived. The Oberammergau Passion Play was first performed in 1634 and the Assumption Play from Elche in Southern Spain has run, apparently without a break, since the late *Middle Ages. Though in different parts of Europe there are vernacular plays from the 12th and 13th centuries (those from the neighbourhood of Arras, for example), the major flowering of religious drama was in the 15th and 16th centuries. It was mainly in the hands of the urban middle class, produced for the honour of God and the city, and telling the stories of the bible and the saints or depicting the struggle of good and evil for the soul of man. Though most plays were almost certainly written by clerics, the extent and nature of the control exercised by the church varied from place to place. In York, for example, the play regularly produced on Corpus Christi Day was completely in the hands of the civic authorities.

For an audience the majority of whom were ignorant of Latin and therefore had little understanding of the *liturgy and no access to theological writing or the Latin bible, the plays were a major source of understanding of the Christian way of life. Their emphasis is not usually on the exploration of complex theological ideas but on retelling the story of redemption in humanly understandable terms, ascribing human motivation and emotions to biblical characters. When there is explication, it is often of *typological links between OT and NT or of the significance of *prophecies or of the meaning of the narrative. The French plays often do this at some length in prologues to plays or to days of performance, the English in brief expositions by doctors or expositors.

Through drama, the bible and the lives of the saints were woven into the fabric of everyday life, not only by where it was performed (city street or square transformed into the streets of Jerusalem or Bethlehem) but also by who organized the performance (town chambers of rhetoric in the Netherlands, craft guilds in England). Sometimes guilds or fraternities were set up specifically for the production of a play (the Pater Noster Guild at York, or, on a different scale, the Confraternité de la Passion in Paris). Involvement in the plays, either as audience or performers, must have created an intimacy with events and characters of the bible or with the saints of a kind that was encouraged in meditation and desired by the pious *laity, as the wide membership of religious fraternities bears witness.

The situation altered in most of Europe in the 16th century. In areas affected by the Protestant *Reformation the plays were eventually brought to an end but often not until late in the century, their emphasis upon straight narrative rather than doctrinal matters perhaps prolonging their lives. But even the attitude of Protestant reformers to religious drama was not universally hostile. In areas that remained Catholic, plays often continued into the 17th century, occasionally even later. Some new ones were created. The text of the Oberammergau play was originally compiled from the 15th-century Augsburg Passion Play but it and its staging have been adapted to suit changing circumstances. The current text is based on one written for the 1810 performance; the most recent revisions were to remove anti-Jewish content. In the 20th century, revivals joined survivals in many places.

In England there were problems. Whereas in the Middle Ages presenting God visibly on stage was not seen as derogatory, now it was considered blasphemous. It was not until 1951 that productions of the York and Chester plays included the later life of Christ. Besides acknowledging the theatrical power of the plays, these productions expressed a belief in the spiritual power of drama. There have been numerous revivals, scholarly and popular, in Europe and America. In England, side by side with the professional theatre's adopting of the mystery plays has gone their nationwide appearance as community plays. What started life as community drama dedicated to religion has ended as religious drama celebrating the community; perhaps the two already coexisted in the Middle Ages.   **Peter Meredith**

Elliott, J. R., Jr., *Playing God: Medieval Mysteries on the Modern Stage* (1989).

Meredith, P., *et al.*, 'Medieval Drama in Europe', in M. Banham (ed.), *The Cambridge Guide to Theatre* (1995).

Muir, L. R., *The Biblical Drama of Medieval Europe* (1995).

mysticism.

It is arguable that there is no such thing as mysticism. At any rate it is the view of the eminent historian of Western mysticism, Bernard McGinn, that 'No mystics (at least before the 20th century) believed in or practised "mysticism".' And though the history of the abstract noun 'mysticism' has yet to be written, there is evidence that in at least one of its contemporary meanings the term is very recent, perhaps entering into usage no earlier than the late 19th century, and then as a term of art within an academic project of comparative *religion.

The typically late 19th- and early 20th-century search for a common element possessed by all the world religions powerfully motivated an argument that runs in outline as follows: though there must be something in common between all religions by virtue of which they come to be recognized *as* religions, that common core cannot consist in such historically and culturally relative elements as *worship, ritual, *symbolism, or doctrine—nor even in theism itself, not all religions being explicitly theistic in belief. For ritual, symbolism, doctrine, and belief-statement are all culturally contingent for the same, general, reason: they all depend for their expression on *language, at least in its broadest sense of a public medium of expression, and all language embodies the particularities of a cultural tradition. Consequently, the common core weaving through the culturally manifold phenomena of the great religious traditions—from Catholic Christianity to Tantric Buddhism—must consist in something not in the same way linguistically dependent, therefore in something *pre*-linguistic (or possibly *post*-linguistic), in some *experience* that cuts either below or above the cultural conditioning that comes with language. 'Mysticism', therefore, is the common core of religiosity constituting world religions *as* religious; it alone meets the condition required, exhibiting the features of an absolute, non-culturally conditioned experience.

Such was the view of William *James, who decisively influenced the 20th-century view of what mysticism consists in. And concerning this view, three things should be noted. First, it is essentially a *theoretician's* view of mysticism. For the term gets its meaning from within a theoretical hypothesis, namely that there is some common core that unites all world religions as religions. It is, moreover, the view of a theoretician with a *philosophical* axe to grind, for the hypothesis depends for its explanatory power on the empiricist philosophical proposition, itself highly contentious, that it makes sense to *talk as if* there are experiences which *ex hypothesi* cannot be *spoken about*.

Secondly, it is a highly abstract view of mysticism, relying not on what practitioners of 'mysticism' say about what they practise—because, again, what they say is culturally conditioned—rather it identifies what they practise in terms that *none* of them recognize. Hence, thirdly, what the theoreticians identify as 'mysticism' is, as McGinn says, nothing which any 'mystic' actually ever practised as thus identified.

More recently this 'experientialist' understanding of mysticism has declined in popularity (James and Stace being its best known proponents in the 20th century) and has long been opposed by the 'constructivists' (such as Katz), who take the view that no common definition of mysticism can be found in any primary datum of 'mystical experience', since experience itself, mystical or otherwise, is necessarily mediated by language, and therefore by historically and culturally specific forms from which it can never be isolated. None the less, there has been common ground in most 20th-century discussions of mysticism in the supposition that even if there is no philosophically definable core of mystical experience, there is a tradition of literature and practice to debate philosophically about, continuous and coherent enough to be worth naming by the common name 'mysticism'. And it is time to ask, at the very least in the name of the western Christian mystical tradition, whether the term is not rather more misleading than helpful even in the identification of a historically continuous reality.

Witness, first, the feelings of arbitrariness aroused by any attempt to *define* 'mysticism' in the western tradition, a sense of unease which is made particularly acute, secondly, by any attempted *canon* of 'mystics'. 'Was St Augustine a mystic?' asks Cuthbert Butler. 'What makes you ask?' one is inclined to reply, since *Augustine himself had no need of an answer, possessing as he did no terms for understanding the question. And problems of definition multiply when one considers the sheer variety of historical phenomena called 'mystical'. In composing a canon of mystics, even within the traditions of the Christian west, any criteria have their price in counter-intuitive results. If we attend to principally *experiential* criteria of the 'mystical' we will readily pick up the signs of it in the 'love' mysticisms of Bernard of Clairvaux, the proponents of the *Braut-mystik* (Bridal mysticism) of the 13th and 14th centuries, particularly the women, Mechtild von Magdeburg, Hadewijch, Gertrude of Helfta; but we will then have to downplay the credentials of Pseudo-*Dionysius, Meister Eckhart, and the Rhineland school, who, however, will come back into the picture, together with Marguerite Porete, the author of the *Cloud of Unknowing*, and Nicholas of Cusa, if we attend to a criterion of 'negative' or 'apophatic' theology. Again, a criterion which gave prominence to visionary phenomena would undoubtedly include *Hildegard of Bingen, Birgitta of Sweden, *Julian of Norwich, or perhaps *Teresa of Avila, but would leave little room for any of the others. Finally, any criterion which, as in some Protestant historiography, associated 'mysticism' with the marginal or with the revolt of the individual against church authoritarianism would remove nearly every name from every canon determined on *any* other criterion.

The problem is general and not trivial. General, because whatever account *we* give of mysticism, however justified by *our* explanatory agendas, 'no mystic ever practised mysticism'. In order to be what they were, these Christians had no need of the term 'mysticism' to describe it. Not trivial: for the reason why no mystics ever saw themselves as 'practising mysticism' was that they saw themselves rather more simply as practising Christianity.

Short of the purely negative and deconstructive solution of abandoning the word as useless and misleading, the most practical way forward is to recognize just *how* misleading the word is, being as it is so bound up with contemporary theoretical agendas and practical preoccupations. On the other hand, there is positive merit in a historical reconstruction of the Christian theological and practical traditions which have led to those present theoretical presuppositions, from the standpoint of which we look back on that tradition and wish to name it 'mystical'—even if that term is a misleading descriptor of it. And in that searching of the historical tradition it is necessary to go back as far as the earliest attempts to articulate the theological bases of the Christian way of life itself.

In western Christianity, two texts from the scriptures seem to be a principal source for the traditions of Christian practice, *prayer, and theology which we call 'mystical': 'It is no longer I who live', says Paul (Gal. 2: 20), 'but Christ who lives in me.' And in 1 John 3: 2 we find, 'Beloved, we are God's children now; it does not yet appear what we shall be, but we know that when he appears we shall be like him, for we shall see him as he is.' These two themes dominate the western Christian mystical tradition: Paul's, of an imitation of Christ such as will end in a complete identity of action and will and life between the Christ and the soul; and John's, of the perfect final vision of God, a vision which ultimately transforms the self into the likeness of God, though here, pre-mortem, it can only be partial and incomplete, achieved 'in a glass darkly'. The emphases vary, as indeed Paul and John differ: for Gregory of Nyssa, Pseudo-Diony-sius, or Meister Eckhart the emphasis is most strongly on the Johannine aspiration to the transforming vision of God, achieved in the presence of a *light so excessive as to produce in the mind a 'brilliant darkness' of unknowing; for Bernard of Clairvaux, Bona-venture, or Julian of Norwich, the emphasis is more Christocentri-cally Pauline, the language borrowing more from the affective metaphors of touch and taste than the visual and cognitive meta-phors of light and darkness. Often both emphases are found to-gether, as in *John of the Cross, who, much influenced as he was by the negative theology of the Dionysian apophatic tradition (indeed, he is probably best known for his imagery of the 'dark nights of the soul'), was as enthusiastic as Bernard of Clairvaux for the thorough-ly carnal, erotic possibilities in the imagery of the *Song of Songs.

If further biblical precedents are sought for this distinctive lan-guage of the Christian mystical tradition, they are found most sig-nificantly in two texts of the Hebrew Scriptures: the narrative of *Moses' ascent of Mount Sinai into the cloud where he meets God, seeing him only 'from behind, for none may see my face and live' (Exod. 33: 20), and in the 'hot and carnal poem' (as a 17th-century Scots divine primly called it) of the Song of Songs. Gregory of Nyssa exploited both texts, Pseudo-Dionysius fused them with late-Plato-nist thought, and in the 9th century John Eriugena transmitted an already established eastern Christian mystical theology to an initial-ly unreceptive western Christendom through his Latin translations of Dionysius and of the commentaries on Dionysius of Maximus the Confessor. By the 12th century, however, the stage was set for those historical and literary phenomena that we now call mysti-cism, the medieval forms of which flourished in the four centuries from Hugh of St Victor to John of the Cross. Whether or not anything is gained or lost by so naming them, there is no doubt that the phenomena so named do constitute a continuous, con-sciously acknowledged tradition.

What characterizes it? First, a complex of imagery, highly depend-ent on these biblical and philosophical sources. Central is imagery of clouds and darkness encountered in the meeting with God, im-agery which in Gregory of Nyssa's Life of Moses fuses elements of Moses' ascent of Mount Sinai with others derived from *Plato's allegory of the mind's ascent from the illusions of the cave to philosophical contemplation of the sun, in Republic, 7. There is

imagery of an ascent to *God driven by the erotic urges to union of the soul with God so amply allegorized in the medieval com-mentary on the Song of Songs, as represented by Bernard of Clair-vaux's eighty-six Sermons on the Song of Songs in the 12th century and by John of the Cross's 16th-century Spiritual Canticle. Dependent on this heavily carnal eroticism is a powerful imagery of the soul's ultimate union in identity with God—Catherine of Genoa's 'I am God' is typical of a certain tradition, though quite how, or how clearly, this 'autotheism' is reconciled with the distinction between creator and creature is a much-contended question, especially in the late Middle Ages. And there is imagery of interiority, this time derived very largely from Augustine's reception of Plotinus' thought, particularly in Confessions and in On the Trinity, generating a model narrative of the Christian soul's ascent to God as a journey of inwardness—typified by Bonaventure's The Journey of the Soul into God. Light and darkness, union with God in erotic ecstasy, ascent to inwardness, these are the defining metaphors of the medi-eval mystical tradition that have left their mark permanently on the western Christian spiritual consciousness, equally in literature and practice. They are discovered fully fledged as metaphors still in later secondary traditions, as in the English poets *Donne, Herbert, and Crashaw and into the late flourishing of the tradition at the end of the 19th and the early years of the 20th century in *Teresa of Lisieux, Elizabeth of the Trinity, and in Simone *Weil. Even today this imagery remains the vernacular of much popular piety and *spirituality, Christian and neo-pagan alike.

Secondly, that tradition is characterized at a secondary level by *paradox. Before God, language breaks down. Much 'mystical' writing is therefore stylistically characterized by a deliberate ex-ploitation of the self-cancelling utterance—the presence of God is a light excessive, dazzling the mind and so is a 'brilliant darkness' as Dionysius puts it; Jesus is our mother and he saves us, as Julian of Norwich says, exploiting gender ambiguities in unselfconscious freedom of spirit; 'you are more within me than I am to myself', as Augustine says in Confessions, very nearly summarizing the whole tradition in one phrase. At this secondary level, the medieval mystical tradition reveals a consciousness of language straining up to the very boundaries of sense itself, attempting to reveal in lan-guage the unknowable and unsayable reality that lies beyond it: for the language of mysticism reaches God precisely at the point where it fails. This conception of theology as teetering on the edge of language, secure as theology only in its insecurity as language, of theology as 'mystical' and 'mysticism' as theology, has so many, at least superficial, resonances with contemporary projects of decon-struction that it hardly surprising that Jacques Derrida himself should feel compelled to consider how his position differs from that of the 'negative theologians' on the matter. For one might very well have supposed it does not.

Thirdly, the tradition is characterized—at any rate until the late Middle Ages—by its exotericism. The common tradition represent-ed the journey to complete union with God as but the ordinary way of following Christ; and the great spiritual masters conceived of their descriptions both of the journey itself and of its outcome in the ecstatic vision of and union with the *Trinity, as but glosses on the Johannine and Pauline texts earlier cited. It was Eckhart, after all, commonly regarded as the most dauntingly esoteric writer of the whole tradition, who was perhaps the clearest of all in insisting that there are no *two* ways about it, an ordinary and a mystical, but only one, Christ; hence, 'those who seek God in ways will find ways and lose God'. And as to that seminal figure, Pseudo-Dionysius, Andrew Louth has pointed out that his elaborate construction of hierarchical ladders of ascent to God are not meant, as they are often read in the west, as a metaphor of the lone individual's journey to God (Plotinus' 'flight of the alone to the alone' is a distinctly *pagan* alternative) but as a theological reconstruction of the phases of the common eucharistic celebration. And that other principal source, Augustine, was not read in the classical medieval period as he is often now read, as a proto-existentialist, for medieval authorities took more from his emphasis on the unity of Christians in the community of charity, than in the personal agonizings of his *Confessions*.

But in the transition from the great medieval period of 'mystical theology' to the modern phenomenon of 'mysticism', much of this changes. Michel *de Certeau has made much of the proposition that it is the 16th-century Carmelites, John of the Cross and Teresa of Avila, who stand at the parting of the ways between the late medieval and early modern conceptions of the mystical, though even if he is right, the tendencies found in late 16th-century mystical writing are clearly exhibited in the late 14th and early 15th centuries. For de Certeau, in any case, the shift is revolutionary and is shown in the sharp distinction he finds in John of the Cross between the 'self of experience' and the 'self of theory', the former being expressed in the vividly carnal, intensely personal eroticism of the poetry, the latter in the detached, impersonal, and objective prose theological expositions that he compiled on the poems.

Be that as it may, the history of mysticism within the Catholic traditions—traditions, because many would find genuine developments of the ancient mystical traditions in the poetry of George Herbert and the prose of the *Caroline Divines Jeremy Taylor and William Law, all Anglicans—shows an increasing tendency to identify mysticism with the personal, experiential, and ineffable, and to separate out a 'mystic way' equally from the development of the theological disciplines and from the common life of Christians. Thus did the practice of 'mysticism' in the 18th and 19th centuries increasingly lend itself to the theoretical constructions placed upon it by William James and, thereby, to the comparativist interests of 19th-century *anthropologists.

Late 20th-century reflection upon 'mysticism' revealed different, often conflicting, theoretical and practical preoccupations. On the one hand, a kind of inter-faith ecumenism led some to seek points of contact particularly between 14th-century European mystical writings and eastern models (as between Meister Eckhart or the *Cloud of Unknowing* and Zen Buddhism), or, more generally, between the parallel eroticisms of eastern and western spiritualities. On the other hand, 'constructivists' on philosophical grounds and historiographers of the Middle Ages on methodological grounds, seemed equally set to deny the possibility of any such ecumenical project, as calculated to produce just another 'third' phenomenon, unrooted in either religio-cultural tradition. It is a paradox that just as there seems to be an enormous revival of interest in 'the mystical' we seem least well equipped conceptually and philosophically to say what 'the mystical' is.   **Denys Turner**

de Certeau, Michel, *The Mystic Fable* (1992).

James, William, *The Varieties of Religious Experience* (1902).

Katz, Stephen, *Mysticism and Philosophical Analysis* (1978).

Louth, A., *The Origins of the Christian Mystical Tradition* (1981).

McGinn, B., *The Presence of God: A History of Western Mysticism*, i. *The Foundations of Mysticism* (1991); ii. *The Development of Mysticism* (1993).

Stace, W. T., *Mysticism and Philosophy* (1961).

Turner, Denys, *The Darkness of God* (1995).

myth. The unequivocal statement in 1 Timothy 4: 7, 'Have nothing to do with profane myths and old wives' tales', might seem to put an end to any further discussion of the matter in Christian circles. As so often, however, it depends how the word 'myth' is understood. In this verse, 'myth' translates, and derives from, the Greek *mythos*. This originally meant simply a word, but then came to be applied to stories, in particular those involving the Olympian gods. By the time the NT came to be written, Greek philosophers, in particular the Sophists, had already turned against these immoral tales of only-too-fallible beings, either rejecting them outright or reading them as allegories of philosophical monotheism. The NT suspicion of myths is in keeping with wider cultural trends, though given a fiercer edge by Jewish hostility to idolatry. The association of 'myth' with fabricated and fanciful stories which are at best the product of ignorance but often deliberately deceptive has a long pedigree. For many centuries, Christian thinkers agreed in dismissing pagan mythology as human folly, the superstitious divinization of ancient heroes, although some went further in detecting demonic influences at work.

It was not until the late 18th and 19th centuries that a new understanding of myth took hold, although this was to some extent anticipated in the work of Giovanni Battista Vico (1668–1744). The change was induced by a new engagement with other cultures as Europe expanded its colonies and the Levant opened up to western scholars. Crucial elements were the encounter with Sanskrit which opened a door into the Vedic traditions and the discovery and decipherment of the literatures of ancient Egypt and Mesopotamia. These made scholars aware of the pervasiveness of myth in human cultures and the striking points of correspondence to be found. Put in this context, the biblical texts began to seem less singular and claims for their uniqueness had to be reformulated.

*Enlightenment scholars, including Hume, saw myth as one explanation of scientific and other puzzles that arose from, and was appropriate to, the infancy of the human race. The German philosopher Schelling (1775–1854) was particularly important in the development of the contrasting *Romantic idea that myths were not just bad science or bad history but were the valid expression of the struggle between the rational and the irrational in the human psyche, which in turn formed humanity's deepest intuitive knowledge of the divine. Such ideas fuelled a fascination with Europe's own legacy of folktale and the Norse, Germanic, and Celtic heritage.

From this point of view, it came to seem almost inevitable that Israel's scriptures would contain mythical elements, which, as in other traditions, had grown up through oral transmission and would reflect themes in common with other cultures. Such topics as the creation of man and woman from the earth, a universal flood, and the dying and rising son of a god, were widely distributed motifs. Some students of myth expressly used these arguments to discredit Christianity's claims to a special *revelation, and, in more sinister fashion, argued for a purging of alien Semitic elements from European culture in favour of a return to the old heroic virtues of the Germanic tradition.

In both OT and NT studies, the acceptance of the mythical nature of key narratives gave Christian thinkers a way to sidestep the assaults of science and historiography on the bible's literal historical truth. For *liberal Protestant theology, narratives whose literal sense was historically or scientifically inaccurate could be defended as truthful without resort being made to what were seen as the discredited techniques of allegorical interpretation. Myth could be claimed to represent a deeper order of insight and to be a form more suited to the communication of spiritual insights than historical accounts. Alternatively, mythical material could be set aside as accommodated to a more primitive level of human thought which too often was crudely equated with Judaism. Either strategy of defence, however, was anathema to conservative thinkers for whom any equivocation over the historicity of scripture was an assault on its revealed authority. Battle lines were drawn which still divide Christians.

In the 1790s Eichhorn and Gabler sought to recover the historical core behind biblical narratives by identifying and then setting aside mythical material. Others, however, for instance De Wette (1780–1849), saw this as too reductive and attempted to discover the symbolic expressiveness of the mythical elements. Yet others denied that the bible contained any purely mythical material, often on the basis of a definition of myth that saw it as intrinsically polytheistic. What it did contain were reworkings of mythic elements, many of which were traced to sometimes overstated Babylonian origins. Genesis 1–11, however, with its tales of interactions between God and humans, its concern with origins and aetiologies and its setting in remote time and places fits wider definitions of myth. The Babylonian story of creation that involved a battle between Marduk and Tiamat, the sea goddess, is echoed in passages in the Psalms and Isaiah where God is praised for his conquest of the sea, a motif that perhaps can be glimpsed in the presence of the waters at the beginning of Gen. 1. Yet many of these comparative efforts, most influentially in the works of J. G. Frazer such as the *Golden Bough* and *Folklore in the Old Testament*, while intriguing, depended on rather tendentious readings of the evidence.

If *anthropological studies proved methodologically difficult enough in relation to contemporary societies, trying to recreate the thought-world of ancient societies proved even more difficult. The prominent 20th-century French anthropologist Claude Lévi-

Strauss pioneered the widely influential structuralist interpretation of myths as attempts to mediate the irreduceable contradictions apparent in any culture's account of the world. He was, however, highly suspicious of the application of his theories to such consciously reworked texts as the bible. The attempts of his follower Sir Edmund Leach to carry out such readings of Gen. 1–3 and the Solomon narratives were, however, suggestive, even if they may have raised as many questions as they answered.

Similar approaches were applied to the rather different material of the NT, which represents a much more compressed and more consciously literary development. The work of D. F. Strauss (1808–74) can be seen in this light and the various subsequent *quests for the historical Jesus have had to wrestle with the ahistorical and mythical elements of the NT accounts. The best known contribution to this debate is that of *Bultmann, whose project of *demythologization first set out in his essay 'The New Testament and Mythology' offered a radical solution and sparked a heated debate.

In theological circles, the rather different approaches of Freud and *Jung to myth have also become part of the argument. Jung's theory of archetypes leads to the view that the creation of myth is a unifying factor underlying all human religious expression. Christianity can be interpreted as one culturally specific variant of a universal human phenomenon, no more nor less true than any other. Freud's scepticism over *religion was greater, but his development of the idea that myths may be expressions of the repressed conflicts of the psyche and of societies have helped to alert scholars to the close but complex links between mythology and ideology (see PSYCHOLOGY). The work of Paul *Ricœur represents a Christian response to these, as he draws attention to the intrinsic importance of *symbol and myth which in his words 'give rise to thought', rather than being the accidental vehicle in which abstract thought is communicated.

The word 'myth' can still act as a red rag to a bull in Christian circles. To continue to set myth and truth in opposition to each other seems to some Christian thinkers entirely to miss the point of how myth operates. Others would see it as crucial on any definition of myth. The argument remains unresolved.

See also RELIGIOUS LANGUAGE; SOCIAL SCIENCES.

Hugh S. Pyper

Bartsch, H. W. (ed.), *Kerygma and Myth*, ET (1953).
Batto, B., *Slaying the Dragon: Myth-making in the Biblical Tradition* (1992).
Rogerson, J., *Myth in Old Testament Interpretation* (1974).
Strenski, I., *Four Theories of Myth in Twentieth-Century History* (1987).

nationalism. The retention of the Hebrew Scriptures within the Christian bible had *political consequences that could not have been anticipated. They provided a powerful precedent for what can be called a national state grounded in religion and, as such, blessed especially by God. The NT had a less obvious political message. It related to people who lacked political power, while the story of the OT centred upon people who sought or possessed such power—*Moses and Joshua, *David and *Solomon.

It is true that when Christians came to power in the 4th century with the triumph of *Constantine, they entered into an imperial polity very different from that of *Israel and endeavoured to consecrate it. It seemed consonant with NT ideals of universality. The Roman Empire and its successors, in the east Byzantium, in the west the Holy Roman Empire of the Middle Ages (the latter both tied to and in tension with papal monarchy), all suggested an ideal Christian political order that was supranational and universalist. Nevertheless, the OT model has often proved the more potent, as well as the more practicable. It was natural for any small Christian state to apply to itself the lessons of Israelite history, to see misfortune in terms of divine punishment, prosperity as proof of divine protection, and to appeal to such 'nationalist' *apocryphal biblical works as the book of Judith to encourage people to resist their enemies. The deep Christian inclination to *translate the bible into a vernacular and to add to that a larger vernacular literature helped establish stable, language-based national identities, a process seen early at work in *Ethiopia and Anglo-Saxon England.

The Israelite sense of being a uniquely chosen nation was little by little transferred to one or another Christian nation from Russia to Portugal. For Joan of Arc, 'all those who fight against the holy kingdom of France fight against the Lord Jesus'; for *Milton, the English were 'a nation chosen before any other'. For each the claim to be a chosen nation had a highly religious connotation: Catholic and monarchical for the one, Protestant and parliamentary for the other. The latter was carried across the Atlantic to shape the political identity of New England. While a vernacularized Christianity easily builds up this sense of national identity, the initial impetus is generally a defensive one. Nationalism springs from a sense that one's cultural, linguistic, or ethnic tradition is imperilled; justified as the desire to defend this may be, the consequence can be to turn national identity, including a highly selective, even mythical, self-history, into an absolute value transcending all others. Once this

has happened, nationalism easily turns aggressive, justifying itself in terms of past grievances, real or imaginary, in pursuit of a 'greater' nation-state at the expense of any other people. While the massacres in the book of Joshua inflicted on the inhabitants of Canaan by the incoming Israelites may, in terms of history, never have happened, in terms of literature, myth, even religious justification, they provide a model for genocide.

Post-Reformation *Protestantism tended, in some of its forms, to glorify both state and nation uncritically. None more so than the English. Thomas *More's appeal against the sovereignty of king in parliament to determine even the nature of the church represented the seemingly archaic voice of a universalist political outlook, centred upon the pope, against the triumph of the nation-state: 'For this one kingdom I have all other Christian realms'—an essentially unacceptable argument for the nationalist. Yet the *French and *Spanish Catholic traditions turned hardly less nationalist. The tendency was common to all the major traditions. While the Protestant free churches rejected ecclesiastical subordination to the nation, they too could be beguiled, as many British Free Churchmen were in the First World War, by a highly simplistic religious nationalism. Only since the 1930s, when faced with National Socialism and its support by the 'German Christian' movement which for a time carried away much of the German Protestant world, has the Christian community developed a more critical evaluation of nationalist rhetoric, recognizing how remote it is from the NT spirit. This was already noticeable at the 1937 *ecumenical Oxford Conference on Church, Community, and State. Nationalism continues to shape attitudes towards the relationship between church and society particularly in many *Eastern Orthodox communities, as was seen to devastating effect in Serb propaganda during the attempted genocide of the Bosnian Muslim population in the early 1990s and later in Kosovo.

The sovereign state and the nation are distinguishable but have tended to coalesce into the sovereign nation-state, consecrated by the post-First World War Versailles Settlement and the cause of numerous 20th-century disasters. While Christianity has no single formula for the shaping of the state, its contribution to the development of national consciousness was all the same an expression deeply characteristic of the way it relates to society, a way very different from that of *Islam. If Christianity's great social and cultural strength is its ability to handle diversity, this very strength, when linked with the temptation to transfer the OT Israel model to a particular Christian people, contributed considerably to the irrational and destructive nationalisms that have damaged the modern world.   **Adrian Hastings**

Dawson, Christopher, *The Judgement of the Nations* (1943).

Hastings, A., *The Construction of Nationhood: Ethnicity, Religion and Nationalism* (1997).

—— 'Special Peoples', *Nations and Nationalism*, 5/3 (1999), 381–96.

Mews, Stuart (ed.), *Religion and National Identity* (1982).

O'Brien, Conor Cruise, *God Land: Reflections on Religion and Nationalism* (1988).

Sells, Michael, *The Bridge Betrayed: Religion and Genocide in Bosnia* (1996).

natural law.

The concept of natural law may be *Aristotle's principal legacy to Christian thought but it was *Aquinas who set out its character in theological terms and his teaching has dominated natural law thinking ever since. Nothing may provide the fault line between classical Catholic and Protestant approaches to *ethical theory better than the former's insistence upon natural law and its rejection or belittlement by the latter.

Aquinas defines natural law as a participation in the eternal law by rational creatures (*ST* I-II q. 91 a. 2). It signifies the very functioning of a person's practical *reason with its inbuilt commitment to seeking good and avoiding *evil. In this the intellect is enlightened by the divine law which it can reject but not escape. From this first inbuilt quest of the good follow other primary principles of natural law relating to *truth, *justice, and the like. We do not discover the existence of natural law as an inference from the study of our bodily functions and needs, although such study undoubtedly helps identify secondary principles and conclusions. The root idea of natural law is that we, being rational, are also inherently moral beings, and that the exercise of moral judgement reflects what *God has made us, and necessarily opens to us an awareness of divine law, whether or not we recognize it as such.

In its primary principles, natural law is absolutely immutable, but not so in its secondary principles. That is to say, people can reasonably conclude in regard to some particulars that what is good or bad in one cultural condition is otherwise in another. Aquinas explicitly agrees that natural law can change in certain particulars (*ST* I-II q. 95 a. 5). Thus polygamy could be against natural law in one society but acceptable to it elsewhere. In conditions of high infant mortality such as long prevailed almost everywhere, *contraception could be morally unacceptable, but, in conditions of low infant mortality and high population increase, the opposite might be the case. While one of the best-known of encyclicals, Paul VI's *Humanae Vitae* (1968), denies that contraception is ever acceptable according to natural law, many upholders of natural law would disagree.

The importance of this concept is that it universalizes *morality, providing a common basis for people of all faiths and none, without wholly standardizing it. It thus grounds the concept of *conscience, establishing a moral link between *humanity and God, present even when the link itself is unrecognized; it upholds a unified moral context for the entire human creation and justifies the claim that *grace perfects nature rather than destroying or ignoring it, while presupposing that the moral judgement is not wholly disrupted by original *sin. It also provides a template for the political order, including a concept of the 'common good', implicit in the construction of positive law, and an ultimate justification for revolution when this is gravely ignored by a tyrannical ruler.

The Thomist concept of natural law was enlarged and applied to establishing a basis for international relations by Francisco de Vitoria, a *Dominican theologian in 16th-century Salamanca, often called the 'father of international law'. Bartolomé de Las Casas, another Dominican, the defender of the native American peoples against Spanish oppression, made use of Vitoria's teaching notably in the famous debate held between him and Gines Sepulveda by royal command at Valladolid in 1551. While Sepulveda appealed to Aristotle's doctrine of '*slaves by nature' to justify the enslavement of Americans, Las Casas, following Vitoria, insisted on the natural rights of everyone. Christian 'natural law' had thus moved far beyond Aristotelian 'natural law'. In the 17th century the Dutch jurist and theologian, Hugo Grotius, wrote his *Law of War and Peace* (1625), which further elaborated this system of ideas so that he has been accorded the same title as Vitoria. After Grotius natural law thinking was increasingly secularized and rewritten as a theory of 'natural rights', understood apart from God. The Universal Declaration of Human Rights (1948) was derived from this tradition, while *John XXIII's encyclical *Pacem in Terris* (1963) well represents its continued Catholic use for interpreting the political order.

The more these ideas were secularized and politicized, the less they appeared to belong to theology. For *Luther and much Protestant thought their presuppositions were anyway unacceptable. Original sin had so corrupted human nature that, without the help of revelation and grace, human reason could not participate in divine law. In the 20th century *Barth forcefully reasserted this view, rejecting natural law together with natural theology and natural religion as falsely pretending to bridge from the creature's side the chasm between humanity and God. Many Protestants, however, have always retained a commitment to natural law from Grotius and *Hooker, who used it in his argument against the *Puritan appeal to the bible alone, through to Reinhold *Niebuhr and William *Temple's *Christianity and Social Order* (1942).

There was a marked revival of natural law thinking among both theologians and jurists in the later 20th century, and with it a revival of the dispute as to whether it can be coherently conceived apart from God. Quite clearly not for Aquinas, but for many modern jurists it can. Some arguments against natural law, though frequently repeated, have little validity. It is said to include an unacceptable inference from 'is' to 'ought', but this is not the case. It does not infer 'ought' from anything but recognizes it as an inescapable element in the practical reason, a pre-inferential part of 'is'. Again, it is said to be unworkable because it implies an ahistorical immobility in morality, but, as we have seen, this is simply a misunderstanding. Finally, it is said to provide an inadequate programme for a Christian ethic. That is true but irrelevant. Christian morality does not deny natural morality but it has to go far beyond it.

                                                                   Adrian Hastings

d'Entrèves, A. P., *Natural Law* (1951).

Finnis, John, *Natural Law and Natural Rights* (1980).

Niebuhr, Reinhold, *The Nature and Destiny of Man* (1964).

Westerman, Pauline, *The Disintegration of Natural Law* (1998).

natural theology

stands in contrast to revealed *theology. Whereas the latter involves reflection upon the content of what is proclaimed as divine *revelation, the former consists in the attempt to prove the existence of *God and to determine his nature using only natural *reason. One may suppose that these two forms of theology are complementary and mutually supportive, but there are those who would deny this.

For most Christian thinkers, however, natural theology has been regarded as having an important role in supporting belief. It may serve to establish the 'preambles of faith', non-religion-specific truths about God, such as that he exists; that he has some or all of the following range of attributes: uniqueness, self-existence, eternity, immutability, *omnipotence, *omniscience, omnipresence, omnibenevolence, immateriality; and that he is the *creator and sustainer of the universe with whose well-being he is concerned. It may also provide refutations of arguments to the effect that God does not, or even that he could not possibly exist. Such arguments usually involve the claim that the existence of God is incompatible with the fact of natural and moral evils, or the proposal that the very idea of God is incoherent or contradictory; for example, it is claimed that nothing could be both immaterial and omnipresent. Natural theology may also be invoked in opposition to sceptical *agnosticism. This is the view that for various reasons there could be no case for the existence of God and hence that belief could never be rationally warranted.

Throughout the recorded histories of *philosophy and of Christianity general experience and natural reason have been invoked in support of theistic claims. About twenty years after the crucifixion, *Paul, writing his Epistle to the *Romans, stated that 'What can be known about God is plain to men for God has shown it to them. Ever since the creation of the world his invisible nature, namely his eternal power and deity, has been clearly perceived in the things that have been made' (Rom. 1: 19–20).

Here Paul is not so much offering a proof as reminding his readers of something that he supposes they do, or should, readily accept. Indeed, viewed as an argument it is open to the charge of begging the question, for whether the natural order is 'something made by God' is precisely what is at issue. It would not be difficult, however, to reconstruct Paul's words so as to form an argument, and many readers have been inclined to interpret them in this way. Certainly such reasoning was familiar in antiquity. A very similar observation to Paul's is reported in Cicero's dialogue On the Nature of the Gods composed around 45 BC but set some thirty years earlier. Cicero has one of the interlocutors, the Stoic philosopher Lucillus, speak as follows: 'The point seems scarcely to need affirming. What can be so obvious and clear, as we gaze up at the sky and observe the heavenly bodies, as that there is some divine power of surpassing intelligence by which they are ordered?' While it is improbable that Paul would have known this dialogue it is very likely that he and many of his Roman readers would have been acquainted with the basic tenets of Stoic philosophy including its natural theology.

It is important to make clear, however, that in its early stages Christianity was not particularly interested in philosophy or in the possibility of deriving support from it. In the Acts of the Apostles we are told that in Athens Paul was invited by Epicurean and Stoic philosophers to expound his beliefs, and that when he spoke about Jesus and the Resurrection he was mocked. In a passage that probably reflects this experience Paul writes to the Corinthians '[When] I was with you … my speech and my message were not in plausible words of wisdom, but in demonstration of the Spirit and power, that your faith might not rest in the wisdom of men but in the power of God' (1 Cor. 2: 4).

Notwithstanding Paul's unfavourable contrast between faith and human wisdom, during the next century Christian writers began to make use of *Hellenic thought in the formulation of their theology. Although some displayed a talent for systematic argument, few Christians, with the notable exception of *Augustine, contributed to philosophy as such. The obvious reason for this was their belief that the most important truths can only be known by revelation: though the existence of a cosmic author may be suggested by reason, of itself the human mind is incapable of determining the nature of the original creator. Even Thomas *Aquinas, the greatest exponent of natural theology and Christian philosophy, held that while reason can establish with certainty that there is a God, it cannot provide knowledge of his essence. In the first part of his Summa Theologiae Aquinas sets out a series of natural proofs each ending with some such phrase as et hoc dicimus deum ('and this we call God'). Yet in the same section he also says that by argument we can know only that God is, not what he is.

The view that reason alone will not allow us to make any definite claims about the divine essence is sometimes termed 'theological agnosticism'. Though clearly the sense of this differs from the usual meaning of the term 'agnosticism', which extends to the question of God's existence, it is related inasmuch as it suggests that where reasoning about God's nature is concerned we must withhold judgement. There is, though, a qualification to this embodied in the idea that Aquinas derived from earlier Christian and Jewish writers, namely the possibility of 'negative theology' (the via negativa). Though we may not prove what God is, we can establish what he is not. In fact the core list of divine attributes is best thought of as a series of concealed negations: unique = not one of many; self-existent = not a dependent being; omnipresent = not limited to any particular time or place, and so on.

In the 'five ways' Aquinas argues (1) from the occurrence of change to an unchanging changer; (2) from series of causes and effects to an uncaused cause; (3) from the existence of contingent things to that of a necessary being; (4) from imperfect instances to a perfect cause of them; and (5) from the regularity and function of natural processes to a cosmic designer. Although these arguments have been much discussed and often criticized they express lines of reasoning still taken seriously today. One difference between Aquinas's position and that of current natural theologians, however, is that while he believed that arguments of the sort he assembled are deductive demonstrations, they generally deny this.

A deductive demonstration is a proof that proceeds from indisputable premisses to a conclusion that is entailed by them and whose truth may therefore be known with certainty. For Aquinas a premiss is indisputable if it is either evident or self-evident. An evident premiss is one apparent from experience, such as that some things are in motion; a self-evident premiss is one apparent from its content, such as that moving objects have spatial properties. A conclusion is entailed by a set of premisses when it is not possible that they be true and it be false. So, Aquinas believed that there are certain propositions that any intelligent person knows are true and from which it follows that there is a God.

The prospect this opens up is certainly exciting, but most present-day philosophers, including advocates of natural theology, would say that this line is not sound. To begin with, contemporary philosophy is in general more sceptically minded, believing that there are few, if any, evident or self-evident propositions. Additionally, contemporary proponents of theistic arguments are disposed to say that the relevant premises make it *likely* that there is a God rather than demonstrating it as true. This attitude is clearly represented in the work of Richard Swinburne, perhaps the most accomplished 20th-century advocate of natural theology. He has written a series of important works in the philosophy of religion, beginning with *The Existence of God*. In this he advances several inductive probability arguments, the general form of which is as follows: we know or have very good reason to believe that so and so is the case; this is not much to be expected unless it is also the case that such and such; therefore it is likely that such and such is the case, 'such and such' being the proposition that there is a God. So, for example, on the basis of observation we have good reason to think that the universe exhibits regularity. This fact is not much to be expected unless there is an author of regularity responsible for it. Therefore it is likely that there is such an author.

Most critics of Swinburne's arguments dispute whether his premisses are true. Thus some would allow that we observe regularities in nature but insist that it does not follow that these are general; and they or others would contend that even if there are such regularities it is not the case that their existence is more probable on a theistic hypothesis than on an atheistic one. Such matters are hard to resolve, but some philosophers still think it is possible that a deductive proof of the existence of God from plausible if not evident premises could be fashioned (Smart and Haldane 1996: pts. 2, 4).

Thus one kind of critic of natural theology allows the possibility of the project but challenges particular attempts to realize it. The most famous of these critics is the Scottish philosopher of the *Enlightenment, David Hume, and most subsequent lines of criticism are indebted to his objections. Hume was a sceptical thinker and launched attacks against many long-standing assumptions. For example, he maintained that inductive inference is invalid: we cannot argue from 'all perceived As have been Bs' to 'all (or even to most) As are Bs'. He furthermore challenged the very idea of real causation. Since most arguments for the existence of God invoke causation and many rely on induction, these points are potentially very damaging. Hume also directed his fire upon arguments from *miracles. His basic claim is that we would never have more reason to believe that a miracle had occurred than to conclude from their reports that witnesses were deluded or deceptive. Unsurprisingly, Hume's views have been subjected to extensive criticism and the fairest summary of discussion thus far is that, as with the case of Aquinas's five ways, scholarly opinion is divided.

A different type of criticism of natural theology also originates, in its modern form, in the ideas of an Enlightenment philosopher, Immanuel *Kant. Hitherto it had generally been supposed that arguments about the existence and nature of God, including atheological arguments, could use the same concepts to characterize the empirical world and any transcendent non-spatial (and perhaps non-temporal) reality. This is what Kant denied. In an effort to synthesize empiricist and rationalist philosophies, he held that we have only two sets of concepts: those acquired *from* experience, e.g. animal; and those presupposed *in* experience as necessary conditions of its possibility, e.g. space and time. In Kant's account these latter concepts cannot be got through experience because experience would not be possible unless we had them. They are, in his terminology, 'a priori concepts' as contrasted with the 'a posteriori' ones acquired by perception.

The point to take from this is that concepts such as 'cause and effect' are attached to what can be experienced. *Ex hypothesi*, the transcendental is beyond experience. Accordingly, it cannot be characterized in empirical terms, and we cannot argue from within experience to beyond it. Unlike Hume who rejected theism (whether he was a strict atheist is harder to say), Kant leaves it as an inexpressible hypothesis. We cannot argue from the world to a cause of it, nor can we speak meaningfully of God—even of what he is not—since our *language is confined by concepts for and of experience. At the same time, however, Kant thought that in aesthetic experience and in our moral reasoning we may have a sense of the transcendent and even of the divine, though this cannot be converted into a direct proof of the existence of God.

In the 20th century, radical empiricists have argued that the only sense that can be attached to statements is that which is related to their empirical verification. 'The cat sat on the mat' is meaningful because it has a verifiable content; 'God exists in eternity' has no empirical content and hence lacks sense. It is entirely vacuous, an empty sigh. Advocates of this view thus go further than Kant, who tried to ground support for religion on intimations from beyond experience. Allowing for this difference in intent, both lines of argument are clearly problematic for natural theology.

Fortunately, however, related difficulties were noticed very long ago and solutions proposed. Prominent among these, and strongly associated with Aquinas and his followers, is the method of *analogy. Although it may not be possible to use observational terms in a literal way to characterize unobservables, the language of physics shows that it is none the less possible to make meaningful claims deploying these terms in analogous ways. Similarly we may conjoin empirical terms so as to apply them beyond experience. A microphysical particle may be described as 'leaping haphazardly', and the infinite may be thought of by extension from the large. Of course much more needs to be said about these matters but once again natural theology has outlived its sceptical undertakers.

There is, though, a further direction from which it has been attacked, surprisingly, that of religious belief. Earlier we saw Paul favour *faith over human *wisdom. Some religious thinkers and those sympathetic to *religion have rejected natural theology precisely because it seeks to give reasons for what they insist can only be a matter of faith and religious practice. This rejection comes in a variety of forms. One such is associated with the Reformed tradition of Christianity. Following Augustine, *Calvin believed that our reason is fallen along with the rest of human nature. *Sin has darkened and disturbed the intellect and so it is not to be trusted. Only faith in Jesus Christ and in the bible can bring us to a knowledge of God. Although the 'seed of religion' lies within all human beings as an innate disposition to religious belief, our fallen nature is such that belief is liable to confusion. Reason, being similarly fallen, is unable to provide sure direction; and thus pure natural theology, belief based on and guided by reason alone, is not a possibility. More dramatically, Karl *Barth, widely regarded as the most important Reformed theologian of the 20th century, viewed philosophical theology as tantamount to idolatry. Related themes, cast in an existentialist-cum-romantic key, are to be found in the writings of Søren *Kierkegaard, who emphasized human finitude and sinfulness to an extent that makes natural theology appear an absurd arrogance.

Less denunciatory but still within the tradition of *Protestant theology is the claim that belief in God need not be held on the basis of evidence or other warranted grounds, either of experience or of reasoning. In its contemporary version this rejection is associated with the 'Reformed epistemology' of American philosophers such as Alvin Plantinga and Nicholas Wolterstorff. For them faith is neither inferred nor otherwise derived. It is (or at least it may be) a matter of basic belief. In some respects this view is reminiscent of ideas expressed by one of the greatest philosophers of the 20th century, Ludwig *Wittgenstein. Although raised a Roman Catholic (and accorded a Catholic burial) he was for most of his life an agnostic. Yet he believed that religion was one of the most important expressions of the human spirit and was concerned to show that it was neither supported by nor vulnerable to attack from philosophical reasoning.

These religious objections are versions of what is sometimes termed *fideism. Although it is certainly right to insist that faith is not a matter of philosophical opinion, most contemporary philosophers of religion would maintain that the two should not be opposed, and many who believe that philosophy supports theism would argue that reason and revelation are complementary. Certainly it is widely held that separating faith from the evaluation of evidence and the marshalling of arguments exposes it to the charge of drifting free of rational thought and action. This invites the thought that if belief is not and cannot be rationally warranted it may be the result of social and other factors, which in turn encourages the idea that it is open to a complete sociological or psychological explanation. It is interesting to speculate whether the dismissive attitude taken towards religion by many intellectuals may be due in part to the insistence by some theologians of earlier generations that faith has nothing to do with reason. If so the fact that natural theology is currently flourishing may promise the prospect of a wide reappraisal of the rational case for religion.

John Haldane

Davies, B., *An Introduction to the Philosophy of Religion*, 2nd edn. (1993).
Evans, C. Stephen, *Philosophy of Religion: Thinking About Faith* (1985).
Gaskin, J. C. A., *Hume's Philosophy of Religion* (1978).
Hick, J. (ed.), *Classical and Contemporary Readings in the Philosophy of Religion*, 3rd edn. (1990).
Hughes, G. J., *The Nature of God* (1995).
Kenny, A., *The Five Ways* (1969).
—— *The God of the Philosophers* (1979).
McDermott, T. (ed.), *Aquinas: Selected Philosophical Writings* (1993).
Mackie, J. L., *The Miracle of Theism* (1982).
Miller, B., *From Existence to God* (1992).
Peacocke, A. R., *Creation and the World of Science* (1979).
Plantinga, A., and Wolterstorff, N. (eds.), *Faith and Rationality* (1983).
Smart, J. J. C., and Haldane, J., *Atheism and Theism* (1996).
Stead, C., *Philosophy in Christian Antiquity* (1994).
Swinburne, R., *The Existence of God*, 2nd edn. (1990).

neo-orthodoxy. Late 20th-century theologians coined this term to define a theological paradigm developed in Europe and *North America in the period after the First World War. What follows refers to this paradigm, not to the new conservatism that emerged within the Christian churches in the 1980s and 1990s, for which the term is also sometimes used.

Despite their considerable differences and theological contexts, Protestant theologians such as Karl *Barth, Emil Brunner, Friedrich Gogarten, Paul *Tillich, H. Richard *Niebuhr, and Reinhold Niebuhr are often grouped under the title 'neo-orthodox' to highlight their common interest in constructing a theology grounded on *Reformation principles. At the time they often described it as 'dialectical theology'. Its major characteristics are the critique of 19th- and early 20th-century *liberal theology with its failure to distinguish sharply between *God and the *world, and the construction of a theology firmly based on the proclamation of God's word in the bible. But despite this emphasis on God's otherness, and stern warnings not to confuse God's realm with the human (dialectical theology), even neo-orthodox theologians are rooted in a particular cultural context. Two world wars, the terror imposed by totalitarian regimes, a technologically organized *Holocaust, together with insights into the ambiguity of *religion, progress, politics, *science, and technology have led to a deep mistrust of all human institutions and culture. God's transcendence must be safeguarded and human brokenness affirmed. *Humanity's only hope is God's saving action in Christ. This strong Christocentrism confronts individuals with the need for a radical decision for or against God's word in Jesus Christ as proclaimed by the church.

The term 'neo-orthodoxy' is also used to define one trend in mid-20th century Roman Catholic theology. Some Roman Catholic theologians, for example Karl *Rahner and Henri *de Lubac, set out to find new and more dynamic ways of approaching classical doctrines through a critical and constructive engagement with both modern thinking and neo-scholastic method. As against a somewhat static, legalistic, and institutional interpretation of Christian existence, they proposed taking human experience seriously in theology, while not going as far as later theologies (for example *liberation theology) which have regarded human experience as a vehicle of divine revelation of equal significance with the bible and tradition. Roman Catholic neo-orthodox theology exerted a strong influence at the time of *Vatican II.

These theologians, labelled neo-orthodox by later generations, have aroused a new interest in the doctrine of God, *christology, and *anthropology. Yet despite their deep insights into God's transcendence and the ambiguity of the human condition, they are felt by some to have failed to make a sufficiently radical critical analysis of the biblical, philosophical, linguistic, hermeneutical, political, and cultural dimensions of Christian faith. They are further criticized for not recognizing the pluralistic nature of both church and world and for their treatment of western and patriarchal theological models as universal without regard to context, culture, history, and experience.

Werner G. Jeanrond

Barth, K., *The Epistle to the Romans* (1918; 1921), ET (1933).
—— *Church Dogmatics* (1932–67), ET (1936–69).
Ford, D., *The Modern Theologians*, 2nd edn. (1997).
Tracy, D., *Blessed Rage for Order* (1975).

Neoplatonism, see PLATO AND PLATONISM.

Nestorianism properly connotes the teaching on the *person of Christ propounded by Nestorius (archbishop of Constantinople

428–31). His authentic doctrine, as studied from primary sources only recently made accessible to scholarship, shows him to have been representing traditional teachings of the *Syrian church, notably of its leading 4th- and 5th-century theologians Diodore of Tarsus and Theodore of Mopsuestia. The most widely used sense of Nestorianism, however, refers to his teaching as it was received by hostile opponents, and denounced by them as the *heretical doctrine of two personal subjects within Christ. Nestorianism is also sometimes used as a misnomer for the Christian church located after the 5th century in Persian and Asian territories, a communion that still regards him as one of its leading figures.

In the *Constantinople of 428, the *Alexandrian tradition of *christology enjoyed high status. The particularly oriental elements of the christological tradition were known in Constantinople (from the time of John Chrysostom, archbishop 398–407) but never until Nestorius came had they received such emphasis. Soon after his enthronement he sponsored a preaching campaign that ridiculed the title *theotokos* (mother of God) as an example of loose and undisciplined thinking about the *Incarnation. *Mary, he said, was the mother of the man *Jesus, or the mother of Christ, not the Mother of God. His concern was to explicate the christological union: the manner in which the divine and human conditions could be conceived as related in Christ. Alexandrian thought was believed by many Syrians still to be tainted with Apollinaris' premisses, whereby the deity of the Logos so overwhelmed and absorbed the *humanity of Jesus that authentic manhood all but disappeared, a model close to *Docetism. The Syrians also resisted the Alexandrian exegetical premiss that all biblical texts represented an 'absolute' perspective (the voice of the Logos spoken over history) and were thus best interpreted by the *allegorical method. They preferred a historical contextualization of scripture which, as applied to the christological problem, gave their thought a realist and 'Pauline' quality that has proved attractive to many modern thinkers. They spoke of human and divine conditions remaining distinct in Christ. The way in which they explained the coming together of such diversity was by the principle of 'God's good favour' (*eudokia*): the *grace of God effecting a dynamic correlation with the life of a man. Nestorius repeated most of Theodore's theology, less originally and brilliantly than his teacher, but with a comparable stress on the foundation of the christological dynamic as 'grace'. The Syrians argued that the concept of 'united natures' implied an abiding compositeness (the plurality endures), whereas the Alexandrians insisted that the logic of the term 'union' demanded a transformation to oneness (plurality is transcended). Syrian theology thus preferred the christological term 'correlation' (*synapheia*, association) to that of 'union' (*henosis*). Nestorius thought he had expressed the manner of the harmony clearly enough by pointing to the single worship the church offered its Lord: 'On account of the one who lies hidden [the Logos], I worship the one who appears [the man Jesus]'; or again: 'Let us confess the God in man, let us adore the man who is to be worshipped together with God because of the divine conjunction (*synapheia*) with God the Creator.'

Many of his critics, both at home and further afield, had never before been presented so starkly with Syrian christology. To some it sounded like an honorific (and thus idolatrous) ascription of deity to a mere man. Others mistook his habit of speaking of the 'man

assumed' for a revival of the adoptionist heresy of earlier centuries. Nestorius' opponents applied these apologetic arguments mercilessly, arguing that the diversity of natures he was proposing had overstepped its mark into a doctrine of 'two Sons', or double subjectivity. This was, perhaps, not his actual intent, more a question of how critics could push his premisses to extremes. The Syrian custom of attributing some biblical actions to the 'man Jesus' and some to 'the Word', delivered Nestorius into the hands of his enemies.

Nestorius' demands for semantic exactness in distinguishing scriptural attributions often led him to regard the traditional pieties of Christian faith as evidence of feeble-mindedness. In the course of arguments with bishops gathering at Ephesus to adjudicate the case between himself and Cyril of Alexandria, he appears to have lost his temper with one who was asking the 'innocent' question: 'Why cannot a Christian simply call Jesus God?' To this he replied: 'We must not call the one who became man for us, God.' and added: 'I refuse to acknowledge as God an infant of two or three months old.' This lack of discretion, and scorn for traditional pieties, went far to alienate the great majority of bishops at the Council of *Ephesus (431), who proceeded to condemn him for heresy.

It might be said that Nestorius' lack of care in propagating Syrian thought caused his downfall. More subtle Syrian theologians active in the same controversy, such as Theodoret of Cyrrhus, Andrew of Samosata, or John of Antioch, eventually came to terms with Cyril's objections, and Cyril himself was always convinced that those Syrians who accepted the necessity of a single subject in Christ were not at all the same as Nestorius whose teaching had failed to secure a proper ground of unity in the divine Christ. Deposed at Ephesus in 431 and later exiled, Nestorius complained that he had been much misrepresented. With the rediscovery for the west, in the early 20th century, of the *Book of Heracleides of Damascus* (formerly mistranslated as *Bazaar of Heracleides*) a primary resource became available for the study of his authentic teaching. It has, however, proved difficult to establish a common scholarly estimate, for much turns on the question to what extent that treatise, composed twenty years after the events, represents hindsight, or the theology he was elaborating at the time. Here Nestorius clearly wishes to demonstrate how the interrelation of divine and human in Jesus may be articulated, and gives a fuller account of personal (prosopic) unity than any of the hostile excerpts cited against him at Ephesus. All told, however, his christological thought in this book remains confused and unclear.

'Nestorianism' has served to inspire much modern christological thought. Nestorius has appealed to several modern commentators who have sympathy for him as a 'wronged thinker', and who find his insistence on the submission of the human Jesus to God more in sympathy with biblical theology and contemporary psychological insights than the orthodox scheme of hypostatic union. And yet, if his picture accords with much of *Paul, it does not fit as well with the christology of the fourth gospel, and critics have pointed out that his understanding of the psychology of Jesus is so thoroughly Hellenist that to claim him, in any sense, as a 'modern' is a gross anachronism.

Nestorianism has been used as a common misnomer for the 'Church of the East', which was centred in antiquity on the archiepiscopal throne of Seleucia-Ctesiphon. This church's theology was rooted firmly in the school of Edessa, and so the tradition over-shadowed in the Byzantine world, in the course of the suppression of Nestorius, continued to hold a dominant place as the church developed outside the imperial boundaries. From its Persian base it extended its influence and missions to Arabia and Egypt, even as far afield as India and *China. Its extent in antiquity was very significant, but by the 14th century it had been depleted by Mongol oppression. In the 16th century certain parts of the church moved for union with Rome, which then declared a Chaldaean *patriarchate. Today the title of Chaldaean is often used of those in Roman communion, while the designation of Suraya (Syrian Christians) refers to the main body. In Britain the title of 'Assyrian Church', popularized by the 19th-century Anglican missionaries, is sometimes applied.   **John McGuckin**

Braaten, C. E., 'Modern Interpretations of Nestorius', *Church History*, 32 (1963).

Brock, S., 'The "Nestorian" Church: A Lamentable Misnomer', in J. F. Coakley and K. Parry (eds.), *The Church of the East: Life and Thought, Bulletin of the John Rylands Library*, 78/3 (1996).

Chesnut, R. C., 'The Two Prosopa in Nestorius' Bazaar of Heraclides', *Journal of Theological Studies*, NS 29 (1978).

McGuckin, J. A., 'The Christology of Nestorius of Constantinople', *The Patristic and Byzantine Review* 7/2–3 (1988).

—— 'Nestorius and the Political Factions of 5th-Century Byzantium: Factors in his Personal Downfall', in J. F. Coakley and K. Parry (eds.), *The Church of the East: Life and Thought, Bulletin of the John Rylands Library*, 78/3 (1996).

New Age

New Age denotes the various beliefs in the non-material and supernatural that do not belong formally to any established mainstream religious tradition, and the practices that are based upon them. The term came into vogue in the 1980s and 1990s, but its roots and precursors are much older. In particular, the term indicates a faith in the immediacy of a new and better phase in the affairs of humanity and the earth. The contemporary New Age includes programmes of self-realization and self-transformation based in general on the concept of a 'true' or 'higher' self transcending the ego, through which a harmony with all beings may be found. It represents a reaction to materialistic *science and looks for spiritual energy and life beyond the empirical, for example the 'channelling' of departed spirits through a medium, the harnessing of the healing power of crystals, plants, and aromas, and the utilization of divinatory techniques of many kinds.

The boundaries of New Age are by no means clear. While some commentators include new religious movements of the tightly organized, sectarian kind, others feel that the term presupposes a liberal, anti-dogmatic view that precludes them. Again, while many observers would include alternative medicine and yoga, many practitioners of these would have no commitment to belief in a supernatural realm.

Christianity is challenged by New Age in so far as the latter flourishes in times and places where Christian and other mainstream religious beliefs and practices have become less popular. It is not surprising, therefore, that it is associated with the urban centres of North America and western Europe, but it is also to be found across the world in countries as diverse as Brazil and Japan. New Age beliefs often draw on eastern *religions, especially *Hinduism, *Buddhism, and Taoism, and native religions suppressed by European colonialism. Its proponents tend to disapprove of the imperialism, formality, hierarchy, exclusiveness, and *dualistic theology of the western religions, while approving their *mystical traditions. New Age is monistic in its theology: it seeks to unite the divine and the human, the cosmic and the terrestrial, the spiritual and the material. One important New Age tenet, inherited from such 19th-century forebears as the Theosophical Society, is that *all* religions are vehicles of an all-encompassing higher *truth even if this is often distorted by their followers. This can lead to a new kind of religious imperialism (Palmer 1993).

Common Christian concerns about New Age beliefs are that the distinction between creator and creature is not maintained; that the focus is on the human world rather than God, and on the self rather than the community; that moral discipline is lacking; that optimistic, 'human potential' ideals fail to take sin and evil seriously. However, there is no standard response to New Age among Christians. For some, it is always misguided, and often harmful and satanic in inspiration, perhaps even the result of a conspiracy to supplant Christianity. For others, New Age does at least demonstrate the continued vitality of the *spiritual quest, and provokes the question of why the churches fail to attract those who turn to New Age. In addition, there are Christians who argue more positively that New Age is in tune with the contemporary Christian rediscovery of underemphasized elements in its tradition, such as: care for the environment (see ECOLOGY); *feminine images for the divine; spiritual discipline as a means of improving human life; the inner mystical journey; *symbol, ritual, dance, and music that inspire and liberate; the importance of experience and intuition.

Heelas's comprehensive and largely sympathetic treatment of the New Age movement (1996) describes it as the 'Celebration of the Self and the Sacralization of Modernity'. Although New Age embodies in part a counter-cultural reaction to negative aspects of modern technological society—such as materialism, meaninglessness, anonymity—it also draws upon the central virtues of *modernity. Heelas includes among these: 'freedom, authenticity, self-responsibility … equality, dignity … harmony, peace, creative expressivity, being positive'. Thus New Age articulates in supernaturalistic, mythical terms a matrix of values widely held in modern western society. Therefore it will endure, and prove effective for the good of the majority of its participants as long as it prioritizes inclusiveness and the common good above self-serving hedonism. Nevertheless, its democratic nature and willingness to value amyriad of personal beliefs militates against a high level of organization, and its effect on society in general is likely to remain marginal, despite the substantial literature that it produces (Bruce 1996).

New Age is a manifestation of a 'common religion' that has continued to exist alongside formalized religious traditions, and it therefore lacks the rational and philosophical rigour that the mainstream Christian tradition has always emphasized. Nevertheless, Christians need to look more closely at the underlying values that New Age, in a variety of ways, ranging from the profound to the ridiculous, draws from modern society at large. Its contemporary form may give clues to the likely social and psychological bases of the spiritual quest of the 21st century. Its general refusal to admit hierarchy and unconditional *authority into its understanding of divinity is appealing to many, in an age when people seek to be citizens rather than subjects, to share skills and experiences rather than defer to an élite.   **Chris Maunder**

Bloom, William, *The New Age: An Anthology of Essential Writings* (1991).

Bruce, Steve, *Religion in the Modern World: From Cathedrals to Cults* (1996).

Carr, Wesley, *Manifold Wisdom: Christians in the New Age* (1991).

Heelas, Paul, *The New Age Movement: The Celebration of the Self and the Sacralization of Modernity* (1996).

Lewis, James and Melton, Gordon J. (eds.), *Perspectives on the New Age* (1992).

Palmer, Martin, *Coming of Age: An Exploration of Christianity and the New Age* (1993).

Newbigin, Lesslie (1909–98).

As rarely in modern times, the church had in Lesslie Newbigin a bishop-theologian whose career was primarily shaped by his evangelistic and pastoral responsibilities and who yet made contributions to Christian thought that match those of the more professionally academic among his brethren. A *Presbyterian from Northumbria, Newbigin was ordained by the Church of Scotland for *missionary service in India. He spent two lengthy periods on the subcontinent: first, 1936–59, as evangelist, ecumenical negotiator, and from 1947 bishop of Madurai in the newly united Church of South India; second, 1965–74, as bishop of Madras. In between he was general secretary of the International Missionary Council at the time of its integration with the World Council of Churches (see ECUMENICAL MOVEMENT). Newbigin's personal writings meshed with his ecumenical draftsmanship: as the author of *The Reunion of the Church* (1948) and *The Household of God* (1953), he was perfectly suited to prepare the description of 'the *unity we seek' for the WCC New Delhi assembly in 1961; having framed the statement on 'the missionary calling of the church' at the IMC's Willingen conference in 1952, he eventually authored the strongly Trinitarian missiology of *The Open Secret* (1978). More broadly, Newbigin's theological reflection was marked by constant interaction with his surroundings: just as in India (where he learned Tamil) he engaged with both the *Hindu religious and the post-independence political cultures, so in Europe (after a brief flirtation with the *secularization theologies of the mid-1960s) he was concerned to assert the public truth of Christianity (*The Gospel in a Pluralist Society*, 1989) amid an apostasizing late modernity ('Can the West be [re]converted?'); and this he did as teacher, local pastor, and national sage after his 'retirement' to England in 1974. Lasting influences on his thought were the presentation of the *Atonement in James Denney's *Romans* (encountered in the early 1930s) and Karl *Barth's *Church Dogmatics* (read in its entirety in the early 1970s). Fascinated with the Fourth Gospel since his scriptural *dialogues with Sanskrit scholars at Kanchipuram, Newbigin's exposition of *John is found in *The Light Has Come* (1982).   **Geoffrey Wainwright**

Newbigin, L., *Unfinished Agenda: An Autobiography* (1993).

Wainwright, G., *Lesslie Newbigin: A Theological Life* (2000).

Newman, John Henry (1801–90).

Newman was the most powerful *theological mind writing in English in the 19th century and the most creative and influential Catholic thinker of his time. Among theologians he was exceptional as a master of language, excelling not only in clarity and the precise formulation of an argument but also, more unexpectedly, in irony, in an up-to-date, almost racy, debating style, as well as in the use of *metaphor and poetic form. Beginning his career as a Calvinist evangelical, he ended it as a Roman cardinal. Entering the Catholic Church in England when it was still a tiny, much-hated minority within a Protestant nation, he transformed their relationship by his long-term influence upon both sides so that, in retrospect, he can be seen as the supreme reconciler.

Newman was born into a middle-class London family. He entered Oxford University when only 16 and in 1822 was elected a fellow of Oriel College. Here he became one of a remarkable group, including John Keble, Edward Pusey, and Hurrell Froude, young men intent on raising educational and moral standards in the university as well as revivifying the Church of England, which they saw as threatened both by traditional lassitude and by the inroads of *liberalism. Newman emerged as the outstanding intellectual leader of this group but no less as a spiritual teacher who, in 1828, was appointed vicar of the University Church of St Mary where his sermons, regularly published, exerted a national influence.

Little by little Newman cut himself free of his early *evangelicalism but not, for many years, of a deep distrust of Rome, which he saw as a profoundly corrupt church. Fascinated by the early fathers, he set himself to map out and defend an Anglican *via media* between *Protestantism and Rome, a doctrinal, sacramental, and episcopal position grounded in patristic scholarship and defensible against *Erastian belittlement of the church's freedom and liberal attacks on its traditional doctrines. Such was the programme of the Tractarian or *Oxford Movement, which did indeed begin to alter the ethos of *Anglicanism but raised intense alarm, especially among the bishops, the more it undermined 'Protestant' and exalted 'Catholic' positions.

'Oxford will want hot-headed men, and such I mean to be, and I am in my place,' wrote Newman in 1831. His first book, *The Arians of the Fourth Century*, appeared the next year. Over the next twelve years it was followed by a massive and creative theological output. *The Prophetic Office of the Church* was published in 1837, the *Lectures on Justification* in 1838, *Tract 90* (defending the compatibility of the Thirty-Nine Articles with the decrees of the Council of Trent) in 1841, and the final major piece in the series, *The Essay on the Development of Christian Doctrine*, in 1845. In the same years no fewer than ten volumes of sermons were published, together with numerous other tracts, articles, letters, and translations. In these years Newman was essentially the university theologian, stimulated by Oxford, a master of both scholarship and controversy.

His position kept changing. The more he devised a comprehensive framework to defend the Church of England, the more he encountered two, both eventually irresolvable, problems. The first was that the leaders of his church did not recognize it. This was particularly striking and painful in the response to *Tract 90*. How can you convincingly defend a church in terms that its own leadership emphatically repudiates? The second was still more fatal. Newman came to lose confidence in the *via media* himself. The more he reflected on the patristic evidence, the more it suggested to him not a basic 'primitive' core from which both Rome and Protestantism had deviated and to which one could confidently return, but a ceaselessly *developing body of doctrine with which modern *Catholicism seemed all in all more validly in line than anyone else. It was essentially the conclusion of a historian. Eventually, after a long period of retreat and silence at the village of

Littlemore just outside Oxford, he entered the Roman Catholic communion on 9 October 1845.

As a convert who was already a famous name, Newman found his position within Catholicism extremely difficult from the start. He had very few Catholic contacts. Rome was not a world he knew or understood though he quickly developed a deep devotion to Philip Neri, who reminded him of Keble and whose 16th-century model of an 'Oratory', a community of secular priests, he determined to follow. Intellectually his stay in Rome (1846–7) horrified him: there was no serious grappling with modern issues. Its university professors, he realized, were unthinking conservatives: 'There was a deep suspicion of change, with a perfect incapacity to create anything positive for the wants of the times.' That would remain true throughout his life. Intellectually Catholicism was in a bad way, reacting against the Reformation, the *Enlightenment, and 19th-century scholarship (see HIGHER CRITICISM) alike with an arid scholasticism, uninterested in the serious study of either patristics or *Aquinas and intensely suspicious of anyone who seemed open to one or another strand of 'liberalism'. While Newman throughout his life depicted himself as an anti-liberal, his greatness in reality derived from a growing refusal to be dominated by a 'suspicion of change'. A historian's conviction about the validity of development had made him a Catholic, but it equally brought him under Catholic suspicion, challenging as it did the profound ahistoricism of *ultramontanism.

After Catholic ordination in May 1847 and a brief Oratorian novitiate he returned to England to found the Oratory in Birmingham where he remained, apart from a few months as rector of the Catholic University in Dublin, for the rest of his life. He lived to be a very old man and was still publishing well into his eighties. His essay 'On the Inspiration of Scripture' appeared in 1884. What is striking, however, is how little he published in the forty years after his conversion when compared with the production of the previous twelve years. These forty years produced only three major books: *The Idea of a University* (1852), the *Apologia pro Vita Sua* (1864), and *A Grammar of Assent* (1870). These may be supplemented by four lesser, but not unimportant publications: the article 'On Consulting the Faithful in Matters of Doctrine', which appeared in the *Rambler* (1859), the *Letter to Pusey* (mostly devoted to Marian theology and devotion) of 1864, the *Letter to the Duke of Norfolk*, replying to Gladstone in regard to *Vatican I (1874), and the article on the inspiration of scripture. Each of these seven works remains significant; nevertheless their quantity is sadly limited and their subjects in several cases are somewhat marginal to theology. It is fully understandable that in his earlier years as a Catholic Newman should have held back from writing anything explicitly theological. Yet it is impossible not to ask how it happened that such an outstanding thinker contributed so little over so many years once he had become a Catholic. In particular, the paucity of sermons from his Catholic years remains perplexing.

The answer can only be that circumstances were intensely unfavourable to his work and remained so until he was too old to profit by the change. As a Catholic he had no allies of any weight, only a few disciples. While English Catholics, lay people and priests, were increasingly proud of him, their own, albeit limited, intellectual tradition was being submerged by a wave of converts who, unlike Newman, mostly adopted in a quite extreme form the beliefs, de-

votions, and political attitudes of Continental ultramontanism. While Newman, for instance, quietly realized that the continued temporal power of the pope over the papal states was anachronistic, damaged the church, and could happily be ended, this was regarded by ultramontanes as an attitude of betrayal. English Catholicism came to be dominated by Manning, a convert of 1851, who had for a time been influenced by Newman but who became an intense *papalist and one of the principal architects of the *infallibility definition of Vatican I, though he had wanted a far less limited definition than was made. But Manning was also, as Newman was not, an ecclesiastical politician of genius and for twenty-seven years the near all-powerful archbishop of Westminster (1865–92). 'I see much danger of an English Catholicism of which Newman is the highest type,' Manning wrote at the time of his appointment to Westminster. 'It is the old Anglican, patristic, literary, Oxford tone transplanted into the church. It takes the line of deprecating exaggerations, foreign devotions, ultramontanism, anti-national sympathies. In a word, it is worldly Catholicism.'

It would be hard to think of anyone much less worldly than Newman. Manning prevented him from opening a house at Oxford to provide support for Catholic students. While Newman was, briefly, rector of the new Catholic University of Dublin in the 1850s, the organizational responsibilities and strains with the Irish hierarchy were too great for someone who had anyway declined to give up his position at the Birmingham Oratory. So there he remained, cut off from any sort of university life, regular theological teaching, or ecclesiastical influence, and continually under suspicion in regard to almost anything he wrote, a suspicion fomented in Rome almost entirely by English converts. As he wrote in his journal in October 1867, 'They have too deeply impressed the minds of authorities at Rome against me, to let the truth about me have fair play while I live … As Almighty God in 1864 cleared up my conduct in the sight of Protestants at the end of twenty years (through the *Apologia*), so as regards my Catholic course, at length, after I am gone hence, *Deus viderit!*' In fact Leo XIII made Newman a cardinal in 1879, as quite deliberately his first creation. 'My Cardinal,' declared Leo proudly. 'It was not easy … they said he was too liberal.' As Newman himself remarked, explaining why he could not refuse, 'for 20 or 30 years ignorant or hot-headed Catholics had said almost that I was a heretic'. Leo's amazing gesture altered that and yet the charge continued to be insinuated long after Newman died. His criticisms of what happened at Vatican I, his insistence on the importance of the *laity, the primacy of *conscience, the acceptability of *evolution, and much else were all far out of line with the dominant attitudes of Victorian clerical Catholicism. But his position on development was far more than that. In principle it involved a revolution in the whole Catholic line of defending the church's position as something unchanging. A hundred years later the line had altered and Newman could be hailed as the father of *Vatican II, just as he was unquestionably the principal father of modern Anglican Catholicism. If there is, inevitably, a simplistic element in such assertions, there is also much truth, although one must sadly acknowledge that if he had been treated differently in the second half of his life he would have given far more. The kind of reconciliation suggested by Vatican II between the Catholic and Protestant traditions had already been realized existentially in the life of the Victorian Catholic who never really forfeited the admiration and affections of the Anglicans he left with so heavy a heart, but for whom it was always true in his own words that 'to remain the same' it is necessary to change: 'to live is to change, and to be perfect is to have changed often'.   **Adrian Hastings**

Newman, J. H., 'On Consulting the Faithful in Matters of Doctrine', ed. John Coulson (1961).
—— On the Inspiration of Scripture, ed. J. D. Holmes and R. D. Murray (1967).
—— The Idea of a University, ed. I. Ker (1976).
—— Apologia pro Vita Sua, ed. Martin J. Svaglic (1967).
—— A Grammar of Assent, ed. I. Ker (1985).
Brown, David (ed.), Newman: A Man for our Time (1990).
Cameron, J. M., John Henry Newman (1956).
Chadwick, Owen, From Bossuet to Newman (1957).
Coulson, John, and Allchin, A. M. (eds.), The Rediscovery of Newman (1967).
Dessain, C. S., 'What Newman Taught in Manning's Church', in Infallibility in the Church: An Anglican-Catholic Dialogue (1968), 59–80.
Hastings, Adrian, 'Newman as Liberal and Anti-Liberal', in The Theology of a Protestant Catholic (1990), 116–32.
Ker, Ian, John Henry Newman: A Biography (1990).
Lilly, William Samuel, A Newman Anthology (1875), 2nd edn. Henry Tristram (1949).
Tristram, Henry (ed.), John Henry Newman: Autobiographical Writings (1956).

New Testament (NT) consists of twenty-seven separate

documents. In the traditional order, it begins with four *gospels (*Matthew, *Mark, *Luke, *John), giving an account of *Jesus' ministry, climaxing in his death and *Resurrection. A history of Christianity's beginnings (Acts of the Apostles), usually attributed to the author of Luke's gospel, provides a link to a body of twenty-one letters. Thirteen are, or claim to be, from the pen of *Paul, the first great missionary to non-Jews, five from the close circle of Jesus' disciples (two from *Peter and three from John), two from brothers of Jesus (James and Jude), and one anonymous tract to the *Hebrews. The collection is rounded off by an *apocalypse, the name given to a writing that unveiled the cosmic secrets behind visible reality and revealed the climax of God's purpose for the world (see REVELATION, BOOK OF).

The period of composition of the twenty-seven documents covers the second half of the 1st century. It is possible that Paul's letter to the Galatians and the letter of James were written before 50 and a few (particularly 2 Peter) may not have been written until after 100. It should be noted also that the traditions behind the gospels relate to the period of Jesus' ministry (30–2). But we may be confident that the bulk of the NT originated in the period 50–100.

To be more precise, only the letters written or dictated by Paul himself can be confidently dated to the first generation (before 65). Opinions vary as to whether that includes only seven of the letters (*Romans, 1 and 2 Corinthians, Galatians, Philippians, 1 Thessalonians, and Philemon), or some more (Colossians and 2 Thessalonians), or the other four as well (Ephesians, 1 and 2 Timothy, and Titus). Mark is usually taken to be the earliest gospel and dated a little before 70. The rest of the documents, including the later 'Pauline' letters (if pseudonymous), are almost all to be dated to the thirty years between 70 and 100. That is to say, the majority of the NT was almost certainly written by second-generation Christians.

Properly speaking, however, the origin of the individual documents is not the origin of the NT. The emergence of the concept of a single coherent collection of Christian writings, and the actual collection of these writings to be bound together as a single codex (the NT), was a lengthy and complex process spanning many decades. In rough terms the deliberate intention to compile such a collection dates from the last decades of the 2nd century, and only with *Origen in the early 3rd century do we begin to hear regular talk of 'the New Testament' referring to a collection of writings. The gospels and the Pauline letters were the first to be fully and widely recognized. Others hovered on the margin (Hebrews, Jude and 2 Peter, 2 and 3 John, Revelation) for a long time, and in fact could be said to have remained marginal ever since. The NT did not reach its final and settled shape until the second half of the 4th century.

Why was the NT put together as a single collection? The most popular view is that it began to be compiled as a norm or rule (canon) for the faith and life of the emerging great (*orthodox/ *catholic) *church over against the less acceptable (*heretical) variations that multiplied in the 2nd century. If there was any single trigger it was probably the publication of a tendentiously edited version of Luke's gospel and the letters of Paul by Marcion in about 150 to serve as justification and scripture for the Marcionite churches. Against this attempt to pre-empt more established claims to these documents, the natural response was to draw up a list of the Christian writings that should be regarded as authoritative. Particularly important was the role of *Irenaeus, who, in the last decades of the 2nd century, was first to argue for the fourfold gospel and to reclaim Paul from those deemed to be heretics (see PRE-CONSTANTINIAN THOUGHT).

The formal criterion by which documents were accepted as canonical was *apostolic authorship. Two of the gospels supposedly met this criterion at once (Matthew and John); Mark was understood to have written as Peter's secretary, and Luke to have been Paul's close companion. Paul himself was not one of the twelve apostles/disciples of Jesus, but his own claim to have been appointed apostle by the risen Jesus (in his conversion on the Damascus road) was not in question. Acts was accepted not least as providing the link between the first disciples of Jesus and Paul. Of the other letters only Hebrews was anonymous and was probably accepted because it could be linked to Paul. And the John who introduces himself as the author of Revelation could be identified as John the apostle.

Few today would agree that all the NT documents met the criterion of apostolic authorship. But that should not be taken as a ground for dismembering or dissolving the NT. For the criterion of apostolic authorship was in effect simply the formalization of more determinative criteria. There were three of these.

First was simply the age of the documents. The culture of the time venerated age and put a high value on origins. The NT writings in fact constitute all the documents surviving from the first decades of Christianity, that is, from the sixty years 40–100. We should also note that some very early documents did not survive. For example, it is generally accepted that one of the two main sources of Matthew and Luke (a collection of Jesus' sayings designated the 'Q' source) was not retained in the mainstream churches except as incorporated in Matthew and Luke. And Paul evidently wrote a number of other letters which did not survive. On the other hand, at least one other early Christian writing can be dated confidently before 100 (*1 Clement*). But that letter itself attests a clear sense of belonging to a sub-apostolic age and so is generally listed as first in a wave of Christian writing that came after the apostles had departed the scene, a derivative and not a primary foundational text of Christianity.

Second, a major criterion was whether the documents in question were widely read, valued, and used in *worship among the Christian churches. Here we should recall that most of these documents were written with a view to some wider distribution and circulation. From one or two references to his letters being passed around, and from the several indications of regular communications between his churches, we may deduce that most of Paul's letters were copied and passed to other congregations by the recipient church. As their teaching and pastoral advice was evidently much appreciated it would hardly be surprising if various churches had their own collections of Paul's letters before the end of the 1st century. Other letters were written with a wider distribution in view from the first (most explicitly the 'catholic' epistles of James and 1 Peter). And though it has been fashionable of late to link each gospel to a particular congregation, it is equally likely that such carefully crafted attempts to encapsulate the memory and teaching of their revered founder and Lord had in view a wider circulation from the first.

It was this expanding circle of influence that was probably crucial in the process of canonization. The fact is that well before the question of canon or of canonical *authority was formally raised, the bulk of the NT documents were already recognized as valuable for worship and authoritative for faith in a wide range of churches. It was not the case that some church assembly or synod lighted on a number of hitherto little-known writings and made them canonical. It was rather that most of the NT writings had been exercising *de facto* authority for some decades and generations, so that their formal recognition was an acknowledgement of canonical authority rather than a bestowal of it. There were some documents which had a more limited, local authority for some time (for example, the *Shepherd of Hermas* and the *Gospel of Peter*), but their lack of wider attestation was a crucial factor in their final rejection. And some have retained a canonical status within particular churches (for example, *1 Enoch* in the Ethiopian Church). Conversely, the recognition and use of Hebrews was just sufficiently widespread for it to be finally counted within the canon of the NT.

This observation is almost sufficient in itself to answer the question often asked: what if Q or a lost letter of Paul were to be discovered? Would they not have to be included in the NT? Moreover, today there are a number of scholars who would argue that some other gospels (particularly the Gospel of *Thomas) have as much claim to be regarded as authoritative accounts of Jesus' teaching as the canonical gospels, implying that the canon of the NT should be revised or that the single volume known as the NT should be expanded. The point, however, is that these documents, however old they may be, did not make it. They did not win enough approval among the earliest churches to become candidates for inclusion within the scriptures of the new covenant. If the historical process whereby the documents of the NT won recognition as definitive expressions of Christian faith and life can be likened to a sieve, then other documents did not pass through that sieve.

All this points to a third criterion for canonicity—what we might call 'apostolicity', rather than apostolic authorship. It was because these documents expressed and embodied the common faith of the early churches, the faith taught by the first disciples/apostles of Jesus, that they were treasured, preserved, and more and more widely valued. They were apostolic because they defined what the apostolic faith was, what Christianity was.

In later centuries the more important factor was the belief that the writing of just these documents had been inspired by the *Holy Spirit. In the early centuries the claim to inspiration was less decisive, since other documents also made the same claim. *Gnostic documents typically claimed to contain the teaching given by Christ after his Resurrection. What was more determinative was the character and content of the claimed document. They were inspiring as well as inspired. Through their words the congregations heard the Word of God.

Putting the same point in other terms, the emergence of the NT coincides with the transition of these documents from personal letters, memories of Jesus' ministry, and so on, to scripture. This was already happening within the period covered by the documents themselves. The late Pauline letter to Timothy seems to refer to the tradition of a saying of Jesus as 'scripture' (1 Tim. 5: 18), and the late 2 Peter refers to all Paul's letters in the same way (2 Pet. 3: 16). But the process of recognizing these writings as scripture, with all that that implied in terms of inspiration and authority, would have covered many years in the course of which the documents would have been read for their spiritual value in countless gatherings for worship.

In short, the NT did not originate as a single entity. It emerged over several decades. It cohered round a core of hardly disputed gospels and epistles. Its boundary only became firm towards the end of the process and has always been rather more fuzzy than the single bound volume of modern publication would seem to imply.

Given such a history, is the NT any more than the collection of the earliest Christian writings that have endured? Does the binding of these variegated documents in a single codex (which does not seem to have happened often or regularly) give a misleading impression of unity? Do these writings have any real coherence? Despite the somewhat accidental nature of the NT's emergence, a positive answer to the last question can be given. The coherence of the NT rests in two features.

The first is indicated by the very title—*new* testament. The first Christians already had their scriptures: the Jewish Scriptures, that is the Torah (Law), the Prophets, and the Writings. This collection had already gone through much the same process as that which would mark the emergence of the NT, that is to say, the *de facto* canonical status of the Torah and the Prophets was already well established. The same was true of the *Psalms, but the limits of the Writings were not yet defined; for example, Psalms were still being written (as the *Dead Sea Scrolls indicate). We cannot yet speak of a *closed* canon for this period. There was also the ambiguous status of the Greek version of the Jewish Scriptures, the Septuagint (LXX), containing as it did further writings such as the Wisdom of Jesus ben Sira (Ecclesiasticus), Judith, and Tobit. It is not irrelevant to recall that these *apocryphal documents are to this day integrated within the *Old Testament in Catholic tradition.

The point is that the documents of the NT were written in the first place to bring out the meaning of *these* scriptures. We might even say that they were originally *midrashim* or commentaries on the Jewish scriptures. This is why the motif of fulfilment is such a prominent feature of the NT writings, most noticeable in Matthew, and particularly intense in several of the letters. At the back of most versions of the Greek NT there is a list of the quotations and allusions to the Jewish Scriptures that have been identified in the NT, a list running to thirty or so double column pages. The Jewish Scriptures formed the NT writers' chief resource and authorization, their vocabulary and idiom and sounding-board; the warp of the NT's weft, the substructure of NT thought and theology.

This means that the NT was (and is) defined as the *new* testament precisely by reference to the *old* testament embodied in the Jewish Scriptures. The NT only makes sense as the new testament because it correlates with the old testament. It assumes and presupposes the old testament and would not make sense without it. The very term 'new testament' is drawn from the scriptures of *Israel—particularly the famous 'new covenant (testament)' prophecy of Jeremiah 31. By its very name the NT claims to complete these scriptures. This is why Christians have continued to regard the Jewish Scriptures as an integral part of the Christian bible. The two are complementary: from a Christian perspective the one cannot be properly understood without the other.

The categories 'new' and 'old' here should not be understood antithetically, nor the claim to be the 'new testament' taken to indicate that the old can be dispensed with. On the contrary, in Christian perspective, the two are two sides of a single coin (the *revelation of the saving purpose of God), marking two phases within the divine plan for humankind.

This means that the NT gains its coherence, in the first place, as the symbiotic other part of a larger whole. Its different writings, in different degrees, are infused with the mindset of its precursor scriptures. It gains its coherence less at the surface level of explicit references, claims, and arguments and more at the level of presupposition and what is taken for granted. Thus, for example, there is little explicit teaching about *God in the NT. This is because the Jewish understanding of God as one, as creator and judge, as God of Israel, was simply assumed. A NT theology in the narrow sense, talk of God, could hardly be written from the NT alone; it is the ways in which the NT works with and reworks this hidden premiss that make NT theology so interesting. But without sensitivity to that older heritage most NT theology would appear to be lacking in coherence.

The second obvious unifying factor bonding the NT into one is the central subject of these writings—Jesus Christ. The foundational claim of the NT as 'new *covenant' is that Jesus himself is the centre and foundation of that new covenant. He is remembered as having celebrated his last meal with his disciples as the symbol and memorial of the new covenant constituted by his death (1 Cor. 11: 25). It is the way in which the future hopes of Jewish lawgiver, prophet, psalmist, sage, and apocalyptist came together and found fulfilment in Jesus that provides the common starting-point for all the NT writings. Christ became the key to understanding the old scriptures, the bridge that links old and new as one, the centre of the new.

The point is most obvious, of course, with the gospels, the accounts of Jesus' ministry, death, and Resurrection. But the structur-

ing of the NT, with the gospels at the beginning and as the first part, establishes the character of the whole. The gospels form and inform the character of the NT as gospel. And in different ways and degrees that opening impression is confirmed throughout. Acts announces itself as the account of the continuation of what had begun with Jesus. The Lord Jesus Christ is indubitably the central and unifying theme of Paul's teaching. Jesus as high priest is the message of Hebrews. Jesus as the lamb that was slain and is alive again is the key figure in Revelation. In contrast, it was the relative absence of Jesus from the epistle of James that made its inclusion in the NT questionable and left *Luther dubious as to its canonical authority. But even in the case of James, it is the allusions to Jesus' teaching and reference to Jesus Christ as 'the lord of glory' (Jas. 2: 1) that ensured the recognition that this was a Christian version of OT teaching.

And if Jesus provided the unifying centre of the NT, we could also say that he served as its excluding boundary. It was the character of Jesus, of his teaching, of the gospel focused in him, that became decisive in ruling out other candidates for inclusion in the NT. The other gospels in particular, not least the *Gospel of Thomas*, did not pass the test: they spoke of Jesus, to be sure, but in comparison with the fourfold gospel it was another Jesus, a different gospel.

In short, the coherence of the NT depends entirely on the Christian understanding of the two words, 'new testament', as denoting a covenant centred on Jesus, which complements and completes the old covenant. As that old covenant could be summed up in the scriptures of Israel, so the new covenant could be summed up in the earliest definitive writings of the new movement that took the first title of Jesus (Christ) as its own name, *Christianity.

How diverse is the NT? Within the Christian tradition there has been a tendency to overemphasize its unity and coherence. This is most clearly evident in the period when the various church confessions were drawn up. For the practice then was to treat the NT as a single quarry from any part of which homogeneous texts could be extracted as of equal value to provide instruction on particular topics. The fact that the bible used in this way provided the basis and justification for *different* and *divergent* church confessions did not provoke the debate that it should. One of the most sobering occasions in the 20th-century *ecumenical movement was when Ernst Käsemann of Tübingen pointed out that the NT canon did not provide a foundation for the *unity of the church so much as for the multiplicity of the confessions.

The diversity of the NT has two main aspects, the first being that of its contents. We may begin by citing the fact that the NT contains *four* gospels and not just *one*; and this, despite the indications that the individual gospels were probably written to be sufficient in themselves. For example, Matthew seems to have absorbed more or less the whole of Mark, and yet Mark was preserved. Luke attempted to provide a more definitive account than his predecessors and yet is retained as only one among four. Most striking of all is the entirely different character of the Gospel of John, where the relatively modest claims of the synoptic Jesus are left far behind by the self-consciously divine claims made consistently and in distinctive language by the Johannine Jesus.

This is countered in part by the early titles given to these gospels—'the Gospel *According to* Matthew', not 'the Gospel *of* Matthew', and so on. In other words, those who put the four together wanted to emphasize that the gospels constituted not four gospels but four witnesses to the one gospel. Equally important is the fact that, despite their differences, they all have the same 'gospel' format, climaxing in the account of Jesus' death and Resurrection. In this way the character of the Christian 'gospel' was fixed, as focused in Jesus' death and Resurrection. And this insight probably provides a further clarification of why writings like Q or the *Gospel of Thomas* were rejected; because they contained only *teaching* attributed to Jesus, they were not, properly speaking, 'gospel' after all.

Nevertheless, the differences cannot be ignored. The clear inference to be drawn is that the gospel of Jesus could be presented in different ways—with different nuances and emphases, as in the first three gospels, and with a very differently presented Jesus in the fourth. In other words, the NT enshrines the fact that the one Jesus, and the one gospel of Jesus, can (and needs to be) presented in diverse ways. In compiling the NT those responsible evidently did not think it desirable to have a single, uniform gospel. The unity of the gospel was important, but so also was the diversity of its presentation.

As a second example we may note the diversity within the other core element of the NT canon, the letters attributed to Paul. This feature is usually considered in terms of the development of Paul's thought and the debate as to whether the development in the latest Pauline letters (the *Pastoral Epistles) is too great for the latter to have been composed or dictated by the same person. For anyone familiar with the Pauline corpus the most marked features of contrast are the developed structure of the church, with the offices of bishop/overseer, deacon, and elder clearly defined, and the more formal structure of 'the faith', with its 'faithful sayings' and 'sound teaching'. Many would see in the pastorals evidence of a second or third generation 'hardening of the arteries', which raises the obvious question: which is the more authoritative, in canonical terms, the early Paul or the late (or post-) Paul?

Here again, however, it is important to recognize the significance of the fact that all these letters were accepted as Pauline. Like 'gospel', so 'Pauline' provides both a unifying feature (others were rejected which might have been attributed to Paul), and a reminder of how rich was the diversity of Pauline theology. That diversity was partly the result of different churches and circumstances addressed, but partly also the result of changing emphases across a span of years (at this point it matters less whether or not the span in question stretched beyond the life of Paul himself). The point is that the Pauline corpus attests the importance of a teaching and pastoral strategy adaptable to the times and circumstances addressed. As Paul's own imagery of the church as the body of Christ emphasized, the unity in view was a unity made possible by and indeed consisting of quite diverse members and functions.

For many, the most striking feature of NT diversity would be the presence of the book of Revelation in the canon. As an apocalypse, Revelation represents a strand of Christianity that most have found unnerving. It is a form of spirituality that depends on the immediacy of *visionary experience, expresses bold claims about the mysteries of heaven, and sees the future in often bizarre *symbolism. Most disturbing of all, over the centuries the apocalypse of John has given rise to not a few cults and revolutionary groups and to not a few episodes disastrous for the reputation of Christianity and catastrophic for the groups themselves.

Yet, the compilers of both the Jewish and the Christian canon evidently thought it necessary to include an apocalypse in each—*Daniel and Revelation. Both Judaism and Christianity have canonized apocalyptic as an integral part of their traditions. This constitutes a reminder that apocalyptic is part of Christianity, that what an apocalypse expresses—awareness of a *heavenly dimension to earthly reality and human 'progress', a sense of history moving towards its divinely ordained climax, a perspective which relativizes the pressing issues of the present—is important in shaping Christian attitudes towards the *world and the tides of *history. This too is part of the diverse coherence of the NT.

Another aspect of the NT's diversity has come to still greater prominence in the last two decades of the 20th century: the diversity of *interpretation* of the NT. This is the other side of Käsemann's observation: whatever the coherence of the NT as a set of 1st-century documents, the fact is that it has given rise to a wide range of interpretations, and these have justified a diverse range of theologies and church orders.

At this point the discussion needs to open out to a consideration of the theory of interpretation, *hermeneutics. In particular, the chief current debate is over the extent to which the meaning read from a text is determined more by the text itself or by the reader. To those who reckon that the reader in greater or less degree 'creates' the meaning, diversity of meanings read from the NT will occasion no surprise. For them the crucial factors will then be the continuance of the NT as the accepted text from which such readings are made, and the particular tradition of interpretation (the reading community) in which they have found themselves or with which they have chosen to identify themselves.

For those, however, who regard the text as providing its own controls and limits on the extent of the diversity of readings that may be regarded as legitimate, the diversity will be so much more limited. In particular, it is important to recall here that the NT is a collection of 1st-century documents written in 1st-century Greek. Before any meaning can be heard from them, the *language and its usage has to be identified. Such unavoidably historical constraints are bound to limit the range of meaning which can justifiably be read from these texts. At the same time, they have functioned for centuries as (part of) the scriptures of Christian faith communities. The resulting dialogue within the reading of the same text as both historical text and scripture is also part of the rich diversity of the NT.

In short, the NT remains a clearly delimited group of 1st-century Christian texts. The recognition of just these texts as canonical itself attests a church that wished its own identity and boundaries to be determined by reference to these texts. Their coherence and the coherence of the Christianity that acknowledged them as canonical was determined by their reference both to the scriptures of the old covenant and to the Christ to which they bore witness. But their usage always takes the form of an interplay of unity and diversity, a recognition both of the diversity within the unity, and of a unity that comes to contemporary expression in inevitably diverse ways.

See also BIBLE, ITS AUTHORITY AND INTERPRETATION.

James D. G. Dunn

Brown, R. E., *An Introduction to the New Testament* (1997).
Campenhausen, H. von, *The Formation of the Christian Bible* (1972).
Childs, B. S., *The New Testament as Canon* (1984).

Dunn, J. D. G., *Unity and Diversity in the New Testament*, 2nd edn. (1990).

Gamble, H. Y., *The New Testament Canon: Its Making and Meaning* (1985).

Hunter, A. M., *The Unity of the New Testament* (1943).

Johnson, L. T., *The Writings of the New Testament* (1986).

Moule, C. F. D., *The Birth of the New Testament*, 3rd edn. (1982).

Reumann, J., *Variety and Unity in New Testament Thought* (1991).

Roberts, C. H., and Skeat, T. C., *The Birth of the Codex* (1983).

Nicaea, Council of,

325 AD, the first and, at least symbolically, the most important of the imperially sponsored synods of bishops designed to solve large-scale problems of organization and doctrine within the *church. These later became known as the ecumenical *councils, and tended to take Nicaea as a paradigm.

The occasion of the synod was *Constantine's desire to settle the *Arian controversy, which he found to be disrupting the unity of the churches when he conquered the east Roman provinces in 324. The disarray in which he found the *episcopate was a setback to his hopes of using the church as a force for social cohesion in the empire. He had already intervened in the cause of western church unity by summoning a large council at Arles in 314, to settle the *Donatist problem. This undoubtedly served him as a model. After the failure of direct action by letter and legation sent to *Alexandria, when he had commanded all parties to cease 'foolish disputes', Constantine decided to summon a large-scale assembly. It gathered at Nicaea (modern Iznik in Turkey), where he had his summer palace. The emperor was determined to impose an eirenic solution, by force if necessary. From the start the council was thus invested with the air of a quasi-senatorial legislature. All the bishops were afforded free use of the imperial post-stations for their travel (though very few western sees were represented), and were given other privileges that dramatically marked their emergence from the era of persecutions. Constantine's management of proceedings at Nicaea provided a pattern for the subsequent involvement of Christian emperors in church affairs. Eusebius of Caesarea, the church historian, in his *Life of Constantine*, gives a vivid, if somewhat sycophantic, account of how influential Constantine's presence was.

The council opened on 19 June 325. Later tradition, following *Athanasius of Alexandria, says that 318 bishops were in attendance, though 250 is probably a truer figure. Very quickly rejecting a pro-Arian creed offered by Eusebius of Nicomedia, the council recognized the orthodoxy of a chief defendant, Eusebius of Caesarea, but promulgated its own credal statement (probably supplied in its original draft form by the standard confession of the church of Jerusalem) to summarize its teachings. At Constantine's insistence this contained the technical term *consubstantial* (*homoousios*) to describe the Son of *God's relationship to the Father and, thus, his full divine status. Into the basic creed the bishops inserted several anti-Arian annotations, and appended five specific anathemas (or denunciations) to proscribe all the major points of Arian teaching. Thus the council affirmed a realist hermeneutic of the biblical analogy of Sonship and *Fatherhood. Explicating the traditional phrase 'begotten from the Father' the council added, as a synonym, 'of the essence [*ousia*] of the Father'. It also specified the traditional statements on the Son's procession from God. To avoid the subordinationist hermeneutic of 'a god from God', or 'a light from the Light', it added its synonym 'true God, from true God'. The five appended anathemas were designed to leave no room for an Arian revival, though this proved a hopelessly optimistic strategy. Constantine

positively discouraged any clarifying debate on the meaning of the key term 'consubstantiality', wishing to use the cipher to forge a broad agreement on the day. Accordingly bishops signed with varying understandings, a factor that contributed to the doctrinal confusions of the next fifty years.

Despite the importance of the Nicene council, a detailed record of proceedings (if there ever was one) did not survive. Historians have only a random collection of letters, indirect testimonies, and later accounts of what happened. The reliability of various sources is a problem. Accounts by ancient historians (some eyewitnesses, but several from later periods) evidently reflect tendentious versions. A Synodical Letter survives, and twenty 'canons' or laws are also attributed to the council. Their common theme is that of raising standards among the clergy and bringing order back into church practice after times of persecution.

The Nicene *Creed which is today recited at the Sunday Eucharists of many different churches is not the original conciliar confession, rather another creed, a development from that of Nicaea, which was adopted after the Council of Constantinople (381). The council and its creed continue to hold a high theological authority in the traditions of oriental Christianity, Orthodoxy, and Catholicism. It represented, for subsequent Christian tradition, a definitive expression of the inspired mind of the church, interpreting its traditional biblical *christology in new and specific categories for the *Greek world; affirming the divinity of Christ by a 'substantive' hermeneutic of the analogy of Sonship. Today there continues to be considerable debate between Christians who regard the creeds as definitive and propositional statements about the nature of Christian revelation, and those who read them more loosely as *typological or *symbolic guides to the theological thought of a particular era.

There was a Second Council of Nicaea, held in 787. This affirmed the validity of the use of *icons in Christian worship; the veneration given to them being understood to pass directly on to the person of Christ (or the saint depicted). Nicaea II is regarded by both Eastern Orthodoxy and Catholicism as the seventh of the ecumenical councils, but it was far more significant in the praxis of the Christian east than ever it was in the west. It continues to exert an influence over the symbolic and sacramental thought of eastern Christian thinkers.

John McGuckin

Hanson, R. P. C., *The Search for the Christian Doctrine of God* (1988).

Kelly, J. N. D., *Early Christian Creeds*, 3rd edn. (1972).

Luibheid, C., *The Council of Nicaea* (1982).

Ortiz de Urbina, I., *Nicée et Constantinople* (1963).

Stead, C., *Divine Substance* (1977), 223–66.

Niebuhr, Reinhold and H. Richard

(1892–1971 and 1894–1962). The Niebuhr brothers, along with the German-American Paul *Tillich, are often regarded as the most influential American theologians of the mid-20th century. In the turbulent theological climate of *North American Christianity, such a judgment is bound to be controversial. Both Niebuhrs broke out of the categories of the *fundamentalist-modernist controversy that shook the American churches in the early part of the century. The combatants in that continuing struggle looked to other intellectual leaders, but often took account of the Niebuhrs as makers and shakers of Christian thought. Ironically, the two were not in the strictest sense theologians. Both did their primary work in Christian *ethics; neither wrote a treatise on the major Christian doctrines. But in a cataclysmic era of world history their response to events and to culture had a considerable impact upon church and society, including more systematic theologians.

The brothers grew up in a parsonage of the Evangelical Synod of North America, a church that inherited both the *Lutheran and *Calvinist traditions of Germany. Both went to a college and theological seminary of that church, then continued studies at the more ecumenical Yale University Divinity School. Both were men in motion, responding in different ways to a changing history. Hence it is appropriate to treat them individually, with attention to their biographical developments, before making some comparisons.

Reinhold Niebuhr

Reinhold Niebuhr began his professional career with a thirteen-year pastorate in Detroit, Michigan (1915–28). There, in the motor capital of the world, he met the problems and conflicts of urban-industrial society. He championed the cause of labour in the automobile industry and chaired the mayor's Race Committee. His book, *Reflections from the Notebook of a Tamed Cynic* (1929), records pastoral experiences from 1915 to 1928 and gives hints of ideas he would later make famous. In 1928 he joined the faculty of Union Theological Seminary in New York and, a little later, the Graduate Faculty of Columbia University. Soon America faced the Great Depression, and Niebuhr entered the ten years that shook his world, as he called them in 1939. At Union he met the British fellow, Ursula Keppel-Compton, whom he married in 1931. The two became devoted marital partners and intellectual companions.

In 1932 Niebuhr published his epochal book, *Moral Man and Immoral Society*. It was a polemic against the '*liberalism' that he had earlier advocated. He argued that people who may be genial and generous in personal relations are often stubborn partisans of their own class or race or nation. He maintained that liberal optimism fails when reason and religion, hailed as the hopes for a better world, become the instruments of power, intensifying rather than moderating factional strife. There was more than a tinge of *Marxism in the book, although Niebuhr kept a critical distance from Marx.

Soon he was urging a more radical politics and more conservative religious convictions than prevailed in American society. That meant a shattering of stereotypes, in which both politics and religion clustered in liberal-radical or conservative groupings. The effect was to disturb conventional thinking and to create new alliances and new debates. Niebuhr ran for Congress as a socialist in 1932, after assuring his seminary president that he would not give up teaching because he had no chance of winning. He founded the Fellowship of Socialist Christians and edited its quarterly, *Radical Religion*, later *Christianity and Society*.

Theologically, he won an international reputation with his address at the Oxford Conference on Life and Work (1937) and enhanced it with his Gifford Lectures at Edinburgh (1939), published as *The Nature and Destiny of Man*. Niebuhr's mature thought drew on many sources, especially three improbable partners in dialogue: *Augustine, Marx, and *Kierkegaard. In Augustine he appreciated the interest in the long drama of history with its ceaseless conflicts between good and evil, never to be resolved this side of the ultim-

ate coming of God's kingdom. In Marx he found the importance of the grubby stuff of economic and political history, too often neglected by Christian thought. In Kierkegaard he found illumination of the anxieties of the self in its frailties, sin, and struggles for faith.

The rise of Nazism led to new moves in Niebuhr's political and theological life. As early as 1933 he resigned from the *pacifist Fellowship of Reconciliation, of which he had been national chairman. In 1940 he left the Socialist Party, which stood aloof from the war. The next year he founded the bi-weekly *Christianity and Crisis*, to oppose the mingled quasi-pacifism and isolationism of much American Christianity and to relate theology to the contemporary world-historical struggles.

The following years brought a stream of writings on theology, politics, American history and culture, and international affairs. These were slowed but not stopped by serious illnesses, beginning with a stroke in 1952. Niebuhr modified his earlier moves towards more radical politics and more conservative theology, in both cases coming to appreciate some elements in the liberalism that he had once attacked.

Politically the evils of Nazism convinced him that the liberal values of *freedom and tolerance, which he had always endorsed, deserved a stronger defence than he had earlier realized. Simultaneously, the social changes brought about by the New Deal in the United States, the Labour Party in Great Britain, and the social democratic parties of continental Europe showed him that liberal democracy had greater capacities for self-correction than he had once supposed. But he sustained his attacks on the liberal faith in progress and the neglect of attention to *sin. Some advocates of neo-conservatism in the United States came to claim the heritage of Niebuhr, although on the American spectrum he remained left of centre and a biting critic of political reactionaries.

Theologically, also, he reclaimed elements of the liberal heritage that he had always taken for granted. Following the First Assembly of the World Council of Churches (Amsterdam, 1948), at which he and Karl *Barth were major speakers, he entered into controversy with Barth, accenting the liberal elements in his own political and theological beliefs. During the Cold War his fierce opposition to Stalinist communism (involving further controversy with Barth) led to greater appreciation of American democracy, even though he continued to criticize its self-righteousness and urged patience in the prolonged coexistence necessary to avoid a nuclear war.

Niebuhr's thinking, never static, responded continuously to historical change. He characteristically advanced by correcting his own earlier thoughts. But four insights remained persistent throughout his mature career. First, he regarded theological language as *symbolic, often *mythological, to be understood 'seriously but not literally'. This brought attacks from conservatives who took literally biblical and traditional beliefs (e.g. original sin) and from liberals who dispensed with such beliefs, regarding Niebuhr as 'neo-orthodox', although he himself disliked that term.

Second, his beliefs about human nature included affirmations of the image of God in human personality, of the power and persistence of sin, and of human dependence on divine *grace, both the common grace that sustains all human life and the special grace described by the bible and Christian tradition.

Third, he was indefatigably activist, an heir of the *social gospel, but anti-utopian. The persistent fact of sin betrays all utopias, which breed fanaticism ('hard' utopias) or ineffective idealism ('soft' utopias). But, against despair, he refused to set limits on the possibilities of improving public life.

Fourth, the love–justice dialectic pervaded all his thought. *Love without *justice degenerates into sentimentality. But when love seeks justice, it moves into the conflicts of power that characterize human social life. Love, which is gracious and voluntary, exercises coercion in the enforcement of law and, most poignantly, in armed defence against aggression or revolution against tyranny. Thus love and justice exist in uneasy tension, yet each is incomplete without the other. Friends of US President Jimmy Carter (1976–80) say that he often quoted Niebuhr's statement that 'the sad job of politics is to bring justice to a sinful world'.

At the time of Niebuhr's death in 1971 the political scientist Hans Morgenthau had acclaimed him as America's 'greatest living political philosopher'. The Federal Bureau of Investigation maintained a file of 635 pages on him, telling more about its follies than about him, yet he was awarded the President's Medal for Freedom in 1964. He was widely known in Europe, and public figures in India and Indonesia acknowledged his influence. A published bibliography of his works ran to more than a thousand items, ranging from articles (some scholarly, some journalistic) to major books. His 'Christian realism', although rejected both by ethical perfectionists and by Christians who abjured political involvement, was the reference point for most Christian debates about social ethics. Although clearly Protestant, he sustained cordial relations with many Roman Catholics and Jews, sometimes joking about his frequent political efforts to get Jews and Catholics to outvote Protestants. Intellectuals quipped about 'atheists for Niebuhr'.

H. Richard Niebuhr

H. Richard Niebuhr, after earning his Ph.D. at Yale—a rite of passage that Reinhold ignored—became for three years president of Elmhurst College, then for four years a professor at Eden Theological Seminary, his alma maters. In 1931 he joined the faculty at Yale Divinity School, where he taught until his death in 1962.

In 1929 he jolted the American church with his first book, The Social Sources of Denominationalism. It was primarily a sociological study in the tradition of Ernst Troeltsch, who had been the subject of Niebuhr's doctoral dissertation. It showed that denominational divisions, often attributed to theology, are actually rooted in social realities—in class and caste, nation, region, and race. But if Niebuhr diminished the historical influence of doctrine, he displayed theological fervour in his attack on the 'hypocrisy' of denominationalism. Those who think of Reinhold as the polemicist and Richard as the quiet sage are still surprised at the sting in his attack on the moral failure of Christianity in its denominational divisiveness.

Eight years later in The Kingdom of God in America he pointed to a more creative role of the American churches. It was their faith in the *Kingdom of God. He showed major variations in this faith: from the *Puritan sovereignty of God to the evangelical reign of Christ in the human soul to the Social Gospel's kingdom on earth; but Niebuhr found in all of these a *prophetic motif. This book includes the most-quoted sentence in all his writings, characterizing one form of liberal theology: 'A God without wrath brought men without sin into a kingdom without judgment through the ministrations of a Christ without a cross' (p. 193).

His next major work was more clearly theological. The Meaning of Revelation (1941) acknowledged the influence of both Troeltsch and Karl Barth. Troeltsch, the pluralist, relativized theological declarations, showing their roots in cultural particularities. Barth declared the radical authority of the *Word of God, addressing and judging human creatures from above. Niebuhr drew together these contrasting themes. Revelation, he said, is the inward appropriation of a particular history, which becomes the centre of a continuing revolution in the religious community. Like Troeltsch he found no superhistorical vantage point from which to judge religions and assert the superiority of one's own. But in Barthian style he said that revelation is self-evidencing, not vindicated by any authority, empirical or rational, outside itself. Thus he affirmed, more modestly than most of the Christian tradition, that Christian insights are limited; yet he reached for universality in holding that God, known by Christians in their limited history, is the God of all histories.

In Christ and Culture (1951), Niebuhr again drew together his sociological and theological interests. Christians, he said, are constantly trying to relate Christ to the culture in which they live. Over the expanse of history he found five principal ways of relating the two. Between two limiting positions, 'Christ against culture' and 'Christ of culture' he discerned three mediating possibilities. Of these, 'Christ the transformer of culture' was his favourite. Yet he found all five to be important partners in a dialogue that is 'unconcluded and inconclusive'. The continuing quest was important to the man who had earlier described revelation as 'continuous revolution'.

All these works reveal a concern for the *church, not always evident in academic theologians. Niebuhr made it quite explicit when he took leave from academia in order to direct a study of theological education in the United States and Canada, sponsored by the American Association of Theological Schools. Once again he brought together his interests in sociology and theology. The study, involving many people and institutions, produced three books, The Purpose of the Church and Its Ministry (1956), and two others assembled by the team that he headed.

The final book published during his lifetime was Radical Monotheism and Western Culture (1960). Here he modified the radical historical accent of earlier works and, in a turn to *metaphysics, described God as 'the principle of being itself' (p. 32). Some scholars saw here the influence of Paul Tillich, whose early book, The Religious Situation, Niebuhr had translated from German in 1932. Others saw the influence of his old love, the American Puritan Jonathan *Edwards.

While friends and admirers were still grieving over Niebuhr's death, The Responsible Self appeared in 1963. Many were surprised to find it a book of 'moral philosophy', in conscious resistance to the neo-orthodoxies that isolated theology from philosophy. He understood moral decisions as the acts of persons responding to other persons and to God in an ever-changing history. He sought to chart a path that avoids both traditional ethical absolutism (which generally absolutizes the particularities of a partisan group) and the glibness of situation ethics.

Continuing influence

Both Niebuhrs fell into some neglect in the 1960s, with the rise of theologies of *liberation and diverse ethical movements. Their self-critical pilgrimages and anti-utopianism seemed tame to more messianic enthusiasts. But with the fading of many partisan hopes came a renewed influence of the brothers. A flurry of posthumous books, by them and about them, thrust both back into the midst of discussion. Republication of their older books kept their ideas in circulation long after the shorter influence of most, though not all, of the thinkers who for a time displaced them.

The brothers had different and complementary styles. Reinhold in his exuberance would seize on an idea, put it forth, then revise or criticize it in later publications. Richard tested his ideas in teaching and reformulated them many times before putting them in print. The two esteemed and admired each other. Occasional dabblers in psychobiography have sought signs of sibling rivalry. Given their searching doctrines of sin, the Niebuhrs probably believed that no brothers since *Cain and Abel have been utterly free of such rivalry. But each dedicated a book to the other. Each occasionally teased the other as each poked fun at himself, and the affection of the teasing was evident to all who observed the smiles and the tone of voice.

On rare occasions they entered into public or semi-public controversy. An example in 1941 was a meeting of the Fellowship of Socialist Christians. Hitler's blitzkrieg had hit Norway, Denmark, and Belgium, made France a puppet state, and bombed British cities. Reinhold publicly advocated American support of Britain at the risk of involvement in *war. Richard said that 'the real issue' for the church was not whether to go to war. It was 'to help the nation to become morally fit either to stay out or to enter into war'. Years later Richard diagnosed the difference: Reinhold was called to the reform of culture while Richard was called to the reformation of the church. A consequence was that Reinhold was the conspicuous public figure, whose opinions were heard (though often rejected) by high government officials. But he sometimes acclaimed Richard as a superior scholar. A later generation would dishonour the Niebuhrs if it fixed their ideas as final truth. Both brothers would rather be known as pilgrims.   **Roger L. Shinn**

Niebuhr, H. Richard, *Faith on Earth*, ed. Richard R. Niebuhr (1989).
—— *Theology, History, and Culture: Major Unpublished Writings*, ed. William Stacy Johnson (1996).
Niebuhr, Reinhold, *The Nature and Destiny of Man*, i. *Human Nature* (1941); ii. *Human Destiny* (1943).
—— *The Children of Light and the Children of Darkness: A Vindication of Democracy and a Critique of its Traditional Defense* (1944).
—— *The Irony of American History* (1952).
—— *The Self and the Dramas of History* (1955).
Brown, Charles C., *Niebuhr and his Age: Reinhold Niebuhr's Prophetic Role in the Twentieth Century* (1992).
Niebuhr, Ursula M. (ed.), *Remembering Reinhold Niebuhr: Letters of Reinhold and Ursula M. Niebuhr* (1991).
Robertson, D. B., *Reinhold Niebuhr's Works: A Bibliography*, rev. edn. (1983).
Stone, Ronald H., *Professor Reinhold Niebuhr: A Mentor to the Twentieth Century* (1992).
Thieman, Ronald F. (ed.), *The Legacy of H. Richard Niebuhr* (1991).

Nietzsche, Friedrich (1844–1900), anti-Christian *philosopher. Nietzsche was the son of a Lutheran pastor. His major writings date from a sixteen-year period of intense creativity, 1872–88, terminated by his lapse into insanity. Nietzsche did not believe in either moderation or modesty. 'I know my fate,' he wrote in *Ecce Homo*. 'One day my name will be associated with the memory of something tremendous—a crisis without equal on earth, the most profound collision of conscience, a decision that was conjured up *against* everything that had been believed, demanded, hallowed so far. I am no man, I am dynamite.' And he is certainly among the most ambitious of the 19th-century critics of *Christianity; in that, unlike the followers of Feuerbach for instance, he did not simply seek to do away with Christian faith whilst preserving Christian *ethics, but instead argued that Christian ethics are immoral.

He attacks Christian ethics in the name of radical honesty. God, he declares, is dead. But that means that moral 'truth' is also dead—in any sense of the word other than the most searching honesty. There is for him no longer any more objective basis for *morality than this.

Along with *Marx and Freud, Nietzsche has been termed (by Paul *Ricœur) one of the three great modern 'masters of suspicion'; but he is the most theologically focused of the three. Christian ethics, he suggests, is essentially the product of *ressentiment* (resentment—he always uses the French term). It is the classic expression of 'slave morality'. The primordial form of ethics was 'master morality': the creation of the ruling class, who defined everything most distinctively characteristic of themselves—glorious ostentation, aristocratic pride, ruthless self-assertion—as 'good', and the uncultivated manners of the herd-like lower classes as 'bad'. But slave morality is the direct reversal of this. It represents the revenge of the lower classes, accomplished through a redefinition of the original master-ethos as 'evil' and the opposing herd-ethos as 'good'; and eventually it prevails, converting even the ruling classes to its precepts. Nietzsche's goal is to go 'beyond good and evil' in this sense—not back to the fragile naivety of master-morality, but on to a new morality of sophisticated free-spiritedness.

Slave morality is the greatest threat to honesty, simply because it must always seek to disguise its true origins in *ressentiment*. It markets itself by offering not only sublimated revenge but also consolation. True honesty demands an absolute renunciation of both. Nietzsche's ideal is a state of wisdom in which the very desire for such revenge or consolation is eradicated. And to the Christian notion of eternal life he therefore opposes the hypothesis of 'eternal return'. Suppose you were faced with the prospect of your whole life, complete with all its sources of grief and all its failures, quite unchanged, recurring eternally, could you bear it? That, he suggests, is the ultimate criterion for truth-as-honesty. For only someone who could seriously answer yes, without reservation, would finally be immune from the fundamental discontents out of which dishonesty springs. In *Thus Spoke Zarathustra* he tells the story of a prophet's wrestling with the true purgative horror of this hypothesis, genuinely taken to heart. In the end, he argues, no mere human could ever fully bear the prospect. To say yes to eternal return, and really mean it, would be the defining quality of the 'overman'.

Nietzsche does not charge *Jesus with promoting slave morality. That is what the *church has done; and the church has thereby betrayed its founder. But his criticism of the original gospel of Jesus is the same as his criticism of Buddhism: that it represents a form of decadent world-weariness. And so it still markets itself with a consoling hope, a promise of release. The 'overman', by contrast, would be fired by a 'Dionysian' creative energy, which simply dispenses with such hopes and promises.

Time and again, in the prefaces to his books, Nietzsche insists that he is writing only for a tiny élite of isolated free spirits, that, indeed, maybe his true readers are not yet born. The rest of us are just eavesdroppers. *Thus Spoke Zarathustra* is, not least, a lyric celebration of intellectual solitude. He has no interest in any doctrine that might directly contribute to the building-up of a community.

This has, however, by no means prevented attempts, by a variety of different existing ideological communities, to appropriate for themselves at any rate certain aspects of his teaching. The Nazis are the most notorious case; marvellously defying his repeated denunciations of *nationalism, *socialism, and, especially, *anti-semitism. But there have also been significant Nietzschean tendencies, for example, within the anarcho-syndicalist tradition; even though he denounced anarchism. Both of these groups warmed, above all, to his anti-Christianity.

In many ways, though, the most interesting communitarian response has been, precisely, on the part of defiantly open-minded *still*-Christian thinkers—interpreting the Nietzschean critique as an exaggerated, one-sided but none the less vital counterbalancing corrective to mainstream church tradition.

No doubt his being linked to *Kierkegaard, in the 19th-century prehistory of *existentialism, has helped. The responsibility for this is largely Karl Jasper's, Nietzsche himself having only ever quite dimly aware of Kierkegaard's work (in his day still untranslated). But perhaps the four most significant of these positive Christian theological responders to Nietzsche, up to now, have been Dietrich *Bonhoeffer, Eberhard *Jüngel, Thomas Altizer, and Don *Cupitt.

Bonhoeffer's enthusiasm for Nietzsche emerges quite clearly in his 1929 Barcelona lecture on 'Basic Questions of a Christian Ethic'. Thereafter, for good tactical reasons relating to the need for church unity in the struggle against Nazism, he ceased to draw attention to it. In this text, however, he takes up two fundamental Nietzschean themes: the idea of going 'beyond good and evil', which later recurs as a key element in his *Ethics* (1940–3); and the demand that we be 'loyal to the earth'. With regard to the former, he argues for a drastic reversal of Nietzsche's hostile verdict on *Paul and *Luther, in particular. The whole Pauline/Lutheran polemic against mere 'works-righteousness', properly interpreted, is, he insists, itself essentially an attempt to go 'beyond good and evil' in very much the Nietzschean sense.

As for 'loyalty to the earth', by this Nietzsche had meant the radical abandonment of what he terms 'metaphysics'. That is, any sort of marketing ploy for one's morality, by appeal to supposed 'ultimate' realities, over and above the actual evidence of observable earthly practice. In the Barcelona lecture Bonhoeffer links such loyalty to the ancient myth of the giant Antaeus—who was the strongest of all mortals, but whose strength flowed into him from the earth, so that, when lifted into the air, he was suddenly rendered quite helpless. Again, amongst his prison writings there is also the draft of a play about Antaeus, in which the giant's earthbound strength seems basically to represent everything required for the most effective possible spiritual resistance to Nazism, undistracted by the operations of mere ecclesiastical self-interest. The 'religionless Christianity' for which Bonhoeffer calls elsewhere in these writings would, he says, be a faith purged of 'metaphysics and inwardness'. But these appear to be just two different aspects of

what Nietzsche simply calls 'metaphysics': ecclesiastical self-interest expressed, on the one hand, in the marketing ploys of the apologetic theologian; and, on the other, in those of the popular evangelist, playing on people's private weaknesses.

Jüngel, in *God as the Mystery of the World* (first published in German in 1977), focuses more directly on the Nietzschean proclamation of the death of God. He accepts the Nietzschean diagnosis to the extent of entirely agreeing that the old God of 'metaphysics', in Nietzsche's sense, is indeed dead. But the true alternative, he argues, is not Nietzsche's *atheism (or, perhaps more accurately, his playful private cult of Dionysius). The fundamental substantive error of 'metaphysics', so defined, is its cosmic projection of a false ideal of impassible imperishability. And, properly understood, the Pauline confession of a crucified God is already, at least in principle, the perfect symbolic antithesis to that. Nietzsche's attack is after all, therefore, only valid with reference to those forms of Christian thought that continue to hold back from the real theological revolution implicit in the original symbolism of the cross.

Altizer and Cupitt, finally, are more flamboyantly provocative. Altizer, an American contributor to the 'death of God' theology of the late 1960s, proclaims a 'gospel of Christian atheism' whose main authorities are Nietzsche, *Hegel, and *Blake. Cupitt, in his writings of the early 1980s, seeks to integrate Nietzschean insight into a form of postmodern 'Christian Buddhism'.

These are certainly bold departures. But no doubt theology, in general, thrives on being confronted by the most awkward possible challenges. And none, perhaps, is more awkward than Nietzsche's.

Andrew Shanks

Nietzsche, F., *Thus Spoke Zarathustra* (1883–4), ET (1961).
—— *Beyond Good and Evil* (1886), ET (1973).
—— *On the Genealogy of Morals* (1887), ET (1967).
—— *The Antichrist* (1895), ET (1968).
Altizer, T. J. J., *The Gospel of Christian Atheism* (1966).
Cupitt, D., *The World to Come* (1982).
Jüngel, E., *God as the Mystery of the World* (1983).
Shanks, A., 'Bonhoeffer's Response to Nietzsche', *Studies in Christian Ethics* (1997).

nineteenth century: an overview. The Christian theological enterprise in Europe and America in the 19th century was a scene of changes unparalleled since the 16th-century *Reformations, changes that set the problems and prefigured most of the directions for theologies in the 20th century. In socio-historical terms, despite the continuing *secularization of the west, the century was notable for the emergence of a powerful *Protestant foreign *missionary enterprise, for popular *Catholic revival on the Continent, and for such distinctive movements in *North America as *Mormonism and Christian Science. But Catholic and Protestant *theologies* alike were deeply troubled as well as creative, characterized by quite new modes of the struggle with *Enlightenment criticism and a rapidly changing social order, as well as by powerful internal tensions between 'liberal' and 'conservative'.

For the beginning of the century, one naturally thinks of *Schleiermacher, the founder of an epoch, whose *Speeches on Religion to its Cultured Despisers* appeared in 1799, and of the contemporary work of *Hegel, Schelling (who was especially important for Catholicism), and *Coleridge. Immediately in the background of their ventures were *Kant's critical philosophy, the French Revolution, and the Napoleonic wars, whose shadows extended long into the century and were important for Roman Catholic and Protestant thought alike. There were independent creative moments elsewhere, notably in Britain and America, but the century's astonishing burst of vitality in the *German faculties reverberated throughout the theological world. *Eastern Orthodox Christianity was hardly participant in novel modes of religious thought, except in *Russia, where the Christian philosopher Soloviev and the profoundly religious novelists *Dostoevsky and *Tolstoy have to be noted.

The theological dramas of the century can usefully be looked at as taking place on three broad and overlapping, almost concentric, stages. The most inclusive, for Catholic and Protestant thought alike in consequence of the Enlightenment, reflects the continuing struggle of the church(es) within the larger society. This framed a network of controversies about the nature of the *church: about *authority within it, its status and rights in relation to the state, and its responsibilities in relation to an increasingly industrialized society, a concern which culminated in 'social gospels' at the end of the century.

Overlaid on this broad scene were restatements of the fundamental nature of the theological enterprise, after the shocks to traditional theology from *Pietism and the Enlightenment. New conceptions emerged most radically among Protestants. In Catholicism the problem was reflected in a new phase of debates over the relation of *faith and *reason, leading eventually to *Vatican I and the *modernist conflict. Correlated with questions of theological method were important problems in conceptualizing the relation between *God and *world.

Equally critical for the reconception of theology was the emergence of a new kind of *historical consciousness, perhaps the most decisive theological development of the century, focusing particularly on the *quest for the historical *Jesus but also including the whole history of Christianity and its relation to other religious traditions. By the end of the century historical questions were at the centre of debate for both Catholics and Protestants.

The question of the church and society

At the beginning of the century, Napoleon drastically reordered the religio-political scene through the destruction of the prince-bishoprics and the reshuffling of the boundaries of the German states to include mixed Catholic and Protestant populations. This meant that the principle of the Peace of Augsburg (1555), that the religion of a state should be the religion of its ruler, was no longer viable. In France the Concordat of 1801 laid the ground for new ways of relating the *papacy to the body of the faithful, particularly through the appointment of bishops. Napoleon's temporary annexation of the papal states (1809) and the exile of Pope Pius VII (1809–12) actually increased the prestige of the papacy and gave an impetus to 'popular *ultramontanism' and the emergence of the papal title 'His Holiness'. However, along with spreading religious indifferentism and rising nationalisms, these actions also indicated threats to the existence of the papacy and of the Catholic church itself.

At the start of the century, movements to assert local authority as against that of the papacy were still significant. Known as *Gallicanism in France, Febronianism in the German-speaking world, and Cisalpinism in Britain, they were modes of 'Catholic Enlighten-

ment' urging the Catholic Church toward decentralization in structure and eclecticism in thought. But as the century wore on, especially after the restoration in 1814 of the Society of Jesus (see JESUIT THOUGHT) and the shift of intellectual gravity to the Gregorian University in *Rome, the power of ultramontanism grew rapidly. It was coupled (especially by Pope Pius IX after the shock of the revolutions of 1848) with a new effort to maintain the rights and freedom of the church, tending to the development of a Catholic 'subculture' as a defence against the onslaughts of modernity, or what was called 'liberalism' in Pius's Syllabus of Errors (1864). Its resistance to various secular intrusions upon the church's rights, especially in regard to *education and the *family as well as internal church affairs, was coupled with rejections of so-called rationalism at several levels. This was carried further (especially in the First Vatican Council, and in Pope Leo XIII's encyclical Aeterni Patris, 1879) with the establishment of the philosophy of Thomas *Aquinas as the great model for Catholic thought, both for theology and for the ordering of society as a whole (see THOMISM, MODERN). Political and theological questions were thoroughly intertwined in these developments. For example, Vatican I was able to deal only with the question of faith and reason (in a Thomistic way) and with the *infallibility of the pope before being interrupted by the Franco-Prussian War.

Quite other ways of reasserting the rights of the church and defining its authority could be found in the form of a strict *Lutheran Confessionalism, shaped in the mid-century by Löhe, Stahl, and others, and in the *Oxford Movement in England, after 1833. The German Confessionalists were committed to the maintenance of state churches (throne and altar together). In this regard it is significant that after the death of Schleiermacher the Prussian king had pressed for the appointment of a 'believing' theologian as his successor at Berlin, to deliver the church from 'rationalism'. Such concern to preserve orthodoxy was also present in a milder way in the German pietist revivals and the *religious-experience orientation of the Erlangen school.

The demand of the Oxford Movement, on the contrary, was for freedom of the church from state control, on the grounds of its ancient traditions and divinely established authority, in continuity with the *apostolic succession. The American experiment of the separation of church and state was unique, being peculiarly related to the pluralism of the US. It was widely noted, even wistfully viewed by an occasional early 19th-century Catholic thinker, for example the *Tübingen school's von Drey and the Cisalpine John Lingard, and enthusiastically appreciated by the German Catholic Hermann Schell at the end of the century, but it was not emulated in Europe or Britain. The final separation of church and state in France in 1905 was quite different. Perhaps the most dramatic proposal about church and state was the contention of the highly original 'speculative' theologian, Richard Rothe of Heidelberg, that Christianity should be freed from the church, whose previously assumed roles should be taken over by a secular-ethical culture. Though understandably never endorsed by any church, by the end of the 19th century Rothe's view could be seen as prophetic of the actual situation.

The *Marxist critique of the church, especially after the Communist Manifesto of 1848, occasioned widely varying theological responses to the emerging industrial social order. On the negative side, these included intransigent opposition both to communist theory and to the programmes of the Social Democrats, a hostility represented by the main line of German Protestant theology (even Harnack thought the church had no responsibility to speak on economic matters) and, apart from the outstanding exception of Bishop Ketteler of Mainz (1811–77), by most Catholic social thought until Leo XIII's *Rerum Novarum* (1891). This became the charter for a Catholic labour movement and for social Catholicism in general.

More positive reactions to Marxism ranged from the mild (and sentimentally utopian) Christian *Socialism of F. D. Maurice and his associates in Britain in the early 1850s, through later vigorous outcries against social injustices, to the radical religious socialism in late 19th-century Swiss Protestantism (Kutter and Ragaz) which hailed the despised Social Democrats for doing what the church ought itself to have been doing. Walter Rauschenbusch in America proposed that theology should be revised so as to be adequate for a *social gospel. By the end of the century, Protestant social gospels were flourishing in Britain and in America, proposing economic and social reforms, from merely palliative measures that would moderate the worst abuses of industrial society to full-scale attacks on *capitalism as incompatible with the Christian gospel.

New views of the theological task

Kant's emphasis on the constitutive role of the mind in all knowledge was reflected in a new and decisive 'turn to the subject' at the cutting edge of 19th-century theology. The religious subject, its point of view, its cognitive structures, its 'interest', its willing and choosing, had to be consciously and systematically recognized as present at the starting-point of theological reflection.

There was continuity here with the Enlightenment confidence in the human. The difference is the rejection of the 18th century's rationalism. This was classically expressed in Schleiermacher's proposal, influenced by *Romanticism and his own early exposure to Moravian Pietism, that *Gefühl*, feeling (or, later, in the *Glaubenslehre*, the 'feeling of utter dependence') is the heart of the religious defined as the deepest level of self-consciousness and awareness, in contrast to the Enlightenment preoccupation with beliefs and morals.

Hegel also took this inward turn, although his view of the self was quite different. He despised the idea of utter dependence. He posited an essentially reasoning and thinking self, but enlarged the idea of the rational to incorporate both the Romantic quest for unity and universality and the dialectic of movement, of subjective and objective moments, in thought and in history. By thus offering a dynamic model of the self, divine or human, Hegel thought he could secure the traditional doctrines of *Incarnation and *Trinity marginalized by Schleiermacher. Not altogether unlike Hegel's idea of reason (though more Schellingian in its roots) was Coleridge's notion of reason as the organ of the 'supersensuous', recalling the Cambridge Platonists. But this reason again transcended Enlightenment fixation on the phenomenal world of sense perception, represented among Coleridge's contemporaries by Bentham and Paley. Reason was to include imagination and will, even the courage to venture beyond the provable. Similarly, Coleridge prophetically redefined the authority of scripture as its power to speak to the deepest needs of the self (see BIBLE, ITS AUTHORITY AND INTERPRETATION).

The turn to the self was reflected in many other ways: in Emerson's focus on religious sentiment; in F. D. Maurice's rejection of every 'system' and his insistence on the partiality and distortion of all apprehensions; in Horace Bushnell's theory of religious language; supremely in *Kierkegaard's recognition of truth as subjectivity; in Albrecht Ritschl's assertion that religious knowledge consists in 'judgments of value'; in the French liberal Auguste Sabatier's emphasis on *psychological religion; in William *James's account of the will to believe and his pragmatic theory of truth; in Cardinal *Newman's 'illative sense'; in the Catholic modernist George Tyrrell's conception of doctrine; and in Ernst Troeltsch's embracing of 'relativism' and of the truth of Christianity 'for us'.

Thus the idea of *revelation itself had to be reconsidered and the former confidence in its truths was dissolved. The question was not *whether* revelation was to be accepted, but rather *what* does 'revelation' mean? And so the old apologetics that took prophecy and *miracle as warrants for 'revealed truth' had to be abandoned.

The 19th-century anthropological turn took its most extreme form in Ludwig Feuerbach's internal critique of theology, in which 'religion' is to be taken with the utmost seriousness, but its talk about God has to be understood as a projection of human attributes and an expression of human wishes (the *Essence of Christianity*, 1840). Thus theology *is* anthropology. Feuerbach insisted that he wanted to celebrate the human, real, sensuous person. His projection theory was later taken up by Freud in the idea of religion as illusion, and his affirmation of the human was to be reflected in Friedrich *Nietzsche's proclamation of the death of God and his bitter polemic against Christianity's slave morality.

More generally in Protestant *liberal theologies, which seemed to be sweeping all before them by the end of the century, the ideas of revelation and of human discovery merged, with religious experience identified as the basis for all theology. A similar appeal to experience was presupposed by Tyrrell, marking a radical change from the earlier Roman Catholic tradition found in the faith/reason discussions, increasingly dominated by the Thomistic view.

Not often so explicitly stated, but widely implicit in the later 19th century's idea of the theological enterprise, was another of Schleiermacher's proposals. In the *Brief Outline on the Study of Theology* (1811; 1830) he argued that dogmatics, or systematic theology, has to be understood as the articulation of the *contemporary* religious consciousness of the church, running parallel to 'church statistics' (i.e. sociology of religion). Thus emerged a new way of ordering the theological enterprise, contrary both to the tradition of the Protestant scholastics and to the '*natural theology' of the 17th and 18th centuries. The theological venture could then be defended on the basis either of its independence and the *sui generis* nature of the religious (Schleiermacher), or of its unity with the whole of human experience and its embodiment of western culture (Hegel, and speculative and idealist theologies generally). Those contrasting perspectives provide an illuminating typology for the century's philosophies of religion.

Intimately related to the reconsideration of the nature of the theological task was the critique of 'supernaturalism', with a new stress instead on immanence in conceptions of the relation of God and the world. The older ideas of theism, dominated by divine transcendence (and carried to an extreme in *deism), were replaced in both Schleiermacher and Hegel by what the 20th century would call panentheism, where God is not identified totally with the cosmos (pantheism) but includes it. More radical immanentism was to emerge in Emerson's light-hearted and happy celebration of the divinity of man, leading in the direction of a thoroughgoing religious naturalism, and in the later Strauss's more heavy-handed evolutionary monism (*The Old Faith and the New*, 1872).

Parallel to these tendencies, traditional conceptions of divine immutability began to be criticized both in a prophetic essay on the subject by the mid-century mediating thinker, Isaak Dorner, and (though for somewhat different reasons) in the emergence of several *kenotic christologies in mid-century Germany and late-century Anglicanism. Some of that critique laid the ground for 20th-century *process theologies and conceptions of a limited God. In William James's pluralistic universe, for instance, the suffocating absolute of idealist philosophy is replaced by a world with real evil and a God genuinely engaged in the struggle for good. These moves were vigorously opposed by Protestant orthodoxy and by the main line of Catholic theology. The charge of 'immanentism' was to be a central theme in Pope Pius X's condemnation of modernism in 1907.

The struggle over Darwin and the theory of *evolution can be viewed partly as a critical focus of the question of how God relates to the world. Certainly in the relation of *science and theology, the 19th was Darwin's century. The theological response to *The Origin of Species* (1859) has been often misconstrued. It did not represent a warfare of science and religion, except in the minds of some interpreters. For the best-known of those, the real conflict was primarily between a new 'scientific history', especially in biblical studies, and institutional religious (especially Roman Catholic) intransigence. There was initially little of the explosion that was to come with the fundamentalist anti-evolution campaign of the 1920s in America, though towards the end of the 19th century Darwin was taken up as ammunition by the Social Democrats in Germany in a battle they were already waging against religion in the name of socialism and materialism.

The variety of serious theological reactions (Catholic as well as Protestant) to Darwin in the 19th century was quite as complicated as the scientific responses (among the latter, Neo-Lamarckism was as widely accepted as Darwin's theory until after 1900). Religious reactions ranged from bitter hostility in some theologians because of the apparent exclusion of *design and the denial of human uniqueness, through qualified acceptance (at least in relation to the development of the human body), to a hearty embrace of evolution as a description of the way God has worked immanently in the world. A God who is only an occasional visitor is an impossible conception: either we banish God altogether or we believe in his immanence in nature from end to end, to summarize Aubrey Moore's classic statement in *Lux Mundi* (1889). Towards the end of the century the idea of evolution (more in a Spencerian than a Darwinian form) could even be heralded as the new paradigm for understanding all things religious and cultural. Martin Kähler claimed that it was easy for German theologians to become Darwinians because 'we were already Hegelians and Hegel anticipated the whole of Darwin'.

In fact, it was conservatives like Charles Hodge in America and Otto Zöckler in Germany who were most attentive to Darwin's own position, which they took to be simply contrary to the biblical

teaching about the origin of humanity. One sees here orthodoxy's tendency to the all-or-nothing view, a way of thinking operating at many levels. These range from Newman's sophisticated commitment to 'dogma' and his contention in the *Apologia pro Vita Sua* (1864) that there was no real middle-ground between Catholic truth and rationalism, to some simplistic fundamentalist objections to any 'higher criticism' on the grounds that, like being only 'a little pregnant', being only a little doubtful of scriptural inerrancy opened the door to scepticism and atheism.

The historical question

The publication of D. F. Strauss's *The Life of Jesus Critically Examined* (1835) was an event of the greatest magnitude both theologically and politically. The work aroused a storm of controversy in Germany, a 'panic-stricken terror' according to the leading contemporary Protestant church historian, F. C. Baur, and it eventually destroyed Strauss's chances of an academic theological career. Politically the work was welcomed by the new left-wing Hegelians as implying radical democratic politics in its conflict with the establishment. The book, translated into English by George Eliot, was so shocking to British sensibilities that, apart from the *Westminster Review* liberals and S. T. Coleridge's posthumous *Confessions of an Inquiring Spirit* (1840), extensive and open debate did not take place in England until the publication of *Essays and Reviews*, a highly controversial engagement with Strauss by a group of more liberal Anglicans, in 1860. In Roman Catholic circles, the new critical perspectives did not come to centre-stage until the modernist controversy at the end of the century.

Strauss proposed a '*mythological' view of the origin of the gospel stories as unconscious poetic products of the early Christian community, which applied the more general idea of humanity united with divinity to the one human figure of Jesus. Both supernaturalist and rationalist interpretations of the gospels were quite implausible in view of the contradictions and repetitions in the texts. Supernaturalism conflicted with the canons of physical science, a consistent chronology, and with any conceivable psychology of Jesus' life. Rationalist explanations simply left out the content of religion, the 'divine'. The question for Strauss as a Hegelian was not whether there was a deep unity between the human and the divine—Hegel stood for that—but whether historical science could justify the identification of the divine–human Christ-figure of orthodoxy with the individual person Jesus.

Strauss thus inaugurated the modern era in critical NT study, which for the most part in the 19th century was the history of German criticism. *Higher criticism developed alongside extensive efforts to establish the Greek text of the NT through analysis of the ancient manuscripts, many newly discovered. At the outset, the gospel of *John, on which the tradition (including even Schleiermacher) had depended so much, had to be rejected as a reliable historical source. This laid the groundwork for subsequent debates over the relation of the Synoptic Gospels, quickly leading to the thesis of the priority of Mark and to the two-source hypothesis (Mark and Q, a sayings source) for the gospels of Luke and Matthew, an explanation dominant by the end of the century. By that time too, the Graf–Wellhausen theory that posited four source documents underlying the Pentateuch had won the day in Britain and America as well as in Germany, undermining claims of Mosaic authorship.

What were the results? One was that the attempt to construct a scientific 'life of Jesus' from the gospel records had to be given up as impossible. As Martin Kähler put it, 'we have no sources for a biography of Jesus of Nazareth which measure up to the standards of contemporary historical science', but only 'a vast field strewn with the fragments of various traditions'. The question was only partly 'what can be known about Jesus?', and there even the argument that there was no such historical person could resurface. The question was equally whether the figure who could be known is appropriate for the faith of modern human beings.

Thus a second result was extended debate over the nature and presuppositions of historical study. Kähler, in his famous 1892 lecture, 'The so-called Jesus of history and the historic biblical Christ', first proposed the distinction between the *historisch* and the *geschichtlich*. The former indicates 'scientific' historical study that abstracts from the presuppositions of faith and operates on the principles of causality and psychological analogy in human experience. The latter characterizes historical work shaped from the outset by faith's confession that Jesus is Lord and that the divine cannot be separated from the human in the gospel stories. This latter kind of history alone is appropriate to the gospels as proclamation.

A third result was the rediscovery of the *apocalyptic in Jesus' teaching about the *Kingdom of God, a theme emphasized by Strauss but recovered at the end of the century by Johannes Weiss and Albert Schweitzer. The apocalyptic interpretation was wholly unacceptable, for example, to the leading Protestant liberal of the day, Adolf Harnack, as making quite impossible the essence of the kingdom as the rule of God in the hearts and souls of individuals. The *eschatological question was to generate the sharpest tensions in Protestant thought for a century. The apocalyptic view was taken up by the Catholic modernists Loisy and Tyrrell, though with vastly different conclusions from their Protestant counterparts. For them, the church was the appropriate fulfilment of the idea of the heavenly kingdom in Jesus' teaching. To say that 'Jesus foretold the kingdom, and it was the church that came', rather than showing the betrayal of Jesus' message as Harnack thought, simply expresses the necessity of the church for the proclamation of the gospel. This attempt to justify the development of Catholicism was hardly acceptable to Rome. Loisy was one of the principal targets in Pope Pius X's condemnation of modernism, and that event, along with the uniformly conservative decisions of the newly reconstituted Biblical Commission (1903), was to shut down the promising beginnings of Roman Catholic critical biblical study and drive it underground for half a century.

Three related dimensions of the new historical consciousness had emerged by the end of the century: the *Religionsgeschichtlichesschule* (history of religions school) looking at *religion as a human phenomenon, the reconsideration of the history of the church and theology, and much more broadly the new study of comparative religion. All of these were reflected in the work of Ernst Troeltsch, as well as of his Catholic contemporary Hermann Schell, who was particularly interested in the work of the great theorist and translator of Eastern religious texts, Max Müller.

The *Religionsgeschichtlichesschule* was especially important for biblical studies. Biblical religion had to be seen as fully a part of general religious history, intimately related to its socioreligious surroundings and influenced by them. This applied to the emergence of early Christianity as a syncretistic movement out of a syncretistic Judaism, as well as, for example, to the creation stories in relation to Babylonian creation myths.

Christian history, especially its theology, had also to be reassessed. For Harnack, in his famous history of dogma, it was to be seen as the corruption of the simple gospel of Jesus by the incorporation of Greek metaphysical categories ('Dogma, in its conception and its construction, is a work of the Greek spirit'), as well as by the emergence of Catholic institutionalism. Though his was an essentially 'ideological-dogmatic' kind of history, Harnack was quite aware of the interplay of social, political, and intellectual influences in the development of theology. But it was Troeltsch, notably in the classic *Social Teachings of the Christian Churches and Groups* (1912), who most clearly articulated the social conditioning of theological ideas and the pluralism within Christianity, so that 'church history' had to become a social history of Christianity, an 'essentially sociological-realistic-ethical' history.

In Troeltsch's lifelong concern with the question of the 'absoluteness' (or the finality) of Christianity, there came a kind of culmination of the 19th century's new recognition of the problem of the relationship between Christianity and other religions, in which the older attitude of exclusiveness and even intolerance was abandoned. Early in the century, the Romantic vision had freed the European mind to become not only curious about other people's religions but also appreciative of them as authentic expressions of the human experience. Both Schleiermacher and Hegel had partly reflected this change of spirit. But in the explosion of knowledge about other religions, including not only the great developed traditions of the Far East but also Egyptian, ancient Mediterranean, and 'primitive' or non-literate religion, a new kind of study of religion flourished by the end of the century. Here the early 19th century turn to the subject developed into an 'objective' study of religious subjectivity itself. This is seen in William James's *Varieties of Religious Experience* (1902), but also the extensive studies of pre-literate religiousness and the attempts to identify the earliest forms of the religious, whether in animism or totemism or even some 'high god' concepts. Frazer's *The Golden Bough* epitomizes the approach. Much of this reflection was dominated by evolutionary notions of development, which often reflected the optimism of the late century.

We owe to Troeltsch a classic formulation of the principles of historical enquiry: criticism (so that all historical judgements prove to be tentative), analogy (so that nothing can be exempted from analogy with our present experience of happenings), and correlation (in which everything is related to everything else). The final result had to be a relativism in which the most that can be said is that the truth of a religious view (in his case the Christian one) is its truth 'for us', inseparable from our particular sociocultural situation.

In sum, by the end of the 19th century one can see both in Protestant liberalism in its struggle with conservatism, and in the suppression of Roman Catholic modernism, unresolved tensions in all the major areas of concern: the relation of church and society; the nature of the theological enterprise and the 'truth' of its faith or the validity of its ethics; and the consequences of the new historical consciousness. These problems were to shape the efforts of the 20th century.   **Claude Welch**

Barth, Karl, *Protestant Theology in the Nineteenth Century* (1946), ET (1972).

Berkhof, Hendrikus, *Two Hundred Years of Theology* (1989).

Chadwick, Owen, *The Secularization of the European Mind in the Nineteenth Century* (1975).

Fitzer, Joseph, *Romance and the Rock: Nineteenth-Century Catholics on Faith and Reason* (1989).

Livingston, James C., *Modern Christian Thought: From the Enlightenment to Vatican II* (1971).

McCool, Gerald A., *Nineteenth Century Scholasticism* (1989).

Misner, Paul, *Social Catholicism in Europe: From the Onset of Industrialization to the First World War* (1991).

O'Meara, Thomas F., *Church and Culture: German Catholic Theology, 1860–1914* (1991).

Pelikan, Jaroslav, *Christian Doctrine and Modern Culture (since 1700)* (1989).

Reardon, Bernard M. G., *Religious Thought in the Nineteenth Century* (1966).

Schoof, T. M., *A Survey of Catholic Theology, 1800–1970* (1970).

Smart, Ninian, *et al.* (eds.), *Nineteenth-Century Religious Thought in the West* (3 vols.; 1985). Extensive bibliographies.

Welch, Claude, *Protestant Thought in the Nineteenth Century* (2 vols.; 1972; 1985). Extensive bibliographies.

North America: an overview.

An enduring mark of Christian thought in North America has been interest in the practicality of *theology. Whether grounded in philosophical and religious traditions nurtured by academic professional theologians or in the democratizing ethos of popular religious movements, this interest in the practical has recurred frequently enough to serve as a convenient organizing principle for an overview.

17th to 19th centuries

It is an interest first expressed in the writings of the Calvinist ministers of colonial New England, who, drawing on medieval and *Reformed scholastics, defined theology as 'the doctrine of living to God', a 'practical' discipline designed to move the will towards its proper end, rather than a 'theoretical' beholding of divine truth as an end in itself. They used this insight to develop a *covenantal theology that received its classic American formulation from Samuel Willard of Boston, in lectures published posthumously as the *Compleat Body of Divinity* (1726). This work employed the distinction between the covenant of works with *Adam and the covenant of *grace through Christ to emphasize that *salvation comes only through grace to the elect.

By the time this book appeared, some of the saints were ready to revise its *Calvinism. The 'Catholick' Congregational writers of the early 18th century preferred a piety of virtue, a theology of divine benevolence, and an admiration for cosmic order. This tendency to equate the practical with the ethical also found expression in the Anglican thought of the southern and middle colonies, where a number of writers argued that religion consisted principally in moral goodness.

Jonathan *Edwards, early America's greatest theologian, opposed such 'enlightened' optimism with a reassertion of Calvinist theology and a defence of 1740s revivalism. By analysing the religious affections, criticizing indeterminist notions of freedom, and discovering different implications in metaphysical idealism, Edwards depicted a sovereign divine beauty that inexorably attracts the wills

of the elect. He emphasized that even 'notional' knowledge had for the elect the 'practical' effect of eliciting the selfless 'consent to being in general' that defined true *virtue.

Edwards set the agenda for a century of debate. His 18th-century disciples, the Edwardean or New Divinity theologians like Samuel Hopkins and Joseph Bellamy, combined the ideal of a selfless 'disinterested benevolence' towards God and neighbour with an analysis of volition that supported the revivalists' call for immediate repentance. Their opponents, the Old Calvinists, argued that this revivalist theology devalued the gradual nurture given by the means of grace in the churches. But by the 1760s a *liberal faction, uneasy with doctrines of depravity and revivalist excesses, distanced itself from both groups.

These mid-century disputes appear tame when compared with the religious turbulence after the Revolution. The rhetoric of democracy helped produce a company of self-taught theologians who disdained the monopoly of the 'learned doctors'. *Universalists, Shakers, *Restorationists, Free-Will *Baptists, *Deists, and *Methodists, all in rebellion against Calvinism, strove for a theology accessible to the common people. On the other hand, the founding of St Mary's Catholic Seminary in Baltimore in 1791 and the Protestant Andover Seminary in 1808 signalled the rise of the full-time professional theologian, who often wrote and taught without assuming ministerial duties.

Under the impetus of revivalist piety, both the populists and the professionals revised the use of the term 'practical'. Instead of denoting a way of knowing God, it came to designate the doctrines that dealt with *sin, *conversion, and *holiness. These practical doctrines generated most of the period's debates. In Boston, William E. Channing and Andrews Norton of Harvard represented after 1819 the *Unitarian insistence that a rational reading of scripture led to a religion of virtue perfecting the soul, rather than to a Calvinism fettered by notions of *Trinity and depravity. In response, some of the Calvinists improvised, as when Nathaniel William Taylor at Yale tried to show that Unitarians misunderstood the Calvinist position: depravity and regeneration were both choices of a will that could theoretically make a contrary choice, even though without grace it would always choose the lesser good. Similar ideas appeared at Oberlin in Ohio, where the former revivalist Charles G. Finney replaced Calvinism with perfectionism, a theme also popular among Wesleyans and utopians.

The old Calvinism endured at Princeton Seminary, where Charles Hodge defined theology as an inductive science grounded in a verbally inspired scripture that taught that God imputed Adam's sin to all humanity and Christ's righteousness to the elect. In an important debate in 1850 with Edwards A. Park of Andover, Hodge criticized the distinction between metaphorical and literal language, which Park had used to soften Calvinist doctrine, arguing that both conveyed propositional truth. His *Systematic Theology* (1871–3) became the classic text of *Princeton theology.

Despite their differences, most of the seminary theologians shared a consensus known as 'rational orthodoxy'. It connoted a confidence in *natural theology and a conviction that time-honoured 'evidences'—miracles, fulfilled prophecies, internal consistency, and religious experience—proved the bible a unique revelation. The yearning for proof helps account for the enthusiastic reception of Scottish *Common Sense philosophy and the scientific theories of Francis Bacon among Americans, who saw them as checks against speculative and sceptical ideas. The parallel trend in Catholicism was the emergence of such works as Martin John Spalding's *General Evidences of Catholicity* (1847).

Many in the antebellum era found the orthodox rationalism stultifying. Ralph Waldo Emerson (see DICKINSON, EMILY) and the Transcendentalists sought immediate experience, not secondary authorities and rational proofs, and, like Theodore Parker in Boston, most of them distinguished between Christianity's transient historical and mythical forms and the eternal truths of the intuitive reason. At the other end of the spectrum, the Catholic Orestes Brownson accused the rational orthodox of simplistic biblicism, while Bishop Ignace Bourget represented the admiration for Roman authority deeply ingrained in the Catholicism of Quebec. Among *Lutherans, Charles P. Krauth spoke for those who preferred the Reformation Confessions to the revivalist piety and evidential theology of the so-called 'American' Lutherans. The theologians at the German Reformed seminary in Mercersburg, Pennsylvania, especially John W. Nevin, adapted conservative forms of German Idealism to define Christian faith as participation in Christ's 'life', incarnate in church and sacraments, rather than either doctrinal assent or revivalist decision. Somewhere between the Transcendentalists and the traditionalists stood the Congregational theologian Horace Bushnell in Connecticut, who contended for a piety of nurture within the family and for a view of *religious language as a poetic gift to the imagination rather than a vehicle of literal propositions.

In the parlours of middle-class homes, readers of popular literature learned new ideas from novelists like Harriet Beecher Stowe, who linked romantic love and Christian *agape*. Democratizing impulses also produced popular theologies that dispensed with evidential preoccupations. The reformer Phoebe Palmer (1845) appealed to her own experience when refining Wesleyan perfectionism and sparking a revival of holiness thought. Alexander Campbell used populist rhetoric in support of his plan to restore primitive Christianity. The Baptist farmer William Miller and his admirer Ellen White touched the popular imagination in the 1840s with *millennial and *adventist themes, while black preachers such as Henry Garnet and Daniel Payne used the bible to support the abolition of *slavery and counter the biblical defence of it. Thousands responded to the 1830 claim of Joseph H. Smith Jr. to have received immediate revelations requiring drastic revisions in historic Christianity and the building of a new *Mormon society.

In his 'Dissertation on Language' (1849), Bushnell had set *religious experience above doctrinal assent. Within decades, thinkers of many different kinds were appealing to experience, and meaning many different things by it. For Catholic Americanists like Isaac Hecker in the 1860s and John Ireland in the 1880s, it meant that the American experience required changes in Catholic thinking about both spiritual formation and democratic societies. For proponents of the Protestant New Theology it meant, as the Baptist William Newton Clarke of Colgate Seminary argued in his *Outline of Christian Theology* (1898), that the theology of any age was largely an expression of the Christian experience of that age.

Advocates of the *social gospel believed that theology also expressed, all too frequently, destructive inherited assumptions about race, class, and gender. A small company of reformers tried to make it more critical of American society. The African Methodist bishop Henry McNeal Turner contended in 1895 for God's 'blackness'; Elizabeth Cady Stanton, editor of *The Woman's Bible* (1895–8), and the Methodist Frances Willard criticized narrowly masculine readings of scripture; and Walter Rauschenbusch of Rochester Seminary wrote his *Theology for the Social Gospel* (1917) as a reformulation of Christian thought in the light of the democratic implications in the idea of the *Kingdom of God. For these reformers, theology became practical by helping to transform society.

1900 to 1960

In the early 20th century, it became popular to argue that theology was practical because it had 'value for life'. For some, this claim had its origins in the pragmatism of William *James and John Dewey, who both argued, in quite different ways, that the meaning and truth of religious statements were to be found in how they functioned. Liberal theologians carried these assumptions about value in different directions. Some took them to mean that theology should promote the value of *persons and personality. The Methodist Borden P. Bowne of Boston University formulated in 1908 a Personalist philosophy that defined reality as a network of persons with a supreme Person at its head, arguing that only such a definition could give the concept of God religious value. The Harvard philosopher Josiah Royce contended, against the Pragmatists, that religion needed metaphysical grounding, and in *The Problem of Christianity* (1913), the best book to come out of the American *liberal Protestant ethos, he shifted attention to a conception of sin, atonement, and community grounded in Absolute Idealism. Yet even Royce observed that he was displaying the presuppositions of an ethic of loyalty and therefore highlighting the 'practical aspects' of religious belief.

Outside the academies, self-taught theological populists still advertised the practicality of their own insights. Drawing on a New Thought movement that sought to tap the hidden sources of cosmic power, Mary Baker Eddy had begun in 1875 a Christian Science movement that offered health and well-being to its followers, while Charles Fox Parham and William J. Seymour expanded a 1901 revival at a Kansas Bible College into a *Pentecostal movement aimed at restoring primitive Christianity, evangelizing the world through speaking in tongues, and recovering the gift of divine *healing.

In the university-related seminaries of the 1920s, the preoccupation with value took an empirical turn. D. C. Macintosh at Yale published in 1919 his *Theology as an Empirical Science*, which defined 'God' as the Reality that produced predictable results when made the object of a right religious adjustment. *Modernist theologians emphasized the functional usefulness of beliefs in adapting persons and groups to their environments. After joining the faculty of the University of Chicago's Divinity School in 1927, Henry Nelson Wieman expounded a theological naturalism that called for adaptation to the value-generating process in nature.

The conservative Protestant reaction against modernism found its most articulate spokesman in J. Gresham Machen at Princeton Seminary. His *Christianity and Liberalism* (1923) described liberal and historic Christianity as two distinct religions. By the time he wrote it, some of the conservatives had begun a *fundamentalist movement marked by adherence to biblical inerrancy and to the premillennial *dispensationalism that had been popularized in the

Scofield Reference Bible (1909) and would remain a perennial mark of one form of popular religious belief.

By the 1930s the modernist agenda was also coming under attack from a Realist movement within the liberal seminaries. H. Richard *Niebuhr at Yale argued in 1937 that the empirical theologians, by defining religion as adjustment to divine reality for the sake of attaining human goods, had made God the preserver of their own values. His 'radical monotheism' sought to define responsible action in the face of the inscrutable power that both created and destroyed all finite values. His brother Reinhold at Union Seminary in New York recovered a doctrine of original sin as a corrective to liberal optimism. His *Nature and Destiny of Man* (1941–3) dissected the dynamisms of pride and sensuality and presented the Kingdom of God, the embodiment of self-sacrificial love, as always a transcendent norm, never a realizable possibility. Neither of the Niebuhrs had the interest in ontology that marked the work of Paul *Tillich, a refugee from Nazism, whose *Systematic Theology* (1951–63) attempted to correlate Christian revelation, interpreted through a metaphysic of being, existence, and life, with questions derived from the analysis of culture.

This Realist movement, influenced by European *neo-orthodoxy, remained separate from the *evangelicals who after 1942 gradually defined their theology as an alternative to liberal, fundamentalist, and neo-orthodox thought. Its most prominent theological voice was Carl F. H. Henry, who still insisted on the inerrancy of scripture but chided separatist fundamentalism for its failure to address social and cultural issues. A second form of evangelical theology emerged at Westminster Seminary in Philadelphia, where Cornelius Van Til argued that all thinking rested, consciously or unconsciously, on the presupposition of a self-revealing triune God. A third evangelical centre was the network of Calvinist colleges and seminaries in the upper Midwest.

1960 to 1999

By the 1960s, a thousand theological flowers were blooming in America, but many of them can be seen as belonging to one of two species. One consisted of thinkers concerned to define Christian identity so as to distinguish the authentically Christian from the cultural values projected onto the tradition.

Proposals about how best to define Christian identity ranged across a remarkable spectrum of options. Within the evangelical culture, Harold Lindsell, editor of *Christianity Today*, led a movement after 1976 to reinstate biblical inerrancy as a defining feature of the faith, but other evangelicals, such as Donald Bloesch of Dubuque Seminary, proposed 'infallibility' (meaning that scripture communicates without error the will of God for salvation) as an alternative. For theologians of liberal or neo-orthodox background, questions about either inerrancy or *infallibility were the wrong ones to ask. One alternative was to turn to the narrative form of the gospel as a clue to its truth and meaning, a turn made in 1975 by Hans Frei at Yale in his *Eclipse of Biblical Narrative*. In a parallel move, his colleague George *Lindbeck argued in 1984 that doctrine, rather than expressing universal human experience or asserting isolated propositions, functioned as the regulative language of a community and derived its force from its relation to communal practices. The concept of narrative proved especially fruitful in the ethical reflections of Alasdair *MacIntyre at Notre Dame and the

Anabaptist John Howard Yoder, while the notion of communal practice informed thinkers like Geoffrey Wainwright at Duke, who took sacramental practice to be the proper context for theological reflection, and the Jesuit Avery Dulles, who attempted to reorient Catholics after *Vatican II to the image of the 'servant church'.

In 1981, the Catholic theologian David *Tracy at the University of Chicago wrote that these narrative and communal theologies had insufficient concern for the intelligibility of their claims to persons outside the tradition, and he called for a 'mutually critical correlation' between the interpretation of the classical Christian texts and the interpretation of general human experience. A similar concern for relating theology to other disciplines marked the writing of the Canadian Jesuit Bernard *Lonergan, whose *Insight* (1957) had examined the structure of the knowing subject as a foundation for theology. Some American *process theologians, adapting Whitehead's metaphysics for theological ends, further exemplified the desire to define a specifically Christian theology that yet remained in conversation with public canons of reasonableness, especially in the natural sciences, while guiding Christian practice in *ethical and *ecological matters.

Not everyone shared the desire to define Christian particularity. Thomas J. J. Altizer's *Gospel of Christian Atheism* (1966) typified the radical theologians who were more inclined to revise the tradition in order to illumine cultural crisis: a motif that gained renewed currency in the writing of religious thinkers in the 1980s, drawn to French deconstruction for philosophical resources. From a different perspective, James Gustafson at Emory attempted in his *Theocentric Ethics* (1981) to draw selectively on Christian tradition for a theological naturalism that acknowledged scientific canons of credibility while exploring the largest possible context for ethical decisions.

The second broad category has been represented by thinkers convinced that Christian thought must be continually tested and transformed through engagement with social oppression and threats to human society and to the planet. From the Trappist monk Thomas *Merton, who in the 1960s explored problems of violence, race, and nuclear weapons, to Gordon Kaufman at Harvard, who argued that theologians should rethink Christian images in ways that help to make life more humane, to Sallie McFague at Vanderbilt, who used studies of *metaphor and *parable to call attention to larger ecological dangers, the engagement with social dilemmas has shaped Christian thinking.

After 1968, a sizeable group of writers was drawn to the notion of 'praxis', the idea that thought and practice intersect and transform each other. They included especially the theologians of *liberation. James *Cone in New York became, after the publication of his *Black Theology of Liberation* (1970), the best-known spokesman for a theological perspective shaped by the history of Black suffering and resistance (see BLACK THEOLOGY). The current interest in *feminist theologies emerged after 1960 and blossomed after Rosemary Radford *Ruether in 1975 published a systematic theology promoting themes of embodiment, connectedness, inclusivity, patriarchal domination, and other dimensions of women's experience to the forefront of theological discussion. Younger theologians have proceeded further by writing on Christian themes from the perspective of Black women (womanist theology), Hispanic cultures, and Asian-American traditions. They share a conviction, reminiscent of the Social Gospel, that theology reflects its social context but can also reveal possibilities of transformation.

Beginning around 1975, a variety of symposia and essays began to lament the decline of Christian thought in North America. The lament referred chiefly to the status of learned, academic theology in the high intellectual culture, where theologians tended to be ignored. Popular theology continues to flourish, and even the professional academics still find readers, especially in the 982 private universities and church-related colleges that teach religion and the 337 Christian seminaries and bible schools. No one pattern of thought has ever dominated the diverse forms of Christian life on the continent: the changing meanings of the 'practical' are only one illustration of the diversity. The outlook for the future is that the diversity will not go away.   **E. Brooks Holifield**

Ahlstrom, S. E. (ed.), 'Theology in America: A Historical Survey,' in J. W. Smith and L. A. Jamison (eds.), *The Shaping of American Religion* (1961).
Bozeman, T. D., *Protestants in an Age of Science* (1977).
Cauthen, K., *The Impact of American Religious Liberalism* (1962).
Cherry, C., *The Theology of Jonathan Edwards* (1966).
Edwards, J., *Ethical Writings*, ed. P. Ramsey (1989).
Ferm, D. W., *Contemporary American Theologies* (1981).
Foster, H. T., *A History of the New England Theology* (1907).
Guelzo, A. C., *Edwards on the Will* (1989).
Handy, R. T. (ed.), *The Social Gospel in America* (1966).
Howe, D. W., *The Unitarian Conscience* (1970).
Hutchinson, W. R., *The Transcendental Ministers* (1959).
—— *The Modernist Impulse in American Protestantism* (1976).
Kuklick, B., *Churchmen and Philosophers* (1985).
Marsden, G. M., *Fundamentalism and American Culture* (1980).
Miller, P., *The New England Mind: The Seventeenth Century* (1939).
Nichols, J. H., *Romanticism in American Theology* (1961).
Noll, M., *The Princeton Theology* (1981).
Reid, D. G., et al. (eds.), *Dictionary of Christianity in America* (1990).
Tilley, T. W. (ed.), *Postmodern Theologies* (1995).

novel, the. The origins of the novel can be traced to ancient Greece and Rome (for example Longus' *Daphnis and Chloe* or Petronius' *Satyricon*), to medieval romances, and to later writers such as Boccaccio, Rabelais, and Cervantes. The genre, however, did not emerge in its present form, which Sir Walter Scott defined as 'a fictitious narrative … accommodated to the ordinary train of human events', until around the middle of the 17th century. In its origins, the novel has little connection with Christianity (unless one lists works like Bunyan's *Pilgrim's Progress* among its ancestors); but by the 19th century the form had attracted many Christian writers, largely because of its scope for psychological understanding and moral discernment, and also perhaps because of questions raised by the role of narratives in Christianity.

There are two kinds of narrative to be considered here: Christianity, having inherited Judaism's understanding of God's purposes as worked out through salvation *history, sees that history as culminating in the redemptive work of Christ, above all in his Passion, *death, and *Resurrection, and as being expressed normatively in the *bible (many books of which are narratives, of different types). It also sees each person's life as a narrative, in which his or her ultimate fate is decided partly by events and choices here and now. Both these narratives involve an *eschatology: they will reach their

fulfilment only when God's ultimate purposes, for his whole *creation and for the individual *person, are worked out.

This cosmic vision suggests the idea that history is divided into three interrelated phases: past salvation history, the subsequent lives of individual men and women, and the final working out of God's purposes. Novelists are concerned with the second phase—though some novels, for instance Thomas Mann's tetralogy *Joseph and his Brothers* (1933–43) or Dan Jacobson's *The Rape of Tamar* (1970), are based on biblical characters. Eschatology is outside the remit of novelists, except in so far as they depict their characters' approaches and attitudes to death. But R. H. Benson's *Lord of the World* (1907) attempted an *apocalyptic theme; and some science fiction can be regarded, perhaps, as a secularized version of eschatology; conversely, C. S. *Lewis used that genre for theological purposes in his trilogy *Out of the Silent Planet* (1938), *Perelandra* (1943), and *That Hideous Strength* (1945).

Although novels are mainly concerned with the second phase of cosmic history, that of individual human lives, Christians see that phase as deriving much of its seriousness from its connection with the other two. Hence the characteristic Christian novel might be described as a novel of *redemption, though that phrase fits several kinds of narrative: accounts of the battle between good and *evil in people's lives, of the slow and hidden working of God's *grace, or of a sudden crisis, illumination, and change. *Tolstoy's *Resurrection* (1899) might be regarded as an example of such a novel, though its author was hostile to the official Christianity of his time; and George Eliot's *Daniel Deronda* (1876) is a novel of redemption by a non-believer who had, nevertheless, been profoundly affected by wrestling with Christianity.

One may also understand the nature of Christian novels by contrasting them with some others. Thomas Hardy's concluding statement in *Tess of the D'Urbervilles* (1891), that ' "Justice" was done, and the President of the Immortals (in Aeschylean phrase) had finished his sport with Tess' reflects the author's hostility to Christian faith and expresses a cosmic pessimism, which is also seen in the ending of *Jude the Obscure* (1896). In a less personal way, Émile Zola's naturalism concentrated on the scientific and documentary character of fiction, and left no room for such ideas as divine grace, redemption, and providence. D. H. Lawrence saw himself as a religious writer, but the salvation that he envisaged was an alternative one to that of traditional Christianity; while, more radically, such works as Samuel Beckett's *Molloy* (1951) wish to exclude from consideration even the desire for redemption.

A more marginal case is that of novelists who write about religious subjects, especially the lives of clergy, without introducing theological themes. Anthony Trollope's Barsetshire novels are the best-known examples. More recently, Susan Howatch's cycle of Starbridge novels seeks to provide a history of the Church of England in the 20th century through the lives of a set of interconnected characters, most of them clergy. Yet she does sometimes introduce theological themes, more often than Trollope; though the latter might, like Jane Austen, be described as a Christian moralist. More marginal cases still are novels which depict characters as shaking themselves free from a religious background, or which use that background as the basis of comedy, like some of the work of Mary Gordon and of David Lodge.

Most significant in terms of Christian thought are those novelists who have sought to convey ideas of grace and redemption in their work. Such writers share the concerns of other novelists for the ways in which human lives develop through time; for psychological truth; and for the analysis of emotions, choices, and moral attitudes. But they seek to delineate the workings of divine grace therein. This concern with the action of grace may well lead them on to other, related topics: the nature of evil (both *sin and *suffering) and of *atonement, saintliness, and the role of representative figures such as priests, ministers, and 'suffering servants'.

The preoccupation with evil is seen most strikingly in the novels of *Dostoevsky, and in those of some 20th-century Roman Catholic writers, for example Georges Bernanos, François Mauriac, Graham *Greene, and Flannery O'Connor. When Mauriac was attacked by some critics who accused him of being preoccupied with the abnormal, the diseased, and the monstrous, he replied, 'There are no monsters. We are not so different from them,' quoting (as did Graham Greene on occasion) Bossuet's remark, 'One must go as far as horror to know oneself.' Mauriac was concerned to penetrate below the surface, to uncover the springs of human conduct and the effects of sin and suffering, but also to discern the subtle movements of grace in the soul. He described himself as 'a metaphysician working in the concrete', finding the novel the ideal medium because it can capture the nature of unseen movements and processes that are worked out only gradually in human lives, and because of its capacity to convey psychological truth.

Thus a seeming preoccupation with evil is often linked closely with a desire to suggest the action of grace. It is difficult to convey the workings of grace in any medium, but the simplest way to start is to imagine a world without grace. Bernanos and Mauriac often attempt this, in their depictions of sad lives set against bleak landscapes. Having shown the absence of grace, the writer may then go on to try to depict its presence, which may produce a sudden illumination or a slow change. The former is easier to describe: one sees it in the scene between the priest and the countess in Bernanos's The Diary of a Country Priest (1936), in Louis's conversion at the end of Mauriac's The Knot of Vipers (1932), and in the scene in prison towards the end of Graham Greene's The Power and the Glory (1940). Mauriac, however, hints that Louis's sudden conversion is the result of unconscious processes continuing for several years. Similarly, Evelyn Waugh gave the heading 'A Twitch upon the Thread' to part three of Brideshead Revisited (1945): the 'twitch' is Lord Marchmain's melodramatic death-bed conversion and its consequences for the lovers Charles and Julia, suggesting the 'thread' of grace that has been there all along.

Many writers depict grace as working in sordid surroundings: Dostoevsky in Crime and Punishment (1866), or Bernanos in several of his works. They seek to bring out the transforming power of grace, by establishing a contrast. Moreover, grace is often depicted as mediated by people who are weak, morally or physically: the prostitute Sonya in Crime and Punishment, or the priests in The Diary of a Country Priest and The Power and the Glory. This conveys the ideas of divine freedom and generosity, and thus again makes a contrast with human limitations. But a further religious motif is introduced if the person who is the channel of grace is depicted as a 'suffering servant', one who is, like Christ, a sacrificial victim, whose sufferings may be vicariously redemptive. Such an idea derives from Isaiah 52–3, which has been regarded as a prophecy of

Christ's Passion, and from *Paul's claim that through one's sufferings one may participate in the sufferings of Christ, helping to complete the latter (Phil. 3: 10; Col. 1: 24). But there may also be an appeal to a particular interpretation of the doctrine of the Communion of Saints, involving the 'co-inherence of souls', the belief that all Christians, living and dead, are interdependent and can therefore assist each other.

One of the main effects of grace is sanctification (see HOLINESS), which probably partly explains the concern of many Christian novelists with saintly characters as well as with flagrant sinners (or, best of all, with sinners who become *saints, like the priest in The Power and the Glory or Fr. Zosima in Dostoevsky's The Brothers Karamazov). But besides the theological concerns with grace and redemption, we need to consider the range of such characters, the roles they play in the narratives, and how successful the authors are in depicting them.

Many of the best-known saintly characters are priests and monks. In any case, as we have seen, clergy often play an important role in Christian novels, because they are 'set apart' from ordinary life (especially if they are celibate), and because they have a special sacramental role, and thereby a peculiar relationship with other people. If they are saintly, this may often be conveyed to some extent by describing their effects on others, as in the case of Dostoevsky's Fr. Zosima. Similarly, in turn, his disciple Alyosha Karamazov's character is depicted partly by describing his relation to others, particularly his family. But Alyosha is presented by the author as an 'innocent': Dostoevsky defers a full decision on his character to the later story of his life in the world, outside the monastery, at which he hints at the end of The Brothers Karamazov (as he hints at the future life of Raskolnikov with his 'redeemer', Sonya, at the end of Crime and Punishment). Likewise, Billy Budd, in Herman Melville's novella of that name (1891) and Ilona in Heinrich Böll's And Where were You, Adam? (1951) are depicted as innocents (and both are put to death). A closely related category is the 'holy fool', a traditional Russian category, transplanted to the west in the character of Guy Crouchback, a knight living in the wrong age, in Evelyn Waugh's Men at Arms trilogy (1952–61), and to Japan in that of Gaston in Shusaku *Endo's Wonderful Fool (1959) or Otsu in his Deep River (1994). There are also ambiguous saints, such as Sarah Miles in Greene's The End of the Affair (1951), and pseudo-saints, like the hypocritical Brigitte Pian in Mauriac's A Woman of the Pharisees (1941), who is contrasted with the real saint, the Abbé Calou, another suffering servant.

Besides pointing a contrast with evil characters and having an effect on others, the saintly character is depicted as Christlike. This is not simply because Christian saints are supposed to be like Christ, being transformed into his image, as Paul says (2 Cor. 3: 18), but also because it is a way of pointing up the connection between salvation history and the present-day life that forms the substance of novels. There may also be parallels between the deaths of characters and Christ's Passion, as in Billy Budd or Nikos Kazantzakis's Christ Recrucified (1954). For if the saintly character is truly Christlike, this is one way of suggesting how the redemptive effects of Christ's work are being manifested continually in the world. The main pitfall for the novelist here is that of forgetting *Aquinas's maxim that 'grace perfects nature', and thus failing to depict a character who is attractive and convincing as a human being.

Novelists may subtly analyse and even moralize about actions and lives, whether they be those of saints or sinners, but first they must present their characters to us convincingly and let us see their lives unfold in the narratives. Thus in *Crime and Punishment* Dostoevsky depicts Raskolnikov as believing at first that the killing of the old moneylender was of no more significance than killing a louse or a cockroach, and indeed was more justifiable, for she actually harmed people. But Dostoevsky persuades us otherwise, by setting forth the true nature of what Raskolnikov has done and its implications. Similarly, Mauriac explores Louis's soul at different phases of his life in *The Knot of Vipers*, ending with his conversion and death. The adoption of a first-person narrative precludes Mauriac from presenting to us his own reflections on Louis. But in any case neither he nor Dostoevsky wish to illustrate theories or simply present us with examples of something more general, for their main concern is to show us life as they see it. Dostoevsky described himself as 'a realist in the higher sense'; and Malcolm Scott argues that the rise of the 'Catholic novel' in France in the late 19th and early 20th centuries came as a conscious response to Zola and other naturalist and realist writers. Their authors were trying to beat the latter at their own game, as it were, by presenting a very different yet 'realistic' account of human life. The reader's decision on which account is truer to life will depend on how convincing he or she finds the characters, worlds, and narratives created by the novelist.

See also FRENCH CHRISTIAN THOUGHT.   **Patrick Sherry**

Dillistone, F. W., *The Novelist and the Passion Story* (1960).

Jasper, David, and Crowder, Colin (eds.), *European Literature and Theology in the Twentieth Century: The Ends of Time* (1990).

Mauriac, François, *God and Mammon* (1929), ET (1936).

—— 'Le Roman' and 'Le Romancier et ses personnages', in *Œuvres Complètes* (1963), viii. 263–84, 287–328.

Nussbaum, Martha, *Love's Knowledge: Essays on Philosophy and Literature* (1990), chs.10–12, 15.

O'Connor, Flannery, *Mystery and Manners* (1984), section v.

O'Donnell, Donat, *Maria Cross: Imaginative Patterns in a Group of Modern Catholic Writers* (1953).

Scott, Malcolm, *The Struggle for the Soul of the French Novel* (1989).

Stratford, Philip, *Faith and Fiction: Creative Process in Greene and Mauriac* (1964).

von Balthasar, Hans Urs, *Bernanos* (1954), ET (1996).

obedience, according to Christian theology, is a moral *virtue that inclines one to respond to the claim(s), intellectual, volitional, behavioural, legitimately made by lawfully constituted *authority (person, institution, law) because and to the extent that such authority expresses the will of *God. Historically obedience has often been oversimplified as the duty of a subordinate to comply with virtually any command issued by a superior. The apotheosis of this misunderstanding was the compliance of much of Christian Europe with Hitler's extermination of millions of Jews and other 'social undesirables' during the Second World War (see HOLOCAUST); and the iniquities of racial *apartheid in South Africa have been justified by appeal to Romans 13: 1–7 as requiring unquestioning obedience to state authority. Any discussion of obedience as a Christian virtue, therefore, requires very careful nuance.

Christian obedience is rooted in the bible. In the OT God made a series of *covenants with Israel according to which God would love and protect the people who, in turn, were to love God and obey the divine laws (cf. Deut. 28–30). The Ten *Commandments, Israel's foundational law, enjoined the honouring of parents (cf. Exod. 20: 12), a recognition of the divinely established social hierarchies that assured the unity and prosperity of the people. The NT offers a very nuanced image of obedience in the person and teaching of *Jesus in the gospels. The rest of the NT demonstrates the first Christians' struggle to follow that example.

Jesus was an observant Jew, obedient to his parents, the Law (see LAW, BIBLICAL), and the religious authorities of Judaism (e.g. Matt. 17: 24–7) but, from his appearance in the gospel of Luke as a 12-year-old, Jesus relativized even legitimate human authority in terms of *conscience. When found after three days by his worried parents, he rebuffed his mother's admonition by claiming that he had to 'be in [his] Father's house' (Luke 2: 49). This same priority of the will of God in his life is expressed at the wedding at Cana (John 2: 1–11) where Jesus claims that he acts only according to God's timetable. Throughout his public life Jesus not only obeyed but counselled obedience to the Law and the authorities (Matt. 23: 1–3). However, he also set aside even the weightiest requirements of the Law, such as Sabbath observance, when his conscience required it (John 5: 1–18; Mark 3: 1–6), and taught his disciples to do the same (Mark 7: 1–23).

The Passion accounts provide the most striking examples of Jesus' attitude towards authority. In John's gospel Jesus is presented as resisting both the demand of the Jewish high priest to defend his teaching (18: 19–24) and that of the Roman governor to give an account of his origin (19: 9–11). He clearly distinguished between God's authority, which claimed his obedience unto death (Matt. 26: 39) for the salvation of the world, and the abuse of office.

In the Acts of the Apostles and the epistles of Paul we see the early church attempting to follow the example and teaching of Jesus in the context of Pharisaic *Judaism and the Roman empire. The story of the apostles preaching Jesus despite explicit prohibition by the Jewish authorities climaxes in their programmatic declaration, 'We must obey God rather than any human authority' (Acts 5: 29). Paul's confronting of Peter, the acknowledged leader of the new Christian community, 'because he [Peter] was clearly wrong' (Gal. 2: 11) shows that authority within the church must be controlled by *truth and *love in the service of the common good and could claim obedience only when properly exercised. However, the Pauline tradition also inculcated the subordination characteristic of patriarchal society, not only of *children to parents, but also of wives to husbands (see MARRIAGE) and slaves to masters (Eph. 5: 21–6: 9; 1 Tim. 6: 1–2) as well as of *women in general to men (1 Cor. 14: 34–6) and of everyone to the state (Rom. 13: 1–7). Throughout Christian history these passages have been used by the powerful to dominate the weak in *family, church, and society.

In short, the biblical teaching on obedience is clear in its insistence that obedience is owed only to God, as manifested first in conscience and secondarily through the legitimate exercise of authority, but the principle is sometimes compromised in scripture itself. Throughout history Christians have demonstrated both heroic obedience even to unworthy civil and ecclesiastical office-holders and heroic resistance to commands that went against conscience or charity. Joan of Arc is a singular example of such resistance in relation to ecclesiastical authority, as was Dietrich *Bonhoeffer to civil authority in Nazi Germany.

True obedience has always been prized in the church as a singularly effective aid to *holiness. Among the earliest *desert ascetics, the medieval *monastics, and modern apostolic religious the vow of obedience has been central to the *asceticism and *spirituality of those seeking to follow Christ in *religious life. The motives and forms of such obedience have been extremely various, pedagogical, familial, and even quasi-military. All have been instrumental in spiritual growth as well as open to abuse.

Basic to a positive understanding of Christian obedience is the desire to do God's will in all things. When few people in a society were educated and access to information was extremely limited, the presumption that those in office knew better what God required in virtually all circumstances made some sense. This conviction was coupled with a deep suspicion of self-will as the proud assertion of the ego against the divine will. At times this led to a simplistic assumption that as long as one did not do one's own will one would be fulfilling God's will. Therefore, it was always better to obey another, especially someone in office, representing God, provided what was commanded was not clearly sinful.

Developments in society, psychology, and theology open ation is much more generally available and no one has superior competence in all matters. Furthermore, the general recognition of the basic equality of persons undermines belief in divinely established social hierarchy in family, society, or even church. It is not at all clear that submission is always healthier or more virtuous than self-determination nor that superiors in virtue of their office represent the will of God in all cases.

Obedience is of various kinds. Pedagogical obedience of child to parent, student to teacher, or novice to formator is obviously salutary provided the superior is competent. Co-operative obedience for the sake of the common good to one charged with the care of the community, even if one does not agree with the directive, is justified and even virtuous. Personal obedience to another can be ascetically and spiritually effective in helping a person to discern between disguised egoism and a true willing of the good. Through generous and free obedience the mind can become humbler, the will more supple, and the determination to please God in all things stronger. True obedience can play an important role, therefore, in formation, promotion of the common good, and personal spiritual development.

But true obedience is the response to genuine authority, which must be based in truth and motivated by love even when it is exercised through office. Consequently, no one is justified in 'blind obedience' which abdicates personal responsibility for discerning in conscience the validity of the exercise of authority. Under some circumstances it may be heroically virtuous to submit, to the extent possible, to the incompetent exercise of office, especially if this promotes the unity of the community and causes no real harm; but it cannot be assumed, without further discernment, that such is the case. Genuine obedience to God arises in the interplay of legitimate authority, discernment, conscience, responsibility, humility, courage, and generous willingness to surrender one's own desires to a higher good. For this very reason obedience to God may well require, under some circumstances, courageous resistance to human commands regardless of the consequences. The Christian is called to be obedient unto death to God in imitation of Christ but always, in cases of conflict, to obey God rather than humans.

See also FREEDOM.   **Sandra M. Schneiders**

Bausch, William J., *Ministry: Traditions, Tensions, Transitions* (1982).
Hill, Edmund, *Ministry and Authority in the Catholic Church* (1988).
Lash, Nicholas, *Voices of Authority* (1976).
Seasoltz, R. Kevin, 'Religious Obedience: Liberty and Law', in Paul J. Philibert (ed.), *Living in the Meantime: Concerning the Transformation of Religious Life* (1994).
Sölle, Dorothee, *Beyond Mere Obedience* (1982).

Old Testament.

In the New Testament the phrase 'old testament' (or '*covenant', the same Greek word) appears only once. *Paul uses it in 2 Corinthians 3: 14 when he speaks of the veil over the mind of the Israelites as they read the 'old covenant'. The immediate context suggests that it is specifically the account of the giving of the law at Sinai that he has in mind. He never uses this expression to indicate the source of any of the numerous passages from the Hebrew Scriptures that he draws on but refers to *ta grammata*, 'the writings'. In this he is followed by the writers of at least the first two centuries.

'Old Testament' as the title for a collection of books is first recorded in the reply that Melito, bishop of Sardis at the end of the 2nd century, wrote to his brother Onesimus who had asked him for extracts from the ancient books that confirmed the Christian faith and also for an accurate list of their number and order. 'Old Testament' presupposes a 'New Testament' and as such is a specifically Christian term. In scholarly contexts, more neutral terms such as Hebrew Scriptures or Jewish bible are now preferred. None of these is quite satisfactory, especially as the number and order of books accepted as belonging to these collections varies between different communities. For much of Christian history, OT has meant the books of the Septuagint or the Latin Vulgate but in Protestant circles it refers to the shorter Hebrew canon. In this article specifically devoted to Christian usage the abbreviation OT is used, but this begs important questions. Where these become pressing, more specific designations are employed.

The NT writers uniformly take for granted the *authority of the Jewish Scriptures which they regard as always having contained the divine *revelation of *salvation. It is, however, only once the key has been given in the person of *Jesus that this can be rightly interpreted. The suggestion that these texts were Jewish rather than Christian would have been an incomprehensible anachronism. They are a common heritage of revelation to Jew and Gentile.

The gospel writers give shape and meaning to the story they tell of Jesus through a complex web of allusions to OT passages. The royal speaker or referent of the *psalms and the enigmatic figure of the servant in *Isaiah, in particular, are threads from which the account of *Jesus' life and ministry is woven. His seeming failure to fit the expected role of the *messiah is shown to be the surprising but inevitable implication of the OT text, properly interpreted. The density of quotations and allusions to the scriptures in *John's gospel, for instance, increases in the account of the Passion, as if to anchor this most unlooked-for event in the Messiah's life all the more firmly in the language and promises of the OT.

The gospels, however, represent Jesus as not only announcing the fulfilment of the scriptures but revising them and even declaring certain provisions outdated. This epitomizes a wider problem for the early church over the significance of the legal and cultic material in the OT. It is not too much of a caricature to define the difference between the Jewish and Christian approaches to this material as follows: Jewish interpretation seeks to clarify how the law and the cult are to be applied in specific and ever-changing circumstances, whereas Christianity has to explain why there is no need to apply what God has clearly commanded. The nascent church is faced with a scripture containing large tracts of direct divine commands which Christians no longer feel any obligation to obey.

On the other hand, the NT contains little specific instruction on key areas of personal and, in particular, political ethics. The narratives as well as the *wisdom traditions of the OT furnish an essential resource for the discussion of such matters. The NT also offers little advice on liturgical matters and contains nothing to compare with the psalms for the expression of both personal and public prayer. Importantly, the church claims that it is the true *Israel: as such it claims to be the heir of the OT *prophecies, and it is the OT that expounds the history of what it is to be Israel. The prophetic traditions point, in Christian interpretation, to Jesus, but there are also prophecies that seem as yet unfulfilled and that therefore can be presumed to have a continued force. Christian thinkers have to evolve ways of mediating this *paradox of difference from Israel and yet continuity with it. How is the authority of a tradition that is only partially adopted to be maintained?

The Epistle to the *Hebrews offers one early and majestic reinterpretation of the scriptural canon in terms of continuity in inspiration but a contrast in plenitude. The prophets, the Law, and the *Temple cult are shadows of what is to come, copies of the heavenly realities. A specific allusion to Jeremiah 31: 31–4, the promise of a new covenant engraved on the hearts of men, in Hebrews 8 conveys the message that the scriptures are to be respected but kept in their place. However, the implicit permission to reinterpret the scriptures was bound to lead to conflict.

By the time of the writing of 2 Peter, the interpretation of the scriptures seems to have become an acknowledged cause of dissent. Not only Paul's letters, but other scriptures have in them matters hard to understand which some 'twist to their own destruction' (2 Pet. 3: 16). In reaction to this internal dissent and growing opposition from other Jews, Christian exegesis develops a polemical rather than a simply expository role. Some of the rather unexpected and at times, to modern thinking, forced exegeses of OT passages in the NT arise because the writers are basing their argument on verses cited by their opponents rather than choosing the most suitable verses for their purpose. This is a powerful *rhetorical ploy, but it also fuels the tendency to go beyond the 'obvious' meaning of the text in order to show how it 'really' lends itself to a Christian interpretation, a tendency already indicated by Paul in his contrast between the letter, which kills, and the spirit, which gives life (2 Cor. 3: 6).

As the church became increasingly Greek-speaking, it inevitably turned from the Hebrew Scriptures to the Septuagint, the translation made in Alexandria in about 200 BC which contained added books with no surviving Hebrew counterparts (see APOCRYPHA, JEWISH). This originally Jewish translation quickly became Christian property to the extent that the rabbis were later to disown it. This meant that Christianity had not only a Jewish text, but a translated one, at its core. The very possibility of *translation implies that there is a meaning to a text that is not unequivocally tied to the actual letters and words of which it is composed. The translated text is already the result of interpretation and this gave further support to the contrast between the letter and the spirit of the text. The way was also open to further translations into Syriac and Latin and eventually into a wider range of languages.

The move to Greek reflects a church that was now addressing audiences and combating opponents who did not share the Jewish community's unquestioning respect for the Hebrew Scriptures. There is a remarkably rapid shift from the argument that Jesus is the messiah because he fulfils the unquestionably authoritative prophecies of the scriptures to one that defends the now threatened status of the OT with the argument that the unquestioned authority of Jesus is foreshadowed in it. For those coming fresh to these texts, problems loomed. How was the irascible anthropomorphic creator of the OT to be reconciled with the *God of the NT, let alone with the unchangeable impassive God of the increasingly assimilated Greek tradition?

The immediate answer was by *allegorical interpretation. Not all were convinced by the elaborate allegorical readings that developed. The most notorious attack on the OT from this perspective was launched around 140 by Marcion, apparently a presbyter of the Roman church. His name still lingers in the term 'Marcionite', which later tradition applies, usually abusively, to anyone who denigrates the OT. Marcion forthrightly ruled out the God of the OT as unworthy to be the father of Jesus Christ. He quite explicitly rejected allegorization as a way to get round this judgement.

Theologically, orthodox insistence on retaining the OT was predicated on the need to maintain the identity between God the Creator and God the Father of Jesus Christ. The reality of *Incarnation, the cosmic scope of *redemption, and the *Resurrection of the material body were the dogmatic truths that could not be surrendered in the face of Marcion and the proliferating *Gnostic sects. The main counter was offered by *Irenaeus who formulated for the first time the importance of the church as a repository of authoritative interpretation against which the readings of heretics could be judged. Put crudely, the OT means what the church has agreed it means and so could not be turned against the dogmatic formulations of the faith.

Rather against the odds, the OT was turned to the church's advantage in its polemics with the *Hellenistic world. The novelty of Christian teaching was not a selling-point in the ancient world which placed a premium on the timelessness of *truth and the antiquity of traditions. Justin Martyr for one claimed that the Greek tradition was derived from the OT. The retention of the OT gave Christianity some grounds, however shaky, to claim the authority of age, something the younger NT texts could not support.

On the other hand, an important strand in the Christian use of the OT has been as a bulwark against the Hellenistic influence on western civilization. Christians have resisted the effects of rationalization and later secularism predicated on the assumptions of Greek philosophical systems by using the OT as the counterweight. The God of Abraham can always be set against the God of the philosophers, whether in Tertullian's famous disjunction of Athens from Jerusalem or the cry of reformers in different ages against the perceived sophistry of the established churches.

Despite Christianity's move out of the Jewish world and development of an anti-Jewish rhetoric, Christian thinkers still needed to be able to prove themselves on Jewish terms. Part of the ambivalent attitude of early, and indeed not so early, Christianity to its Jewish heritage resembles nothing so much as the rebellious child that cannot just ignore its parents but needs their recognition of its rebelliousness and to rub their noses in it. The church insisted its

Jewish contemporaries acknowledge that they were wrong in their own terms and so needed to stake its claim to their Hebrew texts.

When Jerome was commissioned by Pope Damasus to provide a corrected Latin translation of the bible (see LATIN THEOLOGY), the need to produce a text Jews would respect for polemical purposes led him both to propose changes to the received translation and to raise questions over the status of the books in the Septuagint that were not to be found in the Hebrew canon. On both counts he alarmed *Augustine who defended the Septuagint as an inspired translation, using the fact that the apostles cited it to back up his case. Though Jerome's translation, which came to be known as the Vulgate, reached unquestioned status as the bible of the medieval west, it was Augustine's view of the canon that prevailed until the Reformation.

After the fall of Rome in the 5th century and throughout the medieval period, the allegorical tradition held sway and continues to do so in the churches of the east. In the west, Augustine's *On Christian Doctrine* provided the model for biblical interpretation. Augustine himself records that it was only after he heard the allegorical explanations of the OT of Ambrose of Milan that he could rid himself of his Manichaean prejudice against it.

Once the Vulgate became entrenched in the west as the authoritative text of scripture, a specialized but international scholarship in Latin developed, even as the language gave way to various vernaculars. The medieval church was less concerned with apologetics than with the elaboration of its own system. The older issues over the interpretation of the OT now had authoritative solutions enshrined in the church's tradition that were expressed in the form of commentaries or glosses, the most famous of which was the *Glossa Ordinaria*.

The OT was much used in *art and *preaching for its wealth of incident and character which, as types, could enliven and illustrate theological truths. It also provided authoritative backing for the political claims of royal dynasties and was one of the few resources for cosmological and scientific speculation.

An important development in the 12th century was the influence of scholars and ideas from Arabic Spain. Responding to this, Hugh of St Victor showed a reawakening interest in the literal sense of scripture and his followers, especially Andrew of St Victor, studied Jewish interpretation and entered into consultations with rabbis. A growing recognition that the OT came out of a defined and different culture chimed with a renewed emphasis on authorial intention as a determinate of meaning.

A decisive moment came with Thomas *Aquinas who moved theology onto a new footing where *Aristotelian rather than biblical categories provided the framework. Aquinas in no sense repudiated the bible, and indeed insisted on the primacy of the literal interpretation, but his work created a space for later generations to ask questions about the bible that would have been threatening to dogmatics. In the medieval period these were carefully circumscribed, but the rise of humanism in the *Renaissance led to more persistent questioning of the status and authority of biblical texts.

The Renaissance itself arose in response to a trickle and then a flood of rediscovered Greek classics that provided an intellectually sustainable alternative to the biblical world-view. The OT was no longer the only source for history or cosmology but one historical resource which could be checked against others. The developing techniques of critical analysis first applied to the manuscripts of the Greek tradition were turned on the biblical text itself. The interest in Hebrew and in rabbinics also increased and with it an awareness that traditional Christian interpretations were not incontrovertible.

This situation formed the background to the work of *Luther whose break with the authority of the church included a repudiation of the whole structure of scholastic interpretation and allegorization. He provided almost single-handedly the basis for an alternative tradition through his biblical translation and comprehensive series of commentaries. Luther's view of the OT reflects his attitude to the NT. He was prepared to sift through the books of the NT for those which preached Christ and the gift of grace, thereby sidelining James, for instance; how much more so in his use of the OT. He followed Jerome in favouring the Hebrew canon.

In this as in other ways, Protestantism reopened the arguments of the early centuries before Catholic interpretation had been consolidated. In his repudiation of the excesses of allegory, Luther deprived himself of an essential tool for finding Christian meaning in OT passages. In the Law, for instance, what could not be read as a type of Christ had to be interpreted either as general moral law that could be assented to by any right-thinking person on moral principles, or else 'levitical law', specifically designed for the historical situation of Israel and therefore not binding on subsequent generations. In either case, these legal passages are not being read as revelations of an otherwise inaccessible divine will for the reader. The function Law performs is to remind people of their unworthiness and thus act as a spur to the gospel. This opens the way to later questions as to what continuing relevance the OT may have.

Luther provided one answer to this himself. In his preface to the Psalms, he describes how they give a window into the hearts of their writers as they faced the crises of life. They are the record of the struggle of great souls with their God. This subjective view, stressing both the response of the reader and the original experience of the writer, has long consequences.

*Calvin, the other great biblical commentator of the early Reformation, took a different line which stressed the continuity between the OT and NT in that both witnessed to one covenant between God and his people. Calvin was much more prepared to see the positive use of law in the conduct of Christian communities. One consequence of this was a recovery of the political identification of Christian communities with Israel. The price for the moral cohesion and sense of destiny this could offer was in ensuing centuries the exclusivism of such biblically justified political manifestations as South African *apartheid.

The Reformation was accompanied by a new development of sceptical humanism. All the old questions raised by Marcion and other early critics were revived and sharpened by the developing techniques of textual and historical analysis. The works of Spinoza, Hobbes, and Reimarus are only the most enduring of those that raised doubts over the historical accuracy and moral worth of the OT texts.

In this climate of increasing scepticism, a key development is the establishment of a distinct discipline of OT theology. Johannes Gabler in a famous address of 1787 sought to separate the study of the religious ideas evidenced in the OT itself from the dogmatic impositions of Christianity. For Gabler, this was a prelude to a more satisfactory systematics. This is a logical outcome of the Reformation stress on scriptural authority, but it also formalized a new dichotomy between dogma and bible and left unanswered the question of how conflicts between the two were to be adjudicated. A sense of the distinctive cast of the Hebrew mind comes to the fore, either as in earlier times as a counter to the Greek rationalism of the day, or, more ominously, as a way of explaining the deficiencies of the text, an argument that reflected an enduring and developing *antisemitism.

The most influential theologian to tackle the defection of rationalists from Christianity was *Schleiermacher, whose emphasis on the centrality of experience to religion and the universality of that experience led him to see the church's adoption of the OT as a historical contingency. However important the OT was to the early church and to Jesus' own preaching, its job was done once the truths of Christianity were proclaimed. OT proofs were not only no longer necessary, but liable to be misleading. He suggested that the position would be clarified if the OT were printed as an appendix after the NT, and only for the sake of historical fidelity.

Schleiermacher's influence, however, meant that historical enquiry gained a theological justification. His *hermeneutic aim of understanding a writer's works better than the writer himself made it a task with theological significance to identify the authors of particular passages and to elaborate the social and theological milieu in which they worked, without dogmatic presuppositions.

The 19th century thus saw the rise of the great school of *higher criticism in Germany. The importance of this from the point of view of the Christian use of the OT is that though many of its practitioners had a Christian commitment, it was quite consciously *not* a Christian enterprise. Christian thinkers had to work out their reaction to a powerful new reading of the OT texts in which they did not set the intellectual agenda.

Historical criticism brought an awareness of the polyphony of the bible. Not only between books, but between layer on layer of editing, theological and political debates spanning centuries could be seen to be fought out. Rather than a monolithic product of direct revelation, the OT came to be understood as the record of a clamorous and continuing conversation, not to say argument, over the identity of Israel and the nature of its interaction with its God. The explosion in knowledge of the other cultures of the ancient Near East also served to undermine claims of the uniqueness of the OT. Its historical claims were now testable against new *archaeological and literary evidence. For many scholars, this served to displace it once and for all from its claimed authoritative status. Its interest lay in the tendentious record it provided of the religious practice and history of one relatively obscure ancient culture.

For those who sought to defend the place of the OT, the new discoveries meant that the battleground shifted decisively to the historical sphere. A growing interest in the possibility of proving the accuracy of biblical *history and cosmology in secular and rationalist terms emerged in the 19th century and continues unabated in conservative circles. Another response, however, was to pay more attention to the lessons the biblical writers drew from history than to the contested details of what actually happened. For the liberal supporters of the OT, the attempt to defend the literal historicity of many texts had long been abandoned. No argument for its retention that depended on a conservative view of its historical accuracy was likely to convince the sceptics.

More promising was a crucial insight of the historical critics, definitively presented by Wellhausen, that the ethical monotheism of the prophets had historical priority over the Law. This concentration on the creative personalities of the OT was one that chimed with the wider cultural preoccupations of German idealism and Romantic creativity and was seized upon by Christian apologists. The loftiness of the prophets' ideals and beauty of their language gave them the authority of the greatest poets. Unfortunately, this also lent itself to the denigration of ancient and contemporary Judaism as the outgrowth of a process of decline that began with the formalization of the Law and the cult.

These movements in 19th century Protestantism were roundly resisted by the authorities of the Roman church, and *modernist scholars such as Loisy were condemned or, like Lagrange, sidelined and effectively ignored. Unfortunately, the official position on the value of the OT had little hope of persuading those who could not accept the church's authority. The church itself had little interest in providing a defence of the OT in anything other than traditional typological terms. It was not until the 1943 papal encyclical, *Divino Afflante Spiritu*, that there was a loosening of restrictions, so that Catholic OT scholars can now work on the same terms as anyone else, even though official pronouncements continue to show a conservative emphasis.

At the end of the 19th century, Adolf Harnack could proclaim, 'To reject the Old Testament in the 2nd century was a mistake the church rightly repudiated; to retain it in the 16th century was a fate which the Reformation could not yet avoid; but to continue to keep it as a canonical document after the 19th century is the consequence of religious and ecclesiastical paralysis' (*Marcion*, pp. 248–9). Ominously, Harnack's statement coincided with an increasing repudiation of the Jewish heritage in European culture particularly among German intellectuals, but by no means solely confined to them. The OT was represented, for instance by Émile Burnouf, as a Semitic perversion of an originally Aryan spirituality that went back to the Indian Vedas. Jesus himself was claimed as an Aryan. This extreme development of the cross-fertilization between the study of the history of *religions and antisemitic ideology was part of the climate of thought that made the horrors of the *Holocaust possible.

One major counterblast to this came with Karl *Barth's repudiation of the liberal theology in which he had been schooled. His renewed reliance on revelation and his Reformed heritage meant that the OT was given full weight in his thought. His *Church Dogmatics*, whatever its value for systematics, contains some of the 20th century's most penetrating readings of the OT. Barth was no literalist, however, and can best be seen as a pioneer of the literary approach to the bible. What mattered to him was the shape of its stories which, he argued, recorded the baffled response of their writers to the inexorable pressure of revelation that they could hardly understand. Barth drew heavily on the work of Wilhelm Vischer who relied on a modern variation of *typology to read the OT as a Christian book.

In his evaluation of the OT, Barth is at the opposite pole from his contemporary *Bultmann, whose roots were Lutheran. For Bultmann, the OT was a record of failure, a salutary reminder of what can go wrong when eschatological promises are identified with the events of empirical history. He rejected any developmental scheme as depending on a concept of prophecy and fulfilment that can only operate after the event. More serious than this logical flaw, in Bultmann's view, is the theological consequence of trying to soften the scandal of the Christian *kerygma by portraying it as the inevitable result of a historical development.

The two great OT theologies of the 20th century, Walter Eichrodt's and Gerhard von Rad's, appeared at a time when the repudiation of any Jewish heritage was being enacted systematically and brutally. The mere writing of such theologies was an act of defiance. In selecting the concept of covenant on which to centre his OT theology, Eichrodt was following in a tradition that harks back to the so-called federal theology of Cocceius. His systematizing account, for all its datedness, remains a benchmark in its attempt to give a cross-sectional picture of a dynamic religious system. Gerhard von Rad, on the other hand, drew on the concept of salvation history to order his work, arguing that the history of Israel's self-understanding was more theologically significant than whatever events lay behind it. This contrasted with the Anglo-Saxon biblical theology movement, associated with the work of G. Ernest Wright, which returned to a view of the OT as a textbook of examples of God's action in history, with archaeology playing an important role. It foundered on the old problem of relating theological certainty to historical contingency.

After the Holocaust, many Christian scholars made a chastened study of the roots of antisemitism in Christian interpretation of the OT and found a renewed respect for the tradition of rabbinic scholarship. A sense that Christian thinkers have more to learn than to teach in reading these texts has coloured the approach and there has been a renewed appreciation of Paul's insistence in Romans that Israel has its own continuing destiny in God's plan. There has also been a rediscovery of the importance of the wisdom tradition which had tended to be overlooked, given the emphasis on history.

OT theologies continue to be written (Walter Brueggemann's *Theology of the Old Testament* of 1997 is a fine example), though there is a shyness in the *postmodern era over venturing to provide a biblical meta-narrative. The OT itself has been claimed in its diversity and fracturedness as a prime example of a postmodern text. An interesting development has been the burgeoning of works on the bible and especially the OT written by literary critics and artists. This is partly a response to the decline of biblical study in schools. University students were no longer equipped to respond to the all-pervading allusions to the OT in the works of western culture. At the same time there has been a burst of books which reveal the literary artistry of the OT itself.

The OT remains an inescapable but uncomfortable element in Christian thought. Much of the NT is addressed to communities living in the expectation of an imminent end-time. It shows limited interest in the pragmatic concerns of individuals and communities who are trying to ensure their continued survival. The OT, however, is pre-eminently a book about survival, which has itself survived and underpinned the survival of the Jewish people. The Ten *Commandments are still cited as the foundation of civic life and the laws of Leviticus are still pressed into service in contemporary debates on *sexuality and *family life. Whether thereby we are assured of an immovable ethical foundation rooted in God's will or find ourselves shackled with the outdated cultural and political prejudices of an ancient Levantine society is a matter of disagree-

ment amongst Christians. Those concerned with the theological justification of war, the rights of women, the *ecological consequences of what is seen as a biblically based instrumental attitude to the natural world, or with the issue of *homosexuality still argue vehemently over the status of the OT.

A case in point is that of *liberation theology, where the OT has been a particular source of inspiration with its call for social justice and its narrative of exodus and promise of restoration. Oppressed communities identify with Israel in its struggle against Egypt and Babylon. As so often, the OT is a two-edged text in these matters. The settlers in America also saw themselves as a new Israel and some justified the extermination of the native Americans by casting them as the Canaanites. The ideology of *capitalism and colonialism which many liberationists denounce was itself often shored up by images drawn from the OT.

That a motley collection of ancient Semitic texts is still the world's best-selling book is itself an extraordinary fact and testimony to the OT's capacity to answer the needs of diverse communities. What role then does the OT have in the continuing enterprise of Christian thought? The comparison that comes to mind is that of the continued importance of the jungle in the life of the planet. Many of the products we depend on for our civilized lives have their origin there, to our surprise. The jungle may seem chaotic but it teems with diversity and life. Some of its inhabitants are highly dangerous or unpleasant, others have a wild beauty that tame beasts never quite match. It is certainly to be treated with caution and respect. Civilization encroaches constantly on the jungle and seeks to replace it with ordered productivity, but in the process risks losing an essential source of revitalization, a repository of the untameable which may even produce the unexpected cure to an unforeseen disease.

See also BIBLE, ITS AUTHORITY AND INTERPRETATION; JEWISH–CHRISTIAN RELATIONS; JUDAISM IN THE 1st CHRISTIAN CENTURY; LAW, BIBLICAL; PRE-CONSTANTINIAN THOUGHT. **Hugh S. Pyper**

Barr, J., *The Concept of Biblical Theology: An Old Testament Perspective* (1999).

Bray, G., *Biblical Interpretation: Past and Present* (1996).

Childs, B. S., *Introduction to the Old Testament as Scripture* (1979).

Coggins, R., *Introducing the Old Testament* (1990).

Evans, G. R., *The Language and Logic of the Bible* (1984).

Fackenheim, E. L., *The Jewish Bible after the Holocaust: A Re-reading* (1990).

Grant, R. M., with Tracy, D., *A Short History of the Interpretation of the Bible*, 2nd edn. (1984).

Harrisville, R. A., and Sundberg, W., *The Bible in Modern Culture* (1995).

Hayes, J. H., and Prussner, F. C., *Old Testament Theology: Its History and Development* (1985).

Reventlow, H. G., *Problems of Old Testament Theology in the Twentieth Century* (1985).

—— *Problems of Biblical Theology in the Twentieth Century* (1986).

Rogerson, J., *Old Testament Criticism in the Nineteenth Century: England and Germany* (1984).

Smalley, B., *The Study of the Bible in the Middle Ages*, 3rd edn. (1984).

Young, F., *Biblical Exegesis and the Formation of Christian Culture* (1997).

omnipotence, divine.

The doctrine of divine omnipotence has for many centuries been a stock element in most orthodox Christian theology. The claim is, roughly, that *God is all-powerful, so that (in some sense) he can do anything. These formulations are to be taken 'roughly' and 'in some sense' because, as Thomas *Aquinas observed in the 13th century, 'it seems difficult to explain in what his omnipotence precisely consists. For there may be a doubt as to the precise meaning of the word 'all' when we say that God can do all things' (ST I q. 25 a. 3).

There are three main sources for the doctrine. First, certain biblical passages ascribe great power to God (e.g. Gen. 18: 14; Matt. 19: 26; Rev. 19: 6). Second, there is the conviction that unless God had enormous power he would be unable to perform some of the roles that religion assigns to him. Principally, he would not be able to guarantee the eternal blessedness of his people (salvation, resurrection, and eternal life) in the face of the vicissitudes of life and the vast impersonal processes of the universe (see Geach 1973). And third, the doctrine is derived from a speculation within 'perfect-being' theology.

In this latter project, one begins with a very high conception of God: *Anselm's proposal (Proslogion, ch. 2) that God is a being than whom no greater can be conceived, or René *Descartes's claim (in the third Meditation) that God is a being who has all the perfections. Other things being equal, a being with more power would seem to be greater or more perfect than a being with less power. But if God's power were limited, then it would seem that a being with still greater power would be conceivable. And that would amount to conceiving of a being greater than God. That, however, is incompatible with the assumption that God is a being than whom no greater can be conceived. So God must have the greatest conceivable degree of power, that is, omnipotence.

A number of problems arise, however, if we interpret the 'omni' (the 'all' in 'all-powerful') in a completely unrestricted way. We could claim that one of the things that God can do is to create a square circle. It seems then as though square circles could exist. But the latter claim seems to many philosophers and theologians to be false. It is not possible that a square circle exist. But then the scope of divine omnipotence cannot be construed in a completely unrestricted way, so there has been a long project of trying to formulate the relevant limits.

At least since the time of Aquinas, most theologians have thought that divine omnipotence is limited at least to the range of things and projects that are logically possible. 'Things' whose description is self-contradictory—a square circle, a colourless red rose—cannot possibly exist, so even God cannot create them or bring them about. (Perhaps Descartes rejected even this minimum limitation. He suggested, at least in some correspondence, that God could create mountains without valleys and circles with unequal radii; but this is a distinctly minority report. For references and a brief discussion, see Frankfurt 1964.) An important application of limiting the scope of omnipotence to the logically possible occurs in the 'free-will defence' against the problem of *evil, where it is argued that God, even if he is omnipotent, cannot cause a person to perform a particular action by free will, since the action's being done by free will logically entails that it is not determined by an external cause (see Plantinga 1974).

Many philosophers and theologians have thought that there must also be some further restriction on the scope of omnipotence. For there might be things that are not in themselves logically impossible, but which God nevertheless cannot do. These proposals are often put in the form of questions. Some of them generate apparent *paradoxes. Can God make a thing that cannot be destroyed by its maker? Either answer seems to identify something that God cannot do. Some—can God ride a bicycle? Can God do a wicked act?—involve a clash with some other property that is also taken to be essential to the divine nature—incorporeality, or goodness. One group—e.g. can God now prevent Elizabeth II from ever being queen of England?—involve essential reference to *time and to the idea that the past has a special sort of necessity putting it beyond the reach of any possible power, even divine.

Many solutions have been proposed to these problems. Some of them extend the Thomistic strategy, reformulating the doctrine to exclude one or another of these tasks from the proper scope of omnipotence. But others try to show that the puzzling task is within the divine power after all, and that the paradoxes are only apparent (see Mavrodes 1984; Morris 1987; Swinburne 1993; and Wierenga 1989).

Another problem arises from the doctrine of the incarnation, that God somehow 'became' a particular historical human being, who was thus both divine and human (see INCARNATION). But could one person be both omnipotent and human?

This difficulty is not unique. Several divine attributes (pure spirituality, eternity, etc.) seem incompatible with human attributes of material embodiment, and temporality. Paul says that Jesus 'emptied himself' (Phil. 2: 6–8). Perhaps omnipotence is among the easier cases because it is possible to have a power without fully exerting it. So this aspect of the emptying may be a voluntary moratorium on omnipotence, leaving Jesus to lead an essentially human life.

See also OMNISCIENCE; PREDESTINATION; PROVIDENCE.

George I. Mavrodes

Frankfurt, H., 'The Logic of Omnipotence', The Philosophical Review, 73 (1964).

Geach, P., 'Omnipotence', Philosophy, 48 (1973).

Mavrodes, G. I., 'Is the Past Unpreventable?', Faith and Philosophy, 1 (1984).

Morris, T., Anselmian Explorations (1987).

Plantinga, A., God, Freedom, and Evil (1974).

Swinburne, R., The Coherence of Theism (1993).

Wierenga, The Nature of God (1989).

omniscience, divine.

omniscience, divine. The claim that *God is all-knowing has two sources. First, scripture (e.g. Ps. 139) attests to the incomparability of God's knowledge. Second, the conception of God according to which he is the most perfect being possible implies the doctrine, a conception carefully articulated by *Anselm. Besides its theoretical importance, it is of immense personal significance, for there is deep comfort in being loved completely by a magnificent person who understands and knows one completely.

Two kinds of controversy surround the doctrine. The first concerns the range of knowledge required of omniscience, and the second concerns the objects of knowledge. The range issue has focused on the possibility of knowledge of the future. The issue concerning the objects of knowledge arises when we consider whether knowing all *truths is sufficient for being all-knowing.

The traditional account of omniscience claims that God knows everything true. Yet, when we consider the phenomenon of consciousness, it may seem that there is a kind of knowledge that each conscious being has of itself that is inaccessible to anyone else.

There is the knowledge of *what it is like to be me*, and no set of true statements about me can ever fully explain what that is like. If so, knowing all truths is insufficient for knowing everything, and what is worse, perhaps there is knowledge of self that is simply unknowable to anyone else.

The best hope for saving the doctrine, without resorting to pantheistic denials of our distinctness from God, is in recent work on *psychological attitudes. According to some recent theories, an attitude is not simply a relation between a person and a proposition, but includes also a way in which the information contained in the proposition is accessed. If such accounts can be defended, then there is a sense of 'no one else can know what it is like to be me' which does not threaten the doctrine of omniscience. Knowledge of self is unique on such theories because of the unique way we access information about ourselves, not because there are some truths to which only we have access. God still knows everything about us, though not in the same way we know it.

The other difficulty facing the doctrine of omniscience concerns knowledge of those parts of the future not determined by the past. The traditional concern is over actions that result from human *freedom, but in recent times concerns have arisen because of indeterminacies that are implied by our best physical theories of the universe. Some have worried that, if God is aware, in advance, of everything that will happen, then the future is fixed and not open, making freedom and indeterminacy but an illusion that arises from our finite, limited perspective.

In answer to this problem, some either abandon or limit the doctrine, substituting claims to the effect that God knows everything only about certain domains of truth, but not about the undetermined future. Such a move appears to be an abandonment of the doctrine of omniscience, but perhaps it is not. Just as it is a mistake to say that *omnipotence involves the power to do anything (because some things are logically impossible to do, and hence do not count against the claim that some individual is all-powerful), so too is it a mistake to say that omniscience involves knowing everything. Instead, one should at most claim that omnipotence involves the power to do anything that can be done, and perhaps one should at most claim that omniscience involves knowing all that can be known. If the indeterminate parts of the future cannot be known, that fact would not count against God's omniscience.

There are theological costs here, however. God's immutability is compromised since he will have to make adjustments to his plans for unanticipated events. Furthermore, divine sovereignty is endangered, and following God's advice or commands might result in things turning out badly when that advice is based on a prediction of the indeterminate future. The result is a theology in which absolute trust of God outruns one's theology.

Such considerations prompt one to try to save the traditional account. One can do so either by arguing that freedom and *foreknowledge are not incompatible, and defending an account of middle knowledge according to which God's knowledge of future contingents is based on his knowledge of what the beings in question would do (freely) under any possible circumstance. The other, and more widely held, way to save the doctrine grants that God cannot know, in advance, what free individuals will do, but denies that God is in *time. So, strictly speaking, he *foreknows* nothing. On this approach, all of time is present to God in the eternal present of his existence, and he immediately and directly knows what happens at each moment of time by being directly acquainted with it from his perspective in *eternity.

Both of these strategies are controversial. The latter has been criticized for employing a concept that is incoherent, and the former for being unable to explain what makes the contents of God's middle knowledge true. Responses are available to both charges, and there are independent reasons for favouring each position. Advocates of an eternal God have the weight of tradition and the depth of centuries of intellectual exploration and clarification on which to draw. Advocates of middle knowledge can appeal to the cognitive dissonance between the eternality of God, with its origins in Greek thought, and the biblical portrayal of God as a being who intervenes in time and who responds to the needs and concerns of human beings.

See also PREDESTINATION; PROVIDENCE.   **Jonathan L. Kvanvig**

Hasker, William, *God, Time, and Knowledge* (1989).
Helm, Paul, *Eternal God* (1988).
Kvanvig, Jonathan, *The Possibility of an All-Knowing God* (1986).
Ockham, William, *Predestination, God's Foreknowledge and Future Contingents*, ET (1969).
Swinburne, Richard, *The Coherence of Theism* (1977).

ontological argument.

Any argument attempting to prove *God's existence a priori from his nature alone can be called 'ontological', but historically the term refers to that in *Anselm's *Proslogion*, chapter 2, and the variant advanced by *Descartes in his fifth *Meditation*, later developed by Leibniz. Some have claimed that Anselm's argument was anticipated by various classical philosophers (*Aristotle, Parmenides, *Plato, and Zeno of Cition) or by *Augustine, but, although there are suggestive passages in their writings, Anselm's explicit 'proof' of God's existence based on his nature appears to be original.

The scope of Anselm's argument, and its place within his thought, have been much debated; some commentators, notably *Barth, interpret it not as an argument for God's existence starting from a definition of what he is understood to be, but rather as an illumination of God's existence, starting from a revelation of his nature. This interpretation, according to which the argument moves from faith to understanding, corresponds well with the *Proslogion's* original title, *Fides quaerens intellectum*, but threatens to render chapter 2, traditionally seen as the heart of Anselm's argument, otiose: it is hard to see any point in an argument for God's existence starting from the apparently question-begging premiss that God has revealed himself as having a certain nature. However, in chapter 3 Anselm develops his line of reasoning, arguing that God exists in such a way that his non-existence is inconceivable. Hence if chapter 2 is seen not as independent but as a preliminary for chapter 3, these might be taken together as an exploration of God's existence starting from his revealed nature, without rendering Anselm's reasoning trivial or question-begging. Yet the reason why Anselm's argument has fascinated many generations of philosophers and theologians is that it appears to spell out a line of thought that even the unbeliever can follow, starting not from revelation but from the understanding of words, and leading inexorably to God's real existence. Most have dismissed the possibility of such an a priori proof, but the fascination remains because the argument's flaws have been so hard to identify.

Anselm begins with the fool of Psalm 14 who 'says in his heart "There is no God" ', and imagines him hearing and understanding the formula put forward as Anselm's own conception of God: something-than-which-nothing-greater-can-be-thought. His reasoning then proceeds through six steps:

1. The fool understands the phrase 'something-than-which-nothing-greater-can-be-thought'.
2. Hence something-than-which-nothing-greater-can-be-thought exists at least in the fool's mind.
3. It is greater to exist in reality than to exist in the mind alone.
4. So if that-than-which-nothing-greater-can-be-thought existed only in the fool's mind, it would be possible to think of something greater (the same thing existing in reality).
5. But this would be a contradiction, since it is impossible to think of something greater than that-than-which-nothing-greater-can-be-thought.
6. Hence something-than-which-nothing-greater-can-be-thought must exist both in the fool's mind and in reality.

This short paragraph has generated an enormous volume of commentary and criticism. Conceptual points made against it include objections to its alleged Neoplatonic presuppositions; its conflation of the fool's understanding of a phrase with the existence of an entity 'in the mind'; its comparison between existing and non-existing things; its treatment of existence as a property adding to something's greatness (this last criticism is particularly associated with *Kant, though he directed it at Descartes and Leibniz rather than at Anselm). More specifically logical objections include the argument's slide from the thought-properties of an entity to the existence of a thought-entity with those properties; its use of the formula 'that-than-which-nothing-greater-can-be-thought' presupposing that some entity is thus uniquely referred to; and the alleged illegitimacy of its move from claims within the realm of concepts to claims outside it. The most influential objections refrain from identifying any specific flaw, aiming only to show that *something* must be wrong, since similar arguments can be contrived for implausible entities such as a most excellent island (suggested by Anselm's correspondent Gaunilo) or a perfect Pegasus (Gassendi, criticizing Descartes). Such parodies, together with scepticism about the possibility of a priori proof, have led most thinkers to reject Anselm's reasoning while remaining unable to agree on where exactly it goes wrong. The argument's notoriety is based not on its plausibility, but on this lack of agreement.

Anselm's reasoning seems to have proved so difficult to pin down because his formula 'something-than-which-nothing-greater-can-be-thought' is subtly ambiguous, depending on what is accepted as the logical scope of 'can-be-thought'. To examine two possible interpretations: 'something-which-can-be-thought-so-great-that-nothing-can-be-thought-greater' would be a recognizably Godlike nature whose non-existence would not, however, be contradictory (that something *can be thought* supremely great does not imply that *it is* supremely great); whereas 'something-which-*is*-so-great-that-nothing-that-*is*-greater-can-be-thought-of' must indeed exist (since by definition the formula refers to the greatest thing there is), but need not be Godlike. Unfortunately, there is no interpretation of Anselm's formula by which it guarantees both reference to a Godlike nature and the existence of that nature.

More recent types of ontological argument lack the subtlety of Anselm's original and fail more straightforwardly (the best-known are collected in Plantinga (1965), while Oddy (1995) provides an exhaustive survey). Descartes's argument, that God is perfect by definition and so must possess all perfections including existence, succeeds at best in showing that the concept of God is of a being *conceived of as existing*: as Kant pointed out and Mackie has emphasized more recently, no contradiction is implied by the simple denial that this concept has real existence. Twentieth-century proponents like Hartshorne, Malcolm, and Plantinga have turned away from the crude Cartesian pattern, and sought inspiration from the principle of God's *necessary* existence enunciated in *Proslogion*, 3. However the 'modal' form of ontological argument (that if God is understood as a necessary being his existence, if possible, must be actual) has an unfortunate mirror-image; that on the same principles God's *non-existence*, if possible, must be actual. Hence the argument remains unable to convince even if its modal principles are accepted: anyone unsure about the existence of a necessary God should be equally unsure about his mere possibility. As with other versions of the ontological argument its premises appear true only to those already convinced of God's existence.

So the ontological argument fails to establish the existence of God. But, in Anselm's version at least, it remains a fascinating logical conundrum and can, perhaps, for the believer, be a focus for contemplating the special character of God's existence.

Peter Millican

Barth, K. *Anselm: Fides Quaerens Intellectum* (1931), ET (1960).
Hick, J., and McGill, A. (eds.), *The Many-Faced Argument* (1967).
Mackie, J. L., *The Miracle of Theism* (1982).
Oddy, G., *Ontological Arguments and Belief in God* (1995).
Plantinga, A. (ed.), *The Ontological Argument* (1965).

ordination, the rite of setting apart for the ordered *ministry of the *church. The theology and the rite of ordination developed throughout history in relation to changing understandings of the church, its *sacraments, and ministry. The NT offers no blueprint of ministry, nor rite of ordination. Christ's ministry was carried out by all the baptized, all were given gifts of the *Holy Spirit for ministry (Rom. 12: 4–8; 1 Cor. 12: 28–30). Nevertheless, it is clear that there were those designated for certain tasks by *prayer and the laying on of hands (1 Tim. 4: 14; 2 Tim. 1: 6).

A threefold pattern of bishop, presbyter, and deacon (see DIACONATE) which had emerged by the 2nd century soon became general. In *The Apostolic Tradition* of Hippolytus, bishop, *priest, and deacon are appointed by *episcopal laying on of hands and with prayer, all done within the context of a *Eucharist. The integral relation between the community and the one ordained to a distinctive ministry was fundamental. At ordination discernment, election, and presentation by the people, together with their prayer, belonged together. It was not the rite alone that made someone a minister but the call of God discerned by the people. In ancient Roman practice the candidate presented was already vested in the robes of the order and did not put them on at the end as if some change had taken place within the rite. This was expressed in the east by proclaiming the result of the election at the start of the rite. The Greek word translated 'to ordain', *cheirotoneo*, originally meant 'to raise the hand in order to elect'. The relation between ordained and community was further witnessed by the exchange of the kiss of peace. Ancient ordination prayers were for the bestowal of gifts and graces necessary for the discharge of office. Only rarely did prayers list particular powers and functions of office.

In the earliest traditions of east and west only the presiding bishop laid hands on the candidate, but later both the local bishop and the presbyters did so. The Council of *Nicaea stipulated that a minimum of three bishops should lay hands on an episcopal candidate, thus symbolizing the *communion of the local church with the wider church, as well as the relation of the bishop to the college of bishops. The act of ordaining a bishop by one who had himself been ordained by a bishop signified the continuity of ministry back to the apostles. Thus the *catholicity and *apostolicity of the church and its ministry were both symbolized in the rite of ordination.

Up to the 3rd century the complementarity of orders of ministry was stressed. A deacon might become bishop without being ordained presbyter. Gradually a 'lower to higher' ordering emerged, and episcopal candidates would have first to be ordained deacon and then presbyter. Reordination was not countenanced.

Shifts in understanding in the Middle Ages affected the theology and rites of ordination. Ordained ministry came to be seen primarily in terms of its relation to the Eucharist, the priest being the one who had received in ordination the power of offering the eucharistic sacrifice. Sacerdotal language had already become the norm in east and west. The priest came to be understood as different in kind, ontologically different, from the members of the community. The rite of ordination lost its emphasis on the relation between ordained and people which was obscured by anointings, investiture, and the tradition of giving 'instruments' (chalice and paten), all part of an increasingly priestly view of order.

In reaction, the *Reformers of the 16th century formulated rites of ordination that expressed their renewed understanding of the church, its sacraments, and ministry. They emphasized the unity of ministry; the priority of God's call; and the location of ordained ministry in, with, and among the community. They stressed the priestly character of all the faithful while avoiding the use of special priestly language for the ordained. For *Luther the service of ordination was the laying on of hands with the Lord's Prayer. *Calvin emphasized election and the prayer of the people and regarded the laying on of hands as unnecessary. *Baptist and *Congregationalist traditions emphasized the call in and to a local congregation. In some places the giving of the right hand of fellowship replaced the laying on of hands. However, the Moravians, some Lutherans, and the Church of England continued to ordain to a threefold ministry. Furthermore, the latter retained the term 'priest' and stressed the continuity of ordinations with the church through the ages, while omitting sacrificial overtones from the rite.

In the 20th century, through liturgical scholarship and *ecumenical discussions, Christians from many traditions reached a measure of agreement on the doctrine of the church, its ministry, and the rite of ordination. *Baptism, Eucharist and Ministry* (BEM), the report of the broadest ecumenical forum existing, the WCC Faith and Order Commission, sets out agreements on both the understanding and practice of ordination. Ordination denotes an action by God and the community by which the ordained are strengthened by the Spirit for their task and upheld by the acknowledgement and prayer of the people (*BEM* Ministry, 40). The act of ordination, by the laying on of hands with prayer by those appointed to do so, takes place within the context of a Eucharist. Ordination includes an invocation (*epiklesis*) asking God that the ordained be given the power of the Holy Spirit; a sign of the granting of the prayer by the Lord who gives ordained ministry; and the church's acknowledgement of the gifts of the Spirit in the one ordained and its commitment to the new relationship (ibid. 40–4).

The official responses of churches to BEM show that a number of differences in the understanding of ordination still remain. One concerns the understanding of ordination as a 'sacramental sign' and the sense in which 'sacrament' can be applied to ordination. Another concerns the understanding of the 'indelible character' of orders. This notion was, in part, linked to the power (*potestas*) held to be given for life to the one ordained to effect a change in the eucharistic consecration. Ecumenical discussion searches for a fresh way to describe the distinction between ordained and *lay which, while not solely functional, does not entail a stark ontological distinction between the two. *The Final Report of the Anglican–Roman Catholic International Commission* described the ordained ministry as not 'an extension of the common Christian priesthood' but as belonging to 'another realm of the gifts of the Spirit', a distinction not well received by all.

A further issue concerns the validity of orders. Validity is linked, for some, to whether the act of ordination is both in the historic episcopal succession and conveys what the church has always intended to convey. Thus the *Anglican claim to have maintained a valid ministry was officially denied in the papal bull *Apostolicae Curae* (1896) in which Leo XIII declared Anglican orders 'absolutely null and void'. Anglicans omitted from the rite for ordaining priests an explicit conferring of power to consecrate and to offer. This omission was taken to imply an anti-sacrificial view of priesthood and thus to render deficient the continuity and validity of ordinations. Similarly many Anglicans denied the validity of orders conferred in non-episcopal churches.

The question of validity has again been raised in relation to the ordination of *women, an issue central to modern church life both for those who support and those who oppose it. Women may have been ordained to the diaconate in the early church but for most of Christian history they have been entirely excluded from the ordained ministry. Was this due to a culture of patriarchy imposed on the church or to something inherently Christian, such as a deliberate exclusion by Jesus of women from the ranks of the apostles? A move to ordain women to the ministry began in the 19th century. *Reformed, Congregationalist, and *Methodist Churches in Europe and North America were among the first to do so. Some Lutheran, Anglican, and Old Catholic Churches have also taken this step since the 1970s, acting in the light of the experience of the church and the belief that there are no sound theological reasons against it. The community has discerned God's call to women, thus affirming women's own conviction that God is calling them to serve as ordained ministers of word and sacrament. The Orthodox Churches, however, remain opposed to such ordinations and the Roman Catholic Church holds that it has no authority to make such a change in the unbroken tradition of the church. These differences further limit the degree of mutual recognition of ministries and are obstacles to *reconciliation and to a shared rite of ordination. They underline basic divergences as to how the church handles *tradition and how far it can free itself of its own history.

An understanding of ministry and ordination has often been distorted by considering them apart from the life of the whole church. Ordination has thus been understood as something that happens to one person, the transmission of *potestas*, 'power', rather than an act of the whole apostolic church. Ecumenical discussions are restoring an emphasis on the relationship of the community to the person being ordained. There is also a willingness to acknowledge the fruitfulness of the ordained ministries of every church, and their intention to remain faithful to the teaching and mission of the apostles. The sign of ordination, while incorporating an individual in the ministry, may best be seen as an assurance of God's fidelity to the church and the church's intention to be faithful to God's calling, by continuing the apostolic succession of individuals selected for certain specific tasks.   **Mary Tanner**

Baptism, Eucharist and Ministry, Faith and Order Paper, III (1982).

Bradshaw, P., *Ordination Rites of the Ancient Churches of East and West* (1990).

—— 'Ordination as God's Action Through the Church', in D. Holeton (ed.), *Anglican Orders and Ordinals* (1997).

Vos, W., and Wainwright, G. (eds.), *Ordination Rites* (1980).

Warkentin, M., *Ordination: A Biblical and Historical View* (1982).

Origen

(185–*c*.254) was born, probably at *Alexandria, of Christian parents. The education given him by his father Leonides (martyred when Origen was 17) was both Hellenistic and biblical. Origen taught 'grammar' (i.e. literature) and was appointed head of the school of catechetics while still very young. For the first part of his life, to 231, he taught in his native city, but after his ordination as priest at Caesarea in Palestine, Bishop Demetrius' hostility compelled him to leave Alexandria for Caesarea. Here he reopened his school, about which we have abundant evidence from a eulogy by one of his students, the future Gregory Thaumaturgus. He was imprisoned and tortured during Decius' persecution and died about 254 from the after-effects, probably at Tyre, where his tomb in the cathedral was to be seen in the 13th century.

Thanks to one of his Alexandrian converts, Ambrose, who used his wealth to maintain a secretariat and copyists' workshop, Origen left a vast body of work, which survives only partially. Heading the list is the *Hexapla*, a titanic collaborative production on which he worked throughout his life. He set out in six columns (eight or even nine for some books) the entire OT as follows: the Hebrew in Hebrew letters; the Hebrew in Greek letters; the Greek versions of Aquila, Symmachus, the Septuagint (the official Christian text), and Theodotion; plus, for some books, supplementary versions designated Quinta, Sexta, and possibly Septima. Special signs (asterisk and obelus) marked places where the Septuagint had more or less text than others, probably to facilitate Jewish–Christian *dialogue by indicating what was or was not accepted by the other party. The last complete edition of the surviving fragments is Field's (1867; 1870; 1960) but many other fragments have since come to light. Because of the controversies after his death and Justinian's systematic destruction of his manuscripts, most of Origen's work is lost in

the original Greek, though some survives in Latin translations by Rufinus of Aquileia, Jerome, and an unknown translator.

Most of his work is exegetical. We still have in Greek a few books of his *Commentary on John*, possibly his *chef-d'œuvre*, and of his *Commentary on Matthew*, some of which were translated into Latin by an unknown 5th-century writer. Rufinus has left abridged Latin versions of the *Commentary on Romans* and the *Commentary on the Song of Songs*, an early masterpiece of *mystical writing. There are also nearly three hundred homilies on the scriptures, a score (on Jeremiah) surviving in Greek, the others in Latin.

A few non-exegetical works survive: *On First Principles* (*Peri archon*), a first attempt at a synthesis of the Christian faith, complete in Rufinus' Latin translation, one-seventh in Greek; *Contra Celsum*, a refutation of a Platonic philosopher and the most significant of the Apologies, in Greek; also in Greek, two little treatises on *prayer and *martyrdom. We also have two collections of quotations, the *Apologia of Origen* by the martyr Pamphilus in Rufinus' Latin, and the *Philocalia of Origen*, in Greek, attributed to Basil of Caesarea and Gregory Nazianzen.

Origen is an indissoluble combination of exegete, master of spirituality, and speculative theologian; seeing only one of these aspects risks serious distortion. He tends to be seen chiefly as an *allegorizer, whereas he is one of the great literal exegetes of his time. He investigates different readings in the manuscripts and usually explains the literal meaning before allegorizing. His frequent statement that such-and-such a passage has no valid literal sense has been misunderstood: for him the literal sense did not mean what was intended by the author, but just the actual words, the author's intention being included in the spiritual sense. He means that figurative *language has no valid literal meaning. He actually values the literal sense more highly than the most conservative modern exegetes, as witness his defence of the historicity of Noah's Ark against the Marcionite Apelles.

But the literal sense veils a spiritual or allegorical sense intended by *God. The whole *OT is a prophecy of the New, which in turn is a participation in the 'eternal Gospel' of beatitude: such is the intention of the Spirit inspiring the scriptures. All scripture bears a spiritual sense, which the believer must discover on reading. All was written with this intention for us Christians (1 Cor. 10: 11), including the OT, which thus reveals its meaning, as at the Transfiguration Moses and Elijah, symbolizing the law and the prophets, shine with the light of the transfigured Christ. The OT is *revelation only because it is all a prophecy of Christ, while the NT allows us to apply what is said of Christ to the Christian. The 'eternal Gospel' of the state of beatitude will convey, 'face to face', in all their fullness the realities which the 'temporal Gospel', here below, has shown 'in a mirror, as enigma' (1 Cor. 13: 12), but nevertheless as realities, whereas the OT gave us only the 'shadow' of them, not, like the New, a real participation.

Origin is always, in all his exegesis, a master of *spirituality. According to his anthropology, human beings consist of spirit (*pneuma*), *soul (*psyche*), and body (*soma*). The 'spirit which is in man' is a participation in the *Holy Spirit: it is the pedagogue of the soul, which becomes spiritual in proportion to its assimilation to the spirit. But if the soul surrenders to the flesh (*sarx*), thus assimilating itself to the body, it becomes instead wholly carnal. Thus the soul is both the arena and the prize of the spiritual combat.

Starting from scripture, Origen created a number of themes that recur in mystical literature. Thus the Bride in the *Song of Songs, besides the traditional collective interpretation as the *church, bears an individual meaning as the Christian soul, the bride of Christ through membership of the bride-church. The Christian life is the birth and growth of Christ in the soul: if Christ is not born in each one of us, his birth at Bethlehem has no meaning for us. The ascent of the three apostles to the Mount of Transfiguration signifies the *ascetical striving that prepares the soul for the vision of God, with no encroachment on God's absolute freedom. The five spiritual senses, by analogy with the five bodily senses, represent the possibility of an intuitive knowledge of God, by a connaturality revealed as humanity participates progressively in the image of God, that is, his Son, to the point of perfection, the 'likeness' of beatitude. Origen has a comprehensive doctrine of the knowledge of God and identifies it with the union of *love, quoting Gen. 4: 1, 'Adam knew Eve, his wife': knowledge and love are one thing. His too is the theme of the shaft and wound of love, combining Isa. 49: 2, where the Servant of Yahweh (Christ) says of God, 'He has made me a sharp arrow, hidden me in his quiver', with Song of Songs 2: 5, where the Bride says 'I am sick with love'. There are some testimonies in his work to a personal mystical experience (rare, because he says very little about himself), leading Henri *de Lubac to call him 'one of the greatest mystics of the Christian tradition'.

Finally, Origen is a great theologian, *Augustine and *Aquinas his only peers in Christian history. His theology has been seriously misunderstood, leading to his being unjustly branded a *heretic. He has not been judged on his work as a whole, nor even on what remains of it; his accusers have lacked historical sense, not seeing him in the context of his time nor taking the trouble to explain one passage by reference to another in some other work, or even sometimes in the same one. Their excuse, apart from the sheer volume of his work, must be that he was not concerned to 'define' his thought, i.e. to state it with all the nuances and antitheses to be found in other writings. This concern hardly existed for the church fathers of the first three centuries: it arose later under the combined influence of Roman law and controversy with the *Arians, who were good at discovering their own doctrines in their adversaries' statements. Origen's is a theology 'in process of research'—he himself says 'in training'—rather than something finished and elaborated.

One of his main preoccupations was with the numerous heresies, *Gnostic and other, of his time. Against the Marcionites he affirmed the goodness of the creator, his identity with the *Father of Jesus, the agreement of the two Testaments and the value of the Old; against the Valentinians, free will, personal responsibility, rejection of any *predestination arising from differences in human nature; against the modalists, the distinct personality of each of the divine *persons; against the adoptionists, the eternal generation of the *Word; against the *Docetists, the real humanity of Christ. He also combated some tendencies within the Church—anthropomorphists, *millenarianists, and literalists against whom he affirmed the incorporeal nature of God, the soul, and beatitude, and Christ's abolition of the letter of the Jewish Law.

The philosophical basis of Origen's thought is a moderate *Platonism mixed with Stoicism and a touch of *Aristotelianism, as appears from Gregory Thaumaturgus' account of his teaching. But he cannot be called a philosopher, what he drew from these sources being wholly in the service of theology.

He expresses the unity of the divine persons and the personality proper to each dynamically rather than ontologically. The generation of the Son by the Father is both eternal and, from our human point of view, continual; the Spirit derives from the Father through the Son. The Son remains forever in the Father, even when here on earth with his human soul. The statement that 'there is no moment when he (the Son) was not', which occurs three times in Origen's works (*Peri archon*, 1. 2. 9; 4. 4. 1; *Com. Rom.* 1. 5) cannot, as some have suggested, be inauthentic, for the second passage was quoted by *Athanasius (*De doctrina Nicaenae synodi*, 27. 1–2), and explicitly attributed to Origen. The generation of the Son does not imply a division of the Father's substance—*probole*, Latin *prolatio*—as in the doctrine Origen attributes to the Valentinians. The 'subordinationism' with which he is frequently reproached is simply the affirmation that the Father is primary, being the origin of the others and giving them their missions, with no implication of superiority of nature (see TRINITY).

The heart of Origen's *christology is his doctrine of the titles (*epinoiai*) of the Son—the different names he is given in scripture, by allegorical exegesis in the OT, directly in the NT. They correspond to his different activities relating to *humanity and *creation. Origen details about a hundred, the two most important being *Wisdom and Word. As Wisdom the Son is the Intelligible World, containing the seeds and principles of all beings, the mysteries corresponding to the Platonic world of ideas; as Word he is the revealer of the mysteries and the agent of creation. In accordance with Origen's doctrine of the pre-existence of souls, called in this context 'intelligences', the soul of Christ was created with the others, not from all eternity, but from the moment of its creation it was united to the Word and was thus 'in the form of God'. This soul was the spouse of the church, i.e. of the totality of the other intelligences, but it alone did not sin, as the others did to varying degrees. Their *Fall is seen as a diminishing in fervour or a wearying of beatitude, something like the 'acedia' described by the Greek monks. The varying depth of this fall divided the pre-existing intelligences into *angels, men, and demons. They all had ethereal bodies hitherto, but after the Fall those becoming humans took on a terrestrial quality so that they would be in a state of testing, enabling them to redeem their fault. The pre-existing intelligence of Christ also assumed a carnal body, without having sinned, in order to rejoin his fallen spouse, the pre-existing church now fallen into flesh. The OT is like a time of betrothal during which Christ has not yet revealed himself to the spouse, the OT church. In the NT, he has been reunited with his spouse, but this is not yet perfect union, which will be for the end of time.

Thus Christ became *incarnate in *Mary to redeem his fallen spouse and reveal divinity to her. During the Passion his human soul was handed over in ransom to Satan who, not recognizing the bond between Christ and God, took it down to Hades, where it liberated the souls held captive and took them with it in its Ascension. This is how Origen teaches the hypostatic union (for the Word is always with his human soul while still always with the Father) and introduces the concept of the 'communication of idioms' between the Word and the human soul united to him (whereby what is said of the one can be predicated also of the other).

Humanity, like the angels, was created according to the image of God, which is the Word, and participates in the existence and divinity of the Father and the sonship and rationality of the Word. But sin covers over the image of God in humanity with other images, diabolical or bestial, which only the Redeemer can remove. As regards risen bodies, Origen affirms both their identity with and their difference from terrestrial bodies, invoking the Pauline simile of seed and plant (1 Cor. 15: 34–44), in using which he is practically unique at this early period. He does not regard Mary as exempt from all sin, but he is the first to affirm, explicitly, her perpetual virginity, implicit in Justin and *Irenaeus. He sees her as a great exemplar of the spiritual life, and, according to the historian Socrates (*Church History*, 7. 32), he called her *Theotokos*, Mother of God. He gives precise teaching on five of the seven *sacraments (not confirmation or anointing of the sick).

The pre-existence of souls seems to be Origen's only demonstrable 'heresy', which cannot be called heresy in his time, for the church had no teaching on the matter. His vision of *apocatastasis*, i.e. restoration at the end of time, derived from 1 Cor. 15: 23–6, is not pantheistic. As for the salvation of the *devil, he has left contradictory texts, the clearest denial being in his *Letter to Friends in Alexandria*, quoted by both Rufinus and Jerome at the height of their quarrel, and thus, despite being in Latin, difficult to dispute. Other errors with which he is reproached arise from misunderstandings, or from later specialization of terminology.

Attacks on Origen, based on misunderstandings, began soon after his death, for example the two attacks of Methodius of Olympus, at the turn of the 3rd and 4th centuries, about the glorified body and the eternity of the world. These attacks were answered in the *Apologia of Origen* by the martyr Pamphilus of Caesarea, who explained the texts in question by reference to others in Origen's works. The great Doctors of the 4th century are all to a greater or lesser extent his disciples. But Jerome, starting as a fervent Origenist, turned against him after 393 and attacked him in argument with his old friend Rufinus. In the 6th century the Emperor Justinian entered the fray, condemning Origen as interpreted by contemporary 'Origenists', first in a local council in 543, then in a council held some time before the fifth Ecumenical (Constantinople II); this second council is clearly directed against contemporary Origenists. These attacks were made by men lacking in philosophical and theological understanding, but most of all in historical sense, unaware of the change in mentality between the small, persecuted church of Origen's time and the triumphant church of their own. They accuse him in terms of the heresies of their time, not those that he himself faced and that dictated his line of argument. They were unaware of the theological advance stimulated by the Arian crisis, and even of changes in terminology. They projected the 'Origenism' of their time on to Origen, did not explain difficult passages by reference to others, made no distinction between Origen writing 'by way of exploration' and Origen as teacher, and finally judged him by a conception of *orthodoxy increasingly dependent on Roman law. Hence their case against him is without validity.

Ever since the 15th century, with Pico della Mirandola and *Erasmus, Origen has been a subject of serious study, but in the second half of the 20th century interest in him grew among a large number of scholars. Their four-yearly congress brings together as many as 120 people from several European and American countries, and from Japan. After Augustine, Origen is probably at present the most studied of all the church fathers. Now that more exact historical work has revealed his true greatness, unconfused by any later 'Origenism', it seems that his 'exploratory theology', with its basis in scripture and its inspiration drawn from spiritual experience, corresponds very closely to the aspirations of our own age.

See also PRE-CONSTANTINIAN THOUGHT.   **Henri Crouzel**

Origen, *Commentary on Matthew, Books I, II, X–XIV*, ed. J. Patrick (1897).
—— *The Philocalia*, ed. G. Lewis (1911).
—— *Prayer; Exhortation to Martyrdom*, ed. J. J. O'Meara (1954).
—— *The Song of Songs, Commentary and Homilies*, ed. R. Lawson (1957).
—— *On First Principles*, ed. B. W. Butterworth, 2nd edn. (1966).
—— *Contra Celsum*, ed. H. Chadwick, 3rd edn. (1979).
—— *Homilies on Genesis and Exodus*, ed. R. Heine (1982).
—— *Commentary on the Gospel According to John, Books 1–10*, ed. R. Heine (1989); *Books 13–32* (1993).
—— *Homilies on Leviticus 1–16*, ed. G. W. Barkley (1990).
—— *Treatises on the Passover; Dialogue with Heraclides and his Fellow Bishops on the Father, the Son and the Soul*, ed. R. J. Daly (1992).
—— *Homilies on Luke; Fragments on Luke*, ed. J. T. Lienhard (1996).
Bigg, C., *The Christian Platonists of Alexandria* (1913).
Crouzel, H., *Origen* (1984), ET (1989).
—— *Bibliographie critique d'Origène*, with Supplements I and II (1996).
Daniélou, J, *Origen* (1948), ET (1955).
Drewery, B., *Origen and the Doctrine of Grace* (1960).
Hanson, R., *Origen's Doctrine of Tradition* (1954).
—— *Allegory and Event* (1959).
Westcott, B. F., 'Origen and the Beginnings of Christian Philosophy', in *Essays on the History of Religious Thought in the West* (1891).

original sin, see SIN; FALL.

Orthodox churches, see EASTERN ORTHODOX THEOLOGY.

orthodoxy means assent to the *faith of the *church, and is contrasted with *heresy. The earliest expressions of faith were no more than 'Jesus is Lord' (Rom. 10: 9; Phil. 2: 11). As the church grew, uncontrolled by any central authority, its faith was interpreted and developed in different, sometimes contradictory, ways, forcing the production, usually by *councils of bishops, of more extended formulas to distinguish true belief from heresy. Gradually specific points were defined and lengthier *creeds constructed, focusing principally upon *God as *Trinity and Christ as *incarnate. To clarify points at issue a terminology was adopted beyond that found in scripture. The formulation of orthodoxy thus developed across the centuries, the orthodoxy of the 3rd century being different from that of the 4th or 5th. Views still acceptable within the former had become heresies by the latter.

There seems no way, given the Christian commitment to proclaiming revealed *truth and the evolution of culture and ecclesiastical *history, in which a concern with orthodoxy or its ongoing development through *dogma could be avoided. Nevertheless, a seemingly excessive preoccupation with specific theological phrases led to the exclusion of more and more groups of Christians from *communion with one another. Such behaviour became so characteristic of the Greek Church that the title 'Orthodox' became its most cherished badge, but comparable concerns to exclude heresy can be found in all the main ecclesiastical traditions. Modern Catholic orthodoxy was long defined in terms of the dogmatic decrees of *Trent and *Vatican I, *Presbyterian orthodoxy by the *Westminster Confession* (1647). No defence of orthodoxy had a more rending effect than *Chalcedon's definition of the two natures in Christ which resulted in most Christians in Egypt, *Syria, and, later, *Ethiopia and *Armenia being judged unorthodox. In recent times both Rome and Constantinople have, however, accepted their alternative, '*Monophysite', formulation of *christology as adequate. Too narrow a pursuit of orthodoxy, embittered by rivalry between the sees of *Constantinople and *Alexandria, thus unnecessarily divided the churches, to the damage of all concerned, for 1500 years.

In this as in other cases it is increasingly recognized that many of the more scholastically precise statements of doctrine insisted upon in the past, not only in late patristic times but also in the *Reformation era, as a condition for church recognition were both unnecessary and disastrous. In words borrowed from *Vatican II, they were due to a failure to recognize the difference between 'the truths of faith' and 'the manner in which they are formulated', forgetting that diversities in theological tradition are often 'complementary rather than conflicting' (*Gaudium et Spes*, 62; *Decree on Ecumenism*, 17). Orthodoxy has become, in consequence, a concept exceptionally difficult to interpret effectively except in circles, whether *fundamentalist or *ultramontane, dismissive of the approaches just described. For some it has been partially replaced by the idea of orthopraxis: since following *Jesus is more a way of life than adherence to a creed, behaviour such as *antisemitism or support for *apartheid become criteria for denying church membership. The difficulty with this is, however, considerable: if it truly remains a matter of praxis, the church is seen as excluding *sinners; if instead it becomes the subject of a specific formula, it simply adds new, probably transient and certainly debatable, criteria of orthodoxy.

The gap between those who do and those who do not find orthodoxy an easily employable concept may constitute one of the deepest fissures within modern Christian thought. Nevertheless, as recognition of orthodoxy and admission to communion were traditionally correlative, the best criterion for orthodoxy may remain an ability to join in the great amen at the close of the *eucharistic prayer.   **Adrian Hastings**

Hastings, A., 'Community, Consensus, and Truth', *The Theology of a Protestant Catholic* (1990), 9–26.
Kelly, J. N. D., *Early Christian Creeds*, 3rd edn. (1972).
Turner, H. W., *The Pattern of Christian Truth* (1954).

Otto, Rudolf (1869–1937).

In the book by which he is remembered, *The Idea of the Holy*, Otto writes, 'The reader is invited to direct his mind to a moment of deeply-felt religious experience … Whoever cannot … is requested to read no further.' He expected his readers to continue, because human beings share a sense of the uncanny. In an earlier book he spoke of 'the *numen* that loiters in the secret dread of hollows and caves', and from that Latin word for undefined divinity he coined 'numinous', 'the non-rational factor in the idea of the divine'. Published in wartime, in 1917, *The Idea of the Holy*, like *Barth's *Epistle to the Romans*, seemed to side-step the tired good sense of 'culture-Protestantism' that had allowed the world to drift into war. The Latin phrase from Otto, 'mysterium tremendum et fascinans', became general currency. To interpret, the divine is mystery, because it is 'wholly other'. It causes us to tremble with fear: 'How dreadful is this place'. Yet it also draws us in fascination, in delighted rapture. Critics have said that this is too individualist, too experiential.

Otto was an academic theologian in Germany. His own background was *evangelical heart-religion overlaid with *liberalism. In long travels to learn about other *religions, he felt he encountered them on a deeper level than the rational. Hearing 'Kadosh, Kadosh, Kadosh' (Holy, Holy, Holy) sung in a synagogue in Morocco in 1911 was a turning-point. Otto worked to bring religions together, helping set up a World Congress of Faiths, translating Sanskrit texts, and founding a museum of religions at Marburg, where he was professor of theology from 1917.

Otto believed in feeling and the non-rational, but in their place. He was a somewhat constrained person and always stressed the need for 'assiduous and serious study' of *reason first. Individualist experiential Marburg students normally preferred the dialectical existentialism of his contemporary *Bultmann. In an age of *neo-orthodoxy, new light on the religious depths of Hinduism was often unwelcome. A few of his contemporaries, such as Troeltsch, were working on similar lines to Otto. The Swedish Archbishop Söderblom, discussing *holiness in Hastings's *Encyclopaedia* in 1913, said, dangerously to orthodox ears, that it was 'even more essential than the notion of God' and talked about *mana*.

Otto, however, as can be seen from his other books, placed himself in an earlier context. The great theologian of *religious experience was *Schleiermacher. Otto argued, respectfully, that the 'feeling of absolute dependence' was still too much in the realm of cause-and-effect. He chose as his master Schleiermacher's contemporary, the lesser-known philosopher Jacob Fries (1773–1843). Fries's keyword is 'feeling'. 'Knowledge of the eternal in the finite is only possible through pure feeling.' This is *Romantic German idealist philosophy, claiming that feeling is knowing. Most of Otto's readers do not follow his philosophical, or theological, line. He is instead treated as an early phenomenologist, simply describing religious feelings. He became a primary text in the developing discipline of 'religious studies', successfully evoking in generations of readers a sense of the holy.   **Alistair Mason**

Almond, P. C., *Rudolf Otto: An Introduction to his Philosophical Theology* (1984).
Davidson, R. F., *Rudolf Otto's Interpretation of Religion* (1947).

Oxford Movement.

The term, dating from 1839, came to describe the High Church revival in the Church of England between 1833 and 1845. The Movement's principal figure, John Henry *Newman, the greatest 19th-century English theologian, introduced it as 'the religious movement of 1833' in his *Apologia pro Vita Sua* (1864) but he also referred there to the 'Oxford Movement' where he established its chronology between the Assize sermon (14 July 1833) by the Oxford Professor of Poetry, John Keble, and his own conversion to Roman Catholicism in October 1845. The 'Oxford Movement' denotes the inception of the modern *Anglican High Church revival among clergymen-scholars in Britain's oldest university, though it also has the wider connotation of its legacy to Anglican life and thought after 1845, for which more general terms are 'Anglo-Catholic' or 'Tractarian', after the 90

Tracts for the Times published by the leaders of the Movement (1833–41), and 'Puseyite' (usually pejorative and now archaic, after the Movement's greatest scholar, Edward Pusey, canon of Christ Church, and Regius Professor of Hebrew).

The Movement began as a reaction against the passage of the 1829 Catholic Emancipation Bill admitting Catholics to Parliament and so to authority over the *established church, and against the reforming intentions of the Whig government elected in 1830. Its immediate cause was a Whig bill to suppress ten Church of Ireland bishoprics in 1833. Keble and Newman thought that the Church of England could only be defended by renewing its belief in the doctrine of the *church itself, not as a mere national institution but as a divine society with its foundation in heaven; as Christ's *body and bride; and as 'His very self below' in the sacraments conveyed by his *priesthood, exercising his authority through an '*apostolic succession' of bishops (see EPISCOPATE). The Movement's insistence on the necessity of the threefold ministry of bishop, priest, and deacon was explicit in the church's ordinal, though only after 1790 did Anglican High Churchmen, confronted with the growth of *evangelical dissenting churches in England, rigorously apply it to deny the ecclesial character of every *Protestant church except their own. The logic of this position was that *Rome was a church, however corrupt, and that *Geneva was not a church, whatever good might be found there.

Within this position there were those who stressed the threefold ministry and those (like Newman) who thought more in terms of episcopal monarchy, but Newman's own repudiation of the Church of England's Protestant character and redefinition of an Anglican *via media* lying between popery and Protestantism, in place of an older Anglican middle way between popery and *Puritanism, was a rejection of the Protestantism of the High Church tradition. So the Movement was distanced from such traditional High Churchmen as Walter Farquhar Hook, the influential Vicar of Leeds, originally its supporter, but for whom the Church of England's glory was to be both Protestant and Catholic. The result was 'a paper theory', as Newman called it in his *Lectures on the Prophetical Office of the Church* (1837), the chief new attempt to define an Anglican ecclesiology, a theory as yet unrealized in any living church. The theory was a partial reading of Anglican history, and renewed High Church conflict with Anglican evangelicals, foreign Protestants, and English Dissenters as well as with Roman Catholics.

Less rejecting of Protestantism was Pusey, under whose influence the *Tracts for the Times* swelled from flysheets into massive theological treatises. Pusey knew more than his friends about Protestantism, and while increasingly suspicious of its learned *German form, he knew what he was rejecting. The more anti-Protestant members of the Movement like Richard Hurrell Froude looked back admiringly to the theocratic medieval church which they declared to be one with the Church of England, or like the devotional writer Frederick William Faber invoked the contemporary Continental Catholic revival.

Newman, however, was no medievalist, and his work as a student of the church fathers gave the Movement its character. Its first great publication after the *Tracts* was its *Library of the Fathers* (projected in 1836). Its primary appeal, for which it could claim Anglican precedent, was, next to scripture, to the authority of the undivided Catholic Church before 500, and to its abiding definitions of the canon of scripture, *ministry, and *creed. Only secondarily did it appeal to Anglican tradition; its *Library of Anglo-Catholic Theology* began publication in 1841. Newman's meticulous attempt to separate orthodoxy from heresy was rooted in his study of the ancient texts, as in his *Arians of the Fourth Century* (1833), so that the Movement's first crisis occurred when in 1839 he detected analogies between Anglicanism, *Monophysitism, and *Donatism. In 1841, he wrote the final *Tract 90*, which reconciled some of the moderately Protestant Anglican Thirty-Nine Articles not only with primitive Catholicism but with the decrees of the Council of *Trent. This raised a storm of protest, and he retired to Littlemore, near Oxford, to translate Athanasius. His *Essay on the Development of Christian Doctrine* (1845) expressed a *paradox, that the church could only remain the same as a living organism by growth and change, and was a repudiation of the old High Church appeal to the static faith of the early church, as he argued that fundamental doctrines like the Trinity and original sin had developed in history beyond the letter of scripture (see DEVELOPMENT OF DOCTRINE). Newman also carried certain Anglican emphases into the Catholic Church: the role of conscience in the formation of belief, derived from Bishop Butler (1692–1752), the importance of *liturgy to theology, the right of the *laity to a part in defining doctrine, and a constitutional understanding of the church, in which the *papal monarchy was to be tempered by the intellectual office of the theologian. Other converts to Rome once connected with the Movement like William Ward (its greatest philosopher after Newman) and Cardinal Manning (archbishop of Westminster) embodied their dislike of Anglican anarchy in a more thoroughgoing *ultramontanism.

Newman tied doctrine into the church's institutional, moral, spiritual, and pastoral life, and the Oxford Movement illustrated that principle, as it spread through the parishes. It became a movement to renew the beauty of *holiness, especially through the revival of religious orders (see RELIGIOUS LIFE). It made a great pastoral effort to evangelize the neglected poor in the new industrial towns and the countryside; and gave the Church of England a novel religious, aesthetic, and visual symbolic language, by a vast programme of Gothic church building with neo-medieval furnishings (see VISUAL ARTS). These transformed what Newman and Froude had called the Anglican 'ethos', a term that they introduced into modern usage. The leading figure in this transformation was Newman's mentor John Keble, whose book of verse *The Christian Year* (1827), one poem for each Sunday, service, and sacrament of the Book of Common Prayer, invested the Prayer Book with the *Romantic emotions of awe, mystery, and wonder.

Keble was the Movement's model rural pastor, and his scholarship was of a high order. But his remark that if the Church of England were to fail it would be found in his parish gave the Movement from 1841 its *congregationalist character in opposition to Protestant bishops, for all its high conception of episcopal authority. This conflict was little disguised by attempts to regulate High Church doctrine and ritual by what Anglo-Catholics dismissed as the *Erastian state, which tried and failed to uphold Protestant standards by persecuting both George Anthony Denison for asserting a high doctrine of the Eucharist and the ritualists who adapted the Prayer Book to a neo-medieval and Counter-Reformation ceremonial.

This failure to rein in the Anglo-Catholics was a parallel to the church's failure to curb its *liberals. Thus the Anglo-Catholic tradition developed of a priest-pope in every parish, owing not so much obedience to his bishop, as on Newman's original theory, as to the Catholic Church more vaguely defined. From the necessity of episcopacy, High Churchmen deduced that the church subsisted in three great 'branches' or episcopal communions, Orthodox as well as Anglican and Roman Catholic, and an interest in eastern Christianity, explicit in Newman's study of the Greek fathers and in William Palmer's *A Treatise on the Church of Christ* (1838), was carried forward by the polymath and hymnologist John Mason Neale. Yet the appeal to *Eastern Orthodoxy was again a matter of individual inclination; the Movement only survived because the Church of England came to tolerate it on the basis of a Broad Church denial of the right of authority to ban it. In its inability to restore episcopal authority, the Oxford Movement revived every doctrine of the church except *the* doctrine of the church. Paradoxically this permitted the extreme of the Movement to veer to 'Anglo-papalism', in which contemporary Roman Catholic practice counted for more than Anglican tradition.

Newman was the model for Anglo-Catholics to become Roman Catholics, but the generation of High Churchmen after Pusey's death attempted a fusion of liberalism and Catholicism in the Church of England, most notably Charles Gore (1853–1932), one of the greatest of 20th-century Anglican theologians. It had a considerable influence on the Church of England in the 20th century, though this declined with the rise of evangelicalism after 1945. Its more recent division into 'liberal' and 'orthodox' wings, 'Affirming Catholicism' and 'Forward in Faith', over the issue of *ordaining women, reflected both an ambiguity at the heart of its own history and a crisis of authority in the Church of England as a whole.

Sheridan Gilley

Chadwick, O., *The Mind of the Oxford Movement* (1960).
—— *The Victorian Church* (2 vols.; 1966; 1970), esp. i. 167–231.
—— *The Spirit of the Oxford Movement: Tractarian Essays* (1990).
Church, R. W., *The Oxford Movement, Twelve Years, 1833–1845* (1891).
Crumb, L.N., *The Oxford Movement and its Leaders: A Bibliography of Secondary and Lesser Primary Sources* (1988).
Fairweather, E. R. (ed.), *The Oxford Movement* (1964).
Nockles, P. B., *The Oxford Movement in Context: Anglican High Churchmanship 1760–1857* (1994).
Rowell, G., *The Vision Glorious: Themes and Personalities of the Catholic Revival in Anglicanism* (1983).
—— (ed.), *Tradition Renewed: The Oxford Movement Conference Papers* (1986).
—— (ed.), *The English Religious Tradition and the Genius of Anglicanism* (1992).
Vaiss, P. (ed.), *From Oxford to the People: Reconsidering Newman & the Oxford Movement* (1996).

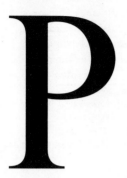

pacifism is the refusal for conscientious reasons to fight in wars or submit to military discipline. Historically speaking pacifism has been predominantly a Christian phenomenon, although today there are many pacifist groups based on other religions (*Buddhism, for instance) or on none. Pacifism is closely linked to, but distinct from, the practice of non-violent action, such as that by Gandhi or Martin Luther King (see BLACK THEOLOGY) to gain political or social objectives.

The 2000-year history of Christian pacifism reveals a constant tension between two opposing impulses: sectarianism and accommodation with the state. NT Christianity emerged as a sect within Judaism, under the eyes of imperial administrators; and *Jesus' teaching, addressed to a people excluded from full participation in the idolatrous paganism of Rome, was of necessity a sectarian appeal. The early church's pacifism was part and parcel of this. But as Christianity spread, its pacifism became less absolute. People with authority and status were becoming Christians. Hence pacifist apologists like Tertullian (see PRE-CONSTANTINIAN THOUGHT) and *Origen felt it necessary to remind fellow-Christians of their obligation to reject the idolatry and bloodshed that was essential to the imperial army. But they were pleading a losing cause: for another, equally fundamental, Christian teaching was now revealing itself, namely *catholicity, or the claim (and vocation) to go out to 'make disciples of all nations'. (Matt. 28: 19–20). Such teaching entailed converting not just individuals with *consciences but the *institutions* that constitute *human civilization. How could this be done without joining the powers that rule this *world?

Pacifist groups have tended to be stronger on conviction and emotional commitment than on theological foundation-building. This is partly because in the past they have often consisted of unlettered groups, becoming easy prey to forms of *fundamentalism. Nevertheless scholars have discovered a theology of pacifism in the NT, going beyond the familiar exhortations not to resist evil (Matt. 5: 39), to turn the other cheek (Luke 6: 29), to refuse to take up the sword (Matt. 26: 52), to love enemies and pray for persecutors (Matt. 5: 44) etc. John *Robinson has shown how *Paul developed this theology of Jesus' own non-violence. He sees Jesus' Passion as a struggle with supernatural powers controlling this world (1 Cor. 2: 8; Col. 2: 15; Eph. 2: 1–2; 6: 12): powers to whom men have wrongly conceded an influence that is God's alone. These 'principalities', 'dominations', and 'powers' always want vio-

lent resistance from any opponent, because violence is something they understand and can deal with. They are governed by what *Augustine called the 'lust for domination' (*libido dominandi*). What they cannot understand, and are literally disarmed by, is absolute non-resistance to the point of death. Jesus saves his own life by losing it, refusing to fight on their terms, and thereby giving them the slip. He offers them his own *death while paradoxically cheating them out of the one thing they really wanted: victory by force.

In Ephesians 6 Paul argues that, to be one with Christ in his struggle against the powers of this world, the Christian has to offer exactly the opposite of what the ordinary Roman soldier is trained for: violence. The Christian must put on the 'whole armour of God' and wield the 'sword of the spirit'. In thus contrasting the Christian 'soldier' with the Roman legionary, Paul is bringing his belief in the 'principalities, dominations, and powers' which rule 'in the air' down to earth, making a devastating, ironic commentary on the machinery by which the Roman empire maintains itself. Tertullian and the other early apologists expanded this insight into a pacifist polemic against the Roman state. But when, by an unforeseen turn of events, the empire itself became Christian, pacifism found itself replaced by Christian accommodation with the temporal order. Augustine gave reluctant expression to this with his teaching that the use of military force could be justified provided it was conducted for the common good by legitimate public authority. This concession, already granted in practice by the post-Constantinian church, legitimized in Christian eyes the power of the state.

The history of pacifism is part and parcel of the story of the *church itself, continually splintering along the fault line between catholicity and sectarianism. Sometimes pacifist groups have turned inwards, endangering their relevance and vitality for this reason. Others, however, have become influential in society and politics, sometimes, as a result, weakening their opposition to state power, for example by being prepared to pay taxes even though these may be used for military purposes. The 12th-century Waldenses, the 15th-century Taborites, the Bohemian *Brethren ('Unitas Fratrum'), the 16th-century Hutterites, all sprang from the sectarian impulse; but eventually compromised, following the lead of new, better-educated, town-based recruits. The 16th-century Anabaptist (see BAPTIST THEOLOGY) movement, which began in Switzerland but soon spread to Germany and elsewhere, was at first a peaceful but *revolutionary sect. Some Anabaptist groups remained steadfast in their separation from the state; but others compromised over the use of the sword to defend civil order, or even (as at Münster, under John of Leiden, 1534–5) became violent revolutionaries. Out of this confusion developed one of the best-known 'peace churches' surviving today: the *Mennonites, founded by Menno Simons in the Netherlands.

The Society of Friends, or *Quakers, founded by George Fox in 1650 in reaction to the militarism of the English Revolution, soon developed its 'peace testimony', although this was not a written document. Nor was subscription to it a condition of membership. In the following decades Robert Barclay and William Penn developed their ideas on the establishment of a new international order of *peace, even including an element of coercive police action under an embryonic 'league of nations'. Thus the Society of Friends became co-operators with, rather than opponents of, the political order as such.

By the time of the First World War conscription had become the norm in most continental European states, but not in Britain or the United States. When the war's massive casualties among volunteer soldiers made conscription unavoidable even in these countries, it was felt necessary to provide for conscientious objection. Some 'absolute' objectors so convinced tribunals of their sincerity and determination that they succeeded in avoiding any kind of conscription into the war effort. But others had to face the consequences of their absolute pacifism: imprisonment. Prison conditions were extremely harsh, and many pacifists suffered permanently as a result. But after the war, with a hoped-for era of peace, Christian pacifist principles gained increasing influence in the churches and in the political sphere: for example in England with the establishment of the Peace Pledge Union by Dick Sheppard, vicar of St Martin-in-the-Fields in London. The 1920s and early 1930s marked the apogee of pacifist thought and activity. But pacifist hopes were soon dashed, as the shadow of fascism fell across Europe. Nevertheless, some good came out of the inter-war pacifist campaigns, for in the Second World War conscientious objectors were better appreciated and better treated than they had been in the First. Hatred of war, engendered in 1914–18, had made pacifism almost respectable.

Yet the mainstream churches were for long *too* respectable to accept widespread pacifism. Roman Catholicism was notoriously hostile to pacifism in practice. And faced by a Hitler or a Stalin, it was understandable that refusals to take part in military defence against these new 'dominations and powers' should be abandoned. Former pacifists like Reinhold *Niebuhr felt obliged to join the military struggle. Dietrich *Bonhoeffer was even drawn into supporting the assassination of Hitler. But with widespread post-1945 consent to strategies of mass 'terror', or 'deterrence', 'nuclear pacifism' soon emerged. This repudiated all specifically nuclear threats. Without explicitly abjuring conventional self-defence, in 1963 Pope *John XXIII, representing the very centre of Catholic universalism, now appeared to come out in support of 'nuclear pacifism', writing that atomic power—the modern world's boast—had rendered war itself no longer apt for putting right the violation of rights (*Pacem in Terris*, 127). In 1965 a key pacifist teaching on the rights of the individual conscience against state conscription was accepted by the Second *Vatican Council (*Gaudium et Spes*, 79). By the mid-1990s, addressing the United Nations, the papacy had gone even further,

repudiating nuclear deterrence itself as a policy for keeping international peace. And in May 1999 an international gathering in the Hague, to celebrate the hundredth anniversary of the first Hague Convention, proclaimed an appeal for peace and for the abolition of war, attracting very large numbers of Christians from peace-groups within the mainstream churches: the Fellowship of Reconciliation, the Anglican Pacifist Fellowship, Pax Christi International, and many others. Perhaps the new millennium will see a new and effective anti-war coalition built within the very citadels of respectable Christianity.

Brian Wicker

Bainton, R. H., *Christian Attitudes to War and Peace* (1960).

Brock, Peter, *Pacifism in the United States: From the Colonial Era to the First World War* (1968).

—— *Twentieth-Century Pacifism* (1970).

—— *Pacifism in Europe to 1914* (1972).

Ceadel, Martin, *Pacifism in Britain 1914–1945* (1980).

Harvey, A. E., *Demanding Peace* (1999).

Martin, David, *Pacifism: An Historical and Sociological Study* (1965).

Robinson, John A. T., *The Body: A Study in Pauline Theology* (1952).

Sharp, Gene, *The Politics of Non-Violent Action* (1973).

Wilkinson, Alan, *Dissent or Conform? War/Peace and the English Churches 1900–1945* (1986).

Pannenberg, Wolfhart (1928–).

Pannenberg was born in north-east Germany (now part of Poland). Although baptized a Lutheran, as a child he had almost no contact with the church. Reading *Nietzsche and the influence of a school literature teacher sparked his interest in *philosophy, Christianity, and *theology. After university studies in Berlin, Basel, and Heidelberg, he occupied teaching posts in Wuppertal (1958–61), Mainz (1961–8), and Munich (1968–93).

In a manner reminiscent of classical theology and in contrast to the widespread contemporary privatization of belief, Pannenberg sees theology as a public discipline. Theological affirmations must be evaluated on the basis of critical canons rather than by appeal to subjective experience, for like the other sciences theology deals with *truth (*Theology and the Philosophy of Science* (1976)). Theology's task is to pursue the truth and thereby place Christian faith on a firm intellectual footing. The truth of Christian theology must be measured according to its ability to illumine all human knowledge. In his *magnum opus*, the three-volume *Systematic Theology* (1991–7), Pannenberg seeks to show the illuminating power of the Christian conception of *God.

Central to Pannenberg's proposal is the understanding of God as the power that determines everything. This means that God's deity is connected to God's demonstration of lordship over all creation (*Basic Questions in Theology* (1970), 3rd volume published separately in the USA as *The Idea of God and Human Freedom* (1973)). Consequently, the entire historical process, in which conflicting (religious) truth claims are struggling for supremacy, is ultimately a demonstration of God's existence and the location of God's self-disclosure as the triune one. Because the final demonstration of the truth of God occurs at the end of *history, all knowledge is provisional (*Revelation as History* (1968)). Nevertheless, God's self-disclosure is proleptically present in *Jesus. Jesus' identity was confirmed by the historical event of the Resurrection (*Jesus—God and Man* (1977)). Because Jesus tasted death for us, we can anticipate participating in God's eternal life beyond death (*An Introduction to Systematic Theology* (1991)).

As God's all-pervasive presence in creation, the *Holy Spirit is the 'field' or environmental network in which and from which all creatures live (*Faith and Reality* (1977)). The Spirit likewise lifts creatures above their environment and orients them towards the future.

The human *person is naturally religious, in that the structure of individual and social life is pervaded by a religious component. The Spirit is operative in human identity formation. Identity develops as we perceive the totality of our personal existence, a perception which becomes the 'field' in which we live. The Spirit's presence also accounts for human self-transcendence and forms the basis for our existence 'in Christ'. *Sin is 'self-love', the 'I' fixating on its own finiteness rather than finding its identity from its true source—existence 'in Christ' (*Anthropology in Theological Perspective* (1985)).

The Christian community lives in hopeful expectation of the coming of God's *eschatological lordship over creation (the *Kingdom of God). En route to that event, the *church is a witness to the temporality of all human institutions. As it gives expression to fellowship among humans and between humans and God, especially in the *Eucharist, the church becomes the sign of God's eschatological kingdom (*The Apostles' Creed* (1972); *The Church* (1983)). This divine reign alone is the hope of the world. Ultimately the future takes precedence in determining all reality. This 'ontological priority of the future' means that all things find their true identity in relationship to God's kingdom (*Metaphysics and the Idea of God* (1990)).

Taken together, these themes witness Pannenberg's unrelenting attempt to maintain the public nature of theology. In a day when theologians have been tempted to retreat into a realm of private or community faith, Pannenberg has pursued the ambitious goal of developing a new synthesis of theology and human learning, a synthesis built upon the conviction that the Christian understanding of God is crucial to the pursuit of knowledge.

Stanley Grenz

Braaten, Carl, and Clayton, Phillip (eds.), *The Theology of Wolfhart Pannenberg: Twelve American Critiques* (1988).
Grenz, Stanley, J., *Reason for Hope: The Systematic Theology of Wolfhart Pannenberg* (1990).

Panikkar, Raimon (Raimundo) (1918–). Panikkar, the son of a Spanish Catholic mother and *Indian *Hindu father, was born in Barcelona. A Catholic priest, he has written significantly and extensively (in at least four major languages) in the areas of comparative religion, *philosophy of religion and *science, and *theology, in a career spanning over fifty years.

Panikkar is said to have described himself as 'fully Indian and fully Spanish'; this illustrates the stimulating paradox that characterizes his thought. Though his views have developed over the years (notably in reinterpreting traditional emphases on the theological primacy of Christ and Christian faith among the world's religions), his abiding passion has been to articulate a 'cosmotheandric vision' (one of many neologisms marking Panikkar's attempts to bridge cultural and religious divides). At the heart of this vision is a 'trinitarian reality', also called an *advaitic* or 'non-dual' unity, in which the human, the cosmic, and the divine exist in an interactive, non-predetermined, and mutually constitutive and irreducible relation-

ship. This '*dialogue', in which there is more than an element of *process theology, is conducted mainly in terms of the Christian, Hindu, *Buddhist and secular-humanist traditions. Where theory of *language is concerned, Panikkar develops another interesting triad: *logos* (the communicated *word), *mythos* (the unexpressed framework for the communication of *logos*), and *pneuma* (that which makes open-ended interaction between *logos* and *mythos* possible). According to Panikkar these ideas must lead to a continuous, fruitful dialectic between contemplation and action that furthers tolerance, *justice, and intercultural co-operation.   **J. J. Lipner**

Panikkar, R., *The Unknown Christ of Hinduism* (1964); rev. edn. (1981).
—— *The Trinity and the Religious Experience of Man*, rev. edn. (1973).
—— *Myth, Faith and Hermeneutics* (1979).
—— *The Silence of God: The Answer of the Buddha* (1989).
Prabhu, J. (ed.), *The Intercultural Challenge of Raimon Panikkar* (1996).

papacy signifies the Church of Rome, and especially its bishops, as claiming and exercising *authority over the universal *church in a way unique to itself and derived from St *Peter. The special position of Peter as it appears in the NT is incontestable. It is also hardly open to doubt that both Peter and *Paul eventually arrived in *Rome and were *martyred there in Nero's persecution. Their tombs soon became shrines of great significance for Christians. This provided the Roman Church with a strongly *apostolic character, superior to that of any other. Whether Peter's authority was of a nature to be passed on, whether, if so, it was necessarily passed to the bishops of Rome and in what—if its transmission be admitted—this authority consists are, however, highly disputable questions.

The church of the first centuries was a network of self-governing local churches held together by a strong but uninstitutionalized sense of shared belief and sacramental *communion. Interference of one church in the affairs of another was rare but advice could be given, common problems discussed and disagreement might lead even to a breaking of communion understood as dechurching the offender. By the late 2nd century a Roman precedence was both claimed by Rome itself and to some extent recognized by others. Thus when Pope Victor (189–98) excommunicated the Asian 'Quartodecimans' for keeping *Easter when they did, he was rebuked by *Irenaeus of Lyons for intolerance rather than for exceeding his authority which, elsewhere, Irenaeus appeared to recognize in a much-discussed phrase: 'With this church on account of her more powerful principality it is necessary that every church should agree.' Irenaeus had lived in Rome and may have imbibed a more Roman ecclesiology than most in the east would have accepted.

While in the early days Rome's 'apostolic' character was linked equally with Peter and Paul (the NT actually referring only to Paul's arrival there), from the mid-3rd century Rome begins to apply to itself the words of Matt. 16: 16, 'Thou art Peter and upon this rock I will build my church.' From then on the Petrine status predominates, and the pope becomes 'the Vicar of Peter'. The 4th century saw two notable, if contrasting, developments. On the one hand, a series of 'ecumenical' *councils held in the east to resolve one doctrinal dispute after another were certainly not called or presided over by popes, though Roman delegates generally played a significant role. On the other hand, Popes Damasus (366–84), Siricius (384–99), and Innocent I (401–17) powerfully developed both the formulation of papal claims and the functioning of the papal Curia with its increasingly far-reaching supervision of Latin-speaking churches everywhere. This process was assisted by increased Christianization of western society, the removal of the imperial capital to *Constantinople, and the gradual collapse of imperial rule in the west. The claim of the bishop of Constantinople, ratified by the ecumenical council of Constantinople in 381, to enjoy 'the privileges of honour after the bishop of Rome, because it is new Rome' was indignantly resisted by old Rome, which denied that its precedence derived from imperial status and described itself instead ever more insistently as 'the apostolic see'. Popes regularly attempted to interfere in controversies within the Greek-speaking churches, but the growing cultural and political divide between east and west ensured that this was often resented or ignored, even though some people, including some emperors, welcomed Roman intervention. While the church of Rome originated inside the Greek-speaking world, it increasingly found itself on the outside, unable quite to understand what was going on, though a number of popes as late as the 8th century were Greeks or Syrians.

In the west, on the contrary, Roman authority, propagated particularly by English *missionaries like Willibrord and Boniface, was virtually unchallenged in the young churches of northern Europe. The papacy was at the same time becoming ruler of central Italy, the 'Patrimony of St Peter' as the papal states came to be called, something that would continue until the 19th century. In the conditions of early medieval Europe this was an almost inevitable development, but it fatefully embroiled the papacy within Italian local politics, while being seen as a providential necessity which every pope had a moral obligation to preserve.

At times, particularly in the 9th century, when it became the plaything of local aristocratic families, the moral collapse of the papacy was appalling but the revival of its authority and moral leadership in the 11th century, connected especially with Gregory VII (1073–85), produced a very different situation and led to the claim that Christendom formed a sort of papal monarchy in which the supreme temporal as well as spiritual authority had been entrusted by God to the pope. The 'vicar of Peter' was now 'vicar of Christ'. The Gregorian Reform produced a greatly enhanced sense of the separateness of the clergy, a stress on higher standards of education and piety, and a Roman curial bureaucracy that endeavoured to respond to appeals from every part of the church for help, not only from bishops but from ordinary Christians. The effects of this on church life in the 12th and 13th centuries were enormous. In general the 'plenitude of power' of the papacy was taken for granted as the very foundation of European Christianity in this age of crusades, *cathedrals, *universities, scholasticism, and canon *law. It was unquestioned by most theologians including *Aquinas, though disputed by rebels such as Marsilius of Padua and William of Ockham. At the same time the ever-greater stress on papal authority profoundly alienated most eastern Christians. Rome's doctrinal authority had always owed much to its conservative adherence to apostolic tradition, but now conservatism seemed to have been abandoned. The ostentatious claims to universal monarchy and, in particular, the introduction of the *filioque into the creed (declaring that the *Holy Spirit proceeds from the Son as well as from the Father: a Gallic innovation that Rome at first resisted) did much to bring about the collapse of the commu-

nion between Greek and Latin churches, which had survived, if at times uneasily, up to the impact of the Gregorian reform.

Medieval papal claims proved politically unsustainable, leading to disaster and long-term powerlessness. They reached their peak in Boniface VIII's bull *Unam sanctam* (1302) defining ('declaramus, dicimus, definimus et pronuntiamus') that 'it is altogether necessary for salvation for every human creature to be subject to the Roman Pontiff'. A few months later Boniface was struck in the face when French soldiers invaded his palace at Anagni. He died of shock, and soon afterwards Pope Clement V, a Frenchman, acknowledged French dominance by settling in France, eventually at Avignon, where the popes remained for seventy years, a 'Babylonian captivity'. Their return to Rome in 1378 was followed by thirty years of *schism in which a disillusioned church was divided between two, and then three, popes. This led to the conciliar movement, which failed largely because the church could not be ruled by councils nationalistically polarized, but papal supremacy could cope no more successfully than *conciliarism with the theological and administrative problems of the late medieval period. The *Reformation was actually triggered by the papal scheme to sell indulgences to raise funds for rebuilding St Peter's, and the subsequent division of western Christendom into two was made inevitable by papal intransigence.

From the 14th to the 19th century the papacy was weak largely because it was embedded within a political power game, struggling to protect its 'independence' in ways that in fact continually undermined that independence. In the 14th century it sanctioned the elimination of the Order of Templars at the behest of the king of France and in the 18th the disastrous abolition of the *Jesuits demanded by various European states. Effective control of most parts of the church that remained Catholic had passed into the hands of monarchies, and popes could be restricted even in their correspondence with bishops. Few indeed were the bishops whose choice depended on the pope though their formal appointment remained his.

The 19th century saw a great change. Hitherto most Catholics were happy enough to be '*Gallican', 'Febronian', or whatever. They saw no need for their churches to be administratively dependent on Rome. The French Revolution altered that, driving more and more Catholics into *ultramontanism. With the growth of antireligious liberalism in the ranks of the powerful, the church's safety appeared to lie in dependence upon Rome. The modern papacy was the result. It consisted, doctrinally, in the dogmas of *Vatican I defining the pope's supreme jurisdictional authority and *infallibility in his solemn teaching; administratively, in a steady increase of curial control of the church worldwide, including the selection of almost all bishops; psychologically, in a popular cult of the reigning pope whose extraordinary qualities were extolled in a mass of devotional literature. The railways made it possible for ceaseless crowds of the faithful to descend on Rome, delighting in the triple crown, the kissing of the pope's toe, and other customs which for both pope and people placed him in a world of almost divine otherness. These developments, dating from the reign of Pius IX (1846–78), were much assisted by the loss of the papal states, finalized in 1870, though a minute papal state comprising the Vatican itself was re-established by the Lateran Treaty with Italy in 1929. While Pius IX bitterly deplored the loss, in fact it led to a new freedom and steadily increasing international authority. It may be added that the nine popes from 1846 to the end of the 20th century have been of a quality (and, in most cases, longevity) greatly to enhance the mystique of papal authority. While the papacy was a principal cause of the division of the church, both between east and west and between Catholic and Protestant, so much so that Paul VI astonishingly admitted that 'The pope, as we all know, is undoubtedly the greatest obstacle in the path of ecumenism,' it should nevertheless be noted that throughout centuries of weakness the papacy has largely fulfilled what many would see as its basic role: to constitute a 'see of unity', ensuring that the majority of Christians, despite many deep divisions, remained within a single communion, consciously sharing a common faith. It has also been a forceful agent for international mission, especially since the establishment of the Congregation of *Propaganda Fide* in 1622.

While *Vatican II brought into question many of the assumptions of ultramontanism, it was careful not to contradict Vatican I. Even so, Paul VI thought it necessary to add the notorious *nota praevia* to *Lumen Gentium*, insisting that *collegiality in no way diminished papal primacy. All talk of 'monarchy', however, disappeared and John Paul I, the first post-Vatican II pope, declined to be crowned, a significant gesture. *John Paul II, on the contrary, reinforced papal authority in numerous ways. By the end of the 20th century it was being exercised universally more than ever before, but it was also being questioned more by Catholics than had been the case for 150 years.

Evaluation of the papacy and its claims must take one of three positions. The first is the ultramontane one, established by Vatican I and formidably reasserted by John Paul II. The papacy possesses by divine decree a unique 'Petrine ministry' that includes total and immediate doctrinal and jurisdictional authority over the church. Though the exercise of this authority has grown with history, the development is providential and fully in conformity with the role entrusted to Peter from the start.

The second position rejects this claim entirely. There is no certain evidence that Peter's authority, whatever it comprised, was passed on to the bishops of Rome and some doubt as to whether there were any 'bishops of Rome' for fifty years after his death. Papal authority derives from the accidental coinciding of the empire's capital with the fact that Peter and Paul died there. The papacy's subsequent history—its politicization, the appalling behaviour of some popes, extravagant claims, suppression of opposition, false teaching, sheer worldliness—suggests that, far from having a divinely appointed mission, the papacy has been the bane of ecclesiastical life, described by some even as Anti-Christ.

The third view rejects both the others as unbalanced. It receives increasing support alike from Roman Catholics (who would almost never have expressed other than the first view between Vatican I and Vatican II) and other Christians who, through both the ecumenical movement and a more irenic reading of history, have come to see the need for an organ of *unity beyond any local church and who recognize the extraordinary ability of the papacy to continue functioning across every crisis. In this view the special role of Peter in the NT church is recognized and seen as requiring continuation. While it may not have been necessary for that continuation to be based in Rome, it appears providential enough and in conformity with much early church history. A see of unity, including a final

court of appeal, is needed to hold a far-spread 'communion' together. That did not, however, require the later politicization of the papacy, the claim to absolute power apart from the wider college of the *episcopate, or any specific papal infallibility. Damaging as the papacy has been at times to the health of Christianity, it remains a necessary organ of the church which will, however, function beneficially only within a context of conciliar collegiality and with a strong application of the principle of *subsidiarity. If the most pressing internal church need remains papal reform, Christianity without the papacy is unimaginable. To quote the conclusion of a sympathetic Anglican scholar, T. G. Jalland, 'It is a strange form of historical blindness which is unable to perceive in its long and remarkable history a supernatural grandeur which no mere secular institution has ever attained in equal measure.... The Papacy must always defy a categorization which is purely of this world.'

Adrian Hastings

Chadwick, O., *A History of the Popes, 1830–1914* (1998).
Duffy, E., *Saints and Sinners: A History of the Popes* (1997).
Giles, E. (ed.), *Documents Illustrating Papal Authority AD 96–454* (1952).
Jalland, T. G., *The Church and the Papacy* (1944).
Kelly, J. N. D., *The Oxford Dictionary of Popes* (1986).
Küng, H., *Infallible?* (1971).
Markus, R., and John, E., *Papacy and Hierarchy* (1969).
Morris, C., *The Papal Monarchy: The Western Church from 1050 to 1250* (1989).
Schatz, K., *Papal Primacy from its Origins to the Present* (1996).
Tillard, J.-M. R., *The Bishop of Rome* (1983).

parable. The origin of the word 'parable' is Greek *parabole*, meaning literally a 'thing cast alongside'. It was used in antiquity to designate certain forms of speech involving resemblance and comparison. Its use was varied and vague. According to *Aristotle *parabole* was not a distinctive literary genre but an invented illustrative parallel.

In the Greek version of the Hebrew bible (the Septuagint), *parabole* translates *mashal*. *Mashal* has a wide range of meaning, covering aphorism, proverb, riddle, fable, and short but complex narrative structures. The common denominator is an element of comparison, of hidden or double meaning.

Early rabbinic literature exhibits much the same variety in its use of the term, and in addition a new application where *mashal* has become a generic designation for an extended comparison. These *meshalim* follow a certain pattern: (1) the point that requires a parable; (2) an introductory formula, 'A parable. Unto what is the matter like? It is like ...', or just the abbreviated form, 'It is like ...'; (3) the parable proper, a fictitious narrative; (4) an explicit application; (5) a concluding citation from scripture which may refer back to the first point, and is the proof-text or the exegetical occasion of the *mashal*. The *meshalim* of the rabbis are preserved not in narrative contexts but in exegetical ones, as part of midrash, the study and interpretation of scripture. They also represent a rather limited set of stereotyped plots, characterizations, and phraseology, perhaps drawing upon a thesaurus of traditional elements. This does not prevent them from showing liveliness and a strong sense of *humour.

The Synoptic *Gospels all claim that speaking in parables was a prominent feature of *Jesus' teaching. The rabbinic *meshalim* represent the only close analogy, though dating from a later period.

The time gap and significant differences such as the narrative context of Jesus' parables should not be underestimated; nevertheless some of them are presented with introductory formulas very similar to those of the rabbinic *meshalim*. In one sense Jesus is a precursor of the later rabbinic tradition. He may indeed have drawn on a style of teaching employed in the Jewish wisdom tradition, and his parables probably draw on well-known characters and plots. Thus the proverbs he quotes, the images he uses, the literary inventory of his stories belong to his time and place in early 1st-century Palestine. However, it is equally clear that he was a master of the art and made extensive and attractive use of it.

The parables were told, not written, and designed for immediate communication. Some have even suggested that in their present form they may be plot summaries, elaborated in various ways in the course of repeated use. Rules common to oral folk narrative apply also to Jesus' parables. They have straightforward plots proceeding through successive scenes with no more than two speakers at a time. The number of characters is usually limited. The parables follow either a threefold pattern with the most important element placed last, or a twofold pattern marked by contrast. The characters are portrayed by no more than one major trait, and, indirectly, by relationships. Emotional features are rare and motivations strikingly absent, except for what is revealed in speech, either monologue or dialogue. Finally, their incompleteness and lack of final resolution invite the hearers to judge for themselves what should happen next. This deliberately concise, economical style of storytelling remains a challenge to interpreters, who tend to fill in and explain what the story leaves open.

Jesus' parables may use stock situations and figures, but they are also close to human life and reflect the realities of a Galilean village. Most have no obvious religious content. Yet they claim to speak about God, and have been called earthly stories with heavenly meaning. They do in fact contain two levels of meaning, and simultaneously reveal and conceal. This tension is obvious already in *Mark's gospel (4: 10–12), which claims that Jesus spoke in parables to conceal his message from those outside. Mark associates parables with the mystery of the *Kingdom and the enigma of Jesus himself. Hence the parables came to be regarded as holding secrets that could be unlocked only by those who possessed the right key. Most Christian interpreters treated Jesus' parables as *allegories needing to be decoded. For example, the Good Samaritan was decoded in this way from the time of Irenaeus (2nd century), through *Origen, *Augustine, and down to the 19th century: the victim is fallen humanity, the thieves the devil, the wounds sin, the priest and Levite the law which cannot save; the Samaritan is Christ, whose fleshly humanity (his beast) carries the sinner to the church (the inn) and who promises to return. Details like wine, oil, two pennies are decoded variously. Though *Luther poured scorn on the allegorical method, he repeated this interpretation, as does Archbishop Trench's *Notes on the Parables* (1841). The only consistent critic until modern times was *Calvin, who read the parable simply as a call to render aid to all in distress.

By the end of the 18th century this long-standing tradition of allegorical interpretation had been broken as scholars, headed by the German Adolf Jülicher, argued that Jesus had not intended his parables to be a means of veiling his meaning. Jülicher introduced a decisive distinction between *metaphor and simile. In a metaphor, one word is substituted for another and of the two things being compared only one is named, the other being known from elsewhere. In a simile, the two things being compared are both named and placed side by side. The simile requires no explanation; the metaphor involves a substitution and must be deciphered—for the uninitiated it remains a riddle. Allegory is made up of metaphors and has as many points of comparison as it has metaphors, but a parable is an extended simile focused on a single point of comparison. So, Jesus' parables were self-explanatory, designed for immediate comprehension, and an excellent aid for popular instruction.

With allegory out of the way, the parables were classified in two major categories: similitudes (aphoristic parables) and parables proper (extended narratives). The similitude uses the present tense to describe a typical or regular event of ordinary life: it is usually briefer than the parable proper, which uses the past tense to describe a particular, invented case. Four parables (the Good Samaritan, the Rich Fool, the Rich Man and Lazarus, the Pharisee and the Tax Collector) fall into a special category called example stories since, despite their likeness to the parables proper, they do not present a comparison, but an example to be imitated or avoided.

These categories have remained a frame of reference for discussion despite some critical revisions. Mixed forms, such as illustrative parables, have been introduced allowing for the one point of comparison to become more complex. Some critics have maintained that all such classification spoils the inclusiveness of the Hebrew *mashal*. The rejection of the parables as allegories has, however, been broadly accepted, even if a few do have allegorical features. These are often an expansion of the so-called stock metaphors: a king signifies God, a vineyard the people of God, a banquet future bliss. In two instances (the Sower and the Net) an interpretation is appended in which the parable is explained feature by feature in allegorical style. Though hardly original, these interpretations show that a tendency to allegorize was at work very early, and that a non-allegorical text may easily be subject to allegorical interpretation. While *Matthew tends to allegorize, *Luke has so strong an interest in ethical instruction that some parables have become example stories.

Recent interpreters of the parables, inspired by the French philosopher Paul *Ricœur, have lifted the ban on metaphor. In their view, however, a metaphor is not a rhetorical ornament or an indirect, coded manner of speech in the service of allegory. It is based not on likeness but on difference. It is not the replacement of one word by another because of an analogy between them, but a linguistic operation at sentence-level. It makes a combination of semantic elements, which, taking the literal sense of each of them, would give no coherent meaning and, to our normal mind and experience, could not be combined.

Thus metaphor shatters the descriptive function of *language and the established system of reference with which we operate. It challenges our accustomed semantic boundaries; it creates rather than reflects meaning. On this interpretation, metaphor violates the conventions of language, but eventually the disorientation leads to reorientation. Metaphors may not succeed, but if they do they instigate and invent similarity. Hence they are not *rhetorical or pedagogical in the sense of being dispensable and superfluous. The semantic collision that they provoke evokes the capacity of language for innovation.

Jesus' parables take on the quality of metaphor by their intertwining of narrative structure and metaphorical process. What is realistic and what is unusual, indeed unimaginable, are woven together as the plot moves through a sequence of scenes. It has long been recognized that the parables have many hyperbolic features and it is often these extravagances that give the metaphorical signals.

As metaphors, the parables work by a tension between the narrated incident and the ordinary well-known world—what we tend to call reality. This is not to deny that Jesus' parables describe daily life and draw on a store of conventional components. But in the course of the story, the familiar world of everyday life and well-known stories is abandoned as the story develops in extraordinary and surprising ways.

Such an interpretation works best for the parables proper, the 'once upon a time' stories that narrate a unique event. The parable proper implies a discrepancy between two stories: the story as already known to the hearers, that is as their experience predicts it, and the unpredictable story being told here. The discrepancy is implicit and has caused endless discussions among interpreters about the realism or the agricultural, cultural, or social accuracy of particular parables. But it is not in most cases a seam or rift in the text caused by different layers of tradition, nor a literary defect, nor a result of our ignorance about life in rural Galilee in the 1st century. It is rather a hermeneutical device whereby we gain access to the meaning of the story. By the power of their literary qualities, the parables convey a truth that is not a mirror of common human experience. By the authority of the storyteller, the parables as metaphors make the boundaries of reality expand, insisting that their narrated world represents the *truth about life as divinely revealed.

Whether a parable has such an effect or not is dependent on the audience who are invited to continue or complete the story. The tension between the ordinary and the extraordinary does not make the inner logic of the story collapse, but it may become unstable. This urges the audience to accept or refuse the extraordinary adventure of this particular story, to respond to it. It becomes a 'language event'.

Metaphors are multivalent. To some extent they hold a potential of meaning inviting retelling. But they may die if they lose their innovative power; they may petrify and end up as literary clichés. This has happened to many of Jesus' parables as they have become fixed allegories or moral tales, or stories that we quite simply know all too well. Yet they never cease to intrigue and challenge us anew.

Turid Karlsen Seim

Boucher, M., 'The Mysterious Parable: A Literary Study', *Catholic Biblical Quarterly*, Monograph Series, 6 (1977).
Crossan, J. D., *In Parables: The Challenge of the Historical Jesus* (1973).
Dodd, C. H., *The Parables of the Kingdom*, rev. edn. (1961).
Jeremias, J., *The Parables of Jesus* (1972).
Linnemann, E., *Parables of Jesus: Introduction and Exposition* (1966).
Ricœur, P., *The Rule of Metaphor: Multi-Disciplinary Studies of the Creation of Meaning in Language* (1978).
Scott, B. B., *Hear Then the Parable: A Commentary on the Parables of Jesus* (1989).
Stern, D., *Parables in Midrash: Narrative and Exegesis in Rabbinic Literature* (1994).

paradise derives from an Old Persian word for a royal park or enclosure which was borrowed by both Hebrew and Greek and through them has entered modern languages. In the Hebrew bible, the word is used sparingly to refer only to the king's park or orchard. It is in the Septuagint that it becomes applied more widely and is associated with the garden of the Lord, both as the setting for the story of *Adam and *Eve and in the vision of restoration in Isaiah 51: 3 and Ezekiel 36: 35.

*Genesis 2 and 3 describes the harmony between human beings, the natural world, and God which characterize Eden, the paradisal garden. Its most precious contents, however, are the trees of life and of the knowledge of good and *evil. Such a primal garden with trees of healing and life appears in many other mythical cycles going back to Sumerian poetry of at least 3000 BC.

Once Adam and Eve forfeit paradise, their return is barred by cherubim and a fiery sword. This reinforces the tradition, not found in Genesis, that the garden is walled, which may also derive from the walled garden of Song of Songs (4: 12). The conception of human life as an *exile with the promise of a restoration pervades subsequent Jewish and Christian thought.

The implication, however, is that despite Adam and Eve's expulsion the garden still exists somewhere, although now hidden. Genesis places Eden between four rivers including the Tigris and Euphrates and non-canonical Jewish writings build on this clue to speculate on its whereabouts. Some sources place it in the extreme east, others in the north, and others, perhaps under Greek influence, seek it in the west. Wherever it was, it was inaccessible and often supposed to be on top of a high mountain, an echo of the OT references to God's holy mountain. Other traditions transferred it to *heaven and saw it as having existed from before the *creation. It was often regarded as the home of righteous souls until the judgement, for instance in *1 Enoch* 61: 12 (see LIMBO). In other sources it became synonymous with heaven itself.

In the NT, the word 'paradise' is used sparingly, though the concept is more prevalent. Rev. 2: 7 contains the clearest NT allusion to the tradition of the restoration of the blessed to paradise: 'To him who conquers I will grant to eat of the tree of life which is in the paradise of God.' These trees (now plural) grow by the river in Revelation 22: 2.

Paul (2 Cor. 12: 3) recounts an experience of being 'caught up into paradise', perhaps, but perhaps not, equivalent to the 'third heaven' of the previous verse, an allusion which tends to deepen the obscurity of this puzzling passage. It does seem to imply a belief in a paradise that exists in parallel to the *fallen earth and Paul can be read as indicating that he had met Christ there. The reticence of this passage contrasts with the elaborate heavenly travelogues of the *apocryphal *apocalypses. Indeed, it may be because of these that the NT writers have consciously exercised caution in such matters.

Jesus' only reference to paradise is his promise to the repentant thief on the cross, 'Truly, I say to you, today you will be with me in paradise' (Luke 23: 43). This is also puzzling. It sits uneasily with prevalent traditions that the dead rest in the earth until the last judgement and with the later tradition of Jesus' descent into hell between his death and *Resurrection. Later writers tend either to assume that the thief is an exception, or to argue that in God's, and Jesus', sight, a day is not simply twenty-four hours.

This combination of reticence with the rich heritage of interpretation inevitably gives rise to *allegorical readings of the paradise narratives of Gen. 2 and 3. So Symeon the New Theologian can speak of the church as a 'new paradise' (*On the Mystical Life*, 107) where the *typology of the primeval garden is reversed: Christ is born of Mary, whereas Eve arose from Adam, and while the tree of life and the tree of knowledge whose fruit brought death are separate in Eden, knowledge and life are brought together on the cross on which life is purchased through death. Ephrem, the great poet-theologian of the *Syrian tradition, uses the imagery of paradise as the spur to a profound meditation on God's promises to the righteous of union with him in a renewed paradise.

The spell of paradise also engenders two of the greatest poetic masterpieces of western culture, *Dante's *Paradiso* and *Milton's *Paradise Lost*. Both bear witness to a long tradition of assimilation between the biblical paradise and its cognates in the classical tradition: the Golden Age, the Elysian Fields, and the Isles of the Blest. Much in the modern popular conception of the afterlife is coloured by these pastoral visions, epitomized in the Victorian painter John Martin's titanic views of a more-than-alpine heavenly landscape. The image of the garden, reconceived as romantic wilderness, sits in tension with the image of the heavenly *city in Christian aspiration.

But the quest for the earthly paradise has never quite died. The discovery of the Americas was often written of in these terms and part of the vision which impelled many to journey westward was the hope of establishing a new paradise. At a more domestic level, the recreation of paradise underlay the development of the great parks and landscape gardening of 18th-century Europe. The rise of biblical literalism at the same time as colonial expansion and the great explorers encouraged the search for Eden, and to this day valleys in Northern Iraq are put forward as competing candidates.

Even for those Christians who would not read the geography of Genesis literally, paradise has lately gained new significance as a reminder of the natural order which has been threatened by human despoliation of the earth. It also holds out a vision of a world restored to *ecological balance and transcending social, sexual, and racial difference. The yearning for paradise, whether conceived of as the goal of mystical union with God, or in pragmatic and materialist terms, is still a powerful theme in contemporary thought.   **Hugh S. Pyper**

Daemmrich, I. G., *The Paradise Myth in Literature* (1997).
Delumeau, J., *History of Paradise: The Garden of Eden in Myth and Tradition*, ET (1995).
McDannell, C., and Lang, B., *Heaven: A History* (1988).
St Ephrem the Syrian, *Hymns on Paradise*, ET (1990).

paradox. Any theistic belief, not just Christianity, generates paradoxes. For instance, could an *omnipotent God create another omnipotent being? If God is *omniscient, and so knows the outcome of every human decision before it is taken, how can human beings be free (see FOREKNOWLEDGE AND FREEDOM)? If God is both entirely benevolent and all powerful, how is it that *evil exists? What makes these questions vexing rather than trivial is that seemingly sound arguments based on reasonable or necessary assumptions lead to a contradiction.

Christianity, however, goes beyond these more general *philosophical conundrums. A monotheistic faith that proclaims that the one God became human, was crucified, and then rose again might be suspected of revelling in paradox. The NT itself is frank about

the bafflement and consequent rage of many of those who encountered Jesus and his followers. 'Scandal' is a word used of the reaction to Jesus' actions and teachings. In John 6, not only the crowd but the disciples are scandalized by his promise of life to those who eat his body and drink his blood. The pragmatic Nicodemus in John 3: 4 is bewildered by Jesus' call that grown men should be born again. Many of Jesus' most pithy sayings take the form of paradoxes: 'He who finds his life will lose it, and he who loses his life for my sake will find it again' (Matt. 10: 39); 'Before Abraham was, I am' (John 8: 58). *Paul has frequent recourse to paradox especially when he is discussing the humiliation and glory of the cross, 'an offence to the Jews and folly to the Gentiles' (1 Cor. 1: 23).

Later theology continues this tendency. A few random examples make the point: the description of Adam's *Fall as *felix culpa* (the happy fault), *Mary's status as *virgin and *mother, the *eucharistic bread which is also the body of Christ, *Luther's vision of humanity as *simul justus et peccator* (at the same time justified and a sinner). The *mystical tradition in particular is replete with paradoxes in their most compressed form, the oxymoron. *Dionysius the Pseudo-Areopagite, whom most later writers draw upon, begins his *Mystical Theology* with a hymn where he speaks of the mysteries of the Word as lying in 'the brilliant darkness of a hidden silence'. His *via negativa*, also known as apophatic or negative theology, asserts that God so far exceeds human categories that he can only be spoken of as what he is not and yet is also beyond any assertion or denial. The use of paradox and oxymoron serves to express the inexpressibility of God.

It can also, of course, be an attempt to mask slack thought or arrant nonsense and can be used by champions of anti-intellectualism as a weapon in the battle to humble the intellect. It is a short but illegitimate step in Christian thought from saying that God is incomprehensible to saying that any effort at comprehension is ungodly, yet it is one that has been taken at many points in Christian history, to the justified scorn of rationalist and humanist thinkers. Christianity has had its share of obscurantists of all sorts who make a virtue of ignorance.

There are two main ways in which Christians have defended themselves against such charges of irrationalism or anti-rationalism. One is to argue that Christianity is in fact rational, which can be done either by redefining Christianity in terms of some rational essence, or by subtly redefining human reason itself as a quality that is dependent on belief in the Christian God. The other, however, makes a virtue of paradox and insists that Christian belief is not accessible to rational proof.

*Pascal is a key figure in this line of thought which is now often labelled *fideism. His often paradoxical *Pensées* reflect his conviction that human reason is beggared before the encounter with God. Partly this arose from an overwhelming experience of God's love, but it is equally a conclusion from his exceptionally rigorous and clear-minded analysis of the philosophical principles of mathematics. It would be quite wrong to view his as an anti-rational stance. It is one thing, as the biblical book of Ecclesiastes shows us, for the fool to abuse, or indeed over-praise, the discipline of *reason, quite another when reason is applied undauntedly to its own limitations.

A more extreme form of fideism follows the 2nd-century writer Tertullian in actively glorying in paradox. *Credo quia absurdam* (I believe because it is absurd) is the expression most often associated with him, but one which he never actually used. He did declare in his *De carne Christi*: 'The son of God died; it must be believed because it is absurd. He was buried and rose again; it is certain because it is impossible.' Not only does he here state the central paradoxes of the faith at their baldest but implies that they are true *because* they are paradoxes (see PRE-CONSTANTINIAN THOUGHT).

Now, this is not the same as arguing that all paradoxes are true, once one acknowledges that there are degrees of absurdity. Some patent contradictions are empty quibbles over words, others are products of deficient understanding of a situation. Some, however, are irreducible and inescapable because the encounter with God pushes reason and the capacities of *language beyond human possibility. The *truth of Christianity is not a matter of rational deduction but of divine *revelation, so those who take this line would maintain. *Kierkegaard is perhaps the most trenchant of the later theologians who insist that the notion of *Incarnation, God become man, is in human terms not just a paradox but the Absolute Paradox, in that it asserts the bridging of two realms that are absolutely other. The realms of *eternity and *time are utterly different, much more so than any seeming mismatch intrinsic to the created universe. Nothing else but the 'impossible possibility' of bringing these two together, however, will effect the radical transformation of salvation in a fallen world.

It is arguable that the importance of paradox in this sense is enshrined in those central declarations of Christian thought, the Nicene *Creed and the *Chalcedonian Definition. These were formulated and adopted in response to fierce quarrels over how the twin paradoxes of a God who is both one and three and a saviour who is both God and man could be understood. The striking thing is that in essence they offer no answer, but instead are carefully worded to present the paradoxes in their starkest form. Jesus is fully human and fully divine. Neither nature can be compromised. Every position deemed heretical seeks to soften the paradox by accommodating the human to the divine or vice versa.

If the biblical tradition and the dynamic of Christian thought can be summed up in one word, that word is 'nevertheless'. It encapsulates an attitude that is not in any simple sense antirational. It implies that the evidence can be, and should be, carefully gathered and subjected to the most rigorous inspection. *Justice, *truth, and integrity demand no less. Yet there is a step beyond: the realm of paradox, of *mercy, *grace, *forgiveness, and *love, in the face of which the world of 'because' retires in confusion.

Christian thinkers have wrestled to understand and uphold the human 'nevertheless' to God, which is epitomized at the end of Habakkuk. Even though crops fail and the herds perish, the prophet proclaims, 'Yet I will rejoice in the Lord' (Hab. 3: 18). Such stubborn faith can seem hard to justify in the face of the pain and lovelessness of so much human experience. Indeed, to those in the extremes of grief and anger, it may seem an inexcusable refusal to see the world as it is. The gospel's answer is to invite this as the only proper response to God's unthinkable 'nevertheless' to humanity, which Paul sums up thus: 'Yet it was while we were still sinners that Christ died on our behalf, this being the proof supplied by God himself of the love he bears us' (Rom 5: 8).   **Hugh S. Pyper**

Hepburn, R. E., *Christianity and Paradox: Critical Studies in Twentieth Century Theology* (1958).

Kierkegaard, S. K., *Practice in Christianity*, ET (1991).

McGaughey, D. R., *Strangers and Pilgrims: On the Role of Aporiai in Theology* (1997).

Russell, D. S., *Poles Apart: The Gospels in Creative Tensions* (1991).

Sainsbury, R. M., *Paradoxes* (1988).

paranormal. The closing years of the 20th century saw an increasing interest in paranormal claims and powers, in both east and west, which shows little sign of abating. While sometimes directly equated with the *New Age, the paranormal is often approached as a distinctive subject although its eclecticism and appeal to supernatural and spiritual agencies locates it partly within New Age territory.

The difficulty in defining the limits of the paranormal reveals much about the subject, which might appear as a smorgasbord of claims with little in common. These include the existence of 'realities' such as extra-sensory perception, psychokinesis (moving objects at a distance without touching them), unidentified flying objects (spacecraft and/or sentient creatures from another planet or dimension), near-death experiences (usually claimed as proving the *immortality of the *soul), reincarnation, clairvoyance, poltergeist manifestations, apparitions, precognition (the ability to gain supernatural knowledge of the future), out-of-body experiences, miraculous healings, spoon-bending by the power of the mind alone, dowsing, fire-walking, *astrology, spontaneous human combustion, kirlian photography (obtaining photographs of 'auras' around plants and humans), the Bermuda Triangle, and the existence of technologically advanced ancient civilizations. This is a typically diverse and far from comprehensive list of claims.

Upon closer inspection, however, a single unifying theme *does* seem to define the limits of the paranormal. Many of its proponents and characteristic features seem to aim at proving that the *scientific 'paradigm' is too narrow to contain, reveal, and explore the whole of reality. Such a unifying (and intriguingly *postmodern) theme has elicited a number of responses, one of the most interesting coming from within scientific humanism. Indeed, some scientists and humanists have sought to shore up scientific 'orthodoxy' against what they perceive as the threat of a return to the dark ages of ignorance, irrationality, and superstition. Such has been the position of the USA-based Committee for the Scientific Investigation of Claims of the Paranormal (CSICOP) an organization that produces the influential (sometimes controversial) *Skeptical Inquirer* magazine. CSICOP has consistently challenged all claims for allegedly paranormal phenomena and argued that the west's—in particular North America's—ready acceptance of irrational and empirically unsupported assertions shows a failure of science education in schools and a need for 'true' science to maintain vigilance against 'pseudo-science'. Overwhelmingly, CSICOP's has been a critical, ultimately condemnatory, approach to the whole area and to paranormal phenomena in particular. It is notable, however, that CSICOP itself has occasionally been accused of violating the spirit and practice of scientific objectivity that it claims to promote.

One outcome of CSICOP's hostile stance has been a polarization of attitudes between believers and sceptics, with unfortunate results. Those who have sought to bypass this polarization prefer to ask questions regarding the *psychological, sociological, existential, and cultural significance of the current popularity of the paranormal. Instead of attempting to understand what it might be telling us about worlds other than this, certain philosophers, theologians, psychologists, *folklorists and cultural historians have sought to understand what it might be saying about *us*. Although this is still a new approach, attempts have been made to show that the paranormal's current popularity and resurgence is evidence of repressed, revitalized, or distorted religiosity, and/or the resurgence of stories and *symbols from the collective unconscious. Such an approach offers much—in particular, to take us beyond the often strident debate between believers and sceptics.

*Theology has been slow in responding to the paranormal. There have, however, been a small number of 'bands of response'. Occasionally, scholarly attention has turned to the parallels between certain types of paranormal claim and their analogues within religious history, for example in Carol Zaleski's comparison of contemporary western near-death experiences with medieval *vision literature in *Otherworld Journeys*. A few texts have attempted a wider overview of a range of paranormal phenomena for a theological audience. On a more popular level, a number of predominantly conservative Christian writers have argued for a view of all paranormal and New Age related claims as evidence of a satanic conspiracy and related 'cosmic seduction'.

Theology and religious studies are in an unusual position as regards the paranormal. There is considerable overlap between many religious claims and those of parapsychology. Indeed, sometimes it is difficult to decide where to locate a particular phenomenon. Does the exploration of the significance of miraculous healing, for example, belong to theology or parapsychology? Is a near-death experience properly defined as religious or paranormal? And what are the implications of the decisions we make over such issues for the ways in which we approach such claims? Indeed, the recognition that the boundaries become blurred at points lies partly behind the activities of, for example, the *Religious Experience Research Centre at Westminster College, Oxford, which has long attempted the systematic investigation of experiences overlapping both disciplines. There is doubt about the existence of reliable or replicable empirical and laboratory evidence for any of the testable claims made by paranormal 'believers'. After over a hundred years of research in Britain alone (including laboratory experiments), this would appear to be of decisive importance in any discussion of the subject. And while it would tend to confirm the validity of the sceptics' position, exponents of the reality and current scientific inexplicability of paranormal phenomena continue to suggest that non-laboratory 'spontaneous' evidence is more impressive. Indeed, many paranormal claims—such as those made on behalf of UFOs and near-death experiences—continue to be solely testimony-driven. The considerable weight of experience and insight afforded by theology to the exploration of testimony, tradition, and religious experience may help towards a greater understanding of the value and significance of the range of claimed paranormal phenomena in the future.
                                                                                                                      Mark Fox

Basil, Robert (ed.), *Not Necessarily the New Age* (1988).

Frazier, Kendrick (ed.), *Science Confronts the Paranormal* (1986).

Hay, David, *Religious Experience Today: Studying the Facts* (1990).

Heaney, John J., *The Sacred and the Psychic: Parapsychology and Christian Theology* (1984).

Zaleski, Carol, *Otherworld Journeys: Accounts of Near Death Experience in Medieval and Modern Times* (1988).

Zollschan, George, Schumaker, John, and Walsh, Greg (eds.), *Exploring the Paranormal: Perspectives on Belief and Experience* (1989).

parousia, see ESCHATOLOGY.

Pascal, Blaise (1623–62), *French mathematician, scientist, religious polemicist, and apologist. Pascal was born in Clermont-Ferrand, the son of Étienne Pascal, a high-ranking officer in the fiscal bureaucracy of the area. His mother died when he was 3, and his father undertook the education of Blaise and his two sisters, Gilberte and Jacqueline, especially after 1631 when the family moved to Paris. Pascal showed precocious scientific skills, which continued in Rouen where his father was appointed tax commissioner for Normandy in 1639. In 1646, two *Jansenist brothers treated Étienne Pascal for a broken hip, which resulted in the whole family converting to Jansenism. This episode is sometimes known as Pascal's 'first *conversion'. In 1647, Pascal secured the condemnation of a former Capuchin, Jacques Forton (Frère Saint-Ange), who had maintained that *reason played an important role in the mysteries of faith. Leaving Rouen in 1648, the family eventually settled in Paris, where Pascal was an active participant in scientific circles. Amongst Pascal's achievements as a scientist in Rouen and Paris are his treatises on conical sections, vacuums, and the arithmetical triangle, as well as the invention of a calculating machine. In 1651, after the death of Étienne Pascal, Jacqueline entered the convent at Port-Royal, against her brother's wishes. On 23 November 1654, Pascal underwent a definitive conversion, known as his 'second conversion', the experience of which he recorded in a document known as the 'Memorial' which he kept sewn into his clothing for the remainder of his life. After this time, Pascal was a frequent visitor to Port-Royal. From 1658 until his death, he was plagued by ill health. Two works in particular distinguish Pascal as a Christian thinker, the *Lettres provinciales* (*Provincial Letters*) and the *Pensées*.

The *Provincial Letters* appeared initially as a series of pamphlets between January 1656 and June 1657, and were published together as eighteen letters in 1657, under the pseudonym of Louis de Montalte. Pascal's decision to write anonymously resulted from the acrimonious dispute between two leading Catholic parties, the *Jesuits (who had the support of the King, Louis XIV) and the Jansenists, named after the Flemish theologian and bishop of Ypres, Cornelius Jansenius, who were based at Port-Royal convent in Paris, and whom Pascal was trying to defend.

The posthumous publication of Jansenius's *Augustinus* (1640), which constituted an attempt to vindicate the teaching of *Augustine against the more recent Jesuit theologians, provoked a debate between a leading theologian at Port-Royal, Antoine Arnauld, and the Sorbonne. Arnauld was about to be censured for taking a stand on five so-called heretical propositions which were allegedly to be found in the *Augustinus*. Because of the risk of imprisonment which Port-Royal sympathizers ran if they were discovered to be attacking the Jesuits, Pascal, who at that time was known only for his mathematical and scientific talents, was chosen to defend Arnauld. The resulting letters, written with the freshness and immediacy of someone not trained in theological intricacies, both appealed to and were understandable by a wider secular audience. Through the use of an interview technique and the selective quotation of Jesuit writers, Pascal manages to make the Jesuits condemn themselves out of their own mouths, which is exacerbated by the comic juxtaposition of an excitable and buffoon-like Jesuit central figure and a quietly reasonable Jansenist. Perhaps the greatest *tour de force* of the early letters is Pascal's ability to maintain the general reader's interest in a complex debate that is focused largely on the Jesuits' use of terms such as 'proximate power' and 'sufficient *grace'. Pascal strongly opposed the Jesuit position that all human beings have *sufficient* grace in them to be saved. The Jansenists believed, on the contrary, that efficacious grace is reserved only for a select few and that this grace cannot be misused. Pascal had elaborated these ideas in his *Écrits sur la grâce* (*Writings on Grace*, written *c*.1657–8), in which he contrasts the Calvinist, Jesuit, and Jansenist views on grace.

The *Pensées*, left unfinished at Pascal's death and first published in 1670, is the work which marks Pascal above all as a Christian *apologist. As the incomplete text comprised various classified and unclassified bundles, the uncertain ordering of the fragments has resulted in numerous editions of the *Pensées*, each with different numbering. There are strong indications that Pascal was intending to give the work a very different structure from that of preceding writers' works, as he reiterates that, whereas his subject-matter has often been treated by others, 'the ordering is new'. Written in order to try and persuade the sceptics and non-believers of Pascal's time of the necessity for religious belief, this collection of fragments and longer passages is still widely read by Christians and non-Christians alike. Many of the fragments, while appearing to be reflections on the human condition without direct reference to Christian thought, are none the less imbued with an Augustinian pessimism that points always to mankind's post-lapsarian corrupt state (see FALL).

One of the most famous passages, known as the Wager, is perceived by many to foreshadow 20th-century *existentialist writers in the discussion of free will and commitment. Although the Wager has often been interpreted erroneously as a mathematical attempt to prove the existence of God, mathematical proofs are demonstrated finally to be inadequate in the realm of religious persuasion. Instead, the reader is shown to be involuntarily involved in the game of wagering either for or against God's existence, as indifference or uncertainty is deemed by Pascal to be akin to betting against God. As the main speaker in the fragment tells his interlocutor, 'you must wager; there is no choice, you are already committed'. Although reason is seen by Pascal to be a sign of man's greatness, he nevertheless strongly opposes *Descartes's belief that human reason alone can comprehend God. According to Pascal, this view does not take into account the role of intuition (called 'the heart' by Pascal) in religious faith, as is evident in another fragment: 'the heart has its reasons that reason cannot know'.

Amongst other longer sections from the *Pensées* that deal directly with the Christian faith, in the fragment known as the Disproportion of Man Pascal makes use of recent scientific discoveries (such as the invention of the telescope and the microscope) to show the contradictions of the human condition. In a world where we find ourselves to be both tiny entities in contrast to the vastness of space and enormous when compared to minute organisms undetectable to the human eye, it is inevitable that we should be in a state of uncertainty, somewhere 'between everything and nothing', as he describes it. Another longer passage is known as the Mystery of Jesus, where Christ is imagined in the Garden of Gethsemane speaking both to his disciples and to an unnamed interlocutor.

Those passages which deal directly with non-believers show Pascal's psychological manipulation of his reader, where often a sceptical interlocutor is flattered before being attacked. Nor is Pascal afraid to use strongly emotive imagery to portray the human condition, as in the fragment where human beings in a godless world are portrayed as prisoners in chains awaiting inevitable death. The terror of the non-believer at the enormity of the universe is captured eloquently in the famous line, 'the eternal silence of these infinite spaces terrifies me'. Other pieces within the *Pensées* concern historical proofs of Christ, prophecies, and miracles.

Pascal's work encompasses many *paradoxes, which makes it impossible to place him in simple categories. Such paradoxes include the fact that, while his scientific work showed his willingness to embrace new and radical ideas, he remained a theological and political conservative. Moreover, although he subscribed to the rigorous Augustinianism of the Jansenists, he still absorbed the writings of secular writers such as Montaigne and Epictetus in his own work, as is evident in the record of his discussions with his spiritual director, *Conversation with M. de Sacy* (*c*.1655). Perhaps most tellingly, Pascal often uses such contradictions to add weight to his arguments. In the *Pensées*, for example, he redirects his initial condemnation of such matters as Imagination, Custom, Diversion, and even Self-love to show their positive use. Pascal has rightly been seen as an innovative Christian thinker whose influence transcends narrow boundaries. Both his ability to introduce complex issues to a lay audience in a readily comprehensible way and his attempt to understand the psychology of his intended readers make him memorable (in a manner that many of his contemporary religious writers were not) and approachable to a modern readership.

Nicholas Hammond

Pascal, B., *Pensées*, trans. A. J. Krailsheimer (1966).
—— *Provincial Letters*, trans. A. J. Krailsheimer (1967).
—— *Pensées*, trans. H. Levi (1995).
Davidson, H. M., *Blaise Pascal* (1983).
Hammond, N., *Playing with Truth: Language and the Human Condition in Pascal's* Pensées (1994).
Krailsheimer, A. J., *Pascal* (1980).
Mesnard, J., *Les Pensées de Pascal*, 2nd edn. (1991).
Norman, B., *Portraits of Thought: Knowledge, Methods and Styles in Pascal* (1988).
Parish, R. J., *Pascal's* Lettres provinciales: *A Study in Polemic* (1989).
Rex, W. E., *Pascal's Provincial Letters: An Introduction* (1977).
Sellier, P., *Pascal et saint Augustin*, 2nd edn. (1995).
Wetsel, D., *Pascal and Disbelief: Catechesis and Conversion in the* Pensées (1994).

Passion, see CROSS AND CRUCIFIXION; EASTER; LENT; SUFFERING.

Pastoral Epistles. The *Pauline corpus includes three documents in letter form addressed to church leaders and concerned to varying degrees with their own spiritual lives (2 Timothy), their oversight of Christian congregations, and the life of these congregations (1 Timothy and Titus). They purport to reflect the situation of Paul as a missionary concerned for the oversight of the congregations and also as a prisoner sending a last message to a colleague. Marked differences in style and thought from the accepted letters of Paul lead most scholars to attribute them to (1) an amanuensis of

Paul; or (2) a close disciple continuing Paul's teaching for the next generation; or (3) a later writer using pseudonymity as a means of reasserting the Pauline faith *c*.100. View 3 is widely held, but there is much to be said for view 2.

The need to refute teaching manifestly different from Paul's forms the immediate occasion for the letters. It was a combination of Jewish speculations based on scripture and a misunderstanding of Pauline teaching on the resurrection of believers leading to a belief in the full realization of salvation here on earth, with a concomitant *asceticism regarding (certain) foods and sexual relationships. A general refusal to submit to *authority of any kind would not have endeared Christians to the surrounding society. Although often characterized as a form of 2nd-century *Gnosticism, there is nothing specifically Gnostic about the teaching; it more probably belongs to the 1st century.

The writer responds to this threat to the Christian gospel and mission. First, he insists on the need to hold fast to the teaching given by Paul and emphasizes the importance of *tradition. The example of Paul's own conversion and the teaching that he gave should guide the church. Second, he regards much of the opposing teaching as nonsensical and giving rise to unprofitable and time-wasting speculations and debates. The leaders' response should not be to enter into futile argument but to teach the truth. Third, he sees the opposing teaching as leading to unethical behaviour of the kind associated with non-Christians and he stresses the importance of *ethical living. His keyword 'piety' embraces a proper attitude towards both God and the world that he has created. The note of sobriety about his understanding of Christian lifestyle suggests that he regarded the teaching that he opposes as essentially frivolous. Fourth, he calls the church to re-establish prayer and teaching at the centre of its activity. Fifth, he sees that the antidote to the *heretical teaching lies in the provision of strong leadership for the congregations through the appointment of men (!) who are godly, blameless in the eyes of society, knowledgeable in the orthodox teaching, and capable of communicating it effectively.

The author relies heavily on traditional teaching but presents this in his own distinctive manner. His understanding of the gospel is thoroughly Pauline, although some Pauline characteristics are absent. In theology he goes along a new path with his concept of epiphany, and in ethics he takes up terminology from the *Hellenistic world, already assimilated by Jewish writers in Greek. He lays a heavy stress on the need for submission to authority (e.g. by *women and *slaves), but the one-sided character of his teaching in this respect may be due to the extremism of the opposition that he faced. Equally, the development of an apparently somewhat rigid form of leadership and ministry is dictated by the anarchic situation that was in danger of developing. The letters have thus to be seen against the background of a specific culture and a situation that required strong discipline. Their actual influence on Christian living and church organization has been greater than their place in the NT may merit; they must be read canonically along with other NT documents which give more place to the *freedom of the *Spirit. Nevertheless, they have a significant function in emphasizing the place of orderliness in the church and in Christian living. Despite their limited aim of equipping church leaders to deal with opposition and heresy, various positive elements—the wonderful mystery of the gospel, the assurance of salvation by grace through faith, the obligation to live the Christian life positively in the midst of a hostile society, the sense of *mission to all people (because Christ died for all) and the glorious hope of the epiphany of the Saviour—all stamp the author's composition with the warmth of a living faith.   **I. Howard Marshall**

Donelson, L. R., *Pseudepigraphy and Ethical Argument in the Pastoral Epistles* (1986).

Marshall, I. H., *The Pastoral Epistles* (1999).

Towner, P. H., *The Goal of Our Instruction* (1989).

Verner, D. C., *The Household of God* (1983).

Young, F., *The Theology of the Pastoral Epistles* (1994).

pastoral theology. The roots of pastoral theology go back to the earliest Christian writings reflecting on Christian *ministry. However, while the dominant strand within the discipline has related to the activities of the ordained pastor and 'the cure of souls', other, broader, strands have always existed. These alternative elements have been recovered and reassimilated within the last three decades of the 20th century, contributing to a significant realignment in pastoral theology. In its emergent form, pastoral theology—in church and academy—is moving towards a self-understanding as the discipline concerned with the practice of the entire Christian community in the *world, not merely practical 'hints and helps' for the clergy.

In their historical survey of pastoral care, Clebsch and Jaekle identify it as the activities of healing, guiding, sustaining, and *reconciling, such tasks being always understood as mediated by various means, in word and *sacrament. Gregory the Great's *Book of Pastoral Rule,* (*c*.590) set the tone and standard for subsequent works, in its appreciation of the personal and *spiritual qualities of the pastor and the efficacy of a discerning and pragmatic insight into human personality. Pastoral care literature was dominated by such manuals until the modern era; theological and cultural context clearly shaped successive writers' characterizations of the effective and godly pastor. While most Roman Catholic traditions emphasized the exercise of priestly discernment in administration of the sacraments, the Reformation brought greater stress on the pastor as moral exemplar and shepherd, themes developed by Protestant divines such as Jeremy Taylor, George Herbert, and Richard Baxter (see CAROLINE DIVINES).

Pastoral theology in the modern era is chiefly associated with the classification of theological education in 18th-century German universities. *Schleiermacher's distinction between 'philosophical', 'historical', and 'practical' *theology established pastoral or practical theology as a discrete discipline and demarcated it as the 'applied' field relating to the practical (and clerical) functions of the *church. This gave rise to the discipline of 'Practical Theology' (the terminology favoured in Germany and the United States), denoting all aspects of ministry, and subdivided into *preaching (homiletics), church administration (jurisprudence), pastoral/personal care (poimenics), *worship (liturgics), and Christian formation, spiritual direction, and education (catechetics). While the Roman Catholic tradition has tended to retain 'pastoral' as pertaining to the corporate mission and ministry of the church, the discipline was effectively dominated for the next two hundred years by what Edward Farley calls 'the clerical paradigm', concentrating on the practical skills and techniques of *ordained ministry.

The development of pastoral theology during the 20th century demonstrates how the discipline has absorbed wider cultural, ecclesial, and theological trends. Thus, following the popularization in Europe and the United States of the *psychological work of Sigmund Freud, William *James, John Dewey, Alfred Adler, and Carl *Jung, pastoral theology has drawn heavily upon various forms of psychological and psychotherapeutic theory. By the 1950s, Rollo May, Seward Hiltner, Carl Rogers, Anton Boisen, and Ross Snyder in the US, and Leslie Weatherhead and Frank Lake in the UK, were transforming the practice and teaching of pastoral ministry through their syntheses of theology and psychology. Later revisionists accused such writers of abandoning the perennial and classical models of pastoral care and eschewing theological themes for humanistic therapies; a closer reading suggests both greater theological diversity and considerable sophistication in attempting a critical dialogue between the insights of secular psychologies and Christian theology.

Within the last three decades of the 20th century pastoral theology has been transformed by a number of factors. The predominance of the ordained minister as sole and exclusive agent of care has been challenged by movements seeking to reclaim a greater role for the laity. Statements from *Vatican II offered models of the church as the presence of the *Kingdom of God in history, shifting attention to pastoral ministry as those activities which facilitate the corporate life and mission of the church in the world. Movements for gender, sexual, and racial *justice in the churches found established clerical models of pastoral ministry neglectful of issues of concern to *women and people of colour, among others. This critique was strengthened by the impact of theologies of liberation from the two-thirds world, exposing further cultural bias within pastoral care and opening new visions of Christian action. Pastoral theology began to question its preference for individualistic therapeutic models, turning to more proactive, public, and critical forms of intervention. *Liberation theology has not only politicized pastoral care: its most enduring influence may prove to be on the epistemological basis of the discipline. The emphasis on theology as *orthopraxis* and the understanding of the primacy of faithful transformation has effected an interest in methodological issues: the discipline no longer regards itself as 'applied' theology concerned with promoting clerical competence, but is gradually being reconstructed as a primary theological discipline relating to the self-understanding of the community of faith in the world. Within this wider undertaking pastoral theology is commissioned to enable the community of faith to practise what it preaches, exploring how action corresponds to belief, how the historical witness of faith relates to contemporary dilemmas, and examining the diversity of practices by which communities of faith embody and enact their theological values. Many contemporary writers use 'pastoral' and 'practical' theology interchangeably, signifying a discipline devoted to the *hermeneutics of Christian practice, or the exercise of theological reflection on the principles informing faithful witness.

See also FEMINIST THEOLOGY; HEALTH AND HEALING.

Elaine Graham

Browning, D. S., *A Fundamental Practical Theology: Descriptive and Strategic Proposals* (1991).

Clebsch, W. A., and Jaekle, C. R., *Pastoral Care in Historical Perspective*, rev. edn. (1994).

Couture, P. D., and Hunter, R. J. (eds.), *Pastoral Care and Social Conflict* (1995).

Duffy, R. A., *A Roman Catholic Theology of Pastoral Care* (1983).

Graham, E. L., *Transforming Practice: Pastoral Theology in an Age of Uncertainty* (1996).

Lartey, E. Y., *In Living Colour: An Intercultural Approach to Pastoral Care and Counselling* (1997).

Lyall, D., *Counselling in the Pastoral and Spiritual Context* (1995).

Pattison, S., *Pastoral Care and Liberation Theology*, 2nd edn. (1997).

patriarchates. In the 6th century, Greek-speaking Christianity came to hold the view that the church was structured on the basis of five patriarchates: *Rome, *Constantinople, *Alexandria, Antioch, and *Jerusalem. Each was seen as an area of the universal *church with its own usages, authoritatively headed by a patriarch who ordained the metropolitans within it.

On a strict view, this concept, still sometimes appealed to as providing a 'primitive' pre-papal pattern of *authority in the church, has little to recommend it, representing only one fairly brief phase in church history. In early Christian times, bishoprics, naturally linked for common decision-making, came to be headed by the bishop of a major town, corresponding to civil administration. At the start of the 4th century, Rome, Alexandria, Antioch, and Carthage most clearly filled this role. Jerusalem, which in *apostolic times could claim an absolute priority, lost it after the city's destruction by Titus. Rebuilt as a Greek town, it became a suffragan of Caesarea. Constantinople, once it became the imperial capital, quickly grew in ecclesiastical importance and the Council of Constantinople (381) accorded it a status next to that of Rome. The Council of *Chalcedon confirmed this, at the same time granting Jerusalem a comparable position. Soon afterwards these five sees came to be called 'patriarchates'. Rome accepted this pattern eventually, if reluctantly, but it did not fit the western church very well, as the Roman jurisdiction was extended here on different, in principle universalist, grounds. Carthage, the only other possible western candidate, had been irreparably weakened by the *Donatist *schism and the Vandal conquest.

A five-patriarchate model never really worked. It was unclear where the Balkans belonged while *Armenia, Persia, and Georgia developed their own comparable jurisdictions whose heads came to be named 'Catholicos'. After Chalcedon, Alexandria and Antioch were divided between rival patriarchates, pro- and anti-Chalcedonian. Constantinople, the late arrival, evolved in two directions. On the one hand, its holder claimed a sort of super-patriarchate, adopting the title of 'ecumenical patriarch'; on the other, it spawned, for long reluctantly, a number of national patriarchates in Bulgaria, Serbia, Russia, and Romania.

In the west, the title has been belittled by attachment in a purely honorific way to sees such as Venice and Lisbon. Nevertheless, even within the Roman *communion, the genuine authority of various uniate patriarchates has survived locally and internationally, as witness the influential, and characteristically eastern, voice of Maximos IV Saigh, patriarch of the Melkites, at *Vatican II.

While any attempt to ground ecclesiology on patriarchates seems unrealistic and unhistorical, they do represent the most characteristic eastern contribution to church order: the salutary conviction that diversity in *tradition and authority should balance *unity. The supreme ecclesiastical authority is seen as a choir in harmony rather than a single voice. It is correct for the Christian community to be divided, along lines of language, culture, liturgy, and theology, into groups larger than an archiepiscopal province. Patriarchates emerged in the later patristic age for geographical reasons as well as theological ones, and comparable divisions may be an appropriate way of containing divergent traditions within the modern church. It might be reasonable to think of the see of *Canterbury as heading an Anglican patriarchate, but it hardly seems sensible to claim that the Roman Catholic communion, apart from its 'Uniate' branches, can consist of a single 'western' patriarchate, including Latin America, Africa, and Asia.   **Adrian Hastings**

Carpenter, E., *Cantuar: The Archbishops in their Office*, 3rd edn., enlarged by A. Hastings (1997).

Every, G., *The Byzantine Patriarchate*, 2nd edn. (1962).

Kane, T., *The Jurisdiction of the Patriarchs of the Major Sees in Antiquity and the Middle Ages* (1949).

patristics, see PRE-CONSTANTINIAN THOUGHT; GREEK THEOLOGY 4TH TO 6TH CENTURIES; LATIN THEOLOGY, 300–1000.

Paul.

There are two sources of information about Paul: his letters and the book of Acts. For an understanding of his theology we need to rely on the letters, but since they were all addressed to particular congregations, and deal with issues that were of concern to them, it is extremely difficult to piece them together into 'a theology'; any attempt to do so must inevitably be incomplete. We have to remember, moreover, that Paul's thinking was anything but static, and that his understanding of the implications of the gospel was developing throughout his life; his experiences and deliberations combined to produce new insights into Christian *faith.

Paul's letters throw very little light on his background and life: about these we find far more information in Acts. The problem is to know how reliable this is. It is impossible, for example, to plot the 'missionary journeys' from Paul's letters, and difficult sometimes to fit the letters into such journeys, either because Paul himself gives us insufficient information, or possibly because *Luke has 'organized' Paul's visits to various cities into an intelligible itinerary. Sometimes details in Acts are confirmed by Paul (Acts 9: 25; 2 Cor. 11: 33); occasionally, as with Paul's account of his visits to *Jerusalem in Galatians 1–2, what Paul tells us appears to be in conflict with Acts. It is therefore necessary to proceed with caution in any attempt to describe his career.

Paul was born into a Jewish family proud of its ancestry, and brought up during the early years of the Christian era; he had been zealous in his own devotion to *Judaism, and scrupulous in his observance of the Law (Phil. 3: 4–6; Gal. 1: 13–14; Rom. 11: 1) (see LAW, BIBLICAL). According to Acts 22: 3, he was born in Tarsus in Cilicia, but was trained in the interpretation of the Law in Jerusalem by Gamaliel, a famous 1st-century rabbi. The reference to Tarsus has often been used to support the belief that Paul must have been a syncretistic, Hellenistic Jew. The view that diaspora Judaism and Palestinian Judaism were essentially different has now been shown to be false, however: there were Jews in both Palestine and the Diaspora who observed the Law, and others who did not, and Paul's claim to have been zealous in his observance should be believed. His exegesis of Jewish scripture supports Luke's statement that he received rabbinic training. From his letters, too, it is clear that he received a Greek education and had a knowledge of *rhetoric.

In the early chapters of Acts Paul is called 'Saul', an appropriate name for someone who claimed to be of the tribe of Benjamin (Phil. 3: 5), but he preferred to use his Roman name. According to Acts, also, he was a Roman citizen, as were many Jews living in the Diaspora (Acts 16: 37; 22: 25–9; his appeal to Caesar, 25: 11–12, almost certainly depends on this). From Acts 18: 3 we learn that Paul was a tentmaker, and we know from the letters that he continued to work at his trade throughout his ministry (1 Thess. 2: 9; 1 Cor. 9: 3–18). Acts 18: 12 provides us with our one clear date for Paul's career, since an inscription at Delphi provides the information that Gallio was proconsul of Achaia in 51–2. Possible dates for other events in his life are calculated from this incident. According to tradition, Paul was beheaded in Rome c.65.

Of the thirteen letters in the NT that are attributed to Paul, seven are generally accepted as authentic. They are *Romans, 1 and 2 Corinthians, Galatians, Philippians, 1 Thessalonians, and Philemon. The authorship of 2 Thessalonians and Colossians is more controversial. Ephesians was probably written in order to present Paul's message to the church of a slightly later day: it is steeped in Pauline vocabulary and shows close dependence on Colossians. The *Pastorals, too, appear to have been written at a later period; although they may contain Pauline fragments, their overall style, vocabulary, tone, approach, and concerns are very different from Paul's.

We do not know when or by whom Paul's letters were first gathered together, but a reference to 'all the epistles' of Paul in 2 Peter 3: 16 indicates that the process had begun when 2 Peter was written (probably during the first half of the 2nd century). Some letters were being quoted as early as 1 Clement (96), and in the 2nd century by Ignatius (d. c.107) and Polycarp (c.69–155). The first person known to have had a collection of all the Pauline letters (with the exception of the Pastorals) is Marcion (c.150). For him, the Pauline letters and Luke's gospel, and not the OT, were the authoritative scriptures of Christianity. By a strange irony, someone whom the church branded a *heretic, and who misunderstood Paul's teaching, may have been the first to give 'canonical' status to his letters.

We know from Paul himself that he had been violently opposed to the Christian faith (Gal. 1: 23; 1 Cor. 15: 9; Phil. 3: 6); to that extent it is correct to describe his experience on the Damascus road (Acts 9: 1–22; 22: 4–21; 26: 9–18) as a '*conversion'. Yet Paul's new faith was in many ways the fulfilment of his earlier beliefs, not their denial. Moreover, Paul's own references to the event view it primarily as his commission to be an *apostle (1 Cor. 9: 1–2; 15: 8–9), and specifically the apostle to the Gentiles (Gal. 1: 16; cf. 2: 7). It was this latter belief that shaped Paul's theology and led to disagreement with some of his fellow Christians. Paul insisted that Gentiles could become members of the Christian community through faith in Christ and *baptism. His opponents maintained that they must also become Jews by circumcision and acceptance of the Law.

Paul's teaching

Basic to Paul's conviction was his understanding of the *death and *Resurrection of Christ as the crucial turning-point in human history. With the Resurrection, a new age had dawned, and the long hoped-for 'end-time' of Jewish expectation had arrived: the purpose of the Law—to bring life—had therefore been achieved. It followed that there was no longer any need to live 'under' Law: indeed, those who believed that there was had, in Paul's view, misunderstood both the gospel and the Law itself. Paul therefore regarded it as a backward step when his converts in Galatia were persuaded that circumcision and obedience to the Law were necessary. Although the Law had been given by God, it belonged to the old era of 'the flesh', which is weak and transient, and so had nothing to contribute to the new era of 'the Spirit', in which the power of God, who is Spirit, is at work. This contrast between flesh and *Holy Spirit is fundamental to the argument of Gal. 3–5 and Rom. 8.

What happened in Christ is part of God's plan, set out in scripture (Rom. 3: 21). Paul's opponents accused him of destroying the Law, a charge which he indignantly denied (Rom. 3: 31). He sees Christ as the true 'end' of the Law, who fulfils its promises and makes its provisions unnecessary (Rom. 10: 4; 8: 3–4; Gal. 4: 4–5). Hence he is able both to quote scripture as a witness to Christ and to insist that Christians are set free from the Law. The Law given to Israel is interpreted as an interim measure until the promises made to Abraham (and accepted by faith) could be fulfilled (Gal. 3: 6–29; Rom. 4: 1–25). It follows that the only requirement from Gentiles is faith.

There is a sense, then, in which Christ replaces the Law. Those who belong to the people of God are now defined as those who have faith in Christ, rather than those who obey the Law. Since the Law was understood in Judaism to be the embodiment of God's purpose, it is hardly surprising if Paul sees Christ in similar terms. The Law was identified in Jewish texts with God's word, and with wisdom, and seen as the embodiment of his glory (Sir. 24: 1–23). By his word (or wisdom) he had created heaven and earth (Gen. 1; Prov. 3: 19; 8: 27–30). We find Paul speaking of Christ as the wisdom of God (1 Cor. 1: 30), and comparing his glory with the (inferior) glory of the Law (2 Cor. 3: 12–18). From this developed the 'Wisdom christology' of Col. 1: 15–20, where Christ is both the agent of creation and its goal.

Paul, then, believed Jesus to be far more than *Messiah (Christ), and the fulfilment of *Israel's hopes. Titles such as 'Son of God', 'image of God' and 'Lord' (the OT name for God) convey his close relationship to God; yet he is obedient to God (Rom. 5: 19; Phil. 2: 8), sent by him (Rom. 8: 3; Gal. 4: 4), and ultimately subject to him (1 Cor. 15: 27–8). It is significant that all these titles can also be used to express what men and women were intended to be—and what they can become through Christ (sonship, Rom. 8: 14–17; Gal. 4: 6; image, 2 Cor. 3: 18; Col. 3.10; Ps. 8: 6, quoted in 1 Cor. 15: 27, describes human lordship). The *sin of *Adam was reversed and the possibility of restoration opened up when Christ lived and died in *obedience and was raised from death to life. Those who are baptized 'into' him are able to share his death to sin (Rom. 6: 4–11) and his status of righteousness before God (2 Cor. 5: 21). Since Adam's sin brought corruption to the world, restoration involved the whole universe (Rom. 8: 19–22; Col. 1: 15–20).

Christ's significance is thus not simply as one who stands over against humanity. He shared our *humanity, and all that means in terms of weakness (Rom. 8: 3; 2 Cor. 5: 21; 8: 9; Gal. 3: 13; 4: 4; Phil. 2: 7–8), in order that we might share in his sonship and righteousness. To do this, however, Christians must share in his death and Resurrection, dying to the realm of flesh and rising to life in the Spirit.

Thus Paul speaks of being crucified with Christ in order that Christ may live in him (Gal. 2: 19–20). This process of death and resurrection is symbolized by *baptism (Rom. 6: 3–4). By baptism 'into Christ', believers are united 'with him', so that they now live 'in him'. These phrases (in particular 'in Christ') express the close relationship between Christ and believers that is so important for Paul. Those who live in Christ are members of the community of God's people, and they in turn are so closely related to one another that they can be described as the *body of Christ (1 Cor. 12: 13, 27). Together they make up 'the temple of God', where the Spirit of God dwells and which is therefore holy (1 Cor. 3: 16–17; 2 Cor. 6: 16–17).

What happens through Christ's death and Resurrection is described in a variety of images. Because of its relevance to the issue of the place of Gentiles in the community, the most common is the verb *dikaioo*, 'justify', an obscure word in modern English, whose basic meaning is 'to bring into a right relationship'. Paul insists that this basic relationship between God and his people is the result of *grace, received by faith; in this, contrary to some later interpretations of his thought, he was fully in accord with the OT.

Other images include *'reconciliation' (Rom. 5: 10–11; 2 Cor. 5: 18–20) and 'redemption' (Gal. 3: 13; 4: 5; Rom. 3: 24; 1 Cor. 1: 30; cf. 6: 20 and 7: 23), implying release from slavery. In 1 Cor. 5: 7 Paul refers to Christ as our passover *sacrifice, implying that his death achieved our redemption. Christ's death is often spoken of as 'for us' without further explanation. In Rom. 3: 25, Paul describes Christ as having been set out by his death as a *hilasterion*, a word used in the LXX of the lid of the ark of the covenant ('mercy-seat'); the meaning (*pace* many translations and interpretations) seems to be that Christ is the place where God is revealed and reconciliation achieved.

These various images refer to something that has already taken place. Final *salvation still lies in the future, however. Christians expect the Day of the Lord, when Christ will return and *judgement take place (1 Thess. 1: 10; 1 Cor. 15: 23–4; Phil. 3: 20); those who belong to Christ will be saved (Rom. 5: 9–10), but they will have to account for what they have done (1 Cor. 3: 10–15; 4: 1–5). The dead in Christ will be raised, and both they and the living will be transformed and share the spiritual body of the risen Christ (1 Thess. 4: 13–17; 5: 1–11; 1 Cor. 15: 35–57; Phil. 3: 21).

In between their reconciliation to God and final salvation, however, those who now live 'in Christ' and who share Christ's righteousness must live accordingly. They are in process of being made what they are called to be, and must live 'as those who have been brought from death to life' (Rom. 6: 13), while being transformed into the image of Christ (2 Cor. 3: 18). Since life comes through death, and glory through *suffering (Phil. 2: 6–11), Christians must expect to share the suffering and dying of Christ (Rom. 8: 17; 2 Cor. 4: 7–18; Phil. 3: 10–11). Unfortunately this aspect of his teaching was overlooked by those who emphasized the benefits of Christ's death and Resurrection and ignored the need to share his suffering (1 Cor. 4: 8–13).

Paul's insistence that Gentile converts should not put themselves 'under Law' was also open to grave misunderstanding. Some of them interpreted his teaching about freedom from Law as meaning that they were free to sin (Gal. 5: 1, 13; Rom. 6: 15). Paul's teaching on faith certainly did not mean that nothing was required of believers: for him, faith involved obedience (Rom. 1: 5), and in all his letters he discusses the implications of faith for behaviour. Paul is true to the Jewish *covenantal pattern: God has saved his people, and they agree to keep his Law. Now, however, obedience to the Law is replaced by 'the law of Christ' (Gal. 6: 2), which means 'living according to the Spirit' (Gal. 5: 16–26); those who so live find that what the Law requires has been fulfilled without their submitting to it (Rom. 8: 4; 13: 8–10; Gal. 5: 14).

The Spirit is the sign that the new age has dawned, and is given to all believers (Gal. 3: 3; Rom. 8: 9; 1 Cor. 12: 3). The Spirit is the power of God at work in the world and in believers. *Virtues are described as 'fruit' of the Spirit (Gal. 5: 22). The gifts of the Spirit are intended for the benefit of the community; hence those that build it up are the greatest. It is noticeable that those Paul singles out in 1 Cor. 13— faith, *hope, and *love—are available to all. The importance of love is stressed elsewhere (Gal. 5: 14, 22; Rom. 13: 8–10; cf. 5: 6–8). Gifts of ministry, on the other hand, though all necessary, are distributed individually (1 Cor. 12: 17–30). Paul mentions apostles, prophets, and teachers in 1 Cor. 12: 29, 'superintendents and ministers' (hardly 'bishops and deacons'!) in Phil. 1: 1. There is, however, no sign of a structured *ministry.

The origins of 'the Lord's supper' are described in 1 Cor. 11.17–34, where it is mentioned only because the Corinthians were abusing it: Paul understands it as a proclamation of the death of Christ, and a symbol of unity in his 'body'.

Paul's influence

Paul's career was marked by controversy, and his letters make frequent reference to opponents. Some of these seem to have been conservative Jewish Christians, who claimed the support of the Jerusalem church (e.g. Gal. 2: 12); Paul was seen by them as out of step, but he insists that on the basic gospel he was in agreement with the Jerusalem church (Gal. 1: 18–24; 2: 15–16; 1 Cor. 15: 1–11). In Corinth, he had to deal with others who questioned his authority as an apostle (2 Cor. 10–13). Both here and in Colossians, Paul warns against the kind of teaching that perhaps developed into the *Gnosticism of the 2nd century.

From the beginning, Paul was clearly influential in *some* areas of the church; the composition of letters in his name is one sign of this, as are Acts and the late 2nd-century *aprocryphal Acts of Paul, though his theological insights were not always understood. At the same time, the language Paul used about Christ appealed to heretical groups such as the Gnostics, who interpreted it to suit their own doctrines; this made Paul suspect to other Christians. In some circles—e.g. among Jewish Christians—he was regarded as the arch-enemy. By the end of the 2nd century, however, his letters were accepted as authoritative.

When read in new situations, Paul's teaching was inevitably interpreted in new ways. When the original debate about the admission of Gentiles was forgotten, Galatians and Romans were understood as attacks on Judaism, and Paul's own Jewish roots were ignored, a process encouraged by Marcion. This tragic misreading of the text became very influential and has contributed to *antisemitism throughout Christian history. The earliest commentators on Paul were the church fathers, who interpreted them from their own viewpoint, which often owed more to Greek culture than to Judaism. Paul's teaching was plundered in support of the

various *christological positions of different commentators, but allowed little scope to the *Alexandrians for *allegorization.

Another important shift that occurred when the controversies of Paul's own time were forgotten was that his teaching was interpreted in far more individualistic terms. With *Augustine, the greatest of the early commentators, 'justification by faith' was seen as the central issue in Paul's teaching, and was understood as the only way for an individual to be accepted by God. Among later commentators Peter *Abelard is noteworthy, since he developed his understanding of the Atonement through his study of Romans. Augustine's interpretation greatly influenced that of *Luther, whose stark opposition between faith and merit, gospel and Law, had a profound effect on Protestant interpretation of Paul for centuries.

The Enlightenment brought attempts to see Paul in historical perspective. F. C. Baur and the *Tübingen school believed that Jewish Christianity was fundamentally opposed to Paul's Law-free gospel and that only those letters that reflected this situation were genuine, while the 'early catholicism' of the 2nd century had brought a synthesis of the two positions.

The early *twentieth century was dominated by a debate between those such as W. Bousset, who saw Paul primarily as a Hellenist, influenced by the mystery religions, and as the founder of a Christianity very different from that of his predecessors, and those like Albert Schweitzer who saw Paul primarily in Jewish eschatological terms. *Bultmann attempted to *demythologize Paul and produced an existentialist version of his theology; like *Barth's commentary on Romans, this offered an interpretation of Paul for the 20th century that was far removed from Paul's original concerns.

In recent years the Jewishness of Paul has been reaffirmed. W. D. Davies pointed to his links with rabbinic teaching, and E. P. Sanders undermined the Lutheran interpretation by attacking the view that 1st-century Judaism had relied upon merit. The issue between Paul and his opponents is now understood by many commentators to be the status of Gentiles within the people of God rather than any question of 'legalism'. Recent work has explored the possible background to Paul's christology in contemporary Judaism, the social context of Paul's churches, his ethical teaching, and the rhetorical structure of his letters.

The most influential of Paul's writings has undoubtedly been the letter to the Romans, which is the closest he came to writing a 'theology'. Within Romans, chapters 1–8 were the most used, because they were interpreted in relation to the life of the individual believer, while chapters 9–11, dealing with the problem of Israel's rejection of the gospel, were for long treated as though an afterthought. The single passage which has been most debated, however, is probably Phil. 2: 6–11, which featured in many patristic christological debates, as well as the 19th-century theory of kenotic christology. Paul has had considerable influence on devotional literature; Charles *Wesley's hymns, for example, are full of Pauline allusions.

It is an irony of history that Paul's writings so quickly became 'canonical'; that the man who protested that his converts must not subject themselves to the Law had his work turned into 'law' and treated as binding on later generations. One example is the use of Romans 13 by some German Christians to justify acceptance of the

Nazi state. Another is the way in which his teaching about *women dressing in a comely way when leading church worship was regarded as authoritative for centuries, even though it was largely based on social convention at the time (1 Cor. 11: 2–16). Here, too, we see the danger of imposing particular beliefs onto the text. Paul's teaching was interpreted in terms of later prejudices, so that his instruction that a woman needed 'authority' on her head when praying or prophesying was understood as a statement that she was '*under* the authority of her husband'! (AV marg., based on Luther.) Paul's assumption that women should take a leading part in worship, together with his statement that men and women are equal in Christ (Gal. 3: 28) were conveniently ignored. Read in the context of the culture of his day (reflected in the Pastorals), he is seen to be the very reverse of a misogynist.

Paul's influence on the development of Christian faith has been greater than that of any other man, for without his conviction that the gospel was intended for Gentiles *qua* Gentiles, Christianity would have remained a Jewish sect. His intellect and training enabled him to see the implications of his new faith, in terms both of belief and behaviour. By fusing old beliefs with new experiences, he developed exciting theological insights that revolutionized the history of the early church, and which continue to challenge the church of today.   **Morna D. Hooker**

Barrett, C. K., 'Pauline Controversies in the Post-Pauline Period', *NTS* 20 (1974).
Beker, J. Christiaan, *Paul the Apostle* (1980).
Bultmann, R., *Theology of the New Testament* (1952), i.
Davies, W. D., *Paul and Rabbinic Judaism*, 2nd edn. (1955).
Dunn, J. D. G., *The Theology of Paul the Apostle* (1998).
Harris, H., *The Tübingen School* (1975).
Morgan, R., with Barton, J., *Biblical Interpretation* (1988).
Pagels, E. H., *The Gnostic Paul: Gnostic Exegesis of the Pauline Letters* (1975).
Sanders, E. P., *Paul and Palestinian Judaism* (1977).
Schweitzer, A., *The Mysticism of Paul the Apostle*, 2nd edn. (1953).
Stendahl, K., *Paul among Jews and Gentiles* (1977).
Stuhlmacher, P., *Biblische Theologie des Neuen Testaments* (1992), i.
Theissen, G., *The Social Setting of Pauline Christianity* (1982).
Westerholm, S., *Israel's Law and the Church's Faith: Paul and His Recent Interpreters* (1988).
Whiteley, D. E. H., *The Theology of St Paul* (1964).
Wiles, M. F., *The Divine Apostle: The Interpretation of St Paul's Epistles in the Early Church* (1967).
Ziesler, J. A., *Pauline Christianity*, rev. edn. (1990).

peace. What is meant by 'peace' in biblical and Christian church tradition? Many different things, at different times. The meaning of the concept may be seen to shift, repeatedly.

Shalom

The first of these shifts occurs to the Hebrew word *shalom*, in the context of post-exilic *prophecy. Thus, at one level this word functions in much the same way as other equivalent words in neighbouring cultures. It has a wide range of usages, all relating to its basic original connotation of wholeness. The enjoyment of personal health; a household's, or a nation's, enjoyment of material *prosperity; the maintenance of *justice, as a precondition for prosperity: all of these are experiences of *shalom*. To return from *war in *shalom*, on the other hand, simply means to return victorious. And *shalom* attained by war by no means precludes the violent coercion

of the defeated (see for example Deut. 20: 10–13). In *mythic terms, Yahweh's 'blessing of peace' in Psalm 29 represents his cosmic victory over the forces of chaos. Here Yahweh is acclaimed in just the same way as Baal-Hadad, the weather god, is acclaimed in a Phoenician hymn.

But in the writings of the post-exilic *prophets there emerges quite another level of meaning; an altogether more distinctive cultural phenomenon. Here, for the first time, true *shalom* is firmly assigned to a historically unprecedented future. In the context of the exiled people's affliction, it becomes the inspirational dream of a new community-bonding social movement. This shift is prepared for in the earlier prophetic denunciations of false *shalom*, especially in *Jeremiah. The new *shalom*-hope is classically encapsulated in the oracle inserted into Isaiah 2: 2–4 and Micah 4: 1–5. It involves the exaltation of Zion as the central unifying focus for all humanity, and the establishment of Yahweh as judge between the nations. Whereupon

> They shall beat their swords into plowshares,
>   and their spears into pruning hooks;
> nation shall not lift up sword against nation,
>   neither shall they learn war any more.

The whole prophecy of Deutero-Isaiah, above all, takes shape as a vision of future *shalom*, tending in the same direction.

Eirene

The *New Testament understanding of *eirene* is likewise multilayered. Partly, it means 'inner peace'. As such, it is one of the primary terms for the immediate blessing which *faith in the gospel conveys to each *convert; virtually equivalent, perhaps, in this sense to 'eternal life'. All the epistles, apart from Hebrews, James, and 1 John, open with a greeting, wishing the recipients *eirene*. This is in straightforward accordance with customary Jewish usage; but the context clearly adds special resonance to the wish. And so too the salutation becomes a standard feature of Christian liturgy: 'peace be with you'.

At the same time, *eirene* is that in the sharing of which the church community is united. *Paul repeatedly invokes the presence of 'the God of *eirene*' in situations of intra-community conflict that need resolving; one of the main immediate purposes of the epistles, in general, is to help maintain peace within the churches. And the great vision of Christ in Colossians 1: 15–20 as cosmic peacemaker appears to be essentially a metaphysical projection of that same dynamic.

Thirdly, however, the NT also recapitulates the *shalom*-hope of post-exilic prophecy in a socially more disruptive manner. *Jesus echoes Jeremiah's denunciation of false *shalom*: 'Do not think that I have come to bring peace on earth; I have not come to bring peace, but a sword' (Matt. 10: 34; Luke 12: 51). And yet this by no means prevents his disciples from appropriating for themselves the formula of Isa. 52: 7: in and through all the conflicts arising from their evangelism, they are essentially the messengers of a 'gospel of *eirene*'.

The early chapters of Luke signal that, with the birth of Christ, the promised last days have arrived; *shalom/eirene* is about to prevail. As appears most explicitly in Luke 19: 38–42, *eirene* here becomes a virtual synonym for the *Kingdom of God. And its pioneers are blessed as 'peacemakers': turning the other cheek to those who offend them, loving and praying for their enemies (Matt. 5: 9, 38–48).

Pax

Arguably, the next great enrichment of the concept, within Christendom, comes with the gradual emergence, during the 19th and 20th centuries, of an organized international *secular civil society; and is a response to the essentially new opportunities which that still ongoing development has opened up. By contrast, the first Christian centuries may be said to have been a period in which the original inspirational energy of the prophetic vision was for the most part simply dissipated.

After all, the more the *church was hierarchically institutionalized the less it needed this visionary mode of community-bonding to define its corporate identity. There remained a few minority groups who kept alive the hope for an imminent new age of peace: the *Montanists from the latter half of the 2nd century onwards; the followers of Joachim of Fiore, and the Brethren of the Free Spirit, in the later Middle Ages (see MILLENARIANISM). But mainstream thinking, by contrast, tended to push it back into a distantly receding future. And meanwhile the real emotional drive of Christian hope was increasingly focused on the immediate post-mortem prospects of the private individual—as expressed in the prayer, 'requiescant in pace' (may they rest in peace).

It is in *Augustine's Latin theology that we find the first systematic Christian discussion of pax (The City of God, 19. 11–17). For Augustine pax is, first of all, a generic term for whatever is attained by the fulfilment of morally proper desire. Hence, its primary manifestation is in the providentially determined structure of the cosmos itself, as a whole, viewed from the perspective of *eternity. But that is then subdivided into two basic contrasting modes: the pax that is the final end of the '*city of God'; and the pax of the 'earthly city'.

Augustine defines the former as 'eternal life in peace', or 'peace in eternal life'. This is the shalom of the post-exilic prophets, or the eirene of the NT; only shorn, it seems, of any immediate worldly hope—other than for the further flourishing of the Catholic church, as an established institution. He defines the pax of the 'earthly city' in terms of a diverse range of goods: wholeness of body; repose of appetite; the achievements of technical proficiency; a healthy lifestyle; observance of the dictates of natural justice; public consensus; and, above all, domestic harmony—based on the patriarchal authority of the benevolent Roman paterfamilias who cares for all the members of his household, slaves included, 'with equal affection'. The highest good—for the citizens of 'the heavenly city in her pilgrimage here on earth'—includes both modes. But, still, the main thrust of Augustine's argument is to stress their absolute separateness and incommensurability.

This has a twofold effect. In the first place, it helps underscore the other-worldly authority of the church, inasmuch as that authority derives precisely from the absolute otherness of the pax the church proclaims, from the pax promoted by other institutions. The earthliness of the pax that belongs to the 'earthly city' lies in its being a form of peace based on sinful individuals' limited perception of their own self-interest; which is therefore radically incomplete. (There is no peace for the wicked, since even the *devil has a natural impulse to righteousness within him, with which his wickedness is at war.) And yet the Augustinian doctrine also tends to allow a real autonomy, at any rate for the foreseeable future, to the 'earthly city's' realpolitik. Augustine simply denies this realpolitik any claim to sacred authority; he does not confront it—on its own level—with any rival model.

Subsequent church history has witnessed various further developments. There was a period, from the late 10th to the 13th century—especially in France, following the breakdown of the Carolingian order—when the church institution's role within the politics of the 'earthly city' was indeed largely that of peacemaker. The feuding nobility were encouraged to swear sacred oaths, that in the course of their struggles they would at any rate not harm church property, the clergy—or the unarmed poor. They also bound themselves to keep certain days and seasons free from warfare: the so-called 'truce of God'. These initiatives, designed to strengthen the internal coherence of Christendom, were often linked with the church's simultaneous promotion of the Crusades.

In other periods the church appeared rather less like a peacemaker. Marsilius of Padua, for instance, in his Defensor Pacis (1324) sees the main threat to peace as coming precisely from what he calls the *papacy's 'perverted desire for rulership'. The pax, or tranquillitas, with which Marsilius is primarily concerned is thus the organic unity of a republican city state, within which the clergy would be fully integrated. Marsilius in fact draws equally on *Aristotle and Augustine as his two leading authorities. But the critical significance of the higher mode of pax in Augustine's thinking—to which the ideologists of papalism appealed—effectively disappears here. Other-worldliness has become irrelevance.

Marsilius seeks to counter papal universalism with civic particularism; other medieval thinkers, such as *Dante, looked to the Holy Roman emperor as a potential guarantor of universal peace. And in the wake of the great 17th-century wars of religion this dream of bringing universal peace to Christendom reappears in the guise of various schemes for a federation of henceforth essentially secular states: notably, the Abbé de Saint-Pierre's Projet pour rendre la paix perpétuelle en Europe (Project for Perpetual Peace in Europe (1712/13)); Rousseau's later reworking of the same; and *Kant's essay Zum ewigen Frieden (Perpetual Peace (1795)).

Meanwhile, the post-Reformation 'historic peace churches'—the *Mennonites, the *Quakers, the Church of the *Brethren—sought to revive the spirit of the *Sermon on the Mount, interpreted in strict *pacifist terms. In the life of these small communities the mainstream approach is rejected in exactly the opposite way to Marsilius's: with the pax of the 'heavenly city' taking shape as a radically un-Augustinian symbolic refusal of the necessary compromises of 'earthly' citizenship.

Peace movements

During the 19th century, however, something new began to appear. 'Peace' became the political project of 'peace movements': spontaneous corporate initiatives from below, which, even when their primary appeal is to the members of a particular Christian denomination, nevertheless systematically detach the larger cause of peace from any mere expression of ecclesiastical self-interest—and thereby open up the possibility of all sorts of *ecumenical, and indeed transconfessional, co-operation.

The first such groups were the Peace Societies founded in 1815/16 in New York and London, with a mostly Quaker membership. In continental Europe the decisive breakthrough came in the years 1848–50, with the holding of Peace Congresses in Brussels, Paris, and Frankfurt. The establishment of the Red Cross in 1864 belongs to the same process. And the following decades witnessed a steadily growing momentum; still further intensified, in the 20th century, by the horrors of the two World Wars. The formation of Pax Christi in 1945, for example, represents a key moment in the development of a free-spirited peace-politics in the Roman Catholic world. Church-based peace groups also played a major role in the great international surge of protest against the nuclear arms race in the early 1980s; above all, in the two Germanies (in West Germany thanks chiefly to the institution of the biennial Kirchentag assemblies), in the Netherlands, and in the USA. Perhaps the chief problem for any future peace-movement theology, on the other hand, is how to confront the—in contemporary conditions—inevitable temptation to cheapen 'peace', for effectiveness' sake, by *propagandizing* it.

Certainly, in the context of the Cold War, 'peace' did become a major theme especially of Eastern bloc propaganda. And the Eastern bloc regimes also made determined efforts to manipulate the work of such groups as the Prague-based Christian Peace Conference for their own purposes. As a result of which, many dissidents in those countries developed an acute—again, rather Jeremiah-like—allergy to the very word. Hence, it is not only the political agenda-defining relationship between 'justice, peace and the integrity of creation' (the favoured triadic formulation of the World Council of Churches) that needs rethinking. But there is also the whole *pre*-political relationship of dependence between *inner* peace and what Václav Havel for instance calls 'living in truth': precisely a radical immunity from all propaganda-ideology, as such. It has to be insisted that—in the end—there can be no authentic political peace either, attained on any other basis than this.

See also GLOBAL ETHICS; RECONCILIATION.   **Andrew Shanks**

Bainton, R., *Christian Attitudes to War and Peace* (1960).
Johnson, J. T., *The Quest for Peace: Three Moral Traditions in Western Cultural History* (1987).
Rasmusson, A., *The Church as Polis* (1994).
Weigel, G., *Tranquillitas Ordinis: The Present Failure and Future Hope of American Catholic Thought on War and Peace* (1987).
Yoder, J. H., *Christian Attitudes to War, Peace and Revolution: A Companion to Bainton* (1983).
—— *Nevertheless: The Varieties and Shortcomings of Religious Pacifism*, (rev. edn., 1992).

Pelagianism

Pelagianism was an *ascetic movement in the *Latin church in the 5th century. In terms of credal confession it was orthodox, as the general councils of the 4th century had understood *orthodoxy, namely, right belief in the doctrines of the *Trinity and the *Incarnation. Its particular tenet, which its supporters maintained was a matter of opinion and not of defined belief, was the denial of any transmission of the guilt of *Adam's primal *sin to his descendants, which meant that every human being comes into the world in the condition of Adam at his creation and able by free choice, through the natural goodness of his divinely created nature, to live according to God's commandments. As a consequence, the Pelagians did not attach the same urgency to infant *baptism—a practice of which they nevertheless approved—as did their opponents, *Augustine of Hippo and his supporters, for whom the death of an unbaptized infant infallibly involved damnation. It was this denial of original sin that conditioned the Pelagian view of human nature. Unlike Augustine, they did not regard Adam as an exceptional human being. For some Pelagians, Adam was created mortal and would have died whether he sinned or not. For others he was like his descendants but had an *immortality conditional upon his obedience to God. In either case, his sin involved himself alone. If his descendants sinned, they sinned by imitation and not through any participation in their ancestor's disobedience, and once cleansed of past sin by baptism they were able, if they chose, to lead a righteous life.

Pelagius (fl. 409–18), a British-born *theologian, is traditionally regarded as the founder and leader of the movement, a view which probably exaggerates his importance. A layman, sometimes called a monk by his contemporaries, Pelagius was a biblical scholar, particularly interested in the Pauline epistles, a moralist and a spiritual director, who converted Caelestius, a Roman aristocrat, from a legal career to an ascetic way of life. Caelestius subsequently showed greater powers of leadership in the movement than did his master.

Pelagius did not, apparently, devise the theological system to which he has given his name. According to the 5th-century Latin theologian Marius Mercator, the inspirer of Pelagianism was a certain Rufinus, called 'the Syrian,' who used Pelagius to propagate his own doctrines. A work ascribed to Rufinus, the *Liber de fide*, denounces the madness of those who, 'because of one man, Adam, convict the entire world of iniquity and crime and assert that Christ destines unbaptized children to the punishment of everlasting fire', in thoroughly Pelagian language. It would appear that Rufinus influenced Pelagius' disciple Caelestius as well as his master. Pelagius, however, had a broader theological vision than a mere denial of original sin. As befitted a student of *Paul, he was concerned with the theology of *grace and was anxious to refute the *predestinarian doctrine of the *dualistic Manichaean *heresy, popular in some Roman circles in the 390s, which held that sin was simply the operation of an evil principle within the individual human being. Pelagius sought to defend human *freedom and to emphasize that divine grace does not destroy it. In consequence, he regarded grace as a help, bestowed upon *humanity in creation, illumination, and *redemption: in creation, by the endowment of a rational will, which enables us to avoid sin; in illumination, in the law of Moses and the teaching and example of Christ; and in redemption in the remission of sins in baptism, by which the benefit of Christ's death is conveyed to the sinner. Such an outlook clearly raises problems about the work of baptism in the case of infants who are, according to Pelagian belief, born without any inherited sin, but these do not seem to have unduly concerned the Pelagians, who permitted infant baptism while regarding the typical baptizand as an adult convert.

It is possible that, but for the influence of secular politics, Pelagianism would have been no more than a passing fashion in theological speculation; but, about 409, when the army of Alaric the Goth menaced Rome, Pelagius and Caelestius fled to North Africa. Pelagius soon went on to Palestine, where many of his aristocratic Roman patrons had settled, but Caelestius remained at Carthage and apparently sought to popularize his theology. In so doing he came into conflict with a theological tradition that, at least from the time of St

Cyprian, had regarded belief in original sin as part of catholic doctrine. The whole human race had sinned in Adam and had thereby justly incurred universal damnation. Out of the *massa peccati*, the lump of sinful humanity so formed, a remnant was elected to salvation by God's *mercy, with the vast majority being left to perdition. Except for the martyrs, no possibility of salvation existed for the unbaptized, though by no means all who received baptism would be saved. Because of the *Fall, Adam's descendants inherited both spiritual and physical weakness. They were free to sin but powerless to do good without the enabling grace of Christ. The guilt inherited from Adam was transmitted to his descendants by sexual concupiscence, the lust that now accompanies procreation even in marriage and that was unknown in Eden. For that reason it was necessary for Christ to be born of a virgin and thus exempted from the awful legacy of Adam's guilt. Such a theology was utterly opposed to that of Caelestius. He defended his views stoutly, appealing to Rufinus of Syria as a witness to his orthodoxy, but was condemned and excommunicated by a Carthaginian local council. He left Africa and went to Antioch, where he was ordained a presbyter.

In 417 Pelagius and Caelestius were both excommunicated by Pope Innocent I under pressure by the African bishops, whose theological spokesman was Augustine of Hippo, after the pair had been acquitted in 415 of charges of heresy by two Palestinian councils. They were condemned again in 418 by the western Roman emperor Honorius; by a pan-African council at Carthage; and finally by Innocent's successor Zosimus, who had initially been sympathetic to their appeal. Pelagius, after an unsuccessful attempt to seek reconciliation with Augustine, fades out of history. Caelestius continued the struggle, only to be condemned again, together with his supporters, at the third Ecumenical Council of *Ephesus in 431. Pelagianism seemed to be wholly crushed, but it had found a new champion in Julian, bishop of Eclanum in Apulia. Julian pointed to Augustine's conception of concupiscence and his insistence on the inevitable damnation of unbaptized infants who had committed no personal sin to charge him with one of the most damaging accusations possible in the later Roman empire, that of Manichaeism, which was a crime as well as a heresy. The foundation of Julian's argument was the principle, taken from Augustine's own anti-Manichaean treatise *De duabus animabus*, that what cannot be avoided cannot be sinful. By this the whole idea of a guilt inherited from an ancestor is invalidated. Julian denied any transmission of original sin and was concerned, like Rufinus the Syrian, to show that the very notion was absurd and repulsive. He rejected with horror the idea of the damnation of unbaptized infants, saying that Augustine's God was a *persecutor infantium*—a divine baby-batterer—thereby provoking Augustine to accuse him (wrongly) of envisaging a 'third place' for them between *heaven and *hell, equivalent to the medieval *limbo. Furthermore, Julian utterly rejected Augustine's notion of *sexual desire as something evil which, in a fallen world, may be directed to good in the begetting of *children in *marriage. For Julian, concupiscence was natural in human physiology, existed in *paradise, and was not brought about, as Augustine held, by a loss of control over the *body resultant on the Fall. Indeed, Julian was prepared to maintain that concupiscence, in the sense of virility and the pleasure that it induces, existed in the humanity of Christ, a suggestion that shocked Augustine.

Julian provoked Augustine more perhaps than any other of his many opponents, but the debate between them was essentially personal. On a wider front was the campaign that Augustine waged against the so-called Semi-Pelagians (a modern name) of Marseilles whose most notable theologian was John Cassian, the popularizer of Egyptian monasticism in the west. The Semi-Pelagians approved the condemnation of Pelagianism but were alarmed by the teaching of Augustine in his later writings that election to salvation is wholly dependent upon grace, so that individual choice plays no part in effecting it. Augustine had come to this belief through a sudden recognition of the significance of 1 Corinthians 4: 7: 'What have you that you did not receive? If then you received it, why do you boast as if it were not a gift?', and it came to determine his predestinarian thinking. For the Semi-Pelagians, Augustine's view was unscriptural and destructive of pastoral ministry, by taking away all motivation for repentance and godly living.

Because of the Pelagian belief that human beings are born today in the condition of Adam before the Fall, with complete freedom of moral choice even after committing a sin, it followed that the human will remains free to live virtuously. From that opinion it followed that sinlessness was possible in this life, if an individual chose to use his God-given freedom of choice. Accordingly, for the Pelagians, divine grace was inevitably seen as existing in our natural endowments and in baptismal regeneration. The doctrine of prevenient grace preceding free choice, which dominated Augustine's thinking, meant nothing to the Pelagians. Hence their view that baptism was essential only for adults, though desirable in the case of infants. Julian of Eclanum, the most effective Pelagian controversialist, laid emphasis on God's justice, which would not damn a child for Adam's sin, and on the innocence of human sexuality, which he held to be impugned by the Augustinian notion of concupiscence. Nevertheless, despite all the efforts of Caelestius and Julian, the overwhelming majority of western Christians accepted the condemnation of Pelagianism. The real opposition to Augustine's predestinarian theology came from the Semi-Pelagians who, while they approved of Pelagius' condemnation, denounced the determinism of Augustine as being a denial of Christian freedom and destructive of any motivation for moral effort. Semi-Pelagian doctrine, expounded by John Cassian and Faustus of Riez, that human free will remained, even in a state of sin, provided a source of orthodox opposition to extreme Augustinian predestinarian theology throughout the Middle Ages.

The writings of Pelagius, often ascribed to other, orthodox authors, had a limited circulation in the Middle Ages and it was only in the 20th century that a more sympathetic evaluation, initiated by Georges de Plinval in 1943, has been undertaken. This has demonstrated the injustice of Harnack's description of Pelagian theology as 'godless'. The recoil from *Calvinism since the *Enlightenment; a deeper appreciation of the concept of synergy ('working with God'), taught by some of the Greek fathers; and a renewed assertion of the freedom inherent in the human will as God's creation, even in the unbaptized, have all combined to rehabilitate Pelagianism in the opinion of some Christian theologians.

Gerald Bonner

Pelagius, *Rufini Presbyteri Liber de Fide*, ed. and trans. M. W. Miller (1964).
—— *The Letters of Pelagius and his Followers*, trans. B. R. Rees (1991).
—— *Commentary on St Paul's Epistle to the Romans*, trans. Theodore de Bruyn (1993).

Bonner, G., *Augustine of Hippo: Life and Controversies*, 2nd edn. (1986).
—— *God's Decree and Man's Destiny* (1987).
—— *Church and Faith in the Patristic Tradition* (1996).
Brown, P., *Augustine of Hippo* (1967).
—— *Religion and Society in the Age of Saint Augustine* (1972).
Evans, Robert F., *Pelagius: Inquiries and Reappraisals* (1968).
—— *Four Letters of Pelagius* (1968).
Rees, B. R., *Pelagius: A Reluctant Heretic* (1988).
Weaver, R. H., *Divine Grace and Human Agency: A Study of the Semi-Pelagian Controversy* (1996).

penance. For the Christian, *Jesus Christ is the source of *reconciliation: 'All have sinned and fall short of the glory of God, they are justified by his grace as a gift through redemption which is in Jesus Christ', 'the expiation for our sins' (Rom. 3: 23–5; 1 John 2: 1), handed over to death for our sins and raised to life for our *justification (Rom. 4: 25). But to be forgiven and reconciled, we must repent, which means conversion of heart and life (Mark 1: 14), *forgiveness of others (Matt. 6: 12), reconciliation with the community (Matt. 18: 17–18) and with God (2 Cor. 5: 18–19). Christ handed over the ministry of reconciliation to his *disciples (Matt. 18: 18; John 20: 22–3). They were 'ambassadors for Christ', urging people to be reconciled to God through Jesus Christ (2 Cor. 5: 20). They could exclude a *sinner from the community (1 Cor. 5: 2–5) but after repentance he could be reconciled (2 Cor. 2: 5–8). The community prays for sinners though some may be beyond the reach of *prayer (1 John 5: 14–16).

The church of the 2nd century had difficulty in coming to terms with the gospel emphasis on *compassion, forgiveness, and reconciliation. Hermas (c.150) held that great sins could be forgiven and the sinner reintegrated into the community, but only once. The end-time was imminent, communities were small, sins were known to all, the body could not risk contamination. Tertullian (c.160–225), even more rigorist in his *Montanist period, denied the church's *authority to forgive great sins. Controversy ensued in both North Africa and Rome where the bishop tended towards lenience. In the mid-3rd-century persecutions some Christians apostatized, others surrendered the sacred writings to government searchers. *Confessores*, those awaiting trial or execution, reconciled even apostates. Cyprian, bishop of Carthage, and Cornelius, bishop of Rome, insisted that apostates should undergo lifelong penance, but allowed others to be reconciled after due penance. An abnormal situation, with untidy solutions, but the principle of lifelong penance for great sins was maintained. It seems, however, that what came to be called canonical penance was already in existence.

In the 4th-century form of penance, the sinner came before the assembly, presided over by the bishop, and acknowledged his sinfulness (*exomologesis*). He was confronted with the gospel demands and enrolled in the order of penitents. He was excluded from communion but could attend the ministry of the word, after which he was dismissed with a blessing. Like all sinners, he was prayed for in the Prayers of the Faithful. The time of penance varied according to the gravity of his offence. The final act of reconciliation could be experienced only once; in Rome it took place on the Thursday of Holy Week. In the Gelasian Sacramentary (6th century), an archdeacon brings the penitents before the bishop and pleads for them as they lie prostrate. The bishop reconciles them in a long prayer and readmits them to the *Eucharist on Easter Day.

Penance was throughout a public, communal action. The bishop presided, he imposed the penance, the status of the penitent was known, the community prayed for him; reconciliation meant public restoration to the community and the Eucharist. As Ambrose (4th century) put it, the church is wounded by its members' sin and made whole again by reconciliation. The lengthy penance was regarded not as 'satisfaction' for sin but as a healing process involving conversion of heart and life.

When, in the 4th century, the 'freedom of the church' brought great numbers to membership, the demands of public penance, involving a virtual withdrawal from social life, proved too great. Penitents had to *fast, to abstain from intercourse with their spouse, almost to lead the life of a religious. Those under 35 were usually excluded for fear of relapse, because of the rule of once-only reconciliation. Despite 6th-century mitigations, the system was breaking down when the barbarian invasions struck Europe and put an end to it.

It was gradually replaced in the west by what has been called tariff penance. This was propagated from the 7th century by Irish and Anglo-Saxon missionaries working in Gaul and the German lands, and can be seen in the Penitentials drawn up at this time. Originating with Celtic *monastic practice, it broke sharply with the past. Except for the more spectacular penances, all—confession to a priest and reconciliation—was now private. The principle of once-only reconciliation for grave sins disappeared, as did the connection with *Lent and *Easter. There was a new emphasis on the penance as satisfaction, with attempts to make the *punishment fit the crime; satisfaction became more punitive than medicinal. Long penances, imposed in an attempt to counter the violence of the times, made daily life difficult, so commutations were made: a sharper, shorter penance might replace one lasting years. A priest could even be made to do his feudal lord's penance.

Tariff penance being too rigorous, the practice of sacramental penance became rare. To correct this situation the Fourth Lateran Council (1215) decreed that all members of the church should, from about the age of reason, confess their sins to their parish priest at least once a year about Easter time. The intention was to *increase* the practice of penance; unfortunately, once a year with holy communion became the norm for many. The rite was now purely private, consisting of contrition (repentance voiced in prayer), confession, absolution, and satisfaction (usually private and often a prayer). A rite of public penance remained in the *Pontificale* but was used only in the most solemn form of excommunication. With the coming of the friars in the 13th century, and the multiplication of handbooks for clergy and people, the practice of confession, for some at least, became more frequent. Nor was penance restricted to the rite. There was the strict fast of Lent and other days of fast and abstinence; works of *mercy and *pilgrimages, supposed to be penitential, were urged upon the people by preachers.

Among the reformers, *Luther retained a rite of penance that had a precarious life in the following centuries. In the 20th century Dietrich *Bonhoeffer regarded private penance as a proper function of the church that would help towards reconciliation (*Sanctorum Communio*, ET (1963), 173). The Church of England showed its concern for repentance in the Commination Service of Ash Wednesday and the exhortations attached to Morning and Evening Prayer. The

Order of the Visitation of the Sick contains a form of absolution for one who 'feels his conscience troubled by any weighty matter'. This was used with counselling in the 17th century; the Tractarians in the 19th (see OXFORD MOVEMENT) revived the practice of private confession, which has spread throughout the Anglican Communion. In 1986 the House of Bishops of the General Synod issued *Lent, Holy Week, Easter*, containing three Services of Penitence for use in Lent and at other times.

The *eastern church's system of public penance resembled that of the west, but was more lenient, allowing reconciliation to be repeated. This made the passage to private penance easier. There was much spiritual counselling, often given by non-ordained monks and other holy men. Present practice, varying in different parts of the Orthodox Church, includes counselling and seeks to heal the sinner. The formula of absolution is 'May God forgive …' (in Russia 'God forgives …'); a penance is not usually imposed. Frequency of use varies. Besides the liturgical form of penance there was, especially from the 17th century, everywhere much *preaching, aimed at stimulating repentance, as in the work of John *Wesley and his followers. In the Catholic Church this took the form of 'internal missions', by Jean Eudes and others in 17th-century France, and by the new orders of Redemptorists and Passionists in 18th-century Italy, and subsequently worldwide. In addition there were the practices of Lenten fasting, prayer centred upon the Passion of Christ, and self-imposed austerities common to many Christians.

With the increasing frequency of communion in the Roman Catholic Church of the 20th century, confession, as it was called, also became more frequent. By the mid-1950s the rite of penance was found unsatisfactory, spiritually and pastorally, by both priests and people. *Vatican II, in its Constitution of the *Liturgy, decreed that the rite should be revised the better 'to express its nature and effects'. The Order of Penance eventually appeared in 1973.

Its introduction exemplifies good pastoral-biblical *theology. Entitled 'The Mystery of Reconciliation in the History of Salvation', it emphasizes the power of God's word to bring about repentance and reconciliation with God, the church, and neighbour. The sinner is restored to union with God and communion with the church which 'he has wounded by his sins'. This Order thus restores an awareness of the communal nature of the sacrament and shows reconciliation as the culmination of repentance. In this context it speaks of the social dimension of sin (which Pope *John Paul II called 'structural sin'); as human beings are solidary in sin and injustice, they should be working for *justice and reconciliation in society and the world.

The Order offers three rites of penance: reconciliation of individual penitents; of many penitents with individual absolution; and of many penitents with general absolution. Though a great improvement on what was available before, all have their defects.

The first obviously lacks the communal element, a normal constituent of liturgical rites, and also the social dimension of sin unless the confessor mentions it in his counsel. Private penance is, however, valued by many; its disappearance would be a serious loss to their spiritual life.

The second can suggest that the service—prayer, song, and homily—is only a prelude to the sacrament proper (private confession and absolution). But it is at least communal, and the presider can, through his choice of scripture texts and homily, make the hearers aware of the social dimension of sin and extend their notions of what is sinful.

The third is liturgically the most satisfactory. It is all of a piece: prayer, song, scripture reading, all lead straight to the general confession and absolution/reconciliation. Unfortunately the restrictions laid down by the Roman authorities make it something of a rarity in pastoral life. Thus those beginning their return to the church community and full reconciliation are excluded. Yet the new Order itself emphasizes that conversion (*metanoia*) is a process and not usually a bolt from the blue. In the catechumenate, *baptism (the primary sacrament of reconciliation) is approached gradually; so also with conversion. This is the context for Lenten services of penitence, also recommended by the Order.

The history of penance displays changing emphases. Canonical penance involved the community, saw conversion as a process, and emphasized reconciliation. Tariff penance highlighted confession and satisfaction. Private penance became purely individualistic, a detailed confession of sins and absolution. The new Order has retrieved the sense of community, emphasizing reconciliation with God, the church, and fellow human beings.

Liturgical reform is one thing, people's needs another. A world that has lost the sense of sin may need a different kind of theological and psychological understanding. Sin is not merely infringement of a law, but the severing of a relationship with God. A sense of sin comes from faith in the living God, not 'the God of the Philosophers' or the legalists but the God of the Lord Jesus Christ. For Thomas *Aquinas, sin is a turning away from God to what is less than God (*aversio a Deo, conversio ad creaturas*). Penance in its various forms offers ways of turning back.   **James Crichton**

Crichton, J. D., *The Ministry of Reconciliation: A Commentary* (1974).
—— *Christian Celebration: Understanding the Sacraments*, rev. edn. (1993).
Dallen, J., *The Reconciling Community: The Rite of Penance* (1986), extensive bibliography.
Dudley, M., and Rowell, G. (eds.), *Confession and Absolution* (1990).
Fitzsimons, J. (ed.), *Penance: Virtue and Sacrament* (1969).
Mortimer, R. C., *The Origins of Private Penance in the Western Church* (1939).
Telfer, W., *The Forgiveness of Sins* (1959).
Tentler, T. N., *Sin and Confession on the Eve of the Reformation* (1977).
Vogel, C., *Le Pécheur et la pénitence dans l'église ancienne* (1966).
—— *Le Pécheur et la pénitence au Moyen Age* (1969).
Watson, O. D., *History of Penance* (1920), repr. (1960).

Pentecost was the Greek name given to Shavuot, the Feast of Weeks, a Jewish pilgrimage festival held seven weeks—on the 'fiftieth day'—after Passover and the Feast of Unleavened Bread to mark the conclusion of the grain harvest (Lev. 23: 9–22; Tob. 2: 1). The Acts of the Apostles (2: 1–11) records that on the day of Pentecost, when after Christ's death and Resurrection the disciples were gathered together in Jerusalem, the *Holy Spirit came among them, resting upon them as tongues of fire and filling their mouths with many languages. This scene became a popular subject for eastern *iconography and western sacred *art, not only on account of the dramatic visual picture painted by the biblical text, but because the event itself is generally considered to be the birth of the *church, born through the pouring out of the Spirit (Acts 2: 17; cf. 1 Cor. 12: 13). Some patristic authors, notably *Augustine (Letter 55: *To Januarius*) and Leo the Great (*Sermon, 75*), connected the rabbinic interpretation of Pentecost as the day on which the law was given at Mount Sinai to the dynamic conferring of the Spirit upon the church: where the first Passover was followed by the old covenant of the Sinaitic law, the Pasch of Christ's sacrifice and Resurrection brought a new covenant written on the heart by the pentecostal Spirit (cf. Rom. 7: 6; 2 Cor. 3; cf. Jer. 31: 31–4).

Many Christian communities of the first four centuries used 'Pentecost' to denote the fifty days following *Easter. There is some suggestion that the fiftieth and final day signalled both Christ's ascent and the Spirit's descent. With the creation of a separate Ascension festival on the fortieth day (Acts 1: 1–11), the bestowal of the Holy Spirit for ministry and mission became the primary focus of the day of Pentecost, and for the eight days (or 'octave') of related celebration that was observed in some regions. The ideal of Christian *unity for the sake of the universal dissemination of the gospel was believed to be displayed by the gift of multilingual capabilities given at Pentecost, regarded by preachers ancient and modern as a reversal of the confounding of speech at Babel (Gen. 11: 1–9).

Tertullian looked on the entire fifty days of Pentecost as a 'most auspicious season (*laetissimum spatium*)' for *baptism (*On Baptism*, 19 (*c.*205)). When the day of Pentecost became a distinct feast, its vigil served after the example of the Easter vigil as an especially suitable baptismal occasion, particularly in the west. The English term 'Whitsunday' popularly substituted for the name Pentecost evokes images of the white garments that were worn by the newly baptized who, through water, the imposition of hands, and chrismation with holy oil, were infused with the power of the Holy Spirit. Another sacramental rite has also been connected with Pentecost: from the 11th century onwards, the Pentecost *hymn 'Veni creator Spiritus, mentes tuorum visita', has been sung at ordinations whatever the season; the 17th-century translation by John Cosin, 'Come, Holy Ghost, our souls inspire', is found in many modern hymn books.

See also CALENDAR. **Karen B. Westerfield Tucker**

Gunstone, J., *The Feast of Pentecost* (1967).

Pentecostalism

Pentecostalism is a *revivalist movement of denominations, independent congregations, and para-church organizations born out of the *Wesleyan-Holiness movement at the beginning of the 20th century. It teaches that all Christians may receive a 'baptism in the *Holy Spirit' that is the source of power for living an 'apostolic' life and engaging in 'apostolic' ministry. Christians should also expect to receive the same evidence of that experience as the earliest Christians received on the Day of *Pentecost, the ability 'to speak in other tongues as the Spirit gave them utterance' (Acts 2: 1–4).

Pentecostalism first attracted attention in January 1901 under the ministry of Charles Fox Parham. Its dynamism, however, came from the three-year revival (1906–9) at the Apostolic Faith Mission, 312 Azusa Street, Los Angeles, led by the African American, William Joseph Seymour (see BLACK THEOLOGY). From Azusa Street the message of *salvation, *holiness, and power was rapidly dispersed around the world by a host of evangelists and *missionaries, and the mission's newspaper, *The Apostolic Faith*. Today the movement, whose strength lies in the 'two-thirds' world, claims 300 million adherents. It has given rise to millions more in the *charismatic movement.

Some Pentecostals have sought to establish continuity with the historic churches by calling attention to earlier Christian *prophetic and *millenarian movements as forerunners to Pentecostalism, groups such as the *Montanists, Camisards, *Quakers, and the Irvingites. More commonly, Pentecostals have highlighted their discontinuity with history by portraying these groups as exceptions rather than the rule. They ignore centuries of Christian history when they, like those in some disparate groups (for example *Mormons and *Adventists) embrace *restorationism. In this scheme, the *church of the NT falls away, though genuine elements of *apostolic faith and life may surface periodically in individuals and movements. With the rise of Pentecostalism, this 'Latter Rain' Movement (Joel 2: 23), however, God has acted to restore the church in purity and power. Thus, the Pentecostal message has clear *eschatological overtones, with strong primitivist convictions, and powerful *evangelistic consequences.

Unlike Protestants, Pentecostals contend that the historic *creeds fail to communicate the essence of Christianity adequately. Apostolic succession is an equally problematic safeguard, since it includes individuals who have not lived exemplary 'apostolic' lives. For Pentecostals, the sole guarantor of apostolic faith, which includes apostolic life, is the Holy Spirit.

Pentecostalism's place in history may be easily located by looking at *The Doctrines and Discipline* of the Azusa Street Mission. Pastor Seymour borrowed heavily from John Wesley's *Doctrines and Discipline*. Wesley, in turn, included an edited version of the Thirty-Nine Articles of the *Anglican Church. The roots of the earliest Pentecostals were planted deeply in Wesleyan-Holiness soil. Pentecostals taught three separate and distinct crisis experiences: *salvation, sanctification, and *baptism in the Holy Spirit. This form of Pentecostalism includes such groups as the Apostolic Faith Movements, the Church of God (Cleveland, Tennessee), the Church of God in Christ, and the Pentecostal Holiness Church.

A second group of early Pentecostals emerged after 1910, led by men such as William H. Durham, who had been affected by Keswick teachings. They encouraged their members to appropriate the 'finished work' of Christ that provides for their positional sanctification and enables them to progress in an 'overcoming' life. Denominations such as the Assemblies of God, the International Church of the Foursquare Gospel, Elim, and the Open Bible Standard Churches embrace this position.

Following a 1913 camp meeting near Los Angeles, where it was noted that in the Book of Acts the apostles baptized only in the 'powerful' name of Jesus Christ (Acts 2: 38), the limits of apostolicity were tested. John G. Schaeppe claimed he received a 'revelation' that genuine Christian baptism must conform to this 'apostolic' pattern. Shortly thereafter, advocates of this position also adopted a modalist understanding of the *Trinity. After 1916, they formed various 'Oneness', 'Jesus Name', or 'Apostolic' groups, including the Pentecostal Assemblies of the World, and the United Pentecostal Church.

A fourth group of Pentecostal organizations may be described as autochthonous. These churches claim a spontaneous origin rather than a developmental one. The oldest such group is La Iglesia Metodista Pentecostal, formed in Santiago, Chile, in May 1910. Its founder, Willis C. Hoover, had been a Methodist missionary. Through a series of letters from a missionary friend in India who had been in contact with the Azusa Street revival, Hoover received his 'baptism in the Spirit'. This led to a break with the Methodist Church, and the formation of an autochthonous Pentecostal community. Other autochthonous groups, including house churches in China and elsewhere, have been founded by those who came to faith in other churches or as a result of missionary activity, but for reasons of nationalism, financial control, leadership, political expediency, or ecclesiological commitments now find themselves living independently.

A case can also be made that a number of the '*African Instituted' or 'African Indigenous' churches are Pentecostal. The Kimbanguist Church may be the best known, but many Zionist churches fit this category, since former members of the Apostolic Faith Mission of South Africa founded them. Pentecostals frequently view such Zionist groups as lying beyond the limits of orthodox Christianity, but their emphasis upon signs and wonders, *miracles, and other charismatic phenomena suggest that the relationship between syncretism and the limits of apostolicity needs further exploration.

Pentecostalism emerged amidst a unique fusion of doctrines and experiences. The field of pneumatology had been infrequently explored, but the emphasis that Pentecostals brought to it also brought a heightened sense of the immanence of *God in a world dominated by transcendence. Pentecostals invoked the power of the Holy Spirit, manifested through signs, wonders, and charisms, to aid in personal transformation, to break down the destructive, sinful structures in individual lives, and to bring relief from misery and death. This was a reality that could still be entered, not merely an abstract doctrine that could only be discussed. The flamboyant evangelist, Aimee Semple McPherson, made this clear in her celebrated sermon, 'Is Jesus the Great "I am", or Is He the Great "I was"?'.

Pentecostalism is highly critical of institutionalization in the church. The church is viewed as transportable, adaptable, indigenizable, and personal. It requires no hierarchy, no buildings, and no mandatory level of education for its leaders. In its best self-understanding, Pentecostalism is a radical experiment in the democratization of the believing community, based upon the promise of Joel 2: 28 that God's Spirit would be poured out on 'all flesh'. As a result, emphasis is placed upon the local, *congregational manifestation of the church. Every member is taken seriously regardless of race, gender, age, or other arbitrary standard of classification. Pentecostalism promises a realized *ecumenism, an end to all forms of discrimination, and the opening up of new possibilities in social relations. Emphasis is placed upon the role of the Holy Spirit to empower each person for some form of ministry, to direct the daily activities of the community, and to provide freedom for cultural creativity. The distinctions between clergy and laity are expected to be minimal.

*Worship becomes an act of praise, hope, and the proclamation of good news. It brings hope to the disenfranchised. A discerning community of faith, carried along and nurtured by the Holy Spirit, fosters vibrant, often spontaneous forms of worship, including the singing of melodies composed by members of the group, clapping, and oral testimonies of what God is doing now. Instruments like drums or tambourines and other creative artistic expressions, like dancing, that may be denied access to worship services in other

traditions, are brought before the community and discerned as genuine forms of spiritual worship. The result is a people's theology in which personal testimony is given a privileged role in the proclamation of the gospel, and the whole is confirmed through signs and wonders. What Pentecostals see clearly as a dynamic situation under the overarching control of the Holy Spirit, the outsider may not understand, viewing it only as chaos or worse (1 Cor. 14: 23).

Pentecostalism provides a redefinition of theological anthropology by criticizing the mind/body or soul/body *dualism that has been common since the Enlightenment. A realized eschatology typified by the already/not yet character of the *Kingdom of God, gives rise to prayer offered for bodily and emotional healing. The material is taken as seriously as the spiritual. The spiritualized nature of much biblical interpretation is supplemented by a literal one, while the contributions of rationalism alone are examined in the light of a hermeneutic of suspicion. The spirit world is viewed as a present reality for which the divinely given charism, the discerning of spirits, is essential to any successful encounter with it. The ability to bind and loose (Matt. 16: 19; 18: 18) takes on new meaning. Spiritual warfare provides not only new insight into that world, but also new weapons that may be used to confront it (Eph. 6: 10–17).

The rediscovery of the human psyche by Pentecostals comes in a most pronounced fashion within speaking in tongues. The conscious and the subconscious seem to be fully integrated under the hand of the Holy Spirit, while a radical decentring of the self, including tears, groanings, apparent babel, even the identification with all of creation (Rom. 8: 26) takes place. Various non-rational (not irrational) phenomena such as *visions, *dreams, speaking in tongues, miracles, and revelations, are integrated alongside a circumscribed rationalism. *Religious experience is valued. *Enthusiasm is openly embraced. Emotions are expressed without shame.

At least four dangers face contemporary Pentecostalism. First among these is its old flirtation with an élitism that undermines its impact. Its claim to possess the 'Full Gospel', as though it were a privileged, self-contained church independent of other Christians, unnecessarily divides the church into two camps, the 'haves' and the 'have nots'. It does not take seriously the contributions of other Christians.

Secondly, Pentecostals risk turning an otherwise dynamic movement of the Holy Spirit into something static, built upon a 'single event theology'. 'Baptism in the Spirit', as an experience of power available to believers from the moment of conversion onwards, is clearly distinctive to Pentecostalism. But Pentecostals disagree among themselves over the appropriate evidence of that experience. Some argue that it is inevitably the ability to speak in other tongues (not to be confused with the charism described in 1 Cor. 12). For others, it may be one of the charisms of the Holy Spirit (1 Cor. 12: 8–10), or a manifestation such as 'dancing in the Spirit'. Whatever else they may believe, Pentecostals must take seriously the spontaneous character of the Spirit's work (John 3: 8), abstain from all frivolous seeking of signs (Matt. 16: 4), and avoid unnecessary division between the people of God (1 Cor. 1: 10).

Thirdly, Pentecostalism is frequently tempted by the allure of broader acceptance. Pentecostalism shares many affinities with evangelicalism. However, the growth in Pentecostal–evangelical relations in the United States has led to the adoption of *fundamentalist views on scripture, and compromises on issues such as *pacifism, *women in ministry, and ecumenism. In Russia, the Pentecostals who chose to be registered under Stalin were required to suppress any marks of their Pentecostalism (for example speaking in tongues), when the Baptists under whom they were placed drafted constitutional guidelines designed to force this suppression. Recognition was more important to these Pentecostals, however, than was a clear Pentecostal witness in solidarity with those Pentecostals who remained unregistered.

Fourthly, as the movement becomes increasingly aware of its size and the power its size portends, it runs the risk of relying more upon its own power than it does on the power of the Spirit that it proclaims. This is particularly tempting in Latin America where Pentecostalism has long occupied the margins of religious and societal life. If the political power of the movement is coupled with its frustration over the oppression it believes it has received from the Roman Catholic Church, it may ultimately yield an equally oppressive Pentecostalism. **Cecil M. Robeck, Jr.**

Burgess, S., and McGee, G. (eds.), *Dictionary of Pentecostal and Charismatic Movements* (1988).
Cox, H., *Fire from Heaven* (1995).
Dayton, D., *Theological Roots of Pentecostalism* (1987).
Hollenweger, W., *The Pentecostals* (1971).
—— *Pentecostalism* (1997).
Synan, V., *The Holiness-Pentecostal Tradition*, 2nd edn. (1997).

person derives from the Latin *persona* which originally meant an actor's mask. By extension it came to mean the character enacted, and then the human individual as it presents itself to others. In contemporary usage, the word has accumulated much deeper psychological, spiritual, and legal resonances. Many secular humanists would concur with the Orthodox theologian John Zizioulas in calling personhood 'the most dear and precious good of human existence', while perhaps remaining unaware that the exploration and deepening of this concept and indeed the word itself are gifts of the Christian theological tradition.

The word itself provides a prime example of the complications that arise in Christian thought when terms from everyday speech or philosophical discourse are adopted to deal with technical problems in theology and then return to common speech. The clashes of usage generate as many questions as answers. In the case of the word 'person', two quite distinct lines of development can be traced in later thought. The traditions fuse and interfere with one another in a fascinating, frustrating, and complex manner.

The primary use of 'person' in theology is as a technical term in the development of the doctrine of the *Trinity. Tertullian in his *Adversus Praxeas* introduced the expression *tres personae in una substantia* (three persons in one substance) to define the unity and triplicity of the Christian God. 'Person' here is a label for whatever accounts for the distinctive identity of Father, Son, and Holy Spirit (see Pre-Constantinian Thought).

On such a definition, the word points to, rather than solves, central theological questions about the nature of God. *Augustine confirms this in his *De trinitate*: 'We say "three persons" not because that expresses just what we want to say, but because we must say something.' *Barth, admitting that he struggled with the term, remarked that it was 'a relief' to discover that his illustrious prede-

cessor Augustine also fought shy of defining it. Attempts to fill it out by human *analogy are fraught with danger. Yet the desire to find a more positive definition is almost irresistible, and, just because it is left unspecified, the term tends to import allusions from its other areas of use.

An added complication is that Tertullian's formula is a Latin equivalent of the later Greek definition put forward by the Cappadocian fathers which spoke of the Trinity as three *hypostases* in one *ousia*. The trouble is that translated literally *hypostasis* and *substantia* have the same root meaning, 'standing under' or 'foundation'. The more natural Greek equivalent of *persona* is *prosopon*, face, or aspect. Translated into Greek, the Latin formula seemed to be saying that the Trinity consisted of three roles performed by one *hypostasis*, a clear example of the *heresy of modalism that gives Father, Son, and Spirit no individual identity. Conversely, if *hypostasis* is translated into Latin as *substantia*, the Greek formula seems to refer to the members of the Trinity as three substances, which leaned a good deal too far towards the equally heretical notion of three separate Gods. The suspicion of *Greek and *Latin theologians over each other's *orthodoxy was heightened by this linguistic confusion until the equivalence between *hypostasis* and *persona* was accepted.

The picture becomes more complicated when we bring in the parallel debates over the constitution of *Jesus Christ. How were human and divine related in the *incarnate Son? Again unity and plurality had both to be asserted. The banal starting-point was that there is only one Jesus, but he was both human and divine. For the orthodox tradition, what was single was the *prosopon*, the presentation, we might say, of Jesus, and what was separate were the 'natures' (*phuseis*). Again it took a long time for the vocabulary to be settled, but the orthodox conclusion was the rather surprising one that Jesus was a person by virtue of being the incarnate *Word. He was not a human person (see Christology).

The seeming oddity of this conclusion serves to strengthen the point that the word 'person' here has nothing to do with the ideas of self-consciousness, responsibility, and identity that modern *psychology, for instance, regards as essential to its definition. Here the term is part of the technical language dealing with the concepts of substance and existence that Christians derived from *Aristotelian philosophy, coloured by the Neoplatonic emphasis on the superior value of mental categories (see Plato). In this formal sense, the Christian philosopher Boethius (c.480–c.545) offered the fundamental definition of a person as 'an individual substance of a rational nature'. *Aquinas later modified this by adding the express indication that this substance is 'incommunicable', i.e. peculiar only to that individual and not interchangeable. Bonaventure (c.1217–47), among others, developed this by saying that personhood can only be predicated of the pre-eminent substance in an entity. In this sense, the human nature of Jesus loses out to his divinity. His human nature is rational, but crucially not pre-eminent, being caught up in the personhood of the Son.

Is *God himself then a person? Aquinas's argument here is that God is certainly not less than a person, as this is the highest category that humans know: 'Person signifies that which is most perfect in all nature' (*ST* I. q. 29 a. 3). Rational thought cannot carry us any further than this and certainly should beware of imposing human personhood on God. Only by revelation can it be known that God's mode of personal existence is as three persons in one substance.

Many of the conclusions of this ontological approach to defining persons seem strange to modern readers. We are steeped in an intellectual heritage which, from the rise of humanism, has agreed with Aquinas in according supreme value to personhood, but accounts for this in terms of self-consciousness and the capacity for relationship rather than metaphysical status. Jesus has been presented as the fullest development of human personality and his uniqueness as the reflection of a profoundly personal and intimate relationship with the God he called 'Abba' ('Father'). The 19th century's *quest for the historical Jesus, and exemplarist theologies that portray *redemption in terms of achieving the same level of personal integration reflect the development of another way of conceiving of the person that also has roots in Christian thought.

This second strand begins from the human person, distinguished by its infinite value and *freedom. Persons are at all times ends in themselves, and never to be regarded as the means to the achievement of some other, greater end. The ground of this regard is the fact that the human person is made in the image of God according to Genesis 1. This biblical idea becomes subtly reconceived in the light of the philosophical tradition. The story of the *Fall, interpreted with an emphasis on knowledge and failures of will, interacts with Neoplatonic ideas to lead to an increasing identification of persons with minds.

This can also be seen in the OT depiction of a God who questions, interacts, laughs, repents, and loves. He is in continual dialogue and interaction with human beings. A book such as Jack Miles's *God: A Biography* testifies to the possibility of writing about this God as a fully formed literary character and to that extent a person. This personal God, however, sits ill with the Platonic image of an unmoved mover that influences later philosophical theology. Much OT imagery is explained by the fathers and later tradition as anthropomorphism and *metaphor. The question is how far that goes. God's hand or eye may be metaphorical, but what about his wrath or, most importantly, his love?

It could be argued that it is Augustine himself who encourages the reconception of the person in psychological terms. He conceived the relations of the Trinity on the analogy of the internal relations of *memory, understanding, and love in the individual consciousness, arguing that the vestiges of the Trinity were most visible in the highest category of entity known to us, the mind and spirit of humanity. Here Augustine is drawing much nearer to the modern conception of personhood based on consciousness which opens the way to the use of such analogies in the later tradition.

With the recovery of aspects of classical thought in the late *Middle Ages and *Renaissance, humanity began to be seen as the measure of the universe, and the exploration and cultivation of what it meant to be truly human became of prime interest. As a result, *anthropology and psychology, rather than theology, become the disciplines which define personhood. In the 17th century, *Descartes brought the concept of consciousness explicitly to the fore. He defined this as an intimate knowledge of one's own mental states, the capacity to reflect on one's own process of thinking.

This self-reflective model of personhood is still highly influential. *Kant, for instance, regarded the consciousness of duty as that which raises the individual from being a phenomenon of the cau-

sally determined natural world to the stature of personhood. The philosophical legacy, however, tends to a view of the person as a discrete, indeed isolated, entity. Another line of thought, which has gained increasing acceptance in modern theology, regards persons as being constituted by their relationships rather than grounded in some more abstract ontology. The argument runs that just as it is absurd to try to dissect out the Father, Son, or Holy Spirit from the Trinity as if it could make sense to speak of one without the other two, so it is absurd to think of some category of human personhood as prior to community, and still more as isolated from God.

This view is the result of an interesting interaction between the development of *existentialist thought in the west, which rejects the idea that some general essential category of humanity has priority over the individual existence of the person, and the recovery of *Eastern Orthodox thought with its deep insights into relationality. The argument has been put forward that the Cappadocian Fathers themselves saw the persons of the Trinity, not the divine substance, as prior. God's unity is an expression of the intimacy of the loving relationships between the three persons, and the Orthodox concept of *theosis* or divinization means that the destiny of the human person is seen in the possibility of being caught up into the relational life of God, not in the persistence of some inherently indestructible discrete entity.

Fundamental to any Christian view of the person is *love. Persons gain their dignity and value from their capacity to give and receive love. God as person represents the infinite source of that love sustained and enduring through the loving relations between Father, Son, and Holy Spirit. Present scientific advances in psychology, socio-biology, medicine, and *reproductive technology (with even the possibility perhaps of cloning) seem to be conspiring with a global reduction of the human individual to the status of consumer in an attack on the concept of the person and its infinite value. The defence of that concept is increasingly difficult but has never been more important. Christianity's attempts to ground that infinite value in the self-disclosure of a God constituted by love, who accords the dignity of personhood to each human individual as caught up in that love, may often have been flawed, but remain an important witness.   **Hugh S. Pyper**

McFadyen, A., *The Call to Personhood* (1990).
Nellas, P., *Deification in Christ: The Nature of the Human Person* (1987).
Schwöbel, C., and Gunton, C. (eds.), *Persons, Divine and Human* (1991).
Torrance, A. J., *Persons in Communion: Trinitarian Description and Human Participation* (1996).
Zizioulas, J. D., *Being as Communion: Studies in Personhood and the Church* (1985).

Peter. The code of Roman Canon Law (1983) starts the section 'Supreme Authority in the Church' by claiming that the responsibility and mission Christ gave to Peter remains in the bishop of the Church of *Rome, adding that the relation of the pope to the college of bishops perpetuates the relation of Peter to the other *apostles in the group (see PAPACY).

Why is Peter so important even today? Consider first one of the last pieces of the NT, the second letter of Peter. This is a pseudonymous document, perhaps c.110, in which a Christian author, using Peter's name and *authority, writes a reminder of many traditions concerning Peter and calls on the readers to continue after his death to follow faithfully his teaching. He concludes, significantly, by commending *Paul's writings. This letter thus shows how Peter's authority was perceived by the author and his early post-apostolic milieu. If 1 Peter is also, as seems, pseudonymous, it provides further evidence for this.

The Pauline epistles are the first witnesses to the place of Peter in the conscience of the Gentile *churches. We know through them that a 'Cephas party' existed in Corinth (1 Cor. 1: 12) and that Paul 'receives' and transmits the tradition that Cephas is the first of the apostles to whom the risen Lord appeared (1 Cor. 15: 5). More explicit is the epistle to the Galatians. Three years after beginning his ministry, Paul came to Jerusalem to meet not all the apostles but only Cephas and to spend fifteen days with him. He also met James, the brother of the Lord (Gal. 1: 18). He returned to Jerusalem fourteen years later, to communicate privately to those 'considered to be pillars' the content of his preaching. Cephas belongs with John to the three pillars, but is named after James. The three endorse the mission of Paul (and Barnabas) to the Gentiles, together with recognition of Cephas as leader of the mission to the circumcised. Later, in Antioch, Paul violently rebukes Cephas in front of the community (2: 11–21), because he ceased to eat with the Gentiles, for fear of James's disciples. So, from this Pauline literature, we know that Peter, called by the official name Cephas (rock), is considered as having important prérogatives (first witness, then leader of the mission to the Jews). But he is not separate from the other ministers of the church (James, John) and, like them, remains under the judgement of the gospel.

In a different way, the twelve first chapters of Acts reveal the same vision. Peter is recognized by the apostolic community as the first of the apostles: leader, not only spokesman. He takes the lead when the good of the church and the mission are at stake. He asks the community to replace *Judas (Acts 1: 15–22). As spokesman of the group he preaches (2: 14–36) and defends the gospel before civil courts (4: 7–12). He judges (5: 1–10), arbitrates (15: 7–11), visits the communities (9: 32–43), works *miracles (3: 1–10; 5: 1–11; 9: 32–42), and is himself miraculously delivered from jail (12: 1–18). Having received from God the authorization to baptize Cornelius and his family he is also the pioneer of the mission to the Gentiles (10: 1–48). At the Council of Jerusalem he defends Paul and Barnabas and the evangelical freedom of converts (15: 7–11). Peter is here portrayed as leader in the apostolic church, but not as a freelance or unaccountable leader. For instance, during the Council of Jerusalem it is James who pronounces the final authoritative speech. The letter sent to the churches of the Gentiles is written in the name of 'the apostles, the elders and the brethren' (15: 13–21, 23). After the meeting with Cornelius, the church in Jerusalem *as such* obliged Peter to justify and defend his decision to preach the Word of God to the Gentiles (11: 1–4). After his release from prison, he asks the disciples to inform James and the brethren (12: 17). It is the apostolic community which sends him, together with John, to Samaria (8: 14).

The authors of the Synoptic Gospels are clearly convinced that Simon who was given by *Jesus the new name of 'Cephas' (rock: in Greek *petros* and thus Peter) received authority and a unique position by Christ's explicit choice. If he is always the first in the list of apostles (Matt. 10: 2–4; Mark 3: 16–19; Luke 6: 14–16), the first of the *disciples called by Jesus (Matt. 4: 18–22; Mark 1: 16–20; Luke 5: 1–11), a member of a small group who seem to have a more intimate relation with Jesus (Mark 5: 35–43; 9: 2–8; etc.), the first of the

apostles to meet the risen Lord (Luke 24: 34; Mark 16: 7), it is certainly with reference to a well-known attitude of Christ himself. This is confirmed by certain signs, such as miraculous interventions (Matt. 14: 28–9; 17: 27). It is also significant that the most important declarations of the gospel are often answers to questions asked by Peter or to situations in which he is involved (Matt. 15: 15; 17: 4; etc.).

This background explains the two major declarations of the synoptic tradition on the role and person of Peter, Luke 22: 31–2 and Matt. 16: 16–19. Luke's context is crucial: the Last Supper, with the apostles discussing which one of them is the first. Having rebuked them, Jesus affirms that the twelve will together judge the twelve tribes of Israel. Then he speaks to Simon alone. He announces that all the disciples will be tempted but that he has prayed for him, that his faith should not fail. This is followed by a specific commission. Once converted, he will have the mission to strengthen his brethren. In spite of this commission Peter will, like the others, betray his Lord. Two elements of this text need stressing: the association of Simon with the twelve in both the eschatological kingdom and in the betrayal of Jesus, the emphasis on his faith which needs to be much more than a fragile enthusiasm.

Matthew's text is the only place in the NT where Peter is identified with the rock on which Christ builds the church. Here again, he is the spokesman for the disciples (16: 13–16) but a spokesman under a personal revelation coming directly from the Father. He receives this revelation in order to confess authentically the faith of the whole group. Since his confession expresses, in the name of all, what Jesus really is, Cephas thus proclaims the faith on which the Church of God has to be for ever constructed. This is the rock which will remain the church's foundation. Accordingly, Peter, the first to proclaim the core of apostolic faith, receives the keys of the kingdom, the power to declare where the faith is or is not, where the gospel is or is not obeyed. How? It is not said. The fathers, especially *Augustine and Leo, refuse to separate this power and the power given to the whole church in Matt. 18: 18–20.

The Johannine dossier is more subtle. In chapter 6, Peter is again seen as the one who confesses the right faith (6: 67–9), although his own faith is always in need of strengthening (13: 6–11). Even the Beloved Disciple, the one who never abandons the Master, the perfect witness of the main events of Christ's life, acknowledges Peter's authority. He lets Simon Peter be the first to enter the sepulchre (20: 1–10). Chapter 21 (certainly an addition to the first redaction of the book) shows the risen Lord formally commissioning Peter, giving him the task of feeding his lambs and sheep, even though he betrayed him during the Passion. This chapter seems clearly intended to teach the Johannine communities, wounded by internal struggles, the need of the kind of authority represented by Peter.

A serious study of the NT thus shows Peter as formally commissioned by Christ to take the lead when fundamental issues concerning the church are at stake. But this commission is always inseparable from that of the whole group of apostles or disciples. It is also inseparable from repeated insistence on Peter's personal weakness, his enduring fallibility, and his capacity actually to provide false witness. Thus it is striking how Mark, while omitting Jesus' saying 'You are Peter and on this rock I will build my church', records a few verses later the vehement rebuke 'Get thee behind me, Satan! Because the way you think is not God's way but man's'

(Mark 8: 33). The story of the Passion is littered with rebukes of Peter, culminating in his own terrible words, 'I know not the man you speak of' (Mark 14: 71). Even after the *Resurrection, it was still necessary to recognize that Peter could be 'manifestly in the wrong', requiring Paul to 'oppose him to his face' (Gal. 2: 11). Insistence upon this side of Peter's NT delineation does not invalidate the other side, but it provides an essential facet of the picture without which any portrayal of Peter's leadership will be gravely misleading.

Nothing is explicitly said, in the NT, of a journey of Peter to Rome and his *martyrdom in this city. But there is, both in the earliest tradition and in archaeological evidence, overwhelming support for his presence and death there. The crucial question remains: was Peter supposed to have successors? Here again the NT is silent. As witnesses of the Resurrection, apostles cannot have real successors. According to the ancients, possession of the bodies of the martyrs creates a profound link between their person, their work, and the place of their burial. This is where they continue to be present and where their authority in a certain way remains. So it is affirmed that Peter and Paul continue to preside over the see of their martyrdom through its bishop, who is their vicar, their 'memory'.

During the first centuries, the bishops of Rome are conscious that by being in communion with them one enters into communion with Peter. Leo I will still proclaim in the 5th century that Peter does not cease to preside on his apostolic chair (*Sermo*, 5. 4), exactly as (in 314) the Council of Arles had declared that Sylvester I was bishop in the city where the two apostles continue to preside and to glorify God by their martyrdom. Around the 5th century, however, another title, that of *successor* (rather than *vicar*) of Peter appears but, until the Middle Ages, it does not supersede the traditional title. Nevertheless, western understanding of *episcopal succession slowly comes to forget the 'once-for-all' transcendence of the apostolic group. Thus Peter comes to have 'successors'. Moreover, since he is now considered to be the *vicar of Christ* as affirmed at the Council of *Florence, his successor also is *vicar of Christ*. Robert Bellarmine, the 17th-century Jesuit theologian, even declared it improper to call the pope 'vicar of Peter'. He is 'the vicar of Christ'. *Vatican I repeated this solemnly.

Such a view opens the door to a cult of the papacy and an uncritical reception of everything coming from the Roman see. It is hardly surprising that the development in the *Middle Ages of a 'monarchical' papacy led both eastern Christians and Protestants to emphatic rejection of Roman claims for Peter's authority. This is not, however, good reason to reject the NT evidence that Peter was accorded both by Jesus and by the early church a position of exceptional authority, a recognition that included considerable stress upon his personal unworthiness.   **J.-M. R. Tillard**

Brown, R., Donfried, K., and Reumann, J., *Peter in the New Testament* (1973).
Brown, R., and Meier, J., *Antioch and Rome* (1983).
Brown, S. K., and Griggs, C. W., *The Apocalypse of Peter: Introduction and Translation* (1977).
Cullman, O., *Peter, Disciple, Apostle, Martyr*, 2nd edn. (1962).
Grappe, C., *Images de Pierre aux deux premières siècles* (1995).
Nau, Arlo J., *Peter in Matthew* (1992).
O'Connor, D. W., *Peter in Rome* (1969).
Smith, T., *Petrine Controversies in Early Christianity* (1988).
Tillard, J.-M. R., *The Bishop of Rome* (1983).

philosophy. In ancient Greece, philosophy included virtually all branches of higher learning. Socrates transformed philosophy so that enquiry was to lead one to a life of virtue and happiness. In the Middle Ages philosophy as a way of life, in contrast to being a Christian, was not a practical alternative. The material available from the ancient world was avidly studied and attempts to advance enquiry were made. The main focus of interest, however, was to use philosophy to increase one's knowledge of *God by stating Christian doctrines in a systematic form and with greater precision. With *Descartes, the father of modern philosophy, it became the source of new, clear, organizing principles for the advancement of knowledge and it sought to supply a unifying world-view. During the 20th century this concept has largely been superseded by new proposals, such as analytic philosophy, phenomenology, *hermeneutics, and most recently *postmodernism. Each conceives of philosophy so differently and uses such different methods, however, that it is virtually impossible for any individual to master more than one of them.

This entry is concerned with philosophy only in so far as it has decisively affected Christian thought, and in turn been decisively affected. First, it will illustrate the fashion in which ancient philosophy affected the foundations of Christian thought, both the bible and the early formulations of Christian *orthodoxy. Then, it will trace the way Christian thought interacted with four major philosophic issues: the notion of the self, the status of the universe, the scope of *reason, and the transition from Greek essentialism to contingency. Finally, it will discuss the relationship between philosophy and Christian believing in recent years.

Greek philosophy and Christian thought

Ancient philosophy was fully formed several centuries before Christianity arose and its impact on it was so immense that 'it helped change the Christian church from an obscure Jewish sect into a worldwide civilizing force' (Stead 1994: frontispiece). Christian *theology is inherently Hellenic because it could not exist as a *discipline* without the kind of intellectual curiosity that was unique to ancient Greece. The ancient Egyptians said that the Greeks were like children always asking, 'Why?' It is not that other ancient people did not ask for the whys and wherefores of many things. It is rather that the Greeks asked questions persistently and systematically as a deliberate programme until they developed the very idea of disciplines—areas of *theoretical* knowledge defined by principles and investigated by appropriate methods of enquiry. A practical problem, such as the need to determine the boundaries of a piece of property, might start an investigation, but the various rules of thumb concerning the relation of lines to angles were not allowed to remain just rules of thumb even though they were perfectly satisfactory for all practical purposes. They were pushed until the theoretical science of geometry was created. So too Socrates persisted in asking people what *justice, courage, *friendship, and piety were, rejecting the examples cited as inadequate for understanding the essential idea they were intended to illustrate.

There are many instances in the *Old Testament of persistent questioning and enquiry, such as, 'Why do the righteous suffer and the wicked prosper?' This arises out of a practical concern over the justice of God, and the yearning for deliverance. It did not lead to formulating the general problem of *evil, how to reconcile divine goodness, power, and knowledge with the existence of evil. That was first done by the Greek philosopher Epicurus (c.300 BC). In addition, the range of questions is much more limited in the OT than in ancient Greece. The early Christian fathers sought to retain a proper sense of mystery, but their minds were Hellenic. They persistently asked of the bible, 'How is that so?' thereby creating the discipline of theology, prizing coherence, organizing principles, and intelligibility. When people today sometimes call for the purging of Greek philosophy from Christian theology, unless they are referring to specific ideas or concepts, they are really calling for the end of the discipline of theology itself, though they may not realize it.

Specific ideas and concepts were indeed of immense importance. Greek ideas that were consonant with Jewish ones were used in the *New Testament itself. Heraclitus' (c.500) *Logos, the principle constituting each individual reality and organizing the cosmos, was used for the Hebrew *dabar* in translating Genesis 1 into Greek, and later in *John's gospel (1: 1–14) for the Word of God by which all things were made, which is said to have become flesh, and is identified with *Jesus.

Some Greek concepts were also used to formulate crucial doctrinal definitions, when all parties to a dispute could affirm the relevant scriptural passages, but interpret them differently. So extra-biblical words were used to formulate the doctrine of the *Trinity as *mia ousia, treis hypostaseis*, translated into English (closely following the Latin) as 'one substance, three persons' (Council of *Nicaea, 325). The controversies concerning the relation of the divine and human in the *person of Christ resulted in the formulation 'one person in two natures,' encouraged by the platonic notion that the human soul as a spiritual substance could exist unembodied. In the *Incarnation, the word of God has, besides a divine nature, a human one as well.

Throughout Christian history the widespread Greek contrasts between being and becoming, the intelligible and the sensible, the *soul and *body—with the former of each pair being more fundamental—have played rich and diverse roles, for good and evil. For example, the Christian pilgrimage towards *holiness and union with God has often included spiritual mastery of the bodily passions in a fashion similar to that of the Stoics, although the aim is not independence, but *obedience to God.

Yet if Christianity was changed by the philosophy that came before its own time so too did it change it. The western philosophical tradition bears the deep impress of Christianity to this day. We will now trace the effects of Christian thought on four major philosophic issues.

The notion of the self

The platonic opposition of spirit–matter, higher–lower, eternal–temporal, immutable–changeable is described by *Augustine in terms of inner–outer. The road from lower to higher passes through attending to our own inwardness. The light of God does not just illumine the order of being, as in *Plato's allegory of the sun, but is also an inner light that illumines that inner space where I am present to myself. This is to experience myself in a way no one else does; it is a first-person standpoint. 'The modern epistemological tradition from Descartes … has made this standpoint fundamental. … It has gone as far as generating the view that there is a

special domain of "inner objects" available only from this standpoint; or the notion that the vantage point of the "I think" is somehow outside the world of things we experience' (Taylor 1989: 131).

Augustine is neither his predecessor (Plato) nor his successor (Descartes). However that may be, Augustine's stress on God's presence to each person as an irreducible individual is rooted in the Christian conviction that because of God's *love each of us is of indefeasible value. The indefeasible value of every person is present in every western ethical philosophy in the Christian era, and underlies our system of jurisprudence and liberal democracy. In spite of *Kant's heroic efforts, no *ethical theory is able to sustain this conviction independently of this Christian belief. In addition, attempts to make ethics autonomous fail to recognize the relevance for ethics of a Christian understanding of the goal of human life.

The status of the universe

The biblical view of God as creator is so familiar to us that its role as the foundation of all Christian theology and its effect on philosophy may not be apparent. The *Genesis stories of *creation make it clear that the universe has a beginning and is therefore not everlasting nor ultimate. The difference between God and the universe is more fundamental than any distinction between any two things that are part of the universe. Things that begin are contingent; that which is everlasting is necessary. Particular beings, such as leaves and trees, may be contrasted to matter and energy which, according to our *science, are conserved in all transformations. But the contrast between members of the universe, such as leaves and trees on the one hand, and matter and energy on the other, is not as fundamental as that between God and the universe. Matter and energy, like leaves and trees, are contingent. Even though they are conserved in all transformations, they and indeed the entire universe began. They and it may end, should God so will. God, moreover, does not need a universe to be complete in himself. God without a universe is not less in being and goodness than God with a universe. God in himself is utterly full and self-sufficient.

Such a view is entirely different from those of all the ancient philosophers for whom the universe always has existed. Even Plato, who in the *Timaeus* describes the origins of the sensible world, has eternal forms as the pattern of the sensible world, and assumes space and a given material for its formation.

The Jewish belief in a creator did not spring from a desire to discover the principles of nature's operations, nor to account for its existence. It is a response to God's initiative, not their investigation of nature's order or origin.

This raises the important question, 'Had God not chosen to reveal himself, would *Israel or anyone else have realized that such a deity existed?' Or, put otherwise, is there anything about the universe, its order or very existence, which gives a basis to the claim that it has an intelligent source? Thomas *Aquinas's treatment of this question led to the category of *natural theology. At its core are Aquinas's 'five ways' to what 'men call God,' and today these are referred to as the traditional proofs of God's existence. They are part of the subject-matter of both philosophy and theology. Philosophers of religion examine what the sheer existence of the universe entails (the cosmological argument), and likewise what its order entails (the teleological, or *design, argument). *Anselm's *ontological argument, by which the idea of God as 'that than which no greater or better can be conceived' is said to imply God's existence, is also to be included among the traditional proofs of God's existence.

Philosophers of religion now generally follow the refutations of those traditional proofs formulated by David Hume in his *Dialogues Concerning Natural Religion* (1779) and by Immanuel Kant in *The Critique of Pure Reason* (1781). Protestant theologians often reject natural theology, following *Pascal's lead. 'What has the God of Abraham, Isaac, and Jacob to do with the God of the philosophers?' Even should any of the traditional proofs be sound, this would not, according to Søren *Kierkegaard, lead one from unbelief to *faith and, according to Karl *Barth, the 'god' whose existence is demonstrated is just the top storey of the universe, not a creator.

Many Protestant and Roman Catholic thinkers, however, do not consider the various proofs of God's existence from nature as rigorous demonstrations, nor as moving the mind from unbelief to belief. They argue that the mind can, none the less, apprehend God to some extent by reflection on God's nature, the natural world, and human experience. General revelation, as it is called, is possible because the created universe, including human beings, bears some indications of dependence on God. This has received some support by recent developments in philosophy and *science.

Thus in philosophy William Rowe has shown that Hume and Kant fail to exclude the questions, why does the universe exist? why does it have this order rather than another? (*The Cosmological Argument* (1975)). Comparable is the realization among many scientists that even an exhaustive knowledge of the laws of nature cannot tell us why the universe has the members it has (and hence their laws), rather than other possible members (and hence different laws). Nature's membership and workings are contingent, not necessary. Nor can we determine why we have a universe at all from a study of what is actually here. Science simply takes the existence of the world as a given.

According to recent *cosmology the order of our universe has a beginning. The biblical story that the world began and exists only because of the divine will is thus supported to the extent that it is clear that the universe is neither necessary nor self-explanatory. This does not prove the existence of God; for the universe may simply have no explanation at all. None the less, God's existence would account for its existence and actual laws.

The scope of reason

The topic of our knowledge of God leads to the third major philosophic issue, the scope of reason. God as fundamentally distinct from all creatures poses a serious issue for a mind that is Hellenized, always asking, 'Why is this so?' This is the case whether the person is a theologian or a philosopher. For a Christian mind the Hellenic attitude must be tempered by reverence for the nature of God. It must recognize that however much it may want fully to understand, God as complete in Godself, inexhaustibly rich, lacking nothing, exceeds such an understanding. The universe consists of beings which we classify according to their likenesses and differences into various kinds of beings. But God is not one being among others, but the continuous source of all other beings. Concepts by which we understand different classes of thing within the world do not enable us to comprehend God fully because God does not fall under any classification within which we place creatures.

For ancient Greeks all reality was in principle comprehensible since the human mind had affinity with the cosmos. Nothing was inherently alien to the human mind. The introduction of the notion of the biblical God meant not only limitations to theological enquiry, but also a tension between theology and philosophy concerning the relation of faith and reason. Even though philosophy itself does not utilize a revelation received by faith, divine transcendence implies that the human mind is limited.

Descartes's effort to render everything (but God) to the clarity of transparency reached its culmination in the 20th century among Logical Positivists, such as Rudolf Carnap, and linguistic philosophers from G. E. Moore to John Austin. In such an atmosphere Christian thinkers have felt pressured to abandon the transcendence of God or reinterpret it along mundane lines. In general, among philosophers it is assumed that to rely on faith is *ipso facto* to have abandoned reason.

In ancient theology, however, faith involves the enlargement, not the abandonment, of reason. As Basil the Great points out (*Hexameron, c.*365), guided by revelation we can read the Books of Nature and direct our lives properly, rather than remain undecided between various speculations. The profound understanding of different *paradoxes of human nature and *history that is possible for a mind exercised by divine revelation is perhaps most impressively exhibited by Augustine. His approach was applied in fresh ways by Pascal (*Pensées* (1670)), Reinhold *Niebuhr (*The Nature and Destiny of Man* (1941–3)), and Simone *Weil (*Waiting For God* (1951)). The light revelation casts on ultimate questions and the spiritual nourishment they mediate lead to intellectual conviction. Few philosophers today are aware of this traditional understanding of the relation of faith and reason. Most continue to treat theological doctrines from an Evidentialist position classically stated by William Clifford (1845–79) in 'The Ethics of Belief'.

From essentialism to contingency

The fourth major philosophic issue Christian thought has affected is that of essentialism. A hallmark of modern and contemporary philosophy is the progressive recognition of the implications of nature's contingency. The ancient Greek notion of theoretical disciplines rested on the conviction that nature was rational through and through, and capable of being understood by human reason. Individuals, as a particular person or the particular colour of a flower, cannot be understood or defined in their particularity. They can be referred to, however, by being grouped into classes according to their similarities, called species by *Aristotle, ('man', 'yellow'). Species, in turn, can be grouped into still larger classes, genera ('animal', 'colour'). These 'general words', universals as they are called, enable us to talk about many individuals and their qualities.

The introduction into western Europe, from the end of the 12th century, of an increasing number of hitherto inaccessible Aristotelian texts led to a rethinking of the entire Christian intellectual tradition. The ontological status of the referents of general words was at the core of the medieval examination of the nature of knowledge. Aquinas rejected the earlier platonic view known as ultrarealism in which the universal is a thing that exists extra-mentally and prior to sense objects.

Aquinas himself endorsed a realism based on Aristotle in which individuals that are like one another have the same common or essential nature which makes them what they are. The intellect is able to abstract from sensible particulars their common natures. These abstractions are the concepts by which we know particulars. Such concepts have no existence independent of the mind, as do Plato's Forms, yet since they refer to common natures in extramental reality, they are not subjective.

The break with ancient and medieval rationalism is largely the result of William of Ockham's rejection of common natures or Forms. This destroys the main causal principle of Aristotle's philosophy, the movement from potency to act; for in Aristotle matter and common natures (Forms) are related as potency and act. With the rejection of Forms matter cannot be a potentiality, but is actual in its own right. Causality becomes efficient cause. One thing is known to be the cause of another if, when it is present, the effect follows, and when it is not present, the effect does not occur. This can be known only by experience, and beyond our experience is only probability. Aquinas' project of natural theology as the crown of all natural knowledge—with philosophy serving as a hand-maiden of theology—is undermined. Ockham relegates the existence of God, along with everything else in theology, to the sphere of faith.

Ockham believed that nature operates in an orderly way because of God's will (Voluntarism), not because God's mind contains exemplars according to which common natures are patterned (Essentialism). Thus the order and structure of the natural world is not necessary. By effectively challenging the hitherto widely held rationalism of Plato and Aristotle, Ockham's Voluntarism opened the door to different possible ways to explain nature's order and movement, and it was far more conducive to a quantitative and experimental approach towards nature. It was fully exploited by *Galileo and Descartes.

Aristotle's view of nature received its fatal wounds primarily from Galileo's work on falling bodies and Descartes's philosophical analysis of the essential properties of bodies. They considered only the mathematical properties of bodies to be essential and objectively present in bodies. All other properties as they appear to our senses, such as colour, texture, smell, taste, are the result of the size, shape, and motion of matter on our sense-organs. Nature is regarded as a vast, impersonal machine, with mechanical causality (impact) as the sole cause of change. Since matter is uniform, all nature can be described by universal laws in contrast to Aristotle's hierarchical universe in which each individual seeks to actualize its own specific form, and heavenly bodies are vastly superior to sublunar ones.

Francis Bacon's *Novum Organum* (1620) popularized the contrast between Aristotle's contemplative attitude towards nature and an experimental approach. The new science Bacon envisioned would uncover 'the springs of nature' so that humans could control it to serve their own purposes. He stressed that it was a divinely given obligation to restore life as far as possible to the original paradise from which it had fallen. The promise of knowledge which could be used to improve life on earth became a widespread and powerful motive for science. At its root lay Christian love for humankind (*philanthropos*).

Universal laws of nature stimulated the search for universal laws for society, politics, law, morals, and religion, as seen in Thomas Hobbes's *The Leviathan* (1651), John Locke's *Second Treatise on Gov-ernment* (1689), and Hugo Grotius. God remained secure as creator and designer of the universe, but with the new mechanistic science he was not needed to keep the clockwork mechanism going. A natural religion (*deism) based solely on nature judged the bible unnecessary for knowledge of God, *miracles to be impossible, and obedience to universal moral laws as encompassing our entire duty towards God.

Never in the history of western culture did the teleological argument enjoy such widespread popularity; for it seemed utterly improbable that 'brute matter,' moving solely by collision, could arrange itself into such intricate order. Some great mind must have arranged its design. But this is also why the problem of evil (attempts to explain how evil is compatible with a benevolent designer) attracted such attention and led to so many theodicies, such as that of Gottfried Leibniz (1710). The proofs for God's existence and the problem of evil have never ceased to be the chief concerns of the philosophy of religion.

In fundamentally different ways Descartes and Locke were confident of our ability to increase our knowledge of a contingent universe because of God. For Descartes, God as perfectly good would not deceive us when our ideas are clear and distinct (his criteria of truth). The mind, however, must be trained to achieve clarity and distinctness in a fashion influenced both by Plato's stress on setting aside the senses and by Christian spiritual practices of meditation. (Descartes's major work is entitled *Meditations on First Philosophy*.) For Locke, there are no innate ideas that allegedly provide the principles of knowledge and morals. Although we must rely on probability for the most part, God has so arranged our world and equipped us that our sense experience and mental operations are sufficient for us to improve our material and social life, learn our duties, and exhibit the reasonableness of Christianity. But Hume's attempts to ground our ideas of material bodies in sense-impressions only, apart from God, released a virulent sense of contingency that has broken out periodically, most recently in 20th-century postmodernism. Indeed Kant's and *Hegel's efforts to reinstate confidence in our knowledge of nature and morality, as well as philosophically acceptable interpretations of Christianity, actually sowed the seeds of their own destruction.

In the *Critique of Pure Reason* Kant argued that experience is an appearance (phenomenon) because sense-impressions are ordered by our faculties of intuition and understanding ('impressions without concepts are blind') and that reason cannot know what is beyond all possible experience (*noumena*) because our faculties must be supplied with raw data to organize ('concepts without impressions are empty'). This 'Copernican Revolution'—objects conform to our minds, rather than our minds to objects—supplied the necessity and universality found in geometry and the principles of science. The price was heavy. It reduced knowledge to appearances with no hope of knowledge of things-in-themselves.

Hegel sought to overcome Kant's dualism of appearances and reality by introducing into philosophy the biblical view of history. Biblical history is directed by divine providence toward the realization of the *Kingdom of God, rather than being cyclical, on the model of the ceaseless repetitions of nature. For Hegel too the events of history are the bearers of ultimate truth and reality. In his *Phenomenology of Spirit* (1807) Hegel gave a narrative account of the rise of human consciousness, which at the same time is the manifestation and realization of Absolute Spirit. The opposition of subject and object in knowing and of finite and infinite in being are progressively overcome in the course of opposition and reconcili- ation in history, with a culmination in the realization by more and more people of their essential unity-in-difference with the Absolute, a consciousness first manifest in Jesus as the God-man.

The emphasis on the human contribution to the process of under- standing in German Idealism encouraged a heightened awareness of the effect of social location on all knowledge claims, values, and interpretations of texts. By the late 20th century this culminated in postmodernism's rejection of the modern world's claim to deter- mine universal principles in all fields of enquiry and activity. Build- ing on a variety of sources—hermeneutics, linguistic philosophy (especially *Wittgenstein), sociology of knowledge (especially Tho- mas Kuhn's *The Structure of Scientific Revolutions*, 1962), *Marxist analysis of ideology—it is asserted that all claims are so rooted in a particular culture or subculture as to lose all possibility of univer- sal validity. This has led to a revival of Friedrich *Nietzsche's total rejection of western values and civilization because its linchpin— God the guarantor of knowledge and value—is 'dead' (no longer a possible option). The future belongs to those who embrace a will to power. Michel Foucault and other postmodernists examine the role of power on knowledge and on social institutions, such as asylums and prisons, as well as on attitudes towards race, gender, and homosexual behaviour. They claim that those in power always suppress and victimize those who are not. Postmodernism, and the forces that have contributed to it, have encouraged pluralism, an increased concern for marginalized and oppressed people, and a heightened awareness of the effects of race, gender, and sexual orientation on social and political structures. At the same time they have led many to discount all claims to absolute knowledge and universal values, including Christian doctrinal and moral teach- ings.

The contemporary philosophical predicament

A major change in the relationship between philosophy and Chris- tian thought in the 20th century was the abandonment of the attempt to justify Christian belief in terms of German and British Hegelian Idealism. This was due in part to Barth's strong rejection of any philosophical justification for theology, but also to the rejec- tion of metaphysics by Logical Positivism, which was developed between the First and Second World Wars, first in Vienna and then in Britain. It regarded all statements as either analytic or synthetic, and claimed that all synthetic statements are empirical. It sought to show how all the statements in science can be reduced to sense observation statements or, when part of a theory, entail some ob- servation statements, which are verifiable. Only what is verifiable is meaningful. Logical Positivism claimed that the language of *meta- physics did not have this relation to sense observation and, accord- ingly, was meaningless. A. J. Ayer's *Language, Truth, and Logic* (1936) is the classic statement.

The main challenge to Christian belief did not come until 1949 in a very brief paper, 'Theology and Falsification', by Anthony Flew. He applied the Falsification Principle to belief in God as the designer of nature's order and to the belief that God loves us. According to the Falsification Principle, an utterance is meaningless unless some sense observation statement could in principle falsify it. To be a

truth-claim an utterance must exclude some state of affairs. If the existence or non-existence of God and God's love are judged com- patible with every imaginable state of affairs, then the words 'God' and 'God's love', however much they might mean emotionally, are empirically vacuous.

The Logical Positivists believed that they had the support of Wittgenstein, yet his *Philosophical Investigations* (1953) became the main source for a defence of the meaningfulness of *religious lan- guage in non-realist terms. R. B. Braithwaite in his essay 'An Em- piricist's View of the Nature of Religious Belief' (1955) used Wittgenstein's claim that language, rather than merely reporting and predicting sense experience, has many functions. Braithwaite argued that Christianity is primarily a commitment to an agapistic way of life, and that Christian beliefs function as stories that help specify and encourage one to adopt that way of life.

After the demise of Logical Positivism, undermined by the non- verifiability of its own principles, philosophy of religion became dominated by Richard Swinburne and Alvin Plantinga. Swinburne argues that the traditional proofs of God's existence may fail as precise demonstrations, but that on balance they indicate the prob- ability of God's existence. Plantinga holds that the ontological ar- gument is valid, but is unclear as to its religious usefulness. For him some Christian beliefs belong to a class of properly basic beliefs which may be rational even when they are not established by evi- dence. He has also elaborated and defended the theory that moral evil is the result of the misuse of our freedom, so that God is not morally culpable.

Much of the recent openness to a range of philosophic approaches is because Marxism, *Existentialism, and Logical Positivism have lost their attraction. A more positive reason is the removal of the absolute embargo on metaphysics. P. F. Strawson was perhaps the first important analytic philosopher to recognize the possibility of metaphysics in *Individuals* (1959) in which he distinguished *descrip- tive* from the hitherto dominant *prescriptive* metaphysics. Not only has this kind of distinction allowed a larger hearing to various neo- Thomist proposals, such as those of Bernard *Lonergan and Karl *Rahner, but it has also allowed contemporary theologians to draw upon a wide variety of philosophic works from ancient times to such contemporaries as Barthes, Foucault, *Ricœur, and Levinas.

See also THOMISM, MODERN; THOMISM, ANALYTICAL.

Diogenes Allen

Allen, Diogenes, *Philosophy for Understanding Theology* (1985).
—— *Christian Belief in a Postmodern World* (1989).
Armstrong, A. H., and Marcus, R. A., *Christian Faith and Greek Philoso- phy* (1960).
Brown, David, *Continental Philosophy and Modern Theology* (1985).
Buckley, Michael, *At the Origin of Modern Atheism* (1987).
Dupré, Louis, *Passage to Modernity* (1993).
Evans, G. R., *Philosophy and Theology in the Middle Ages* (1993).
Foster, Michael, *Mystery and Philosophy* (1957).
Gilson, Étienne, *The Spirit of Medieval Philosophy* (1936).
Mitchell, Basil, *Morality: Religious and Secular* (1980).
Sokolowski, Robert, *The God of Faith and Reason* (1982).
Stead, Christopher, *Divine Substance* (1977).
—— *Philosophy in Christian Antiquity* (1994).
Taylor, Charles, *Sources of the Self* (1989).

Pietism has been claimed as the most intense and profound attempt in the history of the church to realize the power of early

Christianity and has therefore never ceased to inspire. It is normally understood as a reform movement within the German *Lutheran church with Philip Jakob Spener (1635–1705) as its initiator. It could, however, be understood in a wider context as a certain development in piety found in different countries and churches during the 16th, 17th, and 18th centuries: the *Puritans and *Methodists in Anglican England, the *nadere reformatie* in the Reformed Netherlands, the *Jansenists in Catholic France and Belgium, and the Spiritualists and Pietists in *Protestant Germany. What binds them together is a particular personal experience of God known as rebirth, the consequence of which is commitment and growth in individual *holiness. Thus Pietism can be seen, in a narrow sense, as a reform movement within the German Lutheran church, and in a wider sense as an interconfessional development in piety during the centuries after the *Reformation.

To place Pietism in an even wider context one could see it as a consequence of the conflict between the doctrine of *salvation through *grace and God's requirement of individual holiness. The history of Christian thought is in part the history of the effort to maintain both without the one detracting from the other. The origins of every form of Pietism understood as a particular historical development can always be traced to the longing for commitment and individual holiness, wherever this longing is strong.

In Protestant Germany there was a widespread feeling that the Reformation had come to a standstill. Theology had become *orthodoxy. The question was: how is *faith to become real in life? How can we acquire a faith able to cope not only with original *sin but with actual sins and the growing uncertainty created by the disintegration of the *church and increasing *secularization?

The most influential critical voice in the period of post-Reformation orthodoxy was that of the Lutheran clergyman Johann Arndt (1555–1621). His devotional book *Vom wahren Christentum* (1605–9) had an extraordinary influence. Its aim is to lead the reader from orthodox belief in *justification, which is never questioned, to the experience of rebirth and individual holiness. In Arndt we find most of the characteristics of Pietism: revival of the *mystical tradition; life as verifying faith; the need for *penance, and for the experience of rebirth in which justification and individual holiness combine to restore the image of God in human beings.

With Spener Pietism became a sociologically identifiable movement through the practice of gathering the reborn in conventicles and thus establishing a church of true believers within the church (*Collegium pietatis*, 1670). The conventicle has been one of the most significant features of Pietism. Even more decisive was the *eschatology developed by Spener in his *Pia desideria* (1675). He was convinced of the imminent conversion of Israel and the fall of the Roman *Catholic Church, as promised, he believed, in the bible (Rom. 11; Rev. 18–19). He therefore rejected separatism in any form, seeing this vision of the future as involving the fulfilment of the church. He was reviving the old tradition called *chiliasm*, the idea that this age would end with the establishment of the *Kingdom of God, to last for a thousand years.

In *Pia desideria* Spener shows the way forward in six proposals: the centrality of the bible; encouragement of the faithful to exercise their universal *priesthood; realization that Christianity is about doing not knowing: *love is all that matters; avoidance of doctrinal controversies; centrality of bible study to the training for the *ministry; sermons aimed at sowing the faith that bears fruit.

At the centre of Spener's theology was the experience of rebirth, the creation of the new person. This was the passion that united all Pietists. This was the experience that could empower faith. In the concept of rebirth we find the Pietists' main concern: it expresses humanity's absolute passivity in salvation, just as in natural birth; it expresses the total change, the new status as God's child; it focuses on the necessity of development and growth. With this reborn person a new reality has entered the world.

In Spener the eschatological revolution was primarily a matter of *hope and expectation. Under the leadership of August Hermann Francke (1663–1727), professor at the University of Halle, Pietism developed a more active approach to eschatology. Francke aimed at nothing less than reform of the entire world. Barring the way to the Kingdom of God are the actual sins of the individual. The world could be changed by humanity's being changed. Early Christianity demonstrated that this was possible. At Halle, Franke implemented a methodology for education and conversion which became dominant in Pietism: breaking one's own will; intense penance followed by sudden *conversion; rejection of the 'world' and the so-called *adiaphora*; continuous self-testing. Halle Pietism, which became the dominant form of Pietism, put its stamp not only on church life in the greater part of the Lutheran world, even outside Germany and especially in *Scandinavia, but also on society as a whole with its Puritan ethics and lifestyle.

Pietism was a bible movement. The bible was the main means for the re-formation of humanity, the church, and the world. Hence the cultivation of bible study and the establishment of bible societies became task number one. The modern bible society is one of Pietism's most lasting fruits.

The notion of changing the world through changing humanity was an important factor in overcoming the negative attitude to *mission of orthodox Lutheranism. Pietism thus became the driving force in the missionary movement within the Protestant churches. Mission was a sign that the world was being changed.

An *ecumenical attitude was another important consequence of the basic theological principles in Pietism. The focus was on rebirth, the new life of individual communion with the risen Christ. Church institutions, the sacraments, and doctrinal differences were less important. What mattered was the common experience of spanning confessional divisions. Pietism thus became the first major ecumenical force within Protestantism.

Zeal for mission and an ecumenical attitude were especially dominant in one of the most distinctive offsprings of the pietistic movement, the Moravians. A group descended from the Bohemian Brethren and other Protestant emigrants settled in 1722 at an estate in Saxony, belonging to Nikolas Graf von Zinzendorf (1700–60). His idea was to gather all God's reborn children in a non-confessional fraternal society. Though the group was constituted as a separate denomination, they tried to realize the brotherly ideal by founding societies of people who sympathized with Zinzendorf's religion of the heart, without leaving their own church or denomination. Through these societies the Moravians' form of Christianity exerted influence far beyond their own borders.

The Moravians ran into conflict with the dominant Pietism of Halle by rejecting its conversion methodology. Zinzendorf's theology focused instead on intimate fellowship with the Redeemer, stressing the core of Lutheran theology: *atonement and justification by grace. 'We have perfection in Christ, never in ourselves.' This gave the Moravians a *joyful sense of salvation, contrasting with the struggle to achieve and maintain the state of grace characteristic of Halle Pietism. Such a struggle was regarded by Zinzendorf as a threat to the gospel, while the Halle Pietists for their part accused Zinzendorf of not taking individual sanctification seriously enough. It was on this question of Christian perfection that the founder of Methodism, John *Wesley, broke with Zinzendorf, though he was initially very much attracted by the Moravians and their joyful assurance of salvation.

One of the pietistic movement's most important achievements was its ability to channel spiritual *enthusiasm into the existing churches. The more radical elements with their separatist potential (Labadie, Petersen, Arnold, Dippel) were never dominant in Pietism. It is ironic that two movements within the pietistic tradition, Moravians and Methodists, became separate churches against the wishes of their founders.

In its many different forms Pietism has continued to be an important inspiration in the established Protestant churches by its simple bible piety, its focus on *religious experience as the fundamental element in religion, its zeal for mission, its concentration on the essence of salvation, and its ceaseless longing for and striving towards a Christianity that knows only one sort of Christian faith: the living faith that bears fruit.   **Trond Enger**

Brecht, M., Deppermann, K., Gäbler, U., Lehmann, H. (eds.), *Geschichte des Pietismus* (1993–9), i–iv.

Erb, P. C. (ed.), *Pietists: Selected Writings* (1983).

Greschat, M. (ed.), *Zur neueren Pietismusforschung* (1977).

Schmidt, M., Jannasch, W. (ed.), *Das Zeitalter des Pietismus* (1965).

Spener, P. J., *Pia desideria* (1675), ET (1980).

Stein, K. J., *Philipp Jakob Spener: Pietist Patriarch* (1986).

Stoeffler, E. F., *The Rise of Evangelical Pietism* (1965).

—— *German Pietism during the Eighteenth Century* (1973).

Wallmann, J., *Der Pietismus* (1990).

pilgrimage.

The practice of going to a sacred place to make offerings, ask favours, or share in the powers of a holy person, spirit, or deity is universal. The particular character of a pilgrimage varies depending upon theological, cultural, and historical circumstances. Within the Christian tradition the understanding of life as a pilgrimage appears in Hebrews 11: 13 and Philippians 3: 20. Every believer is a pilgrim (*peregrinus* or 'resident alien') whose true home is in heaven. This *ascetic view of pilgrimage was most highly developed in the Eastern and *Celtic churches, through either perpetual wandering or self-enforced exile and life as a hermit. With the conversion of *Constantine and decreased threat of persecution, Christians came to regard both *missionary exile and the hermit's life of prayer as a form of 'white' *martyrdom. Christian pilgrimage is, however, more commonly associated with specific journeys to holy places.

The Holy Land has a pre-eminent place in the history of Christian pilgrimage. Melito of Sardis (*c*.170) journeyed to Palestine to see for himself where *Jesus lived and taught. The 4th-century pilgrim Egeria also saw her visit to Egypt and Palestine as a quest for biblical origins. Like Ignatius Loyola, the 16th-century founder of the Jesuits, Egeria found that standing where Jesus had put his feet

brought the gospel stories alive and intensified her faith. After 372, several Roman women moved to Palestine, including Jerome's friend Paula and her daughter Eustochium. Paula opened a pilgrim hospice in Bethlehem, an important base for Latin Christians visiting the Holy Land. Despite political turmoil and the dangers and hardship of travel, increasing numbers of pilgrims visited Palestine from both eastern and western Christendom throughout the *Middle Ages. In 1384 the Franciscans were officially given the task of caring for the needs of visitors.

*Rome, as the seat of the pope and the site of the tombs of *Peter and *Paul, was a popular pilgrimage venue from the 2nd century. Indulgences (remission of penance, often understood as time remitted from *purgatory) could be gained by visiting the shrines of the apostles, a major motive for pilgrimage in the later Middle Ages. In 1300 Pope Boniface VIII instigated the Holy Year pilgrimage as a centennial event (celebrated every 25 years since 1470); guide books listing the indulgences associated with various shrines were added to the staff and scrip or bag as essential pilgrim's equipment. Pilgrims visiting Rome for the Holy Year in 2000 have probably been motivated by a desire to participate in witness at the centre of western Christendom, rather than to gain indulgences.

Not only sites associated with apostles drew medieval pilgrims. Walsingham, where a replica of the Holy Family's house of Nazareth was built in the 11th century, was known as 'England's Nazareth'. The shrine was destroyed in 1538, and restored only in 1922/3 by the Anglo-Catholic vicar of Walsingham, A. H. Patten. Today Walsingham is again a major pilgrimage centre, welcoming people from many Christian traditions, although the Anglican and Roman Catholic shrines (and gift shops) remain separate.

In *Protestant post-Reformation Europe, pilgrimage became a metaphor for life's spiritual journey; John Bunyan's *Pilgrim's Progress*, describing Christian's progress from 'the City of Destruction' to 'the Holy City', is one of the best-known examples. Greek and *Russian Orthodox, as well as Catholic pilgrims, continued to visit national and international shrines without the rupture caused by the Reformation in the west. In the 19th and 20th centuries places associated with *Marian apparitions have proved extraordinarily popular. Lourdes in France, where *Mary is said to have appeared to Bernadette Soubirous in 1858, Fatima in Portugal (1917), and Medjugorje in Bosnia-Hercegovina (1981 onwards), have all become major centres with highly organized commercial infrastructures. Most shrines are associated with healing, physical and spiritual, and may be visited to petition a favour or in thanksgiving. The hope of witnessing a *miracle cure or non-natural sign (a spinning sun, or weeping statue, for instance) testifies to an enduring faith in theophanies beyond the control of the institutional church.

Pilgrimages have always generated commercial activities. Pilgrims need to travel, to be fed and housed, and usually wish to purchase souvenirs. Shrines may also have guardians who need to be maintained. As Chaucer's *Canterbury Tales* vividly reminds us, the secular and spiritual elements of pilgrimage go hand in hand.

The late 20th century has seen an upsurge in the popularity of pilgrimages amongst all denominations. Papal masses and international youth days draw crowds of millions, while the Protestant monastic community of *Taizé in France hosts tens of thousands of visitors a year, particularly the young, and has spawned liturgical Taizé groups throughout the world. At the other end of the spectrum remote holy wells continue to be venerated, attracting offerings of flowers and other tokens from visitors. It is not always easy to draw the line between Christian and non-Christian pilgrimage. Inter-faith peace walks have many characteristics of a pilgrimage with their devotional intention and veneration of sacred sites. Glastonbury in Somerset, with its rich Christian and pre-Christian associations, is a focus of pilgrimage for increasing numbers of pagans and Christians. Modern pilgrimages frequently combine an interiorized attitude to religion with an element of public witness. To a desire for companionship is added an embodied, as opposed to intellectualized, attitude to faith. Despite the efforts of the Reformers to eradicate such 'superstitious' religious practices, the notion that some places or people mediate the sacred, and that merit can be gained by visiting them, continues to play a central role in religious thought.

See also FOLK RELIGION.   **Fiona Bowie**

Birch, D. J., *Pilgrimage to Rome in the Middle Ages: Continuity and Change* (1998).

Davies, J. G., *Pilgrimage Yesterday and Today: Where? Why? How?* (1988).

Eade, J., and Sallnow, M. (eds.), *Contesting the Sacred: The Anthropology of Christian Pilgrimage* (1991).

Nolan, M. L., and Nolan, S., *Christian Pilgrimage in Modern Western Europe* (1989).

Reader, I., and Walter T. (eds.), *Pilgrimage in Popular Culture* (1993).

Turner, V., and Turner, E., *Image and Pilgrimage in Christian Culture: Anthropological Perspectives* (1978).

Pilgrim's Progress

Pilgrim's Progress (1678), an *allegorical *novel, was written in prison by John Bunyan, a tinker. Unsophisticated Christians loved the book at once; only after a century did educated people discover it was a classic of English literature. Modern students quite often respond to it in 18th-century tones: the man is a narrow *Puritan, consigning us all to *hell; the characters have such obvious allegorical names (the hero is called 'Christian'); and there are even sermons, with numbered points.

Bunyan was a Puritan, in prison for unauthorized *preaching. Puritanism was not a naive peasant religion. Characteristically it involved an almost too logical scheme of *salvation, a rather unnerving psychological insight, and an existential drive for individual authenticity that separated sheep from goats only too well. All this is there in *Pilgrim's Progress*, more or less disconcertingly. But ordinary Christians loved it. Partly this is because the book succeeds as an adventure, a romance: what new terror will Christian meet over the hill? But partly it was because English-speaking Christianity was more Puritan at heart than many people like to think. Christian may not be Everyman, because he arrives at the Celestial City, while most of those he encounters do not, but his experience of struggle, failure, and divine *grace resonated for ordinary Christians. Even if the character the reader identifies with is Ignorance, with his moderate-minded self-justification ('I will never believe that my heart is thus bad'), there will always be a stab of self-doubt at the final terrible paragraph of Part I, when Ignorance is carried off from the gate of the City: 'Then I saw that there was a way to hell, even from the gates of heaven.' Perhaps the Puritans were right.

Earlier literal *pilgrimages were an interlude in life; this pilgrimage is life, and on through *death. The urgency frightens: 'the man began to run ... his wife and children perceiving it, began to cry after him to return; but the man put his fingers in his ears, and ran on, crying, Life! life! eternal life!' Few of those who blame Bunyan for his *Protestant individualism ever read the second part of *Pilgrim's Progress* (1684) where Christian's wife and *family make the journey too. This is social Puritanism, family-minded, travelling as a group. The thumb-nail sketches are of flawed Christians, not hell-fodder. They are often happy. 'So Ready-to-Halt took Despondency's daughter, named Much-Afraid, by the hand, and to dancing they went in the road. True, he could not dance without one crutch in his hand: but, I promise you, he footed it well.' In an allegory, Puritans can dance.

Pilgrim's Progress was second only to the bible in the esteem of Protestant Christianity for three hundred years. In its own country it is now largely read by academics and, with some of the Puritanism removed, by small children. Translated into over a hundred languages, in Africa and elsewhere it has appealed across cultural boundaries and stimulated forms of folk Protestantism less intellectual than Bunyan's Puritanism.

See also HEAVEN.   **Alistair Mason**

Keeble, N. H., *John Bunyan, Conventicle and Parnassus* (1988).

Mullett, M. A., *John Bunyan in Context* (1996).

Sharrock, Roger (ed.), *Bunyan, The Pilgrim's Progress: A Casebook* (1976).

Plato and Platonism.

Plato and Platonism. Whether *Christianity ought to be tied up with Greek *philosophy, and with Platonism in particular, has been an issue since the church's earliest years. The 2nd-century theologian Tatian, who accuses Plato of gluttony and plagiarism, played off Greek thought as a whole against the simple purity of Christianity. A generation later, Tertullian famously asked, 'What has Athens to do with Jerusalem?' But the idea that the true core of Christianity is to be discovered only once we have scraped away the accretions of Greek philosophy does not come to play a prominent part in Christian thought until the modern era. The main figure here is Adolf Harnack (1851–1930), who regarded the early *dogmatic statements of the church as hopelessly contaminated by Hellenism, particularly by Platonism. The most recent major contribution to the controversy has been that of Heinrich Dörrie, who defends the church fathers by arguing that Platonism was known in the ancient church to be incompatible with Christianity and that any apparent Platonism is mere window-dressing, intended to attract educated pagans to the faith and nothing more.

Before addressing these issues, it is necessary to come to some understanding of Plato and Platonism. What is said here must remain rough and approximate, for Plato's philosophy is extremely subtle and the list of philosophers who might be described as Platonists extends from Plato's own times to the present day and includes thinkers of enormous diversity. Plato (429–347 BC) left some twenty-five dialogues plus the *Apology* and a number of letters. The works with the most direct influence upon Christian theology are *Republic*, *Parmenides*, and *Timaeus*. *Republic* contains the famous Myth of the Cave, about nascent philosophers' progress towards the realm of pure Ideas or Forms, and the Myth of Er, which proposes a sort of reincarnation by chance and by choice. Closely associated with the Cave is 'the image of the line' according to which the universe is divided into the sensible and intelligible orders, then each of these divided once again, progress in knowledge thereby being depicted as a graduated separation from the material world. At the highest point, one leaves behind even the intelligible extension that characterizes mentally-posited geometrical objects, and relies only on definitions. This is the realm of the purely intelligible, the realm of immobile pure Ideas (or Forms), in which other things participate. While discussing another image ('the image of the sun'), Plato associates this highest intelligible order with the Good and says that things owe their existence to it, 'although the Good is not being, but superior to it in rank and power' (509b9–10). This latter remark, interpreted as meaning that the highest intelligible order is utterly transcendent, above even being, becomes a shibboleth for a number of later Platonists.

Parmenides, evidently composed after *Republic*, is a work difficult to speak about with any degree of definiteness. It is the ultimate source of the negative (or 'apophatic') theology of many Christian theologians, which looks not to the positive things we can say about God but rather to what we cannot say. In the dialogue, the character Parmenides presents some very telling arguments against the Platonic Theory of Forms, and yet the theory is never retracted. He also puts forward a series of hypotheses which appear to undermine his own position that all is one; but neither is that theory retracted. The upshot of the first hypothesis is that nothing at all can be said about the One; of the second hypothesis, that everything can be said of it. There then follow six other hypotheses, most having to do with what can be said about the things 'other than the One'. It turns out that, similarly, both everything and nothing can be said about these things.

Timaeus includes a very elaborate account of the principles of the universe and another account of the making of man's body and soul, both accounts being presented as inexact myth. In the first, a sort of God, the Demiurge, appears, although he is apparently not the highest of beings since in creating the world he gazes at the Ideas, his models. Nor apparently is his *creation *ex nihilo*; it is rather a bringing of order to a formless mass ('the Receptacle'), the whole process involving the creation of a rational World Soul. Plato enunciates clearly in this account the very important principle of sufficient cause, maintaining that God is the best of all such causes. He also calls God 'the maker and father' of the universe, knowledge of whom is difficult, to speak of whom to all impossible (28c3–5). In the second account, the Demiurge delegates the construction of men to beings whom he begets. These, imitating the Demiurge, accomplish the task by placing immortal rational *souls into *bodies which serve as 'vehicles' (69c5–d6). It is remarks such as this that lead to the frequent characterization of Plato's anthropology as *dualistic.

The influence of Plato arrives in Christianity almost always having been filtered through one or another later version of Platonism. Besides the 'Old Academy', the school established by Plato himself, the two main schools are Middle Platonism and Neoplatonism, Plotinus (205–70) marking the beginning of the latter and being its most prominent figure. There are, however, so many variations among the members of 'Platonic' schools that it is best to regard these groupings as temporal rather than doctrinal. The focus here is upon a few representative figures.

The Old Academy included two philosophers who introduced—or, at least, emphasized for the first time—ideas taken up by later Platonists. The first, Speusippus, holds that the highest principle, the One, is different from the Good and transcendent, even above

being. The second figure, Xenocrates, identifies the highest principle as One, Zeus, Good, Father, and (as in *Aristotle) Mind. Below the One is another, subsidiary God: the Diade (the Two) who is female. Both Speusippus and Xenocrates have a tendency to derive multiple entities from the higher principles, a tendency taken to absurd limits in *Gnosticism, a later religious movement which, at least in some of its manifestations, had connections with Christianity. This tendency to derive 'emanations' is not found in Plato, although his remarks at, for instance, *Timaeus*, 69c, invite such further elaborations.

A representative figure of Middle Platonism is Albinus (2nd century AD). Albinus draws much on Xenocrates and to some extent Aristotle, speaking, in the very important tenth chapter of his *Didaskalikos*, of a 'First God' who is Mind and whose thoughts are the Platonic Ideas, which latter bring order to formless matter (as in *Timaeus*). The First God is also called *Father because he is the cause of all things and 'in accordance with his will, he has filled all things with himself'. Below the Father can be discerned two other entities, Mind and Soul; but the three tend to spill over into one another. Albinus is much concerned with the words we use to name God ('eternally perfect', 'being', 'good'), and identifies three ways of arriving at such knowledge: by negation, by *analogy, and by an ascending from the contemplation of worldly things to immersion in 'the great ocean of the beautiful'.

In Plotinus (the most prominent Neoplatonist), the 'hypostases' within the divine—the One, Mind, and Soul—are more clearly distinct than in Albinus. He explicitly associates the One ('the Father of cause, that is of Mind') with Plato's 'the Good' and Mind with the Demiurge, and the separate existence of the latter is more apparent than it was in Plato's *Timaeus*. In many respects Plotinus is closer to Speusippus than to Xenocrates, putting forward a negative theology according to which God is not—but is rather above being. We can say that the One is one, argues Plotinus, but strictly speaking this is not so; also, it is better not to say that the One is good (as if an attribute might apply to him), but rather that he is the Good. In short, for Plotinus, God is transcendent.

How then did Platonism influence Christianity? Did its use by Christian intellectuals distort the gospel message? These are, of course, huge questions and, as with Platonism itself, we can speak only in generalities. Let us consider three pivotal themes: God's transcendence, the *Trinity, and Platonic anthropology.

With respect to the first, we have already seen that the negative theology which is strong within Christian theology can be traced back to Plotinus, Speusippus, and Plato himself. Certainly these ideas helped Christians—who were, of course, committed to the doctrine that God had become man—to ensure that God was none the less conceived of as comprising in his power the whole of the universe. It is one of the ironies of theology that the more transcendent God becomes the closer he gets to the particular and non-transcendent. By maintaining that God's goodness is not the same as, for example, human goodness we leave room for it to be involved also (indeed, quite intimately) in the good of plants, *animals, and even *angels.

The way in which God's transcendence is expressed by Christians has been influenced by Platonism, but in hardly a straightforward manner. Whereas the 'transcendentalists' among Platonists tend to say that God is above being, Christians have usually felt bound by

Exodus 3: 14, 'God said to Moses, "I am who am." ' Thus, despite his many debts to Plotinus, *Augustine says that 'to be' is proper only to God and that in comparison with God all created things are not; and Thomas *Aquinas says that God is 'subsistent being itself'. This is, in a way, a reversal of the standard Neoplatonic interpretation of Plato's *Republic*, 509b, where the divine is above being; but it also preserves God's transcendence. God's way of being is wholly different from our own.

The question of Platonism's effect on Christian theology of the Trinity is more directly doctrinal. Whereas the early *Councils of the church assert that Christ and the *Holy Spirit are not subordinate to the Father but in some sense equal to him (although begotten by or proceeding from him), for Platonism anything below the highest transcendent object—the Demiurge of Plato's *Timaeus*, for instance, or Mind, the second hypostasis of Plotinus' *Enneads*—must be subordinate to it. As Dörrie points out, in this respect Christianity is directly opposed to Platonism. The Trinitarian formulas ('begotten, not made', for instance) are often deliberate attempts to set out understandings different from those of the Platonists.

And yet Christians certainly employed in this enterprise Platonic terminology; and it is hardly conceivable that, without this terminology and its attendant philosophical tradition, in which the major Christian intellectuals were schooled, the Trinitarian formulas could have been achieved. Consider, for example, an argument by *Athanasius to the ultimate effect that the Son is able to participate in the Father's creative power. A typical Platonist would argue that the work of creation must be excluded from the Godhead as beneath its dignity and that an intermediate is required to serve as creator (as in *Timaeus*). After citing Matthew 10: 29 ('Are not two sparrows sold for a penny? And not one of them will fall to the ground without your Father's will'), Athanasius points out that even a Demiurge's creative power must be traced back to the supreme God; so why not begin by attributing creation to the Father and also to his Son (*Oratio II contra Arianos*, 25–6)? It is unlikely that Athanasius could have realized this feat of bringing something so temporal and various as creation up into the transcendent Godhead had he not been arguing within a Platonic context. On the other hand, it is not insignificant that the motivation for his argument comes from Holy Scripture.

Platonism also often played a part in thought which eventually came to be recognized as *heretical. The most salient example is *Arius, against whom and whose disciples Athanasius spent a lifetime arguing. In his *Thalia* Arius says, 'You must understand that the One was, but the Two was not before it came to be.' We have already seen such language in Xenocrates, according to whom the Two is subsidiary to the One, who is also called Father; but it is likely that Arius got these ideas from the representatives of Middle Platonism and Neoplatonism with whom he was familiar. Schooled in this philosophical tradition and wishing also to protect the simplicity of God, Arius was led to say (immediately before the line just quoted) that 'the Father is alien to the Son in substance, for he has no origin'. This is incompatible, of course, with the credal statement subsequently formulated at *Nicaea, which says that the Son is 'one in substance with the Father'.

What, finally, can we say about the effects of Platonism on Christian anthropology? It is difficult to deny that an excessively dualistic conception of *humanity can lead to the overheated sort of *asceticism in which the body is regarded as evil. But are such excesses among Christians traceable to Platonism? We have already seen that for Plato progress in philosophy (which is equivalent for him to progress in the moral life) involves a gradual separation from the material world. In another dialogue, *Phaedo*, he says that the life of the philosopher is a continual exercise in dying. This ascetical propensity is apparent throughout later Platonism, notably in Plotinus, according to whom the human soul, by nature divine, has fallen into a body and longs to return to 'the One'.

On the other hand, however, we also find in Plato a healthy regard for physical well-being and an appreciation of its place even in the intellectual (i.e. the spiritual) life. In *Timaeus*, for instance, he says, 'With respect to health and disease, virtue and vice, no proportion or lack thereof is more important than that between body and soul' (87d1–3). And Plotinus' asceticism had more to do with charity than with fasting and flagellation. We might also note that in the history of Christianity, the more extreme ascetics have not infrequently been strongly opposed to Platonism. Tatian and Tertullian, mentioned above, are good examples; both also left the church in search of a type of radical asceticism they did not experience within it.

See also BYZANTINE THEOLOGY 6TH–16TH CENTURIES; GREEK THEOLOGY 4TH–6TH CENTURIES; LATIN THEOLOGY, 300–1000; PRE-CONSTANTINIAN THOUGHT.   **Kevin L. Flannery, SJ**

Armstrong, A. H. (ed.), *Cambridge History of Later Greek and Early Medieval Philosophy* (1967).

Armstrong, A. H., and Markus, R. A., *Christian Faith and Greek Philosophy* (1960).

Arnou, R., 'Platonisme des Pères', *Dictionnaire de Théologie Catholique*, xii. cols. 2258–92 (1935).

des Places, E., *Platonismo e Tradizione Cristiana* (1976).

de Vogel, C. J., 'Platonism and Christianity: A Mere Antagonism or a Profound Common Ground?', *Vigiliae Christianae*, 39 (1985).

Dillon, J., *The Middle Platonists* (1977).

Dodds, E. R., *Pagan and Christian in an Age of Anxiety* (1968).

Dörrie, H., *Platonica Minora* (1976).

Klibansky, R., *The Platonic Tradition during the Middle Ages* (1982).

Meijering, E. J., *God being History: Studies in Patristic Philosophy* (1975).

O'Meara, D., *Plotinus: An Introduction to the Enneads* (1993).

Rist, J. M., *Platonism and its Christian Heritage* (1985).

Stead, G. C., 'The Platonism of Arius', *Journal of Theological Studies*, NS 15 (1964).

von Harnack, A., *History of Dogma* (1894), ET (1958).

play. Two contrasting views of play can claim a Christian character, one reproving, the other enthusing. The first could take as its text the gospel condemnation, 'Woe upon you who laugh now, you shall mourn and weep' (Luke 6: 25). Ambrose commented, 'I maintain then that not only loose jokes but jokes of any kind must be avoided,' while John Chrysostom roundly declared, 'It is not God who gives us the chance to play, but the devil.' Graeco-Roman culture was one in which the 'grave-merry' man represented an ideal figure and public games were of huge importance, linked almost inseparably with feasts and gods, the entire system that Christians rejected. The amphitheatre was where games were played and Christians were martyred. It is hardly surprising if early Christianity, with its self-denying *ascetic ideals, appeared inimical to play. Even so, ordinary Christians often danced and sang at the graves of *martyrs on their feast-days, despite episcopal disapproval.

It is, however, in medieval culture that Christian behaviour and play first appear publicly wedded, despite some ecclesiastical qualms, at the popular level of the *mystery play, the carol, the gargoyle, the rituals of the feast of Holy Innocents which could include ball games between clergy and laity. Popular medieval religion became increasingly playful, a quality that *Protestantism turned severely against: the intermingling of play and *worship seemed unacceptable. *Puritanism and its Catholic cousin *Jansenism did not believe in it, and banished 'merriment'. Play, however, was hard to exclude for long and effected many a return, linked especially with more *liberal theologies in the 19th century. Indeed, in some quarters certain kinds of play—football, cricket, Scottish dancing—became almost a badge of sound Christian living, even if the Victorian cult of 'playing the game' was rather too purposeful, muscular, and austere to catch the note of playfulness with high fidelity. *Missionaries in Africa could count their success in the football teams they promoted, but continued exclusion of playing on Sunday indicates that a sense of incompatibility between religion and play still survived.

If playfulness keeps returning in Christian history, however often a stern seriousness seeks to exclude it as a frivolous occasion of *sin, one can ask why. Is it just a sign of backsliding? What does play truly signify and how intrinsically does it relate to Christianity?

In a discussion of purposive action, Thomas *Aquinas remarks that there are two kinds of act which have no end outside themselves: contemplation and play. For each its end is within it (*Summa contra Gentiles*, 3. 2). He follows up this remarkable comparison in a number of discussions of play, notably *ST* II-II q. 168, where three separate articles are devoted to its elucidation. An exploration of this comparison itself may start with the bible, especially Proverbs 9: 27–31, whose relevance depends in part on a variant reading, one often preferred by the Greek fathers. Wisdom 'was at his side each day, his darling and delight, playing in his presence continually, playing on the earth' (NEB).

Emerging from this text is a whole tradition of thinking about *God's relationship with the world in terms of play. For Maximus the Confessor, 'we deserve to be looked upon as a children's game played by God'. Curiously, this idea also seems to derive from *Plato for whom 'Man is ... a plaything in the hand of God, and truly this is the best thing about him' (*Laws*). It is understandable that out of this came a sense that the worship of God is a kind of play as well, and such examples as *David's dancing before the ark come to represent the appropriate response of a playful creature to a playful creator. One can even move from Maximus and Plato to *Teresa (Thérèse) of Lisieux who explained how 'for some time past I had offered myself to the child Jesus, to be his little plaything; I told him not to treat me like one of those precious toys which children only look at and dare not touch, but rather as a ball of no value that could be thrown on the ground, tossed about... or pressed to his heart, just as it might please him' (*Histoire d'une âme*).

Aquinas's calm discussion of whether there is 'virtue in play' is more *Aristotelian but he recalls the story of how some were scandalized to find the evangelist *John playing with his followers.

Aquinas insists that it is right and necessary to seek pleasure in relaxation and wrong to avoid play of any sort. He even explicitly defends professional actors because, while their *work is by definition not play, yet they provide the opportunity for others to relax playfully. Play itself, however, he insists in several places, has no end outside itself. In Donald Nicholl's words, in a game of family cricket on the beach, 'each second of the game is treasured for its own delight, and not as a means towards the next second. In this respect the game on the beach is like contemplation, for in contemplation also there is a suspension of time'. In a sense, then, play both resembles and anticipates heavenly contemplation. Its result really does not matter. 'Who loses, wins' is true of all who know how to play, which is why professional playing is no playing but, instead, a form of work where 'who loses, loses'. The more play is commercialized, the more it ceases to exist. It is with a *children's game in mind that one should read Jesus' words 'Unless you become like little children you will never enter the kingdom of heaven' (Matt. 18: 3), a scene such as Zechariah described as characterizing the New Jerusalem, 'the city will be full of boys and girls playing in the squares' (8: 5).   **Adrian Hastings**

Nicholl, Donald, *Recent Thought in Focus*, Appendix I, 'Play' (1951).
Rahner, Hugo, *Man at Play* (1972).

pneumatology, see HOLY SPIRIT.

poetry. The modern meaning of poetry as a metrical verse composition is little more than three centuries old, and has never been uncontroversial. For much of its history 'poetry', and its cognate 'poesy', spanned the whole of imaginative literature. Until about 1700, critical classification was more often by specific kinds ('epic', or 'lyric'; forms patronized by different Muses in the Greek pantheon) or by *rhetorical styles. It was not until the 18th century, with the rise of the English *novel, that literature was polarized into 'prose' and 'poetry'. At the same time the emergence in Britain, France, and Germany of a new concept of 'literature', attributing aesthetic value to certain writings over and above their contents, coincided with parallel developments in *theology. It is symptomatic of the continuing confusion over the term that while most modern theologians agree that biblical and theological *language is 'poetic', their interpretations of the term range from the primitivist (saying in beautiful language what we all know to be untrue) to the sophisticated (an indissoluble union of deep thought and intense feeling).

Literary aesthetics presented a peculiar problem to the early church. Its classically trained leaders in the 2nd, 3rd, and 4th centuries were appalled by NT *koine* Greek, regarded as a low-status patois. *Augustine, Jerome, Gregory the Great, and Tertullian were all troubled by what they saw as the barbarity of the gospel's language. Some way had to be found of explaining why the *Holy Spirit had such a poor literary style. Tertullian (writing *c*.200) was prepared to reject the whole classical tradition. 'What has Athens to do with Jerusalem? ... We must seek the Lord in purity of heart.... Since Christ Jesus, there is no room for further curiosity, since the gospel, no need for further research.' Similarly, for Gregory, 'the same lips cannot sound the praises of both Jupiter and Christ'. Though Ambrose apparently agreed, he structured his *De officiis ministrorum*, written for the clergy of Milan, on Cicero's *De officiis*. Ambrose's pupil, Augustine, admits in his *Confessions* that it was

Cicero's philosophy that set him on the road to conversion by giving him a passion for true wisdom. Perhaps the most agonizing conflict of aesthetic loyalties was recorded by Jerome, translator of the Vulgate Latin bible, and another avid Ciceronian. Compared with the classics, not just the Greek but even the 'uncultivated language' of the Old Latin bible was so offensive that it made his 'skin crawl'.

Not until the 14th century did a poet dare to suggest that a modern vernacular might equal, or even surpass, the languages of the biblical and classical past. *Dante's De vulgari eloquentia (1303–5?) is an early work, not fully representing the later beliefs of the Divine Comedy; nevertheless, its main thrust clarifies what he was attempting there. He distinguishes between 'language' and what he calls forma locutionis; an almost *Platonic 'linguistic form', neither specifically Hebrew, nor the faculty of language in general, but a particular gift from *God to *Adam, lost after Babel. Dante believed this essentially divine linguistic form could be recaptured and even recreated, not by returning to the Hebrew of the OT, but via the new 'illustrious' Italian language that he was forging for his own great work. The Divine Comedy was conceived and executed as part of a theoretical poetic programme of hitherto unimagined theological and aesthetic boldness.

But if Dante was attempting to produce a Christian work of art that was not merely reflective but creative, and would in some sense rival, or at least complement, scripture itself, he was also seeking to incorporate the world of classical pagan literature which had presented such problems to Christians a thousand years earlier. Hence the presence of Virgil, the greatest poet of the ancient world, as his guide through Hell and Purgatory, who is only superseded when Dante encounters the divine vision in the person of Beatrice at the entry to the Earthly Paradise. Dante's poetry is designed to appropriate not merely the biblical tradition but also that of the pagan classics, and to create from their synthesis a new assertion of the place of poetry in religious experience.

It was an assertion echoed repeatedly throughout the *Renaissance. Sidney in his Defence of Poesy is less cosmically ambitious than Dante, but is also concerned to stress parallels between the pagan Roman poet 'as diviner, foreseer, or *prophet' and King *David, the psalmist, and to demonstrate not merely poetry's excellence over history and philosophy, but (skating skilfully between factual claim and *metaphor) its 'divine' status. Since Sidney was challenging a growing *Puritan attack on the link between *theology and aesthetics, it is the more surprising that it was that Puritan tradition which was to produce in the next generation both the substantial 'metaphysical' talent of Andrew Marvell and the towering genius of *Milton. Like Dante, Milton saw poetry as the natural expression of *religious experience, and used his epic to enrich and revivify the story of the *Fall in ways going far beyond his biblical source: even today, readers can be surprised to discover they are more familiar with Milton's version than with *Genesis. Nevertheless, Paradise Lost is better seen as part of a process of secularization than as a theological work of the stature of Dante's. By attributing 'character' and motive to the protagonists, especially Satan, Milton turns the Hebrew *myth into a human, if cosmic, drama (see DEVIL). It was translated, admired, and imitated all over Europe for two centuries, spawning biblical epics that, consciously or unconsciously, went on

*demythologizing the bible, and included Klopstock's German Messiah (1748) and Philip James Bailey's Festus (1839).

Meanwhile, Protestant/Catholic polemics were making it clear that any 'plain meaning' of scripture was more in the mind of the reader than in the text. By the early 18th century, many critics saw the notion of 'the poetic sublime' as better applied to scripture itself than to psychologized epic paraphrases. For John Dennis, in a much-praised essay (1704), poetry was 'the natural language of religion', the form that expresses the most profound human passion. Similarly, for James Thomson (1726) poetry was 'that divine art' that 'has charmed the listening world from Moses down to Milton' constituting 'the sublimest passages of the inspired writings themselves and what seems to be the peculiar language of heaven.' It was left to Robert Lowth, in his epoch-making Oxford Lectures on the Sacred Poetry of the Hebrews, to give a scholarly basis to Sidney's claim for the prophetic status of the poet in the OT. First delivered in 1741, they were published in the original Latin in 1753, extensively summarized in Blair's Lectures on Rhetoric—a source of much of Wordsworth's Preface to the Lyrical Ballads—and only finally translated into English in 1787. Though Lowth could not have foreseen such developments, his stress on understanding the conditions of the ancient Hebrew world was to launch the new *higher criticism of the bible in Germany; his argument that Hebrew verse worked not by rhyme or metre, but by what he called 'parallelism', suggested that biblical poetry (unlike European) was providentially universally translatable, further blurring boundaries between prose and verse; and his claim for the prophetic status of the poet was to inspire the *Romantic movement: Herder, the Schlegels, and *Schleiermacher in Germany, Chateaubriand in France, and *Blake, *Coleridge, Wordsworth, and even Shelley, in England.

From the German Romantics in particular was to emerge the new concept of 'literature', and the associated idea that '*truth' might be understood not merely in its verifiable relation to the world, but as the capacity to reveal the world in new ways. Poetry (which, in the absence of a developed novel tradition in Germany, still embraced all written art forms) thus became a major source of understanding, independent of any scientific account of things. Not merely was the bible 'poetic' in this sense, but, in a post-*Kantian system, poetry became a key to perception itself. 'No poetry, no reality,' wrote Schleiermacher in the Schlegel brothers' journal, the Athenaeum (1798). For Chateaubriand, in the Genius of Christianity (1802), Christianity was itself 'poetic', and its essential inwardness had transformed poetry (literature) by making possible a new understanding of human character.

Shelley, in his Defence of Poetry (1824), written to counter Peacock's teasing argument in The Four Ages of Poetry (1820) that poetry was the most primitive art-form, and therefore increasingly irrelevant and destined to gradual extinction, saw poets as 'the unacknowledged legislators' of the world, redeeming from decay 'the visitations of the divinity in man', and called all the greatest human thinkers 'poets', including Plato, Jesus, and Bacon. Such a claim went some way to counter the fulfilment of Peacock's ironic prophecy, as the mainstream of creative writing inexorably passed from verse to prose in the course of the 19th century. But this attempt to reclaim the whole of literature as 'poetry' was defeated by the strength of the novel and the associated conventions of 19th-century literary '*realism' and its philosophic equivalent of 'positivism'.

Thus Tennyson, in his immensely popular *In Memoriam*, tacitly abandons traditional assumptions of Christian community, defining '*faith' in purely personal terms as 'believing where we cannot prove'. If his own was ambiguous, for Arnold, Clough, and Hardy the attractions of such 'belief' were even less viable. Arnold's

> Wandering between two worlds
> One dead, the other powerless to be born

articulated the uncertainties of a generation. Though poetry, as Mill was to argue, discovering its healing powers after breakdown, had its place for the cultivation of feelings in a world dominated by the progress of physical science, it represented pure subjectivity. Religious experience seemed correspondingly reducible to a quirk of personal psychology—a view perhaps strengthened rather than diminished by the robust scepticism of the faith of others, like Browning. *Newman's far-sighted recognition, in the *Grammar of Assent* (1878), of the subjective, and indeed 'poetic' nature of all human experience was only narrowly influential.

With the almost simultaneous publication of *Hopkins's work (posthumously) and of T. S. *Eliot's *The Waste Land*, in 1919, following the First World War, poetry took a new role in religious expression. The breakdown of assumptions of objective scientific truth, independent of human perception, reflecting the new *science of relativity and quantum theory, gave renewed vitality to earlier notions of poetic subjectivity. Eliot's conversion to Christianity, celebrated first in *Ash Wednesday* and subsequently in the *Four Quartets*, coincided with a more general aestheticization of 20th-century thought, uniting philosophy, theology, and literature in a poetic synthesis scarcely possible since the Romantic era. At the same time, increasing recognition of the literary and poetic nature of the biblical texts themselves has focused on the narrative continuity of historic Christianity. While some, as different as Derrida and *Cupitt, have argued that what is valuable in such a synthesis is the aesthetic rather than the philosophic or religious, others including Polanyi and Steiner have seen poetry, and even language itself, as essentially religious. Certainly classic distinctions between form and content seem decreasingly relevant as the intimacies of modern religious experience continue to shape new poetic structures for the 21st century.   **Stephen Prickett**

Aarsleff, Hans, *From Locke to Saussure* (1982).

Arnold, Matthew, *Literature and Dogma* (1895).

Bowie, Andrew, *From Romanticism to Critical Theory: The Philosophy of German Literary Theory* (1997).

Chateaubriand, René François Auguste Viscount de, *The Genius of Christianity; or the Spirit and Beauty of the Christian Religion* (1802), ET (1856).

Cupitt, Don, *After God* (1997).

Eco, Umberto, *The Search for the Perfect Language*, ET (1997).

Eliot, T. S., 'Tradition and the Individual Talent'; 'Andrew Marvell'; 'The Metaphysical Poets', in *Selected Essays* (1933).

Farrer, Austen, *A Rebirth of Images* (1944).

Heidegger, Martin, 'Hölderlin and the Essence of Poetry', in *Existence and Being*, ET (1949).

Herder, J. G., *The Spirit of Hebrew Poetry* (1782–3), ET (1833).

Keble, John, *Lectures on Poetry* (2 vols.; 1912 edn.).

Kugel, James L., *The Idea of Biblical Poetry* (1981).

Lowth, Robert, *Lectures on the Sacred Poetry of the Hebrews*, ET (1787).

Polanyi, Michael, *Personal Knowledge* (1958).

Prickett, Stephen, *Words and the 'Word': Language, Poetics and Biblical Interpretation* (1986).

—— *Origins of Narrative: The Romantic Appropriation of the Bible* (1996).

Schlegel, Friedrich, *Dialogue on Poetry and Literary Aphorisms*, ET (1968).

Steiner, George, *Real Presences* (1989).

political theology is a new term, its popularity dating from the 1960s, but its content is as old as Christianity. 'Render to Caesar the things that are Caesar's and to God that things that are God's' (Matt. 22: 21) suggested a *dualism that recognized a sphere of reality proper to Caesar and in some way withdrawn from that of God. Paul in Romans 13 emphatically insisted, however, that Caesar's authority comes from God. That is why it must be obeyed. It is a text which has at times been taken to require obedience even to the worst of governments. A great deal of Christian political thinking can be seen as attempts to square these two texts, combining the idea of a political sphere autonomous from the religious with a basic dependence of the former upon God. Revelation 13, on the other hand, by portraying the Roman empire as satanic, set off a very different line of thought, which has persistently re-emerged in times of crisis. In practice most early Christians were apolitical. They did their best to respect the state but they expected little from it. Their hearts were elsewhere.

With *Constantine everything changed. The empire could now be portrayed as marvellously providential. The *church was to a great extent integrated into the imperial system while the latter was expected to serve Christian purposes. Eusebius provided one 'political theology' in his glorification of Constantine, *Augustine another in his more sober evaluation of the rise and fall of earthly powers in which the *Kingdom of God is far from visible. The Caesaropapism of the Eusebian model was never discarded in the *Byzantine tradition or its successor states of eastern Europe, while Augustine's political outlook for long dominated the western tradition. Meanwhile, in a Christian-run state, all sorts of other issues arose. Christians found themselves responsible for war and peace, the functioning of the judiciary, the granting or withholding of civil rights to non-Christians. As the concept of a 'Christian empire' developed, the shabby treatment of non-Christians, Jews especially, could be justified in terms of their non-participation in the common exercises of society. There was really no room for non-Christians in a strictly defined 'Christendom' and there was a sort of social inevitability in the spread of *antisemitism and the expulsion of Jews in the Middle Ages from country after country of western Europe. The more society was Christianized, the less Christian it might become in its treatment of non-Christians.

At the same time medieval Europe wrestled with many other basically political issues: was Christendom at root a single state or a multitude of states? If the former, was its head the emperor or the pope? Should it demonstrate its Christian unity by engaging in crusades or holy wars against non-Christians? If so, for what exact reason? Could such crusades, initially aimed at freeing the Holy Land from Muslim rule, then be extended to crush the Albigensians or, even, to ravage the Netherlands because they backed a rival pope (as happened in the notorious Despenser crusade in the late 14th century)? The profound politicization of the *papacy and of church life as a whole actually inhibited the development of a coherent political theology with which such questions could be effectively faced, and encouraged the drift towards the sovereignty of the national state and a religious undergirding of *nationalism. Nevertheless in the high Middle Ages a great deal of political theology was being written, from *De regimine principum* of *Aquinas to *Dante's *Monarchy*, the *Defensor pacis* of Marsilius of Padua and much of the work of the 15th-century *conciliarists. Here as elsewhere the most enduring value appears to lie in the work of Aquinas and the development of a *natural law basis for the state, a notable rejection of Augustine's view that it derived from the sinful state of humanity. Aquinas, making much use of *Aristotle, asserted three points that are still with us. The first was that the only proper purpose of political authority is the pursuit of the common good; the second that while authority comes from God it requires also at least the implicit consent of the people; the third that a grossly tyrannical government may justly be overthrown. In the 15th century John Fortescue, the first English constitutional theorist, in defending the advantage of what we can fairly call 'limited monarchy', explicitly appealed to Aquinas. In the 16th century the revived school of Spanish Thomism led by Vitoria and Suarez went on to develop basic concepts of international law, including the political rights of non-Christian peoples. At the same time in England an Anglican Thomist, Richard *Hooker, constructed one of the most coherent, if narrowly national, models of Christian political theory ever conceived.

The grounding of much modern political theory, including the *democratic state, does then lie in medieval theology, but it was grounded too in post-Reformation *Protestant thought, particularly in the *Zwinglian and *Calvinist traditions. Most medieval and *Renaissance political experience was dominated by either papacy or monarchy. It was because Zwinglians and Calvinists effectively rejected both that they were forced, alike in Switzerland, Holland, mid-17th-century England, and North America, to develop in theory and in practice new, more democratic, ways of structuring political experience. In consequence modern Christianity's political debt to this tradition is enormous.

Many other issues, however, were for long almost entirely overlooked. The glaring crime of the slave trade carried on very lucratively by almost all the Christian countries of western Europe for three centuries was comfortably ignored or even justified on various specious religious or Aristotelian grounds. Some Christian societies in America based their entire economy on *slavery and struggled for its retention. If one fully appreciates the work of English *evangelicals of the Clapham Sect in their long struggle to abolish the trade which led on, little by little, to its disappearance almost everywhere, one must at the same time recognize that most Christians (including popes) well into the 19th century accepted the legitimacy of slavery. What is no less striking is how little political theology there was in the 19th century beyond the slavery issue. Christian public doctrine was largely carried away by the attractions of imperialism (justified rather easily by the opportunities it provided for world evangelization), but even on the home front it seldom responded constructively to such matters as the appalling frequency of *capital punishment in early 19th-century Britain. The beginnings of Christian socialism in the middle of the 19th century, followed by the *social gospel school in America and the beginning of papal social teaching with Leo XIII's encyclical *Rerum Novarum*

(1891), are all evidence of a shift, but for long not a very influential one. What is clear is the lack of any coherent political theology able to handle the multitudinous issues of the modern political world from industrialization, secular democracy, and the emancipation of women, to *Marxism, the explosion of colonialism, new forms of nationalism, and the growth of conscientious objection in response to military conscription (see PACIFISM).

The manifest failure of most church leadership in the First World War to do anything other than urge on the opposing sides was proof of a vast omission within Christian thought. There may well have been more coherent political theology available in the 14th century than at the end of the 19th. In reaction to all this the foundation of modern political theology was laid between the wars. It can be located in the 1937 Oxford Conference on Church, Community, and State, and in a number of books by writers like Reinhold *Niebuhr, Jacques *Maritain, and Christopher Dawson, in which a new maturity of Christian political thinking can be recognized. It was a maturity enhanced by the experience of the war, Nazism, and Communism. The participation of Dietrich *Bonhoeffer and other Christians in the plot to kill Hitler challenged long-accepted church political views, especially *Lutheran, which had effectively surrendered to nationalism.

In the post-1945 period, Christianity found itself in an unambiguously new sociopolitical situation, characterizable in the following ways. First, it was democratic. While Anglo-Saxon and Scandinavian countries had long taken this for granted, Christians in Germany, France, and the Mediterranean world had not (and the Latin American and Eastern Orthodox worlds still did not). The monarchist, dictatorial, nationalist, and antisemitic threads in European Christian consciousness (particularly in *French Catholicism and *German Protestantism) were decisively marginalized by the Second World War. Secondly, there was a progressive *secularization of all western societies. It had been proceeding for a long time but the distancing of political and social institutions from religious ones was far more generally taken for granted in the post-1945 world and led to the steady reduction of whatever remained in some countries of a formal ecclesiastical '*establishment'. Thirdly, the decolonization of most of Asia, Africa, the Caribbean, and the Pacific brought to an end, by the early 1960s, the era of Victorian imperial hegemony, while leaving South Africa as a battleground for racialism (see APARTHEID) for another thirty years, and highlighting *Latin America as the home of often still more vicious forms of oppression: a combination of old-fashioned right-wing European Catholic political attitudes, the oppression of native peoples going back for centuries, and a new wave of North American economic imperialism enforced quite as ruthlessly. Fourthly, Christian political thought was at this juncture galvanized by Marxism, both as rival and as exemplar. The political power of the Soviet bloc dominated, and to a greater or lesser extent persecuted, many traditionally Christian societies. But the intellectual power of numerous distinguished western Marxist intellectuals, both philosophers and historians, mattered still more. This galvanization and emulation was made possible by the optimistic and liberationist mood of the 1960s world, the churches included, a mood much strengthened by the campaign for civil rights in America led by Martin Luther King Jr. (see BLACK THEOLOGY). The emerging political theology could in consequence appeal to a new wave of ecclesiastical documents such as *Vatican II's Gaudium et Spes, Paul VI's encyclical *Populorum Progressio* (1967), and the resolutions of the WCC Assembly at Uppsala (1968) with its subsequent 'Programme to Combat Racism' and intensely controversial grants to liberation movements (see ECUMENICAL MOVEMENT).

It was out of all these pressures that a coherent political theology began to emerge, constituting a central theme in the writing of most leading late 20th-century theologians, including *Moltmann and *Pannenberg. Its best-known form, *liberation theology, is discussed separately at length. While this has always remained a primarily Latin American expression of political theology, it has profoundly influenced every other form. Political theology is, in general, like all moral theology, practical as well as speculative. As such it relates to real circumstances. A political theology suitable to the opening of the 21st century is bound to be very different from one suitable for the 12th or the 19th, just because the whole shape of political reality is different. Nevertheless the enduring underlying principles may be clearer after the long traumas of the 20th century than they have ever been before.

Before considering the central themes, however, it is helpful to summarize the three positions against which political theology takes its stand. The first is the widely accepted assertion that *religion and politics have nothing to do with each other. Religion is fine in the personal domain, especially for women, but it must never be allowed to trespass into the public field, except ceremonially. This position may be upheld alike by Marxists and right-wing politicians. The second, definable as an extreme Augustinianism, asserts that politics is so inherently rotten that a good Christian will want to have nothing to do with it. It represents the worst of a fallen world which Christians are condemned to live within but in which they must want to have no part beyond necessity. The third is that of one strand of born-again *evangelicalism, for which Christianity is a matter of accepting Jesus as 'personal saviour' who guarantees *salvation (from hell), health, and prosperity. This type of Christianity, particularly prevalent at the close of the 20th century, represents a form of highly egoistic privatization.

Against all such views, which are themselves interlinked and of varying sorts, political theology reaffirms the public significance of Christian faith for the world as a whole, society as a whole, and history as a whole. Its nature may be considered under four heads:

Justice as an OT concept

It was particularly a *prophetic concept to be found in Amos, *Isaiah, and elsewhere, but it undergirds most of the OT. True religion requires the defence of the poor and the oppressed, the paradigm being either the whole nation's liberation from Egypt in *Exodus or Nathan's denunciation of *David for the death of Uriah. The strength of such a theology lies in its biblical foundation and personal appeal, particularly within the Protestant tradition, but it is hard to use in pluralist contexts or to develop into a coherent, ongoing political doctrine rather than a tirade against public wickedness or a call for *revolution.

The liberation of Christianity from the effects of Constantine

It is roughly true that between the 4th and the 19th centuries the central Christian churches were continuously dominated by the legacy of Constantine. They were 'established' churches in which bishops enjoyed extensive political privileges and were incorpor-

ated into a tiny governing class. The price of privilege was forfeiture of any sort of prophetic voice, something taken over frequently enough by liberal or socialist secularists, but also by the smaller Protestant free churches, such as *Quakers. The collapse of establishment has given the churches back the possibility of a less predictable voice and Amos has never been so often quoted. Part of the task of political theology is to ponder the lessons of the Constantinian centuries to ensure that the church is not once again comfortably politicized. Only a politically liberated church can actually be constructively political.

Natural law

Political theology has to reappraise its relationship to the natural law, human rights, common good, democratic tradition of thought, with its medieval roots, secularized implementation, but relatively weak biblical base. Many modern political theologians, rediscovering the wealth of OT concern for *justice, have appeared unenthusiastic about the natural law tradition. Yet it is out of the latter that the most sustained Christian impact on political life has come; moreover it is only by using such an approach that a Christian political theology can be intelligible to the wider pluralist world. While a specifically biblical and Christian understanding of politics may go well beyond what can be garnered from concepts of the common good or natural law, it does not seem that it can do without them and remain coherent.

Christ as a troubling exemplar

A specifically Christian political theology cannot be achieved either through concentrating on appeals to OT prophecy or by bringing Christian Aristotelianism up to date. The figure of Christ has been returned to the centre of political theology in the work of Moltmann, Pannenberg, and others. At the heart of their doctrine is a figure who is both crucified criminal and lord of *history—not a secret, mystical history but the ascertainable history of the world we know, if admittedly a history that will only be fully understood in an end as yet unattained. Jesus, with all his ambiguity towards temporal power, remains king in Pilate's court, at the world's consummation and in all the time between. That is an affirmation of faith at the heart of the new political theology. It remains a claim which to be meaningful needs to integrate *christology, the thrust of OT prophecy, the pursuit of a nature-based common good, and the sombre lessons of two millennia of Christian history into one coherent whole.   **Adrian Hastings**

Cullmann, Oscar, *The State in the New Testament* (1957).

Davis, Charles, *Theology and Political Society* (1980).

d'Entrèves, A. P., *The Medieval Contribution to Political Thought* (1939).

—— (ed.), *Aquinas: Selected Political Writings* (1959).

Dumas, André, *Political Theology and the Life of the Church* (1978).

Fierro, Alfredo, *The Militant Gospel: An Analysis of Contemporary Political Theologies* (1977).

Forrester, Duncan, *Theology and Politics* (1988).

Hastings, Adrian, 'Christianity', in *The Encyclopedia of Politics and Religion*, ed. Robert Wuthnow (1998), i. 131–42.

Lee, Alistair, *A Reader in Political Theology* (1974).

—— *Domination or Liberation* (1986).

Metz, J. B., *Theology of the World* (1969).

Moltmann, Jürgen, *Theology of Hope* (1967).

Niebuhr, Reinhold, *Moral Man and Immoral Society* (1932).

Sölle, Dorothee, *Political Theology* (1974).

post-Christian thought.

The term 'post-Christian' was first used by the American theologian and thinker Mary Daly in a paper given at the American Academy of Religion in 1973 (and later published in the proceedings of the Working Group on Women and Religion of that body). Daly subsequently would sometimes write 'postchristian'. The term relates to a stage in her career between, on the one hand, attempting as a liberal Catholic to reform the church and, on the other, her more recent wish to make no reference to Christianity (as one does not describe oneself as a divorcee when one has moved beyond a marriage).

In 1973 Daly published her widely influential *Beyond God the Father*. The book represents the first major challenge to Christianity from a feminist perspective. Its driving force is *ethics. Daly argues that from the male *symbolism intrinsic to Christianity it follows that it cannot be liberating for *women. Indeed she speaks of the Christian religion as a hoax by which women have been taken in for two millennia. She urges them in sisterhood to move towards that new 'being' which consists in their empowerment. Christianity manifests a *dualistic ideology in which 'the other' (whether blacks, the Vietcong, or whoever) is excluded. As the paradigmatic other, the coming into their own of women will sound the death knell of the system.

Coming from a *Thomistic Catholic background (she had written two doctoral theses in Thomistic thought) Daly had a fundamental sense, which she still retains, of Be-ing (as she writes to give the sense of a verb) underlying and activating all. In her autobiography *Outercourse* she speaks of childhood experiences of encounter with the transparent beauty of a flower, a hedge, and ice, in which the world lit up. She speaks of an 'intuition of being' (following the Catholic philosopher Jacques *Maritain). As women come to 'be', come to realize themselves (after the non-being they have experienced within patriarchy), they will be at one with Be-ing.

In *Beyond God the Father*, drawing on the many *philosophical and *theological strands that have influenced her, Daly appears to hold a quasi-theological position. Subverting *Aristotle, women become the 'final cause'. Following *process theology she sees unfolding reality as verb (rather than noun). Like *Tillich she speaks of our ultimate concern. But Daly never quite speaks of *God (conceived in whatever terms), or *religious experience. She adapts, or plays with, theological vocabulary, while falling short of affirming the truth of religious claims. However, that the ambience of her thought is religious (particularly Thomist) both in this and later writing is beyond doubt.

In the 1980s in Britain Daphne Hampson came to use the term 'post-Christian', giving it precise connotations as designating a religious position that was definitely theistic but which had abandoned the Christian *myth. Thus *post* Christian in that such a position is no longer Christian; but post *Christian* in that the tradition that has nurtured one and shaped one's thinking was Christianity (not, for example, Buddhism). Subsequent to Hampson's advocacy of such a position in her *Theology and Feminism* (1990) the term came to be widely established in feminist religious circles to designate those who, whilst not Christian, counted themselves in some sense religious or *spiritual people; by contrast with those who still considered themselves insiders to Christianity, thinking it reformable (Christian *feminists). More recently however Hampson has taken to spelling out that she is a theist, in the western tradition, who is not a Christian; for the term 'post-Christian' is confusingly also used as a synonym for *secular.

Women (or men) who have come to a post-Christian position have done so on various counts, which cumulatively led to abandoning Christianity. Hampson considers Christianity epistemologically untenable. Christians hold to a uniqueness surrounding the Christ event. But, given that we have known (at least since the *Enlightenment) that nature and history form an interrelated whole, in which events are one of a type, there can be no such uniqueness. (If there is randomness at the sub-atomic level, that has always been so; there can be no one event—say a resurrection—that fits no category.) It would appear however that the many theologians, students of religion, or for example feminist novelists, who have abandoned Judaism or Christianity (such as Carol Christ, Naomi Goldenberg, or Alice Walker, as well as Daly and Hampson) have alike done so in the conviction that masculinist symbolism for *God (or Christ) is integral to those religious traditions. As Daly remarked, following Marshall McLuhan, the medium is the message. Some of these women have espoused a 'Goddess' religion (Christ), or a 'pagan' position (Walker), to be distinguished from the common understanding of a 'post-Christian' position as here defined.

Furthermore there are profound ethical reasons that lead women to leave behind what they conceive to be patriarchal religions. The idea of a transcendent God (intrinsic to a religion that involves belief in a particular revelation) would seem to limit the moral autonomy of *human beings. Positively, women who are feminists have often believed deeply in a sense of spirit as present within people, in the relationships between them and in the world of nature. Transcendent monotheism, with God conceptualized in masculine metaphors, would appear to be the linchpin of patriarchy. That which is 'other' (women, humanity, or the earth) to the 'One' is held to be 'sinful' and powerless by comparison with that which is defined as good and powerful.

Indeed it can be argued that, far from being incidental to it, the very *raison d'être* of Christianity (and Judaism) is the legitimation and perpetuation of male supremacy over and control of women. The psychoanalytic analyses of the French feminist theorists Luce Irigaray (particularly as interpreted by Elizabeth Grosz) and Julia Kristeva give much food for thought in this regard.

To believe that Christianity is a vehicle that has carried (and distorted) human apprehension of that dimension of reality which is God leaves open the possibility of conceptualizing that reality in other ways. That is to say, human beings have tried to capture that of which they were aware in a symbol system that reflected the male experience under patriarchy. That that symbol system must be abandoned does not invalidate the fact that, in all ages, humans have apprehended that which they named 'God'. Nor does the adoption of a post-Christian position prohibit drawing selectively on theistic strands present in the western tradition that retain their value. Just as in any other discipline (but unlike Christian theology, in which belief in a particular *revelation makes that normative) post-Christians both draw on the past and create anew according to present-day perceptions of truth and their ethical norms.

Indeed the evidence is that at least within British society (witness the work of the Oxford Religious Experience Research Centre), the number of people claiming to have experienced that which is more than themselves (whether or not they call it God) far exceeds the number who are Christians or churchgoers. The evidence of clairvoyance, of the efficacy of *prayer or meditation, of powers that come into play for *healing, suggests to many that, empirically, there is that which we must name, however inadequately. In recent years therefore many (perhaps more particularly women) have come to consider themselves as 'not Christian', but nevertheless as 'spiritual persons' (rather than *atheists).

The term post-Christian as here defined must be distinguished from its use by radicals within the church of non-realist persuasion (see CUPITT, DON). Indeed, the two positions are symmetrically opposed. A post-Christian position may be profoundly '*realist'; no less than in the case of one who conceives of God through Christian symbolism, though the understanding of God will differ markedly. Conversely, such a post-Christian position has abandoned the thought-forms and symbolism of Christianity as detrimental to the interests of women and incompatible with the ethical good of human equality. The post-Christian challenge to 'non-realist Christianity' is that there can be no moral justification for retaining Christian thought-forms if, as a non-realist, one does not believe Christianity true.

A post-Christian position may also be distinguished from *demythologizing Christianity, discovering a message behind the medium of biblical stories, which must today be counted fantastic. A post-Christian is not necessarily a *kerygmatic theology, proclaiming a gospel, as does *Bultmann or indeed much *liberation theology. Thus a post-Christian may well wish to speak in a 'realist' way of that power which is God (drawing on which Jesus of Nazareth, among others, could heal), while considering much of the message of Christianity (as for example the call to self-sacrifice) unhelpful, particularly to women. Again a post-Christian position should be distinguished from a 'liberal' Christianity that has conceived of Christianity as (merely) a social commitment involving good works.   **Daphne Hampson**

Daly, Mary, *Beyond God the Father* (1973).
Hampson, Daphne, *Theology and Feminism* (1990).
—— *After Christianity* (1996).

postmodernism is to be distinguished from postmodernity, which refers to a specific culture, frequently understood as fashioned out of late-capitalism; a culture characterized by mass media, eclecticism, the exaltation of the kitsch and the occasional, and the relativity of values. It is a period concept, and the work of certain writers (John Barth, Thomas Pynchon) and certain architects (Robert Venturi, Frank Gehry) employ an idiom of self-conscious fantasy or exaggerated quotation to announce what the novelist Milan Kundera called the lightness of being. However, where Kundera found this lightness unbearable, many cultural products of postmodernity portray it as humorous, entertaining, even sublime. Postmodernity subverts through irony; it glories in the virtually real, the global hamburger, and the film-set façade. Postmodernity posits itself against the purist, abstract, utopian structures that characterize *modernism. It is consciously a counter-movement. Arnold Toynbee, who was one of the first to employ the term 'post-modern' (within the ironizing inverted commas) in 1939, was describing the crisis of *modernity gathering in Europe throughout the 19th century and erupting after the First World War. More recently, Stephen Toulmin has also seen the avant-garde culture of the 1920s as the early stirrings of postmodern sensibility.

*French writing has frequently been at the epicentre of postmodern thinking, so one date for the onset of postmodernity could be May 1968 with the student riots in Paris against Gaullist conservatism. The thinking of pre-1968 French writers such as Georges Bataille and Jacques Lacan was developed and lionized by the likes of Emmanuel Levinas, Jacques Derrida, and Julia Kristeva. These voices joined a rising group of neo-*Nietzscheans: Gilles Deleuze, Michel Foucault, and Jean-François Lyotard. It was with Lyotard's work, in particular, that the term postmodernism began to announce not a period concept, or a contemporary cultural expression, but a form of philosophical scepticism. With Lyotard, postmodernism does not simply follow modernism, it is the other side of modernism and can be viewed as the condition that precedes it. Modernism is equated with two philosophical (and sociopolitical) projects—*Enlightenment's belief in *reason and liberal humanism's belief in progress. These projects put faith in foundational laws, develop architectonics of the mind and the world, and legitimize certain grand explanations (which Lyotard terms 'narratives') for the way things are (and will be). Postmodernism deflates modernism's self-importance by reminding it of the unpresentable: that which lies outside its scientific and mathematical accounts of the world. Postmodernism is a perennial moment within modernism and vice versa. Postmodernism might well have links then with premodernism—a culture rich with theological *symbolism and resonance. This globalizing philosophy of postmodernism, which views the postmodern condition as before all things and in all things and after them, presents certain problems: not least that it establishes another grand narrative, a monism, albeit a highly indeterminate one. This has enormous implications for the range of theological response to postmodernism.

Postmodernism's anti-metaphysical appeal to surfaces, open-endedness, and contingency is linked to the linguistic turn, *philosophy's turn in the early 20th century towards the analysis of language. Postmodernism's scepticism takes the form of preoccupation with 'discourse' (a specific use of language). The world is viewed as inseparable from the shifting nets of signs that describe and define it. Truth becomes a mobile army of metaphors (and metonymies) locating all knowledge (now knowledges) in cultural production. Against the various *realisms of the 17th to the 19th century—empirical (or metaphysical) realism, scientific realism, moral realism—postmodernism announces a radical non-realism. Hence it sails close to relativism and nihilism, though several postmodern voices (Levinas, Derrida, and Kristeva, for example) would deny they were either relativist or nihilistic. Rather the recognition of difference, the straining to hear, but not appropriate or domesticate, the specific voice of what is other, constitutes a postmodern ethics and politics.

Postmodernity is the age of the consumer; the epoch of the shopping precinct. But the self-conscious superficiality of its market-wares and values is a caustic comment on the dreams of secular humanism and liberalism's *laissez faire*. Postmodernism announces a postsecularism, a re-enchantment of the world, at which point it becomes significant for *theology and religious studies. The work of a number of postmodern thinkers positively re-evaluates *religious language: Levinas explores his Talmudic Judaism; Derrida writes about the negative theologies of Eckhart and Angelus Silesius, and, more recently, about *Augustine and Christ; Kristeva and Irigaray are quizzed by *feminist critics concerning their use of Catholic imagery and terminology; talk about the *soul, *angels, and the divine has become respectable. The immanent logic of secularism is broken open and, while there is a rejection of *dualism and an obsession with embodiment, there are fumbling moves to reassess the role of the transcendent.

Postmodern theologies can be understood as responses to the cultural epoch (postmodernity) in which postmodernism becomes dominant. They share the recognition of the role played by *language in the making of our worlds, a critique of foundationalism, and the acknowledgement that theological discourse is itself culturally embedded and ideologically freighted. Two main forms are distinguishable: postmodern liberal theologies and postmodern radical theologies.

The former have, until recently, held centre-stage and self-consciously announced their projects as postmodern theologies. In North America David Ray Griffin stands somewhat to one side of a group who continually quote each other's texts: Thomas J. J. Altizer, Mark C. Taylor, and Charles Winquist. In Britain, postmodern liberal theology is most clearly evident in the work of Don *Cupitt. The resulting theology or atheology, pushes liberalism's concern with symbol, *metaphor, and *demythologization into a non-realism which embraces the death-of-God and the immanental flux of Being shimmering in the signifying chains of language. Theology is a form of poetry; the promotion of an aesthetics of existence is of paramount importance. Here one can discern the monistic character of much postmodern thinking.

Postmodern radical theologies emphasize the importance of tradition, adhere to a credal grammar, and work through the *orthodoxies of such figures as Augustine, *Aquinas, *Barth, and *von Balthasar. These orthodoxies are read through the critical lens of postmodern thinking (its exaltation of the other, its accounts of desire, the *body, *capitalism, the gift, the politics of knowledge). Frequently these radical theologies are critical of postmodernism's dangers: the nihilistic timbre of its discourses on the sublime, its dissolution of agency, and its potential for endorsing sectarianism. The practitioners of radical postmodern theology are pushing for a more genuine postmodernism, viewing some of the forms of postmodern thinking as born only of modernity's metaphysics and advancing rather than critiquing consumer-driven secularism. The aim here is to write theologies that further post-secularism and give a more profound account of the transcendent in terms of the grammar of a particular faith. In North America, the work of Stanley Hauerwas, George *Lindbeck, and Peter Ochs, and, in Britain, the group of theologians committed to 'Radical Orthodoxy' (including Gerard Loughlin, John Milbank, Catherine Pickstock, and Graham Ward), develop, in their various ways, this radical postmodern theology.   **Graham Ward**

Berry, Philippa, and Wernick, Andrew, Shadow of Spirit: Postmodernism and Religion (1992).
Jameson, Frederic, Postmodernism or the Cultural Logic of Late Capitalism (1991).
Lyotard, Jean-François, The Postmodern Condition (1974), ET (1984).
Taylor, Mark C., Erring: A Postmodern A / Theology (1984).
Ward, Graham (ed.), The Postmodern God (1997).

poverty, in the material sense, has been regarded by Christians as both a virtuous ideal and a just reward for wrongdoing, as central to the concerns of the gospel and as peripheral, as inevitable as well as unacceptable. Opinion has divided more often than not between the poor who struggle to overcome it and the rich who are determined to avoid it. If ever a 'hermeneutic of suspicion' is called for which refuses to take any interpretation of the *bible or account of Christian faith at its face value and asks instead who is commending it and for what reason, then it is needed wherever the issue of poverty is being debated.

The terms of the debate shifted somewhat during the 20th century, partly due to a heightened awareness of the dynamics that drive and shape human society, reflected for example in the *Marxist analysis of history, and partly to the growing influence of the so-called Third World. In the rise of Christian *liberation theology the two joined hands to reinforce one another. Rich Christians in what has been perceived as a 'poor world' have not remained unmoved but their response has often been as subtly protective of their wealth as it has been determined to put an end to the deep and indefensible disparities between countries and the social groups within them.

All the recurring attitudes to poverty in the Christian tradition have claimed biblical support.

1. 'Holy poverty', which renounces material wealth, frees people to serve others and keeps them close to and reliant on God. It was typified by *Francis of Assisi who, suspicious of the growing corporate wealth of the *monastic communities such as the *Benedictines, sent his mendicant friars to live on nothing but the necessities of the moment and the *charity of others. *Jesus' own poverty can be exaggerated but holy poverty finds echoes in gospel sayings about a Son of Man with nowhere to lay his head (Luke 9: 58) and the call of Jesus to the disciples to leave everything and follow him (Matt. 19: 21; Luke 5: 11; 12: 33; 18: 22; cf. 1 Cor. 9: 15) thus replicating his own self-sacrifice and servanthood, becoming poor that we might become rich (see IRENAEUS). In the OT the *psalms are full of admiration for the poor (Ps. 34; cf. Matt. 5: 5). As the pious ones they trust only in God (cf. also Jas. 2: 5) often, one suspects, because there is nothing and no one else left for them to trust. The Tractarians (see OXFORD MOVEMENT) returned to the medieval idea that the poor provided opportunities for the rich to gain *merit for heaven. Complementing this positive assessment of poverty are biblical warnings against riches and the pursuit of riches (Matt. 19: 23), frequently repeated by Christian teachers from the fathers to the *Reformers and just as frequently modified (famously by Clement of *Alexandria in Who is the Rich Man Who is Being Saved, c.190) by insisting that it is the attitude to riches that is decisive not the possession of them (cf. Matt. 5: 3 with Luke 6: 20).

2. The idea that the poor have only themselves to blame dies hard. If *prosperity is a sign of God's blessing (as Abraham and the Psalmist, in 37: 25, and the *Puritans for example thought it was) poverty is due to laziness or lack of intelligence or is a penalty for wrongdoing and, because such human failings persist, will never wholly go away just as heaven will never be built on earth. Many of these ideas were reflected in Victorian attitudes to the poor, turning social welfare provision into something more like a penal code (cf. Poor Law Amendment Act 1834). Contemporary attitudes to poor countries and the 'starving overpopulated millions' are not always

much in advance. In the bible *Job's poverty is thought by his friends to be God's punishment (4: 7–9). Jesus castigates those who lack initiative and bury their talents in the ground (Matt. 25: 26) and, on another occasion, postpones a charity auction with the realistic comment that 'the poor you have always with you' (Mark 14: 7; cf. Deut. 15: 11).

3. That poverty is unacceptable and unjust and ought to be removed by charity, or social change, or both has inspired a whole string of Christian philanthropists and reformers, not to mention *revolutionaries. Some, like John *Wesley, who taught his followers to gain and save and give all they could, would doubtless have combined an appeal to the parable of the talents with another to the Pauline injunction to collect for the poor in Jerusalem (1 Cor. 16: 1–3). Others would go much further, denouncing in prophetic tones the unjust practices which 'sell the needy for a pair of shoes' (Amos 2: 6–7) whilst looking for a reordering of society whereby the last shall be first and, in the words of the Magnificat (Luke 1: 46–55), the mighty are put down from their thrones and the poor are lifted high.

4. Poverty has been seen by liberation movements of the 20th century as a, if not the, central preoccupation of God's mission in Christ and through his church. God opts for the poor (see, for example, the Roman Catholic *Sollicitudo Rei Socialis* 1988), putting them and their freedom from poverty first as the key to the *salvation of the whole, as is made clear in the announcement by Jesus in Nazareth (Luke 4: 18) that he is anointed by the Spirit to preach good news to the poor; all of which is in stark contrast to those who see Christian mission as primarily to sinners, rich and poor alike: they have all broken with God and are reconciled by faith in the redemptive work of Christ. Their salvation may lead to good works and the love of their neighbour, but the acid test of it, no doubt attractive to comfortable Christians, is by no means a drastically different social order or even an experiment in Christian communism within the church (cf. Acts 2: 44; 4: 32; and the Diggers of the 17th century).

Whilst no view of poverty is unaffected by self-interest and personal experience and the issues of the day, we can avoid the worst of distortions by open and constant debate with parties whose interests are other than our own, above all the rich with the poor.

Turning to recent times, in the days of rapid economic growth and increasing affluence in the west, some Christians surmised that the pressing issue for their faith and action would be how to manage wealth rather than how to overcome poverty. Poverty, however, persists. Where it is seen as unacceptable because it is involuntary, or the child of injustice, or because it cramps and diminishes the human spirit and threatens human community, or for whatever reason, Christians have adopted various ways to combat it, often as ambiguous as their attitudes to poverty itself and just as capable of appealing to the bible for support. Charity, the Welfare State, *socialism, and *capitalism, with its alleged links to *Calvinism and the Protestant ethic, are major examples.

In the second half of the 20th century when governments set up the Bretton Woods institutions including the World Bank, the churches created aid and development agencies and set out to redeem the times. The ravages of war (1914–18 and 1939–45) had left millions of destitute refugees in Europe and across the world. Colonialism, often uneasily allied to *missionary endeavours, had ex-

ploited the wealth of the Third World. The fruits of capitalism had been enjoyed by relatively few at the expense of many. Whilst great advances were made, at both government and voluntary levels, in education, healthcare, and the supply of food, for example, the problems did not go away. Conflict, often small-scale but widespread, continued to impoverish. Dependency, whereby the fortunes or misfortunes of poor countries were at the mercy of the rich, continued. Economic development was to be brought about by reproducing and globalizing capitalism and its 'trickle-down' benefits, but it also reproduced its tendency to hand most of the spoils to the strong.

Several complementary or alternative strategies have been adopted. One is to appreciate the technical elegance of the free market (often criticized by Christians as encouraging selfish and competitive individualism) whilst understanding the need to regulate it both within and between countries so that everyone gets a fair chance to trade and earn a living. Another, according to liberation theology, is to free the poor from an oppressive system which cannot be reformed, together with their minds ('conscientization') so that they are capable of initiating and participating in change. The worst of injustice can only be prevented by confronting the issue of power. The Christian tradition recognizes the tendency of any powerful group to look after its own interests (however shortsighted its view of them may be) at the expense of others. The answer is not a revolutionary reversal of power, since that only gives a different group the opportunity to misrule, but a better balance. *Democracy, internalized with regional economies less dependent on the world outside, a strong civil society with international links, a voice for poor countries in the affairs of international institutions, are some of the ways this balance can be achieved. Most important of all is to understand the deep, underlying relationship between poverty, conflict, and insecurity and to tackle conflicts, not only at the level of mediation and peace-keeping but at the level of the scarcity of resources, including the scarcity of land, that provokes them in the first place.

Two ideas have had a particular appeal for Christians at the turn of the century. One is corrective and the other constructive. The biblical idea of Jubilee is described in Leviticus 25 and probably alluded to by Jesus in Luke 4. It required the Israelites to take corrective measures every fifty years in favour of the poor. *Slaves were to be freed. Debts were to be cancelled. Confiscated land was to be handed back. Similar measures have been advocated today including the cancellation of the international debts of the poorest countries (see FORGIVENESS). Of more general and enduring relevance, however, is the recognition that a relentless flow of resources from the poor to the rich is endemic to most societies, local and international, and of the need for built-in mechanisms to reverse it. Global taxes on the movement of capital and on air travel, yielding resources to plough back into the development of poorer countries and the protection of the environment, have been cited as examples. The result is not a periodic jubilee year but a social order permanently characterized by the jubilee principle.

Abject poverty, especially in the wake of disasters, 'natural' or otherwise, is unlikely to disappear, but for the most part poverty is better understood as 'relative'. It adds up to exclusion from the life of the surrounding society, its work and its leisure. The answer is not charity or welfare or aid, though such safety nets are necessary, but 'inclusion': to construct an inclusive order, economic and political, that allows everyone to enjoy a sustainable livelihood as a human right and that consequently can require everyone to take their share of responsibility for others.

'Inclusion' has to come to terms with some of the hard, judgemental words and deeds of the bible and of the church in the name of religion, but it can claim support from the gospel's concern for the outsider, the last and the least. Like any acceptable order however, an inclusive order will not be built on Christian principles alone. The war against unholy poverty must draw on many disciplines, notably those that can harmonize the merits of competition and of co-operation, the claims of the individual and of the community, the benefits of a free market system with corrective mechanisms ensuring fair play, and the accumulation of wealth for investment with its ultimate use to please God and promote all-round human flourishing.

See also GLOBAL ETHICS; JUSTICE.   **Michael H. Taylor**

Brandt, W., *North–South: A Programme for Survival* (1980).
de Santa Ana, J., *Towards a Church in Solidarity with the Poor* (1980).
Dickens, C., *Oliver Twist* (1838).
Finn, D. R., *Just Trading: On the Ethics and Economics of International Trade* (1996).
Munby, D., *God and the Rich Society* (1961).
Russell, H., *Poverty Close to Home* (1995).
Sider, R. J., *Rich Christians in an Age of Hunger*, new edn. (1990).
Taylor, M., *Not Angels but Agencies: The Ecumenical Response to Poverty* (1995).

praise. The practice of praise is central to the Christian tradition of *prayer and *worship. Indeed it is central to the Judaeo-Christian tradition as a whole. The praise *psalms of the OT, said daily, are a vital part of the prayer of praying communities of east and west alike. They form the heart of the *monastic office called Lauds ('praises') which comes at the end of morning prayer. Indeed it seems likely that the practice of praise is central to all religious traditions, and, furthermore, to all human traditions of celebration, whether in *poetry, *music, dance, or song. 'These poems were written for the love of Man and in praise of God and I would be a damn fool if they weren't,' as Dylan Thomas said in the introduction to his *Collected Poems* (1952). To be human is to be able to praise; and in the end that means to praise *God.

Thus in praise we seek to give back true worth to the one praised. This is why there is an inseparable link between praise and worship. If we go on to praise things and people for what they are and for what they do, in the end that is because we praise God both for what he is in himself and for what he does. Above all, however, we praise God for what he is in himself. 'We praise thee, we bless thee, we glorify thee, we give thanks to thee for thy great glory.' When we praise God for what he does, thanksgiving is perhaps the most appropriate term to use. We praise him for what he is, we thank him for what he does. The two things are not mutually exclusive, however, but overlapping.

Christian worship is therefore at its heart a sacrifice of praise and thanksgiving. As those words suggest, praise is as central to our understanding of the *Eucharist and the church's *sacramental life as it is to the prayer of the church sung daily in the office. *Augustine makes clear that *sacrifice is any action in which things are offered to God, made over to him, restored to him, made holy by

being brought into contact with his *holiness (*sacrum facere*, to make holy). This happens in both biblical and sacramental forms of worship.

We do not praise God alone. We praise all things that are, for being, because all things that are reveal to us something of the God from whom they take their being. In particular we praise women and men, made in God's image and likeness, in whom in a particular way God's splendour and beauty, his strangeness and wonder, his grace and glory, are made present and made known. In praising the *saints we praise those who belong to God, the holy ones. But we must not use that word too narrowly or exclusively. All people in some way or other belong to God and in that sense the *communion of saints, which is a sharing in holy things as well as in holy persons, is potentially all-inclusive. In W. H. Auden's words, we 'praise what there is for being'. All creation enters into our praise.

In praising our fellow men and women we are apt to get confused if we do not see the essential God-relatedness involved in all true acts of praise. In a society that does not recognize, or which explicitly denies, the sacred character of poetry and art, praise can very easily be construed as mere idolatrous flattery. If in the end there is no ultimate and eternal source of goodness and beauty to praise, acts of praise may easily be understood as indulgence in illusion or fantasy. In such a view it seems better and more honest to debunk than to praise.

But the praise of God is something quite other than flattery and not a matter of illusion or fantasy. As Philip Toynbee remarks in the last volume of his journal *End of a Journey* (1988), 'true praise of God is quite unlike praising a powerful human being. Far from abasing ourselves in order to flatter the emperor by proclaiming how high he is above us, our adoration of God should be a means of bringing us closer to him. The purer our praise the more we ourselves are filled with the God we are praising.'

*John of the Cross once asked one of the Carmelite sisters what her prayer consisted in. She replied 'in contemplating the beauty of God and rejoicing that he has such beauty'. Writing about the Welsh Methodist *hymn-writer Ann Griffiths, Saunders Lewis speaks of the nature of her prayer as involving 'a selfless vision, a vision wholly appreciative, a vision full of wonder and blessing and rejoicing, without anything of self or any thought of self entering into it' (Allchin 1991: 109).

Such an act of praise is one in which all human faculties are united, love and knowledge, desire and aspiration. The practice of God's praise has a deeply integrating effect on human life. We are united within ourselves and at the same time drawn beyond ourselves into a truly *ecstatic* action which takes us beyond our own limitations and at the same time restores us to our innermost being. We find ourselves in going beyond ourselves. That is true not only here and now in space and time, but beyond this world in the spaces of eternity. We find our true *humanity as we enter into the praise of God, for that is the true end for which we are made: to praise and enjoy him forever.   **A. M. Allchin**

Allchin, A. M., *Praise Above All: Discovering the Welsh Tradition* (1991).
Guiver, George, *A Company of Voices* (1988).
Hardy, Daniel, and Ford, David, *Jubilate: Theology in Praise* (1984).
Stevenson, Kenneth, *Covenant of Grace Renewed: A Vision of the Eucharist in the Seventeenth Century* (1994).

prayer. Christian life has always oscillated between prayer and action, two poles often seen as symbolized by Martha and Mary, the two sisters at Bethany (Luke 10: 38–42). While Mary 'sat at the Lord's feet', Martha was 'distracted by much serving' and asked *Jesus to tell her sister to help her, but he replied, 'Mary has chosen the better part which shall not be taken away from her.' Contemplation, then, is preferable to service. Modern Christianity would appear largely to have sided with Martha, which makes it the more important to do justice to prayer, as central to the entire tradition.

Christian prayer stands in the closest continuity with Jewish prayer. The *psalms constituted the core of the latter, built up across several centuries. They were taken over in their entirety by the church and have remained the core of its official prayer. By far the greater part of the daily office as prayed by monks (see MONASTICISM) and priests in the *Catholic and *Eastern Orthodox churches or as constituting Matins and Evensong for *Anglicans, consists in the recitation of the psalms. Only in very modern times has it been suggested that such lines as 'Happy shall he be who takes your little ones and dashes them against the rock' (137: 9) should be excluded from use. The only words Mark reports Jesus as pronouncing from the cross are taken from Psalm 22.

If the psalms were the regular prayer of Jesus, shared with his *disciples and retained unhesitatingly by the church, he added two personal contributions of no less importance. The first was the *Lord's Prayer (Matt. 6: 9–14 and Luke 11: 2–4). While the Lucan form may be closer to the original, it is the longer Matthean form that has become the single piece of prayer most widely used by Christians, so simple that it can be shared across all denominations and often with non-Christians too. There is nothing in it that does not reflect the deepest Jewish piety. While regularly used within the *liturgy, it is even more a personal and family prayer, effectively the heart of the Christian approach to God.

Less obvious as a creative model of prayer are the words of Jesus at the Last Supper when he took bread, gave thanks, broke it and said, 'This is my body, which is for you. Do this in remembrance of me.... This cup is the new covenant in my blood' (1 Cor. 11: 24–5). Part of a meal, this is something far more unexpected, more difficult to interpret, and open to very diverse continuation, yet this 'giving thanks' (*eucharistia*) in memory of Jesus has remained the central public prayer of the Christian community for all the main traditions, endlessly stimulating theologically. 'As often as you eat this bread and drink this cup, you proclaim the Lord's death until he comes.' It is thus not only a *sacramental re-enactment of Christ's final meal with his disciples and the death that follows with all its sacrificial significance, but also a signal of faith in the future 'until he comes'. The *Eucharist has always been at the heart of theologies of union with Christ as well as with one another within the institutional church, a union which its celebration alone makes fully visible. The church remains, more than all else, a fellowship of prayer. *Lex orandi; lex credendi*: the authorized prayer of the church provides the guide to its belief. The canon of the Eucharist and its related prayers contain Christianity's most fundamental creed.

From these various elements is derived the basic shape of Christian prayer, passed on almost unchanged from apostolic times: on the one hand recital of the psalms and similar canticles, such as the Magnificat, within daily services of prayer and *praise inherited in essentials from the synagogue; on the other, celebration of the Eucharist, primarily on a weekly, *Sunday, basis, a specifically Christian performance. The two together have always constituted the church's public prayer, around which and out of which grows the largely unstructured prayer of the home, the hermit, the monk at work and on his own. Jesus was remembered as someone who prayed alone, often all night long (Luke 5: 16; 6: 12; 11: 1). The disciples are reported by Luke as asking to be taught how to pray when they saw him praying. Matthew records the instruction not to 'heap up empty phrases'. All three Synoptics record his agonized solitary prayer in the garden: 'Abba, Father, all things are possible to thee; remove this cup from me; yet not what I will but what thou wilt' (Mark 14: 36). That, too, has always remained a primary marker for Christian prayer.

From the 4th century these three elements develop, each with its own history. The simple early Eucharist becomes a stately, highly ceremonial occasion for which the great *Constantinian basilicas were constructed; the daily prayer services develop into the extended monastic office with, eventually, eight distinct 'hours' from Matins to Compline, during which the 150 psalms are recited each week in combination with scripture readings and other hymns and prayers (see TIME). From the third element we may trace the growth of personal and *mystical prayer. Paul appears to claim experience of the latter in 2 Cor. 12: 'caught up to the third heaven—whether in the body or out of the body I do not know, God knows'. Here the east was strongest, providing around the start of the 6th century a body of mystical writing by an unknown writer (*Dionysius the Pseudo-Areopagite), devoted to the union of all creation with God; it had a profound influence in the east and, from the 12th century, in the west. Within *Byzantine Christianity there further developed in the following centuries the practice of hesychasm associated particularly with the monasteries on Mount Athos and with Gregory Palamas. Vital for hesychasm was the constant repetition of the Jesus Prayer: 'Lord Jesus Christ, Son of God, have mercy upon me', linked with a particular posture of head and body.

In the west the literature of meditational and mystical prayer grew with *Anselm and Bernard in the 12th century, but still more in the 14th. Two outstanding schools developed, both using the vernacular, the English and the German. To the former belonged Richard Rolle, Walter Hilton, and *The Cloud of Unknowing*, to the latter Meister Eckhart, Henry Suso, and Johann Tauler, all three *Dominicans. Two centuries later the western church produced even more brilliant teachers of mystical prayer in the Spanish school of *Teresa of Avila and *John of the Cross. It is striking that virtually all this literature is in the vernacular. Throughout these writings the concern is for the union of the *soul with God through the practice of prayer growing in simplicity, but this was not a rejection of public liturgical practice. In writers like Rolle and Hilton, it went with a marked concern to help lay people to pray better. Rolle translated the psalms into English (c.1340) and Hilton, in particular, stressed that people in the 'mixed life', other than monks, nuns, and anchorites, can advance in personal prayer. The writings of all these people were popular with the increasing number of lay Christians, such as *Beguines, who sought a way of personal prayer that the stiff, clerical solemnity of Latin high mass and office could not supply. The 'Little Office' of the Blessed Virgin was much used in such circles.

In some ways these movements were confirmed by the *Reformation, with its insistence on praying in the vernacular, its use of the psalms, and its simplification of sacramental and liturgical ritual in public *worship. Cranmer was a master of composition of simple and intellectually satisfying prayers, mostly translations from the Latin liturgy. But the Reformation was in the main not only anti-monastic but anti-mystical, swinging across from Mary to Martha. *Pietism developed in reaction. The master texts of the art of prayer in the 16th and 17th centuries were, however, almost all written by Catholics: from the *Ascent of Mount Carmel* and the *Dark Night of the Soul* of John of the Cross through the *Spiritual Exercises* of Ignatius Loyola to the *Introduction to the Devout Life* of Francis de Sales and the treatise on abandonment to divine providence of Jean Pierre de Caussade, so close to *Quietism. Even members of the small surviving English Roman Catholic minority wrote some remarkable works on prayer in this period, including the *Christian Directory* of Robert Parsons (1582, reprinted over forty times in England before 1640) and *Sancta Sophia* (1657) by the Benedictine Augustine Baker. Much of this literature was used extensively by Protestants even when, as in the case of the Jesuit Parsons, the author was, in political terms, a dangerous enemy.

The psalms can already be classified in terms of different types of prayer as adoration, thanksgiving, propitiation, and petition, and this has remained a basic way of considering content, particularly in regard to public worship. Yet in much Christian prayer it would be hard to separate these different categories, so easily does a single prayer move from one to another or incorporate them all. Prayer is essentially conversation with God and the more it is exercised the less structured it tends to become, as in all good conversations. It can well include long patches of silence. *Quaker prayer meetings may consist of nothing else. Prayer is often associated in the modern mind chiefly with petition, asking for things, and modern-minded philosophical theologians agonize over whether it can be right or reasonable to do so. Can praying for something actually alter the way things are or will be? If one is praying for strength to forgive someone, including oneself, prayer will certainly help alter what otherwise may seem immutable. 'Ask, and it will be given you; seek, and you will find' (Luke 11: 9). In every age people who pray with fervour have found this to be true; it can even include the most inexplicable cure at Lourdes. But they also find that what is given is not necessarily quite what they asked. Entering into prayer with full sincerity means entering God's world unconditionally; when that happens, mind and heart become attuned to a different priority. Not our priorities prevail, but God's: 'Not what I will but what thou wilt.' Of the millions of the sick who go to Lourdes not one in ten thousand is 'cured', but the attitudes of the pilgrims to their sickness may be transformed (see HEALTH AND HEALING).

The practice of prayer begins with the recitation of texts, short or long, but the more it comes alive, the more the texts need to become simpler, to stop holding the mind back from an awareness of God which cannot be verbalized. Oral prayer may at first be supplemented by the meditational practices encouraged particularly by the Ignatian *Spiritual Exercises*, but they in their turn may seem too complicated to be helpful as the mind moves into what is traditionally termed contemplation, an ever simpler relationship

with God, an experience much of which feels like 'dark night' rather than spiritual illumination, but all of which can continue to be nourished by the liturgy and spiritual reading. In the west the religious orders, each with its characteristic *spirituality, have tended to specialize in the practice and exegesis of one or another form of prayer: the *Benedictines of liturgical prayer, the *Jesuits of meditation, the Carmelites, Carthusians, and Dominicans of contemplation. But what is most characteristic of the best modern literature has been encouragement of ways to foster prayer in secular life.

Most Christian prayer has always been directed to God, to the Father, just as was that of Jesus himself. Yet prayer expressly directed to Jesus began already in the NT as with that very early invocation 'Marana tha' (1 Cor. 16: 22 and Rev. 22: 20), 'Come, Lord (Jesus)'. But it has never been extensive within the liturgy, any more than has the invocation of the *Holy Spirit.

Prayer has few absolute rules beyond truthfulness. There seems to be no convincing reason why one should not pray to *Mary, Mother of God, or to other *saints, in the sense of asking for their intercession, or about anything at all. The practice of praying to Mary is very traditional and it fits well into a conversational model of prayer. No one should be left out of the discussion. Nevertheless a pattern of prayer directed mostly to Mary, or still more St Anthony, or even St Philomena (who did not exist!) suggests a misdirection of spiritual effort. But though the medieval practice of the rosary, still in use among many Catholics, may strike an observer as mere mechanical repetition of words addressed to Mary (and may even become just that through inattention), it is in fact intended to be a series of meditations on the events of Christ's life, death, and glorification; at its best a popular form of mental prayer.

The purpose of all prayer is union with God. The best prayer will not wander far from that. But the more mind and heart reach that goal, the more open they will be to bringing with them everyone and everything else in creation in a turning back to 'the world'. In the total geography of Christian living the monastery, the home *par excellence* of a daily round of prayer, is critically important, but not as set apart from the community as a whole. Mary without Martha can make no more sense than Martha without Mary.

Adrian Hastings

Appleton, George, *The Practice of Prayer* (1980).
Baelz, Peter, *Prayer and Providence* (1968).
Bloom, Anthony, *Living Prayer* (1980).
Chapman, John, *Spiritual Letters* (1935).
Davies, J. G. (ed.), *A New Dictionary of Liturgy and Worship* (1986).
Hardy, D. W., and Ford, D. F., *Jubilate: Theology in Praise* (1984).
Jeremias, J., *The Prayers of Jesus* (1967).
Lewis, C. S., *Letters to Malcolm: Chiefly on Prayer* (1964).
Simpson, R., *The Interpretation of Prayer in the Early Church* (1965).
Tugwell, Simon, *Prayer* (2 vols.; 1974).
von Balthasar, H. Urs, *Contemplative Prayer* (1961).

preaching/homiletics.

In its most familiar manifestation, preaching is an occasion for speaking in a *missionary or a cultic setting. The occasion requires a person who is appointed to speak, a congregation of hearers, and an aurally received message. In most settings, the rhetorical situation is sustained by the audience's implicit recognition of the speaker's *authority to convey the things of God, often, though not always, on the basis of a text of scripture.

Beyond this fundamental pattern of elements, Christian preaching has known no theological or rhetorical boundaries.

Some sermons last five minutes, some forty-five. Some are preached beneath the canopied pulpits of great cathedrals, others in store-front meeting halls, hospitals, or cemeteries. Some contain poetic evocations of the divine–human encounter, others follow a style described by the Anglican Robert South, 'plain, natural, and familiar'. Some sermons strive for intellectual stimulation, others for *Pentecostal ecstasy. Some sermons guide the soul's journey to heaven, others, like those of Martin Luther King, Jr., seek to transform the world. Yet all represent Christian preaching.

Of the many purposes for Christian preaching, the four dominant types are missionary preaching, instruction in the *faith, *liturgical preaching, and *moral guidance. The earliest model of the sermon in the NT is not a sermon at all, but the written theology of *Paul, whose single-minded devotion to the 'good news' or the *'kerygma' (proclamation) of the death and *Resurrection of *Jesus supplied a pattern for the missionary sermon and informed the preaching of *Luther, *Calvin, and later *revivalists. However, the *New Testament contains other models as well, including the Epistle to the *Hebrews, which might have been a catechetical sermon, and 1 Peter, which is easily imagined as a liturgical homily at a baptism.

The sermon has its roots in the synagogue. The earliest depiction of a synagogue sermon is found in Luke 4: 16–30 in which the elements of Christian preaching are already present: a setting for *worship; a text from scripture; a speaker whose authority is recognized; an interpretation of scripture (see BIBLE, ITS AUTHORITY AND INTERPRETATION); an application for those assembled; and a congregational response. In this passage we also see the proclaimer becoming the proclaimed: Jesus announces his own mission as the fulfilment or the 'meaning' of the prophetic text.

The close commentary on scripture, or homily-style of preaching, which the church learned from the synagogue, was soon supplemented by the classically inspired oration, or sermon proper, characterized by what George Kennedy (1980: 136) calls a 'more artificial rhetoric addressed to cultured audiences'. Even when the sermon was ostensibly based on the authority of a text, it was nurtured by the classical ideals of *reason, eloquence, and persuasion. The preacher-orator developed themes, which he elaborated and defended by employing the full range of design-schemes, logical inferences, and figures of speech. One of the most famous early sermons was the Easter sermon by Melito of Sardis, preached around 165, which featured 'the most flamboyant literary style imaginable' (ibid.).

The turn to *rhetoric, later validated by *Augustine in On Christian Doctrine, 4, opened preaching to the full embrace of language in all its forms: *metaphor, *poetry, drama, narrative, as well as the ordinary language of common people. The polarity of the simple homily and the more synthetically constructed sermon persisted throughout the Christian centuries. For example, Lancelot Andrewes (see CAROLINE DIVINES) presented a revolutionary alternative to the plain-style sermon with his imaginative recreation of the believer's experience of Christ. Ellen Davis (1995: 21–2) writes, 'Andrewes's terse images contrast with the remarkably extended metaphors so characteristic of John *Donne; but even that flamboyant poet does not exceed the boldness of Andrewes's imagin-

ation. Christ is considered variously as wildcat, grammatical particle, embryo, and herb; the compassionate God as though possessed of multiple wombs filled with the pity of many mothers'. One of Andrewes's Nativity sermons was adopted with little change by T. S. Eliot in his poem Journey of the Magi: Andrewes said of the Magi, 'It was no summer progress. A cold coming they had of it at this time of the year, just the worst time of the year to take a journey, and specially a long journey in. The ways deep, the weather sharp, the days short, the sun farthest off, in solstitio brumali, the very dead of winter'. The effect of such preaching is not to teach a lesson or make a point but to enrol the hearer into the biblical narrative and, in the case of both Andrewes and Donne, to stretch to breaking point the use of ordinary language in order to give utterance to extraordinary truths. In one of his sermons Donne boldly addresses the 'metaphorical God' of the imagination and in another, on the resurrection of the dead, reminds his hearers that 'God knows in what Cabinet every seed-Pearle lies, in what part of the world every graine of every mans dust lies; and … he whispers, he hisses, he beckens for the bodies of his Saints …'.

A century later, George Whitefield found another idiom for preaching. His dramatic performances were not 'witty' in the manner of the metaphysical poet-intellectuals, Andrewes and Donne, but they captured the imagination of the masses by their dramatic evocation of biblical events. Using the device of the privileged witness, Whitefield rhapsodizes on the apostle *Peter, 'Methinks I see him wringing his hands, rending his garments, stamping on the ground and, with the self-condemned publican, smiting his breast. See how it heaves!' Whitefield took his show to America where, according to his biographer, he became 'Anglo-America's first modern celebrity' (Harry Stout, The Divine Dramatist (1991), xii), and his revivals laid the groundwork for the Great Awakenings, the growth of *evangelicalism, and the conversion of Africans in America. Of more dubious value, he was also the proto-celebrity-evangelist whose personal magnetism would in later incarnations outdraw the message itself.

The adaptability of the Christian message to various languages and styles points to two overriding criteria by which a sermon may be evaluated. It is required that a sermon faithfully reflect some authoritative tradition or text, and it must communicate its message in the idiom of its hearers. The bible does not contain rules for achieving these ends. Nor do most preachers reflect on their theological or rhetorical rationale for preaching; they simply preach, week in, week out.

Homiletics is the branch of *pastoral theology that reflects on the church's activity of preaching, asks questions about its practicability, and suggests guidelines for the preparation and delivery of sermons. A synthetic discipline, homiletics (from the Latin for conversation) closely allies itself with several other fields of enquiry and branches of theology, including rhetoric, communications, and *hermeneutics.

On its technical side, homiletics follows the 'rules' of exegesis and adapts them to preaching. It joins its concerns to those of biblical interpretation. Technical homiletics is faith seeking expression in a world far removed from the world of the bible. It asks, how does the contemporary preacher give effective expression to biblical concepts, such as grace, forgiveness, wrath, and the Kingdom of God? How does one speak of 'love' or 'peace' in a culture that uses the same words but empties them of their divine dimension? How does a modern preacher convey the reality of God in a *secular culture?

Interpretation is closely linked with rhetoric. The hymnodist asks, 'What language shall I borrow | to thank Thee, dearest Friend?' Since Augustine, homiletics has employed the classical rhetorical categories of invention, organization, style, memory, and delivery. Invention has to do with discovering the key issue at stake in the text. In the information-gathering stage of sermon preparation, the preacher tries to find out as much as possible about the text. Yet for the preacher, 'invention' is carried out in an attitude of reverence towards the biblical text, as if through it God were searching us, and not vice versa.

Organization, or arrangement, displays the message in as organic a manner as possible. Many contemporary homileticians, inspired by learning theory, have spoken of the sermon as a 'plot' that mirrors the mind's process of discovery. It is not so important to arrange a neatly symmetrical structure, since a sermon is not *seen* as a diagram on paper but is *heard* and experienced like a story or a musical performance. The sermon does not announce its conclusion (or punch-line) at the beginning but gradually unfolds towards it.

*African preachers, as well as African Americans, have sought to transcend the idea-oriented, essaic form of sermon. In place of distilling ideas from a topic or text, which often results in talking *about* religious subjects, preachers have attended to image, rhythm, repetition, and congregational response, in an effort to *execute* the text. The chanted word brings the biblical letter to life. The model here is not explanation but performance. And the ultimate performer is not a single charismatic preacher, but the entire congregation, which enacts the sermon first in the sanctuary, then in the world.

The style of the sermon's language should honour both the integrity of the text and the integrity of contemporary communication. It should not cheaply 'translate' biblical values into slang; nor does it present 'frozen sections' of biblical, Elizabethan, or orthodox traditions to contemporary people who require words they can understand. Two of the most significant developments in modern preaching are the rise of psychology and the communications revolution. Both have influenced the content and style of the sermon. The 19th-century Brighton preacher, F. W. Robertson, pioneered the use of psychological insights in his sensitive portrayals of Jesus and those who struggle to believe in him. He insisted that truth should be taught 'suggestively' not 'dogmatically', and in his evocative studies, for example, 'The Loneliness of Christ', he unveiled a human Christ, one whose suffering seemed to partake of the anxiety and alienation of the modern age. Many of the same interests surfaced in the British Methodist Leslie Weatherhead, minister of London's City Temple from 1936 to 1960. He ministered to the city's wartime anxiety with a simple, caring, pastoral spirit, animated by the question, 'What makes life more meaningful?' In *When the Lamp Flickers* he writes,

> The commonest criticism that I hear of sermons is that they do not deal with the problems ordinary men and women are facing, that they talk a language remote from everyday living, that much of the sermon time is given to biblical and theological problems which do not seem to bear upon life at all, and that the language used is often a preacher's jargon which means little to the layman. In a word, that religion is not apparently related to life. And that is a damning indictment.

Television, mass media, and computer technology have also profoundly affected the sermon. Mass media's clipped and quasi-objective style of presentation has altered the way we think and speak. The average length of a story on a network news programme in America is 45 seconds; the average image lasts 4 seconds. Unrelated stories are strung together by little more than the phrase, 'Now this'. According to Kathleen Hall Jamieson, television, in particular, has 'feminized' public speaking. What the ancients derided as the effeminate style—quiet, experiential, intuitive, narrative, restrained in voice and gesture—has proved quite effective on the small screen, and has become the norm for both female and male communicators.

The church's preaching struggles for its own voice in the new rhetorical atmosphere, or 'sensorium' (Walter Ong). The religious force whose cadences once shaped western culture is now more likely to adapt its own language (and delivery) to its audience's weakened powers of attention and its penchant for images above ideas. Christian preachers increasingly work in a historical vacuum among hearers who come to church with little in the way of theological knowledge or loyalty to tradition. In such an atmosphere, it is likely that in the 21st century the instructional type of sermon will re-emerge with new prominence, and preachers will place renewed emphasis on the communal and human dimensions of the Christian faith.   **Richard Lischer**

Brilioth, Y., *A Brief History of Preaching* (1945), ET (1965).
Craddock, F., *As One Without Authority*, rev. edn. (1974).
Davis, Ellen F., *Imagination Shaped* (1995).
Jamieson, Kathleen Hall, *Eloquence in an Electronic Age* (1988).
Kennedy, G., *Classical Rhetoric and its Christian and Secular Tradition* (1980).
Lash, N., 'Performing the Scriptures,' in *Theology on the Way to Emmaus* (1986).
Lischer, R. (ed.), *Theories of Preaching* (1987).
Ong, W. J., *Orality and Literacy* (1982).
Postman, N., *Amusing Ourselves to Death* (1985).
Willimon, W., and Lischer, R. (eds.), *Concise Encyclopedia of Preaching* (1995).

pre-Constantinian thought.

Christian thought in the 2nd and 3rd centuries, before the change of government policy toward Christianity under *Constantine, provokes differing reactions. The emergence of some consensus in Christian thinking, in the work of such figures as Justin Martyr, Irenaeus, Tertullian, Clement of Alexandria, and Origen, is sometimes hailed as addressing fundamental implications of the gospel, sometimes decried as introducing alien philosophical ideas or imposing ecclesiastical authority in matters of belief.

The developments to which these figures contributed are clear. Despite their differences, they worked towards establishing what would finally become the body of Christian scriptures—the Jewish writings and an eventually recognized collection of Christian writings—as the basis of Christian teaching (see BIBLE, ITS AUTHORITY AND INTERPRETATION). They also agreed in regarding the 'rule (*canon*) of *faith' embodied in the confessions of faith used in preparation for *baptism—the forerunners of later *creeds—as the key to understanding these scriptures. Their exploration of scriptural teaching broadly established the agenda of their successors in the following centuries: the relation of *God to the *world and of the persons of the Godhead to each other, and the nature of *evil, all in the context of the unfolding plan of *salvation now approaching its completion with the coming of Christ and the gift of the *Holy Spirit.

Neither these writers nor their successors were systematic theologians in any later sense. They are treated here in the light of the issues they addressed, with only the briefest reference to contradictory estimates of their work. For instance, we assume that the various confessional forms embodying the 'rule of faith' have their origin in such primitive proclamations and explanations of the new life in Christ, given through the Spirit in baptism, as Romans 6–8 and Matthew 28: 19, rather than that they were contrived to establish ecclesiastical authority over people's beliefs.

Again, when we see them in use, these confessions of faith include themes which differentiate them from the teachings of the various so-called *Gnostic groups: they affirm God as creator of earth as well as heaven, Christ come in the flesh, salvation through the *church, *forgiveness, and *Resurrection rather than 'knowledge'. But our writers are not to be seen as merely rejecting the teaching of their opponents as '*heretical' for questioning common belief. Indeed, much of the interest of the 'orthodox' writing of the period lies in its efforts to understand the secret teaching of the Gnostics and to meet its challenge through interpretation of the scriptures.

Finally, these writers, with their diverse knowledge and differing estimates of the issues discussed in the philosophical schools, were concerned with *philosophy for its usefulness in exploring basic elements of Christian belief, not as constituting a framework within which to interpret the gospel.

The early period

The collection of late 1st- and early 2nd-century writings, which the 17th-century French scholar Cotelier was perhaps the first to call 'apostolic fathers', includes works of considerable and diverse interest: letters of Clement of Rome, Ignatius of Antioch, and Polycarp of Smyrna, the visions of the *Shepherd of Hermas*, and an early liturgical manual called *Didache* (Teaching of the Twelve Apostles). These writings were not eventually included in the body of Christian scriptures, but they are invaluable additions to our knowledge of the life and thought reflected in those contemporary books that were later so included.

The designation of various 2nd-century writers as 'apologists' is justified by its use in the writings of Quadratus, Aristides, and Justin Martyr, and by implication in Theophilus of Antioch, Athenagoras, and Tatian, and certainly reflects the circumstances of a time when growing pagan opposition and government intervention called for reasoned accounts of Christianity. But the 'apologists' addressed not merely pagans but themselves and their Christian readers. It is with them that the processes of Christian thinking that will engage our attention begin to reveal themselves.

Justin Martyr stands out here in view of the extent and influence of his work. Convert from philosophy, catechist of the Greek-speaking Christian community at *Rome, he was martyred *c.*165. His *Apology*, a broadside formally addressed to the co-emperors of the time, while necessarily simplified in presentation, gives a fair summary of his understanding of Christianity. The philosophical tradition has speculated that there is one God, whose *Word is the source of cosmic order and the rational principle in humanity: the God of *Israel is in truth the one whom the philosophers sought, and the Word has now become flesh in Jesus Christ and is responsible for the spread of the church (*Apol.* 9–10, 12–13). For Justin the Jewish writings are the 'scriptures' of the church (the Christian writings are not yet so regarded); and his proof of the truth of Christianity involves showing that what was prophesied in the scriptures is now being fulfilled in the events unfolding through the coming of Christ and, in anticipation, the culmination of the divine plan at the final judgement (ibid. 31–53). Meanwhile, through baptism and *Eucharist we participate in the life of the risen Christ through the Spirit (ibid. 61–6). While Justin does not here refer to a confession of faith, basic elements of his catechetical teaching can clearly be seen behind his explanation of baptism into the triune name; and the account of his trial records the recitation of such a confession as an explanation of Christian belief (*Martyrdom of Justin and Companions*, in Stevenson 1985: 28–30).

Others of Justin's authentic surviving works spell out aspects of his teaching. A *Second Apology*, commonly regarded as an appendix to the first, states clearly that God is the only 'uncreated' reality (2 *Apol.* 6); while the later *Dialogue with Trypho the Jew*, chiefly devoted to showing that the Jewish Scriptures foretell the coming of Christ as understood by Christians, includes an account of his abandonment of the search for salvation through philosophy because he became convinced that the soul is 'created' and thus mortal (*Dial.* 5). It is in treating the issue of 'creation', with its philosophical implications of change, temporality (see TIME), and even physicality, that Justin raises questions that will later be the subject of long debate among Christians. At a time when there is as yet no clear distinction in use between spiritual 'begetting' and 'creation' or 'generation,' Justin calls the Word 'created', unaware of the full dimension of the problem. Nor does he address such issues as the continuance of embodied existence after the Resurrection which the tradition has to deal with later. Nevertheless, with Justin we cross a threshold into a time when the concern of Christians to explain their faith to themselves as well as to others begins to raise rational issues not directly confronted before.

*Irenaeus was bishop of the Greek Christian community at Lyons (Lugdunum) in Gaul. A native of Asia Minor, he was known in the Greek Christian community at Rome, and was a presbyter of Lyons when he succeeded bishop Pothinus on his death in the persecution of 177. He is assumed to have died *c.*195. Of Irenaeus' two surviving works, one is a brief catechetical *Explanation of the Apostolic Faith* (*Demonstratio*), which he described as a summary of the teaching of the other, the massive five books of 'Detection and Refutation of the Knowledge Falsely So-Called', commonly known by the title of its Latin translation: *Against Heresies* (*Adversus haereses*). Irenaeus is especially concerned with the secret teaching of the Christian Gnostic groups of Valentinians (of the western school of Ptolemy), and with the Marcionites. He also gives accounts of a wide variety of teachers, criticizing them for their use of philosophical ideas, while attributing their origin to the teaching of Simon Magus (Acts 8: 9–24), probably in dependence on lost works of Justin.

Irenaeus' treatment of the Valentinians shows them interpreting the same scriptures as used by Christians in general. In the Ptolemaic version of their teaching, they find scriptural evidence for the existence of a vast series of spiritual aeons constituting a divine *pleroma* or 'fullness' beyond the present world. The world was caused by the fall of the last of the aeons, Sophia (*Wisdom), whose envious passion for the highest divine being brings forth a formless offspring, subsequently organized by a lesser creator into three orders: a physical order doomed to destruction, an imperfect psychic order to which the generality of Christians belong, and a spiritual order, the remnant seed of Sophia. Eventually, a saviour from the *pleroma* appears in the form of Jesus, to recall to their true place those who are spirituals by nature.

Irenaeus recognizes the appeal of this scheme when he frequently refers to it as his opponents' *hypothesis*, a plausible but untrue narrative. From Book 1 onwards he opposes to it the 'rule of faith (or truth)' everywhere accepted by the churches (*Adv. haer.* 1. 10. 1–2) as the key to the interpretation of the scriptures, now regarded as including the Christian writings. Though he can speak of the rule as 'our hypothesis', he identifies it as the apostolic *traditio* (*paradosis*) which is 'passed on' in the churches. He constantly insists that the 'rule' identifies the creator not as a lesser but as the only God, and the saviour as the Son of the creator and not an independent aeon. He has also in mind a larger series of issues with which, he suggests ironically, a person of greater insight—a 'Gnostic'—ought to be wrestling instead of denying the essentials of belief (1. 10. 3). Among these is the question of why the same God gave more than one *covenant, and he will later go on to deal with the Marcionite view that the covenant of the *law is the work of an evil God who condemns the disobedient, in contrast to that of the 'God and Father of our Lord Jesus Christ' who accepts sinners who believe.

Irenaeus' work was written in stages, giving rise both to repetition and to the introduction of new subjects. We may notice that Book 2 shows a surprising degree of dependence on rational argument proving that the divine must be one, and that, whether his opponents regard the ground of their *pleroma* or the *pleroma* itself as divine, they are 'rising beyond' human ability to penetrate the divine and erroneously picturing there the diversity of the created order (2. 1. 5, 8. 1–3, 13. 3–8). Book 3, the first of several later instalments, supports the claim of the 'rule' to be *apostolic by pointing to the preservation in the churches, by the succession of bishops (see EPISCOPATE), of the apostolic traditions in contrast to the diversity and lateness of the teachings of his opponents (3. 3–5).

In Book 4 Irenaeus offers his basic reply to his opponents' view of the divine plan or *economy* (*oikonomia*) of salvation. *Humanity, as created, was necessarily imperfect and needed growth and education before it could achieve existence 'according to the image and likeness' of the uncreated God (4. 38. 1–4). Moreover, humanity, as essentially possessed of 'self-determination' (free will), disobeyed and incurred mortality. The plan of salvation must, then, lead humanity freely to its destined perfection as well as reversing the consequences of disobedience. Thus the various stages of God's involvement with humanity lead to the coming of the Son or Word in the flesh in Christ as a *recapitulatio* (a 'new summing up') of humanity (Eph. 1: 10), so that the decrees of the law are cancelled and a renewed humanity is now capable of movement towards perfection 'according to the image and likeness' (e.g. 1. 10. 1; 3. 16. 6; 5. 21). In a phrase which runs through the work in various forms, in Christ 'the divine became human so that humanity might become divine' (e.g. 3. 10. 2, 19. 1; 4. 20. 5; 5 *praef.*).

In the final Book 5, a summary of many themes, Irenaeus looks forward to the outcome of the divine plan, and makes reference to the '*millenarian' tradition of his native Asia Minor, whereby a first resurrection of the saints will be followed by a thousand-year reign on a renewed earth before a final judgement. But his interpretation of the millennium reflects his vision of the perfection of humanity (5. 27–8), so that it serves as preparation for life 'according to the image and likeness of God', the words with which the work concludes.

Irenaeus says that his predecessors had not discovered enough about the teaching of their opponents to answer them (4. *praef.* 2), and he himself not only tries to be clear about that teaching but, despite inevitable rhetoric and invective, to deal with the issues it raises regarding essential elements of belief. He is perhaps most incisive in his treatment of the one divine nature and in his view of the relation of human *freedom and divine initiative in the process of *redemption. But he does not address Justin's outstanding problem of the 'created' Word: while he places Son and Spirit on the divine side of the gulf between divine and created, he avoids discussing their genesis. Similarly, while he clearly sets his anthropology of human freedom against Valentinian determinism, the restoration of the bodily unity of soul and flesh at the resurrection, while insisted upon, remains an unexplored question.

The third century

The writers dealt with so far have belonged to the Greek Christian communities that spread across the eastern Mediterranean and into Italy and Gaul. With Q. Septimius Florens Tertullianus of Carthage (*c*.160–*c*.225), and his early *Apology* of 196, we have evidence of the existence of Latin Christian communities in north-west Africa, already established with Latin translations of the Septuagint and the standard collection of Christian writings. But Tertullian and his Latin Christians did not think theirs a separate tradition of Christian thought. Bilingual himself, familiar with Justin and seemingly already possessing the Latin translation of Irenaeus, *Adversus haereses*, he is consciously dependent on his Greek predecessors. At the same time, attention to some major points will reveal the particular Latin perspective that Tertullian brings to the tradition.

His *Apology* uses themes of Justin's work, but greatly expands on the argument that the scriptures forecast events. These include not only the coming of Christ and the spread of the church but also (a display of the persistent Latin concern for Rome's historical destiny) contemporary troubles reflecting the coming *judgement of God who, rather than the Roman deities, truly controls events (*Apol.* 20, 25–6). Again, using Irenaeus in a summary rejection of Gnosticism in *Concerning the Prescription of Heretics* (*De praescriptione haereticorum*) he employs a legal argument to rule any consideration of Gnostic views of the scriptures out of court since Gnostics do not believe the rule of faith (*Praes.* 15–19). Here too we find the starkest repudiation of reliance on philosophical ideas rather than belief (ibid. 7), though in other places he himself argues at length with the Valentinians and Marcionites, notoriously employs philosophical arguments, and regards religious beliefs as common to all human beings. None the less, the repudiation is an important reflection of ingrained Latin assumptions (as in Cicero and Virgil) that adherence to causes involves and requires unswerving personal commitment. These assumptions are reflected in Tertullian's view of the church as a community of the totally committed. This made him sympathetic to *Montanist claims that a special gift of the Spirit is required for full commitment to Christ. It is also the start of the never-ending struggle among Latin Christians to explain the imperfect character of the body of believers.

Among aspects of Tertullian's thought, note should be taken of his treatment of the status of the Word, a question inherited from his predecessors. In his *Against Praxeas* (*Adversus Praxeam*) in particular, he faces a form of Monarchianism (or rejection of any division within the one divine nature) not dealt with by his Greek sources. Here he confronts more directly than does Irenaeus the problem of what it means that, the Father being the sole ungenerate, the clearly separate Word is generate and the agent of the divine presence in the created order. But here he relies on a Stoic notion of a quasi-physical divine substance in order to argue, one may think unsuccessfully, that the created Word is nevertheless somehow a part of the divine (*Prax.* 8).

If Tertullian marks the reception of major issues of contemporary Christian thought in the Latin Christian world of his time, Clement of *Alexandria, roughly his contemporary (d. *c.*215), witnesses to their reception in the very different cultural and philosophical environment of that city. Clement's surviving trilogy of writings contains an apologetic *Exhortation* (*Protreptikos*), *The Instructor* (*Paidagogos*)—catechetical instruction for those who would follow Christ the pedagogue, the one who leads us to God—and the lengthy books of 'Miscellanies' (*Stromateis*), unsystematic discussions of subtler Christian issues for those capable of advancing to the acquisition of 'true gnosis'.

Attention has often been given to Clement's interest in resonances of Christian belief in Greek literature and philosophy, as well as his belief in a higher knowledge not available to all. It is increasingly clear, however, that he is combating the same opponents as Irenaeus. Thus he teaches that there is no elaborate spiritual *pleroma*, but one divine creator whose Son came in the flesh. There is only one divine economy of salvation embracing both covenants in a lengthy process of overcoming the passions that impede the perfection of the soul. The 'true gnosis' to which not all can aspire does not belong to some élite group of those who are 'spiritual by nature'. Baptism, not knowledge, is the basis of salvation (*Paed.* 2. 6. 25): and true Christian teaching at every level is based on reading the scriptures in conformity with the 'rule of faith' or 'ecclesiastical rule' (e.g. *Strom.* 6. 15. 124-5).

While he is indebted to Irenaeus at many points, Clement is critical of him as well, as in the rejection of the notion that body as well as soul partakes of the divine image (*Strom.* 2. 19. 3. 102). Moreover he recasts Irenaean themes to fit his own presuppositions. The classical theme of *paedeia*, the education of the soul towards full life, is seen in his reworking of the Irenaean dictum regarding the *Incarnation: Irenaeus' 'the divine became human so that the human may become divine' becomes 'the divine became human so that humanity might learn, from a human being, how to become divine' (*Prot.* 1. 8. 4). On the other hand, while Clement opposes the detailed schemes of his Gnostic opponents, he can sympathize with the philosophical concern with human perfection which he finds particularly in the Valentinians. In him we see the now generally received principle of interpreting the scriptures according to the 'rule of faith' as it functions amidst the issues and interests of the intellectual world of Alexandria.

*Origen's career began at Alexandria in the generation after Clement. He left *c.*230 for Caesarea Maritima in Palestine and died in 254. Unquestionably the pivotal Greek Christian theologian of the first half of the 3rd century, his controversial teaching absorbed attention long after his death. The preface to his *On First Principles* immediately reveals the similarities and differences between Origen's and earlier understandings of Christian thought. The apostles delivered certain key teachings in the plainest terms to all believers, but left it to those to whom 'the Holy Spirit gave gifts of language, wisdom, and knowledge' to consider the grounds for these doctrines, and set aside other matters for examination by those with the capacity for it (*praef.* 3). For these key teachings he quotes a threefold baptismal confession of faith (probably that of his Alexandrian congregation), but points out questions left unanswered and matters requiring further consideration.

The preface is crucial: the two major sections of the work (1. 1-2. 3; 2. 4-4. 3) follow this outline, as does the 'recapitulation' (4. 4). From a basic confession of faith issues of scriptural interpretation are approached, but with a profoundly intellectual cast. The apostolic teachings are rational propositions, and the discovery of their basis and investigation of further matters requires deeper intellectual insight. It is assumed that the divine revelation is in the words of the scriptures themselves—of both the 'old' and the 'new' covenants—to be appropriated according to the abilities of the believer. Alexandria's intellectual milieu is clearly visible.

Two subjects preoccupy Origen throughout his writing. His exegetical principles force him to deal with the status of the Son, the divine Word or Wisdom. While only the Father is unbegotten, the spiritual Word or Wisdom is beyond temporality and materiality and thus 'eternally begotten' (1. 2; 4. 4. 1). Hence the Word or Wisdom, and the Holy Spirit, are not assimilated to created things (1. 3. 7-8; 4. 4. 1). On the problem of *evil, Origen, like Irenaeus, ascribes the turning of rational creatures from God to human freedom. He finds, at the spiritual level of scripture, an account of a multitude of pre-existing rational souls turning in varying degrees from God through 'satiety' (*koros*). The present form of embodied existence has been given to them as a place of training and education. The purpose of the divine economy of salvation is the return of all rational creatures to their original state at the 'consummation of all things' (*apokatastasis*) (1. 5-2. 3; 2. 10. 3-6). The incarnation of the Word or Wisdom, in whose image all are created, is the turning-point in the process. In both these subjects, Origen is addressing problems not dealt with before but now seen to be unavoidable; his solutions, however, include difficulties which are also part of his legacy.

The latter part of the 3rd century saw further attempts of the Roman government to destroy the Christian movement, before giving way under Constantine and Licinius to the first stage (313) in the reversal of policy.

The most visible effect of the persecutions on the development of Christian thought is in the Latin west. In the face of widespread apostasy during the persecution of Decius (248-50), and subsequent repentance on the part of apostates, the question of the pure church, a preoccupation of Tertullian, took concrete form in the episcopacy of Cyprian of Carthage (d. 258). With the support of Cornelius, bishop of Rome, Cyprian was willing to restore those who had not actually performed sacrifices. He was confronted with a *schism begun by bishop Novatian, whose followers considered that such restorations revealed Cyprian and his associates as having forfeited any claim to true Christian commitment or to being Christians at all. Cyprian's rejoinder, *On the Unity of the Catholic Church* (*De unitate catholicae ecclesiae*), was that breaking *communion with the authentic episcopal succession was the greater danger to Christian existence (6, 19). This view in turn would be used in 311 by supporters of bishop Donatus to argue that bishops who handed over books and vessels in the final persecution had proved themselves unfit to be called the authentic episcopate as defined by Cyprian and confirmed by his martyr's death. Latin Africa was to wrestle through the 4th century with the issues raised in the *Donatist schism.

The Greek Christian world also faced the issue of apostasy, but was perhaps more open to understanding the mixed motives of the apostates, as witness the *Canonical Letter* of bishop Peter of Alexandria (martyred 311). But, as regards the east, interest must centre on the variety of reactions to the work of Origen. While the *Apology for Origen* (*Apologia pro Origene*) of Pamphilus (martyred *c*.310), in co-operation with Eusebius of Caesarea (d. *c*.340), defends Origen's scriptural work, underlining the speculative character of disputed aspects of his thought, Methodius of Olympus (martyred *c*.310), besides rejecting what he construed as Origen's insufficient commitment to the resurrection of bodies, interpreted his speculations regarding the generation of the cosmos as equivalent to declaring it a second uncreated being (*Creat.* 2–7).

Concluding reflections

The figures of this period should not be seen simply as foreshadowing later issues which they may have anticipated, left to be treated, or provoked. Looked at in themselves, their basic achievement was a rough consensus—so widely accepted as to go largely unrecognized today—regarding Christian thought as the interpretation of the emerging body of Christian scriptures in the light of the baptismal 'rule of faith'. The diverse issues which were taken up in pursuing this task—the relation of God and creation, the status of the Son, Word, or Wisdom, the purpose of the incarnation, the destiny of human embodiment—arose against the background of the challenge of Gnosticism, of issues in current philosophical discussion, and, inevitably, of differences between Christians themselves.

Intersecting these issues, however, and providing their ultimate context, is the assumption that the divine plan of salvation is now entering its final phase with the coming of Christ and the gift of the Spirit. This is arguably the fundamental context of Christian thought from the earliest Christian writings, where the proclamation of Jesus as *Messiah requires a rethinking of Israel's interpretations of the past and expectations of the future. It is this question of the plan of salvation that underlies Justin's explanation of Christianity as the historical fulfilment of the Jewish scriptural promises; which is the basic issue between Irenaeus and his Valentinians; is restated by Tertullian in the light of Roman assumptions about the divine control of history; is rethought in Clement's Christian *paedeia*; and is the source of the problems that Origen sought to resolve through his grand vision of the fall and restoration of souls. Nor would this assumption be lost in the seemingly more dogmatic debates of the period to come.   **L. G. Patterson**

Primary sources: the largest English translation series is the *Ante-Nicene Fathers* (1886), repr. (1994). Wherever possible, translations in the *Ancient Christian Writers* and *Fathers of the Church* series should be used. J. Stevenson, *A New Eusebius*, 2nd edn., (1985) is a useful source book.

Campenhausen, H. von, *The Formation of the Christian Bible* (1972).

Chadwick, H., *Early Christian Thought and the Classical Tradition* (1966).

Crouzel, H., *Origen: The Life and Thought of the First Great Theologian*, ET (1989).

Daley, B. E., *The Hope of the Early Church* (1991).

Evans, R. F., *One and Holy: the Church in Latin Christian Thought* (1972).

Ferguson, E. (ed.), 'Orthodoxy, Heresy, and Schism in Early Christianity', *Studies in Early Christianity*, 4 (1993).

Gonzalez, J., *History of Christian Thought*, 2nd edn. (1988), i.

Grant, R. M., *Gods and the One God* (1986).

—— *The Greek Apologists of the Second Century* (1988).

Hinchcliff, P., *Cyprian of Carthage and the Unity of the Christian Church* (1974).

Jefford, C. N., *Reading the Apostolic Fathers* (1996).

Kelly, J. N. D., *Early Christian Creeds*, 3rd edn. (1972).

Lilla, S. A. C., *Clement of Alexandria: A Study in Christian Platonism and Gnosticism* (1971).

Norris, R. A., *God and World in Early Christian Theology* (1965).

—— 'The Transcendence and Freedom of God in Irenaeus', in W. R. Schoedel and R. L. Wilken (eds.), *Early Christian Literature and the Classical Intellectual Tradition* (1979).

—— 'Theology and Language in Irenaeus of Lyons', *Anglican Theological Review*, 74 (1994).

Orbe, A., *Antropologia de San Ireneo* (1969).

Patterson, L. G., *Methodius of Olympus* (1997).

—— 'The Divine Became Human: Irenaean Themes in Clement of Alexandria', *Studia Patristica*, 31 (1997).

Proctor, E., *Christian Controversy in Alexandria: Clement's Polemic Against Basilideans and Valentinians* (1995).

Trigg, J. W., *Origen: The Bible and Philosophy in the Third Century Church* (1983).

van den Hoek, A., *Clement of Alexandria and his Use of Philo in the Stromateis* (1988).

Vivian, T., *St. Peter of Alexandria: Bishop and Martyr* (1988).

Wilken, R. L., *The Christians as the Romans Saw Them* (1984).

predestination.

predestination. The doctrine of predestination or election is one of the most controversial in the history of Christian thought. Although associated with the *Calvinist tradition, it was set out in uncompromising form by *Augustine whose position was defended in the Middle Ages.

The idea of election is found in the *Old Testament, most explicitly in Deuteronomy but implicitly in the stories that *Israel told of its origins. Yahweh's free act of choosing Israel from amongst the nations accounts for the favour they have received. There is no explanation for this other than Yahweh's choice. This results in a *covenant relationship whereby the law is given to Israel to be obeyed (see LAW, BIBLICAL). Why other nations are not elected in the same way is a problem with which the OT wrestles. Deutero-*Isaiah perceives that the calling of Israel is part of a universal purpose for all the nations. On the other hand, some post-exilic literature refers to a final division between the righteous and the wicked, the chosen and the rejected. Later theologians, following Paul (Rom. 9: 13), were to make much use of Malachi 1: 2–3 'Is not Esau Jacob's brother? Yet I have loved Jacob but I have hated Esau.'

In the NT, Christ himself is spoken of as God's chosen one. In him, Christians are predestined according to Ephesians 1: 4. *Paul, in an important passage at Romans 9–11, wrestles with the apparent unbelief of the majority within Israel. Yet he finally discards the idea that Israel has now been rejected in favour of the view that after the Gentiles have been gathered in Israel will be saved. Thus even in the age of the *church, Israel remains God's chosen people.

Through the early centuries of the church, *theology was marked by an emphasis upon the compatibility of divine *foreknowledge and human *freedom largely to combat Stoic determinism and *astrological fatalism. The freedom of the Christian under the rule of God's *providence represented a release both from the grip of an impersonal fate and the hazards of random fortune. This happy conjunction of human freedom and divine prescience is found in Justin Martyr's *First Apology* (*c.*150). God's control over the future is determined by a foreknowledge of human choices. Divine election is in part a function of this foreknowledge. The manner in which God will determine and govern a human life is fixed by an awareness of the ways in which freedom will be exercised. This position seems to have been the dominant one in the *Eastern Church since the early centuries. In the Longer Catechism of the *Russian Church it is explicitly stated that God's predestination of some to glory and others to damnation is the result of divine foreknowledge of how free wills would be used. This contrasts with the more typically western approach found in *Augustine, Thomas *Aquinas, and the *Reformers.

Against *Pelagius and his followers, Augustine insisted that the will can only incline towards God if it is first released from the ancient bondage of *sin. At root, our nature is corrupt and tainted by the power of evil. Only a *redemption which is sufficient to convert the will can cause a man or a woman freely to will what is good. The prevenient *grace of God must first work upon the human will prior to *conversion and Christian living. If some receive while others resist the gospel, the only theological explanation is that God has decreed that a portion of human beings shall come to the heavenly city to make good the number of *angels that have fallen. The remainder are passed over and consigned to eternal damnation. Thus the doctrine of grace that is forged in the heat of the Pelagian controversy has as its by-product a strong doctrine of predestination. Divine election, instead of tracking foreknowledge as it does in Justin Martyr, now becomes sovereign. The foreknowledge of God ceases to be a function of human freedom and becomes instead a function of predestination. It is God's primary purpose in creation that an elect number shall be redeemed to make good those angels who have fallen from heaven.

The principal difficulties with this doctrine concern its account of human freedom and divine *love. In philosophical terms, Augustine is clearly a soft determinist in so far as he asserts the compatibility between causal necessity and voluntary action. The freedom of the will is consistent with internal causal determination of human action. A voluntary action is to be explained by the necessity of internal rather than external conditions. This enables Augustine to square divine sovereignty with human freedom. The will is governed by the divine decree, but our actions remain voluntary so long as they arise spontaneously from the determined will. However, if a stronger account of freedom is required, an abridgement of divine sovereignty is necessary. Even more problematic is the consequence of Augustine's doctrine for the divine love. The primal decisions of God appear arbitrary and inscrutable. Why

some are chosen and others passed over can only be explained by appeal to the mysterious *justice of God. A universe in which the elect are redeemed and the remainder damned is testimony to the order of *creation and the glory of its Maker. This is a thought from which many have recoiled in horror.

Despite the authority of Augustine, the Roman Catholic Church has never taught predestination as an official dogma. As church teaching it is more characteristically *Reformed. It was no coincidence that when the 16th-century Reformers retrieved the Augustinian doctrine of grace and sin, there was a corresponding recovery of the doctrine of predestination. Although present in *Luther, it exercised a stronger role in Calvin's theology. This was reflected by a departure from the doctrine in later Lutheranism, and its systematic and confessional articulation amongst the Reformed. Calvin judged that the doctrine was plainly taught by scripture and thus he faced it in typically robust fashion. The double aspect of predestination is explicitly stated: if God from all eternity has by grace elected some for *salvation, we cannot but conclude that God has rejected all others. This conclusion is demanded by the particularity of election and the sovereignty of God. As a doctrine that is taught by the church, however, it is to be handled with caution. Its primary purpose is to act as a source of confidence and comfort to the believer.

Calvin defended his corner resolutely but, like Augustine before him, he was driven into a harsher and more forthright exposition of predestination. In the final edition of the *Institutes* and in the essay against Pighius, the double aspect of predestination is given further weight. Divine sovereignty implies that God cannot remain passive in permitting the fall and the damnation of many. God wills that these things come to pass that the divine glory may be fully revealed. Thus he quotes Proverbs 16: 4. 'The Lord has made everything for its purpose, even the wicked for the day of trouble.'

In the subsequent development of the Reformed tradition double predestination comes to greater prominence in the exposition of doctrine. Creation, *Fall, redemption, resurrection, and the last judgement came to be seen as the means by which the divine decrees were executed. None the less, the doctrine continued to be the focus of theological controversy. Disputes between supralapsarians, who held that the decrees logically preceded the divine permission of the Fall, and infralapsarians or sublapsarians, who held that the decrees logically succeeded the permission of the Fall, were generally perceived to lie within the tradition's limits of tolerable disagreement. However, the views of Arminius and the Remonstrants were excluded by mainstream Protestant thought. They taught that the divine decrees were grounded upon foreknowledge of free choices and were compatible with the view that Christ died for all and not only the elect. In condemning *Arminianism, the Synod of Dort (1618–19) reaffirmed the unconditionality of predestination, the irresistible nature of grace, and the limitation of the effect of Christ's work to the elect only. (A doctrine of limited atonement had been expounded in the 9th century by Gottschalk. It was widely condemned at the time.) Arminianism was thus excluded by the Reformed mainstream. The Westminster Confession (1647), the most important Reformed standard of the 17th century, adopts an anti-Arminian stance in reaffirming double predestination in its third chapter. Predestination is not based on foreknowledge of free choices. It is an unconstrained, mysterious, and gratuitous affair. Thus a fixed and immutable number of human beings and angels are predestinated to everlasting life and others foreordained to everlasting death. In the Catholic Church much of the same teaching was given by Cornelius Jansen, the bishop of Ypres, in his prodigiously learned *Augustinus*, published posthumously in 1640, the source of the doctrinal core of *Jansenism.

Since the *eighteenth century, Reformed theology has continued to wrestle with the enigma of predestination. The mainstream *Presbyterian churches in *Scotland and the USA were sufficiently troubled to declare formally, in the face of the doctrine of predestination, their faith in the love of God for all. At the end of the 20th century, the doctrine is maintained in its 17th-century starkness only within the smaller denominations on the margins of Reformed thinking. This shift owes much to Karl *Barth's doctrine of election, expounded in his *Church Dogmatics*, II/2. Barth maintains that election has to be controlled by the person and work of Christ. The events that are constitutive for the Christian faith are the decisive index to the character and purposes of God. The decree, *pace* Calvin, is framed and not merely executed in Christ. There can be no attempt therefore to establish in Christian dogmatics a hidden and incomprehensible divine will behind the words and works of Christ. According to Barth, this incarnate and crucified Word must be thought of as both the electing God and the elected human being. Included in the election of the risen Christ is the election of every man, woman, and child. Each individual is thus determined by the love of God, and it is the vocation of the Christian community to live by the Spirit as the witness to that fact in the world. The double aspect of predestination is thus absorbed by a doctrine of universal election in Christ. The message proffered by the doctrine of predestination is no longer a mixed one of joy and terror, salvation and damnation. It is unequivocally good news of comfort and joy.

This reconfiguration of the doctrine has influenced not only Reformed but also ecumenical theology in the latter part of the 20th century. It removes at a stroke the morally dubious features of the Augustinian-Calvinist doctrine while also facilitating an ecclesiology in which the church is the harbinger of the salvation of the whole world. Its critics, however, claim that Barth's doctrine remains within the grip of theological determinism and leads inevitably to a doctrine of *universal salvation in which individuals can exercise no real choice as to their final destiny.

At its best, the doctrine of predestination has expressed the confidence of a *faith that rests not upon the fragility of human endeavour or the unpredictability of fortune. Its ground is the free, unshakeable will of God which sustains us in life and in death. At its worst, expressions of the doctrine have undermined trust in the love of God and have authorized hostility, sometimes violent, towards those perceived to be outside the circle of the elect.

David A. S. Fergusson

Barth, Karl, *Church Dogmatics*, II/2 (1957).
Berkouwer, G. C., *Divine Election* (1960).
Leith, John H., *An Introduction to the Reformed Tradition* (1978).
McGrath, Alister, *Reformation Thought* (1993).
Pelikan, Jaroslav, *Reformation of Church and Dogma (1300–1700)* (1984).
Weber, Otto, *Foundations of Dogmatics* (1983), ii.

Presbyterian thought. The term 'Presbyterian' denotes a form of ecclesiastical government established within *Reformed churches, particularly in the English-speaking world. Although the *Scottish Reformation in 1560 did not initiate a Presbyterian polity, this emerged in the *Second Book of Discipline* (1578). A hierarchy of church courts gradually replaced the old hierarchy of bishops, yielding a system in which presbyteries, comprising ministers and elders, exercised rule over parishes and kirk sessions within their bounds. The presbytery was in turn accountable to the highest court of the church, the General Assembly. Through emigration Presbyterianism was exported to America and the Australian subcontinent, while missionary endeavour produced Presbyterian churches on African and Asian soil. South Korean Presbyterians now outnumber those in any other country.

Presbyterian theology belongs within the Reformed tradition. Its most significant standard is the Westminster Confession of Faith (1647) which defends a moderate form of federal *Calvinism in its treatment of scripture, *predestination, the work of Christ, *justification, the *church, and the *sacraments. It is particularly marked by a stress upon the Christian life. This practical emphasis is reflected in the history of Presbyterianism through the involvement of its members in civil society. Thus, for example, Presbyterian divines were amongst the leading figures in Scottish society and culture from the late 17th century onwards, while James Madison, the fourth US president and one of the architects of the constitution, was decisively influenced by his education in the Presbyterian environment of Princeton (see DEMOCRACY).

Since the *Enlightenment, Presbyterian theology has experienced the tensions which have characterized Protestant thought more generally. Disputes over the role of philosophy in theological enquiry, *evolutionary science, *higher criticism of the bible, the revision of the tenets of Calvinist orthodoxy, and the powers of the civil state have been keenly felt within the colleges, universities, and seminaries of Presbyterian churches. Thus the conservative Calvinism of Charles Hodge and B. B. Warfield in *Princeton Theological Seminary was counteracted by the liberalism of Union Theological Seminary, New York, in the 19th and early 20th centuries. In Scotland, the *evangelicalism of Thomas Chalmers and the founders of the Free Church in 1843 contrasted with the more moderate views of many within the established church. The Free Church itself was to suffer the trauma of several heresy trials in the late Victorian period. The most renowned of these would lead to the removal of William Robertson Smith from his Old Testament post in the Free Church College in Aberdeen for opinions expressed in an article on the bible in the ninth edition of the *Encyclopaedia Britannica*.

In the 20th century, Presbyterian theology was heavily influenced by the work of Karl *Barth, although other trends ensured that it remained as theologically heterogeneous as at any stage in its history. Its spectrum of theological opinion at the end of the century included figures as distinguished and diverse as Thomas *Torrance and John Hick.

David A. S. Fergusson

Cheyne, A. C., *The Transformation of the Kirk: Victorian Scotland's Revolution* (1983).
Coalter, Milton J., Mulder, John M., and Weeks, Louis B., *The Re-forming Tradition: Presbyterians and Mainstream Protestantism* (1992).
Henderson, G. D., *Presbyterianism* (1954).

presbyters, see MINISTRY; PRIESTHOOD.

priesthood. The story of priesthood in the Christian religion is one that contains both reassurance and disturbance: reassurance, in that the virtually universal religious craving for some form of mediation between the human and the divine has achieved various forms of satisfaction throughout the history of the *church; disturbance, in that the thrust of *Jesus' teaching suggests that no such mediation is necessary; moreover, there is no trace of any priestly institution in the early years of the church that he founded. Yet through the many phases of reaction and counter-reaction to the establishment of priestly practices and a priestly class in the church one factor has been constant: the perennial power of priesthood and *sacrifice as a *metaphor for a profound religious experience.

In respect of the existing institution of priesthood Jesus appears to have been a man of his time. He never calls into question the existence of the *Temple, its daily routine of sacrifices and its complement of priests; indeed on one occasion (Mark 1: 44) he encourages others to respect them. Even his symbolic 'cleansing' of the Temple (Mark 11: 15–17; John 2: 14–22), if it is relevant to the question at all, is likely to have been understood as critical of aspects of the Temple's administration, not of the institution itself. But like the great majority of Jews at that time (who, being widely dispersed throughout the Roman empire, had necessarily to find a more accessible focus for religious observance, namely the synagogue) he shows little interest either in its spiritual significance or in its ritual—which, since it involved constant animal sacrifices, may actually have been a cause of embarrassment to sophisticated Jews and is seldom mentioned in Jewish religious propaganda of the period. Recent scholarly research has placed great emphasis on the importance of the Temple in the religion of Jesus' contemporaries; and it is true that the High Priests were still extremely influential and were largely responsible for the opposition that led to Jesus' condemnation. But the fact remains that Temple and priesthood have no place in his recorded teaching, his participation in the annual pilgrimages to Jerusalem was far from exemplary, and the centre of his religious interest, as with the majority of Jewish thinkers and writers of his time, lay elsewhere (see JUDAISM).

Still less, it seems, did he have any ambition to launch an alternative cult or ritual. Unlike the Covenanters of the *Dead Sea Scrolls, he had no dreams of a purified or reformed priesthood. Variously described as a teacher or a *prophet, he endorsed the prophetic insistence on the priority of virtuous intentions over ritual acts ('I desire mercy, not sacrifice', Matt. 9: 13 (Hos. 6: 6); cf. Mark 12: 33–4). And for generations his followers showed a corresponding lack of interest in any cultic terminology or institution. Their leaders and ministers bore titles—overseer (bishop), presbyter, minister (deacon)—drawn from the synagogue or from secular administration (see EPISCOPATE; DIACONATE). Nowhere in Christian literature of at least the first hundred years is any Christian functionary called 'priest'. When Clement of Rome, at the end of the 1st century, compared Christian ministers to Old Testament priests, he did so only in order to make a case for an ordered and hierarchical structure of responsibility. There is no suggestion that they had any 'priestly' function or significance.

Yet this indifference to ritual did not carry with it any desire to repudiate the power of sacrificial imagery and priestly metaphor.

The author of the Epistle to the *Hebrews, searching for a way of understanding the significance of Christ's death and exaltation into heaven, likened it to the annual ritual by which the high priest entered the Holy of Holies on behalf of the entire nation, having performed atoning sacrifices which, nevertheless, had to be repeated year after year. Jesus could similarly be represented as a high priest, indeed as the destined fulfilment of all high-priestly language in the OT, though he, by contrast, had entered a heavenly, not an earthly, temple, taking with him (instead of leaving outside) those whom he represented, and achieving by the sacrifice of his own life what the offerings of an earthly priest could never accomplish: once for all *atonement and *reconciliation. This powerful application of priestly and sacrificial imagery to the understanding of Christ's self-offering was to have a profound effect on subsequent Christian reflection on priesthood.

Less elaborate instances of such imagery occur elsewhere in the NT. Paul speaks of offering the Gentiles to God 'as an acceptable sacrifice' (Rom. 15: 16); the author of Revelation imagines the prayers of the *saints to be like incense rising from a heavenly altar (8: 3); indeed his visions of the divine presence (ch. 4) are inspired in detail by the mysterious inner chamber, at one time filled by the ark and the cherubim, of the Jerusalem Temple. But the phrase which aroused most resonance in Christian minds and became the centre of centuries of controversy was that in which the author of 1 Peter addressed the Christian congregation as a 'royal priesthood' (2: 9). The words were drawn from Exodus (19: 6), where they expressed the sense of the ancient people of *Israel that they were set apart from other nations by a calling of service and religious observance. In 1 Peter the words convey both the privileged destiny and the serious responsibility of the new people of God. In the context of later church life they were found to be capable of delivering two contrasting messages. On the one hand the whole congregation was a 'priesthood', so that no individual priests were either required or appropriate; on the other hand, since the whole congregation could not effectively discharge its priestly vocation, individual 'priests' must be appointed and authorized to do so on its behalf. Thus the metaphorical use of priestly imagery in the New Testament became enlisted both for the justification and for the repudiation of priestly institutions.

A further potent use of such imagery began to emerge in the 3rd century in connection with the *Eucharist. Here again the influence of the letter to the Hebrews is evident. Christ was like a high priest. The sacrifice he offered was himself. Each time the church celebrated the 'remembrance' of his solemn sharing of the *bread and the *wine (which 'were', or represented, his body and blood), it made its 'offering' and re-enacted and participated in Christ's 'sacrifice'. But if, in some sense, a 'sacrifice' was performed at the Eucharist, it seemed to follow that a 'priest' was required to perform it. This did not immediately result in a priestly definition of the Christian minister (though sacerdotal language does begin to be used of bishops around this time): for it was the entire community that performed the sacrifice, its cohesion and its unity with other congregations being assured by the presidency of a duly ordained and authorized leader—a bishop or his representative. But the sacrificial metaphor, once established, gradually transformed the role of the presiding minister. Though for many centuries it was restrained by the explicit requirement that, to be valid, an *ordination must relate to the service of a particular congregation, the tendency towards the creation of a distinct priestly class in the church gathered momentum until, in the 13th century, it was formally decreed that only an ordained priest had the 'power' to effect the eucharistic sacrifice (Fourth Lateran Council, 1215). By the same token, presiding over the Eucharist (performing the sacrifice) became the fundamental and distinctive office of the priest (though his pastoral responsibilities continued to be recited at his ordination) and remained so in the Roman Catholic Church until a wider definition was adopted by *Vatican II, which in its decree *Presbyterorum Ordinis* deliberately replaced the word *sacerdos* by the less 'priestly' word *presbyter* (a replacement lost in English translations where *presbyter* is rendered 'priest').

It was, of course, far more than this sacerdotalism that was challenged at the *Reformation. The whole structure of clerical power and authority seemed to the Reformers a travesty of any institution that could have been intended by Jesus. But with regard to the transformation of Christian ministry into 'priesthood' they could feel themselves to be on particularly firm ground. Their appeal was to scripture and the early church, and there they found no reference to 'priests'. Elders and deacons were mentioned, and seemed appropriate as ministers to congregations whose 'priesthood' was shared equally by all their members. Pastors were required for the 'shepherding' (see SHEEP AND SHEPHERDS) of the people, bishops (who make a regular appearance only some generations later than the birth of the church) might be tolerated but were generally thought to be dispensable. Only the Church of England (see ANGLICAN THOUGHT), of all the churches stemming from the Reformation, continued to call its ministers 'priests'—the English word, after all, by a curious paradox was derived from 'presbyter'—though firmly rejecting much of the sacerdotal theory and practice that had become attached to it in the preceding centuries.

Reformation was met by *Counter-Reformation. While Protestant churches developed forms of ministry that aspired to reproduce the organization of the early church, the Catholic Church reaffirmed its dogmatic insistence on the necessity of the power of the priest if the *sacrament of the mass was to be validly performed. Not that this preoccupation with priesthood suppressed the recognition of the other historic functions of Christian ministers: the pastoral responsibilities of the priest continued to be recited at every ordination, even if not subsequently performed. That is to say, Christian priesthood was always something very different from its Jewish or pagan predecessors in that it embraced not just sacerdotal functions but also responsibilities for teaching, pastoral care, and leadership. Catholic and Protestant conceptions of ministry were by no means totally polarized. Yet the debate, with its accompanying divisions between denominations, has continued until the present, fuelled on the one side by the power of sacrificial and priestly metaphors and the instinctive place given by traditional cultures to a priestly presence within each community, on the other by faithfulness to the record of a founder and his followers who seem not to have envisaged any such development.

In the late 20th century traditional forms of sacerdotal ministry were placed under strain by a number of new factors. There was a questioning, first, of the extent to which the 'setting apart' of the ordained ministry, in order that it should perform recognizably priestly functions, implied adopting a lifestyle radically different from that of lay men and women. In the Catholic Church the *celibacy of the priest (first made compulsory in 1153) came increasingly into question; in Protestant churches there was anxious discussion on whether ordained ministers serving a society increasingly tolerant of divorce, remarriage, and sexual relationships outside heterosexual marriage were required to set an example of domestic life that seemed to many to belong to a former age.

Related to these questions is that of the power and authority of a priestly class in the church. All churches have found themselves necessarily swept into endorsement and support of democratic principles in government; but strains begin to appear when this is brought to bear on the hierarchical structure that is traditional in most of the historic churches. The 'power' of the priest to celebrate the sacraments was for many centuries reinforced by the superior education, at least in religious matters, available to the clergy. As a result, *authority was exercised and decisions made exclusively by the ordained clergy, so reinforcing the image of a privileged priestly class in the church. Today, given an increasing theological competence among the *laity and strong moral pressure to give expression to democratic values in the life of the church, the scope of clerical authority in the church has undergone significant limitation, with a corresponding withdrawal by lay people of their acquiescence in the unique authority formerly claimed by the 'priest'.

A further social pressure that has influenced and in some cases greatly exacerbated the debate is the claim by *women for equal rights in the church (as elsewhere), extending to qualification for every office in the ordained ministry. This claim is resisted by many on the strength of various theological arguments. But part of the problem is undoubtedly created by the priestly image that continues to attach itself to Christian ministry. This image, with its power to project the 'priest' as a representative of God (traditionally described and pictured in masculine terms) or of Christ (a man), seems to many to be irreducibly male. The word 'priestess', with its pagan connotations, is as offensive to supporters as to opponents of the ordination of women to the priesthood; but the sensitivity it arouses on both sides of the debate indicates something of both the power and the limitations of the priestly metaphor when applied to Christian ministry.

But perhaps the most potent challenge to the priestly image has arisen from *liturgical reform. For many centuries the power of the metaphor has been reinforced by the familiar sight of the priest at the altar at the east end of the church, his back to the people, standing between them and the sacred action in much the same way as a Jewish priest once entered the sacred space of the Temple on behalf of those whom he represented. Today this arrangement has virtually disappeared from the churches of the west (though by no means from *Eastern Orthodox churches, where the separation of priest from people is reinforced by much of the eucharistic action being performed out of sight). The minister now faces the people across what is no longer so easily seen as an 'altar' but rather as a table around which the congregation is gathered. The customary designation of this minister has become the early Christian one of 'president' rather than 'priest': only the brief moments of pronouncing absolution or of giving a blessing remain as liturgical reminders of the priestly role.

Yet the metaphor retains its force. In the early years of this century an Anglican theologian (A. Nairne), inspired by the letter to the Hebrews, proposed the memorable definition of a priest as one who 'stands on the manward side of God and the Godward side of man'. Purged of its non-inclusive language (which might offend many today) this remains a powerful expression of a perennial religious craving for the presence and availability of a person to some degree set apart from the ordinary preoccupations of daily life and given freedom to attend to the things of God and the spiritual needs of fellow human beings. For such a ministry the metaphor of priesthood supplies a rich source of imagery and spirituality, and need create no conflict with the consistently non-sacerdotal teaching and style of Jesus. But taken literally, and given institutional form, it sets up inevitable tensions within a religion that cherishes Jesus' promise of immediate personal access to a heavenly Father to be gained by every believer through repentance and faith.

A. E. Harvey

Congar, Y., *Lay People in the Church* (1953), ET (1964), ch. 4.
Harvey, A. E., *Priest or President?* (1975).
Moberly, R. C., *Ministerial Priesthood*, 2nd edn (1910), repr. (1969).
Nairne, A., *The Epistle of Priesthood* (1913).
Schillebeeckx, E., *Ministry* (1980), ET (1981).
Vanhoye, A., *Old Testament Priests and the New Priest According to the New Testament* (1981).

Princeton theology,

as taught at Princeton Theological Seminary, New Jersey, dominated *nineteenth-century conservative *North American Protestantism. Its leaders refused to admit that there was a 'Princeton theology'. They proudly claimed that 'Princeton had never brought forward a single original thought'. Content with *biblical and *Calvinist orthodoxy, for about a hundred years they taught an untroubled synthesis that seemed to have an answer to everything.

University theology in the Anglo-Saxon world tends to slip into *liberalism. The 'Old School' *Presbyterians felt that even Jonathan *Edwards's university at Princeton was not to be trusted to remain orthodox. So in 1812 they set up alongside it a strictly orthodox seminary. Though the university was sometimes embarrassed that the name 'Princeton' should be tied to a college which set non-academic criteria in appointing staff, the two institutions were closely linked throughout the century. Thus the principal of the seminary was senior trustee of the university. Apart from its insistence on orthodoxy, the seminary was academically rigorous, in the Presbyterian tradition. It became the largest in North America, and by the time of its centenary in 1912 it had taught a thousand more students than any other. The two great professors, Charles Hodge and Benjamin Warfield, had each given a grounding in exegetical, didactic, and polemic theology (to use the titles of their chairs) to more than two thousand students apiece, not all Presbyterians.

Princeton theology was Calvinist: 'Calvinism is just religion in its purity.' They had an unfashionably kind word for scholastic Calvinism, whose 'atmosphere, if wintry and biting, is clear', and Hodge's own *Systematic Theology* replaced the 17th-century scholastic Turretin only in the 1870s. Liberals would try to demonize Princeton as similarly scholastic, but its prevailing tone was one of good-humoured common sense. It was not chance that Princeton itself was home of the Scottish *Common Sense school of philosophy. Dutch Calvinists thought there was too much *natural theology in Princeton. At Princeton, they took human *religious experience

seriously, which meant serious attention to the task of refuting *Schleiermacher, in which they anticipated *Barth. They were polemic and judgemental, but fair. The *Biblical Repertory and Princeton Review* was the best strictly theological review in English. The great American *Lutheran theologian, C. P. Krauth, said that 'next to having Hodge on one's side is the pleasure of having him as an antagonist'.

Princeton theology wanted to be scientific: 'the bible is to the theologian what nature is to the man of science'. Their robust defence of biblical infallibility, which dismissed biblical criticism as needless fuss about proof-reading, to be answered by a claim of 'inerrancy in the original autographs', has outlived their theology. Twentieth-century *fundamentalism, which is seldom Calvinist, and often lacks common sense, is built on selections from Princeton theology. The issue of fundamentalism broke Princeton. Archibald Hodge, Charles's son, worked with liberal scholars; Warfield wrote one of *The Fundamentals* in 1909 while teaching *evolution. In so doing, they demonstrated an intellectual breadth which the increasing polarization of American theology over the issue of biblical literalism could not accommodate. Their natural heir, Gresham Machen, felt he had to leave Princeton in order to safeguard the orthodox tradition.   **Alistair Mason**

Calhoun, David, B., *Princeton Seminary: Faith and Learning 1812–1868* (1994).
—— *The Majestic Tradition 1868–1929* (1996).
Kerr, Hugh T. (ed.), *Sons of the Prophets: Leaders in Protestantism from Princeton Seminary* (1963).
Noll, Mark A. (ed.), *The Princeton Theology 1812–1921* (1983).

process theology.

In wishing to affirm that Christ's divinity is eternal, the *Nicene Creed declares of him that he is 'of the same substance' as the Father. That notion of 'substance' as the unchanging core in things is a concept that has dominated the history of western thought and is to be found in philosophers as diverse as *Aquinas, *Descartes, and Locke. It is this fundamental assumption that is challenged by process theology in its conviction that *science has disclosed all reality to be in the process of change. To the objection that *God as the source of all might be treated as a legitimate exception, A. N. Whitehead (1861–1947), the movement's founder, responded by observing that we have no grounds for believing in any other form of reality than what we experience (what he calls his 'reformed subjectivist principle'). God is therefore to be seen as developing in and through the *world. Room was still found, though, for the more traditional divine attributes which were described as God's 'primordial' nature, and seen as existing independently of the world, but these receive concrete realization only in God's 'consequent' nature. This is the nature that emerges through interaction with the world, as the divine uses persuasion upon all the myriads of concrete 'occasions' or events that help shape the future direction of the world and thus also the very being of God. Each occasion 'prehends' in one way or another the external pressures upon it, and so takes change into itself and thus into the larger processes of which it is part. This is the way in which human beings are also viewed, as aggregates of numerous such occasions. Because of the prior existence of the divine primordial nature Whitehead was reluctant to apply a similar analysis directly to divine *personhood, but his most famous pupil, Charles Hartshorne (d. 1996), exhibited no such hesitations and thereby showed the greater consistency. Certainly, of the two Hartshorne is the more rigorous philosopher; he is even found offering a sustained defence of the *ontological argument for God's existence. That suggests a less empirical approach, and in fact his own preferred contrast is between God's 'necessary' and 'contingent' nature, the latter being what is forged in relationship to the world. Both, however, insisted on a more interactive God than traditional Christian *metaphysics seemed to allow, and so no less important to Hartshorne than to Whitehead was the latter's famous phrase about God as 'the great companion—the fellow sufferer who understands'. The result from both of them is a long series of 'dipolar' (or 'bipolar') opposites as the two aspects of God are contrasted (for example, potential/actual; absolute/relative; unchanging/changing), though this might perhaps have been better expressed in terms of creative tension. So, for instance, God is held to be perfect, but only in the sense that he cannot be surpassed by anything except later versions of himself.

Both Hartshorne and Whitehead were philosophers. John Cobb (b. 1925), who studied under Hartshorne at Chicago, was the person most responsible for giving the movement a more distinctively theological character. His appointment to Claremont in 1957 opened a second major centre for such ideas, where notable support was offered by the work of David Griffin. There have been many advocates outside these two centres, among them Schubert Ogden (b. 1928). Beyond the United States, though, its influence has been mainly indirect, in encouraging those of a fundamentally different persuasion to modify their ideas, such as on the question of divine suffering, development within God, or the image of the world as God's body.

Advocates would argue that such revisions have not gone far enough, and in fact offer a wide variety of further implications. So, for example, in his treatment of the *Trinity Ogden suggests that we view the Father as God's abstract essence with Son and Spirit respectively God's external and internal relation to the world. With *christology he finds the key element to lie in *Jesus' responsive 'prehension' of God. For some that will suggest too subjective an analysis, but one need not necessarily step outside the movement to find a more orthodox alternative. Griffin, for instance, advances a strong claim to Christ's uniqueness through giving a more directive role to God in the processes of Jesus' life. Again, although the absence of a substance or essence in a human being might be thought to tell against any claim to survival beyond death, Griffin challenges whether this is a necessary implication of process thought. Although Cobb's conclusions are perhaps more predictable, he does offer a powerful vision of the 'creative transformation' of the world through the work of the *Logos. Not surprisingly, this has led on his part to strong environmental and social concerns.

Whether in the long run process theology will continue as a distinct movement is unclear. Its main strengths lie in the dynamic character it gives to God, the stress on continuous creation, and the new perspective afforded to the problem of *evil where natural no less than moral evil becomes a question of appropriate 'free' response. But the latter could also be viewed as its main weakness, since it is far from clear what could be meant by talk of God eliciting free responses from sub-atomic 'occasions'. How is this to be distinguished from animism? Fresh vigour, however, might be injected into the movement through its current interest in *dialogue with *Buddhism where a similar stress on the impermanence of things is to be found.

David Brown

Cobb, J. B., *Process Theology as Political Theology* (1982).

Cobb, J. B., and Griffin, D. R., *Process Theology: An Introductory Exposition* (1976).

Cobb, J. B., and Ives, C., *The Emptying God: A Buddhist-Jewish-Christian Conversation* (1991).

Griffin, D. R., *A Process Christology* (1973).

—— *Evil Revisited* (1993).

Griffin, D. R., and Hough, J. C. (eds.), *Theology and the University: Essays in Honour of John Cobb* (1991).

Hartshorne, C., *A Natural Theology for our Times* (1967).

Ogden, S. M., *The Point of Christology* (1982).

Pailin, D., *Probing the Foundations* (1994).

Whitehead, A. N., *Process and Reality* (1929).

prophecy is a crucial component of OT religion but, in some form, is present in almost every religious system. A prophet is someone personally called to speak in the name of God, but both calling and work can take many forms. 'He who is now called a prophet (*nabi*) in time past was called a seer (*roeh*)' (1 Sam. 9: 9). A *nabi* was a spokesman. Thus in Exodus 7: 1 Aaron is described as Moses' *nabi*. But behind the *nabi*, the spokesman, is the *roeh*, the seer, an ecstatic visionary. Groups of spirit-filled attendants at a shrine were a notable feature of early Israelite religion (cf. 1 Sam. 10: 9–12, 2 Kgs. 2: 3). What is stressed here is a collective experience and the spirit's presence which made them 'seers' is demonstrated by their ecstatic dancing. The fully mature OT prophet is a more lonely figure, someone personally called by God as is stressed for Samuel (1 Sam. 3), *Isaiah (Isa. 6) or Amos (Amos 7: 14–15). Amos insists 'I was no prophet nor did I belong to a brotherhood of prophets; I was a shepherd and looked after sycamores, but God called me and said "Go, prophesy".' Unlike an ecstatic seer or diviner, the prophet takes personal responsibility for his message. Delivered in the name of God, it is also very much his own, often spoken at great risk as in Nathan's denunciation of *David (2 Sam. 12) or Elijah's of Ahab for seizing Naboth's vineyard (1 Kgs. 21).

The prophet is often a master of *poetry and *symbolism, a person of imagination. Imaginativeness rather than moral standing may best explain his selection as indeed *Aquinas admits in an interesting discussion of prophecy: *bonitas imaginationis* is more needed than moral goodness (*bonitas morum*) (*De veritate*, 12. 4 and 5). Yet a high spirituality of mind is required as well, argues Aquinas, freed from too great earthly cares if revelation is to be psychologically possible. That, however, raises a problem, because the true prophet's distinctive role seems one of seeing spiritual things less in detachment than in their precise earthly embodiment, in Uriah's wife or Naboth's vineyard. Prophecy's cutting edge is a painful insistence on the relatedness of the spiritual and earthly immediacy. It focuses on justice and injustice with divine *authority but a very human particularity. The prophet is socially a marginal figure, though at times society, and even government, accords him great authority. But it is precisely from the margin that he can speak with such clarity, putting himself necessarily at risk.

The prophetic message was delivered to kings or to society in general but was given under the supposition that the monarchy and Israel as a political entity have a duty to be moral and God-fearing, and it is given by someone who does not himself belong in religious, or any, terms to the establishment. OT prophecy really does presuppose an Israelite state, the exercise of power under God. Once the state disappears, prophecy follows. This is true, even though the morality required by the prophets is really what we might call a '*natural law' morality applicable on occasion to political authorities other than the Israelite (cf. the judgements on neighbouring peoples in Amos 1–2). Morality, personal and political, is common to all peoples because Yahweh is God of all peoples.

In the OT as later there is a problem of criteria: how to tell the true prophet from the false. There can be no single answer but, despite the opinion of Aquinas, much of the true prophet's authentication will come from a moral coherence of person and message. The prophet is totally and manifestly (if sometimes reluctantly) at the service of the word he speaks and from which he gains nothing. Above all, unlike a priest, he is autonomous, empowered from above, independent of any system, human succession, or reward.

Christian theology has often downplayed the characterization of Jesus as prophet. Yet it was above all as such that people saw him; it was how he appears to have described himself and also how Luke, at least, consistently portrays him (Luke 4: 24; 7: 16; 7: 39; 24: 19; Matt. 21: 11 and 46, etc.). His embodiment of God's word, his personal calling, his possession of the *Holy Spirit, his symbolic actions (like the cleansing of the Temple or the Last Supper) even his rejection by Jerusalem, are all prophetic characteristics. A 'prophetic' *christology is not to be despised; it incorporates a historic dynamism unavailable in most other models. If there was no substance to it, the triple 'prophet/priest/king' christology favoured by *Calvin (and by *Vatican II) would not be possible.

Given a relative lack of prophetism other than that of *John the Baptist in the *Judaism of Jesus' time, it is striking how prophet-filled the early NT church appears to have been. The phenomenon of tongues at the first Christian *Pentecost was explained by Peter by quoting the prophet Joel: 'I will pour out my spirit upon all flesh, and your sons and your daughters shall prophesy, and your young men shall see visions, and your old men shall dream dreams' (Acts 2: 17). Presumably it was the prophetic character of Jesus himself which stimulated the prophetism of early Christianity as genuinely part of a succession to his ministry. It looks like a group activity, something conducted within the Christian assembly, and almost anonymous, though a few individual prophets are named (like Agabus, Acts 21: 10). While Paul might well have been categorized as a prophet—his direct personal calling in a vision and intense sense of mission remind one of an OT writing prophet—it is as an *apostle that he establishes himself. The NT prophet is clearly subordinate in status to the apostle. 'Never try to suppress the Spirit or treat the gift of prophecy with contempt,' Paul advises in what may be the earliest of NT writings (1 Thess. 5: 19) but that already suggests how secondary the gift of prophecy really was. Paul may encourage the Corinthian Christians to hope for spiritual gifts 'especially prophecy' (1 Cor. 14: 1)—'the man who prophesies is of greater importance than the man with the gift of tongues'—but one can hardly help feeling that neither matters all that much. It is love that counts for living, and apostolicity for authority. The very completeness of Jesus' prophetic nature renders subsequent prophecy of marginal importance, especially as the very fluid nature of the apostolic charism enables Paul to be included within it. Nevertheless prophets continue in the life of the church for several centuries, even if after *Montanism they come under increasing suspicion.

The firmer grew episcopal government, with its horizontal line of succession, the less room there was felt to be for the 'vertical' authority of prophets personally chosen and Spirit-filled to speak in God's name. Catholic ecclesiology became thoroughly horizontalist: the authority of the Spirit was guaranteed, ex officio, to the holder of episcopal office or, at least, papal office. If Christ was the full and final prophet and the pope the vicar of Christ, then it could be claimed that the spirit of prophecy continued in the church via, and only via, the *papacy. That may be an extreme view, but, in general, institutional ecclesiology left little room for any independent expression of prophetic authority, which could appear almost necessarily heretical. Nevertheless, it did still appear, particularly in the voices of women such as *Hildegard of Bingen and *Catherine of Siena.

When papal authority was challenged at the *Reformation by *Luther, it was done in terms of biblical authority, not an ongoing prophetic voice. Yet Luther had himself many of the characteristics of a prophet and the more radical wing of Protestantism, beginning at Zwickau, erupted into the wildest of prophesying, something which horrified Luther. Much the same happened in the mid-17th-century England of civil war, when numerous radicals, including the first *Quakers, frequently appealed to the direct authority of the Spirit and for freedom to prophesy. As a matter of history institutional leadership alone is usually arid and overcautious; most of the great advances in Christian life have come from the self-authenticating spiritual leadership of individuals who may well be called prophets, such as *Francis of Assisi, John *Wesley, Dietrich *Bonhoeffer, or Trevor Huddleston. It is noticeable that *Newman in his *Prophetic Office of the Church* distinguishes the prophetical office from the episcopal. However exactly the former is conceived, it is something different from the latter, less definable, open to many forms, but no less necessary. That the presence of the Spirit continuing authoritatively in the church should thus be conceived in a twofold way was impressively argued by the Swiss theologian J. L. Leuba in *L'Institution et l'événement: les deux modes de l'action de Dieu dans le Nouveau Testament* (1950)—one operating through a horizontal succession, the other intermittently and vertically through people whose authority is *charismatic and in its way autonomous. They can speak with a forcefulness about the contemporary situation, the failings of the church, the immediate needs of society in a way that hierarchical authority almost never manages. It is the inability of almost any church authority, be it papacy, WCC or whatever, to express painful truths about the use of power, especially when this calls the church's own behaviour into question, that makes the existence of a separate prophetic ministry so necessary. That institutional and prophetic authorities should often be in tension, especially within an institutionally centralized church, is inevitable. But in the church, as in the OT, while prophecy provides a critique of institutional religion, it does not provide a replacement.

The problem remains to identify true prophet from false. It existed in the OT and the NT, and there is no sure criterion. It is intrinsic to the theological sense of prophecy that it is done in God's name or, at least, expresses a judgement on the contemporary from a divine and disinterested standpoint. Prophets are not necessarily fully aware of their role; they are often difficult, testy, apparently over-committed, and repetitive in their insistences. Prophecy is not a gift for life. It is not guaranteed that everything a true prophet says is prophetic or true. It is, moreover, almost impossible to speak prophetically to a given situation without a well-informed understanding. Prophecy only escapes naivety through its grasp of contextuality as well as inspiration. It is characterized by the passionate clarity with which the human predicament is seen in the most ultimate terms. Christian prophecy is normally directed at both the ecclesiastical and the political body, and the two as linked. It is as much a critique of the church for failing to proclaim a relevant gospel of *justice to society and to live that gospel itself, as it is a critique of political society for cruelty, rapacity, and discrimination. Such a voice may not be distinguishable from that of the committed theologian; a mix of 'prophets and teachers' (Acts 13: 1) was already a NT reality. The theological faculty of the University of Paris was seen in the Middle Ages as providing a sort of alternative magisterium, an embodiment of Newman's prophetical office as distinct from the episcopal. Yet Simon Kimbangu or William Wadé Harris among the many prophetic figures of 20th-century Africa may also provide a valid form, and one nearer to the *Pentecostal experience of the early church or of Quakers and Shakers in Cromwellian England. 'Do not suppress the Spirit' refers to a range of phenomena, some of which are far from formally charismatic.

Prophecy points to the reality of tragedy, but it also expresses hope. In this it is emphatically future-orientated. Tragedy may seem absolute. There is little mitigation of it in many of the most blistering OT denunciations of Israel, but the prophet also insists that there remains another way, the way of the living God, and the future is open. Gloomy the prophet may sound but he is far other than a 'prophet of gloom'. **Adrian Hastings**

Brueggemann, Walter, *The Prophetic Imagination* (1978).
Clements, Keith, *Learning to Speak* (1995).
Gill, Robin, *Prophecy and Praxis* (1981).
Hastings, Adrian, *Prophet and Witness in Jerusalem* (1958).
—— *The Shaping of Prophecy* (1995).
Hill, D., *New Testament Prophecy* (1979).
Hooker, Morna, *The Signs of a Prophet: The Prophetic Actions of Jesus* (1997).
Ndiokwere, N., *Prophecy and Revolution* (1981).
Shank, David, *Prophet Harris: The 'Black Elijah' of West Africa* (1994).
Wilson, R. R., *Prophecy and Society in Ancient Israel* (1980).

prosperity. There is no one *Old Testament attitude to prosperity. One salient strand is the theological view that since the earth is the Lord's and the fullness thereof (Ps. 24: 1), *God rewards his faithful followers with a share of his fullness, and withholds his blessings from those who displease him. (See the portrayal of *Abraham in Gen. 12: 1–3, and *Solomon in 1 Kgs. 3: 13.) However this simple equation of wealth with God's favour, and *poverty with his displeasure, expressed very mechanistically in Deuteronomy 28 and other texts, needed rethinking in the light of experience—indeed, the book of *Job is best seen as an example of such rethinking. Some prophets saw that many rich had acquired their prosperity at the expense of the poor (e.g. Amos 2: 6–8; 3: 10; 4: 1). Thus the rich become almost by definition the enemies of God, and conversely the poor become God's special friends; 'the poor' (*anawim*) becomes a theological term, signifying those with a right relationship to God (see Ps. 10; 12; 14; 37; 40; 41; 52; etc.). Alongside such theological positions, there are also common-sense views,

especially in *Wisdom literature, of wealth as the fruit of hard work (e.g. Prov. 10: 4).

For *Jesus, riches constituted a danger liable to distract from the *Kingdom of God, the one thing necessary. 'How hard it is for those who trust in riches to enter the Kingdom of God' (Mark 10: 25; see Luke 12: 16–21, 34). This is the general attitude of the NT, heightened somewhat in Luke (1: 53; 6: 24), James (5: 1–6), and Revelation (18: 11–17). The *New Testament is uniformly more wary of wealth than the OT.

In subsequent Christianity the *ascetic viewpoint tended in theory to dominate. This tendency was institutionalized in *monasticism, in which poverty was one of the 'counsels of perfection'. Throughout the Middle Ages, the profit motive tended to be seen as unchristian, commerce even as the sphere of iniquity. *Usury was a sin. The moral impact of Christianity never encouraged the private accumulation of wealth, a view reinforced through the symbolic significance accorded *Francis of Assisi, 'il Povorello', married by Christ himself to 'Lady Poverty'.

It was the momentous socio-economic changes of the 16th and 17th centuries that effected a rethink in the Christian west. It was particularly a developed form of *Puritanism, stressing *predestination, vocation, and discipline, which viewed prosperity as an indication that *salvation was attained. The enemy was no longer the accumulation of riches, but their misuse for purposes of self-indulgence or ostentation. The admonitions that had been formerly directed against uncharitable covetousness were now directed against improvidence and idleness. Money-making was no longer a danger and nothing else, but something to be engaged in for the greater glory of God. Not sufficiency for the needs of daily life but limitless increase and expansion become the goal of the Christian's efforts. Puritanism did not 'cause' *capitalism, but it did have an 'elective affinity' with the emerging bourgeoisie, legitimating their increasing wealth, reconciling duties of religion and the demands of business.

At the end of the 19th century, North America's 'Gilded Age' saw an essentially Protestant celebration of wealth further developed, this time with an elective affinity with Spencer's social Darwinism. John D. Rockefeller could declare in a Sunday School address: 'The growth of a large business is merely a survival of the fittest … It is merely the working out of a law of nature and a law of God.' The Baptist Russell H. Conwell in his oft-repeated 'Acres of Diamonds' sermon could state: 'I say that you ought to get rich, and it is your duty to get rich … To make money honestly is to preach the gospel.'

In the latter part of the 20th century this 'Gospel of Prosperity' reappeared. God, it is claimed, has met all the needs of human beings in the suffering and death of Christ, and every Christian should now share the victory of Christ over *sin, sickness, and poverty. A believer has a right to the blessings of health and wealth won by Christ, and can obtain these blessings merely by a positive confession of faith: 'Whatever you ask in prayer, believe that you receive it, and you will' (Mark 11: 24). Several figures, all Americans and *Pentecostal, have been influential in creating the doctrine: E. W. Kenyon, A. A. Allen, Oral Roberts, T. L. Osborn, Kenneth Hagin, Kenneth Copeland. Other texts they particularly build on are: Deut. 28–30; 3 John 2; Mark 10: 29–30; Phil. 4: 19. An essential emphasis in most forms of today's prosperity gospel is on the return on investment made to God (Oral Roberts's 'seed faith', underpinned by Mal. 3: 8–11), which has been very helpful in attracting the resources necessary for expensive media ministries.

In the USA this doctrine has all the same proved controversial and been repudiated by large sections of Pentecostalism. It has appeared less controversial in parts of the Third World. Primal religions tend to focus on mundane realities—flocks, crops, lands, children—and religious professionals are expected to ensure the prosperity of their group. Possibly for this reason, Christianity in areas as diverse as Brazil, Korea, and *Africa has proved particularly receptive to 'prosperity' theology. Some observers of Christianity in *Latin America have seen this prosperity doctrine acting as a counter to *liberation theology with its 'preferential option for the poor'; indeed the emphasis on faith in divine intervention seems to be very different from liberation theology's stress on conscientization and political involvement.

The diverse biblical strands have thus given rise to a variety of interpretations, of which some at least seem some distance from the general wariness towards and ambivalence about riches that characterized the original teaching of Jesus.   **Paul Gifford**

Brouwer, Steve, Gifford, Paul, and Rose, Susan, *Exporting the American Gospel* (1996).
Horn, J. N., *From Rags to Riches* (1989).
Tawney, R. H., *Religion and the Rise of Capitalism* (1922).
Troeltsch, E., *The Social Teaching of the Christian Churches* (1931).
Weber, M., *The Protestant Ethic and the Spirit of Capitalism* (1930).

Protestantism.

Sociologically, Protestantism, over against Roman *Catholicism and *Eastern Orthodoxy, is one of the three main groups into which Christian churches have arranged themselves. Historically, it is one of the two main groupings, defined largely in opposition to one another, into which western Christianity formed itself some centuries after the first great *schism between east and west. Formally beginning with *Luther's activities about the end of the second decade of the *sixteenth century, its social and cultural background was in the rise in *national consciousness in Europe while its intellectual basis was in the theological writings and activities of, among others, Duns Scotus, William of Ockham, John Wyclif, and John *Hus, as well as in the humanist studies of the *Renaissance.

The difficulty facing any attempt to define Protestantism is that it is effectively as much a political as a theological term; indeed, the English 'Protestant' is often and misleadingly employed to render the German *evangelisch*, better translated, despite being misleading in other respects, as '*evangelical'. The political origins of the term derive from the 'Protestation' in 1529 of the evangelical princes in face of Catholic attempts to limit their jurisdiction. The developments meant that, as Rupp comments, 'Things could no longer be left to the Word, and what Luther had once denounced as a "mug's game" was now afoot, with all the ominous presentiment of bloody ploys' (*Cambridge Modern History*, ii. 93). Similarly what has come to be called the 'Protestant work ethic' is more cultural than theological in character, an early post-Reformation trend enhanced by *Hegel's programme to use a Protestantism as the social cement of a modernized western world.

At the door of the politicization of Protestantism can also be laid the charge, so glibly repeated in many journalistic pieces, that Protestantism is essentially individualistic, as against the more churchly orientation of *Catholicism. It was, indeed, at the heart of the

Protestation that 'every one must stand and give account before God for himself', but that is not how it began. Luther's first and primary interest was in the renewal of the *church and the purity of her teaching. It is anachronistic to see him as anything other than a Catholic who wished to reform the one church to which he belonged. Things developed as they did because a range of factors drove the two sides into antithetical positions, defined, on the one hand, in the series of *Lutheran and *Reformed Confessions of belief that formed the basis of different national and minority churches; and, on the other, in the writings of the Council of *Trent, which, by establishing Roman polity and *theology on the basis of the thought of Thomas *Aquinas, effectively inoculated the church against other influences from within or without its fold. *Vatican II opened up a process, already begun, in which interaction with other sources has revitalized Catholicism's life, sometimes in ways suspected of being 'Protestant'.

Luther's ecclesiastical conservatism, in wishing largely to restrict reform to doctrine, was overtaken by more radical programmes for reform, particularly in Switzerland, where *Calvin and *Zwingli in different ways sought to reconstitute civic order. But the political outcome was similar, with the widespread acceptance of the principle whereby different forms of Christianity were established in different territories, with Catholicism remaining entrenched in the south of Europe—the parts, that is, which had not been Orthodox—Protestantism in *Scotland, *Scandinavia, and the Baltic in addition to northern Germany and Switzerland. In various places there were more radical attempts, initially Anabaptist (see BAPTIST THOUGHT), to move in the direction of a gathered or believers' church, in which the church is defined over against society, giving rise to a now well-established distinction between the 'magisterial' and radical Reformers. In England further complications were introduced by the rise of *Anglicanism, which sought to be both Catholic and Reformed, but whose settlement under Elizabeth I failed to satisfy various Protestant groups, the forerunners of *Presbyterian, *Congregationalist, and Baptist denominations, themselves with varying attitudes to the establishment of Christianity. The outcome in this case was, in England, the ejection of nonconforming clergy from their livings in 1662 and the legal toleration of non-Anglican Trinitarians by act of Parliament in 1689; in *North America, the establishing of a range of Protestant groups by immigration. Later developments are represented by *Methodism, a more recent splinter movement from Anglicanism; and by the rise during the past century of a large range of *Pentecostal churches, predicated on and seeking to correct the loss or marginalization of the work of the third person of the Trinity in the mainstream churches of all denominations.

One of the just charges of its critics is that Protestantism has historically proved to be highly fissiparous. Protests against Roman centralism and authoritarianism—clearly the occasion for much schismatic behaviour throughout history—have been answered by a kaleidoscopic pattern of authorities and institutional forms. Likewise kaleidoscopic is the range of cultural and political influences claimed by or laid at the door of Protestantism. It clearly had a hand in the development of *democratic institutions, partly by the development in secular congregations of some patterns of *monastic polity. Advocacy of political toleration, sometimes claimed for the *Enlightenment, came first from the protests of

17th-century dissenters and classically in the theology of the *Puritan, John Owen, dean of Christ Church while John Locke studied there. Several studies have traced the links between Reformation thought and the development of early modern *science, in some cases contributing statistics of the predominance of Reformed believers among scientists. While this is scarcely contested, the thesis of Max Weber connecting the rise of *capitalism with Protestant forms of piety has given rise to wide debate. And who can disentangle the theological from the social, cultural, historical, economic, and political strands making up the meaning of 'Protestant' and 'Catholic' in contemporary Northern Ireland?

A theological definition of Protestantism must begin with '*justification by *faith through *grace', the 'article by which the church stands or falls'. According to Luther, calling upon *Paul, God's *justice means that by which he justifies—makes just—rather than punishes the sinner. This justification comes absolutely free and undeserved, through *forgiveness, and is the *basis*, rather than the *result* of Christian *discipleship. It is mediated through scripture rather than the church's sacramental apparatus, which Luther sought to reform, and is appropriated by faith—through a change in the heart, as Melanchthon stressed. While some Protestant groups have subverted this teaching, it remains the touchstone of whether a community remains doctrinally in the evangelical fold. In other respects, although the Reformers were described as *heretics (in the context a social or political rather than a theological charge) they were not, holding as they did unquestioningly to the creeds of the universal church and adopting even on justification a modified form of *Augustine's teaching. (The Reformation is sometimes described as a conflict between Augustine's doctrine of grace and his doctrine of the church.) Their dissatisfaction was not with the creed, but that the church had arrogated to itself the control of divine grace, corruptly offering it for sale, and had subverted the *communion of the church, a particularly glaring instance being the withholding of the eucharistic cup from the *laity.

Despite the dangers of over-schematization, the history of Protestantism can be divided into a number of phases. The first phase of the Reformation consists mainly of varied attempts, met mostly with official rejection, to call the church back to her evangelical purity. The great Reformers did not regard themselves as Protestants but as Catholics effectively driven from a church which refused to heed a call to repentance and renewal. The radical Reformers likewise, though clearly more sectarian in approach, also believed themselves to be restoring the true church, often seeking to replicate biblical patterns, in criticism of the alleged half-heartedness of Luther, Calvin, and their allies.

Undoubtedly there is a real change of atmosphere in the theology of the period, evidenced alike by Luther's insistence on the pastoral function of doctrine and Calvin's *Institutes*, whose deep biblical and patristic learning, oriented on the sources—as he had learned from the humanists—and rhetorical appeal stands in immense contrast to the relatively dispassionate philosophical treatment of themes and often rather wooden appeal to the sources characteristic of the more pedestrian scholastics. But even here there is a deep continuity, Luther drawing on the nominalist tradition of late-medieval theology, Calvin shaped by the tradition of Scotus, mediated through *Scotland·(as Thomas *Torrance has shown).

Ecclesially, the outcome of the failure to contain reformation within the one church was an increasingly entrenched rigidity on both sides. While the Reformers and *Trent treated the question of the relation between scripture and *tradition fairly flexibly—for in essential respects the magisterial Reformers were traditionalists, while the majority at Trent did not wish to give tradition a creative role in dogma—later disputes entrenched a more rigid opposition. Moreover, changing cultural and ecclesiastical patterns generated an intellectual restrictiveness that appears rather impoverished. In Protestantism this involved in later generations a tendency to identify scripture with the word of God and, certainly on the Reformed side, a concentration on formal discussions of *predestination that gave it a prominence far outweighing its place in Calvin's theology. (In any case, his doctrine of predestination was a development of what had been commonplace since Augustine.)

One irony is that a movement that defined itself intellectually in opposition to 'scholasticism' gave rise to one of its own, in some traditions even returning to a form of *Thomism. This and its complicated outcome takes us to the second phase of the story, roughly until the end of the *eighteenth century. It is important to avoid a completely pejorative use of the term 'scholasticism', for in both eras it represented a serious engagement with unavoidable questions. In continental Europe there was a fine tradition of both Lutheran and Reformed theology, some of whose riches were mined in the 20th century by *Barth. In Britain, Protestantism nourished some notable theologians, Knox in Scotland and English *Puritans whose thought is still influential, Perkins, Sibbes, Goodwin, and Owen among them. Significant here is that Owen's *christology was developed in response to the challenge of Socinianism, a libertarian and rationalistic movement that disputed the divinity of Christ and the doctrines of his substitutionary death which had dominated recent Protestant thought. Socinianism was a harbinger of the watershed in European thought that claimed for itself the messianic status of Enlightenment, and whose religious form was a depotentiated form of Christian theism called *deism.

The Enlightenment's relation to Protestantism is generally twofold. First it is a quarrel within the Christian family, and can be understood as a summons to the Christian church to embody the *freedom that it affected to offer. It is here significant that in some Protestant lands the Enlightenment took a less virulently anti-ecclesiastical form than in some Catholic states, appealing as it did to ideals of freedom modelled on the Reformers' independence of spirit. It is not difficult to see in *Kant's moral philosophy a secularized and inverted version of justification by faith—inverted, because it replaces Luther's doctrine of grace with the very autonomous moral striving that he had repudiated. Second, however, the Enlightenment was a rebellion against human dependence on divine *authority of any kind in favour of a stress on individual rational and moral self-determination. Eighteenth-century Protestant theology was deeply marked by both the rationalism of the Enlightenment and the *Pietist reaction against it. Both betray roots in the Reformation, as one-sided versions of the intellectual and affective aspects of belief that the Reformers themselves had maintained in tension. Both, however, unlike the Reformers, sat light to the Christian *dogmatic tradition, which was either subjected to rational critique or subordinated to experiential religion. These were, however, trends rather than fixed positions, as the example of Jonathan *Edwards, America's greatest theologian,

effect of a given entity, is still apparent in our century, for example, in Karl *Barth's *Church Dogmatics*, III/3. 58–288.

The idea of providence has had three contexts in Christian tradition: dogmatics, *natural theology, and spiritual life. Apart from the doctrinal context, there is a strong apologetic tradition. The search for evidence of the divine in the order of nature goes back to Greek natural theology, regained influence in Thomistic tradition in the Middle Ages, and had its heyday in early modernity (1650–1850). Here God's providence was interpreted in the light of an optimistic this-worldly teleology, discarding the eschatological reservations of classic Christian doctrine. Traditional hope in salvation was superimposed upon the fate and fortunes of history. Leibniz conceived of the world as a pre-established harmony, leaving no reason for God to intervene in a world created perfect. Others saw the world as imperfect, but on its way to perfection. This religion of progress was shared by *Kant and *Hegel, by rationalists as well as by romantics.

A third, and neglected, context is that of *spirituality. In continuation of wisdom tradition, God's providence is here related to coping with ordinary life and the individual's special life with God. The aim is not to explain the world in terms of providence (as in natural theology), nor to make a balanced definition of providence (as in dogmatics), but is practical in nature: to discern God's will in accordance with time and circumstance, to attune oneself to his calls, to distinguish between trials sent from God and devilish temptations, and to persevere in faith even through severe struggles. In Christian spirituality, a theology of providence has survived that is relatively unconcerned with the global thought-models of doctrine and apologetics. *Catherine of Siena speaks as a daughter to the Father, whose 'gentle providence' is nourishing and strengthening her faith, hope, and love during her life as a pilgrim (*Dialogues*, 135–53). The 17th-century Jesuit Jean Pierre de Caussade speaks of the demands of God's designs (note the plural) as the 'sacraments of the moment'. *Kierkegaard's wrestling with what older translations refer to as Governance deals with questions of individual destiny. In more typified and public form, the practical aspects of Christian belief in providence are articulated in catechetical instructions (e.g. Heidelberg Catechism, 28) and in numerous hymns. One could argue that the concerns of belief in providence are present always between the Gloria and the Kyrie Eleison in Christian services.

In the 20th century, the concept of providence has been seriously challenged. Scientific determinism, if projected into metaphysical determinism, leaves no room for God's interaction with the natural world. In response to this challenge, *Schleiermacher claimed that God's relation to the world is uniform; so our dependence on him coincides precisely with our determination by the system of nature (*The Christian Faith*, p. 46). Twentieth-century liberal theologians like Maurice Wiles and Gordon Kaufman opt for the same solution. Particular providence is reduced to general providence: creation is one unbroken divine action.

Since the World Wars, a deep sense of the tragedies of history and natural catastrophes has further divested any optimistic historical teleology of its plausibility, while the legitimating use made of providence by the Nazis and proponents of *apartheid theology has led classical theologians like Carl Heinz Ratschow and Jürgen *Moltmann to abandon the concept of providence.

Apart from these strategies of reduction and abandonment, two

other positions are viable. The first is the traditional non-risk view of controlling providence. While conceding that we cannot, from our temporal perspective, understand the meaning of history and existence, we may affirm that God's eternal will is in fact universal, but includes the interactions of history (Peter Geach; Paul Helm; Vernon White). But perhaps the majority of modern theologians support a risk-view of providence. God's plan for creation is not fixed in detail because creation includes a certain self-limitation, motivated by love, to make room for and respect the self-productivity of creatures. History is open-ended; God communicates with humanity throughout history. *Process theology perceives God's presence as offering new possibilities to the free agents in the world, persuading them to make his objectively best proposals their own subjective aims. God proposes; the world disposes. Even if this idea of ontologically uncreated self-creativity contrasts with a classic Christian creation doctrine, the idea of God's persuasive rather than controlling power has been adopted by other types of theology. While rejecting the Pelagian tendency in process thought, Langdon Gilkey distinguishes God as the power of Being (creator) from God as the one who opens the relevant possibilities for the creature (providence). This accords with reinterpreting the majesty of God in terms of the future rather than the past or of *eternity. *Teilhard de Chardin called God the attractant power of the future; Wolfhart *Pannenberg similarly perceives the *Kingdom of God as manifesting God as the power of the future. Creation is unfinished business, and God's inexhaustible power exceeds the forces of nature.

In a similar vein, scientist-theologians Arthur Peacocke, David J. Bartholomew, and John Polkinghorne argue that elements of chance should be re-evaluated as God's providential means for allowing matter to explore its created, inbuilt possibilities. Presupposing that scientific determinism cannot be extended into metaphysical determinism, the classical free-will defence in theodicy is extended into a free-process argument (see OMNIPOTENCE, DIVINE). God takes risks while nurturing, respecting, and redirecting the freedom of creatures.   **Niels Henrik Gregersen**

Ford, Lewis S., *The Lure of God: A Biblical Background for Process Theism* (1978).

Gilkey, Langdon, *Reaping the Whirlwind* (1976).

Helm, Paul, *The Providence of God* (1994).

Polkinghorne, John, *Science and Providence: God's Interaction with the World* (1989).

White, Vernon, *The Fall of a Sparrow* (1985).

psalms.

psalms. The psalms have exercised a profound and lasting influence on the *liturgical traditions and *spirituality of both Judaism and Christianity. They have done so because they give voice to the whole gamut of religious experience from *praise to protest, from quiet confidence to urgent questions, from joyful celebration to the dark night of the soul.

As they now lie before us in the bible, the psalms comprise five books or collections: (1) Psalms 1–41; (2) Psalms 42–72; (3) Psalms 73–89; (4) Psalms 90–106; (5) Psalms 107–50. The relationship between these different collections and their original provenance have been much debated. Two psalms in the first collection, 14 and part of 40, appear again with minor variations in the second collection as 53 and 80, variations that reflect the way in which the first collection uses the personal Hebrew name for the deity, Yahweh, while the second collection uses the more general word God. In the fifth collection Psalm 108 joins together parts of two psalms from the second collection, 57: 7–11 and 60: 5–12. Tradition, as reflected in the psalm headings, associates many of the psalms with *David, but in the second collection a group of psalms, 42–9, are associated with the 'sons of Korah', as are four psalms in the third collection, 84, 85, 87, and 88; and in the third collection Psalms 73–83 are associated with the 'sons of Asaph', with one other Asaph psalm appearing in the second collection, Psalm 50. Both the 'sons of Korah' and the 'sons of Asaph' have, according to Chronicles, close links with the *Jerusalem *Temple (e.g. 2 Chr. 5: 12). Psalm 90 is associated with Moses, Psalms 72 and 127 with Solomon, and Psalm 89 with the otherwise shadowy figure of Ethan. Some of the psalms have been grouped together thematically: for example Psalms 93–9 celebrate the *kingship of God, the 'Songs of Ascents', Psalms 120–34, probably reflect *pilgrimage to the Jerusalem Temple, while the last psalms, 146–50, constitute a concluding hallelujah chorus, 'Praise the Lord'.

That the psalms in their present form owe much to *worship in the post-exilic Jerusalem Temple seems clear. The original provenance of many, however, is a matter of speculation. Some may originally have been associated with festal liturgies in shrines other than the Jerusalem Temple, for example with the northern shrines of Dan and Bethel before the collapse of the northern kingdom of Israel in 721 BC; others may have begun life, as many *hymns have done, as intensely personal poems that, because they reflected common human experience, became part of the shared spirituality of ancient Israel. Many rivulets from many different sources were to flow together before they became the life-giving water for Judaism in both its main stream and sectarian forms.

There is evidence in the *Dead Sea Scrolls for the use of some of the biblical psalms, and other psalms modelled on them, by the Qumran community. Before the Christian era certain psalms were in Jewish tradition linked to some of the major festivals of the Jewish religious year, for example Psalms 111–18 with Passover, while others accompanied the daily sacrifices in the Temple. This tradition is preserved in the Jewish community down to the present day, with the Authorized Daily Prayer Book of the United Hebrew Congregations of the Commonwealth continuing the recital of Psalm 24 on Sunday, Psalm 48 on Monday, Psalm 82 on Tuesday, Psalm 94 on Wednesday, Psalm 81 on Thursday, and Psalm 93 on Friday, with Psalm 90 being traditionally part of the Sabbath service. The destruction of the Temple in 70 AD did nothing to diminish the importance of the psalms in Jewish life since the already established synagogue worship nourished and continues to nourish a spirituality that draws extensively on the psalms.

Within Christian tradition the psalms have been equally influential. The roots of this are clearly there in the NT. Take but two examples. Consider the Passion narratives. In both Mark and Matthew Jesus dies with the opening words of Psalm 22 on his lips, 'My God, my God, why have you forsaken me?', while in Matthew, in particular, verses from Psalm 22 provide building blocks for the whole narrative. In Luke, Jesus' last words, 'Father, into your hands I commend my spirit,' are taken from Psalm 31: 5. In Peter's sermons in Acts 4 we also see something that illustrates and was to pave the way for a new Christian interpretation of the psalms.

Certain psalms, for example Psalm 2, were originally associated with the ruling king, God's anointed, his *messiah, in Israel. Once the monarchy disappeared such psalms were interpreted in Jewish tradition as pointing forward to the king who would one day come to restore the glory of Israel. Such psalms were now applied to Jesus as the fulfilment of that hope. Acts 4: 25–6 uses Psalm 2: 1–2 in this way. Thus a *christological reinterpretation of the psalms begins, and its influence was to embrace the understanding of the entire psalter. The psalms thus became important because of their *prophetic character. They prefigured or pointed forward to the coming of Christ and the life of the Christian community.

This approach lies behind the major commentaries of *Augustine (5th century) and Cassiodorus (6th century). Augustine, for example, argues that the blessing in the opening words of Psalm 1 can only rightly apply to Jesus, while 'the tree planted by the streams of water' in verse 3 is Jesus 'who draws in the water, the sinful people as they course by, into the roots of his moral law'. What commentators declared, however, was but a reflection of the central place that the psalms, christologically interpreted, held in popular Christian devotion and liturgy.

John Chrysostom (4th century) speaks of the well-established practice of meeting together and singing psalms, saying that 'Many who have made little progress in literature, many who have scarcely mastered its first principles, know the psalter by heart.' As Christian liturgy took shape in both east and west certain psalms found a natural home, Psalm 32 in *baptism, Psalm 34 in the *Eucharist, and Psalm 22, not surprisingly, on Good Friday. The antiphonal use of the psalms seems to have come into the west through Ambrose (4th century), and soon there was added to the psalms the Gloria Patri to set, as it were, the Christian seal on OT liturgical material. Emerging Christian lectionaries make extensive use of the psalms, especially in *monastic circles, with the *Benedictine order, through its daily office, reciting the psalter once a week. Although the rigour of this approach was not universally popular or accepted, the principle it enshrines was to be influential across the centuries. The *Anglican Prayer book of 1549 provided for the recital of the psalms once a month, while the Revised Common Lectionary used in most English-speaking churches today has a triennial lectionary in which most of the psalms feature in part or in whole, many of them on more than one occasion.

The *Reformation set the psalms on a new course. Not only were they considered to exhibit Reformation theology, witness the commentaries of *Luther and *Calvin, but in a new form they were to become central to congregational worship. Lutheran tradition focused on *hymns, but many of the finest of them were versions of psalms, such as Luther's rendering of Psalm 46, 'Ein' feste Burg ist unser Gott', later rendered into vigorous English by Thomas Carlyle, 'A safe stronghold our God is still'. In France, Calvinism fostered the production of metrical versions of the psalms in the vernacular. In 1556 there was published One Hundred and Fifty Psalms in English Metre, largely the work of English Reformers who had fled to the Continent. Although Ane Compendium Buik of Godlie Psalmes and Spirituall Sanges, containing metrical versions of twenty-two psalms set to secular tunes, had appeared in Scotland in 1546, John Knox brought the Anglican Geneva Psalter with him to Scotland, and in a revised form it became the accepted metrical version in the Scottish Kirk until replaced in 1650 by what has remained the definitive metrical version. At its best this version is characterized by sublime memorable simplicity, but it also lapses into banal doggerel. The metrical psalms have a continued place in worship in the Church of *Scotland and in other *Presbyterian churches throughout the world, though they never replaced prose psalms in Anglican tradition. They have gradually been replaced by hymns. The *Church Hymnary* (3rd edn., 1973), incorporated just over a third of the metrical psalms, or parts of them, into the hymn book.

The problem of selection from the psalms for use in Christian worship and devotion is not a new one, but it has been given a sharper edge by critical historical scholarship. This has raised questions about the traditional Christian prophetic understanding with its consequent christological and often highly *allegorical interpretations. The traditional approach has and will continue to have its advocates. Liturgical language and poetry in particular are always capable of taking on new meanings. The original meaning of a psalm, even where we can be sure of it, does not necessarily decide its meaning for later worshippers living in different circumstances. Modern scholarship, however, has increasingly sought to understand the psalms in their original setting in the life and worship of ancient Israel. Form Criticism, while clearly delineating hymns of praise, both communal and individual, and royal psalms, the number of which is debatable, has shown that the most common type of psalm is the lament or complaint. Such psalms with their 'Why' and 'How long, O Lord' contain urgent appeals and questions. Sometimes we listen to bitter curses directed against enemies who are held responsible for the community's or the psalmist's plight, for example Psalms 109, 137, 139. The contrast with the words from the cross, 'Father, forgive them, they know not what they are doing' (Luke 23: 34) could not be sharper. In worship selectivity has usually side-stepped this problem. Christians will happily sing Psalm 137: 1–6, but not verses 7–9; selected verses from Psalm 139, but not verses 19–22. There are elements in the psalms to which Christian spirituality may have to say a firm 'No', but selectivity has its dangers. The *Church Hymnary* (3rd edn.), for example, eliminates the elements of lament or complaint from the psalms it selects. It leaves no room in worship for the honest expression of *doubt, and the agonized search for meaning in the attempt to reconcile the goodness and sovereignty of God with the existence of *evil. Such psalms have had an important part to play in Jewish spirituality across the centuries as the Jewish community has faced suffering and persecution, and not least as it has sought to retain faith in the light of the *Holocaust. The honesty of such psalms, the dialogue within them between *faith and doubt, between *hope and unanswered questions ought to have a continuing part to play in Christian spirituality, a part which few traditional hymns adequately address. Because of the catholicity of experience that they enshrine, the psalms will always speak to Jewish and Christian spirituality and find their legitimate place in worship.

See also PRAYER.																							**Robert Davidson**

Among the most useful for both critical and spiritual purposes of the many commentaries on the psalms are: A. Weiser, *The Psalms*, ET (1962), and the three volumes in the Word Bible Commentary series: P. C. Craigie, *Psalms 1–50* (1983); M. E. Tate, *Psalms 51–100* (1990); L. C. Allen, *Psalms 101–150* (1983).
Davidson, R., *The Vitality of Worship* (1998).
Lamb, J. A., *The Psalms in Christian Worship* (1962).
Levine, H. J., *Sing unto God a New Song* (1995).
Millar, P. D., *They Cried to the Lord* (1994).
Mowinckel, S., *The Psalms in Israel's Worship*, ET (1962).
Prothero, R. E., *The Psalms in Human Life* (1904).
Whybray, R. N., *Reading the Psalms as a Book* (1997).

psychology. Christian attitudes to psychology have been very diverse, ranging from the hostile to the enthusiastic. At the negative end, psychology has been seen as a Godless, secular discipline, antipathetic to religion, peddling an unchristian set of self-centred values and assumptions. At the positive end it has been welcomed as enabling the church to plan its work more effectively, and providing the basis for improved *pastoral care. While the extreme suspicions of psychology are misplaced and arise from misunderstandings, caution is needed about the attempts of some Christians to embrace psychology too closely. It is important to remember that psychology and Christianity are distinct and cannot be welded together as though they were the same thing.

Christian responses to psychology have arisen in relation to three main areas: general psychology, the psychology of religion, and pastoral psychology, and these will be considered in turn.

General psychology

Christians have sometimes been sceptical of the assumptions about human nature on which psychology is based. Psychology, in its present form, arose around the end of the *nineteenth century from a long history of philosophical and theological reflection, and sought to take a distinctively *scientific approach to its subject-matter. Though it went through a narrow 'behaviourist' phase, it has recently expanded the range of what it studies and of methods it uses. It is also important to remember the diversity of psychology as a discipline, as a biological science, a *social science, and a cognitive science. Sweeping criticisms of psychology that do not recognize that diversity are misplaced.

The absence of explicit reference does not mean that psychology is incompatible with a religious view. Psychology, like most disciplines, takes a partial view of things in that it omits consideration of the role of *God. However, it still remains possible for psychology to complement theology, from its distinct vantage point.

One approach to reconciling the psychology and theology of the person is that of the 'territorialists' who argue that psychology and Christianity can coexist provided that each stays within its sphere of competence. A more satisfactory resolution is that of the 'perspectivalists', who would see psychology and Christianity as looking at human beings from distinct but complementary perspectives.

Such issues are best pursued by examining the assumptions made about human beings in different branches of psychology. One interesting test case is the neural basis of consciousness. Most scientists now assume that it will be possible to show how consciousness arises from the physical brain. There are several interesting suggestions about how this might occur, but as yet no decisive evidence in favour of any one of them. Francis Crick in *The Astonishing Hypothesis* argued that the eventual success of the enterprise will leave no place for the Christian view of the *soul.

It might seem that we have here a definite clash between secular psychology and Christian thought. However, it is important to remember that, at best, a neural theory of consciousness, *personality, and soul would only show how they were grounded in the physical brain. It would not show, as Crick has claimed, that we are 'nothing more than a bundle of neurones'. Christian thought is not wedded to a *dualist conception of soul in the way that Crick assumes. The grounding of human consciousness in the physical brain is perfectly compatible with the more *Aristotelian concept of soul as the form of the human *body, an important strand in the Christian tradition.

It also seems that there might be a clash between secular psychology and Christian thought over Artificial Intelligence (AI). Here, the claim is that all intelligent human activities could in principle be programmed on a computer. This is linked to the view that the human mind is essentially a computer programme that just happens to run on the biological stuff of the physical brain. This might indeed clash with the Christian view, which emphasizes that human beings are spiritual creatures capable of a relationship with God. However, it would be an exaggeration to say that scientific work in AI implies that all human mental functioning can be programmed in a computer. Detailed scientific work in AI does not need to make that assumption.

There may nevertheless be a case for an emancipation of psychology, to allow it to cope better with the higher aspects of personality with which Christian thought is particularly concerned; indeed there are internal pressures for this arising within psychology itself. In fact, there are many points of contact between psychological and Christian thought about human personality. Peter Morea has drawn out a number of them in a recent book examining parallels in contemporary psychological thought with the approaches of such Christian thinkers as *Augustine, *Kierkegaard, Thomas *Merton, *Pascal, *Teresa of Avila, and Karl *Rahner.

Psychology of religion

Whereas general psychology seems implicitly atheist, this can become explicit in the psychology of religion, and Freud's theory is the most celebrated example. In fact, Freud had several different theories of religion. However, the most coherent and influential was that set out in The Future of an Illusion. Here he sees God as a projection of the human mind, based on the human *father figure. Also, he sees religion as an 'illusion' which, for Freud, is a technical term meaning 'wish fulfilment'. At one point in The Future of an Illusion, Freud makes a distinction between 'illusion' and 'delusion' (or error). Strictly, he is only arguing that religion is illusion, but it is clear that he also thinks it is erroneous.

God is seen as a projection of the human mind, meeting the need for a 'father figure' that is both all-loving and all-powerful. The idea of God as a projection had already been advanced by Feuerbach, but Freud situated it in a more explicit developmental psychology. He gathered no empirical evidence to support his position, though others have subsequently sought to do so. There is, in fact, a reliable but weak correlation between how people describe God and their favourite or ideal parent. This is consistent with Freud's theory but does not prove it. Also, in clinical work, very close similarities have sometimes been found between a client's description of God and of his or her human father that are suggestive of a causal connection. However, that does not show that everyone's ideas of God have such a basis. Neither does it show that God is nothing more than a projection of the human mind.

Freud's theory has, understandably, aroused opposition in Christian circles. However, more striking is the fact that some Christian thinkers have embraced Freud's theory as a positive contribution, though reshaping its implications. The first of such attempts was that of Freud's *Lutheran friend, Oskar Pfister, who argued that Christianity, far from being a refuge of a weak ego, required and promoted the full exercise of the ego functions of love and work. He also saw the application of Freud's theories to Christian pastoral work.

The most important theologian to have made use of Freud's ideas is *Tillich. Tillich's 'method of correlation', which unifies existential questions and theological answers, lends itself to the use of Freudian theory on the existential side. Also, in The Courage to Be, for example, Tillich is happy to embrace Freud's critique of concepts of God as arising through projection, the 'transference God' as he calls it. Tillich's point is, in essence, that though many concepts of God may arise in the way Freud indicates, the religious path involves and requires a liberation from the transference God in favour of the true God who is beyond human knowledge.

There has also been a neo-Freudian stream of thinking about religion, indebted to Winnicott, that sees religion as one of a group of cultural activities that are 'illusionistic', in the sense of occupying a 'transitional' world that is partly objective, partly subjective, and making an important contribution to human adjustment. Psychoanalytic thinking about religion has thus become less suspicious of it than was Freud's own.

Freud's general approach was the springboard for *Jung's much more sympathetic treatment of religion. However, Jung's concept of religion is so broad (virtually equating it with anything 'numinous'), and his theological position so heterodox, that it is debatable how compatible Jungian psychology is with Christianity.

The psychology of religion also includes a more empirical approach to the description and analysis of religious experience and behaviour. William *James's The Varieties of Religious Experience was the early masterpiece in this tradition. The psychological investigation of religion has remained vigorous, with an increasing emphasis on quantitative methods. Some find the application of quantitative methods to religion inappropriate. However, it is not clear that they are doing more than making explicit the comparative judgements that are an almost inescapable part of qualitative discourse.

Empirical psychology of 'religion' in fact focuses almost entirely on contemporary Anglo-American Christianity. Much has been learnt about, for example, the different approaches to religion associated with different personality types, how religious understanding and affiliation develop in *children, the nature of *religious experience, *conversion processes, and much else. This empirical psychology of religion provides much factual information relevant to the ministry and *mission of the churches.

Pastoral psychology

There has been a wide range of different views about the relationship between secular counselling psychology and Christian pastoral psychology. Some have seen the methods of pastoral counselling as similar to those of secular counselling, albeit applied in a different context. Others see the values and assumptions of secular counselling as being fundamentally consonant with those of Christianity, albeit translated to a context which is not explicitly religious. So, for example, talk of 'personal growth' in counselling psychology, or 'individuation' in Jungian psychology, can be seen as equivalent to Christian thought about *salvation. Equally, the qualities of warmth, empathy, and genuineness that Carl Rogers believes that a counsellor needs can be seen as equivalent to the *love that a Christian pastor is needed to show.

In contrast, others have argued that the values of counselling psychology are incompatible with those of Christianity. For example, Kirkpatrick in *Psychological Seduction* argued that counselling psychology promotes a preoccupation with self that is incompatible with the Christian theme of leaving self behind and following God. Moreover, it is alleged that counselling psychology assumes that people can find their way towards some kind of salvation through their own resources, whereas Christianity emphasizes that this can only occur through the grace of God.

Such a rejection of the synthesis of counselling psychology and Christian pastoral care has led to the search for alternative and more distinctively Christian foundations for pastoral practice, drawing more explicitly on the scriptures and the Christian *tradition. This would give a primary place to *ethical values, whereas secular counsellors often think that it is inappropriate to bring their moral views into their counselling work. Further, some Christians might hold that personal problems arise from human *sinfulness, which leads to a view of the role of discipline, repentance, and *forgiveness in Christian pastoral care.

At the extremes, the relationship between secular counselling and Christian pastoral care can thus be seen in terms of assimilation or conflict. A third position, which has much to commend it, would avoid assimilation by carefully distinguishing the two, but would not assume that they were necessarily antagonistic. Rather, it would see them as complementary, and illuminating different aspects of pastoral counselling. Such an approach is implicit, for example, in W. W. Meissner's *Life and Faith*, where he carefully distinguishes the theology and psychology of *grace. He argues that psychology can illuminate how the resources of grace work at the personal level, and draws on the details of 'object-relations' theory to do so.

Similarly, Hunsinger in *Theology and Pastoral Counselling* has recently argued for a relationship between theology and pastoral psychology in terms of 'indissoluble differentiation' (not merely confusing or assimilating theology and psychology), 'inseparable unity' (not separating theology and pastoral psychology so sharply that they bear no relationship to one another), and 'indestructible order' (maintaining a hierarchical view of the relationship between theology and pastoral psychology in which theology is prioritized).

There are parallel issues about the classification of personal problems. Much secular psychology sees these as entirely explicable in psychological terms. At the other extreme, some have argued that all human problems should be seen in specifically Christian or spiritual terms. Amongst those who have seen a place for both perspectives, some have sought to distinguish which particular personal problem should be regarded as psychological and which as spiritual, others have assumed that in most cases there are both psychological and spiritual aspects and have sought to elucidate their respective contributions.

These different approaches are paralleled by different views about the provision of pastoral counselling and spiritual direction.

Though some place exclusive reliance on one or the other, many have seen a place for both. However, there are currently differing views about how sharply they should be distinguished in practice, or whether the same person can provide both pastoral counselling and spiritual direction.   **Fraser Watts**

Benner, D., *Psychotherapy and the Spiritual Quest* (1988).
Brown, L., *The Psychology of Religion: An Introduction* (1988).
Homans, P., *Theology After Freud: An Interpretative Inquiry* (1970).
Hunsinger, D. van D., *Theology and Pastoral Counselling* (1995).
Jeeves, M. A., *Human Nature at the Millennium* (1997).
Meissner, W. W., *Psychoanalysis and Religious Experience* (1984).
—— *Life and Faith: Psychological Perspectives on Religious Experience* (1987).
Morea, P., *In Search of Personality* (1997).
Myers, D. G., and Jeeves, M. A., *Psychology Through the Eyes of Faith* (1991).
Pattison, S., *A Critique of Pastoral Care*, 2nd edn. (1993).
van Loeuwen, M. S., *The Person in Psychology: A Contemporary Christian Appraisal* (1985).
Watts, F., and Williams, M., *The Psychology of Religious Knowing* (1988), reissued (1994).

publishing, the process of making books, journals, and other literature available to as wide a readership as possible. It involves a great many varied activities, from contracting for, preparing, designing, and printing a work to advertising and promotion, distribution, and sales. Because many of these activities can be carried out by separate service organizations, a publishing house can range in size from a few individuals to a vast multinational corporation. However, the publisher controls the process, providing the imagination and the finance, and taking the risks.

The complex network that makes up the world of publishing took some time to develop; for example, it was not until around the end of the 18th century that the functions of the printer, the publisher, and the bookseller were fully differentiated. Publishing antedated the invention of printing; there was a commercial book trade in Athens and Rome. However, for 700 years after the fall of the western Roman empire, at the beginning of the 5th century, the copying of manuscripts took place within the church, emerging again a couple of centuries before the invention which totally changed the intellectual world, the invention of typographic printing by Johann Gutenberg and the first dated printed book in 1457. That this was a psalter shows how closely the book revolution and Christianity were connected, and indeed liturgical, devotional, and morally edifying religious books were a staple trade of the early printers. The developing trade owed much of its success to religious publishing, helped in *Protestant countries by the emphasis on *bible reading and sermons; religious propaganda and instruction also swelled the flood of books.

Such relatively free dissemination of ideas caught the attention of censors in both church and state, since religious and political polemic often went hand in hand; however, what is perhaps most surprising is the degree of freedom there usually was, somewhere, for the printed word, despite temporary draconian measures, for instance in Britain at the time of the French Revolution. Publishing has been crucial to intellectual freedom in religious thought.

Publishing is essentially a commercial activity, and from the start even religious publishing was done within the general activity of the book trade. However, two other types of publisher have also played an important role: the *university presses and the churches or religious societies. The first real university presses were established in Britain during the 17th century, first by Oxford and then by Cambridge. In the next century the newly developing religious societies, like the Society for Promoting Christian Knowledge (founded 1698), saw the potential of publishing for *evangelization and education and set up their own organizations. With the growth of the Free Churches, other societies like the Religious Tract Society (1799) followed, and by the end of the 19th century most religious denominations and churches had their own publishing houses and/or bookshops. Developments in continental Europe and America were similar, leading to a situation in the mid-20th century when these three types of publisher, commercial, university, and religious, existed side by side and often in close association. Even before the modern multinational conglomerates, partnerships developed in the English-speaking world between British and American publishers; combined with the translation of books from foreign languages, this created a worldwide system for the dissemination of ideas.

While publishing is a corporate activity, and substantial capital expenditure and major organizational resources are needed for the publication of great works of scholarship, at its heart lies the creativity of individuals and the resources to carry it through. The famous publishing houses of the world more often than not bear the names of the individuals who founded them, and in many cases they have continued to be family concerns. Despite the growth in the size of firms, the individual editor is still the key figure.

In retrospect, the century between the controversial collection *Essays and Reviews* (1860) and John *Robinson's *Honest to God* (1963) is likely to be seen as the heyday of publishing, and particularly religious publishing. The industry was fully formed, and despite the havoc caused by two World Wars, it offered scope for creativity and new enterprise. The threats from other media were still barely in the making, and the giant organizations that dominate the scene today had not yet been formed. Towards the end of this period the paperback revolution promised even wider dissemination of books, and in the churches was seen as yet another way of promoting Christian belief.

By the time of *Vatican II it was possible for any interested reader to obtain easily and relatively cheaply the classic texts, not only of Christian thought and *spirituality, but of the *theological discussion in Europe and the English-speaking world since the *Enlightenment, and enterprising publishers were encouraging authors who kept the problems of the place of Christian thought in the modern world constantly before the public. The classic instance of this was *Honest to God*, which not only sold more than a million copies in a very short time, but also generated a worldwide debate inside the churches and outside.

Since then, however, the scene has become far more complex, and more difficult, and many factors are emerging that are tending to limit its range of publishing. Since publishing is part of the economy and of society, economic, social, and ideological factors play a role in influencing it. This can be seen particularly within religious and theological publishing. In the last three decades of the 20th century, more and more commercial publishers withdrew from this area. The increasing pressure on them to make good financial returns at a time of an increasing *secularization of society and a sharp decline in church membership were two major reasons. Mergers leading to ever larger groupings constantly threatened editor's creativity and independence. However, commercial textbook and journal publishing continued to thrive in the transatlantic market, not least because of the vast American theological academy.

The main university publishers still play an important part, particularly in major works of reference and, particularly in the United States, in religious studies. However, the demands of academic research assessment exercises have led to the rise of inward-looking, highly specialized houses through which scholars publish books for fellow scholars; here, meeting university requirements and gaining professional advancement are greater priorities than communication with a wider readership and overall quality is often low. Moreover, this development has inevitably reduced the range of good, scholarly, non-technical books and books interpreting developments in scholarship for a wider audience, so that many lessons learned in the past are being forgotten.

By the 1960s, those more mainstream churches and religious societies that had established publishing houses were in increasing difficulties because of financial pressures caused by declining membership. Some of the smaller houses closed or were amalgamated. This decline has continued steadily. At the same time, the involvement of conservative *evangelicalism in publishing increased enormously, and by the 1990s this had given a new complexion to religious publishing. A whole sector of publishing and book-selling grew up calling itself 'Christian' publishing, though representing a very narrow form of Christianity. It has its own publishing houses and its own chains of bookshops and has a marked *missionary aim; this restricts the range of literature which is published and distributed. Moreover the mere existence of this sector has had a notable effect on more general bookshops, most of which now opt for 'body, mind, and spirit' rather than religion and theology.

In this overall situation, the stimulus that has so often come from religious and theological publishing is flagging. Of course imaginative and pioneering books are still appearing; however, even the best religious and theological publishing houses, not only in Britain and America but in continental Europe, find it difficult to maintain high-quality lists. And this has happened in a period in which the churches are showing an increasing antipathy to radical rethinking, exploration of new areas, criticism of tradition, indeed controversy of any kind, and are responding to it with various forms of dissuasion, where authors or publishing houses are under their control.

This is fatal, since down the centuries responsible controversy has kept religious issues in public view. Now, while there is still controversy, all too often it is irresponsible controversy, encouraged by commercial considerations on the one hand and on the other the retreat of the academic world and the churches from their important role of the wider communication of religious and theological issues.

Since the agenda of unanswered questions for religious thought is so great, and there is so much to write about, it is hard to imagine that religious and theological publishing has no future, despite the further challenges presented to book publishing by the Internet and the CD Rom (themselves also a form of publishing, with certain signs of promise). But it is clear that at the end of the 20th century the scene is in great flux, and how it develops in the future will depend mostly on factors outside the publisher's control.

John Bowden

punishment. Though the need to punish offenders is taken for granted by most known societies the concept of punishment remains obscure and complex. In ancient *law codes which go back to almost 2000 BC, the *lex talionis* (retaliation based on like for like) is most probably an attempt to limit indiscriminate revenge. As law developed retaliation was replaced by penalties imposed in the name of society in the interests of protecting social stability, the rights of individuals, or the authority of the state.

Durkheim proposed a variant of this hypothesis that gives religion a central role (see SOCIAL SCIENCES). According to him *morality consists in social solidarity, and the transcendence of the social over the individual finds religious expression. Crime is any action that goes against the collective consciousness, and this calls not just for punishment but for expiation. Expiation differs from propitiation, the attempt to turn away *anger through a gift or promise, in seeking to wipe away guilt. According to Leviticus God has provided the means to deal with guilt through the institution of *sacrifice. In animal sacrifice the *blood of the animal stands symbolically for my life (Lev. 17: 11). I offer it in my place and my guilt is wiped away by the offering. The possibility of this happening rests purely on God's gracious will, but the intention of a new and changed life is implicit in the offering. Serious crimes committed with full deliberation, however, cannot be thus atoned for and in these cases it is either the death or punishment of the offender that is itself the means of expiation. This is what seems to be in view in the common phrase that offenders must 'pay their debt' to society. By serving a prison term, or perhaps by being executed, I make expiation, with my life, for the evil I have done. Here too, as in revenge, the *suffering of the offender is weighed against the suffering of the victim, and this equivalence is symbolically expressed in the scales held by the blindfolded figure of *justice.

Because punishment involves the infliction of what is painful on people it is never a self-evident practice and there have been three main streams of thought that have sought to justify it, roughly retributivist, utilitarian, and welfarist. The most ancient, and still dominant, line of thinking, which draws on ideas both of limiting revenge and of expiation, is that of retribution. At the heart of the retributivist case is the notion of just desert. *Kant, a prominent advocate of this view, insists that punishment must never be inflicted as a means for promoting the good of either the criminal or of society but purely and simply because someone has committed a crime. Punishment is the essential means of maintaining the moral law. Crimes have to be punished because otherwise we all become complicit in their commission. A society without punishment is a society that has given up on the moral law. The difficulty is in explaining how the infliction of harm, which is a breach of the moral law, in fact supports it, and no fully persuasive account of this has ever been forthcoming. In the contemporary debate, where retributivism is again the leading theory, it has been justified in terms of the maintenance of the proper balance of benefits and burdens in society. The criminal is seen as one who takes unfair advantage of the rest of society, and punishment redresses the balance. But it is not clear how it is helpful to think of many of the most serious crimes, such as rape, as representing an improper distribution of burdens and benefits. At bottom the notion that suffering must be met by suffering, that the penalty will give the aggrieved satisfaction equivalent to the harm caused, is difficult to escape from. One theory of the *Atonement has argued that Christ made satisfaction for our sins, that he bore the wrath of God justly incurred by sin, and some philosophers have argued that only theological defences of retributivism are possible. John Mackie, for example, maintains that philosophically retributivism is morally indefensible though inescapable in any foreseeable society.

An attempt to escape from the perceived difficulties of this theory was made by utilitarians who argued that the purpose of punishment was simply to deter others. There have proved to be two crucial objections to this view. The first is that if our aim is deterrence we ought logically to make sentences as harsh as possible, but where this has been tried it leads to a sense of outraged justice. Fundamental to most accounts of justice is the idea that the punishment must fit the crime. The second problem is that crime statistics are against it. Harsh penal regimes seem to have little bearing on rates of offending.

The third main approach to punishment is to understand it in some sense as educational. *Plato suggests that the purpose of punishment is to cure a disorder in the offender's soul, an idea forcefully advocated in the 20th century by Simone *Weil and Elizabeth Moberley. There are strong and weak versions of this view. The weak view is the welfarist account, inclined to trace wrongdoing to bad schooling and environment, and thus understanding punishment as an extension of education. Where this view scores is both in recognizing the high correlation between social deprivation and the more newsworthy forms of crime, and in pointing to a number of well-known success stories. The objection to it is that it can amount to a normalizing form of therapy, where anyone who deviates from the social mainstream is regarded as a case for treatment.

The strong view of Plato and of many Christian writers, on the other hand, takes its stand first on human responsibility, and thus insists that an offender has a right to be punished, but also on the educative value of suffering. The first point is a defence of human dignity. Against those who emphasize the role of circumstances these thinkers insist that it is the capacity to take on responsibility that constitutes true *humanity. Not to punish is not to take the offender seriously as a moral agent. To this is joined the quite different point that it is suffering that is peculiarly adapted to further our moral education. In the words of Simone Weil, the art of punishing is that of awakening in the offender, by pain or even death, the desire for pure good. This view underlies the prophetic and Deuteronomic reading of history. In Christian history reflection on the *cross of Christ and a desire to share in Christ's sufferings has profoundly shaped understandings of the moral life and led to a positive value being ascribed to suffering. Many questions attend the extension of such views to the treatment of offenders, however. Nowhere in the NT is a positive value attached to the cross *as an example of suffering.* Many exegetes would rather understand it as a protest against suffering. Suffering may play a part in the moral economy, but on the other hand it not infrequently embitters and destroys people. Even were it true that suffering were educative, would society have the right to impose it on offenders? Is it not, as Iris Murdoch insisted, something which has to be freely chosen? And does not the valorization of suffering underwrite a morbid view of reality, strangely out of tune with the living God? Notoriously, an insistence on the suffering that is our lot has underwritten many oppressive regimes.

Would it be possible to do away with punishment altogether? This has been argued by some secular and Christian theorists, at the very least as a utopian goal. The NT can be read as a programme for handling breakdown in human relationships in non-alienating ways, without recourse to the law and the battery of punishments that all justice systems have resorted to. Where we have an example of offence within the community, as in the two letters to the Corinthians, it is dealt with by temporary exclusion. It could be argued that church experience very quickly made recourse to other forms of punishment necessary (see PENANCE). On the other hand, the centrality of *reconciliation to the Christian gospel challenges us to find ways of dealing with human folly and wickedness that go beyond the need for satisfaction so deeply implicit in all forms of punishment and to realize in this sphere too the alternative that Jesus sought (Mark 10: 43).

See also CAPITAL PUNISHMENT; CONSCIENCE; NATURAL LAW; SIN.

T. J. Gorringe

Duff, R., *Trials and Punishments* (1986).
Durkheim, E., *The Division of Labour in Society* (1984).
Garland, D., *Punishment and Modern Society* (1990).
Hudson, B., *Justice Through Punishment* (1987).
Moberley, E., *Suffering, Innocent and Guilty* (1978).
Moberly, W., *The Ethics of Punishment* (1968).
Weil, S., *Selected Essays 1934–1943* (1962).

purgatory, a state or place of purification where faithful *souls are prepared for the vision of *God in *heaven, according to Catholic doctrine.

'Whoever speaks against the *Holy Spirit will not be forgiven either in this world or in the next' (Matt. 12: 32). Pope Gregory the Great (c.540–604) concluded from this gospel passage (cf. also 1 Cor. 3: 13–15) that there can be a *forgiveness after death and said that this forgiveness is achieved, before the final judgement, by 'a purifying fire', *purgatorius ignis* (*Dialogues*, 4, 39), from which the term 'purgatory' derives. Clement of *Alexandria, *Origen, and *Augustine had all previously referred to such a purification, this being one way to explain the efficacy of praying for the dead which had become a widespread Christian practice, with a notable OT precedent in 2 Maccabees 12: 39–45 (an *apocryphal book not accepted by Protestants).

These matters first appeared in the formal doctrine of the Catholic Church in the profession of faith proposed to emperor Michael Palaeologus with a view to the reconciliation of Latins and Greeks. Read at the Second *Council of Lyons (1274), it states that repentant sinners who die in charity before having rendered full satisfaction for their sins will be cleansed after death by 'purgatorial and purifying penalties' (strictly speaking, 'purgatory' was not mentioned), which are alleviated by the intercessions of the living faithful, particularly in the *sacrifice of the mass. These penalties were firmly distinguished from the pains of *hell. As Catherine of Genoa's important *Treatise on Purgatory* (c.1490) later emphasized, purgatory has heaven in view. The souls there have an 'instinct' for God, temporarily and painfully restrained, which fundamentally distinguishes them from those in hell. Attempting reconciliation with the Greeks again, the Council of *Florence in 1439 repeated the teaching of Lyons.

On both occasions, the formulation was essentially a Latin one, at odds with the general *Eastern Orthodox view of the soul's state after death. The Latin view, refined by the scholastics, was that, in purgatory, the punishment still due for mortal and venial sins forgiven during life was undergone and expiation was made for unforgiven venial sins. After this purification, souls are received immediately into heaven to enjoy the vision of God with the *angels and the *saints, prior to the final *resurrection on the last day. Both the legalism and the precision of this view were and still are foreign to the east, where it is believed that 'neither the just nor the wicked will attain their *final* state of either bliss or condemnation before the last day'. The Orthodox *liturgy prays for the departed but it is also offered for the apostles and even for the Virgin *Mary. All pray for all in solidarity, because the state of the blessed is not 'a legal and static justification', but 'a never-ending ascent, into which the entire communion of saints—the Church in heaven and the Church on earth—has been initiated in Christ' (Meyendorff 1983: 220–2).

Closely associated with the legalistic doctrine of purgatory in the west were the proliferation of masses for the dead and also the idea of indulgences, by which the temporal punishment due for one's own forgiven sins or for those of the souls in purgatory could be remitted. *Luther rejected the doctrine of indulgences in 1517 and gradually hardened against that of purgatory, considering that it lacked any scriptural warrant and also violated the principle of *justification by *faith alone. The Reformers duly removed the ancient practice of *prayer for the dead from their liturgies. Though, in reply, the Council of *Trent (1563) took the step of declaring 'there is a purgatory', it said nothing about its nature.

If the most famous literary account of purgatory is by *Dante in the *Divine Comedy*, perhaps the most popular is by John Henry *Newman in *The Dream of Gerontius* (1865), thanks to Edward Elgar's magnificent *musical setting. After death, Gerontius eventually comes before Jesu, his judge, and tries to run 'to the dear feet of Emmanuel', but falls because of his sins, 'consumed, yet quickened, by the glance of God'. He needs help and cries, 'Take me away'. It is to the 'golden prison' that he goes to be tended by angels until such time as, released from 'all bond and forfeiture', he can lastingly return to 'the courts of light'.

In more recent times, convinced of the fundamental unity of body and soul, Karl *Rahner developed a theology of *death that contains a remarkably integrated understanding of purgatory, harmonizing the Catholic emphasis on punishment with the Orthodox sense of solidarity and delay until all are ready. In death, he asks, does the soul become strictly 'out of this world' or does she rather, by virtue of the fact that she is no longer bound to an individual body, enter into 'a much closer, more intimate relationship to the universe as a whole'? It is, he suggests, the persistent influence of Neoplatonism that encourages the idea that 'the appearance of the soul before God, which, faith teaches us, takes place at death, stands in some direct opposition to her present relationship to the world, as though freedom from matter and nearness to God must increase by a direct ratio' (Rahner 1961: 27–8). Purgatory's aspect of 'temporal punishment', Rahner suggests, consists of the heightened awareness the soul has of the consequences in the world, as *time continues until the resurrection of the body on the last day, of her own sinful acts (cf. ibid. 31–4).

If the classical doctrine of purgatory, driven by an individualism concerned with what happens to each of us when we die, has encountered much opposition, from Rahner's modern understanding of the interconnectedness of all that exists a surprisingly coherent alternative view of purgatory emerges.

See also LIMBO.   **Paul McPartlan**

le Goff, J., *The Birth of Purgatory* (1981), ET (1984).

Meyendorff, J., *Byzantine Theology* (1983).

Michel, A., and Jugie, M., 'Purgatoire', in *Dictionnaire de Théologie Catholique*, 13/1 (1936), cols. 1163–326.

Ombres, R., *Theology of Purgatory* (1979).

—— 'Latins and Greeks in Debate over Purgatory', *Journal of Ecclesiastical History*, 35 (1984), 1–14.

Rahner, K., *On the Theology of Death* (1961).

Puritanism

Puritanism is one of the most elusive terms in the entire lexicon of religious *history, and yet it carries a heavy ideological freight. Puritanism has been linked to the rise of *capitalism and modern *science, with modern politics, and even with the invention of *North America, as well as of something called the self. Yet 'Puritan' began as no more than a convenient term of abuse, the only *sixteenth-century nickname still carrying some meaning today.

'Puritans' were convinced *Protestants who stood out from the crowd of a population only nominally converted by the legislated *Reformation of the reign of Edward VI (1547–53), reinstated, after the interlude of Catholic Mary (1553–8), by Elizabeth I (1558–1603). It could be said that when most people became Protestants, Protestants became Puritans. Those miscalled Puritans (the label suggested the medieval *heresy of the Cathars) were, in the language of the day, 'singular' and 'precise'. They avoided 'needless' company-keeping, openly reproved swearing and drunkenness, and practised a self-consciously 'godly' way of life, inspired by bible-reading and sermon-going, and undergirded by a *Calvinist faith in God's *providence and *predestinate *grace. For their part, they castigated their enemies as 'carnal worldlings' or, with reference to the covert Catholicism of many Elizabethans, 'church papists'. If there is a language of politics, there is also a politics of language.

Formally, Puritans were defined by dissatisfaction with the deliberately moderated terms of the Elizabethan religious settlement. They agitated for 'further reformation' and refused to conform in all respects to the Prayer Book, or to endorse it by subscription. These were the first 'Nonconformists', another name with a long future ahead of it. At first, the Puritan agenda was dictated by matters ceremonial and *liturgical, including especially vestments, 'popish rags'. But there ensued a more radical movement for the reform, or rather eradication, of the hierarchical *ministry and constitution of the *church, a campaign especially against bishops. These were the first *Presbyterians. Some who found the established church unacceptable, even anti-Christian, seceded to set up separate, 'gathered' churches. Named after one of their founding fathers, Robert Brown, these 'Brownists' were ancestral to Independency, or *Congregationalism. But separatism was a Rubicon too far for the Puritan majority, which practised what might be called semi-separatism, within a kind of church within the church.

In the 1580s, an organized Presbyterian movement challenged the *episcopal hierarchy and, implicitly, the religious policy of the crown. But these efforts suffered defeat, as did a second and carefully moderated attempt to carry a further reformation early in the reign of James I (1603–25). The response to these political disappointments shaped the Puritanism of the *17th century. One reaction took the form of seditious and satirical pamphleteering, the so-called Martin Marprelate Tracts (1588–9). It was the official anti-Martinist response to these libels that helped to create a potent caricature of Puritanism in the sophisticated public eye, the Puritan in literature and on the stage, from Ben Jonson's *Bartholomew Fair* to Samuel Butler's *Hudibras*, serving to define and construct the Puritan in real life. There were further episodes of separatism, the beginnings of an unbroken dissenting tradition. However, the majority of Puritans now made their peace with and within the church, without forfeiting their 'singularity'. Puritanism thus became less a body of opposition to the church than a vigorous force within it.

But fierce local contests between Puritans and their opponents continued, often focused on maypoles, dancing, stage plays and other features of traditional festive culture. Puritanism had not been neutralized as a political force and when, after the accession of Charles I in 1625, control of the church passed into the hands of anti-Calvinist bishops, led by Archbishop William Laud, Puritanism was reactivated, with momentous consequences on both sides of the Atlantic. Either Puritanism, or the effort to suppress it, helped to provoke the great emigration to the eastern seaboard of North America, where the colonies comprising New England engaged in a variety of ecclesiological experiments beyond Presbyterianism. When Charles and Laud attempted to impose their religious model on Presbyterian *Scotland, events were set in train that led to civil war in all three of Charles's kingdoms and the downfall of the episcopal Church of England, together with the monarchy.

Puritanism was triumphantly vindicated, but now fell foul of its own internal contradictions. The principles of Independency, refined in New England, made it impossible to impose a uniform Presbyterian model, while a variety of more radical sects, including *Baptists and *Quakers, proved irrepressible. *Anglicanism, too, was born out of these circumstances. With the restoration of the monarchy and of bishops after 1660, conscientious Presbyterian ministers and their flocks, together with the Independents, Baptists, and Quakers whom they opposed, lost their place in the sun. Dissent was now to be a permanent feature of the religious and political landscape, and after 1689 it was afforded a measure of toleration.

At this point historians have often ceased to talk about Puritanism and have altered their lexicon to refer to 'Dissent'. The semantical adjustment disguises the fact that the Puritan legacy and ideal remained intact and active, both in the dissenting congregations and in the established church, two religious worlds separated by a very permeable membrane, as dissenters continued to attend their parish churches, occasionally, to qualify for public office, or regularly, on Sunday afternoons. That elusive substance, if substance it was, that we conjure up with the very word Puritanism, continued to mould the English character, and the American too. Whether it generated capitalism, *democracy, or modern science, remains a matter for learned debate. It may be more certain that it gave us stewed rhubarb and rice pudding.

Patrick Collinson

Collinson, Patrick, *The Elizabethan Puritan Movement* (1967; 1990).

Coolidge, J. S., *The Pauline Renaissance in England: Puritanism and the Bible* (1970).

Haller, William, *The Rise of Puritanism* (1938), repr. (1957).

Knappen, M. M., *Tudor Puritanism* (1939).

Miller, Perry, *The New England Mind: The 17th Century* (1939), repr. (1954).

Watts, Michael R., *The Dissenters from the Reformation to the French Revolution* (1978).

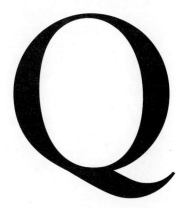

Quaker thought. The story is told of a young Quaker rising to speak for the first time in a Quaker meeting. 'Jesus, I think …' he began, only to be interrupted by a formidable Quaker who rebuked him, 'Friend, thee should not be thinking!' From its inception, members of the Religious Society of Friends, more popularly known as Quakers, have had an ambivalent attitude to the *tradition of Christian thought.

George Fox (1624–91), commonly regarded as the founder of the movement, averred that to be 'bred at Oxford or Cambridge' did not fit a man to be a minister of Christ, and his close colleague Robert Barclay (1648–90) testified that illiterate Quakers had bested academic theologians in arguments over biblical texts by relying on the direct inspiration of the *Holy Spirit. Yet Fox's *Journal*, still regarded as a great spiritual classic, was edited by the Quaker Thomas Ellwood who had been *Milton's amanuensis, not a position for an uneducated man, and Barclay himself was educated at the Scots College in Paris. At the age of 26 he produced his Latin treatise, *Apology for the True Christian Divinity*, which won even Voltaire's admiration of its Latin style and his slightly double-edged compliment that it was 'as good of its kind as it could be'. Quakers were and continue to be eminently capable of thought.

The distrust of the tradition, however, is at one with Fox's fundamental insight which he records as follows: 'And when all my hopes in [priests and preachers] and in all men were gone, so that I had nothing outwardly to help me, nor could tell what to do, then, oh then, I heard a voice which said, "There is one, even Christ Jesus, that can speak to thy condition." ' Fox's experience as he records it is one of abandonment, of a failure of tradition and of argument to 'speak to his condition' (*Journal*, p. 11). He goes on to record a series of deepening insights that depend on no outward influence, not even the bible, because they are directly mediated to him. The bible's place is as a confirmation of these insights. There is no place either for an ordained *priesthood or for theological education. We should recall that Fox reached adulthood in the turmoil of the English Civil War, when all the traditional sources of *authority in matters spiritual had proved unreliable. The Catholic church and its tradition had been ousted, the king had been executed, and the bible itself was manifestly open to a babel of conflicting interpretations. Fox turns from any of these external signs of authority to the unquestionable inward address of God.

This stress on the possibility of direct individual address by God accounts for the lack of interest in the sixteen hundred years of Christian history that Quaker tradition itself evinces. 'Christ is come to teach his people himself', Fox declared, rendering the mediation of the church at best superfluous and at worst a positive barrier to spiritual progress. In Fox's thought, this coming of Christ as teacher represents a peculiar form of realized *eschatology. The Second Coming has been enacted in the development of what William Penn liked to call 'Primitive Christianity Revived'. The coming of Christ into the community means that the community itself is caught up into a restoration of the state before the *Fall. Here is the root of the movement's revolutionary recognition of *women as equal *ministers with men and Fox's insistence on the possibility of human perfection. Even the most demanding requirements of the gospel are entirely within the capacity of those whose lives are lived in the light of Christ. Thus, for instance, the movement quite early embraced *pacifism as such sayings of Jesus as 'Turn the other cheek' and 'Resist not evil' were to be taken literally.

Fox was no systematician, unlike Barclay. The latter's *Apology* was a shot across the bows of the theologically literate opponents of Quakerism. In it, he is at pains to argue that Quakers do not appeal to some private experience or to some human faculty to ground the certainty of their convictions. He appeals instead to a universal conviction of *sinfulness, self-authenticating but itself the result of divine intervention. In this he clearly draws on his contemporary *Descartes who also sought a certain ground for his philosophy in a universal experience, in his case that of doubt, rather than in external or divine authority.

In Barclay's thought, the conviction of sin is a response open to all humankind, but one that derives from divine action. Throughout his exposition Barclay relies on John 1: 4, where the word is described as the *light which enlightens everyone. The experience of the divine light must be universal if it is to be the foundation for the certainty of *religion. If it is universal, however, this must mean that it also illuminates those who have never heard of Christ. The light is Christ, but the human response to it does not depend on acknowledging its nature, but in conforming to its demands. Here we have the root of the continuing debate in Quakerism over the 'scandal of particularity'. Barclay has been read either as a devout follower of Christ or as a proponent of a universal religion of which Christianity is only one local version.

The idea of Fox and Barclay's *thought* is, of course, inescapable. Quakers had to communicate among themselves and to other people to express their convictions, especially in periods when they were severely persecuted. However, underlying the Quaker attitude is a prime example of what Derrida would call the 'logo-centric' tendency in western culture, the attitude that written *language is a pale distortion of living speech, but that this in itself can never be anything but more or less a distortion of unmediated experience. This view of language informs early Quaker thought and still sits uneasily with other, sometimes opposing, trends in contemporary Quakerism.

It had three main consequences. First it put silence at the heart of Quaker *spirituality. In the unmediated stillness of a meeting, Christ was present. The meeting was not entirely silent, however, as out of that silence God might choose to speak directly through anyone present, man, woman, or child. This notion led increasingly to a form of *quietism where the whole effort of the spiritual life was devoted to subduing the human will so that the word of God would not be muddied by human intention.

Secondly, it led to a perhaps *paradoxical concern with words. Credal statements were abandoned because of the inadequacy of their vocabulary, and because they were produced in the 'dark night of apostasy', as the whole of Christian history was known. On the other hand, Quakers were enjoined to take literally the command of Jesus not to swear oaths, and held out a standard of strict verbal and grammatical accuracy and *truthfulness. The Quaker peculiarity of retaining the pronoun 'thou', or in later usage, 'thee', was not just a blow for human equality by refusing to address superiors by what was then the polite form 'you', though undoubtedly this was part of the social background. Fox himself and others searched through treatises on grammar to show that this was 'incorrect' usage as 'you' was strictly a plural pronoun (compare modern French *tu* and *vous*).

Thirdly, it led to an emphasis on sincerity and integrity in all aspects of life. The slippery ambiguities of language were to be mitigated by the directness of charitable action. Steadfastness of character and simplicity of life were the outward signs of a faith anchored in the unchanging nature of God. Quakers never renounced the *world as some similar sects have done but saw it as a field for humanitarian concern. The conviction that none were out of reach of the light meant that Quakers were pioneers in work with those whose humanity was denied, in particular *slaves, prisoners, and the mentally ill.

If verbal *symbols were distrusted, visual and musical symbolism was ruled out of court. The physical symbols of the *sacraments were also deemed superfluous. *Communion and *baptism were spiritual events and the outward signs were a distraction and a source of hypocrisy. Soon every aspect of conduct was regulated and so, for instance, the distinctive Quaker dress developed. This was a sign of a corporate identity in contradistinction to the world and of the equality of the members before God, but also testimony to that plainness and lack of ostentation which was expected in speech.

In this climate, the major form of Quaker religious expression was the spiritual journal, a record of the wrestling of a soul as it sought to conform itself to God's will and to 'live up to the light'. These journals are a fascinating resource and a particular gem is that of

John Woolman, a tailor and Quaker minister in New England who stood out against his fellow Quakers in his concern for slaves. Those which record the struggles of women preachers and missionaries offer a rare glimpse into the spiritual life of women in the 18th and 19th centuries. Such theology as they evidence is implicit and practical. After Barclay, nothing that could be described as systematic Quaker theology was attempted.

Many Quaker ideas had already been promoted by the German Spiritual reformers. What led Quakers to outlast similar contemporary groups was the evolution of a structure of church government that proved flexible enough to endure. Decisions were taken under the guidance of the Holy Spirit in meetings where every member could theoretically take part. Rampant individualism was checked by a strong insistence that personal inspirations should be tested by the meeting as a whole.

Women took full part in such exercises, although in separate meetings until the late 19th century. This accustomed both women and men to the notion of accepting collective responsibility and to the skills of organization and administration. Quaker women were to play important roles in the battles for female emancipation in the 19th and 20th centuries, as much because they had the experience of administering and organizing collectively in a way not open to many of their sisters as because of the relatively high status they enjoyed in the Society.

The practice of these disciplines of discernment in mundane issues was seen as an integral part of religious life, and allowed no distinction between religious matters and daily dealings. One consequence of this is that Quakers have had a disproportionate influence on the development of modern economic life. As a token of their insistence on integrity and truthfulness, they adopted the system of fixed pricing and could be relied on to provide the service they undertook. Their business success was notable and noted and the practice became standard.

Alongside this disciplined pietism, however, Quaker thought has always been open to another line of development. The prioritizing of experience over even the scriptures meant that there has always been a strand of Quaker thought that identifies itself as an experiential faith transcending human religious divisions. The theological liberalism of *Schleiermacher, for instance, bears a striking resemblance to some ways of formulating Quaker thought and his influence becomes apparent in 19th-century Quakerism. Quakers were less distressed by the discoveries of 19th-century *science than many groups as they could afford to take a more relaxed view of biblical authority. Indeed, the meticulousness and facticity of scientific enquiry proved congenial to the many noted Quaker botanists and physicists among whom were John Fothergill (1712–80), John Dalton (1766–1844) pioneer of atomic theory, Arthur Eddington (1882–1944) pioneer of astrophysics, and Kathleen Lonsdale (1909–71) who developed X-ray crystallography. It has been argued, however, that there may have been influence in the other direction. It was predominantly Quaker scientists who promoted the collegial structure of scientific associations, perhaps out of their experience of consensual methods of working within the Society.

A key figure in the further development of modern liberal Quakerism is the American Rufus Jones (1863–1948), who redescribed the Quaker tradition as a development of the Christian mystical tradition, what he called 'practical *mysticism', which issues in a life of committed social service rather than in any *ascetic withdrawal. From this, however, it is a small step to regarding Quakerism as a historically conditioned western form of the universal religion that underlies all the established systems. Its Christian ancestry becomes then merely a historical contingency, one language among many to describe, but also to distort, the primal experience. Its distinctive moral and social stances are understood as the logical outcome of consideration of the unique and equal value of each human being rather than as the manifestations of an eschatologically transformed set of human relations. The 'Inward Light', which for early Friends was the light of Christ shining into the human soul, becomes known as the 'Inner Light'. This small shift may have lent weight to a trend to identify that light with a spark of divinity resident in each human soul, or indeed with the spiritual essence of humanity without reference to an external deity. On this understanding, some contemporary Quakers identify themselves as humanists or even *atheists.

Many Quaker groups around the world are much exercised at present in debates between what are called the Christocentric and the Universalist positions, and the mediation of the apparently conflicting insistence on Christ's uniqueness as against the value of all forms of spiritual expression remains an unresolved problem. The range of positions adopted is diverse. Contemporary Quakerism is a spectrum from the *evangelical, even *fundamentalist, groups of Bolivia, Kenya, and the American West to the *New Age liberalism and humanism of some independent meetings, while a small remnant of Conservative Friends still continues to maintain the peculiarities of dress and language. Institutions such as Woodbrooke College in England and Pendle Hill in the United States provide arenas for discussion and research on Quaker thought in the liberal tradition, and the pastoral and evangelical traditions in the United States and elsewhere have their own training schools. The emphasis, however, is more on developing personal spirituality or on practical action than on developing coherent theological accounts of Quakerism.

Many of what were once the peculiarities of Quaker belief and practice have become widespread in modern Christian identity although any causal link is unprovable. The disuse of titles, the abandonment of the distinction between 'thou' and 'you', the ministry of women, *pacifist convictions, the relaxation of stringencies over the reception of the sacraments, the valuing of the quality of relationships over strict adherence to accepted standards of behaviour, a general feeling that human beings are equal before God and answerable only to their own consciences: none of these can be laid precisely at the door of Quakers, but Quakers have often played more or less public roles in bringing them about. It is notable that, in Britain at least, Quakers form a disproportionately high percentage of the teachers of religion at school and university level. Quaker thought may be an elusive quantity, but what Quakers think has more influence than may at first appear.   **Hugh S. Pyper**

Braithwaite, W. C., *The Beginnings of Quakerism*, 2nd edn. (1955).
—— *The Second Period of Quakerism*, 2nd edn. (1961).
Dandelion, P., *A Sociological Analysis of the Theology of Quakers* (1996).
Fox, G., *Journal*, Nickalls edn. (1975).
Freiday, D., *Barclay's Apology in Modern English* (1967).
Gwyn, D., *Apocalypse of the Word* (1986).
Jones, R., *The Later Periods of Quakerism* (2 vols.; 1921).
Punshon, J., *Portrait in Grey* (1984).
Woolman, J., *The Journal and Major Essays*, ed. P. Moulton (1971).

Quest for the Historical Jesus.

The key term 'historical Jesus' tries to evoke a distinction between the 'real' *Jesus as opposed to some iconic faith-picture of the Christ, and this tension between the received image of Jesus within the church, and the vision of Jesus that might be reconstituted by objectively assessable historical research is at the heart of the issue. The story of the Quest for the Historical Jesus fundamentally represents a series of scholarly movements from the *eighteenth century to the present, trying to reassess the biblical evidence about Jesus in the light of the best critical methods of historical and textual analysis available. It is generally agreed to have been elaborated in four chief stages.

The Old Quest (1778–1906) began with the posthumous publication of the work of Reimarus who proposed to retrieve Jesus from what he thought to be centuries of overlaid dogmatic varnish. The movement thus started with an anti-dogmatic basis. An early opposition was set up between *history and *theology. In retrospect it is easy to see how the postulation of such a division was itself made on post-*Enlightenment *Protestant dogmatic bases. The *nineteenth-century continued the trend of a series of anti-theological lives (usually the 'miraculous' or 'supernatural' elements in the gospel were excised, and an 'essential' character of moral reformer was posited as Jesus' original character and abiding relevance). Of the many Lives of Jesus that were written in this period, most were worthless *Romanticism, though some have lasting scholarly merit. Scholars such as D. F. Strauss, Wrede, and Renan stand out in high relief. But the cumulative effect of the Lives of Jesus movement produced such disparate end-results, and a figure so obviously presented as a *liberal Protestant before his time, that many felt the whole enterprise was fatally flawed. In 1906 Albert Schweitzer called an end to the Quest in his study *Von Reimarus zu Wrede*; English translators renamed it 'The Quest for the Historical Jesus' (1910), and so gave the school a name. Schweitzer ruthlessly exposed the problems of anachronism and bias in previous works, but, while calling for an end to the whole endeavour, he made the telling point that the whole medium of the message and context of Jesus was that of late eschatological *Judaism. Thus eschatology came to the fore throughout the *twentieth-century as a consensus approach to the interpretation of Jesus and his teachings. Recent scholarship has had to raise its voice even to be heard on just how significant is the Jesus material that is not *apocalyptic. To decide, as earlier scholars often did, that the latter material must therefore be secondary and subsequent to Jesus is no longer supportable.

It was the slowly spreading influence of the theological work of Kähler (first issued in 1896), which set the tone for the next stage. This has been called the 'No Quest' era (though in fact several important developments took place in it which refined later stages of the Quest movement). *Bultmann took up the leadership of this phase which had its heyday from 1921 to 1953. It took as a central premiss that the Christ of Faith was the only figure presented in any of the surviving evidence, and that this figure of Christ is therefore the only fit subject for scholarly attention in textual interpretation. The Jesus of History, according to Bultmann, is not capable of being reconstituted. The earliest writers had no interest in him, and nothing survives to allow a scholar to reconstitute an authentic picture.

Bultmann's pessimism was strong and influential. He also pursued dogmatic reasons for advancing it: chiefly that *faith in the Christ alone was salvific. But the dogmatic premiss in his case was based on a powerful and refined historical sense. In the course of his work he significantly refined methods of textual analysis. Form criticism and the birth of tradition criticism are closely associated with him: methods that attempt to trace the prehistory of the various units of *gospel tradition, categorize them, chart their development, and come to a more sensitive system for distinguishing Jesus material from later ecclesiastical adaptations. The advancing refinement of these methods, giving a clearer sense of what could be attributed to individual Christian evangelists, understood as editors of the Jesus tradition, called inevitably for a challenge to be made to Bultmann's pessimism about scholars ever being able to make any reliable statement about Jesus himself.

So it was that in the mid-1950s and through the 1970s the New Quest made its appearance. It was launched with an essay by Bultmann's former disciple E. Käsemann, criticizing Bultmann's scepticism. The New Quest stressed a greater degree of continuity between Jesus and the community of which he was the founder than had been generally admitted in the earlier phase. Large-scale commentaries on the NT gave way to more detailed work on smaller text units. Source, form, and redaction criticism were supplemented as methods by tradition history, narrative, and rhetorical criticism. The general feeling among protagonists of the New Quest was that, by applying ever more refined methods of analysis to the sayings of Jesus, scholars could demonstrate the line of development from Jesus' original teachings to those of the church about him. A set of agreed rules or principles of historical analysis grew up and were collated in this period. In brief these were:

1. The criterion of dissimilarity

If a saying does not fit the period or expectation of a critic it is more likely to be an authentic Jesus saying. This has the advantage of isolating a corpus of material which can be confidently ascribed to Jesus. It has the disadvantage of producing a picture relying on shadows: that is emphasizing a Jesus in discontinuity with his own age, one who is also set against the movement that continues after him, but that is evidently the custodian of his *memory.

2. The criterion of multiple attestation

To have a firm basis for collating the authentic sayings, a critic should rely most on those that were supported by more than one source. Multiple attestation is a mark of the impact of a Jesus saying on the tradition. Solid deductions about Jesus' teaching ought not to be advanced on the basis of a singly attested saying.

3. The criterion of linguistic and environmental assonance

If a saying fits well with the context of Jesus' own day it should be given credibility. If not it should be suspected of being a Hellenized product of the later church. The problem here is not only that it is almost a reverse of principle (1) but also that it tends to presume that commentators already know what would constitute such a 'fit'. The Third Quest was to challenge that presumption quite particularly, and disaffection with this principle in part gave rise to the last stages of the movement.

4. The criterion of coherence

When all the presumed authentic sayings of Jesus are brought together, one ought to witness a coherence of doctrine and intent from the single mind and character who produced them. Jesus was not a dilettante theologian but a deliverer of a message of some force and urgency, and the brief time of his ministry ought to make it clear that major internal contradictions of doctrine or direction cannot be ascribed to the same person. It is clear that this principle too has drawbacks in that it can only operate retrospectively, not as a principle of selection for authentic materials.

The New Quest continued for a long time until, in the 1980s, a renewed awareness of critical difficulties in textual interpretation, brought about in the aftermath of the impact of the French semioticians on schools of literary interpretation, drew it slowly to a close. It had not so much failed, however, as raised new expectations, and from the 1980s to the end of the century a great upsurge of interest in writing about the figure of the Jesus of History could be noticed: so much so that many believe it came to constitute 'The Third Quest.' Others dispute the title in so far as it could produce no commonly agreed set of results. What is common to most of those engaged in the latest phase of the Quest, however, is the optimism that a good deal can now be stated about the historical Jesus. The Third Quest generally tries to remain historical in tenor and principle, rather than becoming 'theological'. To this extent a movement away from issues to do with *miracle or *Resurrection narratives is clearly marked in their studies. It has not, however, seemed to have taken to heart the great problematics witnessed in earlier Quests over the extent to which any historical analysis can ever remain value-free and objective. Some of the more nuanced studies of the New Quest have strictly limited their scope. So, for example, scholars such as E. P. Sanders have attempted to contextualize Jesus as a teacher and activist in as three-dimensional a way as possible within the topography of Second Temple Judaism. Both he and G. Vermes, with differing end-pictures, have argued consistently and illuminatingly how the context of Jesus' Judaism profoundly affects our interpretation of his intent. Others such as S. Freyne or G. Theissen have taken great pains to illuminate the geographical, economic, and political climate of Jesus' own region. W. Telford has described the Third Quest as a search for Galilee as much as for Jesus. The sensitization to Jesus' time and condition has been immeasurably advanced over the last few decades as a result of such a body of scholarly investigation and, whatever the fate of the Third Quest, this achievement cannot be denied. The Third Quest is also characterized by a desire to move away from the preferred methods of the New Quest which focused on individual sayings or small units of gospel tradition. The Third Quest wishes to reconstitute the coherent body of Jesus' teaching as distinct from the developments appended to it by the early disciples. It also attempts to refine the earlier methods of analysis. Some protagonists have also suggested a new (but controversial) criterion: 'plausible tradition' (the earliest form of the tradition ought to be regarded as the sole locus for authentic materials). Not always have the criteria been as coherently applied as many of the Third Questers like to think, however, and the net result is the usual wide disparity of end-results in the various works emerging. The Third Quest has concluded, in turn, that Jesus was 'really': an itinerant Cynic, a Torah Interpreter, a Mystical Visionary, a Magus, an Eschatological Prophet, a Social Reformer, and a Leader of a Peace Party, to isolate just a few of the more notable variants, clearly not all reconcilable with one another. The movement is also marked by a confidence in the use of social-scientific methods of analysis, and attempts at a multidisciplinary approach.

The lasting achievement of the Third Quest will certainly prove to have been the manner in which it has sensitized Christian scholars to the subtleties and complexities of Jesus' Jewish environment. It was something that could rightly have been expected as a Christian response to the horrors of the Second World War, and fitting that it was most productively achieved by focus on the historical figure of Jesus as a Jew. None the less, for all its achievements, the lack of agreement among serious scholars in the Third Quest, the lack, that is, of any coherent end-result about Jesus of Nazareth, is already giving clear signs that the goal of discovering the 'real Jesus' will not be gained by this most recent of the Quests. It is a testimony no less to the difficulty of the interpretation of ancient sources than to the rich nature of the foundational texts of the Christian movement. Perhaps it is also a fit tribute to the enigma of Jesus. Even when one attempts to divest him of any supernatural status, in a supposedly objective purely historical study, elusively he still 'passes through the midst of them' and cannot be grasped (Luke 4: 30).

See also HIGHER CRITICISM.   **J. A. McGuckin**

Chilton, B., and Evans, C. A. (eds.), *Studying the Historical Jesus: Evaluations of the State of Current Research* (1994).

Evans, C. A., *Life of Jesus Research: An Annotated Bibliography* (1989).

Georgi, D., 'The Interest in the Life of Jesus: Theology as a Paradigm for the Social History of Biblical Criticism' *Harvard Theological Review*, 85 (1992), 51–83.

Käsemann, E., 'The Problem of the Historical Jesus', in *Essays On New Testament Themes* (1964).

Tatum, W. B., *In Quest of Jesus: A Guidebook* (1982).

Witherington, B., *The Jesus Quest: The Third Search for the Jew of Nazareth* (1995).

quietism.

'Desire nothing; refuse nothing,' said Francis de Sales (1567–1622). In the century that followed a school of *Catholic *mystics took this advice far enough to be condemned by Pope Innocent XI. These were 'quietists', and some in Naples possibly even claimed the name. A wider use of the term later became quite common, sometimes as a term of abuse by activists of Christians who wanted, for example, to keep religion out of politics, more often of contemplatives by those who insist on busier forms of prayer. The three great names in historic quietism are Miguel de Molinos (1628–97), Madame Guyon (1648–1717), and, a less clear-cut but more famous example, Archbishop Fénelon of Cambrai.

Molinos was a Spanish priest working in Rome, a favourite spiritual director, and the author of a best-selling *Spiritual Guide* (1685). In this he redrew the familiar contrast between meditation and contemplation entirely in favour of contemplation. Only contemplative, indeed purely passive, prayer leads to spiritual perfection. The *Guide* is full of sensible advice on coping with spiritual dryness without fussing about it: 'when thou lackest discourse in prayer, that is thy greatest happiness, because it is a clear sign, that the Lord will have thee to walk by faith and silence in his divine presence'. More in his private advice than in the book, Molinos seems to have encouraged Christians, walking by faith and silence, to side-step the structures of public *worship, of private disciplines of *prayer, and

even of *dogma. This aroused *Jesuit-led suspicion, and Molinos was condemned as a heretic in 1687 and, though he recanted, he spent the rest of his life in prison. His decorous submission was in accordance with his own quietist theology, and does not prove an inner conviction of his errors. There were sexual charges against him, on the lines that spiritual 'indifference' to what befalls the *body leaves open a theoretical opportunity for allowing animal impulses free rein. It was customary to blacken the reputation of opponents in that period, and the Vatican, which has thousands of his letters still locked up, has never published evidence of his sexual misconduct. He deserves the benefit of the doubt. What then was worrying about Molinism? He himself, in fact, encouraged his followers to receive *communion frequently, though he allowed them to cut back on going to confession. He claimed not to disparage the practice of meditation. Almost everything he said had precedents in the great Spanish Carmelite mystics, *Teresa of Avila and *John of the Cross, who in their day had been in trouble too. The problem was that he seemed to be offering a short cut for thousands of the general public to the top of a spiritual ascent which few had ever climbed.

In 1695 in France, Madame Guyon, influenced by Molinos, was also imprisoned for quietism. She had published *A Short and Very Easy Method of Prayer* (1685). Though short and easy, this claimed to supplant all others and to show how so to lose the self as to be utterly in God, like a river reaching the sea. Madame Guyon had a very difficult psychological background and tended to self-dramatize. Critics would call her hysterical. But we must remember the clerical male prejudice she encountered, the fact that she was embroiled, through no fault of her own, in court intrigue, and also that she won over Fénelon, who was very astute and godly. She was in fact a mystic in the classical tradition. She describes powerfully the dark side of *religious experience, when the soul loses all taste for prayer and cannot even 'practise' *virtue. But it is then, when all we have is passivity and failure, that God takes possession of the soul. If this experience is characteristically quietist, then much of Christianity deserves the name, and one understands why the *Catholic Encyclopaedia* (1907–14) called *Luther a quietist. Considering her own experience, she was eager to say, like other mystics, that it went beyond discursive reasoning. It went beyond the control of her own will, and beyond her sense of her own selfhood. This total abandonment and total forgetfulness, which Madame Guyon insisted was the heart of Christianity, was flatly condemned by Bossuet, the greatest orator and theologian of the day, but not a contemplative.

Fénelon, who was a mystic, struggled to defend Madame Guyon, and then, in his *Explication of the Maxims of the Saints on the Interior Life* (1697), tried to distinguish true mysticism from false. He took the list of points where Madame Guyon was condemned, and found in each of them a true and permitted mystical practice. Bossuet would have none of this, and, with the backing of Louis XIV, put pressure on an unwilling Innocent XII to condemn Fénelon. The condemnation in 1699 was the mildest possible, but in consequence Catholic mystics (a term first used in approval of living people by Madame Guyon) were under a cloud for the next century. Both Fénelon and Madame Guyon, like Molinos, submitted to the papal judgement. The encouragement of forms of prayer not far removed from quietism did, however, continue in Catholicism, particularly through the very influential writings of the *Jesuit Jean Pierre de Caussade (1675–1751).

Quietists, like many other early-modern theologians, often sound self-hating. The *Jansenists and the orthodox French school of Bérulle all tend to sound gloomy about *humanity. There are some dark sayings in Fénelon: 'a man's self is his own greatest cross'. Nevertheless, he was a theologian of *love. There was a ladder from the selfish love that wants God's gifts rather than God himself, through love mixed with fear, to that mixed with hope, to the purely disinterested. The hierarchy corresponds to our own make-up: our body, our reasoning powers, our imagination, all are set aside. In the depths of our being we become one with God in pure love.

Fénelon was the most appreciated Catholic thinker among Protestants, where something of the quietist tradition continued. There was a place for a contemplative piety for ordinary people, and Protestantism is more accepting of ways of thought that seem to disparage priests and the visible church. The issues raised by quietism still exist. Can Christians be passive and let God take over? Can they forget everything in God, who is all in all?   **Alistair Mason**

de la Bedoyere, M., *The Archbishop and the Lady* (1956).

Dupré, L., 'Jansenism and Quietism', in L. Dupré and D. Saliers, *Christian Spirituality: Post-Reformation and Modern* (1989).

Knox, R., *Enthusiasm* (1950).

Kolakowski, L., *Chrétiens sans église* (1969).

Laude, P. D., *Approches du quiétisme* (1991).

R

Rahner, Karl (1904–84), one of the most important Roman Catholic theologians of the 20th century and a major influence on *Vatican II.

Born in Freiburg im Breisgau, west Germany, Karl Rahner entered the Society of Jesus in 1922, three weeks after finishing secondary school. He followed the usual pattern of *Jesuit training, and in 1932 was ordained a priest. From 1934 to 1936 he did doctoral work in philosophy at Freiburg, where he also attended the seminars and lectures of the *existentialist philosopher Martin Heidegger. In 1936 he completed a doctorate in theology at Innsbruck in Austria, and subsequently taught at Innsbruck, Munich, and Münster. During the 1950s and early 1960s the orthodoxy of Rahner's work came under suspicion from Rome, but he was appointed as a theological expert at Vatican II by the German bishops, and his role, particularly through the advice he gave them, significantly affected its outcome. Though he retired from teaching in 1971 he continued to publish until his death in 1984.

At the time of Rahner's training the Catholic intellectual world was dominated by neo-scholasticism, a system of *philosophy and *theology based on the thought of Thomas *Aquinas, and in particular Aquinas as seen through the lens of 16th- and 17th-century commentators. Neo-scholasticism offered something very like a closed intellectual system in which everything, or at least everything of any importance, was already worked out. It was the intellectual face of a *Catholicism that had turned in upon itself and adopted a largely negative and defensive attitude towards the developments of the modern world, towards non-Catholic churches, and towards religions other than Christianity. Much of Rahner's work can be understood as an effort to fight the narrowness of this prevailing neo-scholasticism, opening it up from within, showing that the system contained more unresolved issues and open questions than was commonly supposed, and that it in fact left room for positive engagements with contemporary thought and with the modern world.

A variety of influences contributed to the shape of Rahner's theology. One of these was neo-scholasticism itself, which provided the framework within which much of Rahner's thinking took place as well as the framework against which he struggled. Rahner's time studying under Heidegger was also significant, though its influence is arguably more noticeable on the vocabulary than on the content of his thought. Probably the most important philosophical influence on his work came through his study of the writings of Joseph Maréchal, a Belgian Jesuit philosopher of the previous generation. Maréchal interpreted Aquinas in the light of *Kant (which gave rise to the name 'Transcendental Thomists' for his followers) and thereby opened up the possibility of making a positive use of modern philosophy without abandoning the Catholic allegiance to Aquinas (see THOMISM, MODERN). Rahner's theology was also shaped by his immersion in patristic and medieval spirituality, and above all by the Spiritual *Exercises and other writings of Ignatius Loyola, the 16th-century saint and founder of the Jesuits.

Early in his career Rahner produced two significant philosophical works, *Spirit in the World*, which began life as his failed Ph.D. thesis in philosophy, and *Hearer of the Word*, originally a set of lectures in the philosophy of religion. The most important idea to come out of these early volumes is that of the *Vorgriff auf esse*, usually translated the 'pre-apprehension of being'. Undergirding and accompanying every human act of knowing and willing, Rahner argued, there is a certain awareness of the infinity of being, and therefore of *God. God can never be known directly; he can never be an object for the mind in the way that a chair or a table can be; but when we know some particular thing, or will some finite value, we are never *merely* knowing or choosing the particular, finite being, but always at the same time reaching beyond it, towards the whole of being, and therefore towards God. Without this 'reaching beyond', knowledge or choice of individual objects could not occur in the first place: the *Vorgriff auf esse* is a condition of the possibility of all our knowing and willing. Rahner's rather daring claim, then, is that everyone is in some sense aware of God whether they realize it or not, and that all our most pedestrian dealings with the world would in fact be impossible without this awareness.

Apart from these two early philosophical volumes and *Foundations of Christian Faith*, a major systematic work published after his retirement, Rahner's energies were spent on shorter pieces, and it is in his essays and brief monographs that his most characteristic and important work is to be found. Many of the essays are collected in the twenty-three volumes of the *Theological Investigations*.

Rahner dealt with an immense range of themes, and his theology defies summary. The topics on which he published include the Trinity, the Incarnation, the church, the sacraments, Mary, angels, indulgences, heresy, the development of doctrine, concupiscence, poetry, childhood, power, leisure, sleep, pluralism, mystery, symbol, death, devotion to the sacred heart of Jesus, devotion to the saints, asceticism, prayer, Ignatian mysticism, the relationship of Christianity to Marxism, to evolutionary theory, and to psychotherapy (psychology), the relationship between nature and grace, between scripture and tradition, between exegesis and theology, and between the papacy and the episcopate. The list could easily be continued. On the whole this work did not emerge as part of any overarching plan; many of the essays were occasioned by contemporary theological debates or contemporary pastoral problems, by pronouncements of church authorities, by invitations to give lectures, lead retreats or participate in conferences, or simply by Rahner's teaching duties.

In spite of the tremendous range and variety of Rahner's thought, there are certain interlocking themes to which he frequently returns and which play a pivotal role in many, though not all, of his pieces. Key to what could be called the core of his thought are his conception of God's self-communication, his theory of the supernatural existential, and his preoccupation with the relationship between 'transcendental' and 'categorical' experience.

Rahner refers quite frequently to the notion of divine self-communication. God chooses to give himself, to communicate himself, to the world: he does not give some particular thing, or communicate some information *about* himself, but actually gives his very self. This serves as an overarching concept by means of which Rahner can both interpret and unite a variety of traditional topics of theological reflection. *Grace, for instance, is to be understood not, or not primarily, as some particular help or some created gift, but as God's giving of himself to the depths of the individual, and *revelation has to do most fundamentally with God's communication *of* himself rather than a communication of any propositions *about* himself. In the *Incarnation the divine self-communication reaches a point of absolute definitiveness in history. In the beatific vision it reaches its absolute fulfilment. And this self-communication is the purpose of *creation: God creates the world precisely so as to give himself to it; he brings that which is other than himself into being in order to unite it with himself.

The 'supernatural existential' is a related notion: Rahner uses it to specify what this divine self-communication means in the life of the individual. The term itself reflects the unusual interplay of neo-scholasticism and Continental philosophy characteristic of much of Rahner's writing: the notion of an 'existential', a fundamental element in human existence which is a constant feature of experience rather than one among its objects, Rahner derives from Heidegger; 'supernatural', on the other hand, is used as a technical term of scholasticism—the supernatural existential was first introduced, in fact, in Rahner's contribution to a debate among Roman Catholic theologians over the relationship between nature and grace. At issue in this debate was whether human beings have 'by nature' a desire for that which is beyond the capacity of their nature—whether human nature includes an unconditional desire for the beatific vision, for a kind of relationship with God that can only be attained if we are lifted beyond ourselves by grace. Proponents of what was called the *nouvelle théologie*, in particular Henri *de Lubac, defended the existence of such a desire, and accused the traditional neo-scholastics who denied it of making grace irrelevant and superfluous; neo-scholastics countered that the *nouvelle théologie* undermined the gratuity of grace, turning it into something

owed to human beings. Rahner sought to develop a third option acceptable to both sides of the debate. His proposed solution hinged on a distinction between 'pure nature', in the theological sense as that which is distinguished from grace and the supernatural, and 'concrete nature', our human nature as we actually know it. As we concretely experience our nature, Rahner suggested, we do indeed find at its very heart, as the 'central and abiding existential of man', an unconditional desire for grace and for the beatific vision. But this is only because our nature is *already* shaped by its situation in a world created for the sake of God's gracious self-communication. This central existential, then, which is everywhere found as part of our concretely experienced nature, is in fact already *super*natural.

In later writings Rahner presents the supernatural existential not just as an inbuilt *desire* for grace and the beatific vision but as a universal *experience* of grace, or at least of the offer of grace. He maintains that all human beings are not only constantly aware of God by means of the *Vorgriff*, but also that they are constantly experiencing God as graciously offering himself. One does not have to recognize this experience explicitly *as* an experience of grace in order to accept (or reject) it: we accept or reject the offer, according to Rahner, in so far as on some level we fundamentally accept or reject ourselves.

A recurring issue in Rahner's theology is how this grace universally experienced in the depths of consciousness is related to the concrete claims, institutions, and practices of Christianity, to the *bible, the church, and the sacraments, to historical revelation, and to Christ himself. Rahner's reflections in this connection are rich, varied, and developed in a variety of contexts, but in the broadest of terms they revolve around his understanding of the relationship between what he calls transcendental and categorical experience. These terms do not refer to two distinct sets of experiences, but to two levels he takes to be present in all experience. In all our dealings with concrete objects and people, with all that is finite and describable in categories (our categorial experience) we are always at the same time going beyond—'transcending' the finite and the nameable. Our awareness of God, our experience of grace, our sense of responsibility and our freedom, our fundamental choice of who to be, these all belong to the realm of our 'transcendental experience', impossible to pin down precisely and isolate as particular experiences among others and yet ever-present in our most mundane affairs. It is in the nature of transcendental experience, Rahner insists, that it must always somehow find expression and concrete realization on the categorial level, even though the transcendental can never be entirely caught and pinned down in words, categories, or finite realities. And this is true of God's self-communication as well: it is given in our transcendental experience as the supernatural existential, but it must also have a categorial expression. It must be realized and made concrete in history, in particular events, texts, societies, and institutions. Because God's self-communication is everywhere present and active, it finds categorial expression to some degree in all societies and cultures. The definitive and divinely guaranteed expression, however, occurs in Christ, and so also in the society and institution that derive from him, that is in the church.

The theory of the anonymous Christian, for which Rahner is most widely known and most frequently criticized, is closely connected to this core of ideas. Rahner's proposal that *atheists and practitioners of other *religions may in fact be Christians 'anonymously' is not a free-standing attempt to grapple with the problems of religious diversity and interreligious *dialogue, but a proposition that flows directly from some of the central elements of his thought. If grace is universally offered in the depths of consciousness, if it is possible to accept this grace without explicitly realizing that this is what one is doing, and if, as Rahner also maintains, all grace is the grace of Christ, then it becomes possible to suggest that those of any religious persuasion whatsoever may without realizing it be saved through their acceptance of the grace of Christ. There is, it should be noted, no reason to suppose that they will themselves concur in this reading of their situation, given that they do not begin from the same premises as does Rahner, but persuading others to regard themselves as Christians is not the purpose of Rahner's theory.

Like any important and complex thinker, Rahner has come to represent different things to different people. To those interested in problems of religious diversity he is known primarily for the theory of the anonymous Christian, and is presented as the classic exponent of 'inclusivism'. To others he is above all a 'transcendental' theologian, who not only gives a central place to the notion of transcendental experience, but also maintains that theology must follow philosophy in adopting a transcendental method, something which critics see as tending to undermine the historical concreteness and particularity of Christianity. To yet others Rahner represents a particular point on the spectrum of Roman Catholic theology: conservative and tradition-bound in comparison to Hans *Küng, dangerously modern and of questionable orthodoxy from the point of view of Joseph *Ratzinger and Hans Urs *von Balthasar.   **Karen Kilby**

Rahner, K., *Hearer of the Word* (1941), ET (1994).
—— *Spirit in the World* (1957), ET (1968).
—— *Theological Investigations* ET (1963–92), i–xxiii.
—— *Foundations of Christian Faith* (1976), ET (1989).
Dych, W. V., *Karl Rahner* (1992).
Kilby, K., *Karl Rahner* (1997).
O'Donovan, L. (ed.), *A World of Grace: An Introduction to the Themes and Foundations of Karl Rahner's Theology* (1980).
Vorgrimler, H., *Karl Rahner: His Life, Thought and Works* (1966).

Ratzinger, Joseph

(1927–). The only dogmatician of international repute to be simultaneously Prefect of the Roman Congregation for the Doctrine of the Faith, the former Holy Office (*Inquisition), Ratzinger's concern for a renewal of theological doctrine, demonstrated at *Vatican II, derived more from the 1950s-style 'going back to the sources' of la nouvelle théologie than it did from the emerging agenda of post-conciliar 'progressive' Catholicism. While conceding the intellectual strengths of scholasticism, his formation in the Catholic Munich school exposed him to *existentialist personalism in philosophy and the patristic inspiration of *Augustine to whom he would devote the first of his two German doctoral theses, a landmark in the study of Augustine's ecclesiology: Volk und Haus Gottes in Augustins Lehre von der Kirche (1954). For the second, his Habilitationsschrift, he elected to write on the interpretation of history in Bonaventure—an abiding influence, both positively, in his lifelong attempt to produce a specifically Christian evaluation of cultural trends, and negatively, in the disaffection it bred for utopian politics (*The Theology of History in Saint Bonaventure* (1959; ET 1971). Ascending the academic ladder at the universities of, successively, Bonn, Münster, Tübingen, and Regensburg, Ratzinger did not attempt to create an original theology so much as to 'think along with' the intellectual masters of different ages, with the aim of opening a conversation between the revealed word of scripture, as attested in the church fathers, and the voices of his own time: thus his commentary on the Apostles' Creed, *Introduction to Christianity* (1968; ET 1969), and the essay collection *Principles of Catholic Theology* (1982; ET 1987). Appointed archbishop of Munich in 1977, he accepted the post of Prefect of the Doctrine Congregation in 1981 on condition that he be allowed to continue with his personal theological writing, including commentaries on issues raised by his official duties: *Church, Ecumenism, Politics* (1987; ET 1988), and *Called to Communion* (1991; ET 1996).

His disciplining (with the consent, evidently, of Pope *John Paul II) of a number of 'dissenting' theologians, including *Balasuriya and *Boff, was governed by principles he set forth in *The Nature and Mission of Theology* (1993; ET 1995). While *freedom in the *church was chiefly, he held, the positive freedom to participate in the fullness of Christian faith (not the negative freedom to depart from it), the church could only defend the (quite distinct) freedoms desirable in civil society if, through common discipline, she remained internally strong. His guiding hand in the creation of the *Catechism of the Catholic Church* (1992) was exercised to this end, and explained in *Gospel, Catechesis, Catechism* (1995; ET 1997).
                                                                    Aidan Nichols, OP

Nichols, A., *The Theology of Joseph Ratzinger: An Introductory Study* (1988).

realism and antirealism.

Realism, at first approximation, is the view that reality is what it is independently of how we experience it, conceptualize it, know it, or think about it, and independently of our intentions and attitudes towards it. It is neither wholly nor partially constituted by our cognitive and active dealings with it. This is only a first approximation because it cannot hold unrestrictedly. Social institutions like marriage would not be what they are apart from our attitudes and intentions. Marriage bonds would not exist were they not generally recognized as such in the society. By contrast, the denial of realism, antirealism, could conceivably be true unrestrictedly. Many contemporary thinkers hold that anything we can think of is, at least in part, shaped by the way we think of it. We are, however, not concerned here with a global contrast between realism and antirealism, but with its application to Christian thought and belief, more specifically its application to the Christian *God. Thinkers who are not realist or antirealist in general often take one or another of these positions towards a certain domain—physical objects, theoretical entities like electrons and quanta, *moral values, or God. We can call these positions 'domain specific' realisms and antirealisms.

It may seem that, as we have set things up, antirealism with respect to a kind of reality would be incoherent. For if we recognize moral values or God as *real*, does that not amount to taking it to be what it is independent of the way we think or feel about it? Is that not what it is to be real? There undoubtedly is a sense of 'real' in which it is tied to realism in this way. But there is also a sense in which one can recognize, for example, physical objects as real while at the same time taking their nature to be dependent on how we experience and conceptualize them. This is exemplified by *Kant's account of the physical world. On his view we are capable of perceiving the environment only because we conceptually structure the 'manifold of sensation' in terms of our 'categories of the understanding' such as substance and causality. What we perceive has been 'worked up' by our conceptualization to make it possible for us to perceive it. We perceive reality *as it appears to us*, not reality *as it is in itself*. There are, Kant holds, things that are what they are independently of our thought (*noumena*); indeed, it is *noumena* that appear to us in perception. But we know, and can know, nothing about their nature. We can only know reality as it appears to us. Thus, in Kant's famous phrase, the physical world is 'empirically real' but 'transcendentally ideal'. Empirically real because the character of what I perceive is not dependent on what *I* believe about it or how *I* feel about it. It is objective to any particular perceiver. But it is transcendentally ideal because its constitution is shaped by the way human minds conceptualize it, rather than (solely) by the way it is in itself. Thus Kant recognizes the physical world as possessing an objective reality, but not independently of the ways human beings in general experience it and think about it.

Is there any other way of being antirealist about physical objects or God or some other alleged reality? There is, of course, the flat denial that such things exist. This position *vis-à-vis* God is well known under the label of *atheism. But atheists are not generally thought of as antirealists about God any more than those who deny the existence of ghosts, or witches, or phlogiston are thought of as antirealists about those entities. It seems that in order to count as antirealist about a type of entity one must, so to say, take that type of entity more seriously into account than is involved in simply denying its existence. But there is a familiar way in which an atheist can count as an antirealist about God. One might deny that there is any such objective entity as God is typically thought of as being, while at the same time feeling that it is important, perhaps crucially important, to maintain talk and thought and feeling and attitude and practice in which terms such as 'God' and the (or an) idea of God figure prominently. We find this combination in a variety of religiously toned atheisms that have become increasingly prominent during the last two centuries. *Nineteenth-century forms include Ludwig Feuerbach and Auguste Comte. In the 20th century we have George Santayana, an atheist with a strong attachment to Roman Catholic religiosity, of whom it was said that he believed that there is no God and that the Virgin Mary is his mother. Other prominent figures in this camp are Paul *Tillich and such 'Death of God' theologians as Thomas Altizer.

To combine atheism with a positive evaluation of 'God-talk' one must construe the latter as being something other than a series of *assertions* about God. For on that latter construal it would consist solely of false assertions, and what is valuable about that? The most usual idea is that God-talk consists of (1) expressions of feelings and attitudes, (2) commitments to a certain way of life, (3) exhortations to ethical conduct, and/or (4) insights into fundamental aspects of human life, all (or some) of this by means of a pictorial, narrative, or *symbolic presentation. Thus the story of *Jesus' *crucifixion and *Resurrection is taken by Santayana to be a narrative way of expressing the supreme moral value of self-sacrifice, a way that is much more effective than a bare statement that self-sacrifice is of supreme moral worth. It is important to emphasize that realists too

can recognize that religious language has these functions (1) to (4). They differ from this brand of antirealism in holding that religious language can also be used to make truth-claims about God.

Thus we can distinguish two main forms of antirealism about God: (a) God is objectively real in a way, but not in a way that is independent of human thought and discourse; (b) God is not objectively real in any way, but talk that superficially appears to be about God can be understood as playing an important expressive and/or hortatory function.

A prominent view of type (a), that of John Hick, is modelled on Kant's view of the physical world (not on Kant's view of God). Hick considers the objects of worship in a given religion to have phenomenal rather than noumenal reality. Like Kant, he supposes there to be a noumenal reality, 'The Real', which appears to us in various ways. But, again like Kant, he denies that we can know anything about it, except for the way it appears to us. Hick's Kantian interpretation of *religion is relativized. Instead of Kant's picture of a single human schematism of the manifold of sensation by a unique set of categories, we have different appearances of the Real in different religious traditions. As with Kant's view of the physical world, this position is intermediate between unqualified realism and unqualified antirealism. The modes of appearance of the Real in a given religion are objective *vis-à-vis* any particular individual; but their ontological status is that of a way of appearing rather than an independent reality that is appearing. If we use 'God' to refer to the most ultimate being, then Hick is unqualifiedly realistic about that (what he calls 'The Real'). But he denies that we can know anything about it. As the term 'God' is used in theistic religions as a term for a supreme personal agent of whom we can have some conception, Hick ascribes to God only phenomenal reality.

A somewhat more subjective form of type (a) antirealism is the position of Paul Tillich. Like Hick, Tillich recognizes the independent existence of an ultimate reality, which he calls 'Being-Itself', and which, like Hick, he takes to be inaccessible to human conceptualization. Thus both Hick and Tillich are realists about a supreme reality, but they refuse to identify that reality with God as construed in traditional Christianity, since they take the supreme reality to be unconstruable in any way by us. According to Tillich, we can get at Being-Itself only through 'symbols', parts or aspects of the spatio-temporal world which, by virtue of their participation in Being-Itself, serve as media for our experience of the ultimate. They are 'places' in the world where we are 'grasped' by the power of Being. Tillich takes there to be an indefinite plurality of such symbols, which change with different cultural situations.

As for type (b) antirealism, an ideally forthright and extreme example is the British theologian, Don *Cupitt. A close American analogue is Gordon Kaufman. Cupitt presents his view of religion—thought, belief, feeling, attitude, and practice—as part of what he takes to be a powerful movement of *internalization*, a 'mighty historical process by which … meanings and values are withdrawn from external reality and as it were sucked into the individual subject' (1980: 33). He takes the heart of religion to be the cultivation of *spirituality, which involves such things as appraising one's life with unconditional seriousness and honesty, disinterestedness, and purity of heart, the cultivation of meditation and contemplation, and the experience and expression of cosmic thanksgiving and *love. To be sure, spirituality has traditionally been pursued in the context of belief in, and a supposed relation with, a supreme, *omnipotent source of existence. But we have no reason to suppose that any such being exists; such a supposition is dependent on an outmoded *metaphysics. Hence in the quest for a truly spiritual life we are thrown back on ourselves. We can continue to use God-talk, but with the understanding that God is the religious requirement personified. The traditional attributes of God are projections of the main features of human spirituality. Belief in God, in so far as it is possible in this orientation, is simply a commitment to religious values in human life.

So far we have presented some antirealist positions on God but have done nothing to characterize a realist position. It looks as if the tail is wagging the dog. But there is method in this madness. The realist position is the one with which we are all familiar. It is the way all Christians have thought of God until relatively recently. Here are two features of the Christian understanding of God that indicate a deep commitment to realism.

1. God is *ultimate*, that on which all else depends for its being. It is an understatement to say that God is not dependent on human cognition for being what he is. God is not dependent on anything for what he is and does. It is precisely the other way around. A mode of appearance or a symbol or a projection does not have that kind of status. You and I have more creative power than they do.

2. In the Christian story God is active in *history, shaping the destiny of peoples in accordance with his master plan, inspiring the *prophets and other messengers, entering the world in the person of Jesus to save us from *sin and *death, guiding the *church by his *Holy Spirit, and so on. He is pre-eminently a God who acts. And this involves a great variety of interactions with us. In addition to the large-scale historical interactions, God is in constant communication with us in prayer. All this requires that God have an independent mode of reality. A mode of appearance or an imaginative construct or a personification of human ideals cannot be a partner in personal intercourse.

Thus realism is the 'default' position for Christian thought, the position to take in the absence of sufficient reasons against it. The same point can be made about realism in general. Whenever we seem to encounter realities beyond ourselves, the natural supposition is that they have an existence and nature that does not depend on how we think or feel about them. But this presumption is even stronger for the Christian God. (Note that this does not beg the question as to whether we have adequate grounds for various things we believe about God. The presumption in question is that whatever we are justified in believing about God is something we are justified in believing about an independent reality.) Hence the proper way to defend realism is to point out that it is innocent until proved guilty, and then consider whether there are strong enough arguments to overthrow it. This leads us to the arguments that are offered for antirealism about God.

Undoubtedly the main *motive* for taking non-realist construals of God seriously is a conviction that the traditional Christian supports for belief in God as an independent reality that we can, to some extent, truly characterize—primarily *philosophical arguments for the existence of God, the biblical witness, and personal religious experience—have been exposed as radically inadequate. Those so convinced are led to think that the only ultimate being we can take

seriously, if any, is one that is beyond human cognitive grasp, leaving our humanly characterized God in the status of symbol, mode of appearance, or imaginative construction.

As for more specific reasons offered by our antirealists, Tillich argues that it is 'idolatrous' to worship a *being*, however powerful, good, or loving, rather than the absolutely ultimate, Being-Itself. But surely most devout Christians will properly fail to be impressed by the suggestion that it is *idolatrous* to worship a personal being who is infinite in knowledge, power, and goodness and who is the source of existence of everything other than himself.

Hick's distinctive reason for his position is based on the phenomenon of religious diversity. On the one hand, he takes religious experience to put us in genuine contact with the Real, and so he regards it as reasonable to accept what that experience seems to reveal. But he also insists that there is a plurality of religious responses to the Real that are equally supported by experience, and that we have no sufficient reason for picking out one of these as the true one, or as markedly closer to the truth than the others. Hence we must take each of the major world religions to possess a correct account. But since, taken as claims about the Real as it is in itself they contradict each other, we have no alternative but to take each of them as a correct account of the way the Real appears in that religious tradition. Christian thought and belief, like that of other major religions, deals with phenomena rather than with the Real as it is in itself. This is an impressive argument. But it depends on the crucial assumption that there are several systems of religious belief, incompatible with each other, that are equally strongly supported by all relevant considerations. And that is an assumption that, to say the least, is a matter of considerable controversy.

Cupitt, like most other religious antirealists, alleges a lack of rational support for belief in an independently existing deity. But his distinctive reason for rejecting such a deity is his espousal of human autonomy as a supreme value, one that he takes to be an essential feature of *modernity. People nowadays, he says, want to live their own lives, make their own choices, determine their own destinies. And this is incompatible with recognizing the sovereignty of an independently existing deity. For to acknowledge the *de facto* and *de iure* sway of the will and purposes of such a deity is to betray the commitment to autonomy. Since he takes autonomy to be an essential ingredient in a truly spiritual life, this amounts to a *religious* reason against recognizing God as an existent reality. Religious realism, Cupitt contends, is actually irreligious. What are we to say of this argument? Cupitt is certainly right in taking the stress on autonomy to be opposed to traditional attitudes to God. But since he gives no significant reason why the choice between them should go to the extreme autonomy he advocates, his position lacks sufficient support.

Thus, since the reasons given for religious antirealism are unpersuasive, there are no sufficient grounds for abandoning the realist position.   **William P. Alston**

Alston, W. P., 'Realism and the Christian Faith', *International Journal for Philosophy of Religion*, 38 (1995).

Braithwaite, R. B., *An Empiricist's View of the Nature of Religious Belief* (1955).

Bultmann, R., *Kerygma and Myth* (1961).

Cupitt, D., *Taking Leave of God* (1980).

Hick, J., *An Interpretation of Religion* (1989).

Kaufman, G., *The Theological Imagination* (1981).

—— *In Face of Mystery: A Constructive Theology* (1993).

Kelsey, M., *Myth, History, and Faith* (1991).

McFague, S., *Metaphorical Theology* (1982).

Phillips, D. Z., *Faith and Philosophical Enquiry* (1970).

—— *Religion Without Explanation* (1976).

Santayana, G., *Reason in Religion* (1905).

Soskice, J. M., *Metaphor and Religious Language* (1985).

Tillich, P., *Systematic Theology* (1951), i.

—— *Dynamics of Faith* (1957).

reason has been basic to the development of Christian thought but its role remains contested. Its use is already present within the NT. Jesus regularly offers rational arguments in discussion with the Pharisees (for example, Mark 2: 8–10, 17, 19–22, 25–6), while Paul does the same when offering advice to the Corinthian church (1 Cor. 7: 1–16; 10: 23–30). This may reflect rabbinic use of reason in interpreting the law, but in Christian circumstances the scope and need for interpretation grew ever wider. The early church's problems of belief and behaviour were seldom resolved by appeal to new revelations though this occasionally happened, as with Peter's vision at Jaffa (Acts 10: 9–16). The necessity of working out the relationship of this new community to the old law, to Jesus, and to one another stimulated appeals to reason. Sometimes an issue could be settled with something 'from the Lord' (1 Cor. 7: 10) but at others Paul had to admit that what he said was only 'from me', a claim not to additional revelation but to the authority of rational discernment (cf. 1 Cor. 10: 15, 'I speak as to sensible men; judge for yourselves what I say'). Nor was the appeal to rationality, implicit as it mostly was, confined to interpretation of scripture or practical guidance for Christian living. Paul told the Romans that it was rational to acknowledge God (Rom. 1: 19–20) and he attempted the same approach—an appeal to natural reason as preceding *revelation—in his Areopagus speech at Athens (Acts 17: 23–9).

Hellenistic culture stimulated further, more systematic, use of what was then already internal to Christian understanding. In point of fact, without extensive use of reason, Christian *theology as we know it could never have developed. There could only have been the hardening of an original set of beliefs, a moral law, or a plethora of *Gnostic revelations. The occasional denunciation of reason or of any truck with Greek philosophy as found in Tertullian or Tatian is marginal to the tradition and generally close to the heretical. The work of the major Christian thinkers of the early centuries, Justin, *Irenaeus, or *Origen, with its systematic use of logical argument and Greek *philosophical concepts, charts the developing shape of all Christian theology: a set of beliefs drawn by argument from the scriptures on the one hand, a related body of '*natural theology' appealing directly to reason and experience, as in Justin's *Apologies* (*c*.155) on the other. The Logos doctrine (see WORD) implied for Justin a divine reasonableness within the world, incarnate in Christ but present and recognizable elsewhere. So he could appeal to the 'true reason' of Socrates.

While the Councils defined what was to be held of faith in regard to the Trinity and Incarnation, the way they arrived at it was one, as *Newman remarked, in which 'individual reason was paramount' (*Apologia*, 5). Again, it was through the use of reason that the entire system of multiple scriptural meanings, literal and *allegorical, developed. The apparent contradictions within scripture could only

be handled through recognition of a complex pattern of meanings (see HERMENEUTICS). The pattern was not revealed. It was a rational construct. One senses this, for instance, in the way *Augustine wrestled with the first verses of Genesis in the final chapters of the *Confessions*. The need to establish a rational framework of interpretation thus actually controlled the understanding of what was, in principle, a suprarational revealed scripture. Again the earlier books of the *Confessions* have to be read as an account of a rational pursuit of truth in which little by little Manichaean doctrines were dismissed as unscientific and absurd. Orthodox Christian beliefs became plausible for Augustine only with the help of Neoplatonic philosophy (see PLATO). Yet it is often the case that what is first established in an essentially reasonable way later becomes part of a far more *fideistic structure of thought. It becomes merged into revelation as the acceptable way of reading the latter.

The main use of reason by the mature Augustine is, unquestionably, to understand what is already believed. Faith comes first but its comprehensibility depends upon rational analysis. That profoundly Augustinian position was actually most precisely expressed centuries later by *Anselm: *credo ut intelligam* (I believe that I may understand). Never did such understanding take a more rational, indeed logical, form. Anselm endeavoured to demonstrate the existence and Trinity of God, the Incarnation and Atonement, all as rational necessities. Within his argument there is next to no appeal to *authority. That surprised his friends, but for him such appeal was unnecessary. Theology was a matter of precise reason—not, maybe, the reason which would convince a modern secularist but reason as perceived by Anselm himself and judged cogent by numerous disciples across the centuries.

Where Anselm sought to unveil divine rationality, *Abelard half a century later applied a far more secular, dry, scholastic logic, including the analytic comparison of rival views, inaugurating a new, potentially sceptical age of rationalism and forcing more traditional thinkers to re-emphasize the primacy of revelation. Medieval rationalism was grounded in the recovery of *Aristotle's major works and in the Aristotelian identification of reason with nature. As Aristotle's views were at many points well removed from Christian belief, attempts to harmonize the two could seem intensely problematic and Aristotelianism appear to lead to the conclusion of the irrationality of Christianity. The central methodological endeavour of Thomas *Aquinas was, nevertheless, to achieve a profound harmonization, not so much in terms of particular issues, where he was quite willing to admit that Aristotle was mistaken, but in the systematic integration of two ways of thinking. His task was to define the uses of reason, transforming the content of theology by the adoption of Aristotelianism, and yet ensure that the gospel and Augustine were not betrayed in the process. He set out his methodology in question 1 of the *Summa Theologiae*, though less transparently than admirers might desire. Reason, he insisted, is used in a variety of ways. From the analysis of 'nature' it proceeds directly to develop some truths; from 'grace'—that is scriptural revelation—it develops others. The use of reason, therefore, both precedes faith and follows it. Aquinas does not accept Anselm's claims for a total perceived rationality within revelation, but nor does he question that reason can go a long way both without revelation and, still more, in co-operation with it. In practice there is no sustained division in his work between the two. Aristotle and Augustine, as well as scripture, jostle one another throughout the *Summa*. This interplay of faith and reason was never expressed more attractively than in a line in *ST* I q. 1 a. 8 ad. 2: 'As grace does not destroy but perfects nature, it is right that natural reason should serve faith just as the natural loving tendency of the will serves charity.'

After Aquinas this attempted synthesis fell apart. Ockham in particular proved highly influential in his rejection of an Aristotelian model of the natural order as reflecting the nature of God and being itself open to understanding by human rationality. The rationality remained—Ockham was a superb logician—but the claim that the world reflected not the nature but simply the will of God cut the ground from under natural theology and prepared the way for the fideism characteristic of the *Reformation. *Luther violently denounced both Aristotle and the appeal to reason in terms not unlike those of Tertullian. Reason, he thought, was too unreliable in a world so deeply affected by sin. The intellectual and moral appeal had to be to 'faith alone', 'scripture alone'. Other reformers did not go so far. *Calvin had a more rational and orderly mind, *Zwingli remained still closer to the scholastic tradition. Furthermore, scholasticism reappeared in later generations of Protestant theology, while *Hooker emphatically placed the appeal to scripture itself within a Thomist and Aristotelian framework of nature and reason, 'Right Reason' providing the dominant theme of *The Laws of Ecclesiastical Polity*. Nevertheless, the fideism widely characteristic of late medieval and Reformation thought remained for many Protestants almost a mark of orthodoxy. Thus the young, still very Protestant, Newman, preaching on 'The Usurpations of Reason' in 1831, labelled it captious, mere, human, forward, usurping, rebellious, and versatile. Hume, in his *Essay on Miracles*, sneeringly remarked 'Our most holy Religion is founded on Faith, not on Reason'. The anti-fideist reaction of the 17th and 18th centuries, which led through *deism to the claim of rationalism that only what is provable by reason is worthy of retention, fed on an anti-rational streak in Christian thought but, more profoundly, on its commitment to rationality.

'Nothing should be believed, save only what is either self-evident or can be deduced from self-evident propositions,' was one of the statements condemned by the bishop of Paris in 1277. The rationalism of 13th-century academics reappeared, if with a more inductive approach to the rational, in the *Enlightenment theology and philosophy of the 18th. While an early moderate, John Locke, in *The Reasonableness of Christianity as Delivered in the Scriptures* (1695), was prepared to include even *miracles within his definition of 'reasonableness', the crucial point remained that reasonableness had become the controlling principle of faith. The further this was pressed, the less of traditional Christianity was left. With *Kant, no knowledge of God, whether natural or supernatural, remained. For many Enlightenment thinkers and a growing body of 19th-century historical scholars the criterion of reasonableness left less and less in place, for some like Kant as a matter of principle, for others rather as a matter of evidence. The evacuation of faith by reason had become the central dilemma of liberal Protestantism, to be challenged head-on by *Barth in the greatest theological revolution within Protestant history when he reasserted the primacy of faith and initiated 20th-century *neo-orthodoxy with the publication of his *Commentary on the Epistle to the Romans* (1919). There is plenty of reason in his writings: it would be quite impossible to have composed the complex and often profoundly convincing discussion of the *Church Dogmatics* without it, but it is essentially a sort of Anselmian reason, resolutely refusing to function outside the framework of revelation. Natural theology was for Barth a monstrosity.

Catholics meanwhile continued to repeat standard Thomist formulas. However unreasonable papal teaching was becoming on many matters through setting its face against the implications of the political and scientific revolutions of the 19th century, it remains striking that in principle *Vatican I in its first dogmatic constitution emphatically reaffirmed the value of the 'natural light of human reason'. Catholic priests might not use their reason very effectively but until after *Vatican II they invariably began their training by several months' study of formal logic. Chesterton was not mistaken in making the demasking of the counterfeit priest in the first of the Father Brown stories depend on his denouncing reason. 'You attacked reason', said Father Brown, 'it's bad theology.'

If rejection of reason has been somewhat marginal within the tradition of Christian belief and thought, its positive role remains in question. The three areas of contestation are traditional enough. First, is a 'natural theology' possible given the effect of original sin upon rational human nature, the gap in being between creation and creator, or the implications of modern linguistic philosophy? Second, can faith, while not controverting reason, yet get beyond reason, so that theology has a base in revelation which as such escapes rational verification? Third, if there is such a revealed source for both faith and theology, how far can the use of reason carry one in its exploration and extension, and how should its working be envisaged—in Anselmian, Abelardian, or Barthian mode?

Barth has been widely followed among Protestants in his reassertion of the primacy of faith in the given of revelation independent of 'reasonableness', but he has convinced fewer people in his repudiation of any natural theology. This vindication of revelation, when linked with acceptance of the possibility of natural theology (and natural law) has brought much modern theology back to an attitude to the use of reason not far from that of Aquinas. However, whereas for Aquinas reason meant mostly formal deduction, for contemporary theologians it is more a matter of converging probabilities, the weighing of historical evidence, an appeal to experience, even a revindication of allegory. In such ways faith and reason may cease to be contrasted. Whether or not that is right, it is certainly the case that, with relatively minor, if strident, exceptions, Christian thought has used reason extensively and frequently gloried in doing so for two thousand years. Moreover, if it had not, Christian theology could never have existed.   **Adrian Hastings**

Kenny, Anthony, *What is Faith?* (1992).
Lonergan, Bernard, *Insight: A Story of Human Understanding* (1957).
Murray, Alexander, *Reason and Society in the Middle Ages* (1978).
Trigg, Roger, *Rationality and Religion: Does Faith Need Reason?* (1998).

reconciliation in classical theology means much the same as *redemption, *atonement, or, even, *salvation. It refers to the removal of division between *God and *humanity, a division brought by *sin and overcome by *Jesus Christ, both Son of God and new *Adam, in whom divinity and humanity are reconciled.

More than redemption, the word suggests a necessary mutuality of action. Reconciliation cannot be a one-sided achievement. Whatever is offered has also to be accepted, including *forgiveness, an integral element within reconciliation whether human or divine. The *Lord's Prayer with its suggested mutuality linking divine forgiveness with 'as we forgive those who trespass against us' and the injunction of the *Sermon on the Mount, 'first be reconciled to your brother' (Matt. 5: 24) provide a model, but this very sense of mutuality may have resulted in the word 'reconciliation' being less used in theologies that insist on the depravity of humanity and the single-sided character of God's redemptive and forgiving action.

In post-Vatican II Catholicism the sacrament of *penance or 'confession' has been widely renamed the 'sacrament of reconciliation'. It is noticeable in, for instance, the 1994 *Catechism of the Catholic Church* that 'reconciliation with the church' is stressed quite as much as 'reconciliation with God'. The two necessarily go together, but the horizontal dimension remains crucial. It can be harder to feel sincere about reconciliation with erstwhile enemies than with God.

The most striking modern Christian use of the word is, however, in relation to wider social and political issues. A 'ministry of reconciliation' in regard to personal and social conflict has long been seen as a responsibility of the church, but, even in regard to essentially public issues, it functioned largely on the personal level as an attempt to bring people together to shake hands. In consequence, it could seem a cheap response to situations of conflict where longstanding structural injustice was involved and in some modern theology has earned a bad name. Oppression cannot be wished away so easily and well-publicized reconciliatory events at this level simply suggest a lack of socio-ethical realism. From the 1960s *liberation theology and *black theology replaced 'reconciliation' with 'liberation'. Thus in lambasting the weak-kneed 'church theology' which had long appealed for reconciliation while tolerating fairly indulgently the evils of *apartheid, the South African *Kairos* document of 1985 declared that 'The fallacy here is that "Reconciliation" has been made into an absolute principle that must be applied to all cases of conflict or dissension ... Reconciliation, forgiveness, and negotiation will become our Christian duty only when the apartheid regime shows signs of genuine repentance.' True reconciliation cannot be a short cut; in circumstances of profound and continued injustice it cannot be pursued with moral integrity apart from repentance, liberation, and *justice.

'Reconciliation and peace' can, then, be a misleading formula. 'Justice and peace' may be both more realistic and sounder theologically. The danger, however, is to relegate 'reconciliation' to an unrealizable future when 'justice' is fully attained. It never will be. If reconciliation without liberation can be an empty pretence at bringing Christianity into the political forum, the quest for liberation without reconciliation is no more realistic, nor more Christian. Whether in apartheid South Africa, Northern Ireland, or any class-oppressed Latin American regime, what seems needed is a strategy that seriously pursues the two while recognizing that in certain circumstances the one or the other will require a pragmatic priority. In the 1990s South Africa's Truth and Reconciliation Commission, chaired by Archbishop Desmond Tutu, was as apposite a theological contribution as was the *Kairos* document in the 1980s. While the struggle for liberation and justice must often come first in point of time, reconciliation remains prior in point of purpose and moral significance. The mutual forgiveness and acceptance between individuals and social groups hitherto alienated remains the hardest but also the best representation within the sociopolitical world of reconciliatory *love, the highest expression of the will of God. **Adrian Hastings**

Butler, Barbara (ed.), *Open Hands: Reconciliation, Justice and Peace Work around the World* (1998).

de Waal, Victor, *The Politics of Reconciliation* (1990).

Hastings, Adrian, 'Kairos: South African Theology Today', *The Theology of a Protestant Catholic* (1990), 100–15.

The Kairos Document: A Theological Comment on the Political Crisis in South Africa (1985).

redemption. This term, drawn from the world of *slavery and commercial transactions, became a biblical and traditional metaphor for describing the saving work of *Jesus in delivering *humanity from *sin and *evil. It corresponds to a *christological title familiar to many from Handel's *Messiah* ('I know that my Redeemer liveth') and used by *John Paul II as the title of his first encyclical, *Redemptor Hominis* (*Redeemer of Humanity*, 1979). While never giving the title 'Redeemer' (*lutrotes*) to Christ, the NT calls him 'our redemption (*apolutrosis*)' (1 Cor. 1: 30). Unlike the doctrine of the one person of the Son of *God in two natures, the redemption did not provoke theological debate and teaching from general *councils during the church's first centuries. It was simply taken for granted that it was only through Christ that human beings could be saved (Acts 4: 12), and that the purpose of everything from his *Incarnation to his final coming was, as the *creeds stated, 'for us and for our *salvation'.

Two *Old Testament terms had a special role in creating a background for the *New Testament and subsequent Christian language of 'redemption' (or 'buying back'): *padhah* ('ransom', 'free slaves by payment') and *ga'al* ('play the part of a relative or vindicator', 'fulfil a promise or pledge'). The manumission of slaves and the ransoming of prisoners-of-war out of captivity by a purchasing agent also helped to shape the cultural setting in which NT Christians proclaimed Christ as 'redeeming', 'buying', 'ransoming', 'freeing', or 'liberating' 'us', 'you', 'his people', 'Israel', 'many', or 'all'. In a fictitious purchase by some divinity, owners would come with slaves to a temple, sell them to a god, and from the temple treasury receive money which the slaves had previously deposited there out of their savings. Freed from their previous masters, the slaves became the 'property' of the god. At the temple of Apollo in Delphi and elsewhere inscriptions record how 'so and so [the slave being named] was sold to Apollo at the price of [the sum being specified] for freedom'.

This language could still have provided a lively image in the thought world of such early Christian communities as that in Corinth, while being more or less a dead metaphor elsewhere (where few or no slaves and ex-slaves belonged to the community). *Paul wrote of the human race being, along with the whole creation, 'in bondage to decay' and 'groaning' for 'redemption' (Rom. 8: 18–23), of Jews being slaves to the law (Gal. 4: 1–7; 5: 1), and of Gentiles being enslaved to 'gods' and 'elemental spirits' (Gal. 4: 8, 9). Christ has actually and not just fictitiously 'redeemed' or 'bought' us (Gal. 3: 13; 4: 4). At times the NT authors write of Christ 'buying' us at 'a price' (1 Cor. 6: 20; 7: 23), 'ransoming' us with his 'precious blood' (1 Pet. 1: 18–19; see Rom. 3: 24–5), 'becoming a curse for us' on the cross (Gal. 3: 13), 'giving himself to ransom/free us' (Titus 2: 14), and 'giving his life as a ransom (*lutron* or *antilutron*) for many' (Mark 10: 45; 1 Tim. 2: 6). But nowhere does the NT speak of this price or ransom being (literally or metaphorically) paid to someone (e.g. God) or to something (e.g. the law). In the patristic period and later, some Christians expanded the content of this *metaphor, taking 'ransom' as if it described literally some kind of transaction, even a specific price paid to someone (see ATONEMENT, THEORIES OF). Those who failed to observe the limits of the metaphor at times even spoke of human beings as in the possession of the *devil, whose 'rights' of ownership were 'respected' in that the price of Jesus' blood was paid to release them from bondage. For the NT, however, the act of redemption was 'costly', in the sense that it cost Christ his life. The beneficiaries of this redeeming action became 'free' (e.g. Gal. 5: 1) or, by coming under Christ's sovereignty, 'slaves' to him (e.g. Rom. 1: 1; 1 Cor. 7: 22). Nowhere does the NT accept or imply that Satan has any rights over human beings. The metaphor of redemption represents Christ as effecting a deliverance and not as paying a price to anyone.

Why was this redemption deemed to be necessary for everyone? What were human beings to be redeemed from and what were they redeemed for? The pervading presence of evil and sin established the universal need of redemption. Human beings were understood to be enslaved by hostile, cosmic powers (e.g. Eph. 1: 22–3; 2: 1–2; 1 Cor. 15: 24–5) and to live under the shadow of death. Although the Scriptures can also think of death as the natural, normal end of a long and fruitful life (e.g. Gen. 25: 7–11) and even a friend (e.g. Phil. 1: 21–3), they also present death as the effect and sign of sin (e.g. Rom. 5: 12) and as an enemy to be overcome (1 Cor. 15: 26). The heart of evil is personal sin, a condition that affects all people (Rom. 3: 23) and is a tyrannical master enslaving human beings (Rom. 6: 12–7: 25). At times the Bible portrays our sinful condition as that of those who are defiled and in need of cleansing (Ps. 51: 2, 7; 1 Cor. 6: 9–11).

Through *Augustine, Paul's teaching on the inherited need for redemption (Rom. 5: 12–19) became articulated as 'original sin', a doctrine often accompanied by speculations about a state of original justice (graced by 'natural', 'supernatural', and 'preternatural' gifts) which '*Adam and *Eve' lost by falling into sin. The theory of *evolution and other challenges to the view that all human beings are descended from one pair of ancestors have led many Christian thinkers to revise their account of the *creation of the human race and its '*fall' into sin. The heart of Paul's teaching concerns an inherited solidarity in sin that personal sins express and endorse, and that finds abundant suggestive confirmation from human behaviour in the 20th century. In their own secular way, the *novels of Albert Camus depict our universal lack of innocence (e.g. *The Fall*). The fictional works of Flannery O'Connor spell out even more vividly the ubiquitous reality of sin and evil that goes back to human origins. In the *Genesis story, although offered their creator's friendship, 'Adam and Eve' substitute themselves for God by independently deciding on good and evil and determining their destiny for themselves. Alienated from God, 'the man and his wife' become alienated from one another (Gen. 3: 16) and see their world spiralling out of control into murder and vengeful violence (Gen. 4: 24). 'Adam and Eve' symbolize not only the dignity of human beings made in the divine image and likeness (Gen. 1: 26–7) but also their solidarity in sin from which the Redeemer delivers them.

Two verses of a traditional Sussex carol summarize the fruits of redemption:

> Then why should men on earth be so sad,
> Since our Redeemer made us glad,
> When from our sin he set us free,
> All for to gain our liberty?
>
> When sin departs before his grace,
> Then life and health come in its place;
> Angels and men with joy may sing,
> All for to see the new-born King.

In its own way this carol catches some of the major themes of Paul in Rom. 8: redemption as freedom 'from the law of sin and death', new life through the indwelling divine *Spirit, adoption as God's sons and daughters, and the joyful hope of inheriting the eternal life of *resurrection with the risen Jesus. The apostle's language about abounding grace and life coming through 'the one man, Jesus Christ' (Rom. 5: 15–19) coincides even more closely with what the carol celebrates about the consequences of redemption.

When did or does the redemption occur? The carol implicitly associates redemption with the incarnation or 'becoming flesh' of the Son of God, from whose fullness we receive 'grace upon grace' (see John 1: 14, 16). Christian writers, in particular the *Greek fathers, have often stressed the link between the Incarnation and Christ's redemptive 'work' for human beings. In a summary first formulated by *Irenaeus, 'God (or the Son of God or the Word) became human, in order that we humans might become God or be divinized.' On the other hand, not only devotional practices but also many writers in the West—from *Anselm of Canterbury, through the Protestant Reformers, and beyond—have in various ways linked deliverance from the power of sin and death rather with Christ's *crucifixion. Eastern Christians normally go beyond the crucifixion to insist as well on the redemptive impact of Christ's descent to the dead, his resurrection, and the coming of the Holy Spirit.

With his theology of Christ as the new or final Adam 'recapitulating' the whole of human history, Irenaeus offered a way of reconciling the contrasting views in a wider synthesis. He saw redemption as one great drama reaching from creation, through the Easter story, to the final coming, and the end of time. He developed in fuller detail the Pauline view of what Christ has 'already' effected (Rom. 4: 25–5: 11) and of our being saved 'in hope' (Rom. 8: 24) for the full and final redemption which has 'not yet' come. The biblical vision of Irenaeus held together the entire order of creation with that of redemption as two distinguishable but inseparable moments in God's one saving plan for all humanity. John Duns Scotus (d. 1308), *Teilhard de Chardin, and others have maintained this unity in God's creative and redemptive work—a unity challenged by the view encouraged by *Athanasius, *Aquinas, and others that if human beings had not sinned, the Second *Person of the *Trinity would not have become incarnate in our world.

Ever since Paul stressed the obedience of the man Jesus in bringing *justification, *grace, and life (Rom. 5: 12–21), Christian teachers have acknowledged that redemption came through an agent who was not only divine but also truly one with us human beings. After Irenaeus insisted that deliverance from the forces of evil called for the union of divinity and humanity in Christ, Tertullian, *Origen, Gregory Nazianzen, and others endorsed the same conviction. Basil of Caesarea (d. 379) wrote of Christ needing to take on true humanity if he were to destroy the power of sin and death (Epistola, 261. 2). In the next century Leo the Great emphasized that unless Christ had truly assumed our humanity, the redemptive 'battle' would have 'been fought outside our nature' and we would not have experienced what we have experienced, deliverance from the power of evil (Epistola, 31. 2). In the words of J. H. *Newman's Dream of Gerontius, 'A second Adam to the fight | And to the rescue came.'

But how is the connection between the Redeemer and the redeemed to be understood? Christ acted 'for us' in the sense of acting not only for our benefit and to our advantage but also 'in our place'. By acting for our sake, was he our substitute or our representative? There is a major difference between these two ways of envisaging the relationship. A substitute may be simply or even passively and violently put in the place of another person or of other persons. One thinks of hostages executed in the place of escaped prisoners-of-war. The escapees do not wish that this substitution should take place, and they may never even learn about it. Representation, however, is willed by both those represented and the representative, is normally restricted to specific matters, and may well last for only a relatively brief period. Christ freely accepted to represent human beings to God and before God; on their side they are invited to agree to this redemptive representation. Christ's activity brings deliverance but does not constitute an 'unrestricted' representation: human beings may not, for example, hand over to him their duty to praise and thank God. At the same time, this redemptive representation is no brief affair but lasts forever.

From the time of the NT Christians have thought of redemption 'working' to break the curse of *death and the power of sin, so that death now became a passage out of the dominion of sin and into eternal, utterly satisfying life. The viciously cruel crucifixion of Jesus, while symbolizing the weakness and failure of suffering, became the means of human redemption. By dying and rising, Jesus overcame sin, evil, and their tragic consequences and effected a new *exodus from bondage. To celebrate this deliverance, Christian liturgies took over the songs with which *Moses and Miriam led the people in praising God for their victorious liberation from slavery. While the exodus story was the prototype par excellence of such redemptive deliverance, Christian writers and artists from the earliest times found other precedents in such Old Testament stories as Noah and his family being delivered from the flood, *Daniel from the lions' den, the three youths from the fiery furnace, *Jonah from the great fish, and Susannah from the two wicked elders.

From the time of the NT (Rom. 6: 1–11; Col. 2: 12–13), believers understood themselves to re-enact sacramentally the historical redemption effected by the crucifixion and resurrection. *Baptism meant their symbolic dying and being buried with Christ, so as to be freed from sin and rise to a new life. But is this redemption available not only for Christian believers but also for everyone? Does the saving 'work' of Jesus reach beyond the ranks of the baptized? Paul insists that Christ died 'for all' (2 Cor. 5: 14–15), without introducing any exception. Hence he can say that 'God was in Christ reconciling the world to himself' (2 Cor. 5: 19). As Adam brought sin and death to all human beings, so the obedient Christ has led all to justification and life. This redemption has its impact not only on the social and political structures of human society but also on the whole of creation (Rom. 8: 18–23; see Col. 1: 20). The NT claim about Christ's universal redemptive role may well seem arrogant and even outrageous to those who do not share this faith. In the first centuries of Christianity and then in modern times theologians have struggled to interpret and explain how and why Christ functions as the one Redeemer for all men and women of all times and places—or how and why he can be 'the expiation for the sins of the whole world' (1 John 2: 2), even for those who may consciously reject his representative role on their behalf.

Talk of 'redemption' has frequently been associated with Christ's work of expiating sins and lovingly reconciling humanity with God. The NT accepts Jesus as the great high *priest and victim who offered a unique *sacrifice that once and for all expiated sins and brought a new and final *covenant relationship between God and human beings. Some Christians, especially from the late Middle Ages, have interpreted this to mean that Jesus was a penal substitute who was personally burdened with the sins of humanity, judged, condemned, and deservedly punished in our place; through his death he satisfied the divine justice and propitiated an angry God. Anselm's theory about Jesus' offering satisfaction to meet the requirements of commutative justice and set right a moral order damaged by sin acquired, quite contrary to Anselm's explicit statements, elements of *punishment and vindictive justice. Such 'penal' additions to Anselm's theory of satisfaction turn up in the Council of *Trent's teaching on the sacrifice of the mass (from its twenty-second session of 1562) and, even more, in the writings of *Luther and *Calvin. Catholic preachers like J. B. Bossuet (d. 1704) and L. Bourdaloue (d. 1704) also spoke of God's vengeance and anger being appeased at the expense of his crucified Son. As a victim of divine justice, Christ was even held to suffer the pains of the damned. Themes from this penal substitutionary view linger on in the work of Hans Urs *von Balthasar, Jürgen *Moltmann, and other 20th-century theologians.

Many Christian thinkers find this interpretation to entail an unacceptable vision of God, supported only by misinterpretations of the scapegoat ceremony from the Jewish Day of Expiation, the fourth Suffering Servant song (Isa. 52: 13–53: 12), Jesus' cry of abandonment on the cross, and some dramatic passages in Paul's letters. Victimized by human violence and not by a vindictive God, the non-violent Christ, through his self-sacrificing death as our representative, removed the defilement of sin and restored a disturbed moral order.

As regards '*reconciliation', the NT never speaks of redemption as changing and 'reconciling' God to human beings; it is God or God through Christ who brings about redemptive reconciliation by renewing us. Both John and Paul bear eloquent witness to the loving initiative of God the Father in the whole story of the redemptive reconciliation of human beings and their world.

Finally, the blessing of redemption invites the recipients to become in a secondary sense agents. Christ's grace is already victorious (e.g. Gal. 3: 28; Col. 3: 11), yet evil is still present (e.g. 1 Cor. 15: 22–8). The Epistle to the Ephesians begins by blessing God for the grace of redemption (1: 3–23) and ends by encouraging Christians to use their spiritual 'armour' in the ongoing struggle against the forces of evil (6: 10–20). Christ's once-and-for-all sacrifice for sins empowers believers in the daily sacrifice of their lives (Rom. 12: 1). Christ's love, powerfully at work in his crucifixion and Resurrection, calls believers to follow in the way of love.

Gerald O'Collins, SJ

Dillistone, F. W., *The Christian Understanding of the Atonement* (1968).

Gunton, C. E., *The Actuality of the Atonement* (1988).

Hengel, M., *The Atonement* (1981).

Hultgren, A. J., *Christ and his Benefits: Christology and Redemption in the New Testament* (1987).

Jossua, J. P., *Le Salut, incarnation ou mystère pascal* (1968).

Lyonnet, S., *Sin, Redemption, and Sacrifice* (1970).

McIntyre, J., *The Shape of Soteriology* (1992).

O'Collins, G., *Christology* (1995).

O'Collins, G., and Kendall, D., *Focus on Jesus* (1996).

Sesboüé, B., *Jésus-Christ l'unique médiateur: Essai sur la rédemption et le salut* (2 vols.; 1988–91).

Sullivan, F. A., *Salvation outside the Church?* (1992).

reformation. By a process of reification, a number of convulsive and creative movements and events of the *sixteenth century became known as *the* Reformation, especially in the historiography of the 19th century, where, with the *Renaissance, the Reformation became the threshold of the modern world. Thomas Carlyle wrote that if Martin *Luther had not stood his ground before the Holy Roman Emperor at the Diet of Worms in 1521 there would have been no French Revolution, no America. Luther had announced the Reformation when, the story went, on 31 October 1517, he 'posted' on the door of the Castle Church in Wittenberg ninety-five academic theses challenging the power of the Church to dispense 'indulgences' which released sinners from their penitential debts, including, in the case of dead souls, the pains of *purgatory.

Luther's initial protest arose from the acute spiritual anxiety of a professor of biblical theology, obliged to believe what he taught about the process of *salvation. These *anfechtungen* (strenuous temptations) were resolved only when *Paul's teaching in the Epistle to the *Romans persuaded Luther that salvation is by *grace alone and by *faith alone, owing nothing to good and penitential works, sanctification being the product, not the condition, of a *justification that is not progressive but instant. The Reformation thus consists of three 'onlies': *sola scriptura*, *sola gratia*, *sola fide*, scripture alone, grace alone, and faith alone.

From what theologically was a small but critical, and probably original, adjustment to Pauline and *Augustinian doctrine, everything else followed logically. Luther's opinions were condemned in Rome, but he enjoyed immunity in his native Saxony. Under pressure, the full implications of his solifidian ('faith alone') theology were drawn out of him in a ceaseless flow of publications, which attacked the entire fabric of traditional intercessory and *sacramental religion and denounced the *Catholic *priesthood and hierarchy as a 'Babylonish' captivity of the church. All believers were simultaneously both sinners and justified, all equally priests. Luther claimed to be unlike other critics of the prevailing religious system (such as *Erasmus of Rotterdam), in that he struck not at the superficial branches of ecclesiastical abuse but at the doctrinal roots. Evidently this was what distinguished the Reformation from all those earlier attempts to reform the church 'in head and

members'. This was a genuinely new and original brand of Christianity which, however, claimed to be not novel but primitive and biblical. Whatever Carlyle thought, the 16th century looked not forwards but backwards.

Luther's writings evoked a widespread social and political response, which included, to his fury and embarrassment, the chaos of the Peasants' War of 1525. But the authorities, some princes and many cities, were the main protectors, and beneficiaries, of Luther's gospel. At the Diet of Speyer in 1529, the 'Protestatio' of Luther's princely supporters gave to history the name *Protestant, and in the following year, *Lutheranism was set in letters of stone in the Confession of Augsburg, the work, principally, of Luther's lieutenant, Philip Melanchthon.

By this time, other reformers had appeared on the scene. The Swiss Huldrych *Zwingli inaugurated in Zürich a reformation which in its uncompromising biblicism and severe *iconoclasm made a more drastic break with tradition, and denied what Lutherans still affirmed, the real presence of Christ in the *Eucharist, a symbolic point of difference on which Protestant Christianity was to divide into two irreconcilable confessional traditions, Lutheran (or Evangelical) and *Reformed, implying 'best reformed'. The Reformed churches, which ultimately extended from Transylvania to the Scottish Highlands, almost encircling the territorially more circumscribed Lutherans of North Germany and *Scandinavia, derived their distinctive identity from a convergence of reforming currents in Switzerland and the cities of south-west Germany, where a prominent figure was Martin Bucer, the reformer of Strasbourg. But soon Bucer's leadership gave place to the more coherent mind and policy of the Frenchman *Calvin, who made his adopted city of *Geneva, as a reformed community, first among equals. From about the mid-16th century, the label 'Calvinist' began to attach itself to these churches, originally as a stigma. In every part of Europe where the Protestant Reformation gained the upper hand, or, as in France and the Netherlands, struggled vigorously to do so, there was a complex interaction of political, religious, and social forces. In England, the process was primarily political, as Henry VIII sought a solution to marital and dynastic problems by withdrawing the English Church from the Roman obedience and declaring himself its Supreme Head. But an English Protestant movement, inspired in large measure by the bible in English (mostly the work of William Tyndale), eventually gained political control, and by the end of the reign of Elizabeth I (1558–1603) had turned one of the most Catholic countries in Europe into, if not a Protestant, a virulently anti-Catholic nation. By contrast, the *Scottish Reformation was made by its reformers (especially John Knox), its nobility, and its people. Attempts in the 17th century to change the religion of Scotland from above, by royal intervention in the affairs of a church that claimed a large measure of self-government, had explosive consequences.

Two sharply contrasted religious movements that were of great historical importance in their own right, and that, moreover, shaped the emerging identities of the mainstream Protestant churches were the so-called Radical Reformation of the Anabaptists, and the *Counter- or Catholic Reformation. The essence of the Radical Reformation (a term invented by historians) was separation of church and state, its historiographical antitype 'magisterial' Reformation. 'Anabaptist' was another stigma, which strictly speaking applied only to those who had repudiated their *baptism as infants and repeated it. But the principle of adult baptism symbolized the renunciation of that equation of citizenship and church membership on which Christendom had stood foursquare for a thousand years. Beyond that, the Radical Reformation was a spectrum, ranging from congregations resembling modern Baptists (the *Mennonites) to communist utopias and radically spiritualized and unchurched forms of religion. Remorselessly persecuted by Catholic and Protestant governments alike, the sects of the 16th century carried the genes of the pluralistic, tolerant religious world of modern western democracies.

Historians have asked: Counter-Reformation or Catholic Reformation? Counter-Reformation suggests a reactive response to the Protestant Reformation; Catholic Reformation a religious movement which drew upon its own independent sources and impulses for renewal, and which even shared the fundamental aims and concerns of Protestants to evangelize, to instruct, and morally to command, in short, to make society more Christian. So we confront two parallel movements of spiritual rebirth and pastoral improvement. Both terms are helpful as descriptions of what was happening in the 16th and *seventeenth centuries in those territories and churches which had remained faithful to Rome and its doctrine, or which, after episodes of Protestant schism, were recovered for Catholicism, especially in Central Europe, the southern Netherlands, and much of France. The spiritual work was undertaken by reforming popes and bishops, and by new religious orders, especially the Society of *Jesus, founded by Ignatius Loyola, whose missionary ambitions extended to the New World, and to hitherto unevangelized areas of the old, India, Japan, and China.

The political muscle was supplied by Europe's increasingly powerful princely rulers, the majority of whom remained firmly attached to the pope's religion, even while often opposing particular popes. Princely and papal interests were uneasily conjoined in the work of the Council of *Trent, which converted the ideals of the Counter-Reformation into a doctrinal code and a practical pastoral programme, creating the *Catholicism that would prevail until the mid-20th century pontificate of *John XXIII and *Vatican II. It was a paradoxical consequence of the Reformation that Catholicism was now to be defined in terms that Protestantism had dictated, as the negation of its *heresies. Trent and the popes of the Counter-Reformation erected a more consistent and even regimented Catholic Church, the ecclesiastical counterpart of the absolutist states of 17th- and 18th-century Europe. At the same time, the need to defend and define the Protestant confessions, both Evangelical and Reformed, against each other, against the sects, and, above all, against Rome, not to speak of the state-building ambitions of Protestant governments, led to a process of confessionalization, characterized by a neo-scholastic hardening of dogma. German historians call this the Second Reformation. But for English historians, the Second Reformation may mean the *Puritan Revolution of the 1640s and 1650s, and, for *North Americans, the Great Awakening of the mid-18th century, from which the *evangelicalism of more recent centuries derives.

So far, we have assumed that something called 'the Reformation' actually happened in 16th-century Europe, as an event that connected in a kind of seamless web of cause and consequence events and processes: Luther's initial protest logically demanding the emergence of a western Europe divided into Catholic and Protestant nations and communities, sometimes inconveniently intermingled, as in Northern Ireland. But is 'the Reformation' anything more than a piece of periodization? The idea, which we owe to German Lutheran apologists, that Martin Luther was the root-stock from which all other reformers and reforming movements are to be derived is both an optical and a polemical illusion. Religiously, 16th-century Europe was a seething cauldron, and there was no master chef in charge. A leading English historian of the Reformation has written of varied 'patterns of reformation', including the fanatical and the anti-fanatical. But whether, if there had been no Martin Luther, there would have been a John Calvin remains a question to which there is no easy answer.

More fundamentally, students of late medieval theology have called in question the intellectual originality of Luther's Reformation. Luther's teachers belonged to that scholastic tendency labelled 'Nominalist', and arguably Luther's departure from their thought-world was less than absolute. Not only medievalists have said this. Early in the *twentieth century, the German theologian-sociologist Ernst Troeltsch doubted whether authentic Protestantism had much to do with the modern world. Luther's answers may have been new, but the questions, about grace and salvation and church order, were old. It may be better to talk, not of the medieval church, followed by the Reformation, but of the medieval church and its reformation (see MIDDLE AGES).

Increasingly, the concept of 'the Reformation' is found to be an inconvenience. One historian, writing of Christianity in the west from 1400 to 1700, would prefer to do without it. Others collapse the Reformation, as a singular event and watershed, into a multiple sequence of lower-case reformations, or a perennial principle, *ecclesia semper reformanda*. In England, Reformation historians trace the process from the Wyclifite movement (see HUSS AND WYCLIF) of the late 14th century to the end of the 18th century and beyond: the so-called Long Reformation. How different in scale and significance was the Protestant Reformation of the 16th century from those other reformations, the *Methodism of the 18th century, and the *Oxford Movement of the 19th?

In the perception of this writer, it was different. To travel from one end of Belfast to another, or from Geneva to Madrid, one must return convinced that something happened in the 16th century that for the developing history of western civilization was the equivalent of a major earthquake on the Richter scale.

Patrick Collinson

Bossy, J., *Christianity in the West 1400–1700* (1985).

Cameron, Euan, *The European Reformation* (1991).

Delumeau, J., *Catholicism Between Luther and Voltaire* (1977).

Dickens, A. G., *The German Nation and Martin Luther* (1974).

—— *The English Reformation* (1989).

Dickens, A. G., and Tonkin, J., *The Reformation in Historical Thought* (1985).

Haigh, C., *English Reformations: Religion, Society and Politics Under the Tudors* (1993).

Hopfl, Harro, *The Christian Polity of John Calvin* (1982).

Oberman, H. A., *Luther: Man Between God and the Devil* (1986).

Pettegree, A., Duke, A., and Lewis, G. (eds.), *Calvinism in Europe 1540–1620* (1994).

Scribner, R., Porter, R., and Teich, M. (eds.), *The Reformation in National Context* (1994).

Williams, G. H., *The Radical Reformation* (1964).

Reformed theology.

All Protestant churches have a claim to be both evangelical and reformed, but since the 16th century the two major strands have been commonly differentiated as *Lutheran and Reformed. The Reformed tradition began with *Zwingli and *Calvin, so Lutheranism is the older, often seen by the Reformed as not as thoroughgoing in purging all traces of Rome. The issue that split the two sides at the Colloquy of Marburg was *Luther's insistence that in the *Eucharist 'This is my body' is a literal, not merely a symbolic, truth. The Reformed case was that 'is' often means 'represents' in the *bible. This method of argument, not plucking out individual texts but trying to hold all the biblical evidence together in a rationally coherent way, has been characteristic of Reformed theology. Other traditions distrust the way in which the Reformed churches, giving sole authority to scripture, have often ruled out innocent innovations (like *Christmas) as non-scriptural. They have also distrusted the Reformed taste for logic. The difficulty of refuting Calvinist *predestination is almost worse than the horrible decree itself. Calvin, the greatest of Reformed theologians, exemplifies the qualities of his tradition: a thoroughly fair and balanced biblical commentator, a brilliant systematician, unjustly linked with only this one doctrine of predestination, and the deviser, in *Geneva, of a Reformed city-state, admirable and frightening in its single-mindedness. Both Zwingli and Calvin were in some ways nearer *Erasmus's humanism than Luther was; the Reformed tradition loved scholarship, and was notably successful in developing a well-schooled laity and churches where divinity professors ruled.

Lutheran churches tended to be folk churches supported by kings; the churches of the Reform, by contrast, were often struggling minorities. The French Reformed (Huguenots) gained and then tragically lost a limited legal status. When national churches emerged, as in the Netherlands or *Scotland, this was in spite of royal armies. Calvinist *political theology was undeferential, prepared to justify tyrannicide, and is often seen as sowing the seeds of *democracy. Its *presbyterian form of church government avoided autocracy: all ministers were equal, and lay elders had a voice.

Seventeenth-century Calvinist scholasticism was good after its kind. In Germany the smaller Reformed church was more tolerant than the Lutherans, and its characteristic theology was anything but the icy determinism normally associated with later Calvinism. The opening question of the Heidelberg Catechism catches something of the spirit of the German Reformed. 'What is your only comfort, in life and in death? That I belong—body and soul, in life and in death—not to myself but in my faithful Saviour, Jesus Christ, who at the cost of his own blood has fully paid for all my sins.' This Christocentric heart religion was influential in the later rise of *Pietism.

The mainstream of the Reform was Calvinist, defining itself at the Synod of Dort (1618–19) only too clearly against *Arminian innovations. With historical perspective, we can say that the Dutch Remonstrants, who were the Arminian minority, and also the Church of England, were part of the Reformed tradition. The Thirty-Nine Articles are Anglo-Calvinist, and there is a good case for saying that the Elizabethan settlement was a middle way, not between Geneva and Rome, but between Geneva and Wittenberg (see ANGLICAN THOUGHT). Briefly, under the Commonwealth, England experienced, and largely disliked, thoroughgoing Reform, and

after 1660 the Church of England drove out its *Puritan ministers, and the English home of the Reformed tradition became the *Presbyterian and *Congregational churches. Historically more significant for the English-speaking Reform were the successors of the Pilgrim Fathers. The Christianity of the *North American colonies was overwhelmingly Reformed. Puritan theology, for 'wayfaring warfaring Christians', works with ideas of *covenant, but, like the Heidelberg catechism, does not seem to centre round determinism. The custom of the Scottish church of making a great out-door occasion of the holy communion, lasting for several days and many sermons, with people travelling from miles around, is a key part of the history of religious revival. Eucharistic and emotional piety have their place in the Reformed tradition. Nevertheless, the theology of John Owen and the Westminster Confession, as taught with very little change in *Princeton in the 19th century, is a systematic scheme of a inscrutable God, whose ways are not our ways, and who has saved some from the foundation of the world, utterly undeserving as they and all others are.

Not only Arminians but even *Unitarians are historically within the Reformed tradition. The old English Presbyterian church became Unitarian in the course of the *eighteenth century. Somehow the rationality characteristic of the Reformed tradition led some of its people to accept the answers of the *Enlightenment. The Enlightenment itself owed something to the Reform. *Kant turned much of Christian theology on its head, but his moral seriousness went back to his Scottish ancestors. Mainline Presbyterian churches in Scotland and America, without going as far as Unitarianism, split between Old and New Light (or Old and New School, or Side) for and against the 'new light' of the Enlightenment.

The greatest theologian of the 18th century, Jonathan *Edwards, somehow combined Lockean philosophy, the wildfire experiential religion of the Great Awakening, a mystic sense of revelation as beauty, and a sharper denial than Calvin of the existence of free will. This North American synthesis did not hold with his successors, and though churches in the Reformed tradition dominated American culture in the first half of the 19th century, and their divinity faculties are still among the best, they lost out in the democratic free-for-all of the last two centuries of American religion. Lipservice is still paid to the Pilgrim Fathers, but popular American religion, however bible-centred and morally emphatic its rhetoric, is far from the intellectually rigorous Puritanism of the Reformed tradition.

The two greatest European theologians of the 19th and 20th centuries, Friedrich *Schleiermacher and Karl *Barth, also came from the Reformed tradition. As Barth's task in life was largely to counter the work of Schleiermacher, their shared inheritance is somewhat problematic. Should the liberal Schleiermacher count as Reformed? He was in German Reformed orders, but went on to be active in the merger of Lutheran and Reformed in Prussia, and his systematics, the *Christian Faith*, was designed, even in its choice of footnotes, to express the theology of that union. In any case, he was the father of *liberal theology. But, after all, Schleiermacher's 'feeling of absolute dependence' is a description (and he said this himself) of what the Christian who believes the Heidelberg Catechism feels. 'Absolute dependence' may be a more specifically Reformed turn of phrase than it has normally been taken for.

During the 19th century and even later many of the best Reformed biblical scholars and theologians were tried for heresy. Presbyterianism, governed by a hierarchy of courts, had the mechanism to hand, and the theological seriousness to risk contested public debate. In practice, it gave the liberals the martyrs they needed, and changed the minds of many of the laity. Thus John McLeod Campbell (1800–72, removed by his church 1831), unhappy with the image of an angry god who could only be placated with blood, reminded his readers that 'we are here to do with PERSONS—the Father of spirits and his offspring'. With care and subtlety he reworked the Reformed understanding of the *Atonement. Horace Bushnell (1802–76) whose theology of the *family in *Christian Nurture* had cognate insights, was lucky that his Congregational church withdrew from their local association to save him from trial. A string of biblical professors, the most famous probably the OT scholar William Robertson Smith (1846–94, removed 1881), were tried for introducing new methods of biblical criticism (see HIGHER CRITICISM). Most of the Reformed tradition since have accepted the methods of biblical criticism, and some have found the roots of it in Calvin.

Moving in another direction, the American 'Mercersburg theology' of John W. Nevin (1803–86) had a high doctrine of church and sacrament, and, infuriating Princeton, found chapter and verse in Calvin to back this up. Most Protestant churches had drifted towards subjective individualism. Students are often surprised to find how Calvin's doctrine of the Eucharist, and Schleiermacher's doctrine of the church, make higher and more objective claims than are often heard in Reformed pulpits.

Before Barth, P. T. Forsyth (1848–1921) in England was attacking the cheerful culture-Protestantism that canonized humanity's kindlier impulses. As he said of himself, 'I was turned … from a lover of love to an object of grace.' It is not natural, he taught, to human pride to kneel at the foot of the cross. Barth himself, a professor of Reformed theology at a Lutheran university, rediscovered the strength and authenticity of scholastic Calvinism. The successors of scholastic Calvinism saw Barth's theology as a 'new modernism', and, in fact, taking the long view, as a Reformed systematician he had more in common with Schleiermacher than first appears. But at the time Barth was a bombshell to Christian theology. In the old Reformed way, he undercut all human self-reliance. One of his great achievements was a christological reworking of predestination, the key Calvinist doctrine and stumbling-block. Among later Barthians, Thomas *Torrance wrote theology as science, not loving the Enlightenment, but reminiscent of it.

There was a great Dutch tradition of Reformed theology, shaping the culture of the Netherlands. Abraham Kuyper (1837–1920) combined writing neo-Calvinist theology with founding a political party and winning power. Hendrik Kraemer (1888–1965), alongside W. A. Visser't Hooft, was a powerful voice in the *missionary and *ecumenical movement against any tendency towards easy indifferentism. A shadow over this Dutch Reformed tradition was that some of Kuyper's theology underlay the theology of *apartheid in the Dutch Reformed Church in South Africa. It has been claimed that a doctrine of election, more specifically of an elect nation, serves to justify oppression, whether of Boers over blacks or Puritan colonists over Native Americans.

Reformed theology continues, some of it determinedly unchanging. In an ecumenical century the Reformed churches have been no worse than the others at dragging their feet in approaching unity. Their theologians work in interdenominational faculties, and draw on many sources. Some, such as John Hick, like the 18th-century Unitarians, show only a vestigial trace of the tradition that ordained them. Others, like C. H. Dodd, the *Niebuhrs, or Moltmann, though in many ways transcending it, still belonged. Any tradition that gave us the *hymns of Isaac Watts, and the theology of Calvin, Edwards, Schleiermacher, and Barth has done something, but an article on Reformed theology must end not with human beings but with God. 'When I survey the wondrous cross | … [I] pour contempt on all my pride'.

See also REFORMATION.   **Alistair Mason**

Gerrish, B. A., *Tradition and the Modern World: Reformed Theology in the Nineteenth Century* (1977).
McKim, Donald (ed.), *Encyclopedia of the Reformed Faith* (1992).
McNeill, J. T., *The History and Character of Calvinism*, rev. edn. (1967).
Marty, M. E., *Righteous Empire: The Protestant Experience in America* (1970).
Prestwich, Menna (ed.), *International Calvinism 1541–1715* (1985).

religion.

'True religion' has often meant the right form of *Christianity, say Protestantism for a Protestant, contrasted with a false form, superstition, or *heresy, such as Roman Catholicism. Non-Christian beliefs and rituals were not so much 'another' religion as false religion, meaning particularly false worship. In the OT the worship of Baal or Astarte is denounced by the *prophets as worship of nothings. It was false religion. In the Roman empire there was, for the state, a 'true' religion, the Roman *religio*, or official cult, which Christians refused to share in and were therefore persecuted. For Christians, theirs alone was 'true' religion. Much of *Augustine's *City of God* is an argument to demonstrate the falseness of Roman religion. Its gods, Augustine insists, are either empty images or devils. Collectively what the Romans had called their 'religion' was defined by Christians as 'paganism'. That remained, basically, the Christian view of other religions for many centuries. It remained the way Capuchin *missionaries saw the indigenous beliefs and rituals of the Kongo kingdom in the 17th century. In a still more extreme form it was the view of many a 19th-century evangelical missionary. Thus Rufus Anderson, one of the most influential American missionary strategists, wrote in 1869 that there were only two religions, true and false, the latter including Popery, Judaism, Mohammedanism, Buddhism, and 'every form of paganism', all, he declared, 'wonderfully alike'.

The Jews were, nevertheless, in most theological eyes a special case. Though not Christians, they believed in the true God while failing to recognize that their scriptures had been fulfilled in Christ. Their religion was not at all akin to paganism. Still more difficult to categorize from the 7th century had been Muslims. At times *Islam was considered a sort of Christian heresy. Muslims too believed in the God of *Abraham yet accepted no part of the bible and so stood somewhere between Jews and pagans. Ramón Llull (1233–1315), a native of Majorca which had only recently been recovered from Islam, attempted to bring about a world unity of *faith, writing a multitude of works in Arabic, Catalan, and Latin. He started with the monotheistic belief common to Jews, Christians, and Muslims. Llull's intentions were missionary. He longed to convert Muslims but knew that he had first to understand them. The work in which he records a remarkably ecumenical dialogue between a Jew, a Christian, and a Muslim, *Llibre del Gentil e dels tres savis*, is probably the first serious Christian contribution to a *theology of religions.

It would thus be mistaken to imagine that the relationship between 'religions' is only a post-Enlightenment concern. Nevertheless, from the 17th century it grew enormously as philosophically minded theologians shifted their focus from Christian belief on its own to the validity of religion in general and of Christianity as its supreme example. One sees it in the title of books from *De Religione Laici* (1645) of Lord Herbert of Cherbury through to *Schleiermacher's *Reden über die Religion* (1799; ET *On Religion: Speeches to its Cultured Despisers*). Increased western knowledge of Asia led to a new sense of its main religious traditions, *Hindu and *Buddhist. Europe's 19th-century colonial and missionary expansion, greater knowledge of the ancient world, and the development of *anthropology together led to the emergence of a 'science of religion'. It included ancient Egyptian and Mesopotamian rituals and beliefs, and a quickly expanding body of information about non-literate religions in Africa and elsewhere as well as the great scriptural religions, Islamic, Hindu, Buddhist, and Taoist. It became accepted rather easily that there was one genus, 'religion', of which Judaism, Christianity, Islam, Hinduism, and Buddhism were the principal species.

While it would be unreasonable to deny that these and other 'religions' share certain characteristics, such as beliefs about the ultimate meaning of life, the importance of *morality, ritual practices, *mystical experience, it remains true that the differences in the way belief, morality, and ritual are handled are so great between and even within the great traditions that generalizations about religion as such, or religions as such, can prove deeply misleading. Moreover, it is unclear whether Confucianism or even Buddhism should be classified as 'religion' rather than 'philosophy'; where, indeed, the boundary lies between the two categories.

The study of religion and religions profoundly affected modern Christian thought. Thus the religious development of *Israel is seen as having been deeply influenced by the beliefs of neighbouring (Canaanite) peoples. Distinctive as the Israelite tradition undoubtedly was, it cannot be understood in isolation. Nevertheless, increased knowledge might simply mislead. The learned Scottish scholar William Robertson Smith, Professor of Arabic at Cambridge following dismissal from his chair in the Free Church College in Aberdeen, developed in *The Religion of the Semites* (1889) a theory about totemic communion as being the originating motivation in *sacrifice and applied it to the OT. Countless scholars, including Durkheim and Freud, borrowed it from him, but the theory is now generally discredited. In the same period the German History of Religion School (*Religionsgeschichtliche Schule*), led by Wilhelm Bousset, was reinterpreting NT meanings in terms of real or imagined influences from a range of Hellenistic and Middle Eastern religions, Babylonian and Egyptian. While its method was acceptable in principle, its conclusions often far outran the evidence.

Most influential of 20th-century works on religion has undoubtedly been Sir James Frazer's *The Golden Bough* (1st edn. 1890; final edn. 1915), a fascinating but diffuse and weakly argued pilgrimage through the practices of religion. His purpose was to explain why priest-kings need to be killed to give life to the world in *humanity's 'first crude philosophy of life'. By uncovering an almost universal *myth, apparently replicated in the life of Christ, Frazer's thesis could be seen, as he intended, to undermine the central beliefs of Christianity. Yet it could be read another way. C. S. *Lewis had imbibed the Frazer thesis as a confident young atheist, but a few years later found himself convinced instead, as an Oxford don, that 'All that stuff of Frazer's about the Dying God ... it almost looks as if it had really happened once' (*Surprised by Joy*, p. 211). Where old-fashioned believers saw Christianity as both absolutely true and utterly different from all other religions, which were absolutely false, and where Frazer sought to demonstrate that they were in profound ways strangely similar and all, therefore, equally deluded, it could be claimed instead that the central mysteries of Christianity make sense only through taking up the universal myths of religion, responding to them as much as to the OT, so that the sort of similarity Frazer detected helps explain, but does not undermine, Christian belief.

From the latter part of the *nineteenth century Christian thinkers were beginning to wrestle with the theological revolution which a larger knowledge of religions necessitated. One of the most influential pioneers was Frederick Denison Maurice who in 1845–6 delivered the Boyle Lectures on *The Religions of the World and their Relation to Christianity*. Maurice, who looks in retrospect like the wisest of Victorian Anglican theologians but who was at the time marginal, had already written his major two-volume work, *The Kingdom of God* (repr. 1958). In his Boyle Lectures he approached the world's 'other' religions theologically: it was impossible to imagine that God had simply abandoned the greater part of humanity created in his image. If Christianity had something to say to the Muslim, Hindu, or Buddhist, it must be because they were already included within the history of salvation. Genuine faith, responding to the action of God, must be recognized as present in every religious tradition. Maurice's actual knowledge of Asian religions was fairly limited, but probably more than any other mid-19th-century thinker he had proposed the agenda for a new field of theology. Most of the more liberal missionaries of the next seventy years, especially in India, worked to that agenda. One can see the change of attitude in books like T. E. Slater's *The Higher Hinduism in Relation to Christianity* (1902) or J. N. Farquhar's *The Crown of Hinduism* (1913), as in the conclusions of the Edinburgh Missionary Conference of 1910. Christianity is seen as the 'fulfilment' of all other religions, their 'crown'. This implies recognition of a certain continuity between them and acceptance that the *Holy Spirit has been at work in every tradition. Entering into conversation with them, especially with the great religions of Asia, is seen as requiring a profound renewal for Christian thought itself, comparable with what happened in the *Alexandrian school of theology when Clement and *Origen wrestled with *Platonic and *Gnostic thought. It also led to the conviction that western theological formulas could be an impediment to any real meeting of minds and that it was necessary to get behind the conciliar definitions of the 4th and 5th centuries.

Little of this had much immediate effect on theology as written or taught in the west. It remained a preoccupation of Asian missionaries and, while representing a mild form of *liberal Protestantism, never challenged the primacy and ultimacy of Christ which undergirded the basic missionary sense of vocation. In Europe, however, a number of theologians in the last phase of classical Liberal Protestantism went a great deal further (see TWENTIETH CENTURY). Ernst Troeltsch, a close friend of Bousset and the philosopher behind the *Religionsgeschichtliche Schule*, is the most distinguished example. For him there was only one possible approach to the understanding of Christianity: the strict application of a single historical method to the study of all religions, the rejection of any distinction 'between a natural and a supernatural revelation' coupled with a surviving, but diminishing, conviction that the 'strictest, scientific objectivity shows Christianity to be the most profound, the most powerful and the richest expression of the religious idea'. Scientifically, that conviction looks both too subjective in itself and too dependent on prior agreement that 'the religious idea' still means anything when separated from any particular manifestation. One is left with no more than a range of phenomena expressing 'the religious idea'.

The most emphatic repudiation of both the moderate liberal view of Maurice and Farquhar and the full-blown view of Troeltsch came from a Dutch missionary theologian who had worked in Indonesia. Hendrik Kraemer, basically a Barthian, wrote *The Christian Message in a Non-Christian World* by invitation in 1938 as a text for the International Missionary Conference at Tambaram. For *Barth, with his categorical separation of what is of God and what of man, religion is 'the affair of godless man', no less than 'unbelief', to be contrasted absolutely with biblical *revelation. So Kraemer insisted that even the 'highest' elements in other religions were a merely human achievement providing 'no real point of contact for Christian theism ... Fundamentally speaking there is no point of contact'. For Kraemer there is such a 'radical difference between the Christian revelation and the other religions' that any idea that Christianity could be a 'crown' to what is best in them is simply a delusion. He appeals to Barth's theology as a 'merciless war-cry' against any such relativism. For Kraemer, as for Barth, all religions, at their best or worst, are mere human inventions, expressions of human pride, while the core of Christianity, or, to use his own terminology, 'biblical realism', is something quite other, a divine revelation. Kraemer thus represented an exclusivist position, Troeltsch a basically pluralist one, while between them what one may call the Maurice school proposed an inclusivist understanding of religions of which the 'crown' remained a christologically shaped Christianity.

In Catholicism following the First World War there was also a notable development in sympathetic understanding of other religions, particularly in France. Louis Massignon for Islam, Henri *de Lubac for Buddhism, Vincent Lebbe and Dom Célestin Lou for Confucianism, Jean de Menasce for the religions of Persia, *Abhishiktananda, Raimundo *Panikkar, and Bede *Griffiths for Hinduism, all expressed a more positive sense of the relationship between Christian experience and that of other religions without in any way denying the uniqueness of Christ. A profound critique that de Menasce made of Kraemer's theology (*Neue Zeitschrift für Missionswissenschaft*, 1945) as undermining the inner logic of the *Incarnation well expressed the underlying contrast between a *Thomist and a Barthian understanding of the relationship between nature and *grace. Without such developments *Vatican II's *Declaration on the Relation of the Church to Non-Christian Religions* (*Nostra Aetate*, 1965), cautious as it remained, would not have been possible.

The relationship between theology and 'religion' changed de-

cisively in the post-Second World War period. Until then the world in general and the west in particular had retained much of a 'Christendom' character, with political and academic life marked by public recognition of Christianity. The arrival of political independence in 1947 for India and Pakistan, and in 1948 for Ceylon (Sri Lanka), and Burma (Myanmar), coupled with Communist takeover of large parts of Europe and Asia, marks a clear moment of change. This was followed by a rapid advance of *secularization in western societies and the spread of eastern religions in Europe and North America. Until the 4th century Christianity had existed within societies in which other religions were at least as important socially and intellectually. Between Constantine and the Second World War, most Christians lived in states ruled by at least nominal Christians, other religions being encountered only at the fringes of society or in 'mission lands', and hardly at all within an academic setting. Now this changed, and one expression of the change was the multiplication of 'religious studies' departments in western universities and the widespread transformation of the study of theology into that of religion, especially during the 1960s and 1970s. Where theology was studied it had now to place itself within a context of 'other' religions as it had seldom done hitherto: this could only be stimulating.

A Kraemer-like exclusivist viewpoint continued to be urged, chiefly in conservative evangelical circles but also in the World Council of Churches during its early years where Wim Visser't Hooft, another Barthian, was Secretary-General and Kraemer himself first Director of the WCC's Ecumenical Institute at Bossey, Geneva. Elsewhere there was a new determination, especially within Roman Catholicism in the wake of Vatican II, to formulate an inclusivist position which, while retaining the centrality within the divine plan for humanity of Christ and the church, insisted upon God's *universal salvific will. No one is excluded from participating in salvation history. If this is so, it must somehow be through the multiple religious and ethical systems of the non-Christian world. In formulating this position, Karl *Rahner proved particularly influential. While God's salvific grace has been made manifest in and for the whole of humanity in definitive form in Jesus Christ, that grace is also offered to those who do not know him, through the religious and moral traditions they belong to. The latter actually mediate grace rather than, or as well as, being barriers to it as mere expressions of human imaginativeness or pride. All religions may then be seen as human traditions of belief, worship, and behaviour dependent both upon the powers of human nature and upon the working of grace while also containing, no less than Christianity, deformations dependent upon ignorance and *sin. If non-Christians experience salvation, they do so as graced believers in Islam, the Buddha, or whatever, but God's grace remains consequent upon Christ as *Word and Son of God, new *Adam and universal saviour. In the terms of Christian theology, they can then be described as 'anonymous Christians', a reasonable if much-criticized term. It is fully compatible with an assertion that, in Buddhist terms, a devout Christian may be seen as an 'anonymous Buddhist'. Neither statement is derogatory. Each simply implies that a universalist theology must make reference not only to its believers but to everyone.

Inclusivism of this sort has, however, been rejected as an inadequate response to the world's religious diversity. The most forceful spokesman for a full *pluralism has been John Hick, but reference can be made too to Wilfred Cantwell Smith and Paul Knitter, among others. From the early 1970s Hick appealed for what he called a 'Copernican revolution' in theology, from a Christ-centred to a God-centred approach, accepting all the major world religions as equally valid. When it was pointed out that his theism remains recognizably Christian (being formulated in terms of *fatherhood and *love) and that, moreover, some religious traditions are not theistic, he moved towards a definition of religion in terms of a turning from 'self-centredness to Reality-centredness'. The difficulty is to see what cognitive element survives in such an understanding, which seems to reduce theology to a devout *agnosticism with a purely emotional commitment to one's own tradition, to the exclusion of any truth or value judgement between, or even within, traditions. What has held Christianity together from the beginning in all its forms is an affirmation of Christ's uniqueness. If this is abandoned, it is unclear how Christianity could survive recognizably as intelligent belief.

A Christian theology of religion needs somehow to hold together the import of two seemingly contradictory NT texts: 'There is salvation in no one else [than Christ], for there is no other name under heaven given among men by which we must be saved' (Acts 4: 12). 'God our Saviour desires all men to be saved' (1 Tim. 2: 4). 'No other name' on one hand, 'all men' on the other. It seems unthinkable that a God of love so desiring should exclude all the millions of people who have never come near to Christianity from being offered grace or finding salvation. A solution may depend on distinguishing between the causative, normative order and the diversity of human experience. In the former, Christian doctrine has always asserted a certain exclusivity: Christ alone sacramentalizes salvation, that is to say both symbolizes and makes present the grace of God in its fullness within the particularities of history. Religion, however, primarily signifies a human experience. Here pluralism is in order. Grace is received differently by everyone and the reception can be limited by no defined boundaries given God's universal salvific will. The bonding of objective exclusivism and experiential pluralism provides a model that collectively is best described as inclusivism.

Religious experience is not, however, synonymous with the reception of grace or salvation which may happen in a wholly non-religious context. Religion, not excluding Christianity, is always a mix of good and bad. Much in religion has been oppressive, cruel, and inimical to *truth. Nothing would be more misconceived than to imply that an unselfcritical alliance of world religions is necessarily an alliance for righteousness or that all religions 'really' teach the same moral or social code. A Barthian critique of religion remains as necessary as a Rahnerian insistence that grace may be encountered through any religion.   **Adrian Hastings**

Cracknell, Kenneth, Justice, Courtesy and Love: Theologians and Missionaries Encountering World Religions 1846–1914 (1995).

D'Costa, Gavin, Theology and Religious Pluralism (1986).

—— (ed.), Christian Uniqueness Reconsidered: The Myth of a Pluralistic Theology of Religions (1990).

Harrison, Peter, 'Religion' and the Religions in the English Enlightenment (1990).

Hick, John, God and the Universe of Faiths (1973).

Knitter, Paul, No Other Name? A Critical Study of Christian Attitudes Towards the World Religions (1985).

Kolakowski, Leszek, Religion (1982).

Kraemer, Hendrik, The Christian Message in a Non-Christian World (1938).

Küng, Hans, Christianity and the World Religions (1987).

Lane Fox, Robin, Pagans and Christians (1986).

Llull, Ramón, Selected Works, ed. A. Bonner (2 vols.; 1985).

Pailin, David, Attitudes to Other Religions: Comparative Religion in Seventeenth and Eighteenth Century Britain (1984).

Smart, Ninian, The Religious Experience of Mankind (1969).

Smith, Wilfred Cantwell, The Meaning and End of Religion (1963).

Thrower, James, Religion: The Classical Theories (1999).

Troeltsch, Ernst, Writings on Theology and Religion, ed. Robert Morgan and Michael Pye (1977).

religious experience. This term covers a very broad, open class of conscious events—perhaps no single feature runs through all cases. They may be taken as intimations of *God or gods, or stages on a disciplined 'path' leading ideally to a state of enlightenment or bliss. They include, for some, momentous episodes in which items of religious belief become vividly realized and personally appropriated, as in a sudden unheralded *conversion; also a steady, sustained *assurance of being forgiven and accepted by God. They may involve sight or hearing (*visions or voices), emotions or moods (wonder, dread, tranquillity), or may be taken to be predominantly cognitive—as insights into ultimate reality. Characteristically, they can be both profoundly humbling and exalting, through what seems an encounter, immediate and authoritative, with a transcendent source of supreme value and power: in Christian terms, the *Holy.

Religious experiences cannot be restricted to the religious traditions, ancient or contemporary. Isolated experiences of awe or wonder at the cosmos as a whole, or at the development of life and consciousness within it, have sufficient affinity to belong among them. So do other elemental and aesthetic experiences such as the sublime in some of its forms—as a fusion of dread and exhilaration at nature's immensities and energies.

There have been varying attitudes within Christianity towards personal religious experience. When dominant, it may be seen by some as fostering an excessively inward-looking *spirituality: yet others give the highest importance to, for example, experiences of being 'born again', or the prayerful realizing of the presence of a loving God.

Certainly both Old and New Testaments record momentous experiences of the 'numinous' (*Otto 1917), a mystery at once dreadful and exhilarating. Often quoted are those of *Isaiah in the Temple (Isaiah 6): and *Paul on the road to Damascus (Acts 9). Experiences of life-changing theophany are of course prominent also in the scriptures of other faiths, for example Krishna revealed to Arjuna in the Bhagavadgita (ch. 11).

These accounts remind us of the important role played by the doctrinal concepts and categories with which a person interprets religious experiences, thereby importing into an experience *theological and *metaphysical elements of belief. The degree to which a religious experience is so mediated and articulated is highly variable, from the detailed and specific (the Risen Christ, the Virgin *Mary) to the minimally characterized (an unspeakably awesome presence). Again, the nearer the experience is felt to approach to a *mystical closeness or union with the divine, the less describable it becomes. Our concepts, words, cease to fit: fundamental features of normal experience (time, in some cases) seem suspended. Yet the momentousness of the experience prompts one none the less to seek expression for it—inevitably in bold *metaphors and *paradoxes.

The value of religious experience in making a case for Christianity (or indeed other *religions) is not easy to estimate. It can appeal, very understandably, as a turn towards the immediate and direct, away from the uncertainties of *philosophical arguments for God, or (it may be) from forms of *worship that are felt as impersonal or otherwise uncongenial. On reflection, though, we can claim for religious experience only a limited contribution to the case for a particular religious view. Its felt immediacy may be striking, yet it may implicitly draw upon already-learned concepts. Few aspects of religious experience (such as a sense of the presence of another, voices, sense of guilt, sudden reversal of mood) cannot be replicated by psychologically explicable natural causes, some of the more bizarre and dramatic by parallels in psychopathology. On the other hand, that does nothing to prove that the experiences are not properly seen as awareness of the divine. Many of those who testify to religious experiences are free of the syndromes of mental disorders and their destructive effects on the psyche. The causal explicability of everyday perception of things and persons does not rule out our taking these experiences as veridical: so why be more severe and sceptical with *religious* experiences? Mindful, however, of the interpretative ambiguity of religious experience and the peculiar boldness of the believer's claim to be meeting the infinite God, to be visited, touched, addressed directly by the creator of the universe, we may well judge that they do need confirmation through evidence and argument, so as to rule out the many possibilities of error and illusion. Moreover, whether or not we wish to call them 'religious experiences', we do have to note that some people record powerful intimations of the *absence* of God, of cosmic emptiness. Perhaps these could be called 'negative religious experiences'.

Since, in terms of their impact and the strong sense of conviction they engender, quite opposite views of our ultimate situation can be conveyed in religious experiences, whether positive or negative, it is plain that they cannot safely be taken as the sole foundation for a personal world-view. In some instances, *moral* confirmation (or critique) is all-important, since extreme dangers arise if total authority is given to personal religious experience, to the extent that any strong motivation may be taken as God's voice, even when it prompts morally questionable action.

In summary, a religious commitment may be initiated, animated, and renewed by vividly felt and lived-through personal participation. Human fallibility, however, cannot be discounted even here. Religious experience may have to be sifted, respectfully but critically appraised, and reappraised, in the context of our developing synoptic understanding of the *world and ourselves.

Ronald W. Hepburn

Eliade, Mircea, *The Sacred and the Profane*, 2nd edn. (1959).
Franks Davis, Caroline, *The Evidential Force of Religious Experience* (1989).
Hardy, Alister, *The Spiritual Nature of Man* (1979).
James, William, *The Varieties of Religious Experience* (1902).
Otto, Rudolf, *The Idea of the Holy* (1917; 1923).

religious language. From about 1940 to 1970 religious language was much debated in Anglo-American *philosophical theology. *Theology, as discourse about the divine, has always included reflection about the appropriate use of *language in talk of *God: negative terms (*Dionysius the Pseudo-Areopagite), *analogy (*Aquinas), *hermeneutics (*Schleiermacher), indirect communication (*Kierkegaard) being key notions in the history. The agenda of the recent debate, however, was determined largely by the Oxford philosopher Alfred J. Ayer (1910–89), in his *Language, Truth and Logic* (1936).

The central claim was that statements are either analytic or synthetic. Analytic statements are *true because the terms are mutually definable (for example 'All bachelors are unmarried'). Synthetic statements may be true or false if they are verifiable empirically (for example, based on observation). All other utterances, such as those made in *ethics, aesthetics, and *religion, traditionally regarded as asserting something true or false about objects or events, were regarded as expressing attitudes or feelings but having no claim to be true or false about how things are in the world.

As Ayer recognized, the distinction between fact-representing statements and value-ascribing utterances was far more fundamental than any discoveries about language. In retrospect, logical positivism, linguistic analysis, Oxford philosophy (as the movement was successively known), took little account of the variety and complexity of language. From Ayer's book onwards, the debate centred on statements (propositions). What believers themselves, as well as liturgists, historians, and sociologists of religion regard as the primary forms of religious language (story, *parable, *symbol, image, ritual, gesture, chant, etc.) were largely ignored.

Ayer introduced the emotive theory of values (emotivism). In cases where one would once have been thought to be making aesthetic or ethical judgements about something in the world, it turns out, according to the fact/value analysis of language, that the function of the utterance is purely 'emotive'. To say that '*x* is good' means 'I like it'. The same test applied to assertions in religion. What believers regarded as statements about what is or might be the case in this world or the next, it now emerged, were at best expressions of emotion.

Far from challenging this analysis of aesthetic, ethical, and religious utterances, which with hindsight seems the more radical move, many theologians sought instead to reinterpret Christian theism to fit the requirements of the fact/value dichotomy. David Cox, in an extreme example of such reinterpretation, long forgotten but worth recalling as a symptom, made remarks such as the following. The word 'God', rightly used in such expressions as 'encountering God', does not refer to any reality independent of the speaker's subjective experience. The statement that 'God is loving' means that 'no experience of meeting a person who is not someone who loves you can be rightly called "an experience of meeting God"'. The assertion that 'God created the world from nothing' needs to be reinterpreted as meaning that 'everything which we call "material" can be used in such a way that it contributes to the well-being of men'. Christianity, with such reinterpretations, is preserved, according to Cox, 'from the limbo to which metaphysics is being exiled (rightly, as I believe) by the logical positivists' ('The Significance of Christianity', *Mind*, 59 (1950), 209–18). Thomas McPherson, in a severely critical reply, agreed that theological propositions needed clarification but insisted that 'it is more valuable to examine them and find out what their meaning is, than to work on them to make them fit a philosophical view that divides all propositions up according to a rigid principle' (ibid. 545–50). It may be wondered if the dispute advanced much further in the next twenty years.

R. B. Braithwaite, in a famous lecture at Oxford in 1955, argued that Christianity provided a fund of 'stories', expressing attitudes and commitments, that inspire people to have 'an agapeistic frame of mind' (*An Empiricist's View of the Nature of Religious Belief*). There was much else in this vein. Others, such as Ian T. Ramsey, worked hard, within the confines of Ayer's fact/value analysis, to reveal the 'oddity' of religious utterances. Though they are not the fact-representing propositions that they have traditionally seemed, theological statements prove, on closer study, to be neither completely non-cognitive (as Ayer, Cox, and Braithwaite held) nor informative about the world (as traditional believers were assumed to suppose). The significance of some theological utterances lay in their power to articulate or generate 'disclosure situations'. 'The ice breaks', 'the penny drops': such homely expressions in ordinary language should remind us of how a set of facts can suddenly display a different value. Some uses of language, Ramsey insisted, while indeed being expressive of the speaker's subjectivity, are also capable of revealing and transforming a situation in the public world.

In such collective works as *New Essays in Philosophical Theology* (edited by Antony Flew and Alasdair *MacIntyre, 1955) and *Christian Ethics and Contemporary Philosophy* (edited by Ian Ramsey, 1966), it is easy to trace a gradual move from (say) Flew's abrasively anti-theological 'Theology and Falsification' (originally published in 1949), in which it is claimed that an utterance is meaningless unless some empirical observation could falsify it, to (say) 'Vision and Choice in Morality', a discussion (originally in 1956) between R. W. Hepburn and Iris Murdoch, neither of them a believer, where a distinction is drawn, in her words, between 'the man who believes that moral values are modes of empirically describable activity which he endorses and commends and the man who believes that moral values are visions, inspirations, or powers which emanate from a transcendent source concerning which he is called on to make discoveries and may at present know little'.

About the time that Ayer introduced logical positivism, Ludwig *Wittgenstein had discovered from discussion with members of the Vienna Circle that they had radically misread his own early work *Tractatus Logico-Philosophicus* (1922) as an essay in logical positivism. Wittgenstein tried to show what can and cannot be said meaningfully by specifying the form of a proposition within the limits of a truth-functional logic. This greatly restricted what we can meaningfully say. The concerns of ethics and aesthetics but also those of metaphysics and theology became unstatable. But this did not mean that Wittgenstein was the ally of the logical positivists. On the contrary, he believed that there was more than could ever be said, and that what could not be said was far more important than what could be said. The final remark of the *Tractatus*, far from authorizing scientific positivism, suggests on the contrary that 'even if all possible scientific questions be answered, the problems of life have still not been touched at all'.

Wittgenstein initiated the long revolution against the fact/value distinction and thus returned philosophers to a much richer con-

ception of language. His characteristic move is to insist that, when philosophers speak of knowledge, being, the subject, objects, and so on, we should always ask how such words are used in the language where they are at home—'What we do is to bring these words back from their metaphysical to their everyday use' (*Philosophical Investigations* (1953), § 116). This, again, might sound rather like the anti-metaphysical programme of logical positivism, and was indeed often so misunderstood. But Wittgenstein regarded the fact/value distinction as itself a metaphysical invention which recourse to the actual uses of ordinary language would explode.

John Wisdom, following Wittgenstein, strove to show that the concept of *reasoning that is inscribed in our ordinary language does not match the fact/value scheme (cf. *Paradox and Discovery* (1965)). We often have all the facts, as in a court of law (his favourite example); but that does not mean that we have these facts bare of values; on the contrary, the task of judge and jury is precisely to reassess the facts, which does not make their judgement subjective. By simply attending to the ways in which language is actually used, Wittgenstein and Wisdom began to overthrow the grip of the fact/value analysis.

Independently of Wittgenstein, J. L. Austin, the leader of 'Oxford philosophy' in its heyday, distinguished between performatives and constatives in lectures posthumously published as *How to Do Things with Words* (1962). Constative or descriptive utterances are true or false; performatives are 'happy' or 'unhappy' but cannot be either true or false. 'I name this ship "Queen Elizabeth"', for example, cannot be false but if I am not entitled to name ships, or it is not the appropriate occasion, the utterance would be 'unhappy'. To say 'I named that ship' is, in contrast, true or false. In the course of self-criticism, Austin came to distinguish three sentence-using acts: the 'locutionary' act of using a sentence to convey a meaning, as when one is informed that something is the case; the 'illocutionary' act of using an utterance with a certain 'force', as when somebody is warned that something is the case; and a 'perlocutionary' act of producing an effect by the use of a sentence, as when, without actually informing us of some state of affairs, the speaker succeeds in warning us that it has happened. Any single utterance, Austin came to think, combines locutionary and illocutionary functions. Austin soon abandoned these distinctions, except as first approximations to return philosophers to the understanding of language evinced in *Aristotle's *Rhetoric*. In Austin's wake, John Searle published *Speech-Acts* (1969), exploring the logical conditions necessary for the performance of illocutionary acts such as promising, commanding, and so on. In retrospect, Austin's 'ordinary language' philosophy, and Searle's 'speech-act theory' are best read as further attempts to break the grip of the fact/value dichotomy.

By the 1970s, the attention that philosophers of religion were paying to language had begun to connect with 'Continental' philosophy, particularly the work of Paul *Ricœur (then teaching at Chicago). Ricœur extended reflection on language to incorporate the insights of Freud as well as those of the phenomenological tradition of Heidegger and Merleau-Ponty.

More recently, in Anglo-American analytical philosophy at large, there has been a move from concern with language to concern with meaning, truth, and reference (Michael Dummett, Donald Davidson). Philosophers of religion have abandoned problems about the cognitive status of theological language. The move may easily be traced in two widely used textbooks: John Macquarrie's *God-Talk* (1967) has more references to 'language' in the index than to any other concept, whereas Brian Davies's *Philosophy of Religion* (1982) has none.

This particular debate about religious language is over; but there are lessons to be remembered. First of all, the fact/value distinction does great harm, far beyond philosophy. Many people in our culture, who have neither interest nor competence in philosophy, regard judgements in ethics and aesthetics, as well as religious statements, as merely 'emotive'. Whether emotivism as a philosophical theory is cause or effect of this widespread lack of belief in the possibility of true statements in *morals and religion is disputable. Secondly, instead of forcing religious language to fit the requirements of the fact/value dichotomy, it would have been better for philosophers of religion and theologians to highlight the diverse and complex uses of religious language as a way of showing that our messy world simply will not divide neatly into 'facts' and 'values'. Description and evaluation are distinct activities, but most of the time they cannot be entirely disentangled. Thirdly, as Iris Murdoch and others suggested early on, the fact/value dichotomy springs from a highly disputable picture of our psychological make-up: from the notion of 'bare facts' apprehended by a totally neutral faculty of reason, and the notion of a faculty of will that must 'choose values', either arbitrarily or on the basis of instinct. Finally, logical positivism was itself a metaphysical view; it survived in somewhat modified forms in linguistic philosophy; and, not surprisingly, the metaphysical problems eventually returned from the limbo where they had been exiled.   **Fergus Kerr**

Ayer, A. J., *Language, Truth and Logic* (1936).

Donovan, P., *Religious Language* (1976).

Ramsey, Ian T., *Religious Language: An Empirical Placing of Theological Phrases* (1963).

religious liberty.

'The church', said the great 19th-century Catholic historian, Lord Acton, 'began with the principle of liberty, both as her claim and as her rule.' Paul discussed issues of liberty and respect for the *conscience of other Christians even if they were wrong (1 Cor. 8). Primitive Christianity had little chance to oppress dissidents, and often did not want to. 'It is against the nature of religion to force religion' (Tertullian).

From the start, however, there were 'sons of thunder' (Luke 9: 51–6), impatient of the Christian tendency to leave the tares among the wheat. Official state toleration of Christianity under *Constantine was soon followed by persecution of *heretics. *Augustine was at his worst in twisting Luke 14: 23, 'Compel them to come in', against the *Donatists. For centuries, *orthodox Christendom pursued recalcitrant dissidents to death, or if need be dug up their bones for posthumous insult. Heretics, unsurprisingly, were more likely to be in favour of religious liberty.

Practice and theory often differed. The church theoretically punished heretics but not believers in other religions. Unfortunately for the Jews, there were ways of persecuting that were not technically punishment. Sometimes, by contrast, worldly self-interest overruled theological correctness. The roots of the favourite theory of the 18th-century enlightened despots, that toleration was good for trade, go far back.

*Renaissance humanism and the *Reformation had some promising ideas about religious liberty which came to little. *Erasmus was eloquent against burning people, but both Catholics and Protestants thought this merely reflected his basically frivolous half-belief. *More's *Utopia* was tolerant, but not More's England. *Luther was at his most compelling in talking about the freedom of the Christian, but by 1530 he had come round to *Zwingli's policy of drowning Anabaptists (see MENNONITE THOUGHT). Some Reformers, such as Martin Bucer at Strasbourg, continued to be eirenic, but on the whole, churches in power in early modern Europe felt that anarchy loomed, and that the land was polluted by the presence of heresy.

In 1524, Balthasar Hubmaier (1485–1528), the spokesman of the pacifist wing of the Anabaptists, published (perhaps predictably) the first appeal for complete toleration of all heretics: 'let them be and leave them to rage'. God's truth will survive (compare Gamaliel, Acts 5: 38–9). The persecuted Anabaptists themselves policed their own gathered church, people were placed 'under the ban', and there were few hopes for the world outside, so the tolerant temper had limits. A church which by policy withdraws from the world wants nothing more than to be left alone. Understandings of liberty become more troubling when the Christian has to continue to interact with the neighbour.

Other radical Reformers were more open. Caspar Schwenckfeld (1489–1561) and Sebastian Franck (1499–1542) rejected the visible church for an invisible brotherhood of all those of goodwill. 'To me, anyone who wishes my good and can bear with me by his side, is a good brother, whether Papist, Lutheran, Zwinglian, Anabaptist, or even Turk … We know in part … We may be heretics quite as much as our opponents' (Franck). This is not arguing the case for religious liberty for the sake, understandably, of self-preservation, but a new, perhaps ecumenical, theology built round religious liberty. Schwenckfelders, who ended up as a denomination, as often happens with movements intent on blurring boundaries, had slight influence on more dogmatic traditions.

Perhaps more influential was Sebastian Castellio, whose (at first anonymous) book *Concerning Heretics* (1554) was the direct consequence of the burning of Servetus in *Calvin's *Geneva. Castellio challenged the penalty and even the word 'heretic', and his powerful attack has meant that Servetus' death has been held against Calvin ever since. As an anti-Trinitarian, Servetus, if caught, would have been burnt in every Christian country at the time, so this was a little unfair to Calvin. The anti-Trinitarians, more than the Anabaptists, from then on took over the role both of advocates of religious liberty, and of awful warnings of what would then be permitted. In the eyes of orthodox Protestants the most dangerous document of the 17th century was the Socinian Rakovian Catechism (see UNITARIANISM): 'Let everyone be free to express his judgement in religious matters … we are all brothers, and no power, no authority has been given us over the conscience of others.' To this day, a license for *freedom in religious opinion is likely to mean freedom to be Unitarian. Free-thought as such, which came later, is more often than not synonymous with mere unbelief.

With several viable forms of Protestantism, most of them willing to take up arms for their own religious liberty, heresy-hunting diminished in practice during the 17th and 18th centuries. The first step was to give kings religious liberty; dissidents could then move to the nearest like-minded land. Matters were not straightforward: in France, for example, the Protestant minority, whose liberties had been guaranteed by the Edict of Nantes (1598), saw this revoked in 1685, initiating a new period of persecution. The king responsible, Louis XIV, was absolutist in temper and given to superstition; as everyone else saw, he irreparably damaged his country's economy in the process. He found few imitators.

In England there was a state effort to broaden the national church and not to over-define controverted points. The Laudian school in their private piety were genuinely latitudinarian, but spoilt things by bullying the small minorities who would still not come in (see CAROLINE DIVINES). The same could be said of Oliver Cromwell, who had a slightly different wide range of tolerance. *Milton's *Areopagitica* (1644) stood up for freedom to publish as well as think.

The *North American colonies were largely populated by English Puritans who had had enough of Laudian rule. They were not themselves models of religious tolerance: obstinately persistent *Quakers were hanged. The little colony of Rhode Island was different. From its start in the 1630s and 1640s, with a royal charter in 1663, it guaranteed religious liberty (not simply toleration but liberty). Its founder, the Baptist Roger Williams, author of *The Bloudy Tenent of Persecution*, a seeker who distrusted all structured religion, and even more any formal state link, was a Puritan with a difference. In effect he secularized the government of the colony, though it was its religious variety, not its secularity, that was noticed at the time. For slightly less thoroughgoing reasons, the Catholic colony of Maryland and the Quaker colony of Pennsylvania tolerated all comers.

There is a great contrast between Williams and the political philosopher John Locke (1632–1704), who published four *Letters on Toleration* around 1690. His reasoning is human rather than divine, and makes the full case for freedom of worship as well as belief (except for atheism and certain aspects of Catholicism that seemed to threaten the British crown). The argument was won, though even in tolerant England it took many years to remove most of the legal disabilities designed to protect *Anglicanism from its rivals.

In other countries it took a revolution to bring about religious freedom. The French Revolution quite soon turned to persecuting the church, and its heirs in many countries, often in the name of religious liberty, arranged a separation of church and state that involved harassing the former. The mirror image of this was the Catholic Church's continued opposition to religious liberty. Liberty of conscience was still condemned in the papal Syllabus of Errors in 1864. The loophole of 'invincible ignorance', arguing that hereditary Protestants knew no better, widened over the years, and Catholics in the English-speaking world largely adjusted to being a successful denomination in a religious free market, but the official line remained intransigent. This changed with *Vatican II and *John XXIII's encyclical *Pacem in Terris* (1963), which affirms 'man's right to be able to worship God in accordance with the right dictates of his own conscience, and to profess his religion both in private and in public'. There had been a time when the only 'right' dictate of a conscience was to obey one's religious superiors, but the Council now turned away from past intolerance 'hardly in accord with the spirit of the Gospel, and even opposed to it'. There are still some lingering traces of tyranny in the Curia, and many fundamentalist Protestants long to interfere with other people's liberties, but in the 21st century, as in much of the 20th, the issue of religious liberty is not much concerned with Christian

imperialism. Both National Socialism and Marxist Communism posed far greater challenges to religious freedom than any pope. The *Barmen Declaration was a model theological statement of Christian liberty. There are secular and religious governments round the world interfering with people's right to practise the religion they choose. One of the immediate uses of *ecumenism is to provide back-up for oppressed Christian minorities. It is also necessary for Christians to remember the religious rights of Muslims, and not to forget the *Holocaust of the Jews.   **Alistair Mason**

Bainton, R. H., *The Travail of Religious Liberty* (1953).

Cragg, G. R., *Freedom and Authority* (1975).

Jordan, W. K., *The Development of Religious Toleration in England from the Beginning of the English Reformation to the Death of Queen Elizabeth* (1932).

Kamen, Henry, *The Rise of Toleration* (1967).

Shiels, W. J. (ed.), *Persecution and Toleration* (1984).

religious life is a generic term for a variety of forms of Christian life that originated, as a radical response to the gospel, in the 1st century and continue to develop in the present, predominantly among Roman *Catholics and *Eastern Orthodox but also, especially recently, among Protestants and Anglicans. The Protestant community of *Taizé in France has fostered ecumenical exchange.

Religious are Christians who have entered a public and permanent state of life characterized by a full-time and exclusive commitment to living their Christian vocation with an intensity rooted in but beyond that demanded by *baptism. It has sometimes been called 'the life of perfection' or the life of the evangelical counsels—voluntary *poverty, consecrated *celibacy, and radical *obedience—in contrast to the ordinary life of the *Commandments. Such designations can lead to an élitism that is actually contrary to the theology of religious life. The life is distinguished not by superiority to other forms of Christian life but by a total absorption in the quest for *God that excludes other life projects, such as *marriage, the raising of a *family, or *work, from the centrality they might legitimately assume in a Christian's life.

Although 'Religious' is a generic term for all who embrace such a life, historically it has been specified by a variety of terms that emphasize some feature of a particular form of that life. Thus, Religious might be called consecrated *virgins, hermits, *ascetics, monks or nuns, sisters or brothers.

Historically, religious life began when some 1st-century Christians, both women and men, chose perpetual celibacy for the 'sake of the kingdom of heaven' (cf. Matt. 19: 12), a very radical choice in a society in which the *sexuality of its members was a civic resource rather than a purely personal endowment. Originally, these Christians lived as solitaries in their own homes or came together in urban communities, often under the financial patronage and spiritual leadership of wealthy women. While some of these virgins, widows, or celibates pursued a secluded life of *prayer and asceticism others combined their prayer life with active service in the Christian community through direct care of the poor and sick or through scholarship and spiritual ministries.

As Christianity became an acculturated religion in the Roman empire, many Christians withdrew into the *deserts of Egypt, Palestine, and *Syria to live a less worldly Christian life. These first desert dwellers were hermits but, under the leadership of Pachomius (c.290–345), a new cenobitic (communitarian) form of religious life developed. A short time later the great *monastic lawgivers, Basil (c.330–79) in the east and *Benedict in the west, wrote the rules that patterned the form of religious life that was to predominate for the next eight centuries. Monastic life, both male and female, was primarily enclosed and organized around the choral recitation of the Divine Office and manual or intellectual work under the guidance of an abbot or abbess.

In the Middle Ages, largely under the influence of *Francis of Assisi and *Dominic Guzman, a new form of religious life developed. This mendicant form combined monastic life with an *apostolic commitment to *preaching and teaching in the rapidly developing urban centres of Europe. The female branches of the mendicant orders, however, remained strictly cloistered.

After the *Reformation apostolic commitment took precedence in a new form of religious life typified by the *Jesuits. Monastic practices that interfered with *ministry were suppressed to allow fuller involvement in preaching, teaching, and *evangelization at home and in foreign *missions. Although women Religious remained cloistered, their eventually successful struggle for participation in active ministry began with women like Angela Merici (1474–1540), foundress of the Ursulines, Mary *Ward, foundress of the Institute of the Blessed Virgin Mary, Louise de Marillac (1591–1660), foundress with Vincent de Paul of the Daughters of Charity, and other apostolic women. Non-cloistered apostolic women were not canonically recognized as Religious until 1900 (by the papal bull Conditae a Christo of Leo XIII) but most of the religious congregations of women founded in the 19th century were apostolic groups of this type. New forms of community and apostolic life whose canonical status is still undetermined continue to emerge in our own time.

Although no feature except consecrated celibacy undertaken by vow has been characteristic of every form of religious life, certain co-ordinates of the life are in some way common to all. Whether solitary or cenobite, Religious undertake to live Christian community through radical economic and governmental interdependence undertaken through vows of poverty and obedience or some equivalent. Commitment to a regular life of prayer and asceticism beyond that required by the ordinary discipline of the church, and to some form of service of the neighbour, is also virtually universal.

Formation for religious life takes place in a novitiate in which candidates learn how these co-ordinates of the life are understood and practised in the particular institute they are joining. At the end of an extended period of probation and formation candidates make perpetual profession of vows that establishes them in the religious state.

Although they denote some juridical distinctions, such terms as order, congregation, institute, and community tend to be used interchangeably, as do the terms nun and sister, religious and monk, convent and monastery, rule and constitutions. Nevertheless, forms of religious life are distinguished from one another according to various principles and, within each form of the life, institutes are distinguished by their particular spirit or charism.

The most ancient distinction is that between solitaries and cenobites. However, the two forms have always overlapped among such groups as the desert lavra-dwellers, Camaldolese monastics, medieval *Beguines, post-Reformation Carmelites, and contemporary apostolic Religious living singly.

Religious institutes were sometimes distinguished as 'active' or 'contemplative' depending on whether their life was more characterized by ministerial activity outside the monastery or by cloistered life devoted primarily to personal and liturgical prayer. This distinction is perhaps better captured today in terms of community lifestyle in mobile communities that change residence, companions, and ministries according to current apostolic needs or in geographically stable communities exercising primarily spiritual ministries from within the monastery. Monastic orders tend to be organized as federations of autonomous houses while apostolic congregations usually have central governments upon which local houses depend.

Two distinctions that have enormous impact on the life of the members are that between clerical orders in which some or all members are ordained and lay orders of sisters or brothers, and that between international congregations and those which function primarily within a particular culture.

When Religious went to Asia, Africa, and the Americas in the 17th century the essentially European lifestyle that had prevailed since the days of the Roman empire underwent significant changes. These were, however, probably less radical than those instigated by *Vatican II, which called on Religious to renew their life according to the gospel, the distinctive traditions of their institutes, and their historico-cultural settings. A first wave of changes, in the 1960s and 1970s, affected such externals as habit (clothing), titles, and daily horaria (timetables). These were followed in the 1980s and 1990s by more substantive struggles over the very meaning of religious life and the vows, appropriate ministerial involvement, community life, and ecclesial identity.

The renewal brought dramatic decreases in numbers, financial resources, and ecclesiastical power. As numbers declined the median age in congregations rose because of fewer entrants and the departures of professed members. Institutions were relinquished and the high visibility and credibility of religious life diminished. Conflict between Religious committed to conciliar renewal and an increasingly restorationist Vatican discouraged younger Catholics, especially women, from considering a vocation to religious life.

In recent years, as the *laity has become accustomed to Religious living a contemporary lifestyle and prophetically involved in areas of urgent need within and outside the institutional church, there has been a gradual reawakening of interest in religious life, both in full membership and in non-vowed association with religious orders. Although the characteristic co-ordinates of religious life have remained in place, nearly every aspect of the life changed in appearance and functions during the second half of the 20th century. Contemporary candidates for religious life are expected to be mature, educated, employed, able to manage personal finances, make decisions, and handle relationships with members of both sexes. Formation is concerned with deepening the candidate's *spiritual life, developing community skills, and discerning religious vocation and ministerial commitment. Religious no longer function as underpaid ecclesiastical workers or compliant children, but often play major prophetic roles in both church and societal institutions. Religious life continues to undergo significant change but it is, in basic ways, what it has always been, a life of intense search for God focused through consecrated celibacy and expressed in prayer, community, and ministry.   **Sandra M. Schneiders**

Nygren, David J., and Ukeritis, Miriam D., *The Future of Religious Orders in the United States: Transformation and Commitment* (1993).

Philibert, Paul J. (ed.), *Living in the Meantime: Concerning the Transformation of Religious Life* (1994).

Quiñonez, Lora Ann, and Turner, Mary Daniel, *The Transformation of American Catholic Sisters* (1992).

Ranft, Patricia, *Women and the Religious Life in Premodern Europe* (1996).

Schneiders, Sandra M., *New Wineskins: Re-Imagining Religious Life Today* (1986).

Renaissance. The changes in Christian thought during the Renaissance must be understood in the context of the convulsions of European society during the 14th and 15th centuries. Great outrage was directed against the *papacy's residence in Avignon under French domination (1309–76). The pope no longer presided over the physical see of St Peter and, in sentiments that echoed from Petrarch to *Luther, he had subjected the church, the new Jerusalem, to captivity in Babylon. This endangered the ideal of the *imperium christianum*, the melding of church and empire, of religious and political order, through which the medieval papacy had transformed the culture of classical Rome. The papacy's moral standing was damaged further by the forty-year Great Schism (1378–1417), which created rival pontiffs in Rome and Avignon, and the *conciliar movement, while resolving the *Schism, irrevocably placed under dispute the pope's position as supreme ruler of Christendom.

At the inception of this crisis an Augustinian friar, Simone da Cascia, asserted that, 'nothing, no matter how wicked, can put to shame the empire of God, nor confound the order of the universe' (*Ordine della vita christina*). But this belief was nearing exhaustion. The decisive event in the Renaissance reevaluation of Christian thought was the outbreak of the Black Death (1347–50), which killed as much as one-third of Europe's population. As in any social emergency, there were more dogmatic reactions. The Florentine chronicler Matteo Villani saw the scourge as the prefiguration of the Last Judgement. But liturgical processions were no obvious help in restoring sinful humanity to God's favour and the church's spiritual weakness was apparent. The humanists began raising unsettling questions about the clergy's hegemony over matters of *sin and salvation, and about their 'order of the universe'. Referring to the plague in the preface to his first collection of letters, Petrarch stated, 'Time, as they say, has flowed out between our fingers. Our old hopes have gone to the grave with our friends.' The 'old hopes'—of stability, of security—that the plague had buried also carried to the tomb the clergy's pretensions to knowledge about ultimate causes. Petrarch wrote in a second letter that the mouths of those 'who profess all, knowing nothing' are now silent: 'at the end they have been closed by shock' (*Rerum Familiarum Libri*, 8. 7).

At least as regards Italy, clerical commentaries on the Black Death are outnumbered by those of lay chroniclers and humanists. The most vivid description belongs to Boccaccio's *Decameron*. Like his friend Petrarch, Boccaccio refrained from theological speculation about the plague's origin, focusing instead on its physical, social, and psychological effects. In the hundred stories that follow, his lay narrators ridicule the clergy's arrogance, among other vices, and compose a mosaic about human behaviour that transcends any prejudgement based on social class or moral superiority.

The humanists' scepticism about the clergy and their inviolable claim to doctrinal knowledge exhibited those characteristics of the Renaissance identified by Jacob Burckhardt: the state as a work of art, the reawakening of the ancients, the reappraisal of the secular world and man's role within it, and the development of the individual. For as the clergy and their teaching were brought under scrutiny, the 'world', the *saeculum*, no longer bore the same moral subordination to the sacred world of church and cloister. With this moral stigma removed, people explored the natural *world with ambition and delight. The writings of *Aristotle and Cicero could be read not simply for their integration with doctrine, as the scholastics had practised, but with an effort to see more clearly the ethos of the classical age. Neoplatonism, through the work of Ficino and Pico della Mirandola, became a dynamic moral philosophy in its own right, and their Florentine Academy formed a centre for political and artistic discourse. The Latin of the church, the sign of the clergy's educational pre-eminence, was challenged by the vernacular literature, whose language was more resistant to clerical control. *Dante in his Tuscan dialect could summon his beloved Beatrice, Virgil, and the saints as his guides, and his *Commedia* lighted a path for even the friars to follow. The humanists undertook a study of Latin itself on the basis of classical models and desired to examine authoritative texts in their original languages. Boccaccio was one of the first to sponsor the study of Greek in Italy; within a century scholars were investigating the NT and church documents with a more rigorous philology. *Historical analysis revealed the mutability of verbal expression over time. Lorenzo Valla's attention to linguistic development led him to criticize the doctrinal use of Aristotle; his commentary on the Vulgate bible evoked Luther's appreciation in his first lectures at Wittenberg. *Erasmus, the 'Prince of Humanists', inspired the Reformer's reading of Greek scripture and presaged his protest against clerical abuse of power. Whatever the differences in religious outlook between Luther and the humanists, they shared a conviction about the elusive, subjective process of understanding the temporal as well as the spiritual world, and it is this conviction that announces their modernity.

What emerged in the writings of Renaissance humanists and poets, along with their critique of the clergy, was a new understanding of human existence. In the Middle Ages man's pilgrimage was viewed as first and foremost a moral judgement, a sentence of exile for human transgression. In the Renaissance the experience of life's transience was less defined by dogma, and indeed this experience created the very conditions for knowing spiritual truth. A keener sense not only of the instability of all perception, but also of outward change owing to the flow of *time, called forth new assessments of psychology and ontology. These assessments, buttressed by the greater acquisition of classical thought, undermined any fixed knowledge of the eternal verities. Renaissance writings display a heightened sensitivity not only to the influence of mood and emotion on one's perspective but also to the historical nature of thought and action surfacing in the temporal flow. It could not therefore be presupposed that sin blinded man's theological understanding because the impermanence of experience and of the observed world placed in doubt the objective certainty of such moral presuppositions.

The visual *arts witness to this turning away from the church's spiritual certainties. The 'realism' we associate with Renaissance art reflected the waning cultural confidence in traditional representations of the spiritual realm (what Vasari called the 'Greek' or iconic form of painting). Giotto's Virgin possessed an inner life, and the image of Venus by Botticelli or Titian helped liberate art from the conventions of medieval *iconography. Underscoring these new ambiguities in presenting degrees of spiritual enlightenment, artists looked to the physical world to provide the dimensions for the Christian story. The science of single-point perspective offered the means for portraying nature more realistically. It also acknowledged the viewpoint of both artist and viewer, illustrating their subjective investigation of the spatial and temporal bounds of existence. The personality of the artist became the medium and messenger of the Christian *myth, the viewer the active interpreter of the message. As befitted a culture increasingly engaged by the significance of the passing moment, composition was characterized by movement and dramatic tension.

Part of the difficulty in appreciating the Renaissance transformation of Christian thought is that there were so few Renaissance theologians. Both the style and substance of scholasticism fell into disrepute. Petrarch recounted how he physically threw an arrogant schoolman out of his house. It is not clear what disturbed him more, what the scholar said or how he said it. Heralding new avenues of religious discourse, Boccaccio proclaimed Dante a *theologus-poeta*, defending *poetry as a vital means of religious expression against the suspicions of the church. Not until Luther was there a theologian capable of drawing the appropriate doctrinal conclusions from the breakdown of the medieval cosmos. 'By faith alone' and 'every man a priest' are watchwords first intimated by the personal explorations of poets and humanists seeking existential meaning.

In contrast to the theological standpoint of the medieval clergy, Renaissance writers examined human experience from a psychological perspective. The distinction between the transcendent and immanent worlds was upheld, but the focus turned from cosmic order to human folly and restlessness, and hence to the insecurity of all knowledge. The Renaissance undercut medieval theological certainties through its appreciation of the subjective basis of asserting and evaluating truths about the meaning of existence. At the risk of further religious disintegration, the pathway was opened for a deeper epistemological and psychological investigation of Christianity. Christian myth remained the keynote of all Renaissance creative and critical expression. But the medieval image of secure, objective knowledge about spiritual truth capsized with the geocentric model of the cosmos, and the Renaissance searched for new proportions in tune with this shattering discovery.

See also MIDDLE AGES: AN OVERVIEW; PLATO AND PLATONISM; SIXTEENTH CENTURY: AN OVERVIEW. **Timothy Kircher**

Burckhardt, J., *The Civilization of the Renaissance in Italy* (many edns.).
Cassirer, E., *The Individuum and Cosmos in the Philosophy of the Renaissance* (1963).
Kristeller, P. O., *Renaissance Thought and the Arts*, 2nd edn. (1990).
Oberman, H. A. (ed.), *Itinerarium Italicum* (1975).
Panofsky, E., *Renaissance and Renascences in Western Art* (1960).
Trinkaus, C., *In Our Image and Likeness* (1970).

reproductive technology.

Christian thought on assisted reproductive technology (ART) tends to concentrate in two broad areas: (1) the implications of the understanding of *marriage, and (2) the status of the embryo.

1. With its reliance on *natural law, Roman Catholic teaching regards most ART as morally flawed by definition (*Donum Vitae*, 1987). The separation of procreation from sexual intercourse contradicts the God-given meaning of marriage. Similarly, ART's dependence on masturbation for semen collection fails to conform to the moral order. This negative view was already implicit in Catholic teaching on *contraception and, accordingly, is not shared by *Protestant commentators. These generally accept that ART is not in itself morally problematic but is, at best, a case of human co-operation with God in caring for couples experiencing the biblical curse of 'barrenness'. However, there is considerable caution among Protestants about the practical application of ART. Thus the common ground between Catholic and Protestant commentators is greater than might be expected if their perspectives on contraception were taken as a guide.

For example, all Christian traditions view with concern intrusions into the marital relationship. The mutuality and exclusivity of marriage is understood to be an image of the relation between Christ and the church, and also of the unity of the triune God. Some have argued that this image is defaced by medical intervention in procreation, especially when fertilization routinely takes place in the absence of the couple. More commonly church authorities condemn the use of donated sperm or oocytes as an introduction of a third party into the relationship. Surrogacy too is rejected on these grounds, in spite of its biblical precedents, and in addition to concerns over the commodification of the *child and the vulnerability of the parties involved to exploitation. Christian perspectives on marriage have also been challenged by questions of access to ART. The use of ART by unmarried heterosexual couples, lesbian couples, or single women has been controversial. An appeal to natural law as it applies to both procreation and children's rights excludes all these persons from treatment. However, many Christian commentators would accept the legitimacy of helping couples in a stable *de facto* relationship to conceive. Others, aware that lesbian couples and single women already make use of a self-administered form of artificial insemination, argue that to reduce their risk of infection they should be allowed access to medically supervised ART.

2. It is agreed that the embryo comes into existence as soon as the oocyte is fertilized. It is living, human and, in that it is genetically distinct from both parents, an individual. In Roman Catholic teaching, this settles a number of questions concerning the status of the embryo. From the moment of fertilization 'his rights as a *person must be recognized, among which in the first place is the inviolable right of every innocent human being to life'. The deliberate destruction of an embryo is the moral equivalent of *abortion which, in this view, is tantamount to murder. So experimentation on an embryo is unacceptable when it is not intended for the embryo's benefit or poses a risk to its viability. The disposal of embryos surplus to the patient's needs is also condemned. Even the disposal of an embryo found to be imperfectly formed, or carrying a genetic disorder such as cystic fibrosis, is regarded as immoral. Freezing embryos for future use is problematic too since the process risks damage to the embryo, denies it 'maternal shelter and gestation', and prolongs the period of its vulnerability to improper use or disposal.

Alternatively, other Christians argue that while an embryo exists at fertilization, 'conception' cannot be said properly to have taken place until the embryo is transferred to and successfully implants in the woman's uterus. That is, 'conception' takes place when the woman becomes pregnant. This approach resists the reduction of human identity to the genome, obscuring or even denying the inherently relational nature of human being and individuality. At the same time, it counteracts the alienation of the woman from the creation of a new life, which would render her little more than the 'owner' of something of which the embryo has a temporary need, namely, a womb. This definition of 'conception' morally distinguishes the embryo *in vitro* from the embryo *in utero*. The former is to be treated with deep respect, and its use or manipulation limited ethically and legally, but its moral status is not equivalent to that of a foetus. Accordingly, it may be considered unacceptable that a surplus of embryos be created specifically for use in research but experimentation may be permitted on unsuitable or unused embryos donated by the couple for that purpose. So too, the disposal of an embryo on the basis of sex may be prohibited but disposal on the ground that it carries a serious genetic disease would be legitimate. Women would not be obliged or encouraged to have a large number of embryos transferred just because they exist, but imperfect or surplus embryos would be disposed of. Embryo freezing would be permissible as a means of reducing the woman's exposure to the dangers of repeated superovulation and surgery. At the same time every effort would need to be made to estimate the numbers of embryos which she might need over a period of treatment, reducing the likelihood of there being unused embryos when she has finished.

The possible use of cloning in ART has excited much public fascination, but alarmist speculation should be tempered. Advances in the area of human cloning are likely to be slowed by increased ethical supervision of human experimentation, and especially by the prohibition of human cloning in most ART regulations. Christian attitudes to cloning are consistent with those in other areas of ART. Roman Catholic interpreters tend to regard the process as inherently immoral since it radically separates reproduction from sexual intercourse and poses extreme risks to the original embryo and any resultant clones. Protestants would have concerns about the possible misuse of the technology but would accept that cloning in itself is morally neutral. Christians are agreed that any cloned embryo must be accorded the same moral status as all other embryos. So if a couple had difficulty creating a single embryo, it might be acceptable to clone that embryo in the hope of increasing their chances of a pregnancy. But it would be unacceptable to use cloning to create a supply of embryos for experimentation, or to create a new person as a source of genetically identical 'spare parts' for an existing person.

Christian concern for infertile people has been expressed in the critique, especially by feminist scholars, of the traumatic and alienating process of medical treatment. However, the effort which has been expended on ART by Christian thinkers has not yet been matched by the sensitive and skilful investigation of the pastoral issues surrounding the experience of infertility itself.

See also FAMILY; FATHERHOOD; MOTHERHOOD; SEX AND SEXUALITY.

Andrew Dutney

Charlesworth, Max, *Bioethics in a Liberal Society* (1993), 63–106.

Church of Scotland Board of Social Responsibility, *Pre-Conceived Ideas: A Christian Perspective on IVF and Embryology* (1996).

Raymond, Janice G., *Women as Wombs: Reproductive Technologies and the Battle over Women's Freedom* (1993).

restorationism. This 19th-century movement to return to a simple united primitive Christianity gave rise to one more family of denominations. It was American, impatient of *tradition, anticlerical, anti-mystical, wanting nothing but the NT and 'the mind's assent to credible testimony'. If Christians would agree on this minimum then the *millennial dawn would come.

In 1804 the breakaway Springfield Presbytery in Kentucky, led by the revivalist Barton W. Stone, published its 'Last Will and Testament'. 'We will, that this body die, be dissolved, and sink into union with the Body of Christ at large ...' Simple Christians, its candidates for the ministry would henceforth 'obtain license from God to preach the simple Gospel'. In Pennsylvania, Thomas and Alexander Campbell, father and son, renounced any and every hierarchy to read the NT afresh. 'Open the New Testament as if mortal man had never seen it before.'

This unhistorical movement had historical precedents. The Campbells came from Scotland and perhaps owed something to Glasite theology (Glasites or Sandemanians were 18th-century biblicists, with agapes and foot-washing). Certainly they owed much to the philosopher John Locke, who had tried the same approach to the bible. Candid simplicity and *Enlightenment rationalism seem very close twins. 'Restorationist' Christianity rejected the psychic drama of revivalist *conversion. In its place, devised by Walter Scott, was a five-finger exercise, the 'objective' plan of *salvation: (1) have *faith—that is accept the proposition that 'Jesus is Christ'; (2) repent; (3) be *baptized for remission of *sins. Do these, and then (4) you will be *forgiven, and (5) receive the gift of the *Holy Spirit and salvation. There was no 'anxious bench' here for souls awaiting the experience of revival. Without soul-searching, and without intrusive questioning, an individual could do it all in a day. If we choose to be baptized, God is committed.

Pushed out of other churches, the groups from Kentucky and Pennsylvania merged in the 1830s. Their refusal of structure gave power to the articulate. Theirs was the first religious newspaper in the United States, and editors ruled. As the NT was their sole precedent, they stood out against such innovations as music in worship ('Non-Instrumentalist'), missionary associations, and Sunday schools.

At the beginning of the 21st century there are three main continuing strands of restorationism. The *Disciples of Christ are progressive, *ecumenical, a denomination rather than a sect, and open to members of other churches. The *Christian* churches (pronounced as in 'Christ') baptize by immersion, have some national boards, and rather hesitant ecumenism. The conservative Churches of Christ keep to local autonomy, with no co-operation with other churches and a literal biblicism. All would still agree that 'We speak where the scriptures speak; where they are silent, we are silent.' Taken together, they are the sixth largest tradition in the United States.   **Alistair Mason**

Beazley, George, C. (ed.), *The Christian Church (Disciples of Christ): An Interpretative Examination in the Cultural Context* (1973).

Harrell, David E., *Quest for a Christian America: The Disciples of Christ and American Society to 1866* (1966).

Hughes, R. T., and Allen C. L., *Illusions of Innocence: Protestant Primitivism in America 1630–1975* (1988).

Murch, James D., *Christians Only: A History of the Restoration Movement* (1962).

resurrection. The idea that *God would raise from the dead those who had borne faithful witness to him (and that he would raise the wicked in order to punish and humiliate them) does not appear in Jewish thought at all clearly before the Maccabean period, when it is closely connected with the theology of *martyrdom. Those who suffer for their fidelity to God must be vindicated; God will demonstrate that he is pleased with their sacrifice. Daniel 12: 2 is a familiar summary of this: 'And many of those who sleep in the dust of the earth shall awake, some to everlasting life, and some to shame and everlasting contempt.' Earlier references (Isa. 26: 19; Ezek. 37: 12) are more likely to be metaphorical expressions for the hope of the corporate restoration of *Israel.

By *Jesus' time, it seems that 'the resurrection' could be used as pretty well equivalent to 'the age to come' (e.g. Mark 12: 23 and parallels, Luke 14: 14). We know, from Josephus as well as the NT, that the Sadducees denied that there would be a resurrection, and this appears to have been not so much a denial of any kind of afterlife as a denial that the dead would or could return to the life of this earth. Although the language retains much of its connection with the hope of vindication at the end of the age, the usage recorded in the *gospels suggests that it had become somewhat weakened, to not much more than the hope of a particular kind of afterlife. The preaching of Jesus in the Synoptic Gospels has relatively little to say about resurrection as a theme in itself (as distinct from the general hope of God's intervention to bring in the *Kingdom); and this tends to bear out the argument that Jesus' proclamation was not to do with the end of time as such, but only with a decisive act of God inaugurating a new phase of *history. Some have gone further and denied that the original preaching of Jesus could have included any reference to the age to come in any clear or consistent way. But what is clear is that the narratives of the Resurrection of Jesus himself create a decisively new perspective on the whole subject. Jesus is not simply one of the righteous sufferers whose cause will be shown to be just at the end of *time; he has inaugurated a time 'beyond' the time of this world by rising from the dead, and exercises a present and powerful authority in the community of believers because he is alive in the presence of God (Matt. 28: 18; compare Rev. 1: 17–18). From his place in *heaven, he sends the *Holy Spirit to convey *authority to the *church (Luke 24: 48–9; Acts 1: 8). But it is important to note that this idea of the heavenly authority of Jesus would make little sense unless there were a clear belief that Jesus had been vindicated on earth, i.e. that he had in some way tangibly overcome physical *death. The modern tendency to separate the 'exaltation' and glorification of Jesus from the narratives of the empty tomb rather misses the point of what exaltation might have meant concretely for believers of the first Christian generation.

Hence the apparition stories should not be assumed to belong to a late or secondary stage of Resurrection belief. *Paul in 1 Corinthians, the earliest literary witness to a narrative tradition about appearances of the risen Jesus, plainly assumes that the risen Jesus is the one who was buried, and that his visibility to chosen believers—and unbelievers, like Paul himself on the Damascus road—demonstrates his victory over physical death. If Resurrection belief is part of the earliest stratum of Christian discourse (there are some who challenge this), it is hard to avoid the conclusion that Resurrection narrative, involving claims about the empty tomb, is equally primitive. And if Resurrection language is not primitive in Christianity, it is again hard to see why the very specific idea of rising from the dead should have been brought into focus rather than any of the less problematic options available (heavenly assumption, sleeping the sleep of the righteous martyr in expectation of the Resurrection, or whatever). What makes the theology of the risen life in the *New Testament so interesting is that it takes for granted that Jesus is a personal power and agency now active on earth through the Spirit, in a way not completely discontinuous with his historical life in Palestine, though no longer in straightforwardly visible form. It is a complex bundle of ideas, causing many conceptual headaches to writers like Paul, yet it is difficult to identify any strand of early Christian literature that works with different presuppositions—even where, as in the letter to the *Hebrews, the actual language of the Resurrection hardly appears. The narrative tradition is certainly confused: 1 Corinthians 15 suggests divergent accounts, disagreeing over whether *Peter or James the Lord's brother had been the first recipient of a visitation from the risen Lord (extra-canonical sources support the idea that some groups gave priority to James). The witness of the *women at the tomb in the gospels is, as has often been remarked, an odd and potentially weak point in a culture where the evidence of women was disregarded. The gospels are strikingly unclear and inconsistent about the location of the apparitions, *Matthew taking the disciples to Galilee and *Luke keeping them in Jerusalem. But it is noteworthy that efforts to identify a literary model or genre for the Resurrection stories have not been successful, and that their style is markedly different from the Passion narratives, with the latter's strong emphasis on the fulfilment of prophecy. Both the inconsistencies and the lack of clear models suggest that the events behind the narratives were odd enough and unexpected enough to generate new styles and idioms.

Within twenty years of the crucifixion of Jesus, Paul had developed a wide-ranging theological schema to which the Resurrection was central. The risen Christ is alive for ever in the presence of God, sovereign over the power of death: when we are baptized, we share Christ's death, and so pass beyond what death can do to us. His Resurrection assures our own, because to live in his fellowship and under his authority is to inhabit a realm in which death is, in effect, behind us. We have nothing to fear: the death that is a punishment for *sin in fallen humanity is overcome as we accept the 'death' of *baptism, identifying ourselves with Christ's obedient and self-giving death. Once this has been done, new life is ours which physical death cannot touch (Rom. 6: 3–23; 1 Cor. 15: 13–58; 2 Cor. 4: 10–18; etc.). The letters to the Ephesians and Colossians, which may not be from Paul's hand, take this further in emphasizing the idea that Christians are now in some sense with the risen and glorified Christ in heaven (e.g. Eph. 2: 5–6)—a theme also to be found in the Johannine literature (John 5: 19–29; 1 John 3: 14). In 2 Timothy 2: 18 is reflected the unease felt in some quarters about overemphasizing the 'already-achieved' aspect of Resurrection; but it is undeniable that it figures largely in the NT scheme overall, though without removing the concern for future consummation.

The early church maintained a robust belief in the materiality of resurrection for believers. The sacrament of the *Eucharist was understood by some (such as Ignatius of Antioch at the beginning of the 2nd century) as giving the flesh the capacity for everlasting life; those who proclaimed a strongly *dualist account of the human condition, in which the soul was the enduring element, came under frequent attack from Christian apologists. Some have seen in this (very plausibly) a reflection of concerns arising from martyrdom: the torn and degraded body of the martyr is the true spiritual identity of the holy person, their *holiness is inseparable from their bodily fate, so the body cannot be an embarrassing encumbrance needing to be got rid of in the world to come. Even *Origen at the beginning of the 3rd century, who stresses the independent life of the (pre-existent) spirit, concedes the necessity of speaking of a resurrection body, though he does not allow that it is or can be simply a reassemblage of the constituent atoms of the present earthly body. Throughout the *Middle Ages, the same concern is in evidence, in varying degrees of literalism. Bernard of Clairvaux in the 12th century argues that the soul after death is frustrated and incomplete until the last day when it will be reunited to the body; the full enjoyment of heaven depends on a material resurrection, even though the joys of heaven are not material joys. Thomas *Aquinas in the 13th century moves away from a strict commitment to resurrection as the reconstitution of the body's particles: continuity between now and then is assured not primarily by material identity but by continuity of form—by a risen body having the same dimensions and thus expressing the same imagined or understood whole. But neither he nor any other medieval writer abandons the belief that some kind of material continuity is essential to the understanding of resurrection, even though this is not strictly required by Thomist theology or other scholastic schemes.

The early modern period sees few substantial discussions of resurrection as a conceptual issue. This may be partly because early modern philosophy was far less embarrassed than medieval theology about locating essential identity in the mind and distinguishing sharply between the intellectual subject (free to determine its operations) and the material subject (bound by the laws of the material world). This prompts certain questions about how the Resurrection of Jesus is to be conceived. If bodies are invariably law-governed, *miracle in general is suspect; and if what matters and endures is the realm of freedom or spirit or mind, the resurrection that matters is a mental affair, either the survival of a spiritual force or the presence of the dead in the mind of others (whether a divine or a human other).

Reimarus (1694–1768) seems to have been the first modern scholar to deny outright the Resurrection of Jesus conceived as the rising of a body from the tomb (he revived the ancient anti-Christian polemical notion that the apostles deliberately claimed a miracle which they knew had not occurred). Throughout the 19th century, *German NT scholarship continued to wrestle with the possibilities, though more often ascribing the Resurrection stories to delusion than to fraud. As Strauss made abundantly clear in his *Life of Jesus Critically Examined* (1835), miracle could not be admitted into historical record, and claims for miraculous events had to be read in the light of the obsolete cultural conventions, the *mythic idioms, that conditioned the narratives of the pre-modern world. But only

in the 20th century do we find a theological argument against reliance upon the material historicity of the Resurrection of Jesus. Rudolf *Bultmann takes it for granted that modern consciousness cannot with integrity accept the miraculous; but the force of his argument against belief in the historicity of the empty tomb and the apparitions rests upon the profoundly *Lutheran suspicion of basing *faith on anything other than the act of God in the believer's heart, annihilating and recreating. If faith can look to 'proofs' in the material world, it becomes less than itself. The preaching of the Resurrection can be nothing other than the preaching of the *cross as the act of God and the presence of God—the cross unqualified by any hint of a reversal or 'happy ending'. Only so can the Resurrection faith truly be faith, faith in the God who refuses to provide worldly proof and reassurance. Although this proclamation is already compromised in the NT itself by appeals to witness and authority, what Paul in particular has to say about 'the word of the cross', along with John's interiorized version of the coming judgement, points to the necessity of deconstructing the gospel narratives of the Resurrection.

Bultmann's view continued to exercise enormous influence in European and American theology during the 1960s and early 1970s; but a counter-position had been forming as early as the late 1950s, associated especially with younger German theologians like Wolfhart *Pannenberg and Trutz Rendtorff. These writers emphasized that God's *revelation had to have a 'public' dimension, to be enacted in a sphere visible in principle to all human beings. History is therefore an essential dimension of revelation; and the Resurrection is not inaccessible to historical investigation. It can be confirmed or disproved by historical analysis—though Pannenberg is careful to say that, while this is true in principle, the materials may not in fact be there to provide a complete historical demonstration. In short, the Resurrection needs to be a historical fact, whether or not we can firmly establish it as such by the ordinary methods of history. This, it should be noted, is a reaction not only to Bultmann, but also to Karl *Barth, who had argued that the Resurrection was a 'real' event in time, but not the kind of event that historical science could deal with. As God's act, it is not amenable to investigation and cannot be available as a neutral and passive fact for apologetic; but because God has chosen the worldly and historical form of Jesus' identity, the Resurrection cannot be reduced to an internal experience—even the experience of the cross as embodying the act of God.

Debate in the English-speaking world was generally less sophisticated in the post-war period, though the polarization between those who saw the Resurrection as primarily an experience of the Christian community (even if caused by the action of God) and those who insisted on the factuality of the gospel record was no less sharp. Generally there were rather more scholars prepared to take seriously the empty tomb tradition than in Germany; but the overall balance, until recently, favoured a reticent agnosticism about this tradition rather than either a consistent scepticism or an apologetic defensiveness. In the 1990s, the ultra-radical approach of the 'Jesus Seminar' group of scholars in the USA tilted the balance towards a more negative assessment—though, despite the novelty of the textual and narrative analyses (some of which regard the entire Passion-Resurrection complex in the gospels as a relatively late formation: J. D. Crossan, Burton Mack), the underlying models of Resurrection faith simply reproduce the familiar idea that the narratives are a transcription into pseudo-historical terms of the inner *apocalyptic experience of the early community, or parts of it.

The 1990s saw more attention paid to the Resurrection narratives and the Resurrection faith by systematic theologians and philosophers. For some, the very elusiveness of historical certainty is significant as a reminder that the risen Jesus is not a static object or a possession for the church. For others, the revived interest in *Trinitarian theology allows a theology of the Resurrection in which Christ's rising is the sign of the eternal and indestructible relation between *Father and Son which is embodied in the life of Jesus and so must continue to be embodied beyond the physical death of Jesus. This fits well with a common contemporary theological concern about the salvation or transfiguration of the material world as a whole: taking their cue from theologians in the *Eastern Orthodox world, many have found the Resurrection stories suggestive of the destiny of the physical cosmos to be unified and 'sacramentalized' by the priesthood of redeemed humanity. And the significance of the gospel interest in the risen Jesus as calling the *apostles afresh has stimulated reflection on the Resurrection encounters as constitutive for the church's identity as a community summoned into life together.

Thus, by the end of the century systematic theology had developed a fuller investment in the empty tomb tradition than might have been the case earlier; but the world of professional NT scholarship remains deeply divided on this matter, with scepticism being more marked and extreme than previously. It is unlikely that this tension will be quickly resolved: both parties have posed serious methodological questions to each other. But it is still hard to see how a theological acceptance of the most sceptical accounts could do other than throw the emphasis in discourse about the Resurrection on to the interior world of the believer; and it is fair to ask whether that would be a rendering of belief in the Resurrection as the NT and tradition have seen it.

See also ESCHATOLOGY.   **Rowan Williams**

Avis, Paul (ed.), *The Resurrection of Jesus Christ* (1993).

Barton, Stephen, and Stanton, Graham, *Resurrection: Essays in Honour of Leslie Houlden* (1994).

Benoit, Pierre, *The Passion and Resurrection of Jesus Christ* (1969).

Bultmann, Rudolf, *New Testament and Mythology*, ed. S. M. Ogden (1984).

Bynum, Caroline Walker, *The Resurrection of the Body in Western Christianity, 200–1336* (1995).

Carnley, Peter, *The Structure of Resurrection Belief* (1987).

D'Costa, Gavin (ed.), *Resurrection Reconsidered* (1996).

Fuller, Reginald H., *The Formation of the Resurrection Narratives* (1971).

Künneth, Walther, *The Theology of the Resurrection* (1965).

Lampe, G. W. H., and MacKinnon, D. M., *The Resurrection: A Dialogue Between Two Cambridge Professors in a Secular Age* (1966).

Leon-Dufour, Xavier, *Resurrection and the Message of Easter* (1974).

Lüdemann, Gerd, *The Resurrection of Jesus: History, Experience, Theology* (1994).

McDonald, J. I. H., *The Resurrection: Narrative and Belief* (1989).

Martelet, Gustave, *The Risen Christ and the Eucharistic World* (1976).

Marxsen, Willi, *The Resurrection of Jesus of Nazareth* (1970).

Pannenberg, Wolfhart (ed.), *Revelation as History* (1969).

Perkins, Pheme, *Resurrection: New Testament Witness and Contemporary Reflection* (1984).

Torrance, Thomas F., *Space, Time and Resurrection* (1976).

Williams, Rowan, *Resurrection: Interpreting the Easter Gospel* (1982).

revelation. The theological concept of 'revelation' has featured in discussions since the *Enlightenment of the sources and standards of our knowledge of *God. The idea of revelation, however, is embedded in Hebrew and Christian Scriptures with their claims about the way in which God is apprehended by human beings. The Latin term *revelatio* (uncovering, laying bare) was used in the Vulgate to translate the Greek *apokalypsis* (revelation, disclosure). In the *New Testament, *apokalypsis* refers to the revealing by divine agency of matters relating to God and the *world, particularly the future and end of history (see APOCALYPTICISM). Thus the closing book of the NT canon was called the Apocalypse or *Revelation. Behind notions of revelation in the early church there stands the revealing activity of God in the Hebrew Scriptures. This takes place through a variety of media.

The creative activity of God is known through the order and beauty of nature (Ps. 19: 104), though whether this knowledge is attainable by all persons or only those within the *covenant community is disputed by interpreters. In Romans 1: 19–20 *Paul draws upon Stoic arguments that the divine *reason can be perceived in the natural cosmos. Later theologians claimed this as scriptural support for *natural theology, although its context here suggests that its function is intended to be negative in leaving humankind without excuse for its failure to obey the divine *law. The *Wisdom literature of the *Old Testament teaches that much about good practice and right living can be discerned from long experience. The insights of the wise are part of the moral order of God's *creation. These reflect the wisdom by which the world was created. This affirmation is balanced, however, by statements about the limitations of human discernment in *Job and Ecclesiastes. The fear of the Lord, moreover, is said to be the beginning of wisdom (Ps. 111: 10), thus suggesting that knowledge of the God of *Israel is a necessary condition of genuine wisdom. A more immediate form of revelation is found in the inspiration of the *prophets who are compelled to speak the word of God that comes to them. 'The Lord God has spoken; who can but prophesy?' (Amos 3: 8). Similarly, the law given on Sinai comes about through the initiative of God, typically in verbal form. Inspiration can also come through *visions and ecstatic utterances although these, like prophetic claims, have to be tested within the community of faith. In an extended discussion of the charismata in 1 Corinthians 12–14, Paul sets out tests such as the confession of Christ's lordship, the upbuilding of the *church, and the virtue of *love. Revelation is also mediated through *dreams and visions in *Daniel and the book of Revelation. In this apocalyptic genre, these forms of disclosure tend to reveal mysteries that govern the end-times.

These media of revelation can be found in the NT proclamation of Christ as the fullest revelation of God (see CHRISTOLOGY). *Jesus speaks with an authority as immediate as Moses or any of the prophets. He draws upon the ancient wisdom traditions of Israel. He is inspired by God's Spirit to *heal the sick. His teaching reveals *truths about the end-times. He is spoken of as the *Incarnation of God's wisdom and *Word—the rational principle—through whom all things were created, the first and the last, the beginning and end.

In the *Middle Ages, theologians came to distinguish two broad categories of theological knowledge, natural and revealed. *Augustine had tended to identify revelation with the inner divine illumination which attended the act of knowing. Thomas *Aquinas and his successors, in order to accommodate *Aristotelian *philosophy, made a sharper distinction between those truths that could be known through the exercise of natural *reason and those that required the revelation contained in scripture. Natural theology, as practised by the philosophically learned, could establish *inter alia* the existence of God, the *immortality of the *soul, and the freedom of the will. These truths were grasped outside the church by many of the great pagan philosophers. Revealed theology confirmed the findings of natural theology for the unlearned and those who have neither the time nor inclination for philosophy. More importantly, it also disclosed further truths unattainable by reason alone such as the doctrines of the *Trinity, the *person and work of Christ, and the *resurrection of the body. In this respect, *grace does not destroy nature but perfects what is known by unaided reason.

The form of revelation is here understood in terms of the propositions of scripture dictated by the *Holy Spirit to the writers. The veracity of scripture is confirmed by the confirmation of prophecy, the occurrence of *miracles, and the growth of the Christian church. Yet divine grace is required to comprehend that scripture is the Word of God. Revealed theology therefore requires both the preservation of the *bible and the infusion of divine grace to illumine the heart and mind of the believer.

At the time of the *Reformation the distinction between natural and revealed theology persisted. Both *Luther and *Calvin acknowledged the validity of natural theology but tended to minimize its significance. Their stress upon human *sinfulness and the necessity of divine grace led to a lower estimate of the powers of unaided reason to know God. None the less, our natural capacity to know God leaves us without excuse for the corruption and alienation of our minds. Calvin, at the beginning of the *Institutes*, describes the way in which we can know God through both nature and scripture. God's works, from the motion of the planets to the constitution of the human body, testify to the perfections of their creator. Yet this has not led to true piety. So infected are we with sin that even the greatest philosophers are mired in error and illusion. Their profanity knows no bounds. Thus we are wholly dependent upon the medium of scripture which is given to us by divine grace in our fallen condition.

The polemics of the Reformation and *Counter-Reformation were less concerned with the distinction between natural and revealed theology, than with the role of *tradition in accompanying scripture as divine revelation. Luther, appealing to the doctrine of *justification by *faith as he found it in the NT, sought to criticize the institutional church in which he had been nurtured. The Reformation thus took place by going over the heads of bishops and the pope, and appealing to scripture itself. Calvin argued that the church is built on the foundation of the *apostles and prophets who were inspired to write the bible. The church's only legitimate task therefore was to acknowledge the power and authority of scripture. Knowledge of scripture as the Word of God comes not from the church's teaching but from the secret testimony of the Spirit. As in Luther, the appeal is to the illumination of the individual by the Holy Spirit. The role of the church is bypassed.

On the Roman Catholic side the role of tradition was reaffirmed by the Council of *Trent. The revelation of God is contained both in the written books of scripture and in the unwritten traditions of the church. The authority of the tradition provides a way of controlling the interpretation of scripture and of preventing the undeniable fragmentation of Protestantism. The Catholic view, following Trent, tended to assume a two-source theory of revelation. An authoritative book required an authoritative interpreter. This was seen not so much as the church setting itself above scripture but as the only way provided by God for a sure declaration of the meaning of the bible.

More recent *ecumenical dialogue has brought about a greater convergence of positions. In a highly significant development, *Vatican II, in *Dei Verbum* on the Dogmatic Constitution of the Church, articulates the idea that there is only one source of scripture and tradition, namely Christ, whose teachings are handed down by the apostles through the *history of the church. Thus both scripture and tradition share a common 'divine well-spring' and are worthy of the same veneration. Vatican II insists upon the dynamic action of God in the life of the church, while continuing to prioritize the bible by its emphasis upon the centrality of Christ who completes and perfects revelation. The bible, however, may contain error and must be interpreted with the aid of critical scholarship and due attention to its diverse literary forms. On the Protestant side there is a growing recognition that the scriptures themselves are the product of tradition—one might even say different traditions. There is also a developing sense of the ecclesial nature of the reading of the bible. The hearing of the Word of God takes place within the faith, life, and *worship of the Christian community. It has an inescapably social nature.

Following the Reformation, greater attention was devoted to the concept of revelation as rationalism and the Enlightenment raised problems about our knowledge of God. While the traditional distinction between reason and revelation remained, greater weight was accorded the former. John Locke in *The Reasonableness of Christianity* attempted to defend the truths of revelation disclosed in scripture, but this apology rested on the claim that the reasonable person could assent to scripture on the basis of the miracles that were attested therein. These functioned as warrants for rational belief in scripture as divine revelation. The *deists were inclined to place their reliance on reason, regarding revelation as at best a 'republication' of truth, for the benefit of the unlearned, which could be known through the proper exercise of reason. *Kant tended to regard historical revelation as an illustration of truths knowable by universal reason. In his *Religion Within the Limits of Reason Alone* he reinterpreted the revealed doctrines of the Christian faith as aids to a moral understanding of religion which had already been established through the use of practical reason. Though *Hegel was able to assign a greater role to the doctrines of revealed theology such as the Trinity, he argued that revealed truths were only partial and provisional, and would be superseded in the evolution of consciousness by philosophical understanding.

With the growth of historical consciousness in the Enlightenment, questions also arose about the character of the bible. Through the application of the methods of *higher criticism, the texts were studied with reference to the circumstances surrounding their origin. The perspectives and positions of the writers assumed greater importance. The language, literature, and theology of the bible could be seen to reflect the evolution of the religion of Israel in the context of ancient Near-Eastern culture and the growth of the early church within Graeco-Roman civilization. The propositional character of revelation and the theory of the plenary inspiration of scripture were seriously doubted, particularly within *liberal Protestantism. The distinction between general and special revelation—already present in Augustine—came to be favoured, at least in Protestantism, over that of natural and revealed theology. Thus it was recognized that all revelation was dependent upon the influence of the divine upon the human spirit and that the special revelation attested by scripture confirmed and corrected what was known of God in other cultures, traditions, and philosophies.

*Schleiermacher discerned revelation within the distinctive experience of *redemption found in the Christian community. The bible and the church were the media of revelation but it was to be located within an experience of redemption deriving from the consciousness of Jesus imparted to the church. Revelation took not so much a propositional form but more the specifically Christian determination of the universal religious consciousness. In the school of Ritschl, revelation was located in the historical Jesus through moral and religious value judgements made by the church. This presupposed the ability of historical scholarship to demonstrate the uniqueness of the teaching of Jesus about the Kingdom of God. When this was challenged at the beginning of the *twentieth century by work—such as that of Weiss and Schweitzer—indicating the Jewish *eschatological context of Jesus' teaching, theology was forced to reconsider the nature of revelation in relationship to scripture and Christian faith. In this context of reappraisal, the concept of revelation came to the forefront of theological debate in the 20th century.

The dialectical theology that flourished from the 1920s stressed, partly in reaction to the cultural optimism of the late 19th century, the 'wholly other' character of revelation. The Word of God is not to be discerned through historical enquiry or ethical sensibility but in the act of faith through which the transcendent God is apprehended. God speaks through scripture but this is a miraculous event not determined by the inherent properties of the text so much as the divine decision to speak here and now through the proclamation of the biblical writers. In addressing us, God discloses the otherness of the divine character, while pronouncing a verdict both of judgement and forgiveness upon human endeavour. For Rudolf *Bultmann, the proclamation of Christ crucified, when taken up in the act of faith, became the occasion of a new human understanding. The Word of God thus enabled a new life of faith, hope, and love as opposed to revealing a set of cognitive propositions. To articulate this theology he appropriated the categories of *existentialist philosophy. For Karl *Barth, however, the Word of God apprehends the human subject in such a way as to resist reduction to categories of self-understanding. The event of revelation requires the appropriation of language to bear witness to the objectivity of God's act in Christ. Thus the words of scripture and the *dogmas of the church are necessary to the once-for-all action of God in Christ continuing to function as revelation here and now. Yet what is revealed is not information about God but God's own self mediated in this way. In this respect, the Trinity is central to Barth's doctrine of revelation. God is known through Christ by the work of the Holy Spirit. God thus becomes for us in the act of revelation who God is from all eternity. According to Barth, this exposes all forms of natural theology as idolatrous. God is revealed through the divine initiative in *reconciliation and not through any innate human capacity. In this theological climate, biblical theology in the mid-20th century tended to emphasize the distinctiveness of salvation history as a continuum of acts in which God is revealed. This was questioned, however, for its tendency to reduce the diversity of scriptural material to a univocal concept of divine self-revelation.

Other recent theological treatments of revelation include those of *Pannenberg and *Moltmann. Pannenberg, like Barth, locates revelation in the history within which God is revealed. This history, however, is to be described with reference to the non-theological disciplines and can only fully be disclosed at the eschaton. The significance of the resurrected Christ resides in his anticipation and proleptic revelation of the end of all things. In Moltmann, there is a similar stress upon the historical and eschatological character of the revelation of the triune God. The history in which the triune God is revealed is one of promise for the future. It is a history that is not set apart from secular realities but that unfolds in the midst of suffering, injustice, and death. This approach is developed within *liberation theology. Here the event of revelation requires a practical commitment to solidarity with the poor and oppressed. Right practice is an epistemological condition for true belief about revelation.

The concentration of Barth's doctrine of revelation upon the person and work of Christ promotes an understanding of the gospel story as those events by which the divine being determines itself. This has led in more recent theological discussion, in part through the influence of the Yale theologians, Hans Frei and George *Lindbeck, to an emphasis upon the narrative of scripture, and especially the story of Jesus as the one in whom God is reconciled to the world. The trajectory of revelation, moreover, begins with the history of Israel and extends to the life of the church and the formation of its scriptures. The narrative of scripture, as it is read in the church, is thus the medium by which God is revealed and human lives reconfigured.

The distinction between general and special revelation continues to be used to elucidate both the revelation of God throughout the *religions of the world and the particularity of the Incarnation. Something akin to this distinction is employed by Vatican II and Karl *Rahner to make sense of the way in which there can be genuine disclosure to people of other faiths while maintaining the normative status of claims about Christ as a unique and final disclosure of God's purpose for the world. The difficulty, however, is that so-called general or universal revelation is as contextual and particular in other religions as those Christian claims from which it is distinguished and to which it is subordinated. Different attempts to make greater sense of revelation in religions other than the Christian can be found in the recent work of John Hick and Keith Ward. Problems raised by religious plurality are likely to receive greater attention in future accounts of revelation than was the case in those of the leading theologians of the 20th century.

David A. S. Fergusson

Avis, Paul (ed.), *Divine Revelation* (1997).
Baillie, John, *The Idea of Revelation in Recent Thought* (1956).
Barth, Karl, *Church Dogmatics*, I/1 (1956).
Fackre, Gabriel, *The Doctrine of Revelation* (1997).
Gilson, Étienne, *Reason and Revelation in the Middle Ages* (1938).

Gunton, Colin, *A Brief Theology of Revelation* (1995).
Pannenberg, Wolfhart, *Systematic Theology* (1991), i.
Thiemann, Ronald, *Revelation and Theology* (1985).
Ward, Keith, *Religion and Revelation* (1994).

Revelation, book of.

The book opens with the words 'apocalypse of Jesus Christ', the only time the word *apocalypse is used, though elsewhere in the book what is written is described as *prophecy. The contents of the book have parallels in the *eschatological material in the gospels and epistles and, less often noted, the concern with mystery and *revelation in Colossians and Ephesians and the cosmology of the Epistle to the *Hebrews. Its apocalyptic form is unique in the NT and has many distinctive features which cannot be paralleled in related contemporary Jewish literature, though the claim to revelation echoes those made in other parts of both early Christian and Jewish texts.

The first three chapters of Revelation describe the call of John the seer on the isle of Patmos. This is followed by a series of letters to the *angels of the seven churches in Asia Minor in which the Son of Man offers reproof and encouragement. A completely different dimension of John's visionary experience begins in chapter 4, when a door is opened for the seer to witness the acknowledgement of God's sovereignty in *heaven by the heavenly host. The scene, similar in some ways to that found in contemporary Jewish texts, is transformed with the appearance of a Lamb 'standing as though it had been slain', who then receives worship and permission to open the sealed scroll embodying the eternal purposes of God. The opening of the seals which follows the vindication of the slaughtered lamb reveals a scene of devastation resolved only with the establishment of divine justice on earth in chs. 20–2 (see SHEEP AND SHEPHERDS). It is only then that the resolution of the contrary states of heaven and earth, good and evil, takes place in the new *Jerusalem when God dwells on earth with human beings.

The book of Revelation has been interpreted in several ways. First, it has been treated as a prediction of the end of the world, having no connection with present ecclesiastical and political realities. Secondly, the *visions are related to their ancient, 1st-century context. This interpretative approach is concerned with the meaning for the original author and readers and with the need to decipher the complex *symbolism and its relationship to the particular circumstances in which Christians in late 1st-century Asia Minor found themselves. Thirdly, the images are regarded as an *allegory of the struggles facing the individual soul in its quest for God. Finally, there is an application of the text to present realities, whether human or divine, in which the book is used as a lens through which to view contemporary *history. In it the Apocalypse becomes a gateway to a greater understanding of reality, both divine and human, spiritual and political, which includes, but transcends, that offered by the human senses. This way of using the text of the book of Revelation ceases to be solely about the eschaton and becomes a means of interpreting every age of human existence. William *Blake's biblical *hermeneutics offer a particularly good example of such an appropriation of the book.

The book has been used in a variety of ways in the history of the church. In the earliest period Revelation was closely linked with eschatology and a this-worldly hope for the coming of God's kingdom (Justin, *Dialogue with Trypho*; *Irenaeus, *Adv. haer.*). The earliest extant commentary, by Victorinus of Pettau, writing about the beginning of the 4th century, follows in this tradition, though there is also evidence of the application of the text to the present ecclesiastical and political situation. The interpretative approach of Tyconius (late 4th century), which had a profound influence on the mature *Augustine, is a reading that does not consign its message solely to the eschatological future. Augustine's exegesis held sway for much of the next five hundred years, but was challenged by the influential reading by Joachim of Fiore (late 12th century), who broke from the Augustinian tradition, finding eschatological significance in Revelation as a message for his own day. In particular, he suggested that his time was the all-important penultimate period, the time of Antichrist and spiritual renewal. Joachim's historical reading pervaded emerging *Franciscan spirituality and was to influence a variety of *millenarian movements in the later *Middle Ages and beyond.

In the first edition of his German Bible *Luther outlined his reasons for the relegation of the book to a subordinate place within the canon of the NT because it did not adequately preach Christ. Revelation was an important ingredient in the establishment of the millennialist commonwealth in the city of Münster, an event which led to considerable suspicion of the book, evident in the restrictions placed on reading from it. There continued to be a rich tradition of interpretation in which the careful exposition of the book was carried out in a more measured and less heated atmosphere. Most prominent here was Joseph Mede (1586–1638), whose work had enormous influence on subsequent generations of interpreters. Writers and artists, among them Newton, *Coleridge, and Blake for example, turned to Revelation. The rise of historical scholarship led to a different perspective in which the book's meaning was usually related to the circumstances of John's own day. The use of the Apocalypse as a repository of eschatological prophecies was a feature of interpretation from the earliest days, and is very much part of a growing trend in modern, fundamentalist interpretation, in which the book is regarded as unfulfilled prophecy and combined with other scriptural passages to form a horrific eschatological metanarrative.

Even when it is not the actual subject of a commentary, Revelation's influence on Christian theology has been immense. The framework of Augustine's *City of God*, for example, one of the seminal texts of Christian doctrine, is based on the apocalyptic *dualism of Revelation. More recently, Karl *Barth's commentary on the Epistle to the *Romans is dominated by an apocalyptic perspective. Contemporary with Barth and equally concerned with the eschatological inheritance of the Jewish tradition, but with a very different assessment of its significance, Ernst Bloch was committed to the rehabilitation of that millenarian, apocalyptic inheritance on the fringes of orthodox Christianity. Modern *political theology owes a great debt to Bloch's appropriation of the Christian this-worldly apocalyptic tradition. In *liberation theology the book of Revelation offers hope but also stimulates resistance. It encourages those on the margins of society not to remain content with the world as it is nor to accept the ideology of the dominant powers as the ultimate point of reference for reality.

The variety of approaches will come as no surprise to any reader of this tantalizing and bewildering book. Most of them seek to reduce its chaotic, polyvalent imagery to some kind of order and thereby tame it. The problem it poses is that the exercise of imagination conflicts with that desire for an ordered, systematic presentation that lies at the heart of so much theology. As a result of reading Revelation, image and *metaphor can, if one allows them to do so, jar, awaken, and transform action as well as attitudes. Revelation is a book which requires of its readers not so much that they interpret it, as that they allow it to affect them and summon them to the life of prophetic witness that was the vocation of John the seer.   **Christopher Rowland**

Boyer, P., *When Time Shall Be No More: Prophecy Belief in Modern American Culture* (1992).

Bull, M., *Apocalypse Theory* (1995).

Burdon, C., *Apocalypse Unravelling: The Apocalypse in England 1700–1834* (1997).

Cohn, N., *The Pursuit of the Millennium* (1957).

Emmerson, R., and McGinn, B., *The Apocalypse in the Middle Ages* (1992).

Hill, C., *The English Bible and the Seventeenth Century Revolution* (1993).

Rowland, C., *The Open Heaven* (1982).

—— *Radical Christianity* (1988).

—— *Revelation* (1998).

Wainwright, A., *Mysterious Apocalypse* (1993).

revivalism, narrowly defined, is the use of special techniques to awaken interest in religion. More broadly, it embraces those Christian movements whose thought-life and culture honour this formalized pursuit of spiritual renewal. Its distinguishing elements include charismatic evangelists, mass audiences, bible-based *preaching, a gospel of repentance, the elevation of heart and experience over head and theology, and the proliferation of dramatic, often physical, experiences of *conversion. Revivalism has been primarily, but not exclusively, a feature of evangelical *Protestant movements; its roots and characteristic expressions are *North American, but the phenomenon has spread through the globalizing of Anglo-American *evangelicalism. For Christians it has continued to raise questions about divine agency, the role of human instrumentality, and the psychological, sociological, and teleological role of revival in the late-modern world. Concerns over showmanship, evanescence, the manipulation of the vulnerable, questionable spiritual outcomes, and even charlatanism jostle alongside apprehensions of the *Holy Spirit and God's power.

Historians of revivalism generally identify the turn of the *nineteenth century as the era in which the 'instrumentalist' thought-mould of the modern phenomenon was set. If they have tended to overestimate the extent to which Jonathan *Edwards, George Whitefield, and the other leaders of the 18th-century transatlantic 'awakenings' interpreted revivals as miraculous and surprising works of God beyond human contrivance, they are right to highlight Americans' increasingly self-conscious promotion of revivals in the decades after the Revolution. Following the removal of state support, voluntarist churches turned to revivalism as their means of institution-building. *Hellfire preaching, raw emotion, and conversions afflicting the whole neuromuscular system characterized frontier 'camp meetings' in the early 1800s. *Methodists, with their *Arminian emphasis on human enterprise, did more than any others during the second Great Awakening (*c.*1800–*c.*1840) to add the 'ism' to revival and to develop, institutionalize, and market new means of mass conversion: 'protracted meetings', full-time evangelists, and 'anxious benches'. The high priest of the new measures was the charismatic *Presbyterian, Charles Grandison Finney. He, better than any of his generation, faced down the critics of 'worked-up' revivals and 'self-conversionism', those afraid that he had dismissed the Holy Spirit in the cosmic battle to save souls. The classic statement of instrumentalist thought is Finney's technical handbook, *Lectures on Revivals of Religion*.

Since Finney's heyday a host of evangelists have reshaped revivalist practice, but the core of instrumentalist thought has survived unscathed. Trust in human enterprise and organizational ingenuity, and skill in group psychology, have persisted. Revivalists have adapted technological change to religious ends: Finney and his contemporaries brilliantly exploited the new steam press; Dwight L. Moody later adapted revivals to innovations in business practice, consumerism, and popular entertainment; the electronic media have energized revivalists from Aimee Semple McPherson in the 1920s to Oral Roberts, Jerry Falwell, and Pat Robertson in recent decades; Billy Graham led the way in intercontinental satellite link-ups. Revivalist responses to the age of supersonic travel include John Arnott's Toronto Airport Christian Fellowship, to which hundreds of thousands of pilgrims have travelled since the first manifestations of the 'Toronto Blessing' in 1994. That the marks of the Blessing bear a striking resemblance to those of the western revivals two centuries earlier—including large numbers 'slain in the Spirit', groaning, roaring, barking, or laughing unconstrainedly—serves to underscore the instrumentalist linkages between revivalism past and present, as well as its emotional power.

In the modern world revivalism has become almost synonymous with *'fundamentalism', an umbrella term for a movement much more inclusive, even ecumenical, than the early 20th-century conservative *Calvinists who defended a creed of the same name. The present dynamic force, which claims a membership of some 400 million worldwide, embraces Southern *Baptists, *charismatics, and, most significant of all, the burgeoning *Pentecostal movement. Pentecostal revivalism accommodates the exercising of miraculous gifts of the Spirit, including *healing, speaking in tongues, and *prophecy. This in particular has made fundamentalism a potent expansionary force with a global presence, whether in Paul Yonggi Cho's mega-churches of Korea, or the brick and metal tabernacles of Central America and sub-Saharan Africa, or the house churches of Britain and Europe. Religious syncretism may be evident in some of the movements, but the core ingredients of American revivalism continue to characterize the worldwide movement: stress on a born-again relationship with Jesus; the obligation to evangelize; faith in an inerrant bible; strict personal discipline; social conservatism; and, very commonly, *adventist, *millennialist, and *dispensationalist expectations founded on a conviction of God's personal intervention in history.

The history and geography of revivalism suggest a phenomenon closely linked to industrialization and modernization, and to the globalizing of America's culture and economy. On one reading, revivalism has been a way of resisting *modernity. Early transatlantic Methodists sought in *enthusiastic religion a warmth and social network, and an escape from uprootedness, market upheaval, and an emerging factory system. Twentieth-century revivalists have commonly been self-conscious purveyors of an 'old-time religion'. Creationists have resisted *evolutionary theory. The term 'fundamentalism' implies a celebration of cultural origins, and a conservative desire to protect one's identity in the face of potentially overwhelming secular change. The individual's sense of empowerment, central to successful revivalism, provides an anchorage in a plural, relativist world. But neither has revivalism been slow to seize the economic opportunities presented by modern *capitalism. Evangelists have taught self-control, self-discipline, and self-improvement, all adaptive to the capitalist order; the late 19th-century gospel of wealth has its late 20th-century counterpart in an evangel of *prosperity and material rewards on earth; businessmen's prayer meetings illustrate that revivalism has a middle-class and socially aspirant constituency, and is not simply a survival strategy for the poor.

Views differ on the future of revivalism in a diverse, postmodern, syncretist world. Will increasingly variegated localism flourish at the expense of consolidation, and ecumenical music be drowned out by the tunes of individual experience? If revivalism is about power—divine and human—in whose interests and at whose expense will it be exercised? Need a force which in its earlier manifestations provided the moral energy for the abolitionist assault on *slavery be located permanently amongst a cluster of conservative social and political values?   **Richard Carwardine**

Brouwer, S., Gifford, P., and Rose, S. D., *Exporting the American Gospel: Global Christian Fundamentalism* (1996).

Chevreau, Guy, *Catch the Fire. The Toronto Blessing: An Experience of Renewal and Revival* (1994).

Cox, H., *Fire from Heaven: The Rise of Pentecostal Spirituality and the Reshaping of Religion in the Twenty-First Century* (1994).

McLoughlin, W. G., *Modern Revivalism: Charles Grandison Finney to Billy Graham* (1959).

——*Revivals, Awakenings, and Reform: An Essay on Religion and Social Change in America, 1607–1977* (1978).

Percy, M. P., *Words, Wonders and Power: Understanding Contemporary Christian Fundamentalism and Revivalism* (1996).

revolution. Christian support for a political revolution in any state indicates an ultimate crisis in church–state relations. It was never Christian teaching that a government propagating religious or moral ideals hostile to Christianity could, for that reason, be overthrown. The *church was indeed born in just such conditions and decided its own political references in relation to them. The first Christians appear to have had no distinctive political views, and it is as well to remind modern Christians, who are liable to attribute many basic ideas of *freedom to the influence of Christianity, that the early fathers borrowed most of their teaching in this area from the Stoic philosophers. They agreed with Cicero and Seneca in accepting the *authority of *natural law as a test for the legitimacy of government, and that the state must promote *justice and guarantee the conditions in which moral order could be established. It was from the Stoics, too, that they adopted the concept of fundamental human equality—a notion not to be found in the Jewish scriptural tradition. This was the context in which the references of *Paul to civil obedience were received and developed. 'Let every soul be subject to the higher powers. For there is no power but of God: the powers that be are ordained of God,' he declared in Romans 13. *Obedience to civil authority was thus conceived as a duty imposed by God, and obedience was due to the *office* of ruler not to *individual* rulers, whatever their personal moral failings. A corrupt ruler should still be obeyed. It was Pope Gregory I, in the 6th century, who stressed the importance of Christian passive

obedience in his *Pastoral Rule*; for even rulers who were personally wicked could still be the managers of a state structure which preserved order. Government was a remedy for human sin; it was the inherent moral frailty of men and women that required the coercive power of the state to minimize the incidence of anarchy in human affairs. Early Christianity, like Greek thought, was haunted by the fear of primordial chaos returning to the earth.

There was, however, on the matter of civil obedience, one crucial difference between the thinking of the Christians of the first centuries and that of the Stoics. For the Romans as for the Greeks, there could be no real problem of divided loyalty. The Roman civil religion was quite compatible with simultaneous espousal by individuals of all manner of religious cults, and, provided prior acknowledgement was made of the essential divinity of the state, embodied in the person of the emperor, the question of religious *conscience was simply inapplicable. But Christians did not believe that the state was owed *unlimited* obedience. For them, political authority represented the divine will but the state itself was not divine, nor did divinity attach to its magistrates. Christians were members of a spiritual *Kingdom whose claims were exclusive. From the beginning, therefore, Christianity distinguished between temporalities and spiritualities: a distinction unknown to Roman public life. The celebrated solution of *Augustine, in the 5th century, to this difficulty—which had practical implications, since Christians had already been persecuted before the conversion of the empire precisely for their refusal to accept the divinity of the state—was the vision of the two cities. All government, Augustine pointed out, was a remedy for *sin and so was provided by God, but humans were citizens of earthly and of heavenly cities which were not visibly separate. Obedience was due to both within their own spheres. But the problem of what authority, and what set of guidelines, should determine the demarcation of jurisdiction between the two cities remained. In introducing the separation of church and state, Christianity had inaugurated a debate that was intellectually fruitful in western tradition but at the practical level left many issues unresolved.

The broad teaching of acceptance of government and obedience to it, as part of God's providential plan for human life, has been consistently maintained within the historic churches. When half Christendom disappeared under the rule of *Islam in the 7th century, the general response of Christian authorities was to regard obedience to the alien political order as a religious duty. In the *Byzantine empire (or what remained of it), despite the exalted position accorded to the emperor in the determination of Christian practice, the temporal and the spiritual jurisdictions remained ultimately separate. In the Latin West, Pope Gelasius' 5th-century definition of 'the Two Swords', of church and state each functioning within legitimate spheres, remained for centuries the guiding principle of Christian civil obedience. In such a network of understanding the occasions for Christians to contemplate revolution were indeed sparingly distributed. The state, anyway, had very circumscribed purposes, and its affairs were conducted by a small class of people, whether in the court circles of Byzantium or the standing feudal host of the western Holy Roman Empire. Revolution, as a concept, was hardly likely to achieve ideological coherence when the fate of government turned on power conflicts between courtiers or great families. It was, significantly, in relation to the prosecution of *warfare that codes of conduct began to define legitimate and illegitimate uses of force, and therefore, by logical extension, to define the legitimacy of action when a government was in crisis. The 'Just War' theories produced limitations to acceptable actions by authority.

All Christians agreed that usurpers could be overthrown, and so could tyrants. The problem was the absence of an agreed definition of what constituted tyranny. The religious conflicts associated with the *Reformation in Western Europe projected the problem in sharp focus. They also witnessed a general acceptance of the principle—most lucidly argued in the Huguenot treatise of 1579, the *Vindiciae contra Tyrannos*—that tyranny can be distinguished from ordinary government by systematic rule without reference to *law, justice, or piety. To be tyrannical, an evil ruler's actions had to be sustained and habitual. Such a person could be overthrown. The right of revolution belonged to the community as such, and not to any individual or group of people, however numerous they might be. The area of definition therefore moved to the organic concept of a 'community', and to the means of deciding what constitutes the institutional expression of a people's identity. Like the means of determining which ruler is merely corrupt and which is guilty of sustained abuse of power, the problem of deciding what set of civic arrangements adequately incorporates 'the community' itself posits many possibilities of controversy and conflict. And so it has remained. Revolutions occur precisely in those conditions in which there is no consensus about the degree of departure from a previously accepted practice of political virtue.

Christian teaching on the right of rebellion against unjust rulers has been extremely stable; for Aquinas not only a right but a duty, it has been developed in varying circumstances but has produced few particularly radical variations. English *Protestant Dissent, for example, has had a tradition, formulated in reference to its critique of the established Church of England, of scepticism about the notion that political submission is a divine obligation. The Civil War of the *seventeenth century saw the flowering of a number of sects whose radicalism in this regard helped to sustain this tradition. Yet even then the right of rebellion was expressed in terms of a classic definition of tyranny: the king was held to be in violation of his obligations to the people. Religious arguments used to justify the revolt of the thirteen *North American colonies in the 1770s were the same, using the language of contract to describe the nature of the obligation that the civil authority had violated.

It has been changes in the nature of the state, rather than changes of religious thought, that have redefined the issue of revolution in modern times. The collectivist state is expected by its citizens to provide an enormously enhanced range of services and to take responsibility for huge areas of public life. The tests by which it may be judged to have failed in these obligations are accordingly also greatly expanded in number and precision. If a man was poor in traditional society it was regarded as a matter of personal misfortune: he would be cared for by those with a vocation to do so. If a man is poor in the western world today, people conclude that the state is unjust unless it is active in palliative measures. The tests by which a tyranny is recognized have been multiplied. They are applied within the exercise of a mass *democracy that, at any rate in constitutional theory, allows popular and therefore supposedly more authentic tests for the authority of justice to be determined.

Democracy, in this sense, has made revolution more difficult to justify, because the people can be said to have consented to the political arrangements; in another sense, however, revolution has become easier to envisage because weight of numbers, informed by popular education, may sometimes be interpreted as legitimately able to justify rebellion against a government that fails to follow public opinion on some particular matter. The *twentieth century has shown that some truly tyrannous governments have come into existence with democratic assent: fascism in the 1930s rested on mass appeal. Arguments for revolution have increasingly turned on recognizing the existence of such concepts as the *Marxist notions of false consciousness, institutionalized violence, and formal freedoms. Some exponents of actual armed struggle against class society found an identification between Christian teaching and Marxist critiques of the existing order, especially in *Latin American countries in the 1960s and 1970s. Hence the seeds of *liberation theology. In *Africa the politics of race equality echoed the same ideals in a different context, with surviving practices of 'colonialism' replacing economic exploitation by transnational corporations as the springs of oppression. Even in those circumstances, however, traditional teaching about the right to rebel was in general respected, and in each case the right to rebel was argued within very precise conditions. Thus the careful and recognizably traditional points made in, for example, Bishop Donal Lamont's *Speech from the Dock* (1977) in which the white government of former Rhodesia was scrutinized for failing some conventional tests of political legitimacy. Some other Christians, of course, were not persuaded by such appeals, as is always the case in the everlastingly divisive matter of identifying tyranny. In the Republic of South Africa the right of rebellion against the *apartheid state was asserted by some but not conceded by most Christian opponents of the government. That government certainly sustained institutional injustices against the majority of its own citizens, and was guilty of acts of institutionalized oppression, but overall it maintained order and moral stability and so fell short of actual tyranny. That was the opinion of Archbishop Desmond Tutu, and it more or less faithfully represented the view the first Christians had of the Roman imperial power.

The modern state is also a *secular state, and it is a feature of Christian attitudes to revolution today that they have followed secular moral ideals when evaluating the detailed behaviour of rulers. Christians have, for example, identified modern human rights ideology as essentially Christian, just as they have embraced political democracy as a distinctively Christian form of government. When modern Christians acclaim the right of rebellion they are likely to express themselves in the language of human rights rather than in that of Paul. It is in modern Islamic and *Hindu fundamentalism that the right of revolution is now proclaimed for explicitly religious purposes.

See also BLACK THEOLOGY; POLITICAL THEOLOGY.

Edward Norman

Carlyle, R. W. and A. J., *A History of Medieval Political Theory in the West* (6 vols.; 1903–36).

Cone, J. M., *God of the Oppressed* (1975).

Davies, J. G., *Christians, Politics, and Violent Revolution* (1976).

Force in the Modern World, GS 168, A Document Prepared by the Board for Social Responsibility for the General Synod of the Church of England (1973).

Gutiérrez, G., *A Theology of Liberation* (1974).

Huddleston, T., *Naught for your Comfort* (1956).

Kee, A. (ed.), *A Reader in Political Theology* (1974).

Lamont, D., *Speech from the Dock* (1977).

Piediscalzi, N., and Thobaben, R. G. (eds.), *Three Worlds of Christian–Marxist Encounters* (1985).

Populorum Progressio, Encyclical Letter of Pope Paul VI (1967).

Ratzinger, J., *Church, Ecumenism, and Politics: New Essays in Ecclesiology* (1988).

Torres, C., *Priest and Revolutionary: The Text of his Political Programme and of his Messages to the Colombian People* (1968).

rhetoric, a term sometimes used pejoratively to refer to empty language ('mere rhetoric') or to an excessively ornamental style, occasionally used to designate any form of discourse whatsoever. In the ancient world, however, it referred to the art of persuasion, primarily spoken but also written. The Sophists introduced it as a means of communication that might be as effective as epic poetry; later, *Aristotle defined it as 'the faculty of discovering, in the particular case, the available means of persuasion' (*Rhetoric*, 1355^{b}25). Rhetoric encouraged comparative judgements about the effectiveness of particular arguments in moving audiences to action in contingent matters (matters that 'might be otherwise'). Although *Plato criticized it as a mere knack (*Gorgias*, 463a), rhetoric had a profound impact in the *Hellenistic and early Roman eras. It became the standard pedagogical programme in the schools; most educated people would have been exposed to the varying roles of speaker, audience, and argument, and to the use of commonplaces (*topoi*) and figures (*tropoi*).

The NT writers clearly manifest rhetorical influences, employing commonplaces and tropes, and attending to the specificity of their audiences ('I have become all things to all people,' says *Paul, 'that I might by all means save some', 1 Cor. 9: 22). The fathers knew the art of persuasion, as did their opponents; *Origen, in his *Contra Celsum*, demonstrates both. The great 4th-century writers employed tropes and argumentative forms that had been well rehearsed in the schools; obvious examples include the Cappadocians (see GREEK THEOLOGY) and *Augustine, whose *De doctrina Christiana* counsels the appropriation of rhetorical techniques in the service of the gospel.

Christians recognized that their mission ('Go therefore and make disciples of all nations', Matt. 28: 19) required them to speak and write persuasively; hence, rhetoric was a natural ally. It helped preachers and theologians to assess audiences, to weigh alternative argumentative forms, and to speak and write with clarity, grace, and wit. Like advocates in the law courts and Roman senators, Christians sought to *move* their audiences, asking them not just to *think* differently, but to *act* differently (and indeed, to reorder their entire lives). Such appeals are the natural subject-matter of rhetoric, which is thus closely linked with moral philosophy; Aristotle's *Rhetoric* parallels his *Nicomachean Ethics*, while Cicero and Quintilian understood rhetoric as formative for the life of the citizen-orator.

The art of rhetoric thus shaped Christian *preaching and polemic from the very beginning and its influence continued into the medieval and Reformation eras. Although its significance waned with the rise of other approaches to argument (such as 'text and commentary' and scholastic disputation), it significantly shaped the work of writers such as Bonaventure, *Luther, and *Calvin. Rhet-

oric flourished in the *Renaissance (especially in Italian humanism), but until then it underwent little new theoretical development; when Peter Ramus (1515–72) issued his rationalistic attacks on rhetoric, his primary objects of scorn were still Cicero and Quintilian. *Enlightenment rationalism dismissed rhetoric as excessively focused on contingent matters and the emotions, and thus likely to lead to deception and error.

Critiques of rationalism gave new life to rhetorical theory. John Henry *Newman argued that persuasion takes place not through the intellect alone, but by the movement of feeling and the will as well; and not through sheer deduction, but the 'cumulation of probabilities'. Newman's *Essay in Aid of a Grammar of Assent* (1870) is an important post-Enlightenment retrieval of classical rhetorical insights. Friedrich *Nietzsche lectured briefly on classical rhetoric, but is better known as a master of its practice in deconstructing various universalizing pretensions (including those of much Enlightenment theology). In the 20th century, rhetoric re-entered the academy, especially in the United States, in departments of English, Speech, and Communication Studies. Recent influential theorists include Kenneth Burke, Chaïm Perelman, and Brian Vickers, whose magisterial *In Defense of Rhetoric* (1988) is an excellent resource.

Biblical scholars have increasingly employed rhetorical categories, reconstructing hypothetical audiences and examining texts for their use of commonplaces and tropes. An important early work in this field was George Kennedy's *New Testament Interpretation through Rhetorical Criticism* (1984). This approach continues to have its devotees, but has had less impact than, for example, literary criticism, perhaps because of its necessarily speculative hypotheses (concerning, for example, a text's original audience, or an ancient audience's evaluation of a speaker's character).

More significant, perhaps, is the study of rhetoric as formative for various Christian thinkers. Tertullian, Gregory Nazianzen, John Chrysostom, and Augustine have received book-length treatment, as have Calvin, Newman, and Karl *Barth. Most recently, rhetoric has been promoted as a methodological framework for Christian *theology, based on the claim that theology does not rely on universally recognized first principles (as do, for example, logic and lower-order mathematics). Moreover, many objects of theological study are not empirical and cannot be verified to the satisfaction of all parties. Hence, theology bears fewer similarities to analytical enterprises (such as logic) than it does to such activities as politics, *law, and even *poetry. In some quarters rhetoric has again become a focus in theological education.

Rhetoric's adaptability is attested by its use both as a critical tool in deconstructing theological edifices, and as a means of setting the traditional claims of the faith in a brighter and more convincing light. As Aristotle and Augustine both emphasized, the art of rhetoric is itself indifferent; its value depends on the ends to which it is employed. Whatever their theological position, Christians throughout history have sought to persuade their audiences, and rhetoric has helped them do so. Indeed, in describing the goals of theology, Augustine adopted a commonplace from Roman rhetoric: 'to teach, to delight, and to move' (*De doct. Chr.* 4. 27[74]).

David S. Cunningham

Chopp, Rebecca S., *The Power to Speak: Feminism, Language, God* (1989).

Cunningham, David S., *Faithful Persuasion: In Aid of a Rhetoric of Christian Theology* (1991).

Jones, Serene, *Calvin and the Rhetoric of Piety* (1995).

Jost, Walter, *Rhetorical Thought in John Henry Newman* (1989).

Kinneavy, James L., *Greek Rhetorical Origins of Christian Faith* (1987).

Norris, Frederick W. (ed.), *Faith Gives Fullness to Reasoning: The Five Theological Orations of Gregory Nazianzen* (1991).

Ricœur, Paul (1913–),

French Protestant *philosopher and academic. His religious thought has been influenced by *Barth, Jaspers, and Marcel. After a period as a prisoner-of-war in a German camp, Ricœur taught at various French universities, most notably the Sorbonne and Nanterre. From 1980 he was an emeritus professor of the University of Chicago. Profoundly marked by the violence and totalitarianism of the contemporary world, his commitment to social and political *justice has remained constant. A prolific writer and indefatigable lecturer, he practises mediation with the great philosophers of the past and dialogue with his contemporaries. One of the foremost phenomenologists, with major works on free will, *evil, and guilt, Ricœur developed dynamic critiques of *Marx, Freud, *existentialism, and structuralism before exploring with the tools of *hermeneutics the functions of *symbol, *metaphor, and narrative in secular texts as well as in scripture. A Christian who finds the intellectual underpinning to his theological hope in biblical exegesis rather than in dogmatics, he has been at pains to separate his philosophical discourse from his religious conviction, attaining what he called a 'conflictual consensus' between the two. This reflects his increasing concern to emphasize the *fête du sens* (festival of meaning) in the multiplicity and disjunctions of the *bible's variety of modes of discourse, which cannot simply be reduced to narrative. It is this diversity that can spur the imagination to meet the complexity of the human subject. His insights into the hermeneutics of religion have influenced both Catholic and Protestant thinkers.   **Howard Evans**

Ricœur, P., *The Symbolism of Evil*, ET (1967).

—— *Time and Narrative*, ET (1988), i–iii.

—— *Figuring the Sacred: Religion, Narrative and Imagination*, ET (1995).

Hahn, L. E. (ed.), *The Philosophy of Paul Ricœur* (1995).

Robinson John A. T. (1919–83).

John Robinson was a radical, perceptive scholar who held no chair, a creative *Anglican suffragan bishop who was offered no diocese. Apart from his chaplaincy to Wells Theological College (1948–51) and the suffragan bishopric of Woolwich (1959–69), he worked in Cambridge, as Dean of Chapel, Clare College (1951–9) and of Trinity College (1969–83). Influencing scholars, the churches, and a wider public, he understood himself to be where three ways meet: biblical interrogation, *theological exploration, and social responsibility.

Though not in the forefront of NT research, he was an innovative scholar whose technical works spanned his career from *In the End God* (1950) and *The Body* (1952), to the posthumously published *Twelve More New Testament Studies* (1984). Robinson's radical approach to the NT produced surprisingly 'conservative' answers, as in *Redating the New Testament* (1976) and *The Priority of John* (1985).

Honest to God (1963) brought him notoriety. In the language of his contemporaries, for whom traditional images of and *myths about *God no longer 'worked', Robinson affirmed God as 'the ground of being'. This book scandalized many, enabled others to make sense of God-talk, and sold a million copies. He developed it theologically

in *Exploration into God* (1967) and *christologically in *The Human Face of God* (1973).

Reaching millions who would not normally listen to bishops, Robinson's 'social' teaching proved widely influential. *The Roots of a Radical* (1980) illustrates the sweep of his concern: christology, social and *sexual ethics, Christians and violence, nuclear power. As a newly consecrated bishop he published in 1960 *Liturgy Coming to Life*, *On Being the Church in the World*, and *New Ways with the Ministry*.

Robinson was one of the most brilliant, controversial, least-appreciated Anglicans of his time, combining conservative and radical aspects in unexpected, yet self-consistent ways.   **Peter Doble**

James, E., *A Life of Bishop John A. T. Robinson: Scholar, Pastor, Prophet* (1987).

Romans, Epistle to the.

Writing from Greece around 57 AD to Jewish and Gentile Christians in *Rome, *Paul celebrates God's saving 'righteousness' which is now being revealed in the gospel to *all* who believe (1: 16–17). He argues that as Jews and Gentiles are alike under sin (3: 9) they alike need to be put right ('*justified') by *faith in Christ, not on the basis of Torah observance; what God is now doing in Christ is 'apart from law', though witnessed to by scripture (3: 20–5: 11; 9: 30–10: 17). He gives glorious expression to the *grace of God and believers' new life in Christ, gifted with the *Holy Spirit (chs. 5 and 8), free from (or 'dead to') sin and the law (chs. 6–7), and exhorts them to live dedicated lives (chs. 12–15). With arguments from scripture and this account of Christian existence he hopes to persuade his hearers that his Gentile mission without circumcision (cf. Galatians) accords with God's promises and assumes obedience to God's holy will.

Paul's rhetoric has inspired millions who have subsequently heard or read it as Christian scripture, but, as Jewish Christianity became marginal and specifically Jewish requirements were abandoned, the historical context of his argument was forgotten and its antithetical language made the basis of powerful new readings, especially by Marcion, *Augustine, and *Luther. All three generalized Paul's antithesis between faith and works, Christ and the law, to insist in true Pauline manner on God's free grace and believers' loving and trusting response, but directed Paul's antithesis against the Christian moralisms of their own times.

Romans has also been highly valued outside polemical contexts, and even before the NT canon took shape its influence is apparent in several early Christian writings from Ephesians to Christian *Gnosticism. In opposing 2nd-century *heresies, particularly Gnostic *dualism, *Irenaeus then developed Paul's *typology of *Adam and Christ (Rom. 5) to insist on the unity of *creation and *redemption in the history of *salvation. Tertullian could turn Romans *against* Marcion (5. 13. 2), and Paul's greatest ante-Nicene admirers were Clement and *Origen, who had little use for his dialectic of law and gospel. They minimized his ambivalence about the law and interpreted *predestination (Rom. 9) as merely divine *foreknowledge, and through Origen's great commentary (c.247) this exegesis became standard in the east. Greek fathers appealed to Rom. 1: 3 against *Docetism, Rom. 8: 3 in support of subordinationism, and Rom. 9: 5 as referring to the divinity of Christ but the central argument of the epistle made no great impact. They wrote commentaries and preached sermons on Romans, notably the thirty-two *Homilies* of Chrysostom, but these are more about morals than doctrine.

In the west Augustine was inspired by Romans (cf. *Conf.* 8) and advocating his doctrine of grace against *Pelagius he found support in Rom. 5–7, without reference to the apostle's original context. He rightly learned from Romans that righteousness and faith are God's gift; that the law gives knowledge of sin but contributes nothing to the saving act; and that moral action flows from the new life in the Spirit. But he also tied justification to divine election (Rom. 9), paralysing the human will. He explained this human incapacity by a doctrine of original sin which (following Ambrosiaster) misunderstood Rom. 5: 12*d* as saying that 'in *him* (Adam) all sinned' and are guilty.

Augustine's reading of Paul was transmitted by monastic compilers and echoed in such meditations on scripture as St Bernard's sermons on the *Song of Songs. Predestination to evil was rejected but the doctrine of grace became the basis of Catholic *sacramental theology. Paul's thematic phrase 'the righteousness of God' was disputed in medieval exegesis and often misunderstood to imply the punishment of sinners, and through Augustine Romans has continued to influence western thought about the human subject down to *Marx, Freud, *existentialism, and phenomenology.

When *Anselm and *Abelard produced contrasting theories of the *Atonement Romans was again the chief witness. *Aquinas's meticulous commentary feeds into his *Summa Theologiae*, supporting natural theology (Rom. 1: 19–20) and salvation history (Rom. 4), and his *political theory (Rom. 13). Study of Paul led the young Catholic Luther to break with his nominalist teachers and by 1515/16 (*Lectures on Romans*) he had found strong support in Augustine. This academic theology rapidly led to wider social consequences when he applied Paul's antithesis (Rom. 3: 28: justified by faith without works of the law) more radically than Augustine and criticized the medieval sacramental system. Again the Pauline dialectic of law and gospel interpreted a new situation, inspired prophetic protest against perversions of the gospel, and generated new interpretations of the apostolic witness.

The intensive study of Romans continued to underpin the theology of the Reformers, including some who remained Catholic. Melanchthon's *Apology* for the Augsburg Confession (1530) found in Rom. 4 a forensic doctrine of justification, and this became standard in *Protestantism. *Renaissance humanists from Valla to *Erasmus had pioneered NT exegesis and recovered the Greek fathers and the Greek text, but it was the Reformers whose theological interpretations of Romans made history. Predestination again became important, especially for Calvin, whose commentary (1540) and enlarged *Institutes* (1539) made this epistle as central for Reformed Christianity as it was and still is for *Lutheranism. He was more positive about law than Luther and the epistle's ambiguities have underwritten doctrinal, ethical, and political differences between the confessions.

Study of Romans led *Arminius to oppose Calvinism on predestination and later, in the 1770s, John *Wesley took his side. The latter's Aldersgate experience in 1738 had been triggered by Luther's *Preface* to Romans and he recovered justification by faith for English Christianity by his abridgement of Cranmer's 1547 *Homilies*. Protestants of various hues have continued to find Romans 'the clearest gospel of all', whereas for most other Christians the gospels have

been more central. After the brilliant flood of commentaries from all sides in the 1520s and 1530s the Council of *Trent and later the defeat of *Jansenism contributed to a theological depreciation of the epistle within Roman Catholicism.

Modern study of Romans broke out of its confessional moulds with H. Grotius (1646), H. Hammond (1653), and J. Locke (1705–7), but the breakthrough to an interpretation based on its probable historical situation was made by F. C. Baur (1836). Critical historical exegesis provided tools for analysing the NT and discovering mainly from this epistle Paul's anthropology, soteriology, pneumatology, mysticism, and ethics. Since its establishment as a historical discipline in the 19th century, Protestant NT theology has naturally centred on this most systematic epistle of its earliest and theologically most sophisticated witness. The hermeneutical question of its contemporary appropriation was reopened by *Barth's theological interpretation of Romans (1919, 1921), in which Reformation emphases again challenged a more comfortable exegesis. Bultmann's synthesis (1948) combined this theological proposal with the insights of scholarship since Baur, making use also of Heidegger's terms analysing human existence. More recently, Romans has been treasured for its positive attitude to Judaism (ch. 11), and appreciation of Paul's own Jewishness has directed interpretation away from a one-sided emphasis on the discontinuity between his Pharisaism and his messianic faith.

In sum, Romans has played a major part in shaping Christian identity by providing an anthropological and soteriological vocabulary that has interpreted a wide range of experience and stimulated further theological reflection. But it is as much the power of its rhetoric and attractive vision as the cogency of its theological argument that explains its hold on the Christian imagination and its continuing fascination for those who seek to understand this religion, whether from within or without.

See also JEWISH–CHRISTIAN RELATIONS.   **R. Morgan**

Commentaries that attend to the history of interpretation include:
Cranfield, C.E.B., International Critical Commentary (2 vols.; 1976–9).
Dunn, J. D. G., Word Biblical Commentary (2 vols.; 1988).
Fitzmyer, J., Anchor Bible Commentary (1993).
Käsemann, E. (1973 2nd edn. 1982).
Sanday, W. W., and Headlam, A. C., International Critical Commentary (1895).
Wilckens, U., Evangelisch–Katholischer Kommentar (3 vols.; 1978–82).

Romanticism. Before the Romantic Revival it was considered romantic to revel in imagination and emotion. It still is. The Romantic Revival, however, which reached its height in the early 19th century, went further, as an overarching philosophy, a clue to all culture, even a new religion. Great cultural movements are easier to recognize than to define, and Romanticism on principle distrusted and defied definition. It hated the ordering reason of the *Enlightenment. Much of Romanticism is simply rebellion against classical correctness: 'romantic means precisely that it oversteps all bounds' (*Kierkegaard).

All western countries had a Romantic Revival, but possibly the heartland was Germany. Madame de Staël claimed that all German culture, as opposed to French, was Romantic. She could cite the great dramatist Schiller, who depicted outlaw robbers as heroes, or Goethe's lines

> All theory is grey, dear friend,
> Green is the golden tree of life

summing up the Romantic shift from abstract *reason to organic life. But Goethe did not think of himself as a Romantic. In Germany the Romantics were more narrowly defined: first, Early Romantics, the circle of mystic philosophers round the Schlegels and the poet Novalis in Jena and later Berlin, and then High Romantics, in Heidelberg, rediscovering German folk tradition. *Schleiermacher, the father of liberal Protestantism, had shared rooms with one of the Schlegels, and the 'cultured despisers' to whom he addressed his *Speeches on Religion* (1799) were the Early Romantics. Schleiermacher scholars dispute whether he was himself a Romantic, but in any broad definition he certainly was. 'Religion knows nothing of deducing and connecting.' 'True religion is sense and taste for the infinite.' The *Speeches* are, admittedly among other things, a sourcebook of Romantic religious insights.

One heir of the classical tradition called Romanticism 'spilt religion'. A Romantic would answer, like *Blake, that 'the cistern contains; the fountain overflows'. Historically Romanticism arose from Christian *Pietism and *mysticism, and held to a cluster of quasi-religious convictions. The very term Romantic Revival has overtones of religious revival, heart religion as against abstract reasoning. But what a heart religion it is. 'I am certain of nothing except the holiness of the Heart's affections, and the truth of the Imagination' (Keats). Falling in love is holy; imagination is not fiction but truth. The *poets and philosophers of Romanticism claim their inspiration (possible for anyone) is divine. Some Romantics, like Shelley, were categorically non-Christian. Others, like Wordsworth, found a wide readership most appreciative of them when they sounded pantheist, 'a sense sublime | Of something far more deeply interfused'. But orthodox Christianity also benefited from the coming of Romanticism. Keble's best-selling poetry was described, perhaps unfairly, as 'Wordsworth and water'. Christian liturgy, particularly *hymnody, profited from a more affective general culture, and took it at times to melodramatic extremes. Not surprisingly, Romantic church architects preferred the aspiration of Gothic Revival spires to the containment of classical domes. The buildings tell us at once: 19th-century Christianity very largely adopted the romantic tone of darkness and quiet melancholy. Critics might add that this architecture, like much else Romantic, was unreal and self-dramatizing. Why pretend to be in the Middle Ages?

Romanticism rehabilitated the Middle Ages, and thereby undercut much of the Protestant critique of Catholicism. Schools of *art, Nazarenes in Germany, Pre-Raphaelites in England, mirrored religious movements, such as the Oxford Movement or the American Mercersburg Theology, which rediscovered Catholicism in Protestant churches. One side of this is simply part of a wider refusal to accept the modern: let us anoint a Catholic king again in France, as if the French Revolution had never happened. Much conservative political philosophy is deeply Romantic, and much 19th- and 20th-century Christianity had an emotional entanglement with right-wing politics in consequence. The sense of a living, organic link with the past is intuitively true, and serves to authenticate Romantic *nationalism. Catholicism, though an international religion, was very often a successful focus of nationalist feeling. Delight in the local and the particular and the distinctiveness of moments in the past, all characteristic of Romanticism, helped historic churches to revive.

The Romantics had a highly charged encounter with nature. Poets and painters discovered wild landscape, the Lake District, later the Rockies. But even tame, rather ordinary, landscape, like Constable's East Anglia or Turner's Wharfedale, was seen in a new light. Sometimes the religious implications of this were spelt out: 'The Divine is everywhere, even in a grain of sand; here I have represented it as bulrushes' (Caspar David Friedrich). This is a new discovery of divine immanence. In consequence some people would take long walks instead of attending church, but many found God's revelation in nature affirmed their Christianity. Though some Romantic art, for example Delacroix, had little obvious religious feeling, much served to shape Christian sensibility. This is particularly true of *music, the pre-eminent Romantic art-form. 'Music is a revelation of a higher order than any morality or philosophy' (Bettina von Arnim). Wagner, with a later, lusher form of Romanticism, is scarcely Christian in his message, but his Parsifal is a Christian knight.

The Romantics saw Enlightenment man as shallow and superficial. Truth lay in inwardness: 'The way to all mysteries heads inwards' (Novalis). Romantics were self-aware individualists, sometimes Byronic, problematic and ironic to themselves (and to others), willing to identify with Prometheus and Milton's Lucifer. A characteristic literary form was the *Bildungsroman*, the story of a soul's pilgrimage, often spiralling strangely but rightly home. Such self-absorption and pride is strikingly unchristian, yet Christian imagery is there afresh, the infinite value of the individual, the real sense of sin, and the pilgrim's return. 'Each man is meant to represent humanity in his own way,' said Schleiermacher, and this Romantic delight in human diversity has often been liberating.

German idealist philosophy is often seen as Romantic, though one might well think the systematician Hegel less so than his existentialist critic Kierkegaard. More relevant to our theme are actual Romantic theologians. German Protestant theology, very professorial, never was more Romantic than in the work of the young Schleiermacher. The German Catholic theology of the *Tübingen school of Drey and Möhler, which owed much to Schelling, talked of the community of believers as a living organism. In France Lamennais mixed medieval papalism with a Romantic love of the people, writing rhapsodic visionary prose. In England the poet *Coleridge, a convert from *Unitarianism, was one of the founders of modern Anglican theology. His supporters claim to find a greater scheme than German idealism in his more impenetrable fragments. His Romantic reading of the bible, in *Confessions of an Enquiring Spirit*, allowing it to speak to the reader, helped ordinary Christians to cope with biblical criticism. In the United States, Channing led Unitarians from rationalism to Romanticism, and Emerson and the Transcendentalists went on from there. Emerson's 'Divinity School Address' of 1838 sums up the high human claims of Romantic theology: 'Alone in all history, [Jesus] estimated the greatness of man. One man was true to what is in you and me.' Mystic inwardness and individualism could go no further. **Alistair Mason**

Abrams, M. H., *Natural Supernaturalism* (1973).
Cantor, P. A., *Creature and Creator* (1984).
Dabundo, Laura (ed.), *Encyclopedia of Romanticism* (1992).
Morse, David, *American Romanticism* (1987).

Prickett, Stephen, *Romanticism and Religion* (1976).
Reardon, B. M. G., *Religion in the Age of Romanticism* (1985).
Rosenblum, Robert, *Modern Painting and the Northern Romantic Tradition* (1975).
Schenk, H. G., *The Mind of the European Romantics* (1966).

Rome.

The city's significance for Christianity lies in both its imperial and its *apostolic/papal identities. The original gospel story is explicitly linked to the empire within which it happens. A decree of Caesar Augustus, according to *Luke, ensured Jesus' birth at Bethlehem (Luke 2: 1) and it was the Roman governor, Pontius Pilate, who condemned him to death. Moreover, the Acts of the Apostles is framed almost throughout by a sense of the empire within which the church is expanding and it ends, not accidentally, with an account of *Paul's arrival in Rome.

If Rome comes, as persecutor, to represent 'Babylon' in some early Christian thought, that is wholly changed once the emperor *Constantine is converted, although the name of Pilate remains forever in the creed. For the greatest historian of early Christianity, Eusebius, Constantine providentially unites universal *church and universal empire, each meant by God for the other. If Constantine established a new and permanent imperial capital on the Bosphorus, the Roman mystique is not superseded: *Constantinople is not only an intrinsically Christian capital, it is also 'New Rome'. When a thousand years later Constantinople falls to the Ottomans, Moscow quickly claims the succession as the 'Third Rome'. Rome's enduring symbolism in politico-religious terms appears too in the re-establishment of the empire in the west when Charlemagne was crowned emperor by Pope Leo III in St Peter's on Christmas Day 800. This 'Holy Roman Empire' was only finally abolished by Napoleon and, if its reality was always unstable, it still represented a central Christian political ideal for many, notably *Dante.

Rome's specifically Christian identity is grounded, nevertheless, on the *martyrdom there of *Peter and Paul, their burial shrines venerated from a very early time with a sense that their *authority has been inherited by the Roman church. The vast development of the catacombs, underground Christian burial chambers, provided an extraordinary monument to early Christian devotion, *art, and funerary practice. The transformation from a persecuted to a privileged church in the 4th century is strikingly demonstrated by the shift from catacombs to palaces and basilicas. The palaces of the Lateran (formerly owned by Fausta, Constantine's wife) and the Vatican became the bishop of Rome's two official residences. Surviving churches and mosaics from the 4th to the 7th century, such as St Maria Maggiore, St Sabina, and St Pudenziana, represent the religious culture of the high patristic period more richly than anything remaining elsewhere.

The hundreds of Roman churches, constructed and reconstructed in almost every century, provide an incomparable illustration of the history of Christian architecture (Gothic, however, being represented only by St Maria Sopra Minerva) up to, but scarcely beyond, the *Baroque. The 16th-century rebuilding of Constantine's basilica of St Peter's to the design of Michelangelo produced a vast and wonderfully well-proportioned church, symbolic of *Romanitas* and papal self-confidence, but it also precipitated the *Reformation through an unscrupulous campaign of money-raising in Germany based on the sale of indulgences. For many *Protestant Christians, post-Reformation Rome became once more a manifestation of Babylon, the Scarlet Woman, yet in Rome itself spirituality and Baroque architecture went hand in hand, as with St Philip Neri's Chiesa Nuova, mother church of Oratorians, or the Gesù, mother church of the *Jesuits, where St Ignatius lies buried, a masterpiece of High Baroque and a model whose near-replicas were spread worldwide.

In the 16th century the foundation of the Gregorianum, the Jesuit *university, together with a series of national colleges, began a new development—the concentration of clerical education within the city, leading to a multitude of separate ecclesiastical universities and theological colleges. After the destruction of the Napoleonic era, in which both Pius VII and Pius VIII suffered captivity in France, and almost every papal institution in Rome was closed down, this development was renewed and extended in the 19th century, fuelled by *ultramontanism. The larger religious orders moved their generalates and houses of higher study to Rome, whose clerical population vastly expanded as a result. While Rome has seldom produced theological thinkers of the first order, the Biblicum and the Oriental Institute, both attached to the Gregorianum, have a worldwide reputation for their scholarship.

The Lateran and the Vatican were both the scene of 'ecumenical' *councils—the first for five councils, ranging from the 12th to the 16th century, the second for two in the 19th and 20th. The Vatican Library and archives, together with others at Propaganda Fide, the Jesuit Generalate and elsewhere, are easily the most important collections for Christian history in the world. As a centre of *pilgrimage Rome was already thriving in the 4th century and has remained so ever since, an activity enhanced by Boniface VIII's invention of a 'Holy Year' in 1300, something regularly repeated. Major pilgrimages are often planned to coincide with the canonization of *saints. Art, councils, colleges, pilgrimages, canonizations, and archives, all finally depend for their vitality and endurance upon the *papacy and its curial administration which have given Rome—despite its new status since 1870 as capital of a national secular state—a unique stability in religious terms across the centuries, a stability protected since 1929 by the legal independence of the minute Vatican State within the city. Rome remains the most potent and complex of Christian *cities, fascinating for some, repellent for others.

Adrian Hastings

Elling, Christian, *Rome: The Biography of her Architecture from Bernini to Thorvaldsen* (1975).
Galazzi Paluzzi, G. (ed.), *Roma cristiana* (7 vols.; 1962–9).
Kelly, J. N. D., *The Oxford Dictionary of Popes* (1986).
Rodd, Rennell, *Rome of the Renaissance and Today* (1932).

Ruether, Rosemary Radford

(1936–). Ruether is one of the most influential and celebrated of *feminist theologians. Her early work was especially significant in shaping the methodology and concerns of all aspects of Christian feminist theology. Educated at Claremont Graduate School, she is one of the few women of her generation to break into the male-dominated world of theology. She has been dedicated to exposing the sexism inherent in Christianity. However, she is convinced that the Christian tradition is essentially egalitarian and has the potential to become more inclusive of women. As a result she has been involved in debates about the compatibility of feminism and *Christianity.

Her collection of essays *Religion and Sexism* (1974) was one of the first of its kind. It documented the misogyny of the texts, beliefs, and practices of the Judaeo-Christian tradition. She has also engaged in a feminist critique of many doctrinal concerns, for example *Mariology, in *Mary: The Feminine Face of the Church* (1977), *christology, in *Reconstructing the Christ Symbol: Essays in Feminist Theology* (1993), and ecclesiology, in *Women-Church: Theology and Practice of Feminist Liturgical Communities* (1985). Her theology has also been oriented more widely. She coined the phrase 'the interstructuring of oppression', in which she argues that all forms of oppression have common roots in patriarchal thinking. This has been the guiding principle of her work and is the key to her importance. It has led her to examine Christianity's role in *antisemitism, *Faith and Fratricide* (1974), in the *ecological crisis, *Gaia and God: An Ecofeminist Theology of Earth Healing* (1993), and in *political conflict, *God and the Nations* (1995) and *The Wrath of Jonah: Religious Nationalism in the Arab–Israeli Conflict* (1989). Thus she has expanded the horizons of feminist theology far beyond the exclusive concerns of gender.

Linda Hogan

Russian Christian thought.

The early centuries of Christianity in Russia, following the adoption of the faith by the principality of Kiev in or around 988, seem to show relatively few signs of independent intellectual activity compared with the medieval west; but in fact a sturdy local tradition was developing, expressed chiefly in sermons, hagiography, and practical ethical or ascetical treatises. The Monastery of the Caves at Kiev was a significant point of contact between Russia and the *Byzantine world, since it followed the rule of the great Constantinopolitan monastery of Studion. Its founder, Feodosii (d. 1074), was the subject of a very influential Life and the author of some homilies: both Life and homilies suggest a great familiarity with the literature of early *monasticism, a commitment to the service of the poor, and a focus upon the ideal of a Christlike humility and self-emptying—the *kenotic theme that dominates so much Russian Christian theology.

The proximity of the Khazar kingdom in Southern Russia, which had converted to Judaism not long before the Kievan adoption of Christianity, encouraged the production of polemical literature contrasting the dispensation of Jewish Law with that of the grace of Christ; an early example, distinguished by highly polished rhetoric, is the sermon of Metropolitan Ilarion of Kiev (mid-11th century) on Law and Grace. Once again, this was the precursor of much later writing, bequeathing to Russian Christianity a legacy of *antisemitic feeling that was to become increasingly violent and oppressive. Links with the southern Slavonic world were consistently important in the medieval Russian Church, and a good many patristic texts first circulated in Russia in versions translated in Bulgaria. This southern Slav world helped to mediate a number of Byzantine currents in thought and practice to Russia, as well as playing some role, not easy to determine, in the spread of the 'Judaizing' movement of the 14th century. Details of this movement are hard to pin down, but it seems to have involved some questioning of conventional Orthodox exegesis of the OT, perhaps along the lines of the Antiochene exegetes of the early church, who had been reluctant to accept a *typological reading of the OT narratives and prophecies. Other characteristics were a scepticism, perhaps, about aspects of Trinitarian theology; the use of philosophical themes from Maimonides, and indeed al-Ghazali; and a fascination with *astrology. This development gave added impetus to anti-

Jewish polemic, but also stimulated harder and more sophisticated work on OT exegesis.

During the period of Tatar dominance over the Russian principalities in the 13th and 14th centuries, monastic life continued to be an indispensable focus for Russian cultural and intellectual identity. The influence of the hesychast movement in the late 14th century with its revival and development of patristic teaching on contemplative *prayer was felt very early in Russia: Gregory Palamas, the leading figure of this movement in Greece, was venerated as a saint by the middle of the 15th century, and many works on prayer and contemplative experience were translated in this period (see MYSTICISM). However, serious divisions in the Russian monastic world clouded the reception of these influences from Greece and Mount Athos. In the 15th century, there was protracted conflict between those who saw the monastic life (conceived in terms of strict corporate observance) as part of an integral sacred order in society, presided over by the ruler as 'father' of the people, and those who emphasized the need for monastic poverty and detachment. The former, the 'Possessors' (so-called from their defence of the right of monasteries to own estates and serfs) were led originally by Iosif of Volokolamsk (1439–1515), the 'Non-possessors' by Nil of Sora (d. 1508). The latter group were the standard-bearers for hesychasm in Russia; they also opposed religious coercion by the state. When, early in the 16th century, the Muscovite prince Vasilii III gave his unequivocal support to the Possessors, the future direction and emphasis of much of the Russian Christian world was set.

However, although the Possessors enjoyed a measure of political triumph, the contribution of learned monks dedicated to the tradition of monastic detachment continued to be significant for church and state. The Greek scholar Maximos (Maksim Grek, d. 1556) assisted in the translation of many patristic works and introduced some of the interests of Renaissance humanism to Russia. Despite his exile at the behest of the Possessors, he had been an important figure in the public life of Moscow and was canonized in 1591. In the mid-16th century, during the reign of Ivan the Terrible, Metropolitan Makarii of Moscow, not generally a sympathizer with the heritage of Nil of Sora, included in his 'Grand Menology', a collection of 'as many sacred books as were available in Russia', the Slavonic translation of *Dionysius the Pseudo-Areopagite; the mystical tradition was never wholly silenced by the interest of the Possessors in formalizing a comprehensive ritual for both public and domestic life that left little place for the contemplative element. But it was unmistakably this interest that dominated Russian ecclesial life in the late 16th and early 17th centuries, contributing substantially to the great schism of the 1650s and 1660s.

Growing awareness of the new theological developments in western Christianity, and the physical proximity of Protestants in Poland and Lithuania, prompted further scholarly work in the mid-16th century, including more translations of the fathers.

Prince Andrei Kurbskii (1528–83) was a major figure in this movement, though most of his own work was done outside Russia, after he had fled from the enmity of Ivan the Terrible; his correspondence with the tsar (if it is authentic; serious doubts have been raised in recent years) reflects a remarkably high level of patristic and biblical literacy in both men. Kurbskii was not the only Russian to be engaged beyond the frontiers of the Muscovite state in theological and literary work; several Orthodox printing presses flourished in Volhynia and the Ukraine in the late 16th century, fighting on two increasingly beleaguered fronts: polemic against extreme Protestant groups, especially Socinians, and resistance to Roman Catholic pressure. The greatest triumph of Orthodox learning in this region was the publication of a Slavonic bible at Ostrog in Volhynia (1580), a text painstakingly edited with reference to the best Greek texts of the day, to the Masoretic Hebrew, and to recent translations in western Slavic languages. However, the Council of Brest in 1596, which purported to unite the Orthodox communities of Poland and Lithuania with the see of Rome, resulted in the suppression of independent Orthodox activity and the isolation of Byzantine Christians in this region from Russia. Increasingly the theology of the western Russian territories, even among those that did not remain within Polish or Lithuanian territory, came to reflect the controversy between Rome and Protestantism rather than the world of traditional *Eastern theology. The culmination of this trend can be seen in the work of Peter Mogila (1596–1647), Metropolitan of Kiev, who introduced into the Ukraine educational institutions based on the *Jesuit colleges of Poland, using Latin as a medium of instruction. In 1640, Mogila invited a council at Kiev to approve a statement of faith, usually referred to as the *Orthodox Confession*, drawn up by himself and his closest associates, which was derived almost entirely from Catholic textbooks. Although it introduced no strictly doctrinal innovations, its entire style and method of argumentation was alien to the Byzantine tradition. It none the less acquired official status in the Ukraine, and was endorsed by several of the eastern patriarchs, including (eventually) the patriarch of Moscow. For nearly two centuries, the Kiev Spiritual Academy, effectively a seminary of the Tridentine type annexed to a Jesuit-style *collegium*, maintained the same Latinate approach, extending even to a willingness to elide the differences between east and west over the *filioque, to treat this as *almost* entirely a terminological question. The model of the Kiev academy was to spread to Great Russia in the 18th century, and dominated theological education until the beginning of the 19th.

Meanwhile, in the Muscovite tsardom, the 17th century had witnessed the worst conflict yet experienced by the Russian church. Liturgical practice in Russia had come to diverge in a number of ways from the standard in other Orthodox countries, and there were several attempts to restore a more 'correct' usage. Such attempts, however, were always hampered by deep, almost paranoid, suspicion of foreign influences, especially those that emanated from the Lithuanian territories. Furthermore, since the concerns of the Possessors were so closely focused on a solemn and comprehensive ritualizing of practically all aspects of daily life, minor changes in ritual assumed major importance. The theocratic ideology of the Possessors (summed up in the famous claim of a 16th-century monk, Filofei of Pskov, that Moscow was the 'Third Rome', a holy city that would never be overthrown because of its loyalty to integral and unchanging Orthodoxy) made it hard to countenance any reform in custom without somehow undermining the entire symbolic system. When the reforms were taken up and energetically prosecuted by the Patriarch Nikon (1605–81), a man of immense political power and autocratic temperament, fierce conflict broke out. Those who rejected the reforms were persecuted unmercifully; some groups came to believe that the church had apostatized, that the grace of sacraments and priesthood had been withdrawn

from the world, so that all that remained for the faithful community was to await the apocalypse. Some retained a priestly ministry, celebrating an unreformed liturgy. Some concluded that God required a mass self-immolation of the faithful, a literal 'baptism of fire', and encouraged group suicide in the flames (memorably depicted at the end of Mussorgsky's great opera, *Khovanshchina*). Nikon's political pretensions and uncompromising attitude led to his deposition from office in 1666; but the persecution of the dissidents, the 'Old Believers', continued. One of their leaders, the archpriest Avvakum (1621–82), who eventually died a martyr, left an autobiography that is the first great literary work in something like modern Russian: it is a masterpiece of lively narrative, witty and pungent, testifying not only to Avvakum's courage and faithfulness to his beliefs, but to all kinds of details about ecclesiastical and secular life on the Russian 'frontier', the Siberian wastes, in the 17th century.

The old Russia was swept away within a couple of decades of Nikon's death by the reforms of Peter the Great, and the church was subjected to a 'Babylonian captivity' of administration by the direct mandate of the state. The *patriarchate was abolished in 1700, and the German Protestant system of a ruling 'synod' appointed by the monarch replaced it as the supreme authority for the church. Traditional monastic formation was effectively prohibited, and theological education became a curious mixture of scholastic discussion on the Ukrainian model and somewhat moralistic instruction in the reading of the bible along Lutheran lines. Feofan Prokopovich (1681–1736) was the leading figure in the consolidation of this style of education. A man much influenced by the development of Protestant scholasticism, his lack of anything resembling an ecclesiology and his emphasis on the religious duty of passive obedience to the monarch were worthy of some of his contemporaries on the other side of Europe, such as England's Bishop Hoadly. But the new atmosphere in Russian education at least allowed the development of some serious scholarly work in ecclesiastical history, in Greek and in oriental languages. Steps were taken to produce a new critical text of the Slavonic bible in the mid-18th century. On the whole, the alienation of the educated classes from the Orthodox Church was profound—intensified by the general contempt for Slavonic and Russian as languages for civilized discourse. Such piety as was to be found outside the peasantry was heavily influenced by German Pietism and hermetism. Freemasonry spread widely in Russia and the mysticism of Angelus Silesius and Jacob Boehme found many admirers.

However, several factors combined to bring about radical changes in the early years of the 19th century. The last decades of the 18th century had seen something of a revival in the world of classical monastic spirituality. The teaching and example of Tikhon of Zadonsk (1724–82) were a reminder that the tradition could still produce figures of outstanding power. Tikhon combines a history of visionary experience very much in the hesychast mould with a sensibility that has often been compared with that of *John of the Cross, a concern with the burden of the negative and the pain of self-loss in the spiritual life. His near-contemporary, Paisii Velichkovskii (1722–94), who worked mostly in Moldavia, represents a more straightforward reclamation of the Byzantine heritage. In 1793 his (abridged) Slavonic translation of the great spiritual anthology, the *Philokalia* (originating on Mount Athos in the early 18th century), was published in Moscow. It is virtually an independent work, as Paisii had laboured to collate texts and correct earlier Slavonic versions of Greek works on the basis of better manuscript evidence. The impact of this work on Russian spirituality cannot be overestimated: in its Russian version (translated by Ignatii Brianchaninov and published in 1857), it achieved immense popularity, and a further Russian version, including some extra texts and omitting or altering others, was prepared by Bishop Feofan the Recluse and began publication in 1877. The hesychast legacy was made available to a lay readership through this work, and its influence at all levels of society is witnessed to by the deservedly famous *Way of a Pilgrim*, purporting to be the spiritual journal of a 19th-century peasant wanderer, practising the disciplines of hesychast contemplation and communicating them in a variety of delightfully depicted 'everyday' settings. But Paisii's influence was also transmitted more directly through some of his followers, who worked in Russia and helped to provide the impetus for the development of a renewed monasticism at the Optina monastery, not far from Moscow, where a succession of outstanding 'elders' (*startsy*) offered spiritual direction to some of the foremost figures of Russia throughout the 19th century.

Equally influential, though in a totally different way, was the reception of German Idealism in Russia. The work of *Hegel and Schelling was transmitted at first through the Ukrainian academies and was instrumental in creating something of an indigenous Russian philosophy for the first time. The Hegelian system offered not only an ostensibly Christian metaphysic but a schema for understanding a history of violent cultural alternations (as Russia's history had been). Schelling suggested that there might be an epistemology that pointed beyond the deliverances of enquiry and argument to a knowledge by 'participation' in the known. Modified, sometimes simplified, sometimes grotesquely distorted, sometimes deepened, the perspectives of Hegel and Schelling, and, to a lesser extent, Novalis and Fichte, shaped Russian religious philosophy for generations, just as the Hegelian 'Left' was to shape Russian political radicalism and populism, even before *Marx arrived on the scene.

But to speak of 'populism' is to evoke also the movement known as 'Slavophilism', the passionately romantic portrayal of Slavic peasant culture as a kind of moral and political touchstone that influenced so many writers and poets of the 19th century. This too, especially after 1850, profoundly affected the Russian Christian sensibility. Much of the Russian religious philosophy of the mid- and late 19th century is a heady blend of Hegel and Slavophilism. But one of the first serious Russian religious philosophers, Ivan Kireevsky (1806–56), was far more concerned with attempting a philosophical transcription of the wisdom of the monastic tradition, and his system gives primary place to the knowledge of the 'heart', the integral awareness born of relationship and freedom. Aleksei Khomyakov (1804–60) is more clearly wedded to the Slavophil mystique; his major contribution to Russian theology is in his elaboration of the concept of *sobornost* (roughly 'catholicity') as an almost organic basis for the life of the church, a collective yet freely collaborative consciousness, reflected in the life of the peasant commune as an image of the church. The main themes of these two writers—the importance of an intuitive and non-dualistic epistemology and the need for some transpersonal ground of religious

knowing—recur in nearly all the great figures of 19th-century Russian religious writing. Vladimir Soloviev (1853–1900) crystallized these themes in his speculations (influenced by German mysticism, *NOSTICISM and the Jewish cabbala) about divine *Wisdom, Sophia, a kind of world-soul standing between God and creation. In the early 20th century, Pavel Florensky (1882–1937) and Sergii Bulgakov (1871–1944) developed 'sophiology' with great sophistication. Florensky stood close to some representatives of the esoteric and eclectic 'new religious consciousness' at the turn of the century (Blok, Merezhkovsky, and others) so that his version of the doctrine of Sophia is coloured by aspects of Russian Symbolism. Bulgakov, once a Marxist and a teacher of economics, links Sophia with the political task of shaping communities that are able to use the environment meaningfully, as well as with the realm of art and beauty. After his exile from Russia in 1922, he pursued these themes in the context of an exhaustive system of dogmatic theology, covering the Incarnation, the Holy Spirit, and the church, in which Sophia, much demythologized, becomes a way of talking about the divine nature itself as a movement of self-giving or kenosis.

Nineteenth- and early 20th-century Russian religious thought exhibits a sharp tension between, on the one hand, the impulse to metaphysical closure in cosmic pan-unity (*vseedinstvo*, a favourite term of Soloviev) and universal restoration or *reconciliation (dramatically exemplified in Nikolai Fedorov, 1828–1903, with his conviction that it should be possible literally to raise the dead and make all human beings contemporary), and, on the other, the recognition of the unpredictability of individual liberty and its tragic implications. *Dostoevsky wrestles with this tension, most unforgettably in *The Brothers Karamazov* with its simultaneous affirmation of the holiness of the earth and its acknowledgement of the bare incomprehensibility and outrage of suffering in the universe. In many of his novels, Dostoevsky's awareness of the monastic tradition is significant: Tikhon of Zadonsk, the great Serafim of Sarov (d. 1833), and the Optina elders are regularly in the background of his images of sanctity. *Tolstoy, excommunicated after bitter conflicts with the Orthodox Church, shows a similar tension in *War and Peace*, where a deterministic philosophy is asserted in the background while the raw particularity and liberty of personal choice and chance are wonderfully presented in the narrative detail. Tolstoy's own version of Christianity is a distinctive blend of rational moralism with some of the eccentric passions of Russian religious dissidents, egalitarian and *pacifist, at odds with the centralized authorities of church and state. The Dukhobor sect, a Russian parallel to the *Mennonite movement, is of special significance here.

Both Dostoevsky and Tolstoy draw on the folk tradition, going back to Feodosii and the first Russian martyrs, which specially honoured selfless humility as an imitation of Christ's kenosis. A number of 19th-century theologians discussed this in more technical terms; and it was a focal theme for the strange figure of Aleksei Bukharev (1822–71), who abandoned his monastic vocation in order to imitate the powerlessness of Christ and to join him 'on the margins', by which he incurred automatic excommunication. But the figure of Christ occasionally visible in 20th-century Russian literature has many of the same features of marginality and helplessness; the Christ of Zhivago's poetry in Pasternak's *novel; or of the 'Master's' fantasies about the Passion story in Mikhail Bulgakov's *The Master and Margarita*. The greatest of the Russian *émigré* theologians, Vladimir Lossky (1903–58), gives increasing emphasis to the theme. Some have detected it in certain of Solzhenitsyn's characters.

The aftermath of the Revolution of 1917 saw in *émigré* circles a backlash against some features of late 19th-century religious thought. Georges *Florovsky was bitterly critical of the whole sophiological style, arguing for a more systematic retrieval of patristic and monastic theology. Lossky similarly revolted against the older generation and defended not only a more consistently 'personalist' approach, centred on the human person-in-community as image of the Trinity, but also an apophatic stress (speaking of God in negatives: what God is not), linked with the recovery of hesychast theology—sometimes called 'neo-Palamism'. In Russia today, all aspects of the legacy here discussed have their defenders. The extreme voluntarism of Nikolai Berdyaev (1874–1948), a writer much influenced by radical German mysticism, with its concept of an *Urgrund*, a primitive and indeterminate wellspring of freedom, more or less independent of God, had a considerable vogue in the last years of the Soviet regime; and interest in the writers of the Silver Age, the first decade or so of the 20th century, burgeoned. Symposia were published deliberately echoing those of the last days of tsarism, calling for the return of the intelligentsia to religious commitment, so as to bring about an authentic social renewal. Lossky's theology has found many enthusiasts, and some younger Russian writers are attempting a synthesis of patristic theology with currents in modern western philosophy, phenomenological and even postmodernist. The work of the Petersburg School of Religion and Philosophy has been of first importance here, as well as the inspiration provided by Archpriest Aleksandr Men, murdered in 1989. The darker trends of formalism and antisemitism are still well-represented by conservative apologists for a 'folk Orthodoxy' that has little to do with authentic spiritual tradition. The present time is as much one of ferment for the Russian Christian world as was the first decade of the 20th century; there can be little doubt that what will emerge will be no less challenging and important for the rest of Christendom. **Rowan Williams**

Copleston, F. C., *Russian Religious Philosophy: Selected Aspects* (1988).

Fedotov, G. P., *The Russian Religious Mind* (1946).

Florovsky, G. V., *Ways of Russian Theology*, i (1979); ii (1987).

Gorodetzky, N., *The Humiliated Christ in Modern Russian Thought* (1938).

Kontzevich, I. M., *The Acquisition of the Holy Spirit in Ancient Russia* (1988).

Lossky, N. O., *History of Russian Philosophy* (1952).

Lossky, V. N., *The Mystical Theology of the Eastern Church* (1957).

Nicholl, D., *Triumphs of the Spirit in Russia* (1997).

Pascal, P., *The Religion of the Russian People* (1976).

Roberts, E., and Shukman, A. (eds.), *Christianity for the Twenty-First Century: The Life and Work of Alexander Men* (1996).

Solzhenitsyn, A. (ed.), *From Under the Rubble* (1974).

Steiner, G., *Tolstoy or Dostoevsky* (1959).

Zernov, N., *The Russians and their Church* (1964).

—— *The Russian Religious Renaissance of the Twentieth Century* (1963).

S

sabbatarianism designates the view that divine command-ment requires one day a week be set aside for strictly religious use. Within the Christian tradition, such a day includes community gathering, corporate worship, personal devotions, and charitable works.

While sabbatarianism boasts a long tradition, it has remained a point of contention within the *church. Two issues typically arise. The first concerns whether the OT sabbath commandment, while clearly mandating a day of rest for ancient *Israel, applies to the Christian church in the same manner. Most traditions today take the position formulated by the early church in the first two centur-ies, which contends that the sabbath commandment under OT law no longer applies in the same literal sense to Christians under the New Covenant. Through the death and Resurrection of Christ, the church has entered into a new epoch—one characterized by an ongoing, spiritual rest in Christ (Gal. 4: 8–11; Col. 2: 16; Heb. 3: 7–4: 11). While the keeping of *Sunday, especially through celebra-tion of the *Eucharist, in some way replaced the Sabbath, Chris-tians fulfil the sabbath commandment more fundamentally by 'resting' from both sin and self-justifying works. The church thus obeys the original sabbath commandment, but in a spiritual fashion through life in Christ.

Sabbatarians, however, assert that Christians should obey the sabbath commandment more literally. As one of the Ten *Com-mandments, sabbath observance is held, like the others, to be uni-versally binding for the church across time and space. Christians, then, must continue to observe the OT Sabbath, literally resting for a full 24-hour day. While portions of the 4th-century eastern church, the 6th-century Irish church, and medieval *monasticism in Europe and Africa promoted sabbatarianism to varying degrees, a more intense movement began with 17th-century English and Scottish Puritans. The Puritan Sabbath has now all but disappeared, but a few groups such as the Free Church of Scotland, Seventh-Day Baptists, and Seventh-Day *Adventists continue the sabbatarian tradition.

The second debate is among sabbatarians themselves. While they agree that Christians must observe a strict day of rest, they differ on what day of the week that rest should take place. God directed ancient Israel to observe the Sabbath on the seventh day (Saturday) of the week (Gen. 2: 2; Exod. 20: 11; 31: 17). Groups such as the Seventh-Day Adventists thus observe the Sabbath on Saturday, the traditional Jewish Sabbath. This choice is consistent with the literal approach sabbatarians generally take towards sabbath observance.

Most sabbatarians (including the *Puritans), however, observe a day of rest on Sunday. They follow the earliest church tradition in singling out Sunday as the appropriate day for Christians to honour the Lord. On Sunday, Christ rose from the dead, appeared to his disciples, administered the eucharistic meal, and conferred the Holy Spirit.

While strict sabbatarianism remains a minority position, many Christians do combine some aspects of sabbatarianism with a spir-itualized understanding of sabbath rest. Some, following *Luther and *Calvin, emphasize that while a day set aside expressly for rest and worship is important, the commandment has been, strictly speaking, already fulfilled in Christ. Others stress that while Chris-tians have indeed entered into a spiritual rest in Christ, some form of sabbath observance should be promoted as well. Most traditions today offer much latitude for individual members to follow their own conscience. **Joanne C. Beckman**

Carson, D. A., *From Sabbath to Lord's Day* (1982).
Eskanazi, Tamara, *et al.* (eds.), *The Sabbath in Jewish and Christian Trad-itions* (1991).
Strand, Kenneth, *The Sabbath in Scripture and History* (1982).

sacrament is a term whose history and meaning tell us a great deal about what Christians believe and how they see themselves as distinguished from other religious believers. But if your theological vocabulary is virtually restricted to scripture, you will not be able to find the word 'sacrament' in association with the Lord's supper or with *baptism, which were for centuries supposed to have been directly 'instituted' by Christ himself. 'Sacrament' is derived from the Latin *sacramentum*, and Latin is not the original language of the NT. A sacrament could be a sum of money left on deposit for those involved in a legal suit, and could by association be used of the suit itself. New army recruits would initially 'sacrament' themselves, that is agree to serve, and would eventually swear an oath of alle-giance to their commander. They might get a brand on the arm to show whose soldier they were, like a seal on a letter, but marked in human flesh. The sacrament showed to whom they belonged and involved certain commitments. Thus the Roman governor Pliny, reporting to Emperor Trajan in the early 2nd century, recognized that the Christians hauled up before him had switched allegiance.

They had sworn a sacrament, made an undertaking, and at least some of them would rather die than sacrifice so much as a sniff of incense to the Roman gods or to the emperor. Such an undertaking may have been expressed in the creed-like statements to be found in the NT, in the rites of baptism, where words were said and actions performed to mark the change of allegiance, and in the language of 'sealing', as in Revelation 7: 3–8 (cf. Ezek. 9: 4) and Ephesians 1: 13.

'Sacrament' came to be used to translate a word in the Greek NT (*mysterion*) which neatly transliterates into Latin as *mysterium*. It has inescapable connotations of a 'secret' that needs to be revealed. Thus in the resurrection-like appearance of *Revelation 1: 13–20 the one who has the keys of Death and Hades speaks to the seer of 'the mystery of the seven stars which you saw in my right hand'. Without necessarily claiming any such visionary experience Christians clearly believed themselves to have been put 'in the know' about the *revelation of God in Christ 'in whom are hid all the treasures of wisdom and knowledge' (Col. 2: 3), which it was their responsibility to proclaim. None of the texts that translate the Greek *mysterion*, whether as *mysterium* or as *sacramentum*, indicate any direct connection with a rite, and there were good reasons for not doing so. The *mysteria* were the rites of *religions from which Christians wished to be dissociated. One way of distinguishing Christians from others is so to insist on human dependence on the divine that no rite of any kind is required (as in the *Quakers and the Salvation Army today). It may be this conviction that lies behind the problematic attitude even to baptism and *Eucharist that has been discerned in the Fourth Gospel.

It is in the writings of Tertullian (3rd century) that we first find expressions like 'our *sacramentum* of water', and the terminology stayed flexible for some time. In the 4th-century Catechetical Lectures of Cyril of Jerusalem (instruction to adult candidates for baptism) anointing, eating *bread and drinking *wine, and the *liturgy are referred to as heavenly mysteries; and in the work of Ambrose of Milan at the end of that century 'Sacraments' and 'Mysteries' are the interchangeable titles of two versions of his teaching on baptism, chrism, and Eucharist. Isidore of Seville (6th to 7th century) expressed the idea of something material as veiling a mystery by linking sacrament and secret (*sacramentum* and *secretum*). *Augustine had seen the combination of word and matter (water, bread, oil) as being the 'sign' of a sacred reality: thanks to his authority, 'sacrament' could cover the *Lord's Prayer, the *creed, the liturgy, the sign of the cross, the font of baptism, the *water used, ashes, oil, blessing, foot-washing, the reading and exposition of scripture and prayers. The list could be extended, since once the habit of thinking of one's life as 'graced' by divine salvation has taken hold, sacramentalism in its broadest sense, *symbolism, mediated by the prayer of the *church, seems the appropriate way of seeing things. Two 20th-century theologians from very different traditions who think 'sacramentally' are Schmemann and *Tillich. Schmemann thought of the *world as a cosmic sacrament of the divine living presence. Tillich's deep appreciation of human culture meant that for him the sacramental could include everything in which divine presence has been experienced. Certainly discrimination would be needed, and a sense of that need may have been what led to the limitation of the number of the sacraments in the Middle Ages. Moreover there were issues inherited from the early church concerning the 'legal-

ity' of the sacraments, the understanding of what was going on in sacramental action, and what might be called the rationale of the sacraments in relation to the structure of a human life.

Distinguishing 'sacrament' from the 'sacramental' perhaps resulted from reflection on *missionary and *pastoral experience. The list of seven is something held in common by east and west. The proposal to limit 'sacrament' to seven rites is associated in the west with the name of Peter Lombard in the 12th century, but we can see what could be made of it from the reflections of *Aquinas in the 13th. In the third part of his *Summa Theologiae* he discussed which things were to be used to express the grace of Christ's salvation, and how they were to be used. The things that are appropriate were generally available or easily obtainable (an excellent illustration of how to make the common 'holy'). Thinking of the shape of a human life, seven sacraments relate neatly to birth, growth and strength, nutrition, sorting out disorder, relating to other people in one's society, and dying. So baptism, confirmation, Eucharist, *penance, order and presidency, *marriage, and anointing for the transition through death from this life to resurrection would cover everything. This scheme dealt with a whole range of human weakness, and positively fostered *faith, fortitude, *charity, *justice, prudence, *temperance, and above all, *hope (III q. 61 a. 4 and q. 65 a. 1). These were the strengths (virtues) marking the resurrection life of the Christian and providing what one might call a sacramental *morality. By Aquinas's death (1274) the sevenfold scheme was becoming acceptable, as at the Council of Lyons in that year. So far as the later *Reformation movement was concerned, the scheme was to collapse. This was not simply because of unease about whether Christ had authorized seven sacraments and how one could know that he had: there were other difficulties. From a straightforward reading of the NT only baptism and Eucharist could be clearly associated with the actual words of the Saviour. But in any case the place and meaning of Christian rites could be approached in two ways. One could start from proclamation and *preaching and the experience of divine presence through the *Word of the gospel, and then celebrate *salvation in two (or more) rites. Or one could celebrate the rites believed to be divinely authorized to mediate the divine presence, and then by proclamation and preaching convince the hearer of that presence. Given the legacy of the past, and the complications of the period, it became increasingly difficult to hold the two approaches together in one institution. We turn first to the legacy of the past.

From the days of the Roman governor Pliny onwards, some Christians were likely to crumble under the threat of persecution, raising the problem of what procedures had to be observed for readmittance to the Christian community when the persecution was over. As the threat of persecution waned, other difficulties came to the fore. Not so much the issue of relapsing into paganism and then returning, but different understandings of doctrine and life led to splits and dissension which could not always be negotiated. One 3rd-century response was that of Cyprian, who held that there was no salvation outside the church, and that those who took themselves off lost the gifts of the *Holy Spirit. But other Christians believed that those in *schism or deemed to be *heretical could still validly administer baptism, and for them there was a problem about returners. They needed to renew their commitment, but not necessarily by re-baptism, since rites of penance and *reconciliation could be and were developed. There was a further problem about the 'validity' of what was done when a schismatic group celebrated the Eucharist. Augustine's masterly negotiations on this matter distinguished carefully between the activity of the Saviour and that of the mere *minister, between the sacrament and its effect, and between the church as a sacrament of communion here and now and the holy society it would be in the life of resurrection. The distinction reminded Christians that salvation depends entirely upon God and the Passion of Christ, not on the spiritual standing of either the celebrant or the recipient. Whether as well as being valid the sacrament was 'fruitful' (which *would* be affected by the recipient's attitude) was an open question, and, allowing for reasonable church discipline, had to be left to God.

Then there was the problem of continuity with and discontinuity from what had become the '*Old' Testament. What was to be made of *its* 'signs', whether rites, moral instruction, or events (e.g. I Cor. 10: 1–4)? Aquinas used a helpful analogy when he suggested that God could be thought of as the father of a family, giving different directions to his household according to the seasons. Some sacraments were authorized at the time of the old Law and some after the coming of Christ. Drawing on familiar language, he said that the difference between them was that the former 'prefigured' grace, and the latter manifested grace as already present (III q. 61 a. 4). A standard example was that of the passover lamb prefiguring Christ's paschal sacrifice. Sign and sacrament, promise and fulfilment, figure and truth, shadow and reality could be related to one another (see TYPOLOGY). There was disagreement about what was meant by the condemnation of 'works of the law' in Romans 3: 20—did this exclude *all* rites? The universal scope of salvation in Christ stretching throughout time, God's fidelity to his promises, the development of revelation, reading the scriptures in a Christ-centred way—all these were at issue in discussion of sacrament. One solution was to resolve the matter of authorization by working out the proper form of any particular sacrament (the form being the words whose use makes it possible to be sure whether a sacrament is being or has been celebrated). The form showed that Christian sacraments were different from what had preceded them, for they manifest, contain, and even cause grace because of Christ's Passion, Resurrection, and Ascension. Thus a particular terminology developed that largely displaced previous efforts. It came to be held that Christian sacraments were effective *ex opere operato*, that is to say, by virtue of the 'work' having been done. Given Pauline condemnation of 'works' this phraseology was almost bound to create trouble once the point of it was lost. A sacrament seen as a 'work' could be thought of as a human achievement, under human control, a means of grace independent of the trust in divine promise on which alone salvation depends. Among others, *Luther tackled a significant example in his 1520 work on the 'Babylonian Captivity' of the church. Salvation for the dead as for the living depended entirely on the unmerited and gracious *forgiveness of God received as a promise, and in no way on the funding of clerics to say mass for the departed. Again, many penitential practices revealed very deep anxiety about salvation, rather than trust in the divine promise: hence the emphasis of some Reformers on the sacraments (even when reduced to two) as reminders of the grace by which we *have* been cleansed and redeemed.

Attempts at clarity and precision might seem inappropriate in re-

lation to the mysterious and the sacred but natural interest in precisely what happens in a sacramental rite, especially in the Eucharist, was exacerbated by controversy. The options were in view as early as the 9th century. One line was that characteristic of later Reformers: human beings are united in a saving relationship with Christ by faith. The 'sacrament/sign' (bread and wine for instance) remained what it was. The 'reality' was saving union, evident, for instance, in reconciliation with the church. 'Sacrament' meant the rite. For others, however, because what was used in the rite was consecrated by words, including the invocation of the *Trinity, the things used both remained what they appeared to be and also became a different reality. In the case of the Eucharist, the bread and wine now were held to 'contain' the 'real presence' of Christ, so 'sacrament' came to be used not only of the rite but of the consecrated things themselves. Associated with the name of Berengar in the 11th century was the understanding that a sacrament was the visible form of an invisible grace. His understanding of sacrament was transmitted into English-speaking culture via the Book of Common Prayer and the work of Richard *Hooker. So in the 1604 Catechism, the answer to the question 'What meanest thou by this word *Sacrament*?' is 'I mean an outward and visible sign of an inward and spiritual grace given unto us, ordained by Christ himself, as a means by which we receive the same, and a pledge to assure us thereof.'

In the last two hundred years richness of reference has been recovered by the notion of the 'symbolic', as meaning not merely one thing as the 'sign' of another but actually as mediating the divine. This can be found for instance in the work of both Tillich and *Rahner. A major shift, however, has come about as a result of the careful and critical re-evaluation of the tradition prompted by the work of Henri *de Lubac. Attention has moved away from the 'things' used in sacramental worship to the God encountered in Christ in that worship. The continuity of this with earlier understandings may be found in a 12th-century monastic liturgical text: 'O sacred banquet in which Christ is received, the memory of his passion is renewed, the soul is filled with grace, and the pledge of future glory is given us.' Although the primary reference is obviously to the Eucharist, these are the characteristics of any sacrament: the centrality of Christ risen, ascended, and present; the transforming fullness of grace; orientation to the future life of *heaven to which Christ summons his 'body', the church. Sacrament then has to do with Christ's actions in relation to the communion of persons, living and dead, with Christ and with one another; and given his transforming action on bread and wine in the Eucharist, his action may be deemed to embrace the non-human created order as well as the communion of human persons. So theologians as diverse as *Barth, *von Balthasar, and *Schillebeeckx all focus on Christ as the sacrament of God's salvation. Thus there was a renewed theological understanding of Christ as the 'original' or 'primal' or 'primordial' sacrament during the second half of the 20th century. Not only does this emphasis help to resist preoccupation with the 'things' used in the sacraments, or with the past, or with the juridical role of the church as an institution: it makes it possible to focus attention on the mystery of the relation of persons to Christ, who summons them and relates them to each other and to himself. Thus it can be said by Rahner, for example, that the church is the one abiding symbolic presence of Christ's redemptive grace, so that, in relation to particular sacraments, the church is said to be the 'fundamental sacrament' of salvation. So long as it is understood that Christ is the primal sacrament, and that both the church and the sacraments are provisional (since they have no more relevance in the enjoyment of the divine life in heaven) acknowledgement of the church as sacrament need cause no difficulty. Saying that the church is sacrament claims no ultimacy for either in relation to Christ. This is particularly clear in the work of the *Eastern Orthodox theologian John Zizioulas, for whom Christ is present in the church not only as constituting it in those present, but being himself constituted by them, with repeated invocation of the Spirit sustaining freedom for communion with one another. Sensitivity to Orthodox criticism of neglect of the work of the Spirit in the sacraments is no doubt reflected in the work of Jürgen *Moltmann and Leonardo *Boff. Moltmann points to a future kept open for transformation by the gift of the Spirit who acts in Christ; Boff calls for discernment of the Spirit in movements of liberating protest and hope for the future. Liberation movements may be going to have profound effects on the understanding of the church as sacrament, especially in reconsideration of the *laity as sacrament to one another in Christ.

Ann Loades

Brown, D. W., and Loades, A. (eds.), *Christ: The Sacramental Word* (1996).

Chauvet, L.-M., and Lumbala, F. K. (eds.), *Liturgy and the Body* (1995).

de Lubac, H., *The Church: Paradox and Mystery* (1969).

Downey, M., and Fragomeni, R. (eds.), *A Promise of Presence: Studies in Honour of David Power* (1992).

McPartlan, P., *The Eucharist Makes the Church: Henri de Lubac and John Zizioulas in Dialogue* (1993).

—— *Sacrament of Salvation: An Introduction to Eucharistic Ecclesiology* (1995).

Martos, J., *Doors to the Sacred: A Historical Introduction to Sacraments in the Christian Church* (1992).

Moltmann, J., *The Church in the Power of the Spirit* (1991).

Rahner, K., *Studies in Modern Theology* (1965).

sacrifice is one of the most inescapable, impenetrable, and off-putting themes in Christian thought. While the concept is prominent both in *Jesus' own teaching and in the way that his life and *death have traditionally been understood and given meaning by theologians, it has provoked serious divisions between churches and proved repellent to many sensitive Christians. The word 'sacrifice', used both as a verb and as a noun, occurs 213 times in the bible, figures prominently in virtually all *eucharistic liturgies and recurs again and again in the familiar *hymns that have been so important in shaping popular faith. While frequently applied to human offerings of *praise and thanksgiving to *God, or more specific surrenders of self, it is most commonly used in Christian thought to refer to Jesus' death on the *cross, raising a host of questions as to who exactly is making the sacrifice, to whom it is offered, and just where its efficacy lies.

The Christian understanding of the centrality of sacrifice derives in large part from its importance to the ancient Israelites. The cultic slaughter of birds and animals and their presentation as burnt offerings to Yahweh in the *Temple is a prominent theme in the early books of the Hebrew bible. As in other primal religions, the main purpose of these sacrificial rituals seems to have been to provide a means for closer communion between the human and the divine. Giving thanks and making atonement for sin were also important

elements in the Israelite cult although the notion of propitiating an angry deity, which was to be taken up as a major theme in some Christian circles, does not appear to have been a significant motive. The book of *Psalms, and even more the great prophets writing in the 8th and 7th centuries BC, shifted the emphasis away from the ritual slaughter of victims towards the inner sacrifice of the broken heart and the moral qualities of repentance, obedience, and selflessness.

This interiorization and spiritualization of sacrifice is to a large extent confirmed and continued in Jesus' teachings as recorded in the gospels. The emphasis here is on the cost of *discipleship expressed in terms of leading a life of selflessness and even self-abandonment. *John's gospel introduces a more objective and ritualistic element of sacrifice into the treatment of Jesus' death as, for example, in the reference to the flow of *blood and *water from his side. This aspect is more emphatically emphasized in other books in the NT, notably in the Epistle to the *Hebrews which clearly locates Jesus' death in the context of the Israelite cult and presents him as the ultimate high priest who, through shedding his own blood, has made a perfect and all-sufficient *atonement for the *sins of the world. The Pauline epistles, echoing a theme that many scholars find also in John's gospel, firmly identify Jesus with the passover lamb and stress the mystical participation of Christians in his death and *Resurrection. The book of *Revelation in its dramatic portrayal of the lamb slain from the foundation of the world highlights a motif found elsewhere in the NT where sacrifice is presented as revelatory of the eternal and essential character of God.

Efforts to explain the meaning of these complex and sometimes conflicting biblical images have led to bitter argument and division. The fundamental split between liberals and conservatives within the church arises to a large extent from different understandings of the nature of Jesus' sacrifice. While *evangelicals have stressed its substitutionary character and once-for-all efficacy, those of a more liberal persuasion prefer to see it primarily as exemplary or revelatory and stress its ongoing nature. The major division in western Christendom inaugurated by the *Reformation has long centred on disagreement about the sacrificial nature of the Eucharist, with Roman Catholics tending to stress the objective re-presentation of Christ's sacrifice in the mass and Protestants preferring the focus to be on remembering his all-sufficient work on the cross.

In view of all this dissension and dispute it is not surprising that several modern Christian theologians have suggested that the whole notion of sacrifice should be abandoned. They argue that it belongs to a particular era of human evolution and religious development that is now over and takes us back to an unappealing world of ritual slaughter and cultic blood-shedding to appease and pacify an angry deity. It is understandable that many Christians today find notions of penal substitution and propitiation repellent; they are uneasy with a doctrine of atonement that portrays Jesus' death on the cross in crude legalistic or commercial terms as a ransom paid to God for sin. *Feminist and *liberation theologians in particular feel that the connotations of denial and giving up implicit in a sacrifice-centred Christian theology are inappropriate to the life-enhancing and affirming message of the gospel.

The religious value of the notion of sacrifice has also undoubtedly been suspect in the eyes of many 20th-century theologians because of its association with the glorification of *war and *suffering. This reached its apogee at the time of the First World War when thousands of young men were sent off to the carnage of the trenches with sermons about the nobility and heroism of sacrifice ringing in their ears. The 1920s and 1930s saw the gradual abandonment of the gospel of strenuous self-sacrifice that had been preached so vigorously in the Victorian and Edwardian eras. However, significant revisionist work by French Catholic theologians in the area of eucharistic theology helped to rehabilitate the concept of sacrifice. Perhaps the most important study was Eugène Masure's *The Christian Sacrifice* (1944) which made an important connection between sacrifice and order and defined it as the destiny and end of humans as creatures of God.

In the closing decades of the 20th century there was a significant revival of interest in the theology of sacrifice in both Britain and continental Europe. In part this may well have sprung from a prophetic reaction against the prevailing culture of instant self-gratification and conspicuous consumption. Concern with the condition of the environment and with issues of economic and social *justice in an increasingly polarized world prompted a heightened recognition of the urgent need for richer communities to develop more sacrificial lifestyles (see GLOBAL ETHICS). Recent work by patristic scholars, notably Robert Daly and Frances Young, has stressed the importance of sacrifice in the thinking of the early church. The *ecumenical movement may also have made a contribution to rehabilitating the concept of sacrifice by encouraging much closer agreement between Catholics and Protestants on both its character and centrality in eucharistic theology. A significant agreed statement produced by the Anglican and Roman Catholic Commission in 1978 rejected a view of the Eucharist either as a repetition or mere memorial of Christ's sacrifice and spoke rather of 'entering into the movement of his self-offering'.

Stress on the self-offering of Christ, and by analogy on the self-giving of God, was a noticeable and growing theme in late 20th-century Christian thought. In part, it was a dimension of the pervasive and influential doctrine of patripassianism, or the suffering of God. Seminal in the development of this strand was the work of Jürgen *Moltmann, first in his classic *The Crucified God* (1974) and later in *The Trinity and the Kingdom of God* (1981) where he argues that God's eternal nature is best summed up in the phrase 'the self-sacrifice of love'. A number of contemporary theologians, following Moltmann's lead, went beyond the idea of the suffering God and developed the notion of the sacrificing God. In this interpretation, sacrifice, understood in terms of costly self-giving and the bringing about of life through the agency of death, is seen as the most distinctive characteristic of both the being and the work of God. The God who is revealed in Christ is continually sacrificing himself, as much in the activity of *creation as in the work of *redemption through his son. He is the author of life through sacrifice. The Christian revelation points us to the truth that growth and progress are only possible through self-limitation and surrender and that sacrifice, understood as a two-way process of giving and responding, dying and rising again, lies at the heart of our relationship with our creator and redeemer.

This new emerging theology of sacrifice largely steers clear of notions of propitiation and so avoids the profound flaw in the way

that sacrifice has traditionally been presented in the teaching of most churches and understood by many Christians. Instead of being seen primarily as something that is given to God, either by us or by Christ on our behalf, with the object of pleasing him or appeasing his wrath, sacrifice becomes the essential work of God himself, whose very nature is constant and costly self-giving. The notion of the sacrificial nature of God has been important in creation theology, where it has been interpreted in terms of a divine self-withdrawal and self-limitation.

The theme of sacrifice also bulked large in the late 20th-century revival of interest among academic theologians in the theme of atonement. Significant British work in this area includes Colin Gunton's *The Actuality of Atonement* (1988) which finds that of all the metaphors which have been employed to describe the saving action of the cross, 'sacrifice brings us closest not just to the historic action of God in Christ but to the heart of his very being' (p. 197) and Paul Fiddes's *The Creative Suffering of God* (1988) which suggests that 'the sacrifice of God is woven into the whole painful story of human evolution' (p. 29). This theme is also developed in an important and little-noticed work by John Moses, *The Sacrifice of God: A Holistic Theory of Atonement* (1992).

One of the most fruitful and exciting developments arising from this renewed interest in sacrificial theology may well prove to be the construction of a new *natural theology based on the power of sacrifice as the engine that drives all life in the universe as well as the principle eternally at work at the heart of the Godhead. Scientists, particularly biochemists and biologists, are increasingly finding and demonstrating the extent to which life at all levels is dependent on death. An important dimension of this discovery is the phenomenon known as programmed cell death through which the healthy growth and development of all living creatures depends on cells constantly dying and being reborn. This motif of life proceeding out of and through death in the natural world seems to parallel the liberating power of the blood poured out in the sacrificial rituals of primitive religions and the mysterious continuum of crucifixion and resurrection which is at the heart of the Christian faith.

Interfaith *dialogue may also have an important part to play in rehabilitating and refining the theme of sacrifice in modern Christian thought. Other religious traditions testify to the cosmic power of sacrifice to redeem, perfect, and renew creation and to unite all things with their creator. The Vedic texts of *Hinduism, in particular, speak of creation coming out of sacrifice and dramatically portray its costly, all-consuming fire. For Christians, however, this mysterious eternal power will always remain uniquely instanced on the cross, a sacrifice that is at once inclusive, incorporative, and transformative and where victim and priest are one in the supreme moment of divine self-giving and abandonment.

See also PRIESTHOOD.

Ian Bradley

Ashby, G., *Sacrifice: Its Nature and Purpose* (1988).

Bourdillon, M. E. C., *Sacrifice* (1980).

Bradley, I. C., *The Power of Sacrifice* (1995).

Daly, R. J., *Christian Sacrifice: The Judaeo-Christian Background before Origen* (1978).

—— *The Origins of the Christian Doctrine of Sacrifice* (1978).

Dillistone, F. W., *The Christian Understanding of Atonement*, 2nd edn. (1984).

Sykes, S. W. (ed.), *Sacrifice and Redemption: Durham Essays in Theology* (1991).

Young, F., *Sacrifice and the Death of Christ*, 2nd edn. (1983).

saints. The notion of the Christian saint, or holy person, traces its scriptural origins primarily to the Pauline theology of the holiness of the corporate *church, or Body of Christ, in which all its members have their specific gifts and part to play (Rom. 12: 4–8; cf. Eph. 2: 19). A recognizable cult of the saints, however, began to develop only with the 2nd-century *martyrs, and burgeoned from the 4th century, with the emergence of the first great *monastic leaders, such as Antony of Egypt and Martin of Tours. In the early Middle Ages, devotion to the saints took a popular, local, and unregulated form in which the influence of the local bishop was prominent. The first historically attested canonization was that of Ulrich of Augsburg by John XV in 993. In around 1170 Alexander III affirmed in a letter to King Canute of Sweden that no one should be venerated as a saint without the authority of the Roman Church, a position which became canon law in Gregory IX's decretals of 1234. While all Christian traditions recognize the place of the sanctified and exemplary individual, the cult of the saints is particularly associated with Roman Catholic and Orthodox Christianity. At the time of the *Reformation, the *Protestant churches took a sceptical view of the place of devotion to the saints in Christian life, not finding sufficient scriptural warrant. Beatification and canonization in the Catholic Church is pursued by the Congregation for the Causes of Saints, and the conditions for the processes were laid out by Benedict XIV in the 18th century.

The designation of a man or woman as a 'saint' is the judgement by the Christian community of the day, both in its local and universal form, as to the desired qualities of the exemplary Christian life. Saints from different periods therefore stand in sharp contrast to each other. Seventeenth-century philanthropic saints such as Vincent de Paul represent a very different model of *holiness from that of the founding fathers of great 12th-century monastic orders, such as Bernard of Clairvaux or Norbert of Xanten. In the lives of the first monastic founders, for instance, we see the evolution of the early church of martyrdom and social exclusion into a state church for which radical Christian life entailed heroic *asceticism and voluntary withdrawal to *desert places. Likewise the premier saints of the 13th century, like Dominic and *Francis, represented the evangelical activity of the church among new strata of the population, while figures such as Thomas *Aquinas and Bonaventure reflected a recognition of the role of the new learning in the formation of Christian civilization. The official character of canonization, at least in the Roman Catholic Church, adds a further dimension to the construction of the saint. Superimposed upon the spontaneous response of the local population to a man or woman perceived to be holy is the political judgement of the universal church as to whether the qualities of the individual are those which the church of the day would wish to see as universally exemplary.

The role of historiography, which is also a crucial part in the canonization process, has often been precisely to mediate between local records and traditions which reflect the impact of exceptional Christian individuals upon their environment and the more politically charged environment of the institutional church in its universality. Hagiography, with its origins in late classical biography and martyrs' *Acta*, has remained a deeply conservative genre, which has tended to stress the *miraculous effects of an individual's life and to underplay the role of internal struggle and personal development.

Interesting transformations in the institutionalized nature of the saint have taken place in the modern period, with the *Kantian notion of virtue as struggle and with the more nuanced understanding of the human subject as a bundle of internal processes. The case of *Teresa (Thérèse) of Lisieux offers a striking combination of traditional Catholic piety with reflexivity in the implied construction of her identity as a saint within her own lifetime. The notion of the saint, which is common to many religious traditions, has been appropriated at times also within wholly secular contexts. J.-P. Sartre's designation of the playwright Jean Genet as 'saint' in recognition of what Sartre perceived to be his exceptional innocence and unworldliness marks an interesting development in this direction. But it also reflects back in a challenging way upon the Christian tradition of sanctity, which sees in the Christian saint not only an exceptional *moral individual but also a man or woman who exercised a certain detachment from the society of the day and its values. The nomadic and homosexual Genet, victimized and oppressed, but also resourceful, unconventional, and touched by innocence, does to some extent give secular form to the societal awkwardness and unaccountability of the Christian saint, called to a pattern of life and values that transcend the particular, but who is also an individual embedded in specific social, historical, and cultural contexts. A similar blurring of boundaries was seen in the widespread expressions of grief at the death in 1997 of Diana, Princess of Wales, a quasi-cultic phenomenon that contained some of the elements of an early-medieval popular canonization in which the themes of royalty, beauty, personal struggle, and selflessness richly combined.

Oliver Davies

Benedict XIV, *De servorum dei beatificatione et beatorum canonizatione* (4 vols.; 1734–8).

Brown, Peter, *The Cult of the Saints: Its Rise and Function in Latin Christianity* (1980).

Delehaye, Hippolyte, *The Legends of the Saints*, 4th edn., ET (1962).

Furlong, Monica, *Thérèse of Lisieux* (1987).

Heffernan, Thomas, *Sacred Biography: Saints and their Biographers in the Middle Ages* (1988).

Philippart, Guy (ed.), *Hagiographies* (2 vols.; 1994–6).

salvation shares the same basic meaning as *redemption, where it is discussed at greater length. Nevertheless, salvation is too important a word to be omitted, and has, moreover, a wider connotation. *Religions are often somewhat simplistically divided between 'religions of salvation', primarily other-worldly orientated, and religions concerned with nature and the well-being of earthly life. The Israelite is certainly not, narrowly, a 'religion of salvation', but salvation is all the same an important theme within the OT, both for the individual and for the nation: deliverance from danger, ransom from slavery, healing in sickness, victory in battle. The psalms frequently appeal to *God as saviour: 'This poor man cried, and the Lord heard him, and saved him out of all his troubles' (Ps. 34: 6, cf. 7: 10; 18: 27; etc.). The *psalms remained the primary prayer book of Christianity and carried OT concepts of salvation into the church's daily life, but NT usage of the term is far less earthly. It becomes a central term for defining what Christian conversion and belief are all about—'the way of salvation' (Acts 16: 17). Catechetical theology has popularly described the whole of *revelation as 'salvation history'. 'Today salvation has come to this house', declares Jesus when Zacchaeus, a wealthy publican, promises to return fourfold anything he has acquired unjustly (Luke 19: 9), while Paul insists that he is not ashamed of the gospel 'for it is the power of God unto salvation to everyone that believed' (Rom. 1: 16). Both God and *Jesus are named as saviour. Thus 'God our Saviour will have all men to be saved' (1 Tim. 2: 3–4) but Jesus 'became the author of eternal salvation unto all them that obey him' (Heb. 5: 9). Moreover, 'there is no other name under heaven given to men whereby we may be saved' (Acts 4: 12).

While in the gospels the stress is more on the present, something already real for those who believe in Jesus, as time passes the sense of salvation undoubtedly shifts towards the future, the destiny of the faithful after death, and this next-worldly and individualistic dimension came to dominate more and more. But it was increasingly tied to a strong *church base. *Extra ecclesiam nulla salus* (outside the church there is no salvation) became a frequently repeated and near-dogmatic assertion. The so-called Athanasian *Creed (in fact composed in Latin, probably in the 5th century, but much used by most western churches, Catholic and Protestant, until modern times) ends by declaring that no one can be saved who does not faithfully adhere to it as expressing the Catholic faith. The contrast between this and the *universalism suggested by 1 Tim. seems considerable. With salvation being seen as a matter of entry into heaven, such a question as that of the salvation of unbaptized infants (see LIMBO) was entirely about the state after death of people who had never been church members.

A return to less ecclesial, more universalist, and also this-worldly concepts of Christian salvation has been characteristic of the later 20th century. 'Is it not true to say', asked *Bonhoeffer from prison, 'that individualistic concern for personal salvation has almost completely left us all?' (5 May 1944). He went on to suggest that it might be 'a cardinal error' to regard Christianity as 'a religion of salvation'. While Bonhoeffer's prison reflections have been immensely influential, particularly on the 1960s revival of *liberal theology, the larger tendency may be rather to interpret salvation as inherently dualist, a genuine this-worldly deliverance, whether personal or social, being needed to sacramentalize a 'saving' which transcends anything earthly. But is human 'salvation' universally dependent upon Christ? *Vatican II authoritatively rejected the traditional understanding of 'outside the church no salvation' when it affirmed that those who know neither the gospel nor the church but who seek God with a sincere heart 'may achieve eternal salvation' (LG 16). *Rahner attempted to describe such people as 'anonymous Christians'. John Hick, on the contrary, has argued that Jesus is but one point among many through which God 'saves' humankind. While such a view profoundly undermines the whole central theology of Christianity which in one form or another is grounded on the uniqueness of Christ, it involves both a 'Copernican Revolution' (Hick's phrase) in the understanding of all religion and a new sense of what 'salvation' signifies. Few words proper to Christianity's core vocabulary have at present a less defined meaning.

Adrian Hastings

Bonhoeffer, D., *Letters and Papers from Prison* (1953).
Ford, David, *Self and Salvation* (1999).
Hick, John, *God and the Universe of Faiths* (1973).
Rahner, K., 'Salvation' in K. Rahner (ed.), *Sacramentum Mundi* (1970), v. 405–38.

sanctification, see JUSTIFICATION; REDEMPTION; HOLINESS.

Satan, see DEVIL.

Scandinavian Christian thought.

The theological tradition in Scandinavia has many close ties with the rest of Europe. Scandinavian theologians have adopted ideas from Continental *theology but often modified them in an interesting way. There have also been original contributions to Christian thinking from the Scandinavian countries that have influenced theology in other parts of the world. It should be noted, too, that some famous theologians and philosophers from other European countries worked in Scandinavia for part of their lives, for example Samuel Pufendorf, René *Descartes, and Ernst Cassirer. Today there are clear differences in cultural climate, including theology, between the Scandinavian countries, Norway, Sweden, Finland, and Denmark, but it must be remembered that these four have been interrelated in many different ways throughout history, so that national borders have for long periods been without relevance.

During the Middle Ages one person stood out as particularly influential: not a university theologian, but a *woman from the countryside, St Birgitta (1303–73). She was a visionary and mystic who strongly influenced both European politics and the Catholic Church. The order she founded is still active and her name has been mentioned as a possible patron saint for the European Union. Her *visions, recorded in Latin, have been published in a critical edition by the Royal Academy of Letters, History, and Antiquities in Stockholm. It is interesting to see how her working life as the mother of eight children and her concerns with political issues are both reflected in and shaped by her visions.

Universities were founded in Uppsala in 1477 and in Copenhagen in 1478. One of the last Catholic university theologians before the Reformation is important in a European perspective: Poul Helgesen (1485–1535), a Dane, the main representative in Scandinavia of the reform-oriented Catholicism inspired by *Erasmus of Rotterdam. Uppsala and Copenhagen together with Lund, whose university was founded in 1666, would remain the principal centres of Christian thought for a long period.

The *Reformation resulted in the establishment of a *Lutheran theological tradition throughout Scandinavia, closely related to the German. The most theologically significant and influential among the reformers was a Dane, Nils Hemmingsen (1513–1600), who studied in Wittenberg and whose theology clearly shows the influence of Melanchthon. Sweden had Olaus Petri (1493–1552) and Finland, Michael Agricola (1510–57). Close links with Germany were maintained throughout the period of Lutheran orthodoxy.

In the 18th century, connections with England became stronger. Among those who visited England was the great Swedish botanist, Carl Linnaeus (1707–78). He was also a theological thinker, an exponent of a theology with links to the natural sciences. He came more and more under the influence of the book of Ecclesiastes, with a consequent darkening of his theological thinking.

For a Scandinavian theologian from the 18th century who is still read outside Scandinavia and plays a role in the contemporary theological scene, one must abandon mainstream Lutheran theology to focus on Emanuel Swedenborg (1688–1772). He was the son of an orthodox theologian and educated as a scientist. In his theological writing he appears as one of the great visionaries in the European tradition (see BLAKE, WILLIAM). He rejected such central orthodox doctrines as the Trinity, original sin, and salvation through faith alone. He saw the human task as consisting of openness towards God and the transformation of divine influences into practical action.

One 19th-century university professor from Uppsala, Erik Gustaf Geijer (1783–1847), has been of great importance for many modern theologians, especially in Sweden. He was primarily a historian, a philosopher, and a poet in Sweden's living tradition. His theological works develop the idea of an I/thou relationship as the basis both of religious knowledge and of a moral and spiritual life. There are clear similarities between Geijer and such modern thinkers as Martin Buber.

The general religious situation in Scandinavia, however, was not dominated by Linnaeus, Swedenborg, and Geijer. Alongside the still prevailing Lutheran orthodoxy, the influence of *Pietism was far more pervasive within this tradition. The founder of the Swedish congregational church, Svenska Missionsförbundet, was an interesting theologian, P. P. Waldenström. He developed a subjective doctrine of atonement that remains influential.

One alternative to Pietism was offered by the Dane, N. F. S. Grundtvig (1783–1872). He saw culture in its national form as a fertile ground for the Christian message, and the development of the intellectual, moral, and aesthetic potential of every human being as a primary Christian task. His theological programme required a striving towards education and cultural openness. Very little of his work, however, is available in English. This was a golden age for Danish theology.

One of Grundtvig's contemporaries was Søren *Kierkegaard, representing a totally different theological mood and method. Kierkegaard stands out as Scandinavia's most powerful and original contributor to Christian thought. Fiercely opposed to Grundtvig's brand of Christian humanism, he sought, in a series of dazzling and consciously literary works, many of them pseudonymous, to shake contemporary Danish Christians out of their cultural complacency by confronting them with the scandal of Christianity inherent in the idea that God, the 'Absolute Other', became a man. His insistence on the importance of the individual's appropriation of truth and his psychological treatment of the concept of 'angst' (dread) lie behind much of the 'turn to the self' of 20th-century theology, but the breadth of his positive vision of redemption has yet to be fully acknowledged. His importance to modern theology and the philosophy of *existentialism can hardly be overstated. Another Danish theologian of note from the same period is H. L. Martensen, whose work illustrates the importance of Hegel to Scandinavian theology. Attacked by Kierkegaard, he also stood in some opposition to Grundtvig.

At the beginning of the 20th century, a Swedish priest studying Persian religion in Paris moved to Uppsala University as professor and in 1914 he became archbishop of Sweden. This was Nathan Söderblom (1866–1931), best remembered as a key figure in the *ecumenical movement, but his theology is worth reading in its own right. Söderblom was a specialist in comparative *religion and saw all the religions of the world as a function of the meeting between humans and God's self-revelation. God makes himself known not only through the *religious experience of humankind, but also through moral insight and intellectual endeavour of every kind. The *revelation of God gives us access to reality, and there is no conflict between the knowledge of natural *science or history and religious insights. Of special importance for religious thought are the great mystics in different religious traditions. Söderblom introduced a distinction between two kinds of *mysticism—a mysticism of infinity and a mysticism of personality. He attached great significance to the latter and was influenced by the personalist philosophy of Geijer. He saw the great prophets in the biblical tradition as playing a central role in the history of God's revelation and developed a biblical theology from his general view of revelation. It enabled him to be open towards historical biblical criticism; he saw the discovery of influences from other religions in the bible as theologically fruitful. The bible was for Söderblom not unique but the clearest witness of revelation. This experience-related theology was a good basis not only for ecumenism but also for *dialogue with world religions. In his ecumenical vision Söderblom looked forward to the time when Muslims and Christians could understand and respect one another in their common belief in the only God. His Gifford lectures of 1931 are published in English (The Living God (1933)). Söderblom's heritage lives on in Uppsala in the conviction that a primary task for theological thinking is to find models for integrating religious insights and other kinds of knowledge and to analyse the role of religious experience in human life. Söderblom's aim of relating Christian thinking to other religions has been supplemented in recent Uppsala theology by attempts to study connections and conflicts between Christianity and other widespread world-views in modern society.

Later in the 20th century the University of Lund became the centre of theology in Scandinavia. Here emerged what is known in Scandinavia as the Lundensian school of theology, its exponents including Anders Nygren (1890–1978), and Gustaf Aulén (1879–1977).

In his early writing Nygren tried to lay an intellectual foundation for religion and theology. He allied himself with neo-Kantian philosophy in Germany and developed an idea of special categories for religion and morals in the human cognitive apparatus. These categories are at work in human understanding alongside the theoretical ones, analysed by *Kant himself, and are essential for human cognition. To every category there is a corresponding basic question. For the theoretical category it is: what is true? For the religious category the question is: what is eternal? In the moral and religious fields the answer to the basic questions are not directly given by different religions or moral statements. In these fields there is always a leading idea, the answer to the basic categorial question, that holds together the whole system and gives it a special character. Nygren calls it the basic motif. Now the task of Christian theology is to find the basic motif in Christianity. This is called motif research, and became the theological programme of the Lundensian school. In his most famous book, Eros and Agape, Nygren tried to show that the basic motif of Christianity was a special kind of *love, agape, which always comes from God and is bestowed on humans. It is not caused by any good qualities in human beings; on the contrary it creates the value of the beloved person. In Christian *ethics the basic motif is the same as in theology (see MORALITY). A

Christian must transmit the *agape* of God to his fellow-creatures regardless of their merits. In the history of Christianity, however, another kind of love—*eros*—has threatened the basic motif. *Eros* is a demanding love caused by the value of the object. It is directed from humans to God. *Eros and Agape* is a monumental description of the struggles and compromises between the two motifs. Nygren finds clear examples of the *agape* motif in *Paul and *Luther. The mystical tradition, however, consists largely of the *eros* motif, a claim that has often been challenged. Another problem in Nygren's theology lies in the separation of religious insights from the theoretical category and hence from any application of the ordinary question of truth or falsehood. In his last book, *Meaning and Method* (1972), Nygren claimed an affinity between his theory and the philosophy of the later *Wittgenstein, particularly to Wittgenstein's idea of different language games.

Gustaf Aulén shared many of Nygren's basic methodological suppositions. His exposition of Christian doctrine is an attempt to develop in detail the ideas that are basic to the whole Christian tradition (*The Faith of the Christian Church*, ET (1948)). Lutheran influence is clear and chimes with Nygren's theory of Luther as an exponent of the *agape* motif. Especially influential is Aulén's study of the doctrine of *atonement in *Christus Victor*. He found in the early church an alternative both to the objective doctrine of *Anselm and to the subjective theory of *Abelard. This classical understanding of atonement starts from a perspective of conflict. God does not direct everything that happens in the world. He is struggling against evil forces. Through his love embodied in Christ he wins a decisive victory on the cross, and by being united with Christ through faith we participate in this victory, though the struggle will go on until the end of the world. Only from the eschatological perspective can God be seen as the Almighty. Aulén enjoyed a long and active life and published many books in which influences from Nygren played a minor role. He became especially interested in the metaphorical character of religious language and in *The Drama and the Symbols*, ET (1970) he developed the dramatic vision expressed in *Christus Victor*.

An important element in 20th-century Scandinavian theology has been research on Luther. Close historical study of different aspects of Luther's thinking has been seen as a source of inspiration for modern theology. Towards the end of the century this research was perhaps at its most vital in Finland and Norway, as exemplified in the Finn, L. Pinomaa. Gustaf Wingren at Lund also belongs to the group of theologians inspired by Luther studies. He opposed both the philosophical basis for theology developed by the Lundensian school and *Barth's attempt to explain the meaning of the gospel starting from the Incarnation. For Wingren it is necessary to develop an awareness of God as creator of the world and ruler by precepts of the law in order to provide a background and point of connection for God's redemptive and restorative work in Christ. Humans who have realized their guilt in ordinary life can understand and accept the gospel when it is preached to them in church (*Gospel and Church*, ET (1964)).

At Aarhus University in Denmark a highly original Christian thinker, K. E. Løgstrup, worked over a long period, developing his thoughts in clear opposition to the Kierkegaard tradition. His starting-point was a phenomenological analysis of the basic features of life. Human life expresses itself in two ways regardless of all cultural influences. There are spontaneous expressions of trust and compassion whose inherent goodness we can experience. But on the other hand there are elemental forces which are hostile to life, such as envy. The fight between the forces emerging in natural human life as good or bad provides a basis for a religious interpretation of the world, leading to an overall picture of the universe as creation and of humans as dependent on a force greater than themselves. Løgstrup's Christian metaphysics based on phenomenological analysis is an important element in the religious thought of all Scandinavian countries, especially Denmark, and has also been influential in Germany.

This article began with a mystic who combined a deeply religious life with practical work. It ends with someone exemplifying the same characteristics, Dag Hammarskjöld (1905–61), who was Secretary-General of the United Nations. His philosophical and religious diary, *Markings*, is one of Scandinavia's most powerful contributions to Christian thought: the book bears astonishing witness to human openness towards the furthest depths of existence.

Anders Jeffner

Allchin, A. M., *N. F. S. Grundtvig: An Introduction to his Life and Work* (1997).

Aulén, G., *Christus Victor* (1930), ET (1931).

——*Dag Hammarskjöld's White Book: An Analysis of* Markings (1969).

Bergquist, L., *Saint Birgitta* (1996).

Gierow, K., *The Published Writings of Gustaf Aulén* (1979).

Hammarskjöld, D., *Markings* (1963), ET (1988).

Jonsson, I., *Emanuel Swedenborg* (1971).

Kegley, C. W. (ed.), *The Philosophy and Theology of Anders Nygren* (1970).

Løgstrup, K. E., *The Ethical Demand* (1997).

Nygren, N., *Eros and Agape* (2 vols.; 1930–6), ET (1953).

Pinomaa, L. (ed.), *Finnish Theology Past and Present* (1963).

Söderblom, N., *The Living God* (1933).

Stendahl, B., *Søren Kierkegaard* (1976).

Sundkler, B., *Nathan Söderblom: His Life and Work* (1968).

Wingren, G., *Gospel and Church* (1958), ET (1964).

Schillebeeckx, Edward

Schillebeeckx, Edward (1914–). A Flemish *Dominican whose teaching career was spent in the Netherlands, cockpit of avant-garde Catholicism in the 1960s, Schillebeeckx developed his theology from a *Thomism flavoured by additives of *existentialism and phenomenology to an exegetically sophisticated version of *liberation theology, where both modern philosophical *hermeneutics and the critical sociology of the (quasi-Marxian) Frankfurt School played important parts.

He was influenced while studying at Louvain by the epistemologically somewhat agnostic revisionist Thomism of Dominikus de Petter, who elevated 'implicit intuition' above the concept in the evaluation of knowing, and then in *France by the historical theologian and social critic Marie-Dominique Chenu, whose principal concerns he came to share. Appointed professor of dogmatics and the history of theology at the Dutch Catholic faculty of Nijmegen in 1958, he remained there until retirement in 1983. The masterly grasp of *sacramental theology in his first major work, *De sacramentele Heilseconomie* (1952) was achieved by integrating a rich historical knowledge with philosophical acuity in the service of a christological and Trinitarian reading of the sacraments—as became apparent in its briefer continuation, *Christ the Sacrament of the Encounter with God* (1959), ET (1963). Around the time of *Vatican II, which he attended as a theological adviser to the Dutch bishops, Schillebeeckx brought out a series of works uniting self-conscious orthodoxy with an 'open' Thomism: thus *Marriage: Human Reality and Saving Mystery* (1963), ET (1965), the essays collected into two volumes as *Revelation and Theology* (1964), ET (1967–8), and *The Eucharist* (1967), ET (1968).

In 1967, however, struck by the pastoral impact of the *secularization crisis in Western Europe (and, theologically, North America), he abandoned his earlier philosophical scheme. In *God the Future of Man* (1969), he replaced metaphysics by a scanning of contemporary experience. The *hope by which people resist dehumanizing situations constitutes a 'point of insertion' of the gospel. The consequent need to unite the political with the mystical furnishes the key to his later trilogy. There he presented (1) a report on his exegetical probings into the *Jesus of history—*Jesus: An Experiment in Christology* (1974), ET (1979); (2) an enquiry into the New Testament's theologies of *grace—*Christ: The Christian Experience in the Modern World* (1977), ET (1980), and (3) an account of the *church as the 'Jesus movement'—*Church: The Human Story of God* (1990), ET (1990). His later christology, though judged by the Roman authorities to lack doctrinal clarity, escaped more lightly than did his studies of church order where *ministry in the local church, spontaneously gestated, floats alarmingly free from the *apostleship instituted by Christ: thus *Ministry: A Case for Change* (1980), ET (1981) and (more moderately) *Church with a Human Face: A New and Expanded Theology of Ministry* (1985, in both English and Dutch).

Aidan Nichols, OP

Bowden, J., *Edward Schillebeeckx: Portrait of a Theologian* (1983).
Kennedy, P., *Schillebeeckx* (1993).

schism in Greek originally meant a crack or tear. The word appears only three times in the NT, all in 1 Corinthians (1: 10; 11: 18; 12: 25), each time referring to the sort of quarrelling which, Paul believed, had no place in the *church. It has since developed a precise ecclesiastical meaning as a definite rupture in *communion and church life, setting altar against altar, bishop against bishop, but not as such involving doctrinal issues that would turn it into *heresy. It is, then, in its nature something opposed to the church's *unity. For *Aquinas it is a sin against *peace (*ST* II-II q. 39): his treatment of it is followed by a consideration of war. In early Christian thought, schism was seldom clearly separated in theory or practice from heresy and, indeed, most long-lasting schisms developed a doctrinal element.

The traditional western view of schism was largely formulated in the North African church, first by Cyprian and then, in regard to *Donatism, by *Augustine. While Catholics and Donatists disagreed doctrinally about the validity of the *sacraments administered by unworthy priests, they consisted of two networks of bishops present in the same towns, each with their own faithful. This came to be seen as the classic example of a schismatic situation.

The most extensive schisms within Christian history were, first, that dividing the Greek and Latin churches from the early Middle Ages until today and, second, the Great Western Schism (1378–1417) when there were two, and then three, popes simultaneously claiming authority over the church. Each was recognized by part of the church (France, for example, recognizing the pope in Avignon, England the one in Rome) and it was virtually impossible to decide which was the 'true' one. Reflecting on such a destructive situation may, however be usefully constructive. At least it generated *conciliarism.

For Christian thought, schism is not only a painful reality but also presents a theoretical problem. When conflict turns into institutional separation (including mutual excommunications) does this separate one group from the church or are both sides still in the church? 'From' or 'in' becomes a crucial ecclesiological issue. If the church is essentially a 'communion', how can people not in communion all be in one church? The general answer of the early church was 'No, it is impossible'. That remained the answer both of Rome, for whom church membership became synonymous with communion with the *papacy, and of *Eastern Orthodoxy. But the factual reality of a divided Christianity, in which sound ecclesiastical order and the fruits of grace could be discovered on more than one side, has made it hard to sustain, and most modern *ecumenical thinking accepts that schism does not so much separate from the church as exist, however damagingly and even sinfully, within it. Such thinking originated with *Protestants. Belief in the church as primarily 'invisible' and the reality of almost innumerable divisions between different Protestant bodies had undermined a sense of schism's significance until the 20th-century ecumenical awakening. This primarily Protestant movement, in seeking to end Christian divisions, rediscovered the seriousness of schism but needed also to redefine it.

From a Catholic perspective, if the breakdown of communion between bishops could decide the church identity of those subject to them, then maybe all Frenchmen were outside the visible church in the late 14th century, though they had done nothing other than accept that the true pope resided in Avignon. This appears ridiculous: it must be accepted that at least some lengthy schisms are sustainable within what, theologically, remains a single communion. The juridical and institutional cannot dictate to the sacramental. This is increasingly recognized as true of the relationship between the Latin and Greek churches across the centuries. The public feuding and political and cultural divergences, even the arguments over the *filioque, were insufficient to separate either side from the one visible communion of the church. Such schisms should be seen instead as just appallingly blown-up versions of the 'schisms' against which Paul warned the Corinthians.

While this conclusion may sound obvious, its implications are considerable. For instance, no fully ecumenical *council could be thought to have taken place that entirely left out such a large part of the Catholic Communion as either the Greek and Russian churches or, alternatively, the Roman Catholic. A recognition of schism within the church, maiming its unity as it must, is comparable to recognition of sin within the church, maiming its holiness, or of geographical, cultural, and intellectual limitations, maiming its catholicity. Schism should never be condoned, but in a church human and imperfect by nature it may always be there. The unity to which it is opposed is a goal to be achieved as much as a mark to be recognized.

See also LATIN THEOLOGY.   **Adrian Hastings**

Argenti, C., Bruston, H., Congar, Y., and Gouyon, P., *Le Schisme: Sa signification théologique et spirituelle* (1967).
Greenslade, S. L., *Schism in the Early Church*, 2nd edn. (1964).
Hastings, A., 'The Nature of Schism', *One and Apostolic* (1963), 74–86.

Schleiermacher, Friedrich Daniel Ernst (1768–1834), German Protestant thinker, commonly acclaimed 'the father of modern theology'. Schleiermacher's books and unpublished manuscripts range widely over the various philosophical disciplines and every branch of theological studies except Old Testament. He was also an influential public figure through his pulpit in the Trinity Church, Berlin, and has earned high regard for his translations of *Plato's dialogues, thoughts on education, and pioneering work in *hermeneutics. His chief importance for Christian thought lies in his attempt to set the study of *theology on a new footing at a time when the problem was no longer the existence of errors and abuses in the *church, as in the *Reformation era, but rather the alienation of the modern world from the entire Christian tradition.

Schleiermacher lived the problem of *faith and modernity in his own pilgrimage. Born into a family of *Reformed (Calvinistic) preachers, he was sent to a Moravian school, where he underwent a *conversion and learned the love for the Saviour that lay at the heart of Moravian *Pietism. When he moved on to the Moravian seminary, his enquiring mind began to doubt what his teachers told him of Christ's deity and vicarious punishment for sin. What he lost, however, was not his faith in Christ, but his first interpretation of it. He dropped out of the seminary and transferred to the University of Halle, once the home of Pietism but for many years a stronghold of rationalism. Nevertheless, he completed his study for the ministry of the Reformed Church, and a return visit to the Moravian community later drew from him an intriguing testimony: 'I may say that I have become, after all, a pietist again, only of a higher order.'

From apologetics to church dogmatics

Schleiermacher's first book, often said to have inaugurated the modern period in Christian thought, appeared anonymously in 1799, when he was Reformed chaplain at the Charité Hospital in Berlin. A work of Christian *apologetics, On Religion: Speeches to its Cultured Despisers, was written at the urging of his friends, many of whom were disdainful of the church. Since they shared his dislike of *eighteenth century rationalism and moralism, his strategy was to persuade them that their move from the *Enlightenment to *Romanticism actually made them, 'however unintentionally, the rescuers and cherishers of religion'. But what is *religion? To answer, Schleiermacher began on the inside: not with the outward trappings of *dogma and usages that his friends despised, but with what he took to be a universal, if elusive, element in every human consciousness, including the consciousness of religion's cultured despisers. Religion is something antecedent to beliefs and dogmas, which only arise out of second-order reflection on religion.

In the second of the five speeches, Schleiermacher argued that the essence of religion, disclosed to the inward glance of introspection, is 'sense and taste for the Infinite'. He did not mean the Infinite merely as the endless multiplicity of finite things, but rather as the boundless underlying unity that makes the universe a whole. We cannot see or know this unity any more than we can see or know the universe as the sum total of finite existents. The One in the All is accessible only to feeling. To be religious, then, is to feel that everything that affects us is, at bottom, one: which is to say, that our being and living are a being and living through *God. We cannot argue that God is needed as an item in our scientific knowledge of the world, nor that religion provides us with the moral duties requisite to being good citizens. And yet the scientific enterprise fills its sails from the sense of the Infinite, the One in the All, and religion accompanies every human deed like sacred music. In short, religion is an indispensable 'third' in being human, alongside knowing and doing, and the *humanity the Romantics so eagerly cultivated is diminished whenever religion is neglected or despised.

From the second speech one could easily infer that Schleiermacher's religion was individualistic and *mystical. The inference might not be corrected even by a reading of the fourth speech, in which religious community is reduced to mutual exchange between religious individuals. But the final speech discloses that the essence of religion described in speech two is only an abstraction from the concrete mode in which religion actually exists in any society or individual. Introspection tells us what religion is, but not how we have it: we have religion only in the religions. Schleiermacher's apology accordingly reaches its final goal with the case for Christianity as the best we have yet witnessed in the world's great historical religions.

After a brief tenure as professor and university preacher at the University of Halle, Schleiermacher returned to Berlin, where he became Reformed pastor at the Trinity Church (1809) and concurrently (from 1810) professor of theology at the new university. In 1821–2 appeared the second main work on which his reputation as a Christian thinker chiefly rests: The Christian Faith, Presented Systematically According to the Principles of the Evangelical Church. Despite the reservations he had expressed in the Speeches about 'systems', the two-volume Christian Faith is a tight, comprehensive work of systematic theology. More precisely, its genre is church dogmatics. In his Brief Outline of the Study of Theology (1811; 2nd edn., 1830), Schleiermacher offered a classification of the various disciplines requisite for the preparation of church leaders. Surprisingly, he located dogmatics under 'historical theology', which is carefully distinguished from 'philosophical' and 'practical' theology and includes (besides dogmatics) exegetical theology and church history. He also divided dogmatics itself into Glaubenslehre (Christian doctrine) and Sittenlehre (Christian ethics). The Christian Faith is a work of Glaubenslehre, the science of faith. Unfortunately, the companion work on Sittenlehre, the science of morals, was not completed or published in Schleiermacher's lifetime.

Because present-day use of the term 'theology' is much less precise than his, Schleiermacher's careful division of the total field of theological study may strike us as fussy. But for two closely connected reasons it is crucial to a proper understanding of what he was doing in his dogmatic masterwork. First, The Christian Faith does not present the whole of Schleiermacher's theology, but only one division of his dogmatics. Dogmatic theology is not apologetic or philosophical theology (as he understood it). It is not practical theology, immediately transferable to the pulpit, even though it exists solely for the sake of preaching. It is not exegetical theology, which Schleiermacher took to be a co-ordinate discipline distinct from dogmatics. It is always possible to raise on exegetical grounds the question whether a dogmatic proposition is Christian. But dogmatics is concerned with the faith of a particular Christian community at the present time, and no Christian community is ever a mere replica of the apostolic age. Hence the subtitle of The Christian Faith states: 'according to the principles of the evangelical church'. Schleiermacher means the Evangelical Church of the Prussian Union—his own church, created by union of the *Lutherans and the Reformed. The dogmatic question, for him, is whether a proposition is soundly *evangelical. And it is this conception of the particularity of the dogmatic task that led Schleiermacher, secondly, to classify the discipline as 'historical'. Its object of enquiry is something that inevitably undergoes temporal change: not immutable dogma, but the living faith of a particular Christian community, or the way the community has brought the NT norm to bear on its own particular situation and expressed its faith in distinctive creeds or confessions.

Believing that the critical reception of his *Glaubenslehre* (as he liked to call it) was marred by misunderstandings, Schleiermacher paved the way for a new edition (1830–1) with two 'open letters' in a leading theological journal (1829). He was astonished that *The Christian Faith* had been widely read and judged as a philosophical work, a marshalling of proofs and concepts to support a general religiousness and a brave attempt to salvage whatever could be salvaged of church doctrines by assimilating them to a pantheistic philosophy. He insisted, in reply, that the actual aim of the work was to describe the distinctively Christian consciousness. Christians bear their entire consciousness of God as something brought about in them by Christ (see CHRISTOLOGY). Properly so called, Christianity is nothing other than faith in a revelation of God in the person of Jesus. Schleiermacher's aim, therefore, was to describe the need for *redemption and its satisfaction through Christ as actual facts of experience. Of course, it was his intention to present Christian faith more particularly in one of the specific forms it had taken (in the Prussian church). Further, Schleiermacher expressly stated his persuasion that every dogma that represents a genuine element in the Christian consciousness can be so conceived as to avoid conflict with natural and historical science. This, too, belongs to his dogmatic programme. But the substance of the programme outlined in the letters is given as proposition 19 of the new edition of *The Christian Faith*: 'Dogmatic theology is the science of the system of doctrine generally accepted in a Christian church at a given time.' Such a science is not designed to prove the truth of Christian faith. It can only be pursued from within the believing community. For this reason, Schleiermacher set on the title page of *The Christian Faith* epigraphs from *Anselm, ending with the words: 'Anyone who has not experienced will not understand.'

Leading themes in Schleiermacher's dogmatics

Schleiermacher's *Christian Faith* traverses the entire territory of the inherited *Protestant dogmatics. But his main concern was to give an account of the distinctively Christian consciousness of *sin and *grace, the overall theme of the second part of the work. Original sin is not the state into which *Adam and *Eve fell from their created innocence: the doctrines of original perfection (discussed in part one) and original sin are not about two successive stages in the lives of the first human pair, but about two possibilities that coexist in the human nature of every man and every woman. There is the possibility of being conscious of God in every moment, and there is the possibility that the consciousness of God will be inhibited by the lower or sensible self-consciousness in its commerce with the finite objects of daily existence. The strength of the sensible self-

consciousness comes partly from the fact that in each of us it develops first; the God-consciousness emerges later, and only fitfully. There is no progressive ascendancy of the spirit over the flesh. To be sure, the capacity for consciousness of God, which belongs to the *original perfection* of human nature, is never annulled, or else the relative impotence of the God-consciousness could hardly become 'sin', something for which we acknowledge responsibility. And yet, in agreement with the dogmatic tradition, Schleiermacher holds that in all of us there is a sinfulness that has its ground outside individuals, in the common life of sinful humanity into which they are born. This, then, is how we are to understand the *original sin* (German *Erbsünde*, 'inherited sin') that subjects us to a complete incapacity for good, from which we can be set free only by redemption. Actual sin is our voluntary perpetuation of what we thus inherit.

Schleiermacher's treatment of sin is a subtle interweaving of the old Reformation themes of bondage and responsibility. Here, as elsewhere, he attempts to steer between the opposite heresies of *Pelagianism and Manichaeism. His greatest contribution is unquestionably his powerful reinterpretation of original sin in terms of social solidarity. Sin is not merely an individual offence: it is a potent collective force, in each the work of all and in all the work of each. It is the corporate act and the corporate guilt of the entire human race, and we are bound to represent it not simply as a defect, but as a disease. Schleiermacher's design, of course, is to present an understanding of the malady that will correspond with the cure. Indeed, he makes it clear that at every point the doctrine of sin is a proleptic inference from the doctrine of redemption.

The presentation of Christ's person and work, like everything else in part two of *The Christian Faith*, follows in detail the rubrics of the orthodox dogmatics. But Schleiermacher does not merely reaffirm the old doctrines, and it is not difficult to identify the two controlling thoughts in his proposals for revision. In the first place, Christ is the Redeemer because in him, and him alone, the possibility given to human nature by original perfection was realized. He stands apart from us all as the Second Adam, who lived a life of sinless perfection, a life of unbroken *communion with God in total commitment to God's kingdom. This, of course, is an assertion of faith, though Schleiermacher tried in his lectures on the life of Jesus to show its compatibility with the historical sources. And in the dogmatic work he makes the idea of Jesus' perfect God-consciousness the bridge to the orthodox dogma that in Christ we have both true man and true God. For the constant potency of Jesus' consciousness of God must have been nothing less than an actual being of God in him, from which proceeded all his activity. Jesus can redeem us because he needed no redemption for himself, and we are conscious that whatever fellowship we have with God is imparted to us by the Redeemer—which is what we mean by 'grace'.

In the second place, Christ is the Redeemer by bringing into existence a new corporate life that works against the corporate life of sin. His work, to be sure, is the communication of his sinless perfection: he assumes believers into the power of his unique consciousness of God. He does this, however, neither by the kind of immediate encounter that was possible during his earthly ministry, nor merely by his teaching and example, but precisely through the new corporate life that he brought into being. It is not Christ's sufferings and death that redeem us: his passion was the consequence of his redemptive activity in establishing the new corporate life. The objectivity of the *Atonement, for Schleiermacher, lies in the fact that with Christ something entirely new entered human history and created a new humanity and a new world, not just new persons. Although not everyone can be drawn all at once into the sphere of the new corporate life, we can only say of those who are passed over that they are *not yet* regenerated. The distinction between the *elect and the non-elect rests solely on God's good pleasure (Calvin was right about that), but it is a vanishing distinction because there is only one eternal decree, not two, and it embraces all humanity in Christ.

The move from an individual to a corporate perspective on sin and grace makes Schleiermacher pre-eminently a theologian of the church, in which, as he puts it, the redemptive forces of the Incarnation are implanted. (In the 'common' Spirit of the church he acknowledges a second union of the divine essence with human nature and asserts that it is the function of the doctrine of the *Trinity, as the keystone and not the foundation of dogmatics, to affirm and protect this twofold union.) A similar move from part to whole characterizes his discussion of *creation and preservation in part one of *The Christian Faith*, which deals with the more general religious consciousness presupposed by, and contained in, the distinctively Christian religious affections. Here, too, Schleiermacher's dogmatic method enables him to set aside the difficulties posed by the opening chapters of Genesis. He did not assign canonical authority to the Old Testament anyway; but he contends that even if the narrative of the creation were accepted as revealed information about the way the world began, it would have no pertinence to the analysis of the present-day Christian consciousness. The doctrine of creation simply develops the theme of the 'feeling of absolute dependence', which Schleiermacher now (in the introduction to *The Christian Faith*) identifies as the abstract essence of the religious consciousness in every religion.

Everything positive in the doctrine of creation can be subsumed under divine preservation, of which we are conscious as the feeling of absolute dependence is combined with our perception of the world around us. And the word 'preservation' lends itself to Schleiermacher's characteristic desire always to adopt the perspective of the whole. He does not want the concept of divine activity to be construed on the model of special *providences (as we say), by which God performs individual acts of intervention in the course of nature or history. Preservation denotes God's sustaining a total law-governed system that provides an absolutely reliable stage for the Incarnation and redemption. Not only is there no need for the apparent conflict of religion and *science that arises when the doctrine of creation is taken from the book of Genesis; in actual fact, the interests of piety and the interests of natural science coincide, since both presuppose a concept of nature as a seamless nexus of orderly events. But only through the experience of redemption by Christ, explicated in part two, do we understand that the absolute causality of part one is the God of *love, and that by creation everything is disposed with a view to the revelation of God in the flesh and the formation of the kingdom of God. Love is the foundation on which everything else in our consciousness of God is built up.

Schleiermacher did not found a school, but his thoughts on dogmatic method and his reinterpretations of old dogmas have exercised an enduring influence on Christian thought in the modern period. Some of his ideas have passed (often unacknowledged) into the mainstream of Protestant theology; others have been kept alive partly by continuous criticism. Unfortunately, the criticism is still hindered, as it was in Schleiermacher's day, by misunderstandings, or at least by failure to examine closely his own programmatic statements on what he was doing. Despite his express warnings, the progression of topics in *The Christian Faith* has been read as the unfolding of a linear argument, or of the experiential steps on the way to becoming a Christian. He did not in fact see himself advancing from foundations (in the Introduction), through a developed *natural theology (part 1), to revealed Christian theology (part 2); neither did he picture anyone first having a feeling of absolute dependence, then acquiring a general theistic belief, and finally ascending to faith in Christ. Had he wished, he said, he could have reversed the order of the two parts of his system, and he insisted that the introduction strictly lay outside dogmatics proper. The feeling of absolute dependence and the consciousness of God as creator and preserver are abstractions from the Christian faith, whose distinctive affirmations are to be explicated in the main part of the work—whether it comes first or second. The introduction is not part of the explication: it serves only to define its distinctive object and to specify the method to be used. No foundation can be established for the Christian way of believing—unless we wish to say that the explication is itself the foundation.   **B. A. Gerrish**

Blackwell, Albert L., *Schleiermacher's Early Philosophy of Life: Determinism, Freedom, and Phantasy* (1982).

Clements, Keith (ed.), *Friedrich Schleiermacher: Pioneer of Modern Theology* (1987).

DeVries, Dawn, *Jesus Christ in the Preaching of Calvin and Schleiermacher* (1996).

Duke, James O., and Streetman, Robert F. (eds.), *Barth and Schleiermacher: Beyond the Impasse?* (1988).

Forstman, Jack, *A Romantic Triangle: Schleiermacher and Early German Romanticism* (1977).

Funk, Robert W. (ed.), *Schleiermacher as Contemporary* (1970).

Gerrish, B. A., *A Prince of the Church: Schleiermacher and the Beginnings of Modern Theology* (1984).

Gerrish, B. A., *Continuing the Reformation: Essays on Modern Religious Thought* (1993).

Hinze, Bradford E., *Narrating History, Developing Doctrine: Friedrich Schleiermacher and Johann Sebastian Drey* (1993).

Johnson, William Alexander, *On Religion: A Study of Theological Method in Schleiermacher and Nygren* (1964).

Lamm, Julia A., *The Living God: Schleiermacher's Theological Appropriation of Spinoza* (1996).

Niebuhr, Richard R., *Schleiermacher on Christ and Religion: A New Introduction* (1964).

Redeker, Martin, *Schleiermacher: Life and Thought*, ET (1973).

Richardson, Ruth Drucilla (ed.), *Schleiermacher in Context* (1991).

Spiegler, Gerhard, *The Eternal Covenant: Schleiermacher's Experiment in Cultural Theology* (1967).

Thiel, John E., *God and World in Schleiermacher's Dialektik and Glaubenslehre: Criticism and the Method of Dogmatics* (1981).

Williams, Robert R., *Schleiermacher the Theologian: The Construction of the Doctrine of God* (1978).

Wyman, Walter E., Jr., *The Concept of Glaubenslehre: Ernst Troeltsch and the Theological Heritage of Schleiermacher* (1983).

science, an organized body of knowledge, associated since the 17th century with empirical methods of enquiry designed to elucidate the mechanisms underlying physical and mental processes; routinely involving the mathematical modelling of nature, the construction and testing of explanatory hypotheses, and, since the 19th century, increasingly specialized fields of expertise. In the modern era, contrasts between testable scientific propositions and propositions based ultimately on *faith have been exploited in secular critiques of *religion, but also by the faithful in asserting different modes of 'knowing'. In popular literature, the complexity and diversity of relations between Christianity and the sciences are too often reduced to a simplistic formula. For Richard Dawkins (from 1995 Professor of the Public Understanding of Science at Oxford University), religious beliefs are basically primitive forms of scientific explanation rendered obsolete by modern scientific knowledge: human existence and behaviour can be explained, in principle, by genes and memes, without recourse to the transcendent. Dawkins's Oxford colleague Peter Atkins is even more dogmatic in asserting that the sciences can, or will, explain everything, including how the universe could explode out of 'nothing'. In polemical vein Atkins celebrates a rationality, comprehensibility, and simplicity discoverable through the sciences that stand in opposition to the complexities of religion and superstition.

By contrast, the Cambridge physicist and Anglican minister Sir John Polkinghorne offers an entirely different interpretation of the aesthetic satisfaction derivable from science. For Polkinghorne, the beauty of a scientific theory points beyond itself to a genuine harmony in *creation that testifies to its creator. Far from modern physics having rendered theism obsolete, it has redefined, through quantum mechanics and chaos theory, the texture of a reality permeable to divine activity. The elevation of modern physics into a new *natural theology has also served less confessional interests. In the writings of physicist Paul Davies, it has become the basis of an alternative *spirituality seemingly grounded in scientific knowledge alone.

To this contemporary diversity, historical analysis adds at least two complications: competing constructions of the relations between science and religion have regularly served competing political interests; and the very terms 'science' and 'religion' have changed their meanings as boundaries between them have been redrawn. For Isaac Newton, the study of 'natural philosophy' *included* discourse about the deity. Indeed, historical analysis reveals many stories that refuse to lie on a linear trajectory from a past to a present consensus. Each of the positions just identified has roots extending far back in western culture. The view that gods were invented to explain the currently inexplicable was voiced in the 17th century by Thomas Hobbes and very much earlier by the classical Latin poet Lucretius. It surfaced again in the 19th century in the positivist philosophy of Auguste Comte who divided cultural history into three stages: the *theological, succeeded by the *metaphysical, and then triumphantly by the positive facts and laws of science. Similarly the materialism of Peter Atkins has its historical precedent among earlier scientists eager to press their claims for the primacy of physics and chemistry in explaining living systems. An example from the 19th century is Marcellin Berthelot's work on the artificial synthesis of organic compounds, integral to his crusade against vitalism. Like Atkins, Berthelot had an animus against established religion, which permeated even his chemical thinking as he warned other chemists that, in accepting the existence of atoms,

they were behaving as irrationally as those who accepted *transubstantiation during the Catholic mass.

The natural theology of Polkinghorne also has precursors. The new physics of Isaac Newton was once popularized by Anglican clerics such as the Boyle lecturers Richard Bentley and Samuel Clarke. The invisible, immaterial gravitational force was, for Bentley, evidence of direct divine agency in the world; while for Clarke the uniformity of the Newtonian laws was an expression of divine constancy, without prejudice to the deity's power to act otherwise. Newton himself had required a periodic 'reformation' of the solar system to preserve its stability. Though he ascribed this remedial role to comets, he envisaged them as agents of a providential *God with dominion over nature and *history.

Dependence on the sciences alone to construct an alternative and potentially universal religion was mooted both during the *Enlightenment and again in the second half of the 19th century when scientific naturalism became a surrogate religion. Darwin's 'bulldog', Thomas Henry Huxley, preached 'lay sermons', warning that theologians had been extinguished by science like snakes strangled by Hercules. In Victorian Britain, Darwinian biology underscored a surrogate religion of social and technological progress. In Germany the positivist scientist Wilhelm Ostwald composed new carols to old tunes to celebrate not Christmas but the winter solstice.

Another view, favoured by 20th-century *existentialists such as Martin Buber and Rudolph *Bultmann, is that scientific and religious discourses should be separated. There are precedents, too, for this position. *Galileo repeated the adage that the purpose of the bible was to show how to go to heaven, not how the heavens go. Francis Bacon repeated *Augustine's warning that biblical exegesis should not rest on the latest scientific knowledge: how embarrassing it would be were scientific opinion subsequently to change! Witnessing the territorial struggles in 19th-century Oxford, Baden-Powell insisted that it would be to the advantage of both science and theology if their respective spheres of authority were detached: explaining the workings of nature could be safely given to the scientists on the understanding that morality was the preserve of the theologians.

Science and religion in context

There is no single story of convergence towards some 'best account' of the relations between science and Christianity. Historical research also confers importance on local contexts. It would be possible to read texts by Galileo and Cardinal Bellarmine on the relations between Copernican astronomy and scripture and fail to see why they should have been at cross purposes. Both stated that biblical texts would require reinterpretation if the earth's motion were demonstrated and, in one respect, Galileo was the more conservative in allowing the bible jurisdiction over dubious science. But in the context of *Counter-Reformation Rome, Galileo's cavalier pretensions to a rigorous proof and his liberties with biblical texts smacked of disobedience, crypto-Protestantism, and heresy.

Contrasts in receptivity among *Presbyterians in Belfast and *Princeton to Darwin's theory also put the spotlight on local contexts. There was some resistance in Princeton, personified by Charles Hodge who, without rejecting the idea of evolution *per se*, nevertheless found Darwin's mechanism of natural selection effectively atheistic in its evacuation of divine design. But in James

McCosh, Darwinism found a sympathetic ear and a proselyte for theistic evolution. In Belfast, by contrast, there was sustained resentment. A local determinant was John Tyndall's Belfast address of 1874 when, as president of the British Association for the Advancement of Science, he had gone on the offensive proclaiming that science would wrest from theology the entire domain of *cosmological theory. The behaviour of the British Association in excluding a conciliatory paper by the Presbyterian Robert Watts soured relations further. In short, discussions of the mutual bearings of science and Christian theology have not taken place in a philosophical ether: they have a locatedness often ignored in popular narratives. Three such master-narratives have proved sufficiently influential to deserve scrutiny.

Science and theology in conflict

The view that science and Christianity have been permanently locked in combat makes good sport for the media and had its champions in the late 19th century when A. D. White wrote his *History of the Warfare between Science and Theology in Christendom* (1895). Twenty years earlier J. W. Draper had published his *Conflict between Religion and Science* (1874), a popular diatribe against the Roman Catholic Church but hardly sensitive history. Draper castigated the Catholic Church for condemning Galileo, knowing he was *right*—an extraordinary claim when Draper admitted that decisive observational evidence in favour of a moving earth came much later.

White's polemic was inspired by adverse clerical reactions to his non-sectarian charter for Cornell University. Exacting his revenge, he produced a litany of historical examples where clerical obstruction to scientific and technological innovation had proved misguided. Following the electrical researches of Benjamin Franklin in the 18th century, cathedral spires (and many luckless bell-ringers) could have been spared a fatal lightning strike if only clerical authorities had been willing to fit conductors to their buildings. According to White their initial (and in some cases sustained) refusal, on the ground that it was presumptuous to interfere with providence, took a heavy toll in human life. But were the issues as simple, and the opinions as polarized, as he supposed? Was it really a case of warfare between theology and science? Secular bodies were hardly quicker to fit the device: the British government did not immediately protect its munitions depot at Purfleet. There was concern, voiced even by scientific experts such as the Abbé Nollet in France, that conductors, instead of protecting a building, might attract a strike that the edifice would otherwise be spared. As so often in the history of science, the scientific voice was not univocal. In the Boston area of the USA, which had recently suffered an earthquake, there was concern that conducting electricity to earth would generate more tremors. This was no superstition but an expression of the conventional wisdom of the day. It reminds us again how perceptions could be informed by local circumstances. Contrary to White, there is little evidence of concern over meddling with providence. The issue of presumption was occasionally raised; but there were obvious palliatives. As Christian commentators observed, the whole art of medicine, remedial and preventive, involved a form of interference with nature that had been divinely sanctioned. Why should not other preventive and ameliorative techniques be welcomed?

Master-narratives driven by notions of essential conflict between Christianity and science only become remotely plausible by eliminating moderate, intermediate positions. Yet these play a crucial role when scientific innovations are first assessed. For example, it was difficult for Galileo to disprove the intermediate system of Tycho Brahe, in which the earth remained stationary while the sun, circling the earth, became the centre of planetary orbits. Similarly, in the post-Darwinian debates, it was not a straight choice between creation and naturalistic evolution. There were sophisticated alternatives from Richard Owen and Louis Agassiz, who interpreted the history of organic forms as the unfolding of a divine plan. Physical scientists, such as William Thomson and George Stokes, were often critical of Darwin; while some Anglican clergy, notably Charles Kingsley and Frederick Temple, rejoiced in the power of a deity who could make all things make themselves. The triumphalist histories fail because both scientists and religious thinkers could appear on both sides of theological debate.

The warfare histories are also fallible because they neglect the many cases where scientific and religious sensibilities have been complementary. Religious beliefs have sometimes provided presuppositions of science in that creation doctrines have underwritten belief in an intelligible natural order. For Newton, the uniformity of nature and the universality of his law of gravitation were grounded in the omnipresence of the one true God. Religious beliefs have also provided sanction for science, as when Francis Bacon stressed the obligation to study the book of God's works as well as the book of God's words. Even the Christian doctrine of the *Fall could be reinterpreted to provide such a sanction; for Bacon promised, through the application of the sciences, the restoration of a dominion over nature that had been God's original plan for humankind. Religious beliefs have even provided motivation for science in that the perception of design in nature could be enriched through experimental research, as in the microscopic studies of Robert Hooke and Robert Boyle, which excited a sense of awe among Restoration virtuosi. Moreover, throughout the modern period, there have been repeated references to the role of simplicity, elegance, and harmony in guiding theory choice. Undoubtedly with a glint in his eye, Einstein once said that when presented with a mathematical theory he would immediately ask himself whether, had he been God, he would have made the world that way. For his great predecessor of the 17th century, Johannes Kepler, the disclosure of the harmonic structure of the universe through mathematical laws had been a rapturous religious experience.

Science as an outgrowth of Christian theology

Critiques of the warfare thesis have created space for revisionist narratives in which an original dependence of science on Christian theology is stressed. In this alternative historiography it has been claimed that without the Christian doctrine of creation there would have been no modern science. The argument has several twists. The search for 'laws' of nature is said to have been warranted by belief in a divine legislator whose will had been imposed on the world. According to the Cambridge philosopher Michael Foster, a voluntarist theology of creation would also encourage empirical methods of enquiry because, instead of following *Aristotelian canons of rationality, natural philosophers would stress that if God had been free to create whatever world God wished, it was through humble empirical methods alone that one could discover which of the many possibilities had actually been instantiated. In explaining why the scientific movement advanced in Europe, revisionist historians have pointed to the *Protestant *Reformation in creating greater freedom of thought for those unconstrained by the centralized bureaucracy of Rome. More controversially, the American sociologist Robert Merton argued in the 1930s that *Puritan values had been particularly conducive to the expansion of science in 17th-century England: a godly involvement in studying God's creation had been an acceptable calling and a legitimate use of the divine gift of *reason. Ameliorative sciences such as agriculture and medicine were justified in altruistic terms while the imperative to share knowledge for the public good was also a derivative of the Protestant ethic. In this alternative master-narrative, even the secular image of progress towards a science-based utopia had roots in *millenarian speculation about a time when Christ would reign over a reformed earth.

If the warfare thesis has attracted rationalists and humanists, this second account has appealed to religious apologists, pleased by the notion that, at source, scientific and religious values were in unison. Not surprisingly, an alleged harmony between Protestant Christianity and the sciences has had special appeal for Protestant writers. But that can also be an invitation to rehearse reservations. Close study of early 17th-century Puritan sermons often reveals values indifferent rather than conducive to science. Merton's thesis and its derivatives can be spiked on a methodological point: if one examines only those Protestants who were interested in the sciences, it is hardly surprising if a correlation emerges. Equally damaging is a point made by the American historian William Ashworth. After studying prominent Catholic philosophers of the 17th century, he concludes that there was no archetypal Catholic mindset and by implication no archetypal Protestant one either. Natural philosophers, Protestant and Catholic, devised their own individual ways of integrating their faith and science, thwarting our stereotypes. In many cases Catholic philosophers were at the forefront of theoretical innovation: Copernicus, Galileo, Gassendi, Mersenne, Descartes, all contributed to the mechanization of nature in ways that were later adopted by Protestant naturalists. Indeed, a Catholic apologist like Mersenne may have welcomed a mechanical philosophy because it redefined the boundary between the natural and the supernatural, making it easier to distinguish a true *miracle from a natural marvel. The claim that without the Christian doctrine of creation there would have been no modern science has sometimes been buttressed by reference to non-Christian cultures in which incipient scientific movements and institutions proved unsustainable. There has, however, been a degree of cultural chauvinism in such accounts, which also tend to disregard the social and economic preconditions of scientific activity.

There nevertheless remains the possibility, as Peter Harrison has recently argued, that certain Protestant *practices*, as distinct from doctrines and values, could have propitious, if indirect, effects on the sciences. Crucial here is a contrast between two ways of reading the bible, both of which could have serious implications for how the book of nature should be read. The older of the two conventions, prominent in patristic and medieval theology, was characterized by a search for multiple and symbolic meanings of biblical texts, producing a wealth of spiritual *allegory (see HERMENEUTICS).

The correlate of this type of exegesis was the ascription of symbolic meanings to objects in the natural world: the association, for example, of the pelican with piety. By contrast, the newer convention, ostensibly a product of the Reformation, was characterized by the quest for literal, univocal interpretations of the sacred text. This shift in sensibility may have been important for the rise of a mechanistic science because it stripped natural objects of their emblematic accretions. In order to fill the ensuing vacuum, a new language was required for the analysis of nature's objects, one that permitted convergence towards similarly univocal readings. For Galileo, as for Newton later, that new language was mathematics.

Christianity and science in fateful collusion

A third master-narrative deserves comment because it has become fashionable in 'new age' polemics. It appeared in Fritjof Capra's *The Tao of Physics* (1975) and has reappeared in eco-*feminist theologies. Here the contrast is between holistic views of nature, which are virtuous, and mechanistic views that have proved vicious; between monistic views which respiritualize the world and dualistic creeds which have led to its exploitation (see ECOLOGY). In this story *Descartes and Newton are the villains who murdered the natural world with their desiccated models of inert particles driven by pressure or mechanical forces. Allegedly for two hundred years or more the deterministic universe of Newton reigned supreme until, mercifully, in the early years of the 20th century a revolution occurred in physics, introducing indeterminacy and reintegrating the human observer into the cosmic web. Under the old regime nature could be kicked around; now, in keeping with the new physics, we can resume the role of stewards with a greater sensitivity to environmental issues.

There can be nobility in such a vision and we have all had to become better educated on environmental issues. But it is not good history. To conflate Newton with Descartes as villains misses the point that Newton, enthralled by sources of activity in nature, was himself a critic of Descartes. There were 'active principles' in Newton's universe as well as atomic particles and he did not preclude the possibility that nature might be alive. Even the damage done by Descartes's *dualism can be overstated, since he regarded the human being as an integrated whole. It was not a case of the mind in the body like a pilot in a ship. There is even a strand in Descartes's philosophy that commends not the detachment of the human spectator from the cosmic machine but an identification with nature that has a certain spiritual quality: 'If we love God and for his sake unite ourselves in will to all that he has created, then the more grandeur, nobility and perfection we conceive things to have, the more highly we esteem ourselves, as parts of a whole that is a greater work' (Anscombe and Geach 1954: 296). So much for the Descartes who is supposed to be the cause of all modern evils. As for the claim that modern physics has transformed our relation to the natural world, this surely depends on which interpretation one chooses to place on the mathematical formalism of quantum mechanics. Where holistic constructions are favoured, is it not because they are congenial for other reasons?

This question leads to another. Instead of speaking of the implications of modern science for Christian belief, is it not more appropriate to recognize that every scientific innovation has been open to different interpretations? Past debates, so often construed as conflict between science and religion, are better seen as debates about the cultural meaning to be placed on new forms of scientific knowledge. Alternative readings have always been possible. No single implication flows unequivocally from a new discovery.

Finding meaning in the sciences

How the supposed religious 'implications' of scientific innovation are expressed unquestionably depends on personal presuppositions and preferences. As indicated earlier, the mechanistic universe of the 17th century could be attractive as a way of defending the miraculous. It helped to discriminate between natural marvels and true miracles, which Catholic apologists had to do. But a clockwork universe could also appeal to those who wished to exclude divine intervention from nature. If the clock runs by itself, why posit a supernatural power at all? Then again, a clockwork universe might be attractive to Christian apologists because finely tuned clockwork points to intelligent design, to a creator, in Newton's words, very well skilled in mechanics and geometry. But it could equally be invoked by the sceptic. In his posthumous *Dialogues Concerning Natural Religion* (1779) David Hume observed that man-made machines, such as ships and clocks, may have more than one designer and certainly more than one maker: the analogy between nature and human artefact as readily supports polytheism as monotheism.

Innovations in astronomy and geology have sometimes led to the conclusion that the universe itself is meaningless—so vast in both space and *time as to dwarf humanity into insignificance. In his early novel *Two on a Tower*, Thomas Hardy exploited the millions of stars first revealed by Galileo's telescope to argue that their invisibility to the naked eye meant that they had not been made for us and that consequently *nothing* had. But there had long been competing interpretations in which these same stars had been supposed to shine on other worlds, thereby retaining a sense of economy and purpose in creation. Indeed the probability of extra-terrestrial life had become so integrated within Christianity by the mid-19th century, that when William Whewell, Master of Trinity College Cambridge, sought to destroy it, he was rebuked for his eccentricity. Whewell's opponent, the Scottish physicist David Brewster, found special meaning in the successful resolution of nebulae because the conclusion that they were composed of stars created the possibility of countless more extra-terrestrials. And this he believed was consonant with a biblical Christianity in which there were many mansions and other sheep not of this fold.

In evolutionary theory, as in debates about extra-terrestrial life, there are not only internecine divisions between scientists themselves but profound differences concerning whether the products of the evolutionary process should be seen as constrained and inevitable, or whether it is the openness and contingency that should be stressed. In their discussion of divine activity in the world, Christian theologians have also been divided over whether it is better to stress the contingency or the determinacy of the process. And, to complete the paradox, propagandists for secularism have been just as divided over how to maximize capital from the scientific account.

For Stephen J. Gould, as for an earlier interpreter of evolution George G. Simpson, it is the chanciness that is stressed: humans are the product of a process that did not have them in mind. If the dinosaurs had not died out, mammals would not have had the opportunity to develop as they have. The annihilation of the dinosaurs could have depended on some catastrophic event and what a lucky fluke it is that we are here and able to watch the film *Jurassic Park*. It is a chanciness that easily translates into a critique of theistic religions: how can we speak of human beings as purposefully created when the process employed might never have produced us?

In response, some Christian theologians, notably Keith Ward, have recently pressed that same contingency to argue a quite different position. Supposing God did wish to create human beings, God could not have relied on so uncertain a process. Hence the suggestion of a form of divine activity superimposed on evolutionary mechanisms, which turns contingencies into something more like certainties. On this view the more *improbable* it is that humans should appear, the stronger the case for asserting divine agency in making their appearance more certain.

But there is the other side. In sceptical attacks on theism, scientific naturalists have often stressed the inevitability of the emergence of life and its further articulation. If one can show that natural causes alone are quite sufficient to account for the emergence of human qualities, then the deity becomes redundant. This argument usually ignores the consideration that belief in a deity may not depend simply on what is otherwise inexplicable; but when it is advanced, it is often the necessity not the contingency that is stressed. Life as we know it, even human intelligence, was almost bound to evolve given what we now know of the self-organizing power of organic molecules.

That is the naturalistic account; but we find religious apologists on this side too. If the deity did intend to produce human beings then it should not be in the least surprising that the natural processes so devised should be constrained and deterministic in their outcomes. On this view, articulated by John Bowker and Arthur Peacocke, it is the high probability of those outcomes that supports the appeal to a personal agency.

It is hard to avoid the conclusion that whatever the sciences may disclose about the nature of physical (and mental) processes those disclosures will be susceptible of both a naturalistic and a theistic interpretation. Thus the anthropic coincidences concerning the fine-tuning of the universe have been thought by some Christian theists to refurbish the argument from design; while a more secular reading simply involves the reflection that ours is the one among an infinite number of possible worlds that happened to have the propitious parameters. The sciences underline rather than remove what John Hick has called the religious ambiguity of the universe.

J. H. Brooke

Anscombe, E., and Geach, P. T., *Descartes: Philosophical Writings* (1954).
Atkins, P. W., *Creation Revisited* (1992).
Barbour, I. G., *Religion in an Age of Science* (1990).
Barrow, J. D., and Tipler, F. J., *The Anthropic Cosmological Principle* (1986).
Brooke, J. H., *Science and Religion: Some Historical Perspectives* (1991).
Brooke, J. H., and Cantor, G. N., *Reconstructing Nature: The Engagement of Science and Religion* (1998).
Davies, P., *The Mind of God* (1992).
Dawkins, R., *The Blind Watchmaker* (1986).
Drees, W. B., *Religion, Science and Naturalism* (1996).
Funkenstein, A., *Theology and the Scientific Imagination from the Middle Ages to the Seventeenth Century* (1986).
Gould, S. J., *This Wonderful Life* (1989).

Harrison, P., *The Bible, Protestantism and the Rise of Natural Science* (1998).

Hick, J., *An Interpretation of Religion* (1989).

Kaiser, C. B., *Creational Theology and the History of Physical Science* (1997).

Lindberg, D. C., and Numbers, R. L. (eds.), *God and Nature: Historical Essays on the Encounter Between Christianity and Science* (1986).

Moore, J. R., *The Post-Darwinian Controversies* (1979).

Morris, S. C., *The Crucible of Creation* (1998).

Numbers, R. L., *The Creationists* (1992).

Polkinghorne, J., *Belief in God in an Age of Science* (1998).

Russell, C. A., *The Earth, Humanity and God* (1994).

Russell, R. J., Stoeger, W. R., and Coyne, G. V. (eds.), *Physics, Philosophy and Theology: A Common Quest for Understanding* (1988).

Russell, R. J., Murphy, N., and Peacocke, A. R. (eds.), *Chaos and Complexity* (1995).

Ward, K., *God, Chance and Necessity* (1996).

Webster, C., *The Great Instauration* (1975).

Scottish Christian thought.

The Scots, for centuries, have defined themselves against England, their large neighbour to the south. In the Middle Ages, during the Great *Schism when there were rival popes, the Scots took care to back the pope that England did not. For centuries, too, the Scots have been good Europeans, eager to adopt the latest fashions in thought from the Continent. Since the *Reformation this has meant divinity professors trained first in France, later in Holland, and later still in Germany. Finally, also for centuries, Scotland's major export has been people, and links with the Scottish diaspora have served to keep Scottish theology unparochial.

Modern Scots, of almost every tradition, have tried to recover their *Celtic roots in the church of Columba and Cuthbert. The Iona Community, which mixes Scottish radical politics with innovative green liturgy and a Protestant rediscovery of communal life, is a good expression of this (see ALTERNATIVE LIFESTYLES). There is less living continuity with the medieval Catholic church, with most of its cathedrals in ruins, few other ancient churches, and even Highland Catholicism largely the effect of post-Reformation Irish missions. Medieval Scots 'lads of pairts' (promising students) went to Continental universities. John Duns Scotus (c.1266–1308) was a Scot. John Mair (or Major) (d. 1550), professor of theology at Paris before returning to Scotland in 1518, *conciliarist, anti-Lutheran, in favour of popular sovereignty, seems to have influenced the Reformers he opposed. It appears he taught a Scotist (that is, derived from Duns Scotus) intuitive epistemology to *Calvin, and presumably to Calvinists in Scotland.

Scotland had a very thorough Reformation. Modern readers often find themselves in greater sympathy with the more moderate Reformers and with some of the defenders of the old church such as Ninian Winzet (d. 1592) than with John Knox (c.1513–72). Knox was the archetypal Scottish *Presbyterian, trained in *Geneva, eagerly *predestinarian, pugnacious and judgemental. In some ways he Anglified the Scottish church, bringing in the bible in English, and the *sabbatarian ways of English *Puritanism. The 20th-century literary Scottish renascence, rebelling against a Calvinist culture, saw the split between the formal logical English of educated (and religious) discourse and the natural Scots tongue of the heart as the root of much evil, and blamed Knox. Those more historically informed blame Andrew Melville (1545–1622), who went further than Knox. *Barth preferred Knox's old Scots Confession of 1569 to the Westminster Confession of 1647 because it was less cut-and-dried in

its scholastic Calvinist orthodoxy. Melville, a civilized extremist, wrote Latin poetry and reformed the Scottish universities. Knox had been pragmatic about bishops; Melville began a Scottish tradition of anti-*episcopacy, much helped by the crude attempts of Stuart kings to rule their church through bishops. Despite its severely intellectual image, going back to Melville, there is an affective tradition within Scottish Presbyterianism. People still read the *Letters* of Samuel Rutherford (1600–61) for their richly felt metaphors. It was a land of sermon-tasters, not all logicians, and there was a continuing *eucharistic piety.

The normative theology of Scotland became Calvinist. There were other strands. The episcopalian tradition, strong in the north-east, produced the 'Aberdeen Doctors' and Archbishop Leighton (1611–84), eirenic and mystical, beloved by S. T. *Coleridge. The great *Quaker apologist, Robert Barclay (1648–90), was a Scot. The Roman Catholic church in Scotland, first persecuted, and occasionally sombre like its Presbyterian neighbours, surprisingly produced Alexander Geddes (1737–1802), a forerunner of biblical criticism. Part of the imaginative heritage of Scotland has been the martyr tradition of the *Covenanters, eager and extreme Presbyterians suppressed under Charles II. In a mountainous country, these 'hillmen', on the watch for soldiers as they worshipped in the open air, have seemed to exemplify the struggles of Scottish Christianity. The badge of the Church of Scotland is the burning bush, which burned 'and was not consumed'.

Since 1689 Scotland has had a Presbyterian established church, unlike England. The Scots, and the leaders of the Scottish church, embraced the 18th-century *Enlightenment. William Robertson, the leading historian of his day, Adam Ferguson, precursor of *social studies, Hugh Blair, arbiter of literary technique, all were Scottish ministers with an international reputation. Scottish theology as such encountered 'New Light', which, unlike the Covenanters, had misgivings about the state's duty to enforce true religion. The language of instruction in divinity faculties became English instead of Latin, and theology generally became moralized. However, unlike elsewhere in the Reformed world, there was no shift to *Arminianism or even further to *Unitarianism. The standard systematics in the English-speaking Calvinist world for the first half of the 19th century was written by a Scottish 'Moderate', George Hill of St Andrews. The rival 'popular' evangelical party could not fault his Calvinism, and used his book.

Another product of the Enlightenment was the philosophy of 'Scottish *Common-Sense realism', an effort to refute the scepticism of David Hume, devised by Thomas Reid (1710–96), another minister, teaching at Aberdeen and later Glasgow. Taken to North America by John Witherspoon, president of *Princeton, this defence of intuitive truths, more philosophically subtle than it might appear, had great practical use as a natural philosophy for ministers. Right or wrong, it fitted Christianity like a glove. Some have noted the intriguing (hereditary?) resemblance to the Scotist intuitive epistemology.

The orthodoxy of the Westminster Confession might appear unchangeable to an outsider, and debates within Calvinism mere hairsplitting. *Covenant was the keyword in 17th-century Scottish theology, and the strong covenant imagery was overworked. It could sound too legalistic, as if expounding the terms of a series of treaties. On the other side, the heart religion of God's free *grace could sound *antinomian, as in the 'Marrow' controversy (1718–23). Scots worried about the link between election and antinomianism. James Hogg's novel, *Confessions of a Justified Sinner* (1824), played frighteningly with the theme.

The Scottish church split and split again over issues of church and state, largely because of interference in Scottish church affairs by an *Erastian English parliament. Scotland, a nation without its own statehood after 1707, has tended to express its nationality through its religious institutions, and to be protective of them. The catastrophic Disruption of 1843, when about one-third of the Church of Scotland went out to form the Free Church, was led by Thomas Chalmers (1780–1847) who, strangely enough, had made his name arguing the case for ecclesiastical establishment. In the 20th century, a largely reunited Presbyterianism remained conscious of its national role. This was seen at its best in the *political theology of the Baillie Report of the 'Commission for the Interpretation of God's Will in the Present Crisis' (1946).

Even in Scotland the Calvinist hegemony crumbled in the 19th century. Thomas Erskine of Linlathen (1788–1870, though his influential books were published by 1837), a wealthy lay theologian who had no job to lose, and a delightful example of what William *James called a 'once-born', taught of God as a loving Father to all humanity. Each human being has an internal evidence of the truth of revelation, each can choose to be in Christ, and, though Erskine took time to reach this, God's will is that all shall be saved (see UNIVERSALISM).

One of Erskine's circle was John McLeod Campbell (1800–72), probably the greatest Scottish theologian of the 19th century. Campbell was deposed from the ministry of the Church of Scotland in 1831 for teaching that the starting-point of Christian theology and life is the *assurance of God's *love. This was in a period when an orthodox systematics course began with 'The Disease' before it proceeded to 'The Remedy'. Campbell went on to publish *The Nature of the Atonement* (1856) in which he interpreted Christ's death not as a penal substitution but as the offering in solidarity with mankind of a perfect repentance. The work is of deep moral seriousness, and the Scottish churches recognized this. Two great, and basically conservative, theologians of the end of the century, James Denney (1856–1917) and P. T. Forsyth (1848–1921), a Scot working in England, start from McLeod Campbell when discussing the *atoning work of Christ. At their best, Scottish theologians talk about *sin without legalism or rhetoric or frivolity. It may have something to do with the old national tradition of teaching moral philosophy to almost all undergraduates. By the end of the 19th century, the major Scottish churches had drawn back from Calvinism, and published 'Declaratory Acts' allowing their ministers freedom 'on such points in the [Westminster] Confession as do not enter into the substance of the Reformed Faith'. Since then most Scots Presbyterians have not been strict Calvinists, though conscious of their heritage.

A maverick but important figure, Edward Irving (1792–1834) was a great preacher, lionized in London, a *millennialist, encourager of *charismatic gifts (and so a forerunner of *Pentecostalism) and, rather unexpectedly, founder of the Catholic Apostolic Church, with twelve new apostles (not including Irving) and a distinctive and beautiful new *liturgy. Irving was deposed from the ministry of the Church of Scotland because he affirmed, in a way that the 20th

century largely found admirable, that Christ took human nature upon himself even in its sinfulness, though without sin.

Scotland took biblical criticism seriously (see HIGHER CRITICISM). When, in the late 1870s, William Robertson Smith (1846–94), professor of Hebrew at the Free Church college in Aberdeen, was tried for *heresy because of his articles on the bible in the ninth edition of the *Encyclopaedia Britannica*, the full proceedings of his trials were in the Scottish press, and were read avidly. He was dismissed, but convinced the Scottish public. In the history of religious thought, Smith's original but probably misleading ideas on totemism and sacrifice influenced Durkheim and Freud. He was one of several Scottish biblical professors to be hauled before the ecclesiastical courts. Probably the most effective Scottish purveyor of a moderate liberal theology was James Hastings (1852–1923), editor of the periodical *Expository Times* and of the *Encyclopaedia of Religion and Ethics* and many other reference works.

In the Church of Scotland, around 1900, unlike the Free Church, innovation came with the *Hegelian idealism of the Caird brothers, and the high-church Presbyterianism of the Scottish Ecclesiological Society. This had links with the Scots Episcopalians, a church whose scholars have largely been liturgists, interested in Eastern Orthodoxy. Their best theologian, Donald *MacKinnon, a professor at Aberdeen and later Cambridge, agonized creatively over christology, ethics, and tragedy.

Two interwoven concerns of the Scottish tradition were *education and overseas *missions. For a relatively poor country, Scotland was famously well-educated, and overprovided with universities. There was a presumption that any good education helps (Presbyterian) faith. The Scottish missionary movement showed a similar reliance on schools and universities. Such missionary theorists as Alexander Duff (1806–78), J. N. Farquhar (1861–1929), and A. G. Hogg (1875–1954) must be seen against their Scottish background.

Twentieth-century biblical scholarship retained public interest, with the widely read A. M. Hunter (1906–91) and the great preacher J. S. Stewart (1896–1990). Perhaps the best known was William Barclay (1907–78) a NT scholar who popularized liberal theology in a chatty homely style, both on television and in his many writings.

Systematic theologians had a narrower appeal. The best-known were H. R. Mackintosh (1870–1936) and the brothers John (1886–1960) and D. M. (1887–1954) Baillie, all sensible peacemakers who held back from *Barthianism. Though Scotland had some radical 'secular' theologians, like Ronald Gregor Smith (1913–68) of Glasgow, the prevailing theology of the 20th century divinity faculties was *neo-orthodoxy. The greatest of this school, and leader of a clan of Torrances, was Thomas *Torrance. Among Scots working outside Scotland in the 20th century were John Mackay (1889–1983), the ecumenist president of Princeton, and the existentialist theologian John Macquarrie (1919–), professor at Union Theological Seminary in New York and then in Oxford. The divinity faculties remain Scottish in ethos, though no longer specifically Presbyterian, and still convey a sense that Scottish theology is more internationalist than English.   **Alistair Mason**

Brown, S. J., *Thomas Chalmers and the Godly Commonwealth in Scotland* (1982).

Cameron, N. M. de S. (ed.), *Dictionary of Scottish Church History and Theology* (1993).

Cheyne, A. C., *The Transforming of the Kirk* (1983).
—— *Studies in Scottish Church History* (1999).
Drummond, A. L., and Bulloch, J., *The Scottish Church 1688–1843* (1973).
—— *The Church in Victorian Scotland 1843–1874* (1975).
—— *The Church in Late Victorian Scotland 1874–1900* (1978).
Macleod, J., *Scottish Theology in Relation to Church History since the Reformation*, 3rd edn. (1974).
McRoberts, D. (ed.), *Modern Scottish Catholicism 1878–1978* (1979).
Needham, N. R., *Thomas Erskine of Linlathen* (1989).
Sell, A. P. F., *Defending and Declaring the Faith. Some Scottish Examples 1860–1920* (1987).
Torrance, T. F., *Scottish Theology from John Knox to John McLeod Campbell* (1996).
Tuttle, G. M., *So Rich a Soil* (1986).

scripture, see BIBLE, ITS AUTHORITY AND INTERPRETATION.

secularization.

Until the second half of the 19th century 'secularization' had a specific and limited meaning. It denoted the transfer of lands formerly held by the church to lay ownership. In the mid-19th century it began to be used in a wider sense by political reformers who believed that lay control should be extended to other areas where the church was still dominant. Only in the 1860s did the word begin to be used in its modern sense to denote more impersonal and gradual processes whereby *religion or the church played a diminishing role, or vanished entirely, from spheres of life where previously they had been influential. One of the first writers to do this was W. E. H. Lecky, who headed a chapter in his *History of Rationalism* (1865) 'The Secularization of Politics'. From the 1920s the term began to be used quite widely in American sociological literature. Thus Robert and Helen Lynd in a famous study of a small mid-western town (1929) noted a 'secularization of family life', which they saw reflected in a rising divorce rate and increasing use of contraceptives. However it was only in the 1960s that secularization was used more widely to denote the marginalization of religion in modern western societies, and that the term came into general usage. Two books played a decisive role in popularizing the concept: *The Secular City* (1965) by the American *liberal Protestant theologian, Harvey Cox, and *Religion in Secular Society* (1966) by the British sociologist, Bryan Wilson. Wilson's main contention was that although religion may not have disappeared it had become irrelevant: 'Secularization is the process whereby religious thinking, practice, and institutions lose social significance'.

From the later 1960s secularization became the dominant concern of sociologists of religion, as well as being the subject of a considerable historical and theological literature. Discussion of the term and of the phenomena which it denotes has been and continues to be bedevilled, however, by the fact that it has been used to mean many different things. First it is necessary to distinguish between the use of secularization as a *descriptive* term and the *theory of secularization*. In its original form, and indeed in most of the ways in which it was used until the 1960s, 'secularization' described tendencies which happened at a particular time and place or in a particular sphere of life. Writers like Wilson, however, were advancing a *theory* of secularization, namely that the process by which religion loses social significance is a general characteristic of modern societies. Secondly, in looking at the various theories of secularization it is necessary to distinguish between three types of secularization theory, focusing on the relationships of church and state, the social influence of religion, and individual belief and practice. Many theorists of secularization would argue that these three spheres are interconnected. However, it cannot be assumed that this is so. To take the most obvious example, the United States was in 1791 the first western nation to separate church and state, and it continues to be one of the few in which the teaching of religion in the public schools is prohibited, yet the social influence of religious institutions and levels of individual religious belief and practice are far higher than in most European countries.

The idea of secularization was familiar long before the word was widely used. The belief that Christianity is under threat in the modern world goes back at least to the 1690s, and theories of religious decline to the early 19th century. Beginning in England and Holland in the later 17th century there was a movement of religious scepticism, as a result of which many aspects of Christian orthodoxy were challenged, most often in the name of *deism. The influence of these ideas was limited to a relatively small educated public. However, the French Revolution of 1789 and the subsequent conflict between the revolutionary authorities and the Catholic Church inaugurated a new era in European religious history, in which attacks on established churches became a central plank of all progressive political programmes and radicals sought to undermine the influence of the clergy by popularizing religious scepticism. At the same time, major social changes were under way as a result of the Industrial Revolution and mass migrations into cities. Shortages of clergy and church buildings in the fast-growing cities meant that the church lost touch with many of these migrants, and the availability of a wider range of leisure facilities meant that the church was less necessary as a social centre. Meanwhile the progress and growing prestige of *science in the second half of the 19th century gave a further fillip to the development of *agnosticism. At least as influential as the writings of scientists in weakening the authority of the churches and of religious morality was the literary and artistic onslaught which reached a high point in the 1880s and 1890s when such writers as *Nietzsche, Ibsen, Wedekind, and Shaw were pouring scorn on most aspects of conventional religion. In the 20th century, a series of totalitarian governments tried to construct a new kind of society in which religion would have no place, and those who persisted in practising it risked marginalization, or even imprisonment and death. Partly in reaction to developments in Nazi Germany and the Soviet Union, the 1940s and 1950s saw a revival of church influence in many parts of the western world, especially the United States. However in the 1960s there was another severe drop in religious practice, and a rise in the number of declared *atheists and those with no religion, which in most parts of Western Europe has continued to the present.

From at least the 1820s there have been influential secular thinkers who argued that religious decline was an inescapable part of the modern world, and that there was nothing religious believers could do to avert it. Probably the first person to advance this idea in a systematic way was the French philosopher Auguste Comte, who founded a Religion of Humanity to fill the void that would be left by the demise of the older faiths. Comte saw this as the inevitable result of the advance of science and he argued that all areas of human knowledge went through three phases: the theological (which was the most primitive), the metaphysical, and the 'positive' or scientific (which totally superseded all previous forms of understanding). Karl *Marx advanced a more political version of secularization, according to which the final demise of religion would come about when the working class built a world that offered everyone the possibility of a fulfilling life on earth. A third, more sociological, approach was proposed by the French pioneer of sociology Émile Durkheim who introduced the concept known to modern sociologists as differentiation, according to which as society becomes richer and more complex numerous specialized institutions develop to take over areas of life formerly dominated by the church, with the result that the sphere of influence of the clergy and of religious ideas has continuously diminished. In Durkheim's view this process had been going on for as long as human history, but had greatly accelerated in his own day.

Ever since the early 18th century, and more emphatically since the French Revolution, Christian thought has been powerfully influenced by a sense of the strength of the secularizing forces in the modern world and most theologians and church leaders have been aware of the need to respond to this threat. Four characteristic strategies, examples of which can be seen from the 18th century up to the present day, have been (1) partial acceptance of contemporary critiques of Christianity and the church, and restatement of the faith or of the church's agenda in terms likely to make them better understood by critics, (2) total rejection of these criticisms and attempts at a wholesale 'rechristianization' of society, (3) welcoming of secularization as facilitating the removal of harmful aspects of Christian belief and practice and a purification of the faith, and (4) acceptance of the fact of secularization, together with the attempt to establish a Christian subculture within which at least a substantial minority of the population can be protected from harmful influences. At the intellectual level the classic example of the first approach was *Schleiermacher's On Religion (1799), but there have been numerous other examples, of which the most successful in reaching a mass readership was John *Robinson's Honest to God (1963). At a social level, a good example would be such movements as the American *social gospel. Attempts at 'rechristianization' go back at least to the restoration of the power of the monarchies and aristocracies after 1815 and the resulting 'alliance of throne and altar'. Most of the movements, from the French Revolution onwards, that have appeared to undermine Christianity have had their enthusiastic Christian champions, who have seen them instead as the realization of Christian ideals. But the beginning of a more positive evaluation of secularization as such comes (tentatively) with Dietrich *Bonhoeffer's Letters and Papers from Prison and more emphatically with such writers as Harvey Cox who believed that the churches had become too bound up with defending anachronistic traditions and conventions, and that secularization offered an opportunity to rethink Christian practice from first principles. The biggest attempt at creating a Christian subculture was made by the Catholic Church in the later 19th century, when Catholics responded to the growing power of the state by establishing an enormous apparatus of Catholic schools (see EDUCATION), universities, newspapers, trade unions, and leisure facilities. In some countries, the Netherlands for example, these efforts were very successful. In recent years similar tactics have been tried by *evangelical Protestants, most notably in the United States.

Since the 1960s the literature on secularization has grown enormously. The precise terms in which sociologists define and explain it vary considerably, but the most commonly held theory argues that the extent and significance of religion in modern societies declines because of certain general social tendencies, including differentiation, pluralism (undermining the 'taken-for-grantedness' of particular belief-systems and often forcing some degree of compromise between them), individualism (undermining all systems of collective belief and morality), and the development of technology (extending the areas of life under human control). During the 1980s and 1990s theories of secularization have, however, come under considerable criticism. The oldest criticism is the claim that these theories are a form of wishful thinking by the secularist intelligentsia—which may often be true, but does not invalidate the theories. Two other factors have therefore been more important in raising doubts. One has been the continuing strength and rising public profile of religion in the United States. This has led some scholars to suggest that secularization is a product of specifically European conditions. The other factor has been research by historians on religious change in particular countries over the past two or three centuries: this has shown that the patterns of religious growth and decline often bear little relationship to those predicted by the theories of secularization. The fact that most western nations have undergone processes of secularization during the last two centuries is incontestable. But its extent and causes remain unclear.

See also SOCIAL SCIENCES. **Hugh McLeod**

Bruce, Steve (ed.), Religion and Modernization: Sociologists and Historians Debate the Secularization Thesis (1992).

—— Religion in the Modern World (1996).

Chadwick, Owen, The Secularization of the European Mind in the Nineteenth Century (1975).

Cox, Jeffrey, English Churches in a Secular Society: Lambeth 1870–1930 (1982).

Gilbert, Alan, The Making of Post-Christian Britain (1980).

Lehmann, Hartmut (ed.), Säkularisierung, Dechristianisierung, Rechristianisierung im neuzeitlichen Europa (1997).

McLeod, Hugh (ed.), European Religion in the Age of Great Cities c.1830–1930 (1995).

—— Piety and Poverty: Working Class Religion in Berlin, London and New York 1870–1914 (1996).

—— Religion and the People of Western Europe 1789–1989 (1997).

—— Secularisation in Western Europe, 1848–1914 (2000).

Martin, David, A General Theory of Secularization (1978).

Tschannen, Olivier, Les Théories de la sécularisation (1992).

Sermon on the Mount,

a discourse that begins in Matthew 5: 1 with *Jesus sitting on a mountainside and beginning to teach his disciples gathered about him, and ends with the observation that the crowds were astonished at the authority with which he spoke (7: 28–9). In the history of Christian thought—indeed in the history of those observing Christianity—the Sermon on the Mount has been considered an epitome of the teaching of Jesus and therefore, for many, the essence of *Christianity. In common parlance, 'the Sermon on the Mount' is shorthand for 'what Jesus teaches'.

This equation apparently began with *Augustine's treatise, The Lord's Sermon on the Mount (393–6): the Sermon is, 'as measured by the highest norms of morality, the perfect pattern of the Christian life' (ch. 1). Martin *Luther's commentary (1532) followed Augustine's concentration on these three chapters of Matthew. Luther prayed it would 'keep the true, sure, and Christian understanding of this teaching of Christ, because these are such common sayings and texts that are used so often throughout Christendom'. From Luther until the present, the number of works dedicated to the Sermon can scarcely be counted.

Matthew's narrative invites particular attention to this discourse by presenting Jesus as a proclaimer of the kingdom of heaven (Matt. 4: 17), and having the first line of the Beatitudes promise the *Kingdom of God to those who are poor in spirit (5: 3). But Matthew contains other extensive discourses of Jesus pertinent to the same subject (see chs. 10, 13, 18, 24–5). Attention to this discourse as the epitome of Jesus' message derives from premises universally shared in the early church and still operative among Christians unaffected by biblical *higher criticism: that Matthew's *gospel is the first written and comes from an eyewitness; that Matthew reports a discourse actually delivered by Jesus at the very beginning of his ministry; and that this first discourse represents in a particular fashion Jesus' own understanding of the conditions of membership in the kingdom he proclaimed.

Luke's gospel has a much shorter 'Sermon' at the beginning of Jesus' ministry that also opens with beatitudes (Luke 6: 20–49), but differs from Matthew's in length, organization, and setting (the plain, rather than the mountain, Luke 6: 17). The difference in the character of the two versions can be indicated by a schematic summary. Matthew's Sermon starts with ten statements of blessing (the beatitudes, 5: 3–12) and two statements of commission ('you are the salt/light', 5: 13–16). The body of the discourse deals with the proper understanding of righteousness with reference to scripture (5: 17–48), with reference to the practices of piety (6: 1–18), and with reference to everyday conduct (6: 19–7: 12). It concludes with *eschatological warnings (7: 13–23). Matthew's version is marked by an emphasis on piety as well as *morality, and its consistent positioning of Jesus' teaching over against Torah as interpreted by Jewish teachers.

In contrast, Luke's Sermon lacks any explicit reference to scripture or Jewish teachers. It starts with four statements of blessing matched by four statements of threat addressed directly to Jesus' listeners (6: 20–6). The body of the discourse takes up rules for behaviour with regard to outsiders (6: 27–38), and members of the community (6:39–45), before concluding with a rhetorical question and a double *parable describing success and failure (6: 46–9).

Concentration on Matthew's Sermon on the Mount (understood for most of the history of Christianity as Jesus' supreme discourse) included consideration of the perceived incommensurability between the radical *ethics demanded by Jesus, especially in the beatitudes and the antitheses ('you have heard it said, but I say to you', 5: 21–48), and the more moderate moral teaching of other NT writings. Patristic and medieval commentators distinguished between observances demanded of all Christians and more radical teachings offered as 'counsels of perfection' for those who want to follow Christ more closely. Albert Schweitzer, in contrast, considered that the Sermon contained an 'interim ethic' incapable of fulfilment over a long period of time, but demanded by a Jesus expecting the imminent inbreak of God's rule (*The Mystery of the Kingdom of God* (1914), 97). Finally, ethicists like Reinhold *Niebuhr have taken Matt. 5: 48 ('be perfect as your heavenly father is perfect') as indicating that the Sermon has the character of a norm that is impossible of fulfilment by humans but retains its value as a

measure of all human activity and as a goal towards which human behaviour should strive (*The Nature and Destiny of Man* (1943), ii. 40, 84). For all its difficulties, however, the Sermon until very recently was a universally recognized norm for Christian identity, and most Christians continue to read and refer to 'The Sermon on the Mount' as a self-evident, if not necessarily critically assessed, point of reference for Christian life. It was so for non-Christians too: Mahatma Gandhi as well as Martin Luther King, Jr. (see BLACK THEOLOGY) saw his radical social activism as a direct application of the principles enunciated by Jesus in the Sermon on the Mount.

Recent critical scholarship has questioned both the nature and centrality of the Sermon. Source criticism of the Synoptic Gospels compares the Sermons in Matthew and Luke and discovers (1) they share some material; (2) other material found in Matthew's Sermon is used by Luke elsewhere in his narrative (especially in chs. 9–19); (3) Matthew has some material not found elsewhere in Luke. The discourse presents a classic example of the 'synoptic problem' in the twofold tradition.

The minority of scholars who hold the hypothesis of Matthean priority have a simple explanation: Matthew's Sermon was written first, and Luke borrowed from it, using some of the material in his Sermon on the Plain, and some elsewhere. The majority of scholars, holding the so-called 'two-source' hypothesis in which Mark is seen as a source for both Matthew and Luke together with a 'sayings source' designated 'Q', have a number of options from which to choose. How are the two versions connected to Q?

A minimalist position regards Q simply as the material shared by Matthew and Luke but not found in Mark, making no judgement concerning its original textual status. A stronger hypothesis holds that one version of the Sermon was present as a distinct discourse in Q, and was taken over by the respective evangelists from this source. There is no easy solution, but close literary comparison of the gospels reveals how thoroughly each version of the Sermon is integrated into its respective narrative and reflects the themes distinctive to Matthew and Luke.

Whichever source theory is held, the implications of such critical analysis are obvious. The Sermon on the Mount is no longer assumed to be a direct report of an actual discourse delivered in a specific time and place by Jesus himself, but is regarded as a discourse constructed out of discrete sayings either by the anonymous redactors of Q, or by the evangelists. The words and sayings themselves may go back to Jesus, but their fashioning into a discourse as it now stands, particularly in Matthew, must be seen as evidence, not for the historical ministry of Jesus, but for the creative shaping of the memory of Jesus in the church after his death and Resurrection.

There are implications for the authority ascribed to the Sermon by present-day readers. In the light of critical analysis it can no longer simply be assumed that these words have authority because Jesus spoke them this way. Nor can appeal be made to the Sermon as a direct expression of Jesus' intentions that can be used as a measure over against the church. The decision to regard the Sermon as normative must now derive from a prior decision concerning the writings of the NT as the canonical texts of the church. Not a 'historical Jesus' but the Jesus of Matthew's gospel and the Jesus of Luke's gospel speaks in the respective versions of the Sermon.

Some late 20th-century theology has also denied the centrality of the Matthean Sermon on ideological grounds. *Liberation theology finds the Matthean beatitudes too individualistic and spiritualizing, the Matthean strictures against violence too accommodating to evil social structures. Just as late 20th-century 'historical Jesus' research tended to favour the Lucan portrait of Jesus as a prophetic challenge to economic and social oppression, so liberation theology prefers the Lucan version of Jesus' Sermon, with its more obvious social and political edge.

The effect of both source and ideological criticism has been to relativize the importance of that Sermon which for much of the history of Christianity loomed larger even than the gospel in which it appeared. It remains to be seen whether these attempts to displace such a central text represent a scholarly fad or a more fundamental rupture with Christian tradition.

See also BIBLE, ITS AUTHORITY AND INTERPRETATION.

Luke Timothy Johnson

Betz, H. D., *The Sermon on the Mount* (1995).
Davies, W. D., *The Setting of the Sermon on the Mount* (1963).
Jeremias, J., *The Sermon on the Mount*, ET (1963).
Luther, Martin, *The Sermon on the Mount* in *Luther's Works*, xxi, ed. J. Pelikan (1956).

seventeenth century: an overview.

For western Christendom, the century following the *Reformation was more than anything else the century of confessional dogmatics. The separated churches—Roman Catholic, *Lutheran, and *Reformed— drew up their own doctrinal systems, or confessions, and combined this mental consolidation with an organizational one in which the different churches became stable denominations with their own constitutions and lifestyles which they sought to standardize throughout their membership. The confessions—the Decrees and Canons of the Council of *Trent, the Lutheran Formula of Concord, and among the Reformed the Belgic, Gallic, and Helvetic Confessions, the Thirty-Nine Articles, and the Canons of Dort— now stood as basic yardsticks of doctrinal *orthodoxy, against which people's writings and behaviour across a whole range of Christian activities could be scrutinized and (if necessary) condemned. Often born out of immediate problems and struggles, these confessions rapidly became polemically defined credal statements, inflexible to any change. Attempts to adjust or redraft them simply generated more hostility, as the Dutch *Arminians found when they sought to modify the Belgic Confession, and with minor exceptions no new doctrinal statements with genuine 'confessional' status were drawn up after the early years of the century. The *authority of the confessions made compromise or reconciliation between the different confessional groupings all but impossible. It is hardly surprising, in these circumstances, that the century did not give rise to the original genius of a *Luther or *Calvin.

Superficially, the overall picture may thus seem to be one of a loss of vitality and creativity. After the glittering cavalry charges of the Reformation period, religious thinkers would appear to have settled down behind their heavily fortified trenches for a war of theological attrition. In contrast to the freedom and questioning of the earlier period, the 17th century can appear to have retreated into a stale and limited process of endless elaboration and conservative protection (in increasingly ossified forms) of the theological advances of the previous century. But this would be unfair. In fact, for a sup-

posedly arid and conservative forum of religious debate, controversial divinity in this period was an area of constant flux and development. Some of the major alterations and most challenging new developments in Christian thought stem from the confessionally driven controversial divinity of the time, and are inseparable from it.

To begin with, confessionalism proved unable to close down debates within the different communions. On the contrary, a great deal of intellectual energy was devoted to internal conflicts and disputes within the individual confessions and churches. The *Catholic Church was troubled by the *De Auxiliis* controversy between Jesuits and Dominicans and the *Jansenist controversy; the Lutherans by the kenotic and syncretist controversies; the Dutch Reformed churches by the Arminian conflict and the Voetian/Cocceian controversy; the French Reformed by the Amyraldian controversy; while the Church of England was rocked by a seemingly endless series of polemical debates over Arminianism and forms of church government and ceremonies, with a brief wholesale revision of its articles of faith in mid-century. Many of these controversies were concerned in one way or another with the dialectic of *grace and free will, and the eternal problem of balancing God's sovereignty with human agency. For all the implacability of the confessional statements, change and division on this topic continued incessantly in the 17th century. This was partly because, even with a confessional constant, theological formulations change. Confessionalization was just one part of the systematization of earlier writers, and this required theologians to grapple with issues and doctrines which *sixteenth-century authors had not dealt with in any detail. This systematization was accomplished by the increasing use of medieval methods of discourse, disputation, and *philosophy (see MIDDLE AGES). But this revival of scholasticism did not necessarily impose a dead weight of obscurantism on religious enquiry, but was itself a force for change. The increasing use of scholastic method forced an inevitable elaboration of doctrine which was in its way more searching than the less systematic assertions of the early Reformers. An elaboration of doctrine—especially concerning theological prolegomena and the essence and attributes of *God—necessarily brought with it more interest in *metaphysical problems, and the search for a more speculative, philosophically adequate language of theology.

Moreover, the confessions were not quite the inflexible monuments that they might appear. The Council of Trent's doctrinal position was notoriously subtle and ambiguous: it was, as contemporaries called it, a 'nose of wax' on many theological points, phrased in order to head off deep divisions among Roman Catholics themselves. But its very flexibility ensured that it could be read in many different ways, and the theological debates and divisions on the Roman side continued. In the Reformed communion, the idea of confessional community was compromised by a considerable degree of variance between the different confessions, yet at the same time there was much that could potentially be harmonized, thereby making appeal across the confessions possible for the different groups in dispute. When Reformed theologians gathered together at the Synod of Dort (1618–19), they discovered among themselves a rich diversity of views on questions surrounding the doctrine of grace but, despite a good deal of acrimony, they were able to generate sufficient compromises and qualifications to produce an agreed set of doctrinal formulations against Arminianism. The conviction of a shared confessional identity could in these cases often be more vital than doctrinal unanimity in keeping the confessions together.

The continuing controversies between the different confessions were also not the stale, unproductive exercise that they might appear. To begin with, the confessional boundaries erected by polemicists did not necessarily correspond to theological reality. Christians constantly borrowed from different theological traditions, even if they remained formally at variance and on one or two topics always expressed themselves in terms of violent opposition. Participants in the Arminian or *De Auxiliis* controversies could often find their positions closer to those of their confessional rivals than those of their ostensible confessional partners—*Dominican authors and Jansenist divines, for example, were regularly cited by Calvinist theologians in support of their more severely *Augustinian doctrine, against the arguments of Arminian writers.

Moreover, the erection of tightly bound, scholastic theological systems in defence of established confessions did not produce a simple stalemate, or close down creative theological debate. It is true that there may have been little meaningful dialogue between the confessions, and that they continued to clash over the familiar issues of *merit, *justification, *eucharistic doctrine, *papal authority, ubiquitarianism, idolatry, free will, *antinomianism, and so on. The acceptance of the permanent separation of the confessional groupings did nothing to lessen the energy which they devoted to seeking to undermine each other's positions. Nevertheless, this polemical determination meant that the basic assumptions behind the different confessions were subjected to the most searching and damaging scrutiny, so that the very basis of religious knowledge and certainty was called into question.

New scholarly fronts were opened up. Clashes over the different confessions' claims to *catholicity, for example, generated a remarkable surge of interest in patristics and church history, among Protestants as much as Catholics. All confessional groupings claimed to be 'catholic' in the sense of preserving the tradition of the fathers. The views of the church fathers thus became one of the battlegrounds of religious polemic, but in the process patristic scholarship made great strides forward. The first-ever critical patrology was written by the great Lutheran scholar Johann Gerhard (1582–1637), who coined the term. The degree of Protestant enthusiasm for the church fathers did differ, however. Where Georg Calixtus (1586–1656) and the other Lutheran Syncretists taught that the consensus of the first five centuries of church fathers could provide a secondary source of doctrine to supplement scripture, most Lutherans were less convinced, and Gerhard's patrology itself sought more systematically to provide a guide to where the fathers were to be followed and where they had 'erred'. The problem for Protestants in particular was that, as post-Tridentine patristic scholarship became more systematic (exemplified in the voluminous *Annales Ecclesiastici* of Cesare Baronius (1538–1607), but also in many other editions of patristic texts), so it became increasingly difficult to make the fathers fit into later doctrinal divisions. The Huguenot theologian Isaac Casaubon (1559–1614) was deeply troubled when he found himself unable to find patristic support for the French Reformed doctrine of the Eucharist. Another Huguenot theologian, Jean Daillé (1594–1670), sought a more radical solution to this problem when he emphasized the inconsistency of patristic testimony in his *Traicté de l'employ des saincts pères* (1631).

Daillé's work was to be very influential in the long run, but did not secure unanimous Protestant support. In the Church of England a strong emphasis on the importance of the early church fathers as a secondary source both of doctrine and ecclesiology led to attempts by Lancelot Andrewes, William Laud, and other churchmen to adjust aspects of the liturgy and doctrine of the church accordingly. Among Laud's followers were two of Daillé's most prominent Protestant opponents—Henry Hammond (1605–60) and John Pearson (1613–86) (who effectively refuted Daillé's attacks on the reliability of the Ignatian epistles)—although later Anglicans (like other Reformed divines) were strongly influenced by the French theologian.

Daillé's *Traicté* was itself in part a contribution to another increasingly problematic aspect of the Catholic/Protestant debate, and that was concerned with the long-running argument over the 'rule of faith'. Protestants challenged the Catholic claim to *apostolic tradition and papal authority as the criterion for distinguishing true from false faith. In response, Catholics attacked the Protestant claim to scripture as the sole criterion of faith by challenging the notion that scripture was self-authenticating, or that inner persuasion could assure the reader of the truth of the scriptures, and that human reason could serve as the proper mechanism for scriptural interpretation (see BIBLE: ITS AUTHORITY AND INTERPRETATION). Protestants did not simply appeal to enlightened *reason for the interpretation of scripture, and even when it came to the initial conviction that the scriptures were indeed true, not all Protestants simply claimed the importance of inner persuasion. In England, for example, the *Caroline Divines still urged the importance of the church in initially drawing people to the scriptures, and the growing tendency of Church of England divines to emphasize the importance of the physical continuity of the church's witness led their clash with Roman Catholic apologists to concentrate particularly on the succession of the true church via the oft-repeated Catholic demand, 'Where was your church before Luther?'

The debate took an especially critical turn in France, where Catholic controversialists such as François Veron sought to strengthen their assault on Protestantism by turning to forms of 'Pyrrhonism'—a form of undogmatic scepticism that proposed to suspend judgement on a wide range of questions, including whether or not something could be known. In the process, they attacked the very notion that rational faculties could serve as the foundation and support of the faith, seeking to show that Protestants could have no assured faith once they had rejected the church as an infallible judge. This Catholic attack reached its climax in the work of Richard Simon (1638–1712) who endeavoured in his *Critical History of the Old Testament* (1678) to demonstrate that scripture was not self-authenticating, and denied the *Mosaic authorship of the Pentateuch. While Simon sought to use all his scholarship as a club against the Calvinists who claimed religious truth from the bible alone, he was in the process adopting many of the techniques of biblical criticism of Baruch Spinoza (1632–77), who had developed them with a very different intent. Spinoza pushed matters further by insisting on the separation of *theology and philosophy, leaving the role of theology as simply that of teaching piety, obedience, and a moral life. René *Descartes's principle of 'universal doubt' and insistence on a universal method had similarly questioned by implication the immunity of theology and biblical scholarship from the dictates of natural philosophy. While some elements of such ideas could be used to attack Protestantism, they harboured more fundamental dangers for the basis of all Christian confessions (see HIGHER CRITICISM).

The intention of the Roman Catholic Pyrrhonists was to undermine belief in self-authenticating scripture, in order to place the greatest importance on the witness of the Catholic Church. The Protestant response to this challenge could vary, throwing its emphasis variously on scripture, reason, or inner persuasion as offering the key to religious certainty. Lutherans in the later 17th century redoubled their emphasis on the truthfulness of scripture. A more commonly embraced solution, however, for those who took on board some of the assaults on scripture and the fathers, was the championing of a form of mitigated scepticism, which granted the impossibility of infallible certainty but sought instead to elevate human reason as the only means of assessing degrees of probability, in contrast to the scriptural absolutism or patristic confidence of earlier writers. This became especially prominent in Anglican thought in the later 17th century, in the writings of the 'Latitudinarians', including theologians such as John Wilkins (1614–72) who sought to bridge the gap between theological method and the 'new philosophy' by the use of reason.

An alternative approach to the importance of reason emerged in the thought of the Cambridge Platonists. Scholars like Benjamin Whichcote (1609–83) and Henry More (1614–87) attached vital importance in the development of religious knowledge to 'reason', not in the Latitudinarian sense of a natural, impersonal human capacity, but rather in mystical terms as 'the candle of the Lord', a means whereby the individual human soul gained illumination by participation in the divine reason. This equation of human with divine reason, and emphasis on the experiential witness of divine inspiration, offered another response to the 'rule of faith' debate. Here too, the Cambridge Platonists had obvious affinities with the many *evangelical groups throughout the century who emphasized the importance of inner experience as a primary authority in religious life, with an increasing stress on the doctrine of the *Holy Spirit, and a readiness to identify the spirit in scripture with God's Spirit in the individual. It was the *Quakers who moved one crucial step further by their dissociation of the *Word and Spirit, and their insistence that, where there was a discrepancy, the Word should be tried by the Spirit rather than vice versa. There was an enormous difference between the rational Logos theory of the Cambridge Platonists and the theology of the Holy Spirit that humble Quakers worked out from their own religious experience. But both groups, along with the wide range of other *pietistic groups active in the period, were expressive of the crisis of religious authority that the Reformation had unleashed, and that showed no sign of abating in the 17th century.

The involved relationship of scripture to experience and inward revelation was also reflected in the extraordinary flowering of *mystical and *apocalyptic *prophecy and *eschatology in the 17th century. This was the age, not just of confessional dogmatists, but of the German shoemaker-mystic Jacob Boehme (1575–1624), of the extraordinary Rosicrucian manifestos which created such excitement throughout Europe, and of Thomas Venner's attempt in 1661 to overthrow the government of England in order to erect the Fifth Monarchy, as foretold in *Daniel. Nevertheless, a vivid eschatology and prophetical excitement were not simply the preserve of sectarian fanatics, but built on established foundations. Some forces of mystical prophecy and apocalyptic inquiry and prediction were evident in the confessional churches themselves, though in sometimes tense relationship with confessional orthodoxy. In Germany in the late 16th and early 17th centuries prophetic enquiry in both the Lutheran and Calvinist confessions was remarkably intense. Boehme's bizarre fusion of *Gnostic, Christian Platonist, and Paracelsian ideas and influences was *sui generis*, but other writers such as Jacob Arndt (1555–1621) were more mainstream thinkers whose prediction of the imminent end of the world inspired even scholars such as Johann Gerhard. German Calvinism and Lutheranism were alike homes to increasingly eclectic forms of mystical and chiliastic thinking, where eschatological prophecy was combined with *astrology, hermeticism, alchemy, and cabbalistic ideas. Moreover, while Boehme's cosmic vision rejected apocalyptic prophecy and was opposed to historical and literal chiliasm, other groups were more ready to tie prophecies directly to current events and the confessional warfare that was devastating the country.

One particularly potent idea to emerge from this brew of mystical and utopian ideas was a new millennialism. A number of thinkers—most prominently Johann Heinrich Alsted in Calvinist Herborn, and in England Joseph Mede (1586–1638), who had been troubled by Pyrrhonistic inclinations in his youth, broke with past apocalyptic interpretation in reserving the prophesied thousand-year rule of the saints for a future millennial reign on earth, rather than placing it in the past with the binding of Satan in the years between 300 and 1300 AD. This *millenarian doctrine, combined with utopian ideas and heightened expectations, all conveyed in popular tracts and speeches, equipped both mainstream but also more radical prophets with the intellectual gunpowder necessary to fuel an eschatological drive for apocalyptic reform of church, state, and society. Both Germany and England experienced an explosion of apocalyptic writing at times of political crisis—the Thirty Years War and the English Civil War respectively. In both cases earlier apocalyptic and mystical writings were reprinted and applied far more directly to current events, and in both countries such apocalyptic speculation became very heavily politicized as a result. However, in both Germany and England, a reaction against such prophecy set in later in the century. Both Lutheran and Reformed churches became increasingly concerned that key doctrines were being threatened by chiliastic ideas. Both in Lutheran Germany and in England, the politicization of prophecy seems to have been followed by its collapse. There may well be a causal relationship, here: perhaps not so much that increasingly specific prophecies were proved wrong, but that long wars and increasingly complex political crises seemed to defy beliefs that they were to be suddenly and swiftly resolved by divine intervention. In England, moreover, the association of apocalyptic prophecy with political *revolution made it increasingly unpalatable. In both countries, apocalyptic prophecy became spiritualized, the emphasis being placed on Antichrist as a more general force of sin and evil, and the conviction that the kingdom of God was to be erected in the heart of the believer rather than in the national polity. A similar trajectory towards the internalization of reformation and renewal is visible across the Continent and its confessional boundaries, among English Puritans, French Jansenists, and German Lutherans.

This move towards the cultivation of inner piety is as prominent a theme in the Christian thought of the 17th century as the rise of confessionalism. Indeed, enthusiasts of such trends often saw themselves as representing the vital obverse to confessionalism, as upholders of true active faith opposing the stale, 'dead' faith of logic-chopping confessionalism, where dry academic debate had led people to forget and ignore true religion. This urgent desire for a renewal of Christian life is evident time and again throughout the century. What often appears as a vast cross-confessional wave engulfed Europe in the 17th century, with all countries and confessions witnessing the emergence of movements of *ascetic mysticism, moral rigorism, and affective piety that championed a living faith in opposition to mere external show and words. In Catholicism, the writings of the bishop of *Geneva, Francis de Sales (1567–1622), provided a programme for laypeople to pursue spiritual perfection. Several distinctive religious movements also emerged, most notably that of Jansenism—which espoused a sternly Augustinian moral rigorism—and the *quietists, who adopted a less Augustinian form of mystical meditation. The same period also saw a remarkable rise in devotion to the sacred heart of Jesus, which was given a careful theological explanation and justification by Jean Eudes (1601–80). Independently of such developments, in England, Puritan thinkers professed a profound concern for the inward religious life, developing intense forms of personal piety based around assurance of election. The tradition of Puritan spiritual narratives that developed out of such trends continued throughout the century, reaching its apogee in John Bunyan's *Pilgrim's Progress. These forms of Puritan affective piety also manifested themselves in more extreme forms—in the preaching of Scottish and Irish revivalists, in the millenarian and enthusiastic sects of the 1640s and 1650s, and in radical Puritan movements which split apart from Reformed Protestantism altogether, in the shape of the Muggletonians, Quakers, and Antinomians. The Quakers perhaps constituted the logical end of a trend which had insisted on de-emphasizing the significance of all external observances, institutions, and forms in the face of the centrality of the direct individual experience of God. Similar movements emerged in German Pietism and the Dutch nadere reformatie, which in their different strands placed varying emphasis on the importance of mysticism, penance, and the role of the clergy in guiding Christians in the cultivation of true inward holiness.

It is easy to see the rationale of the growth of a stress on inward assurance as an answer to the questioning of the basis of religious knowledge by the epistemology of Descartes and others. But it would be wrong to lump these different streams together, or to depict them in simple opposition to an arid confessional mainstream. To begin with, while these different movements might have been united in their opposition to 'dead faith', they were often deeply divided over the question of how far they should separate from the outside world, and over the role of the Spirit in practical divinity. For example, in contrast to the German Pietists, the 'Dutch Pietists' emphasized practical divinity but were vigorously against mysticism, and were deeply preoccupied with the political aspects of religious renewal, calling for action in every sphere of life. Many English Puritans who were dedicated exponents of practical divinity were similarly determined to reform the government and organization of the church as part of their programme of religious renewal. The different groups also quarrelled violently with one another. Advocates of anxious self-scrutiny and moral rigorism were often the vigorous opponents of those who emphasized the immediate, liberating experience of grace. In this sense, the acrimonious antinomian controversy in Puritan New England found its echo in the hostilities between Jansenists and quietists, and in the almost universal condemnation of the Quakers. The intense vigour with which the different groups opposed each other suggests that they did not see themselves as a single movement, even if their polemic was sometimes motivated by a realization that their antagonists were embarrassingly close to some of their own convictions.

If anything united these different groups, it was their common rejection of formal, 'dead faith'. But the fact that it became fashionable for many to define their religious convictions against cold, dry, hair-splitting theology does not mean that there was also a body of theologians dedicated to 'formalist' emotionless theology. In fact, the latter was a form of theology that was only ever invoked as an 'other' for individuals to define themselves against. In reality, the foremost theological logicians often had a profound concern for spirituality as well, and their fervent desire to uphold the nostrums of orthodoxy sprang in part from a sincere conviction that they thereby protected religious truths that were crucial to the cultivation of a proper and active Christian faith. Many elements of the reaction against mere 'formal, dead faith' were axiomatic to those divines who were themselves at the forefront of confessional scholasticism. Some of the greatest systematic theologians of the century were also prominent devotional writers. The Catholic Cardinal Bellarmine (1542–1621), the Lutheran Johann Gerhard, and the English Puritan William Perkins (1558–1602) were all popular devotional writers whose scholasticism was combined with a deep concern with the practicalities of Christian life and practice. Two of the most prominent early Dutch Pietists, Gisbert Voetius (1589–1676) and William Ames (1576–1633), had been enthusiastic participants at the condemnation of Arminianism at the Synod of Dort. The *predestinarian doctrines of later Calvinism were not arcane and dusty dogmatics, but had a strong *christological foundation and a firm experiential emphasis.

Many of these movements for revival of interior piety emerged naturally out of trends visible within orthodox confessionalism, and it may be most helpful to see them partly as different manifestations of elements of tension and ambiguity within orthodox religion. In essence, the struggle between the 'religion of the heart' and confessional dogmas was not so much a struggle between different religious groups, but rather a conflict that was played out in the mind of every active Christian thinker. Early modern confessionalism created a situation where a hostile observer could easily protest that doctrinal formularies were being prized above Christian living: and it was this perception that generated the urgent demands for an anti-formalist religion, which in themselves created a still more anxious defence of confessional norms that might be violated in such a reaction. What does seem clear, however, is a gradual movement later in the 17th century in all these different pietistic traditions—in England, Germany, France, and the Netherlands—away from attempting to transform society and the church, and instead retreating from the world into the internal, experiential life, and often into separatist conventicles. A more general rejection of theocratic principles is increasingly evident.

Another development associated with the rise of Pietism, and a declining belief in the idea of a godly magistrate, is that of a full-blooded notion of religious toleration. This did not necessarily emerge from any of the ecumenical notions that occasionally found expression among the confessional churches. The reunification of the churches was a regular source of debate and discussion among religious writers of this period, and inspired the actions of committed ecumenists such as John Dury (1596–1680). Various attempts were made by adherents of confessional groups throughout the century to draw up agreed definitions of fundamental articles of faith, and there were amicable discussions between Calvinists and Lutherans at the Leipzig Colloquy (1631), but there was never any real likelihood that confessional barriers would be breached, and nothing was achieved. It was those writers who rejected the precepts of confessionalism—rationalist philosophers or enthusiastic sectaries—who developed the most inclusive views of religious society. But even when increasing numbers of writers were ready to maintain that the Christian magistrate had no right to punish heretics and *schismatics, they usually drew the line somewhere. Even the radically inclusive Roger Williams (c.1604–83), in his The Bloudy Tenent of Persecution (1644) did not allow atheism and blasphemy. Nevertheless, in the writings of Williams and John Locke in England, and of Simon Episcopius (1583–1643) and other Remonstrant divines in the Netherlands, the notion that religious diversity was not merely something that might be reluctantly tolerated for political reasons, but might actually be a positive good, began to be regularly expressed, although it could not yet hope to find a positive reception from society.

The end of the 17th century, then, was marked in many countries by a retreat from the incessant demands of political confessionalization, and of theocratic notions of government. This was a change that was at times combined with the development of new notions of scriptural interpretation and *natural theology that challenged some of the presuppositions of confessionalism, and with the emergence of radically secularizing ideas of toleration and individualism, and of religious ideals that were quietist rather than political, and centred on voluntaristic associations rather than national churches. But these were not developments that carried all before them. It was the impracticalities of confessionalization that more than anything served to subdue it, combined perhaps with a genuine revulsion for the religious upheavals and fanaticism that had characterized the Thirty Years War and the English Civil War. But there was no sudden end to heresy-hunting, or to the general conviction that religious unity was politically desirable. The century ended, not just with the publications of John Locke, but also with the suppression of Socinianism in Poland, and the revocation of the Edict of Nantes in France. Religious censorship continued even in the notoriously liberal Dutch Republic. It would be a long time before the tide of confessionalism truly receded.

Anthony Milton

Barnes, Robin Bruce, Prophecy and Gnosis: Apocalypticism in the Wake of the Lutheran Reformation (1988).

Beeke, Joel R., Assurance of Faith: Calvin, English Puritanism and the Dutch Second Reformation (1991).

Campbell, T., The Religion of the Heart: A Study of European Religious Life in the Seventeenth and Eighteenth Centuries (1991).

Firth, Katherine R., The Apocalyptic Tradition in Reformation Britain, 1530–1645 (1979).

Grell, O. P., and Scribner, R. (eds.), Tolerance and Intolerance in the European Reformation (1996).

Muller, Richard H., Post-Reformation Reformed Dogmatics, i. Prolegomena (1987).

Nuttall, Geoffrey, The Holy Spirit in Puritan Faith and Experience (1946).

Pelikan, Jaroslav, The Christian Tradition: A History of the Development of Doctrine, iv. Reformation of Church and Dogma (1400–1700) (1984).

Popkin, Richard H., The History of Scepticism from Erasmus to Spinoza (1979).

Preus, R. D., The Theology of Post-Reformation Lutheranism (2 vols.; 1970).

Yates, Frances, The Rosicrucian Enlightenment (1972).

sex and sexuality. Any standard introduction to these subjects is likely to employ the distinction between 'sex' as a biological concept classifying living beings as female or male; and 'sexuality' as a sociopsychological concept, expressing how women or men convey their identity as this particular *woman or *man. This distinction has buckled under the weight imposed on it. The biological differences between men and women are much less clear-cut than was previously thought. 'Sex' in the vernacular has acquired many meanings beyond biology. The term 'sexuality' is recent, and was intended to help to classify sexual orientation and behaviour, and thereby the individuals manifesting the behaviour, in relation to assumed norms. Above all, the distinction ignores the huge contribution of gender in shaping sexual expectations, experience, and practice. 'Gendered norms' influence one's self-understanding as a sexual being in relation to others. Once merely a grammatical category, gender now conveys the sense of pre-existing forms of social relations which already permeate a given culture and which require investigation. It is therefore possible to regard sex and sexuality, along with gender, as biological, personal and social, and cultural designations, respectively. Actual usage is more messy, and these distinctions constantly overlap.

All major traditions of Christianity confine sexual intercourse to heterosexual, monogamous *marriage. How far is this insistence open to revision in the light of social/scientific knowledge of sex and sexuality, of the theological grasp of the inevitable dynamics of living historical traditions, of *feminist criticisms of marriage, of *secularization, and of the sexual experience of millions of Christian people which diverges from conveniently simple norms? Early Christian tradition, beginning with *Paul, taught that *celibacy was better than marriage: the value accorded to celibacy and to *virginity in the ancient church required marriage to be defended as a licit, albeit inferior state (see Brown 1988). Defences included the avoidance of fornication and the procreation of *children. When marriage was declared a *sacrament in the 12th century, its sacramental power was thought to convert sexual desire into desire for children. *Protestant Reformers, partly by the denigration of celibacy, heightened the emphasis on marriage as a normative, near-universal state. The requirement that marriage begin with a church ceremony (1563 in Catholic countries, but not until 1753 in England and Wales) heightened the sense of sexual intercourse temporally 'before' the wedding as illicit, and its illicitness is still upheld in most churches as biblical, traditional, and official teaching.

Christian thought has found itself required to respond to theological, social, and intellectual upheavals in the understanding of sex. Feminist theology has convincingly shown that traditional Christian thought in this area, as in all others, is androcentric and so reflects the experience of the male half of the church only. The early Christian vision that in Christ there is neither male nor female (Gal. 3: 28) was soon replaced (see Ruether 1998: ch. 1) by a hierarchy clearly set out in the household rules of the New Testament (Eph. 5: 21–33; Col. 3: 18–19; 1 Pet. 3: 1–7; 1 Tim. 2: 8–15; Titus 2: 2–5) in which men are superior to women, temporally and so ontologically prior to them (1 Cor. 11: 2–16), and married women are to submit to their husbands as to Christ. They are not to teach, and through *Eve they are responsible for bringing *sin into the world. Since theologians were mainly male celibates, it is understandable that women were often depicted in their writings as the source of forbidden desire and temptation, and sometimes as sexually insatiable (see Ranke-Heinemann 1990). Firm control was therefore essential. Given the benefit of hindsight there is no doubt that Christian teaching proclaimed and enforced the social and sexual subjugation of women. The male body was associated with mind, *reason, authority, activity, and culture: the female body with flesh, emotion, submission, passivity, and nature. These beliefs are frequently identified as patriarchal, philosophical, and sexist dualism (Nelson 1978), and may still lead directly to low self-esteem among women in Christian communities where such teaching is upheld. In particular, the expectation of submission to men is undoubtedly a factor in marital rape and familial violence (see Cooper-White 1995). Sexism, discrimination on the grounds of gender, is still practised by the greater part of Christendom, because *ordination and high office are forbidden to women, on questionable theological grounds.

Michel Foucault's analysis of sexuality (*The History of Sexuality: An Introduction* (1976)) is a landmark in 20th-century discussion of sexuality, which presents Christian thought with new opportunities and challenges. The idea of 'disciplinary power' is an important key to his thought. He believes that the social arrangements for the expression of sexuality, such as marriage and indeed the institution of heterosexuality itself, are arrangements of disciplinary power whereby sexual expression is directed into approved forms and activities. The extraordinary consequence of this view is that basic beliefs which passed themselves off as natural or God-given turn out to be social constructions, expressions of control. Both the confession of sexual sins and, in the 18th and 19th centuries, the creation of a vast medical discourse (of which the term 'sexuality' is a product) are understood as edifices of control which, effortlessly, condition whole populations to affirm norms and thereby label deviations as perversions (*homosexuality and masturbation are two of these). The satisfaction of desire is thereby determined in advance by specifying its narrowly legitimate objects. Social constructionists label their opponents 'essentialists', people who hold that there are 'givens' which are derived from universal human norms, or from nature, or, in its religious form, from God, and mediated through sacred text, *tradition, *natural law, or the teaching *authority of the church. These 'givens' may include the complementarity of the sexes (the belief that men and women are essentially incomplete without each other), the heterosexual nature of men and women (rendering lesbian, gay, and bisexual people perverse), the confinement of sexual intercourse to marriage, and

the association of masculinity with power over women. This approach may be contrasted not simply with the 'essentialism' of Christian thought but with the popular 'drive-based' view of much *psychological and medical discourse.

Human sexuality is able to be reconnected to the traditional doctrine of the *imago dei*, based originally on Genesis 1: 26–7, that men and women are made in *God's image. Christian reflection on the *imago dei* posits the triune God who is a *communion of *persons in relation, each coequal, each different from the others, each contributing to who the others are, all of them sharing in the single divine reality which is loving, self-giving communion. While the Christian imagination will refrain from too much specificity in saying in what respects people finitely image their divine Creator, the classical doctrine of the *Trinity suggests real relationality and individuality, identity and belonging, and difference within communion among the *divine* persons which may 'image' what created personhood can and should become. This understanding of the *imago dei* may be contrasted with other versions that compare the human individual person with the divine, bodiless, individual person, God, and look for commonalities mainly in the human *soul, conveniently abstracted from its body. We 'image' God as we reach out in *love to others as embodied beings: our sexuality is thus able to be theorized within Christian faith as God's way of propelling us beyond ourselves in seeking intimacy with others and ensuring that others seek intimacy with ourselves.

A relational understanding of the human person enables sexual desire to be positively experienced and expressed within theology. For celibate men sexual desire often appeared to invade the soul, and the strategies for combating it often led to negative images of women and the reduction of all sexual desire to concupiscence or lust. Desire, including sexual desire, springs from an awareness both of our contingency, and of our many needs, such as companionship, food, knowledge, and art. The acceptance of desire as normative between persons leads to a revaluation of the intense bodily pleasure that results from it. Feminist theologians, rightly sensing that patriarchal theology has been unable to evaluate desire positively, speak of *eros* as a yearning for right relationship and ultimately the yearning for union with God (see Stuart and Thatcher 1997: ch. 8). The possible sinfulness of desire is located in the socio-structural conditions of male power or the commodification and objectification of the *body. The *Song of Songs offers a biblical model of mutual, highly erotic, sexual desire which has been marginalized by being allegorized. There is emphasis in the Song neither on procreation as a justification for love-making, nor on the privileging of the male in initiating or receiving pleasure.

Nelson (1978) has distinguished between theologies of sexuality and 'sexual theology'. Whereas the former required an understanding of scripture and tradition that was then applied to sexual questions in a one-directional manner, the latter begins with the experience of sex and sexuality in all its ambiguity and urgency, and asks how this influences our understanding of scripture and tradition. Tradition and experience can then operate in a dialogical, two-directional inquiry. This prior emphasis on experience is held in common with theologies of *liberation. Nelson (1992) emphasizes the doctrine of *Incarnation in his 'body theology'. That God has become 'enfleshed' in Christ is more than a theological interpretation of who *Jesus Christ historically was; it is the exemplification of how God is normatively discovered and disclosed, in and through the flesh (see CHRISTOLOGY). An incarnational theology must therefore inevitably be body-affirming.

The churches are likely to be divided for some time over sexual relationships between lesbian, gay, and bisexual people. There is a thriving lesbian and *gay theology (see Cleaver (1995) and the bibliography there). At least one well-known theological journal (*Theology and Sexuality*) addresses these issues, yet this growing scholarly, theological output, together with clear 'lesbigay' testimony to the experience and blessing of God, is worryingly ignored by most ecclesiastical authority. While it would be wrong to classify all conservative thought in this area as homophobic, the problem for an account of human sexuality that is both Christian and inclusive (of bisexuality and homosexuality) is that homosexuality (as lesbian and gay Christians are uncomfortably aware) has become the principal site of conflict between conservative and progressive 'mainstream' theological thought. That conservative thought finds lesbian and gay unions condemned in scripture merely raises further problems about what is being done with the bible in order to arrive at such a conclusion. (For a careful account of how the bible should be used in the discussion of human sexuality, see S. Barton, 'Is the Bible Good News for Human Sexuality? Reflections on Method in Biblical Interpretation', in Thatcher and Stuart (1996). Worse, supporters of an inclusive theology of sexuality will think that the virulence of some conservative opponents is based on considerations that are too painful for them to hear. These include the possibility that heterosexual identity is itself precarious; that straight men find gay men a challenge to their masculinity; that straight people may project onto lesbians and gays their dislike and disowning of their homosexual feelings; that lesbians unacceptably remind heterosexual men that they are not necessary for validating all women; that envy may operate against the body-acceptance and ease of intimacy of lesbian and gay people as seen through heterosexual eyes (Nelson 1992: ch. 4). There is a recognized aetiology of heterosexuality which can be shocking to heterosexuals and is liable to be rejected by them for that (inadequate) reason.

Extra-theological discussion of sexuality generally sees compulsory heterosexuality as a classic mediation of disciplinary power, proscribing sexual expression outside it. Christian thought is able to borrow from the social constructionists without conceding the adequacy of constructionism as a whole. That God made *humanity male and female (Gen. 1: 27) may help to explain our procreative powers (as might be expected in an account of the creation of the world). It may also help to explain the desires of heterosexual people for the opposite sex. But since these early aetiologies do not attempt to explain same-sex desire, they should not be used to marginalize it. Still less do they justify an imagined complementarity whereby the need for intimacy, companionship, or 'completion' can *only* be satisfied by a person of the opposite sex (see A. Webster, *Found Wanting* (1995), ch. 1). An inclusive Christian theology of sexuality may posit embodiment and sociality as essential features of being human (see Cahill 1996: ch. 4). Being human cannot happen without being with others, without being born, and for many but not all, without becoming parents. The satisfaction of certain basic human needs such as safety, shelter, food, and companionship may also belong essentially to how we are made.

A sexual theology which is Christian will be based in part on the decisive revelation of the triune God in the gifts of Christ and the *Holy Spirit. The incarnation of God in Christ is the embodiment of self-giving love: the practice of self-giving love is the realization of Spirit. The Christian life is the summons to share in the self-giving and self-receiving communion of the divine Persons. Christians find in lifelong faithful marriage an icon of the *covenant love of God for God's people and Christ's love for the church. Borrowing and transforming a key idea from Foucault, it may be helpful to suggest that life in Christ requires its own 'disciplinary power', one that is chosen rather than imposed, that is the exercise of responsible freedom rather than coercion, or 'power-with' and not 'power-over' (see Cooper-White 1995). The disciplines of *chastity within relationships, lifelong fidelity to one's partner, and (for those with the gift) celibacy, are all best justified by their contributions to the love of God and one's neighbour which is Christian *spirituality. The misuse of power is also the key to much sexual sin, whether the power of socio-economic forces to turn human bodies into objects, the social power of peer pressure which expects and normalizes early sexual experimentation, or the use of power to manipulate or dominate other people. Christian theology sides with the vulnerable and senses the vulnerability of the human body whatever its sex.

Theology must also respond to the near-universal practice of cohabitation and/or sex prior to marriage, the sheer range of *contraceptive devices and products, their use and their consequences, and the immense human dilemmas caused by the new *reproductive technologies. A partial solution to the first problem may lie in the realization that a marriage need not begin with the wedding ceremony marking its solemnization: in other words, the recovery of the premodern distinction between the 'spousals' and the 'nuptials' (Thatcher 1999). The distinction between the prevention of conception and its postponement is a helpful one in assessing the responsible use of contraception. An argument used by *Aquinas against fornication, that it is a sin against the possible child that may result from it (*ST* II q. 154 a. 3), holds good. Indeed a contemporary version of it, based on empirical evidence that children who are born and raised without the long-term care of both biological parents are less likely to thrive, is forcefully presented by J. Davies (see 'A Preferential Option for the Family', in Barton 1996).

What do traditions of faith say to the practices of donor insemination, *in vitro* fertilization with donor gametes, and to surrogacy? The Roman Catholic response, in *Donum Vitae* (1987) forbids them all. Cahill's analyses of these practices (1996: ch. 7) leads her to examine the cultural assumptions on which these practices are predicated, including absolute personal autonomy, absolute freedom of choice with regard to reproduction, the assumed right of childless couples to seek remedy for childlessness, and not least the opportunity for trading in sperm, eggs, and babies. The donation of sperm or eggs by third parties is thought to imperil the unity of the marriage and to cause possibly unforeseen problems for donors and for children. A task for theology will be to contribute to 'open public discussion, to values of parenthood which extend beyond freedom to embodiment, and to see use of reproductive technologies in a larger context of technical reason operating toward unexamined ends' (ibid. 254).

The *postmodern discourse of sexuality regards itself as '*post-Christian', as 'having escaped the ethical codes of the Christian era', for 'there is no longer a hegemonic master discourse telling us how we should behave' (J. Weeks, *Invented Moralities* (1995), chs. 1–2). In dialogue with this, Christian thought is able to create a hearing for itself by offering an alternative based on the experience of life in Christ where 'there is no such thing as Jew and Greek, slave and freeman, male and female' (Gal. 3: 28). But the patriarchal understanding of what it means to be male and female is far from dead in theological thought, and the slowness of pace with regard to on-going problems of gender and orientation may indicate that the Spirit is as active in the *world as in the churches.

Adrian Thatcher

Barton, S. (ed.), *The Family in Theological Perspective* (1996).

Brown, P., *The Body and Society: Men, Women and Sexual Renunciation in Early Christianity* (1988).

Cahill, L. S., *Sex, Gender and Christian Ethics* (1996).

Cleaver, R., *Know My Name: A Gay Liberation Theology* (1995).

Cooper-White, P., *The Cry of Tamar: Violence against Women and the Church's Response* (1995).

Graham, E., *Making the Difference: Gender, Personhood and Theology* (1995).

Heyward, C., *Touching Our Strength: The Erotic as Power and Love of God* (1989).

Moore, G., *The Body in Context: Sex and Catholicism* (1992).

Nelson, J., *Body Theology* (1992).

——— *Embodiment: An Approach to Sexuality and Christian Theology* (1978).

Ranke-Heinemann, U., *Eunuchs for the Kingdom of Heaven* (1990).

Ruether, R. R., *Women and Redemption* (1998).

Stuart, E., and Thatcher, A., *People of Passion: What the Churches Teach about Sex* (1997).

Thatcher, A., *Marriage after Modernity: Christian Marriage in Postmodern Times* (1999).

Thatcher, A., and Stuart, E. (eds.), *Christian Perspectives on Sexuality and Gender* (1996).

Timmerman, J., *Sexuality and Spiritual Growth* (1993).

Whitehead, E. E., and Whitehead, J. D., *A Sense of Sexuality: Christian Love and Intimacy* (1994).

Shakespeare, William

(1564–1616). Shakespeare was born and brought up in Stratford, a place at that time still strongly *Catholic and much affected by the early *Jesuit mission. Almost all those teaching in Stratford Grammar School had Jesuit links and William's father, John, signed an uncompromisingly Catholic 'Spiritual Testament', worded by Charles Borromeo, probably in 1580. At the age of 16 Shakespeare appears to have been taken as one of a group of 'subseminarians', under Edmund Campion's influence, to the secret college and headquarters of the Jesuit mission at Hoghton Tower, Lancashire, under the pseudonym of Shakeshafte, probably with the intention to go later to Douai to study for the priesthood. Campion's arrest and execution in 1581 upset such plans. Shakespeare entered a Lancashire actors' company, the Earl of Derby's, married in 1582, and moved to London. Instead of full-blown recusancy he appears to have spent his working life as a somewhat lapsed Catholic, a 'Church Papist' (one who attended Protestant worship but avoided receiving communion). As a well-known Londoner at a time of considerable anti-Catholicism anything more could have been dangerous, but there is evidence that he died a Catholic. Moreover his personal reticence, indeed the near-invisibility of private life that is so striking and perplexing a characteristic, is well explained by the caution required of someone enduringly influenced by Campion but living in an increasingly *Protestant England where priests were regularly hanged.

The traditional view was that he was born a Protestant, wrote some anti-Catholic plays, and died a Protestant, but there seems little truth in any of these statements. Even the lines in *King John* (*c*.1595) and elsewhere which could appear as expressions of Protestant sentiment are either hard to interpret, given their context, or suggest no more than a kind of anti-papal nationalism which many Elizabethan Catholic laity certainly shared. Moreover, if John, a medieval Henry VIII, asserts his 'great supremacy' against the pope's 'usurped authority' in Act III, he again submits to papal authority in Act V, and it is the Cardinal Legate who, at the end, as John dies, negotiates an honourable peace with the French. The robust assertion of English nationalism in the play's final lines seems consonant with, not in contradiction to, papal authority. That is how most English Catholics would have seen it.

A popular London playwright, in the years after the Armada and around Gunpowder Plot, could hardly not include the occasional sally for a Protestant audience to relish; what is surprising is how sympathetically Catholic ideas are treated and friars, in particular, are portrayed rather pleasingly, while sonnet 73's 'Bare ruined choirs where late the sweet birds sang' suggests nostalgia, not contempt, for a dimension of Catholicism emphatically repudiated by the *Reformation. On the other hand the Lollard martyr Sir John Oldcastle was seemingly caricatured under the guise of Falstaff in a way offensive to Protestant susceptibilities.

All this could suggest a residual cultural Catholicism of slight significance in terms of 'thought'. Most commentators would probably argue that Shakespeare's personal religious preferences hardly matter, given an absence of deeper religious or theological content in his writing. Yet it would seem strange for a genius, influenced in youth by the most brilliant Jesuit of his age and apparently still committed to traditional belief, to avoid attempting anything of theological significance in his own works. The opposite may be the case. The shift in preoccupation from the comedy and history of his first writing decade to theology and *morality in the final years seems incontestable. The mature Shakespeare, it can be claimed, composed a number of striking theological *allegories which have seldom been recognized as such because his religious seriousness has been badly misread by almost all scholars. The literary problem with allegory is that it is generally too obvious, depriving the story of verisimilitude. Shakespeare's are different, in being immersed so subtly that readers may pass them by and never see that here, in Lear's words, we may 'take upon's the mystery of things, as if we were God's spies'.

Consider, then, *King Lear* (1605), a traditional story transformed into a supremely powerful allegory of the tragedy of natural *humanity. Lear as king typifies the human condition, nature fallen, unredeemed, untouched by grace. The theme of 'nature' recurring on page after page fits very well a pre-*Lutheran conception of man's *fallen state. Lear is a man genuinely loved by other good people, far from inherently evil, but he is vain, selfish, pleasure-seeking, irascible, and easily unjust. He turns only too willingly from the unsycophantic honesty of Cordelia and Kent to the lying promises of the thoroughly evil Goneril and Regan and thus precipitates upon himself and society a nightmare of violence, madness, and blindness. 'A very foolish fond old man', he is nevertheless 'more sinned against than sinning'. For both the basically kind Lear and the profoundly evil Edmund 'nature' is 'my goddess', 'dear goddess'. Nature, while far from evil, seems nevertheless so twisted as to allow the Edmunds to prevail. Goneril, Regan, and Edmund have a power, precisely because of their duplicity, denied to the good. In this situation the saviour is she who was at the very beginning of man's odyssey flung out, the Christ figure of the heavenly-eyed, forgiving Cordelia, sent out of Britain dowerless. She returns to save the state but only through her death. *Lear* is a play about the tragedy of natural man, exploring all the subtleties of a Catholic conception of the diversities of nature, fallen but not wholly corrupt, with just the hint of a saviour, but one who only saves through death and not from death, herself immersed within the tragedy. The symbol of *resurrection, so decisively present at the end of the later *Winter's Tale* (1611), a total allegory of *grace, extending from the Fall and its consequences through repentance and *forgiveness to resurrection, cannot be allowed here for this is a story not of grace but nature, and Lear dies still vainly seeking a sign upon Cordelia's lips that she yet lives. The word 'nature' is as pivotal to the one play as the word 'grace' is to the other.

If *Lear* is about an almost unredeemed world, *Measure for Measure* (1604) is emphatically about a Christian one, its themes being central to Christian moral and social theology, interplaying at every level the seemingly irreconcilable demands of *justice and *mercy at once in personal relations and in the shaping and enforcement of *law. This already provided its most serious dimension to the early *Merchant of Venice* (1594) in Portia's appeal:

> Though justice be thy plea, consider this
> That, in the course of justice, none of us
> Should see salvation: we do pray for mercy,
> And that same prayer doth teach us all to render
> The deeds of mercy.

Measure for Measure provides a far more subtle replay of this insight so absolutely central to Christian theology and social theory. Isabella echoes Portia:

> Why, all the souls that were, were forfeit once,
> And He that might the vantage best have took
> Found out the remedy. How would you be
> If He, which is the top of judgement, should
> But judge you as you are? Oh, think on that,
> And mercy will then breathe within your lips
> Like man new made.

Christianity's social and political dilemma has always been that no state can do without law, and law codifies justice, but its central intuition is that, if by justice all must be condemned, justice has been itself replaced by a regime of mercy, established by God but still requiring implementation by man. Angelo's fault is twofold: a particularly double-faced enforcement of justice where he himself has fallen but also complete failure to realize that hard enforcement of law alone, whatever the merits of the law enforcer, is inappropriate. It looks as if Shakespeare depicts him as a spoilt *Puritan and his regime as a Protestant one—part already established, since the Reformation, part still sought for by Puritan contemporaries—while the morally lax regime which preceded it, Pompey's 'merry world' of the past, suggests the 'merry world' that Catholics also liked to look back upon.

But essentially Angelo is us all, as Isabella reminds him. No one is guiltless, no one can wave mercy aside, and that applies to people in authority most of all. *Measure for Measure* is in consequence especially about the corruption of power:

> ... man, proud man,
> Drest in a little brief authority ...
> Plays such fantastic tricks before high heaven
> As make the angels weep.

What can baffle interpreters of *Measure for Measure* most is the Duke—this seemingly grotesque figure who at the beginning invests Angelo with, precisely, 'a little brief authority', then theoretically disappears from the scene while in reality, dressed as a friar, he remains all-seeing, even hearing the confessions of all and sundry, until, the exercise completed, he reappears for the final judgement. The Duke, it can be suggested, represents no less than God's own 'hidden power'. It is God who invests princes with their authority, God alone who sees all that then goes on, God who exercises the definitive, and very merciful, judgement, 'the very mercy of the law'. 'Your Grace, like power divine hath look'd upon my passes', Angelo admits, while Isabella hails his 'unknown sovereignty'. Even the Duke's final invitation to Isabella to marry him would grate less, given her commitment to *chastity and the life of a nun, if he were simply God. It is hard to doubt that we have here Shakespeare's most daring theological allegory: the personification of God in relation to the totality of society.

Only *Cymbeline* (1610) significantly reflects current divisions rather than the common tradition. The overcomplicated story has masked, probably deliberately, the underlying appeal. Cymbeline is Britain misled by an evil, but nameless, queen into refusing to pay tribute to Rome and disinheriting its rightful heirs. Cymbeline's sons meanwhile have been brought up by Belarius, a banished nobleman, in a remote Welsh cave. Across a bizarrely complex plot four elements emerge: the court of Britain claiming 'sovereignty' against *Rome; Rome itself represented by the entirely honourable Lucius; some rather nasty Italians; and a 'Roman' party within Britain, rejected by its crown but utterly loyal. When Britain is invaded by a Roman army, it is the last group that saves the day, rescuing Cymbeline. The queen dies, the king rediscovers his true sons, is reconciled with 'Morgan' (Belarius), and makes peace with Rome. Though Britain has won the war, Cymbeline decides to pay his due tribute once more. It is to be suggested that all this provides an amazing allegory of the post-Reformation ecclesiastical situation and what Shakespeare hoped might still materialize: Britain will recognize the loyalty of its Catholics hidden away in lonely corners of the country (Wales was still a particularly Catholic area in 1610) and be reconciled with the papacy.

> ... let
> A Roman and a British ensign wave
> Friendly together.

The play's ultimate word is 'peace'. Far more profoundly, *Cymbeline* provides a rerun of the reconciliation of Roman authority and nationalism first tackled in *King John*.

Finally, *The Tempest* (1611), Shakespeare's last complete work, an allegory about himself and the world of theatrical imagination he had ruled as he willed. Shakespeare is Prospero, the master of an isle of magic, where, aided by two slaves—Ariel for spiritual things,

Caliban for material ones—he could control all that happened. To end this blissfully tricksy fantasy, his staff broken and the play over (in reality twenty years of play-writing), Prospero speaks a final epilogue: bidding farewell to his own magical land, he looks forward, shorn of 'spirits to enforce, art to enchant', to returning to the dukedom of Milan, or, more prosaic reality, retirement in Stratford. The last lines of epilogue tie so closely with our themes that they require quotation. Here, a century after Luther's protest, he seems with death on the horizon even to be requesting a formal 'indulgence' but, as usual with Shakespeare's theologizing, another meaning remains possible.

> ... my ending is despair
> Unless I be relieved by prayer,
> Which pierces so, that it assaults
> Mercy itself, and frees all faults.
> As you from crimes would pardon'd be,
> Let your indulgence set me free.

The mercy that Portia and Isabella proclaimed and the Duke finally granted, even to Angelo, was now what Shakespeare himself, London life and the compromises of a Church Papist behind him, needed to seek.

Shakespearean theology was basically the common theology of pre-Reformation Christianity little affected by either Protestantism or Counter-Reformation but, if identified, it would have seemed too Catholic to suit the very Protestant society mainstream England was becoming. By the 18th century Shakespeare was indisputably the national bard, but a Protestant nation could not conceive its bard a covert Catholic. Ignoring his Catholicism meant, however, overlooking his theology, so that it became a commonplace that Shakespeare, unlike *Dante or *Milton, was not a religious poet, but only a moral one. It is more than time for Christianity and theology alike to be readmitted into the core of Shakespearean interpretation. This is not a case of reading texts postmodernistically, any way one will, but of being better culturally placed, and better informed, than any generation since Shakespeare's death to detect the half-hidden meanings he intended, portraying the interplay of sin and grace, judgement and mercy, ecclesiastical and national authority, death and resurrection, all the themes central to a Christian understanding of the enigma of human existence.

Adrian Hastings

Duffy, E., 'Was Shakespeare a Catholic?', *The Tablet*, 27 April 1996.
Honigman, E. A. J., *Shakespeare: The 'Lost Years'* (1998).
Hughes, Ted, *Shakespeare and the Goddess of Complete Being* (1992).
Milward, Peter, *Shakespeare's Religious Background* (1973).
—— *The Medieval Dimension in Shakespeare's Plays* (1990).
—— *The Catholicism of Shakespeare's Plays* (1997).
Wilson, R., 'Shakespeare and the Jesuits', *Times Literary Supplement*, 19 December 1997.

sheep and shepherds.

The 23rd *Psalm enjoys a unique status within Christian devotion: 'The Lord is my shepherd, I shall not want; he makes me lie down in green pastures. He leads me beside still waters; he restores my soul.' Shepherding provides the most widely used image in the OT for *God's relationship to his people. It is used too for the forthcoming *messiah, particularly in a text of Ezekiel (34: 23), undoubtedly important for the NT. Here already in the Synoptic Gospels, *Jesus applies the term to himself (Mark 14: 27; Matt. 15: 24; 25: 32–3) most notably in regard to the final

*judgement and the separation of the sheep from the goats. But this theme is greatly expanded in the Fourth Gospel and becomes one of its primary symbols, especially in chapter 10: 'I am the good shepherd. The good shepherd lays down his life for the sheep' (10: 11). Here as elsewhere sheep are necessarily correlative to shepherd; he knows them and is ready to die for them, and will ensure that they form 'one flock'. The *symbolic complexity is, however, denser than that, because Jesus is not only shepherd but also lamb. Indeed, it is precisely as the shepherd who lays down his life for his sheep that he becomes the lamb. So, the author of *Revelation declares, the lamb 'will be their shepherd and will lead them to springs of living water' (7: 17). The *dualism in a sheep/shepherd symbolism is thus overcome. Led by a lamb, the sheep have surely come into their own!

Jesus as 'good shepherd' became one of the most enduring and endearing of images, reappearing in various NT texts and then in much early Christian literature and art. But *John's gospel already added an extension to the pastoral theme in revealing how Jesus' task as shepherd now belongs to the *apostles and elders. The final scene with the moving threefold question to Simon Peter, 'Do you love me?', and the consequent instruction 'Feed my sheep' (John 21: 15–17) is decisively important both for the passing on of the shepherding role to others and for its link with *love. If Jesus remains 'the chief shepherd' it is, therefore, for the elders of the church to 'tend the flock of God' in his name (1 Pet. 5: 2–4). The ecclesiological implications of this for the delineation of the church's subsequent ministry have been far-reaching, especially for the *episcopate. 'Pastor' has become so primary a word for the naming of *ministers, especially within Protestant churches, that its original meaning as shepherd may almost have faded from view. *Pastoral Epistles, pastoral staff, pastoral letters, *pastoral theology—the usage of the term is widespread, even if the underlying symbol has almost disappeared in an urban world where in many countries shepherds hardly exist. This usage has, however, often helped to unbalance clergy–laity relations. The difference between shepherd and sheep suggests an almost total difference in intelligence and function. Ecclesiastical shepherds seldom look like lambs. Instead, an image has been provided which strengthens the unquestioned *authority of the clergy, while making of the *laity a 'flock of sheep', of limited brain-power, fit only to be led and fleeced.

If this side of the shepherd image may have had its day, the attraction of a rewritten Psalm 23 appears as strong as ever. George Herbert's 17th-century 'The God of love my shepherd is, and he that doth me feed', or Henry Baker's 19th-century 'The king of love my shepherd is, whose goodness faileth never,' retain enormous popularity, as do many other versions. It suggests how close Christian devotion remains to the OT. If no other OT text may be so acceptable to Christians in its entirety, no other Christian text may be so universally popular.

Adrian Hastings

sin denotes human disruption of the relationship between humans and *God. Defining sin relationally emphasizes its theological and religious character, as distinct from dealing with the pathology of the human condition in moral or other terms. Sin is what works against God's intention, presence, and action in *creation and *salvation. This disorientation in our relation to God causes immediate confusion concerning *truth, reality, and goodness and thereby in our judgements concerning what is good and right, resulting in disorientation in all our relationships: to ourselves, our bodies, one another, the natural *world.

Both as a reality in the world and as a theme in Christian thought and practice, sin depends on the primary reality to which it is opposed, the good that continually creates possibilities for transforming disfigurement and damage: the creative, sustaining, saving action of God in the world. Sin can only be understood from within the perspective of the Christian story. It is tempting to understand it solely in the context of creation, as counter to the original, good, created order. But the Christian understanding of creation, the original order and orientation of the world, is inseparable from the *eschatological perspective of salvation in Christ. Even as the disorientation of human beings from original, created goodness and blessing, sin must be understood within the whole ecology of Christian faith in which the controlling theme is salvation in Christ (see CHRISTOLOGY).

For Christians, then, the context for understanding sin is faith in God's saving action in Christ. Sin, that which counters the action of God in creation and salvation, can be known only in the context of God's action countering it, working through the damage it causes, to reorient the world towards more abundant possibilities than were available hitherto. The proper function of sin-talk is to relate the world and its pathologies to the dynamics of salvation, not merely in talk but in action. Christians speak of sin in order to understand, participate in, and communicate the reality of salvation, the abundance promised through life in God: the possibility of unmerited *forgiveness and unimagined possibilities for transformation. Sin-talk has to serve the communal and personal practices of confession, penitence, intercession, *love, and forgiveness. A language of blame fixes people in relation to a broken past but authentic sin-talk draws past damage into the liberating future.

A recurrent disagreement concerning the nature of sin arises from seeing relationship with God in terms of *law rather than *grace, or vice versa. Does God deal with the world as giver of a permanent, *static* order? Then sin is breach of law, met by God's reaffirmation of order through *punishment. Or rather as a source of *dynamic* order? Then sin is breach in relationship, constricting the abundance of life before God, and is met by God's working through the resistance of sin, drawing it into more abundant possibilities of life than ever (*resurrection in relation to *cross). The contrast can be overstated. Support for legalism in the OT is illusory. Law in the OT works both as codifying the dynamics of the *covenant relationship and as restoring its benefits to the community when it is breached. The context of law and sin is covenant, intrinsically relational and promissory in character, not a statically constricting, unbending contract. On the other hand, forgiveness, related to the emphasis on grace, is generally understood to require both *judgement and repentance.

Disagreements in the understanding of sin express opposed convictions about the nature of God's relation to the world. Of particular significance is the relationship between divine and creaturely *freedom, as focused in doctrines of grace, creation, and salvation. Understanding freedom as autonomous, exclusive self-determination puts divine and human freedom in competition. There is then a stark choice: either divine sovereignty or human autonomy. *Faith has to be either pure grace working directly on the human

subject or autonomous human will-power. This conception of freedom explains the emphasis on and interpretation of pride, exposes the issues underlying the *Pelagian controversy and subsequent discussions of original sin (see FALL), and illuminates the potential and limitations of recent contributions to the theology of sin.

This non-relational understanding of freedom, profoundly influential throughout Christian history, is hardly consistent with specifically Christian understandings of the *Trinitarian God, humanity, and their interrelation. By forcing a strict either/or between human and divine freedom it generates sharply divergent positions: either defence of divine sovereignty against the incursions of human autonomy or the reverse. Contemporary conservative theologies, like pre-modern orthodoxy, defend divine sovereignty. Modern (especially liberal) positions seek rather to protect human autonomy from God. Being a background assumption shared by both sides, this view of freedom is seldom discussed in theological debate.

This explains traditional emphasis on pride and modern objections to it. Pride elevates one (or that with which one identifies: class, race, sex, political movement) to the ultimate good to which all other goods are to be dedicated. Pride is self-worship: strictly, a form of idolatry. In pride, human beings assert their autonomy and potency in determining and doing the good, thus breaking out of a relation of creaturely dependence. Pride is the insistence that human beings have the kind of self-contained freedom delineated above.

The tradition's emphasis on pride as the root sin affirms divine sovereignty against the creature's refusal of creatureliness, while adopting the conception of freedom as non-relational autonomy. Pride is the creature's attempt to usurp the creator's place, claiming divine power and freedom, claiming to be like God. But this implies that God's freedom is non-relational: the monarchical, coercive power of an isolated, single person.

Given this oppositional and exclusive definition of freedom, the appropriate mode of relation to God would have to be pride's opposite: complete self-abasement. Defining pride in these terms protects God's freedom only by making God everything and humans nothing. The emphasis on pride in the traditional understanding of sin confirms *Enlightenment suspicions that Christianity is incompatible with an adult humanity. The tradition defends divine heteronomy against human autonomy, its critics (humanists and *liberal and *feminist theologians) defend the integrity and autonomy of human beings from the overbearing divine Father. Generally both sides do so in the same terms, assuming the competitive nature of freedom and hence offering only a choice between servile self-abasement and unrestrained self-assertion.

While the traditional emphasis on it is surely misplaced, the sinfulness of pride may be defined on other grounds. It was said in passing that pride is idolatry—wrong worship. This suggests that it might be a type of a more primary sin. In so far as pride is a misdirection of worship it is clearly true to say that the proud self supplants God. Yet this easily misleads. If pride is taken to be usurping the place of God, then the proper order has to be recovered by transposing God and humanity 'back' into their 'correct' positions, which confirms God in the image of the proud human being: an absolute, self-enclosed monarch. But this implies an understanding of God uninformed by the Christian story. The central doctrines of

*Incarnation and *Trinity suggest a God whose identity and freedom are profoundly relational, co-operating with and sustaining the autonomy and integrity of creatures. Worship of the Trinitarian God does not obliterate but empowers human integrity and autonomy while directing them Godwards. The sinfulness of pride cannot lie in the refusal to be nothing, nor can all affirmations of autonomy be sinful pride. It lies rather in unplugging human integrity and autonomy from their proper relation to God, making them self-referring and legitimating. Pride is the attempt to be as we think God must be, when we define divinity and perfection apart from God's self-revelation. Thus pride is rooted in a conceptual falsification of our relation to God even before it enacts its refusal of that relation in which the full goodness, integrity, and freedom of the creature for God and the good are in reality rooted.

Shifting the criterion for identifying sin to worship of the Trinitarian God confirms the sinfulness of pride while ceasing to treat it as paradigmatic and redefining it as a mode of idolatry. It then becomes possible to recognize the opposite of pride as also sin. The emphasis on pride has sometimes led to condemnation of all forms of self-assertion, and celebration of self-denial, self-surrender, and absence of self-regard as intrinsically virtuous. Feminists have pointed out how these 'virtues' collude with forces that systematically deny the *personhood and dignity of the oppressed. If the good that sin disrupts is orientation towards God in worship, in which the self is called and empowered to respond to God on the basis of its own integrity and freedom, then unrelenting self-denial undermines it as much as pride.

The understanding of freedom as competitive also throws light on the Pelagian controversy, for Pelagian and *Augustinian positions were divided by opposed conceptions of freedom and power undergirding their theologies of grace and sin. Pelagius maintained the personal nature of faith and sin by insisting that both were acts of will. Will makes action personal, according to Pelagius, by virtue of its autonomy. In its operation, will is suspended in moral and spiritual neutrality, free from determining influences whether of internal impulses or external pressures. It has no intrinsic attraction towards any particular option and so could always do otherwise. Willed action implies personal causation and responsibility because will has no external relation or reference. It makes no sense to Pelagius to speak of any kind of conditioning or directing of will, whether through grace or the supra-personal dynamics of sin.

In characterizing faith and sin as ventures of the will's inalienable capacity to make free choices, Pelagianism brought both firmly into the sphere of human powers, freedom, and responsibility. This concept of freedom reduces sin to acts capable of moral evaluation (that is, free) and reduces guilt to moral responsibility. Pelagius' understanding of freedom anticipated modern assumptions but his motivation and agenda were more characteristic of his own time. His concern was not to protect human autonomy from overbearing divine power, but to expose people to full accountability for their actions before God. If will operates to the exclusion of other causes, then we are always absolutely culpable for all voluntary action: excusing conditions are eliminated.

Pelagius' dispute with Augustine started from the latter's account of grace. In response, Augustine sharpened his theology of grace and developed a parallel doctrine of original sin. Its defining notion is the inheritance by the entire race of Adam's sin through the

processes of reproduction. It is important to realize that what is communicated is sin itself (guilt), not merely a tendency towards sin or an incapacity for the good. Sin is primarily a state we are in, only secondarily an act. The Fall has effected a fundamental distortion in the biological and social media which give us the means for moral action and decision-making and so make us capable of personal action. Sin is communicated pre-personally, in the basic material out of which we construct our personhood. This explains the traditional reluctance to speak uncomplicatedly of sin in terms of free acts of the will. For the basic insight afforded by the doctrine of original sin (following *Paul) is that the will is not free or neutral but in bondage to it. Sin is not an external choice, but an internal disorientation, infecting the basic structure of intentionality: our sense of what is good, right, true, desirable. It is disorder at the level of desire, not only at the level of action. In naming this communicated disorientation of intentionality 'sin', the tradition maintains that such inheritance incurs guilt. Hence Augustine, when pressed, asserts that even a newly born baby is in the situation of original sin—in a distorted relation to God marked by guilt.

In his development of the doctrine, Augustine applied to sin the understanding of willing that he had developed in relation to faith, when he spoke of the will's being compelled to consent by the indwelling *Holy Spirit. The Spirit so revivifies and reorients the will towards God that alternative motivations no longer operate. The Spirit is a superior field of force influencing the direction in which the personal energy of willing moves. Thus will is not free in Pelagius' sense, but free for God and its own fulfilment, which Augustine called genuine freedom. Original sin is a disorientating field of force that similarly captures our intentionality, binding and bending the will away from God, unplugging all relative goods from their relation to God and therefore from their own true being and freedom.

For Augustine, sin is personal not because we choose it freely by virtue of some neutral inner core but because we are personally incorporated into sin through our willing. Willing is the internal energy through which one's life is directed. It is not directed by a pure, autonomous self, but influenced by fields of force within one's situation, communicated in highly charged ways through the institutions, structures, processes, and relationships in which we live. Hence Augustine can speak in the same breath of bondage and willing. For it is precisely through the contribution of personal energy in willing that the will may be bound to sin, or bound to God through faith. Through willing one both contributes personal energy to the larger pathological dynamic and finds that, in so doing, the power of sin is internalized. One finds one's inner self 'possessed', consenting to, committed to, entrapped by a pathological orientation larger than itself.

For Pelagians, human beings as free causes of what they do have the clear role of perpetrators. Augustine's understanding is much subtler and takes seriously the way in which humans are as much victims of sin and yet, as victims, exercise will. His doctrine of original sin has more to offer *liberation and feminist attempts to see sin from the perspective of victims of oppression (and of the comprehensive disorientation achieved through ideology) than is generally recognized. Victims do not experience free agency, but still exercise will, being coerced into co-operating with the forces oppressing them. Will is not incapacitated, but redirected by the supra-personal dynamics of sin.

Modern reinterpretations of original sin (initiated by *Schleiermacher, but in this century undertaken almost exclusively by Roman Catholics) take the biological frame of reference as symbolic, re-interpreting the doctrine sociologically. Naturally inherited guilt is demythologized into contamination through distorted processes and institutions (from family to polity), as social categories are substituted for the ontological and metaphysical language of the tradition.

On the whole, modern theologies of sin have been marked by the principal cultural assumption of *modernity: the inalienable freedom of the person. This explains the Pelagian impulse of many modern interpretations. In modern culture, a conception of freedom similar to Pelagius' enjoys an ontological and metaphysical status as a basic and enduring structure of human existence. In modern theology it is freedom rather than sin that is an inescapable structure of being. This clashes immediately with the core idea of original sin, that sin is not a phenomenon of freedom but precedes and preconditions individual freedom, lying behind action in the basic intentionality of the agent (indeed, in the biological and social processes behind that). There is thus a strong impulse in modern theology towards rejecting original sin, encouraged by scientific reasons for rejecting the Fall story on which the doctrine appears to depend. The significance of the scientific critique is easily over-played, however. It usually functions as a rationale, preparing the ground for a critique on moral grounds. The consequence tends to be a reduction of sin to individualized moral categories, concerned with free acts alone.

The major sticking-point for modern culture is the idea that guilt may be transmitted by some means other than free personal action. In the end, this applies as much to social reinterpretations as to outright rejections of original sin. While social reinterpretations do speak of social or structural sin, they equivocate over the term: the extension of 'sin' to the supra- and transpersonal is generally said to be by *analogy. Only personal (free) acts are really regarded as sin, and thus able to incur guilt. In social reinterpretation as much as in outright rejection a crucial aspect of the doctrine is given up: that we might inherit guilt through our social and biological inherit-ance. It is assumed that the theological meaning of guilt can be confined to and controlled by moral categories. Not only a strong strand of the OT, but also any orthodox understanding of *atone-ment seems threatened here, for both appear to suggest an account-ability before God not limited to personal, causal agency. That may, in the end, be the function of the Christian language of sin: to call us to take concrete responsibility for our situations in their totality before and towards God's promised future.   **Alistair McFadyen**

Alison, James, *The Joy of Being Wrong* (1998).

Barth, Karl, *Church Dogmatics*, IV/1–2 (1956; 1958).

Brunner, E., *Man in Revolt* (1939).

Dubarle, A. M., *The Biblical Doctrine of Original Sin* (1964).

Gestrich, C., *The Return of Splendor in the World: The Christian Doctrine of Sin and Forgiveness* (1997).

McFadyen, A. I., *Bound to Sin: Abuse, the Holocaust and the Christian Doctrine of Sin* (2000).

Niebuhr, R., *The Nature and Destiny of Man* (1941), i.

Pannenberg, W., *Systematic Theology* (1994), ii.

Plaskow, J., *Sex, Sin and Grace* (1980).

Quell, G., *et al.*, *Sin* (1951).

Ricœur, P, *The Symbolism of Evil* (1969).

——'Original Sin: A Study in Meaning', *The Conflict of Interpretations* (1974).

Ritschl, A., *The Christian Doctrine of Justification: The Positive Development of the Doctrine* (1966).

Schleiermacher, F., *The Christian Faith*, ET (1928), § 66–8.

Schoonenberg, P., *Man and Sin* (1965).

Tennant, F. R., *The Origin and Propagation of Sin*, 2nd. edn. (1906).

Tillich, P., *Systematic Theology* (1978), ii.

Vandervelde, G., *Original Sin: Two Major Trends in Contemporary Roman Catholic Reinterpretation* (1975).

Vanneste, A., *The Dogma of Original Sin* (1975).

sixteenth century: an overview. Most people have inherited vestigial stories of what happened to western *Christianity in the early modern era. Often these take the form of either rejection of 'Roman' errors and uncovering of gospel truth by *Protestants, or rebellion against *Catholic orthodoxy by Protest-ant renegades and defence of the true faith by those remaining in communion with the Apostolic See. To transcend narrow denom-inational accounts and achieve a balanced assessment remains a major challenge. While pure hermeneutical disinterestedness is im-possible to achieve, significant strides have been made by historians and ecumenical theologians in overcoming polemical distortion, and many scholars are looking anew at the interaction of various theologies in the late 15th and 16th centuries, avoiding the carica-tures and simplistic dichotomies of the past.

The wealth and diversity of theological movements in western Europe at this time can seem bewildering. This article aims to give a sense of the main issues dividing Catholics and mainstream Prot-estants, and of the principal ways in which central perceptions in Christianity changed and fragmented. It traces the origins and de-velopment of the three major communities that dominated west-ern Europe by the end of the 16th century, Catholics, *Lutherans, and the *Reformed, and surveys the major doctrinal themes of the era: *grace, the *sacraments, *ministry, the *church, and the cor-rect use of the bible and the writings of early and medieval divines. The theological importance of radical groups, Protestant and other-wise, is not to be underestimated, but because of their numerous divisions and the complex spectrum of views to be found within them, they are treated here only in relation to Catholic and main-stream Protestant positions.

The period from c.1470 to c.1600 was one of immense intellectual fertility. Seminal developments were made in numerous areas, many of which, principally because of the marginalization of *the-ology as an intellectual discipline, now seem remote from the work of the theologian: for example, the theories of the Tübingen the-ology professor, Gabriel Biel (c.1420–95), concerning the nature of money, or the work of the Spaniards, Francisco de Vitoria (c.1485–1546) and Francisco de Suarez (1548–1617) on international *law. Many late-medieval and early-modern Christian writers paid considerable attention to fields, such as cabbalism, hermeticism, and *astrology, that strike the modern reader as bizarre. In addition theologians were profoundly affected by and were often the insti-gators of radical change in linguistic, textual, and critical scholar-ship. Nor did they hold aloof as the dissemination of knowledge was revolutionized by the invention of printing. A large proportion of books printed by the end of the 15th century were theological or devotional, including numerous editions of the bible, both in Latin and in various vernaculars.

In the popular mind the 16th century is associated with the Protestant *Reformation. Yet there was not *one* Reformation, but a number of interrelated but distinct Reformations, including very importantly a *Catholic* Reformation (see COUNTER-REFORMATION). Calls for reform of the church had been widespread in the 15th century, but with no consensus on what needed to be reformed. Contrary to some traditional views that the late-medieval church was in a state of terminal decay and unable to satisfy spiritual needs, recent work on the English church on the eve of the Reformation suggests that parish religion in many parts of the country was vibrant and robust. This complex and luxuriant structure of liturgy and piety was, at least in England, extremely successful in sustaining and communicating particular central truths of medieval Christianity about the bonds of charity binding the living with the living, and the living with the dead. It is difficult to know how far this analysis applies beyond England. While religion on a micro-level may have been in a healthy state, at the macro-level of dioceses, regions, nations, and the international church the situation looked much less rosy: excesses, sanctioned and unsanctioned, in popular piety, distortions of fundamental doctrines, theological confusion, and numerous clerical abuses. Perhaps the late medieval church's very vitality made its flaws all the more glaring.

One practice that certainly required reform was the issue of indulgences. Despite apparently clear official teaching that indulgences were only remissions of the *temporal* punishment for sins already pardoned by God, and that the church could not automatically apply these benefits to those in *purgatory, grotesque distortions and misunderstandings were widely current at the beginning of the 16th century. What is astonishing is that the break-up of western Christianity should be initiated through the publication of a highly technical list of propositions for academic disputation on the subject by an obscure German university professor: Martin *Luther's Ninety-Five Theses (1517). The Theses not only called for reform of indulgences, but presented a radical critique of central elements of medieval religion underpinning the practice. Luther's excommunication did not end the controversy, which released a torrent of reforming zeal and soul-searching throughout Western Europe after almost a century of frustrated expectations of reform. By 1520 Luther had spelled out his radical rejection of the hierarchical church and *priesthood, the dominant theologies of grace and the system of the seven sacraments, proposing instead a priesthood of all believers, freedom for Christians from 'earning' *salvation, and the two sacraments of the gospel, baptism and holy communion, with *penance, at least in the early stages, retaining a semi-sacramental status. How would the church as a whole respond?

Pope Leo X had condemned Luther's teachings using all the force of papal authority, but his bull did not have the desired effect, indicating the lack of consensus in the church on who should ultimately arbitrate in such disputes. There seemed to be a considerable chasm between the papacy's elevated spiritual claims and its more mundane reality: until the reforming popes of the mid-16th century the bishops of Rome often appeared more like Italian princes than 'servants of the servants of God'. Pope Leo seemed unable to bring about the necessary reform of the church. Nor had the Fifth Lateran Council (1512–17) done so. Yet Luther appealed for

adjudication to a truly free ecumenical synod. The bull *Execrabilis* (1460) of Pope Pius II condemning appeals from a pope to a future general *council had failed to eradicate widespread, if inchoate, *conciliarist ideas, particularly the prestige possessed by the initial decrees of the Council of Constance. Much uncertainty remained about the limits of papal authority; the question of the ultimate superiority of an ecumenical council over the *papacy was not definitively settled in Catholic circles during the 16th century. Fear of the threat to papal authority posed by a general council, and the papacy's complex political entanglements, meant that Rome did not call a reforming council until 1537. It did not meet until 1545 at *Trent. Its sessions were so frequently interrupted by tensions between the papacy and the Catholic powers that Trent did not end formally until 1563.

The residual conciliarism of the 16th century was only one element of the complex medieval inheritance concerning *authority in the church. Although the papacy had repeatedly tried to impose a straightforward papal monarchy, medieval Catholicism had never accepted that there was just one locus of authority in the church. Authority remained much more diffused than the papacy wished. The church had to acknowledge the authority not only of popes, cardinals, the Curia, councils, and metropolitan synods, but frequently that of *charismatic reforming figures and movements. Sometimes these succeeded and stayed within the bounds of the church, as did *Catherine of Siena or the Observant movements in various religious orders; sometimes they failed, as did Girolamo Savonarola (1452–98). Luther appeared to many as just such a prophetic figure. There was also the controverted 'teaching authority' of academic theologians: an important example is the central, sometimes independent, role played by the Theology Faculty of the University of Paris in the defence of *orthodoxy and the condemnation of Luther and other 'heretics'.

In many minds the Reformation is intimately connected with 'humanism'. Humanism in the late 15th and 16th centuries was not a unified ideology with a particular perspective on religion, but a collection of new educational techniques: innovative modes of argumentation emphasizing the importance of style and *rhetoric, bypassing commentators, ancient and medieval, to return 'to the sources' of ancient pagan and Christian learning, and hence a renewed interest in early Christian writings, especially the text of scripture. *Erasmus' Greek NT is justly famous, but humanist biblical scholarship was not the preserve of critics of the institutional church: the Complutensian Polyglot produced in Spain under Cardinal Ximénez de Cisneros must not be overlooked. Although Catholics did become more defensive about the authoritativeness of the Vulgate because of radical humanist and, later, Protestant attacks on its reliability, Catholic scholars remained deeply committed to the study of the Hebrew OT and the Greek OT and NT. While some humanists, like Erasmus, were very critical of scholastic theology's barbarous Latin, cumbersome organization of arguments, and supposed obsession with distinctions, there was no necessary opposition between scholasticism and humanism. John Fisher, executed for refusing to accept Henry VIII's supremacy in the Church of England, and one of the forces behind the introduction of humanist techniques into Cambridge University, used the full resources of scholastic theology against Lutheran 'errors'.

Humanistic techniques brought about changes in scholastic theology itself. One of Luther's earliest opponents, Cardinal Cajetan (Tomaso de Vio, 1469–1534), began to write commentaries, not on Peter Lombard's *Sentences*, the almost universal late-medieval practice, but on *Aquinas's writings, especially his more mature works. Rather than any decline of scholasticism in the 16th century, a massive flowering took place, particularly in the Spanish universities where scholasticism and Thomism became so linked that the terms are often treated as synonyms. While their Latin style may still have aroused humanists' ire, Spanish scholastics enthusiastically adopted many humanist critical and historical techniques. Like Erasmus, first- and second-generation Protestant Reformers railed against the evils of scholasticism, but even within the second generation some took a different view; and by the last quarter of the century various scholasticisms, invigorated by the synthesis with humanism, came to dominate Lutheran and Reformed academic theology. Although humanist methods did not necessarily result in particular religious perspectives, leading figures like Erasmus (who never formally broke with Rome) were vehement advocates of reform in the church. The term 'evangelical' is often used to describe groups arising in the late 1510s, 1520s, and 1530s in response to the ferment of reformist ideas, inspired by the scripturalism and piety espoused by Erasmus and others. By no means all attached to such circles, like that around Guillaume Briçonnet (*c.*1470–1534), bishop of Meaux, were proto-Protestants. It is difficult to establish convincing patterns explaining why this or that humanist did or did not become Protestant. Two prominent cardinals, who had been profoundly affected by the Christocentric scripturalism of Italian 'evangelism' were investigated on suspicion of holding Lutheran errors: Reginald Pole, appointed a presiding legate for the Council of Trent, almost elected pope in 1549, archbishop of Canterbury and architect of the Catholic Reformation in England under Mary I; and Giovanni Morone, also at one time a candidate for the papacy, a papal diplomat, and presiding legate at several Tridentine sessions.

A renewed emphasis on the centrality of scripture was part of both Catholic and Protestant Reformations, but mainstream Protestants characterized their position with the term 'scripture alone'. The principle was often applied at face value by radical groups, but magisterial Protestants were at times surprisingly 'traditional'. They defended infant *baptism against Anabaptists, and suppressed those who attacked the doctrine of the *Trinity contained in the ancient *creeds; Michael Servetus was burned in *Calvin's *Geneva for his anti-Trinitarianism. Indeed mainstream Protestants like Luther, *Zwingli, and Calvin never questioned that the Blessed Virgin *Mary was the Mother of God, a title which was an integral part of the *christological teaching of the Councils of *Ephesus and *Chalcedon. They generally accepted the authority of the first four councils, and held the fifth and sixth in high regard. What is more unexpected is their adamant adherence to the much less dogmatically significant perpetual virginity of Mary. It has been argued that the post-Reformation Church of England had a peculiar concern for the authority of the fathers and of medieval writers including Aquinas, to whom the 'Calvinists' and other Continental Protestants supposedly attributed little weight. In fact, both Reformed and Lutherans in the 16th century had as much interest in the early fathers as writers usually construed as 'Anglican'. Not surprisingly, Church of England, as well as other Reformed and Lutheran, theologians rejected the dominant late-medieval teaching (developed largely by canon lawyers, and majority Catholic opinion after Trent) that *tradition contained binding doctrine not found in scripture; but they also rejected the early-medieval and High Scholastic view (to which a minority of post-Tridentine Catholic divines adhered) that the content of scripture and of the church's traditional teaching was identical. Instead they held that the writings of the fathers and medieval divines could not provide any normative key to scripture, but were still an important aid in its interpretation and in demonstrating the antiquity of Protestant doctrines.

Later there was a decisive break in the intellectual continuity of mainstream Protestantism, especially among the Reformed, on the issue of scripture and tradition. Reformed confidence in the usefulness of early and medieval writers as authorities waned, due in part to the writings of Jean Daillé (1594–1670). Daillé argued that the purity of apostolic teaching had degenerated very rapidly; that it was impossible to reach a consensus of patristic opinion on crucial issues; and that the fathers' context was so different from that in which Protestants found themselves that patristic views had little relevance to the construction of sound Protestant theology. This marginalizing of patristics may have been partly a delayed response to the increased sophistication of Catholic scholarship on the early church by the third quarter of the century. As some consensus gradually developed on which ancient texts were authentic and which forgeries, Catholic writers could argue persuasively for the antiquity of doctrines and practices objectionable to Protestants, such as prayer for the dead and veneration of *saints. This crisis also affected the Church of England, although it is a sign of the parting of the ways with the Reformed that took place in the *seventeenth century that some of Daillé's most vehement opponents were English.

The very existence of the collection of documents called the bible was one of the strongest Catholic arguments for authoritative interpretation of scripture by the church; how could one recognize the canon without the witness of the church? Few Protestants were willing to follow Luther in making Christ's gospel (not the gospels) the test of canonicity as he did for the Epistle of James. But the canon also needed careful treatment on the Catholic side. The Council of Trent solemnly declared the complete canonicity of the Hebrew OT, and of the OT books found in Greek and Latin but not in Hebrew; yet it excluded three texts traditionally included in the Vulgate, the Prayer of Manasseh and 3 (1) and 4 (2) Esdras. Earlier, Cajetan had not been alone in advocating the shorter Hebrew canon, and some ambiguity remained implicit in the post-Tridentine distinction between proto- and deutero-canonical books.

Erasmus and many early Protestants had a profound optimism about the clarity of scripture, despite major differences in their exegetical methods. Luther, although he had a flair for innovative scriptural commentary, as in his interpretation of the Pauline concept of justice/righteousness, was quite traditional in his adherence to various forms of allegorical reading. Ironically Cajetan was to cause some shock in traditionalist Catholic circles through his thoroughgoing advocacy of Aquinas's teaching on the primacy of the 'literal sense' of scripture. Naivety about the perspicuity of scripture disappeared rapidly as Protestants confronted the intractability of their own divisions and the even greater threat of radical Protestant exegeses. Although theoretically scripture remained an unnormed norm, in practice Protestant theologians were trained in correct interpretation through an avalanche of catechisms and confessions of faith.

At the heart of Luther's programme was the centrality of God's agency in *salvation. This divine prevenience had been defended in the early church by *Augustine. Though his doctrines had been clouded by lack of complete versions of his works and by a plethora of forgeries, and although there had never been an official endorsement of his controversial later teachings, it is still fair to say that all western theology since Augustine, including that of the 16th century, operated within an Augustinian framework. Augustinian ideas, if not always the text of his writings, were at the centre of Reformation debates. In the late *Middle Ages rigorist Augustinian teachings on grace were not the preserve of radical figures like John Wyclif. An archbishop of Canterbury, Thomas Bradwardine (c.1295–1349), and Gregory of Rimini (c.1300–58), who became the prior general of the Augustinian Hermits, had both vigorously opposed what they perceived as the *Pelagianism of many contemporaries. Recent scholarship has emphasized the significance of Gregory and his disciples for the period just before the Reformation. One of the schools suspected of Pelagianism by the 'Augustinians' was that branch of the 'Modern Way' derived from William of Ockham. Its most significant exponent in the late 15th century was Gabriel Biel, who heavily emphasized the human ability to co-operate with divine grace; for him God and human beings were partners in the work of salvation. One of his central axioms was the scholastic tag that God does not deny grace to those who do their best, which led him to hold that human beings were able in a certain sense to merit forgiveness of sins.

Luther's love of *paradoxes, such as 'righteous and a sinner at the same time', was part of his attempt to encapsulate the human experience of divine forgiveness and union with Christ. Traditional Catholic theological language, before and after Trent, sought rather to express in abstract terms the state of being in or out of friendship with God: states which logically could not coexist. There was in Catholicism an unresolved tension between the abstractions of formal theology and the vigorous tradition, especially in Spain, of reflection on the spiritual life. Traditions of *mystical prayer were tolerated that did not relativize the church's sacraments and hierarchy through the 'subjectivism' of which certain Spanish 'enlightened ones' (alumbrados) were suspected. While Ignatius of Loyola, the founder of the Society of Jesus, had immense devotion to the authority of the institutional church, he successfully defended himself against the *Inquisition's questioning of the authenticity and orthodoxy of the mystical experiences that were to form the basis of his Spiritual *Exercises. *John of the Cross and *Teresa of Avila faced similar hostility. Yet one of the foremost scholastic theologians of his day, the *Dominican Domingo Bañez, was for a time Teresa's confessor and ardent defender. As for mainstream Protestantism, while its first and second generations could confidently proclaim the certitude which the believer should have of being graced, succeeding generations became more divided over the theoretical formulation of this assurance and the problems of its practical application in pastoral situations.

By the second half of the 16th century, Catholic theologians had resolved some of the late-medieval muddle about the human capacity to act virtuously apart from grace, emphasizing that, while fallen human beings could freely perform naturally good acts, they could not, without the assistance of divine grace, perform supernatural acts meriting salvation. For mainstream Protestants, adherence to concepts of merit, however qualified, was at the root of Rome's rottenness: its contamination of the central Christian truth that salvation is by grace alone. Nevertheless Catholic use of 'merit', at least in academic theology, was always within a fundamentally Augustinian framework. The Tridentine decree on *justification relativized all such usage when, alluding to Augustine, it stated that God chooses to crown his gifts as our *merits.

From the perspective of post-Tridentine Catholic orthodoxy Erasmus, in his controversy with Luther on freedom of the will, was still writing in a 'Pelagian' way; 'semi-Pelagian' was coined in the 16th century to describe the theological fuzziness of writers like Erasmus, deemed to have given excessive weight to human initiative in salvation. But Luther obscured the issue for contemporary and later Catholic readers by his penchant for such hyperbolic expressions as 'the enslaved will'. In the more coherently anti-Pelagian context of late 16th-century Catholicism, Thomists could teach (much closer to Luther than to Erasmus) that God's efficacious grace achieves its end by a necessity of infallibility, not a necessity of coercion: the human will is infallibly yet freely moved by grace. Yet at the end of the century the *Jesuit Luis de Molina was developing the novel ideas that human freedom necessarily involved liberty from any external agency, and that God's agency was external. This concept approximates to some modern notions of freedom as autonomy and had radical implications for the doctrine of grace. Thomists in the Dominican order were horrified at what they saw as resurgent semi-Pelagianism attacking the newly formed consensus that Aquinas was the safest guide on such matters. Even Molina's fellow Jesuit, Robert Bellarmine, believed Molina had fallen into grave error. A papal commission, De Auxiliis (concerning forms of grace), was appointed in 1597 to examine Molina's orthodoxy and sat intermittently for almost ten years. Several times he only narrowly escaped condemnation, but in the end the commission was dissolved and a stalemate established that lasted until the present day, with the Thomist and 'Molinist' positions both declared tenable.

It is often assumed that the increasing dominance of scholastic modes of thought in Reformed theology distorted Calvin's more moderate doctrine of grace into an extreme form of determinism as introduced by 'supralapsarians' like Theodore Beza (1519–1605) and the internationally renowned Cambridge divine, William Perkins (1558–1602). In fact their teaching, while more speculative than Calvin's, was in important respects more balanced and moderate. Scholastic categories helped to introduce a careful nuancing of which Calvin had disapproved. Moreover, their doctrine of *predestination cannot properly be called determinist. The majority of the Reformed, in any case, advocated a doctrine of predestination closer to Thomist and Augustinian Catholic positions, and more nuanced and restrained than that of Beza and his followers. Catholic Thomists and Augustinians needed to distort mainstream Reformed positions in order to differentiate them from their own teaching, saying that whereas they merely taught a 'negative antecedent reprobation', 'Calvinists' taught a 'positive antecedent reprobation'. In fact, most infralapsarians, like Roman supporters of absolute predestination, emphasized that reprobation was a purely negative act, the 'passing over' of those in the damnable lump of humanity whose own demerits justly sent them to hell. Many Catholic and mainstream Reformed doctrines of predestination were thus virtually identical. They differed, not in the doctrines of predestination *per se* but, most significantly, in the Reformed affirmation of the complete identity between the number of the justified and the elect (a doctrine known as the golden chain), with the consequent possibility of a believer's knowing that he or she was justified and *ergo* one of the elect.

The Council of Trent reaffirmed the medieval teaching on the seven sacraments without adjudicating on the numerous disagreements in this area among Catholic theologians. Trent repeated the medieval doctrine that the mass is a propitiatory *sacrifice for the living and the dead. Luther and other Protestant theologians rejected this understanding as impinging on the uniqueness and all-sufficiency of Christ's sacrifice. Most late-medieval theologians, like Gabriel Biel, had argued that individual masses, as repetitions of Calvary, did add in some way to the merits of the crucifixion. Similar views remained dominant in 16th-century Catholicism, although a minority, including Cajetan, followed Aquinas in teaching that the mass as a memorial sacrifice is identical with Christ's one sacrifice and gains all its efficacy from it. Luther saw the medieval 'canon' of the mass with its constant reiteration of human offering to God as yet another example of Roman 'works' theology, so he pared it down to what for him was the efficacious proclamation of the gospel's grace, the narrative of the Last Supper. Justification by faith and grace alone had not abolished the crucial significance of the sacraments of baptism and the *Eucharist. While Lutherans rejected the medieval notion of the sacraments dispensing grace 'out of the action performed', baptism and 'the sacrament of the altar' remained very much 'means of grace'. Zwingli's radical teaching that the sacraments were essentially mnemonics of grace already given was anathema to Luther. All mainstream Protestants taught that faith was required to enjoy the benefits of God's gifts in these dominical ordinances, but what sense was to be made of the baptism of infants, so vehemently defended against Anabaptists? Luther and many of his disciples, concerned to protect baptism's efficacy, argued for an 'infant faith', notions ridiculed by Zwingli's followers. But others in the Reformed tradition, such as Calvin, did want to affirm, however cautiously, that baptism had present as well as past and future effects.

While baptism continued to be a contentious issue between Lutherans and the Reformed, the Lord's supper became a geological fault line. Luther and his more zealous disciples held doctrines of the real presence of Christ in the Eucharist as far from Zwinglian minimalism as contemporary Roman doctrines of *transubstantiation. Lutherans objected to the Catholic doctrine, not because it taught the real presence, but because it had elevated an unscriptural piece of scholastic speculation to the level of *dogma. Lutherans never resorted to 'consubstantiation' or 'impanation' to describe their own teaching. All who would not accept the Lutheran shibboleth of 'in, with, and under' the bread and wine, and who did not distance themselves from 'Zwinglianism' were to be condemned. In fact many Reformed found Zwingli's teaching as objectionable as Luther's. Calvin and others taught a real communication of Christ to the believer in the sacrament, but avoided any notion of a 'presence' in the bread and wine. Bullinger in Zurich, while not willing to go as far as Calvin, was ready to moderate Zwingli's extremism; he and Calvin achieved an uneasy and ambiguous consensus on eucharistic doctrine among the Reformed.

Central to Lutheranism and indeed all forms of Protestantism, radical and magisterial, was a desire to remove what were perceived as barriers between the believer and Christ. He was the one mediator between God and *humanity, making all other supposed advocates and mediators unnecessary, whether in heaven (Mary and the saints), or on earth (the sacrificing priesthood). For mainstream Protestants, priesthood, other than the priesthood of all the baptized or of believers, had been abolished. Nevertheless structure in the church, meaning ministers of some sort, remained a necessity, either because good order and decency, and human propensity to sin, required subjection to authority (the dominant position in Lutheranism, also held by some Reformed, including many Church of England, theologians), or because scripture specified the basic elements of church government (the teaching of Calvin and his many disciples). The Swedish and English Protestant churches kept bishops in the historical succession, though the Swedes and initially the English attached no theological significance to them. In the English church the first defences of *episcopacy as 'by divine law' came only towards the end of the century. It is not surprising that there was confusion over the theology of ministry since medieval ideas had been so untidy. It was common teaching that bishops did not form a separate order of minister in the sacrament of orders: the major orders were usually listed as priests, deacons, and subdeacons. Was there an absolute need for bishops? Many seemed more like bureaucratic administrators or temporal lords than 'successors of the apostles' or pastors of their dioceses. Even their absolute necessity for ordaining other ministers could be questioned on the basis of 15th-century papal dispensations to abbots (who were only presbyters) to perform ordinations. Lutheran princes took on many functions of episcopal oversight in their territories. Even among the Reformed, Elizabeth I's supreme governorship of the Church of England was not an unparalleled example of *Erastianism: the views of Thomas Erastus, vehemently attacked by Genevan theologians, were a defence of the model for church–state relations actually existing in Zurich and Basel, where ultimate authority in disputes between church and state lay with the magistrates. In the Catholic sphere, though the papacy, in theory, regained its authority over the 'eldest daughter of the church' through the Concordat of Bologna (1516), in fact it remained a rubber stamp for the royal control of the French church, ironically well before the schism between Henry VIII's English church and Rome.

All the churches resulting from these Reformations claimed to be 'the Catholic church' of the ancient creeds. Luther, in his vernacular of the Apostles' Creed, went so far as to translate Catholic as Christian, to demonstrate that this venerable epithet had nothing to do with 'the papal church'. Papal church, popery, church of Rome were among the ways opponents referred to those communities which had the most direct institutional, liturgical, and doctrinal continuity with the medieval Catholic church of the west. The doctrinal claim of these communities that the 'one, holy, catholic and apostolic church' on earth was identical with themselves was emphatically asserted, despite opposition from other groups, through their use of 'Catholic' as their own name. The modern usage of 'Roman Catholic' was invented in the 17th century by Protestants as a more polite form for use in diplomatic contexts.

The Lutheran churches derived principally from Luther's theological inspiration, and to a lesser extent from that of his friend and associate, Philip Melanchthon. There seems not to have been much opposition to 'Lutheran' as a colloquial self-designation, except possibly in Scandinavia. By the end of the century Lutherans were mainly found there and in northern Germany, with smaller communities in southern and western Germany, and Eastern Europe, although earlier, before divisions with the Reformed had hardened, adherents were more widely scattered.

More formally, Lutherans referred to themselves in variants of 'Evangelical Christians [or Churches] (of the Confession of Augsburg)'. The principal author of the original version of the Augsburg Confession (1530), the most widely accepted of Lutheran confessional documents, was Melanchthon. Most Reformed were willing to subscribe to the Confession, but only in an altered form penned by Melanchthon in 1541. He tried to reunite mainstream Protestants through a more ambiguous formulation of the Confession's teaching on the Eucharist. Numerous colloquies failed to bring about reconciliation and, despite Melanchthon's incalculable impact on the Lutheran tradition, a so-called 'genuine' or Gnesio-Lutheran party relentlessly harried his followers as traitors, referring to them as Philippists or Crypto-Calvinists. The promulgation of the Formula of Concord (1577) and the Book of Concord (1580) were largely a victory in Germany for the hardliners. However, the Scandinavian churches continued to emphasize the primacy of the 1530 Confession of Augsburg, reluctant to accept what they perceived as the burdensome obsession with theological precision of their German co-religionists.

The communities describing themselves as Reformed churches or 'those of the Reformed religion' were by the end of our period mainly located in Switzerland and Geneva (not strictly Swiss), south-west Germany, France, the Low Countries, England, and Scotland, with smaller pockets in Ireland and Eastern Europe. This tradition, characterized by considerable pluralism, developed out of the teachings not only of Zwingli and Calvin but of others with less familiar names: Martin Bucer (1491–1551), Heinrich Bullinger (1504–75), Peter Martyr Vermigli (1500–62) and many others. The term 'Calvinism' is often used for the tradition as a whole, but should be applied to the 16th century only with great caution. 'Calvinist' was essentially a term of abuse, never accepted by the Reformed, except in a most qualified way. We need to remember how diverse and broadly based the Reformed were, not to reduce them to a single brand of 'Calvinism', whether derived from Calvin or his immediate followers.

How did the post-Reformation Church of England fit into the map of mainstream Protestantism? Religion in Henry VIII's reign after his break with Rome has been helpfully, if crudely, described as 'Catholicism without the pope', although the regime did swing spasmodically between humanist-style attacks on traditional piety and traditionalist formulations of doctrine. However, by the end of Edward VI's reign and after the 'settlement of religion' under Elizabeth I, the doctrinal identity of the clerical and lay élites in the Church of England became predominantly Reformed. In the past it was often argued that the English church's doctrinal moderation distinguished it from other Protestant churches: that it was a

via media between the Roman Catholic Church and the extremes of Continental Protestantism. This has had the unfortunate effect of reinforcing the notion that the Church of England embodied a distinctively English tradition, independent of intellectual developments on the Continent. The Church of England after the Elizabethan Settlement saw itself as one of the Reformed churches, but this did not entail any subservience to Calvin's Geneva. Although the 'godly' or 'Puritan' elements who perceived the Church of England as 'but half-reformed' did want it reshaped after foreign templates, especially that of Geneva, those described as 'conformists', committed both to the Church of England's sisterhood with the rest of the Reformed and to upholding the established form of religion, could and did argue, with increasing confidence by the end of the century, that the Church of England was rather the best of the Reformed churches, an exemplar for others.

In the middle decades of the 16th century the theological boundaries between Lutheran and Reformed gradually hardened. The period after the mid-1560s is often called the 'era of orthodoxy' in mainstream Protestantism. Not only Protestant, but also post-Tridentine Catholic, theologians concentrated on careful elaboration of their own 'purified' traditions as well as vitriolic polemic against opponents. Yet, despite all the retrenchment and rigid demarcation, this was a time of theological cross-fertilization: Lutherans and Reformed were avid readers of the end-of-century disputes between Jesuits and Dominicans on grace, freewill, and predestination, and even happily borrowed elements to use in their own intra-Protestant disputes.

Medieval scholasticism, with its precise definitions and careful distinctions, had been criticized by reformers of all hues for its distance from the religion of ordinary people, but it is arguable that the 'new' high theologies produced by the Reformations did not narrow that chasm. Few outside the educated clergy and laity could have grasped the complex issues dividing Christians. But if the masses had only a limited grasp of doctrinal nuances, church authorities were much more adept than their medieval forebears at enforcing formal orthodoxy and rooting out deviance. By the end of the century, Protestant and Catholic traditions had become set around groupings of simple formulas, symbols, and rituals. Although their piety was more streamlined than in the past, and scrutinized with greater zeal by ecclesiastical authority, ordinary Roman Catholics continued to concentrate on what had been central to late-medieval Catholics: the mystery of the mass with its re-enactment of Calvary and the conversion of the host into 'the body of Christ'; devotion to the Mother of God and the saints with their efficacious images and relics; prayer for departed relatives, friends, and benefactors; the forgiveness of sins in baptism, and the sacrament of penance. Ordinary Lutherans came to define their religious identity through the crucifix, the singing of chorales, the presence of Christ in 'the sacrament of the altar', and the exorcism in baptism. Ordinary Reformed on the Continent and in Scotland developed attachments to metrical psalms, plain churches cleansed of idolatry, and long sermons. The 'godly' in the Church of England yearned for larger doses of these Reformed elements. The Edwardine Books of Common Prayer had been largely compiled by a theologian who eventually aligned himself with the Reformed, Thomas Cranmer. Though by their penchant for wordy exhortations, their spare ritual, and general theological content the 1552 and 1559 Prayer Books were definitely Reformed in ethos, they retained more traditional elements than was usual among the Reformed: a fixed structure of worship, little or no room for extempore prayers, an elaborate ecclesiastical calendar, compulsory use of a medieval vestment, the surplice, and signing with the cross in baptism. These and many other matters caused immense irritation to Puritans, but many conservative laity and eventually even theologians, otherwise impeccably Reformed in doctrine, became increasingly attached to them.

By the end of the century great diversity still existed in the Reformed and Lutheran traditions, but what of post-Tridentine Catholicism? We have seen that diversity still existed among Catholic theologians on important doctrines, but the general impression is of a uniformity unheard of in medieval Catholicism. The moderate *Hussites, known as Utraquists or Calixtines, had had a chequered history of grudging toleration or persecution; in the 16th century Rome successfully suppressed their privilege of administering the chalice to the *laity. In the face of the Protestant challenge, Rome was unwilling to compromise on this issue, or clerical *celibacy, or vernacular *liturgy, despite periodic pressure from the Holy Roman Empire for concessions, and the advocacy of compromise by such important figures as Cajetan. However, despite the missal of Pius V (1570), some vestiges of diversity (in liturgy at least) remained, for example, in the Ambrosian rite in Milan, defended by its great reforming archbishop, Charles Borromeo (1538–84). The severest challenge for claims to complete uniformity in post-Tridentine Catholicism came from eastern Catholic churches whose theological and liturgical heritages had received some protection from the decrees of the Council of *Florence. At the end of the century Rome reaffirmed the legitimacy of a degree of pluralism in liturgy and canon law, if not doctrine, in its approval of the union with the Holy See of Byzantine rite Ukrainians in the 1595–6 Union of Brest-Litovsk, and of the East Syrian rite Malabar Christians of St Thomas at the Synod of Diamper (1599). It was not until the 17th century that the *Eastern Orthodox (who rejected *communion with the see of Rome) were forced to respond definitively to the warring camps of Latin Christianity. The richness and energy of the theologies produced by western Christianity in this period are undeniable, but it is arguable that the great tragedy of the 16th-century Reformations is that, however fecund they were with ideas, insights, and zeal, they also produced chasms of doctrine and practice wider than any previous *schism in the Christian community, wider than that between Rome and Constantinople, more unbridgeable even than the divisions that arose from the ancient christological controversies. The mutual recognition of 'one faith, one baptism, one Lord of all' (Eph. 4: 5) and the achievement of a consensus on the legitimate bounds of diversity in the 'One, Holy, Catholic and Apostolic Church' remain, at the beginning of the 21st century, far-off goals.

See also BIBLE, ITS AUTHORITY AND INTERPRETATION.

Seán F. Hughes

Bradshaw, Brendan, and Duffy, Eamon (eds.), *Humanism, Reform and the Reformation: The Career of John Fisher* (1989).
Cameron, Euan, *The European Reformation* (1991).
Donnelly, J. P., 'Calvinist Thomism', *Viator*, 7 (1976), 441–55.
Duffy, Eamon, *The Stripping of the Altars: Traditional Religion in England 1400–1580* (1992).
Gerrish, Brian, *Grace and Gratitude: The Eucharistic Theology of Calvin* (1993).
Hillerbrand, H. J. (ed. in chief), *Oxford Encyclopedia of the Reformation* (4 vols.; 1996).
Jones, Martin D. W., *The Counter-Reformation* (1995).
Kirk, James (ed.), *Humanism and Reform: The Church in Europe, England and Scotland, 1400–1643* (1991).
Küng, Hans, *Justification*, ET (1965).
Lane, A. N. S., 'Scripture, Tradition and Church: An Historical Survey', *Vox Evangelica*, 9 (1975), 37–55.
—— 'Calvin's Use of the Fathers and the Medievals', *Calvin Theological Journal*, 16 (1981), 149–205.
Leith, John H., *Creeds of the Churches*, rev. edn. (1973).
MacCulloch, Diarmaid, *The Later Reformation in England 1547–1603* (1990).
McGrath, Alister, *Reformation Thought: An Introduction*, 2nd edn. (1993).
McSorley, H. J., *Luther Right or Wrong?* (1968).
Muller, Richard, *Christ and the Decree: Christology and Predestination in Reformed Theology from Calvin to Perkins* (1986).
Oberman, Heiko, *The Harvest of Late Medieval Theology: Gabriel Biel and Late Medieval Nominalism* (1963).
Pelikan, Jaroslav, *Reformation of Church and Dogma (1300–1700)* (1989).
Raitt, Jill, *The Eucharistic Theology of Theodore Beza: Development of the Reformed Doctrine* (1972).
Tierney, Brian, *Foundations of the Conciliar Theory*, repr. (1968).
Wicks, Jared, *Cajetan Responds: A Reader in Reformation Controversy* (1978).

slavery in the ancient Mediterranean world seemed to be an economic and social necessity. In classical Greece, voices were raised at times in protest against the ill-treatment of slaves and the enslavement of innocent freemen, but, in the absence of any perceived alternative, ancient thinkers tended to acquiesce in the institution. *Aristotle defended slavery as beneficial to both the master and the slave.

The *Old Testament takes slavery for granted, although it places unusual limits on the master's powers and requires slaves, if fellow Israelites, to be freed after a set period (see Exod. 21: 2–6). On the other hand, the great narrative of Israel's redemption by the Lord from Egyptian slavery offers a powerful model of *liberation for enslaved peoples (see EXODUS).

Against this background, the NT nowhere unequivocally condemns the institution. *Paul advises slaves to accept their status (1 Cor. 7: 21) and sends the slave Onesimus back to his master Philemon with admonitions that he is to be treated as a Christian brother but with a tacit acceptance of Philemon's claim (Philem. 1: 15–16). Paul also calls himself the 'slave of Christ' (Phil. 1: 1; Rom. 1: 1). Since slaves held high positions as stewards in many households, the point here is not servility. The Christian choice is between two masters, either Christ or the powers of the flesh and this *world, not between slavery and *freedom. According to Philippians, Jesus himself took on 'the form of a slave' (Phil. 2: 7) and Christian humility demands that his followers should imitate him.

Yet set against this is Paul's great statement that in Christ 'there is neither slave nor free' (Gal. 3: 28). The rub is the meaning of 'in Christ'. Sharing the *Eucharist is one thing, but no subsequent thinker in the early church takes this verse as a piece of social policy. Gregory of Nyssa is alone in attacking slave-owning as a symptom of the sin of pride. *Augustine saw slavery and its manifest injustices as part of the *punishment humanity had brought on itself in the *Fall and therefore to be accepted. A more sinister line of thought, surfacing in some of John Chrysostom's sermons, for instance, saw slaves as degraded beings deserving nothing better.

With both Augustine and Aristotle in support of slavery, the medieval church had little room for theological manœuvre. The church, however, maintained a stand against the treatment of human beings as mere chattels and in Europe slaveholding had mostly died out by the 11th or 12th centuries, being replaced by the land-based serfdom of the feudal system.

The situation changed with the colonization of the Americas and the demand for cheap labour to exploit their riches. A succession of popes issued condemnations of the virtual enslavement of native populations by Spanish and Portuguese colonists under the system of encomienda, though to little avail. The *Dominican Bartolomé de Las Casas (1484–1566) campaigned against these abuses. Although he later came to condemn any form of slavery, at first he advocated the importation of African slaves instead (see NATURAL LAW).

Such a proposal shows that even he initially fell in with a widespread and theologically defended ideology of racial superiority that justified slavery. Black Africans were seen by many as the cursed children of Ham, condemned to serve his brothers (Gen. 9: 25), and even champions of human equality in the *Enlightenment argued that climatic and racial factors made the African unsuited to freedom. There was unease over this, however, summed up in the French jurist Montesquieu's observation, 'If they [black Africans] are human beings, then we [Europeans] are not Christians.' The notion of inalienable rights found in the writings of Locke, for instance, is hardly compatible with slavery. The subsequent Christian response to slavery is much influenced by these Enlightenment arguments.

The lucrative trade in African slaves to North America was not disturbed by such considerations. The earliest voices of Christian protest seem to have come from *Quakers, arising out of their belief in the universality of Christ's light. George Fox in 1657 already advised Quakers in Barbados to free their slaves, but the facts of economic life saw many wealthy Quakers becoming slave-owners by the middle of the next century. Their consciences were constantly pricked by radicals such as John Woolman and Anthony Benezet, but it was not until 1776 that Philadelphia Friends finally resolved to disown slaveholders. The founders of *Methodism were also strong opponents of slavery and the Great Awakenings in the United States brought a new fervour to anti-slavery protests. Black Christian preachers with similar enthusiasm identified their listeners' situation with that of Israel under Pharaoh.

In Britain an alliance of *evangelical Christians, most notably Granville Sharpe, Thomas Clarkson, and William Wilberforce, with Quakers and others brought about within the empire the abolition of the slave trade in 1807 and of slavery itself in 1838. This considerable achievement, obtained against Britain's economic interests, both set a benchmark for the world at large and provided an important precedent in regard to social and political action for evangelicals ever since. But it was not only evangelicals who were taken up with this matter: in the same year, 1838, Pope Gregory XVI condemned colonial slavery and later Pope Leo XIII was to charge Cardinal Lavigerie to stir up world opinion against the slave trade.

In the Southern United States, however, many Christian apologists for slavery held to the argument that Paul and the OT revealed the servitude of the African to be divinely ordained. Others less dogmatically took the line that slavery was preferable to the social dislocation of abolition. The issue had already split the major Protestant denominations before the Civil War destroyed the institution of slavery, leaving a legacy of bitterness still unresolved.

The abolition of slavery in Europe and the Americas is often seen as a triumph of Christian morality, but the picture is more complex. Christians were ranged on both sides, and the impetus came from Enlightenment principles as much as from Christian conviction. Slavery is a particularly stark example of the problems Christian thinkers have had in distinguishing cultural norms from divinely ordained principles of social ordering and in balancing the need to correct social injustice against the need for stability in the civil order.

See also BLACK THEOLOGY.   **Hugh S. Pyper**

Garnsey, P., Ideas of Slavery from Aristotle to Augustine (1996).

Jakobsson, S., Am I not a Man and a Brother? British Missions and the Abolition of the Slave Trade and Slavery in West Africa and the West Indies 1786–1838 (1972).

Martin, D. B., Slavery as Salvation: The Metaphor of Slavery in Pauline Christianity (1990).

Rodriguez, J. P., Historical Encyclopedia of World Slavery (1997).

social gospel and social teaching.

From the beginning Christianity has had an indirect and a direct impact on society: indirect in as far as the church has offered an alternative form of community and alternative values, based on the belief that God alone deserves our unconditional allegiance; direct because aspects of the church's teaching are inescapably concerned with a social order that is pleasing to God. The history of Christian social teaching is complex, fascinating, and ambiguous. Here we are concerned primarily with social teaching in modern times.

Roman Catholics tend to speak of social teaching or even social doctrine, and refer particularly to the official pronouncements of Rome about the social order. Protestants are more likely to link what the church has to say about the social order to the gospel rather than the *law, *natural or revealed. The *Eastern Orthodox, for their part, tend to avoid doctrinal formulations on social and political matters and suggest that the church, especially when she is celebrating the *liturgy, is presenting a challenging vision of God's purposes for people, society, and the world—almost exactly the point made by the American *Methodist Stanley Hauerwas with his slogan, 'the church does not have, but is, a social ethic'.

The official social teaching of the Roman Catholic Church is generally said to date from the 1891 encyclical Rerum Novarum of Leo XIII. Rerum Novarum, while part of the *papacy's onslaught on liberalism and *modernism, focused on the problems arising from industrialization and urbanization, particularly the sufferings of the poor and the marginalized. Later 'social encyclicals' attacked both unbridled *capitalism and *socialism, and suggested that there could be a third way that protected both *freedom and the interests of the poor and vulnerable. The earlier encyclicals claimed to be propounding timeless moral truths based on natural law; later there was more biblical content, and serious attempts to 'discern the signs of the times', most notably in *John Paul II's encyclical Centesimus Annus in which a chapter provides an interpretation of the events of the remarkable year 1989 when the communist regimes of Eastern Europe collapsed.

Official Roman Catholic social teaching presents, cumulatively, an impressive body of doctrine. It has had considerable impact on policy and practice mainly because of the influence of Christian *Democratic parties which recognize it as authoritative. It is very much teaching delivered from on high, claiming in practice a degree of *infallibility. The *magisterium* or teaching office has in modern times been increasingly centralized in the Vatican, and problems arise when specific hierarchies exercise their own teaching office, as when the US bishops' Pastoral Letter on *war and *peace was felt to take a harder line against nuclear deterrence than the Vatican or certain West European hierarchies. But the most serious tensions arose with the development of *liberation theology in Latin America, with its stress on attending to the voice of the poor and the marginalized and its deep suspicion of the validity of authoritative voices from above. Liberation theology has probably produced the most challenging and effective Christian social teaching in recent times; but Rome has been either negative or deeply ambivalent in its response and remains committed to the development of a cumulative social teaching, which relies on a modified natural law approach to make it both binding on the faithful and recognizable as 'public truth' by other fair-minded people.

Protestant social teaching is an amalgam of sometimes discordant movements, individual or small group theological projects, and church pronouncements by individual denominations or by *ecumenical bodies. Among the movements the most significant were the 'social gospel', initiated in the United States by Walter Rauschenbusch (1861–1918), and the various forms of Christian Socialism or religious socialism in Europe. The social gospel movement rested on an optimistic *liberal theology and saw building the *Kingdom as its task. It was devastatingly criticized for lack of realism and a weak understanding of *sin by Reinhold *Niebuhr, whose 'Christian realism' became perhaps the most influential Protestant social teaching in the 20th century. The Religious Socialist movement on the continent of Europe was part of the movement away from liberal theology and the rediscovery of *eschatology. It called for a radical critique of church and society, and deeply influenced Karl *Barth, Paul *Tillich and many other significant theologians, so that for them it became impossible to do *theology without a constant eye to its social and *political context. The Christian socialist movement (which has recently revived remarkably in Britain) was in the 19th century mainly an English Anglo-Catholic and rather patrician movement, interested primarily in the church as a sign and exemplar of the promised Kingdom, and in efforts to improve the condition of the working class through adult education, housing co-operatives, and so forth.

Individuals who have been significant as social teachers include Karl Barth, Paul Tillich, Reinhold Niebuhr, William *Temple, and R. H. Tawney. In their various ways they and others brought theological insights to bear on the issues of the day. Most denominations also made pronouncements, which were of very variable quality and often ephemeral, on social, economic, and political issues. Occasionally a well-argued and researched church statement, such as the Church of England's *Faith in the City* (1985) or the US Catholic Bishops' Pastoral Letters on war and peace (1983) and on the economy (1985), have had a major impact on public debate and been recognized as making a distinctive contribution.

The mainly Protestant ecumenical movement devoted considerable attention to social *ethics, developing under the influence of J. H. Oldham the middle axiom method and addressing diverse issues from war and peace to unemployment. The Oxford Conference on Church, Community, and State of 1937 was a landmark both in method and in confronting the challenge of Nazism and *antisemitism. The ecumenical movement from the early 1960s became more radical, and committed itself to the support of liberation movements and efforts for thoroughgoing social change, most notably in the World Council of Churches' Programme to Combat Racism which gave support to the struggle against *apartheid in Namibia and South Africa. The subsequent project on Justice, Peace and the Integrity of Creation and the Programme to Overcome Violence have been criticized as diffuse and naive. But despite continuing controversy, the ecumenical movement is committed to exploring the social and ethical dimension of the gospel, and believes that confessing the faith necessarily has implications for lifestyle and for the structures of society.

At a time when in pluralist societies there is a deep uncertainty about goals and values, there is a deeper need than ever for well thought out and clearly expressed Christian social teaching as a contribution to public debate. How far the churches are capable of offering such a constructive contribution is still a moot point.

Duncan B. Forrester

Coleman, J. (ed.), *One Hundred Years of Catholic Social Thought* (1991).
Dorr, Donal, *Option for the Poor: A Hundred Years of Catholic Social Teaching*, rev. edn. (1992).
Forrester, Duncan B., *Beliefs, Values and Policies: Conviction Politics in a Secular Age* (1989).
Preston, Ronald, *Confusions in Christian Social Ethics: Problems for Geneva and Rome* (1994).

socialism is the advocacy of, and the struggle for, a society in which class divisions based on differences of economic and other forms of power are abolished. To achieve this end, socialists believe that minority ownership of the productive, distributive, and service capacities of society must be ended, and that wealth must be held in common. Much Christian social thought historically both reflects and contributes to the socialist project, though there are also strongly anti-socialist elements within the Christian tradition.

In Britain since the 1840s there have been a number of movements called 'Christian socialism', and these too have been diverse, ranging from the authoritarian benevolence of F. D. Maurice and Charles Kingsley, where socialism is a synonym for the co-operative spirit, to the commitment to common ownership of land in Stewart Headlam's Guild of St Matthew (1877), and the communism of Conrad Noel and the Catholic Crusade. A reformist kind of socialism, dominated by the Christian Social Union, became the norm in Anglican social thinking in England around 1900, and reached its peak in the thought of William *Temple, archbishop of York and then of Canterbury. Temple was a key figure in shaping national thought about the welfare state, and his book *Christianity and the Social Order* (1942) influenced the reforms of the Labour government in 1945. Equally influential, both inside and outside the Christian tradition, was the economic historian R. H. Tawney whose writings, such as *Religion and the Rise of Capitalism* (1926) and *Equality* (1931), were of major importance in shaping a Christian socialist tradition.

Much of the thought of the *social gospel movement in the United States, associated with Walter Rauschenbusch and others, and of theologians like Reinhold *Niebuhr and Joseph Fletcher, was affected by socialist ideas. From the 1960s there were new movements for socialism among Christians in Latin America, Africa, and Asia as well as Britain and North America. Key figures in creating an African socialist tradition were Julius Nyerere and Kenneth Kaunda. The works of most *liberation theologians are broadly socialist, and many earlier socialist assumptions have entered the liberal Christian vocabulary. In Britain, the Christian Socialist Movement, formed in 1960, grew enormously in the last decades of the 20th century, attracting many young people and Members of Parliament, including two leaders of the Labour party, the late John Smith and Tony Blair. The 'ethical socialism' associated with Tawney and others seems to have returned in a modern form. However, many Christians in the developed world remain committed to the structures and ideology of *capitalism, and their social thinking takes place within its framework.

Socialism, as a political movement, is quite modern. The word is used throughout the 19th century in a variety of ways. In the 1830s it was seen as the opposite of individualism; much of this early discourse is vague and imprecise. But the concept has certain key elements and parameters. At the heart of its vision has been social or common ownership of the means of production. Common ownership and democratic control of these was far more central to the thought of the early socialists than state control or nationalization, which developed later.

Within the spectrum of socialist thought, a number of key elements can be identified. The 'social question' is seen as political, being inextricably bound up with the structures of capitalism. There is a critique of the oppressive character of labour, of the system of competition and uncontrolled industrial growth, and of the dominance of the market. Notions of community and equality are central, and there has been an international dimension to most forms of socialism.

Socialists have always recognized that there are many possible forms of social ownership of which co-operative ownership is one. Nationalization in itself has nothing particularly to do with socialism and has existed under non-socialist and anti-socialist regimes. Kautsky in 1891 pointed out that a 'co-operative commonwealth' could not be the result of the 'general nationalization of all industries' unless there was a change in 'the character of the state'. The question of the state is central, as Lenin, Tawney, and anarcho-syndicalist thinkers saw, though their understandings were very different. Most socialists have not argued for the abolition of all forms of personal ownership. The Socialist International at its meeting in Frankfurt in 1951 rejected the idea of total public ownership and called for decentralized economic power where this was compatible with planning.

Nevertheless, socialism has throughout its history been inseparable from some form of common ownership. By its very nature it involves the abolition of private ownership of capital; bringing the means of production, distribution, and exchange into public ownership and control is central to its philosophy. It is difficult to see how it can survive, in theory or practice, without this central idea. The maintenance of a socialist philosophy when the economic theory underlying it seems to have died is a major problem, but until recently all socialists have been agreed that socialism could not work simply by patching up the superstructure. Historically, socialism can only be seen as an alternative to capitalism, not a way of managing it.

Thus socialism is at its heart a revolutionary idea. Those who call themselves 'revolutionary socialists' do not believe that socialism is possible without a revolution; a fundamental shift not only in resources, but in economic, political, and social power, a shift that is bound to meet with strong resistance. There are certainly widely differing positions about what can or cannot be achieved by the 'parliamentary road', but many who are attracted by the socialist 'ideal' are disturbed by the prospect of such radical transformation, and, like many members of the Labour Party in Britain, opt instead for a reformed, humanized capitalism. This is a practical issue for all socialist parties who find themselves in power and having to manage a capitalist economy.

Contrary to widespread belief, the Labour Party in Britain has never been a socialist party, rather a party of organized labour; but it has contained socialists and still does. Its commitment to common ownership was embodied until recently in a clause of its constitution and in many other statements. The National Executive policy document For Socialism and Peace (1934) stressed the centrality of common ownership. However, by the end of the 20th century the word 'socialism' had virtually disappeared from Labour documents. The view that socialist values and ideals can be separated from a socialist economic order has been brought out clearly in statements by the British prime minister Tony Blair. 'My kind of socialism is a set of values, based around notions of social justice … Socialism as a rigid form of economic determinism has ended, and rightly.' Blair sees his position as 'within the tradition of social democracy and democratic socialism' and rejects 'the battle between market and public sector'.

So has there been a collapse, or decay, of the very concept of socialism? Certainly the language has largely been abandoned, at least in the British Labour Party. Since the ascendancy of 'new Right' theories, dominated by a reductionist analysis of market exchange, and since the collapse of the Soviet system, many have assumed that the socialist project is now obsolete. Commentators have referred to the 'bankruptcy' of socialism, claiming that the social democratic era itself is drawing to a close, and that we are in a 'post-socialist age'. Some have spoken of the 'burial' of socialism and of the need for 'post-socialist' politics.

Others would argue that what has collapsed is not socialism but the alliance between socialist economics and the repressive authoritarian politics of excessive central control. In many parts of the world, such as South-East Asia, we find a strong commitment to social ownership and co-operation. One of the important questions for the future is whether, and how, markets can be linked with a socialist society. Markets are not intrinsically inimical to socialism, though their dominance certainly is. The idea of a market economy grew up alongside capitalism. But capitalism is about ownership, while markets are allocating mechanisms capable of existing within a variety of systems, including a socialist system. Indeed, they can only operate within some social context.

Socialist thinking and practice has been changed by the growth of the 'new social movements' such as feminism and green movements. Insufficiently analysed notions of class and labour cannot be meaningful in the vastly changed societies of the future, though this is not to deny that class is still very relevant in most societies. The decline of the Labour Party in Britain until its late 20th-century revival was closely linked with the erosion of the traditional working class, especially in the declining urban industrial regions in the north of England upon which Labour traditionally relied. There has certainly been a collapse of the institutional expression of class identity, and the ending of 'class politics' was being discussed as long ago as the 1950s.

Many have spoken of the need to rethink the 'socialist project'. Stuart Hall, one of the founders of the 'New Left' in Britain, asked whether it is 'a word whose historical moment has passed'. Among contemporary left thinkers, some of whom would describe themselves as 'post-socialists', there is a great deal of stress on issues of citizenship, new republicanism, civil society, and pluralism. There is also a shift away from collectivist and statist traditions (central planning, the command economy, the bureaucratic administration of welfare) towards 'associational socialism' or 'socialism from below'.

All the various streams of socialism are reflected in the history of Christian socialism. Much Christian social theory, particularly within the Catholic tradition, has regarded capitalism as a faith or ideology rooted in the mortal sin of avarice, a form of mammon worship. The papal 'social encyclicals' since 1891 have included severe critiques of capitalism but they have, until recently, been pre-socialist critiques. Before the Reformation it was assumed that accumulation, profit, and *usury were in fundamental conflict with religious values, and that such practices corrupted people and impeded the work of redemption. The classical Christian tradition held that inequality and injustice were the results of *pleonexia*, a word usually translated as greed or avarice, but in fact indicating a disposition towards acquisition. But this disposition is essential to the working of the capitalist order, and it is here, according to the Christian social tradition, that capitalism comes into fundamental conflict with Christian ethics and spirituality. For now the purpose of human life is the acquisition of goods, and thus acquisitiveness, *pleonexia*, the vice of avarice, becomes in capitalism a central virtue. Moreover, in order to flourish, capitalism needs to develop individuals who are inclined towards injustice.

Undoubtedly, if there is a socialism of the future, it will have to be reshaped and reconceived in major ways. It has suffered from a narrowness of perspective, being in origin a movement within Western Europe and the nation-state. It has tended to focus on economic issues and to neglect other areas of human life. So we find today that on many important issues—sexuality and gender, race and ethnicity, the Middle East, Ireland, the environment, the whole area of cultural politics—there is no identifiable socialist perspective. As a product of the *Enlightenment, itself under scrutiny, socialism will for the foreseeable future be subjected to serious critique and interrogation. What will emerge from this process remains to be seen. Certainly the struggle for human and ethical alternatives to capitalism will occupy Christians and others well into the 21st century.

See also MARXISM.   **Kenneth Leech**

Atherton, John, *Christianity and the Market* (1992).

Blackburn, Robin (ed.), *After the Fall: The Failure of Communism and the Future of Socialism* (1992).

Bryant, Chris, *Possible Dreams: A Personal History of British Christian Socialists* (1996).

Callaghan, John, *Socialism in Britain Since 1884* (1990).

Cort, John C., *Christian Socialism: An Informal History* (1988).

Dennis, Norman, and Halsey, A. H., *English Ethical Socialism: Thomas More to R. H. Tawney* (1988).

Giddens, Anthony, *Beyond Left and Right: The Future of Radical Politics* (1996).

Leech, Kenneth, *The Sky is Red* (1997).

Leys, Colin, and Panitch, Leo, *The End of Parliamentary Socialism* (1997).

Temple, William, *Christianity and Social Order* (1942).

Wells, Harold, *A Future for Socialism?* (1996).

Wollenberg, Bruce, *Christian Social Thought in Great Britain Between the Wars* (1997).

social sciences. Although the term was first used in English by the *Enlightenment thinker Jeremy Bentham, it is in the latter half of the 19th century and the early decades of the 20th that the modern social sciences took shape. Theoretical and empirical traditions are diverse, though the most influential have been the French and German traditions, particularly those associated with Émile Durkheim and Max Weber.

Much of the unity of the social sciences rests on the assumption that methods arising from the natural sciences can be adapted to the analysis of society. Auguste Comte, who first used the term 'sociology', emphasized that the social sciences should base themselves upon the observation of 'positive', observable facts rather than theological or metaphysical assumptions. This facilitates the emergence of the category of 'religion' as a social phenomenon that needs to be accounted for in a detached and objective manner, reflecting the increasingly secular milieu that made the social sciences possible. It also raises issues of pluralism and the relativization of *truth-claims for Christian theologians. From the very beginning the social sciences have been predisposed towards offering either general theories of *religion, exemplified by Durkheim, or comparative studies, exemplified by Weber.

It would be misleading, however, to suggest that this implies an antireligious character, although this is apparent in the political philosophy of Karl *Marx. The continuity with Enlightenment rationalism is only one significant factor in the development of the social sciences. Robert Nisbet has argued, convincingly, that the social sciences have conservative rather than liberal philosophical sources, reflecting a counter-Enlightenment orientation. This is evident in their central preoccupations: community, authority, status, religion, and alienation. These reflect an ambivalent attitude to *modernity and, in some instances at least, a somewhat nostalgic attitude to the medieval period.

Saint-Simon, Comte's mentor, argued that some sort of common faith was necessary to maintain social solidarity and eventually argued for a reaffirmation of Christianity. Comte, despite his positivism, sought to develop his own 'religion of humanity' complete with sociologist-priests, altars, a calendar of feast days, and modes of worship: a form of religion Nisbet refers to as 'Catholicism minus the Christianity' and 'positivist wine poured into medieval bottles'. Also, as John Milbank has noted, Comteanism was later 're-Catholicized' and gave rise to the 'atheist Catholicism' of the Action française. It is with Durkheim, however, that the *French tradition's concern with religion reaches its finest and most influential expression.

During Durkheim's lifetime, his analysis of religion was opposed by Catholics such as Simon Deploige but was better received by others. According to his contemporary, the Protestant sociologist Gaston Richard, the German Catholic Church enthusiastically greeted Durkheim's argument that Protestants were more likely to commit suicide than Catholics; a result, according to Durkheim, of Protestantism's relatively weaker patterns of social integration. In France, particularly after the Second World War, Durkheim's work was increasingly drawn upon by Catholics, though opposition came from Protestants who objected to his emphasis on the collectivist nature of religion. His final major work, *The Elementary Forms of Religious Life*, remains probably the most impressive attempt to understand religion from the perspective of the social sciences. Not only has this book had a profound impact upon sociology, but also on the work of *anthropologists such as Marcel Mauss, Lucien Lévy-Bruhl, Claude Lévi-Strauss, Victor Turner, and Mary Douglas.

Durkheim argues that religion cannot be explained away as an irrational illusion. Rather than accepting religious participants' own accounts of their experience, however, which refer to non-observable realities, he argues that the 'truth' of religion rests on its capacity symbolically to represent collective life itself, integrating individuals into moral communities. He goes much further than Comte in rejecting simple rationalistic interpretations of religion: the origins of religion, and the origins of society itself, rest in the emotional ferment of 'collective effervescence'. This phenomenon, which recalls Henri Bergson's concept of the *élan vital*, provides the creative social energies that make communal life possible. As a theory of religion and society it has been compared to the crowd psychology of his contemporary Gustave le Bon, whose *Psychologie des foules* greatly interested Freud. Whereas le Bon and Freud interpreted the emotional energies of crowds as dangerous forces, however, reducing the rationality and intelligence of the individuals concerned, Durkheim emphasized their social creativity. Indeed, for Durkheim, society itself would not be possible without religion.

While Durkheim's optimism about the future of religion is indicative of a broader tendency within the French sociological tradition, continued today by writers such as Michel Maffesoli, we find a different viewpoint within the German tradition, especially in the work of Weber. His *The Protestant Ethic and the Spirit of Capitalism* has often been read as a challenge to Marx's reductionist account of religion as an 'epiphenomenal' expression of more important economic realities. Weber attempts to explain why it is that *capitalism developed in Europe, rather than in other contexts where favourable economic circumstances had existed centuries earlier. His argument is that *Protestantism's 'worldly asceticism' encouraged the psychological conditions that allowed capitalism to flourish. This is argued with a particular focus on Calvinism, though he also examines transformations in the thought of *Luther.

The irony in Weber's analysis is that while he emphasizes the influence of religion on the development of modernity, he also argues that the nature of this influence leads to the gradual destruction of religion's social significance. Weber's account of the 'Protestant ethic' emphasizes its rationalism, its individualism, and, with its vision of a radically transcendent God revealed through the bible, its devaluation of the ritualistic and magical dimensions of religion. Taken together, all these processes become part of a pro-

gressive 'rationalization' of the modern world. Weber, himself a disenchanted Lutheran, thus established what became the dominant theoretical model for the interpretation of modern religion in the social sciences: the history of 'rationalization' is that of *'secularization'.

It is Weber's analysis of religion and society that underpins the influential work of Peter Berger, another melancholic Lutheran. Berger's *The Sacred Canopy* develops Weber's idea that, historically, Christianity has been its own gravedigger by examining how the attempts of the Christian churches and theologians to adapt to a secular environment have stimulated further secularization. E. L. Mascall and Robin Gill have argued a similar point: social scientific assumptions about secularization have too often been accepted rather than challenged. *Bultmann's *'demythologization' of the NT was followed by the increasing use of social scientific methods in the analysis of the bible, focusing upon its social contexts, determinants, and the cultural and ideological dimensions of its contents. These encouraged the promotion of a plurality of different 'readings' with their own claims to authority. The rise of various forms of 'secular theology' or 'secular Christianity' in the 1960s, exemplified by Harvey Cox's *The Secular City* and John *Robinson's *Honest to God*, are also examples of a rather uncritical incorporation of the social sciences into *theology. Cox, in particular, explicitly endorses Weber's rationalization thesis and welcomes the opportunities and challenges modernity offers, arguing that theology must adapt to this modern reality. Such enthusiasm about modernity was alien to Weber himself, who referred to it as the 'iron cage'.

Within Roman Catholicism, Gregory Baum has also urged the use of sociology to 'purify' theology of misconceptions about social realities, while Edward *Schillebeeckx's analysis of the ordained ministry led to the accusation that his adoption of sociological assumptions relativized orthodox Catholic theology. Hans *Küng has also attempted to map out a modern theology based on a somewhat sketchy and uncritical reading of Weber's rationalization thesis. The source of Berger's despair at such liberal theological efforts is that he has read Weber rather more carefully and understands that the disenchantment of the modern world cannot be fought with more disenchantment. This argument is also central to the Catholic sociologist Kieran Flanagan's attacks upon theologians for incorporating poorly understood sociological concepts into their theological agendas, and to the anthropologist Victor Turner's Durkheimian deconstruction of the secularizing impact of post-*Vatican II liturgical changes.

On the whole, however, Catholics have perhaps tended to be more cautious about incorporating sociological assumptions into theological analysis, a caution reflected in the tradition of 'religious sociology'. This tradition, influenced by Gabriel le Bras, has tended to use social scientific methods of data collection as a means to a religious end, rather than as a resource for reconstructing Catholic theology. Le Bras was influenced by Durkheim, and believed that the church could use sociology to arrest its decline in France. The strong sociographic tradition among Catholic sociologists in America continues the French pattern to a large extent. Within Anglicanism, David Martin's considerable body of work has also demonstrated a careful separation of sociological and theological methods, reflecting his sensitivity to both the potentialities and the dangers of interaction between the two disciplines.

There is a considerable body of evidence, nevertheless, to support Milbank's assertion that the incorporation of social scientific assumptions into theological reflection has had a generally damaging impact upon Christianity. He argues that Christianity and the social sciences are inevitably in conflict, since the latter express all sorts of philosophical and ideological assumptions contrary to those of Christianity. As he expresses it, Durkheimian analyses essentially conflate the religious and the social, while the Weberian model perpetuates a neo-Kantian conception whereby the two are forever categorically separate realms. Against these, Christianity should develop its own social theory, and not adapt to understandings of social realities promoted by its secularizing opponents. The value of this account rests on its capacity to highlight how various social scientific perspectives are nowhere near as value-free as they appear to be, though whether this necessarily implies their insignificance for theologians is another matter. Within the French tradition, for example, the concern with social solidarity clearly suggests a Catholic influence, but this is precisely what has enabled Catholics to utilize Durkheim's work for their own religious purposes.

An irony in Milbank's position is that he is able to propose this rejection of social science precisely because he has drawn upon social scientific debates about postmodernity that have called into question assumptions about objectivity and value-neutrality. His position is strengthened, however, by *postmodernism's acceleration of a process of fragmentation in the social sciences, so that many traditional boundaries between disciplines have blurred, or broken down, while specialities have arisen which sometimes have a thoroughly conflictual relationship with each other. It is hardly surprising that in such circumstances some theologians have sought to dismiss the relevance of the social sciences. Nevertheless, as debates about postmodernity give way to a reassessment of the enduring insights of the great founding figures of the social sciences, and their counter-Enlightenment aspects, such a dismissive attitude is unlikely to be satisfactory for very long. Weber's picture of the relentless rationalization of modern societies now looks problematic, calling into question those liberal theologies eager to adapt to it, but Durkheim's concern with the persistence of the sacred remains influential. The developing interest of theologians in the insights of writers such as René Girard and Georges Bataille, both of whom owe much to Durkheim, reflects this. The re-emergence of religiously legitimated forms of *nationalism, *fundamentalism, and 'neo-tribalism' have also served to stimulate something of a Durkheimian revival. In consequence, the capacity of the social sciences to stimulate Christian theological thinking about the nature of social life is unlikely to be as redundant as Milbank envisages, and will surely continue to raise challenging questions for Christians.　**Philip A. Mellor**

Berger, P., *The Sacred Canopy* (1967).
Flanagan, K., *The Enchantment of Sociology* (1997).
Gill, R., *Competing Convictions* (1989).
—— (ed.), *Theology and Sociology: A Reader* (1997).
Levine, D., *Visions of the Sociological Tradition* (1995).
Martin, D., *Reflections on Sociology and Theology* (1997).
Martin, D., Orme Mills, J., Pickering, W. S. F. (eds.), *Sociology and Theology: Alliance and Conflict* (1980).
Milbank, J., *Theology and Social Theory* (1990).
Nisbet, R. A., *The Sociological Tradition* (1966).
Pickering, W. S. F., *Durkheim's Sociology of Religion* (1984).

Socinianism, see UNITARIANISM.

Sölle, Dorothee (1929–), German Protestant theologian and political activist. Sölle is one of the leading interpreters of third-world *liberation theology for western audiences, concerned to understand the meaning of 'liberation' for first-world, consumerist, and *secular society. Sölle's own canon of work is deeply informed by her many political commitments—to the *peace movement, green politics, and third-world solidarity—and draws upon literature and poetry (see *Revolutionary Patience* (1974)) as well as biblical and systematic *theology.

Influenced by *Bultmann and the neo-*Marxism of the Frankfurt School, Sölle argues that traditional teachings about the sinfulness of the human condition must be interpreted in materialist terms: *sin is alienation, in which *humanity is separated from its own creativity, and thereby from fellow humans and from *God, who is the source of all life. Like her fellow post-war German *political theologian J. B. Metz, Sölle is scathing in her critique of the privatization and hedonism of consumer *capitalism, which has served to deflect western society from a concern with genuine existence into a banal preoccupation with material possessions. The solution is to 'choose life' (Deut. 30: 19)—to refuse to surrender to the cynicism of materialism severed from the rhythms of *creation (1979).

Sölle rejects *Barthian notions of the otherness of God as implying divine indifference to creation, and favours a model of God as immanent and *incarnational, embodied in communities of relationality and *love (1990). Echoing many Third-World liberation theologians, she emphasizes the historical reality of the crucifixion as a political act of solidarity with the suffering of the world (see CROSS). The Passion of Christ is re-enacted today wherever the integrity of creation is violated; and the *Kingdom of God is realized wherever 'wholeness, trust, ecstasy, and solidarity' (1984) are cultivated.　**Elaine Graham**

Sölle, Dorothee, *Choosing Life* (1979).
—— *To Work and to Love: A Theology of Creation* (1984).
—— *Thinking about God: An Introduction to Theology* (1990).
—— *Against the Wind* (1999).

Solomon, David's son, his heir to the united kingdom of Israel and Judah, and proverbially the wisest man who ever lived, is regarded both as a type of Christ and as a cautionary tale by later tradition. As builder of the *Temple, he holds an indelible place in Jewish tradition, and in later symbolic elaborations of the Temple, for instance, Freemasonry, its design is taken as reflecting his unrivalled insight into the cosmos. Yet there is another side to this. Solomon's imposition of forced labour to carry out his plans is blamed for the tensions that were to split the kingdoms again after his death.

Three books of the Hebrew bible—Proverbs, Ecclesiastes, and *Song of Songs—are traditionally ascribed to him, as is the apocryphal Wisdom of Solomon and two of the psalms. In 1 Kings 4: 32 he is credited with a total of 3,000 proverbs and 1,005 songs. The three canonical books, in the order given above, are regarded as a trilogy by some early commentators: he is seen either as treating successive persons of the Trinity (Father, Son, and Spirit) or else as addressing readers more or less advanced along the path of spiritual maturity. Modern scholarship doubts all these ascriptions, seeing

Solomon as the popular focus of the *wisdom tradition to whom accrue all kinds of texts and legends.

Solomon's proverbial judgement (1 Kings 3: 16–28) where he proposes to halve a disputed child, thereby inducing its real mother to prove her status by renouncing her claim, forms the subject of many paintings. It has been regarded as a type of Christ as judge and the separation of sheep and goats. Solomon's respectful greeting of his mother Bathsheba (1 Kgs. 2: 19), giving her a seat at his right hand, is read as a type of Christ's enthronement of Mary. The subsequent verses, however, show Solomon flatly contradicting his mother's wishes, a telling example of how a single verse out of context can be pressed into *typological service. The visit of the Queen of Sheba bearing gifts and overawed by his wisdom is an OT parallel to the coming of the magi to Jesus' birth. Solomon's wealth was also proverbial, as Jesus himself testifies when he compares Solomon's glory unfavourably to that of the lilies of the field.

The ascription of the Song of Songs to Solomon may reflect his association with the erotic, though the later *allegorical interpretations of the book mean in turn that Solomon gains credentials as a *mystic. Yet he is condemned for turning to idolatry under the influence of his large harem, itself an indulgence later Christian writers would frown upon. Solomon's wisdom, which misreadings of 1 Kgs. 4: 33 even took as far as including knowledge of the language of the animals, is seen to be a great but ultimately partial gift if it is not coupled with humility before God.

Hugh S. Pyper

Conway, M. D., *Solomon and Solomonic Literature* (1972).
Handy, L. K. (ed.), *The Age of Solomon: Scholarship at the Turn of the Millennium* (1997).

Song of Songs.

On the face of it, this enigmatic collection of erotically charged poetry, traditionally ascribed to *Solomon, is a surprising choice for inclusion among the *wisdom books of the OT. Perhaps Solomon's name guaranteed it. Even more surprising is the central place it has had in the development of Christian *spirituality. Its difficulty, however, is the clue. On a principle going back at least to *Origen, medieval thinkers knew that the more perplexing a biblical text seemed the more certain it was that it contained spiritual teaching of the highest order.

Origen himself interpreted the poem *allegorically as a dramatic dialogue written by Solomon to instil understanding of the relations between Christ and the human *soul under the figure of the Bridegroom and the Bride. The discussion of spiritual experience in images of *love drawn from the Song which pervades Origen's homilies and his commentary sets the pattern for subsequent centuries. Not all followed suit. Theodore of Mopsuestia, the representative of the less allegorical Antiochene school, insisted that the Song is a collection of Solomon's love poems to his dark-skinned wife, the daughter of Pharaoh. His condemnation by the second Nicene council for this only strengthened the dominance of allegorical readings.

As illumination for the spiritually advanced, the book was particularly important in the life of religious communities, and hundreds of medieval commentaries were written with this in mind (see MONASTICISM). Bernard of Clairvaux's 86 sermons on the Song, delivered to his brethren over a period of 18 years (1135–53), remain the centrepiece of this tradition. Both *Teresa of Avila and *John of

the Cross draw upon them for their own devotional works. Following Origen, Bernard makes it clear that the Song is addressed to those who are ready for spiritual *marriage to Christ, not to novices who may suppose fleshly delights are being extolled. His purpose as he expounds it is to draw his hearers into the loving relationship between the soul and Christ of which he knows the poem speaks, rather than to uncover its textual niceties. Rupert of Deutz (d. 1129) began a parallel line of interpretation which identified the speakers as Christ and Mary.

The Song left the *Reformers with a quandary. Their desire to break free of allegorical interpretation seldom ran as far as embracing the literal meaning of the Song of Songs. *Luther, in accordance with his general view that biblical texts reflected the spiritual exercises of the author's soul, interpreted the Song as Solomon's allegorical thanksgiving to God for the power and peace of his kingdom. *Calvin defended a traditional reading against his associate Sebastian Castellio who, reading literally, saw the book as lascivious and of little canonical value.

Historical critics came to a general consensus in the 19th century that the book began as a collection of songs sung at weddings and drew parallels with existing marriage practices in Syria. A further development was to regard it as a celebration of sacred marriage between deities. None of this helped Protestant preachers to know what to make of the book. Catholic and Orthodox interpreters held to the traditional view much longer.

Twentieth-century thought on the Song was coloured by a new awareness, sometimes obsessive, of the importance of *sexuality and the *body in human existence. The Song has been reclaimed by commentators as a celebration of sexuality enshrined in the very bible which has been the instrument of sexual repression. *Feminist critics have been particularly taken with the frank expression of female desire in the context of the prevailing patriarchal character of biblical material.

Such critics sometimes imply that the tradition of allegorical interpretation betrays the desire of Christians to repudiate the body and human sexuality. While this may be true of all too many, it misses a point. It is celebration of the ecstacy of union with Christ that drives the best medieval interpreters, a joy that they claim outstrips rather than invalidates bodily pleasure.

Whatever its theological value, there is no doubt that the sometimes bizarre imagery and sheer linguistic exuberance of the Song have had lasting effects. Not only Christian writers and thinkers have been enchanted by the metaphorical shifts between the erotic and the spiritual that it embodies. The novelist A. S. Byatt comments, 'The Song continues to haunt our imaginations, somewhere between the absurd and the sublime' or, we could add, between the human and the divine.

Hugh S. Pyper

Falk, M., *The Song of Songs: A New Translation and Interpretation* (1990).
Matter, E. A., *The Voice of My Beloved: The Song of Songs in Western Medieval Christianity* (1990).
Murphy, R. E., *The Song of Songs* (1990).

soteriology, see REDEMPTION.

soul.

The term is used, primarily, of the subject of inner, mental, and spiritual states. In its widest sense, it is usually contrasted with the body, the physical, animal organism, which, in the human case, has somehow acquired the mental and spiritual capacities that give rise to talk of 'soul'. In this sense, soul includes both mind and spirit, the mental including sensation, desire, belief, and *reason, the spiritual including aesthetic and *religious experience and many other aspects of specifically human life. Philosophers tend to equate soul and mind, religious people tend to equate soul and spirit. (This permits the latter to accuse an intelligent but ruthless criminal of lacking soul.) *Human beings are not simply subjects of mental and spiritual states over and above their bodily condition. They are also intentional agents and conscious participants in interpersonal relations. We tend, however, to speak of the self rather than the soul as agent, and of *persons rather than souls in relation. Both 'self' and 'person', then, are wider terms than 'soul', and more appropriate for use in connection with the human being as a whole. 'Soul' is reserved for certain key aspects of human subjectivity.

In the history of both philosophy and religion, there are strands emphasizing the real distinction between soul and body, as in the various kinds of soul (or mind)–*body *dualism; and there are strands emphasizing the inextricable interconnection of the mental and the physical, as in talk of human beings as psychosomatic unities. More recently, there have been a number of science-based philosophical attempts to explain the mental entirely in physical terms, by advocates of artificial intelligence, for example, who predict that one day advanced computers or robots will be able to exercise and enjoy the same capacities and states as humans.

In the ancient world, the distinctiveness of mind was first observed by Anaxagoras, and the primacy of soul urged by the Orphics and the Pythagoreans. These influences contributed to the first major advocacy of soul–body dualism by *Plato. In the Republic, Plato treats the embodied soul as tripartite, consisting of reason, desire, and spirit (spirit in a rather different sense from that outlined above), but in the Phaedo it is the soul qua reason that is declared to be immortal like the Forms and longing to be released from its temporary imprisonment in the body. *Aristotle, by contrast, takes a much more holistic view. For him, the soul is the form of the body, that is, the way in which a living body is informed by the kind of life peculiar to it. This permits Aristotle to use the term 'soul' in a wider sense than anything so far mentioned and to speak of vegetable and *animal souls as well as human souls. The human soul, however, is specified by rationality, which differentiates humans from the vegetable and animal worlds.

The Jewish/Christian scriptures are often held to exemplify a thoroughly holistic view of the human by contrast with Greek dualism. God breathes the breath of life (Hebrew nephesh) into *Adam, formed from the dust of the ground (Gen. 2: 7). At death this animation is withdrawn. The story of Ezekiel and the valley of dry bones (Ezek. 37) is a story of God's power to reanimate the people, not a parable of *resurrection, still less of *immortality. In the NT, too, the soul (Greek psyche) is more the life principle (e.g. Phil. 2: 30) than a separate creation, and Pauline anthropology is often presented in terms of the psychosomatic unity that constitutes the human person. Yet this contrast between Hebrew and Greek has been overdrawn. Just as Greek thought includes Aristotle as well as Plato, so Judaeo-Christian anthropology contains more dualistic elements than advocates of the Greek/Hebrew contrast allow. James Barr has pointed out how the Hebrew terms nephesh, and, even more, ruah (usually translated 'spirit') are sometimes used, as by Isaiah (see 26: 9) or by the Psalmist (Ps. 86: 13) and

certainly in the Apocrypha's Wisdom of Solomon (12: 7), for a distinct and possibly separable element in human nature. Similarly, in the NT, Jesus warns, in a parable, the rich fool who had been accumulating goods, 'this night your soul is required of you' (Luke 12: 20).

It was the Platonic rather than the Aristotelian tradition that came to influence the theologians of the Christian church during the patristic period when Christian doctrine was being formulated. *Origen went so far as to accept the pre-existence as well as the immortality of the soul, as Plato himself had done. But this was exceptional. A more characteristic Christian Platonism was that of *Augustine, for whom it is indeed the soul, through its *memory, understanding, and will that mirrors the divine *Trinity. But the soul, like the body, is a created substance, wholly dependent on God for being in being.

It is the Judaeo-Christian doctrine of *creation that also accounts for the main differences between western and eastern understandings of the soul. In Vedantic Hinduism, matter is ultimately illusory and so is the individuality of the human soul. Liberation for humans consists in realization of one's ultimate identity with the all-pervasive World Soul. There are echoes of comparable ideas in Aristotle and more clearly in Plotinus and later forms of philosophical idealism, but the doctrine of creation prevents Jews and Christians—and Muslims too—from blurring the distinction between creator and creature, even where, in Christianity's case, the human being, whether as soul or as soul–body unity, is destined to be taken into the life of God, in a transformed state, by the indwelling *Holy Spirit.

The tensions between the holistic and the dualistic strands in Christian anthropology are nowhere more evident than in the thought of Thomas *Aquinas. On the one hand, he accepts the Aristotelian view of the soul as the form of the body. He ascribes agency to the whole person, not just to the soul. On the other hand, the human soul, the seat of our intellectual and volitional capacities, unlike all other kinds of soul, is both subsistent and immortal. As such, it is specially created by God. Human souls, therefore, unlike human bodies, are not the effect of human procreation. But a disembodied soul is not fully human. Our future life as humans requires resurrection.

No such ambiguity attends the thought of the father of modern philosophy, René *Descartes, who is responsible for the most uncompromising mind–body dualism since Plato. For Descartes, the mind or soul is a thinking substance quite distinct from extended matter or body. Moreover, I am essentially my soul in a way in which I am not my body. Animals do not have souls or minds. They, like human bodies, are more akin to complex machines. For a long time Cartesian dualism was regarded as an ally by the Christian church. Not only did the theory of mind or soul as thinking substance favour a doctrine of immortality; it was also held to offer a more intelligible Christian anthropology. Humans are made in the image of God. Rationality and *freedom—the key capacities of thinking substance—could most readily be taken to reflect the incorporeal mind of the creator. (This is comparable, though in less Trinitarian terms, to Augustine's view mentioned above.)

Soul–body dualism retains its advocates today. It is still the official doctrine of the Roman Catholic Church, where it was sharpened in 1869 with the declaration that the soul is infused at conception. It is still maintained not only by Christian philosophers of religion such as H. D. Lewis (see his *The Elusive Mind* (1969)) and Richard Swinburne, but also by secular philosophers such as Karl Popper (see *The Self and its Brain* (1977), written with the neurophysiologist, John Eccles).

The reasons behind such advocacy of the substantial reality of the mind or soul include first-person self-awareness in all its forms, and, correlatively, the inability of science-based materialism to account for consciousness and its subjective and intentional states (the way we focus our minds on purely mental objects and intended projects). But these strong arguments do not necessarily entail dualism in the sense of soul and body as distinct substances. A more common approach today, in both philosophy and theology, is to reject behaviourism, mind–body identity theory, and much so-called cognitive science on just such grounds, but to conclude that what is required is a much broader conception of the powers of nature than strict materialism allows. Thus secular philosophers such as John Searle and Anthony Kenny insist on the mental as an aspect of nature that needs full justice to be done to it, and religious thinkers such as David Braine reaffirm a unitary, holistic view of the human being as a spiritual animal that has acquired over evolution the capacities of subjectivity and self-transcendence. This latter view is attractive to both philosophers and theologians influenced by the later—and specifically anti-Cartesian—work of *Wittgenstein, with its stress on language and culture as constitutive of what it is to be a human being. A similar view of human nature, with its characteristic emphasis on inter-subjectivity, is also to be found in Charles Taylor's work, *Sources of the Self* (1989). Such anti-dualistic, yet non-reductionist, views of human nature also allow for a greater emphasis on the body and its significance for the life of the spirit than does Platonic or Cartesian dualism.

Christian theology, then, is not committed to soul–body dualism, but it is committed to the reality and value of embodied spirit: of human subjectivity in all its affective, mental, rational, volitional, and creative aspects. In this sense it will insist on the retention of the language of soul and spirit. It will also suggest, in dialogue with non-reductionist secular philosophers like Searle and Kenny, that Christian theology is better placed than naturalism to explain the world's capacity to evolve embodied spirits, since it can see the whole of nature and its inbuilt powers as a product of the creator's will.

Does it follow that Christian theology is bound to oppose the very idea of artificial intelligence? Not necessarily. Granted, only 'soft', carbon-based, matter has proved itself capable of evolving organisms with brains of sufficient complexity to give rise to consciousness, rationality, and volition. Only through the procreation of human beings have subjects or selves, of whom the language of mind, soul, and spirit can appropriately be used, in fact appeared upon the scene. 'Hard', silicon-based, matter, despite the awesome calculating power of digital computers, and despite the possibilities of simulating neural networks through 'sophisticated' feed-back mechanisms and built-in randomizers, has shown no signs whatsoever of manifesting even rudimentary forms of awareness, still less affection, imagination, rational thought, or volition. As far as our present knowledge and skill go, artificial 'intelligence' is no more than a metaphor. But if, in the more or less remote future, it were to be discovered that hard as well as soft matter did, after all, have

the capacity to become the vehicle of inner life, including subjectivity, reason, and will, then such artefacts would have acquired selfhood, soul, and spirit, and would require to be treated and related to in just the same way as are our children. It does not look as if God has made the world that way, but we are not in a position to rule the idea out a priori.   **Brian Hebblethwaite**

Barr, J., *The Garden of Eden and the Hope of Immortality* (1992).
Braine, D., *The Human Person* (1993).
Kenny, A., *The Metaphysics of Mind* (1989).
Puddefoot, J., *God and the Mind Machine* (1996).
Searle, J. R., *The Rediscovery of Mind* (1992).
Swinburne, R. G., *The Evolution of the Soul* (1986).
Ward, K., *Defending the Soul* (1992).

Spanish Catholicism.

A humorist observed that Spanish bishops had spoken so much at *Vatican I that they arrived at *Vatican II with their voices still lost. Mgr. Echarren, a well-informed member of the modern Spanish hierarchy, made the same point more soberly when he remarked: 'Perhaps no other group of local churches was so remote theologically, psychologically, pastorally, and vitally, from Vatican Council II and its approach, as the local churches of Spain.' After the prodigious contribution of Spanish divines to the Council of *Trent, galling indeed are such comments for the backward-looking, that is, for those still obsessed with Spain's glorious Catholic past. To this day, in Spanish textbooks pride is taken in the martyrs slain by the Moors, in the medieval Christian Reconquest, and, above all, in the 16th-century Golden Age, when the Catholic monarchy of the Spanish Habsburgs was seen as the bulwark of Tridentine Catholicism and the home of *saints, *mystics, scholars, founders of new religious orders, and evangelizers of new worlds for the one, true church.

Thus it was that before the eruption of the Lutheran protest the Franciscan Cardinal Ximénez de Cisneros (1436–1517), founder of the University of Alcalá and sponsor of the Complutensian Polyglot Bible, had already pursued a vigorous policy of church reform. After Luther, Ignatius Loyola with his Society of Jesus (*Jesuits) and disciples such as Francis Xavier in effect reinterpreted the meaning of *mission. The *Dominicans led by Francisco de Vitoria (1483–1546), from his chair of theology in Salamanca, laid the foundations of international *law through his exploration of the rights of the recently conquered American 'Indians'. His fellow Dominican, Bartolomé de Las Casas (1484–1566) operated a literary and political campaign in their favour, which was to divide both his order and fellow Spaniards. But it is the Spanish contribution to *Counter-Reformation spirituality and mysticism that has attracted most attention. It is not only a question of the influence of Loyola's Spiritual *Exercises. Account must also be taken of the poetry and prose of *Teresa of Avila, founder of the Discalced Carmelites, and above all of the poetry and mystical theology of her disciple, *John of the Cross.

Spanish Catholicism in the Golden Age was not all sweetness and light, as later anticlericals were quick to point out. Above all it was the *Inquisition whose activities ensured for centuries that nothing even remotely like Protestantism took root in Spain. In doing so it created an integralist Catholicism that would dominate the subsequent history of Spanish religion. The most famous cases of inquisitorial perverseness in fact involve two of the Catholic monarchy's most influential orders. The Augustinian Luis de León (1527–91), a gifted poet, prestigious scripturalist, and teacher of John of the Cross at Salamanca, was imprisoned for four years. The Dominican primate, Bartolomé de Carranza, a distinguished theologian and reformer of Oxford University under Mary Tudor, was deprived of his archbishopric of Toledo and spent seventeen years in prison before being released by his fellow Dominican, Pius V.

The dismantling of the old regime in Spain as a result of the Napoleonic invasion of 1808 and the ensuing Peninsular Wars proved to be traumatic for a hitherto closed society. In this painful process no institution suffered more than the church, brought face to face with modernity without prior preparation. There was a direct threat to its privileges, with the loss of its tithes, the abolition of the Inquisition, the expropriation of its property, and the dissolution of its orders, with no fewer than 30,000 male Religious expelled from their houses. Moreover, this disruptive phenomenon was accompanied by spasmodic manifestations of an anticlericalism of horrific virulence that was to persist into the 20th century. There was burning and slaughter in Barcelona during the Tragic Week of 1909 but the climax was reached during the Civil War (1936–9), with the killing of 13 bishops, 4,184 secular priests, and 2,648 members of religious orders, including 283 nuns.

It is self-evidently true that the church in Spain was on the defensive from the first decade of the 19th century. Liberalism was taken to imply, first, the danger of secularism and then of dechristianization. In both halves of the century a layman and a cleric may be singled out as the chief protagonists of an intense national debate. The Estremaduran orator and politician José Donoso Cortés (1809–53) favoured the restoration of the church without concessions to liberalism. The Catalan thinker and theologian, Jaime Balmes, argued in favour of coming to terms with the new situation. In Spain Pius IX's Syllabus was assured of a good reception, and in the later period it was Marcelino Menéndez y Pelayo (1856–1912), the precocious scholar and polymath from Santander, who took up the traditionalist cause with excessive fervour, while the Asturian Dominican primate, Zeferino González (1831–95), took to heart Leo XIII's encyclical Aeterni Patris (1879) and led the restoration of *Thomism. This in turn highlights a factor that conditioned the Catholic response to a complicated and compromising situation at home. The Church in Spain is not autonomous and the influence of *ultramontanism has remained preponderant until the present day. In consequence theological *modernism never became a problem in Spain. The modernist cause was to find expression in literature and journalism, rather than philosophy or theology.

Given this state of affairs, it is impossible to exaggerate the importance of successive nuncios after the Concordat of 1851. Only safe, conformist Romanists were appointed to sees. Equally seriously, thanks to the interference of Barili (nuncio 1857–68), seminarians were to study theology in their diocesan seminaries and not in the universities. There was a disastrous lowering of academic standards. The dispatches of Simeoni (nuncio 1875–6) and Rampolla (nuncio 1882–7) confirm that the Spanish church, overall, lacked leaders of vision. The hierarchy was flawed and divided. The relentless, all-pervading clericalism in power was of a mean disposition and inevitably fostered limited horizons.

The patent failure of the Spanish hierarchy to improve the state of the church did not inhibit all new initiatives. There were 68 new female Institutes of Perfection founded between 1850 and 1899. The Jesuits established Pontifical Universities in Deusto and Comillas and the Augustinians in the Escorial, thus ensuring the church's continuing stake in higher education. The defence of Catholic belief and social values through the Catholic press and confraternities led to the foundation of élitist pressure groups destined to play an outstanding part in Spanish life in general and the church in particular. Leading the way was the National Catholic Association of Propagandists (1908) of Fr. Ayala, with its prestigious national newspaper, El Debate, edited by the remarkable journalist-cum-politician and future cardinal, Angel Herrera Oria, followed by the Teresian Institute (1924) of Fr. Poveda and the Opus Dei (1928) of Fr. Escrivá.

The Holy See was most perturbed by the turn of events in Spain after the fall of the monarchy in 1931 and the proclamation of the Second Republic. Attacks against the religious orders in the Spanish parliament were condemned in Pius XI's encyclical Dilectissima Nobis (1933). The future exile Mgr. Vidal i Barraquer, cardinal archbishop of Tarragona, and Tedeschini (nuncio 1921–36) attempted to reach a modus vivendi with the government. However, prime minister Azaña's reference in parliament to the demise of Catholic Spain presaged a persecution of unprecedented ferocity. The see of Barbastro lost 88 per cent of its secular clergy, Lérida 66 per cent, Tortosa 62 per cent, and Segorbe 55 per cent. Against such an apocalyptic background it was hardly surprising that Catholics should see the *Nationalist cause as a crusade, and the overwhelming majority of bishops, if not all, led by Cardinal Primate Gomá should hail Franco as the saviour of the church, in spite of the Nationalist execution of fourteen Basque priests, two regulars and twelve seculars. Even so, it is telling that although the Civil War ended in 1939, the Concordat with the Holy See was not signed until fourteen years later in 1953, when the Primacy had been held since 1940 by a skilled operator, Cardinal Pla i Deniel.

All students of Spanish ecclesiastical history are agreed that, despite Franco retaining the right to present diocesan bishops, no previous Spanish government had signed a Concordat so favourable to Rome as that of 1953. In return for Catholicism providing the ideological cement for an amorphous coalition that came to power by right of conquest, the church was showered with privileges, which in 1972 the soon-to-be-assassinated Admiral Carrero Blanco estimated to have been worth 300,000 million pesetas. Yet a church that had the largest radio network in Europe, together with 700 magazines, various *publishing houses and newspapers, and more than 7,000 schools and colleges, was, by the late 1960s, wishing to withdraw from the agreement. The short, and from a Spanish point of view, very sharp pontificate of *John XXIII, with its—for Spanish Catholics—almost unthinkably radical encyclicals, Mater et Magistra and Pacem in Terris, all compounded by the aggiornamento advocated by Vatican II, left the Francoist members of the hierarchy high and dry. The Confesiones of Cardinal Tarancón make clear that undivided loyalty to the Holy See was still the one decisive consideration for the hierarchy. The hesitant Mgr. Morcillo, archbishop of Madrid, was deliberately passed over twice for the cardinal's hat. It was Pla i Deniel's successor in Toledo in 1969, Tarancón, later archbishop of Madrid, who was to disentangle and eventually extricate the church from the smothering embrace of the Franco regime and its much flaunted and vaunted National Catholicism. Crucial indeed was the role played by the nuncio, Luigi Dadaglio, a faithful servant of Paul VI, in Madrid from 1967 to 1981 during the critical period of transition from dictatorship to parliamentary *democracy, when in the end the Catholic Church was disestablished (1977). Likewise the creation of a National Conference of Spanish Bishops was used skilfully to strengthen Tarancón.

After Vatican II the contradictions of a self-proclaimed Catholic regime could not be hidden. In spite of the fact that between 1969 and 1973 eleven out of nineteen Franco Cabinet ministers belonged to Opus Dei, the government opened a prison for priestly dissidents in Zamora and threatened to exile a bishop of Bilbao for his outspokenness. The declaration of the Joint Assembly of Bishops and Priests of 1971 begging forgiveness for the church's shortcomings in Spain's hours of need was the clearest signal yet of the church's rejection of National Catholicism. Integrist graffiti demanding that Tarancón be shot by firing squad—*Tarancón al paredón*—did not prevent the Paul VI–Dadaglio–Tarancón alliance from prevailing.

The strength of the church varies in the different regions of Spain. It is dangerous to generalize. Even so, it is clear that churchmen of the calibre of Tarancón were aware of the profound transformation of Spain from a backward rural agrarian society in 1936 to the tenth urban industrial power in 1975. Their sponsorship of the church's withdrawal from party politics may help to explain the virtual disappearance of that rabid anticlericalism that so disfigured the Spanish body politic over the last couple of centuries.

In some circles it is fashionable to question the church's relevance in contemporary Spain. Abundant evidence of ongoing institutional vitality belies this judgement. In this century Spain has produced the strongly conservative *Opus Dei* and Neo-Catechumenate, and the far more ecumenical *Cursillos*—three institutions that continue to influence the development of Catholicism on a global level in more than one direction. Spanish orders, major and minor, still provide missionaries for every continent. Last but not least, the bishops have recovered their voices.   **Ronald Cueto**

Batllorí, Miquel, and Arbeloa, V. M. (eds.), *Arxiu Vidal i Barraquer: Església i Estat durant la Segona República Espanyola 1931–1936* (4 vols.; 1971–86).

Callahan, W. J., *Church, Politics and Society in Spain 1750–1874* (1984).

Díaz de Cerio, Franco, *Regesto de la correspondencia de los obispos de España en el siglo XIX con los nuncios* (3 vols.; 1984).

Díaz de Cerio, Franco, and Núñez y Muñoz, M. F., *Instrucciones secretas a los nuncios de España en el siglo XIX (1847–1907)* (1989).

Enrique y Tarancón, Vicente, *Confesiones* (1996).

García-Villoslada, Ricardo (ed.), *Historia de la Iglesia en España* (5 vols.; 1979).

Hanke, Lewis, *Aristotle and the American Indian* (1970).

Jover, J. M. (ed.), *Menéndez-Pidal Historia de España*, xxv, xxxix, xli (1989; 1993; 1996).

Lannon, Frances, *Privilege, Persecution and Prophecy: The Catholic Church in Spain, 1875–1975* (1987).

Ullman, Joan Connally, *The Tragic Week: A Study of Anticlericalism in Spain, 1875–1912* (1968).

Spirit, see HOLY SPIRIT.

spirituality, forms of.

'Spirituality' is a term much in vogue: it sounds significant, with a touch of mystery, seeming to allow escape from the intellectual quest and wearisome wrestling with mental problems. We turn with relief from *theology to spirituality, but may find ourselves enmeshed in a bewildering variety of techniques, or excitedly following a trail leading nowhere.

For the Christian, spirituality is essentially life in the *Holy Spirit, the life and *love of *God himself, released by the death and glorification of *Jesus Christ. Grounded in a sense of *incarnation, it both transcends and involves the material and physical, the means of subsistence, and the satisfaction of bodily appetites.

The diversities of Christian spirituality are much influenced by the various cultures of Christian history. While all may be comprehended in the Pauline 'life in Christ' or the Holy Spirit, they have taken different forms and involved different techniques. This is already apparent in the NT, despite its common emphasis on a personal relationship with God-in-Christ, a stress on petitionary *prayer modelled on the *Lord's Prayer, and consciousness of the end, both the winding-up of history and the doing of God's will. Over the centuries 'life in Christ' led to very diverse lifestyles. At first the emphasis was on ethics. The way of life of all Christians differed from that of their neighbours essentially in ethical terms: for instance, certain occupations were prohibited. Soon, however, more specialized spiritualities developed, especially with the growth of *monasticism. Since then there has always been tension between seeing Christian spirituality as a common calling of all or as the way of a select few.

In the beginnings of monasticism, the *desert had great influence, a self-denying retreat involving abandonment of 'the world'. God was found in solitude and silence, in prayer and *fasting. Yet complete solitariness was found to be almost impossible and those in the desert banded themselves into communities and, later, even lived near centres of population which they could also assist. Thus, while monasticism did not entirely abandon the ideal of solitariness, its principal form, as encouraged by Basil's rule in the east and *Benedict's in the west, became grounded in the communal prayer of the *liturgy and in labour whether manual or scholarly (see WORK). It was shaped, not indeed for everyone, but for the many rather than the few.

*Mysticism is found in scripture in the sense of longing for union with God. Paul was a mystic, though he came to disparage *visions and revelations as compared with the sharing of Christ's *sufferings and a strength made perfect in weakness (2 Cor. 12). John's is the gospel of union with God though not of mystic states or abnormal phenomena. The influential 5th-century writer called *Dionysius the Pseudo-Areopagite first described the threefold process of purgation, illumination, and union. The last is the goal. The ineffable God is known only in the divine darkness and by the repudiation of ordinary processes of knowing. Entering into the darkness, the *soul relinquishes its own activity and submits to God who himself brings about the union of love. This is the source of the mysticism of an English group of late 14th- and early 15th-century writers, and of that of the 16th-century Spanish Carmelites, *Teresa of Avila and *John of the Cross.

If union is not accomplished without struggle and suffering, entry into the darkness that Christ experienced when he cried out forsaken on the *cross, this suggests similarities between the Catholic John of the Cross and the Protestant Martin *Luther. Mysticism frees Christian spirituality from historical scepticism and uncertainties. Whatever its ladder of ascent, a sense of the immediacy of the divine love with nothing between is its desire and experience. Union with God is no less the focal point of *Calvinism and this too is called 'mystical' in Walter Marshall's *The Gospel Mystery of*

Sanctification (1692), which is pure Calvin. The union is close as vine and branches, bread and eater, but the three stages are here not purgation, illumination, union, but justification, sanctification, glorification.

Dionysius' mysticism was no 'flight of the alone to the alone', unconcerned with a universal order and a human society fulfilling its vocation through the liturgy. He was also aware of 'the glittering beauty of the created order'. There is a spirituality of nature, and *Celtic spirituality, rediscovered in our time, is full of it: the changing seasons, the majesty of storms, as well as the beauty of its peace. In a poem from the Black Book of Carmarthen, God speaks in many images from nature, 'The wind that breathes upon the sea', 'the wave on the ocean, the leaves rustling, trees growing, salmon swimming, the wild boar fighting.' For *Hopkins 'there lives the dearest freshness deep down things', though man has soiled and marred it. Contemporary conservationist creation spirituality, as developed by Matthew Fox, for instance, has links with Meister Eckhart (*c.*1260–1329) and his mysticism of the God without a name. It has as its basis original blessing rather than original sin and four paths rather than the Dionysian three: the positive affirmation of creation; the negative letting go and letting be; the transformative new creation of *compassion; and social justice. It does not think of a ladder of ascent but of a holistic spiral emanating from the creative energy of God. Yet such spirituality must still reckon with terrible natural disasters; cf. Hopkins's wrestling in *The Wreck of the Deutschland*.

There is indeed a thread of anti-nature spirituality too. Evangelical spirituality in its belief that we are saved only by *grace, by God's finding us in Christ and not our search for him, is more conscious of fallen nature than its beauty and splendour. One theologian described nature as 'a grimace': there are no leaves on the tree of the cross. The Cornish poet, Jack Clemo, declared that when Voltaire, moved by sunrise over the Alps, fell to his knees and cried 'O, thou great being', he was no nearer to Christianity than if he had derided the splash of colour in the sky (J. Clemo, *The Invading Gospel* (1958)). Clemo was very different from *Blake, who saw the sunrise not as a golden guinea, as did some he knew, but as the heavenly host praising the Trinity. Clemo too is Trinitarian but asserts that Christianity knows only a righteous Father, an atoning Son, a convicting Spirit: 'the triumph of God's jazz over nature's Dead March'.

At the *Reformation, spirituality broke free of the monasteries, which had had incalculable influence but also implied an élitist model. As Max Weber put it, asceticism became 'intra-mundane', this-worldly. *Pietism represents one form. Leading theologians of the 20th century such as *Barth and Reinhold *Niebuhr have insisted that the Christian life must be lived out in society. Some have allied themselves with freedom fighters and protesters against apartheid and other systems of injustice, combining revolutionary politics with a hidden discipline of prayer. Comparably, from the 'establishment' of the United Nations, Dag Hammarskjöld's *Markings* (1964) are the moving testimony of one who, though not a churchgoer, reaffirmed traditional Christian faith and was always accompanied by Thomas à Kempis's *Imitation of Christ*. He said that 'for many of us in this era the road to holiness necessarily passes through the world of action'.

It is impossible to escape the past and the great figures of history, but different figures speak to different times. Ignatius Loyola's *Spiritual *Exercises* had at the end of the 20th century a popularity unimaginable fifty years before. But one who speaks especially to our time, far more than to previous centuries, is *Julian of Norwich, a *woman of deep theological understanding, aware of the femininity of God in the life of the Trinity. Her 'shewings' of the Passion are horrific, but her belief that God's forgiveness is prior to our sin, itself perhaps necessary that we may see ourselves in the light of the divine reality and love God as we could not otherwise, brings strength to many. Here as elsewhere authentic Christian spirituality rests on a balance between suffering and love.

Diverse as spiritualities remain, there is a movement towards a spiritual ecumenism which can abolish divisions in the sharing of our understandings of God through the practice of prayer. Some would see here the possibility of the reconciliation of all faiths, including Zen *Buddhism, as Thomas *Merton may have done. But in the end spirituality is not a technique but a lived faith, and while it may be an area where diverse *religions approach one another most closely, their reconciliation cannot be achieved through this field alone.

See also RELIGIOUS LIFE.   **Gordon S. Wakefield**

Brooks, Peter (ed.), *Christian Spirituality* (1975).

Demant, V. A., *A Two-Way Religion* (1957).

Dupre, Louis, and Saliers, Don E. (eds.), *Christian Spirituality: Post-Reformation and Modern* (1989).

Jones, Alan, *Soul Making: The Desert Way of Spirituality* (1984).

Jones, C., Wainwright, G., and Yarnold, E. (eds.), *The Study of Spirituality* (1986).

McGinn, B., Meyendorff, J., and Leclerq, J., *Christian Spirituality: Origins to the Twelfth Century* (1989).

Raitt, Jill (ed.), *Christian Spirituality: High Middle Ages and Reformation* (1987).

Sheldrake, Philip, *Spirituality and History* (1991).

Wakefield, G. S. (ed.), *A Dictionary of Christian Spirituality* (1983).

Stein, Edith

Stein, Edith (1891–1942). Edith Stein was born to a Jewish family in Breslau, the youngest of eleven children. In her teens she lost her Jewish faith, returning to religion only in her early twenties. She first studied psychology in Breslau, before moving on to Göttingen, where she studied *philosophy with the distinguished phenomenologist Edmund Husserl. At Göttingen, she showed an outstanding aptitude for philosophy, and became an active member of the circle around Husserl, which included also the leading philosopher and Jewish convert to Catholicism, Max Scheler. Under his influence she became attracted to Catholicism, a trend that gradually took her away from Husserlian phenomenology to the more personalist and value-laden phenomenology of the Schelerian school. In 1916 Stein followed Husserl to Freiburg as his assistant, and submitted her doctoral dissertation *The Problem of Empathy*. This work again shows her concern with questions of interpersonal knowledge, and the role of knowledge in the constitution of *personhood. It particularly shows a prioritization of the other as being not secondarily or phenomenally present to the self but rather primordially so.

Edith Stein was finally baptized in 1922, and took up a teaching position in a school run by Dominican sisters at Speyer. Here she began to study *Aquinas, and was invited by Erich Przywara, a noted *Jesuit philosophical theologian, to undertake a translation of Aquinas's *Quaestiones disputatae de veritate* (*Disputed Questions on*

Truth). This engagement with a medieval theologian led Stein to attempt a synthesis of *Thomism and phenomenology in her major study *Finite and Eternal Being* in which she argued for the primacy of ontology and essence over consciousness and knowledge. During these same years she was very active as a speaker for a number of societies of Catholic women and published a good deal of material in which she argued for fuller recognition of the role of women in German professional life. Again, her perspective was marked by a sense of the unity and integrity of the human person. In 1932, she was appointed to a lectureship at Münster where she was called to specialize in the development of a new Catholic pedagogical theory. After only a year she was dismissed from this post as a result of an antisemitic employment law introduced by the National Socialists from 1933.

In 1934 Edith Stein was clothed as Teresia Benedicta a Cruce in the Carmelite convent at Cologne, where she remained until moving to Echt in Holland in 1938 as a consequence of the acute political insecurity following the violence of Kristallnacht. Together with her sister Rosa, who had also converted to Catholicism, she was arrested and deported from Holland to Auschwitz in August 1942. Her arrest, together with other Jewish Catholics, resulted from the archbishop of Utrecht's proclamation against the deportations read out in Catholic churches in July 1942. She was beatified in 1987, and canonized in 1998. Her canonization has proved a sensitive issue in Catholic–Jewish relations. There is no doubt that Edith Stein was martyred as a Jew, and yet also as a Catholic, inasmuch as it was part of a punishment meted out to the church on account of the protest at the Jewish persecution. She seems herself to have understood her calling to the Passion of Christ as a Carmelite, symbolized by her religious name, to have been intrinsically bound up with her Jewish identity. There is evidence that her death was for her simultaneously an act of solidarity with her people and an imitation of Christ.

See also HOLOCAUST.   **Oliver Davies**

Cargas, Harry James (ed.), *The Unnecessary Problem of Edith Stein* (1993).
Herbstrith, Waltraud, *Edith Stein: A Biography* (1985).
Stein, Edith, *Life in a Jewish Family 1891–1916*, in L. Gelber and R. Leuven (eds.), *Collected Works* (1986), i.

subsidiarity represents an interesting case of an idea developed within a tradition of modern Christian thinking being taken over by the wider world. It begins its history with *Quadragesimo Anno* (1931), the encyclical of Pius XI on social and political affairs, where it was thus explained: 'It is an injustice, a grave evil and the disturbance of right order for a larger and higher association to arrogate to itself functions which can be performed efficiently by smaller and lower societies.' This blast against political and economic centralization was subsequently repeated in various Roman documents, notably by *John XXIII in his encyclical *Mater et Magistra* (1961). He appealed to the 'principle of subsidiary function' to defend the autonomy of 'intermediary bodies and corporate enterprises' and to criticize the extension of state ownership of property beyond what the common good clearly requires. Subsidiarity here represents more or less what recent social theorists have referred to as 'civil society', a crucial intermediate level of organization between the *family and the state necessary for a healthy functioning of *democracy. *Vatican II in *Gaudium et Spes*

(86) further applied the principle internationally. While encouraging the international community to stimulate development worldwide, it warned that the danger in organizing the global economy was to centralize power and so transgress the principle of subsidiarity (see GLOBAL ETHICS).

All of this appears remarkably relevant both to the continued centralization of many state governments and the growing domination of the global economy by the World Bank and the major multinational companies. It is, again, not surprising that within the European Community politicians have appealed frequently to the principle of subsidiarity in criticism of the centralized role of the Brussels bureaucracy. Jacques Delors, when general secretary of the EC, once famously appealed for a definition of subsidiarity. It signifies that no arrangements should be imposed centrally unless there is an overwhelming reason for not taking suitable decisions locally. An idea which seemed confined to a somewhat esoteric Catholic culture in the 1930s had become fashionable in far wider circles by the 1990s. But it is noticeable that the Roman authorities have never suggested that the principle should be applied as well to the Catholic Church, whose administration has grown ever more centralized. Like other things, subsidiarity is easier for those in power to preach than to apply.   **Adrian Hastings**

suffering has become the major objection to belief in *God. Why should this be so when in classical Christian thought suffering had a redemptive role?

Given that so many of the causes of past suffering are now removable, modern anxiety about this problem may seem somewhat ironic. It appears, indeed, to arise partly from dramatically improved expectations. Most people in the west are protected from the sense of life's precariousness with which all previous generations had to reckon. Prior to the arrival of modern medicine people had large families because so many children would not survive into adulthood. Serious poverty was endemic, hygiene barely understood, health insecure: *death happened in the midst of life. Westerners now expect children to be born healthy and to surmount illnesses through vaccination or antibiotics. Death even in old age is sterilized in hospitals. The result is that when things are not perfect people react with horror, cry out for better safety precautions, and demand the development of miracle cures. The notion of a good creator becomes problematic. Yet in contexts with far greater suffering, such as societies in the non-western world or in past history, such a response is rarely found.

There is, however, another factor: greater realization of the scale of human suffering. The advent of radio and television brought atrocities on a scale barely conceivable into every western sitting-room. Even before this, the perception of the issues had shifted for those abreast of ideas through reading and reflection. The 1755 Lisbon earthquake is often cited as the turning-point. Suddenly, for thinkers across Europe, it no longer made sense to speak of a created order ruled by a gracious *providence when tens of thousands had died senselessly. This could hardly be the best of all possible worlds as Leibniz had argued. This event, and the questions about arbitrary and innocent suffering that it raised, haunted subsequent theology. The 20th century hardly alleviated the pressure of the questions. Indeed, the issue raised by human capacity to inflict suffering has been sharpened. The First World War ended the illusion of heroism as warfare was democratized, whole populations becoming involved, millions dying traumatized in the trenches. The *Holocaust has become the symbol of dehumanization and industrialized genocide. How can theology respond convincingly to such a comment as 'If I were God, I wouldn't let my children do to each other what we human beings do.' God's morality is put in question by the creation of a world in which so much horror is perpetrated. Atheism may seem the best option after Auschwitz.

The seriousness of this change in perspective should not be minimized. It challenges the resources for dealing with suffering found in earlier Christian tradition. For much of Christian history biblical Proverbs provided insight, how effectively we can observe by turning to *Hebrews 12. The original readers of this epistle, tempted to give up in the face of suffering and persecution, are accused of having forgotten 'the exhortation that addresses you as children: "My child, do not regard lightly the discipline of the Lord, or lose heart when you are punished by him; for the Lord disciplines those whom he loves, and chastises every child whom he accepts"' (Prov. 3: 11–12). 'Endure trials for the sake of discipline. God is treating you as children; for what child is there whom a parent does not discipline?' (Heb. 12: 5–7). Most pre-modern cultures were, for the good of the child, rigorously strict. God's permission of suffering was treated as analogous. If 'discipline always seems painful rather than pleasant at the time', 'later it yields the peaceful fruit of righteousness' (Heb. 12: 11).

This focus on the benefit of endurance explains why in earlier Christian tradition suffering generally needed no justification. If it did, the same approach could be extended to provide the explanation: this world was meant to be a vale of tears in which we were to be educated morally. Thus, for *Origen, the problem of life's inequities required no explanation. In the *Platonic environment in which he sought a Christian answer, it was natural to presuppose the eternity of the *soul. In fact he argued for the eternity of *creation on the grounds that the unchangeable God could not change and become creator. But this eternal creation was spiritual. The material world was created subsequently when spiritual creatures fell from grace. It was intended as a school for sinners, to discipline and train fallen souls back to rationality and goodness. One's lot in life related to one's training needs. God's *anger was then explicable by *analogy: like a doctor God inflicts pain only to heal. Suffering fitted well into disciplining the body and freeing the soul from the material and fleshly. While some of Origen's ideas did not prove acceptable in the long run, much of Christian history has been shaped by such an other-worldly perspective. Monks and *ascetics across the centuries in east and west have regarded self-inflicted suffering as a means of spiritual discipline.

For John Hick the explanation of suffering lies along similar lines. Against a background of evolutionary thinking, he argues that the purpose of life in this world is 'soul-making'. If created beings were freely to love God, they had to be put at an 'epistemic distance', otherwise God would be overpowering and moral *freedom illusory. So again the universe appears school-like. The *Fall was the condition of human moral growth (here Hick draws on a notion found in Irenaeus—*Adam was an innocent child who had to learn from mistakes); *sin, pain, and suffering emerge as essential components in God's ultimate purpose. Suffering has a teleological role. It is a learning experience.

The analogy with parental discipline is telling. Children whose parents do not expect the best of them, or who grow up undisciplined, apparently have enormous disadvantages. Judgement may well be the reverse side of *love's coin. Furthermore human life is enhanced by challenges: to climb Everest or sail around the world people surmount remarkable levels of pain and hardship. Suffering contributes to character-building. Indeed, a classic distinction in Christian thought was that between moral and physical *evils. The only thing that really counted as evil was sin; physical evils, being either punishment for sin or a means of moral refinement, were not problematic. Famine, earthquake, illness, disability—all were to be accepted as God's judgement or discipline. If the purpose of God is 'soul-making', Hick argues, this must be the only kind of world which could bring about what God intended. Unjust and innocent suffering he justifies on these grounds: no *compassion is felt for one whose suffering results from just and deserved *punishment, yet compassionate love and self-giving for others constitutes the highest value of all; so love requires that suffering be innocent.

But how unfair! The classic example of this reaction of protest is already found in the book of *Job. Job's comforters advance the common wisdom, urging him to repent on the grounds that his suffering in itself shows he cannot be innocent. Job resists this interpretation of his suffering. He protests and argues, begging God to come and vindicate him. But when God does eventually appear, it seems as if Job is simply cowed into submission. Furthermore the narrative within which the dialogues are framed reasserts the view Job so eloquently challenges: God is depicted as allowing Satan to test Job's loyalty, which is then rewarded at the end by a restoration of his fortunes. Many modern readers find the book deeply unsatisfying.

The traditional link between sin and suffering has damaging repercussions, especially when simplistically applied to individuals. Did *Jesus not refuse to make this connection? 'His disciples asked him, "Rabbi, who sinned, this man or his parents, that he was born blind?" Jesus answered, "Neither this man nor his parents sinned: he was born blind so that God's works might be revealed in him"' (John 9: 2–3). But that too seems unfair: why should the man have endured years of suffering just so that Jesus could wave a magic wand? In any case, in the gospels in general, the connection is still implicitly there—Jesus forgives the sins of the paralytic before healing him (Mark 2: 1–12 and parallels); and healing is apparently impossible without faith. These stories can be used to oppress people with disabilities and illnesses: it is their own fault they are in the condition they are in, or they simply do not have enough faith! Nor does the traditional link prove acceptable when it comes to mass suffering, such as the Lisbon earthquake or the Holocaust: the people who were destroyed had no chance of learning from what happened or being morally improved. Is it any wonder that the notion that suffering is either a discipline or a punishment has been increasingly treated as morally repugnant and inadequate as an answer to the problem?

Suffering generates horror in the spectator, not just compassion, and it may prove nothing but destructive for those affected. Yet for participants it may have a deeply ambiguous, indeed mysterious, quality. It may prove a profound challenge to *faith, a reason for atheism, a source of protest and anger, if not against God, certainly against the optimistic theodicy outlined above. On the other hand, it may become the occasion of revelation, the generator of deeper insights into the way in which God is imaged in *humanity through the suffering Christ, and the context in which the fruits of the *Spirit are harvested (Gal. 5: 22–3). This necessitates the observation that Christian thought about suffering cannot be reduced to explaining it away, in however philosophically sophisticated a way. It must rather embrace the fact that suffering lies at the heart of its formative story.

Central to Christianity is Christ's crucifixion, the story of an absolutely innocent person suffering the most extreme form of capital punishment in a context of brutal foreign oppression. How can this possibly be justified by philosophical arguments like those advanced? In fact neither the NT nor Christian doctrine asks that question. Christ is not seen as disciplined or improved by his suffering. Rather his suffering redeems others.

*Atonement through the *cross of Christ must be the starting-point rather than a postscript. The cross redeems humanity from all the 'gonewrongness' of the universe, and this must include not just sin and moral evil, but other kinds of impairment, disability, and suffering. At the very least sufferers have found it possible to believe that the story points to compassionate understanding and experience within the Godhead itself. Furthermore, the suffering of Christ has been exemplary, encouraging believers to endure in *hope, and in the belief that ultimately all will be well. But above all sufferers have been affirmed as bearing the image of God in Christ. If the story of the blind man is set in the whole context of *John's gospel, it is not so much that Jesus waves a magic wand, but that as the *light of the world he enters into the very depth of darkness on the cross and transforms the darkness into light; for this is the hour of glory. The Christian approach to suffering must be by way of atonement.

On the cross Jesus cried out, 'My God, my God, why hast thou forsaken me?' God was absent and yet supremely present. Beginning from the cross, we may gain a different perspective on creation. For, as Simone *Weil observed, creation was itself an act of abandonment. If the infinite divine being is to allow anything to exist that is other than itself, it has to 'withdraw', making space for the 'other', risking exclusion while remaining an enfolding presence and the ultimate condition of any existence at all. Paradoxically, the suffering attendant upon God's absence is necessarily built into the created order. On the cross, God took responsibility for creating such a world by bearing the pain and entering the darkness.

So in Christian thought the redemptive possibilities of suffering outweigh its problematic or educative character.

Frances Young

Fiddes, Paul, *The Creative Suffering of God* (1988).
Hauerwas, Stanley, *Suffering Presence* (1988).
Hick, John, *Evil and the God of Love* (1966).
Moltmann, Jürgen, *The Power of the Powerless* (1983).
Sölle, Dorothee, *Suffering* (1975).
Surin, Kenneth, *Theology and the Problem of Evil* (1986).
Young, Frances, *Face to Face: A Narrative Essay in the Theology of Suffering* (1990).

suicide is the intentional killing of oneself. Intention is crucial in distinguishing it from dangerous activities and forms of self-sacrifice that might be described as suicidal, but whose primary motive is not self-destruction, and that have generally been commended by Christians. *Martyrdom represents the summit of *faith, suicide the nadir of despair.

Intentions, however, are not always clear, nor is the distinction between martyrdom and suicide always unequivocal. The death of *Jesus can in no way be described as suicide, but alongside his shrinking from *death there is also evidence of his intention to die—'laying down his life for his friends'. Captain Oates, walking out into the Antarctic snow on Scott's expedition in 1912, has been much admired for his role in inviting his own death for the sake of his companions (to prevent his frostbite from delaying them). In public suicides designed to draw attention to some deeply felt cause, the intention to die and the implementation of it could not be clearer or more direct, but despite this the language of faith and martyrdom can sometimes seem more appropriate than the language of despair and suicide.

These are extreme and special cases. It is increasingly common, though, for the ambivalence of intention to be acknowledged as a mitigating factor in most instances of suicide. The prevalence of attempted suicide, interpreted as a cry for help rather than a wish to die, raises questions about the number of suicides that may inadvertently have gone too far. There may be psychological or social factors, such as depression, stress, or intolerable circumstances, which reinforce the reluctance to indulge in moral condemnation. The exceptions are when the intention is obvious, rational, and dishonourable, as in the attempt to escape the consequences of a crime. The many coroners' verdicts which add 'while of unsound mind' are evidence of sympathetic public attitudes, as is the 1961 British legislation which, with broad Christian approval, decriminalized suicide.

The traditional Christian condemnation of suicide took shape in a very different social context. *Augustine, who set out the classic arguments in his *City of God* (Book 1), was facing a culture, parts of which regarded suicide as honourable, even in some circumstances admirable. He was writing for Christians tempted to despair at the break-up of the civilized world as they knew it, and he needed to explain why the church honoured martyrs but not suicides. His starting-point was the commandment 'thou shalt not kill', a prohibition that applies no less to ourselves than to the killing of others. To love our neighbours as ourselves implies a proper self-love, that may only be overridden at the direct command of God. There is also a proper fortitude required of Christians, and killing oneself because one has been defiled or abused merely compounds the sin.

Essentially the same arguments are used in most branches of the Christian church today, though usually with greater sensitivity towards the likelihood of diminished responsibility, and without the penalties, such as the refusal of burial in consecrated ground, that previously expressed religious condemnation. To commit suicide with full intention is to lose *hope in God's love, and to that extent to reject God. It is also to place a burden of guilt on relatives and friends, who may see it as a rejection of themselves and of their inadequate attempts to help. The provision of alternative help through counselling services like the Samaritans in the UK has been much praised as a constructive, Christian-inspired response to tragic, and often pitiful, situations.

As in Augustine's day, there are those who commend suicide as the supreme example of self-determination, and this is one of the value judgements that undergird the demand for *euthanasia. There are also latter-day romantics who, like their poetic predecessors, see a peculiar glory in living self-destructively and dying young. The mass suicides in some *apocalyptic sects seem to be expressions of idiosyncratic beliefs about the end of time.

John Habgood

Battin, M., *Ethical Issues in Suicide* (1982).
Varah, C., *The Samaritans* (1984).

Sunday is the principal day of Christian *worship, a day known by several names that reveal its importance and meanings.

Selection of the day is believed to have been done by the Lord himself, for on it he arose from the dead, appeared to his disciples, and conferred the previously promised Spirit. The affiliation of the day with dominical events is reflected in the designation 'the day of the Lord's *Resurrection', first appearing in Tertullian (*On Prayer*, 23), and later abbreviated to 'Resurrection day'. 'The Lord's day' is older (cf. Rev. 1: 10) and associates the day with the central liturgical action of the Christian community: the *Eucharist or Lord's supper (1 Cor. 11: 20; cf. *Didache*, 14). Protestants, particularly those of the Reformed tradition, have preferred the expression 'Lord's Day' as the best indicator of the sacred quality of the day. The Latin form (*dies dominica*) lies behind common parlance for the day of the week (*dimanche*, etc.) in the Romance languages.

Two titles locate the Christian day within the structure of the Jewish seven-day week in which the Sabbath figures as the seventh and last day. There is evidence that early Christians assembled on the first day of the week (1 Cor. 16: 2; Acts 20: 7–12), though some communities apparently continued sabbath observances coupled with first-day prayer until the 4th century, after which seventh-day practices were gradually abandoned by the majority. The first day of the week, following the sequence in Genesis, was interpreted as the day on which, with Christ's Resurrection, a new light dawned, a new order had begun (2 Cor. 5: 17). The theme of new creation was strengthened by the association of the first day with the eschatological eighth day of Jewish *apocalyptic in which the seven days of creation received a millenarian explanation and expansion (cf. Ps. 90: 4). The eighth day, a day superseding the Sabbath, signalled the emergence of a new age. Christian writers from the 2nd century onwards explicitly connected their worship with the eighth day (e.g. *Epistle of Barnabas*, 15. 8–9; Justin Martyr, *Dialogue with Trypho*, 41; Basil, *On the Holy Spirit*, 27. 66), and the number eight, a symbol of completion and fullness, was also linked with *baptism as the new covenant's replacement of circumcision on the eighth day. Eighth-day symbolism has been rediscovered by the church periodically (displayed especially through octagonal architecture and furnishings) and was taken up in *Vatican II's *Constitution on the Sacred Liturgy* (106: *octava quaque die*).

The Christian day of worship did not immediately inherit the Jewish notion of sabbath rest. Civil and ecclesiastical legislation demanding abstention from *work on the day of worship was introduced in the 4th century and continued into the modern age

under the impetus of various *sabbatarian movements. The use of the term 'sabbath' as an equivalent to the 'Lord's Day' is largely a product of the *Reformation, one adopted predominantly by Calvinists and some evangelicals. A different meaning is intended by a few Christian bodies, such as the Seventh-Day *Adventists, whose employment of 'sabbath' refers to their worship on the Jewish Sabbath—Saturday.

The non-biblical term 'Sunday' originates from the Graeco-Roman custom of assigning to each day of the week one of the known planets; the second day of the planetary week was *dies solis*, the day of the sun, which became the first day of the Christian week. Christians of the patristic period capitalized on the solar metaphor in their evangelism, proclaiming through word and art the risen Lord as the 'sun of righteousness' and the 'light of the world'; and in their prayers they turned to the east in anticipation of his return.

Justin Martyr, who already in the mid-2nd century identifies the day of Christian assembly as 'Sunday', gives valuable testimony to the shape of Christian worship on that day: readings 'from the memoirs of the apostles or the writings of the prophets' are followed by an exposition of scripture and exhortation, corporate prayer, eucharistic offertory and prayer, distribution of communion, and the collection of alms for the poor (*First Apology*, 67). This primitive order constituted the basic outline for the subsequent development of Sunday worship, and served as a model for the 20th-century reclamation of the liturgical unity of word and sacrament.

Karen B. Westerfield Tucker

Bacchiocchi, S., *From Sabbath to Sunday* (1977).
Beckwith, R., and Stott, W., *This is the Day* (1978).
Carson, D. A. (ed.), *From Sabbath to Lord's Day* (1982).
Rordorf, W., *Sunday* (1962), ET (1968).

symbolism. The Greek verb from which the term is derived literally means to 'throw together'. The noun *sumbolon* meant the other half of a broken coin or piece of pottery which functioned as a token whereby a guest or ally could reclaim the rights of friendship or hospitality when the two participants next met. In early Christianity *creeds were referred to as 'symbols,' as indeed they still are in some modern European languages (e.g. German *Symbolik*). It is easiest to take this usage as derived from these signs of friendship, with the creeds functioning as the shared token of a common faith. Much more usual, though, is the sense of symbol as that which 'throws together' two different kinds of reality. In the religious case the encounter of the divine and human or earthly may be seen to raise at least seven major issues. Although the examples given are mainly from the 20th century, many of the disputes have strong historical antecedents.

Most basic of all is the question of whether there is any real encounter in one thing standing for another. The more extreme *Protestant view would be that, even if the symbols were divinely chosen, as is the case with *water for *baptism or *bread and *wine for *communion, the connection remains entirely arbitrary: as signs pointing elsewhere without intrinsic worth in themselves. At the other extreme lies the claim that symbols do afford real participation in the divine. Paul *Tillich attempted a mediating position by suggesting that symbols are essentially paradoxical, first offering and then qualifying participation. They differ fundamentally, though, from signs: these are like traffic directions to towns, which offer no sense of the town itself. A difficulty for the realist view is how to distinguish adequately between reverence for such symbols and their worship, which helps to explain the periodic bursts of *iconoclasm that have occurred in most religions, as with early Buddhist attacks on Hinduism, Sikh condemnation of Indian culture, or Islam of Christianity. Yet more realist approaches have usually eventually resurfaced. One might detect some analogy between the solemn way in which the bible is formally brought into church at the beginning of *Calvinist services and processions of the reserved sacrament in *Catholic churches. Similar realist tendencies can be observed in other word-orientated religions such as Judaism and Sikhism. Such moves could be read as sinful regressions, but it is hard to see how a *religion can function as such unless it offers some mediated (and thus symbolic) points of encounter with the divine.

A second and related issue is how the *bible's apparent endorsement of symbols is to be read. In understanding *Reformation attitudes, it is important not to confuse the issues of *sacrament and symbol, though they are closely allied. Both *Luther and *Calvin thought that the Lord's supper (*Eucharist) could mediate the believer's relation to Christ, for Luther through Christ's miraculous presence in association with the bread and wine, and for Calvin by the work of the *Holy Spirit uniting the believer with the exalted Christ in heaven. Where they differed from Roman Catholic thinking was in insisting that the symbols involved acquired no new status. Particularly for Calvin they were to be seen as an acted preaching of *God's promises, which were effected by other means, in the believer's heart. No special reverence was therefore due to the bread and wine outside the immediate context of the service; hence any surplus bread and wine, though consecrated, could be taken home for domestic consumption. Luther required a more reverential attitude, which is also reflected in his more positive attitude to the symbolism of the visual *arts.

Thirdly, one can ask whether any religious symbols are 'natural'. Clearly, in many, perhaps most, cases they are not. Whether one stands or kneels to pray, for instance, will depend on what meaning a particular culture attaches to such postures. The Inuit rub noses as a form of welcome, where westerners would shake hands. Yet seeing God as *creator might be taken to imply that it is part of divine *providence that the *world should carry with it certain readings, and so become another book alongside the bible, 'the book of nature' (an image as old as *Augustine).

Certainly, the height of heaven as a symbol of divine transcendence finds its echo in a number of languages (e.g. Sanskrit, Greek), where the word for 'god' was originally derived from that for 'heaven'. It is being recognized increasingly that Jewish *Temple symbolism has detailed parallels in other cultures. Émile Durkheim and Claude Lévi-Strauss sought to explain such phenomena in purely sociological terms, but some cultural *anthropologists have offered quite different views. Mircea Eliade, for instance, has made much of the human attempt to map microcosm against macrocosm, with sacred sites and festivals deliberately structured as significant points of intersection. Arnold van Gennep noted the virtual universality of initiation rites with their notion of liminality, the move over a threshold into a new form of existence. His work has been developed by Victor Turner who, like Mary Douglas, has

stressed the way in which symbols function as part of a larger social system, deriving their power in part from their ability to bear more than one meaning. That inevitably complicates the question of how much the meaning of any particular symbol comes from the way the world is (nature) and how much from social construction (culture). Yet one might note that Christianity's most basic symbols of water and *blood occur in most religions and with similar connotations. Thus, although water can sometimes be destructive, refreshment and cleansing are surely its two most basic and readily accessible features. Again, the virtual ubiquity of blood *sacrifice raises acute questions of how Christianity's own distinctive theology should be set in the context of this wider background.

A fourth issue concerns the extent to which symbols are dispensable. Lucien Lévy-Bruhl argued that they are part of 'a pre-logical mentality', and in this view he reflected a common *Enlightenment assumption. In the early 19th century *Hegel attempted a major defence, partly through widening the notion in a way that made all religious activity and thought symbolic, but it was a dubious compliment since he none the less insisted that primacy lay with the more abstract concepts of his own philosophy. Hamann (d. 1788) is therefore in some ways a more interesting rebel against the Enlightenment view. For him reality could not be adequately captured except through symbols, and in this he was followed by Herder (d. 1803) with his stress on poetry as the most adequate means of mapping our world (see ROMANTICISM). Similar claims were also canvassed by the Symbolist school of French poetry in the 19th century. Paul Verlaine, a member of the school, and Charles Baudelaire, who can be seen as a precursor of it, both made profound use of Christian symbolism and, particularly in Baudelaire's case, of its inversion.

In the 20th century the American philosopher Susan Langer used the contrast between symbolical and discursive modes of thought to legitimate the symbolical as an alternative mode of knowing. More common, though, as in the writings of Ernst Cassirer or Paul *Ricoeur, has been the claim that all thinking is to varying degrees symbolic. *Language can be seen to face issues very similar to those that confront more concrete symbols. In particular, the common claim that God cannot be adequately captured in language might then be viewed merely as part of a much wider issue about the nature of the world generally. So far as the history of language is concerned, it was once common to treat words as themselves realist symbols. This is seen clearly in Plato's dialogue *Cratylus*, and in the bible's treatment of the significance of the revelation of God's name (Exod. 3: 13–15).

That mention of language raises a fifth issue, the extent to which symbols can ever be seen to act in isolation. As *Wittgenstein emphasized, linguistic symbols seldom function purely by denotation, in a one-to-one correspondence. Rather, they work as part of some wider frame, what he called a 'language game'. Similarly, for Langer the syntax and vocabulary of *music is only intelligible when viewed in relation to a piece as a whole. Much the same might be said about more concrete symbols, whether objects or actions. No religious symbol can be properly understood unless due note is taken of its ritual context. So, for instance, an observer comprehends little if not informed as to why genuflection is made to bread in a church but not to a loaf at home even if a priest blesses it.

A sixth problem is the issue of multivalency. It seems that some cultures are much better than others at appreciating a variety of meanings in the same symbol. Nor is this necessarily anything to do with scientific attitudes to the world. For instance, the ancient Greeks appear to have moved from being largely aniconic in their approach to deity to a superfluity of representations in art. In the history of Christianity perhaps the late Middle Ages and Renaissance are the most marked in contrast to our own times. For us the lion is a symbol of strength and courage, but the Middle Ages added watchfulness (lions were thought to sleep with their eyes open), the resurrection (cubs were born dead until their father breathed on them), evil (cf. Psalm 91: 13), St Mark, and by association the city of Venice. Again, the medieval imagination plundered the OT, and especially the Song of Songs, to portray Mary as enclosed garden, burning bush, lily, fountain, and tower. Modern taste may prefer a Madonna and Child by Henry Moore to a Renaissance painting on the same theme partly because it rejects naturalism, but it may also be affected by resistance to an over-rich symbolic world: the ruined classical arch, Christ toying with a goldfinch, genitals exposed, a lamb playing, the human figures forming a triangle and so forth. Rules of *metaphor allow Christ to be both a rock and a lamb, but perhaps such metaphors are too quickly 'cashed', as though their only value lay in what they literally imply. If so, this might help explain why a proper appreciation of symbols is hampered by such strong resistance to the possibility of even superficial contradictions or apparent overload in meaning.

One last issue may be noted, relating to what theologians have come to label the problem of inculturation. Should different social settings legitimate alternative liturgical symbols? Might one, for example, use beer instead of wine? White wine has in fact been used in some Calvinist churches to counter particular views of eucharistic presence. The practice is not forbidden by Roman canon law, but some might argue that a price is paid, wherever the practice is allowed, in the loss of allusion to the colour of Christ's sacrificial blood. Yet symbols, if themselves unchanged, do in fact alter in their significance. In the Temple the menorah was originally taken as a symbol of God, and later of eternal life, while in medieval Judaism it came to represent the light of the Torah and the sciences that help support its study. Again, the water of baptism has for most of Christian history been taken as symbolic of the washing away of sin, but, as the notion of original sin has declined in popularity, so liturgies have given greater stress to water's still more primal significance as a fount of life.

David Brown

Chupungco, A. J., *Liturgical Inculturation* (1992).
Circlot, J. E., *A Dictionary of Symbolism* (1971).
Dillistone, F. W., *The Power of Symbols in Religion and Culture* (1986).
Dixon, D. W., *Images of Truth: Religion and the Art of Seeing* (1996).
Duchet-Suchaux, G., and Pastoureau, M. (eds.), *Flammarion Iconographic Guide: The Bible and the Saints* (1994).
Eliade, M., *Images and Symbols* (1961).
Farley, E., *Deep Symbols: Their Postmodern Effacement and Reclamation* (1996).
Freedberg, D., *The Power of Images* (1989).
Goodenough, E. R., *Jewish Symbols in the Greco-Roman World* (1953); rev. edn. (1988).
Keel, O., *The Symbolism of the Biblical World* (1978).
Olson, A. M., *Myth, Symbol and Reality* (1980).
Rahner, K., *Theological Investigations* (1966), iv. 221–52.
Ricœur, P., *The Symbolism of Evil* (1967).
Ryken, L., Wilhoit, J. C., and Longman, T. (eds.), *Dictionary of Biblical Images* (1998).

Synoptic Gospels, see MATTHEW; MARK; LUKE–ACTS; GOSPELS.

Syriac Christian thought.

Syriac is a dialect of Aramaic originating in the region of Edessa, now the city of Urfa in south-eastern Turkey. In the early Christian era, it emerged as the lingua franca over a wide area of the eastern Roman empire, the Persian empire, and beyond. It remains a living *language among Christian communities in what is now Syria, Lebanon, south-eastern Turkey, Israel, Iraq, and Iran, and a liturgical language for a sizeable Christian population in south India. Its greatest theological writings were produced between the 4th and 7th centuries, followed by an extraordinary flowering of *mysticism between the 7th and 10th centuries. Western Christians have tended to interpret Christian history through the paradigms of Greek east and Latin west. Syriac Christianity represents a third Christian tradition, one equally ancient but one whose expressions and experiences do not fit those familiar in the west.

Syriac Christian thought found much of its finest articulation in the poetic works of such writers as Ephrem of Nisibis ('the Harp of the Holy Spirit', d. 373), a poet without peer in any Christian language for many centuries, Narsai (d. 502), and Jacob of Serug ('the Flute of the Holy Spirit', d. 521). Whether hymns, verse homilies, or rhythmic prose, *poetry was often the favoured mode of religious reflection for Syriac writers, where Greek and Latin patristic thinkers chose philosophical treatises of a more analytical nature. In the elusive and allusive wordplay of poetry, the startling insights of *metaphor, *paradox, and *symbol, Syriac writers sought to glimpse the divine rather than to define or limit its meaning. From the earliest Syriac texts through the great mystics, one finds a distinctive and powerful understanding of the *Holy Spirit. Because the Syriac term for spirit, *ruha*, is grammatically feminine (as the Hebrew, *ruah*), early Syriac writers generally treated the Holy Spirit as feminine just as they referred to God and Christ in the masculine. Where Greek and Latin writers occasionally employed gendered images when speaking of the divine, in early Syriac texts the understanding of the Holy Spirit as feminine, based within the linguistic structure of the language itself, led to substantive theological developments. However, while no reference to the change survives, after 400 the Spirit in Syriac literature appears almost exclusively in masculine terms. The change occurred in the post-Nicene era when the church throughout its geographical expanse sought greater conformity in doctrinal language and practice. Perhaps the earlier Syriac tradition seemed too discordant in such a climate—a haunting constraint upon the diversity of ancient Christian spirituality.

Yet the Holy Spirit in Syriac thought continued to provide the activity most vividly linking Christian devotional practice with liturgical action and biblical event, an interplay stressed throughout Syriac literature. Thus one finds Syriac writers using the same lexical terms to indicate the action of the Holy Spirit over the waters of *creation, upon *Mary at the Annunciation, upon Christ at the baptism in the Jordan, and upon the disciples at *Pentecost; the same again upon the believer at *baptism, upon the bread and wine at the *epiclesis* (consecration) of the *Eucharist, and upon the heart of the faithful Christian in *prayer.

The rich identification between bible, liturgy, and devotional life also underlies the most notorious aspect of Syriac Christianity, its pervasive and sometimes severe ascetical *spirituality. Yet the extremes of Syrian *asceticism are part of a larger spectrum, in which the individual believer portrayed in bodily actions a symbolism in accordance with that of Syriac poetic theology. From our earliest texts a basic ascetic orientation was expected of every believer: simplicity in food and clothing, *celibacy or *chastity in marriage, care for the poor and sick. By the 3rd century, there emerged a consecrated lay order, the Sons and Daughters of the Covenant (or Covenanters), who took vows of celibacy and *poverty, and devoted themselves to the service of the church community under the direction of priests or bishops; they maintained a visible presence until at least the 10th century. When *monasticism developed over the course of the 4th century as a separated location for devotional practice, in the Syriac realm it did so in close interaction with town and village parishes, and churches in cities. As the 4th-century Syriac writer Aphrahat admonished, care for the sick and poor was also a practice of *prayer—a practice without which prayer was not truly offered.

Syriac ascetic tradition is striking for the tireless immersion of its monks and nuns in service to the poor, oppressed, sick, and suffering of their day. As Christ had done, so too the ascetic battled hunger and weariness in the *body through such disciplines as *fasting and vigils, while ministry to the poor and sick fought against the suffering and injustice of the fallen world. The body both individual and collective could be forged anew, healed, and restored as Christ's own body in its resurrected reality. In the pure prayer taught by the mystics, the body of the ascetic became the church sanctuary, the heart the altar, the tears the incense offered upon the altar. The ascetic body and the ecclesial body could be seen to be one and the same.

The powerfully imagistic theological and ascetic traditions of Syriac Christianity drew upon the metaphorical possibilities of language and behaviour. Both expressions relied upon a sense that divine and human realms are interactive, that spiritual and physical realms are not opposed or incompatible, but rather that human experience in the physical realm is permeated with divine presence and activity. Thus one finds a marked celebration of nature and creation by Syriac writers. In Syriac tradition, there are two books of scripture: the bible itself, and the natural world. Syriac writers delighted to seek God's presence in every nook and cranny of nature, to see God's mark engraved on every aspect of the created order. There was an *ecological celebration that still astounds the reader's senses. Such a sensibility pervaded even the most severe of Syriac ascetic writings, and thus warns against any simplistic charge of *dualistic tendencies. The physical mattered in Syriac Christianity in all its aspects: the body, its actions, the world we inhabit, both civic and natural. To understand its fallen state was also to heed the promise of redeemed existence.

Syriac Christianity is sometimes known for rejecting the theological developments of the Greek east and Latin west. In truth, the heated *christological controversies of the 5th century led to a tragic splintering of Syriac Christianity into separate church families: the Church of the East ('Nestorians'), the Syrian Orthodox (Jacobites or 'Monophysites'), and the Antiochian Orthodox ('Melkites'), each of these families also subsequently dividing into further denominations. Western names for these churches have derogatorily implied heretical status. Yet modern scholarship and the efforts of ecumenism have demonstrated that these traditions grew out of serious christological debates, in which differences in theological terminology and discourse were wrongly interpreted. In the current context of fresh reconsideration, the different Syriac churches provide important correctives in the development of christological doctrine. A further legacy of the divisive theological battles of the 5th and 6th centuries can be seen in Syriac literature itself. From the 6th century onwards, Syriac writers increasingly conform their style, presentation, and terminology to the dictates of Greek philosophical and theological discourse. At their best, Syriac writers like Philoxenus of Mabbug (d. 523) and Isaac the Syrian (late 7th century) combined Semitic and Hellenic traditions to yield a vibrant synthesis. After the 7th century, an even more powerful influence was exerted with the development of Islam, and Christian Arabic in response. Yet Syriac Christian thought preserved its most characteristic aspects in the continuing richness of its liturgical traditions, as well as continuing devotion to the writings of its poets and mystics. Throughout its history, Syriac has been the language of a cultural or religious minority. The brilliance of its Christian thought, produced above all in its first millennium, has been the expression of Christian peoples without the power of kingdoms or empires to further their cause.   **Susan Ashbrook Harvey**

Brock, S. P., 'Mary in Syriac Tradition', in A. Stacpoole (ed.), *Mary's Place in Christian Dialogue* (1982).

—— *The Syriac Fathers on Prayer and the Spiritual Life* (1987).

—— *The Luminous Eye: The Spiritual World Vision of Saint Ephrem the Syrian*, rev. edn. (1992).

Griffith, S. H., 'Asceticism in the Church of Syria: The Hermeneutics of Early Syrian Monasticism', in V. L. Wimbush and R. Valantasis (eds.), *Asceticism* (1995).

Harvey, S. A., 'Feminine Imagery for the Divine: The Holy Spirit, the Odes of Solomon, and Early Syriac Tradition', *St. Vladimir's Theological Quarterly*, 37 (1993).

Moffatt, S. H., *A History of Christianity in Asia*, i. *Beginnings to 1500* (1992).

Murray, R., *Symbols of Church and Kingdom: A Study in Early Syriac Tradition* (1975).

Nedungatt, G., 'The Covenanters of the Early Syriac-Speaking Church', *Orientalia Christiana Periodica*, 39 (1973).

Segal, J. B., *Edessa: The Blessed City* (1970).

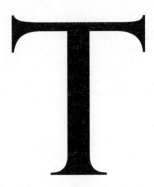

Taizé is an ecumenical community of Christian brothers based at the village of that name near Cluny, France. The community has become famous for hospitality, *liturgy, *ecumenism, and *reconciliation.

Taizé's history of hospitality began during the Second World War when its founder, Roger Schutz, a Swiss Protestant, bought a house there and gave refuge to Jews and others fleeing the Nazis. Betrayal forced him back to Switzerland until after the liberation of France in 1944, when he returned with a small group of companions. The house now welcomed German prisoners-of-war, thus beginning its role of reconciliation.

In the 1960s, the numbers of *pilgrims increased dramatically. The community built a large church that became a gathering place for many young Christians, Europeans at first, for whom Taizé was particularly important during the late 1960s, a time of youth unrest, waning commitment to traditional denominations, and East–West tension. The community provided a symbolic focus in a renewed search for *spiritual roots, ecumenism, and *peace.

Taizé's simple and effective liturgy is based on traditional elements: readings, silence, intercessions, psalms, and chants. The chants have become internationally famous: their simplicity, brevity (allowing for atmospheric repetition), and pleasant harmonies make them suitable for ecumenical or lay-led worship. Various languages are used for the chants: an important feature of a visit to Taizé is that pilgrims sing and hear readings in several tongues other than their own.

Taizé had an ecumenical dimension from the very beginning, when Brother Roger dedicated himself to reconciling the *Catholic and *Protestant traditions. The community avoided the denominational basis of most religious orders, but by its very nature developed close, friendly ties with Roman Catholic and Anglican traditions and others, in addition to the Reformed and Lutheran churches from which its early members were drawn.

Taizé's commitment to reconciliation in the churches is part of a larger commitment to worldwide peace. In various countries, the community has smaller houses of brothers; the French-based brothers also travel periodically in order to live amongst disadvantaged communities, and there has been a close link with the work of Mother *Teresa of Calcutta.

Two important undertakings mark Taizé's recent history. They testify to the ability of the community to influence thousands of Christians worldwide. From the 1970s, large-scale youth meetings were arranged in many countries. These encourage participation especially by minority and marginalized groups. In the 1980s, the 'Pilgrimage of Trust on Earth' was launched, in which pilgrims visit areas of intense community conflict in order to help with work towards reconciliation.

Inspired by the charismatic figure of Brother Roger, Taizé integrates the traditional work of a religious order with new challenges and concerns, such as international peace-making and the youth culture. By so doing, it has created a new model of Christian community for the modern world.   **Chris Maunder**

Balado, J. L. Gonzalez, *The Story of Taizé*, ET (1988).
Brother Roger of Taizé, *No Greater Love: Sources of Taizé*, ET (1991).
Spink, Kathryn, *A Universal Heart: The Life and Vision of Brother Roger of Taizé* (1986).

Teilhard de Chardin, Pierre (1881–1955), a French *Jesuit, was a distinguished scientist of human origins, a fervent Christian *mystic, and a prolific religious writer. Throughout his life he reflected on the meaning of the Christian gospel in the light of modern *science, especially in relation to *evolutionary theory. Born in the volcanic Auvergne in central France into an ancient noble family, and related to Voltaire, he was deeply influenced by his natural environment. Brought up in a traditional Catholic milieu marked by a vibrant faith and strong religious practice, Teilhard was endowed with a deeply pantheistic and mystical orientation, evident from his earliest years. His mystical bent and devotional life, including veneration of the Sacred Heart of Jesus and devotion to Our Lady, were much influenced by the saintly figure of his mother, whereas his scientific interests were initially stimulated by his father, who encouraged his children to collect fossils, stones, and other specimens from nature, thus laying the foundation for Teilhard's scientific studies and career.

After an excellent classical and scientific education at a Jesuit boarding school Teilhard entered the Jesuit novitiate at the age of eighteen. He was torn between his passionate love for God and his equally passionate love for understanding the natural world. He resolved this personal crisis by recognizing that he could combine his search for spiritual perfection with that for greater knowledge and understanding. When the Jesuits were exiled from France, Teilhard continued his theological studies in the south of England, at Hastings (1902–5 and 1908–12), where he was ordained in 1911. From 1905 to 1908 he taught physics and chemistry in a Jesuit school in Cairo where he first discovered his great attraction to the *desert and the east.

It was in Hastings, after reading Bergson's *Creative Evolution*, that Teilhard arrived at his understanding of the meaning of evolution for the Christian faith. Evolution made him see the world anew. All becoming is immersed in a stream of evolutionary creation where every reality is animated by a 'christic element', and the heart of God is found at the heart of the world. The living world discloses itself as an all-encompassing 'cosmic, christic, and divine milieu'. His mystical experiences were followed by scientific studies in Paris, interrupted by the outbreak of the First World War, during which he served as a stretcher-bearer. There he discovered the diversity and powerful tensions of a 'human milieu' not encountered before, an experience that laid the foundations for his future speculations about the oneness of *humanity. Almost daily encounters with *death gave him an extraordinary sense of urgency to leave an 'intellectual testament' to communicate his vision of the world which, with all its turmoil, struggle, and becoming, he saw as animated by and drawn up towards God. Thus he wrote a series of deeply stirring personal essays interspersed with prayers and powerful confessions of faith, published only after his death as *Writings in Time of War*. These relatively little-known essays contain the seeds for all his further writings.

After the war, he obtained a doctorate for his scientific research and was appointed to a lectureship in geology at the Institut Catholique in Paris. This gave him a platform to propound his ideas about evolution and the Christian faith, which soon led him into difficulties with the church, difficulties that never went away, but increased throughout his life. In 1923 he was glad to take up an invitation to join another Jesuit researcher on a fossil expedition to the Ordos desert in China. This year in the Far East was another decisive experience that shaped much of the rest of his life. It also led to the writing of 'The Mass on the World'. Inspired by the vision of the world at dawn transfigured by the rising sun, it expresses a mystical and sacramental offering of the entire cosmos to the energy, *fire, power, and presence of the divine *Spirit.

Over the following years his position in Paris grew more difficult, so that China became a place of exile where he spent the greatest part of his scientific career (1926–46), regularly interspersed with expeditions and travels in east and west. It was in China that he wrote most of his essays and also his two books, *Le Milieu Divin* (1927), and *The Phenomenon of Man* (1938–40). The latter is his best-known, but probably most difficult work, published posthumously. It immediately became a best-seller.

After the Second World War, Teilhard returned to Paris where his situation in regard to the church was still so difficult that he decided to accept a research post in the United States. Lonely and marked by suffering, he spent the last four years of his life mostly in New York, where he died on Easter Sunday 1955. He left a large corpus of writings, but, whereas his scientific papers were published during his lifetime, his religious and philosophical works were banned in his lifetime and became widely known only years later.

Life and thought are closely interwoven in Teilhard's work, which draws integrally on the experiential, emotional, and rational sides of the human being. His central method consists of a combination of outer and inner seeing, leading to a profound transformation of the world as seen, so that *seeing more* also implies *being more*. He often speaks about this 'seeing', especially in *The Phenomenon of Man*. Such seeing involves all the detailed knowledge of the outer world that science has to offer, but combined with a unifying inner vision. Teilhard's vision brought together cosmic, human, and divine dimensions, all centred in Christ and all involved in a process of becoming, or genesis. Whereas cosmogenesis refers to the birth of the cosmos, anthropogenesis and noogenesis refer to the specifically human dimension and the birth of thought. All these processes of growth are studied by modern science, whereas Christogenesis or the birth of God in Christ, as an event of cosmic significance, can only be seen through the eyes of faith. For Teilhard cosmic and human evolution are moving onwards to an ever fuller disclosure of the Spirit, culminating in 'Christ-Omega', because the divine spirit is involved in the evolutionary process at every stage.

This rise is not automatic; its outcome can never be taken for granted. It involves human responsibility and co-creativity, so that Teilhard's mind was much exercised by the moral and *ethical responsibilities for shaping the future of humanity and the planet. He enquired into the spiritual resources needed to create a better quality of life and greater human integration. The heritage of the different world faiths is most important in this context. Human beings are fully responsible for their own further self-evolution, for a higher social and cultural development and a greater unification of the human community, but ultimately these goals are only achievable through the power of *love. Central to his thinking were the ideas of the 'noosphere' and the 'divine milieu'. While interrelated, the first can be seen as belonging to a more secular, the second to a religious context. Given our modern scientific and technological developments, especially in information and media technology, one can see that Teilhard's idea of the noosphere (or sphere of mind) as a layer of thinking and interacting that connects people around the whole globe marks a new stage in human evolution. But the noosphere is not only a thinking layer; it is also an active sphere of love, creating greater bonds of unity between individuals and groups. The model of the noosphere provides a particularly creative perspective on racial, cultural, and religious pluralism in the new context of global complexity. Using an organic metaphor Teilhard sees Christianity, and especially the Catholic Church, as a 'phylum' channelling the unitive power of love. He was convinced that we must study the power of love in the same way that we study all other forces in the world.

Teilhard's *spirituality, a unique blend of science, religion, and mysticism, was forged through much suffering and loss, yet centred on the presence of divine love disclosed through the *Incarnation, creating a 'divine milieu' where God's presence shines through all things. He possessed a deep, intimate love of the human *Jesus and the Christ of the *cross and *Resurrection. A profound panchristic mysticism was the core of his faith and the centre of his worship. As he often used the images of fire and heart, drawn from the bible and the Christian mystics, one can describe his spirituality as a fire and heart mysticism, at once modern and ancient. In its affirmation of and openness to the world as God's *creation it belongs to the kataphatic rather than apophatic type of Christian mysticism. It expresses a creation spirituality 'that acknowledges love as the clearest understanding we have of God, of ourselves, of history, and the cosmos' (David Tracy).

Teilhard spoke of the 'three natures' of Christ: the human, divine, and cosmic. His reflections on the universal, cosmic Christ contain elements for a further development of *christology, never presented in fully systematic form. The 'apostle of the cosmic Christ', as he once described himself, held such a dynamic, innovative, and at the same time faithful view of Christianity that he provided the outlines for a new interpretation of the Christian faith in the modern world. But traditional Christians often find his ideas challenging and unsettling. During his lifetime the Catholic Church found it difficult to accept the scientific teaching on evolution, especially regarding human origins, which contradicted the biblical stories of human creation and the *Fall. It was an early paper on original sin, reinterpreted in the light of evolution, which first brought Teilhard into trouble. Several church authorities dealt rather harshly with him, but he experienced much loyal support and friendship from some members of his order, especially Henri *de Lubac and René d'Ouince, his long-time superior, who described the vicissitudes of Teilhard's life as those of 'a prophet on trial' in the church of his time. He also had much support from several women friends, especially his cousin Marguerite Teillard-Chambon and Lucile Swan.

Teilhard's ideas had some influence on *Vatican II and helped to shape some of its documents, especially *Gaudium et Spes*. Less hostile than before, the Catholic Church has in recent years acknowledged his contribution to Christian life and thought on several occasions. But in spite of the great interest in Teilhard's ideas during the 1960s, he has not been sufficiently valued among Christians, nor have his important ideas been adequately debated and critically evaluated in mainstream academic and intellectual life. Yet like his countryman *Pascal before him, Teilhard attempted to provide an explanation of the Christian faith for the liveliest minds of his age: a modern *apologetic, bringing science, religion, and mysticism together. Often his ideas are cited out of context, and the full extent of his work, most of which is out of print in English, is known and properly appreciated by relatively few. Some critics have accused him of being a *New Age prophet, but this completely ignores the profoundly Christian core of his vision.

What is Teilhard's legacy for Christian thought today? He did not create a great doctrinal synthesis in the manner of traditional theologians but rather provided seminal elements for developing theological and philosophical thinking in new directions. It is his diversity and complexity which many find disconcerting. His work contains challenging reflections on God and the world, the figure of Christ, science and religion, on *ecological responsibilities, interfaith encounter, the greater unification of humanity, the place of the feminine and of love in creating greater unity, and the central importance of spirituality and mysticism in religious life. His new mysticism of action is directed to both the creative transformation of the outer and inner world and the deepest communion with the living God of love, intimately present throughout creation. More than anything else it is his powerful affirmation of the Incarnation and his vision of the universal, cosmic Christ within an evolutionary perspective that reaffirm the core of the Christian faith for our scientific age.   **Ursula King**

Teilhard de Chardin, P., *The Phenomenon of Man* (1959).
—— *Le Milieu Divin* (1960).
—— *The Future of Man* (1964).
—— *Writings in Time of War* (1968).
—— *Science and Christ* (1968).
—— *Human Energy* (1969).
—— *Christianity and Evolution* (1971).
—— *The Heart of Matter* (1978).
—— *Pierre Teilhard de Chardin: Writings Selected with an Introduction by Ursula King* (1999).
Cuénot, C., *Teilhard de Chardin: A Biographical Study* (1965).
de Lubac, H., *The Religion of Teilhard de Chardin* (1967).
King, Th. M., and Wood Gilbert, M. (eds.), *The Letters of Teilhard de Chardin and Lucile Swan* (1993).
King, U., *Spirit of Fire: The Life and Vision of Teilhard de Chardin* (1996).
—— *Christ in All Things: Exploring Spirituality with Teilhard de Chardin* (1997).
Lyons, J. A., *The Cosmic Christ in Origen and Teilhard de Chardin* (1982).
Zaehner, R. C., *Evolution in Religion: A Study in Sri Aurobindo and Pierre Teilhard de Chardin* (1971).

temperance was a virtue among the ancient Greeks. It had overtones of 'nothing too much', of the *Platonic charioteer keeping unruly passions in order, and, perhaps particularly, of Stoic self-control. It was seen at its best in upper-class males. Christianized, it seemed an appropriate quality for bishops (see PASTORAL EPISTLES). As one of the four cardinal *virtues, it was routinely discussed by systematic thinkers, and ranked higher than fortitude. A temperate personality, like a temperate climate, is full of varied and understated delights. Like truth, it is nuanced and can live with shades of grey.

Zeal is intemperate, and quite often leads Christians to hate their ordinary animal appetites. So sometimes talking of temperance loosens Christian behaviour. Pleasures are allowed in moderation that a *Puritan might purge. Good-tempered moralizing Christians of the 18th century liked the word, which did not stop many of them eating too much.

In the 19th century temperance became a matter of stopping people getting drunk. Moral theologians feel their word was stolen from them, and seem almost to gloat in reporting how completely the 'temperance movement' was defeated. In fact the war on drink was often impressive, had some excellent side-effects, and remains instructive.

Among the thousands of do-gooding societies of the early 19th century there were some for suppressing drunkenness. These were middle-class, attacking spirits, but seeing beer as a 'temperance drink'. They were startled and hostile when a working-class movement emerged in the 1830s, from Preston in Lancashire, of teetotallers (named possibly from a stammered 't-t-total abstainer'). The parallel American Temperance Union was founded in 1836. Teetotallers recognized alcohol as a dangerous drug, and hence tried to reverse strong social conventions prescribing alcoholic drinks. They also recognized drunks as prisoners of an addiction, and were kinder to them than the temperate reformers were. This was a successful mass movement, distinctly akin to religious revival. Temperance meetings were fun. By 1844 five and a half million had signed the pledge for Fr. Mathew in Ireland, and whiskey sales had dropped by more than half. In 1846 the state of Maine went dry. The movement failed perhaps because it was too near the churches. Both sides have had reason to regret that teetotalism became a badge of Methodism. Support from bishops, and cardinals, can be a mixed blessing. The policy of catching them young, with the Band of Hope, founded in Leeds in 1846, also was two-edged.

One cannot sufficiently say how important the Women's Christian Temperance Union (1874) was for raising *women's consciousness and politicizing them. They worked by having 'pray-ins' around saloons. Frances Willard pushed outwards the movement's ambitions. Afterwards the women were elbowed aside by the Anti-Saloon League, but it is not by chance that the Eighteenth Amendment (Prohibition) took effect in 1920, the year of the Nineteenth Amendment (Votes for Women). The movements were interwoven.

Prohibition, a serious attempt to do good by law, failed. In practice, punitive taxation worked better. The drink lobby has prospered since. The prohibition temper has turned on cigarettes and recreational drugs. Intemperate temperance fills a need for Christians.   **Alistair Mason**

Blocker, J. S., Jr., *American Temperance Movements: Cycles of Reform* (1989).
Bordin, Ruth, *Women and Temperance* (1981).
Harrison, Brian, *Drink and the Victorians* (1971).

Temple, the.

From its inception, the Temple in *Jerusalem is seen as the dwelling-place of Israel's God but yet never his permanent dwelling. The trouble with temples is that what is built by human hands can be demolished by others. Plundered by successive invaders, in 587 BC the Temple was sacked and the site lay ruined until rebuilding began under Persian rule. This second Temple was remodelled in the grandest manner by Herod, but was finally destroyed by the Romans in 70. Yet Israel, unlike its neighbours, was able to survive these destructions of its central shrine. Ezekiel's visions in Babylon show that Israel's God is unconfined by space, and the elaborate vision of a restored Temple that ends Ezekiel (chs. 40–4) is not an architectural blueprint but an unbuildable ideal with cosmological and spiritual implications.

Even before the rise of Christianity, the Jerusalem Temple was controversial. The *prophets are at times highly critical of the abuses of the cult, though not necessarily of the Temple itself, but other later groups, such as the community at Qumran, seem to have rejected its priesthood as hopelessly tainted. By Jesus' day, regular worship for most Jews was conducted in the local synagogue. In the light of this, the gospel attitude to the Temple is almost surprisingly favourable. Jesus is received there with joy by Simeon and Anna and it is there that he stays to do his father's business. A climax of his ministry is the incident when he cleanses the Temple of merchants which can be read as an act of respect rather than an assault on the Temple itself. In Acts, the early church is recorded as meeting to worship in the Temple.

Yet Jesus also predicts the Temple's overthrow and at his crucifixion (see CROSS) the veil screening the Holy of Holies is ripped in half. The letter to the *Hebrews argues that the repeated *sacrifices to atone for sin in the earthly Temple have been superseded by the one final sacrifice of Jesus' crucifixion. The destruction in 70 was understood by many Christians as a confirmation of the divine rejection of the Jews. Jesus' declaration that he would restore the Temple in three days (John 2: 19) is explained as a reference to his own resurrected *body. The New Jerusalem of Revelation contains no temple, God's presence being immediate. This new understand-

ing is carried over to the *Eucharist by the early church. The divine presence is in the elements rather than any building. The parallel *metaphor of the community itself, and then of the individual believer's body, as Temple (1 Cor. 3: 16; 6: 19) has a powerful effect on later Christian *asceticism. Anything that might defile the body is taken as an insult to the *Holy Spirit.

The biblical descriptions of the Temple become translated into symbolic space, whose proportions and decorations become the subject of mystical contemplation by writers as varied as Bede (*de Templo*), Bunyan, and Herbert. Rather than its stones, the Temple's most enduring legacy is the book of *Psalms, probably compiled for use during the services of the second Temple.   **Hugh S. Pyper**

Barker, M., *The Gate of Heaven: The History and Symbolism of the Temple in Jerusalem* (1991).
Chilton, R., *Jesus in Context: Temple, Purity and Restoration* (1997).
Spatafora, A., *From the Temple of God to God as the Temple* (1994).

Temple, William

(1881–1944). More than any other single person, Temple represented the central thrust within Christianity's public concerns in the *twentieth century. He started at the top of the tree, his father, Frederick, being bishop of London when William was born, and archbishop of *Canterbury soon after. Temple was educated at Rugby School and Balliol College, Oxford, and went on to become a philosophy don at Queen's College and president of the Workers' Educational Association. He was always liberal-minded, good-natured, extremely hard-working, with a photographic memory and a considerable sense of *noblesse oblige*. Once certain doubts about the *Virgin Birth and the historical *Resurrection were resolved, he was ordained in 1908. In 1921 he became bishop of Manchester, in 1929 archbishop of York, and in 1942 archbishop of Canterbury. He died unexpectedly two years later. Few deaths of public figures in modern times appear to have affected people more. Temple's power lay in his ability to hold the confidence of both establishment and reformers. He was for many years a member of the Labour Party (withdrawing when appointed to Manchester) and R. H. Tawney, Labour's chief theorist in the construction of a non-Marxist *socialism, was a close friend. Temple appeared 'modern', 'enlightened', to outsiders in a way unique among senior ecclesiastical leaders: 'To a man of my generation', wrote Bernard Shaw, 'an archbishop of Temple's enlightenment was a realized impossibility.' Yet, unlike his more starkly prophetic contemporary, George Bell, bishop of Chichester, Temple shunned isolated positions. He could never be unpopular, but led in fields where, despite some opposition and incredulity, he could still represent something of a consensus. At Oxford, Temple came under the influence of Neo-Hegelian idealist philosophy. He saw himself as a philosophical theologian all his life, publishing a number of books of which the most important, mature, and least idealist is his Gifford Lectures, *Nature, Man, and God* (1934). Here he endeavoured to construct a 'synthesis' which, he admitted, would in some fundamental ways be nearer the medieval 'thesis' than the modern 'antithesis'. The map provided by *Aquinas, he claimed near the end of his life, needs correction but still provides 'our most hopeful line of advance'.

Social reform and the development of a Christian social conscience were no less important. In his last major book, *Christianity and Social Order* (1942), Temple argued the case once more with an eye on the revolution he hoped for after the war, basing his defence of Christian social responsibility especially on the concept of *natural law and edging forward from it to the conception of an economically fairer society, effectively the welfare state.

The *ecumenical movement was a third great concern, ever since his presence at the 1910 Edinburgh Missionary Conference. More than anyone else he was the steersman of the process whereby in 1937 a World Council of Churches was agreed upon. He then became first chairman of its Provisional Committee. Nothing Temple said has been more quoted than the reference in his enthronement sermon at Canterbury to 'the great new fact of our era', a worldwide ecumenical fellowship.

Especially in these three areas but in others too, notably the internal reform of the Church of England, Temple was the outstanding protagonist for a reconstructed 20th-century Christianity within the Protestant world, one open to the central convictions of medieval and Catholic theology, struggling to overcome the multitudinous divisions of denominationalism in a new ecumenism, and intent on the construction of a new social order, national and international. These were not, for Temple, separate domains, for all his life he sought an integrated 'general system of thought or map of the intellectual world'. His map was, throughout, a Christocentric one, focused on a Christ of *Incarnation rather than *redemption, a Christ who remained the voice with authority beyond, yet still responding to, the *natural theology and law of a created world (see CHRISTOLOGY).   **Adrian Hastings**

Hastings, A., 'William Temple', *The English Religious Tradition and the Genius of Anglicanism*, ed. Geoffrey Rowell (1992), 211–26.
Iremonger, F. A., *William Temple, Archbishop of Canterbury* (1948).
Kent, John, *William Temple* (1992).

Ten Commandments, see COMMANDMENTS, TEN.

Teresa of Avila (1515–82), the Spanish *mystic, also known as

Teresa of Jesus, was born Teresa de Cepeda y Alhumada. Her family could count itself as part of the minor nobility of Avila, though a cloud hung over her background because her paternal grandfather had been a *converso*, found guilty in 1485 at the *Inquisition of Toledo of secretly practising Jewish customs. Teresa was raised in the Catholic orthodoxy of the time, her mind fed by the lives of the *saints if also by the romantic fiction that her mother loved to read. One of the famous stories of Teresa's childhood is how she persuaded her brother Rodrigo to run away to the land of the Moors, 'begging our bread for the love of God, so that they might behead us there'. To the relief of their parents the children were soon found and brought back home.

Her mother died when Teresa was 13, and a year or two afterwards her father, perhaps concerned by her flirtation with a male cousin, sent her to an Augustinian convent. At the time she was set against becoming a nun, but her eighteen-month stay changed her mind. After a period of illness and convalescence during which she read and thought deeply, she entered the Carmelite Convent of the Incarnation, and made her formal profession at the age of 21. The Convent of the Incarnation catered especially for women of the upper classes of society, who had comfortable quarters, their own servants, and a preoccupation with reputation. In spite of this, Teresa felt that at first she made good progress in *prayer. How-

ever, she became seriously ill and fell into a coma which resulted in virtual paralysis for several years. During this time, exhausted and depressed, she gave up private prayer.

Although she returned to the convent in 1540, the laxity of the regime caused her much distress and confusion. Gradually, however, she again took up prayer and *spiritual reading, and in 1554 she was 'reconverted'. From this point onwards, Teresa's life of prayer was ever more closely connected to changes in her life in which she began to adopt *ascetical practices intended to simplify and focus her attention and to work against corruption and towards social justice in the Carmelite order and in the wider society. Teresa began to have intense spiritual experiences: visions, locutions, levitations, transverberations, and so on. One of her greatest fears was that they might all in fact be diabolical deceptions. She sought help from a series of 'learned men', spiritual directors who she felt had little understanding of her condition and who increased her sense of guilt and anxiety. At last, however, she found among the *Jesuits a confessor who took her seriously, and was able to direct her in ways that enabled rather than distorted her spiritual intensity.

Much has been written of these experiences, as though they are what constituted Teresa's life as a mystic. Yet in her own writings Teresa is clear that her experiences of prayer go hand in hand with the transformation of her own life and her work for organizational change of the Carmelite order. Teresa sought to reform the convents from being places where privilege and rank were perpetuated, so that the rule, especially the emphasis on poverty, could be more nearly observed. The symbol of the reform became the wearing of sandals rather than shoes as a sign of humility; and the reform movement in consequence became known as the Discalced (barefoot) Carmelites.

The radical nature of the reform becomes apparent when seen against the backdrop of the *sixteenth century. Spain was at the climax of its triumphalist era, rich with the silver of the New World and brash in the exploits of the *conquistadores* 'for God and for gold'; two of Teresa's brothers were of their number. Yet it was also a Spain that defined itself over against its Other, the Muslims and (secret) Jews who had been required to convert or be expelled in 1492, and the rebellious (and partly Protestant) Netherlands with whom Spain's losing conflict was a running sore. Spanish orthodoxy was safeguarded by the Inquisition bent on rooting out heresy; and the gender stereotypes of the time made it especially likely that *visionary *women of reforming zeal would be among its prime suspects.

In such a context it is hardly surprising either that Teresa's reform should attract serious and committed adherents or that it should meet with violent hostility, both from the Calced Carmelites and from the wider ecclesiastical authorities. Teresa founded a large number of houses of the primitive rule, assisted by *John of the Cross who was for a time her spiritual director. She showed herself a woman of great organizational ability, with energy and insight one would not have expected after the illness and confusion of her earlier years.

Teresa's writings (like those of many another mystic) have often been read as though they fell from heaven, timeless and universal, when in fact her books can be understood only in the context of her life. Several of them were requested by her spiritual directors, and all of them had one eye on the development of the reform and the other on the Inquisition. Teresa was well aware that she was sailing very near the wind, and it can be argued (as Alison Weber has done) that Teresa deliberately used the rhetoric of female ignorance and helplessness as a strategy for claiming her own authority while keeping the Inquisitors at bay.

The books in which her spiritual teaching is most fully set out are *The Way of Perfection* and *The Interior Castle*. *The Way of Perfection* is addressed especially to the nuns of the reform, describing the importance for them of *poverty, discipline, and the forgoing of honour. Teresa discusses her experience of vocal prayer, mental prayer, and the 'prayer of quiet'. She encourages her sisters to use repetitious vocal prayer, the Our Father or the Hail Mary, infusing this outwardly mechanical exercise with a desire for loving communion with God. Another method of prayer by which she sets great store is imaginative meditation on Christ as portrayed through incidents in the gospels. 'If you are happy, look upon your risen Lord, and the very thought of how he rose from the sepulchre will gladden you … If you are suffering trials, or are sad, look upon him on his way to the Garden' (ii. 107). Teresa urges discipline in prayer, but a gentle discipline, offering time and obedient attention to God, and trusting God to open the way forward.

The *Interior Castle* is structured around a sustained metaphor of 'the soul as if it were a castle made of a single diamond or of a very clear crystal in which there are many rooms, just as in heaven there are many mansions' (p. 201). These rooms are organized in seven concentric circles, and in the seventh is God, sitting at the centre of the soul. The way of prayer, then, is by entering more deeply into oneself, integrating all the layers of the personality and recognizing that at our very core, if we 'become what we are' we will be in union with God. Although Teresa has much to say about human *sinfulness, her central conception is of the self as having great dignity and beauty, often unappreciated because of poor self-esteem.

Teresa vividly extends the *metaphor of the castle. The outer court, for example, is occupied by guards who seek to prevent entry: worldly affairs and honour and many other respectable reasons not to engage in prayer. It is also infested with reptiles and poisonous creatures that represent sin and its entanglements. The way into the castle is through prayer: rather than becoming involved with the endless task of killing off these creatures, by entering more deeply into the castle they are gradually left behind.

Another metaphor that Teresa couples with that of the castle is that of spiritual marriage. In her thinking, spiritual marriage is the union with God signified by entry into the seventh, most inward circle (though one should not imagine any of these circles as though they could be left behind once and for all, but rather increasingly integrated with one another). Contrary to the emphasis some commentators have placed on spiritual marriage, its main point is not emotional ecstasy or psychological intensity. Teresa was a passionate woman with strong emotions, and these elements are certainly present in her description. But the central concern is union of the will to the will of God, united with God in loving compassion that seeks divine justice in the world. Thus in her most spiritual writing Teresa can be seen as unifying the energetically practical work and prayer that typified all of her life and thought.

See also COUNTER-REFORMATION; RELIGIOUS LIFE.

Grace M. Jantzen

The Complete Works of Saint Teresa of Jesus, ET (3 vols.; 1946).
The Letters of Saint Teresa of Jesus, ET (2 vols.; 1951).
Slade, Carole, *St. Teresa of Avila: Author of a Heroic Life* (1995).
Weber, Alison, *Teresa of Avila and the Rhetoric of Femininity* (1990).
Williams, Rowan, *Teresa of Avila* (1991).

Teresa of Calcutta (Agnes Gonxha Bojaxhiu, 1910–97).

Mother Teresa, as she was universally known, was probably the most famous Christian of the 20th century, recipient of the Nobel Peace Prize for 1979 and of a state funeral provided by the Government of India. She was an Albanian nun who died in Calcutta, where she had worked for many decades. Born in Macedonia, she joined the Sisters of Loretto, in Ireland, a society derived from Mary *Ward's Institute of the Blessed Virgin Mary, when she was 18. She was sent for her novitiate, as she desired, to India and was soon at work in a high-class girls' school in Calcutta. In 1948 she left her order to serve the very poor, live in a slum, and found a new order, the Missionaries of Charity, to assist her work. The special vow of the members is to render 'wholehearted free service to the poorest of the poor', especially abandoned children, dying vagrants, and lepers. The many thousands of members, mostly Indian, have spread to 122 countries.

Mother Teresa had an entirely old-fashioned *spirituality, uninterested in politics or even the advances of scientific medicine. She was criticized for the poor level of professional care in her hospitals and the lack of medicine, for her willingness to be photographed and receive gifts from some of the world's worst tyrants, producers of *poverty in their subjects, and for the rigidity of her understanding of *obedience and poverty in regard to her own nuns, for whom she made no allowances. She represented an ideal of *religious life especially congenial to *John Paul II, who greatly admired her. It was a spirit almost defiantly in contrast with the tenets of progressives and markedly less 'modern' than that of Mary Ward, three centuries before her, whose audacity and ceaseless travelling she so fully shared. The immense extent of her work worldwide and the impact of her name, face, and simple sari on popular consciousness demonstrate how unremitting love and self-sacrifice can prove more powerful than fashionable ideology. Nevertheless, if her personal spirituality was intensely traditional, her life's work incarnated a central insight of *liberation theology, the preferential option for the poor.   **Adrian Hastings**

Aguiar, Benny, Obituary, *The Tablet*, 13 September 1997.
Egan, E., *Such a Vision of the Street: Mother Teresa—the Spirit and the Work* (1985).

Teresa (Thérèse) of Lisieux (1873–97).

To be both loved and reviled, sometimes simultaneously, does not befall many *saints. It is, however, the case with Saint Thérèse of the Child Jesus and the Holy Face. One reason is that the 19th-century '*Jansenist' spirituality, fearful, negative, and life-denying, that provided the backdrop to Thérèse's life, is now largely out of favour. A second reason lies in the redaction of Thérèse's *spirituality. Thérèse's autobiographical account of her spiritual journey was reworked and interpreted by her elder sister, Pauline, both Thérèse's 'little mother' at home, and for many years her superior, under the religious name Agnes, at the Lisieux Carmel. For many people Pauline/Agnes's *Story of a Soul* and her account of Thérèse's *Last Conversations* remain the mediators of her sister's spirituality.

Thérèse's 'little way' of childlike abandonment to pure love and boundless confidence in God's *mercy sits uncomfortably with Pauline's asceticism, based on reparation and a sense of human sinfulness.

Marie Françoise Thérèse was born into a zealously Catholic family in Alençon (Normandy), the ninth and youngest child of Zélie and Louis Martin. Her mother died when Thérèse was 4, and she attached herself to her favourite sister, Pauline. In the same year the family moved to Lisieux where, in 1882, Pauline entered the local Carmelite convent. Thérèse, only 8, was devastated by this second loss, and fought to be allowed to follow her 'little mother'. She succeeded at the age of 15, having received permission from the pope, as she was still under age.

Thérèse was professed in 1890, and appointed assistant novice mistress in 1893. Among her ambitions were to be a priest (impossible within the Catholic Church) and a missionary in China, but this was prevented by her death from tuberculosis on 30 September 1897, at the age of 24. In 1894 Mother Agnes had ordered Thérèse to write her autobiography, which took the form of three manuscripts, the last completed in June 1897. It is these writings, together with numerous letters, poems, plays, and prayers, that give us such a detailed account of Thérèse's growing confidence in her 'little way' of perfection. It was the smallest actions, performed out of love, which were seen as pleasing to God. Thérèse's spirituality could be grasped and followed by anyone, and has inspired millions of ordinary Christians. It is based on an unshakeable confidence in the *love of God, and in the belief that Jesus himself will make up any deficit in our ability to respond to that love.

Thérèse was canonized in 1925, and is one of the few women to be declared a Doctor of the Church. But which Thérèse was beatified? The rather sugary saint so carefully crafted by her sister and adoring family? Or the more accessible, but also extraordinary, woman who endured the negative spirituality of her day, with its excessive physical privations and low opinion of women, and transcended it through her discovery of the 'abyss of love', which enabled her to place a limitless trust in the goodness and mercy of God?

Fiona Bowie

Thérèse of Lisieux, *Œuvres Complètes* (1992) (contains Thérèse's three main texts, the *Manuscrits autobiographiques* and other texts of Thérèse, plus some texts reworked by Pauline/Agnes, including the *Last Conversations*).
—— *Autobiography of a Saint: The Story of a Soul*, ET (1960).
Furlong, Monica, *Thérèse of Lisieux* (1987).
Six, Jean-Françoise, *Light of the Night: The Last Eighteen Months in the Life of Thérèse of Lisieux*, ET (1996).

theology is reflection about *God, even the 'science' of God. Like all extended human thought it has to make use both of rational processes—the laws of evidence, the avoidance of self-contradiction, processes of deduction and induction—and of imagination within contexts of community, culture, and commitment. Thinking does not happen in a void. Christian theology is a 'science' in that it holds together a large body of conceptions and affirmations, shaped by many minds, in self-consciously rational, internally coherent, ways. But it does not claim that this 'science' is demonstrable, as a whole or in its parts, to someone who does not already hold a prior faith commitment to God as revealed in and through *Jesus Christ.

It is emphatically *Christian* theology. As such its subject is not, in any narrow way, God alone. In Christian *faith, God is *creator and sustainer of everything, and in so far as God can be known it is through the way things are in nature and *history as well as biblical *revelation or *providence. Everything is necessarily the proper subject of theology, but precisely in its Godwardliness.

'Religious studies' is the study of *religion. While such a topic is wide enough, it is not all-embracing. Theology, on the other hand, embraces everything, the secular as much as the sacred, geology and biology as well as church history. All is part of a God-centred reality. Religious studies presupposes no act of faith. It is simply an analysis, as acute as possible, of the phenomena, beliefs, rituals, and moral prescriptions of the many 'religions' of this world. It implies no commitment in regard to them or their *truth content. Theology, on the contrary, involves both a commitment to, and a wrestling with, its subject precisely as truth-laden. It is the rational expression of a person's deepest beliefs about reality. And in so far as any Christian ponders his or her beliefs, reflects upon their relation to other sciences or explores their implications for behaviour, he or she is a theologian.

There has been in the history of Christian theology a continuous oscillation between *unity and diversity. The unity of God, of Christ, of the church and its sacraments, has to be set against a movement towards the multitudinous that has at times seemed preventable only by violent suppression. It is essential for an understanding of theology to see why this has been so and has to be so. The NT itself does not create the necessity, it merely demonstrates it. Each writer sees the mystery through his own eyes, expresses it in his own style, offers it to a specific group of people with needs just a little different from any other. The Christ of Matthew, Mark, Luke, John, and Paul is, indisputably, one and the same Christ, and yet the more they write the more differences appear (see CHRISTOLOGY). Again, the later writings of the NT indisputably reflect presuppositions, gains in structural discipline, losses maybe in imaginative freedom, that distinguish them from what came earlier. Thus already in the NT theological pluralism extends across time as well as place and person. Such is the nature of a '*revelation' that is not dictated, not given to just one person, not even, in most cases, given in such a way that the writers are aware that anything is being given through them. The NT (except for the book of *Revelation) is of its nature wholly different from, for instance, the Qur'an as faithful Muslims believe it to be (see ISLAM).

Having started like this, the Christian tradition of reflection upon God in Christ could only diversify still further, as different *languages were brought into use, not only Greek but Latin, Syriac, German, French, English, Russian; again, as it passed through very different cultures, ancient, medieval, modern, or as it was communicated in strikingly contrasted milieus—urban society, illiterate villages, the *monastic community, the *university. Quite understandably the *church as a single, ever-more widely spreading fellowship struggled to maintain a single core doctrine by *creed and *council, even though that struggle, often unimaginatively and intolerantly sustained, resulted in group after group of Christians being branded *heretical. It could seem impossible that theologians in *Alexandria and Antioch while thinking differently might yet both be within the parameters of genuine theological *development. The formulation of a single doctrinal *orthodoxy seemed at times irreconcilable with the demands of theological pluralism but, somehow, both *de facto* and *de iure* Christianity has had to live with both. There was, and is, no single correct theology.

Five principal types of theology, all valid and even necessary, but each with its own language, methodology, and purpose, can be distinguished.

1. *Liturgical and *pastoral

Its context is the basic celebrations that bring the Christian community together, *Eucharist and *baptism. Its formulations derive from the requirements of these events: liturgical prayers themselves, *hymns, catechetical instructions. While this type of theology is not extensively represented in the NT, it provides some of its most quoted texts: the christological hymn in Philippians 2: 6–11, Paul's instructions on the Eucharist in 1 Corinthians 11: 17–34 and, perhaps, 1 Peter, whose core could be a baptismal homily, and James. Subsequently *sermons have provided a considerable proportion of theological writing, from *Athanasius, Gregory Nazianzen, and *Augustine, to Austin Farrer and Michael Ramsey. It is, of course, a form scripturally grounded, principally in passages chosen from liturgical reading and calling for an exegesis related to the liturgy of a specific feast and suitable for a normally rather mixed congregation. The appropriate note is instructional rather than argumentative or discursive. There is a limit to the appropriate elaboration of a theme even in a long sermon (though some sermons, of Augustine and others, were very long!).

2. Scriptural commentary

The need for reflection on scripture beyond what is practicable in a sermon led to the development of commentaries. The NT writings are to a large extent hidden commentaries on the OT, but the development of formal commentary, moving on chapter by chapter, verse by verse, comes later. *Origen was its first extensive practitioner. Augustine commented no fewer than three times on *Genesis. Some books seem particularly attractive. Commentaries on *Romans from Origen and *Aquinas to Melanchthon and *Barth are legion; hardly less important are those on *John's gospel from Augustine to *Bultmann and Raymond *Brown. The continuing importance of the commentary demonstrates how central scripture remains to the theological enterprise; yet at times it emphasizes one dimension of that enterprise too heavily: the meaning of a specific text, the intentions of its author, the exploration of a cultural context now extremely remote. The nature of the enterprise can rather easily (though it need not) take one out of the present into either the past or some sort of atemporal world in which nothing matters but biblical texts.

3. Thematic

This is already represented in the NT in *Hebrews, Romans, and John's gospel, all of which can be considered as forerunners of systematic theology, the exploration at length of a particular idea. It was both the need to explain Christianity persuasively to nonbelievers and pressure from 'heresy' that led to the expansion of thematic writings, often of an argumentative kind. One sees it already in the 2nd century in *Irenaeus' treatise *Against the Heresies*, then in Athanasius's *On the Incarnation* and Augustine on the *Trinity and *grace. The supreme expression of this type of thematic theology is to be found in *Anselm's *Monologion, Proslogion,* and *Cur deus homo*, where everything is focused on the elucidation of a specific subject. There is little attempt to interpret scripture or instruct a congregation. The intellectual enterprise of 'understanding' a mystery in its own most appropriate terms is here absolutely dominant, but it remains an enterprise imaginable only as a product of faith: *fides quaerens intellectum* (faith seeking understanding) in Anselm's chosen formula.

Systematic theology moves a stage further with the development of the medieval university. *Abelard was here the supreme pioneer. Where Anselm's milieu was a monastery geared to the celebration of the liturgy, the university was a far more secular place, in which the cut and thrust of logical disputation was crucial, and where students in theology had all passed through the school of arts, in which the study of *Aristotelian philosophy had come to dominate. The development of scholastic theology with its dry formality, its heaping up of arguments, its analysis of a question point by point, transformed the way the main theological enterprise was understood for many centuries. Beyond the specific thematic work there developed the generic one, the systematically structured *Summa Theologiae*. The first 'question' of Aquinas's *Summa* consists in a miniature treatise on theological method, one perhaps never surpassed. Aquinas wrote massive commentaries on scripture, Aristotle, *Dionysius the Pseudo-Areopagite, and much else. Only later did the *ST*, composed in his last years and never completed, assume the pre-eminence it has come to retain. Did he order it aright? Is it appropriate for Christian theology to begin with God, turn next to the *angels and *humanity, then in a second part analyse in great detail the *moral life and only, in a third part, consider systematically the person and work of Jesus Christ? Normative as the *ST* has been for much Catholic theology, other systematizations are at least possible; but however much Protestants and some Catholics too have criticized medieval scholasticism, it has proved impossible to escape the powerful attractions of this model. It is present no less in *Calvin's *Institutes* or, for the 20th century, in Barth's *Church Dogmatics*. While Aquinas maintained that the *ST* was a work for beginners (and no one has been quite sure what he meant by that. Was it a joke?) and the first edition of the *Institutes* was brief enough and always pedagogically brilliant, there is no doubt that this type of theology, while benefiting from an academic form preoccupied with clarity, right order, and convincing argumentation, suffers in consequence from a certain remoteness from ordinary life, a professionalization congenial to a clerical élite.

4. Experiential

Reflection upon personal or group experience is at its best perhaps when autobiographical. The NT provides models in the gospels and epistles, especially 1 and 2 Corinthians. What dominates the approach is historical experience, the actual problems of a young church, the personal *angst* of being an apostle. Paul talking about himself in 2 Cor. provides one approach, but any of the evangelists writing about Jesus provides another. Theology here consists in the perception of the divine in and through particular experiences in space and *time. In a weak, at times even corrupt, form, one finds it in the lives of the *saints: Athanasius' Life of Antony, Eusebius' of *Constantine. It is stronger in the best spiritual autobiography, Augustine's *Confessions,* *Newman's *Apologia,* Donald Nicholl's *The Testing of Hearts*, but in another form it includes reflections on the state of Christianity, as fierce as Luther's *Appeal to the German Nobility* or Rosmini's *Five Wounds of the Church*. Both ecclesiology and *mystical theology are predominantly experiential. While this category of theology has as such been largely overlooked, it may be the most influential in shaping and reshaping the mind of the Christian community as a whole.

5. *Allegorical (in a wide sense)

Present all over the OT, its NT representation lies in the parables and the book of Revelation. It includes *The Shepherd* of Hermas, *Dante's *Divina Commedia*, *Shakespeare's *Measure for Measure*, almost everything in *Blake, Chesterton's *The Man who was Thursday*, C. S. *Lewis's *Till We Have Faces*. It is to be found as well in books of *visions and *mythological stories about saints. Its borders are hazy, some of its claimed content dubious. Allegory may penetrate furthest into the meaning of things, the underlying shape of the Christian 'mystery', but it necessarily does so at the cost of some precision. One can never be quite sure what the point of a narrative really is. The bogus can exist in every form of theology but perhaps most evidently here.

Five principles are applicable to the evaluation of theology in general. The first is that, while necessarily far more *personal than doctrine, it be done within the public *worshipping community that provides living expression of '*tradition', though at times it is done in agonized contestation with the community's official leadership, even in a state of formal excommunication. Unlike *philosophy, Christian theology is by its nature corporate, the intellectual organ of the 'Body of Christ'. Secondly its health depends on mutual interaction of scripture and 'world', that is to say, contemporary philosophy and culture. Each affects understanding of the other. A theology that seeks to be solely scriptural surrenders the very factor that makes scriptural interpretation creative, while a theology determined to be primarily 'modern' or world-orientated risks abandoning the principle of its specificity as Christian. Despite the usage of Christian terminology, it has become instead an outcrop of contemporary ideology. Thirdly, while defined through a relationship to faith, theology depends upon *reason, reason operating no differently in its multiple types of argumentation, its use of imagination, its need of freedom and room to make mistakes, from the way it must operate in every other side of human life. Fourthly, in its fullness theology not only can but must make continued use of all five of its principal forms. Its reduction to scholastic systematization, biblical commentary, experiential reflection, or poetic imaginings alone entails a drastic loss of health. Theological vitality lies in diversity and, finally, in the diversity of people who do it. Its reduction to being the property of a single class or group, particularly, as has historically been largely the case, male, clerical, academic, and (within the Catholic tradition) *celibate, maims it appallingly, though even then something was saved by a division into contrasting traditions, *Dominican versus *Franciscan, *German versus *French. Theology is impossible without culture, but the monopolization of theology by any single culture must guarantee its atrophy. It is also impossible without *prayer which provides the affinity between subject and object required for fruitfulness in any science.   **Adrian Hastings**

Aquinas, Thomas, *Summa Theologiae*, i. *Christian Theology*, ed. T. Gilby (1964).

Cross, F. L., and Livingstone, E. A. (eds.), *The Oxford Dictionary of the Christian Church*, 3rd edn. (1997).

Greenslade, S. L. (ed.), *The Cambridge History of the Bible* (3 vols.; 1963–70).

Lonergan, Bernard, *Method in Theology* (1972).

McGrath, Alister, *Christian Theology: An Introduction*, 2nd edn. (1996).

Nichols, Aidan, *The Shape of Catholic Theology* (1991).

Pelikan, J., *The Christian Tradition: A History of the Development of Doctrine* (1971–89).

Rahner, Karl (ed.), *Encyclopedia of Theology* (1975).

Richardson, Alan, and Bowden, John (eds.), *A New Dictionary of Christian Theology* (1983).

Southern, R., *Scholastic Humanism and the Unification of Europe* (3 vols.; 1995–).

Williams, Rowan, *On Christian Theology* (2000).

Thomas, Gospel of (*GTh*), one of the texts discovered in the Nag Hammadi library, a collection of mostly Christian *Gnostic texts. This Coptic version provides the full text of the gospel, Greek fragments of which had been known since the start of the 20th century in three papyri from Oxyrhynchus. The manuscript evidence shows the gospel to have been written no later than mid-2nd century. More precise dating is difficult. The gospel consists of a series of more than 100 sayings attributed to *Jesus, with no narrative element, no account of Jesus' *miracles or Passion. Many of the sayings in *GTh* have parallels in the NT gospels, appearing at times to be more primitive than the NT versions. Hence there is the possibility that *GTh* might provide an early, independent line of the tradition of Jesus' sayings, possibly giving new information about Jesus and perhaps significantly altering both the more traditional picture of him and standard reconstructions of early Christian history.

Several questions about *GTh* remain unresolved, for example how far it can be described as a Gnostic text. Much depends on how one defines 'Gnostic'. There is nothing explicit in *GTh* of a Gnostic myth of the origins of *creation. However, a number of sayings suggest ideas not far from what most would label 'Gnostic' (for instance, *souls imprisoned in the world, awaiting *redemption through the saving knowledge brought by Jesus restoring them to their original state of primordial unity with the deity).

The question of *GTh*'s relationship to the NT *gospels is hotly debated. For some, it is independent of the NT gospels and provides access to original Jesus traditions. For others, *GTh* depends on the Synoptic Gospels (perhaps several stages removed) and thus witnesses primarily to a later stage in the development of the Jesus tradition. Some sayings in *GTh* with no parallel in the NT could be authentic, for example Th. 82, 'He who is near me is near the fire, he who is far from me is far from the kingdom.' However, it is unlikely that material from *GTh* will significantly alter our overall picture of Jesus. It seems clear that, at times, the present text of *GTh* does presuppose the finished texts of the NT gospels, showing links with editorial elements in the latter, possibly because of later assimilation to the texts of the NT gospels as *GTh* was translated into Coptic (cf. Patterson 1993). But it can be shown that at least one of the Greek fragments of *GTh* presupposes an editorial element in the Greek text of the NT gospels (Th. 5 = Luke 8: 17 editing Mark 4: 22). Further, allegedly primitive features in sayings in *GTh* may be due to the gospel's Gnosticizing proclivity to minimize 'allegorical' and other explanatory features.

GTh, therefore, is most probably primarily a 2nd-century text, showing how the tradition of Jesus' sayings was used and adopted within heterodox Christianity.   **Christopher Tuckett**

Robinson, J. M. (ed.), *The Nag Hammadi Library in English* (1977), contains ET of *Gospel of Thomas*.
Patterson, S. J., *The Gospel of Thomas and Jesus* (1993).
Tuckett, C. M., 'Thomas and the Synoptics', *Novum Testamentum*, 30 (1988), 132–57.
Wilson, R. McL., *Studies in the Gospel of Thomas* (1960).

Thomas, M. M. (Madathilparampil Mammen, 1916–96). Thomas was a layman of the Mar Thoma Church, and was one of the most important *Indian theologians of the second half of the 20th century. His theological and ideological quest began during colonial days when India was fighting for her independence and continued afterwards in the new task of nation building. It advanced further during the Indian emergency (1975–7) when he attracted national and international attention, pleading for the necessity of liberal *democracy to enact radical measures that would reshape the lives of the vulnerable (*Responses to Tyranny*). His theological impetus came from wide and often conflicting sources—an initial *Pietism, Gandhism, communist, and ecumenical streams. He moved early into social involvement based on a foundation of the cosmic lordship of Christ. His overtly Christocentric outlook and his concern for the disadvantaged became the basis on which his career as a theologian and as a deeply committed disciple was built. His affection for Christ did not prevent him from repeatedly warning against the church in India becoming another communal institution.

He will be remembered for his leadership at the Christian Institute for the Study of Religion and Society, Bangalore (CISRS), which pioneered studies on social and theological questions and was very influential. He was nourished by the *ecumenical movement of his time, and later was instrumental in shaping its policies, both in the World Student Christian Federation (1947–53) and the World Council of Churches (1968–75) as its moderator. He attracted national recognition when he became the governor of Nagaland (1990–2), an Indian state that is predominantly Christian.

A prolific writer both in English and Malayalam, he produced more than sixty books including twenty-four theological commentaries in his mother tongue. Key texts are: *The Acknowledged Christ of the Indian Renaissance* (1969), *Salvation and Humanisation* (1971), *Man and the Universe of Faiths* (1975), *The Church's Mission and Post-Modern Humanism* (1996). In all these writings he was actively engaged in articulating a theological position that took into account religious pluralism, *secularity, social ethics, globalization, politics, and the Christian *kerygma.   **R. S. Sugirtharajah**

Thomas, M. M., *My Ecumenical Journey* (1990).

Thomism (1), modern. In the middle of the 19th century a movement began in the Catholic Church to revive the scholastic *philosophy and *theology that had largely fallen out of use, and when Leo XIII, one of the principal supporters of the movement, became pope in 1878 he employed his authority to restore them to their former place in clerical education. The encyclical, *Aeterni Patris* (1879), that Leo wrote almost at once to advocate the church's return to 'the wisdom of St. Thomas', has often been called the *magna charta* of the Neo-Thomist movement. Leo encouraged both historical research on the scholastic doctors and the development of a speculative scholastic system capable of serious dialogue with contemporary thought. Consequently, in the next three decades, a programme of textual and historical research on *Aquinas, Bonaventure, and other medieval theologians was carried out in Rome, Germany, Switzerland, France, and Belgium. Franz Ehrle, Heinrich Denifle, Clemens Bäumker, and Pierre Mandonnet were among the notable scholars whose names are associated with that work, and, although a number of their conclusions have been superseded, the lasting value of their pioneering research in medieval studies is undeniable. The speculative results of the Thomist revival, unfortunately, were less impressive and the quality of scholarly output remained uneven. Although the *Dominican faculties of Switzerland and France already showed the promise of their brilliant future, others, including the *Jesuit faculty of the Gregorian University, had not reached the same standard. Teaching and publishing in Latin, as they were obliged to do, for an audience confined to ecclesiastical students, scholastic philosophers and theologians found themselves cut off from the world of secular scholarship. A brilliant exception to that rule, however, was the Higher Institute of Philosophy which Désiré Mercier established at Louvain in 1889. Teaching in a modern university, the Institute's faculty lectured in French, and wrote their books and articles for a lay readership. Furthermore, Mercier and his personally chosen group of colleagues, one of whom was the great medievalist, Maurice de Wulf, addressed themselves directly to the urgent problems raised by contemporary philosophy, history, and science. At Louvain, therefore, thanks to Mercier, speculative Thomism was able for the first time to acquaint a wider audience with its possibilities as a genuinely contemporary form of thought. Thus, by the end of the century, first-class historical research and the speculative openness of pioneers such as Mercier had laid the foundations of a Thomism whose growth in the following decades would justify the hopes that Leo XIII held out for it.

Twentieth-century Thomists were better grounded in their own tradition and much more conversant with modern philosophy. Their leading representatives among the clergy were in contact with the secular universities, and the Thomist movement was strengthened by prominent lay disciples of Aquinas, like Jacques *Maritain, Étienne Gilson, and Josef Pieper, who had been formed in the state university system. Thomists wrote in the vernacular as a matter of course and their books were read by the generally educated public. Shortly before the First World War, the modernist crisis in the Catholic Church had raised a set of ongoing problems on which Thomists were to focus their attention for several decades. Among these were the starting-point of philosophy, the role of the concept and the judgement in the mind's grasp of being, natural knowledge of God, and the rational justification for a free and reasonable act of faith.

Maurice Blondel and Henri Bergson had become very popular with Catholic intellectuals in the years before the First World War. Both had reacted against the antireligious rationalism of French university philosophy and both had shown themselves sympathetic to religion. Nevertheless, attractive as their philosophies might be to Catholics in the aftermath of the modernist crisis, they seemed also problematic. Blondel's philosophy of action, although realistic in its epistemology, had taken over the subjective starting-point of *Kantian idealism that Thomists considered the fundamental flaw in post-Cartesian philosophy. Bergson's process *metaphysics, in which being was grasped through a mobile intuition rather than through the stable concept of Thomist epistemology, threatened the abiding truth of propositions which Catholic *dogma required. Blondel and Bergson therefore both attracted and challenged Thomists and, during the first half of the century, Thomists remained in contact with them. For the leading Jesuit and Dominican Thomists, as for Maritain and Gilson, dialogue with Blondel, Bergson, and, as a consequence, with the whole stream of Cartesian and Kantian philosophy became part of their speculative agenda and that dialogue led to unreconcilable differences among them (see DESCARTES).

Dominican Thomists reacted to Blondel and Bergson by reviving and developing the classical Dominican Thomism of the 15th and 16th centuries. Although acknowledging the significance of Blondel's dynamism of the will and the mind's intuition of itself, on which Bergsonian philosophy relied, Ambrose Gardeil refused to ground the mind's immediate grasp of reality either on its immediate intuition of itself or on the dynamic drive of the human spirit to infinite reality. On the contrary, reality could only be reached through the stable concept of being abstracted from the object of sense experience. None the less, in his remarkable work on mystical experience, La Structure de l'âme et l'expérience mystique, Gardeil showed the influence of Bergson when he drew upon the *Augustinian strand in Dominican spirituality to argue for the soul's intuitive awareness of its own essence, a thesis that more traditional Thomists were unwilling to admit. The best known of the classical Dominican Thomists, however, was Réginald Garrigou-Lagrange. Like Gardeil, Garrigou rejected the Cartesian and Kantian starting-point in consciousness and, like Gardeil, he also grounded the mind's immediate grasp of being through its abstracted concept. On that basis he was able to construct a Thomistic metaphysics and philosophy of God grounded upon the three degrees of abstraction he had inherited from Cajetan, the 16th-century Dominican commentator on Thomas. His systematic theology, supported by the Dominican theology of the act of faith, and a spiritual theology rooted in the classical Thomism of the post-Tridentine period were the crowning elements in his tightly woven synthesis. A prolific writer, whose works were translated into the major European languages, Garrigou-Lagrange was widely read in the English-speaking world. Jacques Maritain, whose own Thomism was in the Dominican tradition, owed a great deal to him.

Maritain had been an enthusiastic Bergsonian before his conversion to Catholicism, and, after it, he blended his Bergsonianism with the Dominican Thomism of Gardeil and Garrigou-Lagrange. The anti-Cartesian starting-point of his The Degrees of Knowledge and the central role played by the three degrees of abstraction in its philosophy of knowledge are reminiscent of Garrigou-Lagrange. The relation between philosophy and theology and the distinction drawn in that early major work between systematic and mystical theology are very similar to those that we find in traditional Dominican Thomism. Nevertheless Maritain was a powerful and original thinker who never forgot his debt to Bergson. That is evident in the brilliant use that he made of intuitive knowledge in Creative Intuition in Art and Poetry. That he had no desire to turn his back on

modern thought and culture was also evident in his Integral Humanism. Maritain's contribution to moral and political philosophy in Moral Philosophy, The Things That Are Not Caesar's, and Man and the State could be called the most original and significant made by any Neo-Thomist, and to Maritain belongs a great deal of the credit for moving his church away from its authoritarian stance towards government to the defence of democracy and religious freedom that it made in *Vatican II. Widely travelled and a prodigious publisher, whose works were translated in all the major languages, Maritain was the best known and most influential of the systematic Neo-Thomists.

While Maritain was hostile to Kant's subjective starting-point, other Thomists were quite open to it. In L'Intellectualisme de saint Thomas, Pierre Rousselot argued that intellectus, the preconceptual form of knowledge by insight, rather than the abstracted concept, was the defining element in Aquinas's theory of knowledge. Far from rejecting idealism out of hand, he claimed, Thomists should incorporate its best elements into their own system. They should also be willing to abandon peripheral and outmoded elements in Aquinas's own corpus. Among these was the Aristotelian scientific method that Thomas had used in his theology and Maritain would later use in The Degrees of Knowledge. In place of the abstracted notion of being, Rousselot and Joseph Maréchal chose to ground metaphysics on the finite mind's dynamic drive to God's infinite intelligibility, and, for that reason, Maréchal, who had a better understanding of Kantianism than most other Neo-Thomists, argued that he could employ the Kantian subjective starting-point and transcendental method and still arrive at the real world of being through relying on the finality of the mind which Kant, he claimed, had overlooked. From Rousselot's and Maréchal's major works, L'Intellectualisme de saint Thomas and Le Point de départ de la métaphysique, came the Transcendental Thomist movement of which Karl *Rahner and Bernard *Lonergan were later well-known representatives.

First-rate historical research went on during the first half of the century. Martin Grabmann and Arthur Landgraf in Germany and Odo Lottin and Fernand van Steenberghen in Belgium made major contributions to it. By far the greatest historian of all, however, was Étienne Gilson, a graduate of the Sorbonne and, for most of his life, a professor in the French university system. His textual studies on Augustine, Bonaventure, Thomas, and Duns Scotus proved that each of these theologians used a radically different philosophy. There had been no common scholastic philosophy, as earlier Thomists had thought. As he explained in The Spirit of Medieval Philosophy, the unity of medieval philosophy came from its 'spirit', its 'way of philosophizing' inside theology. For that reason the Thomist systems of the 17th-century Dominicans, in which philosophy was 'separated' from theology, were not true Thomism, and, as he made clear in Being and Some Philosophers, the Dominican epistemology that grounded our grasp of being through its abstracted concept was not Thomistic either. For Thomas himself, being could only be grasped through the mind's immediate contact with being's concrete act of existence in the judgement. In fact, Gilson claimed in The Philosopher and Theology, none of the contemporary Neo-Thomistic systems could be called authentically Thomistic. The only genuine Thomism was the philosophical theology of the 'Angelic Doctor' himself read in its original text. Gilson, who wrote and spoke English easily and spent extended periods in North America, had many followers there, and, among the Dominicans, one of his disciples, M.-D. Chenu, led the order's movement away from Garrigou-Lagrange's classical Thomism to the more strictly historical study of Aquinas's text in which Dominicans engage today.

Translations made the work of Maritain and Gilson readily available to English readers, and the English Dominicans brought out an admirable translation of the *Summa Theologiae*. In England Daniel Callus and Thomas Gilby ably represented the historical and systematic streams of Dominican Thomism. John Bernard Hawkins's incisive and clearly written expositions of Thomism were popular on both sides of the Atlantic, and the Anglican Thomist, Eric Mascall, whose books were widely read in England and America, emerged as a very talented philosopher in his own right. In the United States, whose network of Catholic colleges and universities featured philosophy in their curricula, all the streams of Neo-Thomism were well represented. The Pontifical Institute of Medieval Studies at Toronto, Marquette, and St Louis University became centres of Gilsonian Thomism. Maritain's influence was strong at Notre Dame while Transcendental, Louvain, and Gilsonian Thomism were all represented at Fordham. Laval University in Québec and Catholic University in Washington developed their own independent Thomism. A number of Thomistic reviews were published and American Thomists, like Anton Pegis and James Collins, made a name for themselves.

Historical research undercut the claim of any one of the Neo-Thomistic systems to represent the authentic thought of the Angelic Doctor and changes in the Catholic Church after Vatican II lessened the influence of Neo-Thomism. Thomism, however, remains vital. Historical research of the first order has been carried out by such scholars as Otto Pesch, James Weisheipl, and Pierre Torrell. Transcendental Thomism provided the inspiration for the work of Karl Rahner and Bernard Lonergan. Personalist Thomism and Thomas's Neo-Platonic participation metaphysics, brought to light by scholars like Cornelio Fabro, were among the sources of William Norris Clarke's independent Thomism. Garrigou-Lagrange as well as Max Scheler influenced the Thomism of Karol Wojtyla, who later became *John Paul II. Thomistic ethics regained their prominence in the work of Alasdair *MacIntyre. Thomists work independently today rather than as members of a movement. Nevertheless, they remain dependent on the work of their Neo-Thomist predecessors.

See also THOMISM, ANALYTICAL.   **Gerald A. McCool, SJ**

Clarke, William Norris, *Explorations in Metaphysics* (1994).
Garrigou-Lagrange, Réginald, *God: His Existence and Nature* (1934).
—— *Reality: A Synthesis of Thomistic Thought* (1950).
Gilson, Étienne, *The Spirit of Medieval Philosophy* (1940).
—— *Being and Some Philosophers* (1952).
—— *A History of Christian Philosophy in the Middle Ages* (1953).
—— *The Philosopher and Theology* (1962).
Hawkins, Daniel John Bernard, *The Essentials of Theism* (1950).
McCool, Gerald A., *From Unity to Pluralism: The Internal Evolution of Thomism* (1989).
MacIntyre, Alasdair, *Three Rival Versions of Moral Inquiry* (1990).
Maréchal, Joseph, *Le Point de départ de la métaphysique* (5 vols.; 1944–9).
—— *A Maréchal Reader*, ed. Joseph Doncell (1970).
Maritain, Jacques, *Creative Intuition in Art and Poetry* (1953).
Mascall, Eric L., *He Who Is* (1943; 1970).
—— *The Openness of Being* (1971).
Rousselot, Pierre, *The Intellectualism of St. Thomas* (1935).

Thomism (2), analytical.

This is not so much a movement as a combination of intellectual style and *philosophical substance shared by a number of philosophers (almost exclusively in Britain and North America). The term was first coined by John Haldane in lectures given under that title at the University of Notre Dame, USA, in the early 1990s and is in increasing use, but the model was provided by the work of an older generation of British philosophers including Elizabeth Anscombe, Peter Geach, Anthony Kenny, and Alasdair *MacIntyre. The first three were Oxford-trained and were influenced by the problem-focused, analytical methods of *Wittgenstein. Anscombe and Geach (her husband) both converted to Catholicism while students at Oxford in the late 1930s, and met Wittgenstein when Anscombe took up a research studentship in Cambridge. Kenny studied first at the Gregorian in Rome and then in Oxford in the 1950s where he encountered Anscombe and Geach who by then had returned there. At the time Kenny was a Catholic priest trained in the scholastic tradition (he subsequently abandoned the priesthood and became an agnostic). MacIntyre proceeded largely independently, though the course of his intellectual journey led him to convert to Catholicism in the 1980s.

The combination of analytical methods and ideas drawn from *Aquinas first appeared in writings by Geach. These greatly influenced Kenny who learnt from him that topics in medieval debates were closely related to issues of contemporary philosophical discussion. Three areas of interest developed: *ethics, philosophy of mind, and philosophical theology, and Anscombe, Geach, and Kenny made important contributions to all three. MacIntyre's contribution was made later when, as a result of his studies of the history of moral philosophy, he came to regard Aquinas as the greatest synthesist of the main elements in the western tradition of ethical thought.

Among US and Canadian academics the situation was different inasmuch as Aquinas had been largely the preserve of neo-scholastics. The modern *Thomism movement, begun in Europe in response to the encyclical *Aeterni Patris* (1879), had been carried to North America in the inter-war years by Étienne Gilson and Jacques *Maritain. There it had taken root in Catholic institutions such as the Pontifical Institute in Toronto, Laval University in Québec, the Catholic University of America in Washington, Fordham in New York, and Notre Dame, Indiana. Modern Thomism tended to be rather uncritical, either historical or, when speculative, somewhat dogmatic. In either case it was largely isolated from, and ignorant of, the mainstream of Anglo-American philosophical thought.

The same has not been true of a school of interpreters of Aquinas emanating from Cornell University. The main figure in this was Norman Kretzmann who died in 1998. Kretzmann and his followers might best be described as analytical historians of philosophy. While most of the members of this group are Christians it is interesting that almost none are Catholics.

The younger generation of philosophers in Britain and America (plus a few in continental Europe) who might describe themselves as 'analytical Thomists' tend to be Catholic and to be interested in issues in philosophy of mind and philosophical theology. The bearing of analytical and in particular Wittgensteinian thought on theology in the Catholic tradition has been explored by Fergus Kerr, and there is some interest among younger theologians in this approach. In his 1998 Oxford Aquinas Lecture, Haldane argued for the need for Thomism to draw from and contribute to main debates in analytical philosophy. It remains to be seen, however, whether 'analytical' thinkers will make any lasting contribution to the history of Thomism. **John Haldane**

Anscombe, G. E. M., *Ethics, Religion and Politics* (1981).

Geach, P., *God and the Soul* (1969).

Haldane, J. (ed.), 'Analytical Thomism', *The Monist*, 80/4 (1997).

—— 'Thomism and the Future of Catholic Philosophy', in *Faithful Reason: Essays Catholic and Philosophical* (2000).

Kenny, A. (ed.), *Aquinas* (1969).

—— *Reason and Religion* (1987).

Kerr, F., *Theology after Wittgenstein* (1997).

—— *Aquinas: Revisionary Versions of Thomism* (1999).

MacIntyre, A., *First Principles, Final Ends and Contemporary Philosophical Issues* (1990).

Tillich, Paul Johannes

Tillich, Paul Johannes (1886–1965), systematic theologian and philosopher of religion. Tillich was born in Starzeddel (now Starosiedle, Poland, then in Brandenburg, Germany), the son of a *Lutheran pastor. He attended the university of Berlin, from which he received his Ph.D., and the University of Halle, from which he received his doctorate in theology. After passing his second theological examination at Halle, he was ordained in 1912.

During the First World War, he served as a military chaplain. These years had a profound impact on Tillich's understanding of human reality. The effect of the war's devastation, physical and spiritual, is reflected in a letter written in November 1916: 'I have become purely an eschatologist [in that] what I, along with others, am experiencing is the actual end of the world of this time.' After completing his military service in December of 1918, Tillich received his qualification for university teaching (*Habilitation*) at the University of Berlin in 1919. That year he published one of his most influential essays, 'On the Idea of a Theology of Culture' ('Über die Idee einer Theologie der Kultur'). The essay presented the principles for interpreting culture theologically that Tillich followed throughout his career and became the basis of a new field of theological study. The guideline that he used for such an interpretation was, in his formulation, that the *Gehalt* (import, or substance) of a cultural work is 'grasped in the content (*Inhalt*) by means of the form and given expression'. Expressionistic art is an example. Here, the forms of everyday reality—for example, the shapes of people or everyday objects—are distorted in such a way as to express a power, or reality, that manifests itself by the very way in which it breaks through the form *and* content of the objects. A theology of culture interprets the meaning of this shattering reality, the 'substance', or depth-content. Accordingly, an interpretation of culture always involves a reference to three elements of cultural works: the form, the content (*Inhalt*), and the substance (*Gehalt*).

In the spring of 1929, Tillich accepted a position teaching philosophy and sociology at the University of Frankfurt. There, in 1933, he published the work that was to lead to his emigration to the United States, *Die sozialistische Entscheidung* (*The Socialist Decision*). It was a cautious analysis of *socialism and a critique of unrestrained *capitalism, based upon the idea of *kairos* (right time)—the idea that, even politically, there are 'right' times for accomplishing certain things—and upon an analysis of German *democracy as only an abstract, not yet a real, democracy. Tillich concluded that the time was ripe for a new socialism, specifically a religious socialism that could incorporate democracy. National socialism not being what he envisaged, the essay also criticized the totalitarian element in the Nazi movement, and, as a result, Tillich became one of the many educated Germans who emigrated under the threat of those years as the movement developed.

Tillich left Germany in October 1933, and in February 1934 began his long teaching career at Union Theological Seminary in New York, remaining there until his retirement in 1955. He then became University Professor at Harvard—a great distinction—and, in 1962, with similar distinction, the Nuveen Professor of Theology at the University of Chicago. His last public address, 'The Significance of the History of Religions for the Systematic Theologian', delivered at the University of Chicago shortly before his death on 22 October 1965, reflected the direction his thought had taken towards the questions raised by the encounter of Christianity with other religions (see DIALOGUE). These differed from the questions he had treated in his earlier works because they involved differences in the religious *symbols themselves.

Tillich's major work is the three-volume *Systematic Theology*, in which he undertakes to interpret Christian symbols as providing answers to ontological questions. Through the 'method of correlation', he shows how the question of the meaning of being (the ontological question) is correlated with the symbol of *God as its answer (the theological answer). The symbol *God* is the reality that answers the question of the meaning of being. In the five divisions of the *Systematic Theology*, Tillich provides, on the one hand, an analysis of the three basic ways in which the ontological question is asked and, on the other hand, an interpretation of religious symbols that shows how these present the reality that answers the question of the meaning of being. Simply put, the three basic questions are these: What is the meaning of being itself? What is the meaning of (human) existence? What is the meaning of life? The first question, answered by the symbol *God*, is occasioned by the finitude of human being. The second question, answered by the symbol of the Christ, is occasioned by the contradictoriness (estrangement) of human being—the fact that things are not what they should and could be. The third question, answered by the symbol of the Spirit, is occasioned by the ambiguity of actual life—its mixture of being and non-being, of the good and the bad, of the creative and the destructive. The symbol *God* presents the meaning of the finitude of being; the symbol *Christ* presents the meaning of the contradictoriness of existence; and the symbol *Spirit* presents the meaning of the ambiguity of actual life. The actual human situation is that of life, in which the finitude of being and the contradictoriness of existence are always ambiguously mixed. To say that 'God', 'the Christ', and 'the Spirit' are symbols means that they actually convey the reality of the answer that they represent. In other words, as a symbol, the word 'God' (or the meaning and image borne by that word) actually presents an ultimate meaning in the finitude of being in the world; as a symbol, the word, or image, or history connected with 'the Christ' conveys a real power to bear the con-traditions and meaninglessness of reality without being over-whelmed by them; and the symbol of 'the Spirit' is the actual presence of an unambiguous meaning discernible through the am-biguities of life.

Through this method of correlation, Tillich intended to assign equal importance to the question of being (the main subject matter of *philosophy or ontology), and to God as the symbol in which the meaning of being is present (the main subject matter of *theology). The correlation between the two is formulated in the statement 'God is being-itself'. That is to say, what is present in the *symbol* God is also the reality to which the ontological *concept* of being-itself refers.

Tillich's distinctive contribution to Christian theology lies in three characteristics of his work. The first is his application of the Prot-estant principle of *justification to the realm of theoretical thought. One who doubts the reality of God knows the *truth despite that *doubt, just as one who sins is justified despite the *sin; the reality of God shows itself to the human mind despite the doubt, just as the goodness of God appears in human actions despite their imper-fection. The second appears in his theology of culture, which is based on the conception that culture itself is capable of expressing, indirectly, the ultimate meaning intended by religious faith. Thus, in his analysis of contemporary culture Tillich showed how it ex-pressed indirectly what religion expresses directly. The third char-acteristic, which is at the basis of the method of correlation used in the *Systematic Theology*, is the idea that philosophy, which asks the question of the meaning of being as such, and *religion, which is based upon the reality shown in the symbol of God, cannot be reduced to each other, and cannot be derived from each other, but can be 'correlated'. What human beings seek when they ask the question of the meaning of being can be correlated with what human beings receive through the meaningfulness of religious symbols. Accordingly, Tillich's definition of faith as 'ultimate concern'—in the sense of one's being ultimately concerned about that which concerns one unconditionally—implies both the onto-logical question of the meaning of being and also the symbol God as the presence of being-itself, which is beyond both being and non-being.

Tillich's wide influence, especially in the United States, is attrib-utable to the ecumenical character of his theology, to the effective-ness of his teaching, the appeal of his work to professionals as well as to the laity, and, no doubt, to his ability to relate theology to the issues of the time.

See also Twentieth Century: An Overview.

Robert P. Scharlemann

Tillich, P., *The System of Sciences according to Objects and Methods* (1923), ET (1981).
—— 'Der Protestantismus als kritisches und gestaltendes Prinzip' (1929).
—— *The Socialist Decision* (1933), ET (1977).
—— *The Protestant Era* (essays), ed. James Luther Adams (1948).
—— *Systematic Theology* (3 vols.; 1951–63).
—— *The Courage to Be* (1952).
—— *Biblical Religion and the Search for Ultimate Reality* (1955).
—— *Theology of Culture* (1959).
—— *Christianity and the Encounter of the World Religions* (1963).
—— *Main Works/Hauptwerke*, ed. Carl Heinz Ratschow *et al.*, Ger./ Eng. edn. with introductions (6 vols.; 1989–92).

Bulman, Raymond F., and Parrella, Frederick J. (eds.), *Paul Tillich: A New Catholic Assessment* (1994).
Kegley, Charles W. (ed.), *The Theology of Paul Tillich*, 2nd edn. (1982).
Wehr, Gerhard, *Paul Tillich zur Einführung* (1998).

time, as *Augustine taught, is both known and unknown, and known only as long as one does not ask what it is. For as soon as one tries to comprehend time, it slips away, leaving only *paradox and puzzlement in its wake. Augustine's prayerful ruminations on time, in Book 11 of his *Confessions*, remain central for Christian thought, because they powerfully address persisting *philosophical problems discussed since *Plato, but set within the theological context of *creation. Augustine asks about time in relation to the biblical God, who made everything out of nothing. Moreover, he understands the frailty of *language when pushed to express the ineffable mystery of *God, the only proper context for thought about time, as about everything else.

It would seem that there is no time, since the past has gone, the future is not yet, and the present moment is no sooner begun than over. Time *is* in so far as it ceases to be. Yet one has a sense of time passing; of a future from which it flows, a past into which it disap-pears, and a present with varying duration. Augustine was much exercised by the apparent reality and unreality of time, as also by the question of its being and measure. He was aware of the idea, held by *Aristotle and others, that time is the change and move-ment of bodies, though not only heavenly bodies, as some sup-posed. Even if there were only the turning of one potter's wheel, there would be time. Yet while he allowed that time depends on motion and change, it differs from them, because they are meas-ured by it. Even though the sun and moon stood still for Joshua, time continued to pass (10: 13). But what is it that measures change, and how? Augustine's answer is that changing bodies, of whatever kind, leave traces in the mind, and it is these that the mind meas-ures, so that past, future, and present are extensions (*distentio*) of the mind, as recollection, anticipation based on present causes, and perception.

Augustine's questing and subtle thought bequeathed to Christian tradition an account of time that relates what is sought to the mind that seeks it, and the limits of language in doing so. While Augus-tine's existential approach would not allow him to reduce time to material change, he nevertheless understood time as a condition of being, as its 'becoming'. Thus the world is not made *in* time, but *with* time. There is no time before the world begins, because both are created together. This ancient teaching has been newly con-ceived by modern *cosmology, which imagines a finite spatio-tem-poral continuum. However, unlike modern cosmology, Christian thought understands temporal being as the creation of an atem-poral, eternal God; the good gift that 'cometh down from the Father of lights, with whom is no variableness, neither shadow of turning' (Jas. 1: 17).

The Christian understanding of *eternity as the atemporal condi-tion of God's being, and so another name for God, can be traced to Augustine, though he drew on the bible read in the light of earlier Christian writers and pagan philosophers. But it was Boethius (*c*.475–*c*.525) who, in *The Consolation of Philosophy*, (5. 6), provided the classic definition of eternity as the 'complete, simultaneous, and perfect possession of everlasting life'. God enjoys a tenseless life, in which there is no past or future, no recollection or expectation, but rather a joyous present, in which everything is known all at once. This concept has endured long in Christian thought, so that even Karl *Barth, who wrote of eternity as God's time and duration, nevertheless held it to be a simultaneous coexistence of what for creatures is past, present, and future. There is thus no succession or change in God. With this understanding, the chief problem is the relation of eternity to temporality. How does an eternal God have knowledge of change and act in time?

The problem is conceptual, but takes narrative form: God appears in the *Old Testament as a character intervening in temporal affairs, often recalling what he has done and announcing what he will do, just as *Israel reminds him of his promises and implores his future benevolence. God appears in the NT as *Jesus Christ, undergoing birth and death. All such events take time, and as the temporal effects of an eternal cause would seem to imply change in God. These considerations were not insurmountable problems for Thomas *Aquinas, who represents the culmination of the Augustinian-Boethian tradition (in the Summa Theologiae, I q. 10). For Aquinas, theological reflection on time, like all theology, is a *mystical, prayerful undertaking, a matter of asking to understand what only God can disclose (I q. 1 a. 1). He held that primary designations for God—as 'being' or 'good'—are used *analogically, poised between univocity and equivocity (I q. 13 a. 5), and he read the bible *typologically, with due attention to its tensed *metaphors, *symbols, and figurations (I q. 1 a. 9 and 10). For him, temporal language is used figuratively of God, and he supposed the possibility of 'transitive' actions, which produce (temporal) effects without changing the (eternal) cause (I q. 13 a. 7). It has become increasingly difficult to sustain this approach in *modernity, which in the wake of Duns Scotus (c.1265–1308) came to favour a univocal language for God and world, and, with the rise of biblical historical criticism, no longer read the bible as divine scripture. Thus many modern thinkers have sought to understand eternity as a special case of temporality, the condition of a changing but endlessly enduring being.

Modernity is not well equipped to understand what lies at the heart of Christian thought, namely the intimacy of eternity and temporality in Jesus Christ. 'I am Alpha and Omega, the beginning and the ending, saith the Lord, which is, and which was, and which is to come, the Almighty' (Rev. 1: 8). The eternal *Word is enfleshed, and the temporal body deified (see INCARNATION). For Christian thought the life of Jesus Christ is the centre and fullness of time, because it is constituted as an eternal temporality. If the divine Word was united with human flesh in Jesus, then the Word always was, is, and will be so united. Indeed, it is this union that constitutes the perfection of creation, and so its telos and foundation. Christ is the 'moving image of eternity', to use a phrase from Plato's Timaeus.

The *Constantinian revolution of the 4th century marked not only the beginning of a new social order, but of a new temporality. Henceforth, time passed differently, imprinting Christ's life on the temporality of the social body through a recurring series of holidays: *Christmas, *Easter, and the more frequent, seven-day return of the *Sun's day (dies Solis), when all but farmers were to cease from labour (see CALENDAR). Through repetition the passage of time is overcome and its creator glorified, in recollection of his rest on the seventh day, after his labours (Gen. 2: 2). More intense patternings of time—chronotypes—would be constructed in

churches, and above all monasteries, where the *monastic body, individual and communal, would repeatedly invoke the eternal God, who gives time for the psalmist's sevenfold offering of praise, as interpreted in the Benedictine rule (ch. 16): lauds, prime, terce, sext, none, vespers, and compline. Liturgical chronotypes order past, present, and future in terms of daily, weekly, and yearly cycles, with the last recapitulating the story of Jesus, from Annunciation to Ascension, so that the centre of all time—Jesus—is also the centre of the church's life. That Jesus is the centre of history was established through calendrical reform. By the 8th century, Dionysius Exiguus' dating of the Christian era, counting from the birth of Christ rather than the accession of Diocletian (284 AD), was generally accepted throughout the Christian world, anno Domini ('the year of the Lord') replacing anno Diocletiani. Even today, Christ remains the covert reference of the Common Era.

From early in Christianity, people, imitating *Daniel, have mapped history in terms of eras, ages, and dispensations. Thus Augustine, fascinated by the mathematical and symbolic gymnastics he could perform with the number 6, suggests in De Trinitate that there are six ages, of which the last dates from the birth of the Lord and continues to the unknown end of time (4. 2). Many of these temporal maps are for the seeking of security in a chaotic world, but Augustine's sixth age is far from secure, since it is the age of the church, stretched between the first and second comings of Christ; between his birth and the end of the world. In Christian thought, the end of time has proved a recurring fascination, especially at the end of centuries and millennia, often resulting in visions of cataclysmic judgement and retribution. But more profound theologies have sought to think about time's ending, like its beginning, in relation to Christ; the one in whom temporality issues from and returns to eternity. Thus the time of the church is the time of Christ's risen life. From the perspective of eternity, Christ's second coming is one with his first, since all of his life is simultaneously embraced in the eternity of God. But from a temporal perspective, Christ becomes fully who he is through the development of his ecclesial body across the passage of time, as each moment gives way to the next. From such an earthly perspective there is an interval between ascension and parousia, in which the church is formed and given time in order to learn eternal life.

It is one of the ironies of history that the monastic desire to order the day, but more especially the night, for the petition and praise of God, led in the 14th century to the monastic embrace, perhaps even the development and promotion, of ever more accurate and reliable mechanical clocks, that would eventually lead to the modern notion of time: a uniform temporality that orders the flight of aeroplanes, the production of factories, and the transfer of capital. Time is no longer patterned by the cycles of heavenly and fleshly bodies, nor measured by sun or water, weight, pendulum, or spring, but, since the introduction of Co-ordinated Universal Time in 1972, by the implacable oscillations of atomic caesium. In the age of electric light and 24-hour commerce, and the almost instantaneous transmission of information, temporal existence has reached the absolute speed of simultaneity. God's gift of time is repudiated in favour of a commodified temporality, which can be bought and sold, lost and wasted, but never purely enjoyed. This cult of simultaneity is like a parody of the classical conception of eternity. Nevertheless, the vagaries of nature resist this 'spatializing' of time: bodies still decay and the speed of the earth's rotation remains inconstant.

The Christian *Eucharist remains the contrary of modern time, as the site where time continues to arrive from eternity. Christ's eucharistic presence arrives from past and future, constituting the present moment through the church's recollection and anticipation of what is promised: the ever-renewed arrival of God's eternity in Christ. The Eucharist eternalizes time, as that which arrives and passes away in order to return again, bearing eternal life with it. The eucharistic celebration teaches the church how to wait upon the arrival of God's gift of time.   **Gerard Loughlin**

Alliez, E., *Capital Times*, ET (1996).

Barth, K., *Church Dogmatics*, II/1 §31. 3; III/2 §47.

Davies, B., *The Thought of Thomas Aquinas* (1992).

Dohrn-van Rossum, G., *History of the Hour: Clocks and Modern Temporal Orders*, ET (1996).

Pickstock, C., *After Writing: On the Liturgical Consummation of Philosophy* (1998).

Sorabji, R., *Time, Creation and the Continuum* (1983).

Tolstoy, Leo

Tolstoy, Leo (1828–1910), Russian novelist and radical. Spurning the doctrine of *Atonement, Tolstoy preached an undogmatic, tolerant, peaceful, and communitarian faith that rejected both ritual and ecclesiastical authority and proclaimed the *Kingdom of God within humanity. Though he himself disdained the many Tolstoyan communities spawned by his teachings, his vision of an essentially earthly *morality has appealed not only to a variety of nonconformist Christians, both within Russia and beyond, but also to eastern gurus, most notably Mahatma Gandhi, whose doctrines of civil disobedience and passive resistance owed much to his correspondent, Tolstoy. Tolstoy's admirers also include secular moralists on the left, though some, seeing his faith in Christ merely in terms of an antidote to his doubts about *God, have wondered whether he may be regarded as a Christian at all.

Tolstoy expressed his doubts about the eternal questions of life and death through the voice of Levin, a noble searcher after truth no less committed to *pacifism than his creator, in the closing pages of his last indisputably great *novel, *Anna Karenina*. Since it appeared during the Russo-Turkish war of 1877–8, a campaign widely proclaimed as a crusade against the infidel, the work was bound to provoke controversy. Rejected by the journal that had serialized earlier parts of the novel, the final passages were attacked in *The Diary of a Writer* by *Dostoevsky, whose *messianic vision conjured up an altogether more militant Russian Christ. From the critics' point of view, worse was still to come. Soon after turning 50, Tolstoy reached the climax of a religious crisis with deep roots in his earlier life. His account of this experience, written in 1878–9, was published as *A Confession* in 1882, when it was promptly banned in Russia. This classic *conversion narrative charts Tolstoy's passage from a childlike belief in spiritual perfection through an immoral phase of pride and self-importance towards a suicidal quest for rational meaning from which he was rescued only by the revelation of an intensely personal form of Christianity. Renouncing his earlier work, Tolstoy found a way forward by attempting to live a merciful and *ascetic existence (he became a vegetarian, he attempted to cobble his own shoes); by rejecting violence (killing was 'evil and contrary to the most fundamental principles of any faith'); and by seeking to separate truth from falsehood in the teachings of the church. Turning from *belles lettres* to an *Investigation of Dogmatic Theology*, a critique of the work of Metropolitan Makarii (Bulgakov) finally published in 1891, Tolstoy reiterated the world-view of his *Confession* in *What I Believe* (1884), which encapsulated his commitment to a literal interpretation of the ethics of the *Sermon on the Mount, *The Kingdom of God is Within You* (1893), and *The Law of Love and the Law of Violence* (1908), in which *love and violence are, naturally, regarded as mutually exclusive. These loosely constructed tracts were complemented by *Resurrection* (1899), a novel written over the course of the 1890s in an attempt to sum up the gospel according to Tolstoy.

Hard to match for emotional power, *A Confession* is unconvincing as intellectual biography. Of course, Tolstoy is not alone in seeing the late 1870s as a significant caesura in his life. Post-revolutionary Russian *émigrés*, rightly convinced that the popularity of his anarchic socioreligious teachings had helped to destabilize an imperial regime increasingly dependent on force, found it convenient to distinguish Tolstoy's wayward *prophecy from his literary genius. Yet, allowing for a widely noted lapse in artistic integrity in Tolstoy's later years, the two are hard to separate. His writings had always crackled with the tension between *reason and *revelation, though Tolstoy insisted on their essential compatibility. 'Reason', conceived as the opposite of intelligence, 'is the divine power of the soul which reveals to it its attitude to the world and to God', he declared in a letter of 1895. 'A return to love is only possible through the removal of temptations, and the removal of temptations is only achieved through the activity of reason. This is the fundamental idea of the Christian teaching, and I have tried to express it in all my writings as well as I could' (Christian 1978: ii, 520–1).

Tolstoy first formulated his 'stupendous idea' of a religion 'purged of dogmas and mysticism' as early as March 1855, while serving in the Sevastopol campaign. But his life was no less riddled with contradictions than his writings. Here was a wealthy landowner who self-consciously donned peasant garb as a model of Christlike simplicity; an intellectual who despised the intelligentsia; a student of Schopenhauer who ultimately concluded that true virtue lay in the Russian tradition of 'holy foolishness' (*iurodstvo*). Here was a devotee of Jesus who condemned churchmen for failing to practise what they preached, and yet himself lived a far from Christlike life—he contracted gonorrhoea from a prostitute when still a student and, locked into a failed marriage, remained 'organically unable to allow his conscience to strike a bargain with his animal nature' (V. Nabokov, *Lectures on Russian Literature* (1981), 140). Here, finally, was a writer uniquely appreciative of life's infinite diversity who nevertheless strove for integration and universal harmony: in Isaiah Berlin's famous terms, Tolstoy was a fox who thought he was a hedgehog. Tensions remained even after he had become a self-proclaimed preacher. Dismissing the elders of the revered monastic community at Optina Pustyn as vainglorious (*Father Sergei*, completed in 1898 but unpublished in his lifetime), Tolstoy himself became the sage of Yasnaya Polyana, his estate in Tula province, which was transformed into a holy place, not only for Russian pilgrims of all social classes, but also for many foreign disciples. Small wonder that one of his most perceptive biographers should have diagnosed a 'split personality' (Wilson 1988: 408).

Within the vast corpus of Tolstoy's writings, structural analysis reveals a persistent search for integrative truth that anchors his thought more firmly in the eastern Christian tradition than the stridently anticlerical tone of his later writings would appear to allow. *Reconciliation, wholeness, and *sobornost*, as personified by the archetypal peasant Platon Karataev in *War and Peace*, are values admired by all *Eastern Orthodox. Indeed, in his insistence on the incomprehensibility of God, Tolstoy was more Orthodox than the scholastic bishop Makarii (a soft target, dismissed as sterile by many churchmen long before Tolstoy published his critique). Yet his dismissal of the ritual which the church so earnestly defended as the sole *apostolically authentic path to salvation unnerved Orthodox already offended by Tolstoy's cavalier scriptural exegesis. In the eyes of a church which saw evangelical sectarianism as the greatest threat to its authority, Tolstoy's teachings amounted at best to moral positivism and at worst to subversive heresy, especially when they took the form of support for the outlawed Dukhobors. Having lampooned the influential synodal over-procurator, K. P. Pobedonostsev, in *Resurrection*, Tolstoy was finally excommunicated in 1901 by bishops who preferred to patronize the radically different form of populist Christianity preached by Father Ioann Sergiev (John of Kronstadt) which was based on the very *miracles that Tolstoy so mistrusted: 'I think that to accept or to believe the miracles of the gospel is a complete impossibility for a sane person in our times' (Christian 1978: ii. 474).

Few of the hundred or so Tolstoyan agricultural colonies established in Bolshevik Russia under the New Economic Policy survived Stalin's collectivization campaign of 1928. Just as a wide readership for Tolstoy's moral tracts lay beyond Russian borders, so did some of the most faithful attempts to rebuild the Kingdom of God on earth along Tolstoyan lines. Severed from its Russian roots, Tolstoyanism generally took the form of a Utopian populist socialism seductive to the anti-establishment. To the radical Nonconformist journalist, W. T. Stead (1849–1912), who made the pilgrimage to Yasnaya Polyana in 1888, Tolstoy's Christianity looked like humanitarianism infused with 'a dash of *Quakerism'. Tolstoy Societies were formed in Manchester and London, inspired by leading lights in the Co-operative Movement. Rejection of force and devotion to physical labour were central commitments of the short-lived Tolstoyan colony established by John Coleman Kenworthy and fellow members of the Croydon Brotherhood Church at Purleigh, in Essex, in 1896. Few today would indulge in such a literal recreation of Tolstoyan ideals. Far more are inclined to mock them. And yet, at the beginning of a new millennium, pacifism and mutual co-operation have not entirely lost their lustre on the left, and Tolstoy's insistence on the need for religious toleration may yet serve a vital purpose in the renascent Russian Federation.   **Simon Dixon**

Tolstoy, L. N., *Polnoe sobranie sochinenii* (90 vols.; 1928–58).

Berlin, I., *Russian Thinkers* (1978).

Christian, R. F. (trans. and ed.), *Tolstoy's Letters* (2 vols.; 1978).

Edgerton, W. (trans. and ed.), *Memoirs of Peasant Tolstoyans in Soviet Russia* (1993).

Florovsky, G., *Ways of Russian Theology* (1937), ET (2 vols.; 1979).

Gustafson, R. F., *Leo Tolstoy: Resident and Stranger* (1986).

Holman, M. J. de K., 'The Purleigh Colony: Tolstoyan Togetherness in the Late 1890s', in W. G. Jones (ed.), *Tolstoi and Britain* (1995).

LeBlanc, R. D., 'Tolstoy's Way of No Flesh: Abstinence, Vegetarianism, and Christian Physiology', in M. Glants and J. Toomre (eds.), *Food in Russian History and Culture* (1997).

Wilson, A. N., *Tolstoy* (1988).

Torrance, Thomas F. (1913–).

One of the leading *Reformed theologians of his generation, Thomas Torrance was born in western China of missionary parents. In 1927 he returned to *Scotland where he studied classics, philosophy, and theology before undertaking doctoral research in Basel under the supervision of Karl *Barth. (Later he organized and edited, with Geoffrey Bromiley, the translation of Barth's *Church Dogmatics* into English.) Following two periods of parish ministry and chaplaincy during the Second World War (for which he was awarded an MBE), he was appointed in 1950 to the Chair of Church History in Edinburgh University and then to the Chair of Christian Dogmatics which he held until he retired in 1979. A committed churchman (appointed moderator of the Church of Scotland, 1976), he has remained actively involved in *ecumenism, working with the *Faith and Order Commission of the World Council of Churches for ten years. His keen conviction that the *Nicene heart of patristic theology provided 'a basis for profound unity' between the Orthodox, Roman Catholic, and Evangelical churches found expression in much of his writing, not least, his *Theology in Reconciliation* (1975), *The Trinitarian Faith* (1988), and the two volumes he edited, *Theological Dialogue between Orthodox and Reformed Churches* (1985 and 1993).

Immensely learned, his prolific writings are characterized by their constructive and creative integration of what are often assumed to be disparate fields of learning. They span not only the history of Christian thought integrating patristic with contemporary debates, but also ecumenical and cross-disciplinary divides, most notably between theology, epistemology, and *science (for which he won the Templeton Prize). His major concern has been to explore the significance of the *Incarnation and the doctrine of the *Trinity for the whole business of understanding the contingent order and our relation to it and thus for the pursuit of truth on the one hand and for the field of natural sciences on the other. Despite his extensive engagement in interdisciplinary debates, his primary interest has remained in Christian dogmatics in which his learning and intellectual commitment find their focus.   **Alan Torrance**

Torrance, T. F., *Theological Science* (1969), repr. (1996).

—— *The Christian Doctrine of God: One Being, Three Persons* (1996).

Tracy, David (1939–),

American Roman Catholic theologian. Tracy studied at the Gregorian University in *Rome and in 1969 became professor of theology at the University of Chicago's Divinity School where he had a great impact on students and faculty because of his intellectual, spiritual, and personal gifts.

Tracy came to prominence with *The Achievement of Bernard Lonergan* (1970). His subsequent work develops from his insight that *Lonergan's assumption of the validity of the truth-claims and relevance of the Christian tradition must be grounded in critical conversation with the broader academy, the church, and society at large. What is entailed in 'grounding' deepens in his career, but always resembles a dynamic conversation. In this vein, *Blessed Rage for Order* (1975) revolves around being loyal to the *God of *Jesus Christ and to the demands of critical thought in a world 'disenchanted with disenchantment'.

Tracy deals with similar issues in *The Analogical Imagination* (1981): given the Catholic commitment to *dialogue with *science, *philosophy, and *art, how can theology articulate the Christian vision of reality in language intelligible outside the community without surrendering Christian particularity? *Plurality and Ambiguity* (1987) and *Dialogue with the Other* (1990) record Tracy's contributions to *hermeneutics and interreligious discussions.

In the late 1970s Tracy became involved with the journal *Concilium*, whose annual meetings afforded opportunities for dialogue with *Gutiérrez, *Schillebeeckx, *Boff, *Küng, Schüssler *Fiorenza and others. His *Concilium* articles were published as *On Naming the Present* (1994), revealing him as a Catholic theologian for whom *feminist and womanist critiques, *spirituality, *pastoral, *liberation, and *justice issues are integral to ecclesiality and theology.

Through the 1980s and 1990s, Tracy wrestled with ways of knowing and speaking of God in a post-Holocaust world. In *On Naming the Present* and *This Side of God* (1999) he suggests that the contemporary experience of presence *and* absence of an uncanny divine gives glimpses both dialectical and analogical of a God beyond God and of ways for Christianity to renew itself spiritually, intellectually, and institutionally.   **William R. Burrows**

Breyfogle, T., and Levergood, T., 'Conversation with David Tracy', *Cross-Currents* (Fall 1994).
Sanks, T. H., 'David Tracy's Theological Project: An Overview and Some Implications', *Theological Studies*, 54 (1993).

tradition is the process of handing on Christian faith and practice. Much in the life of the churches derives from tradition, rather than explicitly from scripture: the canon of scripture itself, the *christological and *Trinitarian doctrines of the early *councils and their *creeds, forms of *ministry and *worship, the *baptism of infants. All Christian churches appeal to tradition but in different and sometimes contradictory ways. Therefore 'tradition' may be seen to contain a hidden principle of selectivity. Furthermore, the grounds on which the selection is made may be suspected as ideological, for as well as handing on the essentials of Christianity tradition can also serve to legitimate privilege, power, and vested interests. It can be shown (Morrison 1969) that in the formative period of Christian theology tradition was invoked selectively, tendentiously, and arbitrarily to support arguments adopted on other grounds. Practices only a generation or so old were elevated to the status of 'tradition' and 'antiquity'. The authority of tradition was subservient to the needs of clerical control.

*Feminist theologians have exposed the inveterate androcentric, patriarchal, and sexist character of the Christian tradition in almost all its forms. *Post-Christian feminist theologians, such as Daly and Hampson, have concluded that this is irredeemably intrinsic to Christianity as a religion that worships a Father-God, based on particular historical episodes embedded in cultures oppressive to *women and centred in the person and authority of a particular man, Jesus of Nazareth. Others, such as Soskice and Coakley, believing that the essence of Christianity is not inextricably wedded to patriarchy and sexism, have remained within the church. Many who have learned from feminist theology have registered the point that broad appeals to tradition are undermined by its pervasive animus against women.

Tradition invites what *Ricœur calls a *hermeneutic of restoration and a hermeneutic of suspicion. We should treat tradition with caution and be alert to ideological uses of it. But this suspicious use depends on a prior receptivity to tradition. We critique

tradition with the tools also provided by tradition. All theological (and other) discourse takes place within the milieu of tradition, for this furnishes all our concepts, images, and models. All enquiry is 'tradition-constituted and tradition-constituting' (*MacIntyre 1981).

The Greek *paradosis* means what has been handed on, handed over, or delivered. *Paul claims to hand on merely what he has received (1 Cor. 11: 23–4; 15: 3). The gospel and the *Word of God are among the things that have been 'traditioned' (Gal. 1: 9; 1 Thess. 2: 12). For Paul the whole Christian mystery has been handed on in tradition. The four gospels are the result of a process of tradition that began with oral testimony. Luke probably refers to oral tradition of the ministry of Jesus as a source for his gospel (Luke 1: 2). John claims to be based on eyewitness testimony (John 21: 24). In these NT texts we have a highly positive view of tradition. However, this has to be set against the negative and pejorative use of the concept of tradition by *Jesus in the gospels. 'For the sake of your tradition you make void the word of God ... by teaching human precepts as doctrines' (Matt. 15: 1–9; cf. 1 Pet. 1: 18).

The early fathers, with their notion of the rule of faith, assume that Christian truth is handed on unchanged from one generation to the next. *Athanasius speaks of 'the actual original tradition, teaching, and faith of the catholic church, which the Lord conferred, the apostles proclaimed and the fathers guarded'. Orthodox, Roman Catholics, and high Anglicans follow those elements in the NT and the early church which uphold tradition as a source and criterion of *truth and tend to idealize it.

The *Eastern Churches revere tradition as unchanging and eternal. Tradition is the rich complexity of all that is normative in the church. In the *eucharistic *liturgy the faithful are caught up in the power of living tradition. Orthodox are generally not inclined to engage in critical analysis of tradition or to distinguish between normative and non-normative elements. Orthodoxy is regarded as the only true and pure form of Christian tradition.

Roman Catholic teaching on tradition is found in the *Dogmatic Constitution on Divine Revelation* (*Dei verbum*) of *Vatican II. This emerged out of sharp conflict between defenders of the pre-Vatican II standard position (which postulated two sources of revelation: scripture and tradition) and the advocates of an integrated and dynamic relationship between scripture and tradition as twin expressions of the one Word of God. The Protestant principle of *sola scriptura* is rejected but the sovereignty of the Word of God is affirmed in a way that won the support of Protestant theologians. Revelation of God's nature and will is mediated through scripture and tradition. Together they form one 'sacred deposit of the word of God'. Tradition is not static since it develops through the guidance of the Holy Spirit, so that the church gains a deeper insight into the abiding meaning of revelation. The body that has divine *authority to interpret the word of God, whether oral or written, is 'the living teaching office of the Church' (the *magisterium*). However, this is not above the Word but serves it. Tradition, scripture, and the teaching office are interlinked and act together—albeit in a way that is not fully explained (*DV* 2). Since Vatican II unchanging tradition has been invoked by Rome to bolster objections to 'artificial' methods of *contraception and to women priests.

*Anglicans give an elevated though not decisive or normative place to tradition. Authoritative tradition is restricted to the period of the early councils or more generally to 'the undivided church', but its role is to serve as a hermeneutic to scripture in secondary matters such as worship and church government (scripture being held to be clear and definitive on essential matters of belief and on the way of salvation), where Anglicans insist only that they be 'not repugnant to holy Scripture'. Anglicanism acknowledges that it derives the canon of scripture, the creeds, and the threefold ministry from tradition. The collective wisdom of the church (the God-given gift of reason, but not conceived in a rationalistic or individualistic way) is employed to interpret the sources, and to adjudicate between what is binding and what is not, in both scripture and tradition.

*Protestants tend to be suspicious of tradition, except where it is embodied in scripture, the early councils, or the Reformation confessions—which gives ample scope for tradition in Protestantism. Protestants do not accept that tradition is a form of the Word of God equal to scripture. *Luther effectively destroyed tradition as a criterion of truth when he burned the canon *law and concluded that General Councils had erred. Luther himself was relaxed about tradition in secondary and inessential matters and Calvin too did not quibble about these. The wholesale rejection of tradition and the insistence on biblical precept or precedent for everything done in the church belongs to the *Puritan strand of the *Reformed faith.

*Ecumenical theology has striven to discover a concept of tradition that overcomes the intractable differences between Christian churches. It recognizes the need for a hermeneutic of tradition. In reality, every act of reception adapts, and every act of transmission reshapes, tradition. *Newman attempted to combine the privileging of tradition with recognition of its dynamic character in his *Essay on the Development of Christian Doctrine* (1845). *Congar has insisted that tradition means development as well as transmission.

The *Faith and Order movement at Edinburgh 1937 suggested a less monolithic, more variegated concept of tradition as 'the living stream of the church's life'. In 1963 (Montreal) it distinguished between Tradition and traditions: the former is the 'living reality' of revelation that is mediated through all the diversity of the latter. *Baptism, Eucharist and Ministry* (Lima 1982) defined 'apostolic tradition' broadly as

> continuity in the permanent characteristics of the church of the apostles: witness to the *apostolic faith, proclamation and fresh interpretation of the gospel, celebration of baptism and the eucharist, the transmission of ministerial responsibilities, communion in prayer, love, joy, and suffering, service to the sick and needy, *unity among the local churches, and sharing the gifts which the Lord has given to each.   (Ministry, 34)

Similarly, Congar says that tradition is not the 'quintessence of primitive Christianity, but the totality of what has been revealed about Christ over long ages'. Von Hügel characterized tradition as 'the greatest multiplicity in the deepest possible unity'. This mystical elevation of tradition, which takes it to embody the whole Christian phenomenon, assimilates it to the holistic understanding of tradition in Orthodoxy but blunts its cutting edge as a criterion of true faith and practice.   **Paul Avis**

Congar, Y., *Tradition and Traditions* (1966).
Hanson, R. P. C., *Tradition in the Early Church* (1962).
McAdoo, H. R., *The Spirit of Anglicanism* (1965).
MacIntyre, A., *After Virtue* (1981).

Morrison, K. F., *Tradition and Authority in the Western Church 300–1140* (1969).
Tavard, G., *Holy Writ or Holy Church* (1959).

translation, biblical. From the very beginning, Christian communities, in their many diverse forms and provenances, have inherited their scriptures in translated forms, along with traditions and beliefs about revelation and inspiration. From their Jewish origins came the Hebrew Scriptures in the Greek translation known as the Septuagint (LXX) together with the custom, dating from at least the time of Ezra, of interpreting readings from the Torah for non-Hebrew-speaking congregations. This unconscious gift bequeathed to the Christian communities the practice of translation without requiring them to debate its necessity or desirability (contrast the Islamic reception of the Qur'an which accords authority only to the original Arabic). Accepting translated scriptures as part of the given, Christians transmitted the sayings of *Jesus in Greek rather than in the Aramaic in which they were presumably originally delivered and were thus able to communicate their message and build communities throughout the *Hellenistic world.

In the west, as Greek gave way to Latin within the church, Christians had to take up the task of translating their inherited scriptures and by the end of the 2nd century Latin versions of the bible had begun to appear. Thus began a complex history of many versions and editions of Latin translations of Christian scripture (loosely incorporated into the term of convenience *vetus latina*, 'Old Latin', for pre-Jerome translations and revisions). It was such versions that constituted the bible of the western fathers of the church and that were the object of their commentaries while the east kept to the LXX.

Many other early translations were of great importance in more delimited areas. The popularity of the LXX among Christians led Jewish exegetes to produce alternative, often more literal, translations of the OT into Greek and these in turn were taken up by Christian scholars, most notably *Origen in his great comparative work, the Hexapla. The production of a gospel harmony (*Diatessaron*) in the 2nd century by Tatian in the Syriac-speaking world of the east contributed to the creation of various Syriac translations, primarily the Peshitta (made from Hebrew) and the Syro-Hexapla (from the Greek of Origen's revision of the LXX). In the 3rd and 4th centuries a Coptic version of the NT was made in the Sahidic dialect, later superseded by a version in the Bohairic dialect. Other notable achievements of biblical translation in that early period include the production of an *Armenian bible in the 5th century, via various stages of translation based on Syriac and Greek texts, and *Ethiopic versions of the bible (via Greek and since the 14th century influenced by Arabic texts).

The most notable individual biblical translator of the early Christian centuries was Jerome, who was also a pre-eminent early biblical exegete (see LATIN THEOLOGY). With papal blessing, he revised the Latin gospels and, seeking to undo what he regarded as the errors of Origen's critically corrected edition of the LXX, he produced Latin translations directly from the LXX of some of the OT books. He also worked on a translation of the OT directly from Hebrew, eventually completing most of it, though he is not responsible for everything in what became the established Latin text, the version known since the 16th century as the Vulgate. This name is a revision of the usage of the Latin fathers among whom the term *vulgata* (Greek *koine*) was applied to the Greek bible and to its Latin versions.

Jerome's translations were not popular at first, even if with time they came to be privileged in Roman Christendom. Disputes about the techniques of translation have contributed to some long-running controversies in Christian history. In particular, there is a famous exchange between Jerome and *Augustine on the nature and practice of translation of the bible from Hebrew and Greek in relation to Latin (see Schwarz 1955: 17–44). While there is much discussion of what precisely was at issue, the crux of the debate seems to be whether it was only the Hebrew text of the OT that had been inspired. If this was so, all translations had to go back to those words. Jerome favoured this position. He had been taught some Hebrew by a Jewish convert and took the view that translators were not prophets. Augustine, however, not a Hebrew scholar, argued that the LXX itself had a special authority. It was a translation that tradition claimed had been produced by seventy-two interpreters who worked independently and yet delivered versions which matched each other word for word, surely evidence of divine inspiration. In addition, it had been hallowed by centuries of use and by apostolic citation. If Jerome was right, was theology not held to ransom by the small group of Christians capable of interpreting the Hebrew text? Jerome's counter was that the copies of the Septuagint used by the churches showed great variation and evidence of textual corruption. Only the linguistic and textual expertise of trained exegetes could preserve the church from doctrinal error and pointless arguments. Looking back on the discussion between these two outstanding early Christian exegetes reminds us that translation, especially of the bible, is a vexed issue, linguistically, culturally, philosophically, and theologically. Built into every translated version of the bible are to be found particular theoretical and practical considerations.

The discussion also presages a fundamental problem that came to a head in the *Reformation but still exercises Christian thinkers: the relationship between the received wisdom of the church and the expertise of the scholar. Long before the Reformation, the Latin bible itself had become an authoritative text, the preserve of the clergy who by and large were the only members of a congregation who could read it, and even they often enough had little comprehension of what they read. To counteract this, parts of the bible were translated into various European vernaculars quite early in the Middle Ages. In the 13th and 14th centuries there was a wave of translations into Dutch, English, German, and French. Such activities became linked with ecclesiastical dissidence. In England John Wyclif oversaw a translation of the Vulgate into the vernacular which became the spur to the reforming group known as the Lollards (see HUSS AND WYCLIF). The increased access to Greek manuscripts after the fall of Constantinople in 1453 and greater interest in the Hebrew tradition all contributed to a growing dissatisfaction with the church's monopoly of the bible and to doubts over the accuracy not only of its interpretations but of the text it hallowed. The publication of *Erasmus' new edition of the Greek NT in 1515 (revised 1519) was one crucial result.

The Reformation set in train a great burst of translation. This brought the bible to a much wider and culturally diverse audience. Furthermore, in rendering some of these versions, it was necessary in the first place to provide a hitherto unwritten *language with a written form or even sometimes an alphabet, as had earlier been the case with Armenian and Slavonic. In the case of languages with a literary tradition, the particular dialect favoured by the translators and the accommodations made to incorporate Hebrew and Greek concepts and syntax attained a new status as linguistic standards. The bible has had a marked effect on the languages and cultures into which it is translated.

Among the best examples of this are German and English. Martin *Luther's translation of the Christian bible into German quickly replaced the previous translations, partly at least on account of its forceful literary artistry, ensuring that his version of High German came to be the dominant linguistic force in German culture from the 16th century. Its all-pervasive influence is one from which some modern Jewish-German translators of the Hebrew bible, notably Buber and Rosenzweig, have since struggled to escape.

The history of the Englishing of the Christian bible is a paradigm for most of the issues involved in bible translation. The most famous of all English versions is the King James Version (KJV) of 1611, but behind that is a history stretching back for centuries. Various Anglo-Saxon renderings of parts of the Vulgate predate the so-called Wyclif Bible, but it is William Tyndale's translation of Erasmus' Greek NT (1526) and his later rendering of parts of the OT directly from the Hebrew which were seminal. The KJV incorporates much of Tyndale through being based on the Bishops' Bible (1568), the version known to *Shakespeare, itself a revision of the earlier Great Bible (1539). It quite explicitly admits to being a palimpsest of a bible rather than a translation *a novo*. Manipulated by King James I through his chosen committee of leading scholarly churchmen, it sought to occupy a mediating position between the radical Presbyterian Geneva Bible (1560) and the Catholic Douai-Rheims Bible (Rheims New Testament 1582; Douai Old Testament 1609–1610) and to replace all other English versions. The KJV abandoned the Genevan and Douai conventions of incorporating explanatory notes in the margins that sought to impose a particular theological slant and, in spite of initial opposition and much criticism (including the petitioning of the English Parliament in the 1660s for a new translation), became over a long time the most popular and influential of all the many Christian bibles in English. It has helped to produce a rich polyglot-textured literature and has been an influence no serious writer of English could escape—a fact that led to this bible being rated a classic of *English* writing.

The KJV evolved through many editions and attained an authoritative status itself. Scholarly disquiet over its inaccuracies and linguistic archaism (cf. Jerome), however, led to the production of the Revised Version towards the end of the 19th century (NT 1881; OT 1885). Further revisions produced the American Standard Version, the Revised Standard Version, and in 1989 the New Revised Standard, all of which retain much of the well-loved language of the older text. It was only after 1945 that the Protestant churches of Britain officially commissioned a new translation that was not dependent on the KJV, though others had steadily appeared. The New English Bible (NT 1961; OT 1970), as it was called, was launched amid protests that Augustine might have uttered over the abandoning of time-honoured phrasing. Subsequently, the Jerusalem Bible (1966) was offered as a replacement for the Rheims-Douai for Catholics and the New International Version (1973) sought to uphold the authoritative tradition of the KJV for evangelicals. These are only some of the most important of the ever-expanding number of English versions available. Older versions still maintain their hold. Individual versions like Heinz Cassirer's *God's New Covenant* (1989) bring particular insights.

The imperial expansion of the various European powers into the non-European world opened up new fields to *missionaries and biblical translators, to some extent consolidated under the aegis of the Bible Societies. To this day the project of translating versions of the Christian bible into the many languages of other cultures continues apace, raising old and new issues of culture and theology (cf. Stine 1990) to do with ideology and imperialism, propaganda and proclamation, as well as shaping the experiences of post-colonialist countries endeavouring to disentangle themselves from such alien influences (see e.g. Homi Bhabha, *The Location of Culture*; Norman Lewis, *The Missionaries: God Against the Indians*; Gayatri Chakravorty Spivak, *Outside in the Teaching Machine*).

Matters relating to bible translation also became entangled with many of the problems of book *publishing and consumerism in the 20th century. The bible is big business and retains its hold even in secularized western cultures, especially the Anglo-Saxon, where legal oaths are still sworn on it and the gift of a bible often accompanies rites of passage such as confirmation or marriage. Under the dual impetus of missionary and publisher the production of new editions and versions of the bible in ever more languages, aimed at ever more specialist audiences, shows no sign of diminishing in the third millennium.   **Robert P. Carroll**

Barnstone, W., *The Poetics of Translation: History, Theory, Practice* (1993).
'Bible, Versions of', *The Anchor Bible Dictionary* (1992), vi. 787–851.
Buber, M., and Rosenzweig, F., *Scripture and Translation* (1994).
Budick, S., and Iser, W. (eds.), *The Translatability of Cultures: Figurations of the Space Between* (1996).
Hargreaves, C., *A Translator's Freedom: Modern English Bibles and their Language* (1993).
Kelly, L. G., *The True Interpreter: A History of Translation Theory and Practice in the West* (1979).
Nida, E. A., *Toward a Science of Translating with Special Reference to Principles and Procedures Involved in Bible Translating* (1964).
Nida, E. A., and Taber, C. R., *The Theory and Practice of Translation* (1969).
Schwarz, W., *Principles and Problems of Biblical Translation: Some Reformation Controversies and their Background* (1955).
Steiner, G., *After Babel: Aspects of Language and Translation* (1975), 3rd edn. (1998).
Stine, P. C. (ed.), *Bible Translation and the Spread of the Church: The Last 200 Years* (1990).
Venuti, L., *The Translator's Invisibility: A History of Translation* (1995).

transubstantiation is a theological term invented in the 12th century to define the effect on *bread and *wine consecrated in the *Eucharist whereby they become really and truly the *Body and *Blood of Christ. While some people, such as the 11th-century theologian Berengar, held that the words 'This is my body' should be understood *symbolically rather than physically, Christians then and now have generally held that what Jesus said is literally true and that this implies something more than symbolism. The belief in a 'real presence' of the living Christ in the Eucharist is common to east and west and very ancient. In what way is such a 'real presence' to be explained? It is clear, and uncontested, that in every detectable

way the bread remains bread, the wine wine, and yet they are now 'really' Christ's body and blood. Medieval theologians believed that they could express what happens in terms of *Aristotle's distinction between substance and accidents. Everything apparent to the sense is an 'accident' but beneath accidents lies the substance of a thing, that which it 'really' is. In the Eucharist, they decided, the accidents remained unchanged but the substance is converted.

The 'Real Presence' of Christ in the consecrated species is a doctrine. Transubstantiation is rather a matter of *theology, a much used and abused interpretation of the mystery of the *sacrament dependent upon the philosophy and physics current in the Middle Ages but now superseded. Lutherans have preferred to call it 'consubstantiation', asserting the substantial coexistence of bread and body. Although the Council of *Trent only asserted that what happens at the eucharistic consecration is 'conveniently and properly called' transubstantiation, the denial or affirmation of transubstantiation became the very touchstone of the *Protestant–*Catholic divide, especially in England. Thus the Test Act of 1673, aiming to exclude Catholics from public life, made a declaration of disbelief in transubstantiation a condition for accepting office and the British sovereign had to do the same in the so-called 'Royal Declaration' until 1910. British Catholics in consequence proudly saw their belief in transubstantiation as the quintessential mark of true faith.

As a theological concept transubstantiation must clearly be dependent on the meaning attached to 'substance', a word that has in fact been used in a great number of ways, and it remains possible to defend use of 'transubstantiation' in other than Aristotelian terms. In common parlance the substance of something is what makes it significant: it is what it most truly is, rather than what it seems to be. A tiny piece of bread is something valueless; consecrated in the Eucharist it becomes supremely valuable: sacramentally Christ is now 'really' present in this bread. In the terms of physics, absolutely nothing has changed but, in the way the believer relates to it in its hidden objectivity, everything has altered. This does justice to the Lutheran point: in one sense it is substantially bread, in another Christ's body. It is in accord with Christian belief in the Real Presence as shared by Catholics, Orthodox, Lutherans, and most Anglicans to speak of transubstantiation in this sense, as is recognized, for instance, by the 1971 ARCIC statement on eucharistic doctrine. *Schillebeeckx suggested 'transignification' as an alternative term, but it may be easier to reformulate the meaning than change the word. On account of the long history of controversy surrounding this term, however ill-informed, it is unlikely and unnecessary that many non-Roman Catholics would wish to use it. Equally long usage and deep historical loyalties fortified by persecution make this a word that many Catholics would not wish to abandon.

                                                        Adrian Hastings

ARCIC, *Final Report* (1982).
Clark, J. T., 'Physics, Philosophy, Transubstantiation, Theology', *Theological Studies*, 12 (1951), 24–51.
Schillebeeckx, E., *The Eucharist* (1968).

Trent, Council of (1545–63). Trent dominated Roman *Catholic theology for four centuries. Although Martin *Luther had appealed to a general *council of the church to resolve the issues brought forward by him, the *papacy long remained unwilling to follow this course. Fear of a revival of *conciliar claims to superiority over the papacy, as propounded by the previous councils of Constance and Basle, as well as disagreement about the place, were major causes of the delay. By the time the council was called, as a result, the divisions between *Protestants and Roman Catholics had hardened. Trent was eventually chosen as a place acceptable to both pope and emperor: to the former as lying in Italy and therefore not too far from his control, to the latter because it was an imperial fief and therefore subject to the emperor's authority. Most of the sessions were held in the cathedral. The council met in the three periods of 1545–7, 1551–2, and 1562–3. In the intervals its continuation was often in doubt. The start, moreover, was far from promising with only thirty or so bishops and others, mostly Italians, attending. Gradually the council gathered momentum and over two hundred members attended the later sessions.

By the third session (February 1546), the council was defining its aims as 'the rooting out of heresy and the reform of conduct'. This twofold purpose dominated the remainder of the council. The *heresy in mind, though it was rarely mentioned by name, was the Protestant *Reformation which, in various forms, had been sweeping across Europe with remarkable success in the preceding decades. Even so, the council, especially in its early stages, was no mere head-on confrontation with Protestantism. There was a party within the council, headed by cardinals Marcello Cervini and Reginald Pole and the head of the Augustinian friars, Girolamo Seripando, who wanted the better elements of the Reformation to be taken on board, and their views were partly represented in the council's decrees. The council, somewhat belatedly, issued three official invitations to Protestants to attend, in 1551, 1552, and 1562.

Trent placed itself in the mainstream of the Christian tradition by affirming the *Niceno-Constantinopolitan *creed in its first doctrinal decree. On *authority, the next issue to be tackled, the council expressed reverence for 'all the books of the Old and New Testaments', but also affirmed the role of *tradition in the church. This stance can be interpreted as a 'two-source' theory of authority, yet scripture and tradition were said to find their one source in the gospel proclaimed by Jesus Christ: a knitting together that was developed further in chapters 2 and 3 of Vatican II's decree on *revelation (see BIBLE). On *justification, another central issue in the Reformation controversies, a long and subtle decree went far in accepting the Protestant position, emphasizing 'the powerlessness of nature and law to justify' and the gratuity of God's saving *grace, but also stressed our role in 'giving free assent to and co-operating with this same grace' and the possibility of further growth in sanctification through 'faith united to good works'.

The rest of the council's doctrinal decrees were mostly taken up with the *sacraments. Detailed expositions affirmed the medieval number of seven—*baptism, *Eucharist, confirmation, *penance, *marriage, orders, and last anointing—against the usual Protestant number of two, baptism and Eucharist. The Eucharist was treated particularly closely and here a rather hardline approach was adopted, with strong emphasis on the doctrine of *transubstantiation. Other doctrinal topics in debate with Protestants received decrees, mostly towards the end of the council: *purgatory, the intercession of *saints, indulgences.

On the 'reform of conduct', the second main thrust, the council's work was extensive but less complete than in the area of doctrine. Instruction and preaching; the suitability and responsibilities of persons appointed to benefices, including the abuses of pluralism and non-residence; religious orders of men and women; various devotional practices, including devotions to *saints and *fasting: these were all treated at some length, though in some cases with too much allowance for papal and other dispensations, too much concern for vested interests, to satisfy the wishes of more thoroughgoing Catholic reformers. An important decree authorized the establishment of seminaries for the training of future priests, preferably one for each diocese.

In its final session, the council entrusted to the pope the task of producing a catechism, revised versions of the breviary and missal, and a list of books that Catholics were forbidden to read. These provisions led to the 'catechism of Trent', the Roman breviary, the Tridentine mass, and *Index librorum prohibitorum*.

Trent was a cornerstone of the *Counter-Reformation and gave Catholic apologists something sensible to say on almost every topic in the Reformation debate. Its range and success was a principal reason why the next general council of the Roman church, *Vatican I, did not take place for more than three centuries: there seemed to be no need for another. Arguably it deepened and prolonged the Reformation divisions but such a view probably does less than justice to the subtlety and sophistication of many of its decrees. The council made points that needed to be stated and it may be seen as the best that could be done, by the Roman Catholic Church, in the circumstances. In this sense it preserved important points in the Christian tradition and may benefit reunion in the end.

Trent's dominance waned in the 1950s and came to an end at *Vatican II. The Roman Catholic Church, however, still struggles with its legacy both internally and in its relations with other churches. Perhaps the best way forward is to value its remarkable achievements without exaggerating its authority: to see it as a general council of the Roman Catholic Church—along with other councils after the east–west schism of the 11th century—rather than an ecumenical council binding on all Christians: a more relaxed attitude that surprisingly few theologians have adopted.

Norman Tanner

Concilium Tridentinum. Diariorum, actorum, epistularum, tractatuum nova collectio. Edidit Societas Goerresiana (11 vols. to date; 1901–).

Jedin, H., *Geschichte des Konzils von Trient* (5 vols.; 1949–75). ET of vols. i and ii, *A History of the Council of Trent* (1957–61).

—— *Crisis and Closure of the Council of Trent* (1967).

Olin, J. C., *Catholic Reform from Cardinal Ximenes to the Council of Trent, 1495–1563* (1990).

Tanner, N. P. (ed.), *Decrees of the Ecumenical Councils* (1990), ii.

Trinity. The character of a religion is chiefly determined by its identification of deity. We may suppose, for a central matter, that all religions 'save'. But this word is a mere place-marker until the saving reality is identified; 'x saves' asserts only that something rescues us from something. Only when 'x' is replaced by a personal proper name or identifying description does the predicate 'saves' become religiously meaningful. Thus, for example, 'Baal saves' means 'Baal sends rain and restores the city'; 'Buddhahood saves' means 'Buddhahood is our refuge from personality'; and 'The Trinity saves' means 'The Trinity takes us into his ineluctable communal personality.'

That some 'salvations' are incompatible appears from the second and third of these examples. The attempt to avoid this by abstracting a deity and salvation in which all religions can be at one only ends with 'x saves' again, that is, with religious and intellectual vacancy. The real question is, *which* claimant do we worship and which salvation do we therefore await?

The doctrine of Trinity is Christianity's answer to this question, its identification of its *God. We turn our worship, says the church, *to* the one whom *Jesus the Israelite called 'my Father'; we worship him *with* this Jesus, as the Son he thus made himself out to be; and we are animated therein *by* that same Spirit who evokes their mutual love (see HOLY SPIRIT). *Just and only so* we have to do with the one God. To proceed at once to the highest pitch of developed doctrine: the God of the church is the one life that occurs between Jesus and his Father by their Spirit, a life that we can sense only as we are admitted into it.

Because the doctrine of Trinity identifies the church's God, the late 20th century required its renewal. In the past in the west, it was generally supposed that when people spoke of 'God' they meant the Christian one. The assumption was always dubious and in the modern world it is clearly untenable. Whom does the Christian gospel propose to be God? is again the urgent question it was for the ancient church. The late 20th-century's strenuous effort to understand and develop the doctrine of Trinity began with the Protestant Karl *Barth and the Catholic Karl *Rahner, and continued in similarly ecumenical fashion.

Deities are identified in different ways. It is itself a specificity of the biblical God that he is not initially identified by timeless predicates, such as 'all-seeing' or 'immortal', or by an image or ritual, but by a narrative. The narrative, moreover, is not *mythic, that is, it cannot be reduced to propositions assigning predicates or interpreting an image or ritual.

In the *Old Testament, God identifies himself as 'the Lord … who brought you out of the land of Egypt, out of the house of slavery' (Exod. 20: 2), and who when he came to do this proclaimed himself the God of the patriarchs. In the *New Testament, God is identified as he 'who raised our Lord Jesus from the dead' (e.g. Rom. 4: 24), and who did it as the God of *Israel to whom this Jesus had committed his life. It is as we attend to the plot of the biblical narrative turning on these two events, and to the *dramatis personae* who appear in them and carry that plot, that we are led to speak of God as Father, Son, and Spirit.

The church's identification of her God by *Resurrection does not replace Israel's by *exodus but rather verifies it. A *narrative* can be an identification of deity only if it is an *eschatological narrative, that is, if it has a dramatic end and if from that end it encompasses all reality. It is because Israel comes to hope for a final act of God that will establish his sole reign, something that involves triumph over *death, over the apparent pre-emption of such completion, that her story with God can claim to identify not only her but her God.

The story of Exodus and Resurrection thus intends to identify not just God's people but God himself. There is then a further question. Histories have more than one agent. In the story of God with his people, do 'God' and 'his people' exhaustively name the agents? That cannot be, for then either God's identity would be determined by mere creatures, or God's own, 'immanent', identity would after all be immune to the biblical events. Thus throughout scripture we encounter *personae* of God's story with his people who are neither simply the same as the story's Lord nor yet other than he. They are precisely *dramatis dei personae*, the personal carriers of a drama that is God's own reality. We turn to their biblical appearance.

The primary sense of 'the Son' in developed trinitarian language may be so stated: he is an other by whom and with whom God is identified, so that what God does to or for this one he does to and for himself, and so that God knows and possesses himself precisely as the one so related to this other—all in a fashion for which the relation of parent and child is the created *analogy. In the OT story of God and Israel, this is the very relation that appears between God and Israel as such, and also between God and figures who appear *within* Israel and share her history. Such figures, fully profiled and repeatedly appearing, include the Lord's '*Angel', 'Name', 'Glory', 'Word', and 'Servant'. Each in some way shares Israel's history and the Lord's being; they belong to the *shekinah*, to God's personal 'settlement' within Israel, which is so ontological that the old rabbis could say that when God redeems Israel he redeems himself because the *shekinah* is with Israel. Thus in the great story of the *Aqedah* (Abraham's sacrifice of Isaac), the 'Angel *of* the Lord' says to *Abraham, 'you have not withheld your son … from *me* (Gen. 22: 11–12, emphases added'). We should note further the way in which especially Deutero-Isaiah's 'Servant of the Lord' is both Israel, to serve the nations, and an individual within Israel, to serve Israel.

'The Spirit of the Lord' is present throughout the OT, to move Israel's history when it stagnates, to make *prophets, and to do the former by doing the latter—his prophets' words 'will not return empty'. We may gain access to the phenomenon of spirit from ourselves, for we too are 'spirited', though only more or less so. A human's spirit is the person himself or herself, in so far as he or she is a life that enlivens others also. Just so, a person's spirit confronts him or her with those others, and so with different possibilities of life, and so with his or her own freedom for a future. Except for ease of understanding, we could have started this chain of characterizations at the other end, and said that a person's spirit is the person as the person's own futurity to him or herself, and so is the person's freedom for community. And it is the second mode that is most appropriate to evoke *God's* Spirit: he is the Power of God as his own Future, the Freedom in which he is community for himself and for us.

Jesus appears in the gospels as the Lord's Prophet, as his incarnate word and glory, and as his servant in and for Israel; simultaneously he appears as the bearer of all Israel's prophetic and serving roles in and for the nations. Thus in him the pattern of divine sonship to which Israel's life is cut steps forward in individual *personhood. The priestly court understood perfectly what Jesus' teaching and acts implicitly claimed: 'Are you, then, the Son of God?' When he said 'Yes', they ruled, 'We have heard the blasphemy …' (Luke 22: 70–1).

Once a historical individual thus appears as the Son, he turns to claim the Lord as 'my Father', and then allows his followers to share this relation by addressing his Father as 'our Father' (Matt. 6: 9). That is, he identifies the Lord as a *persona* of the Lord's own drama, *'the Father'. Contrary to what is often supposed, it is the Father whose personhood fully emerges only in the NT.

The doctrine of Trinity is then fully present in the NT, not, indeed, as a doctrine *about* God but more fundamentally, as a controlling logic: when the NT writers refer to God they regularly mention two or all three of the *personae* (e.g, Jude 20–1; 2 Cor. 1: 21–2; Eph. 2: 18; Rom. 1: 1–4; Rev. 5: 6) usually in some soteriologically meaningful pattern. (e.g. Rom. 8: 11–17). Thus Paul claims 'the grace given me by God to be a minister of Christ Jesus … so that the offering of the Gentiles may be … sanctified by the Holy Spirit' (Rom. 15: 15–16). This logic comes together in the Lord's new personal name on which the church is founded: the church is the community of those initiated into the God named 'Father, Son and Holy Spirit' (Matt. 28: 19).

The formulas we are likely to think of as 'the doctrine of Trinity' are answers to questions this identification of God raised in the Gentile mission, between c.120 and 381. The Greek religious thinkers and the Mediterranean civilization they schooled identified deity by metaphysical predicates: centrally, deity is timelessness, 'impassibility' to *time's contingencies. So soon as the gospel mission reached persons fully at home in this theology, converts carried a heavy burden of cognitive dissonance.

How were they to think of God as timeless, and so as 'impassible', 'immovable', and so on, self-evident characters of deity on all their cultural assumptions, and simultaneously as 'compassionate', 'patient', and so on, as the scriptures display the Lord? Worse, how were they to think of God as identified by and with the blatantly temporal events of a birth and a hanging? Or even with the narratives of the OT? Surely, said Justin Martyr (c.150), God himself did not walk in the Garden or argue with Abraham? (*Dialogue with Trypho*, 1. 11. 127).

If we believe the biblical narrative, but still cling to the dogma that God himself is unsullied by temporal events, only two escapes are open. We can suppose that God himself is a timeless fourth above the temporally implicated Father, Son, and Spirit, and that the latter are deity's manifestations within time, perhaps as 'Creator, Redeemer, and Sanctifier'. Or we can identify the Father with God himself, make him the bearer of the Greeks' deity-predicates, and so have the Son and the Spirit to do the temporal dirty work. Historians call the first 'modalism', the second 'subordinationism'.

From its first appearance at the end of the 2nd century, modalism has been the theology of the pious but unthinking; it seems to find place for the biblical narrative without raising too many problems. Yet its prompt refutation by Tertullian (*Against Praxeas*) was definitive, for modalism in fact makes the Greeks' God the real one (see PRE-CONSTANTINIAN THOUGHT).

Subordinationism is more subtle, and a historically determining line of Christian theologians, from Justin to the first world-class Christian thinker, *Origen of *Alexandria, built a comprehensive subordinationist theology that became the élite theology of the 3rd- and 4th-century church. They adopted a central concept of late-antique religion: 'the Logos', usually translated 'the Word' but here denoting not speech but the meaning which may be expressed in speech. This Logos appears in much philosophy and theosophy of the time as the indwelling divine meaning of the cosmos, and so *mediates* between the sheer atemporality of divinity itself and the temporalities of this world. Justin and his successors thought this 'second God', one step down an ontological ladder from the fully divine Father, was just what was needed as the Son. Only relatively timeless, the Logos could do what the Father could not, condescend to Noah or Abraham; and finally he could even overcome our

alienation from deity by becoming 'incarnate' among us.

The *Arians, whose initiatives split the 4th-century church and occasioned the first great *councils, were simply subordinationists of a blunter than usual sort, who insisted on implications others tried to evade. There are in the bible, they rightly observed, only two kinds of reality, God, who is creator, and creatures. God, they were sure, cannot suffer. But the Son must *suffer for our salvation. Therefore the Son is a, certainly very special, creature. To which first *Athanasius and then the Cappadocians, Basil the Great, Gregory Nazianzen, and Gregory of Nyssa, responded: if the Son is not creator, you must either stop worshipping him or admit to creature-worship. Either way you defect to paganism. Therewith an antinomy was revealed that ran through accepted élite theology, provoking decades of anguished debate.

The church's developed doctrine of Trinity, worked out by Athanasius and the Cappadocians and dogmatized in the *creed laid down at *Nicaea (325) and *Constantinople (381), is simply what Christian theology is compelled to say if the modalist and subordinationist escapes are closed. Christianity had finally to challenge the premiss that God requires a being less divine than himself to mediate his involvement with temporal creatures and their doings. The gospel proclaims a God who is not as God alien to time; the Son who is 'from' God and who lives a temporal life from birth through suffering to death, is not therefore less than 'true God'. Indeed, the Father and this Son are *homoousios*, 'of one being'; that is, as Athanasius gave the word its theological meaning, precisely the relationship between Jesus the Son and his Father determines what it means to be God, and apart from this relationship the biblical God would not be.

The deity of the Spirit became thematic only at the end of the controversy, not for any intrinsic reason but because the subordinationist theology was concerned mostly with the Son, so that its deconstruction began there. So soon as the matter came up, the equal place of Son and Spirit in the baptismal name and throughout Christian worship dictated parallel doctrine. According to Constantinople (381), the 'lordly and life-giving' Spirit is to be worshipped 'with the Father and the Son'. The gospel calls for no spirits, no religious dynamisms, that are not identical with God's own present self; there can be in the church no mere religious 'seeking' for him or general 'spirituality'.

Finally, therefore, it is the *Trinity* who is God. So Gregory Nazianzen: 'Eternal and one is the deity in the Trinity, and one his glory' (*Orations*, 21. 20) We have arrived at the doctrine with which we began. As Basil and the Gregorys worked it out, in the most compressed possible reading: there are three 'hypostases' of God, each of which is distinguishable from the others by the way in which he gives and/or receives one and the same divine 'nature' to or from the others; and this divine nature is but the 'infinity', the eschatological unsurpassability, of the life they thus have together.

Work on the teaching will never come to rest, so long as the gospel continues in cultures in any way descended from the Greeks. In the current effort, four questions perhaps draw most attention.

1. How can the Trinity doctrine, once recognized in its rightful place, be used to solve other theological questions? There is a steady publication-stream of 'trinitarian' theologies 'of' a vast range of matters—and displaying a vast range of competence.

2. Wherein lies the unity of the triune God? From the beginning, the eastern church has found the unity in the position of the Father as the one who gives deity to the Son and Spirit and does not receive it; and the west has found it in the one divine being. The argument is again lively, and is further complicated by the question, 'Can the Trinity as such be called personal?'

3. How can the Spirit's role in the triune life be more fully recognized? Inherited doctrine construes the relations between the persons only as relations of origin. Are there not as fundamentally relations of perfecting?

4. What are the metaphysical implications? If God is not alien to time, and if in standard western doctrine God is Being, what follows for our general grasp of reality?   **Robert W. Jenson**

Barth, Karl, *Church Dogmatics* I/1, ET (1936).
Gunton, Colin, *The Promise of Trinitarian Theology*, 2nd edn. (1997).
Hanson, R. P. C., *The Search for the Christian Doctrine of God* (1988).
Jenson, Robert W., *Systematic Theology* (1997), i.
LaCugna, Catherine M., *God for Us: The Trinity and Christian Life* (1991).
Moltmann, Jürgen, *The Crucified God*, ET (1972).
Pannenberg, Wolfhart, *Systematic Theology*, ET (1991), i.
Rahner, Karl, *The Trinity*, ET (1997).

truth is central to the *christology of *John's gospel: *Jesus says 'I am the way, the truth, and the life' (14: 6). 'Are you a king, then?' asked Pilate … 'For this was I born and came into the world, to bear witness to the truth,' answered Jesus, to which Pilate replied, 'What is truth?' (18: 37).

Pilate's question has been endlessly discussed by philosophers. For the central tradition of western *philosophy, as equally for Christianity, truth is the quality whereby judgements express or correspond with reality, words with world. In *Aristotle's definition, 'to say of what is that it is, and of what is not that it is not, is true'. Truth can also be said to be reality itself, precisely as knowable (what is and what is true being one and the same, a scholastic adage). The first may be called logical (or epistemological) truth, the latter ontological: that is how medieval Christian philosophers tended to formulate it. Logical truth lies formally in a proposition or statement, 'there is a yew tree beside my cottage'. It is the statement that is true, not as such the yew tree, nor the proximity, but it is only true if there is a yew tree so placed. Even if no one makes the statement, its content remains the case. For common sense the truth is unchanged whether or not known by anyone or expressed in a proposition, yet what in that case is true, one can ask, if truth is a quality of statements and there is no statement? Truth theory thus ties itself into knots with a logical conundrum derived from the ambiguity created by the relationship between knowing subject and known object, a relationship founded in the latter but experienced in the former.

Despite various theories of truth that attempt to eliminate the basic sense of correspondence between what is asserted and reality, and to replace this, if never satisfactorily, by some form of constructivism (cf. Michael Dummett's *Truth and Other Enigmas*, 1978), truth remains, especially outside the corridors of university philosophy departments, a supremely realist notion and one upon which human society is totally dependent. The idea of truth grounds order and *justice as much as *science and *history. Did X murder Y? Did A or B obtain more votes? Does this can actually contain the beef its label claims? Courts of law are committed to the

precise evaluation of historic truth as a basis for the administration of justice, as are innumerable other constitutional and commercial processes. Without the conviction that truth matters and can be ascertained, the confidence required to make human society viable must simply disappear. While truth as such first appears as an intellectual matter, it inherently undergirds the ethical order. Telling lies is unethical. It also makes loving personal relationships impossible. Social and moral existence requires, then, an inescapable concept of truth, expressing recognition of the way things actually are, not the way someone would like them to be. The historic reality of the *Holocaust, the Atlantic slave trade, or the crucifixion of Jesus are not myths, creative fantasies, but truths, just as the approximate age of the earth, or the law of gravity is a matter of truth.

The more we get beyond fairly straightforward assertions of fact, nevertheless, the harder it is to formulate truth satisfactorily and the more likely it is that some people will question the formulations of others as mistaken, one-sided, or confused. At that point we move from truth itself to issues of certainty, verification, the criteria for assessing specific truth-claims, differing modes for formulating truth. However, if one interpretation of history, science, or *ethics is challenged by another, it must always be in terms of objective evidence of some sort; each interpretation must claim to be more truthful, that is to say to reflect reality, something given, better than former interpretations.

Far as such ideas may seem from the Johannine claim for Jesus as witnessing to truth, even being truth, it would be mistaken not to understand that claim in this context. While the OT linked truth especially with God and God's word as firm, unchanging, reliable, it uses the same word ('emeth) to indicate the conformity between a human judgement and reality (1 Kgs. 10: 6; 22: 16). Nor are the two separable or unrelated in meaning. If someone speaks the truth, then his word like God's will last: 'Truthful lips endure for ever, but a lying tongue is but for a moment' (Prov. 12: 19). The NT word for truth (*aletheia*) suggests something unconcealed, open to view; this again includes the sense of rightly perceived reality. There is far less of a gap than may be imagined between OT and NT conceptions and the Aristotelian definition of truth as the correct structure of a judgement in relation to reality. What John's gospel claims is that Jesus somehow reveals God, the ultimate reality in which all being and goodness cohere and to which all other judgements have to conform. He is by his very existence a statement about how God is and, therefore, about how everything is.

All truths are compatible while falsehood is detected precisely by its inability to endure on account of its incompatibility with things unquestionably true. For the evangelist the acceptance of truth is a fundamentally moral issue; immediately one consciously leaves the path of truth at any point one puts oneself in danger of multiplying untruths and blocking oneself off from the protection of truth itself. Truth protects because it lasts and because, if one is faithfully committed to it, one cannot be caught out. The claim that truth in this universal and fundamental sense can in any way be identified with Jesus Christ may seem bizarre, but it is a claim implicit within the doctrine of the *Incarnation, the conception of Christ as God's *Word. The Christian sense of truth, drawing as it does on both Hebrew and Greek tradition, is intensely realist, a *realism that goes far wider than its christological centrepiece. Just as non-realism can lead only to chaos in a court of law, so must it in the court of philosophy and religion. It is something inherently non-viable. God is not a concept we can invent and play with; once one believes one has invented it, the only reasonable thing is to discard it. Rather is it essentially the assertion of a given, an existence underlying all other existence, a truth behind all truths.

That is not to say that truth of this sort can be formulated in a neat 'there are only two cows in this field' way, something we can fully claim to understand. Many would indeed claim that truths about God can only be formulated in the negative. The bewildering reality of philosophical *metaphysics, even of what one can term Christian philosophy, should make that clear. The attempts of, for instance, *Anselm, in the De veritate, *Aquinas in his work of the same name, Malebranche's Recherche de la vérité, and so much else may collectively suggest a picture of searching for something in the dark. It remains the case that while modern philosophy has concentrated far more on the conditions for recognizing a true statement, it is hard to escape the basic recognition, as formulated by Schelling, that truth lies in the absolute identity of the subjective and the objective. Truthfulness, in Christ or in ourselves, is the subjective condition of conformity with the objective, but it is surely clear that truthfulness is most complete when it includes what is most ultimate in reality rather than a mass of trivia. If Christ is the embodiment of 'grace and truth' (John 1: 17), he is functioning in regard to ultimate divine reality as Schelling's absolute identification of subjective and objective. In *Kierkegaard's words, 'Christ is the truth in such a sense that to be the truth is the only true explanation of what truth is.' That is the central claim of christology in regard to truth.

Such truth can still not be divorced from any other truth. The accusation of holding a doctrine of 'double truth' (the incompatibility of philosophical truth with theological) was made, perhaps unfairly, against the Christian Averroists in 13th-century Paris. The idea that two assertions can be genuinely incompatible, yet both true, is occasionally resurrected, but it is alien to the central Christian tradition that truth cannot conflict with truth, and that there is a moral duty to cherish all ways, scientific, poetic, prayerful, of arriving at truth. If Christian thought has pursued directly philosophical and rational ways, especially via *analogy, for the expression of truth about ultimate reality, it has also appealed to the roads of *poetry, *allegory, and *metaphor. The gospel of John is poetry compared to the prose of the Synoptics. In terms of historical reportage, it may be less reliable, yet it could be that it expresses the truth about Jesus better than they. It stands back more reflectively from the facts, as, in their different ways, do much modern historical writing as well as poetry. Lear and Othello portray truth, an intensely moral truth, but not a historical one. *Prophecy and *mysticism may open up truth no less genuinely than does philosophy but differently. Yet a recurring weakness in Christian *theology has been an inability to accept pluriformity in the way religious truth is perceived and expressed. John and the Synoptics have often been judged on identical standards of strict literalism. Likewise the use of phrases such as 'true church' and 'true faith' often indicate a too restrictive approach to the way things can be true. Nevertheless, whatever is true, as perceived by any discipline, has finally to represent reality, something given, something we discover, not something we invent. What is invented cannot cohere or endure.

Each invention lies within its own autonomous world of meaning. Where there is deep coherence between things that people imagine and seem to have invented, it must depend upon the invention being actually, despite all the appearance and excitement of creativity, a new port of entry into objective reality.

At the close of the 20th century that was not everywhere a fashionable view, even in Christian circles. In the second half of the century numerous apologists latched on to *Wittgenstein's idea of a 'language game' to suggest that *religious language could be understood and defended as something autonomous: it would be simply one of the linguistic games people play, as valid or invalid as any other. Under the spell of the ethos of *postmodernism, Don *Cupitt and the 'Sea of Faith' group went much further in offering a wholly non-realist view of religious truth or even of all truth. Attractive as this may seem as a defence of religious language and behaviour without any metaphysical claim or assertion of intrinsic universality, it remains in contradiction with the whole objectivist fundament and development of Christian thought, Hebrew and Greek, mystical and philosophical. Realism is not necessarily theistic, but it is unsatisfactory to hold a realist view of truth while defending the utility of a non-realist view of God. If the latter instead leads to a non-realist view of truth as a whole, the practical difficulties, as we have suggested, become overwhelming. Again, while it is not self-evident that reality as we experience it presupposes an ultimate reality that is just another way of saying God, it is the conviction of Christian faith, as well as of *natural theology, that this is in fact the case, however hard it may be to tease it out. Though in the short run it may seem intellectually exciting to assert that we create truth rather than find it, this is essentially a lie, destructive not just of Christianity but of society as well as science. The *devil, declared Jesus, was the father of lies (John 8: 44), but in the words of Coventry Patmore,

> When all its work is done, the lie shall rot;
> The truth is great, and shall prevail,
> When none cares whether it prevail or not.

Adrian Hastings

Brunner, E., Truth as Encounter (1964).
Crowder, Colin (ed.), God and Reality: Essays on Christian Non-Realism (1997).
Gadamer, Hans-Georg, Truth and Method (1960), ET (1975).
Kierkegaard, Søren, Concluding Unscientific Postscript (1846), ET (1945).
Lonergan, Bernard, Verbum: Word and Idea in Aquinas (1967).
Maritain, Jacques, The Degrees of Knowledge (1932), ET (1959).

Tübingen. The theological community in Tübingen is something unimaginable in the English-speaking world: a concentration of over 2,000 students that might claim to form the natural heart of *German theology. Founded in the 15th century by Gabriel Biel, one of the most open-minded of late-medieval theologians, the *university has two faculties of theology, Protestant and Roman Catholic, that have been central to modern European theology since the early 1800s.

The most important theologian in the Stift, the Protestant faculty, in the *nineteenth century was Ferdinand Christian Baur (1792–1860), who worked there almost his entire life. Baur was influenced by both *Hegel and *Schleiermacher, introducing new approaches to biblical criticism that anticipated later historical-critical methods. The founder of the extremely influential Tübingen School of *New Testament criticism, Baur taught both Albrecht Ritschl and David Friedrich Strauss, whose work echoed Baur's in questioning the historical origins of Christianity, and pioneering a historical interpretation of the development of Christian doctrine (see HIGHER CRITICISM).

Baur's writings have remained influential, and through Ritschl in particular he was able to influence the development of 19th-century *liberal Protestantism. In the *twentieth century also Tübingen Protestant theologians have echoed Baur's position. Peter Stuhlmacher and Martin Hengel have maintained the high profile of NT studies. Eberhard *Jüngel and Jürgen *Moltmann have combined Baur's interests in historical criticism and doctrinal interpretation. These theological tendencies remain highly influential in Tübingen's Protestant faculty, even if they are no longer normative, as they were in Baur's time.

The most important Roman Catholic Tübingen theologian was Johann Adam Möhler (1796–1838), professor of church history there until he moved to Munich in 1835. Möhler, not unlike Baur, was influenced by Hegel and Schleiermacher, and wrote persuasively of the challenge of modern thought to traditional Catholicism. Möhler was also committed to the reconciliation of the Protestant and Catholic churches, and looked forward to both the *ecumenical movement, and the work of Karl Adam and Hans *Küng.

Karl Joseph Hefele (1809–93) followed Möhler as a Catholic professor of church history (appointed 1840). Subsequently elected bishop of Rottenburg in 1869, Hefele had a prominent role as consultant in preparations for *Vatican I. He was opposed to the definition of papal *infallibility at the Council, but as bishop relented and published the Vatican Decrees in his diocese in 1871.

Karl Adam (1876–1966) maintained the values of liberalism and *modernism in Tübingen Catholic theology which both Möhler and Hefele had supported and developed (including ecumenism). During his years as professor in Tübingen (1919–49), Adam was arguably the Catholic theologian in Europe with the greatest influence on the laity. He combined a liberal and ecumenical approach with orthodox Catholic teaching, in such works as *The Spirit of Catholicism* helping to prepare the way for *Vatican II.

Adam's influence was continued in the work of Hans Küng, appointed professor of fundamental theology in Tübingen in 1960. Increasingly disillusioned with the *magisterium*, Küng was stripped of his authority to teach as Catholic theologian in 1979, but continued to hold his post at the Institute for Ecumenical Research in Tübingen. From Möhler through Adam to Küng, the tradition of a modernizing Catholic theology remains very strong, highly influential, and faithful to the legacy of Biel.   **Gareth Jones**

Burtchaell, J. T., 'Drey, Möhler and the Catholic School of Tübingen', in N. Smart *et al.* (eds.), *Nineteenth Century Religious Thought in the West* (1985), ii.

Fitzer, J., *Möhler and Baur in Controversy 1832–38* (1974).

Harris, H., *The Tübingen School* (1975).

twentieth century: an overview.

In the winter term of 1899–1900, Adolph Harnack gave a series of open lectures in the University of Berlin on the nature of *Christianity. They were attended by more than 600 students and their text was immediately published and translated into English. *What is Christianity?* went into many editions and, perhaps more than any other book, represents the quintessence of authoritative Christian thought at the start of the 20th century, the high point of *liberal Protestant theology. *Germany had dominated the field throughout the *nineteenth century and Harnack personified that domination in several ways. As Rector of the University of Berlin as well as its Professor of Church History, and a member of the Royal Prussian Academy, he stood at the heart of the German academic, and indeed political, world. His immense learning and the clarity of his teaching made him personally extremely influential, so that many outstanding thinkers of the next generation had been his students. In 1900 he was 50 years old, at the height of his powers, and would continue to be a very active presence in the theological world for another 25 years. No one else so straddled the centuries. Nineteenth-century Germany had rewritten Christian *theology as either *philosophy of a post-*Hegelian sort or as *history. It was the latter approach that Harnack represented and it was so persuasive because it appeared to deal in convincing scholarly detail with the way Christianity had come to be, both in scripture and in the development of church history. It was 'scientific', a word Harnack regularly repeated (using it in its German sense of 'systematic'). His three-volume *History of Dogma* and related works outlined a view of Christianity whose main thrust it seemed hard to deny. Moreover, his was not a sceptical or secular viewpoint. It was an account of 'The Gospel', as he liked to call it, by a believer. But it was essentially 'scientific theology', that is to say 'critical-historical study', which led, he thought, to a view of Christ that could and should lead to faith in the *God and *Father of Christ. For Harnack, in theology science had to come first but good science would lead to true *faith.

He thought that true Christianity must be centred on the Father whom *Jesus preached, and not on Jesus himself. He had little time for any of the dogmatic developments he had researched so skilfully. They almost all led in the wrong direction. The true Jesus was an *ethical teacher whose nature wonderfully reflected that of God and whose guidance could lead the modern world along the paths of a liberal Protestantism. It was essentially spiritual and otherworldly, with no political message whatsoever but not, Harnack believed, anti-worldly. His was an optimistic interpretation of *religion suited to an optimistic age and it did not challenge his own views, which combined confidence in the advance of civilization with conservative, even nationalist, politics. Christianity represented the very best in human religion, no less but little more.

The influence of Harnack was enormous on the thousands of pastors who attended his lectures over the years, but his own *Lutheran Church could not accept a teaching that denied the strictly *miraculous, including the *Virgin Birth, the *Resurrection, and Ascension, as well as the dogmatic value of the *credal affirmations of *Nicaea and *Chalcedon. The Supreme Council of the Evangelical Church had vetoed his appointment to the Berlin Chair, but the veto had been overruled by the emperor with the support of the faculty. Nevertheless, the church denied him official recognition throughout his life.

Much the same tension between a near-consensus of the learned theological world and the authority of the church could be found elsewhere. In 1906 the young William *Temple, son of an archbishop of Canterbury, on a visit to Berlin, wrote back to the bishop of Oxford about his hesitations in regard to the Virgin Birth and the Resurrection. The bishop of Oxford declined to ordain him, although two years later Temple claimed to have come to a sufficient degree of acceptance of both beliefs to be ordained by Randall Davidson, the archbishop of Canterbury and a friend of his father. A few years later (1912) he contributed to *Foundations*, a volume of essays by young Oxford scholars that produced a great deal of tension between ecclesiastical and scholarly viewpoints, symptomatic of a far wider unease between theological thought, traditional belief, and church authority, whether Protestant, Anglican, or Catholic. In *North America the anti-liberal reaction in these same years produced a series of tracts entitled *The Fundamentals* (1910–15), giving its name to the *fundamentalism that would remain throughout the century a principal component of American Christianity.

Nowhere else, however, was the tension so acute as in the *Catholic Church. It was inevitable that Catholic scholars in *France and elsewhere should have shared in the scientific reformulation of church history and biblical studies. Mgr. Duchesne (1843–1922), a professor in Paris and then director of the French School in Rome, was nearly as distinguished an early church historian as Harnack. It was inevitable too that the gap between this growing scholarly consensus and popular devotion should become ever wider: the multitude of dubious relics, the forest of indulgences, the incredible lives of *saints, all cried out for the scathing criticism of historians more interested in precise evidence than in encouraging participation in local feasts and *pilgrimages. The trouble, however, was that such popular devotions had been built into the official ecclesiastical system and an attack on, say, the belief that the Holy House of Loreto had sailed through the air from Nazareth in the 13th century to settle down in Italy was judged at least 'offensive to pious ears'. Duchesne's three-volume history of the early church was placed on the Index in 1912.

The movement of Catholic theological renewal, however, went much further than a criticism of such things. It very largely accepted the biblical and early church analysis of Harnack. Maybe Jesus never instituted the *sacrament of *baptism, maybe *Moses did not write the Pentateuch, all that and much else might be accommodated within a horizon of history in which what mattered was a bond of development, guided by the *Holy Spirit, but shaped by the culture and needs of the age. When Alfred Loisy wrote his *L'Évangile et l'Église* (1902) he saw himself as replying to Harnack from an essentially contrary ecclesiastical standpoint, grounded in *Newman's idea of doctrinal *development, rather than as adopting his viewpoint. While they were often nearer than claimed, the contrast in principle was a real one; but for church authority, especially in the Rome of Pius X and his secretary of state, Cardinal Merry del Val, all this was wholly unacceptable. Loisy and his like were undermining many basic Roman claims and opening the door to the abandonment of a great deal of doctrine and practice judged as the fruit of medieval superstition unacceptable to *modernity. Loisy could in practice be as damning of the way *dogma had actually developed as Harnack himself.

In reality, despite the condemnatory definition given in the encyclical *Pascendi*, there never was a coherent theory of *modernism. There were simply a number of different people, scholars, theologians, thinkers of various sorts, many of them linked in friendship but seldom with quite the same ideas. They included the increas-

ingly radical French priest Loisy, the Anglo-Irish Jesuit George Tyrrell, both arguably heretical enough, but also Friedrich von Hügel, an aristocratic layman, and Tyrrell's close friend, a man as devout as he was learned, the Abbé Brémond, a historian of spirituality, and many others. Possible suspects were myriad. Even Mgr. Duchesne might be numbered among them. In July 1907 the Holy Office issued a decree *Lamentabili*, listing the errors of modernism and followed two months later by *Pascendi*, which presented a systematic account of what it described as the sum total of all the heresies, and prescribing the most rigorous methods to eradicate this threat to Catholicism, including an 'anti-modernist oath' to be taken by all bishops, ordinands, and university and seminary teachers.

While many suspected 'modernists' went to ground avoiding formal condemnation, Tyrrell's temperament required the opposite approach and he accepted invitations from both *The Times* and the *Giornale d'Italia* to write articles criticizing the encyclical, an action equivalent to ecclesiastical suicide. He was excommunicated by papal orders and remained excommunicated until his death. In 1908, Cardinal Mercier of Malines wrote a Lenten pastoral letter, upholding *Pascendi*, remarking somewhat smugly that Belgium was blessedly free of the modernist disease but going on to name Tyrrell as an English priest 'deeply imbued' with modernism. He named no one else. Mercier's gratuitous mention of him in a Belgian pastoral prompted Tyrrell to write a small masterpiece, *Medievalism*, in six weeks. This was by no means the most important of his works: *Christianity at the Crossroads*, published posthumously, was considerably weightier. Tyrrell was not the most profound thinker in the modernist movement, nor its greatest scholar, but he was its most brilliant writer, with the ability to put his finger on the spot that hurt most, as well as the audacity to stand in the breach when almost everyone else was trying to escape attention.

Mercier denounced modernism by branding it a form of Protestantism, than which, it appeared, nothing could be worse: 'The Protestant nations [by which he meant particularly Germany, England, and the United States] are sick.' Their sickness lay, above all, in 'individualism' which he contrasted with the Catholic insistence upon 'authority'. Tyrrell replied that modernism was anything but Protestant and anything but individualistic; it insisted above all on a church which is Catholic because it is the community of many minds and cultures whereas, he declared, the *ultramontanism of *Vatican I and of Mercier himself was the true individualism because it had reduced the shaping of Christianity to a single individual, the pope. Tyrrell died little more than a year later, obstinately Catholic yet excommunicate, denied even burial in Catholic ground. Mercier's pastoral letter and Tyrrell's reply are important partly because Mercier was one of the most intellectual and forward-looking bishops in the Catholic Church, the protagonist and patron of the revival of scholasticism at Louvain, responsible twenty years later for the Malines Conversations with Anglicans. Yet his pastoral of 1908 shows clearly the inability of Catholic leadership to comprehend either modernism or the minimum requirements of historical science for theology.

The gap between ultramontane *orthodoxy and the requirements of a modern (let alone modernist) theology seemed unbridgeable. Tyrrell was not mistaken in characterizing the religion of Mercier and Pius X, in contrast to his own admitted modernism, as 'medievalism'. The result was that *Pascendi* was followed by 25 years of exceptional intellectual aridity within Catholicism. Abbot Cuthbert Butler of Downside wrote to von Hügel in 1922 to explain why he had abandoned serious theological study:

> A priest can publish nothing without 'imprimatur'. The only freedom in Biblical things and the rest is that of a tram, to go ahead as fast as you like on rails, but if you try to arrive at any station not on the line, you are derailed ... When the Biblical Commission got under way, and the *Lamentabili* and *Pascendi* were issued, I deliberately turned away from all this work—my being Abbot made it not apparent.
>
> (*Downside Review* (1979), 298–9).

Cuthbert Butler was hardly a radical. If he could find no other course theologically than to silence himself, there was indeed little room within a Catholicism lying beneath the shadow of the anti-modernist witch-hunt for any significant expression of Christian thought.

Loisy and Tyrrell had hoped to challenge Harnack's interpretation of Christianity in the name of Catholicism but were disqualified from doing so by their own church authority. He was, however, challenged in several other ways. The first and most finally decisive challenge was that produced by his friend and colleague, the philosopher of history, Ernst Troeltsch. Harnack was himself a devout believer. He held, quite simplistically, that scientific history must lead to religious faith, the faith he thought Jesus proclaimed in God's fatherhood and man's brotherhood. But Troeltsch realized that history as such could never found any absolute claim for Christianity in its particularity. One simply cannot establish faith on science, yet for Troeltsch as for Harnack there was no sound theology other than historicism. For Harnack, that remained enough to justify his faith but Troeltsch, to his own deep regret, saw ever more clearly as he approached the end of his life that it must signify the demise of Christianity. 'All I have been able to do for you', he remarked to a grateful student, 'is that I showed you the sunset of Christianity. When the sun has set, it still glows for a long time' (Pauck 1968: 92). A sunset may be inspiring enough, but for Troeltsch whether there would ever be another sunrise was quite uncertain.

Hardly less threatening was the challenge mounted by Albert Schweitzer's *Quest of the Historical Jesus* (1906; ET 1910). The challenge here was less to the central methodological cogency of the Harnackian view than to its content: the delineation of Jesus. Where Harnack believed that you could strip the historical Jesus of later *christological, miraculous, and *mythological accretions to arrive at a moral teacher wholly in accord with the sensibilities of late 19th-century Protestant Europe, Schweitzer powerfully concluded that Jesus' teaching was dominated by an *eschatological conviction that the end was near, not at all what a post-Enlightenment Europe could find congenial. Schweitzer may have overstated his case, but he and numerous other scholars demonstrated how dangerous it is to be overconfident about the religious authority derivable from historicism.

Liberal Neo-Protestantism was challenged yet again by the fact of the First World *War. Such appalling and pointless carnage undermined the comfortable and optimistic cultural context in which it had flourished and for which it could seem a sufficient theology.

Moreover, while the public hegemony of Christianity had mostly survived in the western world up to this point, if in ever more emasculated form, it now largely collapsed, both politically and culturally. The dominant intellectual influences were almost ostentatiously non-Christian: *Marx, *Nietzsche, Freud, Frazer. Christian thought was pushed quite rapidly from the centre to the periphery of intelligent academic debate. In such a *bouleversement* of role, the comfortable, establishmentarian liberalism of a Harnack had lost its social point. Something a great deal more confrontational was called for. Hence the rise of 'dialectical theology', a term used to describe the work of a group who came to dominate the scene in the 1920s and 1930s, all of whom—if in very different ways—accentuated the gap between Christian believing and secular presuppositions rather than the continuities. Already as the war ended the most powerful challenge to the whole stream of Christian thought represented by Harnack had been mounted by one of his former students, the young Swiss theologian Karl *Barth, in his commentary on *Romans, first published in 1919 and then republished in greatly extended form in 1921, a work that, in the words of the Catholic *Tübingen theologian Karl Adam, 'fell like a bomb on the playground of the theologians'. If it fell 'like a bomb' on the theologians, something else a few years earlier had fallen like a bomb on Barth. It was the letter published in August 1914 by ninety-three German intellectuals, including Harnack and almost the entire theological establishment, approving the Kaiser's war aims. For Barth that was a 'black day'. Of what conceivable use was a theology whose leading proponents could so behave? 'So far as I was concerned, there was no more future for the theology of the 19th century.'

Barth was, surely, the most powerful and influential theological mind of the 20th century. To Harnack, courteous gentleman as he was, especially when faced by a young friend, Barth's views were simply incomprehensible, 'naive biblicism'. In the famous and fascinating, if obscure, correspondence between them in 1923, one may pick out the dominant theme. If Jesus Christ stands at the centre of the gospel, how else, asked Harnack, 'can the basis for reliable and communal knowledge of this person be gained but through critical-historical study so that an imagined Christ is not put in place of the real one? What else beside scientific theology is able to undertake this study?' To which Barth replied that 'the "scientific character" of theology' involves 'the recollection that its object *was once subject* and must become that again and again'. The theologian must not begin by studying Paul or Luther as objects but by reliving their experience as subject. We accept the bible uncritically in faith as God's word but then find within it a profound rationality of its own. Barth developed this basic position in his study of *Anselm's theology, *Fides quaerens intellectum*, of 1931. Faith has to come first. For Harnack, writing in 1928 near the end of his life, this constituted the intellectual suicide of theology: 'Barth's reversion to bibliolatry—even Calvin did not go so far—is a piece of scholarly and religious naivety which could only have won the temporary success that it has done at a period like ours, of general despair over reason and scholarship' (to Erik Peterson).

In his total rejection of *natural theology, the insights of other religions, or *religious experience, Barth was opposing himself not only to the central themes of 19th-century Protestantism but no less to Catholicism. His repudiation of a *Thomist *analogia entis*—an analogy of being between creatures and creator allowing us to speak of God—became almost the hallmark of full Barthianism. And yet Barth grew far closer to Catholic theology than he realized, largely because he accepted a fundamental veracity in the gospels and because the christology that was central to his work included within it a strong ecclesiology.

If 'scientific theology' had to its own satisfaction undermined that veracity, leaving in Harnack's view the image of a wonderful God-filled man but in Schweitzer's that of a much mistaken eschatological enthusiast, how could one build a theology of any sort, strong enough to be preached not within the reverential portals of an established church but in the academic market-place against the mounting roar of Marxist, Communist, Nazi, and liberal *atheist? Rudolf *Bultmann was an almost exact contemporary of Barth. He reversed Harnack's position as decisively but in a very different direction. The 'Jesus of History' could not be known and did not matter. Even to bother about his historic character, beyond the one great Daß (that) he died and rose again, is a betrayal of faith. For the true Lutheran, all that need matter is the 'Christ of faith'. Bultmann, one of the greatest of biblical scholars, essentially accepted that scientific study of the NT left one with nothing but a tissue of 'myths' which needed to be '*demythologized' to reveal any message appropriate to the 20th century. But for him it had still to be a 'dialectical' message of faith, not *reason. If such an exercise be accepted, it runs into problems in deciding what are the values left in place by demythologization. If it is personal 'commitment', then to what is one committed? Bultmann filled the content of a demythologized faith with the categories of current *existentialism. While the power of his scholarship and engagement with such a gospel exercised a strong influence in his lifetime, it was a theology bound to wane when, with the passing of time, the content of his demythologized gospel itself proved as culturally dated as he believed the original gospel to have been.

Despite the comparable influence exercised by Paul *Tillich, especially in the USA where he had fled from Nazi Germany, he too displayed the inherent problem of reinventing a workable Protestant theology, neither simply a matter of historical science nor yet almost ostentatiously anti-scientific. In fact the core of his attempt to correlate Christian belief with what was essentially a humanistic ethic and philosophy of history was not so different, as he himself recognized, from late 19th-century German 'scientific' theology as found in Ritschl or Troeltsch.

In his correspondence with Peterson in 1928, Harnack, reflecting upon the identity of Protestantism, distinguished between two elements within it: the one '*Schleiermacherism' including a larger 'illuminist and subjective current', the other 'the Catholic element in primitive Protestantism'. If the former had no future other than a beautiful sunset or sectarianism, then the latter was likely to renew its appeal. Effectively that is what was happening in Barth's case, with his attempt to construct a Church Dogmatics. The case for it would be strengthened by the recovery of intellectual vitality within the Catholic Church itself.

This recovery began to appear fairly cautiously after the traumas of anti-modernism. From Germany came the work of Karl Adam at Tübingen. His Das Wesen des Katholizismus (ET, The Spirit of Catholicism, 1928), focusing on the church as Christ's mystical body, exercised a profound influence on a generation of Catholics world-wide. But the recovery was at first most manifest on the philosophical front and due especially to two remarkable French laymen, Jacques *Maritain and Étienne Gilson. It was they, building undoubtedly on the work of other scholars and thinkers, who chiefly managed to make of the revival of 'scholasticism' so emphatically required by Catholic authority something other than a piece of 'medievalism'. The homogenized scholasticism of the seminaries and Catholic universities appeared at once clerical, backward-looking, and ahistorical. What Maritain did in a number of books devoted to modern culture and politics was to make it seem genuinely serviceable as a tool for coping with the problems of the contemporary world, while Gilson, in the long run possibly even more significantly, worked as a historian of philosophy, historicizing both Thomism and the whole range and variety of thought from *Augustine to *Descartes. In such books as The Spirit of Medieval Philosophy, the Gifford Lectures of 1932, and The Unity of Philosophical Experience (1937), the William James lectures given at Harvard, he succeeded in making Thomism reappear, even in the eyes of non-Catholics, as a system of thought that could be taken with full seriousness in the 20th century. The development of a school of Anglican Thomist theologians, including Austin Farrer and Eric Mascall, shows how impressive this could appear.

But it was not only on the strictly philosophical front that Catholicism was once more influencing Anglicanism. The liturgical movement that had developed in France and Belgium from the early years of the century, to recover lay participation as against the highly clericalized *liturgy that had characterized the Catholic Church for generations, had important reverberations across the English Channel in works like A. G. Hebert's edited volume, The Parish Communion (1937). Equally important in both churches was a wider revival of ecclesiology, demonstrated in Catholicism by the 'rediscovery' of the idea of the church as Christ's 'mystical body' and in Anglicanism by Michael Ramsey's little masterpiece, The Gospel and the Catholic Church (1936), which brought together a whole range of developments: the 'biblical theology' deriving from the Barthian counter-attack against the liberal belittlement of biblical themes with new Catholic insights into liturgy and the church as Christ's Body.

Upon the Protestant side, the 1930s were increasingly dominated by the challenge of Nazism. Within Germany this produced division between the majority whose *nationalism undercut any serious resistance and a minority, originally inspired by Barth and marshalled increasingly by Dietrich *Bonhoeffer, who produced the *Barmen Declaration (1934), insisting on the reality and freedom of the church vis à vis the state, which led to the formation of the 'Confessing Church'. Internationally it was the threat of Nazism, Fascism, and Communism which did much to stimulate the advance of the *ecumenical movement and the decision to merge the two networks entitled *Faith and Order and Life and Work into a proposed World Council of Churches. The basic decisions here were taken in 1937 at the two movements' conferences in Oxford and Edinburgh. The Oxford Conference of Life and Work in July on 'Church, Community, and the State' in particular brought together a highly impressive range of Christian thinkers and church leaders of many countries, concerned to map out the social significance of Christianity in the modern world. It is impossible to imagine so serious a theological conference or such a subject, with committees on Church and State, Economics, War, and similar themes, at any much earlier date. The Oxford Conference marks a decisive turn in the history of modern Christian thinking, completely outdating the individualist piety and uncritical nationalism of a Harnack. The only comparably weighty precedent can be found in *papal encyclicals from Leo XIII's *Rerum Novarum* on. Perhaps the key theological figure here was Reinhold *Niebuhr, but the presence of Barthians or near-Barthians like Hendrik Kraemer and Emil Brunner, as well as of a range of lay intellectuals, from A. D. Lindsay, at the time Oxford University's Vice-Chancellor, to Sir Walter Moberly, Foster Dulles, T. S. *Eliot, and distinguished people from almost every part of the globe, including many *Eastern Orthodox, pointed towards the emergence of something fairly describable as a new Christian intellectual community, emphatic in its commitment to the *creeds, but powerful especially in its sense of mission to the world of economics and politics. In this sense of mission one should again note a new preoccupation with the church as such. 'The first duty of the Church, and its greatest service to the world, is that it be in very deed the Church', declared the conference message, striking a Barthian note. Yet one may note also a degree of consensus about *natural law and *natural theology. Barth indeed was not at Oxford, and his one great division with Brunner, who was there, lay in Brunner's acceptance of the validity of natural theology. Barth had, in his tempestuous way, already written his *Nein! Antwort an Emil Brunner* on this point. It would continue to divide Christian thinkers sharply, but the strong acceptance of the idea of natural law by many, as, for instance, William Temple, at that time archbishop of York and more than anyone else the guiding spirit at Oxford, would again serve to bring the central direction of non-Catholic theology back towards a more Catholic viewpoint. While there were no Catholics at Oxford, the influence of Maritain and Christopher Dawson was considerable.

There were also no German delegates at Oxford. Those who had hoped to come were prevented from doing so and Martin Niemöller was arrested just before the conference began. But the theologian who more than anyone else would in retrospect come to represent the decisive move in 20th-century theology signified by the Oxford conference was a German, Dietrich *Bonhoeffer. He too had been a pupil of Harnack; he had then come under the influence of both Barth and Niebuhr. More than any of these, he struggled as a Lutheran to a position of such full involvement in the political that he became part of the conspiracy to overthrow Hitler and was hanged just before the fall of the Nazi regime. While the turning towards a theology of *politics took very different forms with Barth, Niebuhr, Temple, and Bonhoeffer, the construction of a new vision of church–state relations of a non-nationalist kind was important for all of them, and it would remain important for the rest of the century, despite something of a lull in concern in the 1950s.

The Second World War delayed the launching of the World Council of Churches until 1948 but ensured that when it came it received very wide support from almost all the non-Roman communions. If neither Barth nor the leading Anglican Michael Ramsey attended the 1937 conferences, both took a very active part at Amsterdam in 1948. While the World Council claimed to impose no ecclesiology upon the churches, it inevitably both stimulated its members to think about ecclesiology—why, precisely, as churches, they were divided—and forged a largely new kind of theological community which twelve years later the Catholic Church too would join. While in the Protestant world the 1950s saw the continued dominance of pre-war theologians—Barth, Bultmann, Tillich, the Niebuhrs—in the Catholic world the post-war years witnessed new developments that would prove enormously important. In 1950 the leading inspirer of the French *Dominican school of the Saulchoir in Paris, M. D. Chenu, published his *Introduction à l'étude de saint Thomas d'Aquin*, a work reflecting twenty years of teaching in the richness of its ability to interpret *Aquinas within his historical milieu, the Paris of seven centuries earlier. Why does this matter so much? Because it challenged the still-dominant ahistorical approach to Thomism, regarded as a system belonging to all ages and therefore understandable outside its historical setting. While Gilson had propagated a historicist approach to scholasticism, he had confined himself to the field of philosophy where, as a layman, he did not seem to threaten current theological method too evidently. It was the transference of this approach to theology, something Chenu had already begun with his little 1937 work, *Une école de théologie: Le Saulchoir*, which made the alarm bells ring. It was not that Chenu doubted the supreme intellectual genius of Aquinas. On the contrary, he wanted it understood, but, when placed within its historical milieu, it must require rethinking in every other milieu. Once this line was followed, the underlying post-Tridentine assumption of Catholic theology, that nothing much that mattered had happened either before or after Thomas, was shattered. Chenu's younger colleague Yves *Congar was applying this approach in a variety of ways. His *Chrétiens désunis* (1937) opened up the issue of Catholic ecumenism in a truly foundational way while his *Vraie et fausse réforme dans l'Église* (1950) appealed for a fundamental reform of the church through a 'return to the sources'. Both the Dominican theologians of the Saulchoir and another remarkable group of *Jesuit theologians centred on their house in Lyons and inspired by Henri *de Lubac, whose interests were more patristic, were soon creating a far more diversified theology than the Catholic Church had known for centuries. De Lubac's works on the Eucharist and the Mystical Body (1944) and, still more, *Surnaturel* (1946), his studies of *allegory, making much use of *Origen, of atheistic humanism, and *Buddhism, all published in these years, appeared to challenge aspect after aspect of the current Catholic theological framework.

There had, inevitably, to be a reaction. The Dominican Toulouse province had long been more rigidly Thomist than that of Paris. In 1946 the *Revue Thomiste*, for which it was responsible, published a critique of the work of the Lyons Jesuits—de Lubac, Daniélou, Bouillard, *von Balthasar—to which they quickly responded. Further articles followed, all to be included by M.-J. Nicolas and M.-M. Labourdette, the editors of the *Revue Thomiste*, the following year in a work entitled *Dialogue théologique*. Rather than dialogue it looked like denunciation. For the Toulouse school the 'rigorously scientific character of theology' was at stake. The fondness of the Jesuits for patristic sources demonstrated a 'clear depreciation of scholastic theology', a move towards 'relativism', a lack of true 'fidelity to St Thomas'. The Saulchoir too, by implication, was under attack. In 1950 Pope Pius XII condemned all these tendencies, which had come to be known as the 'nouvelle théologie', though without mentioning names, in the encyclical *Humani Generis* which looked somewhat like a repeat of *Pascendi*. Chenu and Congar in Paris, de Lubac and others in Lyons, were soon removed from their teaching posts. The last great battle against every form of 'modernism' was being waged, but this time it was destined to be lost. There was too much to suppress, and theologians like Congar and de Lubac were too clearly outstanding scholars and devout priests to be discredited. Even Rome itself was divided. Overt anti-modernists like Pietro Parente, Assessor of the Holy Office and then cardinal archbishop of Perugia, had turned their attacks on fellow Romans, such as the Jesuit, Paul Galtier, of the Gregorianum, for his neo-*Nestorian views on the human consciousness of Christ. A vast evolution of theological understanding had in fact been set in motion within Catholicism and nothing could suppress it for long. If, apart from the *Milieu divin*, none of the works of *Teilhard de Chardin were allowed to be published in his lifetime, once he died in 1955 they quickly saw the light and exercised a vast influence. He too was a close friend of de Lubac. It is often implied that a great theological revival was unloosed in the Catholic Church by *Vatican II. In reality, the best of the revival probably came before the Council was even announced. That was certainly true of France, the real power-house behind all that happened, when combined with the work of German theologians such as Karl *Rahner. Important as the role of Pope *John XXIII was in closing an era of repression and inaugurating one of openness, almost unprecedented in Roman history, in terms of thought itself his influence should not be exaggerated. Indeed he appeared not too unhappy with the thoroughly reactionary preliminary draft texts produced in Rome for the Council. When in 1962, in the opening session, they were almost all rejected, it was because the impact of the *nouvelle théologie* and related influences (including, indeed, the earlier, more liberal encyclicals of Pius XII, notably *Divino Afflante Spiritu*, 1943, on the interpretation of scripture, and *Mediator Dei*, 1947, on the liturgy) had had an effect far beyond what theologians in Rome imagined.

The impact of Vatican II, nevertheless, in spreading the new ideas and breaking down practices of repression still current in many parts of the church was enormous. It is to be remembered that in many ways the century separating Vatican I from Vatican II had been for Catholicism an enormously productive one. The *missionary movement had multiplied Catholics and dioceses in Africa and Asia; the *Latin American church had grown still more; in North America Catholicism was now by far the largest single religious body. Everywhere colleges and seminaries had multiplied while the sense of defensive fear, of having the 'true faith' but none the less being an anachronism in the modern, liberal, and Protestant world, still strong at the beginning of the century, had faded away. The church as a whole was ready for intellectual spring-cleaning.

But the impact of Vatican II has also to be seen within the wider culture of the 1960s. Everywhere the 1950s had been a remarkably conservative age: conservatively communist in one part of the globe, conservatively *democratic elsewhere. The values of the church too were inherently restorationist, frozen, perhaps, by the tensions of the Cold War. There seemed little new to say, little reflection even on what had happened during the war, including both the *Holocaust and Hiroshima. Quite suddenly, as the 1950s turned into the 1960s, this changed and a cultural revolution for a time swept all before it—an optimistic revolution in institutional,

intellectual, and sexual attitudes, symbolized as well as anything by President Kennedy's 'Camelot' and the music of the Beatles. 1960 was the 'year of Africa'. The old empires were being hastily wound up and a multitude of new countries were taking their seats at the United Nations. Intellectually, the left seemed to have won—not the tired left of Soviet Marxism, but an exciting new left, fed on the writings of the Young Marx, and a range of Marxist-inclined gurus, from Sartre and Marcuse to Habermas, Ernst Bloch, and Frantz Fanon. Joined to an upsurge of Christian existentialism feeding on a new popularity of the works of *Kierkegaard, all this was to have a very considerable impact on Christian thought, but the most striking phenomenon of the new religious radicalism, John *Robinson's *Honest to God* (1963), owed less to such influences, being an amalgam of ideas derived from Bultmann, Tillich, and Bonhoeffer. What might least be expected was the third. Bonhoeffer had not been a major theological name in his lifetime. As his biographer, Eberhard Bethge, wrote in 1970, 'In 1945 only a handful of friends and enemies knew who this young man had been. In Christian Germany other names were in the limelight. When his name began to emerge from the anonymity of his death, theological faculties and churches felt uncertain and did little. To the present day there are still inhibitions in Germany about fully integrating him and what he stood for' (Preface to English edition of *Dietrich Bonhoeffer*). What excited the 1960s about Bonhoeffer was not just his role as a conspirator against Hitler, but the *Letters and Papers from Prison* which suddenly became, often indeed through misinterpretation, a sort of contemporary gospel of 'religionless Christianity'. *Honest to God* sold more than a million copies and, while it infuriated many firm believers, deeply influenced numerous waverers. This mix of what Barth is unkindly said to have described as the 'froth', mixed together from the 'good beers' of Tillich, Bonhoeffer, and Bultmann (and especially the first), was certainly the standard of a revival of 'liberal' theology over against the previous Barth-dominated years.

The world of 1963 saw not only *Honest to God* but also the height of excitement over the Vatican Council after the almost revolutionary impression of its first session in autumn 1962. In April came Pope John's encyclical *Pacem in Terris*, addressing the issues of peace among the nations in a nuclear age with remarkable freshness. Two months later he died, but, under his successor Paul VI, his council continued. Little of the teaching of Vatican II constituted in itself a major contribution to Christian thought. It could fairly be said that on many points the Catholic Church was only catching up on what Protestantism had recognized either four centuries or one century earlier, although the Council's most carefully shaped document, *Lumen Gentium*, expressed a richness of ecclesiology not easily found elsewhere. With its shift away from preoccupation with the hierarchical, it represented an acceptable Catholic response to the Protestant rediscovery of ecclesiology since the 1930s. The Council's larger impact was immense in a number of ways. Its longest constitution, *Gaudium et Spes*, on 'the church in the modern world', covered a vast range of matters, political, social, cultural, and economic. While much that was said may appear bland or simplistic, what remains significant was that a council should treat of such matters at all, let alone at such length. Comparably significant was the much argued-over and finally very cautiously worded Declaration, *Nostra Aetate*, on non-Christian religions. What is important in both cases is the opening these documents provided for the future. Still more central to the Council's work was the opening of doors between Catholics and other Christians. This was achieved, first, by the invitation of a considerable number of observers from other churches to attend all the Council's sessions. Their presence greatly influenced what was said. It led on through the work of the new *Secretariat of Unity* to the beginning of numerous official 'dialogues' between Rome and other churches, including the WCC. The result was that whereas up to 1960 there had been extremely limited theological contact anywhere between Catholics and other Christians, now it grew not only officially but unofficially to such an extent that the whole public shape of the Christian thought-world was irretrievably altered within a few years, Catholics and Protestants coming to study and teach in many of the same institutions.

While the debates and even some of the decisions of the Vatican Council seemed radical indeed in the eyes of many Catholics, the 1960s saw the development of far more radical radicalisms elsewhere. The 'Death of God' school flourished particularly in America, beginning with G. Vahanian's *The Death of God* (1961) and continuing with such works as T. J. Altizer's *The Gospel of Christian Atheism* (1966). It grew out of a mixture of Hegel, Nietzsche, Bonhoeffer's *Letters and Papers*, and a belief that analytical philosophy had made discourse about God meaningless. While most theologians were not persuaded by the full message, a general break-up of doctrinal coherence seemed to be going on almost everywhere, even in Catholicism where it was widely felt that Aquinas had had his day and must now be replaced by whatever was available in the current market—Barth or Bultmann, Rahner or Altizer. The symposium edited by John Hick, *The Myth of God Incarnate* (1978), with its rather overconfident conviction that the doctrine of the *Incarnation could be debunked, represents a late expression of this form of radical liberalism by people occupying the most senior academic positions.

But the radicalism of the 1960s took other, some more enduring, forms. The fourth assembly of the WCC, Uppsala 1968, made a move from church-centred to world-centred concerns of a fairly radical sort, both mirroring and going well beyond *Gaudium et Spes*. Not unrelated to the Uppsala agenda were developments in Latin America. One of the changes of shape in Christian geography in the post-Second World War period most productive in the field of thought was the advance of Latin America as a giver, and not only receiver, of ideas. The Conference of Latin American Bishops held at Medellín in 1968, a major influence on the reshaping of the South American church, was intended as a follow-up to the Vatican Council for the continent containing the largest numbers of Catholics. It led to the publication in 1971 in Lima of Gustavo *Gutiérrez's *A Theology of Liberation*, which quickly became a classic text, while being the precursor for a great many other works in the same area by such Latin American theologians as Segundo, Sobrino, Míguez *Bonino, and *Boff. Here was a whole new school of *liberation theology coming to grips with the central issues of politics, *justice, and empowerment in a particular social context and considerably influenced by Marxist ideology. Undoubtedly they also owed a good deal to the more theoretical development of 'political theology' by *Moltmann, J. B. Metz, and others. But liberation theology was more context-shaped. If, with some of its proponents,

it represented a large incorporation of Marxist concepts into Christian thought (at times uncritically, at others quite transforming them in the process), this was essentially as a tool for the construction of a public theology relevant to local circumstances and capable of stimulating social change, even *revolution. It was thus both a sociopolitical theology and a local theology, the first considerable example of a coherent theological school outside Europe and North America in modern times (see CONTEXTUAL THEOLOGY).

Whether parallel to, or derived from, liberation theology there developed a range of others: *black, *feminist, *African, Dalit, Minjung. Some of these, fairly temporarily, made use of Marxism; for others that would have been pointless or quite unacceptable. They did, of course, overlap. It had suddenly been rediscovered that not only Latin Americans, but also women and Blacks could be good theologians. What all this had in common was commitment to the theological enterprise from a position quite different from that which had dominated theology hitherto: white, western, male, probably clerical, academic, upper middle-class. What they were all saying is that the way one thinks about God, Christ, the bible, the church, and morality depends enormously on where one is and who one is. Both 19th-century 'scientific' Protestant theology and 'perennial' Catholic scholasticism had forgotten that. *Truth is just truth, theology just theology. The switch to acceptance of not only the fact but also the appropriateness of pluralism in theology (a switch from seeing theology as modelled on mathematics to seeing it as akin to poetry) has been one of the more enduring acquisitions of the 1960s–1970s.

Another has been the incorporation of Christian theology within reflection on 'religion'. In institutional terms departments of theology have been transformed into or joined with departments of religious studies whose subject is world religions. Until the 1960s the theologian who took any other religion as a significant part of his field of study, as de Lubac took Buddhism, was extremely unusual. Christian theology was carried on against a background of the bible and western history, but with minimal consideration of other religious experience except, as in the case of Barthians such as Kraemer, to condemn it. When this changed, the immediate tendency, represented particularly by Wilfred Cantwell Smith and John Hick, was to declare, in the latter's phraseology, that a 'Copernican revolution' had been achieved making impossible continued belief in the 'uniqueness' of Christ or Christianity. Others, no less sensitive to the implications of the human and religious experience of the large non-Christian majority of the world's population, did not believe that Hick's hasty willingness to throw over the central claims of Christianity was necessary or helpful for understanding the religious predicament as a whole.

Religion and religions, liberalism and the 'Death of God', liberation theology and Marxist historical analysis, feminist theology, Catholic abandonment of Thomism as a privileged system, and much else appeared to leave theology a wreck by the later 1970s, a confused mix of tendencies without any clear centre. Yet the theological history of the last quarter of the 20th century was, surprisingly, very different from that. Central to the 1980s and the 1990s was a considerable recovery of orthodoxy, of a Trinitarian and incarnationalist kind, challenged more by the spread of fundamentalism than by the extreme liberalism of previous decades that somehow failed to stick. It was replaced by what might be called a *Nicaean reshaping of Catholic, Orthodox, and Protestant traditions, in which the principal resources are undoubtedly Aquinas, Barth, and the *Greek fathers. German Protestant theology has retained its ascendancy, notably through the work of Moltmann, *Pannenberg, and *Jüngel. While the authority of Bultmann and Tillich has steadily waned, that of Barth has remained remarkably constant, even if it is the later Barth of the *Church Dogmatics*, more willing to be positive about humanity, to which appeal is mostly made. His rejection of 'natural theology' continued to be itself rejected, as notably by Pannenberg, who came to represent the most central position within the Protestant tradition. What is no less striking is the influence of Aquinas. Far from diminishing after Vatican II as anticipated, it has spread very noticeably across the Protestant world. He is now seen not as the formal pillar of Roman Catholic orthodoxy, but rather as the greatest of systematic theologians, yet someone whose teaching has still to be seen as contextually shaped by his own age, one very different from ours. The importance of the Greek fathers is almost as pervasive. It is something shared by the school of Lyons, led by de Lubac and Daniélou, the training ground of von Balthasar, by Barthians like *Torrance, and by Greek Orthodox theologians like Kallistos Ware and John Zizioulas. The massive interest in *Origen, as in *Irenaeus, is evidence of how important the very early patristic witness especially has come to be seen. While Orthodox theology has not played a central role in 20th-century theological thought, it has had an increasingly pervasive influence, from the inter-war writing of such Russian *émigrés* as Berdyaev and Bulgakov in Paris to the ever-wider presence of Greek and *Russian Orthodox churches throughout the world, especially in North America.

Yet this reconciliation of the theological centre has by no means involved totally discarding the legacy of the 1960s and 1970s. On the contrary. The continued context of world religions and a socioethical agenda set in its main lines by political and liberation theology are not in question. Still more important, explicit diversities of viewpoint resulting in a necessary pluralism of theology have been built into the new scheme of things, including a considerable range of viewpoints across the liberal–orthodox spectrum. The perennial theological tension between rationality and *fideism has certainly not disappeared, though it can take on a new look in a world where the values of enlightenment and modernity are under wide attack. The diversities within contemporary theology may be justified by some in *postmodernist terms but by others as in reality characteristic of Christian theology throughout its history: the inevitable consequence of a religion of incarnation and of the otherness of people whose response to God's word must be as diverse as the range of human thought and culture. A return to the narrow agenda and western self-satisfaction of the 1950s would be unthinkable, just as any abandonment of the implications of Vatican II would be unthinkable on the Catholic side, despite curial attempts under *John Paul II to re-establish something like the theological control of the pre-conciliar era. In general, despite notable weaknesses such as the collapse of the French intellectual leadership which mattered so much to Catholicism in the past, Christian theology may well be in a healthier, more internally coherent, and less schismatic state than has been the case for many centuries.

Adrian Hastings

Bowden, J., and Richmond, J. (eds.), *A Reader in Contemporary Theology* (1967).

The Catechism of the Catholic Church, ET (1994).

Chopp, R., *The Praxis of Suffering: An Interpretation of Liberation and Political Theologies* (1986).

Clements, K., *Lovers of Discord: Twentieth-Century Theological Controversies in England* (1988).

Fabella, V., and Torres, S. (eds.), *Irruption of the Third World: Challenge to Theology* (1983).

Ford, D. F. (ed.), *The Modern Theologians* (2nd edn., 1997).

Gill, R. (ed.), *Readings in Modern Theology* (1995).

Hastings, A., *A History of English Christianity 1920–1999* (2000).

—— (ed.), *Modern Catholicism* (1991).

Hastings, C., and Nicholl, D. (eds.), 'A Correspondence: Adolf Harnack and Erik Peterson', *Selection I* (1953), 169–85.

Heron, A., *A Century of Protestant Theology* (1980).

Hodgson, H., and King, R. (eds.), *Christian Theology: An Introduction to its Traditions and Tasks* (1982).

Loades, A., *Searching for Lost Coins: Explorations in Christianity and Feminism* (1987).

Mackey, J., *Modern Theology: A Sense of Direction* (1987).

Macquarrie, J., *Twentieth-Century Religious Thought* (4th edn.; 1988).

Moltmann, J., *Theology Today* (1988).

Pauck, W., *Harnack and Troeltsch* (1968).

Rumscheidt, H. M., *Revelation and Theology: An Analysis of the Barth-Harnack Correspondence of 1923* (1972).

Schoof, T., *A Survey of Catholic Theology 1800–1970* (1970).

Streeter, B. H., (ed.), *Foundations* (1912).

Tracy, D., *Blessed Rage for Order: The New Pluralism in Theology* (1975).

Tyrrell, G., *Medievalism: A Reply to Cardinal Mercier*, new edn. with foreword by Gabriel Daly (1994).

von Harnack, A., *What is Christianity?* (1901).

Wilmore, G. S., and Cone, J. (eds.), *Black Theology: A Documentary History 1966–1979* (1979).

typology is a modern term (perhaps first used by E. B. Pusey in the 1830s) to describe one of the principal forms of scriptural exegesis in the early church, which remained important in the west throughout the Middle Ages, and in the east has continued in use to the present day. It is often distinguished by modern theologians (especially J. Daniélou) from *allegory, although this distinction has no parallel in the language used by the fathers and their successors to describe their method of scriptural exegesis. The origins of typology can be found in the way the early Christians sought to appropriate the writings of what they came to call the Old Testament as their scriptures. Jewish exegesis of these scriptures (by Philo, and especially by the Rabbis) regarded the Pentateuch (the Torah or the Law) as the core of the scriptures, and treated the scriptures as an authoritative source for guidance about how to live a life pleasing to God within the *covenant. Early Christian exegesis, however, saw the OT predominantly as a collection of *prophetic writings foretelling the coming of the *Messiah, who was, they believed, identical with *Jesus of Nazareth. This contrast can be seen by comparing *Paul's use of scripture with that of the evangelists: Paul, in accordance with his rabbinic training, appeals principally to the Torah, the evangelists, writing later, to the prophets, though Paul's appeal to the Torah frequently treats it as prophecy foreshadowing Christ, rather than a source of moral guidance. Very soon Christians came to interpret the whole OT, not just the prophetic books, as prophetic, as can be seen very clearly in Justin Martyr's *Dialogue with Trypho the Jew*. The story of *Adam and the *Fall foreshadowed the reversal of the Fall through the redeeming work of Christ, the second Adam, *Mary being the second *Eve; the story of *Moses bringing the people of Israel out of Egypt foreshadowed Christ's *redemption of the human race, with the crossing of the Red Sea prefiguring Christian *baptism; the *Song of Songs came to be seen as celebrating the relationship between Christ and the *church (or later, between Christ and the individual Christian soul). This foreshadowing was expressed in the language of 'types' (though the Greek word *typos* is probably better rendered 'figure'): the people and events of the OT were understood as types or figures of the Christian story of redemption, focusing on Christ. Such exegesis found expression in sermons and (later) liturgical poetry, a notable example of which, still in use in the western church, is the *Paschal Proclamation*, or *Exsultet*, sung at the *Easter vigil, which celebrates the Resurrection of Christ by recalling events of the OT that foreshadowed it. Such exegesis also found expression from the earliest days in *art: the earliest Christian art, for instance that in the catacombs, dwells predominantly on types of the Christian mystery: Noah's ark, Moses crossing the Red Sea or providing water in the wilderness, Daniel in the lion's den, the Three Children in the fiery furnace.

Gradually Christian exegetes came to formulate their understanding of exegesis as discerning in the stories recounted in the OT the foreshadowing of the redemption wrought by Christ and lived out in the Christian church. It was often, especially in Alexandria and the Latin west, called allegory, borrowing the classical literary term for a method of interpretation in which a text is understood as having a meaning other than its obvious (or surface) one. The meaning thus discerned was sometimes called 'secret' or 'hidden' (Greek *mystikos*, a word also used of the sacraments or *mysteria*, which suggested a parallel between the hidden meaning of scripture and the hidden reality of the *sacraments); sometimes 'contemplative', a usage popular with, though not confined to, the short-lived but influential exegetical school of Antioch, which flourished from the middle of the 4th to the middle of the 5th century. How far such prefigurative exegesis could be extended was disputed. The most prominent Antiochene, Theodore of Mopsuestia, took the conservative view that such exegesis was only valid if there were grounds for thinking that the original author had intended a prophetic meaning: hence he confined prophetic meaning in the psalter to only a very few psalms, and excluded the Song of Songs from the scriptural canon altogether. Very few, even in the Antiochene school, followed Theodore's conservatism. Others maintained that, because the true author of scripture was the *Holy Spirit, the whole of scripture had a potentially inexhaustible meaning, and that every verse had a deeper meaning. *Origen often argued that historical inconsistencies in the biblical narrative proved that scripture had a deeper meaning, since the apparent meaning was self-contradictory—the reader, tripping over these inconsistencies, was thrown into allegory. He held that in this deeper meaning the attentive reader would find himself listening to the living voice of the Word of God. In this context Paul's remark, 'the letter kills, but the spirit gives life', was often cited. *Augustine spoke of the 'wonderful depth' (*mira profunditas*) of scripture.

This sense that the meaning of scripture is many-layered was eventually given formal expression. Origen compared it to a human being: as a human being consisted of spirit, soul, and body, so in scripture there could be discerned a literal meaning (corresponding to the body), a moral meaning (corresponding to the soul), and a spiritual meaning, often concerned with Christian doctrine (corresponding to the spirit). In practice, however, he interpreted scripture as having two meanings: a literal one, and a deeper one. This dual meaning was elaborated by later thinkers, who discerned different layers within the deeper meaning, into a fourfold meaning of scripture, which became the norm in the western Middle Ages. These four meanings were (1) the literal or historical, (2) the allegorical (which usually meant the Christian meaning, doctrinal or sacramental), (3) the moral, or tropological, concerned with Christian conduct, and (4) the anagogical (from the Greek *anagoge*, ascent), concerned with the destiny of the Christian life.

In the progression found in this approach to scripture, advancing from the saving events to their significance, then to the Christian response, and finally to the Christian hope, there is expounded, according to *de Lubac, 'an asceticism and mysticism that may be characterized as christological, ecclesial, and sacramental: a veritable history of the spiritual life, founded on dogma'.

This approach to scripture foundered in the west, partly on the striving after scientific rigour, estranged from the Christian life, found in scholasticism, and finally in the polemic born of the *Reformation. Perhaps *Erasmus' *Ratio verae theologiae* (*An Account of True Theology*) is the last example of an approach to scripture in unbroken continuity with the fathers. For this approach presupposes a shared rule of faith, which was obscured by the claims and counterclaims of the Reformation. To borrow the language of the French poet, Paul Claudel, scripture became, in the early-modern west, an arsenal of ammunition for polemic, rather than a treasury of imagery to be interpreted in the 'magnetic field' of the shared rule of faith. This traditional approach to scripture was rendered still more remote by the *Enlightenment and the rise of the historical-critical method as the only right way of interpreting texts, including the text of the bible, reducing the meaning of a text to what the original writer intended. *Romanticism reinforced the Enlightenment's alienation from the traditional approach to scripture with its distinction between the artificiality of allegory and the natural power of the *symbol. Allegory came to be seen as arbitrary, a method of eisegesis (reading a meaning *into* a text) rather than exegesis (reading a meaning *out of* a text).

Several factors have led to a renewed theological interest in typology or allegory in some quarters in recent times: the revival of interest in the theology of the fathers; the *liturgical movement, with its attempt to rediscover aspects of Christian worship lost to the west since the Middle Ages; and the conviction, sometimes for philosophical reasons, that theology is best expressed in the *language not of propositions, but of metaphor and *poetry. Influenced by all these factors, though especially the first, the French theologian Jean Daniélou became an advocate of what he called 'typology', which he distinguished sharply from 'allegory'. For Daniélou typology was concerned with discerning *analogies between the saving acts of God in the old Covenant and his activity in Christ and the church: as such, it respects, and is based on, historical events and their interpretation; allegory, in contrast, was seen as a way in which a supposedly encoded meaning was elicited from the words of sacred scripture. This chimed in with the widespread modern apologetic concern to emphasize the fundamentally historical character of the Christian faith. Daniélou's distinction was attacked by others (notably de Lubac), especially in so far as Daniélou claimed to find this distinction in the fathers themselves. However, most scholars with any sympathy for patristic exegesis accept some kind of distinction between allegory (or, for Daniélou, typology) as discerning patterns in God's saving activity, and allegory as a kind of play on words. Interpreting the crossing of the Red Sea as prefiguring baptism is an example of the first; interpreting the two swords of Luke 22: 38 as signifying spiritual and temporal authority an example of the second.

The liturgical movement, with its emphasis on the symbolic character of the church's liturgy, also welcomed an approach to scripture that found the themes of the liturgy reflected in the types and symbols of scripture. This has led to liturgical reform which has restored readings from the OT to the eucharistic liturgy, with new lectionaries, often devised to bring out typological links between the scriptural passages. A more fundamental justification of allegorical or typological exegesis may be found in the conviction of the essentially poetic or symbolic nature of theological language: a conviction based on the ultimate unknowability of God and his activity, or the inadequacy of human language to express the ultimate. Developments in literature and literary criticism over the 20th century, with the growing appreciation of the allusive, and the construction of symbolic structures, both in literature (e.g. Mallarmé, T. S. *Eliot, James Joyce) and in literary criticism (William Empson, or more recently Northrop Frye), have created a climate in which typology (and allegory) find more ready acceptance.

See also BIBLE, ITS AUTHORITY AND INTERPRETATION; HERMENEUTICS; HIGHER CRITICISM   **Andrew Louth**

Charity, A. C., *Events and their Afterlife: The Dialectics of Christian Typology in the Bible and Dante* (1966).

Daniélou, J., *From Shadows to Reality* (1950), ET (1960).

de Lubac, H., *Exégèse médiévale: Les quatre sens de l'écriture* (4 vols.; 1959–64).

Farrer, A., *The Glass of Vision* (1948).

Frye, Northrop, *The Great Code: The Bible and Literature* (1982).

Grant, R. M., *The Letter and the Spirit* (1957).

Schneiders, S. M., *The Revelatory Text* (1991).

von Balthasar, Hans Urs, *The Glory of the Lord: A Theological Aesthetic* (1967–9), ET (1989).

ultramontanism signifies a belief in the importance of *papal control of the church of a monarchical kind, together with the Romanization of all aspects of its life. It arose in the 17th and 18th centuries partly in reaction to *Gallicanism and similar attitudes such as Cisalpinism in England and Febronianism in Germany, which stressed the diversity of local churches and the need to limit (but not theoretically exclude) Roman *authority. Ultramontanes appealed 'over the mountains' (the Alps) to Rome. The *Jesuits were supremely ultramontane. Their suppression by the pope in 1773 under pressure from various European powers weakened Roman authority and was a seeming triumph for anti-ultramontanes everywhere. The French Revolution, however, undermined the Gallican power base and seemed to suggest that its 'liberal', mildly *nationalist tendencies had helped bring the church to disaster. In practice Gallicanism involved acceptance of considerable *lay political control of the church, while ultramontanes wanted to free the church by increasing papal control. Ultramontanism was much strengthened by the re-establishment of the Jesuits (1814). As a popular movement it began in France rather than in Italy, but throughout the 19th century, especially in the pontificates of Gregory XVI (1831–46) and Pius IX (1846–78), it came to inspire papal policy and the reshaping of *Catholicism on far more Rome-centred lines than had ever previously been the case. A real cult developed around Pius IX, an 'idolatry of the papacy'. He could even be hailed as 'the Word incarnate still dwelling among us' in Louis Veuillot's influential newspaper, *L'Univers*.

While ultramontanism tended to be markedly anti-liberal and anti-modern, this was not always so. Earlier 19th-century French ultramontanes like Lamennais, Ozanam, and Lacordaire (who refounded the French Dominicans) had combined ecclesiastical ultramontanism with political liberalism, as, in England, did Cardinal Manning, one of its most influential figures. The ecclesiastical triumph of ultramontanism came in 1870 with the definition of papal *infallibility at *Vatican I despite the opposition of many leading Catholic bishops and theologians, although it was expressed in far more restrictive terms than many ultramontanes had wanted. From Pius IX to Pius XII (1938–58), the Catholic Church was so dominated by ultramontane attitudes that many people could no longer imagine any other loyal way of being a Roman Catholic. If ultramontanism was for the most part intellectually anti-modern, it profited immensely from modern developments in communica-

tions which made the church's centralization steadily easier and assisted the popular cult of each pope in turn. *Vatican II, while never repudiating the definitions of Vatican I, nevertheless called for a recognition of pluralism, diversity between local churches, and *collegial rather than monarchical government. Hence many post-Vatican II Catholic theologians have been distinctly anti-ultramontane, but the difficulty of implementing such ideals through a Roman Curia shaped on ultramontane principles has been central to the tensions within Catholicism ever since.

Adrian Hastings

Aubert, R., *The Church in a Secularized Society* (1978).
Chadwick, O., *A History of the Popes 1830–1914* (1998).
Gough, A., *Rome and Paris: The Gallican Church and the Ultramontane Campaign 1848–1853* (1986).
Holmes, J. D., *The Triumph of the Holy See* (1978).

Unitarianism is a belief in *God as a unity, not a *Trinity. Muslims and Jews would say that Trinitarian *orthodoxy compromises the unity of God. Some Christians, either through logic or *mystical insight, have said so too. Moreover, the Jesus of Trinitarian orthodoxy can seem more divine than human, 'only a God'. A love of the man Jesus, conversely, can undercut his divinity. Historically, most Unitarians have believed with Channing, their great 19th-century theologian, that 'the Father sent the Son, and gives, to those that ask, the Holy Spirit', but that neither the Son nor the *Holy Spirit, as such, is God. Unitarians are non-Trinitarian, and orthodox Christians in more fervent times called their chapels Hell and persecuted them. Nowadays they are merely excluded from councils of churches.

After more than a thousand years of Trinitarian orthodoxy, why did anyone question it? In practice, ordinary Christians did not build their faith round the doctrine of the Trinity. There are times in Catholic history when 'Jesus, Mary, Joseph' has had more resonance. The *Protestant reformer Melanchthon, trying to express the heart of Christianity, said 'to know God is to know his benefits', and neglected to expound his nature as Trinity. The great liberal theologian *Schleiermacher left the doctrine to the very end of his systematics, because it was not 'an immediate utterance concerning the Christian self-consciousness'. Preparing a sermon for Trinity Sunday was always a problem.

Actually to set aside the doctrine of the Trinity was another matter. Historians of doctrine point to medieval Scotist and nominalist theology, which said that God could, if he wanted, have saved us by sending a mere human. If there was continuity between this and the fathers of Unitarianism, it was unconscious, because they were heirs of *Erasmus, and despised scholastic theology. The humanism of the *Renaissance thought highly of man, laid stress on conduct, and could well lie behind, though it never spelt out, rationalistic simplifications of theology. The Protestant *Reformation was overwhelmingly orthodox, but 'scripture alone' could, and in time did, subvert Greek technical theology. 'Trinity' is a post-biblical word. The tiny radical reformation in Italy was rational and humanist. A small Anabaptist council in Venice in 1550 agreed that Christ, though filled with the powers of God, was not God but a human being, there were no *angels or *devils, and no *hell but the grave. Other reformed churches grew suspicious of Italians, with their itch for questions. The charming Laelius Socinus (Sozzini) collected testimonials from both *Calvin and Melanchthon, but, with hindsight, his personal creed could be read in an unorthodox sense. For centuries, for safety's sake, the tradition that would become Unitarianism practised equivocation. The famous non-equivocator was the Spaniard Servetus, whom Calvin had burned.

The tradition survived on the margins of Europe. In Poland, where every nobleman was by law a law to himself, dissident Protestants flourished. Men argued at councils in favour of dropping technical Greek philosophy for the language of the *bible alone. This split the Reformed church, and in 1565 the Minor Reformed Church of Poland was the first non-Trinitarian denomination. Its enemies called it *Arian, after the old heresy. The little church, very like the Anabaptists, though more learned, was gently sterner than Calvinism, and never admitted to full membership its greatest theologian, Faustus Socinus (Sozzini) (1539–1604), nephew of Laelius. That church's Rakovian Catechism of 1605, named for their godly commonwealth of Rakow, obsessed orthodox controversialists for a century. 'No Protestant Christian' (said Harnack, much later) 'will read the prefaces … without being stirred to inward sympathy.' These are a classic statement of tolerance and willingness to learn. There is a faint hope that some of the hundreds of scholars who angrily refuted them learnt something themselves. Polish Protestantism, of all sorts, was dispersed by the troops of the *Counter-Reformation.

Ferenc (Francis) Dávid (1510–79) progressed from Catholicism to *Lutheranism to Calvinism to Unitarianism, and won over a king, John Sigismund of Transylvania, a province of Hungary briefly independent, through dangerously playing off the Muslim sultan against the emperor. Dávid and the royal physician Biandrata controversially republished medieval pictures of the Trinity (one with three heads). There was actually a mass movement into Unitarianism, with a popular rallying-cry 'God is one'. Transylvania was Protestant, with Unitarianism (using the name) one of the four Received Religions. Dávid quarrelled with Socinus, who would allow some form of worship to Christ. Despite centuries of bullying, that small church, now largely in Romania, survives, as the national church of the Szeklers, who claim to be descended from the Huns.

Elsewhere, until late in the 18th century, Socinians, as they were usually called, were free-thinking individuals (some famous, like *Milton or Newton), or at best a movement of opinion within other churches. It is possible to over-schematize the move from Calvinism to *Arminianism to Arianism to Unitarianism. These people were more interested in basic human decency than in schemes of correct theology. They were much more emphatic about their cheerful doctrine of humanity than their doctrine of God. In an age of reason, almost all churches tended towards moralism and were impatient of *metaphysics. The English *Presbyterians, as a denomination, chapel by chapel, became effectively Unitarian, but the orthodox Trinitarian divinity faculties of Scotland still gave doctorates to their ministers.

In time, Unitarians came out fighting, first against revivalism, then against the Trinity as such. The first official Unitarian chapels in the United States and England were for ex-Anglicans. The old *Puritan Harvard Divinity School was Unitarian by 1806, but the actual technical name 'Unitarian' was not avowed until the 1820s. It might be thought that to accept the name was to fall in with a Trinitarian choice of vocabulary. Unitarians tended to be middle-class, cultured (a church that bred writers, such as Elizabeth Gaskell and Harriet Martineau) and politically active. Their sympathy with the French *Revolution attracted mob violence in England.

The Romantic Revival challenged all *Enlightenment thought, and saw rationalist Unitarianism as unforgivably cold and cerebral. The two most influential Anglican thinkers of the century, *Coleridge and Maurice, were both converts from Unitarianism. New historical methods of biblical criticism meant that the old arguments based on the 'bible alone', where the Unitarians could hold their own with the orthodox, sounded naive. Nineteenth-century Unitarians tried very hard to find warmth and depth and colour in their theology. Emerson and the Transcendentalists went on beyond Unitarianism, but perceptibly they had been nurtured in a very different Unitarianism from the chilly rationalism depicted in 'Mark Rutherford'. Both James Martineau in England and Theodore Parker in the United States went beyond the 'bible alone' and beyond rationalism. Martineau saw an increase 'of theological doubt and of devotional affection; there is far less belief, yet more faith'. Possibly they went beyond Christianity, as even the 'Lordship of Christ' became doubtful. It is fair to say that just as many mainline Christians should admit that on some matters the Unitarians were there centuries before them, the Unitarians can find themselves anticipated by the *deists, whom their forerunners loathed.

Though the union with the less socially élite *Universalists in 1961 broadened and strengthened the denomination, the 20th century saw a general decline in avowed Unitarianism. Their liberal optimism seemed as dated as their mainline Protestant liturgy and form of government. Somehow cheerful sentences like 'Even in the worst men good feelings and principles are predominant' (Harvard theology) needed too much faith or explanation.

As there are charismatics beyond the Pentecostal churches, are there Unitarians beyond the churches of that name? The prevailing fashion in divinity faculties is undoubtedly Trinitarian. Any mainline theologian who tries to rethink the doctrine of God is likely to be challenged. Those who are happily traditional, or those whom others might call tritheist, often call their opponents Unitarian. Yet it can reasonably be argued that the traditional language owes too much to Greek philosophy. All that really needs to be affirmed is that our experience of God necessarily includes both transcendence and immanence (C. C. Richardson). G. W. Lampe, in *God as Spirit*, leaves Trinitarian language to affirm God as 'personal'. 'I believe in the Divinity of our Lord and Saviour Jesus Christ, in the sense that the one God, the Creator and Saviour Spirit, revealed himself and acted decisively for us in Jesus' (and similarly acts in us in the Spirit). These theologians are not avowedly Unitarian as such. Possibly John Hick, proclaiming a 'Copernican revolution' in the move from a Christocentric to a theocentric theology, goes beyond this. His purpose was to further a wider *ecumenism with the other ethical monotheisms. This might perhaps better be done in other ways than rewriting the creeds, but Unitarians historically remain early models of needful tolerance and modesty. **Alistair Mason**

Ahlstrom, Sydney, and Carey, Jonathan, *An American Reformation* (1997)

Bolam, C. G. *et al.*, *The English Presbyterians from Elizabethan Puritanism to Modern Unitarianism* (1968).

Howe, D. W., *The Unitarian Conscience* (1970).

Schulman, Frank, '*Blasphemous and Wicked*' (1997).

Wilbur, E. M., *A History of Unitarianism* (2 vols.; 1945; 1952).

Wright, Conrad (ed.), *Three Prophets of Religious Liberalism: Channing, Emerson, Parker* (1961).

Young, David, *F. D. Maurice and Unitarianism* (1992).

unity. The understanding of unity in the *New Testament is rooted in the corporate unity of *Israel, *God's chosen people in *covenant relationship with him under the law (see Law, Biblical). *Jesus established a new covenant with his *disciples (Mark 14: 24) which they later realized was not limited to Jews (Acts 10: 47; Rom. 1: 5). His followers understood God's purpose in sending Jesus Christ to reconcile a sinful and divided world to unity with God (2 Cor. 5: 18–20; Eph. 1: 10; Rev. 5: 13). The *church was thought of as a sign, instrument, and foretaste of this unity which would be completed in the *Kingdom of God. Jesus prayed that his disciples might be one as he was one with the Father, so that the world might believe (John 17: 21). The disciples experienced the *Holy Spirit as a powerful presence of God binding them together (Acts 2: 44–6). The source of this unity was the very nature of God, Father, Son, and Spirit, who is love (1 John 4: 7–21).

Of the many images of the church in the NT, some focus on its unity through identity with Christ (e.g. *body of Christ—1 Cor. 12: 4–31; Rom. 12: 4–8), others on its unity through close relationship with him (e.g. bride of Christ—Eph. 5: 23–32; Rev. 19: 7–8 and 21: 2), but even those images which focus on identity also describe the growing relationship and complementarity of the diverse members (Eph. 4: 11–13; 1 Cor. 3: 5–16).

Already in the NT there were threats to the unity of the churches from three causes: (1) failure in relationships (1 Cor. 1: 11–12; Acts 6: 1); (2) differences in behaviour (1 Cor. 5: 1–3; Matt. 18: 15–17); (3) differences in teaching (1 John 4: 1–3; 2 Pet. 2: 1). There are frequent appeals for unity and mutual *love among the followers of Jesus (John 15: 12; 1 Pet. 3: 8; 1 Cor. 1: 10), and many of these refer to the unity of Christians within a local church. However, a serious threat arose to the wider unity between Jewish and Gentile Christians throughout all the churches, and an assembly was held in Jerusalem, including apostles and elders, to settle this dispute (Acts 15). As diverse local churches spread throughout the Roman empire, it was judged necessary to establish norms of identity and visible bonds of unity between them. Gradually a canon of NT writings was accepted everywhere (see Bible): bishops were appointed for each local church and ordained by neighbouring bishops to exercise oversight

and to maintain unity and *communion between all the local churches. Particular respect was given to local churches that had links with the apostles, and especially to *Rome in the west. *Councils of bishops were called to settle disputes, and to establish norms or canons of behaviour and the parameters of orthodox teaching through the Nicene *Creed. Those who accepted the decisions of these councils remained in *sacramental communion with the rest of the church, while those judged not to do so were excluded.

In the course of the fifteen centuries following the Council of *Nicaea *schisms between Christians multiplied for doctrinal, political, and personal reasons, producing a multitude of separated churches, which, therefore, entered the 20th century with different emphases in their understanding of the church and its unity and with distinct identities often partly defined by their differences from one another.

In the first half of the century Roman *Catholic thinking tended to focus upon the institutional unity of the church as a hierarchical society with a legal constitution governed by bishops under the bishop of Rome, the successor of St Peter. All other Christians were regarded as dissidents, and expected to return to union with the 'one true church'. However, the recovery of a more sacramental understanding of unity enabled *Vatican II to recognize members of other churches and ecclesial communities as already sharing a real, although not fully realized, communion with the Catholic Church.

The *Eastern Orthodox Churches understood themselves to be in continuity with the *tradition of the united church of the early fathers and ecumenical councils. The heart of unity was to be found in the *Eucharist, celebrated by the bishop, who was in communion with other bishops in all the autocephalous Orthodox Churches in the world. Unity with other churches depended upon their accepting the tradition in its fullness.

The major churches of the *Reformation believed themselves to be under the authority of scripture, with the duty to preach the pure gospel and to administer the sacraments of the gospel, *baptism, and the Lord's supper. They were increasingly willing to co-operate closely with other churches in pulpit and altar fellowship, if they judged that they faithfully fulfilled these duties.

Independent churches thought of unity as being primarily within each autonomous local congregation, all the members of which had a part in the government of the local church through the church meeting. These local churches, while cherishing their autonomy, increasingly recognized their interdependence, and established federations or alliances of local churches of the same tradition. However, they remained nervous of wider institutional union. The Religious Society of Friends (*Quakers) thought all credal formulae or permanent forms of government to be divisive. They believed in spiritual unity, discovered by waiting together on the presence of the Spirit.

These various patterns of unity, predominating in separate denominational identities, were modified and developed during the 20th century by three factors: (1) the inner renewal of each tradition as it rediscovered its own roots; (2) the interaction of the separate church traditions that became ready to learn from one another and to rediscover their common roots; and (3) the pressures of surrounding society as it reacted against totalitarian authority, discovered the interdependence of the global village, and sought tolerance and *reconciliation in a pluralist and divided world.

The idea of Christian unity as enforced uniformity was widely discredited even before the 20th century began. The model of federal unity was popular among some Protestants who had begun to recognize the self-defeating effect of their mutual competition in mission work.

The pattern that came to dominate the thinking of *Faith and Order, which included *Anglicans, Orthodox, and many Protestants, and from 1971 Roman Catholics, was that of organic unity, based on Paul's image of the church as a body. This claimed that there should be only one church in each place, united in faith and communion with all churches in every other place and time through *conciliar fellowship, so that all could act together as occasion required.

Given the presence in so many places of churches of separate denominations living alongside one another, many Christians today think the pattern of organic unity either to be unrealistic or, if attempted, as inevitably leading to uniformity. With this in mind the Lutheran World Federation in 1977 sought to modify it through the concept of unity in reconciled diversity, by which the distinctive gifts of existing denominations could be preserved as they worked closely together in councils.

The World Council of Churches provides a certain international focus of unity for its 300 member churches. For centuries the Ecumenical Patriarch has had a primacy of honour in Eastern Orthodoxy, and Anglicans and Lutherans have at times expressed willingness to recognize in the bishop of Rome a similar personal primacy, while rejecting his claims to supremacy. A new stage in the discussion about a possible international personal focus of unity began in 1995 when Pope *John Paul II invited other churches to discuss with him how his own primatial ministry of unity might become acceptable to them.

There is virtually universal agreement that the source and substance of Christian unity is the love that God, the Holy *Trinity, has for his people reflected and expressed in their love for one another. The Greek koinonia (Acts 2: 42–7) describes this relationship and is variously translated as communion, fellowship, solidarity, sharing. It is also widely agreed that this koinonia needs to be visible to the world and therefore requires a recognizable, common identity. There is as yet no universal agreement on the facets of that identity. The widest agreement so far reached (in the fifth World Conference on Faith and Order in 1993) focused on (1) a common faith, grounded in scripture and set out in the Nicene Creed; (2) a common life, expressed in one baptism and eucharistic communion, and nurtured by a common ordained *ministry within the ministry of the whole people of God; (3) a common witness, renewing the church as a sign of the Kingdom of God; (4) a way of making common decisions through synodical and primatial structures; and (5) shared ethical living in the struggle for justice, peace, and the integrity of creation.

Perfect unity must await its full realization in the Kingdom of God; but to be faithful to the gospel the disparate Christian communities must seek ever deeper communion (koinonia) with one another locally, regionally, and internationally, as it is only in that way that they will be able to distinguish the diversity that enriches and strengthens unity from that which degenerates into division.

See also ECUMENICAL MOVEMENT.   **Martin Reardon**

Anglican–Reformed Report, God's Reign and our Unity (1984).
ARCIC II, Church as Communion (1991).
Churches Together in England (ed.), Called to be One (1996).
John Paul II, Ut Unum Sint (1995).
Kinnamon, M., and Cope, B. (eds.), The Ecumenical Movement: An Anthology of Key Texts and Voices, Section II (1997).

Universalism.
Universalists believe that everyone will go to *heaven. This contradicts a long-standing Christian *dualism (if heaven, then *hell) and, on the face of it, some of the teaching of Jesus (e.g. Matt. 25: 41, 46).

Early Greek theologians, Clement, *Origen, and Gregory of Nyssa, loving symmetry, spoke of a wonderful return, where everything that had gone wrong would be restored to an original state of perfection (apocatastasis), even the *devil. This was condemned at *Constantinople in 543. *Mystics occasionally had surges of happy insight—for instance *Julian of Norwich's 'and all manner of things shall be well'—but it was only with the coming of the radical wing of the *Reformation that anyone doubted hell. The case was argued by Hans Denck (c.1495–1527), an early Anabaptist; and the Dunkers (Church of the *Brethren) carried it on as a permissible opinion, unexpected for a tiny, rather severe, gathered flock.

In the 18th century others doubted hell. *Deism was congenitally optimistic, and influenced Christians. Protestant mystics and visionaries saw deeper resolutions of biblical truth. A revivalist preacher, John Murray, in 1779 set up a Universalist congregation in Gloucester, Massachusetts. Soon there was a creed, the Winchester Confession (1803), and a denomination.

Murray came from *Calvinism. *Paul can sound universalist: 'even so by the righteousness of one the free gift came upon all men unto justification of life' (Rom. 5: 18). The neat universalist development was: 'Calvinism: God can save all mankind, but will not. *Arminianism: God would save all mankind, but cannot. Universalism: God can save all mankind, and will.' Universalism thus arose to teach a gospel of gratuitous salvation. This was alongside *Unitarianism, which was not hell-minded either. There was a contrast, because Unitarians tended to be better-educated, wealthier, and optimistic about humanity in general, whereas Universalists tended to be poorer, more aware of *sin, and therefore needing a gracious God. They stayed bible-centred longer than the Unitarians. *Socially reformist, with more *women *ministers than any other church, the Universalists at their peak claimed in 1888 to be the sixth largest denomination in the United States.

There were moral questions to Universalism. Would God force hardened unbelievers into heaven? Can Universalists sin boldly, with no sanction of hell? For much of the 19th century most Universalists were 'restorationist', talking of up to 50,000 years of *purgatory. But intuitively the denomination was 'ultra-universalist': sin carries its own punishment in this life; there is enough hell on earth; and then there is *death, which is sufficient purgation. Twentieth-century Universalists, who united with Unitarians in 1961, widened universalism, being humanist and syncretist, and not specifically Christian.

Other Christians have denied eternal punishment. In 1853 F. D. Maurice was dismissed from his professorial chair in London for explaining that the Greek aionios need not be translated as 'everlasting' in that phrase. By 1938 the Doctrine Report of the Church of

England allowed the belief that 'the love of God will at last win penitence' from all. Even the neo-orthodox Karl *Barth can be read as universalist.

It could be said that heaven has faded too.   **Alistair Mason**

Cameron, Nigel M. de S. (ed.), *Universalism and the Doctrine of Hell* (1993).

Cassara, Ernest (ed.), *Universalism in America: A Documentary History* (1971).

Hick, John, *Death and Eternal Life* (1976).

Rowell, Geoffrey, *Hell and the Victorians* (1974).

universities (from Latin, *universitas*, an association or corporation) were a creation of the medieval world (see MIDDLE AGES). The first universities, which appeared in Paris, Bologna, Oxford, and Montpellier at the beginning of the 13th century, were academic associations or syndicates of scholars, in the case of Bologna two syndicates of law students governed by their own student rectors, but in Paris and Oxford associations formed and ruled by teachers. They were not founded or created by any act of sovereign power, but were spontaneous associations, concentrated in a number of cities, entered into by masters or students, who wished to coordinate their teaching arrangements and provide each other with protection and support. The proliferation of schools and the rise of a new class of professional scholars (secular masters who gained a livelihood by teaching) was the outcome of the exuberant intellectual movement of the 12th century associated with the recovery by western scholars of a large part of Greek and Arabic *philosophy and *science and with the revived study of classical Roman law. The masters who formed the early scholastic universities were purveyors of the new learning and expert practitioners of the new scholastic method, which applied dialectic or analytic logic to the study and exposition of the authoritative texts. In northern Europe the teachers of the arts curriculum—the study of logic and the four sciences of the *quadrivium*—were the most numerous, and at Paris took the initiative in forming a self-regulating corporation in the closing years of the 12th century.

The licence to teach had long been a monopoly of the church, and the rise of these autonomous academic societies was at first viewed with misgiving by more conservative prelates. Gradually the canonists and civil lawyers devised a theory to fit them into the existing universalist theories of medieval government. Together with the *regnum* (crown) and the *sacerdotium* (clergy), they formed the *studium* and so were part of the threefold dispensation by which Christian society was ordered and governed. The essence of this doctrine was encapsulated in the term *studium generale* used to designate a university. It meant a school of universal resort, as opposed to a merely regional school, endowed with a special universal status. Its hallmark was the *ius ubique docendi*, the theoretical right of its graduates to teach in any other school of the same status without further examination. Since such a licence could be conferred only by a universal authority, only the pope or the emperor could create a *studium generale*; and in the later Middle Ages a papal bull was the instrument invariably used by princely patrons who sought to raise a school in their dominions to university status. The universities were thus recognized to be the intellectual organs of Latin Christendom.

Although they were clerical corporations, whose heads in northern and central Europe were ecclesiastical dignitaries and whose students enjoyed the immunities of clergy at law, the universities were not seminaries. Not all of them possessed a faculty of *theology and in those that did, such as Paris, Oxford, and Prague, students of theology were greatly outnumbered by those of arts. It was a platitude of the medieval pulpit that theology was queen of the sciences to which every clerk should aspire, but it was in fact a higher faculty to which only a small élite could afford to proceed.

Besides being nurseries of bishops, lawyers, and royal administrators, the university schools served medieval society by providing a think-tank for perplexed rulers and a forum for discussion and creative thought. This was nowhere more active and creative than in theology and canon law. In the international schools of Bologna the teaching of the famous law doctors created and transmitted to students a science of civil and canon *law that affected people of all social levels. Similarly, the debates and *summas* of the Paris theologians clarified and defined the principles of a *sacramental and *moral theology that were universally disseminated through the pulpit and confessional. This was acknowledged by Pope Gregory IX's bull *parens scientiarum* (the great privilege he conferred on the University of Paris in 1231), which averred that by the lectures of the masters 'the corn is ground to feed the whole world'. He was echoed nearly a century later by the masters of Oxford who told the Convocation of Canterbury that 'by scholastic men the grain of saving wisdom is prepared, which in due time is dispensed to the servants of God by the hands of those placed in authority over the Lord's household'. In other words, the university made the theology and the bishops dispensed it.

The *conciliar theories of church government that were invoked in an effort to heal the Great Schism were largely the work of academic canonists and theologians of Paris; similarly the universities played a conspicuous role in the controversies of the *Reformation. But the religious divisions of Europe that followed disrupted the international community of learning. Protestant theology was largely developed in the *German and English universities. In Germany, those universities in principalities with divided confessional allegiance eventually established two distinct faculties of theology, *Lutheran and Catholic (several preserved in modern Germany). In England, Oxford and Cambridge became bulwarks of the *Anglican religious establishment. The *French Revolution and the Napoleonic system had catastrophic consequences for the development of Catholic theology. Under the new, anticlerical regime, church and state were separated, the universities of France, Belgium, and the Netherlands were *secularized and subordinated to the central authority of the state, and theology faculties were abolished. Italian universities suffered a similar take-over by the new secular state after the *risorgimento*,

In these circumstances a leading role in biblical studies and speculative theology fell in the 19th century to German universities. In Berlin, *Tübingen, and elsewhere theologians from *Schleiermacher and Baur in the early 19th century, through Harnack and Troeltsch at the beginning of the 20th, to *Bultmann, *Moltmann, and *Pannenberg, have provided the principal leadership in the development of Christian or at least Protestant thought. It was partly in reaction to the *higher criticism rampant in German universities, as well as to state intrusion into ecclesiastical matters, that the *Oxford Movement, led by a group of dons, began in *Tracts for the Times* a reaffirmation of the dogmas of Catholic orthodoxy, claiming an authentic Catholic identity for the Church of England—a movement that has proved hardly less influential for the shaping of the modern Christian, and not only Anglican, mind. The doctrine of the Tractarians was repudiated by the heads of colleges who governed the university, just as Harnack's was disavowed by the German Evangelical Church, but in each case largely unavailingly. In the 20th century the Divinity Schools of American universities, particularly Yale, Harvard, *Princeton, and Union in New York, with *Tillich and the *Niebuhrs, for example, as professors, were hardly less influential.

For the Roman Catholic Church, the secularization of universities imposed a period of theological stagnation, of which the characteristic product was the seminary manual. The cardinal role of the university as an organ of the *ecclesia docens* (teaching church) was sustained only by the Catholic University of Louvain, revived in 1833 after Belgium gained its independence, the Catholic faculties in Germany, and the Institut Catholique in Paris. Efforts of scholars to apply the methods of historical science to the study of biblical texts and to church history and doctrine encountered increasing opposition from the *ultramontanes and the Roman Curia, culminating in a crushing blow by the Holy Office's decree *Lamentabili* (1907) and Pius X's encyclical *Pascendi*, condemning the asserted errors of *modernism. The subsequent revival of Catholic bible studies, speculative theology, and church history in 20th-century universities, an enterprise in which lay theologians played a significant part, did not escape conflict between the needs of free enquiry and the conservatism of the ecclesiastical hierarchy.

Only with the large role accorded Catholic university theologians at the time of *Vatican II did they recover the position accorded them in the Middle Ages and enjoyed by Protestant theologians ever since. It is a role that hardly fits an ultramontane view of the church and it is unsurprising that it led to Roman moves to re-establish effective control over theological faculties, notably in the cases of Hans *Küng's removal from his chair in the Catholic Faculty at Tübingen and Charles Curran's from Catholic University, Washington.

The university has a vital role in promoting the health of Christian thought, as was famously expounded in *Newman's *The Idea of a University* (1852) and in Walter Moberly's *The Crisis in the University* (1949), the fruit of a discussion among a group of outstanding Christian scholars in the early post-Second World War years. The vocation of the university is the pursuit of *truth and, as Newman argued, it needs 'elbow room' and 'time' to do its work. Its authentic function is undermined if its work (in theological science as well as the physical sciences) is subjected to close outside control. In its own sphere, it alone can 'act as umpire between truth and truth'. Tension between this function and the conservative instincts of an authoritarian church is perhaps inevitable.

See also EDUCATION.   **C. H. Lawrence**

Cobban, A. B., *The Medieval Universities: Their Development and Organization* (1975).

Coulson, John (ed.), *Theology and the University* (1964).

Moberly, Walter, *The Crisis in the University* (1949).

Newman, John Henry, *The Idea of a University*, ed. Frank Turner (1996).

Pelikan, Jaroslav, *The Idea of the University: A Re-Examination* (1992).

Rashdall, H., *The Universities of Europe in the Middle Ages*, ed. F. M. Powicke and A. B. Emden (1936).

usury. The practice of lending money at interest, particularly when the rates charged are high or excessive, was systematically and consistently denounced as immoral in the Judaeo-Christian tradition until the traditional teaching was quietly modified or fell into disuse in modern times.

The opposition to usury depended on two very different types of argument, which were usually thought to be mutually reinforcing. These were arguments derived originally from classical philosophy which at their core relied on a theory of the purpose or end of money, and arguments based on scripture, which rested on the conviction that usury was unjust and disruptive of community because it benefited the wealthy and strong at the expense of the weak and poor (see POVERTY).

*Aristotle was the main source for the philosophical arguments. He argued that usury is hated for good reason because 'it makes a profit from currency itself, instead of making it from the process [of exchange] which currency was meant to serve' (*Politics* 1258^b). Usury is thus to be prohibited as unnatural, because it abuses money, which is intended to enable trade; it is quite improper to use it to 'breed' more money. Money, the scholastics taught, is useful, but 'barren'; it cannot breed.

In the bible usury is denounced as a breach of neighbourly responsibility. The wealthy usurer benefits from the poor person's need. The OT legal codes denounce usury as taking advantage of the misfortune of a fellow *Israelite (Exod. 22: 25; Deut. 23: 19–20; Lev. 25: 35–8). A key passage, which was later to have immense influence in enabling the Jews to become moneylenders in Christendom, was the permission to charge foreigners interest (Deut. 23: 20), and exempting foreigners from the sabbatical remission of debts (Deut. 15: 3). Among Israelites, however, the law was clear: no interest could legitimately be charged, although sureties might be required. In OT times loans in money or kind, like gifts, were seen as a way of helping the unfortunate, and any charging of interest was regarded as exploitation. But the legal prohibitions suggest that usury was in fact practised in Israel, and there is evidence that commercial interest-bearing loans were commonplace in the commerce of some other ancient Middle Eastern societies.

In the NT there is encouragement of lending without expecting to be repaid (Luke 6: 34–5), and the free forgiveness of debts commended in the *Lord's Prayer and elsewhere on the analogy of God's behaviour towards us should not be interpreted in a purely spiritual way (Matt. 6: 12–15; 18: 21–7; Luke 7: 41–2). On the other hand, in the parable of the talents Jesus seems to accept that money can be invested to earn interest (Luke 19: 23; Matt. 25: 27). But the scriptures as a whole were read as strongly opposed to usury as a breach of neighbourliness and as exploitation of the poor and weak by the strong and prosperous.

In very different economic and social conditions, the fathers with near unanimity denounced lending at interest. They still regarded usury as rich people taking advantage of the sufferings of the poor to increase their wealth. Unlike almsgiving or loans without interest which are ways of assisting the poor, usury benefits the lender at the expense of the borrower, and actually means a movement of resources from the poor to the rich.

The medieval scholastics continued to denounce usury, deploying both scriptural and philosophical arguments in a powerful broadside. R. H. Tawney outlined medieval teaching thus:

To take usury is contrary to scripture; it is contrary to Aristotle; it is contrary to nature, for it is to live without labour; it is to sell time, which belongs to God, for the advantage of wicked men; it is to rob those who use the money lent, and to whom, since they make it profitable, the profits should belong; it is unjust in itself, for the benefit of the loan to the borrower cannot exceed the value of the principal sum lent him; it is in defiance of sound juristic principles, for when a loan of money is made, the property in the thing lent passes to the borrower, and why should the creditor demand payment from a man who is merely using what is now his own?   (*Religion and the Rise of Capitalism* (1927), 43)

Usury was probably the most important and contentious issue in Christian social teaching throughout the Middle Ages and early modern times. So sustained and effective was the church's prohibition on usury that it may be that it effectively delayed or constrained the development of a modern economy based on credit and interest (*capitalism).

The traditional teaching came under increasing pressure from the time of the *Reformation. First Protestant churches, particularly *Calvinist ones, began to turn a blind eye to money 'breeding' through interest; Rome took slow steps to modernize its position while denying that any change was taking place. Responsible *moral theologians have argued since the late *nineteenth century that the traditional teaching was incompatible with the development of a modern economy. As a consequence there was a widespread abandonment of any serious attempt to monitor the economy to protect the poor; theology in effect evacuated the economic realm.

The crisis of Third World debt since the 1970s and the explosion of domestic credit/debt in recent years have led many to suggest that the traditional teaching still has validity and should be revived in an effort to defend poor families and poor nations against the effects of uncontrolled debt repayments. Theologians such as Ulrich Duchrow, Timothy Gorringe, and Peter Selby, believing that usury today not only harms quality of life, but kills people, suggest that 'the redemption of money will involve the abolition of usury'. Usury, in the sense of high and uncontrolled levels of interest, causes today a massive flow of resources from poor people and nations to rich people and nations, and makes the condition of the poor much worse, while the already prosperous benefit at their expense. The traditional opposition to usury may have continuing relevance if deployed to curb destructively high levels of interest, and to show that in some circumstances the remission of debt is the wisest and the most positive policy.

See also ANTISEMITISM; GLOBAL ETHICS; JUSTICE.

Duncan B. Forrester

Nelson, B., *The Idea of Usury*, 2nd edn. (1967).

Noonan, J. T., *The Scholastic Analysis of Usury* (1957).

Selby, Peter, *Grace and Mortgage: The Language of Faith and the Debt of the World* (1997).

Viner, Jacob, *Religious Thought and Economic Society*, ed. J. Melitz and Donald Winch (1978).

Vatican I, Council of. The first act of *Vatican II (1962–5) was formally to close the first Vatican Council (1869–70). The latter was adjourned *sine die* on 28 October 1870, after a summer of upheaval as the French troops protecting the pope and his earthly territories from a united Italy were withdrawn to fight the Franco-Prussian war and the Italian forces took over. Facing this crisis, the council's most famous definitions, those of the primacy and *infallibility of the pope, have been likened to a defiant 'no surrender'.

Both Pope Pius XI (1922–39) and Pope Pius XII (1939–58) thought of continuing Vatican I, but Pope *John XXIII wanted a new council, with a fresh approach. The contrast in attitude between the two councils is indicated by the fact that Vatican I, like its predecessors, most immediately the Council of *Trent, summarized its teaching in the form of canons which anathematized any who would disagree. A firm line was thereby drawn, distinguishing the *church from the *world. Vatican II produced no canons and declared no anathemas.

If Trent was the council of the *Counter-Reformation, Vatican I is the keystone of the 19th-century Catholic 'counter-Revolution'. Trent opposed the *Protestant Reformers; Vatican I took up position against the tide of *atheism and irreligion unleashed by the *French Revolution. Consulted by Pope Pius IX (1846–78) about the possibility of a council, the bishops responded that what they most wanted was 'the formal condemnation of the various anti-Christian philosophies of the time, and of the new rationalistic interpretations of Christianity and its sacred books' (Hughes 1961: 300).

Pius opened the council on 8 December 1869, a significant date, the feast of the Immaculate Conception of the Blessed Virgin *Mary, which Pius himself, in 1854, had infallibly declared to be 'revealed by God'. Although papal infallibility had not yet been defined, it had recently been exercised. Its definition was significantly not on the formal agenda of the council, but it was clearly in the air. Many of the bishops, however, thought that defining it was inopportune. Bishops Dupanloup of Orleans, Hefele of Rottenburg, and Ketteler of Mainz were prominent opponents. They were outnumbered, but speculation still continues about the extent to which the bishops gathered for Vatican I, under strong papal and curial pressure, really debated and decided freely and, particularly, about whether they achieved true moral unanimity. Only 535 of the 744 who attended some part of the council were present for the final vote on infallibility, when just two voted against. Many apparently absented themselves. Fifty-five signed a letter to the pope the night before saying that they would stay away rather than offend 'filial piety and respect' by voting against. At issue is the council's ecumenicity (cf. *Küng 1971; Bermejo 1984), though all the opposing or absent bishops subsequently accepted the vote and the resultant papal decree enshrining the dogma.

Only two definitions resulted from 51 draft texts prepared for the council. They are intimately related. Rationalism fundamentally denied the existence of divine *revelation. Accordingly, Vatican I (with 667 voting) promulgated a *Dogmatic Constitution on the Catholic Faith* (*Dei Filius*), which, among other things, declared that, while God can be known with certainty by 'the natural light of human reason', revelation is 'absolutely necessary' because 'God in his infinite goodness has ordained man to a supernatural end'. This was followed by a *Dogmatic Constitution on the Church of Christ* (*Pastor Aeternus*) which identified the pope as possessing 'the infallibility with which the divine redeemer willed his church to be endowed' when he defines 'doctrine concerning faith or morals' as belonging to divine revelation. Thus, revelation exists and the *papacy enables clarity as to its content.

The careful phrasing makes it clear that the pope is not an independent oracle but simply the privileged organ of the church's own infallibility and the guaranteed spokesman for its faith, in certain specific instances (when speaking *ex cathedra*, as 'shepherd and teacher of all Christians'). Thus, the extreme position of the *ultramontane enthusiasts, led by Archbishops Dechamps of Malines and Manning of Westminster (both later cardinals), was not embraced.

Nevertheless, by neglecting to mention the bishops (see EPISCOPATE) whose importance for determining doctrine the first millennium amply showed, Vatican I left Catholic teaching skewed towards the papacy in an unbalanced way that Vatican II would need to correct. The original aim of Vatican I had been to promulgate a broader text. The draft consisted of fifteen chapters, the pope not being encountered until the eleventh, and then only to treat of his *primacy*, his authority to govern. There was no reference to papal *infallibility*. Chapter 9, however, was on the infallibility of the *church*. Christ promised to be with his followers always, even to the end of time (Matt. 28: 20), so the church as a whole could never err in its faith. It was Manning and his associates who pressed to have papal infallibility included and then moved to the top of the agenda. The one original chapter on the pope duly grew into four chapters, ultimately the sum content of Vatican I's teaching 'on the church'.

The model of the church as a pyramid, promoted for the last six or seven hundred years by scholasticism, in contrast with the patristic, communional model of the early centuries, was now complete, with the pope at the summit. Likewise, *Dei Filius* was a final flourish of the scholastic understanding of revelation as *propositional* rather than *personal*, the revelation of supernatural truths rather than of God's own self.

The premature ending of Vatican I may be regarded as providential. Balanced reflection on modernity had time to mature.

Paul McPartlan

Bermejo, L. M., *Towards Christian Reunion. Vatican I: Obstacles and Opportunities* (1984).

—— *Church, Conciliarity and Communion* (1990).

Butler, C., *The Vatican Council* (2 vols.; 1930; 1 vol. edn. 1962).

Hasler, A. B., *How the Pope Became Infallible* (1981).

Hughes, P., *The Church in Crisis: The Twenty Great Councils* (1961), 294–324.

Küng, H., *Infallible?* (1971).

Sweeney, G., 'The Forgotten Council' and 'The Primacy: The Small Print of Vatican I', in A. Hastings (ed.), *Bishops and Writers* (1977), 161–206.

Vatican II, Council of (1962–5). Pope *John XXIII announced his intention to call a general *council on 25 January 1959, feast of St Paul and final day of the octave for Christian Unity, about which he intended the council to be primarily concerned. The idea was apparently a personal inspiration. His announcement came as a complete surprise and was received with considerable hesitation by the Curia and Roman circles generally. Preparations got under way rather slowly. They were placed oddly, if perhaps inevitably, in curial hands, little anxious to move in the directions indicated. There was in consequence a remarkable ambiguity throughout the preparatory period leading to the council's opening in October 1962. On the one hand were many optimistic and irenic speeches by the pope fuelling ever greater world expectations. A Secretariat of Unity was set up, headed by the *Jesuit biblical scholar, Cardinal Bea; invitations to send observers went to all the main churches. In 1961, for the first time, official Catholic observers attended an assembly of the World Council of Churches. A remarkable book by the young German theologian, Hans *Küng, *The Council and Reunion*, circulated in many languages proposals for radical reform. On the other hand, the actual preparation of draft decrees was carried out secretly, dominated by curial conservatives led by Cardinal Ottaviani, Prefect of the Holy Office, who presided over the crucial doctrinal commission, declined to co-operate with Bea's Secretariat, and apparently saw the council as an opportunity to renew the condemnations filling the 1950 encyclical *Humani Generis*. Of the first list of 224 *periti* (theological experts attached to the council and admitted to all its sessions), 85 were Italians, 19 French, 16 Americans, 15 Germans. Many of the non-Italians were, moreover, conservatively minded theologians based permanently in Rome, but a handful of distinguished dissidents, among them *Congar, *de Lubac, and *Rahner, were included. The influence of the non-Roman *periti* steadily grew throughout the council as did that of the observers (forty at the first session, over a hundred by the fourth). Every important section of Christendom, other than

Baptists and Pentecostals, agreed to send representatives, who included many distinguished Orthodox, Anglican, and Protestant theologians.

The direction of the council was decisively shaped by its first weeks in 1962. Hitherto its official planning had been almost wholly Roman and, except in regard to the liturgy, committed to conservatism. The attack on draft after draft was led by senior bishops from northern Europe—Cardinal Suenens of Malines, Frings of Cologne, König of Vienna, and Liénart of Lille—as being scholastic and juridical, unbiblical and unecumenical, offering the world and other Christians condemnation rather than encouragement. This attack infuriated Ottaviani but proved to have the backing of a considerable majority when at a historic moment on 20 November the draft on the sources of *revelation was rejected by 1368 to 822 votes. No draft was approved in the first session and everything of importance (except that on the liturgy) had to be substantially rewritten, some several times. The rewriting was done between sessions, largely by *periti* (who numbered over 400 by the end).

Originally, Pope John hoped that the council's business could be concluded in a single session. By 1962, however, faced with the range of issues raised and wide dissatisfaction with the preparatory drafts, he had realized a second session would be needed. He died before the council could be reopened and it was its continuance by Paul VI for three further sessions that made its achievement possible. Inevitably it was those *periti* who shared (or, indeed, constructed) the outlook of the *episcopal majority who now became most influential. If Rahner, who was still under deep Holy Office suspicion in the summer of 1962, became the council's primary theologian, it was partly because many years as editor of Denzinger's *Enchiridion* (a collection in Latin of all the church's most influential documents) had produced in him a profoundly centralist and responsible frame of mind. But de Lubac, Congar, Mgr. Philips of Louvain, and others took key roles in the shaping of one or another document.

Only two texts received final approval in the second (1963) session, those on *liturgy and the media. The fourteen others were finalized in 1964 and 1965. The theological evolution of the conciliar mind continued so that more relatively radical ideas found expression in the later texts. If liturgy had been delayed until 1965, the council would probably have been less cautious in its reforms than it was two years earlier.

In the run-up to the council, many theologians of various hues connected Vatican II with *Vatican I, never formally closed since the Franco-Prussian war had forced its hasty prorogation. While the original intention at Vatican I was to produce a constitution on the church as a whole, all it actually did was to pick out the topic of papacy, giving an unintentionally one-sided impression. Now was the time to right the balance by treating the church in general and the episcopate in particular, as Vatican I's definitions of papal authority had seemed to undermine the latter's standing. Episcopal *collegiality, as finally described in chapter 3 of Lumen Gentium, can consequently be seen as the council's most premeditated theological contribution. Nevertheless, important as it is, the strength of *LG* lies in the roundedness of its ecclesiology, escaping over-preoccupation with hierarchical ministry of any sort, approached only after two opening chapters on 'the Mystery of the Church' and 'the People of God'. While the first went well beyond Pius XII's encyclical *Mystici Corporis*, it was the second that appeared the more striking and original, so that the idea of 'People of God' developed almost into the theme tune of the council as a whole, at least as received outside Rome itself. It is noticeable that, subsequent to the council, this theme has faded increasingly from Roman terminology, being replaced by that of '*communion' which, while no less significant, was actually treated less explicitly by Vatican II, although it underlay its theology of ecumenism.

What best holds the major theological contributions together is John's original proposal—*unity. It was partly to make the recovery of unity more imaginable that scholastic concepts of revelation, ecclesiastical government, and *religious liberty needed to be spelt out afresh, that *Mary was given no constitution of her own but a chapter devoted to her inserted in the constitution on the church, that the liturgy was to be celebrated in part at least in the vernacular, that the cup might on occasion be given to the *laity, and an order of permanent deacons reinstituted to include married men (see DIACONATE). The council was profoundly committed to a wider pastoral renewal of a kind to escape the heavy legacy of medievalism, yet it can hardly be gainsaid that it showed most insistence and moved most positively at those points that were ecumenically most significant, though always without repudiating any previously held dogmatic position. This was certainly not a matter of simply imitating Protestant models. Thus its most insistent ecclesiological emphasis, repeated throughout the documents, is on the role of the Eucharist as both centre and cause of the church and its unity. While this contrasts noticeably with the teaching of Pius XII's encyclical *Mystici Corporis*, it was certainly not derived from either the theory or practice of Protestantism but from patristic teaching, mediated by de Lubac and the *nouvelle théologie*; nevertheless, the ecumenical significance of shifting from a primarily hierarchical to a sacramental perspective of unity was enormous.

While the council quite deliberately, at Pope John's bidding, eschewed infallible statements, its *dogmatic character, particularly at certain points, should not be underplayed. Both the constitution on the church and that on revelation were described as 'dogmatic'. In them and elsewhere, certain precise statements clearly possess special authority, on account of the way they were formulated and the amount of time given to their preparation and discussion. High among these, besides the passages on collegiality, is the refusal simply to equate the Roman Catholic communion with the Church of Christ (LG 8), again in contrast to *Mystici Corporis* and *Humani Generis*: the change from 'is' to 'subsists in' implies that while the former is certainly in the latter, other communions are not necessarily excluded. No less striking is the one and only use of 'solemnly', a term normally linked with dogmatic statements, to declare that 'the churches of the east, as much as those of the west, fully enjoy the right and are in duty bound to rule themselves' (*Orientalium Ecclesiarum*, 5, exactly repeated in the decree on Ecumenism, 16). While this remarkable admission, so profoundly in contrast with the way Rome has often attempted to 'rule' the east, has been seriously under-noticed, it may prove the council's most far-sighted insistence. What is affirmed for the churches of the east can hardly be denied to those of the south.

If the council's earlier sessions were focused principally on church and revelation, its latter period was on religious freedom (where the influence of Bishop de Smedt of Bruges and the American Jesuit, Courtney Murray, were particularly important) and the wider issues of *modernity tackled in a draft for long cryptically described as 'schema XIII', initially a brainchild of Cardinal Suenens. This finally became Gaudium et Spes, a 'Pastoral Constitution' addressing *family, culture, politics, and economics. By far the longest of conciliar documents, its importance lay in a reorientation outwards from church to *world, from which later sprang, among other things, *liberation theology, but divisions over it prefigured the deep theological rifts within the post-conciliar church. Its rather optimistic view of the world owed much to French Thomists, notably Chenu and Congar. It was the moment at which *Ratzinger with his more pessimistic, even 'Lutheran', approach distanced himself from the north European theological consensus.

The impact of the council was only beginning when it closed in 1965. In the next few years, its liturgical provisions were much extended by Paul VI, while ecumenical relations snowballed, greatly affecting the way in which most other churches regarded Rome and Catholicism. Intellectual, sociopolitical, and emotional attitudes were transformed on both sides. But it may be that the greatest effect was on the internal consciousness of Catholics. The intense debate characteristic of the conciliar years, in which hundreds of theologians were involved, active both in Rome and in explaining and discussing the issues throughout the world, could not be ended with the council. Catholicism became again a community of internal *dialogue rather than monolithic accord, even if after some years Rome endeavoured to rein this in by establishing new norms of post-conciliar theological *orthodoxy, particularly with the 1992 publication of the *Catechism of the Catholic Church*.

The council unquestionably constituted a watershed in Catholic history but its interpretation remains disputed. The 100,000 words of text reflect a variety of viewpoints. Much of it, inevitably, was hardly discussed except in particular commissions and some of it substantially represents pre-conciliar curial attitudes. Some of it (like the Decree on the Media) is absolutely pedestrian. Vatican II never repudiated Vatican I. Whether it implicitly rewrote it or simply provided a range of related teaching is the question. For later curial orthodoxy everything in Vatican II should be interpreted as a single homogeneous block, itself wholly in accord with Vatican I and *Trent. If that is an anti-historicist viewpoint, it simply signifies that the long-standing debate over the interpretation of all past authoritative texts, scriptural, conciliar, and papal, as either reflecting their time and culture or as somehow suprahistorical by virtue of divine guidance, has become extended to the documents of Vatican II.

Adrian Hastings

Alberigo, G. (ed.), *History of Vatican II* (5 vols.; 1995–).
Alberigo, G., Jossua, J. P., and Komanchak, J. (eds.), *The Reception of Vatican II* (1987).
Flannery, A., *Vatican Council II: The Conciliar and Post-Conciliar Documents*, rev. edn. (1992).
Hastings, A., *A Concise Guide to the Documents of Vatican II* (2 vols.; 1968–9).
—— (ed.), *Modern Catholicism: Vatican II and After* (1991).
Hebblethwaite, P., *Paul VI: The First Modern Pope* (1993).
Küng, H., *The Council and Reunion* (1961).
Stacpoole, A. (ed.), *Vatican II by Those Who Were There* (1986).
Vorgrimler, H. (ed.), *Commentary on the Documents of Vatican II* (5 vols.; 1967–9).

via negativa, see GOD.

virgin birth. The doctrine of the virgin birth of Christ has different connotations to different Christians. For *Protestants, and perhaps for most Christians nowadays, the doctrine of the virgin birth means that *Jesus Christ had no human father but was conceived by *Mary through the power of the *Holy Spirit. Traditionally, for Catholics and Orthodox this is the doctrine of the virginal conception, to be distinguished from the virgin birth which affirms that Mary remained a virgin (*virgo intacta*) throughout the process of giving birth to her son. The doctrine of the virginal conception is attested in the infancy narratives of the gospels of Matthew and Luke, and also in a variant reading (known to *Irenaeus at the end of the 2nd century) of John 1: 13 (the accepted reading, which refers to the believers' birth from God, may allude to the virginal conception), but it seems unknown to the rest of the NT. It is, however, attested in most of the rules of faith of the 2nd century (by Ignatius of Antioch, Justin Martyr, and Irenaeus), whence it finds its way into the baptismal and conciliar *creeds of the 4th century (though it is not explicitly mentioned in the creed of the First Ecumenical Council of *Nicaea, 325). The formula of the western Apostles' Creed—'conceived by the Holy Spirit, born of the Virgin Mary'—may be intended to affirm both the virginal conception and the virgin birth. The virgin birth, in the narrower sense, is first attested in the 2nd century in *apocryphal gospels (notably the *Protevangelium of James*) and in Clement of *Alexandria; it was crudely denied by Tertullian. Soon, however, the belief that Mary was virgin before, during, and after childbearing is widely attested, and celebrated by her title 'ever-virgin' (which gained conciliar authority at the Fifth Ecumenical Council of Constantinople in 553). The difficulty posed by the 'brothers of the Lord', referred to in the NT, was answered first by the claim that such brothers were the sons of Joseph by an earlier marriage (an idea that consorts well with the impression given by the Fourth Gospel that Jesus' death left Mary childless), and later, in the west, following Jerome's arguments, that they were Christ's cousins.

Whatever its historical attestation, the virgin birth cannot be reduced to a historical fact, to be established by historical criteria. Like the *Resurrection of Christ, and the *creation itself, it expresses the conviction of the radical newness of God's saving activity. In both the canonical gospels, the story of the virgin birth is the story of a radical new beginning in God's relationship with humanity: from now on he will relate to human beings as one of them, and save them as one of them. In classical *christology, Christ is confessed as one person, of one substance (consubstantial) with God, and of one substance with us: the human substance that he shares wholly with us, he receives from his Virgin Mother. The virgin birth is a *sacrament of the truth that the *Incarnation is, in the words of John Damascene, 'the newest of all new things, the only new thing under the sun' (*De orth. fid.* 45). Mary's virginity is not merely a physical fact, but also an expression of her receptivity, her identification with the poor of the OT, on whom the grace of God is poured.

In Christian history, and especially in Christian devotion, the notion of a Virgin Mother, wholly concerned for the human kind her son came to save, has proved powerful. Only comparatively recently in Christian history has the doctrine of the virgin birth been challenged: even though the *Reformers looked askance at what seemed to them the excesses of devotion to the Virgin Mother of God, the doctrine of the virgin birth itself, with its biblical and credal attestation, was unquestioned. It was only shaken, for some, by the scepticism of historical criticism, and later by the tendency in academic circles in the 19th and 20th centuries to see Christianity as one *religion among many. Historical scepticism drew attention to the lateness of the traditions that attest the virgin birth; scholars of the History of Religions school noticed similar stories of divine parthenogenesis in other religions, not least in the myths of Greek and Roman antiquity. Many Protestant scholars nowadays would treat the virgin birth as a *mythical embellishment of the early Christian story. It is argued, too (and this is undeniable) that there was great enthusiasm for *virginity in early Christianity, an enthusiasm that eventually found expression in organized *monasticism, and that the cult of the Virgin Mother of God is a product of that enthusiasm, rather than of any authentic memory of her human state. More recently it has been argued on biological grounds that the virgin birth of a son is impossible, since a woman, with two X chromosomes, could not on her own bear a child with both X and Y chromosomes. The short answer to these objections is that the virgin birth is believed to be a *miracle, not arbitrarily, but because to speak of God's radical new initiative of *redemption is, on any reckoning, to speak of the miraculous. But all these traditions of thought that attack the virgin birth reject the miraculous on principle. A more strictly theological objection to the virgin birth, drawing strength from the lateness of the historical tradition (in contrast with that attesting the Resurrection), maintains that Christ's full humanity would be impaired, were he not the fruit of normal sexual union between a man and a woman. Such an objection cannot be briefly answered, but it is worth noting that historically it is not independent of the more general factors mentioned above, even though it does not in principle reject the miraculous.

More serious is to rediscover the significance of the virgin birth of Christ in modern terms. There is no doubt that the importance (if not the simple acknowledgement) of the virgin birth for early Christians was bound up with their enthusiasm for virginity. Behind that enthusiasm lay a concern for single-mindedness and simplicity, of which virginity was a physical and social expression. It may be along such lines that the recovery of the significance of the doctrine of the virgin birth may lie.   **Andrew Louth**

Boslooper, T., *The Virgin Birth* (1962).

Brown, R. E., *The Birth of the Messiah: A Commentary on the Infancy Narratives in Matthew and Luke* (1977), rev. edn. (1993).

Campenhausen, H. von, *The Virgin Birth in the Theology of the Ancient Church* (1962), ET (1964).

virginity, the complete and permanent gift of oneself to God, entailing the renunciation of *marriage and *sexual relations. This way of life, undertaken in response to divine grace, out of *love for Christ and in imitation of him (see CHRISTOLOGY), has been significant in the *church from earliest times, and is part of the common heritage of *Catholicism and Orthodoxy.

In the OT the fruitfulness of marriage and the barrenness of virginity were held in antithesis. Only the prophet *Jeremiah explicitly prefigured in his life this aspect of the new order he foretold. NT teaching on virginity, in contrast, occurs in the context of that on marriage (Matt. 19: 3–12; 1 Cor. 7). Matrimony is indissoluble because it is God who joins husband and wife together, and is to be honoured since it foreshadows the 'great mystery' of the union between Christ and the church, his bride (Eph. 5: 23–32). Nevertheless it belongs to the present provisional order, already passing away (1 Cor. 7: 31) (see ESCHATOLOGY). In these end-times some are already called to a love of Christ that transcends marriage and anticipates the coming reality of a new order, 'the *kingdom of heaven', where there will be no death and hence no marriage (Luke 21: 34–6), for the kingdom will not be dependent on what is physical for life. Our future destiny is made known even now through participation in the risen life of Christ in whom 'there is neither male nor female' (Gal. 3: 28). Luke presents as a model the Virgin *Mary, humble and open to the action of the Holy Spirit.

After *martyrdom, virginity is pre-eminent in the church because it is part of the enduring, eternal order. At times it has been idealized, or seen as mere abstinence from sexual relations, even a means of independence for *women. True virginity, like *chastity, requires the integration of sexuality; it is the response of the whole person to the love of Christ, expressed in the gift of the body in addition to heart, mind, and will, according to the grace given.

From the first, Christians of both sexes were found practising lifelong *celibacy, and by the beginning of the 4th century public declaration of virginity had become common in both east and west. The early church recognized three orders of consecrated women: deaconesses, widows, and virgins who were often assigned a place apart in the liturgical assembly. Treatises on the theological and practical aspects of virginity were written by the fathers of the church, notably Basil of Ancyra, Gregory of Nyssa, John Chrysostom, Cyprian, Ambrose, Jerome, and above all *Augustine, whose treatment of the subject is profound. Though physical integrity is a sign of the spiritual reality, virginity of the heart, a gift open to all, is primary.

The rite of consecration of virgins, with its ancient symbol of the veil, developed in the 4th century. The ideal of virginity has never, however, been the sole preserve of women. When Eusebius and *Athanasius used the word 'monk' of a 4th-century Christian ascetic, they were describing him as not primarily a 'solitary' or hermit but someone 'single' and unmarried. *Monastic legislators from Pachomius to Benedict took for granted that virginity, Basil's one monastic vow, was central to profession of monastic life.

As the new *ascetic movement burgeoned, women who wanted to dedicate their lives to Christ in virginity began to leave their homes to live together in monasteries. The 6th-century *Regula Virginum* written by Caesarius of Arles for the nuns of Saint-Jean, Arles, marked a shift in understanding of the vocation of virginity for women from a context of public witness in the local church to that of a hidden, usually strictly enclosed, contemplative life.

The 16th century saw the suppression of the monasteries in England and also in the new Reformed churches on the Continent. Protestant rejection of virginity, hardly in accord with NT teaching but a reaction to late-medieval practices, focused on the issue of religious and clerical vows. In England, where the monasteries had been dissolved for economic and political reasons, *Milton, like his contemporary Jeremy Taylor (see CAROLINE DIVINES), still commended a century later 'the sage and serious doctrine of Virginity'.

The general expansion of *religious life in the 19th century included the emergence of communities, often with a philanthropic basis, in the Reformed, Lutheran, and Anglican churches. Diversification, such as the recognition of the lay, often solitary or individual, vocation to consecrated virginity, marked the pattern of development in the 20th century.

Pius XII's teaching in *Sponsa Christi* (1950) and *Sacra Virginitas* (1954) coincided with a flowering of patristic studies and a renewed understanding of the differentiation of vocation within the universal call to *holiness. This fresh appreciation of the charism of virginity, and its ecclesial role before the formation of religious orders, bore fruit in the teaching of *Vatican II. The *Constitution on the Church*, *Lumen Gentium*, acknowledged the outstanding witness of love given by those committed to the same life of virginity as Christ and his Mother. *Perfectae Caritatis* reminded Religious that the closer they became to Christ, 'virgin and poor', the more fruitful would be the church's apostolate.

Christian virginity, a mystery of love and a powerful reminder of our future destiny, is at the heart of the church's own vocation. 'In saying "I betrothed you to Christ to present you as a pure virgin to her one husband" [2 Cor. 11: 2], St Paul speaks of the whole church' (Augustine, *De bono viduitatis*, 10. 13). Often described as the Body of Christ, and since Vatican II as the People of God, the church is above all the Bride of Christ, united with him by love.

Margaret Truran, OSB

Brown, Peter, *The Body and Society: Men, Women and Sexual Renunciation in Early Christianity* (1988).

Elm, Susanna, *'Virgins of God': The Making of Asceticism in Late Antiquity* (1994).

Flannery, Austin (ed.), *Vatican Council II: The Conciliar and Post Conciliar Documents*, rev. edn. (1992).

John Paul II, *Vita Consecrata: The Consecrated Life and its Mission in the Church and in the World* (1996).

Legrand, Lucien, *The Biblical Doctrine of Virginity* (1963).

Metz, R., *La Consécration des vierges dans l'église romaine* (1954).

virtue. Human beings do not have to be good. Instead, if we turn out to be good it is because we have become so, over time. The virtues are those qualities of character by which we become good. If by *God's *grace we acquire them, they change us; by them we *become* what we once were not.

While recently some have tried (see Pincoffs 1986), it is difficult to imagine the virtues apart from this idea that the human life is a sort of 'becoming'. We are on a journey towards an end, *telos*, as *Aristotle called it. For him the end of life was *eudaimonia*, happiness: not a contented feeling, as moderns think, but engagement in the best activity for which humans are suited. The virtues are the developed capacities that make us capable of this activity. For Aristotle *reason is the highest human faculty; its activity, either theoretically in contemplation, or practically in choosing and acting in the world, constitutes the human *telos*. Corresponding to these activities of reason, he split the virtues in two groups: intellectual and moral.

Generally we mean by 'the virtues' the moral ones; on Aristotle's account, by them reason exercises control over the appetites—control understood as the appropriate modulation, the mean between two extremes. The extremes are the vices. For instance, we can have too much or too little fear, acting in either a cowardly or a rash manner. Courage is the mean between these: just the right amount of fear. Fear, a human emotion, therefore gives courage its specific form. Other virtues are individuated similarly by the appetite or activity to which they obtain as, for example, liberality is a virtue about the use of money.

For Greeks like Aristotle, virtue was a public matter. The person or paragon of virtue was generally determined by the judgement of those of good breeding. He behaved in a dignified, appropriate, even lofty way; Aristotle describes him as the great-souled or high-minded man. Additionally, the success of a community was marked by how well its people exercised and formed their fellow citizens (particularly the young) in virtue.

Christians were rightly suspicious of the high-minded man and his virtues. In fact, they turned parts of Aristotle upside down. Pride, for him the crown of the virtues, became the chief *sin. Moreover, Christians inherited from Jews such terms as 'sin', 'repentance', and 'obedience'; 'virtue' was not really in their earliest lexicon. Nevertheless, the shape of the classical virtue tradition of the Greeks and Romans corresponded to Christians' deep concern about how to live. Human beings were made by God for an end, and a life well lived meant the transformation of the self to Christ's likeness. Hence, before long Christian interpreters spoke explicitly of the virtues of Christ and of the Christian.

The greatest Christian treatment of virtue is found in the *Summa Theologiae* of Thomas *Aquinas. Aquinas's simplest definition of virtue is a good habit of action. It is by acts that the rightful end of the human life is attained. Unlike mice or horses, human beings are not determined to this end. As free creatures they can fail to act well, and so miss their true end. In short, human beings sin. Sin not only brings *evil to the world, it deforms the self since what we do changes us. In fact, we acquire habits, virtuous or vicious, by repeated acts.

His psychology more subtle than Aristotle's, Aquinas held that reason cannot command the passions (Aristotle's 'appetites'), rather it must govern them democratically. Indeed, the passions are key for Aquinas, not just as the spring of action but as what propel us to our ultimate end which, following Augustine, he sees as passionate love of God. Formation in virtue is not just a matter of reason laying out logically patterned behaviour, it is the transformation of our desire to what is truly good.

Likewise, the virtues are not a variety of skills of which we have some and not others, as some people are skilled swimmers but poor musicians. Rather, they unify around the single (but complex) task of perfecting us. The pattern of this unity can be traced. Following the classical emphasis upon the four *cardinal* (Latin *cardo*, 'hinge') virtues, Aquinas notes that since we can be overrun by certain passions (e.g. sexual desire) and held back by certain others (e.g. fear), the life of virtue must begin with the cardinal virtues of *temperance* and *fortitude*. Our passions ordered, we can move towards *justice, the cardinal virtue by which we give to each his due. Finally, we need the highest of the cardinal virtues, *prudence*, that picks out what acts we should do in the midst of life's complexities. Prudence, like Aristotle's practical wisdom, is both a moral and intellectual virtue for it involves knowing the truth about the world in all its contingencies. It perfects the other virtues since 'it is the perfected ability to make right decisions' (Pieper 1966: 6) and to act upon them, and, for Aquinas, by acting rightly we obtain our end.

Aquinas's deeply theological vision refines but also transforms the classical view of virtue. For the cardinal virtues are profoundly changed by *faith, *hope, and *love, the three theological virtues. Prudence is recalibrated by *caritas* (love), for as friends of Jesus we see the world in which we act in a new way: as he sees it. Accordingly, all the virtues are reordered. We receive these theological virtues by infusion, directly from God. By them we are transformed into beings who can exceed the 'natural end' of a life ordered by reason: we commune with God, the end for which ultimately we were created.

Alasdair *MacIntyre has recently argued that Aquinas's remarkably subtle account of the virtues was obscured as Christendom gave way to *modernity. The switch in moral thinking was from virtue and character to theories of right action (e.g. utilitarianism). The change culminated in the 'Enlightenment project of justifying morality' (MacIntyre 1981: 35) by which *philosophers hoped to define right action without answering fundamental questions about the ultimate good for humans. If virtue played a role for Enlightenment philosophers like Immanuel *Kant or Jeremy Bentham (1748–1832), it was motivational. For these thinkers we do not need virtues to identify our obligations, although they might encourage us to fulfil them. Like 'religion', virtue became a private matter. Moral theories described what acts were moral; how a particular person came to do them was up to him.

Recently western intellectual life has departed from this Enlightenment vision. *Postmodernism has declared the Enlightenment hopes for moral objectivity and universality empty; they were merely another form of interest whereby the powerful ensured their prominence. Interestingly, this criticism has stimulated renewed interest in virtue. Relatedly, virtue has returned to popular discourse as William Bennett's best-selling *Book of Virtues* illustrates. In this book Bennett has compiled stories with the express purpose of forming his readers, especially children, in the virtues. It has been widely perceived as advocating a conservative political agenda—a fact that exposes a key difficulty in returning to virtue as the principal language of *morality. Aristotle presumed virtue and the formation of citizens in it was a political matter. Yet today there is widespread divergence—far wider than in Aristotle's *polis*—about what the good life is, and therefore about what the virtues are. Accounts of the moral life in terms of virtue seem destined to vie with one another in the contemporary political arena.

For theologian and virtue *ethicist Stanley Hauerwas, this is hardly surprising. Christians are called to a distinctive way of life in Christ; this way will and should contest other visions of the good. If the church gathers itself around this distinctive vision, its members will have different virtues—a different morality and politics—than those outside it (see POLITICAL THEOLOGY).

As virtue returns to theological discourse, old, yet interesting, theological questions return as well. One can wonder whether the life to which Christians are called, a life as frequently characterized by suffering as by happiness, is not skewed by classical concepts such as virtue. Further, since virtue is acquired through repeated acts and is thought to increase over time, might a return to virtue tempt us to think we can accumulate merit before God by doing good deeds, turning salvation into something we suppose we earn? Despite these potential difficulties, it is clear that contemporary theological accounts of virtue are joining with non-theological ones, reclaiming an ancient discussion about the good. As opposed to those stale moral theories of the more recent past that it is pushing aside, virtue is likely to play an animating role in this ongoing, intriguing, and absolutely fundamental discussion.

Charles Pinches

Aquinas, *Summa Theologiae*, I-II and II-II.
Aristotle, *Nicomachean Ethics*.
Cessario, Romanus, *The Moral Virtues and Theological Ethics* (1991).
Hauerwas, Stanley, *A Community of Character* (1981).
Hauerwas, Stanley, and Pinches, Charles, *Christians Among the Virtues* (1997).
MacIntyre, Alasdair, *After Virtue* (1981).
Meilander, Gilbert, *The Theory and Practice of Virtue* (1984).
Pieper, Josef, *The Four Cardinal Virtues* (1966).
Pincoffs, Edmund, *Quandaries and Virtues* (1986).

visions represent a spectrum of *religious experience. The categories suggested by *Teresa of Avila are useful. A vision may be (1) an apparition that seems physically real to those able to see it, the 'corporeal' vision; (2) an inner picture observed by the mind's eye, the 'imaginary' vision; (3) an inner revelation of God's presence not associated with image or idea, the 'intellectual' vision. These are listed in an ascending order of spiritual importance. Teresa and fellow Spanish Carmelite *John of the Cross especially distrusted the corporeal vision, the most likely to be demonic in origin. In this respect, they anticipated modern psychiatry: realistic apparitions may indicate a pathological condition.

Visions, revelatory *dreams, and locutions (voices) are alike in kind, and have a long history of influence in the Judaeo-Christian tradition. They were fundamental to the *prophetic understanding of God's intervention in ancient *Israel: signs and revelations to be interpreted as guides for action. The most wonderful vision was that of *God (later known as the 'beatific vision'), attested to in the stories of *Moses, *Isaiah, and Ezekiel. Belief in the *Resurrection of Christ began with a series of appearances, and *Paul included his own ecstatic experience on the Damascus road with those of the first apostles.

In medieval Christianity, the age of the flowering of *mysticism, visions were accorded great authority, which often provoked clerical opposition. Visions of God, of the Passion, and revelations of divine truth were common in mystical experiences, for instance the writings of *Hildegard of Bingen, *Julian of Norwich, and Teresa of Avila herself. *Francis of Assisi's stigmata appeared after a vision. The reputation of visionaries such as Birgitta of Sweden (see SCANDINAVIAN CHRISTIAN THOUGHT) and *Catherine of Siena gave them influence in major ecclesiastical matters.

The post-*Enlightenment empirical world-view has devalued subjective experience as a source of *truth. Yet visions have remained popular: for example in the diverse worlds of Romantic poetry; the piety of *Marian apparitions; the *evangelical and *charismatic movements; the psychoanalytical tradition of *Jung; the '*New Age' and its precursors.

As visionary experiences are still influential, it is vital for Christians to maintain the ancient tradition of 'discernment', to attempt a balanced judgement as to whether visions may be profound revelations or the result of wishful thinking, manipulative fraud, or illness. Traditionally, visions have been tested for orthodoxy, effect on visionary, effect on supporters, associated signs and wonders,

such as healing, and fulfilment of prophecies. There is the perennial danger that ecclesiastical judgement may suppress radical ideas out of hand. Thus critical insight is needed as to the agendas operating behind the discernment process.

The vision that is of theological value will, first, challenge the seer and supporters to new commitments—based on gospel values—that may work against self-interest, rather than confirm existing preferences and prejudices. Secondly, it will assure them of the wonder, love, and reality of God.   **Chris Maunder**

Erickson, Carolly, *The Medieval Vision* (1976).
Furlong, Monica (ed.), *Visions and Longings: An Anthology of Women Mystics* (1996).
Rahner, Karl, *Visions and Prophecies*, ET (1963).

von Balthasar, Hans Urs (1905–88). One of the most pro-

lific, creative, and wide-ranging theologians of the 20th century, the Swiss Catholic Hans Urs von Balthasar spent his entire life outside the guild of academic theology. His doctorate was in German literature, not theology, and he never held an academic post or attended theological congresses and the like. This may partly explain why his large volume of writing, expressing a daring originality of vision, has had as yet relatively little impact. Moreover, this very originality makes his work hard to categorize and is thus apt to inhibit any immediate reception and appropriation.

His theological isolation also has certain biographical roots: born into an upper-middle class family of noble stock (hence the *von* in his name), he quickly became known for precocious talents in literature and music and received a doctorate in *Germanistik* from the University of Zürich in 1929. At the time he seemed destined for a career in bourgeois academia until he made a retreat in the Black Forest where he heard a call to become a Catholic priest in the Society of Jesus (*Jesuits). During his pre-ordination philosophical and theological training in the 1930s he acquired an intense aversion for the 'sawdust *Thomism' of the anti-*modernist neo-scholastic manuals that were then standard in seminary teaching. After his ordination in Munich in 1936, he was assigned there to the editorial staff of *Stimmen der Zeit*, the Jesuit monthly; but approaching war and Nazi suspicions of his doctoral thesis *Die Apocalypse der deutschen Seele* (which uncannily anticipated the coming catastrophe) forced his return to Switzerland, where he became chaplain to the students of the University of Basel. There he met the twice-married Protestant physician Adrienne von Speyr, who converted to Roman Catholicism under his tutelage. Much influenced by her *visions and mystical experiences, which he recorded at length, he left the Society of Jesus to join her in founding a 'secular institute', a relatively new form of *religious life under vows but without the traditional external props of distinctive dress or life in common.

One of the major works of this institute was the publishing firm of Johannes Verlag. Besides most of Balthasar's own works, it published Hans *Küng's doctoral thesis, *Justification* (a reconciliation between Karl *Barth and the Council of *Trent), and Karl *Rahner's challenging *Free Speech in the Church*. Balthasar's own study, *The Theology of Karl Barth*, and his *Razing the Ramparts*, an attack on the fortress mentality common in the Roman Catholic Church of that time, combined with these publications to place him among the 'progressive theologians' of the *nouvelle théologie*, under whom he had in fact studied at Lyons before his ordination.

But after *Vatican II—in which, characteristically, he had not taken part—he grew suspicious of certain theological trends claiming support from the Council and founded the journal *Communio* explicitly to counteract the post-conciliar liberal journal *Concilium*. Later in *Cordula* (ET: *The Moment of Christian Witness*), he sharply attacked Rahner's theory of the 'anonymous Christian' and publicly defended the Holy See's withdrawal of Küng's authorization to teach Catholic theology; and towards the end of his life he became known as 'the Pope's favourite theologian'. He died two days before he was to receive the Cardinal's red hat from *John Paul II.

Whatever may have been the effect of these apparent shifts in relation to the climate of opinion, the relatively small response to Balthasar's theology has also been due to its peculiarly anti-systematic bent, a trait that gives his work a strange elusiveness, making it extremely hard to categorize. Perhaps most crucially, the work of assimilation has to clear an additional hurdle: his claim that *modernity's dearest presuppositions must be turned inside out. For Balthasar, the often strained relations between *secular culture and Christian thought stem fundamentally not from Christianity's failure to keep in step with history but from modernity's habit of seeing things from the wrong end of the telescope. Indeed Balthasar's critique of the *Enlightenment bears interesting resemblances to that found in many *postmodernist thinkers—not surprising, considering how greatly he was influenced by *Nietzsche. But in contrast with the extreme perspectivism that has become the standard position of postmodernism, Balthasar will always insist that there is a whole that governs communication across the partial perspectives seen by the finite mind: perspectives are partial *because* there is a whole that exceeds our partial grasp. Indeed, this is the source of his polemic against all systematic thought: that it pretends to have captured the whole in a graspable 'system'.

Soon after leaving the Society of Jesus in 1950 Balthasar conceived the project of writing a theological trilogy that would transpose all of theology into aesthetic, dramatic, and veridical terms, corresponding to the traditional Platonic transcendental properties of Being: the Beautiful, the Good, and the True—*and in that order*. This trilogy was consciously conceived to counteract what Balthasar regarded as the deleterious influence of *Kant's three Critiques, the *Critique of Pure Reason*, *Critique of Practical Reason*, and *Critique of Judgement*, which significantly went in the opposite direction. Balthasar conceived this project because, again like so many postmodernists, he regarded the obsession with epistemological issues that marked modernity, from the time of *Descartes, as a fundamental mistake. Much closer in this regard to *Aristotle, who saw epistemology as reflection on the implications of the knowledge we already know we possess, Balthasar insisted that there can be no reflection on the *truth* of Christian revelation (Part 3) until it is lived out in committed *action* (Part 2), which a Christian will never feel called to do without having first perceived revelation in all its inherent *beauty* (Part 1). For it is the fundamental property of the beautiful to elicit its own quasi-erotic response, a response that will inevitably call the person out of himself and into committed action; and that action will then afford the person a variety of perspectives to serve as the basis for a *later* reflection on the truth of the revelation that elicited the response.

Inside this overarching structure certain other themes emerge, many of which also show Balthasar's deep anti-Kantianism. For

example, it is a fundamental thesis of Kant's that religion must be able to justify itself before the bar of '*reason alone'. But Balthasar's own aesthetic starting-point insists that the Particular (for example, an event of history) gives a deeper insight into reality than does the (abstract) Universal of reason. We see this especially in his *christology, where, in a fascinating image, he insists that the claim of Jesus to be 'the way, the truth, and the life' (John 14: 6) is equivalent to the whitecap on a wave claiming to be the sea itself: one phenomenon inside the world of Becoming has claimed to be Being itself ('before Abraham was, I am').

To understand that claim (in Balthasar's terminology a claim to '*absolute* singularity', defined as one that is, on the face of it, absurd and thus a scandal for universalizing reason), one must first look at such 'relative singularities' as great works of art: 'Great works of art appear like inexplicable eruptions on the stage of history,' he once said in a lecture later published as *Two Say Why*. 'Sociologists are as unable to calculate the precise day of their origin as they are to explain in retrospect why they appeared when they did.... [Art's] unique utterance becomes a universal language; and the greater a work of art, the more extensive the cultural sphere it dominates will be' (pp. 20–1).

The image of wave and sea also proves helpful in trying to understand how Christ's *death and *Resurrection can reach, salvifically, to the ends of the world. How can the impact of one historical figure, *Jesus of Nazareth, reach out to all the rest of *history, both the history that precedes and that follows his life? Altering the metaphor slightly, Balthasar answers that question by comparing the impact of any one human being in history to the ripple effect of a stone dropped into the sea. But with all other human beings the ripple effect eventually fades and dies out; so there must be something about the 'stone' of Jesus that differs in its radiating power.

*Hegel once quoted a Swabian proverb to the effect that 'something has been true for so long it stopped being true'. This is why he insisted that theology, because it is so reliant on an ever-receding historical revelation, must let itself be transposed into the a-historical and universal categories of philosophy. But Balthasar answers Hegel by asserting that the ripple effect of Jesus' stone continues to radiate outwards because, when it plunged all the way to the bottom of the sea on Holy Saturday (that is, when Christ descended into *hell), it landed, so to speak, with a thud that continues to reverberate. And that can only happen if the 'weight' of that single, particular stone serves as the counterweight (*Schwergewicht*) outweighing all the other truths and sufferings of the world, which is impossible unless this 'plunge' takes place within the very life of the *Trinity. Only then does the centre where the stone was dropped continue to reverberate and radiate outwards. Moreover, that outward radiation moves concentrically in such a way as to influence *previous* history as well. This for Balthasar is the real meaning of the scriptural doctrine of Christ's descent into hell, where according to the Petrine tradition he rescues the 'spirits in prison who disobeyed God *long ago*' (1 Pet. 3: 19–20; see also 1 Pet. 4: 5–6).

These fascinating images of stone, wave, and sea clearly lead to a quasi-*Origenistic vision of the possible redemption of *all* these 'disobedient spirits in prison'. This is because in his descent into hell Jesus experiences *all* that is hellish about the world in its otherness and divergence from God—whether that difference was willed through sin or results from creation's finite, non-divine status.

Christ's descent means that ultimately hell is, in Balthasar's famous dictum, 'a christological place,' where finite sinners can, in their finitude, experience in a partial way what Christ himself experienced totally. And since any experience of Christ is by definition salvific, we may at least hope for the salvation of all.

These ideas are indeed daring and highly speculative and have led *Rahner, among others, to accuse Balthasar of indulging in a 'Schelling-esque projection into God of division, conflict, godlessness, and death'. According to Rahner, God must, if the word 'God' is to continue to have any meaning at all, enter history in a way that does not lock God into its horror; whereas for Balthasar God transforms that horror by incorporating suffering and rejection into the trinitarian process itself. And for Balthasar that process was fully realized when God raised Jesus from the dead—that is, when God rescued him from the hell to which he had been condemned *by God*. For 'it was impossible that Hades keep its hold on him' (Acts 2:24, Western text). **Edward T. Oakes, SJ**

von Balthasar, Hans Urs, *Herrlichkeit*; ET, *The Glory of the Lord* (7 vols.; 1982–91).
—— *Theodramatik*; ET, *Theo-Drama* (5 vols.; 1988).
—— *Theologik*; ET *Theo-Logic* (3 vols.; forthcoming 2001).
Capol, C., *Hans Urs von Balthasar: Bibliographie, 1925–1990* (1990).
Chapp, Larry S., *The God Who Speaks: Hans Urs von Balthasar's Theology of Revelation* (1996).
Oakes, E. T., *Pattern of Redemption: The Theology of Hans Urs von Balthasar*, 2nd edn. (1997).
O'Hanlon, G., *The Immutability of God in the Theology of Hans Urs von Balthasar* (1990).
Riches, J. (ed.), *The Analogy of Beauty: The Theology of Hans Urs von Balthasar* (1986).

von Kirschbaum, Charlotte

von Kirschbaum, Charlotte (1899–1975). A Red Cross nurse until she was introduced to Karl *Barth in 1924, von Kirschbaum became his secretary in 1929, inaugurating a personal and creative partnership that lasted until her mental powers declined in the early 1960s. The intimacy of their relationship meant that tensions, sometimes acute, were inevitable both within the family and in wider circles. What bound Barth's wife Nelly together with her husband and von Kirschbaum was their common dedication to a great theological project.

Von Kirschbaum saw it as her vocation to devote herself singlemindedly to the man and the theology she admired. The extent of her influence is hard to estimate, and this is as she would have wished. She acted as his secretary, read and summarized books, prepared lectures, but also contributed to the intellectual development of his work in profound ways. Is it a coincidence that after she entered his life the abortive *Christian Dogmatics* of 1927 was abandoned and replaced by the completely reorganized and significantly retitled *Church Dogmatics*? Reliable reports suggest that increasingly the ageing Barth would merely outline an area of enquiry, leaving von Kirschbaum to work it up for incorporation into the *Church Dogmatics*, particularly in the small print sections.

She was active in theological and church circles in her own right and her writings on *women show a creativity and radicality that goes beyond the comparatively staid stance of Barth's work. Her vision throughout was of the importance of complementarity. She stands as a witness for all those often unacknowledged women thinkers in the Christian tradition whose gifts have been put at the service of men. **Hugh S. Pyper**

von Kirschbaum, C., *The Question of Woman*, ET (1996).
Köbler, R., *In the Shadow of Karl Barth: Charlotte von Kirschbaum*, ET (1997).
Sellinger, S., *Charlotte von Kirschbaum and Karl Barth: A Study in Biography and the History of Theology* (1998).

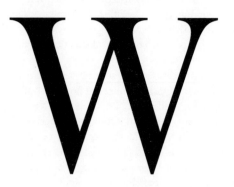

war. Because humans are political animals, their fights tend to become wars. And the more organized society becomes the more complex its wars, which naturally follow the cultural, religious, political, and technological conditions of the time. Nowadays these conditions make war potentially suicidal for humanity. Christians in the past have only interpreted war. But today the point is to prevent it.

The *New Testament says little about war. Soldiering is nowhere forbidden; but *Jesus gives no explicit guidance on how his followers should respond to use of military force. Army life even suggests some profound theological insights. But Jesus' own life preaches absolute non-violence. The NT certainly points towards *pacifism; but military defence of the otherwise defenceless is not specifically excluded.

Early Christian *apologists, like *Origen and Tertullian (c.160–240) preached absolute pacifism, because of the idolatrousness of Roman military practice and/or the bloodshed involved in fighting. Some Christian converts, like Maximilian (d. 295) chose *martyrdom rather than enlisting. But to other Christians the army became an increasingly attractive career. The early apologists never anticipated a Christian emperor, and after *Constantine idolatry in army life melted away. Some (including for a time *Augustine) even came to see the Christian empire as an instrument of divine *providence. But barbarian assaults destroyed this dream. Augustine had always advised his questioners that, while killing in personal self-defence remained unworthy of the Christian (showing excessive attachment to this transitory life) military bloodshed could (tragically) be justified in defence of civilized values. But there were limits. War must be conducted by public authority for the common good, never for sinful purposes such as dominion over others. These concessions to 'realism' were to have fateful consequences Augustine could not foresee.

With the collapse of the empire, competing 'Christian' chieftains in Europe sought security for themselves and their realms by granting lands to loyal warriors in return for military service. Eventually this practice created feudal knighthood; giving much scope for rich men with private armies to settle scores by internecine warfare. Hence the preoccupation of medieval theorists, from Isidore of Seville (d. 636) to Thomas *Aquinas, with defining *justice in war by restricting the authority for conducting it. Aquinas insists (*ST* II-II q. 40, a. 1) that war is licit only if conducted (1) by the sovereign, not a private individual, (2) to correct a real injustice, and (3) with the aim of promoting the good and avoiding the evil. Aquinas quotes older authorities such as Gratian and Augustine to show that the aim enshrined in this third condition of 'right intention' has to be genuine peace. On the other hand, following predecessors such as Innocent IV, Aquinas accepts crusading in the Holy Land when approved by the church as an act of personal penitence in the service of God. He defends the military religious orders on that basis. In the end medieval just-war theory, starting from Augustine's cautious concessions, went far beyond them, permitting some wars without preventing others. On some interpretations it even made plausible the later ideology of 'holy war'.

The next stage in the development of just-war theory arrived when Spanish adventurers in the *sixteenth century, in search of gold and territory overseas, systematically attacked the native 'Indians' of central America. They sought the blessing of the church on these depredations. But academics like the *Dominican Vitoria (d. 1546) disapproved, saying that the Indians had good title to their lands. In any case difference of religion was no just cause of war. Further, Vitoria insisted that those who could not bear arms (women and children, including non-Christians) were 'innocent' and must remain immune from attack. Anyone who seriously believed that a war was unjust should refuse to take part. Here Vitoria's work adumbrated the later development of international law (see NATURAL LAW).

Yet notwithstanding Vitoria's lectures, the expropriations and depredations went on. Soon Dutch trading adventures in the East Indies led to more theorizing, notably by Hugo Grotius (1583–1645) who began his magisterial work on war by considering the question of the freedom of the seas, in the context of Portuguese interference with Dutch trade in the East Indies. Later, in his treatise *De Jure Belli et Pacis* (1625) Grotius broadened his vision, adumbrating the general conditions under which war might be justly conducted in the context of the contemporary international milieu. Though much indebted to Aquinas, Vitoria, and other theological authorities, he effectively secularized the Christian ethic of war, by developing natural *law theory as the universal basis for a new international legal order. He hoped this would restrain warfare in important ways. True, like Aquinas, he held to the belief that natural law was God-given, and that rational persons should and would obey it for this reason. Unfortunately, soon after his death, and in the aftermath of an appalling period of religious warfare ending in the Peace of Westphalia (1648), Europe finally gave public legal recognition to the untrammelled sovereignty of all the emerging European monarchs. The absolute ruler, no longer a warrior himself but the employer of a professional army, could now justify his status as judge and jury in his own cause, not on the basis of 'might is right' but by appeal to law. Believers in divine justice as the foundation of all human law had good reason to fear the worst. Luckily, until Napoleon, the ensuing warfare in Europe remained limited; though not by the writing of more legal textbooks, rather by the economics of maintaining armies too expensive to waste on unnecessary fighting.

The *secularization of Christian just-war thought had divergent consequences. On the one hand, Clausewitz (1780–1831), pondering Napoleon's gigantic post-revolutionary campaigns into which whole nations had been dragged, was forced to conclude that war had nothing to do with correcting injustices. As Augustine had feared, war was motivated simply by the lust for power. It followed, as Clausewitz had to remind his fellow generals, who now constituted an international community of professionals in a specialist military field distinct from that of their civilian rulers, that war was only the continuation of politics—but with the addition of other means.

On the other hand, in the post-Napoleonic period heavy industry and the steam engine were revolutionizing military operations on land and sea. Railways transformed the logistics of land warfare. Armies could now be moved, fed, and supplied all the year round on a scale dwarfing even Napoleon's efforts. And steel battleships, with huge long-range guns, could now project sea-power over an area unimaginable even in the aftermath of Trafalgar. Needle-guns, rifled breech-loading ordnance, magazine rifles using smokeless powder, and the Maxim machine-gun followed each other in quick succession, each adding to the destructiveness of war. So perhaps it was not surprising that following the wars in the Crimea, the USA, and elsewhere, Christians like Francis Lieber (1800–72), Henri Dunant (1828–1910), and Feodor de Martens (1845–1908) worked to make war more humane, laying the foundations of the modern humanitarian laws of war. Lieber wrote a manual of the laws of war for the Union army under President Lincoln (the *Lieber Code* of 1863); Dunant's philanthropic lobbying in Europe for help to the wounded led to the establishment of the International Red Cross; from Russia Martens, at a Hague conference in 1899, produced a statement about the overriding obligations arising from 'the usages established between civilized nations ... the laws of humanity and the requirements of the public conscience', which found its way into international conventions on the restraint of war. Meanwhile, in another quarter, a group round Cardinal Manning was trying, unsuccessfully, to persuade *Vatican I to anathematize the 'massacres far and wide' thought likely to result from the institution of conscription into the armed services of many European states.

With the Hague Convention of 1907 the international community seemed poised to begin eliminating many of war's worst horrors. But the slaughter of 1914–18 disabused them. And Hitler defeated humanitarianism even more decisively in 1939–45. In reaction, after the Second World War and the invention of nuclear weapons, the new hardliners of the nuclear age persuaded themselves and many fellow Christians that the likeliest way of preventing war was by manipulation of the powers of limitless terror, or 'deterrence'. As long as the world remained bemused by the Faustian duel of Cold War, the gamble seemed to work. In 1983 even Pope *John Paul II was prepared to tolerate nuclear deterrence. But by 1993 his strictly conditional acceptance of it had been decisively withdrawn, notably in a speech by his observer to the UN General Assembly that year. In any case, by the late 1980s the politicians had begun to discover a way out. The INF Treaty of 1987 abolished all the intermediate-range nuclear weapons stationed in Europe; and in 1988 Mikhail Gorbachev followed this with a massive withdrawal of Soviet forces from the Warsaw Pact states.

The first ethical conundrum of the nuclear age was: could the west's nuclear weapons ever be licitly used—discriminately and proportionately? But once 'mutually assured destruction' based on a rough balance of forces decisively turned 'hot' war into 'cold', another conundrum appeared: was deterrence possible without conditionally consenting in advance to massacring the innocent to achieve peace? Luckily this question did not have to be answered in military practice. Since then, with reliance on nuclear weaponry fading into the background, the problem has shifted yet again. Campaigns of 'irregular' or 'guerrilla' warfare fought (say) for the gratification of warlords (as in Angola, Sierra Leone), for *national self-determination (as in Palestine and Chechnya) or in self-defence against oppression (as in Bosnia and Kosovo) present even more troubling problems to anyone who believes that just war is still possible. For irregular war seems to break all the ethical rules. And yet it seems at times to be unavoidable.

Today the only legally allowable justification of war, under the UN Charter, is 'self defence'. But this limitation does not solve the problem of 'right intention' when states or coalitions of states intervene in other people's wars. A belligerent fights justly only if his aim is peace. But was the aim of the anti-Saddam Hussein coalition in the Kuwait war of 1990–1 truly *peace*? US President Bush claimed that he was countering aggression and promoting a new world order. But was this the whole truth? What about the diverse purposes of backers and supporters? Could the defence of 'vital interests' (such as oil supplies) to maintain a living-standard sustainable only at the expense of the poor elsewhere in the world, be tolerated as a 'right intention' in Christian terms? Many Muslim citizens of the democratic coalition states certainly thought not. They were convinced that the coalition's real purpose was western dominance of the oil-rich Gulf region by dividing the Islamic world. In theory an issue like this should be settleable by impartial appeal to facts—but, alas, only long after the war has happened (if then). Just-war moralists interpret the world, while what matters is to change it.

These conundrums have led many people, from popes to peace-activists, to insist with increasing urgency that it is war itself that has to be eliminated. At this point, perhaps, just-war theorists and Christian pacifists can at last come together, in a coalition against war. The European Ecumenical Assembly in Basel (1989) insisted that 'efforts should be geared towards *overcoming the institution of war*', and in saying this the assembly may have been echoing *John XXIII, who wrote in *Pacem in Terris* (1963) that 'in this age which boasts of its atomic power, it no longer makes sense to maintain that war is a fit instrument with which to repair the violation of justice'. Nothing has happened since to change the minds of his successors. 'Never again war!' cried John Paul II on the brink of Gulf hostilities in 1991. He was surely right in claiming to be 'voicing the thoughts of millions' then and since when he wrote (to Bush) that 'war is not likely to bring an adequate solution to international problems' but is likely rather to create 'new and worse injustices', and to Saddam that 'experience teaches all humanity that war, besides causing many victims, creates situations of grave injustice which, in their turn, constitute a powerful temptation to further recourse to violence'. Subsequent wars in Bosnia and Kosovo have only reinforced these reservations about the use of military force to solve the world's problems.   **Brian Wicker**

Best, Geoffrey, *Humanity in Warfare* (1980).

Finnis, John, Boyle, Joseph, and Grisez, Germain, *Nuclear Deterrence: Morality and Realism* (1987).

Haleem, H., Ramsbotham, Oliver, Risaluddin, Saba, and Wicker, Brian (eds.), *The Crescent and the Cross: Armed Conflicts and their Resolution—Muslim and Christian Approaches* (1998).

Howard, Michael, *War in European History* (1976).

Hunter, David, 'A Decade of Research on Early Christians and Military Service', *Religious Studies Review*, 18 (1992).

Johnson, James Turner, *Ideology: Reason and the Limitation of War* (1975).

Miller, Richard B., *Interpretations of Conflict: Ethics, Pacifism and the Just War Tradition* (1991).

Murnion, Philip, *Catholics and Nuclear War: A Commentary on 'The Challenge of Peace'* (1983).

Swift, Louis, *The Early Fathers on War and Military Service* (1983).

Walzer, Michael, *Just and Unjust Wars*, 2nd edn. (1991).

Williamson, Roger, *Some Corner of a Foreign Field: Intervention and World Order* (1997).

Windass, Stanley, *Christianity Versus Violence* (1964).

Ward, Mary

Ward, Mary (1585–1645). Mary Ward, who was described by Pius XII as 'that incomparable woman', was born in Yorkshire of steadfast Catholic parentage in a time of great persecution. In 1606 she went to Saint-Omer in France to enter a religious order. After trying the Poor Clares, she felt called in 1609 by a sudden illumination to found a new society and in 1611 she saw that it should take the form of the *Jesuits. For long she enjoyed the support of the bishop of Saint-Omer and various Jesuits, but she would throughout life encounter immense opposition from English secular priests, most Jesuits (who disliked women imitating them), curial cardinals, and others. The reason is clear. What she was proposing, in fact already doing, was revolutionary. While St Jane Frances de Chantal, backed by Francis de Sales, began the Visitation Order at Annecy in 1610, somewhat on the same track, their model for a more active female apostolate was intensely cautious in comparison with Ward's proposals as finally formulated for submission to Rome in 1620.

It was to be a society of *women, ready to go anywhere, directly under papal *authority but ruled by its own General Superior (and therefore free from any immediate male control over individual houses), with no special dress, wholly unenclosed, and committed to teaching girls as well as 'any other ministry of the word of God'. Ward had a very high view of education and believed that women could benefit from it as much as men. Deviating from Jesuit practice, she forbade any imposition of physical *penance. Her critics attacked her on the grounds that 'it was never heard of in the church that women should discharge the apostolic office', and that she and her colleagues were 'but women', too weak for what

they wanted to do. Yet they were denounced too as 'Galloping Girls'.

In an amazing struggle over many years, Ward founded schools in Saint-Omer and Liège, Naples and Perugia, Munich, Prague, Pressburg (Bratislava), and elsewhere. She walked and rode across Europe. When the pope was at length persuaded to dissolve her institute and she was imprisoned for two months in a darkened cell in Munich, she managed to correspond with her company by writing in lemon juice, faithfully transcribed by her secretary, Elizabeth Cotton. Released on the pope's orders and allowed to reopen a house in Rome, she continued the struggle, enabling the society to survive. She died near York, encouraging her companions to the last: 'O fie, fie! What? Still look sad? Come, let us rather sing and praise God joyfully for all his loving kindness.'

Mary Ward was a *prophet, demanding with absolute assurance things that seemed excessively dangerous to most people in a highly patriarchal church but all of which have since been accepted as right, an exceptionally sane prophet, warm, kindly, rational, but tough as nails. The strength of the sisterhood she built up with such women as Mary Poyntz, Barbara Babthorpe, Catherine Smith, Winifrid Wigmore, and Frances Bedingfield was extraordinary, as was the sheer audacity of this group of English women opening up girls' schools across Europe in the conditions of their time. Mary Ward's most memorable words remain her spirited comment in an 'instruction' of 1617 on a priest's remark that 'when all is done, they are but women'. 'I confess, wives are to be subject to their husbands, men are head of the church, women may not administer sacraments nor preach in public churches, but in all other things, wherein are we so inferior to other creatures that they should term us "but women"? As if we were in all things inferior to some other creation, which I suppose to be men! Which, I dare be bold to say, is a lie ...'

See also RELIGIOUS LIFE.   **Adrian Hastings**

Chambers, M. C., *The Life of Mary Ward* (2 vols.; 1882–5).

Littlehales, Margaret Mary, *Mary Ward: Pilgrim and Mystic* (1998).

Orchard, M. E, *Till God Will: Mary Ward through her Writings* (1985).

water

water plays an important part in various OT themes: the Flood, the crossing of the Red Sea, the book of *Jonah, the image in *Isaiah of God's word descending fruitfully upon the world as rain. God was 'the fountain of living waters' (*Jeremiah 2: 13) and washing in water was prescribed especially in Leviticus for many occasions in regard to the priesthood, leprosy, and various forms of pollution. Nevertheless the introduction, probably by *John the Baptist, of a comprehensive '*baptism of repentance for the forgiveness of sins' (Mark 1: 4) is something new. *Jesus, to the embarrassment of many later commentators, was himself baptized by John, and Mark begins his gospel story with Jesus coming 'up out of the water' (Mark 1: 10) to receive the *Holy Spirit and be proclaimed God's son. Passing through water, with its connotations of Flood and *exodus, suggests both dying and rebirth. Jesus at the Samaritan well used water to represent his entire mission: 'Anyone who drinks the water that I shall give will never be thirsty again. The water that I shall give will turn into a spring inside him, welling up to eternal life.' (John 4: 14). Water flows from Christ's side on the cross and becomes one of the 'three witnesses', with the Spirit and *blood, of 1 John (5: 5–8). It is a feminine symbol. Baptismal water, like the womb, engenders life, the life of Christ's bride, the *church, coming forth from the side of the New *Adam as *Eve came forth from the first Adam. Water *symbolism remains hereafter focused on baptism, as the decisive rite of *conversion, abandonment of *sin, and identification with Christ. In Paul's words, 'when we were baptized we were baptized in his death … we went into the tomb with him, so that we too might live a new life' (Rom. 6: 3–4).

For early Christianity water was symbolically central. Baptism was by immersion and, when church building developed from the 4th century, free-standing baptisteries were given an important place. However, as infant baptism became normal and immersion fell into disfavour, the symbolism was reduced, baptisteries ceased to be built, and stress eventually came to be laid instead on the minimum flow of water required for 'validity'.

Water, conversion, and *forgiveness began to fall apart. Forgiveness of sins, mostly post-baptismal, had to be coped with in other ways through developing a *sacrament of *penance in which water played no part. The Anabaptist wing of the Reformation, though disowned by *Luther and *Calvin, attempted to rectify this by a return to both adult baptism and immersion, thus reinvigorating water symbolism, but within most mainline Christianity water has never recovered its original imaginative significance (see BAPTIST THOUGHT). Few bystanders can even see the water in a modern infant baptism. In the *Ethiopian Church, on the other hand, the link with the forgiveness of sins has been maintained by the annual 'rebaptism' of everyone on the feast of Temqat, commemorating Christ's baptism, 6 January. In South African Zionism, as elsewhere, the symbolic power of immersion in sea or river remains the most potent symbol of Christian conversion. Sprinkling water after a 'renewal of baptismal vows' in the *Easter vigil service, a modern Catholic liturgical practice, may not be so impressive but does at least show visible recognition of one of Christianity's originating symbols.   **Adrian Hastings**

Weil, Simone (1909–43).

The thought of Simone Weil, the French *philosopher, *mystic, and Christian Platonist, lies at the heart of much 20th-century *existentialist anguish in regard to Christianity. From her birth in Paris to her lonely death in a sanatorium in Ashford, Kent, Weil lived only thirty-four years. She published only a few articles and was known only to a small circle of friends. Yet some consider her the greatest spiritual thinker that the west has produced in the 20th century. At the same time, others have found her off-putting, even repugnant. Certainly there are few lives that involve as much paradox as hers: born into a comfortable bourgeois family, she became a fanatical supporter of the proletariat; a *pacifist, she fought in the Spanish Civil War; a Jew, attracted to Christianity, she refused to join the church because of its adherence to the Old Testament; she wrote a lot—and beautifully—about love, but abhorred all physical contact with her fellows; her outlook on life and politics was sombre, even pessimistic, yet she was ever ready to propagate Utopian schemes for the reformation of society; finally, she abjured her splendid gifts by refusing existence itself, and her death was caused, at least partially, by self-starvation.

Weil has been called 'the patron saint of all outsiders'. For all her devotion to Christ and her attachment to the liturgy of the church, she resolutely refused *baptism. In part, this was due to her temperament: a supreme individualist, she was just not a joiner. But her rejection of baptism was also founded upon her view that the Christian church was too dogmatic. Rather than saying that what was not Christian was not true, she preferred to say that what was true was Christian. In particular, two aspects of the *dogmas of the church she found objectionable. First, they were intended as *mysteries*, but 'in the church, considered as a social organism, the mysteries inevitably degenerate into beliefs'. Dogmas were not something to be affirmed, but to be regarded with attention, respect, and love. Secondly, the maintenance of dogmas was used to exclude people from the church. Although it was necessary, at certain times, that 'the church should preserve the Christian dogma in its integrity, like a diamond, with incorruptible strictness', this did not entail condemnation of others, still less persecution. It was the use of this *anathema sit* that Weil considered unacceptable.

Weil's doubts about the apparent exclusiveness of Christianity were supported by her enthusiasm for non-Christian religions. Her thinking was tentative and open-ended, enquiring, probing, the very opposite of systematic. She was particularly concerned to link her conception of Christianity with two (at first sight) very different traditions. First, she saw Christianity as emerging out of a rich matrix of Mediterranean spirituality whose centrepieces were Pythagorean thought and Greek philosophy, particularly Plato. The Christian gospel was, for her, 'the last marvellous expression of the Greek genius'. In Greek philosophy, myth, and tragedy she found those prophecies of the gospels that a more orthodox Christianity had been accustomed to see in the OT. Second, Simone Weil saw strong parallels between Christianity and *Hinduism. She learnt Sanskrit to be able to read the Hindu scriptures, particularly the Bhagavadgita, in the original. She found rich material for reflection in the stress on individual action and the doctrine of non-attachment. She was also attracted by the Hindu emphasis on the *im*personal nature of the divine, by the idea of several incarnations rather than the unique *Incarnation of Christianity and, finally, by the lack of a historical dimension in Hindu thought and the preference for the idea of balance over that of progress.

Simone Weil's *God was fundamentally impersonal. From her earliest years she was convinced that the world was governed by necessity, a law-like network of relationships that underlay and knitted together the material world whose author was in some sense God. This dual face of God as present necessity and absent love leads to the problem of creation that lay at the heart of Simone Weil's religious meditation. For her, *creation was itself a contradiction in that God who was infinite, who was all, effected something outside the Godhead that at the same time proceeded from it. Despite all appearances, to remain motionless, 'waiting on God' (the title of her best-known book) was the most effective of all actions. *Atheism could actually be purificatory since religion, in so far as it was a source of consolation, was a hindrance to true faith.

Weil's *ascetic, demanding, always involved lifestyle was the practical counterpart to her thirst for the Absolute. Morbid and perverse to some, to those with a deeper sympathy her very inability to compromise gives to her life and thought a kind of personal authority. In the end, she remains unclassifiable—and therefore perpetually unsettling. Many will think that they have never met anyone with whom they have alternatively agreed or disagreed so violently. But whether we think of her as a 20th-century *saint or condemn her as self-absorbed dreamer, few can refuse to recognize her genius, the challenge her life poses to so many of our own preconceptions, and the unerring instinct with which she managed to go straight to the heart of the problems of our time. As she herself remarked: to be always relevant you have to say things which are eternal. **David McLellan**

Coles, Robert, *Simone Weil: A Modern Pilgrimage* (1987).
McLellan, David, *Utopian Pessimist: The Life and Thought of Simone Weil* (1990).
Miles, Sian (ed.), *Simone Weil: An Anthology* (1986).
Pétrement, Simone, *Simone Weil: A Life* (1976).

Wesley, John and Charles (1703–91 and 1707–88). The two

brothers, although they remained priests of the Church of England to the end of their lives, are regarded by *Methodists as the principal founders of their particular ecclesial tradition that now numbers some 70 million adherents worldwide. Born into the large family of Samuel Wesley and Susanna Annesley at Epworth Rectory, Lincolnshire, John and Charles studied at the University of Oxford, where they became leading members of a group of religiously earnest young men known and mocked for their study of the scriptures, regular prayer, frequent communion, and ministry to prisoners, and nicknamed the Bible Moths, the Holy Club, or the Methodists. In 1735 the Wesleys enrolled with Oglethorpe in Georgia, but their pastorate among the colonists and *mission to the native Americans did not last long. By 1738 they were back in England, having been greatly impressed by the Moravians they encountered at sea, in North America, and again in London.

Under Moravian influence and during gatherings of a 'religious society', the Wesleys each underwent at *Pentecost of that year a spiritual experience described by John in his *Journal* for 24 May: 'I felt my heart strangely warmed. I felt I did trust in Christ, Christ alone, for salvation; and an assurance was given me, that he had taken away *my* sins, even *mine*, and saved *me* from the law of sin and death.' This decisive *assurance, although it did not remain unthreatened, eventually released in John Wesley an energy for *evangelism that began with open-air *preaching near Bristol in March 1739 and continued for 250,000 miles over land and sea until his death (Charles's initial itinerancy gave way upon his marriage to stable pastorates in Bristol and London). Wesley and his helpers (when Methodists use the name Wesley without qualification, they mean John, except in the context of hymn-writing) gathered into tightly structured 'societies' (with smaller 'classes' and 'bands') the people who responded to their preaching of the gospel and their exhortation to 'scriptural holiness', so that by 1791 there were more than 70,000 identifiable 'Methodists' in Britain and over 60,000 in North America, where the movement had been spreading since the 1760s. Methodism left the Anglican womb more gradually in England than in the newly independent United States, where the Christmas Conference of 1784 set up the Methodist Episcopal Church.

While Charles was the chief writer of *hymns, John's theology found expression, not in a single systematic work, but rather in his sermons (the first four published volumes of which remain among the 'doctrinal standards' of Methodism), his *Explanatory Notes upon the New Testament* (again a 'standard'), his occasional treatises (often controversial, and sometimes adapted from the writings of others), his letters and *Journal*, and the decisions taken in the annual conferences of his preachers, which he dominated. Wesley's theology is thus pragmatic in orientation and use; but it would be wrong to detach it from its scriptural basis, its location within the dogmatic tradition of the church, or its use of disciplined reasoning in the service of the faithful proclamation of the gospel and the encouragement of growth in the Christian life.

Wesley called himself 'a man of one book' (*Sermons*, preface), mindful of the Anglican Article VI that 'Holy Scripture containeth all things necessary to salvation'; but the *bible constituted for Wesley, in the formulation of G. C. Cell, not so much 'the boundary of his reading' as 'the centre of gravity in his thinking'. The scriptures must be interpreted in each generation, and always (quoting Thomas à Kempis, *Imitation of Christ*, 1. 5) 'in the same Spirit whereby they were given' (*Explanatory Notes upon the Old Testament*, preface). Guidance was to be sought particularly from the early Christian writers 'the most authentic commentators on Scripture, as being both nearest the fountain, and eminently endued with that Spirit by whom all Scripture was given' (*An Address to the Clergy*). Wesley trusted less the church into which Constantine's imperial favour introduced moral and even religious corruption, but continued to value the ancient *creeds and accepted the dogmatic decisions of the first four ecumenical *councils as hermeneutical keys to the reading of scripture.

For Wesley, the doctrine of the *Trinity was the expression and guarantee of the salvation a believer finds when 'God the Holy Ghost witnesses that God the Father has accepted him through the merits of God the Son—and having this witness he honours the Son and the blessed Spirit "even as he honours the Father"' (Sermon 55, 'On the Trinity'); and final bliss is pictured this way: 'To crown all, there will be a deep, an intimate, an uninterrupted union with God; a constant communion with the Father and his Son Jesus Christ, through the Spirit; a continual enjoyment of the Three-One God, and of all the creatures in him' (Sermon 64, 'The New Creation'). Belief in the divinity of Christ marks a distinction 'from the Socinians and Arians' (*The Character of a Methodist*). 'The Doctrine of the Atonement' is 'the distinguishing point between Deism and Christianity' (letter of 7 February 1778 to Mary Bishop). A 'denial of original sin contradicts the main design of the gospel', which is 'to ascribe to God's free grace the whole of [man's] salvation'; it would be to give up 'justification by the merits of Christ' and 'the renewal of our natures by his Spirit' (*The Doctrine of Original Sin*).

It is in this framework of the doctrine of God and of God's great history of redemption on behalf of humankind that Wesley's declaration is to be understood that 'our main doctrines are three', those 'of repentance, of faith, and of holiness' (*The Principles of a Methodist Farther Explained*). That is a succinct statement of the *via salutis*, or individual appropriation of salvation, whose phases Wesley set out homiletically in his Sermon 43, 'The Scripture Way of Salvation'. All need *salvation (this in accord with the doctrines of original *sin and total depravity). Yet God leaves no one entirely in a state of fallen nature: in virtue of Christ's meritorious work, God stirs the *conscience and restores to everyone a measure of free will sufficient to enable a positive response when confronted by the gospel (a move towards *Arminianism against a teaching of limited *atonement). Then 'the common privilege' of believers is an assurance of present salvation (although this is not a guarantee against lapsing and finally losing). Faith itself 'works through love' (Gal. 5: 6), and so believers strive towards *holiness, having the mind of Christ, and walking as he walked. Wesley liked to cite *Augustine to the effect that 'He who made us without ourselves will not save us without ourselves' (Sermon 63, 'The General Spread of the Gospel'; Sermon 85, 'On Working Out Our Own Salvation'). Entire sanctification consists in single-hearted love of God and neighbour and is attainable, though also capable of being lost, in this life (*A Plain Account of Christian Perfection*).

Wesley endorsed the Westminster Catechism's description of 'the chief end of man' as 'to glorify God, and to enjoy him for ever'. Yet through much of Wesley's presentation of the *via salutis* there is a polemical edge against *Calvinism, and notably against the doctrines of *predestination and final perseverance (themes exegetically and systematically treated in *Predestination Calmly Considered*). In accordance with his reading of the scriptures, Wesley grounded his alternative account in the character of God (whose justice and goodness disallow the 'eternal decrees'), the conditional nature of God's promises, and concern lest moral seriousness be undermined by *antinomianism. In contemporary intellectual terms, Wesley saw systematic Calvinism as aligned with a mechanistic view of the world and a necessitarian view of humankind (*Thoughts upon Necessity*).

Thus while much has been made of Wesley's dictum that 'we think and let think', his magnanimity was limited to those 'opinions' which, in his judgment, did not 'strike at the root of Christianity' (*The Character of a Methodist*). Nor would he surrender what he considered 'essential doctrines': he was quite opposed to doctrinal 'indifferentism' (Sermon 39, 'Catholic Spirit'). Wherever possible he sought to make the most of what Christians held in common on the basis of the scriptures classically interpreted. This is well illustrated by his attitude towards Roman Catholics. While he shared the suspicions of Protestant Englishmen concerning the political loyalty of Catholics, and while he considered that the Church of Rome erred in certain doctrinal matters and encouraged superstitious practices, he set out in his *Letter to a Roman Catholic* a detailed statement of the common faith (an expansion upon the Niceno-Constantinopolitan creed) as the basis for mutual respect, and indeed love, and an endeavour to 'help each other on in whatever we are agreed leads to the kingdom'.

The Wesleyan faith came to its most popular expression in the hymns that were chiefly the work of Charles, although John (who himself made a number of fine translations from German *Pietism) often played a part in their editing and publication. The hymns are characterized by their biblical texture, their dogmatic density, their literary and theological use of *paradox, and their powerful emotivity. Some consist of paraphrase and meditation on particular passages of scripture, but the more effective often weave texts together in a way that relies heavily on the coherence of the canon. Thus a stanza from 'Spirit of faith, come down, | Reveal the things of God' (cf. 2 Cor. 4: 13; 1 Cor. 2:.12–13):

No man can truly say
That Jesus is the Lord,   [1 Cor. 12: 3]
Unless Thou take the veil away,   [2 Cor. 3: 12–18]
And breathe the living word;   [Matt. 4: 4; John 20: 22]
Then, only then we feel
Our interest in his blood,   [1 John 1: 7]
And cry with joy unspeakable   [1 Pet. 1: 8]
Thou art my Lord, my God!   [John 20: 28]

As to the paradoxes of redemption, the dogma of the Council of *Ephesus 431 is succinctly expressed in a couplet from the *Hymns for the Nativity of our Lord*:

Being's Source begins to be,
And God himself is born …

while many of the Passion hymns exploit the communication of properties allowed by the hypostatic union (see CHALCEDON, COUNCIL OF) as they sing of 'a crucified God' and 'the death divine':

The immortal God for me hath died!
My Lord, my Love is crucified.

The *eucharistic revival that accompanied the Methodist movement was served by the Wesleys' *Hymns on the Lord's Supper* of 1745 (166 texts, most of them inspired by Daniel Brevint's treatise on *The Christian Sacrament and Sacrifice* of 1673). The book that formed the backbone of Methodist hymnody throughout the 19th century was the 1780 *Collection of Hymns for the Use of the People called Methodists*, which John Wesley called 'a little body of experimental and practical divinity', of 'scriptural Christianity', in which 'all the important truths of our most holy religion' are 'carefully ranged under proper heads, according to the experience of real Christians' (preface). While Wesleyan hymnody has declined in prominence on its home territory as Methodists have expanded their ecumenical range, several of the best of the Wesleys' hymns have made their way into the repertoire of other churches.

The fate of Wesleyan hymnody may epitomize the significance of the Wesleys' version of the Christian faith: beyond its original context, its importance resides in how far it continues to mark Methodist thought and life, how far Methodism seeks renewal through a return to its particular sources, and how far others find it an enrichment of the tradition of the church. It may count for something that the Wesley brothers have lately been adopted into the commemorative calendars of at least some Anglican and Lutheran churches.

Geoffrey Wainwright

Wesley, John, *Works*, ed. T. Jackson, 14 vols., 3rd edn. (1872), many reprints; now being replaced by the Oxford/Bicentennial Edition (35 vols.; 1975—).
Baker, F. (ed.), *Representative Verse of Charles Wesley* (1962).
——*John Wesley and the Church of England* (1970).
Borgen, O. E., *John Wesley on the Sacraments* (1972).
Campbell, T., *John Wesley and Christian Antiquity* (1991).
Coppedge, A., *John Wesley in Theological Debate* (1987).
Heitzenrater, R. P., *Wesley and the People called Methodists* (1995).
Jones, S. J., *John Wesley's Conception and Use of Scripture* (1995).
Kimbrough, S. T., Jr. (ed.), *Charles Wesley: Poet and Theologian* (1992).
Maddox, R. L., *Responsible Grace: John Wesley's Practical Theology* (1994).
Outler, A. C. (ed.), *John Wesley* (1964); an anthology.
Rack, H. D., *Reasonable Enthusiast: John Wesley and the Rise of Methodism* (1989).
Schmidt, M., *John Wesley: A Theological Biography* (3 vols.; 1962–73).
Tyson, J. R. (ed.), *Charles Wesley: A Reader* (1989).

wine is coupled with *bread in providing the matter of the *Eucharist, Christianity's central *sacrament, performed since *apostolic times weekly, by many even daily. The wine trade may have profited in consequence, yet it represents essentially a common, people's drink. While its Christian usage originates in the cup of the passover celebration, its *symbolic significance is transformed by *Jesus' words at his Last Supper, 'This cup is the new *covenant in my *blood' (1 Cor. 11: 25), although his additional words explicitly referring to wine, 'from now on I shall not drink of the fruit of the vine until the kingdom of God comes' (Luke 22: 18) are less often quoted. A sense of wine as vehicle of spiritual transformation is also engendered by the first *miracle reported in John's gospel (John 2: 1-11), the conversion of *water into wine at the Cana marriage feast, symbol of all that would follow, the world's transformation at the coming of the *Word.

Use of wine for the Eucharist has produced various problems. Does it need to be grape wine? Vines do not grow everywhere. Is it credible that, for centuries, the Eucharist could not be validly celebrated in, say, South India, owing to an absence of grapes? Replacement of grape wine by that of rice or bananas has, nevertheless, been regularly rejected by a sort of sacramental fundamentalism insisted upon above all by Rome. It seems likely that the difficulty of acquiring wine in northern Europe in the Middle Ages contributed to lay exclusion from receiving communion in this form. What may have begun on grounds of scarcity added subsequently to the deep division between clergy and *laity and the privileging of the former, so characteristic of the medieval church, against which *Hussite Utraquists and all 16th-century *Reformers protested. Wine thus helped divide Protestant from Catholic, a separation only overcome when *Vatican II's *liturgy constitution in 1963 began the readmission of Catholic laity to communion of the cup. A further problem derives from *temperance campaigning. Rejection of all alcohol on moral grounds has either to admit an exception for the Eucharist—an exception inevitably undercutting its symbolism—or to celebrate the latter, as do *Methodists, for instance, with a non-alcoholic beverage. But this may seem to diminish the Eucharist's full significance, the hallowing of the whole range of material culture. It can also be diminished by the use of numerous small cups instead of one large one. Drinking wine from a shared cup may constitute the most perfect symbol of *reconciliation and fellowship. **Adrian Hastings**

wisdom, defined as some exceptionally deep insight into the workings of the world, may seem a rather exalted term for much of the biblical book of Proverbs and its like, which could be described as practical common sense. These books are the product of a teaching tradition that is based on and actively encourages the transmission of accumulated experience in the conduct of daily life between father and son, teacher and pupil. Apt imagery is coupled with easily memorable forms to help this process.

The Hebrew wisdom tradition is part of a much wider movement in the ancient world. It is also associated with a literate, scribal culture, though here the evidence in Israel is scanty. Much of the book of Proverbs would be hard to identify as distinctively Israelite if taken out of context. Similar collections can be found in Egypt, Babylon, and throughout the ancient Near East. The lack of interest this strand of biblical writing shows in the events of Israel's history and its specific cultic practices means that the historically based biblical theologies of the 20th century found it hard to deal with, a balance that is beginning to be rectified.

The word wisdom (*hokhma*) in Hebrew has a variety of meanings. It can mean a skill, as of a craftsman. In a wider sense it can mean human cleverness, a quality which is subtly or not so subtly debunked in most of the biblical literature. Even the proverbial wisdom of *Solomon, paragon of this tradition, can be seen to have unwanted and unpredictable results. After all, the most cunning animal of all is the serpent in Eden, and the promise of the knowledge of good and evil is the temptation it offers.

Beyond this, however, wisdom is an attribute of *God, the governing principle of the universe. The natural world, rather than history, reveals God through its ordered and awe-inspiring beauty. From this the wisdom tradition develops its own creation *mythology around the personification of Lady Wisdom, who plays before God and is present at the making of the world (Prov. 8: 30-1) or even an active co-worker in it (Wisd. 7: 22). She has suggestive parallels with other divine female figures of the *Hellenistic world, most importantly Isis. In the Hellenistic period, she is also identified with the Logos.

The opposite of wisdom is folly. For Proverbs, the distinction between the two is clear and the thrust of the book is to guard young men from folly. Both literally and metaphorically folly is associated with the fatal allure of loose women. The wise man is promised security and prosperity and the comfort of a good wife, whereas the fool will perish miserably. Other writers are less sure that things are so neat and here the wisdom tradition reveals a variety of approaches to some of the most vexing problems of religious thought.

The writer of Ecclesiastes (or Qoheleth), with all the resources of wealth and learning behind him, sets up an experiment to test this rigid position. He will try both wisdom and folly as ways of life to see whether the wise man's or the fool's is better. Inevitably, the experiment proves unworkable, as, in order to evaluate the life of the fool, one must retain at least that much wisdom. In any case, both wise and foolish, as Ecclesiastes never tires of pointing out, come to the same end in the grave. Wisdom is not its own reward. Something much more mysterious is going on, and although Ecclesiastes is often read, especially in modern times, as a disappointed cynic whose book contains any hope only in so far as it has been doctored by pious editors, an alternative reading may see it as offering a peculiar liberation from the striving of human wisdom.

The book of *Job is also both a part of the wisdom tradition and a critique of it. Job's comforters appeal to the standard line that Job's sufferings must mean that he has somehow offended God and is undergoing just *punishment. Job's protest is also based on the same tenets. Knowing he is innocent, he appeals to God as the fundamental guarantor of cosmic and moral order to set things right. God overwhelms him with a vision of the uncanniness of his cosmos, reduces him to silence, vindicates him before his friends, and then rewards him, while the reader knows that the whole story revolves around a wager between God and Satan. No brief summary can capture the power and strangeness of this book which seems to subvert every interpretation offered. Still, the wisdom tradition, which at least at one level is here subjected to a devastating critique, manages to persist into the *Apocrypha. Ecclesiasticus, or Sirach, seems to revert to the old paradigm. Yet the book makes a crucial move in tying the specifically religious study of the Torah and the *Temple cult together. The law (see LAW, BIBLICAL) is not to be set against the philosophical traditions of the Hellenistic world, but itself reflects the structure of the cosmos and is Wisdom's gift to Israel. The apocryphal book of Wisdom carries the personification to even greater heights and seems to offer a specific criticism of the attitude of Ecclesiastes.

In the NT, Jesus is seen as a wisdom teacher of a special sort. In Mark 6: 2, his knowledge is a cause of astonishment. Luke's story of Jesus' boyhood discussion with the doctors of the Temple makes clear this is related to knowledge of the Law. Yet Jesus also condemns the scribes and doctors and the whole thrust of his Passion is presented as the paradigm case of the undeserved suffering of the innocent. Wisdom's categories are stretched beyond bearing.

It is this that underlies *Paul's otherwise startling praise of folly and his contention that in crucial respects Christian experience overthrows the structures of worldly wisdom. He reminds the Corinthians that Christ crucified is a contradiction in terms which means that all the terms themselves must be redefined. He dares to speak of the 'foolishness of God' which is 'wiser than men' (1 Cor. 1: 25). Yet he is not complimenting the Galatians when he calls them 'foolish' for abandoning the gospel (Gal. 3: 1). There is a legitimate place for human common sense still, and the *Pastoral Epistles and James provide NT equivalents to the desire for order and the maintenance of the community that Proverbs stands for.

Subsequent Christian thought maintains this tension. Rediscovered *Gnostic texts suggest a suppressed line of devotion to Sophia (Wisdom) as a divine emanation exiled to this world and constantly striving for her own redemption. Salvation is to be found in the union of the believer with Wisdom herself. However, the fact that the great church in the imperial capital *Constantinople was dedicated to Hagia Sophia (Holy Wisdom) reflects the importance of the cult of Wisdom that received legitimation when Sophia was identified with a Roman matron martyred under Hadrian. She is usually depicted as a crowned woman with her three daughters, Faith, Hope, and Charity. The *Eastern Orthodox church especially places great store by the cultivation of true wisdom through contemplation and illumination.

More recently, the dynamic, creative, world- and life-affirming figure of Sophia, personified Wisdom, has had great appeal to Christian *feminist thinkers as offering a biblically grounded vision of God released from the confines of patriarchal imagery and with the nurture of human communities and the natural world at its heart. Wisdom also offers a bridge between biblical religion and other traditions as its appeal is to divine order rather than to divine intervention in the particular history of Israel. Yet Christian thinkers inherit a tradition which maintains an unsettling conviction that even the wisest may be misled into mistaking folly for wisdom and where the arbitrary choice of God may overturn all reasonable assessments.   **Hugh S. Pyper**

Blenkinsopp, J., *Wisdom and Law in the Old Testament* (1995).
Bulgakov, S., *Sophia, the Wisdom of God* (1993).
Davidson, R., *Wisdom and Worship* (1990).
Newbigin, L., *Foolishness to the Greeks* (1986).

Schüssler Fiorenza, E. (ed.), *Searching the Scriptures*, ii. *A Feminist Commentary* (1994).

witchcraft has little to do with Christianity but much to do with Christian *history. Most of the world's cultures appear to have shared the witchcraft fantasy: some people have a secret power to harm or kill their neighbours with invisible means; they meet at night, flying through the air with animals as familiars, to concoct their evil plans. As to how they obtain such powers there is no unanimity and often relatively little interest. It may be a physical element in their bodies, possession by dead ancestors who were similarly endowed, or by other malign spirits, or through a contract with the *devil. Popular conceptions focus on the power to do harm, not its explanation.

Apart from one dangerous line in Exodus (22:18), 'Thou shalt not suffer a witch to live' (and even there 'witch' might well read 'sorcerer'), there is little on the subject in the bible. Christianity long judged belief in witchcraft as simply an example of pagan superstition. Throughout northern Europe, it survived Christian *conversion, just as it does in contemporary *Africa, but seldom led to attacks upon supposed witches when church authorities firmly denied any reality behind such ideas. In accusations of witchcraft, therefore, it was the accuser, not the accused, who was in trouble. Similarly, in modern Africa belief continues unabated but generally stops short of attack on individuals so long as local authorities, civil or religious, refuse to countenance accusations. However, once an authority is willing to do so and punish identified witches, accusations tend to multiply in circumstances of social unrest.

For reasons which remain mysterious, the ecclesiastical and theological attitude to witchcraft changed in the late Middle Ages. Once the *Inquisition was set up to suppress Catharism, c.1233, its *Dominican officials, who understood Catharism as service of the devil, began to revise the standard view about witches, seeing them in a similar light as really existent diabolical servants. They were helped in this by scholastic elaboration of the nature of devils. In 1258, Pope Alexander IV still forbade the Inquisition to bother itself with such cases. While this was altered in 1398, there was no large pursuit of witches until the late 15th century when two Dominican Inquisitors, Heinrich Krämer and Jakob Sprenger, wrote the *Malleus Maleficarum* (*Hammer of Witches*, 1486) and persuaded Innocent VIII, a lax and very ineffectual pope, to give the Inquisition in Germany authority to act. While in the 9th century the idea that witches could fly through the air was dismissed as rubbish by the *canon episcopi*, five centuries later, at the height of the *Renaissance, it was seen as credible and the idea of witches as real people wielding fearful powers and worshipping the devil in Saturday night gatherings on mountain tops became a theological commonplace. In consequence, courts were willing at last to listen to popular accusations, especially in Germany. Though there was little pursuit of witches in the next fifty years, the doctrine of the *Malleus* was entirely accepted by *Luther and early *Protestants generally. The worse outbreaks of witch-hunting took place between 1560 and 1660, mostly in brief localized gusts of hysteria, with sporadic outbursts later still. Thus in countries such as England and Scotland the witch-craze was almost wholly a post-Reformation, Protestant, phenomenon, stimulated by new anti-witchcraft laws passed soon after Protestantism came to power. It was, however, even more violent in many Catholic areas of Germany, France, and, finally, Poland. It was worst of all in the German territories of various Catholic prince-bishops: Trier, Würzburg, Bamberg, and Köln. The outbreak at Salem, Massachusetts, in 1692 when twenty people were executed was a late expression of the craze.

Appalling as the witch-craze was, the number of its victims is often exaggerated; across 250 years there were probably fewer than 500 in England, 1,500 in Scotland, far more in Germany but fewer than 50,000 in Europe as a whole, not the many millions sometimes claimed. Some places, such as Venice, were practically unaffected. If the Inquisition bears heavy responsibility at the start, most experienced Inquisitors grew decidedly sceptical, as did the papacy, which helps explain why so few witches were executed in countries where the Inquisition was powerful, notably Spain and Italy. While the large majority of victims were *women, some 20 per cent were men, including forty-three clergy in Würzburg alone. It is misleading to over-stress any specifically feminine character to the imagined witch.

In the later 17th century, while few people entirely rejected the possibility of a diabolical pact, lawyers increasingly doubted the validity of any evidence produced, especially as much of it was obtained under torture (though not in England). The witch-craze, while essentially a relatively brief, post-medieval, aberration, has served to discredit Christianity and to contrast the theological 'orthodoxy' of the early modern period with a liberal consensus growing from the 18th century that witchcraft theory was no more than a bundle of absurdities—in reality a return to the Christian consensus of the first 1,000 years. In many parts of Africa, however, the debate still continues. **Adrian Hastings**

Briggs, Robin, *Witches and Neighbours* (1997).
Clark, Stuart, *Thinking with Demons: The Idea of Witchcraft in Early Modern Europe* (1997).
Cohn, N., *Europe's Inner Demons: An Enquiry Inspired by the Great Witch-Hunt* (1975).
Larner, Christina, *Enemies of God: The Witch-Hunt in Scotland* (1981).
Levack, Brian, *The Witch-Hunt in Early Modern Europe* (1987).
Sharpe, James, *Instruments of Darkness: Witchcraft in England 1550–1750* (1997).
Thomas, Keith, *Religion and the Decline of Magic* (1971).

Wittgenstein, Ludwig (1889–1951).

Wittgenstein, who was Austrian by birth and early education, studied in Cambridge with Bertrand Russell in 1911–12, gave up *philosophy after completing his *Tractatus Logico-Philosophicus* (German and English, 1922), but returned to Cambridge in 1929, becoming a British citizen and professor of philosophy in 1939. He wrote copiously but published nothing; much has appeared since his death, starting with his *Philosophical Investigations* (German and English, 1953), the second major work which guarantees his place as the leading figure in English-speaking analytic philosophy. Wittgenstein wrote relatively little about religion; the impact of what he wrote, though considerable, has not always been as he might have desired.

Much to his surprise, the *Tractatus* was adopted in the late 1920s by the Vienna Circle as a foundation document in logical positivism. It was assumed that the implication of the book, summed up in the famous final sentence, 'Whereof one cannot speak, thereof one must be silent', was that what cannot be stated in terms verifiable by standard scientific procedures could be neither true nor false. Through A. J. Ayer's *Language, Truth and Logic* (1936) this doctrine was introduced into English-speaking philosophy. Wittgenstein's work thus played a part in encouraging philosophers and others to regard *metaphysics, *ethics, aesthetics, and *theology in reductionist, non-cognitivist, and emotivist terms. What he intended, however, in consigning what cannot be said to silence, was to vindicate a '*mystical' approach to the world: the ineffability of the ethical, metaphysical, and religious would only show that they surpass the capacity of *language to express them. In discussion with members of the Vienna Circle in 1930, for example, he said that he could 'well imagine a religion in which there are no doctrinal propositions, in which there is thus no talking'.

Wittgenstein was brought up as a Roman Catholic. Occasional remarks reveal strong distaste for the kind of *apologetics that he was taught: 'I would be afraid that you would try and give some sort of philosophical justification for Christian beliefs, as if some sort of proof was needed,' he said, typically. Other remarks, however, attest liking for ritual: 'The symbolisms of Catholicism are wonderful beyond words.' In 1931, he scorned what he regarded as J. G. Frazer's rationalistic explanations of religious practices in *The Golden Bough*, declaring that he would rather simply say, admiringly, that 'man is a ceremonious animal'. In 1950, he noted that one might be convinced that God exists, though not by metaphysical arguments but rather through 'a certain kind of upbringing', perhaps by 'life', 'experiences', even 'sufferings of various sorts'. Throughout his life, Wittgenstein reflected on *religion. In 1937, for example, he made notes on Christianity, including predestination and the Resurrection, apparently in the course of reading *Kierkegaard.

Few philosophers, including philosophers of religion, show much interest in Wittgenstein's views on religion. Norman Malcolm, a friend and former student, who wrote on a range of philosophical problems, takes a recognizably Wittgensteinian path by insisting that, whereas believing in God is intelligible when interwoven with certain practices, reactions, and attitudes, it is less clear whether it makes sense to treat belief in God as a hypothesis that can be assessed independently of any such context.

Rush Rhees, another close friend, left a great deal of work on, *inter alia*, philosophy of religion, exploring what kind of reality can be found in religious belief, and how that reality is related to the moral experiences that we value. Peter Winch, in such essays as 'Meaning and Religious Language' and 'Who is my Neighbour?', should also be mentioned (*Trying to Make Sense* (1987)). D. Z. Phillips, the most prolific and best known representative of an approach controversially labelled, by Kai Nielsen, 'Wittgensteinian *fideism', contends that the task of the philosopher who follows Wittgenstein is principally to clear away would-be foundationalist explanations and justifications of religion that get in the way of seeing what is actually there. 'Philosophy may in no way interfere with the actual use of language; it can in the end only describe it. For it cannot give it any foundation either. It leaves everything as it is,' as Wittgenstein said. Following at least one strand in Wittgenstein's thought, Phillips combats traditional theistic apologetics and theodicies as misguided craving for quasi-scientific explanations that distort realities needing simply to be accepted.

While this (much controverted) approach in the philosophy of religion evidently owes a good deal to Wittgenstein, it is less easy to identify his influence on Christian theology. If the *Tractatus* supports verificationism, and the later work a radically anti-intellectualist pragmatism, theologians such as Don *Cupitt may appeal to Wittgenstein. Others, such as George *Lindbeck and Stanley Hauerwas, who show little direct interest in his views about religion, have clearly learned a great deal from some of Wittgenstein's central concerns in philosophy: in particular from the set of remarks known as the Private Language Argument where he insists (against traditional Cartesian dualists as well as contemporary behaviourists) on the incoherence of the idea that we can have knowledge of our own or anyone else's experience independently of our common language (see DESCARTES). These ideas passed into philosophical currency through the work of his friends and former students, Peter Geach (*Mental Acts* (1957)) and G. E. M. Anscombe (*Intention* (1957)), both seminal in the revival of *Thomist moral psychology and ethics of *virtue, in particular in opposition to consequentialism in *moral theology. Openly critical of post-*Vatican II developments in the Roman Catholic Church, of which they are devout members, they have rarely brought philosophy to bear on theological matters; but Geach's *God and the Soul* (1969) and papers on the morality of war and on transubstantiation in Anscombe's *Collected Philosophical Papers III* (1981) show their debt, albeit indirectly, to Wittgenstein's teaching. Michael Dummett, well known for his polemics against liberalism in recent Roman Catholic biblical scholarship, has renewed the ancient metaphysical debate over *realism and its alternatives (*Truth and Other Enigmas* (1978)). Accepting the Private Language Argument, though rejecting Wittgenstein's suspicions of philosophical theorizing, and aligning his later work with anti-realism, Dummett recognizes that the outcome would have theological consequences: realism, and thus objectivity and truth, in metaphysics and ethics, probably depends on some form of theism. Thus, Wittgenstein's impact on Christian thought remains fragmentary and contradictory.

See also RELIGIOUS LANGUAGE.   **Fergus Kerr**

Barrett, Cyril, *Wittgenstein on Ethics and Religious Belief* (1991).

Hacker, P. M. S., *Wittgenstein's Place in Twentieth-Century Analytic Philosophy* (1996).

Monk, Ray, *Ludwig Wittgenstein: The Duty of Genius* (1990).

Phillips, D. Z., *Wittgenstein and Religion* (1993).

Rhees, Rush (ed.), *Recollections of Wittgenstein* (1984).

Sluga, Hans, and Stern, David G. (eds.), *The Cambridge Companion to Wittgenstein* (1996).

woman/femininity.

This topic has, until recently, occupied only a marginal place in Christian thought, particularly within formal theological reflection. The silence is not, however, unbroken. Various elements of the tradition—including its language about *God, its *saints, and its *symbols—have carried powerful implicit messages about womanhood. In addition, certain Christian thinkers have delivered their opinions on woman and femininity clearly and forcefully. *Feminist theology has played a central role in bringing many of these implicit messages to light. In concentrating on Christian theological reflections rather than the actual lives of Christian women, it should be remembered that what a theologian advocates may be very different from what actually occurs. The submission of wives to their husbands, for example, may be presented as God's inalterable command; that fact alone cannot tell us whether or in what ways real wives were actually submissive to real husbands.

Answering the male clerics who disapproved of her *preaching and public ministry, Sarah Grimké (1792–1873), a pioneering American Christian feminist, pointed out that the *Sermon on the Mount was addressed to both sexes. When *Jesus taught that it was wrong to hide one's light under a bushel he was therefore addressing women as much as men. Grimké's mischievous observation makes a serious point. Not only the Sermon on the Mount, but all of Jesus' public teaching seems to have been addressed to both sexes—as indeed is the whole of the bible. By contrast with many of the world's other major religions, Christianity has never restricted access to its scriptures to *men, never developed a separate body of teaching or legislation for women, and never excluded women from its cultus. Its *worship and its two most central rituals, *baptism and the *Eucharist, have always been open to women and men on equal terms.

This lack of discrimination between the sexes is clearly evident in many of the NT documents, including the *gospels and *Paul. Not only was Jesus' teaching addressed to both sexes, it challenged the values and assumptions of a male-dominated society in important ways. The 'good news' that Jesus proclaimed was of the dawning of God's *Kingdom. Not only was this Kingdom open to men and women, but the important players on *Israel's public and religious stages (necessarily male) might not be the first to enter. The Kingdom demanded qualities such as open-heartedness, loving-kindness, fidelity, generosity, and humility in relation to God and neighbour, qualities which were more often associated with women than men. The widow who gives her last mite, the Syro-Phoenician woman, the woman who anoints Jesus' feet—these women of flesh and imagination people the gospels and furnish Christianity with some of its most powerful images of *salvation. Most important of all is *Mary, the mother of Jesus. Present both at the beginning and at the end of the gospel story, her significance within the Christian history of salvation is second only to that of her son Jesus, and she has haunted the Christian imagination ever since. Her various representations, ranging from queen of heaven to humble handmaid of the Lord, or from perpetual virgin to devoted wife and mother, effectively mirror changing Christian concerns.

In many respects Paul's letters display a lack of differentiation between the sexes similar to that of the gospels. Through the death and Resurrection of Jesus, Paul declares, the gift of the *Holy Spirit has been poured into the hearts of all believers, changing them from 'glory into glory' and transforming them into the likeness of Christ. The implications are startling: since the Holy Spirit comes upon both sexes, they stand equal in relation to God and to salvation. Moreover, since the Holy Spirit confers power, *authority, and gifts such as teaching and *prophecy, men and women would also appear to be on an equal footing within the church. Paul's statement in Galatians that 'there cannot be Jew nor Greek, there cannot be slave nor free, there cannot be male and female; for you are one in Christ Jesus' (3: 28) underlines this position. Yet elsewhere Paul seems to draw back from these radical implications of his teaching. In 1 Corinthians, for example, we find him both acknowledging without complaint that women are praying and prophesying in worship (11: 5) *and* declaring that 'women should keep silence in the churches' (14: 34). While this is clearly contradictory, Paul's underlying position may not be. Paul believed that in relation to Christ and salvation there was no difference between the sexes, but *not* that there was no difference between the sexes in other respects. In this life and this body, Paul believes that important differences between the sexes remain, that these are God-given, and that they fit men and women for distinct roles and tasks.

In developing these views on woman/femininity, Paul articulated a position that the majority of later Christian thinkers would affirm: women are equal with men in relation to salvation but different in relation to one another and the roles they should perform here on earth. Later Christian thinkers would disagree, however, about the nature of these differences and their practical implications. Whilst Paul, for example, seems generally to have played down sexual differences, the author of the *Pastoral Epistles places more emphasis on its importance and extent. 'Let a woman learn in silence with all submissiveness. I permit no woman to teach or to have authority over men; she is to keep silent … Yet woman will be saved through bearing children' (1 Tim. 2: 11–15). Together with the story of *Eve in Genesis 2–3, such verses became key texts for those who wished to insist upon the necessary subordination of women and to exclude women from the clerical orders (see ORDINATION).

Even when Christian writers were most insistent upon woman's difference and necessary subordination, their reflections often spring not so much from an interest in the nature of woman *per se*, as from wider concerns—concerns with the *body and the defence of the *family and the social order in particular. In the NT epistles, for example, many of the teachings on women occur within the context of 'Household Codes' that prescribe order within a household (husbands over wives, parents over *children, masters over *slaves). Likewise, the later influential reflections of *Augustine upon women are often driven by his concern to defend *marriage and the family against those who advocated *celibacy as the only truly Christian form of life. Augustine's comments take their place within his wider defence of the whole created order, including what is material and bodily, against a *Gnostic *dualism. For Augustine, the difference between the sexes is part of a good, God-given order that must be respected and honoured by all creatures. While he believed that the *Fall has corrupted human *sexuality and that procreation now represents the only legitimate use for woman's sexuality, Augustine is able to affirm that 'a woman's sex is not a defect' and that it will be restored in the resurrection life (*City of God*, 22. 17).

As in Augustine, so in later Christian thinkers, an insistence on the importance of the body often had the effect of accentuating the difference between the sexes. By contrast, a more spiritual, *Platonic conception of what it is to be *human often had the opposite effect, erasing rather than accentuating sexual difference. Some of the early Christian writers who were most keen to promote the *ascetic life as the highest form of Christian life did so, in part, because of a quasi-Platonic desire to escape from a body regarded as restrictive and corrupting, and it is just such thinkers who are often harsh in their comments on the sinfulness and corruption of women's bodies and sexuality: Jerome (*c*.342–420) is a good example. Yet it was also these thinkers who opened up a new form of equality to women through their advocacy of the celibate life and *monasticism. While wives and *mothers who remained tied to the demands of the body and earthly society were viewed with some disdain, women who took the path of holy *virginity were generally regarded as the equals of their male counterparts.

During the medieval period, the ascetic and *religious life appears to have attracted women in large numbers. Since some of the women who entered the religious life were able to receive an education, it is from this period that we have the first theological documents written by women. As in much male theology, woman/femininity is not normally a direct topic of concern, but its imprint often emerges in other contexts. One interesting example occurs in relation to reflection upon the *Trinity—especially Jesus Christ—where we can observe a feminization of thought in some medieval writers' work. The English anchorite *Julian of Norwich, for example, speaks of 'the Motherhood of God' and, more frequently, of 'Christ as Mother'. Christ is Mother for Julian both through his role in human creation and nurture, and in his taking flesh for our sakes.

Male theologians' reflections upon woman/femininity during the medieval period rarely reveal any comparable feminization of thought. *Aquinas, for example, insisted even more firmly than Augustine on the necessary subordination of women, argued that although woman is made by God she is imperfect compared to man, and maintained that a woman could not be ordained because she is in 'a state of subjection' (*ST* III Supplement, q. 39 a. 1). Despite Aquinas's comments, women played an increasingly influential role within the Christian tradition from the later medieval period, particularly in relation to *spirituality. Like Julian of Norwich, a large number of women claimed authority on the basis of *visions and direct revelations of God, and the association of women with *mysticism stems from this period. Through their mystical insight and their teachings on the spiritual life, women such as *Hildegard of Bingen, *Catherine of Siena, Catherine of Genoa (1447–1510), and *Teresa of Avila assumed an important place in Catholic Christianity. The tradition they established was developed by women like Margaret Mary Alacoque (1647–90) and Thérèse (*Teresa) of Lisieux into the modern period.

The *Reformation's suspicion of mysticism and its attack on the monastic life prevented this tradition of women's mystical theology from continuing unchanged within the Protestant churches. Its exaltation of marriage and the family and its iconoclastic attitude towards Mary and the saints also had a powerful impact on many Christian women's lives. At the level of theological reflection upon woman/femininity, however, the Protestant Reformation was far less revolutionary. Like Paul, *Luther and *Calvin insisted that, though equal in terms of salvation, the sexes are different and have different roles to play, and they defined these roles primarily in terms of women's duties to husband and family. However, whilst some patristic and medieval theologians had maintained that woman was created subordinate, the Reformers tended to stress the equality and perfect companionship of man and woman in creation before the Fall. Radical Protestants (including some *Puritans) who believed in the possibility, through grace, of attaining perfection in this life were therefore able to embrace the ideal of relationships of greater equality and mutuality between the sexes, and to place more stress on partnership and companionship than on childbearing as the chief end of marriage.

What became a typically Protestant stress on the importance of the family for Christian living has been carried through into much modern Protestant thought. As increased affluence and changing economic relations allowed more women to remain in the home, the 19th century saw the development of a popular theology that portrayed woman as the 'angel in the house'—gentle, godly, and pure, but in need of male protection. Yet while an emphasis on woman's sinfulness began to slip away, an emphasis on her proper subordination often remained. Even in the 20th century, major Protestant theologians like Karl *Barth and Dietrich *Bonhoeffer continued to insist upon God-given differences between the sexes that make male leadership appropriate. Though they often speak in terms of a complementarity between the sexes, they retain a typically Protestant insistence that the family is the proper context for human living, and that woman's task is the maintenance of this institution. More popular forms of modern Protestant thought, including that of *fundamentalism, offer an even more strongly subordinationist variant of this message. In much American fundamentalism, the cause of true religion and true godliness has become identical with that of the maintenance of the patriarchal family.

A stress upon the family as woman's proper sphere of operation and responsibility has become typical of much conservative Roman Catholic as well as Protestant thought since the 19th century. True to the influential Pauline current of Christian reflection on woman charted above, modern *papal pronouncements do not deny the fundamental equality of the sexes in relation to salvation, but maintain that there are none the less important differences between men and women that fit woman for the role of wife and mother or, in more exceptional cases, for lifelong celibacy. Gone is any stress on the dangers, corruptions, or limitations of the female condition. In its place there is a new tone of appreciation and even idealization of womanhood, often bound up with a reflection upon the goodness of Mary the mother of Jesus. Unlike much modern Protestant teaching on women which takes scripture as its key authority, conservative Roman Catholic thought continues to appeal to a *natural law tradition that stresses the importance of created, bodily difference between the sexes.

Alongside these more conservative forms of theological reflection, liberal theology has offered alternative Christian reflections on woman/femininity. In the work of *Schleiermacher, often regarded as the father of *liberal theology, we find not only a new turn in theology, but also new reflections upon the relation between the sexes. From *Romanticism Schleiermacher took an emphasis upon the importance of feeling that led him to criticize an exclusively masculine approach as hyper-rational and to express an appreciation of woman's capacities for intuition and affectivity. Schleiermacher commends serious *friendship and conversation between the sexes as the means by which the 'limitations of gender' may be overcome and his ideal of a sexless 'infinite humanity' realized.

In Schleiermacher's twin emphases on the importance of feeling and on the goal of a sexless 'infinite humanity', we find the themes that would become most characteristic of all subsequent liberal Christian theological reflection (both Catholic and Protestant) on woman/femininity—including explicitly feminist reflection. Such reflection has increasingly pressed for full equality between the sexes. This imperative has been couched in terms of an *Enlightenment humanism that insists that the 'humanity' that men and women have in common is far more important than anything that differentiates them. It has also been articulated in terms of a Romantic stress upon the difference between the sexes and the necessity of masculine *reason being complemented (or overridden) by a more feminine reliance on the importance of feeling and experience. As women have gradually been allowed to participate more actively in theological reflection from the 19th century onwards, they have been most prominent in developing these themes. Generally speaking, 19th-century feminist theologians like Elizabeth Cady Stanton (1815–1902), active in the campaign for women's rights, tended to employ the humanistic approach, whilst 20th-century feminist theology combined both approaches, together with a *Marxist-inspired stress on the importance of liberation from structural oppression.

It is interesting then to observe that most liberal and feminist Christian reflection upon woman/femininity has been shaped by influences peripheral or tangential to the Christian tradition. Whilst Christianity maintained a stress on the equality of men and women before God from its beginnings, it is only under the pressure of post-Enlightenment currents of thought that it has developed an explicitly feminist stress upon the proper equality of men and women in this life as well as the next. From a feminist perspective, Christianity's failure to articulate the feminist imperative in terms that are rooted in its own tradition constitutes a serious weakness. It is also directly responsible for the current tension between liberal and conservative Christian reflection on the topic of woman/femininity. On the one hand, much conservative reflection that is rooted in scripture and tradition continues to insist upon a difference between the sexes that makes male leadership appropriate. On the other hand, liberal reflection rejects such subordination, but employs secular conceptualities to do so. Terms like rights, justice, liberation, equality, and humanity are central to such liberal discourse, but are usually construed in ways that owe little to Christian traditions of thought. Within this polarized situation, conservative Christians rightly accuse liberal Christians of failing to produce reflections on womanhood/femininity that have a properly theological basis, whilst liberal Christians rightly accuse the conservatives of defending a hierarchical and patriarchal view of sexual difference. What is needed, it seems, is fresh and creative reflection on the mystery of human sexual difference which is as responsibly related to the Christian tradition as it is to contemporary concerns.

See also PERSON.

Linda Woodhead

Børresen, K. E., *Subordination and Equivalence: The Nature and Role of Woman in Augustine and Thomas Aquinas* (1981).

Bynum, C. W., *Jesus as Mother: Studies in the Spirituality of the High Middle Ages* (1982).

Clark, E. A., *Women in the Early Church* (1984).

Clark, E. A., and Richardson, H. (eds.), *Women and Religion: The Original Sourcebook of Women in Christian Thought*, new edn. (1996).

Fiorenza, E. Schüssler, *In Memory of Her: A Feminist Theological Reconstruction of Christian Origins* (1984).

Irwin, J. L., *Womanhood in Radical Protestantism, 1525–1675* (1979).

Loades, Ann, *Searching for Lost Coins: Explorations in Christianity and Feminism* (1987).

—— (ed.), *Feminist Theology: A Reader* (1990).

Nichol, I. G. (ed.), *Schleiermacher and Feminism: Sources, Evaluations and Responses* (1992).

Roper, L., *The Holy Household: Women and Morals in Reformation Augsburg* (1989).

Ruether, R. R. (ed.), *Religion and Sexism: Images of Women in the Jewish and Christian Traditions* (1974).

Sawyer, D. F., *Women in the First Christian Centuries* (1996).

Warner, Marina, *Alone of All Her Sex* (1985).

womanist theology, see BLACK THEOLOGY; FEMINIST THEOLOGY.

Word/Logos.

The Christian doctrine of the Word (Greek *logos*) developed from the particular emphasis in Judaism on God's speaking to *Israel through the *Law (see also LAW, BIBLICAL) and the *prophets. The idea of scripture as the written Word of God was extended to include, in *apocalyptic circles, disclosures about the future *Messianic Age and, in Hellenistic *Judaism, the revelation of the creator through *creation. Both ideas are found in the *New Testament but with a distinctive concentration on the crucified and risen Messiah, in whom scripture is fulfilled, the future disclosed, and creation renewed. The 'Word' becomes almost a technical term for the *preaching of the gospel, and the *christological focus is so intense that in one or two places in the NT *Jesus is himself identified as God's Word, the *eschatological revelation to Israel and the Gentiles. This last step, from revelation in words to revelation in a person, was to have a long-lasting and dramatic influence on Christian thought.

The prologue to the anonymous sermon 'to the *Hebrews' contrasts 'the many and varied ways in which God spoke to our forefathers through the prophets' with the way in which 'in these last days he has spoken to us in a Son'. The author goes on to exploit the self-confessed incompleteness of the scriptural *revelation as he demonstrates the superiority of revelation in Christ, the origin and goal of creation, the visible radiance of God's glory, the one effective *sacrifice and eternal high *priest, with a status higher than the *angels (Heb. 1: 1–4). Nowhere in Hebrews is any interest shown in words spoken by the earthly Jesus, attention being focused principally on his person and work.

The second key text is the early Christian hymn attached as a preface to the Fourth Gospel. It celebrates the Logos, using the term, here alone in the NT, as an absolute christological title, the One in whom God is revealed in creation (1: 1–5), in the history of God's people (1: 9–13), and in the human person of God's only Son (1: 14, 16–18). The underlying idea combines the *myths of *Wisdom as God's handmaid (Prov. 8: 22–31) and of the prophetic Word as warrior (Wisd. 18: 15; Rev. 19: 13), re-expressing it less mythologically, in language that may owe something to Greek speculation about order and rationality in the universe. The claim that the Word became flesh (1: 14)—philosophically speaking, intolerably *paradoxical—has sometimes been seen, taking one interpretation of the situation of the Johannine writings (see 1 John 4: 2, cf. 2: 18–19), as a rebuke to *Docetic heretics. But since the Fourth Gospel's telling of Jesus' story is itself open to Docetic interpretation, and is chiefly concerned with refuting Jewish denials of the pre-existence and divinity of Christ, it is more likely that the claim that the Word of God became flesh in Jesus was originally a response to these denials (see John 1: 17). The most striking difference between *John and the Synoptic Gospels is the way it replaces the words of the historical Jesus with meditative and sometimes polemic discourses on his own nature by him whom the Prologue identifies as the Word.

The *Greek fathers, from Justin Martyr onwards (see PRE-CONSTANTINIAN THOUGHT), fastened onto the term 'Logos' and made *apologetic capital out of its *philosophical resonances. It enabled the church to assert both the oneness of God and the full deity of the Son, 'consubstantial with the Father', against *Arius' heretical views. It was developed in two contrasting ways in the great intellectual centres of Antioch and *Alexandria. Antioch, typified by Theodore, based its christology on the close conjunction between the Logos and the *man* Jesus, preserving the full *humanity and deity of the Logos-Anthropos at the price of some hesitation about the unity of his *person. Alexandria, typified by Cyril, began from the unity of the person of the Word in human *flesh* (Logos-Sarx) but hesitated about Jesus' human soul and will (see INCARNATION). Elements of both christologies were combined in the Definition of *Chalcedon (451). In patristic discussion, the scriptural, personal, and eschatological aspects of the Logos doctrine become temporarily overshadowed by dogmatic technicalities, and the most significant later developments in the doctrine of the Word may be viewed as the recovery of these three neglected aspects.

Before the formation of the NT canon, early Christianity naturally emphasized what differentiated it from its Jewish matrix: freedom from the law, fulfilment of prophecy, the living authority of the Spirit of the risen Christ. But after the parting of the ways, it inevitably reinvented structures parallel to those in Judaism. Since knowledge of Christ was mediated for later generations chiefly through the apostolic writings, the term 'Word of God' was applied to both Testaments. The 'sacred page' became for medieval theologians the source of that knowledge of God that unaided reason could not provide. The *Reformers reinforced the authority of the *bible in their challenge to the church's hierarchy. Scripture as the Word of God mysteriously mediated *salvation, either by conveying God's transcendent address to the believer, or by interpretation through the inward testimony of the *Holy Spirit. Considering what followed from this assertion of scriptural supremacy (for example, the notions of verbal inspiration and propositional revelation; the defensive reaction of *fundamentalism to scientific discoveries), the move might be thought entirely retrograde; but recovering the scriptural dimension of the doctrine of the Word of God had initially a broadening, humanizing effect on the understanding of revelation. Furthermore, the *translation and dissemination of printed bibles and the freeing of scriptural interpretation from ecclesiastical control were also to have other consequences, very different from those just mentioned.

Historical-critical study of scripture, though it eventually gained its own internal momentum, began in the *Enlightenment's critique of biblical authority, especially regarding OT morality, messianic prophecy, and *miracles. The Word of God, for those critical scholars at the turn of the 19th century who still used the term, was distinguished from scripture and understood as personal revelation, not so much through the person of Christ as by divine self-revelation to human beings through the sense of absolute dependence or through the spirit's coming to know itself as spirit. Liberal theologies of personal revelation have points in common with the early Greek fathers' understanding of the Logos in creation, human history, and religious awareness, but they were moving in the opposite direction, towards severing revelation from classical christology.

The eclipse of liberal Protestantism at the turn of the 20th century was due to the outworking of its own method in two directions, scepticism and eschatology. As historical investigation began casting doubts on whether anything could certainly be known about ancient Israel or Jesus of Nazareth, *neo-orthodox Protestants like Martin Kähler and Karl *Barth rejected historical reason in the name of faith alone. The infinite difference between creator and creature could be bridged only by the sovereign Word of God in scripture, preaching, and the person of Christ. This contrasts starkly with the traditional Catholic understanding of the Logos doctrine, which affirms that transcendent deity is also immanent in nature and history and incarnate in the flesh of Jesus and the church's *sacraments.

The one important exception to the sceptical tendency of historical criticism was the rediscovery of the roots of early Christianity in Jewish apocalyptic hope for the imminent dawn of the age to come, fulfilled and transformed by belief in Christ's Resurrection: this was the very kernel of the faith, not some kind of disposable husk. The Word which Jesus and the first Christians proclaimed, therefore, concerned not just past and present but especially the future: the *Parousia* and the coming *Kingdom of God. It is this insight, revelation as a word of promise, which modern theologies, whether starting from *existentialism, *process thought, or salvation-history, have had to struggle hardest to incorporate within the structures of Christian doctrine.

There are, then, different strands in the concept of the Word/Logos, in some tension with each other. At times the idea has functioned as a way of opening out Christian thought, to embrace all earlier revelation of God and everything rational and good in the universe as the work of the Logos. At others it has functioned in the opposite way, narrowing doctrine within the confines of scripture as its normative expression. It has played an important role in technical discussions about the nature of Christ's person, yet also figured in attempts to replace dogmatic speculation with the lived experience of divine grace. The term has often carried an implicit claim to the finality of Christian faith or one particular form of it; hence it is necessary to understand this finality as eschatological, pointing forwards to a Word of God in *judgement and salvation that has yet to be spoken.   **John Muddiman**

Bultmann, R., *Jesus and the Word*, ET (1934).

Dunn, J. D. G., *Christology in the Making*, rev. edn. (1989).

Ebeling, G., *Word and Faith*, ET (1963).

Holte, R., 'Logos Spermatikos: Christianity and Ancient Philosophy According to St Justin's Apologies', *Studia Theologica*, 12 (1958), 109–68.

Pannenberg, W., *Systematic Theology*, ET (1991), i.

Pittenger, N., *Christology Reconsidered* (1970).

Sellars, R. V., *Two Ancient Christologies* (1940).

work is purposeful, primarily instrumental activity performed for *God, community, and self. As part and parcel of the human condition, work in its widest sense is a perennial theme in Christian thought.

In the bible we first encounter work in the portrayal of God's creative activity and satisfied rest in *Genesis 1 and 2. Human work emerges from God's blessing and mandate to multiply and rule the earth. Genesis, unlike the ancient world, does not split rest and work between gods and humans, or free and slave. Man and woman are co-workers who, as God's image, care for each other and *creation, through productive and reproductive labour.

In *Luther's metaphorical phrase, this idyllic picture lasted about as long as the first afternoon. With *sin's entrance in Genesis 3, pleasant work became hard toil, a site of alienation between *humanity and God, man and woman, and humanity and the earth. But though alienating, work, like childbirth, is not cursed. In Gen. 4–11 God renews the creation commission and still blesses the division of labour despite work's misuse as a means of violence (4: 2–12, 23–4), *slavery (9: 20–7), and technological pride that reaches its pinnacle at Babel (11: 1–9). In *Exodus, *Israel is enslaved by Pharaoh and exploited (1: 8–15). God hears the people's cry and promises an Edenic land of blessed work and rest (3: 7–10) thereby inspiring a bricklayer's strike. The commandment to keep the *sabbath not only echoes God's rest in the beginning, but is also a weekly reminder of that strike. It relativizes human work, for human beings live primarily by God's creative and redemptive work. Part of the *prophetic vision for the future is that the curse of transitoriness and injustice hanging over creation will be lifted, leading to joyful and unalienating work (Isa. 65: 21–3).

In *wisdom literature, Proverbs praises hard work, like the ant's, whereas laziness causes *poverty (6: 6–11; 10: 4; 13: 4). While Ecclesiastes underscores the vanity of the 'work ethic', considering human transitoriness, the book does not advocate a 'shirk ethic' but stresses contentment with one's lot and comradeship in labour (4: 4–10).

In the NT, *Jesus' status as an artisan (Mark 6: 2–3) seems to have been incidental to his mission. He calls disciples away from their ordinary work as fishermen to 'fish for people' for God's kingdom (Mark 3: 16–18) but calls others to stay in their everyday roles (Mark 7: 11–13; 5: 18–20). He offers *eschatological freedom and rest (Matt. 11: 28–12: 8) which his followers must reconcile with their social roles.

*Paul, a theologian of the cross, the community, and the new creation, holds commitments to culture (including work) and God's *Kingdom in tension (cf. 1 Cor. 7). The codes of household economy, which manifest the same tension, teach revolutionary subordination because all, masters and slaves, are accountable to their heavenly Master (cf. Eph. 5: 21; 6: 5–9). Paul's tent-making offers a model for such service (Acts 18: 3; 1 Thess. 2: 9). While his missionary work is the heart of his call, tent-making is integral to it. He linked the Greek perception of the weakness and 'slavery' of his manual and *apostolic work (2 Cor. 11: 21, 27) to God's weakness on the cross (1 Cor. 1: 25). Work is a form of costly *discipleship, but should not be misused to justify meaningless or slavish labour. The new life in the Spirit with its multiple gifts (Rom. 12; 1 Cor. 12; Eph. 4) overflows from the church into the larger society and its activities because of the Spirit's role in new creation (Rom. 8: 18–25; cf. Ps. 104). Christians work within a tension between the present world, where work is often alienating, and the promised new world from which all causes of suffering will be removed (cf. Rev. 20–2).

The Greek exaltation of contemplation over activity, which the bible implicitly challenged, resurfaced in the early and medieval church. After *Constantine's conversion, what had previously been seen as the calling of all Christians became increasingly confined to *monastic life. Most monastic rules combined biblical and Greek views by mixing *prayer, reading, and manual labour, in that order. The best balance was in St *Benedict's rule (6th century), which viewed work as a form of prayer, and in the ideal and practice of skilled communal craftwork in the medieval guilds. But even at its best, medieval work was seen mainly as a material means to intellectual and spiritual ends.

*Protestant Reformer Martin *Luther rejected the medieval confinement of vocation to priests or monks, reclaiming it for ordinary Christian occupations and roles in the household economy, church, and state, which he saw as ways providentially ordered for Christians to love and serve God and neighbour. He identified vocation with social station, which opened the idea to ideological distortion: almost any work, no matter how alienating, should be embraced as an exercise of divine vocation.

The *Puritans' integration of spiritual and worldly vocation with an almost monastic degree of discipline was affected by forces of secularization and individualism after the English Civil War. Work as vocation was gradually separated from the general vocation to live a Christian life and serve the common good: hence in part, Max Weber's thesis that the Puritans' 'Protestant Work Ethic' unintentionally made capital accumulation an end in itself. R. H. Tawney, however, rightly noted that what helped the rise of *capitalism was a *distortion* of the Puritan view. The *deist Benjamin Franklin popularized a purer version of Weber's thesis through such maxims as 'time is money'.

The Industrial Revolution may have raised living standards in the long term, but it also separated work, home, and church. Work belonged increasingly to a technical, male-dominated realm of facts, while church and home became the primary domain of women, a shrinking and privatized area of subjective values. Some Christians employed the resources of their faith to address the problems of increasingly alienating industrialized work through the rising trade union movement, with its echoes of the medieval guilds. However, the *Marxist critique of alienation has been more influential: capitalism turns the workers' creative labour into a mere means to consumption. Frederick Taylor's scientific management principles, popularized by Henry Ford, made alienation into an art form, with workers treated as animated tools. The original Marxian vision notwithstanding, supposedly Marxist societies embraced the same methods. As P. D. Anthony notes (*The Ideology of Work* (1977)), Christian thinkers have often adopted free market or Marxist ideologies without criticizing the ideology of work common to both of them.

At the beginning of the 21st century, prophecies of a leisured society with significant reduction of work have not yet materialized. Instead, many people are working harder than ever and others (about 10% in most western economies), especially the young (about 30%), are without any paid work at all. The absent father syndrome has now become the absent mother syndrome too as women follow the transfer of much of their traditional work into the industrialized service economy. Contemporary societies seem caught in a 'work-and-spend' cycle. The escalating demands of *family, education / career, and desire for new forms of leisure will be crippling unless ways are found to blend active and contemplative elements in people's lives. A theology of work may offer help.

Yet such a theology, necessary though it is, would not suffice to address all the problems of work in contemporary societies. A large-scale critique of the present reality of work and a plausible alternative proposal is needed: a task that can be accomplished only by theologians, economists, political scientists, and cultural anthropologists working together.

Human beings work because God created them to work, to have 'dominion' over creation and to 'till and keep' the garden. Hence work belongs to the very nature of human beings and we find personal fulfilment in meaningful work. Conversely, if we cannot work in a purposeful, non-alienating way our lives are emptied of much, though not all, meaning. Secondly, we work because God imparts gifts appropriate for the various tasks to which we are called. If the whole life of a Christian is life in the *Holy Spirit, work cannot be an exception, whether it is church work or secular work, spiritual or mundane. All human work, complex or simple, is empowered by God's Spirit.

If God created people to work and endows them with gifts for various tasks, two important consequences follow. First, work is no mere means to an end. It is not simply a chore to be endured to satisfy needs and desires. While work, being primarily instrumental, will always remain a means, the best work is more than *just* a means. Because it is essential to our humanity, it also has intrinsic value. Second, 'sacred' and 'secular' work have equal dignity before God. Religious work such as preaching, or teaching in a seminary is not better than secular work such as baking bread or building bridges; both are good if done in response to the gifts and call of God's Spirit. Both are bad or alienating if they ignore his gifts and his call and do violence to our *personhood.

So the *reason* we work lies in our very nature and our specific gifts and callings. What then is the *purpose* of work? (1) To obtain the necessities of life: as Karl *Barth put it, the first thing at issue in all fields of human work is the need of human beings 'to earn their daily bread and a little more'. (2) To provide for the needy: supporting the needy through diligent work is a demand of *justice rather than an act of generosity (2 Cor. 9: 9). (3) For the development of culture: while some ancient cultures saw work as immediate service to the gods, the biblical traditions 'demythologized' human work; it was divorced from its immediate connection with the cult and put into the service of culture. Work is not a cultic, but a cultural activity. (4) Co-operation with God: God and humanity are partners in preserving creation. As Luther put it, human work is 'God's mask behind which he hides himself and rules everything magnificently in the world'. But human co-operation with God in preserving creation is also co-operation in anticipation of God's eschatological transformation of the world. In their daily work humans are 'co-workers in God's kingdom, which completes creation and renews heaven and earth' (*Moltmann). God will purify, transfigure, and receive into his eternal kingdom all good and beautiful things that human hands have created.

Much work, however, does not correspond to God's intention. Work that is reduced to a mere means for survival or that severely restricts freedom and hinders human development is alienating because it is at odds with our personal nature. Work that is self-centred, exploitative, or discriminatory is alienating because it transgresses our communal nature. Yet talk of alienation may strike many unemployed people as a luxury, when they would accept almost any job as a matter of sheer survival. Societies, governments, and companies for whom human labour is an asset not a cost, have a responsibility to provide work fit for human beings. Though at times it may be difficult to achieve the creative distribution of work that would meet that responsibility, to do so is primarily a matter of political will.

Though a fundamental dimension of human existence, even work at its best does not comprise the whole of human life. Life includes other important activities that, unlike work, are not primarily instrumental but have their own intrinsic goals such as *play, *friendship, enjoyment of nature, and especially a relationship to God in *worship. Humans were created not simply to be God's servants and co-workers, but also to be his children and each other's friends. Christian life, unlike much of life as it is experienced, should be lived in a rhythmic alternation between work, worship, and play; between labour, *liturgy, and leisure. Such a balance poses a continuing challenge for Christian thought and practice.

Miroslav Volf
Gordon Preece

Agrell, G., *Work, Toil and Sustenance: An Examination of the View of Work in the New Testament* (1976).

Barth, K., *Church Dogmatics*, III/4 (1961).

Hock, R. F., *The Social Context of Paul's Ministry: Tentmaking and Apostleship* (1980).

John Paul II, *On Human Work* (1980).

Marshall, P., *A Kind of Life Imposed on Man: Vocation and Social Order from Tyndale to Locke* (1996).

Ovitt, G., Jr., *The Restoration of Perfection: Labor and Technology in Medieval Culture* (1987).

Preece, G. R., *Changing Work Values: A Christian Response* (1995).

—— *The Threefold Call: A Trinitarian and Reformed Theology of Vocation* (1998).

Tawney, R. H., *Religion and the Rise of Capitalism: A Historical Study* (1926).

Volf, M., *Work in the Spirit: Toward a Theology of Work* (1991).

Weber, M., *The Protestant Ethic and the Spirit of Capitalism* (1930).

Wingren, G., *Luther on Vocation* (1957).

world, in Greek *kosmos*, is used in several related senses in the NT, all of which derive from its root meaning of 'that which is ordered'. It can be an equivalent of the OT expression 'the heavens and the earth', which means the whole of creation. More specifically, it can denote the inhabited earth as the sphere of human activity. Thirdly, the word may be restricted to human society and its ways.

In any of its meanings, the world is *God's good *creation, established by *covenant, but corrupted by the *Fall. Although God's glory is still reflected in its order, its defining characteristic is impermanence. It is the theatre of the drama of *redemption and the object of God's *reconciling *love (John 3: 16), but also under final *judgement. Both redemption and judgement encompass the highest spheres of heaven and the depths of the humblest human heart.

God's coming in *Jesus into the world shows it in its true colours. The Johannine writings are particularly concerned with this theme. The world owes its existence to the *Word which became flesh (*Incarnation), but the world failed to recognize this and turned against its own creator (John 1). The *disciples and therefore the *church, who do respond in repentance, are chosen out of the world. They become members of the *Kingdom of God which is

'not of this world' (John 18: 36) and come to share the rejection that the world inflicts on its saviour. In turn they are to reject the world. Superficially there seems to be a direct contradiction between passages that speak of God's love of the world and those which enjoin hatred of it. What is to be hated in the world, however, is its rejection of the divine love that seeks its redemption. The love demands the hate.

Often, however, 'the world' has been used as shorthand for everything that Christians should reject, summed up in the slogan 'the world, the flesh, and the devil', which seems to entrench a stark *dualism. As a result, it has proved difficult for Christians not to turn rejection of the world in the more nuanced theological sense into a simplistic rejection of the created order as such. Many *Gnostic and later heretical groups did just this. Steering an orthodox course here requires the same caution as is needed to understand *Paul's strictures against the 'flesh' (*sarx*). He uses this term to refer to the aspect of each of us which is in thrall to the world, but this is not to be equated with the *body as a created entity. As for the *devil, the world, according to John 12: 31 and 16: 11, is given over to a 'ruler', who personifies all that resists Jesus and his message of salvation. Yet this ruler, later identified with the devil, is already defeated and those who follow Christ can be called 'conquerors of the world' (1 John 5: 5) because Christ has conquered the world (John 16: 33).

The NT consistently teaches that Christians are in the world but not of it. Their allegiance to Christ will inevitably draw the world's enmity upon them. Worldly success and popularity are snares. This encourages Christian *asceticism and the rise of *monasticism to provide an alternative order where some, at least, of the world's temptations can be avoided. The concept of the gathered church of those redeemed from the world reflects this impulse in post-Reformation thought. The level of rejection of worldly temptation may vary from something little different from a heightened concern with public respectability to the life of the enclosed orders of the Catholic Church or the distinctive and self-sufficient Amish repudiation of industrialization and its works. Such tendencies can be perverted into the kind of 'other-worldliness' that gives *spirituality a bad name, 'too heavenly-minded to be any earthly use'. This is very different from the robust practicality that characterizes the great contemplative *mystics like *Teresa of Avila. Paul himself has little patience with those who refuse to earn their living in the name of leading a more spiritual life.

In any case, these gospel warnings against the world's temptations have not stopped Christian churches and individuals from accumulating and even priding themselves on the goods and favours of the world. There is a contrary tradition with strong support in some parts of the OT that God's favour is shown in *prosperity and worldly success, taken up by some forms of *Calvinism and blatant in the 'prosperity gospel' of some American evangelists.

This more favourable attitude to the world can be seen also in the development of Christian humanism, which in turn led to the *Renaissance and brought a new appreciation of the autonomy of a world no longer encompassed and subdued by the church. Both the political and the natural worlds were seen as having their own integrity, and it became increasingly clear that the church, however unwillingly, needed to examine and negotiate its relationship with these independent spheres of existence on their own terms. This challenge was embraced particularly by *liberal Protestantism, leading to charges that in some of its forms it has abandoned any distinctive position from which it can offer a Christian critique of the world. The liberal rejoinder is that even if such a position could be formulated, the Christian message will be ignored as irrelevant. The business of the Christian is to be in the thick of the world, following Jesus' example of dealing with the poor, the sick, and the socially and morally outcast.

This is a reminder of the fundamental insight that Christian unworldliness is not an end in itself but directed to the salvation of the world. For contemplative orders, this is effected through *prayer. Others have felt called to risk the inevitable compromises of *political engagement and life in the world as a price which Christians must be prepared to pay in carrying out their responsibilities for the world. *Constantine's adoption of Christianity as the religion of the Roman empire can be regarded as a betrayal of the church's commitment to God's Kingdom rather than Caesar's, or else can be seen as the church rightfully fulfilling its calling to bring order and the news of the gospel to the realities of human society. The whole world must be gathered in, and the *missionary impulse of Christianity was at least an important factor in the drive to explore every corner of the earth that stimulated the colonial expansion of Europe. God's injunction to Adam to 'subdue' the earth (Gen. 1: 28) is also at work here, fostering an attitude that sees the natural world as a resource to be exploited and tamed and human beings as somehow set apart from it.

In wider terms, such Christian visions have contributed both practically and ideologically to the modern development of global consciousness (see GLOBAL ETHICS). This in turn has led to a renewed sense of the precariousness of the world as a finite *ecological system which cannot sustain unfettered human demands. At the same time, the fact that the survival of the human race depends on the maintenance of a nexus of fragile, complex, and imperfectly understood natural systems has become clear. This has brought the concept of human beings as stewards of the world more to the fore.

One aspect of the late 20th-century theologies of *secularism and the death of God was a concern to confront people with their responsibility for the world and to shake them out of a complacent reliance on divine *providence to sort out the consequences of human irresponsibility. A similar concern underlies a seemingly contrasting movement, the recovery by such thinkers as *Teilhard de Chardin and Matthew Fox of the ancient notion of the cosmic Christ and God's work of salvation as involving the whole universe. In an expansion of the theology of creation, the metaphor of the world as God's body has been taken up, leading some more radical Christians to propose something verging on pantheism, where God and the world merge (see NEW AGE). Both these trends bring the importance of the world and human responsibility for its ordered maintenance to the centre of theological concern.

One particularly significant example of this renewed engagement of the church with the world was the pastoral constitution produced by *Vatican II, 'The Church in the Modern World' (Gaudium et Spes, literally 'Joy and Hope'). Disliked by some eminent theologians for its over-optimism, by others for its over-caution, its concerns may already seem rather dated, though this is an inescapable

cost of the attempt to be relevant. Its importance is that it represents a serious attempt by the church to address the world on a comprehensive range of issues in terms that could be understood, if not always assented to. All the mainstream churches have produced strings of public reports on issues such as *poverty, global injustice, and ecology. They can draw on the particular experience of their clergy and their wider membership who live and work in problematic areas and see at first hand what sociologists and politicians may only inspect from a safer distance.

Such endeavours, however, seem doomed to failure and fundamentally misconceived from the standpoint of those many Christians who adhere to the *apocalyptic strand of Christian teaching. Rather than being problems the church is called upon to solve, the ecological and political disasters of the 20th century are irrefutable signs of the world's imminent dissolution in God's final act of judgement. The present world, in this view, is not a precious jewel to be preserved but the realm of sin and death whose destruction is to be prayed for so that the Kingdom can be ushered in.

Paul's great vision of the whole creation groaning as in childbirth (Rom. 8: 22) can be read in these terms, but glee at the pain and destruction involved is no part of his teaching. He looks forward to the entire universe set free from the 'bondage of decay', from the impermanence which characterizes biological and physical systems. In the eyes of its adherents, this biblical vision dwarfs both the vengeful pettiness of much apocalypticism and the sentimental neo-paganism of much eco-theology, but it demands a complete revolution in all the categories by which we understand the world. Christian thinkers are still fundamentally divided over how the present world relates to the Kingdom of God and the respective roles of God and humanity in bringing it about.

See also ALTERNATIVE LIFESTYLES; RELIGIOUS LIFE.

Hugh S. Pyper

Bouyer, L., *Cosmos: The World and the Glory of God* (1988).
Fox, M., *The Coming of the Cosmic Christ* (1988).
Jantzen, G. M., *God's World, God's Body* (1984).
Kortner, U. H. F., *The End of the World: A Theological Interpretation* (1995).
Murray, R., *The Cosmic Covenant* (1992).
Schneider, J., *Church and World in the New Testament* (1983).
Teilhard de Chardin, P., *Hymn of the Universe*, ET (1965).

World Council of Churches, see ECUMENICAL MOVEMENT.

worship.

In the NT the word used is *latreia*, which had its origin in servitude and expressed what a hired servant or slave owed to the master. From this it became the service of God or divine worship. The importance of this derivation is still witnessed to by the common use of the word 'service' to describe an act of worship. The English word derives from Anglo-Saxon *weorthcipe* (worthship), that is, honour.

Worship is *prayer, especially public prayer, the honour expressed through *praise, thanksgiving, and acknowledgement given to God by believing communities in word, symbol, and action. The Westminster Shorter Catechism (1648) declares that 'man's chief end is to glorify God and enjoy Him for ever'. For Christians worship is the pivotal activity that focuses and enriches life, giving meaning and purpose to existence.

In Christian tradition the proper relationship between the created and the creator is best expressed through the relationship of worship. In every assembly for worship Christians express their understanding of the nature of *God and of *humanity's relationship with him. Equally any act of worship reveals their concept of the kind of people that God expects his followers to be.

God is always the gracious initiator of our relationship with himself. It is he who motivates within the human heart the desire for union with himself. So that although worship may seem to be a human activity, true worship, that is 'in spirit and in truth', is a happening in which God comes to us, and the initiative remains God's. Christian worship therefore is always best discussed in terms of response. In worship Christians respond to God. Whatever the form or content, whether *liturgical or extempore, they contribute to an offering continually going on, which existed before them and will continue whether they join it or not.

It is important to recognize the priority of worship over doctrinal formulation. Worship gives rise to *theological reflection rather than the other way round. The law of worship establishes the law of belief. When the *church assembles for worship it is committing an act of believing, which is in turn an act of faith, that it is God who both summons the church and enables its worship. Belief is a consequence of that encounter with the source of the grace of faith in worship. Christians do not worship because they believe, they believe because the one in whose gift faith lies is regularly met in the act of communal worship. Not that the assembly conjures up God, that would always be magic, but because the initiative lies with the God who promised to be 'in the midst'.

The OT contains varying accounts of worship practices from different times, forms of society, and localities going back to a deity conceived anthropomorphically with human wants and appetites which needed to be satisfied by *sacrifice. However, a twofold development can be identified. There is the external, complicated ritual of the Levitical Code, alongside an appreciation of the need for an inward, spiritual dimension. Consequently, there was a temptation to concentrate on the ritual at the expense of the spiritual, an imbalance which earned the condemnation of Jesus.

The Epistle to the *Hebrews argues that since Christ's death was the perfect sacrifice no further sacrifice is needed; Christ became the unique High Priest. In 1 Peter, in the place of the physical structure of the Temple, Christians are to be a spiritual temple and form a holy *priesthood to offer spiritual sacrifices. However, the NT does not offer details about the ways in which Christian worship was to be performed.

The earliest Christians at Jerusalem continued to worship in Temple and synagogue, but in 1 Corinthians things begin to change. Primitive Christian worship, centring in the *Eucharist, was essentially domestic and was celebrated in private houses. Later, after Constantine, worship ceased to be a family gathering and became a public occasion: the church gathered in the basilica, adapted from a pre-existing class of public building. From then on Christians developed those traditions of *iconography, religious *art and architecture, a whole range of human skills, with which we give glory to God visually and aesthetically.

The primacy of the Eucharist for Christian worship—a service of both word and *sacrament—was never seriously challenged in the first 1500 years of Christian time. The 16th-century Reformers, too,

were chiefly concerned with just that, reforming not abolishing the mass, *Luther even retaining the word in his writings. In the churches of the east, as well as throughout the full extent of the Roman church, eucharistic worship was always officially central, even if *lay people rarely received communion and popular devotion was occasionally diverted down other paths. In the 17th and 18th centuries in Great Britain and North America, Anglican and Protestant churches developed other patterns of worship derived from the Divine Office or from non-liturgical structures to such an extent that they came to be accepted as the norm. The *Oxford Movement in Anglicanism, and then the liturgical movement more widely, advocated a return to a eucharistic tradition that increasing ecumenical contacts have encouraged.

Even so, the form and style of Christian worship has always varied. In many places it was formally offered according to fixed rites, but even these developed differently according to various cultures as Christianity spread across and beyond the Roman empire. There was also a measure of improvisation, extemporization, and freedom that received a strong boost at the time of the Reformation and has a particular manifestation in the contemporary *charismatic movement. The result is that worship may be conducted with full and rich ceremonial accompanied by processions, vestments, *music, and incense, or it may have the minimum of ceremonial in surroundings that are bare of *symbols. It may even comprise mainly silence as in a *Quaker meeting. Yet again it may contain the high octane ingredients of the charismatic movement: speaking in tongues, even physical involvement such as the Toronto Blessing, an experience in which it is claimed that the worshipper is thrown to the floor by the Spirit.

Worship comprises common elements, whether they are contained in an established order of service or are part of a 'free' service (although often the latter may be the largely predictable choice of the presiding minister or lay preacher). There will be any or all of six possibilities: (1) adoration: an acknowledgement of God's transcendence made possible by the fact that he is also self-giving, the experience of the *mysterium tremendum et fascinans*; (2) confession of sin: we turn to God with penitence in our hearts and confession of sin upon our lips; (3) proclamation and thanksgiving: the proclamation is addressed to the world while the thanksgiving is Godward; (4) confession of faith, which also comprises an act of commitment; (5) intercession, a plea for the triumph of God's purposes in spite of contrary appearances; (6) expectation: the believer turns to God looking for salvation that comes to human beings 'from beyond', its source being God.

These elements will be expressed by the spoken or sung word, with or without symbolic or ritualistic gesture by priest, minister, or other presider. In some cases, not confined to any particular tradition, forms of clericalism have rendered the congregation passive receivers or, at best, contributors to the singing of hymns and psalms. The liturgical movement, with its origins in Continental Roman Catholicism and comparable developments in all parts of the western church, is in large part a reaction to this, altering attitudes to congregational participation, whose importance has been generally accepted. Worship is recognized as the work of the whole people of God. In the churches of the east there are, however, as yet few indications of a similar acceptance of the principle.

The reading of the scriptures is one important common ingredient. The Reformation, with its fundamental aim of opening the bible to all, created a need for vernacular texts and prompted rubrical instructions that those reading should both turn to the people and speak in a loud enough voice that all might hear.

*Preaching would be considered essential in any act of worship over a wide swath of Christian traditions, in some of which it is regarded as the sacrament of the Word. To neglect it would be an offence in those churches deriving from, or influenced by, the Reformation. Under the influence of the liturgical movement the Catholic tradition has come to recognize the indivisibility of word and table, and Vatican II made it an obligation that Sunday mass should include a homily.

Having come comparatively late to the principle of the use of the vernacular in worship, the Roman Catholic Church has embraced with enthusiasm this and other ways of widening the understanding and appeal of Christian worship. The first major promulgation of Vatican II was the *Constitution on the Sacred Liturgy* (1963), and Catholic scholars have been among world leaders in the study of worship. More recently they have committed themselves to active co-operation in the search for ways in which the churches, sharing the results of scholarship, might also discover ways in which the scandal of separate worship might be removed.

The *Faith and Order movement, an early product of the *ecumenical movement, undertook to produce a survey of the multiplicity of traditions across the denominations, published as *Ways of Worship* (1951). Since then Faith and Order has facilitated further *dialogue that produced a high level of theological agreement in the realm of worship (cf. *Baptism, Eucharist and Ministry*, 1982). Alongside this in Great Britain, North America, and Australia, for instance, more practical co-operation has produced agreed texts for use in worship, so that churches that are still unable (or perhaps able only occasionally) to worship together have the reassurance that they have the words of their (separate) worship in common. This work has also embraced the creation of a common and ecumenical lectionary of scripture, now also used by churches that hitherto have not employed a systematized scheme of scripture reading.

The human capacity for worship does not seem to be in decline. Christians can occasionally be put on the defensive by those who assert they can worship anywhere. While that is true, it is no less the case that Christian worship is authenticated by the presence of fellow worshippers, as part of the Body of Christ.

The Christian church has an important task in interpreting what significance there might be for its future patterns of worship in public reaction to tragic events. In Liverpool, in the wake of the Hillsborough football disaster in 1989, in London following the sudden death of Diana, Princess of Wales, in 1997, and increasingly at the site of accidents, murder, and violence, many find their own ways of expressing their grief, bypassing churches, chapels, and cathedrals, even the popular centres of the charismatic revival, yet using what were recognizably objects and symbols of worship: flowers, candles, votive offerings; making procession and *pilgrimage to their chosen shrine. These are matters that those who plan worship in the 21st century must not ignore.   **Donald Gray**

Crichton, J. D., 'A Theology of Worship', in C. Jones, G. Wainwright, E. Yarnold, P. Bradshaw (eds.), *The Study of Liturgy*, rev. edn. (1992).

Forrester, D. B., McDonald, J. I. H., Tellini, G., *Encounter with God*, 2nd edn. (1996).

Gray, D. C., *Earth and Altar* (1986).

Kavanagh, A., *On Liturgical Theology* (1984).

Lang, B., *Sacred Games: A History of Christian Worship* (1997).

Moule, C. F. D., *Worship in the New Testament* (1961).

Senn, F. C., *Christian Liturgy: Catholic and Evangelical* (1997).

Smart, N., *The Concept of Worship* (1972).

Underhill, E., *Worship* (1936).

Vagaggini, C., *Theological Dimensions of the Liturgy*, ET (1976).

Wainwright, G., *Doxology* (1980).

wrath, see ANGER.

Wyclif, see HUSS.

Zwingli, Huldrych (1484–1531). The *Protestant Reformer, Zwingli, was born in the Toggenburg valley, Lower Alps, now in the Swiss canton of St Gallen. His family belonged to the upper ranks of the peasantry, and Toggenburg had numerous links with the Swiss confederacy. This background explains why Zwingli, throughout his life, felt he had a right and duty to engage in politics, and why he saw Switzerland as his fatherland. Maintaining his country's independence and restoring it to true godliness were supreme goals of his life.

Zwingli studied at Bern, Vienna, and Basel; after a brief period of theological study he was ordained priest and worked from 1506 at Glarus, from 1516 at Maria Einsiedeln. He was influenced by scholasticism, especially that of Duns Scotus, and subsequently by humanism, later above all by *Erasmus, whom he knew personally.

On 1 January 1519 he was appointed people's priest at the Great Minster in Zürich. His battle against the supplying of Swiss mercenaries, especially the contract with France, involved him in Zürich's politics. All his life he fought against this 'commerce', which, while highly profitable to the upper classes, sent many young men, perhaps to a life of adventure, but often to death or permanent injury.

He was fully aware of the *Reformation starting in 1517 in *Luther's circle, but Luther's theology had limited influence on him. Various reformist innovations (such as breach of the *fasting laws) were introduced in Zürich in 1522, and in 1523 the Reformation arrived in the shape of two great Disputations—the first example ever of a successful 'city reformation'. Zwingli had been a decisive influence throughout.

It soon became clear that the people later called Anabaptists (see MENNONITE THOUGHT), while in basic agreement with Zwingli, were prepared to surrender the bond between civic society and the Christian community, a choice that Zwingli would not endorse. While a catholic front was gaining strength in the Swiss Confederation, there was now another opposition in Zürich itself. Doctrinal differences with Luther, particularly over the *Eucharist, became increasingly obvious through their writings. The Colloquy of Marburg (1529) failed to resolve these differences, which severely hampered the formation of a Protestant alliance. Zwingli's entanglement in confessional alliance politics and in the drift towards war in Switzerland resulted in his death at the Battle of Kappel, 11 October 1531.

For the final establishment of the Reformation, Zürich must thank Zwingli's successor, Heinrich Bullinger (1504–75). The *Consensus Tigurinus* between him and *Calvin (1549) led to *Reformed Protestantism's bearing the stamp of Calvinism rather than 'Zwinglianism', despite Bullinger's international reputation.

The starting-point for Zwingli's theology and personal piety is *God's sovereignty. Nothing can hinder God's *foreknowledge and election. His activity embraces even negative factors in history and extends beyond the *church. The working of his *Holy Spirit can be recognized in the pagan philosophers and heroes; it is not confined within *sacramental actions. This is not in any way to question the unique salvific work of Jesus Christ accomplished in his *Incarnation, vicarious death, *Resurrection, and bodily presence in heaven. The dogma of the *Trinity, Father, Son, and Spirit, and the two natures, unconfused and undivided, of the Redeemer are accepted as in the early centuries. Zwingli believed that at that time the principle of scriptural authority, *sola scriptura*, was still in control (see BIBLE).

This concept of God excludes any divinization of creatures such as the Roman Catholic veneration of the *saints, sacramentalism, and hierarchy. For Zwingli, Luther's clinging to the real presence of Christ's body and blood in the supper is 'papistical'. The working of the Spirit in Christians is independent of any rite; it is God's free act, owing nothing to human *merit.

Equally fundamental with God's sovereignty is God's *covenant with humanity. The people of God in the OT and NT is one single covenant people; infant baptism corresponds to circumcision. Hence the Anabaptists are wrong to attach conditions to it. Their separating themselves from the people as a whole is also to be rejected. The word of God, as recovered in the Reformation, is urgently necessary for the well-being of the *res publica*, in Zürich and throughout Switzerland.

Nevertheless, Zwingli is not for theocracy in the proper sense nor for holy war. Divine and human *justice must be clearly distinguished. That which is, without qualification, good in God's sight—in the sense of the *Sermon on the Mount—and our *justification by grace alone are sharply differentiated from political action. Compensatory adjustments to society (care for the poor, including distribution of monastic wealth) and education at school and university level are indispensable for a healthy community life, as is control of *morals, but not, as in Calvin's model, as part of church discipline. Zwingli was not a *puritan.

Some features of Zwingli's teaching that did not pass over into Calvinist orthodoxy are: stress on election rather than rejection in the doctrine of *predestination; restriction of the effect of original *sin to the corruption of nature, with guilt attaching only to actual sins; the possible salvation of pious pagans.

His death in battle immediately prompted hostile polemic from his opponents, and glorification and talk of martyrdom by his supporters. Both are unjustified. His death was more in the nature of an accident. He saw himself as a prophet, meaning one who inter- prets God's word. This makes him neither 'political' nor 'apolitical' in the modern sense. From the Enlightenment onwards, his type of 'rational' Reformation gained in appeal. Particularly as regards eucharistic theology, a large proportion of modern Protestants are in fact Zwinglians. **Alfred Schindler**

Zwingli, H., *Writings*, ET, i. *The Defence of the Reformed Faith*; ii. *In Search of True Religion: Reformation, Pastoral and Eucharistic Writings* (1984).
Gäbler, U., *Huldrych Zwingli: His Life and Work*, ET (1987).
Stephens, W. P., *The Theology of Huldrych Zwingli* (1986).
—— *Zwingli: An Introduction to his Thought* (1992).

INDEX

This index contains only the names of people who do not have their own entry, and is intended to supplement the full list of articles and the cross-references in the text. A name is included if it is cited in more than one article, or if a single entry contains a substantial reference. Once it was decided that a name should be included, all references except the most fleeting were added, so that the reader looking for John Duns Scotus, for instance, will find Franciscan Thought the most helpful article, but the passing reference in Abelard also helps to place Scotus in his context. Citations in bibliographies, however, are not included.

A

Acton, Lord
History; Religious Liberty

Adam, Karl
Tübingen; Twentieth Century

Adams, Robert M.
Divine Command Ethics

Adorno, Theodor
Enlightenment; Existentialism

Aelred of Rievaulx
Friendship; Music

Aetius
Greek Theology

al-Ghazali
Fideism; Jewish-Christian Relations; Russian Christian Thought

al-Hallaj
Islam

Albert the Great (of Cologne)
Analogy; Aristotle; Armenian Tradition; Dominican Thought; Middle Ages

Albinus
Plato and Platonism

Albrecht of Brandenburg
Luther, Martin

Alcuin
Latin Theology

Alexander the Great
Alexandria; Aristotle; Hellenistic World in the 1st Century

Alexander of Alexandria
Arianism; Athanasius; Greek Theology

Altizer, Thomas J. J.
Atheism; Nietzsche, Friedrich Wilhelm; North America; Postmodernism; Realism and Antirealism; Twentieth Century

Amaru, Túpac
Latin American Christian Thought

Ambrose of Milan
Antisemitism; Arianism; Athanasius; Augustine; Baptism; Chastity; David; Hymns; Jewish–Christian Relations; Latin Theology; Lent; Music; Old Testament; Origen; Penance; Play; Psalms; Sacrament; Virginity

Ambrosiaster
Augustine; Romans

Andrewes, Lancelot
Anglican Thought; Caroline Divines; Holiness; Mary; Preaching/Homiletics; Seventeenth Century

Angelico, Fra (Giovanni da Fiesole)
Arts, Visual; Dominican Thought

Anscombe, G. E. M. (Elizabeth)
Thomism, Analytical; Wittgenstein, Ludwig

Antony of Egypt
Athanasius; Monasticism; Saints

Aphrahat of Persia
Armenian Tradition; Greek Theology; Syriac Christian Thought

Apollinaris (of Laodicea)
Chalcedon, Council of; Docetism; Greek Theology; Incarnation; Monophysitism; Nestorianism

Arendt, Hannah
City

Arnauld, Angélique
Jansenism

Arnauld, Antoine
Descartes and Cartesianism; Jansenism; Pascal, Blaise

Arndt, Johann
Holiness; Pietism

Arnold, Matthew
Doubt; Poetry

Athenagoras, Patriarch
Constantinople

Atkins, Peter
Science

Augustine of Canterbury
Canterbury; Folk Religion; Law

Aulén, Gustav
Lutheranism; Scandinavian Christian Thought

Austin, J. L.
Kant, Immanuel; Philosophy; Religious Language

Avicenna (Ibn Sina)
Analogy; Aquinas, Thomas; Jewish–Christian Relations

Avvakum
Russian Christian Thought

Ayer, A. J.
Analogy; Atheism; Philosophy; Religious Language; Wittgenstein, Ludwig

B

Bacon, Francis
Fundamentalism; North America; Philosophy; Poetry; Science

Banerjea, K. M.
Hinduism; Indian Christian Thought

Bañez, Domingo
Faith; Grace; Sixteenth Century

Barclay, Robert
Pacifism; Quaker Thought; Scottish Christian Thought

Baronius, Cesare
Counter-Reformation; Seventeenth Century

Barthes, Roland
Analogy; Philosophy

Basil of Caesarea (the Great)
Armenian Tradition; Asceticism; Athanasius; Episcopate; Greek Theology; Holiness; Holy Spirit; Latin Theology; Marriage; Monasticism; Origen; Philosophy; Redemption; Religious Life; Spirituality, Forms of; Sunday; Trinity

Basilides
Alexandria; Gnosticism

Bataille, Georges
Postmodernism; Social Sciences

Baudelaire, Charles
Symbolism

Baum, Gregory
Holocaust; Social Sciences

Baur, Ferdinand Christian
German Christian Thought; Higher Criticism; History; Liberal Protestantism; Lutheranism; Nineteenth Century; Paul; Romans; Tübingen; Universities

Bautain, Louis
Fideism